P9-CMY-186

JANUARY – DECEMBER 2012

Published by CQ Press, an Imprint of SAGE Publications, Inc.
2300 N Street, N.W., Suite 800, Washington, DC 20037

Photo credits, clockwise from top left: AFP/Getty Images/Bruce Weaver; AFP/Getty Images/Saul Loeb; Ben Powless; AFP/Getty Images/Boris Heger; Getty Images/*The Christian Science Monitor*/Tony Avelar; Getty Images/Kevin Winter

ISBN 978-1-45228-203-9
ISSN 1056-2036

CQ Researcher

CQ Researcher is the choice of researchers seeking accurate, in-depth information on issues in the news. Investigated and written by an experienced journalist, each *CQ Researcher* offers a comprehensive, balanced examination of controversial issues. Now in its 89th year, *CQ Researcher* has received the prestigious Sigma Delta Chi Award for Journalism Excellence for a 10-part series on health care and the American Bar Association's Silver Gavel Award for a nine-part series on liberty and justice issues.

Each *CQ Researcher* report opens with an overview of that issue's topic, followed by a discussion of three key questions that drive the debate surrounding the topic. The answers provided are not conclusive but serve to highlight the range of opinions among different experts and political parties. The overview and issue questions are followed by a "Background" section that places the issue in historical context.

"Current Situation" examines the activities of legislators, citizen groups and others influencing the debate. "Outlook" offers insights by experts on what may happen in the future. Each report also features illuminating photographs, graphs and tables, as well as a presentation of views from representatives on opposing sides of the debate. A chronology identifying milestones in the debate and bibliographies of key sources for further research round out the report.

CITING *CQ RESEARCHER*

Sample formats for citing these reports in a bibliography include the ones listed below. Preferred styles and formats vary, so please check with your instructor or professor.

MLA STYLE

Jost, Kenneth. "Remembering 9/11." CQ Researcher, 2 Sept. 2011: 701–732.

APA STYLE

Jost, K. (2011, September 2). Remembering 9/11. *CQ Researcher*, 9, 701–732.

CHICAGO STYLE

Jost, Kenneth. "Remembering 9/11." *CQ Researcher*, September 2, 2011, 701–732.

ACCESSING *CQ RESEARCHER*

CQ Researcher is available in print and online. For access, visit your library or http://library.cqpress.com/cqresearcher.

CQ Researcher

CONTENTS JANUARY – DECEMBER 2012

Preventing Disease — January 6 1
'Occupy' Movement — January 13 25
Financial Misconduct — January 20 53
Youth Volunteerism — January 27 77
Presidential Election — February 3 101
Patient Safety — February 10 125
Invasive Species — February 17 153
Space Program — February 24 177
Attracting Jobs — March 2 205
Immigration Conflict — March 9 229
Arts Education — March 16 253
U.S.-Europe Relations — March 23 277
Police Misconduct — April 6 301
Internet Regulation — April 13 325
Criminal Records and Employment — April 20 349
Sexual Harassment — April 27 377
Distracted Driving — May 4 401
Celebrity Advocacy — May 11 425
Voter Rights — May 18 449
Traumatic Brain Injury — June 1 477
Alcohol Abuse — June 8 501
Gambling in America — June 15 525
U.S. Oil Dependence — June 22 549

Whale Hunting — June 29 573
Privatizing the Military — July 13 597
Debt Collectors — July 20 621
Smart Cities — July 27 645
Treating ADHD — August 3 669
Farm Policy — August 10 693
Genetically Modified Food — August 31 717
Re-examining the Constitution — September 7 741
Solitary Confinement — September 14 765
Assessing the New Health Care Law — September 21 789
Supreme Court Controversies — September 28 813
Euro Crisis — October 5 831
Social Media and Politics — October 12 865
Understanding Mormonism — October 19 889
Mexico's Future — October 26 913
Managing Wildfires — November 2 941
Indecency on Television — November 9 965
Changing Demographics — November 16 989
Sugar Controversies — November 30 1013
3D Printing — December 7 1037
Future of Homeownership — December 14 1061

CQ Researcher

Published by CQ Press, an Imprint of SAGE Publications, Inc.

www.cqresearcher.com

Preventing Disease

Can lifestyle changes reduce rising health care costs?

The U.S. health care system faces spiraling costs from chronic, or noncommunicable, illnesses such as diabetes, heart disease and preventable cancers. But public health experts are discovering that just pushing people to change bad habits isn't working. Instead, they are placing more focus on "making the healthy choice the easy choice" through such efforts as reformulating processed foods and making streets safe for walkers and bikers. Some in Congress and the Obama administration made a big push for community-based disease prevention approaches, but concerns over the budget deficit could result in major cuts to the Prevention and Public Health Fund enacted as part of the 2010 health reform act. However, some say the government is overreaching in its war on obesity, and studies show that some prevention efforts add to health care costs. The fight against preventable disease is not a U.S. problem alone. In poor countries, the biggest threats are the same ones afflicting Americans: lack of exercise, smoking and unhealthy diets.

First lady Michelle Obama brings her Let's Move campaign to the New York Police Athletic League's Harlem Center on Nov. 18, 2010. The program stresses the importance of exercise and healthy eating in combating childhood obesity, which has more than tripled since 1990.

INSIDE THIS REPORT

THE ISSUES 3
BACKGROUND 10
CHRONOLOGY 11
CURRENT SITUATION 15
AT ISSUE 17
OUTLOOK 18
BIBLIOGRAPHY 22
THE NEXT STEP 23

CQ Researcher • Jan. 6, 2012 • www.cqresearcher.com
Volume 22, Number 1 • Pages 1-24

Los Angeles | London | New Delhi
Singapore | Washington DC

RECIPIENT OF SOCIETY OF PROFESSIONAL JOURNALISTS AWARD FOR EXCELLENCE ◆ AMERICAN BAR ASSOCIATION SILVER GAVEL AWARD

THE ISSUES

3 • Does preventing disease save money?
• Should government encourage behavior change?
• Should the health care system focus more on wellness?

BACKGROUND

10 **Preventable Diseases**
The surgeon general's 1964 report on tobacco was a milestone.

12 **Obesity**
The proportion of obese Americans jumped to 34 percent in 2008.

14 **Community Prevention**
The 2010 health-reform act supports preventive health initiatives.

CURRENT SITUATION

15 **Public Health Targets**
Tobacco and obesity cause the most preventable deaths.

16 **Workplace Wellness**
Programs to improve employees' health are popular.

18 **Other Initiatives**
The Million Hearts Campaign aims to reduce heart attacks, strokes.

OUTLOOK

18 **Two Steps Forward . . .**
Budget cuts may reverse health gains.

SIDEBARS AND GRAPHICS

4 **More Than 30 States Have High Obesity Rates**
One-fourth of adults in 33 states are obese.

5 **Smoking Kills Nearly Half a Million**
Toll includes deaths from secondhand smoke.

7 **Smoking Declined Among Adults, Students**
Twenty percent of adults and high school students smoke.

8 **Smoking and Obesity Are Biggest Killers**
Toll exceeded half a million Americans in 2000.

9 **Are You Getting Enough Exercise?**
Here are guidelines.

11 **Chronology**
Key events since 1789.

12 **Poor Countries Struggle to Curb Preventable Illnesses**
"The world is essentially sleepwalking into a sick future."

14 **Get Out of Your Car, Urban Planners Urge**
"Complete Streets" program promotes bicycling, walking.

17 **At Issue**
Should Americans be penalized for unhealthy behaviors?

FOR FURTHER RESEARCH

21 **For More Information**
Organizations to contact.

22 **Bibliography**
Selected sources used.

23 **The Next Step**
Additional articles.

23 **Citing *CQ Researcher***
Sample bibliography formats.

Cover: Getty Images/Mario Tama

CQ Researcher

Jan. 6, 2012
Volume 22, Number 1

MANAGING EDITOR: Thomas J. Billitteri
tjb@cqpress.com

ASSISTANT MANAGING EDITOR: Kathy Koch
kkoch@cqpress.com

CONTRIBUTING EDITOR: Thomas J. Colin
tcolin@cqpress.com

ASSOCIATE EDITOR: Kenneth Jost

STAFF WRITERS: Marcia Clemmitt, Peter Katel

CONTRIBUTING WRITERS: Sarah Glazer, Alan Greenblatt, Barbara Mantel, Jennifer Weeks

DESIGN/PRODUCTION EDITOR: Olu B. Davis

ASSISTANT EDITOR: Darrell Dela Rosa

FACT CHECKER: Michelle Harris

Los Angeles | London | New Delhi
Singapore | Washington DC

An Imprint of SAGE Publications, Inc.

VICE PRESIDENT AND EDITORIAL DIRECTOR, HIGHER EDUCATION GROUP:
Michele Sordi

DIRECTOR, ONLINE PUBLISHING:
Todd Baldwin

CQ Researcher (ISSN 1056-2036) is printed on acid-free paper. Published weekly, except: (March wk. 5) (May wk. 4) (July wk. 1) (Aug. wks. 3, 4) (Nov. wk. 4) and (Dec. wks. 3, 4). Published by SAGE Publications, Inc., 2455 Teller Rd., Thousand Oaks, CA 91320. Annual full-service subscriptions start at $803. For pricing, call 1-800-834-9020. To purchase a *CQ Researcher* report in print or electronic format (PDF), visit www.cqpress.com or call 866-427-7737. Single reports start at $15. Bulk purchase discounts and electronic-rights licensing are also available. Periodicals postage paid at Thousand Oaks, California, and at additional mailing offices. POSTMASTER: Send address changes to *CQ Researcher*, 2300 N St., N.W., Suite 800, Washington, DC 20037.

BY NELLIE BRISTOL

THE ISSUES

Soon after his election as mayor, Chip Johnson began trying to transform Hernando, Miss., into an oasis of healthy living.

In impoverished Mississippi, that was a challenge worthy of the surgeon general. The state ranks highest in the nation in cardiovascular deaths, obesity and infant deaths and second worst in diabetes. [1]

But if residents exercised and ate right, Johnson figured, future illnesses might be prevented, at the same time saving taxpayers money and making the city of 14,000 a more attractive business environment.

Six years later, Johnson has developed bike paths and lanes with $800,000 in federal, state and private grants, while pushing to require developers to build sidewalks and city engineers to plan roads with walkers and bikers in mind. He even started a farmers market that accepts food stamps. [2]

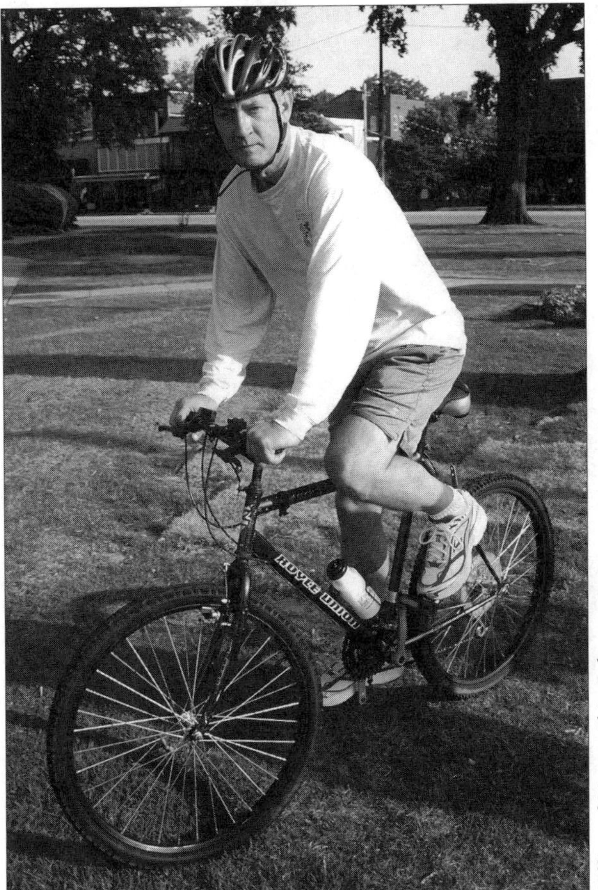

Office of Mayor Chip Johnson

Mayor Chip Johnson, of Hernando, Miss., supports a wide range of projects designed to make residents healthier while saving taxpayers money. In his six years in office he has developed bike paths and lanes while pushing to require developers to build sidewalks and city engineers to plan roads with walkers and bicyclists in mind. A wellness program he approved for city employees reduced health insurance costs 15 percent. "For us, that's a lot of money," he said.

As a Republican, Johnson believes that health and fitness decisions are personal, but he also knows those decisions shape demand for tax-supported health services, influence overall medical costs and help determine the business climate. "We want to recruit corporations to Hernando," he said. "They're not stupid. When they make their decisions, they look at health care costs." [3]

Hernando, a fast-growing bedroom suburb for nearby Memphis, Tenn., is atypical in Mississippi because of its higher rate of affluent and professional residents. Even so, Johnson's efforts are seen as a guide for fostering healthy habits in any community, rich or poor.

Public health experts argue that a locally based, multipronged approach like Hernando's is the only way for communities to reverse the major risk factors for chronic disease: poor eating habits, lack of exercise, smoking and alcohol use, which contribute to cardiovascular and lung disease, diabetes and some cancers.

While there is no hard evidence yet that Johnson's initiatives have improved the town's health, a wellness program Johnson approved for the city's 115 employees helped lead to a 15 percent reduction in health insurance costs. "For us, that's a lot of money," he said. [4]

While Johnson is working to get his town on a better health trajectory, the public health picture nationwide doesn't seem to be improving.

The annual health rankings released recently by the United Health Foundation, an advocacy and philanthropy group, showed that positive health trends in 2011, such as reductions in smoking, preventable hospitalizations and cardiovascular deaths, were offset by increases in obesity, diabetes and childhood poverty. "The country's overall health did not improve between 2010 and 2011," the foundation said. [5]

Negative health trends are taking a toll on the nation's resources. Chronic diseases are responsible for more than three-quarters of U.S. health care costs. [6] The bill is even higher for government health programs, with chronic disease accounting for 96 percent of Medicare spending for the elderly and 83 percent of Medicaid spending for the poor. [7]

Worldwide, chronic, noncommunicable disease is expected to cost the global economy $47 trillion over the next two decades (in today's dollars). [8] The U.N.'s World Health Organization (WHO) estimates that at least 80 percent of heart disease, stroke and Type 2 diabetes cases and more than 40 percent of cancer could be prevented or better managed through smoking cessation, healthy eating and better fitness. [9]

Public health experts say reducing chronic disease requires efforts by a

More Than 30 States Have High Obesity Rates

At least one-fourth of adults in 33 states are obese. In nine states, mainly in the South, 30 percent or more of adults are obese. At least 20 percent are obese in another 16 states. Overall, more than one-third of American adults (more than 72 million people) and 17 percent of children are obese.*

Percentage of Adults Who Are Obese, by State, 2009

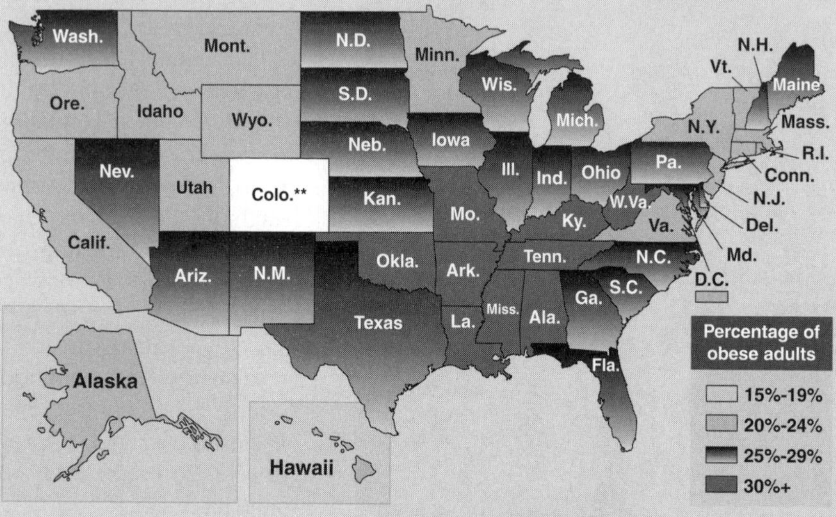

* *Obesity is defined as a body mass index (BMI) of at least 30, or about 30 lbs. overweight for a 5'4" person.*

** *No data available*

Source: "Obesity: Halting the Epidemic By Making Health Easier," Centers for Disease Control and Prevention, 2011, p. 2, www.cdc.gov/chronicdisease/resources/publications/aag/pdf/2011/Obesity_AAG_WEB_508.pdf

broad range of government and private-sector actors. They advocate government actions such as public health messages, limits on salt, sugar and fat in commercial foods and increased sidewalk construction to encourage exercise. They also are encouraging:

- Packaged-food manufacturers to reduce marketing of sugary breakfast cereals and other unhealthy products to children;
- Restaurants to cut portion sizes and post calories counts;
- Communities to build more playgrounds, and,
- The medical system to offer inexpensive or free preventive services and link patients to local support programs.

Some physicians even call for removing severely obese children from their parents. [10] "It should only be used as a last resort," said David Ludwig, a child obesity expert at Harvard University. "It's also no guarantee of success, but when we have a 400-pound child with life-threatening complications, there may not be any great choices." [11]

While many view that idea as extreme, even modest steps can be highly controversial.

Critics of the preventive health movement say, for example, that the "obesity epidemic" has been overblown by public health officials and is a ruse to allow meddling in personal choices and affairs. "This epidemic has been constructed to the benefit of the medical industry that has in part medicalized the treatment of obesity over the years," said University of Houston sociologist Samantha Kwan. [12]

Julie Guthman, an associate professor of community studies at the University of California, Santa Cruz, agrees. "I'm not convinced obesity is the problem it's made out to be," she says. She argues, for example, that a common tool used to determine obesity — the body mass index (BMI) — doesn't effectively take into account muscle mass. She also says the correlation between body weight and sickness is not fully proven.

"People who are overweight or slightly obese actually seem to have longer life expectancy than people who are of so-called normal weight," she says. "There's a lot of panic without really understanding the dimensions of the problem."

Former Gov. Sarah Palin, R-Alaska, took on the issue by bringing cookies to a school in Pennsylvania in reaction to the news report that the state school board was considering limiting sweets brought to the classroom. "I wanted these kids to bring home the idea to their parents for discussion," she said. "Who should be deciding what I eat? Should it be the government or should it be parents? It should be the parents." [13]

Palin also took on the high-profile Let's Move program developed by first lady Michelle Obama to attack childhood obesity, which has more than tripled since 1980. [14] "Instead of government thinking that they need to take over and make decisions for us according to some politician or politician's wife's priorities, just leave us alone, get off our back and allow us as individuals to exercise our own God-given rights to make our own decisions, and then our country gets back on the right track," Palin said. [15]

The food industry also is pushing back, fighting government requirements

Smoking Kills Nearly Half a Million Annually

About 443,000 Americans die each year from smoking, including deaths from secondhand smoke. Smoking-induced lung cancer and heart disease each accounts for about 30 percent of the deaths. Tobacco use is the single most preventable cause of disease, disability and death in the United States.

Annual Smoking-Related Deaths, by Disease, Including Secondhand Smoke, 2000-2004

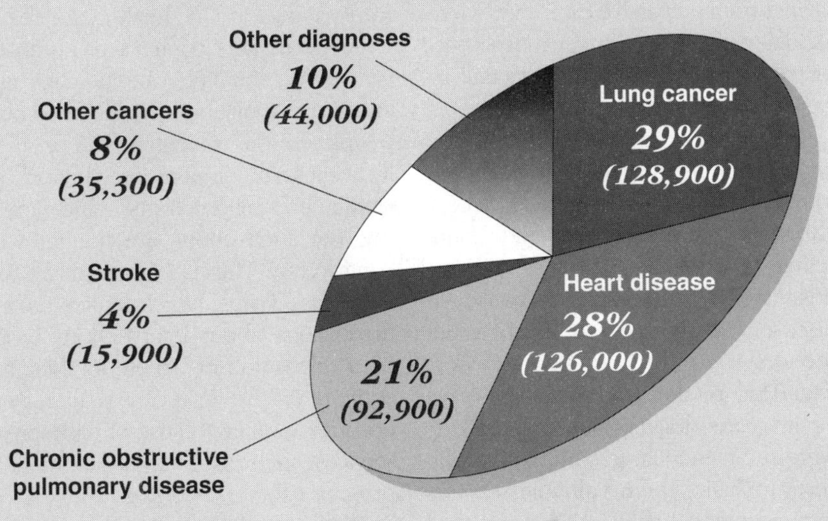

Source: "Tobacco Use: Targeting the Nation's Leading Killer," Centers for Disease Control and Prevention, 2011, p. 2, www.cdc.gov/chronicdisease/resources/publications/aag/pdf/2011/Tobacco_AAG_2011_508.pdf

to limit certain foods, such as potatoes, in school lunches, reformulate products and curtail some types of advertising to children. Industry officials say they prefer a voluntary approach.

But many people think Americans' increasing weight and sedentary lifestyles call for action. A group of retired generals, admirals and other senior U.S. military leaders declared in 2010 that an "alarming" 75 percent of 17-24-year-olds are unfit for military service, citing obesity as a contributing factor. They urged a ban on junk food in schools, improvement in school lunches and greater access for children to obesity-reduction programs. [16]

"If we don't take steps now to build a strong, healthy foundation for our young people, then it won't just be our military that pays the price — our nation as a whole will suffer also," they wrote. [17]

As lawmakers, employers and individuals struggle to find the best ways to prevent or delay chronic disease, here are some of the issues being discussed:

Does preventing disease save money?

Reducing health care costs is a perennial national priority. Health spending in the United States totaled $2.5 trillion in 2009, or an average of $8,086 per person. Spending on health constitutes 17.6 percent of the U.S. gross domestic product (GDP), more than twice the 7.2 percent of GDP in 1970, according to the Kaiser Family Foundation. [18] And unless changes are made, health care costs are expected to keep growing.

The subject is of special concern to congressional lawmakers, particularly in a time of high budget deficits. Medicare, the federal health care program for the elderly and disabled, accounts for 20 percent of national health expenditures. Medicaid, the joint state/federal program for low-income people, makes up 15 percent of national health expenditures. Altogether, the federal government share of national health spending is 27 percent. [19]

Some lawmakers have zeroed in on disease prevention as a cost-cutting measure, reasoning that preventing people from getting sick would save money on future care. But strictly in economic terms and not improvements in longevity and quality of life, the reality is much more complicated.

"Studies have concluded that preventing illness can in some cases save money but in other cases can add to health costs," wrote Joshua Cohen, deputy director of the Tufts University Center for the Evaluation of Value and Risk in Health, and other researchers. "Whether any preventive measure saves money or is a reasonable investment despite adding to cost depends entirely on the particular intervention and the specific population in question." For example, the authors continued, "drugs used to treat high cholesterol yield much greater value for the money if the target population is at high risk for coronary heart disease, and the efficiency of cancer screening can depend heavily on the frequency of the screening and the level of cancer risk in the screened population." [20]

To try to quantify the cost effectiveness of certain disease-prevention services, the Robert Wood Johnson Foundation studied preventive services provided in medical settings, including immunizations and screening for a variety of risk factors such as hypertension and high cholesterol. The researchers drew several conclusions, including that preventive services can reduce prevalence of specific diseases and help people live longer and that many preventive services offer good value for scarce health care dollars.

But they also found that most preventive care does not result in cost savings. "Costs to reduce risk factors, screening costs and the cost of treatment when disease is found can offset any savings from preventive care," they wrote. "Additionally, living longer means people may develop other ailments that increase lifetime health care costs." [21]

In fact, the review of 17 medications/immunizations and screening services found only two that reduced costs: childhood immunizations and counseling of adults on the use of low-dose aspirin to prevent cardiovascular disease. However, a number of other services were found to be cost effective. That is, they didn't directly save health care dollars, but the benefits were sufficiently large compared to the costs to make them valuable services for improving health. These included flu shots for adults, counseling on the use of folic acid for pregnant women and a variety of screening tests, including those for colorectal, breast and cervical cancer, hypertension and cholesterol.

The picture is more positive for what are known as community-based prevention efforts. The Trust for America's Health, a disease-prevention advocacy group, evaluated 84 studies of prevention activities targeted at communities rather than individuals. To be included in the review, interventions could not require medical treatment and had to be proven to reduce disease through improving physical activity and nutrition and preventing smoking and other tobacco use. Programs included, for example, establishment of farmers markets, calorie and nutrition labeling, nutrition education for young mothers and raising cigarette and other tobacco taxes.

Overall, the group found that an investment of $10 per person per year in proven community-based disease-prevention programs could save more than $2.8 billion annually in health care costs in one to two years, more than $16 billion annually within five years and nearly $18 billion annually in 10 to 20 years. [22] The group concluded: "a small strategic investment in disease prevention could result in significant savings in U.S. health care costs."

As lawmakers confront rising health care costs, spiraling obesity rates and an aging population, more focus should be placed on evaluating the cost effectiveness of disease intervention, including prevention efforts, some experts say. But such efforts are fraught with controversy. The U.S. Preventive Services Task Force, which makes recommendations about interventions based on a calculation of benefit to risks, has come under fire in recent years for endorsing more limited use of widespread services such as mammography and prostate cancer screening.

Putting a dollar value on activities aimed at prolonging life has attracted even more heat. The 2009 economic stimulus legislation, for example, included funding for an Obama administration-supported comparative-effectiveness analysis of medical services, but references to calculating cost effectiveness were dropped following objections in Congress. [23]

But some, including Cohen at Tufts, argue that while costs shouldn't be the only consideration, they should be taken into account. "At any given time, we can only spend so much money as a country on health care, so it's not a question of whether we should be spending money only on those things that save money," he says. "If we do things that are less cost effective — have a smaller benefit per dollar invested — we will be taking away, on some level, from those things that are more cost effective, and we will be decreasing overall population health."

Should government encourage behavior change?

Whose responsibility is it to stop Americans from dying from preventable diseases? The question stirs passions deeply tied to opinions on the role of government in society. Many supporters of government involvement say the most effective approach does not focus necessarily on individuals, but rather on creating environments that "make the healthy choice the easy choice."

But not everyone sees the value of getting the government involved. For example, some argue the obesity "epidemic" is overstated and that the government is overstepping when it tells people what to eat.

Nonetheless, government at all levels is actively trying to improve nutrition and increase access to daily exercise. Specific policies adopted include higher taxes on cigarettes to reduce smoking, trans-fat bans to lower the risk of heart disease and healthier school lunch menus.

Many experts concerned about unhealthy eating say the government should better educate consumers about what is in their food, create more access to fresh fruit and vegetables and ban unhealthy foods in schools. "Where the government comes in is when industry is not acting responsibly," said Margo Wootan, director of nutrition policy at the Center for Science in the Public Interest, a consumer advocacy group, and that leaves a lot of potential room for government action, she adds. "The food industry has resisted every meaningful policy I've ever worked on — menu labeling, trans fat labeling, getting soda and candy bars out of schools. The industry's job is not to promote American health, it's to make money."

Scott Kahan, associate director of the Johns Hopkins University Weight Management Center, in Baltimore, said government has long had a role in improving health, starting with upgrading sanitation and water quality. It also steps in when the public is faced with infectious disease, including flu outbreaks. "When we look at how we improved the infectious disease problem in America, structural interventions, policy interventions and government interventions were a really important part of that," he says.

Today, he continues, the nation faces a different set of diseases with different causes, but the need for government action is no less. "We live in an environment right now that in many ways could be called toxic, that's not unlike the toxic infectious environment of a hundred years ago," he says. "In this case, it's sort of a toxic environment around the foods that we eat." The unhealthiest, most high-calorie foods tend to be the cheapest and most heavily marketed, he says, often to young children. As a result, "It's going to be extremely important for government and also the private sector to come together to continue to evolve a set of policies and practices that make the healthier choice just a little bit easier and make the unhealthy choice not so easy."

Former Gov. Parris Glendening, D-Md., now president of the Leadership Institute at Smart Growth America, a coalition of urban advocacy groups, says making changes to the "built environment" to encourage healthier living "is a very legitimate role for state and local governments." Smart growth revolves around the concept that communities should have easy, preferably car-free access to jobs and shopping, and that public policy should encourage sidewalks, bike paths and public transportation to increase daily exercise and reduce air pollution, both of which improve health.

Smart-growth supporters point to a study in Charlotte, N.C., showing that building a light-rail system led users to walk more and lose weight. "The built environment can constrain or facilitate physical activity," said lead investigator John M. MacDonald of the University of Pennsylvania. "Understanding ways to encourage greater use of local environments for physical activity offers some hope for reducing the growth in the prevalence of obesity." [24]

Diane Katz, a research fellow in regulatory policy at the Heritage Foundation, a conservative think tank, says there is nothing wrong with politicians or other leaders encouraging constituents to adopt healthier lifestyles, although she thinks the deficit and other issues should take priority.

But Katz rejects efforts to insert the government into individual food decisions. "Nutrition regulations are commonly justified to defeat an obesity 'epidemic,' " she says, but "both the extent of the problem and the risk it poses are often exaggerated, the product of special-interest propaganda or dubious research." She adds: "Underlying government constraints on food choice is the presumption that individuals are incapable of making dietary decisions and government will do a far better job of it — a conceit that insults the most fundamental principles of limited government and personal freedom."

Katz turns Kahan's argument on its head, saying that since infectious-disease threats are now reduced, health officials have focused on eating and exercise habits because they need to "concoct new menaces to occupy their time."

Meanwhile, many sectors of the food industry are fighting government involvement. Several battles have erupted recently in the policy realm, including one over serving potatoes and pizza in school cafeterias. The Department of Agriculture recently proposed,

Smoking Declined Among Adults, Students

About 20 percent of adults and high school students smoke cigarettes. The percentage has declined by half for students since the mid-1990s and for adults since 1965.

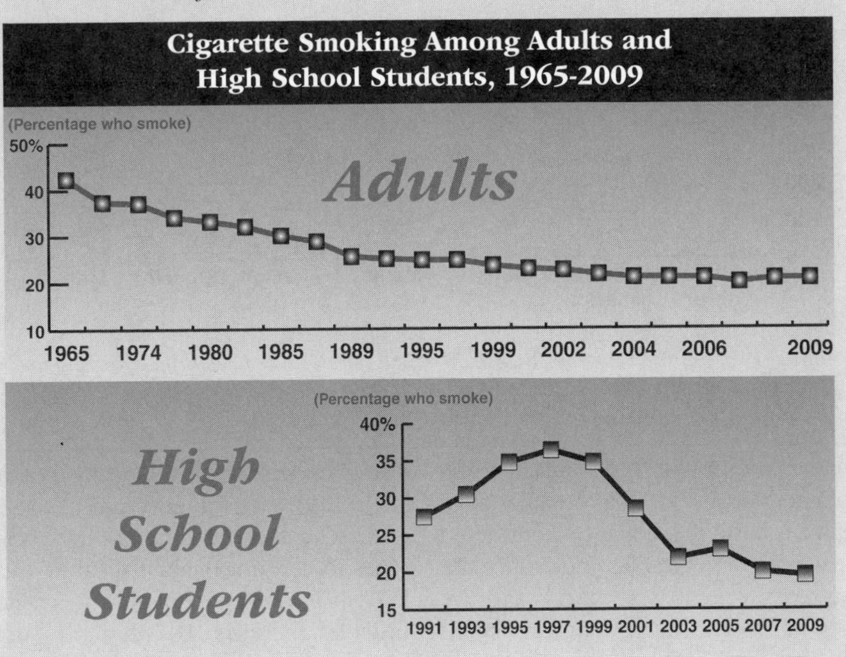

Source: "Tobacco Use: Targeting the Nation's Leading Killer," Centers for Disease Control and Prevention, February 2011, www.cdc.gov/chronicdisease/resources/publications/AAG/osh_text.htm#chart2

Smoking and Obesity Are Biggest Killers

Some 555,000 people died in the United States in 2000 from smoking or obesity. Alcohol abuse was a distant third in the list of behaviors leading to death.

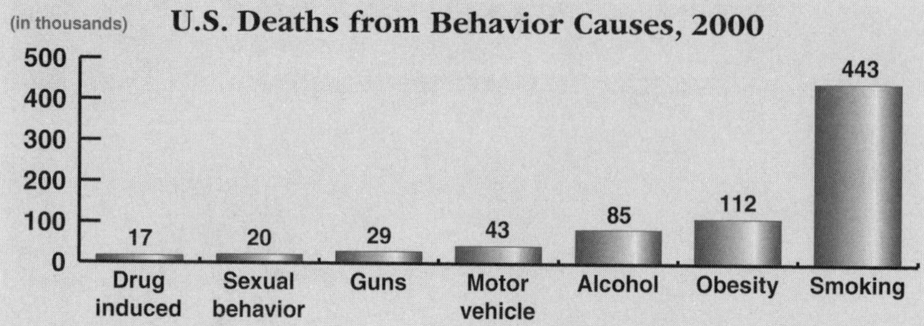

Source: "Preventing Chronic Disease: The New Public Health," Alliance for Health Reform, September 2011, p. 2, www.allhealth.org/publications/Public_health/Preventing_Chronic_Disease_New_Public_Health_108.pdf

based on Institute of Medicine recommendations, to limit the amount of tomato paste that could be considered a serving of vegetables and reduce the starchy vegetables that could be served in schools. [25] Congress altered the tomato paste recommendations spurred by industry groups including, reportedly, the American Frozen Food Institute and Schwan's Food Service, which provides pizzas to schools. Senators from large potato-growing states, Republican Susan Collins of Maine and Democrat Mark Udall of Colorado, worked with the National Potato Council to protest limits on starchy vegetables. [26]

Some companies have begun changing their products to ward off further government action. ConAgra Foods, for example, pledged in 2009 to reduce sodium in about 80 percent of its products by 2015. Kraft Foods said in 2010 it would reduce sodium in its North American products by an average of 10 percent by 2012. [27]

PepsiCo also has been a healthy-products leader. In 2010 it announced 11 goals to improve public health, including product reformulation and changes in marketing. [28] Derek Yach, a former WHO official and now senior vice president of global health policy at PepsiCo, says the government's role is to send the right signals and messages to consumers about healthy eating while industry continues to create healthier products. But that may not be enough to change consumer tastes, he says.

"Even if we put out better products," Yach says, "there's no guarantee they're going to be enjoyed and consumed or whether they're going to displace things with higher salt, sugar and fat, which have been the dietary norm for decades."

Should the health care system focus more on wellness?

The U.S. health care system is designed primarily to treat the sick, not encourage people to stay healthy.

Financial incentives reward health care providers for performing services and procedures, usually after illness has taken hold. But the vast majority of diseases start years and sometimes decades before an affliction drives a patient to a doctor's office. That leaves many experts arguing that caregivers and patients must be given the tools and incentives to stop chronic diseases before they begin.

Several obstacles stand in the way, however:

- An imbalance in the types of services for which physicians are paid;
- A fragmented health system that doesn't give patients comprehensive care;
- A lack of physician training in disease prevention, and;
- An overreliance on technology.

Physicians traditionally have been paid for ordering diagnostic tests, prescribing drugs, performing surgery or conducting other procedures, not for spending time getting to know patients and their potential health risks. As doctors become busier, time with patients has gotten shorter.

"Physicians whom we talk to on a regular basis who truly want to do more health-behavior counseling or coaching with their patients are simply unable to do so because they aren't paid by federal government plans or private insurers to do that kind of preventive medicine work," says Paul Bonta, associate executive director of the American College of Preventive Medicine. Preventive health experts want a system that would pay care providers to delve deeper into lifestyle issues that may be causing disease and to counsel patients on diet modification or smoking cessation.

Other changes also could help, says Georges C. Benjamin, executive director of the American Public Health Association. Insurers should pay for cancer screening without requiring contributions from the patient. In addition, he says, physicians who ensure that patients receive immunizations, blood-pressure screening and other preventive procedures should be financially rewarded.

Preventive health advocates also say physicians need to play matchmaker, linking patients with community programs that offer unique support. "The majority of prevention, especially wellness, probably happens outside the medical system," says Elizabeth Tilson, medical director at Community Care of Wake and Johnston counties in North Carolina. "If you think about it, you may only get into the medical system once or twice a year. The vast majority of the time patients are out in their world."

Medical professionals often aren't aware of community-based support services, such as stop-smoking clinics or nutrition counseling, or don't help patients connect with them, advocates say.

A model of a more comprehensive approach is the "medical home," in which a health care provider tracks a patient's entire care and helps the patient find appropriate programs and specialists. At Martin's Point, a medical center in Portland, Maine, physicians monitor patient care through electronic medical records, and health educators help patients address medication or social issues connected with their disease. [29]

Bonta agrees that physicians need more help in providing ongoing services through their offices or referring patients to community resources. "Often, the patient will go to the physician's office, and the physician will say, 'Start exercising more, we need to get your weight down,' and the patient leaves the office and has no idea how to go about exercising more," he says. "Until we reach the point where we are able to educate or inform physicians about all the work that's going on within their communities, we can't make meaningful inroads in facilitating the behavior change that's needed."

Medical training also needs improvement, says Michael Parkinson, former president of the American College of Preventive Medicine and now a health consultant. He says the centuries-old "false dichotomy" between medical care and "wellness" was made worse in the United States in the early 20th century by the first schools of public health, which Parkinson says split off disease-prevention activities from medical school curricula. As a result, he says, most physicians are not trained in prevention.

Moreover, he adds, the model is outdated in a society in which three-quarters of health care costs could be mitigated through lifestyle changes.

Parkinson says it's unfair to ask doctors who have never been trained in disease prevention and never paid for preventive services to be held responsible for reversing the country's obesity epidemic.

Parkinson also argues that the medical system directs most health spending toward drugs and surgery after disease is present rather than focusing on low-tech strategies of improved diet and exercise. The "medical-industrial complex essentially now consumes nearly 20 percent of the U.S. gross domestic product, and what it lives on is an inherent bias we have for quick fixes with high technology at low or no cost" to consumers, he says.

The payment system also disconnects consumers from the costs of their care, Parkinson says. Patients need to understand, for example, that losing weight could lessen their back pain and risk of arthritis and perhaps help them avoid costly surgery and pharmaceuticals, he says. Those who choose more expensive options should be responsible for some of the extra costs, he adds.

While the increased focus on disease prevention appears to have universal support in the medical field, the shift could create new "winners and losers" in health care reimbursement, Tilson says. "I don't think that conceptually or philosophically anybody is against helping to reimburse for prevention. I just think it's a pure financial argument. There is just not enough money right now," she says.

Investing more in wellness could mean less money for new technologies and could heighten tensions between general practitioners and specialists. Primary-care physicians have argued for years that they aren't afforded the same

Are You Getting Enough Exercise?

To maintain good health, the federal Centers for Disease Control and Prevention recommends the following guidelines:

Recommended physical activity — Moderate-intensity activities — such as brisk walking, bicycling, vacuuming, gardening or anything that causes small increases in breathing or heart rate — for at least 30 minutes per day, five days a week; or vigorous-intensity activities — such as running, aerobics, heavy yard work or anything that causes large increases in breathing or heart rate — for at least 20 minutes per day, three days a week.

Insufficient physical activity — More than 10 minutes total per week of moderate or vigorous-intensity activities, but less than the recommended levels.

Inactivity — Less than 10 minutes total per week of moderate or vigorous-intensity activities.

Leisure-time inactivity — No reported physical activity or exercise in the previous month.

Source: "Physical Activity Statistics: Definition," Centers for Disease Control and Prevention, May 2007, www.cdc.gov/nccdphp/dnpa/physical/stats/definitions.htm.

prestige granted to specialists and can make as little as a fourth of the annual salary of an orthopedist or surgeon.[30] But shifting the advantage to preventive-care practitioners could make today's high earners unhappy. ■

BACKGROUND

Preventable Diseases

Building on the success of the smallpox vaccine, inoculations have been developed for many diseases, and the number keeps growing. In the 19th century, vaccines were developed for rabies and plague. The 20th century saw a host of new vaccines, including those for diphtheria, pertussis, measles and polio.[31] In 2006, a vaccine was approved that prevents the human papilloma virus, which can cause cervical and other cancers.[32]

While immunizations are considered by many to be the most important public health advance ever, some people are concerned about the safety of vaccines and about the growing number of inoculations children receive, which now cover more than a dozen diseases and can require multiple doses.[33]

As public health and medical advances in the early 20th century began to drastically reduce the prevalence of infectious disease and prolong lives, developed countries began to face a different type of disease burden: noncommunicable disease. The significance of cancer, heart disease and other chronic conditions began to be recognized in the 1930s, but according to James Marks, senior vice president and director of the health group at the Robert Wood Johnson Foundation, people didn't think they could be stopped. "Many people thought for a long time that chronic diseases like heart disease and cancer were inevitable and that there wasn't much we could do about them," he says. Doctors made efforts to control high blood pressure and cholesterol levels, but only in extreme cases. Slowly, evidence accumulated showing that some diseases were preventable, including lung cancer and heart disease.

Getty Images/Justin Sullivan

High school and college-level students struggling to lose weight play soccer during fitness training at Wellspring Academy, in Reedley, Calif. More than one-third of American adults and 17 percent of children are obese.

A major milestone in preventing chronic disease came in the form of the U.S. surgeon general's 1964 report on tobacco. Cigarette smoking increased dramatically in the first part of the 20th century, bringing with it a precipitous increase in lung cancer. Annual per capita cigarette consumption jumped from 54 cigarettes in 1900 to 4,435 in 1963. In 1930, the lung cancer death rate for men was 4.9 deaths per 100,000, a rate that increased to 75.6 per 100,000 in 1990.[34]

The ill effects of smoking became more apparent during the 1930s, '40s and '50s as more studies suggested smoking was causing the epidemic rise of lung cancer. In 1957 the U.S. Public Health Service officially declared that evidence pointed to a causal relationship between smoking and lung cancer.[35] In 1964, Surgeon General Luther Terry issued a landmark report on smoking and health that cited cigarette smoking as responsible for a 70 percent increase in the mortality rate of smokers compared to nonsmokers.[36]

The report also estimated the average smoker had a nine- to 10-fold risk of developing lung cancer compared to nonsmokers, and heavy smokers had at least a 20-fold risk. It also connected smoking during pregnancy with lower-weight newborns. In 1965, Congress required health warnings on all cigarette packages. In 1969, cigarette advertising was banned on radio and television. Per capita cigarette consumption began to fall, reaching 1,619 in 2006.[37]

As evidence accumulated showing the hazards of secondhand smoke, jurisdictions began imposing smoking bans. The first was in Minnesota in 1975. The state's Clean Indoor Air Act limited smoking to designated areas in public place and at public meetings.[38]

Continued on p. 12

Chronology

1700s-1800s

Modern vaccine development begins; germ theory attributes diseases to specific organisms and shows they are contagious.

1789
Smallpox vaccine developed by British physician Edward Jenner.

1854
British physician John Snow traces cholera outbreak in London to a water pump, giving a major boost to the science of epidemiology.

1885
Rabies vaccine developed by French scientist Louis Pasteur.

1897
Plague vaccine developed by Russian microbiologist Waldemar Haffkine.

1900-1950

U.S. mortality rates plunge with improvements in clean-water technologies, housing, other living standards.

1917
Cholera vaccine developed by Haffkine, who performs the first human tests of the injection on himself.

1923
Diphtheria vaccine developed by German scientist Emil Adolf Behring.

1924
Tetanus vaccine developed by P. Descombey.

1948
Framingham Heart Study begins; identifies risk factors for chronic disease.

1950-1970

Risk factors for chronic diseases begin to be identified and addressed.

1952
Polio vaccine developed by U.S. medical researcher Jonas Salk.

1964
Surgeon General Luther Terry issues landmark report saying cigarette smoking increases mortality rate of smokers by 70 percent compared to nonsmokers.

1965
Congress requires health warnings on cigarette packages.

1967
World Health Organization (WHO) calls for global eradication of smallpox.

1969
Cigarette advertising banned.

1970-1990

Smallpox eradicated, but new diseases such as HIV/AIDS take hold.

1973
Airplane cabins divided into "smoking" and "no-smoking" sections.

1975
First indoor clean-air law limits smoking to designated areas in public spaces.

1980
WHO declares smallpox eradicated. . . . First cases of HIV/AIDS appear in the United States.

1989
Congress bans smoking on commercial flights.

1990s-2000s

Cancer rates peak and begin to fall; obesity rates rise.

1992
Environmental Protection Agency declares secondhand tobacco smoke a Class A carcinogen.

1998
States get a $246 billion windfall after settling a lawsuit against tobacco companies, but little of the money funds smoking-cessation programs.

2000
Government sets goal of reducing childhood obesity rate, estimated at 15 percent, to 5 percent by 2010.

2003
Study links urban and suburban sprawl with weight gain.

March 2010
President Obama signs the Patient Protection and Affordable Care Act, which includes a $15 billion Prevention and Public Health Fund.

May 2010
White House Task Force sets goal of eliminating childhood obesity in a generation; nutrition labeling of chain-restaurant menus becomes law, effective in 2011.

2011
House of Representatives votes to repeal Prevention and Public Health Fund (April); Obama's deficit-reduction proposals include a $3.5 billion cut in the fund (September); House Republicans propose an $8 billion reduction (December).

Poor Countries Struggle to Curb Preventable Illnesses

"The world is essentially sleepwalking into a sick future."

Malaria and HIV often get the headlines in stories about global health problems, but the biggest threats in poor countries are the same ones afflicting the wealthy and well-fed: lack of exercise, smoking and diets brimming with fat, salt and sugar.

Chronic, or noncommunicable, disease recently became the world's leading killer, accounting for 63 percent of deaths in 2008, according to the U.N.'s World Health Organization (WHO). [1]

The effects of modern lifestyles — including greater reliance on automobiles, pollution, increases in smoking and unhealthy diets are spreading preventable cancers, diabetes and respiratory and heart disease to every corner of the globe. The illnesses are having the greatest impact, however, where poverty is rampant and health systems are inadequate.

The vast majority of cancers in the developing world, for example, are detected in their late stages, but effective treatments are lacking in general. In Uganda, 96 percent of those who die from cancer never see a health care provider. [2] Moreover, in many developing countries, even pain medications for cancer often are unavailable.

Chronic diseases are killing people at earlier ages in developing countries than in the developed world. Nearly 30 percent of deaths from noncommunicable diseases occur among people under age 60 in low- and middle-income countries, compared to 13 percent in high-income countries. [3]

"In wealthy countries, deaths from heart disease and strokes have declined significantly," said Margaret Chan, WHO's director-general. "But this gives a distorted picture. For some countries, it is no exaggeration to describe the situation as an impending disaster — a disaster for health, for society and most of all for national economies." [4]

In September the United Nations unanimously called chronic diseases "a challenge of epidemic proportions" and set out a plan to develop global and national goals for disease reduction, particularly in low- and middle-income areas. [5]

Included in draft targets are recommendations to reduce smoking and decrease salt levels in food. [6] The WHO also developed a list of low- or no-cost disease-prevention steps that countries could adopt, such as promoting public awareness about diet and physical activity. [7]

In addition, the U.N. is working to accelerate implementation of the WHO Framework Convention on Tobacco Control, an international health treaty developed in 2003 that promotes tobacco regulation. [8]

As in the United States, attacking chronic diseases requires a multiprong approach, including strengthening health systems, changing government policies in areas such as urban planning and school physical education requirements and encouraging the involvement of business.

The global food industry has resisted stiffer government regulations, but some companies are participating in voluntary efforts. In 2008, the International Food and Beverage Alliance, which includes such giants as Coca-Cola, Kraft and Kellogg's, committed to five actions over five years to make products healthier: Reformulating food content, providing nutrition in-

Continued from p. 10

More bans followed, and now 3,487 U.S. municipalities restrict smoking. [39] Twenty-five states had comprehensive indoor smoking bans by 2010. [40] Airplanes were divided into smoking and no-smoking sections in 1973; in 1987 Congress began banning smoking on planes. [41]

While lung cancer was the most obviously preventable disease, evidence began to grow in the 1950s and '60s that other conditions could be controlled as well, particularly heart disease. The seminal Framingham Heart Study, launched in 1948 by the National Heart, Lung and Blood Institute, provided the telling data. Researchers recruited 5,209 men and women between the ages of 30 and 62 from Framingham, Mass., to identify risk factors for heart disease and stroke through extensive physical exams and lifestyle interviews. [42]

The study identified high blood pressure, blood triglyceride and cholesterol levels, age, gender, physical inactivity and psychosocial issues as possible drivers of disease. Other studies contributed as well, creating a solid body of evidence that diet, physical activity, smoking and alcohol abuse contribute to chronic diseases including stroke, heart disease, diabetes and cancer.

Focusing on the diseases as well as improvements in medical care began to have an effect. After peaking in the early 1990s, cancer rates have generally fallen since 1998. [43] From 1950 to 1996, deaths from heart disease fell by 56 percent, and deaths from stroke declined 70 percent. [44]

Obesity

As some risk factors for chronic diseases came more under control, including high cholesterol and blood pressure, another major health threat emerged: obesity. In 1960, 13 percent of American adults were obese. By 2008, the figure had risen to 34 percent. During the same period, the percentage of extremely obese adults rose from slightly less than 1 percent of adults to 6 percent. [45]

formation to consumers, advertising responsibly, raising awareness of nutritious diets and promoting physical activity. [9]

But some U.N. officials say such voluntary efforts are too weak to adequately address global health problems.

"World leaders must not bow to industry pressure," said Olivier De Schutter, U.N. Special Rapporteur on the Right to Food, a watchdog role at the international organization. "It is crucial for world leaders to counter food-industry efforts to sell unbalanced processed products and ready-to-serve meals too rich in trans fats and saturated fats, salt and sugars. Food advertising is proven to have a strong impact on children and must be strictly regulated in order to avoid the development of bad eating habits early in life." [10]

Despite the rapid growth in chronic illnesses around the globe, international aid aimed at helping developing countries improve their health systems has been weak. Only an estimated 3 percent of health-related development assistance is devoted to chronic disease. [11] That isn't expected to change any time soon as major donors, including the United States, face their own economic woes and continue to focus on current funding commitments, primarily to fight AIDS, tuberculosis, malaria and afflictions facing children and pregnant women.

Some view the focus as shortsighted. Without a stronger effort to reduce chronic diseases globally, said Ann Keeling, chair of NCD Alliance, an international coalition that focuses on the problem, "the world is essentially sleepwalking into a sick future." [12]

— Nellie Bristol

[1] "Global Status Report on Noncommunicable Diseases 2010," World Health Organization, www.who.int/nmh/publications/ncd_report2010/en/.

[2] "Chronic Disease in Developing Countries: Poor Countries are Developing the Diseases of the Rich, with Lethal Consequences," *The Economist*, Sept. 24, 2011, www.economist.com/node/21530099.

[3] World Health Organization, *op. cit.*

[4] Maddy French, "Why Non-Communicable Diseases Hit the Developing World So Hard," *The Guardian*, June 29, 2011, www.guardian.co.uk/journalismcompetition/why-non-communicable-diseases-hit-the-developing-world-so-hard.

[5] "Political Declaration of the High-level Meeting of the General Assembly on the Prevention and Control of Non-communicable Diseases," U.N. General Assembly, Sept. 16, 2011, www.un.org/ga/search/view_doc.asp?symbol=A%2F66%2FL.1&Lang=E.

[6] Nellie Bristol, "The UN Weighs Solutions to the Plague of Noncommunicable Disease," *Health Affairs*, November 2010.

[7] World Health Organization, *op. cit.*

[8] "Tobacco Control for Global Health and the Development/NCD Summit," Framework Convention Alliance, www.fctc.org/index.php?option=com_content&view=article&id=503:tobacco-control-and-global-health&catid=258:tobacco-control-and-global-health.

[9] "Who We Are," International Food and Beverage Alliance, www.ifballiance.org/about.html.

[10] "World Leaders Must Take Binding Steps to Curb Unhealthy Food Industry-UN Expert," UN News Centre, Sept. 16, 2011, www.un.org/apps/news/story.asp?NewsID=39578&Cr=non+communicable+diseases&Cr1=.

[11] Bristol, *op. cit.*

[12] Kate Kelland, "UN Summit Talks Stalled," Reuters, Aug., 17, 2011, www.idf.org/un-summit-talks-stalled-reuters-interview-ncda-chair-ann-keeling.

Excess weight is associated with a variety of diseases, including heart disease, Type 2 diabetes, some types of cancer, hypertension and stroke. In addition to health consequences, obesity is costly. Medical spending is 42 percent higher for obese people than for those of normal weight. [46] Diagnosed diabetes increased 164 percent from 1980 through 2009, according to the Centers for Disease Control and Prevention (CDC). [47] The disease can cause kidney problems and blindness and require lower-limb amputations. [48]

For many years, the afflictions associated with obesity, including diabetes and cardiovascular disease, were attributed to increased wealth and personal choice. But health experts now say a variety of social, policy and commercial factors are fueling the epidemic and must be addressed by policymakers and the private sector. Contributors to the nation's obesity epidemic include high fat, sugar and salt levels in packaged and fast foods, increased portion sizes and a car-based transportation system.

The public-health response focuses on several areas: increased consumption of fruits and vegetables; increased physical activity; breastfeeding; and decreased consumption of sugary drinks and energy-dense foods, such as meat, processed foods and sweets.

But reducing disease risk factors that are so embedded in society, personal in nature and driven by commercial interests from food manufacturers to tobacco companies has proven daunting. Jeffrey Levi, executive director of the Trust for America's Health, a Washington-based health advocacy group, says addressing current health conditions represents a shift for public health experts. (*See "At Issue," p. 17.*) Prevention traditionally focused on infectious disease, "breaking a chain of infection in some way," he says. Current health efforts, by contrast, focus on more intimate personal behaviors like food choices, "not something public health people traditionally have been terribly comfortable with."

Get Out of Your Car, Urban Planners Urge

"Complete Streets" program promotes bicycling and walking.

State and local lawmakers are trying to accomplish what years of preaching by the President's Council on Physical Fitness and other public health authorities have largely failed to do: Get people moving.

Twenty-five states and 314 city, country or regional jurisdictions have adopted so-called Complete Streets policies, pledging to consider installing bike lanes and sidewalks in future road-construction and major road-rehabilitation projects, according to the National Complete Streets Coalition, a Washington, D.C.-based advocacy group. [1]

The coalition, which encourages people to ditch their cars and build exercise into their daily lives, claims many benefits for the approach beyond disease prevention: improved pedestrian safety, greater use of better-connected commercial centers, fewer traffic jams and better air quality.

"We have this huge infrastructure investment in transportation, and the only thing we do with it is focus on moving cars," says Barbara McCann, the coalition's director.

New Jersey Transportation Commissioner James Simpson is a strong advocate of the approach. The state has its own Complete Streets policy, and 13 municipalities and one county have adopted versions. "A local Complete Streets policy raises awareness among residents, elected officials and the private sector," Simpson wrote. "When projects are proposed, pedestrian, bicycle and transit accommodations are no longer an afterthought — they become an integral feature of the overall investment plan." [2]

But Complete Streets policies don't have universal support. The St. Cloud, Minn., City Council initially rejected a proposal on a tie vote earlier this year because of concerns about redundancy with current policies, effects on new development and costs. [3] The council subsequently approved the proposal, however, when a supportive council member was able to vote a few weeks later. [4]

The New York State Association of Counties recently opposed a Complete Streets proposal in the General Assembly, saying budgets are too tight to give it priority and that the "diversion of effort and funding" mandated by the provision "would further the deterioration of our infrastructure." [5]

In Congress, Complete Streets bills have been introduced in the last three sessions, but none has moved forward.

The Complete Streets approach emerged in the late 1990s, when, McCann says, the President's Council on Physical Fitness was failing in its effort to get more people to exercise. The council brought its concerns to McCann, a writer and transportation expert working on ways to make streets friendlier to walkers and bikers.

"They said, 'OK, we have been trying to get people to go to the gym for years, and it's not working,' " McCann says. " 'There's just a totally flat line on the number of people who are willing to make a special time of day to exercise.' "

The movement got a major boost in 2003 when a report by Smart Growth America, a Washington group that supports better urban planning, equated suburban sprawl — and its reliance on driving rather than walking — with weight gain. "The results show that people in more sprawling counties are likely to

Community Prevention

Federal policies now support the concept of community prevention — developing local efforts to address the leading preventable causes of death and disability, obesity and tobacco use. The health reform bill passed by Congress in 2010 included a Prevention and Public Health Fund totaling $15 billion over its first 10 years. In addition to supporting preventive health initiatives, it funds public health infrastructure and workforce improvements, including research and disease tracking. [49] The fund also supports first lady Michelle Obama's Let's Move campaign, which aims to drastically curtail rising rates of childhood obesity through physical activity and improved nutrition. [50]

But not everyone is convinced. Critics said that by providing greater access to preventive services and disease screening, the reform act would in fact increase health costs. In addition, they said there was no guarantee that changes in communities would decrease health costs. Republican senators tried to remove the fund from the Senate version of the bill. Sen. Michael Enzi, R-Wyo., called the prevention fund "new pork barrel spending," adding, "The bill will pave sidewalks, build jungle gyms and open grocery stores, but it won't bring down health care costs or make quality [health] coverage more affordable." [51]

Doctors and public health experts increasingly focus on "evidence-based medicine," or scientifically proven medical interventions. They use the same strategies for disease prevention as well. The U.S. Preventive Services Task Force reviews evidence and makes recommendations to physicians about which screening tests, counseling, immunizations and preventive medications should be recommended to patients. [52]

The panel's findings are sometimes controversial. For example, in 2009 it raised the age at which it recommended that women with an

have a higher body-mass index," a summary of the research says. In addition, the research showed a "direct relationship" between sprawl and chronic disease, with the odds of high blood pressure increasing 6 percent for every measured increase in sprawl. [6]

Getty Images/Spencer Platt

Bike riders in Brooklyn's Prospect Park West got to keep a controversial bike lane after a judge in August 2011 rejected efforts by local residents to remove the lane. Mayor Michael Bloomberg has sought to make the city more bike and pedestrian friendly.

Some criticized the study's methods and conclusions, however. "This is just another attempt by the report's sponsors to spin research showing only trivial weight differences between city and suburban residents into a national crisis requiring land use restrictions," wrote researchers at the Heritage Foundation, a conservative think tank in Washington. [7]

Even McCann concedes that making a direct connection between planning policy and health has been elusive. "Just on the research side, we aren't quite 100 percent there yet on having a direct link between policy and body weight, but there's certainly a chain that's very clear," she says.

Nonetheless, McCann says the connection makes sense on an intuitive level to many planners, and they've started to respond to it. "We're having tremendous success at the state and local level because they really get it," she says.

McCann argues that despite current fiscal constraints, Complete Streets policies are not necessarily more expensive, but simply require engineers to think about a variety of users when planning transportation routes.

"In a way," McCann says, "you're trying to go back to the way communities used to be built."

— *Nellie Bristol*

[1] "Complete Streets Atlas," National Complete Streets Coalition, www.completestreets.org/complete-streets-fundamentals/complete-streets-atlas/.

[2] James Simpson, "Opinion: N.J. Complete Streets Policy Paves Way for Road Safety," *The Times of Trenton*, Nov. 18, 2011, www.nj.com/times-opinion/index.ssf/2011/11/opinion_nj_complete_streets_po.html.

[3] Kari Petrie, "MN: St. Cloud Votes No to Complete Streets Policy," *St. Cloud* [Minn.] *Times*, Sept. 13, 2011, www.masstransitmag.com/news/10356650/mn-st-cloud-votes-no-to-complete-streets-policy.

[4] Kari Petrie, "St. Cloud Leaders OK Complete Streets Policy," *St. Cloud* [Minn.] *Times*, Nov. 7, 2011, www.sctimes.com/article/20111108/NEWS01/111070061/St-Cloud-leaders-OK-complete-streets-policy.

[5] Noah Kazis, "NY Counties Oppose Complete Streets Bill Without Understanding It," Streetsblog.org, Feb. 8, 2011, www.streetsblog.org/2011/02/08/ny-counties-oppose-complete-streets-bill-without-understanding-it/.

[6] Barbara A. McCann and Reid Ewing, "Measuring the Health Effects of Sprawl: A National Analysis of Physical Activity Obesity and Chronic Disease," Smart Growth America, September 2003, www.smartgrowthamerica.org/report/HealthSprawl8.03.pdf.

[7] Wendell Cox and Ronald Utt, "Sprawl and Obesity: A Flawed Connection," Heritage Foundation, Sept. 19, 2003, www.heritage.org/research/reports/2003/09/sprawl-and-obesity-a-flawed-connection.

average risk for breast cancer should routinely receive mammograms. The change spurred a fierce debate among doctors, women, insurers and politicians. "Their justification: These new guidelines capture 81 percent of mammography's benefits [and] save a lot of resources, with only a 3 percent drop in survivorship from the most common cancer to affect women," said Marisa Weiss, president and founder of BreastCancer.org, a nonprofit cancer awareness and information site.

"But what really is the cost?," Weiss asks. "And who is paying the price? It could be you, your mom, daughter, sister, aunt or grandmother or all of us." [53] ■

CURRENT SITUATION

Public Health Targets

Despite the steady decline in smoking — from 42 percent of adults in 1965 to about 21 percent in 2009 — tobacco remains the primary cause of preventable death in the United States — 443,000 annually. [54] Smoking also is a major focus for public health efforts. [55]

The combination of obesity and inactivity ranks as the nation's second-leading killer, causing 112,000 deaths a year, according to the CDC. [56] While smoking-cessation policies have made progress through increased taxes and smoke-free regulations, public policy to control obesity has proved more difficult.

In order to create environments that support healthier habits, the Obama administration is strongly supporting community prevention efforts. The Prevention and Public Health Fund put $298 million of $750 million doled out in fiscal 2011 toward community efforts. "Prevention is something that can't just happen in a doctor's office," said Health and Human Services Secretary Kathleen Sebelius. "If we are to address the big health issues of our time, from physical inactivity to poor nutrition to tobacco use, it needs to happen in local communities." Funds were targeted toward reducing tobacco use, improving nutrition and increasing physical activity and coordinating efforts to prevent diabetes, heart disease and cancer. [57] The grants support, for example, a network of national telephone "quit lines" for smokers, and increased HIV testing opportunities. [58]

Food and the Workplace

Employers as well as the federal government are grappling with the right approach to curbing chronic diseases. As the insurance providers for nearly two-thirds of Americans under age 65, employers bear a heavy cost for an unhealthy workforce. [59] The cost to employers for all expenses related to health and lost productivity in 2002 was an average of $18,618 per employee. These costs include health insurance premiums, workers' compensation, short-term disability, long-term disability, sick leave and unpaid leave. Expenditures were 228 percent higher for employees with multiple risk factors for heart disease than for employees without the risk factors. Employees who smoke, get inadequate exercise, have high blood pressure and/or poor nutrition cost employers more in health care expenses, absenteeism and overall productivity. [60]

Workplace wellness programs, which try to control costs and improve employees' health, have become popular in recent years. Features include work-site health fairs, screenings and coaching and weight-management programs. Some employers are even developing programs that pay workers to change unhealthy habits. [61] The CDC is conducting a $9 million initiative to encourage workplace wellness programs, which it said could yield an average $3 return for every $1 spent over a two- to five-year period. [62]

Producers of fast food and packaged foods high in fat and sugar also are being targeted in the fight against chronic disease. An earlier Congress and the Obama administration have called on food companies to shift advertising aimed at children to healthier products. [63] Draft guidelines released in April would set voluntary limits on the amount of sodium, sugar and fats in foods advertised to children. Companies spend about $2 billion a year on advertising foods marketed to kids. In 2009, 86 percent of those products were high in calories, sodium, sugar or saturated fat, compared with 94 percent in 2003, when the industry began a self-regulatory program. But experts say the reduction in unhealthy ingredients isn't moving fast enough. [64]

The food and beverage industry is resisting the guidelines, which are now stalled and may be substantially revised. Industry representatives say they are trying gradually to reformulate their products because they worry that quick changes would result in lost customers. [65] "The food industry and the advertising industry have spent billions on reformulating food, changing advertising and putting together public service announcements," said Dan Jaffe, executive vice president for government relations at the Association of National Advertisers. "There is more to be done, but the critics are never going to be satisfied." [66]

Restaurants also are being asked to change. The Food and Drug Administration is drafting regulations to implement calorie count requirements for chain restaurants, a provision included in the health reform act signed into law in 2010. [67] CDC Director Thomas Frieden said the move "empowers people. It gives them information. It also is important because it gets the restaurants to think twice before they put up a 1,500-calorie breakfast. So it both makes the choices healthier and it makes the options healthier by getting some reformulation on the part

Continued on p. 18

Getty Images/Justin Sullivan

Smoking has declined from 43 percent of U.S. adults in 1965 to about 22 percent in 2009, but tobacco remains the nation's primary cause of preventable deaths — nearly half a million annually. Poor diet, lack of physical activity, smoking and alcohol abuse contribute to deadly chronic diseases including stroke, heart disease, diabetes and some cancers. About 4,000 U.S. communities and at least 25 states restrict smoking.

At Issue:

Should Americans be penalized for unhealthy behaviors?

MICHAEL PARKINSON
PAST PRESIDENT, AMERICAN COLLEGE OF PREVENTIVE MEDICINE
WENDY LYNCH
CO-DIRECTOR, CENTER FOR CONSUMER CHOICE IN HEALTH CARE, ALTARUM INSTITUTE

WRITTEN FOR *CQ RESEARCHER*, DECEMBER 2011

yes

Should they be penalized? They already are — and dramatically so. The health and pocketbooks of all Americans already have been hurt by our collective failure to clearly align financial and other incentives — both "carrots" and "sticks" — to help individuals improve health and reduce preventable disease. In truth, those who do not take an active role in their health and health care already are penalized by poor health and higher costs. When we shield consumers from the consequences of their own inaction — by shifting the entire excess cost to their fellow plan members — we compromise their safety and health while costs continue to escalate.

So, let's pose the same question from a reverse perspective: Should we give consumers an opportunity to save money by doing things that are known to improve health and lower costs? We would say yes.

Unsustainable cost trends not only place an unbearable burden on our national debt but also strain the budgets of each family. Some of the overarching drivers of cost are preventable chronic illnesses, medical errors and use of unnecessary or ineffective treatments. All of these cost drivers can be reduced when consumers take an active role in their own care. We can support that active involvement by creating an "environment" (culture, physical spaces, policies and programs) that promotes and sustains better individual choices and actions.

Over a lifetime, one's own behaviors contribute more to health and health care needs than medical treatments will. Individuals who are engaged in their care are less likely to experience errors such as incorrect medications and are more likely to choose appropriate care. Thus, anything that encourages prevention and rewards wise health care choices not only saves money but also averts harm.

Our preferred method of giving people an opportunity to save money is through a funded Health Savings Account. That money serves as a pool of funds to cover expenses before a deductible is reached. If the consumer does not need health care, or can find less expensive alternatives, it accumulates. But consumers can choose to spend it if they want or need to. In this way, each family can choose whether it is worth protecting money (and health) by preventing disease and making wise care choices. That is not punishment, it is personal choice.

JEFFREY LEVI
EXECUTIVE DIRECTOR, TRUST FOR AMERICA'S HEALTH; CHAIR, ADVISORY GROUP ON PREVENTION, HEALTH PROMOTION, AND INTEGRATIVE AND PUBLIC HEALTH

WRITTEN FOR *CQ RESEARCHER*, DECEMBER 2011

no

It is not government's place to ensure that citizens do every last push-up or sit-up. Each of us is personally responsible for making healthy choices for ourselves and our children to prevent illness and promote well-being in our own lives.

However, local, state and federal policymakers can help kids and everyone else, too, by making healthy choices easy choices by providing accessible, safe places to walk, jog, bike, swim, take an exercise class or play sports. In addition, government can improve nutrition and physical-education programs in schools and launch initiatives to reduce tobacco use, especially among children and adolescents.

Ensuring a healthy citizenry isn't about taking punitive measures but, rather, encouraging people to be what they want to be: healthy, productive and happy.

Thankfully, with the creation of the Prevention and Public Health Fund, included in the Affordable Care Act, government has sent the message that it is going to do its best to help people stay healthy in the first place, rather than wait for them to get sick. This is the best, most commonsense way to reduce health care costs and spur economic growth.

A hallmark program of the prevention fund is the Community Transformation Grants (CTGs), which provide communities with the resources needed to work together at the local level to create health initiatives tailored to their specific needs. This can involve small-business owners, faith leaders, youth leaders, employers, community groups, parents, law enforcement officials, schools, and health care providers. Through the CTGs, communities are empowered to create the programs and initiatives that they know will help make the healthy choices easier for all.

You catch more flies with honey than vinegar, as the saying goes. It is government's role to support individuals and communities as they choose to stay active and fit, not penalize them if they fail to do so.

Through support and encouragement, we can spare millions of Americans from developing serious, preventable diseases and, in so doing, shift the paradigm from a sick-care system that focuses on treating disease after it happens to a health care system, where we keep people healthy in the first place.

Continued from p. 16

of the restaurant industry." Nonetheless, Frieden said, calorie labeling remains only a "modestly effective intervention" that can be overrun by things like low prices. He cited a restaurant chain that discounted a high-calorie foot-long sandwich that resulted in an increase in calories consumed per customer. [68]

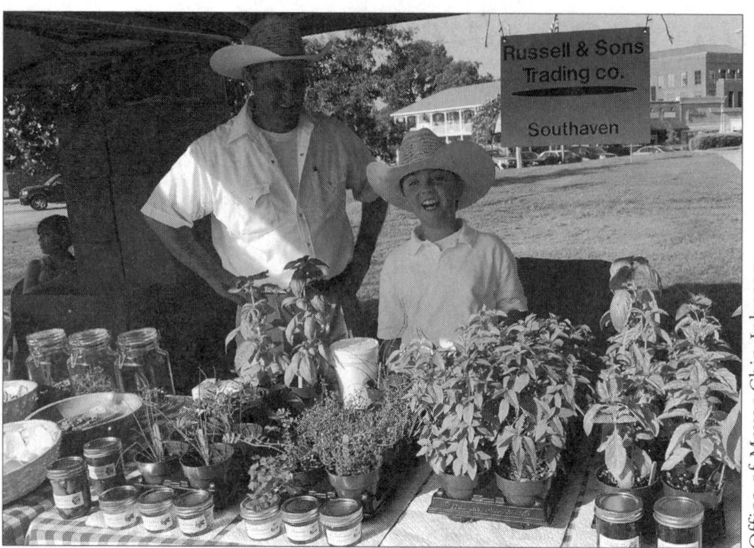

Office of Mayor Chip Johnson

The road to healthier living — and a more business-friendly community — leads to the farmers market in Hernando, Miss. "We want to recruit corporations to Hernando," said Mayor Chip Johnson. "They're not stupid. When they make their decisions, they look at health care costs."

Unhealthy foods are being attacked in others ways as well. In 2004, restaurants in affluent Tiburon, Calif., voluntarily stopped using cooking oil with trans fats, making it the first "trans fat free" city in the country. [69] Other jurisdictions followed, notably, New York City in 2006. [70]

Other Initiatives

In other federal efforts, the CDC and the Centers for Medicare and Medicaid Services (CMS) recently started the Million Hearts Campaign aimed at reducing heart attacks and strokes over the next five years. The program focuses on improving access to effective, quality care, increasing clinical attention to heart attack and stroke prevention, promoting heart-healthy lifestyles and consistent use of high-blood-pressure and cholesterol medications. [71]

Medicare also is focusing more on prevention. CMS announced in November that the program would begin covering obesity screening and counseling in a primary-care setting for beneficiaries whose body mass index (BMI) is 30 or more. Under the change, beneficiaries are entitled to a face-to-face counseling session with a health care provider each week for a month followed by sessions every other week for an additional five months. Participants who lose at least 6.6 pounds during the first six months of counseling are entitled to additional visits every month for six months. [72]

Earlier in the month, CMS announced Medicare coverage of intensive behavioral therapy for cardiovascular disease. The program includes promotion of aspirin use, screening for high blood pressure and intensive behavioral counseling to promote a healthy diet to fight known risk factors for cardiovascular and diet-related chronic disease. [73]

Preventive medicine expert Parkinson is concerned that the level of payment is too low and that many physicians may not have the skills necessary to adequately perform the task. "Beyond wagging their finger at you and saying, 'you really need to lose weight,' most doctors really don't have the cognitive therapy, the motivational skills to do that." Nonetheless, he says, "the physician initiating and asking about how you're doing on weight and saying how important it is to reverse your diabetes is very, very pivotal."

Getting the imprimatur of a health care payer as large as Medicare is an important step in better engaging the health care system to address lifestyle issues, he adds. The coverage changes, he says, "are important landmarks to progress because what Medicare has finally said is the physician and the delivery system have an important role, not a sole role, but a very important role to both initiate and sustain behavior change, which is the only way we're going to get out of this crisis." ■

OUTLOOK

Two Steps Forward . . .

The importance of chronic disease prevention is gaining attention as more people realize both its health and fiscal costs.

Employers are developing new ways to help employees change unhealthy behaviors. Meanwhile, policymakers are paying more attention to the way social environments and commercial forces affect lifestyle choices.

In the policy realm, the Patient Protection and Affordable Care Act — the Obama administration's signature health care law — has given unprecedented attention and funding to prevention activities. "In addition to establishing the Prevention and Public Health Fund, the act also requires Medicare and some private insurers to cover certain preventive services, such as cancer screening, without patient co-pays.

However, the fund is threatened by federal budget cuts, and the health care law's legality is being challenged in the Supreme Court, which will decide that issue this year.

Jud Richland, president and CEO of Partnership for Prevention, a coalition of business, nonprofit and government groups, says even if the health care law is repealed or struck down, insurers are likely to continue to support clinical preventive services but that many community intervention programs are likely to lose funding if the prevention fund is raided or killed.

On the state and local levels, lawmakers could continue to enact policies limiting trans fats, requiring menu labeling and mandating other health-related measures. Richland notes that indoor clean-air laws took years to be passed but became popular once implemented. "The momentum's going in the right direction" for other preventive health laws, he says.

New technologies may encourage prevention as well. Smart-phone applications are coming on line that will help people keep track of their blood pressure, count calories or get fitness coaching. [74] A recent report by ABI Research said the market for health and fitness apps will reach $400 million by 2016. [75]

Nonetheless, despite years of messages about good diet and exercise, experts worry Americans could continue to fall short in those areas.

After dropping consistently for several decades, the proportion of Americans who smoke has stayed relatively steady since 2004. [76] Fewer than 20 percent of adults participate in adequate leisure-time aerobic and muscle-building activity. [77] Only 26 percent eat vegetables three or more times a day. [78]

Overall, the United Health Foundation found that reductions in smoking, preventable hospitalizations and cardiovascular deaths were offset last year by increases in obesity, diabetes and childhood poverty. [79]

A massive culture shift is needed, says North Carolina preventive medicine physician Tilson. "It's hard to get people to change behaviors, especially when their entire environment and culture is against them every step of the way," she says. "It's really hard to be healthy in our society right now."

Tilson says her own office reflects that difficulty. Despite having a workplace wellness plan that promotes a healthy diet and adequate exercise, she says, staff members frequently bring in baked goods, and product sales representatives bring cookies and candy for the staff.

"Even our closest friends undermine us," she says. Love and support is "equated with giving sugar." ■

Notes

1 "America's Health Rankings," United Health Foundation, November 2011, http://statehealthstats.americashealthrankings.org/#/state/US/MS/2011.

2 "Healthy Americas for A Healthier Economy," Trust for America's Health, October 2011, http://healthyamericans.org/report/90/.

3 *Ibid.*

4 *Ibid.*

5 "United Health Foundation's America's Health Rankings Finds Preventable Chronic Disease on the Rise; Obesity, Diabetes Undermining Country's Overall Health," United Health Foundation, Dec. 6, 2011, www.americashealthrankings.org/mediacenter/mediacenter1.aspx.

6 "Chronic Diseases: The Power to Prevent, The Call to Control: At a Glance 2009," Centers for Disease Control and Prevention, Dec. 17, 2009, www.cdc.gov/chronicdisease/resources/publications/AAG/chronic.htm.

7 "An Unhealthy Truth: Rising Rates of Chronic Disease and the Future of Health in America," Partnership to Fight Chronic Disease, www.fightchronicdisease.org/.../UnhealthyTruths_UPDATED.pptx.

8 "Non-Communicable Diseases to Cost $47 Trillion by 2030, New Study Released Today," World Economic Forum, Sept. 18, 2011, www.weforum.org/news/non-communicable-diseases-cost-47-trillion-2030-new-study-released-today.

9 "Preventing Chronic Diseases: A Vital Investment," 2005, World Health Organization, p. 9, www.who.int/chp/chronic_disease_report/full_report.pdf.

10 Dan Harris and Mikaela Conley, "Childhood Obesity: A Call for Parents to Lose Custody," ABC News, July 14, 2011, http://abcnews.go.com/Health/childhood-obesity-call-parents-lose-custody/story?id=14068280.

11 *Ibid.*

12 "Obesity 'Epidemic' May Be Overstated," UPI.com, March 27, 2009, www.upi.com/Health_News/2009/03/17/Obesity-epidemic-may-be-overstated/UPI-50681237311372/.

13 Andy Barr, "Sarah Palin Brings Cookies, Hits 'Nanny State,' " *Politico*, Nov. 10, 2010, www.politico.com/news/stories/1110/44936.html.

14 "Childhood Obesity Facts," Centers for Disease Control and Prevention, www.cdc.gov/healthyyouth/obesity/facts.htm.

15 Nell Katz, "Sarah Palin: Americans Have 'God-Given Right' to be Fat?" CBS, Nov. 30, 2010, www.cbsnews.com/8301-504763_162-20024104-10391704.html.

16 "Too Fat to Fight: Retired Military Leaders Want Junk Food Out of America's Schools," Mission: Readiness: Military Leaders for Kids, 2010, http://cdn.missionreadiness.org/MR_Too_Fat_to_Fight-1.pdf.

17 *Ibid.*

18 "Fast Facts," Kaiser Family Foundation, http://facts.kff.org/.

19 "National Health Expenditure Data," Centers for Medicare and Medicaid Services, www.cms.gov/NationalHealthExpendData/25_NHE_Fact_sheet.asp.

20 Joshua T. Cohen, *et al.*, "Does Preventive Care Save Money? Health Economics and the Presidential Candidates," *The New England Journal of Medicine*, Feb. 14, 2008.

21 Sarah Goodell, *et al.*, "Cost Savings and Cost-Effectiveness of Clinical Preventive Care," Robert Wood Johnson Foundation, September 2009, www.rwjf.org/files/research/48508.costsavings.preventivecare.brief.pdf.

22 "Prevention for a Healthier America: Investments in Disease Prevention Yield Significant Savings, Stronger Communities," Trust for America's Health, July 2008, http://healthyamericans.org/reports/prevention08/Prevention08.pdf.

23 Uwe E. Reinhardt, "Cost Effectiveness Analysis and US Health Care," Economix, *The New York Times*, http://economix.blogs.nytimes.com/

2009/03/13/cost-effectiveness-analysis-and-us-health-care.

[24] "Public Transit Systems Contribute to Weight Los and Improved Health, Study Finds," *ScienceDaily*, June 28, 2010, www.sciencedaily.com/releases/2010/06/100628203756.htm.

[25] Jill U. Adams, "'Pizza Vegetable' Controversy is a Hot Potato: A Law Blocking New Regulations of Tomato Paste, Spuds and Salt in School Meals Causes a Stir," *Los Angeles Times*, Nov. 28, 2011, www.latimes.com/health/la-he-school-lunch-nutrition-20111128,0,4859084,print.story.

[26] *Ibid.*

[27] Derek Yach, *et al.*, "The Role and Challenges of the Food Industry in Addressing Chronic Disease," *Globalization and Health*, 2010, 6:10, www.globalizationandhealth.com/content/6/1/10.

[28] *Ibid.*

[29] Julie Rovner, "Future of Primary Care? Some Say 'Medical Home,' " NPR, Aug. 26, 2010, www.npr.org/templates/story/story.php?storyId=129432707.

[30] Parija B. Kavilanz, "Family Doctors: An Endangered Breed," CNNMoney, July 18, 2009, http://money.cnn.com/2009/07/16/news/economy/healthcare_doctors_shortage/index.htm.

[31] "Immunization Timeline," Keepkidshealthy.com, www.keepkidshealthy.com/welcome/immunizations/immunization_timeline.html.

[32] Rita Rubin, "First-ever Cancer Vaccine Approved," *USA Today*, June 8 2006, www.usatoday.com/news/health/2006-06-08-cervical-cancer-vaccine_x.htm.

[33] Shari Roan, "Despite Concerns, Most Parents Get Their Kids Vaccinated," *Los Angeles Times*, June 9, 2011, http://articles.latimes.com/2011/jun/09/news/la-heb-child-vaccines-20110609. For background see the following *CQ Researcher* reports: Nellie Bristol, "HPV Vaccine," May 11, 2007, pp. 409-432; Kathy Koch, "Vaccine Controversies," Aug. 25, 2000, pp. 641-672 and Sarah Glazer, "Increase in Autism," June 13, 2003, pp. 545-568 (updated July 22, 2010).

[34] "Achievements in Public Health, 1900-1999: Tobacco Use-United States, 1900-1999," *MMWR*, Centers for Disease Control and Prevention, Nov. 5, 1999, 48(43); 986-993, www.cdc.gov/mmwr/preview/mmwrhtml/mm4843a2.htm#fig1.

[35] "The Reports of the Surgeon General: the 1964 Report on Smoking and Health," National Library of Medicine, http://profiles.nlm.nih.gov/ps/retrieve/Narrative/NN/p-nid/60.

[36] *Ibid.*

[37] "Smoking and Tobacco Use, Consumption Data," Centers for Disease Control and Prevention, www.cdc.gov/tobacco/data_statistics/tables/economics/consumption.

[38] Martiga Lohn, "Minnesota Lawmakers Approve Smoking Ban," The Associated Press, May 13, 2007, http://articles.boston.com/2007-05-13/news/29226864_1_bars-and-restaurants-public health experts smoking-ban-limited-smoking.

[39] "Overview List-How Many Smoke Free Laws?" American Nonsmokers' Rights Foundation, www.no-smoke.org/pdf/mediaordlist.pdf.

[40] Mike Stobbe, "Will Every U.S. State Have a Smoking Ban by 2010?" *The Huffington Post*, April 21, 2011, www.huffingtonpost.com/2011/04/21/cdc-predicts-every-us-wil_n_852125.html.

[41] Glenn Kramon, "Smoking Ban Near on Flights in the US," *The New York Times*, April 17, 1988, www.nytimes.com/1988/04/17/us/smoking-ban-near-on-flights-in-us.html.

[42] "History of the Framingham Heart Study," Framingham Heart Study, www.framinghamheartstudy.org/about/history.html.

[43] "Trends Progress Report," National Cancer Institute, http://progressreport.cancer.gov/doc_detail.asp?pid=1&did=2009&chid=93&coid=920&mid=#trends.

[44] "Achievements in Public Health 1900-1999: Decline in Deaths from Heart Disease and Stroke, United States 1900 to 1999," Centers for Disease Control and Prevention, www.cdc.gov/mmwr/preview/mmwrhtml/mm4830a1.htm.

[45] Cynthia Ogden, *et al.*, "Prevalence of Overweight, Obesity and Extreme Obesity Among Adults: United States, Trends 1960-1962 through 2007-2008," Centers for Disease Control and Prevention, June 2010, www.cdc.gov/NCHS/data/hestat/obesity_adult_07_08/obesity_adult_07_08.pdf.

[46] Nellie Bristol, "US Target Disease Prevention in Health Reforms," *The Lancet*, Dec. 12, 2009, http://download.thelancet.com/pdfs/journals/lancet/PIIS0140673609621073.pdf.

[47] "Crude and Age Adjusted Percentage of Civilian, Noninstitutionalized Population with Diagnosed Diabetes, United States 1980-2009," Centers for Disease Control and Prevention, www.cdc.gov/diabetes/statistics/prev/national/figage.htm.

[48] For background, see the following *CQ Researcher* reports: Barbara Mantel, "Preventing Obesity," Oct. 1, 2010, pp. 797-820; Alan Greenblatt, "Obesity Epidemic," Jan. 31, 2003, pp. 73-104; and Adriel Bettelheim, "Obesity and Health," Jan. 15, 1999, pp. 25-48.

[49] "Affordable Care Act: Laying the Foundation for Prevention," HealthReform.gov, www.healthreform.gov/newsroom/acaprevention.html.

[50] Let's Move, www.letsmove.gov.

[51] *Ibid.*, http://articles.chicagotribune.com/2009-08-05/news/0908050021_1_health-care-bike-paths-additional-pork-barrel-projects.

[52] "Recommendations for Adults," U.S. Preventive Services Task Force, www.uspreventiveservicestaskforce.org/adultrec.htm.

[53] Lauren Cox, "Stop Annual Mammograms, Govt. Panel Tells Women Under 50," ABC News, Nov. 16, 2009, http://abcnews.go.com/Health/OnCallPlusBreastCancerNews/mammogram-guidelines-spur-debate-early-detection/story?id=9099145.

[54] "Trends in Tobacco Use," American Lung Cancer Association, July 2011, www.lungusa.org/finding-cures/our-research/trend-reports/Tobacco-Trend-Report.pdf.

[55] "Tobacco Use: Targeting the Nation's Leading Killer At a Glance 2011," Centers for Disease Control and Prevention, www.cdc.gov/chronicdisease/resources/publications/AAG/osh.htm.

[56] "Frequently Asked Questions about Calculating Obesity-Related Risk," Centers for Disease Control and Prevention, undated, accessed Jan. 2, 2012, www.cdc.gov/PDF/Frequently_Asked_Questions_About_Calculating_Obesity-Related_risk.pdf.

[57] "HHS Announces $750 million Investment in Prevention," Department of Health and Human Services, www.hhs.gov/news/press/2011pres/

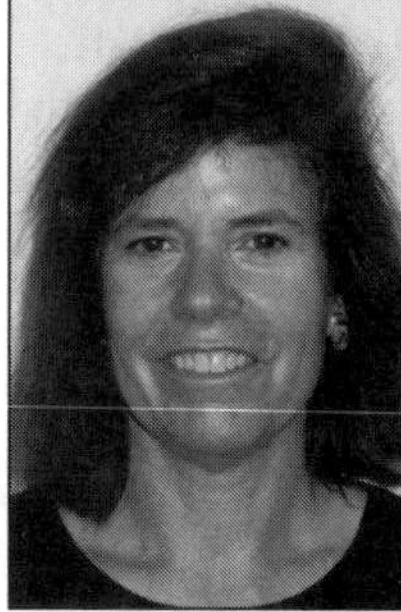

About the Author

Nellie Bristol is a veteran Capitol Hill reporter who has covered health policy in Washington for more than 20 years. She now writes for *The Lancet*, *Health Affairs* and *Global Health* magazine. She recently earned a master's degree in public health/global health from The George Washington University, where she earned an undergraduate degree in American studies.

02/20110209b.html.

[58] "The Affordable Care Act's Prevention and Public Health Fund in Your State," Department of Health and Human Services, www.healthcare.gov/news/factsheets/2011/02/prevention02092011a.html.

[59] "Employer-Sponsored Health Insurance: Trends in Cost and Access," Agency for Healthcare Research and Quality, www.ahrq.gov/research/empspria/empspria.htm.

[60] "Promoting Workplace Health," The Healthy States Initiative, January 2008, www.healthystates.csg.org/NR/rdonlyres/B6FC0AB2-A14A-4321-AAF8-778E57AA9752/0/LPBWorkplaceHealth_screen.pdf.

[61] Lenny Bernstein, "Do Programs that Pay People to Lose Weight Really Work?," *The Washington Post*, Oct. 10, 2011, www.washingtonpost.com/lifestyle/wellness/do-programs-that-pay-people-to-lose-weight-really-work/2011/10/06/gIQAiIABbL_story.html.

[62] "Affordable Care Act Helps Improve the Health of the American Workforce, Increase Workplace Health Programs," Centers for Disease Control and Prevention, press release, Sept. 30, 2011, www.cdc.gov/media/releases/2011/p0930_improve_healthcare.html.

[63] William Neuman, "Ad Rules Stall, Keeping Cereal a Cartoon Staple," *The New York Times*, July 23, 2010, www.nytimes.com/2010/07/24/business/media/24food.html.

[64] Gretchen Goetz, "Obama Urged to Push Kids' Food Marketing Regs," *Food Safety News*, Sept. 29, 2011, www.foodsafetynews.com/2011/09/academics-urge-obama-to-push-child-food-marketing-regulations.

[65] Barbara Mantel, "Preventing Obesity," *CQ Researcher*, Oct. 1, 2010, pp. 977-1000.

[66] *Ibid.*

[67] Jonathan Berman, "Proposed FDA Regulations to Require 'Chain Restaurants' to Post Nutrition Information," Sept. 27, 2011, www.mondaq.com/unitedstates/x/146784/Healthcare+Food+Drugs+Law/Proposed+FDA+Regulations+To+Require+Chain+Restaurants+To+Post+Nutrition+Information.

[68] Eli Y. Adashi, "CDC Director Talks About the Nation's Biggest (and Winnable?) Health Battles," *Medscape Internal Medicine*, Nov. 5, 2010, www.medscape.com/viewarticle/731362.

[69] Jim Staats, "Tiburon's Trans Fat Ban Started National Movement," *The Marin Independent Journal*, Feb. 3, 2007, www.marinij.com/fastsearchresults/ci_5155266.

[70] Thomas J. Lueck and Kim Severson, "New York Bans Most Trans Fats in Restaurants," *The New York Times*, Dec. 6, 2006, www.nytimes.com/2006/12/06/nyregion/06fat.html.

[71] "Million Hearts: About the Campaign," Department of Health and Human Services, htttp://millionhearts.hhs.gov/about-mh.shtml.

[72] Robert Lowes, "Medicare Decision to Cover Obesity Counseling Mostly Praised," *Medscape News*, Nov. 30, 2011, www.medscape.com/viewarticle/754531.

[73] "Decision Memo for Intensive Behavioral Therapy for Cardiovascular Disease," Centers for Medicare and Medicaid Services, Nov. 8, 2011, www.cms.gov/medicare-coverage-database/details/nca-decision-memo.aspx?NCAId=248.

[74] Carla Carter, "Smartphone Apps Keep Health at Your Fingertips, From Fitness to First Aid," *USA Today*, Feb. 2011, http://yourlife.usatoday.com/health/story/2011/02/Smartphone-apps-keep-health-at-your-fingertips-from-fitness-to-first-aid/44130448/1.

[75] Chris Gullo, "By 2016: $400M Market for Health, Fitness Apps," *Mobihealthnews*, Nov. 28, 2011, http://mobihealthnews.com/14884/by-2016-400m-market-for-health-fitness-apps/.

[76] "Trends in Current Cigarette Smoking Among High School Students and Adults, United States, 1965-2010, Centers for Disease Control and Prevention, www.cdc.gov/tobacco/data_statistics/tables/trends/cig_smoking/index.htm.

[77] "Exercise or Physical Activity," Centers for Disease Control and Prevention, www.cdc.gov/nchs/fastats/exercise.htm.

[78] Kim Severson, "Told to Eat Its Vegetables, America Orders French Fries," *The New York Times*, Sept. 24, 2010, www.nytimes.com/2010/09/25/health/policy/25vegetables.html?pagewanted=all.

[79] "America's Health Rankings Finds Preventable Chronic Disease on the Rise; Obesity, Diabetes Undermining Country's Overall Health," United Health Foundation, Dec. 6, 2011, www.americashealthrankings.org/mediacenter/mediacenter1.aspx.

FOR MORE INFORMATION

Centers for Disease Control and Prevention, 1600 Clifton Rd., Atlanta, GA 30333; 800-232-4636; www.cdc.gov. U.S. agency tasked with protecting public health and safety primarily through disease control and prevention.

National Complete Streets Coalition, 1707 L St., N.W., Suite 250, Washington, DC 20036; 202-207-3355; www.completestreets.org. Advocates for the development of state, local and national policies to encourage making streets safe and accessible to all types of transportation, including walking and biking.

Partnership for Prevention, 1015 18th St., N.W., Suite 300, Washington, DC 20036; 202-833-0009; www.prevent.org. A group of business, nonprofit and government leaders advocating evidence-based disease prevention and health promotion.

Robert Wood Johnson Foundation, Route 1 and College Road East, PO Box 2316, Princeton, NJ 08543; 877-843-7953; www.rwjf.org. Provides research and grants for health-improvement activities.

Smart Growth America, 1707 L St., N.W., Suite 1050, Washington, DC 20036; 202-207-3355; www.smartgrowthamerica.org. Advocates neighborhood planning that allows for sidewalks, bike paths and easy access to public transportation.

Trust for America's Health, 1730 M St., N.W., Suite 900, Washington, DC 20036; 202-223-9870; http://healthyamericans.org. Promotes public health and disease prevention.

United Health Foundation, Mail Stop: W150, 9900 Bren Road East, Minnetonka, MN 55343; www.unitedhealthfoundation.org/Main/Default.aspx. Provides funding and resources for programs that lead to better health outcomes and healthier communities.

World Health Organization, Avenue Appia 20m 1211, Geneva, 27, Switzerland; +41 22 791 21 11; www.who.int/en/. United Nations agency that coordinates international public health efforts.

Bibliography

Selected Sources

Books

Duffy, John, *The Sanitarians: A History of American Public Health*, University of Illinois Press, 1990.
A preeminent historian of medicine examines public health in the United States.

Faust, Halley, and Paul Menzel, eds., *Prevention vs. Treatment: What's the Right Balance?*, Oxford Press, 2012.
A preventive medicine physician (Faust) and a philosophy professor (Menzel) review a range of issues on preventive care, including spending on prevention and preventive care's apparent lack of emphasis in the medical field.

Guthman, Julie, *Weighing In: Obesity, Food Justice and the Limits of Capitalism*, University of California Press, 2011.
An associate professor in the Community Studies Department at the University of California, Santa Cruz, takes on the "obesity epidemic," challenging many widely held assumptions about its causes and consequences.

Articles

Kliff, Sarah, "What if Prevention Doesn't Save Money?" *The Washington Post*, Dec. 12, 2011, www.washingtonpost.com/blogs/ezra-klein/post/what-if-prevention-doesnt-save-money/2011/12/11/gIQAM60OnO_blog.html.
A health care reporter considers whether preventive services reduce medical costs.

Konrad, Walecia, "Preventing Sickness, With Plenty of Red Tape," *The New York Times*, Sept. 20, 2011, p. D5, www.nytimes.com/2011/09/20/health/policy/20consumer.html.
Ambiguity persists among consumers and insurers as to what qualifies as preventive care.

Landro, Laura, "Improving Global Health: Focus on Chronic Disease," *The Wall Street Journal*, Nov. 21, 2011, http://online.wsj.com/article/SB10001424052970203699404577042540087339770.html.
Health care experts discuss medical challenges in developing countries.

Lazar, Kay, "Employers Seeing Pluses in Keeping Workers Healthy," *The Boston Globe*, May 31, 2011, p. 1, articles.boston.com/2011-05-31/bostonworks/29604741_1_wellness-programs-health-promotion-programs-professor-of-health-economics.
More employers are embracing wellness programs to foster healthier lifestyles.

Stewart, Kirsten, "Mixed Messages on Health Prevention Baffle Consumers," *The Salt Lake Tribune* (Utah), May 26, 2011, www.sltrib.com/sltrib/home2/51876215-183/cancer-health-prevention-burt.html.csp.
Medicare beneficiaries are taking advantage of new federal regulations that give them free wellness checkups, but few are lining up for high-cost procedures.

Williams, Misty, "Costs Inspire Wellness Plans, Higher Deductibles," *The Atlanta Journal-Constitution*, Nov. 24, 2011, p. A1.
Rising out-of-pocket health care costs are encouraging more and more Atlanta-area workers to join wellness programs.

Reports

"F as in Fat: How Obesity Threatens America's Future," Trust for America's Health, 2011, Robert Wood Johnson Foundation, http://healthyamericans.org/report/88/.
Adult obesity rates increased in 16 states in the past year and did not decline in any state. Twelve states now have obesity rates above 30 percent.

"Global Status Report on Noncommunicable Diseases, 2010," World Health Organization, 2011, www.who.int/nmh/publications/ncd_report2010/en/.
WHO presents the latest global figures on noncommunicable diseases and recommendations for addressing them.

"Healthier Americans for a Healthier Economy," Trust for America's Health, November 2011, http://healthyamericans.org/report/90/.
Six case studies examine how health affects the ability of states and cities to attract and retain employers and how wellness programs can improve productivity and reduce health spending.

"Measuring the Health Effects of Sprawl: A National Analysis of Physical Activity, Obesity and Chronic Disease," Smart Growth America, September 2003, www.smartgrowthamerica.org/report/HealthSprawl8.03.pdf.
An advocacy group discusses research showing connections among urban sprawl, weight gain and high blood pressure.

"Preventing Childhood Obesity: Health in the Balance," Institute of Medicine, Sept. 29, 2004, www.iom.edu/Reports/2004/Preventing-Childhood-Obesity-Health-in-the-Balance.aspx.
A leading medical advisory group offers a comprehensive national strategy that recommends specific actions for families, schools, industry, communities and the government.

"Preventing Chronic Disease: The New Public Health," Alliance for Health Reform, September 2001, www.allhealth.org/publications/Public_health/Preventing_Chronic_Disease_New_Public_Health_108.pdf.
The United States faces "an epidemic of chronic disease," and preventive steps at the community level are an important antidote, says the nonpartisan organization.

The Next Step:

Additional Articles from Current Periodicals

Complete Streets

Adams, Jim, "Down a New, Green Path," *Star Tribune* (Minneapolis), June 11, 2011, p. B1, www.startribune.com/local/south/123670044.html.

About 18 Minnesota cities have adopted "green" street plans intended to make roads safer for all users, according to the state's Complete Streets Coalition.

Garofolo, Chris, "Gov Signs Into Law 'Complete Streets,' " *Brattleboro* (Vt.) *Reformer*, May 19, 2011.

Democratic Vermont Gov. Peter Shumlin has signed into law a bill that ensures that the state's transportation policy accommodates the needs of bicyclists and pedestrians of all ages and abilities.

Murphy, Edward D., "City Seeking a Better Way to Get Around," *Portland* (Maine) *Press Herald*, March 9, 2011, p. A1, www.pressherald.com/news/city-seeking-a-better-way-to-get-around_2011-03-09.html.

The City Council of Portland, Maine, has created a Complete Streets working group to develop a policy that ensures the city's streets can accommodate cars, buses, bikes and pedestrians safely.

Costs

Fox, Staci, "Affordable Preventive Care Saves Women's Lives," *Gainesville* (Fla.) *Sun*, Aug. 25, 2011, www.gainesville.com/article/20110825/OPINION/110829695.

New health care legislation allows women to stop avoiding preventive care services because of their cost, according to the CEO of Planned Parenthood of North Florida.

Madison, Erin, "Prevention Good for Your Health and Your Wallet," *Great Falls* (Mont.) *Tribune*, Aug. 23, 2011, p. 4.

A provision in the Patient Protection and Affordable Care Act requires certain preventive-care services to be fully covered by insurance.

VandeBunte, Matt, "Insurance Price Increase Is a Whole Lot of 'Nothing,' " *Grand Rapids* (Mich.) *Press*, Jan. 3, 2011, p. A1, www.mlive.com/business/west-michigan/index.ssf/2011/01/column_health_insurance_price.html.

New mandated health benefits such as expanded preventive care are causing insurers to pass on the costs to consumers.

Worth, Tammy, "More Care, Less Out-of-Pocket," *Los Angeles Times*, Jan. 24, 2011, p. E3, articles.latimes.com/2011/jan/24/health/la-he-preventive-care-20110124.

The Patient Protection and Affordable Care Act has allowed many Americans to gain access to vaccines, screening and other preventive care services without copayments.

Government Policies

Banjoko, Kimberley, "New Bill to Modify New York State Health Care Laws," *New York Amsterdam News*, July 21, 2011, p. 31, www.amsterdamnews.com/news/article_17f1f786-b306-11e0-9e74-001cc4c002e0.html.

New York lawmakers are working to align the state's policies for preventive care with the new federal guidelines.

Sealover, Ed, "Confusion Slows Compliance in Preventive Services," *Denver Business Journal*, Feb. 18, 2011, www.bizjournals.com/denver/print-edition/2011/02/18/confusion-slows-compliance.html?page=all.

New federal laws requiring insurers to cover preventive medical services are being enforced inconsistently in Colorado, according to the state's Department of Public Health and Environment.

Wellness Programs

Burden, Melissa, "Priority Health Ups Wellness Offerings," *Detroit News*, Oct. 12, 2011, p. D2.

A Michigan nonprofit insurer of more than 625,000 people is offering employers new choices for wellness-based health plans.

Hess, Corrinne, "Health Tax Credits in the Works," *Milwaukee Business Journal*, May 13, 2011, www.bizjournals.com/milwaukee/print-edition/2011/05/13/healthy-tax-credits-in-the-works.html.

Two Wisconsin lawmakers want tax credits for employers that offer employee wellness programs in an effort to lower overall health costs.

CITING *CQ RESEARCHER*

Sample formats for citing these reports in a bibliography include the ones listed below. Preferred styles and formats vary, so please check with your instructor or professor.

MLA STYLE

Jost, Kenneth. "Remembering 9/11," CQ Researcher 2 Sept. 2011: 701-732.

APA STYLE

Jost, K. (2011, September 2). Remembering 9/11. *CQ Researcher, 9*, 701-732.

CHICAGO STYLE

Jost, Kenneth. "Remembering 9/11." *CQ Researcher*, September 2, 2011, 701-732.

CQ Researcher

Published by CQ Press, an Imprint of SAGE Publications, Inc.

www.cqresearcher.com

'Occupy' Movement

Does the protest against inequality have staying power?

Demonstrators protesting income inequality and corporate greed have taken over parks and other public places across the country in the wake of the Occupy Wall Street protest launched in September near New York City's Financial District. Police have shut down many camps following mass arrests, occasional violence and heavy-handed police tactics, including in New York and Oakland, Calif. Still, while top Republicans have condemned the protesters as divisive and dangerous, some Democratic politicians have voiced sympathy for their message. The movement's main claim — that the U.S. political and economic system benefits the richest 1 percent to the detriment of the other 99 percent — has put the issue of economic fairness front and center in the presidential race. But the Occupy movement faces a long, cold winter and a pair of daunting challenges: defining its long-term goals and forming a leadership structure that can chart a sustainable course for the protest effort.

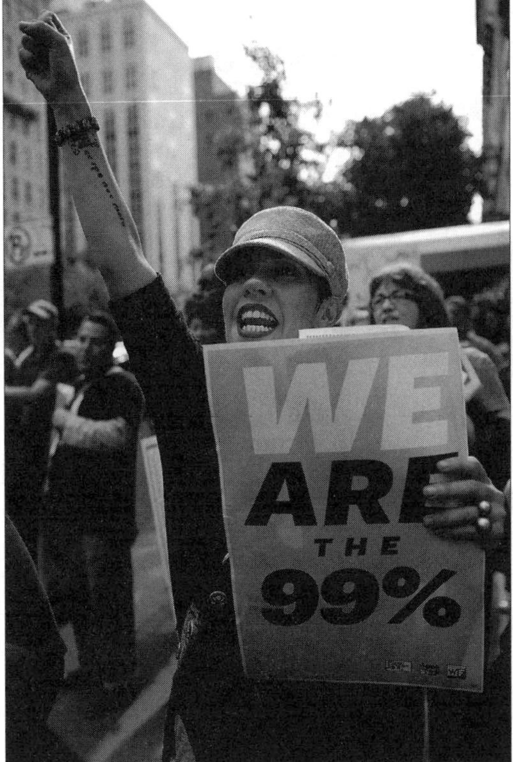

Occupy Wall Street activists demonstrate against income inequality and corporate greed on Oct. 11, 2011, in the Upper East Side Manhattan neighborhood of News Corp. CEO Rupert Murdoch, oil tycoon David Koch and other affluent Americans.

INSIDE THIS REPORT

The Issues 27
Background 33
Chronology 34
Current Situation 42
At Issue 43
Outlook 45
Bibliography 49
The Next Step 50

CQ Researcher • Jan. 13, 2012 • www.cqresearcher.com
Volume 22, Number 2 • Pages 25-52

Los Angeles | London | New Delhi
Singapore | Washington DC

Recipient of Society of Professional Journalists Award for Excellence ◆ American Bar Association Silver Gavel Award

'OCCUPY' MOVEMENT

THE ISSUES

27 • Can the Occupy movement reduce inequality?
• Is Occupy good for the Democratic Party?
• Is the Occupy movement over?

BACKGROUND

33 **Rising Militancy**
A depression in the 1890s sparked activism by farmers, factory workers.

36 **Marching and Occupying**
War veterans demanded aid during the Great Depression.

38 **Civil Rights and Vietnam**
Tumultuous protests marked the 1950s and '60s.

39 **Globalization**
Liberalized trade rules and job outsourcing in the 1990s spurred backlash.

CURRENT SITUATION

42 **'Occupy' Caucuses**
Activists are confronting President Obama and Republican presidential candidates.

42 **'Occupy' Elections**
Activists are backing Elizabeth Warren's Massachusetts Senate campaign.

44 **'Occupy' and Anti-Semitism**
Critics say the movement has become an outlet for haters.

OUTLOOK

45 **New Progressive Era?**
Scholars disagree on whether Occupy will spark changes.

SIDEBARS AND GRAPHICS

28 **Public Backs Occupy's Concerns, Rejects Tactics**
Half of Americans oppose protest methods.

29 **Top 1 Percent Has Biggest Income Gain**
Rich Americans' income rose nearly 300 percent.

34 **Chronology**
Key events since 1885.

35 **Tracking Occupy's Evolution**
The movement began in mid-September and quickly spread.

36 **Surprising Alliance: Union Activists, Union Members**
"We are united in the belief our country needs a change."

40 **Movement Mixes Anarchy and 'Pure' Democracy**
Everybody gets to talk . . . and talk . . . and talk.

43 **At Issue**
Will the Occupy movement continue to affect politics?

FOR FURTHER RESEARCH

48 **For More Information**
Organizations to contact.

49 **Bibliography**
Selected sources used.

50 **The Next Step**
Additional articles.

51 **Citing *CQ Researcher***
Sample bibliography formats.

Cover: AFP/Getty Images/Emmanuel Dunand

CQ Researcher

Jan. 13, 2012
Volume 22, Number 2

MANAGING EDITOR: Thomas J. Billitteri
tjb@cqpress.com

ASSISTANT MANAGING EDITOR: Kathy Koch
kkoch@cqpress.com

CONTRIBUTING EDITOR: Thomas J. Colin
tcolin@cqpress.com

ASSOCIATE EDITOR: Kenneth Jost

STAFF WRITERS: Marcia Clemmitt, Peter Katel

CONTRIBUTING WRITERS: Sarah Glazer, Alan Greenblatt, Barbara Mantel, Jennifer Weeks

DESIGN/PRODUCTION EDITOR: Olu B. Davis

ASSISTANT EDITOR: Darrell Dela Rosa

FACT CHECKER: Michelle Harris

Los Angeles | London | New Delhi
Singapore | Washington DC

An Imprint of SAGE Publications, Inc.

VICE PRESIDENT AND EDITORIAL DIRECTOR, HIGHER EDUCATION GROUP:
Michele Sordi

DIRECTOR, ONLINE PUBLISHING:
Todd Baldwin

CQ Researcher (ISSN 1056-2036) is printed on acid-free paper. Published weekly, except: (March wk. 5) (May wk. 4) (July wk. 1) (Aug. wks. 3, 4) (Nov. wk. 4) and (Dec. wks. 3, 4). Published by SAGE Publications, Inc., 2455 Teller Rd., Thousand Oaks, CA 91320. Annual full-service subscriptions start at $803. For pricing, call 1-800-834-9020. To purchase a *CQ Researcher* report in print or electronic format (PDF), visit www.cqpress.com or call 866-427-7737. Single reports start at $15. Bulk purchase discounts and electronic-rights licensing are also available. Periodicals postage paid at Thousand Oaks, California, and at additional mailing offices. POSTMASTER: Send address changes to *CQ Researcher*, 2300 N St., N.W., Suite 800, Washington, DC 20037.

'Occupy' Movement

By Peter Katel

The Issues

When hundreds of demonstrators suddenly appeared in New York's Financial District last September — along with their tents, sleeping bags and drums — their "1 percent v. 99 percent" buzz-phrase decrying economic inequality caught on immediately.

But sympathizers and critics did have some questions: What did the protesters want to happen? What did they want government to do? Some thought the campers would quickly give up and disperse.

The Occupy Wall Street activists held their ground, however, and the movement grew in strength. And its objectives became a little clearer.

"People are coming out here to voice, you know, their disapproval with the system and to voice themselves in a direct, democratic fashion," said Patrick Bruner, a 23-year-old from Brooklyn. "It's really refreshing for people to think that they can effect change in this system that has essentially made it so that only 1 percent of the population are citizens." [1]

The New York encampment in Zuccotti Park was the seed from which hundreds of Occupy movements sprouted in cities, towns and college campuses across the country. From one coast to the other, activists spoke in similar tones, often with drum circles pounding in the background. "I believe that I am not represented by the big interest groups and the big money corporations, which have increasing control of our money and our politics," Elise Whitaker, 21, a freelance script editor and film director, said at the Occupy Los Angeles site at City Hall Park. Demonstrators want "a more equal economy," she said. [2]

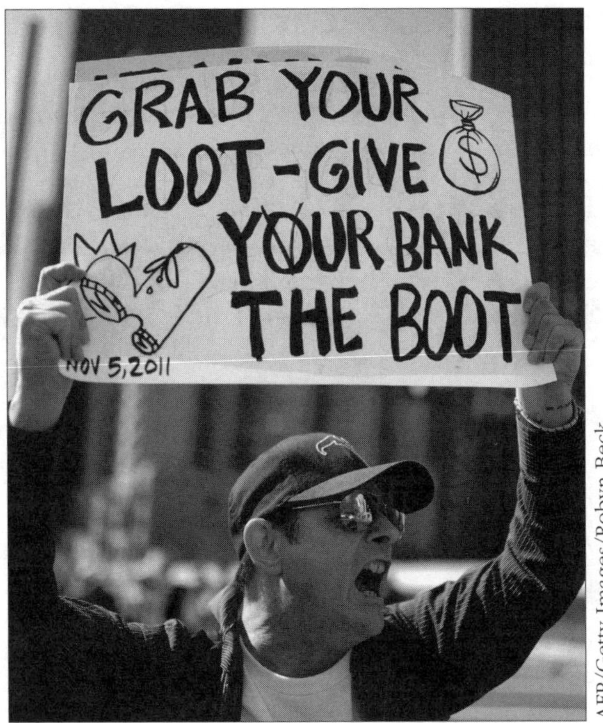

AFP/Getty Images/Robyn Beck

An Occupy protester in Los Angeles on Nov. 5, 2011, urges people to move their money from large banks into small banks or credit unions. "I believe that I am not represented by the big interest groups and the big-money corporations, which have increasing control of our money and our politics," said an activist.

Mayors of Los Angeles, New York and other cities sent police to break up encampments. Winter weather or declining political momentum did in some others, though Occupy Washington was still going in early 2012. And other Occupy groups, including the original New York movement, were still holding meetings as well, though not in a round-the-clock encampment. [3] In addition, the most engaged activists are meeting face-to-face and on the Web, and a major revival of a street presence in the spring seems virtually certain. [4] Already, the movement's image of a country divided between the "1 percent" and the "99 percent" has forced politicians from President Obama on down to confront economic inequality.

"For years, people were saying, 'When are the pitchforks going to come out? When are people are going to get mad?' But no one was doing anything," says Ken Margolies, director of organizing programs at Cornell University's Industrial Labor Relations School. "The Occupy movement caught the imagination of the country."

The occupiers' message was soon buttressed by studies charting substantial income growth for Americans at the top, and relatively meager growth for everyone else. [5] *(See graph, p. 29.)*

Weeks after the Occupy movement took off, the nonpartisan Congressional Budget Office (CBO) reported that from 1979 to 2007 the highest-income 1 percent of the population saw after-tax household income grow 277 percent. By contrast, for the 60 percent of the population in the middle, incomes grew less than 40 percent. [6]

The Organisation for Economic Cooperation and Development (OECD), a policy think tank for industrialized nations, reported that the richest 1 percent of Americans took in 20 percent of national income — a bigger share than in any other industrialized country examined. [7]

Meanwhile, according to a survey released Jan. 11, 2012, by the Pew Research Center, about two-thirds of Americans see "strong conflicts" between rich and poor in the United States, indicating the income inequality message from Democrats and the Occupy movement is seeping into the national consciousness. [8]

The Occupy movement signifies refusal to accept more of the same.

Public Backs Occupy's Concerns, Rejects Tactics

Forty-four percent of Americans support the Occupy Wall Street movement while about half agree with the concerns the protests have raised. A similar percentage, however, disapproves of the movement's tactics, such as staging sit-ins in public places.

Public Views of Occupy Wall Street

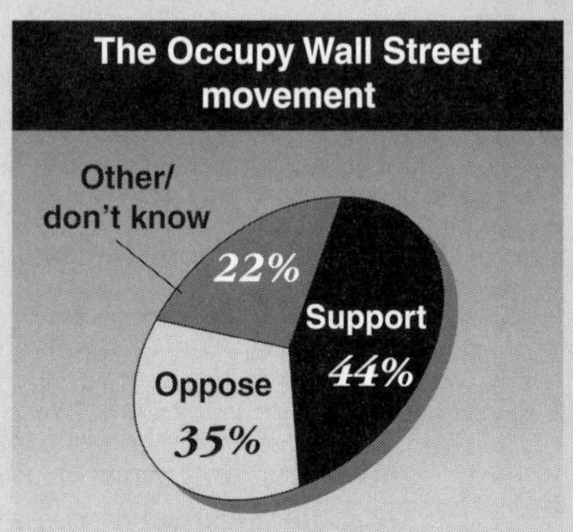

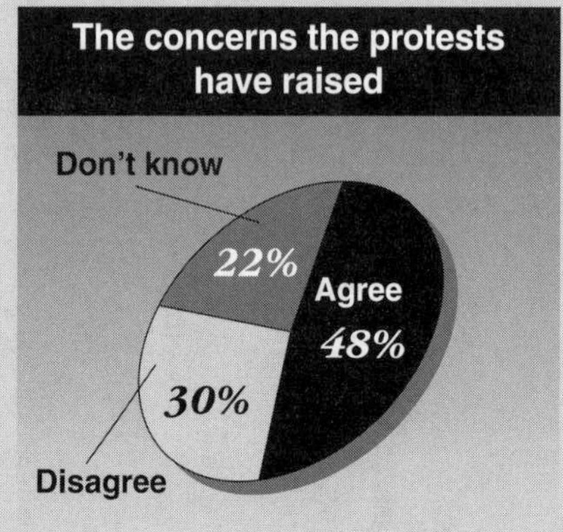

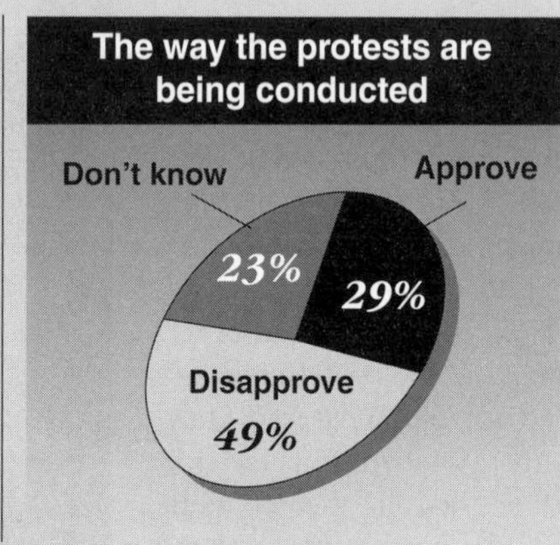

* *Percentages may not total 100 because of rounding.*

Source: "Frustration With Congress Could Hurt Republican Incumbents," Pew Research Center, December 2011, p. 3, www.people-press.org/files/legacy-pdf/12-15-11 Congress and Economy release.pdf

Until it appeared, says Rory McVeigh, director of the Center for the Study of Social Movements at the University of Notre Dame, "The conservative side has been pretty effective in managing public opinion in a way that gets people worried about debt reduction and not really thinking about consequences of joblessness and inequality and stimulating the economy."

Left-wing activists have driven the movement from the beginning, marking the first time since the days of the anti-Vietnam War movement that ideas from the left have helped set the national agenda. "It took three years from the start of the anti-Vietnam War movement to the point when the popularity of the war sank below 50 percent," Todd Gitlin, a professor at the Columbia University journalism school and a participant in and chronicler of the 1960s radical movement, told *New York* magazine in November. "Here, achieving the equivalent took three minutes." [9]

A closer precedent to Occupy arguably lies not in the 1960s but in the 1930s, when the left and unions made common cause — including in the organization of factory occupations. Nevertheless, notes historian Michael Kazin of Georgetown University, "The union movement had no problem with leaders."

The Occupy movement, inspired by anarchist principles, rejects hierarchy in favor of direction by consensus — in other words, "pure" democracy. (*See sidebar, p. 36.*) What's more, the movement lacks a clear-cut program and has little to point to in the way of measurable results. "The Occupy movement is rooted in the idea that the political system is broken to such a degree that we can no longer work through the Republican or Democratic parties," Tim Franzen, an Occupy Atlanta activist, told The Associated Press. [10]

To be sure, Democratic Gov. Andrew Cuomo of New York in December suddenly reversed his avowedly unbending opposition to a so-called "millionaires' tax" on the earnings of high-income New Yorkers. Occupy activists had dubbed Cuomo "Governor 1 Percent." [11]

Survey data make clear that discontent over inequality isn't limited to New York. A substantial majority — 77 percent — of respondents to a November survey by the nonpartisan Pew Research Center agreed that corporations and a small number of rich people wield too much power. And — in a remarkable loss of faith in a bedrock tenet of the American Dream — 40 percent said hard work and determination don't guarantee success. [12]

However, agreeing with some of Occupy activists' points doesn't automatically mean supporting the movement. In December, Pew found that 49 percent of respondents disapproved of the way demonstrations were conducted — almost the exact share that registered agreement with the movement on issues. (*See graphs, above.*)

By then, coverage of the movement had included news accounts of November street clashes in Oakland, Calif. Some featured ultra-radical activists who saw breaking store windows as a form of political action. Others featured aggressive police who in one instance fired a tear gas canister that fractured the skull of an Iraq War veteran. [13]

"Americans usually like the idea of rebellion more than rebellion itself," says Kazin, "not people fighting with cops, even if it's not the fault of the demonstrators. They like protest as long as it's orderly."

Still, for Democrats, the Occupy movement has opened a window of political opportunity. In early December, Obama traveled to historic Osawatomie, Kan., to deliver a major speech on economic inequality. "The typical CEO who used to earn about 30 times more than his or her worker now earns 110 times more," he said. "And yet, over the last decade the incomes of most Americans have actually fallen by about 6 percent. . . . Today, thanks to loopholes and shelters, a quarter of all millionaires now pay lower tax rates than millions of you, millions of middle-class families. Some billionaires have a tax rate as low as 1 percent." [14]

Osawatomie is a political landmark — the site of a 1910 speech by President Theodore Roosevelt urging that corporate power be reined in. "The great special business interests too often control and corrupt the men and methods of government for their own profit," declared Roosevelt, who would soon run again for president as Progressive Party candidate. [15] The White House republished Roosevelt's address simultaneously with the text of Obama's speech. As for the Occupy movement, the president mentioned it only once, and briefly.

Republican primary candidates' responses to Occupy, meanwhile, have ranged from equivocal to hostile. Former Massachusetts Gov. Mitt Romney, who became a multimillionaire in the corporate takeover business, defended Wall Street financiers in October against what he called attempts at "finding a scapegoat, finding someone to blame." [16] But a more recent campaign commercial used hand-written signs bearing gloomy economic statistics, seeming to mimic a well-known Occupy technique. [17]

Meanwhile, former House Speaker Newt Gingrich, R-Ga., offered some mocking advice to demonstrators: "Go get a job, right after you take a bath," he said in November. He went on to disparage them as non-taxpaying freeloaders. [18]

As the Republicans spoke out, the Tea Party faction of their party, which helped the GOP regain control of the House in 2011, was heading downward in public opinion. The trend held true both nationally and in congressional districts represented by lawmakers identified with the faction, the Pew Center reported in November. In those districts, 48 percent of respondents said they viewed the Tea Party unfavorably, and 41 percent favorably — a sharp shift from last March, when the favorability rate was 55 percent. [19]

The Occupy movement could face its own decline — but not for some time, say many observers. "Just when you thought demonstrations and people putting bodies on the line was over," says former Democratic Gov. Madeleine Kunin of Vermont, "it re-emerges."

As debate continues over the impact and future of the Occupy movement, here are some questions being asked:

Top 1 Percent Has Biggest Income Gain

The after-tax income of the top 1 percent of American households rose nearly 300 percent between 1979 and 2007, while that of other groups grew at much slower rates. The bottom 20 percent saw only an 18 percent rise over the period.

Income Gains, by Income Group, 1979 to 2007

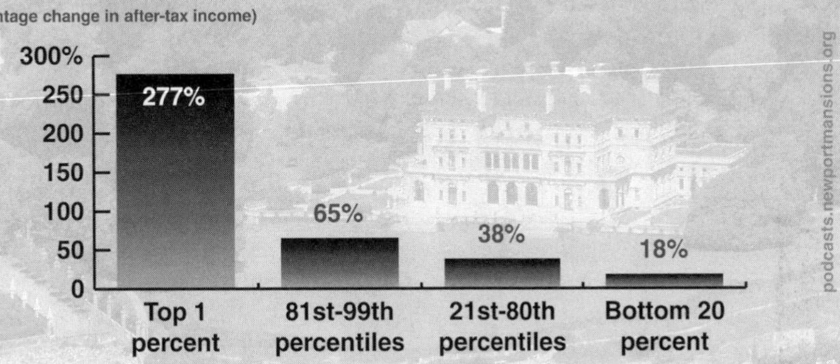

Source: Chad Stone, et al., *"A Guide to Statistics on Historical Trends in Income Inequality," Center on Budget and Policy Priorities, November 2011, www.cbpp.org/cms/?fa=view&id=3629; Congressional Budget Office.*

Can the Occupy movement reduce inequality?

After reading some of the hundreds of stark, personal accounts offered on "We Are the 99 Percent" — a website that offers stories behind the statistics, charts and slogans about economic inequality — Rich Lowry, a prominent Republican commentator and Occupy opponent, acknowledged that the protest movement had raised some legitimate questions. [20]

"There are tales of men losing decent-paying jobs and finding nothing comparable," wrote Lowry, editor of *National Review* magazine, the flagship of Republican conservatism since 1955. "Such downward mobility is a dismaying constant. . . . The recession has added a layer of joblessness on top of punishingly dysfunctional and expensive health-care and higher-education systems." [21]

The accounts on the website are by low-paid workers, unemployed people with experience but no job prospects, students accumulating debt and sufferers of chronic illness with inadequate health insurance — or none at all.

Lowry's take on the issue animating the movement may be a minority view among conservatives. But his commentary — though critical of the Occupy movement's politics — illustrated a point made by reporter Dylan Byers of *Politico*, an influential Washington newspaper. He noted that the term "income inequality" had soared in frequency in news stories, from 91 appearances before the demonstrations began to 500 a week in early November. [22]

Occupiers "already can take credit for starting a national conversation about the increasingly inequitable distribution of growth that stands as a profound economic problem in our country," wrote Jared Bernstein, a senior fellow at the liberal Center on Budget and Policy Priorities and former chief economist for Vice President Joseph Biden. [23]

Generating attention and debate, though an important achievement, might mark the limit of what the Occupy movement can do, some sympathizers acknowledge.

"We've had a wave of columns and news stories based on inequality," says Dean Baker, an economist and co-founder and co-director of the Center for Economic and Policy Research. "But I don't think anyone is going to say that he changed his position based on the movement."

The very nature of the Occupy movement may limit its direct political effects, Baker says. "It's an amorphous group; it doesn't want to embrace politicians," he says. "One can argue about whether that is the most effective way to proceed."

However, activists can point to one example of a politician who appears to have responded to the Occupy message by reversing himself on an important piece of legislation with a direct effect on income inequality.

Cuomo, the New York governor, in early December suddenly embraced and pushed to legislative approval a so-called "millionaires' tax" on individuals who earn more than $200,000 a year.

Getty Images/Mario Tama

Occupy Wall Street activists gather in New York City's Duarte Square on Nov. 15, 2011, after police removed them from Zuccotti Park. The police action, endorsed by Mayor Michael Bloomberg, followed similar moves in Oakland, Calif., and Portland, Ore.

In the weeks leading up to his move, Cuomo had declared unbendable opposition to the tax. Said Tim Dubnau, an organizer for the Communication Workers of America (CWA) who has been working closely with Occupy Wall Street, "There is no doubt in anyone's mind that that is a result of the Occupy Wall Street movement educating people" about tax policy.

And Dubnau noted that the tax debate that Occupy amplified is being echoed in the nationwide focus on equality. "In every single paper in the country almost every single day for months there have been stories about how we have an unequal society," he says. "I can't see that as a bad thing."

Nevertheless, New York, where labor unions still carry political weight and leftwing activism is deeply embedded in the state's history and political culture, may not be a national indicator of Occupy influence. "A movement is likely to get concessions in a sympathetic environment," says McVeigh of Notre Dame.

From a national perspective, "The polls are showing a fair number of people are fairly sympathetic to what Occupy Wall Street is putting forward, but without an intense commitment," McVeigh says. "So it's risky for anybody in power to completely embrace the movement and call it his or her own."

Even so, says Cornell University's Margolies, congressional Republicans' internal disagreement over Obama's efforts to extend the payroll tax cut may reflect confusion over how to deal with the inequality issue that Occupy activists have emphasized. "The movement has certainly changed the debate," Margolies says. "The Republicans realized they're getting caught by their own rhetoric; they finally found a tax cut they don't like." (He spoke before House Republicans caved to pressure from the White House and their own Senate partners, backing a two-month extension of the tax cut.)

But Margolies qualifies his favorable reading of the movement's effects. "A real test would be if it helps a union win a major strike or get a contract in a tough situation, or helps change labor law, or helps a group of workers organize."

Is Occupy good for the Democratic Party?

In his Kansas speech in December, President Obama drew on themes sounded by Occupy members, connecting them to longstanding political traditions that energized the early 20th-century wave of political and financial regulation known as the Progressive Era.

Obama made much of the fact that the politician who laid the groundwork for those changes, President Theodore Roosevelt, had been a Republican.

But the president went on to underline the difference between Roosevelt and his party descendants of today. "Thanks to some of the same folks who are now running Congress, we had weak regulation, we had little oversight, and what did it get us?" he asked rhetorically.

Whether Obama can draw on the anger that has fed the Occupy movement remains unclear, however. A cautionary example comes from the recent experience of the Republican Party with its Tea Party faction. The Tea Party propelled a number of Republican congressional candidates to victory in 2010, giving the GOP the House majority. But in the GOP presidential primaries, many candidates arguably have tacked so far to the right to appeal to the Tea Party that they may have alienated mainstream Republican voters.

"Republicans now are growing very nervous" because Tea Party freshman in the House have been so adamant against compromise, Norman Ornstein, a resident scholar at the American Enterprise Institute (AEI), a conservative think tank, said in December. "By standing so firm against taxing the rich . . . they lost sight of where the zeitgeist was, and it hurt them." [24]

But Obama faces problems within his own party, most notably disillusion among many Democrats over what they see as a lack of progress on social and economic reforms. That disillusion has helped animate the Occupy movement. "People went through the experience of 2008 and had their hopes raised significantly by Obama in a way we haven't seen in this generation," says Amy Muldoon, a CWA union member participating in an Occupy Wall Street working group on organized labor. "And now the Occupy movement in part is people who went through that experience and said, 'it didn't deliver for me.' "

Muldoon, speaking for herself and not the union, says a significant number of the most engaged Occupy activists are "looking past elections as a way of changing society." Democrats' attempts to "utilize what Occupy has exposed — with rhetoric about a candidate for the 99 percent, meaning Obama — I don't think will fly with the people who are most involved with Occupy."

To voters at large, however, argues Georgetown's Kazin, the Occupy movement has provided an appealing narrative "as long as people see the economy in serious trouble and are worried about their futures."

Moreover, the electoral alienation of the most committed Occupy activists doesn't pose an active threat to Democratic prospects, Kazin says. In the 1960s, "The antiwar movement saw Democrats and [President Lyndon B. Johnson, a Democrat who escalated the Vietnam War] as prime villains," he says. "I haven't seen that same hostility and hatred for Obama. A lot of core activists clearly think there is no difference between Republicans and Democrats, but that's not the same as saying that it's the Democrats' fault that we have economic inequality and a financial crisis."

But Nick Schulz, a fellow at AEI and editor of its online magazine, argues that the nature of the Occupy movement itself poses a potential problem for Democrats in general and Obama in particular. "I come from the school that says that being positive in your politics is a winning formula," he says. "That's not what emerged from Occupy. I understand why people in Occupy are angry, but if the negative animating spirit of Occupy comes to dominate the Democratic Party, that's a political loser."

Obama owes much of his success to his ability to convey optimism, Schulz says. But in the coming election, he argues, if voters see the president's message as intertwined with Occupy grievances, "The moderately conservative, college-educated cohort that went in large numbers for Obama because they liked his upbeat, aspirational message. If it becomes a negative — 'we're going after the rich and the top 1 percent' — that will turn them off."

Baker of the Center for Economic and Policy Research suggests that Occupy likely will benefit some Democrats and hurt others. "It's bad news for the more business-oriented Democrats," he argues, pointing to Robert Rubin — a Wall Street financier, former director of Citigroup and former Treasury secretary in the Clinton administration who still wields considerable influence on administration economic policy. "Their room to maneuver has been sharply reduced by the Occupy movement; they certainly don't see it as good news." [25]

On the other hand, Baker says, "The labor-progressive wing of the Democratic Party certainly does see it as good news." Even so, adds Baker, repercussions from Occupy attacks on business-oriented Democrats could hurt the movement's liberal allies. "The Rubin types provide money for campaigns," Baker says. "Do you run the risk that you're going to so antagonize the business wing of the party that you won't be able to run effective campaigns?"

Is the Occupy movement over?

The onset of winter, and police evictions, have deprived the Occupy name of its emotional punch — the occupations themselves — lending new strength to questions about the movement's goals. Those questions have been circulating virtually ever since it began: What exactly does the movement want to achieve? And does it have staying power?

Some observers see change within the political system as a waste of time. Many call themselves disenchanted after investing their political energies. "Obama syndrome: lost hope," says Sri Louise, who is active in Occupy Oakland. "I feel like I've been there and done that. I have no interest in the electoral process."

Others argue that improving that process is the movement's natural goal.

"If you want to get at the root of what's wrong with this system, in my opinion the way we fund and run elections has become skewed in the direction of powerful money interests," says Kunin, the former Vermont governor, summarizing a column she wrote for *The Huffington Post* website. [26] "If we're going to have the voice of the 99 percent back, we have to change that system and find a way to do public financing or limit contributions."

The tension between reformers and revolutionaries — a natural condition in all social movements — remains unresolved. "At some point, movements must take on some form, some identifiable agenda," the Rev. Jesse Jackson, a veteran of the 1960s civil rights movement, told *New York* magazine. "At some point, water must become ice." [27]

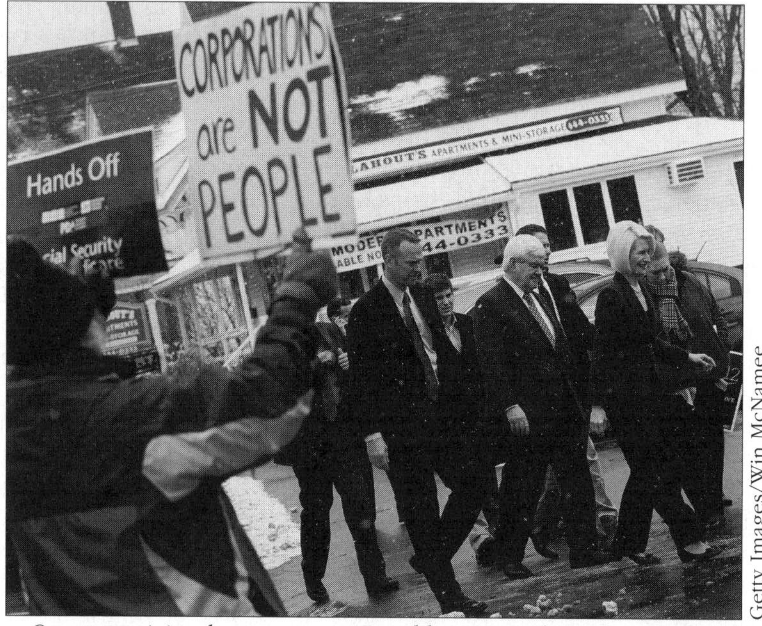

Occupy activists demonstrate as Republican presidential candidate Newt Gingrich and his wife Callista, both at right, arrive at a town hall meeting in Littleton, N.H., on Jan. 5, 2012. In November, he told Occupy demonstrators: "Go get a job, right after you take a bath." He went on to disparage them as non-taxpaying freeloaders.

Getty Images/Win McNamee

Whether many people like camping in city parks when water turns to ice is another question. Nevertheless, some argue that the loss of New York's Zuccotti Park did take a toll on Occupy Wall Street — the national movement's starter motor. "The fact that people were willing to sleep out in the cold rain and snow was inspiring," says the CWA's Dubnau. "There are some signs the movement is fizzling with the physical space of Zuccotti Park lost."

Activists reoccupied the park in early January after city authorities removed barricades and checkpoints that had limited the number of people allowed in; but a ban on tents and sleeping bags remained in force.

But Dubnau, like many others, expects open-air demonstrations to revive with the coming of warm weather. The movement has struck a chord, he says. "Everyone is anxious about jobs in America; everyone knows what the occupiers are talking about."

Nevertheless, Artur Davis, a former Democratic congressman from Alabama and now a Washington lawyer who writes political commentary for *Politico*, argues that maintaining a physical presence "is a low bar to meet." The real test of lasting influence, he says, will be the Occupy movement's ability to accomplish political goals.

One obstacle so far, Davis says, is that the "99 percent" versus "1 percent" paradigm is too broad and vague. "It equates the interests of a hungry child in the Mississippi Delta with a stockbroker who makes six figures but whose mortgage is underwater," he says. "It's as if the civil rights movement had said in the 1960s, 'We're not going to make this about African-Americans, we're going to make it about people who are struggling all over the country; we're going to equate our interests with those of white suburbanites who are paying too much property tax.' "

From within the movement, though, some lifelong activists who've seen other political waves rise and fall argue that skeptics are thinking too small. Adam Hochschild, a journalist and author who co-founded the left-wing *Mother Jones* magazine in 1976 and who has written on the 18th- and 19th-century campaign to abolish slavery in the British Empire, likened that effort to Occupy. "By 1792 at least 400,000 people in the British Isles were refusing to eat slave-grown sugar," Hochschild wrote in the "Occupied Wall Street Journal," published by New York activists. [28]

"In combating entrenched power of a different sort — a system with obscene profits for the 1 percent and hardship and a downward slide for many of the rest — I think we're now at about 1792 in this process," Hochschild wrote. [29]

Hochschild and others who see the movement reaching for changes in how wealth and power are distributed agree — in a sense — with some of their most fervent foes. "The philosophical political movement that these extreme leftists have decided to participate in will try to continue," says David Bossie, president and board chairman of Citizens United, a conservative advocacy group that specializes in producing politically charged documentary-style movies.*

The encampments reflected the movement's philosophical underpinnings, Bossie says. "It's the closest form of communal living," he says, tracing the tent cities to "socialism, communism — you name the institutions by which they believe. They believe in taking from everyone and giving it to them." ■

* Bossie's lawsuit challenging a Federal Election Commission decision to limit advertising for a Citizens United work, "Hillary: The Movie," led to a landmark U.S. Supreme Court decision overturning restrictions on corporate political contributions.

BACKGROUND

Rising Militancy

Economic transformation capped by major depression marked the late 19th century, prompting a wave of activism among farmers and factory workers. Wall Street financiers, industrialists and politicians who served business interests were their common targets. [30]

In the 1880s, a wave of labor organizing spread across manufacturing, shipping and mining centers throughout the country. Twelve-hour work days, paltry pay, child labor, the right to collectively bargain and the often hazardous nature of the work spurred workers to demand change. Many went further, demanding that society be reordered so that the fruits of labor were distributed more equitably.

Workers had been forming and joining unions for decades, but they were made up of craftspeople whose skills gave them considerable power in dealing with employers. As industrialization advanced in the latter decades of the 1800s, a new kind of union arose.

The Knights of Labor, founded in secret in 1869, grew into an open organization for all skilled and unskilled members of the "producing classes." (Members included African-Americans and, eventually, women — revolutionary policies at the time.) "We declare an inevitable and irresistible conflict between the wage system of labor and republican system of government," the Knights said, vowing to fight big-business domination of government. [31]

In 1885, the Knights led a successful strike against one of the country's leading corporations, the Southwestern Railroad, whose majority owner was fabled Wall Street financier Jay Gould. By 1886, as many as 1 million members, about 10 percent of the country's nonagricultural workforce, had joined the union.

A five-year depression that began in 1893 saw labor-business conflicts escalate into armed confrontations between workers and police and military forces deployed against them. President Grover Cleveland sent 10,000 Army troops to Chicago to quell a nationwide strike against the Pullman Palace Car Co., which manufactured sleeping cars for railroads. Thirteen strike supporters were killed in clashes with anti-union forces. [32]

Newly unemployed workers mounted campaigns of their own. The most well-known centered on a march from Ohio to Washington led by evangelical businessman Jacob S. Coxey, who advocated a major road-building program to put jobless men to work. "Coxey's Army" was met in Washington by U.S. marshals, who arrested Coxey and other leaders, snuffing out the effort. [33]

Shortly before the 1893 depression struck, a mass movement arose featuring rural Americans demanding better prices from companies that bought their crops, as well as a host of other improvements in conditions in the countryside. The movement evolved quickly into a political organization — from the Farmers' Alliance to the People's Party, founded in 1892, and soon dubbed "Populists."

In 1892, populist candidates around the country earned more than 1 million votes. Colorado and Kansas elected Populist governors, and Populist presidential candidate James Weaver captured three states, thus winning electoral votes. But ultimately, the third-party effort benefited the Republicans. In the 1896 presidential election, Republican William McKinley defeated William Jennings Bryan, who ran as both Democrat and Populist. And in 1912, Woodrow Wilson beat William Howard Taft, thanks partly to Theodore

Continued on p. 36

Chronology

1880s-1920s

Organizing drives and strikes by industrial workers provoke repression.

1885
Knights of Labor leads successful strike against Southwestern Railroad.

1894
Workers strike at Pullman Palace Car Co. in Chicago; President Grover Cleveland sends troops to break the labor action. . . . Men demanding jobs march on Washington.

1905
Left-wing unionists found anti-capitalism Industrial Workers of the World.

1910
President Theodore Roosevelt denounces corporate power in speech in Osawatomie, Kan.

1929
Wall Street crash marks beginning of Great Depression.

1930s

Nation's worst depression sparks massive discontent, rise of new unions.

1932
"Bonus Army" of 20,000 jobless World War I veterans sets up camp in Washington but is eventually routed by Army troops and police.

1934
Wagner Act restricts employer interference in union activities.

1936
"Sitdown" tactic spreads to General Motors factories; company recognizes the United Automobile Workers union.

1950s-1960s

Civil rights and anti-Vietnam War movements make mass protest a major political force.

1955
The Rev. Martin Luther King Jr. leads bus boycott in Montgomery, Ala.

1956
Montgomery desegregates buses.

1957
President Dwight D. Eisenhower orders Army troops to enforce desegregation in Little Rock, Ark.

1960
Black students sit in at Greensboro, N.C., lunch counter to challenge segregated seating; tactic spreads.

1961
"Freedom Riders" defy segregation in interstate buses and terminals.

1964
Civil Rights Act prohibits racial discrimination in public accommodations, public education and most employment.

1965
Voting Rights Act outlaws racial discrimination in election process.

1967
Tens of thousands march in Washington to protest Vietnam War.

1968
The Rev. King is assassinated in Memphis.

1970
As demonstrations against U.S. invasion of Cambodia sweep campuses and cities, National Guard troops kill four students at Ohio's Kent State University, and police kill two students at Jackson State College in Mississippi.

1990s-Present

Left-wing activism targets liberalized trade rules, job outsourcing and Iraq War.

1993
Over strong opposition from unions and the left, President Bill Clinton pushes North American Free Trade Agreement (NAFTA) through Congress.

1997
College students organize boycott to protest athletic-wear companies using sweatshops.

1999
Anti-globalization protesters in Seattle battle with police at World Trade Organization meeting.

2003
Iraq War sparks a new anti-war movement.

2007
Richest 1 percent of population sees after-tax income grow by about 275 percent since 1979 while middle-income sector sees modest growth. . . . Recession begins.

2008
Obama presidential campaign awakens hope for rebirth of left-Democratic Party alliance that collapsed during Vietnam War.

2010
Energized by Tea Party faction, Republican candidates sweep House elections, gaining majority. . . . Left-wing Obama supporters grow disillusioned with economic policies seen as too timid.

2011
"Arab spring" in Tunisia, Egypt and elsewhere, and protests against austerity programs and inequality in Spain and Israel prompt U.S. activists to consider similar efforts.

Tracking Occupy's Evolution

The "Occupy" movement began in September in New York City to protest economic inequality and corporate greed. Since then the movement has spread across the U.S. Here is a timeline of its evolution:

2011

July 13 — Canadian anti-consumerist magazine *Adbusters* calls for a Sept. 17 protest on Wall Street demanding "democracy not corporatocracy."

Zuccotti Park

Sept. 17 — Protests begin as about 1,000 participants walk up and down Wall Street. Protesters settle into Zuccotti Park.

Sept. 20 — Police arrest mask-wearing protesters under state law banning non-entertainment masked gatherings.

Sept. 24 — About 80 arrested in Manhattan after marching without permit. The use of pepper spray against women earns Occupy movement its first major media coverage. Occupy protests begin in Chicago.

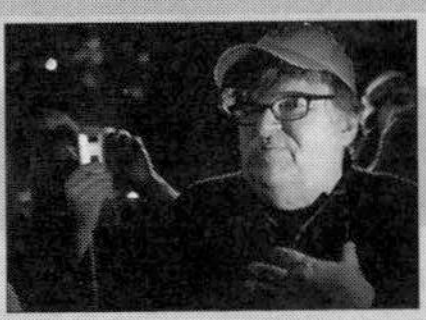
Moore

Sept. 26 — Filmmaker and activist Michael Moore addresses crowd at Zuccotti Park.

Sept. 28 — Transport Workers Union Local 100 in New York City becomes first large union to support Occupy protest.

Oct. 1 — Nearly 700 protesters arrested in march across Brooklyn Bridge. Protests begin in Los Angeles, Washington, D.C.

Oct. 3 — Protests begin in Boston, Memphis, Minneapolis, St. Louis, Hawaii and Maine.

Oct. 5 — New York labor unions join march through N.Y. Financial District.

Obama

Oct. 6 — Protests begin in Austin, Houston, San Francisco and Tampa. President Obama says the movement "expresses the frustrations the American people feel."

Oct. 7 — New York Mayor Michael Bloomberg says protesters are taking jobs from people and discouraging tourism.

Oct. 10 — Bloomberg softens criticism, saying protesters can stay if they obey the law.

Oct. 25 — Oakland police clear about 170 protesters from a City Hall encampment, use tear gas when protesters return.

Nov. 5 — "Bank Transfer Day" protesters encourage Americans to move their money out of big banks.

Nov. 15 — Police evict protesters from Zuccotti Park under orders from Bloomberg. A judge rules protesters do not have a First Amendment right to camp in the park, but can return without tents.

Cuomo

Nov. 17 — Protesters march in front of the New York Stock Exchange to mark movement's two-month anniversary.

Dec. 17 — Protesters mark three-month anniversary of Occupy Wall Street by marching across the city.

Dec. 20 — Hacker group Anonymous exposes personal information of police officers who have arrested protesters.

2012

Jan. 1 — Nearly 70 protesters arrested after attempt to resettle into Zuccotti Park. Protesters march at the end of Rose Bowl parade in Pasadena, Calif., on float made of plastic bags.

Romney

Jan. 2 — Protesters interrupt speech by Republican presidential candidate Mitt Romney in Des Moines, Iowa.

Jan. 4 — Protesters attend New Hampshire town hall meeting with Romney prior to state's primary Jan. 10. Organizers say they plan protests at future primaries, caucuses.

Jan. 10 — Protesters are permitted back into Zuccotti Park.

All photos/Getty Images

Surprising Alliance: Activists and Union Members

"We are united in the belief that our country needs a change."

As he marched through Lower Manhattan last October leading telephone workers side by side with Occupy Wall Street activists, Tim Dubnau, a union organizer for the Communications Workers of America (CWA), could tell that the OWS movement's message was reaching beyond its natural left-wing constituency.

"When we passed the World Trade Center, "I chanted, 'Every job a union job,' and the hard-hat people [working on the site] were giving us the thumbs up," says Dubnau, one of a number of unionists across the country building ties with the movement.

A salute from New York City "hard-hats" carries special significance for left-wing activists. Ever since a contingent of construction workers beat up anti-Vietnam War protesters (only blocks from the eventual World Trade Center site) in 1970, the building trades have been considered a bastion of working-class patriotism and contempt for the left and the counterculture. [1]

But the hardhat reception witnessed by Dubnau during the march to the headquarters of communications giant Verizon — which is locked in a contract fight with the CWA — was only one sign of a budding Occupy-union alliance.

CWA donated thousands of dollars' worth of walkie-talkies and air mattresses to occupiers and also provided meeting rooms. Other unions have supplied ponchos and storage space. Unions elsewhere have been generous as well. [2]

Top union leaders have been showering the movement with praise since shortly after the first OWS encampment, at Manhattan's Zuccotti Park, went up. "Across America, working people are turning out with their friends and neighbors in parks, congregations and union halls to express their frustration — and anger — about our country's staggering wealth gap," Richard Trumka, president of the AFL-CIO, declared in October, vowing continued union support for the Occupy movement. [3]

Mary Kay Henry, president of the Service Employees International Union (SEIU) declared her solidarity in *The Wall Street Journal*. "While unions cannot claim credit for Occupy Wall Street," she wrote, "SEIU members are joining the protesters in the streets because we are united in the belief that our country needs a change." [4]

Amy Muldoon, a phone worker who also works part time with the Occupy movement for the CWA, says activism focused on social and economic inequality creates a political climate favorable to organized labor.

"The unions recognize," she says, "that it's beneficial to negotiate contracts at a time when people are saying the rich and banks and corporations get away with whatever they want, and politicians are bought and sold by them."

Nevertheless, union-Occupy ties could fray when the presidential race intensifies. Already, some Occupy activists have made plain their distance from unions' long and close ties to the Democratic Party.

"There will be debates in the movement about whether people should put their energy into supporting Democrats," says Jackie Smith, a University of Pittsburgh sociology professor and Occupy activist. In that atmosphere, she says, "It will be difficult to maintain coalitions with labor."

Relations were tested on the West Coast by Occupy-initiated attempts to shut down two ports on Dec. 12. "U.S. ports have become economic engines for the elite; the 1 percent these trade hubs serve are free to rip the shirts off the backs of the 99 percent who turn their profits," the organizers of the West Coast Port Blockade announced online. [5]

In addition to the port of Oakland, Calif., the shutdowns targeted SSA Marine, a West Coast port operator, and EGT, which runs a grain shipping terminal in Longview, Wash., that is in a contract dispute with the International Longshore and Warehouse Union (ILWU). SSA is also partly owned by Goldman Sachs, a major Wall Street firm, making it an even more tempting target for Occupy activists. [6]

Continued from p. 33

Roosevelt's third-party candidacy.

The labor movement divided as well, with more radical unionists (including anarchists) forming the Industrial Workers of the World (IWW), in 1905, to fight for the overthrow of capitalism.

The years of union and populist activism, as well as the depression of 1893, presaged the early-20th-century "progressive" era, embodied by Presidents Theodore Roosevelt and Wilson. The period was marked by federal and state moves to improve working conditions. By 1912, 38 states prohibited or limited child labor, and the federal government had imposed regulations on the banking industry.

Often forgotten today is the extent of death and destruction — some of from the radical side — that accompanied the rise of the labor movement and the enactment of laws that granted legal protection to unions. "For more than half a century, between the 1870s and the 1930s," writes historian Beverly Gage of Yale University, "labor organizers and strikers regularly faced levels of violence all but unimaginable to modern-day activists." [34]

Marching and Occupying

The Great Depression that began in 1929 brought massive unem-

But union leadership opposed the Longview shutdown. "Support is one thing, organization from outside groups attempting to co-opt our struggle in order to advance a broader agenda is quite another," ILWU President Robert McEllrath said in a letter to local unions a week before the shutdown attempts, "and one that is destructive to our democratic process and jeopardizes our over-two-year struggle." [7]

Getty Images/Kevork Djansezian

Long Beach police arrest an Occupy protester on Dec. 12, 2011, for blocking the road leading to SSA Marine, a shipping company partially owned by investment bank Goldman Sachs.

In the end, port shutdowns in Longview, Oakland and Portland, Ore., cost union longshoremen all or most of their day's pay. Non-unionized truck drivers weren't paid at all. "This is a joke," driver Christian Vega told The Associated Press. "What are they protesting? It only hurts me and the other drivers." [8]

Some union longshoremen were happy with the protests. The website of the Southern California ILWU local carried a video in which Anthony, a shutdown-supporting longshoreman in Oakland, says that members were split 50-50 on the matter. "Some are upset because they lost a day's pay," he said. [9]

Anthony supported the shutdown as a "warning that the working class is serious." But, he added, the Occupy movement "probably has to get away from that 99 percent slogan, because then a lot of people say, 'You're hurt by the 99 percent not letting you go to work.' " [10]

Even some leftwing union activists found the shutdown troubling in ways that suggest that maintaining union-Occupy relations may take some work. "The IlWU is not a corrupt, stodgy union," says Dubnau of CWA. "If they're saying this is not a good tactic, you don't from the outside say this is a good tactic; you can't disrespect them," he says. "Yeah, it feels good to shut down ports; it's relatively easy to do — that doesn't mean it's a good strategy. You can't do it just because it's militant."

— Peter Katel

[1] For newspaper articles and other documentary material on the event, see "The HardHat Riots, an Online History Project," George Mason University, http://chnm.gmu.edu/hardhats/homepage.html.

[2] Quoted in David B. Caruso, "Occupy movement accepts modest help from the left," The Associated Press, Nov. 1, 2011.

[3] "Statement by AFL-CIO President Richard Trumka on Occupy Wall Street," AFL-CIO, press release, Oct. 5, 2011, www.aflcio.org/mediacenter/prsptm/pr10052011.cfm.

[4] Mary Kay Henry, "Why Labor Backs 'Occupy Wall Street,' " *The Wall Street Journal*, Oct. 8, 2011, http://online.wsj.com/article/SB10001424052970203476804576615200938120050.html.

[5] "Wall Street On the Waterfront?" West Coast Port Blockade, undated, http://westcoastportshutdown.org/content/wall-street-waterfront.

[6] "Occupy protesters seek to shut West Coast ports," The Associated Press, Dec. 12, 2011; Terry Collins, "Protesters halt operations at some western ports," The Associated Press, Dec. 13, 2011.

[7] "Message from Pres. McEllrath: We share Occupy's concerns about America, but EGG battle is complicated," ILWU Local 13, Dec. 6, 2011, www.ilwu13.com/message-from-pres.-mcellrath-we-share-occupy's-concerns-about-america-but-egt-battle-is-complicated-4580.html.

[8] Quoted in Collins, *op. cit.*

[9] "Anthony from ILWU on OccupyOakland.TV," OccupyOaklandTV, Dec. 12, 2011, www.ilwu13.com/dec.-12th — -anthony-from-ilwu-on-occupyoakland.tv-4800.html.

[10] *Ibid.*

ployment and widespread misery. In 1932, as the administration of Republican President Herbert Hoover drew to a close, following years in which he minimized the Depression's effects and refused to mount a major government response, thousands of jobless World War I veterans demanded assistance. Specifically, they wanted the government to immediately pay a cash bonus they had been promised. When no help was offered, a group of vets began marching on Washington from Portland, Ore. As the idea caught on, "bonus marchers" from across the country headed for the capital. Their encampments eventually housed about 20,000 people, including some vets' families.

After Congress — with Hoover's support — defeated resolutions to make early payments of the bonus, Washington police and then the U.S. Army heavy-handedly destroyed the bonus marchers' camps. Most notoriously, Army Chief of Staff Douglas A. MacArthur ignored orders to the contrary and sent troops across the Anacostia River to break up the vets' biggest tent city. [35]

Occupation tactics proved far more successful in the workplace. Following a wave of strikes in 1934 that descended into armed conflict in several cities, Congress passed the landmark Wagner Act, endorsed by President Franklin D. Roosevelt. The law authorized unions to organize and to strike. With factory production resuming as the economy slowly revived, workers at the Firestone tire factory in Akron, Ohio, hit on a new tactic in response to the company's suspension of a union activist. [36]

Instead of leaving the factory and mounting a picket line, the workers stopped working but stayed in place. The union won: The suspended worker was reinstated, and the occupiers were paid (though at a lower rate) for the time they'd spent on strike.

The occupation — or "sitdown" — tactic spread rapidly through the entire automobile industry (and even to department stores and smaller shops in Detroit and Chicago). It generally was designed to pressure companies into recognizing and negotiating with unions. Factory takeovers were marked by workers' discipline in preventing damage to machinery.

Factory takeovers reached their peak in 1936. The standout was the occupation of General Motors factories in Flint, Mich., where GM employed about 80 percent of the workforce. The company fought back, on at least one occasion sending police to try to retake a Chevrolet plant. That move failed. And after sitdown strikes spread to GM factories elsewhere, the company gave in, formally recognizing the United Automobile Workers (UAW) as bargaining agent for workers in the occupied factories.

By late 1937, the union's victory against the world's major carmaker brought an influx of members that swelled UAW rolls to nearly 400,000, from 30,000 the previous year. And the union's example encouraged workers in other industries: 4.7 million took part in strikes in 1937, including 400,000 who joined sitdowns. That same year, total union strength reached 7 million.

Businesspeople and politicians who saw the hand of the Communist Party in the labor upsurge weren't entirely wrong, although major sectors of the movement were led by strongly anti-communist socialists. Communist Party members occupied important positions in the Congress of Industrial Organizations (CIO), the labor federation to which the new breed of more militant unions belonged, as well as in steel, automobile, maritime and electrical unions. [37]

Time Life Pictures/Getty Images/Francis Miller

Arkansas National Guard troops block Minnijean Brown, center, and other black students from entering Central High School in Little Rock on Sept. 4, 1957. After President Dwight D. Eisenhower sent U.S. Army troops to enforce desegregation at the school, a white mob resisted, unsuccessfully. Arkansas Gov. Orval Faubus charged the troop deployment had turned Little Rock into "an occupied territory."

Civil Rights and Vietnam

The movement for black equality, which had been building steadily throughout the 20th century, grew into an irrepressible force in the 1950s as it adopted the tactic of mass defiance of segregation.

In 1954, the U.S. Supreme Court outlawed school segregation. The following year, the Rev. Martin Luther King Jr. led a boycott of city buses in Montgomery, Ala., in response to the arrest of NAACP activist Rosa Parks for defying the back-of-the bus law and occupying a "white" seat. The boycotters won their demand to abolish segregated seating on the buses.

In 1957, President Dwight D. Eisenhower sent Army troops to enforce the desegregation of Central High School in Little Rock, Ark. — a move that a mob of white residents resisted, unsuccessfully. Arkansas Gov. Orval Faubus charged that after the troop deployment, all of Little Rock was "an occupied territory." [38]

These dramatic events set the stage for the politically and socially tumultuous 1960s. The decade was only a month old when 20 black students from North Carolina Agricultural & Technical College in Greensboro challenged segregation in public places with a new tactic aimed at lunch counters.

After lunch counter sit-ins spread throughout the South — soon forcing stores to desegregate — activists refusing to obey state "Jim Crow" laws in buses and bus stations in the South began mounting "freedom rides" in 1961. By year's end, after the Freedom Riders had braved mob violence, the federal Interstate Commerce Commission issued a categorical ban on racial segregation in interstate trains, buses and terminals. [39]

The next major civil rights campaign — challenging exclusion of black people from voting in southern states — followed demonstrations throughout the South that sparked police violence and killings and bombings by hardcore segregationists. The campaign resulted in the Civil Rights Act of 1964 and the Voting Rights Act of 1965, which outlawed racial discrimination in public accommodations, public education and most jobs, as well as voting procedures. [40]

King and some other civil rights leaders followed those victories by shifting their focus to poverty, including in northern cities. King was assassinated in Memphis in 1968 as he lent support to sanitation workers, all of them black, striking over discriminatory pay and working conditions. A more radical wing of the civil rights movement embraced a black nationalist doctrine in which economic goals were subordinated to political objectives, especially a rejection of racial integration. [41]

As debate raged over the civil rights movement's future, opposition to the Vietnam War was expanding, especially on college campuses. Tens of thousands of male students were becoming eligible for the draft upon graduation (or dropping out), ensuring that the escalating war commanded their attention.

By the late 1960s, the anti-war movement became polarized between ultra-leftist radicals and traditionally minded leftist activists who wanted to focus on electoral politics.

On the radical left, the only anti-war mass organization — Students for a Democratic Society (SDS) — imploded in 1969 after a bitter conflict between the "Weatherman" faction,* which preached immediate armed struggle, and a Maoist group, the Progressive Labor Party, which advocated organizing workers. Less fanatical activists fell away and SDS vanished.

At the peak of anti-war activism, news in May 1970 of a U.S. military invasion into Cambodia brought millions of war opponents into the streets throughout the country. Student demonstrations at some 1,350 colleges and universities involved an estimated 4.3 million people — 60 percent of the country's total student population. Four students at Kent State University in Kent, Ohio, were shot and killed by National Guard troops during a demonstration; and two students at predominantly African-American Jackson State College in Mississippi were shot to death by police. [42]

The anti-war movement faded away with the U.S. military withdrawal from Vietnam in 1973. Many members whose goals transcended an end to the war — that is, they sought a more equitable society — continued their activism. (An SDS founder, Tom Hayden, was a California legislator from 1982-2000.) But since the draft ended in 1973, America's military campaigns haven't mobilized an opposition even close to the size and intensity of the anti-Vietnam War movement. [43]

Globalization

Issues that aroused the left in the post-Vietnam years included nuclear power (opposed), U.S. policy in Central America (opposed) and environmental protection (supported). In the 1990s, these concerns largely gave way to opposition to the package of liberalized foreign trade rules and job outsourcing known as "globalization."

Opposition had been building for years among unions and residents of industrial areas in the Northeast and Midwest, which were losing jobs to foreign factories. When the North American Free Trade Agreement (NAFTA) came before Congress for approval in the early 1990s, the globalization question went national. [44]

At first, the NAFTA debate took place almost entirely in the political arena, not the streets. Both the Democratic and Republican parties backed NAFTA; Democratic President Bill Clinton pushed it through Congress in 1993 after his Republican predecessor, George H. W. Bush, tried but failed to do so. [45]

Opposition to globalization simmered through the 1990s, drawing much of its inspiration from movements in more politicized societies in Latin America, Asia and Africa. In the United States, one major form of activism, starting on campuses in 1997, centered on boycotts of firms whose running shoes, sweatshirts and other apparel were made in foreign and domestic sweatshops. Garment-workers unions played a major role as well, an early sign that unions and the left were rebuilding their historic alliance. [46]

A more significant sign of that convergence came in 1999 during street demonstrations in Seattle that disrupted a meeting of the World Trade Organization (WTO) convened to negotiate international commerce rules. The demonstrations, which attracted as many 50,000 globalization opponents, included a small contingent of self-styled anarchists who smashed windows in chain stores and committed other acts of vandalism.

Seattle police were by their own accounts unprepared and overwhelmed. They responded by declaring a 50-block area of the city a "no-protest" zone, at one point declaring an all-night curfew in the area and deploying massive amounts of tear gas. Police Chief Norm Stamper, who resigned following the event, said recently that he unwittingly escalated conflict by using tear gas. Police who have recently used pepper spray against Occupy demonstrators are repeating his error,

* The name came from a line in a Bob Dylan song, "Subterranean Homesick Blues:" "You don't need a weatherman to know which way the wind blows."

Movement Mixes Anarchy and 'Pure' Democracy

Everybody gets to talk . . . and talk . . . and talk.

What's the difference between pure democracy and anarchy? The Occupy movement's decision-making process offers some answers. But one thing is certain: The process isn't neat and tidy. And sometimes it can be pretty raw.

At each occupation site, a General Assembly (G.A.) of all the activists present makes decisions through a process of "direct" democracy: Everyone votes on everything, everyone gets to speak. And speak. And speak. . . .

Some of them shout as well. At a December meeting of Occupy Oakland, one G.A. attendee periodically yelled four-letter obscenities during the assembly.

But occasional shouts are a price that the anarchist-inspired activists behind Occupy have been willing to pay. They launched Occupy Wall Street as a deliberately anti-hierarchical movement, providing a model for the entire nationwide movement and its sometimes chaotic decision-making process.

During preparations for a G.A. meeting in Manhattan in late October, a man approach the Facilitation Working Group, which would run the meeting, and proposed that the G.A. demand jobs for everyone. "The G.A. already said this is a movement without demands," another man said. "So how can there be a working group on demands?" [1]

In reality, the entire Occupy movement embodies a demand for change in an economic and political system that activists view as deeply unequal. "We come to you at a time when corporations, which place profit over people, self-interest over justice and oppression over equality run our governments," says the "Declaration of the Occupation of New York City," adopted by the Occupy Wall Street G.A. last Sept. 29. [2]

How to change the system? The declaration isn't specific: "Create a process to address the problems we face, and generate solutions accessible to everyone." [3]

That hard-to-disagree-with goal reflects organizers' initial vision of a movement that welcomed all comers and gave them all equal voice. But anarchists, while opposed to hierarchy and political domination, don't necessarily oppose leadership and structure.

"The G.A. is beautiful, but it's not an effective decision-making body," an Occupy Wall Street organizer, filmmaker Marisa Holmes, told *The New Yorker.* [4] She developed a proposal for a "Spokes Council" that would run the encampment's day-to-day affairs. In late October, the G.A. approved the plan. (Though the 24-hour Wall Street camp no longer exists, the G.A. and the Spokes Council are still meeting.) [5]

Anarchism is popularly linked with wild-eyed bomb-throwers, who were indeed a presence in the late 19th and early 20th centuries. But anarchism as a political philosophy that traced social ills to hierarchical control had a deep influence on the early labor and radical movements, including the militant Industrial Workers of the World (IWW). Its accomplishments included a landmark victory in a textile workers' strike in Lawrence, Mass., in 1912, led in part by anarchists. [6]

Later, the antifascist side in the Spanish Civil War — which inspired generations of U.S. leftwingers — had a major anarchist presence. Though anarchism in theory rejects state power, four Spanish anarchist leaders became ministers in the Republican government that was under attack by right-wing military forces. [7]

Many European anarchists had become convinced years before, says Stephen Schwartz, a historian of the Spanish conflict, that their movement needed strong leaderships because "the anarchist workers could not attain on their own the necessary quality of leadership they needed to prevail in a major political conflict." [8]

Among U.S. radicals, anarchist influence has more recent roots as well. "There were strong anarchist streaks in the New Left of the 1960s," wrote Todd Gitlin, a professor at the Columbia University School of Journalism who was president of the radical Students for a Democratic Society (SDS) in 1963-64. [9]

An SDS slogan, "Let the people decide," Gitlin added, "meant in practice, 'Let's have long meetings where everyone gets to talk.' " The eventual effect, he adds, was that "tiny hierarchies" of highly ideological Marxist-Leninists were able to take over the organization, which eventually splintered and fell apart. [10]

But that outcome only encouraged even deeper suspicion of hierarchies in later radical movements. And when the collapse

he told the BBC. "Today it is being used indiscriminately," he said, "and that is really appalling." [47]

The Seattle demonstrations were a forerunner of the Occupy movement in other respects as well. Activists used email, Web chat rooms and cell phones — all in their infancy at the time — to mobilize and strategize. And they welcomed the participation of labor unions, which saw globalization as a job-killer. "We told people, if you pick up a CD or a paper cup or a stereo, under this [WTO] system, this product has more protections than the workers producing it," Ron Judd, executive secretary of the King County Labor Council in Washington state, told the *Los Angeles Times*, describing outreach to union members. [48]

In 2001, the Sept. 11 terrorist attacks transformed the political landscape. Left-liberal activists — those not transformed into hawks by the attacks — threw themselves into anti-Iraq War organizing, as well as civil liberties work and opposition to the George W.

of the Soviet Union seemed to spell the end of Marxism-Leninism as a viable model, and Western European socialist governments failed as well, Gitlin wrote, "Anarchism's major competitors for a theory of organization imploded." [11]

But none of that makes running a non-hierarchical organization any easier. One question already prompting debate is whether Occupy activists will work in the 2012 presidential campaign — conducted within a hierarchical, centralized, corporate-influenced political system. Many, anarchists or not, are disinclined. "A lot of activists, myself included, we vote, but we don't necessarily put much energy into the electoral process," says Jackie Smith, a University of Pittsburgh sociology professor who is working with the Occupy movement in her city.

OFF/AFP/Getty Images

Vladimir Lenin, main founder of the Soviet state, clashed with anarchists. In the 1960s, young American radicals inspired by Lenin clashed with anarchist-inspired counterparts, hastening the eventual collapse of Students for a Democratic Society.

Some activists, members of small groups formed under the Occupy umbrella, are more interested in what anarchist theoreticians call "direct action" — the other side of the sometimes cumbersome G.A. process.

In Oakland, one young group of activists who constituted Occupy Oakland's Tactical Action Committee took over a foreclosed house in a tough section of West Oakland, intending to use it as a base to organize resistance to foreclosures (as Occupy activists have done in Brooklyn, Chicago and Atlanta). [12]

Occupying homes to prevent foreclosure reflects a classically anarchist approach — the opposite of, say, asking a bank not to foreclose, or a sheriff not to evict occupants.

"The reason anarchists like direct action is because it means refusing to recognize the legitimacy of structures of power," David Graeber, an American professor of anthropology at the University of London and a Wall Street occupation planner, said before the movement began. "Nothing annoys forces of authority more than trying to bow out of the disciplinary game entirely and saying that we could just do things on our own. Direct action is a matter of acting as if you were already free." [13]

— Peter Katel, with reporting in Oakland by Daniel McGlynn

[1] Quoted in Mattathias Schwartz, "Pre-Occupied," *The New Yorker*, Nov. 28, 2011, www.newyorker.com/reporting/2011/11/28/111128fa_fact_schwartz.

[2] "Declaration of the Occupation of New York City," New York City General Assembly, www.nycga.net/resources/declaration.

[3] *Ibid.*

[4] Schwartz, *op. cit.*

[5] New York City General Assembly, /www.nycga.net/events/event/general-assembly-2012-01-05/.

[6] Dorothy Gallagher, *All the Right Enemies: The Life and Murder of Carlo Tresca* (1988), pp. 35-40; Michael Kazin, *American Dreamers: How the Left Changed America* (2011), pp. 127-129.

[7] Hugh Thomas, *The Spanish Civil War* (1961), pp. 44, 318.

[8] For background see Victor Alba and Stephen Schwartz, *Spanish Marxism Versus Soviet Communism: A History of the P.O.U.M. in the Spanish Civil War* (2009).

[9] Todd Gitlin, "The Left Declares Its Independence," *The New York Times*, Oct. 9, 2011, Section SR, p. 4.

[10] *Ibid.*

[11] *Ibid.*

[12] Jason Cherkis, "Occupy Atlanta Helps Save Iraq War Veteran's Home From Foreclosure," *Huffington Post*, Dec. 19, 2011, www.huffingtonpost.com/2011/12/19/occupy-atlanta-saves-iraq-veterans-home-from-foreclosure_n_1158097.html; Adam Martin, "Occupy Our Homes Takes Over Properties in New York and Chicago," *The Atlantic Wire*, Dec. 6, 2011, www.theatlanticwire.com/national/2011/12/occupy-our-homes-occupies-its-first-home/45832/.

[13] Ellen Evans and Jon Moses, "Interview With David Graeber," *The White Review*, 2011, www.thewhitereview.org/interviews/interview-with-david-graeber.

Bush administration.

Many commentators saw the 2008 Obama presidential campaign and the early phase of his administration as the rebirth of a liberal movement in sync with the Democratic Party — an alliance not seen since before the Vietnam War. "President Obama has a historic opportunity to restore an alliance that was crucial to the success of twentieth-century liberalism," Julian Zelizer, a Princeton historian, wrote in the liberal *Dissent* magazine in 2010. "The 2008 election depended on a broad Democratic coalition that bridged left and center." [49]

But the consensus is that the coalition is, at best, badly frayed. "For two years," wrote Columbia University's Gitlin after Occupy Wall Street began, "Barack Obama got the benefit of the doubt from fervent supporters — I'd bet that many of those in Lower Manhattan during these weeks went door-to-door for him in 2008 — and that support explains why no one occupied Wall Street in 2009." [50] ■

Current Situation

'Occupy' Caucuses

As the 2012 presidential race moves into full swing, Occupy demonstrators are trying to turn the primary-election process for evaluating presidential candidates into the latest theater of action.

The Iowa caucuses, held Jan. 3 and narrowly won by Romney by just eight votes over former Pennsylvania Sen. Rick Santorum, provided a preview of the Occupy efforts. Activists who organized "Occupy Iowa Caucuses" vowed to confront both Republican contenders and supporters of President Obama. "President Obama and the other bought-and-paid-for candidates who give us the brush-off when we try to ask real questions will be forced to hear us as we converge upon their campaign headquarters," organizers said on a website set up for the occasion. "We will chase the candidates and their Wall Street cronies around the state of Iowa. . . . We are taking American democracy back!" [51]

When the Republican primary road show moved to New Hampshire in early January, Occupy activists followed. Their numbers were not large, though Occupy New Hampshire members did manage to draw attention by attending GOP candidates' campaign events, sometimes chanting slogans. One of their targets, Romney, won the primary with 39.3 percent of the vote. Rep. Ron Paul, R-Tex., came in second, with 22.9 percent, followed by former Utah Gov. Jon Huntsman, 16.9 percent; Gingrich, 9.4 percent; and former Sen. Rick Santorum, 2.2 percent. All vowed to pursue their candidacies in the South Carolina Republican primary. [52]

In Iowa, activists' main targets were Republican candidates for the presidential nomination. For them, the Iowa caucuses — that state's more complicated version of a primary election — were a critical step in the process by which the list of contenders gets narrowed down.

On the last day of 2011, 18 Occupy protesters were arrested in separate episodes outside the Iowa headquarters of Republican candidates Michele Bachmann, a Minnesota representative who subsequently dropped out of the presidential race after finishing sixth in the state's caucuses; and former House speaker Gingrich, who finished fourth, and Santorum. [53]

Most of those arrested — members of a contingent small enough to fit in three rented buses — were arrest-hardened veterans of previous Occupy demonstrations. One of them, 16-year-old Heaven Chamberlain, had been arrested at an Occupy demonstration at the Iowa state capitol in October. She professed pride in her record. "It shows that I'm active with the community," she told *The New York Times*, "and that I care about people's opinions." [54]

Her mother and fellow Occupy activist shares that view of the teenager's rap sheet. "For her record I don't worry, because she's standing up for what's right," Heather Ryan told *The Times*. [55]

Iowa is not the only place in which the movement has been trying to demonstrate a 2012 presence. "Whose year? Our year!," chanted several hundred people gathered in New York's Zuccotti Park on New Year's Eve. [56] Their attempt to reclaim the park ended as did several of the Occupy events of 2011 in New York — with arrests, including at least one police use of pepper spray. [57]

Activists reoccupied the park in early January after city authorities removed barricades and checkpoints that had limited the number of people allowed in; but a ban on tents and sleeping bags remained in force.

But while the New York events resembled past confrontations between Occupy and the New York Police Department, the attempt to bring the movement to the caucuses apparently represented the first collision between Occupy and the electoral process.

Occupy activists aren't neglecting events that may enjoy higher visibility than primary elections. On New Year's Day, several thousand Occupy marchers followed the Rose Bowl parade in Pasadena, Calif., with a parade of their own. Their props included a 250-foot banner that said "We the People," and a 70-foot plastic octopus intended to represent the tentacles of corporate greed. [58]

'Occupy' Elections

One political campaign stands out as the best test case so far of the Occupy movement's effect on voters and candidates.

Elizabeth Warren, the front-runner for the Democratic nomination for the 2012 Senate election in Massachusetts, is the closest thing to an Occupy candidate within the two-party system.

A Harvard Law School professor of commercial law who gained national attention as a fierce critic of the financial industry, Warren launched her candidacy after President Obama backed off nominating her to head the new Consumer Financial Protection Bureau. He bowed to massive opposition from Republicans, echoing the position of industries the bureau is charged with overseeing. Warren, a specialist in consumer debt, largely wrote the legislation that created the bureau. [59]

The Oklahoma-born Warren's advocacy on behalf of ordinary consumers who sign up for credit cards and take out mortgages has done wonders for the campaign treasury of her possible general-election oppo-

Continued on p. 44

At Issue:

Will the Occupy movement continue to affect American politics?

DEAN BAKER
CO-DIRECTOR, CENTER FOR ECONOMIC AND POLICY RESEARCH

WRITTEN FOR *CQ RESEARCHER*, JANUARY 2012

yes

The Super Committee, the big topic of conversation in Washington in early October, was the longstanding dream of many D.C. deficit hawks. It had the power to produce a deficit-reduction plan that would be fast-tracked through Congress.

But as it turned out, the Super Committee produced no plan to send to Congress for a vote. Its deadline passed, and the committee became just another deficit-reduction plan to be tossed into history's dustbin.

Part of the committee's story was undoubtedly the intransigence of Republican members who refused to go along with anything that could raise taxes. However, part of the story was the constraints perceived by Democrats who were openly willing to include cuts to Social Security and Medicare as part of a deal.

As the Occupy Wall Street movement spread across the country, the obsession with deficit reduction dwindled. Almost every major news outlet ran one or more major stories on the rise in income inequality over the past three decades. The distinction between the "1 percent" who were the big gainers in the economy over the last three decades and the "99 percent" who had almost nothing to show became a standard feature of political debate.

In this context, it became almost inconceivable for the Democrats on the Super Committee to "reward" the 99 percent with big cuts in Social Security and Medicare. The party that has pretenses of protecting working people and the poor could not be seen slashing these two essential programs at a time when the country is still suffering from the recession.

President Obama's December speech in Osawatomie, Kan., which focused on inequality and helping ordinary workers get ahead, should also be seen in this context. There is a renewed commitment — at least in rhetoric — to pursue an economic agenda that advances the interest of the vast majority.

In this context it is striking to see the surge in interest in a financial-speculation tax. This is the sort of measure that gets to the heart of the Occupy agenda. It would strike a big blow directly against the financial speculation that has dominated Wall Street in the last few decades, while raising hundreds of billions of dollars over the next decade. The fact that this tax and other comparable measures are now part of the national debate is directly attributable to the Occupy movement.

NICK SCHULZ
DEWITT WALLACE FELLOW, AMERICAN ENTERPRISE INSTITUTE

WRITTEN FOR *CQ RESEARCHER*, JANUARY 2012

no

The current movement protesting income inequality aims its guns at the wrong targets. As long as that is so, it will not have much of an effect on American politics.

Most Americans aren't interested in redistributing income from the rich to the poor as a way of addressing inequality. They are more interested in living in a society with adequate social mobility — where a person can climb the socioeconomic ladder through talent and hard work. To the extent that envy animates today's anti-inequality movement, it will fail to gain sufficient political traction.

Upward mobility in America today requires an individual to possess adequate amounts of human, social and cultural capital. In order to address the obstacles to upward mobility, we could start by thinking about what I call a different kind of "home economics": the economic consequences of America's changing family structure. The collapse of intact families over the last half-century, manifest in rising numbers of single-parent homes and rising out-of-wedlock birthrates, has eroded vital human and social capital, and it has had baleful economic consequences as a result. This is a problem for which there is no easy solution, but it is a mistake to ignore it as a driver of economic outcomes.

We could also think creatively about another critical institution for inculcating and developing essential human and social capital — schools. There are good ideas across the ideological spectrum for reforming and strengthening schools. But genuine reform will require a period of messy experimentation and trial and error. As a nation we must be open to radical ways of thinking about education as entrepreneurs find new ways of educating students; develop new business, academic and management models; and build new technology.

To the extent that today's movement to protest inequality is comfortable with the educational status quo, it will fail to make a genuine difference.

While relative income and living standards matter, absolute living standards matter most of all. Ask yourself if you'd prefer to live in an unequal country with the living standards of the United States or an equal country with the living standards of Congo. The point is that snapshots of a nation's income inequality matter less over time to a nation's welfare than economic growth and increases in productivity. It's not that income inequality doesn't matter; it's just that many things matter a great deal more.

Continued from p. 42

nent. Finance-industry executives are pouring money into the campaign of Sen. Scott Brown, R-Mass., whom Warren would oppose in the November election if she wins the primary race in September. [60]

"Elizabeth is about 99-1-99," a Wall Street executive, Anthony Scaramucci, managing partner of Skybridge Capital, told *The New York Times*, referring to former Republican presidential primary candidate Herman Cain's "9-9-9" tax plan. "She thinks the 99 percent want to tax the 1 percent 99 percent. It is a failed strategy." [61]

The Center for Responsive Politics reports that the securities and investment, law and real-estate industries are among the top five sectors of Brown's campaign contributors. They account for about $3.2 million of $5.3 million in donations Brown has received since he began his national political career, winning a special election in January 2010 for the Senate seat vacated by the death of Democratic Sen. Edward M. (Ted) Kennedy. [62]

If her Wall Street enemies didn't suffice to link Warren with the Occupy movement, she herself drew the connection in late October soon after entering the primary race. "I created much of the intellectual foundation for what they do," she said of the movement, then in its second month. [63]

Republicans leapt to attack. A National Republican Senatorial Campaign Committee spokesman, Brian Walsh, noted that two Occupy Boston demonstrators had been arrested for allegedly selling heroin. "Professor Warren has yet to comment on whether these were also some of the individuals that she's now claiming to have provided the 'intellectual foundation' for as well," Walsh said in a press release. [64]

Warren then followed up her remark by drawing a line between her campaign and the Occupy movement. "What I meant to say was I've been protesting Wall Street for a long time," she told The Associated Press. "The Occupy Wall Street [Movement] is organic, it is independent, and that's how it should be." And she pointedly opposed law-breaking by demonstrators. [65]

Getty Images/Alex Wong

Elizabeth Warren, front-runner for the Democratic nomination for the 2012 Senate election in Massachusetts, is a favorite of the Occupy movement. The Harvard Law School professor gained national attention as a fierce critic of the financial industry. She launched her candidacy after President Obama bowed to massive opposition from Republicans and backed off nominating her to head the new Consumer Financial Protection Bureau, which she largely created.

But Republicans kept up their strategy of portraying Warren as comrade-in-arms of radical demonstrators. One TV ad produced by an affiliate of American Crossroads, a so-called "super PAC" not subject to funding or spending restrictions for its political advocacy, juxtaposed images of Warren with those of demonstrators, to illustrate that she "sides with extreme left" demonstrators who "attack police, do drugs and trash public parks." [66]

Strikingly, the next ad in the Crossroads campaign took an entirely different tack. Apparently responding to poll data showing voter discontent with banks and big business, the follow-up commercial depicted Warren as overly friendly to Wall Street. The ad focused on Warren's role as staff director of a congressional investigation of Treasury Department administration of the $700 billion financial industry bailout. "Congress had Warren oversee how your tax dollars were spent, bailing out the same banks that helped cause the financial meltdown," Crossroads declared. [67]

Warren shot back, calling the charge "ridiculous" in an ad of her own. [68]

'Occupy' and Anti-Semitism

Of all the accusations hurled at the Occupy movement, the potentially most damaging is that it's become an outlet for haters who follow a classic anti-Semitic script by arguing that Jews pull the strings on Wall Street.

Jewish supporters of Occupy responded immediately, noting that an author of the accusation is a Republican strategist. But that conflict has morphed into a debate within the amorphous movement itself over what role it should take, if any, on the conflict between Israel and Palestinians.

The anti-Semitism charge surfaced almost as soon as the movement began. A Web-broadcast video featured clips of anti-Jewish statements and placards from people at Occupy Wall Street. [69]

The video — which also featured cautious expressions of sympathy for the demonstrators by President Obama, former House Speaker Nancy Pelosi, D-Calif., and former New York Attorney General Eliot Spitzer — was produced by the Emergency Committee for Israel (ECI), whose chairman, William Kristol, editor of the *Weekly Standard*, is a prominent Republican of the hawkish neoconservative school. [70]

Aimed at rallying opposition to the movement, the video prompted immediate counterattacks from within the Jewish community.

"It's an old, discredited tactic: find a couple of unrepresentative people in a large movement and then conflate the oddity with the cause," said a statement signed by 15 prominent liberal Jewish Occupy supporters. "Occupy Wall Street is a mass protest against rising inequality in America." [71]

The nonpartisan Anti-Defamation League, a nearly century-old organization that fights anti-Semitism, declared in October that "anti-Semitism has not gained traction more broadly with the protesters, nor is it representative of the larger movement at this time." [72]

Before long, however, the issue of Occupy and anti-Semitism shifted from an argument between politically opposed foes and supporters of the movement. Activists began arguing over whether the Occupy movement should involve itself in the fight between Israel and the Palestinians. That debate reawakened the original conflict over Occupy as a refuge for anti-Jewish sentiment, given the long-running debate over when anti-Israel, pro-Palestinian politics cross the line into anti-Semitism. That highly charged issue runs through all debate over Israel, especially on the left and most especially among Jews.

One of the events that prompted the conflict was a Nov. 4 sit-in at the Israeli consulate in Boston by about 20 Occupy members who had marched from a downtown encampment in Dewey Square. [73]

The action was intended to support a failed attempt to bring supplies by ship to Gaza, a Palestinian enclave under Israeli military control, in defiance of an Israeli maritime blockade. In New York, Occupy Wall Street issued a Nov. 3 tweet of support for the blockade-running effort. But the tweet was deleted, on the grounds that the entire Occupy Wall Street movement hadn't taken a position on the matter, the nonpartisan JTA news service on Jewish affairs reported. [74]

Some in the movement were demanding that it oppose Israeli policies. But Daniel Sieradski, an Occupy activist who organized Occupy Judaism, which held Jewish services at Zuccotti Park, has been working to keep Occupy open to supporters as well as foes of Israeli policy by keeping the movement out of Middle Eastern matters. "We are being sidetracked by some in our community and some outside our community who are insisting on integrating this into the Occupy Wall Street platform," Sieradski told JTA. [75]

A long piece in the neoconservative monthly *Commentary* criticized that approach as a dodge to avoid grappling with the challenges posed by anti-Israel sentiment on the left — often, the Jewish left. "The blind quest for 'social justice' in its left-wing understanding, despite the onslaught of leftist hatred for the Jewish people and the Jewish state, demonstrates the degree to which too many Jews overlook or excuse the indefensible," wrote Jonathan Neumann, a fellow at the magazine who specializes in the Middle East. [76]

One of the targets of Neumann's criticism, staff writer Marc Tracy of *Tablet*, an online magazine on Jewish affairs, responded: "The main reason I did not enjoy seeing certain OWS [Occupy Wall Street] protests adopting an anti-Zionist agenda is because I saw neither the relevance nor the connection between anti-Zionism and OWS's '1 percent' message, and I didn't see the connection because I am in fact a Zionist who also supports OWS's economic message." [77] ■

OUTLOOK

New Progressive Era?

Of all the forecasts about the possible future of the Occupy movement, one of the most far-reaching comes from Jeffrey D. Sachs, an influential economist who directs the Earth Institute at Columbia University.

"A third progressive era is likely to be in the making," Sachs wrote in *The New York Times* in November. The Occupy movement, he argued, is harbinger and engine of a 21st-century version of the periods of the late 1800s and early 1900s and the 1930s characterized by sweeping social and regulatory legislation. [78]

"Twice before in American history, powerful corporate interests dominated Washington and brought America to a state of unacceptable inequality, instability and corruption," Sachs wrote. "Both times a social and political movement arose to restore democracy and shared prosperity." [79]

Kazin, the Georgetown University historian and veteran of the 1960s antiwar movement, offers a more cautious assessment. "Movements of this kind," he says, "especially ones that are this fluid and rise quickly, may also fragment quickly." He adds, however, that the large community of activist young people suddenly made visible by Occupy is likely to remain engaged, given the persistence of the economic conditions underlying the movement.

If Kazin is wary of declaring the dawn of a new age, he has the experience of having written in 1999 that the anti-globalization demonstrations in Seattle likely represented the birth of a new populist movement. [80] Yet Kazin in that piece may simply have been ahead of his time. "Something like Occupy would have come much sooner if not for 9/11," says Muldoon, the CWA union member working with the Occupy movement in New York. "It was like someone threw the emergency brake."

As for the future, Muldoon says, "I think you'll be able to look back and say that things shifted." She adds, "Some of this is up to us about how significant a shift."

Also up to the movement and its tentative allies in the Democratic Party is whether and how to bridge the profound differences between believers and nonbelievers in the two-party system.

Columbia University's Gitlin acknowledged: "Of course, it's also conceivable that the structural divergences are so great that they can't be bridged. Sometimes these things blow up and leave everything in ruins." [81]

Among Occupy opponents, Bossie of Citizens United, the producer of conservative videos, describes in a tone of deep satisfaction what he says will be the short and unremembered life of Occupy. "I don't think the movement had any effect except to tell the American people just what they don't want America to become," he says.

Alliances with conventional politicos are doomed, Bossie says. "The leftist politicians are now trying to distance themselves from it, because they understand the American people are so turned off by this really sick movement."

Davis, the former Democratic congressman, who describes himself as a centrist, argues that the movement's future depends on whether activists decide to remain outside the conventional political system. "You can influence society simply by making a point over and over again, which is relatively easy to do," he says. "Influencing politics is much harder. It requires mobilizing people, keeping them energized, raising money, building a structure."

Moreover, he says, the movement will have to develop a clearer analysis of America's ills — moving beyond frequently voiced complaints about the burdens of college loans. "I haven't heard Occupy Wall Street spend any time talking about 35 million children being income-insecure," he says, "Those children have a higher moral priority than people paying student loans."

Occupy's future also depends on the nature of authorities' response, argues the CWA's Dubnau. Repression, he notes, has been known to radicalize its targets.

Dubnau cites widely circulated video footage of a University of California, Davis, police officer squirting pepper spray into the faces of students conducting a peaceful sit-in on campus. [82] "You get pepper-sprayed," he says, "you're going to come out a different person." ■

** Freelance writer Daniel McGlynn contributed reporting from Oakland.*

Notes

[1] Quoted in "Inside Occupy Wall Street: A Tour of Activist Encampment at the heart of Growing Protest," "Democracy Now," Sept. 30, 2011, www.democracynow.org/2011/9/30/inside_occupy_wall_st_a_tour.

[2] Quoted in Erik Eckholm and Timothy Williams, "Anti-Wall Street Protests Spreading to Cities Large and Small," *The New York Times*, Oct. 4, 2011, p. A18.

[3] Paul Courson, "Occupy DC demonstrators bolstered by migrating NYC Occupiers," CNN, Jan. 3, 2012, www.cnn.com/2012/01/02/us/occupy-migration/?hpt=us_c2; New York City General Assembly, www.nycga.net/events/event/general-assembly-2012-01-05/.

[4] John Heilemann, "2012=1968," *New York* magazine, Nov. 27, 2011, http://nymag.com/news/politics/occupy-wall-street-2011-12; Sean Captain, "Occupy Geeks Are Building a Facebook for the 99%," *Wired* (Threat Level blog), Dec. 27, 2011, www.wired.com/threatlevel/2011/12/occupy-facebook.

[5] For background, see the following *CQ Researcher* reports: Peter Katel, "Child Poverty," Oct. 28, 2011, pp. 901-928; Maryann Haggerty, "Business Ethics," March 6, 2011, pp. 409-432; Marcia Clemmitt, "Income Inequality," Dec. 3, 2010, pp. 989-1012; Marcia Clemmitt, "Financial Industry Overhaul," July 30, 2010, pp. 629-652; Peter Behr, "Fixing Capitalism" (*CQ Global Researcher*), July 1, 2009, pp. 177-204; and Thomas J. Billitteri, "Middle Class Squeeze," March 6, 2009, pp. 201-224.

[6] "Trends in the Distribution of Household Income Between 1979 and 2007," Congressional Budget Office, October 2011, p. ix, www.cbo.gov/ftpdocs/124xx/doc12485/10-25-Household Income.pdf.

[7] "Divided We Stand: Why Inequality Keeps Rising — An Overview of Growing Inequalities in OECD Countries," OECD, 2011, p. 38, www.oecd.org/dataoecd/40/12/49170449.pdf.

[8] Sabrina Tavernise, "Survey Finds Rising Perception of Class Tension," *The New York Times*, Jan. 11, 2012.

[9] Heilemann, *op. cit.*

[10] Quoted in Beth Fouhy, "Democrats see minefield in Occupy protests," The Associated Press, Nov. 17, 2011; Michael Kazin, "Anarchism Now: Occupy Wall Street Revives an Ideology," *The New Republic*, Nov. 7, 2011, www.tnr.com/article/politics/97114/anarchy-occupy-wall-street-throwback.

[11] Thomas Kaplan, "Albany Tax Deal To Increase Rate For Top Earners," *The New York Times*, Dec. 7, 2011, p. A1; Andrew Rosenthal, "Fighting the 'Governor One Percent' Label," The Loyal Opposition blog, *The New York Times*, Nov. 30, 2011.

[12] "Frustration with Congress Could Hurt Republican Incumbents," Pew Research Center, Dec. 15, 2011, pp. 3-4, www.people-press.org/files/legacy-pdf/12-15-11%20Congress%20and%20Economy%20release.pdf.

[13] Adam Gabbatt, "Scott Olsen injuries prompt review as Occupy Oakland protests continue," *The Guardian*, Oct. 26, 2011, www.guardian.co.uk/world/2011/oct/26/scott-olsen-occupy-

oakland-review; Joshua Holland, "Who's Behind the Mayhem at the Occupy Oakland Protests?," *AlterNet*, Nov. 11, 2011, www.alternet.org/media/153053/who's_behind_the_mayhem_at_the_occupy_oakland_protests/?page=entire.

[14] "Remarks by the President on the Economy in Osawatomie, Kansas," The White House, Dec. 6, 2011, www.whitehouse.gov/the-press-office/2011/12/06/remarks-president-economy-osawatomie-kansas.

[15] "From the Archives: President Teddy Roosevelt's New Nationalism Speech," The White House Blog, Dec. 6, 2011, www.whitehouse.gov/blog/2011/12/06/archives-president-teddy-roosevelts-new-nationalism-speech.

[16] Nicholas Confessore, Christopher Drew and Julie Creswell, "Buyout Profits Keep Flowing to Romney," *The New York Times*, Dec. 18, 2011, www.nytimes.com/2011/12/19/us/politics/retirement-deal-keeps-bain-money-flowing-to-romney.html?pagewanted=all. See also Sarah B. Boxer, "Mitt Romney zings 'Occupy Wall Street' and praises Herman Cain in N.H.," CBS News, Oct. 11, 2011, www.cbsnews.com/8301-503544_162-20118511-503544.html.

[17] Meg Handley, "Romney Conjures Occupy Wall Street in New Campaign Video," *U.S. News & World Report*, Dec. 28, 2011, www.usnews.com/news/blogs/ballot-2012/2011/12/28/romney-conjures-occupy-wall-street-in-new-campaign-video; "We Are the 99 Percent," http://wearethe99percent.tumblr.com.

[18] Quoted in "Newt Gingrich on Occupy Wall Street: Protesters Should 'Get a Job' and 'Take a Bath,' " *Huffington Post*, Nov. 19, 2011, www.huffingtonpost.com/2011/11/19/newt-gingrich-occupy-wall-street-job-bath_n_1103172.html.

[19] "More Now Disagree With Tea Party — Even in Tea Party Districts," Pew Research Center, Nov. 29, 2011, www.people-press.org/2011/11/29/more-now-disagree-with-tea-party---even-in-tea-party-districts.

[20] "We Are the 99 Percent," http://wearethe99percent.tumblr.com.

[21] Rich Lowry, "Heed the 99 Percent," *National Review*, Oct. 14, 2011, www.nationalreview.com/articles/280104/heed-99-percent-rich-lowry.

[22] Dylan Byers, "Occupy Wall Street is winning," *Politico*, Nov. 11, 2011, www.politico.com/blogs/bensmith/1111/Occupy_Wall_Street_is_winning.html#.

[23] Jared Bernstein, "On Inequality: Why Now?," *On the Economy* (blog), Dec. 6, 2011, http://jaredbernsteinblog.com/on-inequality-why-now/.

[24] "A Report Card for the Tea Party," "Weekend Edition Sunday," NPR, Dec. 25, 2011, www.npr.org/2011/12/25/144248297/a-report-card-for-the-tea-party-2011.

[25] Neil Irwin, "Hamilton Project relaunches in a more friendly environment," *The Washington Post*, April 22, 2010, p. A17.

[26] Madeleine Kunin, "Occupy Congress," *The Huffington Post*, Dec. 9, 2011, www.huffingtonpost.com/madeleine-m-kunin/occupy-congress_b_1138870.html.

[27] Heilemann, *op. cit.*

[28] Adam Hochschild, "Common Threads: We Are Not Alone," *Occupied Wall Street Journal*, Nov. 18, 2011, http://occupiedmedia.us/2011/11/wearenotalone.

[29] *Ibid.*

[30] Stephen Brier, *et al.*, *Who Built America?: Working People & the Nation's Economy, Politics, Culture & Society* (1992), pp. 68-154.

[31] *Ibid.*, pp. 111-112.

[32] Richard Schneirov, "The Pullman Strike and Boycott," *Illinois During the Gilded Age* (2007), http://dig.lib.niu.edu/gildedage/pullman/events3.html.

[33] Amanda Wisner, " 'General' Jacob S. Coxey," Massillon (Ohio) Museum, 2006, www.massillonmuseum.org/research_massillonhistory_coxey.html.

About the Author

Peter Katel is a *CQ Researcher* staff writer who previously reported on Haiti and Latin America for *Time* and *Newsweek* and covered the Southwest for newspapers in New Mexico. He has received several journalism awards, including the Bartolomé Mitre Award for coverage of drug trafficking, from the Inter-American Press Association. He holds an A.B. in university studies from the University of New Mexico. His recent reports include "Child Poverty" and "Reviving Manufacturing."

[34] Beverly Gage, "Lessons for Occupy Wall Street," *Slate*, Nov. 2, 2011, /www.slate.com/articles/business/moneybox/2011/11/occupy_wall_street_how_how_the_protesters_should_respond_to_esca.single.html.

[35] "The Bonus March," "American Experience," PBS, undated, www.pbs.org/wgbh/amex/macarthur/peopleevents/pandeAMEX89.html.

[36] Jim Pope, "Worker Lawmaking, Sit-Down Strikes, and the Shaping of American Industrial Relations, 1935-1958," *Law and History Review*, Spring 2006, www.historycooperative.org/journals/lhr/24.1/pope.html.

[37] *Ibid.*

[38] Quoted in "Desegregation of Central High School," National Park Service in *Encyclopedia of Arkansas History and Culture*, updated Sept. 28, 2011, http://encyclopediaofarkansas.net/encyclopedia/entry-detail.aspx?entryID=718.

[39] "Freedom to Travel," in "Freedom Riders," PBS, 2011, www.pbs.org/wgbh/americanexperience/freedomriders/issues/freedom-to-travel.

[40] "Major Features of the Civil Rights Act of 1964," Dirksen Congressional Center, undated, www.congresslink.org/print_basics_histmats_civilrights64text.htm; "The Voting Rights Act of 1965," U.S. Justice Department, undated, www.justice.gov/crt/about/vot/intro/intro_b.php.

[41] "1968 AFSCME Memphis Sanitation Workers' Strike Chronology," AFSCME, undated, www.afscme.org/union/history/mlk/1968-afscme-memphis-sanitation-workers-strike-chronology; Daniel Levine, *Bayard Rustin and the Civil Rights Movement* (2000), pp. 191-192.

[42] Jerry M. Lewis and Thomas R. Hensley, "The May 4 Shootings at Kent State University: The Search for Historical Accuracy," Prof. Jerry M. Lewis website, http://dept.kent.edu/sociology/lewis/lewihen.htm; Kirkpatrick Sale, *SDS* (1974), pp. 635-636.

[43] Drummond Ayres Jr., "Political Briefing; System Catches Up With Tom Hayden," *The New York Times*, Aug. 27, 2000, www.nytimes.com/2000/08/27/us/political-briefing-system-catches-up-with-tom-hayden.html?src=pm.

[44] For background, see Peter Katel, "Reviving Manufacturing," *CQ Researcher*, July 22, 2011, pp. 601-624.

[45] "NAFTA and Democracy," Public Citizen, undated, /www.citizen.org/trade/nafta/votes; "NAFTA," *Duke Law Library & Technology*, updated January 2011, www.law.duke.edu/lib/researchguides/nafta.

[46] Liz Featherstone, "Students Against Sweatshops: A History," in Daniel E. Bender and Richard A. Greenwald, eds., *Sweatshop USA:*

The American Sweatshop in Historical and Global Perspective (2003), pp. 247-264.

[47] Quoted in Chloe Hadjimatheou, "Ex-Seattle chief: 'Occupy' police used 'failed' tactics," BBC News, Nov. 28, 2011, www.bbc.co.uk/news/magazine-15929017.

[48] Quoted in Kim Murphy and Nancy Cleeland, "Labor Unions Revive Powerful Past as WTO March Looks to New Future," *Los Angeles Times*, Dec. 4, 1999, p. A18.

[49] Julian E. Zelizer, "Carter, Obama, and the Left-Center Divide," *Dissent*, June 9, 2010, www.dissentmagazine.org/online.php?id=361.

[50] Todd Gitlin, "The Left Declares Its Independence," *The New York Times*, Oct. 9, 2011, Opinion Section, p. 4.

[51] "First in the Nation Caucus Occupation," Occupy Iowa Caucuses, undated, www.occupyiowacaucuses.org.

[52] "New Hampshire Primary Results," *The New York Times*, Jan. 10, 2012, http://elections.nytimes.com/2012/primaries/results/live/2012-01-10.

[53] Brian Bakst, "Occupy Protesters Arrested Outside Republican Presidential Candidates' Iowa Campaign Headquarters," The Associated Press (*Huffington Post*), Dec. 31, 2011, www.huffingtonpost.com/2011/12/31/occupy-protests-iowa-caucuses-2012_n_1177997.html?ref=occupy-wall-street.

[54] Quoted in Will Storey, "For 'Occupy the Caucus' Protesters, a Successful Day of Arrests," *The New York Times* (The Caucus blog), Dec. 31, 2011, http://thecaucus.blogs.nytimes.com/2011/12/31/for-occupy-the-caucus-protesters-a-successful-day-of-arrests.

[55] Quoted in *ibid*.

[56] Quoted in Colin Moynihan and Elizabeth A. Harris, "Surging Back Into Zuccotti Park, Protesters Are Cleared by Police," *The New York Times* (City Room blog), updated Jan. 1, 2012, http://cityroom.blogs.nytimes.com/2011/12/31/protesters-surge-back-into-zuccotti-park.

[57] *Ibid*.

[58] "Rose Bowl parade gets occupied," The Associated Press (CBS News), Jan. 2, 2012, www.cbsnews.com/8301-201_162-57350999/rose-bowl-parade-gets-occupied.

[59] Samuel P. Jacobs, "Warren Takes Credit for Occupy Wall Street," *Daily Beast*, Oct. 24, 2011, www.thedailybeast.com/articles/2011/10/24/elizabeth-warren-i-created-occupy-wall-street.html; Jim Puzzanghera "U.S. Senate race puts spotlight on Wall St.," *Orlando Sentinel*, Dec. 30, 2011, p. A13.

[60] Quoted in Nicholas Confessore, "Vilifying Rival, Wall St. Rallies for Senate Ally," *The New York Times*, Nov. 18, 2011, www.nytimes.com/2011/11/19/us/politics/wall-street-rallies-around-scott-brown-for-senate-race.html?pagewanted=all.

[61] Quoted in *ibid*.

[62] "Total Raised and Spent, 2012 Race: Massachusetts Senate," Center for Responsive Politics, updated Dec. 30, 2011, www.opensecrets.org/races/summary.php?cycle=2012&id=MAS1.

[63] Quoted in Jacobs, *op. cit.*

[64] Quoted in Andrew Miga, "Warren claims credit for Occupy Wall St. protests," The Associated Press, Oct. 25, 2011.

[65] Quoted in Bob Salsberg, "US Senate hopeful Warren clarifies protest remark," The Associated Press, Oct. 27, 2011.

[66] Quoted in Andrew Miga, "Outside groups air barrage of ads in Mass. Race," The Associated Press, Dec. 27, 2011.

[67] Quoted in Puzzanghera, *op. cit.*

[68] Miga, *op. cit.*, "Outside groups."

[69] "Hate at Occupy Wall Street," Emergency Committee for Israel, Oct. 13, 2011, www.youtube.com/watch?feature=player_embedded&v=NIlRQCPJcew#!.

[70] "Emergency Committee for Israel," www.committeeforisrael.com.

[71] "Jewish Leaders Denounce Right-Wing Smears of Occupy Wall Street," Jewish Leaders Against Smears, Nov. 1, 2011, http://jewishleadersagainstsmears.wordpress.com.

[72] " 'Occupy Wall Street' Demonstrations: Anti-Semitic Incidents Surface," Anti-Defamation League, updated Nov. 1, 2011, www.adl.org/main_Extremism/occupy_wall_street.htm.

[73] Dennis Trainor Jr., "Occupy Boston Occupies Israeli Consulate," ncftv, YouTube, Nov. 4, 2011, www.youtube.com/watch?v=xd1uO29UwzY.

[74] Dan Klein, "Pro-Palestinian activists push cause within Occupy Wall Street movement," JTA, Nov. 15, 2011, www.jta.org/news/article-print/2011/11/15/3090241/pro-palestinian-activists-face-pushback-within-occupy-wall-street-movement?TB_iframe=true&width=750&height=500.

[75] Quoted in *ibid*.

[76] Jonathan Neumann, "Occupy Wall Street and the Jews," *Commentary*, January 2012, www.commentarymagazine.com/article/occupy-wall-street-and-the-jews.

[77] Marc Tracy, "How Jewish is Occupy Wall Street?," *Tablet*, Dec. 29, 2011, www.tabletmag.com/scroll/87123/how-jewish-is-occupy-wall-street/.

[78] Jeffrey D. Sachs, "The New Progressive Movement," *The New York Times*, Nov. 12, 2011, www.nytimes.com/2011/11/13/opinion/sunday/the-new-progressive-movement.html.

[79] *Ibid*.

[80] Michael Kazin, "Saying No to W.T.O.," *The New York Times*, Dec. 5, 1999, Sec. 4, p. 17.

[81] Heilemann, *op. cit.*

[82] "UC Davis Protesters Pepper Sprayed," Aggie TV, Nov. 18, 2011, www.youtube.com/watch?v=6AdDLhPwpp4.

FOR MORE INFORMATION

Center for the Study of Social Movements, University of Notre Dame, Notre Dame, IN 46556; http://nd.edu/~cssm. The center's blog includes discussion and analysis of developments in the Occupy movement.

Center on Budget and Policy Priorities, 820 First St., N.E., Washington DC 20002; 202-408-1056; www.cbpp.org. Liberal think tank and major center of research on inequality, unemployment, and policies to counteract them.

Citizens United, 1006 Pennsylvania Ave., S.E., Washington, DC 20003; 202-547-5420; www.citizensunited.org. The conservative media-production and advocacy group is preparing a movie on the Occupy movement.

Congressional Budget Office, Ford House Office Building, 2nd and D Streets, S.W., Washington DC 20515; 202-226-2602; www.cbo.gov. Nonpartisan agency that has conducted research on inequality and other issues raised by the Occupy movement.

New York City General Assembly, www.nycga.net. Website has information on meetings of the Occupy Wall Street General Assembly and of many single-topic working groups.

Bibliography

Selected Sources

Books

Flank, Lenny, ed., *Voices From the 99 Percent: An Oral History of the Occupy Wall Street Movement*, Red and Black, 2011.

Participants tell the movement's brief story thus far.

Gessen, Keith, et al., eds., *Occupy: Scenes from Occupied America*, n+1, 2011.

A series of reports and essays by sympathetic observers chronicle the movement and examine its possibilities.

Kazin, Michael, *American Dreamers: How the Left Changed a Nation*, Knopf, 2011.

A Georgetown University historian, sympathetic but not naive, examines the role of the left in U.S. history.

Articles

Abelson, Max, "Bankers Join Billionaires to Debunk 'Imbecile' Attack on Top 1%," Bloomberg, http://mobile.bloomberg.com/news/2011-12-20/bankers-join-billionaires-to-debunk-imbecile-attack-on-top-1-.html.

Wealthy Americans explain their anger at, in their view, being vilified for their success.

Colin, Chris, "A teepee grows in Oakland," *Salon*, Nov. 30, 2011, www.salon.com/2011/11/30/a_teepee_grows_in_oakland/.

A writer chronicles Occupy Oakland activists' search for direction after the forcible closing of their encampment.

Dupuy, Tina, "The Occupy Movement's Woman Problem," *The Atlantic*, Nov. 21, 2011, www.theatlantic.com/politics/archive/2011/11/the-occupy-movements-woman-problem/248831/.

A journalist sympathetic to the Occupy movement reports on gender imbalance in the encampments.

Gage, Beverly, "Occupy Wall Street: How the protesters should respond to escalating violence," *Slate*, Nov. 2, 2011, www.slate.com/articles/business/moneybox/2011/11/occupy_wall_street_how_how_the_protesters_should_respond_to_esca.html.

A Yale historian puts repression of Occupy demonstrations in the context the violent birth of the labor movement.

Lowry, Rich, "Heed the 99 Percent," *National Review Online*, Oct. 14, 2011, www.nationalreview.com/articles/280104/heed-99-percent-rich-lowry.

Though critical of the Occupy movement, a conservative magazine editor acknowledges the economic and social distress that prompted its rise.

Meighan, Patrick, "My Occupy LA Arrest," myoccupylaarrest.blogspot.com/2011_12_01_archive.html.

An Occupy LA demonstrator gives a long, angry account of his arrest and contrasts the gratuitous brutality he says he and others suffered with the non-prosecution of bankers.

Packer, George, "All the Angry People," *The New Yorker*, Dec. 5, 2011, www.newyorker.com/reporting/2011/12/05/111205fa_fact_packer.

A writer specializing in political movements covers Occupy New York through the experience of a previously apolitical participant, a high-tech specialist who lost his job in the recession.

Wallsten, Peter, "Lending a little organized labor to Occupy Wall Street," *The Washington Post*, Oct. 21, 2011, p. A1.

Ties are growing between Occupy and unions.

Whoriskey, Peter, "Growing wealth widens distance between lawmakers and constituents," *The Washington Post*, Dec. 26, 2011; and Lichtblau, Eric, "Economic Downturn Took a Detour at Capitol Hill," *The New York Times*, Dec. 26, 2011.

In two major and similar reports, reporters detail lawmakers' increasing affluence.

Reports and studies

"Trends in the Distribution of Household Income Between 1979 and 2007," Congressional Budget Office, October 2011, www.cbo.gov/ftpdocs/124xx/doc12485/10-25-Household-Income.pdf.

In painstaking detail, the nonpartisan congressional agency documents the growth and extent of the wealth gap.

"Frustration with Congress Could Hurt Republican Incumbents," Pew Research Center, Dec. 15, 2011, www.people-press.org/files/legacy-pdf/12-15-11%20Congress%20and%20Economy%20release.pdf.

One section of the nonpartisan center's report analyzes survey responses on the Occupy movement and inequality.

On the Web

***Occupy Wall Street page, Huffington Post*, www.huffingtonpost.com/news/occupy-wall-street.**

Daily coverage by the liberal-leaning news site.

***Occupy Videos*, http://occupyvideos.org.**

Videos sympathetically documenting Occupy activities.

***We Are the 99 Percent*, http://wearethe99percent.tumblr.com.**

Individual accounts by those who call themselves part of the "99 percent."

The Next Step:

Additional Articles from Current Periodicals

Democratic Party

Bierman, Noah, "Warren Walks Fine Line on Occupy Movement," *The Boston Globe*, Oct. 26, 2011, p. 1, articles.boston.com/2011-10-26/news/30324894_1_tea-party-movement-elizabeth-warren-protesters.

Elizabeth Warren, a Democratic Massachusetts candidate for the Senate, has backed the Occupy movement's message but has avoided close ties with the movement itself.

Kochakian, Charles, "OWS Golden Ticket for Democrats?" *New Haven* (Conn.) *Register*, Oct. 22, 2011, p. A8.

Occupy protesters' demand for "economic justice" may provide Democrats with political capital to enact more Wall Street reforms.

Lorber, Janie, "Occupy, Liberals Can't Get Together," *Roll Call*, Dec. 14, 2011, www.rollcall.com/issues/57_74/Occupy_Liberals_Tensions-211034-1.html.

Democrats are adopting the Occupy movement's "99 percent" language but retreating from its anti-capitalist rhetoric.

Robinson, Eugene, "Occupy Movement Is a Largely Undeserved Windfall for Democrats," *Contra Costa* (Calif.) *Times*, Oct. 18, 2011, www.contracostatimes.com/ci_19139409.

Democrats may reap benefits from the Occupy movement even though President Obama hasn't sought many fundamental Wall Street reforms.

Rothenberg, Stuart, "Do Democrats Face More Trouble From OWS?" *Roll Call*, Dec. 8, 2011, www.rollcall.com/issues/57_71/democrats_face_more_trouble_occupy_wall_street-210865-1.html.

The Occupy movement may have yet to redefine the country's politics, but it could still be a factor in the 2012 elections.

Scherer, Michael, "Inside the Organized Left's Courtship of Occupy Wall Street," *Time*, Oct. 13, 2011, swampland.time.com/2011/10/13/inside-the-organized-lefts-courtship-of-occupy-wall-street/#ixzz1ahIhcspA.

The potential of the Occupy movement has already been discussed at the highest levels of the Obama administration.

Ward, Louis C., "Can Wall Street Protests Help Obama?" *Orlando Sentinel*, Oct. 31, 2011, p. A23, articles.orlandosentinel.com/2011-10-31/news/os-ed-wall-street-obama-myword-103111-20111028_1_republican-front-runner-mitt-romney-obama-wall-street-s.

Using the Occupy movement as a strategy against Republicans comes with risks for Obama because many of his senior advisers have ties to the financial industry.

Wolfgang, Ben, "Parties See Protests As Two Sides of Coin," *The Washington Times*, Oct. 10, 2011, p. A1, www.washingtontimes.com/news/2011/oct/9/parties-see-protests-as-two-sides-of-coin/?page=all.

Many Democrats and Republicans see many similarities between the Occupy and Tea Party movements.

Young, J.T., "Democrats' Buy-In to Occupy Is a Risky Bet," *The Washington Times*, Nov. 28, 2011, p. B4, www.washingtontimes.com/news/2011/nov/26/democrats-buy-in-to-occupy-is-a-risky-bet/?page=all.

The potential for violent conflict makes the Occupy movement a risky association for Democrats, according to a former Republican congressional staffer.

Inequality

Filice, Carlo, "Protesters Complaining About a Lack of Social Equality," *Buffalo* (N.Y.) *News*, Oct. 19, 2011, p. A6, www.buffalonews.com/editorial-page/from-our-readers/another-voice/article599544.ece.

Wealth inequality does not necessarily mean the economic system is unfair as the Occupy movement suggests, according to a philosophy professor at the State University of New York at Geneseo.

Schulz, Nick, "Three Inconvenient Truths for Occupy Wall Street," *Los Angeles Times*, Nov. 30, 2011, p. A27, articles.latimes.com/2011/nov/30/opinion/la-oe-schulz-occupy-20111130.

The Occupy Wall Street movement is not fully aware of the factors that contribute to income inequality, according to a fellow at the conservative American Enterprise Institute.

International Protests

Adam, Karla, "United in Anger, Occupy Wall Street Protesters Go Global," *The Washington Post*, Oct. 16, 2011, p. A20, www.washingtonpost.com/world/europe/occupy-wall-street-protests-go-global/2011/10/15/gIQAp7kimL_story.html.

Occupy protests have been held in more than 900 cities across Europe, Africa, Asia, Latin America and the United States as a rallying cry against the global financial system and corporate greed.

Chu, Henry, "Brits Protest With Cheeky Creativity," *Chicago Tribune*, Oct. 20, 2011, p. 23.

The British public has been staging rallies similar to Occupy Wall Street but with more unconventional forms of protest.

Gardner, Daniel K., "China Is Ripe For Its Own Occupy Protests," *The Christian Science Monitor*, Nov. 8, 2011, www.csmonitor.com/Commentary/Opinion/2011/1108/

China-is-ripe-for-its-own-Occupy-protests.
Occupy protests have yet to spread to China, but the Chinese government has already cracked down on media coverage of the movement.

Preston, Jennifer, "Occupy Wall Street, And Its Global Chat," ***The New York Times*****, Oct. 17, 2011, p. B7, query.nytimes.com/gst/fullpage.html?res=9F05E3D61238F934A25753C1A9679D8B63.**
The Occupy Wall Street movement has gone global largely because of the online conversations facilitated by Twitter, Facebook and YouTube.

Labor Unions

Fagan, Kevin, "Occupy, Labor Look At Forming Alliance," ***The San Francisco Chronicle*****, Nov. 6, 2011, p. A1, articles.sfgate.com/2011-11-06/news/30368140_1_labor-unions-organized-labor-labor-movement.**
The Occupy movement and labor unions both support taxing wealthy corporations and boosting the rights of working people.

Fletcher, Ed, "Unions Press for Alliance With Occupy Sacramento," ***Sacramento*** **(Calif.)** ***Bee*****, Nov. 18, 2011, p. B1, www.sacbee.com/2011/11/18/4063788/unions-press-for-alliance-with.html.**
Unions have organized "we are the 99 percent" rallies as a sign of solidarity with the Occupy movement in Sacramento, Calif.

Greenhouse, Steven, "Standing Arm in Arm," ***The New York Times*****, Nov. 9, 2011, p. B1, www.nytimes.com/2011/11/09/business/occupy-movement-inspires-unions-to-embrace-bold-tactics.html?pagewanted=all.**
Unions are starting to embrace some of the bold tactics and social-media skills of the Occupy Wall Street movement.

Greenhouse, Steven, and Cara Buckley, "Seeking Energy, Unions Join Wall Street Protest," ***The New York Times*****, Oct. 6, 2011, p. A1, www.nytimes.com/2011/10/06/nyregion/major-unions-join-occupy-wall-street-protest.html?pagewanted=all.**
Labor union leaders believe they can tap into Occupy Wall Street's vitality, while protesters think they can benefit from the unions' money, membership and stature.

Johnson, O'Ryan, "'Occupy,' Unions Connect in Protest," ***Boston Herald*****, Oct. 14, 2011, p. 4, bostonherald.com/news/regional/view/2011_1014occupy_unions_connect_in_protest_local_labor_workers_join_forces_to_blast_verizon.**
The protesters of Occupy Boston have joined forces with organized labor to support electrical workers in a stalemate over negotiations with Verizon.

Wallsten, Peter, "Lending a Little Organized Labor to Occupy Wall Street," ***The Washington Post*****, Oct. 21, 2011, p. A1, www.washingtonpost.com/politics/occupy-wall-street-and-labor-movement-forming-uneasy-alliance/2011/10/19/gIQAkxo80L_story.html.**
Some Occupy activists regard their protests as a chance to push the increasingly weak union movement into a more aggressive posture.

Leadership

Braun, Bob, "Why a Movement Defined By Equality May Be Undone By It," ***Star-Ledger*** **(Newark, N.J.), Oct. 9, 2011, p. 1, blog.nj.com/njv_bob_braun/2011/10/braun_why_a_movement_defined_b.html.**
Occupy's long-term chances of effecting change are uncertain amid the movement's lack of a coherent strategy and leadership structure.

Brisbane, Arthur S., "Who Is Occupy Wall Street?" ***The New York Times*****, Nov. 13, 2011, p. SR12, www.nytimes.com/2011/11/13/opinion/sunday/who-is-occupy-wall-street.html.**
Occupy Wall Street is a movement that naturally abstains from leadership structures and formal demands.

Davis, Paul, "Occupy Wall Street Needs Leadership to Be Politically Relevant," ***American Banker*****, Oct. 27, 2011.**
Occupy Wall Street must develop a leadership structure if it wants to influence the 2012 presidential race, according to a University of Virginia political analyst.

Wood, Daniel B., and Gloria Goodale, "Does 'Occupy Wall Street' Have Leaders? Does It Need Any?" ***The Christian Science Monitor*****, Oct. 10, 2011, www.csmonitor.com/USA/Politics/2011/1010/Does-Occupy-Wall-Street-have-leaders-Does-it-need-any.**
Politicians and the media are scrambling to identify Occupy's leaders, but the movement wonders whether it needs any.

Citing *CQ Researcher*

Sample formats for citing these reports in a bibliography include the ones listed below. Preferred styles and formats vary, so please check with your instructor or professor.

MLA Style

Jost, Kenneth. "Remembering 9/11," CQ Researcher 2 Sept. 2011: 701-732.

APA Style

Jost, K. (2011, September 2). Remembering 9/11. *CQ Researcher, 9*, 701-732.

Chicago Style

Jost, Kenneth. "Remembering 9/11." *CQ Researcher*, September 2, 2011, 701-732.

CQ Researcher

Published by CQ Press, an Imprint of SAGE Publications, Inc.

www.cqresearcher.com

Financial Misconduct

Is government action tough enough?

The United States is slowly coming out of the worst financial crisis since the Great Depression, but many Americans want tougher law enforcement against the companies and executives they say created the mess. Four years after the crisis began, no prominent financial executives have been prosecuted. Civil charges were brought against major banks for misleading investors by packaging subprime mortgages with insufficient disclosure, but a federal judge recently rejected a proposed settlement as too lenient. Meanwhile, major mortgage lenders are negotiating a potential multibillion-dollar settlement over allegations of improper home foreclosures. Some states, however, are balking at banks' request for protection from subsequent lawsuits. Many experts say the government has failed to devote adequate resources to prosecuting wrongdoers. But some also acknowledge that certain activities that triggered the crisis were not necessarily illegal.

Raj Rajaratnam, founder of the now-defunct Galleon Group, leaves court on May 11, 2011, after his conviction on fraud and conspiracy charges. Prosecutors said he used insider information from Wall Street contacts to make more than $70 million over six years at his once high-flying hedge fund. He was sentenced to 11 years in prison.

INSIDE THIS REPORT

THE ISSUES 55

BACKGROUND 62

CHRONOLOGY 63

CURRENT SITUATION 68

AT ISSUE 69

OUTLOOK 70

BIBLIOGRAPHY 74

THE NEXT STEP 75

CQ Researcher • Jan. 20, 2012 • www.cqresearcher.com
Volume 22, Number 3 • Pages 53-76

Los Angeles | London | New Delhi
Singapore | Washington DC

RECIPIENT OF SOCIETY OF PROFESSIONAL JOURNALISTS AWARD FOR EXCELLENCE ◆ AMERICAN BAR ASSOCIATION SILVER GAVEL AWARD

FINANCIAL MISCONDUCT

THE ISSUES

55 • Was illegal conduct a major cause of the financial crisis?
• Was government action tough enough in prosecuting wrongdoing?
• Should mortgage lenders be punished for their role in improper foreclosures?

BACKGROUND

62 **Policing the Markets** Regulation of banking, housing and securities dates from the Great Depression.

65 **Losing Control** Widespread financial misconduct hit the U.S. beginning in the 1980s.

66 **Digging Out** After the financial crisis, prosecutors pursued wrongdoers, and lawmakers sought to prevent another financial meltdown.

CURRENT SITUATION

68 **Blaming Fannie, Freddie?** Top executives of the two mortgage giants are charged with fraud.

70 **New Agency Under Way** Republicans are challenging Richard Cordray's appointment to head the Consumer Financial Protection Bureau.

OUTLOOK

70 **No Way to Know?** The financial industry insists it could not have known the bubble would burst.

SIDEBARS AND GRAPHICS

56 **SEC Targets Insider Trading** More than 500 cases have been brought by the Securities and Exchange Commission.

57 **Financial Crisis Sparks SEC Charges** Misconduct laid to executives, companies.

58 **Madoff Eluded SEC for 16 Years** Despite tips, agency failed to halt his $18 billion Ponzi scheme.

60 **Financial Fraud Prosecutions on the Decline** Number of cases dropped sharply in past 20 years.

63 **Chronology** Key events since 1933.

64 **'Test Drive' for Wiretaps in Insider-Trade Case** Galleon Fund founder made more than $70 billion illegally.

69 **At Issue** Will the Financial Protection Bureau help consumers?

FOR FURTHER RESEARCH

73 **For More Information** Organizations to contact.

74 **Bibliography** Selected sources used.

75 **The Next Step** Additional articles.

75 **Citing *CQ Researcher*** Sample bibliography formats.

Cover: AFP/Getty Images/Emmanuel Dunand

CQ Researcher

Jan. 20, 2012
Volume 22, Number 3

MANAGING EDITOR: Thomas J. Billitteri tjb@cqpress.com

ASSISTANT MANAGING EDITOR: Kathy Koch kkoch@cqpress.com

CONTRIBUTING EDITOR: Thomas J. Colin tcolin@cqpress.com

ASSOCIATE EDITOR: Kenneth Jost

STAFF WRITERS: Marcia Clemmitt, Peter Katel

CONTRIBUTING WRITERS: Sarah Glazer, Alan Greenblatt, Barbara Mantel, Jennifer Weeks

DESIGN/PRODUCTION EDITOR: Olu B. Davis

ASSISTANT EDITOR: Darrell Dela Rosa

FACT CHECKER: Michelle Harris

Los Angeles | London | New Delhi
Singapore | Washington DC

An Imprint of SAGE Publications, Inc.

VICE PRESIDENT AND EDITORIAL DIRECTOR, HIGHER EDUCATION GROUP: Michele Sordi

DIRECTOR, ONLINE PUBLISHING: Todd Baldwin

CQ Researcher (ISSN 1056-2036) is printed on acid-free paper. Published weekly, except: (March wk. 5) (May wk. 4) (July wk. 1) (Aug. wks. 3, 4) (Nov. wk. 4) and (Dec. wks. 3, 4). Published by SAGE Publications, Inc., 2455 Teller Rd., Thousand Oaks, CA 91320. Annual full-service subscriptions start at $1,054. For pricing, call 1-800-834-9020. To purchase a *CQ Researcher* report in print or electronic format (PDF), visit www.cqpress.com or call 866-427-7737. Single reports start at $15. Bulk purchase discounts and electronic-rights licensing are also available. Periodicals postage paid at Thousand Oaks, California, and at additional mailing offices. POSTMASTER: Send address changes to *CQ Researcher*, 2300 N St., N.W., Suite 800, Washington, DC 20037.

Financial Misconduct

BY KENNETH JOST

THE ISSUES

The Securities and Exchange Commission (SEC) exuded confidence last fall when it announced a $285 million settlement with the financial conglomerate Citigroup for misleading investors about a $1 billion package of toxic mortgages sold in early 2007.

In its 25-page complaint filed Oct. 19, the federal agency depicted Citigroup as hatching a devious scheme to offload around $500 million of subprime mortgages to institutional investors without disclosing that Citi would be betting that the package would go bust.

Which it did. The investors — hedge funds and others — lost "several hundred millions of dollars" when the package defaulted in November 2007, according to the SEC. But Citigroup pocketed $160 million in profits by selling the mortgages with the expectation they would plunge in value — along with the original $34 million management fee for structuring and marketing the package.

AFP/Getty Images/Tim Sloan

Angelo Mozilo, founder of Countrywide Financial Corp., testifies before a congressional committee in 2008. The next year the Securities and Exchange Commission charged Mozilo with securities fraud and insider trading for selling off his Countrywide stock despite his worries about the quality of subprime loans Countrywide had helped create and popularize. In 2010, Mozilo agreed to pay a $67.5 million fine and never again serve as a director or officer of a publicly traded company.

The SEC had successfully brought similar securities-fraud complaints within the past 15 months against two other Wall Street giants: Goldman Sachs and JP Morgan Chase. The allegations underscored one dark side of the housing-market bust that led to the financial crisis of 2008. Big financial firms trading in securitized mortgages tried to profit or shield themselves from losses by concealing their own fears that many of the mortgages were likely to default.

Some news accounts, however, noted one potential stumbling block for the SEC's enforcement action against Citigroup. The case had been assigned to a federal judge in New York, Jed Rakoff, who — *The New York Times* pointed out — had previously "taken a hard line on SEC settlements." In February 2010, Rakoff had approved a $150 million settlement the agency negotiated with Bank of America for inadequate disclosure about the details of its acquisition of the former investment firm Merrill Lynch, but only after criticizing the deal as "half-baked justice at best."

The caveat proved to be prophetic. On Nov. 28, Rakoff stunned the SEC and Citigroup alike by refusing to sign off on the accord. In a 15-page decision, Rakoff blasted the agency for allowing Citigroup to resolve the complaint without admitting allegations that, the judge added, had been inadequately laid out. The settlement was "pocket change" for Citigroup, Rakoff said, while the agency was seeking only "a quick headline" instead of fulfilling its "statutory mission to see that the truth emerges." [1]

Rakoff's rebuff to one of the key federal agencies charged with protecting the public from financial misconduct came just six days before a nationally televised news program blasted the U.S. Justice Department for failing to prosecute high-level executives responsible for the financial crisis. The CBS program "60 Minutes" showcased would-be whistleblowers from Citigroup and Countrywide Financial, the nation's largest mortgage lender until its collapse in 2008. Former Countrywide executive Eileen Foster and former Citigroup vice president Richard Bowen told correspondent Steve Kroft that the Justice Department had shown no interest in hearing their accusations. [2]

The unrelated episodes exemplify a sentiment widely shared by the public that the financial crisis stemmed at least in part from violations of the law and that the government has failed to bring the wrongdoers to justice. "We know there are insiders within the companies who say there is strong evidence that the companies committed criminal wrongdoing that should have warranted prolonged investigations and that should have resulted in actions by now," says Russell Mokhiber, editor of

SEC Targets Insider Trading

The Securities and Exchange Commission has brought more than 500 insider-trading cases against individuals and entities over the past 10 years, including 57 in fiscal 2011. Defendants include hedge fund managers, corporate insiders, attorneys and government employees who allegedly traded securities on nonpublic information.

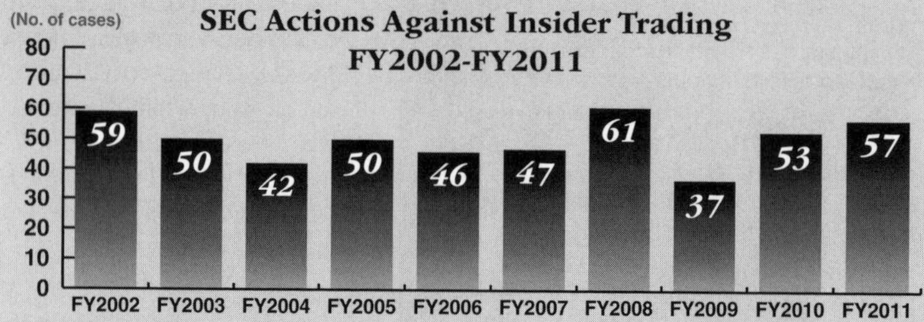

Source: "Year-by-Year SEC Enforcement Actions," Securities and Exchange Commission, www.sec.gov/news/newsroom/images/enfstats.pdf

Corporate Crime Reporter, a Washington, D.C.-based newsweekly founded in 1987. "And we have no actions."

The SEC and Justice Department both reject the criticism. The SEC has brought charges against 87 companies and individuals stemming from the financial crisis, including 39 CEOs, chief financial officers or other senior officers. The agency, which can bring civil but not criminal charges, said financial penalties and "other monetary recovery" in the actions total nearly $2 billion. [3] (*See graph, p. 57.*)

In the "60 Minutes" program, Assistant Attorney General Lanny Breuer, who heads the department's Criminal Division, insisted the government was pursuing investigations without any outside interference, but noted the difficulties of making a criminal case.

"I find the excessive risk-taking to be offensive," Breuer said. "I find the greed that was manifested by certain people to be very upsetting. But because I may have an emotional reaction and I may personally share the same frustration that American people all over the country are feeling, that in and of itself doesn't mean we bring a criminal case." [4]

Legal experts acknowledge some of the difficulties of bringing criminal prosecutions in cases based on complex and arcane financial transactions. Indeed, the government suffered a black eye in its most high-level prosecution when a federal jury acquitted two hedge fund managers at the defunct investment firm Bear Stearns of obstructing justice in November 2009.

Still, many experts agree with the public perception that the government could and should do more. "They aren't bringing as many cases against public firms for [misleading] financial statements as they could," says Jennifer Arlen, a securities law expert at New York University Law School. "And they haven't been as aggressive in going against senior individuals as they could."

William Black, an associate professor of economics and law at the University of Missouri-Kansas City and a former federal regulator, strongly seconds Rakoff's criticism of the SEC practice of allowing defendants to settle complaints without admitting wrongdoing. "When something doesn't work and doesn't work profoundly, you really should reconsider," says Black, who worked with the former Office of Thrift Supervision in cleaning up the savings and loan crisis of the 1980s. "And the SEC hasn't worked for a very long time."

Some experts, however, dispute the widespread assumption that criminal conduct was at the heart of the financial crisis. "People think that because there's a scandal that people ought to go to jail," says Thomas Gorman, a Washington lawyer who publishes a blog on SEC litigation. "That's not necessarily true."

The SEC has helped win prison sentences for some Wall Street figures by referring insider-trading cases to the Justice Department for prosecution. Most notably, Raj Rajaratnam, the head of the Galleon Group hedge fund, was sentenced to 11 years in prison in October for orchestrating a large insider-trading scheme at Galleon over a six-year period. Rajat Gupta, a prominent Wall Streeter formerly at Goldman Sachs, was indicted later that month for tipping off Rajaratnam to valuable inside information about corporate deals. (*See sidebar, p. 64.*)

In the latest insider-trading case, the U.S. attorney's office in Manhattan announced charges on Jan. 18 against a prominent hedge fund manager and six others in a scheme that allegedly netted nearly $62 million in illicit profits in 2008 and 2009 — rivaling the $70 million-plus in illicit gains that Rajaratnam was alleged to have realized. Anthony Chiason, co-founder of Level Global Investors LP, was charged along with others in a plot that allegedly used inside information from a paid tipster at Dell, the big computer maker, to trade in Dell stock. The tipster and two others pleaded guilty and were cooperating with authorities, the U.S. attorney's office said. [5]

Apart from the insider-trading cases, however, the only prominent Wall Street figure to be prosecuted successfully since the financial crisis hit is Bernard Madoff, who is now serving a 150-year prison sentence for turning his wealth-management business into a Ponzi scheme that cost investors $18 billion or more. Madoff's prosecution brought no kudos to the SEC, however. A report by the SEC's inspector general showed the agency failed to detect Madoff's crimes despite a succession of ever-more-detailed tips going as far back as 1992. (*See sidebar, p. 58.*)

Madoff's offenses were tangential, however, to the financial crisis. To date, no prominent executive who played a central role in the events leading up to the crisis has been prosecuted. The SEC did file civil complaints in December, however, against the former chief executives and four other top managers of the two government-sponsored mortgage lenders: Fannie Mae and Freddie Mac. The complaint, announced on Dec. 17, charges the executives with misleading investors about the extent of subprime mortgages in their portfolios.

Financial Crisis Sparks SEC Charges

The Securities and Exchange Commission has charged 87 entities and individuals — including 45 CEOs or other senior corporate officers — with financial misconduct in connection with the financial crisis that began in 2008. Penalties and other monetary relief total nearly $2 billion.

SEC Enforcement Actions Related to Financial Crisis*	
Number of entities and individuals charged	87
Number of CEOs, CFOs and other senior corporate officers charged	45
Total penalties, disgorgement and other monetary relief	$1.97 billion

* *As of Dec. 16, 2011*

Source: "SEC Enforcement Actions Addressing Misconduct That Led to or Arose From the Financial Crisis," Securities and Exchange Commission, December 2011, www.sec.gov/spotlight/enf-actions-fc.shtml

The SEC is appealing Rakoff's rejection of its proposed Citigroup settlement, but at the same time somewhat revising its policy of allowing defendants to avoid admitting wrongdoing in resolving civil complaints. Under a new policy announced Jan. 6, the SEC will not allow a defendant to stand mute on the substance of a civil complaint if it already has admitted wrongdoing in a related criminal case. [6]

Meanwhile, the nation's biggest banks are squared off with attorneys general from all 50 states over legal remedies for allegedly having used improper procedures to evict delinquent borrowers from their homes as the financial crisis deepened. The banks had been close to an agreement last summer, calling for a $20 billion settlement, but some states balked at their demand to be shielded from any further liability.

Another federal agency also is entering the field of policing financial misconduct with President Obama's appointment of a director for the newly established Consumer Financial Protection Board (CFPB). Obama named former Ohio Attorney General Richard Cordray to head the new agency on Jan. 4, using his power to make a recess appointment after Senate Republicans had stalled action on the nomination. GOP senators disputed the move, saying the Senate was technically in session. The legal wrangling masks a bigger issue, however, about whether the agency's powers to regulate nonbank financial institutions — such as payday lenders — will actually benefit consumers. (*See "At Issue," p. 69.*)

As the various legal proceedings continue, here are some of the questions being debated:

Was illegal conduct a major cause of the financial crisis?

Ralph Cioffi and Matthew Tannin were pulling down seven-figure salaries for managing hedge funds for the Wall Street firm Bear Stearns until the funds, heavily invested in mortgage securities, went belly up in July 2007. Federal prosecutors charged the two with securities fraud in June 2008, alleging that they knowingly misled investors about the funds' exposure to potentially toxic assets.

Cioffi and Tannin defended themselves in a three-week trial in fall 2009 by contending that they and their funds were victims of an unforeseeable market meltdown. Federal court jurors apparently agreed, finding the pair not guilty after barely six hours' deliberation. Columbia University securities law expert John Coffee called the result "a total rebuff to the prosecution." [7]

The too-clever-by-half financial deals that came crashing down in the summer and fall of 2008 naturally led many of the victims — investors left holding the bag, homeowners stuck with underwater mortgages — to assume that laws had been violated. But experts and financial-crisis watchers from President Obama down caution that illegal conduct was not necessarily to blame.

Answering a question at a press conference on Oct. 6 about the lack of major prosecutions, Obama replied: "One of the biggest problems about the collapse of Lehmans" —a reference to the investment bank Lehman Brothers, which declared bankruptcy in September 2008 —"and the subsequent financial crisis and the whole subprime lending fiasco is that a lot of that stuff wasn't necessarily illegal, it was just immoral or inappropriate or reckless." [8]

Assessing the verdict in the Bear Stearns case, financial journalists Bethany McLean and Joe Nocera voiced a similar view.

Madoff Eluded SEC for 16 Years

Despite tips, agency failed to halt $18 billion Ponzi scheme.

The Securities and Exchange Commission (SEC) got its first tip about something fishy in Bernard Madoff's investment operations in 1992. The next, very detailed tip came in 2000, followed by four more reports before Madoff sons' accusations against their father in December 2008 finally got the agency to stop what appears to have been the largest Ponzi scheme in U.S. history.*

The missed opportunities to stop a scheme that bilked investors out of $18 billion in cash — and higher amounts in claimed but nonexistent profits — are catalogued in a damning report issued in late August 2009 by the SEC's inspector general. SEC investigators repeatedly failed to grasp the significance of tipsters' information, according to the 450-page report, and never took some rudimentary steps that could have verified the suspicions. [1]

Two years later, the agency confirmed on Nov. 11 that it had disciplined eight employees for mishandling the investigation, but fired no one. A ninth employee resigned before disciplinary action could be taken, according to *The Washington Post*'s account. Victims of Madoff's fraud denounced the disciplinary steps as inadequate. [2]

Madoff, now 73, is serving a 150-year sentence in a federal prison in North Carolina even as a court-appointed trustee seeks to recover and return to victims some of the misappropriated funds. As of December, an estimated $11 billion had been recovered. [3]

The inspector general's report clears the SEC of any conflicts of interest or inappropriate interference in the investigations but ends with an understated critique of the agency's thoroughly botched response to tips it received.

"The SEC never properly examined or investigated Madoff's trading and never took the necessary, but basic, steps to determine if Madoff was operating a Ponzi scheme," the report states. "Had these efforts been made with appropriate follow-up at any time beginning in June 1992 until December 2008, the SEC could have uncovered the Ponzi scheme well before Madoff confessed."

The report prompted sharp criticism of the agency from members of Congress from both parties. Sen. Charles E. Schumer, D-N.Y., said the report showed "a level of incompetence unseen since [the Federal Emergency Management Agency's] handling of Hurricane Katrina." Sen. Charles Grassley, R-Iowa, said the agency's "utter failure" to follow up on the tips was "further evidence of a culture of deference toward the Wall Street elite." [4]

"The SEC was properly chastised," says Thomas Gorman, a Washington lawyer who publishes a blog on SEC litigation. "They had multiple opportunities to find that case. They simply failed to analyze the information."

Jennifer Arlen, a securities law professor at New York University, is more sympathetic to the agency's investigators' difficulties in dealing with what she calls "huge numbers of tips" of varying quality and credibility. "They're making tradeoffs between, 'Here are these things that I know something wrong's going on,' and 'Here's something big but it could be something or it could be nothing.' "

The first of the tips against Madoff came in June 1992 from customers of an investment firm suspicious that the firm was claiming "100%" safe investments with "extremely high and consistent" rates of return. The firm's investments, it turned out, were managed exclusively by Madoff. "Inexperienced" investigators suspected a Ponzi scheme, the inspector general's report states, but failed to conduct a thorough investigation.

Eight years later, the SEC received the first of three detailed complaints about Madoff from Harvey Markopolos, a securities executive-turned-independent financial fraud investigator in Boston. Markopolos' reports grew from an eight-page complaint in May

* A Ponzi scheme, named after the early 20th-century swindler Charles Ponzi, is a fraudulent investment operation in which investors are paid gains from money deposited by new investors. The schemes typically collapse when new investors cannot be recruited or a large number of investors try to cash out all at once.

"Much of what took place during the crisis was immoral, unjust, craven, delusional behavior—but it wasn't criminal," McLean and Nocera write in their book, *All the Devils Are Here.* [9]

Other experts, however, are less inclined to give a legal pass to the companies and individuals whose actions helped topple respected Wall Street firms, forced the government to bail out the nation's biggest banks, caused millions of homeowners to lose their homes and left hundreds of thousands of others owing more than their homes were worth.

"Accounting-control frauds drove this financial crisis, as they did the two prior financial crises: the Enron era fraud [of the early 2000s] and the S&L debacle," says Black, the former regulator from the S&L crisis. "What caused the crisis was overwhelmingly garden-variety fraud, which can and should be prosecuted."

Fraud was widely seen as a major factor in the 1980s S&L crisis, but the extent to which fraud caused the collapse of so many thrift institutions defies simple calculation. Early on, the government suggested that fraud was a factor in 70 to 80 percent of the thrift failures. But a study by the Resolution Trust Corporation, the government-

2000 to a longer version in October 2005 with the headline, "The World's Largest Hedge Fund Is a Fraud."

In each report, Markopolos said he had attempted but failed to replicate Madoff's claimed returns based on Madoff's reports of his investment strategy. Markopolos has forcefully criticized the agency in interviews and in his first-person account, *No One Would Listen*, published in 2010. [5]

AFP/Getty Images/Timothy A. Clary

Bernard Madoff, once a prince of Wall Street, pleaded guilty to running a Ponzi scheme that bilked investors out of $18 billion. He is serving a 150-year prison sentence.

By the third of his reports, Markopolos was being taken seriously by SEC investigators, according to the inspector general's report. They focused, however, more on the question of whether Madoff needed to register as an investment adviser than on whether he was operating a Ponzi scheme as Markopolos believed.

In addition, the report states, SEC investigators failed to take the basic step of attempting to verify through third parties whether Madoff actually was making the trades that he said he was making. "A simple inquiry . . . could have immediately revealed the fact that Madoff was not trading in the volume he was claiming," the report states.

Other complaints came to the SEC from "a respected hedge fund manager," an anonymous informant and a "concerned citizen," who first contacted the agency in December 2006 and again in March 2008. The last communication included the damning detail — later confirmed — that Madoff kept two sets of records, "the most interesting of which is on his computer which is always on his person."

Even when SEC investigators began probing his operations, Madoff, the one-time chairman of the NASDAQ stock exchange, fended them off in an interview, according to the report, by lording his credentials and knowledge over the less experienced agency personnel. Supervisors closed the investigation in January 2008 and declined to reopen it after receiving the report about double sets of books two months later.

Madoff's scheme finally unraveled when he confessed in December 2008 to his sons, Andrew and Mark, who reported him to federal authorities. Madoff was arrested on Dec. 10; he pleaded guilty on March 12, 2009, to 14 federal felonies, including securities fraud. In court, Madoff said he began his Ponzi scheme in 1991. Judge Denny Chin sentenced him three months later.

Madoff has apologized for his conduct, but his son Andrew has said he will never forgive his father. Mark Madoff committed suicide by hanging himself in his Manhattan apartment. He was found dead on Dec. 11, 2010, two years to the day after his father's arrest.

— Kenneth Jost

[1] "Investigation of Failure of SEC to Uncover Bernard Madoff's Ponzi Scheme — Public Version," U.S. Securities and Exchange Commission's Office of Investigations, Aug. 31, 2009, www.sec.gov/news/studies/2009/oig-509.pdf. The executive summary is found at pp. 20-41. For coverage, see David Stout, "Report Details How Madoff's Web Ensnared S.E.C.," *The New York Times*, Sept. 3, 2009, p. B1; Zachary A. Goldfarb, "The Madoff Files: A Chronicle of SEC Failure," *The Washington Post*, Sept. 3, 2009, p. A1.

[2] See David S. Hilzenrath, "SEC disciplines 8 employees for Madoff failures," *The Washington Post*, Nov. 12, 2011, p. A1; "SEC's disciplinary steps in Madoff case enrage fraud victims," *The Washington Post*, Nov. 17, 2011, p. A17.

[3] See Diana B. Henriques, "A Lasting Shadow," *The New York Times*, Dec. 12, 2011, Business, p. 1.

[4] See Sean Lengell, "Schumer: Boost SEC's budget to fight fraud," *The Washington Times*, Sept. 4, 2009, p. 9; Marcy Gordon, "SEC bungled Madoff probes, agency watchdog says," The Associated Press, Sept. 3, 2009.

[5] Harry Markopolos with Frank Case, Neil Chelo, Gaytri Kachroo, and Michael Ocrant, *No One Would Listen: A True Financial Thriller* (2010).

owned company organized to manage the assets of the failed thrifts, estimated more conservatively that fraud played a significant role in the failure of about a third of the institutions. Officials estimated that fraud was to blame for about 10 percent to 15 percent of net losses from the crisis. [10]

Any firm conclusion about how much fraud or other illegal conduct was to blame for the latest financial crisis is years away. For now, Arlen, the New York University professor, acknowledges uncertainty. "It does seem to me clear that there were disclosure problems," Arlen says, "but I'm not yet in a position to know whether the problems relate to judgment calls that are inherently part of the accounting profession or to actual fudging."

Lawyers who defend white-collar-crime cases voice doubts about the extent of fraud in the recent events. "In most of these cases, I don't see fraud," says David Douglass, a Washington lawyer and chair of the government enforcement and compliance committee of the defense bar organization DRI. "In most of these cases, I see why people would be unhappy with the results, but it's not fraud."

"You're talking about companies taking huge risks, companies being hugely

Financial Fraud Prosecutions on the Decline

Federal prosecutions for financial institution fraud have declined sharply over the past 20 years. They totaled 1,251 in the first 11 months of fiscal 2011 and were projected to reach 1,365 for the full year if trends continued. That would be 29 percent fewer than in 2006 and 58 percent fewer than a decade ago.

Criminal Fraud Prosecutions of Financial Institutions FY1991-FY2011

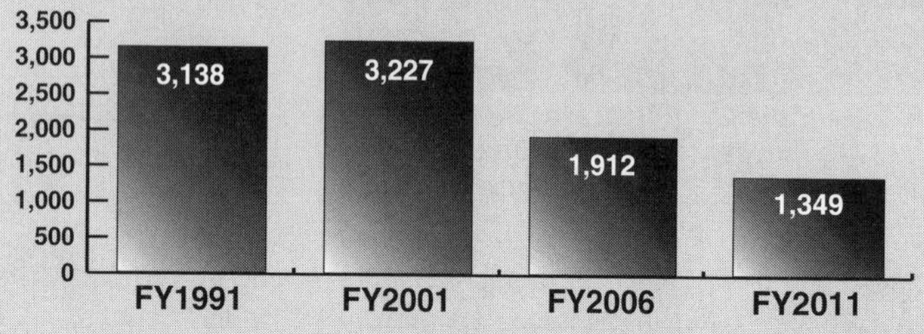

Source: Transactional Records Access Clearinghouse, Syracuse University, November 2011, trac.syr.edu/tracreports/crim/267/

leveraged," says Gorman, the lawyer with the securities litigation blog. "You might categorize that as reckless mismanagement or breach of fiduciary duty, but it's not criminal."

Even years from now, any assessment of the issue may be elusive, in part because of the difficulties of proving fraud or financial wrongdoing in court. "It is enormously problematic for prosecutors to prove beyond a reasonable doubt that the executives of a company acted with fraudulent intent," says Michael Perino, a professor at St. John's University School of Law in Jamaica, N.Y., and a former Wall Street litigator. "That is what you need to show a criminal prosecution under the federal security law."

But Black points out that federal regulatory agencies have referred far fewer cases for possible prosecution in the current scandal than the 10,000-plus criminal referrals that were made during the S&L crisis. As of November 2011, Black counted no referrals from the Office of Thrift Supervision, three from the Office of the Comptroller of the Currency and three from the Federal Reserve. [11]

"Yes, these are difficult cases," Black says. But, he adds, "Without criminal referrals there are no police on elite white-collar criminals."

Have federal agencies been tough enough in prosecuting financial wrongdoing?

Angelo Mozilo helped found Countrywide Financial in 1969 and built it over the next three decades into the largest lender of single-family home loans in the country. By 2006, however, Mozilo was worrying about a possible decline in home prices and the quality of some of the subprime loans his company had helped create and popularize.

Publicly, however, Mozilo voiced confidence in his company right up to its collapse in late 2007 and acquisition in January 2008 by Bank of America at the fire-sale price of $4 billion. As the storm clouds grew, the SEC in June 2009 charged Mozilo in a civil suit with securities fraud and insider trading for selling off his stock in Countrywide.

In October 2010, the SEC negotiated a settlement with Mozilo that included a $67.5 million fine and a permanent ban on his serving as a director or officer in a publicly traded company. Robert Khuzami, director of the SEC's Division of Enforcement, said the "record penalty" was a "fitting outcome" in the case. But observers noted that the agreement allowed Mozilo to avoid any admission of wrongdoing. And the government's criminal investigation was quietly shelved a few months later. [12]

The decision to bring no criminal charges against Mozilo exemplifies what *The New York Times* called in a 4,000-word overview last spring the "dearth of prosecutions" in connection with the financial crisis. [13] The story by two of the *Times'* veteran financial reporters, Gretchen Morgenson and Louise Story, noted that under President George W. Bush, Attorney General Michael Mukasey declined to create a nationwide task force on financial crimes — as was done during the S&L crisis. A task force created by Obama's attorney general, Eric Holder, was given a broad mandate but no additional resources.

Black, who was prominently quoted in the story, continues to speak out about the lack of prosecutions. "There has been no prosecution of an elite Wall Street figure who played a major role" in the crisis, Black says today. "That's an astonishing fact."

Statistics compiled by the private Transactional Records Access Clearinghouse at Syracuse University show an uninterrupted, decade-long decline in the number of federal prosecutions for financial institution fraud. In a report in late 2011, the clearinghouse showed more than 3,000 such prosecutions per year in the 1990s but only 1,349 for fiscal 2011. [14] (*See graph, above.*)

In the "60 Minutes" segment, former Countrywide vice president for fraud investigations Eileen Foster said there was "systemic" fraud at the company — specifically, loan officers approving mortgages based on forged or manipulated statements of borrowers' incomes and assets. However, she told correspondent Kroft, she was never interviewed by the Justice Department.

In the second part of the segment, Richard Bowen, a former senior vice president in Citigroup's consumer-lending division, said he warned Citi's top executives in November 2007 that a high percentage of mortgages in its portfolio were "defective" and that the company was understating its financial risks. Kroft went on to suggest that Citi's CEO Vikrim Pandit and Chief Financial Officer Gary Crittenden may have violated a central provision of the post-Enron Sarbanes-Oxley Act by certifying inaccurate financial statements to the SEC. Kroft quoted the company as defending the statements.

Commenting generally, New York University's Arlen sharply criticizes the failure to bring legal actions against individual executives. "You can't safeguard the market unless securities fraud doesn't pay, and it has to not pay for the individuals who do it," Arlen says. "You need people to be personally afraid of the consequences of lying."

SEC officials insist the agency is not shying away from going after individual executives. In announcing the civil suit against the former Fannie Mae and Freddie Mac executives, enforcement chief Khuzami promised that "all individuals" would be held accountable for financial misrepresentations "regardless of their rank or position." [15]

The SEC also is touting its recent crackdown on insider-trading cases. In testimony to congressional committees in December, Khuzami described insider trading as "one of the Division of Enforcement's highest priorities" and listed several initiatives aimed at spotting suspicious trading patterns and abusive market practices. [16]

Private lawyers Douglass and Gorman both give the SEC credit for its insider-trading initiatives. "It's aggressive and innovative," says Douglass. "It captured the attention of the business community." Overall, however, Douglass, an assistant U.S. attorney before going into private practice, calls the government's prosecution policies in the financial crisis "feckless."

"Insider trading should be prosecuted, but I don't think you can link insider-trading cases to these other kinds of fraud," Douglass says. "It undermines people's faith in the legal system when prosecutors say they're going to hold people accountable and they fail to do so."

Should mortgage lenders be punished for their role in improper foreclosures?

Among the more than 5 million home foreclosures since the financial crisis, banks and other mortgage lenders are now known to have completed a substantial number with procedures more akin to a factory assembly line than to a court of law. Banks, lenders and mortgage-servicing companies acknowledge the practice — dubbed "robo-signing" when first disclosed in October 2010 — where loan officers routinely signed foreclosure papers en masse without having read them.

Consumer advocates and some state attorneys general say the procedures amounted to "foreclosure fraud." Major banks admitted but somewhat minimized the problems even as they halted foreclosures for a while in order to clean up procedures. Investigations by news organizations and others, however, indicate that robo-signing and other documentation discrepancies continue. [17]

Banks hoping to put the issue behind them have been negotiating with representatives of state attorney general offices since spring 2011, looking to a multibillion-dollar settlement that would also limit their liability in further investigations. An accord looked close last fall, but the likelihood of agreement dimmed as some state attorneys general split off from the talks to take a tougher line.

In the most significant development, Massachusetts Attorney General Martha Coakley sued the nation's five largest mortgage lenders in state court on Dec. 1. The 57-page complaint charges the banks — Bank of America, Citigroup, GMAC Mortgage and its parent company Ally Financial, JP Morgan Chase and Wells Fargo — with having seized properties unlawfully. It asks for a court order that they change their practices and correct defects in previous foreclosures. [18]

In announcing the suit, Coakley said she pulled out of the settlement talks because the banks had failed to take responsibility for what she called "the devastation" on individual homeowners and communities. Critics of the lenders' practices similarly say the proposed settlement — which is being pushed by the Obama administration — would allow the banks to escape accountability for throwing people out of their homes without proper procedures.

"We should have prosecutions," says Yves Smith, who writes critically about financial industry news on the popular blog *Naked Capitalism*. "You don't settle unless you know what the crime was," she continues. "The attorneys general don't know what they're settling for, so they don't have any bargaining leverage."

Smith sharply criticizes the banks' effort to limit further legal exposure. "The banks have continued to ask for more and more and more," she says. Black, the law professor and former S&L regulator, agrees. "I would not have believed it possible in the United States that we would actually immunize them," Black says.

Banks involved in the negotiations have generally declined to comment about the talks. Spokesmen for three of the banks — Bank of America, JP Morgan Chase and Wells Fargo — all expressed disappointment with the filing of the Massachusetts suit. "We continue to believe that the collaborative resolution rather than continued litigation will most quickly heal the housing market and help drive economic recovery," BofA spokesman Lawrence Grayson said.

GMAC was more combative. "GMAC Mortgage believes it has strong legal and factual defenses," the company said in a statement, "and "will vigorously defend its position in court." [19]

The value of the proposed settlement as reported could reach $25 billion if all 50 states participate, most of it apparently in the form of principal write-downs, interest-rate reductions and other benefits to homeowners. Some cash penalties could be imposed on the banks. The settlement would be reduced if some states — most notably, California — balk at the accord. [20]

California is one of five states — all with Democratic attorneys general — that have pulled out of the talks to pursue separate legal actions. Besides Massachusetts, the others are Delaware, Nevada and New York.

Obama administration officials, including Treasury Secretary Timothy Geithner and Housing and Urban Development Secretary Shaun Donovan, have been pushing the settlement in the interest of stabilizing the banks and the housing market. Without commenting on the specifics of the proposed settlement, Christopher Mayer, a real estate finance expert at Columbia Business School, agrees on the importance of resolving the issues.

"Settling this is incredibly important because there's an enormous backlog of delinquent mortgages," Mayer says. "The process of doing nothing is a loser for everybody. We need to reduce uncertainty."

Mayer says most of the foreclosures are justified in economic terms. "The vast, vast majority of people who are involved are people who are not paying their mortgages," he says.

But Smith insists that the banks' actions are more than "innocent" mistakes. "These are not mistakes," she says. "They happened on too large a scale to be mistakes." ■

BACKGROUND

Policing the Markets

Federal regulation of the banking, housing and securities industries dates from the Great Depression, the economic calamity touched off by the stock market crash of 1929 that cost millions of Americans their homes, farms, jobs or life savings. The legislative and regulatory regimes set up to insure bank deposits, protect investors and support home mortgages appeared to serve the country's financial system well for half a century. By the 1970s, however, the Supreme Court began to balk at some of the SEC's expansive applications of anti-fraud rules. Since then, marketplace changes have combined with deregulatory initiatives and out-and-out dishonesty to jolt the financial system, first in the 1980s and twice already in the 21st century. [21]

The stock market crash of October 1929 — a 25 percent drop in two days — came unexpectedly after a decade of boom times. The subsequent congressional investigation documented abuses that, if known, might have foretold the collapse — in particular, risky investments in securities by banks. Over a four-year period, 43 percent of the 24,970 U.S. banks failed or were merged out of existence. [22]

The investigation by the so-called Pecora Commission — named after its lead investigator, Ferdinand Pecora — helped build support for new laws regulating banking and securities. The Glass-Steagall Act, passed in 1933, separated commercial from investment banking and also established the Federal Deposit Insurance Corporation (FDIC) to insure individual depositors' accounts. In the same year, Congress passed the Securities Act, which required disclosure of financial information by companies issuing stock or other securities. A year later, the Securities Exchange Act created the SEC, regulated securities trading and gave the SEC power to write anti-fraud rules.

Congress also sought to bolster home mortgages. The Federal Home Owners' Loan Corporation was created in 1933 to repurchase foreclosed homes and reinstate former mortgages; the Federal Housing Administration was established in 1934 to insure those mortgages. Meanwhile, deposit insurance was extended in 1934 to savings and loan associations, the main source of mortgage funds. Then in 1938, the Federal National Mortgage Association — dubbed "Fannie Mae" — was founded as a government-sponsored enterprise to invest in mortgages. Fannie Mae was transformed into a private corporation in 1968; that change prompted Congress two years later to create a competitor: the Federal Home Loan Mortgage Corporation, dubbed "Freddie Mac."

Despite congressional and law enforcement investigations, the Depression-era financial turmoil spawned only a "small handful" of criminal prosecutions, according to St. Johns professor Perino. "The point of the Pecora Commission was to show that the laws and regulations were inadequate," he explains. The highest profile prosecutions failed. Bank executive Charles Mitchell of National City Bank was found not guilty of tax evasion; utility tycoon Samuel Insull of Commonwealth Edison was acquitted of mail fraud and antitrust charges. The only big name to go to prison was Richard Whitney, president of the New York Stock Exchange from 1930 to 1935, who embezzled money from the exchange's gratuity fund to cover heavy investment losses. He pleaded guilty to state charges in 1938 and served three years in prison.

The banking and securities regulations remained controversial through the 1930s. In a memoir, Pecora warned in 1939 against allowing Wall Street to

Continued on p. 64

Chronology

Before 1960
Federal regulation of banks, securities established.

1933, 1934
Financial disclosure required to offer stock, other securities (Securities Act). . . . Commercial, investment banking separated; federal deposit insurance instituted (Glass-Steagall Act). . . . Securities and Exchange Commission (SEC) established.

1938
Federal National Mortgage Association ("Fannie Mae") created by Congress; becomes private company in 1968; Federal Home Loan Mortgage Corporation ("Freddie Mac") established as competitor in 1970.

1960s-1970s
SEC becomes more aggressive, meets Supreme Court resistance.

1961
SEC prescribes "disclose or abstain rule" to bar insider trading.

1976
Supreme Court rules that securities fraud requires intent to deceive, not mere negligence.

1980s-1990s
Savings and loan crisis: government bailout, tightened rules.

1980, 1982
Congress passes, two presidents sign legislation to deregulate thrift industry to aid competition with commercial banks.

Mid-1980s
Hundreds of S&Ls fail; speculative loans, looting by executives blamed.

1989
Congress reregulates thrift industry, approves bailout of failed S&Ls (Financial Institutions Reform, Recovery and Enforcement Act). . . . Bailout cost later put at $88 billion; more than 1,800 S&L officials prosecuted, more than 1,000 sent to prison.

1996, 1998
Congress limits private securities-fraud suits in federal, state courts.

1999
Congress repeals Glass-Steagall; allows banks, securities firms to merge (Gramm-Leach-Bliley).

Early 2000s
Enron, accounting scandals followed by reforms.

2001
Enron forced into bankruptcy after accounting frauds; top executives later prosecuted, convicted.

2002
Congress requires top executives to personally certify financial statements, creates agency to oversee accounting profession (Sarbanes Oxley).

2008-Present
Financial crisis freezes markets, brings financial overhaul, calls for tougher government action.

2008
Government forces Bear Stearns fire-sale to JP Morgan Chase (March 16). . . . Government takes over Fannie Mae, Freddie Mac (Sept. 7). . . . Lehman Brothers declares bankruptcy (Sept. 15). . . . Treasury Secretary Henry Paulson strong-arms major banks to agree to bailout; Congress OKs plan (Emergency Economic Stabilization Act) (September/October). . . . Bernard Madoff charged with Ponzi scheme (Dec. 10).

2009
Madoff pleads guilty (March 12); later sentenced to 150 years in prison. . . . SEC Office of Inspector General says investigators could have stopped Madoff after first tip in 1992 (Aug. 31). . . . Bear Stearns hedge fund managers acquitted (Nov. 9).

2010
Goldman Sachs agrees to $550 million penalty in marketing subprime mortgages (July 15). . . . Dodd-Frank Act gives government more power to seize failing banks; creates Consumer Financial Protection Bureau (July 21). . . . Countrywide founder Angelo Mozilo settles with SEC for $67.5 million (Oct. 15).

2011
Meltdown could have been avoided, Financial Crisis Inquiry Commission says; Republican members file dissent (Jan. 27). . . . Hedge fund manager Raj Rajaratnam convicted in insider-trading case (May 11); later draws 11-year sentence; two dozen others convicted. . . . JP Morgan Chase agrees to $154 million penalty for rigged subprime mortgage package (June 21). . . . Citigroup agrees to $285 million settlement in toxic mortgage deal (Oct. 19), but judge balks at deal (Nov. 28).

2012
President Obama uses recess appointment to name Richard Cordray to head Consumer Financial Protection Bureau; Republican senators object (Jan. 4).

'Test Drive' for Wiretaps in Insider-Trading Case

Galleon hedge fund founder made more than $70 billion in illegal gains.

Federal prosecutors in New York City have used wiretaps and a wired informant to help win more than two dozen convictions in a sprawling insider-trading investigation, including a record-setting prison term against the billionaire hedge-fund founder at the center of the case.

Dozens of recorded telephone calls provided the critical evidence that netted Raj Rajaratnam an 11-year prison sentence after his May 11 conviction in federal court in New York on nine counts of insider trading and five counts of conspiracy.

Rajaratnam, founder of the now defunct Galleon Group, made more than $70 million in illegal profits over a six-year period, according to prosecutors, by trading on inside information gathered from multiple contacts in Wall Street and corporate circles. [1]

One of Rajaratnam's major sources is alleged to have been Rajat Gupta, a friend and former head of the giant consulting firm McKinsey & Co. Gupta was charged in a six-count indictment unsealed on Oct. 26 with passing valuable inside information to Rajaratnam from his position as a director with Goldman Sachs, a big investment firm constantly involved in potential corporate mergers and acquisitions.

Among the lesser figures in the investigation was Brien Santarlas, formerly a patent attorney with a New York law firm, whose secretly recorded conversations with other conspirators helped win convictions in June of a key stock trader linked to Rajaratnam and two other defendants. Santarlas, who pleaded guilty to securities fraud charges in November 2009, was given a reduced, six-month sentence on Nov. 30, 2011, based on his cooperation with the prosecution. [2]

The government's first extensive use of wiretaps in an insider trading case — a tactic usually associated with organized crime and public corruption investigations — is one of the issues being raised on appeal by lawyers for Rajaratnam. Patricia Millett, a Washington lawyer and veteran appellate litigator, previewed her argument in an unsuccessful attempt in late November to win bail for Rajaratnam pending appeal.

Millett told a panel of the Second U.S. Circuit Court of Appeals on Nov. 30 that the government had not filed a proper request for the taps. Assistant U.S. Attorney Jonathan Streeter said the requests had been proper and noted that the trial judge had considered the issue before admitting the tapes at the start of Rajaratnam's seven-week trial. The appeals court denied bail for Rajaratnam the next day without comment. [3]

The prosecution made the most of the tapes during the trial. "You heard the defendant commit his crimes time and time again in his own words," Assistant U.S. Attorney Reed Brodsky said in closing arguments. Former government lawyers had praise after the verdict for the tactic. Prosecutors "took wiretaps for a test drive, and I'd say it was a resounding success," Stephen Miller, a former federal prosecutor in private practice in Philadelphia, told The Associated Press. [4]

Continued from p. 62

go back to the time "before Uncle Sam stationed a policeman at its corner." [23] Over the next several decades, however, the regulatory regimes appeared to gain general acceptance. With FDIC insurance, runs on banks by worried depositors became a relic of history. Investors grew accustomed to the financial disclosures required from companies issuing securities. By the 1950s and '60s, the SEC was being criticized not for over- but for under-regulating. President John F. Kennedy responded to a report by former SEC Chairman James Landis that called for strengthening regulatory agencies by increasing the SEC staff and appointing an activist-minded corporate law expert, William Cary, as chairman.

Cary laid the basis for the SEC's insider-trading enforcement with an administrative ruling in November 1961 sanctioning a broker who sold a company's stock based on advance word of a dividend cut that he learned from a partner who was on the company's board of directors. The ruling in *In re Cady, Roberts & Co.* established a so-called "disclose or abstain" rule: insiders had to disclose material information about a company's finances or abstain from trading on the basis of the information. In 1968 the rule gained judicial endorsement from the New York-based Second U.S. Circuit Court of Appeals in a case, *SEC v. Texas Gulf Sulphur Co.*, where company insiders had bought up stock and stock options in advance of an announcement of a major discovery of copper and zinc deposits. The appeals court interpreted the anti-fraud Rule 10b-5 to require that all investors have "relatively equal access to material information." [24]

The Supreme Court, which left the Texas Gulf Sulphur ruling in place by rejecting the company's appeal, had been generally supportive of SEC authority since the 1930s but began to shift in the 1970s. In a succession of rulings, the court cut back on SEC litigating positions. In 1976, for example, the court ruled 6-2 that the SEC's anti-fraud rule required proof of an intent to deceive, not mere negligence. A 1980 ruling rejected the SEC's attempt to expand the definition of insider to include people with no fiduciary relationship to the company. [25] Despite the adverse court rulings, however, the SEC increased its insider-trading enforcement, thanks in part to the creation of a computerized tracking system to monitor stock trading, corporate filings and news items. [26]

Santarlas, who got into the insider-trading racket in October 2007 as a young associate at the New York office of the Boston-based firm Ropes & Gray, agreed to cooperate with the government in his first meeting with FBI agents in November 2009. He admitted being paid for tips about pending corporate deals gathered from confidential information at his firm. In the later trial, Santarlas testified that he was instructed to use a prepaid cell phone to relay information and then to cut the phone into pieces and throw the pieces into the river.

Getty Images/Spencer Platt

Former Goldman Sachs director Rajat Gupta is facing charges of passing inside information to hedge fund founder Raj Rajaratnam, who was convicted on fraud and conspiracy charges in connection with his making $70 million in illegal profits.

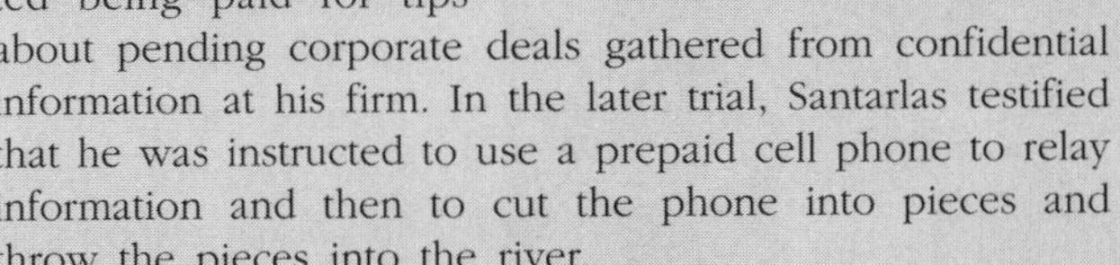

Santarlas testified, along with fellow lawyer-turned-tipster Arthur Cutillo, in the trial of stock trader Zvi Goffer, who had worked for Rajaratnam before starting his own firm. Goffer and two others who worked for him — his brother Emanuel and lawyer Michael Kimelman — were convicted on June 13 on multiple counts of securities fraud and conspiracy. Zvi Goffer later received a 10-year prison sentence, Emmanuel Goffer a three-year term, and Kimelman a 30-month sentence.

Cutillo, who like Santarlas pleaded guilty to a single count of conspiracy, was sentenced on June 30 to 30 months in prison. Both lawyers apologized at sentencing for their offenses. "I know what I did was terribly wrong," Cutillo said in the June 30 hearing. Five months later, Santarlas said he was "ashamed," "embarrassed" and "humiliated" about what he had done. "It's something I'll never forgive myself for," he said.

— Kenneth Jost

[1] Press releases on individual developments in the case can be found by date on the website of the U.S. attorney for the Southern District of New York: www.justice.gov/usao/nys/pressreleases/. Details on Rajaratnam's trial and conviction taken from Tom Hays and Larry Neumeister, "Hedge fund founder convicted in inside-trade case," The Associated Press, May 11, 2011.

[2] See Larry Neumeister and Tom Hays, "NY jury convicts 3 in NYC hedge fund trial," *ibid.*, June, 13, 2011; Tom Hays, "Tipster sentenced in NYC insider trading case," *ibid.*, Nov. 30, 2011.

[3] Larry Neumeister, "Fund boss loses bid to stay free during appeal," *ibid.*, Dec. 1, 2011.

[4] Quoted in Larry Neumeister and Tom Hays, "Wiretaps key in conviction of ex-hedge fund giant," *ibid.*, May 11, 2011.

Losing Control

Twice over the next quarter century, the United States experienced seeming epidemics of financial misconduct, followed each time by strengthened federal regulation and criminal prosecutions of prominent corporate executives. The savings and loan crisis of the 1980s required a $100 billion federal bailout to stabilize the thrift industry. By one count, more than 100 executives were prosecuted for various offenses. The accounting scandals of the early 2000s forced thousands of companies to revise their financial statements and led to prison terms for several top corporate managers. Meanwhile, Congress and the Supreme Court significantly tightened the rules governing civil suits for securities fraud while Congress also approved legislation to loosen regulation of abstruse financial instruments known as derivatives.

The S&L crisis stemmed from the competitive pressure on the thrifts created by the rise in interest rates in the late 1970s and a regulatory cap on interest they could pay on deposits. To aid the thrifts, Congress in 1980 and 1982 passed deregulatory legislation that, among other provisions, uncapped interest rates for most deposits, permitted adjustable-rate mortgages and allowed more speculative investments. Initially, the thrifts seemed to fare well, but many investments went bad as the real estate boom subsided. The thrifts also fell prey to high-flying entrepreneurs, some of whom simply looted the funds for personal benefit. By the end of the decade, more than 1,000 had failed, sticking the government with a $100 billion bailout bill. By 1995, the Justice Department had conducted 1,852 prosecutions of S&L officials, with 1,072 sentenced to prison. [27]

Congress and President George H. W. Bush responded to the S&L crisis by enacting the Financial Institutions Reform, Recovery and Enforcement Act of 1989. In addition to authorizing the $100 billion bailout by the newly established Resolution Trust Corporation, the law revamped deposit insurance, raised capital requirements for thrifts and placed them under the authority of the newly established Office of Thrift Supervision within the Treasury Department.

In contrast to the heightened regulation of the thrift industry, Congress and the Supreme Court were erecting barriers in the 1990s to private lawsuits aimed at enforcing federal securities laws. Congress responded to business-community complaints about supposedly baseless securities class action suits by enacting, over President Bill Clinton's veto, the Private Securities Litigation Reform Act of 1996. The act raised the initial burden of proof for private securities-fraud suits to proceed and tightened various rules governing federal class action suits. When plaintiffs' lawyers tried to circumvent the law by bringing suits in state courts, Congress responded with a second law, the Securities Litigation Uniform Standards Act, effectively preempting state court jurisdiction over securities cases.

Earlier, the Supreme Court in 1994 had issued a closely divided ruling that barred extending civil liability for aiding and abetting securities fraud to outsiders, such as accountants, attorneys or other professionals. [28] In 1997, however, the court boosted both private and criminal enforcement against insider trading by endorsing the SEC's so-called misappropriation theory, which barred anyone — not just corporate insiders — from trading on confidential company information. The ruling in *United States v. O'Hagan* upheld the 57-count conviction of a Minneapolis lawyer who made $4.3 million in profits while trading in Pillsbury stock in advance of a planned tender offer by a corporate client of his firm. [29]

As the decade ended, Congress approved two additional deregulatory initiatives that helped set the stage for the later financial crisis. The Gramm-Leach-Bliley Act of 1999 effectively repealed the Glass-Steagall Act by allowing banks and financial holding companies to own both commercial banking and securities firms as well as insurance companies. A year later, the Commodity Futures Modernization Act blocked the Commodity Futures Trading Commission from asserting regulatory authority over the complex financial instruments known as over-the-counter derivatives. Clinton signed both measures after they had won bipartisan support in Congress.

Getty Images/Michael Reynolds-Pool

With Richard Cordray at his side, President Obama addresses staffers at the new Consumer Financial Protection Bureau on Jan. 6, 2012. Obama used a recess appointment to install the former Ohio attorney general as the agency's head after Republicans blocked action on the nomination. Cordray is laying out an aggressive initiative for the agency despite potential legal challenges to his appointment.

The financial scandals of the early 2000s were embodied most dramatically in the story of Enron, a Houston-based energy trading company that used creative accounting tricks to conceal shaky finances until being forced late in 2001 to issue financial restatements and then seek bankruptcy protection. Top Enron executives were prosecuted, along with the company's outside accounting firm Arthur Andersen. Similar accounting scandals forced a succession of other companies to issue restatements, and a few other top executives faced criminal charges. The image of a corporate crime wave was heightened by a spike in unrelated cases of garden-variety insider trading and misappropriation of corporate funds. [30]

Even as criminal prosecutions were getting under way, Congress and President George W. Bush responded by overhauling corporate accounting practices. The bipartisan Sarbanes-Oxley Act — named after its principal Senate and House sponsors — included provisions to strengthen auditors' independence from corporate boards and to require top executives to take individual responsibility for the accuracy of financial statements. It also established a new, quasi-independent agency, the Public Company Accounting Oversight Board, to oversee accounting firms' compliance with the act. In signing the bill, Bush called it "the most far-reaching reforms of American business practices since the time of Franklin D. Roosevelt."

Digging Out

The financial crisis of 2008 formed under the surface for several years before emerging into public view in March when the government forced the sale of cash-strapped Bear Stearns to JP Morgan Chase for a paltry $2 a share. By year's end, Lehman Brothers had collapsed, Fannie Mae and Freddie Mac had been nationalized and the nation's nine biggest banks had been ordered to take billions in bailouts in exchange for a commitment to unfreeze the frozen credit markets. Government regulators and federal prosecutors then went to work, looking for culpability. The government won some significant victories but endured constant second-guessing from critics about the pace of investigations and the penalties imposed. [31]

Meanwhile, Congress was working on legislation aimed at preventing another financial meltdown. As signed into law by President Obama on July 21, 2010, the Wall Street Reform and Consumer Protection Act — more commonly, the Dodd-Frank Act after its principal Senate and House sponsors — gives the government more power to seize and wind down big financial firms. It also requires companies that sell mortgage-backed securities generally to retain at least 5 percent of the risk of the products. The bill also mandates regulation of over-the-counter derivatives and requires hedge funds to register with the SEC. And it established the Consumer Financial Protection Bureau as an independent agency within the Federal Reserve to enforce consumer-protection laws against not only banks and mortgage lenders but also credit card issuers, payday lenders and other financial-service companies. [32]

The charges against the ex-Bear Stearns hedge fund managers Cioffi and Tannin in June 2008 marked the first financial crisis-related prosecution to hit Wall Street directly. The pair were arrested June 19 on a fraud and conspiracy indictment based largely on e-mails showing undisclosed doubts about their funds' strength. Mark Mehrson, head of the FBI's New York office, told reporters the case was about "premeditated lies to investors and lenders." Lawyers for Cioffi and Tannin foreshadowed their successful defense by insisting their clients were victims of an unexpected crisis in financial markets. After the acquittals, a former Enron fraud prosecutor told *The New York Times* that the verdict showed the weakness of relying on " 'smoking gun' e-mails" to make a white-collar crime case. [33]

Once in office, the Obama administration made a public show of going after financial misconduct with the creation of an interagency task force on financial fraud in November 2009. Holder, accompanied by SEC Chairwoman Mary Schapiro and Cabinet colleagues Geithner from Treasury and Donovan from HUD, promised that the task force would be "relentless" in investigating and prosecuting corporate and financial wrongdoing. But Black, the Missouri law professor, notes that in addition to the task force getting no additional resources, its mission was extended beyond Wall Street. In April 2011, for example, a task force working group was formed to study the causes of rising oil and gas prices. [34]

The SEC, meanwhile, was achieving some success with civil actions carrying nine-figure settlements in cases against Goldman Sachs and JP Morgan Chase. Both companies were charged with securities fraud by misleading investors in subprime mortgage packages. The $550 million settlement that Goldman agreed to in July 2010 was described as one of the biggest penalties in SEC history. The agency charged Goldman with marketing a package of mortgages picked by the prominent hedge fund manager, John Paulson, who later bet against the bonds. News reports after the settlement disclosed that the five-member agency had split along party lines in initiating the complaint and approving the settlement, with three Democrats in favor and two Republicans against. Almost a year later, the agency won a $154 million settlement against Morgan in a similar case. In both cases, the firms neither admitted nor denied wrongdoing. [35]

Despite complaints in the press and from observers about the lack of prosecutions, the government was winning some significant convictions. It won a big case in April 2011 when a federal jury in Alexandria, Va., convicted Lee Farkas, the former majority owner of the big mortgage company Taylor, Bean & Whitaker, in a $3 billion fraud that toppled the Florida-based firm as well as the Alabama-based Colonial Bank. Farkas was sentenced on June 30 to 30 years in prison. [36]

In May 2011, the government notched a higher-profile victory with the conviction of prominent hedge fund manager Rajaratnam on 14 counts of securities fraud and conspiracy. Rajaratnam received an 11-year prison sentence in October — said to be the longest ever for insider trading — even as Gupta, one of his sources, a former chief executive of the giant consulting firm McKinsey & Co., was awaiting trial himself for insider trading. [37]

The SEC was still basking in the publicity glow from the Rajaratnam and Gupta cases when Judge Rakoff caught the agency by surprise by rejecting the proposed settlement with Citigroup. Two weeks later, on Dec. 15, the SEC announced that it would ask the Second U.S. Circuit Court of Appeals to overturn Rakoff's decision. "We believe the district court committed legal error by announcing a new and unprecedented standard that inadvertently harms investors by depriving them of substantial, certain and immediate benefits," enforcement chief Khuzami said in a statement accompanying the court filing. [38]

The next day, the agency shifted from defense to offense with its civil complaint charging the former Fannie and Freddie executives with fraud. The executives misled investors by understating their exposure to subprime mortgages, Khuzami said. In a briefing, Khuzami said the case was the 38th action brought by the commission in connection with the financial crisis. [39] ■

Current Situation

Blaming Fannie, Freddie?

The SEC's fraud complaint against the former Fannie Mae and Freddie Mac executives is renewing the debate over the government-sponsored mortgage companies' responsibility for the subprime mortgage crisis, even as lawyers for the defendants call the charges baseless.

The parallel complaints, filed in federal district court in New York City, charge the former chief executives and two other ranking executives at each of the companies with making "materially false and misleading public disclosures" by understating the companies' exposure to subprime mortgage loans.

Named in the 59-page complaint against Fannie Mae executives are former CEO Daniel Mudd; Enrico Dallavecchia, former chief risk officer; and Thomas Lund, former executive vice president of Fannie's single-family mortgage business. The 49-page complaint against Freddie Mac executives names former CEO Richard Syron; Patricia Cook, former executive vice president and chief business officer; and Donald Bisenius, executive vice president for its single-family business.

The suits both seek disgorgement of profits, unspecified civil penalties and "other necessary and appropriate relief," which could include bans on their serving as officers or directors of publicly traded companies. The Fannie Mae case was assigned to Judge Robert Carter, the Freddie Mac case to Judge Richard Sullivan. [40]

None of the defendants has filed any response to the complaints, but Mudd and lawyers for Syron denied the allegations after the SEC announcement. "The SEC is wrong, and I look forward to a court where fairness and reason — not politics — is the standard for justice," Mudd said. Representing Syron, attorneys Thomas Green and Mark Hopson contended Freddie's filings had "no shortage of meaningful disclosures." They called the SEC's case "fatally flawed" and "without merit." [41]

The cases apparently will turn on how broadly to define the risks of unconventional loans offered by the two mortgage companies during the two-year period covered in the complaints up to their takeover by the government in August 2008. A chart accompanying the SEC's news release depicts Fannie as reporting $8 billion and Freddie $6 billion in subprime exposure as of second-quarter 2008, when their actual exposure to risky loans was $110 billion and $250 billion, respectively.

In the Fannie Mae complaint, the agency elaborates that its disclosures did not include so-called Alt-A reduced-documentation mortgages and loan products targeted to borrowers with weaker credit histories — also known as Expanded Approval or EA loans. Such loans, the complaint states, "were exactly the type of loans that investors would reasonably believe Fannie Mae included when calculating its exposure to subprime loans." Similarly, the Freddie Mac complaint says the company failed to include loans referred to internally as "subprime," "otherwise subprime" or "subprime-like."

The role played by the two mortgage giants — sometimes referred to as "government-sponsored enterprises" or GSEs — had been a partisan issue on Capitol Hill and elsewhere since the financial crisis emerged. Republicans and conservative experts argued that Fannie and Freddie led mortgage lenders into the subprime swamp in order to satisfy 1990s-era statutory and regulatory mandates to provide access to affordable housing. Democrats generally defended the affordable-housing mandates and depicted the mortgage companies' problems as due to profit-driven recklessness. Days after the SEC filing, Peter Wallison, a longtime critic of the GSEs and a senior fellow at the conservative American Enterprise Institute (AEI), wrote in an op-ed in *The Wall Street Journal* that the legal actions vindicated his critique. "For the first time in a government report, the complaint has made it clear that the two government-sponsored enterprises (GSEs) played a major role in creating the demand for low-quality mortgages before the 2008 financial crisis," Wallison wrote. [42]

In a sharp reply to Wallison's argument even before the op-ed appeared, *New York Times* columnist Joe Nocera argued that Wallison was wrong in blaming the two GSEs for what he called "imagined" mistakes. "Fannie and Freddie got into subprime mortgages, with great trepidation, only in 2005 and 2006, and only because they were losing so much market share to Wall Street," Nocera wrote. He went on to call the SEC's case "extraordinarily weak," insisting that the agency was exaggerating the amount of risky loans and ignoring the companies' relatively low default rates. [43]

As part of the legal action, the SEC agreed not to prosecute the two companies, and both agreed to cooperate with the agency in pursuing the case. The filing appeared to be drawing generally positive reaction. Appearing on the PBS "NewsHour," Lynn Turner, a former SEC chief accountant, called the complaints "a very positive development" that showed the government "is willing to go after and hold accountable the people at the very top." [44]

Less approvingly, Black, the former regulator from the S&L crisis, acknowledges that the agency has a lower burden of proof in a civil case than the government would have in a criminal case. But he still complains about the lack of criminal prosecutions. "The Department of Justice still has failed to prosecute any of the elite accounting-control frauds that drove this crisis," he says.

Continued on p. 70

At Issue:

Will the Financial Protection Bureau benefit consumers?

ROBERT L. BOROSAGE
CO-DIRECTOR, CAMPAIGN FOR AMERICA'S FUTURE

WRITTEN FOR *CQ RESEARCHER*, JANUARY 2012

yes

The best tribute to the potential of the Consumer Financial Protection Bureau (CFPB) is the millions the banking lobby expended in an unrelenting campaign to block its creation and cripple it once it was established. The reason for the resistance is simple. The CFPB has one mission: to protect consumers against abuse by large banks and other previously unregulated nonbank financial institutions.

The CFPB consolidates consumer protections previously scattered across the federal government into one agency devoted to their enforcement. Every other financial regulatory agency gives priority to protecting the "safety and soundness" of the banks they supervise. The result, witnessed to catastrophic effect in the housing bubble, has been an utter failure to protect consumers, allowing what the FBI called an unchecked "epidemic of fraud" in subprime mortgages that cost consumers trillions and drove the economy into recession.

One of CFPB's priorities will be to police nonbanking institutions, particularly the payday lenders that levy obscene charges — effective interest rates of 400 percent or more and onerous penalties and fees — on the most vulnerable workers who live paycheck to paycheck. If it simply exposes the big banks engaged in these practices, while requiring and enforcing clear notice of costs, the CFPB can make a dramatic difference.

Already the CFPB is stepping up scrutiny of lenders peddling loans to students at profit-making colleges, many of which project 50 percent default rates. The CFPB also has set up special sections to monitor abuses of seniors and active-duty military personnel who are often targeted by predatory lenders.

The CFPB already has begun to develop clear "know before you owe" notifications of terms for mortgages, credit cards and student loans. Currently consumers sign forms that are purposefully too long, detailed and arcane to be read or understood. By forcing simplification, the CFPB will allow consumers to police the tricks and traps now used on unwary borrowers.

Despite the claims of the bank lobby and Republicans, the concern about the CFPB isn't that it is unaccountable, but that it will be constrained by budgetary limits and unique oversight requirements. Its rule-making can be overturned by a Financial Oversight Council, made up of traditional banking regulators, all more concerned about protecting the solvency of banks than fairness to consumers.

But an active CFPB will garner immense public support as it cracks down on financial predators. No wonder the banking lobby continues to try to weaken it.

DIANE KATZ
RESEARCH FELLOW IN REGULATORY POLICY, HERITAGE FOUNDATION

WRITTEN FOR *CQ RESEARCHER*, JANUARY 2012

no

Some unknown number of individuals may benefit from the Consumer Financial Protection Bureau (CFPB). But the new agency's unparalleled powers — magnified by an absence of accountability — bodes ill for most consumers.

President Obama's recess appointment of Richard Cordray to direct the bureau demonstrates the indiscretion to which the CFPB is prone. To the extent its regulations unduly restrict the availability of financing, economic growth will be constricted. And when unnecessarily stringent regulation raises the cost of credit, consumers are forced to find alternatives that entail greater cost and risk than conventional sources.

Researchers have long documented these dynamics, which are also inherent in other provisions of the Dodd-Frank regulatory statute. For example, the so-called Durbin amendment, which imposed price controls on the fees that banks charge retailers to process debit card transactions, has led to higher fees for checking accounts and other bank services. Higher fees, in turn, force low-income Americans from banks and to less conventional lenders of the very sort regulatory advocates warn against.

Imbued with ill-defined powers and unparalleled independence, the bureau is the epitome of regulatory excess. Well-intended or otherwise, its proponents are wholly invested in saving us from ourselves, and thus disposed to overreach. That increases the likelihood that consumers will be lulled into a false sense of security and makes the absence of bureau oversight all the more problematic.

The CFPB is ensconced within the Federal Reserve, its funding set by statute. Therefore, its budget is not subject to the same congressional control as most other federal agencies. And the bureau's status within the Fed also effectively precludes presidential oversight.

Its accountability is also minimized by the vague language of its statutory mandate. It is empowered to punish "unfair, deceptive and abusive" business practices. While *unfair* and *deceptive* have been defined in other regulatory contexts, the term *abusive* is largely undefined, granting the CFPB officials inordinate discretion.

The financial crisis did not result from any lack of regulation over consumer financial products. Therefore, creation of the CFPB will not help to prevent a future crisis. But it will limit consumer choices. Congress should abolish the CFPB's funding mechanism and subject it instead to congressional control, strike the undefined term *abusive* from the list of practices under CFPB purview, and require the bureau to apply definitions of *unfair* and *deceptive* practices in a manner consistent with consumer choice.

Continued from p. 68

New Agency Under Way

The head of the new Consumer Financial Protection Bureau is promising to make full use of the agency's regulatory and enforcement powers even as Republicans and industry groups challenge his recess appointment to the post.

"It's a valid appointment," Richard Cordray said in remarks to the Brookings Institution on Jan. 5, the day after President Obama named him to the position. "I'm now director of the bureau." [45]

Cordray, a former Ohio attorney general, is signaling an initial priority to extend federal regulation to what he calls in a press release the "thousands" of so-called nonbanks. The non-depository financial businesses include mortgage lenders, mortgage servicers, payday lenders, consumer reporting agencies, debt collectors and money-services companies such as currency exchanges and traveler's check and money order issuers.

"This is an important step forward for protecting consumers," Cordray said in a Jan. 5 release. "Holding both banks and nonbanks accountable to consumer financial laws will help create a fairer, more transparent market for consumers. It will create a better environment for the honest businesses that serve them. And it will help the overall economic stability of our country." [46]

The debate over Obama's invocation of his recess-appointment power adds to the controversies surrounding the new agency, created as part of the Dodd-Frank Act passed by the Democratic-controlled Congress and signed by the president in 2010. Senate Republicans had blocked action on Cordray's nomination and Obama's previous selection of Harvard law professor Elizabeth Warren in an effort to change the structure and powers of the agency as provided in the law. Warren, now running as a Democrat for the U.S. Senate seat from Massachusetts, was a prime architect of the new agency.

Obama named Cordray the day after the Senate formally convened on Jan. 3 (as required by law) and then resumed a long holiday break. But the Senate had been conducting pro forma sessions every two to three days during the interval. Minority Leader Mitch McConnell of Kentucky and other GOP senators say the Senate's pro forma sessions during the period barred the president from invoking his power under the Constitution to fill positions while the chamber is in recess.

A week after the appointment, the Justice Department released a memorandum from the Office of Legal Counsel supporting Obama's action. "[T]he convening of periodic pro forma sessions in which no business is to be conducted does not have the legal effect of interrupting an intrasession recess," assistant attorney general Virginia Seitz wrote in the 23-page opinion. Administration officials said Seitz had summarized her conclusion to Obama before his appointment.

Seitz acknowledged "substantial arguments" on the opposite side and possible "litigation risks" to the action. Sen. Charles Grassley of Iowa, ranking Republican on the Judiciary Committee, called the memorandum "unconvincing." [47]

The law establishes the CFPB as an independent agency within the Federal Reserve to be headed by a single director. Senate Republicans want to provide instead for a multimember board, comparable to other regulatory agencies. They also criticize the agency's independent budget authority. Democrats counter that Republicans should have tried to amend the law instead of blocking action on the nomination. If valid, Obama's recess appointment would allow Cordray to stay in the post through the remainder of the year.

In assuming the office, Cordray is making special efforts to solicit input from consumers and whistleblowers. In a two-minute video posted on the CPFB web site (www.consumerfinance.gov), Cordray personally invites consumer complaints. "Tell us your story today," he says in closing. In his remarks at Brookings, Cordray said the agency "will make clear that there are real consequences to breaking the law."

A week later, Cordray briefed reporters on plans to scrutinize the student loan business, particularly nontraditional lenders to students at for-profit and trade schools. Cordray said the bureau has seen evidence of loans made by lenders even though they knew borrowers would be unlikely to be able to pay off the loans. [48] ■

OUTLOOK

No Way to Know?

Ben Bernanke wrapped up his first meeting as chairman of the Federal Reserve Board of Governors in March 2006 with cautious optimism about what he described as the "cooling" in the housing market. Transcripts of the March 27-28 meeting — released in accord with the Fed's practice five years afterward — show Bernanke expected the economy's "strong fundamentals" to offset any reduced spending from homeowners as house prices sagged. "I think it would take a very strong decline in the housing market to substantially derail the strong momentum for growth that we are currently seeing in the economy," Bernanke concluded. [49]

Instead of the "soft landing" that Bernanke predicted, the United States' decades-long housing bubble burst dramatically and plunged the nation into recession by the end of 2007. Four years later, the economy has yet to recover. Many victims of the recession — those who lost their jobs, homes or both — naturally blame mortgage lenders and other financial institutions for driving the market catastrophically to unsustainable levels.

The financial industry has responded in general by insisting that it did not know — and could not have known — that the bubble would burst as it did. In the industry's view, all of the people at banks and investment firms who sliced and diced mortgages into marketable investment packages hardly could have known that they were selling what turned out to be "toxic assets."

The law enforcement agencies going through the wreckage — chiefly, the SEC and Justice Department at the federal level — have found plenty of cases of unmistakable financial misconduct, such as Bernard Madoff's giant Ponzi scheme or the flurry of insider-trading cases. In one of the most recent cases, the government is trying to determine what happened to $1.2 billion in customer money when the New York-based brokerage firm MF Global headed into bankruptcy in October 2011. [50]

The SEC also has found evidence of deception at some of the nation's banks in marketing securitized mortgages — deception that could amount to fraud under federal securities law. Two banks, Goldman Sachs and JP Morgan Chase, agreed to nine-figure payments to resolve such charges, and Citigroup was prepared to do the same until Judge Rakoff balked at the settlement. But the SEC may face an uphill fight in making a similar case against the former Fannie Mae and Freddie Mac executives if they contend that they cannot be held responsible for failing to spot the housing market crash that Bernanke and his Federal Reserve colleagues did not see coming.

Based on his experience in the S&L crisis, Black thinks the evidence of prosecutable "garden-variety fraud" is there for the looking. He sees a lack of political will to pursue cases. "It's the Wall Street folks who were the frauds, and nowadays they are the leading contributors to both parties," he says.

At the Justice Department, Breuer denies any political interference. "This Department of Justice is acting absolutely independently," he told correspondent Kroft in the "60 Minutes" interview. "Every decision that's being made by our prosecutors around the country is being made 100 percent based on the facts of that particular case and the law that we can apply." [51]

Gorman, the Washington lawyer and SEC litigation blogger, thinks the critics are exaggerating the extent of criminal activity involved. "It's one thing to run your business in a reckless way," Gorman says. "It's another thing to actually violate the law."

Washington defense lawyer Douglass thinks the government itself is to blame for feeding the public perception of serious wrongdoing. "If they think there's fraud, they should go out and build those cases," he says. "It's not that hard. It's just a heavy lift."

The government has been "pretty ineffective," says David Skeel, a professor of corporate law at the University of Pennsylvania in Philadelphia. "The pattern of enforcement and nonenforcement has been depressing, to put it mildly."

When Skeel was interviewed for *The New York Times* overview in March 2011, he said the lack of prosecutions led to "the whole perception that Wall Street was taken care of, and Main Street was not." Today, he says he is "hopeful but pessimistic" that the government will improve on its record.

"My fear is that two years from now the 2007-2008 crisis will seem to have been a long time ago," Skeel says. "The sense of urgency that regulators ought to have about stepping in will have dissipated." ■

Notes

[1] The decision is *U.S. Securities and Exchange Commission v. Citigroup Global Markets, Inc.*, 11 Civ. 7387 (JSR), U.S. Dist. Ct., S.D.N.Y., Nov. 28, 2011, www.scribd.com/doc/74040599/Rakoff-Citigroup. For coverage, see Edward Wyatt, "Judge Rejects an S.E.C. Deal With Citigroup," *The New York Times*, Nov. 29, 2011, p. A1; David S. Hilzenrath, "Judge rebukes SEC on Citigroup deal," *The Washington Post*, Nov. 29, 2011, p. A1. For the SEC press release, and links to the complaint, see "Citigroup to Pay $285 Million to Settle SEC Charges for Misleading Investors About CDO [Collateralized Debt Obligation] Tied to Housing Market," Oct. 19, 2011, www.sec.gov/news/press/2011/2011-214.htm. For coverage, see Edward Wyatt, "Citigroup to Pay Millions to End Fraud Complaint," *The New York Times*, Oct. 20, 2011, p. B1. For coverage of the Bank of America case, see Louise Story, "Bank's Deal With S.E.C. Is Approved," *The New York Times*, Feb. 23, 2010, p. B1.

[2] "Prosecuting Wall Street," "60 Minutes," Dec. 4, 2011, www.cbsnews.com/8301-18560_162-57336042/prosecuting-wall-street/?tag=contentMain;cbsCarousel (video, script, and 'Web extras').

[3] "SEC Charges Stemming From Financial Crisis," Oct. 19, 2011, www.sec.gov/news/press/2011/2011-214-chart-stats.pdf. For background on the financial crisis, see these *CQ Researcher* reports: Marcia Clemmitt, "Financial Industry Overhaul," July 30, 2010, pp. 629-652; Thomas J. Billitteri, "Financial Bailout," Oct. 24, 2008, pp. 865-888, updated July 30, 2010; Kenneth Jost, "Financial Crisis," May 9, 2008, pp. 409-432.

[4] "Prosecuting Wall Street," *op. cit.* The interview with Breuer ends the segment.

[5] "Manhattan U.S. Attorney and FBI Assistant Director-in-Charge Announce Charges Against Seven Investment Professionals for Insider Trading Scheme That Allegedly Netted more than $61.8 Million in Illegal Profits," U.S. Attorney, Southern District of New York, Jan. 18, 2012, www.justice.gov/usao/nys/pressreleases/January12/newmantoddetalchargespr.pdf; Jenny Strasburg, Michael Rothfeld and Susan Pulliam, "Federal Officials Charge Seven in Insider Probe," *The Wall Street Journal*, Jan. 18, 2012, http://online.wsj.com/article/SB10001424052970204468004577168450897919374.html?mod=WSJ_hp_LEFTTopStories.

[6] See Edward Wyatt, "S.E.C. Changes Policy on Firms' Admissions of Guilt," *The New York Times*, Jan. 7, 2012, p. B1.

[7] Quoted in E. Scott Reckard, "Pair are cleared of fraud charges," *Los Angeles Times*, Nov. 11, 2009, p. B1; see also Zachery Kouwe and Dan Slater, "2 Bear Stearns Funds Leaders Are Acquitted," *The New York Times*, Nov. 11, 2009, p. A1. For an account of the rise and fall of the funds, see Bethany McLean and Joe Nocera, *All the Devils Are Here: The Hidden History of the Financial Crisis* (2010), pp. 285-295.

[8] "News Conference by the President," Oct. 6, 2011, www.whitehouse.gov/the-press-office/2011/10/06/news-conference-president.

[9] McLean and Nocera, *op. cit.*, p. 362. McLean is a contributing editor at *Vanity Fair*, Nocera a columnist with *The New York Times*.

[10] See Kitty Calavita, Henry N. Pontell, and Robert H. Tillman, *Big Money Crime: Fraud and Politics in the Savings and Loan Crisis* (1997), p. 29.

[11] Quoted in Bruce Maiman, "Occupy protest should focus on the bank," *Sacramento* (Calif.) *Bee*, Nov. 8, 2011.

[12] For coverage, see Gretchen Morgenson, "Leading Magnate Settles Charges for $67 Million," *The New York Times*, Oct. 16, 2010, p. A1; Walter Hamilton and E. Scott Reckard, "Countrywide execs settle fraud charges," *Los Angeles Times*, Oct. 16, 2010, p. A1. Under an indemnification agreement, Bank of America will pay $20 million of Mozilo's fine. Background drawn from McLean and Nocera, *op. cit.*, *passim*, esp. pp. 219-221, 230-31.

[13] Gretchen Morgenson and Louise Story, "A Financial Crisis With Little Guilt," *The New York Times*, April 14, 2011, p. A1.

[14] "Criminal Prosecutions for Financial Institution Fraud Continue to Fall," Transactional Records Access Clearinghouse, Nov. 15, 2011, http://trac.syr.edu/tracreports/crim/267/. The report showed 1,251 prosecutions for the first 11 months of fiscal 2011; a separate update for the final month (September 2011) showed 98 more, for a total of 1,349. The pictured chart projected 1,365 cases.

[15] "SEC Charges Former Fannie Mae and Freddie Mac Executives With Securities Fraud," Dec. 16, 2011, www.sec.gov/news/press/2011/2011-267.htm. For coverage, see David S. Hilzenrath and Zachary Goldfarb, "SEC charges ex-Fannie, Freddie chiefs," *The Washington Post*, Dec. 17, 2011, p. A1; Azam Ahmed and Ben Protess, "Ex-Fannie, Freddie Chiefs Accused of Deception," *The New York Times*, Dec. 17, 2011, p. A1.

[16] "Statement on the Application of Insider Trading Law to Trading by Members of Congress and Their Staffs," testimony to Senate Committee on Homeland Security and Government Affairs, Dec. 1, 2011, www.sec.gov/news/testimony/2011/ts120111rsk.htm. Khuzami delivered similar testimony to the House Committee on Financial Services on Dec. 6.

[17] Background drawn in part from " 'Robo-Signing' Paperwork Breakdown Leaves Many Houses in Foreclosure Limbo," PBS "NewsHour," Oct. 6, 2010, www.pbs.org/newshour/bb/business/july-dec10/foreclosures_10-06.html; Scot J. Paltrow, "Banks Continue 'Robo-Signing' Foreclosure Practices In Spite Of Promises to the Contrary: Investigation," Reuters Thomson, July 18, 2011, updated Sept. 17, 2011, published in *Huffington Post*, www.huffingtonpost.com/2011/07/18/robo-signing-foreclosure-banks_n_902140.html?page=1/.

[18] The lawsuit is *Commonwealth v. Bank of America et al.*, Suffolk County Superior Court, B.L.S. 1-4363, www.mass.gov/ago/docs/press/ag-complaint-national-banks.pdf. The suit is also against Mortgage Electronic Registration System Inc., a widely used mortgage recording firm, and its parent company. For coverage, see Jenifer B. McKim, "State sues big US lenders," *Boston Globe*, Dec. 2, 2011, p. 1; Gretchen Morgenson, "Massachusetts Sues 5 Major Banks Over Foreclosure Practices," *The New York Times*, Dec. 2, 2011, p. B1.

[19] Reactions from McKim, *op. cit.*, and Morgenson, *op. cit.* (Dec. 2, 2011).

[20] See Ruth Simon, Nick Timiraos and Dan Fitzpatrick, "Banks in Push for Pact," *The Wall Street Journal*, Dec. 13, 2011, p. C1.

[21] Some background drawn from "Fair to All People: The SEC and the Regulation of Insider Trading," Nov. 1, 2006, www.sechistorical.org/museum/galleries/it/.

[22] Cited in Robert J. Samuelson, "Fed bashing slander," *The Washington Post*, Dec. 12, 2011, p. A21. For background, see Hoyt Gimlin, "Wall Street: 40 Years After the Crash," *Editorial Research Reports*, Oct. 8, 1969, and Richard Boeckel, "Stock Exchanges and Security Speculation," *Editorial Research Reports*, Feb. 1, 1930; both available in *CQ Researcher Plus Archive*.

[23] Ferdinand Pecora, *Wall Street Under Oath: The Story of Our Modern Money Changers* (1939), p. xi. For Perino's account of the commission's investigation, see *The Hellhound of Wall Street: How Ferdinand Pecora's Investigation of the Great Crash Forever Changed American Finance* (2010).

[24] The citation is 401 F.2d 833 (2nd Cir. 1968). The Supreme Court declined to hear the company's appeal.

[25] The cases are *Ernst & Ernst v. Hochfelder*, 425 U.S. 185 (1976); *Chiarella v. United States* — 445 U.S. 222 (1980).

[26] See story by Judith Miller, no headline available, *The New York Times*, March 7, 1980, sec. 4, p. 1 (SEC begins crackdown on 'insiders').

[27] U.S. Department of Justice, "Attacking Financial Institution Fraud: A Report to the Congress of the United States," June 30, 1995, June 30, 1995, cited by incomplete name in Gillian Tett, "Insight: A Matter of Retribution," *Financial Times*, Sept. 30, 2009.

[28] The decision is *Central Bank of Denver v. First Interstate Bank of Denver*, 511 U.S. 164 (1994). For coverage, see Kenneth Jost, *Supreme Court Yearbook*, 1993-1994.

[29] The citation is 521 U.S. 642 (1997). For coverage, see Jost, *Supreme Court Yearbook, 1996-1997*.

[30] For background, see "Corporate Crime," *op. cit.* For a later listing of some companies implicated, see Perry E. Wallace, "Accounting, Audit and Audit Committees After Enron, *et al.*: Governing Outside the Box Without Stepping Off the Edge in the Modern Economy," *Washburn Law Review*, Vol. 94 (January 2004), pp. 102-103 & accompanying notes.

[31] For a dramatized overview of the events of 2008, see Frontline, "Inside the Meltdown," PBS, originally aired Feb. 17, 2009, www.pbs.org/wgbh/pages/frontline/meltdown/.

[32] See Brady Dennis, "Obama ushers in new financial era," *The Washington Post*, July 22, 2010, p. A13; "Historic Financial Overhaul Creates Bureau, Expands Oversight of Banks," *2010 CQ Almanac*, pp. 3-3 to 3-9.

[33] Mehrson, defense lawyers Edward Little (Cioffi) and Susan Brune (Tannin) quoted in Tom Hays, "2 Former Bear Stearns Hedge Fund Managers Charged," The Associated Press, June 20, 2008; ex-Enron prosecutor John

About the Author

Associate Editor **Kenneth Jost** graduated from Harvard College and Georgetown University Law Center. He is the author of the *Supreme Court Yearbook* and editor of *The Supreme Court from A to Z* (both *CQ Press*). He was a member of the *CQ Researcher* team that won the American Bar Association's 2002 Silver Gavel Award. His previous reports include "Financial Crisis" and "Corporate Crime." He is also author of the blog *Jost on Justice* (http://jostonjustice.blogspot.com).

Hueston quoted in Kouwe and Slater, *op. cit.*

[34] Government releases: SEC, www.sec.gov/news/press/2009/2009-249.htm; Justice Department: www.justice.gov/opa/pr/2011/April/11-ag-500.html.

[35] See Sewell Chan and Louise Story, "S.E.C. Settling Its Complaints With Goldman," *The New York Times*, July 16, 2010, p. A1; David S. Hilzenrath, "J.P. Morgan to pay $153.6 million to settle fraud suit," *The Washington Post*, June 22, 2011, p. A14.

[36] For the trial, see Matthew Barakat, "Jury convicts exec in $3B mortgage fraud case," The Associated Press, April 19, 2011.

[37] For the trial, see Tom Hays and Larry Neumeister, "Hedge-fund founder convicted in inside-trade case," The Associated Press, May 11, 2011.

[38] See Edward Wyatt, "Citing 'Legal Error,' S.E.C. Says It Will Appeal Rejection of Citigroup Settlement," *The New York Times*, Dec. 16, 2011, p. B3.

[39] Quoted in Ahmed and Protess, *op. cit.*

[40] The cases are *SEC v. Mudd et al.*, Case No. 11 CIV 9202 (S.D.N.Y., Dec. 18, 2011), www.sec.gov/litigation/complaints/2011/comp-pr2011-267-fanniemae.pdf; *SEC v. Syron et al.*, Case No. CIV 9201 (S.D.N.Y., Dec. 18, 2011), www.sec.gov/litigation/complaints/2011/comp-pr2011-267-freddiemac.pdf.

[41] Mudd quoted in Andrew Strickler and Josh Bernstein, "FBI Launches Probe of Fannie, Freddie," *The Daily*, Dec. 17, 2011, www.thedaily.com/page/2011/12/17/121711-news-fannie-fredie-1-2/; Syron's lawyers quoted in Ahmed and Protess, *op. cit.*

[42] Peter J. Wallison, "The Financial Crisis on Trial," *The Wall Street Journal*, Dec. 21, 2011, p. A19. Wallison served under President Ronald Reagan as general counsel for the Treasury Department and White House counsel and played a significant role in the administration's unenacted proposals to deregulate the financial services industry. As a member of the Financial Crisis Inquiry Commission, he joined with other Republican appointees in dissenting from the majority report.

[43] Joe Nocera, "An Inconvenient Truth," *The New York Times*, Dec. 20, 2011, p. A33. See also Joe Nocera, "The Big Lie," *ibid.*, Dec. 24, 2011, p. A21.

[44] "Former Fannie, Freddie Officials Face 'Significant' Fraud, Lying Charges," PBS "NewsHour," Dec. 16, 2011 (interview by Judy Woodruff), www.pbs.org/newshour/bb/business/july-dec11/fanniefreddie_12-16.html.

[45] See Edward Wyatt, "New Consumer Chief Promises Strong Agenda," *The New York Times*, Jan. 6, 2012, p. B3; Suzh Khimm, "Cordray Proceeds Despite Appointment Challenges," *The Washington Post*, Jan. 6, 2012, p. A16. See also Edward Wyatt, "Appointment Clears the Way for Agency to Act," *The New York Times*, Jan. 5, 2012, p. A16.

[46] "Consumer Financial Protection Bureau launches nonbank supervision program," Jan. 5, 2012, www.consumerfinance.gov/pressrelease/consumer-financial-protection-bureau-launches-nonbank-supervision-program/. See also Peggy Twohig and Steve Antonakes, "The CFPB launches its nonbank supervision program," Jan. 5, 2012 (blog), www.consumerfinance.gov/the-cfpb-launches-its-nonbank-supervision-program/.

[47] The memorandum is entitled "Lawfulness of Recess Appointments During a Recess of the Senate Notwithstanding Periodic Pro Forma Sessions," Jan. 6, 2012, www.justice.gov/olc/2012/pro-forma-sessions-opinion.pdf. Grassley is quoted in Charlie Savage, "Justice Dept. Defends Obama Recess Appointments," *The New York Times*, Jan. 13, 2012, p. A19. See Lyle Denniston, "First challenge on new Obama appointees," SCOTUSBlog, Jan. 13, 2012, www.scotusblog.com/2012/01/first-challenge-on-new-appointees/.

[48] See Edward Wyatt, "Some Lenders to Students to Face Greater Scrutiny," *The New York Times*, Jan. 13, 2012, p. B3. For background, see Marcia Clemmitt, "Student Debt," *CQ Researcher*, Oct. 21, 2011, pp. 877-900; and Barbara Mantel, "Career Colleges," *CQ Researcher*, Jan. 7, 2011, pp. 1-24.

[49] "Meeting of the Federal Open Market Committee, March 27-28, 2006, www.federalreserve.gov/monetarypolicy/files/FOMC20060328meeting.pdf. Bernanke's concluding comments begin at p. 95. For coverage, see Zachary A. Goldfarb, "As financial crisis brewed, Fed appeared unconcerned," *The Washington Post*, Jan. 13, 2012, p. A1; Binyamin Appelbaum, "Inside the Fed in '06: Coming Crisis, and Banter," *The New York Times*, Jan. 13, 2012, p. A1.

[50] See Ben Protess and Azam Ahmed, "U.S. Inquiry of MF Global Gains Speed," *The New York Times*, Jan. 10, 2012, p. B1.

[51] "Prosecuting Wall Street," *op. cit.*

FOR MORE INFORMATION

American Bankers Association, 1120 Connecticut Ave., N.W., Washington, DC 20036; 1-800-226-5377; www.aba.com. Nation's largest banking trade association.

Campaign for America's Future, 1825 K St., N.W., Suite 400, Washington, DC 20006; 202-955-5665; www.ourfuture.org. Progressive political organization that opposes the influence of financial institutions in politics.

Consumer Financial Protection Bureau, 1500 Pennsylvania Ave., N.W., Washington, DC 20220; 202-435-7000; www.consumerfinance.gov. Independent agency within Federal Reserve that enforces consumer-protection laws against banks, mortgage lenders, credit card issuers, payday lenders and others.

Department of Justice, 950 Pennsylvania Ave., N.W., Washington, DC 20530; 202-514-2000; www.justice.gov. Federal executive department responsible for enforcing laws against financial misconduct.

Heritage Foundation, 214 Massachusetts Ave., N.E., Washington, DC 20002; 202-546-4400; www.heritage.org. Conservative think tank working to repeal financial reforms it says interfere with free enterprise.

Mortgage Bankers Association, 1919 Pennsylvania Ave., N.W., Washington, DC 20006; 202-557-2700; www.mbaa.org. National association promoting residential and commercial real estate markets and increased homeownership.

Securities and Exchange Commission, 100 F St., N.E., Washington, DC 20549; 202-942-8088; www.sec.gov. Federal agency that oversees publicly traded companies and enforces securities laws.

U.S. Chamber of Commerce, 1615 H St., N.W., Washington, DC 20062; 202-659-6000; www.uschamber.com. Lobbying group for businesses and trade associations.

Bibliography

Selected Sources

Books

McLean, Bethany, and Joe Nocera, *All the Devils Are Here: The Hidden History of the Financial Crisis*, Portfolio/Penguin, 2010.

Veteran business journalists trace the origins and course of the financial crisis of 2008 from the invention of securitized mortgages through the proliferation of subprime mortgages and their dispersal to financial institutions and investors with limited disclosure of the financial risks. McLean is a contributor editor to *Vanity Fair*, Nocera a columnist for *The New York Times*. No notes or bibliography.

Morgenson, Gretchen, and Joshua Rosner, *Reckless Endangerment: How Outsized Ambition, Greed, and Corruption Led to Economic Armageddon*, Times Books, 2011.

The book focuses critically on the role played by Fannie Mae, the giant, government-sponsored mortgage company, in marketing subprime mortgages, especially loans written by its primary partner, Countrywide Financial. Morgenson is a Pulitzer Prize-winning reporter and columnist for *The New York Times*; Rosner is a consultant and early critic of the role of Fannie Mae and the other government-sponsored mortgage company, Freddie Mac. No notes or bibliography.

Articles

"Prosecuting Wall Street," 60 Minutes (Steve Kroft, correspondent; James Jacoby, producer), CBS News, Dec. 4, 2011, www.cbsnews.com/8301-18560_162-57336042/prosecuting-wall-street/?tag=contentMain;cbsCarousel.

Two whistleblowers — former executives with Countrywide Financial and Citigroup — tell Kroft that they know of financial misconduct at their former companies but have not been questioned by government investigators.

Morgenson, Gretchen, and Louise Story, "A Financial Crisis With Little Guilt," *The New York Times*, April 14, 2011, p. A1.

The 4,000-word story details, in text and informative graphics, the lack of criminal prosecutions against companies or individuals involved in the financial crisis.

Reports and Studies

"The Financial Crisis Inquiry Report: Final Report of the National Commission on the Causes of the Financial and Economic Crisis in the United States," January 2011, www.gpoaccess.gov/fcic/fcic.pdf.

The congressionally appointed panel concluded that the financial crisis could have been avoided if the financial industry and public officials had heeded warnings and properly understood and managed evolving risks in the financial system. Republican members of the commission did not support the conclusions.

On the Web

"Chasing the Devil Around the Stump: Securities Regulation, the SEC, and the Courts," SEC Historical Society, Dec. 1, 2011, www.sechistorical.org/museum/galleries/ctd/.

The "gallery" in the SEC Historical Society's virtual museum and archive provides a compact, up-to-date overview of the Securities and Exchange Commission's regulatory activities and philosophy in the context of court decisions that alternately approve or disapprove of the agency's efforts at expansive enforcement. For a longer historical account, see the earlier gallery, "Fair to All People: The SEC and the Regulation of Insider Trading," Nov. 1, 2006, www.sechistorical.org/museum/galleries/it/.

Books on the Financial Crisis

The financial crisis of 2008 and the developments that led up to it have been chronicled and analyzed in a veritable flood of books. Here is a list of some that have drawn the most attention, with brief notations of the topics covered; all have been republished in paperback.

Cohan, William E., *House of Cards: A Tale of Hubris and Wretched Excess on Wall Street*, Doubleday, 2009. [Bear Stearns]

—, *Money and Power: How Goldman Sachs Came to Rule the World*, Anchor, 2011.

Lewis, Michael, *The Big Short: Inside the Doomsday Machine*, W.W. Norton, 2010. [bond and real estate derivative markets]

Lowenstein, Roger, *The End of Wall Street*, Reed Elsevier, 2010. [2008 financial collapse]

Sorkin, Andrew Ross, *Too Big to Fail: The Inside Story of How Wall Street and Washington Fought to Save the Financial System — and Themselves*, Viking, 2009. [2008 financial collapse]

Tett, Gillian, *Fool's Gold: How the Bold Dream of a Small Tribe at J.P. Morgan Was Corrupted by Wall Street Greed and Unleashed a Catastrophe*, Free Press, 2009.

Wessel, David, *In Fed We Trust: Ben Bernanke's War on the Great Panic*, Crown Business, 2009. [Federal Reserve]

Zuckerman, Gregory, *The Greatest Trade Ever: The Behind-the-Scenes Story of How John Paulson Defied Wall Street and Made Financial History*, Broadway Books, 2009. [hedge fund manager Paulson].

The Next Step:

Additional Articles from Current Periodicals

Financial Crisis

Chan, Sewell, "Crisis Panel's Report Parsed Far and Wide," *The New York Times*, Jan. 28, 2011, p. B1, www.nytimes.com/2011/01/28/business/economy/28inquiry.html.
The government-appointed Financial Crisis Inquiry Commission has concluded that the crisis was caused by a bias toward deregulation by government officials and mismanagement by financiers who failed to perceive risks.

Thomas, Bill, *et al.*, "What Caused the Financial Crisis?" *The Wall Street Journal*, Jan. 27, 2011, p. A21, online.wsj.com/article/SB10001424052748704698004576104500524998280.html.
Critics say the financial crisis stemmed from more than a simple lack of Wall Street regulations.

Insider Trading

Harris, Larry, "Don't Let the Insiders Rule," *Los Angeles Times*, Oct. 17, 2011, p. A15, articles.latimes.com/2011/oct/17/opinion/la-oe-harris-rajaratnam-20111017.
Lifting restrictions on insider trading would make problems related to financial disclosure worse, argues a University of Southern California finance professor.

Lattman, Peter, "In Galleon, Prison Term Seen As Test," *The New York Times*, Sept. 20, 2011, p. B1, dealbook.nytimes.com/2011/09/19/in-galleon-insider-case-prison-term-is-seen-as-test/.
The prosecution of hedge-fund magnate Raj Rajaratnam is widely seen as a litmus test of how serious an offense insider trading will be regarded.

Sandy Smith, John F., "Insider Trading Still an Issue," *Atlanta Journal-Constitution*, May 22, 2011, p. D2.
Insider trading is wrong and illegal because other investors don't get access to the same beneficial information, says the chair of the Institute for Research in the Social Sciences at Stanford University.

Legal Action

Avalos, George, "Feds File Charges Against Execs of Failed United Commercial Bank," *Contra Costa* (Calif.) *Times*, Oct. 11, 2011.
Federal authorities allege that top executives of a San Francisco-area bank concealed the extent of loan losses during the height of the financial crisis.

Gordon, Marcy, "SEC May Act Against S&P for '07 Debt Rating," *The Boston Globe*, Sept. 27, 2011, p. 8, www.boston.com/realestate/news/articles/2011/09/27/sec_may_act_against_sp_for_07_debt_rating/.
The Securities and Exchange Commission is considering legal action against Standard & Poor's for an inflated rating of a 2007 mortgage debt offering.

Holan, Angie Drobnic, "Bankers Largely Escape Prosecution," *St. Petersburg* (Fla.) *Times*, Oct. 10, 2011, p. A1, www.tampabay.com/news/politics/national/michael-moores-corporate-crime-claim-mostly-true/1196036.
Filmmaker and activist Michael Moore told Occupy Wall Street protesters that no bankers or CEOs have been arrested for bringing down the economy in 2008.

Regulations and Reforms

Frank, Barney, "A Thousand Cuts," *The Boston Globe*, July 30, 2011, p. 11, articles.boston.com/2011-07-30/bostonglobe/29833822_1_financial-reform-wall-street-reform-consumer-financial-protection-bureau.
Republicans are trying to undo financial reform that the public broadly supports, says the former chairman of the House Financial Services Committee.

Isaac, William M., "Deregulation Gone Awry," *The Washington Times*, April 11, 2011, p. B4, www.washingtontimes.com/news/2011/apr/8/deregulation-gone-awry/?page=all.
Repealing the Dodd-Frank law without delivering a serious alternative would have negative consequences for Republicans, says a former chairman of the Federal Deposit Insurance Corporation.

Wichert, Bill, "Senator Underestimated Wall Street Reforms," *Star-Ledger* (Newark, N.J.), Dec. 19, 2011, p. 3.
A New Jersey state senator has criticized the lack of effective reforms following the collapse of major investment banks.

CITING *CQ RESEARCHER*

Sample formats for citing these reports in a bibliography include the ones listed below. Preferred styles and formats vary, so please check with your instructor or professor.

MLA STYLE

Jost, Kenneth. "Remembering 9/11," CQ Researcher 2 Sept. 2011: 701-732.

APA STYLE

Jost, K. (2011, September 2). Remembering 9/11. *CQ Researcher, 9*, 701-732.

CHICAGO STYLE

Jost, Kenneth. "Remembering 9/11." *CQ Researcher*, September 2, 2011, 701-732.

In-depth Reports on Issues in the News

Are you writing a paper?

Need backup for a debate?

Want to become an expert on an issue?

For more than 80 years, students have turned to *CQ Researcher* for in-depth reporting on issues in the news. Reports on a full range of political and social issues are now available. Following is a selection of recent reports:

Civil Liberties
Remembering 9/11, 9/11
Government Secrecy, 2/11
Cybersecurity, 2/10
Press Freedom, 2/10

Crime/Law
Eyewitness Testimony, 10/11
Legal-Aid Crisis, 10/11
Computer Hacking, 9/11
Class Action Lawsuits, 5/11
Cameras in the Courtroom, 1/11
Death Penalty Debates, 11/10

Education
Digital Education, 12/11
College Football, 11/11
Student Debt, 10/11
School Reform, 4/11
Crime on Campus, 2/11

Environment/Society
Fracking Controversy, 12/11
Water Crisis in the West, 12/11
Google's Dominance, 11/11
Managing Public Lands, 11/11
Prolonging Life, 9/11

Health/Safety
Military Suicides, 9/11
Teen Drug Use, 6/11
Organ Donations, 4/11
Genes and Health, 1/11
Food Safety, 12/10
Preventing Bullying, 12/10

Politics/Economy
'Occupy' Movement, 1/12
Reviving Manufacturing, 7/11
Foreign Aid and National Security, 6/11
Lies and Politics, 2/11

Upcoming Reports

Youth Volunteering, 1/27/12
Presidential Election, 2/3/12
Medical Errors, 2/10/12

ACCESS

CQ Researcher is available in print and online. For access, visit your library or www.cqresearcher.com.

STAY CURRENT

For notice of upcoming *CQ Researcher* reports or to learn more about *CQ Researcher* products, subscribe to the free e-mail newsletters, *CQ Researcher Alert!* and *CQ Researcher News*: http://cqpress.com/newsletters.

PURCHASE

To purchase a *CQ Researcher* report in print or electronic format (PDF), visit www.cqpress.com or call 866-427-7737. Single reports start at $15. Bulk purchase discounts and electronic-rights licensing are also available.

SUBSCRIBE

Annual full-service *CQ Researcher* subscriptions—including 44 reports a year, monthly index updates, and a bound volume—start at $803. Add $25 for domestic postage.

CQ Researcher Online offers a backfile from 1991 and a number of tools to simplify research. For pricing information, call 800-834-9020, or e-mail librarymarketing@cqpress.com.

CQ Researcher ***Plus*** *Archive*

Get Online Access to Vital Issues from 1923 to the Present

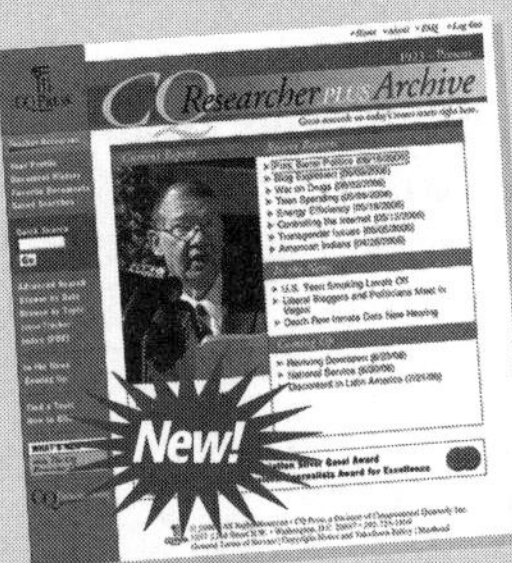

CQ Researcher Plus Archive delivers fast, online access to every *CQ Researcher* report from 1991 to the present, *PLUS* lets you explore the complete archive of *Editorial Research Reports** from 1923-1990. Search and browse more than 3,600 in-depth reports.

Loaded with handy online features, *CQ Researcher Plus Archive* provides the trustworthy reporting and the advanced online functionality today's researchers demand. The new "Issue Tracker" feature provides quick links to past and present reports on the specific topics you need.

For a free trial, visit http://library.cqpress.com/trials.

For pricing information, call 1-800-834-9020, ext. 1906 or e-mail librarymarketing@cqpress.com.

**Editorial Research Reports*, the predecessor to *CQ Researcher*, provides the same expert, nonpartisan reporting on the vital issues that have shaped our society.

CQ Press • 2300 N Street, NW, Suite 800 • Washington, DC 20037

CQ Researcher

Published by CQ Press, an Imprint of SAGE Publications, Inc.

www.cqresearcher.com

Youth Volunteerism

Should schools require students to perform public service?

After Hurricane Katrina hit New Orleans in 2005, Tulane University made volunteering for community projects in the ravaged city, such as restoring parks or tutoring grade-school students, a requirement for graduation. Since then, applications to Tulane have shot up. Schools and colleges nationwide have increased volunteer opportunities for students, and nearly 90 percent of colleges offer service-learning programs that tie class work with volunteer activities. Researchers see ample evidence that at least some service programs encourage students to participate in civic life as they grow older. Experts worry, however, that volunteer opportunities are far more prevalent for middle-class and affluent students than for those from low-income families. Meanwhile, many school districts continue to mull whether to require volunteer service for high school graduation. Courts have upheld the constitutionality of such requirements, but some students and parents resist them.

Students check their net during a water-quality test in Charleston, S.C. The project was organized by Earth Force, a national organization sponsored by the Corporation for National and Community Service that teaches youth how to improve the environment.

INSIDE THIS REPORT

THE ISSUES 79
BACKGROUND 86
CHRONOLOGY 87
CURRENT SITUATION 92
AT ISSUE 93
OUTLOOK 94
BIBLIOGRAPHY 97
THE NEXT STEP 98

CQ Researcher • Jan. 27, 2012 • www.cqresearcher.com
Volume 22, Number 4 • Pages 77-100

Los Angeles | London | New Delhi
Singapore | Washington DC

RECIPIENT OF SOCIETY OF PROFESSIONAL JOURNALISTS AWARD FOR EXCELLENCE ◆ AMERICAN BAR ASSOCIATION SILVER GAVEL AWARD

YOUTH VOLUNTEERISM

THE ISSUES

79 • Does community service spur civic engagement?
• Should students be required to perform community service?
• Are more young people volunteering today?

BACKGROUND

86 **Volunteers of America**
Grassroots community volunteers date back to America's earliest history.

88 **University Service**
Early American philosophers theorized about integrating real-world experience into schooling.

90 **Schools and Service**
A drop in teen volunteering beginning in the 1970s sparked interest in service learning.

91 **AmeriCorps Questioned**
Opposition began building after President Obama took office in 2009.

CURRENT SITUATION

92 **Federal Phase-Out**
The Republican-led House wants to end AmeriCorps.

92 **Changing Landscape**
The recession and declining worker pool are changing volunteerism.

OUTLOOK

94 **Good Citizenship**
Many youths value service over voting.

SIDEBARS AND GRAPHICS

80 **Where College Students Volunteer**
Educational or youth service organizations attract the most volunteers.

81 **Teen Volunteerism Declined**
Rates dropped 4 percentage points from 2005 to 2007.

82 **'Voluntourists' Mix Pleasure and Altruism**
But doing good in exotic lands has a downside.

84 **Older Americans Volunteer Most**
Americans between 35 and 54 lead the pack.

87 **Chronology**
Key events since 1736.

88 **Volunteer Programs Lacking for Low-Income Kids**
"It's not because adolescents aren't interested."

91 **Service-Learning Programs Aid Students, Nonprofits**
Linking schoolwork and volunteerism is the biggest challenge for programs.

93 **At Issue**
Should AmeriCorps be eliminated?

FOR FURTHER RESEARCH

96 **For More Information**
Organizations to contact.

97 **Bibliography**
Selected sources used.

98 **The Next Step**
Additional articles.

99 **Citing *CQ Researcher***
Sample bibliography formats.

Cover: Corporation for National and Community Service

CQ Researcher

Jan. 27, 2012
Volume 22, Number 4

MANAGING EDITOR: Thomas J. Billitteri
tjb@cqpress.com

ASSISTANT MANAGING EDITOR: Kathy Koch
kkoch@cqpress.com

CONTRIBUTING EDITOR: Thomas J. Colin
tcolin@cqpress.com

ASSOCIATE EDITOR: Kenneth Jost

STAFF WRITERS: Marcia Clemmitt, Peter Katel

CONTRIBUTING WRITERS: Sarah Glazer, Alan Greenblatt, Barbara Mantel, Jennifer Weeks

DESIGN/PRODUCTION EDITOR: Olu B. Davis

ASSISTANT EDITOR: Darrell Dela Rosa

FACT CHECKER: Michelle Harris

Los Angeles | London | New Delhi
Singapore | Washington DC

An Imprint of SAGE Publications, Inc.

VICE PRESIDENT AND EDITORIAL DIRECTOR, HIGHER EDUCATION GROUP:
Michele Sordi

DIRECTOR, ONLINE PUBLISHING:
Todd Baldwin

CQ Researcher (ISSN 1056-2036) is printed on acid-free paper. Published weekly, except: (March wk. 5) (May wk. 4) (July wk. 1) (Aug. wks. 3, 4) (Nov. wk. 4) and (Dec. wks. 3, 4). Published by SAGE Publications, Inc., 2455 Teller Rd., Thousand Oaks, CA 91320. Annual full-service subscriptions start at $1,054. For pricing, call 1-800-834-9020. To purchase a *CQ Researcher* report in print or electronic format (PDF), visit www.cqpress.com or call 866-427-7737. Single reports start at $15. Bulk purchase discounts and electronic-rights licensing are also available. Periodicals postage paid at Thousand Oaks, California, and at additional mailing offices. POSTMASTER: Send address changes to *CQ Researcher*, 2300 N St., N.W., Suite 800, Washington, DC 20037.

Youth Volunteerism

BY MARCIA CLEMMITT

THE ISSUES

After Hurricane Katrina devastated New Orleans in 2005, Tulane University began requiring students to work on community projects closely tied to their coursework as a condition of graduation. Education majors might tutor elementary students, for instance, and architecture students could help restore parks.

The aim, says Vincent Ilustre, executive director of the university's Center for Public Service, is "to engage our students in rebuilding New Orleans."

Some worried the graduation requirement would send applications to Tulane into a nose dive. Instead, it has been a huge hit, Ilustre says. Before it was added in 2006, "we had about 18,000 applications for 1,500 slots" in the freshman class, he says. "Last year we had 44,000 applications for the same 1,500 places." Anecdotal evidence suggests the remarkable increase is closely related to the school's new mandate.

Tulane is far from alone in requiring — or at least encouraging — public service. *

Over the past two decades, schools and colleges nationwide have increased the number of volunteer opportunities they provide for students. Today, 89 percent of colleges sponsor some form of service learning, in which volunteer work such as helping at a homeless shelter, is linked to studies in, for example, urban policy, says Andrew Furco, associate vice president for public engagement at the University of Minnesota. Meanwhile, volunteer rates among youths ages 16 to 19 soared from 13.4 percent to 24.5 percent between 1989 and 2007, largely because a rising number of high schools sponsor or require service. [1]

Still in question, however, is how many programs are of high enough quality to improve students' learning, help communities and encourage greater civic and social commitment as students grow into adulthood.

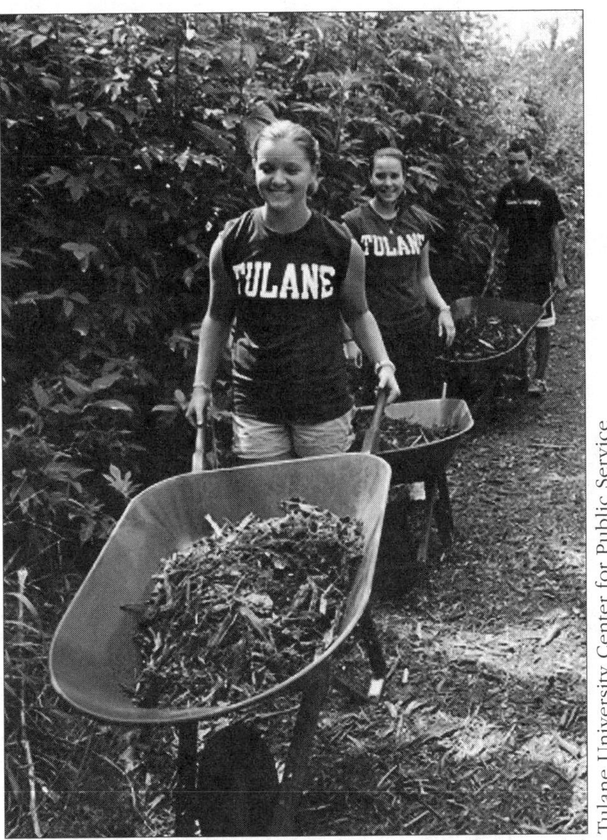

Tulane University Center for Public Service

Students from Tulane University in New Orleans volunteer at City Park as part of efforts to restore the devastated city following Hurricane Katrina in 2005. Tulane made community service a graduation requirement after the disaster and saw applications to the school shoot up. Nearly 90 percent of the nation's colleges provide service-learning opportunities.

Researchers see ample evidence that at least some service programs encourage students to participate in their communities later. "I'm working on a paper right now about whether willingness to serve on a jury" relates to an earlier history of volunteerism, and data suggest that "yes, it does," says sociology professor Marc A. Musick, associate dean for student affairs in the College of Liberal Arts at the University of Texas (UT), Austin. Volunteering makes people more civic minded," says Musick, coauthor of the 2008 book *Volunteers: A Social Profile*. For example, he says, young people who have volunteered are likely "to look at government organizations in a different way because they've done some of the same kinds of service" for the community.

Students who do community-service projects "meet people unlike those they know" and "learn to know them as individuals," says Steven Meyers, a professor of psychology and social justice at Roosevelt University, in Chicago. That, he says, "can lead to a much more informed worldview" that encourages engagement in civic and community life later on.

But Leslie Lenkowsky, a clinical professor of public affairs and philanthropic studies at Indiana University, in Bloomington, argues that it's not so much service experiences as education that spurs civic engagement. "People don't just wake up one morning and say, 'How can I get engaged in something today?' " says Lenkowsky, who during the George W. Bush administration headed the Corporation for National and Community Service, a federal agency that runs AmeriCorps and other pro-

* Campuswide service requirements at the college level are rare. Some schools have them, however, including Catholic-affiliated Belmont Abbey College, in Belmont, N.C.; Methodist-affiliated Centenary College, in Hackettstown, N.J.; historically black Benedict College, in Columbia, S.C.; and at least one public university, California State University at Monterey Bay.

Where College Students Volunteer

Educational or youth service organizations attract the most college student volunteers, followed by religious programs.

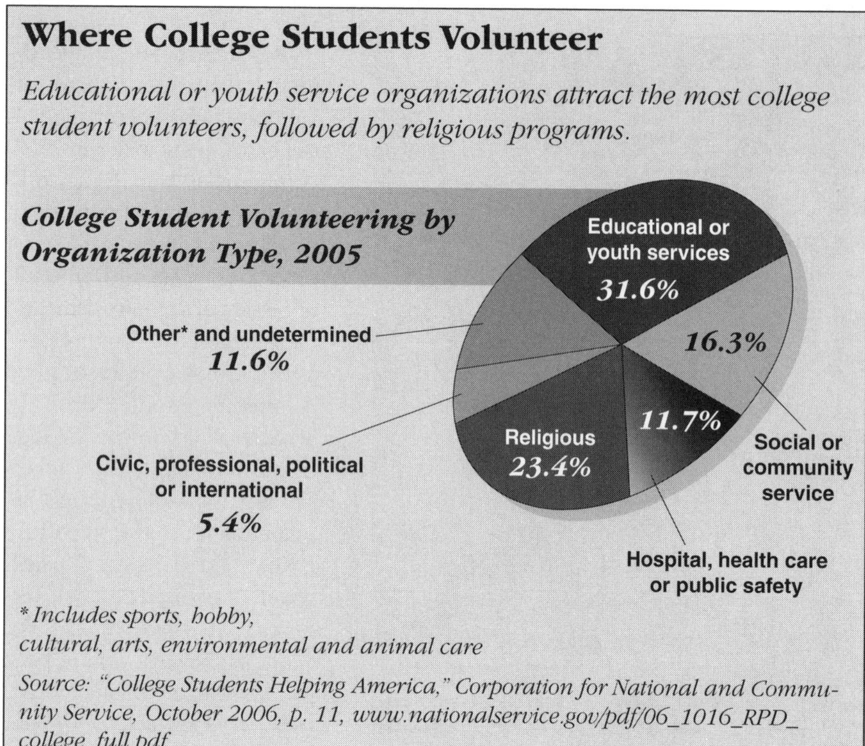

* *Includes sports, hobby, cultural, arts, environmental and animal care*

Source: "College Students Helping America," Corporation for National and Community Service, October 2006, p. 11, www.nationalservice.gov/pdf/06_1016_RPD_college_full.pdf

grams that place volunteers in nonprofit organizations and help support their service with stipends and other assistance.

Lenkowsky says people pursue volunteer opportunities mainly "because they're concerned about something" — such as abortion, taxation or homelessness. "And how do people get involved in issues? It depends on the quality of education," he says. "The ability of young people to see public issues as important to their own concerns" — and thus worth committing themselves to through voting, volunteering or the like — "is less than it used to be," he says.

In the 1990s, some high schools began adding community service to their graduation requirements, but the practice remains controversial. Skeptics argue that so many students already have the motivation to volunteer that requirements are overkill.

"I don't see the necessity for a mandate," said Brett Fortin, a senior at Mansfield High School, in Mansfield, Mass., where instituting a requirement was discussed last fall. "I do believe that most of the student body is actively involved," said Fortin, president of the student-run Student Service Corps, which has researched and helped organize voluntary student participation in more than 50 projects in the Mansfield area, including helping out at Special Olympics events and joining a community leaf-raking effort. [2]

Some researchers say the opinions about service that students draw from school programs depend almost entirely on how well the programs are structured and managed, not on whether the service is required or not. After decades of research on the mandate question, "the data's clear on this, although people haven't really listened," says James Youniss, a research professor of psychology at Catholic University, in Washington. Numerous studies demonstrate that student attitudes after they'd performed service depended on the structure and quality of the programs they participated in, not on whether they'd chosen to volunteer or been required to do so, he says. [3]

Youniss and other researchers caution that unless volunteer programs actively promote thoughtful analysis of students' experiences and issues involved in their service, the programs' effects on students' attitudes and behavior will be nil.

"We studied one Catholic school where kids went to a soup kitchen" and through observation and discussion worked out theories for themselves about how homelessness originates and what things might help it, Youniss says. Data show that only programs that include such follow-up work affect student attitudes and behavior in the long term, he says.

Effective service experiences can be integrated into all kinds of subject matter, Youniss says. In two public schools in Iowa, he says, "kids looked at the disposal of oil filters from cars" in a science class, collected data, analyzed it in light of the science they learned, and ultimately "got a bill passed" directing proper disposal methods.

Community-service participation is particularly high among students at selective colleges and among college-bound high school students, a trend that reveals a troubling socioeconomic divide in who gets access to volunteer opportunities. Critics worry that volunteer opportunities are more prevalent among wealthier students and that those facing financial challenges often lack the time for public service because they are working to pay for school.

"There is a huge socioeconomic gap" for the poor in service opportunities, as there is for most other educational opportunities, says Youniss. "If a school has low-income students [or] many immigrants," for example, "it's less likely to have" programs known to improve students' civic involvement, including volunteer-service programs and even student government, he says.

The socioeconomic gap not only deprives young people of community-engagement opportunities but also likely discourages activities such as voting, Youniss says. He notes that people with high school diplomas or less, and especially poor people, vote at much lower rates than college graduates. "You might want to trace that back to poor civics" education and fewer opportunities to build engagement among youth, at least partially, he says.

As lawmakers, colleges and school districts mull whether to expand or limit community-service programs, here are some of the questions that are being asked:

Teen Volunteerism Declined

Teen volunteerism rates have fluctuated drastically in the nearly four decades beginning in 1974. After declining to a low of 13.4 percent, volunteering more than doubled, to 28.4 percent in 2005, but then dropped nearly 4 percentage points in the next two years.

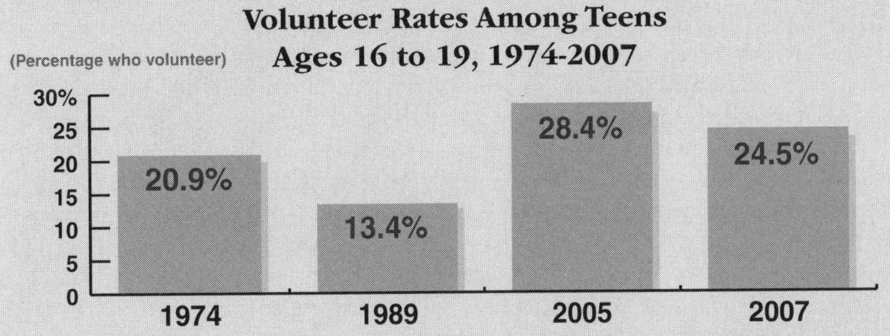

Sources: "Reaching Our Goals: An Overview of Research in Support of the Strategic Initiatives," Corporation for National and Community Service, March 2009, p. 3, www.nationalservice.gov/pdf/08_1113_rpd_reachingourgoals.pdf; "Volunteer Growth in America: A Review of Trends Since 1974," Corporation for National and Community Service, December 2006, p. 2, www.nationalservice.gov/pdf/06_1203_volunteer_growth.pdf

Does community service lead to greater civic engagement?

Supporters of volunteerism argue that community work encourages people to become more willing to help others and to fulfill civic duties such as voting later in life. The jury is out on how effectively service programs accomplish those goals, however. Researchers report that some programs appear very effective while others don't lead to long-term improvement in community engagement.

History provides strong evidence that at least some volunteer experiences — notably on behalf of a political cause, such as civil rights — can spur young people to remain socially engaged, says Youniss of Catholic University. "Young people who were involved in the civil rights movement" as well as Vietnam-era anti-war activities are "still very much engaged" in community life today, and even their children show high degrees of civic engagement, he says. "It's very clear that activism on behalf of these justice causes remains" with people throughout life.

Youniss sees two main reasons for the long-lasting effects. Civil rights and anti-war activists "were very effective" and thus saw the fruits of their labors in society, which likely encouraged them to remain engaged, he says. Furthermore, young civil rights volunteers saw themselves as part of a historical tradition stretching back centuries. This gave them a sense of belonging and a feeling that their work had meaning beyond themselves, both factors that encourage continued involvement in community causes, Youniss says. Civil rights volunteers "saw themselves as jumping into history to participate in the abolition movement" against slavery that dated back 200 years.

In fact, simply belonging to any group in which service is the norm can lead to a longer-term interest in volunteering, even when the group's main function isn't service, says Musick. For example, at UT, Austin, and on other campuses where "students volunteer in groups," often through fraternities and sororities, the phenomenon "creates a little culture of volunteering that's self-reinforcing" and encourages future involvement, he says.

Similarly, church-related service is fostered not just by religious principles but by the notion of "fellowship — getting together with other believers" to serve, Musick says. "To get civic engagement, you need structures like this — situations where, if you're not volunteering, you're left out," he says.

Many advocates of service-learning courses argue that volunteering frequently brings students into contact with people from very different backgrounds and circumstances than their own, which can spur civic engagement by broadening students' understanding of the world and its problems.

"Our students are more privileged, and when they go into inner-city schools and students begin to talk to them, the takeaway is, 'Those kids have the same dreams I did, but they have challenges in their lives that I hadn't even imagined,' " says Sandra Enos, an associate professor of sociology at Bryant University, in Smithfield, R.I. "They get into conversations that disrupt their thinking" and, usually for the first time, learn things from experience without the learning being "mediated" by parents, teachers or textbooks, she says. Students regularly report that "their parents kept

'Voluntourists' Mix Pleasure and Altruism

Doing good in exotic lands has an allure — but also a downside.

In an era of easy worldwide travel and the ubiquitous, information-packed Internet, new kinds of volunteering have grown quickly over the past decade. There's voluntourism — in which travel is combined with service work — and computer-based volunteering initiatives that invite Internet users to participate in social-issues campaigns. Reactions to both are mixed, however.

Combining volunteering with travel as an alternative to traditional vacations is growing in popularity, partly because of some other trends in volunteer behavior, wrote Beth Gazley, an associate professor in the School of Public and Environmental Affairs at Indiana University. More people are volunteering today, including more young people, "but for fewer average hours" than the typical volunteer committed in the past, she wrote.

Spending a week's vacation performing service in a potentially exotic location — such as a wild-elephant preserve or a remote village abroad — fits in well with the shrinking time frame of modern volunteering, Gazley said. Furthermore, "potential volunteers often cite lack of available leisure time as one barrier to service," so "volunteer vacations neatly circumvent this problem." [1]

Volunteer vacations also can last from a few days to months, most involve hands-on helping, such as building a trail or helping conduct research, and tourist volunteers pay their own way and, in some cases, also make additional financial contributions. [2]

Earthwatch, one of the oldest voluntourism organizations, began sponsoring environmental voluntourism in 1973. "We began with rocks and stars, where amateurs couldn't hurt anything," said founder Brian Rosborough. [3] Now Earthwatch projects enable volunteers to help conduct scientific research and protect endangered animals and fragile habitats, Rosborough said. [4]

Nevertheless, since many, if not most, "voluntourists" are attracted more by the exotic travel than by the service itself, there's a danger that trips will be created "just for the travelers," and that is "usually a waste of money and not a lasting solution to any problem," said Daniela Papi, founder of PEPY Tours, which arranges voluntourism in Cambodia. "The hardest part is finding projects that both make the volunteers feel 'needed' and really ARE needed," said Papi. A good project, for example, would be to have volunteers clear land for a new school in a community "already organized in a way that will take care" of the land when the tourists depart, she said. [5]

While some web-based volunteerism initiatives draw criticism as promoting a dangerously shallow view of what constitutes useful service, others provide substantive help to those in need.

In the Thurston school district of Lacey, Wash., the Intergenerational Grandfriend Project helped students, including those with special needs, link online with older people in nursing homes or retirement communities. The elders mentored the teens, while the teens provided stimulating youthful companionship. "Silver [Web] surfers and high-school students exchanged e-mails," and most were extremely enthusiastic about the project, wrote teacher Martin Kimeldorf, who directed the project. [6]

Some websites link volunteers with service projects that need help. At San Francisco-based Sparked.com, for example, nonprofit service organizations post "challenges," or projects where added assistance and expertise are needed. For example, Cincinnati's Ronald McDonald House — which houses families of sick children during hospitalizations — used the site to find Arabic translators for its written materials, while Chimpanzee Sanctuary Northwest found computer experts to help figure out how to prevent hacks of its website. [7]

For volunteers who can't travel, some websites post do-at-home opportunities. The Extraordinaries, another San Francisco-based website, developed a mobile phone app that alerts users to small volunteer tasks that can be "completed in small snatch-

them in a bubble" that a service experience has broken.

However, many scholars say that while there's good evidence that some volunteer programs increase the likelihood of long-term civic engagement, others don't.

"There's no evidence that anything happens, that anything takes" when students participate in volunteer programs that don't help them think about the underlying causes of community problems they observe or don't encourage them to see themselves as part of a solution, says Youniss.

"There's nothing wrong with going to a soup kitchen to help out, but it won't have a long-lasting effect on you" if "you just end up thinking of yourself as a sweet, little individual do-gooder," Youniss says. Only students who actively think about the issues their service raises and see those issues in a historical and philosophical perspective are likely to parlay service into long-term community engagement, he says. Often, that deeper perspective grows out of volunteering with a group that holds certain beliefs about social problems, such as a church or environmental organization, Youniss notes.

"People think of service as an individual action that by itself can somehow modify something inside a kid's head" to increase his or her civic-mindedness, says Youniss. "But that's not it." Change in future behavior comes only when a young volunteer is induced to consider volunteering as part of some larger vision of society and one's place in it, he says.

For example, if a young person in the mid-Atlantic region gets involved with one of the "hundreds of local

es of time," wrote Mike Bright, founder of a British microvolunteering site, Help from Home. Microvolunteering "invites quick actions" such as signing up to donate your hair for wigs for sick children suffering from hair loss, making a "micro loan" to someone in a developing country, signing an online petition, or counting plants or birds in your back yard for a biodiversity project. Evidence is accumulating that microvolunteers can make "meaningful contributions," Bright wrote.[8]

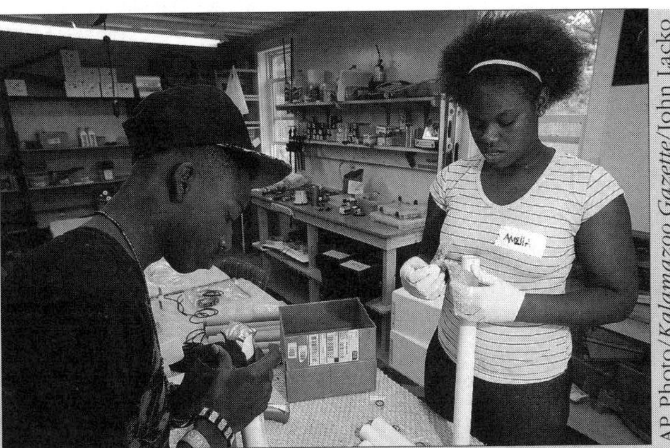

AP Photo/*Kalamazoo Gazette*/John Lacko

Teenagers Cranston Mitchell and Amelia Hampton assemble parts for a water filtration system for use in Senegal last June. Eight students from Kalamazoo, Mich., spent 15 days in the West African nation last year doing community service as part of the Urban Youth for Africa program sponsored by the Kalamazoo Deacon's Conference.

Others aren't so sure. "My favorite pet peeve at the moment is . . . the notion that you can volunteer spontaneously via your cell phone for tiny periods of time — saving the world in 10-second intervals," wrote Steve McCurley, editor of the online journal *e-Volunteerism*. "It's an idea that is emotionally endearing and intellectually absurd."[9]

Other trends attract similar criticism. For example, some analysts worry that a shallow view of service may arise from high-profile volunteerism-related activities such as "sporting colorful empathy ribbons" or forwarding social-media messages — such as Twitter posts calling attention to a dangerous disease or environmental threat. "It's legitimate to worry that public displays of emotion run the danger of diverting people from a more complex message . . . or course of action," wrote *e-Volunteerism* Editor-in-Chief Susan J. Ellis.[10]

Nevertheless, wrote Ellis, even such shallow service participation presents an opportunity. "Public outpourings of emotion imply reservoirs of desire to affiliate and make a difference," and service organizations and longtime volunteers could help to turn ribbon-wearers and message-forwarders into active volunteers, said Ellis.[11]

— Marcia Clemmitt

[1] Beth Gazley, "Volunteer Vacationers and What Research Can Tell Us About Them," *e-Volunteerism*, January 2001, www.e-volunteerism.com/quarterly/01win/facintro.

[2] *Ibid.*

[3] Quoted in "The Growth of Voluntourism," *e-Volunteerism*, July 2007.

[4] For background, see Earthwatch Institute, www.earthwatch.org.

[5] Quoted in "The Growth of Voluntourism," *op. cit.*

[6] Martin Kimeldorf, "Wiring Friendships Across Time, Space, and Age: An Evaluation of Intergenerational Friendships Created Online," *e-Volunteerism*, October 2001, www.e-volunteerism.com/quarterly/01fall/kimmeldorf.

[7] Kivi Leroux Miller, "Microvolunteering: Small Jobs on Your Own Time," *Kivi's Nonprofit Marketing Guide blog*, June 22, 2011, www.nonprofitmarketingguide.com/blog/2011/06/22/microvolunteering-small-jobs-on-your-own-time-mds11.

[8] Mike Bright, "Micro-Volunteering: Quickies, Quandaries and Questions," *e-Volunteerism*, October 2010, www.e-volunteerism.com/volume-xi-issue-1-october-2010/feature-articles/812.

[9] Steve McCurley, "Reflections on a Decade of e-Volunteerism," *e-Volunteerism*, October 2009, www.e-volunteerism.com/quarterly/09oct/09oct-points.

[10] Susan J. Ellis and Steve McCurley, "Public vs. Private Compassion: Colored Ribbons, T-shirts and SUVs," *e-Volunteerism*, April 2004, www.e-volunteerism.com/quarterly/04apr/04apr-points.

[11] *Ibid.*

and regional conservation organizations that have strong philosophies of protecting the environment" of the Chesapeake Bay, volunteering with the group "provides values education" and makes the student see himself or herself "as an actor in a larger story," he says. It's by "working your way into some civic tradition" rather than just engaging in individual "character-building activities" that long-term civic commitment is fostered, says Youniss.

"Focusing on trying to solve a particular problem, seeing that problem in a historical perspective" and, often, working with long-standing, service-oriented groups "who have a ready-made identity and offer a part that the kid can play" are the key elements of programs that change behavior in the long run, he says.

Should students be required to perform community service?

Over the past two decades, school districts around the country — including the entire Maryland system — have added community service as a high school graduation requirement. Critics argue that the requirements are a burden and disliked by so many students that they may decrease interest in volunteering later in life. Some studies find, however, that similarly structured service programs — whether voluntary or required — have basically the same effect on most students.

Students who face service requirements often approach the jobs halfheartedly and may become turned off to service altogether, some college students told University of Maryland researchers in a 2008 study. The "bad side" of a requirement is that it "reduces feelings of being altruistic, kind and loving, because it is seen as just

Older Americans Volunteer Most

Nearly one-third of Americans between ages 35 and 54 — the highest rate — participate in volunteer activities. Youths ages 16-19 are in the next-highest participation bracket, along with people from 54 to 74. Young adults ages 20-24 have the lowest volunteerism rate.

Volunteer Rates by Age Group, 2008-2010

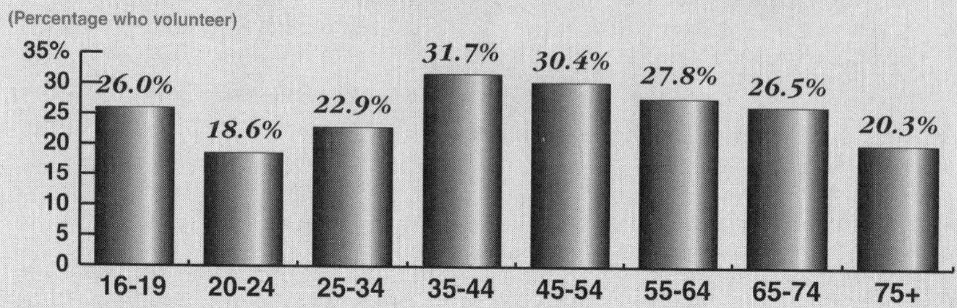

Source: "Volunteering in the U.S.," Corporation for National and Community Service, August 2011, www.volunteeringinamerica.gov/national

a mandate that I'll just get done and it will be over with," said one. "This cuts down motivation to want to go out and help others." [4]

Requirement supporters argue that "everyone born owes a debt to society," said Barbara Moralis, a librarian whose son attended high school in Bethlehem, Pa., which instituted a requirement in 1990. (*See Background, p. 90.*) But "I don't think it's up to government to decide who owes a debt and how it should be paid." Mandates are "spreading like a cancer. Someone has to stand up for an American's right to freedom," Moralis said. [5]

Requirements sour some but not all students on service, according to a study by scholars from the University of Northern Colorado and two other colleges. Specifically, students who were inclined to volunteer before they faced a requirement still said, after completing the service, that they were open to volunteering in the future. Students who originally were "less inclined to volunteer of their own free will" and who felt they were "being controlled" by the requirement, however, told researchers that the mandate made them even less likely to volunteer in the future. [6]

"I'm not in favor of community service for everyone," says Tulane's Ilustre. When schools require a certain number of service hours for graduation, "I think it's too easy for volunteering to lose its flavor and turn people off against service" and, potentially, against community engagement generally, he says. "I don't like it when universities penalize students with service hours," for example. "That's penalizing the community as well by sending them students who don't want to be there." Volunteering "should be done by those who want to do it," Ilustre says.

Even though Ilustre runs the office that manages student placements under Tulane's mandatory service program, he says he sees no conflict between his job and his opposition to requirements elsewhere. For one thing, he says, many if not most Tulane students actually choose the school because of its commitment to community involvement. And, most important, service to fulfill requirements is always tightly linked to students' own curricular interests. For example, a Tulane student taking pre-med courses to prepare for a career in cancer medicine will get a volunteer placement in a hospital oncology department, doing work that's closely tied to classwork.

Some researchers find that required or voluntary service can turn students into more engaged citizens.

In research comparing two groups of college-bound high school students in Ontario, Canada — one that attended before service was required for graduation and one afterward — scholars at Wilfrid Laurier University, in Waterloo, Ontario, found that mandating service is beneficial for the community because it "draws students into the volunteer sector who probably would not go there if not required to do so." Furthermore, the study of more than 1,200 students concluded that even those who said their personal experience wasn't very rewarding still ended up holding "mandatory volunteering in high regard" as a way to create more "engaged citizens." [7]

Another study by the Wilfrid Laurier researchers found that, at least in the short term, most "students who were mandated to perform community service exhibit the same attitudes and perspectives about community engagement as those who" didn't face a requirement. "Requiring community service . . . does not detract from" young people's "motivation to volunteer in the future," and the quality of the service experience is likely a much more important determinant of young people's attitudes toward volunteering than is the mandated or non-mandated nature of the experience," the Canadian analysts said. [8]

Are more young people volunteering today?

School and government programs have led to steep increases over the past two decades in the number of young people who volunteer. But there is a significant socioeconomic divide in volunteering, with high rates concentrated among certain groups, such as college-bound high school students. Community-service participation remains low among people in their early 20s. (*See graph, p. 84.*)

The volunteer rate among people ages 16 to 19 soared from 13.4 percent to 24.5 percent between 1989 and 2007, according to the Corporation for National and Community Service. [9]

Getty Images/Scott Olson

Student volunteers clear debris around a tornado-damaged apartment complex in Joplin, Mo., on July 30, 2011. A twister that hit the city on May 22 killed more than 150 people and destroyed some 7,500 homes. Nationwide, volunteer rates among youths ages 16 to 19 soared from 13.4 percent to 24.5 percent between 1989 and 2007, largely because a rising number of high schools sponsor or require service.

Service learning — courses that require students to do a service project and analyze the experience in the light of ideas studied in class — continues to rise around the country. Between 2008 and 2010, for example, the average number of service-learning courses offered per campus rose from 43 to 64 among colleges that responded to a survey by the college service consortium Campus Compact. [10]

Furthermore, more young people heading for college and graduate school are adding volunteer activities to their résumés, says Musick of UT. Many more people attend college today than in past decades, but because selective schools aren't significantly expanding their enrollments applicants must try harder than ever to gain an edge over the competition, he points out. Volunteering is one way to do that, he says.

But Musick cautions that the way colleges count volunteerism in admission decisions can lead to inequities between wealthy and low-income students.

"I look at these kids' résumés and see that some are doing an enormous amount of volunteering," he says. "But colleges have to be very careful" about how they compare students' records in this regard because many impressive-sounding volunteer opportunities are available for students who don't have to help out at home or take paying jobs to cover their school costs, says Musick. "If a kid lists going abroad to build clinics, it's likely that his or her family has paid for this," making it unfair to count it much in the student's favor because it's an opportunity that isn't available to most applicants, he says.

While volunteering rates among older teens have soared over the past two decades, a longer historical look reveals that recent rates, hovering around 24 percent, aren't much higher than they were decades ago. That's because between the mid-1970s and late 1980s teen community-service rates dropped substantially, from 20.9 percent in 1974 to 13.4 percent in 1989. That decline helped spur the recent rise in school community-service programs. [11]

The dropoff raised concerns that schools were not turning out graduates who were likely to be involved in their communities or fulfill civic responsibilities, such as voting, when they became adults. What's more, Lenkowsky of Indiana University says concerns grew that laissez-faire policies promulgated during the administration of President Ronald Reagan (1981-89) "were causing people to grow too self-interested." Those worries fueled establishment of programs to build a new spirit of service among American students, he says.

And while young volunteers showed the greatest percentage gain since 1989, young people still lag behind their parents when it comes to volunteering. The proportion of 16- to 19-year-olds performing service remained lower in 2007 than among the baby-boom generation born between 1946 and 1964, whose volunteer rates grew from 24.1 percent in 1989 to 29.9 percent in 2007. Among those over 65, the volunteering rate rose from 16.9 percent to 23.8 percent from 1989 to 2007. [12]

In 2010, people in their early 20s volunteered at the lowest rate — 18.4 percent — while 35- to 44-year-olds volunteered at the highest rate — 32.2 percent — according to the U.S. Bureau of Labor Statistics. [13] The rate for people ages 16 to 24 hovered around 22 percent between 2006 and 2010, the lowest of any age group and well below the average volunteer rate for all people age 16 and over, which was about 27 percent. [14]

Low volunteering rates among the older part of the 16-24 age group account for the low overall rate in that segment of the population, says Lenkowsky. "We have data showing that over 90 percent of college-bound high school students" perform some kind of service, but the 18- to 24-year-old contingent "has the lowest rates of any age group" for several reasons, Lenkowsky says.

Students in that age group who are enrolled in selective colleges have high service rates, around 50 percent in some cases, he says. But very low rates of volunteering prevail among "many who aren't going to college and thus are less engaged" in the community. Meanwhile, 20-somethings who are just out of college or who didn't attend are busy with the "Sex and the City" scene — socializing and looking for jobs and careers — and thus have very low community-service rates, Lenkowsky says. Beginning around age 25, volunteer rates increase as people settle into jobs, have families and become more settled members of their communities, he says.

Furthermore, the country "is very stratified" when it comes to volunteerism opportunities for young people, says UT's Musick. Volunteering among college students and college-bound high school students is at high levels, but "there's too much tendency to focus on these populations," which inflates the overall picture of whether volunteering is actually becoming more prevalent in our society, Musick says.

Based on his extensive study of factors that lead to volunteering, Musick says, even though rates have risen at selective colleges and among college-bound high-school students, "in the rest of the population, I'll bet it hasn't changed very much." Churches are the main center of American volunteering, "and are they fundamentally changing in ways that would lead to more volunteering? No." ■

BACKGROUND

Volunteers of America

From volunteer firefighting to street-cleaning brigades, grassroots voluntary efforts to serve and improve communities date back to America's earliest history. Starting in the mid-20th century, however, the federal government, schools and colleges began establishing formal volunteerism programs, sometimes integrated into class work, as education theorists found that real-life work enhanced learning. [15]

In 1736, young men in Philadelphia signed up for the first American volunteer firefighting company, founded by Benjamin Franklin. In the early 1800s, a Protestant religious revival in the United States known as the Second Great Awakening spurred many young people to work for the abolition of slavery and for the temperance movement to discourage drunkenness. In the early 19th century, juvenile anti-slavery societies collected signatures of teens and children on petitions they forwarded to Congress, urging lawmakers to abolish slavery.

In New York City in 1915, 25,000 children in neighborhood groups picked up litter, reported overflowing trash cans and urged adults to keep communities tidy. In the 1920s, the National Safety Council — a nonprofit group founded by volunteers in 1915 to tackle safety issues — helped students form school-based committees to study safety hazards and propose solutions. [16]

Beginning in the 1920s, volunteers conceived of and built the Appalachian Trail — the wilderness pathway for hikers that spans the mountain ranges of the East Coast. And in 1954, Philadelphia volunteers opened the first U.S. Meals on Wheels programs — begun in Britain in 1939 — to deliver food to homebound people; the initiative soon spread nationwide, with high school and college students making many of the deliveries.

During emergencies such as wars and natural disasters, many children and teens helped out because adults were busy elsewhere. During the Civil War, child volunteers sewed bandages and bedding for soldiers and collected money to buy them food. During World War II, the city of Chicago established 30,000 small plots in parks where fifth- through eighth-graders cultivated "victory gardens" to boost the nation's food supply. Communities around the country followed suit. [17]

American membership organizations, such as the business-networking group Kiwanis, founded in 1915 in Detroit, routinely included volunteer service as a top activity, "and many had youth auxiliaries," says Catholic University's Youniss.

The Great Depression of the 1930s saw students as well as adults volunteer in soup kitchens and breadlines for the jobless and homeless, says Youniss. "The thought was that if you were well enough off to be in school, then you should help" those in greater need.

The 1930s Civilian Conservation Corps (CCC), established by President Franklin D. Roosevelt, provided work and a small stipend for young men who couldn't find other jobs. The program was the first in a long line of government service projects for young people that have offered stipends. Others include today's AmeriCorps and Teach for America programs. Despite its modest pay, mainly sent home to the young men's families, the CCC was widely viewed as a volunteer program because the work benefited the community rather than private interests.

Beginning in the 1960s, some policymakers' interest grew in government-sponsored volunteerism. Government service programs have had two main goals, says Indiana University's Lenkowsky. "One is to get more people involved in working on society's problems," and the other "to encourage a lifetime of civic engagement."

In 1961 President John F. Kennedy proposed and Congress approved establishment of the Peace Corps. The goal was to place volunteers of all ages — although mainly young adults — in less industrialized countries, to help with community-development projects and

Continued on p. 88

Chronology

1700s-1910s

Americans form volunteer groups to tackle social problems from disease to drunkenness.

1736
Benjamin Franklin enlists young Philadelphia men as the first American volunteer firefighters.

1835
In his classic book *Democracy in America*, French historian Alexis de Tocqueville reports on Americans' many voluntary groups promoting "public safety, commerce, industry, morality and religion."

1916
In *Democracy and Education*, American philosopher John Dewey argues that children's minds are formed only in the context of their experiences in society.

1930s-1970s

Beginning in the Great Depression, the federal government creates community-service programs.

1933
President Franklin D. Roosevelt creates the Civilian Conservation Corps, in which young unemployed men get modest stipends to restore public lands.

1961
President John F. Kennedy establishes the Peace Corps.

1964
President Lyndon B. Johnson establishes domestic volunteer programs, including VISTA, Job Corps, Neighborhood Youth Corps and the Teacher Corps.

1971
White House Conference on Youth calls for schools to link studies to community service.

1979
Volunteer rate among 16- to 19-year-olds is 20.9 percent.

1980s-1990s

As young people's volunteering rates drop, colleges, schools and the federal government seek ways to encourage community service.

1985
The presidents of Brown, Georgetown and Stanford universities promote community service.

1989
Volunteer rate for 16- to 19-year-olds hits a low of 13.4 percent.

1990
National Service Act authorizes funds for independent Points of Lights Foundation, proposed by President George H. W. Bush, to encourage volunteerism.

1992
Democratic presidential candidate Bill Clinton promises to create a young people's service corps and give college aid to anyone serving for at least a year.

1993
Congress enacts AmeriCorps, as proposed by President Clinton. . . . Federal appeals court declares that schools may require community service for graduation (*Steirer v. Bethlehem Area School District*).

1994
Led by House Speaker Newt Gingrich, R-Ga., congressional Republicans begin an unsuccessful multi-year campaign to end AmeriCorps.

1996
Two more federal appeals courts rule that service requirements don't violate students' constitutional rights.

2000s

Volunteer service becomes a standard feature of high school and college life.

2005
After Hurricane Katrina, volunteers clear debris and begin rebuilding New Orleans.

2007
Volunteer rate for 16- to 19-year-olds rises to 24.5 percent.

2009
President Barack Obama signs a law to triple AmeriCorps in eight years.

2010
People ages 20 to 24 continue to have the lowest volunteer rate.

2011
Congressional Republicans vote to phase out AmeriCorps, but Senate Democrats block the move. . . . House Education and the Workforce Committee warns AmeriCorps against politicization after some volunteers are found to have worked in advocacy positions for Planned Parenthood. . . . AmeriCorps volunteers perform energy audits to aid conservation in Iowa and help police in Albany, N.Y., collect information from neighbors about a crime wave.

2012
White House says summer jobs program for disadvantaged youth will include 4,000 AmeriCorps positions.

Volunteer Programs Lacking for Low-Income Kids

"It's not because adolescents aren't interested."

Volunteer opportunities are much scarcer for students from low-income families than for those from wealthy backgrounds — a problem that can have life-long impacts, including low participation in voting and other civic engagement, scholars say.

"There is a huge socioeconomic gap" in service opportunities, as there is for most other educational opportunities, says James Youniss, a research professor of psychology at Catholic University, in Washington.

"If a school has low-income students or many immigrants," for example, "it's less likely to have" programs known to improve students' civic involvement, including service-learning programs that link classroom work with volunteer opportunities, Youniss says. It's well known — and often lamented — that poor people generally vote at lower rates than better-off people, and fewer opportunities to build civic engagement during youth are partly to blame, he says.

Robert Atkins, an associate professor of nursing and childhood studies at Rutgers University, runs STARR, a multi-faceted youth-development program for teens in Camden, N.J., which consistently ranks among the nation's poorest cities. In 2009, for example, 36 percent of residents lived below the poverty level and 18 percent of those had incomes 50 percent or more below the poverty threshold. [1] The gulf between volunteerism opportunities for low-income and middle- and upper-income students mirrors many other socioeconomic gaps in society, such as health-care access, Atkins says.

Volunteerism among low-income young people isn't rare "because adolescents aren't interested," Atkins says. His program, which he launched in 1995, includes various service opportunities that "the kids love," he says.

For example, "we deliver turkey baskets" each Thanksgiving to needy families, Atkins continues. A church donates a room, "and the adolescents put the baskets together," then "we sit in the car while they go to the door and say, 'Happy Thanksgiving.' It's great for them, and they love doing the turkey baskets. They're often the recipients of giving, so the opportunity to give themselves" is rare.

Other activities have included tree planting, voter-registration drives and walkathons for causes such as the immune-system disease lupus. "They don't know in advance that they're going to love doing these things," Atkins says. "But once they do it, they volunteer to do it again. And it's very good for the communities they're part of" because it gives everyone a different view of the teens, he says.

A low ratio of adults to young people in low-income areas is one of the biggest obstacles to improving the rate of youth volunteering in poverty-stricken neighborhoods, Atkins says. "There are just simply fewer adults to pitch in and help" kids get involved, he says.

Continued from p. 86

spread goodwill for the United States; volunteers received modest stipends. [18]

In 1964, as part of his War on Poverty, President Lyndon B. Johnson created VISTA — Volunteers in Service to America — which placed volunteers in community organizations to help educate and train low-income people. VISTA workers got a modest living stipend and either a small cash payment or an education grant after a year's service.

Individual programs came and went, but presidents Richard M. Nixon (Republican, 1969-1974), Jimmy Carter (Democrat, 1977-1981) and George H. W. Bush (Republican, 1989-1993) all supported and worked to maintain at least some federal role in youth volunteerism.

In 1993, Democratic President Bill Clinton created AmeriCorps — which places young people in community-based nonprofit organizations to help with education, health, environmental and other projects — and the Corporation for National and Community Service to manage government volunteerism efforts.

During the Clinton years, however, Republican lawmakers increasingly argued that public-sector activity was damaging in arenas where private-sector initiatives existed.

"The program distorts the true sense of volunteerism and perpetuates the notion that the solution to every problem is just one big-government program away," said Rep. Todd Tiahrt, R-Kan., pitching repeal of AmeriCorps in 1997. [19]

AmeriCorps won more Republican friends in the late 1990s and 2000s, however. Sen. John McCain, R-Ariz., who had voted against establishing the program in 1993, said in January 2000 that "overall, the program has been a success. And it was a failure on my part not to recognize that earlier." [20]

To the surprise of some, when Republican President George W. Bush took office in 2001, he urged every American to devote 4,000 hours over a lifetime to community service and won substantial conservative backing for doubling Peace Corps membership and increasing AmeriCorps membership by 50 percent. At Bush's urging, Congress increased funding for both programs, although Peace Corps funds fell short of Bush's goal. [21]

University Service

Around the turn of the 20th century, some American philosophers

Atkins says low-income urban communities tend to be "child-saturated," with 30 to 40 percent of the population under age 18, making a ratio of only about two adults per child, compared to three in middle-income towns such as nearby Cherry Hill, where Atkins lives.

STARR Program/Bill Cramer

Tree planting draws eager volunteers from the STARR program at Rutgers University's campus in Camden, N.J. STARR President Robert Atkins is at right.

The high ratio of children to adults also "makes the kids seem more like a problem to be dealt with and kept out of trouble," not "a resource that could do some service," he adds. As a result, communities are more likely to organize activities they hope will keep teens off the street, such as "midnight basketball leagues," and less likely to come up with ideas for adolescents to perform community service.

"There's been a national effort to get kids more engaged, but I'm not sure if that can trickle down to Camden," says Atkins. "Instead of helping these kids get involved in actively doing things, people are more likely to talk to them about what not to do, such as avoiding pregnancy."

Adults in low-income neighborhoods generally "are less educated, and they're working a lot. And . . . many don't have any volunteering experience of their own" to draw on, he says.

Urban adults also tend to be younger, and many have young children of their own. Older adults are more likely to have the time and ability to engage in volunteer work and help out youngsters, Atkins says. Younger adults also "have less confidence in their ability to structure these opportunities," and if adults aren't there to provide the foundation, "it's not surprising that it doesn't happen."

Atkins is pushing one potential solution: "micro" projects serving perhaps a dozen kids rather than hundreds.

"You don't need to build a big community center but just get individuals who are interested in something" — participating in the arts or fixing up a local park, for example — and encourage adults "to find a way to share that interest with some kids," he says.

— Marcia Clemmitt

[1] "Camden, New Jersey, Poverty Rate Data — Information About Poor and Low-Income Residents," City-Data website, www.city-data.com/poverty/poverty-Camden-New-Jersey.html.

theorized that real-world experience integrated into schooling would improve learning and society. John Dewey (1859-1952), a professor of psychology and philosophy at the University of Chicago and Columbia University, developed the theory that lies behind many of today's university programs. "All genuine education comes about through experience" that the learner then reflects on, Dewey wrote. [22] When education fosters "membership within . . . a little community, saturating" students "with the spirit of service, . . . we shall have the deepest and best guarantee of a larger society which is worthy, lovely and harmonious." [23]

These ideas percolated in the education community throughout the 20th century. A follow-up report to a 1971 White House Conference on Youth, for example, recommended that schools and colleges utilize the service-learning link to improve education.

But the movement among campuses to foster student service really took off in the 1980s, says Enos, of Bryant University. At the time, social analysts had christened the current generation of students the "Me Generation," focused on furthering careers and making money and unconcerned with being good citizens and neighbors. In response, new organizations emerged to promote service. [24]

Notably, in 1985, the presidents of Stanford, Brown and Georgetown universities joined the president of the Education Commission of the States — an information-exchange forum consisting of the governments of 49 states, three territories and the District of Columbia — to form Campus Compact, a group that would help colleges develop systems to foster student service. As of 2011, more than 1,100 colleges and universities are members. [25]

"The most important thing an institution does is not to prepare a student for a career but for life as a citizen," said Campus Compact co-founder Frank Newman, former president of the University of Rhode Island. [26]

Initially, Campus Compact mainly helped schools establish extracurricular service programs, but around 1990 the group began to focus on integrating volunteer work into academic courses — "service learning," wrote Enos. [27] Also in 1990, President George H. W. Bush signed into law Serve America — now called Learn and Serve America, a federal grant program to establish service learning on campuses.

As usually defined, "service learning" means incorporating service, such as working in a homeless shelter, into a class in a subject such as urban policy. But service done without a class tie-in also may fall under the definition if students are required to analyze the service by, for example, writing about it. Some schools, such as Kentucky's Berea College, have decades-long service-learning traditions, and in the 1990s the idea spread nationwide.

Today, 89 percent of colleges and universities sponsor service learning, says the University of Minnesota's Furco. Key to successful programs is integrating service into academic goals, he says. For example, tutoring might be good service experience in a math class if "one of a professor's learning objectives for students is how to communicate technical information so that it can be understood by lay people."

"The knowledge from the class informs what students do in the community, and what they do in the community makes information come alive in class," providing specific examples "to illuminate general concepts being studied," says Roosevelt University's Meyers.

But creating service-learning experiences that benefit both students and the community is difficult, many analysts say.

Some programs mainly provide good publicity for the school and résumé padding for students without meeting community needs, charged John W. Eby, a professor of sociology at Messiah College in Grantham, Pa. [28] For example, a semester's worth of course-related service may encourage a potentially harmful habit among young volunteers: pursuing service on a given issue only briefly, wrote Eby. Short-term service "has potential to do actual harm to individuals," especially children who become attached to a young volunteer who disappears a few months later, he wrote.

Schools and Service

Beginning in the late 1980s, interest in service learning, along with general volunteerism, increased in high schools and even in some middle and elementary schools. A sharp drop-off in teen volunteering between the early 1970s and the late 1980s sparked the interest.

Habitat for Humanity/Steffan Hacker

Students from the Habitat for Humanity campus chapter at the University of Wisconsin, Madison, spent their week-long spring break building houses in Miami as part of Habitat's Collegiate Challenge program for high school and college volunteers.

In 1979, 92 percent of high schools reported making some extracurricular community-service options available to students, mostly informally, but only 15 percent offered service learning. By 1999, though, 83 percent of high schools offered service opportunities, many actually required it, and 46 percent offered some service learning. [29]

In the 2000s, volunteer programs, including requirements, persist in schools but service learning has been decreasing. In the 2003-04 school year, 44 percent of high schools offered service learning, but by 2008 only 35 percent did. Budget cuts and the need to prepare students for high-stakes standardized tests may explain the decrease. In a 1999 government study, almost all principals whose schools offered service learning said the programs helped the community and promoted altruism, but only 12 percent said they helped with academics and only 19 percent said they taught critical thinking. [30]

California, Vermont and Wisconsin no longer put many resources into what were strong public school service-learning programs several years ago, and Florida's may be the only remaining volunteerism effort that truly weaves service and learning goals together, says the University of Minnesota's Furco.

In the 1990s, students brought three major lawsuits claiming that service requirements are unconstitutional. Federal courts decided all three in the schools' favor.

In a 1993 decision in *Steirer v. Bethlehem Area* [Pennsylvania] *School District*, the Third U.S. Circuit Court of Appeals rejected the argument that a district's 60-hour service requirement amounted to "involuntary servitude," banned under the 13th Amendment outlawing slavery. The amendment bans "forced labor through physical coercion," not service that is "primarily designed for the students' own benefit and education" by teaching them about the value of community work, said the court. [31]

While battles over service requirements grab headlines, researchers say

Service-Learning Programs Aid Students, Nonprofits

Linking schoolwork and volunteerism is biggest challenge.

Service-learning programs, which tie students' volunteer work to their academic studies, are growing in popularity on college campuses, but they can be challenging to set up and administer effectively.

Schools must help both the students and the service organizations where they volunteer to understand what to expect from one another, says Vincent Ilustre, executive director of the Center for Public Service at Tulane University, in New Orleans.

On the volunteer end, "we encourage students to find something they love and stick to it, because we don't want the nonprofits to have to keep training new people," Ilustre says. Then "we need to educate the community about what these students can do," a challenge that generally requires a dedicated campus office, Ilustre and other experts say.

At Tulane, "I look at our community partners not just in terms of placement but as partners in educating our students," Ilustre says. "We run workshops that allow the community to understand the students, the university calendar" and so on.

Tulane has 420 nonprofits in its database, but with 1,200 to 1,500 students participating per semester, about two-thirds of the organizations won't get a placement at any given time, says Ilustre. To keep local organizations involved, the university provides workshops on topics such as nonprofit fundraising and budgeting.

Steven Meyers, a professor of psychology and social justice at Roosevelt University, in Chicago, says service-learning programs are most successful when they are "promoted by a university office that supports them" using "an up-to-date, well-vetted database of suitable programs for professors to use."

"It's unreasonable to expect" individual professors to delve into the community to find service-learning opportunities unaided, Meyers says.

Developing service projects that both serve the community and advance learning goals is a challenge for nonprofits as well as faculty.

Different schools and courses can take different approaches to doing this, says Sandra Enos, an associate professor of sociology at Bryant University, in Smithfield, R.I. Bryant, which began as a business school but recently added liberal-arts majors, generally favors projects in which students make specific, practical use of their class work, Enos says. For example, students might work with a community "client" to make the organization's marketing message more effective. Or students might help a school enhance the math-readiness of its kindergarteners.

For service learning to be effective, students must analyze their experiences and tie them to material they learn in class, says James Youniss, a research professor of psychology at Catholic University, in Washington.

"Discussions are a very effective tool" for fostering such learning, he says. For example, high-school students who volunteer in a daycare center should afterward be encouraged to discuss such issues as whether a pregnant 16-year-old should get a job, be allowed to go on welfare or be given an incentive to finish her education, he says.

Course-based service learning can work across the curriculum, says Meyers. For example, he describes an English composition course in which students worked with an anti-domestic-violence group, interviewed workers and then developed an effective way to write and post a blog to help inform people how to cope with domestic violence.

— Marcia Clemmitt

the more important question is whether programs are well managed.

For example, "the state of Maryland has this crazy 74-hour requirement" of service for graduation, "but they don't want to put resources into it," so that the quality of individual programs is all over the map, says Catholic University's Youniss. Furthermore, it's not even clear that such large programs are feasible, Youniss says. If every Maryland senior were to participate even in the most well-structured service programs, "organizations in the state couldn't absorb them all," he says.

AmeriCorps Questioned

Soon after Barack Obama took office in 2009, conservative opposition to AmeriCorps began building again.

Midway through 2009, his first year in office, Obama raised congressional eyebrows when he abruptly fired AmeriCorps' Inspector General Gerald Walpin. Inspectors general are government officials appointed to be independent watchdogs over federal programs. The administration said that the then-77-year-old Walpin had been "confused, disoriented" and "unable to answer questions" at a Corporation for National and Community Service board meeting, raising doubts about "his capacity to serve." [32]

Walpin argued that he was fired because he'd stated that an Obama supporter, Kevin Johnson, now mayor of Sacramento, Calif., had misused AmeriCorps grants at his nonprofit community-development agency, St. HOPE. [33]

"While firing an investigator who uncovered the abuse of funds by a political ally might be considered an act of 'political courage' in Chicago politics, for most Americans it raises troubling questions," said Rep. Darrell Issa, R-Calif., chairman of the House

Committee on Oversight and Government Reform. [34] (In November 2009, however, a Republican inquiry failed to find evidence that Walpin's dismissal was politically motivated. [35] In January 2011, a federal appeals court ruled against Walpin in a lawsuit he filed claiming wrongful firing.) [36]

Also in 2009, Obama signed a bill passed by the Democratic-led Congress to triple AmeriCorps' size in eight years. [37]

But AmeriCorps remains controversial, especially among staunch conservatives. As AmeriCorps expands, "there is a very strong chance that we will see that young people will be put into mandatory service," said Rep. Michele Bachmann, R-Minn., who campaigned unsuccessfully for the Republican presidential nomination. "There are provisions for what I would call re-education camps . . . where young people have to go and get trained in a philosophy that the government puts forward," she said. [38] ■

CURRENT SITUATION

Federal Phaseout?

The Republican-led House of Representatives is pushing to phase out AmeriCorps, arguing that the program wastes public money to accomplish community service that the private sector would effectively and willingly handle on its own.

In 2011 the House Appropriations Committee proposed cutting funding by about 70 percent, leaving money to support the National Senior Volunteer Program but gradually eliminating young-adult programs. Appropriators in the Democratic-led Senate, however, forced a compromise that resulted in only a minimal funding cut — about 2 percent — for the Corporation for National and Community Service. [39]

Allegations continue to surface of left-wing politicization of AmeriCorps and were the subject of a June 2011 hearing in the House. Lawmakers queried Robert Velasco, the corporation's acting CEO, about two incidents, in New York City and Tacoma, Wash., in which AmeriCorps apparently violated laws against the use of federal funds to place volunteers in positions related to "advocacy, lobbying, protesting, union organizing" or "partisan political activity." In both incidents, volunteers' work was related to the advocacy functions of Planned Parenthood, the reproductive-health provider and advocacy organization. [40]

City Year/Seattle/King County

City Year volunteer Daniel Curme clears brush on a trail in Seattle on Oct. 7, 2011. The education-focused organization partners with public schools to provide full-time intervention for at-risk students.

How the placements "could possibly abide by the spirit of volunteerism is beyond me," said Rep. Virginia Foxx, R-N.C., chairman of the Education and the Workforce Subcommittee on Higher Education. "I appreciate that once notified of these situations, the corporation acted swiftly to stop the prohibited activities," said Foxx. "However, our goal should be to prevent these kinds of activities before they take place." [41]

Both the corporation and AmeriCorps actively monitor local organizations that host volunteers for compliance with laws, but the large number of volunteers and organizations makes it difficult to spot all problems before they start, Velasco said. [42] From now on, he said, the corporation would require organizations that host volunteers to reaffirm each year that they're following regulations. [43]

Changing Landscape

The nature of volunteerism may be changing.

The worker pool has declined for some services traditionally provided by volunteers. Volunteer fire and emergency personnel, long a rural mainstay, have become harder and harder to find, for example.

Continued on p. 94

At Issue:

Should AmeriCorps be eliminated?

DOUG BANDOW
SENIOR FELLOW, CATO INSTITUTE

WRITTEN FOR *CQ RESEARCHER*, JANUARY 2012

yes

Americans always have organized to help their neighbors. The government should stop paying for service through AmeriCorps. The budget crisis is reason enough to terminate AmeriCorps — and even the Corporation for National and Community Service, which oversees AmeriCorps.

Washington has funded many service, training and "volunteer" initiatives, which usually achieve some good but also plenty of bad. Journalist Jim Bovard has documented political abuse, waste and low priority work at AmeriCorps. Inexplicably, the Obama administration fired the corporation's inspector general while Congress cut funding for his office.

Waste and inefficiency are inevitable because free labor will be treated like a free good. But even seemingly productive jobs won't necessarily produce significant social benefits.

The critical question is not the cost-benefit ratio but the opportunity cost of AmeriCorps funding. Could the resources be better spent elsewhere? There is no reason to believe that a dollar for "national service" yields more good than an additional dollar spent on medical research or business investment.

Indeed, service comes in many forms. Being paid by Uncle Sam to shelve books in a library or teach in a public school is no more laudable than being paid by the local used book store or private school. Moreover, who should do the giving? It might be simpler if Washington empties pockets nationwide, giving either grants or labor to charity. But the right way is for individuals to directly aid deserving groups.

Nor is dependence on government healthy for private charities. Although charities get to train publicly funded volunteers, government inevitably will favor some activities. Such preferences subtly pressure organizations to adjust their mission to ensure eligibility for funding. An early review by Public/Private Ventures, a nonprofit that seeks to improve the effectiveness of anti-poverty programs, noted that the corporation aggressively shaped service programs. An assessment in the *Journal of Public Administration Research and Theory* found that those involved sought to "influence the type of implementation process that fits their own political interests."

Moreover, AmeriCorps is likely to encourage people to further abdicate their civic responsibilities. Federally funded service makes it less necessary for people to contribute and volunteer. People won't do more if they perceive no need to do so, and they will see less need if Washington provides charities with "volunteers."

Never content to wait for government to act, Americans always have worked with families, friends and neighbors to help those around them. Uncle Sam should stop paying them to help today.

SHIRLEY SAGAWA
VISITING FELLOW, CENTER FOR AMERICAN PROGRESS; FOUNDING MANAGING DIRECTOR, CORPORATION FOR NATIONAL AND COMMUNITY SERVICE

WRITTEN FOR *CQ RESEARCHER*, JANUARY 2012

no

The vast majority of volunteers act without support from government, and that's the way it should be. Every year, 63 million Americans strengthen their communities by leading scout troops or coaching soccer, raising money for band uniforms or leading museum tours. These are good things, and government doesn't need to interfere.

On the other hand, many functions widely understood to be public priorities are in desperate need of an affordable source of dedicated human capital. For example, providing a quality education is labor intensive, particularly in high-poverty schools where many children need extra supports. National service can be a key part of a strategy to turn around failing schools. That's why the widely acclaimed Diplomas Now initiative deploys City Year corps members to take action when middle school students exhibit early warning signs of dropping out.

In other cases, national service members play a critical role organizing community volunteers. For example, in Madison, Wis., the Schools of Hope initiative has wiped out racial disparities in reading with community and college volunteer tutors recruited and supervised by national service members. This kind of low-cost intervention saves significant public funding down the road.

AmeriCorps funding is key to both City Year and Schools of Hope. AmeriCorps members serve full time (or make a substantial part-time commitment) and receive a modest stipend and education award in return. In addition to serving in schools, AmeriCorps members address a wide range of locally determined needs, including community health centers, early-childhood programs and college access initiatives. In fact, AmeriCorps figures prominently in a Joplin, Mo., monument to the volunteers who helped its post-tornado recovery.

Not only is AmeriCorps a low-cost way to direct human resources to public problems but it also creates badly needed entry jobs for priority populations. Most AmeriCorps positions are filled by young adults — a group facing the highest rates of unemployment. Older adults who have more to give after retirement also serve — and by so doing, stay healthy and independent. A new priority for AmeriCorps is to engage veterans, a population suffering from high rates of unemployment and a strong desire to serve their communities.

At a time when nonprofit organizations are stretched thin with the weak economy, too many schools are struggling and millions of Americans are out of work and ready to serve, we should be expanding AmeriCorps, not eliminating it.

Continued from p. 92

Thomas F. O'Hara, coordinator of the Firemen's Association of the State of New York volunteer programs, noted last summer that the number of volunteer firefighters in New York "has declined over the past two decades — from nearly 100,000 in the 1990s to a little over 88,000 today," even as the population needing service has increased. [44]

Largely thanks to school and university programs, young people volunteer more today than in the past. Studies also report, however, that young people tend to perform their service with less regularity than adult volunteers and don't volunteer for the same causes for years, as adults often do, so organizations and causes may benefit less, long term, from youth service. [45]

"Religion is the best predictor we have of both giving and volunteering, including for non-religious causes," and religious affiliation is in a long decline, says Lenkowsky of Indiana University. Alongside the long, slow drop in religious affiliation, "we see giving and volunteering declining too." [46]

Participation is sharply up for some community-service programs. Applications for AmeriCorps rose from 360,000 for 80,000 available slots in 2008-2009 to 536,000 applications for 2009-2010. Teach for America, which places graduates of selective colleges in high-need schools for two-year teaching stints, received 25,000 applications in 2008 and 48,000 in 2011. [47]

The recession and resulting bad job market cloud the meaning of these statistics, however. The federal programs offer modest payment, a possible draw in a tough job market. In addition, volunteer service offers a chance to network and learn new skills, and "people might recognize this more in the recession . . . because they don't have a job and they are looking for ways to build their résumés," said Peter Levine, director of CIRCLE — The Center for Information on Research Learning and Engagement, a research group based at Tufts University, in Medford, Mass. [48]

But Teach for America Executive Vice President Elissa Kim is skeptical of that analysis. "I don't think people are just jumping on the bandwagon . . . because the economy is shaky." Teach for America applicants make the choice based on whether "this is the right thing for them," she says. [49] ■

OUTLOOK

Good Citizenship

Schools and colleges have built volunteer programs partly in hopes of creating a more involved citizenry. Research suggests that participating in thoughtfully structured service makes people more likely to participate in activities such as voting, which is traditionally seen as the key responsibility of citizenship.

Recently, however, some scholars have spotted an unforeseen trend that may change that equation. Young people, especially, say some researchers, have begun to view volunteer service itself as a far more important part of being a good citizen than political activities such as staying informed on public issues and voting.

"In the 1960s and '70s, young people's involvement [in society] tended to be political," as when they fueled the civil-rights and anti-war movements, says Catholic University's Youniss, "but now when kids think of doing service to society, they think of doing good deeds" — acts of charity, essentially — "not any kind of political acts."

Over the past three decades, numerous political analysts have raised alarms about Americans becoming too disconnected from society. They have pointed to evidence such as low voting rates, especially among younger people, and surveys showing that many people have lost faith in government's ability to tackle important problems, wrote Russell J. Dalton, a political science professor at the University of California, Irvine. But alongside the drop in some traditional measures of active citizenship has come a rise in young people's affinity for volunteer service as a primary form of social engagement, wrote Dalton, one of the main researchers following that trend. [50]

Despite the alarms of some, the new view of citizenship is not necessarily something to fear, since it replaces interest in politics with more concern about "the welfare of others," Dalton said. He describes a conversation he had with a college student who helped out in New Orleans in 2005, after Hurricane Katrina. While the young man "was active on a variety of social and political causes," including poverty in Africa and the Iraq War, he had "a stark lack of interest" in political parties and voting. That's typical of the "many Americans" who now "believe they are fully engaged in society even if they do not vote." Dalton said. Still, he argues, the rise in volunteerism can be used to turn young people on to voting as well. [51]

It's unclear whether the new trend relates to schools' emphasis on volunteer work or exactly how it will affect political and social life. However, the trend does mean that traditional groups such as political parties will have to retool their messages to appeal to young nonvoters who are nevertheless interested in public service, Dalton wrote. For example, a political campaign could explain "how elections can have an even greater impact on the issues for which youth now volunteer" than volunteering itself can have, he said.

Many experts on volunteerism would like to see it continue to rise among young people but wonder how to accomplish that. "We don't call on young people enough," says Indiana University's Lenkowsky. Rebranding might help, according to some social-marketing experts, he says. "The word 'volunteer' sounds like something your grandmother would do. You need to make it cool" to continue to entice a new generation. [52] ■

Notes

[1] "Reaching Our Goals: An Overview of Research in Support of the Strategic Initiatives," Corporation for National and Community Service, March 2009, p. 3, www.nationalservice.gov/pdf/08_1113_rpd_reachingourgoals.pdf.

[2] Quoted in Heather Harris, "Community Service Requirement Mulled for MHS," *Wicked Local Mansfield*, Nov. 16, 2011, www.wickedlocal.com/mansfield/features/x1821246343/Community-service-requirement-mulled-for-MHS#axzz1g3WqP0n8. Jeff Sullivan, "Mansfield School Committee Discusses Mandated Community Service," *Mansfield* [Mass.] *Patch*, Nov. 18, 2011, http://mansfield-ma.patch.com/articles/mansfield-school-committee-mulls-madated-community-service.

[3] For background, see Jeffrey A. McLellan and James Youniss, "Two Systems of Youth Service: Determinants of Voluntary and Required Youth Community Service," *Journals of Youth and Adolescence*, February 2003, pp. 47-58.

[4] Quoted in Susan R. Jones, Thomas C. Segar and Anna L. Gasiorski, " 'A Double-Edged Sword'; College Student Perceptions of Required High School Service-Learning," *Michigan Journal of Community Service Learning*, Fall 2008, pp. 5-17, http://quod.lib.umich.edu/cgi/t/text/text-idx?c=mjcsl;view=toc;idno=3239521.0015.101.

[5] Quoted in Michael Winerip, "Required Volunteerism: School Programs Tested," *The New York Times*, Sept. 23, 1993, www.nytimes.com/1993/09/23/us/required-volunteerism-school-programs-tested.html?pagewanted=all&src=pm.

[6] Arthur A. Stukas, Mark Snyder and E. Gil Clary, "The Effects of 'Mandatory Volunteerism' on Intentions to Volunteer," *Psychological Science*, Jan. 1, 1999, p. 59.

[7] Marlene Ritchie, "Volunteering Trends Including Required Volunteer Experience for Ontario High School Students," Child Research Net website, www.childresearch.net/RESOURCE/RESEARCH/2010/RITCHIE2.HTM; Steven Brown, S. Mark Pancer, Alisa Henderson and Kimberly Ellis-Hale, "The Impact of High School Mandatory Community Service Programs on Subsequent Volunteering and Community Engagement," Draft Research Report to the Knowledge Development Centre, Imagine Canada, January 2007, www.lispop.ca/PDF%20working%20paper/WPS6.pdf.

[8] Alisa Henderson, Steven Brown, S. Mark Pancer and Kimberly Ellis-Hale, "Mandated Community Service in High School and Subsequent Civic Engagement: The Case of the 'Double Cohort' in Ontario, Canada," Working Paper, Laurier Institute for the Study of Public Opinion and Public Policy, www.lispop.ca/PDF%20working%20paper/WPS3.pdf.

[9] Reaching Our Goals: An Overview of Research in Support of the Strategic Initiatives, Corporation for National and Community Service, March 2009, p. 3, www.nationalservice.gov/pdf/08_1113_rpd_reachingourgoals.pdf.

[10] "Annual Membership Survey Results: Executive Summary 2010," Campus Compact, 2011, p. 3, www.compact.org/wp-content/uploads/2008/11/2010_Annual-Survey_Exec_Summary-4-8.pdf.

[11] "Volunteer Growth in America: A Review of Trends Since 1974," Corporation for National and Community Service, December 2006, p. 2, www.ideaencore.com/item/volunteer-growth-america-review-trends-1974-1.

[12] "Reaching Our Goals," *op. cit.*, p. 3.

[13] "Volunteering in the United States — 2010," news release, U.S. Bureau of Labor Statistics, Jan. 26, 2011, www.bls.gov/news.release/volun.nr0.htm.

[14] *Ibid.*

[15] For background, see Susan J. Ellis and Katherine H. Campbell, *By the People: A History of Americans as Volunteers* (2006).

[16] Susan J. Ellis, "The Legacy of Volunteering by Children," *e-Volunteerism*, January 2008, www.e-volunteerism.com/quarterly/08jan/08jan-voices.

[17] *Ibid.*

[18] For background, see John Greenya, "National Service," *CQ Researcher*, June 30, 2006, pp. 577-600; H. B. Shaffer, "Voluntary Action: People and Programs," *Editorial Research Reports*, 1969, Vol. 1; H.B. Shaffer, "Domestic Peace Corps," *Editorial Research Reports*, 1963, Vol. 1; "National Service Timeline," AmeriCorps website, www.nationalservice.gov/about/role_impact/history_timeline.asp; Harris Wofford, "The Politics of Service: How a Nation Got Behind AmeriCorps," Brookings Institution, Fall 2002, www.brookings.edu/articles/2002/fall_civilsociety_wofford.aspx.

[19] "H.R. 993, 'The AmeriCorps Program Elimination Act: What It Does," National Center for Public Policy Research, www.nationalcenter.org/AmeriCorps597.html.

[20] Quoted in "AmeriCorps Is Changing the Minds of Congressional Republicans," press release, Clinton White House, Jan. 15, 2001, http://clinton5.nara.gov/library/hot_releases/January_15_2001_7.html.

[21] Wofford, *op. cit.*

[22] Quoted in Dwight E. Giles, Jr., and Janet Eyler, "The Theoretical Roots of Service Learning in John Dewey: Toward a Theory of Service Learning," *Michigan Journal of Community Service-Learning*, 1994, p. 79, http://quod.lib.umich.edu/m/mjcsl/3239521.0001.109/1?page=root;rgn=full+text;size=100;view=image.

[23] Quoted in *ibid.*, p. 82.

[24] For background, see Sandra Enos, "Service-Learning on American Campuses: Challenges for Pedagogy and Practice," *Issues in Teaching and Learning*, 2003, www.ric.edu/itl/volume_02_enos.php.

[25] "Who We Are," Campus Compact website, www.compact.org/about/history-mission-vision.

[26] "Quotes to Use," Campus Compact website, www.compact.org/resources-for-presidents/quotes-to-use.

[27] Enos, *op. cit.*

[28] John W. Eby, *Why Service-Learning Is Bad*, March 1998, www.messiah.edu/external_programs/agape/servicelearning/articles/wrongsvc.pdf.

[29] "Community Service and Service-Learning in America's Schools," Corporation for National and Community Service, November 2008,

About the Author

Staff writer **Marcia Clemmitt** is a veteran social-policy reporter who previously served as editor in chief of *Medicine & Health* and staff writer for *The Scientist*. She has also been a high school math and physics teacher. She holds a liberal arts and sciences degree from St. John's College, Annapolis, and a master's degree in English from Georgetown University. Her recent reports include "Reading Crisis?" and "Computer Hacking."

www.nationalservice.gov/pdf/08_1112_lsa_prevalence.pdf.
[30] *Ibid.*
[31] For background, see *Steirer v. Bethlehem Area School District*, 987 F. 989 (3rd Cir. 1993), http://openjurist.org/987/f2d/989/steirer-steirer-v-bethlehem-area-school-district; *Immediato v. Rye Neck School District*, 873 F. Supp. 846 (2nd. Cir. 1996), Jan. 2, 1996, http://caselaw.lp.findlaw.com/scripts/getcase.pl?navby=search&case=/data2/circs/2nd/957237.html; *Herndon v. Chapel Hill School District*, 89 F.3d 174 (4th Cir. 1996), http://caselaw.findlaw.
[32] Quoted in Josh Gerstein, "W.H.: Fired IG 'Confused, Disoriented,' " *Politico*, June 16, 2009, www.politico.com/news/stories/0609/23831.html.
[33] *Ibid.*; for background, see "Kevin Johnson (Politician)," Times Topics, *The New York Times*, April 10, 2009, http://topics.nytimes.com/topics/reference/timestopics/people/j/kevin_johnson/index.html.
[34] Quoted in "Republicans not Satisfied With White House Explanation for Walpin Firing," Fox News.com, June 18, 2009,www.foxnews.com/politics/2009/06/18/republicans-satisfied-white-house-explanation-walpin-firing.
[35] Justin Elliott, "GOP Inquiry Fails to Show Obama's Firing of AmeriCorps IG Was Politicized," *Talking Points Memo*, Nov. 20, 2009, http://tpmmuckraker.talkingpointsmemo.com/2009/11/issa_grassley_inquiry_hits_white_house_on_walpin.php.
[36] "Ex-AmeriCorps IG Loses Appeal in Wrongful Firing Suit," *Talking Points Memo*, Jan. 5, 2011, http://tpmmuckraker.talkingpointsmemo.com/gerald_walpin.
[37] For background, see Justin Ewers, "Congress Sends Obama a Bill to Boost Community Service," *U.S. News & World Report*, April 8, 2009, www.usnews.com/news/obama/articles/2009/04/08/congress-sends-obama-a-bill-to-boost-community-service, and "Money for College for Volunteers Under New Obama Service Bill," *Edu in Review*, April 21, 2009, www.eduinreview.com/blog/2009/04/obama-to-triple-size-of-americorps-by-signing-national-service-bill/.
[38] Quoted in Chris Steller, "Bachmann Fears 'Politically Correct Re-education Camps for Young People,' " *The Minnesota Independent*, April 6, 2009, http://minnesotaindependent.com/31237/bachmann-reedcuation-camps.
[39] For background, see "Legislative Update," Save Service in America website, www.saveservice.org/pages/legislative-update, and FY 2012 Appropriations Update: "House Appropriations Committee Releases Draft Labor, Health and Human Services, Education, and Related Agencies Bill," Lewis-Burke Associates LLC, Sept. 29, 2011, http://research.brown.edu/ovpr/HouseAppropriationsBill_092911.pdf; *Policy News*, Afterschool Alliance, Jan. 11, 2012, www.afterschoolalliance.org/PolicyFedNewsArchive.cfm.
[40] For background, see "Demanding Accountability in National Service Programs," hearing transcript and report, House Committee on Education and the Workforce, 2011, http://frwebgate.access.gpo.gov/cgi-bin/getdoc.cgi?dbname=112_house_hearings&docid=f:66967.pdf.
[41] Quoted in *ibid.*, p. 2.
[42] *Ibid.*, p. 15.
[43] *Ibid.*
[44] Jaegun Lee, "Ohio Fire Chief Addresses Shortage of Volunteers," *Watertown Daily Times* [NY], Aug. 19, 2011, www.watertowndailytimes.com/article/20110819/NEWS03/708199918.
[45] Mark Hugo Lopez and Karlo Barrios Marcelo, "Volunteering Among Young People," The Center for Information & Research on Civic Learning and Engagement, April 2007, p. 2, www.civicyouth.org/PopUps/FactSheets/FS07_Volunteering.pdf.
[46] For background, see Marcia Clemmitt, "Protestants Today," *CQ Researcher*, Dec. 7, 2007, pp. 1009-1032.
[47] Natalie DiBlasio, "College Students and Graduates Volunteering for Longer Terms," *USA Today*, Nov. 28, 2011, www.usatoday.com/news/nation/story/2011-11-23/sharing-college-students-volunteering/51447910/1.
[48] Quoted in *ibid.*
[49] Quoted in *ibid.*
[50] Russell J. Dalton, *The Good Citizen: How a Younger Generation Is Reshaping American Politics* (2008), p. 2-3.
[51] *Ibid.*, p. 1.
[52] *Ibid.*, p. 173.

FOR MORE INFORMATION

AmeriCorps, 1201 New York Ave., N.W., Washington, DC 20525; 202-606-5000; www.americorps.gov. Federal program that places volunteers in community-service organizations around the country.

Bureau of Labor Statistics, Volunteering in the United States, www.bls.gov/news.release/volun.toc.htm. Federal agency that tracks volunteering rates.

Campus Compact, 45 Temple Place, Boston, MA 02111; 617-357-1881; www.compact.org. National coalition of 1,100 colleges that promote community service by students.

CIRCLE (The Center for Information and Research on Civic Learning and Engagement), Jonathan M. Tisch College of Citizenship and Public Service, Lincoln Filene Hall, Tufts University, Medford, MA 02155; 617-627-4710; www.civicyouth.org. Conducts research on civic education in schools, colleges and community settings and on young Americans' voting habits and political and civic involvement.

Corporation for National and Community Service, 1201 New York Ave., N.W., Washington, DC 20525; 202-606-5000; www.nationalservice.gov. Agency that manages all federal domestic community-service programs, including AmeriCorps and the service-learning program Learn and Service America.

International Association for Research on Service-Learning and Community Engagement, Tulane University Center for Public Service, Alcee Fortier Hall, 6823 St. Charles Ave., New Orleans, LA 70118; 504-862-3366. Nonprofit association of service-learning and community-engagement researchers.

National Service Learning Clearinghouse, 866-245-7378; www.servicelearning.org. Website operated by a federal contractor that provides information for schools, colleges and others running service-learning programs.

Voluntourism.org, www.voluntourism.org/index.html. Private group that provides information on how the tourism industry and nonprofit service organizations can coordinate volunteer activity.

Bibliography

Selected Sources

Books

Butin, Dan W., *Service Learning in Theory and Practice: The Future of Community Engagement in Higher Education*, Palgrave Macmillan, 2010.
An associate professor of education at Merrimack College, in North Andover, Mass., argues for focusing more on service learning's intellectual content and embedding it more formally into school curricula.

Ellis, Susan J., and Katherine H. Campbell, *By the People: A History of Americans as Volunteers*, Energize Inc., 2006.
Ellis, the editor of a journal on volunteerism, and Campbell, a consultant, chronicle the service projects and organizations that American volunteers have participated in throughout the nation's history.

Youniss, James, and Miranda Yates, *Community Service and Social Responsibility in Youth*, University of Chicago Press, 1997.
A psychology professor at the Catholic University of America (Youniss) and a psychology and public-health researcher describe how a social-justice class that included work in a soup kitchen led urban high school students to examine their political and moral convictions and develop a sense of themselves as participants in the community.

Articles

Giegerich, Elizabeth, "A Look at Tulane's Service-Learning Post-Katrina," *The Nation*, Aug. 25, 2008, www.thenation.com/article/look-tulane-universitys-service-learning-post-katrina.
The process was difficult, but after a 2005 hurricane devastated its home city of New Orleans, Tulane University transformed its curriculum to include a strong emphasis on social service for all students.

Tugend, Alina, "The Benefits of Volunteerism, if the Service Is Real," *The New York Times*, July 30, 2010, www.nytimes.com/2010/07/31/your-money/31shortcuts.html?pagewanted=all.
Researchers find that high school students who perform community service and have a chance to analyze and discuss their experiences are more likely to remain civically involved and think in terms of larger-scale solutions to social problems.

Reports and Studies

***Community Service and Service-Learning in America's Schools*, Corporation for National and Community Service, November 2008, www.aces4kids.org/public/uploads/research-news/service_learning_corporation_for_national_and_community_service_.pdf.**
Elementary, middle and high schools continue to offer students volunteer opportunities. But interest by school leaders in establishing service-learning programs dropped off during the 2000s, and schools in low-income communities are especially unlikely to offer service learning.

***Serving Communities: How Four Organizations Are Using National Service to Solve Community Problems*, Abt Associates/Corporation for National and Community Service, December 2011, www.nationalservice.gov/pdf/servingcommunities_11_30.pdf.**
Based on interviews at service organizations that employ federally sponsored youth and senior volunteers from the AmeriCorps and Senior Corps programs, the report explains how four such groups manage their volunteers and the benefits and challenges they see in the programs.

Enos, Sandra, "Service-learning on American Campuses: Challenges for Pedagogy and Practice," *Issues in Teaching and Learning*, Rhode Island College, 2003, www.ric.edu/itl/volume_02_enos.php.
An associate professor of sociology at Bryant University, in Smithfield, R.I., explains what's led to a recent increase in service learning.

Hart, Daniel, Thomas M. Donnelly, James Youniss and Robert Atkins, "High School Community Service as a Predictor of Adult Voting and Volunteering," *American Educational Research Journal*, March 2007, pp. 197-219, http://aer.sagepub.com/content/44/1/197.full.
Researchers find that high school students who perform community service during high school, whether the service is freely chosen or mandatory, are more likely to vote and do volunteer work as young adults.

Jones, Susan R., Thomas C. Segar and Anna L. Gasiorski, " 'A Double-Edged Sword': College Student Perceptions of Required High School Service-Learning," *Michigan Journal of Community Service Learning*, Fall 2008, pp. 5-17, http://quod.lib.umich.edu/cgi/p/pod/dod-idx?c=mjcsl;idno=3239521.0015.101.
Researchers from the University of Maryland find that many Maryland high school students consider their state's community-service requirement burdensome but often develop a more positive opinion of the experience once they enter college.

From CQ Researcher *Archives:*

Thomas, W.V., "Volunteerism in the Eighties," *Editorial Research Reports*, 1980, Vol. II.

Clark, Charles S., "The New Volunteerism," *CQ Researcher*, Dec. 13, 1996, pp. 1081-1104.

The Next Step:

Additional Articles from Current Periodicals

Civic Engagement

Lipman, Harvy, "Surge in Volunteerism Has Not Lasted," *The Record* (Bergen County, N.J.), Sept. 2, 2011, p. A1.

Rates of volunteerism and the sense of civic responsibility have waned since the Sept. 11 attacks, according to the Center for Information and Research on Civic Learning and Engagement at Tufts University.

Metcalf, Todd, "Civic Engagement Makes a Difference," *Eureka* (Calif.) *Times Standard*, Aug. 16, 2011, www.times-standard.com/lifestyle/ci_18690489?source=rss.

Civic engagement taps into a wellspring of generosity and empathy that can be both energizing and gratifying, says the director of a California senior center.

O'Connor, Sandra Day, and Bob Graham, "Jobs and U.S. Civics Go Hand in Hand," *USA Today*, Nov. 2, 2011, p. A9, www.usatoday.com/news/opinion/forum/story/2011-11-01/economy-civics-participation-voting/51031150/1.

Unemployment has risen less in cities and states where more people volunteer and work with neighbors to address community challenges, according to a retired Supreme Court justice (O'Connor) and a former Florida governor.

Shenkman, Rick, and Alexander Heffner, "Fighting Civics Ignorance," *St. Petersburg* (Fla.) *Times* (now *Tampa Bay Times*), March 22, 2011, p. A11, www.tampabay.com/opinion/columns/fight-civics-ignorance/1158754.

A Presidential Civics Commission would bolster civic engagement and galvanize leaders already engaged in grassroots volunteer efforts, according to a George Mason University professor and a Harvard student.

College Applications

Albers, Katherine, "Do Teens Volunteer for Altruism or College?" *Naples* (Fla.) *Daily News*, June 3, 2011, p. A3, m.naplesnews.com/news/2011/jun/02/altruism-or-college-requirement-more-local-teens-f/.

College admissions counselors say volunteering allows students to become aware of the world around them instead of remaining internally focused.

Garn, Gregg, "Summer Offers Options for Students," *The Oklahoman*, June 12, 2011, p. C2, newsok.com/students-can-make-summer-count-...-twice/article/3576471.

Summer vacations offer high school students the opportunity to volunteer and enhance their college applications.

Kahane, Audrey, "Setting Yourself Apart Is Key," *The Record* (Bergen County, N.J.), May 28, 2011, p. L2, www.northjersey.com/news/122763338_Setting_yourself_apart_is_key.html.

Community service is a good way for high school students to set themselves apart on college applications, says an independent college counselor.

Netburn, Deborah, "Teens Opt for Good Deeds in Town," *Los Angeles Times*, July 30, 2011, p. E2, articles.latimes.com/2011/jul/30/home/la-hm-volunteer-vacations-20110730.

Increased competition for college admissions has spawned an international travel industry focused on placing students in volunteer positions overseas.

Rosenhall, Laurel, "UC Berkeley's 'Holistic' Application Review Sets the Standard for System," *Sacramento* (Calif.) *Bee*, March 24, 2011, p. A1, www.sacbee.com/2011/03/24/3499621/uc-berkeleys-holistic-application.html.

Admissions officers at the University of California at Berkeley look for a dedication to community service among applicants in addition to good grades and high test scores.

Seidman, Carrie, "Teenager Starts Website to Help Others Volunteer," *Sarasota* (Fla.) *Herald Tribune*, Aug. 5, 2011, p. BS1, www.heraldtribune.com/article/20110804/ARTICLE/110809803.

A Florida high school senior has started a website to help fellow students find volunteer opportunities that will enhance their college applications.

Requirements

Gehlke, Roni, "Community Service Program Could Be on Chopping Block," *Contra Costa* (Calif.) *Times*, April 13, 2011.

A California school district may have to cut its community service program for students due to potential funding shortfalls.

Javier, Jeffrey, "Peoria District's Students Could Earn Activity Points," *Arizona Republic*, June 8, 2011, p. 12, www.azcentral.com/news/articles/2011/06/08/20110608peoria-unified-school-district-may-consider-out-of-classroom-programs.html.

An Arizona school district may require its students to get involved in experiences — such as volunteering — that will help them succeed in college and the workplace.

LeFevre, Rachael, "Should High School Students Be Forced to Volunteer?" *Kalamazoo* (Mich.) *Gazette*, Aug. 13, 2011, p. A9, www.mlive.com/opinion/kalamazoo/index.ssf/2011/08/should_high_school_students_be.html.

High schools should require students to volunteer because the experience helps them to expand their knowledge of the world, according to a Michigan high school senior.

Mills, Sarah, "College Educations Include Learning While Lending a Hand," *San Antonio Express-News*, May 29, 2011, p. B3, www.mysanantonio.com/news/education/article/College-educations-includelearning-while-lending-1400586.php.

Many colleges are requiring students to engage in community service because they consider it a form of learning through experience.

Moore, Jean Cowden, "Las Virgenes Schools Want to Give Back," *Ventura County* (Calif.) *Star*, June 19, 2011, www.vcstar.com/news/2011/jun/18/making-volunteering-a-requirement-to-graduate/.

A California school district is considering mandating community service for its high school students despite concerns over costs, liability and logistics.

Pina, Kimberly, "Students Gain Skills, Knowledge at Hospital," *Houston Chronicle*, Sept. 15, 2011, p. 6, www.chron.com/neighborhood/katy-news/article/Students-gain-skills-knowledge-at-hospital-2168846.php.

Volunteers at a Houston-area hospital are permitted to count their volunteer hours toward fulfilling their high school graduation requirements.

Plummer, Sara, "Scholarship Meets Service," *Tulsa* (Okla.) *World*, April 28, 2011, p. A13, www.tulsaworld.com/news/article.aspx?subjectid=11&articleid=20110428_11_A13_CUTLIN302962&rss_lnk=11.

Students partaking in a financial-aid program at Tulsa Community College in Oklahoma are required to volunteer 40 hours per year to remain eligible for assistance.

Trends

DiBlasio, Natalie, "Longer-Term Volunteering Is the Drill for Collegians," *USA Today*, Nov. 29, 2011, p. D3, www.usatoday.com/news/nation/story/2011-11-23/sharing-college-students-volunteering/51447910/1.

Students who are volunteering are doing so more regularly or on a longer-term basis, according to an officer with the Corporation for National and Community Service.

Driscoll, Jessica, "Students Help Launch School Pantry," *Gloucester County* (N.J.) *Times*, Oct. 12, 2011, www.nj.com/gloucester-county/index.ssf/2011/10/clayton_school_district_partne.html.

The Food Bank of South Jersey is working with local high school students to open and operate pantries throughout the area.

Matchan, Linda, "Volunteering Spirit Catches Fire," *The Boston Globe*, Feb. 1, 2011, p. 1, articles.boston.com/2011-02-01/news/29339349_1_young-adults-college-students-national-service.

Community service applications are soaring in Boston, where college students abound and volunteer opportunities are plentiful.

Rampell, Catherine, "In Service to the Public," *The New York Times*, March 2, 2011, p. B1, www.nytimes.com/2011/03/02/business/02graduates.html?pagewanted=all.

Applications for AmeriCorps and Teach for America positions have increased in recent years as corporate job offerings have dried up.

Santana, Marco, "Kids With a Conscience — and a Camera," *Chicago Daily Herald*, April 8, 2011, p. 4, www.dailyherald.com/article/20110407/news/704079897/.

An Illinois volunteer group is encouraging youth volunteers to videotape their work in hopes of persuading other students to engage in community service.

Thomas, Emma, "A Yearning to Give Back," *News Sentinel* (Knoxville, Tenn.), May 15, 2011, p. B1, www.knoxnews.com/news/2011/may/15/a-yearning-to-give-back/?print=1.

Previous volunteer experience is encouraging many college students to pursue public-service jobs upon graduation.

Trevizo, Eddi, "Youth Group Uses Social Media to Encourage Involvement," *Arizona Republic*, Feb. 12, 2011, p. 3, www.azcentral.com/community/swvalley/articles/2011/02/14/20110214arizona-project-five-community-involvement.html.

A group of Arizona high school students has created a social media campaign to encourage youths to volunteer and participate in community activities.

Tumulty, Brian, "New York State Has Lowest Rate of Volunteerism, Report Shows," *Journal News* (Westchester County, N.Y.), Aug. 14, 2011, p. AWP14.

New York ranks last among states in volunteerism, according to a report from the Corporation for National and Community Service.

Citing *CQ Researcher*

Sample formats for citing these reports in a bibliography include the ones listed below. Preferred styles and formats vary, so please check with your instructor or professor.

MLA Style

Jost, Kenneth. "Remembering 9/11," CQ Researcher 2 Sept. 2011: 701-732.

APA Style

Jost, K. (2011, September 2). Remembering 9/11. *CQ Researcher, 9*, 701-732.

Chicago Style

Jost, Kenneth. "Remembering 9/11." *CQ Researcher*, September 2, 2011, 701-732.

In-depth Reports on Issues in the News

Are you writing a paper?

Need backup for a debate?

Want to become an expert on an issue?

For more than 80 years, students have turned to *CQ Researcher* for in-depth reporting on issues in the news. Reports on a full range of political and social issues are now available. Following is a selection of recent reports:

Civil Liberties
Remembering 9/11, 9/11
Government Secrecy, 2/11
Cybersecurity, 2/10
Press Freedom, 2/10

Crime/Law
Financial Misconduct, 1/12
Eyewitness Testimony, 10/11
Legal-Aid Crisis, 10/11
Computer Hacking, 9/11
Cameras in the Courtroom, 1/11
Death Penalty Debates, 11/10

Education
Digital Education, 12/11
College Football, 11/11
Student Debt, 10/11
School Reform, 4/11
Crime on Campus, 2/11

Environment/Society
Fracking Controversy, 12/11
Water Crisis in the West, 12/11
Google's Dominance, 11/11
Managing Public Lands, 11/11
Prolonging Life, 9/11

Health/Safety
Military Suicides, 9/11
Teen Drug Use, 6/11
Organ Donations, 4/11
Genes and Health, 1/11
Food Safety, 12/10
Preventing Bullying, 12/10

Politics/Economy
'Occupy' Movement, 1/12
Reviving Manufacturing, 7/11
Foreign Aid and National Security, 6/11
Lies and Politics, 2/11

Upcoming Reports

Presidential Election, 2/3/12 | Patient Safety, 2/10/12 | Invasive Species, 2/17/12

ACCESS
CQ Researcher is available in print and online. For access, visit your library or www.cqresearcher.com.

STAY CURRENT
For notice of upcoming *CQ Researcher* reports or to learn more about *CQ Researcher* products, subscribe to the free e-mail newsletters, *CQ Researcher Alert!* and *CQ Researcher News*: http://cqpress.com/newsletters.

PURCHASE
To purchase a *CQ Researcher* report in print or electronic format (PDF), visit www.cqpress.com or call 866-427-7737. Single reports start at $15. Bulk purchase discounts and electronic-rights licensing are also available.

SUBSCRIBE
Annual full-service *CQ Researcher* subscriptions—including 44 reports a year, monthly index updates, and a bound volume—start at $803. Add $25 for domestic postage.

CQ Researcher Online offers a backfile from 1991 and a number of tools to simplify research. For pricing information, call 800-834-9020, or e-mail librarymarketing@cqpress.com.

CQ Researcher **PLUS** *Archive*

GET ONLINE ACCESS TO VITAL ISSUES FROM 1923 TO THE PRESENT

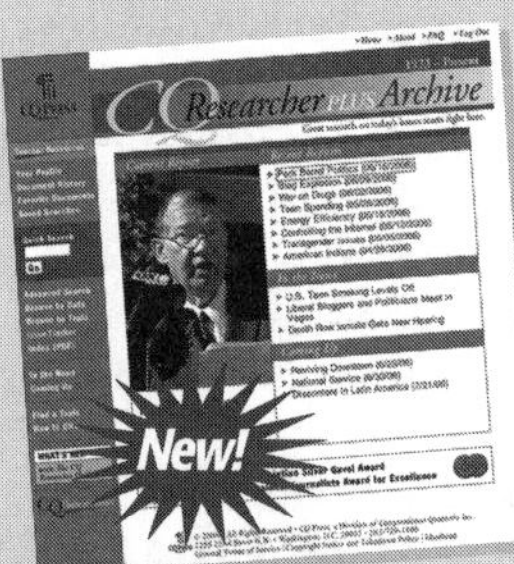

CQ Researcher Plus Archive delivers fast, online access to every *CQ Researcher* report from 1991 to the present, *PLUS* lets you explore the complete archive of *Editorial Research Reports** from 1923-1990. Search and browse more than 3,600 in-depth reports.

Loaded with handy online features, *CQ Researcher Plus Archive* provides the trustworthy reporting and the advanced online functionality today's researchers demand. The new "Issue Tracker" feature provides quick links to past and present reports on the specific topics you need.

For a free trial, visit http://library.cqpress.com/trials.

For pricing information, call 1-800-834-9020, ext. 1906 or e-mail librarymarketing@cqpress.com.

**Editorial Research Reports*, the predecessor to *CQ Researcher*, provides the same expert, nonpartisan reporting on the vital issues that have shaped our society.

CQ Press • 2300 N Street, NW, Suite 800 • Washington, DC 20037

CQ Researcher

Published by CQ Press, an Imprint of SAGE Publications, Inc.

www.cqresearcher.com

Presidential Election

Can Obama withstand the Republican challenge?

The 2012 contest pitting President Obama against a yet-to-be-determined Republican challenger ranks as one of the most intriguing presidential campaigns in history. Two powerful populist factions — the conservative Tea Party movement and Occupy Wall Street protest against income inequality — are helping to shape campaign ideologies and stump speeches. An unusually large field of Republican candidates, including multimillionaire Mormon Mitt Romney and thrice-married Newt Gingrich, have fought each other as aggressively as they have Obama, leaving the GOP so fractured that some think a nominee won't emerge until the party convention in August. Meanwhile, following a controversial Supreme Court ruling on campaign finance, wealthy donors are pouring millions of dollars into TV attack ads through so-called SuperPACs. And overshadowing the entire spectacle is the shaky U.S. economy and the question of which candidate is best equipped to turn it around.

President Obama stops for a campaign photo op in Phoenix on Jan. 25. Fewer than half of Americans approve of his job performance, but polls show his re-election odds are better, partly because of many voters' dissatisfaction with the Republican Party and its increasingly vocal conservatism.

INSIDE THIS REPORT

THE ISSUES 103
BACKGROUND 110
CHRONOLOGY 111
CURRENT SITUATION 116
AT ISSUE.........................117
OUTLOOK 119
BIBLIOGRAPHY 122
THE NEXT STEP 123

CQ Researcher • Feb. 3, 2012 • www.cqresearcher.com
Volume 22, Number 5 • Pages 101-124

CQPRESS

Los Angeles | London | New Delhi
Singapore | Washington DC

RECIPIENT OF SOCIETY OF PROFESSIONAL JOURNALISTS AWARD FOR EXCELLENCE ◆ AMERICAN BAR ASSOCIATION SILVER GAVEL AWARD

PRESIDENTIAL ELECTION

THE ISSUES

103 • Will the economy decide the election?
• Do voters share responsibility for political gridlock?
• Will unregulated campaign funding determine the outcome of the GOP primaries?

BACKGROUND

110 **The First Tea Party**
The American Revolution grew out of the founders' ability to inspire popular outrage against British rule.

113 **Resentment and Reform**
Economic populism exploded in the late 19th century, fueled by farmers' dissatisfaction.

113 **Party Rebellion**
The centrist establishments in both major parties faced increasing dissension.

115 **Partisan Divide**
Today's electorate is deeply divided along partisan lines.

CURRENT SITUATION

116 **Income Inequality**
Economic fairness, more than any other issue, may bolster Obama's re-election chances.

118 **Senate Battles**
Democrats may need a strong Obama victory to hold on to the Senate.

119 **House Comeback?**
A Democratic resurgence cannot be ruled out.

OUTLOOK

119 **Seizing the Opportunity**
Obama's campaign will capitalize on the intensifying discussion of income inequality.

SIDEBARS AND GRAPHICS

104 **Mixed Views on Obama's Performance**
The president gets a low rating on fixing the economy, but he garners more trust than Republicans.

105 **Romney SuperPACs Pull in Most Money**
Gingrich is distant second.

111 **Chronology**
Key events since 1854.

112 **Polling Trends Can Be Uncannily Accurate**
But politicians believe them at their peril.

114 **Nominating Process Has Come a Long Way**
Populist demands broke the grip of party bosses.

117 **At Issue**
Should campaign-finance regulations be tightened?

FOR FURTHER RESEARCH

121 **For More Information**
Organizations to contact.

122 **Bibliography**
Selected sources used.

123 **The Next Step**
Additional articles.

123 **Citing *CQ Researcher***
Sample bibliography formats.

Cover: AFP/Getty Images/Jewel Samad

CQ Researcher

Feb. 3, 2012
Volume 22, Number 5

MANAGING EDITOR: Thomas J. Billitteri
tjb@cqpress.com

ASSISTANT MANAGING EDITOR: Kathy Koch
kkoch@cqpress.com

CONTRIBUTING EDITOR: Thomas J. Colin
tcolin@cqpress.com

ASSOCIATE EDITOR: Kenneth Jost

STAFF WRITER: Marcia Clemmitt

CONTRIBUTING WRITERS: Sarah Glazer, Alan Greenblatt, Peter Katel, Barbara Mantel, Jennifer Weeks

DESIGN/PRODUCTION EDITOR: Olu B. Davis

ASSISTANT EDITOR: Darrell Dela Rosa

FACT CHECKER: Michelle Harris

Los Angeles | London | New Delhi
Singapore | Washington DC

An Imprint of SAGE Publications, Inc.

VICE PRESIDENT AND EDITORIAL DIRECTOR, HIGHER EDUCATION GROUP:
Michele Sordi

DIRECTOR, ONLINE PUBLISHING:
Todd Baldwin

CQ Researcher (ISSN 1056-2036) is printed on acid-free paper. Published weekly, except: (March wk. 5) (May wk. 4) (July wk. 1) (Aug. wks. 3, 4) (Nov. wk. 4) and (Dec. wks. 3, 4). Published by SAGE Publications, Inc., 2455 Teller Rd., Thousand Oaks, CA 91320. Annual full-service subscriptions start at $1,054. For pricing, call 1-800-834-9020. To purchase a *CQ Researcher* report in print or electronic format (PDF), visit www.cqpress.com or call 866-427-7737. Single reports start at $15. Bulk purchase discounts and electronic-rights licensing are also available. Periodicals postage paid at Thousand Oaks, California, and at additional mailing offices. POSTMASTER: Send address changes to *CQ Researcher*, 2300 N St., N.W., Suite 800, Washington, DC 20037.

Presidential Election

BY BOB BENENSON

THE ISSUES

Meet the 2012 candidates: A Hollywood-handsome Mormon multimillionaire, a former House speaker who was fined for ethical lapses and has been married three times, a 76-year-old libertarian with a youthful cult following, a former senator fond of sweater vests and family-values speeches, and last but not least the first African-American president, struggling to persuade the nation that he can revive its damaged economy.

With that cast of characters — all at each others' throats — it's no wonder the media are focusing on the horse-race nature of the contest. But interest in the race goes way beyond who's up and who's down.

The 2012 campaign comes amid an historic level of congressional gridlock and the most intense partisan rancor in memory. The populist "Occupy" movement against income inequality and the conservative Tea Party are shaping campaign rhetoric and could sway the election's outcome. [1] Disarray dogs the Republican Party as an unusually crowded field of GOP rivals snipe at each other as much as at Obama.

Meanwhile, wealthy donors are pouring millions of dollars into so-called SuperPACs, technically independent political action committees that can raise and spend unlimited amounts of money in support of both individual candidates and partisan causes. The new financing phenomenon arose on the heels of the Supreme Court's controversial 2010 ruling on campaign finance in the *Citizens United* case.

And overshadowing the entire 2012 election is the one issue that could well decide the race: the struggling U.S. economy.

Polls show that fewer than half of Americans approve of President Obama's job performance. [2] Yet political analysts put his re-election odds no worse than 50-50, partly because Americans are even less enamored with the Republican Party and its increasingly vocal conservatism.

Getty Images/Win McNamee

Mitt Romney, left, and Newt Gingrich, shown at a South Carolina debate on Jan. 19, are fighting over the Republican presidential nomination. The two candidates, along with Ron Paul and Rick Santorum, are survivors of what started as a nine-member pool of GOP hopefuls. Despite Romney's big win in the Florida primary on Jan. 31, analysts say the race is still so tight the nominee may not be chosen until the GOP convention in late August.

"There's no magic number that gets President Obama re-elected," says Nathan Gonzales, deputy editor of the *Rothenberg Political Report* in Washington. "People have to feel the economy getting better. Until their neighbor, cousin and brother get jobs, the president is going to struggle."

Indeed, the stakes are especially high for Obama. Conservatives view him as a socialist ideologue dangerous to the nation's future, while, conversely, some far-left liberals within his own Democratic party accuse him of failing to deliver on promised social and economic reforms or more aggressively use federal funds to put people back to work.

In addition, many mainstream voters also are frustrated with Obama's handling of the economy, and he faces opposition in some quarters to his signature health-care overhaul that he pushed to enactment in 2010.

Yet many analysts say Republican infighting, combined with frustration with Congress and a growing backlash against the wealthy, could give him the edge.

Meanwhile, five major polls conducted in early- to mid-January showed approval of Congress's job performance at between 11 percent and 13 percent. While voters assign blame for congressional dysfunction to both major parties, polls show it falls heaviest on Republicans. [3]

This might not matter as much for the GOP's hopes of defeating Obama if the party's nominating process was coalescing around a single highly popular challenger. But that has not been the case, at least so far.

Mixed Views on Obama's Performance

Sixty percent of Americans believe President Obama hasn't made any real progress in fixing the economy, but he garners more trust than congressional Republicans to make the right decisions concerning the economy and job creation. Forty-six percent of Americans blame Republicans for congressional gridlock, compared with 30 percent who blame Obama and other Democrats and 16 percent who blame both parties. Obama also gets higher marks than Republicans on willingness to compromise.

Public Views on Obama and Congressional Republicans, January 2012

Economy

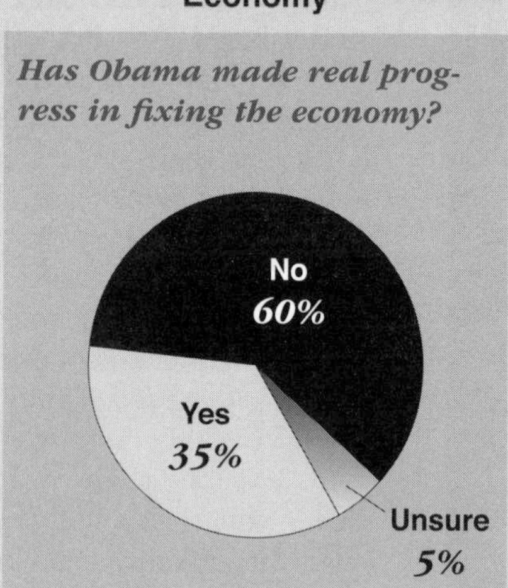

Who do you trust more to make the right decisions . . .

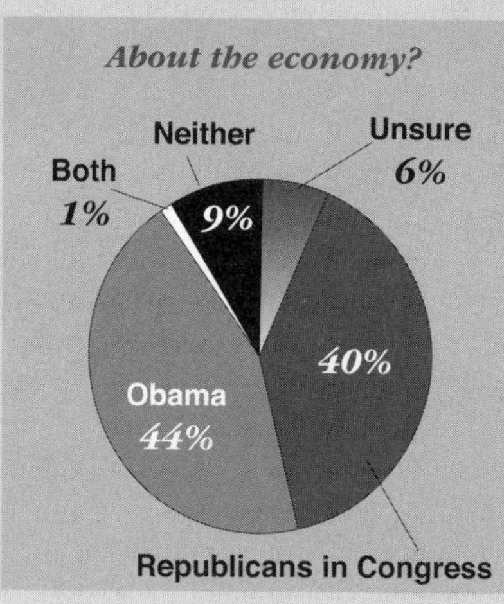

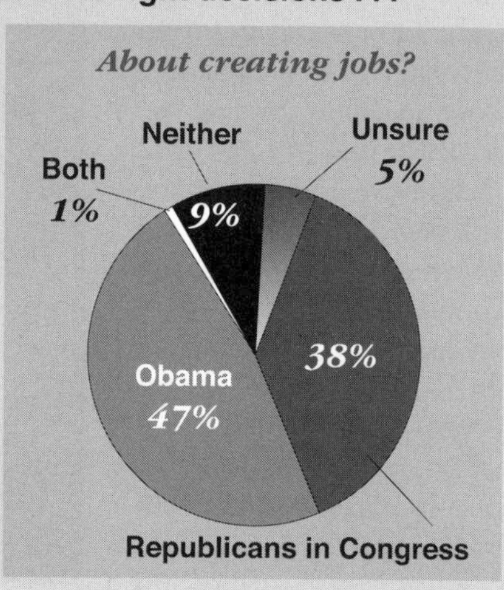

Gridlock

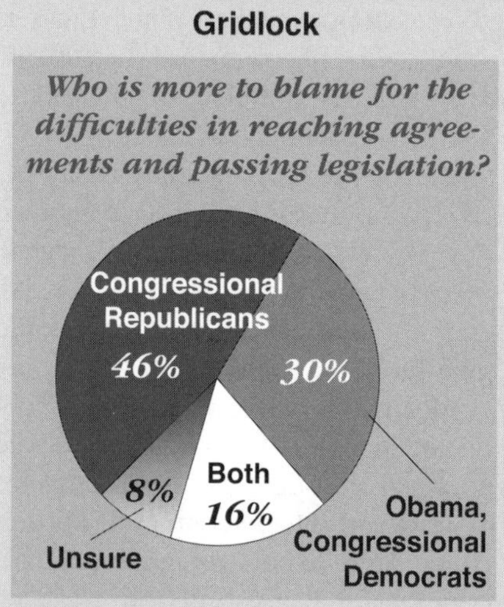

Do you think . . .

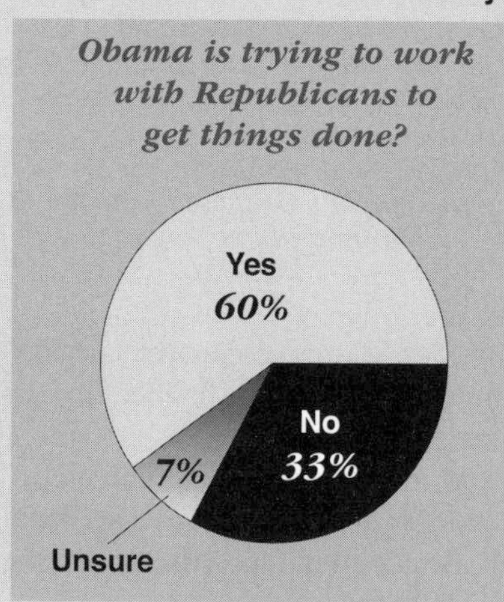

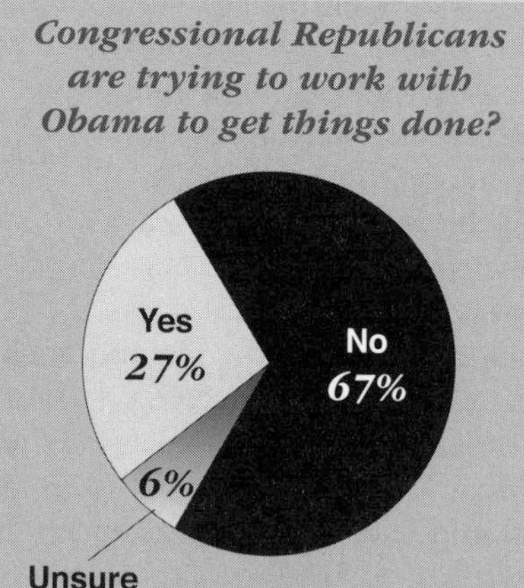

Source: "President Obama and the Obama Administration," PollingReport.com, January 2012, www.pollingreport.com/obama_ad.htm

A furious campaign for the Republican nomination has raged among four principal contenders: former Massachusetts Gov. Mitt Romney, a multi-millionaire business executive who lost a bid for the Republican presidential nomination in 2008; former House Speaker Newt Gingrich, who quit Congress to become a highly paid consultant after being ousted from his House leadership position following GOP losses in the 1998 midterm elections; social conservative Rick Santorum, a former Pennsylvania senator who lost his seat in 2006; and libertarian Ron Paul, a veteran House member from Texas who ran unsuccessfully for the White House in 2008.

The four are survivors of what started as a nine-member pool of GOP hopefuls, yet none has emerged as the clear leader. Romney, widely regarded as the front-runner coming into the contest, won the New Hampshire primary Jan. 10, but only after he lost to Santorum in the Iowa caucuses a week earlier. Gingrich stomped Romney in the South Carolina primary Jan. 21, coming from behind to take first place despite unflattering coverage of marital infidelities, including a late-breaking allegation by his second wife that he had asked for an open marriage. [4]

Romney rebounded 10 days later when he won the Florida primary by a big margin, out-running Gingrich by 46 percent to 32 percent after a campaign sprint in which he put his leading rival on the defensive by portraying him as a Washington "influence peddler." The outcome spurred speculation from some quarters that Romney had regained his footing and was reinstated as the odds-on favorite for the nomination, but the visceral dislike building between the candidates — and Gingrich's stated intention to fight all the way to the Republican convention Aug. 27-30 — left the situation cloudy. (*See sidebar, p. 114.*)

Romney SuperPACs Lead Funding Race

SuperPACs — political action committees that can accept unlimited contributions from individuals, corporations or unions and use them to promote candidates — grew out of a controversial 2010 U.S. Supreme Court ruling on campaign finance. The top 12 SuperPACs in the current election cycle supporting specific presidential candidates together spent about $40 million as of Jan. 31, nearly half of it backing Republican Mitt Romney.

Top SuperPACs in 2012 Election Cycle Supporting Specific Presidential Candidates as of Jan. 31, 2012

SuperPAC	Candidate supported	Independent expenditures
Restore Our Future	Mitt Romney	$17,485,658
Winning Our Future	Newt Gingrich	$8,829,797
Make Us Great Again	Rick Perry	$3,959,824
Endorse Liberty	Ron Paul	$3,339,583
Our Destiny PAC	John Huntsman	$2,453,204
Red, White and Blue	Rick Santorum	$1,954,534
Citizens for a Working America PAC	Mitt Romney	$455,000
9-9-9 Fund	Herman Cain	$418,445
Priorities USA Action	Barack Obama	$321,229
Santa Rita Super PAC	Ron Paul	$317,542
Leaders for Families	Rick Santorum	$231,376
Strong America Now	Newt Gingrich	$189,459

Source: "Super PACs," Center for Responsive Politics, January 2012, Open Secrets, www.opensecrets.org/pacs/superpacs.php?ql3

"Romney made an impressive showing among practically every element of his party except the most conservative of voters and swept to victory in practically every corner of the sprawling state," wrote Eric Pianin of *The Fiscal Times* in a Florida primary analysis. "But whether his strong comeback after a disastrous loss to Gingrich in South Carolina is the beginning of the wrap-up of the GOP presidential nomination battle or simply a milestone in a growing blood feud between him and Gingrich that may tear their party to shreds is far from clear." [5]

A protracted battle of attrition would be a far cry from early expectations that Romney would sweep the field. He entered the race as the best-organized and best-funded candidate but ran into resistance over his Mormon faith — a longstanding issue particularly for doctrinaire evangelical Christians — and a lack of enthusiasm for his platform and personality among many staunch GOP conservatives.

While Romney has sought to project a solidly conservative image, his critics have reminded voters of more liberal views he has voiced in the past on social issues, such as abortion and gay rights, and his role in pushing through a state health-care overhaul in Massachusetts widely described — over Romney's strong denials — as a model for Obama's health plan.

Romney's critics also have accused him of being out of touch with middle-class Americans. They cite his background as a corporate takeover specialist who profited by buying and sometimes shutting down struggling companies and firing workers. Critics also cite Romney's prodigious wealth — he earned $45 million in 2010 and 2011 from investments and was likely to pay $6.2 million in taxes for the two years; his roughly 14 percent tax rate was considerably lower than what many affluent Americans pay. [6] Romney has put his net worth at between $150 million and $200 million. [7]

Romney is not alone, however, in his mix of political strengths and weaknesses:

• Gingrich, who masterminded the 1994 "Contract With America," a policy blueprint that enabled the Republicans to break a 40-year Democratic hold on the House, has exhibited strong command of issues during Republican presidential debates. But he has taken fire for having been ousted as speaker by his Republican colleagues; earning millions of dollars as a Washington insider after quitting Congress in the 1990s; and marrying his third wife after divorces preceded by extramarital affairs.

• Santorum has displayed a steadfast social conservatism that made him a surprise winner in Iowa. But many Republicans fear his image as a crusader on issues such as abortion and gay marriage limits his appeal to the broader general electorate in November.

• Paul, who first gained a serious national following during his quixotic 2008 campaign for the Republican presidential nomination, espouses sharp cuts in the size and scope of government and an isolationist foreign policy. His popularity has grown during the 2012 campaign, especially among young voters. But Paul's foreign policy views run counter to the traditional GOP core principle of supporting robust U.S. military power, and he has had a hard time explaining newsletters published under his name in the 1990s that contained racist and anti-Israel sentiments.

Meanwhile, analysts say Obama also presents a mixed bag of pluses and minuses — populist appeal and success in eliminating 9/11 terrorist plotter Osama bin Laden, for example, but also a stagnant economy, staggering federal debt and lingering controversies over his health care plan, the future of which is now in the hands of the U.S. Supreme Court.

Still, analysts see multiple reasons why Obama's electoral prospects may not be as bleak as his job-approval numbers might suggest. They point to his strengths as one of the most charismatic candidates in recent U.S. political history, a trait Democrats hope will help him make a better case for his policies on the campaign trail than he has in the daily grind of Washington's politics.

Obama also has exhibited epic fundraising prowess. He brought in a record $779 million for his 2008 campaign, and his re-election organization already reported raising $141 million by the end of 2011, ahead of the pace set four years earlier.

Moreover, Obama's support among his party's liberal base, though hardly unanimous, remains strong. Unlike the two most recent incumbents defeated for re-election — Democrat Jimmy Carter and Republican George H. W. Bush — Obama drew no serious challenger to his renomination bid.

Getty Images/John W. Adkisson

Ron Paul is a veteran Republican House member from Texas who ran for the White House in 2008. A libertarian, he espouses sharp cuts in government and an isolationist foreign policy. Recently, Paul has been confronted with newsletters published under his name in the 1990s that contained racist and anti-Israel sentiments.

Even the weak economy, which appears to be the single biggest threat to Obama's re-election, is showing tentative signs of life. Unemployment fell to 8.5 percent in December, down from 9.2 percent in June 2011 and a peak of 10 percent in October 2009. Still, in late January the Federal Reserve indicated it did not think the economy would completely recover from the 2008 crash until at least late 2014. [8]

"If things remain stagnant, Obama and the Democrats will have a more difficult time," says Timothy M. Hagle, a political science professor at the University of Iowa. "On the other hand, even slight improvements will help Obama."

But perhaps the most important factor keeping Obama's hopes for re-election alive is that the 2012 contest is not just about him but about his Republican Party adversaries as well.

"The election boils down to whether the contest is a referendum or a choice," says Gonzales. "With an incumbent president, the election starts as a referendum on Obama. But Democrats will do everything in their power to take the focus off the president and shine the light on the GOP agenda. President Obama probably couldn't win a referendum election but he could win a choice election."

As the race for the White House heats up, here are some of the issues being debated:

Will the state of the economy decide the election?

In a CBS News-*New York Times* poll in mid-January, 56 percent of respondents said the economy was the most important issue in the presidential race. Ranking second and third were two other issues with big economic implications: the federal budget deficit (15 percent) and health care (14 percent). [9]

The focus on "kitchen-table" issues is common in American politics, even in better circumstances. "Except in times of war or massive scandal, the state of the economy drives most votes and tips elections one way or the other," says Larry Sabato, a political scientist at the University of Virginia and publisher of the *Crystal Ball* political website.

But this year, with unemployment stuck above 8 percent, the nation's economic difficulties have cast a long shadow over presidential contenders in both political parties.

Heightening the political stakes is the Occupy movement, a grassroots protest against income inequality that began last September near New York City's Financial District and has spread nationwide. [10]

Occupy demonstrators have not formulated a cohesive political message so far, and they have waged protests against Republican and Democratic policies and candidates alike. But their chief argument — that the political and economic system benefits the nation's wealthiest 1 percent to the detriment of the other 99 percent — has thrust the issue of economic fairness to the forefront of the presidential race.

A survey by the Pew Research Center for the People and the Press found that while nearly half of respondents disapproved of the movement's tactics, a nearly equal proportion agreed with the concerns raised by the protesters. [11]

In his State of the Union address on Jan. 24, Obama reinforced the inequality theme, saying that people who make more than $1 million per year should pay at least 30 percent of their earnings in income tax. "When Americans talk about folks like me paying my fair share of taxes, it's not because they envy the rich," Obama said, making his remarks just after Romney reluctantly disclosed that he'd paid an effective tax rate of about 14 percent. "It's because they understand that when I get a tax break I don't need and the country can't afford, it either adds to the deficit, or somebody else has to make up the difference. . . . That's not right." [12]

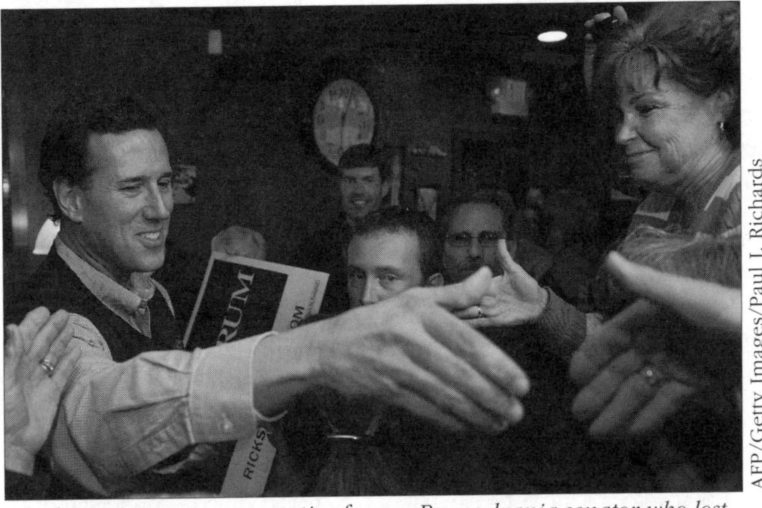

AFP/Getty Images/Paul J. Richards

Rick Santorum, a conservative former Pennsylvania senator who lost his seat in 2006, narrowly beat Romney in the Iowa caucuses. But many Republicans fear that his image as a crusader on issues such as abortion and gay marriage limits his appeal to moderate voters.

Political analysts have differing views on how the Occupy movement's inequality message might play at the ballot box.

"It has helped to frame the issue of the '1 percent vs. the 99 percent,' which is already a powerful part of the political lexicon," says elections expert Rhodes Cook, who publishes a bimonthly political analysis. "That could have even more resonance if Mitt Romney is the GOP nominee."

But G. Evans Witt, CEO of Princeton Survey Research Associates International, says the Occupy movement's impact has been "very mixed." "If the Democrats can successfully take one element of the movement — 'we are the 99 percent' — and craft a positive message around that approach, it could be a positive for them," Witt says. "If the GOP can paint the Occupy movement as [a group of] meaningless extremists, that could be a help to their candidates."

However the Occupy theme plays out, millions of Americans struggling with the recession's fallout are demanding answers from both political parties.

For Obama and his GOP rivals, however, persuading a skeptical electorate that they have solutions is an uphill struggle.

Obama's critics accuse him of stifling job growth with government regulation and adding to the federal debt by pushing an $830 billion economic stimulus plan through a Democratic-controlled Congress in 2009. While several nonpartisan studies found that the stimulus created or saved as many as 3 million jobs, many voters think the measure either didn't work or didn't do enough. [13]

"When the Democrats say that the stimulus helped to prevent the economy from slipping into an even worse recession, they are absolutely right," says Charles Ballard, an economics professor at Michigan State University. "Even very conservative economists agree with that. But of course, 'it could have been worse' isn't an easy sell, even if it's true."

A CBS News-*New York Times* poll showed only 40 percent of respondents approved of Obama's handling of the economy while 54 percent disapproved.

Such sentiment leaves Obama vulnerable in November, especially if the unemployment rate remains, as many economists expect, above 8 percent, analysts say. The 7.2 rate when Ronald Reagan was re-elected in 1984 was the highest for any president who won a second term since Democrat Franklin D. Roosevelt won in 1936 despite a 17 percent rate amid the Great Depression.

"Even though we have three branches of government, I think the average voter believes the president is in control of everything, and he gets a disproportionate share of credit and blame," says Gonzales of the *Rothenberg Political Report*. "So if the economy continues to sputter into next year, I believe the president and his party are more at risk of being punished on Election Day."

But the Republicans have plenty of image-building to do too. House resistance last December to extending a payroll-tax exemption aimed at helping poor and middle-class families and Republican brinksmanship last summer that nearly led to a government debt default have left the party open to accusations of obstructionism.

Polls underscore public mistrust of the GOP's ability to turn around the economy. The CBS News-*New York Times* poll showed Obama — despite his low approval rating on the economy — with a slight edge (44 percent to 40 percent) over congressional Republicans on the question, "Who do you trust more to make the right decisions about the nation's economy?"

Meanwhile, a mid-January ABC News-*Washington Post* poll found that most respondents, while skeptical about Obama's actions, still largely blame the nation's financial problems on his predecessor, George W. Bush. The poll showed 54 percent of respondents blamed Bush more, while 29 percent said Obama was more to blame.

Few political observers think Obama could weather an election-year setback on the economy, however. "If the economy isn't at least improving a little bit, it can't be good for President Obama," says Ballard. But many also caution against assuming that unemployment must drop below the 7.2 percent Reagan threshold for Obama to win. As long as enough voters believe the economy is moving in the right direction, they contend, that may be enough to put him over the top.

Do voters share responsibility for political gridlock?

Bitter partisanship has been intensifying for years, and it's seen as a major contributor to both Congress's abysmal job-approval ratings and skepticism that whoever occupies the White House can effect substantive change.

Americans, by and large, favor cooperation and negotiation over unflinching partisanship. The CBS News-*New York Times* poll found that more than 80 percent of respondents said they wanted lawmakers to compromise on at least some issues.

Yet, elected officials in each party — but moreso among Republicans with the rise of the Tea Party movement — have responded to rising demands from the most ideological voters that they stick to "party principles," even if that means resisting compromise.

This split political personality could be seen over the first two years of Obama's presidency, which was coupled with Democratic control of both chambers of Congress.

The passage of the economic stimulus and health care overhaul, over nearly unanimous Republican opposition, contributed to what Columbia University historian Alan Brinkley called "probably the most productive session of Congress since at least the '60s." [14]

But many voters didn't see things that way. In the 2010 congressional elections, House Democrats received the worst shellacking of either party in 62 years and suffered a deep cut in their Senate majority as well.

The battle lines drawn in the current Congress suggest that members of both parties are most responsive to their activist bases rather than to voters demanding compromise. A "party unity" study by *CQ Weekly* for the 2011 House session — measuring how often each member voted with most colleagues of his or her own party against most members of the other party — showed a median score of 95 percent in both the Republican and Democratic parties. [15]

Still, opinions among political experts are mixed concerning whether voters bear responsibility for the gridlock that many Americans strongly criticize.

George C. Edwards III, a distinguished professor of political science and presidential scholar at Texas A&M University, thinks they do. "Politicians don't cause gridlock, voters do," he says. "The real problem is that some voters, particularly Republicans, vote for candidates who will not compromise. Moreover, these same voters do not want their representatives in Congress to compromise."

Darrell West, director of governance studies at the Brookings Institution, agrees that voters are partly to blame for congressional stalemates. "Voters share responsibility for gridlock when they elect ideologues who refuse to compromise," he says. "They need to understand that negotiation is not a sign of lack of principle."

But Ronald A. Faucheux, president of Clarus Research Group, in Washington, believes gridlock stems mainly from failed political leadership. "Voters may be responsible for electing a government that's divided between the parties, but it's not their fault when Democrats and Republicans in Congress refuse to find common ground," he says.

"Both parties have been living off of the weaknesses and mistakes of one another for a long time now," Faucheux adds. "There is no reason to think that will change this year. That is a tragedy, because good government can also be good politics. Voters hunger for a practical, positive agenda."

Hagle, the University of Iowa political scientist, agrees that a leadership deficit is at the heart of the problem.

"The idea is that because of increased partisanship, voters have sent members to Congress who are less likely to compromise for fear of losing their seats," Hagle says. "What that really means is that those Congress members have failed in one way or another. It could mean that they are more interested in their personal political ambition than in getting things done. It could also mean that they just lack the leadership skills necessary."

Will unregulated campaign funding determine the outcome of the GOP primaries?

The high-stakes contest for the Republican nomination has been a proving ground for a new variant of political action committees called SuperPACs. (*See chart, p. 105.*) These organizations can accept unlimited financial contributions from individuals, corporations or unions and use them to clearly promote candidates for public office — or, more often, to attack their opponents with barrages of negative advertising.

The newest wrinkle in the ever-evolving efforts by groups outside the political parties to influence election outcomes, SuperPACs resulted from a controversial January 2010 Supreme Court ruling in *Citizens United v. Federal Election Commission.* [16]

The court, on a 5-4 vote, overturned a provision of the Bipartisan Campaign Reform Act of 2002 that had barred "electioneering communications" by corporations and unions within 60 days of a general election or 30 days of a primary. The court's narrow majority established as a matter of law that corporations and unions have a First Amendment right to make unlimited political expenditures if not coordinated with any candidate's campaign.

The first SuperPACs, which sprang up quickly to leverage this new avenue for political spending, were formed by supporters of each of the major parties during the campaigns for the 2010 midterm elections and were seen essentially as adjuncts to the parties' efforts to elect more of their candidates. But it was not long before the emergence of SuperPACs dedicated to a much narrower purpose: the election of individual candidates.

Federal law imposes only one major restriction on SuperPACs: They cannot directly coordinate with a candidate's election campaign. But some SuperPACs come close. The biggest player in the campaign's earliest stages was Restore Our Future, which advocated for Mitt Romney's presidential candidacy and is headed by several longtime Romney associates.

Through Jan. 26, Restore Our Future had spent $16.7 million, according to the Center for Responsive Politics, a nonpartisan group in Washington that tracks campaign spending. [17] (*See graphic, p. 105.*) According to a *New York Times* analysis of Federal Election Commission (FEC) data, most of that was used to finance negative advertising aimed at Gingrich, who after a slow start had surged in polls in weeks before the Jan. 3 Iowa caucuses. [18]

The ads against Gingrich played off controversies from his political career — including ethics violations for which the House fined him $300,000 when he was Speaker — and his personal life.

But the ads didn't appear to be effective in boosting Romney, who narrowly lost in Iowa to Santorum and was trounced by Gingrich in South Carolina. By the time the campaign arrived in South Carolina, the SuperPAC playing field had leveled. Winning Our Future, a committee backing Gingrich, received a $5 million donation from Sheldon Adelson, a Las Vegas casino and hotel owner who is a longtime Gingrich ally. By Jan. 21, Winning Our Future had spent almost $4 million, more than three-quarters of that on negative ads and almost all of those aimed at portraying Romney as a corporate vulture who made big profits at Bain Capital by buying up struggling companies and laying off many of their workers. It quickly became clear that there would be no let-up, as the pro-Gingrich SuperPAC received an addi-

Getty Images/Michael Reynolds-Pool

Sheldon Adelson, a Las Vegas casino and hotel owner, donated $5 million to a SuperPAC backing Newt Gingrich. The PAC received an additional $5 million from Adelson's wife Miriam shortly after Gingrich's victory in South Carolina. The Supreme Court's Citizens United *decision in 2010 allows corporations and unions as well as individuals to make unlimited contributions to political committees operating independently of candidates' campaigns.*

tional $5 million from Miriam Adelson, Adelson's wife, shortly after Gingrich's victory in South Carolina.

The pro-Romney PAC came roaring back in Florida, though, with its almost non-stop barrage of negative advertising aiding in halting and reversing Gingrich's momentum.

Political insiders differ sharply on their view of the *Citizens United* decision and the role of SuperPACs in the 2012 election.

Common Cause, a government watchdog organization, has formed a satellite group called Amend 2012 that aims to overturn the Supreme Court ruling through a constitutional amendment. (*See "At Issue," p. 117.*)

Chairing the effort is Robert Reich, former Labor secretary in the Clinton administration. Reich called Romney "Son of Citizens United" in a recent essay, saying that Restore Our Future "reveals the grotesque result of the Supreme Court's decision . . ., which reversed more than a century of efforts to curb the influence of big money on politics.

"If income and wealth in America were as widely shared as in the first three decades after World War II, we'd have less reason to worry. But now, with an almost unprecedented concentration of money at the very top, *Citizens United* invites the worst corruption our democracy has witnessed since the Gilded Age." [19]

But John Samples, director of the Center for Representative Government at the Cato Institute, a libertarian think tank in Washington, contends that SuperPACs fit perfectly within the definition of the nation's constitutional guarantee of free speech. "SuperPACs fund political speech. The First Amendment protects such speech," he wrote. [20]

Indeed, supporters of SuperPACs generally argue that unfettered campaign spending enhances the quantity of information about candidates. They also generally dismiss complaints that such spending promotes the use of distorted or false attacks on candidates, arguing instead that voters are capable of filtering information and determining what is and is not fair.

"The First Amendment does not allow anyone to pursue his vision of a better world through censorship," argued Trevor Burrus, a legal associate with Cato's Center for Constitutional Studies. "Although we'd all love the liars and shouters to be silenced, the First Amendment forbids such censorship precisely because there is no way to agree on who is a liar and who is 'too loud.' Those determinations are too intertwined with our ideological commitments." [21]

Yet even some of those who are heavily engaged in the SuperPAC phenomenon have qualms about it.

Prior to the Jan. 31 Florida primary, the pro-Gingrich Winning Our Future group spent millions of dollars on TV ads that attacked Romney, mainly to try to persuade the strongly conservative Republican voting base that he is actually a liberal. But Rick Tyler, a leading operative of Winning Our Future, told the *Tampa Bay Times* days before the primary that SuperPACs are "terrible."

In a refrain about negative campaigning often heard in other contexts over the years, Tyler said the Gingrich side was not going to "unilaterally disarm" while the pro-Romney Restore Our Future PAC was slamming Gingrich with its own negative ads. But he added, "We didn't make the rules. We don't like the rules. But these are the rules. I'm hopeful we've learned enough from this wretched experiment to fix it." [22] ■

BACKGROUND

The First Tea Party

The adoption of the "Tea Party" label by some conservatives and their use of Revolution-era slogans such as "Don't Tread on Me" illuminate the thread of angry populism that runs from the nation's founding all the way to this year's presidential race.

The success of the American Revolution rested on the ability of the nation's founders to inspire popular outrage against excesses in British rule. Protesting "taxation without representation," radicals reacted to duties on imported tea by dumping crates of tea into Boston Harbor in December 1773.

Public anger escalated when Britain, reacting to colonial rebellion, suspended home rule in Massachusetts and imposed martial law, acts that led to the Revolutionary War. Yet some of the founders who created the U.S. Constitution and Bill of Rights resisted populism. They worried that democracy would degenerate into mob rule.

In most states during the nation's early decades, only white, male property owners could vote. State legislators chose the members of the U.S. Senate (a system maintained until ratification of the 17th Amendment in 1913 mandating that all senators be elected by voters). State legislators also chose the electors who decided which candidate each state would support for president; states only gradually tied their votes in the Electoral College to a popular vote for president.

Yet as the nation's population grew and its borders expanded westward, the people excluded from the political process grew restive, and they found a champion in Tennessee's Andrew Jackson. A hero of the War of 1812 with Great Britain, Jackson narrowly lost a bid for president in 1824 but was elected in 1828 and 1832 with the support of many white males who lacked substantial property holdings but had nonetheless attained voting rights.

Jacksonian democracy would sound familiar to many of today's activists on both the right and the left. "He certainly made a great deal of his

Continued on p. 113

Chronology

1850s-1860s

Voting rights expand; the nation splits violently and a new Republican Party rises.

1854
Whig Party dissolves; Republicans oppose expansion of slavery.

1861-65
Election of first Republican president, Abraham Lincoln, in 1860 prompts 11 Southern states to secede, sparking Civil War.

1865
Lincoln assassinated, but Republicans begin long period of dominance; South stays Democratic for generations. . . . Jim Crow laws suppress civil rights for blacks.

1930s-1950s

Populist movement leads to Progressive activism.

1932
Election of Franklin D. Roosevelt begins Democratic Party dominance, growth of government.

1945-1950s
Prosperity and national confidence follow World War II.

1960s-1980s

Scandals and an unpopular war erode faith in presidency.

1963
President John F. Kennedy assassinated in Dallas.

1964-65
President Lyndon B. Johnson signs laws barring racial discrimination.

1965
Johnson escalates Vietnam War, dividing American society.

1968
The Rev. Martin Luther King Jr. and Sen. Robert F. Kennedy are assassinated. Republican Richard M. Nixon elected president on law-and-order platform.

1974
Nixon resigns amid Watergate scandal.

1980
Republican Ronald Reagan elected president as conservatives gain dominance in GOP.

1990s-Present

Economic insecurity and partisanship shift party control of Congress, White House.

1992
Democrat Bill Clinton elected president after Republican incumbent George H. W. Bush breaks "no new taxes" pledge.

1994
Republicans take over Congress.

1996
Economic rebound helps Clinton win re-election.

1998
House impeaches Clinton in sex scandal but Senate acquits him.

2000
Republican George W. Bush elected president over Democrat Al Gore, following disputed vote count.

2002
Bush wins broad support for Iraq invasion.

2003
President's approval plummets as U.S. troops become bogged down.

2004
Bush narrowly wins re-election.

2005
Bush administration's disorganized response to Hurricane Katrina criticized.

2006
Democrats gain control of Congress.

2008
Democrat Barack Obama becomes first black president.

2009
Democratic-controlled Congress passes $830 billion economic stimulus over GOP objections. . . . Tea Party movement emerges.

2010
Supreme Court hands down *Citizens United* decision (Jan. 21). . . . Obama pushes his signature health-care overhaul bill through Congress; GOP regains control of House.

2011
Obama and congressional Republicans agree to $38 billion in budget cuts, averting government shutdown. . . . Republicans block increase in federal debt limit until White House agrees to major deficit reduction. . . . Congressional "super-committee" fails to craft deficit-reduction plan. . . . House Republicans balk at extending payroll tax reduction, but reverse course.

2012
Mitt Romney enters the year as the GOP front-runner but faces stiff opposition from former House Speaker Newt Gingrich; Rep. Ron Paul and former Sen. Rick Santorum survive early primaries. . . . Super Tuesday (March 6). . . . Republican Convention (Aug. 27-30).

Polling Trends Can Be Uncannily Accurate

But politicians believe them at their peril.

Optimists love the phrase, "The trend is our friend." They use it so frequently — in politics, business, sports and many other areas — that a Google search shows nearly 100 million hits.

But the phrase comes with a big caveat: "unless it's not." In other words, trends are dependable, unless they aren't.

If President Obama's poll numbers begin improving, the trend certainly could turn out to be his friend. That's because he started the 2012 election year with relatively weak job-approval ratings. On the other hand, if Obama's numbers drop, he could be facing an "unless it's not" scenario.

The Gallup polling organization reported Jan. 16 that Obama's average job-approval rating for the first half of January was just 44 percent — well below the 50 percent threshold that Gallup "considers determinant for re-election." [1]

Yet the analysis accompanying that report suggests Obama's chances of winning in November would improve significantly if his approval ratings show any significant uptick — even if they don't end up greatly exceeding 50 percent.

It also shows that one of the worst things that can happen to a president seeking re-election is to peak too soon. Some of Obama's recent predecessors who appeared more popular a year out from Election Day either lost or struggled to eke out a narrow victory.

The role model for an Obama election-year comeback is fellow Democrat Bill Clinton, whose approval average in early January 1996 was a dismal 42 percent. By October, though, Clinton's approval rating had bounded up to 58 percent, and he ended up winning re-election with relative ease.

On the other hand, Democrat Jimmy Carter — whose approval ratings had sunk to 28 percent in July 1979 because of economic problems, energy shortages and international challenges — appeared in much better shape as 1980 began, with a mid-January job-approval average of 56 percent. However, that proved to be an artificial "bounce" in the polls, mainly reflecting a "rally around the flag" response after Islamic radicals in Iran took 52 Americans hostage in November 1979. Carter's approval ratings dropped to near his all-time low, and he ended up losing badly to Republican Ronald Reagan.

Reagan himself appeared somewhat vulnerable entering his re-election campaign in 1984, with an average approval rating of 52 percent. But by October, that rating was up to 58 percent, and he ended up winning one of the biggest landslides in presidential history, thrashing Democrat Walter F. Mondale, Carter's vice president.

The data above show presidents since Richard M. Nixon ran for a second term in 1972 who gained ground in job-approval polling during their re-election campaigns and those who lost ground. All three presidents whose trend lines rose during their re-election bids won second terms. Two of the three presidents whose popularity was declining during the re-election campaign lost their contests, while the other won a narrow victory. [2]

— ***Bob Benenson***

The Trend Was Their Friend	The Trend Was Not Their Friend
1972: Richard M. Nixon (Republican) Won Mid-January Job-Approval Average: ***49%*** June Job-Approval Average: ***59%**** Election Result: ***Nixon 61.1%***, ***George S. McGovern*** (D) ***37.5%***	**1980: Jimmy Carter (Democrat) Lost** Mid-January Job-Approval Average: ***56%*** June Job-Approval Average: ***32%*** Election Result: ***Reagan 50.7%***, ***Carter 41%***, ***John B. Anderson*** (Independent) ***6.6%***
1984: Ronald Reagan (Republican) Won Mid-January Job-Approval Average: ***52%*** October Job-Approval Average: ***58%*** Election Result: ***Reagan 58.8%***, ***Walter F. Mondale*** (D) ***40.6%***	**1992: George H. W. Bush (Republican) Lost** Mid-January Job-Approval Average: ***46%*** October Job-Approval Average: ***33%*** Election Result: ***Clinton 43%***, ***Bush 37.4%***, ***Perot*** (Independent) ***18.9%***
1996: Bill Clinton (Democrat) Won Mid-January Job-Approval Average: ***42%*** October Job-Approval Average: ***58%*** Election Result: ***Clinton 49.2%***, ***Bob Dole*** (R) ***40.7%***, ***Ross Perot*** (Reform) ***8.4%***	**2004: George W. Bush (Republican) Won** Mid-January Job-Approval Average: ***60%*** October Job-Approval Average: ***50%*** Election Result: ***Bush 50.7%***, ***John Kerry*** (D) ***48.3%***

** Because of changes in how late in the year Gallup conducted its daily tracking polls on presidential job approval, its averages run through June up to Carter's presidency and then are through October for subsequent elections.*

[1] Lydia Saad, "Obama Faces Challenging Re-Election Climate," Gallup, Jan. 16, 2012, www.gallup.com/poll/152051/Obama-Faces-Challenging-Election-Climate.aspx.

[2] Democrat Lyndon B. Johnson, who ran in 1964 after succeeding assassinated President John F. Kennedy in 1963, and 1976 Republican incumbent Gerald R. Ford, who moved up from vice president in 1974 after the Watergate scandal, were included in the Gallup report, but are excluded here because they were not technically running for re-election. Johnson, whose approval ratings slipped marginally from 77 percent in January 1964 to 74 percent that June, defeated Republican Barry Goldwater by 61.1 percent to 38.5 percent. Ford, whose approval ratings plummeted from 56 percent in January 1974 to 32 percent that June, regained ground before Election Day but still lost to Democrat Carter by 50.1 percent to 48 percent.

Continued from p. 110

humble frontier roots, engaged in heated rhetoric, and drew class distinctions," wrote Henry Olsen, a vice president of the American Enterprise Institute, a conservative Washington think tank. "In 1832, he campaigned against the Second Bank of the United States — a forerunner of the Federal Reserve — arguing that it was a scheme of the elite and the rich to despoil the people." [23]

Resentment and Reform

Populist sentiment played a role in the Civil War (1861-1865), as North and South clashed in a bitter ideological fight over slavery, states' rights and other issues. But economic populism didn't explode onto the national scene in full force until the late 19th century, fueled by struggling farmers' resentment toward bankers, rich businessmen and railroad interests.

In 1892, James B. Weaver, a former House member from Iowa, ran for president on the upstart People's Party (also known as the Populists) ticket. He took 8.5 percent of the popular vote and carried Kansas, Colorado, Idaho and Nevada.

In 1896, the Democratic Party, which had thrown in with the Populists, nominated William Jennings Bryan for president. A congressman and fiery orator from Nebraska, Bryan blasted "the idle holders of idle capital" who, he charged, victimized the struggling masses. His diatribes prompted his Republican opponent, William McKinley, to brand him a dangerous radical.

Bryan lost the 1896 election, a 1900 rematch with McKinley and a 1908 contest with Republican William Howard Taft. Yet many ideas initially dismissed as radical — tighter business regulation, child-labor laws and popular election of U.S. senators, for example — later were adopted by the political establishment, a pattern repeated in future populist movements.

Not all populist uprisings are viewed today in a positive light. For example, the federal government's post-Civil War efforts to provide civil liberties for blacks spawned a populist backlash from white Southerners that resulted in the Ku Klux Klan and so-called Jim Crow laws that institutionalized racial discrimination in the region for generations.

The American Enterprise Institute's Olsen noted a unique — and positive — feature of American populism, however: Even in the worst of times, he said, it has never metastasized into the kind of mass fanaticism that produced communist and fascist regimes overseas.

"Americans are a self-governing people through and through, and American populism reflects the American passion for self-determination," he wrote. "That passion certainly leads some Americans to respond powerfully against overbearing elites, and so causes some populist movements to form. But it has also often allowed these responses to be channeled in constructive directions — keeping our politics in balance, and over time giving rise to enduring political coalitions." [24]

Public faith in government remained strong during the two decades after World War II, a time of rapidly spreading prosperity. Nearly three-fourths of respondents to a 1958 poll said they trusted the government to do the right things. [25]

The past half-century, though, has presented a series of polarizing events that have eroded public trust in government and specifically the presidency. That erosion was reflected in a poll released in March 2010 by the Pew Research Center for the People and the Press that found trust in the federal government had fallen to 22 percent. [26] The figure ticked up to 29 percent in a Pew poll released a year later mainly because the GOP upsurge in the 2010 elections had eased the level of distrust among Republicans. [27]

The 1963 assassination of President John F. Kennedy and the 1968 killings of his brother, Sen. Robert F. Kennedy, and civil rights leader the Rev. Martin Luther King Jr. rocked the nation's sense of security. At the same time, President Lyndon B. Johnson's escalation of the Vietnam War in the mid-1960s deeply divided the electorate.

Party Rebellion

Meanwhile, the relatively centrist establishments in both major parties faced increasing dissension.

The Republican Party, which then had a large segment of liberal to moderate members, mainly from the Northeast, first faced a populist rebellion leading up to the 1964 presidential election. Conservative activists expressed frustration with what they saw as acquiescence to the expansion of the federal government. This faction succeeded in nominating Arizona Sen. Barry Goldwater for president that year. Though Goldwater lost to Johnson in a landslide, the conservative upsurge was a harbinger of Ronald Reagan's election 16 years later amid a strong GOP shift to the right.

The Democratic Party, whose coalition historically had included many Southern conservatives, faced demands by liberals for greater representation. That division, on vivid display at the tumultuous 1968 Democratic National Convention in Chicago, ultimately would lead to a shift of the party to the left.

The 1970s brought more turmoil. The Watergate political scandal, which forced Republican President Richard M. Nixon to resign in disgrace in 1974, shattered public faith in government more than any other event. Meanwhile, oil boycotts by Arab nations retaliating against U.S. support for Israel, growing economic competition from overseas and periods of economic stagnation eroded Americans' confidence

Nominating Process Has Come a Long Way

Populist demands broke the grip of party bosses.

It wasn't so long ago — 40 years to be exact — that political party bosses, not citizens voting in party caucuses and primaries, used to select presidential candidates. Since the 1972 campaign, however, a series of state-by-state contests — which begins with the Iowa caucuses and New Hampshire primary in early winter and runs until June — has invariably produced a candidate who has clinched his party's nomination well before the summertime national conventions.

But this system is, in fact, relatively new in the context of the history of presidential elections in the United States.

From the first presidential convention in 1831 right through 1968, nominations were tightly controlled by national party leaders and state and local officials. The public was largely excluded from the deal-making (also known as "horse-trading") that determined the nominee.

Presidential primary elections were first held by a few states in the early 20th century, a product of Progressive Era reforms. But most states stuck with the traditional system, in which party insiders reigned supreme.

Change came rapidly, though. Longstanding complaints from dissidents about tight control of the selection process by party "bosses" were amplified in the 1960s by the anti-establishment sentiment stirred up by the anti-Vietnam War and civil rights movements.

This sentiment crystallized after the 1968 Democratic convention in Chicago was marked by shouting and shoving matches in the convention hall — between party regulars who succeeded in nominating Vice President Hubert H. Humphrey and anti-war insurgents who favored Sen. Eugene McCarthy of Minnesota — and violent clashes in the streets between police and protesters.

Demands for a more open system prompted the Democratic Party, following Humphrey's narrow defeat by Republican Richard M. Nixon, to empanel a commission, chaired by Sen. George S. McGovern of South Dakota and Rep. Donald M. Fraser of Minnesota, to recommend changes. The McGovern-Fraser commission called on state parties to invite more women, minorities and young voters into the process and remove impediments to their participation.

The commissioners wanted to make the Democratic Party's organizations more inclusive and thereby temper sentiment for a radical overhaul of the party's structure. But, like many political reforms, those instituted 40 years ago had an unintended consequence.

Most state parties decided that substituting primaries for their traditional process was the easiest way to meet the new requirements for broadened participation. The number of states holding primaries nearly doubled from 17 in 1968 to 30 in 1976.

According to the late Austin Ranney, a political scientist who served on the commission, "We hoped to prevent any such development by reforming the delegate-selection rules so that the party's non-primary processes would be open and fair, participation in them would greatly increase, and consequently the demand for more primaries would fade away. . . . We achieved the opposite of what we intended." [1] By 2008, when Barack Obama outran Hillary Rodham Clinton for the presidential nomination, 40 states held Democratic presidential primaries. While populist demand to overhaul the process was not as great among Republicans, the GOP went along with the changes in most states: This year, Republican delegates will be allocated based on primary results in 39 states.

The nominating campaign as we know it today developed in stages. The caucuses in Iowa nudged ahead of the New Hampshire primary — the first major event in each party since 1948 — after McGovern in 1972 and Jimmy Carter in 1976 each used a strong showing there as a springboard to the Democratic nomination. Then, in the 1980s, several states began scheduling their events for a single day early in the campaign, dubbed "Super Tuesday."

in the future. The rise of a radical Islamic regime in Iran, where 52 Americans were held hostage for more than a year starting in November 1979, contributed greatly to Reagan's presidential victory over Democratic incumbent Jimmy Carter in 1980.

After weathering a deep recession early in his presidency, Reagan benefited from a sharp economic rebound, and his optimistic evocation of America as a "shining city on the hill" led to a temporary uptick in the public's faith in government. But even on Reagan's watch, the once-dominant manufacturing sector was losing major ground to foreign competition, and middle-class economic woes shaping today's presidential election were beginning to grow.

By 1992, public distrust of politicians was solidifying. George H. W. Bush, Reagan's Republican successor, was denied a second term by Democrat Clinton, who garnered 43 percent of the popular vote to Bush's 37 percent. H. Ross Perot, a quirky billionaire playing on voters' dissatisfaction with both parties, took 19 percent.

The political pendulum then took a quick swing in 1994, as conservative Republicans broke the Democrats' 40-year hold on the House and gained control of the Senate.

Clinton rebounded and won re-election, aided by strong economic growth and a sense among most Americans that congressional Republicans, led by Gingrich, were pushing too fast

In more recent years, the competition for clout intensified, resulting in a practice called "frontloading," in which more and more states crowded their nominating events into the early months of the election year.

Resentment in some states toward the outsized influence of Iowa and New Hampshire prompted an increasing number to try to leapfrog to the head of the calendar. Iowa, which held its 2012 caucuses on Jan. 3, and New Hampshire, which held its primary a week later, responded by moving their events earlier and earlier.

Frontloading also pushed up Super Tuesday. In 2008, the busiest primary and caucus day — when Democratic parties in 22 states and Republican parties in 20 states held events — came on February 5.

Julian Wasser/Time-Life Pictures/Getty Images

Police remove a demonstrator from a statue in Grant Park during the 1968 Democratic National Convention in Chicago.

In every election since its inception 40 years ago, the primary-driven process has enabled a candidate in each party to clinch the party's nomination well before its convention. While the 2008 Democratic campaign lasted all the way to the end of the primary season in June before Clinton conceded to Obama, that was an exception: Sen. John McCain, who won the 2008 Republican nomination, gained unstoppable momentum by running well in the February Super Tuesday contests and eliminated his last serious challenger by early March.

The early-decision tendency, in turn, stripped the summer conventions of their decision-making role, turning them into what has been described as "four-day infomercials" for the parties.

Most political analysts expect one of the candidates in this year's crowded Republican field to galvanize enough support to lock up the nomination. But a month into the primary and caucus season, none of the Republican contenders had yet been established as the runaway favorite. (In fact, former Pennsylvania Sen. Rick Santorum won in Iowa, former Massachusetts Gov. Mitt Romney won in New Hampshire and former House Speaker Newt Gingrich won in South Carolina.)

This creates at least the potential for the Republican convention in Tampa Aug. 27-30 to be thrust into a now-unaccustomed role of deciding who the party's nominee will be.

At the least, it should take longer than has become usual for anyone to clinch the nomination. Though previous efforts to comprehensively overhaul the process have failed, the GOP did take steps to reverse the frontloading trend.

As a result, this year's Super Tuesday has 10 state events scheduled, only half as many as in 2008, and, California, the nation's most populous and delegate-rich state, moved its primary all the way back from Feb. 5 in 2008 to June 5 this year.

— Bob Benenson

[1] Bob Benenson, ed., "Presidential Selection Reforms," in *Elections A to Z*, 3rd ed. (2007), CQ Press.

on their conservative agenda. But revelations that Clinton lied about an extramarital affair with White House intern Monica Lewinsky, which led to his impeachment by the House and acquittal by the Senate, again rocked Americans' confidence in the presidency.

Partisan Divide

Given the weak foundation of support with which public officials entered the new century, it may not be hard to see why the electorate is so deeply divided along partisan lines today.

The terrorist attacks in 2001 temporary rallied the nation around President George W. Bush, who was less than a year into his first term. His decision to use military force to evict the Islamist Taliban government in Afghanistan, which had harbored al Qaeda leader Osama bin Laden, drew strong popular support. But national unity evaporated after Bush decided to invade Iraq in 2003 on grounds that dictator Saddam Hussein was stockpiling weapons of mass destruction. When that claim proved false, public opinion turned strongly against Bush, who won a narrow re-election victory in 2004 but saw his approval ratings plummet.

Bush also faced severe criticisms over a delayed and faltering response to Hurricane Katrina, which devastated New Orleans in August 2005.

Meanwhile, many Republican activists had become increasingly dissatisfied with what they viewed as "big-government conservatism" under Bush, embodied by a rising national debt, an increased federal oversight role in state and local education and the creation of an expensive prescription-drug benefit for Medicare recipients.

Liberals' rejection of Bush and policies of his fellow Republicans helped spark a Democratic recapture of Congress in 2006 and propelled Obama into the White House in 2008. But the glow of victory was short-lived, as many Americans resisted Democrats' assertions that they had a mandate to push for a progressive political agenda. The economic crash, which unfolded as Obama was elected and prepared to take office, only added to the pressure on the Democrats.

In Congress, partisanship was in full bloom. Despite the Republicans' big gains in the 2010 midterm elections, they controlled only the House, setting up a climate of bitter confrontation with the Democratic-controlled Senate and Obama White House. Pitched battles in spring 2011 over a much-delayed spending bill for the remainder of that fiscal year threatened to cause a shutdown of non-essential federal government operations. Republicans ultimately agreed to a measure that would cut about $40 billion from current spending levels but made it clear that they regarded that as a small down payment on bigger cuts.

Obama and Republican leaders, most prominently House Speaker John A. Boehner of Ohio, held negotiations on a possible "grand bargain" that would have mainly featured spending reductions but also some tax increases. But the effort failed amid plenty of finger-pointing.

The possibility of a bipartisan agreement to slash the deficit got another airing after Republicans balked last summer at raising the federal debt ceiling to enable the government to pay its bills. Obama administration officials and many economists warned that failing to raise the ceiling would cause a default, tarnish the nation's creditworthiness and possibly set back the economic recovery. But House Republicans held firm almost to the end. They agreed to raise the ceiling at the 11th hour, and only after the White House committed to $2.4 trillion in deficit reduction over 10 years.

How those reductions were going to be made was left uncertain, however. A bipartisan congressional "super-committee" charged with reaching a deal broke down along party lines in late November.

The final partisan confrontation of 2011 came in December, and it was one in which Obama and his fellow Democrats appeared to gain an unusually clear political advantage that may yet pay dividends in this year's election. A Social Security payroll-tax reduction that had been part of Obama's economic stimulus program was due to expire at the end of the year. When it became clear that agreement on how to pay for a long-term extension could not be reached before that date, Obama and Senate Republican leaders agreed on a two-month extension of the payroll tax break, but House Republicans rejected the plan.

That stance proved problematic, especially in a presidential election year. Some Republicans worried that the House majority, which staunchly opposed efforts to raise taxes on the wealthiest Americans, was picking the wrong fight on a tax issue that affected most of the nation's workers.

Boehner and the other House Republican leaders ended up yielding, and a two-month extension was approved, but not before political damage was done. Conservative columnist Charles Krauthammer wrote that "the Democrats set a trap and the Republicans walked right into it. By rejecting an ostensibly bipartisan 'compromise,' the Republican House was portrayed as obstructionist and, even worse, heartless — willing to raise taxes on the middle class while resolutely opposing any tax increases on the rich." [28] ■

CURRENT SITUATION

Income Inequality

Many observers believe that economic fairness, more than any other issue, may bolster Obama's re-election chances.

"The Obama campaign has at least one major card to play," says Michigan State's Ballard. "They can emphasize issues regarding income inequality. The No. 1 weapon of the Obama camp is the steady Republican opposition to higher taxes on millionaires. They would say, 'the Republicans are looking out for the fat cats; we need someone to look out for the average guy.' "

The backlash against income inequality has at least complicated Romney's efforts to win the Republican nomination. He has argued that his business background makes him uniquely qualified to get the nation's economy back on track as president. But his longstanding reluctance to disclose the extent of his wealth, his reluctant release of tax-return data showing he made $45 million in two years from investments and his work at Bain that sometimes cost workers their jobs have all put him on the defensive.

Obama has sought to mine political capital from Romney's wealth. While he did not mention Romney by name in his State of the Union address, Obama seemed to have the GOP candidate in his sights when he called for "an economy where everyone gets a fair shot, and everyone does their

Continued on p. 118

At Issue:

Should campaign-finance regulations be tightened?

BOB EDGAR
PRESIDENT AND CEO, COMMON CAUSE

WRITTEN FOR *CQ RESEARCHER*, FEBRUARY 2012

yes

It's only February, and we're neck deep in presidential campaign sludge. Winning Our Future, a SuperPAC supporting Newt Gingrich, has produced a 30-minute "documentary" film brimming with half-truths, and absolute lies, about Mitt Romney. Restore Our Future, run by friends of Romney, is airing an ad falsely accusing Gingrich of supporting the Chinese government's "one-child" policy. The U.S. Chamber of Commerce is running ads that the nonpartisan website FactCheck.org says deliver false attacks against at least two Democratic senators.

Everyone understands that much more, and much worse, is still to come.

Thank the Supreme Court. Its *Citizens United* decision two years ago opened the floodgates for corporations to dump hundreds of millions of dollars — as much as they want, really — into our elections. All that corporate money, plus donations from super-rich individuals turned loose by an earlier court ruling that money is speech, is behind the falsehoods now polluting our airwaves.

Between *Citizens United*, the dysfunctional Federal Election Commission, a Congress deadlocked over disclosure requirements and a year of presidential dawdling over a draft executive order on disclosure of political spending by government contractors, special interests essentially are running loose in the 2012 campaign. Just wait until next year, when all these political investors come to Washington to collect on their gifts to the new Congress: The corruption will make Watergate look like petty crime.

At Common Cause, we're persuaded we need long- and short-term fixes to address the flood of corporate money in politics. In the immediate future, we need to push for more disclosure around political spending and for passage in Congress of a clean elections-style federal public-financing system. We need to push for shareholder resolutions to assure that shareholders have a say, and are knowledgeable about, corporate political spending.

In the long term, the way to start fixing this broken system is a constitutional amendment declaring that corporations aren't people, money isn't speech and Congress has authority to set limits on political spending. Common Cause recently launched Amend 2012, a national campaign to put people back in charge. We're hoping to force a vote, eventually in every state, on a ballot question in which Americans could instruct their senators and representatives in Washington to pass an amendment and submit it to the states for ratification. We're convinced, sadly, that Congress won't act until the people demand it.

HANS A. VON SPAKOVSKY
SENIOR LEGAL FELLOW, HERITAGE FOUNDATION; FORMER MEMBER, FEDERAL ELECTION COMMISSION

WRITTEN FOR *CQ RESEARCHER*, FEBRUARY 2012

no

Campaign-finance regulations should not be tightened. The greatest liberty we have is the ability to engage in political speech and political activity, individually or in association with others, as well as to "petition the Government for a redress of grievances" (in modern terms, lobbying). The *Citizens United* decision restored vital First Amendment rights.

The federal ban on independent political expenditures and restrictions on "electioneering communications" (broadcast ads that simply mentioned a candidate close to an election) were some of the worst restrictions on political activity since the Alien and Sedition Acts of 1798. We should welcome more political speech by corporations and labor unions. The more speech we have in the political marketplace, the better off we are. No government agency or bureaucrat should be empowered to censor political speech — which is exactly what the Federal Election Commission did prior to the *Citizens United* decision.

As for the alleged "secrecy" regarding SuperPAC spending — balderdash. SuperPACs have to disclose political expenditures and all $200-plus donors just like candidates and other PACs. Certain nonprofit associations like the NAACP and the NRA don't have to disclose all of their donors (although they have to disclose their political spending).

But they are membership organizations composed of individuals who associate together because they share common beliefs. Election politics is not their primary activity as it is for political PACs. As the Supreme Court said in *NAACP v. Alabama*, the privacy of donating to issue organizations is "indispensable to preservation of freedom . . . particularly where a group espouses dissident beliefs."

Through such organizations, average Americans with limited means can make their voices heard. Does anyone watching a political ad from the NRA or the NAACP really not know who those organizations are?

And if labor unions or corporations believe a particular candidate's position on issues will harm their members, employees or shareholders, shouldn't they be able to inform voters of their opinions? The response of critics should not be to censor that speech but to inform voters of their countervailing views.

Campaign-finance restrictions help incumbents and stifle competition. It was in 2010, after *Citizens United*, that we had the most competitive congressional elections since the 1930s.

And don't forget, the government actually argued that Congress could extend the "electioneering communication" restriction to books. Imagine Americans imprisoned for writing political books.

Continued from p. 116

fair share, and everyone plays by the same set of rules." [29]

"Romney, whom the president's aides still view as his most likely opponent in the fall, was the unspoken adversary in Mr. Obama's call for a more equitable society," *The New York Times* said. [30]

Yet the economy will remain a cloud over Obama's re-election chances unless the recovery accelerates quickly, which appears unlikely. A day after Obama's speech, the Federal Reserve said it was likely to keep short-term interest rates near zero until the end of 2014, signaling that a full recovery from the 2008 crash remains distant. [31] An unfolding economic crisis in Europe makes the economic outlook especially dicey.

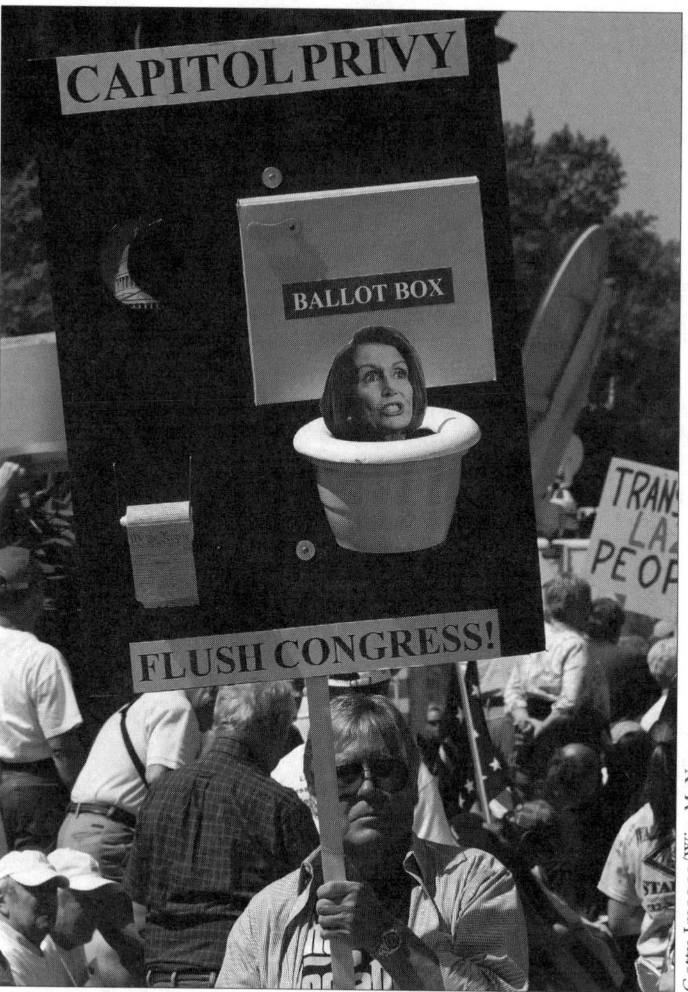

Getty Images/Win McNamee

Tea Party supporters protest in Washington, D.C., on April 15, 2010 — the deadline for Americans to file their income tax returns. The conservative Tea Party and populist Occupy movement against income inequality are shaping campaign rhetoric and could sway the election's outcome.

Republicans are wasting no time in capitalizing on the nation's persistent economic woes, however. In the GOP response to the State of the Union address, Indiana Gov. Mitch Daniels said that while Obama "did not cause the economic and fiscal crises," he "cannot claim that the last three years have made things anything but worse."

"The president's grand experiment in trickle-down government has held back rather than sped economic recovery," Daniels said. "He seems to sincerely believe we can build a middle class out of government jobs paid for with borrowed dollars. In fact, it works the other way: A government as big and bossy as this one is maintained on the backs of the middle class, and those who hope to join it." [32]

The political environment in which Obama is seeking a second term is starkly different from the one in which he ran four years ago. In his 2008 election, Obama capped a meteoric political rise that began only four years earlier when he delivered a dynamic keynote address to the Democratic National Convention and then won an election that sent him from relative obscurity in the Illinois state Senate to a U.S. Senate seat. With his rhetorical emphasis on "hope," "change" and a "Yes We Can" attitude, along with the historic nature of his bid to become the nation's first African-American president, Obama inspired millions.

But this time around, his GOP rivals have sought to use his political legacy against him. Gingrich, campaigning in Florida in late January on the heels of his big win in South Carolina, said Obama should stop blaming his Republican predecessor for the nation's economic problems. "This is the fourth year of his presidency," Gingrich said. "He needs to get over it. A friend of mine says, 'He has shifted from Yes We Can to Why We Couldn't.' " [33]

Senate Battles

Democrats may need not only an Obama victory, but a strong one, to hold on to their fragile majority in the Senate. They must defend 23 seats compared with only 10 for the Republicans.

The Democrats' majority in the Senate of 53 seats to the Republicans' 47 is narrow enough that it would be considered tenuous under most circumstances. The Republicans would need a modest net gain of three seats to gain control if their nominee for president defeats Obama. That is because vice presidents serve as president of the Senate and can cast a tie-breaking vote in favor of their party.

Should Obama win re-election and keep the vice presidency in Democratic hands, the Republicans would need a four-seat gain.

Democrats are defending three seats they won in 2006 by very narrow margins: in Virginia, where Jim Webb upset incumbent George Allen by four-tenths of a percentage point; Montana, where Jon Tester edged incumbent Conrad Burns by less than 1 point; and Missouri, where Claire McCaskill unseated Jim Talent by a bit more than 2 points.

Complicating Democrats' efforts to maintain their Senate majority are the pending retirements of seven of 23 Democratic incumbents.

Most at risk are the open seats in two Farm Belt states that otherwise lean strongly Republican: Nebraska, where Ben Nelson is retiring after 12 years in the Senate; and North Dakota, where Kent Conrad, chairman of the Senate Budget Committee, is ending a 26-year Senate career.

"Democrats look like underdogs in North Dakota and Nebraska," says Gonzales of the *Rothenberg Political Report*.

In addition, Webb's decision to serve only one six-year term appeared to raise the Democrats' vulnerability in Virginia, where Republican Allen is angling for a comeback. Republican strategists also hope to make a serious run at seats left open by retiring Democrats Herb Kohl of Wisconsin, Daniel K. Akaka of Hawaii and Jeff Bingaman of New Mexico, who would have been heavy favorites had they run again.

And while Connecticut leans strongly Democratic, Republicans are eying the seat of retiring Joseph I. Lieberman, an Independent since 2006 who caucuses in the Senate with the Democrats, his former party.

On top of these contests, Republicans are banking on the partisan tide continuing to run in their favor as they prepare for serious challenges to Democratic incumbents Bill Nelson of Florida, Debbie Stabenow of Michigan and, possibly, Sherrod Brown of Ohio.

It is far from certain, though, that the Republicans will be able to achieve the gains they need to wrest control of the Senate from the Democrats. While the Senate majority is definitely in play, it is too early to predict the outcome of key races, analysts say.

"Lopsided exposure is a killer," says Faucheux of Clarus Research, referring to the fact that the Democrats have more than twice as many seats to defend as the Republicans. "There are more than enough pick-up opportunities for Republicans to win a majority, although many of these opportunities remain close calls."

House Comeback?

It is symbolic of this particularly volatile period that a Democratic comeback in the House cannot be ruled out, even as the party faces a mighty challenge to maintain its control of the Senate.

The Republicans hold 242 House seats to the Democrats' 192. A bare majority of 218 seats is needed to claim control of the House, so the Republicans have a 24-seat cushion, pending the outcome of an upcoming Arizona special election to replace Democrat Gabrielle Giffords, who resigned to continue her recovery from a gunshot wound.

By the standards of more stable eras, a 25-seat gain would be a daunting target for the Democrats. In the five House election cycles after 1994 — when the Republicans surged to a net gain of 52 seats — the biggest switch was a six-seat gain for the Republicans in 2002.

But, in comparison to the wild swings over the past six years, a 25-seat Democratic gain does not seem inconceivable. Democrats gained 30 seats in 2006 and 21 in 2008. Republicans enjoyed a 63-seat rebound in 2010.

Because that 2010 Republican surge was so big, many election analysts do not believe the GOP has room for significant additional House gains this year. "Republicans are probably at their high-water mark in the House, so I think it's natural that they lose some seats and come back to reality," Gonzales says.

The Democrats' hopes in their "Drive for 25" could well be tied to whether an improved economy and other issues enable Obama to enjoy a timely election-year rebound in public approval.

"If the economy is still down or people are unhappy with [the Obama-backed health care plan passed in 2010] or if it's going to be a tough race, candidates may want to distance themselves from Obama," says the University of Iowa's Hagle. "If the economy is improving, then they will want him to campaign with them. The point is that without that enthusiasm for the top of the ticket, it would be that much harder for the minority party to regain control of the House." ■

OUTLOOK

Seizing the Opportunity

Obama's State of the Union address sent strong signals about the strategy he intends to employ in his re-election campaign. His calls for greater economic fairness made it clear that he would try to seize the opportunity presented by the increased discussion of income inequality. But he also touted some proposals that appeared aimed at softening the hard-line opposition he has faced from Republicans.

For instance, he promoted expanded extraction of domestic energy resources, including oil, natural gas and clean coal; proposed a new trade-enforcement unit with an emphasis on Chinese practices that harm American businesses, an issue that Romney and some other Republicans have been hitting hard; and called for increased use of public-private partnerships to better target job-training and career-development programs.

While it is highly unlikely that partisan infighting in Washington is going to suddenly cease, especially in the midst of a bitterly contested election campaign, Obama's proposals seem oriented to at least put his Republican adversaries on the defensive. From that perspective, they are part of an ongoing effort that included his address to Congress last Sept. 8 in which he laid out a multipart jobs package with the refrain "Pass this bill now!" and his push in December to persuade House Republicans to drop their resistance to extending the payroll tax cut.

Conservatives, however, were largely unimpressed by Obama's State of the Union address. "It made Bill Clinton's notoriously endless lists of poll-tested banalities look like artistry by comparison," wrote Rich Lowry, editor of the conservative *National Review.* [34]

Should Obama win re-election, it will give him leverage in dealing with Congress, even if the Republicans end up with control of the House, the Senate, or both. And there is the possibility that a strong rebound by Obama could restore Democrats to full control of the federal policymaking apparatus — just as a bad showing by Obama could result in Republican control.

Both recent history and the unpopularity of both parties at this moment suggest that some form of divided government is the most likely outcome. Over the past 32 years since Reagan's 1980 election, there has been one-party control of the federal government for only nine and a half years.

But both parties and political pundits will be closely watching polls to see if there is a major shift in sentiment among the politically crucial constituency of independent voters, the group some pundits said Obama's State of the Union speech targeted most specifically. Obama does not necessarily need to win back everyone who voted for him in 2008, as he won the overall popular vote by 53 percent to 46 percent and took 365 electoral votes to McCain's 173. But it appears he needs to reconnect with at least some of the independents who have turned against him if he is to avoid a very close election — or even a loss.

Republicans, though, have their own worries, not the least of which is the possibility that their combative presidential nominating campaign will not deliver a clear winner — producing the first "brokered" convention in either party since 1952.

Many political observers think a nominee will emerge before the GOP holds its convention in Tampa in August, but Michael Steele, the former Republican Party chairman, laid down 50-50 odds of a brokered convention.

"The [Republican] base wants its chance to have their say," Steele said on the night of the South Carolina primary. "They aren't going to want it to end early." [35] ■

About the Author

Bob Benenson is a freelance journalist who specializes in political analysis. Before recently moving with his wife to Chicago, he covered presidential and congressional politics at Congressional Quarterly (now CQ Roll Call), where he served as CQ's politics editor and head of its election coverage team from 1998 to 2009. He also worked for ABC Radio News in New York City and as a reporter at *Editorial Research Reports* (now *CQ Researcher*). He graduated from Michigan State University.

Notes

[1] For background see Peter Katel, "Tea Party Movement," *CQ Researcher*, March 19, 2010, updated May 23, 2011, pp. 241-264; and " 'Occupy' Movement," *CQ Researcher*, Jan. 13, 2012, pp. 25-52.

[2] "President Obama: Job Ratings," *The Polling Report*, www.pollingreport.com/obama_job.htm.

[3] *The Polling Report* compiles multiple polls on congressional job approval at www.pollingreport.com/CongJob.htm. An ABC News-*Washington Post* survey, conducted Jan. 12-15, showed just 21 percent of respondents approved of congressional Republicans, while 75 percent disapproved. Ratings for congressional Democrats were also poor, but better: 33 percent approval and 62 percent disapproval. See also, Gary Langer, "Congress Hits a New Low in Approval; Obama Opens Election Year Under 50 Percent," ABC News, Jan. 16, 2012, http://abcnews.go.com/blogs/politics/2012/01/congress-hits-a-new-low-in-approval-obama-opens-election-year-under-50/.

[4] ABC News, http://abcnews.go.com/Blotter/video/marianne-gingrich-says-newt-gingrich-wanted-open-marriage-15392793.

[5] Eric Pianin, "Romney Clobbers Gingrich in Florida Blood Feud," *The Fiscal Times*, Feb. 1, 2012, www.thefiscaltimes.com/Articles/2012/02/01/Romney-Clobbers-Gingrich-in-Florida-Blood-Feud.aspx#page1.

[6] Michael D. Shear, Jeff Zeleny and Jim Rutenberg, "Romney Tax Returns Show 2-Year Income of $45 Million," *The New York Times*, Jan. 24, 2012, http://thecaucus.blogs.nytimes.com/2012/01/24/romney-tax-returns-to-give-view-of-family-wealth/?hp.

[7] Glen Johnson, "Mitt Romney says net worth is about $200 million," *The Boston Globe*, Jan. 25, 2012, www.boston.com/Boston/politicalintelligence/2012/01/mitt-romney-says-net-worth-about-million/QYUE2XtKi7rrMubEGYrnwL/index.html.

[8] Binyamin Appelbaum, "Fed Signals That a Full Recovery Is Years Away," *The New York Times*, Jan. 25, 2012, www.nytimes.com/2012/01/26/business/economy/fed-to-maintain-rates-near-zero-through-late-2014.html?hp.

[9] Jeff Zeleny and Dalia Sussman, "Poll Shows Obama's Vulnerability With Swing Voters," *The New York Times*, Jan. 18, 2012, www.nytimes.com/2012/01/19/us/politics/poll-shows-obamas-vulnerability-with-swing-voters.html?scp=1&sq=%22poll%20shows%20obama's%20vulnerability%22&st=cse.

[10] For background, see Peter Katel, " 'Occupy' Movement," *CQ Researcher*, Jan. 13, 2012, pp. 25-52.
[11] "Frustration with Congress Could Hurt Republican Incumbents," Pew Research Center for the People and the Press, Dec. 15, 2011, www.people-press.org/2011/12/15/frustration-with-congress-could-hurt-republican-incumbents/.
[12] "Remarks by the President in State of the Union Address," White House, Jan. 24, 2012, www.whitehouse.gov/the-press-office/2012/01/24/remarks-president-state-union-address.
[13] See for example, "Estimated Impact of the American Recovery and Reinvestment Act on Employment and Economic Output from July 2011 to September 2011," Congressional Budget Office, November 2011, www.cbo.gov/ftpdocs/125xx/doc12564/11-22-ARRA.pdf.
[14] Lisa Lerer and Laura Litvan, "No Congress Since '60s Makes As Much Law As 111th Affecting Most Americans," Bloomberg News, Dec. 22, 2010, www.bloomberg.com/news/2010-12-22/no-congress-since-1960s-makes-most-laws-for-americans-as-111th.html.
[15] Emily Ethridge, "Ever More Polarized, Parties Set Records," *CQ Weekly*, Jan. 16, 2012, pp. 111-121.
[16] For background, see the following *CQ Researcher* reports: Kenneth Jost, "Campaign Finance Debates," May 28, 2010, pp. 457-480; Thomas J. Billitteri, "Campaign Finance Reform," June 13, 2008, pp. 505-528; and Kenneth Jost, "Campaign Finance Showdown," Nov. 22, 2002, pp. 969-992.
[17] "Super PACs," Center for Responsive Politics, January 2012, www.opensecrets.org/pacs/superpacs.php?ql3.
[18] "Independent Spending Totals," Election 2012, *The New York Times.com*, http://elections.nytimes.com/2012/campaign-finance/independent-expenditures/totals.
[19] Robert Reich, "Mitt, Son of Citizens United," *The Huffington Post*, Jan. 16, 2012, www.huffingtonpost.com/robert-reich/mitt-romney-restore-our-future-citizens-united_b_1189024.html.
[20] John Samples, "Super PACs Enhance Democracy," *U.S. News & World Report*, Jan. 13, 2012, www.usnews.com/debate-club/are-super-pacs-harming-us-politics/super-pacs-enhance-democracy-super-pacs-enhance-democracy.
[21] Trevor Burrus, " 'Wrong' Speech Is Also Free Speech: Citizens United at Two," *The Huffington Post*, Jan. 24, 2012, www.huffingtonpost.com/trevor-burrus/citizens-united-anniversary_b_1229013.html.
[22] Alex Leary, "Super PACs Reshaping 2012 Presidential Campaign," *Tampa Bay Times*, Jan. 27, 2012, www.tampabay.com/news/politics/national/super-pacs-reshaping-2012-presidential-campaign/1212559.
[23] Henry Olsen, "Populism, American Style," *National Affairs*, summer 2010, www.nationalaffairs.com/publications/detail/populism-american-style.
[24] *Ibid.*
[25] "Public Trust in Government: 1958-2010," Pew Research Center for the People and the Press, www.people-press.org/2010/04/18/public-trust-in-government-1958-2010/.
[26] *Ibid.*
[27] "Fewer are Angry at Government, But Discontent Remains High," Pew Research Center for the People and the Press, March 3, 2011, www.people-press.org/2011/03/03/section-1-attitudes-about-government/.
[28] Charles Krauthammer, "The GOP's Payroll-Tax Debacle," *National Review Online*, Dec. 23, 2011, www.nationalreview.com/articles/286595/gop-s-payroll-tax-debacle-charles-krauthammer.
[29] White House, *op. cit.*
[30] Mark Landler, "Critiques for Capitalists in Obama's Speech, With One in Particular in His Sights," *The New York Times*, Jan. 25, 2012, www.nytimes.com/2012/01/25/us/politics/obama-sets-sights-on-romney-in-state-of-the-union.html?hpw.
[31] Appelbaum, *op. cit.*
[32] "Mitch Daniels' Republican response to State of the Union Speech," NBC Politics, Jan. 24, 2012, http://nbcpolitics.msnbc.msn.com/_news/2012/01/24/10229239-mitch-daniels-republican-response-to-state-of-the-union-speech.
[33] Brian Bakst, "Drawing thousands, Gingrich goes hardest at Obama," The Associated Press, Jan. 24, 2012, www.boston.com/news/local/massachusetts/articles/2012/01/24/drawing_thousands_gingrich_goes_hardest_at_obama/.
[34] Rich Lowry, "Obama's Proposals Evasive and Irresponsible," Fox News.com, Jan. 24, 2012, http://nation.foxnews.com/state-union-address/2012/01/25/opinion-obama-state-union-proposals-evasive-irresponsible#ixzz1kfY1xJrx.
[35] Howard Fineman, "Republican Convention Has '50-50' Chance Of Being Open: Former GOP Chair," *The Huffington Post*, Jan. 21, 2012, www.huffingtonpost.com/2012/01/21/republican-convention-mitt-romney-south-carolina-primary_n_1221350.html.

FOR MORE INFORMATION

Cato Institute, 1000 Massachusetts Ave., N.W., Washington, DC 20001; 202-842-0200; www.cato.org. Libertarian think tank supporting less regulation of campaign fundraising and spending.

Center for Responsive Politics, 1101 14th St., N.W., Suite 1030, Washington, DC 20005; 202-857-0044; www.opensecrets.org. Nonpartisan group that collects, analyzes and publishes campaign-finance data.

Common Cause, 1133 19th St., N.W., Ninth Floor, Washington, DC 20036; 202-833-1200; www.commoncause.org. Public-interest group favoring tighter regulation of campaign fundraising and spending; promotes a constitutional amendment to rein in SuperPACs.

Democratic National Committee, 430 S. Capitol St., S.E., Washington, DC 20003; 202-863-8000; www.democrats.org. Central governing organization of the national Democratic Party.

Federal Election Commission, 999 E St., N.W., Washington, DC 20463; 202-694-1000; www.fec.gov. Government agency regulating campaign finance spending.

Gallup Organization, 901 F St., N.W., Washington, DC 20004; 202-715-3030; www.gallup.com. One of the nation's oldest public-opinion polling firms.

Pew Research Center for the People and the Press, 1615 L St., N.W., Suite 700, Washington, DC 20036; 202-419-4300; www.people-press.org. Nonpartisan public opinion research organization studying attitudes toward politics and public policy issues.

Republican National Committee, 310 First St., S.E., Washington, DC 20003; 202-863-8500; www.gop.com. Central governing organization of the national Republican Party.

Bibliography

Selected Sources

Books

Barone, Michael, and Chuck McCutcheon, *The Almanac of American Politics 2012*, The University of Chicago Press, 2011.
The biennial guide to Congress and U.S. politics includes analysis of the big Republican sweep in the 2010 elections, profiles of each member of Congress and political statistics about each state and district.

Bicknell, John, and David Meyers, eds., *Politics in America 2012: 112th Congress*, CQ Roll Call, 2011.
A counterpart to the *Almanac of American Politics*, this biennial edition also provides analysis of the 2010 elections, profiles of congressional members and data.

Heilemann, John, and Mark Halperin, *Game Change: Obama and the Clintons, McCain and Palin, and the Race of a Lifetime*, Harper, 2010.
Veteran political journalists Heilemann of *New York* magazine and Halperin of *Time* provide a narrative of Barack Obama's historic 2008 presidential campaign.

O'Hara, John M., *A New American Tea Party: The Counterrevolution Against Bailouts, Handouts, Reckless Spending and More Taxes*, Wiley, 2010.
A Tea Party organizer and activist discusses the conservative movement's rise and its policy agenda.

Plouffe, David, *The Audacity to Win: The Inside Story and Lessons of Barack Obama's Historic Victory*, Viking Adult, 2009.
Obama's chief campaign strategist wrote this insider's perspective on the 2008 campaign. The title plays off Obama's 2006 book, *The Audacity of Hope: Thoughts on Reclaiming the America Dream* (Crown).

Zernike, Kate, *Boiling Mad: Inside Tea Party America*, Times Books, 2010.
A *New York Times* reporter who covered the rise of the Tea Party examines the movement.

Articles

Ethridge, Emily, "Ever More Polarized, Parties Set Records," *CQ Weekly*, Jan. 16, 2012, pp. 111-121.
An analysis of the votes cast by House and Senate members in 2011 underscores the deep divisions between Republican and Democratic lawmakers.

Olsen, Henry, "Populism, American Style," *National Affairs*, summer 2010, www.nationalaffairs.com/publications/detail/populism-american-style.
A vice president of the conservative American Enterprise Institute reviews the history of populist movements in the United States and concludes that the public's inherent aversion to extremism has allowed radical factions to influence the nation's political system without overturning it.

Reich, Robert, "Mitt, Son of Citizens United," *The Huffington Post*, Jan. 6, 2012, www.huffingtonpost.com/robert-reich/mitt-romney-restore-our-future-citizens-united_b_1189024.html.
The former Labor secretary under President Bill Clinton takes a negative view of SuperPACs.

Samples, John, "Super PACs Enhance Democracy," *U.S. News & World Report*, Jan. 13, 2012, www.usnews.com/debate-club/are-super-pacs-harming-us-politics/super-pacs-enhance-democracy-super-pacs-enhance-democracy.
An executive at the libertarian Cato Institute defends SuperPACs as representing the constitutional guarantee of free speech.

Silver, Nate, "On The Maddeningly Inexact Relationship Between Unemployment and Re-Election," *The New York Times*, June 2, 2011, http://fivethirtyeight.blogs.nytimes.com/2011/06/02/on-the-maddeningly-inexact-relationship-between-unemployment-and-re-election/.
A leading statistical analyst of election trends explores the degree to which the unemployment rate is a leading indicator of an incumbent's re-election prospects.

Reports and Studies

"Distrust, Discontent, Anger and Partisan Rancor," Pew Research Center for the People and the Press, April 18, 2010, www.people-press.org/2010/04/18/distrust-discontent-anger-and-partisan-rancor/.
The nonpartisan center analyzes the history and reasons for widespread public anger with government, with polling data on trust in government dating to 1958.

"Fiscal Year 2012 Historical Tables," Budget of the U.S. Government, U.S. Office of Management and Budget, www.whitehouse.gov/sites/default/files/omb/budget/fy2012/assets/hist.pdf.
This addendum to the Obama administration's fiscal year 2012 budget proposal contains rich historical detail about federal spending and revenues.

"Frustration with Congress Could Hurt Republican Incumbents," Pew Research Center for the People and the Press, Dec. 15, 2011, www.people-press.org/2011/12/15/frustration-with-congress-could-hurt-republican-incumbents/.
The center analyzes the nation's political landscape entering the 2012 election campaign, including the unpopularity of Republicans in Congress, the public's top policy priorities and the political impact of the Occupy Wall Street movement.

The Next Step:

Additional Articles from Current Periodicals

Economy

Bennett, George, "Historical 'Keys' Favor Obama Despite Economy," *Palm Beach* (Fla.) *Post*, Aug. 21, 2011, p. A1, www.palmbeachpost.com/news/state/despite-weak-economy-history-professors-system-predicts-obama-1768593.html.
More than 150 years of electoral precedent make Obama a strong favorite for re-election whether or not the economy improves, according to a political historian.

Geiger, Kim, and Dan Eggen, "Obama Hangs His Reelection on the Economy," *Los Angeles Times*, Aug. 22, 2011, p. A7, articles.latimes.com/2011/aug/21/nation/la-na-obama-economy-20110822.
President Obama doesn't foresee another recession but says his re-election hopes hinge on an economic recovery.

Sommer, Jeff, "Through an Economic Lens, an Election Too Close to Call," *The New York Times*, Jan. 8, 2012, p. BU4, www.nytimes.com/2012/01/08/your-money/an-election-too-close-to-call-as-seen-in-an-economic-lens.html?pagewanted=all.
The economy will be a significant factor in determining which party wins the election.

Nominating Process

Gitz, Bradley R., "No More People Power," *Arkansas Democrat-Gazette*, Jan. 16, 2012.
The vast majority of Republicans have no real power in the presidential nominating process because results from Iowa and New Hampshire essentially determine the nominee, according to a freelance columnist.

Hallow, Ralph Z., "New Rules Turn GOP Race From Sprint Into Marathon," *The Washington Times*, Nov. 21, 2011, p. A1, www.washingtontimes.com/news/2011/nov/20/new-rules-turn-gop-race-from-sprint-into-marathon/?page=all.
Less frontloading in the GOP primary calendar will make it tougher to quickly clinch the nomination.

Jakubowicz, Robert, "This Is No Way to Choose a President," *Berkshire Eagle* (Pittsfield, Mass.), Jan. 11, 2012.
The GOP nominating process is dominated by political activists with extreme conservative views in early primary states, according to a Massachusetts attorney.

Political Gridlock

Dunkelman, Marc, "Gridlock: Maybe It's Our Fault," *Pittsburgh Post-Gazette*, July 17, 2011, p. F1, www.post-gazette.com/pg/11198/1160646-109-0.stm.
Gridlock is partly a result of Americans' unwillingness to familiarize themselves with the struggles of fellow citizens, according to a former Democratic House staffer.

Eachus, Ron, "Senate Democrats Can Blame Only Themselves," *Statesman Journal* (Salem, Ore.), Feb. 1, 2011, p. C5.
Some Republicans say Democratic Senate leaders have rejected filibuster reforms that could have ended partisan gridlock.

Trumbull, Mark, "Obama Casts Congress As the Problem, Tells Americans to 'Let Them Know,'" *The Christian Science Monitor*, Aug. 13, 2011, www.csmonitor.com/USA/Politics/2011/0813/Obama-casts-Congress-as-the-problem-tells-Americans-to-let-them-know.
Obama says Americans "deserve better" than the partisanship and gridlock exhibited in Congress, perhaps aligning himself with a frustrated public as a means for political gain.

SuperPACs

Farnam, T. W., "After a Candidate Drops Out, Few Rules Control Super-PAC Cash," *The Washington Post*, Jan. 5, 2012, p. A15, www.washingtonpost.com/politics/few-rules-control-super-pac-donations-after-a-candidate-withdraws-from-a-race/2012/01/04/gIQAe6ZObP_story.html.
SuperPACs face few regulations on spending campaign contributions after a presidential candidate drops out.

Fouhy, Beth, "Mogul Gives $5M to Pro-Gingrich Group," The Associated Press, Jan. 8, 2012, www.sfgate.com/cgi-bin/article.cgi?f=/n/a/2012/01/07/national/a200758S32.DTL.
Las Vegas casino mogul Sheldon Adelson has contributed $5 million to a SuperPAC run by Gingrich allies, bolstering the former House speaker's presidential campaign.

CITING *CQ RESEARCHER*

Sample formats for citing these reports in a bibliography include the ones listed below. Preferred styles and formats vary, so please check with your instructor or professor.

MLA STYLE

Jost, Kenneth. "Remembering 9/11," CQ Researcher 2 Sept. 2011: 701-732.

APA STYLE

Jost, K. (2011, September 2). Remembering 9/11. *CQ Researcher, 9*, 701-732.

CHICAGO STYLE

Jost, Kenneth. "Remembering 9/11." *CQ Researcher*, September 2, 2011, 701-732.

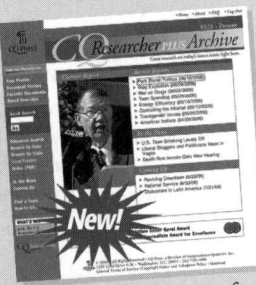

CQ Researcher

Published by CQ Press, an Imprint of SAGE Publications, Inc.

www.cqresearcher.com

Patient Safety

Are health care providers doing enough to prevent harm?

More than 12 years have passed since a groundbreaking report on preventable patient deaths in hospitals alerted the nation to a crisis in patient safety. Galvanized into action, the federal government poured money into research and training, patients and families formed advocacy groups, private and government insurers began refusing to reimburse medical institutions for the most serious preventable injuries and hospitals developed systems to track patient harm at the insistence of accreditation agencies. Yet patients continue to suffer high levels of death and injury from medical errors, and the health care industry, government regulators, insurers and patient advocates are struggling to figure out how to tackle the problem. Bloodstream infections caused by contaminated catheters are among the most dangerous threats, and hospitals are taking strong steps to prevent them. Meanwhile, medical experts are debating the value of patient involvement in safety procedures.

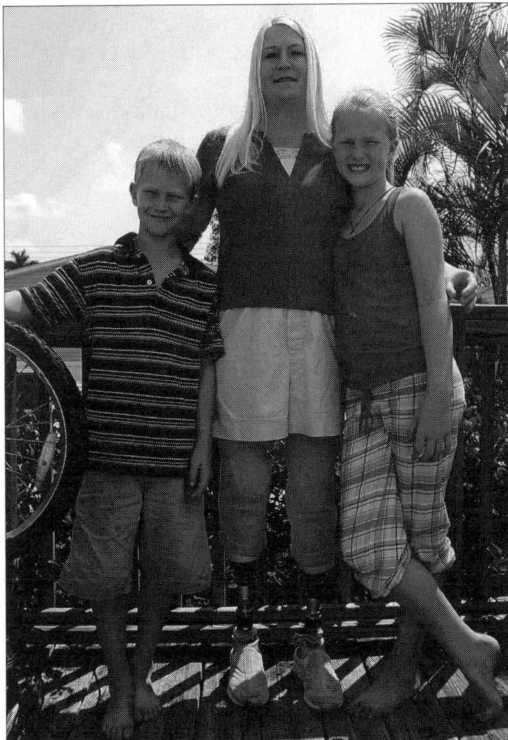

Lisa Strong of Davie, Fla., went to a hospital in severe pain from kidney stones. When she developed life-threatening septic shock after a misdiagnosis, doctors were forced to amputate her lower arms and lower legs to save her life. A jury rejected her claim for $75 million in damages.

INSIDE THIS REPORT

THE ISSUES 127
BACKGROUND 134
CHRONOLOGY 135
CURRENT SITUATION 139
AT ISSUE........................143
OUTLOOK 144
BIBLIOGRAPHY 148
THE NEXT STEP 149

CQ Researcher • Feb. 10, 2012 • www.cqresearcher.com
Volume 22, Number 6 • Pages 125-152

RECIPIENT OF SOCIETY OF PROFESSIONAL JOURNALISTS AWARD FOR EXCELLENCE ◆ AMERICAN BAR ASSOCIATION SILVER GAVEL AWARD

THE ISSUES

127 • Should the government use financial penalties to force hospitals to improve patient safety?
• Does the country need mandatory national reporting for serious adverse events?
• Does information technology prevent medical mistakes?

BACKGROUND

134 **Early Advocates**
Pioneering promoters of patient safety initially were spurned.

138 **Groundbreaking Report**
Report on patient deaths captured media and health care industry attention.

139 **Government Policy**
In 2001 Congress appropriated funds for patient-safety research.

139 **Private Initiatives**
Several nonprofits have made patient safety a priority.

CURRENT SITUATION

139 **Partnership for Patients**
Administration proposals aim to reduce patient deaths.

142 **Medical Education**
Patient safety is poorly covered by textbooks, medical schools.

142 **Resident Hours**
Cuts in interns' shift lengths have been controversial.

OUTLOOK

144 **Budget Pressure**
No-pay rules for Medicare will apply to Medicaid.

SIDEBARS AND GRAPHICS

128 **Infection-Reporting Laws**
Hospitals in 27 states must disclose infections.

129 **Hospital Employees Hold Mixed Views on Safety**
Many fear raising questions.

132 **Infections Declined**
Fewer incidences reported for several common infections.

135 **Chronology**
Key events since 1989.

136 **Patients Urged to Help Prevent Mistakes**
But can sick patients and family members really help?

137 **Tips for Preventing Medical Errors**
Hospital stays, surgery and medications are covered.

140 **Fighting Central-Line Infections with a Checklist**
"For decades we thought they were inevitable."

143 **At Issue**
Does hospital reporting of adverse events improve patient safety?

FOR FURTHER RESEARCH

147 **For More Information**
Organizations to contact.

148 **Bibliography**
Selected sources used.

149 **The Next Step**
Additional articles.

151 **Citing *CQ Researcher***
Sample bibliography formats.

Cover: AP Photo/J. Pat Carter

CQ Researcher

Feb. 10, 2012
Volume 22, Number 6

MANAGING EDITOR: Thomas J. Billitteri
tjb@cqpress.com

ASSISTANT MANAGING EDITOR: Kathy Koch
kkoch@cqpress.com

CONTRIBUTING EDITOR: Thomas J. Colin
tcolin@cqpress.com

ASSOCIATE EDITOR: Kenneth Jost

STAFF WRITER: Marcia Clemmitt

CONTRIBUTING WRITERS: Sarah Glazer, Alan Greenblatt, Peter Katel, Barbara Mantel, Jennifer Weeks

DESIGN/PRODUCTION EDITOR: Olu B. Davis

ASSISTANT EDITOR: Darrell Dela Rosa

FACT CHECKER: Michelle Harris

Los Angeles | London | New Delhi
Singapore | Washington DC

An Imprint of SAGE Publications, Inc.

VICE PRESIDENT AND EDITORIAL DIRECTOR, HIGHER EDUCATION GROUP:
Michele Sordi

DIRECTOR, ONLINE PUBLISHING:
Todd Baldwin

CQ Researcher (ISSN 1056-2036) is printed on acid-free paper. Published weekly, except: (March wk. 5) (May wk. 4) (July wk. 1) (Aug. wks. 3, 4) (Nov. wk. 4) and (Dec. wks. 3, 4). Published by SAGE Publications, Inc., 2455 Teller Rd., Thousand Oaks, CA 91320. Annual full-service subscriptions start at $1,054. For pricing, call 1-800-834-9020. To purchase a *CQ Researcher* report in print or electronic format (PDF), visit www.cqpress.com or call 866-427-7737. Single reports start at $15. Bulk purchase discounts and electronic-rights licensing are also available. Periodicals postage paid at Thousand Oaks, California, and at additional mailing offices. POSTMASTER: Send address changes to *CQ Researcher*, 2300 N St., N.W., Suite 800, Washington, DC 20037.

Patient Safety

BY BARBARA MANTEL

THE ISSUES

It was orthopedist David Ring's last surgery of the day at Massachusetts General Hospital, a straightforward procedure to treat carpal tunnel syndrome on the left wrist of a 65-year-old woman, using local anesthesia.

Everything seemed to go smoothly, but back in his office 15 minutes after the operation, Ring realized he had performed the wrong procedure. The woman was actually scheduled for surgery on a painful, stiff finger.

Ring immediately notified the operating staff — and then hospital administrators — and asked the patient if she wanted him to perform the correct surgery. She did, and he completed the operation without complication. [1]

"Just imagine the worst thing that's ever happened to you and that's how it feels," said Ring of the back-to-back surgeries in 2008. "I don't want anybody to make the same mistake I made." [2]

Sebastian Ferrero Foundation

A series of catastrophic mistakes led to the death of Horst and Luisa Ferrero's 3-year-old son Sebastian at a Gainesville, Fla., hospital. After he received a lethal overdose of a growth hormone in 2007, his parents brought him to the hospital, where personnel waited four hours before treating him, then misread his CT scan. His parents donated their $850,000 settlement toward construction of a new children's hospital in the community.

So Ring took an unusual step. He and two colleagues from Mass General wrote in *The New England Journal of Medicine* about the string of errors that led up to that day's wrong surgery.

Ring had become distracted by an emotional encounter with an earlier patient; a nurse marked the patient's hand at the wrist, not at the surgical site; the patient was moved to a new operating room with new staff because other surgeons were behind schedule; and just before operating, Ring spoke to the non-English-speaking patient in Spanish, leading the staff to mistakenly conclude he was conducting a "time-out," a standard procedure to verify one last time the patient's identity, surgical site and procedure. But no verification had occurred. [3]

Other medical mistakes — tens of thousands each year — have far more serious consequences, including injury and death due to post-surgical infections, overmedication, contaminated catheters, in-hospital falls and oversight by overworked staff.

In 2002, journalist Michael Hurewitz died at Mt. Sinai Medical Center in New York City after donating part of his liver to his brother. He choked on his own blood three days after the operation. A state probe found that the transplant unit in which Hurewitz died lacked adequate staff, staff experience and supervision. The ward had 34 postoperative patients under the care of a single first-year resident. Following the episode the State Health Department in New York called for beefed-up staffing in transplant units and frequent checks of patients by experienced doctors, among other rules. [4]

Just over 12 years ago, the Institute of Medicine, an independent organization that provides advice to the federal government and public, released a game-changing report, "To Err is Human: Building a Safer Health Care System," capturing the public's attention with blunt language and grim statistics: Between 44,000 and 98,000 Americans die in hospitals each year because of medical mistakes. [5] "These stunningly high rates of medical errors . . . are simply unacceptable," said William Richardson, chair of the committee that wrote the report. [6]

The committee's solution was revolutionary: It was time to stop blaming individual health care practitioners and to start changing the systems that allowed human error to result in patient harm. The report criticized hospital wards stocked with full-strength drugs that are toxic unless diluted; a lack of communication between specialists treating the same patient; and hand-written prescriptions that nurses and pharmacists cannot read. All were systems and procedures that could be changed, the committee said. [7]

But despite federal, state, and private efforts since then, many experts say health care remains unsafe. "If we only improve care as much in

Infection-Reporting Laws on Rise

Twenty-seven states require hospitals and sometimes other health care facilities to report infections. Only five states had infection-reporting laws in 2005.

States Requiring Public Reporting of Infection Rates by Health Care Facilities, 2010

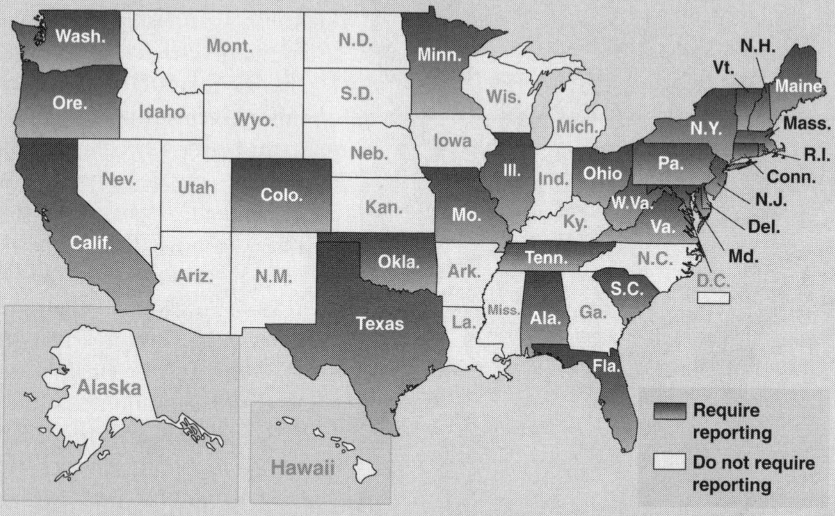

Source: "Methicillin-Resistant Staphylococcus aureus (MRSA) and Other Healthcare-Associated Infections," National Conference of State Legislatures, 2012, www.ncsl.org/issues-research/health/healthcare-associated-infections-homepage.aspx

the next decade as we have in the last, we are failing the American public," Kathleen Sebelius, secretary of the U.S. Department of Health and Human Services (HHS), said last October. [8]

While doctors, hospitals, patient advocates and researchers are trying to solve what seems to be an intractable problem, however, they disagree on some important fundamentals: whether, for example, hospital reporting of patient injuries and near misses eats up valuable time or improves patient safety; whether states should require public reporting of serious patient injuries; and whether financial penalties against hospitals are the best way to improve care.

There are bright spots. The Centers for Disease Control and Prevention (CDC) has reported progress in reducing some hospital-acquired infections in 2010, such as those associated with urinary catheters and central lines.* Still, the CDC estimates that one in 20 patients — or 1.7 million a year — will get an infection in the hospital. [9]

The real number, patient advocates say, is probably much higher. In fact it is difficult to know the full extent of patient injuries because many are never reported or recognized.

In 2010, the Office of the Inspector General (IG) at HHS released a study that found nearly one in seven Medicare patients suffered serious harm in the hospital in a one-month period, and almost half of those events were preventable. The researchers had reviewed a random sample of patient charts nationwide. [10] A year later, in a follow-up analysis, the IG determined that hospital staff had not reported 86 percent of those incidents to their superiors, partly because they were confused about what constitutes harm. [11] All hospitals that receive Medicare reimbursement must "track medical errors and adverse patient events, analyze their causes, and implement preventive actions," the IG noted. [12]

A more recent study used a streamlined form of chart review called the Global Trigger Tool. It allows reviewers to look for any of 52 triggers, such as use of an antidote medication, that would indicate something had gone wrong and would prompt a closer look at the chart. In a study of three hospitals, researchers reported that reviewers found serious adverse events in one-third of hospital admissions, at least 10 times more than staff reports. [13]

"We need this kind of data going forward if we are going to understand what's out there, what is working and where we need to make improvements," says pediatrician Christopher Landrigan, director of Harvard Medical School's Sleep and Patient Safety Program at Brigham and Women's Hospital in Boston. Landrigan would like to see every hospital use the trigger tool. Even just using it on a small sample of patient charts in every hospital would yield "far better information than we have today about how often harm is taking place and what to do about it," says Landrigan.

The private nonprofit National Quality Forum (NQF) in Washington, D.C., lists 34 "safe practices," such as procedures known to reduce hospital-acquired infections, checklists to reduce surgical errors and practices to reduce serious pressure ulcers, commonly known as bedsores. [14] But neither the NQF nor the federal government consistently tracks which hospitals are implementing them.

---

* A central line is a flexible tube placed in a large vein in a patient's arm, chest or neck to give medicines, fluids, nutrients, or blood products over a long period of time. Central lines can become freeways for germs if not kept clean.

Moreover, "it has become apparent that it is difficult to make these changes because it really requires teamwork," says physician Lucian Leape, a member of the Institute of Medicine committee that released "To Err Is Human" and a professor at the Harvard School of Public Health in Boston. "But physicians aren't trained in teamwork. What we are looking for is a very big culture change in medicine."

The traditional hierarchy of hospitals, where everyone defers to the doctor, has been a major impediment to patient safety, Leape says. The increasing complexity of medical care makes it imperative that doctors consult with other physicians, nurses and health care providers, he says.

In addition, many physicians don't treat co-workers with respect, Leape says. "Once you have humiliated a nurse, you can be sure she's not going to call a doctor about a problem if she knows she's going to get chewed out."

In fact, in a government survey of patient safety culture in just over a thousand hospitals, fewer than half of staff said they felt free to question the decisions or actions of those with more authority. [15]

Leape says several hospitals have successfully created a patient-safety culture, including the Mayo Clinic in Rochester, Minn.; Ascension Health, the nation's largest nonprofit health system, with hospitals in 20 states and Washington, D.C.; and Virginia Mason Medical Center in Seattle.

Ever since an accidental injection of antiseptic rather than dye during a brain aneurysm procedure caused the death of patient Mary McClinton in 2004, Virginia Mason has been trying to transform itself into a defect-free health care system. It has adopted many of the NQF's safe practices, and it has instituted a Patient Safety Alert System, based on a Toyota program that allows assembly line workers who spot problems to "stop the line." [16]

Hospital Employees Hold Mixed Views on Safety

Most hospital employees believe patient-safety procedures are good at preventing errors and that safety is never compromised to get more work done, according to a federal government survey of nearly 568,000 staff members at 1,128 hospitals. More than half say mistakes are reported always or most of the time whether or not they harm patients. Only 47 percent, however, believe they can freely question their superiors' decisions.

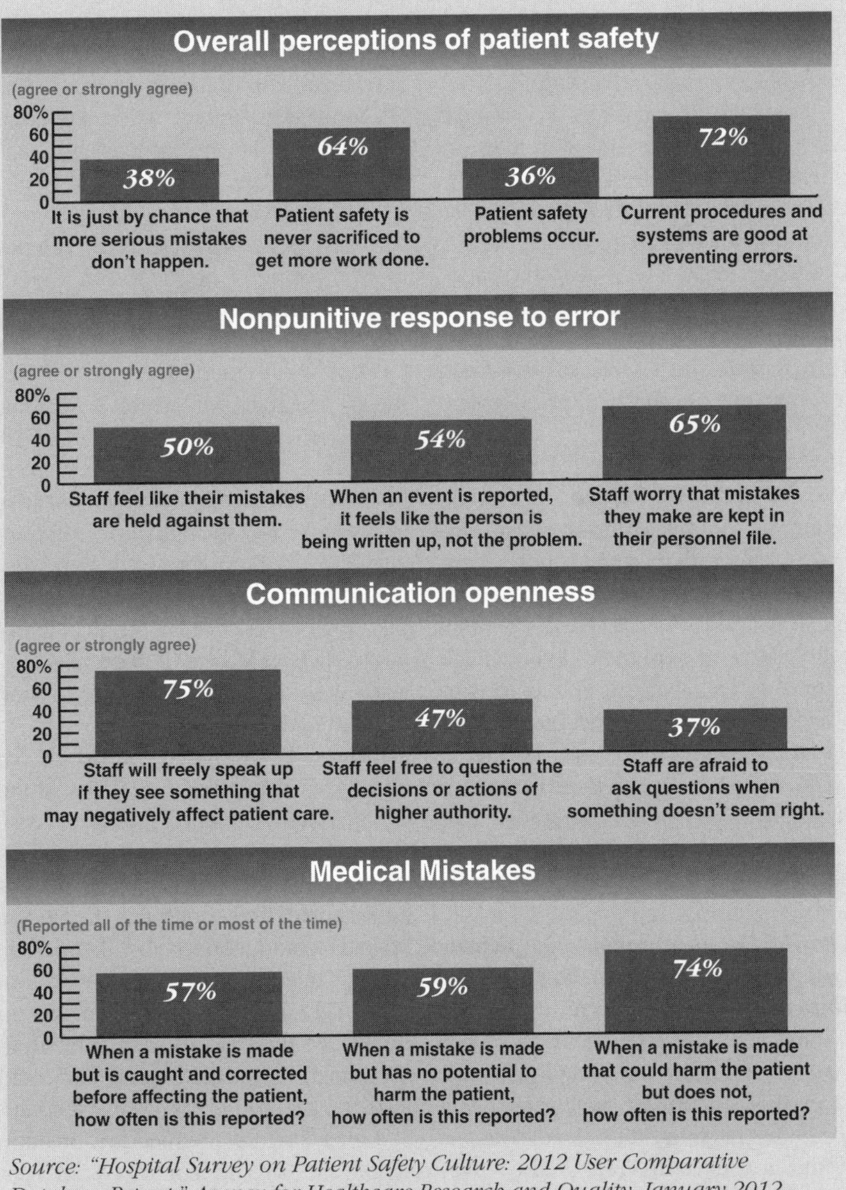

Hospital Staff Perceptions of Patient Safety Culture, January 2008-June 2011
Overall perceptions of patient safety
(agree or strongly agree)
80%
60
40
20
0
38%
64%
36%
72%
It is just by chance that more serious mistakes don't happen.
Patient safety is never sacrificed to get more work done.
Patient safety problems occur.
Current procedures and systems are good at preventing errors.
Nonpunitive response to error
(agree or strongly agree)
50%
54%
65%
Staff feel like their mistakes are held against them.
When an event is reported, it feels like the person is being written up, not the problem.
Staff worry that mistakes they make are kept in their personnel file.
Communication openness
(agree or strongly agree)
75%
47%
37%
Staff will freely speak up if they see something that may negatively affect patient care.
Staff feel free to question the decisions or actions of higher authority.
Staff are afraid to ask questions when something doesn't seem right.
Medical Mistakes
(Reported all of the time or most of the time)
57%
59%
74%
When a mistake is made but is caught and corrected before affecting the patient, how often is this reported?
When a mistake is made but has no potential to harm the patient, how often is this reported?
When a mistake is made that could harm the patient but does not, how often is this reported?

Source: "Hospital Survey on Patient Safety Culture: 2012 User Comparative Database Report," Agency for Healthcare Research and Quality, January 2012, www.ahrq.gov/qual/hospsurvey12/hosp12chart5-2.htm

"Whether they are a housekeeper or a neurosurgeon, they can and should report concerns," says Cathie Furman, senior vice president for quality and compliance at the medical center. When Virginia Mason began the program, it had three patient safety alerts a month; in December it had 559. "They can be anything from an expired tuna fish sandwich to 'I almost operated on the wrong person' and everything in between," Furman says. The hospital's goal is to reach 1,000 alerts a month, she says. "That's how we learn about all the system issues that allow a doctor or person to make a mistake."

So far, the program has shown good results, Furman says. Infection rates are down, the number of patient falls is down and the hospital's professional liability insurance premiums have shrunk by double digits every year, she says.

But persuading staff to participate in the alert system hasn't always been easy, Furman says. The key, she says has been a commitment from the medical center's top executives.

Massachusetts General Hospital also learned from Dr. Ring's mistaken operation on his patient's wrist. Surgeons rather than nurses now mark the surgical site; the surgical scrub nurse is not allowed to hand the knife to the surgeon until the time-out check is finished; all staff are encouraged to speak up with any concerns; and an auditor monitors the entire process. [17]

As hospitals try to improve safety, here are some of the questions that practitioners, regulators and patient advocates are asking:

Should the government use financial penalties to force hospitals to improve patient safety?

Since October 2008, the federal Centers for Medicare and Medicaid Services (CMS) stopped paying hospitals for the cost of treating Medicare patients for certain "reasonably preventable" conditions acquired after admission. That list has grown to 12, including falls resulting in fractures; transfusion of the wrong blood type; pressure ulcers; and infections associated with a urinary catheter or central line. [18]

CMS also does not pay for three so-called "never event" surgeries: wrong body part, wrong patient and wrong procedure. Medicare collects this information through automated reviews of hospital discharge data.

Financial penalties work, according to Sebelius, the HHS secretary. When it came to eliminating infections from central lines placed in patients in intensive-care units, for instance, "many hospitals only got serious when Medicare added them to the no-pay list," she said late last year. [19]

But there is a set of medical procedures backed by scientific evidence that, if properly applied, can reduce those infections to close to zero. (*See sidebar, p. 140.*)

Many in the medical community say the preventability of several other hospital-acquired conditions on the CMS list is not as clear and that penalizing hospitals when such conditions arise is wrong. "We strongly oppose nonpayment" for conditions "that are not reasonably preventable through the application of evidence-based guidelines," wrote Michael Maves, CEO of the American Medical Association (AMA) in a letter to CMS last June. [20]

Nancy Foster, vice president for Quality and Patient Safety Policy at the Chicago-based American Hospital Association (AHA), a major lobbying group for the hospital industry, cites falls as an example. To reduce falls to zero, a hospital could conceivably keep frail, elderly patients in bed, says Foster, "but that might mean the hospital has to catheterize them [to urinate], which patients might find uncomfortable and could lead to other problems, like infection."

Foster also says sometimes pressure ulcers are hard to control. "Some patients come to us with very fragile skin, and many medications we put them on impinge on the integrity of their skin, and so they may get a pressure ulcer in a blink of an eye," Foster says.

But only stage III and IV pressure ulcers, the most serious, are on the CMS list, and Leah Binder, CEO of the Leapfrog Group, whose members are large employers and group purchasers of health care benefits, says there is no excuse for them. "They are horrible, and the suffering is unimaginable," says Binder, "and if stage I and II pressure ulcers are properly cared for, stage III and IV don't happen."

Matthew Wynia, director of the AMA's Center for Patient Safety, agrees with Foster that many conditions on the CMS list lack proven prevention guidelines. Wynia says he is concerned that nonpayment could lead to unintended consequences. CMS does not adjust for patient risk in its nonpayment policy, and, as a result, hospitals might refuse to treat the sickest or most complex cases, he says. For example, Wynia says, Medicare does not pay for the additional care caused by mediastinitis, an infection of the chest cavity after open-heart surgery. Such infections are more likely to occur in patients who are obese or diabetic or have emphysema, says Wynia, "and some of these things hospitals cannot do anything about.

"What you would hate to see happen is a hospital saying we are going to be more reluctant to do open-heart surgery on these type of patients because they are high risk," he continues. "The data show that some of the time this does happen."

Some patient-safety experts, including Binder, want the CMS to expand its list. "Deep-vein thrombosis [blood clots] and pulmonary embolism [arterial blockages in the lung] are only on the list for a small, select number of procedures, and that could be expanded," says Donna Woods, a professor at Northwestern University's Institute for Healthcare Studies. But regulators must be careful to add only hospital-acquired conditions that are clearly preventable and that truly occurred only after admission, she says.

In any case, hospitals have incurred relatively little in financial penalties so far because many of the hospital-acquired conditions targeted by the CMS policy are rare. But much larger financial penalties are scheduled to follow. So for example, the Affordable Care Act — the landmark health care law championed by the Obama administration and passed by Congress in 2010 — instructs CMS, beginning in 2015, to rank hospitals from best to worst based on their rates of the current set of "reasonably preventable" hospital-acquired conditions. CMS would then penalize the worst-performing one-fourth of hospitals by withholding 1 percent of their total Medicare payments.

The AHA has complained about the mathematical formulas to be used to calculate the rates of occurrence, saying they will penalize hospitals that treat the sickest patients. In addition, hospital groups say that while it is right to hold all hospitals to the same high safety standards, using across-the-board financial penalties to achieve that goal could cause some hospitals to close.

"We have 13 very small, very rural hospitals that struggle financially," says Paula Bussard, senior vice president for policy and regulatory services at the Hospital and Healthsystem Association of Pennsylvania, a Harrisburg-based trade group. The loss of 1 percent of their Medicare payments could send them in a downward spiral, jeopardizing their ability not only "to assure access to needed care but also to continually improve quality and safety," she says.

Woods shares that concern. "In general I'm more in favor of targeting particular [hospital-acquired conditions] than across-the-board payment cuts," she says. But Leapfrog's Binder says plenty of financially strapped hospitals in poor communities have been able to significantly improve patient safety. Leapfrog has a set of quality and safety measures that hospitals, which volunteer to participate in its surveys, must meet to receive, in essence, the group's seal of approval.

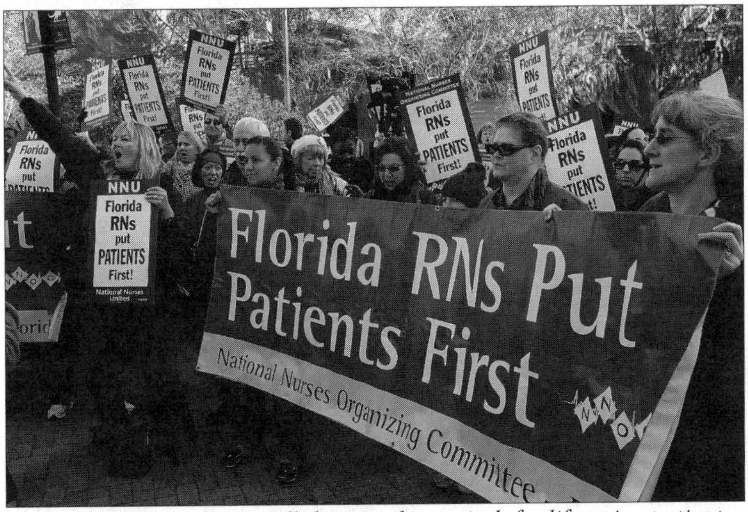

AP Photo/Phil Coale

Florida nurses rally in Tallahassee, the capital, for lifesaving patient-safety improvements on Feb. 17, 2010. The traditional hierarchy of hospitals, where everyone defers to the doctor, has been a major impediment to patient safety, according to Lucian Leape, a professor at the Harvard School of Public Health. With medical care increasingly complex, it is vital that doctors consult with other physicians, nurses and health care providers, he says.

"My experience with Leapfrog is that there is no correlation between the quality of a hospital and its financial health," says Binder. "You cannot predict the quality of a hospital by the amount of money it has."

Does the country need mandatory national reporting for serious adverse events?

"To Err Is Human" recommended that Congress create both a voluntary system for hospitals to report near misses and actual patient harms and a mandatory nationwide reporting system for serious adverse events. In 2005 Congress passed legislation to create the voluntary system, but it has largely left mandatory reporting up to the states. Medicare's data is limited to 12 hospital-acquired conditions and to patients age 65 and older, and it consists of discharge data, which studies have shown to be an unreliable gauge of patient injury.[21]

"We don't have anybody in charge, and so the states are all over the map," says Harvard's Leape. Only 27 states and the District of Columbia require hospitals to report serious adverse events, with half those states using their own lists of events while the other half use a list from the National Quality Forum. The NQF's 29 largely preventable "serious reportable events" include incorrect surgical procedures or surgeries on the wrong patient or body part; patient death or serious injury from contaminated drugs or a medication error; death or serious injury from a fall; and advanced pressure ulcers.[22]

A key aim of mandatory reporting is to hold hospitals accountable to their peers and to consumers. Twenty-three states make the data publicly available, but most release it in aggregate form without identifying individual hospitals. Only seven release facility-specific information or plan to do so. Mandatory reporting also is intended to allow states to require hospitals to take corrective action and track trends.

"So for instance, are pressure ulcers more commonly reported, are falls more commonly reported?" asks

Health Care-Associated Infections Decline

Four common infections acquired in hospitals declined in 2010, according to the Centers for Disease Control and Prevention. "Hospitals and state health departments need to translate this progress to other areas of health care delivery and health care infections, such as dialysis and ambulatory surgery centers, and diarrheal infections," said CDC Director Thomas R. Frieden.

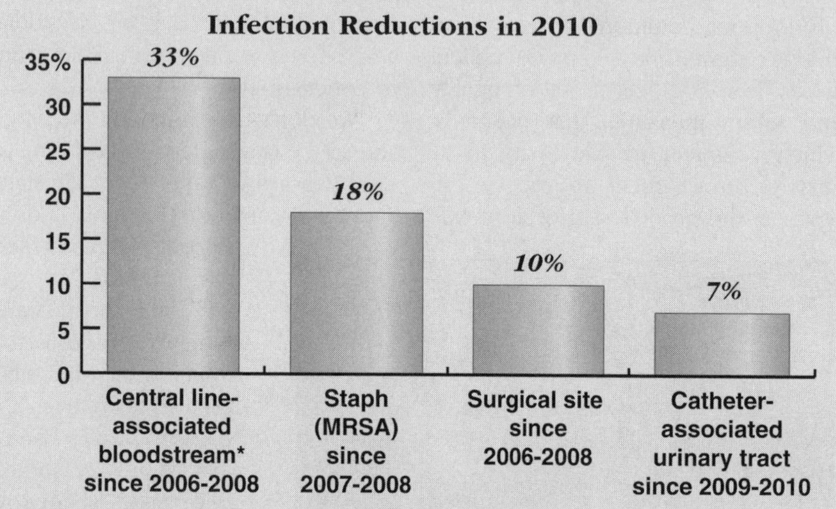

** A central line is a tube placed inside a patient's vein to deliver medicine or other treatment. Bloodstream infections can occur when lines are improperly inserted.*

Source: "Health Care-Associated Infections Declined in 2010," Centers for Disease Control and Prevention, October 2011, www.cdc.gov/media/releases/2011/p1019_healthcare_infections.html

Jill Rosenthal, a program director at the National Academy for State Health Policy (NASHP), a research organization based in Portland, Maine. "The states can use that information to collaborate with hospitals to make improvements."

Some patient advocates reject this piecemeal approach and want a nationwide mandatory public reporting system, although there is disagreement about its shape.

"We believe that every state and every consumer should have access to this kind of information about their hospitals and other health care facilities," says Lisa McGiffert, director of the Consumers Union Safe Patient Project, based in Austin, Texas. "Public disclosure is what drives change."

Denise Cardo, director of the CDC's Division of Healthcare Quality Promotion, agrees. "If it weren't for Consumers Union pushing public reporting, we wouldn't be here now," said Cardo as she announced the 2010 reduction in hospital-acquired infection rates last October. [23] As a result of prodding by advocacy groups like Consumers Union, 27 states now require reporting of hospital-acquired infections and release that facility-specific data to the public.

McGiffert would like to see every state adopt such infection-reporting legislation as well as similar laws regarding all other serious patient harm. "The states can be the laboratories before we do a national model, to show what works," says McGiffert.

But other patient advocates favor a federal rather than state-by-state approach.

"It's nice to allow states to be laboratories," says Martin Hatlie, co-founder of the Chicago-based nonprofit Consumers Advancing Patient Safety. "But the only way Americans will know the basic safety records of their health care providers," he says, is if Congress requires all hospitals to maintain the same list of serious patient injuries and deaths and report them to a federal patient-safety agency. "You'll find that it is a pretty radical point of view," Hatlie acknowledges.

Bussard says the Hospital and Healthsystem Association of Pennsylvania supports that state's current confidential reporting system. Pennsylvania requires hospitals to report on a broad array of harms and even near misses to its Patient Safety Authority (PSA), which analyzes trends and issues advisories but does not publicly identify specific hospitals. "It is designed to be a learning, not a punitive, system," says Bussard, who says she is concerned that publicly releasing hospital-specific data would discourage medical staff from reporting mistakes.

Foster of the AHA says the current national voluntary reporting system "seems to be the best bet" and that "the thought of having another national data-collection system is challenging." Like Bussard, she worries that making facility-specific information public will discourage reporting and that consumers will misinterpret the information.

The federal government does not fund the voluntary system, which it rolled out in 2009. Instead, the Agency for Healthcare Research and Quality (AHRQ) at HHS approves patient-safety organizations (PSOs) that collect and analyze information voluntarily supplied by hospitals, which pay for the service and receive feedback and advice. By law, the information is kept confidential. There are currently 77 PSOs across 30 states and the District of Columbia; they range from hospital chains and trade associations to nonprofit groups and private companies. [24]

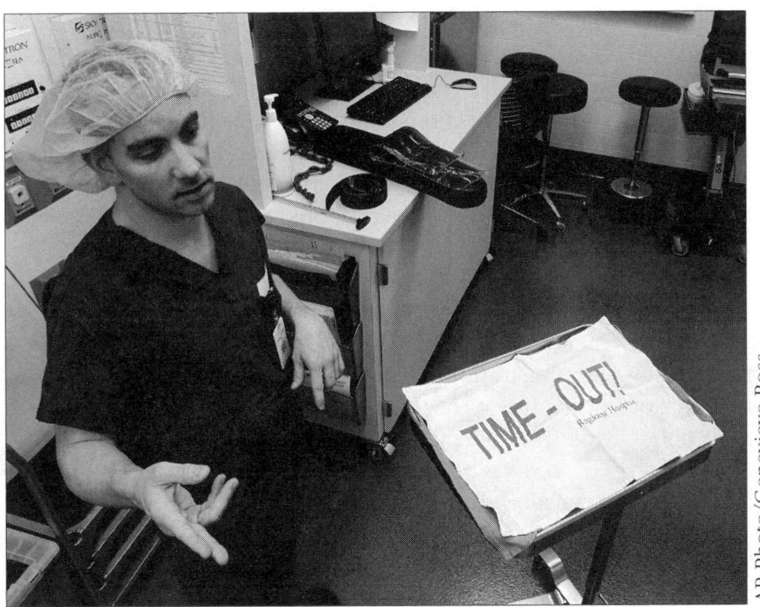

AP Photo/Genevieve Ross

Gary B. Collins, head of the Surgery Department at Regions Hospital in St. Paul, Minn., explains how the "Time-Out!" towel reduces wrong procedures. The towel is placed over surgical instruments, and surgery team members cannot remove it and proceed with an operation until a safety checklist has been completed.

"We have been impressed by some of the PSOs out there and their effectiveness in helping hospitals make their care even safer," says Foster.

But no one knows how many hospitals are working with PSOs. The American Hospital Association does not track it, and AHRQ has just begun collecting data. "AHRQ expects the number of hospitals working with PSOs to increase over the next few years," says William Munier, director of AHRQ's Center for Quality Improvement and Patient Safety. That's because the Affordable Care Act requires health insurance plans that operate in insurance exchanges — a centerpiece of the law — to contract only with hospitals that report events to a PSO.

Hatlie runs a small nonprofit PSO in Chicago and would like a national mandatory reporting system to run parallel to the voluntary one. McGiffert, on the other hand, says the federal government should not be supporting a confidential, voluntary system. "They are building on a theory that we believe is flawed," says McGiffert, "that if you allow hospitals to keep things secret they will come forward and confess and try to change, but we haven't seen this theory to be supported."

Does information technology prevent medical mistakes?

When doctors Rushika Fernandopulle and Neil Patel opened their primary-care practice in southern New Jersey in 2007, they designed it to be paper-free. They purchased a widely used electronic health-records system and equipped work areas with desktop computers and clinicians with electronic tablets.

The doctors enter each patient's demographic and clinical data into the system, which not only alerts them to mistakes, such as incorrect dosages, patient allergies and drug interactions, but is designed to receive reports from laboratories and send prescriptions to pharmacies.

The system was supposed to save time and money and reduce errors, but it didn't turn out that way. The system was "so riddled with bugs," the two physicians wrote, that they had to patch together fixes using outside software.

There were also benefits to the electronic system: no hunting down documents or trying to decipher a colleague's illegible handwriting, and records could be accessed remotely. But the interface between the laboratory and the practice never worked, document creation actually took longer, software design flaws led to medical errors and drug alerts were so constant that Fernandopulle and Patel eventually disabled that feature. [25]

A little less than a year ago, the federal government began to distribute money from a potential $27 billion incentive program to encourage doctors and hospitals to switch from paper to electronic health records by 2014. The money comes from the 2009 American Recovery and Reinvestment Act — the so-called economic stimulus bill aimed at shoring up the beleaguered U.S. economy — and flows to health care providers as bonuses on their payments from Medicare and Medicaid.

They must, however, attest that the software they've installed meets a majority of government-designated "meaningful use benchmarks." Requirements include maintaining a list of each patient's medications and medication allergies, communicating with a patient's multiple physicians electronically and using computerized provider order entry (CPOE), a system that allows clinicians to enter medication orders electronically and alerts them to potential complications. [26] About one-third of office-based physicians report having a "basic" electronic health records system in 2011 — one that meets many but not all the government benchmarks — and about half plan to eventually apply for incentive payments. [27] Eight out of 10 hospitals plan to apply. [28] Five years ago, one-tenth of office-based doctors had an electronic records system.

But a recent Institute of Medicine (IOM) report on information technology and patient safety warns that while potential benefits are great, so are possible harms. The report calls for greater government oversight. "To protect patients, industry and government have a shared responsibility to ensure greater transparency, accountability and reporting of health [information technology]-related medical errors," said Gail Warden, president emeritus of Detroit's Henry Ford Health System and chair of the IOM committee behind the report. [29]

Currently there is no oversight, and there is little research quantifying risk, in part because no central repository exists for collecting information about such errors and injuries and because vendor contracts usually prohibit users from publicly sharing it. [30]

One research study comes from the Leapfrog Group. A total of 214 hospitals participated in a simulation of their CPOE systems, running intentionally harmful drug orders for a set of fictitious patients.

"The results were disturbing," says Leapfrog's Binder. On average, the systems failed to flag about half of the routine errors and missed a third of the potentially fatal ones. Most of the hospitals improved on a second round of simulations after making changes to software and the way clinicians use the systems.

Leapfrog wants the federal government to require health care providers not only to have electronic health records systems in place but also to test them for safety and accuracy. The government so far has not done that, "and we think that is a problem," says Binder.

The IOM committee recommends that the federal government create an independent watchdog agency, along the lines of the National Transportation Safety Board (NTSB). The agency would collect mandatory reports of deaths and serious injuries from software vendors and voluntary reports from clinicians, analyze the data to make safety recommendations and conduct investigations. However, it would have no enforcement powers. The IOM also stopped short of recommending that the U.S. Food and Drug Administration (FDA) regulate and pre-approve health-information technology products.

Vendors have argued against FDA regulation for years. "Regulation will not necessarily create a safer [electronic health record] system and might actually limit innovation and responsiveness when it is needed most," said Carl Dvorak, executive vice president of Epic Systems Corp., a software manufacturer in Verona, Wis. [31]

"There is no strong evidence that regulation stifles innovation. None, zero," says physician Richard Cook, a member of the IOM committee and the director of the University of Chicago's Cognitive Technologies Laboratory in the Department of Anesthesia and Critical Care. "What regulation does is require people to think through the consequences of their innovations."

Cook wrote a dissent to the IOM report arguing that health information technology is a medical device and so, by statute, must be regulated by the FDA. "The fact that the FDA has not done this tells you that this is an incredibly sensitive issue. They regulate tongue depressors, for God's sake," says Cook.

Tongue depressors are class I devices, a hearing aid is class II and cardiac defibrillators are class III. Cook argues that health information technology is a class III device, which the law defines as one that "is of substantial importance in preventing impairment of human health or presents a potential, unreasonable risk of illness or injury." [32]

The IOM committee did recommend that the HHS secretary monitor the safety and reliability of health information technology and, if in the future the agency determines that progress is insufficient, that it "direct the FDA to exercise all available authority" to regulate it. [33] ■

BACKGROUND

Early Advocates

The medical establishment often disregarded or spurned early advocates of patient safety.

In 1847, while working at a maternity clinic at Vienna General Hospital, Hungarian physician Ignaz Philipp Semmelweis instructed interns who had performed autopsies to wash their hands with chlorinated lime solutions before working on the ward. As a result, the incidence of "childbed fever," at the time a fairly common, potentially fatal bacterial infection contracted during childbirth or miscarriage, dropped dramatically. However, Semmelweis' hypothesis of the importance of cleanliness, coming two decades before French chemist Louis Pasteur helped establish the germ theory for disease, "was extreme at the time and was largely ignored, rejected or ridiculed" by other doctors, according to one biography. [34]

More than 60 years later, a Boston physician suggesting that hospitals and doctors track their patients' outcomes was also met with ridicule. Orthopedic surgeon Ernest Amory Codman defined his revolutionary idea this way: "The common sense notion that every hospital should follow every patient it treats, long enough to determine whether or not the treatment has been successful, and then to inquire, 'If not, why not?' with a view to preventing similar failures in the future." [35]

Continued on p. 137

Chronology

1980s-1990s

Tragic medical errors and a government report put patient safety on public's radar.

1985
American Society of Anesthesiologists (ASA) launches Anesthesia Patient Safety Foundation. The combination of a shift in attitude among practitioners and the adoption of new procedures and technology leads to marked improvement in anesthesia safety.

1989
New York state limits medical residents' maximum work week to 80 hours after systemic failures lead to death of 18-year-old Libby Zion in a Manhattan hospital emergency room.

1991
Researchers find that 3.7 percent of sampled hospitalizations in New York state resulted in adverse events, more than half due to preventable medical errors.

1994
Boston Globe health columnist Betsy Lehman dies of chemotherapy overdose at Dana-Farber Cancer Institute in Boston.

1996
Institute for Healthcare Improvement begins national collaborative effort to reduce adverse drug events in hospitals.

1999
Institute of Medicine (IOM) report, "To Err is Human: Building a Safer Health System," publicizes the large number of preventable patient injuries and deaths in U.S. hospitals. . . . Healthcare Research and Quality Act requires Agency for Healthcare Research and Quality (AHRQ) to support research to identify causes of preventable health care errors and patient injury; develop strategies for reducing errors and injuries; and disseminate effective strategies throughout the health care industry.

2000s

Government funds patient-safety efforts, yet rates of many patient injuries do not improve.

2001
AHRQ publishes "Making Health Care Safer," detailing patient safety practices that reduce health care errors and patient injury. AHRQ awards nearly 100 grants to study patient safety.

2003
Accreditation Council for Graduate Medical Education (ACGME) sets 80-hour work week for medical residents and maximum shifts of 30 consecutive hours.

2004
AHRQ releases "Hospital Survey on Safety Patient Culture," which allows hospitals to assess their patient safety culture.

2005
Patient Safety and Quality Improvement Act of 2005 establishes patient-safety organizations (PSOs), which can collect voluntarily reported patient-safety events from hospitals and clinicians without fear of legal repercussions. Regulations are finalized in 2009.

2006
New England Journal of Medicine reports that bloodstream infections dropped 66 percent over 18 months at 77 Michigan hospitals that adopted a safety checklist when inserting central-line catheters, saving an estimated $200 million and 2,000 lives. . . . IOM's "Preventing Medication Errors" estimates that, on average, a hospital patient is subject to at least one medication error per day.

2008
Only half of the most recent editions of core medical textbooks reviewed cover patient safety, and only 10.4 percent of U.S. medical schools formally offer specific courses covering patient safety.

2009
Medicare stops paying for certain serious hospital-acquired conditions. A similar Medicaid program goes into effect in 2012. . . . American Recovery and Reinvestment Act provides a potential $27 billion in incentives to health-care providers who adopt electronic health records.

2010
Affordable Care Act requires Department of Health and Human Services (HHS), starting in 2015, to rank hospitals based on hospital-acquired conditions and penalize the worst-performing institutions by withholding 1 percent of their Medicare payments. . . . HHS reports that one in seven Medicare beneficiaries is harmed during a hospital stay, costing the government an estimated $4.4 billion annually.

2011
ACGME reduces shifts for first-year interns to 16 hours. . . . Centers for Disease Control and Prevention reports hospital-acquired infections drop substantially in 2010. . . . Obama administration launches Partnership for Patients, a set of collaborative hospital programs designed to drastically lower patient injury.

2012 (July)
All states must stop making Medicaid payments for 12 hospital-acquired conditions.

Patients Urged to Help Prevent Mistakes

But can sick patients and stressed family members really help?

The spouse of a patient allergic to Heparin stops a nurse from flushing a catheter with the anticoagulant, possibly avoiding a serious or fatal reaction. The allergy had not been entered in the patient's chart.

A parent prevents a surgeon from removing a child's tonsils and adenoids. The child was to have had a polyp excised, but the surgeon's office had placed an incorrect reservation on the operating room schedule.

A patient's husband asks a nurse if the band around his wife's arm should be so tight. Two hours earlier, another nurse had forgotten to remove the tourniquet when inserting an IV.

Hundreds of such reports were submitted to the Pennsylvania Patient Safety Reporting System over a six-month period. "Patients and family members who speak up about patient-care issues have not only identified medical errors but have also prevented errors and injuries," according to the Pennsylvania Patient Safety Authority, which created the reporting system. [1]

Campaigns now exist to recruit patients and family members as watchdogs to ensure safe care. In 2000, the federal Agency for Healthcare Research and Quality (AHRQ) created a fact sheet for consumers called "20 Tips to Help Prevent Medical Errors" (*see box, p. 137*), and the private Joint Commission, which accredits hospitals, in 2002 launched its Speak Up initiative to encourage patients to be vigilant. [2] But some experts think such campaigns ask too much of sick patients and stressed family members and might actually do more harm than good. And patients are not always willing.

Both the AHRQ and Joint Commission urge patients to ask health care providers if they have washed their hands, and the Joint Commission suggests asking if they should be wearing gloves. Hospital-acquired infections are a major problem in health care, and hand washing is the primary preventive. Yet studies show that nurses, physicians and other health care workers wash their hands far less frequently than is recommended. [3] Patients are also encouraged to confirm their identity with surgeons before an operation, along with the body part being operated on.

While surveys show that patients are often willing to ask for more information, they are less inclined to engage in behaviors they perceive as challenging doctors and nurses. For example, people in one survey were quite willing to ask for an explanation of something they didn't understand or to ask the reason for a hospital procedure, but they were much less willing to ask health care providers about washed hands or whether they had the right patient before a procedure. [4] Researchers recommend educating physicians and nurses about the value of patient participation so they will accept questions and concerns raised by patients and encourage patients to speak up. Researchers also recommend that patients themselves be educated about the value of their contributions. [5]

But some experts don't believe this kind of patient participation is worthy of long-term investment and instead should be seen as a sporadic, unexpected source of help in reducing medical errors. According to Melinda Lyons, an engineer specializing in the study of human capabilities in Great Britain, all patients are not equally suited to the role of safety watchdog because of their varying ages, cultures, backgrounds, personalities, levels of intelligence and languages.

In addition, it's unreasonable to burden patients suffering from fatigue, stress, pain or discomfort with additional responsibilities when any other industry would consider someone suffering from even one of those factors "too high risk to be trusted with any critical decisions," said Lyons.

Lyons also worried that clinicians and hospitals, in an effort to save time and costs, could try to inappropriately shift the safety burden to patients and that clinicians could be lulled into a false sense of security if they view patients as a reliable backup to catch errors. [6]

In fact, the Pennsylvania Patient Safety Reporting System received many reports of health care providers accepting a patient's word too hastily. In one case, an anesthesiologist asked a patient if she was having surgery on her left shoulder, to which the patient replied, "Yes." After the anesthesiologist administered a local anesthetic to that shoulder, the nurse informed the anesthesiologist that it was the right shoulder being operated on.

That error, and others like it, could have been prevented if the entire team had marked the surgical site beforehand, a standard practice in some hospitals. [7]

— ***Barbara Mantel***

[1] "When Patients Speak — Collaboration in Patient Safety," PA PSRS Patient Safety Advisory, March 2005, http://patientsafetyauthority.org/ADVISORIES/AdvisoryLibrary/2005/Mar2(1)/Pages/01b.aspx.

[2] "20 Tips to Help Prevent Medical Errors," AHRQ. www.ahrq.gov/consumer/20tips.htm, "Speak Up Campaign," www.jointcommission.org/speakup.aspx.

[3] W.E. Bischoff, *et al.*, "Handwashing compliance by healthcare workers: the impact of introducing an accessible, alcohol-based hand antiseptic," *Archives of Internal Medicine*, April 10, 2000, www.ncbi.nlm.nih.gov/pubmed/10761968.

[4] William M. Marella, "Health Care Consumers' Inclination to Engage in Selected Patient Safety Practices: A Survey of Adults in Pennsylvania," *Journal of Patient Safety*, December 2007, p. 186, http://csr.hbg.psu.edu/LinkClick.aspx?fileticket=WrFeoFs7W-E%3D&tabid=856.

[5] *Ibid.*, p. 188.

[6] Melinda Lyons, "Should patients have a role in patient safety? A safety engineering view," *Quality and Safety in Health Care*, April 2007, www.ncbi.nlm.nih.gov/pmc/articles/PMC2653153.

[7] "When Patients Speak," *op. cit.*

Continued from p. 134

According to the American Academy of Orthopaedic Surgeons, "Common sense it may have seemed, but it was simply not done." Local surgeons rejected Codman's idea, and he resigned from Massachusetts General Hospital to open Codman Hospital, where staff members were required to study the results of their care. In three pamphlets "stunning in their honesty," Codman published the outcomes of his own cases, going so far as to classify errors as those due to lack of judgment and those due to lack of technical skill. [36]

"For his cutting-edge posture, Codman was ostracized by his colleagues, died a pauper and is buried in an unmarked grave in Boston," according to a report of the Lucian Leape Institute Roundtable on Reforming Medical Education. [37]

The approach to patient safety began to change in the late 1970s, when chemical and biomedical engineer Jeffrey Cooper borrowed a tool from aviation called the critical incident technique, which involves collecting and analyzing stories of pivotal events to understand system failures, and applied it to health care. "We set out to interview anesthesiologists, residents, and nurse anesthetists, seeking to learn from them about their own mistakes or those they had observed," wrote Cooper. [38]

In 1985, Cooper and the leadership of the American Society of Anesthesiologists (ASA) launched the Anesthesia Patient Safety Foundation to help avoid preventable adverse clinical outcomes. But according to Cooper, the foundation would not have succeeded, despite his published research documenting serious problems in anesthesia safety, if it hadn't been for "a malpractice crisis that was markedly reducing the incomes of anesthesiologists." Rather than fight for an overhaul of the malpractice laws, ASA leaders persuaded members to focus on decreasing harm instead. As a result, a marked improvement in anesthesia safety began, through a combination of a shift in attitude among practitioners and the adoption of new procedures and technology, Cooper wrote. [39]

But the rest of medicine did not immediately follow. At the time, there

Tips for Preventing Medical Errors

Medications

- Alert your doctor to all medications you are taking and bring all of your medications and supplements to your doctor visits.
- Notify your doctor of any allergies or adverse reactions to any medications.
- Make sure you can read your doctor's handwriting on prescriptions.
- Ask your doctor or pharmacist how medications should be taken, make sure you understand the directions on medicine labels and ask about potential side effects.
- Ask your pharmacist for advice on measuring liquid medications.
- Make sure your pharmacy gives you the correct medications prescribed by your doctor.

Hospital Stays

- Ask all health care workers who will touch you whether they have washed their hands.
- Have your doctor explain your home-treatment plan before you are discharged.

Surgery

- Make sure you, your doctor and your surgeon agree on exact procedures.
- If possible, choose a hospital where many patients have had the same surgeries or procedures.

Other Steps

- Speak to your health care professionals if you have any questions or concerns.
- Make sure that someone, such as your primary-care doctor, coordinates your care.
- Make sure your doctors have your important health information.
- Ask a family member or friend to accompany you to appointments.
- Find out the purpose behind additional tests and treatments.
- Ensure you get the results for your tests, for better or worse.
- Learn about your condition and treatments from doctors, nurses and other reliable sources.

Source: "20 Tips to Help Prevent Medical Errors," Agency for Healthcare Research and Quality, September 2011, www.ahrq.gov/consumer/20tips.pdf

was no national policy on patient safety, no uniform methods for collecting systematic, detailed data on medical injuries, and little attention paid to patient safety in medical education, researchers noted. [40] The public seemed uninterested as well.

Groundbreaking Report

The disinterest began to change in 1995, with sustained media attention to the case of *Boston Globe* health columnist Betsy Lehman, who died of a chemotherapy overdose at the Dana-Farber Cancer Institute in Boston. Combined with other media reports of tragic medical mistakes and research indicating that the great majority of adverse drug events in hospitals went unreported, "a gripping picture began to emerge of an industry at odds with itself," wrote physicians Stephen Small and Paul Barach. The health care industry, they said, was unaccountable to the public and under extreme pressure to cut costs while sorely needing to improve its safety systems. [41]

Research on patient safety accelerated. Studies examined the impact of sleep deprivation and the costs of adverse drug events. Evidence mounted on the efficacy of computerized physician order entry and bar coding to prevent medication errors. And the nonprofit Institute for Healthcare Improvement, based in Cambridge, Mass., began to train hospital teams on how to implement safe practices, according to Leape, the Harvard professor.

"Still, patient safety was not a major concern for most hospitals or doctors, nor for the public, until November of 1999," wrote Leape, when the IOM released its landmark "To Err is Human" report. [42] Physicians Robert M. Wachter and Kaveh G. Shojania, in their 2004 book *Internal Bleeding: The Truth Behind America's Terrifying Epidemic of Medical Mistakes*, called the prose of the IOM report's book jacket, with its references to "stunning statistics" and the "startling truth about medical error," more like the "trailer for a Hollywood blockbuster than the synopsis of an academic report." [43]

AP Photo/Chitose Suzuki

Massachusetts Public Health Commissioner Christine Ferguson announces the creation of the Betsy Lehman Center for Patient Safety and Medical Error Prevention in Boston, on Jan. 12, 2004. Lehman, pictured in framed photo at left, died in 1994 after receiving a chemotherapy overdose at the Dana-Farber Cancer Institute, where she was being treated for breast cancer. She had been a Boston Globe *health reporter.*

The report estimated that medical errors at U.S. hospitals kill 44,000 to 98,000 people each year, more than motor vehicle accidents, breast cancer or AIDs. And that was just "a modest estimate" since medical errors occur at outpatient surgical centers, physicians' offices, clinics and retail pharmacies as well, the report said. [44]

Wachter and Shojania noted that after two days of saturation media coverage, followed by a spate of TV specials, magazine articles and congressional hearings, medical mistakes "joined airline and food safety (and two years later, terrorism) as omnipresent sources of angst in the American zeitgeist." [45]

Yet the IOM report did not reveal new data. Instead, it extrapolated information from two earlier studies, one conducted in Colorado and Utah and the other in New York state. The New York study, called the Harvard Medical Practice Study I, reviewed 30,121 randomly selected records from 51 hospitals and found that 3.7 percent of hospitalizations resulted in an adverse event and that more than half of those events were preventable and due to error. The results were reported in *The New England Journal of Medicine* in 1991. [46]

Besides publicizing its frightening statistics, the IOM report had a second message: Rather than continuing to blame individuals for their medical mistakes, the focus must shift to "preventing future errors by designing safety into the system." [47] It called for a major national initiative and recommended, among other things, that:

- Congress establish a Center for Patient Safety to set national goals for patient safety and develop a research agenda;
- Both a nationwide mandatory system for reporting serious adverse events due to medical error and a confidential, voluntary reporting system of adverse events be established;
- Regulators and accreditors require health care organizations to implement meaningful patient-safety programs and

third-party payers provide incentives for patient-safety improvement;

• Health care organizations and their providers establish patient-safety programs and implement proven medication-safety practices. [48]

Government Policy

The IOM report galvanized Congress, which in 2001 appropriated $50 million annually to the Agency for Healthcare Research and Quality for patient-safety research. AHRQ established a Center for Quality Improvement and Patient Safety to educate and train health care professionals and to develop safety measures and help set standards. [49] One of AHRQ's most notable efforts is a program that has successfully taught health care providers in more than 1,000 hospitals how to reduce hospital-acquired bloodstream infections.

In 2009, AHRQ finalized rules to set up a voluntary reporting system for serious patient injuries. Private patient-safety organizations (PSOs), certified by AHRQ, collect voluntarily reported adverse events from hospitals and then help hospitals learn and improve. The information is kept confidential and cannot be used in litigation, with the idea that this protection will encourage reporting. However, there is no public data on how many hospitals are participating, and patient advocates complain it is too secret.

Congress eventually decided that research, education and training were not enough to reduce medical errors, which were costing third-party payers such as Medicare billions of dollars a year. It passed the Deficit Reduction Act of 2005, which required the HHS secretary to identify at least two preventable hospital-acquired conditions, the additional care for which Medicare would no longer pay, beginning in 2009. [50] There are now a dozen such conditions on the list. Many private insurers have followed suit.

But there are carrots as well as sticks. The 2009 federal stimulus bill provides a potential $27 billion in incentives for health care providers to adopt electronic health records. And last year the Obama administration launched Partnership for Patients, which has awarded grants to collaborations between hospitals to spread the best patient-safety practices.

States have also played an important role, with more than half requiring some form of mandatory reporting of adverse patient events.

As of yet, there is no national, mandatory state reporting system, as recommended in the IOM report more than 12 years ago.

Private Initiatives

Several nonprofit organizations have made patient safety a priority. The National Quality Forum (NQF) was established in 2000 to set voluntary standards in the health care industry. It has since defined a list of adverse patient events that many states use as the basis of their mandatory reporting systems, and it also created a list of evidence-based safe practices that hospitals can implement to reduce harm to patients.

The Joint Commission accredits and certifies more than 19,000 health care organizations and programs in the United States, and it "has been one of the most effective instruments of change for safety," according to Harvard's Leape, "first by changing to unannounced accreditation audits" and more recently by requiring hospitals to implement many of the NQF's safe practices. [51]

Since 2003, the Accreditation Council on Graduate Medical Education (ACGME) has been limiting the workload for residents and requiring tighter supervision, although some sleep experts would like to see the ACGME go even further. ACGME followed the lead of New York state, which in 1989 limited the number of hours residents could work after the highly publicized death five years earlier of 18-year-old Libby Zion in a busy emergency room under the care of two residents.

Hospitals and their trade associations have made significant changes as well, hiring patient-safety officers, instituting internal adverse-event reporting systems, participating in collaboratives across the country to learn how to reduce hospital-acquired infections and working with PSOs and state agencies to analyze mistakes and make improvements.

Large employers have also been active. In 2000 they established the Leapfrog Group to demand that the health care industry improve patient safety and quality. More than a 1,000 hospitals nationwide volunteer to participate in the Leapfrog Hospital Survey, which assesses hospital performance based on four quality and safety practices that are proven to reduce preventable medical mistakes and are endorsed by the NQF. Leapfrog makes the results public.

Despite all these efforts and progress in reducing certain hospital acquired infections, however, health care facilities remain dangerous places for many patients. ■

CURRENT SITUATION

Partnership for Patients

The Obama administration is proceeding with an ambitious plan to sharply reduce preventable patient injuries, deaths and rehospitalizations.

Fighting Central-Line Infections with a Checklist

"For decades we thought they were inevitable."

Every day in hospitals around the country, doctors insert a flexible tube into a large vein in the arm, chest or neck of some of their sickest patients. These central-line catheters are essential for delivering medicines, fluids, nutrients or blood products, but if not inserted properly, they can become lethal highways for germs.

An estimated 41,000 blood-stream infections associated with central lines occur annually in hospital intensive care units (ICUs) and wards, and an additional 37,000 occur among patients receiving outpatient hemodialysis for kidney failure. As many as a fourth of the patients with the infections will die. [1]

"These catheter infections are an enormous public-health problem," says critical-care physician Peter Pronovost, director of the Armstrong Institute for Patient Safety at Johns Hopkins Medicine in Baltimore, "and for decades we thought that they were inevitable."

Not anymore, thanks to Pronovost's work over the past decade. First he developed a five-step safety checklist based on Centers for Disease Control guidelines for inserting central lines. He then demonstrated, initially at Johns Hopkins and then at more than 100 hospitals in Michigan, that using the checklist and changing an institution's safety culture can virtually eliminate the infections in hospital ICUs. [2]

Not only were central-line-associated bloodstream infections in Michigan ICUs driven nearly to zero, but infection rates stayed low for three years. [3] "It is a remarkable success story of what is possible when you are guided by science, when the efforts are led by clinicians and when you have good measurements," says Pronovost.

Since 2009, the federal government has been underwriting an effort to spread this success to hospitals nationwide. Called "On the CUSP: Stop BSI [blood stream infection] Project," the program has enlisted 1,055 hospitals — about one-fifth of the nation's total — across 45 states. The first step of the project is to get hospitals to adopt what Pronovost says is his relatively simple checklist. Doctors must:

- Wash their hands,
- Clean the insertion site with the antiseptic chlorhexidine,
- Drape themselves and the patient,
- Avoid placing catheters in the groin, and
- Ask every day if the catheter is still needed.

The other step is to improve the hospital's safety culture so that the checklist is used consistently, properly and forever. "Cultural improvement is harder to institute than the checklist," says Sam Watson, director of the Keystone Center for Patient Safety and Quality at the Michigan Health and Hospital Association, a partner in the federal program. It involves training people how to communicate and work as a team, Watson says.

But without top hospital executives making this change a chief priority, it probably won't happen, he adds. "I can have a group of nurses who are extremely excited about doing something, but without support of a physician champion or senior leadership, they are not going to have much traction," Watson says.

The progress made in the program's first two years may persuade other hospital CEOs to get onboard. Adult ICUs in more than 750 hospitals have reduced their central-line-associated bloodstream infection rates by an average of one-third, and the percentage of ICUs with zero quarterly infection rates increased from 27.3 percent to 69.5 percent. "That is an incredible change," says Watson.

There also is a business case to be made. A study of six Michigan hospitals that are using the checklist and have gone through staff training shows they avoided on average 30 central-line infections a year and averted about $1.1 million in associated costs. [4] That far outweighs the expense of implementing the program.

In April 2011, the administration launched Partnership for Patients, a public-private partnership that it hopes will accomplish what a decade of patient-safety efforts has failed to do. With as much as $1 billion provided by the Affordable Care Act, the program seeks to achieve two goals by the end of 2013:

- A 40 percent decrease in preventable hospital-acquired conditions compared to 2010, which would translate into 1.8 million fewer patient injuries and more than 60,000 fewer deaths.
- A 20 percent reduction in hospital readmissions, which would translate into 1.6 million fewer patients suffering a preventable complication requiring rehospitalization within 30 days of discharge.

The administration projects savings up to $35 billion across the health care system, including up to $10 billion in Medicare savings, over three years. Over 10 years, achieving these goals could reduce Medicare costs by $50 billion, according to the administration. [52]

But at a hearing of the Senate Committee on Health, Education, Labor and Pensions in November, Sen. Mark Kirk, R-Ill., questioned those projections, saying that the Centers for Medicare and Medicaid Services has "no way of backing that up." Kirk indicated the Obama administration's goals could be out of reach. [53]

Dennis Wagner, co-director of Partnership for Patients, however, called the goals ambitious but attainable. "There are individual hospitals and, in fact, entire hospital systems that have already generated these kinds of results," said Wagner last December. [54] That month the program awarded

Yet a substantial number of such infections continue to occur in outpatient hemodialysis centers and inpatient wards, and even in ICUs.

In states that publicly report infection rates by facility, there are some hospitals with rates 10 to 12 times the national average, according to Pronovost, who calls that "a travesty." They are all accredited by the Joint Commission, an independent group, he says.

"At these hospitals, I'll walk around the ICU and I'll say, 'Do you have all the equipment you need?' and they'll say, 'No, the hospital tells us we need to do this checklist, but the equipment is not available,' " says Pronovost. Or he'll ask a nurse " 'If you saw a senior doctor not complying with the checklist, would you speak up?' and they say, 'Peter, are you nuts? What hospital do you work in?' " says Pronovost.

Peter Pronovost, director of the Armstrong Institute for Patient Safety at Johns Hopkins Medicine in Baltimore, has developed a safety checklist that virtually eliminates central-line infections.

Pronovost wants the Joint Commission to hold these hospitals accountable. If their central-line-associated infection rates in the ICU are much higher than the national average, the hospitals should be given three months to bring them down or be subject to a commission investigation, says Pronovost.

But the commission's current focus is on prevention strategies, not outcomes, according to Kelly Podgorny, project director in the Division of Healthcare Quality Evaluation at the Joint Commission. The commission requires its accredited hospitals to follow the checklist, among other practices, as part of its National Patient Safety Goals, and when its surveyors visit hospitals they evaluate how it's being done. "That may include direct observation, and it may include interviewing staff," says Podgorny, as well as talking to patients and sometimes reviewing documentation.

As far as infection rates, "we do not have in our National Patient Safety Goal a particular national average percentage that organizations are held to at this time," she says. That may change. Podgorny says Pronovost's suggestion is "something that we are discussing."

However, the discussion is limited to hospital ICUs. Both Podgorny and Pronovost agree that there is not enough research to know how far central-line infection rates can be reduced in burn units and other inpatient wards.

— Barbara Mantel

[1] "Vital Signs: Central Line — Associated Blood Stream Infections — United States, 2001, 2008, and 2009," Centers for Disease Control and Prevention, www.cdc.gov/mmwr/preview/mmwrhtml/mm6008a4.htm.

[2] Peter Pronovost, *et al.*, "An Intervention to Decrease Catheter-Related Bloodstream Infections in the ICU," *The New England Journal of Medicine*, Dec. 28, 2006, www.nejm.org/doi/full/10.1056/NEJMoa061115.

[3] Peter J. Pronovost, *et al.*, "Sustaining reductions in catheter related bloodstream infections in Michigan intensive care units: observational study," BMJ, Feb. 4, 2010, www.bmj.com/content/340/bmj.c309.abstract?sid=2b4d73f5-78da-42df-a7ce-7709e2aba8a0.

[4] "New Report: Michigan Hospitals Prove Business Case for Quality," Michigan Health and Hospital Association, Aug. 23, 2011.

two-year contracts totaling $218 million to 26 private collaboratives, officially called Hospital Engagement Networks. "You only will achieve goals if you set them," says Bussard of the Hospital and Healthsystem Association of Pennsylvania. The association received one of the 26 contracts, for $5.2 million.

The Hospital Engagement Networks are to serve as "mobile classrooms," sharing the best patient safety practices among hospitals. The networks will work at the regional, state, national or hospital-system level and be required to conduct intensive training programs in hospitals, provide technical support and monitor hospitals' progress in meeting goals.

Besides preventable readmissions, the networks will work to reduce nine areas of preventable harms:

- adverse drug events;
- catheter-associated urinary tract infections;
- central line-associated bloodstream infections;
- injuries from falls;
- obstetrical adverse events;
- pressure ulcers;
- surgical-site infections;
- deep-vein thrombosis and pulmonary embolisms; and
- ventilator-associated pneumonia. [55]

"If you look at the Centers for Disease Control's recent reports on rates of infection, Pennsylvania has already made progress in that area," Bussard says. "But can we make more progress? Absolutely."

Each network will determine how to measure problems and improvement. So for instance, many Pennsylvania hospitals have already participated in collaboratives to reduce bloodstream infections. "What we are finding now is that to keep that infection rate at basically zero, we need to look at factors around the maintenance of the line," says Bussard. "Whereas in another state or another network, they still may be looking at the insertion of lines, and their measures will relate to that."

Out of 216 Pennsylvania hospitals eligible to participate in the state association's Hospital Engagement Network, 108 have signed up so far, while 17 have signed up for national networks, says Bussard, who adds that recruitment is ongoing. Nationwide, more than 3,200 hospitals, a little more than half the nation's hospitals, have become partners in networks to date. [56]

Medical Education

There is no better place to begin training doctors in patient safety than in medical school and the residency programs that follow, say safety experts. Yet, change has been slow.

"Despite the increased attention to patient safety after publication of the IOM ["To Err Is Human"] report, only half of the most recent editions of core medical textbooks reviewed contained any patient safety-related content," wrote researchers in 2008.

The researchers also discovered that only 10.4 percent of all U.S. medical schools formally offered specific courses covering patient safety. And while the Accreditation Council for Graduate Medical Education mandated that residents at teaching hospitals learn about patient safety, the council did not say how that was to be done. [57]

That changed in July 2011, when the council beefed up its requirements, specifying that patient-safety education move out of the lecture hall and become integrated into clinical instruction and supervised patient care. [58] "There are general safety practices that all residents should understand, and then there are those that are specialty-specific," says Woods of Northwestern. For example, they all should know patient-identification procedures and medication allergy assessment, but surgical residents would need to know the surgical checklist as well, says Woods.

The accreditation council also said residents must learn how to work in teams to coordinate patient care. It also said they must learn to participate in identifying systemic problems that can lead to patient injury and to implement solutions. [59] All residents should also understand how to test a suggested solution "to make sure it doesn't lead to significant unintended consequences," says Woods.

Pediatrician Jason Kane is the patient-safety officer for the pediatrics department at Rush Children's Hospital in Chicago and one of the authors of the 2008 study on patient safety and medical education. Kane says his department is incorporating patient safety into resident training by changing the traditional morbidity and mortality conference, where cases with poor or avoidable outcomes are reviewed. These meetings at many hospitals tend to have "a culture of blame and shame. They tend to be hostile, with finger-pointing," says Kane.

The meetings in his department, recently relabeled patient-safety conferences, no longer "focus on who did what" but "on the process of care and how the system allowed this to happen," says Kane. It's called root-cause analysis. His department also does something called failure modes and effects analysis, borrowed from manufacturing, which looks forward and tries to identify fail points before patients are harmed.

In addition, since the summer of 2008 all health care professionals in the hospital, including residents, are trained in crew resource management, borrowed from aviation. "We bring everyone into a workshop and we literally give them the scripting and the language for when they have a concern," says Kane. That way people higher up in the chain of command know to listen. It's important, says Kane, because research has shown that communication failure is the leading root cause of medical errors.

Resident Hours

Extended shifts and little sleep have long been the bane of medical residents. But research has shown that sleep deprivation and fatigue among residents may cause patient harm, and so the Accreditation Council for Graduate Medical Education has changed its rules for the second time in a decade.

In 2003, it imposed a maximum 80-hour work week for residents and a duty shift of no more than 30 consecutive hours. Last July, it reduced the maximum shift for first-year residents, or interns, to 16 hours and slightly shortened shifts for all other residents to a maximum of 28 hours.

The council also now requires residency programs to educate residents and faculty about sleep deprivation and fatigue management, increase supervision of residents and ensure effective hand-offs of patients between shifts. [60]

Some teaching hospitals oppose the reduction in shift hours, concerned about the impact on cost, resident education and the continuity of care now that there will be more hand-offs as interns work shorter shifts. Poor communication during hand-offs is itself a source of medical errors. But sleep experts worry that the changes did not go far enough. "If you put 10 physicians in a room, you'll get 12 opinions on duty hours," said internist Thomas Nasca, chief executive of the accreditation council. The council tried to balance granting residency programs as much education time as possible while protecting patients from harm, he said. [61]

Continued on p. 144

At Issue:

Does hospital reporting of adverse events improve patient safety?

WILLIAM M. MARELLA
DIRECTOR, PATIENT SAFETY REPORTING PROGRAMS, ECRI INSTITUTE; PROGRAM DIRECTOR, PENNSYLVANIA PATIENT SAFETY AUTHORITY

WRITTEN FOR *CQ RESEARCHER*, FEBRUARY 2012

yes

Reporting patient-safety concerns makes the health care system safer by highlighting the vulnerabilities in how we deliver care and providing insight into why adverse events occur and how we can prevent human errors from harming patients. Sharing the reports among hospitals through state reporting programs or patient-safety organizations enables hospitals to learn from one another and to address their own latent hazards. Reporting programs generate actionable information.

In our work with the Pennsylvania Patient Safety Authority, these reports guided our analysis of the causes of wrong-site surgery and determined the most effective preventive strategies. This enabled us to help one group of 30 hospitals reduce these errors by 73 percent and a second group of 19 facilities to go for one year with no wrong-site procedures in their operating rooms. These reports helped to convince regulators to revise labeling requirements for hydromorphone, a powerful narcotic which, when confused with morphine, can cause a fatal overdose. We have used these reports to help reduce infections from central lines-catheters used to deliver drugs directly into the heart. Pennsylvania's rate of central line infections is one-third the national average, and over the past few years our hospitals have reduced these infections by 24 percent.

Reviewing medical records or analyzing billing data may produce better estimates of the underlying rate of adverse events, because reporting systems suffer from under-reporting and confusion about what types of events to report. However, counting events isn't the point of reporting programs. Their unique contribution is the contextual detail about why these events occur and how we might prevent them. Medical charts and billing data fail miserably at this.

Critics often cite the amount of time reporting takes from staff. However, even if regulations didn't require it, hospitals would collect staff reports to identify potential liability claims. Virtually all commercial electronic reporting systems, which hospitals purchase voluntarily, incorporate near misses. Hospitals wouldn't demand this feature if they didn't value the insights these reports provide. Most of these reports can be transferred electronically to reporting programs from hospitals' internal systems without taking any additional time from clinicians.

While hospital reporting is a critical part of the solution, improving safety also requires that the reports be analyzed by experts, that the resulting guidance is useful and timely and that the hospitals implement that guidance effectively. Reporting is a necessary, but not in itself sufficient, condition for improvement.

ROBERT M. WACHTER, MD
ASSOCIATE CHAIRMAN, DEPARTMENT OF MEDICINE, UNIVERSITY OF CALIFORNIA, SAN FRANCISCO

FROM "WACHTER'S WORLD" BLOG, SEPT. 20, 2009; ACCESSED FEB. 6, 2012

no

Our unquestioning support for "report everything" incident reporting has created a bureaucratic, data-churning, enthusiasm-sucking, money-eating monster.

At my hospital, we now receive about 20,000 incident reports (IRs) a year. And believe me, we don't report everything. If we did, I'd estimate that my one hospital would receive at least five times as many IRs.

Is this a problem? Yes, it is. First of all, IRs are all but useless in determining the actual frequency of errors. If the number of a hospital's IRs has gone up over the past year, they breathlessly proclaim, "This is great. We've succeeded in creating a reporting culture. We're getting safer!"

That would sound more credible if hospitals with downward trends didn't invariably shout, "This is great, we have fewer errors! Our efforts are paying off!"

But the bigger problem is that IRs waste huge amounts of time and energy that could better be used elsewhere in patient safety or care. Let's return to my hospital for a moment. Each of our IRs probably generates 20 minutes of reporting and 60 minutes of reading and analysis. That's 26,667 hours of work a year.

If we value the time of our people doing the reporting, reading, analyzing and acting on IRs at an average of $60 per hour, we're talking about a yearly investment of $1.6 million in my one hospital.

Even that expenditure wouldn't be so horrible if this work was yielding useful insights, but, for the most part, it's not.

I'd limit complete, year-round IR reporting to only those errors that cause temporary or serious harm, along with a small number of reporting categories that require complete data. . . . For the remainder of the categories, I'd switch to a monthly schedule: All medication errors get reported in January, all falls in February, all serious pressure ulcers in March, and so on.

I'd estimate that this change would cut the number, and cost, of IRs by at least 50 percent. Risk managers would still hear about the worst errors, sentinel events would come to light to generate root-cause analyses, and a month of complete data for each of the error categories would easily provide sufficient information to explicate more subtle problems. More importantly, caregivers would be more enthusiastic about reporting, and hospital administrators would have the time to analyze the reports and develop meaningful action plans.

Wachter is author of *Understanding Patient Safety.*

Continued from p. 142

"While the changes they made for first-year residents really are transformational and are a major step forward, I personally was disappointed that those changes were limited to interns," says Landrigan of Harvard Medical School. No data suggest that with experience one suddenly becomes immune to the effects of sleep deprivation or fatigue, he says.

"These types of long shifts have been deeply entrenched in the fabric of medicine for a century," says Landrigan, "so it's hard to make change happen" despite some positive research.

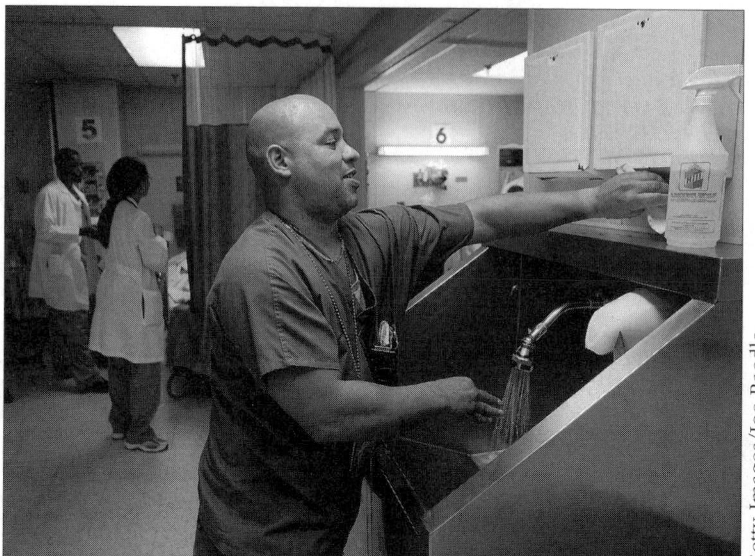

Getty Images/Joe Raedle

Registered nurse Rafael Sepulveda washes his hands in the emergency room at the VA Medical Center Hospital in Miami. Patient-safety experts encourage patients to be actively involved in their medical care, including asking all health care workers who will touch them whether they have washed their hands.

For instance, a 2010 review of available studies found that "reduction or elimination of resident work shifts exceeding 16 hours did not adversely affect resident education and was associated with improvements in patient safety and resident quality of life in most studies." [62]

But each of the studies was limited to a single location and not broad-based, and many physicians say there are still good reasons to be cautious about reducing resident hours. For one thing, it's essentially an unfunded mandate.

"Restricting hours is a mixed bag," says Kane of Rush Children's Hospital. "Hospitals aren't necessarily hiring any new people, so residents are working harder when they do work." Kane says another concern is that if the resident isn't there, the attending physician has to do more work.

"So what's ironic is that you have protected the trainees from fatigue but you're deferring that fatigue to the supervising attending physicians, who are not only responsible for patient care but for all other administrative and academic activities that need to be done in a teaching hospital," says Kane.

"Obviously we don't want an exhausted supervisor," says David Dinges, associate director of the Center for Sleep and Circadian Neurobiology at the University of Pennsylvania's School of Medicine. "It has to be figured into a hospital's budget and costs."

Dinges served on an IOM committee that produced a report on resident duty hours in 2008. The committee recommended that all residents work either a maximum shift of 16 continuous hours or a 30-hour shift with an uninterrupted five-hour break for sleep after 16 hours. [63] ACGME did not adopt the five-hour nap.

It may have been because there is no guarantee that residents would use that nap time. "A resident who says to the senior, 'I'm going to take my nap now,' will they be seen as not hard-working even if they are mandated to do so?" says Kane.

Research into the effectiveness of naps for residents is scarce. Dinges is currently conducting research at two hospitals, tracking how many residents would use protected sleep time, how long would they sleep, the impact on alertness and the cost.

Even without the nap, the costs of the accreditation council's new rules concern many hospitals. One study has estimated the total direct annual costs at close to $400 million nationwide, although that could go lower or higher depending on how these changes are implemented. But if the changes reduce preventable patient injuries, which also cost hospitals money, by at least 11 percent, teaching hospitals would actually come out ahead. [64] ■

OUTLOOK

Budget Pressure

Under the 2010 health care reforms, Medicaid — the state- and federally funded health insurance program for the poor — will be covered by the same no-pay rule applying to Medicare, in which hospitals are not reimbursed for care stemming from a dozen preventable patient harms. Seventeen states already have such a policy, and by July all states must comply. [65]

But the Medicaid no-pay policy has the potential to be much broader than Medicare's because the Centers for Medicare and Medicaid Services is allowing states to expand it beyond hospitals. States could refuse to pay for avoidable health care conditions acquired in nursing homes, outpatient surgery centers, inpatient rehabilitation facilities and health clinics.

The American Medical Association is opposed to the expansion. "There are practical, logistical problems figuring out who is responsible for what," says the AMA's Wynia, because patients may see multiple physicians. And the American Hospital Association has said that the Centers for Medicare and Medicaid Services is exceeding "its statutory authority." [66]

But Baltimore health care lawyer Mark Stanley expects states to take full advantage of the new authority to expand the no-pay rules beyond hospitals. "The rules are being implemented as cash-strapped states look to balance their budgets without the aid of federal stimulus dollars," said Stanley. "Medicaid providers can therefore expect the nonpayment provisions to have some teeth." [67]

The hospital association is hoping to modify another requirement under the health care law that, starting in 2015, hospitals be ranked on their safety record and the bottom 25 percent be penalized through withholding 1 percent of their Medicare payments. The hospitals will be ranked according to their rates of certain hospital-acquired conditions, and the association wants those rates risk-adjusted, so that hospitals that admit sicker patients at higher risk of these conditions aren't "unfairly" penalized. [68]

"The political pressure to reduce the impact of this is going to be immense," says Binder of the Leapfrog Group, which opposes risk adjustment for avoidable hospital conditions.

Budget pressures are having an impact on other areas of reform. Creating an independent agency to oversee the health care information-technology industry, as recommended in a recent IOM report, would require funding. Michael Ettlinger, vice president for economic policy at the Center for American Progress, a left-leaning research organization based in Washington, says it is hard to imagine Congress approving such funding in a presidential election year. "If the administration is for it, then the Republicans are going to be against it," he says.

States that require mandatory reporting of avoidable adverse patient events fund their programs in different ways. Some state legislatures appropriate money for the program, general funds are used in other states and some impose a fee on health care facilities. "However, it is definitely a question of whether they have adequate funding," says Rosenthal of the National Academy for State Health Policy. As a result, many states collect minimal data and lack the resources to track and analyze it and issue advisories to hospitals.

Pennsylvania, whose Patient Safety Authority is funded by a hospital fee, is well known nationally for collecting a broad spectrum of information about patient injuries, including near misses, and working with hospitals and other health care facilities on programs to improve patient safety. But South Dakota and South Carolina, for example, have "bare-bones programs, and I think it is related to the funding that is available," says Rosenthal. Neither state has a dedicated fee.

But creating some kind of national mandatory reporting system to supplement the patchwork of state systems is going to be subject to the same pressures. "In the current political environment, there is certainly not going to be any national reporting requirement," says Leape, the Harvard professor, with disappointment. ■

Notes

[1] David C. Ring, James H. Herndon and Gregg S. Meyer, "Case 34-2010: A 65-Year-Old Woman with an Incorrect Operation on the Left Hand," *The New England Journal of Medicine*, Nov. 11, 2010, p. 1951, www.nejm.org/doi/full/10.1056/NEJMcpc1007085.

[2] JoNel Aleccia, "Surgery error leads doc to public mea culpa," msnbc.com, Nov. 11, 2010, www.msnbc.msn.com/id/40096673/ns/health-health_care/t/surgery-error-leads-doc-public-mea-culpa/#.TxXpxpg7-pE.

[3] Ring, *et al.*, *op. cit.*

[4] Lydia Polgreen, "State to Give Liver Donors Safeguards In Transplants," *The New York Times*, Sept. 26, 2003, www.nytimes.com/2003/09/26/nyregion/state-to-give-liver-donors-safeguards-in-transplants.html?ref=michaelhurewitz.

[5] "To Err is Human: Building a Safer Health System," Institute of Medicine, November 1999, Chapter 2, pp. 26, 34, www.iom.edu/Reports/1999/To-Err-is-Human-Building-A-Safer-Health-System.aspx.

[6] "Preventing Death and Injury from Medical Errors Requires Dramatic System-Wide Changes," press release, National Academy of Sciences, Nov. 29, 1999, www8.nationalacademies.org/onpinews/newsitem.aspx?RecordID=9728.

[7] *Ibid.*

[8] "The Richard & Hinda Rosenthal Lecture 2011: New Frontiers in Patient Safety," IOM, October 2011, p. 5, www.nap.edu/catalog.php?record_id=13217.

[9] Health care-associated infections declined in 2010," press release, CDC, Oct. 19, 2011, www.cdc.gov/media/releases/2011/p1019_healthcare_infections.html. Maggie Fox, "Hospital Infection Rates Drop, CDC Says," *National Journal*, Oct. 19, 2011, www.nationaljournal.com/healthcare/hospital-infection-rates-drop-cdc-says-20111019.

[10] "Adverse Events in Hospitals: National Incidence Among Medicare Beneficiaries," Office of the Inspector General, HHS, November 2010, pp. I-II, http://oig.hhs.gov/oei/reports/oei-06-09-00090.pdf.

[11] "Hospital Incident Reporting Systems Do Not Capture Most Patient Harm," Office of the Inspector General, HHS, January 2012, http://oig.hhs.gov/oei/reports/oei-06-09-00091.pdf.

[12] *Ibid.*

[13] David C. Classen, *et al.*, " 'Global Trigger Tool' Shows That Adverse Events in Hospitals

May Be Ten Times Greater Than Previously Measured," *Health Affairs*, April 2011, p. 1, http://content.healthaffairs.org/content/30/4/581.abstract.

[14] "Safe Practices for Better Healthcare — 2010 Update," National Quality Forum, April 2010, www.qualityforum.org/Publications/2010/04/Safe_Practices_for_Better_Healthcare_-_2010_Update.aspx.

[15] "Hospital Survey on Patient Safety Culture: 2012 User Comparative Database Report," Agency for Healthcare Research and Quality, January 2012, www.ahrq.gov/qual/hospsurvey12/hosp12chart5-2.htm.

[16] Charles Kenney, *Transforming Health Care: Virginia Mason Medical Center's Pursuit of the Perfect Patient Experience* (2011), p. xviii.

[17] Ring, *et al.*, *op. cit.*, p. 1956.

[18] "Improving quality of care during inpatient hospital stays," Fact Sheet, Centers for Medicare and Medicaid Services, Aug. 1, 2011, http://nasuad.org/documentation/newsroom/friday_updates/CMS%20Acute%20Care%20Fact%20Sheet%203.pdf.

[19] "The Richard & Hinda Rosenthal Lecture 2011," *op. cit.*

[20] Michael D. Maves, "Re: Proposed Changes to the Hospital Prospective Payment Systems for Acute Care Hospitals, 76 Fed. Reg. 25,787, May 5, 2011," American Medical Association, June 15, 2011.

[21] Classen, *op. cit.*, p. 2.

[22] "NQF Releases Updated Serious Reportable Events," press release, NQF, June 13, 2011, www.qualityforum.org/News_And_Resources/Press_Releases/2011/NQF_Releases_Updated_Serious_Reportable_Events.aspx.

[23] Fox, *op. cit.*

[24] "Alphabetical Directory of Listed Patient Safety Organizations," AHRQ, www.pso.ahrq.gov/listing/alphalist.htm.

[25] Rushika Fernandopulle and Neil Patel, "How The Electronic Health Record Did Not Measure Up To The Demands of Our Medical Home Practice," *Health Affairs*, April 2010, pp. 622-624, 628, http://content.healthaffairs.org/content/29/4/622.abstract.

[26] "Eligible Professional Meaningful Use Table of Contents Core and Menu Set Objectives," CMS EHR Incentive Programs, www.cms.gov/EHRIncentivePrograms/Downloads/EP-MU-TOC.pdf.

[27] "Electronic Health Record Systems and Intent to Apply for Meaningful Use Incentives Among Office-based Physician Practices: United States, 2001-2011," CDC, www.cdc.gov/nchs/data/databriefs/DB79.pdf.

[28] "Surveys show significant proportions of hospitals and doctors already plan to adopt electronic health records and qualify for federal incentive payments," news release, HHS, Jan. 13, 2011, www.hhs.gov/news/press/2011pres/01/20110113a.html.

[29] "To Improve Patient Safety, Health Information Technology Needs Better Oversight, Accountability," IOM, Nov. 8, 2011, www8.nationalacademies.org/onpinews/newsitem.aspx?RecordID=13269.

[30] Lena H. Sun, "Panel seeks monitor for health IT," *The Washington Post*, Nov. 9, 2011.

[31] "Statement of Carl Dvorak, Epic Systems Corporation, before the HIT Policy Committee Adoption/Certification Workshop," HHS, Feb. 25, 2010.

[32] "Health IT and Patient Safety: Building Safer Systems for Better Care," IOM, November 2011, p. E-2, www.nap.edu/catalog.php?record_id=13269.

[33] *Ibid.*, p. S-10.

[34] See semmelweis.org/about/dr-semmelweis-biography.

[35] William J. Mallon, "E. Amory Codman," American Academy of Orthopaedic Surgeons, www.aaos.org/news/bulletin/janfeb07/research1.asp.

[36] *Ibid.*

[37] "Unmet Needs: Teaching Physicians to Provide Safe Patient Care," Lucian Leape Institute Roundtable on Reforming Medical Education, 2010, www.delawarehsa.org/downloads/kbpc/L%20Leape%20Unmet%20Needs.pdf.

[38] Jeffrey B. Cooper, "Getting Into Patient Safety: A Personal Story," Agency for Healthcare Research and Quality, www.webmm.ahrq.gov/perspective.aspx?perspectiveID=29.

[39] *Ibid.*

[40] Stephen D. Small and Paul Barach, "Patient safety and health policy: a history and review," Hematology/Oncology Clinics of North America, December 2002, http://hcdesign.coa.gatech.edu/paper/session1/Small_Barach.pdf.

[41] *Ibid.*

[42] Lucian Leape, "Scope of Problem and History of Patient Safety," Obstetrics and Gynecology Clinics of North America, October 2008, p. 4, www.obgyn.theclinics.com/article/S0889-8545(07)00118-0/abstract.

[43] Robert M. Wachter and Kaveh G. Shojania, *Internal Bleeding: The Truth Behind America's Terrifying Epidemic of Medical Mistakes* (2004), pp. 55-56.

[44] "To Err is Human: Building a Safer Health System, Institute of Medicine," *op. cit.*, pp. 1-2.

[45] Wachter and Shojania, *op. cit.*, pp. 56-57.

[46] Troyen A. Brennan, *et al.*, "Incidence of Adverse Events and Negligence in Hospitalized Patients — Results of the Harvard Medical Practice Study I," *The New England Journal of Medicine*, Feb. 7, 1991, www.nejm.org/doi/full/10.1056/NEJM199102073240604.

[47] "To Err is Human: Building a Safer Health System," *op cit.*, p. 5.

[48] *Ibid.*, p. 6.

[49] Leape, *op. cit.*, p. 5.

[50] "Medicare Nonpayment for Hospital Acquired Conditions," National Conference of State Legislatures, www.ncsl.org/issues-research/health/medicare-nonpayment-for-hospital-acquired-conditio.aspx.

[51] Leape, *op. cit.*, p. 6.

[52] "Partnership for Patients: Better Care, Lower Costs," HealthCare.gov, www.healthcare.gov/compare/partnership-for-patients.

[53] "Senate Committee on Health, Education, Labor and Pensions Holds a Hearing on Health Care Delivery System Reform," *Political Transcript Wire*, Nov. 11, 2011, www.highbeam.com/doc/1P3-2508605501.html.

[54] Suzanne Hoholik, "2 Ohio Efforts; Feds push hospitals to improve safety," *The Columbus Dispatch*, Dec. 21, 2011, www.dispatch.

About the Author

Barbara Mantel is a freelance writer in New York City. She is a former correspondent and senior producer for National Public Radio and has won several journalism awards, including the National Press Club's Best Consumer Journalism Award and the Front Page Award from the Newswomen's Club of New York for her April 18, 2008, *CQ Researcher* report "Public Defenders." She holds a B.A. in history and economics from the University of Virginia and an M.A. in economics from Northwestern University.

com/content/stories/local/2011/12/21/feds-push-hospitals-toimprove-safety.html.

[55] "Hospital Engagement Networks: Connecting Hospitals To Improve Care," Fact Sheet, CMS, Dec. 14, 2011, www.cms.gov/apps/media/press/factsheet.asp?Counter=4219&intNumPerPage=10&checkDate=&checkKey=&srchType=1&numDays=3500&srchOpt=0&srchData=&keywordType=All&chkNewsType=6&intPage=&showAll=&pYear=&year=&desc=&cboOrder=date.

[56] "Partnership for Patients Pledgers," http://partnershippledge.healthcare.gov. "Fast Facts on U.S. Hospitals," AHA, www.aha.org/research/rc/stat-studies/fast-facts.shtml.

[57] Jason M. Kane, Melissa Brannen and Emily Kern, "Impact of Patient Safety Mandates on Medical Education in the United States," *Journal of Patient Safety*, June 2008, http://journals.lww.com/journalpatientsafety/Abstract/2008/06000/Impact_of_Patient_Safety_Mandates_on_Medical.7.aspx.

[58] "Common Program Requirements Effective: July 1, 2011," ACGME, pp. 10, 12, www.acgme.org/acWebsite/dutyhours/dh_dutyhourscommonpr07012007.pdf.

[59] *Ibid.*

[60] *Ibid.*, pp. 12-14, 17.

[61] Teresa Chin, "New doctors have shorter hours, better work-life balance," *Cleveland Plain Dealer*, Aug. 6, 2011, www.cleveland.com/healthfit/index.ssf/2011/08/new_doctors_have_shorter_hours.html.

[62] Adam C. Levine, *et al.*, "Effects of Reducing or Eliminating Resident Work Shifts over 16 Hours: A Systematic Review," *Sleep*, August 2010, www.journalsleep.org/ViewAbstract.aspx?pid=27858.

[63] "Resident Duty Hours: Enhancing Sleep, Supervision, and Safety," IOM, Dec. 15, 2008, p. 13. http://books.nap.edu/openbook.php?record_id=12508.

[64] Teryl Nuckols and José J. Escarce, "ACGME Common Program Requirements: Potential Cost Implications of Changes to Resident Duty Hours and Related Changes to the Training Environment Announced on September 28, 2010," pp. 4-5, www.acgme-2010standards.org/pdf/dh-CostAnalysisfor2011CPRs.pdf.

[65] Doug Trapp, "Medicaid to reduce hospital pay for preventable conditions," *American Medical News*, June 13, 2011, www.ama-assn.org/amednews/2011/06/13/gvsc0613.htm.

[66] Rick Pollack, "RE: Medicaid Program; Payment Adjustment for Provider-Preventable Conditions Including Health Care-Acquired Conditions," AHA comment, March 18, 2011, www.aha.org/advocacy-issues/letter/2011/110318-cl-hac.pdf.

[67] "CMS Proposes Rule for Medicaid Nonpayment in the Event of Health Care Acquired Conditions," *Payment Matters Newsletter*, Ober Kaler Attorneys at Law, March 10, 2011, www.ober.com/publications/1283-cms-proposes-rule-medicaid-nonpayment-event-health-care-acquired-conditions.

[68] Rick Pollack, "RE: CMS-3239-P, Medicare Program; Hospital Inpatient Value-Based Purchasing Program; Proposed Rule (Vol. 76, No. 9), Jan. 13, 2011," AHA comment, March 1, 2011, www.aha.org/advocacy-issues/letter/2011/11031-cl-cms-3239-p.pdf

FOR MORE INFORMATION

Accreditation Council for Graduate Medical Education, 515 North State St., Suite 2000, Chicago, IL 60654; 312-755-5000; www.acgme.org. Private, nonprofit organization that evaluates and accredits U.S. residency programs.

Agency for Healthcare Research and Quality, U.S. Department of Health and Human Services, 540 Gaither Road, Suite 2000, Rockville, MD 20850; 301-427-1104; www.ahrq.gov. Sponsors research into improving the quality, safety, efficiency and effectiveness of health care.

American Hospital Association, 155 N. Wacker Dr., Chicago, IL 60606; 312-422-3000; www.aha.org. Membership organization committed to shaping and influencing federal legislation and regulation on behalf of the nation's hospitals.

American Medical Association, 515 N. State St., Chicago, IL 60654; 800-621-8335; www.ama-assn.org. Membership organization promoting public health and the interests of physicians and their patients.

Centers for Medicare & Medicaid Services, U.S. Department of Health and Human Services, 7500 Security Blvd., Baltimore, MD 21244; 877-267-2323; www.cms.gov. Administers Medicare, Medicaid and the Children's Health Insurance Program.

Consumers Union Safe Patient Project, 506 West 14th St., Suite A, Austin, TX 78701; 512-477-4431. Seeks to eliminate medical harm and improve FDA oversight of prescription drugs.

Institute for Healthcare Improvement, 20 University Road, 7th Floor, Cambridge, MA 02138; 617-301-4800; www.ihi.org. Nonprofit working with healthcare stakeholders to ensure adoption of best practices and effective innovations.

Joint Commission, One Renaissance Blvd., Oakbrook Terrace, IL 60181; www.jointcommission.org. Nonprofit that accredits and certifies more than 19,000 health-care organizations and programs in the U.S.

Leapfrog Group, 1150 17th St., N.W., Suite 600, Washington, DC 20036; 202-292-6713; www.leapfroggroup.com. Employer-sponsored program alerting health care industry that big leaps in safety, quality and customer value will be recognized and rewarded.

National Academy for State Health Policy, 10 Free St., Second Floor, Portland, ME 04101; 207-874-6524; www.nashp.org. State health policymakers dedicated to helping states achieve excellence in health policy and practice.

National Quality Forum, 1030 15th St., N.W., Suite 800, Washington, DC 20005; 202-783-1300; www.qualityforum.org. Nonprofit working to improve health care quality by endorsing standards for measuring and publicly reporting on performance.

Bibliography

Selected Sources

Books

Kenney, Charles, *Transforming Health Care: Virginia Mason Medical Center's Pursuit of the Perfect Patient Experience*, Productivity Press, 2011.
Administrators, clinicians, front-line workers and hospital trustees seek to transform a Seattle medical center into a defect-free facility.

Wachter, Robert M., and Kaveh G. Shojania, *Internal Bleeding: The Truth Behind America's Terrifying Epidemic of Medical Mistakes*, Rugged Land, 2004.
Two professors at leading medical schools reveal the inner workings, dilemmas and tragedies of an overburdened, understaffed health care system.

Articles

Aleccia, JoNel, "Surgery error leads doc to public mea culpa," msnbc.com, Nov. 11, 2010, www.msnbc.msn.com/id/40096673/ns/health-health_care/t/surgery-error-leads-doc-public-mea-culpa/#.TxXpxpg7-pE.
A Massachusetts General Hospital surgeon performs the wrong procedure on a woman's hand and goes public with the errors that preceded the blunder.

Chin, Teresa, "New doctors have shorter hours, better work-life balance," *Cleveland Plain Dealer*, Aug. 6, 2011, www.cleveland.com/healthfit/index.ssf/2011/08/new_doctors_have_shorter_hours.html.
The accreditation counsel for medical residency programs limits interns' shifts to 16 hours but leaves hours for senior residents largely unchanged.

Fox, Maggie, "Hospital Infection Rates Drop, CDC Says," *National Journal*, Oct. 19, 2001, www.nationaljournal.com/healthcare/hospital-infection-rates-drop-cdc-says-2011 1019.
The Centers for Disease Control and Prevention reports that hospital-acquired infections declined in 2010 thanks to a concerted effort to prevent them.

Hoholik, Suzanne, "2 Ohio Efforts; Feds push hospitals to improve safety," *The Columbus Dispatch*, Dec. 21, 2011, www.dispatch.com/content/stories/local/2011/12/21/feds-push-hospitals-toimprove-safety.html.
The Ohio Hospital Association receives a grant from the federal government to help Ohio hospitals improve patient safety as part of a broad national program.

Sun, Lena H., "Panel seeks monitor for health IT," *The Washington Post*, Nov. 9, 2011.
An influential Institute of Medicine committee recommends federal oversight of the rapidly growing health care information-technology industry.

Reports and Studies

"Adverse Events in Hospitals: National Incidence Among Medicare Beneficiaries," Office of the Inspector General, Department of Health and Human Services, November 2010, http://oig.hhs.gov/oei/reports/oei-06-09-00090.pdf.
A government study finds that one in seven Medicare hospital patients experienced a serious adverse event.

"Health IT and Patient Safety: Building Safer Systems for Better Care," Institute of Medicine, November 2011, www.nap.edu/catalog.php?record_id=13269.
An influential panel of patient-safety experts recommends government oversight of health care information technology.

"Hospital Incident Reporting Systems Do Not Capture Most Patient Harm," Office of the Inspector General, Department of Health and Human Services, January 2012, http://oig.hhs.gov/oei/reports/oei-06-09-00091.pdf.
A government study finds that hospital staff do not report 86 percent of patient incidents of harm.

"Leapfrog Group Report on CPOE Evaluation Tool Results June 2008 to January 2010," Leapfrog Group, June 2010, www.leapfroggroup.org/media/file/NewCPOEEvaluationToolResultsReport.pdf.
A simulation study finds that specially designed computer software failed to pick up half of common medication errors.

"To Err is Human: Building a Safer Health System," Institute of Medicine, November 1999, www.iom.edu/Reports/1999/To-Err-is-Human-Building-A-Safer-Health-System.aspx.
A panel of patient-safety experts releases a landmark report on the dangerous state of U.S. hospitals and triggers congressional and state action.

Classen, David C., *et al.*, "'Global Trigger Tool' Shows That Adverse Events in Hospitals May Be Ten Times Greater Than Previously Measured," *Health Affairs*, April 2011.
Researchers study three hospitals and find that reviewing patient charts uncovers 10 times more patient incidents of harm than staff reports.

Fernandopulle, Rushika, and Neil Patel, "How The Electronic Health Record Did Not Measure Up To The Demands of Our Medical Home Practice," *Health Affairs*, April 2010.
Two doctors describe their disappointing experience with electronic health records in their private practice.

Ring, David C., James H. Herndon and Gregg S. Meyer, "Case 34-2010: A 65-Year-Old Woman with an Incorrect Operation on the Left Hand," *The New England Journal of Medicine*, Nov. 11, 2010.
The authors describe the series of medical staff and system errors that led to a surgical mistake.

The Next Step:

Additional Articles from Current Periodicals

Assessments

Burden, Melissa, "Hospital Safety Rises," *Detroit News*, Oct. 25, 2011.
Michigan hospitals are continuing to make improvements in patient safety and quality, according to the Michigan Health and Hospital Association.

Feinstein, Karen Wolk, "Hospitals Are Still Killing Patients," *Pittsburgh Post-Gazette*, Feb. 27, 2011, p. F1, www.post-gazette.com/pg/11058/1127982-109.stm.
The Pennsylvania Health Care Cost Containment Council says health care continues to be unnecessarily dangerous for patients because needless mistakes are still being made.

Freeman, Liz, "Mistakes More Common in Hospitals Than Estimated," *Naples* (Fla.) *Daily News*, April 8, 2011, p. A3, www.naplesnews.com/news/2011/apr/07/lee-county-hospitals-will-join-nch-using-method-ad/?print=1.
Medical mistakes may occur 10 times more than previously estimated and could occur in a third of all patient admissions, according to a University of Utah study.

May, Heather, and Sheila R. McCann, "Falls, Trauma Most Common Injuries Inside Utah Hospitals," *Salt Lake Tribune*, April 6, 2011, www.sltrib.com/sltrib/news/51576301-78/hospitals-utah-reported-center.html.csp.
Falls, burns and other types of trauma are the most common injuries sustained by patients in Utah hospitals.

McNeill, Ryan, and Daniel Lathrop, "Parkland in Dallas Has Been Among Texas' Worst Hospitals for Patient Safety for Years, Analysis Shows," *Dallas Morning News*, Oct. 16, 2011, www.dallasnews.com/investigations/patient-safety/headlines/20111015-parkland-in-dallas-has-been-among-texas-worst-hospitals-for-patient-safety-for-years-analysis-shows.ece.
A Dallas-area hospital has been put under government monitoring because of systematic failures in patient care.

Osby, Liv, "Study: More Care Needed to Improve Outpatient Safety," *Greenville* (S.C.) *News*, June 26, 2011.
Medical errors happen in outpatient settings as often as they do in hospitals, and experts say it points to the need for enhanced safety initiatives in ambulatory care.

Piper, Ben, "Birmingham Hospitals Rank Low in Patient Safety Report," *Birmingham* (Ala.) *Business Journal*, March 11, 2011, www.bizjournals.com/birmingham/print-edition/2011/03/11/birmingham-hospitals-rank-low-in.html?page=all.
Birmingham, Ala., ranks near the bottom of 68 metropolitan areas for patient safety, according to a study that used three years of data from Medicare patient records.

Rojas-Burke, Joe, "No Gains Against Hospital Mistakes," *The Oregonian*, June 2, 2011, www.oregonlive.com/health/index.ssf/2011/06/oregon_hospitals_reported_136.html.
At least 34 patients died as a result of preventable mistakes in Oregon facilities, in 2010, according to the state's patient-safety commission.

Timko, Nicholas I., "Make Patient Safety a Priority," *Post Standard* (Syracuse, N.Y.), Feb. 7, 2011, p. A13, blog.syracuse.com/opinion/2011/02/commentary_make_patient_safety.html.
There has been little improvement in the rates at which hospitals are infecting, injuring and killing patients, according to the president of the New York State Trial Lawyers Association.

Ulene, Valerie, "When Errors in Care Occur," *Los Angeles Times*, Feb. 28, 2011, p. E1, articles.latimes.com/2011/feb/28/health/la-he-doctors-malpractice-20110228.
The flawed nature of the medical malpractice system often fails to help victims of medical errors, according to a physician columnist.

Wiehe, Jeff, "Study Reveals Hospital Visit Safety Issues," *Fort Wayne* (Ind.) *Journal Gazette*, May 23, 2011, p. A1, www.jg.net/article/20110523/LOCAL/305239970/1002/LOCAL.
Nearly 600 out of 500,000 Medicare patients suffered some sort of ailment after being admitted to an Indiana hospital between October 2008 and June 2010.

Disclosure

Bernhard, Blythe, "Hospitals Want Errors Kept Private," *St. Louis Post-Dispatch*, Feb. 27, 2011, p. A1, www.stltoday.com/news/local/metro/article_9403fd2a-b2f4-5aed-9f08-1d92dc9165b7.html.
Many Missouri hospitals don't want to disclose mistakes because they believe placing blame doesn't make patients safer.

Collins, Lois M., "Most of Us Want Hospitals to Tell Public About Errors, Infections," *Deseret* (Utah) *Morning News*, March 31, 2011, www.deseretnews.com/article/700123138/Consumer-Reports-poll-Most-of-us-want-hospitals-to-tell-public-about-errors-infections.html.
Consumers want to know how individual hospitals are working to prevent medical errors and infections, according to a survey by *Consumer Reports.*

Deed, Martha, "Daughter's Death Gives Mother a Cause," *Buffalo* (N.Y.) *News*, Aug. 13, 2011, p. C1, www.buffalonews.com/life/article521177.ece.
Disclosing medical mistakes can strengthen a community's determination to improve patient safety in local hospitals,

according to the mother of a victim who died from a hospital infection.

Judd, Alan, "A Hidden Shame," ***Atlanta Journal-Constitution*****, Nov. 20, 2011, p. A1.**
Georgia law prohibits public review of reports that hospitals submit following incidents of patient suicides, surgical errors and sexual assaults by hospital staff.

Okeson, Sarah, "Hospital Errors Could Be Public," ***Springfield*** **(Mo.)** ***News-Leader*****, Jan. 13, 2012, p. B1, www.news-leader.com/article/20120113/NEWS01/201130337/hospital-errors-Medicaid.**
Proposed new rules in Missouri could make it possible for serious medical errors to become public record.

Smith, Tammie, "Federal Data Report Errors Made in Hospitals," ***Richmond*** **(Va.)** ***Times Dispatch*****, April 9, 2011, p. B1, www2.timesdispatch.com/business/2011/apr/09/TDBIZ01-federal-data-report-errors-made-in-hospita-ar-960895/.**
Virginia is among several states that have developed error-reporting systems that collect and disclose data on bloodstream infections.

Error Prevention

Cohn, Meredith, "Hopkins Turns to Patient Safety," ***Baltimore Sun*****, May 27, 2011, p. A1, articles.baltimoresun.com/2011-05-26/health/bs-hs-hopkins-patient-safety-20110526_1_patient-safety-medical-mistakes-patient-deaths.**
The Johns Hopkins University School of Medicine plans to use a $10 million gift to launch an institute of patient safety that will conduct research and develop methods that could reduce infections and improper treatments.

Hethcock, Bill, "Hospitals Aim to Cut Injuries, Complications," ***Dallas Business Journal*****, May 13, 2011, www.bizjournals.com/dallas/print-edition/2011/05/13/hospitals-aim-to-cut-injuries.html.**
North Texas hospitals are likely to spend more than $3 million a year combined in a pledge to cut hospital-acquired ailments by 40 percent, according to health care experts.

Jackson Jr., Jodie, "Careful Hand-Washing Shown to Save Lives," ***Columbia*** **(Mo.)** ***Daily Tribune*****, March 3, 2011, p. A6, www.columbiatribune.com/news/2011/mar/03/a-simple-remedy-hand-washing/.**
Good hand-cleansing policies and enforcement have been shown to reduce or eliminate hospital infections.

Kestin, Sally, and Bob LaMendola, "Efforts to Improve Patient Safety Not Enough, Critics Say," ***Orlando*** **(Fla.)** ***Sentinel*****, Aug. 8, 2011, p. A1.**
Technological advances and a national emphasis on preventing mistakes have made little impact on patient safety, says the CEO of a health care software company.

Mullen Jr., Frank X., "System Fail-Safes Key to Reducing Hospital Errors," ***Reno*** **(Nev.)** ***Gazette-Journal*****, June 21, 2011, www.rgj.com/article/20110621/NEWS/106190363/System-fail-safes-key-reducing-hospital-errors.**
Northern Nevada hospital officials say they are working to improve safety systems and creating more opportunities to prevent serious medical mistakes.

Pho, Kevin, "How Doctors Can Reduce Medical Errors, Lawsuits," ***USA Today*****, Jan. 18, 2012, p. A9, www.usatoday.com/news/opinion/forum/story/2012-01-17/doctors-malpractice-errors/52621714/1.**
Doctors must maintain open communication with patients to reduce mistakes, says a primary care physician in New Hampshire.

Ratnayake, Hiran, "Health Law Takes Aim At Hospital Infections," ***News Journal*** **(Wilmington, Del.), April 21, 2011.**
The Partnership for Patients is a federal initiative designed to improve patient safety by forging a bond between hospitals, patient-advocacy groups and government agencies.

Rowe-Peplinski, Lisa, "Patients Play a Key Role in Medication Safety," ***Wisconsin Rapids Daily Tribune*****, March 21, 2011, p. WRT4.**
Patients can help reduce medical errors by listing the medications that they use each time they seek medical care.

Sewell, Abby, "UCI Hospital to Boost Drug Pump Safety," ***Los Angeles Times*****, Dec. 23, 2011, p. A4, articles.latimes.com/2011/dec/23/local/la-me-1223-uci-20111223.**
The University of California at Irvine Medical Center has promised to correct problems with the operation of drug-infusion pumps.

Shelton, Deborah L., "Medical Mistake Spurs Relatives to Join Hospital Panel, Not Sue," ***Chicago Tribune*****, Oct. 7, 2011, p. A1.**
The family of a victim who died from a medical error has chosen to join the Chicago hospital's safety review committee to help prevent future errors.

Thomas, Monifa, "Make Sure Hospital Stay Doesn't Leave You Sicker," ***Chicago Sun-Times*****, April 26, 2011, p. 15, www.suntimes.com/lifestyles/health/4992961-423/make-sure-hospital-stay-doesnt-leave-you-sicker.html.**
The Agency for Healthcare Research and Quality has provided tips to help patients avoid becoming victims of medical errors.

Information Technology

Amaro, Yesenia, "Bar Code System Tracks Hospital's Medications," ***Merced*** **(Calif.)** ***Sun-Star*****, Feb. 8, 2011, www.mercedsunstar.com/2011/02/08/1762569/bar-code-system-tracks-hospitals.html.**

A California hospital has implemented a bar code scanning system intended to increase patient-medication safety.

Graham, Judith, and Cynthia Dizikes, "Technology May Be Risky for Patients," *Chicago Tribune*, June 27, 2011, p. A1, articles.chicagotribune.com/2011-06-27/news/ct-met-technology-errors-20110627_1_electronic-medical-records-physicians-systems.

Computers often present a slew of disorganized data, making it difficult for physicians to quickly find crucial information about patients.

Gulliver, David, "Digital Doctors: Will Technology Help or Harm?" *Bradenton* (Fla.) *Herald*, Sept. 4, 2011, www.bradenton.com/2011/09/04/3467295/digital-doctors-will-technology.html.

Supporters of digitizing medical records say the practice will lead to fewer mistakes and duplicate tests.

Karkaria, Urvaksh, "Piedmont Health to Invest $180M in IT Overhaul," *Atlanta Business Chronicle*, Sept. 16, 2011, www.bizjournals.com/atlanta/print-edition/2011/09/16/piedmont-health-to-invest-180m-in-it.html?page=all.

A large health care provider is investing $180 million in an information technology overhaul designed to improve patient care and control operating costs.

Toland, Bill, "Electronic Records No Panacea," *Pittsburgh Post-Gazette*, Aug. 7, 2011, p. A1, www.post-gazette.com/pg/11219/1165767-114-0.stm.

Studies show that errors and inefficiencies persist in health information technology services.

Ward, Getahn, "Doctors' Shift to Electronic Record Keeping Brings Short-Term Pain," *The Tennessean*, Dec. 13, 2011.

More and more doctors are using electronic records to improve patient safety, but some say the process leads to lower productivity and higher labor costs.

Wilson, Kathleen, "County Shifts to Electronic Health Data," *Ventura County* (Calif.) *Star*, Oct. 7, 2011, p. A1.

A California county has entered into a $32 million contract for an electronic health records system intended to improve patient care and cut costs.

Young, Jeffrey, "GE Unit Targets Medical Errors," Bloomberg, Feb. 14, 2011, www.bloomberg.com/news/2011-02-09/ge-s-healthcare-unit-joins-u-s-medical-error-avoidance-program.html.

General Electric's health care unit — a leading provider of health information technology systems — has joined a government initiative designed to reduce medical errors.

Penalties

Gorman, Anna, "Medical Centers Fined Over Errors," *Los Angeles Times*, Sept. 8, 2011, p. AA3, articles.latimes.com/2011/sep/08/local/la-me-0908-medical-errors-20110908.

California public health officials have fined 12 medical centers for errors that have harmed or killed patients.

Japsen, Bruce, "Death Prompts Action," *Chicago Tribune*, April 15, 2011, p. A27.

The U.S. Centers for Medicare and Medicaid Services terminated the University of Chicago Medical Center's Medicare payments after a death exposed deficiencies deemed threatening to patient health and safety.

Lundberg, Carol, "So Sorry? So What?" *Michigan Lawyers Weekly*, April 29, 2011.

Republican Gov. Rick Snyder has signed a law that allows health care providers in Michigan to apologize for mistakes without fear that their words will be used against them in court.

McKinney, Maureen, "Going Beyond Saying You're Sorry," *Modern Healthcare*, March 28, 2011, p. 32, www.modernhealthcare.com/article/20110328/MAGAZINE/110329968.

More and more hospitals are allowing full transparency of medical errors in an effort to avoid potentially large financial penalties.

Melvin, Joshua, "Seton Hospital Fined $100,000 After Patient Suffocates," *Contra Costa* (Calif.) *Times*, Jan. 31, 2012, www.contracostatimes.com/breaking-news/ci_19860419.

A California medical center has been fined $100,000 — the maximum state penalty — after a nearly comatose patient suffocated because of the hospital's error.

Woodards, Shantee, "State Fines BWMC for Radiation Error," *Maryland Gazette*, Aug. 6, 2011, p. A2, www.mdgazette.com/content/state-fines-bwmc-radiation-error.

A Maryland hospital was fined $14,000 by state regulators for giving a patient an improper dose of radiation.

CITING *CQ RESEARCHER*

Sample formats for citing these reports in a bibliography include the ones listed below. Preferred styles and formats vary, so please check with your instructor or professor.

MLA STYLE

Jost, Kenneth. "Remembering 9/11," CQ Researcher 2 Sept. 2011: 701-732.

APA STYLE

Jost, K. (2011, September 2). Remembering 9/11. *CQ Researcher, 9*, 701-732.

CHICAGO STYLE

Jost, Kenneth. "Remembering 9/11." *CQ Researcher*, September 2, 2011, 701-732.

In-depth Reports on Issues in the News

Are you writing a paper?
Need backup for a debate?
Want to become an expert on an issue?

For more than 80 years, students have turned to *CQ Researcher* for in-depth reporting on issues in the news. Reports on a full range of political and social issues are now available. Following is a selection of recent reports:

Civil Liberties
Remembering 9/11, 9/11
Government Secrecy, 2/11
Cybersecurity, 2/10
Press Freedom, 2/10

Crime/Law
Financial Misconduct, 1/12
Eyewitness Testimony, 10/11
Legal-Aid Crisis, 10/11
Computer Hacking, 9/11
Cameras in the Courtroom, 1/11
Death Penalty Debates, 11/10

Education
Youth Volunteerism, 1/12
Digital Education, 12/11
College Football, 11/11
Student Debt, 10/11
School Reform, 4/11
Crime on Campus, 2/11

Environment/Society
Fracking Controversy, 12/11
Water Crisis in the West, 12/11
Google's Dominance, 11/11
Managing Public Lands, 11/11

Health/Safety
Military Suicides, 9/11
Teen Drug Use, 6/11
Organ Donations, 4/11
Genes and Health, 1/11
Food Safety, 12/10
Preventing Bullying, 12/10

Politics/Economy
Presidential Election, 2/12
'Occupy' Movement, 1/12
Reviving Manufacturing, 7/11
Lies and Politics, 2/11

Upcoming Reports

Invasive Species, 2/17/12
Space Program, 2/24/12
Attracting Jobs, 3/2/12

ACCESS
CQ Researcher is available in print and online. For access, visit your library or www.cqresearcher.com.

STAY CURRENT
For notice of upcoming *CQ Researcher* reports or to learn more about *CQ Researcher* products, subscribe to the free e-mail newsletters, *CQ Researcher Alert!* and *CQ Researcher News*: http://cqpress.com/newsletters.

PURCHASE
To purchase a *CQ Researcher* report in print or electronic format (PDF), visit www.cqpress.com or call 866-427-7737. Single reports start at $15. Bulk purchase discounts and electronic-rights licensing are also available.

SUBSCRIBE
Annual full-service *CQ Researcher* subscriptions—including 44 reports a year, monthly index updates, and a bound volume—start at $1,054. Add $25 for domestic postage.

CQ Researcher Online offers a backfile from 1991 and a number of tools to simplify research. For pricing information, call 800-834-9020, or e-mail librarymarketing@cqpress.com.

CQ RESEARCHER ***PLUS*** *ARCHIVE*

GET ONLINE ACCESS TO VITAL ISSUES FROM 1923 TO THE PRESENT

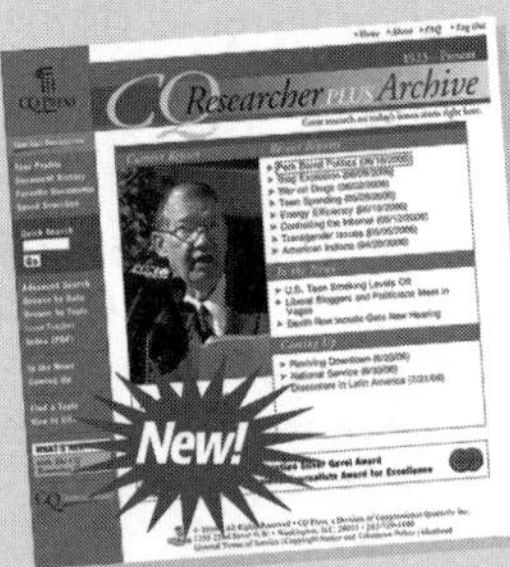

CQ Researcher Plus Archive delivers fast, online access to every *CQ Researcher* report from 1991 to the present, *PLUS* lets you explore the complete archive of *Editorial Research Reports** from 1923-1990. Search and browse more than 3,600 in-depth reports.

Loaded with handy online features, *CQ Researcher Plus Archive* provides the trustworthy reporting and the advanced online functionality today's researchers demand. The new "Issue Tracker" feature provides quick links to past and present reports on the specific topics you need.

For a free trial, visit http://library.cqpress.com/trials.

For pricing information, call 1-800-834-9020, ext. 1906 or e-mail librarymarketing@cqpress.com.

**Editorial Research Reports*, the predecessor to *CQ Researcher*, provides the same expert, nonpartisan reporting on the vital issues that have shaped our society.

CQ Press • 2300 N Street, NW, Suite 800 • Washington, DC 20037

CQ Researcher

Published by CQ Press, an Imprint of SAGE Publications, Inc.

www.cqresearcher.com

Invasive Species

Should non-native species be screened at U.S. borders?

Non-native plants and animals have invaded major areas of the United States, including the Great Lakes and Rocky Mountains, causing billions of dollars in damage yearly. Many imported species are harmless in new locations, but some thrive, altering ecosystems and killing off native wildlife. In the Florida Everglades, thousands of Burmese pythons — many the progeny of pets released illegally by owners — are devouring native animals, and wildlife officials are at a loss as to how to eradicate the giant snakes. Moreover, climate change has allowed both non-native and native species, such as the Western bark beetle, to spread at high rates and cause widespread environmental damage. To stem the tide of invasive species, conservationists want to tighten U.S. import laws. But the exotic pet industry — a major source of invasives — argues that stricter laws would undercut private rights. Meanwhile regulators with limited resources face hard choices about which species to control.

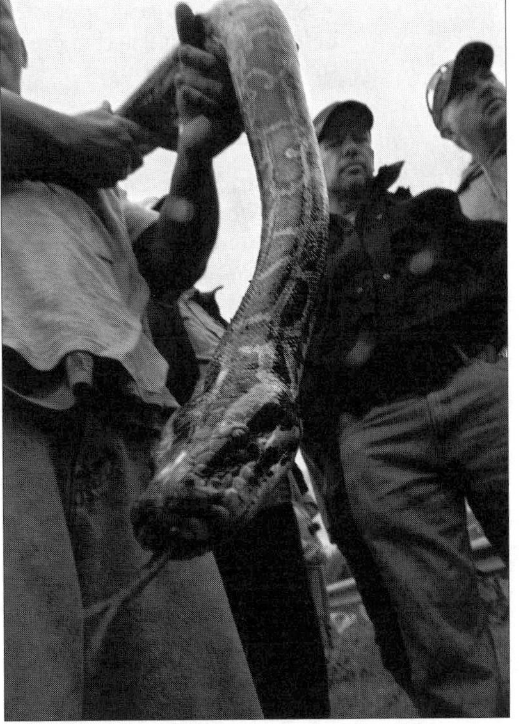

More than 1,300 Burmese pythons were removed from the Everglades between 2000 and 2010, but thousands more remain in South Florida. Last year a 16-foot python that had swallowed a deer whole was killed in Everglades National Park.

INSIDE THIS REPORT

The Issues 155
Background 161
Chronology 163
Current Situation 166
At Issue........................169
Outlook 170
Bibliography 174
The Next Step 175

CQ Researcher • Feb. 17, 2012 • www.cqresearcher.com
Volume 22, Number 7 • Pages 153-176

SAGE | CQPRESS
Los Angeles | London | New Delhi
Singapore | Washington DC

Recipient of Society of Professional Journalists Award for Excellence ◆ American Bar Association Silver Gavel Award

THE ISSUES

155 • Should invasive species be eliminated?
• Is climate change promoting the spread of invasive species?
• Should the exotic pet industry be regulated more strictly?

BACKGROUND

161 **Exploring the New World**
Europeans triggered ecological invasions in the 1500s.

162 **Early Controls**
In 1900, Congress passed the first federal wildlife-protection law

165 **Grappling With Invasions**
The 1973 Endangered Species Act protected plants, animals and habitats.

165 **Altered Communities**
In the 1990s, the new field of invasion biology focused on environments such as Chesapeake Bay.

CURRENT SITUATION

166 **Border Quarantines**
Many scientists advocate tighter import restrictions, but others say such laws would be too broad.

166 **New Strategies**
Amnesty days and other creative approaches are being used to control non-native species.

170 **Backyard Wildlife**
As suburbs spread to wooded areas, they attract wild animals.

OUTLOOK

170 **Tighter Restrictions**
Experts call for better enforcement of existing laws.

SIDEBARS AND GRAPHICS

156 **Wildlife Refuges Threatened**
More than 150 million acres are affected.

157 **Efforts Grow to Eradicate Everglades Pythons**
More than 1,300 were removed since 2000.

159 **Invasives Cost Billions**
Insects alone destroy crops worth $13 billion.

160 **Non-Indigenous Aquatic Species on the Rise**
Two-thirds of the 1,600 species are in lakes and rivers.

163 **Chronology**
Key events since 1889.

164 **Native Species Suffer When Invasives Thrive**
Exotic newcomers contribute to "environmental apocalypse."

167 **Aquatic Invaders Corrupting World's Waters**
"They crowd out other species."

169 **At Issue**
Should imports of large constricting snakes be banned?

FOR FURTHER RESEARCH

173 **For More Information**
Organizations to contact.

174 **Bibliography**
Selected sources used.

175 **The Next Step**
Additional articles.

175 **Citing *CQ Researcher***
Sample bibliography formats.

Cover: *The Miami Herald*/McClatchy Times/Getty Images/Tim Chapman

CQ Researcher

Feb. 17, 2012
Volume 22, Number 7

MANAGING EDITOR: Thomas J. Billitteri
tjb@cqpress.com

ASSISTANT MANAGING EDITOR: Kathy Koch
kkoch@cqpress.com

CONTRIBUTING EDITOR: Thomas J. Colin
tcolin@cqpress.com

ASSOCIATE EDITOR: Kenneth Jost

STAFF WRITER: Marcia Clemmitt

CONTRIBUTING WRITERS: Sarah Glazer, Alan Greenblatt, Peter Katel, Barbara Mantel, Jennifer Weeks

DESIGN/PRODUCTION EDITOR: Olu B. Davis

ASSISTANT EDITOR: Darrell Dela Rosa

FACT CHECKER: Michelle Harris

Los Angeles | London | New Delhi
Singapore | Washington DC

An Imprint of SAGE Publications, Inc.

VICE PRESIDENT AND EDITORIAL DIRECTOR, HIGHER EDUCATION GROUP:
Michele Sordi

DIRECTOR, ONLINE PUBLISHING:
Todd Baldwin

CQ Researcher (ISSN 1056-2036) is printed on acid-free paper. Published weekly, except: (March wk. 5) (May wk. 4) (July wk. 1) (Aug. wks. 3, 4) (Nov. wk. 4) and (Dec. wks. 3, 4). Published by SAGE Publications, Inc., 2455 Teller Rd., Thousand Oaks, CA 91320. Annual full-service subscriptions start at $1,054. For pricing, call 1-800-834-9020. To purchase a *CQ Researcher* report in print or electronic format (PDF), visit www.cqpress.com or call 866-427-7737. Single reports start at $15. Bulk purchase discounts and electronic-rights licensing are also available. Periodicals postage paid at Thousand Oaks, California, and at additional mailing offices. POSTMASTER: Send address changes to *CQ Researcher*, 2300 N St., N.W., Suite 800, Washington, DC 20037.

Invasive Species

BY JENNIFER WEEKS

THE ISSUES

Last October, a work crew made its way to a tree island in Florida's Everglades, aiming to cut down lygodium vines, an invasive species native to Asia and Australia. Growing as high as 90 feet, the thick vines have taken over thousands of Florida acres, shading out native vegetation.

But as crew members carefully explored the island — on the lookout for alligators — they found much bigger quarry than invasive vines: a 16-foot Burmese python dangling from a tree, with an enormous bulge in its midsection. After the snake was killed with a shotgun, an autopsy showed that it had swallowed a 76-pound deer. [1]

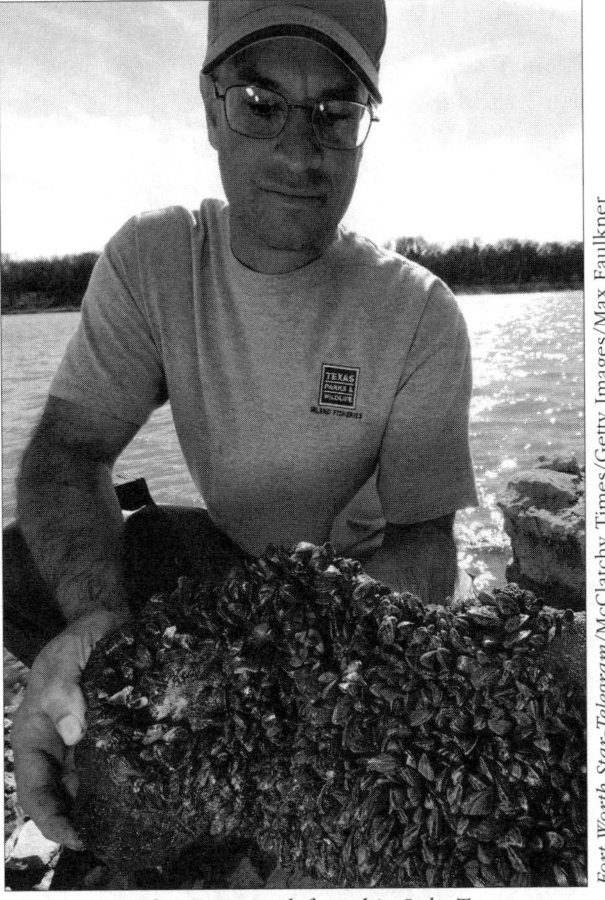

Fort Worth Star-Telegram/McClatchy Times/Getty Images/Max Faulkner

Zebra mussels cover a rock found in Lake Texoma, on the Texas-Oklahoma border. Brought to the United States from Russia on ship hulls or in their ballast tanks, the mussels clog water intake valves at power plants and factories and compete with native species. Many of the thousands of plants and animals imported to the United States are harmless, but some endanger native species and cause billions of dollars in damage.

Florida's lush climate, thriving exotic pet industry and role as a global cargo entry point make it a hotspot for invasive species. Burmese pythons are just one of many non-native organisms that have become established and are preying on local wildlife. [2] Some of the huge snakes escaped from captivity near the Everglades during Hurricane Andrew in 1992; others were released later by owners who could not manage the snakes once they grew to full size.

State officials removed more than 1,300 Burmese pythons from the Everglades between 2000 and 2010, and press reports estimate that thousands more pythons and other large constrictors live in the wild in South Florida today. [3] The huge predators threaten Florida's endangered animals and birds — and, some say, its human residents. In 2005 a python swallowed a 6-foot alligator in the Everglades and then burst open; four years later a pet python strangled a 2-year-old girl in her home in central Florida. [4]

Florida's invasive snakes generate lurid headlines, but they are just one example of thousands of invasive animals and plants that are ravaging waterways, forests and grasslands across the United States. For example, carnivorous Asian carp are on the verge of colonizing the Great Lakes, where they could devastate the region's fisheries. Nutria — semi-aquatic rodents similar to muskrats — are accelerating erosion along the Gulf Coast, making the region more vulnerable to storms and floods. And fast-spreading and highly flammable cheatgrass is increasing the frequency and intensity of prairie fires in many Western states.

"Non-native invasives are coming in from all corners of the globe, and they're affecting land, wildlife and forests," says Bill Toomey, director of forest health protection for The Nature Conservancy, a conservation group that works to protect ecologically important lands and waters in the United States and more than 30 other countries. "They are a major threat to forests, which cover one-third of the U.S., filter or store half of our water supply and provide jobs to millions of people."

Humans have moved plants and animals around the globe for centuries but began to realize the potential consequences of doing so only in recent decades. Many organisms flourish in a new setting without causing harm and are known as exotic or non-native species. But when transplants have no natural predators or controls in their new locations, they can thrive and multiply aggressively, crowding out or preying on native species and disrupting local ecosystems.

More than 6,500 non-indigenous species have become established in the United States and are causing environmental or economic damage or threatening public health, according to the U.S. Geological Survey. [5] One widely cited analysis estimates that invasive species cause nearly $120 billion in damages in the United States every

Invasive Species Threaten Wildlife Refuges

Invasive species ranging from rodents and ants to climbing vines and noxious weeds imperil marshes, meadows, dunes and grasslands within the National Wildlife Refuge System, a 150-million-acre network of public lands managed by the U.S. Fish and Wildlife Service, including 556 refuges. The Audubon Society, a national conservation organization, has identified several particularly vulnerable "hot spots."

Invasive Species "Hot Spots" in the National Wildlife Refuge (NWR) System

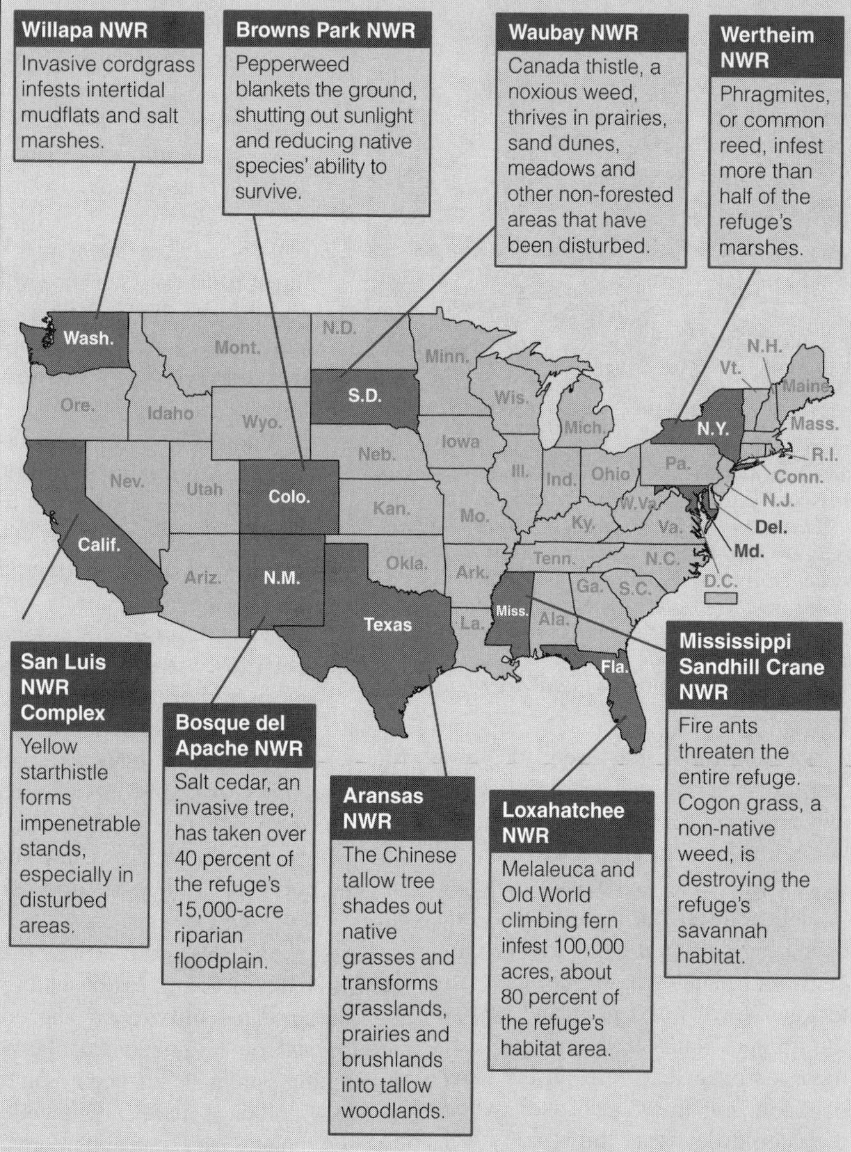
Willapa NWR
Invasive cordgrass infests intertidal mudflats and salt marshes.
Browns Park NWR
Pepperweed blankets the ground, shutting out sunlight and reducing native species' ability to survive.
Waubay NWR
Canada thistle, a noxious weed, thrives in prairies, sand dunes, meadows and other non-forested areas that have been disturbed.
Wertheim NWR
Phragmites, or common reed, infest more than half of the refuge's marshes.
San Luis NWR Complex
Yellow starthistle forms impenetrable stands, especially in disturbed areas.
Bosque del Apache NWR
Salt cedar, an invasive tree, has taken over 40 percent of the refuge's 15,000-acre riparian floodplain.
Aransas NWR
The Chinese tallow tree shades out native grasses and transforms grasslands, prairies and brushlands into tallow woodlands.
Loxahatchee NWR
Melaleuca and Old World climbing fern infest 100,000 acres, about 80 percent of the refuge's habitat area.
Mississippi Sandhill Crane NWR
Fire ants threaten the entire refuge. Cogon grass, a non-native weed, is destroying the refuge's savannah habitat.
Wash.
Ore.
Calif.
Idaho
Nev.
Mont.
Wyo.
Utah
Ariz.
Colo.
N.M.
N.D.
S.D.
Neb.
Kan.
Okla.
Texas
Minn.
Iowa
Mo.
Ark.
La.
Wis.
Ill.
Mich.
Ind.
Ohio
Ky.
Tenn.
Miss.
Ala.
Ga.
Fla.
S.C.
N.C.
Va.
W.Va.
Pa.
N.Y.
Vt.
N.H.
Maine
Mass.
R.I.
Conn.
N.J.
Del.
Md.
D.C.

Source: National Audubon Society, 2012, policy.audubon.org/invasive-species-hot-spots-national-wildlife-refuge-system

year. [6] Another study calculates that in the Great Lakes alone, ship-borne invasive species cause at least $200 million in damage to fisheries, wildlife and water quality annually. [7] And a study funded by The Nature Conservancy estimates that damage from invasive forest insects costs local governments nearly $1.7 billion and private property owners about $830 million yearly. [8]

Invasive species are so widespread that some have penetrated into popular culture. Wild pigs, which are scourges in California, Hawaii and the South, inspired a 2009 Discovery Channel series called "Pig Bomb." ("Moving into our towns. Attacking our animals — and even coming after us," a narrator intoned ominously in a preview.) [9] Videos of Asian carp, which can leap 10 feet or more out of the water when they are disturbed by boat noise, have become a staple on YouTube. And acclaimed writer T.C. Boyle's latest novel, *When the Killing's Done*, is a fictional account of controversies over eliminating invasive rats and feral pigs from California's Channel Islands. [10]

Raising public awareness is a start, but conservationists say the United States needs to tighten laws and regulations. The most important steps, they contend, are prescreening imported plants and animals to keep potential invaders out of the country; creating stronger requirements for ships to treat ballast water before discharge; and providing more funding for agencies that prevent and control invasive species. [11]

However, some businesses that import and sell exotic species resist new regulations, arguing that the harm is overstated, stricter rules threaten profits and private owners help protect threatened species. (*See "At Issue," Page 169.*) Other businesses that trade in non-native species support tighter restrictions, though. The U.S. horticulture industry — which introduced many exotic plants to the nation over more than a century — now is helping to shape standards to help prevent new invasions, conservationists say.

Global climate change is worsening the picture, according to environmental advocates and numerous research studies. Many invasive species are well positioned to profit from climate change. For example, tamarisk (a shrub also known as salt cedar) grows well in hot, dry locations. Drought in Western states is expanding zones suitable for tamarisk, which is crowding out cottonwood trees and other native plants along streambeds. And red fire ants, which sting humans and damage trees and crops, are spreading northward as average annual temperatures rise. [12]

To confront these challenges, government agencies and outdoor advocates are trying creative strategies. Some states offer amnesty days when owners can turn in exotic pets to government handlers with no questions asked — an alternative to releasing them outdoors. In another approach, some regulators and conservationists are appealing to the ultimate predator — humans — to hunt down and serve up edible species such as lionfish, carp and feral pigs.

As government officials, conservationists and businesses debate how to curb the spread of invasive species, here are some questions they are considering:

Efforts Grow to Eradicate Everglades Pythons

More than 1,000 invasive pythons were removed from Florida's Everglades and surrounding areas between 2008 and 2010. A recent study suggests the giant snakes may have virtually eliminated racoons, possums, deer and bobcats in the park. The invasion resulted from animals that escaped from captivity and pet owners releasing snakes into the wild.

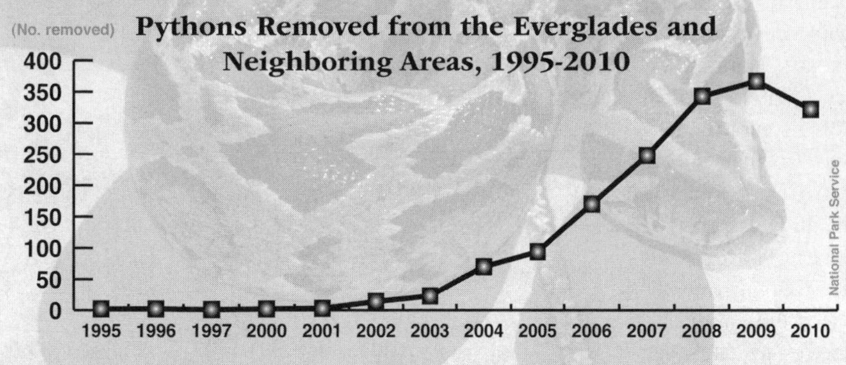

Source: Michael E. Dorcas, Department of Biology, Davidson College

Should invasive species be eliminated?

Executive Order 13112, issued by President Bill Clinton in 1999, defines an invasive species as "an alien species whose introduction does or is likely to cause economic or environmental harm or harm to human health." [13] U.S. policy states that invasive species should be stopped or at least contained, and that species and ecosystems affected by invasions should be restored to make them more resilient. [14]

But some scientists argue that this approach is based on a misleading distinction between native and non-native species and assumes that native species are desirable but non-native species are harmful. Instead, they contend it is time to accept the fact that humans have drastically altered many of the world's ecosystems and that conservation efforts should target species that are harmful, whether native or not.

Nineteen scientists made this argument in an article last June in the British science journal *Nature*. "[M]any of the claims driving people's perception that introduced species pose an apocalyptic threat to biodiversity are not backed by data," they argued. Further, the authors asserted, "It is impractical to try to restore ecosystems to some 'rightful' historical state. . . . We must embrace the fact of 'novel ecosystems' and incorporate many alien species into management plans, rather than try to achieve the often impossible goal of eradicating them or drastically reducing their abundance." (They acknowledged, however, that some invasive species, such as zebra mussels — small shellfish that cover ship hulls and clog water intake valves at power plants and factories — cause serious damage and should be controlled.) [15]

"The term 'invasive' is applied too easily and liberally, and it's often based on assumptions of harm instead of scientific evidence," says Mark Davis, a biology professor at Macalester College in St. Paul, Minn., and the *Nature* article's lead author. "A lot of policy has been made on beliefs that were not solidly backed up with scientific data."

As one example, Davis argues that the impact of invasive plants in Midwestern and Northeastern forests has been exaggerated and that actions such as spraying to kill these plants in national parks have been ineffective. "The assumption was that these plants were choking out natives and reducing biodiversity, but recent studies show that the ecosystems were changing anyway. The drivers were more likely factors like over-browsing by deer and invasions of earthworms — these plants were just taking advantage of the opportunities. They're more like passengers than pilots," he says.

Other scientists, however, reject the charge that they are too quick to condemn every exotic or non-native species. "Plenty of exotic plants are useful. The corn on my table is exotic to North America," says Damon Waitt, senior director and botanist at the Lady Bird Johnson Wildflower Center at the University of Texas in Austin. "Invasive is about the ability of a species to take over. It's not about where it came from, it's about what it does when it gets here."

Many scientists stress that they are not reflexively against all non-native species, just the harmful ones. "There is no campaign against all introductions," 141 scientists argued in response to the *Nature* article. Moreover, they contended, it is important to assess new species very carefully because some might have harmful impacts that only become apparent over time. "Pronouncing a newly introduced species as harmless can lead to bad decisions about its management," they warned. [16]

The idea of accepting invasives — at least, those that have become well-established — has divided scientists in biodiversity hotspots like Puerto Rico, Panama and the Galápagos Islands, an archipelago in the Pacific Ocean west of Ecuador. Hotspots are zones that have especially high concentrations of plants and animals found nowhere else and that some scientists and environmental groups say should be conservation priorities. [17] But many of these hotspots have also been heavily colonized by invasive species, and some researchers say it makes more sense to accept those that are not harmful as "new natives" instead of trying to eliminate them.

Archaelogical Institute of America/Lindblad Expeditions

Invasive species have become well-established in the Galápagos Islands and other biodiversity hotspots — zones that have especially high concentrations of plants and animals, such as the giant tortoise, found nowhere else. Some researchers say it makes more sense to accept exotic species that are not harmful as "new natives" instead of trying to eliminate them. For now, however, that is a minority view.

"As scientists and conservationists, we need to recognize that we've failed: Galápagos will never be pristine," said Mark Gardener, head of restoration at the Charles Darwin Research Station on the Galápagos island of Santa Cruz. For now, however, this is a minority view. Conservation biologists typically argue that altered ecosystems are not as diverse or healthy as they were in their original states, although some studies suggest novel ecosystems can also be diverse and healthy. [18]

Toomey of The Nature Conservancy says that these discussions are useful. "We all want to use our resources as efficiently as we can," he says. "We're not trying to combat invasives everywhere — we're focusing on species that could cause the most serious damage to species or populations." In his view, invasive species control efforts can succeed only if they have clear goals and carefully estimate the resources that will be needed to get the job done. "It makes a big difference whether your goal is eradicating a species or containing it," he says.

Is climate change promoting the spread of invasive species?

Non-native organisms have the potential to become invasive if they encounter favorable conditions for growth and reproduction in their new settings, such as suitable temperature ranges, moisture levels and food sources, and a lack of predators. Many environmentalists have warned that climate change will promote the spread of invasive species — particularly plants and insects that thrive in tropical climates — and cause native pests to multiply at invasive rates.

For example, the National Wildlife Federation, a national conservation advocacy group, warned in 2010, "As climate change causes winters to warm and seasons to shift, a host of exotic invasives and destructive natives are marching their way into our lives at an ever-increasing rate." Species that the study predicted would expand their ranges, become more toxic or increase in numbers included deer ticks (which carry Lyme disease), poison ivy, cheatgrass, fire ants and mosquitoes. [19]

In Western states and Canada, bark beetles have killed millions of pine and spruce trees over the past decade, leaving vast hillsides covered with brown stands of dead conifers. Although the beetles are native to the West, these outbreaks are the largest and most severe ever recorded. After years of research, the U.S. Forest Service has concluded that climate change is a factor fueling the destruction.

"We view climate change as a very strong accelerator of beetle disturbances," says David Cleaves, a senior adviser with the Forest Service. "We would probably have had a situation without it, but it might not have been as big." If temperatures sink to around -40 degrees Fahrenheit for several weeks during winter, beetle populations normally do not explode during warm weather. However, winter temperatures have been rising across the West in recent decades, so more beetles are surviving through the year.

What's more, bark beetles are moving up to higher elevations than they have occupied in the past, so the Forest Service expects that the insects may start attacking new species of trees. "The context is changing, and checks on the beetles are relaxing, so we're getting surprised," says Cleaves.

Climate change is also driving the spread of some invasive plants, scientists say. One study used data initiated over 150 years ago by famed author and conservationist Henry David Thoreau that tracked spring temperatures and the first bloom of various species of flowers around Concord, Mass. Contemporary researchers found that over that time, non-native species were better able than native species to adapt to climate change through adjustments such as blooming earlier as winters became shorter. [20]

Another study found that yellow starthistle, an invasive weed in Western states, was better able to respond to increased carbon dioxide levels than native grasses. (Climate change is driven by increasing levels of carbon dioxide and other greenhouse gases in the atmosphere.) "It was an impressive increase in growth," said Purdue University forestry professor Jeff Dukes, lead author of the study. [21]

But other researchers warn that such findings are very specific to individual species and may not signal a broad trend. "All species are going to be influenced by climate change, not just the non-natives, and some native species may become much bigger problems than they have been in the past," says Macalester College's Davis. "It's very hard to generalize about the

Invasive Species Cost Billions

Invasive species cause billions of dollars in damage annually in the United States. Invasive insects alone destroy $13 billion worth of crops each year, and the U.S. Fish and Wildlife Service and its partners have spent more than $6 million since 2005 to control invasive constrictor snakes in Florida.

Cost of Selected Invasive Species

- Sudden oak death, an invasive forest pathogen, is projected to cost $7.5 million in tree treatment, removal and replacement from 2010 to 2020.
- Salt cedar, an invasive tree, costs Western states between $450 and $2,800 annually per hectare (2.47 acres) in water and flood-control losses; eradication and revegetation projects cost about $7,400 per hectare.
- Black and Norway rats annually consume stored grains and destroy other property valued at more than $19 billion.
- Invasive species in ship ballast or on hulls cost the Great Lakes region $200 million annually to control.
- Invasive insects destroy $13 billion worth of crops annually.
- The Fish and Wildlife Service, along with other organizations, has spent more than $6 million since 2005 combating invasive constrictor snakes in Florida.

Sources: "The Cost of Invasive Species," U.S. Fish and Wildlife Service, January 2012, www.fws.gov/home/feature/2012/pdfs/CostofInvasivesFactSheet.pdf; "The Economic Cost of Large Constrictor Snakes," U.S. Fish and Wildlife Service, January 2012, www.fws.gov/home/feature/2012/pdfs/EconImpact.pdf

Non-Indigenous Aquatic Species on the Rise

About 1,600 non-indigenous aquatic species have been introduced into the United States, with the total more than tripling since 1950. About half are fish and plants, and the rest are reptiles, amphibians, corals, shellfish, sponges, bacteria and viruses. About two-thirds are found in freshwater lakes and rivers, and the rest in oceans and bays.

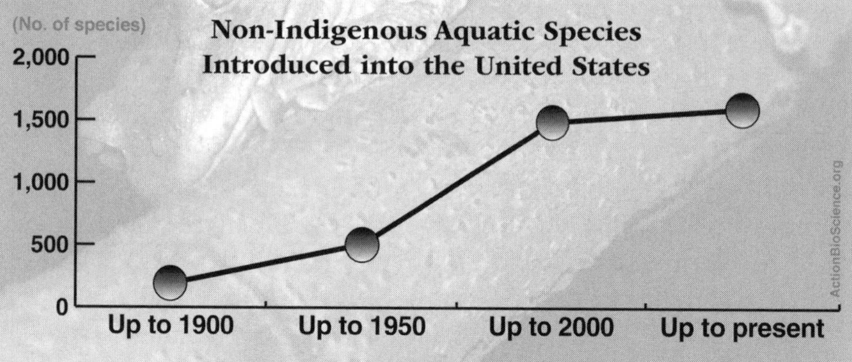

Source: "NAS Graphs and Charts: All Introduced Aquatic Species in the US," U.S. Geological Survey, February 2012, nas.er.usgs.gov/graphs/All.aspx

natural world because each species will respond differently based on its own traits. Some native species will move easily, and so will some non-natives."

Princeton University researchers recently tested the impact of climate change on the ranges of five widespread invasive plants: yellow starthistle, tamarisk (salt cedar), cheatgrass, spotted knapweed and leafy spurge. The study found that the first two plants will probably expand their range in a warming world. However, cheatgrass and knapweed will likely expand in some areas and contract in others, and leafy spurge is likely to contract. The researchers suggested that native plants might be able to occupy sites where invasives lost ground if land managers re-introduced the natives at the right time. [22]

Similarly, impacts will vary among insect pests, says Toomey of The Nature Conservancy. "A lot of these pests are very specific to certain species of trees, so impacts are very species-specific. Emerald ash borers prey on ash trees, but Asian long-horned beetles attack multiple species," Toomey notes.

What's more certain, many experts say, is that climate change will make many regions more vulnerable to invasives because they will already be coping with difficult conditions. "New pests that arrive in the future may find more susceptible trees," Toomey predicts. "These systems are stressed enough now, and climate change will just make the problem worse."

Should the exotic pet industry be regulated more strictly?

Many invasive animals and fish that have become established in the United States were imported here by exotic-animal dealers who sold them to pet stores, zoos, aquariums and private owners. Burmese pythons in the Everglades are just one example of exotic pets that have escaped or whose owners have released them to the wild and that have become established in their new settings.

According to a recent study by scientists and state regulators in Florida, 137 species of non-native reptiles and amphibians were introduced in Florida between 1863 and 2010 (three additional species were intercepted in transit). More than 80 percent of these animals came in via the pet trade — far more than any other source. An importer in Broward County (Fort Lauderdale) was the likely source of at least 32 species. [23] Although state law forbids releasing any non-indigenous animal in Florida without a state permit, no one has ever been caught doing so.

Some pet dealers have released animals directly into the wild, according to Kenneth Krysko, a senior biologist at the Florida Museum of Natural History in Gainesville and lead author of the study. "They'll open up the back door and throw an animal out if it's missing a toe or something," Krysko says. "If an animal escapes on your watch, that's illegal, but the law is unenforceable."

The main federal law that governs imports of live wild animals is the Lacey Act, enacted in 1900. The law includes a list of "injurious wildlife" that cannot be imported into the United States without a permit from the U.S. Fish and Wildlife Service (FWS). More than 200 species are listed under the act, including fruit bats, brushtail possums, zebra mussels, several types of Asian carp and brown tree snakes. [24] But the exotic pet industry brings numerous non-native species into the U.S. every year. In 2009 FWS regulated imports of more than 177 million live animals, including reptiles, mammals, insects, birds, worms, shellfish and other organisms. FWS has about 120 wildlife inspectors who screen wildlife shipments at 49 entry points nationwide. [25]

"There's something new every day," says Krysko. "We recorded 10 new species of reptiles and amphibians [in Florida] in 2011 alone."

Conservationists say that listing species under the Lacey Act takes too long and often happens after harmful species have already entered the country. Instead, they argue that FWS should be required to carry out detailed screenings of animals to see whether they may be harmful before they enter the United States. [26] But animal dealers contend that harmful impacts from exotic animals are exaggerated, and that tighter regulations would cut into a highly lucrative industry.

Last month, after several years of debate, the Obama administration adopted a rule that added Burmese pythons, North African pythons, South African pythons and yellow anacondas to the list of injurious wildlife, out of nine species proposed. Snake dealers strongly opposed the measure and said owners of exotic pets were helping to preserve rare species.

"The captive population of boas and pythons in the United States is an excellent example of a decentralized, nongovernmental economic model of conservation," argued Andrew Wyatt, president of the U.S. Association of Reptile Keepers, in comments on the proposed rule. "The time has come around the world to work to establish as many animal species in captivity as possible." [27]

Many opponents of the proposed snake listing saw it as an example of excessive government regulation. "They are wanting to take people's rights away from them," said Larry Groskey, owner of a 10-acre Florida reptile farm. "They don't believe the public should have wildlife — period." [28]

But animal specialists say the new limits are warranted. "We try to be very discriminating and focus on species that pose the greatest risk," says Scott Hardin, exotic wildlife species coordinator for Florida's Fish and Wildlife Conservation Commission. Florida banned private ownership of large constricting snakes several years before the federal rule was adopted.

By comparison, the U.S. horticulture industry — which has been a major source of invasive plants over the past two centuries — is starting to address the invasive species problem. Imports of hundreds of invasive plants are regulated by the Agriculture Department's Animal and Plant Health Inspection Service (APHIS) and by states, but many of these restrictions are inconsistent. Moreover, new plants are popular with many gardeners, so plant dealers have an incentive to seek out new species from global sources. [29]

Asian Carp Regional Coordinating Committee

Asian carp, which can leap 10 feet or more out of the water when they are disturbed by boat engine noise, are on the verge of colonizing the Great Lakes, where they could devastate the region's fisheries. In one of the more creative approaches to controlling invasive species, some regulators and conservationists are urging humans to hunt and serve up edible species such as carp and lionfish.

Nonetheless, dozens of city and state gardening associations have adopted codes of conduct that call for reducing or eliminating use of invasive plants and educating members about their impacts. [30] "Once people understand that invasive plants are a problem, it's pretty easy to mobilize them to do something about it," says Waitt of the Lady Bird Johnson Wildflower Center. "Naturalists and native plant societies know about native flora and want to protect it. And once homeowners know what to do and not do, they'll take steps that are ecologically friendly." ■

BACKGROUND

Exploring the New World

Large-scale ecological invasions in North America were set in motion in the 1500s, when European explorers began crossing the Atlantic to seek land and wealth in the New World. They brought crops such as oats, wheat, barley and rye; products imported from farther-flung regions, such as sugar, citrus fruits and coffee; and domesticated animals, including horses, cattle, goats, sheep and hogs. French settlers brought domesticated pigeons as pets, and English colonists imported European honeybees to Jamestown and Williamsburg to make honey and wax.

Unknowingly, the settlers also brought vermin. Rats crossed the ocean in the holds of ships, and colonists carried germs such as smallpox, whooping cough and influenza in their bodies. Indigenous peoples in North and South America had little ability to resist these diseases, and untold numbers died in epidemics triggered by European settlement.

A thriving seed-import industry developed in the young United States, where plants were used not only for agriculture but also in cooking, medicine and ornamental gardens. In 1827 President John Quincy Adams declared that national policy should encourage the entry of "plants of whatever nature whether useful as food for man or the domestic animals, or for purposes connected with manufactures or any of the useful arts." [31] Some of today's important invasive plants, including purple loosestrife, salt cedar and musk thistle, were deliberately imported during this era. Other modern invasives, such as Canada thistle, were accidentally introduced as contaminants in seed shipments. [32]

As settlers pushed across the continent, growing networks of roads, canals and drainage ditches created new pathways for invasive species. Canadians started work in 1825 on the Welland Canal, a link between Lake Erie and Lake Ontario that bypassed Niagara Falls. The canal enabled ships — and invasive aquatic species — to travel from the Atlantic Ocean up the St. Lawrence River into all five Great Lakes.

Railroads, which spread across the continent starting in the 1860s, also promoted the spread of invasive species. Rail commerce made it possible to ship crops and timber over long distances and to distribute cargo from a single train to many different areas. And laying railroad tracks uprooted native plants, creating corridors where invasive plants spread easily.

The impacts of global commerce soon became clear. In the late 1870s, for example, gypsy moth outbreaks began to occur in suburban Boston, where an amateur scientist had imported eggs and attempted to culture them in his backyard. [33] The moths, which fed on the leaves of many North American trees, quickly spread beyond the Northeast.

AFP/Getty Images/Luis Robayo

Passage of the Lacey Act in 1900, the first federal wildlife protection law, barred importation of the mongoose, a small carnivore, and other "injurious" species, including fruit bats, English sparrows and starlings. The law was designed to regulate trade in animals and birds and to prevent the "unwise" introduction of non-native species, but advocates say it takes too long to list species that may become invasive.

Thousands of miles west, Hawaii's native bird populations were also falling victim to invasive species — in this case, diseases such as avian malaria and bird pox. The diseases were carried by mosquitoes, which reached the islands in water casks on visiting ships. [34]

Early Controls

In 1900 Congress enacted the first federal wildlife protection law, the Lacey Act, which regulated trade in wildlife. Rep. John Lacey, R-Iowa, argued that the U.S. Department of Agriculture (USDA) should have power to regulate trade in animals and birds and to prevent the "unwise" introduction of non-native species. Lacey's main concern was protecting agriculture, which was harmed by declines in native bird species that preyed on insects. [35]

The Lacey Act imposed a number of limits on importing, exporting and transporting wildlife across state lines. It also barred imports of four species that had already spread rapidly after being introduced in the United States — the mongoose (a small carnivore), fruit bats, English sparrows and starlings — and any other animals that USDA should designate as "injurious." [36] However, more than 50 years would pass before another species was added to the injurious wildlife list. [37]

More laws followed as the United States sought to prevent harmful organisms from crossing its borders. The Plant Quarantine Act of 1912 authorized USDA to inspect all agricultural imports and bar any goods infested with insect pests from entry. The act evolved into a system, administered by USDA's Animal and Plant Health Inspection Service (APHIS), in which many agricultural products were required to go through quarantine and treatments (such as cold storage or fumigation) before they could enter the country.

In 1931 Congress passed the Animal Damage Control Act, which empowered APHIS to study and control species that were harming agriculture, ranching, forestry, wild game populations

Continued on p. 165

Chronology

1600s-1900

European settlers bring animals, plants and seeds to North America to colonize the New World. Early Americans import still more species for agriculture and commercial uses.

1889
Nutria (large semi-aquatic rodents) are imported to the United States from South America for fur production.

1900-1950s

Congress authorizes federal agencies to control harmful organisms, but industrial development speeds the spread of invasive species.

1900
Congress passes the Lacey Act, prohibiting imports of "injurious" animals, fish and birds.

1921
Parasitic sea lampreys penetrate from Lake Ontario into the other Great Lakes through the Welland Canal, a Canadian ship canal that bypasses Niagara Falls.

1931
Animal Damage Control Act gives Interior Department broad authority to investigate and control "injurious" animal species.

1937
Nutria escape from captivity in Louisiana, multiply to an estimated 20 million within two decades.

1959
St. Lawrence Seaway opens, creating a shipping channel from the Atlantic Ocean to the Great Lakes and increasing transmission of invasive species into the lakes in ballast water.

1960s-1980s

Environmentalists call for protecting endangered species, but invasive plants and animals remain a low priority until impacts become severe in Great Lakes.

1963
Arkansas imports grass carp from Asia for aquaculture and research, followed by bighead and silver carp to control weeds in fish ponds.

1973
Endangered Species Act calls for protecting species that are endangered or threatened by "disease or predation" or other factors.

1974
Federal Noxious Weed Act prohibits imports of harmful non-native weeds.

1985
Congress transfers Animal Damage Control Act authority to the Agriculture Department.

1986
Zebra mussels detected in the Great Lakes.

1990s-Present

Congress acts to control some invasive species, but climate change and global trade drive new outbreaks.

1990
Congress passes the Non-Indigenous Aquatic Nuisance Species Prevention and Control Act, regulating ballast water and other pathways for introduction of aquatic nuisance species into the Great Lakes.

1993
Coast Guard issues first mandatory regulations controlling ballast water discharges in Great Lakes.

1996
National Invasive Species Act authorizes steps to protect the Great Lakes from non-native species and creates an international framework to prevent the spread of invasive species in ballast water. . . . Bark beetle outbreak begins in Rocky Mountain states.

2002
All snakehead species are listed as injurious. Two years later the predatory fish are found in the Potomac River.

2007
Three types of Asian carp are listed as injurious species under the Lacey Act.

2010
Federal scientists launch an "Eat Lionfish" campaign to publicize threats from the fish and encourage fishermen to target it as a food product. . . . Florida bans new private ownership of large constricting snakes.

2011
Bighead carp (an Asian species) listed as injurious under the Lacey Act. . . . Damage from mountain pine beetles in Colorado and Wyoming covers more than 4 million acres.

2012
Obama administration bans imports of four species of large constricting snakes but defers decision to list imports of five others.

Native Species Suffer When Invasives Thrive

Exotic newcomers contribute to "environmental apocalypse."

Invasive species and endangered ones are two sides of the same coin: When invasives move in, native species suffer — sometimes to the point of extinction.

"From prehistory to the present time, the mindless horsemen of the environmental apocalypse have been overkill [excessive hunting], habitat destruction, introduction of animals such as rats and goats, and diseases carried by these exotic animals," eminent Harvard biologist E. O. Wilson wrote in his prize-winning 1992 book *The Diversity of Life*. In the modern era, Wilson argued, habitat destruction and introduction of exotic animals were the top threats to the world's biodiversity, and these two pressures often reinforced each other. [1]

One notorious invader, the brown tree snake, is native to the South Pacific but was introduced to the island of Guam in the 1950s, probably as a stowaway on cargo planes. Predation by brown tree snakes has eliminated 10 of Guam's native forest bird species and reduced the last two to fewer than 200 birds apiece.

Predation also could alter the composition of Guam's forests, because forest birds play an important ecological function: When they eat fruits and eliminate the seeds, they scatter the seeds so that trees reproduce over broad areas. With fewer native birds, scientists say, Guam's forests could become less diverse because there will be less mixing of tree species. [2]

Another endangered species, the Indiana bat, is threatened by habitat loss and white-nose syndrome, a disease that may have been introduced from Europe. The bats hibernate in winter in caves and abandoned mines in the Midwest and Southeast, then roost in wooded areas in summer. Habitat loss from human activities — development, cave exploration and blasting in old mines — is a serious threat to the bats, whose population has fallen by half since the late 1960s. [3] Bats play many important ecological roles. For example, they eat huge quantities of insects and also pollinate plants.

White-nose syndrome is an infectious disease that has killed an estimated 5.7 to 6.7 million Indiana bats and other, more common species across 16 states over the past five years. [4] One recent study projects that white-nose syndrome could drive several bat species — including a previously common type known as the little brown bat — to extinction in the Eastern United States as early as 2015. [5]

Many invasive species are highly adaptable and can flourish in settings that have been disturbed — attributes that help them out-compete native species. Disturbances may be natural processes such as floods or fires, or may result from human actions, such as plowing up prairie grasslands, introducing cattle or sheep onto grazing lands or building roads, bridges, canals and other infrastructure.

Ecosystems often recover after invasions, although it may take many years, depending on how severely they have been affected. University of Michigan researchers have found that invasive zebra and quagga mussels are causing "astounding changes" in the food webs of Lakes Huron and Michigan by consuming microscopic algae, which form the base of the lakes' food webs. As levels of these algae drop, creatures such as small crustaceans that feed on them are affected. In turn, these organisms are prey for many types of fish.

The scientists called for Great Lakes management agencies to take urgent action against these shifts. "Ecological changes that formerly occurred over decades are now happening in just a few years," said Donald Scavia, director of the University of Michigan's Graham Environmental Sustainability Institute. [6]

Making ecosystems more resilient against invasions can be a long-term process. Last summer the U.S. Fish and Wildlife Service announced that the whitebark pine tree — an important species that stabilizes mountain slopes in Western states and provides food for animals and birds — was a candidate for listing under the Endangered Species Act, partly because of unprecedented predation by pine beetles over the past decade. The trees' natural range is also shifting with global climate change, which is raising average temperatures and decreasing rainfall across the West.

U.S. Forest Service researchers are conserving genetic material from whitebark pines and analyzing whether to plant them in new zones where they will be better able to grow. "Sometimes it's not how hard you get hit, it's how well you roll and what you can do for the next forest that grows back," says David Cleaves, a senior adviser with the Forest Service. "The next forests will have to be more resilient in a different environment. That could mean new planting strategies, or supporting transitions to new types of forests."

— Jennifer Weeks

---

[1] Edward O. Wilson, *The Diversity of Life* (1992), p. 253.

[2] "Where Have the Birds of Guam Gone?" Smithsonian National Zoological Park, http://nationalzoo.si.edu/Animals/Birds/Facts/FactSheets/fact-guambirds.cfm; "Brown Tree Snake Could Mean Guam Will Lose More Than Its Birds," *ScienceDaily*, Aug. 8, 2008, www.sciencedaily.com/releases/2008/08/080808090313.htm.

[3] "Endangered Species: Indiana Bat," U.S. Fish and Wildlife Service, www.fws.gov/midwest/Endangered/mammals/inba/inbafctsht.html.

[4] Louis Sahagun, "Fungus Killing More Bats Than Previously Thought," *Los Angeles Times*, Jan. 18, 2012, www.latimes.com/news/local/la-me-bats-20120118,0,5306951.story.

[5] Winifred F. Frick, *et al.*, "An Emerging Disease Causes Regional Population Collapse of a Common North American Bat Species," *Science*, Vol. 329, no. 6, Aug. 6, 2010, pp. 679-682.

[6] "Invasive Mussels Causing Massive Ecological Changes in Great Lakes," *Science Daily*, April 13, 2011, www.sciencedaily.com/releases/2011/04/110413171331.htm.

Continued from p. 162

or other resources. And the 1939 Federal Seed Act regulated interstate and international trade in seeds and authorized APHIS to ban shipments containing "noxious-weed seeds" from entering the country.

In 1958 Charles Elton, an ecologist at Oxford University, published *The Ecology of Invasion by Animals and Plants*, one of the first scientific studies to focus attention on invasive species as a serious threat to biodiversity. Citing examples such as mitten crabs, chestnut blight and gypsy moths, Elton showed how invasives altered food chains, changed population balances and disrupted local ecosystems in many other ways. "We must make no mistake, we are seeing one of the great historical convulsions in the world's flora and fauna," Elton wrote. [38]

AFP/Getty Images/Karen Bleier

A freighter enters Lake Superior after passing through the Soo Locks at Sault Ste. Marie, Mich. A recent study calculates that in the Great Lakes alone, ship-borne invasive species such as zebra mussels cause at least $200 million in damage to fisheries, wildlife and water quality annually. At least 100 exotic species are established in the Great Lakes, about half of them brought in oceangoing ships' ballast tanks.

Grappling With Invasions

Invasive species had not become a major public focus by 1970, when concerns about pollution and waste led to the first Earth Day and a wave of national environmental conservation laws. But the impact of invasives was recognized indirectly in the 1973 Endangered Species Act (ESA), which was enacted to protect threatened and endangered fish, wildlife and plants and the habitats that they depended on to survive. As conservationists pressed federal regulators to list species for protection under the ESA, it became increasingly clear that competition from non-native species was one of the top threats pushing endangered plants and animals to the edge.

In the 1980s researchers began finding invasive organisms in the Great Lakes, including spiny water fleas (tiny crustaceans that fed on plankton, competing with fish), Eurasian ruffles (fish that fed on native fish species' eggs) and, most alarming, zebra mussels. [39]

A 1990 study by two government commissions estimated that at least 100 exotic species had become established in the Great Lakes and about half of them had been transported there in oceangoing ships' ballast tanks. "The health and integrity of the Great Lakes Basin Ecosystem, including the 40 million humans who live in the basin, are jeopardized by an immediate and growing problem: the rampant colonization by shipborne exotic organisms," the study warned. [40]

In 1990 Congress passed the Non-indigenous Aquatic Nuisance Prevention and Control Act, which required federal agencies to work jointly to monitor and control risks from aquatic invasive species. The law authorized the Coast Guard to regulate ballast water discharges in the Great Lakes and directed the Army Corps of Engineers to study methods for controlling zebra mussels.

Altered Communities

During the 1990s scientists flocked to the fast-expanding field of invasion biology and found plenty of subjects. For example, non-native fish, shellfish, worms and microorganisms had colonized San Francisco Bay, the Chesapeake Bay and numerous rivers and lakes in between. [41] And invasive plants such as cheatgrass and knapweed were moving across the Rocky Mountain states, displacing native species such as sagegrass that provided food and habitat for many animals and birds. [42]

In 1996 Congress enacted the National Invasive Species Act, which created a program for regulating ballast water nationwide, although critics argued that the law was patchy and did not address problems in major rivers such as the Colorado and Rio Grande. [43] Three years later President Clinton signed an executive order that sought to elevate the issue by creating a National Invasive Species Council that included the Agriculture, Commerce, Interior, Defense, Health and Human Services, State, Transportation and Treasury departments and Environmental Protection Agency (EPA). The order also directed all federal agencies to address invasive species issues and refrain from actions that would worsen problems with invasives. [44]

Asian carp were an urgent concern at this time. The fish had escaped from Southern aquaculture facilities during heavy floods in the early 1990s and were moving up the Mississippi River toward the Great Lakes. State regulators worried the voracious predators would attack native species in a region where sport fishing and boating generated more than $20 billion in annual revenues. [45]

In 2002 the Army Corps of Engineers installed a system that generated an electrical field across the Chicago Sanitary and Ship Canal, which connects the Mississippi River to Lake Michigan, to prevent carp from moving upstream. Two more electric barriers were activated in 2009 and 2011. [46] But in 2010 carp were detected in the canal beyond the first two electric barriers. [47]

Meanwhile legal battles raged among Great Lakes states, with Michigan suing to force Illinois to close locks that would keep carp out of the Great Lakes. The U.S. Supreme Court rejected Michigan's plea in 2010, but state leaders continued to press for legal or political action and denounced the Corps of Engineers for failing to take more aggressive action. "Their failure and lack of responsibility is the sorriest thing I've ever seen," Michigan Attorney General Bill Schuette said last December. [48] ■

CURRENT SITUATION

Border Quarantines

Many scientists, regulators and advocates working to control invasive species say the nation needs tighter controls on plant and animal imports. It is easier and cheaper to block invasive species from entering the country than to contain them once they are loose in the environment, experts say. Therefore, they argue, the nation should adopt more regulations that require non-native organisms to be quarantined at the borders and analyzed to determine whether they may become invasive or carry invasive organisms.

Last year the Agriculture Department amended regulations covering nursery plant imports for use in gardening and landscaping, creating a new category called "not authorized for importation pending pest risk analysis," or NAPPRA. Now the agency has proposed listing 148 species of plants as either pests or hosts for quarantine pests. [49]

"Importing plants into the U.S. is kind of a free-for-all now, so this will help stem the tide," says Waitt of the Lady Bird Johnson Wildflower Center. Many groups and agencies agree. "Prevention is the most cost-effective method of stopping the spread of invasive plants," California Invasive Plant Council officials wrote in comments on the proposed lists. [50]

However, many nurseries and horticultural groups worry that the list is too broad. Some, for example, object to including cut flowers and greenery as possible pest carriers because cut flowers pose less risk of being introduced into the environment than plants purchased for cultivation in gardens. [51] Others say that some of the proposed species are already present in the United States and thus do not meet the legal definition of exotic plants. [52]

Environmental groups want Congress to update the Lacey Act to similarly require imported animals to be quarantined and screened. [53] The FWS appears to support the idea. FWS "has not been able to make injurious wildlife listings under the Lacey Act into the nimble, timely and proactive tool needed to address the current rate of importation and transport of potentially invasive, non-native species," agent George Phocas testified at a hearing in Hawaii last October. "Having the opportunity to evaluate non-native species that are proposed for importation could be an invaluable tool" to prevent introduction of new invasive species, Phocas said. [54]

However, the Obama administration has not proposed to amend the Lacey Act. And many environmental and animal welfare groups saw the administration's recent decision to list only four species of large constricting snakes as injurious species under the act, instead of the nine proposed, as conceding to pressure from the pet trade. "[T]he Obama administration caved in," said Humane Society of the United States President Wayne Pacelle. [55]

New Strategies

Regulators and activists are seeking creative ways to contain non-native species that are already present in the United States. Florida's Fish and Wildlife Conservation Commission (FWC), working with other state and federal agencies, holds amnesty days across the state when overwhelmed owners can turn over non-native pets, free of charge, to officials who work to place the animals with qualified adopters and sanctuaries. Officials also help owners learn about exotic pet care and offer low-cost microchipping so animals can be traced back to their owners. (For some exotic species, such as large snakes, microchipping has been required under Florida law since 2008). [56]

"We haven't closed off all options for people who want to own exotic pets responsibly. That's the key word — responsibly," says Hardin, FWC's exotic wildlife species coordinator.

Through late 2011 Florida had collected more than 600 exotic pets, including lizards, snakes, rats, scorpions, birds, fish, tortoises and small monkeys. [57] At an event last November a

Continued on p. 168

Aquatic Invaders Corrupting World's Waters

"They crowd out other species and restructure the environment."

Many animal and plant invasions on land are highly visible, but the situation underwater – though not easily seen — is equally dire. Scientists warn that invasive species are major threats to healthy rivers, lakes and oceans and already are altering many marine zones around the globe.

"Marine invaders are out of sight and out of mind, but they're just as problematic as weeds in your backyard," says Judith Pederson, advisory leader and regional coordinator of the Sea Grant program at the Massachusetts Institute of Technology. [1]

According to the U.S. Geological Survey, nearly 1,600 non-native species have been introduced to U.S. waters. About half are fish and plants; the rest range from reptiles and amphibians to corals, shellfish, sponges, bacteria and viruses. About two-thirds are found in freshwater lakes and rivers and the rest in oceans and bays. [2]

Kstk.org/Lily Mihalik

Tunicates are among the aquatic invasives that compete with or prey upon native species. The small, rubbery-looking organisms, some known as sea squirts, attach themselves to rocks, piers and other underwater surfaces.

As on land, many aquatic invasives compete with or prey upon native species. "Often it happens in subtle ways," says Pederson. As one example, she cites tunicates — small rubbery-looking organisms that feed by siphoning water through their sac-like bodies. Many kinds of tunicates (including sea squirts) attach themselves to rocks, piers and other underwater surfaces. "They slowly increase their areas and become very dominant," says Pederson. "We still don't know whether they have any significant predators. Other organisms like crabs and starfish don't seem to feed on them. So they crowd out or overgrow other species like shellfish and sponges and restructure the environment." [3]

In addition to the Great Lakes and Mississippi River basin, many other major U.S. water bodies have been invaded. Hundreds of non-native shellfish, sea slugs, plankton, parasites and other organisms have become established in San Francisco Bay, many of them carried in cargo ships' ballast tanks. [4] Dozens of invasive species are also present in and around the Chesapeake Bay, including mute swans, nutria and phragmites, a fast-spreading plant that crowds out cattails and other native marsh plants. The most-impacted zones of oceans are along coastlines, which are heavily used by humans for trade, development, aquaculture and recreation.

Shipping is one of the main routes by which aquatic invasive species spread, not just by ships emptying their ballast tanks but also when organisms stick to ships' hulls. Other sources include releases of baitfish or live seafood, such as fish and plants that escape from aquaculture facilities. Asian carp were first introduced to the United States when they were imported for aquaculture in the 1970s; they later escaped into the Mississippi River during heavy flooding. [5]

Dealers who sell and ship numerous species around the globe also contribute. In one widely known case, a large aquarium in Monaco dumped water that contained a fast-spreading species of bright green algae called *Caulerpa taxifolia* into the Mediterranean Sea. By 2000 the plant had spread over 10,000 acres of coastline in Spain, France and Italy and had come to be known as "killer algae" because it spread aggressively and smothered native aquatic plants. [6] In that year it also turned up in a lagoon near San Diego, where state and federal agencies spent more than $3 million to remove it before it could spread farther along the California coast. [7]

The International Council for Exploration of the Sea (ICES), which promotes marine research in the North Atlantic, has published a voluntary code of practice for introducing and transferring marine organisms. The code calls for live organisms to be quarantined and analyzed for harmful impacts before they are released into the natural environment. [8] "If you did it correctly, it would probably take a year or two to get a permit, and that's how it should be," says Pederson.

— ***Jennifer Weeks***

---

[1] Sea Grant is a federally funded research and outreach program on marine issues that operates at 32 U.S. universities and research laboratories.

[2] "Non-Indigenous Aquatic Species Graphs and Charts," U.S. Geological Survey, http://nas.er.usgs.gov/graphs/All.aspx.

[3] See "Invasive Sea Squirt Potential Threat to Connecticut's $30M Shellfish Industry," University of New Haven, Sept. 14, 2011, www.newhaven.edu/news-events/190707/, and "Invasive 'Tunicate' Appears in Oregon's Coastal Waters," *ScienceDaily*, May 13, 2010, www.sciencedaily.com/releases/2010/04/100513 143546.htm.

[4] Malia Wollan, "An Underwater Fight Is Waged for the Health of San Francisco Bay," *The New York Times*, Aug. 1, 2009, www.nytimes.com/2009/08/02/science/earth/02seaweed.html; Lauren Sommer, "Foreign Species Invade San Francisco Bay," National Public Radio, May 11, 2011, www.npr.org/2011/05/11/136212105/foreign-species-invade-san-francisco-bay.

[5] Rosamond L. Naylor, *et al.*, "Aquaculture — A Gateway For Exotic Species," *Science*, Vol. 294, Nov. 23, 2001, pp. 1655-1656.

[6] David Perlman, "'Killer Algae' Migrates to California Coast," *San Francisco Chronicle*, July 6, 2000, www.sfgate.com/cgi-bin/article.cgi?f=/c/a/2000/07/06/MN79725.DTL.

[7] "Eradication and Surveillance of Caulerpa taxifolia within Agua Hedondia Lagoon," Carlsbad, California, Fifth Year Status Report (2005), pp. 10-11, http://swr.nmfs.noaa.gov/hcd/caulerpa/Year5StatusReport.pdf.

[8] "ICES Code of Practice on the Introductions and Transfers of Marine Organisms," (2005), p. 6, www.ices.dk/reports/general/2004/ices%20code%20of%20practice%202005.pdf.

Continued from p. 166

woman handed over two dozen sugar gliders — small opossums native to Australia and the Pacific that are similar to flying squirrels. "Things just got out of control" for the owner, a FWC official said. "She ended up turning in about 25 of them — they are prolific breeders." [58]

Another increasingly popular approach for certain species can be summed up, "If you can't beat 'em, eat 'em." Federal and state officials, sometimes working with conservation groups and celebrity chefs, are urging Americans to kill and cook up targeted invasives.

Hunting is not always an appropriate strategy, even if an animal is edible. For example, feral hogs have become invasive across the United States precisely because they are popular as game. Over the past several decades breeders have relocated and released hogs in many areas to establish wild populations for hunting. [59] Biologists estimate that there are roughly 4 million feral pigs nationwide, mainly in the Southeast, Texas and California, and they are starting to appear in other areas. [60]

Feral hogs eat practically anything, including plants, crops, birds and small animals, and can heavily damage property by trampling and rooting up native plants. But although many people hunt hogs for food, some states with hog problems such as Tennessee have reclassified them from a game species to a nuisance and strictly regulate hog hunting. Wildlife experts have found that trapping is a more effective way of regulating hogs than hunting, which cannot keep up with their breeding rates. Moreover, they say, promoting sport hunting encourages breeders to release more hogs as targets. [61]

AFP/Getty Images/Karim Sahib

In Florida and the Caribbean, lionfish prey on native reef fish and compete with larger native species such as grouper and snapper. Conservation groups are encouraging scuba divers to spear the striped predators, which are native to the Indo-Pacific region. "Lionfish were introduced here through the aquarium trade, so they're like a form of biological pollution," says Lad Akins, at the Reef Environmental Education Foundation. "It's up to us to minimize those impacts and clean up our mess."

In other cases, officials are willing to promote eating invasives. Some Midwestern chefs have touted Asian carp, and Illinois recently launched a campaign to encourage residents to serve the fish, which are raised in China for food. [62] On the plus side, the fish are large (up to 100 pounds), but they also are very bony, which makes ready-to-cook carp portions expensive. And some Americans have trouble seeing Asian carp as an attractive food source, even though the fish are not bottom-feeders like other carp species. Some advocates have suggested new names such as "silverfin" and "Kentucky tuna" — a strategy that has helped make other fish species popular menu choices. [63]

In Florida and the Caribbean, the National Oceanic and Atmospheric Administration (NOAA) is working with fishermen, conservationists and chefs to promote consumption of lionfish — showy striped predators native to the Indo-Pacific region, that are preying on native reef fish and competing with larger native species such as grouper and snapper. "Eat sustainable, eat lionfish!" a NOAA brochure urges readers. [64]

Encouraging scuba divers to spear colorful fish might seem out of character for a conservation group. But Lad Akins, special project director for the Florida-based Reef Environmental Education Foundation (REEF), sees no conflict. "Our members are strongly in

Continued on p. 170

At Issue:

Should imports of large constricting snakes be banned?

JOHN KOSTYACK
VICE PRESIDENT FOR WILDLIFE CONSERVATION, NATIONAL WILDLIFE FEDERATION

WRITTEN FOR *CQ RESEARCHER*, FEBRUARY 2012

Giant constrictor snakes have slithered, crushed, killed and terrified their way across movie screens for years. The real horror story, however, is much closer to reality — and to home. Non-native constrictors are decimating wildlife in the Florida Everglades, changing the very fabric of that rich but sensitive ecosystem. Moreover, as pets constrictors have also been responsible for a number of human deaths, including the strangulation of a 2-year-old in her crib. These predators may start out small, but they can grow up to 200 pounds and 20 feet long. When they become too big, too hungry and too overwhelming, irresponsible owners dump them. As a result, these invasive species become a threat to our ecosystem, wildlife and safety.

Following a lengthy review, the U.S. Fish and Wildlife Service (FWS) recently prohibited the importation and interstate transport of four non-native species of constrictors: Burmese python, yellow anaconda, northern African rock python and southern African rock python. While the National Wildlife Federation supports these long-overdue restrictions, it is disappointing that the Obama administration dropped five other harmful large constrictors recommended by the FWS for inclusion in the importation ban. As a result, the reticulated python, DeSchauenee's anaconda, green anaconda, Beni anaconda and boa constrictor will continue to audition for reoccurring roles in the invasive species assault on America's ecosystems.

There is no scientific or statutory basis to justify allowing these lethal creatures to continue being imported into the United States. A small but vocal sector of the pet industry, using spurious arguments about purported "job losses," has placed a stranglehold on a sensible rule. Unfortunately, when it came to weighing the interests of a tiny population of animal breeders against the enormous economic and ecological damage these snakes can cause, the administration was sold a bottle of snake oil.

Controlling the constrictors that have already escaped is costing taxpayers millions. To make matters worse, well-documented shifts in climate will help these cold-blooded creatures thrive farther north, affecting more states and increasing their ecological damage and costs to taxpayers.

The National Wildlife Federation supports banning imports not only of the four exotic snake species now regulated, but also the five additional species of large constrictors targeted by federal wildlife managers. Keeping these deadly "pets" from invading America's backyards and natural habitats must be a priority and will save wildlife, money and human lives.

DAVID G. BARKER
MEMBER, U.S. ASSOCIATION OF REPTILE KEEPERS

FROM TESTIMONY BEFORE THE HOUSE COMMITTEE ON OVERSIGHT AND GOVERNMENT REFORM, SEPT. 14, 2011

The U.S. reptile industry has grown rapidly over the past two decades. The number of U.S. households that own a reptile rose from 2.8 million to 4.7 million from 1994 to 2008, an increase of 68 percent. In contrast, the number of households that own any kind of pet increased only 35 percent over that same period. Today, this sector of the pet industry has become increasingly complex, generating annual revenues approaching $1.4 billion.

The prime movers fueling this growth are small, predominantly American businesses. . . . Of the overall market for reptiles, the component comprising the nine species proposed to be listed is estimated to [represent] about 11 percent, generating over $100 million a year in economic activity. It is [composed] of importers; captive breeding operations such as my own; specialized herpetological veterinarians; rodent breeders and distributors; manufacturers of food pellets, lighting, terrariums, terrarium decorations, heating products, vitamins and supplements, thermostats, snake hooks, sexing tools and humidity products; specialized transport companies; trade show organizers and promoters; and others. Ninety-nine percent of the affected businesses qualify as small businesses under the Regulatory Flexibility Act.

Under the proposed rule, a significant portion of this business will be lost. This industry is driven by high-valued snakes specially bred for unique colors, patterns, albinism and other traits. These so-called "morphs" can fetch hundreds and even thousands of dollars from collectors, both domestically and abroad. At the highest end, prices rise to the tens of thousands of dollars for an animal. If the Lacey Act listing is adopted, this sector will die, and thousands of small breeding operations will be left with inventories of snakes and specialized equipment that will be virtually worthless. . . .

I, like many others who are passionate about snakes and reptiles and who have made this their life's work, spend a large amount of time in educational activities. . . . We introduce students to these magnificent creatures, assist zoos and aquariums in care, maintenance and supply, aid conservation efforts, and publish articles, both for the scientific community and the general public. If this rule is adopted, all these valuable services will be lost, along with American jobs and the American dream for thousands of people. These "costs" — both human and monetary — are not offset one iota by this misguided rule that utterly lacks a single benefit. With this rule, we will be a poorer nation in all senses.

Continued from p. 168

favor of it," he says. "Lionfish were introduced here through the aquarium trade, so they're like a form of biological pollution. Humans created it, and it's causing significant impacts. It's up to us to minimize those impacts and clean up our mess."

REEF sponsors lionfish derbies, in which teams compete to collect as many lionfish as possible, and educates the public about how to handle and fillet the fish. Lionfish have venomous spines that can easily be removed, and cooking neutralizes their toxin. Restaurants in the Florida Keys are using the mild white fish in such dishes as nachos and ceviche.

Few divers seem worried about getting stung for a good cause. "We're taking a part in the battle," said Robert Hickerson, a diver from Vero Beach, Fla., competing in a lionfish derby. "I've killed over a hundred of them. I try to kill them even when I'm on vacation." [65]

Getty Images/Newsmakers/Chris Hondros

No, Fido, that's not a wild Nile monitor lizard out for a stroll in Manhattan. It's just one of the many exotic pets found on the street or given up for care and adoption to Robert Shapiro, operator of Social Tees Animal Rescue. The big reptile was sent to a rescue facility in Arizona after the New York City Health Department banned lizards, pythons, iguanas and other exotic pets. "It's a great regulation," says Shapiro. "Most people who keep exotic pets don't know how to care for them. It's really a shame."

Backyard Wildlife

Many suburban communities are feeling impacts not only from invasive species but also from expanding populations of native wild animals, such as beaver, wild turkey, coyote, mountain lion and black bear. Although many stories describe these clashes as wildlife "invasions," there are important differences between backyard wildlife expansions and the spread of invasive species.

Backyard wild animals typically are native species that were hunted to near-regional extinction through the early 20th century and then rebounded in recent decades — some of them protected by the Endangered Species Act, others by state and local hunting limits. Another trend promoting their spread is the regrowth of forests in the Northeast and Midwest on abandoned farmland. And as suburbs spread into once-wooded areas, they alter the environment in ways that attract animals.

"Human-sourced foods like crops and garbage cans attract populations of some species, such as deer, bear and raccoon," says Timothy van Deelen, a professor of wildlife ecology at the University of Wisconsin. "We're giving native animals subsidies that encourage them to expand beyond natural population limits."

Suburban wildlife can disrupt local ecosystems in ways similar to invasive species or can help invasive species spread. For example, heavy grazing by white-tailed deer in Northeastern and Midwestern forests is opening areas for invasive plants that are less palatable to deer, altering the mix of plants in many forests and reducing biodiversity. [66]

Other wild animals in suburbs may disrupt human activities without altering the ecology of an entire area, as when beavers dam local streams and flood nearby roads and basements. Unlike dealing with invasive species, regulators and animal advocates typically advise homeowners to learn to live with suburban wildlife when possible, instead of trying to remove it. Some experts also point out that in suburbs humans alter the environment more radically than animals.

"Now that we humans are a major ecological driving force on earth, we create conditions that will be favorable to some species but not to others," writes biologist Stephen DeStefano. "In many ways you cannot pick your neighbors, regardless of species — they establish residency if they like the neighborhood and the conditions are right." [67] ■

OUTLOOK

Tighter Restrictions

Although limiting invasive species can seem like an overwhelming mission, many experts are optimistic that the nation can make progress over the next decade.

"Awareness will really increase in the next 10 years," says Waitt of the Lady Bird Johnson Wildflower Center. "There are so many groups doing education about invasive species, and that's very positive. I also expect tighter restrictions on imports allowed into the U.S. Those two trends should start making a dent in the issue."

Along with tighter import restrictions, The Nature Conservancy's Toomey says that better enforcement of existing laws — and more funding for inspectors and regulators — should also be priorities. "When you think of these restrictions as an ounce of prevention, they are extremely cost-effective," he says.

Much more research is needed on potential invasives, especially obscure species, cautions Judith Pederson, advisory leader and regional coordinator of the Sea Grant program at the Massachusetts Institute of Technology. "The more we know about the life histories of organisms, the easier it is to understand their impacts" on native species, she says. "We still don't know how to predict the impacts of many invasives and how they'll behave out of their own areas without predators. And we don't know what impact climate will have, although we know it will affect natives and non-natives together."

Scientific research is not the only arena for further action. Experts widely agree that Americans' personal choices can make a major difference in slowing invasions. And many steps are easier than spearing lionfish underwater. For example, people can choose not to buy exotic pets or non-native plants; not to transport firewood, pets, produce or other items that can carry pests from state to state; and to follow state guidelines on activities such as washing and decontaminating boats when they are moved from one water body to another.

Another helpful step is to volunteer with local conservation groups for projects such as removing invasive plants from parks and other public lands. "Citizens are out there birding, hiking and biking, so they can keep a lookout for things," says Waitt, who has helped develop a plan for managing invasive plants on city-owned land in Austin, Texas. "We've had several citizen scientists [non-scientist volunteers] who have been the first to find invasive plants. They're our eyes in the field."

Davis, the Macalester College biologist, believes that American perceptions of invasive species will evolve away from a perspective that casts native species as benign and alien or exotic species as bad. "We'll definitely move toward a more sensible, less ideological view of non-native species, although there will be a lot of pushback because people have invested a lot of time and work in the nativist perspective," he says. "The world is globalizing fast, and young people are growing up in a globalized world. Being surrounded by all kinds of cultures and colors and species is normal for them." ■

Notes

[1] David Fleshler, "Adult Deer Found Inside Python in Everglades," *South Florida Sun-Sentinel*, Oct. 28, 2011, http://articles.sun-sentinel.com/2011-10-28/news/sfl-python-digesting-a-deer-captured-in-everglades-20111028_1_burmese-python-scott-hardin-snake.

[2] "Non-Native Snakes Are Taking a Toll On Native Birds in Florida, Scientists Find," *ScienceDaily*, March 10, 2011, www.sciencedaily.com/releases/2011/03/110310131100.htm.

[3] Dan Thayer, testimony before the House Natural Resources Committee, Subcommittee on National Parks, Forests and Public Lands and Subcommittee on Insular Affairs, Oceans and Wildlife, March 23, 2010, p. 5, http://naturalresources.house.gov/UploadedFiles/ThayerTestimony03.23.10.pdf; Virginia Chamlee, "Lawmakers Urge Obama Administration to Ban Trade in Large Snakes," *Florida Independent*, Dec. 19, 2011, http://floridaindependent.com/61466/obama-burmese-pythons.

[4] Tamara Lush, "Python Problem Tough To Swallow," *Tampa Bay Times*, Oct. 16, 2005, www.sptimes.com/2005/10/16/State/Python_problem_tough_.shtml; "Girl, 2, Strangled By Pet Python, Police Say," MSNBC.com, July 1, 2009, www.msnbc.msn.com/id/31684161/ns/us_news-life/t/girl-strangled-pet-python-police-say/#.TwthDvkx1kg.

[5] "Ecoystems — Invasive Species Program," U.S. Geological Survey, http://ecosystems.usgs.gov/invasive/.

[6] David Pimentel, Rodolfo Zuniga, and Doug Morrison, "Update on the Environmental and Economic Costs Associated With Alien-Invasive Species in the United States," *Ecological Economics*, Vol. 52 (2005), pp. 273-288, www.mendeley.com/research/update-environmental-economic-costs-associated-alieninvasive-species-united-states-3/.

[7] David Lodge and David Finnoff, "Annual Losses to Great Lakes Region by Ship-Borne Invasive Species at least $200 million," July 2008, www.glu.org/sites/default/files/lodge_factsheet.pdf.

[8] Juliann E. Aukema, *et al.*, "Economic Impacts of Non-Native Forest Insects in the Continental United States," *PLoS One*, Vol. 6, No. 9, e24587 (Sept. 9, 2011), www.plosone.org/article/info%3Adoi%2F10.1371%2Fjournal.pone.0024587.

[9] "Sneak Peek: Pig Bomb," Discovery Channel, www.discoverychannel.ca/article.aspx?aid=16572.

[10] T.C. Boyle, *When the Killing's Done* (2011).

[11] "An Action Plan on Invasive Species," National Environmental Coalition on Invasive Species, February 2011, www.necis.net/wp-content/uploads/2011/02/NECIS-brochure-2011.pdf.

[12] "They Came From Climate Change!" National Wildlife Federation, April 2010, p. 8, www.nwf.org/~/media/PDFs/Global-Warming/Reports/They-Came-From-Climate-Change-WEB.ashx; Texas Agricultural Extension Service, "Fire Ants and Their Management," p. 1, http://gallus.tamu.edu/library/extpublications/B-1536.PDF. For summaries of current studies on invasive species, see www.sciencedaily.com/news/plants_animals/invasive_species/.

[13] Executive Order 13112, Feb. 3, 1999, http://frwebgate.access.gpo.gov/cgi-bin/getdoc.cgi?dbname=1999_register&docid=99-3184-filed.pdf.

[14] "2008-2012 National Invasive Species Management Plan," National Invasive Species Council, August 2008, pp. 4-6, www.invasivespecies.gov/home_documents/2008-2012%20National%20Invasive%20Species%20Management%20Plan.pdf.

[15] Mark Davis, *et al.*, "Don't Judge Species on Their Origins," *Nature*, Vol. 474, June 9, 2011, pp. 153-154, www.nature.com/nature/journal/v474/n7350/full/474153a.html.

[16] Daniel Simberloff, *et al.*, "Non-Natives: 141 Scientists Object," *Nature*, Vol. 475, No. 36, July 7, 2011, www.nature.com/nature/journal/v475/n7354/full/475036a.html.

[17] For more information see Norman Myers, *et al.*, "Biodiversity Hotspots for conservation Priorities," *Nature*, Vol. 403, Feb. 24, 2000, pp. 853-858, and Conservation International, "Biodiversity Hotspots," www.nature.com/nature/journal/v403/n6772/abs/403853a0.html.
[18] Gaia Vince, "Embracing Invasives," *Science*, Vol. 331, March 18, 2011, pp. 1383-1384.
[19] "They Came From Climate Change!," *op. cit.*
[20] Charles G. Willis, *et al.*, "Favorable Climate Change Response Explains Non-Native Species' Success in Thoreau's Woods," *PLoS One*, Vol. 5, Issue 1, January 2010, www.plosone.org/article/info:doi%2F10.1371%2Fjournal.pone.0008878.
[21] "Climate Change Allows Invasive Weed to Outcompete Local Species," *ScienceDaily*, May 31, 2011, www.sciencedaily.com/releases/2011/05/110531155351.htm.
[22] Bethany A. Bradley, *et al.*, "Climate Change and Plant Invasions: Restoration Opportunities Ahead?," *Global Change Biology*, Vol. 15, 2009, pp. 1511-1521, www.princeton.edu/step/people/faculty/michael-oppenheimer/research/Bradley-et-al.-2009.pdf.
[23] Kenneth L. Krysko, *et al.*, "Verified Non-Indigenous Amphibians and Reptiles in Florida from 1863 through 2010: Outlining the Invasion Process and Identifying Invasion Pathways and Stages," *Zootaxa*, Vol. 3028, 2011, pp. 1-64, www.flmnh.ufl.edu/herpetology/kk/pdf/2011_Krysko_et_al_Verified_herps_in_Florida.pdf.
[24] "Species Listed as Injurious under the Lacey Act," U.S. Fish and Wildlife Service, updated Sept. 29, 2011, www.fws.gov/fisheries/ANS/pdf_files/Current_Listed_IW.pdf.
[25] "Live Animal Imports: Agencies Need Better Collaboration to Reduce the Risk of Animal-Related Diseases," U.S. Government Accountability Office, GAO-11-9, November 2010, pp. 7, 44-45, www.gao.gov/new.items/d119.pdf.
[26] "Broken Screens: The Regulation of Live Animal Imports in the United States," Defenders of Wildlife, 2007, pp. 29-31, www.defenders.org/programs_and_policy/international_conservation/u.s._imports_of_live_animals/broken_screens.php.
[27] "USARK Reptile Industry Economic Summary for the Office of Management and Budget," March 1, 2010, www.usark.org/uploads/Economic%20OMB%20Testimony.pdf.
[28] Skyler Swisher and Dinah Voyles Pulver, "Fangs come Out Over Snake Bans," *Daytona Beach News-Journal*, Jan. 22, 2012, www.news-journalonline.com/news/local/west-volusia/2012/01/22/fangs-come-out-over-snake-bans.html.
[29] Alex X. Niemiera, "Invasive Plants — A Horticultural Perspective," Virginia Cooperative Extension, 2009, http://pubs.ext.vt.edu/426/426-080/426-080.html; Jennifer Drew, *et al.*, "Conundrums of a Complex Vector for Invasive Species control: A Detailed Examination of the Horticultural Industry," *Biological Invasions*, Vol. 12, 2010, pp. 2837-2851.
[30] "Linking Ecology and Horticulture to Prevent Plant Invasions," undated www.centerforplantconservation.org/invasives/endorsementN.asp.
[31] Quoted in "Predicting Invasions of Nonindigenous Plants and Plant Pests," National Research Council, 2002, p. 27, www.nap.edu/openbook.php?record_id=10259&page=27.
[32] "Missouri River: Invasive Plants," National Park Service, www.nps.gov/mnrr/planyourvisit/upload/Invasive-plants.pdf; National Invasive Species Information Center, "Species Profiles: Leafy Spurge," www.invasivespeciesinfo.gov/plants/leafyspurge.shtml.
[33] "Gypsy Moth in North America," U.S. Forest Service, www.fs.fed.us/ne/morgantown/4557/gmoth/, and "E. Leopold Trouvelot, Perpetuator of Our Problem," www.fs.fed.us/ne/morgantown/4557/gmoth/trouvelot/.
[34] Deborah M. Finch, *et al.*, "Terrestrial Animals as Invasive Species and as Species at Risk From Invasions," in "U.S. Forest Service, A Dynamic Invasive Species Research Vision: Opportunities and Priorities 2009-2029," p. 52, www.fs.fed.us/rm/pubs_other/gtr_wo79_83_043_054.pdf; U.S. Geological Survey, "Feral Pigs, Introduced mosquitoes, and the Decline of Hawai'i's Native Birds," February 2006, http://biology.usgs.gov/pierc/Fact_Sheets/Pigs_and_mosquitoes.pdf.
[35] Robert S. Anderson, "The Lacey Act: America's Premier Weapon in the Fight Against Unlawful Wildlife Trafficking," *Public Land Law Review* (1995), online at www.animallaw.info/articles/arus16publlr27.htm#1.
[36] *Ibid.*
[37] The fifth species to be listed was the myna, a bird related to the starling, in 1952. Andrew J. Fowler, *et al.*, "Failure of the Lacey Act to Protect U.S. Ecosystems Against Animal Invasions," *Frontiers in Ecology and the Environment*, Vol. 5, No. 7 (2007), pp. 353-359, http://nd.edu/~lodgelab/Lodge_Lab_Website/Research_files/Failure%20of%20the%20Lacey%20Act%20to%20protect.pdf.
[38] Quoted in David M. Richardson, ed., *Fifty Years of Invasion Ecology: The Legacy of Charles Elton* (2011), p. xi.
[39] "Aquatic Invasive Species: Then and Now," International Joint Commission and Great Lakes Fishery Commission, undated, www.ijc.org/rel/ais-timeline/.
[40] "Exotic Species and the Shipping Industry: The Great Lakes-St. Lawrence Ecosystem at Risk," International Joint Commission and Great Lakes Fishery Commission, September 1990, pp. 1-2, www.glfc.org/pubs/SpecialPubs/ExoticSpecies.pdf.
[41] Andrew N. Cohen and James T. Carlton, "Nonindigenous Aquatic Species in a U.S. Estuary: A Case Study of the Biological Invasions of the San Francisco Bay and Delta," report for the U.S. Fish & Wildlife Service, December 1995, http://nas.er.usgs.gov/Publications/SFBay/sfinvade.html; Rona Kobell, "Officials Swap Stories of Battles Against Invasive Species," *Bay Journal*, January 2010, www.bayjournal.com/article.cfm?article=3743.
[42] Dan Louie Flores, *The Natural West: Environmental History in the Great Plains and Rocky Mountains* (2001), pp. 196-199.
[43] M. Lynne Corn, *et al.*, "Invasive Non-Native Species: Background and Issues for Congress," Congressional Research Service, Nov. 25, 2002, pp. 31-32, www.nationalaglawcenter.org/assets/crs/RL30123.pdf.
[44] Executive Order 13112, Feb. 3, 1999, http://fr

About the Author

Jennifer Weeks is a Massachusetts freelance writer who specializes in energy, the environment and science. She has written for *The Washington Post, Audubon, Popular Mechanics* and other magazines and previously was a policy analyst, congressional staffer and lobbyist. She has an A.B. degree from Williams College and master's degrees from the University of North Carolina and Harvard. Her recent *CQ Researcher* reports include "Gulf Coast Restoration" and "Energy Policy."

webgate.access.gpo.gov/cgi-bin/getdoc.cgi?dbname=1999_register&docid=99-3184-filed.pdf.

[45] "Charting Asian Carp's Course," Circle of Blue, undated, www.circleofblue.org/waternews/2010/world/charting-asian-carps-course/.

[46] "Chicago Sanitary and Ship Canal Electric Fish Barrier," U.S. Army Corps of Engineers, www.asiancarp.org/documents/BarrierBrochure.pdf.

[47] Emily Chung, "Stopping the Asian Carp Invasion," CBC News, Aug. 6, 2010, www.cbc.ca/news/technology/story/2010/08/04/f-asian-carp-invasive-species.html.

[48] Monica Davey, "What to Do About Asian Carp? Great Lakes States Can't Agree," *The New York Times*, Dec. 20, 2011, www.nytimes.com/2011/12/21/us/in-great-lakes-states-a-divide-over-the-asian-carp.html.

[49] "Proposed Rules and other Federal Register Notices," U.S. Department of Agriculture, Noxious Weeds program, www.aphis.usda.gov/plant_health/plant_pest_info/weeds/newregs.shtml.

[50] Comments from Elizabeth Brusati, Docket APHIS-2011-0072-0011, Aug. 22, 2011, www.regulations.gov/#!documentDetail;D=APHIS-2011-0072-0011.

[51] See comments from the American Nursery & Landscape Association and the Society of American Florists, www.regulations.gov/#!documentDetail;D=APHIS-2011-0072-0038.

[52] See comments from North American Rock Garden Association, www.regulations.gov/#!documentDetail;D=APHIS-2011-0072-0015.

[53] "Invasive Species Solutions," National Environmental Coalition on Invasive Species, www.necis.net/intro-to-invasive-species/invasive-species-solutions/.

[54] George Phocas, testimony before the Senate Homeland Security and Governmental Affairs Committee, Subcommittee on Oversight, Oct. 27, 2011, p. 6, www.hsdl.org/?view&did=691182.

[55] "Exotic Animal Industry in the U.S.," "The Diane Rehm Show," National Public Radio, Feb. 1, 2012, transcript at http://thedianerehmshow.org/shows/2012-02-01/exotic-animal-industry-us/transcript.

[56] "Nonnative Amnesty Day Events," Florida Fish and Wildlife Conservation Commission, www.myfwc.com/wildlifehabitats/nonnatives/amnesty-day-events/.

[57] Martin E. Comas, "Exotic Pet Amnesty Day: SeaWorld Event to Collect Unwanted Exotic Critters," *Orlando Sentinel*, Oct. 30, 2011, http://articles.orlandosentinel.com/2011-10-30/news/os-exotic-pets-amnesty-20111031_1_exotic-animals-exotic-critters-scott-hardin.

[58] Erin McLaughlin, "Florida Opens Door for Owners to Surrender Exotic Pets," ABC News, Nov. 6, 2011, http://abcnews.go.com/US/pythons-giant-turtles-flying-marsupials-florida-holds-event/story?id=14893228#.Tyq_EfnW6Bo.

[59] "Coping With Feral Hogs," Texas A&M University, http://feralhogs.tamu.edu/faq/.

[60] "Feral Pigs," Wisconsin Department of Natural Resources, http://dnr.wi.gov/org/land/wildlife/publ/wlnotebook/pig.htm.

[61] "Coping With Feral Hogs," Texas A&M, *op. cit.*; Tennessee Wildlife Resources Agency, "New Wild Hog Regulations," http://tn.gov/twra/feralhog.html.

[62] Lauren Etter, "Asian Carp Fix: Just Eat It," *The Wall Street Journal*, April 26, 2010, http://online.wsj.com/article/SB10001424052748704388304575202612308114130.html; "Illinois Launches Campaign to Improve Asian Carp's Image (For Eating)," Associated Press, Sept. 22, 2011, www.chicagotribune.com/news/local/breaking/chi-illinois-launches-eat-asian-carp-campaign-20110922,0,4550212.story.

[63] Troy Reimink, "Would You Eat Asian Carp? What If It Was Called Silverfin?" *Grand Rapids Press*, May 19, 2010, www.mlive.com/news/index.ssf/2010/05/would_you_eat_asian_carp_what.html.

[64] "Eat Lionfish pull card," www.ccfhr.noaa.gov/docs/EatLionfishPullCard.pdf.

[65] Erik Olsen, "Florida Keys Declare Open Season on the Invasive Lionfish," *The New York Times*, Nov. 22, 2010, www.nytimes.com/2010/11/23/science/23lionfish.html.

[66] Thomas J. Rawinski, "Impacts of White-Tailed Deer Overabundance in Forest Ecosystems: An Overview," U.S. Forest Service, June 2008, http://na.fs.fed.us/fhp/special_interests/white_tailed_deer.pdf; William J. McShea, "Ecology and Management of White-Tailed Deer in a Changing World," *Annals of the New York Academy of Sciences*, online version, Jan. 23, 2012, http://onlinelibrary.wiley.com/doi/10.1111/j.1749-6632.2011.06376.x/full.

[67] Stephen DeStefano, *Coyote at the Kitchen Door: Living With Wildlife in Suburbia* (2010), p. 73.

FOR MORE INFORMATION

Florida Fish and Wildlife Conservation Commission, 620 S. Meridian St., Tallahassee, FL 32399; 850-488-4676; www.myfwc.com. Manages hundreds of species of fish and wildlife for the state of Florida, which has been severely impacted by invasive species.

Lady Bird Johnson Wildflower Center, 4801 LaCrosse Ave., Austin, TX 78739; 512-232-0100; www.wildflower.org. A garden complex and research center founded by former first lady Lady Bird Johnson to promote plant diversity and advocate for native plants.

MIT Sea Grant College Program, Massachusetts Institute of Technology, 292 Main St., 3rd Floor, Cambridge, MA 02142; 617-253-7041; www.seagrant.mit.edu. One of a network of federally funded ocean and coastal research programs at U.S. universities and research institutes.

The Nature Conservancy, 4245 North Fairfax Dr., Suite 100, Arlington, VA 22203; 800-628-6860; www.nature.org. A U.S.-based group that works to preserve lands and waters at home and in 33 other countries.

REEF, P.O. Box 246, Key Largo, FL 33037; 305-852-0030; www.reef.org. An organization of scuba divers and marine enthusiasts working to advance marine conservation and protect the oceans, mainly by monitoring fish populations.

U.S. Fish and Wildlife Service, Department of the Interior, 1849 C St., N.W., Washington, DC 20240; 202-208-3100; www.fws.gov. Federal agency charged with conserving fish, wildlife, plants and their habitat.

U.S. Forest Service, 1400 Independence Ave., S.W., Washington, DC 20250; 800-832-1355; www.fs.fed.us. An agency within the U.S. Department of Agriculture that manages 193 million acres of national forests and grasslands across the United States.

Woods Hole Oceanographic Institution, 266 Woods Hole Road, Woods Hole, MA 02543; 508-548-1400; www.whoi.edu. The world's largest private, nonprofit ocean research, engineering and education organization.

Bibliography

Selected Sources

Books

Boyle, T.C., *When the Killing's Done*, Viking, 2011.
The acclaimed novelist sets his latest story on California's Channel Islands, where animal-rights activists oppose plans to eliminate invasive rats and feral pigs.

DeStefano, Steve, *Coyote at the Kitchen Door: Living With Wildlife in Suburbia*, Harvard University Press, 2010.
An urban ecologist analyzes why moose, coyotes, alligators, and other wildlife are increasingly showing up in suburban areas and argues that humans should learn to coexist with wild animals.

Mabey, Richard, *Weeds: In Defense of Nature's Most Unloved Plants*, HarperCollins, 2010.
The British naturalist says weeds can be destructive but also play many important roles, such as regreening areas ravaged by human actions.

Nikiforuk, Andrew, *Empire of the Beetle: How Human Folly and a Tiny Bug Are Killing North America's Great Forests*, Greystone, 2011.
An award-winning Canadian journalist investigates bark beetle outbreaks that have killed more than 30 billion pine and spruce trees across North America since the late 1980s.

Articles

"New Quantitative Method Enables Researchers to Assess Environmental Risks Posed by Non-Native Species," *ScienceDaily*, Dec. 26, 2011, www.sciencedaily.com/releases/2011/12/111226093008.htm.
Norwegian researchers have developed a formula that classifies invasive species according to their biological characteristics and environmental impacts, making it possible to rank them according to the overall risks they pose.

Gallo, Travis, and Damon Waitt, "Creating a Successful Citizen Science Model to Detect and Report Invasive Species," *BioScience*, Vol. 61, No. 6, June 2011, pp. 459-465.
The Invaders of Texas program has trained volunteers to work as "citizen scientists," cost-effectively gathering data and monitoring the spread of invasive plants across the state.

Gillis, Justin, "With Deaths of Forests, a Loss of Key Climate Protectors," *The New York Times*, Oct. 1, 2011, www.nytimes.com/2011/10/01/science/earth/01forest.html?pagewanted=6&ref=temperaturerising.
Bark beetle outbreaks are among many factors causing large-scale forest die-offs and could sharply alter the world's carbon balances.

Maher, Kris, "The Vexing Bugs in the Global Trade System," *The Wall Street Journal*, Jan. 25, 2010, http://online.wsj.com/article/SB10001424052748704362004575000883982322608.html.
As global trade increases, more destructive insects and plants are entering the United States along with imported goods.

Pittman, Craig, "When pythons take over Everglades, raccoons, rabbits and other small mammals vanish," *Tampa Bay Times*, Jan. 30, 2012, www.evergladescisma.org/v1_ch9.pdf.
Between 2003 and 2011, areas of Everglades National Park where pythons had proliferated experienced a steep drop in the number of raccoons, opossums, deer, rabbits and other animals, scientists found.

Reynolds, Glenn Harlan, "The Perfect Way to Get Rid of Invasive Species — Eat Them," *Popular Mechanics.com*, Sept. 26, 2011, www.popularmechanics.com/outdoors/recreation/fishing/the-perfect-way-to-get-rid-of-invasive-species-eat-them.
Caribbean divers are promoting invasive lionfish to restaurants and also feeding the speared fish to sharks and groupers.

Reports and Studies

"Inventory of Available Controls for Aquatic Nuisance Species of Concern, Chicago Area Waterway System," U.S. Army Corps of Engineers, December 2011, http://glmris.anl.gov/documents/docs/ANS_Control_Paper.pdf.
Options are presented for preventing nuisance species of fish, shellfish, plants and microorganisms from moving between the Great Lakes and Mississippi River Basin.

Burgiel, Stanley W., and Adrianna A. Muir, "Invasive Species, Climate Change and Ecosystem-Based Adaptation: Addressing Multiple Drivers of Global Change," Global Invasive Species Programme, 2010, www.gisp.org/whatsnew/docs/Climate_Change_ReportA4.pdf.
A study funded by the World Bank contends that climate change is compounding the impact of invasive species worldwide and recommends steps to make ecosystems more resilient against the twin threats.

Rodgers, LeRoy, et al., *2011 South Florida Environmental Report, Chapter 9: Status of Nonindigenous Species in the South Florida Environment*, March 1, 2011, www.evergladescisma.org/v1_ch9.pdf.
Florida faces "significant and diverse threats" from hundreds of invasive species of animals and more than 1,300 species of plants, according to an annual report by the South Florida Water Management District.

The Next Step:

Additional Articles from Current Periodicals

Climate Change

April, Kelly, "Scientists Plan for a Changed Climate," *Chicago Tribune*, Aug. 28, 2011, p. A6, articles.chicagotribune.com/2011-08-28/news/ct-met-climate-change-conservation-20110828_1_climate-change-warmer-winters-great-lakes.

Chicago-area scientists are planning ways to address potential growth in invasive species due to climate change.

Begley, Janet, "Experts Warn of Invasive Plants, Animals Spreading to Treasure Coast," *Press Journal* (Vero Beach, Fla.), Jan. 4, 2012, p. 1, www.tcpalm.com/news/2012/jan/03/forestry-experts-warn-of-invasive-plants-animals/.

Florida's Treasure Coast — a 70-mile stretch on the state's eastern side — is a target for at least 10 invasive plant and animal species because of its hot climate, forestry experts say.

Scott, Michael, "Scientists See Plants, Insects Warming to Climate Change," *Plain Dealer* (Cleveland), May 26, 2011, p. A1, blog.cleveland.com/metro/2011/05/ohios_plants_and_insects_are_a.html.

Ohio's plants and insects are adapting to climate change, but a warming climate may also make living conditions more favorable for invasive species more suited to warmer temperatures.

Elimination

Funes, Juliette, and J.D. Velasco, "Invasive and Potentially Dangerous Asian Mosquitoes Found to Be Widespread in El Monte," *San Gabriel Valley* (Calif.) *Tribune*, Sept. 23, 2011, www.sgvtribune.com/news/ci_18962556?source=rss.

Invasive Asian mosquitoes in El Monte, Calif., should be eliminated because of their danger to humans, officials say.

Lynch, James Q., "In Battle Against Invasive Species, Iowa DNR Fighting for Time," *The Gazette* (Cedar Rapids, Iowa), Feb. 8, 2012, thegazette.com/2012/02/08/in-battle-against-invasive-species-iowa-dnr-fighting-for-time/.

Iowa's Department of Natural Resources is having trouble curbing zebra mussels in a way that won't kill native species.

Exotic Pets

Gamiz Jr., Manuel, "What Should People Do With Their Unwanted Exotic Pets?" *Morning Call* (Allentown, Pa.), March 9, 2011, p. A21, articles.mcall.com/2011-03-08/opinion/mc-explain-it-exotic-20110308_1_exotic-pets-owners-alligators.

Some exotic pets turned in by owners go to rescue homes.

Grau, Charlie, "Pet Amnesty Day to Offer Break for Owners of Exotic Pets," *South Florida Sun-Sentinel*, Jan. 5, 2012, articles.sun-sentinel.com/2012-01-06/news/fl-pet-amnesty-day-20120105_1_exotic-pets-pet-amnesty-day-nonnative-pet.

Palm Beach County, Fla., is offering exotic-pet owners a Pet Amnesty Day when they can turn in their pets without penalty.

Marine Invaders

Fredrickson, Leif, "The Aliens Are Coming!" *Missoula* (Mont.) *Independent*, April 21, 2011, p. 14, missoulanews.bigskypress.com/missoula/the-aliens-are-coming/Content?oid=1432982.

Aquatic invasive species can alter the food webs of rivers and lakes.

Gibson, William E., "Mass Invasion of Lionfish Threatens East Coast Waters," *Los Angeles Times*, July 10, 2011, p. A11, articles.latimes.com/2011/jul/10/nation/la-na-lionfish-20110710.

Scientists say lionfish are gobbling up other reef fish in the Caribbean, Gulf of Mexico and Florida estuaries.

Schmitt, Glen, "We Must Regulate Invasives," *St. Cloud* (Minn.) *Times*, March 20, 2011, p. D8.

Invasive aquatic species can't be eliminated in Minnesota, but their growth can be slowed, an outdoor columnist says.

Wood, Pamela, "Fighting Aquatic Invaders," *Maryland Gazette*, Oct. 8, 2011, www.mdgazette.com/content/fighting-aquatic-invaders.

Baltimore officials have unveiled a research barge that will be used to test technologies for removing marine invaders from ballast water.

CITING *CQ* RESEARCHER

Sample formats for citing these reports in a bibliography include the ones listed below. Preferred styles and formats vary, so please check with your instructor or professor.

MLA STYLE

Jost, Kenneth. "Remembering 9/11," CQ Researcher 2 Sept. 2011: 701-732.

APA STYLE

Jost, K. (2011, September 2). Remembering 9/11. *CQ Researcher, 9*, 701-732.

CHICAGO STYLE

Jost, Kenneth. "Remembering 9/11." *CQ Researcher*, September 2, 2011, 701-732.

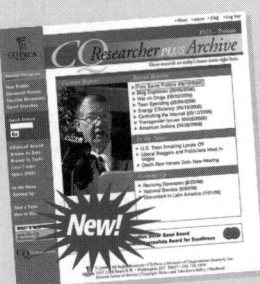

CQ Researcher

Published by CQ Press, an Imprint of SAGE Publications, Inc.

www.cqresearcher.com

Space Program

Can NASA set a new course for human exploration?

More than 40 years after astronauts first walked on the moon, the U.S. space program is in search of direction. With the end of the space shuttle program last year, the United States must rely on Russian *Soyuz* rockets to send Americans into space. Private contractors are building spacecraft to ferry astronauts to the International Space Station and beyond, but those won't be ready for years. Meanwhile, budget cutters have pared NASA spending, and President Obama has angered some space enthusiasts by proposing to shift funds from two international Mars missions to a new telescope slated to replace the aging Hubble observatory. Mars remains a tantalizing destination, and a sophisticated rover is scheduled to land there in August to search for signs of life. But a human landing may be decades away. Obama has rejected returning to the moon as a stepping stone to Mars, preferring to send astronauts to an asteroid.

End of an Era: The space shuttle Atlantis *lifts off from Kennedy Space Center on July 8, 2011, carrying four astronauts to the International Space Station. It was the shuttle program's last flight. The United States now must depend on Russian* Soyuz *spacecraft to ferry Americans to the orbiting laboratory.*

INSIDE THIS REPORT

THE ISSUES 179
CHRONOLOGY 189
BACKGROUND 190
CURRENT SITUATION 195
AT ISSUE.........................197
OUTLOOK 199
BIBLIOGRAPHY 202
THE NEXT STEP 203

CQ Researcher • Feb. 24, 2012 • www.cqresearcher.com
Volume 22, Number 8 • Pages 177-204

Los Angeles | London | New Delhi
Singapore | Washington DC

RECIPIENT OF SOCIETY OF PROFESSIONAL JOURNALISTS AWARD FOR EXCELLENCE ◆ AMERICAN BAR ASSOCIATION SILVER GAVEL AWARD

SPACE PROGRAM

THE ISSUES

179 • Is the space program justified?
• Should a human mission to Mars be the next big objective?
• Is the space station worth the cost?

BACKGROUND

190 **Obama's Course Change**
Privately built spacecraft will replace President Bush's Project Constellation.

192 **New Approaches**
A new launch vehicle and spacecraft will support flight to an asteroid.

193 **'Mission Complete'**
The last space shuttle touched down July 21, 2011.

CURRENT SITUATION

195 **Private Sector's New Role**
Companies will handle routine missions.

198 **NASA's Budget**
The space agency faces fiscal tightening.

198 **Scientific Missions**
NASA has 94 active missions, including orbiting Mercury and Pluto.

OUTLOOK

199 **Leadership in Space**
Critics ask: Can we afford to do more exploration? Supporters respond: Can we afford not to?

SIDEBARS AND GRAPHICS

181 **Many See U.S. Space Leadership as Essential**
More Republicans favor continued exploration.

182 **Is There Life on Mars?**
NASA's mission to find out is nearing touchdown.

184 **Mars Missions Date Back Nearly 50 Years**
More than a dozen successful ones preceded *Curiosity*.

185 **Mars Rover Poised for Touchdown**
The SUV-size vehicle is set to land in August.

189 **Chronology**
Key events since 1957.

190 **Webb Telescope Reaches for the Heavens**
Delays and funding fights cloud its development.

192 **Obama Seeks to Shift Funds to Webb Telescope**
Spending would also increase for space station.

194 **Countdown for Private Spaceflight Has Begun**
Space entrepreneurs include Virgin Galactic's Richard Branson.

197 **At Issue**
Is the United States in danger of losing a space race to China?

FOR FURTHER RESEARCH

201 **For More Information**
Organizations to contact.

202 **Bibliography**
Selected sources used.

203 **The Next Step**
Additional articles.

203 **Citing *CQ Researcher***
Sample bibliography formats.

Cover: AFP/Getty Images/Bruce Weaver

CQ Researcher

Feb. 24, 2012
Volume 22, Number 8

MANAGING EDITOR: Thomas J. Billitteri
tjb@cqpress.com

ASSISTANT MANAGING EDITOR: Kathy Koch
kkoch@cqpress.com

CONTRIBUTING EDITOR: Thomas J. Colin
tcolin@cqpress.com

ASSOCIATE EDITOR: Kenneth Jost

STAFF WRITER: Marcia Clemmitt

CONTRIBUTING WRITERS: Sarah Glazer, Alan Greenblatt, Peter Katel, Barbara Mantel, Jennifer Weeks

DESIGN/PRODUCTION EDITOR: Olu B. Davis

ASSISTANT EDITOR: Darrell Dela Rosa

FACT CHECKER: Michelle Harris

Los Angeles | London | New Delhi
Singapore | Washington DC

An Imprint of SAGE Publications, Inc.

VICE PRESIDENT AND EDITORIAL DIRECTOR, HIGHER EDUCATION GROUP:
Michele Sordi

DIRECTOR, ONLINE PUBLISHING:
Todd Baldwin

CQ Researcher (ISSN 1056-2036) is printed on acid-free paper. Published weekly, except: (March wk. 5) (May wk. 4) (July wk. 1) (Aug. wks. 3, 4) (Nov. wk. 4) and (Dec. wks. 3, 4). Published by SAGE Publications, Inc., 2455 Teller Rd., Thousand Oaks, CA 91320. Annual full-service subscriptions start at $1,054. For pricing, call 1-800-834-9020. To purchase a *CQ Researcher* report in print or electronic format (PDF), visit www.cqpress.com or call 866-427-7737. Single reports start at $15. Bulk purchase discounts and electronic-rights licensing are also available. Periodicals postage paid at Thousand Oaks, California, and at additional mailing offices. POSTMASTER: Send address changes to *CQ Researcher*, 2300 N St., N.W., Suite 800, Washington, DC 20037.

Space Program

BY JOHN FELTON

THE ISSUES

If all goes as planned next August, a NASA rover about the size of a small SUV will be gently lowered from a spacecraft onto the surface of Mars and begin searching for signs that the "red planet" once supported life — and perhaps still does.

The $2.5 billion mission — the most ambitious to Mars ever mounted — marks a bright spot on an otherwise cloudy horizon for the U.S. space program. Beset by disagreements over the next destination for human spaceflight and squeezed by budget cuts, the U.S. space program faces more uncertainty than at any time in its storied history. [1]

"We are in a real mess right now with our space program, and it's not clear how we're going to get out of it," says Alex Roland, a professor emeritus of history at Duke University and longtime critic of NASA, where he was an historian in the 1970s.

Some critics are especially upset at cancellation of the space shuttle program, leaving the United States to depend on Russian *Soyuz* spacecraft to bring Americans to the International Space Station (ISS), the only current destination for American astronauts.

"I am not at all happy with some of the directions the space program is going, in particular retiring the space shuttles before we have a new heavy-lift launching system in place," pioneering astronaut John Glenn, who became the first American to orbit Earth 50 years ago this month, told *The New York Times*. "If the Russians had a hiccup with *Soyuz*, our manned space program would be ended, maybe for years." [2]

National Aeronautics and Space Administration

NASA's Mars Science Laboratory, carrying the rover Curiosity, *is lifted into position before being attached to an Atlas rocket at Cape Canaveral on Nov. 3, 2011. The mission to Mars was launched on Nov. 26 and is due to arrive at the "red planet" Aug. 6. Critics say the Obama administration's proposed withdrawal from participation with the European Space Agency on two unmanned follow-up expeditions to Mars threatens U.S. leadership in space research. But NASA says it is considering future Mars missions.*

Indeed, China and Russia are the only countries currently capable of putting humans into Earth orbit. [3] Private companies, operating under NASA contracts, might begin taking cargo to the space station this year, but commercial flights to ferry astronauts to the station are several years away.

Spaceflight emerged as an issue in the Republican presidential primaries in January when former House Speaker Newt Gingrich, campaigning in Florida, proposed a major commitment to colonize the moon. A small number of space advocates have pushed such a plan, but Gingrich's political opponents mocked it, and his appeal for votes along Florida's Space Coast, where NASA has launched rockets since the 1950s, failed to help him win the Florida primary. [4]

A much more serious debate about the future of the space program likely will take place this year in Congress. The starting point will be President Obama's fiscal 2013 budget request, submitted Feb. 13, which would continue most current programs and give NASA about the same amount — $17.8 billion — as for the current fiscal year. (*See chart, p. 192.*) However, the administration would eliminate two unmanned scientific missions to Mars, scheduled for 2016 and 2018, that had been high-profile examples of cooperation in space between the United States and Europe.

Roger Handberg, a political science professor at the University of Central Florida who has written extensively about space policy, is deeply skeptical about NASA's ability to continue its programs without reshaping them to fit a new era of reduced budgets. "I don't think NASA will survive doing what it is doing — and wants to do on the scale it has been at — because the money won't be there," he says.

NASA has courted members of Congress by scattering installations and contracts around the country, Handberg says, but "the problem is that they don't have the kind of public support they need to survive a major cutback in the budget."

NASA officials say, however, that the space program is well-charted for years to come. NASA and private contractors are spending billions of dollars on research and other programs that NASA says could return Americans to deep space as early as 2025.

Citing a series of recent decisions, notably the selection of a design for a new launch vehicle intended eventually to take humans to Mars and beyond, NASA Administrator Charles Bolden said last September that "NASA is not only alive and well" but is "poised to take the next big leaps into both human space exploration and scientific discovery." [5]

AFP/Getty Images/Bruce Weaver

A Falcon 9 *rocket lifts off from Cape Canaveral, Fla., on Dec. 8, 2010, carrying the* Dragon *space capsule. The launch was sponsored by SpaceX, the firm founded by PayPal co-founder Elon Musk. SpaceX (Space Exploration Technologies) is one of two firms NASA has contracted with to build rockets and spacecraft that will take food, fuel, scientific equipment and other supplies to the space station. The Hawthorne, Calif., firm has a $1.6 billion contract for 12 cargo flights through 2016.*

Scientific discovery is the one aspect of the U.S. space program that has continued relatively unabated. NASA currently runs more than 90 unmanned scientific missions, some operated with other countries. One of the most famous is the spunky golf cart-sized *Opportunity* rover on Mars, which is still roaming eight years past its original 90-day lifespan. *Opportunity*'s twin, the *Spirit*, got mired in sand in 2009 and went silent in 2010. The *Mars Odyssey* has been orbiting the "red planet" since 2001; among its achievements is the detection of hydrogen just beneath the Martian surface, suggesting the presence of frozen water. [6]

The new Mars mission, the Mars Science Laboratory, with its bigger, more complex rover, *Curiosity*, launched last Nov. 26, is due to arrive at Mars Aug. 6. [7] However, the Obama administration has decided, for budget reasons, to withdraw U.S. participation from two unmanned follow-up scientific expeditions to Mars, both in cooperation with the European Space Agency. Outraged advocates of planetary science missions say the United States risks losing its leadership in an important area of research. Bolden, however, said NASA is not abandoning scientific exploration of Mars and suggested that some kind of mission might be possible in 2018-20, when the planet will be relatively close to Earth. [8]

NASA also has two telescopes in space that have produced copious information. The orbiting Kepler telescope has discovered more than 1,000 planet candidates. [9] The better-known Hubble Space Telescope, repaired in space four times because of design and production flaws, has looked into remote areas of the universe; it has been capturing light emitted 13 billion years ago and discovered the largest black holes yet observed. [10] NASA plans to replace Hubble in 2018 with the much more powerful James Webb Space Telescope — that is, if Congress continues funding it. The House of Representatives tried unsuccessfully to kill the Webb program in 2011, but Obama has called on Congress to keep it alive. (*See sidebar, p. 190.*)

The single biggest and most expensive space endeavor ever — the International Space Station — is still operating. The ISS, a $100 billion project by the United States, Russia, Europe, Japan and others, was finally completed last year and has been occupied by astronauts since 2000. Current plans call for it to continue operating at least until 2020 and possibly as late as 2028. [11]

Russia also is active in Mars exploration but has failed 17 times compared with two partial successes. [12] The latest failure came when its Phobos-Grunt mission failed to push past Earth orbit last November and crashed into the Pacific Ocean Jan. 15. [13] The mission was supposed to land on the Martian moon Phobos and send a small soil sample back to Earth. Russian officials at first suggested a U.S. military radar might have damaged the spacecraft but later said it suffered a software malfunction. [14]

China put its first astronaut into space in 2003 and last year launched the first element of what it says will be a space station, possibly manned, by 2020. [15] A five-year plan issued in Beijing last December repeated talk of preliminary planning for a "human lunar landing" — an event most U.S. experts say is at least a decade off. [16]

Another opportunity that was nearly inconceivable at the dawn of the space age but is now nearing reality is private space travel. At least three companies are building spacecraft to take paying customers for suborbital flights (about 60 miles in space) lasting about three to six minutes. Several hundred people already have put down deposits of up to $200,000 for a flight. [17] But the companies — all U.S.-based — have experienced repeated delays, and predictions of a booming private space business have yet to pan out.

The two companies with the most advanced programs are hoping to launch their first test flights (without paying customers) late in 2012. [18] (*See sidebar, p. 194.*)

As debate continues over the direction and funding of the U.S. space program, here are some of the questions being asked:

Is the space program justified?

When the Pew Research Center asked Americans in a poll last June whether it was essential "that the United States continue to be a world leader in space exploration," most said yes, but more than a third said no. (*See graph, above.*) Republicans and people with family incomes above $75,000 were somewhat more likely to answer yes than Democrats, independents, and people with lower family incomes. [19]

The survey points up a huge divide in American society over whether space exploration is worth the cost, particularly during a time of staggering federal deficits.

NASA spends $5 billion to $8 billion of its annual $17.8 billion budget on programs related to human spaceflight. (*See chart, p. 192.*) The biggest

Many See U.S. Space Leadership as Essential

Nearly 60 percent of Americans say it is crucial for the United States to remain a world leader in space exploration. The highest percentages with that view are Republicans and those with annual household income of more than $75,000.

Views on U.S. Space Leadership, June 2011

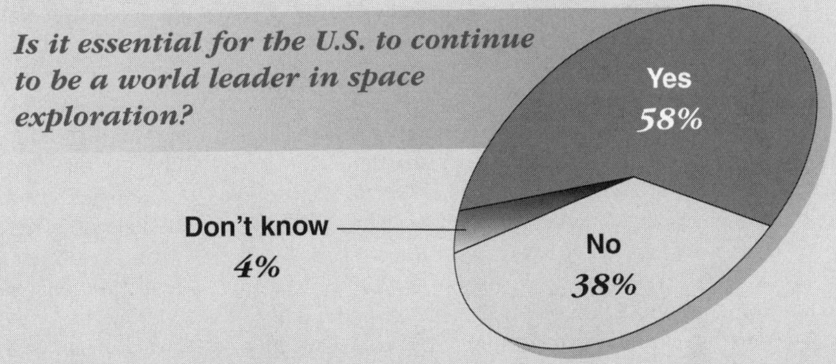

Is it essential for the U.S. to continue to be a world leader in space exploration?
Yes 58%
No 38%
Don't know 4%

By family income

Income level	Yes	No	Don't know
$75,000+	63%	35%	2%
$30,000-$75,000	55%	42%	4%
<$30,000	57%	37%	6%

By party affiliation

Party	Yes	No	Don't know
Republican	67%	30%	3%
Democrat	54%	42%	4%
Independent	57%	40%	3%

** Figures may not total 100 because of rounding.*

Source: "Majority Sees U.S. Leadership in Space as Essential," Pew Research Center, July 2011, www.people-press.org/2011/07/05/majority-sees-u-s-leadership-in-space-as-essential/

Is There Life on Mars?

NASA's mission to find out is nearing touchdown.

It's been called the "rover on steroids," a one-ton mobile geology lab bristling with instruments that will help determine whether conditions on Mars have ever been favorable for life. [1]

The rover — named *Curiosity* — is the heart of NASA's Mars Science Laboratory, a $2.5 billion mission that is the most sophisticated effort to date to look for signs of microbial life — past or present — on the so-called "red planet."

Launched last Nov. 26, a spacecraft carrying *Curiosity* will land on Mars Aug. 6 if all goes according to plan. The craft will descend in a series of S-curves through the Martian atmosphere, and three minutes before touchdown a parachute will slow it down. Then, retro rockets attached to an upper stage will fire, and in the final seconds the upper stage will act as a sky crane, gently lowering *Curiosity* on a tether to the ground. [2]

The Mars Science Laboratory is the latest in a long line of U.S. scientific missions to Mars dating back to 1965, when Mariner 4 flew past the planet and transmitted 21 images back to Earth. [3]

One of NASA's greatest achievements so far has been the mission of the twin Mars rovers *Opportunity* and *Spirit* that began in January 2004. Both about the size of golf carts, the solar-powered vehicles were scheduled to roam just a few miles of the Martian surface, examining soil and rocks, for only 90 days. But they kept going, and NASA repeatedly extended their missions based on the enormous quantity of information they sent back to Earth about Mars' geology.

Spirit drove 4.8 miles before ceasing communications in 2010. *Opportunity* is still at work, eight years after landing, having driven more than 21 miles — it was built to drive less than one mile. *Opportunity* has examined four craters, including one 14 miles in diameter known as Endeavour, where it has been positioned since last fall. [4]

Curiosity, which is about five times the size of *Spirit* and *Opportunity*, will use its instruments, including a rock-vaporizing laser, to collect and examine rock and soil, then send technical information back to Earth. [5] Among other things, it will look for evidence of methane gas, which might suggest Mars has some form of life. [6]

Despite its eight years on the job, *Opportunity* is not the longest-serving spacecraft to visit Mars. That distinction is held by *Mars Odyssey*, which has been in orbit around the "red planet" since 2001 and will continue for the indefinite future. In December 2010 *Odyssey* surpassed the previous record for Mars service held by the *Mars Global Surveyor*, which orbited the planet from 1997 to 2006. Among *Odyssey*'s achievements has been the detection of hydrogen beneath the Martian surface, leading scientists to believe water might also be present. [7]

Another major Mars program, planned by the United States in conjunction with the European Space Agency, may have fallen victim to budget cuts. [8] Known as ExoMars, it is supposed to have two components: the Trace Gas Orbiter, to be launched in 2016, with a mission of examining the Martian atmosphere in greater detail than previous orbiters could; and two rovers, to be launched in 2018, which would dig up soil samples to be retrieved by later missions. The goal is to learn much more than is currently possible about the planet's geological history. [9]

However, the proposed NASA budget issued Feb. 13 by the Obama administration eliminated funding for U.S. participation in ExoMars. Administration officials for months had signaled that such a cut was likely, leading the European and Russian space agencies in late 2011 to begin discussions about a joint program without U.S. participation. [10]

The proposed withdrawal from the mission has angered Mars exploration advocates, including Robert Zubrin, founder and president of the Mars Society. Zubrin says the Obama administration "is reneging on a deal we had with the Europeans. Not only are they wrecking our own program, but they are wrecking the European program as well."

Unless reversed by Congress, the U.S. withdrawal likely will affect a subsequent mission to retrieve the soil samples. Known as the Mars Astrobiology Explorer-Cacher (MAX-C), it was the highest-priority project in a NASA-sponsored survey of planetary science projects for the coming decade, according to the independent National Research Council. Cost estimates for the project have ranged from $2.2 billion to $4.7 billion. However, the council suggested deferring or even canceling the pro-

chunk, about $3 billion in fiscal 2012, is earmarked for a new rocket — or "space launch system" — to carry humans deep into space and a multipurpose crew capsule. [20]

The U.S. space community, ranging from scientists to technicians to business people with a commercial interest in the space program, is more uniformly positive than Americans in general about the merits of the space program. But it is divided over two basic issues: how to justify human spaceflight and what the next destination for manned missions, if any, should be. Helping to drive that debate are worries about how mission costs can be explained to taxpayers.

"Money is the root of the problem," says Jeffrey A. Hoffman, a five-time shuttle astronaut and now a professor of aeronautics and astronautics at MIT. He adds that concerns about money come at a time when "clearly, there is a lack of consensus about what we should be doing" with the space program.

Historically, political leaders and space

ject if it could not be done for under $2.5 billion. [11]

NASA said last June that it concurred with that recommendation and was examining "a significant cost reduction" to enable the project to proceed. [12]

NASA/JPL-Caltech

A sky crane lowers the Curiosity *rover to the surface of Mars in this artist's rendering.*

While most of the past and current U.S. explorations of Mars have been successful, the same cannot be said for the other great space power of the past 50 years. Since the 1960s, Russia (and its predecessor, the Soviet Union) have enjoyed partial successes in only two of 19 attempts to send spacecraft to Mars. [13] Moscow's best result came in 1971, when its *Mars 3* orbiter collected data for eight months, and a related lander got safely to the Martian surface but sent back only 20 seconds of data, according to NASA. [14]

Russia's latest stumble came in November, when the ambitious Phobos-Grunt mission failed to get out of Earth orbit. Russian engineers tried unsuccessfully for weeks to save the spacecraft, which eventually plunged into the Pacific Ocean on Jan. 15. Russian officials initially were quoted as suggesting that a U.S. military radar installation in Alaska might have damaged Phobos-Grunt, but subsequent reports said cosmic radiation damaged the spacecraft's software. [15]

The spacecraft included a probe that was supposed to land on the small Martian moon Phobos, scoop up soil, and then return it to Earth. If successful, the mission would have marked the first time that any object from Mars had been returned to Earth for scientific examination. [16]

— John Felton

1 "NASA Launches Sophisticated Rover on Journey to Mars," The Associated Press, *The New York Times*, Nov. 26, 2011, www.nytimes.com/2011/11/27/science/space/nasas-curiosity-rover-sets-off-for-mars-mission.html?scp=1&sq=nasa%20launches%20sophisticated%20rover%20on%20journey%20to%20mars&st=cse. See also, "Mars Science Laboratory," NASA, www.jpl.nasa.gov/news/fact_sheets/mars-science-laboratory.pdf.

2 "Mars Science Laboratory," *ibid.* See also "Rover Mission," NASA, http://mars.jpl.nasa.gov/msl/mission/rover/.

3 Mars Exploration Program, "Historical Log," Jet Propulsion Laboratory, http://mars.jpl.nasa.gov/programmissions/missions/log/.

4 Chris Gebhardt, "Opportunity's eight years on Mars: A story of science and endurance," NASASpaceflight.com, Jan. 25, 2012, www.nasaspaceflight.com/2012/01/opportunitys-eight-years-mars-story-science-endurance/.

5 "Mars Science Laboratory Overview," Jet Propulsion Laboratory, http://marsprogram.jpl.nasa.gov/msl/mission/overview/.

6 Kenneth Chang, "On Mars Rover, Tools to Plumb a Methane Mystery," *The New York Times*, Nov. 22, 2011, www.nytimes.com/2011/11/23/science/space/aboard-mars-curiosity-rover-tools-to-plumb-a-methane-mystery.html?ref=marsplanet.

7 "NASA's Odyssey Spacecraft Sets Exploration Record on Mars," Jet Propulsion Laboratory, Dec. 15, 2010, http://mars.jpl.nasa.gov/odyssey/news/whatsnew/index.cfm?FuseAction=ShowNews&NewsID=1091.

8 Jeff Foust, "Tough decisions ahead for planetary exploration," *The Space Review*, April 4, 2011.

9 "The ESA-NASA ExoMars Program 2016-2018," European Space Agency, http://exploration.esa.int/science-e/www/object/index.cfm?fobjectid=46048.

10 Amy Svitak, "ESA, Roscosmos See ExoMars Without NASA," *Aviation Week*, Feb. 10, 2012, www.aviationweek.com/aw/generic/story_channel.jsp?channel=space&id=news/awx/2012/02/10/awx_02_10_2012_p0-423750.xml&headline=ESA,%20Roscosmos%20See%20ExoMars%20Without%20NASA.

11 "Vision and Voyages for Planetary Science in the Decade 2013-2022," Committee on the Planetary Science Decadal Survey; National Research Council, The National Academies Press, pp. 9-15. www.nap.edu/catalog.php?record_id=13117.

12 Letter from Edward J. Weiler, NASA associate administrator for science mission directorate, to Dr. Charles F. Kennel, chair, Space Studies Board of the National Research Council, July 29, 2011, p. 6.

13 Dwayne A. Day, "Red Planet blues," *The Space Review*, Nov. 28, 2011, www.thespacereview.com/article/1980/1.

14 "Mars Exploration Program: Historical Log," *op. cit.*

15 "Russia blames Phobos-Grunt failure on cosmic radiation," spacetoday.net, Feb. 1, 2012, www.spacetoday.net/getsummary.php?id=55170.

16 Jonathan Amos, "Phobos-Grunt: Failed Probe 'Falls Over Pacific,' " BBC News, Jan. 15, 2012, www.bbc.co.uk/news/science-environment-16491457.

advocates have cited numerous reasons why the United States should lead the world in human spaceflight — everything from asserting global power, inspiring new generations of scientists and satisfying the human yearning for exploration to providing high-skill, high-paying jobs for tens of thousands of aerospace workers. [21]

Yet, while these justifications remain valid, space enthusiasts say, there seems to be little agreement on which are the most compelling in today's political and budgetary environment.

In 2010 Congress ordered NASA to contract with the independent National Research Council to review "the goals, core capabilities, and direction of human spaceflight" through 2023. [22] The study is unlikely to be finished until next year, says analyst Marcia Smith, founder and editor of *Space Policy Online*, which tracks space programs and spending. It could "profoundly" influence the direction of

Continued on p. 185

Mars Missions Date Back Nearly 50 Years

The launch of the sophisticated rover Curiosity *last November was the latest of more than a dozen successful U.S. scientific missions to Mars dating back to* Mariner 4 *in 1964. The* Odyssey *and* Opportunity *rovers and* Mars Reconnaissance Orbiter *continue to explore the planet.*

Successful U.S. Mars Missions, 1964-present

Mission	Launch date	Purpose	Results
Mariner 4	Nov. 28, 1964	First Mars flyby	The first successful flight past Mars, on July 14, 1965, returned 21 photos
Mariner 6	Feb. 24, 1969	Mars flyby	Returned 75 photos on July 31, 1969
Mariner 7	March 27, 1969	Mars flyby	Returned 126 photos on Aug. 5, 1969
Mariner 9	May 30, 1971	Orbiter mission	Orbited Nov. 13, 1971-Oct. 27, 1972; returned 7,329 photos
Viking 1	Aug. 20, 1975	Orbiter/lander mission	Orbiter operated June 19, 1976-1980; lander in operation July 20, 1976-1982
Viking 2	Sept. 9, 1975	Orbiter/lander mission	Orbiter operated Aug. 7, 1976-1987; lander in operation Sept. 3, 1976- and 1980; more than 50,000 photos returned
Mars Global Surveyor	Nov. 7, 1996	Orbiter mission	Arrived Sept. 12, 1997; detailed mapping through January 2000; third extended mission completed Sept. 2006; last communication Nov. 2, 2006
Mars Pathfinder	Dec. 4, 1996	Lander/rover mission	Landed July 4, 1997; completed prime mission and began extended mission Aug. 3, 1997; last transmission Sept. 27, 1997
Mars Odyssey	March 7, 2001	Orbiter mission	Arrived Oct. 24, 2001; completed prime mission Aug. 25, 2004; currently conducting extended science and communication relay mission
Mars Exploration Rover Spirit	June 10, 2003	Rover mission	Landed Jan. 4, 2004, for three-month prime mission inside Gusev crater; completed several extended missions; last communication March 22, 2010
Mars Exploration Rover Opportunity	July 7, 2003	Rover mission	Landed Jan. 25, 2004, for three-month prime mission on Meridiani Planum plain region; currently conducting extended mission
Mars Reconnaissance Orbiter	Aug. 12, 2005	Orbiter mission	Arrived March 12, 2006; completed prime mission Sept. 26, 2010; currently conducting extended mission of science and communication relay
Phoenix Mars Lander	Aug. 4, 2007	Lander mission	Landed May 25, 2008; completed prime mission and began extended mission Aug. 26, 2008; last communication Nov. 2, 2008
Mars Science Laboratory	Nov. 26, 2011	Rover mission with analytical laboratory	Curiosity rover scheduled to arrive August 2012

Sources: "Mars Science Laboratory Launch," National Aeronautics and Space Administration, November 2011, pp. 60-61, www.jpl.nasa.gov/news/press_kits/MSLLaunch.pdf; Mars Science Laboratory Mission, Jet Propulsion Laboratory

Introducing the New and Improved Mars Rover

The new Mars mission rover Curiosity *is a one-ton mobile geology lab bristling with cameras and instruments designed to determine whether climate and other conditions on Mars are, or ever have been, capable of supporting life. Using cameras, lasers, a spectroscope and other instruments,* Curiosity *will chemically analyze rock, soil and other samples. The dynamic albedo of neutrons, at right, analyzes minerals under the rover for possible water content. Actions by the rover will be controlled by scientists and technicians on Earth. Previous Mars rovers have sent back strong evidence that the planet has water and thus could host some form of life. The rover is powered by a multimission radioisotope thermoelectric generator (top right), a nuclear battery that converts heat into electricity.*

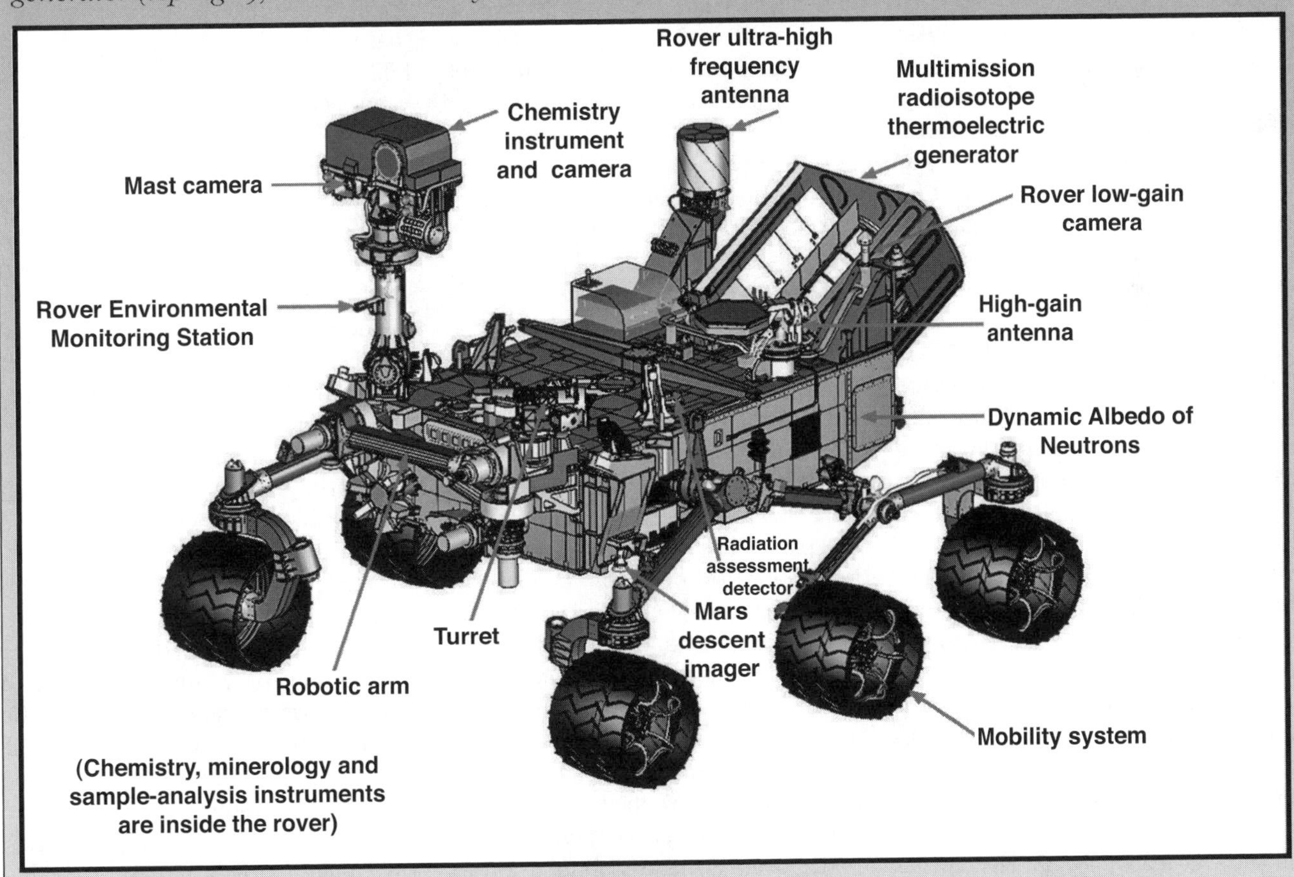

Source: Mars Science Laboratory Launch press kit, NASA, November 2011

Continued from p. 183

U.S. space policy, according to University of Texas astronomer Dan Lester.

Paul Spudis, senior staff scientist at the NASA-funded Lunar and Planetary Institute in Houston, says demonstrating global leadership is justification enough for the U.S. human spaceflight program. "One aspect of being a great power is the obligation to behave as one, to possess the ability to freely come and go and project power anywhere it might be challenged," he says. "If we abandon space, we will no longer possess that ability and, hence, our global stature will decline."

But Lester says that while human spaceflight has a role in future mission, using robots and other scientific instruments to explore space might be the better approach in some cases.

In the past, he notes, NASA and others compared human spaceflight to such great historical explorations as Columbus's journeys to the New World and the Lewis and Clark expedition to the uncharted American West in the early 1800s. "We're trying to be modern-day versions of all these guys who did noble things by going places that were off the map," says Lester. "But that historical template doesn't work that well anymore because we are in an era with sophisticated communications and robotic systems. We send rovers to drive around on Mars, and they send back thousands of pictures, so how can we say we don't know what is there and we have to go find out for ourselves? It's a harder case to make."

Roland, the former NASA historian, says robotic capabilities have reduced the need to send humans deep into space. "Virtually anything we can identify to do in space, we can do more economically, more safely, and more reliably with automated spacecraft controlled by human operators," he says. "This does not mean, however, that humans will not or should not fly in space. It means simply that with our existing technology, sending humans into space is more expensive, more dangerous and more unreliable than it is worth."

Many advocates of human spaceflight disagree that robots can always be as effective as humans in space. "Robots can be incredibly valuable, but if you are talking about really exploring the moon or Mars, both of which are so complex, that is where the value of humans as observers and scientists becomes so much greater," former astronaut Hoffman says.

But even the most avid supporters of human spaceflight say they are frustrated with the lack of a concrete plan for where astronauts will go once the next generation of rockets and space capsules is ready. "NASA literally has no goal," charges Robert Zubrin, president of the Mars Society, a group in Lakewood, Colo., that advocates human exploration and settlement of Mars. "They are spending $10 billion a year on human space flight and have no idea where they are going with it."

NASA says it is following Obama's space policy released in June 2010. That policy calls for a mission to an asteroid by 2025 and to Mars in the 2030s. [23] NASA administrator Bolden insisted to reporters on Feb. 13 that "we have a solid plan, a sustainable plan, and we're moving out to implement it . . . opening the next great chapter of American exploration." [24]

Edward Hudgins, advocacy director for the Atlas Society, a libertarian think tank in Washington, argues that the government should get out of the space business as much as possible and leave it to private enterprise. "The answer is to wait for costs to come down and allow natural market process to come into play," he says. It might be years before entrepreneurs can develop the necessary technology to send humans deep into space, even as far as the moon or Mars, he acknowledges. "But why the rush? Mars will still be there."

Should a human mission to Mars be the next big objective?

For more than a century, Mars has been the focal point for speculation about other life forms in the solar system. [25] U.S. orbiting observatories and rovers on the surface of Mars have sent back strong evidence that the planet has water and thus could host some form of life. [26]

For many space enthusiasts, the ultimate goal is sending humans to Mars, initially to explore it in greater depth than has been possible with machines and eventually to settle humans there. Some advocates argue that a Mars outpost could preserve the human species if it were destroyed on Earth.

The Mars Society's Zubrin, a former aerospace engineer for Martin-Marietta Corp., is among the most avid proponents of human missions to Mars. He insists that sending humans to the "red planet" need not be a massive, decades-long undertaking. Several years ago Zubrin developed his own plan for a relatively low-cost mission, called Mars Direct, which involves three successive flights to Mars, the third of which would carry astronauts who would spend up to 18 months on the planet before returning home. [27]

The most recent version of Zubrin's plan envisions using a launch rocket (the *Falcon-9 Heavy*) and crew capsule (*Dragon*) being developed by the private company SpaceX, led by PayPal co-founder Elon Musk. A decision to use these systems could put humans on Mars by 2020 or even earlier, Zubrin says, at a possible cost of about $50 billion — about the same amount, he says, that NASA plans to spend over that period on systems that will not be ready to launch until billions more have been spent many years later. [28]

NASA is "designing a completely fancy spaceship, like *Battlestar Galactica*, which is absolutely not needed," Zubrin says. "They have gone from the realm of, 'let's set a goal and then go do it,' into the realm of, 'let's dream about it, and maybe some time in the future we might get around to doing it.' It's not a mission. It's just being used as propaganda to justify a technology program."

Zubrin also advocates a much more ambitious concept than just one or two exploratory missions to Mars. He believes humans eventually can settle on Mars, assuming the planet actually has the buried frozen water that NASA orbiters suggest is there. "I believe that if we can establish the first human foothold on a new world, 200 years from now there will be branches of human civilization on Mars, with their own dialects, their own cultures. If you have it within your power to do something grand like this, why not do it?"

Former astronaut Buzz Aldrin, one of the first two humans to walk on the moon in July 1969 as part of *Apollo 11*, also backs settlements on Mars, saying the idea "seems central to the vision many Americans have for the country." Moreover, he said it "uniquely protects U.S. leadership in space exploration, provides insurance for our national security, uniquely presses the envelope of science and is certain to trigger a fusillade of economic opportunities here on Earth." [29]

But others disagree that a human expedition to Mars makes sense. "A human mission to Mars would no doubt make some people feel good and inspire some people to bold or creative ventures," says Duke University's Roland. "It would not, however, improve upon the scientific research that could be done more economically, safely and effectively with automated spacecraft. And it would alienate and discourage those who think that the hundreds of billions of dollars could be better invested in economic development on Earth." In short, he says, "going to Mars, like going to the moon, would be a stunt with no payoff and no potential for further use."

AFP/Getty Images

A Chinese AsiaSat 7 *communications satellite sits atop a Russian* Proton-M *rocket on a launch pad at the Baikonur cosmodrome in Kazakhstan. With the retirement of the U.S. space shuttle system last year, China and Russia are now the only countries capable of putting humans into Earth orbit.*

Scott Pace, director of the Space Policy Institute at George Washington University and a former NASA executive, says going to Mars might be worthwhile in the future, but not anytime soon. The technical and budgetary challenges posed by a Mars mission actually are incentives, he says, because "it's in working on things that are hard that one learns new skills, discovers new things and builds relationships." However, he adds, "I wouldn't make a near-term national commitment to go to Mars. I would focus more on returning to the moon."

Pace says the moon should be the priority because it "is already challenging enough since it's been more than a generation since we left low-Earth orbit." Moreover, he says, the moon "is a subject of interest to many non-traditional, potential partners, particularly in Asia, and thus the moon is likely to be the most acceptable common goal for international cooperation."

Lester, the University of Texas astronomer, suggests a compromise between a full-scale human mission to Mars and not going at all. Lester notes that robots and rovers have become increasingly sophisticated, but their movements still need to be controlled by scientists and technicians on Earth. In the case of rovers, it takes as long as 40 minutes between the time a human gives a command and it arrives at the equipment on Mars — a lag that reduces the amount of work both the human researcher and the rover can accomplish. "If I want to turn over a rock, it can take an hour. That is a major impediment to research," he says.

On the other hand, sending humans to the surface of Mars "would be really cruel," Lester says, because it would expose them to intense cosmic radiation and other danger. In addition, landing astronauts on a planetary object and getting them back to the spacecraft for the return trip constitute a significant share of the cost (up to one-half by some estimates) and technical challenge of any human mission, he says.

As an alternative, Lester proposes that astronauts fly to Mars but only robots and rovers land on the surface. From orbit, the astronauts would control the machines, cutting to a minimum the lag time for sending and receiving instructions. "This would be the equivalent of putting human cognition on another world, but without having humans actually being there and being in danger," Lester argues.

Is the space station worth the cost?

Over nearly 30 years, the United States, Russia, European Union, Japan and 10 other countries worked on the largest-ever global collaborative project in space: the International Space Station (ISS). At an estimated cost of $100 billion (about half for modules and related equipment and half for travel to and from the orbiting station), the ISS has been both costly and controversial.

Supporters argue that the station is worth its cost because it promotes international collaboration, hosts sustained scientific research in a zero-gravity environment and allows scientists to examine the human-health effects of living for months in space. [30] But critics argue that these benefits are not worth the cost and that the money spent on the space station would be better spent on other space programs.

Getty Images/NASA/Paolo Nespoli

The International Space Station — the biggest and most expensive space endeavor ever — is still operating. The $100 billion project by the United States, Russia, Europe, Japan and others has been occupied by astronauts since 2000 and finally was completed last year. It will continue operating at least until 2020 and possibly as late as 2028, according to current plans. Companies operating under NASA contracts might begin taking cargo to the space station this year, but commercial flights to ferry astronauts to the station are several years away.

The ISS is the third long-term facility in space. U.S. *Skylab* was in service from 1973 until it was allowed to fall into the Indian Ocean in July 1979. [31] Russia's *Mir*, completed in 1996, remained in service until 2001 despite numerous problems. It was allowed to fall back into the atmosphere, where most of it disintegrated. [32]

The space station remains one of the single most costly items in NASA's budget: Congress appropriated $2.8 billion in the current fiscal year, about $500 million more than two years earlier. [33] Obama has proposed an increase to $3 billion for fiscal 2013. In addition, NASA is spending $406 million this fiscal year to help private companies develop systems to take cargo, and eventually human crews, to the space station, ending U.S. reliance on Russian spacecraft. [34]

The George W. Bush administration proposed to stop funding the station in 2016, just a few years after its completion. However, the Obama administration has called for keeping it in service at least until 2020 and possibly 2028. [35] Some components probably would need to be updated or replaced for the station to operate into the 2020s, MIT's Hoffman says.

The beginnings of a second space station already are in Earth orbit. Last Sept. 29, China launched the first module, known as *Tiangong-1*, for what it has said will be an unmanned space laboratory by "around" 2016 and a full-scale station "around" 2020. The Chinese government has offered few details about its plans, however. [36]

Glenn, the first American to orbit the Earth and the oldest person to fly in space — he flew on a shuttle mission at age 77 in 1998 — is an avid space station supporter. [37] "One of the things our country needs most is more innovation, more research, more of the new that has been the hallmark of this country," says Glenn, who served four terms as a Democratic U.S. senator from Ohio. "That's where the station fits in. It's the most unique laboratory ever put together, and I think we need that kind of research. We should be leading the world in that."

However, some space scientists are not convinced of the space station's research capabilities. The University of Texas' Lester lauds the "enormous success" of international collaboration that resulted in assembly of a large structure in space. But he says the station has been a disappointment in terms of scientific research. "We have never gotten enough science out of the space station, and it appears likely we never will," he says.

An even harsher assessment came from Nobel Prize-winning physicist Steven Weinberg, a university colleague of Lester. He told an American Astronomical Society conference in January that "the International Space Station was sold as a scientific laboratory, but nothing interesting has come from it." [38]

One of the primary justifications for the space station is its role as a platform for conducting research into the

Continued on p. 190

Chronology

1950s-1960s

Space race with Soviet Union yields huge gains for NASA.

1957
Soviet Union launches *Sputnik* satellites.

1958
NASA formed.

1961
Soviet cosmonaut becomes first human in space; U.S. astronaut Alan B. Shepard Jr. takes suborbital flight. . . . President John F. Kennedy sets landing an astronaut on the moon as a national goal.

1962
John Glenn becomes first American to orbit Earth.

1964
U.S. launches *Mariner 4*; returns 21 photos of Mars.

1969
Mariner 6 and *7* Mars missions launched. . . . *Apollo 11* astronauts Neil Armstrong and Buzz Aldrin land on moon.

1970s-1980s

Apollo moon missions end; space shuttle program begins.

1971
Mariner 9 launched; returns 7,329 photos of Mars.

1972
Final U.S. moon landing occurs as NASA budget shrinks. . . . President Richard M. Nixon agrees to reusable space shuttle system. . . . *Landsat*, first Earth-observing satellite, launched.

1973
Skylab space station launched; three crews occupy it for 171 days and perform 300 experiments before it is allowed to disintegrate.

1975
Viking 1 and *2* Mars orbiters and landers launched; together they return more than 50,000 photos of the planet.

1981
Space shuttle begins flying.

1984
President Ronald Reagan calls for a "permanently manned space station . . . within a decade."

1986
Shuttle *Challenger* explodes during liftoff, killing all seven astronauts, including teacher Christa McAuliffe.

1990s-Present

Private space industry emerges as shuttle program ends.

1996
Mars Global Surveyor launched. . . . *Mars Pathfinder* lander and rover launched; they return more than 17,000 images, plus scientific information on Mars.

1998
Space station assembly begins.

2001
Mars Odyssey orbiter launched; conducts extended scientific mission.

2003
Space shuttle *Columbia* disintegrates during re-entry, killing all seven astronauts. . . . NASA launches Mars rovers *Spirit* and *Opportunity.*

2004
President George W. Bush proposes Mars mission. . . . Privately financed SpaceShipOne claims $10 million Ansari X Prize by making two successful trips into space.

2005
NASA establishes Constellation program. . . . NASA launches Mars reconnaissance orbiter.

2007
Mars Phoenix lander launched.

2009
President Obama orders review of human spaceflight program; panel says Constellation program is "not viable" because of budget restraints.

2010
Obama announces decision to cancel Constellation, use private industry to ferry U.S. crews to the space station after shuttle is retired. . . . Obama also says he wants to send astronauts to an asteroid by 2025 and Mars by 2030. . . . Congress opposes Constellation cancellation.

2011
Space shuttle ends. . . . Congress allows Obama administration to cancel Constellation except for Orion program to build craft to ferry astronauts into Earth and lunar orbit and possibly deep space. . . . NASA announces plan for new launch vehicle but destination remains uncertain. . . . China launches what it says is first component of an eventual space station, reaffirms plan for a manned lunar mission.

2012
Obama's $17.8 billion 2013 budget request for NASA would shift more funding to the new Webb Space Telescope, eliminate U.S. participation in two unmanned missions to Mars. . . . First commercial cargo flight to space station delayed until April.

Webb Telescope Reaches Uncertainly for the Heavens

Delays and funding fights cloud its development.

For nearly two decades, the Hubble Space Telescope has opened a window on the universe, providing startling images of planets, galaxies, quasars, and nebulae.

Now, a far more powerful celestial observatory — the $12 billion James Webb Space Telescope — is in development. But whether, literally, it gets off the ground depends on a very down-to-Earth issue: money.

The telescope, named for a former NASA administrator and under development for most of the past decade, has encountered more than its share of problems. Work has taken much longer than expected because of technical problems, repeatedly delaying the launch date from the original 2014 to 2018, at the earliest. Moreover, the costs have skyrocketed, from an original budget of about $2.4 billion. [1]

The project, in development since 2004 with financial or technical support from 14 other countries, went through a near-death experience in 2011, after the powerful House Appropriations Committee voted in July to stop funding it. [2] The vote deeply distressed space scientists, who launched a broad campaign to save the Webb, including a letter to *The New York Times* signed by 32 Nobel laureates. They argued that canceling the program "would deal a fatal blow to large and ambitious space science missions for the foreseeable future and would deny the public access to new and exciting images of the type that have captured the imagination of people of all ages." [3]

The Webb had more support in the Senate, which voted $529.6 million for it in fiscal 2012 — about 42 percent more than President Obama had requested in his budget. The final NASA budget, approved by Congress in November, included the Senate-approved amount, thus guaranteeing at least another year for construction of the Webb. [4] Obama's fiscal 2013 budget requested $627 million and projected comparable funding for the following four years. [5]

Unlike Hubble, which has both optical and infrared cameras, the Webb will be an all-infrared telescope that will see even deeper and more sharply into the universe. Also important, according to its advocates, the Webb will cut through the clouds of dust that sometimes obscure Hubble's vision. [6]

While the Webb's development has been rocky, it doesn't compare — at least so far — with the Hubble Space Telescope's long road to celestial superstardom. When it was launched from the space shuttle *Discovery* in April 1990, Hubble was supposed to be a miracle instrument for astronomers: capable of peering deep into the universe where the vision of Earth-bound telescopes was distorted by gases and atmospheric particles.

The miracle quickly evaporated, however, because Hubble's 94.5-inch mirror turned out to be distorted and incapable of producing crisp images. Space shuttle astronauts began repairing the Hubble in 1993 and eventually fixed or replaced most of its equipment. [7]

The renovated Hubble has been even more productive than astronomers had hoped, generating thousands of images and other observations about the deep recesses of the universe. Hubble has collected information about planets orbiting other stars and light that originated some 13 billion years ago, not long after what scientists believe was the genesis of

Continued from p. 188

effects of long-term weightlessness on humans. Handberg, at the University of Central Florida, says "data on long-term endurance in space is absolutely necessary before we even think of going to places like Mars. We don't have that data yet."

But Zubrin of the Mars Society dismisses that role for the space station. "This idea of sending people to space to study the health effects of zero gravity is absurd," he says, comparing it to laboratory experiments on animals. "It would not pass a medical ethics test if someone proposed it here on Earth." ■

BACKGROUND

Obama's Course Change

The current — if highly uncertain — status of the U.S. human spaceflight program results from decisions made in the past eight years by President Obama and his predecessor, George W. Bush.

In 2004 Bush laid out what he called a "vision" for long-term human exploration of space, beginning with a return to the moon by 2020 and use of the moon as a base for a human expedition to Mars about a decade later. [39]

If Bush hoped his vision would capture the nation's imagination — as had President John F. Kennedy's ringing 1961 call to land a man on the moon and return him safely — he must have been disappointed, because neither the public nor Congress seemed overly excited by his pronouncement. Bush himself rarely mentioned his space vision afterward. [40]

Even so, NASA incorporated Bush's idea into a program called Project Constellation. The plan: build two new rockets to ferry astronauts to and from the space station following the end of the space shuttle, then use the technology to take humans well beyond Earth orbit. Congress endorsed Constellation in 2005 and 2008. [41]

the universe, the so-called Big Bang. [8]

The Hubble's original lifespan, planned to last 20 years, was extended by its many replacement parts. Even so, NASA says the Hubble will need to be replaced soon. Its technology is dated, and its parts are wearing out. That means an opening for the more powerful Webb — if, that is, it makes it into the heavens.

National Aeronautics and Space Administration

Launch of the $12 billion James Webb Space Telescope, shown in an artist's rendering, has been postponed from 2014 to 2018. It will replace the Hubble Space Telescope.

Jeff Foust, publisher of *The Space Review*, an online publication that covers space exploration, wrote in January that the budget battle over the Webb "may be one sign of a much bigger issue: that government willingness to fund big science projects may be waning."

Although top NASA officials have said they are committed to the Webb and other space science research, they have acknowledged that budget pressures will cause some cutbacks, Foust noted. For example, officials have said NASA will have to cut from other planetary science programs to provide enough money for Webb. Foust quoted Steven Weinberg, a Nobel laureate physicist at the University of Texas, as saying, "We may see in the next decade or so an end to the search for the laws of nature which will not be resumed again in our own lifetimes." [9]

— John Felton

[1] Brian Verstag, "Budget fight rages over James Webb Space Telescope," *The Washington Post*, Oct. 26, 2011, www.washingtonpost.com/national/health-science/budget-fight-rages-over-james-webb-space-telescope/2011/10/13/gIQALjYLKM_story.html.

[2] Dennis Overbye, "Panel Proposes Killing Webb Space Telescope," *The New York Times*, July 6, 2011, www.nytimes.com/2011/07/07/science/07webb.html?_r=1&ref=hubblespacetelescope.

[3] "Keep the Webb Telescope, 32 Nobel Laureates Say," *The New York Times*, Aug. 26, 2011, www.nytimes.com/2011/08/27/opinion/keep-the-webb-telescope-32-nobel-laureates-say.html?_r=1&ref=space&pagewanted=print.

[4] Denise Chow, "NASA's Webb Survives Funding Battle, But Challenges Remain," *Space News*, Jan. 23, 2012, www.spacenews.com/civil/nasa-webb-survives-funding-battle-but-challenges-remain.html.

[5] "Fiscal 2013 Budget Estimates," NASA, p. 12, www.nasa.gov/pdf/622655main_FY13_NASA_Budget_Estimates.pdf.

[6] "Science on the Edge," WebbTelescope.org, http://webbtelescope.org/webb_telescope/science_on_the_edge/.

[7] "Hubble Space Telescope," *The New York Times*, http://topics.nytimes.com/top/news/science/topics/hubble_space_telescope/index.html.

[8] "Hubble Discoveries," Hubblesite, http://hubblesite.org/hubble_discoveries/.

[9] Jeff Foust, "Big science in an era of tight budgets," *The Space Review*, Jan. 16, 2012, www.thespacereview.com/article/2007/1.

But after taking office in 2009, Obama asked senior aerospace industry executives and space specialists to evaluate the Bush plan. In October 2009 they determined that it was "not viable" under the pared-back budget Obama had proposed. [42] With their conclusion in hand, Obama said in his fiscal 2011 budget, released in February 2010, that he had decided to cancel Constellation. Instead, he said NASA would contract with private industry to build new spacecraft to take astronauts and cargo to the space station after the shuttle program ended. [43]

In June 2010, Obama issued a new National Space Policy calling for the United States to build a new rocket and spacecraft that could take astronauts to a near-Earth asteroid by 2025 and then to Mars by the mid 2030s — skipping the moon altogether. [44]

Obama's decisions sparked huge controversy in Congress and among enthusiasts of human spaceflight, partly because of the shift from Bush's plan and partly because NASA already had spent billions of dollars on Constellation. Spudis, of the Lunar and Planetary Institute, charges that Obama "discarded the existing strategic direction, for which we had a hard-won bipartisan consensus, and replaced it with, literally, nothing."

Some in Congress also said private industry was not ready to build spacecraft that could substitute for the shuttle on missions to the ISS, as Obama proposed, and that relying on Russia to get to the space station was a mistake.

"Not only would we be turning our backs on 40 years of American space superiority, we would be giving up vital national security and economic interests to other nations that are eager to exploit this situation," Sen. Kay Bailey Hutchison, R-Texas, whose state includes the Johnson Space Center in Houston, told NASA officials in a February 2009 hearing. [45]

As a compromise, Congress in October 2010 passed a new authorization act that, in essence, told NASA to continue work on Constellation while adding the new elements Obama had proposed, including commercial

Obama Seeks to Shift Funds to Webb Telescope

The Obama administration has requested a fiscal 2013 NASA budget of $17.71 billion, slightly less than the 2012 level. Obama proposes to spend about $5 billion on science missions, with an increase of more than $100 million on the James Webb Space Telescope, being built to replace the Hubble observatory, but less on planetary science projects. Spending would also increase for the International Space Station.

National Aeronautics and Space Administration Budget, FY2012-FY2013
(in $ millions)

	FY2012*	FY2013 (requested)
Science	**$5,073.7**	**$4,911.2**
Earth science	$1,760.5	$1,784.8
Planetary science	1,501.4	1,192.3
Astrophysics	672.7	659.4
James Webb Space Telescope	518.6	627.6
Heliophysics	620.5	647.0
Aeronautics	**569.4**	**551.5**
Space technology	**573.7**	**699.0**
Exploration	**3,712.8**	**3,932.8**
Exploration systems development	3,007.1	2,769.4
Commercial spaceflight	406.0	829.7
Exploration research and development	299.7	333.7
Space operations	**4,187.0**	**4,013.2**
Space shuttle	556.2	70.6
International Space Station	2,829.9	3,007.6
Space and flight support	800.9	935.0
Other	**3,653.4**	**3,603.7**
Total NASA Budget	**$17,770.0**	**$17,711.4**

** Figures for fiscal 2012 are estimates and may vary slightly from actual spending.*
Source: "FY 2013 President's Budget Request Summary," National Aeronautics and Space Administration, 2012, www.nasa.gov/pdf/622655main_FY13_NASA_Budget_Estimates.pdf

flights to the space station. But the new law did not propose additional money. [46]

Finally, in one of a series of "continuing resolutions" that kept government appropriations flowing while Congress worked on regular spending bills, Congress in April 2011 allowed Obama to cancel Constellation, more than a year after he had proposed doing so. [47] In subsequent action, congressional committees have settled on an annual budget for new human spaceflight programs of about $3.7 billion — not enough for NASA to do all it wants to do, says Smith of *Space Policy Online*, which tracks NASA programs and spending. Obama's proposed budget for fiscal 2013 would continue about the same level of funding.

"Congress and the administration have reached an accommodation with each other on their different approaches," Smith says.

But that does not mean that congressional supporters of the space program, and of NASA in particular, are happy. Hutchison, for one, immediately denounced Obama's fiscal 2013 budget plan, saying it cut by "hundreds of millions of dollars" NASA's new rocket system and crew capsule. [48] The result of these proposals and congressional legislation is that NASA has moved on two tracks for human spaceflight, one intended to continue U.S. participation in the space station at least through 2020 and the other to build new systems to take humans deeper into space, including eventually to Mars and possibly even beyond. [49]

New Approaches

On the final space shuttle mission last July, the *Atlantis* delivered the last set of materials needed to finish construction of the space station, which had been under way since 1998. The $100 billion orbiting base has hosted human crews since November 2000 and has three major scientific laboratories, run by the United States, Japan and the European Space Agency. [50]

In addition to deliveries by the shuttles and European and Japanese cargo craft early in 2011, much of the space station's components, supplies and astronauts have been ferried by Russian *Soyuz* rockets, workhorses dating to the late 1960s.

The Obama administration's plan to continue relying on Russia for the next few years has been thrown into question in recent months, however. Concerns were raised last August when a *Soyuz* rocket carrying an unmanned cargo ship (called *Progress*) with three tons of food and fuel for the space station failed to achieve orbit and crashed in a Siberian forest. [51] Two *Soyuz* missions did reach the space station in September and December 2011, but a failed test of a *Soyuz* descent capsule in late January could delay the next cargo shipment to the station. [52]

Over the longer term, NASA plans for deliveries of supplies and humans to the space station to be handled by vehicles designed and built by private companies, under NASA contracts. The first commercial cargo deliveries, which have been postponed repeatedly, are expected to take place this year. (*See sidebar, p. 194.*)

The other major part of the current U.S. plan for human spaceflight is development of a new launch vehicle and a spacecraft capable of carrying humans and cargo much deeper into space than ever before: to a near-Earth asteroid by 2025 and then Mars by 2030. This incorporates some aspects of Bush's Project Constellation and thus represents another part of a compromise between Obama (who wanted to cancel that project entirely) and Congress (which wanted to keep it going).

The launch vehicle, which NASA calls a Space Launch System, is intended to be the largest rocket built since the *Saturn V*, which delivered *Apollo* astronauts to the moon in the late 1960s and early '70s. Under pressure from Congress to move ahead with the program, NASA on Sept. 14 announced that it had selected a design for the booster rocket, which initially would be capable of lifting 70 to 100 metric tons into space. Eventually the rocket could handle 130 metric tons — the weight expected to be needed for a flight to and from Mars. NASA said the rocket's first test flight could be in 2017. [53]

Technical challenges aside, the biggest hurdle facing the new launch vehicle might be its price: A top NASA official estimated the initial development and construction cost at $3 billion a year for six years. [54]

Sitting atop that new rocket will be a new spacecraft, the *Orion Multi-Purpose Crew Vehicle*. The *Orion* will be similar to the *Apollo* spacecraft that took three astronauts into lunar orbit but will carry four crew members. The *Orion* is the one major component of Constellation that has survived relatively intact, although its mission has changed from Bush's plan for it to take crews to the space station and then to the moon; under Obama's plan, the *Orion* will ferry astronauts to an asteroid, which could be a launching pad for a later trip to Mars. [55]

However, some space advocates are unenthused by the prospect of a trip to an asteroid. "There are few to no asteroid targets that are both reachable and scientifically attractive," says Pace, at the Space Policy Institute at George Washington University.

AFP/Getty Images/Karen Bleier

The space shuttle Enterprise *served as the prototype for future shuttles. Though it never flew in space, it proved shuttles could fly in the atmosphere and land like a glider — without power. Now at the Smithsonian Institution's Udvar-Hazy Center in Northern Virginia,* Enterprise *will be moved to the Intrepid Sea, Air and Space Museum in New York City; another shuttle will take its place. Other shuttles are at space museums around the country.*

'Mission Complete'

At dawn on July 21, 2011, the space shuttle *Atlantis* rolled to a stop at the Kennedy Space Center in Florida, and Capt. Christopher J. Ferguson, the shuttle's commander, immediately radioed to the Johnson Space Center halfway across the country: "Mission complete, Houston." It was the final mission, not just for *Atlantis* but for the famed, and often trouble-plagued, shuttle program, which for 30 years had represented America's once-vaunted commitment to sending humans into space but which Presidents Bush and Obama had both decided to end. [56]

The shuttle program was the compromise result of competing visions for U.S. space efforts after the end of the *Apollo* program in the early 1970s. Eventually, the shuttle ended up being a cargo workhorse with two main missions: taking into space the major components, and later the supplies for and occupants of, the space station; and repairing the Hubble telescope four times after design and production flaws hampered its usefulness.

The shuttles flew 135 missions, two of which remain seared into the nation's

Countdown for Private Spaceflight Has Begun

Space entrepreneurs include Virgin Galactic's Richard Branson.

Ever since the privately financed SpaceShipOne claimed the $10 million Ansari X Prize in 2004 by making two successful trips into space (but not into orbit) within two weeks, the once far-fetched idea of private space travel has seemed closer to reality than ever. [1]

Two companies claim to be almost ready to put rockets with passengers into space, possibly by the end of 2012. They would be the first private space flights since the prize-winning flights almost eight years earlier.

But private enterprise is not a new thing in space. Most of NASA's spacecraft have been built by commercial companies or, at least, assembled from parts produced commercially. Moreover, private companies have operated all of the U.S.-based commercial satellites that beam to Earth everything from weather observations to most of what appears on the Internet.

Now NASA and a handful of space entrepreneurs are betting that commercial uses of space are about to take off in much bigger ways — possibly just as government-run programs diminish because of budget cuts in Washington. In addition to satellites, two other private space enterprises are poised for launch. One is funded entirely by private investors and aimed at promoting travel to low-Earth orbit for those with Jupiter-size bank accounts; the other is more of a joint venture between NASA and private companies to promote the government's space endeavors.

Virgin Galactic, the brainchild of British entrepreneur Richard Branson, is using an updated version of *SpaceShipOne* (dubbed *SpaceShipTwo*). Branson plans to charge $200,000 for a flight 60 miles above the Earth that includes about three minutes of weightlessness. Also competing for space-tourism business are XCOR Aerospace of Mojave, Calif., which hopes to begin flights with two customers each in 2013, and Space Adventures Ltd. of Vienna, Va., which is working with a Texas company to develop a pilotless spacecraft that can carry two passengers into space, briefly. [2]

Much more extensive involvement in space by private companies is likely to happen as a result of collaboration with NASA. The space agency already is working with private firms under two major programs intended to take supplies, and later, astronauts, to the International Space Station.

During the George W. Bush administration, in 2008, NASA awarded contracts, in a program called Commercial Orbital Transportation System, to two companies to deliver cargo to the space station after the shuttle program ended: Space Exploration Technologies (SpaceX) of Hawthorne, Calif., received a $1.6 billion contract for 12 cargo flights through 2016, and Orbital Sciences of Dulles, Va., won a $1.9 billion contract for eight supply flights.

Both companies have experienced repeated delays. The first commercial cargo flight to the space station by SpaceX's *Dragon* unmanned cargo capsule — originally scheduled for December 2011 — was first pushed back until February 2012, then in mid-January was delayed again until April for "additional work," according to a company spokeswoman. [3] Until SpaceX and Orbital can make regular cargo runs, NASA will continue using Russian *Soyuz* spacecraft to transport cargo and U.S. astronauts to the station. [4]

The Obama administration also has developed a separate program of paying private companies to develop new launch vehicles and spacecraft to deliver humans, as well as cargo, to the space station and into low-Earth orbit. NASA calls the program "commercial crew" and says the goal is to have the spacecraft ready for flight by the middle of the decade. NASA's stated rationale for relying on commercial contractors is that spacecraft development will be cheaper if the government and private companies split the costs. [5]

Commercial crew has generated widespread opposition in Congress, where members in both parties worry about relying too much on profit-driven contractors. Appropriations commit-

collective memory: the 1986 explosion of the *Challenger* shortly after liftoff, killing all seven astronauts on board, including school teacher Christa McAuliffe; and the 2003 break-up of the *Columbia* as it returned to Earth, also killing its seven astronauts.

Aside from those two tragedies and high-profile missions to repair the Hubble, most of the shuttle flights took place in relative obscurity. Shuttle astronauts, unlike their famed predecessors, were little-known to the public. *The Economist* magazine observed last summer that the shuttle eventually "made space travel seem routine, almost mundane — which helped to dampen public interest" in the space program. [57]

The shutdown of the shuttle program already has put about 7,000 people out of work, notably at the Kennedy Space Center in Florida. [58] Some advocates say they wish some way could have been found to keep the shuttles flying, if only as the one means for the United States to keep putting people into space until the next spacecraft are ready. "The shuttles were expensive, but I think that it was a mistake to not keep the shuttles going," says former astronaut Glenn.

The remaining space shuttles are being readied for their final resting places: not in space, but in museums. NASA administrator Bolden announced last April that the *Atlantis* would be displayed at the Kennedy Space Center in Florida; *Discovery* at the National Air and Space Museum's Steven F. Udvar-Hazy Center in Northern Virginia; the *Endeavor* at the California Science Center in Los Angeles; and a shuttle

AFP/Getty Images/Nicholas Kamm

PayPal co-founder Elon Musk unveils the Falcon-9 Heavy *launch rocket developed by his firm, SpaceX.*

tees in the House and Senate substantially trimmed the administration's $850 million request for the program in fiscal 2012, and in the end Congress approved only $406 million.[6] Eventually, says Marcia Smith, editor of *Space Policy Online*, which tracks space programs and spending, "If push comes to shove, Congress would probably keep money for NASA programs and drop the commercial crew component."

The commercial crew program also has generated controversy outside Congress, including from what might seem an unlikely source: Christopher Caldwell, a senior editor of the conservative *Weekly Standard*. Caldwell wrote in *The Financial Times* recently that private investors "need to be watched like hawks" when it comes to the use of tax dollars. "The public should remain vigilant . . . that these space entrepreneurs do not come to resemble the railroad-building industry in the time of the robber barons," he wrote.[7]

Meanwhile the first privately funded space station might also reach orbit in the next few years, according to American entrepreneur Robert Bigelow. He is developing lightweight components for an inflatable structure he says can be built in space at a fraction of the cost of the $100 billion International Space Station. The company's *Genesis I* and *Genesis II* spacecraft have been orbiting Earth since 2006 and 2007, giving Bigelow the data he says he needs to prove that a full-scale station is possible.[8]

Some supporters say Bigelow and other commercial entrepreneurs, rather than governments, might represent the best chance for the United States to return to and remain active in space — if not in the next few years, then in the decades to come. But other space enthusiasts are skeptical that private companies will ever represent more than a part of the nation's future in space.

Says Paul Spudis, senior staff scientist at the NASA-funded Lunar and Planetary Institute in Houston, "None of them have a positive cash flow from commercial customers yet, and it remains to be seen whether their markets develop or not."

— John Felton

1 "Ansari X Prize," http://space.xprize.org/ansari-x-prize.

2 Kenneth Chang, "Booking a Flight to Space With Travel Insurance," *The New York Times*, Jan. 3, 2012, www.nytimes.com/2012/01/04/science/space/space-flights-prepare-to-expand-customer-base.html?ref=space.

3 "SpaceX Postpones Station-bound Dragon Launch," *SpaceNews*, Jan. 16, 2012, www.spacenews.com/venture_space/011612-spacex-postpones-station-bound-dragon-launch.html.

4 "NASA Commercial Partners: Cargo," www.nasa.gov/exploration/commercial/cargo/index.html.

5 "NASA Commercial Partners: Crew," www.nasa.gov/exploration/commercial/crew/index.html.

6 "NASA's FY2012 Budget Request and Final Action," *SpacePolicyOnline.com*, Jan. 11, 2012, Table 1, p. 2, www.spacepolicyonline.com/pages/images/stories/NASA's%20FY2012%20Budget%20Request.pdf.

7 Christopher Caldwell, "The folly of private space travel," *Financial Times*, Dec. 16, 2011, www.ft.com/cms/s/0/15aede0e-2713-11e1-b9ec-00144feabdc0.html#axzz1isZhCSIo.

8 "Genesis I," Bigelow Aerospace, www.bigelowaerospace.com/genesis-1.php.

prototype, *Enterprise*, would be moved from the Udvar-Hazy Center (where it has been on display since 2003) to the Intrepid Sea, Air and Space Museum in New York City.[59]

Some museums that lost bids for the shuttles — and members of Congress and other politicians representing those locations — complained about Bolden's selections. But NASA's inspector general concluded last August that NASA followed proper procedures and had not been unduly influenced by political or other considerations.[60] ■

CURRENT SITUATION

Private Sector's New Role

The Obama administration plans to rely on private companies to handle routine missions, such as trips to the space station, leaving NASA to concentrate on more ambitious goals, such as manned and unmanned scientific missions to Mars and other deep-space destinations.

Private companies have long been significant actors in all aspects of the U.S. space program. Working under NASA contracts, hundreds of private firms have built launch vehicles and spacecraft and performed much of the necessary logistical work to put, and keep, objects and people in space.

The Obama administration has extended this traditional relationship be-

Continued from p. 166

tween government and private industry to a new level. Building on a program started by the previous Bush administration, NASA under Obama is paying private companies — some with little experience — not only to build but also to operate vehicles that will carry cargo and, eventually, human crews to the ISS. Besides freeing up NASA for more ambitious projects, the administration hopes to reduce dependence on Russia for trips to the space station.

NASA's new relationship with private industry has two components:

AFP/Getty Images

John Glenn, the first American to orbit Earth, receives a Congressional Gold Medal at the Capitol Rotunda on Nov. 16. The crew of the first moon landing, Neil Armstrong, Buzz Aldrin and Michael Collins, also were honored. "They will tell you that they are not heroes. Don't listen to them," said Senate Republican Leader Mitch McConnell. "America is only as strong as the citizens we produce, and here are four of the best."

• Under a program initiated by the Bush administration and known as the Commercial Orbital Transportation System, NASA has contracted with two companies to build rockets and spacecraft that will take food, fuel, scientific equipment and other supplies (but not people) to the space station. Space Exploration Technologies (SpaceX) of Hawthorne, Calif., has a $1.6 billion contract for 12 cargo flights through 2016; Orbital Sciences of Dulles, Va. has a $1.9 billion contract for eight supply flights. [61] Both companies have experienced repeated delays, the most recent in January, when SpaceX postponed its first cargo flight to the space station. It also had postponed the flight from 2011 until Feb. 7, 2012. The company did not explain the delays but did set a new schedule of late April. [62]

• A program initiated by the Obama administration in 2010 called "commercial crew" will use private companies to send cargo and astronauts to the space station. NASA and the companies will share the cost of developing launch vehicles and spacecraft, and the companies will operate the flights under NASA contracts. The companies also can use the technologies they create for private commercial purposes.

Four companies are developing systems under the second of two rounds of NASA grants: the Boeing Corp., SpaceX, Sierra Nevada Corp. and Blue Origin (headed by Amazon.com founder Jeff Bezos). Representatives of the first three companies told a House subcommittee last October that they would be ready to launch their vehicles by 2015, but only if they receive what they called "adequate" funding from NASA. NASA's plan has been to pick two winners from among the four companies. [63]

Commercial crew has been highly controversial in Congress. Obama requested $850 million for the program in fiscal 2012, but lawmakers slashed that to $406 million. It remains uncertain how that cut will affect the program. [64] Obama has asked for $830 million for the program in fiscal 2013. [65]

"The irony is that you have a Democratic administration that wants to rely on private industry for a key element of the space program, while members of Congress, Republicans included, very much want this to be a government program," says Smith of *Space Policy Online*. She and others say most of the resistance has come from members of both parties who represent districts in states such as Alabama, Florida and Texas with large NASA installations or the facilities of other private contractors. "This about jobs and money, not about ideology," Smith says. Despite the congressional opposition, the administration's plan has won substantial support from within the space community. Last November, 23 retired astronauts asked Congress and the administration for full funding of Obama's request. [66] Among them was MIT's Hoffman, who says he sees the commercial crew concept as "one of

Continued on p. 198

At Issue:

Is the United States in danger of losing a space race to China?

PAUL D. SPUDIS
SENIOR STAFF SCIENTIST, LUNAR AND PLANETARY INSTITUTE

WRITTEN FOR *CQ RESEARCHER*, FEBRUARY 2012

yes

Are we in a race back to the moon? Should we be? The Apollo program achieved not only its literal objective of landing a man on the moon (propaganda, soft power) but also its more abstract objective of intimidating our Soviet adversary (technical surprise, hard power) and thus played a key role in the end of the Cold War.

Its two follow-on programs, the space shuttle and space station, although fraught with technical issues, had significant success in pointing the way toward a new paradigm for space. That new path involves getting people and machines to satellite assets in space for construction, servicing, extension and repair.

We cannot access satellites now with people and machines because we do not have a transportation system that allows us freedom of movement in the space between Earth and the moon. Recent data from the moon show that it has not only near-permanent sunlight near the poles but also abundant water. This water would allow us to make fuel on the moon to power rockets. Such a system is the logical next step in both space security and commerce. A return to the moon for resource utilization thus contributes to national security and economic interests as well as scientific ones.

What societal paradigm shall prevail in the new space economy? What shall the organizing principle of society be in the new commerce of space resources: the rule of law or authoritarian oligarchy? An American win in this new race for space does not guarantee that free markets will prevail, but an American loss could ensure that free markets would never emerge on this new frontier.

In one of his early speeches defending the Apollo program, President John F. Kennedy laid out the reasons that America had to go the moon. Among the many ideas he articulated, one stood out. He said, "Whatever men shall undertake, free men must fully share."

We explore new frontiers not to establish an empire but to ensure that our political and economic worldview prevails — the system that has created the most freedom and the largest amount of new wealth in the hands of the greatest number of people in the history of the world.

By leading the world into space, we guarantee that space does not become the private domain of powers who view humanity as cogs in their ideological machine rather than as individuals to be valued and protected.

ROGER B. HANDBERG
PROFESSOR OF POLITICAL SCIENCE, UNIVERSITY OF CENTRAL FLORIDA

WRITTEN FOR *CQ RESEARCHER*, FEBRUARY 2012

no

China's ongoing advances in its space program have raised the question of whether the United States will become engaged in a space race similar to that which occurred in the 1960s.

That race began in 1961 when President John F. Kennedy announced that the United States would reach the lunar surface and return to Earth within the decade. The Apollo program was one fruit of that challenge, which the United States won in July 1969 when the Eagle landed on the moon with two crew members. To achieve that goal, the United States spent billions of dollars in a field of competition that had only come into existence in 1957 when the Soviet Union launched *Sputnik 1* into orbit.

Now, some say that China poses an equivalent challenge to the United States, meaning that a space race will be the logical outcome. I would suggest that the calls for a space race are overinflated because the conditions for such an endeavor do not presently exist.

First, China's rise to prominence has not been cast as a prelude to a weapons race in space; that occurred in the late 1950s when Nikita Khrushchev announced the Soviets would "bury" the United States. That threat was based on the Soviets' possession of nuclear weapons to which were added missiles to reach the United States. China's space program has been cast as a peaceful analogue to earlier American, European, Japanese and Russian/Soviet programs after the successful conclusion to the Apollo program. Weapons in outer space are often cited as a reason for a space race, but such weapons are not as useful as many think.

Second, China's space activities are tracking the earlier U.S.-Soviet space programs with no direct security threats. The Chinese, like the Americans, have a military space program, but that alone does not generate the political support for a space race. Instead, the Chinese are catching up because the United States finds manned space exploration a desired goal but not an overwhelming one into which billions must be poured in order to be first.

Third, human space-exploration efforts are becoming more international — an endeavor the Chinese at some point will join as full members based on their technological achievements and capabilities.

Putting humans in outer space remains a long-term process that crash projects do not in the end advance as readily as systematic efforts incorporating the world's talents most efficiently.

Continued from p. 196

the potentially most exciting things going. It might be a real game changer" for the space program. "If NASA could buy those services at a marginal cost, it would save a lot of money and allow NASA to concentrate its resources on exploration, where the private sector is not going to be involved."

NASA Budget

Except for politically sensitive items such as the commercial crew program, NASA escaped the 2011 congressional budget wars relatively unharmed. Of Obama's overall $18.5 billion request for the space agency, Congress approved $17.8 billion, with nearly all the $700 million cutback the result of resistance from the House of Representatives, where budget-cutting demands were most intense.

Two big hurdles face NASA in the near future, however. The first is Obama's fiscal 2013 budget, which proposed a small overall reduction to about $17.8 billion but kept most programs — except for the future Mars exploration missions that were to be conducted with the Europeans — relatively intact. Once again, the big battle in Congress could be over the "commercial crew" budget, which Congress has cut in each of the past two years, and the space launch vehicle and *Orion* crew capsule, both of which many in Congress want to fund at a higher level than Obama has proposed.

NASA also faces possible automatic budget cuts stemming from Congress's failure to deal effectively with budget issues in 2011. Up to $1.2 trillion in cuts in "discretionary" programs (which would include NASA) are to take effect in January 2013 unless Congress takes action this year to avert them. [67] NASA administrator Bolden told space advocates in December he was confident Congress would act. [68]

Scientific Missions

NASA currently has 94 active missions in space, and only one — the space station — is manned. [69] All the others are scientific endeavors using telescopes, X-ray observatories, robotic rovers and other pieces of scientific equipment.

Many of these missions orbit the Earth, sending back information intended to increase understanding of climate change, the oceans and other natural features. Most missions are exploring the solar system, from the moon to Pluto, whose planetary status is still being debated. Other missions are focused on deep space well beyond the solar system, looking for information about how the universe was formed and whether other Earth-like planets might exist.

Among NASA's most notable current missions:

• In March 2011, NASA's *MESSENGER* (short for MErcury, Surface, Space ENvironment, GEochemistry and Ranging) became the first spacecraft to orbit Mercury, after a trip of more than six-and-a-half years covering 4.9 billion miles. The probe was scheduled to continue for one year, but in November NASA announced an extension until March 2013. *MESSENGER* is supposed to answer six questions about the smallest planet, including why it appears to be at least twice as dense as Earth and how it formed geologically. [70]

• The *New Horizons* spacecraft was launched in 2006 and will fly past Pluto and its moon, Charon, in July 2015. Last year the spacecraft sped by Uranus. It will be only the fifth spacecraft to travel so far from the sun and, NASA says, the first to come so close to a planet-like body at that distance. Its mission is to map and determine the composition of Pluto and Charon. After passing Pluto, the spacecraft will continue to the Kuiper Belt, the enormous collection of icy bodies (some nearly half the size of Earth's moon) that orbit just beyond Neptune, the most distant planet. [71]

• The *Cassini* spacecraft continues its observations of Saturn and its moons. It has sent back startling information that has altered much of what scientists thought they knew about the Saturnian system. Among *Cassini*'s recent discoveries are the potential existence of an underground saltwater ocean on the moon Enceladus (suggesting that some form of life might be possible there) and seasonal "rain showers" of liquid methane that change the surface of the large moon Titan. *Cassini* was launched in 1997 and reached Saturn in 2004. [72]

• The mission known as GRAIL consists of twin spacecraft that were launched last September and reached lunar orbit Dec. 31, 2011, and Jan. 1 this year. During their planned 82-day mission, they are intended to conduct the most detailed study ever of the moon's surface and inner core. NASA scientists have said that understanding the makeup of the moon will provide information about how the Earth and other solid planets in the solar system were formed. [73] The spacecraft are named *Ebb* and *Flow*, based on entries from fourth-grade students in Bozeman, Mont. [74]

• *Juno*, launched last August, is scheduled to arrive at Jupiter in July 2016. The craft will orbit for 14 months, examining the giant planet's magnetic field, electrical and gas emissions and other features, including determining how much water is in the atmosphere. It is the most ambitious scientific mission to Jupiter since the highly successful *Galileo* probe, which orbited for nearly eight years, until September 2003. [75] ■

OUTLOOK

Leadership in Space

In the 1960s and '70s, the U.S. space program was driven as much by the Cold War rivalry with the Soviet Union as by the traditional American ambition to explore new frontiers. The Cold War ended two decades ago, however, eliminating that driving force and leading space advocates to search for new justifications for their ambitions. Into the foreseeable future, the nation's budget and long-term deficit problems could pose even greater hurdles to the space program than the technical obstacles that the Americans and Russians raced each other to overcome a half-century ago.

"Can this democracy continue to fly in space? I don't know that we can," says Handberg of the University of Central Florida. "It requires a long-term funding commitment, and there is no payoff except to say that we've been there, and given our budget problems the political support is not there for that type of commitment."

Some other observers are not quite so pessimistic. Smith of *Space Policy Online* notes that the space program faces little outright opposition on Capitol Hill or among the public at large. But even the optimists acknowledge that the space program will struggle to compete for increasingly scarce public dollars.

Smith recalls that the space program has gone through periods of retrenchment in the past, including after the end of the *Apollo* flights to the moon in the early 1970s, and managed to survive. Former NASA executive Pace and many of his counterparts point out that NASA's entire budget represents less than 0.5 percent of federal spending.

Spudis of the Lunar and Planetary Institute says "the idea that we cannot afford space is ludicrous. We could triple the NASA budget with no significant impact on the overall federal budget." Even so, the space program is one of the "discretionary" budget items that could be easier for Congress to cut than entitlement programs such as Medicare and Social Security. NASA's public support, Handberg says, "is a mile wide and an inch deep."

Privately funded spaceflight could represent at least part of the future in space, although few experts seem to believe it can take the place of government programs anytime soon. Even Hudgins, of the libertarian Atlas Society, acknowledges that without government contracts, space entrepreneurs Elon Musk, Jeff Bezos and others, for all their billions, will have trouble doing more than "tourism and honeymoon suites in space until they can figure out a way to make the economics work."

Many space advocates in the United States are paying attention to China, the up-and-coming superpower that is developing an ambitious program of space exploration — including the possibility of landing humans on the moon in the 2020s. [76] Spudis says China's ambitions should spur the United States not just to return to the moon but also to establish "the permanent presence of people on the moon."

Former astronaut Hoffman of MIT says he is not particularly concerned about China's space plans. "By the time China is ready to go to the moon," he says, "hopefully we will be doing more interesting things, and we can look back and say, 'Congratulations, and welcome to the moon.' "

Hoffman, however, says there is more reason to worry about what the Chinese military might be doing in space. [77] "China has clearly demonstrated that it will become a full space power, just like the United States and Russia, and that will include a military component. That has a lot of our military people concerned, as they should be." ■

Notes

[1] For background, see the following *CQ Researcher* reports: Thomas J. Billitteri, "Human Spaceflight," Oct. 16, 2009, pp. 861-884; David Masci, NASA's Future, May 23, 2003, pp. 473-496; Mary H. Cooper, "Space Program's Future," April 25, 1997, pp. 361-384; and Richard L. Worsnop, "Mission to Mars: Benefits Vs. Costs," Oct. 1, 1969.

[2] John Noble Wilford, "50 Years Later, Celebrating John Glenn's Feat," *The New York Times*, Feb. 13, 2012, www.nytimes.com/2012/02/14/science/space/50-years-later-celebrating-john-glenns-great-feat.html?hpw. Glenn orbited the Earth three times on Feb. 20, 1962.

[3] Kenneth Chang, "The Shuttle Ends Its Final Voyage and an Era in Space," *The New York Times*, July 21, 2011, www.nytimes.com/2011/07/22/science/space/22space-shuttle-atlantis.html?_r=1&ref=atlantis.

[4] Marcia Smith, "Gingrich Wants Moon Base by 2020, Mars Colony, New Propulsion, Prizes-UPDATE," *SpacePolicyOnline*, Jan. 25, 2012, www.spacepolicyonline.com/news/gingrich-wants-moon-base-by-2020-mars-colony-new-propulsion-private-investment-UPDATE.

[5] Charles Bolden, NASA administrator, Air Force Association Air & Space Conference and Tech Exposition, Washington, DC, Sept. 19, 2011, www.nasa.gov/pdf/593460main_Bolden_IAC.pdf.

[6] "NASA's Odyssey Spacecraft Sets Exploration Record on Mars," Jet Propulsion Laboratory, Dec. 15, 2011, http://mars.jpl.nasa.gov/odyssey/news/whatsnew/index.cfm?FuseAction=ShowNews&NewsID=1091.

[7] "NASA Launches Most Capable and Robust Rover To Mars," Jet Propulsion Laboratory, Nov. 26, 2011, http://mars.jpl.nasa.gov/news/whatsnew/index.cfm?FuseAction=ShowNews&NewsID=1189.

[8] Charles Bolden, Remarks at NASA fiscal 2013 budget presentation, Feb. 13, 2012, www.nasa.gov/pdf/622812main_12_0213_Final_Bolden_FY13_Budget.pdf.

[9] Sindya N. Bhanoo, "Kepler Finds More Planets Orbiting Two Stars," *The New York Times*, Jan. 11, 2012, www.nytimes.com/2012/01/17/

science/scientists-find-more-planets-orbiting-two-stars.html?ref=space.

[10] Dennis Overbye, "Astronomers Find Biggest Black Holes Yet," *The New York Times*, Dec. 5, 2011, www.nytimes.com/2011/12/06/science/space/astronomers-find-biggest-black-holes-yet.html?_r=1&ref=hubblespacetelescope.

[11] William H. Gerstenmaier, NASA associate administrator for human exploration and operations, statement to the House Subcommittee on Space and Aeronautics, Oct. 12, 2011.

[12] Mars Exploration Program, Historical Log, Jet Propulsion Laboratory, http://mars.jpl.nasa.gov/programmissions/missions/log/.

[13] "Russia's Failed Mars Probe Crashes Into Pacific," *The New York Times*, Jan. 15, 2012, www.nytimes.com/2012/01/16/science/space/russias-phobos-grunt-mars-probe-crashes-into-pacific.html.

[14] "Software glitch likely cause of Phobos-Grunt failure," *SpaceToday.net*, Jan. 20, 2012, www.spacetoday.net/Summary/5504.

[15] Andrew Jacobs, "China's Space Program Bolstered by First Docking," *The New York Times*, Nov. 3, 2011, www.nytimes.com/2011/11/04/world/asia/chinas-space-program-boosted-by-first-docking.html?ref=space&pagewanted=print.

[16] "China's Space Activities in 2011, State Council Information Office of the People's Republic of China, December 2011, www.scio.gov.cn/zxbd/wz/201112/t1073727.htm.

[17] David Warmflash, "About Those Space Joyrides," *Air and Space*, Jan. 6, 2012, www.airspacemag.com/space-exploration/About-Those-Space-Joyrides.html.

[18] Jeff Foust, "Caution and optimism about the future of human spaceflight," *The Space Review.com*, Jan. 23, 2012, www.thespacereview.com/article/2011/1.

[19] "Majority Sees U.S. Leadership in Space as Essential," Pew Research Center, July 5, 2011, www.people-press.org/2011/07/05/majority-sees-u-s-leadership-in-space-as-essential/.

[20] "NASA's FY2012 Budget Request and Final Action," *SpacePolicyOnline.com*, Jan. 11, 2012, Table 1, p. 2, www.spacepolicyonline.com/pages/images/stories/NASA's%20FY2012%20Budget%20Request.pdf.

[21] "The Future of Human Spaceflight," Massachusetts Institute of Technology, Space, Policy, and Society Research Group, December 2008, http://web.mit.edu/mitsps.

[22] NASA Authorization, fiscal years 2011-13 (PL 111-267), section 204.

[23] "National Space Policy of the United States," The White House, June 28, 2010, p. 11, www.whitehouse.gov/sites/default/files/national_space_policy_6-28-10.pdf.

[24] Charles Bolden, "Remarks at NASA fiscal 2013 budget presentation," Feb. 13, 2012, www.nasa.gov/pdf/622812main_12_0213_Final_Bolden_FY13_Budget.pdf.

[25] Pat Duggins, *Trailblazing Mars: Nasa's Next Giant Leap* (2010), p. 1.

[26] "NASA Spacecraft Data Suggest Water Flowing on Mars," Mars Reconnaissance Orbiter, www.nasa.gov/mission_pages/MRO/news/mro20110804.html.

[27] Robert Zubrin, *The Case for Mars* (2011).

[28] Robert Zubin, "How We Can Fly to Mars in this Decade — And on the Cheap," *The Wall Street Journal*, May 14, 2011, http://online.wsj.com/article/SB10001424052748703730804576317493923993056.html.

[29] Buzz Aldrin, American Space Exploration Leadership — Why and How," *The Huffington Post*, Jan. 5, 2012, www.huffingtonpost.com/buzz-aldrin/american-space-exploration_b_1184554.html.

[30] Roger Handberg, "ISS Next: chasing humanity's future in space and the "next logical step," *The Space Review*, Dec. 19, 2011, www.thespacereview.com/article/1993/1.

[31] "Skylab Operations Summary, Kennedy Space Center, www-pao.ksc.nasa.gov/history/skylab/skylab-operations.htm.

[32] Mir Space Station, NASA History, http://history.nasa.gov/SP-4225/mir/mir.htm.

[33] "NASA's FY2012 Budget Request and Final Action," *op. cit.*

[34] Marcia S. Smith, "Adequate Funding Key to Commercial Crew Timing," *Space Policy Online*, Oct. 27, 2011, www.spacepolicyonline.com/news/adequate-funding-key-to-commercial-crew-timing.

[35] Statement of William H. Gerstenmaier, *op. cit.*

[36] "Tiangong-1 orbiter enters long-term operation management," Xinhua News, Nov. 19, 2011, http://news.xinhuanet.com/english2010/china/2011-11/19/c_131257600.htm.

[37] STS 95, NASA, http://spaceflight.nasa.gov/shuttle/archives/sts-95/.

[38] Jeff Foust, "Tough decisions ahead for planetary exploration," *The Space Review*, April 4, 2011.

[39] President George W. Bush, "Remarks at the National Aeronautics and Space Administration," Jan. 14, 2004, www.gpo.gov:80/fdsys/pkg/PPP-2004-book1/pdf/PPP-2004-book1-doc-pg56.pdf.

[40] Zachary Coile, "Bush's space vision finds few boosters: Costly proposal faces rebuff from GOP, Democrats," *San Francisco Chronicle*, Jan. 22, 2004, www.sfgate.com/cgi-bin/article.cgi?f=/c/a/2004/01/22/MNGD64F5M71.DTL.

[41] "NASA's Project Constellation And The Future Of Human Spaceflight," *Space Policy Online*, May 24, 2011, www.spacepolicyonline.com/images/stories/Constellation_Fact_Sheet_May_2011.pdf.

[42] "Seeking a Human Spaceflight Program Worthy of a Great Nation," Review of Human Spaceflight Plans committee, Oct. 8, 2009, www1.nasa.gov/pdf/396093main_HSF_Cmte_FinalReport.pdf.

[43] "Launching a New Era in Space Exploration," Feb. 2, 2010, www.nasa.gov/pdf/421063main_Joint_Statement-2-1.pdf.

[44] "National Space Policy," June 28, 2010, www.whitehouse.gov/sites/default/files/national_space_policy_6-28-10.pdf.

[45] Senator Kay Bailey Hutchison, "Challenges and Opportunities in the NASA FY 2011 Budget Proposal," Feb. 24, 1010, http://commerce.senate.gov/public/index.cfm?p=Hearings&ContentRecord_id=1fe8aef1-3b71-4380-921f-828311451d7e&Statement_id=f0457665-7571-4d01-977e-ad3367ce7d05&ContentType_id=14f995b9-dfa5-407a-9d35-56cc7152a7ed&Group_id=b06c39af-e033-4cba-9221-de668ca1978a&MonthDisplay=2&YearDisplay=2010.

About the Author

John Felton has been a journalist for more than 40 years, specializing primarily in international affairs. After covering education and politics for newspapers in Ohio and Delaware, he covered foreign policy for Congressional Quarterly, then was a foreign editor at National Public Radio. He is now a freelance writer and editor, living in the Berkshires of Western Massachusetts.

[46] Marcia S. Smith, "NASA's Project Constellation And The Future Of Human Spaceflight," *Space Policy Online*, May 24, 2011, www.spacepolicyonline.com/free-fact-sheets-and-reports/nasas-project-constellation-and-the-future-of-human-spaceflight-a-spacepolicy online-com-fact-sheet.

[47] "NASA's FY2012 Budget Request and Final Action," *op. cit.*

[48] "Senator Hutchison To Work with Colleagues to Restore NASA Human Exploration Funding," Office of Senator Kay Bailey Hutchison, Feb. 13, 2012, http://hutchison.senate.gov/?p=press_release&id=975.

[49] Doug Cooke, "Plans for Human Exploration Beyond Low Earth Orbit," NASA, March 4, 2011, www.nasa.gov/pdf/524774main_COOKE.pdf.

[50] "NASA International Space Station Facts and Figures," www.nasa.gov/mission_pages/station/main/onthestation/facts_and_figures.html.

[51] "Russian Rocket Set for Space Falls in Woods," *The New York Times*, Aug. 24, 2011, www.nytimes.com/2011/08/25/science/space/25space.html?_r=1&ref=space.

[52] "Soyuz problem may delay next ISS mission," *Spacetoday.net*, Jan. 28, 2012, www.spacetoday.net/.

[53] "NASA Announces Design For New Deep Space Exploration System," NASA, Sept. 14, 2011, www.nasa.gov/exploration/systems/sls/sls1.html.

[54] "NASA Unveils New Rocket Design," *The New York Times*, Sept. 13, 2011, www.nytimes.com/2011/09/15/science/space/15nasa.html?ref=nationalaeronauticsandspaceadministration&pagewanted=all.

[55] "Orion MPCV," www.nasa.gov/exploration/systems/mpcv/index.html.

[56] "The Shuttle Ends Its Final Voyage and an Era in Space," *The New York Times*, July 21, 2011, www.nytimes.com/2011/07/22/science/space/22space-shuttle-atlantis.html?ref=space.

[57] "Into the Sunset," *The Economist*, July 2, 2011, p. 67.

[58] Mike Schneider, "Space Coast feels ripple effect as 7,000 jobs are lost to the canceled space shuttle program," Associated Press, July 10, 2011, www.theday.com/article/20110710/OP03/3071 09983.

[59] "NASA Announces New Homes For Shuttle Orbiters After Retirement," April 12, 2001, www.nasa.gov/home/hqnews/2011/apr/HQ_11-107_Orbiter_Disposition.html.

[60] "NASA Chose the Right Museums for Retired Space Shuttles, Report Finds," Space.com, Aug. 27, 2011, www.collectspace.com/news/news-082711a.html.

[61] "NASA Commercial Partners: Cargo," www.nasa.gov/exploration/commercial/cargo/index.html.

[62] "SpaceX COTS launch delayed to late April," *Spacetoday.net*, Feb. 11, 2012, www.spacetoday.net/Summary/5529.

[63] Marcia Smith, "Congressional Hearing Notes: NASA's Commercial Crew Development Program: Accomplishments and Challenges," *Space Policy Online*, Oct. 26, 2011, www.spacepolicy online.com/images/stories/Commercial_Crew_Hrg_Oct_26_2011.pdf.

[64] "NASA's FY2012 Budget Request and Final Action," *op. cit.*

[65] "Fiscal 2013 Budget Estimates," NASA, p. 19, www.nasa.gov/pdf/622655main_FY13_NASA_Budget_Estimates.pdf.

[66] Group Letter To Congress and the Obama Administration Regarding NASA's Commercial Crew Program, SpaceRef.com, Nov. 8, 2011, www.spaceref.com/news/viewnews.html?id=1585.

[67] Jennifer Steinhauer And Robert Pear, "The Deficit Deal That Wasn't: Hopes Are Dashed," *The New York Times*, Nov. 20 2011, www.nytimes.com/2011/11/21/us/politics/deficit-deal-fell-apart-after-seeming-agreement.html?ref=politics#.

[68] Marcia S. Smith, "Bolden: NASA Not Budgeting for Sequestration," *Space Policy Online*, Dec. 5, 2011, www.spacepolicyonline.com/news/bolden-nasa-not-budgeting-for-sequestration.

[69] Current Missions, NASA, www.nasa.gov/missions/current/index.html.

[70] Mercury: the Key to Terrestrial Planet Evolution, NASA, http://messenger.jhuapl.edu/why_mercury/index.html.

[71] New Horizons: Mission to Pluto and the Kuiper Belt, NASA, http://pluto.jhuapl.edu/mission/whereis_nh.php.

[72] Cassini: Unlocking Saturn's Secrets, NASA, www.nasa.gov/mission_pages/cassini/main/index.html.

[73] GRAIL: Gravity Recovery and Interior Laboratory, NASA, www.nasa.gov/mission_pages/grail/overview/index.html.

[74] Montana Students Pick Winning Names for Moon Craft, NASA, www.nasa.gov/mission_pages/grail/news/grail20120117.html.

[75] Juno: Unlocking Jupiter's Mysteries, Jet Propulsion Laboratory, www.nasa.gov/mission_pages/juno/main/index.html.

[76] Edward Wong and Kenneth Chang, "Space Plan From China Broadens Challenge to U.S., *The New York Times*, Dec. 29, 2011, www.nytimes.com/2011/12/30/world/asia/china-unveils-ambitious-plan-to-explore-space.html?ref=space&pagewanted=all.

[77] For background, see Konstantin Kakaes, "Weapons in Space," *CQ Global Researcher*, Aug. 16, 2011, pp. 395-420.

FOR MORE INFORMATION

Mars Society, 11111 West 8th Ave., Unit A, Lakewood, CO 80215; 303-980-0890; www.marssociety.org/home. Advocates human and robotic exploration of the red planet.

NASA, Public Communications Office, NASA Headquarters, Suite 5K39, Washington, DC 20546-0001; 202-358-0001; www.nasa.gov. Conducts human and scientific exploration and aeronautical research.

National Space Society, 1155 15th St., N.W., Suite 500, Washington, DC 20005; 202-429-1600; www.nss.org/. Advocacy group that promotes the United States as a "spacefaring civilization."

The Planetary Society, 65 N. Catalina Ave., Pasadena, CA 91106-2301; 626-793-5100; www.planetary.org. Advocacy group for space exploration.

Space and Technology Policy Group, LLC, 2503D N. Harrison St., Arlington, VA 22207; 571-286-9168; www.spacepolicyonline.com. Provides news, information and analysis about space program policy, international space activities and space law.

The Space Review, www.thespacereview.com. Website that publishes analysis and commentary pieces about space and space programs globally.

Bibliography

Selected Sources

Books

Duggins, Pat, *Trailblazing Mars: NASA's Next Giant Leap*, University Press of Florida, 2010.
A veteran space journalist covers the history and potential of Mars missions.

Moltz, James Clay, *Asia's Space Race: National Motivations, Regional Rivalries and International Risks*, Columbia University Press, 2011.
An associate professor at the Naval Postgraduate School analyzes the forces driving space developments in China and other Asian nations.

Pelton, Joseph N., and Angelia P. Bukley (eds.), *The Farthest Shore: A 21st Century Guide to Space*, Collector's Guide Publishing, 2010.
The detailed reference work features essays by scientists, astronauts and other experts on topics dealing with space and spaceflight.

Seedhouse, Erik, *The New Space Race: China vs. USA*, Springer Praxis Books, 2010.
An aerospace scientist examines China's intentions in space.

Zubrin, Robert, *The Case for Mars: The Plan to Settle the Red Planet and Why We Must*, Free Press, 2011 (2nd ed.).
The founder of the Mars Society advocates an all-out U.S. effort to put humans on Mars.

Articles

"Into the sunset: The final launch of the space shuttle brings to an end the dreams of the Apollo era," *The Economist*, July 2, 2011, pp. 66-68.
The British journal insightfully analyzes what the end of the shuttle program means for the U.S. space program.

"Space 2012: What's Ahead," *The Daily Planet blog, Air & Space*, Dec. 29, 2011, http://blogs.airspacemag.com/dailyplanet/2011/12/space-2012-what's-ahead/.
The list of likely or possible space events in 2012 includes the reassuring news that "the world won't end" during the year.

Broad, William J., "With the Shuttle Program Ending, Fears of Decline at NASA," *The New York Times*, July 3, 2011, www.nytimes.com/2011/07/04/science/space/04nasa.html?_r=1&ref=space.
The report details concerns about the future of spaceflight.

Foust, Jeff, "Caution and optimism about human spaceflight?," *The Space Review*, Jan. 23, 2012, www.thespacereview.com/article/2011/1.
An aerospace analyst examines the challenges facing the U.S. human spaceflight program.

Handberg, Roger, "American human spaceflight and future options, short- and long-term," *The Space Review*, Nov. 21, 2011, www.thespacereview.com/article/1974/1.
A longtime observer of the space program puts NASA's current challenges into historical and political context.

Reports and Studies

"America's Future in Space: Aligning the Civil Space Program with National Needs," National Research Council, 2009, www.nap.edu/catalog.php?record_id=12701.
Experts on space conclude that the U.S. civilian space program is "a national imperative today, and will continue to grow in importance in the future."

"Recapturing a Future for Space Exploration: Life and Physical Sciences Research for a New Era," National Research Council, 2011, www.nap.edu/catalog.php?record_id=13048.
Scientists in biology and other life sciences set out their priorities for space exploration in the coming decade.

"The Scientific Context for Exploration of the Moon: Final Report," National Research Council, 2007, www.nap.edu/catalog/11954.html.
Top lunar scientists analyzes what can be learned, and what might not be, from more extensive exploration of the Moon.

Ansdell, M., L. Delgado, and D. Hendrickson, "Analyzing the Development Paths of Emerging Spacefaring Nations," Capstone Research, April 2011, www.gwu.edu/~spi/assets/docs/Ansdell_Delgado_Hendrickson.pdf.
Researchers examine the opportunities and challenges facing a wide variety of nations that are developing space programs.

Pace, Scott, and Giuseppe Reibaldi, eds., "Future Human Spaceflight: The Need for International Cooperation," International Academy of Astronautics, 2010.
"Human space exploration can and should be guided by questions that promote international collaboration and cooperation," the editors write.

On the Web:

***Hubble Space Telescope: NASA provides photos, background and other information on the celestial observer*, www.nasa.gov/mission_pages/hubble/main/index.html.**

***Mars Science Laboratory: NASA's Jet Propulsion Laboratory provides an overview of the ongoing mission to land the Curiosity rover on Mars*, http://mars.jpl.nasa.gov/msl/mission/rover/.**

***International Space Station: NASA provides images, videos and other information on the orbiting station*, www.nasa.gov/mission_pages/station/main/index.html.**

The Next Step:

Additional Articles from Current Periodicals

Human Spaceflight

Berger, Eric, "Laying Groundwork or a Gravestone for Spaceflight?" *Houston Chronicle*, Jan. 29, 2012, p. B1, www.chron.com/news/houston-texas/article/Laying-groundwork-or-a-gravestone-for-spaceflight-2795090.php.

Scientists are unsure whether a new rocket being produced by NASA will benefit future human spaceflight.

Dean, James, "NASA, Companies Offer Reassurance to Those Wary of Spaceflight's Future," *Florida Today*, April 29, 2011, p. A9.

NASA has awarded $269 million in contracts to four companies to develop commercially operated spacecraft.

Griffin, Gerry, "As Shuttle Retires, a Vote for Commercial Space Flight," *USA Today*, April 6, 2011, p. A9, www.usatoday.com/printedition/news/20110406/column06_st1.art.htm.

Human spaceflight is necessary for U.S. leadership, a former director of the Johnson Space Center says.

Mars

Kaufman, Marc, "NASA's Future Could Hinge on $2.5 Billion Mars Rover Mission," *The Boston Globe*, Nov. 26, 2011, p. A5, articles.boston.com/2011-11-26/news/30445105_1_mars-science-laboratory-mars-missions-nearest-planetary-neighbor.

Analysts say the *Curiosity* rover must make substantial discoveries on Mars in order for NASA to justify its cost.

Mangels, John, "Mars Mission Topic of Talks By NASA Engineer, a Local Native," *Plain Dealer* (Cleveland), Aug. 24, 2011, p. B1, www.cleveland.com/science/index.ssf/2011/|08/nasa_engineer_and_cleveland_na.html.

The presence of water on Mars opens the possibility for more groundbreaking discoveries, says a NASA engineer.

Vastag, Brian, "Obama's Space Budget Would Scale Back Mars Program," *The Washington Post*, Feb. 9, 2012, p. A2, www.washingtonpost.com/national/health-science/presidents-next-budget-to-cut-mars-solar-system-exploration/2012/02/08/gIQAvrm3zQ_story.html.

President Obama's budget plan includes a decrease in funding through 2017 for the NASA division that launches rovers to Mars.

Private Sector

Hennigan, W. J., "SpaceX Delays Rocket Mission," *Los Angeles Times*, Jan. 17, 2012, p. B2, articles.latimes.com/2012/jan/16/business/la-fi-0117-spacex-launch-delay-20120117.

SpaceX has delayed the launch of its *Dragon* capsule.

Palmer, Michael, "What's Next for Space Program? NASA Looks to Private Sector," *The Record* (Bergen County, N.J.), July 9, 2011, p. A1, www.northjersey.com/news/125257184_WHAT_S_NEXT_FOR_SPACE_PROGRAM__NASA_looks_to_private_sector.html.

NASA is shifting low-Earth-orbit missions and human spaceflight to the private sector after the shuttle program ends.

Werner, Debra, "NASA Must Change How It Works With Private Sector, Exec Says," *Federal Times*, Aug. 8, 2011, p. 12.

NASA must work with private sector partners to make them more innovative and cost-effective amid budget setbacks.

Webb Telescope

Leone, Dan, "Lawmaker, NASA Defend Beleaguered Webb Space Telescope Program," *Federal Times*, July 18, 2011, p. 12.

Sen. Barbara Mikulski, D-Md., says that any attempts to deny funding for the Webb telescope are "shortsighted."

Matthews, Mark K., "Sky-High Costs Threaten Smaller NASA Projects," *Los Angeles Times*, Sept. 11, 2011, p. A24, articles.latimes.com/2011/sep/10/nation/la-na-nasa-budget-20110911.

Scientists are worried that funding for the Webb telescope could devour much of NASA's shrinking budget in the coming years.

Roylance, Frank D., "Astronomers Split Over Webb Telescope's Future," *The Baltimore Sun*, Oct. 3, 2011, p. A1, articles.baltimoresun.com/2011-10-03/news/bs-md-webb-telescope-20111002_1_webb-telescope-webb-project-nasa.

Astrophysicists are worried that a lack of funding for the Webb telescope could lead to a 20-year setback for the field.

CITING *CQ RESEARCHER*

Sample formats for citing these reports in a bibliography include the ones listed below. Preferred styles and formats vary, so please check with your instructor or professor.

MLA STYLE

Jost, Kenneth. "Remembering 9/11," CQ Researcher 2 Sept. 2011: 701-732.

APA STYLE

Jost, K. (2011, September 2). Remembering 9/11. *CQ Researcher, 9*, 701-732.

CHICAGO STYLE

Jost, Kenneth. "Remembering 9/11." *CQ Researcher*, September 2, 2011, 701-732.

In-depth Reports on Issues in the News

Are you writing a paper?

Need backup for a debate?

Want to become an expert on an issue?

For more than 80 years, students have turned to *CQ Researcher* for in-depth reporting on issues in the news. Reports on a full range of political and social issues are now available. Following is a selection of recent reports:

Civil Liberties
Remembering 9/11, 9/11
Government Secrecy, 2/11
Cybersecurity, 2/10
Press Freedom, 2/10

Crime/Law
Financial Misconduct, 1/12
Eyewitness Testimony, 10/11
Legal-Aid Crisis, 10/11
Computer Hacking, 9/11
Cameras in the Courtroom, 1/11
Death Penalty Debates, 11/10

Education
Youth Volunteerism, 1/12
Digital Education, 12/11
College Football, 11/11
Student Debt, 10/11
School Reform, 4/11
Crime on Campus, 2/11

Environment/Society
Invasive Species, 2/12
Fracking Controversy, 12/11
Water Crisis in the West, 12/11
Google's Dominance, 11/11

Health/Safety
Patient Safety, 2/12
Military Suicides, 9/11
Teen Drug Use, 6/11
Organ Donations, 4/11
Genes and Health, 1/11
Food Safety, 12/10
Preventing Bullying, 12/10

Politics/Economy
Presidential Election, 2/12
'Occupy' Movement, 1/12
Lies and Politics, 2/11

Upcoming Reports

Attracting Jobs, 3/2/12 | Immigration Controversies, 3/9/12 | Arts Education, 3/16/12

ACCESS
CQ Researcher is available in print and online. For access, visit your library or www.cqresearcher.com.

STAY CURRENT
For notice of upcoming *CQ Researcher* reports or to learn more about *CQ Researcher* products, subscribe to the free e-mail newsletters, *CQ Researcher Alert!* and *CQ Researcher News*: http://cqpress.com/newsletters.

PURCHASE
To purchase a *CQ Researcher* report in print or electronic format (PDF), visit www.cqpress.com or call 866-427-7737. Single reports start at $15. Bulk purchase discounts and electronic-rights licensing are also available.

SUBSCRIBE
Annual full-service *CQ Researcher* subscriptions—including 44 reports a year, monthly index updates, and a bound volume—start at $1,054. Add $25 for domestic postage.

CQ Researcher Online offers a backfile from 1991 and a number of tools to simplify research. For pricing information, call 800-834-9020, or e-mail librarymarketing@cqpress.com.

CQ RESEARCHER ***PLUS*** *ARCHIVE*

GET ONLINE ACCESS TO VITAL ISSUES FROM 1923 TO THE PRESENT

CQ Researcher Plus Archive delivers fast, online access to every *CQ Researcher* report from 1991 to the present, *PLUS* lets you explore the complete archive of *Editorial Research Reports** from 1923-1990. Search and browse more than 3,600 in-depth reports.

Loaded with handy online features, *CQ Researcher Plus Archive* provides the trustworthy reporting and the advanced online functionality today's researchers demand. The new "Issue Tracker" feature provides quick links to past and present reports on the specific topics you need.

For a free trial, visit http://library.cqpress.com/trials.

For pricing information, call 1-800-834-9020, ext. 1906 or e-mail librarymarketing@cqpress.com.

**Editorial Research Reports*, the predecessor to *CQ Researcher*, provides the same expert, nonpartisan reporting on the vital issues that have shaped our society.

CQ Press • 2300 N Street, NW, Suite 800 • Washington, DC 20037

CQ Researcher

Published by CQ Press, an Imprint of SAGE Publications, Inc.

www.cqresearcher.com

Attracting Jobs

Do tax breaks for business spur employment?

Tax-supported subsidies aimed at luring companies to relocate or retain offices and factories in specific locations have proliferated. Local and state governments, engaged in fierce competition for jobs, are giving businesses up to $70 billion annually in tax breaks, new roads and training facilities and other incentives. Economic-development officials and companies that have relocated for subsidies say the incentives have spurred employment growth and helped some businesses stay profitable. But critics, who include many economists, argue that the incentives generate relatively few new jobs and instead lead many companies merely to shift operations from one place to another, depending on where they can broker the best deal. Among the most controversial subsidies are those supporting professional-sports stadiums. Supporters say new sports facilities help cities raise their profile and attract growth, while critics charge the subsidies fail to pay for themselves.

Fans stream into the Yankees' brand-new $2 billion stadium in the Bronx, built with substantial public funding, on Oct. 29, 2009, for game two of the World Series. Skeptics of taxpayer-funded business subsidies, including many economists, disagree about the claimed jobs and other benefits of subsidies.

INSIDE THIS REPORT

THE ISSUES 207
BACKGROUND 214
CHRONOLOGY 215
CURRENT SITUATION 220
AT ISSUE........................221
OUTLOOK 222
BIBLIOGRAPHY 226
THE NEXT STEP 227

CQ Researcher • March 2, 2012 • www.cqresearcher.com
Volume 22, Number 9 • Pages 205-228

SAGE | CQPRESS
Los Angeles | London | New Delhi
Singapore | Washington DC

RECIPIENT OF SOCIETY OF PROFESSIONAL JOURNALISTS AWARD FOR EXCELLENCE ◆ AMERICAN BAR ASSOCIATION SILVER GAVEL AWARD

THE ISSUES

207 • Do state and local tax incentives for businesses create jobs?
• Are location-based business incentives good for communities?
• Should states and localities compete for business locations?

BACKGROUND

214 **Early Competition**
The first property-tax break in North America was awarded in 1640.

217 **Economics vs. Politics**
Location-based tax incentives are inefficient, but politicians love them.

219 **Regional Cooperation and Accountability**
At least 37 states post online information about subsidies to business.

CURRENT SITUATION

220 **Tight Times**
Policymakers are hoping richer incentives will lead to more jobs.

222 **Right to Work**
Many states ban contracts requiring workers to join or pay dues to unions.

OUTLOOK

222 **Beyond Incentives**
Will growing concern about the environment make relocation incentives obsolete?

SIDEBARS AND GRAPHICS

208 **'Right-to-Work' Laws Enacted in 23 States**
Most are in the South.

209 **Development Subsidies Take Many Forms**
Programs range from revenue bonds to enterprise zones.

210 **Rural Areas Hit Barriers to Job Creation**
"Before incentives can matter, fundamentals have to be strong."

212 **More Companies Receiving Tax Breaks**
Number of property tax abatements increased threefold.

215 **Chronology**
Key events since 1967.

216 **Subsidies Spark Debate — and New Ideas**
"At least give them to companies that reflect your values."

218 **If Cities Build Stadiums, Will Fans Come?**
Critics view sports subsidies as waste of tax dollars.

221 **At Issue**
Do "right-to-work" laws help states attract businesses?

FOR FURTHER RESEARCH

225 **For More Information**
Organizations to contact.

226 **Bibliography**
Selected sources used.

227 **The Next Step**
Additional articles.

227 **Citing *CQ Researcher***
Sample bibliography formats.

Cover: Getty Images/Mario Tama

CQ Researcher

March 2, 2012
Volume 22, Number 9

MANAGING EDITOR: Thomas J. Billitteri
tjb@cqpress.com

ASSISTANT MANAGING EDITOR: Kathy Koch
kkoch@cqpress.com

CONTRIBUTING EDITOR: Thomas J. Colin
tcolin@cqpress.com

ASSOCIATE EDITOR: Kenneth Jost

STAFF WRITER: Marcia Clemmitt

CONTRIBUTING WRITERS: Sarah Glazer, Alan Greenblatt, Peter Katel, Barbara Mantel, Jennifer Weeks

DESIGN/PRODUCTION EDITOR: Olu B. Davis

ASSISTANT EDITOR: Darrell Dela Rosa

FACT CHECKER: Michelle Harris

Los Angeles | London | New Delhi
Singapore | Washington DC

An Imprint of SAGE Publications, Inc.

VICE PRESIDENT AND EDITORIAL DIRECTOR, HIGHER EDUCATION GROUP:
Michele Sordi

DIRECTOR, ONLINE PUBLISHING:
Todd Baldwin

CQ Researcher (ISSN 1056-2036) is printed on acid-free paper. Published weekly, except: (March wk. 5) (May wk. 4) (July wk. 1) (Aug. wks. 3, 4) (Nov. wk. 4) and (Dec. wks. 3, 4). Published by SAGE Publications, Inc., 2455 Teller Rd., Thousand Oaks, CA 91320. Annual full-service subscriptions start at $1,054. For pricing, call 1-800-834-9020. To purchase a *CQ Researcher* report in print or electronic format (PDF), visit www.cqpress.com or call 866-427-7737. Single reports start at $15. Bulk purchase discounts and electronic-rights licensing are also available. Periodicals postage paid at Thousand Oaks, California, and at additional mailing offices. POSTMASTER: Send address changes to *CQ Researcher*, 2300 N St., N.W., Suite 800, Washington, DC 20037.

Attracting Jobs

BY MARCIA CLEMMITT

THE ISSUES

Shocking news greeted the 2,160 employees at Boeing's military aircraft plant in Wichita, Kan., in early January. After 80-plus years as a centerpiece of the city's economy — and two years after Kansas spent $43 million to build a training center for aerospace workers — Boeing announced it was shutting down the plant.

Republican Gov. Sam Brownback, a former U.S. senator, called Boeing's decision "very disappointing," noting that, "no one worked harder for the success of the Boeing Company than Team Kansas." [1]

But according to a company executive, "Business costs in Wichita are not competitive" for Boeing's operations. [2]

Kansas is far from alone in offering millions of dollars in tax breaks, plus millions more for training centers, roads and other incentives aimed at enticing companies to relocate to an area or keep jobs from moving elsewhere. Such tax-funded perks have proliferated over the past decade as the economy has cratered and unemployment has soared.

But serious questions are being raised about the effectiveness of incentives, which can put a big dent in state and local revenues. Economists say many companies that receive perks fail to deliver promised jobs. And many also question whether the intense rivalry for jobs among states leads to little more than an economic shell game, with jobs moving from one place to another without a significant net national gain in employment.

In the case of Boeing, it eliminated most of its jobs in Wichita and moved the rest to company operations in Oklahoma and Texas.

AP Photo/*The Witchita Eagle*/Brian Corn

Boeing's 2,160-worker plant in Wichita, Kan. — centerpiece of the local economy — is closing. Just two years after the state spent $43 million to build a training center for aerospace workers, Boeing announced the plant would shut down by year's end because of high operational costs. States and localities spend up to $70 billion annually on business subsidies. Proponents say they generate prosperity. Critics say they often fail to deliver promised jobs and end up losing money.

"In a given year, it is estimated that, on average, some 15,000 communities vie for roughly 1,500 major industrial projects available nationally," wrote Jonathan Q. Morgan and David M. Lawrence at the University of North Carolina, Chapel Hill. [3] "This creates an intensely competitive and often costly situation in which the odds of success are low for many communities." [4]

Estimates of how much states and localities spend on location incentives annually range between $40 billion and $70 billion. [5] The amounts have skyrocketed nationwide. In Arizona, for example, businesses in 1994 claimed just $5 million in state tax credits, which reduce companies' state tax bill. By 2008 the credits had grown 17-fold, to $86 million. [6]

Proponents of business subsidies insist, however, that they generate jobs and help localities prosper.

Kentucky is seeing large effects from new tax breaks enacted in 2009, said Larry Hayes, who heads the Kentucky Cabinet for Economic Development, the state's main economic-development agency. Those breaks include a tax credit for filmmakers that shoot in the state and job-creation incentives for companies both existing and new to Kentucky. The more than 200 companies working their way through the new programs' approval process could potentially generate more than 13,500 jobs and help retain 4,800 existing ones in Kentucky, he said. [7]

But Kentucky isn't the only state attracted by Hollywood's glitter. About 45 states offer tax credits to filmmakers. Rhode Island's filmmaker credits, which totaled $56.7 million between 2005 and 2009, created 4,184 full-time jobs in that period — including jobs directly connected to movie production and in other industries such as food and lodging that saw increased business while the movies were made, wrote Edward M. Mazze, a business professor at the University of Rhode Island. [8]

Although tax incentives can give an area an economic boost, focusing on a quick local hit misses some big-picture

'Right-to-Work' Laws Enacted in 23 States

Twenty-three states, mostly in the South and Midwest, have enacted laws that bar companies and unions from signing contracts requiring employees to join or pay fees to a union. Some industries, such as federally regulated airlines, are exempt. Proponents say the laws give states a business-friendly advantage in competing for jobs, but critics say they reduce wages and don't promote job growth.

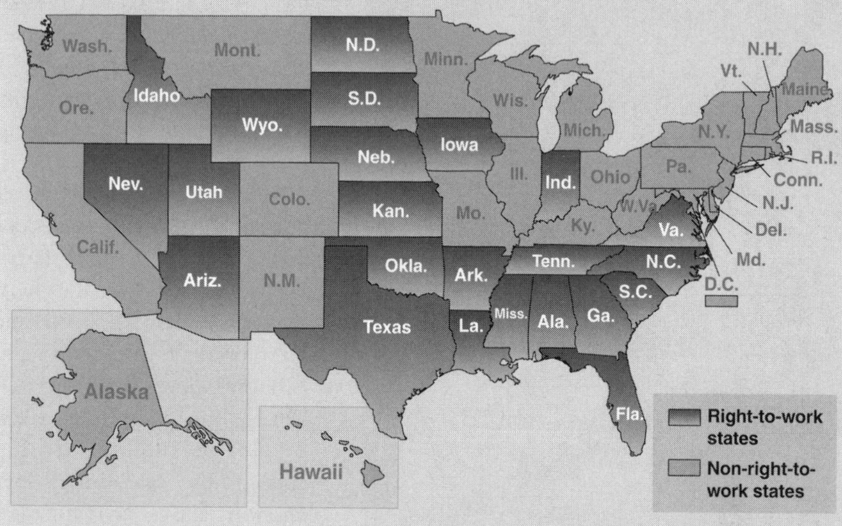

Source: "Right to Work States," National Right to Work Legal Defense Foundation, 2012, www.nrtw.org/rtws.htm

questions, says Joseph J. Seneca, a professor of economics at the Edward J. Bloustein School of Planning and Public Policy at Rutgers University in New Jersey. What's seldom asked — but probably should be — is "whether those jobs are taken away from, say, Brooklyn, or whether they're jobs the company would have created anyway," even if it hadn't received an incentive, he says.

Many communities, especially rural ones, have offered incentives to lure so-called "big box" retail stores such as Walmart and Home Depot. Those transactions can be as pricey — and as uncertain in their effects — as incentives to lure manufacturing companies.

Last year, towns that had provided significant incentives to lure Borders book stores were left high and dry when the retailer went bankrupt. Pico Rivera, an eastern suburb of Los Angeles, for example, had spent $1.6 million in federal grant money to get a Borders outlet, including helping to pay the store's rent for eight years. When the chain went bust, the town lost more than just jobs and a bookstore that was a center of economic activity. It also will be on the hook for rent until a new tenant is found for the vacated 18,100-square-foot site, plus for other costs, the *Whittier Daily News* reported. [9]

In 2009 alone, Walmart stores got $1.8 million in tax credits to build five stores in Louisiana. Bridgeton, Mo., approved a $7.2 million deal in 2010 to bring a single Walmart outlet to town. [10]

Businesses are growing accustomed to incentives and often tell states and localities to "fight amongst yourselves" to win our favor, says Katherine Chalmers, an assistant professor of economics at California State University, Sacramento.

Yet, the ammunition communities often use to outgun their rivals, including so-called business-climate rankings, can be suspect. Many such rankings give top billing to states that offer generous business tax breaks and go easy on environmental or workplace regulations. But some economists say a high ranking on such lists doesn't necessarily equate with a strong or competitive economy.

South Dakota, for example, ranks second in a 2012 index from the Tax Foundation, a business-oriented think tank in Washington, and 17th — comfortably in the top half of states — in a *Forbes* ranking. [11] The state's unemployment rate was 4.2 percent in December, compared to 8.2 percent nationally. [12]

But South Dakota contains four of the nation's 15 poorest counties, including the three poorest, according to the latest census data. [13] Moreover, South Dakota's economy rests largely on only two legs: agriculture and public employment at Ellsworth Air Force Base, the state's second-largest employer, near Rapid City. [14]

Robert W. Wassmer, a professor of economics also at Cal State, Sacramento, points to South Dakota as typical of many states that may rank high in some economic-climate measures but "don't have other things" that businesses need to thrive, such as access to markets and raw materials, good infrastructure and a skilled workforce. Rank, Wassmer says, doesn't necessarily translate to overall economic strength.

The disjoint exists because breaks on taxes and regulation have less influence on business-location decisions than many think, Wassmer argues. California, with relatively high business taxes and tough regulations, has a good record of retaining companies and jobs, he says. "Not that many businesses are being driven out," Wassmer asserts. Meanwhile, low-tax, lightly regulated Reno in neighboring Nevada "should be booming right now. Everybody should be flooding there, but they're not," Wassmer says.

"There's a consensus among economists that smokestack chasing is not effective," says Laura Kalambokidis, an associate professor of applied economics at the University of Minnesota, St. Paul. For one thing, "using tax incentives to chase employers is pretty much universal now, so they're not going to be effective" because businesses can get similar breaks from virtually any state, she says.

Policymakers who promote location incentives intend to boost job prospects for local residents, but the measures can fail on that score even when they bring jobs, says Robert Greenbaum, a professor of public policy at Ohio State University. If the targeted companies are suitable to a different — that is, a mobile or more educated — workforce than the local one, for instance, "people coming in from out of state take the jobs."

Nevertheless, lawmakers are very reluctant to give up the incentives because they "are good politics," wrote Terry F. Buss, a professor of public policy at Carnegie Mellon University's Heinz School of Business campus in Adelaide, Australia. "There is little risk to politicians when incentives fail because failure can be blamed on . . . market forces" or other hard-to-control factors. Then, when economic times are good, "policymakers can claim credit" — but only if they've enacted incentives, said Buss. [15]

Economists see things very differently. "I think the academic consensus would be, 'It would be best if we didn't have interstate competition' " to offer incentives, says Seneca, at the Bloustein School of Planning and Public Policy. "The real things that incentivize [business] investment" are states' long-term commitment to providing good "infrastructure, effective and efficient regulation and taxation, research and development spending, education and quality of life" that apply to all residents and businesses, not specially targeted efforts.

"In a sense, you do want states to compete with one another — but to be able to say that 'we are the best-run state,' " says Kalambokidis, at the University of Minnesota.

As policymakers and taxpayers consider how best to bring jobs to their towns and cities, here are some of the questions being asked:

Do state and local tax incentives for businesses create jobs?

Over the past few decades, states and metropolitan areas have offered an increasing number of special tax breaks for businesses that pledge to bring new jobs to their areas. Economic-development officials say the incentives are effective in leading businesses to create local jobs. Most economists, however, argue that often the tax breaks don't create jobs but merely induce companies to move them from one place to another, often rewarding companies for location decisions that they would have made anyway.

"Incentives do work," said Alex Labeau, president of the Idaho Association of Commerce and Industry, a business lobby. Idaho recently learned a hard lesson when Boeing bypassed

Development Subsidies Take Many Forms

States and local governments offer a variety of subsidies to attract businesses ranging from tax cuts to cash grants.

Common Types of Economic Development Subsidies

Tax abatements — Reduce or eliminate taxes paid to state and local governments. Often apply to property, inventory or sales taxes.

Tax credits — Reduce or eliminate corporate income taxes by allowing companies to deduct a percentage of certain expenses, such as research-and-development or new-equipment costs.

Industrial revenue bonds — Bonds with tax-free interest, giving companies what amounts to low-interest loans.

Infrastructure assistance — Reduces construction costs by giving local governments the responsibility for improving roads, sewers, water lines and other utilities.

Grants — Cash subsidies that companies may use for general or specific purposes.

Land-price write-downs — Reduce land-purchasing costs typically through third-party transfers. Local governments may also pay for such expenses as eminent domain or environmental cleanup.

Tax-increment financing — Uses property tax collected on the appreciation value of a new development to pay for infrastructure, land acquisition or other related costs.

Enterprise zones — Economically depressed areas in which companies are eligible for multiple subsidies.

Source: "Beginner's Guide," Good Jobs First, 2010, www.goodjobsfirst.org/accountable-development/beginners-guide

Rural Areas Find Barriers to Job Creation

"Before incentives can matter, fundamentals have to be strong."

Hard as it is to generate jobs in cities, it's even tougher in rural areas. An aging workforce and less easy access to markets and suppliers are among the barriers to expanding employment in rural counties. Even so, economic-development experts say some strategies show promise.

In North Carolina, for example, "metro areas are doing well income-wise, but the other 90 counties aren't," says Jason Jolley, senior research director of the Carolina Center for Competitive Economies at the University of North Carolina, Chapel Hill. North Carolina's core economy has shifted from tobacco, textiles and furniture to high-tech industries such as pharmaceuticals, but many jobs in new industries have gone to people moving into the state, Jolley says, while native rural residents lack access to similar opportunities.

In economists' perfect world, people would simply move where jobs are. "But people aren't as mobile as economic theory would argue" — especially since the housing crash left many with houses they can't sell, says Robert Greenbaum, professor of public policy at Ohio State University. That makes finding ways to develop rural jobs crucial, he and others say.

Rural areas lose young, educated workers at a high rate, another factor making those areas less attractive to employers, wrote Jonathan Q. Morgan, associate professor of public administration at the University of North Carolina (UNC), Chapel Hill, and colleagues. Nationwide, the median age in rural counties was 40.1 years in 2007, compared to 36.1 in metropolitan areas. Moreover, 16.3 percent of rural residents were 65 or older, compared to 11.9 percent in metro areas. [1]

Like most states that provide incentives to businesses, North Carolina gives larger ones to companies that put jobs in high-need areas, says Morgan. But if fundamentals such as adequate sewers and transportation infrastructure are lacking — often the case in rural areas — most businesses aren't interested, he says. "Before incentives can matter, fundamentals have to be strong."

"For the longest time, rural areas did what everybody else did — try to recruit big industry," says Morgan. "Some had success, but even they are realizing that they need a more diversified base so they are not dependent on one big company that might move offshore."

Options exist, though none is close to foolproof, and different areas need different approaches, economists say.

Localities shouldn't necessarily disdain retail and service jobs, despite their low wages and a prevailing view that only exporting industries can sustain an economy, says Katherine Chalmers, an assistant professor of economics at California State University, Sacramento. "With computer manufacturing, for example, you worry that it'll be outsourced, but it's hard to outsource your hairdresser."

In West Texas, where Chalmers grew up, retailing essentially is an export industry for towns where it's clustered, "because people drive long distances to shop there," she says.

Policymakers waste effort using strategies suited only for urban areas in rural places, says Thomas G. Johnson, a professor of development economics at the University of Missouri's Harry S Truman School of Public Affairs in Columbia. "Urban areas exist because there is value in clustering; rural areas exist because there's a value in space," he says.

For rural jobs, "you should look at sparsity-based businesses" such as forestry and tourism as well as manufacturing that doesn't depend on having complementary industries nearby.

its capital, Boise, as the site for a new $750 million plant the state had hoped to snag thanks to its proximity to Boeing's Seattle headquarters. Instead, the plant went to South Carolina, which will pay Boeing approximately $3,100 in incentives per job created, said Labeau. [16]

The Charleston, S.C., *Post and Courier* reported that the total incentive package, which the state government did not officially announce, totaled more than $900 million, twice as much as state officials announced. [17] By contrast, Idaho, with its small population, offers companies that create jobs only a small tax credit, worth thousands, not millions, of dollars, a harsh economic reality that may have doomed Boise in this case, according to the *Idaho Statesman.* [18]

"When it comes down to two or more equally satisfactory sites, a superior incentive package and 'red carpet treatment' can clinch a deal," wrote Bill Schweke, who recently retired as a senior fellow at the Corporation for Enterprise Development, a group in Washington that focuses on low-income communities. [19]

Alabama, Louisiana and Texas, widely considered to be "leading in the economic recovery" from the recession, "excel in their incentive offerings" to business, according to *Area Development*, a magazine for corporate site-selection professionals. The Texas Development Fund, for example, offers cash grants and tax breaks to companies making a final location decision between Texas and another state. [20] (Many large and medium-sized Texas cities, along with some in Alabama and Louisiana, have repeatedly topped lists of cities showing strong recession recovery.) [21]

Timothy J. Bartik, senior economist at the W.E. Upjohn Institute for Employment Research, an independent group in Kalamazoo, Mich., acknowledged that some critics of incentives argue that they are "too small" compared to a company's total costs "to

In North Carolina, some coastal and mountain towns are trying to start clusters of heritage-based enterprises by helping artisans such as potters and woodworkers strengthen their businesses and enticing more artisans to the area. Morgan says those efforts often begin with "revitalizing Main Streets," which "are the heart and soul of towns," then using "quality of life to attract entrepreneurs who are located elsewhere," as well as tourists and, possibly, retirees looking for an interesting place to settle.

How well this approach works "is not fully documented," but there is evidence that it has encouraged some communities to pull together with a "can-do attitude" to try to revitalize themselves, says Morgan. "At issue is whether such approaches "can make a dent, when you realize how many jobs aren't coming back."

Nevertheless, "there's a lot of literature showing that small businesses are job creators if they can stay alive," says Karen Chapple, associate director of the Institute of Urban and Regional Development at the University of California, Berkeley. So providing help to local small businesses, such as assistance with tax analysis and preparation, might help sustain entrepreneurs, she says.

One oft-heralded economic-development tool is the cluster — a geographical concentration of companies that are interconnected by being in the same industry, being part of the same supply chain or using the same set of job skills, for example. But while clusters can work for rural areas, they're no silver bullet, economists say.

"If there is a misperception" about clusters "it's that these programs have the potential to be adopted almost everywhere," says David L. Barkley, professor emeritus of applied economics at South Carolina's Clemson University.

Existing businesses with solid growth potential to form the seed of the cluster are essential, Barkley says. Sometimes creativity is required to discover growth potential. For example, while American textile manufacturing has moved offshore, in South Carolina the industry has "spotted growth in the 'miracle fiber' sector," such as athletic apparel that wicks away moisture and extra-warm lightweight hikers' clothing, he says.

Even then, Barkley says, "you still have to be introspective and ask, 'Do we have the resources needed' " to compete with other places to attract companies, including areas that have a head start. In the current economy, especially, "many communities aren't likely to be able to do it."

Despite difficulties, however, "there are lots of interesting" small-scale clusters sustaining local economies, including rural ones, Barkley says. Montana sports a high-end custom log cabin industry, Kentucky has houseboat builders and an area in Mississippi manufactures custom upholstered furniture.

In North Carolina, a group of four distressed rural counties hopes to piggyback on an existing cluster in a nearby metropolitan area — the high-tech Research Triangle Park area, near Durham, just to their south, says Morgan. "They are trying to get economies of scale by collaborating on a large industrial park" that might attract complementary businesses "interested in the lower-cost" living of the rural counties.

— Marcia Clemmitt

[1] Jonathan Q. Morgan, William Lambe and Allan Freyer, "Homegrown Responses to Economic Uncertainty in Rural America," *Rural Realities*, Mid-year [Issue 2] 2009, http://ruralsociology.org/StaticContent/Publications/Ruralrealities/pubs/RuralRealities3-2.pdf.

affect business location." But, he wrote, that argument is "unpersuasive." "Many states and metropolitan areas will be close substitutes" as sites, "offering similar access to markets and suppliers," so that "even small . . . cost differentials" such as what might come from a tax credit "could prove decisive for a particular . . . decision," he said. [22]

Many economists who criticize location-based tax and cash incentives for businesses, however, argue that such incentives don't create jobs but simply cause them to shift from one place to another — and generally don't do that as efficiently as economic-development officials claim.

One of the oldest forms of tax incentive are so-called enterprise-zone programs, in which businesses get tax breaks for locating in distressed areas. "There is really no evidence that these zones boost employment," says David Neumark, a professor of economics at the University of California, Irvine. Research findings on enterprise zones are clear enough, he says, that policymakers have only two realistic choices — "either kill them, or scale them way back to test" whether some specific tweaks and applications may make them work better.

Shawn M. Rohlin, a University of Akron assistant professor of economics, says his research shows enterprise zones do attract some businesses, especially retail and service operations. "However," he adds in an email interview, "the overall effect is smaller than one would anticipate, making the program quite expensive per new firm/employee." Furthermore, areas neighboring enterprise zones "seem to have lost almost as many firms as the zone gained, indicating that the zones improved at the expense of the neighboring areas."

In a study of North Carolina's tax credits, "We found that slightly more than half of companies had more jobs" after receiving a credit, but "45 percent had fewer," says Jason Jolley, senior

More Companies Receiving Tax Breaks

Forty-two states offered companies multiyear property tax breaks known as abatements in 2007, a nearly threefold increase from four decades earlier. The incentives reduce or eliminate property taxes paid to state and local governments in exchange for doing business in the area.

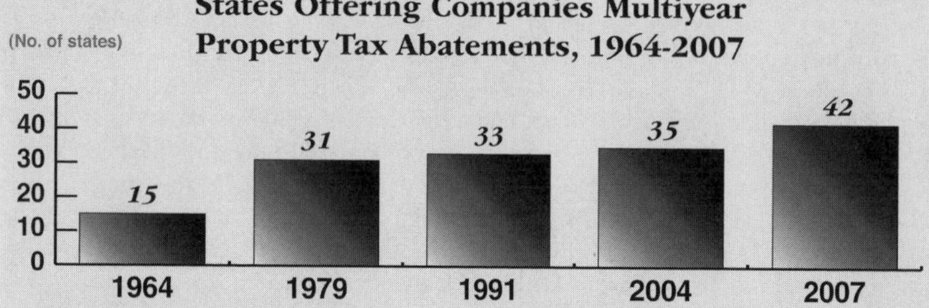

Source: Robert W. Wassmer, "The Increasing Use of Property Tax Abatement as a Means of Promoting Sub-National Economic Activity in the United States," Social Science Research Network, December 2007, papers.ssrn.com/sol3/papers.cfm?abstract_id=1088482

research director of the Carolina Center for Competitive Economies at the University of North Carolina, Chapel Hill. "Many companies told us that they didn't even know they were getting" some of the state credits, which seriously undercuts the argument that they are a vital factor in attracting and retaining companies, says Jolley.

"Firms that relocate are typically in declining industries" that must keep cutting costs to stay afloat, and this can mean successful job-luring efforts are short-lived victories, wrote Scott Loveridge, a professor of agricultural economics at Michigan State University. [23]

"For example, North Carolina gave away $240 million in tax credits to Dell in 2004 to lure them . . . while the closest competitor offered only $30 million," according to the Institute on Taxation and Economic Policy (ITEP) a Washington think tank that studies tax fairness. But six years later, as the market for personal computers became increasingly cost-focused, a struggling Dell announced that it would shut the North Carolina plant, "leaving at least 400 people without jobs," according to ITEP. [24]

"Several good studies . . . suggest that well-run, customized job training and manufacturing extension services" — government- or university-run initiatives that provide expertise to help local businesses improve their practices — "are far more cost-effective in creating jobs than is true of general business tax cuts or business tax incentives," wrote Bartik at the Upjohn Institute. [25]

Are location-based business incentives good for communities?

Critics of incentives offered to attract businesses to new locations say that many of the tax breaks actually have a reverse effect, siphoning public funds needed to provide roads, airports and other infrastructure and services that businesses need to thrive. The effect, critics say, is that the incentives may actually discourage job growth in the long run.

Supporters of incentives argue, however, that even when companies don't quite meet job goals, bringing businesses to an area and helping them stay profitable improves communities in many ways.

After the Sears Holdings Corp., in Hoffman Estates, Ill., announced in December that it would close more than a 100 Sears and Kmart stores, officials in Jackson, Miss., and other towns said that tax breaks to keep their stores would be worth the cost. Should its Sears store close, Jackson stands to lose $129,000 annually in property taxes plus one of only two large "anchor" stores that bring in enough customers to a Jackson shopping mall to keep it alive for other businesses. [26]

Many businesses argue that a valid purpose for incentives is helping local companies stay competitive by lowering their costs, says UNC's Jolley.

In Tulsa, Okla., some taxpayers cried foul when McLean, Va.-based media giant Gannett Co. moved a 500-worker call center out of state last year after receiving $260,000 in tax breaks from the city. But the fact that Gannett had supplied 500 jobs at the center for four years means that "the state gave Gannett nothing" and has no spilt milk to cry over, said Mike Neal, president of the Tulsa Chamber of Commerce. Gannett supplied jobs, "paid taxes, and they, in return, have got a little bit of that tax returned to them," making the situation a win for Tulsa, despite the move, he said. [27]

Many economists call the relocation of jobs from state to state or city to city a "zero-sum" game with no net benefits for the national economy. But Upjohn's Bartik argues that "such reshuffling may benefit the nation," at least in some cases. If jobs move to a high-unemployment area — as they may under enterprise-zone programs, for example — those areas "will benefit more" from the jobs than the business' previous location would have, since "the social benefits from hiring the average unemployed person are higher" than the benefits derived from hiring a less needy person, Bartik wrote. [28]

Critics of incentive programs argue that the economic improvements they spur are often short-lived and benefit the wrong people while the tax breaks drain needed public funds.

Incentives such as the tax credits that states often give to moviemakers filming on location are intended to produce only temporary jobs. Critics of the program say that this and other common features of incentives raise questions about their value.

Massachusetts' filmmaker credits allow moviemakers to take the credits in cash or sell them to others if their state tax bills aren't high enough to need the full credit as an offset, even though the movie jobs won't "even be there next year," said Peter Enrich, a professor at Northeastern University School of Law, in Boston. In 2008, the state issued $100 million in film credits, but only $100,000 was used to reduce filmmakers' own tax liabilities, while "the rest was paid out in cash or to reduce the taxes of insurance companies and banks" that bought the credits. [29] It's not clear that taxpayers would see that result as much of a boon to the community, Enrich says.

But taxpayers, and even lawmakers, often don't know the details of incentives that have been in place for years, says UNC's Jolley. Many incentives come in the form of tax credits or other tax breaks that are not included in state budgets, so they don't face annual legislative review as other government programs do, he says.

Some of North Carolina's filmmaker subsidy will go to the company that's filming the action movie "Iron Man 3" in Wilmington this year, says Jolley. And because the state basically hands over the credit, with no say in how it's used, "for all we know we could be subsidizing [lead actor] Robert Downey Jr.'s salary for up to $1 million," he says. "This makes you say, 'Wait a minute. Shouldn't we consider whether this is what we really want to do?' "

Even when monetary caps and so-called "sunset" provisions — which require lawmakers to reauthorize credits periodically — are written into credit programs most lawmakers uncritically extend the credits and raise the caps when businesses ask them to, said Missouri state Sen. Jason Crowell, a Republican. "History has shown" that "we will just raise those caps in exchange for campaign contributions." [30]

TheHungerGamesMovie.com/Murray Close

Jennifer Lawrence waits for her cue during filming of "The Hunger Games" in North Carolina, one of more than 40 states offering tax subsidies and other inducements to filmmakers. Critics call for more transparency for incentives. Since they often come in the form of tax credits or other tax breaks that are not included in state budgets, they don't face the annual legislative reviews given to other government programs.

Some analysts argue that incentives ostensibly designed to bring jobs to high-need areas can actually end up increasing inequality of opportunity.

A study of Ohio's enterprise zones, for example, found that "higher-income districts reap most of the jobs and investment," even though the program aims to improve economies in low-income areas. [31]

Another Ohio study, by Good Jobs First, a Washington, D.C.-based national policy resource center that seeks accountability in subsidies, found that many taxpayer-funded relocations in the Cleveland and Cincinnati areas moved jobs away from public-transit-accessible neighborhoods, potentially putting the jobs out of reach of residents who cannot afford cars. [32]

Some praise tax credits as a valuable counterbalance to high business tax rates, which they argue inhibit economic growth, but many economists disagree. "People say, 'Taxes distort markets,' and I agree. But then they say, 'Tax credits will offset that distortion,' and I say, 'No, it just gives you two distortions,' " says Thomas G. Johnson, a professor of development economics at the University of Missouri's Harry S Truman School of Public Affairs, in Columbia. "Unless tax credits are really well designed, they get people to do things they don't want to do," which promotes economic inefficiency, not improvement, he says.

Should states and localities compete for business locations?

Some analysts say interstate business-incentive competition has become a "race to the bottom" in which governments undermine their neighbors and even themselves by giving away more than they can afford. Others argue, however, that interstate competition has always been a valuable spur to improvement.

"Competition for economic growth is undeniably, irrevocably American — and therefore unavoidable. In some ways, the whole history of the United States is the history of communities competing with each other," wrote William Fulton, an economic-development expert and a former mayor of Ventura, Calif. [33]

Tax competition "is an effective restraint on state and local taxes," keeping them at business-friendly levels, says a 2012 study by the conservative The Tax Foundation. [34]

AFP/Getty Images/Mandel Ngan

Borders stores in cities around the country, including this one in Washington, D.C., closed after the retailer declared bankruptcy last year. Many of the communities had provided incentives to lure the stores. Pico Rivera, a suburb of Los Angeles, for example, had spent $1.6 million, including helping to pay the store's rent for eight years.

"There is a role for competition" when each state strives to create the best "general tax-and-spend policy," said Arthur J. Rolnick, a former research director of the Federal Reserve Bank of Minneapolis and now a senior fellow at the University of Minnesota's Humphrey School of Public Affairs. "Such competition leads states to provide a more efficient allocation of public and private goods." [35]

"I do believe that states and localities should compete but not in superficial ways," says the University of Missouri's Johnson. "They should compete to be better hosts to jobs," mainly using longer-term strategies such as beefing up transportation and other infrastructure and workforce training, and creating an efficient tax system.

Competition on infrastructure and education can constitute a race to the top, rather than to the bottom, says Ohio State's Greenbaum. "If a business you brought in leaves, tax breaks may be wasted, but human and infrastructure investments" remain.

But much interstate competition takes the form of location-based incentives and has grown so intense that "politicians aren't acting rationally, and they're giving away too much," says Wassmer at California State University.

Competition on giveaways — unlike competition to improve state systems and services — quickly becomes an inescapable trap, even for states that believe it may not be in their best interest, said Rolnick. "As long as a single state engages in this practice, others will feel compelled to compete." [36]

When state competition "takes the form of preferential treatment for specific businesses," it undercuts the goal of having a strong national economy by causing some businesses to locate in places that might not be the best sites for them in the long run and also may decrease tax revenues so that money can't go to transportation projects or schools, for example, said Rolnick. [37]

"Ideally, you would expect a firm to locate where things are most efficient for it," not in the place that fought hardest to attract it, says Tonya Hansen, an assistant professor of economics at Minnesota State University Moorhead. "If a firm is only local because of an incentive," then it may not be operating in the most efficient business mode, she says.

Federal-level programs generally are more efficient than state competition because "they bring in more money, the money is more stable, and it blankets the 50 states" with similar incentives "so it's not pitting state against state," says Chalmers, at Cal State. In addition, the most blighted, neediest areas may have a better chance of capturing federal dollars because when decisions are made on the state level "the self-interest of politicians to get reelected" sometimes shifts dollars toward communities with more votes rather than high needs. ■

BACKGROUND

Early Competition

The first property-tax break for a North American business was awarded in 1640 — more than 125 years before the United States was founded. Given in the region that later became Connecticut, it started a persistent tradition. Along the way, doubts arose about whether interstate competition for business was an effective strategy. But local self-interest has won the day, and competitive use of business incentives has steadily increased. [38]

In 1791, Treasury Secretary Alexander Hamilton and other investors persuaded the New Jersey Assembly to exempt from state and county taxes a group called the Society for Useful Manufactures. They argued that the tax break

Continued on p. 217

Chronology

1960s-1970s

As the nation's hot economy slows, policymakers look for ways to create jobs.

1967
Sen. Robert F. Kennedy, D-Mass., introduces a bill to award tax credits to businesses for bringing jobs to low-income urban "enterprise zones," but Congress doesn't act.

1975
Fantus Corp. publishes first rankings of advantageous locations for facilities, including analysis of tax breaks and other incentives.

1980s-1990s

As manufacturing jobs dwindle, lawmakers hope tax-advantaged "enterprise zones" in low-income areas can create jobs.

1980
Prime Minister Margaret Thatcher's conservative government introduces enterprise zones in the United Kingdom. Presidential candidate Ronald Reagan and two New York representatives, Republican Jack Kemp and Democrat Robert Garcia, propose enterprise-zone bills, but they are not enacted. . . . Connecticut and Louisiana adopt enterprise-zone legislation in 1981.

1985
Early evidence that enterprise zones attract business to depressed areas — although sometimes only through relocation from nearby neighborhoods — spurs at least 40 states to enact enterprise-zone laws.

1993
First federal enterprise zones created in cities including Atlanta and Baltimore and rural areas including Mississippi's Delta region and Texas's Rio Grande Valley.

1997
Spurred by research showing that fierce state job competition doesn't create jobs but merely moves them, progressive lawmaker Rep. David Minge, D-Minn., proposes legislation to impose a heavy federal tax on states' location-based tax credits to business; Congress doesn't act on the measure.

2000s

State competition for business relocations heats up, but studies find most programs are ineffective.

2005
Sen. George Voinovich, R-Ohio, and bipartisan list of cosponsors introduce a bill to guarantee states the right to compete for business sites using tax incentives. Congress doesn't act on the measure.

2007
U.S. cities have built 28 major-league stadiums and arenas since 2000, as teams encourage cities to compete for them using taxpayer-funded incentives.

2008
As recession begins, some states require businesses to forgo incentive funds if job-creation goals aren't met.

2009
Walmart gets $1.8 million in tax credits to build five stores in Louisiana. . . . South Carolina attracts new Boeing plant by offering financial incentives and a lower-wage workforce because the state's right-to-work law makes unionization less likely. . . . In fierce competition to attract conventioneers, American cities have spent $23 billion since 1993 to build convention centers; 320 cities now have them.

2010
Reflecting the growing trend of transparency for subsidies, 37 states post some information online about business-subsidy recipients, up from 23 states in 2007.

2011
Jackson, Miss., officials propose tax breaks to keep a Sears store open after Sears Holdings Corp. announces closures of about 100 Sears and Kmart stores. . . . Newspaper publisher Gannett moves a 4-year-old call center out of Oklahoma despite receiving $260,000 in tax credits. . . . North Carolina lures Chiquita Brands International's headquarters from Cincinnati to Charlotte with $22 million in incentives.

2012
Boeing closes Wichita military aircraft plant, moves jobs to Texas and Oklahoma, two years after Kansas built a $43 million aerospace training center. . . . Proposal for a new Minnesota Vikings football stadium, with about $700 million in taxpayer funding, may reach state lawmakers this spring. . . . Indiana becomes first Rust Belt state and 23rd nationwide to enact business-friendly "right-to-work" legislation banning contracts requiring workers to join or pay dues to a union. . . . Louisiana Republican Gov. Bobby Jindal proposes allowing localities to offer 10-year tax abatements for facilities such as corporate headquarters and data centers.

Subsidies Spark Debate — and New Ideas

"At least give them to companies that reflect your values."

Public officials aren't likely to stop using tax incentives and other benefits to lure businesses and jobs to their communities. But experts see ways to make such subsidies more effective.

"It's hard to end the incentives, but you can try to mend them," says economist Robert W. Wassmer, a professor at California State University, Sacramento.

Step one might be for policymakers to expand their vision of where jobs come from, says Jonathan Q. Morgan, associate professor of public administration at the University of North Carolina, Chapel Hill. Recruiting businesses to a location by offering subsidies and other inducements has been at the top of most states' agendas, he says.

But "business retention and expansion and figuring out how to help" businesses grow that are already in a community is "an important and under-appreciated tool of job creation." Finding ways to help residents who want to "create new businesses from scratch" is another, Morgan says.

Public officials should consider offering tax breaks to lure business relocations only under very specific circumstances, Wassmer says. "Do a benefit-cost assessment" for any incentive under consideration, he says: "Am I just being played by this plant?" Only a company known to face a real choice between very suitable, profit-making locations should be offered an incentive package, Wassmer wrote. Otherwise, he argued, taxpayer dollars will go to companies that would have moved in anyway.

Furthermore, Wassmer advised sober analysis to make sure businesses receiving incentives will generate enough tax revenues, jobs and other benefits to more than compensate for the cost of the inducements. [1]

But it's not always easy to persuade local politicians to cast a skeptical eye on business incentives, Wassmer says.

"Asking those questions goes against the whole political movement" that's driven increased state competition on subsidies for decades, he says. "If more politicians would do it, though, we'd see the end of those bidding wars" between states and cities that consume public money.

Some researchers note that emotions can get in the way of making realistic decisions about which job-building strategies to use.

It's "enormously difficult to do economic development" with analysis done just by local policymakers and officials, says David L. Barkley, professor emeritus of applied economics at South Carolina's Clemson University. A person has a tendency to "exaggerate both the good and the bad of one's own area, saying, 'We have great schools' or 'Woe is me, we have no possibilities here,'" he says. Bringing in outside analysts who can be objective and know what competing regions are doing is necessary, he says.

"A public-private partnership" that includes scholars who study the regional economy could "figure out what kinds of business could thrive in a region, and that, I think, could be beneficial," says Laura Kalambokidis, associate professor of applied economics at the University of Minnesota, St. Paul. "Pitfalls include the fact that every state wants to be the next 'green revolution' state or the next Silicon Valley, but that simply won't work everywhere."

"If you're going to use incentives, at least give them to companies that reflect your values," such as paying workers well and having environmentally sustainable practices, says Jason Jolley, senior research director of the Carolina Center for Competitive Economies at the University of North Carolina, Chapel Hill. To accomplish that, states are better off requiring the legislature or another official body to choose each incentive recipient, rather than automatically offering incentives to any company that meets statutory requirements, Jolley says.

Research shows that some types of incentives are simply more effective at expanding employment and strengthening economies, scholars say.

Tax credits that simply reward companies for hiring the unemployed are relatively efficient and effective, partly because they have relatively low administrative costs, says David Neumark, professor of economics at the University of California, Irvine.

Tax credits that go only to new companies or companies with definite plans to expand also have promise, says Jolley.

Building in accountability provisions also matters. A periodic vetting process involving both the legislature and a state bureaucracy should be part of all incentive programs, to ensure "that they're worth doing long term," Jolley says.

A strong requirement for firms to report their employment numbers is also vital, says Tonya Hansen, assistant professor of economics at Minnesota State University Moorhead. Accurate performance data can be a basis for awarding further incentives and studying program effectiveness, she says.

States are getting smarter, says the University of North Carolina's Morgan. Incentive agreements that impose performance standards and force companies to return incentive money to the government if they don't meet agreed-upon goals will grow more common, "slowly but surely," he says.

— Marcia Clemmitt

[1] For background, see Robert W. Wassmer, "The Increasing Use of Property Tax Abatement as a Means of Promoting State and Local Economic Activity in the United States," in *Erosion of the Property Tax Base: Trends, Causes, and Consequences*, Nancy Augustine, Michael Bell, David Brunori and Joan Youngman, eds., 2009, pp. 221-259.

Continued from p. 214

would provide, "by moderate calculation," jobs for "20,000 persons" in the state. [39]

Nearby states reacted with horror. The "powers, rights and privileges, given to this company would be . . . very injurious to this state as well as other states," complained a member of the Pennsylvania House of Representatives. [40]

As the country grew, competition for businesses spread. After the Civil War, Southern states excused some companies from property taxes in an attempt to get Eastern and Midwestern industries to relocate.

In the 1920s, a wealthy industrial real estate executive, Felix Fantus, founded the Fantus Corp., the first consultancy to specialize in helping companies find the most advantageous locations for facilities — a service that included analysis of tax breaks and other incentives. By the 1950s, the company advised businesses to encourage state competition for lucrative incentive packages. [41]

Beginning in 1975, Fantus published the first state "business climate" rankings, which helped drive interstate competition on incentives. [42]

In the 1980s, worries began about American industrial jobs "getting slashed" by automation and foreign, low-wage competition, says Ohio State's Greenbaum. In hopes of bringing jobs back to the United States and placing them in struggling neighborhoods, the states and later the federal government established enterprise-zone programs. The zones "had appeal in a time when government budgets were limited, since they targeted" high-need areas with the incentives, he says.

Economics vs. Politics

The University of North Carolina's Jolley says that while studies show that location-based tax incentives don't work well, researchers "have failed to convince policymakers" of that.

"Our political and government structure is not set up for the most efficient economic policies," says Kalambokidis, of the University of Minnesota. Business supply chains and markets relate to geographic and demographic features that span regions rather than stop at city or state borders.

Most tax breaks decrease government revenues in later years — leaving "the cost to fall on future office-holders" — but demonstrate to voters that today's politicians are working to bring in jobs, says Greenbaum. As a result, he says, many lawmakers are reluctant to end them.

"One legislator told us, 'This is the best study we've ever ignored,' " says Jolley, whose legislature-requested 2008 study showed that North Carolina's incentives aren't effective. [43] "There was excitement" in the legislature when Jolley and colleagues said that scaling back the tax breaks would allow the state to lower corporate tax rates. But lawmakers so far have opted to keep the incentives. "They wouldn't be able to demonstrate" immediate budget savings if they traded the incentives for lower corporate tax breaks, and economic-development officials insist that "there's value in staying in the game," Jolley says.

Getty Images/Spencer Platt

Many communities, especially rural ones, offer substantial incentives to lure "big box" retail stores such as Walmart. In 2009, Walmart got $1.8 million in tax credits to build five stores in Louisiana. Bridgeton, Mo., approved a $7.2 million deal in 2010 to bring a single Walmart outlet to town. Above, a Walmart store in Valley Stream, N.Y.

Lawmakers and courts have long been ambivalent about location-based incentives.

Prior to 1789, when the Articles of Confederation governed the United States, "the states were very autonomous, and the standard was to impose tariffs" on out-of-state business to protect in-state companies, says Enrich, of Northeastern Law School. Part of the impetus to adopt the Constitution's stronger central government was to keep "interstate commerce" flowing, since "the Framers recognized that tariff competition between the states didn't make sense" for a country that needed to establish a strong national economy, he argues.

Under the Commerce Clause of the Constitution, Congress alone has the power to "regulate commerce . . . among the several states." The clause has been interpreted as banning states from regulating — including imposing taxes — in ways that interfere with interstate business dealings. [44]

If Cities Build Stadiums, Will Fans Come?

Critics view sports subsidies as waste of tax dollars.

The Minnesota Vikings ended the 2011 football season with three wins and 13 losses, but they could end the year victorious anyway. The Vikings may finally come out on top of a years-long battle to score a new, mostly public-funded stadium if state lawmakers approve a plan this spring supported by Democratic Gov. Mark Dayton. [1]

Minnesotans have wrangled for years over which jurisdiction should house the facility and how to cover two-thirds of the stadium's estimated $1 billion cost using public funds. Last fall, for example, Minneapolis and nearby Ramsey County both tried to sweeten their bids by proposing to levy new sales taxes without first getting voters' approval. But the legislature upheld a Minnesota law requiring a vote, and those plans, like earlier ones, went back to the drawing board. [2]

The push for tax-subsidized stadiums is happening not only in Minnesota. Professional sports teams and their supporters, who include some lawmakers, repeatedly argue that new arenas create jobs and spur economic activity. Regions from Los Angeles to Tampa Bay are locked in struggles over proposed facilities for both major- and minor-league teams. [3]

Between 2000 and 2007, 28 new arenas for Major League Baseball, basketball, football and hockey teams were built around the country at a total cost of about $9 billion, with at least $5 billion paid by taxpayers. [4]

"There is likely no major metropolitan area in this country that has not been held hostage at some point by the owner of a sports franchise" who threatened to move the team if taxpayers didn't ante up, Arthur J. Rolnick, former research director of the Federal Reserve Bank of Minneapolis, told Congress in 2007, when the Vikings battle was already under way.

At the time, construction had just begun for a new Minnesota Twins baseball stadium after a 10-year fight in which the team finally secured "about $400 million in public financing" from "a previously reluctant state legislature," said Rolnick, now a senior fellow at the University of Minnesota's Humphrey School of Public Affairs. [5]

Proponents say the public funding has value for communities. When jurisdictions in the Washington area vied for a Major League Baseball team that was set to come in 2005, supporters of a Northern Virginia site predicted their plan would give the state more than a $287 million annual boost. The National Football League urges cities to build large, updated stadiums partly to snag the annual Super Bowl, which the league claims brings about $400 million in business to the host city. [6]

Skeptics of taxpayer-funded business subsidies, along with many academic economists, disagree about the benefits, however.

The New York Yankees' stadium that opened in the Bronx in 2009 with substantial public funding created jobs, but most "are part time and low wage" and of little help to the neighborhood, argued Bettina Damiani, project director of Good Jobs New York, an advocacy group that seeks accountability in business subsidies.

"Few fields of empirical economic research offer virtual unanimity of findings. Yet independent work on the economic impact of stadiums and arenas has uniformly found there is no statistically positive correlation between sports facility construction and economic development," wrote Andrew Zimbalist, a professor of economics at Smith College, in Northampton, Mass. [7]

The Supreme Court has repeatedly upheld states' right to discriminate between in-state and out-of-state businesses by actions such as buying services from local rather than out-of-state businesses, since those aren't regulatory acts, just market activity, Enrich says. Rulings in regulation- and tax-related cases have been mixed.

In a case that reached the Supreme Court in 2006, Enrich and attorney Terry Lodge, working on behalf of some Michigan and Ohio residents, challenged tax incentives the city had offered to keep a DaimlerChrysler Jeep plant in town. They argued, among other things, that a property-tax exemption in the package interfered with interstate commerce because it favored the Ohio plant over other businesses, including out-of-state companies. The court didn't rule on the merits of the case, however, but dismissed the challenge on the grounds that the citizens who brought it had not suffered actual harm and therefore had no standing to sue. [45]

Congress should enact legislation clarifying which incentives are allowable and which are not, many say — and have said for decades.

"Congress alone can provide for a full and thorough canvassing of the multitudinous and intricate factors which compose the problem of the taxing freedom of the states and the needed limits on such state taxing power," Supreme Court Associate Justice Felix Frankfurter wrote in 1959. [46]

During the 1990s, Rep. David Minge, D-Minn., tried several times to blunt the effect of state incentives. His bills would have levied high federal taxes on any "preferential" state subsidies, thus making them worthless to businesses. [47]

Conversely, in 2005, two Ohio Republicans — U.S. Sen. George Voinovich and Rep. Patrick Tiberi — introduced legislation, with bipartisan support, to allow most subsidies. Their bill would have barred commerce clause-based legal challenges of "all state and local tax incentives," with seven narrow exceptions. [48]

No bill on incentives has made it out of committee.

The controversy extends beyond sports. Many cities use public funds to build convention centers, museums and similar venues in hopes of attracting paying visitors to town.

U.S. cities have poured more than $23 billion into convention centers from 1993 to 2009, when there were 320 throughout the country, reported *Next American City* magazine. [8]

As with sports arenas, hopes that a business boom will follow can be misplaced. As the number of convention centers rose between 1996 and 2003, attendance at many declined, the magazine reported. In response, many cities actually undertook major facility expansions, competing to snag the very biggest conventions, which previously found only a few cities with facilities large enough to host them, such as Las Vegas.

But that strategy has proved disappointing in many cities. A 420,000-square-foot expansion of Houston's George R. Brown Center, for example, was expected to bring 600,000 single-night visits to Houston in 2005. But it yielded only 220,000 — just over a third of expectations. [9]

— Marcia Clemmitt

Getty Images/Hannah Foslien

The Minnesota Vikings and Denver Broncos play at the Hubert H. Humphrey Metrodome in Minneapolis on Dec. 4, 2011. Minnesota lawmakers are considering long-debated plans to build a new $1 billion stadium, mostly with public funds.

[1] Mike Kaszuba, "Vikings Stadium Plan East of Dome Now on Fast Track," *Star Tribune* [Minneapolis], Feb. 5, 2012, www.startribune.com/politics/statelocal/138721284.html.

[2] Tom Scheck, "Dayton and Legislative Leaders Say Sales Tax Increase Won't Work for Stadium," MPR News, Minnesota Public Radio, Nov. 1, 2011, http://minnesota.publicradio.org/collections/special/columns/polinaut/archive/2011/11/dayton_and_legi.shtml.

[3] For background, see Michael Hunt, "NFL Teams Are Bold Because They Can Be," *Journal Sentinel* [Milwaukee], Feb. 9, 2012, www.jsonline.com/sports/nfl-teams-are-bold-because-they-can-be-iv44veu-139067354.html; Barry Wilner, "Goodell: 34 Teams Likely if LA Included," Associated Press/Globe [Boston], Feb. 3, 2012, http://articles.boston.com/2012-02-03/sports/31022006_1_concussion-research-la-stadium-brain-trauma.

[4] Sarah Wilhelm, "Public Funding of Sports Stadiums," Policy Perspectives, Center for Public Policy and Administration, University of Utah, April 30, 2008, www.imakenews.com/cppa/e_article001083889.cfm?x=b11,0,w.

[5] Arthur J. Rolnick, "Congress Should End the Economic War Among the States Testimony," The Federal Reserve Bank of Minneapolis website, Oct. 10, 2007, www.minneapolisfed.org/publications_papers/studies/econwar/rolnick_testimony_2007.cfm.

[6] Robert A. Baade, Robert Baumann, and Victor A. Matheson, "Selling the Game: Estimating the Economic Impact of Professional Sports Through Taxable Sales," *Southern Economic Journal*, January 2008, pp. 794-810, www.allbusiness.com/government/public-finance-taxes-taxation/7068215-1.html.

[7] Quoted in "Build It and They Will Come: Do Taxpayer-Financed Sports Stadiums, Convention Centers and Hotels Deliver as Promised For America's Cities?" Hearing transcript, House Oversight and Government Reform Domestic Policy Subcommittee, March 29, 2007, www.gpo.gov/fdsys/pkg/CHRG-110hhrg38037/html/CHRG-110hhrg38037.htm.

[8] Josh Stevens, "Unconventional Thinking," *Next American City*, Summer 2009, http://americancity.org/magazine/article/unconventional-thinking.

[9] *Ibid.*

Regional Cooperation and Accountability

Regional cooperation on economic development is still rare, but some states seek greater accountability for subsidies.

Some multistate economic-development programs do exist, says Rutgers' Seneca. For example, the New York/New Jersey Port Authority opened in 1921, with congressional authorization, to develop the harbor region the states share. [49] Since economic regions don't stop at state boundaries, "that's the kind of thing that gives a positive return on investment," Seneca said.

Two jurisdictions in the Columbus, Ohio, area recently "agreed to disarm from competition" after the headquarters of the Bob Evans restaurant chain "got a lot of state incentives to move from a depressed area" in the region "to a higher-income area nearby," says Ohio State's Greenbaum. To avoid an escalating economic arms race — and to limit the harm to the lower-income area that lost the facility — the towns agreed to share tax revenues from the project, he says.

Regional agreements are tough to enforce, however, says Enrich. In the 1990s, Illinois, Indiana and Wisconsin agreed not to discriminate against employers based in any of the states, but after one state was suspected of doing so, the compact broke down, he says.

Some advocacy groups, such as Good Jobs First, are pushing for greater accountability for subsidies, such as requiring public disclosure and periodic legislative scrutiny of tax credits or other incentives. [50]

Some state programs have accountability features. New Jersey's Business Employment Incentive Program "has some very attractive elements that other states have emulated" such as paying companies only if they create a net number of new jobs, based on verifiable tax records, says Seneca. [51]

As of December 2010, 37 states posted online information about what companies received at least one major state subsidy, up from only 23 states that did so in 2007, according to Good Jobs First. [52]

Yet, many politicians continue to resist transparency. In 2010, for example, Gov. Arnold Schwarzenegger, R-Calif., vetoed a bill that would have disclosed tax-credit recipients. [53]

"This is public money and there is a big accountability issue, but you can't make the negotiation public; your prospects" — businesses considering a move to one's state — "will walk away and just laugh at you," said Graham Toft, president of the Indiana Economic Development Council. [54]

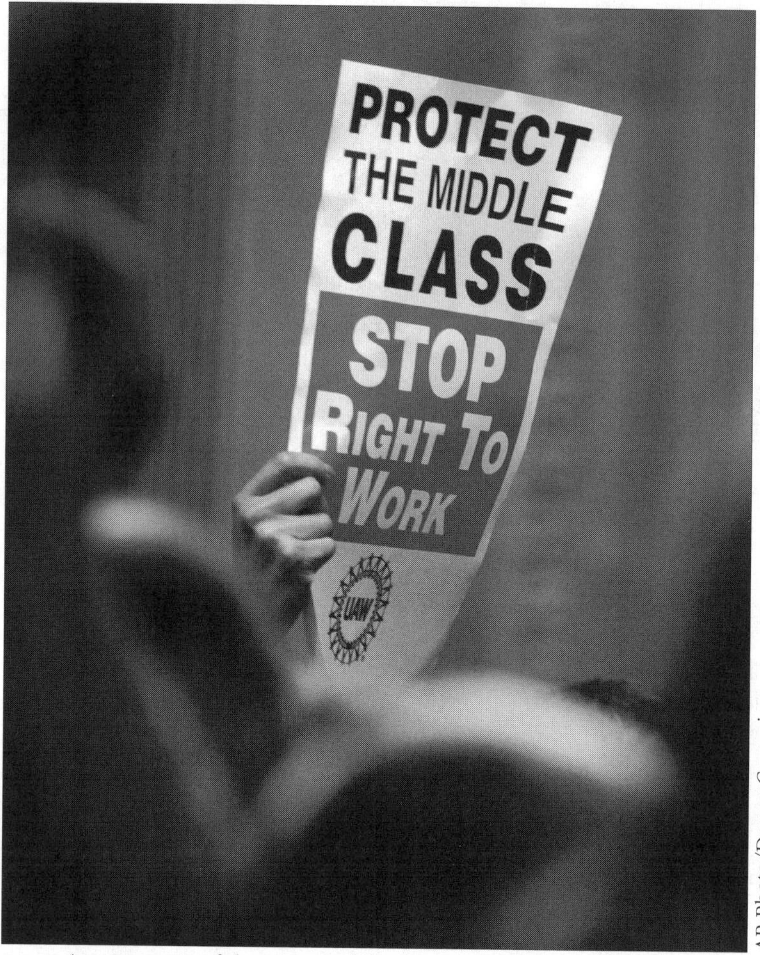

AP Photo/DarronCummings

An opponent of the proposed "right-to-work" law in Indiana demonstrates outside the State House on Jan. 23, 2012. On Feb. 1 Indiana became the 23rd state to enact such legislation, which bans workplace contracts requiring people to join or pay dues to a union. Republican governors and state legislators have pushed the laws, which they say give states a business-friendly edge in jobs competition.

Current Situation

Tight Times

With jobs on voters' minds, many policymakers are pushing new incentive competition in 2012.

In February, Louisiana's Republican governor, Bobby Jindal, proposed allowing localities to offer up to 10 years of tax breaks to facilities such as corporate headquarters, data centers and research-and-development operations. The move would ultimately bring 10,000 jobs, Jindal said. [55]

Last December, the Illinois legislature and Democratic Gov. Pat Quinn approved at least $100 million in tax breaks to keep Sears Holdings Co. and the Chicago Mercantile Exchange, a financial and commodities trading market, in the state. [56] "If Ohio is offering $400 million to Sears . . . we will defend ourselves," said Quinn. [57]

States are adopting many kinds of tax incentives. "Tax stabilization agreements" — which guarantee a business's tax rates won't rise — are used in 12 states, says Hansen, of Minnesota State University. "Nearly everything else" in the way of tax incentives is used by at least 40 states today, she says. *(See graph, p. 212.)*

Some states are courting not just employers but the site-location consultants who advise corporations about where to locate. Last spring, New Jersey economic-development officials entertained executives from the top 12 site-location firms. From the comfort of a hotel suite, they watched the NCAA basketball tournament and met with New Jersey's governor. [58]

Concerns are building about whether incentives deliver.

A group of local governments in the St. Louis area recently determined that more than $5.8 billion in public funds had gone to business incentives over the past 20 years, more than 80 percent of it to develop big-box stores and shopping centers. Despite the huge outlay, the number of retail jobs ticked up only slightly, "retail sales or per capita spending have not increased in years" and more than 600 small businesses closed, eliminating nearly as many jobs as the new stores brought in, said the group. [59]

Continued on p. 222

At Issue:

Do "right-to-work" laws help states attract businesses?

PAUL KERSEY
DIRECTOR OF LABOR POLICY, MACKINAC CENTER FOR PUBLIC POLICY

WRITTEN FOR *CQ RESEARCHER*, MARCH 2012

yes

Under a state right-to-work law, an employee cannot be forced to pay union dues or fees as a condition of employment; individual workers can support a union or withhold their support. The law does not change the process for recognizing a union or lessen the obligation to bargain with a union once it has proved it has majority support in the workforce. Since the evidence indicates that most workers join the union in their workplace voluntarily in right-to-work states, right-to-work is actually a fairly modest change.

Yet unions treat right-to-work with alarm, while employers respond very positively to the provision of worker choice.

The attraction of right-to-work for employers is hard to deny. Between 2002 and 2010, employment was up 3 percent on average in right-to-work states and down 3 percent in non-right-to-work states. Union apologists have argued that the job gains in right-to-work states have been due to weather or other factors, but research into economic growth along the borders between right-to-work and non-right-to-work states shows that job growth is one-third higher in counties that have right-to-work than in neighboring counties that don't.

In a right-to-work state, employers know that unions will have the resources workers want them to have, no more and no less. Union officials must pay close attention to the desires of workers who can leave the union and keep their dues money if they are not happy.

Without that protection, unions are tempted to substitute their own ideological agenda for workers' real-world interests. Most employers accept the need for bargaining with employees and understand that over the long term they are better off if employees are happy with their wages and working conditions. If workers prefer to bargain collectively, so be it, but employers want to know that the union they bargain with will pursue the best interests of their employees, not the preferences of union officials.

But the real reason why states should pass right-to-work laws is because they respect the First Amendment right of workers to associate as they see fit, to join a union or not, to give or withhold support from an institution that they may or may not support. If political leaders really value workers, in terms of both recognizing their rights and respecting their judgment, they won't hesitate to give workers that choice. There is every reason to have confidence that workers will use that choice responsibly, to the benefit of both businesses and workers themselves.

GORDON LAFER
ASSOCIATE PROFESSOR, LABOR EDUCATION AND RESEARCH CENTER UNIVERSITY OF OREGON

WRITTEN FOR *CQ RESEARCHER*, MARCH 2012

no

In 2011-12, statehouses across the country saw renewed battles over so-called "right-to-work" (RTW) laws. Contrary to what the public might assume, right-to-work does not guarantee anyone a job. Rather, it makes it illegal for unions to require each employee who benefits from the terms of a contract to pay his or her fair share of the costs of administering it.

The aim of RTW — according to its backers — is to cut wages and benefits on the gamble that this will bring more jobs into a state. As the Indiana Chamber of Commerce explains, "unionization increases labor costs," and therefore "makes a given location a less attractive place to invest new capital." By giving up unions and lowering wages, workers are supposed to increase their desirability in the eyes of manufacturers.

Research shows that RTW cuts wages and benefits — but fails to promote job growth. According to multiple studies, RTW laws lower average income by about $1,500 a year and decrease the odds of getting health insurance or a pension through your job — for union and nonunion workers. But RTW does not boost job growth.

It may be that companies in the 1980s moved to RTW states in search of lower wages. But in the globalized economy, companies looking for cheap labor overwhelmingly look to China or Mexico.

In this sense, the most important case study for any state considering RTW in 2012 is that of Oklahoma, which adopted RTW in the post-NAFTA era.

When Oklahoma debated RTW in 2001, corporate location consultants told legislators that if the state adopted RTW, it would see "eight to 10 times as many prospects." What happened? The number of new companies coming into the state has fallen by one-third in the 10 years since RTW was adopted. Manufacturing employment has decreased 30 percent.

Surveys of manufacturers confirm that RTW is not a significant draw; in 2010 manufacturers ranked it 16th among factors affecting location decisions. For higher-tech, higher-wage employers, nine of the 10 most-favored states are non-RTW.

RTW is promoted as providing a competitive advantage to a state. But to the extent more states go RTW — or a national bill passes — wages will be lowered in all states, no one will have an advantage and the number of jobs in the country will be exactly the same as before. This is how RTW undermines the American middle class.

Continued from p. 220

Right to Work

Republican governors and state legislators have pushed to enact "right-to-work" laws that ban workplace contracts requiring people to join or pay dues to a union. Proponents argue that the laws give states a business-friendly edge in the jobs competition. (*See "At Issue," p. 221.*)

On Feb. 1, Indiana became the 23rd state to enact right-to-work legislation and the first in the once-vibrant Midwest and Northeastern industrial heartland to do so. [60] New Hampshire, Michigan, Wisconsin and Ohio also are considering such measures. [61]

Opponents see no relationship between right-to-work laws and job creation. "Both the highest and the lowest unemployment rates in the country are found in states" with right-to-work laws, wrote Gordon Lafer, an associate professor of political economics at the University of Oregon's Labor Education and Research Center. The auto industry's continued commitment to Michigan — traditionally a union bastion — shows that workforce skills and state technology-development projects are more important to at least some companies, he wrote. [62]

But James Hohman, assistant director of fiscal policy at the Mackinac Center for Public Policy, a free market-oriented think tank in Midland, Mich., argued that because Michigan has no right-to-work law, the state was forced to offer millions of dollars in incentives to retain the car companies. That would not have been necessary had the state had "an attractive business environment," with a right-to-work law, Hohman said. [63]

Even as some proponents of location-based incentives question their value, fierce struggles among states to lure employers are likely to continue. "It's like a nuclear-arms standstill. No one is willing to blink first."

—Jon Shure

Director, State Fiscal Strategies, Center on Budget and Policy Priorities

Tax incentives have made an appearance in the 2012 presidential race. In January, former House Speaker Newt Gingrich, R-Ga., blasted former Sen. Rick Santorum, R-Pa., for endorsing 1997 Pennsylvania legislation that gave the Pittsburgh Steelers football team and Pittsburgh Pirates baseball team taxpayer dollars for stadiums — often touted as job creators — without requiring repayment. [64] (*See sidebar, p. 218.*)

Meanwhile, another contender for the Republican presidential nomination, former Massachusetts Gov. Mitt Romney, approved at least one location-based tax break for job creation as governor: a tax rebate for biotechnology companies. [65]

President Obama is proposing a new federal "growth zone" plan to replace the longstanding enterprise zone program. Under the new plan, which Congress so far has not approved, 20 rural and urban areas with economic-growth potential would get federal funds for business tax credits and other incentives for job creation. [66]

Some economists say such federally administered programs work better than state incentives in part because they're less politicized. However, any locality offering incentives, no matter how they're administered and paid for, feeds the fevered competition, says Hansen at Minnesota State. "No state or locality will unilaterally disarm" unless federal policy simply eliminates the use of incentives altogether, she says. ■

OUTLOOK

Beyond Incentives

Even some incentive proponents now question whether interstate competition for jobs is the best strategy. Hanging over the whole enterprise, meanwhile, is the question of whether the United States can actually expand the number of good jobs.

Fierce struggles among states to lure employers are likely to remain the norm for some time, many say.

"It's like a nuclear-arms standstill. No one is willing to blink first," said Jon Shure, director of state fiscal strategies at the Center on Budget and Policy Priorities, a liberal think tank in Washington. [67]

Among state officials, "a few more are skeptical than 10 years ago, but an awful lot still say, 'We need this tool,' " says Enrich, of Northeastern University Law School.

Still, says the University of North Carolina's Morgan, incentive agreements that impose performance standards and force companies to return incentive money to the government if they don't meet agreed-upon goals will grow more common "slowly but surely," he says.

Congress has the constitutional right to either ban or authorize incentive competition, but while legislation giving a green light to it seemed a strong possibility several years ago, the current Senate's Democratic leadership reportedly wouldn't support such a move, says Enrich.

Even without location-based incentives, localities engaged in fierce competition for jobs can still spur employment in their areas, says Karen Chapple, associate director of the Institute of Urban and Regional Development at the University of California, Berkeley. For example, governments might offer various kinds of targeted assistance to businesses that try to create entirely new labor-intensive industries, she says.

Meanwhile, with the environment a growing concern, localities might offer expert assistance and even cash to business startups interested in "green retrofitting" of buildings or in recycling throwaway materials into new products such as carpets, she says. Recycling-based manufacture could be a net job creator because it would require more workers than the old throwaway economy, and "states and local economies can do something to help develop these new capacities and help develop markets" for new products, she says.

Offshore competition has made it more and more difficult to create jobs in America, "but energy and climate change could someday change that," bringing manufacturing and agriculture back to America so that states no longer have to engage in such bitter rivalries for a dwindling number of good jobs, adds California State's Wassmer. "Shipping all these containers from China" may become too costly and environmentally damaging, "and you might end up with more domestic goods production" — and the jobs that go with it. ■

Notes

[1] For background, see Aubrey Cohen, "Boeing Closing Wichita Plant," *Seattle Post-Intelligencer*, Jan. 4, 2012, www.seattlepi.com/business/boeing/article/Boeing-closing-Wichita-plant-2440784.php; and Emily Knapp, "Governments Rob Taxpayers of Billions to Fund Ill-advised Incentive Programs," *Wall St. Cheat Sheet*, Jan. 19, 2012, http://wallstcheatsheet.com/stocks/governments-rob-tax-payers-of-billions-to-fund-ill-advised-incentive-programs.html.

[2] Cohen, *ibid.*

[3] Jonathan Q. Morgan and David M. Lawrence, "Economic Development," County and Municipal Government in North Carolina, Chapel Hill School of Government, 2007, p. 2, http://sogpubs.unc.edu/cmg/cmg26.pdf. Morgan is an associate professor of public administration; Lawrence is now retired as a professor of government.

[4] *Ibid.*

[5] For background, see "Boeing Tax Grab Shows Peril of Offering Tax Dollars for Growth," Bloomberg, Jan. 19, 2012, www.bloomberg.com/news/2012-01-19/boeing-job-grab-shows-peril-of-offering-tax-dollars-for-growth.html, and "Money-Back Guarantees for Taxpayers," Good Jobs First, January 2012, www.goodjobsfirst.org/moneyback. Alan Peters and Peter Fisher, "The Failures of Economic Development Incentives," *Journal of the American Planning Association*, Issue 1, 2004, pp. 27-37.

[6] Ronald J. Hansen, "Arizona Tax Credits Rising for Business," *The Arizona Republic*, Nov. 22, 2011, www.azcentral.com/news/articles/2011/11/21/20111121arizona-tax-credits-rising-for-business.html.

[7] "Kentucky Business Climate Boosted by State Incentives," *BusinessClimate.com*, http://businessclimate.com/kentucky-economic-development/kentucky-business-climate-boosted-state-incentives.

[8] Edward M. Mazze, "The Economic Impact of the Motion Picture Production Tax Credit on the Rhode island Economy for the Years 2005-2009," www.film.ri.gov/MazzeStudy.pdf.

[9] Ruby Gonzales, "Pico Rivera Faces Paying Rent Even With Borders Leaving," *Whittier Daily News* [Calif.], March 19, 2011, www.whittierdailynews.com/news/ci_17652157.

[10] Stacy Mitchell, "Don't Subsidize Big Boxes at Local Shops' Expense," *Bloomberg BusinessWeek*, Sept. 9, 2011, www.businessweek.com/small-business/dont-subsidize-big-boxes-at-local-shops-expense-09092011.html.

[11] Mark Robyn, "2012 State Business Tax Climate Index," Jan. 25, 2012, www.taxfoundation.org/news/show/22658.html; "The Best States for Business," *Forbes*, www.forbes.com/pictures/mli45ggdd/17-south-dakota/#content.

[12] "Unemployment Rates — Most Current Available," South Dakota Department of Labor and Regulation, http://dlr.sd.gov/unemploymentrate.aspx; "Employment Situation Summary," U.S. Bureau of Labor Statistics news release, Feb. 3, 2012, www.bls.gov/news.release/empsit.nr0.htm.

[13] "The Poorest Counties in the America," MSN Money, http://money.msn.com/family-money/the-poorest-counties-in-america.

[14] Vincent Fernando and Betty Jin, "10 States With Ridiculously Low Unemployment," MSNBC/Business Insider, www.msnbc.msn.com/id/38838429/ns/business-us_business/t/states-ridiculously-low-unemployment/#.TzLAcoH0izV.

[15] Terry F. Buss, "The Effect of State Tax Incentives on Economic Growth and Firm Location Decisions: An Overview of the Literature," *Economic Development Quarterly*, February 2001, http://edq.sagepub.com/content/15/1/90.abstract.

[16] Quoted in Kiersten Valle Pittman and Tim Funk, "In Scramble for New Jobs, Incentives Play a Key Role," *Idaho Statesman*/McClatchy Newspapers, Dec. 13, 2011, www.idahostatesman.com/2011/12/13/1914317/in-scramble-for-new-jobs-incentives.html.

[17] David Stade and Katy Stech, "Boeing's Whopping Incentives," *The Post and Courier* [Charleston], Jan. 17, 2010, www.postandcourier.com/news/2010/jan/17/boeings-whopping-incentives.

[18] Pittman and Funk, *op. cit.*

[19] Bill Schweke, "Major Questions About Economic Development, Part V," CFED website, Dec. 2, 2009, http://cfed.org/blog/inclusiveeconomy/major_questions_about_economic_development_part_v.

[20] Mali R. Schantz-Feld, "Top Site Selection Factors: Tax Rates, Exemptions, and Incentives — Keeping an Eye on the Competition," *Area Development*, November 2011, www.areadevelopment.com/laborEducation/November2011/site-selection-factors-skilled-labor-220743.shtml.

[21] For background, see "2011 Best-performing Cities," Milken Institute, http://bestcities.milkeninstitute.org.

[22] Timothy J. Bartik, "Boon or Boondoggle? The Debate Over State and Local Economic Development Policies," in *Who Benefits from State and Local Economic Development Policies?* W.E. Upjohn Institute for Employment Research, pp. 1-16, http://research.upjohn.org/up_bookchapters/88.

[23] Scott Loveridge, "Local Industrial Recruitment: Boondoggle or Boon?" May 1995, www.rri.wvu.edu/pdffiles/wp9510.pdf.

[24] "Taxes and Economic Development 101," Institute on Taxation and Economic Policy, September 2011, www.itepnet.org/pdf/pb42.pdf.

[25] Timothy J. Bartik, "State Economic Development Policies: What Works," presentation at the Center on Budget and Policy Priorities Annual State Fiscal Policy Conference, Washington, D.C., Nov. 30, 2011, http://research.upjohn.org/presentations/27.

[26] Alice Hines, "As Sears Plans Closings, Cities Fight to Keep Stores," *Huffington Post*, Jan. 26, 2012, www.huffingtonpost.com/2012/01/26/sears-closes-cities_n_1231326.html?ref=most-popular.

[27] Quoted in Ashli Sims, "Tulsa Taxpayers Upset After Company Receiving State Rebate Shuts Down," NewsOn6 website, April 11, 2011, www.newson6.com/story/14426304/quality-jobs-program.

[28] Bartik, "Boon or Boondoggle?" *op. cit.*

[29] Quoted in Penelope Lemov, "Is the Hollywood Tax Credit Under Attack?" *Governing*, March 16, 2011, www.governing.com/columns/public-finance/hollywood-tax-credit-under-attack.html; for background, see "Tax Credits for Filmmakers — By U.S. State and Canadian Province," Making the Movie website, http://makingthemovie.info/2006/07/tax-credits-for-filmmakers-state-by-state.html.

[30] Quoted in Brian R. Hook, "Critics Blast Tax Credit Proposals by Missouri Review Panel," Missouri Watchdog website, Dec. 2, 2010, http://missouri.watchdog.org/7972/critics-blast-tax-credit-proposals-by-missouri-review-panel.

[31] Mark Cassell, "Zoned Out; Distribution and Benefits in Ohio's Enterprise Zone Program," Policy Matters Ohio, October 2003, www.kent.edu/cpapp/research/upload/eco-enterprise-zones.pdf.

[32] Greg LeRoy and Leigh McIlvaine, "Paid to Sprawl: Subsidized Job Flight for Cleveland and Cincinnati," Good Jobs First, www.goodjobsfirst.org/paidtosprawl, July 2011.

[33] William Fulton, *Romancing the Smokestack: How Cities and States Pursue Prosperity* (2010), p. 4.

[34] Robyn, *op. cit.*

[35] Arthur J. Rolnick, "Congress Should End the Economic War Among the States," The Federal Reserve Bank of Minneapolis website, Oct. 10, 2007, www.minneapolisfed.org/publications_papers/studies/econwar/rolnick_testimony_2007.cfm.

[36] Quoted in "Professional Sports Stadiums: Do They Divert Public Funds From Critical Public Infrastructure?" Hearing transcript, House Oversight and Government Reform Domestic Policy Subcommittee, Oct. 10, 2007.

[37] *Ibid.*

[38] For background, see Robert W. Wassmer, "The Increasing Use of Property Tax Abatement as a Means of Promoting State and Local Economic Activity in the United States," in Nancy Augustine, Michael Bell, David Brunori and Joan Youngman, eds., *Erosion of the Property Tax Base: Trends, Causes and Consequences* (2009), pp. 221-259, and P.G. Marshall, "Do Enterprise Zones Work?" *Editorial Research Reports*, 1989 (Vol. 1).

[39] Joseph J. Seneca, James W. Hughes and George R. Nagle, "An Assessment of the New Jersey Business Employment Incentive Program," July 27, 2004, www.policy.rutgers.edu/reports/beip/beip_report.pdf.

[40] Quoted in *ibid.*

[41] Ann R. Magnusen and Katherine Nesse, "Institutional and Political Determinants of Incentive Competition," in *Reining in the Competition for Capital*, W.E. Upjohn Institute for Employment Research, 2007, pp. 1-42, http://research.upjohn.org/up_bookchapters/237.

[42] *Ibid.*

[43] Brent Lane and G. Jason Jolley, "An Evaluation of North Carolina's Economic Development Incentive Programs: Summary of Analysis, Findings and Recommendations," University of North Carolina Center for Competitive Economies, Jan. 21, 2009, www.kenan-flagler.unc.edu/kenan-institute/about/organization/competitive-economies/~/media/Files/kenaninstitute/UNC_KenanInstitute_NCIncentivesStudy.ashx.

[44] For background, see David G. Savage, *Guide to the U.S. Supreme Court* (5th ed.) (2010), Vol. 1, p. 142.

[45] The decision is *DaimlerChrysler v. Cuno*, 547 U.S. 332 (2006). For background, see Russell Mokhiber and Robert Weissman, "Corporate Shakedown in Toledo," *Common Dreams*, Feb. 8, 2000, www.commondreams.org/views/021000-105.htm, and Chris Atkins, *Cuno v. DaimlerChrysler: A Pyrrhic Victory for Economic Neutrality*, Fiscal Facts, Tax Foundation, April 18, 2005, www.taxfoundation.org/publications/show/344.html.

[46] *Northwestern States Portland Cement Co. v. Minnesota*, 358 U.S. 450 (1959) (Frankfurter, J. dissenting). "Dissent of Justice Felix Frankfurter," http://caselaw.lp.findlaw.com/scripts/getcase.pl?court=us&vol=358&invol=450.

[47] Quoted in "Professional Sports Stadiums: Do They Divert Public Funds From Critical Public Infrastructure?" Hearing transcript, House Oversight and Government Reform Domestic Policy Subcommittee, Oct. 10, 2007, Government Printing Office, www.gpo.gov/fdsys/pkg/CHRG-110hhrg51756/html/CHRG-110hhrg51756.htm; for background, see H.R. 3044.IH, Thomas, Library of Congress, http://thomas.loc.gov/cgi-bin/query/z?c105:H.R.3044.IH:.

[48] For background, see "S. 1066: Economic Development Act of 2005," govtrack.us, www.govtrack.us/congress/bill.xpd?bill=s109-1066&tab=summary; Michael Mazerov, "Should Congress Authorize States to Continue Giving Tax Breaks to Businesses?" Center on Budget and Policy Priorities, June 30, 2005, www.cbpp.org/files/2-18-05sfp.pdf; "Voinovich, Tiberi, Stabenow and Chandler Propose Bill to Protect Key Economic Development Tools," press release, website of Rep. Pat Tiberi, May 19, 2005, http://tiberi.house.gov/News/DocumentSingle.aspx?DocumentID=32632.

[49] For background, see "History of the Port Authority," The Port Authority of New York & New

About the Author

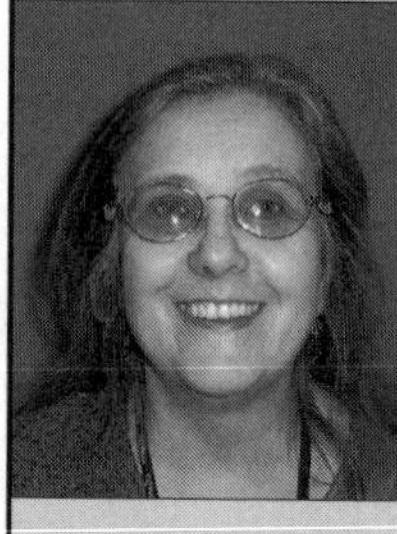

Staff writer **Marcia Clemmitt** is a veteran social-policy reporter who previously served as editor in chief of *Medicine & Health* and staff writer for *The Scientist*. She has also been a high school math and physics teacher. She holds a liberal arts and sciences degree from St. John's College, Annapolis, and a master's degree in English from Georgetown University. Her recent reports include "Income Inequality" and "Financial Industry Overhaul."

Jersey, www.panynj.gov/about/history-port-authority.html.

[50] For background, see "Key Reforms: Overview," Good Jobs First website, www.goodjobsfirst.org/accountable-development/key-reforms-overview.

[51] For background, Seneca, Hughes and Nagle, *op. cit.*

[52] "Show Us the Subsidies," Good Jobs First, December 2010, www.goodjobsfirst.org/sites/default/files/docs/pdf/showusthesubsidiesrpt.pdf.

[53] Ronald J. Hansen, "Ariz. Tax Credits Rising for Business," *Arizona Republic*, Nov. 22, 2011, www.azcentral.com/arizonarepublic/news/articles/2011/11/21/20111121arizona-tax-credits-rising-for-business.html.

[54] Quoted in David Fettig, "A Report from the Battlefield," *The Region*, Minneapolis Federal Reserve Bank, June 1, 1996, www.minneapolisfed.org/publications_papers/pub_display.cfm?id=3660.

[55] Ed Anderson, "Proposed Business Tax Breaks Could Produce 10,000 Jobs, Gov. Bobby Jindal Says," *The Times Picayune* [New Orleans], Feb. 2, 2012, www.nola.com/business/index.ssf/2012/02/proposed_business_tax_breaks_c.html.

[56] Christopher Wills and David Mercer, "In the Game of Tax Breaks, States Play at Their Own Risk," Associated Press/*Salt Lake Tribune*, Dec. 17, 2011, www.sltrib.com/sltrib/money/53126758-79/tax-illinois-state-companies.html.csp.

[57] Quoted in Kathy Bergen, "Tax Breaks for Sears, CME Head to Governor," *Chicago Tribune*, Dec. 14, 2011, http://articles.chicagotribune.com/2011-12-14/business/ct-biz-1214-cme-sears-20111214_1_corporate-income-tax-tax-rate-business-tax.

[58] Alejandra Cancino and Julia Wernau, "States Go All Out With Tax Incentives, Deals to Hook Firms," *The Chicago Tribune*, May 15, 2011, http://articles.chicagotribune.com/2011-05-15/business/ct-biz-0515-incentives-20110515_1_tax-incentives-state-incentives-illinois-companies.

[59] "An Assessment of the Effectiveness and Fiscal Impacts of the Use of Development Incentives in the St. Louis Region," East-West Gateway Council of Governments, January 2011, www.ewgateway.org/pdffiles/library/dirr/TIF-FinalRpt.pdf, and Stacy Mitchell, "Don't Subsidize Big Boxes at Local Shops' Expense," *Bloomberg Businessweek*, Sept. 9, 2011, www.businessweek.com/small-business/dont-subsidize-big-boxes-at-local-shops-expense-09092011.html.

[60] For background, see Mary Beth Schneider and Chris Sikich, "Indiana Becomes Rust Belt's First Right-to-Work State," *The Indianapolis Star/USA Today*, Feb. 2, 2012, www.usatoday.com/news/nation/story/2012-02-01/indiana-right-to-work-bill/52916356/1.

[61] For background, see Steven Greenhouse, "Strained States Turning to Laws to Curb Labor Unions," *The New York Times*, Jan. 3, 2011, www.nytimes.com/2011/01/04/business/04labor.html?pagewanted=all; Kyle Maichle, "Midwest States Are Focus of a New Push for Right-to-Work in 2011," Dec. 10, 2010, http://ballotpedia.org/wiki/index.php/Midwest_states_are_focus_of_a_new_push_for_Right-To-Work_in_2011.

[62] Gordon Lafer, 'Right to Work': The Wrong Answer for Michigan's Economy, *EPI Briefing Paper*, Economic Policy Institute, Sept. 15, 2011, www.epi.org/publication/right-to-work-michigan-economy. Garry Rayno, "Hundreds Gather to Fight Right-to-work Bill," *UnionLeader.com*, Feb. 10, 2012, www.unionleader.com/article/20120210/NEWS06/702109989.

[63] Quoted in Tom Gantert, "Debate: Could Union Costs Be Pricing Michigan Out of Auto Jobs?" CAPCON: Michigan Capitol Confidential, Mackinac Center for Public Policy, Oct. 13, 2011, www.michigancapitolconfidential.com/15873.

[64] Pema Levy, "Newt Goes Ballistic on Pretty Much Everyone," *Talking Points Memo*, Jan. 9, 2012, http://2012.talkingpointsmemo.com/2012/01/newt-is-not-here-to-make-friends.php; for background, see Kevin Clark Forsythe, "The Stadium Game Pittsburgh Style: Observations on the Latest Round of Publicly Financed Stadia in Steel Town, USA, and Comparisons With 28 Other Major League Teams," *Marquette Sports Law Review*, Spring 2000, http://scholarship.law.marquette.edu/cgi/viewcontent.cgi?article=1470&context=sportslaw.

[65] Jeanne Sahadi, "Mitt Romney's Tax Record: Tax Cutter or Tax Hiker?" *CNNMoney*, Jan. 23, 2012, http://money.cnn.com/2012/01/23/news/economy/Romney_tax_record/index.htm.

[66] For background, see "2012 Federal Budget Proposals," CCH Group, Feb. 17, 2011, http://tax.cchgroup.com/downloads/files/pdfs/legislation/treasury-greenbook.pdf.

[67] Quoted in Cancino and Wernau, *op. cit.*

FOR MORE INFORMATION

Area Development, www.areadevelopment.com. Advertising-supported magazine for the site-location industry.

Good Jobs First, 1616 P St., N.W., Suite 210, Washington, DC 20036; 202-232-1616; www.goodjobsfirst.org. Research and advocacy group that tracks accountability in economic-development subsidies.

HandMade in America, P.O. Box 2089, Asheville, NC 28802; 828-252-0121; www.handmadeinamerica.org. Group that works to revitalize small towns in North Carolina through small-scale economic development.

International Economic Development Council, 734 15th St., N.W., Suite 900, Washington, DC 20005; 202-223-7800; www.iedconline.org. Membership group for the economic-development profession.

New Carolina, 1411 Gervais St., Suite 315, Columbia, SC 29201; 803-760-1400; www.newcarolina.org. Group that works on public and private projects to strengthen industry clusters in South Carolina.

Site Selection, 6625 The Corners Parkway, Suite 200, Norcross, GA 30092-2901; 770-446-6996; www.siteselection.com. Magazine of the Industrial Asset Management Council; covers corporate real estate and economic development.

The Tax Foundation, National Press Building, 529 14th St., N.W., Suite 420, Washington, DC 20045-1000; 202-464-6200; http://taxfoundation.org. Research group that publishes state business-climate rankings.

W.E. Upjohn Institute for Employment Research, 300 S. Westnedge Ave., Kalamazoo, MI 49007-4686; 269-343-5541; www.upjohninst.org. Research group that studies ways to prevent unemployment.

Bibliography

Selected Sources

Books

Fulton, William, *Romancing the Smokestack: How Cities and States Pursue Prosperity*, Solimar Books, 2010.
In a collection of articles, a longtime economic-development analyst describes the many methods cities use to attract and retain jobs and businesses.

LeRoy, Greg, *The Great American Jobs Scam: Corporate Tax Dodging and the Myth of Job Creation*, Berrett-Koehler Publishers, 2005.
The head of the advocacy group Good Jobs First, which promotes accountability for tax subsidies, argues that case studies demonstrate community harm from interstate and inter-local subsidy competition, including deteriorating infrastructure and sprawl.

Articles

Johnston, David Cay, "On the Dole, Corporate Style," Tax.com, Jan. 4, 2011.
Tax breaks for business are increasing worldwide, but Canada and the European Union are trying to curb the trend. Some sought-after businesses, such as companies that store data for Internet giants Yahoo! and Google, produce few jobs and therefore may be particularly questionable recipients of subsidies.

Pittman, Kirsten Valle, and Tim Funk, "In Scramble for New Jobs, Incentives Play a Key Role," *Idaho Statesman*/McClatchy Newspapers, Dec. 13, 2011, www.idahostatesman.com/2011/12/13/1914317/in-scramble-for-new-jobs-incentives.html.
Some Idaho economic-development officials say they lost a Boeing aircraft plant to South Carolina because their state wouldn't give the company a big enough financial incentive, but other analysts argue that states should be cautious about such interstate competition.

Schantz-Feld, Mali R., "Top Site Selection Factors: Tax Rates, Exemptions and Incentives — Keeping an Eye on the Competition," *Area Development Online*, November 2011, www.areadevelopment.com/taxesIncentives/November2011/site-selection-factors-taxes-incentives-224443.shtml.
Some states that offer location incentives to meet specific companies' wish lists are emerging from the recession with stronger job growth than average, according to a magazine for business site-selection professionals.

Spathelf, Christof, "First Person: The Site Selection Process Behind VW's First U.S. Manufacturing Facility," *Area Development Online*, November 2011, www.areadevelopment.com/Automotive/November2011/VW-Christof-Spathelf-Overseas-manufacturing-77780192.shtml.
A training partnership with a local university and community college played a role in bringing a Volkswagen plant to Chattanooga, Tenn.

Reports and Studies

"Money-Back Guarantees for Taxpayers," Good Jobs First, January 2012, www.goodjobsfirst.org/sites/default/files/docs/pdf/moneyback.pdf.
With states and cities spending an estimated $70 billion annually on economic-development subsidies, governments are monitoring the outcomes of subsidy programs more closely but are far from requiring real accountability, says a subsidy watchdog group.

"Report of the Missouri Tax Credit Review Commission," Missouri Tax Credit Review Commission, Nov. 30, 2010, http://tcrc.mo.gov/pdf/TCRCFinalReport113010.pdf.
A panel of Missouri lawmakers and business and community representatives concludes that "there currently exists a problem in interstate competition where states manipulate the marketplace with incentives and cannibalize each other's industries."

"Show Us the Subsidies," Good Jobs First, December 2010, www.goodjobsfirst.org/showusthesubsidies.
Analysts for a nonprofit group that advocates for subsidy accountability finds that states are disclosing more information about who gets business incentives but that complete transparency is a long way off.

Bartik, Timothy J., "State Economic Development Policies: What Works?" Upjohn Institute, Nov. 30, 2011, http://research.upjohn.org/presentations/27.
Research shows that well-administered customized job-training programs are much better than tax cuts and tax incentives at creating good-paying jobs in a state.

Coates, Dennis, and Brad R. Humphreys, "The Stadium Gambit and Local Economic Development," *Regulation*, Cato Institute, Summer 2000, www.cato.org/pubs/regulation/regv23n2/coates.pdf.
In a report for a libertarian magazine, two University of Maryland economists say that evidence over the years demonstrates that bringing a professional sports team to a city doesn't increase residents' per capita income and isn't worth the taxpayer dollars spent.

Fisher, Peter S., "Corporate Taxes and State Economic Growth, Iowa Fiscal Partnership," February 2011, www.iowafiscal.org/2011docs/110209-IFP-corptaxes.pdf.
A University of Iowa professor emeritus of urban and regional planning argues that because taxes make up a relatively small portion of business costs, tax breaks have much less effect than policymakers believe in influencing companies' location decisions.

The Next Step:

Additional Articles from Current Periodicals

Competition

"KC Leaders Want End to 'Poaching' of Businesses," The Associated Press, April 12, 2011, www.newstribune.com/news/2011/apr/12/kc-leaders-want-end-poaching-businesses.
Kansas City business leaders want the governors of Kansas and Missouri to end incentives that lure businesses from one state to the other.

Pittman, Kirsten Valle, "Economic Incentives Tied to Job Creation," *Buffalo* (N.Y.) *News*, Dec. 12, 2011, p. B7.
Economic incentives for businesses are becoming more common as states and localities compete for jobs.

Sunnucks, Mike, and Jan Buchholz, "Phoenix Shoots But Misses Short List for New Sears HQ," *Phoenix Business Journal*, Dec. 7, 2011, www.bizjournals.com/phoenix/blog/business/2011/12/phoenix-shoots-but-misses-short-list.html?page=all.
Phoenix is out of the running to become the new headquarters of Sears Holdings as the company considers leaving suburban Chicago.

Location-Based Incentives

Hopkins, Kyle, "Group Calls for Changes to Alaska Filmmaking Subsidy," *Anchorage* (Alaska) *Daily News*, Nov. 17, 2011, www.adn.com/2011/11/16/2174879/17-alaska-films.html.
Alaska filmmakers say they have not benefited from the nation's movie boom because of the state's weak film subsidy program.

Kukec, Anna Marie, "Not All Towns Offering Incentives to Lure Businesses," *Chicago Daily Herald*, April 4, 2011, p. 1, www.dailyherald.com/article/20110403/news/704039913/.
Several Chicago suburbs are using aggressive marketing techniques instead of financial incentives to lure national retailers and other businesses.

Raletz, Alyson, "Data Center Incentives Effort Gets New Life," *Kansas City Business Journal*, July 29, 2011, www.bizjournals.com/kansascity/print-edition/2011/07/29/missouri-special-session-data-center.html.
Low-cost power in the Midwest has turned the region into a competitive market for data-center relocations.

Verrier, Richard, "Film Tax Credits Extended Briefly," *Los Angeles Times*, Sept. 14, 2011, p. B3, articles.latimes.com/2011/sep/14/business/la-fi-ct-onlocation-20110914.
California lawmakers have granted a one-year extension for the state's film tax credit program.

Tax Incentives

Alaimo, Jessica, and Russ Zimmer, "Analysis: Breaks on Taxes Good for Ohio Jobs," *Newark* (Ohio) *Advocate*, Oct. 16, 2011, www.newarkadvocate.com/article/20111016/NEWS01/110160302/Analysis-Breaks-taxes-good-Ohio-jobs.
Ohio companies that have benefited from tax-incentive programs have largely kept their promises to add and keep jobs.

Crabb, Peter R., "Government Incentives for Business Are Useless," *Idaho Statesman*, May 4, 2011.
Special tax incentives for businesses have done little to promote job growth, according to a finance professor at Northwest Nazarene University in Idaho.

Erickson, Kurt, "Tax Credit Yields Few Jobs," *The Pantagraph* (Bloomington, Ill.), Dec. 17, 2011, p. A9.
A tax incentive program launched by Democratic Illinois Gov. Pat Quinn has fallen far short of its job-creation goal.

Marsteller, Duane, "Tennessee's Job-Creation Subsidies Lack Scrutiny, Study Finds," *The Tennessean/Knoxvillbiz.com*, Jan. 19, 2012, www.knoxnews.com/news/2012/jan/19/tns-job-creation-subsidies-lack-scrutiny-study-fin/.
Tennessee ranks 29th among all states in how well it monitors, verifies and enforces the terms of job-creation subsidies.

White, Cliff, "More to Courting Firms Than Offering Incentives," *Centre Daily Times* (State College, Pa.), Feb. 12, 2012, www.centredaily.com/2012/02/12/3098230/more-to-courting-firms-than-offering.html.
Critics say tax incentives waste state revenue on companies that would likely relocate anyway.

CITING *CQ RESEARCHER*

Sample formats for citing these reports in a bibliography include the ones listed below. Preferred styles and formats vary, so please check with your instructor or professor.

MLA STYLE

Jost, Kenneth. "Remembering 9/11," CQ Researcher 2 Sept. 2011: 701-732.

APA STYLE

Jost, K. (2011, September 2). Remembering 9/11. *CQ Researcher, 9*, 701-732.

CHICAGO STYLE

Jost, Kenneth. "Remembering 9/11." *CQ Researcher*, September 2, 2011, 701-732.

CQ Researcher

Published by CQ Press, an Imprint of SAGE Publications, Inc.

www.cqresearcher.com

Immigration Conflict

Should states crack down on unlawful aliens?

Americans are very concerned about illegal immigration but ambivalent about what to do about it — especially the 11 million aliens currently in the United States illegally. Frustrated with the federal government's failure to secure the borders, several states passed laws allowing state and local police to check the immigration status of suspected unlawful aliens. Civil rights organizations warn the laws will result in ethnic profiling of Latinos. The Obama administration is suing to block several of the laws for infringing on federal prerogatives. Advocates of tougher enforcement say undocumented workers are taking jobs from U.S. citizens, but many business and agricultural groups say migrant workers are needed to fill jobs unattractive to U.S. workers. Two years ago, the U.S. Supreme Court upheld an Arizona law providing stiff penalties for employers that knowingly hire illegal aliens. Now, the justices are preparing to hear arguments on the controversial, new Arizona law that inspired other states to crack down on illegal immigration.

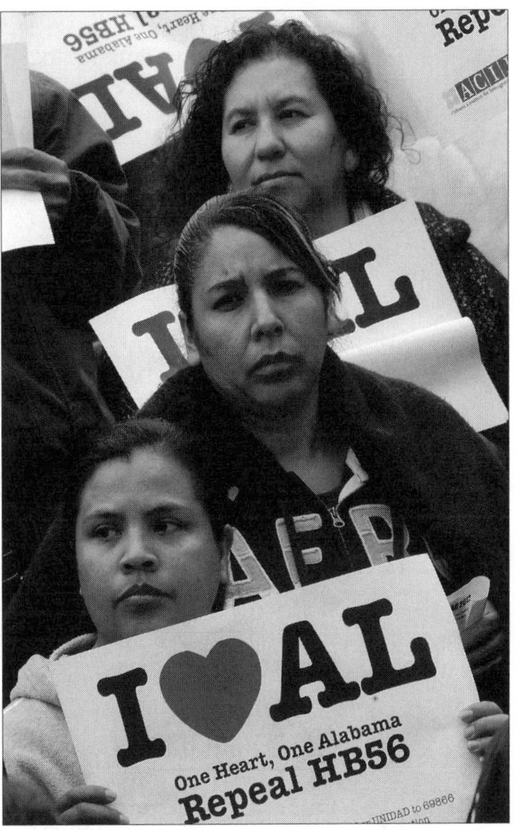

Opponents of Alabama's tough, new immigration law protest in Montgomery on Feb. 14, 2012.

INSIDE THIS REPORT

The Issues 231
Background 238
Chronology 239
Current Situation 243
At Issue 245
Outlook 247
Bibliography 250
The Next Step 251

CQ Researcher • March 9, 2012 • www.cqresearcher.com
Volume 22, Number 10 • Pages 229-252

Los Angeles | London | New Delhi
Singapore | Washington DC

Recipient of Society of Professional Journalists Award for Excellence ◆ American Bar Association Silver Gavel Award

THE ISSUES

231 • Is illegal immigration an urgent national problem?
• Should state and local police enforce immigration laws?
• Should Congress make it easier for illegal immigrants to become citizens?

BACKGROUND

238 **Constant Ambivalence** Americans have been alternately critical and supportive of immigrants through history.

241 **Cracking Down?** Illegal immigration has been increasing, despite tougher laws and enforcement.

242 **Getting Tough** President Obama has stepped up enforcement while backing some reforms.

CURRENT SITUATION

243 **Obama's Approach** His mix of firm and flexible policies is drawing critics from both sides.

246 **Supreme Court Action** Arguments on Arizona's tough law are set for April 25.

OUTLOOK

247 **A Broken System** Public opinion on immigration is conflicted.

SIDEBARS AND GRAPHICS

232 **West Has Highest Share of Unlawful Aliens** In several states they comprise 6 percent of the population.

233 **Americans Want Less Immigration** More than 40 percent favor lower levels.

234 **Immigration Law Basics** Here are key points on issues such as quotas, visas and refugees.

235 **Major State Immigration Laws in Court** Six states give police a role in enforcing U.S. laws.

236 **Unlawful Immigration High Despite Dip** The number increased by one-third in last decade.

239 **Chronology** Key events since the 1920s.

240 **Journalist Reveals His Immigration Secret** "There's nothing worse than being in limbo."

245 **At Issue** Should Congress pass the DREAM Act?

FOR FURTHER RESEARCH

249 **For More Information** Organizations to contact.

250 **Bibliography** Selected sources used.

251 **The Next Step** Additional articles.

251 **Citing *CQ Researcher*** Sample bibliography formats.

Cover: AP Photo/Dave Martin

CQ Researcher

March 9, 2012
Volume 22, Number 10

MANAGING EDITOR: Thomas J. Billitteri tjb@cqpress.com

ASSISTANT MANAGING EDITOR: Kathy Koch kkoch@cqpress.com

CONTRIBUTING EDITOR: Thomas J. Colin tcolin@cqpress.com

ASSOCIATE EDITOR: Kenneth Jost

STAFF WRITER: Marcia Clemmitt

CONTRIBUTING WRITERS: Sarah Glazer, Alan Greenblatt, Peter Katel, Barbara Mantel, Jennifer Weeks

DESIGN/PRODUCTION EDITOR: Olu B. Davis

ASSISTANT EDITOR: Darrell Dela Rosa

FACT CHECKER: Michelle Harris

Los Angeles | London | New Delhi
Singapore | Washington DC

An Imprint of SAGE Publications, Inc.

VICE PRESIDENT AND EDITORIAL DIRECTOR, HIGHER EDUCATION GROUP: Michele Sordi

DIRECTOR, ONLINE PUBLISHING: Todd Baldwin

CQ Researcher (ISSN 1056-2036) is printed on acid-free paper. Published weekly, except: (March wk. 5) (May wk. 4) (July wk. 1) (Aug. wks. 3, 4) (Nov. wk. 4) and (Dec. wks. 3, 4). Published by SAGE Publications, Inc., 2455 Teller Rd., Thousand Oaks, CA 91320. Annual full-service subscriptions start at $1,054. For pricing, call 1-800-834-9020. To purchase a *CQ Researcher* report in print or electronic format (PDF), visit www.cqpress.com or call 866-427-7737. Single reports start at $15. Bulk purchase discounts and electronic-rights licensing are also available. Periodicals postage paid at Thousand Oaks, California, and at additional mailing offices. POSTMASTER: Send address changes to *CQ Researcher*, 2300 N St., N.W., Suite 800, Washington, DC 20037.

Immigration Conflict

BY KENNETH JOST

THE ISSUES

Micky Hammon minced no words when he urged his fellow Alabama legislators to enact what would become the toughest of a batch of new state laws cracking down on illegal immigrants. "This bill is designed to make it difficult for them to live here so they will deport themselves," Hammon, leader of the Alabama House of Representatives' Republican majority, said during the April 5, 2011, debate on the bill. [1]

Immigrant-rights groups say the law, which took effect Sept. 28 after partly surviving a court challenge, is as tough as Hammon hoped — and more. "It's been pretty devastating," says Mary Bauer, legal director of the Southern Poverty Law Center in Montgomery, Alabama's capital. "Tens of thousands of people have left, and the people who remain are completely terrorized by this law."

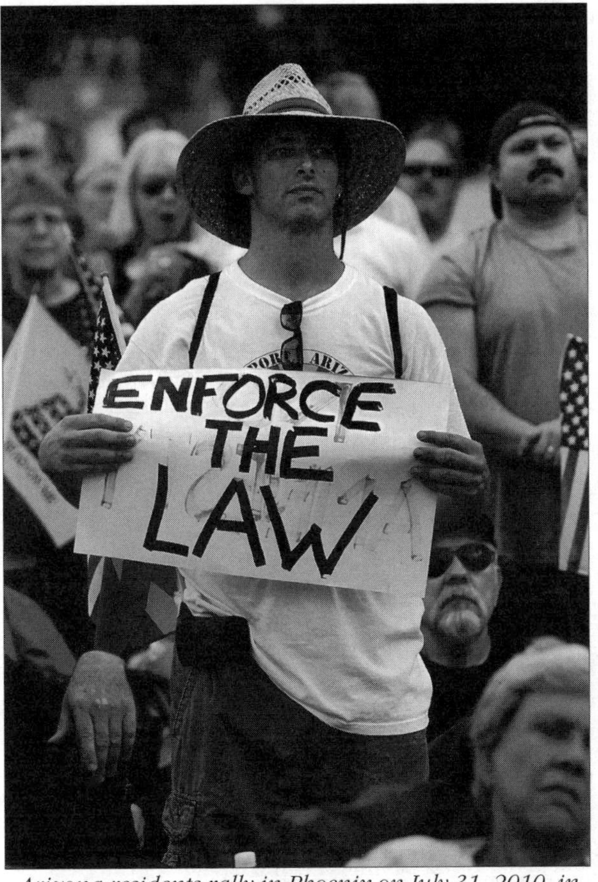

Getty Images/John Moore

Arizona residents rally in Phoenix on July 31, 2010, in support of the state's hard-hitting immigration law, which gives police new responsibilities to look for immigration law violators. Five states last year followed Arizona's lead. The U.S. Supreme Court will hear arguments on the disputed Arizona measure on April 25.

Among other provisions, Alabama's law requires state and local law enforcement officers to determine the immigration status of anyone arrested, detained or stopped if there is a "reasonable suspicion" that the person is an alien "unlawfully present" in the United States. Failure to carry alien-registration papers is made a state crime, punishable by up to 30 days in jail for a first offense.

Alabama, with an estimated 120,000 unlawful aliens living within its borders as of 2010, was one of five states that last year followed Arizona's lead a year earlier in giving police new responsibilities to look for immigration law violators.* Republican-controlled legislatures in each of the states said they were forced to act because the federal government was not doing enough to control illegal immigration at the border or in U.S. workplaces. Opponents warned the laws risked profiling Latinos, including U.S. citizens and aliens with legal status.

All six of the laws are being challenged in federal court, with the "stop and check" provisions blocked except in Alabama's case. In the most important case, the Arizona measure is scheduled to be argued before the U.S. Supreme Court on April 25 after a federal appeals court struck some of the law enforcement provisions as interfering with federal immigration policy. [2] (*See chart, p. 235.*)

Alabama's law includes a unique provision that prohibits unlawful aliens from entering into any "business transaction" with state or local governments. Some public utilities in the state interpreted the provision to require proof of immigration status for water or electricity service. Until a federal judge's injunction on Nov. 23, some counties were applying the law to prevent unlawful immigrants from renewing permits for mobile homes. [3]

Once the law went into effect, school attendance by Latino youngsters dropped measurably in response to a provision — later blocked — requiring school officials to ascertain families' immigration status. The fear of deportation also led many immigrants in Alabama to seek help in preparing power-of-attorney documents to make sure their children would be taken care of in case the parents were deported, according to Isabel Rubio, executive director of the Hispanic Interest Coalition of Alabama. "You have to understand the sheer terror that people fear," Rubio says.

The law is having a palpable effect on the state's economy as well, according to agriculture and business groups. With fewer migrant workers, "some farmers have planted not as much or not planted at all," says Jeff Helms, spokesman for the Alabama Farmers Federation. Jay Reed, president of Associated Builders and Contractors of Alabama, says it has been harder to find construction workers as well.

---

* The others were Utah, Indiana, Georgia and South Carolina.

West Has Highest Share of Unlawful Aliens

Undocumented immigrants comprise at least 6 percent of the population of Arizona, California, Nevada and Texas and at least 3.8 percent of the population of New Mexico, Oregon and Utah. Unlawful immigrants also make up sizable percentages of several other states' populations, including New Jersey and Florida. The nationwide average is 3.7 percent.

Unauthorized Immigrants as a Share of State Population, 2010

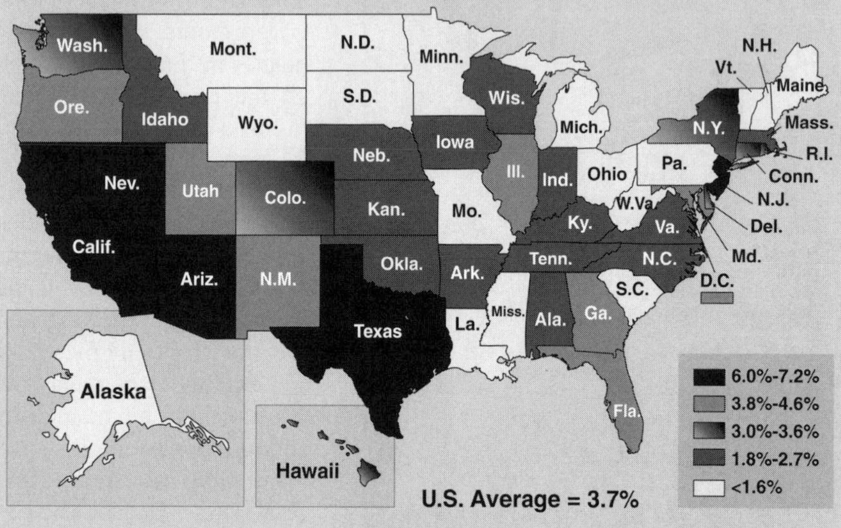

Source: Jeffrey Passel and D'Vera Cohn, "Unauthorized Immigrant Population: National and State Trends, 2010," Pew Research Center, February 2011, p. 29, www.pewhispanic.org/files/reports/133.pdf

Reed, co-chair of the multi-industry coalition Alabama Employers for Immigration Reform, wants to soften provisions that threaten employers with severe penalties, including the loss of operating licenses, for hiring undocumented workers. He and other business leaders also worry about the perception of the law outside the state's borders. "Some of our board members have expressed concern about our state's image and the effect on economic-development legislation," Reed says.

Reed says the state's Republican governor, Robert Bentley, and leaders in the GOP-controlled legislature are open to some changes in the law. But the two chief sponsors, Hammon and state Sen. Scott Beason, are both batting down any suggestions that the law will be repealed or its law enforcement measures softened.

"We are not going to weaken the law," Hammon told reporters on Feb. 14 as hundreds of opponents of the measure demonstrated outside the State House in Montgomery. "We are not going to repeal any section of the law." [4]

On the surface, Alabama seems an improbable state to take a leading role in the newest outbreak of nativist concern about immigration and immigrants. Alabama's unauthorized immigrant population has increased nearly fivefold since 2000, but the state still ranks relatively low in the proportion of unauthorized immigrants in the population and in the state's workforce.

Alabama's estimated 120,000 unauthorized immigrants comprise about 2.5 percent of the state's total population. Nationwide, the estimated 11.8 million unauthorized immigrants represent about 3.7 percent of the population. Alabama's estimated 95,000 unauthorized immigrants with jobs represent about 4.2 percent of the workforce. Nationwide, 8 million undocumented workers account for about 5.2 percent of the national workforce. [5]

Nationwide, the spike in anti-immigrant sentiment is also somewhat out of synch with current conditions. Experts and advocates on both sides of the immigration issues agree that the total unauthorized immigrant population has fallen somewhat from its peak in 2007, mainly because the struggling U.S. economy offers fewer jobs to lure incoming migrant workers.

"The inflow of illegals has slowed somewhat," says Mark Krikorian, executive director of the Center for Immigration Studies (CIS) in Washington. The center describes its stance as "low-immigration, pro-immigrant." [6]

Jobs were a major focus of the debate that led to Alabama's passage of the new law. "This is a jobs bill," Beason said as the measure, known as HB 56, reached final passage in June. "We have a problem with an illegal workforce that displaces Alabama workers. We need to put those people back to work." [7]

Today, Beason, running against an incumbent congressman for the U.S. House seat in the Birmingham area, credits the law with helping Alabama lower its unemployment rate from 9.8 percent in September to 8.1 percent in December. "I promised that the anti-illegal immigration law would open up thousands of jobs for Alabamians, and it has done that," Beason said in a Jan. 26 statement.

A University of Alabama economist, however, doubts the law's claimed effect on unemployment. Samuel Addy, director of the university's Center for Business and Economic Research in Tuscaloosa, notes that unemployment actually has increased, rather than declined, in the four sectors in the state viewed as most dependent on immigrant labor: agriculture, construction, accommodation and food and drinking places. [8]

In a nine-page study released in January, Addy contends instead that the immigration law is likely to hurt the state's economy overall. After assuming that 40,000 to 80,000 workers leave the state, Addy calculated that the law could reduce the state's gross domestic product by $2.3 billion to $10.8 billion. State income and sales taxes could take a $56.7 million to $265.4 million hit, Addy projected, while local sales tax revenue could decline by $20.0 million to $93.1 million. Hammon dismissed the report as "baloney." [9]

Five months after it took effect, however, the law's impact may be ebbing. Police appear not to have enforced the law vigorously, perhaps stung by the nationwide embarrassment when a visiting Mercedes-Benz executive from Germany carrying only a German identification card was held after a traffic stop until he could retrieve his passport. With police enforcement lagging, some of the immigrants who left appear to be coming back. "Some people have returned," Rubio says. [10]

Meanwhile, attorneys for the Obama administration and the state were preparing for arguments on March 1 before the federal appeals court in Atlanta in the government's suit challenging the state law on grounds of federal pre-emption, the doctrine used to nullify state laws that conflict with U.S. laws and policies. The Hispanic Interest Coalition had challenged the law on broader grounds in an earlier suit, represented by the American Civil Liberties Union and other national groups.

In a massive, 115-page ruling, U.S. District Court Judge Sharon Blackburn upheld major parts of the law on Sept. 28 and then allowed the upheld parts to go into effect even as the government and civil rights groups appealed. Blackburn blocked half a dozen provisions on pre-emption grounds but found no congressional intent to prevent states from checking the immigration status of suspected unlawful aliens. [11]

With the legal challenges continuing, the political debates over immigration are intensifying. Republican presidential candidates generally agree on criticizing the Obama administration for failing to control illegal immigration even though the administration has increased the number of immigrants deported to their home countries. The Republican hopefuls disagree among themselves on the steps to deal with the problem.

For his part, Obama concedes that Congress will not approve a broad immigration overhaul in this election year. But he used his State of the Union speech to call for passage of a bill — the so-called DREAM Act — to allow legal status for some immigrants who have served in the U.S. military or completed college. (*See "At Issue," p. 245.*)

As the immigration debates continue, here are some of the major questions being considered:

Americans Want Less Immigration

More than 40 percent of Americans say they favor a lower level of immigration, reflecting a view that has prevailed over most of the past half-century. About one in six want immigration to increase, while about one-third favor the current level.

Should immigration be kept at its present level, increased or decreased?

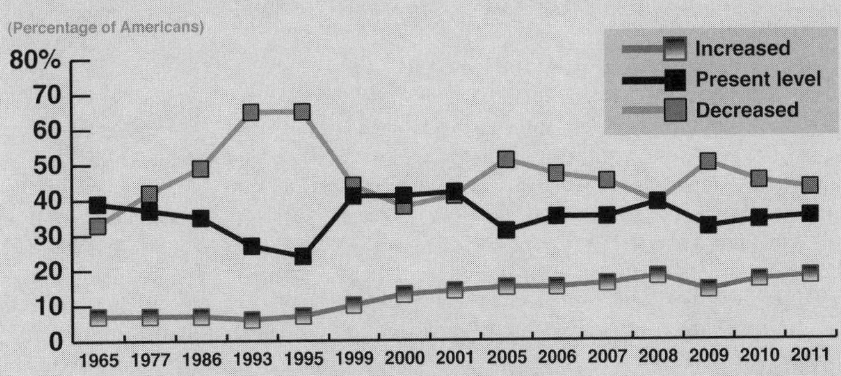

Sources: Jeffrey M. Jones, "Americans' Views on Immigration Holding Steady," Gallup, June 2011, www.gallup.com/poll/148154/americans-views-immigration-holding-steady.aspx; Roger Daniels, Guarding the Golden Door, Hill and Wang Press, December 2004, p. 233

Is illegal immigration an urgent national problem?

As the anti-illegal immigration bill HB 56 was being signed into law, Alabama's Republican Party chairman depicted the measure as needed to protect the state's taxpayers and the state's treasury. "Illegal immigrants have become a drain on our state resources and a strain on our taxpaying, law-abiding citizens," Bill Armistead declared as Republican governor Bentley signed it into law on June 9, 2011. [12]

Today, Republican officials continue to defend the law in economic terms. "Unemployment was sky high, especially in areas where there's high concentration of these undocumented workers," says Shana Kluck, the party's

Immigration Law Basics

Even experts find it confusing.

Immigrating legally to the United States is difficult at best for those who fit into categories defined in mind-numbing detail by federal law and impossible for those who do not. Here is a primer on a body of law that is complex and confusing even to immigration experts, and all the more so for would-be Americans.

The Immigration and Nationality Act — sets an overall limit of 675,000 permanent immigrants each year. The limit does not apply to spouses, unmarried minor children or parents of U.S. citizens, but the sponsoring U.S. citizen must have an income above the U.S. poverty level and promise to support family members brought to the United States.

Who gets visas — Out of the 675,000 quota, 480,000 visas are made available under family-preference rules, and up to 140,000 are allocated for employment-related preferences. Unused employment-related visas may be reallocated to the family-preference system.

The family-sponsored visas are allocated according to a preference system with numerical limits for each category. Unmarried adult children of U.S. citizens are in the first category, followed, in this order, by spouses and minor children of lawful permanent residents; unmarried adult children of lawful permanent residents; married adult children of U.S. citizens; and brothers and sisters of U.S. citizens. No other relatives qualify for a family preference. Again, the sponsor must meet financial and support requirements.

Visa categories — The employment-based preference system also sets up ranked, capped categories for would-be immigrants. The highest preference is given to "persons of extraordinary ability" in the arts, science, education, business or athletics; professors and researchers; and some multinational executives. Other categories follow in this order: persons with professional degrees or "exceptional" abilities in arts, science or business; workers with skills that are in short supply and some "unskilled" workers for jobs not temporary or seasonal; certain "special immigrants," including religious workers; and, finally, persons who will invest at least $500,000 in a job-creating enterprise that employs at least 10 full-time workers.

In addition to the numerical limits, the law sets a cap of 7 percent of the quota for immigrants from any single country. The limit in effect prevents any immigrant group from dominating immigration patterns.

Refugees — Separately, Congress and the president each year set an annual limit for the number of refugees who can be admitted based on an inability to return to their home country because of a fear of persecution. Currently, the overall ceiling is 76,000. The law also allows an unlimited number of persons already in the United States, or at a port of entry, to apply for asylum if they were persecuted or fear persecution in their home country. A total of 21,113 persons were granted asylum in fiscal 2010. Refugees and asylees are eligible to become lawful permanent residents after one year.

Debate over the rules — An immigrant who gets through this maze and gains the coveted "green card" for lawful permanent residents is eligible to apply for U.S. citizenship after five years (three years for the spouse of a U.S. citizen). An applicant must be age 18 or over and meet other requirements, including passing English and U.S. history and civics exams. About 675,000 new citizens were naturalized in 2010, down from the peak of slightly more than 1 million in the pre-recession year of 2008.

Applying for citizenship — Immigration advocates say the quotas are too low, the rules too restrictive and the waiting periods for qualified applicants too long. Low-immigration groups say the record level of legal and illegal immigration over the past decade shows the need to lower the quotas and limit the family-reunification rules.

— Kenneth Jost

spokeswoman. Kluck also points to the cost on public treasuries. "The public-assistance budgets were bursting at the seams," she says. "That's why HB 56 was necessary."

Nationally, groups favoring tighter immigration controls make similar arguments about immigrants' economic impact, especially on jobs and wages for citizen workers. "We need to slow down immigration," says Dan Stein, president of the Federation for American Immigration Reform (FAIR), pointing to the current high levels of unemployment and underemployment.

"Immigration helps to decimate the bargaining leverage of the American worker," Stein continues. "If you use a form of labor recruitment that bids down the cost of labor, that leads you to a society where a small number are very, very rich, there's nobody in the middle, and everyone is left scrambling for crumbs at the bottom."

"The longer this economic doldrum continues, the more likely you are to see some real pushback on immigration levels as such, not just illegal immigration," says Krikorian with the low-immigration group Center for Immigration Studies. The group's research director, Steven Camarota, said if illegal immigrants are forced to go back to their home countries, there is "an ample supply of idle workers" to take the jobs freed up. [13]

Pro-immigration groups say their opponents exaggerate the costs and all but ignore the benefits of immigrant labor. "They never take into account the contributions that undocumented immigrants make," says Mary Giovagnoli, director of the American Immigration Council's Immigration Policy Center.

"We've had an economy that depends on immigration," says Ali Noorani, executive director of the National Immigration Forum. "It would be an economic and social disaster for 11 million people to pick up and leave."

Madeleine Sumption, a senior labor market analyst with the pro-immigration Migration Policy Institute in Washington, acknowledges that immigration may have what she calls a "relatively small" impact on employment and wages for citizen workers. But the costs are more than offset, she says, by the benefits to employers, consumers and the overall economy.

The benefits can be seen particularly in sectors that employ large numbers of immigrants, according to Sumption. "The United States has a large agriculture industry," she says. "Without immigration labor, it would almost certainly not be possible to produce the same volume of food in the country." The health care industry also employs a high number of immigrants, especially in low-end jobs, such as home-health aides and hospital orderlies. "These are jobs for which there is a growing demand and an expectation of an even more rapidly growing demand in the future," Sumption says.

In Alabama, Rubio with the Hispanic coalition and the leaders of the agriculture and construction groups all discount Camarota's contention that citizen workers are available to take the jobs currently being filled by immigrants. "We did not have a tomato crop [last] summer because the immigrants who pick that crop weren't there," Rubio says. "This is hard work, and many people don't want to do it."

Major State Immigration Laws in Court

Five states have followed Arizona's lead in giving state and local police a role in enforcing federal immigration law. With some variations, the laws authorize or require police after an arrest, detention or stop to determine the person's immigration status if he or she is reasonably suspected of being unlawfully in the United States. In legal challenges, federal courts have blocked major parts of five of the laws; the Supreme Court is set to hear arguments on April 25 in Arizona's effort to reinstate the blocked portions of its law.

State	Bill, date signed	Legal challenge
Arizona	S.B. 1070: April 23, 2010	*United States v. Arizona* Major parts enjoined; pending at Supreme Court
Utah	H.B. 497: March 15, 2011	*Utah Coalition of La Raza v. Herbert* Major parts blocked; suit on hold pending Supreme Court ruling in Arizona case
Indiana	SB 590: May 10, 2011	*Buquer v. City of Indianapolis* Major parts blocked; suit on hold pending Supreme Court ruling in Arizona case
Georgia	HB 87: May 13, 2011	*Georgia Latino Alliance v. Deal* Major parts blocked; on hold at 11th Circuit
Alabama	HB 56: June 9, 2011	*United States v. Alabama* Major parts upheld; on hold at 11th Circuit
South Carolina	S20: June 27, 2011	*United States v. South Carolina* Major parts blocked; suit on hold pending Supreme Court ruling in Arizona case

Sources: National Conference of State Legislatures, http://www.ncsl.org/issues-research/immig/omnibus-immigration-legislation.aspx; American Civil Liberties Union; news coverage.

Reed, president of the state's builders and contractors' organization, says construction companies similarly cannot find enough workers among the citizen labor force. "Traditionally, in our recruitment efforts we have unfortunately not found those that are unemployed are ready and willing to perform these kinds of jobs that require hard labor in extreme weather conditions," Helms says.

The claimed costs and benefits from immigration for public treasuries represent similarly contentious issues. Low- or anti-immigration groups emphasize the costs in government services, especially education and medical care. Pro-immigration groups point to the taxes that even unlawful aliens pay and the limits on some government benefits under federal and state laws. In an independent evaluation of the issue, the nonpartisan Congressional Budget Office in 2007 found a net cost to state and local governments but called the impact "most likely modest." [14]

The cost-benefit debates are more volatile in stressed economic times, according to David Gerber, a professor of history at the University of Buffalo and author of a primer on immigration. "People get angry when they feel that

Unlawful Immigration High Despite Dip

Despite a dip beginning in 2007, an estimated 11.2 million unauthorized immigrants live in the United States, one-third more than a decade ago (top graph). An estimated 8 million are in the civilian labor force, a 45 percent increase since 2000 (bottom graph).

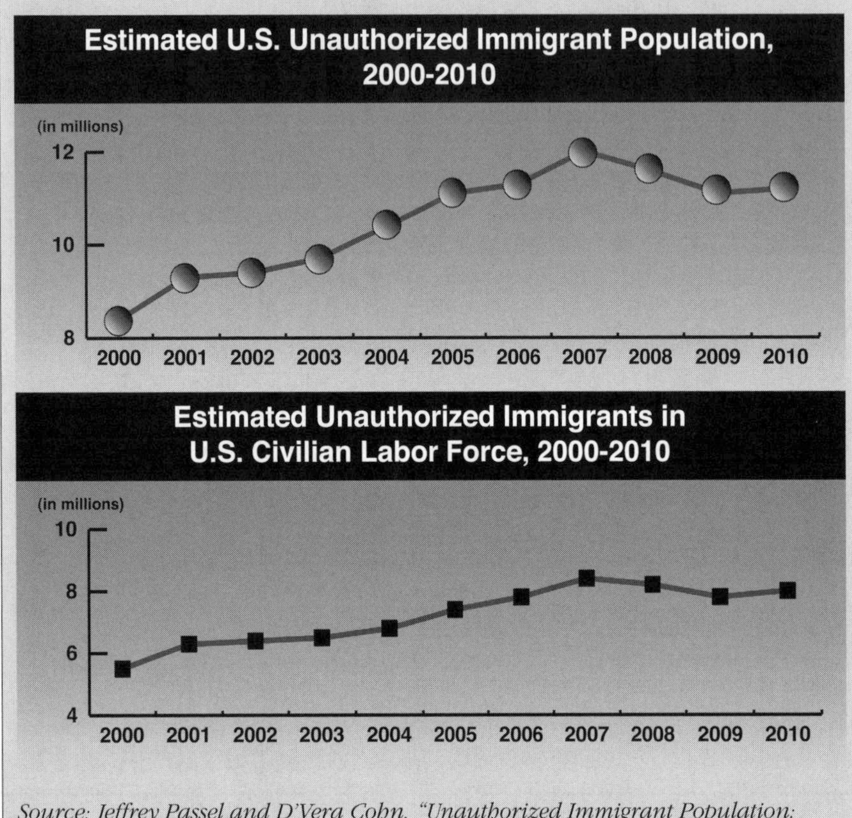

Source: Jeffrey Passel and D'Vera Cohn, "Unauthorized Immigrant Population: National and State Trends, 2010," Pew Research Center, February 2011, pp. 1, 17, www.pewhispanic.org/files/reports/133.pdf

immigrants are competing for jobs of people in the United States or when they feel that immigrants are getting access to social benefits that the majority is paying for," Gerber says. "In harder times, it makes people angrier than in times of prosperity." [15]

Even so, David Coates, a professor at Wake Forest University in Winston-Salem, N.C., and co-editor of a book on immigration issues, notes that fewer undocumented workers are entering the United States now than in the peak year of 2007, and the Obama administration has been deporting unlawful aliens in significantly greater numbers than previous administrations. Asked whether illegal immigration should be less of an issue for state legislators and national politicians, Coates replies simply: "Yes, in terms of the numbers."

Should state and local police enforce immigration laws?

Alabama's HB 56 was stuffed with more provisions for state and local governments to crack down on illegal immigrants than the Arizona law that inspired it or any of the copy-cat laws passed in four other states. Along with the stop-and-check section, the law includes provisions making it a state crime for an unauthorized alien to apply for work and barring unauthorized aliens from court enforcement of any contracts. Another provision made it illegal to conceal, harbor or rent to an illegal immigrant or even to stop in a roadway to hire workers.

Opponents harshly criticized the enforcement provisions as they were signed into law. "It turns Alabama into a police state where anyone could be required to show their citizenship papers," said Cecillia Wang, director of the ACLU's Immigrant Rights Project. Noorani, with the National Immigration Forum, called the law "a radical departure from the concepts of fairness and equal treatment under the law," adding, "It makes it a crime, quite literally, to give immigrants a ride without checking their legal status." [16]

Today, even with the harboring provision and several others blocked from taking effect, opponents say the law is having the terrorizing effect that they had predicted on immigrants both legal and illegal as well as U.S. citizens of Hispanic background. "We've heard numerous accounts of people who have been stopped under very suspicious circumstances, while driving or even while walking on the street," says Justin Cox, an ACLU staff attorney in Atlanta working on the case challenging the law.

The law "has had the effect that it was intended to have," Cox says, "which was to make immigration status a pervasive issue in [immigrants'] everyday lives."

Supporters of the law are defending it, but without responding to specific criticisms. "We've seen an awful lot of illegal immigrants self-deport," House Majority Leader Hammon said as opponents rallied in Montgomery on Feb. 14. "We're also seeing Americans and legal immigrants taking these jobs." [17]

When questioned by a Montgomery television station about critical documentaries prepared for the progressive group Center for American Progress, Hammon declined to look at the films but attacked the filmmaker. "We don't need an activist director from California to come in here and tell us whether this law is good or not," Hammon said. "The people in Alabama can see it for themselves." [18]

Nationally, immigration hawks view the new state laws as unexceptionable. "They're helping the feds to enforce immigration laws," says Center for Immigration Studies executive director Krikorian. "The question is [whether] local police use immigration laws as one of the tools in their tool kit to help defend public safety."

"Every town is a border town, every state is a border state," Krikorian continues. "Immigration law has to be part of your approach, part of your strategy in dealing with some kind of a significant problem."

FAIR president Stein strongly objects to the Obama administration's legal challenges to the state laws. "It should be a massive, industrial-strength issue that the Obama administration" has attacked the laws on grounds of federal pre-emption. But Giovagnoli with the pro-immigration American Immigration Council says the state laws should be struck down. "Congress has established that immigration enforcement is a federal matter," she says. "The more states get into the mix, the more you create a real patchwork of laws that don't make sense together."

As Krikorian notes, federal law already provides for cooperative agreements between the federal government and state or local law enforcement agencies to enforce immigration laws. U.S. Immigration and Customs Enforcement (ICE), the successor agency to the Immigration and Naturalization Service, touts the so-called 287(g) program on its website as one of the agency's "top partnership initiatives." The program, authorized by an immigration law overhaul in 1996, permits the federal agency to delegate enforcement power to state or local law enforcement after officers have received training on federal immigration law. [19]

AP Photo/Montgomery Advertiser/Mickey Welsh

Republican Alabama Gov. Robert Bentley addresses lawmakers at the state capitol on June 9, 2011, before signing the state's new immigration law. Republican cosponsors of the law, Sen. Scott Beason (left), and state Rep. Micky Hammon (right), both oppose softening or repealing the law. But state business interests want to ease provisions that threaten employers with severe penalties for hiring undocumented workers. They also worry about the perception of the law outside the state.

Pro-immigration groups say the training requirement distinguishes 287(g) programs from the broader roles being given state and local police by the new state laws. "State and local law enforcement officers are not trained to do this kind of work," says Cox. "Inevitably, they're going to rely on pernicious stereotypes about what an undocumented immigrant looks like." The result, Cox continues, "is a breakdown of trust between the immigrant community and law enforcement, which ultimately affects all of us. It undermines public safety."

Alabama Republicans, however, insist that the state law fulfills a 2010 campaign pledge that helped the GOP gain control of both houses of the state legislature and that it remains popular despite the criticisms and legal challenges. "We've definitely been criticized," party spokeswoman Kluck acknowledges, but she blames the criticisms on "misinformation." As for possible changes in the law, Hammon and other legislative leaders are guarding details until a bill with proposed revisions can be completed by late March.

Should Congress make it easier for illegal immigrants to become citizens?

With many Republican primary and caucus voters viewing illegal immigration as a major issue, presidential candidate and former Massachusetts Gov. Mitt Romney says he has a simple solution: Get undocumented immigrants to "self-deport" to their home countries and then get in the legal waiting line for U.S. citizenship. But one of his rivals for the Republican nomination, former House speaker Newt Gingrich, pushing stronger enforcement at the border, mocks Romney's belief that 11 million unlawful aliens will go back home voluntarily. Speaking to a Spanish-language television network in late January on the eve of the Florida presidential primary, Gingrich called Romney's plan "an Obama-level fantasy." [20]

Pro-immigration groups agree that Romney's stance is unrealistic. "It's a fantasy to think that people are going to self-deport," says the National Immigration Forum's Noorani. Unlike border-control advocates, however, Noorani and other pro-immigration advocates and experts say the solution is "a path to legal citizenship" for the undocumented.

"We need a functioning legal immigration system, a system that has the necessary legal channels for a person to immigrate here whether for a job or his family," Noorani says. "That doesn't exist here." Without "a solution," Noorani says, "the only ones who are winning are the crooked employer who is more than happy to exploit the undocumented, poor third-country worker."

Immigration hawks quickly denounce any broad legalization proposal as an "amnesty" that they say is neither workable nor deserved. "All amnesties attract future immigration," says the CIS's Krikorian. "All amnesties reward lawbreakers." As evidence, immigration critics point to the broad amnesty granted under the 1986 immigration act to some 3 million immigrants — and its evident failure within a matter of years to stem the flow of illegal immigrants from across the country's Southern borders.

As an alternative to broader proposals, pro-immigration groups are pushing narrower legislation that in its current form would grant conditional legal status to immigrants who came to the United States before age 16 and have lived in the United States for at least five years. The so-called DREAM Act — an acronym for the Development, Relief and Education for Alien Minors Act — had majority support in both chambers of the Democratic-controlled Congress in 2010 but failed to get a Senate floor vote in the face of Republican opposition.

The DREAM Act starts with the assumption that immigrants who came to the United States as children have grown up as Americans and are innocent of any intentional immigration violations. They would be eligible for a conditional permanent residency and could then earn a five-year period of temporary residency by completing two years in the U.S. military or two years in a four-year college or university.

"The intent of the DREAM Act is to provide legal status for individuals who are enlisting in our armed services or pursuing higher education," says Noorani. "Whether they came here at age 5 or 15, I think we only stand to benefit."

"It's a good way to show that if you provide legal status to folks like this, the world is not going to fall apart," says Giovagnoli with the American Immigration Council. "In fact, the country would be better off if these people were in the system."

Similar proposals have been introduced in Congress since 2001. Immigration hawks acknowledge the proposals' appeal and argue over details. "The concept that people who have been here from childhood, that it might be prudent to legalize people in that position, is a plausible one," says Krikorian. But, he adds, "As it exists, it is not a good piece of legislation."

As one change, Krikorian says the eligibility age should be lowered, perhaps to age 10 or below. "The reason they pick 16 is it legalizes more," he says. Paradoxically, Krikorian also says the bill is too narrow by allowing temporary residency only by joining the military or going to college. "What if you're not college material?" he asks.

Krikorian also dismisses the idea of absolving those who arrived as youngsters of any responsibility for immigration violations. "The parents . . . did know what they were doing," he says. The bill needs to be changed, he says, "to ensure that no parent would ever be able to benefit" under family-reunification rules.

Gingrich and some GOP lawmakers favor a narrower version of the DREAM Act that would extend legal status for serving in the military but not for going to college. Supporters oppose the narrower version. "If you read the bill carefully, it would actually allow a fewer number of immigrants to enlist in the military than the original," Noorani says. Krikorian also dismisses the alternative. He calls it "phony," adding that it would help "only a few thousand people a year."

The White House pushed hard for the bill in the Democratic-controlled Congress's lame-duck session in December 2010 but fell short in the Senate. Obama continues to speak out for the bill, most prominently in his State of the Union address. "[I]f election-year politics keeps Congress from acting on a comprehensive plan, let's at least agree to stop expelling responsible young people who want to staff our labs, start new businesses, defend this country," Obama said near the end of the Jan. 24 speech. "Send me a law that gives them the chance to earn their citizenship. I will sign it right away." [21] ■

BACKGROUND

Constant Ambivalence

The United States is a nation of immigrants that has been ambivalent toward immigration through most of its history. Immigrants are alternately celebrated as the source of diversity and criticized as agents of disunity. Immigrants were recruited to till the soil, build the cities and labor in the factories, but often criticized for taking jobs from and lowering wages for the citizen workforce. The federal government reflected popular sentiment in restricting immigration in the late 19th and early 20th century, only to draw later criticism for exclusionary policies. Today, the government is drawing criticism for liberalized policies adopted in the 1960s and for ineffective border enforcement from the 1980s on. [22]

African slaves were the first source of immigrant labor in America, but Congress banned importation of slaves

Continued on p. 240

Chronology

Before 1960

Congress establishes immigration quotas.

1920s
Quota Act (1921), Johnson-Reed Act (1924) establish national-origins quota system, favoring Northern European immigrants over those from Southern Europe, elsewhere.

1952
McCarran-Walter Act retains national-origins system but adds small quotas for some Asian countries.

1960s

Congress opens door to immigration from outside Europe.

1965
Immigration and Nationality Act of 1965 abolishes national-origins quota system dating from 1920s; allows dramatic increase in immigration from Central and South America, Asia.

1980s-1990s

Illegal immigration increases, becomes major public issue.

1986
Immigration Reform and Control Act allows amnesty for many unlawful aliens, prohibits employers from employing undocumented workers; enforcement proves elusive.

1996
Illegal Immigration Reform and Immigrant Responsibility Act seeks to strengthen border security, streamline deportation proceedings; creates optional E-Verify system for employers to electronically check immigration status of workers and job applicants.

2000-Present

Illegal immigration increases; immigration reform falters in Congress; state laws to crack down on illegal immigration challenged in court.

2001
Al Qaeda 9/11 attacks on U.S. soil underscore national security threat from failure to track potential terrorists entering United States (Sept. 11); USA Patriot Act gives immigration authorities more power to exclude suspected terrorists (Oct. 26).

2005-2006
Immigration reform measures fail in GOP-controlled Congress despite support from Republican President George W. Bush; Congress approves Secure Fence Act, to require double-layer fence on U.S.-Mexico border.

2007
Immigration reform measure dies in Senate; three motions to cut off debate fail (June 7). . . . Arizona legislature passes employer-sanctions law; companies threatened with loss of operating license for knowingly hiring undocumented aliens, required to use federal E-Verify system; signed into law by Democratic Gov. Janet Napolitano (July 2). . . . Unauthorized immigrant population in United States peaks near 12 million.

2008
Democrat Barack Obama elected president after campaign with little attention to immigration issues (Nov. 4); Obama carries Hispanic vote by 2-1 margin.

2009
Obama endorses immigration reform, but without specifics; issue takes back seat to economic recovery, health care.

2010
Arizona enacts law (S.B. 1070) to crack down on illegal immigrants; measure requires police to check immigration status if suspect or detainee is reasonably believed to be unlawful alien; makes it a crime to fail to carry alien registration papers; signed by Republican Gov. Jan Brewer (April 23); federal judge blocks parts of law (July 28). . . . DREAM Act to allow legal status for unlawful aliens who entered U.S. as minors approved by House of Representatives (Dec. 8) but fails in Senate: 55-41 vote is short of supermajority needed for passage (Dec. 18).

2011
Utah, Indiana, Georgia follow Arizona's lead in giving state, local police immigration-enforcement powers (March, May). . . . Federal appeals court upholds injunction against parts of Arizona's S.B. 1070 (April 11). . . . Supreme Court upholds Arizona's employer-sanctions law 5-3 (May 21). . . . Alabama enacts nation's toughest state law on illegal immigrants, HB 56 (June 9). . . . Federal judge blocks some parts of HB 56, allows others to take effect (Sept. 28).

2012
Immigration is flashpoint for Republican presidential candidates. . . . Obama urges passage of DREAM Act (Jan. 24). . . . Alabama, Georgia laws argued before U.S. appeals court (March 1). . . . Supreme Court to hear arguments on Arizona's S.B. 1070 (April 25); ruling due by end of June.

Journalist Reveals His Immigration Secret

"There's nothing worse than being in limbo."

When journalist-turned-immigration rights activist Jose Antonio Vargas traveled to Alabama with a documentary filmmaker, he found a Birmingham restaurant patron who strongly supported the state law cracking down on undocumented aliens. "Get your papers or get out," the patron said.

"What if I told you I didn't [have papers]?" Vargas is heard asking off camera. "Then you need you get your ass home then," the patron rejoined. [1]

Journalist Jose Antonio Vargas disclosed in The New York Times *in June 2011 that he was an undocumented immigrant.*

Getty Images/Justin Sullivan

Vargas says he is home — in America, where he has lived since his Filipina mother sent him, at age 12, to live in California with his grandparents in 1993. "I'm an American without papers," says Vargas, who came out as an undocumented immigrant in dramatic fashion in a 4,300-word memoir in *The New York Times Magazine* in June 2011. [2]

In the story, Vargas recounts how he learned at age 16 that he was carrying a fake green card when he applied for a driver's license. The DMV clerk let him go. Back home, Vargas confronted his grandfather, who acknowledged the forgery and told Vargas not to tell anyone else.

For the next 14 years, Vargas kept his non-status secret from all but a handful of enablers as he completed high school and college and advanced rapidly from entry-level newspaper jobs to national-impact journalism at *The Washington Post, Huffington Post* and glossy magazines. His one attempt at legal status ended in crushing disappointment in 2002 when an immigration lawyer told him he would have to return to the Philippines and wait for 10 years to apply to come back.

Vargas was inspired to write about his life by the example of four undocumented students who walked from Miami to Washington, D.C., in 2010 to lobby for the DREAM Act, the status-legalizing proposal for immigrants who came to the United States as minors. Vargas's story, published by *The Times* after *The Washington Post* decided not to, quickly went viral in old and new media alike.

In the eight months since, Vargas has founded and become the public face for a Web-based campaign, Define American (www.defineamerican.org). "Define American brings new voices into the immigration conversation, shining a light on a growing 21st century Underground Railroad: American citizens who are forced to fill in where our broken immigration system fails," the mission statement reads. "Together, we are going to fix a broken system."

The DREAM Act fell just short of passage in Congress in December 2010 and has gotten little traction since. Broader proposals to give legal status to some of the 11 million unlawful aliens are far off the political radar screen. Vargas is critical of Alabama's law cracking down on illegal immigration but acknowledges the states' frustration with federal policies. "At the end of the day, the federal government hasn't done anything on this issue," he says.

In the meantime, Vargas waits. "There's nothing worse than being in limbo," he says.

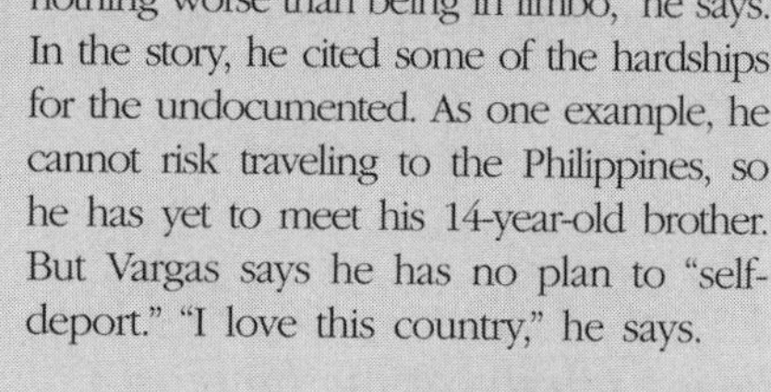

In the story, he cited some of the hardships for the undocumented. As one example, he cannot risk traveling to the Philippines, so he has yet to meet his 14-year-old brother. But Vargas says he has no plan to "self-deport." "I love this country," he says.

— Kenneth Jost

[1] "The Two Faces of Alabama," http://isthisalabama.org/. The films by director Chris Weitz were prepared under the auspices of the Center for American Progress. Some comments from Vargas are from a Feb. 15, 2012, screening of the videos at the center.

[2] Jose Antonio Vargas, "Outlaw," *The New York Times Magazine*, June 26, 2011, p. 22. Disclosure: the author is a professional acquaintance and Facebook friend of Vargas.

Continued from p. 238

in 1808. Otherwise, the United States maintained an open-door policy on immigration until the late 19th century. Europe's mid-century agricultural crisis drove waves of German and Irish peasants to the United States in the 1840s and '50s. Many were met by ethnic and anti-Catholic hostility, embodied in the first nativist political movement: the American or so-called Know-Nothing Party. The party carried one state in the 1856 presidential election and then faded from history.

Significant Chinese immigration began with the California Gold Rush of 1849 and increased with the post-Civil War push to complete the transcontinental railroad. Stark warnings of the "Yellow Peril" led to a series of restrictions at the federal level — most notably, the

Chinese Exclusion Act of 1882, which suspended immigration of Chinese laborers and barred citizenship for those already in the United States. Significantly for present-day debates, efforts to deport those in the country or to seal the borders against new Chinese immigrants were no more than partly successful. [23]

Congress laid the basis for present-day immigration law and policy in a series of increasingly restrictive enactments from the 1890s through the early 1920s that coincided with the great waves of immigration from Europe, including regions previously unrepresented in the American polity. The Immigration Act of 1891 established the Bureau of Immigration, then under the Treasury Department, and provided for border inspections and deportation of unlawful aliens. Additional laws prescribed admission procedures, created categories of inadmissible immigrants and tightened the exclusion of immigrants from Asia.

The restrictive policies drew support from nativists worried about assimilation, pro-labor groups concerned about the impact on jobs and wages and progressive leaders fearful of the impact on the urban environment. The restrictions culminated in the passage of the first and second Quota Acts in 1921 and 1924, which established the first quantitative limitation on immigration (350,000, lowered to 150,000) and a national-origins system that favored immigrants from Northern and Western Europe. In reporting the bill in 1924, a House committee stated: "If the principle of liberty . . . is to endure, the basic strain of our population must be preserved." [24]

The Quota Acts' exception for Western Hemisphere immigrants combined with the unrest associated with the Mexican Revolution (1910-1929) to produce what Stanford historian Albert Camarillo calls "a tsunami" in immigration across the United States' Southern border. Camarillo says 1.5 million Mexicans — one-tenth of the country's population — relocated to the United States by the end of the 1930s. [25] The influx fueled ethnic prejudice embodied in the derogatory term "wetback" to refer to the Mexican immigrants, most of whom actually entered by crossing arid regions rather than fording the Rio Grande River.

During the Great Depression of the 1930s, the federal and state governments — concerned about the impact on jobs for Anglo workers — sent tens of thousands of Mexicans back to their home country, sometimes with force and little regard for due process. During World War II, however, the government worked with Mexico to establish the so-called bracero program to use temporary immigrant labor for agricultural work. The "temporary" program continued into the 1960s.

Congress liberalized immigration law with a 1952 statute that included restrictionist elements as well and then, dramatically, with a 1965 law that scrapped the Eurocentric national-origins system and opened the gate to increased immigration from Latin America and Asia.

The 1952 law preserved the national-origins system but replaced the Chinese Exclusion Act with very small quotas for countries in the so-called Asia-Pacific Triangle. The act also eliminated discrimination between sexes. Over the next decade, immigration from European countries declined, seemingly weakening the rationale for the national-origins system. Against the backdrop of the civil rights revolution, the national-origins system seemed to many also to be antithetical to American values. The result was the Immigration Act of 1965, which replaced the national-origins system with a system of preferences favoring family reunification or to lesser extents admissions of professionals or skilled or unskilled workers needed in the U.S. workforce.

Quickly, the demographics of immigration shifted — and dramatically. Immigration increased overall under the new law, and the new immigrants came mostly from Latin America and Asia. By 1978, the peak year of the decade, 44 percent of legal immigration came from the Americas, 42 percent from Asia and only 12 percent from Europe. [26]

Cracking Down?

Immigration to the United States increased overall in the last decades of the 20th century, and illegal immigration in particular exploded to levels that fueled a public and political backlash. Congress and the executive branch tried to stem the flow of undocumented aliens first in 1986 by combining employer sanctions with an amnesty for those in the country for several years and then a decade later by increasing enforcement and deportations.

Then, in the wake of the Sept. 11, 2001, terrorist attacks on the United States, Congress and President George W. Bush joined in further efforts to tighten admission procedures and crack down on foreigners in the country without authorization.

Estimates of the number of immigrants in the United States illegally are inherently imprecise, but the general upward trend from the 1980s until a plateau in the 2000s is undisputed. As Congress took up immigration bills in the mid-1980s, the Census Bureau estimated the number of those undocumented at 3 million to 5 million; many politicians used higher figures. The former Immigration and Naturalization Service put the number at 3.5 million in 1990 and 7.0 million a decade later. Whatever the precise number, public opinion polls registered increasing concern about the overall level of immigration. By the mid-1990s, Gallup polls found roughly two-thirds of respondents in favor of decreasing the level of immigration, one-fourth in favor of maintaining the then-present level and fewer than 10 percent for an increase. [27]

The congressional proposals leading to the Immigration Reform and Control Act in 1986 sought to stem illegal immigration while recognizing the reality of millions of undocumented immigrants and the continuing need for immigrant labor, especially in U.S. agriculture. The law allowed legal status for immigrants in the country continuously since 1982 but aimed to deter unauthorized immigration in the future by forcing employers to verify the status of prospective hires and penalizing them for hiring anyone without legal status. Agricultural interests, however, won approval of a new guest worker program. Some 3 million people gained legal status under the two provisions, but illegal immigration continued to increase even as civil rights groups warned that the employer sanctions would result in discrimination against Latino citizens.

The backlash against illegal immigration produced a new strategy for reducing the inflows: state and federal laws cutting off benefits for aliens in the country without authorization. California, home to an estimated 1.3 million undocumented aliens at the time, blazed the path in 1994 with passage of a ballot measure, Proposition 187, that barred any government benefits to illegal aliens, including health care and public schooling. The education provision was flatly unconstitutional under a 1982 ruling by the U.S. Supreme Court that guaranteed K-12 education for school-age alien children. [28]

The measure mobilized Latino voters in the state. They contributed to the election of a Democratic governor in 1998, Gray Davis, who dropped the state's defense of the measure in court in his first year in office. In the meantime, however, Congress in 1996 had approved provisions — reluctantly signed into law by President Bill Clinton — to deny unauthorized aliens most federal benefits, including food stamps, family assistance and Social Security. The law allows states to deny state-provided benefits as well; today, at least a dozen states have enacted such further restrictions.

The centerpieces of the 1996 immigration law, however, were measures to beef up enforcement and toughen deportation policy. The Illegal Immigration Reform and Immigrant Responsibility Act authorized more money for the Border Patrol and INS, approved more funding for a 14-mile border fence already under construction and increased penalties for document fraud and alien smuggling. It sought to streamline deportation proceedings, limit appeals and bar re-entry of any deportee for at least five years. And it established an Internet-based employer verification system (E-Verify) aimed at making it easier and more reliable for employers to check legal status of prospective hires. The law proved to be tougher on paper, however, than in practice. The border fence remains incomplete, deportation proceedings backlogged and E-Verify optional and — according to critics — unreliable. And illegal immigration continued to increase.

A Maricopa County deputy arrests a woman following a sweep for illegal immigrants in Phoenix on July 29, 2010. The police operation came after protesters against Arizona's tough immigration law clashed with police hours after the law went into effect. Although the most controversial parts of the law have been blocked, five other states — Utah, Indiana, Georgia, Alabama and South Carolina — last year enacted similar laws.

AFP/Getty Images/Mark Ralston

The 9/11 attacks added homeland security to the concerns raised by the nation's porous immigration system. In post-mortems by immigration hawks, the Al Qaeda hijackers were seen as having gained entry into the United States with minimal scrutiny of their visa applications and in many cases having overstayed because of inadequate follow-up. [29] The so-called USA Patriot Act, enacted in October 2001 just 45 days after the attacks, gave the INS — later renamed the U.S. Citizenship and Immigration Service and transferred to the new Department of Homeland Security — greater authority to exclude or detain foreigners suspected of ties to terrorist organizations. The act also mandated information-sharing by the FBI to identify aliens with criminal records. Along with other counterterrorism measures, the act is viewed by supporters today as having helped prevent any successful attacks on U.S. soil since 2001. Illegal immigration, however, continued to increase — peaking at roughly 12 million in 2007.

Getting Tough

Congress and the White House moved from post-9/11 security issues to broader questions of immigration policy during Bush's second term, but bipartisan efforts to allow legal status for unlawful aliens fell victim to Republican opposition in the Senate. As a presidential candidate, Democrat Obama carried the Hispanic vote by a 2-1 margin over Republican John McCain after a campaign with limited attention to immigration issues. In the White House, Obama stepped up enforcement in some respects even as he urged Congress to back broad reform measures. The reform proposals failed with Democrats in control of both the House and the Senate and hardly got started after Republicans regained control of the House in the 2010 elections.

Bush lent support to bipartisan reform efforts in the Republican-controlled Congress in 2005 and 2006 and again in the Democratic-controlled Congress in his final two years in office. Congress in 2006 could agree only on authorizing a 700-mile border fence after reaching an impasse over a House-passed enforcement measure and a Senate-approved path-to-citizenship bill. Bush redoubled efforts in 2007 by backing a massive, bipartisan bill that would have allowed "earned citizenship" for aliens who had lived in the United States for at least eight years and met other requirements. As in the previous Congress, many Republicans rejected the proposal as an unacceptable amnesty. The bill died on June 7 after the Senate rejected three cloture motions to cut off debate. [30]

Immigration played only a minor role in the 2008 presidential campaign between Obama and McCain, Senate colleagues who had both supported reform proposals. Both campaigns responded to growing public anger over illegal immigration by emphasizing enforcement when discussing the issue, but the subject went unmentioned in the candidates' three televised debates. McCain, once popular with Hispanics in his home state of Arizona, appeared to have paid at the polls for the GOP's hard line on immigration. Exit polls indicated that Obama won 67 percent of a record-size Hispanic vote; McCain got 31 percent — a significant drop from Bush's 39 percent share of the vote in 2004. [31]

With Obama in office, Congress remained gridlocked even as the president tried to smooth the way for reform measures by stepping up enforcement. The congressional gridlock had already invited state lawmakers to step into the vacuum. State legislatures passed more than 200 immigration-related laws in 2007 and 2008, according to a compilation by the National Conference on State Legislatures; the number soared to more than 300 annually for the next three years. [32]

The numbers included some resolutions praising the country's multi-ethnic heritage, but most of the new state laws sought to tighten enforcement against undocumented aliens or to limit benefits to them. Among the earliest of the new laws was an Arizona measure — enacted in June 2007, two weeks after the Senate impasse in Washington — that provided for lifting the business licenses of companies that knowingly hired illegal aliens and mandated use of the federal E-Verify program to ascertain status of prospective hires. Business and labor groups, supported by the Obama administration, challenged the law on federal preemption grounds. The Supreme Court's 5-3 decision in May 2011 to uphold the law prompted several states to enact similar mandatory E-Verify provisions. [33]

The interplay on immigration policy between Washington and state capitals is continuing. In Obama's first three years in office, the total number of removals increased to what ICE calls on its website "record levels." Even so, Arizona lawmakers and officials criticized federal enforcement as inadequate in the legislative debate leading to SB 1070's enactment in April 2010. Legal challenges followed quickly — first from a Latino organization; then from a broad coalition of civil rights and civil liberties groups; and then, on July 6, from the Justice Department. The most controversial parts of the law have been blocked, first by U.S. District Court Judge Susan Bolton's injunction later that month and then by the Ninth Circuit's decision affirming her decision in April 2011. The legal challenges did not stop five other states — Utah, Indiana, Georgia, Alabama and South Carolina — from enacting similar laws in spring and early summer 2011. Civil rights groups and the Justice Department followed with similar suits challenging the new state enactments.

As the 2012 presidential campaign got under way, immigration emerged as an issue between Republican candidates vying for the party's nomination. The issue posed difficulties for the GOP hopefuls as they sought to appeal to rank-and-file GOP voters upset about illegal immigration without forfeiting Latino votes in the primary season and in the general election. Presumed front-runner Mitt Romney took a hard stance against illegal immigration in early contests but softened his message in advance of winning the pivotal Jan. 31 primary in Florida with its substantial Hispanic vote.

Despite differences in details and in rhetoric, the three leading GOP candidates — Romney, Newt Gingrich and Rick Santorum — all said they opposed the DREAM Act in its present form even as Obama called for Congress to pass the bill in his State of the Union speech. ■

CURRENT SITUATION

Obama's Approach

The Obama administration is claiming success in increasing border enforcement and removing unlawful aliens while injecting more prosecutorial discretion into deportation cases. But the mix of firm and flexible policies is resulting in criticism from both sides of the issue.

U.S. Immigration and Customs Enforcement (ICE) counted a record 396,906 "removals" during fiscal 2011, including court-ordered deportations as well as administrative or voluntary removals or returns. The number includes a record 216,698 aliens with criminal convictions. [34]

Meanwhile, Homeland Security Secretary Janet Napolitano says illegal border-crossing attempts have decreased by more than half in the last three years. In a Jan. 30 speech to the National Press Club in Washington, Napolitano linked the decline to an increase in the number of Border Patrol agents to 21,000, which she said was more than double the number in 2004.

"The Obama administration has undertaken the most serious and sustained actions to secure our borders in our nation's history," Napolitano told journalists. "And it is clear from every measure we currently have that this approach is working." [35]

Immigration hawk Krikorian with the Center for Immigration Studies gives the administration some, but only some, credit for the removal statistics. "They're not making up the numbers," Krikorian says. But he notes that immigration removals increased during the Bush administration and that the rate of increase has slowed under Obama.

In addition, Krikorian notes that new figures compiled by a government information tracking service indicate the pace of new immigration cases and of court-processed deportations slowed in the first quarter of fiscal 2012 (October, November and December 2011). A report in early February by Syracuse University's Transactional Records Access Clearinghouse (TRAC) shows 34,362 court-ordered removals or "voluntary departures" in the period, compared to 35,771 in the previous three months — about a 4 percent drop.

A separate TRAC report later in the month showed what the service called a "sharp decline" in new ICE filings. ICE initiated 39,331 new deportation proceedings in the nation's 50 immigration courts during the first quarter of fiscal 2012, according to the report, a 33 percent decline from the 58,639 new filings in the previous quarter. [36]

"The people in this administration would like to pull the plug on enforcement altogether," Krikorian complains. "They refuse to ask for more money for detention beds and then plead poverty that they can't do more."

From the opposite perspective, some Latino officials and organizations have been critical of the pace of deportations. When Obama delivered a speech in favor of immigration reform in El Paso, Texas, in May 2011, the president of the National Council of La Raza tempered praise for the president's position with criticism of the deportation policy.

"As record levels of detention and deportation continue to soar, families are torn apart, innocent youth are being deported and children are left behind without the protection of their parents," Janet Murguía said in a May 10 press release. "Such policies do not reflect American values and do little to solve the problem. We can do better." [37]

Latinos disapprove of the Obama administration's handling of deportations by roughly a 2-1 margin, according to a poll by the Pew Hispanic Center in December 2011. Overall, the poll found 59 percent of those surveyed opposed the administration's policy while 27 percent approved. Disapproval was higher among foreign-born Latinos (70 percent) than those born in the United States (46 percent). [38]

Napolitano and ICE Director John Morton are both claiming credit for focusing the agency's enforcement on the most serious cases, including criminal aliens, repeat violators and recent border crossers. Morton announced the new "prosecutorial discretion" policy in an agency-wide directive in June 2011. [39]

TRAC, however, questions the claimed emphasis on criminal aliens. The 39,331 new deportation filings in the first quarter of fiscal 2012 included only 1,300 against aliens with convictions for "aggravated felonies," as defined in immigration law. "Even this small share was down from previous quarters," the Feb. 21 report states. Aliens with aggravated felony convictions accounted for 3.3 percent of deportations in the period, compared to 3.8 percent in the previous quarter. [40]

The administration is also being questioned on its claim — in Obama's El Paso speech and elsewhere — to have virtually completed the border fence that Congress ordered constructed in the Secure Fence Act of 2006. [41] The act called for the 652-mile barrier to be constructed of two layers of reinforced fencing but was amended the next year — with Bush still in office — to give the administration more discretion in what type of barriers to use.

As of May 2011, the barrier included only 36 miles of double-layer fencing, according to PolitiFact, the fact-checking service of the *Tampa Bay Times*. The rest is single-layer fencing or vehicle barriers that critic Krikorian says are so low that a pedestrian can step over them. PolitiFact calls Obama's claim "mostly false." [42]

Meanwhile, the administration is preparing to extend nationwide its controversial "Secure Communities" program, which tries to spot immigration law violators by matching fingerprints of local arrestees with the database of the Department of Homeland Security (DHS). A match allows U.S. Immigration and Customs Enforcement (ICE) to issue a so-called detainer against violators, sending their cases into the immigration enforcement system. The administration

Continued on p. 246

At Issue:

Should Congress pass the DREAM Act?

WALTER A. EWING
SENIOR RESEARCHER, IMMIGRATION POLICY CENTER AMERICAN IMMIGRATION COUNCIL

WRITTEN FOR *CQ RESEARCHER*, MARCH 2012

yes

The Development, Relief and Education for Alien Minors Act is rooted in common sense. To begin with, it would benefit a group of unauthorized young people who, in most cases, did not come to this country of their own accord. Rather, they were brought here by their parents. The DREAM Act would also enable its beneficiaries to achieve higher levels of education and obtain better, higher-paying jobs, which would increase their contributions to the U.S. economy and American society. In short, the DREAM Act represents basic fairness and enlightened self-interest.

More than 2 million young people would benefit from the DREAM Act, and their numbers grow by roughly 65,000 per year. They came to the United States before age 18, many as young children. They tend to be culturally American and fluent in English. Their primary ties are to this country, not the countries of their birth. And the majority had no say in the decision to come to this country without authorization — that decision was made by the adult members of their families. Punishing these young people for the actions of their parents runs counter to American social values and legal norms. Yet, without the DREAM Act, these young people will be forced to live on the margins of U.S. society or will be deported to countries they may not even know.

Assuming they aren't deported, the young people who would benefit from the DREAM Act face enormous barriers to higher education and professional jobs because of their unauthorized status. They are ineligible for most forms of college financial aid and cannot work legally in this country. The DREAM Act would remove these barriers, which would benefit the U.S. economy.

The College Board estimates that over the course of a working lifetime, a college graduate earns 60 percent more than a high school graduate. This higher income translates into extra tax revenue flowing to federal, state and local governments.

The DREAM Act is in the best interest of the United States both socially and economically. It would resolve the legal status of millions of unauthorized young people in a way that is consistent with core American values. And it would empower these young people to become better-educated, higher-earning workers and taxpayers. Every day that goes by without passage of the DREAM Act is another day of wasted talent and potential.

MARK KRIKORIAN
EXECUTIVE DIRECTOR, CENTER FOR IMMIGRATION STUDIES

WRITTEN FOR *CQ RESEARCHER*, MARCH 2012

no

The appeal of the DREAM Act is obvious. People brought here illegally at a very young age and who have grown up in the United States are the most sympathetic group of illegal immigrants. Much of the public is open to the idea of amnesty for them.

But the actual DREAM Act before Congress is a deeply flawed measure in at least four ways:

- Rather than limiting amnesty to those brought here as infants and toddlers, it applies to illegal immigrants who arrived before their 16th birthday. But if the argument is that their very identity was formed here, age 7 would be a more sensible cutoff. That is recognized as a turning point in a child's psychological development (called the "age of reason" by the Catholic Church, hence the traditional age for First Communion). Such a lower-age cutoff, combined with a requirement of at least 10 years' residence here, would make a hypothetical DREAM Act 2.0 much more defensible.
- All amnesties are vulnerable to fraud, even more than other immigration benefits. About one-fourth of the beneficiaries of the amnesty granted by Congress in 1986 were liars, including one of the leaders of the 1993 World Trade Center bombing. But the DREAM Act specifically prohibits the prosecution of anyone who lies on an amnesty application. So you can make any false claim you like about your arrival or schooling in America without fear of punishment. A DREAM Act 2.0 would make clear that any lies, no matter how trivial, will result in arrest and imprisonment.
- All amnesties send a signal to prospective illegal immigrants that, if you get in and keep your head down, you might benefit from the next amnesty. But the bill contains no enforcement provisions to limit the need for another DREAM Act a decade from now. That's why a serious proposal would include measures such as electronic verification of the legal status of all new hires, plus explicit authorization for state and local enforcement of immigration law.
- Finally, all amnesties reward illegal immigrants — in this case including the adults who brought their children here illegally. A credible DREAM Act 2.0 would bar the adult relatives of the beneficiaries from ever receiving any immigration status or even a right to visit the United States. If those who came as children are not responsible, then those who are responsible must pay the price for their lawbreaking.

Continued from p. 244

touts the program as "a simple and common sense" enforcement tool. Critics note, however, that it has resulted in wrongful detention of U.S. citizens in a considerable but unknown number of cases. One reason for the mistakes: The DHS database includes all immigration transactions, not just violations, and thus could show a match for an immigrant with legal status. [43]

Supreme Court Action

All eyes are on the Supreme Court as the justices prepare for arguments on April 25 in Arizona's effort to reinstate major parts of its trend-setting law cracking down on illegal immigrants.

The Arizona case is the furthest advanced of suits challenging the six recently enacted state laws that give state and local police responsibility for enforcing federal immigration laws. After winning an injunction blocking major parts of the Arizona law, the Obama administration filed similar suits against Alabama's HB 56 as well as the Georgia and South Carolina measures.

The ACLU's Immigrants Rights Project, along with Hispanic and other civil rights groups, has filed separate challenges on broader grounds against all six laws. Federal district courts have blocked parts of all the laws, though some contentious parts of Alabama's law were allowed to take effect.

District court judges in the Indiana, South Carolina and Utah cases put the litigation on hold pending the Supreme Court's decision in the Arizona case. Alabama and Georgia asked the Eleventh U.S. Circuit Court of Appeals to postpone the scheduled March 1 arguments in their cases, but the court declined.

Judge Charles R. Wilson opened the Atlanta-based court's March 1 session, however, by announcing that the three-judge panel had decided to withhold its opinion until after the Supreme Court decides the Arizona case. "Hopefully, that information will help you in framing your arguments today," Wilson told the assembled lawyers. [44]

Wilson and fellow Democratic-appointed Circuit Judge Beverly B. Martin dominated the questioning during the three hours of arguments in the cases. Both judges pressed lawyers defending Alabama and Georgia on the effects of their laws on the education of children, the ability of illegal aliens to carry on with their lives while immigration courts decided their cases and what would happen if every state adopted their approach to dealing with immigration violations. The third member of the panel, Richard Voorhees, a Republican-appointed federal district court judge, asked only three questions on technical issues.

Opening the government's argument in the Alabama case, Deputy Assistant U.S. Attorney General Beth Brinkmann said the state's law attempts to usurp exclusive federal authority over immigration. "The regulation of immigration is a matter vested exclusively in the national government," Brinkman said. "Alabama's state-specific regulation scheme violates that authority. It attacks every aspect of an alien's life and makes it impossible for the alien to live."

Alabama Solicitor General John C. Neiman Jr. drew sharp challenges from Wilson and Martin even before he began his argument. Wilson focused on the law's Section 10, which makes it a criminal misdemeanor for an alien unlawfully present in the United States to fail to carry alien registration papers.

"You could be convicted and sent to jail in Alabama even though the Department of Homeland Security says, 'You're an illegal alien, but we've decided you're going to remain here in the United States?' " Wilson asked.

Neiman conceded the point. "If the deportation hearing occurred after the violation of Section 10, then yes," Neiman said. "Someone could be held to be in violation of Section 10 and then later be held not removable."

Wilson also pressed Neiman on the potential effects on the federal government's ability to control immigration policy if states enacted laws with different levels of severity. "These laws could certainly have the effect of making certain states places where illegal aliens would be likely to go," the state's attorney acknowledged.

Representing the ACLU in the separate challenge, Immigrants Rights Project director Wang sharply attacked the motive behind the Alabama law. The law, she said, was written to carry out the legislature's stated objective "to attack every aspect of an illegal immigrant's life so that they will deport themselves." *

In Washington, lawyers for Arizona filed their brief with the Supreme Court defending its law, SB 1070, in early February. Among 20 *amicus* briefs filed in support of Arizona's case is one drafted by the Michigan attorney general's office on behalf of 16 states similarly defending the states' right to help enforce federal immigration law. A similar brief was filed by nine states in the Eleventh Circuit in support of the Alabama law.

The government's brief in the Arizona case is due March 19. Following the April 25 arguments, the Supreme Court is expected to decide the case before the current term ends in late June.

Meanwhile, legal challenges to other parts of the state's law are continuing in federal court in Arizona. In a Feb. 29 ruling, Bolton blocked on First Amendment grounds a provision prohibiting people from blocking traffic when they offer day labor services on the street. [45] ■

* The appeals court on March 8 issued a temporary injunction blocking enforcement of two provisions, those prohibiting unlawful aliens from enforcing contracts in court or entering into business transactions with state or local government agencies.

OUTLOOK

A Broken System

The immigration system is broken. On that much, the pro- and low-immigration groups agree. But they disagree sharply on how to fix it. And the divide defeats any attempts to fix it even if it can be fixed.

Pro-immigration groups like to talk about the "three-legged stool" of immigration reform: legal channels for family- and job-based immigration; a path to citizenship for unlawful aliens already in the United States; and better border security. Low-immigration groups agree on the need for better border controls but want to make it harder, not easier, for would-be immigrants and generally oppose legal status for the near-record number of unlawful aliens.

Public opinion is ambivalent and conflicted on immigration issues even as immigration, legal and illegal, has reached record levels. The nearly 14 million new immigrants, legal and illegal, who came to the United States from 2000 to 2010 made that decade the highest ever in U.S. history, according to the low-immigration Center for Immigration Studies. The foreign-born population reached 40 million, the center says, also a record. [46]

Some public opinion polls find support for legal status for illegal immigrants, especially if the survey questions specify conditions to meet: 66 percent supported it, for example, in a Fox News poll in early December 2011. Three weeks earlier, however, a CNN poll found majority support (55 percent) for concentrating on "stopping the flow of illegal immigrants and deporting those already here" instead of developing a plan for legal residency (42 percent). [47]

Other polls appear consistently to find support for the laws in Arizona and other states to crack down on illegal immigrants — most recently by a 2-1 margin in a poll by Quinnipiac University in Connecticut. [48] "Popular sentiment is always against immigration," says Muzaffar Chishti, director of the Migration Policy Institute's office at New York University School of Law and himself a naturalized U.S. citizen who emigrated from his native India in 1974.

Pro-immigration groups say the public is ahead of the politicians in Washington and state capitals who are pushing for stricter laws. State legislators "have chosen to scapegoat immigration instead of solving tough economic challenges," says Noorani with the National Immigration Forum. "There are politicians who would rather treat this as a political hot potato," he adds, instead of offering "practical solutions."

From the opposite side, the Federation for American Immigration Reform's Stein says he is "pessimistic, disappointed and puzzled" by what he calls "the short-sighted views" of political leaders. Earlier, Stein says, "politicians all over the country were touting the virtues of engagement in immigration policy." But now he complains that even Republicans are talking about "amnesty and the DREAM Act," instead of criticizing what he calls the Obama administration's "elimination of any immigration enforcement."

Enforcement, however, is one component of the system that, if not broken, is at least completely overwhelmed. In explaining the new prosecutorial discretion policy, ICE director Morton frankly acknowledged the agency "has limited resources to remove those illegally in the United States." [49] The nation's immigrant courts have a current backlog of 300,225 cases, according to a TRAC compilation, double the number in 2001. [50]

Employers' groups say the system's rules for hiring immigrants are problematic at best. In Alabama, Reed with the contractors' group says employers do their best to comply with the status-verification requirements but find the procedures and paperwork difficult. The farm federation's Helms says the same for the rules for temporary guest workers. "We're working at the national level to have a more effective way to hire legal migrant workers to do those jobs that it's hard to find local workers to do," he says.

The rulings by the Supreme Court on the Arizona law will clarify the lines between federal and state enforcement responsibilities, but the Center for Immigration Studies' Krikorian says the decision is likely to increase the politicization of the issue. A ruling to uphold the law will encourage other states to follow Arizona's lead, he says, but would also "energize the anti-enforcement groups." A ruling to find the state laws pre-empted, on the other hand, will mobilize pro-enforcement groups, he says.

The political and legal debates will be conducted against the backdrop of the nation's rapidly growing Hispanic population, attributable more to birth rates than to immigration. [51] "Whoever the next president is, whoever the next Congress is, will have to address this issue," says Giovagnoli with the American Immigration Council. "The demographics are not going to allow people to ignore this issue.

"I do believe we're going to reform the immigration system," Giovagnoli adds "It's going to be a lot of work. Even under the best of circumstances, it's a lot of work." ■

Notes

[1] Quoted in Kim Chandler, "Alabama House passes Arizona-style immigration bill," *The Birmingham News*, April 6, 2011, p. 1A.

[2] The case is *Arizona v. United States*, 11-182. Background and legal filings compiled on SCOTUSblog, www.scotusblog.com/case-files/cases/arizona-v-united-states/?wpmp_switcher=desktop.-

[3] See Human Rights Watch, "No Way to Live: Alabama's Immigration Law," December 2011, www.hrw.org/news/2011/12/13/usalabama-no-way-live-under-immigrant-law.

[4] Quoted in David White, "Hundreds rally at State House seeking immigration law repeal," *The Birmingham News*, Feb. 15, 2012, p. 1A.

[5] See "Unauthorized Immigrant Population: State and National Trends, 2010," Pew Hispanic Center, Feb. 1, 2011, pp. 23, 24, www.pewhispanic.org/files/reports/133.pdf. The U.S. Department of Homeland Security estimates differ slightly; for 2010, it estimates nationwide unauthorized immigrant population at 10.8 million.

[6] For previous *CQ Researcher* coverage, see: Alan Greenblatt, "Immigration Debate," pp. 97-120, updated Dec. 10, 2011; Reed Karaim, "America's Border Fence," Sept. 19, 2008, pp. 745-768; Peter Katel, "Illegal Immigration," May 6, 2005, pp. 393-420; David Masci, "Debate Over Immigration," July 14, 2000, pp. 569-592; Kenneth Jost, "Cracking Down on Immigration," Feb. 3, 1995.

[7] Quoted in David White, "Illegal immigration bill passes," *The Birmingham News*, June 3, 2011, p. 1A.

[8] See Dana Beyerle, "Study says immigration law has economic costs," *Tuscaloosa News*, Jan. 31, 2012, www.tuscaloosanews.com/article/20120131/news/120139966. For Beason's statement, see http://scottbeason.com/2012/01/26/beason-statement-on-the-impact-of-hb-56-on-alabama-unemployment-rate/.

[9] Samuel Addy, "A Cost-Benefit Analysis of the New Alabama Immigration Law," Center for Business and Economic Research, Culverhouse College of Commerce and Business Administration, University of Alabama, January 2012, http://cber.cba.ua.edu/New%20AL%20Immigration%20Law%20-%20Costs%20and%20Benefits.pdf; Hammon quoted in Brian Lyman, "Studies, surveys examine immigration law's impact," *The Montgomery Advertiser*, Feb. 1, 2012.

[10] See Alan Gomez, "Immigrants return to Alabama," *USA Today*, Feb. 22, 2012, p. 3A; Jay Reeves, "Immigrants trickling back to Ala despite crackdown," The Associated Press, Feb. 19, 2012.

[11] The decision in *United States v. Alabama*, 2:11-CV-2746-SLB, U.S.D.C.-N.D.Ala. (Sept. 28, 2011), is available via *The New York Times*: http://graphics8.nytimes.com/packages/pdf/national/112746memopnentered.pdf. For coverage, see Brian Lyman, "Judge allows key part of immigration law to go into effect," *The Montgomery Advertiser*, Sept. 29, 2011; Brian Lawson, "Judge halts part of immigration law," *The Birmingham News*, Sept. 29, 2011, p. 1A. The Alabama Office of the Attorney General has a chronology of the legal proceedings: www.ago.state.al.us/Page-Immigration-Litigation-Federal.

[12] Quoted in Eric Velasco, "Immigration law draws praise, scorn," *The Birmingham News*, June 10, 2011, p. 1A.

[13] Steven A. Camarota, "A Need for More Immigrant Workers?," Center for Immigration Studies, June 2011, http://cis.org/no-need-for-more-immigrant-workers-q1-2011.

[14] "The Impact of Unauthorized Immigrants on the Budgets of State and Local Governments," Congressional Budget Office, Dec. 6, 2007, p. 3, /www.cbo.gov/sites/default/files/cbofiles/ftpdocs/87xx/doc8711/12-6-immigration.pdf.

[15] David Gerber, *American Immigration: A Very Short Introduction* (2011).

[16] Quoted in Velasco, *op. cit.*

[17] Quoted in White, *op. cit.* Hammon's office did not respond to several *CQ Researcher* requests for an interview.

[18] "Alabama's Illegal Immigration Law Gets Hollywood's Attention," WAKA/CBS8, Montgomery, Feb. 21, 2012, www.waka.com/home/top-stories/Alabamas-Illegal-Immigration-Law-Gets-Attention-From-Hollywood-139937153.html. The four separate videos by Chris Weitz, collectively titled "Is This Alabama?" are on an eponymous website: http://isthisalabama.org/.

[19] See "Delegation of Immigration Authority 287(g) Immigration and Nationality Act," www.ice.gov/287g/ (visited February 2012).

[20] See Sandhya Somashekhar and Amy Gardner, "Immigration is flash point in Fla. Primary," *The Washington Post*, Jan. 26, 2012, p. A6.

[21] Text available on the White House website: www.whitehouse.gov/the-press-office/2012/01/24/remarks-president-state-union-address.

[22] General background drawn from Gerber, *op. cit.*; Otis L. Graham Jr., *Unguarded Gates: A History of America's Immigration Crisis* (2004). Some country-by-country background drawn from Mary C. Waters and Reed Ueda (eds.), *The New Americans: A Guide to Immigration Since 1965* (2007).

[23] Roger Daniels, *Guarding the Golden Door: American Immigration Policy and Immigrants Since 1882* (2004), pp. 19-22.

[24] Quoted in Graham, *op. cit.*, p. 51.

[25] Albert M. Camarillo, "Mexico," in Waters and Ueda, *op. cit.*, p. 506.

[26] Figures from *INS Statistical Yearbook*, 1978, cited in Daniels, *op. cit.*, p 138.

[27] Polls cited in Daniels, *op. cit.*, p. 233.

[28] See *Plyler v. Doe*, 452 U.S. 202 (1982).

[29] See Graham, *op. cit.*, Chap. 17, and sources cited therein.

[30] "Immigration Rewrite Dies in Senate," *CQ Almanac 2007*, pp. 15-9 — 15-11, http://library.cqpress.com/cqalmanac/cqal07-1006-44907-2047763.

[31] See Julia Preston, "Immigration Cools as Campaign Issue," *The New York Times*, Oct. 29, 2008, p. A20, www.nytimes.com/2008/10/29/us/politics/29immig.html; Mark Hugo Lopez, "How Hispanics Voted in the 2008 Election," Pew Hispanic Research Center, Nov. 5, 2008, updated Nov. 7, 2008, http://pewresearch.org/pubs/1024/exit-poll-analysis-hispanics.

[32] "Immigration Policy Report: 2011 Immigration-Related Laws and Resolutions in the States (Jan. 1- Dec. 7, 2011)," National Conference of State Legislatures, www.ncsl.org/issues-research/immigration/state-immigration-legislation-report-dec-2011.aspx.

[33] The decision is *Chamber of Commerce v. Whiting*, 563 U.S. — (2011). For coverage, see Kenneth Jost, *Supreme Court Yearbook 2010-2011*, http://library.cqpress.com/scyb/document.php?id=scyb10-1270-72832-2397001&type=hitlist&num=0.

[34] See "ICE Removals, Fiscal Years 2007-2011," in Mark Hugo Lopez, *et al.*, "As Deportations Rise to Record Levels, Most Latinos Oppose Obama's Policy," Pew Hispanic Center, Dec. 28, 2011, p. 33, http://pewresearch.org/pubs/2158/latinos-hispanics-immigration-policy-deportations-george-bush-barack-obama-administration-democrats-republicans. The report notes that

About the Author

Associate Editor **Kenneth Jost** graduated from Harvard College and Georgetown University Law Center. He is the author of the *Supreme Court Yearbook* and editor of *The Supreme Court from A to Z* (both *CQ Press*). He was a member of the *CQ Researcher* team that won the American Bar Association's 2002 Silver Gavel Award. His previous reports include "States and Federalism" and "Bilingual Education vs. English Immersion." He is also author of the blog *Jost on Justice* (http://jostonjustice.blogspot.com).

ICE's statistics differ somewhat from those released by DHS, its parent department.

35 "Secretary of Homeland Security Janet Napolitano's 2nd Annual Address on the State of America's Homeland Security: Homeland Security and Economic Security," Jan. 30, 2012, www.dhs.gov/ynews/speeches/napolitano-state-of-america-homeland-security.shtm.

36 "Share of Immigration Cases Ending in Deportation Orders Hits Record Low," *TRAC Reports*, Feb. 7, 2012, http://trac.syr.edu/immigration/reports/272/; "Sharp Decline in ICE Deportation Filings," Feb. 21, 2012, http://trac.syr.edu/immigration/reports/274/. For coverage, see Paloma Esquivel, "Number of deportation cases down by a third," *Los Angeles Times*, Feb. 24, 2012, p. AA2, http://articles.latimes.com/2012/feb/24/local/la-me-deportation-drop-20120224.

37 Text of La Raza statement, www.nclr.org/index.php/about_us/news/news_releases/janet_murgua_president_and_ceo_of_nclr_responds_to_president_obamas_speech_in_el_paso_texas/. For coverage of the president's speech, see Milan Simonich, "In El Paso, President Obama renews national immigration debate, argues humane policy would aid national economy," *El Paso Times*, May 11, 2011.

38 Lopez, *op. cit.*, p. 16.

39 U.S. Immigration and Customs Enforcement: Memorandum, June 17, 2011, www.ice.gov/doclib/secure-communities/pdf/prosecutorial-discretion-memo.pdf. For coverage, see Susan Carroll, "ICE memo urges more discretion in immigration changes," *Houston Chronicle*, June 21, 2011, p. A3.

40 "Sharp Decline," *op. cit.*

41 For background, see Reed Karaim, "America's Border Fence," *CQ Researcher*, Sept. 19, 2008, pp. 745-768.

42 "Obama says the border fence is 'now basically complete,' " PolitiFact, www.politifact.com/truth-o-meter/statements/2011/may/16/barack-obama/obama-says-border-fence-now-basically-complete/. The original rating of "partly true" was changed to "mostly false" on July 27, 2011.

43 See "Secure Communities," on the ICE website: www.ice.gov/secure_communities/; Julia Preston, "Immigration Crackdown Snares Americans," *The New York Times*, Dec. 14, 2011, p. A20, www.nytimes.com/2011/12/14/us/measures-to-capture-illegal-aliens-nab-citizens.html?pagewanted=all.

44 Coverage of the hearing by contributing writer Don Plummer. For additional coverage, see Brian Lawson, "11th Circuit won't rule on Alabama/Georgia laws until after Supreme Court rules on Arizona," *The Huntsville Times*, March 2, 2012; Jeremy Redmon, "Court to rule later on Georgia, Alabama anti-illegal immigrant laws," *The Atlanta Journal-Constitution*, March 2, 2012.

45 See Jacques Billeaud, "Judge blocks day labor rules in AZ immigration law," The Associated Press, March 1, 2012.

46 Steven A. Camarota, "A Record-Setting Decade of Immigration, 2000-2010," Center for Immigration Studies, October 2011, www.cis.org/articles/2011/record-setting-decade.pdf.

47 Fox News poll, Dec. 5-7, 2011, and CNN/ORC International poll, Nov. 18-20, 2011, cited at www.PollingReport.com/immigration.htm.

48 Quinnipiac University poll, Feb. 14-20, 2011, cited *ibid.*

49 ICE memo, *op. cit.*

50 "Immigration Court Backlog Tool," Transactional Records Access Clearinghouse, http://trac.syr.edu/phptools/immigration/court_backlog/ (visited March 2012).

51 "The Mexican-American Boom: Births Overtake Immigration," Pew Hispanic Center, July 24, 2011, www.pewhispanic.org/files/reports/144.pdf. The report depicts the phenomenon as "especially evident" among Mexican-Americans; it notes that Mexican-Americans are on average younger than other racial or ethnic groups and that Mexican-American women have more children than their counterparts in other groups. For background, see David Masci, "Latinos' Future," *CQ Researcher*, Oct. 17, 2003, pp. 869-892.

FOR MORE INFORMATION

American Civil Liberties Union, Immigrant Rights Project, 125 Broad St., 18th floor, New York, NY 10004; 212-549-2500; www.aclu.org/immigrants-rights. Seeks to expand and enforce civil liberties and civil rights of immigrants.

American Immigration Council, 1331 G St., N.W., 2nd floor, Washington, DC 20005; 202-507-7500; www.americanimmigrationcouncil.org. Supports sensible and humane immigration policies.

America's Voice, 1050 17th St., N.W., Suite 490, Washington, DC 20036; 202-463-8602; http://americasvoiceonline.org/. Supports "real, comprehensive immigration reform," including reform of immigration enforcement practices.

Center for Immigration Studies, 1522 K St., N.W., Suite 820, Washington, DC 20005-1202; 202-466-8185; www.cis.org. An independent, nonpartisan research organization that supports what it calls low-immigration, pro-immigrant policies.

Define American, www.defineamerican.com/. Founded by journalist and undocumented immigrant Jose Antonio Vargas, the web-based organization seeks to fix what it calls a "broken" immigration system.

Federation for American Immigration Reform, 25 Massachusetts Ave., N.W., Suite 330, Washington, DC 20001; 202-328-7004; www.fairus.org. Seeks "significantly lower" immigration levels.

Migration Policy Institute, 1400 16th St., N.W., Suite 300, Washington, DC 20036; 202-266-1940; www.migrationpolicy.org. A nonpartisan, nonprofit think tank dedicated to analysis of the movement of people worldwide.

National Council of La Raza, 1126 16th St., N.W., Suite 600, Washington, DC 20036-4845; 202-785-1670; www.nclr.org. The country's largest national Hispanic advocacy and civil rights organization.

National Immigration Forum, 50 F St., N.W., Suite 300, Washington, DC 20001; 202-347-0040; www.immigrationforum.org. Advocates for the values of immigration and immigrants to the nation.

Pew Hispanic Center, 1615 L St., N.W., Suite 700, Washington, DC 20036; 202-419-4300; www.pewhispanic.org/. Seeks to improve understanding of the U.S. Hispanic population and to chronicle Latinos' growing impact on the nation.

Bibliography

Selected Sources

Books

Coates, David, and Peter M. Siavelis (eds.), *Getting Immigration Right: What Every American Needs to Know*, Potomac, 2009.
Essays by 15 contributors representing a range of backgrounds and views examine, among other issues, the economic impact of immigration and proposed reforms to address illegal immigration. Includes notes, two-page list of further readings. Coates holds a professorship in Anglo-American studies at Wake Forest University; Siavelis is an associate professor of political science there.

Daniels, Roger, *Guarding the Golden Door: American Immigration Policy and Immigrants Since 1882*, Hill and Wang, 2004.
A professor of history emeritus at the University of Cincinnati gives a generally well-balanced account of developments and trends in U.S. immigration policies from the Chinese Exclusion Act of 1882 through the immediate post-9/11 period. Includes detailed notes, 16-page bibliography.

Gerber, David, *American Immigration: A Very Short Introduction*, Oxford University Press, 2011.
A professor of history at the University of Buffalo gives a compact, generally positive overview of the history of immigration from colonial America to the present. Includes two-page list of further readings.

Graham, Otis L. Jr., *Unguarded Gates: A History of America's Immigration Crisis*, Rowman & Littlefield, 2004.
A professor emeritus at the University of California-Santa Barbara provides a critical account of the United States' transition from an open-border policy with relatively small-scale immigration to a system of managed immigration that he views today as overwhelmed by both legal and illegal immigration. Includes notes.

Reimers, David M., *Other Immigrants: The Global Origins of the American People*, New York University Press, 2005.
A New York University professor of history emeritus brings together new information and research about the non-European immigration to the United States, emphasizing the emergence of "a new multicultural society" since 1940. Individual chapters cover Central and South America, East and South Asia, the Middle East, "new black" immigrants and refugees and asylees. Includes extensive notes, six-page list of suggested readings.

Waters, Mary C., and Reed Ueda (eds.), *The New Americans: A Guide to Immigration Since 1965*, Harvard University Press, 2007.
The book includes essays by more than 50 contributors, some covering broad immigration-related topics and others providing individual portraits of immigrant populations by country or region of origin. Includes detailed notes for each essay, comprehensive listing of immigration and naturalization legislation from 1790 through 2002. Waters is a professor of sociology at Harvard University, Ueda a professor of history at Tufts University.

Articles

"Reap What You Sow," *This American Life*, Jan. 27, 2012, www.thisamericanlife.org/radio-archives/episode/456/reap-what-you-sow.
The segment by reporter Jack Hitt on the popular public radio program found that Alabama's law to encourage undocumented immigrants to self-deport was having unintended consequences.

Kemper, Bob, "Immigration Reform: Is It Feasible?," *Washington Lawyer*, October 2011, p. 22, www.dcbar.org/for_lawyers/resources/publications/washington_lawyer/october_2011/immigration_reform.cfm.
The article gives a good overview of recent and current immigration debates, concluding with the prediction that any "permanent resolution" will likely prove to be "elusive."

Reports and Studies

"No Way to Live: Alabama's Immigrant Law," Human Rights Watch, December 2011, www.hrw.org/reports/2011/12/14/no-way-live-0.
The highly critical report finds that Alabama's law cracking down on illegal immigrants has "severely affected" the state's unlawful aliens and their children, many of them U.S. citizens, as well as "the broader community linked to this population."

Baxter, Tom, "Alabama's Immigration Disaster: The Harshest Law in the Land Harms the State's Economy and Society," Center for American Progress, February 2012, www.americanprogress.org/issues/2012/02/pdf/alabama_immigration_disaster.pdf.
The critical account by journalist Baxter under the auspices of the progressive Center for American Progress finds that Alabama's anti-illegal immigration law has had "particularly harsh" social and economic costs and effects.

Passel, Jeffrey S., and D'Vera Cohn, "Unauthorized Immigrant Population: National and State Trends, 2010," Pew Hispanic Center, Feb. 1, 2011, www.pewhispanic.org/files/reports/133.pdf.
The 32-page report by the Washington-based center provides national and state-by-state estimates of the unauthorized immigrant population and the number of unauthorized immigrants in the workforce.

The Next Step:

Additional Articles from Current Periodicals

Arizona and Alabama Laws

Rawls, Phillip, "Ala. Split Over Immigration Law's Fairness," The Associated Press, Dec. 15, 2011, www.chron.com/news/article/Poll-Ala-split-over-immigration-law-s-fairness-2405167.php.

Alabama residents are sharply divided over the fairness of the state's new immigration law, according to a survey.

Richey, Warren, "Supreme Court Takes Arizona Immigration Law Case in Key Test of Federal Power," *The Christian Science Monitor*, Dec. 12, 2011, www.csmonitor.com/USA/Justice/2011/1212/Supreme-Court-takes-Arizona-immigration-law-case-in-key-test-of-federal-power.

The Supreme Court's decision to review Arizona's immigration law could determine whether states have rights to set immigration policy.

Williams, Roy L., "Construction Job Drop Linked to State Law on Immigration," *Birmingham* (Ala.) *News*, Nov. 30, 2011, p. D1, blog.al.com/businessnews/2011/11/alabama_immigration_law_blamed.html.

Some analysts say job losses in Alabama's construction industry are partly due to the state's new immigration law.

Citizenship

Gonzalez, Daniel, and Dan Nowicki, "A Change to Citizenship Would Have Wide Effects," *The Arizona Republic*, March 20, 2011, www.azcentral.com/news/articles/2011/03/20/20110320birthright-citizenship-illegal-immigration.html.

Supporters of amended birthright citizenship rules say illegal immigrants would be less likely to come to the United States if children born to them in the future didn't automatically become citizens.

Ho, James C., "Ban on Birthright Citizenship Unconstitutional," *The Washington Times*, April 11, 2011, p. B1, www.washingtontimes.com/news/2011/apr/8/ban-on-birthright-citizenship-unconstitutional/?page=all.

Efforts to repeal birthright citizenship for children born to undocumented persons are unconstitutional, says the former Texas solicitor general.

Economic Impact

Lawson, Brian, "Study: Law Will Cost State Billions," *Huntsville* (Ala.) *Times*, Feb. 1, 2012, p. A1, blog.al.com/breaking/2012/02/immigration_law_sponsor_disagr.html.

Alabama's immigration law will cost the state billions of dollars in lost production and state sales and income taxes, according to a study by the University of Alabama's Center for Business and Economic Research.

Smith, Lamar, "Give Immigration Enforcement a Try," *The Washington Times*, April 14, 2011, p. B3, www.washingtontimes.com/news/2011/apr/13/give-immigration-enforcement-a-try/.

Jobs open up for Americans when immigration laws are administered, says the Republican House member from Texas.

Tures, John A., "Farming and Immigration: Foreigners Will Pick Our Food — But Where?" *Columbus* (Ga.) *Ledger-Enquirer*, Dec. 11, 2011.

A Georgia immigration law has cost farmers $140 million.

Enforcement

Arpaio, Joe, "We're Enforcing the Law," *USA Today*, Dec. 28, 2011, p. A8, www.usatoday.com/news/opinion/editorials/story/2011-12-27/Joe-Arpaio-illegal-immigration/52245530/1.

The top law enforcement officer in Maricopa County, Ariz., says he is obliged to enforce his state's immigration laws.

Couch, Aaron, "State Illegal Immigration Laws: What Have They Accomplished?" *The Christian Science Monitor*, March 23, 2011, www.csmonitor.com/USA/Politics/2011/0323/State-illegal-immigration-laws-What-have-they-accomplished.

State immigration laws have yielded few arrests while creating a populist backlash, says the Migration Policy Institute.

Stein, Dan, "State Enforcement Policies Work," *USA Today*, July 15, 2011, p. A10.

The failure to enforce immigration laws imposes fiscal and social burdens on states, says the president of the Federation for American Immigration Reform.

CITING *CQ RESEARCHER*

Sample formats for citing these reports in a bibliography include the ones listed below. Preferred styles and formats vary, so please check with your instructor or professor.

MLA STYLE

Jost, Kenneth. "Remembering 9/11," CQ Researcher 2 Sept. 2011: 701-732.

APA STYLE

Jost, K. (2011, September 2). Remembering 9/11. *CQ Researcher, 9*, 701-732.

CHICAGO STYLE

Jost, Kenneth. "Remembering 9/11." *CQ Researcher*, September 2, 2011, 701-732.

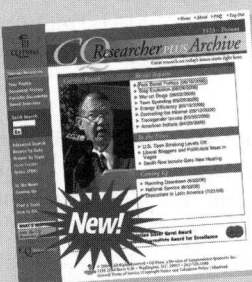

CQ Researcher

Published by CQ Press, an Imprint of SAGE Publications, Inc.

www.cqresearcher.com

Arts Education

Does arts training improve social and academic skills?

Arts education faces serious challenges, even as teachers and business leaders recognize its value to students as never before. A growing body of research suggests that the arts offer students a unique, valuable way to grow intellectually, socially and emotionally. Some researchers suggest high-quality arts education helps improve test scores and reduce tardiness and truancy. Others argue that even without such benefits, the arts are inherently good because they help children grow into creative, problem-solving adults with skills necessary for the 21st-century economy. But arts education — on the decline for more than two decades — is now threatened by shrinking school budgets and a narrowing of the curriculum because of federal and state testing and accountability mandates. Meanwhile, a small but growing number of schools are integrating the arts into academic courses and using the arts to help students overcome learning disabilities.

A proud artist shows off her artwork at Inner-City Arts, which provides a wide range of arts activities — during school hours and after school — at a modern campus in the heart of Los Angeles' Skid Row neighborhood.

Inside This Report

The Issues 255
Background 261
Chronology 263
Current Situation 268
At Issue........................269
Outlook 271
Bibliography 274
The Next Step 275

CQ Researcher • March 16, 2012 • www.cqresearcher.com
Volume 22, Number 11 • Pages 253-276

Los Angeles | London | New Delhi
Singapore | Washington DC

Recipient of Society of Professional Journalists Award for Excellence ◆ American Bar Association Silver Gavel Award

THE ISSUES

255 • Does arts education improve academic performance?
• Does the No Child Left Behind Act harm arts education?
• Should the arts be integrated into science and math education?

BACKGROUND

261 **'Revolutionary Accomplishment'**
The arts played a key role in humans' intellectual development.

262 **Creativity Rationale**
Education pioneer John Dewey argued arts help give life meaning.

262 **Doughnuts and Drama**
Young actors sent plays to soldiers during World War II to raise morale.

265 **Federal Role**
U.S. policy supports arts education, but schools still focus mainly on basics.

CURRENT SITUATION

268 **Inequities in Access**
Low-income and ethnic communities often lack arts education.

270 **21st-Century Workforce**
Educators and policymakers say arts education fosters innovation.

OUTLOOK

271 **'Schizophrenic' Future?**
State budgets are tight, but arts education is valued.

Cover: Inner-City Arts

SIDEBARS AND GRAPHICS

256 **Childhood Arts Education Declined**
Education in music, visual arts and creative writing plummeted.

257 **Most Parents Say 'Right' Emphasis Put on Arts**
Nearly a third says it gets too little attention.

259 **Americans Strongly Back Arts Education**
Big majority say it improves communication skills.

260 **Arts Education for Minorities on Decline**
Levels for whites were higher, largely unchanged.

263 **Chronology**
Key events since 1907.

264 **Arts Education Program Wins Supporters**
"The kind of place you'd want for your own child."

266 **Strong Support for Music in Schools**
More than 90 percent want music in regular curriculum.

267 **Art Opens Vistas for Kids With Disabilities**
"It's motivational, it's inspirational, it helps with attention."

269 **At Issue**
Should the arts be integrated with science education?

FOR FURTHER RESEARCH

273 **For More Information**
Organizations to contact.

274 **Bibliography**
Selected sources used.

275 **The Next Step**
Additional articles.

275 **Citing *CQ Researcher***
Sample bibliography formats.

CQ Researcher

March 16, 2012
Volume 22, Number 11

MANAGING EDITOR: Thomas J. Billitteri
tjb@cqpress.com

ASSISTANT MANAGING EDITOR: Kathy Koch
kkoch@cqpress.com

CONTRIBUTING EDITOR: Thomas J. Colin
tcolin@cqpress.com

ASSOCIATE EDITOR: Kenneth Jost

STAFF WRITER: Marcia Clemmitt

CONTRIBUTING WRITERS: Sarah Glazer, Alan Greenblatt, Peter Katel, Barbara Mantel, Jennifer Weeks

DESIGN/PRODUCTION EDITOR: Olu B. Davis

ASSISTANT EDITOR: Darrell Dela Rosa

FACT CHECKER: Michelle Harris

Los Angeles | London | New Delhi
Singapore | Washington DC

An Imprint of SAGE Publications, Inc.

VICE PRESIDENT AND EDITORIAL DIRECTOR, HIGHER EDUCATION GROUP:
Michele Sordi

DIRECTOR, ONLINE PUBLISHING:
Todd Baldwin

CQ Researcher (ISSN 1056-2036) is printed on acid-free paper. Published weekly, except: (March wk. 5) (May wk. 4) (July wk. 1) (Aug. wks. 3, 4) (Nov. wk. 4) and (Dec. wks. 3, 4). Published by SAGE Publications, Inc., 2455 Teller Rd., Thousand Oaks, CA 91320. Annual full-service subscriptions start at $1,054. For pricing, call 1-800-834-9020. To purchase a *CQ Researcher* report in print or electronic format (PDF), visit www.cqpress.com or call 866-427-7737. Single reports start at $15. Bulk purchase discounts and electronic-rights licensing are also available. Periodicals postage paid at Thousand Oaks, California, and at additional mailing offices. POSTMASTER: Send address changes to *CQ Researcher*, 2300 N St., N.W., Suite 800, Washington, DC 20037.

Arts Education

BY BETH BAKER

THE ISSUES

Two dozen kindergarteners hop, skip, jump and gallop to the beating of a drum at Joe's Movement Emporium, a dance studio in Mount Rainier, Md. A petite instructor leading the controlled chaos gently exhorts the children to turn their bodies into straight lines or curvy shapes, which most do with gusto.

The youngsters, students at Mount Rainier Elementary School, participate in the program thanks to principal Janet Reed's passionate commitment to the arts. Without the grants Reed raises from government and philanthropic sources, her students would lack almost all arts instruction, except for music.

"All of the research shows the arts advance academic excellence," Reed says. But providing arts education isn't easy for schools to do, she says. "It comes down to money."

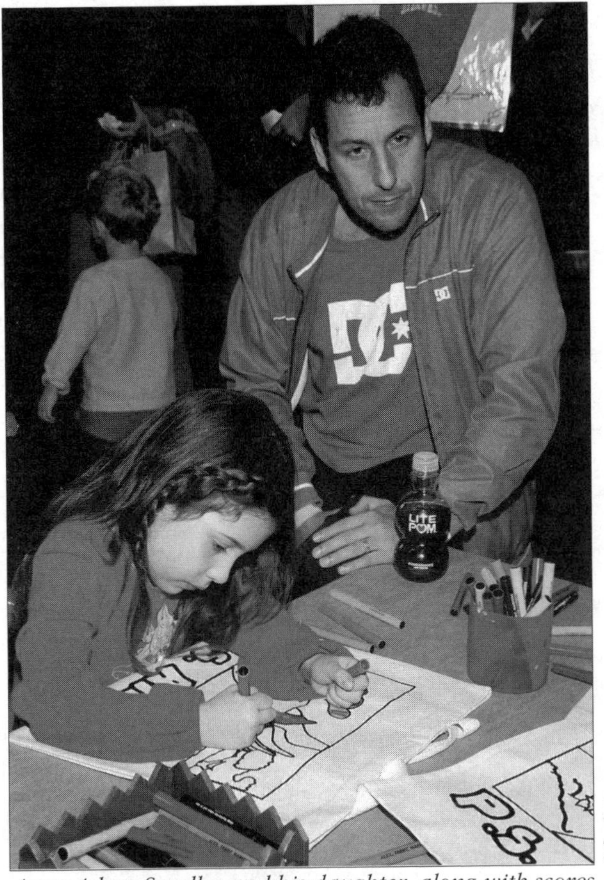

Actor Adam Sandler and his daughter, along with scores of other celebrities, attend a fundraiser in Santa Monica, Calif., last November for PS Arts, a 20-year-old program that brings arts education to underserved schools and their communities and offers arts-related workshops for classroom teachers.

Indeed, many educators and researchers argue that the arts, whether music, dance, drama or visual arts, enhance learning and foster critical-thinking skills.

"The research shows there are many direct benefits from all of the art forms, in different ways," says Sandra Ruppert, executive director of the Arts Education Partnership, a coalition of education, arts, government, business and philanthropic organizations. "In music we see a lot of connections between studying keyboards and understanding mathematical concepts. We see drama as a way to help early readers develop their comprehension skills. When they have an opportunity to act out the story, they gain a greater comprehension in reading."

Still, the strength of the link between arts education and academic achievement remains an open question. Ellen Winner, a psychology professor at Boston College who specializes in arts-education research, says that while "studies are showing kids who take a lot of arts are also doing well in school," a variety of factors may explain why. For example, she says, some students "come from families who want them to achieve." And some "go to schools that are strong in both" arts and core subjects like math and reading.

Whether or not the arts translate directly into higher academic achievement, many educators and parents see an inherent value in arts training. For example:

- Ninety-three percent of respondents to a public opinion survey said the arts are vital to a well-rounded education. [1]
- A third of K-12 parents said schools placed "too little emphasis" on art and music, while 61 percent said the "right amount" was placed on those subjects; only 5 percent said they received "too much emphasis." [2]
- Ninety-five percent of Americans said they considered music part of a well-rounded education, and 79 percent said music education should be mandatory. [3]

"The arts are absolutely crucial because these are the subjects and activities that bring children to school," says Diane Ravitch, research professor of education at New York University. "They're highly motivating, and they expand students' ability to think and feel and get connected to other students."

Yet schools are struggling to maintain arts programs in the face of eroding school budgets and government mandates to concentrate on raising math and reading test scores.

"Back in the old days, [school administrators] had more latitude to be more supportive of programs like art and music, and science even, that are not part of reading and math," says Daniel A. Domenech, executive director of the American Association of School Administrators. "School districts cannot run on a deficit like our government. So it's their obligation to be financially responsible, and if they don't

Childhood Arts Education Declined

The percentages of 18-year-olds who received childhood education in music, visual arts and creative writing — the most popular forms of arts education — dropped significantly from 1982 to 2008. Levels for theater and dance education remained largely unchanged.

Percentage of 18-Year-Olds Who Received Arts Education During Childhood By Type of Art, 1982-2008

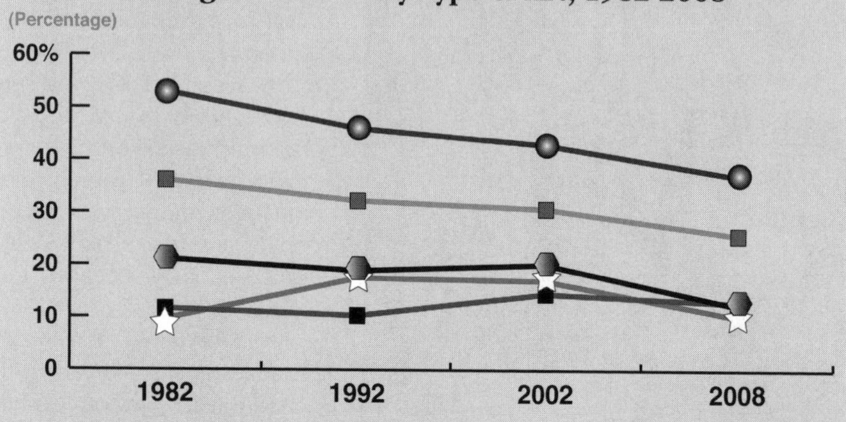

Source: Nick Rabkin and E. C. Hedberg, "Arts Education in America: What the Declines Mean for Arts Participation," National Endowment for the Arts, February 2011, p. 44, www.nea.gov/research/2008-SPPA-ArtsLearning.pdf

have the money, they don't have the money."

In Westerville, Ohio, school officials recently cut back arts education, among other programs, as they struggled to deal with a $23 million budget deficit in the school system. On March 6, voters supported a special property-tax levy, by a 51%-49% margin, that will restore $8 million in funding for arts classes, athletics, band, remedial reading and gifted classes. A similar levy was defeated in November. [4]

While arts education is widely viewed as important, data are hard to come by. School districts are not required to report to the federal government the status of their arts education programs.

"There's very little national-level research on the status and condition of arts education," says Narric W. Rome, senior director for federal affairs and arts education at Americans for the Arts, an advocacy organization based in Washington. Results of the last federal survey on access to arts education came out in 2002, and data from a new survey are expected in April. But even that survey will not include key information, such as how many students have access to arts classes, says Rome.

The President's Committee on the Arts and the Humanities, which advises the White House on cultural issues, in 2011 found "a complex patchwork" of arts programs, "with pockets of visionary activity flourishing in some locations and inequities in access to arts education increasing in others." [5] Other studies have found that cuts in arts education have disproportionately affected African-American and Latino youngsters.

Advocates argue that rather than cutting exposure to the arts, students should have contact with the field in multiple ways. "The richest experiences for children are ones where you have an arts specialist who isn't just teaching kids in isolation but who acts as a coach or mentor to a classroom teacher," Ruppert says. Children also learn from visiting artists who expose them to professional-level work.

Education professor Mariale Hardiman, chair of the Department of Interdisciplinary Studies at Johns Hopkins University, is exploring whether teaching other subjects through the arts can improve memory and comprehension. In a randomized, controlled experiment at a low-income school in Baltimore, Hardiman hopes to learn if art can improve fifth-graders' understanding of astronomy and ecology. Art is "a way to improve pedagogy and give kids the opportunity to manipulate information and have more fun with it," she says.

Learning art — whether by making pottery, playing an instrument or choreographing a dance — encourages open-ended inquiry, proponents say. "The arts teach children that problems can have more than one solution and that questions can have more than one answer," writes Elliot W. Eisner, a professor emeritus of art at Stanford University. [6]

At the same time, advocates say, the arts can require discipline and set a high bar for excellence. "There are so many benefits," says Michael Blakeslee, deputy executive director of the National Association for Music Education. "One is the idea of learning something in depth and sticking to it and going for perfection. If children take a math test and get 85 percent, they think they did well. If they go to a concert and play 85 percent of the notes right, they don't think they did so well."

Moreover, children simply enjoy participating in the arts — which may be one of art's greatest strengths. "When there's strong emotional content to the learning — when it's fun or engaging or gratifying — it's more likely to take hold," says Lois Hetland, an associate professor of art education at the Massachusetts College of Art in Boston. "It gets tied into memory. Being engaged is a critical factor in learning."

As educators, researchers, arts specialists and school-reform advocates debate the merits of arts education, here are some of the questions being asked:

Most Parents Say 'Right' Emphasis Put on Arts

More than 60 percent of parents say schools place the right amount of emphasis on art and music, while nearly a third say the arts get too little weight. Only 5 percent say schools place too much importance on the arts.

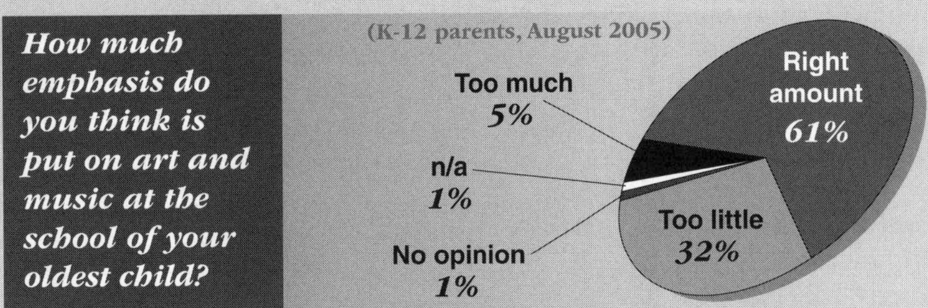

Source: "Education," Gallup, March 2012, www.gallup.com/poll/1612/education.aspx#2

Does arts education improve academic performance?

Speaking in 2010 at a conference of the Arts Education Partnership, Education Secretary Arne Duncan said the arts teach students teamwork and help them "practice collaborative learning with their peers.

"They develop skills and judgment they didn't know they had — whether it is drumming in time or acquiring the knowledge to differentiate between Pavarotti and the tenor in the choir loft at the Sunday service," he said. [7]

For decades, arts education advocates have been amassing evidence aimed at convincing education policymakers and school superintendents that the arts should be a basic part of the curriculum for every child. Hundreds of studies suggest the arts contribute to cognitive and academic improvement, though the extent to which that may be true remains a matter of debate within the education field.

Perhaps the most famous study — and one that is still being debated — suggested there is a "Mozart effect" on learning for those who listen to classical music. In a 1993 experiment, college students performed better on a test for spatial reasoning after listening for 10 minutes to a Mozart sonata. The effect lasted only 15 minutes. [8] But the experiment, which others have tried to replicate with mixed results, sparked intense public interest, even prompting Democratic Gov. Zell Miller of Georgia to include the cost of a classical music CD for every baby born in the state in his 1998 budget.

A promising new avenue of research comes from neuroscience, using brain imaging to delve into how the arts might affect learning in other realms. "Is it simply that smart people are drawn to 'do' art — to study and perform music, dance, drama — or does early arts training cause changes in the brain that enhance other important aspects of cognition?" asked Michael Gazzaniga, director of the Arts and Cognition Consortium, made up of researchers from seven major institutions, that was established by the Dana Foundation in 2004. [9]

Gazzaniga spoke at a consortium summit in 2009 at Johns Hopkins University, where researchers reviewed new findings emerging from brain imaging. In a published summary of the summit's key findings, Gazzaniga identified links between "high levels of music training and the ability to manipulate information" in both working memory, which allows people to reason and collect information, and long-term memory even beyond the domain of music training. The researchers found that interest in performing arts leads to high levels of motivation and sustained attention that in turn improves cognition generally. [10]

Other researchers are looking at how arts involvement might affect attendance, dropout and graduation rates. The Center for Arts Education, an advocacy organization, looked at graduation rates at more than 200 New York City schools over two years. Schools in the top third in graduation rates offered their students the most access to arts education and the most arts resources, while schools in the bottom third offered the least. [11]

"We can't say it's a direct correlation, but we do believe the arts influence that," says Lori Sherman, the center's development director. "Principals will tell you the arts have changed the culture of their schools, from teachers working more collaboratively to kids being happier, to kids showing up at school."

In a long-term study, James Catterall, a professor emeritus of education at the University of California, Los Angeles, found that children who were engaged in the arts showed many positive academic improvements. Drawing on a wealth of data from the National Education Longitudinal Study, he looked at how several hundred low-income students did over time.

Those with high arts involvement graduated from college and completed post-graduate degrees at higher rates than their peers with low arts involvement, he found. [12]

But other researchers question the evidence suggesting the arts lead to student success. "Another explanation could be that the types of students attracted to the arts are the types more likely to achieve these benefits rather than the arts causing them," Dan Serig, an associate professor of art education at the Massachusetts College of Art and Design, wrote in a review of Catterall's work. [13]

Eisner, of Stanford University, has pointed out that if students take more coursework in any subject — whether art, science, foreign languages or history — their SAT scores will rise. [14]

Hetland, of the Massachusetts College of Art, who has collaborated with Boston College's Winner, says, "There are some studies that have shown positive results and others have failed to. The ones that have failed to tend to be more rigorously designed and also tend to be less known because people don't want to know those results."

Winner says she'd like to see more experimental studies, such as one conducted by E. Glenn Schellenberg, a professor of psychology at the University of Toronto. Schellenberg administered IQ tests to 144 6-year-olds before they entered first grade. During the coming year, the children were randomly assigned to one of four groups for 36 weeks. Two groups received after-school music instruction (keyboard or vocal), one received drama instruction and one had no special arts class. The children's IQ's were then retested. Those with music instruction had a greater increase in IQ than the other two groups, regardless of their socioeconomic background, and the drama group had better adaptive social skills.

Inner-City Arts

A youngster works on her art project at Inner-City Arts, which provides arts education for elementary, middle and high school students through a partnership with the Los Angeles Unified School District and local charter and parochial schools. Founded in 1989, the program has served more than 150,000 children living in the city's poorest neighborhoods.

"I get pretty consistent effects between music lessons and IQ," Schellenberg says in an interview. Moreover, he has found music training can improve language. In his study, he concluded: "Does music make you smarter? The answer is a qualified yes." [15]

Schellenberg suggests several possible reasons for that. For example, he says, music lessons are "school-like" and have similar benefits. And music training, he says, improves a "constellation of abilities," among them memorization, expression of emotions, attention and fine-motor skills. Still, he says more research is needed, and he stresses that to see real benefit, students likely need more music instruction than is possible during the school day.

Whether or not the research on linking arts to academic achievement bears out, say Eisner and others, educators should focus chiefly on art's inherent value.

"It's too utilitarian an argument to say that test scores will grow if you do the arts," says New York University's Ravitch. "I don't think it's relevant, and it doesn't matter. They're important for our spirit and soul and humanness. No one with any means, who can pick the best school in the nation, would pick a school without the arts."

Does No Child Left Behind harm arts education?

When President George W. Bush unveiled the No Child Left Behind Act (NCLB) in 2001, arts educators were pleased that the arts were among the 10 core subjects that all children should learn, along with math, reading and other basics. But with schools being assessed primarily by their students' reading and math scores, many feel the arts and other subjects are getting short shrift.

"Testing of reading and math became the basis for determining whether school districts were making annual yearly progress, whether they'd be failing or excellent," says Domenech, of the American Association of School Administrators. "This put a lot of pressure on educators, from classroom teachers to principals to superintendents. I think it's fair to say the emphasis on reading and math deemphasized other areas, including art, music and physical education, that we as educators feel are important to a comprehensive education. Reading and math are basic skills, but they hardly compromise the totality of the curriculum."

Gail Connelly, executive director of the National Association of Elementary School Principals, agrees. "NCLB, we felt, really starved the education of the whole child and forced the focus to be much more narrow," she says.

Liza Linder, an art teacher in Prince George's County, Md., in suburban Washington, also is critical of NCLB. "I don't get it," she says. "Every child that is musically inclined, every child who is visually inclined, they are left behind. I've seen instrumental music being taught in a hallway or in the cafeteria during lunch."

But others say the jury on NCLB is still out.

"One of the positive things about NCLB is that the arts are listed as a highly qualified area, meaning you have to have highly qualified teachers teaching those subjects," says Linda Adams, supervisor of fine arts for Montgomery County Public Schools in Maryland, also in suburban Washington. In her county, which includes affluent communities such as Bethesda and Chevy Chase, every elementary school has art and music weekly for all students, and high school students must take at least one art credit to graduate.

A 2010 survey of visual arts teachers by F. Robert Sabol, president of the National Art Education Association, found mixed views of NCLB's effects on visual arts education. "Yes, NCLB has caused negative impacts," he says. "However, being fair, there were some positive effects as well. Teachers . . . focused a great deal more time on assessment of learning. Arts educators know they are held accountable. They're looking at national standards, improving their instructional techniques, looking at areas of strength, and also areas where improvement was needed." [16]

Lynn Tuttle, director of arts education for the Arizona Department of Education and president of the State Education Agencies' Directors of Arts Education, a national association, says NCLB is a mixed blessing. Her position in Arizona is funded with NCLB money, although she acknowledges this may not be true across the nation. In addition, she says, "I have had access to $6-7 million of NCLB funds which I've used to fund arts integration and arts education [in Arizona schools]. So it can be a catalyst."

Inspired leadership that can use the law to good ends is the key, she says. "I credit our Title I director, who is a big believer in arts education and arts integration as a tool for achievement in other parts of the curriculum," she says.

Education scholar Chester E. Finn Jr., president of the Thomas B. Fordham Institute, a conservative think tank, questions whether the arts should even have been elevated to their status as a core subject under NCLB. "The big four are English, math, history and science," he says. "It's the central obligation to get kids competent in those four subjects. It's desirable to get kids competent in other things, but I don't think it's imperative."

Finn says he's not the only one who wants the focus to be on fewer subjects. "I've heard principals say with some justice that students have got to read before they can do much else in school," he says. "They've got to master basics first or they'll never get the broad-based education."

Should the arts be integrated into science and math education?

In recent years, arts advocates began pushing for a closer link between the arts and science, technology, engineering and math (known as STEM) — thus turning STEM to STEAM. (*See "At Issue," p. 269.*)

Support for STEM itself has gained ground and is viewed by many as fundamental to global competitiveness and innovation. In his 2011 State of the Union address, President Obama called for 100,000 new STEM teachers to be trained over the next decade. In December, the White House Office of Science and Technology Policy (OSTP) released an inventory of federal STEM education programs, the most

Americans Strongly Back Arts Education

More than 80 percent of Americans believe arts education improves children's attitudes toward school and teaches them to communicate effectively with adults and peers.

Americans' Views on Arts Education, 2005

- **86 percent** agree arts education improves a child's attitudes toward school.
- **83 percent** believe arts education teaches children to communicate effectively with others.
- **79 percent** say incorporating arts into learning is the first step in addressing what's missing in public education.
- **79 percent** believe it's important for them to get personally involved in improving arts education.

Source: "New Harris Poll Reveals That 93 Percent of Americans Believe That the Arts Are Vital to Providing a Well-Rounded Education," Americans for the Arts, June 2005, www.artsusa.org/news/press/2005/2005_06_13b.asp

Arts Education for Minorities on Decline

Fifty-eight percent of whites ages 18 through 24 reported receiving arts education during childhood, about the same percentage in 2008 as in 1982. African-Americans and Hispanics received less arts education than whites, and the level declined significantly over the same period, falling below 30 percent in 2008.

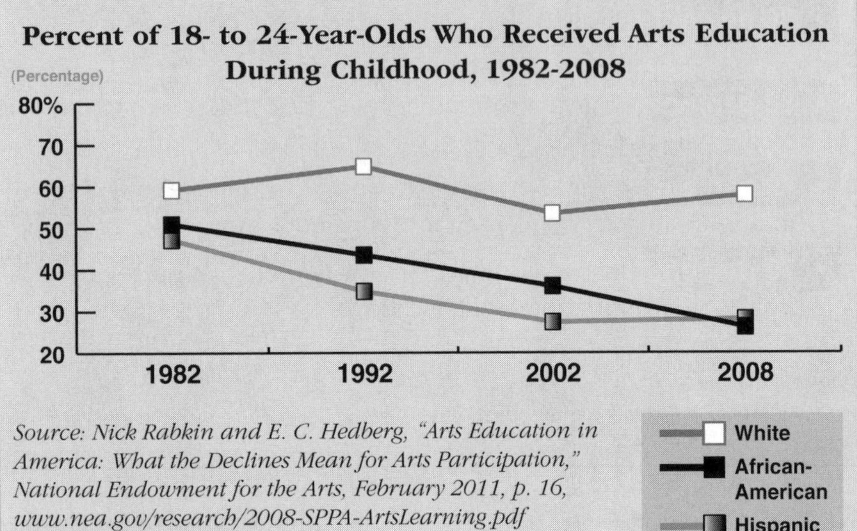

Source: Nick Rabkin and E. C. Hedberg, "Arts Education in America: What the Declines Mean for Arts Participation," National Endowment for the Arts, February 2011, p. 16, www.nea.gov/research/2008-SPPA-ArtsLearning.pdf

comprehensive to date, identifying $3.4 billion spent on 252 projects in 2011. This spring OSTP will release a five-year strategic plan for STEM education. [17]

Using the arts to strengthen learning in science, technology, engineering and math would foster greater innovation in scientific research and draw more students to the STEM field, STEAM proponents say.

Bill O'Brien, senior adviser for program innovation at the National Endowment for the Arts (NEA), supports the linkage. "In the last decade or so we have really narrowed our focus on certain types of learning that we felt were entwined with technology, and we may have missed how important imagination and creativity were," he says. "The whole notion of STEM to STEAM allows us to think of the mind as a holistic organ that needs all of this stuff to work together in order to function at the highest levels."

In January 2011, NSF and the Rhode Island School of Design (RISD) brought together artists and designers with STEM researchers. At the conference, RISD President John Maeda asked, "How do we make innovation happen? It happens through science, technology, engineering and mathematics. Could it be missing something that is actually quite important? It's missing the arts — the right-brain innovation that has propelled our country, made us competitive."

The Rhode Island School of Design is actively pushing STEM to STEAM. It hosted a congressional briefing in Washington in June 2011 and sent a delegation to the Massachusetts Institute of Technology last October to promote RISD's STEM-to-STEAM initiative. Maeda points to studio art skills such as creative problem solving, flexible thinking and risk-taking as fundamental to innovative research.

Although the National Science Foundation has given small grants to explore the intersection of the arts and STEM, it's not a major focus for the foundation, says Al DeSena, a program director in NSF's education and human resources directorate. But, he adds, "Some of us would make a claim that the fundamental processes of the human mind are pretty similar in terms of arts and sciences, and you can see that in the lives of artists and scientists."

Robert Root-Bernstein, a professor of physiology at Michigan State University and winner of a MacArthur "genius" Fellowship, says the arts and science used to be much more closely linked. "We need to go back to the way people used to be trained," he says. "Until you were 10 or 12, you would go out and explore nature, make collections, draw them, compare them, learn how to classify, look at them through a microscope, paint them, do all these things so you actually have observed them and handled them and smelled them, you literally know what they are."

Too often, he says, today's students have not been taught essential scientific skills. "The arts are really, really good at teaching people," he says. "Artists learn how to observe acutely, how to abstract something to get at the essence, how to make models of things" — all skills which help scientists figure out problems and express their ideas.

Root-Bernstein studied Nobel laureates and found almost all were engaged in artistic pursuits. Compared with other scientists, they were 25 times more likely to sing, dance or act and 17 times more likely to be a visual artist. (*See "At Issue," p. 269.*)

High-achieving science and technology graduates of the Michigan State University Honors College also had an artistic bent, he found. "Arts-and-crafts experiences are significantly correlated among these graduates with producing patentable inventions and founding new companies," Root-Bernstein and colleagues wrote in 2011 on how arts education could boost Michigan's economy.

But others think the idea of turning STEM to STEAM is misguided. Susan Singer, a biology professor at Carleton College, in Northfield, Minn., worries the merger would mean dilution, rather than cross-fertilization. Although she agrees that the scientific pursuit involves "a huge amount of creativity," she worries that "both art and science could potentially be diluted if we can't be clear about both the similarities and the differences.

AFP/Getty Images/Mandel Ngan

Students at Booker T. Washington High School in Memphis, Tenn., perform at graduation ceremonies on May 16, 2011. With a graduation rate that went from 55 percent in 2007 to 81.6 percent in 2010, the school won the Obama administration's 2011 Race to the Top High School Commencement Challenge. Ninety-five percent of Americans consider music as part of a well-rounded education.

"For example, if you took an approach that was rigorous and valid in science, you could end up with something really dismal in terms of the world of art, because they have different ways of framing and seeing the world — not that one is better than the other, or that one has cornered any kind of truth compared to the other."

Physicist Alan Friedman, a consultant on museum development and communicating science to the public and former director of the New York Hall of Science, has long been interested in the intersection of science and literature. But he says that while the arts are valuable, they should be studied not as part of science but parallel with it.

"In STEM there are clear, rigorous measures," he wrote in an email. "For example, an idea in science must be 'falsifiable' — i.e., built into an idea must be a way to show how it could be tested and found wanting. There is nothing remotely like this measure of value in the arts. Deciding what is good and what's not in the arts is a more subjective, changing notion. That flexibility over time and culture is one of the great strengths of the arts, but there is nothing remotely like that notion in STEM." (*See "At Issue," p. 269.*)

Root-Bernstein, both an artist and a historian of science, disagrees. "If you ask any scientist, he wants to come up with something unique — certainly it has to be replicated, but they want to come up with something unique," he says. "The theory of thermodynamics was invented by 12 different people, and each formulation was different. What we call thermodynamics was a consensus, but each had a unique stamp of the inventor on it, just as an artist has a unique stamp on a painting."

But Friedman responds that all the liberal arts are worthy. "Why privilege STEM and art uniquely by merging them but not put history in too (SHTEAM)? I'd argue that art and history are both essential to understanding life and the universe, both illuminate STEM and both can be illuminated by STEM. But we couldn't stop there. How can we deny the fundamental connections between STEM and civics, religion, anthropology, archeology, philosophy?"

Finn, the education scholar, agrees. "I think that what we're dealing with here is a kind of goals inflation or mission creep," he says. "It's fine for schools also to teach the arts, but I don't think the argument here is much more compelling than that of the other subjects that want to get on this bandwagon." ■

BACKGROUND

'Revolutionary Accomplishment'

Dance, music, and storytelling have been part of every culture and time period in human history. The earliest humans drew pictures on caves and carved statues from stone, marking "a revolutionary accomplishment in the intellectual development of humankind," according to the Metropolitan Museum of Art. [18]

As the first National Standards for Arts Education, developed by a consortium of arts educators in 1994, put it, "All peoples, everywhere, have an abiding need for meaning — to connect time and space, experience and event, body and spirit, intellect and emotion. People create art to make these connections." [19]

But despite the arts' universality, their place in education has fluctuated over time.

In ancient Greece, Aristotle believed the elite should focus on intellectual pursuits rather than crafting works of art. Aristotle put "what are now called the 'fine' arts, music painting, sculpture, in the same class with menial arts so far as their practice is concerned," wrote John Dewey (1859-1952), a prominent American philosopher and educator. The intellectual class should appreciate music — but not perform it, Dewey said of Aristotle's view. Aristotle viewed painters, sculptors, and musicians as hirelings, much like cooks. [20]

But that began to change during the Renaissance, a period spanning roughly the 14th to 17th centuries during which the arts flourished. In 15th-century Florence, practitioners of visual arts moved from being viewed as technicians to being revered as creators and were supported by wealthy patrons. The first art schools were created, the arts became an intellectual pursuit and the seeds of "art for art's sake" were planted. [21]

In the United States, while fine art has long been seen as integral to a liberal arts education, the public seems to have always been ambivalent about its place in K-12 schools.

"The arts . . . have never enjoyed a secure place in American public education," said the National Endowment for the Arts. "There have been earnest debates about the value of the arts in education throughout our history, and the rationale for their inclusion in the curriculum has rarely been based on the value of learning the arts themselves. Rather, it has focused on their value in achieving other broadly accepted goals of public education." [22]

In the past, some of those goals furthered societal interests beyond the school walls. For example, the first public school curricula included music, aimed at advancing the quality of church singing.

The notion that skills learned in arts classes might transfer to other academic areas — still being debated today — appears to date back to the 1800s. According to the NEA, "An influential report in 1836 urged the new [public] schools to include music instruction to 'promote [students'] progress in other subjects.' " [23]

Even in the 19th century, global economic competition influenced what should be included in the curriculum. Public schools began including drawing in the 1800s not for aesthetic reasons but to help U.S. manufacturers keep pace with other countries during the Industrial Revolution. The idea was to foster a generation of designers to compete with factories in Europe.

In 1870, the Massachusetts Drawing Act mandated drawing in public education. Soon after, educator Walter Smith arrived in Massachusetts from England to direct drawing in public schools in Boston. He later founded the nation's first normal school, which included his method for teaching drawing as part of the curriculum. [24]

At the turn of the 20th century, art history and the study of master works were added to public school coursework, in part to teach moral values and cultural traditions.

Creativity Rationale

In the early 1900s, Dewey, the architect of modern progressive education, argued that children need to experience and make art as well as learn how to appreciate it. The arts "are not only intrinsically and directly enjoyable, but they serve a purpose beyond themselves," he wrote. "They reveal a depth and range of meaning in experiences which otherwise might be mediocre and trivial. . . . They are not luxuries of education, but emphatic expressions of that which makes any education worthwhile." [25]

Throughout much of the 20th century, arts education enjoyed a steady rise, although the data are far from complete. In 1930, 20 percent of students took some arts in school; that number grew to 50 percent in the 1970s, as students completed more years of schooling than in the past. [26]

Early childhood education was also blossoming, led by pioneers such as Jean Piaget and cultural psychologist Jerome Bruner. Bruner identified two main ways humans manage knowledge of their world: logical-scientific thinking and narrative thinking — including drama, song and fiction. Schools have focused on the former, but Bruner argued, "It is only in the narrative mode that one can construct an identity and find a place in one's culture. Schools must cultivate it, nurture it, cease taking it for granted." [27]

In the 1940s educator Viktor Lowenfeld of Pennsylvania State University and others developed the creativity rationale for arts education. Lowenfeld would later write that its goal was "not the art itself or the aesthetic product or the aesthetic experience but rather the child who grows up more creatively and sensitively and applies his experience in the arts to whatever life situations may be applicable." [28]

Doughnuts and Drama

As scholars analyzed the merits of arts education, teachers of the arts were organizing as professionals. In 1907, the Music Supervisors Conference (now the National Association for Music Education) was founded. The association continues to work to include music in public school curricula and advance the music-teaching profession.

Continued on p. 264

Chronology

1900s-1920s

New progressive education movement calls art crucial for children's development.

1907
Music Supervisors Conference is precursor of the first professional arts educator association.

1915
American education reformer John Dewey writes *Democracy and Education*, calling for students to create art as well as appreciate it.

1929
Three West Virginia teachers form National Thespians to foster theater education.

1930s-1950s

Arts education gains popularity as children's creativity is recognized.

1930s
Twenty percent of school children receive some arts education.

1942
Museum educator Victor D'Amico's *Creative Teaching in Art* helps to develop the creativity rationale for arts education.

1959
British scientist and novelist C. P. Snow delivers "The Two Cultures," lecture, bemoaning the separation of science and literary arts.

1960s-1970s

Research on benefits of arts education grows.

1967
Project Zero established at Harvard to study arts education. . . . Tanglewood Symposium says music in schools should include songs of all cultures.

1970s
Half of U.S. school children receive at least some arts education. . . . Stanford's Elliot Eisner urges schools to teach the arts for their unique contribution "to human experience and understanding," rather than as a means to an end.

1977
Philanthropist David Rockefeller Jr. convenes national panel to explore how arts can be integrated into the school curriculum.

1980s

Access to arts education in public schools begins to decline.

1982
President Ronald Reagan establishes first President's Committee on Arts and the Humanities. . . . Getty Center for Education in the Arts develops "discipline-based arts education."

1983
Harvard developmental psychologist Howard Gardner develops theory of multiple intelligences.

1988
National Endowment for the Arts' "Towards Civilization" study warns the arts in schools are in jeopardy.

1989
Kentucky Supreme Court orders state schools to include the arts to teach appreciation of students' cultural heritage.

1990s

Arts recognized as core subjects as research on arts and intelligence picks up.

1992
Chicago Arts Partnerships in Education is founded to lead school reform.

1993
Researchers identify "Mozart effect," linking music to improved spatial-reasoning skills.

1994
President Bill Clinton signs Goals 2000 Act, including the arts as a core subject. . . . First National Standards for Arts Education published.

1998
National Dance Education Association established.

2000-Present

Arts confirmed as core subject but threatened by budget cuts.

2002
President George W. Bush signs No Child Left Behind Act, confirming the arts as a core subject. . . . Partnership for 21st Century Skills identifies creativity and innovation as critical workforce skills.

2009
Brain imaging shows arts training boosts cognitive abilities.

2011
President's Committee on the Arts and the Humanities calls for schools to include high-quality arts programs.

April 2012
Department of Education to release first national survey in a decade on status of arts education in schools.

Arts-Based School Wins Supporters

"The climate is the kind of place you'd want for your own child."

Jana Jean teaches science at a charter high school in Oklahoma City. But sometimes it seems she's more of an arts teacher.

In her advanced chemistry class, for example, Jean taught a six-week unit on metals in which students learned about heat treating, a process that changes a metal's physical or chemical properties. Jean linked the lesson to artistic design. Students "had to design a metal bookmark," she says. "They had to know what heat treatment to use and what metal to choose to get the properties they needed." Similarly, after a unit on ceramics, the students designed glass jewelry.

Combining science and art lessons is a hallmark of a small but growing innovation in elementary and secondary education called A+ Schools. As education reformers seek ways to transform public schools, the model is gaining adherents, with 124 A+ Schools in three states by this summer.

The model was created in 1995 in Winston-Salem, N.C., by the Kenan Institute for the Arts. Today, there are A+ Schools in North Carolina, Oklahoma and Arkansas. In February, Arkansas A+ Schools received former President Bill Clinton's endorsement.

As noted by the President's Committee on the Arts and the Humanities, "More than 12 years of research about A+ Schools in North Carolina tracked consistent gains in student achievement, the schools' engagement of parents and community and other measures of learning and success." Most notably, the report continued, "A+ Schools with higher proportions of disadvantaged and minority students performed as well on statewide reading and mathematics assessments as students from more advantaged schools. This is doubly impressive considering that while other schools have focused on basic skills in response to high-stakes testing, the A+ Schools have been able to achieve reading and mathematics gains on statewide accountability tests without narrowing the curriculum." [1]

Jean Hendrickson, executive director of Oklahoma A+ Schools, says she'd long sought a transformational model, especially for schools with high numbers of impoverished students, such as Mark Twain Elementary in Oklahoma City where she was principal. In 2001, she was selected as national principal of the year from Oklahoma and was part of a group sent to North Carolina to investigate A+ Schools. "I came back convinced I had found the model I'd been looking for my entire professional career," she says. Today Oklahoma has 70 A+ Schools, with four more scheduled to be added soon.

"We're committed to arts every day, for every child," says Hendrickson. Some Oklahoma A+ Schools have specialists for all four art forms — visual arts, music, drama and dance — while others have none, Hendrickson says. "Arts every day has to reflect the community in which it resides," she says. "If there's not an arts specialist on staff, how do we provide the capacity to deliver a genuine arts connection that supports broader learning?"

The arts are one of eight interrelated components that form the basis of A+ Schools. The model draws from Harvard be-

Continued from p. 262

In 1929, in a small town in West Virginia, three educators came up with the idea of an honor society for high school theater students. National Thespians (now the Educational Theatre Association) grew rapidly, with 350 troupes formed by 1935. After the start of World War II, the young actors raised money to buy play scripts to send to troops overseas. "Doughnuts and coffee are provided to these soldiers by many sources, but the special privilege of providing them with dramatic literature is ours," the thespian troupes were told in a fund-raising appeal. [29]

Soon after the war, the National Art Education Association was founded, to promote visual arts education. The National Dance Education Organization, representing the youngest and smallest of the arts education fields, was formed in 1998.

Over time, art and music became a regular part of an elementary school education. By secondary school, arts courses generally became electives, though in some school systems they were required for graduation.

In 1982, the rise in arts education came to an abrupt halt and began a steady decline. In the preceding decades, a long line of academic theorists had promoted the study of the arts and its role in child development.

In 1967 American philosopher Nelson Goodman founded Project Zero at Harvard University to study arts education. According to the project's website, "Goodman believed that arts learning should be studied as a serious cognitive activity, but that 'zero' had been firmly established about the field; hence, the project was given its name." [30]

Throughout the 1960s and '70s, there was a growing acceptance of a whole-child approach to education that included a robust arts-rich environment. Harvard developmental psychologist Howard Gardner, who served as co-director of Project Zero from 1972-2000, developed his theory of multiple intelligences: linguistic, logical-mathematical, spatial, musical, bodily-kinesthetic, interpersonal and intrapersonal. "The purpose of school should be to develop intelligences and to help people reach vocational and avocational goals that are appropriate to their particular spectrum of intelligences," he wrote. [31]

havioral psychologist Howard Gardner's multiple intelligences concept and recent brain research. "We want there to be experiential, hands-on learning," says Hendrickson. "We want enriched assessment that says a standardized test score one day does not tell me everything about what my students need to know and understand." Collaboration — among teachers, students, parents and other schools is key, she says.

Oklahoma A+ Schools

Jean Hendrickson of Oklahoma A+ Schools says combining science and arts lessons is "the model I'd been looking for my entire professional career."

The model is kept affordable, she says, by developing a cadre of A+ Fellows within each school who then train others. The fellows receive on-site training by arts specialists and attend summer institutes.

Susan Brewer, a 40-year education veteran and A+ Fellow, teaches third grade at Linwood Elementary in Oklahoma City, integrating arts throughout the curriculum. In reading, for example, she focuses on getting pupils to see detail. At the same time, the art teacher will encourage the children to develop detail in their drawings. "She'll say, 'this is a nice tree, but where's the bark? Where are the leaves?' " Other concepts, such as texture, are reinforced across the curriculum, whether it's in art or on a topographical map.

Oklahoma A+ Schools show modest test score improvement over other schools that have not adopted the model. In 2010-2011, for example, the state's A+ Schools average Academic Performance Index score was 1,151, compared to 1,113 for schools in the district and 1,138 for Oklahoma statewide. [2]

Test scores, though, are not how A+ Schools measure success, says Hendrickson. "Whether it's a good day or bad, whether the test scores came out higher or lower, everybody is working toward the best student outcomes that we can get," she says. "Teacher and student attendance goes up, parent engagement goes up, there is evidence of creative learning and the climate is the kind of place you'd want for your own child."

— Beth Baker

[1] "Reinvesting in Arts Education — Winning America's Future Through Creative Schools," President's Committee on the Arts and the Humanities, 2011, pp. 20-21, The report cites D. Corbett, *et al.*, "The A+ schools program: school, community, teacher, and student effects," 2001, Kenan Institute for the Arts.

[2] Data compiled by Oklahoma A+ Schools, based on test scores published annually by the Oklahoma State Department of Education.

Gardner and colleagues developed the Arts PROPEL program as a way to teach the arts and assess students' work. Students were given the chance to compose works of art and to reflect on how artistic masters made choices in creating their works.

In 1982 the Getty Center for Education in the Arts, based in Los Angeles, began pushing for more rigor in arts education through "discipline-based arts education." The idea was that the arts curriculum should include four interrelated disciplines — art making, art history, art criticism and aesthetics. [32]

In contrast, says Boston College's Winner, also a principal investigator at Project Zero, she and her colleagues argued that the core of arts education is the making of art. Only by making art will students become interested in art history or appreciation, they argued.

On another front, E. D. Hirsch, a retired professor of education and the humanities at the University of Virginia, and others argued that the arts and art appreciation should be part of a core curriculum to help all students become culturally literate. William Bennett, a conservative former Secretary of Education, and colleagues wrote, "When we hold up to students true masterpieces of art and music, we teach them to discriminate between what is fine and what is mediocre, between the sublime and the mundane. We cultivate in their hearts a love for beauty." [33]

Federal Role

Over the last 35 years, arts education has reflected changes in national education policy generally.

In 1977, a blue-ribbon panel of artists, educators, business leaders and foundations endorsed "a curriculum that puts 'basics' first, because the arts are basic. And we suggest not that reading be replaced by art but that the concept of literacy be expanded beyond word skills." [34]

That view was eclipsed in 1983, however, by "A Nation at Risk," a landmark report by President Ronald Reagan's National Commission on Education Excellence that warned that American schools faced a "rising tide of mediocrity." The report laid the

Strong Support for Music in Schools

More than 90 percent of Americans consider music part of a well-rounded education and feel schools should offer it as part of their regular curriculum. About 80 percent say music education should be mandated for every student.

American Attitudes Toward Music in Education, 2003

- ***95 percent*** consider music part of a well-rounded education.
- ***93 percent*** feel schools should offer music as part of regular curriculum.
- ***79 percent*** say music education should be mandated for every student.

Source: Linda Lyons, "Americans Want Music Students to Play On," Gallup, May 2003, www.gallup.com/poll/8434/americans-want-music-students-play.aspx

foundation for today's focus on reading, math and, to some extent, science. The arts were de-emphasized.

"To compound the uphill struggle the arts encountered in the early 1980s, the visibility of the arts within the federal education department was eliminated," wrote Doug Herbert, special assistant in the Office of Innovation and Improvement in the U.S. Department of Education. "The former Arts and Humanities Office, responsible for a relatively small but innovative set of annual grants to school districts for curricular and instructional improvements, was abolished in 1981." [35]

In 1988, NEA renewed the focus on arts education, arguing that it was in trouble — considered by many a frill, with no common standards of what should be taught. [36]

In response, arts education advocates, including NEA Chairman John Frohnmayer, promoted the arts at hearings around the nation as a core part of the National Education Goals being developed under the administration of President George H. W. Bush and the nation's governors in 1989. The goals were an attempt to raise education standards and achievement nationally.

"The word got out that the National Education Goals [including the core subjects to be covered] didn't have arts listed," Herbert recalls. "People started showing up at public hearings en masse, saying, 'you have to have the arts in that list of subjects.' "

Meanwhile the Consortium of National Arts Education Associations began developing national voluntary standards for schools in dance, music, theater and visual arts. At the same time, NEA and the Getty Center for Education in the Arts donated $1.25 million to develop a framework for including the arts in the National Assessment of Educational Progress (NAEP), better known as the "nation's report card."

All these efforts paid off. By 1994, when President Bill Clinton unveiled Goals 2000 for education, a set of nine subjects in which students were to demonstrate competency, the arts were among them.

Clinton also "allocated a lot of funding for the arts," says Jane Bonbright, executive director of the National Dance Education Association. "Our people used that funding galore to get the arts established. That's one reason why now we have 37 states that are certifying teachers in dance."

Also in 1994, the first National Standards for Arts Education were published, an important step in legitimizing arts education. The standards, which included detailed content for each art form, called for graduating high school students to be able to:

- Communicate at a basic level in the four arts disciplines [visual arts, music, drama and dance];
- Communicate proficiently in at least one art form;
- Develop and present basic analyses of works of art;
- Have an informed acquaintance with exemplary works of art from a variety of cultures and historical periods; and
- Relate various types of arts knowledge and skills within and across the arts disciplines. [37]

To encourage school systems to adopt high-quality arts programs, the U.S. Department of Education launched the Arts Education Model Development and Dissemination Grants program in 2002. In 2009, for example, the program awarded $265,000 to help Milwaukee Public Schools integrate arts education into the curriculum at four high-poverty schools. [38]

The Obama administration has used the bully pulpit to call attention to the arts and subjects other than reading and math, which have been the focus of many schools due to testing requirements. At a speech to the Arts Education Partnership in April 2010, Duncan, the Education secretary, said, "For decades, arts education has been treated as though it was the novice teacher at school, the last hired and first fired when times get tough."

Nevertheless, the administration's Race to the Top education policy continued NCLB's focus on reading and math testing.

In 2011, the President's Committee on the Arts and the Humanities released a major report, "Reinvesting in Arts Education — Winning America's Future through Creative Schools," the

Continued on p. 268

Art Opens Vistas for Kids With Disabilities

"It's motivational, it's inspirational, it helps with attention."

At Zane North Elementary School in Collingswood, N.J., all classes — including two for students with autism — study visual art once a week and music twice a week.

"The arts are huge for special-ed kids," says principal Thomas Santo, who majored in special education in college. He recently invited a music therapist to visit the special-education classes. "It was a huge hit," he says. "The kids responded to guitar, singing, drama. From what the teachers have told me, it's motivational, it's inspirational, it helps with attention."

Although research is limited on whether the arts can help students with learning disabilities succeed in school, studies show promise, says Christine Mason, associate executive director for research and development for the National Association of Elementary School Principals, in Alexandria, Va.

"Overall, most of the research is showing that you can get gains in student achievement and literacy by using the arts as a tool to integrate learning for all children, including those with disabilities," she says. "Even if it may not get a tremendous jump up in test scores, those of us who have done research in this area feel, for the most part, you want to look [not only at] art's impact on literacy and student achievement but also art for art's sake."

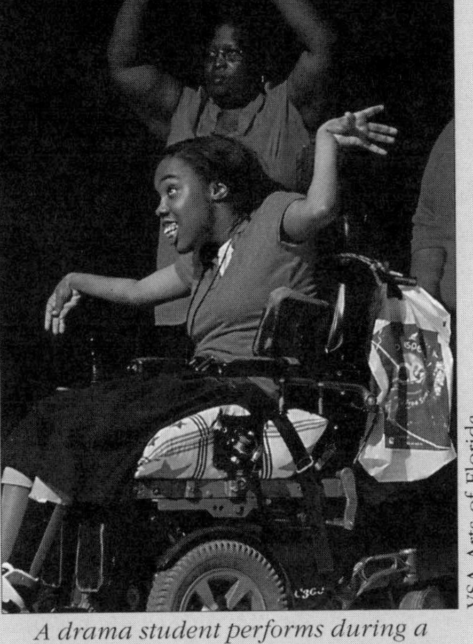
VSA Arts of Florida

A drama student performs during a showcase in Miami sponsored by VSA Arts, which provides arts-intensive programs for students with disabilities.

In a 2005 study, Mason and her colleagues held 34 focus groups of teachers in 16 states to better understand how educators perceived the value of the arts for students with disabilities. The teachers felt the inherent flexibility of the arts help students express emotion in appropriate ways, exercise problem-solving and decision-making skills and access content through multiple avenues.

The arts also provide teachers "with opportunities to meet the unique needs of their students," according to a summary of the study, which was conducted for VSA Arts, a division of the John F. Kennedy Center for the Performing Arts in Washington that provides arts and education opportunities to people with disabilities. [1]

In an earlier study for VSA Arts (formerly called Very Special Arts), other researchers observed three model arts-intensive schools aimed at students with learning disabilities. They found "significant opportunity for documenting the use of the arts as a primary strategy for meeting the learning goals of students with special needs," according to the study. [2]

The role of drama in helping children with learning disabilities improve their language and social skills also has been examined. In a 1995 study, 35 students ages 5 to 11 were divided into two groups — 21 were assigned to creative drama classes and 14 were a control group and had their regular speech therapy sessions. The drama group had four three-week units aimed at enhancing four behaviors and skills: courtesy, self-control, focus and social compliance (following written instructions). After 12 weeks, members of the drama group had improved in all four areas and also had significantly improved their oral expressive-language skills, compared to the control group. The researchers tested the children two months later and found that the beneficial effects of drama held up over time. [3]

Jane Bonbright, executive director of the National Dance Education Organization, has used dance to teach literacy and math skills to children with Down syndrome. "They didn't understand concepts like over, under, up, down, one versus four," she says. Through dance, she showed the children how to "perform the concepts."

"Kids first and foremost are kinesthetic learners," she says. "What is 'over'? You put shoes out and say jump over these shoes. They begin to feel in their body what is 'over.' Same with counting. You can teach them to jump once, jump twice, jump four times. They begin to get these concepts of math and relationships in a very fundamental way."

— ***Beth Baker***

---

[1] For a summary of the study by Arts Education Partnership: C.Y. Mason, *et al.*, "Impact of Arts Integration on Voice, Choice, and Access. Teacher Education and Special Education," *The Journal of the Teacher Education Division of the Council for Exceptional Children*, 31 (1), 2008, p. 36.

[2] Dr. Carol Keirstead and Wendy Graham, "VSA Arts Research Study: Using the Arts To Help Special Education Students Meet Their Learning Goals," National Endowment for the Arts, VSA Arts and RMC Research Corp. (2004), p. 1, www.kennedy-center.org/education/vsa/resources/VSAarts_Research_Study2004.pdf.

[3] A summary of the study, "The Effects of Creative Drama on the Social and Oral Language Skills of Children with Learning Disabilities," is found in *Critical Links — Learning in the Arts and Student Academic and Social Development*, Arts Education Partnership, 2002, p. 20, www.aep-arts.org/publications/info.htm?publication_id=10.

Continued from p. 266

federal government's first substantive examination of arts education in more than a decade. The commission argued that every school should offer an arts-rich environment.

But with schools by and large controlled locally, there's only so much the federal government can do to implement its vision. New York state law, for example, states that high school students must complete one year of art education, taught by a certified art teacher. But at least 20 percent of schools don't have a certified art teacher. "The federal government does say the arts are a core subject, [but] they are not treated as a core subject," says Sherman of New York's Center for Arts Education. "There's no accountability." ■

Think 360 Arts/Renee Fajardo-Anstine

A student shows off the mask she made to celebrate Dia del los Muertos — the Day of the Dead, a Mexican holiday — at Think 360 Arts. The statewide organization provides arts education programs and services throughout Colorado, including programs for students and professional development for teachers.

CURRENT SITUATION

Inequities in Access

A number of studies confirm that schools in lower-income communities and those with high concentrations of racial or ethnic minorities often lack arts education.

A 2009 survey by the Government Accountability Office on the effects of the No Child Left Behind Act found that "teachers at schools identified as needing improvement and those with higher percentages of minority students were more likely to report a reduction in time spent on the arts." [39]

In 2008 the NEA asked respondents ages 18-24 if they had had arts education in childhood. Compared to a survey done in 1982, the declines for African-American and Hispanic children were "quite substantial" compared to white respondents. (*See graph, p. 260.*) "There's a big inequity as far as racial and ethnic groups as well as lower socio-economic groups and geographical areas — both rural and inner city, although we haven't done a thorough analysis on this," says Sunil Iyengar, who directs the NEA's Office of Research and Analysis.

The 2008 National Assessment of Educational Progress — the most recent federal "report card" for the arts — found that students from lower-income families — those eligible for free or reduced-price school lunches — scored 28 points lower in music and nine points lower in visual arts than students ineligible for school-lunch aid. Moreover, scores for white and Asian/Pacific Islander students were significantly higher in music and visual art compared to African-American and Hispanic students' scores. [40]

Tuttle, of Arizona's arts education department, says rural schools, because of their small size and remoteness, have a hard time funding arts classes. "I have some very small districts," she says. "One has 70 kids in the whole district. The superintendent is the special-education teacher, the bus driver — her ability to provide music or art is not going to happen." Arizona is also home to many charter schools, which often are smaller and unable to hire arts specialists.

Continued on p. 270

At Issue:

Should the arts be integrated with science education?

ROBERT ROOT-BERNSTEIN
MACARTHUR FELLOW,
PROFESSOR OF PHYSIOLOGY
MICHIGAN STATE UNIVERSITY

FROM "THE ART OF SCIENTIFIC AND TECHNOLOGICAL INNOVATIONS," SCIENCEBLOGS.COM, POSTED APRIL 11, 2011

yes

Most people are at a loss to be able to identify any useful connections between arts and sciences. This ignorance is appalling. Arts provide innovations through analogies, models, skills, structures, techniques, methods, and knowledge. Arts don't just prettify science or make technology more aesthetic; they often make both possible.

That cell phone or PDA you're carrying? It uses a form of encryption called frequency hopping to ensure your messages can't easily be intercepted. Frequency hopping was invented by the composer George Antheil in collaboration with the actress Hedy Lamarr. Yeah, really.

The first programmable device was invented by J. M. Jacquard to control the looms that made his tapestries, and exactly the same technique was used to program the first computers. He also made the first digital image — out of black and white threads. In fact, the computer chips that run virtually all our devices today are made using a combination of three classic artistic inventions: etching, silk screen printing, and photolithography.

Oh, and that bridge you drove over on the way to work: Good chance its design was invented by an artist. Princeton engineering professor David Billington and Smithsonian historian Brooke Hindle have shown that most of the innovations in bridge design have originated with artistically trained engineers.

In fact, I've just published a study that shows that almost all Nobel laureates in the sciences are actively engaged in arts as adults. They are 25 times as likely as average scientists to sing, dance, or act; 17 times as likely to be an artist; 12 times more likely to write poetry and literature . . . four times as likely to be a musician; and twice as likely to be a photographer. Many connect their art with their scientific creativity.

Moreover, those folks who produce the new patentable inventions and found the new companies to produce them — they, too, are artistically trained: They are far more likely to have continuous participation in drawing, painting, dancing, woodworking, metal working, and mechanics than their less innovative peers. Ninety percent of them, in interviews, expressed the opinion that the arts should be part of every scientists' and technologists' education. Eighty percent of them could point to specific ways in which their arts training directly enhanced their innovative ability.

In sum, successful innovators in sciences and technology are artistic people. Stimulate the arts, and you stimulate innovation.

ALAN FRIEDMAN
CONSULTANT, MUSEUM DEVELOPMENT AND SCIENCE COMMUNICATION

WRITTEN FOR *CQ RESEARCHER*, MARCH 2012

no

Integrating science and the arts in education curricula would do a disservice to both realms. Now, I do believe strongly that the arts should be used to strengthen science education and vice versa. And I believe just as strongly that history, philosophy, civics, geography, math, engineering and other fields can and should illuminate science, and again vice versa.

What I object to is, first, singling out the arts as the one cultural enterprise that should be blended with the sciences; and, two, attempting to integrate disciplines, which may be mutually enlightening but also may have profound differences that tend to be downplayed in integrated curricula.

What are some of these profound differences between the arts and the sciences?

• The two decide what's good and what's not in incompatible ways.

In science there are clear, rigorous measures. For example, an idea in science must be "falsifiable" — that is, built into an idea must be a way to show how it could be tested and found wanting. This tough test is a reason why scientists have been able to correct themselves.

There is nothing remotely like this measure of value in the arts, and there is no reason there should be. Deciding what is good and what's not in the arts is a subjective, changing notion. That flexibility allows art dismissed in one milieu to be hugely appreciated in another.

• Science demands that its ideas be completely replicable by others, while the arts celebrate uniqueness.

If other science practitioners cannot soon reproduce the same results using the same ideas, those ideas are rejected. The arts have quite the opposite criterion: Uniqueness is highly desirable and increases value, while easy replicability is a devaluing quality.

I believe in a liberal arts education in which every one of the great cultural enterprises — art, engineering, history, languages, math, science, and so on — is given its place in the curriculum. Let's make sure they all get good introductions, and then let's help learners to put together any pairs, trios or combinations that appeal to them. We can do this institutionally as well, with museums devoted to a combination of art and science, history and technology or math and civilizations. There are valuable insights to be won in every combination.

But fully integrating any of these combinations in the curriculum runs the risk of losing the unique, fundamental distinctions that are behind the glories of each field.

Continued from p. 268

Low-income parents may find it difficult to pay for extra programs for their children. "We often see things like band programs or orchestras requiring parents to do more, to pay a fee — not just in the arts, we see it with athletic programs as well," says Ruppert of the Arts Education Partnership. "Student fees for participation are increasing. The problem is, the wealthier schools that have parents who have resources can afford to donate more and raise more money."

At Mount Rainer Elementary in Maryland, like other schools in Prince George's County, visual arts were slashed 30 years ago during a county budget crunch and not restored. As a result, each visual arts teacher serves four schools, seeing each class only two or three times a year for one hour. There is no art room, and the teachers bring supplies on a cart. "[The students] love art, and they're very proud of it," says first-grade teacher Greg Pugliese. "When I make the announcement that we're having art class, they all cheer."

Art teacher Linder is responsible for teaching more than 2,000 students in her four schools. "The students are missing a chance to show what they're capable of, and that's tragic," she says. "I've had so many teachers tell me [of students], 'I had no idea that he had an imagination like that, that she could express herself, that she knew deep things about the human condition that you can't show in a math problem.' "

Even as many lower-income students are losing out, research suggests they may benefit the most from arts education. "Our research has shown that the arts can be most helpful to those children, and we see their opportunity to participate in arts education is limited," says Ruppert. "Kids who are struggling in reading and in mathematics and in persistence and attendance, the beneficial effects of arts education are greater for those children." Studies have shown that the arts especially help students who feel isolated or marginalized, in part by better engaging them with school. A U.S. Department of Justice study found the arts reduced delinquency and drug use and increased self-esteem. [41]

Teachers and administrators who are committed to the arts are finding ways to mitigate the inequities.

AFP/Getty Images/Mandel Ngan

Grammy award-winning musicians Sharon Isbin and Joshua Bell perform during a student music workshop at the White House on Nov. 4, 2009. The event is a part of a series created by first lady Michelle Obama to highlight arts education. In 2011, the President's Committee on the Arts and the Humanities released the federal government's first substantive examination of arts education in more than a decade; it argued that every school should offer an arts-rich environment.

At Mount Rainier, principal Reed is not able to hire arts specialists, but she's doing what she can to bring the arts to her students — 90 percent of whom are eligible for the free or reduced-cost lunch program and over half are immigrants. School walls are painted with bright primary colors rather than institutional beige ("I got in trouble for that," says Reed) and hung with murals and pictures made by the children, including sophisticated botanical drawings of seed pods that older students made. The school choir and a "Mad Hot Ballroom" dancing group compete with other schools. Visiting artists, from poets to dancers and puppeteers, regularly come to the school to perform and to offer professional development sessions for classroom teachers.

Without the arts, says Reed, "We're not allowing children the broad spectrum of opportunities they need."

21st-Century Workforce

As the United States seeks to remain globally competitive, arts education advocates, business leaders and policymakers are looking to arts education as a vehicle for fostering creativity and innovation in tomorrow's workforce.

The National Endowment for the Arts is leading a task force of 13 federal agencies and departments to encourage more and better research on how the arts help people reach their full potential at all stages of life, including in school and on the job.

"A lot of people for quite a while have devalued the real benefits of arts education," says O'Brien of NEA. "It's not just a fun activity or something you'd like to give to your kids if you could, but it has a real function in learning that has real consequences in industry and our economy."

A survey of *Fortune* 500 companies found that 400 companies were using "arts-based learning" in workforce development. [42] For example, jazz saxophonist Michael Gold uses jazz improvisation to teach business improvisation and collaboration. [43]

Daniel Windham, director of the arts for the New York City-based Wallace Foundation, which supports research on arts education, says education reform should be shaped with the ultimate goal in mind. "If we want children as they approach adulthood to be able to think expressively and creatively and have experience in creative domains and innovation — not only in the industrial model but in a broader way of thinking — if we want them to be successful in the workplace, looking for new ways of solving problems," he says, "then the 12 years that you have them in schools need to prepare them for those outcomes." The arts, he says, are fundamental to that goal.

A leader in this effort is the Partnership for 21st Century Skills, founded in 2002 by the U.S. Department of Education, the National Education Association — a major teacher's union — and large corporations. Its leadership today includes Ford, Apple, Dell, Crayola, Verizon and LEGO Education, among many others.

The partnership seeks to serve as a catalyst for school systems to transform what and how they teach. It wants to "fuse" the traditional core subjects listed in No Child Left Behind (which includes the arts) with what it calls "the 4Cs:" critical thinking and problem solving; communication; collaboration, and creativity and innovation.

In a public opinion poll the partnership commissioned in 2007, a wide majority (88 percent) of respondents thought these skills should be part of the curriculum for all students. While the public supported reading as its top priority, "voter attitudes clearly have shifted away from the 'back to basics' movement that was a strong theme for school improvement during the 1990s." [44]

Arts educators see "the 4Cs" as a golden opportunity to elevate the arts in the eyes of school systems and the public. Adams, the supervisor of fine arts in Montgomery County, Md., says her school system's new curriculum is based on these 21st-century skills. "They understand that the arts are important," she says, and that through the arts "the learning is going to be deeper."

"At a national policy level, it would be a missed opportunity to not place the arts in the center" of 21st-century skills," says Rohit Burman, program director for the MetLife Foundation, which supports arts programs for young people. "What better way for a teenager to think of connections, to think of different ways to present information than to be on stage or to think about the music. There are so many different pieces where arts can play a role in creative thinking."

The Conference Board, a business membership and research organization, is conducting a series of studies to learn more about how — or if — arts education nurtures creative workers. In 2008, it partnered with Americans for the Arts and the American Association of School Superintendents to survey business executives and school superintendents. They found a disconnect between the two groups.

Most superintendents thought graduating students met or exceeded all 11 skills or behaviors identified as being linked to creativity; most business executives thought new employees met or exceeded only seven. At the same time, executives ranked the ability to identify problems as the most important skill, while superintendents ranked it ninth. Superintendents ranked problem solving as No. 1, while executives ranked it eighth.

"These discrepancies bolster the view that while schools teach students how to solve problems put before them, the business sector requires workers who can identify the problems in the first place," a report on the study stated. [45]

Mary Wright, program director for human capital with the Conference Board, says the business group's next step will be to ask executives to look at their most creative, innovative employees: Are there commonalities in their education, such as a strong background in the arts? "We do not have empirical evidence that says, 'Gee, as I look at my 15 most creative people, these are the classes that they have taken.' That is what we are hoping to do," she says. She expects that research to be conducted next year. ■

OUTLOOK

'Schizophrenic' Future?

Research on the value of arts education will likely accelerate, if funding can be found. But that's a big if.

"I think we're at the infancy stage," Sabol of the National Art Education Association says of such research. "Neuroscience as a field is making remarkable strides. They're still exploring the brain. We don't understand how certain things happen. As advances occur, we'll be able to make firm connections, we'll see areas of the brain light up during engagement with art."

Also on the horizon is a fifth form of art — media arts — which may soon be included under the arts education umbrella. Media arts encompass all sorts of technology applications, whether for Web design, animation, software graphics, sound engineering, film or communications.

"The use of technology for self-expression has its own design considerations and equipment," says Sabol. "It's gone through remarkable growth and development in the last decade and has just ballooned."

The emphasis on school accountability is not likely to wane. The major arts associations are collaborating to update the national standards published in 1994. They also are working with the Partnership for 21st Century Skills to explain how the arts contribute to critical thinking and problem solving, communication, collaboration and creativity and innovation.

The Internet helps school systems and arts associations quickly, widely and inexpensively disseminate successful programs. "There are many wonderful models on which to draw," says Tuttle of Arizona. She anticipates a growing emphasis on teacher evaluation and a challenge to arts educators to develop assessment measures for student progress in the arts, as a complement to the testing of reading and math.

Ruppert of the Arts Education Partnership feels "schizophrenic" about the future. On the one hand, state budgets may continue to face the ax, threatening arts programs. "But," she says, "I'm feeling optimistic because I do believe there is a lot of persuasive evidence we're gathering for the difference learning through the arts can make in the lives of children."

The push for more research, better assessment, standards and accountability will likely intensify in education generally, and the arts need to find their place in order to be taken seriously, experts say.

"From a policy point of view, as you allocate dollars in a fiscally conservative environment, you have to make smart decisions," says Iyengar of NEA. "Just like any other social service or activity, we need to have the information that arts matter to the community and show its worth." ■

Notes

[1] "New Harris Poll Reveals That 93% of Americans Believe That the Arts Are Vital to Providing a Well-Rounded Education," Americans for the Arts, news release, 2005, www.AmericansForTheArts.org/news/press/2005/2005_06_13b.asp.

[2] "Education," Gallup Poll, undated, www.gallup.com/poll/1612/education.aspx.

[3] Linda Lyons, "Americans Want Music Students to Play on," Gallup, May 20, 2003, www.gallup.com/poll/8434/americans-want-music-students-play.aspx. The poll was conducted for the International Music Products Association.

[4] Jennifer Nesbitt, "Westerville School Levy Barely Passes — by 585 Votes," This Week Community Newspapers, March 7, 2012, www.thisweeknews.com/content/stories/2012/03/06/election-issues/issue-no-10-westerville-school-levy.html.

[5] "Reinvesting in Arts Education — Winning America's Future Through Creative Schools," President's Committee on the Arts and the Humanities, 2011, p. v, www.pcah.gov/sites/default/files/PCAH_Reinvesting_4web_0.pdf.

[6] Elliot Eisner, *The Arts and the Creation of Mind* (2002), pp. 70-92. See "10 Lessons the Arts Teach," National Art Education Association, www.arteducators.org/advocacy/10-lessons-the-arts-teach.

[7] Arne Duncan, "The Well-Rounded Curriculum," speech to the Arts Education Partnership National Forum, April 9, 2010, www2.ed.gov/news/speeches/2010/04/04092010.html.

[8] Ellen Winner and Lois Hetland, eds., "Beyond the Soundbite: Arts Education and Academic Outcomes Conference Proceedings," J. Paul Getty Museum Publications, 2000, pp. 56-57, www.getty.edu/foundation/pdfs/soundbite.pdf.

[9] Mariale Hardiman, *et al.*, "Neuroeducation: Learning, Arts, and The Brain," The Dana Foundation, 2009, p. 13, www.dana.org/news/publications/publication.aspx?id=23964.

[10] *Ibid.*, pp. 13-14.

[11] Douglas Israel, "Staying in School: Arts Education and New York City High School Graduation Rates," The Center for Arts Education, 2009, p. 2, www.cae-nyc.org/arts-education-report.

[12] "Doing Good and Doing Well by Doing Art," Arts Education Partnership, March 9, 2010, www.aep-arts.org/files/AEPWireDoingWell.pdf.

[13] Dan Serig, "Research Review: 'Doing Well and Doing Good by Doing Art,' " *Teaching Artist Journal*, Vol. 8, No. 2, pp. 113-121, 2010.

[14] Eisner, *op. cit.*, p. 218.

[15] E. Glenn Schellenberg, "Music and Cognitive Abilities," *Current Directions in Psychological Science*, 2005, pp. 317-320, www.erin.utoronto.ca/~w3psygs/SchellenbergCDPS2005.pdf.

[16] F. Robert Sabol, "No Child Left Behind — A Study of Its Impact on Arts Education," National Art Education Foundation, 2010, www.arteducators.org/research/NCLB_Summary_of_Findings_2-10_3.pdf.

[17] "The Federal Science, Technology, Engineering and Mathematics Education Portfolio," December 2011, www.whitehouse.gov/sites/

About the Author

Beth Baker is an award-winning freelance journalist in Takoma Park, Md., who writes on the arts and health care and whose articles have appeared in numerous publications, including *The Washington Post, AARP Bulletin, Ms.* and *BioScience*, where she is features editor. She has received two National Mature Media Awards for her reporting on aging and media fellowships to study aging and cancer issues from, respectively, Case Western Reserve University and the National Press Foundation. Her books include *Old Age in a New Age — The Promise of Transformative Nursing Homes* (Vanderbilt University Press, 2007).

default/files/microsites/ostp/costem__federal_stem_education_portfolio_report.pdf.

[18] From Heilbrunn Timeline of Art History, Metropolitan Museum of Art, www.metmuseum.org/toah/hd/lasc/hd_lasc.htm.

[19] "Dance, Music, Theatre, Visual Arts — What Every Young American Should Know and Be Able to Do in the Arts," Consortium of National Arts Education Associations, 1994, p. 5.

[20] John Dewey, *Democracy and Education* (1916), quoted here from 1944 edition, p. 253.

[21] *The New Encyclopedia Britannica*, University of Chicago Press, 1987, Vol. 25, p. 343.

[22] Nick Rabkin and E. C. Hedberg, "Arts Education in America: What the Declines Mean for Arts Participation," National Endowment for the Arts, 2008, p. 41, www.nea.gov/research/2008-SPPA-ArtsLearning.pdf.

[23] *Ibid.* The report cites a quote from E. B. Birge, *History of Public School Music in the United States* (1928).

[24] Paul E. Bolin, "The Massachusetts Drawing Act of 1870: Industrial Mandate or Democratic Maneuver?" in Donald Soucy and Mary Ann Stankiewicz, "Framing the Past: Essays on Art Education," National Art Education Association, 1990, pp. 58-68. See "Notes for a Perspective on Arts Education," www.noteaccess.com/APPROACHES/ArtEd/History/MADrawingAct.htm.

[25] Dewey, *op. cit.*, p. 238.

[26] Rabkin and Hedberg, *op. cit.*, p. 14.

[27] Jerome Bruner, *The Culture of Education* (1996), p. 42.

[28] Rebecca S. New and Moncrieff Cochran, *Early Childhood Education: An International Encyclopedia* (2007), p. 494. The authors cited John A. Michael, "The Lowenfeld lectures: Viktor Lowenfeld on art education and therapy," 1982.

[29] Educational Theatre Association, http://schooltheatre.org/about/history.

[30] www.pz.harvard.edu/History/History.htm.

[31] Howard Gardner, *Multiple Intelligences — The Theory in Practice* (1993), p. 9.

[32] Ralph A. Smith, "The DBAE Literature Project," undated, www.arteducators.org/research/DBAE_Lit_Project.pdf.

[33] William J. Bennett, Chester E. Finn, and John T. E. Cribb, Jr., *The Educated Child — A Parent's Guide from Preschool through Eighth Grade* (1999), p. 263.

[34] Doug Herbert, "Finding the Will and the Way to Make the Arts a Core Subject," *The State Education Standard*, Winter 2004, p. 5. The author is citing The Arts, Education and Americans Panel, "Coming to our Senses: The Significance of the Arts for American Education," 1977.

[35] Herbert, *Ibid.*

[36] *Ibid.*, p. 5.

[37] Consortium of National Arts Education Associations, *op. cit.*, pp. 18-19.

[38] See U.S. Department of Education, www2.ed.gov/programs/artsedmodel/2009awards.html.

[39] "Access to Arts Education," Government Accountability Office, February 2009, p. 3, www.gao.gov/new.items/d09286.pdf.

[40] "The Nation's Arts Report Card — Summary of Results," Arts Education Partnership, 2008, p. 4, www.aep-arts.org/NAEP.html.

[41] President's Committee, *op. cit.*, p. 18.

[42] Harvey Seifter and Ted Buswick, "Special Issue: Creatively intelligent companies and leaders: Arts-based learning for business," *Journal of Business Strategy*, 2010, p. 8.

[43] See the "Art of Science Learning" website for this and other examples, www.artofsciencelearning.org/conference-reports/118-education-practice-working-group-notes.html.

[44] "Voter Attitudes towards 21st Century Skills," Partnership for 21st Century Skills, 2007, www.p21.org/storage/documents/p21_pollreport_2pg.pdf.

[45] "Ready to Innovate — Key Findings," The Conference Board, 2008, www.otis.edu/creative_economy/download/ready_to_innovate.pdf.

FOR MORE INFORMATION

American Alliance for Theatre and Education, 4908 Auburn Ave., Bethesda, MD 20814; 301-200-1944; www.aate.com. Connects theater artists, educators and researchers. Offers advocacy toolkit and the scholarly *Youth Theatre Journal*. Website summarizes benefits of arts education for student achievement.

Americans for the Arts, 1000 Vermont Ave., N.W., 6th Fl., Washington, DC 20005; 202-371-2830; or One E. 53rd St., New York, NY 10022; 212-223-2787; www.artsusa.org. Website provides a wealth of information on the arts and arts education, including research, webinar series, news and professional development and ways to get involved.

Arts Education Partnership, One Massachusetts Ave., N.W., Suite 700, Washington, DC 20001-1431; 202-326-8693; www.aep-arts.org. Provides access to 25-plus publications, most free or at nominal cost, plus a searchable database of arts education state policies and report cards.

Educational Theatre Association, 2343 Auburn Ave., Cincinnati, OH 45219-2815; 513-421-3900; http://schooltheatre.org. Offers professional development and advocacy for theater teachers, *Dramatics* magazine and a national theater festival for high school students. Website has research, state resources and news.

National Art Education Association, 1806 Robert Fulton Dr., Suite 300, Reston, VA 20191; 703-860-8000; www.arteducators.org. Advances visual arts in schools. In addition to professional-development resources, website offers downloadable research reports on benefits of arts education.

National Association for Music Education, 1806 Robert Fulton Dr., Suite 300, Reston, VA 20191; 703-860-4000 or 800-336-3768; www.nafme.org. Largest and oldest arts education association; provides information on programs and scholarships for students and fact sheets on benefits of music education. Includes ordering information for a sing-along linking students around the globe in a huge virtual concert.

National Endowment for the Arts, 1100 Pennsylvania Ave., N.W., Washington, DC 20506-0001; 202-682-5400, www.nea.gov. Arts Education section of the website provides several reports free for download, on topics such as research, programs for juvenile offenders, after-school programs and introducing children to the arts.

Bibliography

Selected Sources

Books

Catterall, James S., *Doing Well and Doing Good by Doing Art — The Effects of Education in the Visual and Performing Arts on the Achievements and Values of Young Adults*, CreateSpace, 2009.

A professor of education follows students into adulthood and analyzes how the arts affect their long-term progress.

Davis, Jessica Hoffman, *Why Our Schools Need the Arts*, Teachers College Press, 2007. Also, *Why Our High Schools Need the Arts*, 2011.

A cognitive psychologist and former Harvard researcher makes a compelling case for why arts education is important.

Deasy, Richard J., and Lauren M. Stevenson, *Third Space: When Learning Matters*, Arts Education Partnership, 2005.

The former executive director (Deasy) and a senior researcher (Stevenson) with the Arts Education Partnership profile 10 schools in low-income neighborhoods that used arts education to transform themselves into great schools.

Donahue, David M., and Jennifer Stuart, eds., *Artful Teaching — Integrating the Arts for Understanding Across the Curriculum, K-8*, Teachers College Press and National Art Education Association, 2010.

A professor (Donahue) and a school arts coordinator (Stuart) show how visual arts, music, drama and dance can be used to teach English, social studies, science and math.

Articles

Robelen, Erik W., "Schools Integrate Dance into Core Academics," *Education Week*, Nov. 7, 2010, p. 1.

Schools use dance to teach everything from photosynthesis to phonetics.

Robelen, Erik W., "STEAM: Experts Make Case for Adding Arts to STEM," *Education Week*, Dec. 1, 2011, p. 8.

Experts debate whether the arts should be closely linked to science and math education.

Smith, Fran, "Why Arts Education is Crucial, and Who's Doing it Best," *Edutopia*, Jan. 28, 2009, www.edutopia.org/arts-music-curriculum-child-development.

The author provides a useful overview of the state of arts education, including links to several studies and examples from local districts.

Winner, Ellen, and Lois Hetland, "Art for Our Sake," *The Boston Globe*, Sept. 2, 2007, www.boston.com/news/globe/ideas/articles/2007/09/02/art_for_our_sake/?page=full.

Two leading arts education researchers make their case for the intrinsic benefits of the arts for student development and learning.

Reports and Studies

"Re-Investing in Arts Education — Winning America's Future through Creative Schools," President's Committee on the Arts and Humanities, 2011, www.pcah.gov/resources/re-investing-through-arts-educationwinning-americas-future-through-creative-schools.

An up-to-date summary of research emphasizes the benefits of arts integration.

Asbury, Carolyn, and Barbara Rich, eds., "Learning, Arts, and the Brain — The Dana Consortium Report on Arts and Cognition," The Dana Foundation, 2008, www.dana.org/news/publications/publication.aspx?id=10760.

Neuroscientists present research that seeks to answer: Are smart people drawn to the arts or does arts training make people smarter?

McCarthy, Kevin, Elizabeth H. Ondaatje, Laura Zakaras and Arthur Brooks, "Gifts of the Muse-Reframing the Debate about the Benefits of the Arts," Wallace Foundation, 2004, www.rand.org/pubs/monographs/2005/RAND_MG218.pdf.

Researchers from the Rand Corp. review the research on arts education, explaining what is known and what has yet to be determined.

Rabkin, Nick, and E. C. Hedberg, "Arts Education in America: What the Declines Mean for Arts Participation," National Endowment for the Arts, 2008, www.nea.gov/research/2008-SPPA-ArtsLearning.pdf.

The authors analyze results of the Survey of Public Participation in the Arts and document parallel downward trends in arts education and adult attendance at concerts, plays and ballet performances.

Ruppert, Sandra, "Critical Evidence-How the Arts Benefit Student Achievement," Arts Education Partnership, 2006.

A review of the research on arts education places it in a broader education-policy context.

On the Web

"Champion Creatively Alive Children," www.crayola.com/educators/naesp/.

The National Association of Elementary School Principals and Crayola worked together to create free resources for teachers and parents to nurture creativity in kids and transform their schools' culture.

ArtsEdSearch, www.aep-arts.org.

A new online clearinghouse of research on the educational outcomes of learning in and through the arts will be launched on April 12 by the Arts Education Partnership.

The Next Step:

Additional Articles from Current Periodicals

Academic Performance

Beldon, Sanford, "Cutting Allentown Arts Programs Ignores Benefits to Students," *Morning Call* (Allentown, Pa.), April 7, 2011, p. A18, articles.mcall.com/2011-04-06/opinion/mc-alletown-school-arts-beldon-yv-04020110406_1_arts-programs-students-allen-high-school.
Arts can have a tremendous impact on children's ability to do well in school, says the chairman of the Allentown Art Museum in Pennsylvania.

Hines, Robin, "Well-Rounded Education Is Found in Houston Schools," *Macon* (Ga.) *Telegraph*, Sept. 28, 2011, www.macon.com/2011/09/28/1720352/well-rounded-education-is-found.html.
Arts education benefits academic achievement largely because it gives students motivation, confidence and a better understanding of teamwork, says a school superintendent.

Strauss, Valerie, "The Problem With Linking Arts Education to Test Scores," *The Washington Post*, May 30, 2011, p. B2.
Critics say linking arts education to higher test scores undermines the importance of creativity in student development.

Funding

Evans, Tim, "Arts Program Struggles to Fund the Gift of Expression, Creativity," *USA Today*, Nov. 29, 2011, p. D6, www.usatoday.com/news/nation/story/2011-11-21/sharing-indiana-disabled-art-program/51446368/1.
Staff members of VSA Indiana, which provides arts programs to the disabled, have taken pay reductions in order to avoid major service cuts.

Hiaasen, Scott, and Kathleen McGrory, "Miami-Dade School District to Restore Funds to Charter School," *The Miami Herald*, Nov. 4, 2011, www.miamiherald.com/2011/11/04/2487712/miami-dade-school-district-to.html.
A Florida school district has decided to partially restore funds for a charter school devoted to arts education.

Seidman, Carrie, "A Boost to Arts in Sarasota," *Sarasota* (Fla.) *Herald Tribune*, June 16, 2011, p. A1.
The Kennedy Center in Washington, D.C., has chosen Sarasota, Fla., for a program aimed at expanding arts education in elementary and middle schools.

Wereschagin, Mike, "Endangered Arts Have Powerful Advocate in Pa.," *Pittsburgh Tribune Review*, June 17, 2011, www.pittsburghlive.com/x/pittsburghtrib/news/state/s_742542.html.
Susan Corbett, wife of Republican Pennsylvania Gov. Tom Corbett, wants more funding for the state's arts council.

Learning Disabilities

Pollak, Suzanne, "Special School for Special Students," *Washington Jewish Week*, Jan. 19, 2012, p. B9.
The Diener School in Potomac, Md., emphasizes arts education as a means to overcome learning disabilities for children from K-fifth grade.

Putterman, Rebecca, "Parents With ADHD Children Support Each Other," *Clayton* (N.C.) *News-Star*, Feb. 5, 2012, www.claytonnewsstar.com/2012/02/05/1831482/parents-with-adhd-children-support.html.
A group of parents with ADHD-diagnosed children in Clayton, N.C., are turning to art therapy to keep their children's hyperactive minds focused.

STEAM

Genellie, Kate, "A Pair of Reshaped Schools Reopen in Benton Harbor," *Herald-Palladium* (St. Joseph, Mich.), Aug. 19, 2011.
A Michigan school district has opened two magnet schools that will focus on the STEAM education method, which incorporates arts with Science, Technology, Engineering and Math.

Whitlow, Joan, "So Many New High School Choices, So Much Confusion," *Star-Ledger* (Newark, N.J.), May 13, 2011, p. 15, blog.nj.com/njv_joan_whitlow/2011/05/so_many_new_high_school_choice.html.
The Newark STEAM Academy in New Jersey is designed to offer nontraditional curricula for families wanting a different approach to education.

Citing *CQ Researcher*

Sample formats for citing these reports in a bibliography include the ones listed below. Preferred styles and formats vary, so please check with your instructor or professor.

MLA Style

Jost, Kenneth. "Remembering 9/11," CQ Researcher 2 Sept. 2011: 701-732.

APA Style

Jost, K. (2011, September 2). Remembering 9/11. *CQ Researcher, 9*, 701-732.

Chicago Style

Jost, Kenneth. "Remembering 9/11." *CQ Researcher*, September 2, 2011, 701-732.

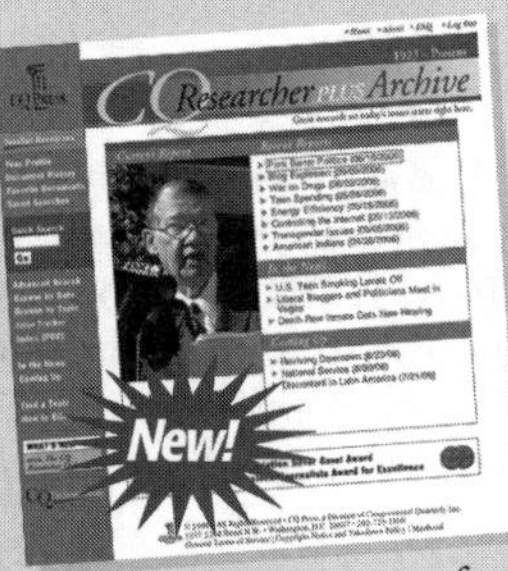

Researcher PLUS Archive
New!

CQ Researcher

Published by CQ Press, an Imprint of SAGE Publications, Inc.

www.cqresearcher.com

U.S.-Europe Relations

Is the historic trans-Atlantic alliance still relevant?

Following World War II, the U.S. alliance with Western Europe stood as the cornerstone of American foreign policy in the face of Cold War threats from what was then the Soviet Union. Forged in the North Atlantic Treaty Organization (NATO) — the alliance's enduring defense pact — the partnership is rooted in the shared values of democracy, rule of law and free-market principles. But with the emergence of China and India as global economic powers, the Arab Spring revolutions and Iran's uncertain nuclear ambitions, the United States has shifted its political and security priorities to the Asia-Pacific region, leaving Europe worried that its historic ties with the United States are fraying. In May, President Obama will host two meetings of European leaders that could help define the trans-Atlantic alliance for years to come: a NATO summit in Chicago and a summit of the Group of 8 industrialized nations at Camp David, the presidential retreat.

President Obama and British Prime Minister David Cameron arrive at the White House Rose Garden for a press conference on March 14, 2012. After discussing global economic woes and other shared problems, Obama said of America's alliance with Britain, "We stand together and we work together and we bleed together and we build together."

INSIDE THIS REPORT

THE ISSUES 279
BACKGROUND 285
CHRONOLOGY 287
CURRENT SITUATION 292
AT ISSUE 293
OUTLOOK 295
BIBLIOGRAPHY 298
THE NEXT STEP 299

CQ Researcher • March 23, 2012 • www.cqresearcher.com
Volume 22, Number 12 • Pages 277-300

SAGE | CQPRESS
Los Angeles | London | New Delhi Singapore | Washington DC

RECIPIENT OF SOCIETY OF PROFESSIONAL JOURNALISTS AWARD FOR EXCELLENCE ◆ AMERICAN BAR ASSOCIATION SILVER GAVEL AWARD

U.S.-EUROPE RELATIONS

THE ISSUES

279 • Should the U.S. pull its forces out of Europe?
• Is Asia the new focus of U.S. foreign policy?
• Is a U.S. drift away from Europe reversible?

BACKGROUND

285 **North Atlantic Treaty**
The postwar pact ensured a U.S. role in Europe.

285 **Marshall Plan**
U.S. efforts to rebuild Europe aided 17 nations.

286 **Missile Crisis**
The U.S. urged Europe to answer the Soviet's threat.

288 **Afghanistan and Iraq**
The U.S. invasion of Iraq hurt U.S.-Europe relations.

290 **European Union**
The confederation has solidified U.S.-European ties.

CURRENT SITUATION

292 **EU and Iran**
The U.S. and Europe are pressuring Iran over suspected nuclear weapons.

292 **Debt Crisis**
The EU is tightening its belt amid the need for economic stimulation.

294 **Afghanistan Tensions**
NATO's patience with the deadly war is running thin.

OUTLOOK

295 **NATO Summit**
The top priority will be an Afghan war exit strategy.

Cover: AFP/Getty Images/Mandel Ngan

SIDEBARS AND GRAPHICS

280 **How the U.S. and E.U. Compare**
The E.U.'s gross domestic product exceeds the U.S. GDP.

281 **U.S.-European Trade on the Decline**
Both imports and exports are down.

283 **Debt Plagues European Nations**
Economies of Greece, Italy Ireland and Portugal threatened.

284 **Few NATO Members Meet Defense Obligations**
Only four European members hit spending benchmarks.

287 **Chronology**
Key events since 1947.

288 **EU Tribunals Trump National Courts on Key Issues**
Critics worry that they wield too much clout.

291 **Once Spurned, 'Old Europe' Makes a Comeback**
U.S ties shift away from Eastern Europe.

293 **At Issue**
Should the NATO alliance continue?

FOR FURTHER RESEARCH

295 **For More Information**
Organizations to contact.

298 **Bibliography**
Selected sources used.

299 **The Next Step**
Additional articles.

299 **Citing *CQ Researcher***
Sample bibliography formats.

CQ Researcher

March 23, 2012
Volume 22, Number 12

MANAGING EDITOR: Thomas J. Billitteri
tjb@cqpress.com

ASSISTANT MANAGING EDITOR: Kathy Koch
kkoch@cqpress.com

CONTRIBUTING EDITOR: Thomas J. Colin
tcolin@cqpress.com

ASSOCIATE EDITOR: Kenneth Jost

STAFF WRITER: Marcia Clemmitt

CONTRIBUTING WRITERS: Sarah Glazer, Alan Greenblatt, Peter Katel, Barbara Mantel, Jennifer Weeks

DESIGN/PRODUCTION EDITOR: Olu B. Davis

ASSISTANT EDITOR: Darrell Dela Rosa

FACT CHECKER: Michelle Harris

Los Angeles | London | New Delhi
Singapore | Washington DC

An Imprint of SAGE Publications, Inc.

VICE PRESIDENT AND EDITORIAL DIRECTOR, HIGHER EDUCATION GROUP:
Michele Sordi

DIRECTOR, ONLINE PUBLISHING:
Todd Baldwin

CQ Researcher (ISSN 1056-2036) is printed on acid-free paper. Published weekly, except: (March wk. 5) (May wk. 4) (July wk. 1) (Aug. wks. 3, 4) (Nov. wk. 4) and (Dec. wks. 3, 4). Published by SAGE Publications, Inc., 2455 Teller Rd., Thousand Oaks, CA 91320. Annual full-service subscriptions start at $1,054. For pricing, call 1-800-834-9020. To purchase a *CQ Researcher* report in print or electronic format (PDF), visit www.cqpress.com or call 866-427-7737. Single reports start at $15. Bulk purchase discounts and electronic-rights licensing are also available. Periodicals postage paid at Thousand Oaks, California, and at additional mailing offices. POSTMASTER: Send address changes to *CQ Researcher*, 2300 N St., N.W., Suite 800, Washington, DC 20037.

U.S.-Europe Relations

BY ROLAND FLAMINI

THE ISSUES

When British Prime Minister David Cameron visited Washington on March 14, President Barack Obama directed a few light-hearted zingers his way, ribbing him over Britain's burning of the White House during the War of 1812. "It's now been 200 years since the British came here . . .," Obama joked. "They made quite an impression. They really lit up the place."

Joshing back, Cameron replied: "I can see you've got the place a little better defended today. . . .You're clearly not taking any risks with the Brits this time."

The kidding around reflected the growing friendship between Obama, 50, and Cameron, 45. Indeed, the night before, Obama took the conservative British leader to an NCAA basketball playoff game in Dayton, Ohio, during the March Madness tournament. (By coincidence, Ohio just happens to be a key state in the president's upcoming re-election bid.)

But Cameron's visit was far from all fun and games.

He and the president talked about a range of weighty and shared problems — the war in Afghanistan, unrest in the Middle East and global economic woes. "We stand together and we work together and we bleed together and we build together," Obama said of America's historical alliance with Britain. [1]

In some respects, Obama's comments could apply to America's ties with much of Europe. Despite India and China's rising economic and political power, U.S. trade and financial ties with Europe remain strong. But in other ways, the link between the two continents is increasingly strained and uncertain. Not only do Europe's fiscal problems threaten the U.S. economy, but the vaunted, 63-year-old military alliance binding the U.S. and Europe — the North Atlantic Treaty Organization (NATO) — must seek a new direction, analysts say.

These and other issues will confront President Obama and European leaders when they meet in May — in Chicago for the first NATO summit in the United States in 13 years and at the Camp David presidential retreat in Maryland two days earlier for a summit of the Group of 8 (G8) industrialized nations.* Dominating the agenda will be Europe's debt crises, the war in Afghanistan and the global response to Iranian nuclear ambitions.

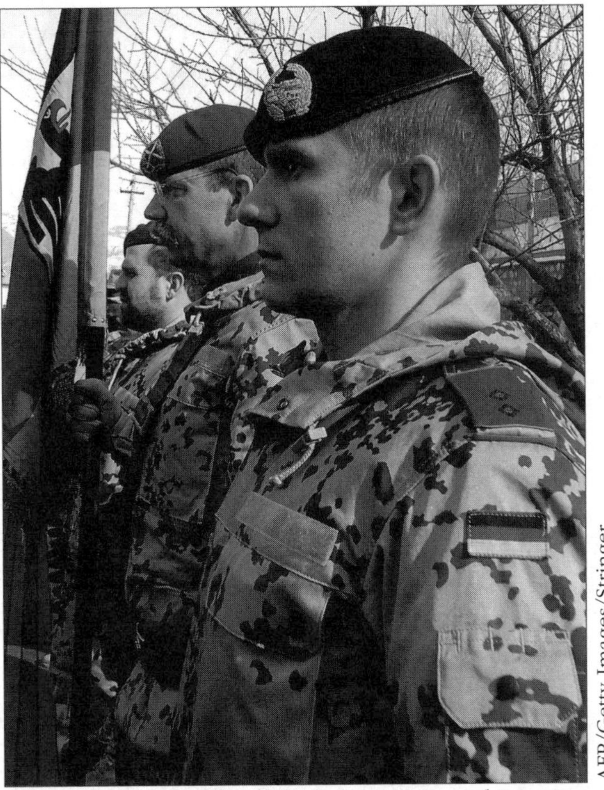

AFP/Getty Images/Stringer

German troops in the NATO-led International Security Assistance Force hand over security in Afghanistan's Badakhshan Province to Afghan forces during a ceremony on Jan. 24, 2012. Tensions over Afghanistan will be on the agenda when President Obama and European leaders meet in May in Chicago for the first NATO summit in the United States in 13 years. Some 130,000 NATO forces are engaged in combat, military training and peace-building missions in Afghanistan.

And overshadowing both summits will be the question of whether the NATO alliance can survive in its current form as the focal point of geopolitics shifts to the emerging Asia-Pacific region, particularly China. "This is a time of change in the U.S.-European relationship," says Frances Burwell, director of trans-Atlantic relations and studies at the Atlantic Council think tank in Washington. "I think we're really at a crucial point, but it may be a turning point."

Defining NATO's 2014 Afghan exit strategy will weigh on the Chicago summit, centered on the question of how many of the 130,000 Alliance forces will remain in the country to continue fighting the Taliban insurgents, training Afghan security forces and building its institutions.

Tensions with the Afghan government and people increased this winter, first when copies of the Quran were inadvertently burned at Bagram Airfield, and six U.S. military personnel were killed in the wave of protests. [2]

Then, on March 11, a U.S. Army staff sergeant allegedly murdered 16 Afghan villagers, mostly women and

* The G8 is composed of the United States, Canada, France, Germany, Italy, Japan, Russia and the United Kingdom.

How the U.S. and EU Compare

The United States is more than twice the size of the 27-nation European Union but has about 200 million fewer people. The EU's gross domestic product (GDP) of $16.4 trillion is about $2 trillion more than that of the United States. Productivity is higher in the United States, however, with per capita GDP of $46,437, about 40 percent more than in the EU.

GDP and Population, EU and United States

KEY METRICS	EU	U.S.
GDP (2009)	$16.4 trillion	$14.3 trillion
Percent of global GDP	28.19%	24.52%
Population (2010)	501 million	309 million
Percent of global population	7.31%	4.51%
Per capita GDP (2009)	$32,842	$46,437
Total area (sq. miles)	1,634,757	3,536,310

Source: "The European Union and the United States: A Long-Standing Partnership," EU Focus, European Union, December 2010, p. 4, www.eurunion.org/eu/images/stories/eufocus-eu-usrels-dec-2010.pdf

children, in their homes. [3] The incidents add urgency to the effort to define NATO's 2014 Afghan exit strategy.

Since its formation in April 1949 in the aftermath of World War II and the start of the Cold War, the NATO alliance has been in the diplomatic and foreign policy DNA of the United States and its Western European allies. Charles Kupchan, a senior fellow at the Council on Foreign Relations think tank in Washington and professor of international affairs at the School of Foreign Service at Georgetown University, calls NATO "an institution vital to preserving the coherence and effectiveness of the West as a potential community."

But the end of the Cold War and the global shift in attention toward the Asia-Pacific region have profoundly changed the nature of U.S.-European relations. The question is how the strategic partnership can be strengthened and made more relevant to geopolitical and economic realities.

Some critics argue that the United States has let its commitment to the alliance slip as it has focused more on China. Others contend that Europe has been so preoccupied with managing the European Union (EU) that it hasn't paid sufficient attention to the alliance either.

For all the speculation about the trans-Atlantic alliance, however, the United States and Europe still seem united on fundamental issues of war and peace. The best example is Iran, which has sparked global tensions over what many believe are plans to build nuclear weapons. Since 2010, the European Union has imposed progressively tougher sanctions on Iran, culminating in January in a ban on Iranian oil imports to Europe — measures that brought U.S. and European sanctions policies against Iran into broad alignment.

It's hard to find anyone on either side of the Atlantic, especially in Europe, who favors abolishing NATO. Instead, the discussion tends to focus on the search for relevance. "NATO's institutional setup may be the offspring of another age," says Riccardo Alcaro, a specialist in trans-Atlantic affairs at the Institute of International Affairs think tank in Rome. "But the core interest that its member states have in it — being party to a permanent military alliance between Europe and North America — has not diminished an inch."

The NATO summit will bring together the heads of state of the alliance's 28 member countries, plus Russia and Japan. Two days earlier, on May 18-19, Obama will host the G8 summit. The major challenge facing that group is how to resolve Europe's debt crisis, now in its third year.

The crisis has put the economies of Greece, Portugal, Ireland, Spain and Italy in jeopardy and threatened the viability of the euro — the EU's common currency. European leaders have introduced austerity measures but resisted U.S. pressure to increase stimulus spending. Many economists say that by not pumping more money into the European economy, European nations are making the continent's economic woes worse and undermining the United States' recovery from its own financial crisis.

The European debt crisis is all the more serious because trans-Atlantic trade and investment are the backbone of the global economy. Combined EU and U.S. economic output, or gross domestic product (GDP), amounts to about 53 percent of the world total. U.S. investments in Europe easily top those in Asia. Together, the EU and United States command more than 40 percent of world trade, and their bilateral economic relationship was worth $898 billion in trade of goods and services in 2010 just short of $3 billion per day. [4]

The rise of China and other Asia-Pacific nations on the global economic and geopolitical scene has spurred concerns that the United States is losing interest in Europe. Obama himself, visiting Australia in November, assured Asian allies that America would stand by them in a crisis. "Let there be no doubt: In the Asia-Pacific of the 21st century, the United States is all in," he said. [5] Almost at the same moment, Washington announced it will station 2,500 U.S. Marines in Darwin, Australia, possibly open a base in the Philippines and will withdraw two U.S. Army brigades (5,000-6,000 men each) from Europe by the end of 2014 as a cost-cutting measure. [6]

"The Pacific focus inescapably means fewer resources for the traditional Atlantic partnership, symbolized by NATO," wrote *Washington Post* foreign policy columnist David Ignatius. "Given its recent economic jitters, Europe may feel abandoned." [7]

Secretary of State Hillary Rodham Clinton and Defense Secretary Leon Panetta in February both attended the annual Munich Security Conference, a gathering of defense ministers and foreign policy experts, where they reaffirmed America's commitment to the alliance with Europe. "Europe is and remains America's partner of first resort," Clinton declared.

Even so, "there's no question that the [Obama administration] sees Asia Pacific as the most challenging area," says Xenia Dormandy, a specialist on America's international role at Chatham House, a London think tank. "There's a real sense that America doesn't see Europe as a problem but as part of the solution. But the Europeans are still very much watching" developments.

As U.S. and European leaders weigh the future of the NATO alliance and the economic ties between the two continents, here are some of the questions being asked:

U.S.-European Trade on the Decline

European Union exports to the United States accounted for 19 percent of the EU's total exported goods — or about 206 billion euros — in 2009, down from 28 percent in 2000. EU imports from the United States fell from 21 percent of total European imports in 2000 to 13 percent in 2009.

EU Trade in Goods with the United States, 2000 and 2009
(in millions of euros)

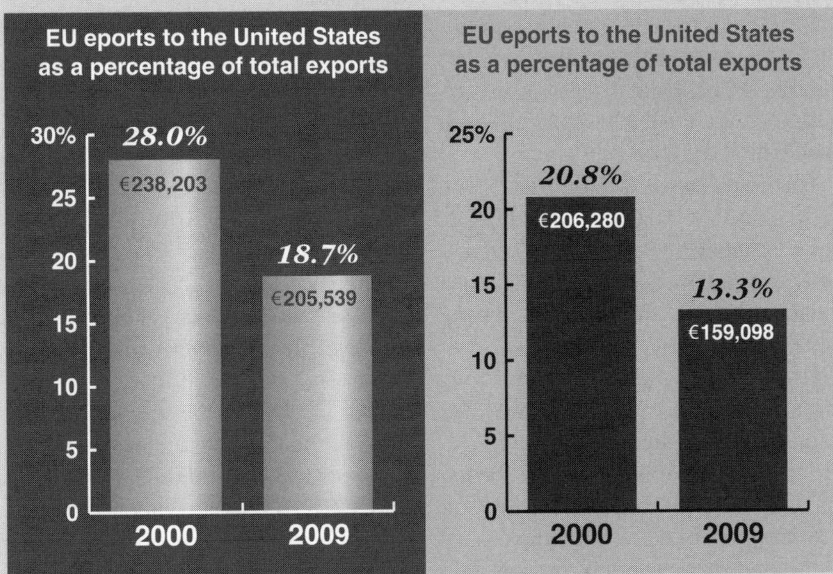

Source: "EU27 Surplus in Trade in Goods With the USA Almost Doubled in the First Six Months of 2010," Eurostat, European Union, November 2010, www.eurunion.org/eu/EU-US-Relations/EU-US-Facts-Figures.html

Should the U.S. pull all its forces out of Europe?

"Europe's GDP is greater than that of the United States, and its population is greater than the United States, so the notion that we need to continue to defend a continent that is eminently capable of defending itself is absurd," declares Christopher Preble, vice president for defense and foreign policy studies at the Cato Institute, a libertarian think tank in Washington.

The American military is not likely to be leaving Europe anytime soon. But questions are now being asked about how many of the 80,000 troops currently in Europe will still be there after 2014. The expected withdrawal of the two infantry brigades, beginning in late 2012, from Germany as part of Pentagon budget cuts has sparked speculation in Europe that a long but final drawdown of the U.S. presence may be beginning. And stirring such speculation, some observers say, may be part of an American plan.

Recent defense cuts combined with plans for leaner, more flexible, hi-tech American forces are factors behind the pullout. But the subtext may reflect growing impatience with Europe's habitual reliance on the U.S. military to do the heavy lifting when it comes to defense — combined with the hope that the Europeans might be goaded or scared into fending for themselves to a greater degree than they have in the past under the American security umbrella.

Every NATO country is required to spend at least 2 percent of GDP on defense. In reality, only four members besides the United States currently meet that obligation — the United Kingdom, France, Albania and — oddly — financially ailing Greece.

By contrast, the United States spends 5 percent. (See chart p. 284). In 2010, combined European spending on defense dropped to $275 billion, from $314 billion in 2008.

The euro crisis is partly to blame for the decline. But the other reason, argued Stephen Hadley, national security adviser in the George W. Bush administration, is that Europe has become a "free rider."

Hadley said the Europeans have been taking the United States for granted in providing defense and filling military-capability gaps. "Europe has become so enamored with soft power" — persuasion and diplomacy — "that it has stopped investing in hard power" — military action, he said. "In terms of hard security, it makes Europe a free rider." [8]

Dana Allin, senior fellow for trans-Atlantic affairs at London's International Institute of Strategic Studies, told the British House of Lords, "The history of U.S. relations with Europe ever since [World War II] has been trying to develop a semi-autonomous organization and alliance that can balance whatever the threat is. . . . Going back to the 1950s there was always a view that this should be possible. Europeans were becoming rich democracies and had a martial tradition." [9]

Today, says Charles Heyman, a defense analyst and former editor of *Jane's World Armies*, "The European Union as a whole is 10 percent richer than the United States based on GDP, and that is making a lot of American planners scratch their heads and say, 'What are we doing?' "

The U.S. presence in Europe is being questioned more widely than just by military planners. "Since the Cold War ended 20 years ago, the 80,000 troops still in Europe can be reduced to 20,000," wrote Laurence Korb, a defense analyst at the Center for American Progress, a liberal Washington think tank. [10]

"We now have a military alliance where many of the members do not want to engage in military operations . . .," wrote Robert Guttman, director of the Center on Politics and Foreign Relations at the Johns Hopkins University School of Advanced International Studies.

"Maybe we should call NATO a huge success, pat everyone on the back and dissolve the military organization and move on," he said. [11]

But the U.S. military could be staying on the continent simply because hot spots in the Middle East, Africa and Western Asia are much more easily reached from bases in Europe than in the United States. Indeed, the U.S. European Command (EUCOM) covers 93 countries in all and includes North Africa and parts of the Middle East. It also provides backup for the U.S. Africa Command. On the fringes of Europe are some explosive areas, including Georgia's border with Russia, Kosovo's border with Serbia, and Turkey and its Arab neighbors, Iraq and Syria, to say nothing of other areas of the Middle East.

There's also the influence factor. Alcaro of the Institute of International Affairs points out that it's a lot easier for the United States "to exert influence on European affairs and to keep European countries on its side on a number of issues, regional as well as global," if the American flag is flying in Europe.

Has Asia become the new focus of U.S. foreign policy?

Early in January, President Obama visited the Pentagon to introduce a new U.S. defense strategy employing advanced military technology to complement what, in the words of *The New York Times*, he described as "a smaller, more agile force across Asia, the Pacific and the Middle East." Obama's presence was highly unusual — presidents don't often visit the Pentagon — but it had a broader significance: It signaled the end of a decade of global politics shaped by the aftermath of the Sept. 11, 2001, terrorist attacks on New York City and the Pentagon. [12]

Obama called it "turning the page on a decade of war . . . the end of long-term nation-building with large military footprints." [13] That approach had dominated strategic thinking in the George W. Bush administration. Under Obama, two major conflicts (Iraq and Afghanistan) were being declared over, and a decade of global military expansion was coming to an end.

Driving the new defense strategy was a fiscal crisis requiring a deep 8 percent cut in the Pentagon budget ($487 billion over 10 years) and a geographic reorientation toward Asia and the Pacific. "Mostly there is agreement that a more focused response . . . is needed to counter China's fast-growing military capabilities and address the concerns of allies in the region about how the emerging superpower will behave," noted *The Economist*. In short, China's emergence and the economic significance of Asia as a whole have made the region America's security priority. "We will be strengthening our presence in the Asia Pacific, and budget reductions will not come at the expense of that critical region," the president declared. [14]

But the budget cuts had to come from somewhere. And though Obama added the assurance that the United States intended "to continue investing in our critical partnerships and alliances, including NATO," analysts were speculating that the U.S. presence in Europe would shrink further.

The president left further explaining to senior Pentagon officials, including Gen. Martin E. Dempsey, chairman of the Joint Chiefs. "All of the trends, demographic trends, geopolitical trends, economic trends and military trends are shifting toward the Pacific," Dempsey said. "So our strategic challenges will largely emanate out of the Pacific region, but also the littorals of the Indian Ocean." [15]

Dempsey sees how China's submarines and missile platforms, soon to be backed up by an aircraft carrier taskforce, are projecting naval power into regions where the U.S. has dominated since 1945," commented *The Guardian* in Britain. "In short, he can read the writing on the Chinese wall." The general can foresee the United States having to stare down China the way it once did the Soviet Union, the paper said.

Panetta drove the point home. The Asia-Pacific region "is growing in importance to the future of the U.S. economy and our national security," he said. "This means, for instance, improving capabilities that maintain our military's technological edge and freedom of action." [16]

Nobody actually mentioned China, but Beijing noticed. "As promised, China would unwaveringly stick to its path of peaceful development," commented the Chinese government news agency Xinhua. It quoted Chinese Vice President Xi Jinping as saying that "a sound and stable China-U.S. relationship is not only vital to both sides but also crucial to peace, stability and prosperity of the Asia-Pacific region and that of the world as well."

And the *Global Times*, an English language offshoot of the Communist Party's *People's Daily*, swiftly made it clear China would be ready to match the United States step for step, wherever that uncharted path might lead. "Of course we want to prevent a new Cold War with the United States, but at the same time, we must avoid giving up China's security presence in the neighboring region," it said in an editorial.

Debt Plagues European Nations

Debt held by the governments of Greece, Italy, Ireland and Portugal exceeds the countries' gross domestic product, threatening their economic stability.

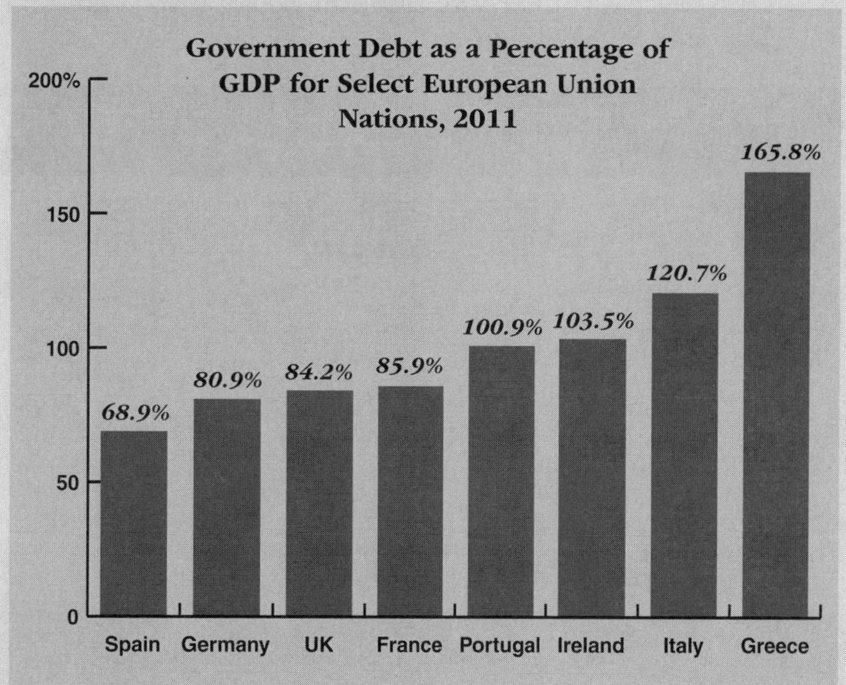

Source: "General Government Gross Debt (Maastrict Debt) in % of GDP — Annual Data," Eurostat, European Union, March 2012, epp.eurostat.ec.europa.eu/tgm/table.do?tab=table&init=1&language=en&pcode=tipsgo10&plugin=0

A strong argument why the United States should focus on Asia-Pacific came in the form of a warning from Australian Foreign Minister Kevin Rudd, a Mandarin-speaking sinologist. Rudd pointed out at the Feb. 1 Munich Security Conference that within the next decade China's economy is likely to be bigger than America's and that "there is analysis around that China's military expenditure may pass that of the United States by 2025." It will be, he said, "the first time in 200 years that the world has a non-democracy as the world's largest economy."

That will have a profound effect because the Chinese do not necessarily share "the longstanding liberal, international values which underpin the architecture of the post [World War II] global order," Rudd said. For the past 50 years, he said, the American military presence has ensured "Pax Pacifica" — the Asian-Pacific security balance — and it will remain the indispensable balancer throughout the region. [17]

Is a U.S. drift away from Europe reversible?

When the Soviet Union collapsed in 1989, there were 213,000 U.S. troops deployed in Western Europe, mainly

Few NATO Members Meet Defense Obligations

The North Atlantic Treaty Organization (NATO) requires members to spend at least 2 percent of their gross domestic product (GDP) on defense. The United States spends the most, at 5.4 percent. Only four European members — Greece, the United Kingdom, Albania and France — meet the benchmark.

Defense Expenditures as a Percentage of GDP for NATO Members, 2010 estimates

Country	% of GDP	Country	% of GDP
United States*	5.4%	Czech Republic	1.4%
Greece	2.9	Denmark	1.4
United Kingdom*	2.7	Germany	1.4
Albania	2.0	Italy	1.4
France	2.0	Netherlands	1.4
Poland	1.9	Romania	1.3
Turkey	1.9	Slovakia	1.3
Estonia	1.8	Belgium	1.1
Bulgaria	1.7	Hungary	1.1
Portugal	1.6	Spain	1.1
Slovenia	1.6	Latvia	1.0
Canada	1.5	Lithuania	0.9
Croatia	1.5	Luxembourg	0.5
Norway	1.5		

** Figures include military pensions.*
Iceland is not listed because it has no armed forces.

Source: "Financial and Economic Data Relating to NATO Defence," North Atlantic Treaty Organization, March 2011, p. 6, www.nato.int/nato_static/assets/pdf/pdf_2011_03/20110309_PR_CP_2011_027.pdf

in Germany, but also in the United Kingdom, Italy and Turkey. By 2011, U.S. troop levels in Europe had been pared to around 80,000.

When the planned pullout of the two Army brigades begins later this year, more American troops will still be deployed in Europe than anywhere else in the world — even though hardly a shot has been fired in anger in Western Europe since the end of World War II in 1945.

The military presence in Europe has symbolized America's enduring commitment to the trans-Atlantic alliance of shared values and — U.S. critics will say — allowed Europeans to develop complacent, "leave-it-to-the-Americans" attitudes toward security. Defense Secretary Panetta's predecessor, Robert Gates, called it "the demilitarization of Europe, where large swaths of the general public and political class are averse to military force and the risks that go with it." [18]

In Eastern Europe and the Baltic states, however, the American presence "provides the ultimate guarantee of protection from a resurgent Russia," according to Alcaro of the Institute of International Affairs — and the 2008 Russian incursion into Georgia, which is outside the NATO shield, underlined its importance. Alcaro argues that had Georgia been a NATO country, the Russians would not have risked a confrontation with the West by attacking.

The European Union's fledgling Common Security and Defense Policy envisions a standing multilateral force but is now on hold because of the continent's economic problems. The policy doesn't inspire the same confidence as the Atlantic alliance, in part because NATO has tended to perceive it as an inferior rival.

The U.S. view is that there has been no drift away from the American commitment in Europe. The new defense strategy unveiled by President Obama in January stresses that view. The United States, the strategy document explains, is turning economic necessity to its advantage "to rebalance the U.S. military investment in Europe." That way it can structure "future capabilities" to create a lean, mean military suitable for a "resource-constrained era" (that is, one with budget pressures) and capable of meeting new military challenges wherever and whatever they may be, such as cyber warfare. [19]

The geopolitical center of gravity has been shifting toward the Asia-Pacific region for some time. "Many observers see the shift . . . as a natural, if long overdue, transition for the United States as it draws down in Iraq and Afghanistan," wrote Jonathan Masters an associate staff writer at the Council on Foreign Relations. [20]

But as German journalist Christoph von Marschall explained in the *German Times*, "in this subdued atmosphere of pervasive European self-doubt, a speech by President Obama convinced people a tectonic shift was under way in international politics." [21]

The U.S. troop drain from Europe is likely to continue even after 2014 because of Pentagon plans to reduce the military significantly and use the

U.S. Air Force and Navy more forcefully than in past operations. The success of the Libyan operation, with NATO planes bombing Libyan forces, supported by a maritime blockade but no ground forces, is cited by American strategists as a model for future operations. Still, Dormandy of Chatham House says the Atlantic alliance will continue to exist foremost because "it gives more legitimacy (for countries) to come together under the banner of NATO."

AFP/Getty Images/Louisa Gouliamaki

Greek pensioners protest in Athens on Sept. 28, 2011, against further government austerity measures, including pension cuts and reduced health benefits. Greece, recently rescued from the brink of bankruptcy, is at the heart of the European debt crisis. The crisis has exposed huge government debts and threatened the eurozone economies of Spain, Portugal, Italy and Ireland as well as Greece.

Besides, as a report on the trans-Atlantic alliance by the Chicago Council on Global Affairs recently put it, a United States with economic problems and with its power "diluted by other centers of influence around the world . . . will be hard pressed to . . . preserve the openness and influence of the U.S.-led international order" and is going to need more, not less, support from its allies. [22]

The days of the unilateral U.S. force that can fight two major ground wars simultaneously are over, to be replaced by what the new strategy calls "fight and deter," meaning fight one war and prevent another. "The future is going to look at more collaborations of larger diverse groups of [NATO] member states with the will, the assets and the interest to take action," says Dormandy. ■

BACKGROUND

North Atlantic Treaty

By the end of World War II in Europe on May 8, 1945, more than three million Americans had fought in the conflict against Nazi Germany. [23] G.I.'s had been welcomed as liberators in Paris, Rome and elsewhere. But when the celebrations stopped and the Americans began to embark for home, Europeans realized they faced a new threat from the East.

The Soviet Union had at least 700,000 troops under arms and capable of overrunning war-weary Western Europe. Another fear was a ghost from the past: a possibly resurgent Germany.

To nail down a protective U.S. presence in Europe, the Western allies formed NATO — the North Atlantic Treaty Organization — in 1949.* NATO's first secretary general, Britain's Lord Ismay, is purported to have said the purpose of the alliance was "to keep the Russians out, the Americans in, and the Germans down." [24]

At the heart of the treaty is Article 5, which ensures that "an armed attack against one or more of [the parties to the treaty] in Europe or North America shall be considered an attack against them all." In the face of such a threat, the article goes on, NATO will take "such action as it deems necessary, including the use of armed force, to restore and maintain the security of the North Atlantic area." [25]

Marshall Plan

NATO was actually the second U.S. postwar intervention in Europe. The alliance's participating European countries needed first to be rescued from the war's wreckage to their economies. So in 1947, the United States offered the Marshall Plan, named after Secretary of State George Marshall, who first proposed it in a commencement speech at Harvard University. [26]

Representatives from 17 European countries — including the Soviet Union — met in Paris and formulated a $22 billion plan (in 1947 dollars) for consideration by the United States. The plan focused on help to rebuild industry and agriculture and included requests for basic foods, such as sugar. Congress pared the request to $13 bil-

* The 12 original NATO members were the United States, Great Britain, France, Italy, the Netherlands, Belgium, Luxembourg, Norway, Denmark, Portugal, Iceland and Canada.

lion in grants and loans, and Marshall Plan aid began flowing to Europe in 1948. Stalin rejected it for Russia and its satellite countries, so 17 European countries received aid. [27]

Marshall Plan aid, an analyst wrote, was "the decisive kick that pushed Western Europe beyond the threshold of sustained recovery." [28] Britain was the top recipient with $2.7 billion; West Germany came second with $1.7 billion.

Marshall aid ended in 1951, but the North Atlantic Alliance is still in business six decades later.

With Russia "out" and Germany no longer regarded as a threat to European peace, many felt that NATO's role had come to an end and the alliance would be dissolved. Instead, NATO has expanded across Central and Eastern Europe, doubling in size. During the Cold War, NATO's anti-Soviet line of defense had extended from the Turkish border with the USSR in the south to Norway in the north, but the alliance never fired a shot against the potential enemy.

Since the 1990s, "NATO is not just about Europe and in Europe, but is increasingly seen as the hub of a global network of security," Ivo Daalder, U.S. permanent representative to NATO, said recently. [29] Since the end of the Cold War, the alliance has "focused on operations," Daalder said, in the Balkans (1992) and more recently in its first out-of-area missions in Afghanistan and Libya.

At times across the years, the NATO alliance has looked more like a misalliance. Its history is full of spirited — but eventually resolved — disputes. For example, in the 1960s it took NATO nearly a decade of internal debate to adopt and develop the so-called U.S. strategy of flexible response to an enemy attack: conventional forces first; if that failed, tactical nuclear weapons (short-range missiles for battlefield use); and if the enemy still wasn't pushed back from NATO territory, a strategic nuclear response would entail intercontinental rockets, which would bring the United States into direct conflict with the Soviets. Skeptical Europeans wondered whether the United States would ultimately be prepared to go to war for Europe. [30]

In 1966, French President Charles de Gaulle pulled France out of NATO's military command structure because he felt the United States was too dominant in the decision-making. At de Gaulle's insistence, NATO's headquarters moved from Paris to Brussels. Only intense damage control by the other allies prevented NATO's possible collapse.

In the end, no other country followed France's lead. Indeed, according to a recent analysis, the French departure was "a catalyst for action that actually strengthened the alliance in the long run." [31]

Missile Crisis

In the late 1970s Washington pressed its European allies to deploy 108 U.S.-supplied Pershing II medium-range missiles and 462 ground-launched cruise missiles in response to Soviet deployment of the medium-range SS-20 missile, capable of carrying nuclear warheads to cities in Europe. Violent public opposition to the missiles erupted in Germany, Italy and elsewhere, and the issue became a critical test of the alliance's political resolve. [32]

Moscow worked hard to open a rift between the United States and its European allies. Ailing Soviet leader Leonid Brezhnev flew to Bonn, the West German capital, in an attempt to persuade Chancellor Helmut Schmidt to reject the U.S. missiles. The Germans gave Brezhnev a new Mercedes to add to his car collection but stood firm on the missiles, as did other NATO countries.

Following the collapse of the Soviet empire, NATO began expanding its membership to include former Soviet satellite countries, starting with Poland, the Czech Republic and Hungary in 1999. Moscow's one-time dominions, still nervous about their old master, welcomed NATO's (that is, America's) protective shield.

NATO troops saw action for the first time in the Balkans in the 1990s. In 1995, the alliance launched its first peacekeeping operation: the Implementation Force (IFOR) in Bosnia. Approximately 60,000 troops from the 16 NATO members and 17 non-NATO countries, including Russia, were tasked with making sure that the conditions of the Bosnia peace agreement, brokered by the United States and including a cease-fire, were observed. The main challenge was to keep Serb and Bosnian factions from renewing hostilities. Another was to create safe and secure conditions for repatriation of refugees and other humanitarian efforts.

Then in 1999, NATO planes began bombing targets in the former Republic of Yugoslavia (Serbia and Montenegro), and NATO forces were deployed in Kosovo to halt a Serbian ethnic-cleansing (genocide) campaign against Albanian Muslims. President Bill Clinton called the air strikes "a moral imperative." [33] Inevitably, the two offensives — and especially the air strikes — brought out the problems of waging war by consensus, since the 17 member states often disagreed on strategy.

"These problems included making war without admitting that it was war, and a clash of confused notions of how to use force effectively," according to an article in *Foreign Affairs* based on a published account of the war by U.S. Army Gen. Wesley Clark, the NATO commander at the time. Clark even had to take into account what NATO's legal advisers had to say

Continued on p. 288

Chronology

1940s U.S. establishes postwar connection with Western Europe through North Atlantic Treaty Organization (NATO) and Marshall Plan.

1947
U.S. Secretary of State George C. Marshall announces extensive aid program for European recovery.

1949
NATO treaty signed in Washington by United States, Great Britain, France, Italy, the Netherlands, Belgium, Luxembourg, Norway, Denmark, Portugal, Iceland and Canada.

1950s-1960s

Cold War Europe divided by "Iron Curtain", with NATO forces in West and opposing Warsaw Pact nations in the East.

1955
West Germany joins NATO; Soviet Union and seven Eastern European nations form Warsaw Pact.

1956
Israel, Britain and France invade Egypt after Egyptian leader Gamal Abdul Nasser nationalizes the Franco-British-owned Suez Canal. President Dwight D. Eisenhower pressures allies to pull out.

1957
Belgium, France, West Germany, Italy, Luxemburg and the Netherlands sign Treaty of Rome, founding document of European Union.

1961
East Germany begins Berlin Wall.

1966
France leaves NATO military structure; alliance moves to Brussels.

1970s-1980s

U.S. plan to deploy intermediate-range missiles sparks protests in Europe, tension with America's allies.

1973
Denmark, United Kingdom and Ireland join European Community.

1987
United States and Russia sign Intermediate-Range Nuclear Forces Treaty (INF), removing U.S. and Russian missiles from Europe after less than a decade of deployment.

1989
Berlin Wall falls, allowing free travel between East and West Germany and leading to the formal reunification of Germany.

1990s-2000s

Europe, in further steps toward unification, establishes European Union, a unified currency (the euro) and a European single market.

1990
Trans-Atlantic Declaration formalizes common goals of the United States and European Community.

1994
NATO planes enforce no-fly zone to protect Bosnian civilians from the Serbs. NATO eventually sends ground troops as well. Bosnia is NATO's first combat operation.

1999
Euro currency officially launched.

Sept. 12, 2001
Following the 9/11 terrorist attacks, NATO — for the first time in its history — invokes Article 5 of the treaty, holding that an armed attack against one state will be considered an armed attack against all. . . . Rift opens between Bush administration and France and Germany over Iraq War, but Britain, Spain and Eastern Europe support the conflict against Saddam Hussein.

2007
U.S.-EU Trans-Atlantic Economic Council formed to coordinate bilateral economic decision-making.

2009
Faced with a global debt crisis, G20 summit agrees to increase International Monetary Fund aid for European economies.

2010-Present

Economic crisis, wars, political upheavals cause global tension.

2010
NATO summit in Lisbon agrees on establishing a missile defense shield for Europe acceptable to Russia. NATO also endorses 2014 as date for withdrawal of NATO forces from Afghanistan.

2011
NATO leads aerial offensive to protect civilians in Libya following uprising against the regime of Libyan leader Moammar Gadhafi.

2012
Discovery of charred copies of the Quran inadvertently burned at Bagram air base in Afghanistan sparks anti-NATO demonstrations in which 30 Afghans and six U.S. soldiers die. . . . EU sovereign debt crisis eases somewhat after Greece successfully negotiates 50 percent reduction of its debt to private creditors and receives $130 billion EU bailout.

EU Tribunals Trump National Courts on Key Issues

Critics worry that they wield too much clout.

British pub owner Karen Murphy wanted to keep her soccer-crazy customers happy — but she also wanted to cut down on expenses. So with a major soccer championship coming, she opted to bypass Sky Television, the big European media company that had an exclusive contract with the British soccer organization to broadcast its games in the U.K., and use a cheaper Greek satellite broadcaster to show the game.

The soccer organization filed and won a copyright infringement case against her, claiming exclusive rights to the game. But Murphy won on appeal to the European Union Court of Justice, which said the soccer authority's exclusive deal was "contrary to EU law." [1]

The Court of Justice and two lower EU courts — the General Court and the EU Civil Service Tribunal — form an increasingly potent legal force in European affairs. They hear hundreds of cases annually involving EU citizens, corporations and national courts seeking guidance on EU issues. Among the General Court's cases this year is a request from Microsoft Corp. for a reduction in an 899 million euro ($1.3 billion) fine imposed by the court in a 2008 antitrust case.

The Court of Justice, based in Luxembourg, is the highest in the European Union on issues covered by EU law, outranking national supreme courts. EU court decisions are binding on all 27 member countries.

In March, Spanish courts asked the Court of Justice to clarify an important addition to an EU online privacy-protection law. Called "the right to be forgotten," the new rule enlarges people's right to request the removal of personal data from Google and other search engines. Though the inquiry came from Madrid, the EU court's reply will be applicable throughout the European Union. [2]

"If today there exists something called [European] law, with its own particular features, characteristics, and issues, all this is due to the [European] Court's work," wrote Oreste Pollicino, a lecturer in public law at Bocconi University in Milan. [3]

And as far back as 1993, an American law professor and an Oxford University scholar called the European Court of Justice "an unsung hero" of European unification. Anne-Marie Burley, a University of Chicago law professor, and Walter Mattli, a professor of political economy at Oxford, wrote that "thirteen judges quietly working in Luxembourg, managed to transform the Treaty of Rome . . . into a constitution. They thereby laid the legal foundation for an integrated European economy and polity." [4]

But critics say the courts wield too much power over the courts of individual nations. Dutch law professor Henri de Waele of Radboud University in Nijmegen said a "visible attempt at more balanced interpretation [of European law] could do wonders." [5] Sir Patrick Neill, a leading British jurist, once famously called the Court of Justice "uncontrollable, skewed, and dangerous." [6]

In 2011 the Court of Justice completed 638 cases — a 10 percent increase over the previous year — and the General Court around twice that number.

Continued from p. 286

on tactical options, according to the magazine. [34]

At one phase of the bombing, said *Foreign Affairs*, "Germany wanted to stop bombing Serbia's cities, Americans worried about bombing within Kosovo, and France wanted to stop the bombing in northern Serbia." [35] The Europeans were afraid continued attacks would derail peace negotiations. [36]

After almost four months of bombing, Serbian President Slobodan Milosevic ordered his troops to withdraw, but only because he believed that a NATO ground attack was imminent. In fact, *Foreign Affairs* said, such an attack wasn't even in the planning stage. [37]

Afghanistan and Iraq

Following the Al Qaeda terrorist attacks on New York and the Pentagon, NATO for the first time in its history invoked Article 5. Initially, the Bush administration rejected NATO's help in Afghanistan, preferring to work "with a more flexible international coalition" that was "unencumbered by the institutional constraints of alliance decision-making," wrote a British analyst, "while the U.S. was able to pick and choose only what it wanted — and needed — from NATO assets and member states." [38]

Subsequently, however, ISAF (International Security Assistance Force), a multinational coalition in Afghanistan deployed in December 2001, morphed into the NATO force deployed in Afghanistan, with U.S. forces as a separate command called Operation Enduring Freedom.

Two years later, France and Germany, although engaged in Afghanistan, refused to support the Bush administration's war in Iraq, and the United States put together what President Bush called the "coalition of the willing," which still included several NATO members.

"Passionate differences over the invasion of Iraq pushed trans-Atlantic and inter-European relations to an historic low point in 2003-2004," stated a recent study of U.S.-European relations prepared for members of Congress by the Congressional Research Service

Most corporate cases are on a smaller scale than the Microsoft antitrust action but can still have broad impact. In a famous 1979 ruling involving *Crème de cassis* (the French cordial), for example, the Court of Justice said a product approved for sale in one European country must be accepted by others. The so-called *Cassis de Dijon* case established the principle of Europewide product standards and was a cornerstone of the European single market.

Each EU member country appoints a judge to each of the three courts, but the full bench at plenary sessions consists of only 13 judges. Eight advocates-general deliver legal opinions on the cases, but the judges don't necessarily accept their interpretation.

Unlike in the U.S. Supreme Court, judges serve not for life but for six-year terms, and dissenting opinions are not made public. Yet, in the impact of its rulings, the European Court of Justice bears a strong similarity to its American counterpart.

Much of the court's work involves action against member states for failing to comply with regulations or treaty obligations. The European Commission (the EU's executive branch in Brussels) announced Feb. 28 that it was suing the French government in the Court of Justice for allegedly failing to prevent pollution of drinking water by agricultural chemicals in rural areas of France. [7]

The EU court's broad portfolio has given it a key role in the recent European social compact signed in March by 25 EU members and intended to bring national budgets under control. The compact mandates a maximum debt of less than 3 percent of the gross domestic product, and the court is charged with imposing fines of 0.1 percent of GDP on countries that fail to comply.

In the past few years the court has emerged from the shadows. "The (court's) accomplishments have long been the province only of lawyers," wrote Burley and Mattli more than a decade ago. No longer.

— Roland Flamini

---

[1] "Pub landlady Karen Murphy wins TV football court case," *BBC News*, Feb. 24, 2012, www.bbc.co.uk/news/business-17150054.

[2] Loek Essers, "Spain seek jurisdiction guidance from EU for Google privacy complaints," *Computer World*, March 6, 2012, www.computerworlduk.com/news/it-business/3342444/spain-seeks-jurisdiction-guidance-from-eu-for-google-privacy-complaints/.

[3] Oreste Pollicino, "Law Reasoning of the Court of Justice etc.," *German Law Journal*, Vol. 5, No. 03, 2004, www.germanlawjournal.com/article.php?id=402.

[4] Anne-Marie Burley and Walter Mattli, "Europe Before the Court: A Political Theory of Legal Integration," World Peace Foundation and Massachusetts Institute of Technology, 1993, www.seep.ceu.hu/alpsa/articles/burley.pdf.

[5] Henri de Waele, "The Role of the European Court of Justice in the Integration Process...,"*Hanse Law Review*, 2010, www.hanselawreview.org/pdf9/Vol6No01Art01.pdf.

[6] "Biased Referee," *The Economist*, May 15, 1997, www.economist.com/node/149581.

[7] Helene Roques, "Dis-moi ce que tu peux depolluer, je te dirai ce que je vais fabriquer," *Le Monde*, March 13, 2012, www.lemonde.fr/idees/article/2012/03/13/dis-moi-ce-que-tu-peux-depolluer-je-te-dirai-ce-que-je-vais-fabriquer_1656463_3232.html.

(CRS). "Iraq was the unforgettable defining element in their perceptions of President George W. Bush — too unilateral, too reliant on military force, too dismissive of international treaties and norms." But, CRS said, Iraq became shorthand for other areas of dispute between the United States and various European governments, such as U.S. rejection of the Kyoto climate treaty and the International Criminal Court, which pursues war crimes worldwide. [39]

The Iraq debate also revealed a deep division within Europe "between states that seek European identity through confrontation with America and those, led by Britain and Spain, that seek in it an instrument of co-operation," former U.S. Secretary of State Henry Kissinger wrote. He blamed the split on a resurgence of Gaullism — a reference to de Gaulle's nationalist philosophy — that, he wrote, "insisted on a Europe with an identity defined in distinction from the United States." [40]

But in 2005, Christian Democrat Angela Merkel replaced Socialist Gerhard Schröeder as chancellor of Germany, and relations with the Bush White House improved. Then in 2007, the pro-American Nicolas Sarkozy was elected president of France. Two years later, Sarkozy reintegrated France into all structures of the NATO alliance, 43 years after de Gaulle had broken away from military affairs. [41]

NATO'S presence in Afghanistan was not without friction because some countries, including Germany, tried to limit combat risks by imposing so-called caveats: Its troops were permitted to fire only in self-defense. "There's no question that there [were] exasperations with Germany in Afghanistan due to caveats and limitations," Allin of the International Institute of Strategic Studies told the House of Lords. [42]

On balance, however, NATO's deployment in Afghanistan was "a success for the cohesion of the alliance," argued Karl-Heinz Kamp, director of research at the NATO Defense College in Rome. When NATO took over in Afghanistan in 1973, "hardly anyone had assumed that the alliance would be able to remain fully engaged in the region for more than eight years (and still committed to stay until an acceptable level of stability is achieved)" and would have "successfully maintained unity of all members in Afghanistan." [43]

European Union

Meanwhile, the U.S. and Europe have other significant ties besides the North Atlantic alliance. Chief among them is U.S. support for the European process of integration culminating in the emergence of the European Union (EU), a political and economic confederation of nations established in 1992, and its subsequent expansion to 27 members. The United States supported moves toward European political and economic integration after World War II, beginning with the 1957 Treaty of Rome. Following the Soviet Union's collapse, the United States favored inclusion of East European and Baltic countries into the European Union. Like NATO membership, EU membership helped speed up the restoration of democracy in such countries as Poland and Lithuania, because a democratic system was a prerequisite for membership in both institutions.

"Europe is more united, more democratic and more peaceful than it has ever been in history," said Daalder, the U.S. NATO representative. "That is an accomplishment that NATO and the European Union and the countries [that make up these organizations] can be proud of." [44]

But the EU's plans for a Common Security and Defense Policy, including the creation of a European force parallel to NATO, drew strong U.S. opposition. John Bolton, the George W. Bush administration's U.N. ambassador, called the proposal "a dagger pointed at the heart of NATO." Madeleine Albright, President Clinton's secretary of state, warned that alliance members should avoid what she called the three "Ds" — decoupling, duplication and discrimination.

As the European Common Market of the 1960s became the European Economic Community of the 1970s and then the European Union and the EU Single Market in the early 1990s, the continent's economic integration was at first seen as a rising challenge to U.S. industrial and commercial interests. Touring European cities in 1989, Carla Hills, the U.S. trade representative, expressed concern about "actions taken, threatened or merely implied that discriminate against American and other non-European firms, forcing them to locate in Europe or lose sales." Hills said she hoped the emerging EU Single Market would result in "a freer (market), not a fortress Europe." [45]

The New York Times warned that "through import quotas, antidumping actions and requirements of reciprocity, a fortress might just be taking shape, brick by brick." [46] But despite some remaining differences, the relationship was quickly perceived to be mutually beneficial.

NATO Photo

Delegates to the North Atlantic Treaty Organization meet in Washington, D.C., for the organization's first meeting on Sept. 17, 1949. Today every NATO country is required to spend at least 2 percent of GDP on defense, but only four members besides the United States currently meet that obligation – the United Kingdom, France, Albania and Greece. The heart of the treaty is Article 5, which ensures that "an armed attack against one or more [members] in Europe or North America shall be considered an attack against them all."

The two economies represent 54 percent of the world's output or gross domestic product and nearly one-third of world trade. In 2010, nearly 93 percent of global foreign exchange holdings were in dollars, euros or pound sterling. In 2009, the two-way flow of goods, services and income receipts from investments totaled $1.25 trillion. In 2007, Washington and Brussels set up the Transatlantic Economic Council, a high-level body of government officials and economists who meet yearly to reduce nontariff barriers and increase regulatory convergence.

The 2008 global financial meltdown shook this strong economic axis to its foundation. A collapse of the housing and banking sectors in the United States and Europe exposed huge government debts, threatening the eurozone economies of Spain, Portugal, Italy, Ireland, and Greece and even the viability of the European currency itself.

The close relationship made the United States vulnerable to the eurozone crisis, but differences over how to confront the crisis made it hard to adopt a coordinated response. Europeans rejected Treasury Secretary

Continued on p. 292

Once Spurned, 'Old Europe' Makes a Comeback

U.S ties shift away from Eastern Europe.

After France and Germany came out strongly against the use of force in the run-up to the U.S.-led Iraq War in 2003, U.S. Defense Secretary Donald Rumsfeld scornfully dismissed the two countries as anachronisms.

"You're thinking of Europe as Germany and France," he told journalists. "I don't. I think that's old Europe. . . . If you look at the entire NATO Europe today, the center of gravity is shifting to the East." [1]

The new Europe was Eastern Europe's former Soviet satellites, which joined President George W. Bush's "coalition of the willing" in the Iraq War, earning them praise from the president. In 2004, Poland deployed 1,700 troops to Iraq, Romania sent 700 and smaller numbers came from Bulgaria, Hungary and the Czech Republic. [2]

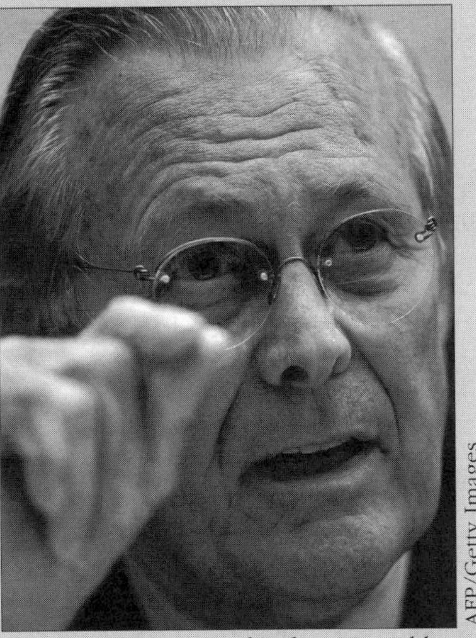

AFP/Getty Images

Former Secretary of Defense Donald Rumsfeld dismissed France and Germany in 2003 as remnants of "old Europe."

But eight years later, "Old Europe" is new again. The balance of U.S.-European ties has reverted to more traditional lines, with the larger and more important nations, such as the United Kingdom, Germany and France, again Washington's foremost allies. By contrast, U.S. ties to Eastern Europe have soured, largely because of what the East Europeans perceive as Washington's failure to live up to their expectations as allies.

Michael Rubin, a resident scholar at the American Enterprise Institute, a conservative think tank in Washington, recently wrote that "the Obama administration has, at various times, thrown Poland, the Czech Republic and Georgia under the bus." As a result, said Rubin, these countries "increasingly doubt the commitment of the United States to them." [3]

President Obama's decision in 2009 to cancel the Bush administration's agreement with Poland and the Czech Republic to deploy an anti-missile defense system on their territory was a major disappointment for Eastern Europe. The system's main purpose was to intercept missiles fired by a rogue state hostile to the United States — Iran or North Korea, for example. For the Eastern Europeans the plan would have meant enhanced security and a potentially useful bilateral link with Washington.

But the plan drew protests from Russia, which considered it a security threat. [4] The Obama administration denied that in canceling the plan it was kowtowing to Moscow's objections and said a more efficient system was being developed that did not require deployment in Eastern Europe.

But the Eastern Europeans saw the cancelation as the United States giving precedence to Moscow, their old nemesis.

And on the eve of Obama's visit to Poland in May 2011, the English-language *Warsaw Business Journal* said, "Relations between Poland and the United States are at a low point, as Warsaw has grown dissatisfied with Washington's level of commitment to Poland's security." [5]

U.S. relations with Hungary are strained following the election in 2010 of right-of-center Prime Minister Viktor Orbán, who, *The New York Times* said, is drifting "toward authoritarian government . . . in defiance of mounting criticism from Europe and the United States." [6]

In December, Secretary of State Hillary Rodham Clinton wrote to the Hungarian government to express concern "about constitutional changes under consideration in your country" and to push "for a real commitment to the independence of the judiciary, freedom of the press and transparency of government. . . . Our concerns are significant and well-founded." [7]

Orbán replied that all the changes were being made "in constant dialogue" with the European Commission, the executive body of the European Union, and interested parties in Hungary. But analysts pointed out that the European Union had been equally critical of what it considers the authoritarian drift of Orbán's government. [8]

— Roland Flamini

---

1 "Outrage at 'Old Europe' remarks," *BBC News*, Jan. 23, 2003, http://news.bbc.co.uk/2/hi/europe/2687403.stm.

2 Brookings Institution "Iraq Index," Nov. 21, 2005, "Non-U.S. troop deployment," www.brookings.edu/fp/saban/iraq/index20051121.pdf.

3 Michael Rubin, "Afghanistan Exposes Old vs New Europe," *Commentary*, March 14, 2012, www.commentarymagazine.com/2012/03/14/afghanistan-exposes-old-vs-new-europe/.

4 Douglas Lytle and Lenka Ponikelska, "Obama to drop Poland and Czech Missile Defense Proposal," *Bloomberg*, Sept. 17, 2009, www.bloomberg.com/apps/news?pid=newsarchive&sid=awZyw2fptKCQ.

5 "Obama's visit to Poland," *Warsaw Business Journal*, May 27, 2011, www.wbj.pl/article-54714-stratfor-obamas-visit-to-poland.html?typ=ise.

6 "Hungary," *The New York Times*, March 15, 2012, http://topics.nytimes.com/top/news/international/countriesandterritories/hungary/index.html.

7 "Hillary Clinton letter to the Hungarian Government," *Scribd*, Dec. 23, 2011, www.scribd.com/doc/77009957/Letter-from-Hillary-Clinton-to-the-Hungarian-government.

8 "Prime Minister Viktor Orbán's answer to Secretary of State Clinton's letter," *Hungarian Spectrum*, Feb. 25, 2012, http://esbalogh.typepad.com/hungarianspectrum/2012/02/prime-minister-viktor-orb%C3%A1ns-answer-to-secretary-of-state-hillary-clinton.html?cid=6a00e009865ae58833016762fbd947970b.

Continued from p. 290

Timothy Geithner's calls for greater stimulus spending in preference for austerity programs. ■

Current Situation

EU and Iran

The United States and Europe are struggling — together and separately — with a host of economic, military and national-security issues.

Both have imposed economic sanctions against Iran in hopes of halting what is widely suspected to be an effort by Tehran to develop nuclear weapons. The European Union, Iran's second-largest oil customer after China, halted all Iranian oil imports, effective July 1. (The United States has not imported oil from Iran for more than 30 years.)

In addition, U.S. and European leaders have sought to persuade Israel, which is considering a pre-emptive attack on Iran's nuclear facilities, to give the sanctions more time to work. In February, Israeli Defense Minister Ehud Barak bluntly warned that time quickly was running out for stopping Iran's nuclear program, which Israel appears convinced is weapons oriented.

After visiting Iranian nuclear sites, which Tehran claims are for peaceful energy-generation purposes, inspectors from the U.N. nuclear-monitoring organization, the International Atomic Energy Agency (IAEA), declared that the agency "continues to have serious concerns regarding possible military dimensions to Iran's nuclear program." But the IAEA stopped short of accusing the Iranians of planning to develop a nuclear arsenal. [47] U.S. intelligence officials say they remain unsure of Iran's intentions.

As 2011 ended, President Obama signed legislation barring foreign banks that did business with Iran's central bank from dealing with U.S. financial institutions. Afterward, the European Union froze the central bank's assets and halted Iranian oil imports.

The EU's oil cutoff represents a potentially significant hit to Iran's economy, which derives half its earnings from oil revenue. China, Japan and South Korea, which could conceivably cover the EU shortfall, have said they don't plan to increase oil imports from Iran. In response to Iranian threats to retaliate by closing the Strait of Hormuz — through which 20 percent of Gulf oil exports flow — Britain and France have sent warships to the Gulf to support the U.S. aircraft carrier *Abraham Lincoln*.

The Israelis argue that the sanctions, even if effective economically, will not halt Iran's nuclear program. Iran has been moving its nuclear enrichment program — the key factor in its nuclear development — to a hardened underground facility in Fordow, near the holy city of Qom; Barak said that once the bunker-like site is finished, an attack on it could come "too late."

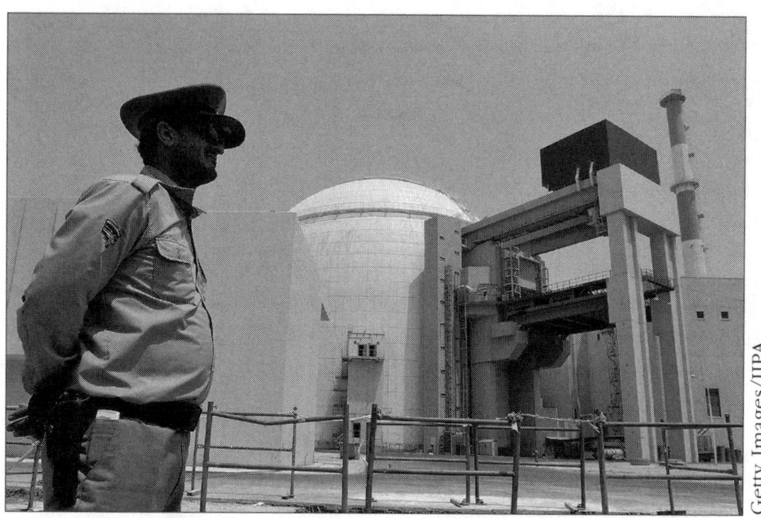

Getty Images/IIPA

Iran's first nuclear facility, the Russian-built Bushehr nuclear power plant, uses uranium fuel well below the enrichment level needed for weapons-grade uranium. Concern that Iran may be enriching fuel for nuclear weapons prompted the United States and Europe to impose strict economic sanctions on Iran. In January the European Union banned Iranian oil imports to Europe – aligning U.S. and European sanctions policies. The U.S. has not imported oil from Iran for 30 years.

Debt Crisis

In an effort to neutralize the debt crisis, 25 members of the European Union in March signed a "fiscal compact" requiring governments to run balanced budgets and write the agreement into their nations' constitutions. The compact calls for capping annual deficits at 0.5 percent of each country's GDP and the tracking of their economies by the EU Commission in Brussels. The European court can impose fines on any country failing to observe that rule. The U.K. and Czech Republic refused to accept the pact. [48] Cameron, the British prime minister, said it meant giving up too much operational independence.

Many analysts, however, fear that the move came too late because the Europeans still have to dig out of their present fiscal plight. Greece,

Continued on p. 294

At Issue:

Should the NATO alliance continue?

XENIA DORMANDY
SENIOR FELLOW, U.S. INTERNATIONAL ROLE, CHATHAM HOUSE, LONDON

WRITTEN FOR *CQ RESEARCHER*, MARCH 2012

yes

Among other factors, new technologies, diverse communications channels, more-integrated problems and a rising number of actors are all increasing the complexity and speed of change in the world today. Amid this cacophony and potential confusion, it would be only sensible to propose that the methods of responding to today's events need to be updated.

The United Nations will be 67 this year. NATO will be 63. While there are many valid questions regarding their constituent memberships, given their relatively broad inclusiveness and their long and respected histories, their activities invoke a certain legitimacy.

Nations will continue to choose, where possible, to undertake operations under the banner of these institutions according to the situation and their specific capabilities, responsibilities and strategic concerns. Recent efforts by European, Gulf and U.S. powers to gain a U.N. resolution on Syria are indicative of this. However, these efforts also demonstrate that such institutions, precisely because of their broad membership, can be dysfunctional. Different values and ideologies can stymie decisions and progress on vital issues.

If international institutions are to continue to be effective tools for multilateral action, they will have to find new ways of working. The likely path will mirror patterns already seen in structures like the Proliferation Security Initiative (PSI) or the post-2004 East Asian tsunami response, in which five countries came together to provide immediate relief as the U.N. mounted its operations and subsequently disbanded when its job was done. These are ad hoc groups of nations with the will, capabilities and interests to act to achieve specific objectives, which, when attained, break up. The future lies with such groups.

If current organizations like the U.N. and NATO want to continue to remain effective, they too will have to adopt similar mechanisms. We are already seeing this to be the case. The operation in Libya had NATO cover but involved only a subset of NATO members in its activities, in coordination with some non-NATO actors. The ISAF (International Security Assistance Force) operations in Afghanistan are another such example.

NATO is already finding ways to act effectively according to this new ad hoc method, within its more formal constructs. It is unlikely, however, that the members will formalize this methodology, instead letting it take place implicitly. One should not expect the current debate within NATO for all members to "pull their weight" to end anytime soon.

JUSTIN LOGAN
DIRECTOR OF FOREIGN POLICY STUDIES, CATO INSTITUTE, WASHINGTON

WRITTEN FOR *CQ RESEARCHER*, MARCH 2012

no

The United States should form military alliances to fight wars. NATO was formed because after World War II Western Europe was devastated, and Washington feared that Moscow might be able to plunge into Western Europe and capitalize on the devastation.

In 1951, however, President Dwight D. Eisenhower remarked that "if in 10 years, all American troops stationed in Europe for national defense purposes have not been returned to the United States, then this whole project will have failed." According to Ike, the purpose of NATO was to help the Western European countries "regain their confidence and get on their own military feet."

NATO's broader purpose in Europe was summed up in an apocryphal quote attributed to Lord Ismay: The alliance was to keep "the Russians out, the Americans in and the Germans down." The Russians are out, and they are going to stay out. Poland faces no threat of Russian attack, to say nothing of countries to her west.

Instead, today NATO constitutes a system of transfer payments from U.S. taxpayers (and their Chinese creditors) to bloated European welfare states. It also serves as a make-work project for the think tankers, bureaucrats and journalists who make a living off the "trans-Atlantic relationship."

All of this might be waved off as harmless had the alliance not expanded eastward three times to include an array of countries that no major member has any intention of defending militarily, should it come to that. There simply aren't the funds in member-state accounts to cover the checks NATO has written.

In the past decades there has been talk in Europe of promoting autonomous European defense capabilities. (Indeed, talk of autonomous European cooperation goes back nearly to the founding of NATO.) However, Washington has consistently scuppered European attempts at creating a third force because it views NATO as a vehicle for controlling Europe's security policy. The result has been a militarily infantile Europe that found it impossible even to fulfill its desire to change the regime of Moammar Gadhafi without help from Washington.

Despite Washington's misgivings, a more powerful, more autonomous Europe would be a good thing for America. It would allow the United States to shrink its armed forces and save money. Sixty years after Eisenhower's admonition, surely it is time to declare the alliance a relic of the past and put NATO out to pasture.

> **"There is no question that the patience of America's NATO allies with the expensive, deadly Afghan war has been running out. They joined the war alongside the United States, which had been attacked by Al Qaeda on Sept. 11, 2001, from its sanctuaries in Afghanistan. But the Taliban government is long gone, Osama bin Laden is dead, and Al Qaeda has been diminished and mostly pushed into Pakistan."**
>
> ***— The New York Times, Jan. 21, 2012***

Continued from p. 292

which is at the heart of the European debt crisis, was rescued from the brink of bankruptcy — at least for the moment — when its private creditors were persuaded to forgo 50 percent of their debt, thus opening the way for a second EU bailout of 130 billion euros. The debt reduction brought Greece's overall indebtedness down from 120 percent of GDP to 117 percent. Greece needed the money for a bond payment by March 30 to avoid defaulting. The slight improvement in Greece's situation had a salutary effect on Italy and Spain.

The United States has watched these developments warily. "For the longer term, analysts are concerned that economic difficulties in Europe could act as a brake on U.S. growth and the world economy," the Congressional Research Service stated. "A dawning age of austerity in Europe could also impact trans-Atlantic cooperation on international issues including defense and development assistance." [49]

But the EU is slowly coming around to the Obama administration's view that Europe needs to stimulate economic growth and create jobs rather than focusing exclusively on austerity measures, which have resulted in riots and protests across the continent from the United Kingdom to Greece — particularly in the latter.

Afghanistan Tensions

The U.S.-EU alliance in Afghanistan appears increasingly fragile. French President Sarkozy, reacting to the killings of four unarmed French soldiers by an Afghan soldier, threatened to pull France's contingent out of Afghanistan by the end of the year.

"If security conditions are not established clearly, then the question of an early return of the French army will arise," Sarkozy declared. Under the current plan, NATO began handing over security duties to Afghan forces last year, with the target date for completing the transition set for the end of 2014. [50]

Accomplishing the transition does not necessarily mean withdrawal from Afghanistan. In the view of Kamp, of the NATO Defense College, Obama was wrong to peg NATO's departure to 2014. This is "a myth" that helps the insurgents plan in advance and raises public expectations in alliance countries, Kamp argued. A long-term commitment needs to follow NATO's departure, both in terms of financial help and also physical presence on the ground, he said. [51]

"There is no question that the patience of America's NATO allies with the expensive, deadly Afghan war has been running out," *The New York Times* said. "They joined the war alongside the United States, which had been attacked by Al Qaeda on Sept. 11, 2001, from its sanctuaries in Afghanistan. But the Taliban government is long gone, Osama bin Laden is dead, and Al Qaeda has been diminished and mostly pushed into Pakistan." [52]

The situation was not helped when on February 20 charred copies of the Quran were found in an incinerator at the Bagram Airfield, Afghanistan's largest military base. A military investigation found that the books were destined for disposal but that three U.S. service personnel on garbage detail inadvertently placed them in the incinerator before a decision had been made. President Obama publicly apologized for the incident amid an upsurge of protest demonstrations and attacks on NATO personnel, resulting in the death of 30 Afghans and six U.S. soldiers in separate attacks by Afghan security personnel. [53]

In a separate incident that further undermined the fragile relationship between the Afghans and NATO, a U.S. Army staff sergeant allegedly went on a dawn rampage and killed 16 Afghan villagers, mostly women and children, before giving himself up. [54] ■

Outlook

NATO Summit

NATO's summit in Chicago in May will be the first in the United States in 13 years. The last one, in Washington in 1999, celebrated the alliance's 50th anniversary. Given the problems facing Europe, neither the NATO summit nor the G8 meeting is likely to be celebratory. Casting ominous shadows over the deliberations will be the war in Afghanistan and the European debt crisis.

What's more, the Iranian nuclear controversy could reach crisis proportions in the event of Israeli military action and the retaliatory closing of the Strait of Hormuz. In March, without going into detail, Obama told *The Atlantic* magazine that if sanctions failed, the United States itself would take action. "I think that the Israel government recognizes that as president of the United States, I don't bluff," he said. It was, Obama went on, "unacceptable for Iran to have a nuclear weapon. We mean what we say." [55]

For now, however, NATO's top priority is spelling out in greater detail the Afghanistan exit strategy and its aftermath. In listing four main discussion areas for the Chicago summit recently, Daalder, the NATO representative, spoke of preliminary consultations currently under way to determine "how a shift in mission can occur most effectively." At the summit, he said, "President Obama and the other leaders will make a final decision on the transition and how the next phase will be implemented . . . and how we can support a sustainable and sufficient Afghan security force and how we can further strengthen our strategic partnership with Afghanistan in 2015 and beyond." [56]

All of which sounds like less of a done deal than Vice President Joseph Biden's "drop dead date" for a U.S. and allied withdrawal in 2014. [57]

Daalder also said NATO will be advancing plans for its long-proposed missile defense system or shield to protect Europe from a Middle East attack — a presumed reference to Iran. "New threats require new defense responses that are just as capable, just as immediate, just as agile as the ones that we had before," he said.

As a third summit issue, Daalder cited NATO'S Smart Defense program, designed to encourage allies to coordinate their defense spending better in an era of fiscal austerity. Daalder cited the example of Sweden paying for half of the purchase of three C-17 Globemaster transport planes and 11 other countries paying the rest. The arrangement entitles the Swedes to one-sixth share of the huge planes' flying time, he said.

NATO also will address the participation of non member countries in NATO operations, as has happened in both Libya and Afghanistan, Daalder said. "All these countries have come to recognize that NATO is a hub for building security; not that NATO is the

FOR MORE INFORMATION

Atlantic Council, 1101 15th St., N.W., 11th Floor, Washington, DC 20005; 202-463-7226; www.acus.org. Nonpartisan institution working to promote trans-Atlantic cooperation on such issues as security, business, energy and the environment.

Cato Institute, 1000 Massachusetts Ave., N.W., Washington, DC 20001; 202-842-0200; www.cato.org. Libertarian think tank advocating for U.S. troop reductions in Europe.

Chatham House, 10 St James's Square, London, England SW1Y 4LE; +44 (0) 20 7957 5700; www.chathamhouse.org. Non-governmental organization analyzing major international issues.

Council on Foreign Relations, 58 E. 68th St., New York, NY 10065; 212-434-9400; www.cfr.org. Nonpartisan think tank specializing in U.S. foreign policy and international affairs.

Court of Justice of the European Union, Boulevard Konrad Adenauer, Kirchberg, L-2925 Luxembourg; +352 4303 1; curia.europa.eu. Interprets laws of the European Union to ensure they are applied consistently across member nations.

European Union Delegation to the USA, 2175 K St., N.W., Washington, DC 20037; 202-862-9500; www.eurunion.org. European Union's representative body in the United States.

German Marshall Fund of the United States, 1744 R St., N.W., Washington, DC 20009; 202-683-2650; www.gmfus.org. Public policy institution promoting better understanding between North America and Europe on trans-Atlantic issues.

International Institute for Strategic Studies, 13–15 Arundel St., Temple Place, London, England WC2R 3DX; +44 (0) 20 7379 7676; www.iiss.org. Research institute specializing in political-military conflict.

North Atlantic Treaty Organization, Boulevard Leopold III, 1110 Brussels, Belgium; +32 (0) 2 707 41 11; www.nato.int. Intergovernmental military alliance of North American and European countries.arts.

world policeman, which it is not, but that it is a forum for dialogue and a forum for bringing countries together for collective action," he said.

Others see coalition-building as an effective way for the Atlantic alliance to stay in business. Says Dormandy of Chatham House: "You're going to see more and more coalitions because they answer problems more effectively. NATO will survive if it continues to show a willingness to move in this direction." The issue needs to be discussed, she says, because "the rhetoric is still behind the action. In people's minds they're not there yet."

Analysts say President Obama will also need to calm European anxiety about America's continued commitment to NATO. He will need to elaborate on whether America's first ever decision not to take the lead in a NATO action — in Libya — is to become an option in U.S. military planning, and if so, how that will change the geometry of the alliance.

By May, the leaders of the G8 industrialized nations may have to confront a fresh setback in Greece, Portugal on the edge and other aspects of the crisis in Europe. But on a more hopeful note, they are expected to discuss — and perhaps even agree on — a comprehensive, bilateral U.S.-EU trade agreement.

"Suddenly, there's a lot of support for an agreement," says the Atlantic Council's Burwell. "The United States and Europe have parallel economies, each is the other's main economic partner, and they have huge levels of investment," she says. A trade partnership will help resolve some of the pending issues, such as coordinating standards, she adds. "It's an achievable arrangement." ■

Notes

[1] "Remarks by President Obama and Prime Minister Cameron of the United Kingdom at Arrival Ceremony," *White House*, March 14, 2012, www.whitehouse.gov/the-press-office/2012/03/14/remarks-president-obama-and-prime-minister-cameron-united-kingdom-arriva. For background, see the following *CQ Researcher* and *CQ Global Researcher* reports: Sarah Glazer, "Future of the Euro," *CQ Global Researcher*, May 17, 2011, pp. 237-262; Roland Flamini, "U.S.-British Relations," *CQ Researcher*, Nov. 5, 2010, pp. 917-940; Roland Flamini, "Future of NATO," *CQ Global Researcher*, January 2009, pp. 1-26; Brian Beary, "The New Europe," *CQ Global Researcher*, August 2007, pp. 181-210; Kenneth Jost, "Future of the European Union," *CQ Researcher*, Oct. 28, 2005, pp. 909-932; Philip M. Seib, "U.S. British Relations," *CQ Researcher*, Jan. 30, 1998, pp.73-96.

[2] Deb Riechmann, "2 U.S troops are killed in Afghanistan: Quran backlash claims 6," *Detroit Free Press*, March 2, 2012, www.freep.com/article/20120302/NEWS07/203020383/2-U-S-troops-are-killed-in-Afghanistan-Quran-burning-backlash-claims-6.

[3] Mirwais Khan and Sebastian Abbot, "Afghan official: Video shows soldier surrendering", *The Associated Press*, March 14, 2012, http://hosted.ap.org/dynamic/stories/A/AS_AFGHANISTAN?SITE=AP&SECTION=HOME&TEMPLATE=DEFAULT.

[4] European Commission, Trade, United States, http://ec.europa.eu/trade/creating-opportunities/bilateral-relations/countries/united-states/.

[5] "U.S. President Barack Obama addresses the Australian Parliament," Youtube, Nov. 17, 2011, www.youtube.com/watch?v=8_hSqLEtX_Y.

[6] Jackie Calmes, "U.S. Marine Base in Australia Irritates China," *The New York Times*, Nov. 16, 2011, www.nytimes.com/2011/11/17/world/asia/obama-and-gillard-expand-us-australia-military-ties.html?pagewanted=all.

[7] David Ignatius, "Defense 'pivot' with big consequences," *Commercial Appeal*, Jan. 7, 2012, www.commercialappeal.com/news/2012/jan/07/david-ignatius-defense-pivot-with-big/?print=1.

[8] Judy Dempsey, "U.S. Sees Europe as Not Pulling Its Weight Militarily," *The New York Times*, Feb. 6, 2012, www.nytimes.com/2012/02/07/world/europe/07iht-letter07.html?pagewanted=all.

[9] "Military Capabilities available to the EU," *House of Lords Select Committee*, Nov. 3, 2011, www.iiss.org/whats-new/iiss-experts-commentary/military-capabilities-available-to-the-eu/.

[10] Laurence Korb, "Invitation to a Dialogue: the Military Budget," *The New York Times*, Nov. 9, 2011, www.nytimes.com/2011/11/10/opinion/invitation-to-a-dialogue-the-military-budget.html?_r=1.

[11] Robert Guttman, "Happy 60th Birthday NATO; Time to Go Out of Business?," *Huffington Post*, April 1, 2009, www.huffingtonpost.com/robert-guttman/happy-60th-birthday-nato_b_181734.html.

[12] Elizabeth Bumuller and Tom Shanker, "Obama Puts His Stamp on Strategy for a Leaner Military," *The New York Times*, Feb. 5, 2012, www.nytimes.com/2012/01/06/us/obama-at-pentagon-to-outline-cuts-and-strategic-shifts.html.

[13] "Obama's Remarks on Military Spending," *The New York Times*, Jan. 5, 2012, www.nytimes.com/2012/01/06/us/text-obamas-remarks-on-military-spending.html?pagewanted=all.

About the Author

Roland Flamini is a Washington-based correspondent who specializes in foreign affairs. Fluent in six languages, he was *Time* bureau chief in Rome, Bonn, Beirut, Jerusalem and the European Common Market and later served as international editor at United Press International. While covering the 1979 Iranian Revolution for *Time*, Flamini wrote the magazine's cover story — in which Ayatollah Ruhollah Khomeini was named Man of the Year — and was promptly expelled because authorities didn't like what they read. His books include a study of Vatican politics in the 1960s, *Pope, Premier, President*. His most recent report for *CQ Global Researcher* was "Rising Tension Over Iran."

[14] *Ibid.*
[15] Simon Tisdall, "China Syndrome dictates Barack Obama's Asia-Pacific strategy," Jan. 20, 2011, *The Guardian*, www.guardian.co.uk/commentisfree/2012/jan/06/china-barack-obama-defence-strategy.
[16] *Ibid*
[17] Kevin Rudd, speech at the 48th Munich Security Conference, Feb. 2, 2012, www.securityconference.de/Activities.192+M52087573ab0.0.html.
[18] Brian Knowlton, "Gates calls European mood a Danger to Peace," *The New York Times*, Feb. 23, 2012, www.nytimes.com/2010/02/24/world/europe/24nato.html.
[19] "Sustaining Global Leadership," Department of Defense, January 2012, www.defense.gov/news/Defense_Strategic_Guidance.pdf.
[20] Jonathan Masters, "The Pentagon points to Asia," Council on Foreign Relations, *Analysis Brief*, Jan. 6. 2012, www.cfr.org/united-states/pentagon-pivots-asia/p26979.
[21] Christoph von Marschall, "Fear not, Europe!" *The German Times*, Feb. 2, 2012, www.german-times.com/index.php?option=com_content&task=view&id=41618&Itemid=25.
[22] Thomas Wright and Richard Weitz, "The Transatlantic Alliance in a Multipolar World," *The Chicago Council of Foreign Affairs*, November 2010, www.thechicagocouncil.org/userfiles/file/task%20force%20reports/The%20Transatlantic%20Alliance%20in%20a%20Multi-polar%20World.pdf.
[23] T. Dotson Stamps and Vincent Esposito, "A Military History of world War II," Vol. 1, *U.S. Military Academy*, 1953.
[24] "What Comes after Europe?" *The Wall Street Journal* online, Sept. 19, 2011, http://online.wsj.com/article/SB10001424053111904106704576580522348961298.html?mod=WSJ_Opinion_carousel_2.
[25] "The North Atlantic Treaty, Washington, April 4, 1949," (text), *North Atlantic Treaty Organization*, www.nato.int/cps/en/natolive/official_texts_17120.htm.
[26] Brookings Institution, "The Marshall Plan," http://www.brookings.edu/about/History/marshallplan.aspx.
[27] *Ibid.*
[28] Albrecht Ritschl, "The Marshall Plan, 1948-1951," EH.net, Feb 5, 2010, http://eh.net/encyclopedia/article/Ritschl.Marshall.Plan.
[29] Ivo Daalder, "NATO and the Transatlantic Alliance: The American Perspective," speech at Chicago Council on Global Affairs, March 1, 2012, www.thechicagocouncil.org/files/Event/FY_12_Events/Transcripts/NATO_and_the_Transatlantic_Alliance_The_American_Perspective.aspx.
[30] "NATO strategy of flexible response," *Bulletin of the Atomic Scientists*, April 1963, http://books.google.com/books?id=3QUAAAAAMBAJ&pg=PA19&lpg=PA19&dq=nato+strategy+of+flexible+response&source=bl&ots=PNAGKyQ-zO&sig=3dp571exsYrlhnKAZdTzr4etkQs&hl=en&sa=X&ei=fyxRT8GpHePl0QHUzO-jNDQ&ved=0CEAQ6AEwBjgo#v=onepage&q=nato%20strategy%20of%20flexible%20response&f=false.
[31] Christian Nuenlist and others, "Globalizing de Gaulle: International Perspectives on French Foreign Policy 1958-1969," *Harvard Cold War Studies Book Series*, 2010; see introduction by Mark Kramer.
[32] "U.S. will deploy Missiles if Soviets Balk," *Ocala Star-Banner*, Nov. 19, 1981, http://news.google.com/newspapers?nid=1356&dat=19811119&id=TbRPAAAAIBAJ&sjid=LgYEAAAAIBAJ&pg=2600,3550543.
[33] "Clinton: 'We must act now,'" *BBC Online Network*, March 25, 1999, http://news.bbc.co.uk/2/hi/europe/303052.stm.
[34] Richard K. Betts, "Compromised Command," *Foreign Affairs*, July/August 2001, www.foreignaffairs.com/articles/57062/richard-k-betts/compromised-command.
[35] *Ibid.*
[36] *Ibid.*
[37] *Ibid.*
[38] Ellen Hallams, "The Transatlantic Alliance Renewed: the United States and NATO since 9/11," *Journal of Transatlantic Studies*, Vol. 7, Issue 1, 2009, www.tandfonline.com/doi/full/10.1080/14794010802658823.
[39] Derek E. Mix, "The United States and Europe: Current Issues," Congressional Research Service, May 4, 2011, http://fpc.state.gov/documents/organization/168024.pdf.
[40] Barry D. Wood, "There is no clear line between 'Old' and 'New' Europe," *European Institute*, Spring 2003, www.europeaninstitute.org/20030302351/Spring-2003/there-is-no-clear-line-between-qoldq-and-qnewq-europe.html.
[41] Stefan Simons, "Sarkozy breaks with de Gaulle and tradition," *Spiegelonline*, March 13, 2009, www.spiegel.de/international/europe/0,1518,612840,00.html.
[42] "Military Capabilities available to the EU," House of Lords Select Committee, Nov. 3, 2011, www.iiss.org/whats-new/iiss-experts-commentary/military-capabilities-available-to-the-eu/.
[43] Karl-Heinz Kamp, "NATO Chicago Summit: A Thorny Agenda," *NATO Defense College*, November 2011, www.ndc.nato.int/research/series.php?icode=1.
[44] Daalder, *op. cit.*
[45] "Carla Hills Voices Concern on 'Fortress Europe,' " *Los Angeles Times*, Sept. 11, 1989, http://articles.latimes.com/1989-09-11/business/fi-1616_1_fortress-europe.
[46] Steven Greenhouse, "The growing fear of Fortress Europe," *The New York Times*, Oct. 23, 1988, www.nytimes.com/1988/10/23/business/the-growing-fear-of-fortress-europe.html?pagewanted=all&src=pm.
[47] Scott Peterson, "IAEA report on Iran: 'serious concerns' about nuclear program," *The Christian Science Monitor online*, Feb. 24, 2012, www.csmonitor.com/World/Middle-East/2012/0224/IAEA-report-on-Iran-serious-concerns-about-nuclear-program.
[48] William Boston, "Fiscal Pact Huge Step Toward European Stability: Merkel," *The Wall Street Journal*, March 1, 2012, http://online.wsj.com/article/BT-CO-20120301-708211.html.
[49] Mix, *op. cit.*
[50] Steven Erlanger and Alissa J. Rubin, "France Weighs Pullout After 4 of Its Soldiers Are Killed," *The New York Times*, Jan. 20, 2012, www.nytimes.com/2012/01/21/world/europe/sarkozy-weighs-afghan-withdrawal-after-4-french-troops-killed.html?pagewanted=all.
[51] Kamp, *op. cit.*, November 2011.
[52] Erlanger and Rubin.
[53] Patrick Quinn, "Afghanistan Quran Burnings: Conflicting Accounts Emerge," *Huffington Post*, March 12, 2012, www.huffingtonpost.com/2012/03/03/afghanistan-quran-burnings_n_1318297.html.
[54] Richard Engel, "Soldier accused of killing 16 Afghans relocated," *NECN/NBC*, March 15, 2012, www.necn.com/03/15/12/Soldier-accused-of-killing-16-Afghans-re/landing_newengland.html?blockID=670288&feedID=4207.
[55] Jeffrey Goldberg, "Obama to Iran and Israel: "As President of the United States, I Don't Bluff," *The Atlantic*, March 2, 2012, www.theatlantic.com/international/archive/2012/03/obama-to-iran-and-israel-as-president-of-the-united-states-i-dont-bluff/253875.
[56] Daalder, *op. cit.*
[57] "Joe Biden: 2014 Afghanistan Pullout is 'Drop Dead Date,' " *Huffington Post*, May 25, 2011, www.huffingtonpost.com/2010/11/19/afghanistan-2014-withdrawal-biden_n_785904.html.

Bibliography

Selected Sources

Books

Goldgeier, James, *The Future of NATO*, Council on Foreign Relations, 2010.

A professor of political science and international relations at George Washington University examines NATO's options for remaining relevant in the 21st century.

Lewis, Michael, *Boomerang: The Meltdown Tour*, Penguin Books, 2011.

A best-selling author and journalist examines developments in the United States and Europe that led to the global debt crisis. He contends the Goldman Sachs investment bank helped the Greek government rig the books to hide the true nature of its economy from other European Union members.

Lundestad, Geir, ed., *Just Another Major Crisis? The United States and Europe Since 2000*, Oxford University Press, 2008.

Scholars on both sides of the Atlantic discuss the state of trans-Atlanticism; historian Lundestad is director of the Norwegian Nobel Institute.

Ross, Robert S., Tuosheng Zhang, *et al.*, *U.S.-China-EU Relations: Managing the New World Order*, Routledge, 2009.

A professor of political science at Boston College (Ross), the director of the Center for Foreign Policy Studies, Beijing, and other international scholars examine how U.S.-China-EU relations will shape the future of international politics, playing a key role in establishing and managing a new world order.

Sloan, Stanley R., *Permanent Alliance? NATO and the Transatlantic Bargain from Truman to Obama*, Continuum, 2012.

A longtime writer and lecturer on the Atlantic Alliance traces its development and reasons for its failures and successes.

Articles

Brezezinski, Zbigniew, "An Agenda for NATO: Toward a Global Security Web," *Foreign Affairs*, October 2009.

A former White House national security adviser, marking the Atlantic Alliance's 60th anniversary, notes that during its history NATO has united the West, secured Europe and ended the Cold War, and discusses its future role.

Hao, Li, "European Recession 2012: How would it affect the U.S. economy?" *International Business News*, March 7, 2012, www.ibtimes.com/articles/310705/20120307/european-recession-2012-exports-fdi-eu.htm.

In a recession, says the writer, bond investors will sell European debt, which would only exacerbate the current crisis.

Ifeany, K.C., "Euro debt crisis could cripple U.S. business travel," *Inc.*, Feb. 17, 2012, www.inc.com/kc-ifeanyi/european-debt-crisis-could-cripple-us-business-travel.html.

With Greece on the verge of bankruptcy and other European countries ailing, the economic climate abroad has potentially severe ramifications for U.S. business travel as executives lose interest in European business opportunities.

"European Debt Crisis: Recent Developments," *The New York Times*, March 2, 2012, http://topics.nytimes.com/top/reference/timestopics/subjects/e/european_sovereign_debt_crisis/index.html.

The Times summarizes recent developments in the European debt crisis.

Soros, George, "How to Save the Euro," *The New York Review of Books*, Feb. 23, 2012.

A noted financier and philanthropist argues against Germany's austerity policy and says that what Europe needs to extract itself from the euro crisis is growth, not more belt-tightening.

Reports and Studies

Dewan, Selwa, and Christian E. Weller, "When Europe's Sovereign Debt Crisis Hits Home," Center for American Progress, Sept. 22, 2011, www.americanprogress.org/issues/2011/09/europe_debt.html.

Two economists at the liberal Washington think tank warn that the United States will not escape the backwash from Europe's sovereign debt crisis and outline ways in which America can minimize the impact.

"Economic Crisis in Europe: Causes, Consequences, and Responses," European Union, Directorate General of Economic and Financial Affairs, July 2009, http://ec.europa.eu/economy_finance/publications/publication15887_en.pdf.

This detailed and surprisingly frank official assessment of how the European Union got into its current fiscal mess explores the prospects for effectively resolving the crisis while offering useful background on the financial mechanisms of the EU.

Vasconcelos, Alvaro de, and Marcin Zaborowski, eds., "The Obama Moment," European Union Institute of Security Studies, 2009, www.iss.europa.eu/uploads/media/The_Obama_Moment__web_A4.pdf.

The election of Barack Obama occasioned this in-depth evaluation of European-American relations by leading analysts and political figures from both sides of the Atlantic; much of it is still relevant.

The Next Step:

Additional Articles from Current Periodicals

Asia

Haass, Richard N., "Continental Drift," ***The Washington Post*****, June 19, 2011, p. B1.**

The United States should play a greater role in Asia because of a lack of political and security arrangements among Asian nations, says the president of the Council on Foreign Relations think tank.

LaFranchi, Howard, "Obama Seeks to Reassure Asia of US Interest," ***The Christian Science Monitor*****, Nov. 11, 2011, www.csmonitor.com/USA/Foreign-Policy/2011/1111/Obama-seeks-to-reassure-Asia-of-US-interest.**

A potential European financial meltdown and other global crises are unlikely to divert U.S. attention from Asia.

Nakamura, David, "Asian Trip Shows Where Obama Is Focusing Job Hopes," ***The Washington Post*****, Nov. 8, 2011, p. A4.**

Europe remains the United States' top trading partner, but Asia is becoming more central to American economic and strategic interests.

Debt Crisis

Cooper, Helene, "U.S. Leverage Is Limited as Greek Debt Drama Dominates G-20 Meeting," ***The New York Times*****, Nov. 4, 2011, p. A12, www.nytimes.com/2011/11/04/world/europe/obama-urges-european-solution-to-debt-crisis.html.**

President Obama was merely a bystander as Greek officials figured out the details on how to protect the euro.

Crutsinger, Martin, "Geithner Sees Encouraging Progress in Europe," The Associated Press, Dec. 7, 2011, articles.boston.com/2011-12-07/news/30486967_1_geithner-mario-draghi-imf-support.

U.S. Treasury Secretary Timothy Geithner says he is encouraged by Europe's progress in crafting plans to shore up the euro.

Irwin, Neil, "E.U. Crisis Touches Wallets in U.S.," ***The Washington Post*****, Oct. 1, 2011, p. A1, www.washingtonpost.com/business/economy/us-economic-recovery-tied-to-european-debt-crisis/2011/09/29/gIQAAIAEBL_story.html.**

The European debt crisis is influencing the business decisions of major players in the U.S. economy.

Wolf, Richard, "Obama Tackles Europe's Debt Crisis," ***USA Today*****, Nov. 29, 2011, p. A7, www.usatoday.com/news/washington/story/2011-11-28/obama-summit-europe-debt-crisis/51450186/1.**

President Obama says the United States is ready to help Europe solve its debt crisis because the problem is of significant importance to the American economy.

European Court of Justice

"Court: Anheuser-Busch InBev Can Continue Bud Fight," ***St. Louis Business Journal*****, March 29, 2011, www.bizjournals.com/stlouis/news/2011/03/29/court-a-b-inbev-can-continue-bud-fight.html.**

The European Court of Justice has referred back to a lower court Anheuser-Busch's fight over the "Bud" trademark with Czech brewer Budejovicky Budvar.

"U.S. Opposes EU Airline Emission Tax Plan," United Press International, Dec. 21, 2011, www.upi.com/Top_News/US/2011/12/21/US-opposes-EU-airline-emission-tax-plan/UPI-89841324516528/.

The U.S. State Department has expressed disappointment in a ruling by the European Court of Justice that allows the European Union to charge airlines an emission tax on flights in EU countries.

Military

Bumiller, Elisabeth, and Steven Erlanger, "Panetta and Clinton Seek to Reassure Europe on Defense," ***The New York Times*****, Feb. 5, 2012, p. A4, www.nytimes.com/2012/02/05/world/europe/panetta-clinton-troops-europe.html.**

Defense Secretary Leon Panetta and Secretary of State Hillary Rodham Clinton said the United States will maintain a military presence in Europe despite troop cuts.

Huntley, Steve, "A Well-Timed Warning to Europe," ***Chicago Sun-Times*****, June 14, 2011, p. 21.**

The United States should maintain a common military defense in Europe, but allies should also stop shirking their NATO responsibilities, says a columnist.

CITING *CQ RESEARCHER*

Sample formats for citing these reports in a bibliography include the ones listed below. Preferred styles and formats vary, so please check with your instructor or professor.

MLA STYLE

Jost, Kenneth. "Remembering 9/11," CQ Researcher 2 Sept. 2011: 701-732.

APA STYLE

Jost, K. (2011, September 2). Remembering 9/11. *CQ Researcher, 9*, 701-732.

CHICAGO STYLE

Jost, Kenneth. "Remembering 9/11." *CQ Researcher*, September 2, 2011, 701-732.

Researcher PLUS Archive
New!

CQ Researcher

Published by CQ Press, an Imprint of SAGE Publications, Inc.

www.cqresearcher.com

Police Misconduct

Will excessive force, racial profiling be curbed?

The U.S. Department of Justice is stepping up its oversight of local police departments, pressuring them to limit the use of force in civilian encounters and eliminate racial profiling during traffic stops and other enforcement. Over the past year, the Justice Department's civil rights division has criticized long-troubled police agencies in such places as New Orleans, Seattle and Maricopa County, Ariz., which includes Phoenix. The department's power stems from a 1994 law allowing the federal government to identify a "pattern or practice" of constitutional violations and threaten court action to force police agencies to adopt changes. Seattle officials have proposed a detailed plan to answer the government's criticisms, but negotiations are stalled in New Orleans and Maricopa County, where Sheriff Joe Arpaio is balking at the government's demand for court supervision of policy changes. Meanwhile, the racially charged shooting death of a Florida teenager by a neighborhood watch volunteer has focused attention on police handling of the case.

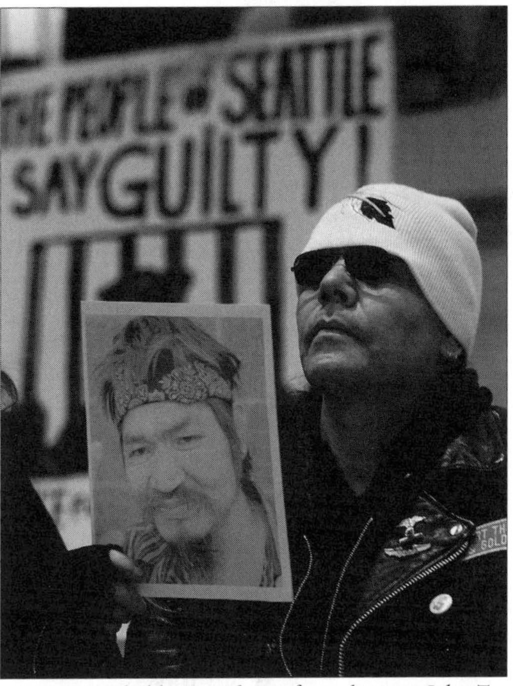

A protester holds up a photo of wood carver John T. Williams, a hearing-impaired Native American killed by Seattle Police Sgt. Ian Birk in 2010. A fixture at a nearby social service center, Williams was shot after failing to respond to Birk's order to drop an open carving knife. The Feb. 16, 2011, demonstration was to protest the King County prosecutor's decision not to charge Birk, who later resigned.

INSIDE THIS REPORT

THE ISSUES 303
BACKGROUND 310
CHRONOLOGY 311
CURRENT SITUATION 316
AT ISSUE 317
OUTLOOK 319
BIBLIOGRAPHY 322
THE NEXT STEP 323

CQ Researcher • April 6, 2012 • www.cqresearcher.com
Volume 22, Number 13 • Pages 301-324

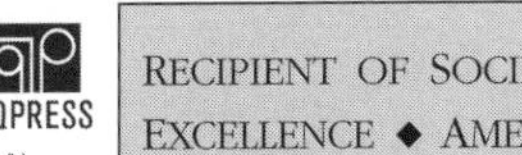

Los Angeles | London | New Delhi
Singapore | Washington DC

RECIPIENT OF SOCIETY OF PROFESSIONAL JOURNALISTS AWARD FOR EXCELLENCE ◆ AMERICAN BAR ASSOCIATION SILVER GAVEL AWARD

THE ISSUES

303 • Should police do more to control excessive force?
• Should police do more to prevent racial and ethnic profiling?
• Should police adopt stronger disciplinary measures for misconduct?

BACKGROUND

310 **Police Problems**
Police misconduct has been a problem since the 1800s.

313 **Police Accountability**
Major police departments were beset by scandals during the final decades of the 20th century.

313 **Changing Priorities**
Oversight of police conduct took a more aggressive stance under President Obama.

CURRENT SITUATION

316 **Investigations Urged**
Citizens groups in several cities want the Justice Department to examine police agencies with records of fatal shootings.

318 **Reforms Outlined**
Seattle is preparing to adopt a plan to overhaul its police procedures, but reform efforts in New Orleans have hit a snag.

OUTLOOK

319 **Police Under Pressure**
Budget cuts and homeland security concerns add to the pressures on police.

SIDEBARS AND GRAPHICS

304 **Justice Department Targets Police Misconduct**
The federal government has found police misconduct in such localities as New Orleans, Seattle and East Haven, Conn.

305 **Killings of Arrestees by Police on Rise**
Police committed 2,931 arrest-related killings from 2003 through 2009.

307 **Police Handle Tense Situations in Steps**
Agencies employ a "use of force continuum."

308 **Half of Arrest-Related Killings Are of Minorities**
Blacks and Hispanics made up more than half of those killed while under arrest from 2003 through 2009.

311 **Chronology**
Key events since 1960.

312 **Supreme Court Eases Rules on Police Searches**
Evidence gleaned illegally allowed in criminal trials.

314 **Police Under Scrutiny in Trayvon Martin Case**
Critics question handling of shooting.

317 **At Issue**
Is the exclusionary rule needed to deter illegal police searches?

FOR FURTHER RESEARCH

321 **For More Information**
Organizations to contact.

322 **Bibliography**
Selected sources used.

323 **The Next Step**
Additional articles.

323 **Citing *CQ Researcher***
Sample bibliography formats.

Cover: AP Photo/Ted S. Warren

CQ Researcher

April 6, 2012
Volume 22, Number 13

MANAGING EDITOR: Thomas J. Billitteri
tjb@cqpress.com

ASSISTANT MANAGING EDITOR: Kathy Koch
kkoch@cqpress.com

CONTRIBUTING EDITOR: Thomas J. Colin
tcolin@cqpress.com

ASSOCIATE EDITOR: Kenneth Jost

STAFF WRITER: Marcia Clemmitt

CONTRIBUTING WRITERS: Sarah Glazer, Alan Greenblatt, Peter Katel, Barbara Mantel, Jennifer Weeks

DESIGN/PRODUCTION EDITOR: Olu B. Davis

ASSISTANT EDITOR: Darrell Dela Rosa

FACT CHECKER: Michelle Harris

Los Angeles | London | New Delhi
Singapore | Washington DC

An Imprint of SAGE Publications, Inc.

VICE PRESIDENT AND EDITORIAL DIRECTOR, HIGHER EDUCATION GROUP:
Michele Sordi

DIRECTOR, ONLINE PUBLISHING:
Todd Baldwin

CQ Researcher (ISSN 1056-2036) is printed on acid-free paper. Published weekly, except: (March wk. 5) (May wk. 4) (July wk. 1) (Aug. wks. 3, 4) (Nov. wk. 4) and (Dec. wks. 3, 4). Published by SAGE Publications, Inc., 2455 Teller Rd., Thousand Oaks, CA 91320. Annual full-service subscriptions start at $1,054. For pricing, call 1-800-834-9020. To purchase a *CQ Researcher* report in print or electronic format (PDF), visit www.cqpress.com or call 866-427-7737. Single reports start at $15. Bulk purchase discounts and electronic-rights licensing are also available. Periodicals postage paid at Thousand Oaks, California, and at additional mailing offices. POSTMASTER: Send address changes to *CQ Researcher*, 2300 N St., N.W., Suite 800, Washington, DC 20037.

Police Misconduct

BY KENNETH JOST

THE ISSUES

Wendell Allen was wearing only pajama bottoms when New Orleans police officers on a marijuana raid broke into his house in the city's middle-class Gentilly neighborhood on the evening of March 7. Armed with a search warrant, six officers, clad in plain clothes covered by jackets identifying them as police, announced their presence and, after receiving no response, barged in.

Allen, a 20-year-old former high school basketball star with a previous marijuana-related conviction, was in the stairwell, unarmed, when Officer Joshua Colclough fired a single gunshot that hit Allen in the chest. The bullet penetrated Allen's heart, aorta and lungs. He died "almost instantly," New Orleans Parish Coroner Frank Minyard said later. [1]

Allen's death, the second fatal shooting of an African-American youth by New Orleans police within a week, remains under what Superintendent Ronal Serpas promises will be "a complete and thorough" investigation. Colclough, in his fifth year with the force, gave a voluntary statement to investigators a week after the shooting. His attorney, Claude Kelly, says an "honest" investigation will show the shooting was justified.

Allen's family and leaders of the city's African-American community, however, have no doubt that the shooting was unwarranted. "There have been egregious wrongs done to the black community of New Orleans," W. C. Johnson, leader of the United New Orleans Front, declared as protesters massed outside police headquarters two days after the shooting. Helen Shorty, Allen's grandmother, called for Colclough to be booked for murder. [2]

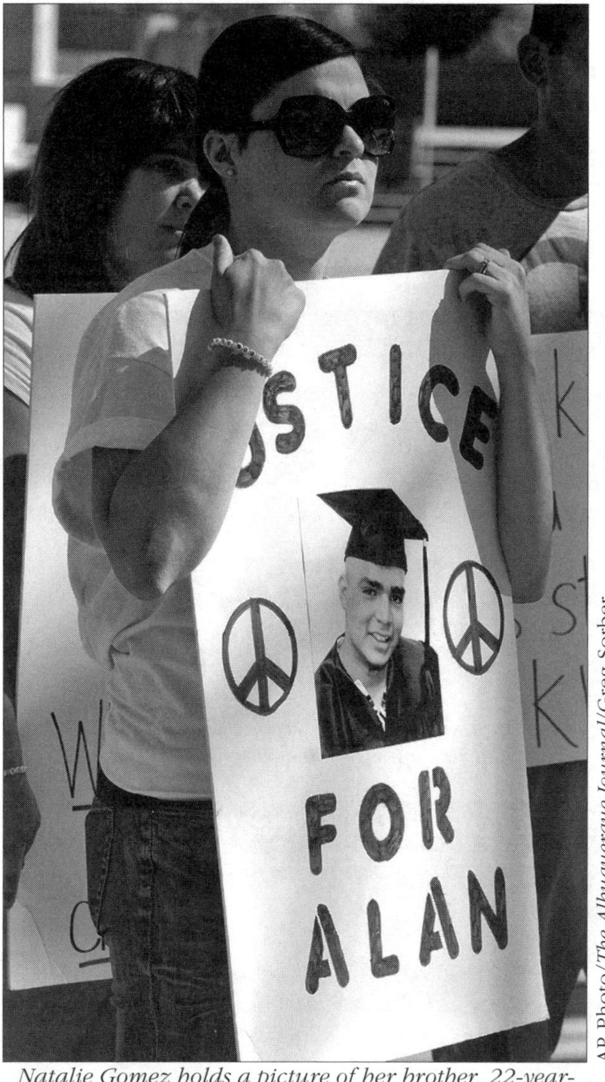

AP Photo/The Albuquerque Journal/Greg Sorber

Natalie Gomez holds a picture of her brother, 22-year-old Alan Gomez, who was killed last year by Albuquerque, N.M., police. Ms. Gomez participated in a rally on June 14, 2011, protesting the police department's use of lethal force. The department's police union was found to have been giving officers involved in fatal shootings $500 to help them recover from stress. Critics have called the payments a bounty system for killing suspects.

The shootings come as the long-troubled department is negotiating with the U.S. Department of Justice (DOJ) the terms of a possible agreement on wide-ranging reforms to be supervised by a federal court. The negotiations follow a scathing report by the Justice Department's civil rights division in March 2011 that accused the New Orleans police of routine constitutional violations, including use of excessive force, improper searches and racial and ethnic discrimination. [3]

The 158-page report is one of nine published so far by the civil rights division's so-called "special litigation section" under President Obama that have held police departments around the country up to highly critical scrutiny. In three reports published within five days in mid-December, Justice Department investigators upbraided Seattle police for use of excessive force and the Maricopa County, Ariz., sheriff's office and East Haven, Conn., police department for ethnic profiling of Latinos. (*See graphic, p. 304.*)

Racial profiling is also at the heart of the nationwide controversy over the Feb. 26 fatal shooting of a black Florida teenager by a white neighborhood watch volunteer. (*See sidebar, p. 314.*) Trayvon Martin, 17, was shot as he was returning from a convenience store to the house of his father's girlfriend in Sanford, an Orlando suburb. George Zimmerman, whose mother is Hispanic, claims he shot the unarmed Martin in self-defense after following the youth because of what he regarded as suspicious behavior. The incident has touched off nationwide debate not only over racial profiling but also over Florida's so-called Stand Your Ground law, which allows someone to use deadly force when feeling threatened, with no duty to attempt to retreat.

Justice Department Targets Police Misconduct

U.S. Department of Justice investigators have examined the policies and practices of more than two dozen law enforcement agencies over the past decade and found a range of illegal or otherwise improper practices, ranging from harsh treatment of suspects and racial profiling to failure to probe allegations of sexual assault. Here are highlights from five recent Justice Department reports.

New Orleans

(March 17, 2011) *Use of excessive force; unconstitutional stops, searches and arrests; biased policing; racial, ethnic and sexual-orientation discrimination; failure to provide effective policing services to persons with limited English proficiency; systemic failure to investigate sexual assaults and domestic violence.*

Puerto Rico

(Sept. 7, 2011) *Excessive force; unreasonable force, other misconduct designed to suppress exercise of First Amendment rights; unlawful searches and seizures; evidence of frequent failure to police sex crimes and incidents of domestic violence; evidence of discriminatory practices targeting individuals of Dominican descent; "staggering level" of crime and corruption.*

Maricopa County, Ariz. (includes Phoenix)

(Dec. 15, 2011) *Racial profiling of Latinos; unlawful stops, detentions and arrests of Latinos; unlawful retaliation against individuals who complain about or criticize the office's policies or practices; reasonable cause to believe the office operates its jails in a manner that punishes Latino inmates with limited English proficiency for failing to understand commands given in English and denying critical services provided to other inmates.*

Seattle

(Dec. 16, 2011) *Use of unnecessary or excessive force; lack of adequate training on use of force; failure of supervisors to provide oversight on use of force; serious concerns about possible discriminatory policing, particularly relating to pedestrian encounters.*

East Haven, Conn.

(Dec. 19, 2011) *Systematic discrimination against Latinos, including targeting Latinos for discriminatory traffic enforcement, treating Latino drivers more harshly than non-Latino drivers after a traffic stop and intentionally and woefully failing to design and implement internal systems of control that would identify, track and prevent such misconduct.*

Source: U.S. Department of Justice, www.justice.gov/crt/about/spl/findsettle.php.

The most recent reports by the Justice Department's police accountability unit exemplify its more aggressive stance after an eight-year period of dormancy under President George W. Bush. "They've been very assertive," says Samuel Walker, a professor of criminal justice, emeritus, at the University of Nebraska-Omaha and the nation's senior academic expert on police-accountability issues. In all, the unit is conducting 20 investigations of state or local law enforcement agencies.

Local police officials sometimes challenge the Justice Department's findings. "The department is not broken," a defiant Seattle Police Chief John Diaz declared as the DOJ's report was being released on Dec. 16. The city's mayor, Mike McGinn, backed him up.

Over time, however, local officials generally yield to federal authorities. In East Haven, Police Chief Leonard Gallo retired on Jan. 30 in the wake of DOJ criticism. In Seattle, McGinn rethought his initial skepticism about the report in the face of public criticism and directed Diaz to begin carrying out some of the Justice Department's proposed changes.

In Arizona, however, the outspoken Maricopa County Sheriff Joe Arpaio is refusing the Justice Department's insistence for court supervision of changes in police and jail policies. "None of us agreed to allow a federal monitor to come remove my authority as the elected sheriff of Maricopa County," Arpaio declared on April 3. The government now has the option of going to federal court on its own to force changes. [4]

Holding police departments accountable to the law has been an intractable problem since the era of urban police departments began in the 1830s. [5] The 20th century saw a succession of efforts to reduce or eliminate police misconduct, starting with a movement to professionalize policing and continuing through the mid-century criminal-law revolution under Chief Justice Earl Warren.

In the decades since, civilian review boards or other independent auditing mechanisms have advanced from objects of fierce debate to structures viewed by police organizations themselves as "best practices." Congress in 1994 also gave the Justice Department a direct role in police reform by passing a law authorizing the federal government to sue state or local law enforcement agencies if it found a "pattern or practice" of violations of constitutional or federally protected rights.

The reforms have borne fruit in a general strengthening of policies and improved conduct by police officers in the nation's nearly 18,000 state or local law enforcement agencies nationwide. "We've seen a progressive improvement in the professionalism of law enforcement over the last 30 years," says Andrew Scott, a police consultant since his retirement as Boca Raton, Fla., police chief in 2006, after 30 years in law enforcement.

"Police departments have come a long way, both in terms of the officers and the leadership in policing," says Hubert Williams, president of the Police Foundation, a Washington-based research organization, and a former Newark, N.J., police chief.

Walker, a civil liberties-minded researcher on police practices and policies since the 1970s, agrees that police behavior has generally improved over the past few decades. But he says there is a continuing gap between the country's best and worst departments. "Some departments are taking up what I call the new accountability measures, moving forward, doing the right thing, and reducing misconduct," Walker says. "And there are some that slip back."

The New Orleans department, by common agreement, ranks low on those measures. "The New Orleans Police Department has never been a model of good behavior so to speak," says Marjorie Esman, executive director of the American Civil Liberties Union of Louisiana (ACLU-La.).

Killings of Arrestees by Police on Rise

From 2003 through 2009, law-enforcement officials committed 2,931 arrest-related killings, whether criminal or justifiable, of people in their custody. Some experts caution that the upward trend over the seven-year period may reflect improvements in data reporting.

Arrest-Related Killings by Law Enforcement Personnel, 2003-2009

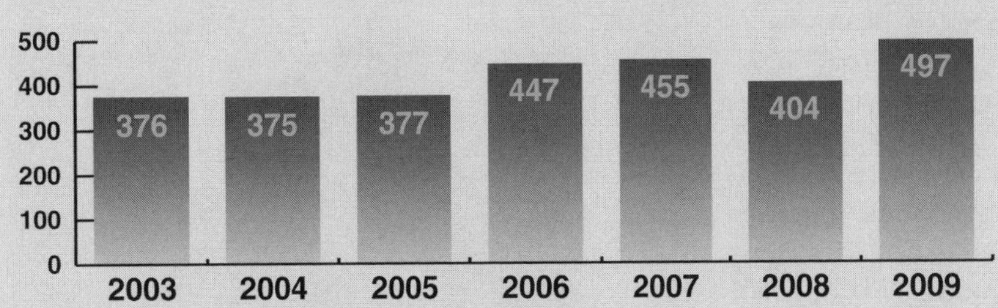

Source: Andrea M. Burch, "Arrest-Related Deaths, 2003-2009 — Statistical Tables," Bureau of Justice Statistics, U.S. Department of Justice, November 2011, p. 4, bjs.ojp.usdoj.gov/content/pub/pdf/ard0309st.pdf

Walker is even blunter: New Orleans is "everybody's candidate for the worst police department."

Far from fighting the Justice Department's findings, New Orleans superintendent Serpas joined the DOJ's civil rights chief Thomas Perez in the March 17, 2011, news conference to release the report. Serpas said it contained few surprises and went on to pledge improvement. "I am convinced we will be a world-class police department," he said. A week later, Serpas said many of the reforms were already being put into effect. [6]

The Justice Department launched its investigation in May 2010 at the request of the city's newly inaugurated mayor, Mitch Landrieu. The investigation came on top of ongoing federal prosecutions of officers implicated in the attempted cover-up of the shooting of six unarmed black civilians on the Danziger Bridge six days after Hurricane Katrina devastated the city in September 2005.

By May 2010, four officers had already pleaded guilty to obstruction-type charges in connection with the shooting. In addition to one other guilty plea, five officers were convicted in August 2011 on federal civil rights charges after a seven-week trial. U.S. District Court Judge Kurt Engelhardt imposed sentences ranging from 38 to 65 years on four of the five defendants after an emotional sentencing hearing on April 4; a fifth defendant drew a six-year term. One other defendant is awaiting a retrial, set to begin in May, after a mistrial in January. [7]

As in previous investigations, Justice Department lawyers are negotiating with New Orleans officials on possible reforms. The changes would be included in a consent decree to be overseen by a federal court for a specified period. The department has followed the same procedure since the mid-1990s in such major cities as Pittsburgh, Cincinnati, Detroit and Los Angeles.

A one-day roundtable with police officials, experts and others convened by the Justice Department in June 2010 concluded the procedure has been effective in reforming police department practices. Experts generally agree. "Departments have come out of this much better than they went in," says David Harris, a professor at the University of Pittsburgh School of Law.

Some of the officials at the roundtable, however, complained that the process creates a "negative stigma" that takes time for a department to overcome. [8]

As assistant attorney general for civil rights, Perez has pushed the "pattern or practice" process more vigorously than any of his predecessors. In addition to New Orleans, Perez personally attended news conferences to announce the reports in Seattle and Maricopa County. "When police officers cross the line, they need to be held accountable," Perez told *The Washington Post.* "Criminal prosecutions alone will not change the culture of a department." [9]

One of the supposed deterrents to police misconduct, however, is being weakened by the Supreme Court under Chief Justice John G. Roberts Jr., according to civil liberties advocates. The Roberts Court has issued three decisions in the past six years that somewhat narrow the exclusionary rule — the court-created doctrine that prohibits the use of evidence police find during illegal searches. (*See story, p. 312; "At Issue," p. 317.*)

Meanwhile, the New York City Police Department, the nation's largest, is under a national spotlight after news reports, particularly by The Associated Press, detailing the department's secret infiltration and surveillance of Muslim and some liberal groups as part of counterterrorism investigations. The AP stories, dating from summer 2011 and continuing, show that the department investigated hundreds of mosques and Muslim student groups and infiltrated dozens. City officials are defending the practice, but some Muslim leaders are calling for the resignation of Police Commissioner Raymond Kelly. [10]

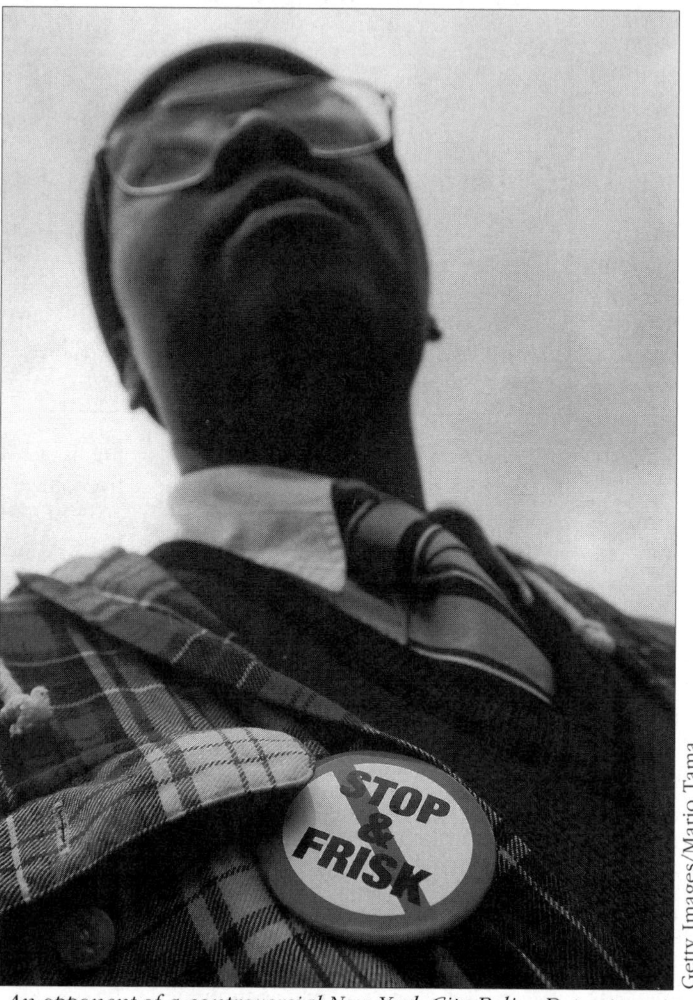

Getty Images/Mario Tama

An opponent of a controversial New York City Police Department "stop and frisk" policy marches in the Bronx borough on Jan. 27, 2012. The NYPD says the policy helps to prevent crime, but critics accuse the police of racial profiling and civil rights abuses. Out of 684,330 persons stopped by NYPD officers in 2011, the vast majority — 87 percent — were black or Hispanic.

The Justice Department investigations, coupled with the recurrent local controversies over police behavior, focus increased national attention on such issues as use of force, racial profiling and police accountability. Here are some of the arguments being heard as those issues are debated:

Should police do more to control excessive force?

John Williams was carrying a board and an open wood-carving knife at an intersection near Seattle's Pioneer Square on Aug. 30, 2010, when Police Sgt. Ian Birk spotted him, got out of his patrol car and ordered him to drop the knife. When the hearing-impaired Williams failed to respond, Birk fired four shots from about nine feet away. Williams, a fixture at the nearby social service center for Native Americans, died at the scene.

Williams' death added to long simmering concerns about use of force by Seattle police forces. Led by the ACLU of Washington State, a coalition of 34 community groups asked the Justice Department to investigate. The department's devastating report, released on Dec. 16, found routine violations of constitutional rights when force was used, with a small number of officers responsible for a disproportionate number of instances and with scant internal review of the incidents. "Seattle cannot control its own officers," says Jennifer Shaw, deputy director of the ACLU affiliate. [11]

Statistics are hard to come by, but experts appear to agree that police use force less frequently today than in the past. "Overall, it is less frequent than it was in the 1960s," says the Police Foundation's Williams. A study by the International Association of Chiefs of Police

(IACP), published in 2001, found that police used force 3.6 times per 10,000 service calls during the 1990s. Citing the IACP's and a more recent study, the National Institute of Justice, the Justice Department's research arm, concluded in 2011 that use of excessive force is "rare," even while conceding the difficulty of defining "excessive." [12]

As in Seattle, a small number of officers are typically found most likely to resort to force or to use excessive force in encounters with civilians. "The vast majority of officers do not engage in excessive use of force," says former chief Scott. "It is the small minority of officers who abuse their power."

The U.S. Supreme Court has given only limited guidance on use of force by police. The court ruled in 1985 that police can use deadly force when pursuing a fleeing suspect only if the suspect poses a significant threat of death or serious physical injury to the officer or others. In a broader ruling, the court held in 1989 that any use of force by an officer must be objectively reasonable. Factors to be considered include the severity of the crime, whether the suspect poses "an immediate safety threat" and whether the suspect is "actively resisting arrest" or attempting to escape. The court added that the "calculus of reasonableness" should take into account an officer's need to make "split-second judgments." [13]

"The legal standards are pretty loose," says Robert Kane, an associate professor at the University of Baltimore's School of Criminal Justice and co-author of a forthcoming book on police accountability issues. "There's a lot of gray in terms of trying to judge the appropriateness of force."

City governments are occasionally hit with five-, six- or even seven-figure damage awards in suits by victims of police beatings or shootings. As one dramatic example, Rodney King was awarded $3.8 million for the beating he suffered from Los Angeles police officers in 1991 after a high-speed car chase. Criminal prosecutions are more difficult. The King case ended in state court acquittals of four officers and a federal civil rights trial that ended with two convictions and two acquittals.

Internally, police departments appear to reject most citizen complaints of excessive force. In a recent study of eight local police departments, researchers at Michigan State University and Central

Police Handle Tense Situations in Steps

Most law enforcement agencies have policies that guide their use of force. Such policies describe an escalating series of actions an officer may take to resolve a situation. Officers are instructed to respond with a level of force appropriate to the situation. An officer may move from one part of the continuum to another in a matter of seconds.

A typical use-of-force continuum:

Officer Presence — No force is used. Considered the best way to resolve a situation.

- The mere presence of a law-enforcement officer works to deter crime or defuse a situation.
- Officers' attitudes are professional and nonthreatening.

Verbalization — Force is not physical.

- Officers issue calm, nonthreatening commands, such as "Let me see your identification and registration."
- Officers may increase their volume and shorten commands in an attempt to gain compliance. Short commands might include "Stop" or "Don't move."

Empty-Hand Control — Officers use bodily force to gain control of a situation.

- *Soft technique.* Officers use grabs, holds and joint locks to restrain an individual.
- *Hard technique.* Officers use punches and kicks to restrain an individual.

Less-Lethal Methods — Officers use less-lethal technologies to gain control of a situation.

- *Blunt impact.* Officers may use a baton or projectile to immobilize a combative person.
- *Chemical.* Officers may use chemical sprays or projectiles embedded with chemicals to restrain an individual. Pepper spray is an example.
- *Conducted Energy Devices (CEDs).* Officers may use a device such as a Taser to immobilize an individual. Such devices discharge a high-voltage, low-amperage jolt of electricity at a distance.

Lethal Force — Officers use lethal weapons to gain control of a situation. These should be used if a suspect poses a serious threat to an officer or other individual.

- Officers use deadly weapons such as firearms to stop an individual's actions.

Source: www.nij.gov/nij/topics/law-enforcement/officer-safety/use-of-force/continuum.htm

Half of Arrest-Related Killings Are of Minorities

More than half of the 2,958 people who were killed while under arrest from 2003 through 2009 were black or Hispanic. Whites comprised 42 percent of the total. All but 27 of the deaths were at the hands of law enforcement officers.*

Racial Origin of Those Killed While Under Arrest, 2003-2009

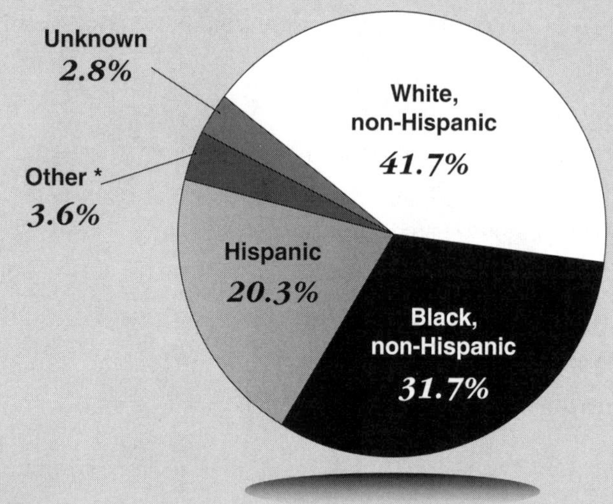

** Includes American Indians, Alaska Natives, Asians, Native Hawaiians, other Pacific Islanders and persons of two or more races.*

Figures do not total 100 because of rounding.

Source: Andrea M. Burch, "Arrest-Related Deaths, 2003-2009 — Statistical Tables," Bureau of Justice Statistics, U.S. Department of Justice, November 2011, p. 6, bjs.ojp.usdoj.gov/content/pub/pdf/ard0309st.pdf

Florida University found that six took no action on at least 90 percent of the complaints during the two-year period studied. Only three officers were suspended and one terminated because of use-of-force complaints during the period. [14]

The IACP's model policy on use of force largely restates the general guidelines from the Supreme Court, with added advisories against firing warning shots or shooting at a moving vehicle. Many departments provide more detailed guidance, including a so-called use of force continuum that correlates the level of force to be used with the suspect's level of resistance or threat to safety. (*See graphic, p. 307.*)

Walker says policies and training are the keys to reducing excessive force by police. "If you have a bad use-of-force incident, it's a mistake to focus on the officer because the underlying cause is some failure by the department: lack of proper training or lack of proper supervision," he says.

Should police do more to prevent racial and ethnic profiling?

Many studies over the past two decades have shown that African-American and Hispanic drivers are more likely to be stopped for traffic enforcement than white motorists. In a mammoth journalistic project, the *Hartford Courant* took the issue one step further earlier this year by analyzing what happened in Connecticut to drivers after they were stopped by local police.

The newspaper's analysis of more than 100,000 traffic stops found that blacks and Hispanics were far more likely to get a citation than whites stopped for the same offense. As one example, blacks were twice as likely and Hispanics four times as likely to be ticketed for improper taillights as whites stopped for the same reason. "This is beyond profiling," Glenn A. Cassis, executive director of the state's African-American Affairs Commission, told the newspaper. "This goes to actually a level of discrimination, and who gets the wink and who doesn't get the wink." [15]

The Justice Department's recent reports found similar evidence of racial or ethnic profiling in New Orleans, Maricopa County and East Haven. In New Orleans, investigators found that police shot 27 civilians during a 16-month period, all of them African-Americans. In Maricopa County, Latino drivers were four to nine times more likely to be subjected to traffic stops than similarly situated non-Latino drivers. In East Haven, Latinos make up about 10 percent of the population, but accounted for nearly 20 percent of traffic stops. [16]

The tensions between police departments, historically predominantly white, and African-American and Hispanic communities are of long standing. The U.S. Supreme Court's initial decision, in 1936, limiting police conduct during interrogations came in the case of three black tenant farmers who confessed to murder only after being tortured. Los Angeles police tacitly abetted white servicemen attacking Latinos in the "Zoot Suit" riots in 1943. The Kerner Commission report on urban riots of the 1960s listed the "deep hostility between police and ghetto communities as a primary cause of the disorders."

Racial profiling advanced to the top of the national agenda in the mid- and late-1990s — as seen in the popularizing of the grimly ironic phrase "driving while black." In litigation that documented the experiences of many African-Americans, ACLU affiliates in several states filed suits contesting the practice. Some states, including Connecticut, responded by passing laws requiring demographic statistics-gathering on traffic stops to try to spot signs of racial profiling.

Racial and ethnic profiling appears to be continuing despite increasing diversity on local police forces. The New Orleans police force is now majority black. In New York City, a majority of the police officers are black, Latino or Asian; whites comprise only 47 percent. Out of 684,330 persons stopped by NYPD officers in 2011, however, the vast majority — 87 percent — were either black or Hispanic. [17]

Harris, the Pittsburgh law professor and author of a book on racial profiling, says the practice "is a police issue, not a race issue." Profiling, he says, "is a product of the training, culture and customs within that department. Black officers are going to be trained like all others. They're going to want to fit in just like all officers."

Other experts say profiling results naturally from the demographics of crime. "This is a social issue," says the University of Baltimore's Kane. "We know that race and class are strongly tied up with crime, perceptions of crime and urban disorder. Crime and race are not randomly distributed across America."

"It is a problem, and it will continue to be a problem," says police consultant Scott. "But it may not be extending from a police officer's bigotry. If you have a particular segment of the community that is particularly involved in a particular crime, part of the profiling has to be the ethnicity of the offender."

Identifying impermissible profiling can also be difficult, Scott adds. "It may be insidiously nontransparent as to why an officer has stopped a particular individual," he says. In its report on East Haven, the Justice Department accused the force of "intentionally and woefully failing to design and implement internal systems of control that would identify, track, and prevent such misconduct." The report on Maricopa County faulted Sheriff Arpaio by name for using "unverified tips or complaints" that were "infected with bias against Latino persons."

Police Foundation president Williams says the responsibility for stopping the practice rests with police officials. "Are chiefs dealing with the problem?" he asks rhetorically. "I think they have policies that prohibit it, and from that perspective they're dealing with it. It's the enforcement of those policies that's the big question mark. In that area, there's more of a question mark."

Should police adopt stronger disciplinary measures for misconduct?

Jason Mucha has had a checkered career with the Milwaukee Police Department since being hired as an aide in 1996 while still a teenager. He was promoted to sergeant in 2005, but over the next few years was accused by 10 different suspects of either beating them or planting drugs or both. Although he was never disciplined, a state appeals court explicitly questioned Mucha's credibility as a witness, and the U.S. attorney's office dropped one case rather than put him on the stand.

The department's disciplinary procedure has now caught up with Mucha, however, after he and fellow squad members were accused of invasive body searches in drug investigations. Mucha and seven officers in his unit were stripped of police powers and reassigned to desk duties in March because of the accusations, according to the *Journal Sentinel.* Without confirming the report, Chief Edward Flynn told a news conference on March 22 that if the allegations were true, the searches would have violated state law. [18]

The *Journal Sentinel* has been on the department's case over discipline for years. A three-part series in October 2011 criticized the department for allowing "at least" 93 officers to remain on the force despite offenses such as drunken driving and domestic violence. A similar, nine-part series by the *Sarasota Herald Tribune* in December found that "thousands" of officers remain on the job in Florida police departments despite "arrests or evidence" implicating them in crimes punishable by prison sentences. [19]

Despite such newspaper investigations, some experts give police departments generally good marks for disciplining rogue cops. "Internal discipline is taken seriously by most if not all American police departments," the University of Baltimore's Kane says. "Police commanders and departments can often determine that a police officer is not good for the department and not good for the public."

Police Foundation president Williams gives a mixed review. "Some police departments are very good at discipline — a lot, not just a few," he says. "But I wouldn't want to say that all police departments are like that."

ACLU officials are more critical. "We have found problems with internal disciplinary procedures around the country," says Vanita Gupta, deputy legal director for the national ACLU. "To say that they are an adequate remedy for these violations is a real problem. It's just not how it plays out."

The disciplinary procedures that exist today are the culmination of decades of pressure from outside groups — in particular, groups such as the ACLU and other civil rights organizations — for more effective oversight of police practices in general and in specific cases. "Some form of citizen oversight exists in almost every city," according to the University of Nebraska's Walker.

In contrast to civilian review boards — perhaps the most common oversight mechanism — Walker says he prefers the appointment of an independent auditor for a department. "They have authority to review the operations of an agency and to make public reports," Walker explains. "That's the best solution for improving the department, not just finding guilt or innocence in a particular incident."

Roger Goldman, a professor at St. Louis University School of Law who has specialized in police accountability issues, notes that even when an officer has been removed from a force, he or she often looks for — and sometimes finds — a job with another law enforcement agency. To remedy the problem, Goldman favors a system of "decertifying" an officer for any police work after a finding of misconduct — akin to disbarment for lawyers, for example. "The problem can't be left up to local municipalities and police departments to handle," he says.

Police consultant Scott says police unions represent a big obstacle to strengthened discipline. "The unions can protect the incompetent, and the malicious, and allow them to get back on the streets," Scott says. "The unions have lost their way as to who they're supposed to represent in the bigger picture of law enforcement."

Other experts, however, stress the role of leadership at the top in improving discipline. "What you've got to have," says Williams, "is commitment at the highest levels of the department." The ACLU's Gupta agrees. "We know and police experts know how to implement best practices in this area," she says. "There are best practices out there, but there still remains a lot of work to be done." ■

BACKGROUND

Police Problems

Police misconduct has been a persistent problem since full-time police forces were first organized in the United States in the mid-19th century. Political patronage and financial corruption were dominant concerns in the 1800s; use of force and other coercive tactics and racial and ethnic discrimination became major issues in the 1900s. A reform movement to professionalize policing dates from the early 20th century. The Supreme Court began to exercise oversight by the 1930s and then brought about significant changes in police practices with decisions in the 1960s establishing new limits on interrogations and searches. [20]

The constables and night watches of the colonial and early post-independence years proved inadequate for law enforcement by the mid-19th century. The emergence of urban centers brought with it the breakdown of law and order due to interethnic clashes, economic discontent and conflict over political issues, including slavery. Philadelphia and Boston created police forces in the 1830s — not long after Sir Robert Peel in 1829 had created the first urban police force in London, England. New York City followed in 1845.

The 19th century officer was typically unarmed and untrained, inefficient and largely ineffective in preventing crime. He was likely chosen on the basis of political patronage and afforded no job security.* Corruption was "epidemic," according to a textbook by the University of Nebraska's Walker and Arizona State University professor of criminology Charles Katz, but reform efforts typically consisted merely of replacing supporters of one political faction with those of another. And "no attention" was given to the two issues that would dominate the 20th century: excessive force and racial discrimination. [21]

More serious reform efforts began in the early 20th century as part of Progressive Era movements to replace spoils-system, moneyed-interest politics with popular democracy and professional government services. Walker and Katz credit August Vollmer, chief of the Berkeley, Calif., police force from 1905 to 1932, as the father of the movement to define policing as a profession. He created college-level courses in police work and, along with other reformers, favored raising standards for hiring officers, eliminating political influence and placing control in the hands of qualified administrators.

But police reform "progressed very slowly," Walker and Katz write. And in 1931 Vollmer co-authored a critical report by the presidentially appointed National Commission on Law Observance and Enforcement, commonly called the Wickersham Commission. Among its findings: Physical brutality was "extensively practiced" by police departments around the country.

The Supreme Court first entered the field in 1936 with a unanimous decision, *Brown v. Mississippi*, declaring the use of confessions obtained by torture-like interrogation to be a violation of the Due Process Clause. Over the next three decades, the court adopted a case-by-case approach that barred confessions if induced by either physical or psychological coercion.

By the 1960s, the court saw the need to adopt a stronger, preventive safeguard. The result was the controversial but now largely accepted decision, *Miranda v. Arizona* (1966), which required police to advise a suspect of his or her rights, including the right to remain silent, before any custodial interrogation — that is, any interrogation during which the suspect is not free to leave. Five years earlier, in *Mapp v. Ohio* (1961), the court had established another landmark limitation on police conduct by requiring states to enforce the exclusionary rule, which bars the use of evidence obtained by police during an unconstitutional search or arrest. [22]

Continued on p. 312

* Chicago is now believed to have hired the first female officer in 1891; Portland, Ore., followed in 1905, Los Angeles in 1910.

Chronology

1960s Supreme Court lays down rules for police searches, interrogation.

1961
Supreme Court says states must adopt exclusionary rule to bar use of evidence found by police during unconstitutional searches (*Mapp v. Ohio*).

1966
Supreme Court requires police to advise suspects of rights before in-custody interrogation (*Miranda v. Arizona*).

1968
National Advisory Commission on Civil Disorders (Kerner Commission) report says distrust between police and "ghetto communities" was major cause of urban riots. . . . Law Enforcement Assistance Administration is established to provide federal grants to state, local law enforcement agencies; in 14-year lifetime, agency promotes accreditation standards, provides funds for officer training.

1990s Justice Department gains power to investigate state, local law enforcement agencies.

1991, 1992
Videotaped beating of Rodney King by Los Angeles police officers provokes debate over use of force, leads to riots in African-American neighborhoods after officers are prosecuted but acquitted.

1994
Congress authorizes Justice Department (DOJ) to investigate state, local law enforcement agencies for "pattern or practice" of violations of constitutional or statutory rights (42 U.S.C. § 14141).

Mid- to late '90s
Justice Department uses new law to get Pittsburgh and Steubenville, Ohio, police departments to agree to reforms; launches investigations in other cities, including Washington, D.C.

1999, 2000
Los Angeles Police Department is rocked by disclosures of corruption, excessive force by antigang unit in predominantly Latino Rampart neighborhood; Justice Department, city agree in 2000 on reforms, court supervision.

2001-Present Bush administration pulls back on police department investigations; Obama administration takes aggressive stance.

2003
Detroit agrees to institute police reforms after investigation initiated in December 2000.

2005
Two African-American civilians killed, four others wounded by New Orleans police officers while crossing Danziger Bridge to flee post-Katrina flooding.

2006
Supreme Court allows use of evidence found in Detroit drug raid despite officers' failure to follow knock-and-announce rule (*Hudson v. Michigan*); first of Roberts Court rulings weakening enforcement of exclusionary rule.

2009
Eric Holder is named first African-American attorney general; chooses Thomas Perez to head Justice Department's civil rights division.

2010
Roundtable convened by Justice Department finds police investigations "effective" in promoting reform; some police officials complain of "negative stigma."

2011
Justice Department report sharply criticizes New Orleans Police Department for excessive force, discriminatory policing; police chief promises reforms (March 17). . . . Five New Orleans officers are convicted in federal civil rights trial in Danziger Bridge case (Aug. 5); five others had pleaded guilty earlier. . . . DOJ report lambasts Puerto Rico Police Department for excessive force, other issues (Sept. 7). . . . Three more DOJ reports fault police in Maricopa County (Phoenix), Ariz.; Seattle; East Haven, Conn. (Dec. 15, 16, 19).

2012
East Haven Police Chief Leonard Gallo retires (Jan. 30). . . . African-American teenager Trayvon Martin is shot and killed by neighborhood watch coordinator George Zimmerman in Sanford, Fla. (Feb. 26); death touches off debate over authorities' failure to arrest Zimmerman, Florida law easing rule on self defense. . . . Seattle mayor, police chief adopt plan to revise use-of-force policies, review racial profiling (March 29). . . . Puerto Rico Police Chief Emilio Díaz Cólon resigns to avoid hurting reforms (March 29). . . . Maricopa County Sheriff Joe Arpaio rejects Justice Department demand for court-supervised consent decree (April 3). . . . Justice Department weighs requests for formal investigations of police in Albuquerque, Omaha, elsewhere.

Supreme Court Eases Rules on Police Searches

Evidence gleaned illegally allowed in criminal trials.

Detroit police officers thought they were raiding a big crack-cocaine house when they converged, seven strong, on Booker Hudson's home on the afternoon of Aug. 27, 1998. Wary of being shot, Officer Jamal Good shouted, "Police. Search warrant," and then paused only a moment before barging in.

Good's nearly instantaneous entry violated a Supreme Court decision issued three years earlier, in *Wilson v. Arkansas*, that imposed a so-called knock-and-announce rule requiring police to wait a reasonable period after the initial knock before entering a private home.

When Hudson was tried on cocaine charges, he sought to exclude the evidence that police found in their search: five individually wrapped "rocks" of crack cocaine that he had in his pants pockets. Michigan courts refused, and so did the U.S. Supreme Court — in the first of three decisions under Chief Justice John G. Roberts Jr. that critics say have seriously weakened the so-called exclusionary rule against using evidence found during an illegal police search. (*See "At Issue," p. 317.*)

Writing for the majority in *Hudson v. Michigan* (2006), Justice Antonin Scalia said the costs of applying the exclusionary rule to knock-and-announce violations in terms of releasing criminals would outweigh any benefits in terms of protecting privacy or deterring improper police behavior. As one reason, Scalia pointed to what he called the "substantial" existing deterrents to police violations of search rules.

David Moran, then a Wayne State University law professor who represented Hudson before the Supreme Court, sharply disagreed. "It's a joke to say that the police will comply with the knock-and-announce rule without the exclusionary rule as a sanction," he said. [1]

The exclusionary rule, a distinctively U.S. legal doctrine, dates from a 1914 Supreme Court ruling applying it to federal court cases. The Supreme Court forced the same rule on state courts in 1961 in one of the first decisions under Chief Justice Earl Warren that expanded the rights of suspects and criminal defendants. The court trimmed but did not eliminate the rule under the next two chief justices, Warren E. Burger and William H. Rehnquist.

Supporters of the exclusionary rule, criminal defense attorneys and civil liberties advocates among others, echo Moran's view that the only effective deterrent to police misconduct in conducting searches is to exclude the evidence from trial. Critics say there are other deterrents, including police disciplinary procedures and civil damage suits.

As a White House lawyer under President Ronald Reagan, Roberts helped lay the basis for a series of attacks aimed at either amending or abolishing the exclusionary rule. Now, as chief justice, Roberts leads a five-vote conservative majority that critics say is transforming those broadsides into legal precedent. [2]

The *Hudson* case came in Roberts' first full term as chief justice. Three years later, Roberts wrote for the same 5-4 majority in a second decision cutting back on the exclusionary rule. The decision in *Herring v. United States* (2009) allowed the use of evidence that an Alabama man was carrying when he was arrested in 2004 on the basis of what was later found to be an outdated arrest warrant. Roberts said the exclusionary rule applies only to police conduct that is "sufficiently deliberate that exclusion can meaningfully deter it, and sufficiently culpable that such deterrence is worth the price paid by the justice system." [3]

In a third decision, the court in June 2011 held that the exclusionary rule does not require suppression of evidence obtained by police if they relied in good faith on an established court precedent, even if it was later overruled as violating the Fourth Amendment's protections against unreasonable searches and seizures (*Davis v. United States*). In January, however, the court gave defense lawyers and civil liberties advocates a significant victory by limiting the authority of police to attach a GPS tracking device to a vehicle for surveillance purposes. The unanimous ruling in *United States v. Jones* apparently requires police to get a search warrant unless they can show a reason for an exception. [4]

— ***Kenneth Jost***

[1] Account taken from Kenneth Jost, *The Supreme Court Yearbook 2005-2006*.

[2] See Adam Liptak, "Justices Step Closer to Repeal of Evidence Ruling," *The New York Times*, Jan. 31, 2009, p. A1.

[3] See Kenneth Jost, *The Supreme Court Yearbook 2008-2009*.

[4] For coverage, see Adam Liptak, "Justices Reject GPS Tracking in a Drug Case," *The New York Times*, Jan. 24, 2012, p. A1.

Continued from p. 310

The 1960s also saw agreement between Congress and the president to increase the federal role in professionalizing state and local police agencies. Since the 1930s, the FBI had been allowing local police officers to enroll in what was originally called the FBI Training School, now the FBI National Academy, in Quantico, Va. In 1968, Congress created, as part of the Omnibus Crime Control and Safe Streets Act, a new agency to support state and local law enforcement: the Law Enforcement Assistance Administration (LEAA).

In its 14 years of existence, LEAA funneled about $8 billion in grants to state and local police agencies. It was abolished in 1982, unpopular in Congress and among some experts, in part because of a penchant for funding expensive gadgetry. But it also is credited with helping establish standards for police and corrections agencies and with providing funds for training state and local police officers.

"LEAA was the catalyst that promoted the education of police officers by creating a significant amount of money for police officers to get educated," Police Foundation president Williams says today. [23]

Police Accountability

Despite widely acknowledged improvements in professionalism and accountability, major police departments around the country were beset by high-profile scandals during the final decades of the 20th century. Major controversies in New York City and Los Angeles resulted in the formation of blue-ribbon commissions that recommended significant changes, some eventually adopted. In Washington, Congress laid the foundation for increased police accountability with two legislative enactments: the 1994 provision authorizing Justice Department suits against rights-violating police departments and a 2000 provision requiring data collection on arrest-related deaths.

Financial corruption of the sort widespread in earlier eras continued as a recurrent issue. In the most dramatic episode, New York City police detective Frank Serpico blew the whistle on widespread bribery and extortion in the NYPD in a newspaper expose in 1970 and a year later as a witness before the blue-ribbon Knapp Commission. [24] The city's response to the commission's recommendations for internal reforms was criticized as timid. Two decades later, however, Mayor Rudy Giuliani established a standing independent commission to combat police corruption. Today, critics in New York continue to highlight allegations of misconduct, but the commission credits the department's Internal Affairs Bureau generally with "thorough and diligent investigations" of accusations. [25]

In the 1990s, the Los Angeles Police Department experienced two major scandals, each of which made national headlines. In the first, an onlooker captured on videotape the seemingly unjustified beating of an African-American suspect, Rodney King, by LAPD officers on the night of March 3, 1991, after a high-speed automobile chase. The blue-ribbon Christopher Commission created in the wake of the incident found that "a significant number" of officers repetitively used excessive force against suspects. The acquittals of the officers charged in the King beating in 1992 touched off riots in the city's largely African-American neighborhoods and helped force the resignation of Police Chief Daryl Gates. He was succeeded by Willie Williams, the LAPD's first African-American chief.

The King beating also led to the federal law authorizing the Justice Department to sue local police departments for rights violations. Members of Congress from California pushed the proposal unsuccessfully in 1991 and 1992; it was enacted in 1994 as a provision in the omnibus Violent Crime Control and Law Enforcement Act, thanks in part to a push from then-Senate Judiciary Committee Chairman Joseph Biden. Despite its later importance, the provision attracted little attention. A detailed Justice Department fact sheet on the law failed to mention the provision.

By 1996, however, the department's civil rights division was beginning to use the new powers with investigations initiated in response to citizen complaints of police departments in Pittsburgh and Steubenville, Ohio. By the end of the decade, those cases had resulted in consent decrees requiring organizational changes. Nine other investigations were pending as the decade ended, including one in Washington, D.C., requested in 1999 by a new chief of police.

The department had already investigated the Los Angeles Police Department for three years when a new scandal erupted in 1999, featuring wide-ranging excessive force, corruption and obstruction of justice accusations against members of an antigang unit assigned to one of Los Angeles' predominantly Latino communities. The wide-ranging allegations of misconduct by Rampart Division officers included unprovoked shootings and beatings, planting of evidence, stealing and dealing in narcotics and covering up of the offenses. The scandal led to disciplinary actions against 58 officers, but an independent commission later criticized the department's response as inadequate.

The Justice Department intensified its investigation of the LAPD after the scandal. By mid-2000, government lawyers were threatening to sue the city in federal court unless it agreed to wide-ranging internal reforms. Mayor Richard Riordan resisted any agreement, but painstaking negotiations eventually resulted in the city's agreement to an enforceable consent decree that the city council approved by a vote of 11-2 on Nov. 2, 2000. Among other provisions, the agreement required creation of a new division to investigate all uses of force. The decree, formally entered in June 2001, was terminated in 2009. [26]

Meanwhile, Congress gave the federal government an additional tool for police accountability by passing the Death in Custody Reporting Act to collect data on deaths of inmates in prisons and jails and of suspects in police custody. The bill was approved by voice vote in the House of Representatives in June 2000 and by the Senate in September; President Bill Clinton signed it into law on Oct. 13. After setting up procedures, the Bureau of Justice Statistics began collecting reports on police-custody deaths in fiscal 2003.

Changing Priorities

The Justice Department's oversight of local law enforcement agencies lagged under President George W. Bush. Investigations and cases already initiated were

Florida Police Under Scrutiny in Trayvon Martin Case

Critics question handling of shooting by armed civilian.

The fatal shooting of an African-American teenager by a volunteer neighborhood watch coordinator in a gated suburban community in Florida has ignited a racially charged debate over the police department's handling of the case. The episode also puts a national spotlight on Florida's controversial Stand Your Ground law, which allows a civilian to use potentially lethal force in self-defense in public places without first trying to retreat to safety. [1]

Some six weeks after the Feb. 26 death of Trayvon Martin, a special state prosecutor is set to present evidence in the case on April 10 to a Seminole County grand jury. [*Update*: Special prosecutor Angela Corey announced on April 9 that the case would not be presented to the grand jury on April 10, but specified that the investigation was continuing.] The U.S. Justice Department is also reviewing the case. The moves have come, however, only after local and national protests over the authorities' decision that night not to file charges against George Zimmerman, a neighborhood watch volunteer since August 2011.

Martin, 17, was returning from a convenience store to the home of his father's girlfriend in the Retreat at Twin Lakes community in Sanford, Fla., shortly after 7 p.m. when he drew Zimmerman's suspicions. Martin was unarmed; he was carrying a bag of candy and a can of iced tea and wearing a gray hoodie to protect himself from the rain. Zimmerman, 28, a resident of white and Hispanic ancestry, was carrying a 9 mm handgun — despite earlier instructions from the Sanford police department's neighborhood watch liaison that volunteers should not be armed.

Zimmerman had volunteered for the neighborhood watch in August 2011 because of several burglaries in the gated community of some 260 homes. Suspicious of Martin, he placed a 911 call to the Sanford Police Department. Zimmerman said Martin was "just walking around" and appeared to be "up to no good." The police dispatcher advised Zimmerman not to follow Martin and to wait to meet a patrol officer. Later in the recorded four-minute call, Zimmerman is heard saying something listed on the police transcription as "unintelligible" and interpreted by others in the subsequent debate as a racial epithet.

An altercation of some sort ensued after Zimmerman — 5-foot-10, 170 pounds — got out of his vehicle and Martin — 6-foot-1, 150 pounds — realized he was being surveilled. An unidentified girlfriend of Martin's says Martin called her to complain about being followed. Zimmerman's father says his son told police that Martin challenged him, used a racial epithet, forced him to the ground and pummeled him with his fists.

Whatever the exact course of the dispute, Zimmerman fired a single shot that hit Martin in the chest. Martin died at the scene. The police officers who arrived handcuffed Zimmerman and took him to the police station, where he was questioned and released without having been tested for drugs or alcohol. A video appears to show a gash on the back of Zimmerman's head but no serious injury to his face despite Zimmerman's claim to have suffered a broken nose during the altercation. A funeral director who examined Martin's body said it showed no scrapes, bruises or other signs of a fight other than the single gunshot wound to his chest.

Martin's death drew no news coverage for almost two weeks until his father, Tracy Martin, held a news conference on March 8 to call for Zimmerman's arrest and demand the release of the tapes of Zimmerman's 911 call. The tapes, released over the next weekend, turned the episode from an overlooked local story into a round-the-clock nationwide controversy.

In the weeks since, Martin has been described as a typical teenage boy, with good manners and good attitude, but a record of three suspensions from his high school in north Miami-Dade County, where he lived with his mother. In February, he was staying with his father in Sanford after having been hit with a 10-day suspension because of marijuana residue found in his backpack.

continued, but reports on newly opened investigations took a deferential tone toward police policies. Obama's selection of civil rights-minded officials for key posts at the Justice Department signaled a likely change in priorities. Even before Perez's confirmation to head the civil rights division, the special litigation section's report on one local department took a sharper tone than those in the Bush years. By the end of 2011, the section's activist stance was evident with a record number of investigations open and stinging reports issued on five law enforcement bodies within four months.

As a presidential candidate in 2000, Bush said he believed police matters should be handled locally. Under Bush, the civil rights division became highly politicized, morale declined sharply and career lawyers left in droves. A later report by the Government Accountability Office found that the special litigation section suffered an attrition rate of 31 percent in 2005, 24 percent in 2006 and 18 percent in 2007. [27]

The special litigation section had achieved important victories early in the Bush years in investigations begun by the Clinton administration of police forces in Washington, D.C.; Detroit; and Prince George's County, Md. The investigation in Washington found "a pattern . . . of excessive force" by officers in the 1990s and applauded new efforts to reduce the problem. Police officials agreed to the appointment of a monitor to oversee the department for five years. In Detroit, a consent decree agreed to in

Zimmerman is described as a former altar boy with unrealized ambitions of becoming a police officer, capable of kindness but also with a volatile temper. He was arrested in summer 2005 after pushing a Florida state alcohol agent during a raid at a college-area bar; the charge was dropped after Zimmerman agreed to a pretrial diversion program. A month later, he and his ex-fiancée obtained reciprocal domestic violence injunctions based on mutual accusations of physical violence.

AFP/Getty Images/Joe Klamar

Protesters in downtown Los Angeles mark the one-month anniversary of the Feb. 26, 2012, killing of unarmed black teenager Trayvon Martin by a neighborhood watch volunteer in Florida.

From the outset, authorities in Sanford and Seminole County explained that Zimmerman had not been charged in the shooting in part because of a law Florida enacted in 2005 making it harder to prosecute individuals in the face of a claim of self-defense. The Stand Your Ground law extends the long-established "castle doctrine" — allowing the use of deadly force in self defense inside one's home — to any setting, private or public.

In its central provision, the 1,000-word statute provides that someone in a place where he or she has a right to be "has no duty to retreat and has the right to stand his or her ground and meet force with force, including deadly force if he or she reasonably believes it is necessary to do so to prevent death or great bodily harm to himself or herself or another or to prevent the commission of a forcible felony." The law specifically provides immunity from criminal or civil liability if the use of force is justified. [2]

Similar laws are on the books in about half the states. Coverage of the Florida episode has led to a national debate over the laws. Prosecutors in Florida said the law had made it harder to bring charges in homicides where the suspect claimed self-defense. Police organizations have criticized the laws, but gun-rights groups have defended them.

Only after a full month had passed since the shooting was it reported that Sanford Detective Chris Serino, the lead investigator in the case, had initially recommended charging Zimmerman with manslaughter only to be overruled by his chief and by state's attorney Norman Wolfinger, who has declined to comment on the report. Wolfinger was removed from the case after Gov. Rick Scott and Attorney General Pamela Bondi appointed Angela Corey, the state's attorney from the Jacksonville area, as special prosecutor.

— Kenneth Jost

---

[1] For a comprehensive overview, see Dan Barry, Serge F. Kovaleski, Campbell Robertson and Lizette Alvarez, "In the Eye of a Firestorm: In Florida, an Intersection of Tragedy, Race and Outrage," *The New York Times*, April 2, 2012, p. A1, www.nytimes.com/2012/04/02/us/trayvon-martin-shooting-prompts-a-review-of-ideals.html?_r=1&hp. The rapidly changing, heavily annotated Wikipedia entry on the case includes links to the 911 call made on the night of Trayvon Martin's shooting, to other police documents and to collections of news and commentary in *The New York Times* and *Wall Street Journal*, http://en.wikipedia.org/wiki/Shooting_of_Trayvon_Martin. Background details drawn from both accounts.

[2] See Title XLVI, Chap. 0776, www.flsenate.gov/Laws/Statutes/2011/Chapter 0776/All.

June 2003 similarly provided for an outside monitor to check compliance with changes that included new steps to track officers named in excessive-force complaints. In Prince George's County in suburban Washington, D.C., the police agreed in January 2004 to curb excessive force by officers and restrict the use of police dogs, with compliance to be tracked by an outside monitor. [28]

In later years, however, reports on police departments appeared to steer clear of pointed criticism or threats of litigation. Instead, reports, such as one in August 2008 suggesting the Orange County (Fla.) Sheriff's Office adopt new policies on the use of Tasers, generally included language specifying that the "technical assistance" being provided was viewed "as recommendations and not mandates." [29]

Obama's appointment of Eric Holder as the first African-American to serve as attorney general signaled a likely reinvigoration of the Justice Department's role in civil rights enforcement, including police-accountability investigations. As deputy attorney general in the Clinton administration, Holder had helped oversee police department investigations, including the filing of the suit against the Los Angeles Police Department in 2000. To head the civil rights division, Obama and Holder picked Perez, a former criminal prosecutor in the division from 1988 to 1995 who had gone on to hold political posts as deputy to the head of the division (1998-1999) and head of the Office of Civil Rights in the

Department of Health and Human Services (1999-2001). Perez drew Republican opposition because of his work with the immigrant rights group CASA de Maryland, but eventually won Senate confirmation on Oct. 6, 2009, by a vote of 72-22. [30]

Even before Perez took office, a slight change of tone was seen in the section's report on the Yonkers, N.Y., police department. The June 2009 report included the same "not a mandate" language used in earlier reports, but followed with a sentence "strongly" urging the department to adopt the recommendations listed. A report on the Inglewood, Calif., department issued in December "strongly" urged adoption of the recommended changes.

Stronger reports came in quick succession in 2011, beginning with the one on New Orleans in March. A report on Puerto Rico, issued on Sept. 7, found a pattern of "unreasonable force" along with "other misconduct" aimed at limiting free speech rights as well as "troubling evidence" of "discriminatory policing practices" targeting persons of Dominican descent. In releasing the report, Perez told reporters that the section had 17 investigations under way. The investigations are "really a cornerstone of our work," Perez said. Three months later, he elevated the issue further by personally attending December news conferences releasing the Seattle and Maricopa County reports. [31] ■

CURRENT SITUATION

Investigations Urged

With 20 investigations already under way, the Justice Department is being urged by citizen groups in several other cities to look into police departments with troubling records of fatal shootings and other uses of force against arrestees and suspects.

In the most recent request, the Omahans for Justice Alliance asked the Justice Department and U.S. Attorney Deborah Gilg on March 13 to investigate the Omaha Police Department. The 10-page letter cited an alleged pattern of excessive force, illegal arrests, disregard of state law and department polices and other misconduct.

"The kind of incidents that we've had are very, very serious and appear to get worse," University of Nebraska professor Walker, one of three co-signers of the letter, said at a news conference to announce the request. Supporting organizations include the ACLU of Nebraska, Nebraskans for Peace, Black Men United of Omaha, the NAACP's Omaha Branch and the Progressive Research Institute of Nebraska. [32]

In a prepared statement, Lt. Darci Tierney, a police spokeswoman, noted that the Justice Department had previously reviewed use-of-force incidents as part of "normal business practices." She voiced no objection to scrutiny of the additional incidents noted in the letter. "We strive to be a transparent agency, and if a citizen group feels the need for the Department of Justice to review these events, we welcome the review," Tierney said. [33]

Also in March, an Albuquerque citizens' group stepped up its calls for a federal investigation of the city's police department after two fatal shootings in mid-March brought the total to 18 over the past two years. Most of those killed have been young Hispanic men, according to Jewell Hall, executive director of the Martin Luther King Jr. Memorial Center. "I hope that they will do an investigation to get deep inside the Albuquerque Police Department," says Hall, a retired teacher.

The Albuquerque department drew national attention with the disclosure that the police union has had a practice for several years of giving officers involved in fatal shootings $500 to help them take time off to recover from stress related to the incidents. Critics said the payments appeared to be a bounty for killing a suspect. Police Chief Ray Schultz said he was unaware of the practice. With the controversy raging, two top officers of the Albuquerque Peace Officers Association resigned on March 27; their successors joined Schultz and Mayor Richard Berry on March 30 in announcing an end to the practice. [34]

Walker, who co-authored a study of the Albuquerque police department in 1997, says the number of deaths at the hands of police appeared to warrant a Justice Department investigation. "That's a lot of shootings," he told The Associated Press. [35]

The Justice Department has acknowledged the preliminary inquiry into the Albuquerque department but says it has made no decision on whether to open a formal investigation. The Justice Department had no response to the Omaha request in news coverage immediately afterward. Investigations are being sought in other cities, including Las Vegas, The Associated Press reported. Justice Department officials did not respond to a request from *CQ Researcher* for a complete list of current investigations.

In both Omaha and Albuquerque, the groups pressing for federal investigations complained that civilians involved in police shootings or use-of-force incidents were predominantly people of color. The Omaha group also cited figures from a state commission showing that black drivers are stopped almost as often by the Omaha Police Department as white drivers are.

Both forces are predominantly white. In 2000, about 80 percent of the Omaha officers were white, and the Albuquerque department was 60 percent Anglo and 36 percent Hispanic, according to federal Bureau of Justice Statistics data. [36]

Continued on p. 318

At Issue:

Is the exclusionary rule needed to deter illegal police searches?

NORMAN L REIMER
EXECUTIVE DIRECTOR, NATIONAL ASSOCIATION OF CRIMINAL DEFENSE LAWYERS

WRITTEN FOR *CQ RESEARCHER*, APRIL 2012

yes

While it is true that the Supreme Court has at times over the past decade treated the exclusionary rule with disdain, fortunately the court has not yet completely disavowed it. It is perhaps the only tool the courts have to circumscribe police behavior that violates the Fourth Amendment. Let me give you an example.

The Supreme Court in January decided a case — *U.S. v. Jones* — that is sure to be the first of many that will test the limits of government's ability to use modern technology to invade individual privacy. The court unanimously upheld the suppression of GPS tracking data, rejecting the government's sweeping claim that it can track a person's movements without spatial or temporal limitation, and without a warrant or any judicial oversight.

The idea that such surveillance could occur solely at the government's discretion prompted Chief Justice John G. Roberts Jr. to ask in astonishment whether, in the government's view, the FBI could put GPS monitors on the cars of every member of the court. The government's position was a resounding "yes." Fortunately for the future of privacy in a world in which technology now permits once unfathomable invasions of privacy, the court's decision was an equally resounding "no."

How massively was this taking place before the court's decision? During the oral argument, the deputy solicitor general acknowledged that the federal government alone has been using GPS devices "in the low thousands annually." Separate from that, state and local law enforcement authorities frequently employ GPS tracking devices — subjecting untold thousands to surveillance.

Was the court's invocation of the exclusionary rule, a venerable remedy that will soon celebrate its 100th anniversary in American jurisprudence, an effective tool to vindicate fundamental rights guaranteed by the Fourth Amendment? You bet it was. Within weeks, the FBI's general counsel, Andrew Weissmann, said the ruling in *U.S. v. Jones* caused a "sea change" in law enforcement. Following the oral argument and in anticipation of the ruling, the FBI scrambled to ensure that the government had warrants for 3,000 active GPS tracking devices.

After the decision, 250 of those tracking devices remained shut down. Many may eventually be reactivated where there is legal cause — as they should be. No doubt, states and localities are responding similarly to ensure compliance with the dictates of the Fourth Amendment. Thus, once again, the power of the exclusionary rule to rein in governmental abuse is vindicated.

WILLIAM J. FITZPATRICK
DISTRICT ATTORNEY, ONONDAGA COUNTY, N.Y.

WRITTEN FOR *CQ RESEARCHER*, APRIL 2012

no

As a prosecutor for 35 years, I have never met a cop who was deterred by a judicial opinion written five years after he or she made a split-second decision. The Supreme Court-crafted exclusionary rule has morphed from its intended restraint on police misconduct into a judicially sanctioned version of roulette.

Antoine Jones, a Washington, D.C., nightclub owner, was making money the old-fashioned way, entertaining his customers with hip-hop music and running the District's largest cocaine distribution ring. Rather than spend countless hours legally following Jones, police in 2005 decided to place a GPS tracking device on his wife's car, and even though not required, they actually got a search warrant to track the location of this vehicle.

This innovative tactic resulted in Jones' arrest and conviction as well as the seizure of five kilos of cocaine and $850,000 in ill-gotten drug proceeds.

Inexplicably, when the U.S. Attorney's office authorized the installation of the tracking device, the police did so one day beyond the sanctioned 10-day window.

In *United States v. Jones*, the Supreme Court ruled — for the first time — that the installation of a GPS device by the authorities on a suspect's car constituted a search under the Fourth Amendment. Thus the evidence obtained in the case was suppressed, despite the fact that, prior to the decision, the prevailing law was murky at best. Pardon me if I'm confused as to how this deters police misconduct. Would it not make more sense to punish the appropriate grammar school teachers who failed to properly train the future attorneys on how to read a calendar?

My colleagues have no problem with the GPS warrant requirement. What concerns us is the uncertainty and Draconian response to what may be charitably called a technical error. If we track EZ-Pass holders to locate an abducted child or trace a terrorist by using cell-tower records, do the criminals go free? While technology is changing rapidly, police who make life-and-death decisions do not have the luxury of waiting for the courts to delineate these constitutional boundaries before they take action.

Even the learned justices in *Jones* had little consensus on the grounds for the decision. Prosecutors merely want a rational approach to evidence suppression where concepts such as proportionality and good faith have some standing. You do not "deter" cops with a system that is, as Justice Lewis Powell said, "intolerably confusing." You only confuse cops and make the public less secure.

Continued from p. 316

In Omaha, the citizens' group also is urging the city to re-establish the office of Public Safety Auditor. The office was created in 2001, but Mayor Mike Fahey fired Tristan Bonn from the post in October 2006, barely a week after she delivered a report sharply critical of the department. The city fought Bonn's lawsuit to regain the position and has failed to refill the position, according to the citizens' group. [37]

The current mayor, Jim Suttle, says there is no need for an auditor. "We have a lot of faith in our police chief," he told an Omaha television station in September 2011 in the midst of a controversy over the videotaped beating and kicking of a suspect in police custody. [38]

In Albuquerque, an officer involved in a November 2009 shooting was fired the next year after the department's internal affairs unit and the Independent Review Officer found the shooting unjustified. Schultz said he fired Brandon Carr because the officer lied to investigators about the events.

The city paid the victim's family $950,000 to settle a civil suit, but on March 30 the district attorney's office announced no criminal charges would be brought against Carr. Out of 29 police shootings since 2009, eight are awaiting grand jury action, but no criminal charges have been brought in the other 21, according to the *Albuquerque Journal*. [39]

Reforms Outlined

The Seattle Police Department is preparing to adopt a 20-point reform plan aimed at answering criticisms from citizens' groups and the Justice Department and perhaps avoiding federal court supervision for several years.

The plan, released by Mayor McGinn on March 29, includes steps to revamp use-of-force policies, strengthen the role of a newly established Force Review Board, collect data on possible racial profiling and improve diversity training. In one specific change, the plan responds to criticism of how police dealt with Occupy Seattle protesters in November by prohibiting the use of pepper spray except in self-defense or as "a last resort."

Seattle and Justice Department officials met behind closed doors the next day to discuss the plan. Seattle officials appeared to hope the department would back away from insisting that the city agree to a court order giving a federal judge supervisory authority over the plan's implementation for a specified number of years. [40]

Progress on a reform plan in Seattle came after negotiations between the Justice Department and New Orleans officials had stalled because of a bizarre incident involving the federal government's point person in the talks. Sal Perriccone withdrew from the talks and then resigned from the U.S. Attorney's office in New Orleans in March after he acknowledged having used a pseudonym to post hundreds of online comments about law enforcement-related stories on the *Times-Picayune*'s website, nola.com. [41]

Two of the major groups involved in requesting the Justice Department investigation of the Seattle Police Department reacted approvingly to what McGinn called the 20/20 plan — 20 steps to be put into effect over 20 months. Estela Ortega, executive director of the Hispanic advocacy group El Centro de la Raza, appeared at the news conference with McGinn and Chief John Diaz and praised their willingness to work with community leaders on the plan.

In a brief statement, Kathleen Taylor, executive director of ACLU of Washington State, said the civil rights organization was "encouraged" by the plan. But she said a court-supervised consent decree "is critical to ensure that reforms are thoroughly implemented and are sustained for the long term."

The plan's use-of-force provisions call for developing "updated, clear policies" on the use of "lethal, less-lethal and non-lethal tools available to officers." Officers would be trained annually on the policies and on "de-escalation" of "low-level encounters." Sergeants and commanders are also to be given annual training on how to investigate and document use-of-force incidents.

Seattle's Force Review Board, established after the release of the Justice Department report in December, would be given a formal role. Some form of civilian review of the board's work would be instituted.

Issues of "biased policing" are to be addressed by streamlining race-data collection related to traffic stops and initiating the collection of race data for pedestrian encounters. The University of Washington's African-American Studies Department is to be engaged to review the department's practices as related to the issue.

In New Orleans, Perricone took himself out of the federal-local negotiations on March 16 after his role as pseudonymous online commentator came to light. Mayor Landrieu said Perricone's participation had "poisoned" the negotiations, but U.S. Attorney Jim Letten insisted the removal would not cause a delay.

ACLU official Esman says the ongoing talks are "very guarded," but she expects eventual agreement on a court-supervised consent decree. "Something will come of it," Esman says. "Whether it will be enough, whether it will work is anybody's guess."

Meanwhile, another of the police forces sharply criticized in Justice Department reports last year got new leadership in late March in a move that may ease the way for reforms. Puerto Rico Gov. Luis Fortuño named former FBI official Hector Pesquera as superintendent of the commonwealth's 17,000-person police department on March 29 following the resignation of Emilio Díaz Cólon from the post.

Díaz had been superintendent for only three months when the Justice

Department report was released in September. He responded by denying any constitutional violations by the force. Over the next six months, Díaz was criticized for failing to offer an anti-crime program. Fortuño quoted Díaz as saying he was resigning to avoid hurting prospective reforms. [42] ■

OUTLOOK

Police Under Pressure

Popular trends in law enforcement push police departments in opposite directions. Police departments use high-tech tools to surveil suspects, crack down on drugs and try to spot terrorists, even as officers are being urged to get out of their cars, walk the streets and engage the public in "community policing." [43]

Along with these competing visions of good policing come financial pressures as fiscally strapped local governments cut back on police departments' staffing, pay and services. In Detroit, police precincts are open only during daytime hours, and nonemergency reports have to be made through a central call center. To save $80 million in 2011, the Los Angeles City Council cut overtime pay for cops, but the department still had to find $41 million more in savings. And police departments around the country have been dealing with layoffs by taking reports on many property crimes over the phone instead of sending officers to investigate. [44]

The financial pressures lead police consultant Scott to worry about cutbacks in the training needed to ensure that officers live up to professional standards. "Law enforcement is not training its personnel the way it should," the former police chief says. "This is where I see many, many lawsuits that could be avoided if we as a public demanded to have better trained police officers."

Police accountability is being enhanced, however, by new technology, such as the video cameras now installed on many police cars to record officer-suspect encounters. "The way to encourage police reform and police accountability is [with] sunlight," says University of Baltimore professor Kane, "making these practices known to the public."

Technology at the same time increases the potential for police abuse of individual privacy and safety. Civil liberties groups complain that local police now are using cell phone tracking routinely and aggressively, often without much judicial oversight. Tasers, once seen as a non-lethal alternative to firearms for subduing suspects, are linked by the human rights group Amnesty International to hundreds of deaths of suspects — a risk that the manufacturer acknowledges but calls exaggerated. [45]

The high-power, high-tech weaponry provided to SWAT teams, especially for drug raids, is viewed disapprovingly, even by police-friendly experts. "In some cases, you've got this hypercoercion being used in situations that don't require this kind of force," Kane says. "It's almost like a toy that needs to be played with."

Even without high-power weaponry, the risk of unnecessary and excessive force, sometimes lethal, persists in police-civilian encounters. Review procedures in place, as in Albuquerque, often find officers' conduct justifiable, even as outside groups and victims' families disagree. But national police organizations appear to devote little attention to the subject. In assuming the presidency of the International Association of Chiefs of Police in November 2011, Quincy, Fla., Police Chief Walter McNeil said the group's highest priority would be "to continue a comprehensive violence-against-police-officers reduction strategy." McNeil did not address the issue of excessive force against civilians, nor has he mentioned the issue in his monthly column in the association's magazine despite the spate of critical Justice Department reports in December. [46]

Walker, the veteran of police accountability issues, worries that the post-9/11 emphasis on homeland security has been a setback for best police practices. "Your primary focus is not community policing, which tells you that the major things we have to do is work with people in the community," he says. And he worries about the impact of budget-imposed layoffs. "If the economy worsens," Walker says, "things could be very, very worse."

Still, Walker believes that excessive force and racial profiling are not intractable problems. "If these problems are persisting, it's just because [police leaders] are not paying attention," Walker says. "We have a much clearer picture of possible things we can do. It's just finding the will do to do them." ■

Notes

[1] Account drawn primarily from coverage by Brendan McCarthy in *The Times-Picayune* (New Orleans): "Raid details show focus on weed," March 10, 2012, p. A1; "Man killed by cops was not armed," March 9, 2012, p. A1. Some other information drawn from other *Times-Picayune* articles, most of them by McCarthy.

[2] Johnson, Shorty quoted in McCarthy, *ibid.*, March 10.

[3] The New Orleans report is available on the Justice Department's website: www.justice.gov/crt/about/spl/nopd.php. A complete list of Special Litigation Section cases and matters, including "Conduct of Law Enforcement Agencies Investigations" and "Conduct of Law Enforcement Agencies Complaints," is found here: www.justice.gov/crt/about/spl/findsettle.php.

[4] Diaz quoted in Mike Carter, Steve Miletich, and Jennifer Sullivan, "City faces possibility of court intervention," *The Seattle Times*, Dec. 17, 2011, p. A1; Gallo's retirement reported in Denise Buffa and Josh Kovner, "Chief Steps Down," *Hartford Courant* (Conn.), Jan. 31, 2012, p. A1;

Quoted in J. J. Hensley, "Negotiations between MCSO, DOJ fall apart," *The Arizona Republic* (Phoenix), April 4, 2012, p. A1.

[5] For previous coverage, see these *CQ Researcher* reports: Kenneth Jost, "Policing the Police," March 17, 2000, pp. 209-240; Sarah Glazer, "Police Corruption," Nov. 24, 1995, pp. 1041-1064; Richard L. Worsnop, "Police Brutality," Sept. 6, 1991, pp. 633-656; and earlier reports in *CQ Researcher-plus Archives*.

[6] See Brendan McCarthy and Laura Maggi, "NOPD deeply defective, report says," *The Times-Picayune*, March 18, 2011, p. A1; Brendan McCarthy, "Reforms in place, Serpas says," *ibid.*, March 24, 2011, p. B1. See also Laura Maggi, " 'Clear pattern' of excessive force cited," *ibid.*, March 18, 2011, p. A14.

[7] See Brendan McCarthy, "Judge imposes stiff sentences on 5 NOPD officers convicted in Danziger shootings," nola.com, April 4, 2012, www.nola.com/crime/index.ssf/2012/04/judge_imposes_sentences_on_5_n.html. The defendants and their sentences are Robert Faulcon Jr., 65 years; Kenneth Bowen, 40 years; Robert Gisevius Jr., 40 years; Anthony Villavaso II, 38 years; Arthur "Archie" Kaufman, six years. For an overview of the case in advance of the trial, see Brendan McCarthy and Laura Maggi, "Federal prosecutors allege civil rights abuses," *The Times-Picayune*, June 19, 2011, A1; for a post-verdict account, see Katie Urbaszewski and Brendan McCarthy, "Danziger evidence outweighed chaos theory," *ibid.*, Aug. 23, 2011, p. A1.

[8] "Taking Stock: Report from the 2010 Roundtable on the State and Local Law Enforcement Police Pattern or Practice Program (42 USC § 14141)," National Institute of Justice, September 2011, https://ncjrs.gov/pdffiles1/nij/234458.pdf.

[9] Quoted in Jerry Markon, "Justice Dept. is policing the police," *The Washington Post*, Sept. 18, 2011, p. A3.

[10] See "Highlights of AP's probe into NYPD intelligence operations," http://ap.org/media-center/nypd/investigation.

[11] See "Investigation of the Seattle Police Department," U.S. Department of Justice, Civil Rights Division/U.S. Attorney's Office, Western District, Washington, Dec. 16, 2011, www.justice.gov/crt/about/spl/documents/spd_findletter_12-16-11.pdf. The letter requesting the investigation is on the ACLU's website: www.aclu-wa.org/re-request-investigate-pattern-or-practice-misconduct-seattle-police-department. For initial coverage of Williams' death, see Sara Jean Green and Steve Miletich, "Police have questions about shooting by cop," *The Seattle Times*, Sept. 1, 2010, p. A1.

[12] "Police Use of Force in America," International Association of Chiefs of Police, 2001, www.theiacp.org/Portals/0/pdfs/Publications/2001useofforce.pdf; "Police Use of Force," National Institute of Justice, www.nij.gov/topics/law-enforcement/officer-safety/use-of-force/welcome.htm#note2 (modified January 2012).

[13] The decisions are *Tennessee v. Garner*, 471 U.S. 1 (1985); *Graham v. Connor*, 490 U.S. 386 (1989).

[14] William Terrill, Eugene A. Paoline III and Jason Ingram, "Final Technical Report Draft: Assessing Police Use of Force Policy and Outcomes," National Institute of Justice, February 2012, p. 159, www.ncjrs.gov/pdffiles1/nij/grants/237794.pdf.

[15] Matthew Kauffman, "In Traffic Stops, Police Tougher on Blacks, Hispanics," *Hartford Courant* (Connecticut), Feb. 26, 2012, p. A1.

[16] New Orleans data cited in Kenneth Jost, " 'Black on Black' Racial Profiling: Why?" *Jost on Justice* (blog), March 11, 2011; Justice Department findings on Maricopa County, www.justice.gov/crt/about/spl/mcso.php; East Haven; and www.justice.gov/crt/about/spl/documents/easthaven_findletter_12-19-11.pdf.

[17] Figures from the New York Civil Liberties Union cited in Sean Gardiner, "Stop-and-Frisks Hit Record in 2011," *The Wall Street Journal*, Feb. 14, 2012, p. A21.

[18] Gitta Laasby, "Flynn addresses inquiry into strip searches," *Journal Sentinel* (Milwaukee), March 23, 2012, p. B1. Background on Mucha drawn from past coverage by Gina Barton: "Gun Case Falls Apart With Cop's Testimony," *ibid.*, Aug. 8, 2010, p. A1; "Forceful Impact: Suspects have accused Sgt. Jason Mucha 10 times of beating them or planting drugs. He wasn't disciplined, but courts took notice," *ibid.*, Sept. 29, 2007, p. A1.

[19] Anthony Cormier and Matthew Doig, "Unfit for Duty," *Herald-Tribune* (Sarasota, Fla.), December 2011 (nine parts), http://cops.htcreative.com/; Gina Barton, "At least 93 Milwaukee police officers have been disciplined for violating the law," *Journal Sentinel*, Oct. 23, 2011 (1st of 3 parts), www.jsonline.com/watchdog/watchdogreports/at-least-93-milwaukee-police-officers-have-been-disciplined-for-violating-law-132268408.html.

[20] Background drawn in part from Samuel Walker and Charles M. Katz, *Police in America: An Introduction* (5th ed., 2005), chapter 2 (pp. 23-58). The sixth edition (2011) was not available for use before deadline.

[21] *Ibid.*, pp. 33-34.

[22] The major cases are *Brown v. Mississippi*, 297 U.S. 278 (1936); *Miranda v. Arizona*, 384 U.S. 436 (1966); *Mapp v. Ohio*, 367 U.S. 463 (1960). For background, see David G. Savage, Guide to the U.S. Supreme Court (5th ed., 2011), pp. 740-748 (confessions), 725-726 (exclusionary rule).

[23] For an official assessment, see "LEAA/OJP Retrospective: 30 Years of Federal Support for State and Local Criminal Justice," U.S. Department of Justice, Office of Justice Programs, July 11, 1996, p. 3, www.ncjrs.gov/pdffiles1/nij/164509.pdf.

[24] For background, see Glazer, *op. cit.*; Peter Maas, *Serpico* (1973), and the cinemazation of the same title, also 1973, with Al Pacino in the title role.

[25] "14th Annual Report," City of New York Commission to Combat Police Corruption, February 2012, www.nyc.gov/html/ccpc/downloads/pdf/14th_annual_report.pdf.

[26] See Tina Daunt and Jim Newton, "City OKs Police Reform Pact With U.S.," *Los Angeles Times*, Nov. 3, 2000.

[27] See Ryan J. Reilly, "Report Delivers Hard Numbers on Bush Civil Rights Division," Main Justice, Dec. 7, 2009, www.mainjustice.com/2009/12/07/report-delivers-hard-numbers-on-

About the Author

Associate Editor **Kenneth Jost** graduated from Harvard College and Georgetown University Law Center. He is the author of the *Supreme Court Yearbook* and editor of *The Supreme Court from A to Z* (both *CQ Press*). He was a member of the *CQ Researcher* team that won the American Bar Association's 2002 Silver Gavel Award. His previous reports include "Eyewitness Testimony" and "Prosecutors and the Law." He is also author of the blog *Jost on Justice* (http://jostonjustice.blogspot.com).

bush-civil-rights-division/.

[28] See David A. Fahrenthold, "U.S. Faults D.C. Police Use of Force in the '90s," *The Washington Post*, June 14, 2001, p. B1; "Findings Letter re Use of Force by the Washington Metropolitan Police Department," U.S. Department of Justice, June 13, 2001, www.justice.gov/crt/about/spl/documents/dcfindings.php; M.L. Erlick and Ben Schmitt, "U.S. Demand to Detroit: Stop Police Abuses Now," *Detroit Free-Press*, June 13, 2003; "Investigation of the Detroit Police Department" (technical assistance letters, 2002), U.S. Department of Justice, www.justice.gov/crt/about/spl/documents/dpd/detroit_cover.php; Jamie Stockwell and Ruben Castaneda, "Pr. George's Agrees to Curb Excessive Force by Police," *The Washington Post*, Jan. 23, 2004, p. A1; U.S. Department of Justice, "Investigation of the Prince George's County Police Department," Jan. 22, 2004, www.justice.gov/crt/about/spl/documents/pgpd/pgpd_cover.php.

[29] "Investigation of the Orange County Sheriff's Office Use of Conducted Energy Devices," U.S. Department of Justice, Aug. 20, 2008, www.justice.gov/crt/about/spl/documents/orangecty_ta_ltr.pd.

[30] Andrew Ramonas, "Senate Confirms Tom Perez," Main Justice, Oct. 6, 2009, www.mainjustice.com/2009/10/06/senate-confirms-tom-perez/. For a profile, see Jerry Zremski, "Former area man takes top civil rights post," *Buffalo News*, Nov. 14, 2009, p. A1.

[31] Perez quoted in Markon, *op. cit.*

[32] Quoted in Sarah Te Slaa, "Group Calls for Federal Investigation Into Police Department," KMTV (Omaha), March 13, 2012, www.kmtv.com/news/local/142578935.html. See also Roseann Moring, "Groups seek federal probe of Omaha police," *Omaha World-Herald*, March 14, 2012.

[33] The statement is cited in full in "Police Respond to Complaint," WOWT, March 13, 2012, www.wowt.com/home/headlines/Police_Respond_to_Complaint_142541525.html?storySection=story.

[34] See Jeff Proctor, "Cop Payments to Stop," *Albuquerque Journal*, March 30, 2012, p. A1; and earlier coverage by same reporter. For national coverage, see Manny Fernandez and Dan Frosch, "Payments to Albuquerque Officers Are Called a 'Bounty System,' " *The New York Times*, March 25, 2012, p. A20.

[35] See Russell Contreras, "Albuquerque activists seek federal probe of police," The Associated Press, March 27, 2012. Some other background drawn from article.

FOR MORE INFORMATION

American Civil Liberties Union, 125 Broad St., New York, NY 10004; 212-549-2500; www.aclu.org. Has been active on racial profiling, use of force and other police-practices issues.

Fraternal Order of Police, Grand Lodge, 1410 Donelson Pike, A-17, Nashville, TN 37217; 615-399-0900; www.grandlodgefop.org. Largest membership organization representing rank-and-file law enforcement officers.

International Association of Chiefs of Police, 515 North Washington St., Alexandria, VA 22314; 703-836-6767; www.theiacp.org. Represents operating chief executives of international, federal, state and local law enforcement agencies of all sizes.

National Association of Civilian Oversight of Law Enforcement, 638 E. Vermont St., P.O. Box 1737, Indianapolis, IN 46206; 1-866-462-2653; www.nacole.org. Brings together individuals and agencies working to establish or improve oversight of police officers in the United States.

National Association of Criminal Defense Lawyers, 1025 Connecticut Ave., N.W., Suite 901, Washington, DC 20036; 202-872-8600; www.crimdefense.org. The largest organization exclusively representing criminal defense lawyers.

National District Attorneys Association, 44 Canal Center Plaza, Suite 110, Alexandria, VA 22314; 703-549-9222; www.ndaa.org. Represents criminal prosecutors in state, district, county and city attorneys' offices.

National Sheriffs' Association, 1450 Duke St., Alexandria, VA 22314; 1-800-424-7827; www.sheriffs.org. Represents and assists sheriffs' offices nationwide through education, training and information resources.

Police Foundation, 1201 Connecticut Ave., N.W., Washington, DC 20036-2636; 202-833-1460; www.policefoundation.org. Established by the Ford Foundation in 1970; sponsors research to support innovation and improvement in policing.

[36] See "Law Enforcement Management and Administrative Statistics, 2000," Bureau of Justice Statistics, April 2004, pp. 31, 32, http://bjs.ojp.usdoj.gov/content/pub/pdf/lema001a.pdf.

[37] See Lynn Safranek, "Future of police auditor post under review," *Omaha World-Herald*, Oct. 31, 2006, p. 1B.

[38] Liz Dorland, "Ernie Chambers Requests Federal Investigation Into Omaha Police Department," KMTV, Sept. 7, 2011, www.kmtv.com/news/local/129429963.html.

[39] Jeff Proctor, "Fired Cop Cleared in Death of Vet," *Albuquerque Journal*, March 30, 2012, p. 41.

[40] See "SPD 20/20: A Vision for the Future," City of Seattle, www.seattle.gov/mayor/media/PDF/SPD2020.pdf. For coverage, see Mike Carter, "Seattle mayor announces broad initiative to improve police force," *The Seattle Times*, March 29, 2012; Sara Jean Green, "Mayor's initiatives seem to address complaints of biased policing," *ibid.*

[41] See Michelle Krupa and Gordon Russell, "Prosecutor bows out of NOPD talks," *The Times-Picayune*, March 17, 2012, p. A9.

[42] "Former FBI director named Puerto Rico police chief," The Associated Press, March 29, 2012.

[43] For background, see Richard L. Worsnop, "Community Policing," *CQ Researcher*, Feb. 5, 1993, pp. 97-120.

[44] See Joe Rossiter, "Godbee: Virtual police precinct plan to go into effect Monday," *Detroit Free Press*, Jan. 31, 2012, p. A7; Kate Linthicum, "L.A. council cuts millions from budget," *Los Angeles Times*, May 19, 2011, p. AA1; Kevin Johnson, "Home burglarized? Fill out a form," *USA Today*, Aug. 25, 2010, p. 1A.

[45] On use of cell phone tracking, see Eric Lichtblau, "Police Are Using Phone Tracking as Routine Tool," *The New York Times*, April 1, 2012, p. A1; on Tasers, see CBS News, "Taser: An officer's weapon of choice," 60 Minutes (David Martin, correspondent; Mary Walsh, producer), Nov. 13, 2011, www.cbsnews.com/8301-18560_162-57323531/taser-an-officers-weapon-of-choice/.

[46] See Walter A. McNeil, "The Year Ahead," *Police Chief*, November 2011, www.policechiefmagazine.org/magazine/index.cfm?fuseaction=display_arch&article_id=2519&issue_id=112011.

Bibliography

Selected Sources

Books

Delattre, Edwin J., *Characters and Cops: Ethics in Policing* (6th ed.), AEI Press, 2011.
A professor of philosophy, emeritus, at Boston University and an adjunct scholar at the American Enterprise Institute combines two decades of studying police behavior to examine a full range of ethics issues for law enforcement. Includes detailed notes, short bibliography.

Kane, Robert J., and Michael D. White, *Jammed Up: Bad Cops, Police Misconduct, and the New York City Police Department*, New York University Press, 2012 (forthcoming: Nov. 19).
The book examines the causes of — and responses to — alleged police misconduct based on unprecedented, complete access to the confidential files of more than 1,500 New York Police Department officers over a 20-year period. Includes detailed notes, bibliography. Kane is an associate professor at the University of Baltimore's School of Criminal Justice, White an associate professor at Arizona State University's School of Criminology and Criminal Justice. For an earlier article on their findings, see Robert J. Kane and Michael D. White, "Bad Cops: A study of career-ending misconduct among New York City police officers," *Criminology and Public Policy*, Vol. 8, No. 4 (November 2009), pp. 737-769. The issue includes three other policy essays on police misconduct.

Roberg, Roy, Kenneth Novak, and Gary Cordner, *Police & Society* (3d ed.), Roxbury Publishing, 2005.
The college textbook includes lengthy chapters on "Behavior and Misconduct," "Force and Coercion" and "Accountability and Ethics." Each chapter includes notes, suggested websites for further study. The book also comes with an interactive student study guide. The authors are professors, respectively, at San Jose State University, University of Missouri-Kansas City and Eastern Kentucky University.

Walker, Samuel, and Charles M. Katz, *Police in America: An Introduction* (6th ed.), McGraw-Hill, 2011.
The college textbook includes overviews of the history and current structure of U.S. law enforcement and individual chapters on police corruption and accountability, plus chapter notes, a glossary and an interactive student study guide. Walker is a professor of criminal justice, emeritus, at the University of Nebraska-Omaha and a longtime expert on police issues; Katz is an associate professor at Arizona State University's School of Criminology and Criminal Justice.

Walker, Samuel, *The New World of Police Accountability*, SAGE, 2005.
The book synthesizes major developments in police accountability over the previous decade. For an earlier account, see *Police Accountability: The Role of Citizen Oversight* (Thomson Learning, 2001). Walker maintains an informative website on police accountability issues, including a page covering developments in New Orleans (http://samuelwalker.net/). His other books include *Popular Justice: A History of American Criminal Justice* (2d ed.) (Oxford University Press, 1998); and *A Critical History of Police Reform: The Emergence of Professionalism* (Lexington, 1977).

Articles

Kocher, Charles, *et al.*, "Sustaining Police Operations at an Efficient and Effective Level under Difficult Economic Times," *Police Chief*, March 2012, www.policechiefmagazine.org/magazine/index.cfm?fuseaction=display&article_id=2621&issue_id=32012.
The article, co-authored by a retired deputy Camden, N.J., police chief, in the monthly magazine of the International Association of Chiefs of Police examines the need for adapting police department structures and operations in times of layoffs, cutbacks and consolidated services.

Reynolds, Dawn, "Coast to Coast — the Public and the Justice Department is Demanding More Accountability," National Association of Civilian Oversight of Law Enforcement, spring 2012, www.nacole.org/sites/default/files/NACOLE_Review_Spring2012.pdf.
The article in the association's quarterly newsletter reviews the Justice Department's reports on Seattle; Maricopa County, Ariz., and East Haven, Conn.

Reports and Studies

"Taking Stock: Report from the 2010 Roundtable on the State and Local Law Enforcement Police Pattern or Practice Program (42 USC § 14141)," National Institute of Justice, September 2011, https://ncjrs.gov/pdffiles1/nij/234458.pdf.
The report includes a 10-page summary of the views expressed at a roundtable convened to assess the impact of the Justice Department's pattern or practice of police misconduct program. The report includes notes, a list of all participants and a list of settlements and investigations as of July 2010.

Weisburd, David, Rosann Greenspan, Edwin E. Hamilton, Kellie A. Bryant and Hubert Williams, "The Abuse of Police Authority: A National Study of Police Officers' Attitudes," Police Foundation, 2001, www.policefoundation.org/pdf/AOANarrative.pdf.
The first-ever national survey of police officers' attitudes found that most believe extreme abuse-of-authority cases are infrequent and that the public and the media are too concerned with such incidents.

The Next Step:

Additional Articles from Current Periodicals

Excessive Force

McCoppin, Robert, and Dan Hinkel, "Many Complaints, Little Discipline," *Chicago Tribune*, Feb. 10, 2012, p. A1, articles.chicagotribune.com/2012-02-10/news/ct-met-north-chicago-brutality-20120210_1_excessive-force-jack-frost-police-misconduct/2.
Excessive-force cases against North Chicago police have steadily increased, but not many officers have been disciplined.

McGhee, Tom, "Spike in Cops' Lawsuit Payouts," *Denver Post*, Jan. 13, 2012, p. B1, www.denverpost.com/breakingnews/ci_19730217.
Denver paid $1.34 million in 2011 to settle lawsuits alleging that city police officers engaged in excessive force.

Walter, Donna, "8th Circuit: Minor Injuries Can Come From Excessive Force," *Missouri Lawyers Media*, June 6, 2011.
Plaintiffs do not have to sustain major injuries in order to prove the use of excessive force by police, according to a U.S. appeals court ruling.

Discipline

Coe, Jackee, "Interim Chief Earns Praise for Tougher Policies," *Arizona Republic*, Aug. 10, 2011, p. 3, www.azcentral.com/community/swvalley/articles/2011/08/10/20110810goodyear-interim-chief-earns-praise-improving-department.html.
The interim police chief of Goodyear, Ariz., has been praised for establishing a consistent professional-standards policy outlining misconduct violations and disciplinary measures.

Furst, Randy, "Dolan Panned on Cop Discipline," *Star Tribune* (Minneapolis), Dec. 20, 2011, p. B1, www.startribune.com/local/minneapolis/135898668.html.
The Minneapolis Civilian Review Authority says it has "no confidence" that the city's police chief would discipline officers who engage in misconduct.

Grossman, Daniel J., "Atlanta Officers Escape Discipline," *Atlanta Journal-Constitution*, May 13, 2011, p. A19, www.ajc.com/opinion/atlanta-officers-escape-discipline-944221.html.
The failure of the Atlanta Police Department to discipline its officers for misconduct exposes the city to direct financial liability, says a civil rights attorney.

Klein, Robert L., "Police Must Be Accountable to the People," *Hartford* (Conn.) *Courant*, May 1, 2011, p. C1, articles.courant.com/2011-05-01/news/hc-op-klein-poice-brutality-misconduc20110501_1_police-officers-police-misconduct-police-force.
Connecticut needs an agency to hear complaints of police misconduct and to discipline officers accordingly, says a former state assistant attorney general.

Profiling

Hanna, Bill, "Fort Worth Councilman Says Report Suggests Appearance of Racial Profiling," *Fort Worth* (Texas) *Star-Telegram*, May 25, 2011, www.star-telegram.com/2011/05/24/3101314/fort-worth-councilman-says-report.html.
A Fort Worth, Texas, council member has asked the city's police chief to provide more data justifying the arrests of alleged victims of racial profiling.

Pinkerton, James, "A Trend Not in Decline: More Blacks Pulled Over," *Houston Chronicle*, May 9, 2011, p. A1, www.chron.com/cars/article/More-black-motorists-pulled-over-according-to-1691304.php.
Houston police say race plays no part in traffic stops, but black residents continue to be pulled over more often than any other racial group.

Rubin, Joel, "Latinos Targeted in Traffic Stops By LAPD Officer," *Los Angeles Times*, March 27, 2012, p. A1, www.latimes.com/news/local/la-me-lapd-racial-profile-20120326,0,6544493.story.
An inquiry by the Los Angeles Police Department concluded that one of its officers targeted Latinos for traffic stops.

Vock, Daniel C., "Racial Profiling Data Often Unstudied," *The Washington Post*, Aug. 9, 2011, p. A13.
Illinois state police hardly ever study racial profiling information, says the state chapter of the American Civil Liberties Union.

CITING *CQ RESEARCHER*

Sample formats for citing these reports in a bibliography include the ones listed below. Preferred styles and formats vary, so please check with your instructor or professor.

MLA STYLE

Jost, Kenneth. "Remembering 9/11," CQ Researcher 2 Sept. 2011: 701-732.

APA STYLE

Jost, K. (2011, September 2). Remembering 9/11. *CQ Researcher, 9*, 701-732.

CHICAGO STYLE

Jost, Kenneth. "Remembering 9/11." *CQ Researcher*, September 2, 2011, 701-732.

In-depth Reports on Issues in the News

Are you writing a paper?

Need backup for a debate?

Want to become an expert on an issue?

For more than 80 years, students have turned to *CQ Researcher* for in-depth reporting on issues in the news. Reports on a full range of political and social issues are now available. Following is a selection of recent reports:

Civil Liberties
Remembering 9/11, 9/11
Government Secrecy, 2/11
Cybersecurity, 2/10
Press Freedom, 2/10

Crime/Law
Immigration Conflict, 3/12
Financial Misconduct, 1/12
Eyewitness Testimony, 10/11
Legal-Aid Crisis, 10/11
Computer Hacking, 9/11
Death Penalty Debates, 11/10

Education
Arts Education, 3/12
Youth Volunteerism, 1/12
Digital Education, 12/11
College Football, 11/11
Student Debt, 10/11
School Reform, 4/11
Crime on Campus, 2/11

Environment/Society
Space Program, 2/12
Invasive Species, 2/12
Fracking Controversy, 12/11

Health/Safety
Patient Safety, 2/12
Military Suicides, 9/11
Teen Drug Use, 6/11
Organ Donations, 4/11
Genes and Health, 1/11
Food Safety, 12/10
Preventing Bullying, 12/10

Politics/Economy
U.S.-Europe Relations, 3/12
Attracting Jobs, 3/12
Presidential Election, 2/12

Upcoming Reports

Regulating the Internet, 4/13/12
Criminal Records, 4/20/12
Sexual Harassment, 4/27/12

ACCESS

CQ Researcher is available in print and online. For access, visit your library or www.cqresearcher.com.

STAY CURRENT

For notice of upcoming *CQ Researcher* reports or to learn more about *CQ Researcher* products, subscribe to the free e-mail newsletters, *CQ Researcher Alert!* and *CQ Researcher News*: http://cqpress.com/newsletters.

PURCHASE

To purchase a *CQ Researcher* report in print or electronic format (PDF), visit www.cqpress.com or call 866-427-7737. Single reports start at $15. Bulk purchase discounts and electronic-rights licensing are also available.

SUBSCRIBE

Annual full-service *CQ Researcher* subscriptions—including 44 reports a year, monthly index updates, and a bound volume—start at $1,054. Add $25 for domestic postage.

CQ Researcher Online offers a backfile from 1991 and a number of tools to simplify research. For pricing information, call 800-834-9020, or e-mail librarymarketing@cqpress.com.

CQ Researcher **PLUS** *Archive*

Get Online Access to Vital Issues from 1923 to the Present

CQ Researcher Plus Archive delivers fast, online access to every *CQ Researcher* report from 1991 to the present, *PLUS* lets you explore the complete archive of *Editorial Research Reports** from 1923-1990. Search and browse more than 3,600 in-depth reports.

Loaded with handy online features, *CQ Researcher Plus Archive* provides the trustworthy reporting and the advanced online functionality today's researchers demand. The new "Issue Tracker" feature provides quick links to past and present reports on the specific topics you need.

For a free trial, visit http://library.cqpress.com/trials.

For pricing information, call 1-800-834-9020, ext. 1906 or e-mail librarymarketing@cqpress.com.

**Editorial Research Reports*, the predecessor to *CQ Researcher*, provides the same expert, nonpartisan reporting on the vital issues that have shaped our society.

CQ Press • 2300 N Street, NW, Suite 800 • Washington, DC 20037

CQ Researcher

Published by CQ Press, an Imprint of SAGE Publications, Inc.

www.cqresearcher.com

Internet Regulation

Are stiffer rules needed to protect web content?

Lawmakers are struggling with tough questions about how to regulate digital media and the Internet. With digitized versions of feature films and recorded music playable on personal computers and cell phones, the film, television and music industries have repeatedly complained that global "pirates" use cheap, widely available computer technology and the Internet to steal their intellectual property and profits. A bill to require Internet service providers (ISPs) to shut down websites suspected of posting or distributing copyrighted material stalled in Congress. Meanwhile, ISPs are fighting government attempts to bar them from discriminating against certain websites. Advocates say such "net neutrality" rules are needed to prevent situations in which, for example, a cable TV-owned ISP that also sells video content might slow the flow of video that customers buy from other companies. But ISPs argue that it wouldn't be in their financial interest to conduct business that way.

The heavy-metal band Metallica raised early concerns about digital copyright protection. In 1999 the group sued Napster, the first website for music sharing, after Metallica's unreleased music appeared on the now-defunct site. Above, the group performs in Indio, Calif., on April 23, 2011.

INSIDE THIS REPORT

The Issues 327
Background 334
Chronology 335
Current Situation 340
At Issue 341
Outlook 343
Bibliography 346
The Next Step 347

CQ Researcher • April 13, 2012 • www.cqresearcher.com
Volume 22, Number 14 • Pages 325-348

Los Angeles | London | New Delhi
Singapore | Washington DC

Recipient of Society of Professional Journalists Award for Excellence ◆ American Bar Association Silver Gavel Award

THE ISSUES

327 • Is Internet piracy harming the economy?
• Should Congress crack down harder on piracy?
• Should the government require Internet-service providers (ISPs) to treat all websites the same?

BACKGROUND

334 **Communication Wars**
Owners of older technologies always fight innovation.

334 **Copyright Disputes**
Emerging technologies threaten owners of intellectual property.

334 **Media Converging**
Digital media intensified threats to copyright owners.

337 **Net Neutrality**
New rules ban "discrimination" among websites.

CURRENT SITUATION

340 **Going Dark**
Thousands of websites shut down on Jan. 18 in protest of proposed copyright protection legislation.

342 **Net Neutrality in Court**
Several lawsuits are challenging new federal rules regulating the Internet.

OUTLOOK

343 **Continuing Battles**
Wrangling will continue over control of digital intellectual property and Internet traffic.

SIDEBARS AND GRAPHICS

328 **Top-Speed Internet Options Limited**
This year only 15 percent of Americans will have the fastest Internet connections.

329 **One-Fourth of Downloads Are Illegal**
In the United States about 18 percent of downloads are illegal.

330 **New Technology Spurs Innovation — and Resistance**
Critics say "dinosaurs" seek veto power over the future.

332 **U.S. Internet Use Soars**
More than three-fourth of Americans are online.

335 **Chronology**
Key events since 1996.

336 **'Remix' Culture Worries Copyright Owners**
Software allows anyone to manipulate works of art.

338 **Entertainment Industry Seeks New Business Plan**
"There is a slow and grudging march toward progress."

341 **At Issue**
Should lawmakers support the FCC's net-neutrality rules?

FOR FURTHER RESEARCH

345 **For More Information**
Organizations to contact.

346 **Bibliography**
Selected sources used.

347 **The Next Step**
Additional articles.

347 **Citing *CQ Researcher***
Sample bibliography formats.

Cover: Getty Images/Kevin Winter

CQ Researcher

April 13, 2012
Volume 22, Number 14

MANAGING EDITOR: Thomas J. Billitteri
tjb@cqpress.com

ASSISTANT MANAGING EDITOR: Kathy Koch
kkoch@cqpress.com

CONTRIBUTING EDITOR: Thomas J. Colin
tcolin@cqpress.com

ASSOCIATE EDITOR: Kenneth Jost

STAFF WRITER: Marcia Clemmitt

CONTRIBUTING WRITERS: Sarah Glazer, Alan Greenblatt, Peter Katel, Barbara Mantel, Jennifer Weeks

DESIGN/PRODUCTION EDITOR: Olu B. Davis

ASSISTANT EDITOR: Darrell Dela Rosa

FACT CHECKER: Michelle Harris

Los Angeles | London | New Delhi
Singapore | Washington DC

An Imprint of SAGE Publications, Inc.

VICE PRESIDENT AND EDITORIAL DIRECTOR, HIGHER EDUCATION GROUP:
Michele Sordi

DIRECTOR, ONLINE PUBLISHING:
Todd Baldwin

CQ Researcher (ISSN 1056-2036) is printed on acid-free paper. Published weekly, except: (March wk. 5) (May wk. 4) (July wk. 1) (Aug. wks. 3, 4) (Nov. wk. 4) and (Dec. wks. 3, 4). Published by SAGE Publications, Inc., 2455 Teller Rd., Thousand Oaks, CA 91320. Annual full-service subscriptions start at $1,054. For pricing, call 1-800-834-9020. To purchase a *CQ Researcher* report in print or electronic format (PDF), visit www.cqpress.com or call 866-427-7737. Single reports start at $15. Bulk purchase discounts and electronic-rights licensing are also available. Periodicals postage paid at Thousand Oaks, California, and at additional mailing offices. POSTMASTER: Send address changes to *CQ Researcher*, 2300 N St., N.W., Suite 800, Washington, DC 20037.

BY MARCIA CLEMMITT

THE ISSUES

Wikipedia, the online encyclopedia written by its users, has become a dependable web presence — always there to answer questions on just about every conceivable subject, from aardvarks to Zoroaster. But on Jan. 18 Wikipedia disappeared, abruptly shutting down its U.S. site in a self-proclaimed "day of darkness."

The blackout came in protest of two Hollywood-backed proposals in Congress — the Stop Online Piracy Act (SOPA) and the Protect Intellectual Property Act (PIPA) — aimed at combating the unauthorized use or reproduction of movies, TV shows, recorded music and other copyrighted material.

Such pirating, which typically occurs on foreign-based rogue websites, has mushroomed into a global enterprise costing the entertainment industry and others billions of dollars a year in lost revenues and royalties.

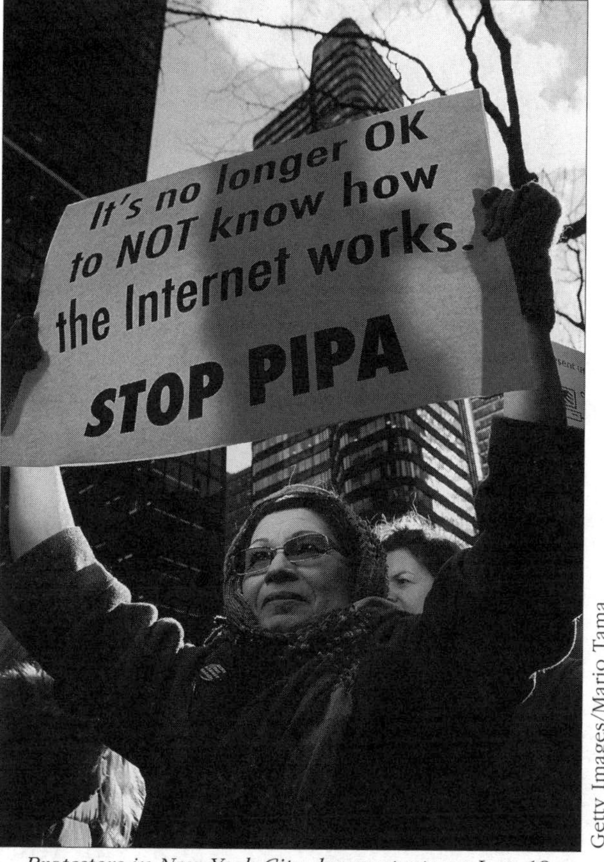

Getty Images/Mario Tama

Protesters in New York City demonstrate on Jan. 18, 2012, against the proposed Protect Intellectual Property Act (PIPA) and the Stop Online Piracy Act (SOPA), which would block the unauthorized use of movies, TV shows, recorded music and other copyrighted material. The bills' opponents — including Wikipedia co-founder Jimmy Wales — argue they are too draconian and will lead to censorship.

But opponents of the proposed bills — including Wikipedia co-founder Jimmy Wales — argued they were so vague and draconian that they would force any website carrying user-generated content perceived to violate copyright laws to shut down at nearly a moment's notice.

What's more, opponents said, the bills would effectively block search engines from connecting to those sites and allow copyright owners to stop advertisers from doing business with them.

"I hope we send a broad global message that the Internet as a whole will not tolerate censorship in response to mere allegations of copyright infringement," said Wales. [1] Thousands of other websites also shut down in protest, while Google and Facebook, among others, remained in operation but expressed support for Wikipedia's stand.

Debates on Internet regulation are heating up as cyber companies gain clout in Washington and the Internet penetrates every area of life. Besides the fight over copyright enforcement, a battle is raging over government attempts to bar Internet-service providers (ISPs) from delivering some websites' content to customers more slowly than others.

Government advocates argue that such "net neutrality" rules are needed to keep broadband ISPs — mostly cable TV and phone companies that provide high-speed Internet services but also are interested in supplying content to customers — from hurting small or upstart competitors in the content business. But the ISPs argue that such legislation impinges on their free-speech rights: After all, they argue, they own the transmission lines that carry the data. And besides, they say, slowing the flow of online traffic wouldn't be in their financial interest because it might make customers go elsewhere.

While the net neutrality debate can descend into the technical and arcane, Internet piracy is a subject that anyone who has knowingly watched a bootleg movie or illegally downloaded a Top 10 hit song can understand. Two days after Wikipedia's online protest, on Jan. 20, Congress postponed long-expected floor votes on House and Senate bills requiring online-payment companies, search engines and ISPs to cut their ties with websites alleged to be posting copyrighted material.

"The growing number of foreign websites that offer counterfeit or stolen goods continues to threaten American technology, products and jobs," said Rep. Lamar Smith, R-Texas, chief sponsor of the House bill. "Congress cannot stand by and do nothing while some of America's most profitable and productive industries are under attack." [2]

The 1998 Digital Millennium Copyright Act (DMCA) currently governs copyright infringement. Advocates of new legislation say it is outmoded because it doesn't cover the full range of Internet-piracy issues that have emerged over the past decade.

Top-Speed Internet Options Limited

Only about 15 percent of Americans will have a choice among top-speed broadband Internet service providers (ISPs) in 2012. Advocates of net neutrality, which would prevent ISPs from slowing delivery of some websites' content, say consumers won't be able to pressure ISPs to treat all content equally if they can't threaten to switch their business to other providers.

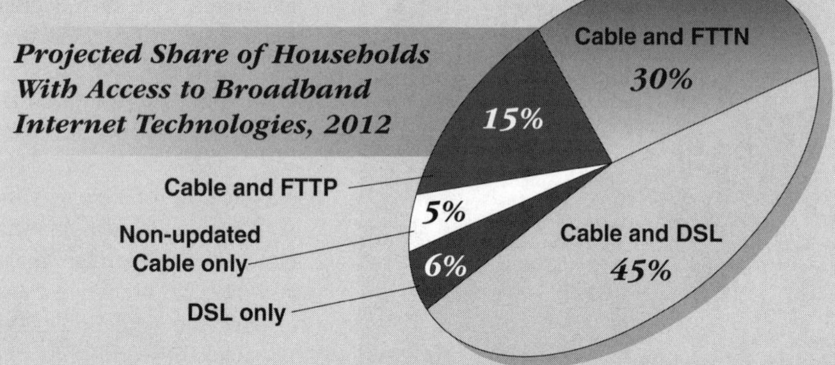

** Some telephone companies offer very high-speed broadband, but most service is slower. Fiber-to-the-premises (FTTP) is fastest — roughly as fast as current, upgraded cable. Fiber-to-the-node (FTTN) is somewhat slower, and digital subscriber line (DSL) is about a third as fast as top-speed cable and FTTP.*

*** Figures do not total 100 because of rounding.*

Source: "Broadband Competition and Innovation Policy," Federal Communications Commission, 2010, www.broadband.gov/plan/4-broadband-competition-and-innovation-policy/

But others say the new bills go too far. "I'm not exactly a fan" of the DMCA, but it "has a process that at least gives people a hearing," says Jon Ippolito, an associate professor of new media at the University of Maine, in Orono. In contrast, proposed legislation risks "poisoning the very nature of the Internet" as a participatory medium by authorizing near-immediate shutdowns of websites with user-generated content, he says.

Meanwhile, after years of wrangling, the Federal Communications Commission (FCC), the federal agency that writes and enforces rules for telecommunications, last November required ISPs that deliver high-speed Internet service to observe "net neutrality" in managing their networks. While it's understood that ISPs may sometimes need to slow some data to avoid network congestion, they must publicly disclose the methods they use to manage traffic and may not block lawful websites or "unreasonably" discriminate among sites.

A congressional resolution to stop the regulation passed the House last year, but not the Senate, and lawmakers continue to fight over the issue.

The net neutrality rules are an unwarranted intrusion into an Internet market that functions well, wrote Gerald R. Faulhaber, professor emeritus of business and public policy at the University of Pennsylvania's Wharton School, and David J. Farber, professor of computer science and public policy at Carnegie Mellon University in Pittsburgh. The FCC's "successful policy of no regulation" for the past two decades has led to "the wildly successful Internet we have today" and should not be abandoned, they said. [3]

But net-neutrality advocates argue that broadband ISPs might have significant business motives for slowing some websites' traffic. The ISPs, too, would like to get into the Internet content game, which has brought big financial rewards to companies such as Facebook and Amazon. But the online services they could offer — video and phone service — also have competitors, such as the video company Netflix and the Internet phone company Skype.

Therefore, regulation advocates say, ISPs might consider it in their financial interest to slow content traffic to those competitors to gain an edge over them. For example, a phone company that offers broadband might be motivated to slow delivery of Internet-telephone services such as VoIP, and, in fact, several ISPs have been accused of such blocking in the past. [4]

"I don't pay Comcast for making Netflix inferior to [Comcast's] pay-per-view," says Robert Frieden, a professor of telecommunications and law at Pennsylvania State University, in University Park. "I don't want the intermediaries tilting things to favor their own content."

Edward W. Felten, a professor of computer science and public affairs at Princeton University and chief technologist at the Federal Trade Commission, says it remains an "open question whether government can police favoritism by Internet network operators." Nevertheless, he says that keeping the Internet neutral by some means would help small Internet providers get off the ground or thrive against their bigger rivals.

"The next generation of innovators, who need neutrality the most, are not at the bargaining table. They're hard at work in their labs or classrooms, dreaming of the next big thing, and hoping that the Internet is as open to them as it was to the founders of Google." [5]

As lawmakers, entrepreneurs and policy analysts consider the future of Internet regulation, here are some of the questions being debated:

Is Internet piracy harming the economy?

For advocates of tougher copyright regulation, the domino effect may be the most compelling argument for toughening anti-piracy laws: Piracy of copyrighted material not only robs creative artists of due compensation but harms the whole economy as lost revenues in one industry decrease sales in others, they argue.

However, many analysts argue that economic- and job-loss estimates cited by copyright-owners' groups such as the Recording Industry Association of America (RIAA) and the Motion Picture Association of America (MPAA) are inflated and based on minimal data.

"The accumulative impact of millions of songs downloaded illegally . . . is devastating" to a whole group of workers, including "songwriters, recording artists, audio engineers, computer technicians, talent scouts and marketing specialists, producers, publishers and countless others," said the RIAA. [6]

"More than 2.2 million hard-working, middle-class people in all 50 states depend on the entertainment industry for their jobs, and many millions more work in other industries that rely on intellectual property," Michael O'Leary, MPAA senior executive vice president, said in lauding the House Judiciary Committee's strong bipartisan support for SOPA. [7]

"Rogue websites that steal America's innovative and creative products . . . threaten more than 19 million American jobs," wrote Mark Elliot, executive vice president of the U.S. Chamber of Commerce. [8]

"The independent music community is impacted by . . . illegal downloading, even more so in many cases than major music labels or movie studios because [profit] margins are so thin for independent labels," according to the American Association for Independent Music (A2IM), a trade group that represents smaller, independent record labels. "Because we are not part of larger corporations which might be able to offset losses during leaner years, making a living becomes that much more difficult." [9]

One-Fourth of Downloads Are Illegal

Roughly one-fourth of global Internet traffic, and about 18 percent of U.S. traffic, illegally accesses copyrighted media through downloading methods that include file-sharing, video streaming and use of torrents, which are files that reveal the online location of copyrighted items.

Internet Traffic Illegally Accessing Copyrighted Media

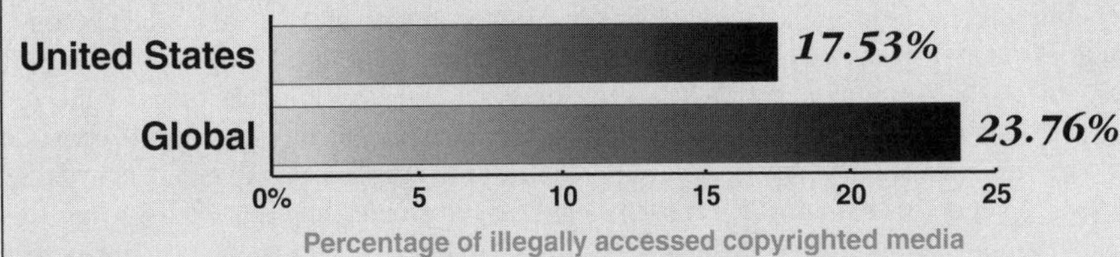

** Percentages do not include pornography because its status can be difficult to assess.*

Source: "Technical Report: An Estimate of Infringing Use of the Internet," Envisional, January 2011, pp. 2-3, documents.envisional.com/docs/Envisional-Internet_Usage-Jan2011.pdf

Recorded-music sales have declined significantly in most years since the advent of Internet downloading. In 2010, for example, worldwide music sales dropped by 8.4 percent — $1.45 billion. The decrease comes "as the industry continues to struggle with piracy and winning consumers over to legal download models," observes *The Guardian* newspaper in Britain. [10]

"The demand for new music seems as insatiable and diverse as ever, and record companies continue to meet it. But they are operating at only a fraction of their potential because of a difficult environment dominated by piracy," said Frances Moore, chief executive of the music-industry trade group International Federation of the Phonographic Industry (IFPI). [11]

"Piracy remains an enormous barrier to sustainable growth in digital music," according to IFPI. "Globally, one in four internet users (28%) regularly access unlicensed services," said the group. [12]

"I made a film called 'Naked Ambition: An R-rated Look at an X-rated Industry' " that Apple, Netflix and Warner Brothers distributed but that was widely pirated anyway, wrote photographer and independent filmmaker Michael Grecco. He received 107 Google alerts about online references to his movie that each named multiple websites where his film was available for free. The sites, which Grecco had not authorized to host his film, "made all the money; I have never seen a dime," he wrote. [13]

Piracy-related monetary and job losses are difficult to estimate, but the conservative, Lewisville, Texas-based think tank, Institute for Policy Innovation (IPI), founded by former House Majority Leader Dick Armey, R-Texas, has published perhaps the most oft-cited statistics. In 2005, industries that sell material whose copyrights they own, such as the film, TV and recording industries, lost at least $23.5 billion to piracy of music, video games and software, and retailers lost another $2.5 billion, the IPI calculated. The group also estimated that lost sales from pirating cost the United States the chance to add 373,375 jobs to the

New Technology Spurs Innovation — and Resistance

Critics say "dinosaurs" seek veto power over the future.

Jesse Jordan, a freshman at Rensselaer Polytechnic Institute in Troy, N.Y., got the idea for his new search engine in 2003. It would be a useful and harmless way for his fellow students to search each others' files in the "public file" section of the school's internal computer system.

But after some searches turned up copyrighted music files that students had stowed on the system, the Recording Industry Association of America (RIAA) — the music-industry trade group — sued Jordan for music piracy, demanding millions of dollars in damages. Ultimately, Jordan — who said his program wasn't intended for sharing music — paid $12,000 to settle the suit, without admitting wrongdoing. [1]

Jordan wasn't alone. In the early 2000s, RIAA filed or threatened dozens of lawsuits against college students around the country. The campaign was needed, said RIAA General Counsel Steven Marks, because "the enormous damage compounded with every illegal download is alarming — thousands of regular, working class musicians . . . out of work, stores shuttered, new bands never signed." [2]

But there was more to the lawsuit blitz than simply an effort to scare pirating students straight, says Kevin J. Greene, a professor at Thomas Jefferson School of Law, in San Diego. Among the schools where lawsuits were threatened were many that produce highly skilled technology majors, including Rensselaer, the Massachusetts Institute of Technology (MIT) and Carnegie Mellon University, in Pittsburgh. "That was not by chance," says Greene. RIAA officials "were trying to send a message to these high-tech kids" to back off from inventing new technology that would make it easier to copy and share music.

Attempts to slow the commercial impact of new communications technology have a long history.

In the 1930s, AT&T banned one of its engineers, Clarence Hickman of the telephone giant's famous research facility, Bell Labs, from continuing to work on an answering machine he'd invented that used magnetic tape to record messages. Worried that having conversations recorded would "lead the public to abandon the telephone," AT&T shut down Bell research on magnetic tape — the eventual source of audiocassettes, videocassettes and the first computer-storage systems. Eventually, "magnetic tape would come to America via imports of foreign technology, mainly German," wrote Tim Wu, a professor at Columbia Law School who specializes in technology issues. [3]

Also in the 1930s, the young broadcast industry — at the time limited to AM radio — stymied the emergence of FM radio. David Sarnoff, president of RCA, a radio manufacturer and broadcast company, assigned noted inventor Edwin Armstrong of Columbia University to devise a way to eliminate the static that plagued AM broadcasts. Armstrong went one better, inventing an entirely new form of transmission that reduced broadcast noise and made high-fidelity music broadcasts possible. It did so by mod-

economy, about 120,000 in media- and software-creating industries and the rest in jobs that would have been supported by the 120,000 new media-industry workers. [14]

Skepticism about those estimates abounds, however. The Government Accountability Office (GAO), Congress' nonpartisan auditing arm, concluded in 2010 that while economic losses likely are "sizable," no existing estimates can be trusted. No public agencies collect their own data on piracy, industry groups often don't disclose the methods behind their estimates and numerous uncertainties cloud such questions as how much pirated material actually translates into lost sales, the GAO said. For example, a consumer who pays a low price for a counterfeit DVD wouldn't necessarily have paid the price of a non-counterfeit copy, it noted. [15]

Essentially, IPI argued that when a movie studio makes $10 selling a DVD, then passes on $7 to the company that manufactured it and $2 to the trucker who shipped it, the total value of the DVD is $10 plus $7 plus $2, or $19, wrote Timothy B. Lee, an adjunct scholar at the Cato Institute, a libertarian think tank in Washington. "Yet some simple math shows that this is nonsense," he wrote. After paying its subcontractors, "the studio is $1 richer, the trucker . . . $2, and the manufacturer . . . $7. . . . That adds up to $10." [16]

Sales of music CDs dropped steadily in the 2000s, but while the RIAA pins the blame on Internet piracy, the conclusion doesn't hold up because too many other factors likely play into the decrease, argued Lawrence Lessig, a Harvard Law School professor. For example, in the early 2000s, when RIAA reported a substantial drop in the number of CDs sold, fewer CDs than previously were being released and the per-CD price was rising, both solid reasons to expect fewer sales, Lessig wrote. [17]

Free downloading does sometimes replace a music sale, but it's misleading to count every free Internet download as an act of piracy that deprives a copyright owner of dollars, Lessig argued. For example, a large number of "pirated" downloads are of older music that has been taken off the market and is impossible to obtain legally, he wrote.

"This is still technically a violation of copyright, though because the copyright owner is not selling the content anymore, the economic harm is zero — the same harm that occurs when I

ulating radio waves' frequency, rather than their amplitude. It was called FM (frequency modulation) radio.

Because FM radio also operates at a much lower power, Armstrong's invention opened the way for more small broadcasters to get into the game. "You might think that the possibility of more radio stations with less interference would be generally recognized as an unalloyed good," wrote Wu. But, he added, "by this point the radio industry . . . had invested heavily in the status quo of fewer stations," which pleased advertisers by reaching many listeners with one ad buy.

To preserve their business model, industry leaders convinced federal regulators that FM transmission was not ready for prime time, and for six years the government banned its commercial use and limited its experimental use to one narrow band of frequencies. "There was no way for an FM station even to get started without breaking the law," Wu wrote.

In the 21st century, the RIAA successfully fought for new music-licensing rules to hamper expansion of so-called "Internet radio," wrote Harvard Law School Professor Lawrence Lessig. Internet technology allows a virtually unlimited number of "Internet radio stations" to "broadcast," potentially allowing a much wider range of musicians to find a worldwide audience.

But what technology does not limit, laws can, according to Lessig. The RIAA fought to expand copyright law to require Internet stations to pay licensing fees to both composers and the recording artists who perform their songs. Ordinary broadcast-radio stations pay composers only. (In an earlier amendment to the law, Congress had reasoned that radio play acts as advertising for singers and bands, so payment isn't needed.) [4]

The financial burden Internet stations face from the rule "is not slight," Lessig wrote. By one estimate, an Internet station delivering "ad-free popular music to ten thousand listeners, twenty-four hours a day," would owe $1 million a year in recording-artists' fees, while a traditional station doing the same thing would not, he argued.

It's not surprising that existing businesses fight technological change, Lessig wrote. But, he added, the resistance comes with a cost: "It gives dinosaurs a veto over the future."

— Marcia Clemmitt

[1] For background, see "Music Settlement," transcript, "American Morning," CNN.com, May 6, 2003, http://transcripts.cnn.com/TRANSCRIPTS/0305/06/ltm.03.html.

[2] "RIAA Sends More Law Pre-Lawsuit Letters to Colleges With New School Year," press release, RIAA, www.riaa.com/newsitem.php?id=36CA9067-8061-3114-41BB-491B8B32A357.

[3] Tim Wu, *Master Switch: The Rise and Fall of Information Empires* (2010), p. 106.

[4] Lawrence Lessig, *Free Culture: The Nature and Future of Creativity* (2005), p. 197.

sell my collection of 1960s 45-rpm records to a local collector." [18]

Figures about lost jobs from piracy don't add up, wrote Cato Institute Research Fellow Julian Sanchez. Research suggests that, for as many as 80 percent of free music downloads, the consumer would not actually have bought the music, even if a pirated copy had been unobtainable, he wrote. Those acts of piracy, then, cost the industry nothing, since they didn't replace potential sales, he said.

Meanwhile, in the 20 percent of cases in which piracy does replace a sale, the result is a loss to the music industry, "but not a [net] loss to the economy, since the money just ends up being spent elsewhere," Sanchez argued. That being the case, "there is no good reason to think eliminating piracy by U.S. users would yield any jobs on net." [19]

Should Congress crack down harder on digital piracy?

The entertainment industry argued forcefully over the past year that a much tougher system of copyright enforcement is imperative. However, critics of the stalled SOPA and PIPA bills contend that the legislation gives a few large businesses unwarranted power to shut down websites without due process.

SOPA and PIPA "would provide needed tools to combat foreign rogue websites," said MPAA's CEO, former Sen. Christopher Dodd, D-Conn. [20]

PIPA puts "muscle behind closing down foreign sites whose main purpose is to steal" and that cost "working professionals (not just corporations) hundreds of millions of dollars every year," wrote Grecco, the photographer and independent filmmaker. [21]

"Let's all agree that doing nothing is not an option any intellectual property creators can live with," said the independent-label group A2IM. [22]

Even some SOPA/PIPA critics want Congress to quickly craft tougher laws to combat piracy.

"While I'm relieved that the flawed SOPA and PIPA bills seem unlikely to pass in their current forms . . . rogue websites dedicated to the infringement of U.S. copyrights pose a public policy problem that merits . . . prompt (albeit prudent) legislative action," said Ryan Radia, associate director of policy studies at the Competitive Enterprise Institute, a free-market-oriented think tank. [23]

Others argue for more caution, however.

Trying to simply shut down sources of content is "bound to fail in today's

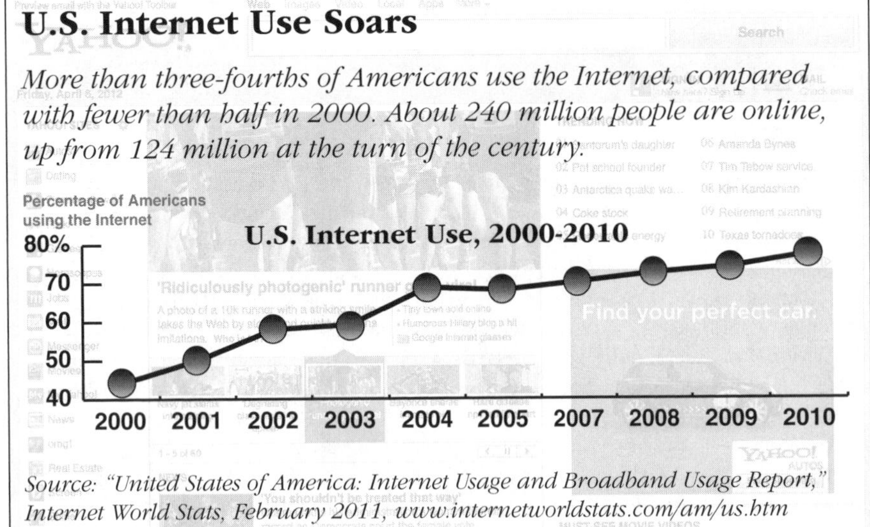
U.S. Internet Use Soars
More than three-fourths of Americans use the Internet, compared with fewer than half in 2000. About 240 million people are online, up from 124 million at the turn of the century.
Percentage of Americans using the Internet
U.S. Internet Use, 2000-2010
80%
70
60
50
40
2000
2001
2002
2003
2004
2005
2007
2008
2009
2010
Source: "United States of America: Internet Usage and Broadband Usage Report," Internet World Stats, February 2011, www.internetworldstats.com/am/us.htm

increasingly interactive world," where new technologies and channels that facilitate information sharing come along continually, said Cato's Sanchez. "As the success of services like [the ad-supported video-streaming site] Hulu and [movie and TV-program distributor] Netflix suggests, consumers are only too happy to pay for content that's made available in a convenient form, and at a reasonable price," he said. "If the content industries want a genuinely effective way to reduce global piracy, they should spend less time and money lobbying for new regulations and focus on providing innovative services that make piracy unattractive." [24]

Many SOPA/PIPA critics view the bills as part of a long-running power grab by big media companies.

"I have first-hand knowledge of what the large media companies think of the Internet. They will never like it until they can control it 100 percent; of course ruining it in the process," wrote Joe Escalante, an entertainment lawyer and bassist for the punk band The Vandals. Escalante's band is being sued by the entertainment newspaper *Daily Variety* because websites unconnected to the band have posted images of album-cover art that the band withdrew from the market and scrubbed from their own website after *Variety* complained that it constituted trademark infringement. [25]

"The *Daily Variety* will claim in front of a jury, presumably with a straight face, that mere 'links' to a site that posted artwork from a discontinued CD displaying an 'infringing parody' should result in the four members of the Vandals paying . . . upwards of a million dollars" in damages, Escalante said. "If the fear is that under SOPA, the media companies will take advantage of a legal anomaly that will permit them to shut down entire websites, with the burden of proving innocence placed on the defendant, based on trumped up claims and theories, I can tell you, it's not paranoia. It is a real-world certainty." [26]

Historically, media and entertainment companies have sought legal protection against every technology that has given the public freer access to copyrighted content, wrote Clay Shirky, a professor at New York University's interactive-telecommunications program, in New York City. "This is an industry that tried to kill Tivo [a device for recording TV shows]. . . . They tried to kill player pianos. They do this whenever a technology increases user freedom over media. Every time. Every single time." [27]

Should the government require Internet-service providers (ISPs) to treat all websites the same?

The FCC and some technology analysts want the government to enforce rules preventing ISPs, mainly phone and cable companies, from treating different websites differently by slowing data from some websites. The aim of the enforcement, they say, would be to prevent ISPs from slowing the flow of content from companies such as video distributors or Internet phone companies that compete with an ISPs' other lines of business or with its business partners. But others argue that such "net neutrality" rules would violate ISPs' rights to conduct business as they see fit over wires and cables they own.

Advocates of net-neutrality regulation have turned traditional arguments for free-speech protections on their head, said Adam Thierer, a senior research fellow in technology policy at George Mason University's Mercatus Center, which researches free markets. They argue that barring ISPs from treating different websites differently would guarantee free speech to website owners that supply content to users. But this is a "twisted theory" of the Constitution's free-speech guarantee, said Thierer. The Constitution is written to stop government from becoming the enemy of free speech and doesn't envision "private platforms" such as ISPs taking that role, he wrote. [28]

In fact, new rules would abridge ISPs' freedom of speech, Thierer said. ISPs are in the business of delivering content to consumers, and "the First Amendment . . . was not intended as a tool for government to control the editorial discretion of private . . . institutions." [29]

"Disappointing one's paying end-user customers is unlikely to be a great business model over time," so "it seems unlikely that broadband ISPs are going to intentionally make a practice of slowing or blocking access to select websites," wrote technology analyst Barbara Esbin, a former special counsel at the Federal Communications Commission. Thus net-neutrality rules are unnecessary, she said. [30]

The 2005 horror movie "Snakes on a Plane," starring Samuel L. Jackson, received a major marketing boost from bloggers and Internet movie-fan communities. After advance word of the movie leaked out, online fans distributed parodies, doctored photographs and mock videos, which the producers used to market the film and shape its plot.

The so-called "takings clause" in the Fifth Amendment to the Constitution bars the government from taking private property "for public use, without just compensation" to the owner, says Daniel Lyons, an assistant professor at Boston College Law School. Cable- and phone-company ISPs own the wires and cables that bring Internet data into individual homes and businesses — the so-called "last mile" of Internet-content delivery — and because of that, the takings clause may apply to Internet regulations, Lyons says. "Since the 1920s there's been a branch of law that says regulations that go too far are like a taking," and net-neutrality rules may fall into that category, meaning that the government would have to pay ISPs to abide by them, he argues.

(In 1982, the Supreme Court ruled that the public interest required a New York landlord to give a cable-TV company access to his roof to install a cable box, as state law required, but that he was entitled to "just compensation" for doing so. The court deemed "just compensation" in the case to be just one dollar; nevertheless, the court established the principle that regulatory requirements are similar to an actual taking, says Lyons. [31])

Many net-neutrality advocates argue that ISPs have solid business reasons for slowing some data relative to others, but that rules to control the behavior are necessary.

A cable-TV company that offers broadband might be strongly motivated to slow the online delivery of movies from a competing video vendor such as Netflix, for example, says Frieden, of Pennsylvania State.

Furthermore, it's already been done, Frieden says. ISPs have said, "We'll never do this. We have no incentive to throttle" traffic. But in 2007, when Comcast was accused of deliberately slowing data transmitted with peer-to-peer file-sharing technology — computer programs that allow individuals to send and receive digital-media files, including music and games — first the company "said it didn't do it, then it said it did. Players do have incentives to distort the market," says Frieden.

(Comcast has argued that many users of file-sharing technology were transferring very large files and that slowing them was necessary in order to keep Internet traffic overall flowing. Subsequently, the company has worked to develop methods of traffic management that would not depend on blocking content from specific websites. [32])

Furthermore, such distortion can be consequence-free for an ISP, Frieden says. "All the consumer knows is that Netflix isn't working well, and they'll blame Netflix," even if the real culprit were an ISP slowing traffic, he says.

ISPs enter contracts with consumers to deliver certain amounts of Internet content at certain rates of speed, and the government could establish some kind of consumer-protection system for those contracts, says Frieden. For example, Congress could explicitly give the FCC authority to do "light-handed" conflict resolution of specific consumer complaints about ISPs hindering traffic, he says.

Opponents of net-neutrality regulation argue that the consumer marketplace is the proper place to handle such problems, but that may not be feasible, says Jonathan Zittrain, a Harvard Law School professor of Internet law.

"If access to Facebook is important to you, and an ISP provides poor (or no) connectivity to Facebook, you can fire your ISP. That is how markets work." But there's a catch, he continues. "There have to be meaningful alternatives" to your nonperforming ISP, and "you have to *know* that you are getting less than you want so you are motivated to switch. Both assumptions may turn out to be wrong." There is less ISP competition than many had hoped for, and rather than blaming one's ISP for slow connections, "you might just think the site itself doesn't have its act together." [33] ■

BACKGROUND

Communications Wars

Struggles over control of communications and media businesses have been among the most intense in economic history. Owners of older, dominant technologies have repeatedly fought innovations that threatened their businesses. [34]

In the mid-19th century, for example, Americans communicated long distances using a single technology — the telegraph — controlled by a single company, Western Union. When, around 1880, the fledgling telephone caused telegraphy to lose its role as virtually the only swift, viable distance-communications technology, Western Union faced potential collapse. Thus, "no sooner had the firm realized the potential of the Bell company's technology to overthrow the telegraph monopoly" than it made an all-out attempt "to kill or devour Bell," wrote Tim Wu, a professor of Internet, media and communications law at Columbia Law School in New York. [35]

Western Union's effort failed, but the pattern would repeat itself many times, frequently slowing development of innovations, sometimes for decades. [36] (*See sidebar, p. 338.*)

At times, the government has stepped in to keep communications companies from snuffing out new competitors.

Beginning in the 1890s, some entrepreneurs strung their own wires through communities — attaching them to supports such as farms' barbed-wire fences — to provide local phone service. The companies prospered, especially in rural areas and small remote towns not served by the Bell system, and in the early 1900s began banding together into larger systems.

AT&T President Theodore Vail feared for his business and believed the small companies would provide inferior service. He began offering independent companies membership in the Bell system, on the condition that they adopt its technical standards and pay to use its long-distance lines. Many companies, which knew they were hamstrung without long-distance service, took the deal, even though AT&T did not promise to connect any calls to non-Bell customers.

The federal government, however, viewed the deals as antitrust violations, intended to snuff out AT&T's competition. To avoid sanctions, Vail agreed to allow independents access to AT&T's lines without joining the company and, more important, to operate AT&T henceforth as a "common carrier" — a company deemed so important to the public good that it must be required to do business in a nondiscriminatory way. [37]

Copyright Disputes

Over the years, numerous legal fights have arisen over protecting the rights of copyright owners, such as composers and filmmakers, when emerging technology has provided new ways for others to copy, alter or publish their intellectual property.

In 1909, Congress amended copyright law for music to ensure that composers were paid for "mechanical reproductions" of their works, such as phonograph records and player-piano rolls. Previous law had granted composers the exclusive right to control whether, when and how their music was performed in public. Under the new law, however, once a composer authorized any recording of a composition, subsequent musicians had the right — the "license" — to record and distribute new recordings of the piece, as long as they paid the composer a fee set by law.

Such licensing arrangements still prevail, and over time lawmakers have expanded their use in an attempt to balance the interests of original intellectual-property owners and those of others who want to use the works. Without such balance, "the monopoly power of rights holders . . . would stifle follow-on creativity," such as the creativity of musicians arranging old music into a new style, wrote Harvard's Lessig. [38]

In recent years, intellectual-property owners have argued for controlling or even banning the use of some technology.

Soon after VCRs — machines that could record TV shows and play tapes of movies for home viewing — hit the market in the 1970s, for example, the movie and television industries sought a ban. "The VCR is to the American film producer and the America public as the Boston strangler is to the woman home alone," Motion Picture Association of America (MPAA) President Jack Valenti told Congress in 1982. [39]

Movie studios sued VCR inventor Sony Corp., alleging that the machines were made for the sole purpose of copyright infringement. In 1984, the Supreme Court narrowly decided the case in Sony's favor, ruling that the recorders were most likely to be used to record TV programs to watch when convenient, a benign purpose that wouldn't harm original creators. [40]

Media Converging

The birth of digital media intensified past struggles.

When the digital revolution began, communications and media executives, like most people, viewed computers as calculating tools and scientific instruments. They missed the fact that, as computers gained more memory, everyday users not only would be able to access all kinds of media — including sound, graphics and video — through a single computer but also could manipulate those media as they wished.

Continued on p. 336

Chronology

1990s *Introduced in 1969 as a network linking a few research centers, the Internet attracts millions of users.*

1996
Phone companies unsuccessfully seek congressional ban on Internet telephone service. . . . Congress passes the Telecommunications Act, classifying cable-TV broadband Internet providers as lightly regulated "information services" but saying little else about the Internet.

1998
Congress passes Digital Millennium Copyright Act, toughening penalties for online piracy.

1999
Millions of users begin sharing music, much of it copyrighted, on Napster, first peer-to-peer file-sharing website.

2000s *Copyright owners worry as online file-sharing booms. Advocates push for requiring broadband Internet service providers (ISPs) to practice "net neutrality" by not blocking lawful content.*

2000
Judge orders Napster to shut down in wake of lawsuits by musicians and the Recording Industry Association of America (RIAA).

2003
RIAA sues or threatens lawsuits against thousands of students for alleged music piracy; Rensselaer Polytechnic Institute freshman Jesse Jordan is among those sued.

2005
Supreme Court rules that cable broadband providers don't have to open their lines to competitors. . . . FCC announces that phone companies providing broadband Internet service can operate under the same rules as cable broadband ISPs. . . . FCC will monitor all broadband ISPs to ensure that consumers can access the websites and applications they choose.

2006
Congress considers net-neutrality legislation.

2008
FCC orders cable broadband provider Comcast to stop blocking peer-to-peer file-sharing programs; Comcast complies but sues, arguing the FCC had no authority to issue the order. . . . RIAA announces it will end mass lawsuits against college students.

2009
Congress is split on net neutrality. Sen. John McCain, R-Ariz., introduces legislation to prohibit the FCC from regulating the Internet; Rep. Edward Markey, D-Mass., introduces a bill to make net neutrality national policy.

2010s *As Internet speeds rise and video streaming increases, movie and TV studios worry about illegal downloads.*

2010
Federal appeals court overturns FCC ruling in 2008 Comcast case. . . . FCC announces an "Open Internet Order," requiring ISPs to disclose their methods for managing Internet traffic and to not discriminate among websites; because of their capacity limitations, wireless broadband providers get more leeway to slow traffic.

2011
FCC Open Internet Order takes effect. . . . House passes resolution calling for the order to be rescinded; a similar measure fails in the Senate. . . . Phone company ISP Verizon sues the FCC over the order, arguing that the agency has no authority to issue it. . . . Countries including the United States, Australia, Canada, Japan and South Korea sign the Anti-Counterfeiting Trade Agreement (ACTA), requiring stronger cross-border antipiracy enforcement.

2012
Motion Picture Association of America urges Congress to toughen anti-piracy legislation. . . . Congress puts two anti-piracy bills, the Stop Online Piracy Act (SOPA) and the Protect Intellectual Property Act (PIPA), on a fast track, but House and Senate leaders pull the measures from consideration two days after Wikipedia and other websites close for a day to protest them. . . . After protests, several European countries delay signing the Anti-Counterfeiting Trade Agreement (ACTA). . . . Department of Justice shuts down Hong Kong-based Megaupload file-sharing site for violating the Digital Millennium Copyright Act. . . . Comcast announces that traffic from its Xbox streaming video service won't count against users' monthly data caps, but other video-streaming will; net-neutrality advocates say Comcast's policy endangers the Internet's standing as a neutral medium fostering economic competition.

'Remix' Culture Worries Copyright Owners

Software allows anyone to manipulate works of art.

After young fans of British author J. K. Rowling began posting renditions of her wildly popular *Harry Potter* story on their own Potter-related websites, Warner Brothers — producer of the book's film version — fought back.

Even though Rowling and her publisher, Scholastic, said they supported the young fans' creative impulses, Warner Brothers tried to block some of the websites, many of them run by children or teenagers, arguing that it wanted to prevent audience confusion about which sites were official. [1]

Heather Lawver, a young American fan, circulated a petition to stop Warner's crackdown and debated a company executive on television. "There are dark forces afoot, darker even than [Potter's evil nemesis] He-Who-Must-Not-Be-Named, . . . daring to take away something so basic, so human, that it's close to murder," she wrote. "They are taking away our freedom of speech." [2]

Warner Brothers backed off.

The episode underscored the increasingly uneasy relationship between copyright owners and others with a financial stake in creative works and a so-called "remix" culture that creates new art by copying, building upon and altering older art.

"Remix culture is in fact not an invention of the digital age," noted Edward W. Felten, a professor of computer science and public affairs at Princeton University. [3] Shakespeare, after all, famously borrowed virtually every plot twist of his play "Julius Caesar" from the Roman historian Plutarch.

New, however, is the breadth of older works that artists can incorporate, now that all art can be digitized and software allows virtually anyone to access, remix and manipulate it, altering visual art pixel by pixel, for example.

Furthermore, while the ability to publish was once the province of professionals, today everyone can publish their creations online.

As a result, traditional distinctions between artist and audience are breaking down.

"Once upon a time . . . the edge of the stage was there. The performers are on one side. The audience is on the other side, and never the twain shall meet," said Eric Kleptone, a Brighton, England-based producer of mashups — recordings that blend tracks from other songs into new music. As media-manipulating software such as Pro Tools, for music, and Photoshop, for graphics, allows people to put their own stamp on art they love, the creator-audience dichotomy is changing, he said. Increasingly, the media-buying public expect "that they should be able to personalize [purchased media] or manipulate it in some way. Or at least have the freedom to do so." [4]

By allowing amateurs to share their creations and get feedback, the Internet spurs more amateur remixes — and makes it easier for copyright owners to find — and object to — such uses of their creative output, according to Henry Jenkins, a professor of communications at the University of Southern California. In the past, "nobody minded, really, if you copied a few songs and shared the dub tape with a friend," he wrote. "But, as those transactions came out from behind closed doors, they represented a visible, public threat to the absolute control the culture industries asserted over their intellectual property." [5]

Continued from p. 334

The secret is "digitization" — the fact that a photograph, audio recording or any other piece of information can be converted into a two-digit "binary code" that computers can store, process and manipulate.

Coded digital information, no matter how complex, is expressed as a sequence containing only zeroes and ones. Digital technology means that "I don't use . . . different kinds of digits for representing music than I use for representing video or . . . documents," said Princeton's Felten. So "where I previously had . . . separate sets of technology" for producing and viewing video and audio, for example, a home computer now becomes "a universal machine" that can access any media and "cause a great earthquake in the media business." [41]

Peer-to-peer file-sharing (P2P) was one of the quake's first tremors.

Via cassette tapes and photocopiers, people have long shared their favorite copyrighted media with friends, but in 1999, the first P2P website for music sharing, Napster, came on the scene. Within months millions were using the site. Some downloaded others' copies of hard-to-obtain music, such as older songs that record companies had taken off the market, and amateur recordings, such as bootleg concert recordings.

But many also downloaded new music without paying for it. Heavy-metal band Metallica sued Napster after leaked copies of their unreleased music appeared on the site. The trade association Recording Industry Association of America (RIAA) also sued Napster for copyright infringement, and in 2000 a federal court ordered the website to close. [42]

The universal power of digital computing has led to a boom in the so-called "remix" culture — the creation of new art by copying and manipulating the old. Amateur and professional artists can manipulate photographs and paintings to create their own collages and animated videos, and young movie buffs intercut scenes from digitized commercial films with their own video to create unauthorized sequels to classic movies such as "Star Wars." (*See sidebar, above.*)

For the most part, copyright owners' response has been to ask Congress to "massively" increase "regulation of creativity in America," wrote Lawrence Lessig, a professor at Harvard Law School. As a result, "To build upon or critique the culture around us one must ask . . . for permission first. Permission is, of course, often granted — but it is not often granted to the critical or the independent." [6]

Young fans of Harry Potter *author J. K. Rowling posted their own* Harry Potter *spin-offs, raising copyright concerns.*

Crackdowns on amateur expression risk snuffing out a vital source of cultural progress, argued Lessig. In the past, "The ordinary ways in which ordinary individuals shared and transformed their culture — telling stories, reenacting scenes from plays or TV, participating in fan clubs, sharing music, making tapes — were left alone by the law." It was "a tradition that, for at least the first 180 years of our Republic, guaranteed creators the right to build freely upon their past." [7]

As the realization dawns that the Internet is nearly impossible to control, some copyright holders may be casting a friendlier eye on remixers, some analysts say.

Warner Brothers' subsidiary New Line Cinema, for example, actually collaborated with bloggers and Internet movie-fan communities in the making and marketing of the 2005 horror movie "Snakes on a Plane," wrote Aram Sinnreich, an assistant professor at Rutgers University's School of Communication and Information.

"After advance word of the film was leaked . . . the one-two punch of its absurd title and a star turn by Samuel L. Jackson (perhaps the most remixed and mashed-up actor in cyberspace) attracted legions" of fans to share online "video mash-ups and remixes, doctored photographs," parodies and more, which the studio used to shape both its marketing campaign and the plot of the film itself, Sinnreich said. [8]

— Marcia Clemmitt

[1] Henry Jenkins, *Convergence Culture: Where Old and New Media Collide* (2006), p. 137.

[2] Quoted in *ibid.*, p. 87.

[3] Edward Felten, quoted in Carlos Ovalle, transcript, "Rip, Mix, Burn, Sue: Technology, Politics and the Fight to Control Digital Media," a lecture, Oct. 12, 2004, (transcript by Carlos Ovalle), www.cs.princeton.edu/~felten/rip.

[4] Quoted in Aram Sinnreich, *Mashed Up: Music, Technology, and the Rise of Configurable Culture* (2010), p. 109.

[5] Jenkins, *op. cit.*, p. 137.

[6] Lawrence Lessig, *Free Culture: The Nature and Future of Creativity* (2005), p. 71.

[7] *Ibid.*, p. 8.

[8] Sinnreich, *op. cit.*, p. 79.

To blunt computers' power to share and remix media, one bill introduced in Congress — but not enacted — would have required that computers come with software that can determine whether online content is copyrighted and keep copyrighted material from being shared. [43]

Such attempts are doomed, however, according to Lessig. Any technological fix "will likely be eclipsed" in short order by new technologies that make it even easier for consumers to access and adapt media, he wrote. [44]

Net Neutrality

The Internet was born in the 1960s when engineers at the Rand Corp., a think tank that focused on military issues, sought to devise a communications network that could survive a nuclear war.

Traditional networks — like the phone system and U.S. Postal Service — route messages through central switching points and can break down completely if vital nodes are knocked out. Rand's Paul Baran proposed a network with no central switch points but merely many smaller, widely dispersed nodes, each of which could route data to another node until a message finally reached its destination. Each message would be chopped into tiny "packets" of digital code, and each separately addressed packet would travel on its own to the destination, where a computer would reassemble all the packets into a coherent message.

Each digital packet "would be tossed like a hot potato from node to node to node, more or less in the direction of its destination, until it ended up in the proper place," explained technology and science fiction writer Bruce Sterling. "If big pieces of the network had been blown away, that simply wouldn't matter; the packets would still stay airborne, lateralled wildly across the field by whatever nodes happened to survive." [45]

Soon the fledgling network was up and running, with packets traveling over telephone wires. The seven research-university computers that constituted the entire network in 1969 expanded to thousands by the early 1970s and millions by the early 1990s. Users paid to use phone lines to transmit their

Entertainment Industry Seeks New Business Plan

"There is a slow and grudging march toward progress."

You might say the pirate hunters engaged in a little piracy of their own. At the Sundance Film Festival, in Park City, Utah, this past January, VEVO — a video website owned by music-industry giants Sony Music Entertainment and Universal Music Group — streamed a pirated ESPN football game for guests, according to technology writer Jason Kincaid. Like many who pirate, VEVO likely streamed the game illegally because doing so was convenient and because a legal stream at a reasonable price wasn't available, Kincaid said. [1]

Sony and Universal have been at the forefront of protecting profits and fighting music and movie piracy, but as VEVO's display of the game underscores, they could be fighting a losing battle. Eventually, the Internet could make a wide variety of media — movies, TV programs, music CDs and other offerings — more easily and cheaply accessible to everyone, on demand, even if it means streaming content illegally.

Yet, while conventional wisdom says that such a trend would be financially devastating for media companies, the sales effects of piracy — and of laws that crack down on it — aren't as clear-cut as they might seem, some experts argue.

For example, in one study, researchers found that while pirated movies released before a film's debut significantly reduce opening-weekend box-office revenues, the piracy had no impact on the box-office take after that. That might have been because only fervent fans who attend openings want to see movies pre-release. [2]

In France, where an ultra-tough three-strikes-and-you're-banned-from-the-Internet law was adopted in 2009, aimed at individual users, piracy rose after enactment, as illegal downloaders switched to websites not explicitly targeted by the law. Furthermore, some of the most active music pirates in the study were also among the most frequent music buyers, so banning them from the Internet could wind up depressing sales, the researchers said. [3]

Of course, big media companies that rely on above-the-board sales of movies and music would rather see piracy disappear. But Internet sales of creative works may not be as gloomy as some may think, thanks in large part to an expanding online marketplace.

"It's true that CD sales are down precipitously," but the size of the music sector overall "actually grew last year," says Aram Sinnreich, an assistant professor at Rutgers University's School of Communication and Information. While some growth came from a rebounding economy, he said, the rest was likely due to the growing universe of online venues for accessing music conveniently and economically.

At Apple's iTunes site, listeners can buy the exact songs they like for a wallet-friendly $1.29 per tune. At the London-based ad- and subscription-supported website Spotify, users can stream and share songs the company has licensed from record labels, without buying, if they choose, says Sinnreich.

data, but, otherwise, phone companies showed no interest in the medium.

As a result, the Internet initially developed without the strife that attended the early spread of such technologies as the telephone.

"There were no . . . Internet service providers . . . no commercial anything. So nobody . . . saw the original Internet initiative as a threat to their business," said Robert Kahn, an early Internet developer. [46]

In 1972, AT&T actually turned down an offer from the federal government to run the Internet. [47]

As late as 1996, when Congress undertook its first major overhaul of telecommunications law since 1934, lawmakers, too, ignored the Internet, mentioning it only a handful of times. Instead, the Telecommunications Act of 1996 focused on provisions lawmakers hoped would create more competition within each of the different forms of data transport, such as cable-TV or local landline phone service. The law also set up different regulatory structures for the various modes of information transfer, with cable companies operating under a completely different set of rules than telephone companies. [48]

Lawmakers failed to grapple with the rapidly materializing prospect that the Internet would soon become a competitor to cable-TV and phone companies, transmitting video and audio data. They also did not foresee that Internet data would soon be carried by numerous modes, including TV cables, phone wires, high-speed wires, fiber-optic cables and wireless transmitters, some of which their new law had put under separate, very different, systems of regulation.

The main Internet-related provision in the 1996 law, which continues to have significant consequences, stems from these different levels of regulation. Specifically, the law states that cable-TV companies' broadband — or "high-speed" — Internet service will operate as a loosely regulated "information service" rather than a tightly regulated "telecommunications carrier," such as a phone company.

"Telecommunications carriers" — like the "common carriers" of old — must offer access to their lines to anyone who seeks it, including competing businesses. For this reason, slow, dial-up Internet service — which travels over regular phone lines — has been offered by many independent ISPs to whom phone companies are required to open their lines.

By contrast, in dubbing cable broadband Internet an "information service,"

In addition, "music publishers are having a field day," as downloads provide an unprecedented opportunity to sell the reams of older music to which they own rights, Sinnreich says. "Back catalogs used to be a hassle. You wouldn't distribute [CDs by 1970s singer-songwriter] Dan Fogelberg to Walmart" because too few would buy them, he says. But the CDs can be sold as downloads because no manufacturer or store shelf space is needed. And with computer tools that break recorded music into individual tracks and put it back together in new ways, "you can have [digital music producer] Danger Mouse do a remix of Dan Fogelberg" that may sell to a new generation.

What's needed, say many Internet experts, are new business and copyright models that reasonably compensate artists while helping consumers take advantage of online streaming, sharing and buying.

Such models might involve "licensing" — with websites buying the right to distribute songs, films or TV shows by selling ads or subscriptions and forwarding payment to industry groups such as the Recording Industry Association of America (RIAA) to distribute among the artists in proportion to how much their creative works were used.

Historically, that's been the solution to disputes between copyright holders and new technology, says David Touve, an assistant professor of business administration at Washington and Lee University, in Lexington, Va. "Radio is a massive infringer of copyright — except that they have a license," he quips. The challenge is "figuring out at what license value both copyright owners and others will be willing to participate," then devising an appropriate licensing scheme, he says.

Online technologies could help more artists get paid for their work, says Sinnreich. According to the RIAA, under "today's copyright-intensive system, only one in 10 albums make back their money" and, "if they don't, artists don't get paid. Can we develop a model that compensates a greater number of musicians?"

Websites such as TuneCore, which helps musicians place music on retail download sites such as Amazon, and CD Baby — a sales site for independent artists — show that payment can be distributed more widely and fairly among individual copyright holders, Sinnreich says. "There is a slow and grudging march toward progress on the economic front."

— Marcia Clemmitt

[1] Jason Kincaid, "Music Labels' Joint Venture, VEVO, Shows Pirated NFL Game at Sundance," *TechCrunch*, Feb. 9, 2012, http://techcrunch.com/2012/02/09/music-labels-joint-venture-vevo-shows-pirated-espn-game-at-sundance.

[2] "Selected Research Findings," "Digital Media," Heinz College iLab website, www.heinz.cmu.edu/ilab/research/digital-media/index.aspx.

[3] For background, see David Murphy, "French Anti-Piracy Law Actually Increasing Piracy," *PC Magazine*, March 28, 2010, www.pcmag.com/article2/0,2817,2361925,00.asp.

Congress lumped it with "luxuries, nonessentials that don't need the same level of protection," says Pennsylvania State's Frieden. That decision — plus fast-moving technological change — set up the so-called "net neutrality" debate that has raged ever since.

For one thing, soon after passage of the 1996 law, phone companies joined cable TV companies as providers of high-speed Internet, laying down their own technologically advanced networks — DSL, or digital subscriber lines, and, later, wireless networks and fiber-optic cable.

Furthermore, in the late 1990s and accelerating in the 2000s, the Internet's importance to public life and business soared as it became a one-stop shop for media and communications, as well as business functions such as shopping and banking. For many observers, this raised the question of whether the public's growing political and economic dependence on online access required all ISPs to operate as a kind of common carrier.

Further complicating matters, so-called packet-sniffing technology was developed that gave ISPs the ability to find out what kind of data a website was transmitting and, to some degree at least, slow or speed up that data.

In the early 2000s, calls began for the government to require all ISPs — including the lightly regulated cable companies — to abide by a principle of "net neutrality," treating data from all websites the same. In 2005, however, the Supreme Court and the FCC moved the other way. In a key ruling based on Congress' classification of cable broadband as an "information service," the Supreme Court ruled 6-3 that a cable company had no obligation to open its lines to a competing, independent ISP. [49]

The ruling opened the door for telephone companies to argue that if cable broadband was not obliged to follow common-carrier-type rules, their broadband services shouldn't be required to do so either.

In 2005, the FCC agreed. Beginning in August 2006, phone companies would no longer be required to offer competing ISPs, such as AOL, free access to their DSL connections. Dial-up Internet would still travel free over regular phone lines, however. [50]

The FCC was not entirely comfortable with leaving ISPs with so much discretion to block competitors, however. It announced that it would monitor ISPs to protect consumers' right to access and run any lawful websites, applications or services and link to the Internet any devices that would not harm the ISP network.

In 2008, the U.S. Court of Appeals for the District of Columbia ruled that cable giant Comcast had violated those policies when it selectively blocked some users' peer-to-peer file-sharing, which Comcast said it did to prevent Internet bottlenecks. In 2010, however, the same court decreed that, under the 1966 law, the FCC had no authority to impose common-carrier-type rules on cable broadband. [51]

German Web entrepreneur Kim Dotcom, founder of Megaupload.com, a file-sharing website, leaves an Auckland, New Zealand, court on Feb. 22, 2012, after being released on bail. He was arrested at the request of the U.S. Justice Department, which is seeking to extradite him on online piracy charges.

Lawmakers are sharply divided. In 2009, Sen. John McCain, R-Ariz., introduced a bill that, with a few exceptions, would have banned the FCC from issuing any rules governing the Internet. That same year Rep. Edward Markey, D-Mass., introduced legislation to establish net neutrality as national policy.

Technical complexity hampers the progress, says Princeton's Felten. "There's a general consensus" that requiring ISPs to be evenhanded has value, "but how do you draw the line between reasonable network management and discrimination? That's hard to talk about" in legislative language, he says.

In December 2010, the FCC adopted an "Open Internet Order," proposing to maintain net neutrality through three rules. Network operators must:

• publicly disclose methods for managing network traffic;

• not block legal applications or websites, except as required for network management;

• not practice "unreasonable discrimination" among websites.

Only the "no blocking" and public-disclosure rules will apply to wireless broadband. Unlike wired transmission, wireless leaks a large amount of its signal into the air, experiences significant signal interference and can't easily add more capacity, as wired networks can. Therefore, as Internet traffic increases, wireless networks might become hopelessly congested without aggressive traffic management, the agency noted. [52]

The order took effect on Nov. 20, 2011. ■

CURRENT SITUATION

Going Dark

After seeming to be on the fast track toward enacting strict new online copyright enforcement, Congress has backed away amid protests by individuals and some major Internet players, including Google and Wikipedia. Meanwhile, some lawmakers are vowing to stop the FCC's net-neutrality order.

In January, Congress postponed long-expected floor votes for SOPA (H.R. 3261), introduced last year in the House by Smith, the Texas Republican — and PIPA — the Protect Intellectual Property Act (S. 968), introduced last year by Sen. Patrick Leahy, D-Vt. [53]

The bills were intended to help copyright owners fight media piracy that websites such as the Swedish site The Pirate Bay facilitate. The Pirate Bay and other sites host so-called bit-torrent files and other software that allow users to share massive audio and video files, many of which are copyrighted. Entertainment industries want enhanced enforcement to stop it.

Posting copyrighted files online without paying is already illegal under the 1998 Digital Millennium Copyright Act (DMCA). [54] The entertainment industry argues, however, that, because the law is tougher on individual copyright infringers than on websites where the material is posted, it goes after small-time pirates while passing up the chance to shut off piracy at its source by forcing entire piracy-facilitating websites offline.

SOPA would give the government a quick path to order advertising networks and online-payment companies such as PayPal to cut off service to websites where copyright infringement is alleged to occur. It would bar search engines from linking to those sites and require ISPs to block access to them. Copyright owners themselves could order advertising and payment companies to stop doing business with websites that post copyrighted material and sue if companies don't comply.

PIPA takes a similar approach but differs in some particulars. For example, it would not require search engines

Continued on p. 342

At Issue:

Should lawmakers support the FCC's net-neutrality rules?

GIGI B. SOHN
PRESIDENT, PUBLIC KNOWLEDGE

FROM TESTIMONY BEFORE THE HOUSE JUDICIARY SUBCOMMITTEE ON INTELLECTUAL PROPERTY, COMPETITION AND THE INTERNET, FEB. 15, 2011

yes

An open Internet is vitally important to political discourse, societal interactions, commercial transactions, innovation, entrepreneurship and job creation in the United States. However, past actions by incumbent broadband Internet access providers have threatened the preservation of an open internet resulting in the need for clear, enforceable baseline network-neutrality rules.

Network-neutrality rules are necessary to protect consumers against the monopoly and duopoly behavior of broadband Internet access providers in our country. Contrary to assertions by industry incumbents that consumers enjoy competition when it comes to broadband access choice and can simply switch, the Federal Communications Commission's (FCC's) National Broadband Plan reported that 13 percent of Americans have only one broadband access provider, and 78 percent of Americans have only two broadband Internet access providers.

Cable and telephone incumbents have asserted that network-neutrality rules are unnecessary and that the market has never demonstrated the need for rules. However, there is a documented history of harmful actions taken by broadband Internet access providers. The commission observed that it had acted on two high-profile incidents of blocking but recounted evidence of numerous other incidents. . . .

AT&T blocked certain applications, such as SlingBox video streaming, Skype and Google voice, from its mobile network while permitting its own streaming and voice products to use the same network. Cox and RCN both admitted to slowing or degrading Internet traffic at times. Both providers deny wrongdoing and claim that these practices are designed to handle congestion, but in neither case did providers disclose their traffic-management practices to subscribers. It is ironic that providers which publicly proclaim they have no intention of ever actually blocking or degrading content routinely include statements in their terms of service that would allow them to engage in precisely these practices — and without prior notice to consumers.

I want to mention Public Knowledge's concern with recent discussions in Congress to invoke the Congressional Review Act (CRA) to repeal the FCC network-neutrality rules. Enactment of a CRA repeal of the FCC's network-neutrality rules would virtually eliminate the agency's authority to protect an open Internet.

I urge members of the committee to recognize that the economic benefits of the Internet are entirely based on ensuring that it remains an open and free marketplace and that the federal government has an integral role to play in that regard.

LARRY DOWNS
SENIOR ADJUNCT FELLOW, TECHFREEDOM

FROM TESTIMONY BEFORE THE HOUSE JUDICIARY SUBCOMMITTEE ON INTELLECTUAL PROPERTY, COMPETITION AND THE INTERNET, FEB. 15, 2011

no

Proponents of net-neutrality regulation argue that the Internet's defining feature — and the key to its unarguable success — is the content-neutral routing and transport of individual packets throughout the network by Internet service providers, Internet backbones and other individual networks that make up the Internet.

As evidenced in all of my writings on the digital revolution, I share the enthusiasm for the open internet. I just don't believe there is any evidence of a need for regulatory intervention to "save" this robust ecosystem, or that the Federal Communications Commission (FCC) had the authority to do so.

As with any lawmaking involving disruptive technologies, moreover, the risk of unintended consequences is high.

There was no need for new regulation. Despite thousands of pages of comments from parties on all sides of the issue, in the end the [FCC] majority could only identify four incidents in the last 10 years of what it believed to be non-neutral behavior. All four were quickly resolved outside the agency's adjudication processes. Yet these four incidents provide the sole evidence of a need to regulate. With no hint of market failure, the majority instead has issued what it calls a "prophylactic rule" it hopes will deter any actual problems in the future.

But maybe these four incidents are not what's really driving the push for FCC regulation of Internet access. Maybe the real problem is, as many regulatory advocates argue vaguely, the lack of "competition" for broadband. According to the National Broadband Plan, 5 percent of the U.S. population still doesn't have access to any wireless broadband provider. In many parts of the country only two providers are available, and in others the offered speeds of alternatives vary greatly, leaving users without high-speed alternatives.

If lack of competition is the problem, though, why not solve the problem? Multiple technologies have been used to deliver broadband access to consumers, including DSL, coaxial cable, cellular, wireless and broadband over power lines (BPL). But rather than promote multiple technologies, the FCC has done just the opposite. For example, the agency has sided with some state governments who argued successfully that they can prevent municipalities from offering telecommunications service. And the commission has dragged its feet on approving trials for BPL.

Why does anyone believe the FCC can "prophylactically" solve a problem dealing with an emerging, rapidly evolving new technology that has thrived in the last decade in part because it was unregulated?

Continued from p. 340

to remove infringing sites from their indexes and would set up a different legal process for seeking court orders.

PIPA is "a strong and balanced approach to protecting intellectual property through a . . . system that leverages the most relevant players in the Internet ecosystem," Leahy said in early January. [55]

Only a few days later, though, thousands of website owners staged a dramatic protest against what many called copyright owners' overreach. On Jan. 18, sites including Wikipedia, the social-media site Reddit, and Boing Boing shut down for the day, redirecting visitors to explanations of their objections to the bills. Other sites, including Google, expressed support for the protests, and millions signed online petitions against the legislation. [56]

"It's not hard to imagine . . . that a service provider, acting with abundance of caution and out of its own self-interest, will simply cut off services to entire sites that have been accused of infringement, even if the court order only applies to a portion of the site," wrote Christine Montgomery, president of the Online News Association, a digital journalists' organization. [57]

The ferocity of the fight is driven by the movie industry, says Kevin J. Greene, a professor of intellectual-property and entertainment law at Thomas Jefferson School of Law, in San Diego. The MPAA spent around $1 million a month fighting for the legislation during the last four to six months before Congress dropped the bills, he says. "Their fears are legitimate," though, especially when it comes to how piracy affects global sales, he says. "In the online world, it's said that if you have a video game to sell in China, you'll sell one copy" because the rest will be pirated.

Nevertheless, the MPAA "said that the problem they were going after was foreign websites, but the language in the bill was so broad" that it casts doubt on that claim, says Greene. "It looks more like they just wanted more weapons in their arsenal" against copyright infringement in general, even though "that arsenal has been getting bigger and bigger for years." (The MPAA did not respond to *CQ Researcher*'s request for comment.)

On Jan. 20, congressional leaders withdrew the bills from consideration. [58]

The protests themselves were a kind of watershed in Internet history — "the first time the Internet rose to defend itself," says Ippolito, of the University of Maine.

Others doubt that grassroots activism played much of a role, however. In the end, the dispute was "monopoly against monopoly, a clash of very big players," with Google and Facebook pitted openly against entertainment-industry giants such as Sony for the first time, says Robert W. Gehl, an assistant professor of communication at the University of Utah, in Salt Lake.

Progress toward an anti-piracy treaty once thought to be on the fast track to adoption also slowed this year.

In October 2011, countries including Australia, Canada, Japan, Morocco, New Zealand, Singapore, South Korea and the United States signed the Anti-Counterfeiting Trade Agreement (ACTA), which would set tough international standards for pursuing copyright enforcement and other anticounterfeiting actions. [59] This year, however, protests in countries such as the U.K., Germany, Poland and the Netherlands have led several European countries to postpone signing the measure. [60]

The White House Office of the U.S. Trade Representative promises that the compact will "support American jobs in innovative and creative industries." [61]

But opponents argue that while the treaty targets "commercial-scale piracy," its language is so vague that it might criminalize small-scale noncommercial file-sharing that involves no financial gain and is handled in civil courts today. [62]

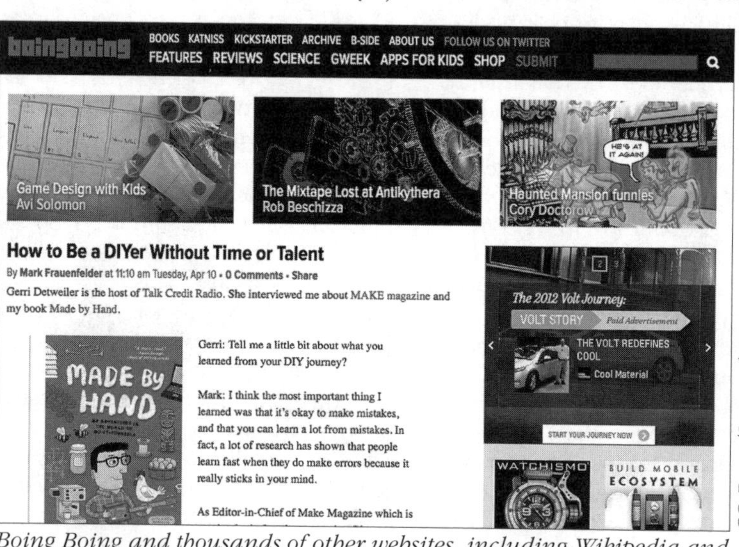

CQ Press/Screenshot

Boing Boing and thousands of other websites, including Wikipedia and Reddit, shut down on Jan. 18, 2012, to protest proposed legislation to block pirating of online copyrighted material. The sites oppose the Stop Online Piracy Act and the Protect Intellectual Property Act, which they claim would amount to censorship. Posting copyrighted files online without paying is already illegal, but supporters of the legislation, principally the entertainment industry, argue tougher laws are needed to stop piracy at its source.

Net Neutrality in Court

The FCC's plan to monitor ISPs for possible discrimination against particular websites remains under fire. In 2011, a joint congressional resolution disapproving the rule — and ordering the agency to refrain from regulating the Internet altogether until Congress issues directions for how to do so — passed the House but failed in the Senate. [63]

Lawsuits questioning the order are proceeding.

On Sept. 30, 2011, New York City-based Verizon Communications filed suit, arguing that the order is unnecessary and that the FCC had no legal authority to promulgate it. "We are deeply concerned by the FCC's assertion of broad authority to impose potentially sweeping and unneeded regulations on broadband networks and services and on the Internet itself," said Senior Vice President Michael E. Glover. [64]

Yet, the Massachusetts-based media-reform advocacy group Free Press also has filed suit, arguing that the rule doesn't go far enough. "The final rules . . . fail to protect wireless users from discrimination," an "arbitrary distinction" between regulations for wireless and wired Internet that is "unjustified," said Policy Director Matt Wood. [65]

Some analysts say Congress must act to clarify the situation for consumers, the FCC and the courts.

ISP subscribers "don't expect anybody to mess with" their data delivery, says Frieden, of Pennsylvania State. For that reason, "Congress needs to clarify the law," stipulating exactly what power the FCC has to settle disputes between consumers and ISPs, he says. "You can revile government and hate the courts but you need some kind of referee here." ■

OUTLOOK

Continuing Battles

It's anybody's guess how the ongoing battles over control of digital intellectual property and management of the Internet's traffic flows will turn out.

This year's heated debate over SOPA and PIPA, however, did reveal something new, says Greene, of Thomas Jefferson Law School. For the first time in a fight over copyrights, "the motion picture industry was up against somebody as well financed as they are" — Internet giants such as Google and Facebook — and that fact is what slowed the bills down, he says.

If SOPA or PIPA were enacted, it would break a "deal cut in 1998" when Congress, the entertainment industry and Internet businesses negotiated the Digital Millennium Copyright Act, Greene says. At that time, everyone agreed that "there's a lot of piracy online but also that we don't want ISPs to actually have to police it," he says.

Recently, however, MPAA came back with new proposals, asking Congress to require ISPs to do just that. In the past, they've gotten what they wanted through backroom channels, Greene says. This time, though, the Internet industry "has more power and money than the entertainment industry."

Many analysts worry that the concerns of the public and of small business won't be heard in the debates.

"Nobody, except for some poorly funded organizations" such as the San Francisco-based Electronic Frontier Foundation — which advocates on civil-liberties issues related to computers — "are standing up for the consumer and citizen," says Aram Sinnreich, an assistant professor at Rutgers University's School of Communication and Information. And those groups have trouble enlisting support "since it's difficult to make these arguments in terms that make sense to non-policy wonks," he says.

Ironically, while the goal of net-neutrality advocates is ensuring that new, small organizations with good ideas get a chance to grow online, such organizations are left out of legislative discussions, says Felten, of Princeton. "When it comes to small companies in the start-up culture, and small business as an engine of growth, there's less understanding than there could be" of what's needed. "People in government look to large, established companies" for guidance on shaping the laws, he says.

Most alarming to some is the likelihood that powerful industries' desire to control online behavior — such as by detecting downloads of copyrighted media — "will overlap with a political interest in overseeing citizens' online behavior," says Sinnreich.

"As committed as we are to freedom, our government and every other government in the world has a prevailing interest in surveillance and control, which is truly scary if it aligns with corporate interest in the same thing." ■

Notes

[1] Quoted in Emma Barnett, "Wikipedia Founder Jimmy Wales Defends SOPA Protest Blackout," *The Telegraph* [UK], Jan. 17, 2012, www.telegraph.co.uk/technology/wikipedia/9020053/Wikipedia-founder-Jimmy-Wales-defends-SOPA-protest-blackout.html.

[2] Lamar Smith, "Why We Need a Law Against Online Piracy," CNN.com, Jan. 20, 2012, www.cnn.com/2012/01/20/opinion/smith-sopa-support/index.html.

[3] Gerald R. Faulhaber and David J. Farber, "The Open Internet: A Customer-Centric Framework," *International Journal of Communication*, 2010, pp. 302-342, http://ijoc.org/ojs/index.php/ijoc/article/view/670/388.

[4] For background, see "10 ISPs and Countries Known to Have Blocked VoIP," *VoIP Providers List*, Feb. 2, 2009, www.voipproviderslist.com/articles/others/10-isps-and-countries-known-to-have-blocked-voip.html.

[5] Edward Felten, "'Neutrality' Is Hard to Define," Room for Debate blog, *The New York Times*, Aug. 10, 2010, www.nytimes.com/roomfordebate/2010/8/9/who-gets-priority-on-the-web/net-neutrality-is-hard-to-define.

[6] "Who Music Theft Hurts," Recording Industry Association of America, www.riaa.com/physicalpiracy.php?content_selector=piracy_details_online.

[7] "MPAA Statement on Strong Showing of Support for Stop Online Privacy Act," Motion Picture Association of American, Inc., press release, Dec. 16, 2011, www.mpaa.org/resources/

5a0a212e-c86b-4e9a-abf1-2734a15862cd.pdf. See also, "Intellectual Property and the U.S. Economy: Industries in Focus," U.S. Commerce Department, March 2012, www.esa.doc.gov/sites/default/files/reports/documents/ipandtheuseconomyindustriesinfocus.pdf.

[8] Mark Elliot, letter to the editor, *The New York Times*, Nov. 18, 2011, www.nytimes.com/2011/11/19/opinion/rogue-web-sites.html.

[9] "Protect IP and SOPA Legislation — Obama Administration Announcement," A2IM website, Jan. 16, 2012, http://a2im.org/tag/sopa.

[10] Mark Sweney, "Global Recorded Music Sales Fall Almost $1.5 bn Amid Increased Piracy," *The Guardian* [UK], March 28, 2011, www.guardian.co.uk/business/2011/mar/28/global-recorded-music-sales-fall.

[11] Quoted in *ibid.*

[12] "IFPI Publishes Digital Music Report 2012," press release, International Federation of the Phonographic Industry, Jan. 23, 2012, www.ifpi.org/content/section_resources/dmr2012.html.

[13] Michael Grecco, "Michael Grecco Is Pro Protect IP and SOPA," MichaelGrecco.com, Jan. 20, 2012, http://michaelgrecco.com/michael-grecco-blog/michael-grecco-is-pro-protect-ip-and-sopa.

[14] Stephen E. Siwek, "The True Cost of Copyright Industry Piracy to the U.S. Economy," Institute for Policy Innovation, October 2007, www.ipi.org/IPI%5CIPIPublications.nsf/PublicationLookupFullTextPDF/02DA0B4B44F2AE9286257369005ACB57/$File/CopyrightPiracy.pdf?OpenElement.

[15] "Observations on Efforts to Quantify the Economic Effects of Counterfeit and Pirated Goods," Government Accountability Office, April 2010, www.gao.gov/new.items/d10423.pdf.

[16] Tim Lee, "Texas-sized Sophistry," The Technology Liberation Front website, Oct. 1, 2006, http://techliberation.com/2006/10/01/texas-size-sophistry.

[17] Lawrence Lessig, *Free Culture: The Nature and Future of Creativity* (2005), p. 71.

[18] *Ibid.*, p. 67.

[19] Julian Sanchez, "How Copyright Industries Con Congress," Cato at Liberty blog, Jan. 3, 2012, www.cato-at-liberty.org/how-copyright-industries-con-congress.

[20] Christopher Dodd, "These Two Bills Are the Best Approach," Room for Debate blog, *The New York Times*, Jan. 18, 2012, www.nytimes.com/roomfordebate/2012/01/18/whats-the-best-way-to-protect-against-online-piracy/these-two-bills-are-the-best-approach.

[21] Grecco, *op. cit.*

[22] "Protect IP and SOPA Legislation — Obama Administration Announcement," *op. cit.*

[23] Ryan Radia, "Are Rogue Websites Really So Bad After All?" The Technology Liberation Front, Jan. 23, 2012, http://techliberation.com/2012/01/23/are-rogue-websites-really-so-bad-after-all.

[24] Julian Sanchez, "Focus on Innovation Instead," Room for Debate blog, *The New York Times*, Jan. 18, 2012, www.nytimes.com/roomfordebate/2012/01/18/whats-the-best-way-to-protect-against-online-piracy/the-content-industry-should-focus-on-innovation-instead.

[25] For background, see Vickie Chang, "Painful Parody," *OC Weekly*, Sept. 9, 2010, www.ocweekly.com/2010-09-09/music/vandals-vs-daily-variety/.

[26] Joe Escalante, "Does Daily Variety Validate SOPA Fears?" *Huffington Post*, Jan. 23, 2012, www.huffingtonpost.com/joe-escalante/sopa-copyright_b_1222058.html.

[27] Clay Shirky, "Pick up the Pitchforks: David Pogue Underestimates Hollywood," Shirky.com, Jan. 20, 2012, www.shirky.com/weblog/2012/01/pick-up-the-pitchforks-david-pogue-underestimates-hollywood.

[28] Adam Thierer, "Net Neutrality Regulation & the First Amendment," The Technology Liberation Front, Dec. 9, 2009, http://techliberation.com/2009/12/09/net-neutrality-regulation-the-first-amendment.

[29] *Ibid.*

[30] Barbara Esbin, "Net Neutrality: A Further Take on the Debate," The Progress & Freedom Foundation, December 2009, http://papers.ssrn.com/sol3/papers.cfm?abstract_id=1529090.

[31] For background, see *Loretto v. Teleprompter Manhattan CATV Corp.*, 458 U.S. 419, 434-35 (1982), http://caselaw.lp.findlaw.com/cgi-bin/getcase.pl?navby=case&court=US&vol=458&invol=419&pageno=436.

[32] For background, see K. C. Jones, "Comcast Removes Blocks on File Sharing," *Information Week*, Jan. 7, 2009, www.informationweek.com/news/internet/policy/212701122; Ryan Paul, "FCC to Investigate Comcast BitTorrent Blocking," *Ars Technica*, http://arstechnica.com/tech-policy/news/2008/01/fcc-to-investigate-comcast-bittorrent-blocking.ars.

[33] Jonathan Zittrain, "Net Neutrality as Diplomacy," Jan. 23, 2011, http://papers.ssrn.com/sol3/papers.cfm?abstract_id=1729424.

[34] For background, see Tim Wu, *Master Switch: The Rise and Fall of Information Empires* (2010); Marcia Clemmitt, "Controlling the Internet," *CQ Researcher*, May 12, 2006, pp. 409-432; Kenneth Jost, "Copyright and the Internet," *CQ Researcher*, Sept. 29, 2000, pp. 769-792.

[35] Wu, *op. cit.*, p. 27.

[36] *Ibid.*, p. 10.

[37] *Ibid.*, p. 58.

[38] Lawrence Lessig, *Free Culture: How Big Media Uses Technology and the Law to Lock Down Culture and Control Creativity* (2004), p. 57.

[39] Quoted in Carlos Ovalle, transcript, "Rip, Mix, Burn, Sue: Technology, Politics and the Fight to Control Digital Media," a lecture by Edward Felten, Oct. 12, 2004, www.cs.princeton.edu/~felten/rip.

[40] *Sony Corp. v. Universal City Studios*, 464 U.S. 417 (1984), http://supreme.justia.com/cases/federal/us/464/417.

[41] Ovalle, *op. cit.*

[42] For background, see Steve Knopper, "Napster Wounds the Giant," *Rocky Mountain News*, Jan. 2, 2009, www.rockymountainnews.com/news/2009/jan/02/napster-wounds-the-giant.

[43] Lessig, *Free Culture: How Big Media Uses Technology*, *op. cit.*, kindle location 5476, Chap. 12, footnote 11.

[44] *Ibid.*, p. 193.

[45] Bruce Sterling, "Internet," *The Magazine of Fantasy and Science Fiction*, February 1993, archived at Electronic Frontier Foundation website, w2.eff.org/Net_culture/internet_sterling.history.txt.

[46] Quoted in "Putting It All Together With Robert Kahn," Computer and Computer History website, http://66.14.166.45/history/network/

About the Author

Staff writer **Marcia Clemmitt** is a veteran social-policy reporter who previously served as editor in chief of *Medicine & Health* and staff writer for *The Scientist*. She has also been a high school math and physics teacher. She holds a liberal arts and sciences degree from St. John's College, Annapolis, and a master's degree in English from Georgetown University. Her recent reports include "Digital Education" and "Computer Hacking."

Robert%20Kahn%20Interview%20-%20Putting%20it%20all%20Together%20with%20Robert%20Kahn.pdf.

[47] For background, see Scott Bradner, "Blocking the Power of the Internet," *Network World*, Jan. 16, 2006, www.networkworld.com/columnists/2006/011606bradner.html.

[48] For background, see Charles B. Goldfarb, "Telecommunications Act: Competition, Innovation, Reform," Congressional Research Service, Aug. 12, 2005, http://digital.library.unt.edu/ark:/67531/metacrs7798/m1/1/high_res_d/RL33034_2005Aug12.pdf.

[49] For background, see *National Cable & Telecommunications Assn. v. Brand X Internet Services*, 545 U.S. 967 (2005), www.law.cornell.edu/supct/html/04-277.ZS.html.

[50] For background, see Angele A. Gilroy, "Access to Broadband Networks: The Net Neutrality Debate," Congressional Research Service, Oct. 25, 2011, www.fas.org/sgp/crs/misc/R40616.pdf.

[51] For background, see *Comcast Corp. v. FCC*, 600 F.3d 642, www.cadc.uscourts.gov/internet/opinions.nsf/EA10373FA9C20DEA85257807005BD63F/$file/08-1291-1238302.pdf.

[52] For background, see Matthew Lasar, "It's Here: FCC Adopts Net Neutrality (Lite)," *Ars Technica*, 2011, http://arstechnica.com/tech-policy/news/2010/12/its-here-fcc-adopts-net-neutrality-lite.ars, and Elliott Drucker, "Tech Insights — Sizing Up Wireline Vs. Wireless Performance," *Wireless Week*, Jan. 16, 2011, www.wirelessweek.com/Articles/2011/02/Drucker-Sizing-Up-Wireline-Vs-Wireless-Performance.aspx.

[53] For background, see bill text, H.R. 3261, Thomas, Library of Congress, http://thomas.loc.gov/cgi-bin/query/z?c112:H.R.3261:, and bill text versions, S. 968, Thomas, Library of Congress, http://thomas.loc.gov/cgi-bin/query/z?c112:S.968.

[54] For background, see "The Digital Millennium Copyright Act of 1998," U.S. Copyright Office, December 1998, www.copyright.gov/legislation/dmca.pdf.

[55] Quoted in Mike Masnick, "Senator Leahy Hopes to Rush Through PIPA By Promising to Study DNS Blocking . . . Later?" *TechDirt*, Jan. 12, 2012, www.techdirt.com/articles/20120112/14322317392/senator-leahy-hopes-to-rush-through-pipa-promising-to-study-dns-blocking-later.shtml.

[56] For background, see Sean Poulter and Rob Waugh, "Wikipedia Protest Hits Home: U.S. Senators Withdraw Support for Anti-piracy Bills as 4.5 Million Sign Petition," *Daily Mail Online* [UK], Jan. 19, 2012, www.dailymail.co.uk/news/article-2087673/Wikipedia-blackout-SOPA-protest-US-senators-withdraw-support-anti-piracy-bills.html.

[57] Christine Montgomery, "Letter from the President: Why ONA Opposes Sopa," Online News Association website, Jan. 5, 2012, http://journalists.org/2012/01/05/ona-on-sopa.

[58] For background, see SOPA/PIPA Timeline, *Pro Publica*, http://projects.propublica.org/sopa/timeline.

[59] For background, see "Anti-Counterfeiting Trade Agreement," www.mofa.go.jp/policy/economy/i_property/pdfs/acta1105_en.pdf.

[60] For background, see "Timeout for Finland in Ratifying ACTA," *Valtioneuvosto*, Finnish Government, March 9, 2012, http://valtioneuvosto.fi/ajankohtaista/tiedotteet/tiedote/fi.jsp?oid=352766&c=0&toid=1802&moid=1803; Dave Lee, "ACTA Protests: Thousands Take to Streets Across Europe," BBC News, Feb. 11, 2012, www.bbc.co.uk/news/technology-16999497; Raphael Satter and Venssa Gera, "Anonymous Protests ACTA, Attacks FTC and Other U.S. Agencies' Sites," Associated Press/*Huffington Post*, Feb. 17, 2012, www.huffingtonpost.com/2012/02/17/anonymous-acta-ftc_n_1285668.html; Anti-Counterfeiting Trade Agreement, Foreign Affairs and International Trade Canada, www.international.gc.ca/trade-agreements-accords-commerciaux/fo/intellect_property.aspx?view=d; Glyn Moody, "Brazil Drafts and 'Anti-ACTA': A Civil-Rights-Based Framework for the Internet," *Tech Dirt*, www.techdirt.com/articles/20111004/04402516196/brazil-drafts-anti-acta-civil-rights-based-framework-internet.shtml.

[61] "Anti-Counterfeiting Trade Agreement," Office of the U.S. Trade Representative, www.ustr.gov/acta.

[62] Dan Mitchell, "Meet SOPA's Evil Twin, ACTA," CNN Money, Jan. 26, 2012, http://tech.fortune.cnn.com/2012/01/26/meet-sopas-evil-twin-acta.

[63] For background, see S.J.Res. 6, Open Congress, www.opencongress.org/bill/112-sj6/show.

[64] Quoted in Marguerite Reardon, "Verizon Sues Again to Block Net Neutrality Rules," CNET, Sept. 30, 2011, http://news.cnet.com/8301-30686_3-20114142-266/verizon-sues-again-to-block-net-neutrality-rules.

[65] Quoted in Grant Gross, "Free Press Files Lawsuit on FCC's Net Neutrality Rules," *Computer World*, Sept. 28, 2011, www.computerworld.com/s/article/9220367/Free_Press_files_lawsuit_on_FCC_s_net_neutrality_rules.

FOR MORE INFORMATION

Chilling Effects Clearinghouse, www.chillingeffects.org. University-supported website that provides information on and analysis of digital-media issues.

Electronic Frontier Foundation, 454 Shotwell St., San Francisco, CA 94110-1914; 415-436-9333; www.eff.org. Advocates for media-related civil liberties, such as open access to the Internet.

Federal Communications Commission, 445 12th St., S.W., Washington, DC 20554; 888-225-5322; www.fcc.gov. Federal agency that sets rules for communications industries.

Motion Picture Association of America, 1600 Eye St., N.W., Washington, DC, 20006; 202-293-1966; www.mpaa.org. Trade association that represents the major American motion-picture and television studios.

Progress and Freedom Foundation, www.pff.org. Archives of a free-market-oriented think tank that analyzed digital media policy until October 2010.

Public Knowledge, 1818 N St., N.W., Suite 410, Washington, DC 20036; 202-861-0020; www.publicknowledge.org. Advocates for net neutrality and copyright policies that balance the interests of intellectual-property owners and media consumers.

Recording Industry Association of America, 1025 F St., N.W., 10th Floor, Washington, DC 20004; 202-775-0101; www.riaa.com. Trade association that represents major music-recording companies.

Technology Information Front, http://techliberation.com. Website of commentary by libertarian analysts that opposes government regulation of the Internet.

Bibliography

Selected Sources

Books

Downes, Larry, *The Laws of Disruption: Harnessing the New Forces that Govern Life and Business in the Digital Age*, Basic Books, 2009.

A business and legal consultant describes how digitization and the Internet are disrupting the traditional economy. He argues against hasty government regulation of new technologies and for allowing a new legal system suitable to the digital era to emerge on its own.

Lessig, Lawrence, *Free Culture: The Nature and Future of Creativity*, Penguin, 2004.

A Harvard University law professor argues that copyright law favors copyright owners, empowering media companies to strangle creative digital opportunities.

Wu, Tim, *The Master Switch: The Rise and Fall of Information Empires*, Vintage, 2011.

A Columbia University law professor describes the history of American communications industries as one in which inventors create powerful industries that then fight to suppress competing innovations.

Articles

Ferreira, Heather, "What Do Directors Think When People Make a Torrent for Their Movie?" *Huffington Post*, Feb. 22, 2012, www.huffingtonpost.com/quora/what-do-directors-think-w_b_1292760.html.

An independent filmmaker argues that anti-piracy legislation serves the interests of big film studios and the highest-paid tier of Hollywood talent but not those of independent creators.

Hachman, Mark, "Comcast's Xfinity-on-Xbox Plans Draw Net Neutrality Fire," *PCMag.com*, March 26, 2012, www.pcmag.com/article2/0,2817,2402149,00.asp.

Net-neutrality advocates say Comcast's policy of not counting video streaming from its Xbox subsidiary toward customers' monthly data-usage caps violates the principle of an open Internet.

Jardine, Nick, "Meet the Man Who Founded the Pirate Party That Is Spreading Through European Parliaments," *Business Insider*, Dec. 5, 2011, http://articles.businessinsider.com/2011-12-05/europe/30477454_1_new-movement-young-voters-protest.

A Swedish-based political movement that aims to legalize online file-sharing is gaining support, especially among young people.

Wortham, Jenna, and Amy Chozick, "The Piracy Problem: How Broad?" *The New York Times*, Feb. 8, 2012, www.nytimes.com/2012/02/09/technology/in-piracy-debate-deciding-if-the-sky-is-falling.html?pagewanted=all.

Copyright-owning industries such as the movie and music businesses cite huge financial losses from piracy, but many consumers say they resort to pirating only when they can't conveniently access what they want at a reasonable price.

Reports and Studies

Benkler, Yochai, "Seven Lessons from SOPA/PIPA/Megaupload and Four Proposals on Where We Go From Here," Techpresident, Jan. 25, 2012, http://techpresident.com/news/21680/seven-lessons-sopapipamegauplaod-and-four-proposals-where-we-go-here.

A Harvard law professor argues that anti-piracy bills in Congress this year were an over-reach by copyright-owning industries and that protests that slowed the bills' progress show how consumers are learning to use the Internet to accomplish political goals.

Esbin, Barbara S., "Net Neutrality: A Further Take on the Debate," Progress on Point, The Progress and Freedom Foundation, December 2009, http://papers.ssrn.com/sol3/papers.cfm?abstract_id=1529090.

A media lawyer and former Federal Communications Communication official argues that the fast-evolving nature of the Internet and its openness to new businesses and new ideas would be hampered if the government chose to regulate it.

Felten, Edward W., "Rip, Mix, Burn, Sue: Technology, Politics, and the Fight to Control Digital Media," video lecture, Princeton University, Oct. 12, 2004, www.cs.princeton.edu/~felten/rip; transcript, www.ischool.utexas.edu/~i312co/copyright/felten.html.

A Princeton University professor of computer science and public affairs discusses how digitization changes the game for media and communications businesses.

Gilroy, Angele A., "Access to Broadband Networks: The Net Neutrality Debate," Congressional Research Service, April 15, 2011, http://opencrs.com/document/R40616.

An analyst for Congress' nonpartisan research office describes the history and legislative, regulatory, judicial and commercial issues involved in the debate over net neutrality.

Thierer, Adam, "Net Neutrality Regulation & the First Amendment," The Technology Liberation Front, Dec. 9, 2009, http://techliberation.com/2009/12/09/net-neutrality-regulation-the-first-amendment.

A libertarian telecommunications analyst argues that net-neutrality advocates turn the Constitution's First Amendment on its head when they argue that in order to preserve freedom of speech Internet service providers (ISPs) must treat all content the same. In fact, he writes, net-neutrality rules would assault ISPs' free-speech rights by substituting government rules for ISPs' own editorial judgment.

The Next Step:

Additional Articles from Current Periodicals

Economy

Gaudiano, Nicole, and Elizabeth Bewley, "Songwriters Sing Praises of Bill to Fight Online Piracy," *The Tennessean*, Dec. 14, 2011, www.knoxville.com/news/2011/dec/14/songwriters-sing-praises-bill-fight-online-piracy/?partner=RSS.

Several Nashville-based songwriters say they have lost a large portion of their royalty income on copyrighted songs because of online piracy.

Lynch, Brendan, "Backlash Over Piracy Bills," *Boston Herald*, Jan. 15, 2012, p. 8, bostonherald.com/business/technology/general/view/20220115backlash_over_piracy_bills_websites_spar_over_rules_for_internet.

Experts say curbing piracy would hurt the economy by stifling technological innovation.

Selby, W. Gardner, "Smith's Estimates of Billions Lost to Piracy Don't Add Up," *Austin* (Texas) *American-Statesman*, Feb. 7, 2012, p. B1.

Rep. Lamar Smith, R-Texas, says the United States loses $100 billion annually to illegal counterfeiting and piracy.

Internet-Service Providers

Flint, Joe, "Coalition Forms to Crack Down on Internet Piracy," *Los Angeles Times*, July 8, 2011, p. B3, articles.latimes.com/2011/jul/07/business/la-fi-ct-piracy-20110708.

The Center for Copyright Information has formed a coalition to fight online piracy.

Sisario, Ben, "Net Providers Plan Penalties to Slow Piracy," *The New York Times*, July 8, 2011, p. A1, www.nytimes.com/2011/07/08/technology/to-slow-piracy-internet-providers-ready-penalties.html?pagewanted=all.

Several Internet providers plan to develop a system to identify customers suspected of digital copyright infringement.

'Remix' Culture

Barnhart, Aaron, "Sample This! Authors Say Use of Fair Use Is Growing," *Kansas City Star*, Sept. 20, 2011, p. D1, www.kansascity.com/2011/09/19/3153835/sample-this-show-authors-say-use.html.

Proponents of video and music remixing say sampling past works, whether or not they are copyrighted, is a legitimate form of artistic expression.

Johnson, Stephon, " 'Creative License' Tackles the Murky World of Sampling in Music," *New York Amsterdam News*, June 30, 2011, p. 19.

Legal debates over music sampling and copyright issues didn't emerge until the birth of hip-hop culture and rap music.

Kaufman, Sarah, "Beyoncé: 'Countdown' Video and the Art of Stealing," *The Washington Post*, Nov. 18, 2011, p. E1.

A Belgian choreographer accused pop star Beyoncé of copying dance moves in a recent music video without permission.

Stop Online Piracy Act

Atkinson, Claire, "Tinseltown Offensive: Studios Strike Back With $3M SOPA Blitz," *New York Post*, Jan. 20, 2012, p. 28, www.nypost.com/p/news/business/tinseltown_offensive_cVgdYVB2xwiBselYnBxLpI.

Major Hollywood studios are launching a $3 million campaign to back the Stop Online Piracy Act.

Caristi, Dom, "Congress Blocks Path for Evolving Technology," *Indianapolis Star*, Dec. 24, 2011, p. A11, www.indystar.com/article/20111224/OPINION01/112240317/My-View-Congress-blocks-path-evolving-technology.

The Stop Online Piracy Act is an example of Congress impeding evolving technology, says a telecommunications professor at Ball State University in Muncie, Ind.

MacInnis, Laura, "Concerns for Online Piracy Measure," *The Washington Post*, Jan. 15, 2012, p. A20.

Several White House advisers say the Stop Online Piracy Act could make many Internet businesses vulnerable to litigation.

Wadhwani, Anita, "Music Row Spent $4 Million on Lobbying in 3 Months," *The Tennessean*, Nov. 20, 2011, www.tennessean.com/article/20111120/BUSINESS/311200042/Music-Row-spent-4-million-lobbying-3-months.

Nashville's country-music industry has spent at least $4 million to lobby Congress to pass the Stop Online Piracy Act.

Citing *CQ Researcher*

Sample formats for citing these reports in a bibliography include the ones listed below. Preferred styles and formats vary, so please check with your instructor or professor.

MLA Style

Jost, Kenneth. "Remembering 9/11," CQ Researcher 2 Sept. 2011: 701-732.

APA Style

Jost, K. (2011, September 2). Remembering 9/11. *CQ Researcher, 9*, 701-732.

Chicago Style

Jost, Kenneth. "Remembering 9/11." *CQ Researcher*, September 2, 2011, 701-732.

CQ Researcher

Published by CQ Press, an Imprint of SAGE Publications, Inc.

www.cqresearcher.com

Criminal Records and Employment

Should barriers be eased for ex-prisoners?

Many former prisoners are turned away from jobs because of their criminal records. The federal government, more than 30 cities and at least 26 states limit the kind of criminal-background information employers can obtain or when they can request it. Advocates for ex-prisoners say such restrictions don't go far enough in making it easier for former offenders to find work. But employers note that they can be sued for failing to check out an employee who harms fellow workers or customers. Further complicating the picture is new research suggesting that an old criminal history doesn't predict behavior. Meanwhile, the vast majority of the 92 million criminal records covering an estimated 65 million people are accessible online. And companies selling criminal histories may number in the thousands.

Ex-offender Urick Phillips works at Goodwill Industries in Colorado Springs on March 2, 2011. He and other former prisoners in the area receive health care services from a local nonprofit.

INSIDE THIS REPORT

The Issues 351
Background 358
Chronology 359
Current Situation 364
At Issue........................367
Outlook 369
Bibliography 373
The Next Step 374

CQ Researcher • April 20, 2012 • www.cqresearcher.com
Volume 22, Number 15 • Pages 349-376

Los Angeles | London | New Delhi
Singapore | Washington DC

Recipient of Society of Professional Journalists Award for Excellence ◆ American Bar Association Silver Gavel Award

CRIMINAL RECORDS AND EMPLOYMENT

THE ISSUES

351 • Should government control employers' access to job-seekers' criminal records?
• Is deleting records effective in the Internet age?
• Should employers have access to old criminal records?

BACKGROUND

358 **The Pardon Route**
U.S. presidents often issued pardons to cancel sentences they considered unfair.

360 **Social Integration**
In the early 1950s, rehabilitation gained acceptance as the objective of incarceration.

362 **War on Crime**
Rising crime beginning in the 1960s led to harsh penalties.

363 **Re-entry with Records**
Hiring decisions based on criminal records were challenged.

CURRENT SITUATION

364 **Top-Down Change**
Ohio Gov. Kasich wants sweeping reforms of employment policies.

366 **New EEOC Guideline**
The commission is considering new rules on use of criminal records.

368 **Warning on Apps**
Mobile applications for criminal-record searches may violate federal law.

OUTLOOK

369 **More Screening?**
Fingerprints may become part of job-applicant scrutiny.

SIDEBARS AND GRAPHICS

352 **States Ease Job Barriers for Ex-Prisoners**
Thirteen states sought to expunge records for low-level offenses.

353 **Minorities Dominate U.S. Prison Population**
Sixty percent of inmates are black or Hispanic.

356 **'Ban the Box' Policies Adopted in 20 States**
New York is among cities with reformed policies.

359 **Chronology**
Key events since 1910.

360 **Studies Challenge Views on Race, Recidivism**
Criminal records don't always predict future conduct.

364 **In Pennsylvania, Arrest Records Can Vanish**
"Why are they there? Only so employers can use them illegally."

367 **At Issue**
Are more limits needed on employers' access to criminal records?

FOR FURTHER RESEARCH

372 **For More Information**
Organizations to contact.

373 **Bibliography**
Selected sources used.

374 **The Next Step**
Additional articles.

375 **Citing *CQ Researcher***
Sample bibliography formats.

Cover: AP Photo/*The Gazette*/Jerilee Bennett

CQ Researcher

April 20, 2012
Volume 22, Number 15

MANAGING EDITOR: Thomas J. Billitteri
tjb@cqpress.com

ASSISTANT MANAGING EDITOR: Kathy Koch
kkoch@cqpress.com

CONTRIBUTING EDITOR: Thomas J. Colin
tcolin@cqpress.com

ASSOCIATE EDITOR: Kenneth Jost

STAFF WRITER: Marcia Clemmitt

CONTRIBUTING WRITERS: Sarah Glazer, Alan Greenblatt, Peter Katel, Barbara Mantel, Jennifer Weeks

DESIGN/PRODUCTION EDITOR: Olu B. Davis

ASSISTANT EDITOR: Darrell Dela Rosa

FACT CHECKER: Michelle Harris

Los Angeles | London | New Delhi
Singapore | Washington DC

An Imprint of SAGE Publications, Inc.

VICE PRESIDENT AND EDITORIAL DIRECTOR, HIGHER EDUCATION GROUP:
Michele Sordi

DIRECTOR, ONLINE PUBLISHING:
Todd Baldwin

CQ Researcher (ISSN 1056-2036) is printed on acid-free paper. Published weekly, except: (March wk. 5) (May wk. 4) (July wk. 1) (Aug. wks. 3, 4) (Nov. wk. 4) and (Dec. wks. 3, 4). Published by SAGE Publications, Inc., 2455 Teller Rd., Thousand Oaks, CA 91320. Annual full-service subscriptions start at $1,054. For pricing, call 1-800-834-9020. To purchase a *CQ Researcher* report in print or electronic format (PDF), visit www.cqpress.com or call 866-427-7737. Single reports start at $15. Bulk purchase discounts and electronic-rights licensing are also available. Periodicals postage paid at Thousand Oaks, California, and at additional mailing offices. POSTMASTER: Send address changes to *CQ Researcher*, 2300 N St., N.W., Suite 800, Washington, DC 20037.

Criminal Records and Employment

BY PETER KATEL

THE ISSUES

By age 58, Edward Collins of Detroit had accumulated the kind of record that tends to go over badly in a job interview. In fact, he had spent most of his life behind bars for armed robbery, car theft and other crimes. "I never hurt anyone physically," Collins says. "But eventually, from being a parasite, I became a criminal."

Upon release, he joined the 700,000 people who leave federal and state prisons every year. [1] But Collins was luckier than most of them: He managed to get a job — as a part-time, minimum-wage janitor. He figured he'd get no further. "Once a guy gets a record," he says, "some doors are just shut unless you happen to know someone."

But a chance visit to a soup kitchen run by a Roman Catholic order, the Capuchin Franciscans, led to Collins getting involved in a baked-goods project that the Capuchin friars had started. Collins, who learned baking in prison, now helps run what has become a full-fledged bakery — On The Rise. He mentors younger workers who have criminal records, instilling what he calls the values of "sobriety and changing your social life, being an honest citizen and helping out the community and the neighborhood."

All of the young workers leave the bakery with jobs. "Some guys really do want to change," Collins says.

Whether all employers recognize that a criminal past doesn't necessarily predict a criminal future is another matter. It's a pressing question in a country where at least 50 percent of males have been arrested at some point in their lives and state governments have criminal records on an estimated 65 million people. Most of those records — which may show arrests that led no further or that resulted in convictions and prison sentences — are automated and searchable online, making them accessible to the hundreds, or perhaps thousands, of companies that sell criminal-background checks. [2]

Given the expense and social cost of keeping people locked up, lowering the reincarceration rate is becoming increasingly urgent. And an ex-prisoner who finds a job is considered less likely to return to crime.

On The Rise

Thanks to bakery skills he learned in prison, Edward Collins landed a job in Detroit with the On The Rise bakery, where he mentors young men with criminal records. To give former prisoners a better chance at employment, 32 cities and counties require government employers to postpone criminal-record questions until job-seekers pass the application stage; the trend hasn't caught on in the business world.

Thirty-two cities and counties across the country recently have passed "ban the box" laws that apply to applicants for government jobs. (*See map, p. 356.*) The laws require employers to postpone criminal-record questions until job-seekers get past the application stage; in the past, applicants would have been required to check a box if they'd been arrested or convicted. The trend hasn't caught on in the business world, however: Only Massachusetts and Hawaii, along with the city of Philadelphia, now apply "ban the box" to private-sector employment. [3]

Race and ethnicity play a prominent role in the criminal-records issue. Their influence is inescapable: As the United States has become the world incarceration leader — with 2.3 million people behind bars in 2010 — about 38 percent of federal and state prisoners are black and 22 percent Hispanic. (*See graphic, p. 353.*) Given the disproportionate representation of blacks and Latinos in the inmate population, an employer's blanket policy on criminal records tends to disproportionately affect those groups of applicants and job-holders. [4]

For that reason, the U.S. Equal Employment Opportunity Commission (EEOC) has long sought to regulate criminal-record use by employers. Now, with attention to the issue growing, the EEOC is considering broadening its guidelines to deal more extensively with records of conviction as well as arrest. (*See Current Situation, p. 364.*) And 26 states have enacted laws over the past two years aimed at limiting or postponing employer access to criminal records, allowing removal —

States Ease Job Barriers for Ex-Prisoners

Twenty-one states adopted laws and policies in 2010 or 2011 that address employment challenges facing people with criminal records, including 13 states that took steps to expunge or seal records of low-level offenses.

Employment Reforms for People with Criminal Records, 2010-2011

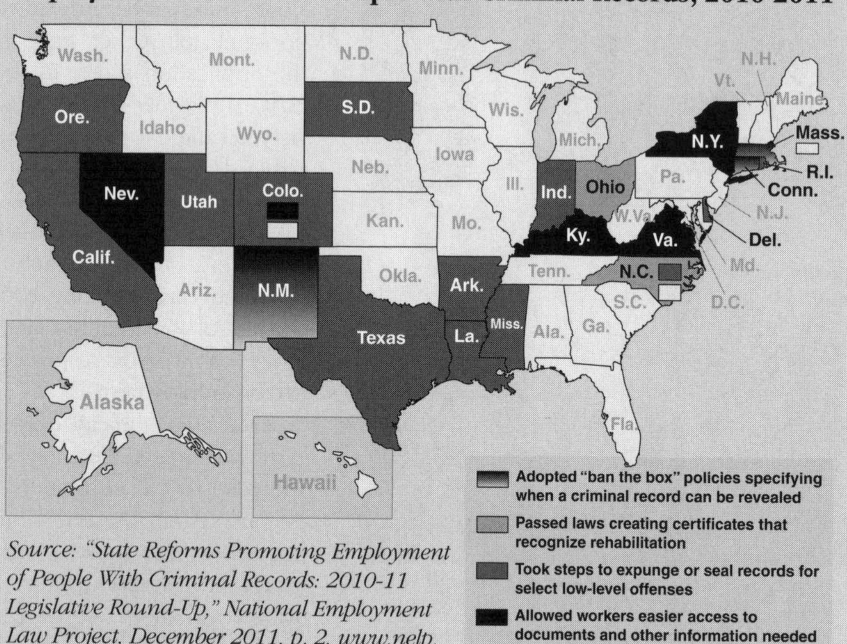

Source: "State Reforms Promoting Employment of People With Criminal Records: 2010-11 Legislative Round-Up," National Employment Law Project, December 2011, p. 2, www.nelp.org/page/SCLP/2011/PromotingEmploymentofPeoplewithCriminalRecords.pdf?nocdn=1

"expungement"* — of some records of minor offenses or establishing ways that people with records can prove they're rehabilitated. [5] (*See sidebar, p. 364.*)

Further efforts by states are under way. In Ohio, Republican Gov. John Kasich is pushing for legislation this year to give people with records a chance at employment, including in licensed occupations — such as electrical contractor — that now bar anyone with a felony record for life.

"All we're saying is that there's got to be some reasonable assessment of risk and not to make blanket assessments," says Maurice Emsellem, policy co-director of the New York-based National Employment Law Project (NELP), which advocates measures that, in the organization's view, give job-seekers with records a chance at being considered. "You want policy to reward good behavior. If you have a blanket disqualification, you're not promoting rehabilitation."

Another dimension of the issue concerns the accuracy of background reports. An April report by the Boston-based National Consumer Law Center argues that regulation of screening firms is lax to nonexistent, despite the fact that an adverse — and possibly inaccurate — report can wreck an individual's job prospects. [6]

Some on the employers' side argue that a growing thicket of restrictions and limitations on background screening could be superfluous because many companies don't want to impose blanket restrictions in the first place. "Across the board, generally speaking, employers don't want to hire someone who is a threat to their business or to their customers or other employees," says Pamela Quigley Devata, a Chicago-based employment lawyer who represents employers. "But they don't necessarily care that someone had a drug-possession conviction seven years ago as long as someone is not intoxicated on the job."

Still, she adds, "If someone has engaged in rape or violence or drug manufacturing, most employers would be concerned."

EEOC guidelines bar employers, when deciding on hiring, promotion and retention, from considering arrests that didn't lead to conviction That's one reason some major background-investigation firms don't even report on arrests that didn't lead to criminal proceedings.

"We do that because we know that employers typically cannot use that information," says Frederick G. Giles, senior vice president of Carco Group, a Holtsville, N.Y.-based screening and investigation company. He adds that if employers did get information on arrests that went no further, the information would be difficult to disregard. "It's hard to put the toothpaste back in the tube," says Giles, who is incoming chairman of the National Association of Professional Background Screeners, based in Schaumburg, Ill.

Nevertheless, many employers want arrest information and use it to screen out applicants, advocates for job-seekers say. In many cases, "An employer looks at arrest and conviction in the same light," says Anthony Lowery, policy director of the Safer Foundation, a

* Expungement (or expunction) is a legal term used in criminal law denoting the legally sanctioned destruction or eradication of records or other information in databases, written files and archives pertaining to criminal charges against an individual.

Chicago-based organization that helps people with criminal records rejoin society.

One of those employers is the U.S. Census Bureau, according to lawyers for applicants who were rejected for temporary jobs collecting data for the 2010 Census. The bureau rejected anyone whose name showed up in the FBI's national arrest database and couldn't produce, within 30 days, "official court documentation" showing, for instance, that charges had been dismissed. The effect was to bar anyone who'd been arrested — about 700,000 people, a 2010 lawsuit said. [7]

Government attempts to have the suit dismissed have failed. In March, U.S. Magistrate Judge Frank Maas of New York, who is overseeing the case, denied a government motion for dismissal of some claims, and he allowed some plaintiffs to claim they represented a class of would-be census workers. [8]

Advocates for job-seekers say the Census Bureau isn't alone in using arrest as a disqualifier. NELP surveyed job ads on Craigslist, a major source of employment ads, and found that more than 300 ads, including by major firms, rejected applications from anyone who had even been arrested, regardless of whether the arrest led to a conviction. [9]

In early January, Pepsi paid $3.1 million to settle EEOC charges over the company's use of arrest records in screening job-seekers. The company vowed to take a more "individualized approach" in distinguishing between applicants' backgrounds. [10]

Some employers advocate the individualized approach, partly because they've seen people with criminal records perform ably. In testimony before the EEOC last July, Victoria Kane, Los Angeles-based area director for labor relations for Portfolio Hotels & Resorts, cited employees who "had already been working at the hotel 10, maybe even 20, years in some cases, and you come to find out that, hey, they do have a criminal history and they're working just fine and they've been successful for years in this position. How could we as an employer have this very standard policy that if you have a conviction we're not going to hire you?" [11]

Yet the criminal-records issue affects more than simply those with decades-old convictions. People recently released from prison are flooding job markets, hobbled by a lack of education and training and the absence of a track record that would allow an employer to conclude that they're worth taking a chance on.

A turn away from crime — "desistance" in criminology parlance — takes place in many people with recent records, criminal justice professors Shawn D. Bushway of the University of Albany and Robert Apel of Rutgers University wrote in a recent study. Still, most ex-prisoners are reincarcerated within three years of release. "Desistance is

Minorities Dominate U.S. Prison Population

Sixty percent of the nation's 1.5 million state and federal prisoners are black or Hispanic, and more than 90 percent are male. The United States has the highest incarceration rate in the world, with 731 people per 100,000 residents in jail or prison. The prison population has increased 15 percent over the past decade.

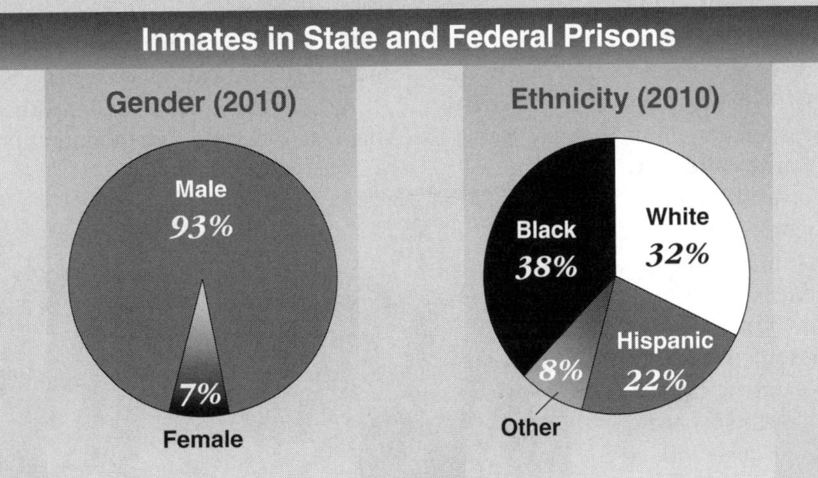

- The state and federal prison population increased by 15 percent from 2000 to 2010, from 1.3 million to 1.5 million. Local jails held an additional 748,728 inmates in 2010.
- A total of 7.1 million Americans were under some form of criminal-justice supervision in 2010, with 4.9 million on probation or parole.
- One in 10 black Americans ages 30 to 34 were incarcerated in 2010, as were one in 26 Hispanics and one in 61 whites in that age group.
- Forty-seven percent of state prisoners in 2009 were convicted for non-violent drug, property or public-order crimes.

Source: "Facts About Prisons and Prisoners," The Sentencing Project, January 2012, www.sentencingproject.org/doc/publications/publications/inc_factsAboutPrisons_Jan2012.pdf.

fundamentally unobservable to employers and others who might wish to identify good employees from the group of people who have criminal records," they concluded. But participation in a return-to-society — or "reentry" — job-training program could serve as a "signal" of desistance. [12]

The On The Rise bakery in Detroit operates according to that principle. "You've got to want to change," says Collins, the ex-prisoner who helps run the operation. "But if a guy wants to change, he can. Everybody wants to know your background, but in food service, if you've got the skill and it's needed, some people will give you a chance."

As employers, policy makers and advocates for ex-prisoners consider the impact of criminal records, here are some of the questions they are debating:

Should government control employers' access to job-seekers' criminal records?

Job-seekers with old or minor records — perhaps with arrests but no convictions — have an interest in preventing a potential employer from seeing that information. A potential employer has a stake in knowing everything about a potential employee that could affect workplace safety and company profitability.

Between these clashing interests lie a tangle of federal guidelines, state laws and city and county ordinances that determine what criminal data employers can see and when they can see it.

These restrictions cover only certain types of information. And, advocates for job-seekers say, tough enforcement isn't the norm. At the federal level, they cite the lawsuit charging the Census Bureau with effectively barring nearly all applicants for 2010 census jobs who had ever been arrested.

Lawyers for the plaintiffs — originally seven and now five — cited a 2010 letter to Commerce Department and Census Bureau officials from Stuart J. Ishimaru, then acting EEOC chairman, warning that the hiring policy was "overbroad," apparently violating an EEOC guideline against using arrest records alone to bar employment. "The Census Bureau should not rely on arrest records for which there was no conviction, and the Census Bureau itself should inquire as to whether the alleged conduct took place," he wrote. [13]

NAACP

Philadelphia Mayor Michael A. Nutter, flanked by city and NAACP leaders, signs into law on April 18, 2012, a so-called "ban the box" bill that will prohibit private employers from requiring job applicants to disclose their criminal history until after the initial stages of the hiring process. "This legislation will make it easier for ex-offenders to be judged by their abilities as opposed to their past," Nutter said. Only Philadelphia, Massachusetts and Hawaii apply "ban the box" to private-sector employment.

Advocates for job-seekers with criminal records say the smallest bit of information can easily disqualify an applicant from even being considered for employment. Federal, state and local governments should go beyond merely prescribing standards for employers' handling of arrest or criminal-record information, some advocates say.

They cite Pennsylvania law as a model. In 1979, the state's General Assembly barred private employers from considering criminal records that are irrelevant to the applicant's qualifications for a particular job. [14]

But despite the specificity of the law, not all employers heed it, says Sharon M. Dietrich, managing attorney for employment and public benefits at Community Legal Services of Philadelphia. "My experience is that you can't count on employers to follow the law," she says. Specifically, she adds, "Though mostly they should not be considering arrests, our experience is mostly that they do. If they consider information that they should not, a good percentage of people will be rejected. I would very much like to see a situation in which information was restricted."

Employers, however, face a situation in which knowing as much as possible about a job-seeker could head off legal problems if the applicant is hired and creates problems on the job. A company that had researched an applicant's past would be able to show that it didn't make the hiring decision carelessly.

"We're coming from a position that employers need information to make the best business decisions," says Michael Burns, executive vice president of the American Society of Employers, based in Livonia, Mich. "They're seeking information about whether the record of a person presenting himself to be employed may affect the workplace.

"Criminal history is not a protected class" of information, Burns says. The idea of limiting employer access to it is "not a good thing."

Yet, argues Roberta Meyers-Peeples, director of the New York-based National H.I.R.E Network (Helping Individuals with criminal records Reenter through Employment), criminal records can be filled with irrelevant and misleading data. "In many states, everything related to that record is released, including arrest charges — and law enforcement agencies are known for throwing as much as possible into the mix in terms of original charges in the hope of something being allowed to stick."

Practically speaking, Meyers-Peeples says, "I refuse to believe that for the employer sitting there with all this information, that judgments are not going to be based on the original arrest record." Criminal-record information, she says, should be limited to data about recent convictions.

But James Jacobs, a law professor at New York University who is writing a book about criminal-records issues, argues that limiting access to public information is probably an illegal interference with the First Amendment right of free speech. "I don't like censorship," he says. "In the United States, arrests have always been public information. To have a law that said no employer could ask for or receive information about a person's arrest — I don't think that would pass a constitutional test."

Jacobs acknowledges that information can be misused. "People will say that about all kinds of information," he says. "Some will say, 'We don't want information about evolution.' I think we are best served by a free flow of information."

Is deleting records effective in the Internet age?

As more data have gone online, Web-based businesses selling criminal-record searches have proliferated. The growing availability of digitized and highly accessible information is spurring debate over the employment effects of criminal-record information.

Keith Finlay, an economics professor at Tulane University in New Orleans, traces the origins of the digital data explosion to a federal initiative. From 1995 to 2007, Finlay wrote in 2009, the federal government channeled about $400 million to state governments to automate their criminal records.

The immediate purpose was to enable compliance with the Brady Handgun Violence Prevention Act of 1993, which required handgun buyers to undergo a criminal background check within five days of initiating a weapon purchase. "In the late 1990s, some states began to make these records available over the Internet," Finlay wrote. "Internet-based criminal background checks are significantly more convenient than any other method." [15]

Whether convenience equals accuracy and completeness is another issue. The question has become pressing as more states offer opportunities to seal or expunge some criminal records. At least 45 states plus the District of Columbia now offer the opportunity to seal the records of long-ago or minor crimes. [16]

In nearly all cases, experts of differing perspectives agree, juvenile records tend not to turn up in background searches. Most states require that those files be sealed unless a juvenile offense was serious enough to be prosecuted as an adult crime or the juvenile was initially charged as an adult. With that exception, says Adam T. Klein, a New York lawyer specializing in employee-side employment law, "It's unlikely that a private background check would report a juvenile arrest."

Where adult records are concerned, expungement in practical terms may mean withdrawing data that previously was available.

And a company that sells criminal-background checks that hadn't updated information might include details of a record even though it had been ordered expunged, some experts say. In Illinois, where only records of non-conviction arrests can be expunged, and only a small number of low-level drug offenses can be sealed, "Updating doesn't happen," says Lowery of the Safer Foundation. [17]

Even official records aren't always updated, experts say. Burns of the American Society of Employers says that as president of the organization's for-profit HRMG Services, which does background screenings, he has run into cases in which records ordered expunged "are still sitting there." In these cases, he says, employers or prospective employers get the information.

"We will provide anything in the database as long as it's accurate," Burns says. "The fact that the database hasn't been expunged — who has the problem? I would argue that it's the person whose record is sitting there. It's incumbent on him to get it fixed." An employer would, nevertheless, be told of an expunction order, Burns says.

His assessment would seem to support the arguments of advocates such as Margaret Colgate Love, a Washington-based lawyer specializing in pardons. "Expungement . . . has fallen victim to modern technology," she wrote in the *Howard Law Review* last year. "It is at least misleading to encourage people whose convictions have been expunged or sealed to deny that they have ever been convicted, as do many 1970s-era laws that are still on the books." [18] Love was U.S. pardon attorney in 1990-1997, during the George H. W. Bush and Bill Clinton administrations.

Instead of what she calls the futile hope of putting some records out of

Ban the Box Policies Adopted in 20 States

Thirty-two cities and counties in 20 states — including Chicago and New York — have "ban the box" policies that bar state and municipal employers from requiring applicants to reveal an arrest or conviction record during the initial stages of the hiring process.

States and Localities with "Ban the Box" Policies for Public-Sector Workers

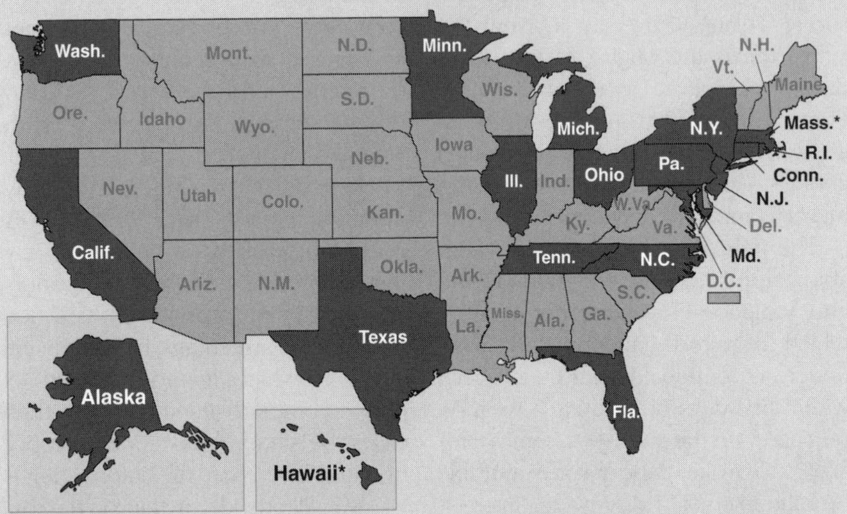

* *The policies cover both private- and public-sector employers throughout the state.*

Note: California, Connecticut, Hawaii, Massachusetts, New Mexico and Minnesota have adopted statewide "ban the box" policies for either state government jobs alone or all government and private-sector employment.

Source: "Ban the Box: Major U.S. Cities and Counties Adopt Fair Hiring Policies to Remove Unfair Barriers to Employment of People With Criminal Records," National Employment Law Project, February 2012, p. 1, www.nelp.org/page/-/SCLP/2011/CityandCountyHiringInitiatives.pdf?nocdn=1

employers' reach, Love advocates adoption of a procedure proposed by the American Bar Association and the Uniform Law Commission, a 120-year-old organization that promotes consistency in state laws. The proposal calls for a judge or official body to issue a Certificate of Restoration of Rights after an ex-convict has lived a law-abiding life for a given period of time. Certification "should encourage public and private entities to give convicted persons a second chance," Love writes. [19]

But Dietrich of Philadelphia's Community Legal Services argues against the certificate approach. "It would take such a mind-change for employers to accept that sort of thing," she says, given the "stigma that is attached to those criminal records."

Though the expunction process may not be 100 percent reliable in the digital age, Dietrich says, "If you asked 20 of my clients whether they'd prefer expungement or some other mechanism for dealing with their records, they'd prefer expungement."

Practical issues crop up for the proposed certificate approach, experts also note. "It could be a fairly cumbersome process to get one of these certificates," says Marc Mauer, executive director of the Sentencing Project, which has long advocated alternatives to mass incarceration. "Depending how much paperwork is involved, or time in court, if it could be done efficiently that's one possible resolution, but the sheer numbers make it challenging."

At the same time, Mauer acknowledges that expungement presents its own obstacles. "It's awfully difficult to actually do that these days," he says. For it to be effective in the digital age, he adds, removal of records from databases should be combined with penalties for anyone who found and used the information in an employment matter, along with a campaign to educate the business community about criminal records and their use.

Should employers have access to old criminal records?

The Fair Credit Reporting Act (FCRA) prohibits companies that sell background reports for employment from reporting arrests without convictions that are older than seven years. [20]

But advocates for job-seekers with criminal records are urging a broader approach, arguing that even convictions, if they are decades old, don't reliably predict a criminal future. That argument has gathered force from a 2010 Justice Department-funded examination of people who had been arrested.

Alfred Blumstein, a professor of urban studies and operations research at Carnegie Mellon University, and Kiminori Nakamura, a professor of criminology at the University of Maryland in College Park, studied the records of 88,000 people arrested for the first time in New York state in 1980. Among the results: 18-year-olds arrested for aggravated assault had the same chance, within 4.3 years of that first arrest — if they hadn't been arrested for anything else in the meantime — of being arrested again as someone with no criminal record. Those arrested for burglary attained that status after 3.8 years. The chance of subsequent arrests for 18-year-olds arrested for robbery fell to the norm at 7.7 years. [21]

The data led Blumstein and Nakamura to challenge reliance on criminal records.

"We believe it is unreasonable for someone to be hounded by a single arrest or conviction that happened more than 20 years earlier," they wrote in an op-ed in *The New York Times*, advocating restricting access to older criminal records and ending lifetime bans in some occupations for anyone with any sort of criminal record. "Policies that encourage employers to hire people who made a mistake in the past but have since rebuilt their lives would not only help those people but also our economy and our society," they wrote. [22]

To be sure, the data that the two academics developed have complications. Those first arrested at age 16 took longer to achieve the same likelihood of re-arrest as anyone else — 8.5 years. The authors acknowledged that their results were limited by their one-state, one-year data. These wouldn't show if a person had been re-arrested outside of New York. And the inclusion of people whose arrests were dismissed probably lowered the period in which the subjects ran a higher risk of re-arrest. Overall, Blumstein and Nakamura wrote in their op-ed, the time in which a once-arrested person falls into the normal range for re-arrest is 10 to 13 years. [23]

Some employer advocates note the preliminary nature of the Blumstein-Nakamura study. In addition, says Devata, the Chicago-based lawyer, "The question is not whether or not a person is more likely to engage in a certain activity after a certain time." Instead, she says, employers' concern typically comes from direct experience.

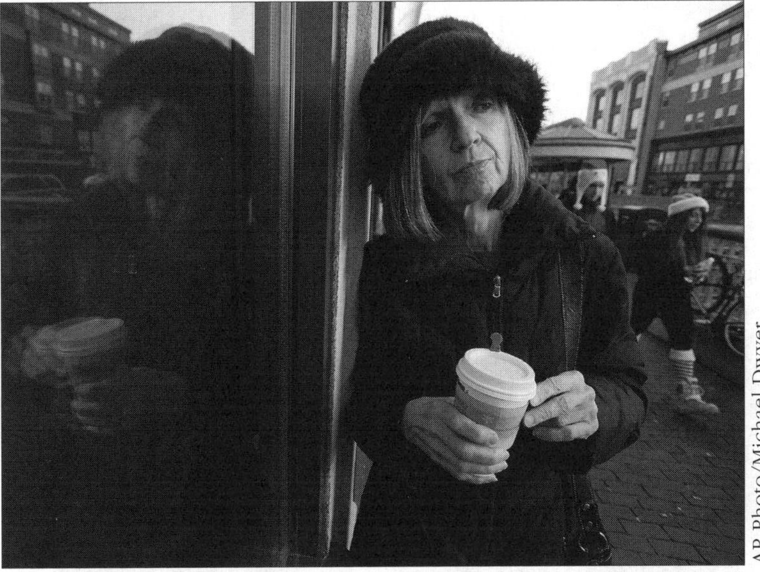

AP Photo/Michael Dwyer

A company hired to conduct a background check on Kathleen Casey, of Cambridge, Mass., mistakenly found a different woman with the same name who lived nearby — but who had a criminal record. Unable to land a job, Casey ended up homeless. An April report by the Boston-based National Consumer Law Center argues that regulation of screening firms is lax to nonexistent, despite the fact that an adverse — and possibly inaccurate — report can wreck an individual's job prospects.

"They had empirical evidence that they gave a person a chance and they engaged in fraud or violent behavior," Devata says. Employers are deeply concerned about being sued for "negligent hiring," because an employee with a record harmed someone. "One lawsuit is devastating," she says.

But looked at from a job-seeker's perspective, says Meyers-Peeples of the National H.I.R.E. Network, permanent access to criminal records has the effect of making past errors inescapable. "You have people out here being judged for something they did when they were 18 years old," she says. "After a certain amount of time it becomes irrelevant. It's insane that we think it's OK for peoples' records of stuff they did long ago to be left open, and not recognize that people change, grow, mature."

Meyers-Peeples, like others on her side of the issue, acknowledges that for some jobs, some records are permanently relevant; the classic example is convicted sex offenders in jobs involving children. But overall, she says, keeping records forever accessible runs counter to the trend to lower recidivism. "Discussions around re-entry, recidivism," she says, "always come back to, 'How do we get people working?'"

A veteran background investigator counters that time limits can create more problems than they solve. "Some states in their well-meaning quest have created a nightmare," says Giles of Carco Group and the National Association of Professional Background Screeners. In California, where state law prohibits reporting any criminal information that's more than seven years old, he says, "We can report the fact that a person is on the sex offender registry, but if the offense occurred more than seven years ago, we can't report why." Yet, he says, the underlying offense could be a serious one.

The California law also complicates hiring for banks, which are required by the Federal Deposit Insurance Corp. (FDIC) to know whether an employee has ever been convicted of a crime involving a breach of public trust. [24] Banks can't afford to do without that information, so instead of relying on background-search companies to collect it, they look for it on their own, Giles says. He argues that companies like his are more knowledgeable in interpreting data. That aside, he says, the conflict between laws demonstrates the inconsistencies and complications that mark the background-checking issue. ■

BACKGROUND

The Pardon Route

From the earliest days of U.S. history, presidents issued pardons, often to cancel sentences they considered excessive or unfair. Presidential doubts about the fairness of sentencing laws paved the way for criminal-law innovations, including the doctrine of innocence by reason of insanity, according to documents cited by Love, the former U.S. pardon attorney. [25]

Early U.S. presidents often plunged into the details of cases underlying pardon requests. Drawing on research by journalist George Lardner Jr., formerly of *The Washington Post*, Love writes that President James K. Polk, who served from 1845 to 1849, read indictments and trial records. His pardons referred to a judge's acknowledgement that a key prosecution witness was unreliable, to false testimony in another case and to the details of a steamboat inspection at issue in a prosecution of the boat's captain.

During the Civil War, President Abraham Lincoln devoted considerable time to studying pardon requests from soldiers and their families, in some cases hearing them in person at the White House. He also issued 331 pardons in civil cases.

Lincoln was considered so softhearted, pardon clerk Edmund Stedman wrote, that the attorney general "soon discovered that my most important duty was to keep all but the most deserving cases from coming before the kind Mr. Lincoln at all; since there was nothing harder for him to do than put aside a prisoner's application." [26]

AFP/Getty Images

New sentencing laws in the early 20th century set the stage for an increasing number of presidential pardons to restore rights to people who had served their sentences. Democratic President Franklin D. Roosevelt issued more than 3,000 pardons during his four terms (1933-1945), the vast majority aimed at restoring rights to people who already had served their sentences. Roosevelt's successors, Harry S Truman, a Democrat, and Dwight D. Eisenhower, a Republican, compiled similar records.

But putting aside Lincoln's kindheartedness (which had its limits — he also authorized executions), he was also a lawyer. And the pardon system was so crucial in 19th- and early 20th-century America, Love writes, because convictions were so frequently based on flimsy evidence. She cites research showing that from 1885 through 1931, a total of 181 pardon requests were based on doubt about guilt; another 93 flatly said the convicted persons were innocent or the victims of mistaken identification; and 46 cited deathbed confessions to murder by people who hadn't been convicted.

But at the dawn of the 20th century, lawyers and judges were becoming more professional, and new laws began providing alternatives to imprisonment, as well as a way to shorten prison terms. In 1910, Congress instituted a parole system, allowing qualified prisoners to be released after serving one-third of their sentences. (Each of the country's three federal penitentiaries had its own parole board.) And in 1925, federal judges were authorized to sentence some convicted defendants to probation instead of prison. [27]

As a result of these new sentencing-policy laws, official pardon became, above all, a route to restoring rights to people who had served their sentences. By 1931, post-sentence pardons accounted for the vast majority of pardons.

President Franklin D. Roosevelt issued more than 3,000 pardons during his four terms, 1933-1945, but only 488 of those were commutations that reduced a convicted person's sentence; the rest were aimed at restoring rights to people who'd already served their time in prison. Roosevelt's successors, Harry S Truman, a Democrat; and Dwight D. Eisenhower, a Republican, compiled

Continued on p. 360

Chronology

1910-1945
Sentencing laws become less rigid and the criminal-justice system more professional.

1910
Federal parole system established, allowing qualified prisoners to be released after serving one-third of sentence.

1925
Congress authorizes federal judges to sentence some defendants to probation instead of prison.

1931
Post-incarceration pardons now account for majority of pardons.

1945
At his death, President Franklin D. Roosevelt has issued more than 3,000 pardons, most for people who have completed their sentences.

1955-1996
As crime rises, emphasis in criminal-justice policy shifts from rehabilitation and restoration of ex-convicts' rights to punishment.

1955
National Council on Crime and Delinquency urges that ex-offenders have all civil rights restored.

1967
Presidential commission criticizes deprivation of rights to ex-convicts.

1970
Rates of violent and nonviolent crimes have doubled from their 1960 levels.

1984
President Ronald Reagan attacks "liberal approach of coddling criminals" in urging passage of Comprehensive Crime Control Act, with "mandatory minimum" sentences. . . . FBI anti-drug funding increases more than 10-fold from 1980 level.

1986
Congress passes Anti-Drug Abuse Act, including "mandatory minimum" sentences with especially harsh penalties for crack cocaine offenses.

1987
U.S. Equal Employment Opportunity Commission (EEOC) issues first guideline on employers' use of criminal records.

1991
Because of sentencing-law changes, drug offenders serve average sentences of 80 months, two-and-a-half times longer than in 1985.

1995
Federal government begins distributing money to states to automate criminal records to meet background-check rules for handgun purchasers.

1996
Fourteen states bar ex-convicts from voting, up from 11 in 1986.

2001-2012
Increased accessibility of criminal records and new security worries prompt rise in background screening.

2001
Sept. 11 attacks prompt new concern over employees' and job applicants' backgrounds.

2002
Congress requires credentials for port workers.

2004
Boston enacts first "ban the box" ordinance, prohibiting questions about criminal records in first stage of job-application process.

2007
Port-worker credentialing process begins; workers whose records include certain felony convictions are required to seek waivers. . . . Federal aid on state criminal-record automation reaches $400 million. . . . Third U.S. Circuit Court of Appeals in Philadelphia upholds firing of public transit van driver for 40-year-old second-degree murder conviction.

2010
Prison and jail population reaches 2.3 million, 38 percent black and 22 percent Latino. . . . Applicants rejected for temporary Census jobs claim that 700,000 applicants were barred simply because they had been arrested but not necessarily convicted.

2011
Three states have enacted "ban the box" laws; two have created rehabilitation certificates for ex-convicts; 13 have enacted criminal-record expungement laws. . . . EEOC holds hearing on possible expansion of its guidelines on criminal-record use.

2012
Number of cities and counties with "ban the box" laws reaches 32. . . . Pepsi pays $3.1 million to settle lawsuit over use of arrest records in screening job applicants. . . . Federal Trade Commission warns three Web-based criminal-records search firms that they may be violating federal law. . . . Republican Ohio Gov. John Kasich demands legislation to give people with criminal records better job possibilities.

Studies Challenge Views on Race, Recidivism

Misdeeds don't always predict future conduct.

At first, Alfred Blumstein, one of the nation's leading criminologists, was certain he was right. Ex-convicts were considerably more likely to commit crimes than people who had never been in trouble with the law, Blumstein, of Carnegie Mellon University, told a federal judge presiding over a 2004 lawsuit in Philadelphia. The suit had been brought by a van driver who was fired from his job ferrying handicapped people on grounds that he had been convicted of second-degree murder 40 years earlier, when he was 15 years old. [1]

In a report to the judge, Blumstein said it was "entirely prudent and reasonable" for the Southeastern Pennsylvania Transportation Authority (SEPTA) to fire the long-ago-convicted Douglas El, because of its duty "to do whatever it can to protect the vulnerable population that uses its paratransit services." Drivers, he said, must "be free of any such [violent] convictions." [2]

The judge agreed, but in the years following his testimony, Blumstein immersed himself in data on prisoner re-entry into society and came to a more nuanced conclusion: that a criminal past doesn't necessarily predict future conduct.

That view has come to be repeatedly cited by advocates for job-seekers with criminal records. And new studies by sociologists, economists and criminologists have lent credence to it.

At an Equal Employment Opportunity Commission (EEOC) meeting last year, Amy Solomon, a senior adviser on prisoner re-entry to the Justice Department, cited Blumstein's study of people with arrest records. "After staying clean for some period of time," she said, "these individuals are no more likely than anyone else to have another arrest in the future. I believe this research has important and very practical implications." [3]

In his first report of an ongoing study of the subsequent lives of New Yorkers first arrested in 1980, Blumstein and a collaborator cited previous evidence that recidivism — or re-offending — tends to occur within the first few years of an initial arrest. But for those who don't get back into trouble, the study found, their likelihood of recidivism eventually declines to that of the general population. [4]

To be sure, Blumstein and his collaborator, Kiminori Nakamura, a criminology professor at the University of Maryland, College Park, noted that people arrested for violent crimes take longer to present an average risk, as do those who are arrested at young ages. "Employers . . . serving vulnerable populations like children and the elderly would be particularly sensitive to a prior record involving violence," they wrote. [5]

Meanwhile, other researchers have been studying how race affects employer perceptions of job applicants. Devah Pager, a Princeton University sociology professor who studies the effect of criminal records on employment, has found evidence that many employers screen out African-American job applicants at a higher rate than white applicants, regardless of whether they have a criminal record.

In 2001, while at Northwestern University in Evanston, Ill., Pager set up an experiment in which black and white subjects applied for job openings in Milwaukee. Some subjects disclosed fictitious criminal records invented for the experiment.

Of Pager's white subjects, 34 percent without criminal records received callbacks from prospective employers. For those with records, the callback rate was 17 percent. For black subjects, 14 percent without records were called back — compared with a mere 5 percent for those with records. [6]

"This is a startling result," Pager told the EEOC in 2008, "and I think it points to some of the ways in which high incarceration rates among African-Americans may have strengthened the association between race and crime in the minds of many Americans and many employers. So in some ways all black men pay a penalty for their membership in a group with such high levels of incarceration." [7]

The same point was made, in a different way, in a study by three academics led by Harry J. Holzer, co-founder of the

Continued from p. 358

similar records: 1,900 pardons, 118 commutations; and 1,100 pardons and 47 commutations, respectively. [28]

Social Integration

During Eisenhower's two terms, 1953-1961, policymakers came to accept the idea that rehabilitation should be the objective of the criminal justice system. Federal and state laws reflected that view, to some extent.

In 1955, the National Council on Crime and Delinquency, an influential research and advocacy organization founded in 1907, recommended that offenders should have all their civil rights restored when they completed their sentences. The council later proposed a law that included procedures to expunge a criminal record. [29]

The following year, the National Conference on Parole — convened by Attorney General Herbert Brownell Jr. — resolved that "the present law on deprivation of civil rights of offenders is in most jurisdictions an archaic holdover from early times and is in contradiction to the principles of modern correctional treatment."

In 1967, Democratic President Lyndon B. Johnson's Commission on Law Enforcement and Administration of Justice criticized in a 342-page report the "whole system of disabilities and disqualifications" applied to released prisoners. "Little consideration has been given to the need for particular deprivations in particular cases." [30]

Georgetown University Center on Poverty, Inequality and Public Policy in Washington. Holzer and his colleagues — Steven Raphael of the University of California, Berkeley, and Michael A. Stoll of the University of California, Los Angeles — studied the effects of background screening on African-American job applicants. They concluded that employers who screen job applicants' backgrounds are more likely to hire African-Americans than those who don't screen prospective employees. They theorized that screening helps educate employers and cancel out negative stereotypes they may harbor.

www.search.org

Changing his views, criminologist Alfred Blumstein of Carnegie Mellon University concluded that a criminal past doesn't necessarily predict future conduct.

"Employers who perform criminal background checks are more likely to hire black applicants than employers who do not," Holzer and his colleagues concluded. The reason seemed to be, they wrote, "that employers with a particularly strong aversion to ex-offenders may be more likely to overestimate the relationship between criminality and race and hire too few African-Americans as a result." [8]

The study has been cited by background-screening companies as evidence of their value.

Frederick G. Giles, senior vice president of the Carco Group, a screening firm in Holtsville, N.Y., says the moral of the study is that "when you are trying to end discrimination, you use those tools that have proven effective in ending discrimination. By vilifying background screening, you're creating a climate in which there's a higher propensity for discrimination."

But, says Sharon Dietrich, managing attorney for public benefits and employment at Community Legal Services of Philadelphia, "If employers are presuming that black men commit crime, that is a matter of racial discrimination and should be dealt with as a matter of racial discrimination — not by background checking."

— Peter Katel

---

[1] Quoted in *El v. Southeastern Pennsylvania Transportation Authority*, Memorandum and Order, U.S. District Court for the Eastern District of Pennsylvania, 2:02-cv-03591-JCJ, July 12, 2005, p. 17, www.reentry.net/library/folder.152902-El_v_SEPTA_Litigation; *El v. Southeastern Pennsylvania Transportation Authority et al*, 3rd Circuit Court of Appeals, No, 05-3857, March 19, 2007, pp. 4-5, www.ca3.uscourts.gov/opinarch/053857p.pdf.

[2] Quoted in *ibid.*, U.S. District Court.

[3] U.S. Equal Employment Opportunity Commission, transcript of meeting, July 26, 2011, www.eeoc.gov/eeoc/meetings/7-26-11/transcript.cfm.

[4] Alfred Blumstein and Kiminori Nakamura, "Redemption in the Presence of Widespread Criminal Background Checks," *Criminology*, May 1, 2009, p. 330, http://onlinelibrary.wiley.com/doi/10.1111/j.1745-9125.2009.00155.x/abstract; (shorter version) Alfred Blumstein and Kiminori Nakamura, "Redemption in the Presence of Widespread Criminal Background Checks," *NIJ Journal*, National Institute of Justice, updated June 1, 2010, www.nij.gov/journals/263/redemption.htm.

[5] *Ibid.*, *NIJ Journal*, p. 2.

[6] Devah Pager, "The Mark of a Criminal Record," *American Journal of Sociology*, March 2003, pp. 955-960, www.princeton.edu/~pager/pager_ajs.pdf.

[7] U.S. Equal Employment Opportunity Commission, transcript of meeting, Nov. 20, 2008, www.eeoc.gov/eeoc/meetings/11-20-08/transcript.cfm.

[8] Harry J. Holzer, *et al.*, "Perceived Criminality, Criminal Background Checks, and the Racial Hiring Practices of Employers," *Journal of Law and Economics*, October 2006, p. 473, www.jstor.org/discover/10.1086/501089?uid=3739640&uid=2&uid=4&uid=3739256&sid=47698810486547.

The idea of easing an ex-convict's reintegration into society persisted into the early 1980s. In 1981, the American Bar Association (ABA) proposed eliminating the automatic civil penalties imposed on ex-convicts. Only those additional penalties directly related to an offender's crime — such as withdrawing driver's licenses from people with multiple drunken-driving convictions — should be authorized, the ABA said.

Reports and model laws didn't amount to actual changes in law. However, in the 1960s and '70s, legislatures in a number of states adopted laws that automatically restored civil rights after offenders served their sentences or after a set period of time. [31]

The attitudes underlying all these developments were largely a product of the social and political transformations produced by the civil rights movement, which played a growing role in U.S. society during the 1950s through the '70s. With its eventual partnership with the federal government, and some state and local governments as well, the movement gave rise to confidence that humane policies and laws could play a powerful role in reducing crime.

"Liberals . . . insisted that social reforms such as the War on Poverty and civil rights legislation would get at the 'root causes of criminal behavior' . . . and stressed the social conditions that predictably generate crime," writes civil rights lawyer Michelle Alexander, a professor at Ohio State University's Moritz College of Law in Columbus, in an influential book on incarceration and the drug war. [32]

The approach she summarizes permeated the 1968 report of the National Advisory Commission on Civil Disorders, a blue-ribbon commission headed by Gov. Otto Kerner Jr. of Illinois, formed after the outbreak of summertime uprisings in black inner cities, the most serious of them in Newark and Detroit in 1967. [33]

Criminal records had not yet emerged as an employment issue, but joblessness in the African-American population was acknowledged as a major problem. "Pervasive unemployment and underemployment are the most persistent and serious grievances in minority areas," the commission concluded. "They are inextricably linked to the problem of civil disorder." The panel urged "immediate action" to create 1 million private-sector and 1 million public-sector jobs. [34]

Reuther Library/Detroit News Staff

Detroit's 12th Street descends into chaos on July 23, 1967, during rioting in several U.S. inner cities. A year later the National Advisory Commission on Civil Disorders linked the riots to "pervasive unemployment and underemployment . . . in minority areas." The panel urged "immediate action" to create 2 million private- and public-sector jobs.

War on Crime

Formation of the national commission on civil disorders reflected growing awareness of another trend — a rising crime rate.

In 1960, the violent-crime rate stood at 160.9 violent crimes per 100,000 people, and the property-crime rate at 1,726.3 property crimes per 100,0000. By 1970, rates in both categories had more than doubled, to 363.5 and 3,621 per 100,000, respectively. [35]

Crime rates kept increasing in the 1970s, peaked in 1980, dipped slightly, then resumed the climb after 1985. By then, the violent crime rate stood at 558.1 per 100,000, and the property crime rate at 4,666.4 per 100,000. [36]

As crime became a political issue, the clear advantage went to politicians of both parties perceived as tough on criminals. The first president to capture the new public mood was Ronald Reagan, a Republican who served two terms, from 1981 to 1989. "The liberal approach of coddling criminals didn't work and never will," he said in a 1984 radio address. [37]

Reagan was urging passage of the Comprehensive Crime Control Act, which had passed the Senate but was stuck in the Democratic-controlled House. The bill eventually passed, with provisions including the scrapping of "indeterminate" sentencing in which judges had wide discretion over the length of prison terms; a requirement of "mandatory minimum" sentences for offenders defined as career criminals; and other measures designed as tough anti-crime steps. [38]

Meanwhile, law enforcement budgets skyrocketed. The FBI alone saw its antidrug funding soar from $8 million to $95 million from 1980 to 1984. [39]

Major changes to federal and state sentencing laws, including post-sentence measures, continued in the 1990s, during Democrat Bill Clinton's two terms, 1993-2000. One impetus was a headline-grabbing escalation of street drug-dealing and violence growing out of the crack cocaine epidemic, a trend that took off in the latter 1980s. [40]

The crack boom prompted a rash of tough-on-crime measures, including, at the federal level, the Anti-Drug Abuse Act of 1986, which ordered "mandatory minimum" sentences for certain drug crimes based both on the nature of the offense and the specific drug involved. Where crack was involved, even first-time simple possession of 5 grams or more required a minimum five-year sentence, a policy that largely affected blacks. [41]

As the new laws took effect, people convicted of drug offenses were serving sentences two-and-a-half times longer in 1991 than in 1985, more than 6.5 years on average. [42]

State legislatures enacted comparable laws and added post-conviction or post-incarceration penalties. A 1996 survey found that, measured against 1986, the number of states permanently barring ex-convicts from voting rose from 11 to 14, while the number of states allowing termination of parental rights rose from 16 to 19. [43]

And a series of federal measures barred those convicted of some crimes (usually involving drugs) — or authorized states to bar them — from a wide range of federally funded benefits, including food stamps, public housing, student loans and driver's licenses. [44]

Re-Entry with Records

Nationwide, the crime increase of the 1960s-1980s, and the massive law-enforcement, prosecution and imprisonment boom that began in the 1980s gave the United States the world's highest incarceration rate, 731 people behind bars per 100,000 population. From 1972-2010, federal and state prison and jail populations grew uninterruptedly. By 2010, the total prisoner population reached more than 1.5 million in state and federal prisons, plus about 749,000 in city and county jails — a total of almost 2.3 million people. [45]

Sheer rates and numbers aside, the other notable feature of the incarceration boom was its racial and ethnic dimension. By 2010, nearly 38 percent of federal and state prisoners were black and 22 percent Hispanic. The disproportion was glaring — 12.6 percent of the total U.S. population was black, and 16.3 percent Latino. [46]

One early sign of awareness of the criminal-records issue, and its race-ethnicity aspect, came in 1985 from the EEOC, then under the chairmanship of Clarence Thomas, now an associate justice of the U.S. Supreme Court. Citing the disproportionate numbers of African-Americans with criminal records, the commission ruled that a business that was legally challenged for turning away an applicant or firing an employee based on a criminal record had to show that it considered not just the record itself but the nature and seriousness of the offenses involved; the length of time since the person was convicted or released from jail or prison; and the nature of the job involved. [47]

The EEOC reasoned that hiring or firing decisions arising from records alone would have a discriminatory effect on African-Americans and Latinos. For the same reason, the commission had ruled in 1987 that only records of convictions — not arrests that didn't lead to convictions — provided valid grounds for employment decisions. [48]

Getty Images/Alex Wong

Headed by then-Chairman Clarence Thomas, now an associate Supreme Court justice, the Equal Employment Opportunity Commission in 1987 took action to compensate for the disproportionate number of African-Americans with criminal records. The commission ruled that a business that was legally challenged for turning away an applicant or firing an employee based on a criminal record had to show that it considered not just the record itself but the nature and seriousness of the offenses involved; the length of time since the person was convicted and the nature of the job involved.

Meanwhile, the numbers of prisoners released from prisons and jails each year began to climb, reaching more than 500,000 by the early 2000s. [49] Accordingly, policy experts, academics and some politicians were calling for greater attention to what became known as "re-entry." A key element was the employment problems that people with criminal records faced. Once again, race played a role, according to some research.

As a growing number of people began to report being affected by records checks, the issue began to resound politically. In 2004, Boston became the first city to enact a "ban the box" ordinance for city government jobs.

That same year, the nonprofit Legal Action Center in New York reported that 37 states allowed employers and occupational licensing agencies to take into account for employment decisions arrests that never led to convictions. Forty-five states had no standards on private employers' use of criminal records in job decisions. [50]

By then, another factor had emerged. The Sept. 11 attacks created worries over employee backgrounds among companies whose businesses touched on some aspect of national security. Under a law passed soon after the attacks, all workers in shipping and transportation, including port workers, had to qualify for security credentials by submitting to background investigations.

The National Employment Law Project (NELP) represented about 500 port workers around the country who had been denied credentials. Most felony convictions less than seven years old could disqualify workers, but the Transportation Security Administration (TSA) effectively issued preliminary denials for all workers whose arrests showed up on an FBI database — a database in which about half the entries don't indicate if arrest charges were dismissed. [51]

The law allowed workers with records to apply for waivers. All but two of the workers NELP assisted received waivers, says Executive Director Emsellem. "There hasn't been a

In Pennsylvania, Arrest Records Can Vanish

"Why are they there? Only so employers can use them illegally."

The Philadelphia woman had accumulated a nine-page criminal record by age 24. Combing through it, lawyer Ryan Hancock quickly realized that for all its length, the rap sheet contained only one conviction, for simple assault.

That conviction will remain on her record. But thanks to a Pennsylvania law, the woman could apply for the other arrests to be expunged, or erased, from state records. The law allows expungement of records of nonconviction arrests. Records of minor, or "summary offenses," such as disorderly conduct, shoplifting and harassment, may also be expunged for people who have had no other run-ins with the law for five years. [1]

If the woman's request is granted, her assault conviction still will remain and could be a problem if she applies for jobs. However, with the other arrests cleared, "She has a much better chance of getting employed," Hancock says. "Employers don't know how to read docket sheets; they see, 'Oh my God, a person has been arrested nine times.' "

Hancock is chairman of the Criminal Record Expungement Project (C-REP), which is designed to make the legal procedure available to people who can't afford to hire a lawyer to clear their records.

"An attorney in Philadelphia would charge $750 to $2,000 to do expungement," Hancock says. "We call the expungement law a legal luxury — something for rich white kids in the suburbs who get a DUI."

Whoever the private clients might be, they're numerous enough to account for an abundance of websites by Pennsylvania lawyers offering expungement services.

"A criminal conviction can hurt your employment opportunities, career advancement, educational opportunities and even your personal relationships," a typical Web ad says. "With the rise of the Internet, anyone from a prospective employer to a fiancé can find out if you have been arrested or convicted of a crime." [2]

Hancock and his colleagues on the project, who include 28 law students from the University of Pennsylvania and elsewhere, do the work for free, thanks to a grant from the Philadelphia-based Bread & Roses Community Fund. The subsidy is essential because, as reflected in the fees that private lawyers charge, expungement is not a simple bureaucratic procedure.

Each request takes the form of a petition to the court. And each petition can be opposed by the district attorney, though if the prosecution doesn't challenge a request, it's automatically granted. So far, C-REP has won 496 of the 505 expungements it has filed; appeals have been filed on the nine denials. A district attorney could argue against expunging a record that contained nothing but arrests, with no convictions. But, Hancock says, Pennsylvania law requires prosecutors to prove that the state interest in preserving a record outweighs the harm it does to an individual. In those circumstances, refusal to expunge an arrest-only record is "highly unlikely," he says.

Pennsylvania law treats expunged records as though they never existed and bars them from being attached to an individual's name. [3]

At least 45 states allow expungement under widely varying circumstances. Recent years have seen efforts in several states to make the procedure more widely applicable. Rhode Island, for instance, is one of several states in which legislators have debated allowing expungement of nonviolent felonies as well as nonviolent misdemeanors. [4]

Employers haven't campaigned against expungements. "If a record is expunged, employers don't want to know about it," says Pamela Quigley Devata, a Chicago-based lawyer who works with employers. "I've never had an employer say they want to take action based on an expunged record."

An employer may encounter an expunged record if it turns up in law enforcement databases and a background-checking firm used by the company fails to follow up on it, says Frederick G. Giles, executive vice president of Carco Group, a Holtsville, N.Y.-based background investigation firm. "We re-verify,"

single problem with folks they waived in," he adds. "People who are working are not inclined to turn around and jeopardize their work situation."

As advocates for job-seekers with records mobilized in states and cities, they achieved some successes. In 2010 and 2011, key years for political action on the issue, three states enacted "ban the box" laws (in two cases affecting government employment only); two states created certificates of rehabilitation to ease employers' fears of hiring people with records; 13 states adopted laws allowing some criminal records to be expunged; and three states limited the liability of employers who hire people with criminal records, under certain circumstances. [52]

Meanwhile, 32 cities and counties had passed "ban the box" ordinances and laws by early 2012. Philadelphia applied the ban to all private employers. Seven of the measures affect employers doing business with the local governments involved. [53] ■

CURRENT SITUATION

Top-down Change

Ohio's Gov. Kasich wants people with criminal records to have a better chance at employment. He's

adds Giles, incoming chairman of the National Association of Professional Background Screeners. "If it is expunged, it is not available to us when we go to court records. It doesn't go in our report."

In Philadelphia, the appeal of clearing a record is strong enough, and the number of people with records large enough, that C-REP cautions on its website that it can't accept all applicants whose incomes are low enough to qualify for the free service. "We are unable to handle all of the expungements for everyone with a record in Philadelphia," the group says. "We may reject applicants with records that, while expungeable, will not leave the applicant in a substantially better position to find employment or qualify for public benefits." An example is an applicant with several serious convictions in addition to several minor arrests that did not lead to convictions. [5]

Pennsylvania law also allows a lesser form of expungement, called "redaction." In this procedure, charges for which someone was arrested, but which weren't prosecuted, can be removed from the publicly available record but remain accessible to law enforcement, even while the resulting conviction remains.

The option is valuable, Hancock says, because police often arrest people on major charges that are then dismissed in plea bargains. "In Philadelphia, if you're young and black and get arrested for one joint on your person, you'll all of a sudden be charged with 15 offenses, serious offenses — and ultimately plead out to simple possession, a misdemeanor," he says.

The stories of those who qualify for the procedures testify to their value. One C-REP client had been barred from a nursing home because he'd been arrested in a fight in the 1970s. Another said an arrest for shoplifting as a teenager had blocked her from any sort of stable job. [6]

Another client told *The Philadelphia Inquirer* that employers who'd turned her down for about 40 jobs informed her that the reason was her 1999 arrest for aggravated assault and related charges arising from a fight with her drug-addicted brother. The charges had been dropped, a check of the record by C-REP confirmed, but that didn't seem to matter. [7]

"Some said I couldn't get hired because I would deal with money," said the woman, a former assistant manager of a self-storage facility. She had run through her unemployment insurance and was scraping by — selling bottled water on the street and doing some moving and hauling work. [8]

Tales of employers using such arrests to bar employment are familiar at C-REP. "There is no doubt that employers should have the right to use criminal records to make employment decisions if it deals with a job," Hancock says. "But arrests — it's actually illegal under Pennsylvania law for an employer to use them. So why are they there in the record? They're only there so employers can use them illegally."

— Peter Katel

[1] Brian Zeiger, "Summary Offenses in Pennsylvania," *Criminal Defense Lawyer Blog*, Jan. 22, 2009, www.criminallawyerphiladelphia.com/blog/2009/01/22/summary-offenses-in-pennsylvania.

[2] Patrick Artur & Associates, undated, www.willdefend.com/Criminal-Defense-Overview/Expungements-and-Pardons.shtml.

[3] Pennsylvania Code, Chapter 195.1, www.pacode.com/secure/data/037/chapter195/chap195toc.html.

[4] "State Reforms Promoting Employment of People with Criminal Records," National Employment Law Project, December 2011, pp. 8-12, www.nelp.org/page/-/SCLP/2011/PromotingEmploymentofPeoplewithCriminalRecords.pdf?nocdn=1; "Expungement," undated, Electronic Privacy Information Center, http://epic.org/privacy/expungement/.

[5] "Philadelphia Criminal Record Expungement Project," updated 2012, www.paexpungementproject.org/get-help.

[6] Kia Gregory, "Legal Volunteers Help Those Seeking a Clean Slate" (*Philadelphia Inquirer*), *Pittsburgh Post-Gazette*, Nov. 27, 2011, p. B-4, http://articles.philly.com/2011-11-21/news/30425011_1_sanchez-clean-slate-law-students.

[7] *Ibid.*

[8] Quoted in *ibid.*

making the matter a priority. "We have rules that are overly punitive," he told the *Columbus Dispatch* in February. "That's just not right." [54]

Ohio law now includes restrictions that are especially problematic to people with records. They include lifetime bans on anyone with a felony record of any kind for occupations including licensed construction trades.

So far, Kasich's administration has eliminated questions on criminal background from applications for state jobs. Applicants will be checked out, but only after the initial phase of a job search in which they show valid qualifications.

"Kasich has been terrific," says Love, the pardon-law expert. "You need somebody in the bully pulpit who can rally the troops, persuade the legislature. It takes leadership."

Last year, Kasich signed a sentencing-law overhaul that is projected to reduce the state's prison population by 6,000 compared to what it would have been without the legislation. Ohio's inmate count currently stands at 50,000. The new law also grants "achievement and employability" certificates to ex-prisoners who satisfactorily completed vocational training and behavioral improvement programs while incarcerated and who complete community service requirements when released. Companies that hire certificated ex-prisoners can't be sued for "negligent hiring." (They can be sued for keeping an employee who shows "incompetence or dangerousness.") [55]

But Kasich has a more ambitious plan. He wants legislation drafted this year that would alter Ohio's severe employment restrictions on people with records of any kind. Criminal-record barriers on jobs that involve contact with children would remain. But, he said last November, "We think there is a way to find a middle ground, to give people who are felons an opportunity to reclaim their lives." [56]

Stephen JohnsonGrove, deputy director for policy at the Ohio Justice and Policy Center, a Cincinnati-based advocacy group, who is contributing to a draft of the anticipated legislation, says he expects it to include a provision to allow individual consideration of occupational license applicants; a "ban the box" system in the private sector, and a requirement that employers acquiring criminal-record information be given only the final disposition of a case.

The latter provision would ensure that someone arrested for a serious felony, but who then pleaded guilty to a misdemeanor, would have a record for employment purposes of only the lesser charge.

A conservative Republican, Kasich by some accounts has shown more determination to make changes that would give ex-offenders a chance than Democrats whose rhetoric tends to be more liberal. "Democrats were so incredibly afraid of doing anything about this," JohnsonGrove says, recalling recent years in which Democrats held the governor's office and one legislative chamber. Both chambers are now controlled by Republicans.

"Republicans controlled the tough-on-crime dialogue so much that they can violate it, because they control the conversation," JohnsonGrove says. "When Democrats are in charge, they know that Republicans will use it against them."

Getty Images/Chip Somodevilla

Republican Gov. John Kasich of Ohio is pushing for legislation this year to give people with records a chance at employment, including in licensed occupations — such as electrical contractor — that now bar anyone with a felony record for life. "We have rules that are overly punitive. That's just not right," he said.

He adds, "For me as a fairly progressive, activist lawyer, it's Republicans who are totally my friends on this issue."

New EEOC Guideline

The EEOC has been considering whether to expand its guidelines on employers' use of criminal records. EEOC guidelines set a national standard for non-discriminatory practices by employers.

At a hearing last summer, some commission members expressed strong interest in keeping guidelines current with conditions that have changed since the EEOC first weighed in on the subject in 1987.

Most notably, the size of the incarcerated population mushroomed since then. Federal and state prison populations totaled about 585,000 in 1987, less than half the 2010 population of 1.5 million (not counting jail prisoners). [57]

As the prisoner count has grown, so has the number released each year — about 700,000 — commission chairwoman Jacqueline A. Berrien said at the July 26, 2011, hearing called to gather testimony on whether to revise EEOC guidance. "After release, the vast majority of these people will return to communities they came from; and it is in the interest not only of those communities, but public safety in general, to help them reconnect with society, find gainful employment, stay out of trouble and avoid returning to jail to the extent we can do that consistently with any public safety concerns." [58]

Something else has changed since the EEOC last weighed in on criminal records. A 2007 decision by the Third U.S. Circuit Court of Appeals in a criminal-records case arising from the firing of a Philadelphia van driver named Douglas El suggested to at least one commissioner that guidelines could be more specific. (*See sidebar, p. 360.*) "The Third Circuit decision . . . is further indication that it's important for us to update our guidance," said Commissioner Stuart J. Ishimaru. [59]

Extending that point, Juan Cartagena, president and general counsel of LatinoJustice PRLDEF (formerly the Puerto Rican Legal Defense and Education Fund) said in written testimony to the EEOC that the ruling "provides

Continued on p. 368

At Issue:

Are more limits needed on employers' access to criminal records?

ROBERTA MEYERS-PEEPLES
DIRECTOR, NATIONAL H.I.R.E. NETWORK

WRITTEN FOR *CQ RESEARCHER*, APRIL 2012

yes

The federal government should ensure that states prohibit the dissemination and use of arrest records that did not result in a conviction as well as limit access to old or minor convictions. Government should do everything in its power to make sure everyone, including individuals who have paid their debt to society, has a fair chance to compete for jobs.

Because of the disproportionate representation of people of color in the criminal justice system, the U.S. Equal Employment Opportunity Commission (EEOC) issued guidance to employers nearly three decades ago discouraging employers from considering arrest records that did not lead to conviction and from having blanket bans against hiring individuals with conviction records. Unfettered use of criminal records in employment perpetuates the injustice.

Many employers blatantly discriminate against qualified job-seekers with criminal records, no matter how minor or old the record. Employers routinely post job notices that say, "People with criminal records need not apply." Therefore, it's safe to assume they will consider any and all information they obtain from background-check sources in their hiring decisions. In fact, a recent case brought against Pepsi Co. by the EEOC is evidence that criminal record-based discrimination happens, even with companies that have a plethora of employment lawyers at their disposal to advise them about fair hiring standards. Employers should conduct individualized assessments of prospective employees and consider such factors as the relationship between the person's record and the duties of the job; the age of the person at the time of the conviction, and evidence of rehabilitation.

Permitting the use and consideration of arrest records that did not result in a conviction flies in the face of the bedrock of our legal system of the "presumption of innocence in favor of the accused." Additionally, research shows that when an individual has been crime-free for a period of time, it is reasonable to presume the individual is less likely to reoffend.

Criminal records have become the Scarlett Letters of our time. They are brands that rest on the backs of millions of people. Many skilled and highly educated people with criminal records are unemployed and overlooked because they have been relegated to a new underclass that is excluded from participating in our highly competitive labor market simply because they have a record.

FREDERICK G. GILES
SENIOR VICE PRESIDENT, CARCO GROUP; CHAIRMAN-ELECT, NATIONAL ASSOCIATION OF PROFESSIONAL BACKGROUND SCREENERS

WRITTEN FOR *CQ RESEARCHER*, APRIL 2012

no

Censorship in any form always has unintended consequences, and rarely are those positive. Unfettered access to our courts is a fundamental right shedding light on the process to ensure equal and fair treatment for all. Censorship is both pernicious and subjective. Once allowed by any means and for any well-meaning purpose, it tends to spread and morph beyond the original intended purpose, and its application shifts with individual ideology or bias.

Advocates for limiting employers' access to court records argue that when unfettered access is permitted, employers are unfairly disqualifying applicants who have long since paid their debt to society, and are thereby creating a permanent underclass of unemployables who will be "forced" to re-offend when no honest employment is available. They argue that older records must therefore be declared "stale" and censorship enforced to prevent this societal harm.

It is true that former offenders must be able to fairly compete for appropriate jobs and that after a period of time certain crimes should not be held against ex-offenders for certain positions, if at all. But censorship is not the answer for a number of reasons. The first and simplest is that already-overburdened court staff, faced today with shortened hours and layoffs due to budgetary constraints, are not equipped to add another responsibility that is not directly related to the running of the courts. Nor do courts have the budgets to establish special filters and access for newly defined classes of public-record seekers.

Even if budget were not an issue, censorship is unworkable because by its very nature it assumes that "one size fits all." The reality is that different jobs have different risks, so that the same offense may be irrelevant to one job but very relevant by statute for another many years later. Further, each work environment is different, and if one employer has a serious workplace issue related to a specific offense type (be it drugs, theft or violence), that employer may have a business necessity to avoid those ex-offenders while another employer with the same job type but a more healthy environment can safely overlook that offense.

Finally, there already exist law and EEOC guidance that require the employer to consider the seriousness, job relevance and time since the offense before making an employment decision. Legal guidance is the answer, not censorship.

Continued from p. 366

the EEOC with an opportunity to reissue its guidance on criminal convictions and arrests so as to support its clear mandate that employers must substantiate and document their reasoning behind criminal-conviction bars to employment." [60]

A bus company that had a contract with the Southeastern Pennsylvania Transportation Authority (SEPTA) to drive vans for mentally and physically disabled people hired El as a driver in 2000. But it fired him within weeks after discovering a 1960 conviction for second-degree murder that occurred during a gang fight when El was 15 years old. [61]

The circuit court judges ruled that SEPTA had made a valid case for firing El — but only because his lawyers didn't provide evidence to counter the main justification for dismissal. Justice Department data show convincingly that recidivism within three years of release from prison is a strong possibility, the judges wrote. "But what about someone who has been released from prison and violence-free for 40 years?," they added.

SEPTA did present expert witnesses who testified that even someone with a long-ago conviction was more likely to commit a crime than someone with a clean record. The appeals judges said they were not "convinced that SEPTA's expert reports are ironclad." But there was no evidence to the contrary. [62]

Likewise, the judges wrote, an EEOC staff decision in El's favor — which didn't lead to an EEOC lawsuit because the Justice Department declined to pursue the case — cited no evidence to back up the argument that El's conviction was too old to be relevant. "The EEOC determination is terse and simply asserts the relevance of El's youth and the remoteness of his conviction without explanation, analysis, or authority," the judges concluded. "It provides nothing of substance on which the jury could rely." [63]

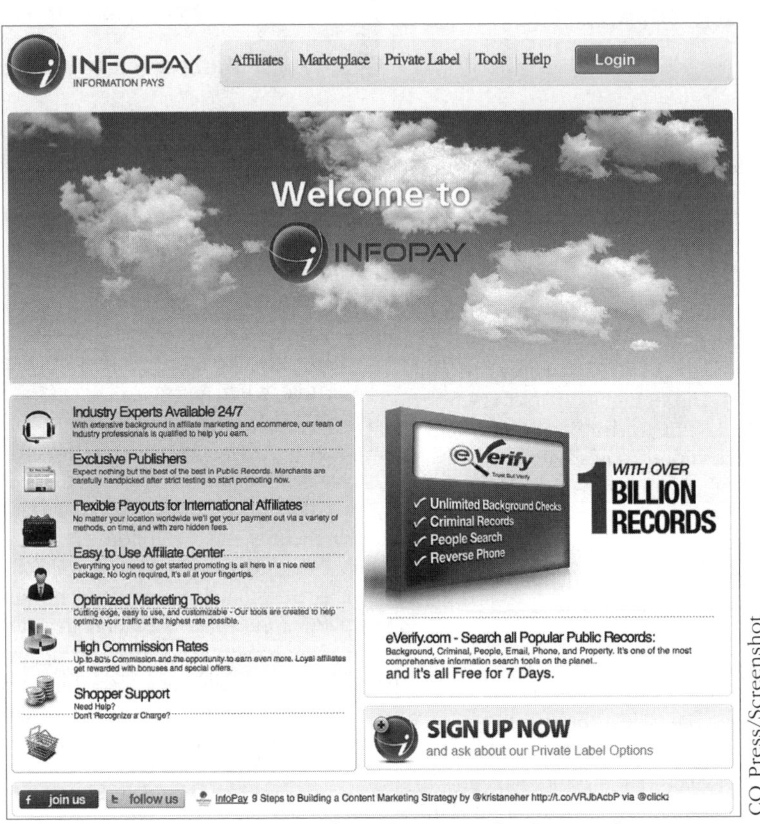

The Fair Credit Reporting Act (FCRA) requires background-screening firms such as Infopay and Everify to take steps to ensure accuracy and to notify those being screened of any adverse information, giving them a chance to correct errors. Both firms use mobile apps, but the Federal Trade Commission is warning that some apps may violate federal laws designed to regulate background-screening practices.

CQ Press/Screenshot

Warning on Apps

As smartphones and tablets have taken the Web mobile, some criminal-record search firms have been adapting. But the Federal Trade Commission (FTC) is warning that some mobile applications (apps) through which customers can order searches may violate the federal law designed to regulate background-screening practices.

In identical letters last January to three firms, the FTC said the mobile app-initiated searches for criminal records had to comply with the Fair Credit Reporting Act (FCRA).

"Employers are likely to use such criminal histories when screening job applicants," FTC Associate Director Maneesha Mithal wrote. "If you have reason to believe that your reports are being used for employment or other FCRA purposes, you and your customers who are using the reports for such purposes must comply with the FCRA. This is true even if you have a disclaimer on your website indicating that your reports should not be used for employment or other FCRA purposes." [64]

The FCRA requires background-screening firms to take steps to ensure accuracy and to notify those being screened of any adverse information, offering an opportunity to correct possible errors.

Mithal wrote that FTC staff hadn't decided if the firms were violating the FCRA, but would take legal action against them if the agency concludes they were breaking the law.

The letters went to Everify Inc., which runs an app called Police Records; InfoPay Inc., with an app called Criminal Pages; and Intelligator Inc., which markets apps named Background Checks, Criminal Records Search, Investigate and Locate Anyone, People Search and Investigator.

None of the companies responded to e-mail queries from *CQ Researcher* about their responses to the FTC warning. The FTC also failed to respond to two inquiries about company responses, if any.

Questions surrounding Web-based search firms go beyond their mobile apps. Giles, at the National Association of Professional Background Screeners, cites a tendency among some companies to try to find a loophole through the FCRA. "I do think it's a problem that some companies are offering Web-based checks and putting tiny disclaimers on the bottom that say 'not to be used for pre-employment screening.' "

How many such firms exist seems to be anybody's guess. In 2005, a Justice Department-funded study by a task force of experts from the background-checking industry, state law enforcement and the Justice Department, could not come up with a hard number for the field as a whole. "In addition to a few large industry players, there are hundreds, perhaps even thousands, of regional and local companies." [65]

But the task force had no question about why the field was so large. "Some end-users place a premium on being able to obtain almost instant results on demand," it noted. "An executive with a temporary-staffing company, for example, emphasized the need for being able to conduct speedy background checks in a business where staff is often needed with little prior notice." [66]

Some advocates for job-seekers with criminal records don't have a lot of confidence in the FTC's ability to systematically ensure widespread compliance with the FCRA.

"You can put 'regulation' in quotation marks," says Dietrich of Philadelphia's Community Legal Services. "They're pretty unregulated at this point."

"I do think it's a problem that some companies are offering Web-based checks and putting tiny disclaimers at the bottom that say 'not to be used for pre-employment screening.' "

— Frederick G. Giles
Incoming Chairman
National Association of Professional Background Screeners

But Devata, the Chicago lawyer who represents employers, says her dealings with screening firms leave her "absolutely" convinced that regulation is rigorous. "In my experience and my practice, more often than not background screening companies take painstaking procedures to follow the law." ■

OUTLOOK

More Screening?

In coming years, job candidates who are asked for the key information that would allow a background check to start — name, birthday, Social Security number — might be asked for one other thing: fingerprints.

Improvements in the technology of transmitting fingerprint images are likely to find their way into the background-screening industry, the task force studying the industry predicted in 2005. "A fingerprint-based check virtually eliminates the occurrence of a 'false positive,' " it said approvingly. "False positives are easy to come by. It is estimated, for example, that there are 23,000 individuals with the name 'Michael Smith' in the United States." [67]

The task force also posited that the public is becoming more accustomed to the use of "biometric" identifiers but acknowledged grounds for concern. Among them, "whether biometrics and biometric-supported databases will be consensual, and whether these technologies could encourage surveillance activities or the development of a national identification system." [68]

Already, the use of social media in job-applicant screening — including by law-enforcement agencies — is leading to resistance.

In March, several employers, including the Maryland Department of Corrections, were reported to have demanded Facebook passwords from job applicants. [69] After the ACLU complained about the corrections department, it dropped the practice. But employees were asked to "voluntarily" provide their Facebook logins, the ACLU reported. [70]

The civil liberties group is pressing the Maryland legislature to prohibit the practice. In Illinois, where several sheriff's departments have been demanding passwords, a lawmaker is working on a similar bill. And Facebook itself announced that it might take legal action to oppose the practice, which arguably is prohibited by the company's terms of service. [71]

Precisely how widespread the trend has become isn't known. Giles of CARCO says the practice seems largely confined to jobs requiring security clearances. "From our perspective," Giles said in an e-mail, "employers . . . should NEVER ask for passwords." His company's policy on the matter notes that a social network account holder "may post pictures or thoughts intended as humor for their friends that the employer might find offensive, juvenile or perhaps immoral by their own code, which . . . are in fact neither illegal nor even immoral."

The hubbub over social-networking passwords, though not directly related to criminal records, illustrates the expansion of background checking — a development that some advocates say has been advancing faster than regulation of the industry. "In terms of impact on workers, it's really going to depend on what happens now and in the next couple of years to get a handle on ensuring that background checks are more fair and more accurate," says Emsellem of the National Employment Law Project.

NYU's Jacobs argues that the emphasis on criminal records as an employment factor diverts attention from a pressing need to attend to problems of ex-convicts that are far greater than the existence of their records. "You have a large number of people who have been chronically involved in criminal activities who have so many deficiencies, mental and emotional," he says. "I don't think this can be wished away as a figment of the imagination that would be solved if employers would just get their act together."

One of the fundamental problems, Jacobs says, is that too many people have been incarcerated. "There has to be something done about reintegrating them into society and not just assigning them to the criminal underclass."

JohnsonGrove of the Ohio Justice and Policy Center foresees a lessening of absolute employment prohibitions on people with criminal records, "The day when you just say, 'Felons will never do this job' — we'll grow beyond that."

Nevertheless, he acknowledges that he has heard arguments that measures he advocates could give ex-offenders an edge over others in competition for jobs, as opposed to simply helping them get past an automatic rejection. "We're talking about giving a guy with a 10-year-old drug offense who's demonstrated he turned his life around an opportunity," JohnsonGrove says.

In any case, a terrible jobs climate is only one factor in the debate. Another, some point out, is the enormous number of people with criminal records of some kind. Against that backdrop, says Dietrich of Community Legal Services, "I am oddly optimistic. Even as more restrictions keep developing, I feel that there is more public understanding of the consequences of these restrictions and the lack of public-policy sense that some of them make." ■

Notes

[1] Christy A. Visher, *et al.*, "Employment After Prison: A Longitudinal Study of Former Prisoners," *Justice Quarterly*, Dec. 10, 2010, p. 699, www.tandfonline.com/doi/abs/10.1080/07418825.2010.535553; for background, see Peter Katel, "Prisoner Reentry," *CQ Researcher*, Dec. 4, 2009, pp. 1025-1028.

[2] Alfred Blumstein and Kiminori Nakamura, "Redemption in the Presence of Widespread Criminal Background Checks," *Criminology*, May 1, 2009, p. 330, http://onlinelibrary.wiley.com/doi/10.1111/j.1745-9125.2009.00155.x/abstract; "Survey of State Criminal History Information Systems," U.S. Bureau of Justice Statistics, 2008, pp. 2-4, www.ncjrs.gov/pdffiles1/bjs/grants/228661.pdf; "Report of the National Task Force on the Commercial Sale of Criminal Justice Record Information," p. 7, www.search.org/files/pdf/RNTFCSCJRI.pdf.

[3] "Ban the Box: Major U.S. Cities and Counties Adopt Fair Hiring Policies to Remove Unfair Barriers to Employment of People with Criminal Records," National Employment Law Project, Feb. 6, 2012, www.nelp.org/page/-.

[4] "Facts About Prisons and Prisoners," Sentencing Project, January 2012, www.sentencingproject.org/doc/publications/publications/inc_factsAboutPrisons_Jan2012.pdf.

[5] "EEOC Policy Statement on the Issue of Conviction Records," U.S. Equal Employment Opportunity Commission, Feb. 4, 1987, www.eeoc.gov/policy/docs/convict1.html, "State Reforms Promoting Employment of People with Criminal Records," National Employment Law Project, December 2011, www.nelp.org/page/-/SCLP/2011/PromotingEmploymentofPeoplewithCriminalRecords.pdf?nocdn=1.

[6] Peris S. Yu and Sharon M. Dietrich, "Broken Records: How Errors by Criminal Background Checking Companies Harm Workers and Businesses," National Consumer Law Center, April 2010, www.nclc.org/issues/broken-records.html.

[7] *Eugene Johnson, et al. v. Gary Locke*, secretary, U.S. Department of Commerce, U.S. District Court, Southern District of New York, Aug. 5, 2010, 10-cv-3105(FM); Larry Neumeister, "Lawsuit: Census Bureau discriminated in hiring," The Associated Press, Aug. 5, 2010.

[8] Decision and Order, 10 Civ. 3105 (FM), U.S. District Court, Southern District of New York, March 22, 2010 (emailed to *CQ Researcher*).

[9] Michelle Natividad Rodriguez and Maurice Emsellem, "65 Million Need Not Apply: The Case for Reforming Criminal Background Checks for Employment," National Employment Law Project, March 2011, pp. 13-14, http://nelp.3cdn.net/e9231d3aee1d058c9e_55im6wopc.pdf.

[10] Sam Hananel, "Pepsi Beverages pays $3.1M in racial bias case," The Associated Press, Jan. 11, 2012.

[11] U.S. Equal Opportunity Commission hearing transcript, July 26, 2011, www.eeoc.gov/eeoc/meetings/7-26-11/transcript.cfm.

[12] Shawn D. Bushway and Robert Apel, "Overview of: 'A Signaling Perspective on

Employment-Based Reentry Programming: Training Completion as a Desistance Signal,' " *Criminology & Public Policy*, February 2012, http://onlinelibrary.wiley.com/doi/10.1111/j.1745-9133.2012.00785.x/abstract.

[13] *Eugene Johnson et al. v. Gary Locke*, secretary, U.S. Department of Commerce, U.S. District Court, Southern District of New York, Aug. 5, 2010, 10-cv-3105(FM); Larry Neumeister, "Lawsuit: Census Bureau discriminated in hiring," The Associated Press, Aug. 5, 2010.

[14] "New State Initiatives Adopt Model Hiring Policies Reducing Barriers to Employment of People with Criminal Records," National Employment Law Project, Sept. 21, 2010, www.nelp.org/page/-/SCLP/ModelStateHiringInitiatives.pdf?nocdn=1.

[15] Keith Finlay, "Effect of Employer Access to Criminal History Data on the Labor Market Outcomes of Ex-Offenders and Non-Offenders," National Bureau of Economic Research, 2009, www.nber.org/chapters/c3587.pdf.

[16] "State Reforms Promoting Employment of People With Criminal Records: 2010-11 Legislative Round-Up," National Employment Law Project, *et al.*, December 2011, www.nelp.org/page/-/SCLP/2011/PromotingEmploymentofPeoplewithCriminalRecords.pdf?nocdn=1; "Expungement," Electronic Privacy Information Center, undated, http://epic.org/privacy/expungement/.

[17] "How to Clear Your Illinois Criminal Record," Office of the State Appellate Defender, pp. 1-2, January 2012, www.state.il.us/defender/expforms/2012%20InstGuide.pdf.

[18] Margaret Colgate Love, "Paying Their Debt to Society: Forgiveness, Redemption, and the Uniform Collateral Consequences of Conviction Act," *Howard Law Journal*, Nov. 3, 2011, pp. 777-778, http://papers.ssrn.com/sol3/papers.cfm?abstract_id=1802180.

[19] *Ibid.*, p. 788.

[20] "The Fair Credit Reporting Act," U.S. Federal Trade Commission, July 30, 2004, www.ftc.gov/os/statutes/031224fcra.pdf.

[21] Blumstein and Nakamura, *op. cit.*, *Criminology*, Nov. 2, 2009, and Blumstein and Kiminori Nakamura, "'Redemption' in an Era of Widespread Criminal Background Checks," *NIJ* [National Institute of Justice] *Journal*, June 1, 2010, (shorter version), www.ncjrs.gov/pdffiles1/nij/226872.pdf.

[22] Alfred Blumstein and Kiminori Nakamura, "Paying a Price, Long After the Crime," *The New York Times*, Jan. 9, 2012, www.nytimes.com/2012/01/10/opinion/paying-a-price-long-after-the-crime.html.

[23] Blumstein and Nakamura, "Redemption," *op. cit.*; *ibid.*

[24] "Employment Background Checks in California: New Focus on Accuracy," Privacy Rights Clearinghouse, updated February 2012, www.privacyrights.org/fs/fs16a-califbck.htm. "FDIC Law, Regulations, Related Acts," Federal Deposit Insurance Corp., amended May 10, 2011, www.fdic.gov/regulations/laws/rules/5000-1300.html.

[25] Except where otherwise noted, this subsection is drawn from Margaret Colgate Love, "The Twilight of the Pardon Power," *Journal of Criminal Law and Criminology*, June 22, 2010, www.law.northwestern.edu/jclc/symposium/v100/n3/1003_1169.Love.pdf.

[26] Quoted in *ibid.*, p. 1178.

[27] Peter B. Hoffman, *History of the Federal Parole System* (2003), pp. 6-7.

[28] Love, "Twilight of the Pardon Power," *op. cit.*

[29] Except where otherwise noted, this subsection is drawn from Jeremy Travis, *But They All Come Back: Facing the Challenges of Prisoner Reentry* (2005).

[30] Quoted in *ibid.*, p. 66.

[31] *Ibid.*, p. 67.

[32] Michelle Alexander, *The New Jim Crow: Mass Incarceration in the Age of Colorblindness* (2010), p. 45. Concerning the book's influence, see: Jennifer Schuessler, "Drug Policy as Race Policy: Best Seller Galvanizes the Debate," *The New York Times*, March 6, 2012, www.nytimes.com/2012/03/07/books/michelle-alexanders-new-jim-crow-raises-drug-law-debates.html?ref=books.

[33] John Herbers, "Panel on Civil Disorders Calls For Drastic Action To Avoid 2-Society Nation," *The New York Times*, Feb. 29, 1968, www.nytimes.com/learning/general/onthisday/big/0229.html#article; "Kerner Commission Reports on U.S. Racial Inequality," The Learning Network — *The New York Times*, Feb 29, 2012, http://learning.blogs.nytimes.com/2012/02/29/feb-29-1968-kerner-commission-report-details-racial-inequality-in-u-s/.

[34] "Report of the National Advisory Commission on Civil Disorders — Summary of Report," Eisenhower Foundation, (pages not numbered), www.eisenhowerfoundation.org/docs/kerner.pdf.

[35] "State and national crime estimates by year(s)," FBI Uniform Crime Reporting Statistics data tool, updated March 29, 2010, www.ucrdatatool.gov/Search/Crime/State/StateCrime.cfm.

[36] *Ibid.*; for background see Sarah Glazer, "Declining Crime Rates," *CQ Researcher*, April 4, 1997, pp. 289-312.

[37] "Radio Address to the Nation on Proposed Crime Legislation," Ronald Reagan, Feb. 18, 1984, www.presidency.ucsb.edu/ws/index.php?pid=39541#axzz1oealhFKg.

[38] Paul J. Hofer, *et al.*, "Fifteen Years of Guidelines Sentencing," U.S. Sentencing Commission, November 2004, pp. 3-6, www.ussc.gov/Research/Research_Projects/Miscellaneous/15_Year_Study/15_year_study_full.pdf.

[39] Alexander, *op. cit.*, p. 49.

[40] *Ibid.*, pp. 50-53.

[41] Lisa M. Seghetti, "Federal Crime Control: Background, Legislation, and Issues," Congressional Research Service, June 12, 2007, p. 9, www.fas.org/sgp/crs/misc/RL32824.pdf.

[42] Hofer, *et al.*, *op. cit.*, pp. 48, 53.

[43] Travis, *op. cit.*, pp. 67-68.

[44] *Ibid.*, pp. 69-71.

[45] "Facts About Prisons and Prisoners," Sentencing Project, January 2012, www.sentencingproject.org/doc/publications/publications/inc_factsAboutPrisons_Jan2012.pdf.

[46] *Ibid.*; "USA Quickfacts," U.S. Census Bureau, updated Jan. 17, 2012, http://quickfacts.census.gov/qfd/states/00000.html.

[47] "EEOC Policy Statement on the Issue of

About the Author

Peter Katel is a *CQ Researcher* staff writer who previously reported on Haiti and Latin America for *Time* and *Newsweek* and covered the Southwest for newspapers in New Mexico. He has received several journalism awards, including the Bartolomé Mitre Award for coverage of drug trafficking, from the Inter-American Press Association. He holds an A.B. in university studies from the University of New Mexico. His recent reports include "Prisoner Reenty" and "Downsizing Prisons."

Conviction Records under Title VII of the Civil Rights Act of 1964," U.S. Equal Employment Opportunity Commission, Feb. 4, 1987, www.eeoc.gov/policy/docs/convict1.html.

[48] "Written Testimony of Barry A. Harstein," U.S. Equal Opportunity Commission, July 26, 2011, www.eeoc.gov/eeoc/meetings/7-26-11/hartstein.cfm.

[49] Devah Pager, "The Mark of a Criminal Record," *American Journal of Sociology*, March 2003, p. 937, www.princeton.edu/~pager/pager_ajs.pdf.

[50] "After Prison: Roadblocks to Reentry: A Report on State Legal Barriers Facing People With Criminal Records," Legal Action Center, 2004, www.lac.org/roadblocks-to-reentry/upload/lacreport/LAC_PrintReport.pdf.

[51] Maurice Emsellem, *et al.*, "A Scorecard on the Post-9/11 Port Worker Background Checks," National Employment Law Project, July 2009, http://nelp.3cdn.net/0714d0826f3ecf7a15_70m6i6fwb.pdf; "The Attorney General's Report on Criminal History Background Checks," U.S. Department of Justice, June, 2006, pp. 3, 21, www.justice.gov/olp/ag_bgchecks_report.pdf.

[52] "State Reforms Promoting Employment of People with Criminal Records: 2010-11 Legislative Round-Up," National Employment Law Project, *et al.*, December 2011, www.nelp.org/page/-/SCLP/2011/PromotingEmploymentofPeoplewithCriminalRecords.pdf?nocdn=1.

[53] "Ban the Box Resource Guide," National Employment Law Project, updated Feb. 6, 2012, www.nelp.org/page/-/SCLP/2011/CityandCountyHiringInitiatives.pdf?nocdn=1.

[54] Quoted in Alan Johnson, "Disqualifications; States tries to ease job hunts of ex-cons," *Columbus Dispatch*, Feb. 20, 2012, p. A1, www.dispatch.com/content/stories/local/2012/02/20/state-tries-to-ease-job-hunts-of-ex-cons.html.

[55] Alan Johnson, "Sentencing Overhaul; Law will open prison doors for thousands," *Columbus Dispatch*, Sept. 30, 2011, p. A1; "Certificates of Achievement and Employability (fact sheet)," Ohio Justice and Policy Center, 2011, http://webcache.googleusercontent.com/search?q=cache:u-xmX2-k304J:www.opnff.net/Files/Admin/Certificates%2520of%2520Achievement%2520and%2520Employability.pdf+%E2%80%9DCertificates+of+Achievement+and+Employability+(fact+sheet),%E2%80%9D&hl=en&gl=us; "Application for certificate of achievement and employability," Ohio Laws and Rules, 2011, http://codes.ohio.gov/orc/2961.22; "Individualized consideration; civil liability," Ohio Laws and Rules, 2011, http://codes.ohio.gov/orc/2961.23.

FOR MORE INFORMATION

American Society of Employers, 19575 Victor Parkway, Suite 100, Livonia, MI 48152; 248-353-4500; www.aseonline.org. Trade association representing management; includes a for-profit spinoff that performs background investigations.

National H.I.R.E. Network, 225 Varick St., New York, NY 10014; 212-243-1313; www.hirenetwork.org. Advocacy organization for ex-prisoners; website offers information on criminal record-related laws and regulations, as well as manuals on record expungement.

National Employment Law Project, 75 Maiden Lane, Suite 601, New York, NY 10038; 212-285-3025; www.nelp.org. Advocacy organization that litigates on behalf of people with criminal records; publishes detailed reports on state public-records laws.

U.S. Equal Employment Opportunity Commission (EEOC), 131 M St., N.E., Washington, DC 20507; 202-663-4900; www.eeoc.gov. Federal guidelines on employer use of criminal records available on commission's website.

National Association of Professional Background Screeners, 1901 N. Roselle Road, Suite 920, Schaumburg, IL 60195; 888-686-2727; www.napbs.com. Trade group for companies that check background records of job applicants, others; website offers information for the public.

Safer Foundation, 571 W. Jackson, Chicago, Ill., 60661; 312-922-2200; www.saferfoundation.org. Advocates for ex-prisoners seeking to reintegrate into society; limits its work to Illinois but provides information that applies nationally.

[56] Quoted in Laura A. Bischoff, "Kasich seeks to help ex-cons find jobs," *Dayton Daily News*, Nov. 29, 2011, p. A1, http://dayton-daily-news.vlex.com/vid/kasich-seeks-cons-hurdles-offenders-335559566.

[57] "One in 100: Behind Bars in America 2008," Pew Center on the States, February 2008, www.pewcenteronthestates.org/uploadedFiles/8015PCTS_Prison08_FINAL_2-1-1_FORWEB.pdf; "Facts About Prison and Prisoners," *op. cit.*

[58] U.S. Equal Employment Opportunity Commission hearing transcript, *op. cit.*

[59] *Ibid.*; Cristin Schmitz, "Ban on Hiring Ex-Convicts Raises Title VII Concerns," *Inside Counsel*, June 2007.

[60] "Written Testimony of Juan Cartagena," July 26, 2011, www.eeoc.gov/eeoc/meetings/7-26-11/cartagena.cfm.

[61] *El v. Southeastern Pennsylvania Transportation Authority et al.*, Third U.S. Circuit Court of Appeals, No, 05-3857, pp. 4-5, March 19, 2007, www.ca3.uscourts.gov/opinarch/053857p.pdf.

[62] *Ibid.*, pp. 33-34.

[63] *Ibid.*, p. 36.

[64] "FTC Warns Marketers That Mobile Apps May Violate Fair Credit Reporting Act," Federal Trade Commission, press release (links to letters included), Feb. 7, 2012, www.ftc.gov/opa/2012/02/mobileapps.shtm.

[65] "Report of the National Task Force on the Commercial Sale of Criminal Justice Record Information," *op. cit.*, p. 7.

[66] *Ibid.*, p. 34.

[67] *Ibid.*, p. 86.

[68] *Ibid.*, p. 87.

[69] Meredith Curtis, "Want a Job? Password, Please!," ACLU Blog of Rights, Feb. 18, 2011, www.aclu.org/blog/technology-and-liberty/want-job-password-please.

[70] "Your Facebook Password Should Be None of Your Boss' Business," Blog of Rights, ACLU, March 20, 2012, www.aclu.org/blog/technology-and-liberty/your-facebook-password-should-be-none-your-boss-business.

[71] Doug Gross, "ACLU: Facebook password isn't your boss' business," CNN, March 22, 2012, www.cnn.com/2012/03/22/tech/social-media/facebook-password-employers/index.html; Doug Gross, "Facebook speaks out against employers asking for passwords," CNN, March 23, 2012, http://articles.cnn.com/2012-03-23/tech/tech_social-media_facebook-employers_1_passwords-facebook-friends-chief-privacy-officer?_s=PM:TEC.

Bibliography

Selected Sources

Books

Alexander, Michelle, *The New Jim Crow: Mass Incarceration in the Age of Colorblindness*, New Press, 2010.
A civil rights lawyer analyzes the racial dimensions of law-enforcement policy and sentencing law, including the effects of criminal records on employment.

Pager, Devah, *Marked: Race, Crime, and Finding Work in an Era of Mass Incarceration*, University of Chicago, 2007.
A Princeton sociologist expands on a study that showed that the stereotypical association of African-Americans with criminality affects black job-seekers without criminal records and is devastating for those with records.

Articles

Armon, Rick, "Crime Can Have a Life Sentence of Joblessness," *Akron Beacon Journal*, Nov. 7, 2011.
In Ohio, where the employment effects of criminal records have become a major political issue, a reporter chronicles the consequences of ordinary people having a record.

Gambacorta, David, "Ex-cons can no longer be boxed out of jobs," *Pittsburgh Post-Gazette*, Jan. 12, 2012, p. 10.
The first municipal "ban the box" ordinance applied to private employers takes effect.

Gregory, Kia, "Legal Volunteers Help Those Seeking a Clean Slate," *Pittsburgh Post-Gazette*, Nov. 27, 2011, p. B-4.
Philadelphians who can't afford private attorneys for criminal-record expungement proceedings rely on volunteer lawyers.

Lee, Anita, "Casino dealer loses fight for permit," *Biloxi* (Mississippi) *Sun-Herald*, April 28, 2011.
A working casino dealer loses his job after a background check turns up a 30-year-old conviction for marijuana possession with intent to distribute.

McCulloch, Debra M., "Commentary: Refresh what you need to know about background checks in the electronic age," *Michigan Lawyers Weekly*, Nov. 29, 2011.
An employment lawyer explains laws applying to background checks of criminal records and other biographical details.

Pender, Kathleen, "When pot possession is made an infraction," *San Francisco Chronicle*, Nov. 7, 2010, p. D1.
California's softening of its marijuana-possession law means a conviction for possession of less than one ounce won't go on a criminal record or have to be disclosed on job applications.

Simmons, Andria, "More companies check for arrests," *Atlanta Journal-Constitution*, Aug. 21, 2011, p. D1.
A story aimed at job-seekers offers advice on how to handle background checks and questions about criminal records.

Suarez, Paul, "In tough economy, convicts struggle for jobs," The Associated Press, Sept. 14, 2011.
Criminal records affect job applicants at a time when jobs are hard to find in Washington state.

Walberg, Matthew, and Joe Mahr, "Sex offenders paid to baby-sit," *Chicago Tribune*, p. C1.
A danger of inadequate background checking surfaces in an investigative report on child-care workers with violent-felony records.

Reports and Studies

Blumstein, Alfred, and Kiminori Nakamura, "Redemption in the Presence of Widespread Criminal Background Checks," *Criminology*, May 1, 2009, p. 330, http://onlinelibrary.wiley.com/doi/10.1111/j.1745-9125.2009.00155.x/abstract; (shorter version) Alfred Blumstein and Kiminori Nakamura, "Redemption in the Presence of Widespread Criminal Background Checks," *NIJ Journal*, National Institute of Justice, updated June 1, 2010, www.nij.gov/journals/263/redemption.htm.
This widely cited work shows that the recidivism risk of once-arrested people who don't immediately reoffend eventually declines to that of the general population.

Bushway, Shawn D., and Robert Apel, "A Signaling Perspective on Employment-Based Reentry Programming: Training Completion as a Desistance Signal," *Criminology & Public Policy*, February 2012, http://onlinelibrary.wiley.com/doi/10.1111/j.1745-9133.2012.00785.x/abstract.
Scholars examine how employers can distinguish between ex-offenders who have renounced crime and those likely to break the law again.

Holzer, Harry J., Steven Raphael and Michael A. Stoll, "Perceived Criminality, Criminal Background Checks, and the Racial Hiring Practices of Employers," *Journal of Law and Economics*, October 2006, p. 473, www.jstor.org/discover/10.1086/501089?uid=3739640&uid=2&uid=4&uid=3739256&sid=47698810486547.
A widely cited study concludes that background checks apparently benefit African-Americans without criminal records because the checks undermine the common misperception that most black males have records.

Yu, Peris S., and Sharon M. Dietrich, "Broken Records: How Errors by Criminal Background Checking Companies Harm Workers and Businesses," National Consumer Law Center, April 2010, www.nclc.org/issues/broken-records.html.
Advocates argue that regulation hasn't kept pace with expansion of the background-checking industry.

The Next Step:

Additional Articles from Current Periodicals

Expungement

Champagne, Denise M., "New York State Bar Association Recommends Criminal Record Sealing," *Daily Record of Rochester* (N.Y.), Jan. 27, 2012, nydailyrecord.com/blog/2012/01/27/nysba-recommends-criminal-record-sealing/.

The New York State Bar Association says sealing criminal records for certain low-level offenses is preferable to expungement because sealing allows reopening if a person gets into trouble again.

D'amico, Diane, "Charter Tech Founder Seeks Expungement of 37-Year-Old Pot Arrest, Return to Board of Trustees," *Press of Atlantic City* (N.J.), Jan. 6, 2012, www.pressofatlanticcity.com/communities/northfield_linwood_somers-point/charter-tech-founder-seeks-expungement-of--year-old-pot/article_a438c668-3806-11e1-9d4a-001871e3ce6c.html.

The founder of a New Jersey charter school is working to expunge his record of a 1974 marijuana arrest so he can remain on the school's board of trustees.

Evans, Elizabeth, "Woman Falsely Charged With Murder Has Record Expunged," *York* (Pa.) *Dispatch*, Oct. 21, 2011.

A Pennsylvania woman is getting her criminal record expunged 11 years after murder charges against her were dropped.

Finley, Ben, "Acquitted, But Not Completely Cleared," The Associated Press, April 23, 2011, www.phillyburbs.com/news/local/courier_times_news/acquitted-but-not-completely-cleared/article_0a2266df-fcb7-5d8d-9aeb-3893533564c0.html.

Experts say expungements have become less valuable over time because a lot of background information is available online.

Gillham, Omer, "Dismissed, Expunged Cases Can Stay on File," *Tulsa* (Okla.) *World*, Sept. 4, 2011, p. A1, www.tulsaworld.com/news/article.aspx?subjectid=11&articleid=20110904_11_A1_Indivi551487.

The expungement of criminal records in Oklahoma does not always mean a person's record is wiped clean.

Harding, Margaret, "Expunging Arrest Record Comes With a Price Tag," *Pittsburgh Tribune Review*, July 5, 2011, www.pittsburghlive.com/x/pittsburghtrib/news/s_745204.html?_s_icmp=NetworkHeadlines.

Pennsylvania courts can collect fees for clearing the arrest record of anyone who hasn't been convicted of a crime.

Kelly, Niki, "Shielding Criminal Past Fires Debate," *Fort Wayne* (Ind.) *Journal Gazette*, June 26, 2011, p. A1, www.journalgazette.net/article/20110626/NEWS07/306269938.

Indiana residents are split over a new law that allows nonviolent criminal histories to be shielded from public view.

Mgbatogu, Ike, "Online Tool Able to Assist Convicts in Expunging Criminal Records," *Call & Post* (Ohio), Oct. 26, 2011, p. A3.

The Ohio Poverty Law Center has released an online tool designed to help those with criminal records assess their chances of expungement.

Montero, David, "Bill Would Remove Minor Traffic Offenses From Criminal Records," *Salt Lake* (Utah) *Tribune*, Feb. 17, 2012, www.sltrib.com/sltrib/politics/53521155-90/bill-minor-records-criminal.html.csp.

Utah legislators are considering a bill that would allow minor traffic violations to be expunged from criminal records.

Phillips, Noelle, "Workshop Helps Clear Records," *The State* (Columbia, S.C.), Feb. 1, 2012, www.thestate.com/2012/02/01/2135813/workshop-helps-clear-records.html.

A South Carolina solicitor is working with people who qualify to have items expunged from their criminal records.

Rankin, Bill, "Bill Would Hide Arrest Information," *Atlanta Journal-Constitution*, March 25, 2012, p. B7.

A bill in the Georgia House of Representatives would help exonerated individuals to have their criminal records shielded from public view.

Rourke, Bryan, "Legal Aid Helps Homeless Clear Police Records," *Providence* (R.I.) *Journal*, Sept. 30, 2011, p. 6.

A Rhode Island nonprofit is working with the homeless to navigate the court process for expunging criminal records.

Swift, Aisling, "Law That Erases Past Rarely Used," *Naples* (Fla.) *Daily News*, Nov. 15, 2010, p. A1, m.naplesnews.com/news/2010/nov/14/florida-law-expunction-enpunge-arrest-record-clear/.

A seldom-used Florida law allows the wrongfully accused to expunge everything relating to their arrests and court cases.

Internet

Agar, John, "Beware of the Erroneous Background Check," *Grand Rapids* (Mich.) *Press*, April 11, 2011, p. A1, www.mlive.com/news/grand-rapids/index.ssf/2011/04/lawsuit_draws_attention_to_pot.html.

A Michigan man had a job offer wrongly rescinded after an employer ran an online background check and discovered a felony conviction belonging to a different man with the same name.

Bremmer, Cathleen Bell, "Employers Take Risks When Asking for Access to Social Media Sites," *Tampa Bay* (Fla.) *Business Journal*, July 1, 2011, www.bizjournals.com/tampabay/print-edition/2011/07/01/employers-take-risks-when-asking-for.html?page=all.

Employers could face lawsuits when asking applicants for access to their social media accounts because it may divulge information that is off-limits during a job interview.

Goode, Erica, "Internet Lets a Criminal Past Catch Up Quicker," ***The New York Times*****, April 29, 2011, p. A17, www.nytimes.com/2011/04/29/us/29records.html.**
The Internet has made it easy and inexpensive for employers to search the criminal histories of applicants.

Johnson, Kevin, "Cops Get Screened for Digital Dirt," ***USA Today*****, Nov. 12, 2010, p. A1, www.usatoday.com/tech/news/2010-11-12-1Afacebookcops12_ST_N.htm.**
Many law-enforcement agencies are asking job candidates to sign waivers that allow investigators access to their social media accounts.

Kilbride, Kim, "Background Checks Deep Enough?" ***South Bend*** **(Ind.)** ***Tribune*****, Jan. 22, 2012, p. A1.**
Employment screening experts say it is difficult to authenticate a prospective employee's background information if it is found on the Internet.

Kwoh, Leslie, "Phone App's Background Checks Spur Privacy Fear," ***Star-Ledger*** **(Newark, N.J.), July 29, 2011, p. 1, www.nj.com/business/index.ssf/2011/07/app_background_checks.html.**
A new mobile application allows users to perform background checks with their smartphones.

Preston, Jennifer, "Social Media History Becomes a New Job Hurdle," ***The New York Times*****, July 21, 2011, p. B1, www.nytimes.com/2011/07/21/technology/social-media-history-becomes-a-new-job-hurdle.html?pagewanted=all.**
Social Intelligence, a California-based startup, searches the Internet for everything prospective employees may have done online in the past seven years.

Ring, Dan, "Patrick Inks Criminal Records Law," ***The Republican*** **(Springfield, Mass.), Aug 7, 2010, p. 4, www.masslive.com/chicopeeholyoke/republican/index.ssf?/base/news-28/1281165634122660.xml&coll=1.**
Democratic Gov. Deval Patrick of Massachusetts has signed a law allowing employers to obtain criminal records of job applicants over the Internet.

Sixel, L. M., "Employers Ferret Out Online Lives," ***Houston Chronicle*****, April 28, 2011, p. 1, www.chron.com/business/sixel/article/Working-Employers-ferret-out-online-lives-1687748.php.**
A growing number of employers are searching the social media accounts of applicants for signs of criminal activity.

Wagner, Daniel, "Data in Background Check May Be Wrong," ***Detroit Free Press*****, April 11, 2012, p. C2, www.freep.com/article/20120411/BUSINESS07/204110343/Data-in-background-check-may-be-wrong.**
Many employers are checking faulty background data drawn from shoddy online records, says the National Consumer Law Center.

Job-Seekers

Curry, Lynne, "Don't Let Inaccurate Background Check Hinder Job Search," ***Anchorage*** **(Alaska)** ***Daily News*****, March 26, 2012, www.adn.com/2012/03/25/2390736/dont-let-inaccurate-background.html.**
The Fair Credit Reporting Act allows job applicants to ask for details when employers turn them down due to problematic background checks.

Guillen, Joe, "Dance Instructor's Criminal Past Raises Issue of Background Checks," ***Plain Dealer*** **(Cleveland), July 26, 2011, p. B1, www.cleveland.com/open/index.ssf/2011/07/state_law_requires_background.html.**
Ohio requires criminal background checks for many state and private-sector jobs and professional licenses, but checks are not required for most private-sector positions.

Luna, Taryn, "Law Students Help Job-Seekers Trying to Clear Records," ***Pittsburgh Post-Gazette*****, Feb. 19, 2012, old.post-gazette.com/pg/12050/1211277-298.stm.**
Duquesne University Law School students in Pittsburgh are helping job-seekers with criminal pasts navigate a pardon process that would clear their records prior to their applying for jobs.

Vanaski, Nafari, "Ban on Box Could Open Pandora's Box of Woe," ***Pittsburgh Tribune Review*****, April 28, 2011, www.pittsburghlive.com/x/pittsburghtrib/s_734313.html.**
A columnist questions whether Pittsburgh could be at legal risk if it adopts a "ban the box" policy barring it from asking job applicants, using a checkoff box on employment applications, whether they have a criminal record.

Citing *CQ Researcher*

Sample formats for citing these reports in a bibliography include the ones listed below. Preferred styles and formats vary, so please check with your instructor or professor.

MLA Style

Jost, Kenneth. "Remembering 9/11," CQ Researcher 2 Sept. 2011: 701-732.

APA Style

Jost, K. (2011, September 2). Remembering 9/11. *CQ Researcher, 9*, 701-732.

Chicago Style

Jost, Kenneth. "Remembering 9/11." *CQ Researcher*, September 2, 2011, 701-732.

In-depth Reports on Issues in the News

Are you writing a paper?

Need backup for a debate?

Want to become an expert on an issue?

For more than 80 years, students have turned to *CQ Researcher* for in-depth reporting on issues in the news. Reports on a full range of political and social issues are now available. Following is a selection of recent reports:

Civil Liberties
Remembering 9/11, 9/11
Government Secrecy, 2/11
Cybersecurity, 2/10
Press Freedom, 2/10

Crime/Law
Police Misconduct, 4/12
Immigration Conflict, 3/12
Financial Misconduct, 1/12
Eyewitness Testimony, 10/11
Legal-Aid Crisis, 10/11
Death Penalty Debates, 11/10

Education
Arts Education, 3/12
Youth Volunteerism, 1/12
Digital Education, 12/11
College Football, 11/11
Student Debt, 10/11
Crime on Campus, 2/11

Environment/Society
Internet Regulation, 4/12
Space Program, 2/12
Invasive Species, 2/12
Fracking Controversy, 12/11

Health/Safety
Patient Safety, 2/12
Military Suicides, 9/11
Teen Drug Use, 6/11
Organ Donations, 4/11
Genes and Health, 1/11
Food Safety, 12/10
Preventing Bullying, 12/10

Politics/Economy
U.S.-Europe Relations, 3/12
Attracting Jobs, 3/12
Presidential Election, 2/12

Upcoming Reports

Sexual Harassment, 4/27/12
Distracted Driving, 5/4/12
Celebrity Advocacy, 5/11/12

ACCESS

CQ Researcher is available in print and online. For access, visit your library or www.cqresearcher.com.

STAY CURRENT

For notice of upcoming *CQ Researcher* reports or to learn more about *CQ Researcher* products, subscribe to the free e-mail newsletters, *CQ Researcher Alert!* and *CQ Researcher News*: http://cqpress.com/newsletters.

PURCHASE

To purchase a *CQ Researcher* report in print or electronic format (PDF), visit www.cqpress.com or call 866-427-7737. Single reports start at $15. Bulk purchase discounts and electronic-rights licensing are also available.

SUBSCRIBE

Annual full-service *CQ Researcher* subscriptions—including 44 reports a year, monthly index updates, and a bound volume—start at $1,054. Add $25 for domestic postage.

CQ Researcher Online offers a backfile from 1991 and a number of tools to simplify research. For pricing information, call 800-834-9020, or e-mail librarymarketing@cqpress.com.

CQ RESEARCHER ***PLUS*** *ARCHIVE*

GET ONLINE ACCESS TO VITAL ISSUES FROM 1923 TO THE PRESENT

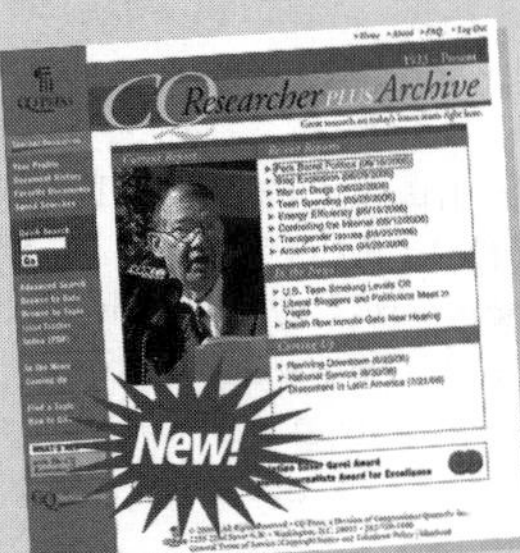

CQ Researcher Plus Archive delivers fast, online access to every *CQ Researcher* report from 1991 to the present, *PLUS* lets you explore the complete archive of *Editorial Research Reports** from 1923-1990. Search and browse more than 3,600 in-depth reports.

Loaded with handy online features, *CQ Researcher Plus Archive* provides the trustworthy reporting and the advanced online functionality today's researchers demand. The new "Issue Tracker" feature provides quick links to past and present reports on the specific topics you need.

For a free trial, visit http://library.cqpress.com/trials.

For pricing information, call 1-800-834-9020, ext. 1906 or e-mail librarymarketing@cqpress.com.

**Editorial Research Reports*, the predecessor to *CQ Researcher*, provides the same expert, nonpartisan reporting on the vital issues that have shaped our society.

CQ Press • 2300 N Street, NW, Suite 800 • Washington, DC 20037

CQ Researcher

Published by CQ Press, an Imprint of SAGE Publications, Inc.

www.cqresearcher.com

Sexual Harassment

Do training programs reduce offenses?

Workplace sexual harassment dominated the news last fall when four women accused presidential hopeful Herman Cain of sexual misconduct in the late 1990s — accusations Cain vigorously denied. Employment lawyers say the widespread adoption of anti-harassment policies and training programs over the past decade has led to a decline in workplace sexual harassment charges filed with federal, state and local government agencies. But plaintiffs' attorneys say sexual harassment remains a persistent and under-reported problem that boiler-plate corporate policies and training programs often fail to address. And worker-rights advocates say the numbers of charges may be declining for other reasons, including a move by employers to require potential employees to agree to binding arbitration of workplace disputes. Companies say arbitration benefits everyone by speeding up the dispute process, but workers' advocates strongly disagree.

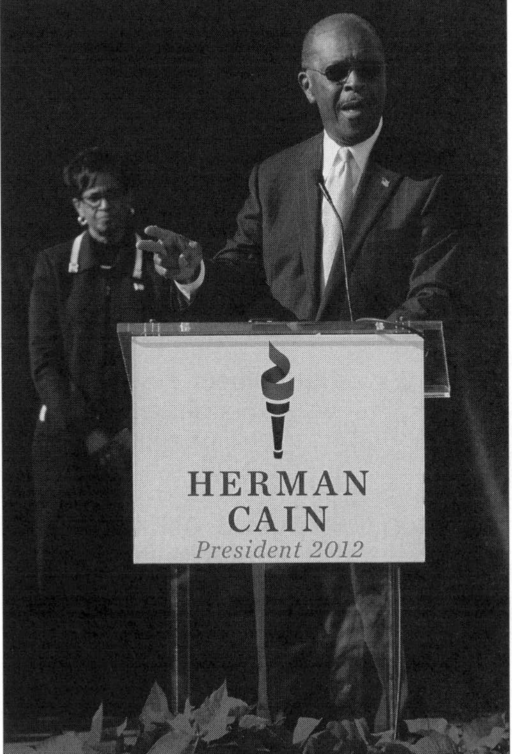

Facing charges of infidelity and sexual harassment, Herman Cain — his wife behind him — announces in Atlanta on Dec. 3, 2011, that he is suspending his campaign for the Republican presidential nomination.

INSIDE THIS REPORT

The Issues 379
Background 386
Chronology 387
Current Situation 392
At Issue 393
Outlook 395
Bibliography 398
The Next Step 399

CQ Researcher • April 27, 2012 • www.cqresearcher.com
Volume 22, Number 16 • Pages 377-400

Los Angeles | London | New Delhi
Singapore | Washington DC

Recipient of Society of Professional Journalists Award for Excellence ◆ American Bar Association Silver Gavel Award

Sexual Harassment

The Issues

379 • Do workplace anti-discrimination policies and training programs reduce harassment?
• Should employers be allowed to mandate arbitration for resolving sexual harassment complaints?
• Do university sexual harassment policies erode civil liberties on campus?

Background

386 **Naming the Behavior** The term sexual harassment was coined in 1975.

389 **Harassment Lawsuits** Women began challenging sexual harassment in court in the 1970s.

389 **Expanded Definition** A legal scholar in 1979 suggested expanding the meaning of sexual harassment.

390 **Evolving Case Law** Several federal and Supreme Court decisions involved sexual harassment.

Current Situation

392 **Defining 'Supervisor'** The Supreme Court is being asked to define the term.

394 **Same-Sex Harassment** Complaints are on the rise.

394 **Retaliation** More people are claiming retaliation for reporting employment discrimination.

Outlook

395 **Surveying the Climate** Companies are encouraged to survey employees about workplace problems.

Sidebars and Graphics

380 **Complaints Decline** Sexual harassment charges fell 28 percent since 1997.

381 **Defining Sexual Harassment** It involves unwanted sexual advances in the workplace.

383 **How to Handle Sexual Harassment** Victims should document the incident.

387 **Chronology** Key events since 1964.

388 **Workplace Romances Challenge Employers** Some dating employees are asked to sign "love contracts."

391 **Military's Harassment Policies Seen as Weak** Fewer than 5 percent of alleged victims file complaints.

393 **At Issue** Do university sexual harassment policies threaten students' due-process rights?

For Further Research

397 **For More Information** Organizations to contact.

398 **Bibliography** Selected sources used.

399 **The Next Step** Additional articles.

399 **Citing *CQ Researcher*** Sample bibliography formats.

Cover: Getty Images/Scott Olson

CQ Researcher

April 27, 2012
Volume 22, Number 16

Managing Editor: Thomas J. Billitteri tjb@cqpress.com

Assistant Managing Editor: Kathy Koch kkoch@cqpress.com

Contributing Editor: Thomas J. Colin tcolin@cqpress.com

Associate Editor: Kenneth Jost

Staff Writer: Marcia Clemmitt

Contributing Writers: Sarah Glazer, Alan Greenblatt, Peter Katel, Barbara Mantel, Jennifer Weeks

Design/Production Editor: Olu B. Davis

Assistant Editor: Darrell Dela Rosa

Fact Checker: Michelle Harris

Los Angeles | London | New Delhi
Singapore | Washington DC

An Imprint of SAGE Publications, Inc.

Vice President and Editorial Director, Higher Education Group: Michele Sordi

Director, Online Publishing: Todd Baldwin

CQ Researcher (ISSN 1056-2036) is printed on acid-free paper. Published weekly, except: (March wk. 5) (May wk. 4) (July wk. 1) (Aug. wks. 3, 4) (Nov. wk. 4) and (Dec. wks. 3, 4). Published by SAGE Publications, Inc., 2455 Teller Rd., Thousand Oaks, CA 91320. Annual full-service subscriptions start at $1,054. For pricing, call 1-800-834-9020. To purchase a *CQ Researcher* report in print or electronic format (PDF), visit www.cqpress.com or call 866-427-7737. Single reports start at $15. Bulk purchase discounts and electronic-rights licensing are also available. Periodicals postage paid at Thousand Oaks, California, and at additional mailing offices. POSTMASTER: Send address changes to *CQ Researcher*, 2300 N St., N.W., Suite 800, Washington, DC 20037.

Sexual Harassment

BY BARBARA MANTEL

THE ISSUES

With his wife Gloria by his side, an unapologetic Herman Cain told supporters in Atlanta last December that he was suspending his presidential campaign in the face of an accusation of infidelity and escalating allegations of sexual harassment. Insisting that the charges were all untrue, he said, "I'm at peace with my God. I'm at peace with my wife, and she is at peace with me." [1]

The charges against Cain first surfaced in October, rocking his campaign and propelling sexual harassment back onto the nation's front pages. Cain called the press coverage "a high-tech lynching," echoing the words used by Supreme Court justice Clarence Thomas a little more than 20 years earlier to describe his Senate confirmation hearings, when law professor and former Thomas employee Anita Hill accused him of sexual harassment in televised Senate hearings that riveted the nation for days. [2]

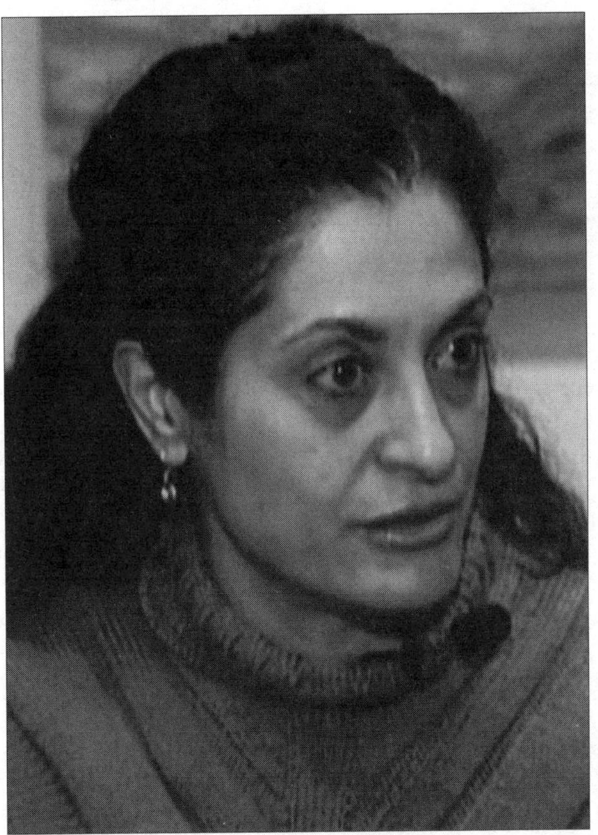

ABC News

Ani Chopourian, a surgical assistant in Sacramento, Calif., is believed to have won the largest individual workplace harassment judgment in U.S. history. A jury earlier this year awarded her $168 million — $125 million in punitive damages and $42.7 million for lost wages and mental anguish. Her employer, Mercy General Hospital, is appealing. Chopourian said she had filed 18 complaints with the hospital over two years, alleging sexual harassment, bullying and intimidation by cardiac surgeons.

Chicago resident Sharon Bialek was the first woman to speak publicly, saying Cain had sexually harassed her 14 years ago when he headed the National Restaurant Association. Eventually three more women, two anonymously, made similar accusations, including Karen Kraushaur, a U.S. Treasury Department spokeswoman, who said she had left her job at the association because of Cain's alleged misconduct.

"When you are being sexually harassed in the workplace, you are extremely vulnerable," she said. [3] Cain had denied the charges at the time, and the association settled with Kraushaur and one other woman for the equivalent of a year's salary.

Now a decade and a half later, much about sexual harassment in the workplace has changed. Allegations of sexual harassment are less often about an obvious "quid pro quo" — in which a supervisor's unwanted sexual advances affect a subordinate's employment — and more often about creating an intimidating work environment. (*See box, p. 381, for legal definition.*)

Most large companies and many smaller ones now have explicit sexual harassment policies, grievance procedures and anti-harassment training programs. And the number of formal charges of workplace sexual harassment filed with government agencies has been declining for the past four years. State and local governments and the U.S. Equal Employment Opportunity Commission (EEOC) — which investigates employment discrimination under Title VII of the Civil Rights Act — received a total of 11,364 complaints of sexual harassment last year, nearly 30 percent fewer than the peak of 15,889 reached in 1997. [4]

Sexual harassment charges in industries once notorious for such behavior — such as banking and finance — have declined significantly over the past decade. According to an analysis by FINS, an online career site affiliated with *The Wall Street Journal*, harassment charges by employees in the finance, insurance and real estate industries dropped from 641 in 2001 to 266 in 2010. [5] Some say that's because more women are entering those fields.

Michelle Caiola of Legal Momentum, a New York-based organization that provides legal support for women, says the worst behavior today tends to be in industries such as construction or firefighting, where women are still a minority, or where workers are young, such as the restaurant industry. [6]

But fewer charges filed doesn't necessarily mean fewer incidences of sexual harassment on the job, nor does it mean there are no high-profile sexual harassment cases. In February a Sacramento surgical assistant was awarded $168 million in a case against the hospital where she worked and complained of sexual harassment, bullying and

Sexual Harassment Complaints Decline

Employees filed more than 11,000 sexual harassment charges with federal, state and local anti-discrimination agencies in 2011 — down about 28 percent since 1997. But the percentage of complaints filed by males increased — from 11.6 percent in 1997 to 16 percent, in 2011. Agencies don't track the gender of the accused, but some officials say charges by males mostly involve same-sex incidents. It is unknown whether sexual harassment of men is rising or whether men are just more likely to report it than in the past.

Sexual Harassment Charges Filed with Federal, State and Local Agencies, 1997-2011
(and percentage filed by men)

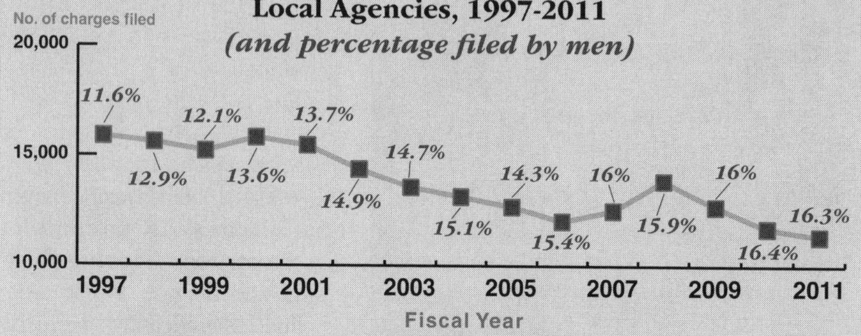

Source: "Sexual Harassment Charges: EEOC & FEPAs Combined: FY 1997-FY 2011," U.S. Equal Employment Opportunity Commission, 2012, www.eeoc.gov/eeoc/statistics/enforcement/sexual_harassment.cfm

intimidation by cardiac surgeons. And in 2011, a St. Louis woman was awarded $95 million, the largest sexual harassment award in history, but after the company appealed, the parties settled for $6 million. (*See box, p. 389.*)

There is wide disagreement about the causes for the decline in charges filed. Some observers emphasize improvement in workplace environments, and some stress other factors, such as employees' sense that reporting discrimination may be futile, fears of retaliation for reporting discrimination, job insecurity in a weak economy and pressure from companies to keep complaints in-house.

An ABC News/*Washington Post* poll last November supports the notion that there has been real, though perhaps modest, improvement in the workplace for women. While one in four women said they had experienced sexual harassment at work, that is down from 32 percent in 1994. Additionally, among those who have been sexually harassed, 41 percent now say they reported it to their employer — up from 33 percent in 1994. [7]

"Employers have gotten more harsh about how they deal with it," said Laura Schnell, a New York attorney who has represented employees in sexual harassment cases since 1985. "If they can verify that something happened, they do fire people." [8]

Moreover, said Steven Foster, president and CEO of Business Controls, a Denver-based consultant to employers, many harassers now use company email and corporate cell phones, making it "a hell of a lot easier for organizations to investigate" allegations. Foster said he is astonished at what people will say in electronic communications. [9]

Others say that the decline in charges filed with government agencies may be the result of a growing number of companies requiring potential employees to agree to mandatory, binding arbitration of workplace disputes. While companies say arbitration benefits everyone by speeding up the process, advocates for workers' rights strongly disagree.

"You are being forced to sign away your rights to go to court should your employer violate the law down the road," says Sarah Crawford, director of workplace fairness at the Washington, D.C.-based National Partnership for Women and Families.

Some lawyers who represent plaintiffs say the decline in sexual harassment charges could also be linked to fear of retaliation in a weak job market. "There's absolutely no doubt that claims are going down because people are more reluctant to bring claims against companies in this economy," said Janice Goodman, a New York attorney specializing in anti-discrimination law. [10]

But while a sluggish economy may increase fears of retaliation, it also may reduce the underlying misconduct, according to the Ethics Resource Center, a nonprofit research organization in Arlington, Va., which tracks workplace ethics. "Many employees feel even less secure now than they did two years ago," the center states in its latest ethics survey. And so they are "more careful to avoid misconduct." In fact, 30 percent of employees agree that "bad actors" in their company are laying low because of fears about the weak economy.

Meanwhile, about a third of employees say management watches them more closely than two years ago, and 42 percent say their company has increased its efforts to raise awareness about ethics. [11]

Some critics say corporations have gone overboard, creating policies that forbid a broader set of behaviors well beyond the legal definition of sexual harassment. "In our effort to create a wholly unhostile work environment, have we simply created an environment that is hostile in a different way?"

Katie Roiphe, a professor of journalism at New York University, wrote in an opinion piece during the Cain controversy last November. "Maybe it's better to live with colorful or inappropriate comments, with irreverence, wildness, incorrectness, ease." [12]

There are similar complaints about speech restrictions at universities and fears that academic debate is being compromised in the name of eradicating sexual harassment on campus.

But no matter the true extent of sexual harassment in society, its consequences are undisputed. Studies clearly show that women and men who experience frequent sexual harassment have significantly higher levels of depression, and that the impact can be long-term. [13] Employers suffer costs as well, ranging from decreased employee productivity and higher staff turnover to poor staff moral, damaged company reputation and possible legal costs.

As Americans try to understand the changing climate around sexual harassment, here are some of the questions being asked:

Defining Sexual Harassment

Under federal law, sexual harassment is any unwelcome sexual advance, request for sexual favors or other verbal or physical conduct of a sexual nature that explicitly or implicitly affects an individual's employment, unreasonably interferes with his or her work performance or creates an intimidating, hostile or offensive work environment.

Sexual harassment is a form of sex discrimination that violates Title VII of the Civil Rights Act of 1964, which applies to employers with 15 or more employees, including federal, state and local governments. The anti-discrimination statute does not prohibit simple teasing, offhand comments or isolated incidents that are not "extremely serious."

Sexual harassment can occur in a variety of circumstances, including but not limited to the following situations:

- The victim and the harasser may be a woman or a man. The victim does not have to be of the opposite sex.
- The harasser can be the victim's supervisor, an agent of the employer, a supervisor in another area, a co-worker or a non-employee.
- The victim does not have to be the target of the harassment but could be anyone affected by the offensive conduct.
- Unlawful sexual harassment may occur without economic injury to or the firing of the victim.
- The harasser's conduct must be unwelcome.

Sources: www.eeoc.gov/eeoc/publications/fs-sex.cfm and www.eeoc.gov/policy/docs/harassment.pdf; standards of evidence are from www.LegalMatch.com; http://dictionary.lp.findlaw.com

Do workplace anti-discrimination policies and training programs reduce harassment?

A typical day for women employees at the manufacturing and distribution center of music publisher Hal Leonard Publishing Co., in Winona, Minn., involved more than just routine office work. An EEOC investigation determined the women were subjected to unwelcome grabbing of breasts, exposure of genitalia by male co-workers and sexual comments, while management ignored multiple complaints. In March, the company settled a sexual harassment charge, agreeing to pay a total of $150,000 to 10 women, conduct annual anti-discrimination training and provide the EEOC with documentation of all sexual harassment complaints for three years. [14]

Many companies already have such training in place. According to the Alexandria, Va.-based Society for Human Resource Management, 59 percent of businesses provide sexual harassment training for their employees at least every other year. [15] In fact, an entire industry of anti-discrimination trainers has evolved, ranging from lawyers to nonprofits to multinational corporations. Nearly all large employers also have explicit sexual harassment policies and formal grievance procedures. [16] Twenty-five years ago, that was rare.

"Both policies and training programs are critical tools to stop and prevent sexual harassment," says Linda Meric, executive director of 9 to 5, a national organization for working women based in Milwaukee, Wis. "Good policies and training programs make sure that everyone in the workplace understands what sexual harassment is and isn't, their rights and responsibilities, the consequences for violating the policy and how to go about making a complaint."

But evidence that they reduce the incidence of sexual harassment is scant. "As far as I am aware, there have not been any systematic studies," says Ariane Hegewisch, a study director at the Institute for Women's Policy Research in Washington, D.C. "And that means we don't know either way."

Some believe they barely make a dent. "You would think that if policies and training were terribly effective . . . you would have seen dramatic change," says Joanna Grossman, a professor at Hofstra Law School in Hempstead,

N.Y., specializing in sex discrimination. "But there is not any good reason to believe, based on available survey data, that sexual harassment is gone."

Trying to figure out the answer by examining the number of complaints is difficult, because the EEOC doesn't release individual company data. "We could not make public any 'before and after' examinations of the effect of training because to do so we would have to publish the number of discrimination charges filed against a specific employer, which is impermissible," says Justine Lisser, a senior attorney-adviser in the EEOC's office of communications.

Most human resource (HR) departments don't keep track either, for fear it could be used as evidence in a lawsuit, says Ingrid Fredeen, director of content development at ELT, a leading provider of online training products headquartered in San Francisco. "If you have an HR person aggregating harassment complaints, litigation and [EEOC] charges and creating all these wonderful and beautiful charts, that can be discovered in litigation unless it is a done by a lawyer," says Fredeen. But, even with attorney-client privilege, company lawyers are reluctant, she says. "Working with numbers and statistics and percentages isn't something that a lot of lawyers enjoy doing."

In the 1990s, the Supreme Court ruled that employers were automatically liable for quid pro quo sexual harassment, such as when a supervisor asks a subordinate for sexual favors and demotes her if she doesn't comply. If there is no quid pro quo but the supervisor's harassment creates a hostile work environment, the employer can offer an affirmative defense* by showing that it tried to prevent and promptly correct the supervisor's behavior and that the employee unreasonably failed to take advantage of preventive and corrective opportunities. When it comes to harassment between co-workers, employers are only liable if the accuser can prove the employer either knew or had reason to know about it and didn't take appropriate action.

As a result, Grossman says, companies have mixed incentives. An employer whose sole motivation is minimizing liability, she says, would want a policy "that looks good on paper but does not, in fact, invite complaints." She says she hopes "there aren't that many employers where that is the case."

But even more of a problem, Grossman says, is incompetence. "Studies of investigations — and the investigations I've seen as an expert witness [for plaintiffs] — show that the way many employers conduct investigations into harassment complaints is haphazard," says Grossman.

"I have to disagree with that strongly," says Judy Lampley, vice president for operations at the Washington, D.C.-based Equal Employment Advisory Council, a nonprofit association of large employers. "Our companies' investigative processes are very robust. Companies don't want harassment in the workplace. They know they are not going to get highly skilled employees where harassment is going on."

The group 9 to 5 has a model corporate policy to stop and prevent sexual harassment, and Meric says many companies could stand to improve. Some written policies, she says, just repeat the legal definition of sexual harassment, which can be difficult for most employees to interpret. Or the policies are written only in English or not readily available. And some grievance procedures have only one avenue for complaints.

"It is common to say that the complaint needs to be reported to your supervisor, and that doesn't take into account that the supervisor may be the harasser or that the harasser could be someone close to the supervisor," says Meric.

Fredeen says it's important for training programs to use examples to explain the law. Her firm, ELT, films news anchors reporting on fictional stories of harassment produced with actors and inspired by case law and experience.

But Grossman says even perfect policies, exemplary complaint procedures and gripping training programs — while of important symbolic value — have limited impact on reducing sexual harassment at work. They may help in a small way, where individual perceptions are skewed, she says, such as when a man believes his behavior is flirtatious but women see it as harassing.

But such programs won't change someone whose behavior is pathological, says Grossman. And they won't reduce harassment that results from structural problems, such as strict hierarchies, the lack of workplace diversity or limited opportunities for female advancement. "I would hope that bigger companies would have auditors come in and look at the workplace and its gender dynamics," says Grossman.

Grossman would like to see Congress pass legislation that would abolish the affirmative defense so companies focus less on policies and training and more on figuring out how to fix these structural problems. "But I don't think this is a hot button issue for Congress," she says.

That's just fine with Fredeen. "You want to encourage an employer to prevent sexual harassment and to respond when complaints come up, and I think the system works that way right now," she says. However, she would like to see states follow the lead of California, Connecticut and Maine, which require employers larger than a certain size to provide sexual harassment training.

Should employers be allowed to mandate arbitration for resolving sexual harassment complaints?

Over the past 12 years a growing number of companies have begun requiring employees to submit all job-

* An affirmative defense is a defense in which the defendant introduces evidence, which, if found to be credible, will negate civil liability, even if it is proven that the defendant committed the alleged acts.

related disputes, including discrimination complaints, to a private arbitrator rather than seek legal redress through the courts. The Supreme Court paved the way for this surge in mandatory binding arbitration agreements in a landmark ruling in March 2001. In *Circuit City Stores, Inc. v. Saint Clair Adams*, the court said the 1925 Federal Arbitration Act applies not only to commercial contracts but to employment contracts as well. [17]

"It's very troubling to see employers single-handedly having the authority to prevent workers from going to court," says Crawford of the National Partnership for Women and Families.

But proponents of mandatory arbitration say it has benefits for both employers and employees. "First would be the lower costs associated with arbitration versus litigation as well as the relative speed in resolving cases in arbitration as opposed to protracted litigation," says Rae Vann, general counsel for the business group Equal Employment Advisory Council.

Another advantage, say proponents, is the expertise of arbitrators. "You don't have generalists, you have specialists," says Richard Naimark, a senior vice president at the nonprofit American Arbitration Association (AAA), a leading provider of arbitration services in the United States. Arbitrators know the statutes, the technicalities and the latest case law — a level of expertise that juries don't have, he says, and "most judges have to be generalists."

But San Francisco corporate attorney Steve Blackburn says speed and lower costs have "pretty minimal value." Moreover, he says, what employers initially perceived to be the many advantages of arbitration have "evaporated" in California and in many other states. Blackburn says after the Supreme Court's 2001 decision, many companies began overreaching in imposing arbitration. They began limiting the availability of punitive damages allowed under law, requiring employees to cover part of the costs of arbitration and restricting the recovery of attorney fees if the employee prevailed.

"Virtually all of those efforts . . . have been struck down by the courts," says Blackburn. So while half of the large corporations he represents have a mandatory arbitration clause, "if you came to me as an employer today and asked if mandatory arbitration is a good idea, I would probably tell you no, not really," says Blackburn.

Yet, according to Naimark, companies continue to adopt mandatory arbitration policies, often after having the arbitration association review their policies to ensure they conform to the association's due-process protocols.

While companies in most states can no longer limit damages or shift arbitration costs — in fact, the AAA requires employers to cover an employee's arbitration fees — critics say

How to Handle Sexual Harassment

When confronted with unwanted sexual advances in the workplace, an employee should follow some basic steps, according to the American Association of University Women. Here are some guidelines to help remedy the situation and deter future misconduct:

Tell harassers:

- That their attention is unwanted.
- What they have done. Name the behavior and be specific.
- That he or she should stop the offending behavior.

Keep records, with dates and times, of:

- Each incident of harassment, and list all witnesses.
- Any negative actions you experience as a result of your refusal to submit to sexually harassing behavior.
- Any meetings you have with your employer regarding the harassment.
- Any retaliation you may experience after complaining about the harassment.

File a complaint through:

- Formal channels in the workplace. Check the employee handbook and speak with the human resources department to review the policies.
- Your supervisors as soon as possible. Tell them in writing, and keep a copy with you.

Contact:

- The human resources department to determine the next course of action.
- An attorney to determine your rights and your employer's obligations.

Source: "Sexual Harassment: Strategies," American Association of University Women, www.aauw.org/act/laf/library/workplaceharassmentstrategies.cfm

Victims Received $52 Million in 2011

Victims of sexual harassment collected more than $52 million in fiscal 2011 in payouts in non-litigated settlements of cases filed with federal, state and local agencies that monitor compliance with civil rights and fair-labor laws.

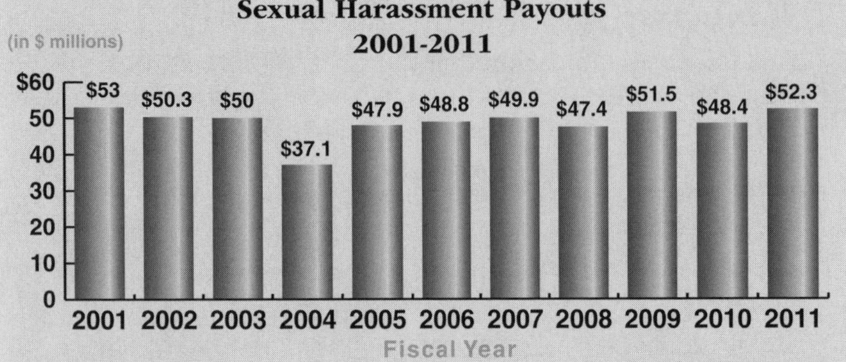

Source: "Sexual Harassment Charges: EEOC & FEPAs Combined: FY 1997-FY 2011," U.S. Equal Employment Opportunity Commission, 2012, www.eeoc.gov/eeoc/statistics/enforcement/sexual_harassment.cfm

employers still have unfair advantages, which they say account for arbitration's continued popularity among employers. "There aren't the same kinds of subpoena and discovery powers available in an arbitration process as there are in court," says Meric from 9 to 5, "and that negatively impacts an employee's ability to prove their case."

Typically, the employer holds the relevant records on the accused harasser, such as past disciplinary information and reports from managers and witnesses, and the arbitrator determines the plaintiff's level of access to those documents.

But Vann says the whole point of arbitration is to resolve a dispute more expeditiously than in court. "Limiting both sides to five depositions as opposed to 20 depositions . . . is consistent with the whole notion of more expeditious resolution," she says.

Yet, a recent empirical study of the outcomes of more than 1,200 AAA-administered arbitration cases found that the employee "win rate" and the size of damage awards in arbitration were substantially lower than after court trials. That effect was magnified when the same arbitrator was involved in more than one case with the same employer, "a finding supporting some of the fairness criticisms directed at mandatory employment arbitration," the study found. [18]

That finding is curious given AAA policy, which does not allow employers to unilaterally select the arbitrator. AAA provides a list of arbitrators and their résumés to both parties and selects one that is most mutually agreeable. "The key thing is that the arbitrators must disclose — we push them hard on this — any previous contact with either party or anything that . . . might cause somebody to be concerned about their impartiality," says Naimark.

Nevertheless, the study's author said employers could be more expert than employees at selecting friendly arbitrators or there could be hidden arbitrator bias. [19]

In court, on the other hand, "the makeup of the jury would be subject to all the protections that are available by law," says Raymond Peeler, an attorney-adviser in the EEOC's Office of Legal Counsel.

The EEOC has another objection to mandatory binding arbitration. "One purpose of Title VII is to provide a deterrent effect, both to the employer and to put other employers on notice when there is a violation," says Peeler. But since arbitration decisions are confidential, "that deterrent effect is gone," he says.

"Respectfully, that is ridiculous," says Vann. "Having to defend itself in any type of forum is a disincentive to engaging in practices and policies that may be considered discriminatory or unlawful." In addition, word gets around, at least within the workplace, she says. "Employees talk to one another, people find out about problems."

Dozens of consumer and employee-rights groups support the proposed Arbitration Fairness Act, which would ban pre-dispute, mandatory binding arbitration in employment and consumer contracts. The act would not eliminate arbitration agreed to voluntarily after a dispute arises. Versions of the act have been pending in both the U.S. House and the Senate for a year.

The bills' supporters are particularly concerned about a Supreme Court decision last year that held that California — despite its own contract law to the contrary — must enforce arbitration agreements that require consumers to settle disputes individually and not as a class. [20] The ruling, *AT&T v. Concepcion*, would apply to employment arbitration agreements as well. It's unknown how many workplace arbitration clauses ban class action, but workers' rights advocates say class action can be more effective than individual claims when there is a pattern of discrimination.

The matter could eventually end up back at the Supreme Court. That's because the National Labor Relations Board (NLRB), a government agency that enforces labor law, ruled in early January that residential developer D.R. Horton could not prohibit workers from going through arbitration as a class. Horton has appealed the decision to the Fifth U.S. Circuit Court of Appeals.

Do university sexual harassment policies erode civil liberties on campus?

During the past year, some of the nation's top universities have lowered the standard of proof they use to investigate complaints of sexual harassment, including sexual violence, bringing them in line with procedures used in the vast majority of universities in the United States. But critics say the changes erode students' due-process and free-speech rights.

The schools' actions are a direct response to a letter that the U.S. Department of Education's Office for Civil Rights (OCR) sent a year ago to universities and colleges across the country.[21] The OCR enforces Title IX of the Education Amendments of 1972, which prohibits sex discrimination, including sexual harassment, at schools receiving federal funds. Among other things, the letter said that in dealing with sexual harassment investigations, schools must use the preponderance-of-evidence-standard (meaning, it is "more likely than not" that the accused is guilty). Using the more rigorous clear-and-convincing standard (meaning that it is "highly probable or reasonably certain" that the accused is guilty) violates Title IX, the OCR said.

Title IX does not specify a standard of proof, but the OCR had been communicating to schools individually for decades that they should be using the preponderance-of-evidence standard. This was the first time that the office had said as much to all schools at once.

Applying the preponderance-of-evidence standard "absolutely makes sense because you are talking about grievance procedures and a process to ensure that a hostile environment, if created, is alleviated quickly and that the victim is afforded all of their rights so that they can continue to learn," says Russlynn Ali, the Education Department's assistant secretary for civil rights.

AFP/Getty Images/Tim Sloan

The U.S. Supreme Court, shown here in October 2010, has issued several key decisions on sexual harassment in the past quarter-century. In 1986, in its first ruling on the issue, the court in Meritor Savings Bank v. Vinson *ruled that sexual harassment is illegal if it is "sufficiently severe or pervasive to alter the conditions of the victim's employment and create an abusive working environment." In 1993, feminists won another victory when the Court ruled in its second sexual harassment case,* Harris v. Forklift Systems, Inc., *that plaintiffs need not show psychological harm to establish that sexual harassment caused a hostile work environment.*

Allison Kiss, executive director of the nonprofit Security on Campus, headquartered in Wayne, Pa., agrees with enforcing the use of the lower standard. "We know that sexual harassment is so underreported," she says, "and lowering the standard would encourage people to report. Pretty much the top reasons we hear from students for not coming forward to complain about stalking and verbal sexual harassment is that they think it will not be taken seriously and that it is difficult to prove."

But Ann Green, chair of the Committee on Women in the Academic Profession at the Washington, D.C.-based American Association of University Professors, which objects to the lower standard of proof, says there are other reasons that prevent students from registering harassment complaints, especially if the harassment is coming from a professor. "In my experience, they are concerned about their grade, they don't want to 'cause a problem' and often they are not sure what sexual harassment is," says Green.

William Creeley, director of legal and public advocacy at the Philadelphia-based Foundation for Individual Rights in Education (FIRE), says reducing the burden of proof for sexual violence "will inevitably undermine the integrity, accuracy and reliability of the proceedings" and lowering the evidentiary standard for nonviolent sexual harassment "is equally problematic [because of] the widespread and stubborn persistence of overly broad and vague harassment codes at many of our nation's universities." It will result in "more students wrongly found guilty of sexual harassment for expression that is protected by the First Amendment," says Creeley.

The OCR, however, points out that the preponderance-of-evidence standard is the standard of proof used in civil proceedings for alleged Title VII sexual harassment violations.

But Creeley calls this a "deeply flawed argument." Civil courts have checks and balances to ensure fairness and impartiality, he says, such as rules governing jury selection, discovery, witnesses, admissible evidence and jury instructions. "It is simply wrong, then, to pretend that importing the low standard of evidence from this context into the university setting — where none of these safeguards are in place and hearings are conducted by students and university administrators, often without training or education — is appropriate," says Creeley.

The stakes are high for a false conviction: expulsion, suspension or a disciplinary record that says one is guilty of sexual misconduct, says Creeley.

Green makes a similar argument for allegations involving professors. "A false charge can ruin a career," she says. "Generally, if your tenure is revoked for any reason, no one else will hire you. And part-time and non-tenure-track faculty have fewer protections [from dismissal] than tenured faculty, and so a higher standard of evidence protects them as well."

But W. Scott Lewis, a partner at the National Center for Higher Education Risk Management, a law and consulting firm based in Malvern, Pa., says, "Their biggest argument is that getting kicked out of school is forever stigmatizing in life, that it is going to ruin your life, and it's just not true. There are open-enrollment schools, and there are plenty of schools that would take a good student." As for faculty members, he says, "they are employees, just like every other employee in the U.S. They should not get additional protections in this case."

According to FIRE, 39 of the top 100 American colleges have changed or will be required to lower their standard of evidence. [22] Since the OCR letter came out, several schools have done so, including Duke University, Stanford University and the University of Virginia. [23] After concerns about due process were raised during a public comment period, UVA also required that its Sexual Misconduct Board reach a unanimous verdict rather than a majority vote.

These recent changes in the standard of proof for sexual harassment have led to a discrepancy on some campuses. The evidentiary standard for all other disciplinary proceedings at UVA and Stanford remains proof beyond a reasonable doubt, the highest standard; at Duke it remains clear and convincing. So, for example, a student accused of a drug offense would be held to a higher burden of proof than a student accused of sexual assault.

"It is a terrible idea to have a different standard for different disciplinary offenses. It doesn't happen in the workplace," says Lewis, who would like to see the preponderance-of-evidence standard used in every disciplinary case on campus.

Other schools are still reviewing their policies. "We prefer not to comment publicly until the process is complete," says Harvard Law School's public information office. ■

BACKGROUND

Naming the Behavior

In the late 19th century and the early 20th century, a growing number of women entered the labor force in a wide range of occupations — from waitresses, factory workers and shop girls to, less frequently, typists, secretaries and stenographers. Many were young, single, immigrant and uneducated. [24]

In 1908, *Harper's Bazaar* published a collection of stories about these new entrants into the workplace, "stories that reveal widespread and extensive [sexual] harassment. Other historical accounts tell of a broom factory in which women carried knives to protect themselves," wrote Louise Fitzgerald, a psychology professor at the University of Illinois at Urbana-Champaign. [25]

But the term sexual harassment wasn't coined until March 1975, when a group of women's-rights activists at Cornell University in Ithaca, N.Y., decided to put a name to something "they had all experienced but rarely discussed — unwanted sexual demands, comments, looks or sexual touching in the workplace," wrote Carrie Baker, author of *The Women's Movement Against Sexual Harassment.* [26]

Their inspiration was Carmita Wood, a 44-year-old mother of four and administrative assistant to a Cornell physics professor, who, Wood said, continually made unwanted sexual advances. Wood and other women complained to the head of the lab where they worked, whose response, said Baker, was typical of the times. He told the women they could take care of themselves and should "try not to get into those situations." Wood finally resigned because of the stress of fending off her boss and applied for unemployment compensation, but her claim was denied. A hearing officer said the reasons she left her job were "personal" and "not compelling." [27]

Wood sought help from three feminists working in Cornell's Human Affairs Program, which offered courses on topics such as prison reform and urban redevelopment. These women located attorneys for Wood and, along with others, succeeded in politicizing the issue by writing press releases, appearing on local television and radio, distributing pamphlets, testifying at a government hearing, organizing a speak-out event and popularizing a name for the problem. As a result, serious articles about "sexual harassment" began to appear in national media, including *The New York Times* and *The Wall Street Journal.* [28]

But skepticism in the popular press soon followed, according to Baker, first by commentator Rhoda Koenig in the February 1976 issue of *Harper's*

Continued on p. 388

Chronology

1960s-1970s

Sexual harassment cases reach courts.

1964
Title VII of the Civil Rights Act of 1964 prohibits employment discrimination. . . . Congress creates the Equal Employment Opportunity Commission (EEOC) to investigate employment discrimination claims.

1975
Feminists at Cornell University coin the term "sexual harassment" to describe sexual misconduct in the workplace.

1976
First successful sexual harassment case, *Williams v. Saxbe*, is argued in federal district court in Washington, D.C.

1977
In *Barnes v. Costle*, D.C. Court of Appeals rules that sexual harassment violates Title VII when the victim experiences economic loss or tangible job-related harm, so-called quid pro quo harassment.

1980s ***Government defines sexual harassment. Supreme Court issues landmark ruling.***

1980
EEOC defines sexual harassment as discriminatory when it involves a quid pro quo or creates a "hostile work environment."

1984
In *Barrett v. Omaha National Bank*, Eighth U.S. Circuit Court of Appeals finds that a single incident, if severe enough, can constitute sexual harassment.

1986
In landmark *Meritor Savings Bank v. Vinson*, Supreme Court says sexual harassment that creates a hostile work environment is discriminatory.

1990s ***Courts expand definition of sexual harassment and clarify employer liability.***

1991
In *Robinson v. Jacksonville Shipyards*, a federal district court in Florida rules that crude language, sexual graffiti and pornography create a hostile work environment. . . . Law professor Anita Hill accuses Supreme Court nominee Clarence Thomas of sexual harassment in televised hearings. One month later, Congress strengthens Title VII to give sexual harassment plaintiffs the right to seek a jury trial and compensatory and punitive damages.

1993
In *Harris v. Forklift Systems, Inc.*, Supreme Court says plaintiffs need not show psychological harm to establish that a hostile work environment exists. The court says a hostile environment exists if both the plaintiff perceives it and a "reasonable person" would agree.

1996
EEOC files largest sexual harassment suit to date against Mitsubishi Motor Manufacturing of America Inc., on behalf of hundreds of female employees at a Normal, Ill., plant.

1998
In *Oncale v. Sundowner Offshore Services, Inc.*, Supreme Court says Title VII prohibits same-gender sexual harassment. In *Faragher v. City of Boca Raton*, the court says an employer is not liable if supervisor sexual harassment causes a hostile work environment but the employer has programs to prevent and respond to sexual harassment that the victim failed to use. . . . Mitsubishi settles EEOC case for $34 million.

2000s ***Sexual harassment charges filed with government agencies decline.***

2000
Nearly 16,000 charges of sexual harassment are filed with the EEOC and state and local government agencies, up from 10,532 in 1992 and just shy of the 1997 peak.

2011
Sexual harassment charges filed with government agencies decline to 11,364. . . . Four women reveal they had made sexual misconduct accusations in the 1990s against presidential candidate Harman Cain; Cain denies them but drops out of race.

2012
On Feb. 29 a Sacramento, Calif., jury awards surgical assistant Ani Chopourian $168 million, believed to be largest award for a single victim of workplace harassment in U.S. history ($125 million in punitive damages and $42.7 million for lost wages and mental anguish). Mercy General Hospital plans to appeal.

Workplace Romances Challenge Employers

Some companies ask dating employees to sign 'love contracts.'

"One of American society's most cherished beliefs is that the workplace is — or should be — asexual," wrote Yale Law School professor Vicki Schultz, a belief she traces to American prudishness and management gurus. Sexual harassment policies, she noted, "now provide an added incentive and an increased legitimacy for management to control and discipline relatively harmless sexual behavior." [1]

To control such workplace behavior, employers sometimes either discourage or ban intimate relationships among employees, Schultz wrote. But such policies are probably unrealistic, says Rosemary Haefner, vice president of human resources at Career Builder.com, one of the country's largest online job-search sites. Work is where "many people spend most of their time and form most of their acquaintances," she says.

CareerBuilder publishes an annual office romance survey conducted by Harris Interactive. This year, 38 percent of 7,000 respondents nationwide said they have dated a co-worker at least once in their careers, and nearly a third of those workers said their office romance led to marriage, "something we didn't see as much a generation ago," says Haefner. The hospitality industry — lodging, restaurants and tourism — saw the most workplace romances, with nearly half of respondents saying they had dated a co-worker. Financial services was a close second. [2]

Workplace romance is fine, says Haefner, as long as "romance never gets in the way of professionalism, fairness and, of course, business."

Romance between bosses and subordinates gives employers the most pause. According to the CareerBuilder survey, one in five of those who dated on the job said they had dated their boss. More than one in four had dated someone higher up the corporate ladder. [3] But because of potential conflict-of-interest issues, "Employers with the best practices in place do not allow a supervisor and a subordinate to be in a dating relationship," says Ingrid Fredeen, director of content development at ELT, a provider of online training products in San Francisco.

For instance, says Fredeen, suppose "I'm a supervisor and I need to pick one employee to go on this really fabulous trip that's going to be with a client, and it's a great career opportunity . . . and I choose the one I'm dating. Is that a legitimate decision?" Such a situation is bound to create "a sense of favoritism and distrust in the organization."

The other concern, she says, is the potential for a quid pro quo-style harassment claim. If the relationship sours, the employee may claim that he or she was forced into the relationship because of the power dynamic. The alleged victim may also claim that anything negative that happens post-breakup was in retaliation for breaking up.

On the other hand, Fredeen says, banning romance between co-workers who do not have a supervisor-subordinate relationship would be "a bit aggressive," because potential company liability would be less of a problem.

Some employers require supervisor-subordinate couples to sign a "love contract." According to Philadelphia employment-law attorneys Jonathan Bloom and A. Nicole Stover, such contracts typically state that a relationship is consensual, both parties will behave professionally and there will be no preferential treatment.

But contracts raise several practical concerns. If the relationship is not disclosed, human resources personnel can be placed "in the untenable position of approaching employees with proposed contracts to sign based on mere office rumor," said Bloom and Stover. And at what point, they ask, should the couple be asked to sign such a contract. "When they sneak away for their first happy hour?" [4]

"A love contract is merely evidence of intent," says Fredeen. "It doesn't shield the employer, it just challenges the credibility of the person who is now saying I felt coerced into the relationship and the employer should now be strictly liable."

Of course, the employee could also say that she or he was coerced into signing the love contract.

— Barbara Mantel

---

[1] Vicki Schultz, "The Sanitized Workplace," *The Yale Law Journal*, June 10, 2003, www.yalelawjournal.org/pdf/112-8/SchultzFINAL.pdf.

[2] "Nearly One-Third of Workers Who Had Office Romances Married Their Co-Worker, Finds Annual CareerBuilder Valentine's Day Survey," CareerBuilder.com, Feb. 9, 2012, www.careerbuilder.com/share/aboutus/pressreleasesdetail.aspx?id=pr678&sd=2%2f9%2f2012&ed=12%2f31%2f2012&siteid=cbpr&sc_cmp1=cb_pr678.

[3] *Ibid.*

[4] Jonathan F. Bloom and Nicole Stover, "Love Among the Cubicles," *Metropolitan Corporate Counsel*, Sept. 1, 2011, www.metrocorpcounsel.com/articles/15332/love-among-cubicles.

Continued from p. 386

Magazine. Koenig wrote that "a lot of women would feel deprived without a reasonable quota of sexual harassment per week" and condemned feminists for perpetuating the "myth of women as oppressed." [29]

A survey of 9,000 women, published that November by the women's magazine *Redbook* told a different story. The article, entitled, "What Men Do to Women on the Job," said sexual harassment was "not epidemic, it is pandemic — an everyday, everywhere occurrence." Nine out of 10 women said they received unwanted sexual attention, especially sexual remarks. Only 15 percent found men's sexual advances flattering. Nearly half said that she or a woman she knew had quit work because of sexual harassment. [30]

Harassment Lawsuits

In the early 1970s, women began challenging sexual harassment in federal court by filing lawsuits under Title VII of the Civil Rights Act of 1964, which prohibits employment discrimination based on race, color, religion, national origin or sex.

"Arguing that an employer's demand for sexual favors was a form of sex discrimination was a novel idea," wrote historian Julie Berebitsky in *Sex and the Office*, and plaintiffs lost all but one of the first six cases. Defense attorneys successfully argued that courts "should not be concerned with the social life of company employees" and that sexual harassment was not sex discrimination because it could happen to both men and women. [31]

In 1976, Diane Williams became the first successful plaintiff in a sexual harassment case. Williams said she had a good working relationship with her boss when she began working in the U.S. Department of Justice's Community Relations Service in January 1972. But within six months he began making sexual advances to her, which she said she rejected. Williams claimed he then began to humiliate and harass her, and in September 1972 he fired her.

The defense argued that since both men and women could be asked for sexual favors, a supervisor who retaliates against a subordinate for rejecting such advances could not be found to have discriminated based on sex. In other words, Williams was not fired because she was a woman but because she had spurned her boss.

However, Judge Charles Richey of U.S. District Court for the District of Columbia rejected that line of argument, stating that a finding of sex discrimination under Title VII "does not require that the discriminatory policy or practice depend upon a characteristic peculiar to one of the genders." [32] The landmark case established quid pro quo sexual harassment — in which a supervisor's unwanted sexual advances affect a subordinate's employment — as a form of sex discrimination.

An explosion of mostly critical press coverage followed Williams' victory. "Editorials mocked this effort to regulate 'office hanky-panky,' " wrote Berebitsky. "Sexual shenanigans at work were becoming so wrapped in 'ridiculous red tape,' one lamented, 'that they no longer seemed worth the trouble.' " [33]

Harassment Lawsuits Cost Companies Millions

Several sex harassment cases have resulted in large damage awards in recent years, including the largest in history.

Recent Notable Sexual Harassment Lawsuits:

- **Ani Chopourian**, 45, a surgical assistant in Sacramento, Calif., was awarded $168 million — $125 million in punitive damages and $42.7 million for lost wages and mental anguish — by a California jury earlier this year. It is believed to be the largest award in U.S. history for a single victim of workplace harassment. She had filed 18 complaints with her employer, Mercy General Hospital in Sacramento, over two years, alleging sexual harassment, bullying and intimidation by cardiac surgeons. The hospital is appealing.
- **Ashley Alford**, 26, an employee at the rent-to-own company Aaron's, was awarded $95 million by a St. Louis jury in 2011 after claiming her supervisor sexually assaulted her after a year of escalating sexual harassment in a workplace rife with sexual jokes and lewd propositions. A federal legal cap on damages reduced the award by more than half. The company appealed, and the parties settled for $6 million in late March.
- Former UBS Financial Services sales associate **Carla Ingraham**, 51, was awarded $10.6 million in 2011 by a Kansas City, Mo., jury after claiming she was fired for complaining that her supervisor sexually harassed her. A judge reduced the award to $8.4 million.
- Six women working for Ralph's grocery store in Escondido, Calif., were awarded a total of $30.6 million in punitive damages and hundreds of thousands of dollars for economic damages and emotional distress in 2002 after alleging a store director inappropriately touched and verbally abused them. After an appeal by Ralph's, two of the women settled out of court. A state appeals court reduced the award for the remaining women to $1.5 million.

Source: News reports

Expanded Definition

In 1981, the Equal Employment Opportunity Commission (EEOC), created by Congress in 1964 to investigate employment discrimination, amended its guidelines on sex discrimination to add a section devoted to sexual harassment. It recognized two forms of workplace sexual harassment: the quid pro quo harassment that Williams had experienced at the Justice Department, as well as "unwelcome sexual advances, requests for sexual favors, and other verbal and physical conduct of a sexual nature" that unreasonably interferes with "an individual's work performance" or creates "an intimidating, hostile or offensive working environment." [34]

This controversial two-pronged definition was first proposed by legal scholar Catharine MacKinnon in her 1979 book *Sexual Harassment of Working Women*. Its adoption by the EEOC caused a flurry of critical press. The guidelines require companies to "police innocent flirtation," said *The Wall Street Journal*. A *Fortune* magazine column said the EEOC bureaucracy was looking for new ways to create work for itself. [35]

MacKinnon responded in a *Washington Post* editorial that "objection to sexual harassment is not a neopuritan protest against . . . compliments, flirtation or touching on the job. It's a protest against sex that is one-sided, unwelcome or comes with strings attached . . . coming from someone with the economic power to hire or fire, help or hinder, reward or punish." [36]

In 1986, the expanded definition of sexual harassment became part of case law when the Supreme Court issued its first ruling on sexual harassment. In the landmark *Meritor Savings Bank v. Vinson* case, the court ruled that sexual harassment is illegal if it is "sufficiently severe or pervasive to alter the conditions of [the victim's] employment and create an abusive working environment." [37]

But the concept of sexual harassment did not seep deeply into the national consciousness until the uproar over the 1991 Senate hearings to confirm Clarence Thomas for the Supreme Court. As the nation watched the live broadcasts, law professor Anita Hill testified that Thomas had graphically discussed pornography and "his own sexual prowess" on several occasions when she worked for him at two government agencies a decade earlier. Thomas adamantly denied the allegations, calling the proceedings "a circus" and a "high-tech lynching." The Senate voted largely along party lines, 52-48, to confirm him, the slimmest margin in a century. [38]

In the wake of the hearings, President George H. W. Bush signed the sweeping Civil Rights Act of 1991, after having vetoed an earlier version of the bill. Previously, plaintiffs alleging employment discrimination could sue only for injunctive relief such as reinstatement, back pay, lost benefits and interest. The 1991 act gave plaintiffs the right to sue for compensatory and punitive damages and the right to request a jury trial.

Encouraged by the prospect of additional damages and emboldened by the memory of the Senate hearings, employees filed a record number of charges of sexual harassment with the EEOC and state and local agencies the following year. By 1997, charges had reached 15,889, more than double the 6,127 received in 1990. Over that same period, the amount of money the EEOC helped employees recover, outside of litigation, grew sevenfold — from $7.1 million to $49.5 million. [39]

Evolving Case Law

Throughout the 1990s, sexual harassment case law evolved rapidly through a series of important federal and Supreme Court decisions.

In the groundbreaking case *Robinson v. Jacksonville Shipyards, Inc.*, a Florida district court judge ruled in 1991 that "pictures of nude and partially nude women" posted throughout the workplace constitute sexual harassment, even if the plaintiff was not targeted. Some refer to this as "ambient" sexual harassment. The court found that the testimony of Lois Robinson, a welder at the shipyards, "provides a vivid description of a visual assault on the sensibilities of female workers at JSI that did not relent during working hours." [40]

But Robinson was awarded just one dollar in nominal damages, an amount she called "a slap in the face." Her case had been one of the catalysts for the Civil Rights Act of 1991 and its expansion of damages. [41]

In 1993, feminists won another victory, when the Supreme Court ruled in its second sexual harassment case, *Harris v. Forklift Systems, Inc.*, that plaintiffs need not show psychological harm to establish that sexual harassment caused a hostile work environment. Writing for the court, Justice Sandra Day O'Connor said: "Title VII comes into play before the harassing conduct leads to a nervous breakdown. A discriminatorily abusive work environment, even one that does not seriously affect employees' psychological well being, can and often will detract from employees' job performance, discourage employees from remaining on the job, or keep them from advancing in their careers." [42]

The court also stated that a hostile environment exists if both the plaintiff subjectively perceives it and if a "reasonable person" would agree, admitting that "this is not, and by its nature cannot be, a mathematically precise test." [43]

Then in 1998, the Supreme Court both expanded and reduced the reach of Title VII, according to Minneapolis attorney Kristin Berger Parker in an article in the *Northwestern University Law Review*. In *Oncale v. Sundowner Offshore Services, Inc.*, the court resolved a split among circuit courts when it ruled that same-sex harassment is sex discrimination under Title VII. But at the same time the justices said that in order to be discriminatory, sexual harassment must be shown to be "because of sex." In other words, if a supervisor, for example, treats both men and women badly, there is no sex discrimination. [44]

The impact of *Oncale* in lower court rulings has been widespread, said Berger Parker. Many federal courts have rejected claims of ambient sexual harassment. Some have reasoned that if the displayed pornography or general

Continued on p. 392

Military's Harassment Policies Seen as Weak

Fewer than 5 percent of alleged victims file complaints.

The vast majority of non-violent sexual harassment in the military may go unreported, according to a U.S. Government Accountability Office (GAO) study. Fourteen percent — about one in seven — of surveyed service members said they were sexually harassed in the preceding year, and of those, fewer than 5 percent made a formal complaint. [1]

Such underreporting makes it difficult to know the true extent of sexual harassment in the military, but Brenda Farrell, director of defense capabilities and management at the GAO and the study's author, says "it is definitely a problem." Farrell cites a Department of Defense (DoD) survey in which 41 percent of service members indicated that in their work group, people would be able to get away with sexual harassment, even if it were reported. "That's pretty high," says Farrell.

U.S. Air Force/File Photo

Air Force Chief Master Sgt. William Gurney pleaded guilty on Jan. 24, 2010, to criminal sexual misconduct with subordinates. In a recent survey 14 percent of service members said they were sexually harassed, but fewer than 5 percent formally complained.

The military has had sexual harassment policies and training programs for several decades, but the GAO found several deficiencies:

- The DoD has only one person providing oversight;
- The military has no clear goals, objectives, milestones or metrics for measuring progress on reducing sexual harassment;
- Not all military installations and commands report sexual harassment complaint data;
- The DoD does not hold commanders accountable for implementing sexual harassment policies. [2]

"Sexual harassment can lead to psychological harm, and the DoD has a study under way to see if there is a connection between those who commit sexual harassment and those who then commit sexual assault," says Farrell.

The good news, she says, is that the DoD concurred with the GAO report and its recommendations. According to the DoD, it is working to improve collection of both formal and informal sexual harassment complaints; hold military commanders responsible for promoting, supporting and enforcing sexual harassment policies and programs; and beef up oversight.

But some experts are skeptical that significant reforms are on the way.

"The DoD likes to study things, but they don't like to implement things," says Greg Jacob, who served in the Marines before becoming policy director for the Service Women's Action Network, a New York-based advocacy organization. Jacob doubts the DoD will follow through on its promises.

"Commanders' authority is absolute," says Jacob. "It's very difficult to get any kind of institutional change that hints at taking any kind of authority away from commanders," he says.

The military needs to make sexual harassment a "show stopper" just like drunken driving, says Jacob. "If you drink and try to drive through the base gate, your career is over. You'll never get promoted, or they'll take active measures to get you out."

And the DoD needs to get women into immediate supervisory roles over the rank and file in combat units, he says. "We're talking about company commanders, platoon commanders, platoon sergeants and first sergeants," Jacob says.

While combat units are exclusively male, same-sex harassment can occur, and combat troops can harass women in support units, he says. [3]

Jacob argues that men in combat units need to have female leaders and see that women are not second-class soldiers. But, he says, that would mean the DoD would have to rescind its combat exclusion policy — a move it so far has resisted but that many in and outside the military recommend, in large part to lessen the stress on recruitment and best utilize all members of the military.

— ***Barbara Mantel***

[1] Brenda Farrell, "Preventing Sexual Harassment: DOD Needs Greater Leadership Commitment and an Oversight Framework, Highlights," Government Accountability Office, Sept. 21, 2011, www.gao.gov/products/GAO-11-809.

[2] *Ibid.*

[3] For background, see Marcia Clemmitt, "Women in the Military," *CQ Researcher*, Nov. 13, 2009, pp. 957-980.

Continued from p. 390

sex talk predated the appearance of women in the workplace, it is not discrimination against a female plaintiff on the basis of her sex. Many courts, said Berger Parker, "have simply noted that ambient harassment is visible and offensive to persons of both genders and therefore is not discriminatory." [45]

In two other cases that year the Supreme Court clarified under what conditions employers are liable for discriminatory sexual harassment. In *Faragher v. City of Boca Raton* and *Burlington Industries, Inc. v. Ellerth*, the court ruled that an employer is automatically liable when a supervisor sexually harasses a subordinate and there is a quid pro quo. But the employer can defend itself in hostile-environment cases by showing it exercised reasonable care to prevent and promptly correct the harassing behavior and that the employee unreasonably failed to take advantage of any preventive or corrective opportunities. [46]

When the harasser is not a supervisor, the employer is liable only if it was negligent, a standard that places a greater burden on the employee, according to Melanie Herman, executive director of the Nonprofit Risk Management Center in Leesburg, Va., which advises nonprofits. The employee must prove the employer either knew or had reason to know about the harassment and didn't take proper action before he or she can collect damages. [47]

In *Pennsylvania State Police v. Suders* in 2004, the Supreme Court reaffirmed that when an employee has been forced to quit her job because of a supervisor's sexual harassment — quid pro quo harassment — the employer is automatically liable and can offer no affirmative defense. [48]

These rulings prompted businesses to adopt formal sexual harassment policies and training programs. Since 2000, the number of charges of sexual harassment received by the EEOC and state and local agencies has declined by nearly 30 percent, although there is little consensus about the reasons why and whether that drop reflects an actual decline in harassment. ■

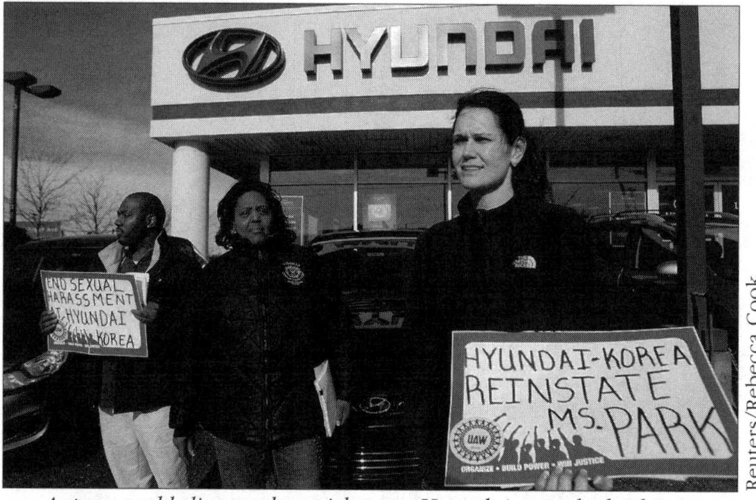

Reuters/Rebecca Cook

Auto assembly line workers picket at a Hyundai auto dealership in Dearborn, Mich., on Nov. 30, 2011, in support of an auto worker in South Korea who was fired after filing a sexual harassment complaint with Korea's National Human Rights Commission. The woman worked for a Hyundai subcontractor. Demonstrators picketed at 75 Hyundai dealers.

CURRENT SITUATION

Defining 'Supervisor'

The Supreme Court has been asked to take a case that could determine once and for all how to define a "supervisor," a critically important issue because the degree of company liability for workplace harassment depends upon that definition. Federal courts have not always agreed, and now the Supreme Court is being asked to set the record straight.

The confusion lies in Title VII of the Civil Rights Act, which says a "supervisor is someone with power to directly affect the terms and conditions of the plaintiff's employment." Some U.S. circuit courts have interpreted that to mean a supervisor must have the power to "to hire, fire, demote, promote, transfer or discipline an employee." Other courts have said "the authority to direct an employee's daily activities" is enough to establish supervisory status. [49]

Maetta Vance, a dining service employee at Ball State University in Muncie, Ind., and the only African-American in her department, began filing complaints with the school in 2005 alleging that co-workers were using racial epithets against her, referring to their Ku Klux Klan ties and making veiled threats of physical harm. Vance eventually filed suit in federal district court, alleging that a co-worker and three supervisors harassed her on account of her race, but the court dismissed her case. She appealed to the Seventh U.S. Circuit Court of Appeals.

The Chicago court found that the behavior of the co-worker and two of the supervisors was not severe or pervasive enough to qualify as racial harassment. As for the third supervisor, Saundra Davis, the court found that although Davis held the title of supervisor, she did not have supervisory authority over Vance because she did not have the right to hire, fire, demote, promote or transfer Vance.

Continued on p. 394

At Issue:

Do university sexual harassment policies threaten students' due-process rights?

TREVOR BURRUS
LEGAL ASSOCIATE, CENTER FOR CONSTITUTIONAL STUDIES, CATO INSTITUTE

WRITTEN FOR *CQ RESEARCHER*, APRIL 2012

yes

By lowering protections given to university students accused of sexual harassment, the Office for Civil Rights (OCR) has rolled back centuries-old due-process and First Amendment rights. Colleges should be teaching students the history of the struggle against oppressive regimes that led to our due-process and free-speech rights, not re-enacting that history.

Given the irreparable damage to a student's reputation that an accusation of sexual harassment can bring, it is important that alleged perpetrators get the protections of due process. Such protections should include, at minimum, a higher standard of proof than the "preponderance of the evidence" standard promulgated by the OCR, which assumes that the allegation is more likely true than not, but also the right to confront witnesses — a right enshrined in our Constitution.

The OCR has curtailed the right for the accused to confront his or her accuser because the experience "may be traumatic or intimidating" for the accuser. Astoundingly, the OCR has even requested that the few remaining due-process rights of the accused "not restrict or unnecessarily delay" the alleged victim's complaint and that investigators "minimize the burden on the complainant." Thus, the accuser is regarded presumptively as the victim, and the presumption of innocence for the accused — a fundamental tenet of our justice system — has been eliminated.

Moreover, because sexual harassment usually comes in the form of spoken or written communication, the preponderance-of-the-evidence standard of proof threatens to chill free expression in the place where it should be most important: on college campuses. Coddling women to protect them from misogynistic or sexually charged speech undermines female equality because it presumes that women cannot "deal with it" or protect themselves. Furthermore, the lower standard of proof ensures that students will excessively self-censor, for fear of being accused of sexual harassment, thus shielding students not only from speech that actually is harassing but also from speech anyone could construe as harassing, a much larger category.

College campuses should be the bastions of freedoms we hold dear. All speech should be given the full First Amendment protections, but offensive speech even more so. After all, if the First Amendment does not protect speakers who offend or challenge the prevailing standards, what good is it? Finally, teaching students that due-process and free-speech rights are contingent upon the government granting those rights undercuts the core principles of a free society. We must demand more from our universities.

LISA M. MAATZ
DIRECTOR, PUBLIC POLICY AND GOVERNMENT RELATIONS, AMERICAN ASSOCIATION OF UNIVERSITY WOMEN

WRITTEN FOR *CQ RESEARCHER*, APRIL 2012

no

Title IX clearly is about creating a safe learning environment, and this trumps other considerations. The Department of Education's April 2011 Dear Colleague Letter (DCL) on schools' Title IX obligations to prevent and deal with sexual harassment and violence reasserts an old standard of proof: the preponderance-of-the-evidence standard, which is appropriate for campus proceedings.

Often referred to as "more likely than not," this standard has been used for prosecuting violations of civil rights laws, including proceedings involving discrimination based on gender under Title VII of the 1964 Civil Rights Act, by the Office of Civil Rights in resolving complaints and by schools dealing with allegations of harassment based on race, ethnicity and disability. It follows that the same standard would be appropriate in proceedings pursuant to allegations of sexual harassment or violence.

Grievance procedures that use the stricter "clear and convincing standard" (i.e., that it's highly probable or reasonably certain that sexual harassment or violence occurred) are not equitable under Title IX. This seems especially perverse in the case of alleged sexual harassment or assault in which the victim inherently lacks power over the aggressor. Proceedings should be fair and not give a clear advantage to either party. The preponderance-of-the-evidence standard is the best one to ensure a safe learning environment.

The argument that civil proceedings in Title IX sexual discrimination cases should use a different standard than other civil-rights proceedings flies in the face of precedent and prevents a reduction in student sexual harassment and violence cases. School grievance proceedings under Title IX are not criminal proceedings. As the DCL makes clear, schools should move forward with their Title IX obligation to investigate and resolve any grievances. This action should be taken by schools independent of whether or not criminal charges are filed or a subsequent police investigation is conducted or concluded.

Pervasive sexual harassment and violence on college and university campuses contributes to a hostile environment that interferes with every student's right to an education free of discrimination. The correct and timely application of Title IX's protections strengthens campus communities as a whole. This is not a time for shortcuts; not when the safety of students is at stake.

Continued from p. 392

The court also found that Ball State had taken prompt and remedial action in response to Vance's complaints. Although Davis continued to make inappropriate remarks to Vance on occasion, the court said, "Title VII does not require an employer's response to 'successfully prevent subsequent harassment,' though it should be reasonably calculated to do so." Thus, the court said, there was no basis for Ball State to be found liable.

In February Vance petitioned the U.S. Supreme Court to accept her case and determine once and for all the legal definition of a supervisor. The court asked the U.S. solicitor general to file a brief expressing the government's view in the case, *Maetta Vance v. Ball State University, et al.*

"If the Supreme Court takes the case and adopts the broader definition of supervisor . . . it could result in heightened liability for employers," Jennifer Craighead, a Pennsylvania employment attorney, wrote in a recent blog post. [50] Its impact would be felt not just in racial harassment but in sexual harassment cases as well. The Supreme Court's decision on whether to take the case is pending.

Same-Sex Harassment

John Cherry worked on a surveying crew for Shaw Coastal, a civil engineering and surveying firm in Houma, La. Cherry claimed that in March 2007, shortly after he joined the crew, supervisor Michael Reasoner began touching him, commenting on his looks and sending him sexually suggestive text messages. Both men were married.

Cherry complained to Reasoner's supervisor, who at first viewed the behavior as "horsing around" and failed to notify human resources, as was required by company policy. When human resources did eventually investigate, the company took no action because it said there was not enough evidence of harassment, despite the availability of other witnesses. [51]

Cherry sued the company, and the case ended up in the Fifth U.S. Circuit Court of Appeals. In January, the New Orleans court found Shaw Coastal liable and reinstated a jury award of $500,000, which had been reversed in circuit court.

"If a female employee complained about a male supervisor inappropriately touching her and sending her lewd and obscene messages, most employers would response promptly and thoroughly," said Milwaukee employment attorney Ryan Parsons. "This case provides a strong reminder that employers must take *all* sexual harassment claims seriously," said Parsons. "Failure to do so could be costly." [52]

In fact, complaints of same-sex harassment are on the rise. Between 1992 and 2011, the percentage of charges of sexual harassment filed with the EEOC by men has climbed from 9.1 percent to 16.3 percent. While the commission does not keep track of the gender of the alleged harasser, it believes that the increase is due mainly to reports of men harassing men. "While some people may think sexual harassment of male employees is a joke, the issue is real," EEOC spokesman David Grinberg told the news website *The Daily Beast*. "We are seeing more of it, and such conduct has serious legal consequences for employers." [53]

"It's certainly possible that there's more sexual harassment of men going on, but it could just be that more men are coming forward and complaining about it," said Ernest Haffner, a lawyer in the EEOC's office of legal counsel. [54]

Fewer than 3 percent of sexual harassment lawsuits make it to trial as Cherry's did, according to a study by the American Bar Foundation, a Chicago-based research organization. Many are dismissed; the majority are settled. [55]

In one high-profile same-sex sexual harassment case, the Cheesecake Factory restaurant chain settled a suit in November 2009 brought by the EEOC on behalf of six employees in Phoenix, Ariz. The six men claimed they were repeatedly subjected to sexual fondling, simulated rape and physical abuse at the hands of other male workers. The company denied the charges but agreed to pay $340,000 to the plaintiffs.

"Sexual harassment is about using power in a way to hurt somebody," said Marcia McCormick, a professor at Saint Louis University School of Law. The Cheesecake Factory defendants were never alleged to be attracted to men. The sexual harassment was a form of intimidation, McCormick said. [56]

Retaliation

In March a state panel in Maine agreed with the claims of Windham police officer Danielle Cyr that a male co-worker touched her, urinated in front of her and sexually harassed her. It also found that when she reported the harassment to higher-ups and eventually to the EEOC, other members of the police department retaliated against her, giving her the silent treatment and shunning her at work.

"Danielle's life depends on her not being alone," said Rebecca Webber, Cyr's attorney. "Danielle's life depends on other people being willing to risk their lives to make sure she is not on her own." [57]

While sexual harassment charges filed with the EEOC and state and local agencies fell for the fourth straight year in 2011, charges of retaliation for reporting employment discrimination of all types — racial, age, sex, etc. — continue to climb. For the first time in EEOC history, retaliation was the most frequently filed complaint in 2010, and it trumped all other employment discrimination complaints again in 2011. [58]

Part of the increase may be due to a Supreme Court decision in 2006 that expanded the scope of employee's protections from retaliation. Title VII forbids employers from retaliating against an employee who opposes discriminatory practices. But prior to the Supreme Court decision, U.S. circuit courts were divided on how to define retaliation. Did the employee have to be fired or denied a promotion? Demoted? Or would a transfer qualify?

Sheila White was a forklift operator and the only woman working in the maintenance department at a rail yard in Memphis, Tenn., when she complained to management that her supervisor was sexually harassing her. The company reassigned her to a more physically demanding track-laborer position at the same pay and later temporarily suspended her. In *Burlington Northern & Sante Fe Railway Co. v. White* the Supreme Court ruled that the transfer, even at equal pay, and the temporary suspension were retaliation for White's sexual harassment complaints. [59]

"The Supreme Court ruling has made employees more confident in filing a [retaliation] charge," said Adam Klein, a plaintiff's attorney in New York City specializing in the financial industry. During hard economic times, "employers are less willing to tolerate [discrimination] complaints, leading to more retaliatory actions, and employees are fighting back," Klein said. [60]

According to the Ethics Resource Center's survey, 22 percent of employees who reported workplace misconduct experienced some form of retaliation. That's an all-time high and compares to 12 percent in 2007 and 15 percent in 2009. Heading the list of retaliatory actions are exclusion from decision-making by supervisors, a cold shoulder from co-workers, verbal abuse from a manager and co-workers, denial of promotions or raises and threat of job loss. ■

OUTLOOK

Surveying the Climate

In its latest survey, the Ethics Resource Center says the percentage of employees who claim to have witnessed misconduct at work fell to a new low of 45 percent. But the center predicts that ethical behavior in the workplace will deteriorate in the years ahead as business prospects slowly improve. "Historically, when the economy is good, workplace ethics tend to suffer: Profit takes precedence over proper behavior," said the survey. [61]

According to the center, retaliation and pressure to break the rules are increasing at an alarming rate. Pressure to break the rules climbed five points — to 13 percent, "just shy of the all-time high of 14 percent in 2000." [62]

Certain categories of lawbreaking behavior already are increasing, including sexual harassment. Eleven percent of surveyed employees said they observed sexual harassment at work in 2011 — up from 7 percent in 2009. [63]

If companies want to reverse that trend, they must pay closer attention to the ethical climate at work, just as some companies track employee satisfaction through anonymous "climate surveys," says Hegewisch of the Institute for Women's Policy Research. "There is a whole industry doing those. It is a quite a developed HR market."

Hegewisch would like to see companies include questions about sexual harassment in those internal surveys, such as: If you felt there was sexual harassment, do you know what to do? Has this ever happened to you? Is this a problem in the workplace? It would allow companies to gauge the extent of the problem and whether their policies and training programs are understood and effective, she says.

But companies are resistant. "We raised this as an idea with someone at EEOC, and she said that they tried to negotiate that in some consent decrees, but employers were hostile. Employers are afraid that anything they collect could be turned against them in future litigation," says Hegewisch. "It's a problem because it really stops activities that allow you to capture the problem before it becomes too big."

Surveys have pitfalls, however. Perhaps the biggest problem is defining sexual harassment. Do you define it, or allow survey participants to supply their own definition? Or do you ask about particular behaviors?

A survey by the American Association of University Women (AAUW) made national headlines last November when it revealed that nearly half of the students surveyed in grades 7-12 experienced "some form of sexual harassment" from their peers in the 2010-11 school year, and 87 percent of those said the behavior had affected them negatively. Verbal harassment "made up the bulk of the incidents," although physical harassment was "far too common," the study said. [64]

The high percentages could be partly the result of the study methodology. The survey did not ask students specifically about "sexual harassment" but asked if they had experienced different unwanted behaviors, which study authors then defined as sexual harassment. For instance, students were asked, "Has anyone ever made unwelcome sexual comments, jokes, gestures to or about you?" Or "Have you ever been touched in an unwelcome way?"

"It's surprising it's only half," wrote Roiphe of New York University in her opinion piece last November, after complaining about the broad array of behaviors included in the survey.

"We did define it broadly, and I want to be clear about that," says study co-author Catherine Hill, the director of research at AAUW. "We intentionally wanted to look at all kinds of behaviors that might affect the climate at the school. This is not a survey about legal cases. This is a survey about how students feel."

It's not just fear of future litigation that is keeping companies from surveying their employees about sexual harassment, says Hoftra's Grossman. The way many judges handle sexual harassment lawsuits doesn't provide much of an incentive either, she says.

"Most courts want to know: 'Did you adopt a policy?' and 'Do you have a procedure?' They aren't willing to look at the subtleties of 'Was this policy calculated to invite complaints?' or 'Did it invite complaints? How did you treat people when there were complaints?' Those questions don't get asked.

"Employers at this point don't have much of an incentive to engage in self-reflective activities," says Grossman. ■

Notes

[1] Susan Saulny, "A Defiant Herman Cain Suspends His Bid for Presidency," *The New York Times*, Dec. 3, 2011, www.nytimes.com/2011/12/04/us/politics/herman-cain-suspends-his-presidential-campaign.html.

[2] Vanessa Beasley, "Anita Hill-Clarence Thomas Hearings," The Museum of Broadcast Communications, www.museum.tv/archives/etv/H/htmlH/hill-thomash/hill-thomas.htm.

[3] Michael D. Shear, Jim Rutenberg and Mike McIntire, "Cain Speaks Out to Deny Accusations; 2nd Voice Heard," *The New York Times*, Nov. 8, 2011, www.nytimes.com/2011/11/09/us/politics/cain-to-respond-to-allegation-after-vowing-to-move-on.html?scp=1&sq=karen%20kraushaar&st=cse; http://abcnews.go.com/Blotter/herman-cain-accuser-identified/story?id=14905460.

[4] "Sexual Harassment Charges: EEOC & FEPAs Combined: FY1997-FY2011," Equal Employment Opportunity Commission, www.eeoc.gov/eeoc/statistics/enforcement/sexual_harassment.cfm.

[5] Julie Steinberg, "Sexual Harassment Falls, Retaliation Rises," FINS, April 28, 2011, www.fins.com/Finance/Articles/SB130220514090402381/Sexual-Harassment-Falls-Retaliation-Rises.

[6] "Sexual Harassment: Nasty, but rarer," *The Economist*, Nov. 12, 2011, www.economist.com/node/21538157.

[7] "One in Four U.S. Women Reports Workplace Harassment," ABC News/*Washington Post* Poll, Nov. 16, 2011, www.abcnews.go.com/blogs/politics/2011/11/one-in-four-u-s-women-reports-workplace-harassment.

[8] Jeff Green, "The Silencing of Sexual Harassment," *Bloomberg Businessweek*, www.businessweek.com/magazine/the-silencing-of-sexual-harassment-11172011.html.

[9] Hilary Stout, "Less 'He Said, She Said' In Sex Harassment Cases," *The New York Times*, Nov. 6, 2011, www.nytimes.com/2011/11/06/jobs/in-sex-harassment-cases-less-he-said-she-said.html?pagewanted=all.

[10] *Ibid.*

[11] "2011 National Business Ethics Survey," Ethics Resource Center, 2012, pp. 13, 25-26, www.ethics.org/nbes.

[12] Katie Roiphe, "In Favor of Dirty Jokes and Risque Remarks," *The New York Times*, Nov. 12, 2011, www.nytimes.com/2011/11/13/opinion/sunday/sex-harassment-what-on-earth-is-that.html.

[13] Jason N. Houle, *et al.*, "The Impact of Sexual Harassment on Depressive Symptoms During the Early Occupational Career," *Society and Mental Health*, July, 2011, www.asanet.org/images/journals/docs/pdf/smh/Jul11SMHFeature.pdf.

[14] Paul Walsh, "Hal Leonard Publishing settles sex suit," *StarTribune*, March 15, 2012, www.startribune.com/local/142772395.html.

[15] "SHRM Poll: Is Workplace Sexual Harassment on the Rise?" Society for Human Resource Management, April 16, 2010, www.shrm.org/Research/SurveyFindings/Articles/Pages/SexualHarassmentontheRise.aspx.

[16] "Sex Discrimination and Sexual Harassment," Catalyst, July 2011, www.catalyst.org/publication/213/sex-discrimination-and-sexual-harassment.

[17] *Circuit City Stores, Inc. v. Saint Clair Adams*, U.S. Supreme Court, March 21, 2001, www.law.cornell.edu/supct/html/99-1379.ZO.html.

[18] Alexander J. S. Cohen, "An Empirical Study of Employment Arbitration: Case Outcomes and Processes," *Journal of Empirical Legal Studies*, March 2011, p. 1, http://onlinelibrary.wiley.com/doi/10.1111/j.1740-1461.2010.01200.x/abstract.

[19] *Ibid.*, p. 15.

[20] *AT&T v. Concepcion*, U.S. Supreme Court, April 27, 2011, www.scotusblog.com/case-files/cases/att-mobility-v-concepcion. For background, see Kenneth Jost, "Class Action Lawsuits," *CQ Researcher*, March 13, 2011, pp. 433-456.

[21] "Dear Colleague Letter," Office of Civil Rights, U.S. Department of Education, April 4, 2011, www2.ed.gov/about/offices/list/ocr/letters/colleague-201104.pdf.

[22] "Standard of Evidence Survey: Colleges and Universities Respond to OCR"s New Mandate," Foundation for Individual Rights in Education, Oct. 28, 2011, http://thefire.org/article/13796.html.

[23] Karin Kapsidelis, "U.Va. revising sexual-misconduct policy," *Richmond Times-Dispatch*, May 6, 2011, www2.timesdispatch.com/news/news/2011/may/06/tdmain01-uva-revising-conduct-policy-ar-1020303.

[24] Mary Bularzik, "Sexual Harassment at the Workplace, Historical Notes," p. 6, bcrw.barnard.edu/archive/workforce/Sexual_Harassment_at_the_Workplace.pdf.

[25] Louise F. Fitzgerald, "Science v. Myth: The Failure of Reason in the Clarence Thomas Hearings," *University of Southern California Law Review*, 1992, http://heinonline.org/HOL/LandingPage?collection=journals&handle=hein.journals/scal65&div=62&id=&page=.

[26] Carrie N. Baker, *The Women's Movement Against Sexual Harassment* (2008), p. 27.

[27] *Ibid.*, pp. 27-28.

[28] *Ibid.*, pp. 31-32, 35-36.

[29] *Ibid.*, p. 36.

[30] Julie Berebitsky, *Sex and the Office: A History of Gender, Power, and Desire* (2012), p. 225.

[31] *Ibid.*, p. 239.

[32] *Williams v. Saxbe*, http://dc.findacase.com/research/wfrmDocViewer.aspx/xq/fac.19760420_0000062.DDC.htm/qx.

[33] Berebitsky, *op. cit.*, p. 241.

[34] Francis Achampong, "The Evolution of Same-

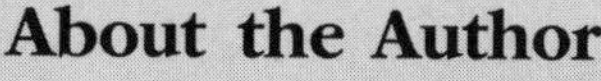

About the Author

Barbara Mantel is a freelance writer in New York City. She is a former correspondent and senior producer for National Public Radio and has won several journalism awards, including the National Press Club's Best Consumer Journalism Award and the Front Page Award from the Newswomen's Club of New York for her Nov. 1, 2009, *CQ Global Researcher* report "Terrorism and the Internet." She holds a B.A. in history and economics from the University of Virginia and an M.A. in economics from Northwestern University.

Sex Sexual Harassment Law: A Critical Examination of the Latest Developments in Workplace Sexual Harassment Litigation," *St. John's Law Review*, Summer 1999, p. 703, http://scholarship.law.stjohns.edu/lawreview/vol73/iss3/3.
[35] Baker, *op. cit.*, p. 119.
[36] *Ibid.*, p. 146.
[37] *Meritor Savings Bank v. Vinson*, U.S. Supreme Court, http://caselaw.lp.findlaw.com/cgi-bin/getcase.pl?court=us&vol=477&invol=57.
[38] Joel Siegel, "Clarence Thomas-Anita Hill Supreme Court Confirmation Hearing 'Empowered Women' and Panel Member Arlen Specter Still Amazed by Reactions," ABC News, Oct. 24, 2011, http://abcnews.go.com/US/clarence-thomas-anita-hill-supreme-court-confirmation-hearing/story?id=14802217#.T38zrO07-pE.
[39] "Sexual Harassment Charges," *op. cit.* Also see Sarah Glazer, "Crackdown on Sexual Harassment," *CQ Researcher*, July 19, 1996, p. 640.
[40] *Robinson v. Jacksonville Shipyards, Inc.*, U.S. District Court, Jacksonville, Florida, www.leagle.com/xmlResult.aspx?page=2&xmldoc=19912246760FSupp1486_12018.xml&docbase=CSLWAR2-1986-2006&SizeDisp=7.
[41] Kristin H. Berger Parker, "Ambient Harassment Under Title VII: Reconsidering the Workplace Environment," *Northwestern University Law Review*, 2008, p. 955, www.law.northwestern.edu/lawreview/v102/n2/945/LR102n2BergerParker.pdf.
[42] *Harris v. Forklift Systems, Inc.*, U.S. Supreme Court, www.law.cornell.edu/supct/html/92-1168.ZO.html.
[43] *Ibid.*
[44] Parker, *op. cit.*
[45] *Ibid.*, p. 961.
[46] Melanie Herman, "Managing The Risks of Sexual Harassment," The National Legal Aid & Defender Association, 2011, www.nasams.org/Insurance/Insurance_LossPrevention_Sexharassment?printable=yes.
[47] *Ibid.*
[48] "Major Supreme Court Decisions on Women's Rights," American Civil Liberties Union, www.aclu.org/files/interactive/womensrights_scotus_0303a.html.
[49] *Maetta Vance v. Ballstate University, et al.*, Seventh Circuit Court of Appeals, June 3, 2011, www.law.com/jsp/tal/PubArticleTAL.jsp?id=1202496921129&slreturn=1.
[50] Jennifer Craighead, "Racial Harassment Plaintiff Asked Supreme Court to Clarify Supervisor Liability Under Title VII," Pennsylvania Litigation Blog, March 2, 2012, www.palitigationblog.com/2012/03/articles/labor-and-employment-litigatio/racial-harassment-plaintiff-asked-supreme-court-to-clarify-supervisor-liability-under-title-vii.
[51] *Cherry v. Shaw Coastal, Inc.*, Fifth Circuit Court of Appeals, Jan. 19, 2012, www.ca5.uscourts.gov/opinions/pub/11/11-30403-CV0.wpd.pdf.
[52] Ryan N. Parsons, "Appeals Court Finds Employer Liable for Supervisor's Same-Sex Sexual Harassment," *Legal News: Employment Law Update*, Feb. 13, 2012, www.foley.com.
[53] Krista Gesaman, "Abuse of Power: An Increase in male-on-male sexual harassment shows larger truths about abuse in the workplace," *The Daily Beast*, Jan. 12, 2010, www.thedailybeast.com/newsweek/2010/01/12/abuse-of-power.html.
[54] Sam Hananel, "More men filing sexual harassment claims; Many cases involve abuse for not fitting male stereotypes," *The Washington Post*, March 21, 2010.
[55] "Contesting Workplace Discrimination in Court," American Bar Foundation, Oct. 29, 2008, p. 32, www.americanbarfoundation.org/uploads/cms/documents/nielsen_abf_edl_report_08_final.pdf.
[56] Gesaman, *op. cit.*
[57] Heather Steeves, "Panel finds Maine cop was sexually harassed, retaliated against," Police one.com, March 26, 2012.
[58] "Charge Statistics, FY 1997 Through FY2011," Equal Employment Opportunity Commission, www.eeoc.gov/eeoc/statistics/enforcement/charges.cfm.
[59] *Burlington Northern & Santa Fe Railroad Co. v. White*, *LII Supreme Court Bulletin*, Legal Information Institute, April 17, 2006, www.law.cornell.edu/supct/cert/05-259.
[60] Steinberg, *op. cit.*
[61] "2011 National Business Ethics Survey," *op. cit.*, p. 15.
[62] *Ibid.*, pp. 12,15.
[63] *Ibid.*, p. 29.
[64] Catherine Hill and Holly Kearl, "Crossing the Line: Sexual Harassment at School," American Association of University Women, November 2011, p. 2, www.aauw.org/learn/research/crossingtheline.cfm.

FOR MORE INFORMATION

American Arbitration Association, 1501 M St., N.W., Suite 400, Washington, DC 20005; 202-629-5650; www.adr.org. Provides arbitration, mediation and other alternative dispute-resolution services.

American Association of University Professors, 1133 19th St., N.W., Suite 200, Washington, DC 20036; 202-737-5900; www.aaup.org. Promotes academic freedom and professional standards for higher education.

Cato Institute, 1000 Massachusetts Ave., N.W., Washington, DC 20001; 202-842-0200; www.cato.org. Promotes individual liberty, limited government and free market policies.

Equal Employment Advisory Council, 1501 M St., N.W., Suite 400, Washington, DC 20005; 202-629-5650; www.eeac.org. Advises member companies on compliance with equal employment opportunity and affirmative action regulations.

Equal Employment Opportunity Commission, 131 M St., N.E., Washington, DC 20507; 202-663-4900; www.eeoc.gov. Enforces federal employment-discrimination laws.

Foundation for Individual Rights in Education, 601 Walnut St., Suite 510, Philadelphia, PA 19106; 215-717-3473; http://thefire.org. Promotes individual rights at U.S. colleges and universities.

Institute for Women's Policy Research, 200 18th St., N.W., Suite 301, Washington, DC 20036; 202-785-5100; www.iwpr.org. Promotes women's issues, policies to strengthen families and communities.

9 to 5 National Association of Working Women, 207 East Buffalo St., Suite 211, Milwaukee, WI 53202; 414-274-0925; www.9to5.org. Advocates for working women.

National Partnership for Women and Families, 1875 Connecticut Ave., N.W., Suite 650, Washington, DC 20009; 202-986-2600; www.nationalpartnership.org. Promotes workplace fairness, reproductive health and access to affordable health care.

Service Women's Action Network, P.O. Box 1758, New York, NY 10156; 212-683-0015; http://servicewomen.org. Advocates for female service members and veterans.

Bibliography

Selected Sources

Books

Baker, Carrie N., *The Women's Movement Against Sexual Harassment*, Cambridge University Press, 2008.
A women's studies professor at Smith College recounts how a diverse social movement put sexual harassment on the public agenda in the 1970s and '80s.

Berebitsky, Julie, *Sex and the Office: A History of Gender, Power and Desire*, Yale University Press, 2012.
The director of women's studies at Sewanee, the University of the South, in Sewanee, Tenn., explores how American attitudes toward sexuality and gender in the office have changed since the 1860s, when women first took clerical jobs at the U.S. Treasury.

Articles

Gesaman, Krista, "Abuse of Power: An Increase in male-on-male sexual harassment shows larger truths about abuse in the workplace," *The Daily Beast*, Jan. 12, 2010, www.thedailybeast.com/newsweek/2010/01/12/abuse-of-power.html.
The Cheesecake Factory restaurant chain settles a same-sex sexual harassment claim while denying the charges.

Green, Jeff, "The Silencing of Sexual Harassment," *Bloomberg Businessweek*, www.businessweek.com/magazine/the-silencing-of-sexual-harassment-11172011.html.
More companies require workers to arbitrate sexual harassment claims and give up their right to have their cases heard in court.

Hananel, Sam, "More men filing sexual harassment claims; Many cases involve abuse for not fitting male stereotypes," *The Washington Post*, March 21, 2010.
Men account for a growing percentage of sexual harassment cases filed with government agencies.

Kapsidelis, Karin, "U.Va. revising sexual-misconduct policy," *Richmond Times-Dispatch*, May 6, 2011, www2.timesdispatch.com/news/news/2011/may/06/tdmain01-uva-revising-conduct-policy-ar-1020303.
The University of Virginia has revised its sexual misconduct policies and procedures in the wake of newly clarified standards from the Department of Education.

Saulny, Susan, "A Defiant Herman Cain Suspends His Bid for Presidency," *The New York Times*, Dec. 3, 2011, www.nytimes.com/2011/12/04/us/politics/herman-cain-suspends-his-presidential-campaign.html.
Presidential candidate Herman Cain dropped out of the presidential race amid mounting charges of sexual harassment during the 1990s, when he ran a restaurant trade organization.

Stout, Hilary, "Less 'He Said, She Said' In Sex Harassment Cases," *The New York Times*, Nov. 6, 2011, www.nytimes.com/2011/11/06/jobs/in-sex-harassment-cases-less-he-said-she-said.html?pagewanted=all.
The number of charges of sexual harassment filed with government agencies is declining, but observers don't agree on why.

Walsh, Paul, "Hal Leonard Publishing settles sex suit," *StarTribune*, March 15, 2012, www.startribune.com/local/142772395.html.
A music publisher settles a sexual harassment case by agreeing to pay aggrieved female employees and provide anti-discrimination training in the workplace.

Reports and Studies

"Standard of Evidence Survey: Colleges and Universities Respond to OCR's New Mandate," Foundation for Individual Rights in Education, Oct. 28, 2011, http://thefire.org/article/13796.html.
The survey documents the response of colleges to a Department of Education mandate requiring a lower standard of evidence in campus sexual harassment proceedings.

"2011 National Business Ethics Survey," Ethics Resource Center, 2012, www.ethics.org/nbes.
An employee survey shows ethical behavior in the workplace improves as the economy declines.

Berger Parker, Kristin H., "Ambient Harassment Under Title VII: Reconsidering the Workplace Environment," *Northwestern University Law Review*, 2008, www.law.northwestern.edu/lawreview/v102/n2/945/LR102n2BergerParker.pdf.
Some courts have been reluctant to find employers liable for hostile-environment sexual harassment that doesn't target a particular victim.

Cohen, Alexander J. S., "An Empirical Study of Employment Arbitration: Case Outcomes and Processes," *Journal of Empirical Legal Studies*, March 2011, http://onlinelibrary.wiley.com/doi/10.1111/j.1740-1461.2010.01200.x/abstract.
Employees win less often and receive smaller damage awards in arbitration than through litigation.

Houle, Jason N., *et al.*, "The Impact of Sexual Harassment on Depressive Symptoms During the Early Occupational Career," *Society and Mental Health*, July 2011, www.asanet.org/images/journals/docs/pdf/smh/Jul11SMHFeature.pdf.
Men and women suffer from long-term depression when they endure continuous sexual harassment early in their careers.

The Next Step:

Additional Articles from Current Periodicals

Lawsuits

Hammack, Laurence, "Va. Tech, Employee Settle Lawsuit Claiming Sexual Harassment," *Roanoke* (Va.) *Times*, Oct. 11, 2011, p. A9, www.roanoke.com/news/roanoke/wb/299532.
A former Virginia Tech employee has settled a lawsuit in which she claimed her supervisor acted as if a five-day training session with her was an "extended date."

Horowitz, Ben, "Teacher Says She Got Boot After Reporting Male Student's Suggestive Comments," *Star-Ledger* (Newark, N.J.), Nov. 22, 2011, p. 13.
A former English teacher at a New Jersey high school who says she was fired for reporting sexually harassing language by a student is suing the board of education and the superintendent.

Rosynsky, Paul, "Former Warriors Employee Files Sexual Harassment Suit Against Monta Ellis," *Contra Costa* (Calif.) *Times*, Dec. 21, 2011, www.thestar.com/sports/basketball/nba/article/1105808–former-employee-files-sexual-harassment-suit-against-monta-ellis-warriors.
The former community relations director for the Golden State Warriors basketball team says a player sexually harassed her for a month.

Military

Brown, Matthew Hay, "Sex Assault Reports Double at Naval Academy," *The Baltimore Sun*, Dec. 28, 2011, p. A2, articles.baltimoresun.com/2011-12-27/news/bs-md-naval-academy-sexual-violence-20111227_1_unwanted-sexual-contact-naval-academy-percentage-of-female-midshipmen.
Officials say more awareness has led to an increase in the reporting of sexual assaults and harassment at the U.S. Naval Academy.

Davidson, Joe, "GAO Faults Pentagon's Will to Prevent Sex Harassment," *The Washington Post*, Nov. 2, 2011, p. B4.
The Government Accountability Office says the Pentagon needs "greater leadership commitment" in creating an environment free from sexual harassment.

Kime, Patricia N., "Group Seeks More Awareness in Wake of 'Don't Ask' Repeal," *Military Times*, July 11, 2011, p. 10.
The Defense Advisory Committee on Women says the military should step up sexual harassment awareness and monitoring after the repeal of "don't ask, don't tell."

Reporting

Healy, Vikki Ortiz, *et al.*, "Sexually Harassed Interns Often Feel All Alone," *Chicago Tribune*, Nov. 25, 2011, p. A1.
Interns seldom report sexual harassment because they feel powerless in the workplace.

Yung, Katherine, and Patricia Montemurri, "Fewer Report Being Harassed," *USA Today*, Nov. 10, 2011, p. B5, www.usatoday.com/money/workplace/story/2011-11-09/sex-harassment-incidents-down-still-prevalent/51144798/1.
Experts say a poor economy makes people less likely to report sexual harassment for fear of being viewed unfavorably by their employers.

Workplace Policies

Bober, Daniel, "Firm Sexual Harassment Policies Benefit Business," *The Miami Herald*, March 11, 2012, www.miamiherald.com/2012/03/11/2688163/firm-sexual-harassment-policies.html.
Strong policies against workplace sexual harassment increase productivity, says a Miami-area psychiatrist.

Haq, Husna, "Two Decades After Anita Hill: How Workplaces Are Handling Sexual Harassment," *The Christian Science Monitor*, Nov. 12, 2011, www.csmonitor.com/USA/Justice/2011/1114/Two-decades-after-Anita-Hill-how-workplaces-are-handling-sexual-harassment.
Twenty years after Anita Hill accused Supreme Court nominee Clarence Thomas of sexual harassment, workplaces have become more vigilant in combating harassment.

Messenger, Brian, "Zanni Enforces New Sexual Harassment Policy," *Eagle Tribune* (North Andover, Mass.), Jan. 29, 2012, p. 9, www.eagletribune.com/local/x1669706454/Zanni-enforces-new-sexual-harassment-policy.
A Massachusetts mayor is enforcing a new sexual harassment policy after an expensive legal battle involving two former city employees.

CITING *CQ RESEARCHER*

Sample formats for citing these reports in a bibliography include the ones listed below. Preferred styles and formats vary, so please check with your instructor or professor.

MLA STYLE

Jost, Kenneth. "Remembering 9/11," CQ Researcher 2 Sept. 2011: 701-732.

APA STYLE

Jost, K. (2011, September 2). Remembering 9/11. *CQ Researcher, 9*, 701-732.

CHICAGO STYLE

Jost, Kenneth. "Remembering 9/11." *CQ Researcher*, September 2, 2011, 701-732.

CQ Researcher

Published by CQ Press, an Imprint of SAGE Publications, Inc.

www.cqresearcher.com

Distracted Driving

Should driver texting and cellphone use be banned?

Drivers have long tried to manage any number of distractions ranging from eating a snack and reading a map to dealing with unruly children in the backseat and putting on makeup. But with the increasing popularity of cellphones and texting, distracted driving has emerged as a central concern of safety experts. Studies indicate that distractions are involved in more than 5,000 traffic fatalities every year. Most states have enacted laws to restrict texting or talking on handheld cellphones, and policymakers face calls for a near-total ban even on hands-free communications devices — including those that are built into the dashboards of new cars and heavily marketed by automakers. But even if more restrictive laws were passed, many motorists would find it hard to set aside the devices they have come to rely upon to make business and personal calls and also to check websites or update their Facebook pages.

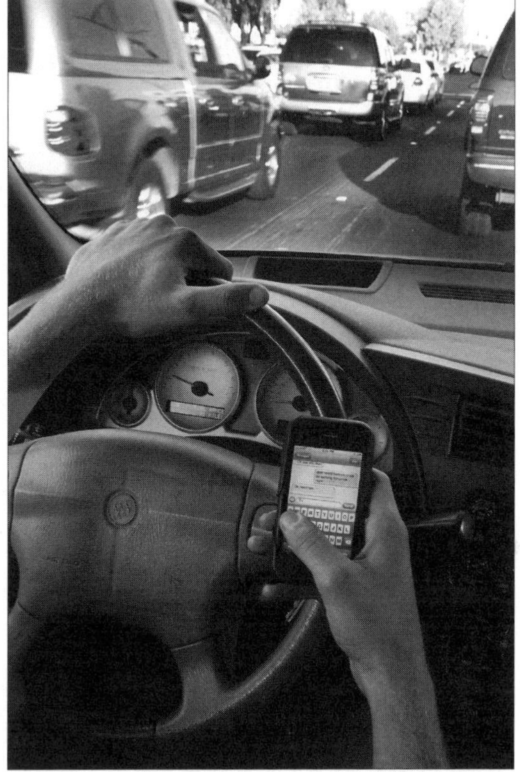

Cellphone-using drivers in the United States under age 20 and ages 30-39 had the highest rates of fatal accidents. More than 5,000 people were killed and nearly half a million injured in crashes involving distracted driving in 2009, the most recent data available.

INSIDE THIS REPORT

THE ISSUES 403
BACKGROUND 410
CHRONOLOGY 411
CURRENT SITUATION 415
AT ISSUE........................417
OUTLOOK 419
BIBLIOGRAPHY 422
THE NEXT STEP 423

CQ Researcher • May 4, 2012 • www.cqresearcher.com
Volume 22, Number 17 • Pages 401-424

Los Angeles | London | New Delhi
Singapore | Washington DC

RECIPIENT OF SOCIETY OF PROFESSIONAL JOURNALISTS AWARD FOR EXCELLENCE ◆ AMERICAN BAR ASSOCIATION SILVER GAVEL AWARD

DISTRACTED DRIVING

THE ISSUES

403 • Should drivers be banned from talking on cellphones?
• Should drivers be banned from texting?
• Are drivers' distractions getting worse?

BACKGROUND

410 **Calling While Driving**
Scientists developed the technology in the 1940s.

412 **Growing Concerns**
Mobile phone-safety issues were raised as early as the 1960s.

413 **New Distraction**
In 2008, Ford introduced a computer built into the dashboard that gave drivers access to the Web.

CURRENT SITUATION

415 **Action in Chapel Hill**
It passes nation's toughest cellphone restrictions.

416 **Action in Washington**
The National Transportation Safety Board weighs in.

418 **Action in the States**
Midwestern states are eyeing cellphone bans.

OUTLOOK

419 **Enter Google**
It's developing cars that drive themselves.

SIDEBARS AND GRAPHICS

404 **Many States Ban Driver Texting and Cellphone Use**
Ten states and Washington, D.C., ban hand-held phones.

405 **Distracted Drivers Under 20 Had Top Fatality Rate**
Drivers ages 30-39 were most distracted by cellphones.

407 **Fatalities Linked to Distracted Driving Rose**
Rate rose from 10 percent in 2005 to 16 percent in 2009.

408 **Eating/Drinking Top List of Distracting Behaviors**
Cellphone use is also widespread.

411 **Chronology**
Key events since 1903.

412 **Distracted Drivers Take Astonishing Risks**
"If I wasn't there, I wouldn't have believed it."

414 **Apps Put Barriers Between Drivers and Phones**
But overcoming "addiction" to texting is difficult.

417 **At Issue**
Are integrated devices safer than using hand-held devices while driving?

FOR FURTHER RESEARCH

421 **For More Information**
Organizations to contact.

422 **Bibliography**
Selected sources used.

423 **The Next Step**
Additional articles.

423 **Citing *CQ Researcher***
Sample bibliography formats.

Cover: Getty Images/*The Christian Science Monitor*/Tony Avelar

CQ Researcher

May 4, 2012
Volume 22, Number 17

MANAGING EDITOR: Thomas J. Billitteri
tjb@cqpress.com

ASSISTANT MANAGING EDITOR: Kathy Koch
kkoch@cqpress.com

CONTRIBUTING EDITOR: Thomas J. Colin
tcolin@cqpress.com

ASSOCIATE EDITOR: Kenneth Jost

STAFF WRITER: Marcia Clemmitt

CONTRIBUTING WRITERS: Peter Katel, Barbara Mantel, Jennifer Weeks

DESIGN/PRODUCTION EDITOR: Olu B. Davis

ASSISTANT EDITOR: Darrell Dela Rosa

FACT CHECKER: Michelle Harris

Los Angeles | London | New Delhi
Singapore | Washington DC

An Imprint of SAGE Publications, Inc.

VICE PRESIDENT AND EDITORIAL DIRECTOR, HIGHER EDUCATION GROUP:
Michele Sordi

DIRECTOR, ONLINE PUBLISHING:
Todd Baldwin

CQ Researcher (ISSN 1056-2036) is printed on acid-free paper. Published weekly, except: (March wk. 5) (May wk. 4) (July wk. 1) (Aug. wks. 3, 4) (Nov. wk. 4) and (Dec. wks. 3, 4). Published by SAGE Publications, Inc., 2455 Teller Rd., Thousand Oaks, CA 91320. Annual full-service subscriptions start at $1,054. For pricing, call 1-800-834-9020. To purchase a *CQ Researcher* report in print or electronic format (PDF), visit www.cqpress.com or call 866-427-7737. Single reports start at $15. Bulk purchase discounts and electronic-rights licensing are also available. Periodicals postage paid at Thousand Oaks, California, and at additional mailing offices. POSTMASTER: Send address changes to *CQ Researcher*, 2300 N St., N.W., Suite 800, Washington, DC 20037.

Distracted Driving

BY DAVID HOSANSKY

THE ISSUES

Yvonne Mondragon of Longmont, Colo., was driving home from work one evening when she glanced down to read a message that a friend had just sent her. When she looked back at the road, she saw that traffic had stopped — and there was no time to brake.

So she swerved into the next lane without looking and then onto the shoulder. Fortunately, there was no car in her way. Afterwards, Mondragon sat for several minutes in her car, shaking.

Now, she tucks her phone inside her purse when she gets behind the wheel.

"That really changed things for me," she says. "Sometimes I want to look at my phone, but then I remember that moment."

Mondragon is hardly alone when it comes to distracted driving. But many are unable to stop their potentially lethal behavior, even after near accidents.

The National Highway Traffic Safety Administration (NHTSA) concluded that 5,474 people were killed in the United States in accidents involving distracted driving in 2009, the latest year for which it has such figures. That represents 16 percent of all U.S. traffic fatalities — up from 10 percent from four years earlier. In addition, 448,000 people were injured in accidents involving a distracted driver. [1]

Teen drivers appear to be especially susceptible to distraction, with the NHTSA estimating that 16 percent of all drivers younger than 20 involved in fatal crashes were believed to be distracted — the highest proportion of any age group.

FocusDriven

Taylor Sauer, 18, knew the danger of texting and driving. Moments before the Utah State University student slammed into a tanker truck at 80 mph, dying instantly, she texted to a friend: "I can't discuss this now. Driving and Facebooking is not safe! Haha."

Distracted driving can be traced almost to the dawn of automobiles, and these days it can take many forms, from adjusting the radio and looking at a map to daydreaming or even shaving or putting on makeup. But it is the widespread and apparently growing use of cellphones while driving that has galvanized safety advocates and policymakers, many of whom support laws prohibiting texting or, in some cases, even talking on a cellphone while behind the wheel.

NHTSA last year estimated that about 120,000 drivers were sending text messages or physically manipulating phones at any given time during the day, up 50 percent from 2009. And the number of drivers talking on cellphones at any one time was even higher: an estimated 660,000. [2]

Although experts are uncertain about the extent to which cellphone use distracts drivers, research suggests that talking on a phone can be as impairing as having a blood alcohol concentration at the legal limit. Texting is even more distracting.

The National Transportation Safety Board (NTSB) last year called for a ban on the use of both handheld and hands-free devices by drivers, contending that years of research had clearly demonstrated motorists could not use a cellphone and focus on the road at the same time.

"Our nation is at a deadly intersection of mobility and connectivity," NTSB chairwoman Deborah Hersman said in March. "We don't need another decade of investigations and recommendations. . . . It's clear that we need to act now. Too much is at stake." [3]

Although the board lacks the authority to impose a ban, the issue has generated debate across the nation. Over the last decade, most states have called for at least some restrictions on handheld electronic devices, ranging from prohibiting novice drivers from using cellphones to banning all drivers from calling or texting except in emergencies. Now safety advocates, emboldened by the NTSB's recommendation, are pressing to expand the prohibitions to hands-free devices.

"Whether it's hands-free or handheld doesn't matter: These devices are a distraction," says Rob Reynolds, executive director of Focus Driven, a national advocacy group that favors a ban on cellphone use by motorists. Reynolds, whose 16-year-old daughter was killed in an accident with a distracted driver, adds: "They're an im-

Many States Ban Driver Texting, Cellphone Use

Although lawmakers at the federal, state and local level are examining a wide variety of issues related to driver distraction, the most common concern is cellphones and other technology in the car. Ten states and the District of Columbia have banned hand-held phone use by all drivers. Legislatures in other states have prohibited cellphone use by younger drivers and school bus drivers. More than 220 million people in the United States subscribe to wireless services, and up to 80 percent of those subscribers use their phones while driving.

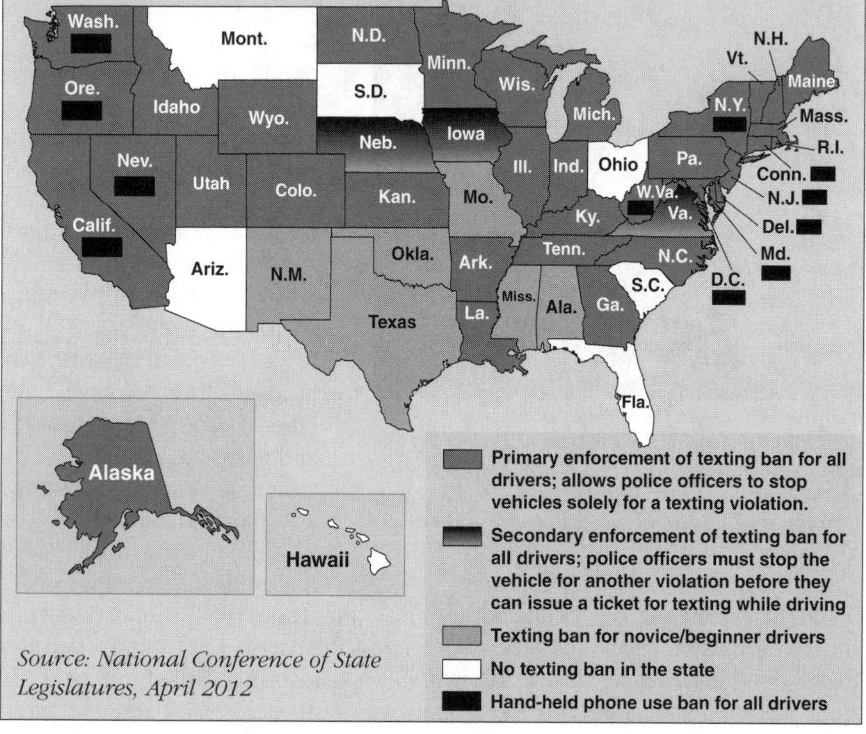

Source: National Conference of State Legislatures, April 2012

pairment while they're being used, and that's what's causing accidents and what's causing people to die."

But business executives who rely on their phones while behind the wheel say they can safely drive while talking, especially if they are using a hands-free device.

"We use Bluetooth, which means all I have to do is press one button on my earpiece and I can talk," says Dave Cotton, owner of AdvantaClean, a Huntersville, N.C.-based disaster-restoration and cleaning business that could be affected by a new local ordinance banning motorist use of virtually all portable electronic devices. "Don't take away my earpiece because someone says I can't drive at the same time."

Many policymakers also are reluctant to impose restrictions on cellphone use. Republican Texas Gov. Rick Perry vetoed a bill in 2011 that would have curbed texting while driving, calling it "a government effort to micromanage the behavior of adults." [4]

Despite concerns that distracted behavior is increasing, the overall accident rate in the United States has dropped in recent years, with total fatalities declining from 43,510 in 2005 to 32,885 in 2010. [5] While there are many possible reasons for the decline, including improved road engineering and automotive design, including safety features such as air bags, some experts wonder if cellphones are supplanting older distractions instead of creating new ones.

"The reality is that distracted driving has been with us since we started driving cars," says Russ Rader, spokesman for the Insurance Institute for Highway Safety, an organization funded by auto insurers and associations that conducts research into safety issues. "We keep inventing new ways of being distracted. It could be that cellphones are just replacement distractions."

Researchers who study distracted driving, however, worry that cellphones are especially dangerous because their use is so widespread and because they impose particularly demanding mental tasks on a driver.

"There are all kinds of distractions, but they're not all equally impairing," says David Strayer, a psychologist at the University of Utah who uses driving simulators and other tools to study the impact of distractions on motorists. "If you're passively listening to a radio or a book on tape, that doesn't increase your crash risk. If you've got another adult in the car, they will help out a driver by saying, 'Hey, here's the exit or look out for this hazard,' " and they'll stop talking when driving becomes difficult.

"But if you're talking on a cellphone and actively involved in generating speech, that is pretty impairing. Once you get to an interesting conversation, the brain can't process all the details in the driving environment."

And the distractions don't stop with cellphones. Carmakers are adding new technologies to the dashboard, such as Web browsers and GPS units. Carmakers say that such technologies are designed very carefully for safety, but safety advocates worry that they are creating even more hazardous driving conditions.

"The cautionary thing I will say about these systems is they are not safety devices," says Reynolds. "They have nothing to do with the safety of the car." They have nothing to do with operation of the car. They are purely entertainment devices."

Some psychologists liken the desire to constantly check messages or call friends to an addiction.

"This technology is socially addicting and maybe even addicting in the same way that gambling is addicting," Strayer says.

Experts say it will take a combination of laws and enforcement, more driver education and possibly new technology — including call-blocking programs and high-tech safety features in cars — to reduce the threat of using cellphones while driving.

As policymakers consider how to keep the roads safe from distracted drivers, here are some issues being considered:

Drivers Under 20 Had Top Fatality Rate

The age group with the greatest proportion of distracted drivers in fatal crashes (16 percent) was the under-20 group, followed by the 20-29 group (13 percent). Among drivers distracted by cellphones, the 30-39 age group had the highest proportion of fatal crashes (24 percent), followed by the under-20 group.

Driver Age and Cellphone Use in Distracted Driving Fatalities, 2009

	Total Drivers	Distracted Drivers		Drivers with Cellphone	
Total	45,230	5,084	11%	1,006	20%
Age Group					
Under 20	3,967	619	16%	138	22%
20-29	10,719	1,378	13%	293	21%
30-39	7,633	832	11%	196	24%
40-49	7,930	811	10%	161	20%
50-59	6,559	631	10%	124	20%
60-69	3,968	367	9%	56	15%
70+	3,778	408	11%	37	9%

Source: National Highway Traffic Safety Administration, "Traffic Safety Facts," September 2010.

Should drivers be banned from talking on cellphones?

Those who favor banning motorists' phone conversations say the issue comes down to the basic priority of keeping people safe.

"Unfortunately, cell phones cause a real distraction — a distraction we can't afford on our roadways," said Democratic West Virginia Gov. Earl Ray Tomblin as he signed legislation banning motorists from talking on cellphones or texting except in emergencies. [6]

Opponents of cellphone bans, however, say they are concerned about the government telling drivers what they can and cannot do, especially given the amount of business that people feel they must conduct behind the wheel in an increasingly fast-paced society.

"I'm on the phone from when I leave the Capitol to when I get home, and that's a two-hour drive," said Tad Jones, who, as majority floor leader in the Oklahoma House, worked to block cellphone legislation in 2009. "A lot of people who travel are used to using the phone." [7]

Extensive research over the past two decades indicates cellphone use is a significant contributor to highway accidents and deaths nationwide. Some studies also indicate that using hands-free phones is not significantly safer than hand-held phones.

Experts in psychology and sociology who study the issue say that talking on a cellphone while driving is far more distracting than talking with an adult passenger because it consumes additional cognitive resources, including creating a mental picture of the person on the other end of the conversation. Although some people may think they can safely talk and drive, researchers who observe people in driving simulators as well as in actual cars on the road find that a cellphone conversation will invariably intrude on a driver's attentiveness.

"We haven't found anybody who is not negatively affected," says Clifford Nass, a professor of communication at Stanford University who studies multitasking. "The research is unequivocal and clear. When the person you're talking with is not physically present, you use brain resources to essentially create a mental picture of the person, and that takes cognitive capacity away from other tasks."

This "brain drain" comes as little surprise to most drivers. A 2011 survey by the AAA Foundation for Traffic Safety found that 71 percent of respondents considered it unacceptable for drivers to hold and talk on their cellphones, and 58 percent considered themselves seriously threatened by other cellphone-using drivers.

At the same time, however, two-thirds of the survey respondents admitted to talking on a cellphone recently while behind the wheel. [8]

Part of the reason has to do with human psychology: People tend to believe they can multitask safely even if others cannot.

"People who support laws that would outlaw the use of cellphones are basically wanting other people to be not allowed to use cellphones," says Strayer of the University of Utah. "It turns out one of the byproducts of talking on a cellphone is you tend to be blind to your own impairments."

textingndriving.com

Safety officials have estimated that 120,000 U.S. drivers are sending text messages at any one time during the day and that 660,000 are talking on cellphones. Research suggests that talking on a phone while driving can be as impairing as being legally drunk. Texting is even more distracting.

The impact of cellphones on accidents is uncertain. Many states do not record whether an accident involved cellphone use. Even if they do, a police officer might not differentiate between talking on a cellphone or texting.

Studies using driving simulators have indicated that drivers using cellphones are up to four times more likely to cause an accident as other drivers and are as impaired as someone with a .08 blood alcohol level — generally the level of legal intoxication. Other research, using cameras that record drivers on the road, concludes that the crash risk may be about 30 percent greater than non-distracted driving — and that the risk increases substantially while the driver is dialing a cellphone.

Beginning with New York in 2001, 10 states, plus the District of Columbia and some other cities, have prohibited hand-held cellphones.

Additional states restrict novice drivers from talking on cellphones. But many legislators oppose a blanket ban on driver use of cellphones, given that so many of their constituents rely on them.

"It's a balancing act with personal freedoms and doing your business, and weighing that with traffic safety," says Anne Teigen, senior policy analyst with the National Conference of State Legislatures. "With some legislators, it's the slippery slope argument. Next thing you know, you're not allowed to have kids in the back seat anymore."

Experts caution that laws can have limited effects on stopping drivers from using cellphones unless the laws are vigorously enforced. In New York City, for example, an informal 2009 survey by *The New York Times* study found that cab drivers routinely disregarded a prohibition on using cellphones while driving. And a 2010 study by the Highway Loss Data Institute, which is sponsored by the automobile insurance industry, found that cellphone bans in four jurisdictions did not reduce accident rates. [9]

On the other hand, California's ban on hand-held cellphones substantially improved road safety and cut cellphone-related traffic fatalities by almost half, according to the University of California, Berkeley. [10]

Safety advocates say it can take years for laws to change behavior, and they must be supported by vigorous enforcement and public information campaigns.

"Do people generally drive 20 mph over the speed limit?" asks Nicholas Ashford, director of the Technology and Law Program at the Massachusetts Institute of Technology. "No, because there are consequences for doing so. It's a question of enforcement."

The U.S. Department of Transportation has waded into the debate, approving regulations that took effect early this year prohibiting interstate bus and truck drivers from talking on hand-held cellphones while driving. The department, which doesn't regulate passenger vehicles, acted after several major truck accidents. In 2008, three people were killed and 15 injured when a tractor-trailer crashed into a line of stopped traffic in eastern Missouri. The trucker admitted to being distracted by a cellphone. [11]

"When drivers of large trucks, buses and hazardous materials take their eyes off the road for even a few seconds, the outcome can be deadly," said Transportation Secretary Ray LaHood in announcing the ban. "I hope that this rule will save lives by helping commercial drivers stay laser-focused on safety at all times." [12]

But neither LaHood nor state lawmakers have taken on the potentially contentious issue of restricting hands-free devices for all drivers. Although research indicates that such devices may be as distracting as hand-held cellphones, only one jurisdiction in the country — Chapel Hill, N.C. — has such a restriction.

"Part of the challenge is that people from citizens through legislators don't necessarily appreciate the cognitive risk that remains with hands-free devices," says Justin McNaull, director of state relations at the AAA Foundation. "There's not the same degree of public support for that as for a hands-held ban."

Should drivers be banned from texting?

In the last minutes of her life, Taylor Sauer, 18, showed that she knew the dangers of texting while driving-even if she was unable to stop.

As the Utah State University student was driving late at night on Jan. 12, 2012, along Interstate 84 to see her family in Idaho, she passed the time texting — sending one about every 90 seconds. Her final message, sent to a friend on Facebook during an exchange about the Denver Broncos: "I can't discuss this now. Driving and Facebooking is not safe! Haha."

Just seconds later, as she drove more than 80 mph, she slammed into a tanker truck that was climbing a hill at 15 mph. Sauer died instantly. An investigation indicated that she had not applied the brakes. "I think she was probably [texting] to stay awake, she was probably tired," said her father. "But that's not a reason to do it, and the kids think they're invincible. To them, [texting] is not distracting; they're so proficient at texting that they don't feel it's distracted driving." [13]

At the time of Sauer's death, Idaho was one of just 15 states that did not prohibit texting by drivers. Although state lawmakers had rejected previous attempts at curbing the activity, publicity over Sauer's case and personal appeals to legislators by her parents helped lead to a new Idaho law imposing an $85 fine on texting while driving.

Safety experts say that texting by motorists is far more dangerous even than talking on a cellphone. That is because drivers not only have the cognitive distraction of communicating with someone but also must take their hands off the wheel and their eyes off the road. "Clearly, if there's a perfect storm with distraction, it's texting," says Clarence Ditlow, executive director of the Center for Auto Safety, which supports restrictions of cellphone use behind the wheel. "Your hands and eyes are off the road, and it's a very intense mind distraction as well."

Indeed, a 2009 study by the Virginia Tech Transportation Institute that focused on drivers of larger vehicles and trucks concluded that texting increased the risk of a crash by 23 times compared with non-distracted driving. Shockingly, texting drivers took their eyes off the road for each text an average of 4.6 seconds — which, at 55 mph, means they were driving the length of a football field without looking. [14]

Given such research, even some organizations that have a neutral position on cellphone restrictions say texting should be banned.

"Texting is completely incompatible with safe driving," says John Walls, vice president of public affairs for CTIA, an association of wireless companies. "We support text-messaging bans for all drivers."

But texting remains prevalent among drivers and may even be on the rise. A 2010 study, for example, found that 25 percent of New Jersey voters admitted sending a text while driving, compared with 15 percent just two years earlier. While young drivers ranked among the worst offenders, the increase since 2008 was largely due to middle-aged drivers. [15]

Safety officials warn that texting bans can be extremely difficult to enforce, partly because it is difficult to spot drivers who are texting.

"How do you know the person was texting and not dialing a number?" asked Alberto Gutier, director of the Arizona Governor's Office of Highway Safety. "We need to go after distracted driving, but distracted driving can be so many things. I see people doing all kinds of stupid things. . . . People reading their mail. I see people putting in contact lenses." [16]

Experts also are divided over whether bans are effective in preventing drivers from texting or in reducing crashes.

A 2010 study by the Highway Loss Data Institute indicated that texting bans fail to make roads safer. In fact, the study concluded that states that enacted texting bans actually experienced a slight increase in insurance claims associated with accidents,

Fatalities Linked to Distracted Driving Rose

The number of crashes and fatalities linked to distracted driving rose from 10 percent in 2005 to 16 percent in 2009. More than 5,400 fatalities occurred in the nearly 4,900 crashes in 2009 linked to distracted driving.

Crashes Involving Distracted Driving, 2005-2009

	Overall Crashes in U.S.		Crashes Involving Distraction		
	Crashes	Fatalities	Crashes	Fatalities	Injuries
2005	39,252	43,510	4,026 (10%)	4,472 (10%)	604,000
2006	38,648	42,708	5,245 (14%)	5,836 (14%)	503,000
2007	37,435	41,259	5,329 (14%)	5,917 (14%)	448,000
2008	34,172	37,423	5,307 (16%)	5,838 (16%)	466,000
2009	30,797	33,808	4,898 (16%)	5,474 (16%)	448,000

Source: National Highway Traffic Safety Administration, "Traffic Safety Facts," September 2010.

Eating/Drinking Top List of Distracting Behaviors

Most adults who drive regularly engage in a wide range of distracting behaviors, with eating and drinking by far the most prevalent, according to a recent poll. Large numbers of drivers also admitted to inattentive driving habits, such as driving after having two or more drinks or driving while feeling sleepy and even briefly dozing off.

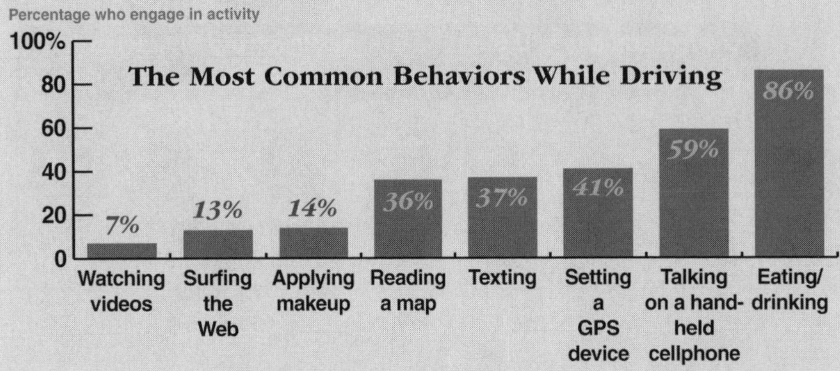

Source: Harris Interactive/HealthDay, Nov. 30, 2011, www.harrisinteractive.com/NewsRoom/HarrisPolls.aspx

possibly because drivers were trying to conceal the activity by holding their cellphones lower down — thereby taking their eyes off the road for even longer periods. [17]

Other studies have come to different conclusions. In 2011, the U.S. Department of Transportation announced that texting behind the wheel dropped by almost three-quarters in Hartford, Conn., and Syracuse, N.Y., after pilot programs in the two cities combined strict enforcement of cellphone and texting laws with high-profile public education campaigns. [18]

Safety experts note that it took decades of enforcement and public education before large number of motorists complied with drunken-driving and mandatory seat belt laws.

"These things can take years," says Reynolds of FocusDriven. "In the short term, it's very easy to say that it's not moving the needle immediately, so let's abandon it. But as with any safety campaign, if you have education and you have laws and you have enforcement, then it does very well."

As of April 2012, three-quarters of the states prohibited drivers from texting on hand-held devices. The penalty in most cases is a fine, but in Utah texting drivers face misdemeanor charges, and they could be treated as harshly as drunken drivers and sent to prison after a fatal accident. [19]

Yet lawmakers in some states remain reluctant to prohibit texting while driving. The South Dakota legislature this year failed to advance a texting ban amid concerns about singling out texting when drivers experience other distractions as well.

"If a bill was brought forward to prohibit texting and cellphone and makeup and eating and etc., I'd be for it," said Rep. Gene Abdallah, R-Sioux Falls. [20]

Secretary LaHood and some members of Congress would like the federal government to expand the ban on trucker and bus driver texting and place a national ban on texting on handheld devices.

"The dangers posed by texting while driving are the same whether you're behind the wheel of an 18-wheeler or a four-door sedan," said Sen. Charles Schumer, D-N.Y. [21]

Schumer in 2009 co-sponsored legislation that would have slashed federal highway funds for states that refuse to enact texting bans. Congress, however, declined to take action.

Are drivers' distractions getting worse?

Drivers who want to update their Facebook pages or make an online restaurant reservation no longer need their smartphone or laptop. Automakers are integrating the technology into the dashboards of new cars.

For several years, new models have boasted electronic gadgets, such as GPS devices and video screens that display information such as the fuel level and temperature. But automakers now are beginning to roll out "connected cars" enabling motorists to tweet, check stock prices, download music and perform other online tasks while driving.

The new options, which use new types of chips that are smaller and consume less energy, represent an enormous marketing opportunity for auto makers and their suppliers.

"We have always looked at the PC market with envy," said Sachin Lawande, chief technology officer at Harman, a maker of high-end car-audio equipment. "They've always had these great chips we could not use, but now that's changing." [22]

But safety advocates say the dashboard technologies are creating dangerous new distractions.

"It's an outrageous application of technology to be putting more distractions into the car," says MIT's Ashford. "When we all know from either direct experience or statistics how dangerous cellphones are to drivers, why in hell's name would you ever place an additional distraction in the cabin of a car? It's simply unjustified profiteering at the price of public safety."

Automakers, however, contend that their systems will actually reduce the risks of distracted driving. Unlike cellphones and other portable electronic devices, they argue, dashboard technology is specifically designed for drivers and therefore contains critical safety features.

"When we're designing technology, it's designed from the very beginning to be used in one environment, and that's the driving environment," says Wade Newton, a spokesman for the Alliance of Automobile Manufacturers. "We design things to allow consumers to do what they're going to do anyway, but to make sure they do it as safely as possible."

For example, Newton says, devices that are built into cars offer hands-free use. In addition, they are designed for very simple operation — as opposed to smartphones and other electronic devices that may have complex controls — and wait on the operator instead of reverting to a previous screen if there is a delay in inputting new data. The technology can also be designed to reduce the number of buttons to manipulate. A driver, for instance, may be able to look at a convenient place on the dashboard to see the identity of an incoming caller and then both accept that call and turn down the radio with a single button.

Certain features, such as a Web browser in newer Mercedes-Benz models, cannot be activated while the car is in motion.

Some drivers say they appreciate the new technology, both because of the convenience it offers and the attention to safety.

"I like the way it looks," said Jamie Kaye Walters, a television production company executive who recently bought a 2012 Ford with a voice-activated SYNC system. "It's a little bit distracting, but it kind of allows me to do work while I am driving without having to look down at my phone. I can do the whole thing with voice activation." [23]

The automakers say that drivers will remain connected regardless of whether cars offer such features. With new dashboard technology, the connectivity can be accomplished as safely as possible.

"It isn't possible to stop it," said Michael Sprague, marketing director at Kia Motors America. "Consumers are going to continue to drive with phones, and all we can do as a manufacturer is to provide what the consumers are asking for and make it as safe as possible." [24]

Indeed, there are cases of drivers who took their laptops or other devices into their vehicles, sometimes with disastrous results. A driver in Alaska in 2003 was so focused on watching a movie on a video monitor perched on his dashboard that he killed two motorists. [25]

Some auto executives also take issue with the assertion that new forms of hands-free technology will necessarily endanger motorists. Louis Tijerina, a senior technical specialist with Ford's Advanced Engineering Department, asked why safety advocates might assume that it is more dangerous to use

The Faces of Distracted Driving

Alison Holden, Washington, D.C.
The single mom was driving to work on April 27, 2009, when a driver sending a text message rear-ended her vehicle at a stoplight. She suffered traumatic brain injury.

Alex Brown, 17, Wellman, Texas
Brown was killed Nov. 10, 2009, when she crashed her truck on a rural road while on the way to school. She was texting at the time of the crash.

Xzavier Davis-Bilbo, 7, Milwaukee, Wis.
Then 5-year-old Xzavier was crossing the street near his home on Oct. 10, 2010, when he was struck by a young woman who was texting while driving. Xzavier, who had dreamt of becoming a football player, was paralyzed from the diaphragm down.

Linda Doyle, 61, Oklahoma City
Doyle was killed Sept. 3, 2008, when a young driver talking on a cellphone ran a red light and smashed into her vehicle.

Casey Feldman, 21, Ocean City, N.J.
Feldman was struck and killed by a distracted driver July 17, 2009, as she crossed the street.

Source/Credit: National Highway Traffic Safety Administration

a voice-controlled navigation system than trying to study traditional maps "or simply driving around lost and confused." [26]

But safety experts worry that the ready availability of the dashboard features may further distract drivers no matter how carefully they are designed.

"By making it easier for people to engage in these behaviors, you're inviting them to do it, you're encouraging them," says McNaull of the AAA Foundation.

Some experts say that our lives have become so oriented around the distractions of social media and the Internet that it has become more difficult than ever for drivers to focus on driving.

"What we're seeing in younger drivers is what we call a desire for distraction," says Stanford's Nass. "We may have to rethink the distraction issue to now ask the question: 'How can we help drivers who want to be distracted not to be? How can you design interfaces that lure them back to the road?' "

For example, he says, if a driver is staring at the instrument panel, the word "CAR" can pop up if there is an approaching vehicle. Or a message can occasionally flash in the windshield to provide enough stimulation to keep a driver's attention on the road without being overly distracting.

"You provide the driver with things that seem like distractions, but aren't," Nass explains. ■

BACKGROUND

Calling While Driving

Distracted driving has been a concern since at least the first decade of the 20th century, when the invention of windshield wipers spurred concerns that the hypnotic movement would make it difficult for motorists to concentrate. [27] A generation later, the growing popularity of car radios raised new concerns. Policymakers in Massachusetts and St. Louis briefly weighed efforts to make them illegal because they could be mentally distracting as well as contribute to "one-arm driving."

The emergence of fast food in the 1950s made it easier to eat behind the wheel. At the same time, companies began developing more complex audio systems. Early attempts by Chrysler and RCA to put phonographs into cars failed, but audio companies successfully sold four-track and then eight-track tapes to a generation of drivers. By the 1970s, cassette tapes were taking hold, and motorists found themselves sorting through stacks of tapes and sometimes trying to fast forward or rewind to find a favorite song while cruising down the highway. [28]

Such distractions, however, were overshadowed by the emerging popularity of mobile phones.

Phoning from a car was an early dream of inventors. In the first decade of the 20th century, an early experimenter in wireless telephony named Archie Fredrick Collins unsuccessfully tried to invent a mobile telephone for automobiles. But other inventors pursued the idea. [29]

In the 1940s, engineers at Bell Labs developed the transmitters and other technology needed for in-car calls. On June 17, 1946, a motorist in St. Louis used a handset from under his car's dashboard to place the first mobile telephone call — although the phone, described as a radio telephone, was far more primitive than later car phones. Truckers and other professional drivers used such devices for the next couple of decades, but the limitations were so severe that a metropolitan area might be serviced by just a single transmitter on a central tower, and no more than three people could make a call at any one time. [30]

Car phones became more convenient after 1962, with the emergence of automatically switched wireless networks. But within a couple of decades, the cumbersome, car-mounted devices would face a mortal threat from an en-

Continued on p. 412

AutoBlog.com

Many new vehicles have dashboard-equipped communication systems, including Ford's voice-activated SYNC, shown above. Automakers say drivers will remain connected to the Web regardless of whether cars offer such features, and that new dashboard technology will make the connectivity as safe as possible. But safety experts worry that the ready availability of the dashboard features may further distract drivers.

Chronology

1900s-1940s

Safety advocates worry that new devices added to cars, such as windshield wipers and radios, could distract drivers.

1903
Windshield wiper is patented.

1930s
Officials in Massachusetts and St. Louis consider banning car radios.

1940s-50s

Early radiophones enable drivers to make the first calls from behind the wheel. Engineers begin laying the groundwork for cellphone technology.

1946
Motorists use radio telephones.

1947
Cellphones are conceptualized by a Bell Lab researcher.

1950s-1970s

Rise of fast food and cellphones draws warnings about driver distractions.

Early 1960s
Motorola cellphone engineer Martin Cooper recommends a lock to prevent drivers from using phones.

1970
Bell Labs develops system allowing calls to continue even if the phone moves through several cell areas.

1977
AT&T builds the first cellular network, in Chicago.

1980s-1990s

Large-scale commercial cellphone service is launched. Research begins to warn about the risks of using cellphones.

1983
An Ameritech executive in a car in Chicago calls a great grandson of telephone inventor Alexander Graham Bell in Germany, marking the beginning of large-scale cellphone service.

1984
AAA advises motorists to park before using cellphones.

1991
Research shows that cellphone use can hinder the reactions of motorists, especially older drivers. . . . Mitsubishi warns customers not to use cellphones while driving.

Feb. 13, 1997
New England Journal of Medicine reports that collisions are four times more likely among drivers on the phone.

2000-Present

Policymakers take steps to rein in cellphone use by drivers.

2000
Wireless industry association runs ad campaign highlighting danger of distracted driving and urging use of hands-free devices.

2001
California lawmakers reject ban on hand-held cellphones by drivers; wireless industry opposes bill. . . . Gov. George Pataki, R-N.Y., signs first legislation in country prohibiting drivers from using hand-held cellphones except in emergencies.

2003
Verizon Wireless switches positions and supports California legislation to ban drivers from using cellphones.

May 11, 2007
Washington becomes first state to ban texting while driving. Dozens of states enact similar bans over next several years.

Sept. 12, 2008
Concerns about texting crystallize after a California commuter train driven by a texting engineer crashes and kills 25 people.

2008
Ford develops dashboard equipped with Internet access and hands-free calling, ushering in an era of new automotive technology.

Sept. 30, 2009
President Obama signs executive order banning federal employees from texting and driving.

Feb. 26, 2010
Transportation Secretary Ray LaHood announces that truck and bus drivers will be banned from texting behind the wheel.

Nov. 23, 2011
LaHood announces new regulations banning truck and bus drivers from talking on hand-held cellphones. . . . Dec. 13, 2011: National Transportation Safety Board calls for nationwide ban on drivers using portable electronic devices, including hands-free devices.

March 26, 2012
Town Council in Chapel Hill, N.C., votes 5-4 to ban motorists from using hand-held or hands-free electronic devices, but state's attorney general says the town lacks the authority to enforce such a law.

Distracted Drivers Take Astonishing Risks

One motorist was feeding a macaw — perched on the steering wheel.

Most parents, if they are honest, can tell some pretty startling tales on themselves — and the bad child-care decisions they have made on occasion. And then there's the busy mom in Dayton, Ohio. She was not just breast-feeding her baby, whom she had pushed against the steering wheel. She was also talking on a hand-held cellphone — all the while driving on rain-slick roads. [1]

A passing motorist called police, who tracked the woman down. They could not ticket her for a driving infraction, since they had not seen it. But after the woman admitted she had been breast-feeding, she was charged with child endangerment.

While much of the concern around distracted driving has focused on cellphones and texting, motorists engage in many other distracting activities. Among the most common that are cited by safety-oriented websites:

- Adjusting the car stereo
- Reading a map, book or newspaper
- Putting on makeup
- Shaving
- Combing or brushing hair
- Reaching for an object on the floor, backseat or elsewhere
- Looking at something on the side of the road
- Eating, drinking or smoking
- Talking to children in the backseat, or passing objects to them.

Experts note that not all these activities are equally distracting.

"There's a huge difference between someone who's eating a banana versus someone who tried to dip sushi in soy sauce and mix it just right with ginger," says Justin McNaull, director of state relations at the AAA Foundation for Traffic Safety. A 2011 poll found that most adults who drive regularly admit to engaging in distracting behaviors, including 86 percent of Americans who say they eat and drink while driving. Large numbers of respondents also admitted to inattentive driving habits, such as driving after having two or more drinks or driving while feeling sleepy and even briefly dozing off.

"The number of drivers who engage in potentially dangerous, in some cases extremely dangerous, behaviors while driving is terrifyingly high," said Humphrey Taylor, chairman of The Harris Poll. "While we have some information on how dangerous some of these behaviors are . . . we can only speculate as to the numbers of accidents and deaths that are caused by the many millions of people who drive while setting their GPS, eating or drinking, surfing the Internet, watching videos, combing their hair, reading or applying makeup." [2]

In addition to the common types of distracting behavior, some are, simply, mind-boggling. *Washington Post* columnist Marc Fisher wrote about three motorists on I-95 driving at about

Continued from p. 410

tirely new technology: handheld phones that relied on cellular networks.

The early cellphones were limited, however, in that they could not be moved very far without dropping the call because each coverage area was served by one base station, and there was no continuity of service if a phone moved through different cell areas.

In 1970, however, Amos E. Joel Jr. of Bell Labs invented an automatic call handoff system that allowed a call to continue uninterrupted even if the phone moved through several cell areas. The technology continued to evolve in the 1990s, as the industry adopted digital transmission, and ever-larger amounts of data could be moved on high-speed networks.

Increasingly, cellphone users — including drivers — could use their devices to access more and more information. The first text message was sent in 1992, and text messaging emerged as a popular way of communicating, especially among young users, by the end of the decade. Around the same time, manufacturers began combining the functions of traditional cellphones with those of a personal digital assistant. These so-called smartphones became hugely popular in the first decade of the 21st century, enabling users to talk on the phone, text, check email, browse the Web or engage in numerous other activities in any place where they had cellphone reception — including most roadways. By the end of 2011, Americans owned an estimated 96 million smartphones. For the first time, the number of wireless subscriber connections (327.6 million) surpassed the nation's population (315.5 million). [31]

Growing Concerns

The early mobile phones, which could be used only by a limited number of truckers and other workers, generated little concern about distracted driving. But when engineers began to work on developing the first portable cellphones, some experts started taking notice.

Martin Cooper, a Motorola engineer who developed the first portable cellphone, spoke frankly of the risks of the new technology to a Michigan state commission in the early 1960s,

65 mph while engaging in unexpected activities. One was engrossed in a novel perched against the top of his steering wheel, a second had rigged a laptop on the dashboard so he could watch a movie and a third kept his thighs pressed against the steering wheel for stability while leaning forward and playing a trumpet. [3]

Patrick Rothfuss

Cellphones and texting are not the only distracting activities by drivers.

Fisher invited readers to submit examples they had witnessed of distracted drivers. Among the more bizarre:

- A man driving at highway speed with a can of beer in one hand and a fried chicken leg in the other
- A driver scratching off lottery tickets
- A woman knitting, steering with her elbows
- A driver holding a cellphone in one hand and taking pictures of other cars with a camera in the other hand while driving at 70 mph
- A driver looking through a camcorder viewfinder videotaping nearby monuments
- A truck driver sharing a bag of sunflower seeds with a blue-and-gold macaw perched on the steering wheel
- A woman putting on pantyhose while driving in rush hour traffic

"As astonishing and frightening as such sights can be on the highway, I feel obliged to report that all three of these fellas [on I-95] were driving fairly well," Fisher wrote. "The swervers and drifters I encountered on this trip were all — every single one of them — deeply engrossed in cell conversations."

— David Hosansky

1 Stacey Garfinkle, "Multitasking Gone Too Far?" *The Washington Post*, March 3, 2009, http://voices.washingtonpost.com/parenting/2009/03/multitasking_gone_too_far.html.

2 Amanda Gardner, "Most U.S. Drivers Engage in 'Distracting Behaviors,'" *USA Today*, Dec. 1, 2011, www.usatoday.com/news/health/story/health/story/2011-12-01/Most-US-drivers-engage-in-distracting-behaviors/51544554/1.

3 Marc Fisher, "Driving While Trumpeting: Car as Living Room," *The Washington Post*, July 18, 2007, http://voices.washingtonpost.com/rawfisher/2007/07/driving_while_trumpeting_car_a.html.

saying common sense dictated that drivers keep their hands on the wheel and their eyes on the road. Decades later, he recalled telling them: "There should be a lock on the dial so that you couldn't dial while driving." [32]

Despite such concerns, the cellphone industry developed into a $150 billion business in the United States partly by marketing to drivers. Cellphones initially were referred to as cellular car telephones, and ads stressed their benefits to motorists.

In 1984, the AAA advised motorists to park before using their cellphones. The AAA Foundation for Traffic Safety followed up by funding a 1991 study warning that cellphone use — especially intense conversations — hindered the reaction of motorists and was especially deleterious to older people.

That same year, the operating instructions for a Mitsubishi car phone advised that drivers "place calls only when the vehicle is stopped." [33] Other cellphone companies adopted similar cautions over the next several years.

Concerns mounted as cellphone use mounted. In 1995, Rochester Institute of Technology researchers concluded that cellphone use increased the risk of traffic accidents. A 1997 study in *The New England Journal of Medicine* showed that collisions were four times more likely when a driver was on the phone. But the cellphone industry touted the benefits of the devices. A 2000 Harvard University study, funded by AT&T, pegged the economic benefits of drivers using cellphones at $43 billion. [34]

New Distraction

The issue of whether drivers should use cellphones became a point of debate in state capitals. In 2001, cellphone companies lobbied against a California bill that would have required drivers to use hands-free devices. But the New York legislature that year banned the non-emergency use of hand-held cellphones despite a multimillion-dollar advertising campaign by the cellphone industry that called for education about the risks of distracted driving but not a ban. The new law, the first of its kind in the nation, imposed a fine of up to $100 on violators. "Driving a car is a serious responsibility that requires the attention, the full attention, of the driver," said

Apps Put Barriers Between Drivers and Phones

But overcoming "addiction" to texting is difficult.

If anyone should be able to put down his cellphone while driving, it would be David Teater of Spring Lake, Mich. Teater's son died in a 2004 accident when he was hit by a young woman talking on her cellphone. But Teater, who works on transportation issues for the National Safety Council, said he has had trouble setting aside his cellphone while driving even after the accident.

"With all the motivation in the world, I couldn't do it," he said. Eventually, he needed to create a physical barrier between himself and his phone: "I put the cellphone in the trunk." [1] If cellphone technology has made it so difficult for drivers to focus on the road, can the same technology also help solve the problem?

Wireless-industry executives think so. They see the opportunity for apps that help motorists resist using their cellphones in a risky fashion.

For example, AT&T is marketing an app called DriveMode that allows for the disabling of emails, incoming and outgoing calls and Web browsing during driving. It includes an option for an auto-reply to text messages, notifying senders that the user is driving and will reply when it is safe. So drivers will not feel uncomfortable about being disconnected, they can select up to five contact numbers to send and receive calls, and they also can access 911.

The app "offers an easy way for wireless users to make a decision to not text and drive without making them feel completely disconnected," says Charlene Lake, AT&T senior vice president of public affairs and chief sustainability officer.

DriveMode is just one of numerous such options for motorists trying to overcome the urge to use their cellphones while driving. The apps generally work by partially disabling a phone when sensing movement beyond certain speeds.

"The beauty of the industry is that it is competitive, and there are a number of options and many different ways that they can be deployed," says John Walls, vice president of public affairs for CTIA, an association of wireless companies. "There is a wave of solutions out there."

Such apps are popular among parents, who can use them to block their children from calling or texting while driving and would be notified if the child disabled the app. Companies also deploy them if they want to prevent employees from using company cellphones for conversations while behind the wheel.

But some safety experts question whether they can make a substantial difference to drivers who are trying to overcome their compulsion to use their own cellphones while behind the wheel.

"How do you convince people to spend money on something that will restrict their use of their own phone when the phone already has a power button on it to accomplish the

Republican Gov. George Pataki as he signed the bill into law. [35]

Three years later, however, the Insurance Institute for Highway Safety showed that New York drivers, who had initially reduced their cellphone use, were disregarding the ban and using their phones as much as before the law was passed. Safety experts said the state needed to put a greater emphasis on publicizing and enforcing the law. "If you look at the experiences with other laws in highway safety like seat belt and drunken-driving laws, what seems to make a difference in the long term is publicized enforcement," said Anne McCartt, the study's lead author. [36] New York eventually increased the penalties for cellphone use, including a 2011 decision to impose two points on the driving records of offenders.

As more studies demonstrated the risks of cellphone use — a 2002 Harvard study estimated that distracted drivers caused 570,000 accidents yearly, with 2,600 deaths — additional states advanced cellphone restrictions and the industry began putting a greater focus on safety. [37] The year after the Harvard study, Verizon Wireless broke with the industry in supporting a California proposal to ban hand-held cellphone use behind the wheel. In 2009, the cellular industry adopted a neutral stance on laws restricting cellphone use by motorists. It now supports bans on texting.

As attention turned to the risks of texting, Washington became the first state to impose a texting ban in May 2007. Dozens of states followed over the next several years. The laws generally exempted emergency situations, and they also allowed drivers to use hands-free devices.

Even as lawmakers focused on texting, however, drivers began to face a new distraction. In 2008, Ford introduced a computer built into the dashboard that gave drivers access to the Web, enabled hands-free phone conversations, and featured a GPS device. Other automakers followed with their own computer systems. They also urged drivers to remain focused on the road. A 2009 Ford ad for the company's voice-activated SYNC system included this warning: "Driving while distracted can result in loss of vehicle control. Only use mobile phones and other devices, even with voice commands, when it is safe to do so." [38]

With all states allowing hands-

same thing?" asks Justin McNaull, director of state relations at the AAA Foundation for Traffic Safety. Part of the problem, experts say, is that the compulsion to stay connected is like an addiction. Psychologists liken the desire to talk or text while driving or to engage in social-media activities such as updating a Facebook page to a gambler who is unable to walk away from a slot machine or poker table.

"There's concern that some of these activities may in fact be addicting," says David Strayer, a psychologist at the University of Utah. "When your phone rings, you may be getting a little bit of adrenaline, a burst of dopamine, that's a bit of a reward in your brain. Someone cares about me enough to want to call me and chat."

Deborah Hersman, chairwoman of the National Transportation Safety Board, likens using cellphones behind the wheel to getting hooked on nicotine.

Getty Images/Brendan Hoffman

Deborah Hersman, chairwoman of the National Transportation Safety Board, compares cellphone use behind the wheel to nicotine addiction.

"Addiction to these devices is a very good way to think about it," she said. "It's not unlike smoking. We have to get to a place where it's not in vogue anymore, where people recognize it's harmful and there's a risk and it's not worth it." [2]

Although the wireless industry has been criticized for marketing its devices to drivers for many years, AT&T's Lake says it can play a major role in helping drivers to kick the habit.

"It's not just the application itself, but the awareness the app itself creates," she says. "There is no question this is a complex issue. It will take time and many voices joining in the cause to help change behavior."

— *David Hosansky*

[1] Matt Richtel, "Drivers and Legislators Dismiss Cellphone Risks," *The New York Times*, July 18, 2009, www.nytimes.com/2009/07/19/technology/19distracted.html?pagewanted=all.

[2] Matt Richtel, "Reframing the Debate Over Using Phones Behind the Wheel," *The New York Times*, Dec. 17, 2011, www.nytimes.com/2011/12/18/us/reframing-the-debate-over-using-phones-while-driving.html?pagewanted=all.

free devices, researchers launched a number of studies to investigate whether they were actually safer than hand-held devices. Some research showed that hands-free devices provided little benefit, including a 2008 study at Carnegie Mellon University that showed engaging in a phone conversation, even while not holding the phone, caused a deterioration in driving performance. [39]

Experts said more research was needed into the issue. But with studies pointing to hands-free devices having at least some impact on drivers — and possibly distracting them as much as hand-held devices — Chapel Hill, N.C., in March 2012 became the first city in the country to ban virtually all cellphone and wireless use, including hands-free devices. ■

CURRENT SITUATION

Chapel Hill Leads Way

Drivers in Chapel Hill, N.C., are facing the nation's toughest restrictions on cellphone use. Beginning June 1, not only will they face restrictions on picking up their phones to make a call or send a text but they also will not be allowed to use hands-free devices.

The Town Council's 5-4 vote on March 26 on the new ordinance generated immediate controversy over the wisdom and even the legality of banning hands-free devices. Safety advocates hailed the move, citing research indicating that hands-free devices may be just as distracting as handheld ones.

"In passing a total ban, Chapel Hill has taken a significant step toward making their roads safer," said Janet Froetscher, president and chief executive of the National Safety Council, in a written statement. "Passing total cellphone bans — that include hand-held and hands-free use — makes our roads safer. [40]

Some local company owners, however, warned that the restriction would contribute little to safety and could make it much more difficult to conduct their business.

"If I follow the law to the letter, it will hurt my business," says Cotton of AdvantaClean, who uses Bluetooth technology so he can keep his hands on the wheel while talking. "My vehicle is my office. I drive from site to site, and when I'm driving, I'm talking to customers."

The controversy, which has received substantial attention in the national news, may be a sign of things to come in the debate over distracted driving. Already, there are signs that more jurisdictions may follow Chapel Hill's lead. For example, the Evanston, Ill., City Council will consider a ban on hands-free devices this spring. No state has moved to ban the increasingly popular technology for all drivers, but 31 states and Washington, D.C., ban novice drivers from using hands-free as well as hand-held devices.

FocusDriven

Sixteen-year-old Cady Reynolds of Omaha, Neb., died when a distracted under-18 driver ran a red light and hit her car, above. Her death spurred her father, Rob Reynolds, to help found FocusDriven, a support organization for the families of victims of distracted driving that opposes all cellphone use by drivers. "Whether it's hands-free or hand-held doesn't matter: These devices are a distraction," he says.

Action in Washington

Researchers are continuing to examine the risks of hands-free devices, using video cameras to observe drivers. But several studies already have examined how people respond in driving simulators, and the results generally do not show that hands-free technology offers much, if any, safety advantage. The reason, psychologists say, is that drivers invest a lot of mental focus in a conversation over a phone regardless of whether they are holding the phone or the steering wheel. That takes away from their attention to the road.

"We've done a number of studies in the simulator, and we see no safety advantage for hands-free vs. hand-held," says Strayer of the University of Utah. "It's not even that you're a little bit better. You're no better at all."

The issue is dividing policymakers in Washington. The National Transportation Safety Board in December called for a ban on hands-free devices, even though there appears to be little appetite in Congress or among state legislators for such a restrictive approach. "Whether it's hand-held or hands-free, touching the dashboard, or waving at a windshield, it can be distracting," said NTSB chairwoman Hersman. [41]

But the five-member board is an independent advisory body with no rulemaking authority. Transportation Secretary LaHood, who on April 26 called for federal action to stop cellphone use in all 50 states, responded coolly to the recommendation. [42] "The problem is not hands-free," LaHood said in December. "That is not the big problem in America." [43]

Instead of pursuing a ban, the department is focusing on working with automakers to develop voluntary guidelines for new dashboard technologies. Those guidelines could include disabling a number of features while the car is in motion, including calling, texting and Internet browsing. They could also include additional safety elements, such as limiting the amount of time that a device would cause a driver to look away from the road to no more than two seconds at a time.

Once those guidelines are established, Transportation Department officials say they may consider additional guidelines for electronic devices brought into a car, such as smartphones.

Safety advocates, who have generally applauded LaHood's emphasis on distracted driving, are disappointed that the department is allowing automakers to continue to install increasingly complex dashboard technologies.

"They're taking a side on this issue that doesn't line up with the facts," says Reynolds of FocusDriven. "They are supporting the auto industry's push to put more of these devices in cars. And that's going to be a very costly mistake in terms of lives."

Automakers, who are rolling out high-profile marketing campaigns around the new dashboard technologies, say voluntary guidelines made more sense than government mandates.

"It just seems that guidelines are a quicker, more nimble way to do this with technology evolving so quickly," says Newton of the automakers alliance.

The technology has become so complex that, experts say, it may be difficult for the government to regulate hands-free devices even if policymakers wanted to. That is because different devices fall under the purview of different agencies: smartphone technology, for example, is generally regulated by the Federal Communications Commission while a Bluetooth device installed in a car would generally be

Continued on p. 418

At Issue:

Are integrated devices safer than using hand-held devices while driving?

MITCH BAINWOL
PRESIDENT AND CEO, ALLIANCE OF AUTOMOBILE MANUFACTURERS

WRITTEN FOR *CQ RESEARCHER*, MAY 2012

There is no debate about whether distracted driving is a concern. It is. The salient question is how best to ameliorate it in the real world where drivers demand connectivity — and with the prevalence of portable smartphones, they have it.

Technology has transformed our society forever. According to CTIA, The Wireless Association, at the end of 2011 there were 331.6 million wireless subscriber connections — more than the entire U.S. population.

We share Transportation Secretary Ray LaHood's conviction that drivers should not use handheld devices to communicate when driving. Looking away from the road to dial, surf, text or navigate is dangerous. Research confirms that 80 percent of crashes involve the driver looking away from the roadway just prior to the crash.

We can put our heads in the sand and demand a behavioral shift — as some policymakers advocate — or we can find ways to make communication in the car safe.

Automakers are relying on integrated systems to operate as a "safety filter" to channel driver behavior in a way that mitigates accident risk and saves lives.

Consumers are going to communicate; the only viable path to make that activity safe is to provide a technological answer that addresses the visual distraction. Built-in communications systems are that answer. They rely on the cellphone passively and only for connectivity — so with the integrated system, you can lock that phone up in the glove box as you depart.

Whether it's for communicating or listening to music or getting travel information, the objective of policymakers should be to encourage drivers to utilize the vehicle's hard-wired system rather than looking away from the road to concentrate on a handheld's small display screen — a screen never designed for use while driving.

In contrast — and by definition — auto displays, and other in-vehicle technologies, are designed from the very beginning to facilitate safe travel. They're easier to read and less distracting — much like tuning a car radio.

All this is covered in the Alliance's guidelines on in-vehicle technologies. They've been in place for a full decade now, serving as the base for the National Traffic Highway Safety Administration's recently proposed guidelines.

We know drivers are going to insist on staying connected behind the wheel. Our shared challenge is to construct policy and rely on technology that enables drivers to keep their eyes on the road and hands on the wheel.

ROB REYNOLDS
EXECUTIVE DIRECTOR, FOCUSDRIVEN

WRITTEN FOR *CQ RESEARCHER*, MAY 2012

The growing use of electronic devices built into car dashboards mostly grows out of studies that have found a greater risk from holding a cellphone and conversing over talking "hands free." Automakers use some of these studies to explain how adding hands-free texting, emailing, web surfing, social networking and talking apps into their infotainment systems make you "safer."

However, these so-called naturalistic studies have inherent characteristics that make relying on their results as the basis for these assumptions problematic, at best.

The studies themselves rely on observation and measurement of physical data using vehicles rigged with expensive cameras and monitoring equipment in the hopes that "events" (crashes) and "near events" can be recorded and later examined in detail.

But several points should be raised about their results:

- Participants know they are driving rigged vehicles, so it's questionable whether they are driving "naturally."
- The cost of the equipment and the fact that crashes/near crashes are infrequent events in most drivers' experience make both the sample size and the target for the study (crash causation) too small to draw widespread conclusions from.
- None of the monitoring equipment measures so called "cognitive distractions of the brain caused by the cellphone and other applications."

The majority of research on distractions with cellphones and smartphones has been done with epidemiological and lab research. In fact, at least 30 studies put the increased risk of conversing on a cellphone while driving (handheld or hands-free) at four times the risk of driving alone. All of this is being ignored by automakers in lieu of a select few studies that create a favorable argument for these applications.

In addition, automakers have said that "drivers will use these apps anyway; we just want to make it safer." I recall cigarette makers using similar arguments for adding filters to cigarettes (that doesn't work either — the behavior is unsafe regardless).

Think if we had used naturalistic studies to address intoxicated driving. Would we really rig cars with cameras and just wait and see or would/did we rely upon actual crash data and blood alcohol concentration (BAC) levels?

Impairment is impairment, whether it's temporary or constant. Four times increased crash risk is equal to the crash risk of driving at .08 BAC, the legal limit in most states. We can only reduce distracted-driving crash rates by banning the activity — not by trying to enhance the experience.

Continued from p. 416

regulated by the Transportation Department.

Indeed, Chapel Hill's ambitious new ordinance may face legal challenges. North Carolina's Democratic attorney general said regulating car phone use is a state issue, not a local one. Even if the ordinance stands, it contains so many exemptions that it may be difficult to enforce. For example, drivers on cellphones can be stopped only if they are violating another traffic law. The $25 fine doesn't apply if the driver is talking to emergency officials, with a doctor's office or with an immediate family member. If also exempts electronic mail.

Some business leaders say they will simply disregard it. Frank Coker, owner of Senior Helpers in Chapel Hill, says he often gets phone calls from elderly clients who have fallen or are facing some other crisis.

"I need to answer those calls right away," he says. "I don't want to wait four or five minutes until I find an exit on the highway. That can seem like an eternity to them.

"I will continue to use my phone."

Action in the States

Illinois this spring appears to be on its way to becoming the first state in the Midwest to ban drivers from talking on their cellphones. The state House of Representatives narrowly approved a ban on using hand-held phones, 63-58, in March, and observers think the plan has a good chance to win approval in the state Senate, where it is supported by Senate President John Cullerton, D-Chicago.

"I want to make sure that people understand that drivers need to be responsible, because they're taking other people's lives into their hands when they're driving a car and using a handheld cellphone," said Rep. John D'Amico, D-Chicago, the bill's sponsor. [44]

If Illinois moves ahead, it will provide a major boost to advocates of tougher distracted driving laws. Before this year, the nine states that had banned virtually all drivers from talking on cellphones were in the Northeast and far West. (*See map, p. 404.*) But with West Virginia last month imposing such a ban and Illinois very possibly headed down that road, the prohibitions on handheld cellphone use are reaching into the South and Midwest.

In addition, Idaho and Pennsylvania approved texting bans this year — although the Pennsylvania measure became law only after legislators stripped out language that also would have banned cellphone use and included a provision overriding local ordinances prohibiting talking on cellphones.

Other states, however, seem unlikely for the moment to impose new restrictions. In Ohio, for example, a bill that would prohibit drivers from texting remains stalled in a Senate committee. "We're discouraged," said Brian Newbacher, director of public affairs at AAA East Central, "but not defeated." [45]

Several Ohio cities, such as Columbus and Toledo, ban texting by drivers, creating a potentially confusing situation on the roads.

While most states or cities have some restrictions on cellphone use, such as prohibiting novice drivers from texting, a handful of states have declined to pass such laws, and in some cases they even prohibit local jurisdictions from imposing restrictions. In Florida, for example, where drivers can freely text or talk on their cellphones anywhere in the state as long as they obey traffic laws, the legislature adjourned in March without passing a bill that would have banned texting while driving.

House Speaker Dean Cannon, an opponent of the proposed legislation, said there are several other behaviors that distract drivers at least as much as text messaging while driving, and he expressed concerns about "one more layer of prohibitive behavior" from state government. He and other opponents of texting laws also point to laws already on the books that target careless driving.

"Look, I think a lot of our members have concerns about both the remedy

"We haven't found anybody who is not negatively affected [by talking on a cellphone while driving]. The research is unequivocal and clear. When the person you're talking with is not physically present, you use brain resources to essentially create a mental picture of the person, and that takes cognitive capacity away from other tasks."

— Clifford I. Nass

Professor of Communication, Stanford University

and the structure of any bill that regulates individual behavior," he said. "I've got personal-liberties concerns." [46] ■

OUTLOOK

Enter Google

In the last text she ever wrote, Canadian Emy Brochu, 20, responded to a message of love from her boyfriend by writing: "I love you too and I will try my best to make you happy Mr. Fortin."

Moments later, Brochu slammed into a truck as she drove east of Montreal. She died instantly. Her grief stricken boyfriend, Mathieu Fortin, would later garner international headlines when he posted their final, romantic exchange on Facebook to draw attention to the dangers of texting while driving. [47]

If such poignant reports about the hazards of texting cannot get motorists to kick the habit, and if laws also fall short (every province in Canada has banned texting while driving), what is the solution to such distractions?

Some experts are looking to crash-avoidance systems, which offer the potential to prevent accidents involving drivers who are not paying attention.

"If laws aren't working, one thing that does have some potential is technology itself," says Rader of the Insurance Safety Institute. "Crash-avoidance systems have the potential to address the wide range of distracted driving situations, not just when drivers are using their phones." Crash avoidance systems generally rely on a network of sensors in a car that detect other vehicles, road conditions, and other information that can be helpful to a driver. Carmakers are just beginning to offer such systems as options in higher-end models. Within the next couple of years, most models are expected to offer them.

A recent study by the Highway Loss Data Institute gave hope that such systems can significantly reduce the number of accidents, although they may not eliminate them entirely. The 2011 study focused on Volvo XC60 midsize SUVs outfitted with a system known as City Safety, which uses an infrared laser sensor built into the windshield to detect vehicles in slow-moving, heavy traffic and automatically applies the brakes when necessary. The study found that the number of insurance claims filed under property damage liability coverage, which pays for damage to vehicles struck by an at-fault driver, were 27 percent less for the XC60 than other midsize luxury SUVs.

"This is our first real-world look at an advanced crash-avoidance technology, and the findings are encouraging," said institute President Adrian Lund. "City Safety is helping XC60 drivers avoid the kinds of front-to-rear, low-speed crashes that frequently happen on congested roads." [48]

Experts caution that the technology is still years away from being able to reliably bail out drivers who are not paying attention, and it may never prevent all accidents involving distracted drivers. Furthermore, some wonder if the technology may cause drivers to become complacent.

"Drivers still have to pay attention and react," says McNaull of the AAA Foundation. "If we become overly reliant on new technologies, are there some unintended consequences?"

Even as automakers seek to refine crash avoidance systems, engineers are beginning to eye the next generation in technology — vehicles that drive themselves. Google has tested several such cars, which use artificial intelligence software with information gathered from Google Street View and input from car-mounted sensors and cameras. Google officials believe that these types of vehicles offer the potential to prevent accidents and improve traffic efficiency.

Although such automated cars are many years away from being widely used, policymakers are beginning to discuss how that could affect transportation law, including restrictions on distracted drivers. And Nevada legislators don't intend to be left in the dust. Indeed, in 2011 they approved legislation allowing "drivers" of autonomous vehicles to send text messages, although the state prohibits texting while driving.

"We see autonomous technology as the future of the automobile," said Bruce Breslow, director of the Nevada Department of Motor Vehicles. "Certainly within two to five years there will be autonomous, self-driving cars sold to people in our country. And we look at it as a safety system to avoid crashes, to avoid deaths." [49] ■

Notes

[1] "Distracted Driving 2009," *Traffic Safety Facts Research Note*, National Highway Traffic Safety Administration, September 2010, www.distraction.gov/research/PDF-Files/Distracted-Driving-2009.pdf. For background, see the following *CQ Researcher* reports: Marcia Clemmitt, "Cyber Socializing," July 28, 2006, pp. 625-648; Sarah Glazer, "Cell Phone Safety," March 16, 2001, pp. 201-224; and Brian Hansen, "Auto Safety," Oct. 26, 2001, pp. 873-896.

[2] *Ibid.*; see also "Driver Electronic Device Use in 2010," National Highway Traffic Safety Administration, *Traffic Safety Facts Research Note*, December 2011, www.distraction.gov/download/research-pdf/8052_TSF_RN_DriverElectronicDeviceUse_1206111_v4_tag.pdf.

[3] Deborah A. P. Hersman, chairwoman, National Transportation Safety Board, opening remarks, Attentive Driving Forum: Countermeasures to Distraction, Washington, D.C., March 27, 2012, www.ntsb.gov/news/speeches/hersman/daph120327.html.

[4] Susan Carroll, "Texas not likely to follow feds' call to ban cellphone use while driving," *Houston Chronicle*, Dec. 14, 2011, www.chron.com/news/houston-texas/article/Texas-not-likely-to-follow-feds-call-to-ban-2401263.php.

[5] Traffic fatality statistics are drawn from *Fatality Analysis Reporting System* encyclopedia, www-fars.nhtsa.dot.gov/Main/index.aspx and

National Highway Traffic Safety Administration's "2010 Motor Vehicle Crashes: Overview," *Traffic Safety Facts Research Note*, February 2012, www-nrd.nhtsa.dot.gov/Pubs/811552.pdf.

[6] Carrie Cline, Michael Hyland and Josh McComas, "NEW INFO: Gov. Tomblin Signs Bill to Ban Texting, Cellphone Use while Driving," WSAZ, April 4, 2012, www.wsaz.com/news/charlestonnews/headlines/Dealing_with_Distracted_Drivers_112698089.html.

[7] Matt Richtel, "Drivers and Legislators Dismiss Cellphone Risks," *The New York Times*, July 19, 2009, www.nytimes.com/2009/07/19/technology/19distracted.html?pagewanted=all.

[8] "2011 Traffic Safety Culture Index," AAA Foundation for Traffic Safety, January 2012, www.aaafoundation.org/pdf/2011TSCIndex.pdf.

[9] "Hand-held cellphone laws and collision claims frequencies," Highway Loss Data Institute, Jan. 29, 2010, www.iihs.org/news/rss/pr012910.html.

[10] The findings by the University of California, Berkeley's Safe Transportation Research and Safety Center were announced on March 2, 2012, in a lengthy memo by the center's director, David Ragland, to the California Office of Traffic Safety, www.safetrec.berkeley.edu/news/Memo_CellPhoneBan.pdf.

[11] Ken Leiser, "Interstate Truck Drivers Face Cellphone Ban on Jan. 3," *St. Louis Post-Dispatch*, Dec. 10, 2011, www.stltoday.com/news/local/metro/interstate-truck-drivers-face-cellphone-ban-on-jan/article_c2e61739-c27c-5f8f-ac54-0b5adf902a9f.html.

[12] "U.S. Transportation Secretary LaHood Announces Final Rule that Bans Hand-Held Cell Phone Use by Drivers of Buses and Large Trucks," press release, U.S. Department of Transportation, Nov. 23, 2011, www.dot.gov/affairs/2011/fmcsa3511.html.

[13] Michael Inbar, "Parents of teen who died texting and driving: 'Kids think they're invincible,' " MSNBC Today News, March 5, 2012, http://today.msnbc.msn.com/id/46627015/ns/today-today_news/t/parents-teen-who-died-texting-driving-kids-think-theyre-invincible/.

[14] "New data from Virginia Tech Transportation Institute provides insight into cellphone use and driving distraction," news release, Virginia Tech Transportation Institute, July 29, 2009, www.vtnews.vt.edu/articles/2009/07/2009-571.html.

[15] "Jersey Drivers Text More; Say New Yorkers Are Worse," news release and statistics, Fairleigh Dickenson University and N.J. Division of Highway Traffic Safety, July 19, 2010, www.nj.gov/oag/newsreleases10/pr20100719-Texting.pdf.

[16] Larry Copeland, "Feds ban texting by truck, bus drivers," *USA Today*, Jan. 27, 2010, www.usatoday.com/tech/wireless/2010-01-26-texting-driving-commercial-ban_N.htm.

[17] "Texting Laws and Collision Claim Frequencies," *Highway Loss Data Institute Bulletin*, September 2010, www.iihs.org/research/topics/pdf/HLDI_Bulletin_27_11.pdf.

[18] "Four High-Visibility Enforcement Demonstration Waves in Connecticut and New York Reduce Hand-Held Phone Use," *Traffic Safety Facts Research Notes*, National Highway Traffic Safety Administration, www-nrd.nhtsa.dot.gov/Pubs/811845.pdf.

[19] Information about state laws on texting and cellphone use is tracked by the National Conference of State Legislatures on web pages such as www.ncsl.org/issues-research/transport/cellular-phone-use-and-texting-while-driving-laws.aspx.

[20] David Montgomery," Bill banning texting while driving fails to pass House committee," *Rapid City Journal*, Feb. 2, 2012, http://rapidcityjournal.com/news/bill-banning-texting-while-driving-fails-to-pass-house-committee/article_c44ae2b0-4cf1-11e1-a42b-0019bb2963f4.html#ixzz1shQO4Ees.

[21] Copeland, *op. cit.*

[22] Ashlee Vance and Matt Richtel, "Despite Risks, Internet Creeps Onto Car Dashboards," *The New York Times*, Jan. 6, 2010, www.nytimes.com/2010/01/07/technology/07distracted.html.

[23] Mike Ramsey, "Don't Look Now: A Car That Tweets," *The Wall Street Journal*, Feb. 10, 2012, http://online.wsj.com/article/SB10001424052970203824904577213041944082370.html.

[24] *Ibid.*

[25] Matt Richtel, "Utah Gets Tough With Texting Drivers," *The New York Times*, Aug. 28, 2009, www.nytimes.com/2009/08/29/technology/29distracted.html?pagewanted=all.

[26] Paul A. Eisenstein, "Distracted Driving: Deadly Epidemic or 'Storm in a Teacup?' " Today.com, March 31, 2011, www.msnbc.msn.com/id/42338592/ns/business-autos/t/distracted-driving-deadly-epidemic-or-storm-teacup/.

[27] Early concerns about the potentially distracting effects of windshield wipers on drivers can be found at several online sources, such as a Massachusetts Institute of Technology website about inventions, http://web.mit.edu/invent/iow/anderson.html.

[28] The history of audio in cars and its potential distractions is briefly summarized by Gerry Kobe, "Death by Distraction — Statistical Data Included," in the CBS Interactive Business Network Resource Library, http://findarticles.com/p/articles/mi_m3012/is_5_180/ai_62685785/pg_3/?tag=content;col1.

[29] The early history of car phones can be found at several websites, including the Dead Media archive of New York University's Department of Media, Culture, and Communications, http://cultureandcommunication.org/deadmedia/index.php/Car_Phone#A_Brief_Technological_History_of_the_Car_Phone and "The History of Car Phones" by Dmitry Rashnitsov, www.ehow.com/about_5426865_history-car-phones.html.

[30] AT&T provides a history of early mobile phones at www.corp.att.com/attlabs/reputation/timeline/46mobile.html.

[31] Chris Gullo, "CTIA: 96 million smartphones in US," MobiHealth News, http://mobihealthnews.com/13796/ctia-96-million-smartphones-in-us/.

[32] Matt Richtel, "Promoting the Cell Phone Despite Risks," *The New York Times*, Dec. 6, 2009, www.nytimes.com/2009/12/07/technology/07distracted.html?pagewanted=all.

[33] *The New York Times* timeline, www.nytimes.com/interactive/2009/12/07/technology/07distracted-timeline.html.

[34] *Ibid.*

[35] "New York hand-held cell phone bill signed into law," CNN, June 28, 2001, http://articles.cnn.com/2001-06-28/us/cellphones_1_hand-held-cell-cell-phone-enormous-threat?_s=PM:US.

[36] Alicia Chang, "Study: Drivers ignore N.Y. cell phone ban," MSNBC, Feb. 4, 2004, www.

About the Author

David Hosansky is a freelance writer in the Denver area who specializes in environmental issues. He previously was a senior writer at *CQ Weekly* and the *Florida Times-Union* in Jacksonville, where he was twice nominated for a Pulitzer Prize. His previous *CQ Researcher* reports include "Food Safety" and "Youth Suicide."

msnbc.msn.com/id/4162174/ns/technology_and_science-games/t/study-drivers-ignore-ny-cellphone-ban/.

[37] Ricardo Alonso-Zaldivar, "Cell Phones and Driving a Lethal Mix, Study Finds," *Los Angeles Times*, Dec. 2, 2002, http://articles.latimes.com/2002/dec/02/nation/na-fones2.

[38] *The New York Times* timeline, *op. cit.*

[39] Marcel Adam Just, Timothy A. Keller and Jacquelyn Cynkar, "A decrease in brain activation associated with driving when listening to someone speak," *Brain Research*, 2008, www.distraction.gov/download/research-pdf/carnegie-mellon.pdf.

[40] Mark Hachman, "Chapel Hill Enacts Total Cellphone Ban on Drivers," *PC Magazine*, March 29, 2012, www.pcmag.com/article2/0,2817,2402374,00.asp.

[41] David Shepardson, "NTSB Defends Car Call Ban Plan," *The Detroit News*, March 28, 2012, www.detroitnews.com/article/20120328/AUTO01/203280331/1148/auto01/NTSB-defends-car-call-ban-plan.

[42] Jim Forsyth, "U.S. ban sought on cell phone use while driving," Reuters, April 26, 2012, www.msnbc.msn.com/id/47197722/ns/us_news/.

[43] *Ibid.*

[44] Matthew Walberg, "Data fail to show much difference in cellphone ban on road safety," *St. Louis Post-Dispatch*, March 30, 2012, www.stltoday.com/news/national/data-fail-to-show-much-difference-in-cellphone-ban-on/article_4f5d1adf-e20d-54ab-a2e0-fe037729d567.html.

[45] John Horton, "Ohio Senate not ready to hit send on texting-while-driving law," *Cleveland Plain Dealer*, Feb. 2, 2012, www.cleveland.com/roadrant/index.ssf/2012/02/ohio_senate_not_ready_to_hit_s.html.

[46] "Texting While Driving: Florida Sends Wrong Message," *The Ledger*, March 27, 2012, www.theledger.com/article/20120327/EDIT01/120329402?p=2&tc=pg.

[47] Julie Marcoux, "Romantic text sent moments before deadly crash," *Toronto Sun*, March 14, 2012, www.torontosun.com/2012/03/14/romantic-texts-sent-moments-before-deadly-crash.

[48] "High-tech system on Volvos is preventing crashes," news release, Highway Loss Data Institute, July 19, 2011, www.iihs.org/news/rss/pr071911.html.

[49] Sarah Rich, "Nevada DMV Approves Regulations for Testing Driverless Vehicles," *Governing*, Feb. 28, 2012, www.governing.com/news/technology/nevada-dmv-approves-regulations-for-testing-driverless-vehicles.html.

FOR MORE INFORMATION

AAA Foundation for Traffic Safety, 607 14th St., N.W., Suite 201, Washington, DC 20005; 202-638-5944; www.aaafoundation.org/multimedia/Distracteddriving.cfm. Conducts education programs and sponsors research on distracted driving and other safety issues.

Alliance of Automobile Manufacturers, 1401 Eye St., N.W., Suite 900, Washington, DC 20005; 202-326-5500; www.autoalliance.org. Advocacy group for the auto industry; endorses use of integrated electronic communication systems in car dashboards.

Center for Auto Safety, 1825 Connecticut Ave., N.W., Suite 330, Washington, DC 20009-5708; 202-328-7700; www.autosafety.org. Founded by Consumers Union and consumer activist Ralph Nader, advocates for improved auto safety and so-called lemon laws on behalf of consumers.

Centers for Disease Control and Prevention, 1600 Clifton Road, Atlanta, GA 30329; 800-232-4636; www.cdc.gov/Motorvehiclesafety/Distracted_Driving/index.html. The principal Department of Health and Human Services agency that oversees public health.

CTIA, 1400 16th St., N.W., Suite 600, Washington, DC 20036; 202-736-3200; www.ctia.org/advocacy/policy_topics/topic.cfm/tid/17. An international association representing cellphone companies. Favors laws to ban texting behind the wheel and has a neutral position on other issues such as talking on cellphones while driving.

FocusDriven, P.O. Box 45333, Omaha, NE 68145; 630-775-2405; www.focusdriven.org. An advocacy group overseen by people who have lost family members to distracted driving; presses for laws to curb cellphone use and other potential motorist distractions.

Governors Highway Safety Association, 444 N. Capitol St., N.W., Suite 722, Washington, DC 20001; 202-789-0942; www.ghsa.org/index.html. Represents state highway safety offices and provides information about distracted driving to state policy makers.

Insurance Institute for Highway Safety, 1005 N. Glebe Road, Suite 800, Arlington, VA 22201; 703-247-1500; www.iihs.org/research/qanda/cellphones.aspx. Funded by auto insurance companies, argues that distractions have been an issue for drivers long before cellphones and questions whether laws to ban drivers from using cellphones are effective; Highway Loss Data Institute is an affiliated organization.

National Conference of State Legislatures, 7700 East First Pl., Denver, CO 80230; www.ncsl.org/issues-research/transport/spotlight-distracted-driving.aspx. Provides authoritative background and updates on state laws that restrict phoning and texting by motorists.

National Safety Council, 1121 Spring Lake Dr., Itasca, IL 60143-3201; 630-775-2199; www.nsc.org/safety_road/distracted_driving/pages/distracted_driving.aspx. Public service organization that warns of the dangers of both hands-free and hand-held cellphone use by motorists.

U.S. Department of Transportation, 1200 New Jersey Ave., S.E., Washington, DC 20590; 202-366-9742; www.distraction.gov. Emphasizes the dangers of distracted driving on its website; maintains that laws and enforcement can significantly reduce cellphone use by drivers but does not focus on the potential risks of hands-free devices.

Bibliography

Selected Sources

Books

Kiesbye, Stefan, ed., *Cell Phones and Driving*, Greenhaven Press, 2011.
This slim volume from the At Issue Series provides a collection of articles from newspapers and other sources about the risks of cellphone use and texting by drivers.

Articles

Carroll, Susan, "Texas not likely to follow feds' call to ban cellphone use while driving," *Houston Chronicle*, Dec. 14, 2011, www.chron.com/news/houston-texas/article/Texas-not-likely-to-follow-feds-call-to-ban-2401263.php.
This article summarizes the resistance of Texas policymakers to imposing restrictions on cellphone use by drivers.

Copeland, Larry, "Feds ban texting by truck, bus drivers," *USA Today*, Jan. 27, 2010, www.usatoday.com/tech/wireless/2010-01-26-texting-driving-commercial-ban_N.htm.
The article discusses differing approaches by policymakers to regulate cellphone use by drivers.

Cruz, Gilbert, and Kristi Oloffson, "Distracted Driving: Should Talking, Texting Be Banned?," *Time*, Aug. 24, 2009, www.time.com/time/magazine/article/0,9171,1916291,00.html.
The article succinctly summarizes key controversies and studies surrounding the risks of using cellphones behind the wheel.

Eisenstein, Paul A., "Distracted Driving: Deadly Epidemic or 'Storm in a Teacup?' " *Today.com*, March 31, 2011, www.msnbc.msn.com/id/42338592/ns/business-autos/t/distracted-driving-deadly-epidemic-or-storm-teacup.
This thoughtful discussion of the key debates over cellphone use includes conflicting views on the risks they present.

Gardner, Amanda, "Most U.S. Drivers Engage in 'Distracting Behaviors," *USA Today*, Dec. 1, 2012, www.usatoday.com/news/health/story/health/story/2011-12-01/Most-US-drivers-engage-in-distracting-behaviors/51544554/1.
Gardner summarizes poll data indicating the extent to which drivers engage in potentially dangerous distracting behavior.

Inbar, Michael, "Parents of Teen who Died Texting and Driving: 'Kids Think They're Invincible,' " *Today.com*, March 5, 2012, http://today.msnbc.msn.com/id/46627015/ns/today-today_news/t/parents-teen-who-died-texting-driving-kids-think-theyre-invincible.
Inbar's detailed account tells the story of an Idaho teen driver whose final text message warned of the dangers of texting while driving. She died in a car wreck moments later.

Ramsey, Mike, "Don't Look Now: A Car That Tweets," *The Wall Street Journal*, Feb. 10, 2012, p. B1, http://online.wsj.com/article/SB10001424052970203824904577213041944082370.html.
Ramsey takes a detailed look at the new technologies that automakers are adding to dashboards, enabling drivers to engage in such tasks as updating Facebook pages and buying movie tickets.

Richtel, Matt, "Driven to Distraction," *The New York Times*, 2009-2010, http://topics.nytimes.com/top/news/technology/series/driven_to_distraction/index.html#.
Richtel's massive body of work on distracted driving earned him a Pulitzer Prize in 2010. His series of articles that began in 2009 touches on virtually every aspect of the issue, including new developments in technology, the psychological impacts of multitasking and the challenges faced by policymakers who try to restrict cellphone use.

Reports and Studies

"Distracted Driving 2009," *Traffic Safety Facts Research Note*, National Highway Traffic Safety Administration, September 2010, www.distraction.gov/research/PDF-Files/Distracted-Driving-2009.pdf.
This federal report provides estimates of the number of people killed and injured in distracted accidents in 2009, the most recent year for which such data were available.

"Driver Electronic Device Use in 2010," Traffic Safety Facts Research Note, National Highway Traffic Safety Administration, December 2011, www.distraction.gov/download/research-pdf/8052_TSF_RN_DriverElectronicDeviceUse_1206111_v4_tag.
Although authorities do not monitor the number of drivers who use portable electronic devices, these estimates by the National Highway Traffic Safety Administration indicate that hundreds of thousands of drivers are texting or talking on hand-held cellphones every moment during the day.

"2011 Traffic Safety Culture Index," AAA Foundation for Traffic Safety, January 2012, www.aaafoundation.org/pdf/2011TSCIndex.pdf.
This report summarizes polling data indicating that most drivers believe cellphones are dangerous, even as they continue to use them.

"Texting Laws and Collision Claim Frequencies," *Highway Loss Data Institute Bulletin*, September 2010, www.iihs.org/research/topics/pdf/HLDI_Bulletin_27_11.pdf.
This much-discussed study concludes that texting laws in four states failed to improve road safety. A companion study has similar findings regarding states that banned motorists from talking on cellphones.

The Next Step:

Additional Articles from Current Periodicals

Cellphones

Halsey III, Ashley, "Police Link Work-Zone Crashes, Cellphones," *The Washington Post*, April 26, 2012, p. B5, www.washingtonpost.com/local/trafficandcommuting/nva-police-accidents-caused-by-cellphones-have-increased/2012/04/25/gIQAxSYxgT_story.html.

Cellphone use is to blame for one-third of work-zone accidents, according to a survey of Northern Virginia police officers.

Shepardson, David, "Group: Wait on Cellphone Ban," *Detroit News*, July 7, 2011, p. B4.

The Governors Highway Safety Association wants more research before states pass new restrictions on cellphones.

Von Quednow, Cindy, "Cellphone Ban Shows Results," *Ventura County* (Calif.) *Star*, March 19, 2012, p. A1, www.vcstar.com/news/2012/mar/18/study-shows-fewer-cellphone-related-crashes/?print=1.

Deadly crashes caused by driver cellphone use have declined in California since the state outlawed the practice.

Legislation

Adams, Glenn, "Maine Gov Signs Bill Banning Texting While Driving," The Associated Press, June 3, 2011, bangordailynews.com/2011/09/25/politics/maine-texting-while-driving-ban-to-start-this-week/.

Maine now outlaws text messaging while driving.

Bumsted, Brad, "Corbett Asks Legislature for Bill That Bans Texting While Driving," *Pittsburgh Tribune Review*, Oct. 26, 2011.

Republican Pennsylvania Gov. Tom Corbett has asked the legislature to ban texting while driving.

Spector, Joseph, "Cuomo Pushes for Stricter Texting-While-Driving Legislation," *Poughkeepsie* (N.Y.) *Journal*, June 11, 2011, p. APJ1.

Gov. Andrew Cuomo, D-N.Y., has introduced legislation that would crack down on distracted driving.

Other Distractions

"Cell Phones Aren't Drivers' Only Distraction," *Mobile* (Ala.) *Register*, Dec. 19, 2011, p. A5.

Drivers often take their eyes off of the road when eating, arguing with passengers and petting their dogs.

Walberg, Matthew, "Drivers Distracted By More Than Calls, Texts," *Chicago Tribune*, March 26, 2012, p. A10, articles.chicagotribune.com/2012-03-26/news/ct-met-distracted-driving-sidebar-20120326_1_hand-held-cell-phones-inattentive-actions-texting.

Adjusting the radio and painting fingernails are among driving distractions not involving cellphones, according to a 2010 report.

Texting

Cary, Annette, "Formula Detects Texting Drivers," *Tri-City Herald* (Kennewick, Wash.), March 21, 2012, p. A1, www.tri-cityherald.com/2012/03/21/v-print/1873247/pnnl-team-finds-formula-for-cellphone.html.

A Washington state physicist is working on a program that would allow parents to determine whether their children are driving while distracted.

Collier, Anne, "Peer Pressure Is Part of Texting and Driving — Teens Can't Say No," *The Christian Science Monitor*, April 19, 2012, www.csmonitor.com/The-Culture/Family/Modern-Parenthood/2012/0419/Peer-pressure-is-part-of-texting-and-driving-teens-can-t-say-no.

The pressure on teens not to ignore their friends is leading to increased texting while driving.

Norris, Toraine, "Police: Text Ban Tough to Enforce," *Birmingham* (Ala.) *News*, Sept. 5, 2011, p. A1, blog.al.com/spotnews/2011/09/police_texting_bans_are_hard_t.html.

Enforcing bans on texting is difficult because it's hard to tell what drivers are doing in their vehicles, Birmingham, Ala., police say.

Tadjdeh, Yasmin, "Texting Bans Don't Reduce Crash Numbers," *Centre Daily Times* (State College, Pa.), July 8, 2011, tlc.centredaily.com/2011/07/08/2823840/texting-bans-dont-reduce-crash.html.

Many states that have banned texting while driving have seen slight upticks in texting-related accidents.

CITING *CQ RESEARCHER*

Sample formats for citing these reports in a bibliography include the ones listed below. Preferred styles and formats vary, so please check with your instructor or professor.

MLA STYLE

Jost, Kenneth. "Remembering 9/11," CQ Researcher 2 Sept. 2011: 701-732.

APA STYLE

Jost, K. (2011, September 2). Remembering 9/11. *CQ Researcher, 9*, 701-732.

CHICAGO STYLE

Jost, Kenneth. "Remembering 9/11." *CQ Researcher*, September 2, 2011, 701-732.

CQ Researcher

Published by CQ Press, an Imprint of SAGE Publications, Inc.

www.cqresearcher.com

Celebrity Advocacy

Do stars influence issues, politics?

More and more, celebrities are using their star power to promote causes ranging from fighting poverty and protecting the environment to safeguarding human rights and working for world peace. More than 2,800 celebrities now support slightly more than 1,800 causes. In a celebrity-obsessed society, entertainers and athletes can help focus public attention on global trouble spots, raise funds for disaster relief or increase public awareness of little-known diseases or medical conditions. The idea of looking to celebrities to educate the public about important issues may seem paradoxical, but some celebrities work hard to master difficult issues. The singer Bono has met with world leaders on global poverty issues, for example, while actor George Clooney has helped document Sudan's war against the breakaway state of South Sudan. Celebrity advocacy is likely to increase, experts say, with social media such as Facebook and Twitter increasingly used to air views, raise money and engage supporters.

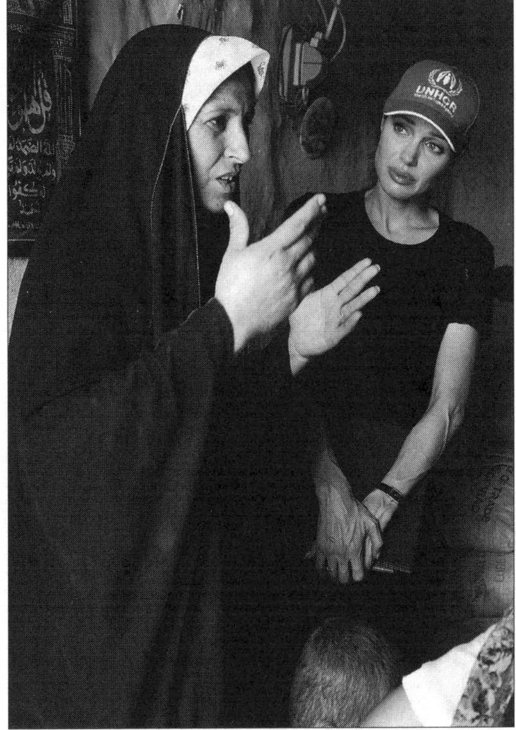

Actress Angelina Jolie listens to an Iraqi woman's story at a refugee camp northwest of Baghdad on July 23, 2009. Since being named a United Nations goodwill ambassador in 2001, she has met with refugees in more than 20 countries.

INSIDE THIS REPORT

THE ISSUES 427
BACKGROUND 433
CHRONOLOGY 435
CURRENT SITUATION 440
AT ISSUE.........................441
OUTLOOK 443
BIBLIOGRAPHY 446
THE NEXT STEP 447

CQ Researcher • May 11, 2012 • www.cqresearcher.com
Volume 22, Number 18 • Pages 425-448

SAGE
Los Angeles | London | New Delhi
Singapore | Washington DC
CQPRESS

RECIPIENT OF SOCIETY OF PROFESSIONAL JOURNALISTS AWARD FOR EXCELLENCE ◆ AMERICAN BAR ASSOCIATION SILVER GAVEL AWARD

CELEBRITY ADVOCACY

THE ISSUES

427 • Do celebrity advocates help educate the public about issues?
• Is celebrity advocacy mostly about self-promotion?
• Is celebrity advocacy slanted in favor of liberal causes?

BACKGROUND

433 **Star Power**
The birth of motion pictures made celebrities more influential.

434 **Leading Roles**
Celebrities moved to starring roles in politics at the 20th century's end.

437 **Multiple Causes**
Rising numbers of celebrities now support a wide range of causes.

CURRENT SITUATION

440 **Tweets Among Friends**
Celebrities are promoting their causes with social media.

442 **Official Engagements**
George Clooney uses his fame to try to influence policymakers on Sudan.

OUTLOOK

443 **Fascinated With Fame**
Celebrity advocacy is likely to increase, given the public's interest.

SIDEBARS AND GRAPHICS

428 **Entertainers on the Political Stage**
Performers have won election to a wide range of offices in recent years.

429 **Children's Issues Top List of Celebrity Causes**
Celebrities support more than 500 charities for children.

432 **Some Celebrity Charities Spend Little on Programs**
Elton John's AIDS Foundation is highly rated.

435 **Chronology**
Key events since 1944.

436 **Actors Seek Electoral Limelight**
For some the political stage is the place to be.

438 **Advocacy Films Have a Long History**
"The most effective sneak their message in in subtle ways."

441 **At Issue**
Are Hollywood celebrities politically out of touch with mainstream America?

FOR FURTHER RESEARCH

445 **For More Information**
Organizations to contact.

446 **Bibliography**
Selected sources used.

447 **The Next Step**
Additional articles.

447 **Citing *CQ Researcher***
Sample bibliography formats.

Cover: AFP/Getty Images/Boris Heger

CQ Researcher

May 11, 2012
Volume 22, Number 18

MANAGING EDITOR: Thomas J. Billitteri
tjb@cqpress.com

ASSISTANT MANAGING EDITOR: Kathy Koch
kkoch@cqpress.com

CONTRIBUTING EDITOR: Thomas J. Colin
tcolin@cqpress.com

ASSOCIATE EDITOR: Kenneth Jost

STAFF WRITER: Marcia Clemmitt

CONTRIBUTING WRITERS: Peter Katel, Barbara Mantel, Jennifer Weeks

DESIGN/PRODUCTION EDITOR: Olu B. Davis

ASSISTANT EDITOR: Darrell Dela Rosa

FACT CHECKER: Michelle Harris

Los Angeles | London | New Delhi
Singapore | Washington DC

An Imprint of SAGE Publications, Inc.

VICE PRESIDENT AND EDITORIAL DIRECTOR, HIGHER EDUCATION GROUP:
Michele Sordi

DIRECTOR, ONLINE PUBLISHING:
Todd Baldwin

CQ Researcher (ISSN 1056-2036) is printed on acid-free paper. Published weekly, except: (March wk. 5) (May wk. 4) (July wk. 1) (Aug. wks. 3, 4) (Nov. wk. 4) and (Dec. wks. 3, 4). Published by SAGE Publications, Inc., 2455 Teller Rd., Thousand Oaks, CA 91320. Annual full-service subscriptions start at $1,054. For pricing, call 1-800-834-9020. To purchase a *CQ Researcher* report in print or electronic format (PDF), visit www.cqpress.com or call 866-427-7737. Single reports start at $15. Bulk purchase discounts and electronic-rights licensing are also available. Periodicals postage paid at Thousand Oaks, California, and at additional mailing offices. POSTMASTER: Send address changes to *CQ Researcher*, 2300 N St., N.W., Suite 800, Washington, DC 20037.

Celebrity Advocacy

BY KENNETH JOST

THE ISSUES

George Clooney spent three busy days in Washington in mid-March, but the Hollywood superstar was not promoting a movie or scouting a film location. Instead, Clooney was testifying before Congress and meeting with President Obama on a subject far removed from Hollywood glitz and glamour: the war being waged by Sudan against its own people in the mountainous region bordering the breakaway nation of South Sudan.

Despite a decade's worth of headlines — including the deaths of an estimated 2 million civilians — Sudan is unfamiliar to most Americans, the reasons for its turmoil dimly understood at best. Clooney was on a mission to change that. One of his tools: a dramatic video of the perilous trek he had made into the volatile border region just the week before. On the video, and again before the Senate Foreign Relations Committee, Clooney described suffering children filled with shrapnel, the sound of rockets flying overhead and the reality of hundreds of people hiding in caves to escape the bombardments. "That happens every day," he told committee members. [1]

AFP/Getty Images/Paul J. Richards

Actor George Clooney is arrested for trespassing at the Sudanese Embassy in Washington on March 16, 2012. Earlier, he urged the Senate Foreign Relations Committee to take action against Sudan's "campaign of murder and fear and displacement and starvation" against South Sudan. "I'm not a policymaker," Clooney says. "My job is to try and bring attention to places that don't have it."

After meeting with Obama the next day, Clooney told reporters he was encouraged by the president's level of interest. "We feel like there's a commitment at the high level" to address the Sudanese situation, Clooney told reporters. But Clooney got even more attention the next day as TV cameras provided live coverage of his arrest for trespassing onto the grounds of the Sudanese Embassy to protest what he had described to the senators as Khartoum's "campaign of murder and fear and displacement and starvation." Hauled away in plastic handcuffs, Clooney later settled the charge by paying a $100 fine. [2]

Clooney's three-day media blitz in the capital was just the most recent example of the influential role that star power can play in contemporary affairs. "We live in a society, whether we like it or not, that is celebrity-obsessed," says Robin Bronk, chief executive officer of the New York City-based Creative Coalition, an entertainment industry social-advocacy organization founded in 1989 by activist actor Ron Silver.

"Celebrities have become carriers of cultural meaning," says David Blake, a professor of English at the College of New Jersey. "We increasingly come to rely on them to have public discussion, to have discourse about what matters to our society."

Blake, who is writing a book on the role of celebrity in the 1950s, notes that celebrities' influence is far greater today because of the large number of news and social media outlets and the often instantaneous transmission of high-profile events. "George Clooney is arrested, and we're aware of it instantly," Blake says.

Yet Clooney himself acknowledges the ambiguous nature of his role as celebrity advocate. "I'm not a policymaker," Clooney told co-anchor Judy Woodruff on the "PBS NewsHour." "My job is to try and bring attention to places that don't have it." Two days later, in advance of his arrest, he told The Associated Press: "It's such a silly thought to think you're actually succeeding in any of this. But if it's loud enough and you keep making it loud enough, at the very least people will know about it, and you can't say we didn't know. That's the first step." [3]

Celebrities are by no means new to politics and causes in the United States. Prominent entertainers dabbled in politics as early as the mid-19th century. In the 20th century, thanks to the wider recognition they could gain through movies, radio and television, many more entertainers took on advocacy roles. Today, thousands of celebrities from the worlds of entertainment, politics and sports promote charitable causes on virtually every topic under the sun — from animal rights to weapons reduction. The web-

Entertainers in Politics

Actors and other performers have won election in recent years to offices at all levels of government: local, state and federal. Here are some of those who made the transition from entertainment to politics:

Entertainer	Office(s) held	Major Credits
Sonny Bono	Mayor, Palm Springs, Calif. (1988-1992) U.S. House, Calif. (1995-1998)	Sonny & Cher
Clint Eastwood	Mayor, Carmel, Calif. (1986-1988)	Play Misty for Me, Dirty Harry
Al Franken	U.S. Senate, Minn. (2011 -)	Saturday Night Live
Fred Grandy	U.S. House, Iowa (1987-1995)	The Love Boat
Ben Jones	U.S. House, Ga. (1989-1993)	The Dukes of Hazzard
Sheila Kuehl	Legislature, Calif. (1994-2008)	The Many Loves of Dobie Gillis
Arnold Schwarzenegger	Governor, Calif. (2003-2011)	Conan the Barbarian, Terminator
Fred Thompson	U.S. Senate, Tennessee (1994-2003)	Die Hard 2, The Hunt for Red October
Jesse Ventura	Governor, Minn. (1999-2003)	World Wrestling Federation

Credit: Getty Images (all)

site *Look to the Stars* counts more than 2,800 celebrities supporting slightly over 1,800 charitable organizations. (*See chart, p. 429.*)

"There's a whole level of celebrity advocacy," says Steven J. Ross, a professor of history at the University of Southern California in Los Angeles and author of *Hollywood Left and Right: How Movie Stars Shaped American Politics.* "There's less than the public would expect for explicitly political issues, but more than the public might expect for non-controversial celebrity advocacy, let's say, for diseases." "It's not necessarily that there's more celebrity involvement in politics," says Blake. "It's just that we're more aware of it."

For candidates or causes, celebrities' value comes from their ability to attract attention. "The public is fascinated with celebrity, and they have a reach that can be significant," says Alia McKee, a principal with Sea Change Strategies, a research and marketing firm that works with nonprofit organizations. If correctly chosen and used, celebrities also enhance the stature of the organizations they are backing. "There is a cachet that nonprofits get when they have a celebrity speaking on their behalf," McKee says.

Conversely, a celebrity may increase the bad publicity when missteps occur either on the organization's part or the celebrity's. "If a celebrity gets involved in some sort of scandal, it can have a negative impact on the charity," says Sandra Minutti, marketing director for Charity Navigator, a major charity-evaluation service. The group gives high marks to many of the charities personally founded by or associated with celebrities, but marks others down for high fundraising and administrative costs or poor financial controls. (*See chart, p. 432.*)

Celebrities can also provoke suspicions that they are supporting a charitable cause as much to promote their own careers as to serve the public good. "There's quite a bit of skepticism about celebrities in the public eye," says Joshua Gamson, a sociology professor at the University of San Francisco and author of *Claims to Fame: Celebrity in Contemporary America*. "It always carries the risk that people will perceive the celebrity's actions as motivated by the gain in celebrity and industry value."

Celebrities can avoid such insinuations if they know their cause and devote serious effort to it, according to Tom Sheridan, president of the Sheridan Group, a Washington lobbying firm that represents nonprofit and philanthropic organizations. Sheridan has been the principal strategic adviser for the singer Bono in the last decade in his advocacy work on AIDS and global poverty.

Sheridan likens Clooney's involvement on Sudan to Bono's work. "He's been there, he brought his cameras with him," Sheridan says. "It actually showed a level of personal commitment."

Celebrity advocates have their politically motivated critics as well. Conservative commentators complain that celebrities inevitably flock to liberal politics and causes. "They tend to skew left on every conceivable issue, particularly on social issues," says Ben Shapiro, editor at large for the conservative website Breitbart.com and author of a critical look at what he says is leftist television programming, *Prime Time Propaganda: The True Hollywood Story of How the Left Took Over Your TV.*

Others discount but stop short of completely rejecting the critique. "There's some of that," Minutti says of the perceived liberal bias. But she also sees a blurring of ideological lines in charity-related advocacy. "I don't think we see the left or the right," she says.

In the age of Facebook groups and Twitter blasts, celebrities have more and more ways to make their influence felt in supporting political candidates or raising public consciousness on social and environmental issues.

Children's Issues Top List of Celebrity Causes

More than 1,700 celebrities support 566 charities that focus on children's welfare, making it the leading cause among celebrity advocates. Celebrities support another 221 charities focusing on at-risk and disadvantaged youths. Health, education and poverty are also among the leading celebrity causes. Overall, more than 2,800 celebrities support over 1,800 charitable organizations.

Leading Causes Supported by Celebrities, May 2012

Cause	Number of charities	Number of celebrities
Children	566	1,755
Health	451	1,537
Education	255	790
At-risk/disadvantaged youths	221	720
Poverty	187	932
Cancer	160	863
Environment	160	609
AIDS	142	972
Women	131	517
Human rights	130	855
Animals	125	518
Family/parent support	121	525

Source: "Celebrity Causes," Look to the Stars, May 2012, www.looktothestars.org/category

With celebrity advocacy seemingly on the rise, here are some of the questions being debated:

Do celebrity advocates help educate the public about issues?

Inspired by a documentary about child prostitution in Cambodia, the now estranged celebrity couple Demi Moore and Ashton Kutcher established a foundation in 2010 to take on the issue of child sex slavery, around the world and in the United States. Focusing on the demand side, Kutcher put together a series of semi-satiric public service announcements ending with the message, "Real men don't buy girls."

The campaign drew favorable attention — Kutcher and Moore were invited to appear at a United Nations event on the issue — but Kutcher took some flak for claiming on a prime-time talk show that there were "between 100,000 and 300,000" child sex slaves in the United States. Under the headline "Real Men Get Their Facts Straight," *The Village Voice* effectively debunked the figure in June 2011.

The newspaper showed that Kutcher got his figure from an academic study that estimated 100,000 to 300,000 girls *at risk* of sexual exploitation in the United States. Law enforcement records reviewed by the newspaper showed only 8,263 underage girls as having been arrested for child prostitution over the previous decade. Kutcher replied to the story by launching a Twitter war with the *Voice* for allegedly abetting child prostitution through the sex ads carried by the newspaper. [4]

The episode illustrates one of the dangers of celebrity advocacy — the risk of factual misstatements. "When celebrities go off like loose cannons, nobody can stop them one way or another," says Ross of USC.

"When you have the capacity to get a lot of attention on a subject, you have the responsibility to really know what you're talking about," remarks the University of San Francisco's Gamson. Even though the erroneous six-figure estimate had been reported in mainstream media earlier, it was Kutcher's interview that prompted a critical look. "When he was using it, people were actually listening," Gamson says.

Despite the risks, celebrities undoubtedly have the ability to bring public attention to issues and mobilize public engagement. Ernie Allen, president and CEO of the National Center for Missing & Exploited Children, says the Real Men campaign "elevated public knowledge around the issue and advanced the cause." [5]

Sheridan, the Washington lobbyist, agrees, but stresses the importance of a serious commitment of time and effort by the celebrity. "Celebrities have a tremendous capacity to educate the public about issues, but that capacity is directly relevant to their credibility," Sheridan says. "If you hear a celebrity talk about an issue only once or twice, it's water off the duck."

A personal connection to an issue helps keep celebrity advocates engaged. Among recent examples, Christopher Reeve and Michael J. Fox have helped raise funds and public awareness by struggling in public with debilitating conditions — a paralyzing spinal injury for Reeve, who died in 2004, and Parkinson's disease for Fox. Elton John was moved to establish his AIDS foundation by the deaths of many friends during the height of the epidemic in the 1980s.

In its campaigns, the Creative Coalition stresses careful preparation with the celebrity. "When the coalition gets involved, our people get involved," says Bronk, the CEO. "We don't just pick a celebrity. It has to be a thoughtful reason why the celebrity is involved."

The risks of missteps by celebrities may be minimized somewhat by the rise of social media, according to David Mindich, an associate professor of journalism and mass communication at St. Michael's College in Colchester, Vt. "It used to be [that] celebrity endorsements for causes really were important because you might not have known what your friends were advocating for or endorsing," Mindich says. "Nowadays we can find out what our friends on Facebook care about. We are swayed a lot by that."

Moore and Kutcher are continuing their advocacy work despite their impending divorce. They traveled together in December to a U.N.-sponsored conference in Egypt on human trafficking. A U.S. expert on child prostitution gives them credit for focusing on an issue that needs more public attention, but faults Kutcher for his statistical misstep.

"We don't really have good statistics about how big a problem it is," says David Finkelhor, director of the Crimes Against Children Research Center at the University of New Hampshire in Durham. "All the available numbers are wild speculation."

The numbers cited by Kutcher are "just guesstimates that have gotten credibility by being repeated by reputable people but aren't recognized by any scientific methodology," Finkelhor says. "It's always good when people want to take on social problems," he adds, "but it behooves them to work with evidence-based approaches."

Getty Images/Kevork Djansezian

Actress Olivia Wilde visits a settlement camp for displaced persons in Port-au-Prince, Haiti, on April 12, 2010. Soon after an earthquake devastated the country in January, actor Sean Penn set up a relief organization to oversee the camp, where thousands of Haitians now live. The organization has become a leader in helping Haiti recover.

Is celebrity advocacy mostly about self-promotion?

Los Angeles Lakers basketball star Kobe Bryant drew about 20 reporters to a homeless shelter in Hollywood last summer to hear him announce the formation of a foundation dedicated to helping disadvantaged youth and families. But when a magazine writer accompanied Bryant's philanthropy adviser to My Friend's Place a few months later, Bryant was not along for the visit. Instead, Trevor Neilson, president of Global Philanthropy Group, told the writer that Bryant and his wife Vanessa were "on vacation somewhere exotic." [6]

The Kobe & Vanessa Bryant Family Foundation continues, despite the couple's impending divorce, but its website is thin on concrete accomplishments since the June 7 news conference. The site's news page has four entries: Bryant's trip to China to visit U.S. students, his sponsorship of a trip to China for 11 disadvantaged students from Los Angeles, his service as honorary co-chair of a United Way 5K walk and his appearance on the television show "Extreme Makeover" to support a campus clothing drive.

Bryant made the connection with Neilson's philanthropy group in January 2011 after having been "spottily associated" with charitable works up till then, according to *New Yorker* staff writer John Colapinto. He had started two foundations earlier, but they had gone dormant. And Colapinto notes that Bryant's image needed rehabilitation because of a rape charge in 2003 — eventually dropped — and his use of an anti-gay epithet in April 2011.

Celebrities may help the charitable organizations and causes they support, but they also benefit from the reflected light of their good works. "Celebrities understand that they are a brand, and they want to enhance that brand, and they understand that affiliating with a charity can help do that," says Minutti with Charity Navigator. "And most charities are glad to have that help."

"I don't see anything inherently wrong in that," says Gamson, the San Francisco professor. "It's a system in which they're operating, and they're making use of the system in a variety of ways."

Conservative commentator Shapiro, however, has little use for celebrities who portray themselves as experts on complex or contentious public policy issues. "People think these celebrities are obnoxious, and they are obnoxious," Shapiro says. "What makes them experts?"

Sheridan, the Washington lobbyist, similarly disdains the celebrity who turns to good deeds to counteract bad publicity. "If you're looking for a way to distract people from your last affair or your drug rehabilitation, this is not for you," he says.

But Sheridan cites his work as a counterexample to the unfavorable image of spotlight-seeking, policy-skimming celebrities. He says he did little press with Bono for the first several years after taking on the global rock star as a client to work on debt relief and trade issues.

Even while promoting his causes at concerts and elsewhere, Bono puts in "a significant amount of time" on the issues, often out of the spotlight, Sheridan says. "Bono goes to Africa every year," Sheridan says, and not just for a flyover. "It's not a 30,000-foot approach for him."

The typical celebrity endorser, however, is by no means self-effacing, according to those who work with them. Celebrities "require a lot of hand-holding," says McKee with Sea Change Strategies. Working with a celebrity's schedule and through a celebrity's own staff essentially requires an organization to have a staff member "completely devoted" to coordinating with the celebrity. "A good celebrity staffer will be able to set expectations and leverage the relationship," McKee says.

Zack Brisson, who formerly worked for the Enough Project, the anti-genocide organization that Clooney is working with, agrees. Celebrities may be cost-effective, he says, but they are not cost-free. "There's a staffing cost, there's an intellectual cost, there's a time cost, there's a brand-risk cost," Brisson said. [7]

Despite the benefits to celebrities in most instances, there are some risks, according to Bronk with the Creative Coalition. "Getting involved in an issue is not free for an entertainer's career," she says. "There are always fans who won't agree with us. It's not easy to get involved, but getting involved is an important part of citizenship."

"Just because you're an entertainer or celebrity," Bronk adds, "doesn't mean that you should check your citizenship at the stage door."

Is celebrity advocacy slanted in favor of liberal causes?

In a quarter-century of global philanthropy, Bono has received praise and honors of nearly every description, including a knighthood in Britain, designation as *Time* magazine's "Person of the Year" and three Nobel Peace Prize nominations. But in his native Ireland, Bono and his band, The Edge, draw criticism for their tax-planning decision several years ago to move their accounts to the Netherlands to avoid what would have been a seven-figure euro tax bill on album sales and royalties. [8]

Bono and the other band members note that the move was perfectly legal. But conservative commentator Shapiro, like some of Bono's countrymen, views the tax move as inconsistent with the singer's call for more government aid to developing countries. "It's easy for him to talk about how we should have higher taxes to pay for this while he's a tax evader," Shapiro says.

Shapiro voices the widely held view that most of the celebrities visibly engaged in political or charitable advocacy espouse liberal, often far-left, viewpoints. And he attributes the political slant to the financial and social advantages that celebrities enjoy. "They're extraordinarily wealthy," says Shapiro. "So there's no risk for them in saying things that are politically extreme."

Several experts largely dismiss the view of a liberal slant among celebrity advocates. "I don't think you can make that generalization anymore," says

Some Celebrity Charities Spend Little on Programs

Spending on programs varies widely among charities associated with celebrities, according to Charity Navigator, an organization that evaluates American charities. The Michael J. Fox Foundation for Parkinson's Research and the Elton John AIDS Foundation received the highest rating of 4, with at least 90 percent of their revenues going toward program expenses. By contrast, Operation Lookout National Center for Missing Youth, whose international spokesperson is actress Dyan Cannon, received a 0 rating, with only about 10 percent of revenue used for programs.

Ratings and Program Expenses for Select Celebrity-Endorsed Charities

Charity and associated celebrities	Rating (0-4, with 4 being best)	Program expenses (as a percentage of total revenue)
Michael J. Fox Foundation for Parkinson's Research	4	91%
New York Restoration (Bette Midler)	4	88%
Elton John AIDS Foundation (Elton John, Jane Fonda, Whoopi Goldberg)	4	95%
United Nations Foundation (Ted Turner)	4	88%
Tony LaRussa's Animal Rescue Foundation	4	91%
Baltimore Reads (Cal Ripken Jr.)	3	84%
Tiger Woods Foundation	3	86%
Doug Flutie Jr. Foundation for Autism	3	80%
Farm Aid (Willie Nelson, Neil Young, John Mellencamp, Dave Matthews)	3	75%
Christopher and Dana Reeve Foundation	2	84%
Save the Manatee Club (Jimmy Buffett)	2	85%
Joe Torre Safe at Home Foundation	2	63%
Teammates for Kids Foundation (Garth Brooks)	1	76%
Larry King Cardiac Foundation	1	69%
Operation Lookout (Dyan Cannon)	0	10%

Source: Charity Navigator, www.charitynavigator.org

Bronk with the Creative Coalition.

"Somehow the arts became this political football," Bronk continues. "I think more and more people are becoming more independent. I think more people are crossing political lines."

"There may be more liberals in the entertainment industry in the same way that there are more conservatives in the defense industry," says College of New Jersey professor Blake. "But to say that all of Hollywood is liberal and they can't be trusted — that's an argument that goes back to the late 1940s."

USC professor Ross says that even if liberals outnumber conservatives in present-day Hollywood, industry conservatives have had the larger impact over time. "Conservatives have a longer political history," Ross says, pointing to the close ties that the legendary film producer Louis B. Mayer had with the Republican Party in the 1920s and '30s. Mayer, he notes, introduced George Murphy to politics, who in turn recruited Ronald Reagan into the political sphere. Both first won office in the 1960s: Murphy to the U.S. Senate from California in 1964, Reagan to the governorship two years later, and later the presidency.

Today, Hollywood celebrities can be found on both sides of the political aisle. BuzzFeed, the social-content tracking website, includes on its list of 40 Republican celebrities quiz show hosts Drew Carey and Pat Sajak, singers Gloria Estefan and Wayne Newton and film actors Bo Derek, Chuck Norris and Sylvester Stallone. The list of 40 Democratic celebrities includes television hosts Regis Philbin and Oprah Winfrey, singers Eminem and the Dixie Chicks and film actors Tom Hanks, Jack Nicholson and Gwyneth Paltrow. [9]

With no partisan labels, the compilation of celebrity-supported causes on the Look to the Stars website does appear to have something of a liberal tilt. Some of the top causes, such as children and health, may seem to be non- or cross-ideological, but several of the others draw much of their support from liberals, including poverty and the environment. Support for veterans and service members is low down on the list, with 36 charities supported by 174 celebrities. And criminal justice or crime victims' rights does not appear at all.

"Maybe they do skew left," says McKee with Sea Change Strategies, "but there are celebrities who speak to the right side of the aisle."

Shapiro, however, continues to insist his ideological side is out-advocated in the celebrity world. One reason, he says, is a prevalent anti-conservative bias in Hollywood. Conservatives get a backlash when they talk politics, he says. In addition, conservatives have less reason to get into political advocacy, he says. "Most conservative celebrities are saying, 'Leave me the hell alone,' " Shapiro says, "which isn't something that needs a lot of backing." ■

Getty Images/NBAE/Andrew D. Bernstein

Basketball star Kobe Bryant of the Los Angeles Lakers drills Chinese exchange students at a clinic supported by his foundation on Jan. 31, 2011, in Bell Gardens, Calif. Questions have been raised about his commitment to charitable causes. Some argue that Bryant's image needed rehabilitation because of a rape charge in 2003 — eventually dropped — and his use of an anti-gay epithet in April 2011.

BACKGROUND

Star Power

Celebrities from the world of entertainment have taken on increasingly prominent roles in political and charitable causes since the beginnings of the modern era of mass media in the early 20th century. Celebrities promoted war bonds and the war effort generally in both of the last century's worldwide conflicts. With the advent of motion pictures, actors discovered that their visibility and popularity allowed them to influence public opinion both through and apart from their films. By midcentury, Hollywood had clusters of stars on both the political right and left, and they helped shape national debates on such issues as internal security, civil rights, the Vietnam War and the environment. [10]

The United States had celebrities before the 20th century, including evangelists, authors and road-show performers such as the Wild West figures Buffalo Bill and Annie Oakley. Two entertainers even foretold the late 20th-century phenomenon of actors as politicians, according to College of New Jersey professor Blake. The actor Edwin Forrest (1806-1872) was "a vibrant speaker" and "hero to the working classes" who became an important speaker for the Democratic Party in fundraising events. Circus clown Dan Rice (1823-1900) flirted with running for Congress, lost a race for a state Senate seat in Pennsylvania and waged a short-lived campaign for the Democratic nomination for president in 1868.

The birth of motion pictures in the early 20th century helped entertainers rise to national prominence more quickly than before. With Hollywood in its infancy, the government enlisted early superstars Charlie Chaplin, Mary Pickford and Douglas Fairbanks, among others, to sell war bonds during World War I. A quarter-century later, many stars of the more mature film industry were pressed into similar roles. By then, Hollywood figures had also learned the political uses of movies. On the left, Chaplin mocked industrial life in "Modern Times" (1935) and Adolf Hitler in "The Great Dictator," which premiered in October 1940 with the nation still ambivalent about the war in Europe. By contrast, the series of Andy Hardy films in the late 1930s and early '40s, produced at MGM under the legendary Mayer, embodied what USC professor Ross describes as a conservative ideology critical of an expansionist federal government.

Hollywood's political divisions emerged more sharply in the post-World War II debate over internal security. Many Hollywood figures on the political left had helped mobilize anti-fascist opinion in the 1930s; some were communist sympathizers or outright supporters. In 1944, some on the political right, including Walt Disney, John Wayne and many others, formed the Motion Picture Alliance for the Preservation of American Ideals with a mission of combating both fascism and communism.

With the Cold War just getting under way, the House Un-American Activities Committee (HUAC) convened a hearing in 1947 to examine allegations — made by, among others, Reagan, then president of the Screen Actors Guild — of communist influence on movie industry unions and movies themselves. Among more than 40 witnesses summoned, 10 actors and directors refused to testify; for their refusal, the Hollywood 10 were found in contempt and sentenced to jail. Despite a vigorous defense by the Hollywood-organized Committee for the First Amendment, the episode marked the start of the blacklist that damaged or destroyed the careers of many Hollywood actors and screenwriters through the 1950s.

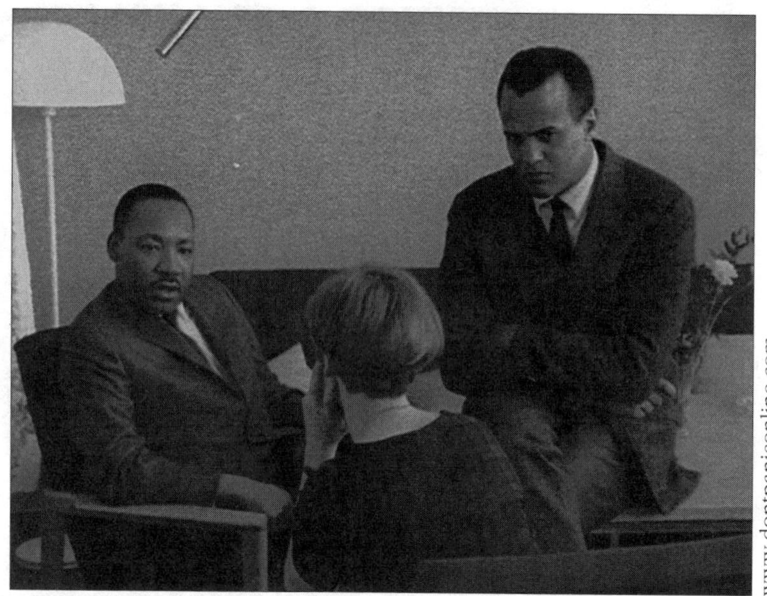

Singer Harry Belafonte, the nation's first black television star (right), played a largely behind-the-scenes role in the civil rights movement as a friend and adviser to the Rev. Martin Luther King Jr. (left). Belafonte helped organize support for the famous 1963 March on Washington from such stars as Marlon Brando, Burt Lancaster and Charlton Heston.

Hollywood was more closely united on the next major domestic issue: civil rights. Movie studios and producers began introducing audiences to African-American actors and racially themed films, tentatively at first in the 1950s and more overtly by the mid-1960s as in the interracial romance depicted in "Guess Who's Coming to Dinner" (1967). Singer Harry Belafonte, the nation's first black television star, played a largely behind-the-scenes role in the civil rights movement as a friend and adviser to the Rev. Dr. Martin Luther King Jr. And Belafonte helped organize public support for the famous 1963 March on Washington from a contingent of recognizable stars that included Marlon Brando, Burt Lancaster and Charlton Heston, two decades before Heston's evolution into an outspoken conservative.

The Hollywood community divided sharply, however, on the other major issue of the 1960s: the Vietnam War. Heston traveled to Vietnam in January 1966 with doubts and came back a confirmed supporter of the war. He joined with Bob Hope and Henry Fonda in a televised Independence Day special in 1967 to explain the goals of the war. A year later, the release of the anti-communist film "The Green Berets" helped fortify hawkish support for the war.

On the opposite side, left-leaning celebrities such as Paul Newman and Leonard Nimoy backed the anti-war candidate Eugene McCarthy in 1968, and Warren Beatty became a close adviser to Democratic presidential nominee George McGovern in 1972. Counterculture musicians such as Joan Baez and Phil Ochs sang for the anti-Vietnam march on Washington in 1967. Most memorably, perhaps, Jane Fonda traveled to North Vietnam in 1972 to dramatize the impact of U.S. bombing and became a lasting symbol to conservatives of what they regard as Hollywood's ambiguous stance on patriotism issues.

Leading Roles

Celebrities moved from supporting to leading roles in politics and cause-related advocacy in the closing decades of the 20th century. Reagan's advance from B-list films to the White House validated the political aspirations of other actors, some of whom took the plunge while others merely dipped their toes into political waters. Musical celebrities were put to good use in a succession of cause-related concerts beginning with the spectacular Live Aid concert for the Ethiopian

Continued on p. 436

Chronology

1940s-1950s
Hollywood is roiled by Red Scare, blacklist.

1944
Walt Disney, John Wayne, others form Motion Picture Alliance for Preservation of American Ideals to combat fascism, communism.

1947
Hollywood Ten refuse to answer questions about Communist Party affiliations in hearing by House Un-American Activities committee; sentenced and sent to jail for contempt of Congress.

1949
Comedian Milton Berle hosts TV telethon for cancer research; format later used for countless celebrity-hosted charity drives.

1950s
Many actors, screenwriters blacklisted for prior communist sympathies.

1960s-1970s
Hollywood united on civil rights, divided on Vietnam.

1963
Hollywood stars help organize, enlist support for pro-civil rights March on Washington for Jobs and Freedom.

1964, 1966
Song-and-dance man George Murphy elected to U.S. Senate from California; serves one term (1965-1971). . . . Ronald Reagan elected governor of California; serves two terms (1967-1975), becomes leader of conservative movement within Republican Party.

1967
Charlton Heston co-hosts pro-Vietnam War TV special. . . . Joan Baez, Phil Ochs, others perform at anti-Vietnam War March on Washington.

1968
Liberal Hollywood stars have high profile in. unsuccessful anti-war presidential campaign of Sen. Eugene McCarthy, D-Minn.

1972
Warren Beatty is behind-the-scenes adviser to Democratic presidential nominee Sen. George McGovern of South Dakota.

1980s-1990s
Celebrities take starring roles in politics, advocacy.

1981
Reagan sworn in as president; helps pave way for other film, TV actors to transition to politics in succeeding years.

1985
Live Aid concert simultaneously in London and Philadelphia raises $284 million for Ethiopian famine relief with performances by the Rolling Stones' Mick Jagger and other big stars. . . . Elizabeth Taylor heads American Foundation for AIDS Research. . . . First Farm Aid concert held, organized by Willie Nelson, John Mellencamp and Neil Young.

1989
Creative Coalition is founded to enlist celebrities

1995
Christopher Reeve suffers paralyzing spinal cord injury in horse-riding accident; later, lends name to foundation to support research, treatment.

1998
Michael J. Fox discloses he has Parkinson's Disease; establishes foundation in 2000 to support research, treatment.

1999
Beatty flirts with possible run for president, but backs off.

2000-Present
Celebrities use social media for advocacy, fund-raising.

2002
Bono helps launch "debt, trade, AIDS, Africa" campaign; merges with other global poverty groups in 2007 to form ONE campaign.

2005
Brad Pitt, other celebrities help raise funds for Gulf Coast relief after Hurricane Katrina.

2006
George Clooney visits Sudanese region of Darfur, calls for humanitarian aid to refugees there. . . . Angelina Jolie and Brad Pitt establish Jolie Pitt Foundation, dispense multimillion-dollar grants annually to U.S., international charities. . . . Look to the Stars is founded to track celebrities' support for charities, causes; by May 2012 counts 2,844 celebrities backing 1,806 charities.

2010
Demi Moore and Ashton Kutcher establish foundation to combat child sexual slavery; Kutcher later criticized for exaggerating extent of child prostitution in United States.

2012
Clooney testifies before Congress, meets with President Obama on Sudan/South Sudan conflict (March 14-15); is arrested for protest at Sudanese Embassy (March 16).

Actors Seek Electoral Limelight

For some, the political stage is the place to be.

Superstar Warren Beatty wrote, directed and played the title role in the 1998 film "Bulworth" as a disillusioned senator who decides to come clean with his constituents about the corruption of present-day politics. A year later, urged on by supportive friends, Beatty took on a real-life role in fall 1999 as a disillusioned citizen who publicly ponders the idea of running for president himself.

The four-month flirtation ended on Jan. 3, 2000, when *Vanity Fair* magazine hit the newsstands with Beatty's "not now, maybe later" decision. "I'm not running now," Beatty told the magazine. "I think the question is: Can I be effective at another time? Whether that is in a year, or two years, who knows?" [1]

A half-century earlier, Beatty's possible candidacy might have been dismissed as a Mittyesque daydream. But that was before Ronald Reagan showed that in the United States, even a B-list film star could grow up someday to be president — for two terms, even.

By the end of the 20th century, one-time actors had served in elective office at every level of government, including at least four in Congress: Reps. Sonny Bono (R-Calif.), Fred Grandy (R-Iowa) and Ben Jones (D-Ga.) and Sen. Fred Thompson (R-Tenn.).

All four of the actors-turned-lawmakers had creditable records in Congress that, for some of them, belied their TV roles. Grandy, the bumbling bursar on the TV show "The Love Boat," was described in 1992 as "one of the most able of the younger generation of House Republicans." Jones, on the other hand, was said to be "popular with colleagues" because of a "real-life folksy manner" that matched that of his character on "The Dukes of Hazzard." [2]

Today, Al Franken is a serious voice for liberal Democratic politics as junior senator from Minnesota decades after he started in show business as a comedy writer and performer on the NBC program "Saturday Night Live."

Reagan and fellow actor George Murphy were by no means taken seriously at first when they ventured into electoral politics in California in the 1960s. But Steven J. Ross, author of the book *Hollywood Left and Right: How Movie Stars Shaped American Politics*, says reporters mistook the one-time film stars to be political neophytes. "These guys had been in the political trenches," Ross says.

Ross says the two conservatives were "absolutely fundamental to unseating the liberal Republican stronghold in the state." Murphy bested an establishment candidate to win the GOP primary for a U.S. Senate seat in 1964 and then defeated former White House press secretary Pierre Salinger in the general election. Reagan similarly beat a more liberal Republican in 1966 to gain the party's gubernatorial nomination and went on to win over two-term incumbent Edmund G. (Pat) Brown. [3]

Like Reagan before him, Beatty was far from a political amateur when he toyed with a presidential candidacy in 1999. Beatty had been a close adviser in 1972 to Democratic presi-

Continued from p. 434

famine in 1985. Meanwhile, Hollywood and Broadway figures, with Elizabeth Taylor in the lead, played a prominent role in AIDS-related advocacy from the mid-1980s on, and Reeve and Fox demonstrated in the 1990s the potential impact of a celebrity's personal story in focusing attention on major health issues. [11]

Reagan's evolution from New Deal Democrat to conservative Republican began in the 1950s. In the face of doubts and derision, Reagan proved his abilities as a political candidate and elected official in two terms as governor of California (1967-1975) and then two terms as president (1981-1989). With Reagan as example, other TV and movie actors tried out for political roles. By the end of the 20th century, one-time actors had served or were serving as mayors in several cities, in the California legislature, in the Minnesota statehouse and in the U.S. Congress. And as the 1990s ended, Beatty publicly flirted with a possible run for the presidency as a liberal Democrat, but decided in the end to stick with movies.

Celebrity fundraising dates from the earliest days of television: Comedian Milton Berle hosted a telethon that raised $1.1 million for cancer research in 1949. The model continued most famously with the Muscular Dystrophy Association Labor Day telethon hosted for 45 years by actor-comedian Jerry Lewis (1966-2011). In the 1980s, musical producers and performers updated the concept with fundraising concerts — beginning with Live Aid, organized by the now-legendary music producer Bob Geldof. The star-packed, simultaneous concerts in London and Philadelphia on July 22, 1985, raised an estimated $284 million for famine relief in Ethiopia. In the United States, singers Willie Nelson, John Mellencamp and Neil Young adapted the idea for the Sept. 22, 1985, Farm Aid concert to help family farmers; similar concerts were staged four times over the next six years and have been annual events since 1992.

Fundraising for AIDS has drawn immeasurable support from countless celebrities from Hollywood and Broadway but from no one more prominent than Taylor. Moved by the death from AIDS of her one-time costar Rock Hudson, Taylor agreed in 1985 to be the founding chair of the American

dential nominee George McGovern, who later praised his political instincts. Later, Beatty worked for Gary Hart in his two unsuccessful campaigns for the Democratic presidential nomination, in 1984 and 1988. Unlike Reagan, however, Beatty backed away from seeking office himself. He was jealous of his privacy, according to Ross, and ill-suited for governing as well. [4]

Getty Images/The White House/Michael Evans

Ronald Reagan transitioned from a B-list film star into leading political roles, first as governor of California and eventually as president of the United States.

Ross says actors still risk being belittled when they decide to delve into politics. David Blake, a professor of English at the College of New Jersey, agrees, but finds the public's doubts ironic given the blurring line between entertainment and politics. "It's an odd dynamic," says Blake, who is writing a book on celebrity in the 1950s. "On the one hand, we resent entertainers who become political, but we are also becoming more and more accustomed to politicians who become entertainers."

Today, many successful politicians are also finding it necessary to prove themselves in the world of entertainment. Richard Nixon's appearance as presidential candidate in 1968 on the NBC comedy "Laugh-In" is famous, in part, because it was so unusual at the time. But candidate Bill Clinton's saxophone gig on the "Arsenio Hall Show" set a new standard for politicians, who now routinely appear on entertainment as well as TV news programs. In August 2003, actor-turned-politico Arnold Schwarzenegger went so far as to announce his candidacy for governor of California on "The Tonight Show" with Jay Leno.

— Kenneth Jost

[1] Quoted in "Beatty Tells Magazine He Won't Run for President Now, but He Isn't Ruling Out Later," The Associated Press, Jan. 3, 2000. For background, see Steven J. Ross, *Hollywood Left and Right: How Movie Stars Shaped American Politics* (2011), pp. 348-359.

[2] See CQ's *Politics in America 1992*, pp. 544 (Grandy), 365 (Jones).

[3] For background, see Ross, *op. cit.*, pp. 131-183.

[4] *Ibid.*, p. 345.

Foundation for AIDS Research (amfAR), the first mainstream AIDS organization. Through the years, she testified before Congress, spoke to the U.N. General Assembly and founded her own foundation to support AIDS research and treatment. At her death in 2011, Taylor was credited with raising more than $100 million. Many other film stars and movie industry groups have helped keep the spotlight on the issue. [12]

The New York theater community has also helped fight AIDS through the merged organizations Broadway Cares/Equity Fights AIDS, founded respectively by producers in 1988 and actors in 1987. Through 2011, the organizations have distributed $123.5 million in grants to AIDS organizations nationally and internationally. [13]

Reeve and Fox gave their names to foundations on the health issues that affected them directly. Reeve became a public spokesman for research about and treatment of spinal cord injuries in his years of rehabilitation after a horse-riding injury in 1995 left him a quadriplegic. By demonstrating that one could continue a public life even while forced to use a wheelchair and breathing apparatus, Reeve provided information and inspiration about a subject not well covered before. [14] Somewhat similarly, Fox sought out the public spotlight in 1998 by disclosing that he had Parkinson's disease, first diagnosed in 1991. While forced into semiretirement from acting after 2000, he has written books, given interviews and testified before Congress about his experience with the disease. The foundation he established in 2000 has become the single largest funder of Parkinson's research, with $179 million distributed through 2011. [15]

Multiple Causes

An ever-growing number of celebrities found an ever-growing number of causes to support in the early 21st century through an ever-growing number of platforms, including social media. Natural and man-made disasters drew major responses from entertainers and others. Celebrities also sprang into action to help raise awareness of — and research and treatment funds for — diseases both well known and obscure. And global issues, including human

Advocacy Films Have a Long History

"The most effective sneak their message in in subtle ways."

With a record $2.8 billion in box office receipts and three Oscars among other awards, "Avatar" ranks among the most successful movies in history. It won critical acclaim from reviewers as well as from Academy Award voters for cinematography, visual effects and art direction. But director James Cameron made the movie as more than entertainment. He also wanted to convey an anti-colonialist, pro-environment message to audiences in the United States and around the world.

The villains in "Avatar" (2009) are evident surrogates for Western colonizers and corporate exploiters; the heroes are indigenous peoples who are at peace rather than at war with nature. The movie, one environmentalist wrote, sends "an urgent message" against "the atrocities . . . being carried out right now against our own planet." [1]

"Avatar" takes its place among a century's worth of movies with politically themed messages dating from Charlie Chaplin's "The Jungle" (1914) and D. W. Griffith's "The Birth of a Nation" (1915) and continuing to the present day. Within the past decade or so, filmmakers have put strong messages in movies dealing with such issues as gay rights ("Milk," 2008), sexual harassment ("North Country," 2005), genocide ("Hotel Rwanda," 2004) and toxic dumps ("Erin Brockovich," 2000).

Message-sending filmmakers do best, however, by embedding their points of view in movies that succeed as entertainment as well, according to Steven J. Ross, a professor of history at the University of Southern California and author of the book *Hollywood Left and Right: How Movie Stars Shaped American Politics*.

"The most effective message movies are those that are not openly didactic, those that sneak their message in subtle ways," says Ross. "You don't get many movies that hit you over the head — not if they want to be effective."

Ross lists Chaplin as Hollywood's "first political movie star," beginning with his adaptation of the Upton Sinclair novel that portrayed the meatpacking industry as indifferent to public health. Chaplin subtly used comedy in later films to convey anti-authoritarian, anti-capitalist themes, but in "The Great Dictator" (1940) he ended a mocking satire of Mussolini and Hitler by coming on screen to personally deliver a passionate plea for world peace.

"The Birth of a Nation" marked the first time a film itself became a political controversy. The adaptation of the post-Civil War novel *The Clansman* stirred a strong protest from the NAACP for its stereotyped depictions of freed slaves and exaltation of the Ku Klux Klan. Griffith made amends of sorts with his next film, "Intolerance" (1916), which depicts the effects of prejudice through four story lines from different historical eras.

International affairs put their stamp on films in successive decades. Ross notes "Confessions of a Nazi Spy" (1939) as the first film to depict the Nazis as a threat to the United States. [2] With the Cold War under way, anti-communist themes emerged in the 1950s in movies such as "I Married a Communist" (1949), most of them unmemorable except for their propagandistic excess. [3] In the 1960s, the excesses of the Cold War were starkly critiqued in "Fail Safe" (1964) and savagely mocked in "Dr. Strangelove or How I Learned to Stop Worrying and Love the Bomb" (1964). Explicitly anti-war films came to the fore in the 1970s, including the satiric Korean War comedy "M*A*S*H" (1970) and the haunting Vietnam War epic "Apocalypse Now" (1979).

Domestic issues can also be seen in any number of movies from the 1950s on. "12 Angry Men" (1957) famously exalts a hold-out juror who helps save an innocent defendant from a

rights, poverty and the environment, became major focuses for such A-list film stars as Angelina Jolie and Brad Pitt, Leonardo DiCaprio and Matt Damon. [16]

Bono, lead singer of U2, achieved perhaps the most visible success among the early 21st-century celebrity advocates as he took his ONE campaign for global poverty relief directly to political and financial leaders. On the eve of a concert in Washington, Bono lunched at the White House with President George W. Bush on Oct. 19, 2005, to discuss debt relief, trade, AIDS and malaria. Early in 2008, the Irish singer had a similar tête-à-tête with French President Nicolas Sarkozy. Before the White House meeting, Bono had voiced gratitude to Bush for anti-AIDS funding. But in Paris he had what he called a "feisty" meeting about lagging French aid. Sarkozy responded with an on-the-spot pledge to restore 20 million euros to disease-fighting efforts. [17]

Pitt and Jolie — dubbed "Brangelina" by the tabloids — shared Bono's interest in global issues and possibly outpaced him in visibility. Together, the glamour couple established the Jolie Pitt Foundation in 2006 and used it through the years to make multimillion-dollar grants annually to an array of charities. Jolie took a special interest in refugees after being named a U.N. goodwill ambassador on the issue in 2001; over the next decade, she visited more than 20 countries to meet with refugees. Pitt has focused in particular on sustainable architecture and design. And they have traveled together to disaster sites — for example, to Pakistan-controlled Kashmir after the 2005 earthquake there.

Disasters in or near the United States also galvanized U.S. celebrities. A long list of performers — including Neil Young,

wrongful conviction. Two 1967 movies, "In the Heat of the Night" and "Guess Who's Coming to Dinner," show the triumph of racial tolerance over prejudices held by otherwise respectable figures. The conservative era of the 1980s spawned a stinging critique of ruthless corporate raiders in "Wall Street" (1987). The AIDS epidemic was movingly portrayed in "Philadelphia" (1993) through the death of a gay lawyer fired after his symptoms became evident.

One of the most successful movies ever made, "Avatar" conveyed director James Cameron's clear anti-colonialist, pro-environment message.

While those and other films conveyed liberal viewpoints, conservatives saw their views represented in such movies as "Dirty Harry" (1971), with its unrelenting law-and-order stance, the hawkish action-film Rambo series that began with "First Blood" (1982) and the epic science-fiction series of "Terminator" films starring the future governor of California, Arnold Schwarzenegger.

Today, "there seems to be an overabundance" of message movies, writes Alison Hill, a freelance journalist and documentary producer who compiled her own list of 10 films in the genre for the website Listosaur. Hill concedes that message movies have an uncertain impact. She credits "The Killing Fields" (1989) with informing the public about one of the bloodiest genocides in history — the slaughter of more than a million Cambodians by the Khmer Rouge regime in the 1970s. But she says that "Blood Diamond" (2006), a fictionalized account of the sale of "conflict diamonds" to finance insurgencies in war-torn African countries, appears to have had little if any impact on the sale of diamonds in the West. [4]

Hill says she is "partial" to movie messages and says there is "a niche market" for such films. But she concedes that many do not succeed at the box office. "People want to go to movies to escape rather than be confronted with harsh reality," she says.

— ***Kenneth Jost***

[1] Mike Adams, "James Cameron's Avatar delivers a powerful message of connectedness with Mother Nature," *NaturalNews.com*, Dec. 26, 2009, www.naturalnews.com/027810_Avatar_James_Cameron.html#ixzz1tptrQ6FJ. Some information on individual films taken from entries on Wikipedia or IMDB (Internet Movie Data Base). Some background from Steven J. Ross, *Hollywood Left and Right: How Movie Stars Shaped American Politics* (2011).

[2] *Ibid.*, p. 104.

[3] See Philip J. Landon, "Films of the Cold War: 1948-1990," http://userpages.umbc.edu/~landon/Local_Information_Files/Films%20of%20the%20Cold%20War.htm. Landon, now deceased, was a professor of English at the University of Maryland-Baltimore County.

[4] Alison Hill, "10 Movies with a Message," June 8, 2011, http://listosaur.com/politics/10-movies-with-a-message.html.

Paul Simon, Alicia Keys, Sheryl Crow, the Dixie Chicks, Rod Stewart and Randy Newman — staged an all-day concert for Gulf Coast relief on Sept. 9, 2005, in the wake of Hurricane Katrina. A wire-service compilation two weeks later listed two dozen other celebrity-driven efforts, including a $10 million contribution by Oprah Winfrey. Haiti's devastating Jan. 12, 2010, earthquake sparked a similar response, including a prime-time telethon on Jan. 22 hosted by Clooney and fundraising appeals by, among others, the Haitian singer Wyclef Jean. [18]

Celebrities also continued to raise money for disease research and prevention, often after personal interactions with individuals suffering from the conditions. Julianne Moore began raising awareness of tuberculosis sclerosis complex after the father of a 3-year-old boy with the condition accosted her on a New York City street. Ben Stiller's work on amyotrophic lateral sclerosis — ALS or Lou Gehrig's disease — began after a longtime friend came down with the condition. And Ben Affleck became an advocate on the rare genetic disease ataxia telangiectasia (A-T or Louis-Bar syndrome) after he noticed 10-year-old Joe Kindregan among the spectators at a movie shoot in 1998; nine years later, Affleck spoke at Kindregan's graduation from Falls Church High School in Virginia. [19]

Environmental issues became causes for any number of celebrities. DiCaprio established a foundation in 1998 to work on various environmental issues; he also produced and narrated the 2007 documentary "The 11th Hour," on the threats to global survival. Damon also turned to filmmaking advocacy with "Running the Sahara," a 2006 documentary on the water crisis in North Africa. And Pierce Brosnan has been active on several environmental issues, with a special interest in ocean protection. [20] ■

Current Situation

Tweets Among Friends

Celebrities and the charitable and political organizations they support are using social media to expand their reach and to communicate directly with supporters in appeals for action or contributions.

Social media such as Facebook and Twitter allow celebrity advocates to bypass traditional news media, tailor messages specifically for supporters and build interactive relationships between an organization's leaders and followers. But strategists also caution that the new instruments of communication can mislead organizations into slighting the traditional nuts-and-bolts work of building support and galvanizing supporters into concrete actions.

Without doubt, social media speed up the process of getting news and information out to interested audiences. Twitter users reacted almost instantly to Clooney's arrest at the Sudanese Embassy on March 16, with tweets bearing the hashtag "#FREEClooney." [21] The rock group Green Day drew 622,838 views of three environmental videos less than a year after posting them on the group's website, according to a study of celebrity advocacy and social media by political scientist A. Trevor Thrall. [22]

Thrall, an associate professor of government and politics at George Mason University in Fairfax, Va., says celebrity advocates are often "almost invisible" in what he calls the "gatekept media," but can use social media to reach and communicate with their followers. "They have trouble making it past the media gatekeepers in *The New York Times* or other mainstream media, but they're very compelling characters," Thrall says. "When people have the opportunity to reach out directly to find out what celebrities are doing, they do so."

Washington consultant Sheridan says social media have had a "seismic" effect on celebrity advocacy. "The ability to use that network as aggressively and on the scale that we've been able to do to reach out to their fan base is seismically different — faster, cheaper and bigger than anything we've ever had before," he says.

Despite the potential for good works, both Thrall and Sheridan acknowledge that celebrities use social media mainly to advance their careers. "Celebrities are using Twitter and those things to promote themselves," Sheridan says. A Twitter-follower ranking of the 100 top celebrities — with Lady Gaga at the top with more than 23 million — includes only a few who are strongly associated with political or cause-related advocacy. [23]

"Anecdotally, they tweet all the time," Thrall remarks. "Normally, this is pretty awful," he says, "but they also do a lot of advo-tweeting. They often include links, and the links are to nonprofit websites."

Facebook gives an organization both visibility and interactivity, and some make

Continued on p. 442

AFP/Getty Images/Paul J. Richards

Michael J. Fox, who suffers from Parkinson's disease, waits to testify on Sept. 28, 1999, before a Senate subcommittee studying research and treatment for the neurological disorder. Fox helped lead the way in demonstrating how a celebrity's personal story can focus attention on a major health issue. The organization he established in 2000 has become the single largest funder of Parkinson's research, with $179 million distributed through 2011.

At Issue:

Are Hollywood celebrities politically out of touch with mainstream America?

BEN SHAPIRO
***EDITOR AT LARGE,* BREITBART.COM; *AUTHOR,* PRIMETIME PROPAGANDA: THE TRUE HOLLYWOOD STORY OF HOW THE LEFT TOOK OVER YOUR TV**

WRITTEN FOR *CQ RESEARCHER*, MAY 2012

yes

The question is only slightly less preposterous than "Is the sky blue?" Before answering it, however, we have to define just who "mainstream Americans" are. To go by opinion polls, most Americans believe in relatively low taxation, a basic social safety net, traditional marriage and some restrictions on abortion. Americans are uniquely religious and believe in the morality of the Constitution and in American exceptionalism. Most Americans believe more heavily in equality of opportunity than in equality of result.

For the most part, those in Hollywood oppose each of these positions on principle. Hollywood writers, producers, executives and actors are drawn from the major coastal cities; they have spent most of their adult lives in liberal milieus. Like most industries, the Hollywood industry is quite parochial, with friends hiring friends.

Hollywood, however, differs from other industries in that its greatest celebrities are "creative types." This means that evaluation of talent is largely subjective, allowing more room for friendship and cliquishness to cloud hiring and firing decisions than in other industries. Hollywood, therefore, has an informal blacklist — if you do not believe in certain basic political positions (right now, the bright line is same-sex marriage), you will not work in Hollywood.

Hollywood celebrities — think Michael Moore and his private jet, or Barbra Streisand and her private beach — don't want to give up the perks of the wealthy. Instead, they want to use their wealth, at least publicly, to stump for the liberal causes in which they are supposed to believe. Kanye West can, with a straight face, attend Occupy Wall Street rallies decrying the 1% while simultaneously wearing a $300 designer shirt.

Not that Hollywood is entirely out of touch. Hollywood celebrities have a symbiotic relationship with social change. They're completely in touch with the politics of Los Angeles or New York or San Francisco. They then trumpet those values out to the rest of America, shaping it in the process. It's no wonder that Vice President Joe Biden recently proclaimed that "Will & Grace" had done more than any single thing to shape American views of same-sex relationships.

Overall, though, Hollywood is not reflective of American society. It is transformative of it. Celebrities seek to mold America to reflect their more "cosmopolitan" worldviews. They have deep scorn for Americans in flyover country, or at the very least, a nasty sort of paternalism.

STEVEN J. ROSS
***PROFESSOR OF HISTORY, UNIVERSITY OF SOUTHERN CALIFORNIA; AUTHOR,* HOLLYWOOD LEFT AND RIGHT: HOW MOVIE STARS SHAPED AMERICAN POLITICS**

WRITTEN FOR *CQ RESEARCHER*, MAY 2012

no

Are Hollywood celebrities politically out of touch with mainstream America? If we take a broad look at American politics, the answer is no. For more than 100 years, movie stars on the left and the right have spoken out on behalf of the most important political issues of the day. Since the late 1920s, the Hollywood right preferred pursuing electoral power while the Hollywood left focused on promoting issues of national concern. Causes that seemed out of touch with public sentiment at one moment often became the dominant opinion of another time.

The conservative revolution of the 1980s, for example, could not have happened without the groundwork laid by Metro-Goldwyn-Mayer head Louis B. Mayer; his protégé, former actor and California Sen. George Murphy; and Murphy's protégé, former actor, governor and president, Ronald Reagan. During the 1950s and '60s, Murphy and Reagan helped build an insurgent grassroots constituency by speaking to conservative groups throughout the nation. Aided by the likes of Robert Montgomery and John Wayne, the two stars had their finger on the pulse of Americans who were unhappy with what they saw as Big Government and creeping federal socialism.

The Hollywood left, whose activists have stretched from Charlie Chaplin to George Clooney, concentrated on issues of broad national importance rather than running for office. And they often did so at times when their pronouncements were unpopular among political opponents. During the isolationist 1930s, Hollywood liberals such as Chaplin, Edward G. Robinson and Melvyn Douglas publicized the dangers posed by Nazism and fascism.

During the 1950s and '60s, Harry Belafonte, Sidney Poitier and then-liberal Charlton Heston helped awaken a nation to the importance of the civil rights movement. Recent appearances by Susan Sarandon, Mark Ruffalo and other liberal stars at Occupy Wall Street protests, while not popular with conservatives, have drawn national attention to the problems of economic inequality.

These stars of past and present have always been in touch with the sentiments of millions of Americans. Whether their opinions have been the mainstream opinions of the moment is debatable, but over the long run their ideas and causes have become important parts of national life. Rather than attack them, we should praise celebrities for risking their careers and box-office fortunes by speaking out on behalf of issues and causes of great concern. They have proved to be citizens first and movie stars second.

Continued from p. 440

active use of their Facebook pages. A recent post on the Michael J. Fox Foundation page asked followers to suggest questions that ABC newscaster Diane Sawyer could ask Fox in a scheduled interview. The Robin Hood Foundation, a New York City anti-poverty organization, was asking supporters to order a Mother's Day card, with proceeds to benefit the foundation.

Organizations can be listed on Facebook even if they do not actively maintain their pages. Bono's ONE campaign has a Facebook page with a description from Wikipedia, 4,500 "likes" and no posts other than a note from a "friend" saying that proceeds from the sale of Glee's 2011 Christmas album would benefit the campaign. Clooney's Satellite Sentinel project similarly has a Wikipedia description and 340 likes.

Both Facebook and the photo-sharing site Flickr give organizations the capacity to add visuals to their informational displays. The Enough Project posted photos on April 29 showing the continuing fighting between the Sudanese armed forces and the Sudanese People's Liberation Army. As of May 1, the project's Flickr photostream included 1,260 images dating from April 2007.

Strategist McKee agrees that social media are a "game-changer" for nonprofit organizations but also cautions against exaggerating their potential. "Somewhere along the line, many nonprofits become over-reliant on the Internet as a communication tool," McKee says. "They think of it as the easy button. It's easy to forget that there's no easy button to building a relationship with your supporters and donors."

The Internet creates "weak ties," McKee explains. "Very few of those people are truly, meaningfully bonded to the cause or movement." Clicking a "like" button, she says, "is very different from attending a meeting, very different from lobbying a legislature, very different from working in a neighborhood organization or writing a letter for a human rights organization calling for the release of a political prisoner."

Getty Images/Nike/(Red)/Chris Jackson

U2 lead singer Bono and British soccer star Didier Drogba call for increased funding for HIV/AIDS research and treatment in Africa during a charity event in London on Nov. 30, 2009. Bono has achieved perhaps the most visible success among contemporary celebrity advocates, taking his ONE campaign for global poverty relief directly to political and financial leaders. In 2005, for example, the Irish singer lunched at the White House with President George W. Bush to discuss debt relief, trade, AIDS and malaria. Early in 2008, he had a similar meeting with French President Nicolas Sarkozy.

Sheridan acknowledges the need to tend to traditional organization-building steps. "Matching the political process with this ever-changing, fast-breaking need to keep communicating sometimes creates this lag," he says. "We sometimes feel, 'how do we keep up with this demand in order to keep them active?' But that's a problem we love having."

Official Engagements

George Clooney is continuing to use his celebrity status to engage with Washington officials on the conflict between Sudan and South Sudan even as the two countries move perilously close to all-out war.

Clooney returned to Washington on April 28 as a guest of *Time* magazine at the annual White House Correspondents Association dinner. Along with posing for countless photographs with fans or acquaintances, Clooney found time to buttonhole policymakers on his issue: Sudan.

"If you're going to commit to do something, you need to do it," Clooney told *The Washington Post*'s Reliable Source gossip columnists at an after-party held at the French Embassy, "and my job is Sudan."

The gossip columnists reported that Clooney "cornered" CIA Director Leon E. Panetta for 10 minutes and also praised former Secretary of State Colin Powell for his work in the region. Powell was the first U.S. official, back in 2004, to label Sudan's killings of indigenous peoples in the western region of Darfur as genocide.

Clooney told *The Post*'s columnists that he had had "long conversations" with policymakers at the dinner and after-party. But he demurred on whether he had made any progress. "Nothing, nothing, gets solved at the correspondents' dinner," Clooney said. "Ever." [24]

Meanwhile, the Enough Project continues to chronicle the fighting along the ill-defined, 1,200 mile border that separates Sudan and its predominantly Arab population from South Sudan, populated almost completely by African tribal groups. In an April 30 blog post written from inside South Sudan, field researcher Nenad Marinkovic describes how he and a group of international journalists embedded with a division of the Sudan People's Liberation Army were caught in crossfire as the SPLA came under attack from Sudanese armed forces.

"The experience gave me and my compatriots a firsthand account of what civilians and SPLA soldiers, alike, have experienced almost daily in [South Sudan's] Unity state over the past several weeks," Marinkovic wrote. As they traveled to the SPLA encampment, Marinkovic said, "we encountered trucks of soldiers rushing in both directions, to and from the frontline. There was nothing but soldiers to be seen in the area, as civilians have fled and moved to the relative safety of Bentiu [about 50 miles from the border] and neighboring villages."

Marinkovic added a link to a CNN video of the attack to the entry, which was cross-posted on the Satellite Sentinel website. He also posted on May 1 some of his own pictures on the Enough Project's Flickr photostream, including one showing the effects of Sudanese bombing of the South Sudan village of Rubkona.

With fighting continuing, efforts to find a diplomatic solution to the conflict are intensifying. The U.N. Security Council approved a resolution on May 2 threatening both Sudan and South Sudan with sanctions unless the two countries stopped the fighting and resumed negotiations on contentious issues, including sharing of oil revenues. Significantly, Russia and China voted for the resolution after having previously balked at voting against Sudan. [25]

China, seen as a significant player in the conflict because it gets 6 percent of its oil from South Sudan, came under increased pressure to help broker a cease-fire when U.S. Secretary of State Hillary Rodham Clinton visited Beijing May 3-5. Clinton voiced hope that Washington and Beijing would join in sending "a strong message" that Sudan must halt all cross-border attacks, "particularly its provocative aerial bombardments." [26]

Clooney has also stressed China's pivotal role in the conflict and has met with leaders there to discuss the situation. "China is the issue here," Clooney told *Time* magazine's Africa bureau chief Alex Perry in late April. "And they can be the hero here." [27]

Meanwhile, Sudan agreed to a seven-point roadmap proposed by the African Union (AU) that called for Khartoum and Juba to begin negotiation by May 7. In accepting the roadmap, however, the Sudanese foreign ministry called on South Sudan to halt fighting and to withdraw from disputed areas. [28] ■

OUTLOOK

Fascinated With Fame

The New York City premiere of the 1991 film "Once Around" was staged as a benefit for the then still new Creative Coalition. Along with the film's stars, Christopher Reeve made an appearance, making a pitch to the A-list crowd to support the coalition and its causes: abortion rights, the environment, homelessness and the arts.

> **"The old fear that people are blank canvases who are going to be manipulated by Hollywood . . . hasn't been true. . . . People are very effective at blocking out celebrities they disagree with and listening to those they do agree with."**
>
> ***— David Blake***
>
> ***Professor of English, College of New Jersey***

Writing up the event later, *The New York Times*' cultural critic, Richard Bernstein, reflected on the ambiguous nature of what he called the public's "fascination with fame." Stars such as Reeve, Sting, Barbra Streisand and others "may be brilliant performers," Bernstein wrote, "but are they qualified to guide Americans on complex political and social questions? And does their presence make a media circus out of what should be sober reflection on complicated problems?" [29]

Bernstein wrote when it was still relatively new for celebrities to form free-standing advocacy organizations or hire full-time aides to coordinate their advocacy work. Two decades later, more than a few celebrities have their own charities, even more have established relationships with charities or advocacy groups and the position of celebrity liaison is a well recognized job title in the nonprofit world.

Has it gone too far? Blake, the College of New Jersey professor, thinks so. "We definitely have celebrity overload," he says. "I think we're definitely there."

In his overview, Bernstein quoted author Paul Fussell, then a professor at the University of Pennsylvania, as worrying that the public would be "hoodwinked" by the stars, "deluded by a lot of circuses." But despite Fussell's complaints, Blake says today that he is confident in the public's discernment and judgment.

"The old fear that people are blank canvases who are going to be manipulated by Hollywood . . . hasn't been true," Blake says. "Average citizens are really quite savvy about receiving all this hoopla and framing things so that it's meaningful for them. People are very effective at blocking out celebrities they disagree with and listening to those they do agree with."

A recent study of television advertising provides some support for Blake's sanguine view about the public's ability to separate celebrity fluff from substantive information. Out of 2,600 TV commercials studied, the research firm Ace Metrix found that fewer than 12 percent of the spots using celebrities achieved a 10 percent effectiveness "lift" versus regular ads. "This research proves unequivocally that, contrary to popular belief, the investment in a celebrity in TV advertising is very rarely worthwhile," Peter Daboll, CEO of Ace Metrix, told *AdWeek*. [30]

Advertisers continue to use celebrities, however, and advocacy groups do the same. And Gamson, the San Francisco professor, thinks the organization benefits in terms of added visibility. "It seems to work pretty regularly," Gamson says. "The cameras that are following [celebrities] around are amoral and neutral. They don't really care where George Clooney is or what he's doing. They just want to capture it and sell it."

With the value of celebrity support viewed as a given, advocacy groups need to work hard and be smart in lining them up, according to McKee at Sea Change Strategies. "It's hard to round up A-list celebrities," McKee says. "The Angelina Jolies, George Clooneys, they're already taken."

One strategy, McKee says, is for organizations to latch on to rising stars and get them deeply involved in hopes they will stay engaged after becoming A-listers. As one example, she cites the new print and video campaign by the environmental group Oceana that uses Adrian Grenier, a rising star from the eight-season HBO series "Entourage" (2004-2011), to plead for saving bluefin tuna. A 30-second video shows Grenier in wetsuit, swimming under water and then surfacing to make an appeal: "Go to Oceana.org. Save bluefin before they're gone."

For now, practitioners and observers expect celebrity advocacy to continue to increase. "We will see more of it because the line between politics and entertainment has disappeared," says Darrell West, director of governance studies at the Brookings Institution, a Washington think tank, and co-author of *Celebrity Politics*.

West also sees celebrities' influence extending across ideological lines. "Celebrities are able to attract attention to an issue regardless of where an individual is on the issue," he says. "Everybody pays attention to what George Clooney has to say even if they don't share that political perspective." ■

About the Author

Associate Editor **Kenneth Jost** graduated from Harvard College and Georgetown University Law Center. He is the author of the *Supreme Court Yearbook* and editor of *The Supreme Court from A to Z* (both *CQ Press*). He was a member of the *CQ Researcher* team that won the American Bar Association's 2002 Silver Gavel Award. His previous reports include "Human Rights Issues" and "Blog Explosion." He is also author of the blog *Jost on Justice* (http://jostonjustice.blogspot.com).

Notes

[1] For Clooney's testimony, see Senate Foreign Relations Committee, "Sudan and South Sudan: Independence and Insecurity," March 14, 2012, www.foreign.senate.gov/hearings/sudan-and-south-sudan_independence-and-insecurity; Clooney's testimony starts at 84:00. The four-minute video, "Witnessing War Crimes," is on the website of the Satellite Sentinel Project: http://satsentinel.org/. For print coverage of Clooney's testimony, see Karen DeYoung, "Clooney visits Hill to urge action on Sudan," *The Washington Post*, March 15, 2012, p. A10; Ashish Kumar Sen, "Clooney accuses Sudan of war crimes," *The Washington Times*, March 15, 2012, p. 10.

[2] "Clooney's DC blitz on Sudan reaches Oval Office," The Associated Press, March 15, 2012; Brett Zongker, "Clooney arrested in protest at Sudanese embassy," The Associated Press, March 16, 2012.

[3] See "George Clooney Puts 'Spotlight' on Bloodshed, Crisis in Sudan's Nuba Mountains," "PBS NewsHour," March 14, 2012, www.pbs.org/newshour/bb/world/jan-june12/sudan_03-

14.html?print; Zongker, *op. cit.*

[4] For coverage, see Russ Baker, "Fact Wrestling: Ashton Kutcher v. Village Voice," *Business Insider*, July 9, 2011, http://articles.businessinsider.com/2011-07-09/politics/30034209_1_penn-study-actor-ashton-kutcher-ashton-and-demi; Sofia M. Fernandez, "Ashton Kutcher in Twitter War with the Village Voice," *The Hollywood Reporter*, July 1, 2011. See Demi and Ashton Foundation, http://demiandashton.org/. Kutcher's interview was on CNN's "Piers Morgan Tonight" on April 18. Kutcher and Moore announced that they were divorcing in November 2011.

[5] Quoted in John Colapinto, "Looking Good," *The New Yorker*, March 26, 2012, p. 60.

[6] See Colapinto, *op. cit.* Some background drawn from article. For coverage of the June 7, 2011, news conference, see Mark Medina, "Kobe Bryant in research stages in helping to reduce homelessness," *Lakers Now* (blog), *Los Angeles Times*, June 7, 2011, http://lakersblog.latimes.com/lakersblog/2011/06/kobe-bryant-in-research-stages-in-helping-to-reduce-homelessness.html?cid=6a00d8341c506253ef01538f081153970b. The story includes a 2:15-minute video clip.

[7] See Mark Harris, "How to Train Your Celebrity: Five Hollywood Charity Myths," FastCompany.com, June 29, 2011, www.fastcompany.com/magazine/157/how-to-train-your-celebrity.

[8] See Conor O'Clery, "Is Bono a tax evader?," globalpost, March 3, 2009, updated May 30, 2010, www.globalpost.com/dispatch/ireland/090303/bono-tax-

[9] See www.buzzfeed.com/mjs538/40-celebrities-who-are-republicans; www.buzzfeed.com/mjs538/40-celebrities-who-are-democrats.

[10] Steven J. Ross, *Hollywood Left and Right: How Movie Stars Shaped American Politics* (2011). For previous *CQ Researcher* coverage, see Howard Altman, "Celebrity Culture," March 18, 2005, pp. 245-268.

[11] Some information on individual celebrities drawn from Look to the Stars: www.looktothestars.org/.

[12] See Phoebe Connelly, "Elizabeth Taylor and AIDS: A Brief History of AIDS," *The Awl*, March 24, 2011, www.theawl.com/2011/03/elizabeth-taylor-and-aids-a-brief-history-of-the-80s.

[13] BroadwayCares/Equity Fights AIDS web site: www.broadwaycares.org/history_of_bcefa. The two organizations merged in 1992.

[14] See Christopher and Dana Reeve Foundation: www.christopherreeve.org. The foundation was established in 1982 as the American Paralysis Foundation and renamed after Reeve became a supporter. Reeve died in 2004 of heart failure; his wife Dana died in 2006 of lung cancer.

[15] Michael J. Fox Foundation: www.michaeljfox.org/index.cfm.

[16] Some information on individual celebrities taken from entries on the web site Look to the Stars.

[17] Nedra Pickler, "Bono Discusses the World's Poor With Bush," The Associated Press, Oct. 20, 2005; Bono quoted in "Bono Charity Work, Events and Causes," Look to the Stars, *op. cit.*

[18] See "Celeb Benefits Continue After Katrina," The Associated Press, Sept. 23, 2005; Freida Thomas, "Haiti's Earthquake Tragedy: How Are Celebrities Helping in Relief Efforts?," yahoo.com, http://voices.yahoo.com/haitis-earthquake-tragedy-celebrities-5288001.html.

[19] See Jill Smolowe and Jason Lynch, "Touched by a Star," *People*, Sept. 8, 2003, www.people.com/people/archive/article/0,,20140992,00.html.

[20] DiCaprio, Damon information from "Putting Star Power to Work," *Newsweek*, Feb. 28, 2011, p. 23.

[21] See Samantha Murphy, "Twitter Users Show Support for George Clooney After Arrest," *Mashable*, March 16, 2012, http://mashable.com/2012/03/16/george-clooney-arrested/. For background, see Marcia Clemmitt, "Social Networking," *CQ Researcher*, Sept. 17, 2010, pp. 949-772.

[22] See A. Trevor Thrall, *et al.*, "Star Power: Celebrity Advocacy and the Evolution of the Public Sphere," *The International Journal of Press/Politics*, Vol. 13, No. 4 (October 2008), pp. 362-385, http://hij.sagepub.com/content/13/4/362.short?rss=1&ssource=mfc.

[23] The Twitaholic.com Top 100 Twitterholics Based on Twitter Followers, http://twitaholic.com/ (visited May 2012).

[24] See Roxanne Roberts and Amy Argetsinger, "Clooney's got his game face," *The Washington Post*, April 30, 2012, p. C2.

[25] See Josh Kron, "Council Resolution Threatens Sanctions Against Sudan and South Sudan," *The New York Times*, May 3, 2012, p. A14.

[26] Matthew Lee, "Clinton presses China to help on global challenges," The Associated Press, May 4, 2012.

[27] Quoted in "Q&A with George Clooney: Hollywood Legend Talks Sudan, Satellites and How to Stop Atrocities," *Time Global Spin* (blog), April 27, 2012, http://globalspin.blogs.time.com/2012/04/27/qa-with-george-clooney-hollywood-legend-talks-sudan-satellites-and-how-to-stop-atrocities/.

[28] "Sudan agrees to AU roadmap, must meet South Sudan," The Associated Press, May 3, 2012.

[29] See Richard Bernstein, "Should Stars Set the Agenda?," *The New York Times*, March 10, 1991, sec. 2, p. 11.

[30] Steve McClellan, "Study: Celebrity Ads Not So Effective After All," *AdWeek*, Jan. 13, 2011, www.adweek.com/news/advertising-branding/study-celebrity-ads-not-so-effective-after-all-125383.

FOR MORE INFORMATION

Charity Navigator, 139 Harristown Rd., Suite 201, Glen Rock, NJ 07452; www.charitynavigator.org. Provides evaluations of more than 5,000 charities based on financial controls and accountability and transparency.

Enough Project, 1333 H St., NW, 10th floor, Washington, DC 20005; 202-682-1611; 202-682-1611; www.enoughproject.org. Founded in 2006, seeks to end genocide and crimes against humanity by focusing on areas where some of the worst atrocities occur. The Satellite Sentinel Project, an affiliated organization, has documented the conflict in Sudan and South Sudan.

Look to the Stars, P.O. Box 6147, Oroville, CA 95966; www.looktothestars.org. Founded in 2006, compiles celebrity charity news and information.

ONE, www.one.org. Founded in 2004 as a nonpartisan campaign to mobilize Americans to help fight poverty and preventable disease in Africa. Founding groups include DATA (Debt, AIDS, trade, Africa), the anti-poverty organization established two years earlier by the singer Bono, among others.

Bibliography

Selected Sources

Books

Brownstein, Ronald, *The Power and the Glitter: The Hollywood-Washington Connection*, Pantheon, 1990.
A political journalist details the history of the Hollywood-Washington connection from the age of the moguls in the 1920s and '30s through the Reagan era and the backlash against the era's conservative politics. Brownstein, national political correspondent for the *Los Angeles Times* when he wrote the book, is now editorial director for *National Journal*. Includes notes, eight-page bibliography.

Gamson, Joshua, *Claims to Fame: Celebrity in Contemporary America*, University of California Press, 1994.
A professor of sociology at the University of San Francisco examines the phenomena of celebrity and celebrity-watching in the 20th-century United States from historical, political and sociological perspectives. Includes detailed notes and a list of works cited.

Ross, Steven J., *Hollywood Left and Right: How Movie Stars Shaped American Politics*, Oxford University Press, 2011.
A professor at the University of Southern California relates the history of Hollywood's influence on U.S. politics through individual chapters profiling major figures, such as actor Charlie Chaplin and producer Louis B. Mayer from the early days of the film industry and more recent celebrities such as Jane Fonda, Charlton Heston, Warren Beatty and Arnold Schwarzenegger. Includes detailed notes.

West, Darrell, and John Orman, *Celebrity Politics*, Prentice Hall, 2003.
Two political scientists provide a compact overview of celebrities in politics and in issue-related advocacy. Includes chapter notes. West is director of governance studies at the Brookings Institution; Orman was a professor of politics at Fairfield University until his death in 2009.

Articles

"Bono: The 'Rolling Stone' Interview," *Rolling Stone*, Nov. 3, 2005, pp. 48ff.
U2's lead singer traces the origins and explains the motivations of his activism in an interview with *Rolling Stone* publisher Jann Wenner. For an account of the launching of his Africa campaign, see Anthony DeCurtis, "Bono's Crusade: U2 Singer Takes on African AIDS, Debt Issues at World Economic Forum," *Rolling Stone*, March 14, 2002, pp. 25, 28.

Avlon, John, "A 21st-Century Statesman," *Newsweek*, Feb. 28, 2011, pp. 16-23.
The article favorably details George Clooney's involvement in Sudanese issues over a five-year period, including what the writer depicts as pivotal support for the successful referendum on independence for South Sudan. An accompanying chart details cause-related advocacy by 10 other celebrities. For a recent interview with Clooney, see "Q&A with George Clooney: Hollywood Legend Talks Sudan, Satellites and How to Stop Atrocities," *Time Global Spin*, April 27, 2012, http://globalspin.blogs.time.com/2012/04/27/qa-with-george-clooney-hollywood-legend-talks-sudan-satellites-and-how-to-stop-atrocities.

Bernstein, Richard, "Should Stars Set the Agenda?," *The New York Times*, March 10, 1991, sec. 2, p. 11.
The *Times*'s cultural critic gives a good overview of celebrity advocacy as the practice was becoming "less ad hoc and more a permanent presence on the scene."

Colapinto, John, "Looking Good: The new boom in celebrity philanthropy," *The New Yorker*, March 26, 2012, pp. 56-64.
Staff writer Colapinto uses a profile of Trevor Neilson, president of the Global Philanthropy Group, to critically examine the role that celebrities play in philanthropy.

Harris, Mark, "How to Train Your Celebrity: Five Hollywood Charity Myths," *FastCompany.com*, June 29, 2011 (July/August print edition), www.fastcompany.com/magazine/157/how-to-train-your-celebrity.
A writer for the business-oriented print and online magazine analyzes the ways in which celebrities can help charity and advocacy organizations and the steps that organizations need to follow to maximize the benefits.

Thrall, A. Trevor, *et al.*, "Star Power: Celebrity Advocacy and the Evolution of the Public Sphere," *International Journal of Press/Politics*, Vol. 13, No. 4 (October 2008), pp. 362-385, http://hij.sagepub.com/content/13/4/362.short?rss=1&ssource=mfc.
A study led by political scientist Thrall finds that the news-making abilities of celebrities has been "significantly" overstated and suggest instead that social media are increasingly important forums for celebrities to exercise influence. Thrall wrote the article while at the University of Michigan-Dearborn; he is now an associate professor of government and politics at George Mason University.

Traub, James, "The Celebrity Solution," *The New York Times Magazine*, March 9, 2008, pp. 38ff.
The article thoroughly explores what contributing writer Traub calls "the celebrity-philanthropy complex."

Reports and Studies

"Philanthropy Resource Guide," *The Hollywood Reporter*, June 17, 2011.
The comprehensive list of charities supported by celebrities includes hundreds of organizations, with descriptions and contact information.

The Next Step:

Additional Articles from Current Periodicals

Advocacy Films

Adams, Sam, "Power of a Light," *Los Angeles Times*, Dec. 22, 2011, p. E10, articles.latimes.com/2011/dec/22/news/la-en-paradise-lost-20111222.

The directors of "Paradise Lost" say the film has brought celebrity attention to three teenagers who were allegedly wrongly convicted of murdering three boys in West Memphis, Ark.

Cohen, Sandy, "Depp, Streep Join Call to Lower 'Bully' Rating," The Associated Press, March 14, 2012, www.insidesocal.com/outinthe562/2012/03/johnny-deep-meryl-streep-join-call-to-lower-bully-film-rating.html.

Johnny Depp and Meryl Streep are pushing for a PG-13 — instead of R — rating for the advocacy film "Bully" so that more people would be allowed to watch it.

Daysog, Rick, "Hollywood Jumps Into Fight Against Efforts to Suspend Climate Change Law," *Sacramento* (Calif.) *Bee*, Oct. 15, 2010.

Director James Cameron, whose "Avatar" film features a pro-environment message, is fighting for a clean energy future for California.

Stehle, Vincent, "How Documentaries Have Become Stronger Advocacy Tools," *The Chronicle of Philanthropy*, Oct. 2, 2011, philanthropy.com/article/article-content/129202/.

Documentary films are using the power of investigative journalism, social media and celebrity to influence public policy.

Education

Haggerty, Ryan, "Giving to Chicago and Beyond," *Chicago Tribune*, May 22, 2011, p. A13, articles.chicagotribune.com/2011-05-20/entertainment/ct-ae-0522-oprah-causes-metro-20110520_1_philanthropy-harpo-janice-peck.

Oprah Winfrey has made large charitable gifts around the world, but she is also working to bring awareness to several Chicago-based programs.

Howell Jr., Tom, "Redskins, Celebrities Get Behind City's Rights," *The Washington Times*, Oct. 7, 2011, p. A13, www.washingtontimes.com/news/2011/oct/6/redskins-celebrities-get-behind-dc-rights/.

Three Washington Redskins players have taped public-service announcements to educate Americans about the District of Columbia's lack of congressional voting rights.

Preston, Caroline, "Matt Damon's Mission to Promote Clean Water," *The Chronicle of Philanthropy*, July 24, 2011, philanthropy.com/article/article-content/128333/.

Matt Damon is educating the public on microfinance tools that help small clean-water projects in the developing world.

Politics

Branch, John, "In Rarity, a Player Speaks Out for Gay Rights," *The New York Times*, May 8, 2011, p. SP6, www.nytimes.com/2011/05/08/sports/hockey/08avery.html.

New York Rangers hockey player Sean Avery has recorded a video asking politicians for more gay rights.

Dillingham, Maud, "Daryl Hannah Arrested for Protesting Proposed Keystone XL Oil Pipeline," *The Christian Science Monitor*, Aug. 31, 2011, www.csmonitor.com/Environment/2011/0831/Daryl-Hannah-arrested-for-protesting-proposed-Keystone-XL-oil-pipeline.

Actress Daryl Hannah was arrested outside the White House during a protest against the Keystone oil pipeline.

Glanton, Dahleen, "Celebrity Do-Gooders Don't Always Win Hearts," *Chicago Tribune*, May 1, 2012, p. A2.

The public often questions what celebrity advocates know.

Jackson, Herb, "Lights, Camera, Political Action," *The Record* (Bergen County, N.J.), June 6, 2011, p. A1, www.northjersey.com/news/123209473_Lights__camera__political_action.html.

Celebrities can be effective in bringing issues to the attention of Congress because politicians often get starstruck.

Kuhnhenn, Jim, "Seeking the Limelight, With the Help of Star Power," The Associated Press, March 17, 2012, www.salon.com/2012/03/16/seeking_the_limelight_with_the_help_of_star_power/.

Many celebrities align themselves with political candidates in order to bring attention to issues the celebrities are supporting.

CITING *CQ RESEARCHER*

Sample formats for citing these reports in a bibliography include the ones listed below. Preferred styles and formats vary, so please check with your instructor or professor.

MLA STYLE

Jost, Kenneth. "Remembering 9/11," CQ Researcher 2 Sept. 2011: 701-732.

APA STYLE

Jost, K. (2011, September 2). Remembering 9/11. *CQ Researcher, 9*, 701-732.

CHICAGO STYLE

Jost, Kenneth. "Remembering 9/11." *CQ Researcher*, September 2, 2011, 701-732.

CQ Researcher

Published by CQ Press, an Imprint of SAGE Publications, Inc.

www.cqresearcher.com

Voter Rights

Should photo IDs be required at the ballot box?

A partisan conflict over voter identification is intensifying as this year's presidential election approaches. Republican state lawmakers have promoted voter-ID requirements in the name of instilling confidence in the electoral system and reducing what they argue is rampant voter fraud. The strictest laws require voters to produce an unexpired, government-issued photo ID at the polls. Studies have found little evidence of "impersonation" fraud in which someone casts a ballot under somebody else's name, but Republicans say the practice is common enough to warrant concern. Democrats, however, maintain that such fraud is rare and argue that photo-ID laws are aimed at reducing turnout by voters who lean Democratic — including minorities, students and the elderly. Some studies show disproportionately lower ID possession among those groups, but Republicans say minority turnout in states requiring a photo ID has increased.

NAACP members demonstrate in New York City on Dec. 10, 2011, against voter-ID requirements, which they equate with poll taxes many states once imposed to block African-Americans from voting.

INSIDE THIS REPORT

THE ISSUES 451
BACKGROUND 460
CHRONOLOGY 461
CURRENT SITUATION 466
AT ISSUE........................467
OUTLOOK 469
BIBLIOGRAPHY 473
THE NEXT STEP 474

CQ Researcher • May 18, 2012 • www.cqresearcher.com
Volume 22, Number 19 • Pages 449-476

Los Angeles | London | New Delhi
Singapore | Washington DC

RECIPIENT OF SOCIETY OF PROFESSIONAL JOURNALISTS AWARD FOR EXCELLENCE ◆ AMERICAN BAR ASSOCIATION SILVER GAVEL AWARD

VOTER RIGHTS

THE ISSUES

451 • Is election fraud a significant problem?
• Do voter-ID laws reduce turnout by minorities, other Democratic-leaning sectors?
• Should federal or state governments conduct a massive voter-registration effort and provide photo IDs if required?

BACKGROUND

460 **Race and Income**
Early voting rights were largely limited to white, male property owners.

463 **Restricting Immigrants**
A flood of newcomers in the mid-19th century led to restrictive voting requirements.

464 **Southern Battleground**
In the early 20th century, voting restrictions largely targeted Southern blacks.

465 **Identity Issues**
A succession of strict voter ID laws was passed beginning in 2002.

CURRENT SITUATION

466 **Minnesota Battle**
Voters will decide on a constitutional amendment calling for voter photo IDs.

466 **Voting Rights Act**
Texas is challenging the Justice Department's authority over states' voting statutes.

469 **Florida Registration**
Tough voter-registration standards are being challenged.

OUTLOOK

469 **Deeply Rooted Views**
Opinions about voter fraud follow party lines.

SIDEBARS AND GRAPHICS

452 **Thirty States Require ID at the Polls**
Five have strict photo-ID requirements.

453 **Study Finds Error-Riddled Voter Registration**
About one in eight registrations are no longer valid.

454 **Charges of Rampant Election Fraud Fall Flat**
"Voter fraud is rare," says a researcher.

456 **Obama Election Sparked Minority Turnout**
Roughly 65 percent of registered blacks voted in 2008.

461 **Chronology**
Key events since 1792.

462 **Conservative Group Drops Push for Voter-ID Laws**
Retreat follows growing liberal opposition.

467 **At Issue**
Do photo-ID laws disenfranchise racial and ethnic minorities?

FOR FURTHER RESEARCH

472 **For More Information**
Organizations to contact.

473 **Bibliography**
Selected sources used.

474 **The Next Step**
Additional articles.

475 **Citing *CQ Researcher***
Sample bibliography formats.

Cover: NAACP

CQ Researcher

May 18, 2012
Volume 22, Number 19

MANAGING EDITOR: Thomas J. Billitteri
tjb@cqpress.com

ASSISTANT MANAGING EDITOR: Kathy Koch
kkoch@cqpress.com

CONTRIBUTING EDITOR: Thomas J. Colin
tcolin@cqpress.com

ASSOCIATE EDITOR: Kenneth Jost

STAFF WRITER: Marcia Clemmitt

CONTRIBUTING WRITERS: Peter Katel, Barbara Mantel, Jennifer Weeks

DESIGN/PRODUCTION EDITOR: Olu B. Davis

ASSISTANT EDITOR: Darrell Dela Rosa

FACT CHECKER: Michelle Harris

Los Angeles | London | New Delhi
Singapore | Washington DC

An Imprint of SAGE Publications, Inc.

VICE PRESIDENT AND EDITORIAL DIRECTOR, HIGHER EDUCATION GROUP:
Michele Sordi

DIRECTOR, ONLINE PUBLISHING:
Todd Baldwin

CQ Researcher (ISSN 1056-2036) is printed on acid-free paper. Published weekly, except: (March wk. 5) (May wk. 4) (July wk. 1) (Aug. wks. 3, 4) (Nov. wk. 4) and (Dec. wks. 3, 4). Published by SAGE Publications, Inc., 2455 Teller Rd., Thousand Oaks, CA 91320. Annual full-service subscriptions start at $1,054. For pricing, call 1-800-834-9020. To purchase a *CQ Researcher* report in print or electronic format (PDF), visit www.cqpress.com or call 866-427-7737. Single reports start at $15. Bulk purchase discounts and electronic-rights licensing are also available. Periodicals postage paid at Thousand Oaks, California, and at additional mailing offices. POSTMASTER: Send address changes to *CQ Researcher*, 2300 N St., N.W., Suite 800, Washington, DC 20037.

Voter Rights

By Peter Katel

The Issues

The 2012 presidential campaign is taking place against the backdrop of a bitter partisan fight over how to run elections. Building in intensity since the early 2000s, the conflict pits Republicans who insist that safeguards against voter fraud need strengthening against Democrats who counter that Republicans are trying to suppress Democratic turnout.

At the center of the fight are laws recently enacted in 16 states requiring voters to show a government-issued photo ID — usually a driver's license — in order to cast ballots. Under the strictest laws, a voter without a proper ID may cast a "provisional" ballot that can be counted later only if the voter has produced the correct form of identification. The less stringent laws allow regular voting for people who produce other forms of ID or swear to their identities. All but two of the ID laws were passed in the 2000s by GOP-controlled legislatures. [1]

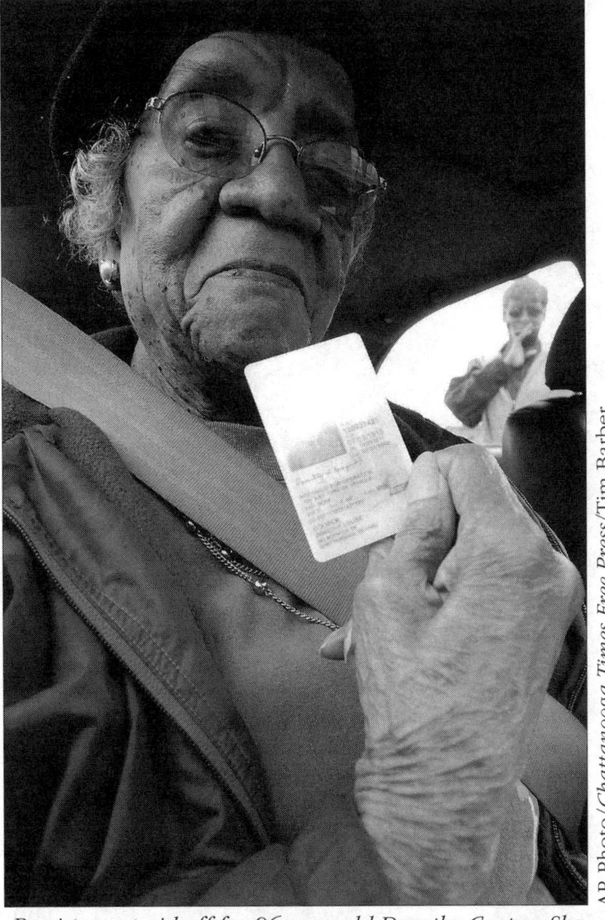

AP Photo/*Chattanooga Times Free Press*/Tim Barber

Persistence paid off for 96-year-old Dorothy Cooper. She got her voter ID card at the Driver Safety Center in Chattanooga, Tenn., on Oct. 20, 2011, after initially being turned away because she did not have her marriage certificate. Critics, mainly Democrats, say voter IDs will be difficult for many people to obtain, but Republicans say they are needed to block voter fraud.

The biggest push for voter-ID laws followed a Republican sweep in state legislative elections in 2010 that produced a GOP majority in 25 legislatures. [2]

"There is a fundamental philosophical difference between the parties: access versus integrity," says Doug Chapin, director of the Program for Excellence in Election Administration at the University of Minnesota's Humphrey School of Public Affairs. "Democrats tend to worry about access, about whether John Q. Voter has access to the system; and they're especially concerned about disparate impacts on racial and demographic minorities. Republicans care about voting rights, but they view it through the lens of, 'Does the system itself have integrity?' "

Pennsylvania enacted photo-ID legislation most recently. Its new law, which Republican Gov. Tom Corbett signed in March, has been challenged in federal court by the ACLU of Pennsylvania and several other voting-rights organizations. [3] Earlier challenges of voter-ID laws, in Indiana and Georgia, failed.

Elsewhere, Democratic Gov. Mark Dayton of Minnesota vetoed a photo-ID law, which led the Republican-controlled legislature to submit it to voters as a proposed state constitutional amendment on this November's ballot. Mississippi voters approved a similar amendment last year. In Wisconsin, the state Supreme Court in April declined to consider for now appeals of two rulings that suspended a tough photo-ID law on grounds that it could deprive eligible voters of their right to vote. [4]

And the Justice Department, which oversees balloting in several states with histories of racially discriminatory election-law abuse, rejected photo-ID laws in Texas and South Carolina on the grounds that racial and ethnic minorities disproportionately lack the required credentials. Both states are fighting back in federal court. Texas also is demanding elimination of the 1965 Voting Rights Act provision — known as preclearance — requiring Justice Department approval of its law.

But a 2008 U.S. Supreme Court decision that upheld Indiana's photo-ID law, one of the nation's strictest, has encouraged GOP legislators to maintain their drive to implement stricter rules on voting. Voter ID laws are pending in an additional 14 states, and another 10 are considering laws to toughen existing voter-ID requirements. [5]

Republicans argue that photo-ID laws protect against voter fraud. Democratic politicians, voter-advocacy groups and a number of academic analysts of voting practices maintain that investigations have produced little evidence of fraud involving voting under someone else's name.

Thirty States Require ID at the Polls

Thirty states require or request voters to show some form of identification before voting. Five require an acceptable photo ID. Six ask voters to show a photo ID but allow them to vote if they can confirm their identity through other means. Nineteen require identification that can include bank statements or utility bills instead of a photo ID.

Voter-ID Requirements by State, 2012

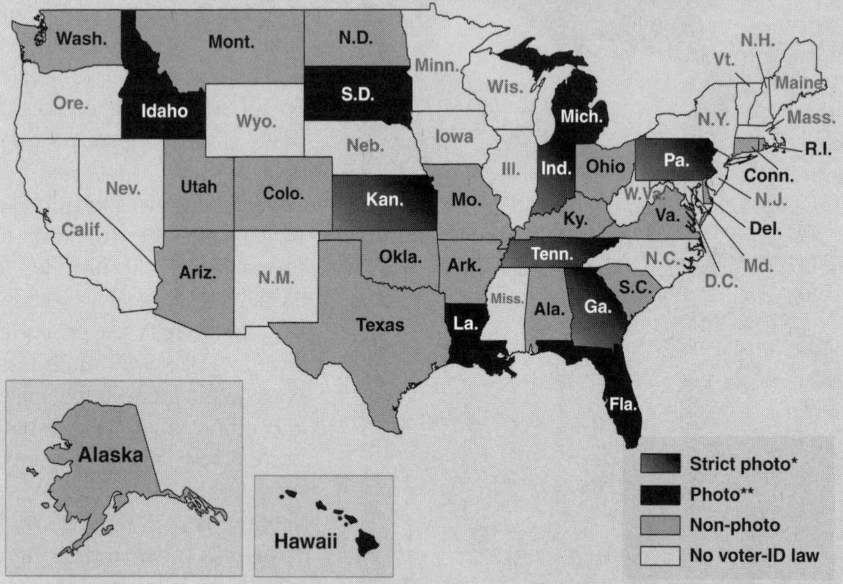

** Voters unable to show a photo ID may vote on a provisional ballot, which is counted only if the voter shows a photo ID to an election official within several days of the election.*

*** Voting criteria for those without a photo ID vary by state. Some states ask voters to provide personal information such as a birth date. Others require a signed affidavit confirming identity. Those without a photo ID are asked to present one to an election official within several days of the election.*

Source: "Voter Identification Requirements," National Conference of State Legislatures, 2012, www.ncsl.org/legislatures-elections/elections/voter-id.aspx

"There is no evidence that voter impersonation at polls is a real problem at any kind of scale that would cause a need for any kind of [new] ID requirement," says Richard L. Hasen, a professor of law and political science at the University of California, Irvine. "It seems like an unnecessary solution to a nonexistent problem," says Hasen, a founding editor of *Election Law Journal* and author of a widely cited election-law blog. [6]

But photo-ID advocates argue that — investigation results aside — tougher identification requirements are still needed to rebuild faith in the state-run election system.

Voter impersonation is "a kind of fraud that's very hard to prosecute," Rep. Todd Rokita, R-Ind., told the Senate Judiciary's Constitution, Civil Rights and Human Rights Subcommittee last September. "But that doesn't mean it doesn't exist, and the bottom line — it's not a matter of how many cases or convictions there are, gentlemen. It's a matter of confidence." [7]

Subcommittee Chairman Sen. Dick Durbin, D-Ill., hit back at the confidence argument in an exchange with another witness, Hans A. von Spakovsky, a senior legal fellow at the conservative Heritage Foundation and the leading national advocate of tougher voter-ID laws. (*See "At Issue," p. 465.*)

"What impact does disenfranchising people who can't make it to these DMV [Department of Motor Vehicles] offices because of inconvenient locations or inconvenient opportunities — what impact does that have on public confidence in elections?" Durbin asked. [8]

Von Spakovsky retorted: "Those claims are quite frankly bogus, senator." Two federal court challenges to photo-ID laws failed because challengers couldn't produce people whom the laws had prevented from voting, he said. [9]

Academics disagree about the effects of photo-ID laws on voting. But some who have asked registered voters whether they have credentials that would meet strict photo-ID standards have concluded that racial and ethnic minorities, as well as students and the elderly, are disproportionately less likely to possess the required documents. Moreover, minorities, students and the elderly are less likely to have the documents now needed in most states — above all, a birth certificate — needed to obtain a new ID under post-9/11 laws requiring definitive proof of citizenship and identity, the academics have found. [10]

"When you get into the footnotes of most of these laws, the ID has to be 'valid,' so the underlying documents become problematic," says Gabriel R. Sanchez, a professor of political science at the University of New Mexico. "If you don't have a driver's license, you might need a birth certificate."

ID standards do vary. (*See map, above.*) In Texas, a photo ID can't have expired more than 60 days before the election. Indiana allows an ID that expired after the most recent general election. (That limitation doesn't apply to military IDs). But for people who have never had a driver's license or passport, the birth certificate issue can pose a major problem, critics say. In the lawsuit against Pennsylvania's new photo-ID law, six of the 10 mostly elderly plaintiffs — most of them longtime voters — said they'd been unable to obtain birth certificates. In one case, an 86-year-old woman born at home in rural Virginia said she was told the state has no birth record for her. [11]

Because of state and federal litigation and pending Justice Department actions in some states, it is unclear how many of the strict photo-ID laws will be in effect by this year's Election Day, Nov. 6. But President Obama's reelection campaign is operating on the assumption that they all will be and that Democrats are the laws' intended targets. "They are clearly put forward for partisan political gains," Jeremy Bird, the Obama campaign's field director, told *The New York Times*. [12]

But Republican National Committee Chairman Reince Priebus said the criticism "reeks of desperation and represents the worst in modern politics."

Ironically, although the photo-ID conflict is being fought along partisan lines, it stems from attempts in the early 2000s to forge bipartisan consensus on election reform. That effort in turn grew out of the turmoil that surrounded the 2000 presidential election, when a battle over vote counting in Florida led to the U.S. Supreme Court certifying George W. Bush as the winner.

Two blue-ribbon commissions — the first co-chaired by former Democratic President Jimmy Carter and former Republican President Gerald R. Ford, the second by Carter and former Republican Secretary of State James A. Baker III — helped propel the photo-ID movement. But the latter commission proposed a photo-ID system as part of a comprehensive modernization package that would have amounted almost to a national voting system, as well as massive voter-registration campaigns. [13]

The commission called photo identification a vital confidence-building measure, saying that government-issued photo IDs have become part of modern life and that voting shouldn't be an exception. That reasoning underlies the most important legal decision on the issue so far. In his 2008 Supreme Court opinion upholding Indiana's strict photo-ID requirement, Justice John Paul Stevens quoted approvingly from the Carter-Baker commission. The panel's report said photo-ID cards "currently are needed to board a plane" and called voting "equally important." [14]

But a photo-ID opponent tested the airplane analogy last year and found it unsubstantiated. Justin Levitt, a professor at Loyola Law School, Los Angeles, showed up at Los Angeles International Airport last year without a photo ID. He was taken out of line, asked additional questions, then allowed to board his flight. The Transportation Security Administration's (TSA) own website, Levitt notes, warns travelers that they'll get "additional screening" if they lack a photo ID — but the TSA doesn't say they'll be prevented from boarding. [15]

Though he demonstrated that the TSA shows more flexibility in its ID procedures for travel than strict photo-ID states do for voting, Levitt's deeper point is that any analogy between the two activities is flawed. "Voting isn't a right for most people," he says. "It's a right we secure for all eligible citizens. Government and the private sector have figured out simple ways to accommodate those who don't have the single form of ID that's preferred. The electoral apparatus ought to be able to do that."

Most travelers do show photo IDs, though, a fact that helps build support for photo IDs for voters. "I'll be

Study Finds Error-Riddled Voter Registration

The nation's voter registration system is "plagued with errors and inefficiencies that waste taxpayer dollars, undermine voter confidence and fuel partisan disputes over the integrity of our elections," according to a study this year by the Pew Center on the States. Among Pew's findings:

- ***About one in eight — or 24 million —*** voter registrations are no longer valid or are significantly inaccurate.
- ***More than 1.8 million*** deceased people are listed voters.
- ***About 12 million*** voter records list an incorrect address.
- ***Approximately 2.7 million*** people are registered in more than one state.
- ***About one in four — or 51 million —*** eligible citizens are not registered to vote.

Source: "Inaccurate, Costly, and Inefficient," Pew Center on the States, February 2012, pp. 1-4, www.pewtrusts.org/uploadedFiles/wwwpewtrustsorg/Reports/Election_reform/Pew_Upgrading_Voter_Registration.pdf

Charges of Rampant Election Fraud Fall Flat

"Voter fraud is rare," says scholar who tracked a decade's worth of allegations.

Ever since Republican leaders alleged widespread "impersonation" fraud, in which someone casts a ballot using another person's name, they've launched investigations to prove it.

But critics say the results have been underwhelming.

Among them is Lorraine C. Minnite, a political scientist at Rutgers University's Camden, N.J., campus, and a senior fellow at Demos, a liberal advocacy group in New York that opposes laws requiring people to produce a photo ID at polling places.

Minnite tracked every case during the past decade in which politicians, almost invariably Republicans, alleged voter fraud. "I spent a number of years engaged in painstaking research, aggregating and sifting all the evidence I could find," she wrote in a book presenting the results. "Voter fraud is rare," she concluded. And the notion that it's pervasive is a "politically constructed myth." [1]

www.demos.org

Political scientist Lorraine C. Minnite, of Rutgers University, says widespread voter fraud is a "politically constructed myth."

Yet, charges of ballot fraud have persisted. In January 2011, Colorado Secretary of State Scott Gessler, a Republican, announced that more than 6,000 noncitizens might have registered to vote in the state. "Fact is, my office has every reason to believe that thousands of noncitizens are registered to vote in Colorado," he said three months later. [2]

His office released a six-page report that wound up stating that the number of voting noncitizens might amount to more than 4,000 — or to as few as 106. The report recounted a process of comparing names on driver's licenses granted to foreigners residing legally in the United States with names on the state's registered-voter list. [3]

The comparison yielded 11,805 people who seemed to be on both lists. "This number does not prove that all 11,805 noncitizens were registered improperly," the report said. It then narrowed the field further to 4,947 of those people said to have voted in the 2010 general election, then to 106 people said to have presented noncitizen documents in obtaining driver's license and to have registered to vote "on or before they applied for a licensing noncitizenship document."

One source of uncertainty, the report acknowledged, is that the department didn't know if someone who obtained a license as a foreign national later became a U.S. citizen.

The report said Gessler's department "is virtually certain" that the 106 noncitizens are illegally registered to vote, along with an unknown number of the remaining 11,699. "But it cannot accurately determine the number of noncitizens improperly registered to vote," the report concluded.

The uncertainties appear to go even deeper. An analyst at the liberal Brennan Center for Justice, a voting-rights advocacy group at New York University School of Law, found that Gessler's report is "utterly silent" on the method used to determine that the approximately 4,000-plus foreigners had voted in 2010.

"Since 2006, the same time period Gessler used to identify noncitizens, 32,140 individuals became citizens in Colorado," Keesha Gaskins of the Brennan Center wrote, citing immigration data from the Department of Homeland Security. "It is certainly reasonable to assume that some, if not many, of the over 4,000 individuals who the report alleged were noncitizens when they voted in 2010 were, in fact, citizens at the time of the election." [4]

In New Mexico, Republican Secretary of State Dianna Duran told state legislators last year that 117 noncitizens had registered to vote and that an unknown number had voted. In November, after checking voter registration records, Duran's office reported that nine registrants had identified themselves using foreign documents and might have voted. Another 10 had done so as well — but might have become citizens afterward. [5]

The recent Colorado and New Mexico episodes match results elsewhere during the approximately 10 years that Re-

the first to acknowledge that this issue polls very well," says Minnesota state Rep. Steve Simon of the Democratic-Farmer-Labor Party (the state's version of the Democratic Party), which opposes the state's proposed voter-ID constitutional amendment. "I completely understand the surface appeal. Most people think of their own circumstances — when they buy a six-pack of beer or board an airplane, they always show photo ID."

As debate continues over requiring photo IDs at the ballot box, here are some of the questions being asked:

publicans have insisted that U.S. elections are riddled with fraud.

While Minnite, in her lengthy study, found no evidence of an epidemic of voter fraud, she did find instances in which the registration and election process was not administered well.

For example, she wrote, the election for Washington state governor in 2004 was marked by major allegations of fraud, made largely by Republicans, before and after Democrat Christine Gregoire was declared the winner. And a state court concluded in 2005 that 1,678 illegal votes had been cast. Among them were 1,401 votes cast by people with felony convictions who hadn't regained the right to vote. Another 19 were cast in the names of dead people and six by people who had voted twice. In addition, 175 provisional ballots were filed by people whose eligibility to vote couldn't be determined; another 77 ballots exceeded the number of voters. [6]

The Washington state judge in the case concluded that bad administration, not fraud, was the reason for the illegal votes. "Neither the act of fraud nor the causation arising there from were proved," he said. [7]

U.S. Supreme Court Justice John Paul Stevens, writing an opinion upholding Indiana's photo-ID bill, cited different figures from the same Washington state election — 19 "ghost voters" who upon investigation were found to include one person who had committed in-person voting fraud. [8]

The Washington state election took place during a period when officials of the George W. Bush administration were spurring U.S. attorneys throughout the country to investigate election fraud. In fact, one of nine U.S. attorneys — all administration appointees — whom the Bush administration fired in 2006 was the top federal prosecutor in Washington state. He said at the time that he was dismissed for insufficient zeal in investigating fraud in that gubernatorial election.

"They wanted me to go out and start arresting people," John McKay of Seattle told *Newsweek* in 2007. He didn't, he said because there was "no evidence." [9]

A report by the Bush administration's Justice Department was "not able to conclude . . . whether complaints about McKay's handling of voter-fraud cases either did or did not contribute" to his firing. [10]

Allegations that another U.S. attorney, David Iglesias of New Mexico, was dismissed in part because he was seen as inattentive to voter fraud did not hold up under reinvestigation by the Obama administration. "There . . . was insufficient evidence that anyone in the [Bush] White House or DOJ [Department of Justice] sought to influence Mr. Iglesias to bring a voter fraud or public corruption case," an investigator concluded in 2010. (The reference to alleged public corruption was not election-related.) [11]

Still, Iglesias had said in 2007 that the pressure to prosecute election fraud was unmistakable and intense. He said an Albuquerque lawyer — an officer of the now-defunct American Center for Voting Rights Legislative Fund, which pressed Republican demands for stricter voter identification — demanded more action from him. The lawyer was "obsessed" and "convinced there was massive voter fraud going on in this state, and I needed to do something to stop it," Iglesias said. [12]

— Peter Katel

---

[1] Lorraine C. Minnite, *The Myth of Voter Fraud* (2010), p. 6.

[2] Quoted in Michael Roberts, "Scott Gessler's push for voter verification is a solution in search of a problem, says ProgressNow," *WestWord*, March 8, 2011, http://blogs.westword.com/latestword/2011/03/scott_gessler_voter_citizenship_verification_hb_1252.php; "Voting ID bill rejected in CO Senate," The Associated Press, Jan. 27, 2011. In addition, 175 provisional ballots were filed by people whose eligibility to vote couldn't be determined; and 77 ballots exceeded the number of voters and could have been the result of double voting.

[3] "Comparison of Colorado's Voter Rolls With Department of Revenue Non-Citizen Records," Colorado Department of State, March 8, 2011, pp. 1-3, www.scribd.com/fullscreen/50368826.

[4] Keesha Gaskins, "Smoke and Mirrors: Alleged Non-Citizen Voting in NM and CO," Brennan Center for Justice, blog, April 1, 2011, www.brennancenter.org/blog/archives/smoke_and_mirrors_alleged_non-citizen_voting_in_new_mexico_and_colorado/.

[5] "Interim Progress Report: Ongoing Efforts by the Secretary of State to Improve the Accuracy and Integrity of the Statewide Voter File," New Mexico Secretary of State, Nov. 16, 2011, p. 12, http://nmpolitics.net/Documents/SOSVoterFileReport.pdf.

[6] Minnite, *op. cit.*, p. 125.

[7] Quoted in *ibid.*, p. 125.

[8] *Crawford, et al. v. Marion County Election Board, et al.*, U.S. Supreme Court, 553 U.S. 181 (2008), n. 12, www.law.cornell.edu/supct/html/07-21.ZS.html.

[9] Quoted in Michael Isikoff, "Fuel to the Firings," *Newsweek*, March 19, 2007, p. 42.

[10] Quoted in Mike Carter, "McKay likely fired because he angered boss, report finds," *Seattle Times*, Sept. 30, 2008, p. A1.

[11] Letter, Assistant Attorney General Ronald Welch to Rep. John Conyers Jr., July 21, 2010, http://legaltimes.typepad.com/files/conyers.dannehy.ola.resp.pdf.

[12] Quoted in "Not-for-profit behind ID push," McClatchy Newspapers (*Columbia Daily Tribune*), July 1, 2007.

Is election fraud a significant problem?

The voter-ID fight grows out of the longer-running conflict over fraud and ballot access. These disputes center on a paper-based voter registration system plagued by errors and outdated entries — including 1.8 million records of voters who have died but are still included on registration records — the nonpartisan Pew Center on the States reported in February. Inefficient and inaccurate, the systems "can lead to problems with the rolls, including the

Obama Election Sparked Minority Turnout

Roughly 65 percent of registered black and white voters and 50 percent of registered Hispanics voted in the 2008 presidential contest between Democrat Barack Obama, the nation's first African-American presidential candidate, and Republican Arizona Sen. John McCain. In the 2004 presidential election, by comparison, 60 percent of blacks, 47 percent of Hispanics and 65 percent of whites voted.

Voting and Registration by Demographic Group, November 2008 Presidential Election (in millions)

Group	No. of voting-age citizens	Percent registered	Percent who voted
Total	**206.0**	**71.0%**	**63.6%**
Male	98.8	69.1	61.5
Female	107.2	72.8	65.7
White	169.4	72.0	64.4
Black	24.9	69.7	64.7
Asian	7.1	55.3	47.6
Hispanic	19.5	59.4	49.9

Sources: "Voting and Registration in the Election of November 2008 — Detailed Tables," U.S. Census Bureau, November 2010, www.census.gov/hhes/www/socdemo/voting/publications/p20/2008/tables.html

perception that they lack integrity or could be susceptible to fraud," the report said. [16]

Republican politicians have been insisting since the early 2000s that the election system is riddled with fraud — particularly "impersonation fraud" in which someone casts a ballot under somebody else's name.

But proponents of photo-ID legislation also argue that such laws would prevent other kinds of voter fraud. Von Spakovsky of the Heritage Foundation told Durbin's subcommittee that photo-ID policies would also stop voting under fictitious voter registrations, double voting by individuals registered in more than one place and voting by foreigners. [17]

In Colorado and New Mexico, Republican secretaries of state who had announced suspicions that foreigners had voted in the states' elections eventually published inconclusive reports. (*See sidebar, p. 454.*)

The U.S. Supreme court, in its 2008 decision upholding Indiana's strict photo-ID law — the key legal decision in the debate so far — noted that the record contained no evidence of impersonation fraud in Indiana. But, Justice Stevens wrote, "Such fraud has occurred in other parts of the country." [18]

Stevens acknowledged in a footnote that instances of voter impersonation in modern times were "scattered." He cited evidence of 19 "ghost voter" cases in Washington state's 2004 gubernatorial election. But a state investigation later found only one voter had committed impersonation fraud. [19]

Still, Rokita, the Indiana representative and photo-ID advocate, maintained that his state has not been spared. "Whether or not you agree that in-person voter fraud exists . . . , it does exist," Rokita told the Senate panel, citing his eight years as Indiana's secretary of state, the state's top elections administrator. Rokita said there is "a lot of evidence" of voter fraud but that it is hard to pin down. He said he had referred cases to prosecutors who didn't follow up because evidence was lacking — as Rokita himself acknowledged. "It's something that happens in an instant, and then it's gone," he said of voter impersonation "It's not a domestic-violence case; it's not something that leaves visible scars. [20]

But other election experts say "impersonation fraud" is not only rare but also ineffective at manipulating election results.

"Photo ID addresses identification issues at polling places, for which there is not a lot of evidence there is a problem," says Michael Pitts, a professor at Indiana University's law school in Indianapolis who specializes in election law. Absentee ballots present a much greater potential for abuse, Pitts says, but photo-ID requirements don't deter fraud involving voting by mail. "Is it hard to catch an individual who impersonates somebody else at the polling place? I think that's probably true. The other side of that coin is, what is the incentive for one person to commit voter-ID fraud? Rarely does one vote make a difference. Then you have to think about a conspiracy, but that creates more opportunity to catch people."

But Dan McGrath, executive director of Minnesota Majority, a conservative advocacy group promoting a state constitutional amendment requiring photo IDs for voting, says his group turned up evidence of large numbers of unauthorized voters casting ballots. Approximately 6,000 voters had signed up to vote under Minnesota's same-day registration procedure, but then didn't return non-forwardable postcards sent to them to verify that their names and addresses were correct, he says. Postcards that come back as undeliverable can indicate that whoever registered to vote doesn't live at the address listed, at least under that name. "In 2008, our Senate election was decided by 312 votes," McGrath says.

As for those 6,000 voters, "It's impossible to know who they were," McGrath says. "All we know is they don't live where they say they lived."

Office of Gov. Mark Dayton

Democratic Gov. Mark Dayton of Minnesota vetoed a photo-ID law passed in April by the Republican-controlled legislature. But Dayton was unable to prevent lawmakers from putting it on the state ballot as a proposed constitutional amendment, which requires only a simple majority under Minnesota law. Voters will decide the issue in November.

But Beth Fraser, government affairs director for Minnesota Secretary of State Mark Ritchie, a Democrat and photo-ID opponent, charges that McGrath's group "consistently misconstrues data." More than 1,800 of the 6,000 did in fact live at the addresses they'd listed, but the postcards had been misdelivered, Fraser says. About 2,000 more of the allegedly missing registrants had moved after voting without leaving forwarding addresses to which separate postcards could be sent, she says. And the remainder included 700 who had not voted in 2008 and registrants whose cards were returned undelivered because of illegible handwriting and other reasons.

"In every election, there are a handful of people who vote who shouldn't have," Fraser says. "But fraud is not a significant issue in Minnesota elections."

McGrath dismisses Fraser's criticism, however. "We're definitely sticking to our report," he says. Still, responding to the Secretary of State's office, McGrath has acknowledged that the office "differs in their analysis of the data" compared with the way Minnesota Majority views the numbers. The approximately 6,000 voters could amount to about 3,000, McGrath's report said. [21]

Do voter-ID laws reduce turnout by minorities, youths and other Democratic-leaning sectors?

For opponents of voter-ID laws, the near-absence of definitive proof that impersonation fraud is occurring on a large scale means advocates must have another reason for pushing such laws. Opponents argue that such laws are actually an effort to reduce the number of likely Democratic votes.

Exclusion of specific blocs of voters based on their presumed political sympathies, social status or gender has a deeply rooted history in the United States. Women didn't get the right to vote until 1920, and it took the Voting Rights Act of 1965 to outlaw practices designed to keep African-Americans and other minorities from the ballot box. (*See Background, p. 465.*) [22]

Voter-ID opponents cite the historical record as well as studies showing that minorities, very young adults and the very old are less likely than others in the population to have the documents — including birth certificates — that the strictest voter-ID laws require.

Backers of these laws counter that the opponents have not been able to point to more than a handful of cases in which members of groups said to be disproportionately affected by ID laws have been kept from voting. An absence of plaintiffs who had been prevented from voting was a factor in the Supreme Court's 2008 decision on the Indiana law. The record of the case, Justice Stevens wrote, "does not provide any concrete evidence of the burden imposed on voters who currently lack photo identification." [23]

Indiana's law was challenged before its requirements took effect, photo-ID opponents noted at the Senate subcommittee hearing, so no one had yet been affected. But Rokita and von Spakovsky noted that no such people filed later lawsuits alleging they'd been prevented from voting. "Where are the lawsuits making that claim?" von Spakovsky asked. [24]

Election-law expert Hasen of the University of California, a harsh critic of Republicans' insistence on the threat of fraud, says photo-ID critics cannot point to hard evidence of how many people the laws may keep from voting. "Just as Republicans use the scare of voter-ID laws as a wedge issue to boost Republican turnout, Democrats use the scare of voter suppression to boost Democratic turnout," Hasen wrote on his blog in February. "Social science has a lot of work to do now to track whether voting laws passed by Republican legislatures actually depress much turnout. There's been some work on voter-ID laws, the best of which shows likely a very small effect, but very hard to measure." [25]

Some academics argue that research points convincingly to a voter-suppression effect, however.

Political science professors Matt A. Barreto of the University of Washington, Stephen A. Nuño of the University of California, Irvine, and Sanchez of the University of New Mexico, who are working with photo-ID opponents on legal challenges to the law, have published several papers based on their own surveys of voters in states with and without photo-ID requirements. Their findings roughly match those of a 2008 national survey of registered voters, which reported that 90 percent of the African-Americans, 89 percent of the Latinos and 86 percent of the Asian-Americans polled had up-to-date driver's licenses or non-driver ID cards. By contrast, 95 percent of white voters had the documents. [26]

Defining compliance with ID standards as a "cost" of voting, Sanchez says, "One consistent finding in political science literature is that whenever you increase the costs of voter participation, participation goes down, particularly among vulnerable segments of the population."

In 2008, researchers from American University — led by the Carter-Baker commission's executive director — concluded that the share of voters without IDs required by law is far smaller — 1.2 percent. And some of those people did have proof of citizenship. "These data suggest that access to IDs and the documents necessary to obtain a valid photo ID, for registered voters, is not a serious problem," that study said. [27]

However, Sanchez criticizes that study because the sample was selected using responses to postcards — a system he says is more likely than others to produce larger numbers of people with up-to-date drivers' licenses.

Under the Help America Vote Act of 2002 (HAVA), passed in the wake of the disputed 2000 presidential election — prospective voters who lack a required ID can cast a provisional ballot, but Sanchez argues that is not as much of a benefit as it may appear. The reason, he says, is that individual voters don't believe they are going to decide elections except those voting in tiny jurisdictions. "Given that the benefits of voting are pretty minuscule," Sanchez says, "any time you tweak the costs for folks that aren't mobilized to a great extent to begin with, you're going to impact turnout."

Yet, a leading national advocate of photo-ID laws argues that the vote-suppression argument is disabled not only by a lack of definitive evidence but also by data that point in the opposite direction. "What I am disputing is that voter ID depresses their [African-Americans'] turnout," von Spakovsky, manager of the Heritage Foundation's civil justice reform initiative, told Durbin's subcommittee last September. "Actual numbers in Georgia and Indiana since voter-ID laws have been passed show that that's not true." [28]

Von Spakovsky, who oversaw elections as assistant attorney general for civil rights in the George W. Bush administration, said African-Americans' share of the vote in Georgia increased from 25 percent in 2004, before the state instituted its voter-ID law, to 30 percent in 2008, after the law took effect. In Indiana, he said, less than 54 percent of the black voting-age population voted in 2004, before the Indiana

www.oyez.org

A U.S. Supreme Court decision in 2008 that upheld Indiana's photo-ID law, one of the nation's strictest, has encouraged GOP legislators to maintain their drive to implement stricter rules on voting. Voter-ID laws are pending in an additional 14 states, and another 10 are considering laws to toughen existing voter-ID requirements. Justice John Paul Stevens, who wrote the majority opinion, is in front row, second from left, in this 2006 photo. He retired in 2010.

law passed, compared with 59 percent in 2008. [29]

Photo-ID opponents challenged von Spakovsky's use of statistics, though. "The 2008 election is a particularly bad example," Levitt of Loyola Law School told the committee. "The minority turnout in those states would have been buoyed through the roof with a presidential candidate at the top of the ticket for a major party who was himself a minority. Under any circumstances in Georgia and Indiana, the turnout should have shot up." [30]

In any event, Levitt says in an interview, turnout statistics provide an inadequate gauge of ID laws' effects. "Over one-third of eligible American citizens aren't registered to vote at all," he says. "When people just look at turnout they are completely missing all these folks. When we design rules for our election system, we ought to be designing them considering the eligible American public, not just individuals who turned out in . . . the last election."

Still, Henry E. "Eddie" Mahe, a San Diego-based Republican political consultant and former deputy chairman of the Republican National Committee, points to a difference between arguing that voter ID suppresses turnout and championing greater access to voter registration. Referring to neighborhoods in which IDs are relatively scarce, Mahe says ID laws made no difference: "Look at turnout in those areas."

As for Democratic-leaning citizens who are already on the voter rolls, Mahe says, they should have no problem obtaining whatever new ID a recent law may require. "These people are already registered voters. They can't turn out if they're not registered voters. In my book, if you're a registered voter, by definition somebody has said, 'You're a citizen, so get your ID.' I just don't think it's that big a burden for most people."

Should federal or state governments conduct a massive voter-registration effort and provide photo IDs if required?

The photo-ID conflict grows out of an even deeper ideological split between advocates of universal voter registration and those who believe signing up to vote is an individual responsibility.

In 2005, the blue-ribbon commission headed by Carter and Baker tried to bridge the gap. The panel advocated a virtually national registration system in which state voter lists would be placed on a shared electronic network and photo-ID cards would be made available to all citizens wanting them. [31]

That same year, Republicans were stepping up their demands for tougher ID laws. Though voter fraud hadn't been shown to alter any modern election results, GOP leaders argued that the value of legitimate votes was lessened when they were accompanied by ballots cast by people unauthorized to vote. "The votes of Americans of every background are . . . diluted or canceled out when fraudulent votes are cast and counted," the Senate Republican Policy Committee said in a 2005 paper calling for a federal photo-ID election law. [32]

Those on the open-access side argue that the best way to end disputes over who can vote is for the federal government to ensure that every eligible American is registered to vote. State governments could do the job if deeply rooted objections to a national ID card made that approach unworkable, open-access advocates say.

"You could streamline the system of registration, even forget doing it on a national basis, with a card that has a little chip in it," says Alexander Keyssar, a historian at Harvard University's Kennedy School of Government who wrote a history of the right to vote. "As a person moves from, say, one Illinois town to another, he would remain registered."

Numerous paths toward universal registration have been proposed, including the Carter-Baker commission's idea that high schools instruct their students on how to register. Montana adopted that approach in 2006. [33]

Sanchez, of the University of New Mexico, says, however, that a high school-oriented system would effectively exclude dropouts, who, he noted, come disproportionately from racial and ethnic minority populations. (In New Mexico, about 40 percent of Hispanic students, an equal share of African-American students and 44 percent of American Indian students don't graduate from high school.) [34]

Sanchez favors a "system of national IDs or a system of voter IDs; you could say that everybody has got to get one of these."

In the early years of that sort of system, Sanchez says, "If somebody shows up at the polls and doesn't have an ID, they cast a provisional ballot and apply for their ID right there."

But voting is not about convenience, those on the other side say, applying that argument to the ID issue as well to registration procedures. "I've heard today that people have to leave their jobs to come and vote — why make it harder?" Indiana's Rokita told the Senate panel last September. "I would take the opposite end of that."

The key to encouraging more people to vote is to tighten the voting process, not loosen it, Rokita said. In states that don't require an ID to vote, he said, speaking in the persona of a voter, " 'These people didn't even care enough to find out who I was, yet they ask me to leave my life and go vote.' " Rokita added, "We want to instill confidence in the system to drive up turnout."

But Mahe, the Republican political consultant, argues for wider registration on practical as well as philosophical grounds. "My goal would be to have every citizen be registered and have a voter ID," says Mahe, who suggested putting registration offices in vans and driving them to areas with low registration. "I want to make it as easy as possible for people to vote."

New Mexico, where Mahe lives when not at his San Diego office, established a system in 2010 to comply with the National Voter Registration Act of 1993, enabling Motor Vehicle Department offices to offer voter registration or registration address changes.[35] "That was seen as helping Democrats, but in point of fact I don't see that we suffered any as a consequence," Mahe says. Later that year, Republican Susana Martinez won election as governor, succeeding two-term Democrat Bill Richardson.

Dred Scott was an American slave who sued to obtain freedom for himself, his wife and their two daughters in 1857. The U.S. Supreme Court ruled in the infamous Dred Scott *decision that black people, whether free or enslaved, were not and could not become citizens. The Union victory in the Civil War led in 1870 to ratification of the 14th Amendment — which overturned the decision — and to the 15th, which prohibited denial of the vote on "account of race, color or previous condition of servitude."*

But McGrath of Minnesota Majority opposes anything resembling a mass-registration system, especially on the national level. "Voting is an option in the United States," he says, noting a difference with countries such as Australia, where voting is mandatory. "If you want to vote, you have to proactively take that step."

And, like many people of varying political persuasions, McGrath rejects any sort of national ID, preferring instead for ID cards to be issued by local or state governments. "The Carter-Baker commission had the right idea about photo ID," he says, "but I do not agree with national ID or a federal election system." ■

BACKGROUND

Race and Income

Voting and other citizenship rights for African-Americans have been on the national agenda since the United States was founded. Delegates to the Constitutional Convention in 1787 agreed that slaves couldn't vote. But they decided that three-fifths of the slave population could be counted for political representation purposes — a way to keep Southern states from losing congressional representation as a consequence of having large numbers of nonvoting slaves.[36]

During the early 1800s the nation's estimated 500,000 free blacks were excluded from voting in nearly all states. In many cases, qualifications for voting were limited to white, male property owners.

Five states — Massachusetts, Maine, Vermont, New Hampshire and Rhode Island — allowed all free, black, adult males to vote. New York restricted the black vote to property owners — a practice that, theoretically, allowed some black voters, but in practice kept all but a few from casting ballots.

On the federal level, African-Americans were prohibited from voting in nonstate U.S territories. That policy was validated in 1857, when the U.S. Supreme Court ruled in the infamous *Dred Scott* decision that black people, whether free or enslaved, were not and could not become citizens.[37]

In the North as well as the South, justifications for prohibiting black people from voting were, in today's terms, explicitly and unapologetically racist. "Every Negro was a thief and every Negro woman far worse," said a Wisconsin delegate to his state's constitutional convention of the late 1840s.[38]

American Indians fared nearly as badly. Because they were classified as members of separate nations, they had to rely on treaties or special acts of Congress to become U.S. citizens and, thereby, voters.

Meanwhile, another set of state laws prohibited voting rights for "paupers" — roughly the equivalent of

Continued on p. 462

Chronology

1792-1870

Restrictions based on race and class mark early voting laws.

1792
Prohibitions on voting by "paupers" begin, eventually pass in 12 states.

1845
Start of immigration wave from Ireland sparks "Know Nothing" movement.

1857
U.S. Supreme Court's *Dred Scott* decision denies citizenship to African-Americans. . . . Massachusetts requires voters to be able to read the Constitution and sign their names.

1870
Fourteenth Amendment to Constitution overturns *Dred Scott* decision, and 15th Amendment prohibits denial of vote based on race, color or previous enslavement.

1879-1944

Southern states, and some others, perpetuate racial exclusion at the polls, but tide begins to turn as World War II ends.

1879
California constitutional convention bans voting by native Chinese.

1890
Mississippi includes in state constitution a "poll tax" and literacy test, both designed to keep blacks from voting; the measures become a model for other Southern states.

1927
Supreme Court rejects whites-only Democratic primary in Texas.

1935
Texas Democrats limit party membership to whites; Supreme Court approves the policy.

1944
Supreme Court reverses itself, prohibits racial discrimination in political party membership.

1960s *Civil rights movement forces enactment of strong voting-rights law.*

1961
U.S. Civil Rights Commission reports that 100 counties in eight Southern states use violence or other means to bar blacks from voting.

1964
Twenty-fourth Amendment, banning poll tax, is ratified. . . . Three voter-registration volunteers are murdered in Mississippi. . . . Supreme Court rules (*Wesberry v. Sandders*) against legislative redistricting aimed at reducing black political representation.

1965
At urging of President Lyndon B. Johnson, Congress passes Voting Rights Act.

1993-2012 *Voter rolls expand, and conflict arises over voting rights and election administration.*

1993
National Voter Registration Act — so-called "motor voter" law — adds about 9 million people to voter rolls.

2000
Supreme Court decides outcome of Bush-Gore presidential race.

2001
Carter-Ford commission recommends upgrading states' voter lists and linking them to driver's license records.

2002
Help America Vote Act requires new voters and those who have moved to document their identities, but doesn't require government-issued photo IDs.

2004
Arizona, Georgia, Indiana and Missouri pass strict photo-ID voting laws.

2005
Carter-Baker commission proposes use of driver's licenses to prove voter identification.

2006
Three of nine U.S. attorneys fired by Bush administration allege they were pressured to mount voter-fraud prosecutions.

2008
U.S. Supreme Court approves Indiana photo-ID voting law.

2011
Voter-ID bills introduced in 34 legislatures; photo-ID laws passed in eight states. . . . Governors in Minnesota and four other states veto photo-ID laws. . . . U.S. Justice Department denies "preclearance" for South Carolina photo-ID law.

2012
South Carolina challenges Justice Department action in federal court. . . . Justice Department denies "preclearance" for Texas photo-ID law; Texas takes department to court. . . . Minnesota legislature puts photo ID on ballot as proposed constitutional amendment.

Conservative Group Drops Push for Voter-ID Laws

Retreat follows liberal opposition.

Under pressure from liberals, a powerful conservative organization backed by some of the nation's biggest corporations has apparently dropped efforts to persuade states to adopt several of its positions, including requiring voters to show a photo ID at the polls.

The American Legislative Exchange Council (ALEC), a key proponent of voter-ID laws, announced in April that it shut down a Public Safety and Elections Task Force. The task force's focus included the voter-ID issue along with so-called "Stand Your Ground" laws that expand the circumstances in which people can claim self-defense after using lethal force during a physical conflict.

"We are refocusing our commitment to free-market, limited government and pro-growth principles and have made changes internally to reflect this renewed focus," the Washington-based organization said in a press release. [1]

The move, which followed announcements by some major consumer companies that they were resigning from ALEC, was significant partly because ALEC, which has prepared models for hundreds of conservative bills for introduction in state legislatures, was highly influential in shaping conservative thinking on the voter-registration issue. In 2009, ALEC's election task force approved a model photo-ID bill shaped to withstand legal challenges from opponents, who argue such laws discourage minorities and the poor from voting. [2]

ALEC's model law would have required voters to have a current, government-issued photo ID. However, unlike the strictest ID laws, such as Wisconsin's, the ALEC bill wouldn't have required voters to document their address. [3]

ALEC's board approved the model law about six years after the voter-ID push began in 2003, when new laws were enacted in five states. [4] The model was drafted in time for the 2010 Republican sweep in state legislative races, in which the GOP gained majority control in 20 new legislatures, giving them the majority in 25 statehouses and the power to pass new voter-ID laws. [5]

Liberal opposition to ALEC's views, in part related to the ID issue, had been growing for months before the conservative group refocused its work in April. ColorofChange, an advocacy organization that presses for expanded African-American political representation, led efforts to pressure corporations to quit ALEC over the photo-ID bill. ColorofChange began hosting a free Web app that photo-ID opponents could use to protest the corporate involvement. [6]

The organization didn't launch a boycott of ALEC, but based on the activist group's messages, corporations may have seen that move as the next step. "Major companies that rely on business from Black folks shouldn't be involved in suppressing our vote," ColorofChange said. [7]

Whether the photo-ID conflict by itself would have been enough to spur the corporate pullouts and ALEC's announced change of direction isn't clear.

Opposition to ALEC gathered considerable force because of the organization's influence in getting states to adopt so-called "Stand Your Ground" laws. Such a law passed by the Florida legislature in 2005 is expected to play a key role in the defense of George Zimmerman, a Sanford, Fla., neighborhood watch coordinator who killed African-American teenager Trayvon Martin after a confrontation in February. [8]

As outrage over the shooting intensified, the boycott threat against ALEC's corporate supporters encouraged such companies as Pepsi, Kraft Foods, McDonald's and Intuit, along with Coca-Cola, to end their ALEC memberships. [9]

Ever since its formation more than 30 years ago, ALEC had deliberately kept a low profile and had barely been known outside political circles. But political analysts had been watching the organization closely. [10]

In 2011, *Bloomberg Businessweek* described ALEC as a network of corporations and state legislators, virtually all of them Republicans. The companies want certain bills introduced in state legislatures, and ALEC-member legislators have the clout and connections to see the corporate agendas carried out, the magazine said.

The network approach "allows companies to work directly with legislators for many states, rather than having to lobby in each state individually to get language into a bill," the magazine reported. [11]

More than convenience, ALEC offered companies the opportunity to shape legislation without being publicly identified with it. "Corporations drop bills off at one end, and they come out the other, stamped with the imprimatur of a nonprofit, 'nonpartisan' group of state legislators," the article said. [12]

But anti-ALEC activism made membership a liability for some corporate sponsors. "The proliferation of bills enacting immi-

Continued from p. 460

today's welfare recipients. From 1792 until the late 1800s, they were denied the right to vote in 12 states.

Of all the restrictions and prohibitions, those covering African-Americans were the most politically volatile, relating as they did to the conflict over slavery.

The Union victory in the Civil War led in 1870 to ratification of the 14th Amendment — which overturned the *Dred Scott* decision — and to the 15th, which prohibited denial of the vote on "account of race, color, or previous condition of servitude." [39]

But the wording of the 15th Amendment left loopholes large enough to allow suppression of the black vote, based on prohibitions that weren't explicitly racial.

gration crackdowns, expanded self-defense rights and voter-ID requirements brought unwanted heat to brand-conscious, public-facing companies like Coca-Cola and Kraft," journalist Adam Sorensen wrote in *Time*. [13]

Nevertheless, whether ALEC will continue its pullback from controversial social and political issues remains unclear. Republican state Rep. Jerry Madden of Texas, who had chaired the now-disbanded public-safety and elections task force, told a conservative religious news website that the closure "won't impact the important issues we've worked on." He added that opponents were targeting ALEC "because when conservatives get together, we influence state and federal policy in a major way, and these groups are scared of us — and should be." [14]

That statement led ColorofChange to call the ALEC move to shut down its safety and elections task force a "publicity stunt." On its blog, the group added, "We'll continue to make sure that major corporations with ties to ALEC are aware that they're funding a toxic agenda." [15]

In addition to ColorofChange, *The Nation*, a New York-based liberal magazine, and the Center for Media and Democracy — a Madison, Wis.-based advocacy organization funded by the Ford Foundation and Rockefeller Family Foundation, among others — had also weighed in on ALEC and its photo-ID agenda. They put up an "ALEC-Exposed" website that included not only the complete library of once-secret ALEC-drafted legislation but also the template for ALEC's photo-ID bill, which legislators could use in drafting their own versions. [16]

The trove also included a copy of a magazine for ALEC members with advice on crafting photo-ID legislation to withstand legal challenges. Steps should include programs to distribute free ID cards, and a major advertising campaign to inform voters of new requirements, it said. "Taking these precautions," it said, "may be the difference between success and failure." [17]

— Peter Katel

---

[1] "ALEC Sharpens Focus on Jobs, Free Markets and Growth — Announces the End of Task Force that Dealt with Non-Economic Issues," American Legislative Exchange Council, April 17, 2010, www.alec.org/2012/04/alec-sharpens-focus-on-jobs-free-markets-and-growth-announces-the-end-of-the-task-force-that-dealt-with-non-economic-issues.

[2] *Ibid.*; Stephen Elzinga, "The Challenge of Photo ID," Inside ALEC, June, 2009, http://images2.americanprogress.org/campus/web/Inside_alec_June09.pdf; "Voter ID Act," (model bill), 2009, http://alecexposed.org/w/images/d/d9/7G16-VOTER_ID_ACT_Exposed.pdf.

[3] *Ibid.*, "Voter ID Act;" "Details of Voter ID Requirements," in "Voter Identification Requirements," National Conference of State Legislatures, updated regularly, www.ncsl.org/legislatures-elections/elections/voter-id.aspx.

[4] "2003-2010 Legislative Action," in "Voter Identification Requirements," National Conference of State Legislatures, regularly updated, www.ncsl.org/legislatures-elections/elections/voter-id.aspx#Legislation.

[5] Tim Storey, "GOP Makes Historic State Legislative Gains in 2010," *Rasmussen Reports*, Dec. 10, 2010, www.rasmussenreports.com/public_content/political_commentary/commentary_by_tim_storey/gop_makes_historic_state_legislative_gains_in_2010.

[6] "Stop corporate-funded voter suppression," colorofchange.org, undated, http://act.colorofchange.org/sign/alec.

[7] "Tell corporations: stop funding ALEC," colorofchange.org, http://colorofchange.org/campaign/alec/original_email.

[8] For background, see Kenneth Jost, "Police Misconduct," *CQ Researcher*, April 6, 2012, pp. 301-324. See also, Lizette Alvarez, "A Florida Law Gets Scrutiny After a Teenager's Killing," *The New York Times*, March 20, 2012, www.nytimes.com/2012/03/21/us/justice-department-opens-inquiry-in-killing-of-trayvon-martin.html?pagewanted=all; Eric Lichtblau, "Martin Death Spurs Group to Readjust Policy Focus," *The New York Times*, April 17, 2012, www.nytimes.com/2012/04/18/us/trayvon-martin-death-spurs-group-to-readjust-policy-focus.html; Mike Baker, "Legislative group turns focus amid Martin backlash," The Associated Press, April 17, 2012.

[9] Barbara Liston and Martinne Geller, "Coke withdraws from group that backs Stand Your Ground law," Reuters, April 6, 2012, http://uk.reuters.com/article/2012/04/05/usa-coke-alec-idUKL2E8F54P120120405; Brendan Greeley, "Why Are McDonald's, Coca-Cola, and Intuit Fleeing ALEC?," *Bloomberg Businessweek*, April 13, 2012, www.businessweek.com/articles/2012-04-13/why-are-mcdonalds-coca-cola-and-intuit-fleeing-alec.

[10] "Legislative group turns focus . . . ," *op. cit.*

[11] Brendan Greeley and Alison Fitzgerald, "Pssst . . . Wanna Buy a Law?," *Bloomberg Businessweek*, Dec. 1, 2011, www.businessweek.com/printer/magazine/pssst-wanna-buy-a-law-12012011.html.

[12] *Ibid.*

[13] Adam Sorensen, "ALEC Scraps Gun-Law, Voter-ID Task Force," *Swampland blog, Time*, April 17, 2012, http://swampland.time.com/2012/04/17/alec-scraps-gun-law-voter-id-task-force.

[14] Quoted in Paul Stanley, "Coca-Cola, Procter & Gamble, Kraft Dump Conservative Nonprofit ALEC," *Christian Post*, April 24, 2012, www.christianpost.com/news/wal-mart-procter-gamble-kraft-dump-conservative-nonprofit-alec-73752/.

[15] "ALEC leader admits last week's announcement was a PR stunt," Colorof Change blog, April 24, 2012, http://colorofchange.org/blog/2012/apr/24/alec-admits-internal-changes-wont-impact-their-wor/.

[16] "ALEC Exposed," Center for Media and Democracy, updated May 1, 2012, http://alecexposed.org/wiki/ALEC_Exposed; "Voter ID Act," Alec Exposed, http://alecexposed.org/w/images/d/d9/7G16-VOTER_ID_ACT_Exposed.pdf.

[17] Elzinga, *op. cit.*

Indeed, in the years following ratification of the amendment, white Southern politicians took full advantage of its limits. Following experiments with restrictions in various states, Mississippi in 1890 enacted what became the model for a comprehensive approach to barring African-Americans (and, in Texas, Mexican-Americans) from voting. Included in a new Mississippi state constitution were a $2 "poll tax" — a fee for voting — and a literacy test on knowledge of the Constitution and its interpretation.

Restricting Immigrants

In 1845-1855, about three million German and Irish immigrants poured into the young United States — a number equivalent to about 15 percent of the entire U.S. population. Most of the Irish were poor and uneducated, and as Roman Catholics they were considered adherents of a menacing, foreign-controlled faith. [40]

Their arrival in huge numbers in cities in the Northeast, and as far west as Chicago, prompted a backlash by Protestants. Politically active immigration foes organized a movement that became known as the Know-Nothing Party, which began as a secret society (hence the nickname, which referred to a vow of silence about the group to outsiders).

The Know-Nothings resolutely opposed voting rights for Catholic immigrants. Fear of the political and social power of the immigrants was strong enough to propel Know-Nothing candidates to victory in nine gubernatorial elections and ensure Know-Nothing majorities in at least six state legislatures.

Know-Nothings were able to effectively block immigrants from voting in New York City, prevent naturalization of Irish immigrants in four New England states and have voting limited to property owners in Georgia (where Irish immigrants had settled in Savannah and Augusta).

The Know-Nothing surge didn't last. Nor did a Know-Nothing-imposed two-year waiting period after naturalization for voting in Massachusetts, which was repealed during the Civil War (though the literacy test remained, in both Massachusetts and Connecticut). The newly formed Republican Party of President Abraham Lincoln opposed the law's anti-immigrant character.

At about the same time that nativists were barring Irish immigrants from voting in the Northeast, states in the Midwest were allowing German immigrants to vote — even before they became citizens. Under laws designed to apply to German immigrants, they had to have lived in the United States for two years and formally declared their intention to apply for citizenship.

The liberal voting laws didn't survive the next big immigrant wave, which began in the late 1800s. These newcomers were from Southern and Eastern Europe — and, on the West Coast, from China. They aroused considerable xenophobia even in states that had welcomed Germans and other Northern Europeans.

Also during the late 1800s, states widely adopted voter-registration systems, in some cases designed to prevent or delay voting by newly naturalized U.S. citizens. The restrictions included a New Jersey requirement that non-native voters present their naturalization papers when registering or voting. Legislators knew that many immigrants had lost their papers or wouldn't have realized they were needed for voting. Other states imposed waiting periods between naturalization and voting.

One aim of registration was fraud prevention, which reformers were sure was pervasive, especially in cities teeming with immigrants. Election fraud did exist in those locales. Justice Stevens, in a footnote to his 2008 opinion in the Indiana case, cited a quote by a 19th-century New York machine politician on how to ensure that repeat voters weren't recognized on multiple visits: Start them off with beards, then have the whiskers gradually shaved for each time the repeaters voted. [41]

But Keyssar, the Harvard historian, writes that documented cases of fraud during the late 19th century are scarce. What's more, he noted, recorded cases of fraud extend beyond cities to rural communities. In Adams County, Ohio, in the 1890s, for instance, 90 percent of voters were paid for their votes. And during a violent union-management fight in Huerfano County, Colo., in 1914, company-allied Republicans swept to victory thanks to election-rigging that excluded union members.

Southern Battleground

Prohibitions against "paupers" voting, along with various other restrictions, existed throughout the country into the early 20th century. But as in the pre-Civil War years, conflict and debate focused largely on laws and procedures that kept Southern blacks from casting ballots. [42]

The poll tax was only one such device. Restricting voting in Democratic Party primaries to whites was another. Because the post-Civil War Republican Party was still the party of Lincoln — reviled in the white South — the region was overwhelmingly Democratic, making its primaries the only significant political contests.

In 1927, the U.S. Supreme Court ruled that it was unconstitutional to bar blacks from voting in primaries. The decision arose from a challenge to the exclusion of a black voter from a Democratic primary in Texas. [43] Texas Democrats eventually responded by limiting party membership to whites, which had the effect of barring black citizens from voting in primaries. In 1935, the U.S Supreme Court accepted that policy. [44]

But only nine years later, the high court reversed itself. "Constitutional rights would be of little value if they could be thus indirectly denied," the court said. [45]

After World War II, the South remained the major arena of voting-rights conflict. Despite the 1944 Supreme Court decision, African-Americans couldn't vote in much of the region. In 1961, the U.S. Civil Rights Commission reported that outright physical violence or legalistic devices prevented blacks from voting in 100 counties in eight Southern states.

These devices included the poll tax, aimed at impoverished black citizens, that remained in effect in Alabama, Arkansas, Mississippi, Texas and Virginia until the early 1960s. In addition, seven states — Alabama, Georgia, Louisiana, Mississippi, North Carolina, South Carolina and Virginia — used "literacy tests" as racial barriers.

The poll tax was outlawed in federal elections by the 24th Amendment, which was ratified in early 1964. That same year, a coalition of civil rights organizations sent as many as 1,000 volunteers to Mississippi — the state that civil rights activists deemed the heart of Southern resistance to civil rights — to help African-Americans register to vote. [46]

Two of the white civil rights workers, Andrew Goodman and Michael Schwerner, were murdered in Neshoba County, Miss., together with a black activist from the area, James Chaney. [47] National indignation over their deaths, coupled with TV news footage of Selma, Ala., police beating civil rights demonstrators, made voting rights a national priority. "It is wrong — deadly wrong — to deny any of your fellow Americans the right to vote," President Lyndon B. Johnson told Congress in March 1965. [48]

The Voting Rights Act was enacted soon thereafter. In addition to effectively eliminating literacy tests and similar devices, the law also included a "pre-clearance" provision requiring the Justice Department to approve changes in voting procedures in states or political subdivisions with a history of discriminatory practices or where fewer than 50 percent of eligible voters weren't registered or hadn't voted in the 1964 presidential election. [49]

Identity Issues

The next major increase in registration came in 1995 in the form of the National Voter Registration Act. Vetoed earlier by Republican President George H. W. Bush, the bill became law under his Democratic successor, Bill Clinton. Known as the "motor voter" law because it allowed voter registration at state driver's license and motor vehicle offices, the measure added 9 million registrants to the rolls. As Republicans had expected, the new registrants tended to be young, black and Democratic-leaning. [50]

If the "motor voter" debate presaged the voter-ID fight, the direct impetus was the 2000 presidential election, which took a U.S. Supreme Court decision to resolve and prompted widespread concern that electoral systems across the country needed improvement. [51]

The blue-ribbon commission headed by former Presidents Carter and Ford suggested establishing statewide — as opposed to county- or city-level — computerized registered-voter lists in each state, linked to lists of licensed drivers. Each registration by a new applicant should include a "separate and specific affirmation that the applicant is a U.S. citizen," the panel said. [52]

The recommendations underpinned the Help America Vote Act of 2002 (HAVA). The law required prospective voters new to a given jurisdiction to provide documentation of their identities. Acceptable credentials included a photo ID, without a requirement that it be government-issued, as well as utility bills, paychecks and similar documents. [53]

Notably, HAVA did not include a proof-of-identity requirement for voters at the polls, leaving the states with their existing identity-certification procedures. HAVA also left out the boldest Carter-Ford commission recommendation — that people with felony convictions be allowed to vote after serving their sentences and any probation or parole terms. [54]

When the law was enacted, 11 states already required voters to identify themselves at polling places through such means as a driver's license, utility bill, hunting and fishing license or Social Security card. [55]

A second blue-ribbon commission — headed by Carter and former Secretary of State Baker, urged a more rigorous identification system. It proposed the use of driver's licenses issued under the REAL ID Act of 2005, which penalizes states whose driver's license standards don't require proof of identity and U.S. citizenship or legal status. Under the act, licenses issued by noncompliant states are invalid outside those states. After several postponements, the compliance deadline now is Jan. 15, 2013.

"There is no evidence of extensive fraud in U.S. elections or of multiple voting, but both occur, and it could affect the outcome of a close election," the commission said in explaining its ID proposal, which helped launch the movement for photo-ID laws. [56]

But Republicans insisted that the electoral system was beset by widespread and systematic fraud. "In certain parts of America," Karl Rove, then the top political adviser to President George W. Bush, said in 2006, it was "beginning to look like we have elections like those run in countries where the guys in charge are colonels in mirrored sunglasses." [57]

The Republican campaign that Rove was leading took the form of pushing for law-enforcement investigations as well as legislation. Those investigations didn't produce the desired results. When the Bush administration fired nine U.S. attorneys in 2006, three of them had run afoul of White House-supported efforts to mount prosecutions against what Republican activists claimed were systematic, large-scale vote fraud conspiracies — of which the ousted prosecutors said no evidence existed. [58]

The Republican drive proved much more successful on the legislative front. Following the 2004 elections, GOP state legislators pushed through strict photo-ID laws in Georgia, Indiana and Missouri, although a Missouri court struck down the state's photo-ID law in 2006. A federal court upheld Georgia's in 2007. [59]

Indiana's law required voters to show a government-issued photo ID that can have expired no later than the previous general election. Lacking that, a voter could cast a provisional ballot — which would be counted only if the voter presented valid documentation of identity to the county clerk within 10 days of the election.

A challenge to that law reached the U.S. Supreme Court, which ruled 6-3 in 2008 that the ID requirement was a legitimate measure to counteract the risk of fraud and strengthen voter confidence in election integrity. [60]

By 2012, 14 more states had passed photo-ID laws, seven of which the National Conference of State Legislatures categorized as "strict" measures, in which showing a photo ID was required to cast a ballot, though all allowed provisional balloting by people who would then have several days to document their identities. [61] ■

CURRENT SITUATION

Minnesota Battle

The fight over voter rights is playing out in a number of states, and with special intensity in Minnesota, where citizens are scheduled to vote up or down this year on strict ID requirements.

The Republican-controlled legislature passed a voter photo-ID bill in April. Democratic Gov. Mark Dayton promptly vetoed it. But he couldn't prevent lawmakers from putting it on the state ballot as a proposed constitutional amendment, a legislative move that requires only a simple majority under Minnesota law. Voters will decide the issue in November.

Minnesota is considered a stereotypical clean-politics state, lacking the histories of racial division and real or mythical political corruption that drive much of the debate over photo-ID laws. But a hard-fought U.S. Senate election in 2008 between incumbent Republican Norm Coleman and his Democratic challenger, Al Franken, led to a legal battle of more than seven months in which Franken — a former "Saturday Night Live" comedian — was finally declared the winner by 312 votes. [62]

"I'm not saying that every Republican is trying to avenge a loss," says state Rep. Simon of the Democratic-Farmer-Labor Party. "But I think that what we're seeing in part is a reaction to losing an achingly close election." McGrath of Minnesota Majority, a leader of the campaign for a photo-ID law, says the episode "punctuated how important election integrity is."

The legislative votes that placed the photo-ID issue on the state ballot were strictly partisan. The only exception was a sole Republican senator who voted with Democrats against the proposal. [63]

Photo-ID advocates, for their part, accuse their opponents, including Secretary of State Mark Ritchie, of trying to scare Minnesota voters by arguing that changes accompanying the proposed system would disrupt an election system that Minnesotans like.

"For the secretary of state to be fear-mongering like that to the entire state of Minnesota — that's pretty blatant politics," said Republican state Rep. Keith Downey. [64]

Ritchie has been warning that the proposed amendment's establishment of a provisional ballot system for the first time in Minnesota history would effectively end a practice under which Minnesotans can register and vote on the same day. The same-day system, in effect since 1974, is widely popular, accounting for about 550,000 votes per election in recent years. [65]

But the photo-ID proposal seems popular as well. A survey last year by the *Minneapolis Star-Tribune* showed 80 percent support for a photo-ID requirement in Minnesota. Not surprisingly, among Republicans approval was nearly unanimous at 94 percent. But 64 percent of Democrats supported the idea as well. "The public wants it, but the governor doesn't," says McGrath. "Across every major political group there is strong support for voter ID." [66]

He adds, "When you've got 80 percent of voters who want voter ID, the vast majority don't have full confidence in our system. Our election law is the loosest in the nation. We don't require any sort of ID to register and vote on Election Day."

According to the Minnesota secretary of state's office, same-day registrants without ID can be accepted on the basis of a sworn affidavit by another voter who is already registered in the same precinct. [67]

McGrath argues that that provision, which allows one person to vouch for up to 15 individuals, can in practice allow groups of voters to travel from precinct to precinct, getting "vouched" at each one. No such cases have been reported, though Republicans in 2008 did report that Obama campaigners in college neighborhoods were vouching for strangers in order to ensure that they could vote. [68]

Voting Rights Act

Texas is challenging not only the Justice Department's rejection of the state's photo-ID law but also the department's very authority over some states' voting statutes.

That "preclearance" authority, spelled out in Section 5 of the Voting Rights Act of 1965, "violates the Constitution," Texas Attorney General Greg Abbott said in a lawsuit filed in March, citing

Continued on p. 468

At Issue:

Do photo-ID laws disenfranchise racial and ethnic minorities?

JUSTIN LEVITT
PROFESSOR, LOYOLA LAW SCHOOL, LOS ANGELES

FROM TESTIMONY TO SENATE JUDICIARY COMMITTEE'S SUBCOMMITTEE ON THE CONSTITUTION, CIVIL RIGHTS AND HUMAN RIGHTS, SEPT. 8, 2011

yes

There is no question that most eligible citizens have government-issued photo identification. The right of the franchise — and the responsibility to ensure its continued reasonable access — is not limited to the majority of the American public. Voting is a fundamental right for more than just most of us. It is a right that must be zealously safeguarded for every eligible American citizen.

It is important to note that even choosing the most conservative estimate . . . 1.2 percent of registered voters do not have the identification required by the most restrictive states. Even this substantially conservative result amounts to an impact reaching more than two million registered voters if applied nationwide. And the larger estimates show an impact reaching more than 22 million voting-age citizens.

Even if turnout provided an accurate assessment of the impact on past voters, it would cover only the impact on past voters, without any assessment at all of the impact on eligible Americans who have not yet [voted].

Those without government-issued photo identification are not evenly spread across the electorate. The available data clearly show that those without government-issued photo identification are more likely to be nonwhite, more likely to be either younger voters or seniors, more likely to be from low-income households and more likely to have less formal education.

These impacts are both substantial and statistically significant. For example, one 2008 survey found that while 3.7 percent of responding white registered voters nationwide did not have current, valid government-issued photo identification, 7.3 percent of Latino voters and 9.5 percent of African-American voters lacked this ID. And among voting-age citizens rather than registered voters, a 2006 national survey found that 8 percent of white citizens but 16 percent of Latino voting-age citizens and 25 percent of African-American voting-age citizens do not have current, valid government-issued photo identification.

These statistics are not merely important for their reflection of the status quo but for their reflection of significant impact into the future. It often takes [an] ID to get [an] ID. For example, most native-born citizens in Arkansas seem to require an official copy of a birth certificate to get a government-issued photo identification card . . . and seem to require government-issued photo identification to get an official copy of a birth certificate.

The restrictions are unnecessary and unjustified, and even potentially counterproductive. Our most fundamental constitutional right deserves better.

HANS A. VON SPAKOVSKY
SENIOR LEGAL FELLOW, HERITAGE FOUNDATION

FROM TESTIMONY TO SENATE JUDICIARY COMMITTEE'S SUBCOMMITTEE ON THE CONSTITUTION, CIVIL RIGHTS AND HUMAN RIGHTS, SEPT. 8, 2011

no

Despite tiresome false claims to the contrary, there is no evidence that voter ID decreases the turnout of voters or has a disparate impact on minority, poor or elderly voters. The overwhelming majority of Americans have photo ID or can easily obtain one.

In the 2008 general election, Georgia, with one of the strictest voter-ID laws in the nation, had the largest turnout in its history. Democratic turnout was up an astonishing 6.1 percentage points from the 2004 election, when there was no photo-ID requirement. Just as has happened in every state that has considered voter-ID legislation, organizations in Georgia like the ACLU and the NAACP made apocalyptic claims that there were hundreds of thousands of Georgians without photo-ID. Yet when the federal district court dismissed all of their claims, the court pointed out that after two years of litigation, none of the plaintiff organizations had been able to produce a single individual who did not have a photo ID or could not easily obtain one.

In Indiana, which the U.S. Supreme Court said has the strictest voter-ID law in the country, turnout in the Democratic presidential preference primary in 2008 quadrupled from the 2004 election, when the photo-ID law was not in effect. In the general election in November, the turnout of Democratic voters increased by 8.3 percentage points from 2004, the largest increase in Democratic turnout of any state in the nation. According to Census Bureau surveys, 59.2 percent of the black voting-age population voted in the 2008 election compared to only 53.8 percent in 2004, an increase of over 5 percentage points.

Voter ID and proof of citizenship requirements do not affect the turnout of voters. The claims that the implementation of such laws is vote suppression is completely unsupported and a libel on the American people and their elected representatives who understand these are commonsense reforms easily complied with. If these were the equivalent of "Jim Crow" as has been outrageously and inaccurately claimed, then the security requirements imposed by the [Transportation Security Administration] and Congress itself must also be categorized as "Jim Crow."

Polls show overwhelming support for voter ID across all ethnic and racial lines. Americans have to use a photo ID to obtain a library card, drink a beer, cash a check, board an airplane, buy a train ticket or check into a hotel. They understand that requiring voter ID is a commonsense reform.

Continued from p. 466

the 10th Amendment to the Constitution, which reserves to the states powers not explicitly delegated to the federal government. [69]

That battle could reach the Supreme Court, where considerable skepticism already exists over whether the Justice Department should continue to have election-law oversight powers.

Federal approval of election-law changes in states and localities with histories of discrimination in election administration — mostly in the South — was extended by Congress in 2006. But three years later, Chief Justice John G. Roberts wrote: "Things have changed in the South. . . . Blatantly discriminatory evasions of federal decrees are rare. And minority candidates hold office at unprecedented levels." [70]

The high court didn't throw out Section 5 on that occasion. But the provision's supporters took no comfort from the justices' signals. "Section 5 is living on borrowed time," Nathaniel Persily, a Columbia University law and political science professor, told the U.S. Commission on Civil Rights in February. [71]

Texas' challenge, arising from the Justice Department's photo-ID action, joined two other lawsuits urging elimination of Section 5. Those suits, which don't involve the photo-ID issue, were filed by Arizona and North Carolina. [72]

The Texas case began in March, when the Justice Department concluded that Texas' own data showed that the state's new photo-ID law would have a discriminatory effect.

According to the Justice Department's reading of the data, nearly 604,000 and potentially about 795,000 of Texas' approximately 12 million voters lacked driver's licenses or state non-driver ID cards — with Hispanic voters at least 46 percent more likely to lack the credentials. "The state has failed to demonstrate why it could not meet its state goals of ensuring electoral integrity and deterring ineligible voters from voting in a manner that would have avoided this retrogressive effect," Assistant Attorney General Thomas E. Perez wrote to Texas' secretary of state in March. [73]

In Texas' lawsuit, state Attorney General Abbott called the federal data analysis flawed. The Justice Department calculated effects on Hispanics by counting Spanish surnames, the Texas lawsuit said, thereby overlooking large numbers of Hispanic citizens with Anglo last names. In any case, he added, even if minorities are disproportionately less likely to have a government-issued photo ID, that doesn't reflect intentional discrimination. [74]

The Justice Department's rejection of Texas' photo-ID law followed a similar denial of South Carolina's law in December. In that case, the department concluded from state data that non-white voters accounted for about 34 percent of voters who did not possess a photo-ID that met state requirements for voting. And non-whites made up about 30 percent of South Carolina's overall registered-voter population. "Non-white voters were therefore disproportionately represented, to a significant degree, in the group of registered voters who, under the proposed law, would be rendered ineligible to go to the polls and participate in the election," Perez wrote. [75]

South Carolina, in its legal challenge to the Justice Department's denial under the Voting Rights Act, argued that the department hadn't recognized the state's efforts to help voters without proper identification. These included allowing those voters to cast provisional ballots and providing free ID cards. "These exemptions . . . render any temporary disparity in the racial composition of the group of individuals without qualifying voter IDs entirely transitory," the state said in a suit signed

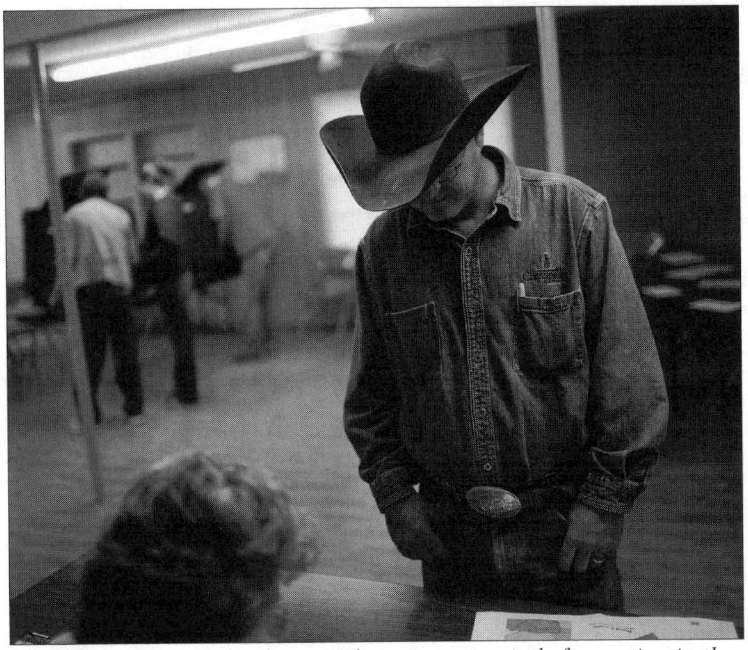

Getty Images/Tom Pennington

A voter in Lipan, Texas (pop. 425), waits to sign in before voting in the 2008 presidential contest between then-Sen. Barack Obama, D-Ill., and Sen. John McCain, R-Ariz. Texas is challenging the Justice Department's rejection of the state's photo-ID law as well as the department's basic authority over some states' voting statutes. The department has so-called "preclearance" authority over new election laws in Texas and eight other states under the Voting Rights Act of 1965.

by Paul D. Clement, a Washington lawyer who specializes in Supreme Court cases. [76]

The lawsuit didn't directly challenge Section 5. But South Carolina did argue that its law met the standards laid out by the Supreme Court in 2008, when it upheld Indiana's photo-ID law. Approving the Justice Department's action against South Carolina would treat laws differently based purely on whether they were subject to federal approval. [77]

Florida Registration

An election-law conflict in Florida, one of the country's major swing states, centers on voter registration. Although the state's Republican-controlled legislature this year rejected a strict photo-ID requirement, a 2011 state law imposed tough new standards on the voter-registration process. The nonpartisan League of Women Voters and other groups are challenging the standards in two federal court lawsuits on the grounds that they hamper registration drives, which they say play a disproportionately large role in building turnout in black and Hispanic communities. [78]

The new requirements led the League to quit voter-registration work in the state. Registration workers themselves must register with the state and must turn in their lists of newly registered voters within 48 hours or face fines of up to $1,000. Other measures include use of tracking numbers that allow the names of registrants to be traced to the organizations that helped them sign up to vote. [79]

Republicans backed the registration law, saying the restrictions are essential to combat voter fraud. State officials are now investigating thousands of registrations of people who may not be U.S. citizens. [80]

"You cannot have people that are not eligible to vote casting votes in our election," state Republican Party Chairman Lenny Curry told NPR. "It completely undermines the integrity of our system." [81]

The volume of registrations has dropped since the law took effect. From May 2011 to March of this year, 81,471 fewer Floridians signed up to vote than during the same period before the 2008 election, *The New York Times* calculated using state registration data. [82]

A state election official disputed the idea that the new law caused the apparent registration drop, arguing that in 2008 Floridians were facing an opportunity to vote in Democratic and Republican presidential primaries (there is no Democratic presidential primary this year), as well as on proposed constitutional amendment on property taxes. "To suggest the new election law had a greater impact on voter registration than the election ballot itself is a leap of logic," Chris Cate, communications director for Florida's Department of State, told *The Times*. [83]

For opponents of the law, the question of who is not registering is as important as the statistical drop in registrations. Camila Gallardo, a spokeswoman for the National Council of La Raza (NCLR), told NPR: "Minorities are more likely to register through a third-party voter organization like NCLR. So, you know, you can't help but think that this is in some way targeted." [84] ■

> **"You cannot have people that are not eligible to vote casting votes in our election. . . . It completely undermines the integrity of our system."**
>
> ***— Lenny Curry***
> ***Chairman,***
> ***Florida Republican Party***

OUTLOOK

Deeply Rooted Views

Experts of varying views see no quick end to the photo-ID fight. Views about fraud, on the one hand, and vote suppression on the other, seem too deeply embedded, they say.

That assessment is consistent with the conclusions of a 2008 study on whether ID requirements improve voters' confidence in the election system. "We find that voters who have been forced to show identification are no less likely to perceive fraud than those not similarly subject to an ID requirement," wrote Stephen Ansolabehere, a political science professor at the Massachusetts Institute of Technology, and Persily of Columbia University, citing survey data. [85]

Nationwide, they wrote, 13 percent of respondents in 2008 believed that voter fraud was very common, and 9 percent believed that impersonation was frequent. In the four states with the strictest photo-ID laws, 14 percent considered voter fraud very common and 10 percent believed impersonation occurred often. And in the seven states with the loosest ID requirements, the percentages were similar: 11 percent believed voter fraud was common, and 8 percent believed impersonation was frequent. [86]

Political affiliation and belief played a bigger role than ID laws in voters' beliefs about fraud, Ansolabehere and Persily concluded. In 2008, for example, "58 percent of Republicans said fraud occurs somewhat often or very often, compared with 39 percent of Democrats," they wrote. In 2007, "Forty-six percent of those . . . who describe themselves as very conservative believe fraud is very common, [but] only 16 percent of those who describe themselves as very liberal hold a similar view." [87]

Given the ideological underpinnings of the photo-ID fight, says Harvard's Keyssar, the key to the future of the conflict lies in the outcome of state legislative elections. "Right now, Republicans control a remarkable number of state legislatures. If that were to continue, we'll see more and more of these laws."

If the Republicans aren't as successful, Keyssar says, Democrats might be able to ensure that ID laws don't keep citizens from voting. "That's a more optimistic vision," he adds.

But in Minnesota, photo-ID supporter McGrath says he's confident that public sentiment will propel more states into the photo-ID camp. "That is my hope and expectation," he says.

From the opposing side in the Minnesota fight, Simon, the Democratic lawmaker, expresses hope that an electronic voter registry, which could include a digital photo of each registered voter, could offer a way to resolve the conflict. "That could help split the burden, rather than put it all on the voter," he says, "so that somebody who lost their ID or maybe just moved two weeks before the election can be identified easily."

Loyola's Levitt argues that expansion of that model is not inevitable. "I think the majority of states will continue to realize that it's better worth their time trying to fix real problems rather than offering fake solutions to problems that don't exist."

Chapin of the University of Minnesota speculates that the conflict could resolve itself. "Maybe Republicans will have to accept some limits on who needs to show ID," he says, "and Democrats are going to need to accept that ID will be necessary under conditions — a new voter, or a voter who is new to a jurisdiction."

Rhode Island, whose ID law requires voters to show some form of identification, but not necessarily a photo ID, might be another possibility, Chapin says. In the absence of compromise, "We could see ID laws yo-yo back and forth depending who's in control of the legislature." ■

About the Author

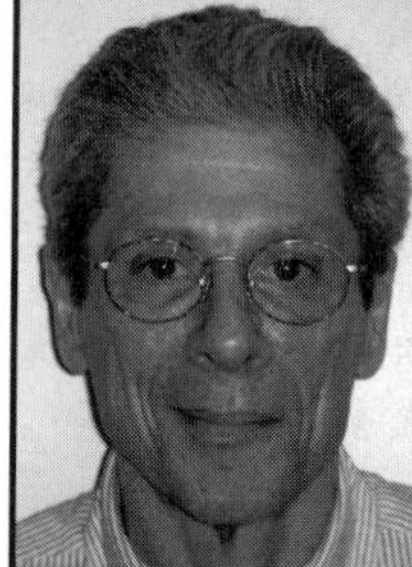

Peter Katel is a *CQ Researcher* staff writer who previously reported on Haiti and Latin America for *Time* and *Newsweek* and covered the Southwest for newspapers in New Mexico. He has received several journalism awards, including the Bartolomé Mitre Award for coverage of drug trafficking, from the Inter-American Press Association. He holds an A.B. in university studies from the University of New Mexico. His recent reports include "Prisoner Reenty" and "Downsizing Prisons."

Notes

[1] "Voter Identification Requirements," National Conference of State Legislatures, regularly updated, www.ncsl.org/legislatures-elections/elections/voter-id.aspx; "2012 State and Legislative Partisan Composition," National Conference of State Legislatures, April 28, 2012, www.ncsl.org/documents/statevote/2012_Legis_and_State.pdf.

[2] Tim Storey, "GOP Makes Historic State Legislative Gains in 2010," Rasmussen Reports, Dec. 10, 2010, www.rasmussenreports.com/public_content/political_commentary/commentary_by_tim_storey/gop_makes_historic_state_legislative_gains_in_2010.

[3] "Groups File Lawsuit in Commonwealth Court to Overturn Unconstitutional Voter Photo ID Law," ACLU of Pennsylvania, press release, May 1, 2012, www.aclupa.org/pressroom/groupsfilelawsuitincommonw.htm.

[4] Patrick Marley, "Supreme Court refuses to take up voter ID cases," JSOnline, *Milwaukee Journal-Sentinel*, April 16, 2012, http://m.jsonline.com/topstories/147608115.htm; Karen Langley, "Lawsuit seeks to overturn Pennsylvania ID law," *Pittsburgh Post-Gazette*, May 1, 2012, www.post-gazette.com/stories/local/state/lawsuit-seeks-to-overturn-pennsylvania-voter-id-law-633820; Karen Langley, "Law Is Enforceable for April Primary," *Pittsburgh Post-Gazette*, March 15, 2012, p. A1; "Recent Litigation," in "Voter Identification Requirements," *op. cit.*

[5] "2012 Legislative Action," in "Voter Identification Requirements," *op. cit.*

[6] Richard L. Hasen, "Election Law Blog," http://electionlawblog.org/.

[7] "Hearing of the Subcommittee on the Constitution, Civil Rights and Human Rights of the Senate Judiciary Committee," Federal News Service, Sept. 8, 2011; for video: "New State Voting Laws: Barriers to the Ballot?," Senate Judiciary Committee, Subcommittee on the Constitution, Civil Rights and Human Rights, Sept. 8, 2011 (Webcast), www.judiciary.senate.gov/hearings/hearing.cfm?id=2072649339b2bb3b19d320ce62f6c1b8.

[8] *Ibid.*

[9] *Ibid.*

[10] For background, see Peter Katel, "REAL ID," *CQ Researcher*, May 4, 2007, pp. 385-408.

[11] "Voter ID Clients," ACLU of Pennsylvania, undated, www.aclupa.org/legal/legaldocket/applewhiteetalvcommonwealt/voteridclients.htm; "Details of Voter Identification Requirements," in "Voter Identification Requirements," *op. cit.*

[12] Quoted in Michael D. Shear, "Obama Campaign Confronts Voter ID Laws," *The New York Times*, April 29, 2012, www.nytimes.com/2012/04/30/us/politics/obama-campaign-confronts-voter-id-laws.html.

[13] "To Assure Pride and Confidence in the Electoral Process," National Commission on Federal Election Reform, August 2001, pp. 31-39, http://web1.millercenter.org/commissions/comm_2001.pdf; "Building Confidence in U.S. Elections," Commission on Federal Election Reform, September 2005, pp. 18-20, www1.american.edu/ia/cfer/report/full_report.pdf.

[14] Quoted in *Crawford et al v. Marion County Election Board et al.*, U.S. Supreme Court, 553 U.S. 181 (2008), www.law.cornell.edu/supct/html/07-21.ZS.html.

[15] Quoted in "Travel Assistant," U.S. Transportation Security Administration, undated, www.tsa.gov/travelers/airtravel/assistant/index.shtm.

[16] "Inaccurate, Costly, and Inefficient," Pew Center on the States, Feb. 14, 2010, p. 4, www.pewtrusts.org/uploadedFiles/wwwpewtrustsorg/Reports/Election_reform/Pew_Upgrading_Voter_Registration.pdf.

[17] "Hearing of the Subcommittee," *op. cit.*

[18] *Crawford et al v. Marion County Election Board et al., op cit.*

[19] *Ibid.*, pp. 11-12, n. 12.

[20] "Hearing of the Subcommittee," *op. cit.*

[21] Dan McGrath, "Unverifiable Voters in Minnesota's Elections," Minnesota Majority, Jan. 17, 2012, p. 5, http://wewantvoterid.com/documents/2012_PVC_Report_Final.pdf.

[22] Alexander Keyssar, *The Right to Vote: The Contested History of Democracy in the United States* (2009 ed.)., p. 175.

[23] *Crawford et al v. Marion County Election Board, et al., op. cit.*

[24] "Hearing of the Subcommittee, *op. cit.*

[25] Rick Hasen, "How many voters actually deterred by new Republican voting laws?," *Election Law Blog*, Feb. 16, 2012, http://electionlawblog.org/?p=29665.

[26] Gabriel R. Sanchez, Stephen A. Nuño, Matt A. Barreto, "The Disproportionate Impact of Photo-ID Laws on the Minority Electorate," *Latino Decisions*, May 24, 2011, http://latinodecisions.wordpress.com/2011/05/24/the-disproportionate-impact-of-stringent-voter-id-laws; "Details of Voter Identification Requirements," in "Voter Identification Requirements," *op. cit.*

[27] Robert Pastor, *et al.*, "Voter IDs Are Not the Problem: A Survey of Three States," Center for Democracy and Election Management, American University, Jan. 9, 2008, p. 9, www1.american.edu/ia/cdem/pdfs/VoterIDFinalReport1-9-08.pdf.

[28] "New State Voting Laws . . . ," *op. cit.*

[29] More details in von Spakovsky's written testimony, www.judiciary.senate.gov/pdf/11-9-8SpakovskyTestimony.pdf.

[30] "Hearing of the Subcommittee," *op. cit.*

[31] "Building Confidence in U.S. Elections," Commission on Federal Election Reform, September 2005, pp. 18-20, www1.american.edu/ia/cfer/report/full_report.pdf.

[32] "Putting an End to Voter Fraud," Republican Policy Committee, U.S. Senate, Feb. 15, 2005, www.votelaw.com/blog/blogdocs/Voter%20Fraud%20Paper%20(no%20sig).pdf.

[33] "Building Confidence in U.S. elections," *op. cit.*, p. 51; "Case Studies on the Impact of the Help America Vote Act's Identification Requirements for First-Time Voters," U.S. Election Assistance Commission, May 2008, p. 26, www.eac.gov/assets/1/workflow_staging/Page/63.PDF.

[34] "4-Year Graduation Rates, Cohort of 2011, Statewide," New Mexico Public Education Department, undated, www.ped.state.nm.us/Graduation/2012/Webfiles%20Graduation%20Cohort%20of%202011%20-%204%20Year_2012-05-04_1120.pdf.

[35] "New Mexico Settles Lawsuit, Agrees to Implement 'Motor Voter' Law," Advocates for Justice, May 16, 2010, www.advocatesforjustice.net/new-mexico-settles-lawsuit-agrees-to-implement-motor-voter-law/.

[36] Unless otherwise indicated, this subsection is drawn from Keyssar, *op. cit.*; for background, see Peter Katel, "Voting Controversies," *CQ Researcher*, Sept. 15, 2006, pp. 745-768.

[37] "Missouri's Dred Scott Case," Missouri Digital Heritage, Missouri Office of the Secretary of State, undated, www.sos.mo.gov/archives/resources/africanamerican/scott/scott.asp.

[38] Quoted in Keyssar, *op. cit.*, p. 46.

[39] Quoted in *ibid.*, pp. 79-80.

[40] Except where otherwise indicated, this subsection is drawn from Keyssar, *ibid.*

[41] "Crawford, et al. v. Marion County Election Board et al.," *op. cit.*, n. 11.

[42] Except where otherwise noted, this subsection is drawn from Keyssar, *op. cit.*

[43] *Nixon v. Herndon*, 273 U.S. 536 (1927), http://supreme.justia.com/cases/federal/us/273/536/case.html.

[44] *Grovey v. Townsend*, 295 U.S. 45 (1935), http://supreme.justia.com/cases/federal/us/295/45/case.html.

[45] *Smith v. Allwright*, 321 U.S. 649 (1944), http://supreme.justia.com/cases/federal/us/321/649/case.html.

[46] "Mississippi Freedom Summer Events," Civil Rights Movement Veterans, 2011, www.crmvet.org/tim/tim64b.htm#1964fs.

[47] Eighteen men were tried in 1967 on charges of depriving the three of their civil rights. Seven (including a deputy sheriff) were convicted. In 2005, after the *Clarion-Ledger* newspaper in Jackson, Miss., uncovered evidence, the state filed a murder charge in 2005 against a former Ku Klux Klan leader, Edgar Ray Killen. He was convicted of manslaughter and sentenced to 60 years in prison. Ariel Hart, "41 Years Later, Ex-Klansman Gets 60 Years in Civil Rights Deaths," *The New York Times*, June 24, 2005, www.nytimes.com/2005/06/24/national/24killen.html; Robert D. McFadden, "First Murder Charge in '64 Civil Rights Killings of 3," *The New York Times*, Jan. 7, 2005, www.nytimes.com/2005/01/07/national/07mississippi.html.

[48] Quoted in Keyssar, *op. cit.*, p. 211.

[49] The states covered in their entirety are: Alabama, Alaska, Arizona, Georgia, Louisiana, Mississippi, South Carolina, and Texas; Virginia had been included, but 18 subdivisions were removed from coverage over recent decades. "About Section 5 of the Voting Rights Act," U.S. Department of Justice, undated, www.justice.gov/crt/about/vot/sec_5/about.php; "Section 4 of the Voting Rights Act," undated, www.justice.gov/crt/about/vot/misc/sec_4.php#bailout_list.

[50] Keyssar, *op. cit.*, pp. 255-256.

[51] For background, see Peter Katel, "Voting Controversies," *CQ Researcher*, Sept. 15, 2006, pp. 745-768.

[52] "To Assure Pride and Confidence," *op. cit.*, pp. 6-18.

[53] "Case Studies on the Impact of the Help America Vote Act's Identification Requirements for First-Time Voters," U.S. Election Assistance Commission, May, 2008, p. 1, www.eac.gov/assets/1/workflow_staging/Page/63.PDF; "Help America Vote Act of 2002," 107th Congress,

p. 116, STAT 1713, www.fec.gov/hava/law_ext.txt.
[54] *Ibid.*, "Case Studies," p. 1; "To Assure Pride and Confidence . . . ," *op. cit.*, p. 8.
[55] *Ibid.*, p. 1.
[56] "Building Confidence in U.S. Elections," *op. cit.*, p. 18; "REAL ID Implementation, Center for Immigration Studies, Feb. 21, 2012, www.prnewswire.com/news-releases/real-id-implementation-139798783.html.
[57] Quoted in Keyssar, *op. cit.*, p. 280.
[58] Quoted in "Not-for-profit behind ID push; Group partners with GOP on voting laws," McClatchy Newspapers (*Columbia Daily Tribune*), July 1, 2007.
[59] "Recent Litigation" in "Voter ID Requirements," *op. cit.*
[60] *Crawford et al. v. Marion County Election Board et al.*, *op. cit.*
[61] "Voter Identification Requirements," National Conference of State Legislatures, regularly updated, www.ncsl.org/legislatures-elections/elections/voter-id.aspx.
[62] Brian Montopoli, "Coleman Concedes; Franken Wins Senate Seat," Political HotSheet, CBS News, June 30, 2009, www.cbsnews.com/8301-503544_162-5126051-503544.html.
[63] Bill Salisbury, "Minnesota voter ID measure going on fall ballot," *St. Paul Pioneer Press*, April 3, 2012.
[64] Quoted in Alexandra Tempus, "Sec. of State Ritchie steps into voter ID battle," The Associated Press, April 14, 2012.
[65] Lori Sturdevant, "Same-day registration for voters is on the block," *Minneapolis Star-Tribune*, March 25, 2012, p. 1OP.
[66] Eric Roper, "Minnesota Poll: Big show of support for voter photo ID," *Minneapolis Star-Tribune*, May 13, 2011, www.startribune.com/politics/statelocal/121678219.html.
[67] "Registering to Vote," Office of the Minnesota Secretary of State, undated, www.sos.state.mn.us/index.aspx?page=204.
[68] Dave Orrick, "Republicans to target Minnesota's easy-to-vote laws," *St. Paul Pioneer Press*, Dec. 4, 2010.
[69] *Texas v. Holder*, First Amended Expedited Complaint for Declaratory Judgment, 1:12-cv-00128RMC-DST-RLW, March 12, 2012, https://docs.google.com/file/d/0BxeOfQQnUr_gb2t4blV3bIFUZHFGZ0hvSEIwSlhHUQ/edit?pli=1; "Tenth Amendment," *FindLaw*, http://caselaw.lp.findlaw.com/data/constitution/amendment10/.
[70] Quoted in Robert Barnes, "States line up to challenge stringent Section 5 voting rights provision," *The Washington Post*, Feb. 9, 2012, www.washingtonpost.com/politics/states-line-up-to-challenge-stringent-section-5-voting-rights-provision/2012/02/01/gIQA5aYE1Q_story.html.
[71] Quoted in *ibid.*
[72] *Ibid.*
[73] Letter, U.S. Justice Department, Civil Rights Division, March 12, 2012, https://s3.amazonaws.com/s3.documentcloud.org/documents/324586/justice-departments-decision-on-the-texas-voter.pdf.
[74] *Texas v. Holder*, United States District Court for the District of Columbia, First Amended Expedited Complaint, March 12, 2012, 1:12-cv-00128, www.scribd.com/doc/85611907/Amended-Voter-ID-Complaint.
[75] Letter, U.S. Justice Department, Dec. 23, 2011, http://brennan.3cdn.net/594b9cf4396be7ebc8_0pm6i2fx6.pdf.
[76] *State of South Carolina v. United States of America and Eric H. Holder*, Feb. 7, 2012, United States District Court for the District of Columbia, 1:2012cv00203, http://docs.justia.com/cases/federal/district-courts/district-of-columbia/dcdce/1:2012cv00203/152606/1/0.pdf?1328811750.
[77] *Ibid.*
[78] "League of Women Voters v. Browning," Brennan Center for Justice, case summary, Dec. 15, 2011, www.brennancenter.org/content/resource/league_of_women_voters_of_florida_v._browning/.
[79] Scott Powers, "Groups register voters — carefully," *Orlando Sentinel*, April 26, 2012, p. A1.
[80] Greg Allen, "In Florida, Registering Votes A Whole New Game," NPR, May 14, 2012, www.npr.org/2012/05/14/152517589/in-florida-registering-voters-a-whole-new-game.
[81] Quoted in *ibid.*
[82] Michael Cooper and Jo Craven McGinty, "Florida's New Election Law Blunts Voter Drives," *The New York Times*, March 27, 2012, www.nytimes.com/2012/03/28/us/restrictions-on-voter-registration-in-florida-have-groups-opting-out.html.
[83] Quoted in *ibid.*
[84] Quoted in "In Florida, Registering Voters . . . ," *op. cit.*
[85] Stephen Ansolabehere and Nathaniel Persily, "Vote Fraud in the Eye of the Beholder: The Role of Public Opinion in the Challenge to Voter Identification Requirements," *Harvard Law Review*, May 2008, p. 1740, www.harvardlawreview.org/issues/121/may08/ansolabehere_persily.pdf.
[86] *Ibid.*, p. 1758.
[87] *Ibid.*, pp. 1747-1748.

FOR MORE INFORMATION

ACLU Voting Rights, 125 Broad St., New York, NY 10004; 212-549-2500; www.aclu.org/voting-rights. Active in litigation against photo-ID laws; provides news, analysis and research reports.

Brennan Center for Justice at NYU School of Law, 161 Avenue of the Americas, New York, NY 10013; 646-292-8310; brennancenter@nyu.edu. Liberal think tank that publishes litigation documents, research and analysis.

Heritage Foundation, Civil Justice Reform Initiative, 214 Massachusetts Ave., N.E., Washington, DC 20002; 202-546-4999; www.heritage.org/issues/legal. Conservative think tank that advocates for more stringent ID requirements for voting.

National Conference of State Legislatures, 7700 East First Place, Denver, CO 80230; 303-364-7700; www.ncsl.org. Nonpartisan organization that furnishes the most complete and up-to-date information on states' voter-ID laws.

True the Vote, P.O. Box 27368, Houston, TX 77227; http://truethevote.org. Web-based organization that supports photo-ID laws. It is organizing a nationwide network of election-watchers.

U.S. Department of Justice, Civil Rights Division, Room 7254 — NWB, Department of Justice, 950 Pennsylvania Ave., N.W., Washington, DC 20530; voting.section@usdoj.gov. Federal agency involved in reviewing photo-ID laws in some states under Voting Rights Act of 1965.

Bibliography

Selected Sources

Books

Fund, John H., *Stealing Elections: How Voter Fraud Threatens Our Democracy*, Encounter, 2008.
A senior editor at the conservative *American Spectator* magazine lays out the Republican argument that the election system is riddled with fraud.

Hasen, Richard L., *The Voting Wars: From Florida 2000 to the Next Election Meltdown*, Yale, 2011.
A leading election-law expert at the University of California, Irvine, chronicles this century's voting-rights conflicts and treats the voter-ID controversy in detail.

Keyssar, Alexander, *The Right to Vote: The Contested History of Democracy in the United States*, Basic Books, 2009.
A historian at Harvard's Kennedy School of Government traces voting-rights disputes to the nation's beginning.

Minnite, Lorraine C., *The Myth of Voter Fraud*, Cornell, 2010.
A Rutgers University political scientist concludes after years of research that voter fraud is not a serious problem.

Articles

Blake, Aaron, "The GOP's Voter ID gambit," The Fix (politics blog), *The Washington Post*, March 29, 2011, www.washingtonpost.com/blogs/the-fix/post/the-gops-voter-id-gambit/2011/03/28/AFhk1YuB_blog.html.
As newly elected GOP majorities in a number of states began pushing voter-ID laws, a political reporter examined Republicans' reasons and their prospects.

Bowes, Mark, "Va. investigates voter fraud," *Richmond* (Va.) *Times-Dispatch*, April 22, 2012, www2.timesdispatch.com/news/2012/apr/22/tdmain01-va-investigates-voter-fraud-ar-1859666/.
A major Virginia daily reports that 38 people have been criminally charged as a result of alleged election irregularities in 2008, but that none of the cases involves voters casting ballots in the names of other people.

Burnett, Sara, "Secretary of State ready, willing to pick a fight," *Denver Post*, Dec. 24, 2011, p. A1.
Colorado's major daily profiles the state's top election official, who has alleged major election fraud.

Davenport, Jim, "SC voter ID law hits some black precincts harder," The Associated Press, Oct. 19, 2011.
An analysis by the news service concludes that a disproportionate number of residents in majority-black voting districts couldn't meet new ID requirements for voting.

Gamboa, Suzanne, "Voter ID laws target rarely occurring voter fraud," The Associated Press, Sept. 24, 2011.
Gamboa reports on the relative scarcity of the kind of voter fraud that ID laws are designed to prevent.

Gillman, Todd J., "Supreme Court could be receptive to Texas' challenge of Voting Rights Act," *Dallas Morning News*, March 18, 2012.
Texas' challenge to a provision of the Voting Rights Act of 1965 may be well received at the U.S. Supreme Court.

Marley, Patrick, "Supreme Court refuses to take up voter ID cases," *Milwaukee Journal Sentinel*, April 16, 2012, www.jsonline.com/news/statepolitics/supreme-court-refuses-to-take-up-voter-id-cases-1b51335-147608115.html.
Declining to rule on challenges to the state's new photo-ID law, the Wisconsin Supreme Court effectively kept the law from applying in critical elections in May and June.

Salisbury, Bill, "Minnesota voter ID measure going on fall ballot," *St. Paul Pioneer Press*, April 3, 2012.
A Minnesota political reporter recounts how the Republican-controlled legislature placed before the voters an idea that the Democratic governor had vetoed.

"Waging a Battle Over Voter ID Laws," "PBS NewsHour" (Web video), March 14, 2012, www.pbs.org/newshour/bb/politics/jan-june12/voterid_03-14.html.
Leading advocates debate the photo-ID issue.

Reports and Studies

"Inaccurate, Costly, and Inefficient: Evidence that America's Voter Registration System Needs an Upgrade," Pew Center on the States, February 2012.
The nonpartisan research group concludes that about 24 million voter registrations are invalid or significantly inaccurate and that more than 1.8 million deceased persons are listed as voters.

Von Spakovsky, Hans A., "Lessons from the Voter ID Experience in Georgia," Heritage Foundation, March 19, 2012, www.heritage.org/research/reports/2012/03/lessons-from-the-voter-id-experience-in-georgia.
A prominent photo-ID advocate reports that Georgia's experience shows no disenfranchisement of minority-group voters.

Weiser, Wendy R., and Lawrence Norden, "Voting Law Changes in 2012," Brennan Center for Justice, 2011, http://brennan.3cdn.net/92635ddafbc09e8d88_i3m6bjdeh.pdf.
Staff members of a liberal New York-based think tank opposed to photo-ID laws lay out state-by-state results of recent voting-law changes.

The Next Step:

Additional Articles from Current Periodicals

Election Fraud

Caswell, Cheryl, "Lincoln Officials Plead Guilty in Election Fraud," *Charleston* (W.Va.) *Daily Mail*, March 8, 2012, p. A1, dailymail.com/News/201203070032?page=2&build=cache.
Two county officials in West Virginia pleaded guilty to engaging in an election-fraud scheme that involved stuffing ballot boxes in the 2010 primary election.

Clary, Mike, "Steven Lippman, Colleague of Convicted Ponzi Schemer Scott Rothstein, Charged With Election Fraud," *South Florida Sun-Sentinel*, April 10, 2012, articles.sun-sentinel.com/2012-04-09/news/fl-lippman-fraud-charge-20120409_1_rra-scott-rothstein-steven-lippman.
A colleague of a convicted Ponzi schemer has been charged with conspiracy to violate federal election laws by funneling money from his bosses into Sen. John McCain's failed 2008 presidential campaign.

Davenport, Jim, "Group Seeks Those Impacted By New SC Voter ID Law," The Associated Press, July 8, 2011.
Opponents of South Carolina's voter ID law say there is no proof that people were previously engaging in election fraud by not having to show a photo ID.

Grimm, Fred, "Absentee Ballots Still Source of Election Fraud," *The Miami Herald*, June 27, 2011.
Florida's new election-fraud law ignores the fraud created by absentee ballots, says an editorial columnist.

Jordan, Bob, "2 Plead Not Guilty in Campaign Scam," *Asbury Park* (N.J.) *Press*, May 31, 2011.
Two New Jersey men pleaded not guilty to six counts of election fraud after being accused of funding an unsuccessful 2006 congressional campaign with more than $30,000 in illegal contributions.

Owen, Sue, "Abbott Touts Voter Fraud Convictions That Weren't," *Austin* (Texas) *American-Statesman*, April 27, 2012, p. B1.
Texas Attorney General Greg Abbott has allegedly inflated his office's number of election-fraud convictions.

Vielmetti, Bruce, "Voter Fraud Verdict: Not Guilty," *Milwaukee Journal Sentinel*, May 26, 2011, p. B1, www.jsonline.com/news/crime/122632359.html.
A jury found a Milwaukee couple not guilty of election fraud after they were accused of voting twice in the 2008 presidential election.

Florida Law

Bousquet, Steve, "Senators Blast Voting Law," *Tampa Bay* (Fla.) *Times*, Jan. 28, 2012, p. A1, www.tampabay.com/news/politics/national/senators-question-new-florida-election-law-at-tampa-hearing/1212709.
Sens. Bill Nelson, D-Fla., and Dick Durbin, D-Ill., say Republican-backed changes to Florida's election law will suppress Democratic turnout in the upcoming presidential election.

Brandon, Robert M., "Protect Access to Polls," *Tampa* (Fla.) *Tribune*, Jan. 27, 2012, p. 13, www2.tbo.com/news/opinion/2012/jan/27/naopino2-protect-access-to-polls-ar-351854/.
Florida's new election law will suppress voter turnout on Election Day, says the president of the Fair Elections Network.

Cerabino, Frank, "Teacher Tried to Register Kids — And Broke Law," *Palm Beach* (Fla.) *Post*, Oct. 28, 2011, p. B1, www.palmbeachpost.com/news/state/cerabino-civics-teacher-tried-to-register-kids-to-1937702.html.
A Florida teacher had no idea she had become "a third-party voter registration organization" when she passed out registration applications to her high school seniors.

Cooper, Michael, and Jo Craven McGinty, "Florida's New Election Law Blunts Voter Drives," *The New York Times*, March 28, 2012, p. A1, www.nytimes.com/2012/03/28/us/restrictions-on-voter-registration-in-florida-have-groups-opting-out.html.
Prominent civic organizations in Florida have suspended voter-registration drives because of what they say are onerous restrictions in the new election law.

Lantingua, John, "Registration Groups Fight Voter Law in Court," *Palm Beach* (Fla.) *Post*, March 2, 2012, p. A1, www.palmbeachpost.com/news/state/u-s-judge-hears-registration-groups-case-against-2210864.html?printArticle=y.
The League of Women Voters and other nonprofit organizations that undertake voter-registration campaigns are challenging Florida's election law in federal court.

Moseley, Charles, "Broward County Supervisor of Elections Dr. Brenda Snipes Outlines Voting Changes During NAACP Meeting," *Westside Gazette* (Fort Lauderdale, Fla.), Nov. 3, 2011, p. 1.
The supervisor of elections in Broward County, Fla., reached out to the local NAACP chapter to educate voters on changes in the state's election law.

Powers, Scott, "Groups Register Voters — Carefully," *Orlando* (Fla.) *Sentinel*, April 26, 2012, p. A1, articles.orlandosentinel.com/2012-04-26/news/os-florida-voter-registration-20120423_1_voter-registration-league-of-women-voters-registration-drives.
Several Hispanic nonprofit groups are staging voter-registration drives throughout Florida to reach out to more Hispanic voters despite worries of possibly violating the state's new election law.

Wasserman Schultz, Debbie, "GOP's New Voting Law in Florida Now Punishes Teachers, Too," ***The Miami Herald*****, Nov. 12, 2011.**
There is no indication of foul play when Florida teachers give their students voter-registration applications, says the Democratic representative.

Minorities

Bakeman, Jessica, "Ga. Voter ID Law Used to Refute Fear of Lower Turnout," ***Clarion-Ledger*** **(Jackson, Miss.), Oct. 16, 2011, p. A4.**
Georgia's secretary of state says voter turnout increased among all groups — including blacks — when the state adopted a voter ID law in 2006.

Eversley, Melanie, "Black Voter Registration Down to 59% From 2008," ***USA Today*****, May 14, 2012, p. A3, www.usatoday.com/news/nation/story/2012-05-09/naacp-voter-registration-drives/54889184/1.**
The NAACP and other civil rights organizations are launching their registration drives earlier than in past presidential elections because of low registration levels among blacks.

Haman, Ansley, "Groups Prepare for Voter ID Law," ***Chattanooga*** **(Tenn.)** ***Times Free Press*****, Aug. 23, 2011, p. A1, timesfreepress.com/news/2011/aug/23/groups-prepare-for-voter-id-law/.**
Voter ID laws will eventually curtail voter fraud, says a Tennessee county election administrator.

Ingram, Sommer, "Democrats Fault State for Inability to Detail Impact of Voter ID Law on Hispanics," ***Dallas Morning News*****, Oct. 7, 2011, www.dallasnews.com/news/state/headlines/20111006-democrats-fault-state-for-inability-to-detail-impact-of-voter-id-law-on-minorities.ece.**
Democrats say Texas' voter ID law could keep minorities from the polls.

Pettus, Emily Wagster, "NAACP Seeking to Block ID Law," ***Huntsville*** **(Ala.)** ***Times*****, May 11, 2012.**
The Mississippi NAACP is asking federal officials to block the state's new voter ID law because they say it would violate the 1965 Voting Rights Act by diminishing the voting strength of minorities.

Richey, Warren, "In Voter ID Case, South Carolina Fights Back Against Obama Administration," ***The Christian Science Monitor*****, Feb. 8, 2012, www.csmonitor.com/USA/Justice/2012/0208/In-voter-ID-case-South-Carolina-fights-back-against-Obama-administration.**
South Carolina's attorney general has asked a three-judge panel in Washington to overturn a Justice Department decision that blocks the state's voter ID law.

Thompson, Krissah, "Minority Voter Registration Has Dropped Since '08," ***The Washington Post*****, May 5, 2012, p. A4, www.washingtonpost.com/politics/voter-registration-down-among-hispanics-blacks/2012/05/04/gIQAOqEY1T_story.html.**
The number of black and Hispanic voters has fallen sharply since 2008, posing a challenge to the Obama campaign.

Outreach

Brandon, Robert, "Universities Can Help Make Voting Easier for Students," ***Michigan Chronicle*****, Nov. 23, 2011, p. B4.**
Several universities are taking steps to make voter registration and compliance with new voter ID laws easier for students.

Finkelmeyer, Todd, "Major Efforts Afoot to Help Students Navigate Voter ID Law," ***Capital Times*** **(Madison, Wis.), Nov. 30, 2011, p. 13, host.madison.com/ct/news/local/education/campus_connection/campus-connection-major-efforts-afoot-to-help-students-navigate-voter/article_9d356770-17b5-11e1-a276-001cc4c03286.html.**
Major efforts are under way to ensure that Wisconsin students can vote under the state's new voter-ID law.

Shear, Michael D., "Obama Campaign Workers Try to Prepare for New Voter ID Laws," ***The Boston Globe*****, April 30, 2012, p. A6, articles.boston.com/2012-04-30/news/31500816_1_voter-identification-voter-registration-new-voter.**
Obama campaign workers are letting voters know about new laws that discourage precinct workers from guiding voters who show up at the wrong precinct.

Sher, Andy, "Education Pushed on Tennessee Voter ID Law," ***Chattanooga*** **(Tenn.)** ***Times Free Press*****, Nov. 1, 2011, p. A1, timesfreepress.com/news/2011/nov/01/education-pushed-on-tennessee-voter-id-law/.**
Tennessee election officials are conducting outreach programs to explain a new law that requires a photo ID to vote.

CITING *CQ RESEARCHER*

Sample formats for citing these reports in a bibliography include the ones listed below. Preferred styles and formats vary, so please check with your instructor or professor.

MLA STYLE

Jost, Kenneth. "Remembering 9/11," CQ Researcher 2 Sept. 2011: 701-732.

APA STYLE

Jost, K. (2011, September 2). Remembering 9/11. *CQ Researcher, 9*, 701-732.

CHICAGO STYLE

Jost, Kenneth. "Remembering 9/11." *CQ Researcher*, September 2, 2011, 701-732.

Researcher PLUS Archive
New!

CQ Researcher

Published by CQ Press, an Imprint of SAGE Publications, Inc.

www.cqresearcher.com

Traumatic Brain Injury

Is an effective cure possible?

About 1.7 million Americans suffer a traumatic brain injury (TBI) every year, about three-quarters of them mild TBIs, or concussions. Yet, while they affect so many people, TBIs received little medical-research funding until brain injuries from the wars in Iraq and Afghanistan — often caused by shock waves from explosions — began to mount in recent years. Nearly 20 percent of veterans deployed in those wars have returned with a TBI, often severe enough to require intense physical, psychological and emotional aid. Since 2007 Congress has poured millions of dollars into TBI research, but most patients still cannot pay for the expensive rehabilitative services that severe brain injuries require. Meanwhile, researchers have found that even a series of mild TBIs, such as those suffered by many football players, substantially raises the risk of severe dementia and depression.

Quarterback Aaron Garcia of the now-defunct New York Dragons rests after receiving a mild concussion in an Arena League game against the Philadelphia Soul on June 22, 2008. The kinds of repetitive head injuries received by athletes such as football players and boxers can lead to degenerative brain disease.

INSIDE

THIS REPORT

THE ISSUES 479
BACKGROUND 486
CHRONOLOGY 487
CURRENT SITUATION 492
AT ISSUE........................493
OUTLOOK 495
BIBLIOGRAPHY 498
THE NEXT STEP 499

CQ Researcher • June 1, 2012 • www.cqresearcher.com
Volume 22, Number 20 • Pages 477-500

CQPRESS
Los Angeles | London | New Delhi
Singapore | Washington DC

RECIPIENT OF SOCIETY OF PROFESSIONAL JOURNALISTS AWARD FOR EXCELLENCE ◆ AMERICAN BAR ASSOCIATION SILVER GAVEL AWARD

Traumatic Brain Injury

The Issues

479 • Are TBIs being diagnosed accurately?
• Are TBI patients getting adequate treatment?
• Do TBIs predispose people to violence or suicide?

Background

486 **Old Wounds**
Suspicions began long ago that brain trauma could result from mere proximity to an explosion.

489 **Costs of Recovery**
Hospital rehabilitation for Rep. Gabrielle Giffords, wounded in an assassination attempt, cost roughly $8,000 a day.

490 **New Wars**
During the 1990s, civilian medicine moved ahead of military medicine in TBI treatment.

Current Situation

492 **Maintaining Momentum**
Advocates are pressing for better access to services for people with brain injuries.

494 **Sports Injuries**
Athletic organizations are increasingly aware of the dangers of brain trauma.

Outlook

495 **Dementia Epidemic?**
Studies seek to determine if blast injuries lead to degenerative brain disease.

Sidebars and Graphics

480 **Most States Require Motorcycle Helmets**
Nineteen states and the District of Columbia mandate use for all riders.

481 **Falls Cause the Most TBIs**
Americans suffered about 1.7 million brain injuries annually between 2002 and 2006.

483 **Military Faces Growing TBI Caseload**
TBIs more than doubled during the past decade as combat increased in Iraq and Afghanistan.

484 **Most States Target Youth Sports Concussions**
All but two have enacted or are considering legislation.

487 **Chronology**
Key events since 1987.

488 **Brain Trauma Often Unfolds in Stages**
Some seemingly mild injuries worsen quickly.

490 **Researchers Explore Frontiers of Brain Injury**
"The more I learn, the more questions I have."

493 **At Issue**
Should states require all motorcycle riders to wear helmets?

For Further Research

497 **For More Information**
Organizations to contact.

498 **Bibliography**
Selected sources used.

499 **The Next Step**
Additional articles.

499 **Citing *CQ Researcher***
Sample bibliography formats.

Cover: Getty Images/New York Dragons/Mike Stobe

CQ Researcher

June 1, 2012
Volume 22, Number 20

Managing Editor: Thomas J. Billitteri
tjb@cqpress.com

Assistant Managing Editor: Kathy Koch
kkoch@cqpress.com

Contributing Editor: Thomas J. Colin
tcolin@cqpress.com

Associate Editor: Kenneth Jost

Staff Writer: Marcia Clemmitt

Contributing Writers: Peter Katel, Barbara Mantel, Jennifer Weeks

Design/Production Editor: Olu B. Davis

Assistant Editor: Darrell Dela Rosa

Fact Checker: Michelle Harris

Los Angeles | London | New Delhi
Singapore | Washington DC

An Imprint of SAGE Publications, Inc.

Vice President and Editorial Director, Higher Education Group:
Michele Sordi

Director, Online Publishing:
Todd Baldwin

CQ Researcher (ISSN 1056-2036) is printed on acid-free paper. Published weekly, except: (March wk. 5) (May wk. 4) (July wk. 1) (Aug. wks. 3, 4) (Nov. wk. 4) and (Dec. wks. 3, 4). Published by SAGE Publications, Inc., 2455 Teller Rd., Thousand Oaks, CA 91320. Annual full-service subscriptions start at $1,054. For pricing, call 1-800-834-9020. To purchase a *CQ Researcher* report in print or electronic format (PDF), visit www.cqpress.com or call 866-427-7737. Single reports start at $15. Bulk purchase discounts and electronic-rights licensing are also available. Periodicals postage paid at Thousand Oaks, California, and at additional mailing offices. POSTMASTER: Send address changes to *CQ Researcher*, 2300 N St., N.W., Suite 800, Washington, DC 20037.

Traumatic Brain Injury

BY MARCIA CLEMMITT

THE ISSUES

Nick Toon was 4 when his father — New York Jets wide receiver Al Toon — was forced to leave football after suffering as many as nine concussions during his eight-year pro career. The blows led to years of problems for the star player: impaired movement, oversensitivity to light, inability to concentrate, emotional difficulties and other symptoms.

"I remember vividly, right after he retired and he got his last concussion, [lying] on the bed with him and hanging out and we couldn't turn the lights on or anything," Nick Toon said recently. Nevertheless, the injuries didn't discourage him from following in his father's footsteps. Now 23, he is preparing to play this fall as a newly drafted wide receiver for the New Orleans Saints. Looking back, he said, "I think my mom and dad did a good job of handling the situation because it didn't scar me." [1]

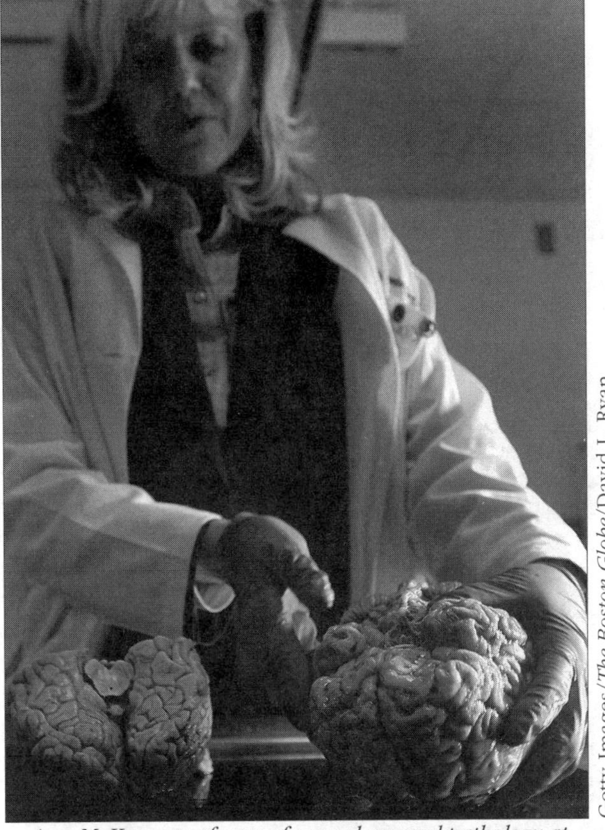

Getty Images/*The Boston Globe*/David L. Ryan

Ann McKee, a professor of neurology and pathology at Boston University, examined the brains of two recent military veterans and found the same brain patterns as in athletes with chronic traumatic encephalopathy (CTE), a degenerative brain disease apparently caused by repeated traumatic brain injury (TBI). About 1.7 million American civilians suffer TBIs annually, mainly mild concussions. In addition, more than 300,000 military personnel have returned from Iraq and Afghanistan with TBIs, typically caused by improvised explosive devices (IEDs).

Concussions and a wide range of other traumatic brain injuries (TBIs) — from blows received in falls and car accidents to devastating battlefield wounds — have incapacitated millions of Americans, leading scientists and medical professionals to push for a deeper understanding of the brain, its proneness to damage and its capacity for healing. Multiple studies have found that suffering one severe TBI, several mild ones or, for some people, even a single mild or moderate TBI raises the risk of permanent brain damage — and problems ranging from memory loss to heightened emotional responses that can make it difficult to cope with life's ups and downs. At the same time, with today's improved emergency care, more and more people are surviving serious TBIs.

About 1.7 million American civilians suffer a TBI annually, with three-quarters or more of the injuries of the mild variety known as a concussion. Children up to about age 4 and the elderly, both susceptible to falls, and people in their late teens and early 20s, most prone to injuries in car crashes or sports, are most likely to suffer TBIs. [2] In addition, about 20 percent of service members — more than 300,000 military personnel — have returned from Iraq and Afghanistan with TBIs. (*See graph, p. 483.*) In fact, with the widespread use of improvised explosive devices, or IEDs, whose blasts can cause TBIs even if no shrapnel hits the person, TBIs are now considered the signature injury of the current wars. Improved battlefield medicine enables more service members to survive severe TBIs. [3]

Meanwhile, at least 1,300 former pro players are suing the National Football League, charging that it ignored evidence for years that repeated mild or moderate TBIs can create long-term brain damage, including memory loss and depression. [4] The players want the NFL to provide close medical monitoring of all head injuries and lifetime health coverage for brain conditions. Even in the most recent NFL collective-bargaining agreements, signed last year, "physical injury benefits were covered but . . . not . . . cognitive monitoring, prevention and treatment," said Craig Mitnick, a New Jersey-based plaintiff's lawyer. [5]

TBIs include any injury in which an object penetrates the brain, the head sustains a hard hit or the head and body suffer quick acceleration and/or deceleration — as in a car crash — so that the gelatin-like brain moves and stops rapidly inside the skull, often causing bleeding and swelling. TBIs also can result from the shock waves of a big explosion. Military personnel, especially, have long suffered so-called "blast injuries" — strong force waves from nearby explosions, such as bombs or cannon shots, that surge through the body and

Most States Require Motorcycle Helmets

Nineteen states and the District of Columbia mandate helmet use for all motorcyclists regardless of age. Twenty-eight states require helmets for youths. Three states — Illinois, Iowa and New Hampshire — have no helmet law.

Motorcycle Helmet Laws, May 2012

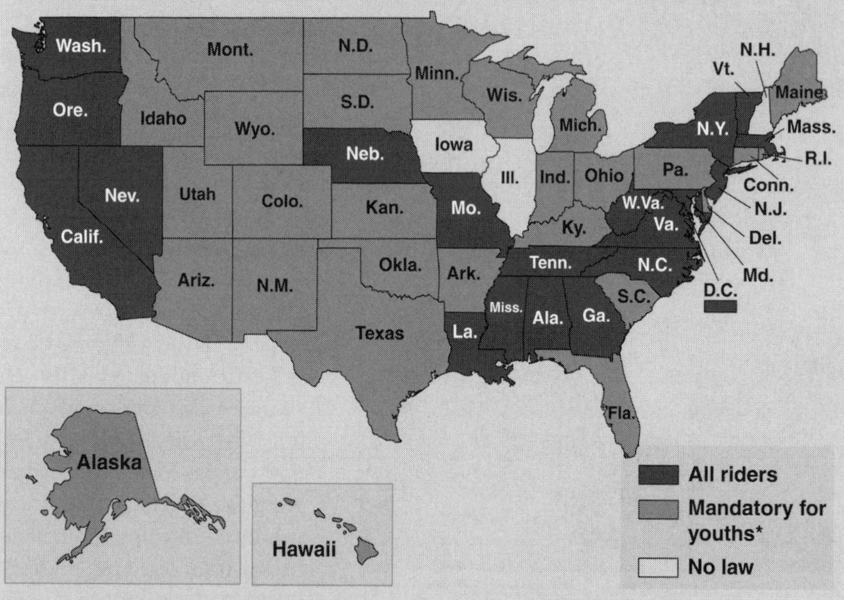

** Laws vary by age. Eight states require helmet use for riders 20 and younger. Nineteen require use for those 17 and younger. Delaware requires use for riders 18 and younger.*

Source: "Motorcycle and Bicycle Helmet Use Laws," Insurance Institute for Highway Safety, May 2012, www.iihs.org/laws/HelmetUseCurrent.aspx

damage the brain and other organs, even when no shot or shrapnel touches the person. [6] (*See sidebar, p. 490.*)

While every injury is different, just as every brain is different, "if you follow TBI long enough you see recurring patterns of neurobehavioral consequences," says Thomas McAllister, a professor of psychiatry and neurology at Dartmouth Medical School, in New Hampshire.

"People will tell you, 'My mind just doesn't work as well as it used to' " and point to problems such as trouble concentrating, McAllister says. And because TBIs generally affect the whole brain, not just part of it, personality and mood changes are common. "A spouse will say, 'This is not the person I knew before' " and point to changes such as heightened emotionalism, McAllister says. "Things that once made them sad now make them quite tearful," and once-minor irritations lead to rage.

Certain areas of the brain are at particular risk for TBI damage. Those regions — mainly but not entirely in the front of the brain — are linked to humans' "higher functions," such as the regulation of mood and behavior and the management of cognitive functions such as reasoning and memory, McAllister says.

Meanwhile, among elite athletes in contact sports such as boxing and football, where multiple TBIs are common, scientists now find strong links between TBIs and Alzheimer's disease as well as a unique form of dementia called chronic traumatic encephalopathy (CTE). [7]

CTE is "a rare, midlife dementia you get in your 40s, and it's fatal," says Elaine Peskind, a professor of psychiatry and behavioral sciences and associate director of the Alzheimer's Disease Research Center at the University of Washington, in Seattle, who is studying whether blast injuries may raise the risk of CTE.

In a May 16 paper, an international team including researchers from Boston University and the Department of Veterans Affairs announced that the autopsied brains of four veterans of the current Mideast conflicts showed the same signs of neurodegeneration as those found in some contact-sport athletes. Furthermore, in studies on mice, the scientists reported that a single blast trauma was found to be sufficient to lead to dementia-related degeneration in the brain. [8]

As knowledge increases about TBI, the search for ways to help patients intensifies. There is no pharmaceutical or surgical fix. Instead, patients need intensive help relearning lost or damaged physical, mental, behavioral and emotional capabilities.

"We know that rehab works, as does cognitive therapy" — assistance in relearning lost mental skills and developing workarounds for mental capacities that don't function as well as they used to — says David Hovda, director of the Brain Injury Research Center at the University of California, Los Angeles. Scientists now know that "behavior will change the brain," and although it's not clear how that process works, it is clear that rehab and therapy in some way constitute a literal rebuilding of damaged brains, he says.

But rehab and therapy are difficult and expensive. Rehab in the hospital following a severe TBI can cost as much as $8,000 a day, and post-hospitalization rehab from $600 to $2,500 a day. [9]

Partly as a result of the high costs, access to care is the biggest problem TBI patients face, says Susan Connors, president and CEO of the Brain Injury Association of America (BIAA), an advocacy group in Vienna, Va.

"It's easier and cheaper to get somebody a wheelchair than to get them to walk again" through rehab, "but it's not better for the patient," says Connors. "And we also need people to understand that rehabbing a brain is not the same as rehabbing a hip — that's it's very complex."

As policymakers, athletes and military personnel grapple with emerging research about TBIs, here are some of the questions being asked:

Are TBIs being diagnosed accurately?

Medical advances over the past few decades have improved diagnosis of TBI. Nevertheless, many factors make diagnosis tricky.

Around 1975, hospitals began installing a new kind of machine for a diagnostic procedure called X-ray computerized tomography — the now familiar CT scan. A computer hooked to an X-ray machine gathers data from multiple scans of a patient's head, then assembles a three-dimensional image that can distinguish between brain tissue and blood in the brain by the different ways in which the two materials block the X-ray beams. [10] CT scanners in emergency rooms can reveal deadly brain bleeding in some patients before irreversible damage occurs, for example.

Some organizations have instituted programs to improve diagnosis for high-risk groups, such as athletes and service members.

The National College Athletic Association (NCAA) now bases sideline scrutiny of potential TBIs on widely accepted medical standards. Coaches are advised not to rely on their own judgment of whether a player is concussed but to get a clinician's evaluation. [11]

Falls Cause the Most TBIs

Americans suffered about 1.7 million traumatic brain injuries (TBIs) annually from 2002 through 2006. Falls caused more than a third of the injuries, and traffic accidents 17 percent.

External Causes of Traumatic Brain Injury, 2002-2006

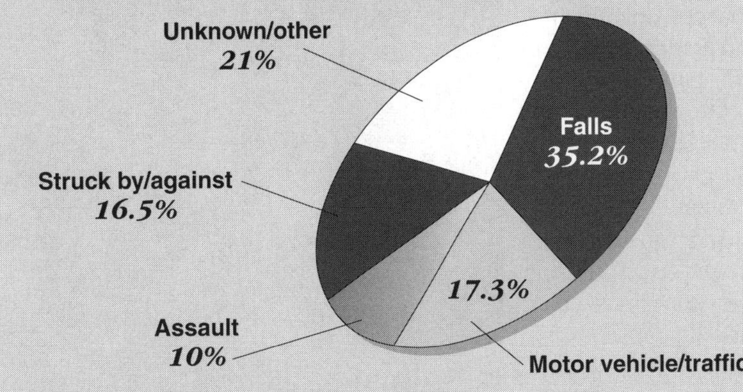

Source: "Traumatic Brain Injury in the United States," Centers for Disease Control and Prevention, March 2010, pp. 17-18, www.cdc.gov/traumaticbraininjury/pdf/blue_book.pdf

The military is going further. In 2008 the Pentagon mandated "baseline predeployment neurocognitive testing" for all service members, to give medics an assessment of each person's normal, noninjured brain and facilitate later TBI diagnosis. Brains are ultra-complex and highly individual, so it helps to know how an individual's normal brain functions before declaring that a bomb blast, for example, has indeed created abnormalities that point to a TBI.

Using in-depth interviews along with CT scans, clinicians can accurately diagnose TBIs and differentiate them from other conditions, such as post-traumatic stress disorder (PTSD), an anxiety disorder that can also result from a bad accident or other trauma, says Robert Sbordone, a neuropsychologist in Laguna Hills, Calif., and long-time scholar in the field. For one thing, an accident victim with PTSD but no TBI will remember the accident clearly, but a TBI sufferer won't, he says. "I ask, 'What happened when you first got into the car? What was the weather?' " — questions that can establish whether there's a period for which the patient has no memories.

Diagnosing mild TBIs in service members can be difficult because the military's tendency to maintain a stiff upper lip in the face of physical challenges makes many reluctant to discuss symptoms, says Rodney Vanderploeg, supervisory psychologist for neuropsychology and polytrauma at the James A. Haley Veterans' Hospital, in Tampa. To correctly diagnose and heal, both patients and clinicians "need patience and to be open, honest and forthright," he says. "That takes trust and time," elements that the VA has tried to build into its TBI care system, he says.

Despite progress, diagnosis of milder TBIs remains spotty, however.

"There's no question that we're not capturing all the injuries," says Alisa Gean, a professor of radiology, neurology and neurosurgery at the University of California, San Francisco.

In one study, for example, trauma centers missed mild TBIs in "over half" of patients, says Ronald Ruff, a clinical neuropsychologist and rehabilitation psychologist in San Francisco. Many TBI patients come to the hospital with multiple injuries, and if a patient answers "I'm fine" to doctors' cursory questioning about concussion, physicians may dismiss the TBI possibility and get busy treating injuries that seem more pressing, such as a spinal-cord injury, Ruff says.

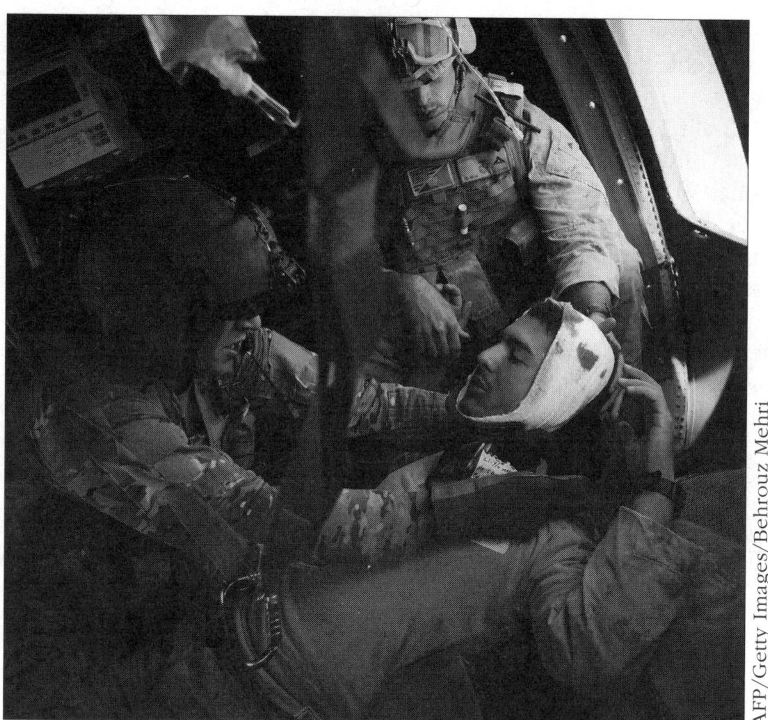

AFP/Getty Images/Behrouz Mehri

A Marine who suffered a concussion and other injuries after his vehicle struck an improvised explosive device (IED) in Afghanistan's Helmand Province is airlifted for treatment on Nov. 4, 2011. The shock waves from IEDs can cause TBIs even if no shrapnel hits the person. Improved battlefield medicine enables more service members to survive severe TBIs, which are now considered the signature injury of the wars in Afghanistan and Iraq.

TBI symptoms can be slow-developing and thus easily missed in trauma care, says Sbordone. Some emergency rooms lack CT scanners, and sometimes "a scan comes back normal" in the early going, if bleeding in the brain is slow, he says.

An accurate diagnosis can hinge on a patient interview, but "we know that patients can look and feel normal and say they're back to their baselines when they're not," says Gean.

There's no "simple lab test" that provides a sure diagnosis or distinguishes TBI from PTSD, for example, says David Cifu, national program director for physical medicine and rehabilitation (PMR) services at the VA and a professor of PMR at Virginia Commonwealth University, in Richmond. For this reason, the VA uses a team of clinicians from different specialties, including neurology and psychology, he says.

Clinical tools currently available don't give a clear picture of TBIs' many possible nuances, and few emergency-room personnel are TBI specialists.

One standard tool, the Glasgow Coma Scale, classifies TBIs as mild, moderate or severe based on emergency personnel's assessments of patients' behaviors, such as whether and how often they blink, for example, says Connors at the Brain Injury Association of America. "But that initial score doesn't take into account the cascade of secondary injuries" that occur in the hours and days after a TBI and doesn't even distinguish between wounds in which an object penetrates the brain and so-called "closed-head" injuries, she says.

"I've seen some people with [bad] Glasgow Coma Scale [ratings] do very well and people [who rate as only 'mildly' injured on the] scale do very badly," says Brent Masel, president of Transitional Learning Center, a rehabilitation center in Galveston, Texas, and national medical director for the BIAA. "As of yet, we have no good way of surely categorizing" TBIs, so "all we can do is be vigilant" about how patients' conditions develop.

"With TBI, the trauma can be of different magnitudes and can come from the front, from the back or side of the head. So there's not really a predictable pattern" that imaging machines, such as CT scans and MRI machines, can pick up, as there is with most other brain ills, such as multiple sclerosis or stroke, says Michael Weiner, a professor of medicine, radiology and psychiatry at the University of California, San Francisco, and director of the VA's Center for Imaging of Neurodegenerative Diseases.

Furthermore, scientists now know that psychological problems such as PTSD can change the brain in much the same way that TBIs can. As a result, "it is often unclear if a service member," for example, "is suffering primarily from biological damage . . . or a psychological injury," says the advocacy group Iraq and Afghanistan Veterans of America (IAVA). [12]

Are TBI patients getting adequate treatment?

The past three decades have seen many new treatment strategies that keep TBIs from killing patients in the first hours. Furthermore, the brain is resilient, and most people with mild TBIs recover on their own. But medicine still doesn't have adequate answers for some patients with long-lasting symptoms, and many patients have trouble getting access to rehab care.

Several decades ago, half of those who suffered severe TBIs died at the accident scene, but today the number has dropped to fewer than one-fifth, thanks to better emergency care, says Connors, of the BIAA.

Intensive-care practices developed in the last quarter-century have greatly reduced the incidence of death or vegetative states from TBI, says UCLA's Hovda. Those practices include careful monitoring of blood flow to the brain, as well as such aggressive procedures as removing part of the skull to give space to a swelling brain. "These things improve people's outcomes by not allowing the situation to worsen," Hovda says.

"There's been extraordinary advancement in physical rehabilitation" for TBIs that affect patients' ability to move, says Connors. Two patients who suffered TBIs of that sort, one 20 years ago and one today, likely have very different outcomes, with the earlier-injured patient "stuck in a wheelchair" and today's patient mobile and back on a job, she says.

Many new treatments are available for symptoms such as pain that TBIs share with other ills. The treatments, including helping patients sleep, improve recovery chances by giving the brain a better chance to heal, says Jeffrey Barth, director of the Brain Injury and Sports Concussion Institute at the University of Virginia Health System, in Charlottesville.

With mild TBIs — concussions — "the average person will get well on his own," says Cifu, of the VA.

So resilient is the brain that recovery goes on for years, contrary to previously accepted medical wisdom that, after two years at most, recovery ceased, says California neuropsychologist Sbordone. "Years ago, when I was a professor . . . I used to tell people this, but then I went into private practice and heard people say things like, 'You ought to see my son. It's been six years now, and he keeps getting better.' I'm not saying they recover completely, but most continue to improve for decades . . . in all areas, including how they interact with others, how they solve problems."

"It's hard to get well from this, just like it's hard to lose weight," but "there are well-established ways" of treating the condition, "and the people who work at it succeed," says Cifu.

Nevertheless, TBIs remain daunting to both understand and treat.

"People who have had a concussion will describe sensitivity to light, headache, lethargy, emotional problems," says Hovda. "Over the course of days to weeks, if they are allowed to rest — not bed rest but no extraordinary mental activity — then these symptoms usually clear" for about 80 percent of patients, he says. "For the other 20 percent — the under-appreciated minority — they don't clear, they can last for months. And there's no scientific understanding of why."

"An enormous number of people get better and plateau, but I've watched people deteriorate," developing additional serious illnesses such as dementia and Parkinson's disease, says Masel at the Transitional Learning Center.

"People with brain injuries are at very great risk" for developing psychiatric conditions such as depression and anxiety disorders, says Dartmouth's McAllister. "And it's pretty clear that if a brain-injured person gets a psychiatric illness, the symptom pattern is magnified."

"A good portion [of TBI patients] do well" with treatment, but that doesn't mean that many patients' concept of a normal life won't have to change, post-injury, says Ruff, the San Francisco neuropsychologist. He describes a psychologist at a top university hospital who couldn't return to the job after suffering a TBI because the caseload was too much for a damaged brain. "I can't process things as fast as I used to" is a common complaint, Ruff says.

"Instead of trying to make somebody 'normal,' " by their pre-injury standards, it's important to recognize that "the brain has changed. You will never be the same person," says Hovda. "Instead of trying to force them to play

Military Faces Growing TBI Caseload

Nearly 28,000 military personnel were diagnosed with a traumatic brain injury (TBI) in 2009, about two-and-a-half times more than in 2000. The rise in cases coincides with the level of U.S. military engagement in Iraq and Afghanistan and rising use of IEDs (improvised explosive devices).

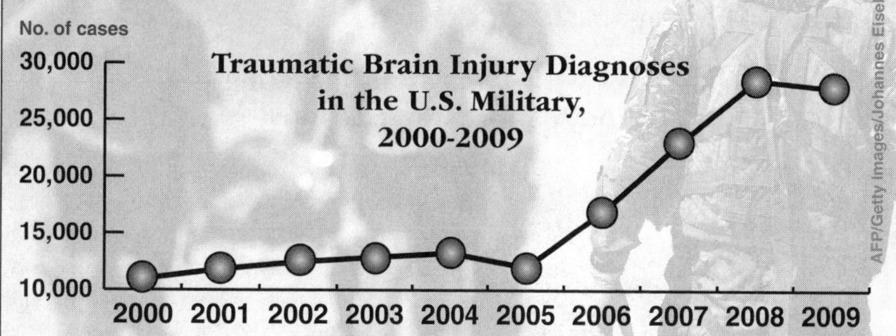

Source: Hannah Fischer, "U.S. Military Casualty Statistics: Operation New Dawn, Operation Iraqi Freedom, and Operation Enduring Freedom," Congressional Research Service, September 2010, p. 3, www.fas.org/sgp/crs/natsec/RS22452.pdf

Most States Target Youth Sports Concussions

Almost all the states and the District of Columbia have or are considering laws addressing concussions in youth sports, such as requiring schools to distribute information on concussions to families and coaches or pull athletes from the field when a concussion is suspected. Only two states — Arkansas and Montana — have no laws on the books or under discussion.

States With Legislation Targeting Youth Sports Concussions

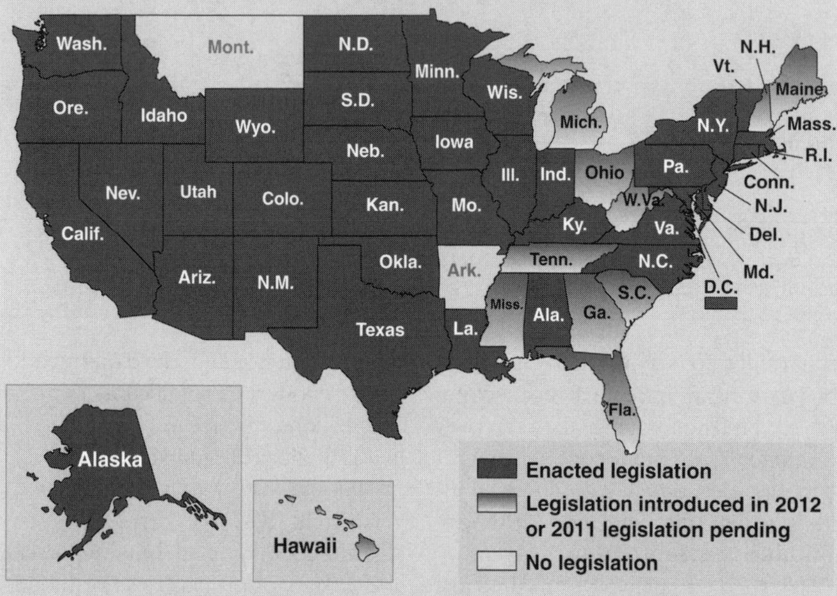

Source: "Traumatic Brain Injury Legislation," National Conference of State Legislatures, April 2012, www.ncsl.org/issues-research/health/traumatic-brain-injury-legislation.aspx

with the same cards, let's see what the new cards are" and figure out how to optimize the patient's potential, given the new way the person's brain operates, he says.

People with a severe TBI are "lucky" if they work, but they typically need such help as counseling to "harden" themselves against some things that non-brain-injured people take for granted, says the BIAA's Connors. Something as simple as "adjusting to the fluorescent lights" in an office or factory may be a tough challenge, she says.

In the first hours after a TBI, doctors know that cells in some areas of the delicate brain "are damaged and are going to die, and you'd like to get in there and stop them," says Hovda. But there have been between 150 and 200 clinical trials on such early-stage interventions, "and they just haven't worked out."

A key reason is likely that so many biochemical and physical changes occur in a brain just after injury that "trying to intervene at any one point" with, for example, medication, "is like putting up an umbrella in Hurricane Katrina," McAllister says.

While the vagaries of immediate treatment continue to confound medical specialists, access to care in the days, weeks and months following a TBI remains what Connors calls "the biggest problem in brain injury."

Data show that "the severity of your injury determines how long you stay in the hospital," but insurance and economic status determine what level of care, if any, is provided after hospital discharge, she says. That's a problem because reaching one's full recovery potential is a long-term project, usually requiring numerous kinds of rehabilitation.

"In this country, if you have a brain injury, you go into rehab as soon as you come out of the coma, and they bombard you with all of these things" to learn and do, says Sbordone. "Then the money runs out, and they stop completely," he says.

"I went to Russia in 1980, and they did the exact opposite" — giving patients plenty of rest in the early going, then providing long-term therapy, he says. Patients desperately need the therapy but "aren't ready right at first" for the intensive brain work that rehabilitation entails, Sbordone says. "If you had a heart attack or broke your leg, what would you think if the next day your doctor said, 'Run 10 miles'?"

Do TBIs predispose people to violence or suicide?

In March, after U.S. Army Staff Sergeant Robert Bales allegedly murdered 17 Afghan civilians and wounded six others, some commentators posited that a TBI Bales reportedly suffered in an unspecified accident during earlier duty in Iraq — along with PTSD — may have predisposed him to violence. [13]

Details about Bales' background "suggest that brain damage . . . might have been a contributing factor" to the event, said a report on the website of *Wired* magazine. "No one factor could possibly lead to the kind of rampage seen in Afghanistan," it said. But, the report added: "Myriad studies have concluded that a connection between TBI and violence does seem to exist." [14]

On the cover of its March 13 issue, the *New York Daily News* dubbed Bales

"Sergeant Psycho" and noted in a subhead: "Killer G.I. had suffered traumatic brain injury." [15]

Some veterans reacted with outrage at the implied connection, however.

After a guest on physician Drew Pinsky's HLN-network cable-TV talk show suggested that "a combination of traumatic brain injury and PTSD" might have influenced Bales, Paul Rieckhoff, founder of Iraq and Afghanistan Veterans of America, responded that the "ignorant, irresponsible comment reveals the scary underbelly of raising awareness of invisible wounds" of battle such as TBI: a high risk of pinning an undeserved negative stereotype on vets. [16]

More than a million U.S. vets have served in Iraq and Afghanistan, and many suffer from brain injuries and stress conditions, yet "so far only one person . . . went out and killed [17] civilians," proving that the stereotype is wholly undeserved, argued Iraq War veteran Jason Fritz on the national-security blog Ink Spots. [17]

Yet, experts say a TBI can substantially change some patients' intellect, personality and even character. "Cancer may take your life. But a brain injury takes your soul," says Masel, the Galveston rehab center president.

In the past, when clinicians submitted papers on TBI to medical journals, reviewers would press them to specify exactly where in the brain the injury occurred, Masel says. With TBI, "the answer was that it was everywhere." Other nervous-system injuries, including strokes, are more localized, dimming some capacities but generally leaving more of the person unscathed. The late actor Christopher Reeve, for example, who suffered a severe spinal-cord injury in 1995 when he was thrown from a horse, "could direct movies," Masel says. "Cognitively he was intact."

Studies have linked TBIs to a wide range of emotional, psychological and serious coping difficulties for some people. In a study of 3,000 persistently homeless people, for example, "at least half" reported "histories of blows to the head sustained in the context of severe childhood physical abuse" or accidents, wrote Jennifer Highley, a nurse practitioner in New York specializing in psychiatric and mental health. [18]

Getty Images/Chip Somodevilla

Katherine Brearley, the mother of the late University of Pennsylvania football player Owen Thomas, told a congressional committee on Sept. 23, 2010, that repeated blows to his head over the many years he played football may have caused traumatic brain injury (TBI) and contributed to his depression and suicide. An autopsy found early signs of TBI-induced dementia in Thomas's brain.

A large Swedish study found that TBIs were linked to a significantly higher risk of committing violent crime, although only among two groups of TBI patients: those who also abused alcohol or drugs or who had family members who'd committed violence. While the findings show that violence is not a risk with most TBI patients, the study demonstrates that "certain groups of patients . . . would benefit from violence risk assessment" and do have an increased risk of violence from TBI, researchers concluded. [19]

The brain's frontal lobes, key to regulating thoughts and behavior and controlling runaway emotions, are among the areas most likely to suffer damage from a TBI, says Sbordone, the Laguna Hills neuropsychologist. "If the mechanic looks at your car and says, 'The engine's fine, but your brakes are out,' you have a problem."

"I've got a case with a severe brain injury from 1983, and the poor guy has no control. He'll masturbate in public," Sbordone says. "How many times have you felt like telling somebody off, but you don't?" But, he adds, if the brain system that regulates behavior is damaged, "then you will."

Emotional problems often accompany a TBI because "emotions aren't in the heart, as people used to think, but in the brain," says Ruff, the clinical neuropsychologist in San Francisco.

TBI symptoms can include physical, cognitive or emotional disruptions, and unlucky "synergies" among the three can intensify problems, Ruff says. "If a TBI leads to a lot of headaches, you may not schedule a date" for fear you'll be sick and unable to keep it. "Then you'll get frustrated, and you'll wake up at night and have trouble sleeping," which may lead both to more headaches and to errors in judgment by a brain that's both damaged and, now, overtired, and so on.

Some TBI patients find their previously excellent coping abilities deeply challenged, says the University of California's Gean. She describes a young

Iraq veteran who suffered an apparently mild blast TBI, with only a brief loss of consciousness. "He didn't have any wounds that you can see," she says. "But he was motivated and very sharp before the injury, and now he is struggling unbelievably, just keeping it together." ■

BACKGROUND

Old Wounds

Death from penetrating brain wounds — and efforts to prevent it — has been a feature of battle since ancient days. Around 400 BC the Greek physician Hippocrates, often called the father of Western medicine, declared that "no head injury is too severe to despair of or too trivial to ignore." [20]

And in a controversy that continued well into the modern era, suspicions began long ago that grave brain injury and other organ damage might result from simply being near an explosion, such as a cannon shot, without ever being touched by a projectile. Whether such mysterious "blast injuries" existed was debated for centuries.

Sir Thomas Longmore, a 19th-century British military surgeon, described the controversy over whether the mere "breath of the cannonball" could cause injury. "Many eminent surgeons" once believed that it was so, he wrote. But by the late 19th century majority opinion had shifted to what Longmore considered the modern, solidly scientific view: that internal injuries had to be caused not by an invisible blast force but by a projectile that actually grazed a soldier's skin without visibly scraping or bruising it. [21]

Subsequent wars have demonstrated that Longmore's "modern" opinion was wrong, however, while earlier physicians who believed in a powerful but unseen blast wave — or "breath of the cannonball" — were correct. Serious blast injuries, to the brain and other organs, can indeed be caused by an invisible force that radiates from an explosion, without any contact or near-contact with shrapnel or any other solid object. (*See sidebar, p. 490.*)

Whether even a mild TBI can produce continuing symptoms also has been long debated, says Dartmouth's McAllister. "Back 100 years you'll find that discussion," which shifted from a focus on war wounds to debate over civilian injury during the Industrial Revolution of the early-to-mid 19th century.

With train travel came the first civilian accidents at high enough speed for "acceleration-deceleration forces" on the head to slosh the delicate brain about in the skull, wrote Andrew Robertson, an Australian psychiatrist. Physicians were soon called upon to distinguish in the courts between passengers and railway workers who had "genuine complaints and those who feigned disease" and sought compensation after an accident, he wrote. By the early 1860s, the railroads were paying out "very large sums" in such cases, he wrote. [22]

The question of whether blast TBIs were "real" injuries — and thus compensable — took center stage in the wars of the 20th century.

During World War I, many British troops suffered blast injuries, "particularly before the introduction of the steel helmet at the beginning of 1916," wrote Edgar Jones, a professor of the history of medicine and psychiatry at King's College in London. "Increasing numbers of soldiers who had been close to a detonation without receiving a [visible] head wound" complained of "puzzling symptoms," including "amnesia, poor concentration, headache, . . . [and] dizziness" that often didn't respond to treatment. The term shell shock arose to describe such cases. However, controversy soon raged as similar symptoms began turning up in other soldiers who "had been nowhere near an explosion." [23]

By 1917, 10 percent of British war casualties reported shell-shock-like symptoms, encompassing soldiers who had been near strong blasts and others who had not. By war's end, in November 1918, the British government had awarded some 32,000 disability pensions for these conditions. [24]

During World War II (1939-1945), confusion reigned about whether shell shock apparently suffered by soldiers near blast explosions was a real injury. Questions also arose over whether similar symptoms reported by soldiers who had not been near a blast also denoted a real condition, but different from blast injuries.

The only thing clear was that paying disability pensions to soldiers claiming these two conditions — both hard to verify by medical means at the time — was extremely expensive. As a result, in an attempt "to avoid another epidemic of shell shock," British authorities banned the use of the term by the military. Squelching the words did not make the problem go away, however. "Despite this precaution, soldiers exposed to blast injury continued" to report symptoms, even though their condition — shell shock — had effectively been ruled out of existence by the British government, wrote Jones. [25]

Most of the progress in diagnosing and treating TBIs has come in the past half-century.

By the 1960s, autopsies on accident victims had "revealed that many deaths after head injury, and by implication disabilities in survivors, were avoidable because they resulted from potentially preventable secondary brain damage" — changes in the brain that occur in the hours and days following the initial TBI incident, wrote Bryan Jennett, a neurosurgeon in Glasgow, Scotland. In 1970, Jennett convened an international group of physi-

Continued on p. 488

Chronology

1980s-1990s

More people survive severe traumatic brain injuries (TBIs) because of improvements in trauma care.

1987
Young people with TBI-related disabilities become eligible for state special-education services under the Individuals with Disabilities Education Act.

1990
Dubbing the 1990s the Decade of the Brain, President George H. W. Bush pledges more federal research funding for TBIs and other conditions.

1991
Public awareness of brain injuries grows when Harrison Ford stars in "Regarding Henry," a film about a lawyer whose life is turned upside down after a gunshot wound to the head.

1992
Sen. Edward M. Kennedy, D-Mass., introduces Traumatic Brain Injury Act, to boost research and access to care; the bill gets a committee hearing but is not enacted. . . . Congress establishes a TBI research and care program for active-duty service members and veterans.

1996
Traumatic Brain Injury Act enacted; authorizes federal funds for research, prevention, data collection on the number of injuries and grants to states to provide services.

2000s-Present

TBIs become the signature injury of the Iraq and Afghanistan wars. Concerns grow about long-term brain damage from mild TBIs.

2001
Reps. James C. Greenwood, R-Pa., and William Pascrell, D-N.J., establish the Congressional Brain Injury Task Force to increase lawmakers' awareness of TBI.

2002
About 12,500 U.S. service members suffer TBIs.

2003
A public-private Blue Ribbon Panel on Amusement Park Rides, formed in response to congressional requests, finds that reckless riders, not the rides, bear most blame for TBIs suffered on roller coasters.

2006
Reporting from Iraq, ABC News correspondent Bob Woodruff suffers a severe TBI from an improvised explosive device (IED). His injury helps to focus congressional attention on war-related TBIs.

2007
Nearly 20 percent of Iraq and Afghanistan veterans have suffered TBIs. . . . Congress increases funds for civilian and military TBI research.

2008
Defense Department begins requiring predeployment cognitive testing for service members, using a computer-based assessment later criticized as inaccurate. . . . IEDs grow more common in Iraq and Afghanistan; more than 28,500 service members suffer TBIs.

2009
A Pentagon team finds that most military clinicians at the front lines aren't aware of TBI-diagnosis guidelines distributed in 2006. . . . Actress Natasha Richardson suffers a head injury in a ski accident; initially refusing medical treatment, she dies two days later after the TBI worsens.

2010
Autopsy finds early signs of TBI-induced dementia in the brain of football lineman Owen Thomas, a University of Pennsylvania junior who committed suicide.

2011
Rep. Gabrielle Giffords, D-Ariz., survives a devastating TBI from an assassination attempt. . . . New research on veterans and retired football players increases the certainty that TBIs raise dementia risk. . . . Institute of Medicine says TBI patients should continue to receive cognitive rehabilitation therapy (CRT) despite the lack of clear statistical data on its value.

2012
Controversy flares when some commentators suggest Army Staff Sergeant Robert Bales' alleged massacre of Afghan civilians may relate to a TBI he suffered. . . . College and professional athletic leagues join the National Sport Concussion Outcomes Study, which will trace TBIs and brain changes in more than 1,000 athletes. . . . TRICARE, the health plan for active and retired service members, will cover CRT in some cases. . . . More than 1,300 former National Football League players have joined lawsuits charging that the NFL ignored evidence of long-term health risks from TBIs. . . . TBI-related brain damage is suspected as a factor in the suicide of retired NFL middle linebacker Junior Seau. . . . Researchers find more evidence of dementia-related degeneration in the autopsied brains of young veterans.

Brain Trauma Often Unfolds in Stages

Injuries that seem mild can lead to death.

The roughly three-pound mass inside the human skull has the consistency of not-quite-set Jello, and it's just as fragile.

The brain is highly vulnerable to shakes, shock waves from nearby blasts and other trauma, and while some injuries can seem mild at first, the brain's intricate chemical and biological makeup can still go haywire over time, leading to long-term or permanent impairment — or death.

"The brain is exquisitely sensitive to rapid movement," and that's partly why this most complex of all organs is so vulnerable to damage, says David Cifu, national program director for physical medicine and rehabilitation (PMR) services for the Department of Veterans Affairs (VA) and a professor of PMR at Virginia Commonwealth University. Because of this sensitivity, traumatic brain injury (TBI) occurs not just when the head hits a hard object but in numerous other scenarios, such as when whiplash snaps the head back and forth in an auto accident, or an invisible blast wave from a nearby explosion sweeps through a soldier's body.

While much of the brain is gelatinous, some parts are more dense than others. The differences in density increase the brain's sensitivity to injury because trauma causes certain areas to move, start and stop at different rates, stressing and straining the organ.

The brain's "gray matter" — consisting of what are sometimes called brain cells, or neurons — is somewhat less dense than the "white matter," which is composed of fat-coated cells that carry out functions vital to the brain's operation. These cells include axons, or nerve fibers, that carry signals through the brain.

"Some areas of the brain are more elastic and flexible whereas other regions are stiffer and less compliant to stretching," wrote David Hovda, director, and Richard Sutton, an adjunct associate professor, at the Brain Injury Research Center at the University of California, Los Angeles. As a result, "the signature of anatomical damage in TBI reflects this complicated interaction" between the exact trauma a brain suffers and the organ's physical characteristics, they wrote. [1]

But the complications go far deeper. The initial trauma-induced sloshing and tearing is only the "primary injury," says Thomas McAllister, a professor of psychiatry and neurology at Dartmouth Medical School, in New Hampshire. The brain functions partly by sending neurotransmitters — different chemicals that act as signaling devices — among its cells, and "in the hours, days and weeks" that follow a TBI "a complicated cascade of neurochemical events is set off that amplify" the initial trauma by changing the brain's chemical environment, says McAllister.

For example, part of the chemical cascade causes more calcium than usual to enter the cells, producing an "energy crisis" in the injured brain, says Hovda. "You don't store energy in the brain," Hovda explains. Instead, small parts of the brain cells called mitochondria manufacture the energy from glucose in the blood. In the case of calcium overload, the mitochondria "suck up the calcium, and if there's too much they die" or at least stop functioning. That "energy crisis" can be dire because, while the brain accounts for a mere 2 percent of the body's weight, it requires at least 20 percent of all the energy the body produces.

"This is why people can't think hard" and have trouble coping with "fear, stress, anything that causes an increase" in the brain's energy needs following a TBI, Hovda says. "During the time the brain is expressing this neurobiology, it is very vulnerable to a second insult or a challenge" such as a seizure, hard mental or emotional work or a second, even mild, TBI, which among young people, especially, can even be fatal.

Also occurring after the initial trauma is a continuing breakdown of the signal-carrying axons, which are crucial to a functioning brain. That's because "a disconnected neuron is a useless neuron," says David Brody, an associate professor of neurology at Washington University School of Medicine, in St. Louis.

In experiments with mice, Brody's lab found that in severe TBIs, axons "were broken immediately," but "in the milder concussive injury, it does not look like they break right away. They're abnormal right away but not broken," suggesting that subsequent changes in the brain cause a continued breakdown of axons after the initial trauma.

In the past, "it was thought that the biomechanical load on the brain" during a TBI "produced shearing forces that literally pulled apart the connections between brain regions," Hovda and Sutton wrote. But newer research suggests that "stretching of axons at the time of trauma" sets neurochemical and other reactions in motion. Over time, they wrote, that leads to "axon disconnection."

— Marcia Clemmitt

---

[1] David A. Hovda and Richard L. Sutton, "30 Years of Scientific Discovery on a Path of Hope," *The Challenge*, Brain Injury Association of America, Fall 2010, p. 13, www.biausa.org/brain-injury-publications.htm.

Continued from p. 486

cians to develop injury classifications to help physicians determine which patients had head injuries that were potentially treatable and which were likely to die of their wounds despite medical intervention. The resulting Glasgow Coma Scale was a first step in using behavioral clues, such as how patients respond to touch, to determine which patients could be successfully treated. [26]

Physicians returning from the Vietnam War in the 1960s and '70s reported saving many more lives of injured soldiers, including TBI patients, than in past conflicts, says San Francisco-based neuropsychologist Ruff. For example, military medicine uncovered the principle of the "golden hour" — the short period of time after an injury when immediate treatment increases a person's chances of recovery.

But the path from knowledge to practice wasn't smooth, Ruff says. "Imagine telling the old guard that you need to have a helicopter on top of the hospital" to ensure that patients arrive in time for effective treatment, he says. Nevertheless, innovations such as the designation of hospitals within a geographical region as level 1, 2 or 3 trauma centers, depending on how severe an injury each can handle, eventually came about based on military medics' findings.

In the 1980s, the National Institute of Neurological Diseases and Stroke, along with a group of hospitals that specialized in TBI, collected long-term data on hundreds of patients with severe closed-head TBIs, to track their progress over time. The researchers found that some patients in a vegetative state — who, unlike comatose patients, are seemingly awake, open their eyes and move their limbs, but are apparently not aware of their surroundings — could still recover two years after injury. [27]

Getty Images/Scott Wintrow

Actress Natasha Richardson died after suffering a head injury in a skiing accident in 2009; she initially refused medical treatment and died two days later, after her traumatic brain injury worsened. Multiple studies have found that suffering one severe TBI, several mild ones or, for some people, even a single mild or moderate TBI raises the risk of permanent brain damage. At the same time, with today's improved emergency care, more and more people are surviving serious TBIs.

Costs of Recovery

As more patients survive TBIs, attention has turned to the development of rehabilitation strategies — and how rehab care should be paid for.

It's clear that intensive rehab helps patients regain at least some of their cognitive, physical and emotional brain function, even after severe TBIs, many experts say. Take the case of Rep. Gabrielle Giffords, D-Ariz., recovering after a bullet passed entirely through the left side of her brain during an assassination attempt on Jan. 8, 2011. Giffords has recovered to a remarkable degree, learning to walk and talk again, after an injury that many initially thought she might not survive. [28]

Because Giffords was wounded on the job, workers' compensation insurance for federal employees has paid for her care. Her rehabilitation during hospitalization cost roughly $8,000 a day, and post-hospitalization rehab can range from $600 to $2,500 a day. [29]

If she had fallen off a horse, her federal Blue Cross medical insurance wouldn't have paid for nearly this level of rehab, says Masel, the BIAA medical director.

Few TBI patients can pay for their own rehab, and insurance coverage is spotty at best, says the BIAA's Connors. Workers' compensation, which is administered state-by-state except for a federal-worker policy, is the most consistent payment source. Some accident and health policies cover some level of rehabilitation, and auto-insurance policies pay in some states.

Michigan, for example, has no-fault auto insurance that covers the full range of rehab services, and Texas requires insurers to provide brain and nervous-system rehabilitation services, as well as the physical-rehab services that are more frequently covered, Connors says. In some states, funds from taxes or, more often, fees added to drunken-driving citations or speeding tickets are set aside for TBI care. Funding is low, however, Connors says.

"The key issue really tripping us up is how to conduct rehab research" to produce clear evidence on which insurers can base decisions about which treatments are worth their cost, she says.

In medicine, the gold standard of research is the so-called double-blind clinical trial used to test pharmaceuticals, Connors says. In such trials, neither trial participants nor researchers know which patients receive a drug and which a placebo. But "any treatment that has to be done by a human" — such as rehab — "can't be double-blinded," she says.

"I have papers in my files dating back to 1987 with NIH [the National Institutes of Health] saying, 'We need more re-

Researchers Explore Frontiers of Brain Injury

"The more I learn, the more questions I have."

In the quest to understand traumatic brain injury (TBI), scientists are following many paths, from studying how blast waves interact with brain tissue to researching how TBI patients' brains change with age.

Autopsies of people who die of other causes after suffering a TBI show brain changes that current diagnostic technologies can't detect. That leads many researchers to hope for medical-imaging breakthroughs that can reveal more about living brains.

When traditional scans are taken of people with mild concussive injury, the brain "looks totally normal," says David Brody, an associate professor of neurology at Washington University School of Medicine, in St. Louis. "But if they die of a heart attack or something, at autopsy it becomes very clear that there is injury to the axons" — the slender extensions of nerve cells that carry messages among them — "that are the most brittle thing in the brain."

Brody is among scientists working to refine an imaging technique called DTI — diffusion tensor imaging. It is a form of magnetic resonance imaging (MRI) that uses a magnetic field and pulses of radio-frequency electromagnetic waves to sense how water molecules diffuse — or spread — through axons. A clear image of how the water travels should reveal whether and how an axon is damaged.

DTI has clinical promise "because you can do it on a regular scanner and just reprogram it," potentially putting the technology within reach of most medical facilities, says Brody. Evidence that the technology can detect injured axons came from analysis, first by DTI and then by autopsy, of the injured brain of a mouse. "We found that what the DTI revealed was the same thing that the autopsy revealed," he says.

Currently, however, DTI is "not ready for prime time" in clinical use, in part because its results aren't fully consistent from one MRI machine to another. Researchers aren't sure why.

Brody's lab also studies the relationship between TBI — in particular, how it damages axons — and the abnormal accumulation of so-called Tau proteins, a hallmark of Alzheimer's disease and other forms of dementia.

"The job of Tau is to stabilize the microtubules" — tiny structures that are a key part of axons' structural scaffolding, or cytoskeleton. "I do not think it's a coincidence that they're broken and the Tau is accumulating," Brody says. Tau-protein disorders found in TBI patients' brains include both "normal proteins accumulating in the wrong places" and proliferation of abnormal Tau proteins — "ones that are folded the wrong way," for example, he says.

Other researchers are trying to figure out exactly what happens to brains that suffer so-called blast injuries from nearby explosions, such as those caused by roadside bombs in Afghanistan.

"When a combustible solid substance is detonated, it goes from a solid to a gas and releases an enormous amount of energy," says Alisa Gean, a professor of radiology, neurology and neurosurgery at the University of California, San Francisco. "It can break windows." But beyond that, she says, things get murky. Traveling at supersonic speed, an explosion's blast wave consists of a trough of extremely low atmospheric pressure followed by a very high-pressure area that together pack a force that can toss Humvees like matchsticks and cause havoc in air-filled human organs such as the lungs and stomach.

Furthermore, strong blast waves are accompanied by even less-well-understood phenomena, such as an electromagnetic

search, but we can't find a way to do it,' " Connors says. "It kind of drives me crazy that nothing in the emergency room [ER] is subject to this scrutiny. There was no double-blinded study for the first [emergency] craniotomy" — removal of bone to allow an injured brain to swell, she says. Nevertheless, the surgery was paid for, "and now it's become standard." In ERs, "professionals learn from one another what works," and it's frustrating that a similar process doesn't exist to verify rehab therapies, she says.

For years, the federal government's TBI programs were in the Department of Education, not the NIH. [30] "The idea was that all you could do was to train people" to adapt after injury, not heal them by actually improving some brain functions, says Masel.

Efforts are under way to develop research methods that will work for nondrug treatments such as rehab. President Obama's 2009 economic-stimulus legislation, as well as the 2010 health-care reform law, established programs on "comparative-effectiveness" studies, which compare treatment regimens as they're used in ordinary medical practice. [31]

New Wars

The prevalence of TBIs in the Afghanistan and Iraq wars that began in 2001 and 2003, respectively, have pushed the field forward.

"Twenty years ago, [TBI] wasn't on people's radar. But the military context with the blast explosions has brought it to everybody's attention," says Dartmouth's McAllister.

Until five years ago, NIH funding for TBI-related research totaled less than $10 million annually, far below funding levels for other conditions that affect equivalent numbers of people, says Connors.

But when the realization struck that huge numbers of service members were TBI patients, Congress pumped in dollars. At the NIH, funding rose to more than $80 million annually in fiscal 2010, 2011 and 2012. [32] The Depart-

pulse that might affect the brain's electrical signaling. "The more I learn, the more questions I have," Gean says.

Working with neuroscientists and biologists who study the brain's physical makeup and the effects of physical events on its structure and processes, Raul Radovitzky, associate professor of aeronautics and astronautics at the Massachusetts Institute of Technology, has developed a computer model to examine how a brain changes as a blast wave spreads through it.

Computer simulations have allowed researchers to examine the multiple, complex, interacting forces unleashed by blast waves and to study such questions as how electrical forces are transmitted and what happens when fluids interact with solids, Radovitzky says. Researchers formulate those multiple factors as a set of "impossibly complicated equations," enter specific values, then turn the work over to "supercomputers with 10,000 processors crunching numbers for a day, two days, or even a week," he says. "Eventually you get what happens, the stresses" that occur at individual points in the brain, he says.

One important finding so far: "The big problem areas" for a brain exposed to a blast wave are those not protected by bone or other tissue but instead are "where the wave goes directly into the brain," such as through the mouth, eyes, ears or hollow sinus cavities that surround the nose, Radovitzky says.

What happens to service members in the years following blast-induced TBI is another area of investigation. Research confirms that TBIs caused by physical contact, such as blows to a boxer's head, are linked to the development of Alzheimer's disease and another form of dementia: CTE, or chronic traumatic encephalopathy. That connection raises the question whether Iraq and Afghanistan veterans exposed to multiple blast injuries face a similar risk of dementia, says Elaine Peskind, a professor of psychiatry and behavioral sciences and associate director of the Alzheimer's Disease Research Center at the University of Washington, in Seattle.

Peskind is studying veterans who were injured by blasts and, while not cognitively impaired, display some TBI symptoms, such as irritability and forgetfulness. She hopes to find out whether their brains already show changes that could predispose them to dementia in coming years.

"You obviously don't want to raise alarms that aren't justified, but we are definitely finding changes" in the brain structure and function, she says, using methods such as positron emission topography — PET scans. In a PET scan, an injected radioactive chemical enters the tissues and gives off energy that provides data about bodily functions, such as how the brain metabolizes glucose, its vital fuel.

In key brain areas that control movement, cognition, emotion and sleep, the brains of blast-injured veterans show lower glucose metabolism than normal brains, Peskind says. Lower conversion of glucose to energy reflects reduced levels of some brain activity, she says.

Concerned about what may lie ahead, veterans are highly supportive of the research, Peskind says. That's despite the fact that, as she notes, participants in the studies must undergo a gauntlet of tests: four different kinds of medical imaging, including lengthy stints in MRI machines, a spinal tap, genetic studies, neuropsychology testing and more.

"In lots of studies," she says, "recruitment [of research subjects] is your biggest obstacle. On this one it's not."

— Marcia Clemmitt

ment of Defense's (DOD) Congressionally Directed Medical Research Programs provided no funds specifically for TBI between 1999 and 2006 but allotted $150 million in 2007. [33]

During the 1990s and early 2000s civilian medicine moved far ahead of military medicine in TBI care, especially for cognitive and psychological problems, says Connors. Most TBIs occur among civilians, for whom they're among the most complex and challenging injuries, and the civilian injury rate varies little over time, thus calling for consistent effort, she says.

For the military, by contrast, wartime brings not only TBIs but many similarly devastating wounds, such as lost limbs, and the number of TBI patients varies widely from peacetime to wartime. As a result, the VA has long been "the undisputed leader in orthotics and prosthetics" for bodily injuries, but "they knew quite a bit less about the cognitive side of rehab" when the current Mideast conflicts began, Connors say.

In fact, to conserve resources, the VA formerly contracted out most cognitive rehabilitation for TBI patients — mainly injured in training accidents — to civilian facilities, she says.

In Iraq and Afghanistan, however, enemy attacks that relied heavily on improvised explosive devices (IEDs) — plus improved emergency care that allowed severe-TBI patients to survive — drastically increased the number of military TBI cases. By October 2007, an estimated 19 percent of service members from the Iraq and Afghanistan campaigns — about 320,000 people — had suffered traumatic brain injury. [34]

TBI's profile rose even higher in January 2006, when ABC News correspondent Bob Woodruff suffered a severe TBI from an IED while reporting in Iraq. [35] Congress quickly handed the VA and DOD "a big chunk of cash" for TBI research and care, and "they tried to ramp up quickly," Connors says.

The money and effort have begun to lead to changes, researchers say.

"The military has been very responsive to some people like me" —

civilian researchers whose findings provide direction about TBI care, says the University of Virginia's Barth. For example, alerted to the need for brain rest in the hours following even a mild TBI, the Pentagon directed that people within 50 meters of a blast be evaluated for concussion and held out of combat for a period to avoid further injury, he says.

Getty Images/Mike Coppola

Awareness of traumatic brain injury increased significantly after ABC News correspondent Bob Woodruff was severely wounded by an improvised explosive device (IED) in Iraq in January 2006. Woodruff, shown here with his wife, Lee, in November 2010, recovered and returned to TV. His brain injury helped prompt Congress to give the Veterans Administration and Pentagon more funding for TBI research and care.

What's more, in 2006, DOD distributed to military medical facilities a Military Acute Concussion Evaluation protocol, jointly designed by civilian and military researchers. [36] And in 2008 the Pentagon began requiring universal pre-deployment testing — with a computer-based measurement tool, the Automated Neuropsychological Assessment Metrics (ANAM) — to establish a baseline neurocognitive profile of each service member for use in assessing later changes in brain function that might indicate a TBI. [37]

Unlike for civilians, TBIs among service members are often just one piece of a "polytrauma" — a complex of severe injuries, such as burns, shrapnel injuries, missing limbs and even psychological injuries such as anxiety disorders — that occur in a single incident, says the VA's Vanderploeg. For that reason, the VA is working to create an interconnected system in which patients have access to multidisciplinary teams to diagnose and manage multiple ills. That's especially helpful for patients who have both TBI and PTSD, he says. "People are more likely to walk through the TBI door" — because a physical brain injury is easier to admit to than a psychological wound — but the team approach means both conditions get attention.

Still there have been bumps in the road. For example, worried that TBIs might still not be adequately addressed, Joint Chiefs of Staff Chairman Adm. Michael Mullen in 2009 sent scientists and clinicians to investigate TBI care at the battlefront. In Afghanistan, the group found that instead of regularly using the concussion-evaluation assessment tool disseminated three years earlier, "doctors couldn't tell you the first thing about it, even though they had all the training materials," said Army physician Col. Christian Macedonia, an adviser to Mullen. [38]

Meanwhile, as experts continue to praise the Pentagon for instituting pre-deployment screening in 2008, critics charge that in hurrying to meet a congressional mandate for better TBI diagnosis, DOD chose a particular screening test, the ANAM, that doesn't work. Part of the problem is that no all-computerized testing system so far devised is up to the job, many analysts say. "It is incredibly frustrating because I can see first-hand the soldiers that we've missed," said Col. Mary Lopez, the now-retired former manager of the Army's TBI testing program. [39]

Critics also have charged that bureaucratic hurdles have slowed veterans' switch from the DOD medical-care system, which covers active-duty military personnel, to VA care for post-discharge veterans, setting back recovery. "The hand-off . . . was very slow," said Jonathan Barrs, a young Marine veteran who suffered successive blast-injury TBIs in Iraq. "The VA care has been very good, but this whole time of waiting was very hard," said Barrs, who received a medical retirement because of TBI-related symptoms in May 2009 but didn't get VA care until April 2010 — nearly a year's wait. [40] ■

CURRENT SITUATION

Maintaining Momentum

This year, advocates hope to see federal TBI-related funding remain strong, despite a weak economy. Advocates also say they will continue to press for better access to services for people suffering from brain injuries.

Many experts are pleased that TBI has made it onto the national agenda. "I'm thrilled by how much progress has been made," says San Francisco

Continued on p. 494

At Issue:

Should states require all motorcycle riders to wear helmets?

ANNE T. MCCARTT
VICE PRESIDENT, RESEARCH, INSURANCE INSTITUTE FOR HIGHWAY SAFETY

WRITTEN FOR *CQ RESEARCHER*, MAY 2012

Until the recession hit, motorcycle ridership was on the upswing, and so were motorcyclist deaths. The number killed reached a record of 5,112 in 2008 before declining with less riding during the economic downturn. Numbers for 2010 (the most recent available) indicate deaths are once again increasing. In contrast, the number of passenger vehicle-occupant crash deaths has declined to historic lows.

Motorcycles are inherently risky, and when crashes occur, head injury is a leading cause of death. The most effective way we know to reduce head injury risk is to wear helmets that meet federal safety standards. Wearing a helmet would have saved at least 730 motorcyclists' lives in 2009, according to the National Highway Traffic Safety Administration (NHTSA).

Unhelmeted motorcyclists are three times as likely as helmeted ones to suffer traumatic brain injuries in crashes. NHTSA estimates that helmets reduce the likelihood of fatalities by 37 percent.

Laws covering all motorcyclists are effective, but only 19 states and the District of Columbia have such laws. Twenty-eight other states require only some riders to wear helmets.

During the late 1960s and early '70s, when the government tied highway construction funding to state highway safety laws, nearly every state had a universal helmet law, and helmet use approached 100 percent. But fueled by pressure from motorcyclist-rights groups, state legislators continue to introduce bills to repeal or weaken helmet laws. In April, Michigan became the latest to drop its universal law.

Watered-down laws are associated with sharp declines in helmet use and increases in deaths. Florida is a case in point. In 2000, the state weakened its universal law to exempt riders 21 and older who have at least $10,000 of medical insurance coverage. An Insurance Institute for Highway Safety study found that the motorcyclist death rate per crash subsequently increased by about 25 percent.

Universal laws are crucial not only for safety but also for economic reasons. Governments spend vast amounts of public money to treat people who get injured in motorcycle crashes, especially those with brain injuries. Such injuries can last a lifetime — and so can the treatment costs.

Motorcyclist groups often tout skills training as an alternative to wearing helmets; however, there's no evidence that training reduces crashes. Antilock brakes are the only proven way to reduce crash risk. Nevertheless, motorcycles will still crash, and helmets prevent injuries and deaths when crashes happen. States should require all riders to wear them.

WAYNE ALLARD
VICE PRESIDENT, GOVERNMENT RELATIONS, AMERICAN MOTORCYCLIST ASSOCIATION

WRITTEN FOR *CQ RESEARCHER*, MAY 2012

Motorcycle helmet mandates don't prevent crashes. The American Motorcyclist Association (AMA) strongly encourages riders and passengers to wear a properly fitted motorcycle helmet certified to meet federal standards. However, the AMA believes that adults should have the right to voluntarily decide when to wear a helmet.

Every comprehensive motorcycle safety program must focus on prevention of motorcycle crashes. Helmets reduce injuries when a crash happens but do nothing to prevent crashes. Sadly, helmet-mandate lobbyists seem less concerned with promoting policies that prevent motorcycle crashes and more concerned with reducing insurance payments after crashes occur.

The AMA promotes strategies to reduce motorcycle crashes, such as rider training and motorist-awareness programs.

The federally funded motorcycle crash causation study, conducted by Professor Hugh "Harry" Hurt Jr., documented the efficacy of rider education. The 1981 report said: "The basic Motorcycle Rider Course of the Motorcycle Safety Foundation is effective in training motorcycle riders, and those trained riders are both less involved and less injured in motorcycle accidents."

The National Highway Traffic Safety Administration also cited rider education as effective in its 2005 report, "Promising Practices in Motorcycle Rider Education and Licensing." The report states: "Although evidence of the effectiveness of rider education on crash reduction is mixed, several studies have shown that trained riders tend to have fewer crashes, less severe crashes and overall lower cost of damage resulting from crashes."

Motorist awareness programs have become an increasingly valuable strategy in reducing motorcycle crashes. One of the most frequent causes of motorcycle accidents cited by the Hurt study was the violation of motorcyclists' right-of-way by other drivers. As traffic density, the prevalence of large SUVs and the frequency of distracted vehicle operation have increased, motorcyclists benefit when drivers are regularly reminded in the media and on highway signs to watch for motorcyclists.

One of the common arguments against voluntary helmet use is that injured motorcyclists disproportionately rely upon the public to pay for their care, yet studies by Harborview Medical Center (1988) and the University of North Carolina Highway Safety Research Center (1992) do not support this claim.

Rider training and motorist-awareness programs can reduce motorcycle crashes, yet in today's austere environment they are often underfunded — tragically so — when scarce resources are redirected toward helmet-mandate enforcement, as the history of federal intervention on this issue teaches us.

Continued from p. 492

neuropsychologist Ruff. Clinicians "are getting better trained, and many more are showing interest." In the '80s, TBI was dubbed a "silent epidemic," but it's no longer overlooked, he says.

Many needs remain, however. Among items on the 2012 wish list of the Brain Injury Association of America is an outlay by Congress of an additional $10 million for the CDC to disseminate TBI-care guidelines to primary-care physicians and other medical professionals in communities around the country and for regulators implementing the 2010 health-care reform law to ensure that a full slate of rehab services is covered for all patients. [41]

Controversy continues to simmer around a form of rehab known as cognitive rehabilitation therapy (CRT). In CRT, which can take many forms, patients relearn intellectual skills, such as focusing attention; practice strategies such as list-making to compensate for lost memory skills; and cultivate awareness of the way their mind works, in a learning strategy called metacognition. [42]

TRICARE, the health-insurance system that covers active-duty military personnel, their families and some military retirees, once refused to cover CRT, arguing that evidence had not established its effectiveness. But now it covers it in some circumstances, including for some retirees. [43] In late 2011, the Institute of Medicine (IOM), a congressionally chartered nongovernmental advisory group, announced that, despite "methodological shortcomings" in rehab research, the evidence of CRT's effectiveness is strong enough to recommend its continued use, as research goes on. [44] BIAA is working with TRICARE to ensure that military patients learn how they can get CRT. [45]

Sports Injuries

This year, headlines about TBI-related cognitive and emotional problems in elite contact-sport athletes just keep coming.

"With each bone-breaking, head-injuring hit, NFL players are killing themselves slowly," wrote a *Washington Post* sports columnist after the May 2 suicide, at age 43, of former San Diego Chargers linebacker Junior Seau. [46] Seau's position entailed making many skull-rattling hits, and many believe brain damage from TBIs likely contributed to his apparent suicidal depression. [47]

At least two players have decided to leave the game, in the wake of Seau's death.

Linebacker Andrew Sweat, who had recently signed on with the Cleveland Browns, announced May 14 that health consequences he experienced from concussions suffered as a Ohio State University player convinced him to attend law school instead of play pro ball. [48] After a recent concussion, "I was not myself. My mind was not there. Some of the thoughts that were out there, I was getting worried about that," Sweat told the *Cleveland Plain Dealer.* [49]

Veteran NFL offensive lineman Jacob Bell, who'd recently signed to play next season with the Cincinnati Bengals, also is leaving the game in the wake of Seau's suicide. "We sell our soul to a game for money, for fame, for glory. And at some point, you've kind of got to sit there and say, 'Is this still worth what I'm doing?' " In his case, the answer was no, Bell said. [50]

Athletic organizations are increasingly aware of TBIs' dangers, and "a lot of groups are trying hard to make their sports more safe," including the World Boxing Council and the NFL, says Hovda of UCLA.

Still, especially worrisome is the total number of brain-rattling hits a football player may sustain in a career, since evidence now suggests that repeated concussions can lead to chronic traumatic encephalopathy (CTE), a severe form of dementia, says Barth, of the University of Virginia.

There has been some progress on that front, however. Last summer, NFL team owners and the players' union agreed in a new collective-bargaining agreement to strictly limit the number of full-contact practices, to reduce players' exposure to the hardest hits. Teams now are limited to 14 such practices per season, and only three in the season's final six weeks. [51]

But people concerned with TBIs agree that plenty remains to be done.

"In my discipline, we'd like people not to be blasé about mild TBIs," says Ruff. "When my kids and I see a James Bond movie, we count the concussions. And then the guy who gets the concussion turns up dancing in a tuxedo in the next scene, and he always gets the girl." Such cultural clichés send a dangerous message, San Francisco clinical neuropsychologist Ruff says. The brain needs rest after even a mild TBI to prevent the injury from getting worse. A second concussion quickly following the first can actually be fatal, especially for a young person, he says. [52]

"The United States is the only advanced country where there is organized opposition to motorcycle helmet laws," says Russ Rader, senior vice president for communications at the Insurance Institute for Highway Safety, an Arlington, Va.-based nonprofit funded by the auto-insurance industry. As a result, since the 1970s, when "just about every state had a mandatory helmet law," today only 19 states and the District of Columbia require all riders to wear a helmet. (*See graphic, p. 480.*) Evidence makes clear that helmet requirements save lives, Rader says. [53]

Nevertheless, "the push to repeal is constant," he says. On April 13, Michigan Republican Gov. Rick Snyder signed a repeal of that state's 35-year-old helmet requirement. [54] (*See "At Issue," p. 493.*)

Meanwhile, neither medical nor psychology training includes enough attention to TBI, some clinicians say.

"My oldest kid is a neurologist, and the only place he learned about this is at the kitchen table," not in med school, says BIAA medical director Masel. "There's never really been a specialty that's embraced it" except among rehabilitation specialists.

"The challenge going forward is to maintain momentum" despite the unlikelihood that a "silver bullet" to repair or prevent TBI damage will be found, says Dartmouth's McAllister. "In science there are 'Aha!' moments. But they always occur on the back" of slow, unglamorous studies that don't compel the public's and lawmakers' interest. "The momentum now is awesome, but I fear there may be disheartenment" as findings turn out to be incremental, he says. ■

OUTLOOK

Dementia Epidemic?

In contact sports such as boxing and football, researchers have found strong links between TBIs and dementia as well as mood and behavior problems. Now, studies are under way to determine whether blast injuries of the kind prevalent in Iraq and Afghanistan also increase those risks. If they do, providing care for veterans will become even more challenging.

Many retired boxers develop CTE, a progressive, degenerative brain disease apparently caused by repeated head injuries, with symptoms including memory loss, depression and poor impulse control. In autopsies, the disease shows up as a distinctive buildup of certain proteins in the brain, and football, soccer and hockey players also are known to develop it. [55]

So far, evidence hasn't established what level and amount of trauma are needed to put someone at risk of CTE. Debate is intense between researchers who believe that a few mild TBIs are enough to endanger a person and others who doubt that, says Dartmouth's McAllister. The skeptics say, "Whoa! Whoa! So many people have played contact sports over the years. Why don't we see oceans of people with dementia?" he says.

It's already known that "a single moderate-to-severe TBI at any time of your life also increases your risk of Alzheimer's," which "raises the concern that our vets may be at increased risk" for Alzheimer's and CTE related to blast injuries, says Peskind, of the University of Washington.

Ann Mckee, a professor of neurology and pathology and co-director of the Center for the Study of Traumatic Encephalopathy at Boston University, examined the brains of two recent military veterans who died before middle age. She found the same brain patterns as in athletes with CTE. "It's not conclusive" evidence of the blast-injury connection, "but it's two out of two," says Peskind. If further studies continue to confirm the link, "the VA will have to be prepared to take care of these people," since the condition would be service-related.

Meanwhile, many veterans with troubling TBI symptoms wonder where to turn for support and advice, says Will Wilson, a retired Army colonel who now is a North Carolina-based psychologist specializing in military psychology. "You won't go to your chaplain, you won't go to your family, because you fear you're letting them down," he says. But "you will go to other vets."

As the government ponders the pricey — and sometimes emotionally fraught — logistics of providing help to brain-injured vets, grassroots veterans' organizations, of which there are many, would be an effective "and money-saving place" to base services, Wilson says. ■

Notes

[1] Quoted in Gary Myers, "Former NY Jets WR Al Toon's concussions haven't kept son Nick from following in his dad's footsteps," *New York Daily News*, Oct. 15, 2011, http://articles.nydailynews.com/2011-10-15/sports/30303682_1_nick-toon-al-toon-larry-grantham. See also, Mike Florio, "Disconnect Grows Between Former, Current Players Regarding Concussions," ProFootballTalk blog, NBC Sports, April 29, 2012, http://profootballtalk.nbcsports.com/2012/04/29/disconnect-grows-between-former-current-players-regarding-concussions; for background, see T. J. Simers, "A No-Brainer: Football Leads to Concussions: Al Toon Will Attest that Symptoms Can Remain for Years," *Los Angeles Times*, Oct. 20, 1995, http://articles.latimes.com/1995-10-20/sports/sp-59156_1_concussions-year-toon.

[2] "Traumatic Brain Injury," Centers for Disease Control and Prevention, www.cdc.gov/traumaticbraininjury.

[3] Vanessa Williamson and Erin Mulhall, "Invisible Wounds: Psychological and Neurological Injuries Confront a New Generation of Veterans," Iraq and Afghanistan Veterans of America, January 2009, p. 5, http://iava.org/files/IAVA_invisible_wounds_0.pdf.

[4] For background, see Gary Milhoces, "Players Call for Immediate Testimony in Concussion Suits," *USA Today*, April 25, 2012, www.usatoday.com/sports/football/nfl/story/2012-04-25/NFL-concussions-lawsuits-hearing/54532472/1, and "Battling with Memory Loss, Dorsett Joins Concussion Lawsuit Against NFL," CBS Sports, Feb. 2, 2012, www.cbssports.com/nfl/story/17085305/battling-with-memory-loss-dorsett-joins-concussion-lawsuit-against-nfl.

[5] Quoted in Malena Caruso, "NFL and Retired Players Want Multiple Concussion Related Lawsuits Rolled Into One," *Medill Reports*, Jan. 27, 2012, http://news.medill.northwestern.edu/chicago/news.aspx?id=199387. For background, see Kenneth Jost, "Professional Football," *CQ Researcher*, Jan. 29, 2010, pp. 73-96 (update, Oct. 11, 2011), and Jost, "College Football," *CQ Researcher*, Nov. 18, 2011, pp. 977-1000.

[6] For background, see the following *CQ Researcher* reports by Peter Katel: "Wounded Veterans," Aug. 31, 2007, pp. 697-720; "Caring for Veterans," April 23, 2010, pp. 361-384; and "Military Suicides," Sept. 23, 2011, pp. 781-804.

[7] For background, see "Often Misdiagnosed as Alzheimer's Disease, Chronic Traumatic En-

cephalopathy Could Play a Role in Veterans' Dementia," *U.S. Medicine*, 2011, www.usmedicine.com/compendium/often-misdiagnosed-as-alzheimers-disease-chronic-traumatic-encephalopathy-could-play-a-role-in-veterans-dementia.html.

[8] Lee E. Goldstein, *et al.*, "Chronic Traumatic Encephalopathy in Blast-Exposed Military Veterans and a Blast Neurotrauma Mouse Model," *Science Translational Medicine*, May 16, 2012, p. 134, http://stm.sciencemag.org/content/4/134/134ra60; Greg Miller, "Blast Injuries Linked to Neurodegeneration in Veterans," *Science*, May 18, 2012, p. 790.

[9] Liz Borkowski, "Who's Paying for Gabrielle Giffords' Rehabilitation?" *The Pump Handle blog*, June 16, 2011, http://scienceblogs.com/thepumphandle/2011/06/whos_paying_for_gabrielle_giff.php.

[10] For background, see "CT Scan," netdoctor.co.uk, www.netdoctor.co.uk/health_advice/examinations/ctgeneral.htm.

[11] For background, see Peter Pollack, "Ringing the Bell on Concussion Management," *AAOS Now*, American Academy of Orthopaedic Surgeons, September 2011, www.aaos.org/news/aaosnow/sep11/cover1.asp; "Concussion: A Fact Sheet for Coaches," NCAA/Centers for Disease Control and Prevention, http://fs.ncaa.org/Docs/health_safety/ConFactSheetcoaches.pdf; "Consensus Statement on Concussion in Sport 3rd International Conference on Concussion in Sport Held in Zurich, November 2008," *Clinical Journal of Sport Medicine*, May 2009, pp. 185-200, http://journals.lww.com/cjsportsmed/fulltext/2009/05000/consensus_statement_on_concussion_in_sport_3rd.1.aspx.

[12] Williamson and Mulhall, *op. cit.*

[13] For background, see Martha Raddatz, Muhammad Lila and Nick Schifrin, "Soldier Held in Afghan Massacre Had Brain Injury, Marital Problems," ABC News, March 12, 2012, http://abcnews.go.com/International/us-soldiers-alleged-deadly-rampage-taliban-vow-revenge/story?id=15900289#.T7PTAlLdeUl.

[14] Katie Drummond, "What Role Did Accused Soldier's Brain Injury Play in Afghan Massacre? (Updated)," *Wired, Danger Room blog*, March 13, 2012, www.wired.com/dangerroom/2012/03/afghan-massacre-tbi.

[15] Helen Kennedy, "Sergeant Psycho: Killer GI Suffered Traumatic Brain Injury," *New York Daily News*, March 13, 2012, p. 1; http://timemilitary.files.wordpress.com/2012/03/picture-1.png; for background, see Paul Rieckhoff, "How to Stereotype Our Military as Drunken Beggars: A Case Study in #MediaFail by Dr. Drew," *Huffington Post*, March 21, 2012, www.huffingtonpost.com/paul-rieckhoff/how-to-stereotype-our-mil_b_1371590.html.

[16] Rieckhoff, *op. cit.*

[17] Jason Fritz, "Robert Bales Is Not the Victim," *Ink Spots*, March 19, 2012, http://tachesdhuile.blogspot.com/2012/03/robert-bales-is-not-victim.html.

[18] Jennifer L. Highley and Brenda J. Proffitt, "Traumatic Brain Injury Among Homeless Persons: Etiology, Prevalence and Severity," June 2008, p. 2, www.nhchc.org/wp-content/uploads/2011/12/TBIAmongHomelessPersons_2008.pdf.

[19] Seena Fazel, Paul Lichtenstein, Martin Grann and Niklas Långstrom, "Risk of Violent Crime in Individual with Epilepsy and Traumatic Brain Injury: A 35-year Swedish Population Study," *PLoS Medicine*, December 2011, www.plosmedicine.org/article/info%3Adoi%2F10.1371%2Fjournal.pmed.1001150/.

[20] Quoted in Bryan Jennett, "The Glasgow Coma Scale: History and Current Practice," *Trauma*, April 1, 2002, p. 91.

[21] Thomas Longmore, *Gunshot Injuries: Their History, Characteristic Features, Complications, and General Treatment; With Statistics Concerning Them as They Have Been Met in Warfare*, 2nd Edition (1894), pp. 132-136, http://books.google.com/books?id=xhwLAAAAIAAJ&printsec=frontcover#v=onepage&q&f=false.

About the Author

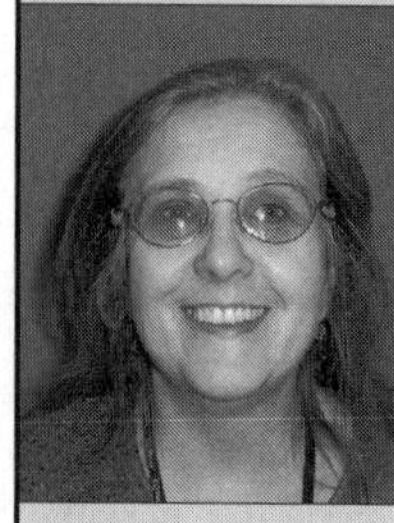

Staff writer **Marcia Clemmitt** is a veteran social-policy reporter who previously served as editor in chief of *Medicine & Health* and staff writer for *The Scientist*. She has also been a high school math and physics teacher. She holds a liberal arts and sciences degree from St. John's College, Annapolis, and a master's degree in English from Georgetown University. Her recent reports include "Genes and Health" and "Animal Intelligence."

[22] Andrew Robertson, "The Post-concussional Syndrome Then and Now," *Australian and New Zealand Journal of Psychiatry*, Dec. 1, 1988, p. 396.

[23] Edgar Jones, Nicola T. Fear and Simon Wessely, "Shell Shock and Mild Traumatic Brain Injury: A Historical Review," *American Journal of Psychiatry*, Nov. 1, 2007, pp. 1641-1645, http://ajp.psychiatryonline.org/article.aspx?articleid=99147.

[24] *Ibid.*

[25] *Ibid.*

[26] Jennett, *op. cit.*

[27] J. Piek, "Lessons to be Learnt from the Traumatic Coma Data Bank," *European Journal of Anaesthesiology*, January 1998, pp. 35-37, http://journals.lww.com/ejanaesthesiology/Fulltext/1998/01001/Lessons_to_be_learnt_from_the_Traumatic_Coma_Data.23.aspx.

[28] For background, see Zain Shauk and Todd Ackerman, "Giffords Ordeal Came at Dawn of New Medical Era," *Houston Chronicle*, Jan. 8, 2012, www.chron.com/news/housto n-texas/article/Giffords-ordeal-came-at-dawn-of-new-medical-era-2448624.php#page-2, and Daniel J. DeNoon, "Gabrielle Giffords' Brain Injury: FAQ," WebMD, Jan. 27, 2011, www.webmd.com/brain/news/20110109/gabrielle-giffords-brain-injury-faq.

[29] Borkowski, *op. cit.*

[30] "Remembering BIAA: A Digest of Events and Accomplishments," *The Challenge!*, Brain Injury Association of America, Fall 2010, p. 3.

[31] For background, see "Comparative Effectiveness Research Funding," U.S. Department of Health and Human Services website, www.hhs.gov/recovery/programs/cer/index.html; Initial National Priorities for Comparative Effectiveness Research, Board on Health Care Services, The National Academies Press, 2009, www.nap.edu/openbook.php?record_id=12648&page=29, and "Comparative Effectiveness Research," *Health Affairs* website, Oct. 8, 2010, www.healthaffairs.org/healthpolicybriefs/brief.php?brief_id=27.

[32] "Estimates of Funding for Various Research, Condition and Disease Categories," Research Portfolio Online Reporting Tools, National Institutes of Health, Feb. 13, 2012, http://report.nih.gov/categorical_spending.aspx.

[33] Sharon Weinberger, "Bombs' Hidden Impact: The Brain War," *Nature*, Sept. 21, 2011, pp. 390-393, www.nature.com/news/2011/110921/full/477390a.html.

[34] Terri Tanielian and Lisa H. Jaycox, eds, "Invisible Wounds of War: Psychological and Cognitive Injuries, Their Consequences, and

Services to Assist Recovery," Rand Center for Military Health Policy Research, 2008, p. xxi, www.rand.org/pubs/monographs/2008/RAND_MG720.pdf.

[35] For background, see Denise Mann, "Bob Woodruff's Traumatic Brain Injury Recovery," WebMD, www.webmd.com/brain/features/bob-woodruff-after-traumatic-brain-injury.

[36] For background, see "Validation of the Military Acute Concussion Evaluation (MACE) for In-Theater Evaluation of Combat-Related Traumatic Brain Injury," October 2009, www.dtic.mil/dtic/tr/fulltext/u2/a515492.pdf.

[37] "Automated Neuropsychological Assessment Metrics," Defense and Veterans Brain Injury Center, Winter 2012, www.dcoe.health.mil/Content/Navigation/Documents/About%20ANAM.pdf.

[38] Quoted in Weinberger, *op. cit.*

[39] Joaquin Sapien, T. Christian Miller and Daniel Zwerdling, "Testing Program Fails Soldiers, Leaving Brain Injuries Undetected," Pro Publica/NPR, Nov. 28, 2011.

[40] Quoted in Kelly Kennedy, "TBI Vets Face Delays, Poor Access to Care," *Air Force Times*, May 6, 2010, www.airforcetimes.com/news/2010/05/military_traumatic_braininjury_050610w.

[41] For background, see Advocacy and Government Affairs, Brain Injury Association of America, www.biausa.org/biaa-advocacy.htm.

[42] "What Is Cognitive Rehabilitation Therapy?" The Society for Cognitive Rehabilitation, www.societyforcognitiverehab.org/patient-family-resources/what-is-cognitive-rehab.php.

[43] "Cognitive Rehabilitation Therapy," Covered Services, TRICARE website, www.tricare.mil/mybenefit/jsp/Medical/IsItCovered.do;jsessionid=PgBWhQpQGVzJT176QhJPfKBRJN9YRLN3nKWjplXdMnyz2jLzXytb!67060548?kw=Cognitive+Rehabilitation+Therapy.

[44] "Cognitive Rehabilitation Therapy for Traumatic Brain Injury: Evaluating the Evidence," Institute of Medicine, October 2011, www.iom.edu/~/media/Files/Report%20Files/2011/Cognitive-Rehabilitation-Therapy-for-Traumatic-Brain-Injury-Evaluating-the-Evidence/CRTforTBIreportbrief2.pdf.

[45] "Ensure Returning Service Members Receive Access to Effective TBI Treatments," Issue Brief, Brain Injury Association of America, 2012.

[46] Jason Reid, "Junior Seau's Death Should Force Fans to Ask Uncomfortable Questions," *The Washington Post*, May 12, 2012, www.washingtonpost.com/sports/redskins/junior-seaus-death-should-force-fans-to-ask-uncomfortable-questions/2012/05/12/gIQAFJfGLU_story.html.

[47] Jarrett Bell, "Junior Seau's Suicide Sparks Memories of Another NFL Death," *USA Today*, May 4, 2012, www.usatoday.com/sports/football/nfl/story/2012-05-03/junior-seau-suicide-death-larry-bethea/54739400/1.

[48] Chris Greenberg, "Andrew Sweat Turns Down Browns, NFL Career for Law School Over Concussion Concerns," *Huffington Post*, May 14, 2012, www.huffingtonpost.com/2012/05/14/andrew-sweat-browns-nfl-concussions-law-school_n_1515343.html.

[49] Doug Lesmerises, "Concussion Symptoms End Football Career for OSU's Andrew Sweat," *Plain Dealer* [Cleveland], May 15, 2012, www.cleveland.com/browns/index.ssf/2012/05/concussion_symptoms_end_footba.html.

[50] Quoted in Bill Whitaker, "NFL Veteran Quits, Fearing Future Brain Damage," CBS News, May 16, 2012, www.cbsnews.com/8301-505270_162-57435281/nfl-veteran-quits-fearing-future-brain-damage.

[51] Peter King, "Making Sense of the New CBA and How It Will Affect the Game," *SI.com*, July 25, 2011, http://sportsillustrated.cnn.com/2011/writers/peter_king/07/24/labor/index.html#ixzz1bp6uBWoM.

[52] For background, see Marcia Clemmitt," Extreme Sports," *CQ Researcher*, April 3, 2009, pp. 297-320.

[53] "Motorcycle and Bicycle Helmet Use Laws," Insurance Institute for Highway Safety, May 2012, www.iihs.org/laws/HelmetUseCurrent.aspx.

[54] Mark Guarino, "Look, Ma, No Helmet! Michigan Repeals Helmet Law for Motorcyclists," *The Christian Science Monitor*, April 13, 2012, www.csmonitor.com/USA/Politics/2012/0413/Look-ma-no-helmet!-Michigan-repeals-helmet-law-for-motorcyclists.

[55] For background, see "Often Misdiagnosed as Alzheimer's Disease, Chronic Traumatic Encephalopathy Could Play a Role in Veterans' Dementia," *op. cit.*

FOR MORE INFORMATION

American Motorcyclist Association, 13515 Yarmouth Dr., Pickerington, OH 43147; 614-856-1900; www.americanmotorcyclist.com. Membership group that advocates voluntary, but not mandatory, helmet use.

Brain Injury Association of America, 1608 Spring Hill Rd., Suite 110, Vienna, VA 22182; 703-761-0750; www.biausa.org. Principal advocacy organization for traumatic brain injury (TBI) patients; provides information on research and policy.

Center for Neuroscience and Regenerative Medicine, Uniformed Services University of the Health Sciences, 4301 Jones Bridge Rd., Bethesda, MD 20814-4799; www.usuhs.mil/cnrm. Medical-research program on TBI and post-traumatic stress disorder run jointly by the Department of Defense and National Institutes of Health.

Defense and Veterans Brain Injury Center, 11300 Rockville Pike, Suite 1100, Rockville, MD 20852; 866-966-1020; www.dvbic.org. Federal agency that conducts research on military-related TBIs, provides care to patients and informs the public about TBI.

Insurance Institute for Highway Safety, 1005 N. Glebe Rd., Suite 800, Arlington, VA 22201; 703-247-1500; www.iihs.org. Research group funded by auto-insurance companies that promotes highway safety.

Matthew A. Gfeller Sport-Related Traumatic Brain Injury Research Center, 2207 Stallings-Evans Sports Medicine Center, Campus Box 8700, Chapel Hill, NC 27599-8700; 919-962-0409; www.tbicenter.unc.edu. University-based clinical and research organization for sports-related TBIs.

National Institute of Neurological Disorders and Stroke, NIH Neurological Institute, P.O. Box 5801, Bethesda, MD 20824; 301-496-5751. Federal agency that conducts and sponsors TBI research.

One Mind for Research, info@1mind4research.org, www.1mind4research.org. Ten-year, privately funded campaign to foster multidisciplinary research collaborations on brain disorders, including TBI, reduce the stigma of such disorders and advocate for federal research funding.

Bibliography

Selected Sources

Books

Cassidy, John W., and Lee Woodruff, *Mindstorms: Living With Traumatic Brain Injury*, Da Capo Lifelong Books, 2009.
Cassidy, a neuropsychiatrist, tells stories of real-life patients to explain diagnosis and treatment. Co-author Woodruff is the wife of ABC News correspondent Bob Woodruff, who suffered a serious brain injury in Iraq in 2006.

Crimmins, Cathy, *Where is the Mango Princess?*, Vintage, 2001.
A humor writer chronicles the agonizing aftermath of her lawyer husband's traumatic brain injury.

Articles

"Often Misdiagnosed as Alzheimer's Disease, Chronic Traumatic Encephalopathy Could Play a Role in Veterans' Dementia," *U.S. Medicine, 2011 Compendium*, www.usmedicine.com/compendium/often-misdiagnosed-as-alzheimers-disease-chronic-traumatic-encephalopathy-could-play-a-role-in-veterans-dementia.html.
A Boston University neurologist and neuropathologist has found a unique pattern of likely dementia-inducing proteins in the autopsied brains of contact-sport athletes.

Borkowski, Liz, "Who's Paying for Rep. Gabrielle Giffords' Rehabilitation?" *The Pump Handle*, June 16, 2011, http://scienceblogs.com/thepumphandle/2011/06/whos_paying_for_gabrielle_giff.php.
A public-health analyst discusses the state of insurance coverage for TBI rehabilitation for civilian and military patients.

Caponigri, Paul, "The Concussion Issue, From a Player's Point of View," Slap Shot blog, *The New York Times*, Dec. 22, 2011, http://slapshot.blogs.nytimes.com/2011/12/22/the-concussion-issue-from-a-players-point-of-view.
High-speed action is key to hockey's appeal, but it means TBIs will likely never be completely eliminated from the game.

Cotsonika, Nicholas J., "NHL Players to Participate in Ambitious Concussion Research Project," *Yahoo! Sports*, April 5, 2012, http://sports.yahoo.com/news/nhl-players-participate-ambitious-concussion-210500736--nhl.html.
The National Hockey League is one of several athletic organizations that will participate in a long-term study of what kind of TBIs elite athletes encounter.

Hovda, David A., and Richard L. Sutton, "30 Years of Scientific Discovery on a Path of Hope," *The Challenge!* Brain Injury Association of America, Fall 2010, www.biausa.org/brain-injury-publications.htm.
Three decades of medical research shows that TBIs involve brain damage that accumulates over time.

Miller, T. Christian, and Daniel Zwerdling, "Army Plans New Guidelines to Resolve Denials of Purple Hearts to Brain-injured Soldiers," ProPublica/NPR, March 16, 2011, www.propublica.org/article/army-plans-new-guidelines-ro-resolve-denials-of-purple-hearts.
Because many TBIs come from bloodless head injuries, some service members find it difficult to make the case that they qualify for the Purple Heart, awarded for combat injuries.

Miller, T. Christian, and Daniel Zwerdling, "Critical Shortage of Army Neurologists for U.S. Troops in Iraq and Afghanistan," ProPublica/NPR, April 20, 2011, www.propublica.org/article/critical-shortage-of-neurologists-for-us-troops-in-iraq-and-afghanistan.
A shortage of brain specialists hinders treatment of service members who suffer TBIs.

Miller, T. Christian, and Daniel Zwerdling, "Pentagon Health Plan Won't Cover Brain-Damage Therapy for Troops," ProPublica/NPR, Dec. 20, 2010, www.npr.org/2010/12/20/132145959/pentagon-health-plan-wont-cover-brain-damage-therapy-for-troops.
TRICARE, the health plan that covers active-duty and retired military personnel, has been reluctant to cover cognitive rehabilitation.

Weinberger, Sharon, "Bombs' Hidden Impact: The Brain War," *Nature*, Sept. 21, 2011, www.nature.com/news/2011/110921/full/477390a.html.
The military has been scrambling to understand blast-induced TBIs and put together a workable system of diagnosis and treatment.

Reports and Studies

Parker, Kevin Kit, "The Blasted Brain: Traumatic Brain Injury on the Battlefield," The Science Network/One Mind for Research, May, 24, 2011 (video, audio and transcript at http://thesciencenetwork.org/programs/one-mind-for-research).
A Harvard University professor of bioengineering and applied physics and Afghanistan war veteran argues that academic and government scientists should develop new scientific tools for TBI-drug research to tempt reluctant pharmaceutical companies into the game.

Tanielian, Terri, and Lisa H. Jaycox, eds., "Invisible Wounds of War: Psychological and Cognitive Injuries, Their Consequences, and Services to Assist Recovery," RAND, 2008, www.rand.org/pubs/monographs/2008/RAND_MG720.pdf.
The psychological and cognitive toll on men and women who served in the Iraq and Afghanistan wars could be huge in decades to come.

The Next Step:

Additional Articles from Current Periodicals

Diagnoses

Dao, James, "Athletes' Brain Disease Is Found in Veterans," *The New York Times*, May 17, 2012, p. A14, www.nytimes.com/2012/05/17/us/brain-disease-is-found-in-veterans-exposed-to-bombs.html.

Scientists who have studied degenerative brain disease in athletes have found the same condition in veterans exposed to roadside bombs in Iraq and Afghanistan.

Fitzgerald, Sharon C., "Diagnosing Troops' Brain Injuries Faster," *Daily Progress* (Newport News, Va.), June 7, 2011, p. A9, www2.dailyprogress.com/news/2011/jun/05/uva-researchers-eye-technology-improve-diagnosis-t-ar-1087382/.

University of Virginia researchers are developing technology that could diagnose soldiers with traumatic brain injury right on the battlefield.

Walker, Monique, and Chelsea Conaboy, "Brain Trauma Cited," *The Boston Globe*, Aug. 17, 2011, p. 6, articles.boston.com/2011-08-17/sports/29897228_1_bedford-va-medical-center-brain-trauma-traumatic-encephalopathy.

Traumatic brain injury can be diagnosed only through a brain autopsy, but there are behavioral signs indicating the presence of the disease, says a Boston University neurologist.

Research

Grady, Denise, "Advanced Scans Reveal Veterans' Brain Injuries," *The New York Times*, June 2, 2011, p. A16, www.nytimes.com/2011/06/02/health/02brain.html.

Researchers hope new medical-scanning technologies will do a better job of picking up the early signs of blast injuries to the brain suffered on the battlefield.

Jackson Jr., Harry, "Research Targets Veterans' Brain Damage in the Lab," *St. Louis Post-Dispatch*, Aug. 11, 2011, p. B1, www.stltoday.com/lifestyles/health-med-fit/fitness/article_e5452d06-3ac7-5f78-a05a-7f05dbce8310.html.

The Defense Department has funded a $5.3 million St. Louis University study to analyze the brains of soldiers with traumatic brain injury.

Suicide and Violence

Brown, David, "Weak, Murky Links Found Between PTSD and Violence," *The Washington Post*, April 1, 2012, p. A4, www.washingtonpost.com/national/health-science/link-between-ptsd-and-violent-behavior-is-weak/2012/03/31/gIQApYFZnS_story.html.

Scientists have not established a strong link between such brain disorders as post-traumatic stress disorder and traumatic brain injury and violent behavior.

Kime, Patricia, "Experts Downplay Possible Role of Head Injury in Afghan Attack," *Military Times*, March 26, 2012, p. 8.

Psychiatric experts are unsure whether complications from traumatic brain injury played a role in an American soldier's shooting spree in Afghanistan.

Tamari, Jonathan, "Seau's Death Re-ignites Debate on Violent Hits," *Philadelphia Inquirer*, May 3, 2012, p. D3, articles.philly.com/2012-05-04/sports/31556716_1_cte-brain-injury-suicide.

Following the death of pro football player Junior Seau, doctors cautioned that nobody has yet established a definitive link between brain injuries and suicide.

Treatment and Prevention

Carey, Benedict, "Treatment of Trauma to Brain Is Studied," *The New York Times*, Oct. 12, 2011, p. A13, www.nytimes.com/2011/10/12/health/12brain.html.

Techniques used to treat psychological lapses from traumatic brain injury are helpful but lack significant scientific support, says a government-appointed panel.

Colliver, Victoria, "S.F. General Treatment for Brain Injuries Lauded," *The San Francisco Chronicle*, Oct. 4, 2011, p. C3, www.sfgate.com/cgi-bin/article.cgi?f=/c/a/2011/10/03/BAGP1LCVCC.DTL.

San Francisco General Hospital has become the first in the nation to be certified for treatment of traumatic brain injury, a recognition that is expected to set the standard for all other hospitals.

CITING *CQ RESEARCHER*

Sample formats for citing these reports in a bibliography include the ones listed below. Preferred styles and formats vary, so please check with your instructor or professor.

MLA STYLE

Jost, Kenneth. "Remembering 9/11," CQ Researcher 2 Sept. 2011: 701-732.

APA STYLE

Jost, K. (2011, September 2). Remembering 9/11. *CQ Researcher, 9*, 701-732.

CHICAGO STYLE

Jost, Kenneth. "Remembering 9/11." *CQ Researcher*, September 2, 2011, 701-732.

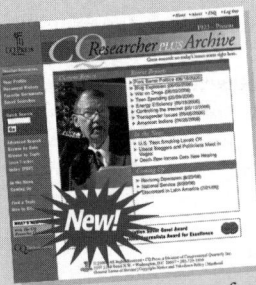

CQ Researcher

Published by CQ Press, an Imprint of SAGE Publications, Inc.

www.cqresearcher.com

Alcohol Abuse

Can underage drinking be curbed?

Americans are abusing alcohol less than in the past with one exception: college students, who drink more and binge drink more often than nonstudents of similar age. And alcohol continues to extract a high toll from those who abuse it at any age, killing 80,000 Americans a year and draining more than $220 billion from the economy. Although high school students drink and binge less, bingeing accounts for 90 percent of the alcohol consumed by teens who drink. Health experts also worry about the effects of new products, especially flavored alcoholic drinks, which seem to encourage young women and girls to drink and drink more. To combat alcohol abuse, many educational institutions, community organizations and government agencies are stepping up efforts to promote abstinence among the young and responsible drinking by adults who do imbibe.

Health experts worry about flavored alcoholic beverages with names that suggest drunkenness, such as Four Loko, which has been called "a binge in a can." Some researchers say the proliferation of such beverages contributes to girls now drinking as much or more than boys.

Inside This Report

THE ISSUES 503
BACKGROUND 510
CHRONOLOGY 511
CURRENT SITUATION 515
AT ISSUE........................517
OUTLOOK 518
BIBLIOGRAPHY 522
THE NEXT STEP 523

CQ Researcher • June 8, 2012 • www.cqresearcher.com
Volume 22, Number 21 • Pages 501-524

CQPRESS

Los Angeles | London | New Delhi
Singapore | Washington DC

RECIPIENT OF SOCIETY OF PROFESSIONAL JOURNALISTS AWARD FOR EXCELLENCE ◆ AMERICAN BAR ASSOCIATION SILVER GAVEL AWARD

THE ISSUES

503 • Should the legal drinking age be lowered?
• Should governments make it more difficult to obtain alcoholic beverages?
• Should colleges ban alcohol from campus?

BACKGROUND

510 **Taxing Booze**
During the Renaissance, beer taxes often were a chief revenue source.

512 **Banning Booze**
Prohibition in the United States and 11 other countries eventually was repealed.

515 **Advertising Booze**
Voluntary bans on broadcast liquor ads ended by 2011.

CURRENT SITUATION

515 **Banning Ads**
Activists want to ban or reduce all alcohol promotion, especially if it reaches children.

516 **Discouraging Abuse**
Governments, colleges and private institutions discourage alcohol abuse.

OUTLOOK

518 **Continuing Debate**
Activists don't expect big changes in alcohol policy in the near future.

SIDEBARS AND GRAPHICS

504 **Heaviest Binge Drinking Occurs in 19 States**
Drinkers ages 18-20 have the highest proportion of binge drinking.

505 **Highs, Lows of U.S. Alcohol Consumption**
Beer drinking has declined since its peak in 1981.

506 **Student Drinking Haunts University**
Communitywide effort helps, but alcohol abuse persists at Maryland's Frostburg State.

508 **Teen Alcohol Abuse Worse in Europe**
The rate of U.S. teen drunkenness is one-third Europe's.

511 **Chronology**
Key events since 8000 B.C.

512 **Health Benefits — or Not — of Alcohol**
"Alcohol is both a tonic and a poison," according to the Harvard School of Public Health.

517 **At Issue**
Would raising alcohol taxes reduce abuse?

FOR FURTHER RESEARCH

521 **For More Information**
Organizations to contact.

522 **Bibliography**
Selected sources used.

523 **The Next Step**
Additional articles.

523 **Citing *CQ Researcher***
Sample bibliography formats.

Cover: AFP/Getty Images/Paul J. Richards

CQ Researcher

June 8, 2012
Volume 22, Number 21

MANAGING EDITOR: Thomas J. Billitteri
tjb@cqpress.com

ASSISTANT MANAGING EDITOR: Kathy Koch
kkoch@cqpress.com

CONTRIBUTING EDITOR: Thomas J. Colin
tcolin@cqpress.com

ASSOCIATE EDITOR: Kenneth Jost

STAFF WRITER: Marcia Clemmitt

CONTRIBUTING WRITERS: Peter Katel, Barbara Mantel, Jennifer Weeks

DESIGN/PRODUCTION EDITOR: Olu B. Davis

ASSISTANT EDITOR: Darrell Dela Rosa

FACT CHECKER: Michelle Harris

Los Angeles | London | New Delhi
Singapore | Washington DC

An Imprint of SAGE Publications, Inc.

VICE PRESIDENT AND EDITORIAL DIRECTOR, HIGHER EDUCATION GROUP:
Michele Sordi

DIRECTOR, ONLINE PUBLISHING:
Todd Baldwin

CQ Researcher (ISSN 1056-2036) is printed on acid-free paper. Published weekly, except: (March wk. 5) (May wk. 4) (July wk. 1) (Aug. wks. 3, 4) (Nov. wk. 4) and (Dec. wks. 3, 4). Published by SAGE Publications, Inc., 2455 Teller Rd., Thousand Oaks, CA 91320. Annual full-service subscriptions start at $1,054. For pricing, call 1-800-834-9020. To purchase a *CQ Researcher* report in print or electronic format (PDF), visit www.cqpress.com or call 866-427-7737. Single reports start at $15. Bulk purchase discounts and electronic-rights licensing are also available. Periodicals postage paid at Thousand Oaks, California, and at additional mailing offices. POSTMASTER: Send address changes to *CQ Researcher*, 2300 N St., N.W., Suite 800, Washington, DC 20037.

Alcohol Abuse

By Tom Price

The Issues

Earlier this year, a jury found former University of Virginia lacrosse player George Huguely V guilty of second-degree murder in the death of his ex-girlfriend, Yeardley Love, also a UVA lacrosse player.

The prosecution's case had been straightforward: Huguely — in a drunken rage — kicked in the door of Love's off-campus apartment shortly before midnight on May 2, 2010, beat her, then left her to die, her head bleeding into a pillow on her bed. Jurors recommended Huguely be sentenced to 26 years in prison. Final sentencing by the judge is Aug. 30. [1]

Huguely and his teammates had begun drinking the day before to celebrate a victory, and Huguely continued almost nonstop until he broke into Love's room. She, too, had been drinking. Her blood-alcohol content was estimated at around 0.14 percent — nearly twice Virginia's limit for driving.

www.pennlive.com

Former University of Virginia lacrosse player George Huguely V faces 26 years in prison after his second-degree murder conviction in the death of his girlfriend, Yeardley Love. Prosecutors said he killed her in a drunken rage after drinking continuously for hours. While drinking and alcohol abuse are generally declining in the United States, they are rising among college students, especially student athletes.

Love's murder may have captured national attention, but the alcohol abuse that fueled it was hardly unusual on college campuses. By many measures, alcohol consumption and abuse are declining in the United States, with one exception: college students, especially student athletes. And alcohol continues to extract a high toll from those who abuse it at all ages.

Nationally, 65 percent of college students told researchers they recently had consumed alcohol, and 44 percent said they had gotten drunk. [2] College students drink more alcohol and binge drink more often than nonstudents of similar ages. While binge drinking by their nonstudent peers and by high-schoolers has declined in recent years, college bingeing has held constant since 1993. [3]

A Health and Human Services Department report suggests that the college environment encourages drinking and that intercollegiate athletics also seem to contribute. [4] Athletes tend to drink more than other students, and lacrosse players tend to drink more than other athletes. [5]

Susan Bruce, who runs UVA's Gordie Center for Substance Abuse Prevention, said athletes may feel pressured to drink if they see teammates drinking. [6] Athletes may have a "work hard, play hard personality type," said Ana Abrantes, an assistant professor at the Brown University Medical School, in Providence, R.I.

Besides worrying about those who overindulge, health experts also are concerned about the effects of new products, especially flavored alcoholic beverages with names that suggest drunkenness, such as Four Loko, Blast and Tilt. Critics say Blast, promoted by rap artist Snoop Dog, is marketed to young African-Americans, noting that it is not generally sold in predominantly white and affluent neighborhoods.

David Jernigan, director of Johns Hopkins University's Center on Alcohol Marketing and Youth, in Baltimore, calls Four Loko "a binge in a can," because the 12 percent alcohol content, sold in 23.5-ounce cans, delivers the kick of four to five beers.

Four Loko and Tilt originally contained caffeine, which made them particularly potent because caffeine counters over-drinkers' tendency to pass out, enabling them to drink more and suffer more harm. [7] Under heavy criticism, the manufacturers removed the stimulants, but students seek the same buzz by mixing alcoholic beverages with stimulant-packed energy drinks, such as Red Bull. [8]

Compared with the trends among college students, drinking statistics for children are almost universally encouraging, although significant numbers of eighth- through 12th-graders still do drink and get drunk. University of Michigan surveys found the percentage of eighth-graders who reported

Heaviest Binge Drinking Occurs in 19 States

Adult bingers in 19 states consume between 7.9 and 9 drinks at one sitting, the nation's heaviest binge-drinking rate. Drinkers ages 18 to 20 have the highest proportion of binge drinking. Binge drinking accounts for 90 percent of the alcoholic beverages consumed by teens, according to the Centers for Disease Control and Prevention.*

No. of Drinks Consumed by Binge Drinkers, 2010
(among adults age 18 and older)

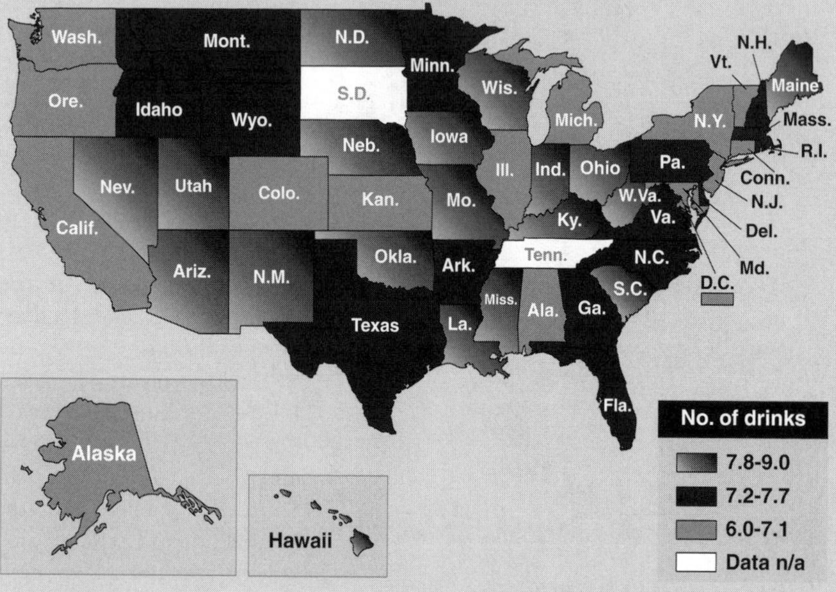

** Binge drinking is commonly defined as consuming five or more drinks at one sitting (four for a woman).*

Source: "Vital Signs: Binge Drinking Prevalence, Frequency, and Intensity Among Adults — United States, 2010," Centers for Disease Control and Prevention, January 2012, www.cdc.gov/mmwr/preview/mmwrhtml/mm6101a4.htm?s_cid=mm6101a4_w.

having consumed alcohol in the previous 30 days fell by nearly half — from 25.1 percent in 1991 to 12.7 percent in 2011. The percentage who said they had gotten drunk in the previous month declined from 7.6 to 4.4. Twelfth-grade drinking dropped from 54 to 40 percent and drunkenness from 31.6 percent to 25. [9]

Scholars worry about the habits of those who do drink, however. According to the Centers for Disease Control and Prevention (CDC), binge drinking accounts for 90 percent of alcohol consumed by teens, and more than half by adults. [10]

Some researchers suggest that the proliferation of flavored alcoholic beverages contributes to girls now drinking as much or more than boys. American Medical Association surveys found that girls are more likely than boys to drink flavored beverages, and 82 percent of girls who tried flavored alcohol said it tastes better than other alcoholic drinks. [11] Four Loko "tastes like candy" and is "a faster way to get drunk," a 17-year-old female high school junior said. [12]

But young people are not the only population segment with excessive drinking problems. While drinkers 18 to 20 have the highest proportion of drinkers who binge, older bingers — age 65 and above — binge more often. [13] And adult women — especially those who exercise and are more highly educated — are imbibing more than in the past. [14]

Excessive drinking kills 80,000 Americans each year and drains more than $220 billion from the economy, according to the CDC. [15] About 4,700 young Americans die each year because of underage drinking. [16] But heavy drinkers hurt more than themselves. Excessive drinking killed 10,228 people on American roads in 2010, a number that's been on a fairly steady decline since 1982, when 26,173 died in alcohol-related crashes. [17]

Tragically, hard-drinking parents often pass alcohol abuse and other ailments on to their children. "Children from addictive families tend to drink at earlier ages, tend to have more problems as a result of their drinking and tend to cross the line over to addiction at younger ages," says Jerry Moe, national director of children's programs at the Betty Ford Institute, in Palm Desert, Calif., which fights addiction through research, prevention and education programs.

A mother who drinks during pregnancy may have a newborn with fetal alcohol syndrome — central nervous system damage that can lead to deficiencies in academic performance, communication, memory, attention and decision-making. But children of heavy drinkers can suffer the greatest problems, such as physical and mental defects that leave them more likely to abuse alcohol themselves, commit crimes and wind up in jail. [18]

As government, education and health leaders grapple with problem drinking, here are some of the questions they're asking:

Should the legal drinking age be lowered?

A group of college presidents — now numbering 136 — raised a lot of eyebrows in 2008 when they signed a petition calling for the United States to lower the drinking age from 21.

The educators, organized by Middlebury College President Emeritus John McCardell Jr., argued that the higher drinking age encourages under-age college students to get drunk at clandestine parties rather than learn to drink responsibly in public. The presidents suggested that states be allowed to issue drinking licenses to 18-year-olds who complete an alcohol-education program. They would lose the license if they violated drinking laws.

"I don't believe one wakes up on a particular birthday and is automatically capable of exercising mature judgment about alcohol," McCardell says. "When a young person reaches driving age, we don't simply toss them the keys to a car and say go figure it out."

McCardell, now vice chancellor of the University of the South in Sewanee, Tenn., complains that current law prevents colleges from teaching students to drink responsibly, because teachers and administrators only can preach abstinence to students.

The National Youth Rights Association attacks the current drinking age as unfair to individuals who are considered adults for other purposes. "What does it say about us as a country that we're willing to send our young people overseas to fight and defend our freedom, but when they get home we target them as not responsible enough to enjoy a drink with friends or family?" association Vice President Jeffrey Nadel asks.

Citing what he calls the "forbidden fruit effect," the 19-year-old University of Pennsylvania freshman calls current law counterproductive. "Other countries don't stigmatize alcohol as we do," he says. "People drink healthily and responsibly and don't binge drink."

Highs, Lows of U.S. Alcohol Consumption

Measured by the amount of actual alcohol (ethanol) in each drink, Americans drink less beer per capita than they did in 1981, when consumption peaked, but considerably more than in 1850. Wine consumption hovers near its 1986 peak and is more than five times its low point, in 1934 — the year after Prohibition ended. Liquor consumption is about a third of its peak in 1860.

Estimated Per Capita Alcohol Consumption*
(in gallons, 1850-2009)

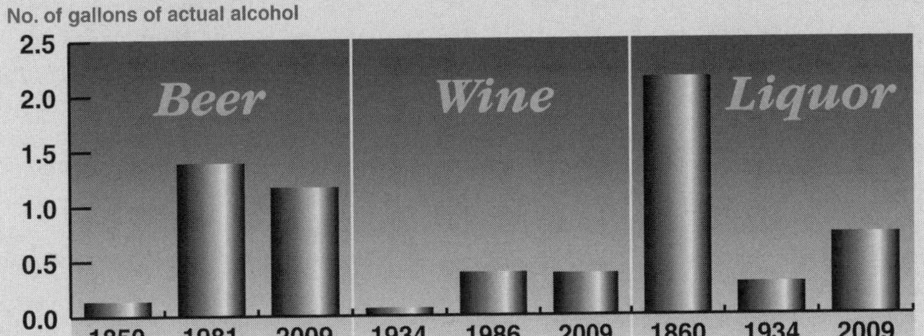

** Based on reported use by those age 15 and older prior to 1970 and age 14 and older thereafter.*

Source: "Apparent Per Capita Ethanol Consumption, United States, 1850-2009," National Institutes of Health, August 2011, pubs.niaaa.nih.gov/publications/Surveillance92/tab1_09.htm

Although individual states have the authority to set their own minimum drinking age, all 50 states adopted a 21-year-old minimum age after Congress passed the National Minimum Uniform Drinking Age Act in 1984, at the urging of President Ronald Reagan. Under that law, states with a lower drinking age lose 10 percent of their federal highway funding. [19] Within four years all the states had complied, and none has lowered its drinking age since.

However, Rep. Jack Kingston, R-Ga., has introduced legislation to lower the drinking age to 18 on military bases, and several state lawmakers introduced similar bills in 2011 and 2012, according to the National Conference of State Legislatures. [20] The moves have been opposed by military officials, including former Defense Secretary Robert Gates. [21] None has become law.

The proposals also have faced stiff opposition from health and safety experts, government officials and even the head of the Distilled Spirits Council of the United States. Lowering the drinking age would increase alcohol abuse by youths under 21, including those younger than 18, they warn.

"All the seniors in high school would be of legal drinking age," Jennifer Salerno, who runs the University of Michigan's Regional Alliance for Healthy Schools, points out. As a result, "the 18-year-olds may be buying 15- and 16-year-olds alcohol."

Timothy Naimi, an associate professor at the Boston University School of Medicine, says damage would occur at even younger ages. At college, 21-year-olds buy alcohol for their younger classmates, he says. Young teenagers aren't likely to score booze from college students, Naimi points out, but "13- and 14-year-olds do know 18-year-olds."

Student Drinking Haunts University

Communitywide effort helps, but alcohol abuse persists.

The costs of student alcohol abuse became tragically clear to Jonathan Gibralter in September 2006, shortly after he became president of Frostburg State University (FSU) in western Maryland. A local resident was assaulted and nearly killed by a student who had been at an off-campus party where drinking occurred. [1] Earlier that year, before Gibralter took office, an inebriated student drowned in his own vomit in his off-campus house. [2]

The incidents led Gibralter to launch a comprehensive campaign against alcohol abuse. The efforts have garnered national recognition for the president and the school.

The National Institute on Alcohol Abuse and Alcoholism appointed Gibralter to its College Presidents Working Group, created to help determine what research and informational materials would be most effective in combating alcohol abuse among students. A group of national educational organizations gave Gibralter its Presidential Leadership Award, which came with a $50,000 grant to support college projects to combat alcohol problems. [3] The state has given the school special grants to fund anti-alcohol activities. And Frostburg State was invited to join 31 other colleges in a nationwide project to test the effectiveness of anti-alcohol-abuse strategies.

Despite it all, alcohol-related tragedy continues to haunt Frostburg State.

Students still attend alcohol-centered parties in off-campus housing, sometimes paying an admission fee for the opportunity to enter and drink. [4] In November, a student stabbed another to death outside such a party, and police said alcohol likely played a role. [5]

Brandon Busteed, founder of one of the organizations that presented the Presidential Leadership Award, said it's not surprising that Frostburg students still drink to excess. "Even on campuses that are doing some of the best work, the issue is still such a big problem that all of us are a heartbeat away from potential disaster," he said. [6]

Gibralter himself lamented that "we don't always have control over where [students] are and what they do." [7] The campaign against alcohol abuse is an endless task, he said. "Every year, we get a new group of students, and we have to start all over again."

The incidents at Frostburg State — in 2006 and last year — highlight the fact that the challenge of student drinking extends beyond campus. The broader community contributes to the problem and must be part of the solution, Gibralter says. To bridge the town-gown gap, Gibralter created a community task force to guide the university's campaign against alcohol abuse. Members include students, faculty, administrators and local residents — among them a bar owner and a rental-property manager. Gibralter and other university representatives also meet regularly with local residents to discuss mutual concerns.

One such meeting, in late 2008, demonstrated the community's interest in the college and Gibralter's style of leadership. Gibralter had invited bar owners and beverage distributors to campus to discuss how they could help reduce student alcohol abuse. "I was told nobody would show up," he recalls. But "it was standing room only." Among the attendees: bar owners, bar managers, bartenders, beer distributors, the mayor, police chief and members of the Allegany County Liquor Board.

A local newspaper described Gibralter's requests of the group, including putting all bartenders through Training for Intervention Procedures (TIP), which teaches servers' legal responsibilities, how to recognize intoxication, how to refuse service to inebriated customers without instigating a confrontation and how to spot fake IDs.

Training all servers would be a significant expense, one bar owner noted, saying: "It would help if FSU would sponsor a training session or something to help offset the costs."

"Consider it done," Gibralter replied. [8]

Now, a university employee is studying to become a TIP instructor, so Frostburg State can offer free training on a regular

There also are scientific reasons to oppose younger drinking, the Betty Ford Institute's Moe says. "We're learning that brains aren't fully developed until about age 25," he explains, so underage drinking can interfere with healthy brain development.

In addition, say opponents of a lower drinking age, alcohol-related traffic fatalities fell significantly when the drinking age was raised. And, they argue, evidence from other countries shows that early drinking leads to more alcohol abuse. Most countries allow 18-year-olds (or younger) to drink, and many have worse drinking problems than the United States. (*See graph, p. 508.*) [22]

According to the World Health Organization, for instance, Europe has the world's highest per-capita illness and death caused by alcohol. European Union residents are the world's heaviest-drinking people, and binge drinking is common among all age groups across the continent. [23]

The European School Survey Project on Alcohol and Other Drugs, an ongoing research effort in more than 40 European countries, found last year that 57 percent of 15- and 16-year-olds reported drinking within the previous 30 days, and 39 percent reported "heavy episodic drinking." [24] In a comparable U.S. survey last year, 13 percent of eighth- and 27 percent of 10th-graders reported drinking at all, while 4 percent of eighth- and 14 percent of 10th-graders said they got drunk. [25]

basis. To combat increasingly sophisticated fake IDs, the school will use a state grant to supply bars with ID scanners that read magnetic strips, bar codes and other information on cards to search for evidence of counterfeiting.

Prevention begins with incoming freshmen, who are required to take an online alcohol-education class; parents can take the class as well. The university also conducts a "social-norming" campaign, in which results of student surveys are used to demonstrate that drinking and bingeing are less common than many students assume. The message is splashed on posters, T-shirts, bracelets and in the campus newspaper, explains Associate Dean of Students Jeff Graham. Students also run an anti-drinking peer-education program.

According to the Centers for Disease Control and Prevention's Community Preventive Services Task Force, when students overestimate how much their peers drink, they're more likely to drink excessively themselves. [9]

The university offers alcohol-free housing and activities, such as laser-tag tournaments that begin at about 10 p.m., when many students would be headed for drinking parties or bars. Administrators also encourage faculty to offer more Friday classes to discourage students from beginning weekend partying on Thursday afternoons.

It's also "critically important to combine prevention efforts with enforcement efforts," Gibralter says. That includes "giving clear messages about high-risk behavior and the resulting consequences," Graham adds.

University policy permits students over 21 to have alcoholic beverages in their rooms, but nowhere else in the residence halls. A first violation of alcohol rules brings a $75 fine and requires participation in a $25 alcohol-education program and notification of parents or guardians. Subsequent offenses carry heavier penalties, including possible suspension from school. Students also can face additional fines for violating state law.

Because most problem drinking occurs off campus, the university pays for extra Frostburg Police Department patrols and has obtained authority from the city for university police to enforce the law off campus.

Gibralter says alcohol use is down, based on student surveys, indicating that the university's efforts have helped to reduce drinking and bingeing. In 1997, 90 percent of Frostburg students said they drank in the previous 30 days. This year, 64 percent said they did. Bingeing during the previous two weeks dropped from 59 percent to 41 percent. The average number of drinks consumed per week by students who did drink dropped by more than half, from 9.5 to 3.9. [10]

— Tom Price

[1] Robin Wilson, "Despite Alcohol Crackdown, the Party Goes On," *The Chronicle of Higher Education*, Dec. 5, 2008, p. 1.

[2] "Regional Digest," *The* (Annapolis) *Capital*, March 28, 2006, p. 4.

[3] Jennifer Raley, "FSU president receives award for diminishing role of alcohol," *Cumberland Times-News*, Sept. 5, 2008, http://times-news.com/archive/x1540432728.

[4] Wilson, *op. cit.*

[5] Susan Reimer, "Frostburg student fatally stabbed at off-campus party," *The Baltimore Sun*, Nov. 7, 2011, http://articles.baltimoresun.com/2011-11-07/news/bs-md-student-frostburg-killed-20111106_1_stab-wound-frostburg-student-witnesses; and Peter Hermann, "Officials: Drinking likely played a role in slaying of Frostburg student," *The Baltimore Sun*, Nov. 7, 2011, http://articles.baltimoresun.com/2011-11-07/news/bs-md-frostburg-killing-20111107_1_shanee-liggins-binge-drinking-back-to-back-parties.

[6] Wilson, *op. cit.*

[7] Reimer, *op. cit.*

[8] Kristin Harty, "Frostburg bar owners meet with university president," *Cumberland Times-News*, Dec. 14, 2008, http://times-news.com/archive/x1540440018.

[9] "4 Tiers," National Institute on Alcohol Abuse and Alcoholism, July 11, 2007, www.collegedrinkingprevention.gov/StatsSummaries/4tier.aspx.

[10] "Core Survey," in "Comparison of Alcohol and Other Drug Use," Frostburg State University.

McCardell says he could accept forbidding drinking for 18-year-olds still in high school. But he and Nadel reject the other arguments against the presidents' proposal. For instance, McCardell asks, if the brain doesn't mature until age 25, why aren't proponents of the higher drinking age recommending that it be raised to 25? And although drinking among college students has declined, he points out, binge drinking has not.

"Alcohol-related traffic fatalities have gone down in every age group" for many reasons — not just the higher drinking age, he says. Tougher drunken-driving laws have helped, he says, as have stricter enforcement, increased seat-belt use, safer cars and improved emergency medical care. [26]

Should governments make it more difficult to obtain alcoholic beverages?

Some of the world's most prestigious health agencies want governments to raise barriers between drinkers and alcohol.

The World Health Organization last year called for hiking alcohol taxes, restricting sales and banning some alcohol advertising. [27] In the United States, the CDC's Community Preventive Services Task Force recommended six actions to reduce alcohol abuse:

- Raising alcohol taxes;
- Cracking down on sales to minors;

Teen Alcohol Abuse Worse in Europe

About 14 percent of U.S. 10th-graders said in 2011 that they had been drunk in the past 30 days, compared with nearly 40 percent in Europe, where the legal drinking age is 18 or younger.

Percentage Drunk Within the Past Month, 2011

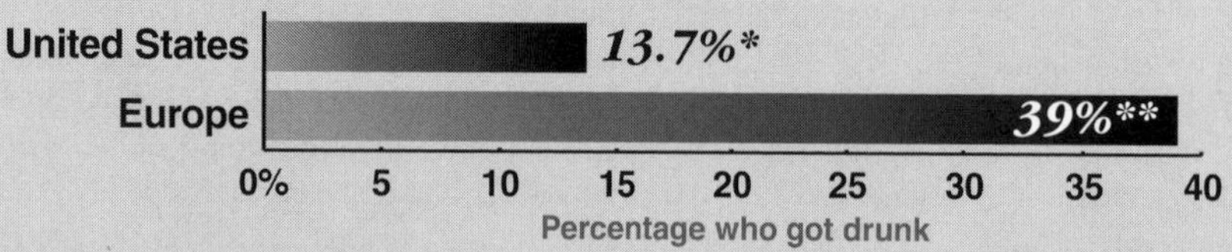

* *10th-graders who had "been drunk"*

** *15- and 16-year-olds who participated in "heavy episodic drinking"*

Sources: "The 2011 ESPAD Report: Substance Abuse Among Students in 35 Countries," European Monitoring Centre for Drugs and Drug Addiction, 2012; "Trends in Annual Prevalence of Use of Various Drugs in Grades 8, 10, and 12," Monitoring the Future, 2011, www.monitoringthefuture.org/data/11data/pr11t2.pdf

• Limiting the number of places that sell alcoholic beverages;

• Holding servers or owners of alcohol-dispensing establishments liable for customers who drink too much and then injure or kill others in drunken-driving accidents;

• Limiting the hours or days when alcohol can be sold;

• Retaining government monopolies on distribution of alcoholic beverages. [28]

Industry representatives say restrictive measures aimed at the total population don't reduce alcohol abuse. Studies cited by advocates of restrictions show correlations but don't prove cause and effect, the industry argues. And tax hikes would be unfair and damage the economy, they say. In fact, the Beer Institute is trying to roll back the $18-a-barrel federal excise tax to its pre-1991 level of $9. [29]

When Maryland raised its sales tax on alcoholic beverages to 9 percent from 6 percent last year, Sarah Longwell, managing director of the American Beverage Institute, complained that the higher levy "burdens Maryland's poorest consumers with a highly regressive tax" and could have a "serious adverse impact" on restaurant jobs. [30]

And, in a letter to state legislators, the heads of the Beer Institute, the Distilled Spirits Council and the Wine Institute warned that the tax hike would hurt Maryland businesses because out-of-state consumers would stay away. [31]

"History has shown that, as prices go up, sales go down — and jobs go away," they wrote. [32]

But supporters of higher taxes argue that reducing sales leads to reduced consumption, which makes for a healthier population and lower costs for alcohol-related medical care and emergency room visits.

However, Distilled Spirits Council President Peter Cressy contends that reducing sales has little impact on alcohol abusers. "They simply drink down," he says. "They drink a lower-priced product." Higher taxes, however, hit the responsible drinker who is price-conscious, he argues.

Cressy also contends that abusers are not affected by reducing the hours alcohol can be sold or the number of premises that can sell it. "You can't demonstrate in the . . . real world that [limiting] access has had a negative impact on social indices [of alcohol abuse] or that curtailing access in the future will," Cressy says. "Correlation is not causation."

What works, he says, is action that specifically targets the abuser. "The evidence suggests that education, tough laws [such as those against drunken driving] and tough enforcement are far more effective."

However, the CDC task force cited studies that support its recommendations, and other proponents of restricting access say there's plenty of evidence to back their positions.

For instance, Philip Cook, senior associate dean for faculty and research at Duke University's Sanford School of Public Policy, who has studied alcohol economics for 30 years, says his first paper in a peer-reviewed journal in 1982 documented that state liquor taxes reduced cirrhosis mortality rates.

"Among economists who study this topic, it is now well established that drinking decisions are influenced by price, and people who drink heavily will particularly be influenced by price," says Cook, a professor of public policy studies, economics and sociology at Duke. "When the tax or price goes up, we see reductions in the consequences of alcohol abuse."

Young people are especially responsive to price or tax hikes, according to the National Institute on Alcohol Abuse and Alcoholism. "Higher beer prices tend to decrease drinking and binge drinking among U.S. college students," the institute reported.

Taxes need to be raised because their effectiveness has eroded over time, argues Boston University's Naimi. Most alcohol taxes are levied on the volume sold rather than on the price, so they've stayed constant even though inflation has pushed prices much higher, he explains. Returning the federal beer tax to its 1991 level is the opposite of what needs to be done, Naimi says.

Jernigan at The Johns Hopkins Center on Alcohol Marketing and Youth contends that, because of inflation, the alcohol industry essentially gets a tax cut every year.

Toben Nelson, an assistant professor of public health at the University of Minnesota, says studies clearly link alcohol abuse to the number of sales outlets and how long they're open. "We know from a lot of research that the problems associated with alcohol use are really a function of how available alcohol is," he says. "Make alcohol less available and people will drink less of it and cause fewer problems."

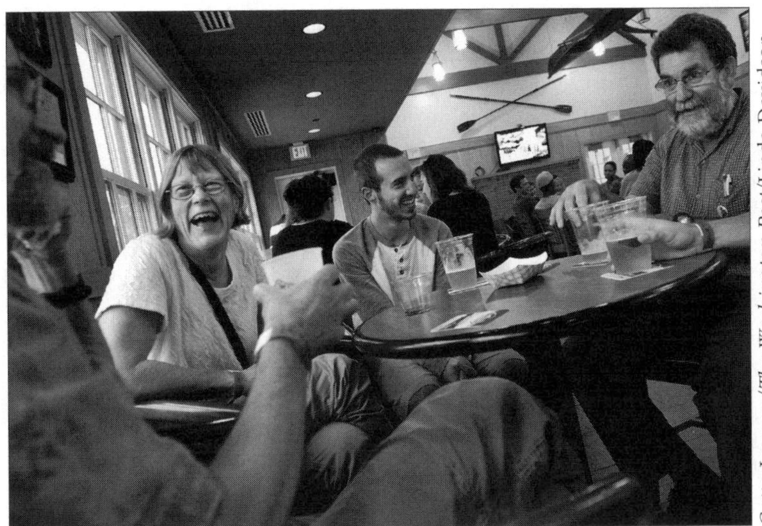

Getty Images/*The Washington Post*/Linda Davidson

Zach Alexander, a senior at St. Mary's College, in Maryland, enjoys a beer with his professors at an on-campus bar, on May 9, 2012. More than 130 college presidents have signed a petition calling for lowering the drinking age from 21, arguing that the higher threshold encourages under-age college students to get drunk at clandestine parties rather than learn to drink responsibly in public.

Furthermore, privatizing state alcohol-distribution monopolies increases consumption, Naimi says, because state stores tend to spend less on advertising and operate fewer outlets than private liquor stores.

The CDC task force cited a 2011 review of 11 studies showing "strong evidence" that motor vehicle fatalities and other alcohol-rated harm are reduced by holding bartenders and establishment owners liable for their inebriated customers' behavior. [33]

Should colleges ban alcohol from campus?

When Robert Carothers became president of the University of Rhode Island in 1991, his first challenges were erasing the institution's party-school reputation and raising students' academic performance.

"I found I wasn't going to achieve that with a significant portion of the community hung over from Thursday to Monday," he said. So in 1996, after five years of failing to overcome those challenges, he banned alcohol at all campus events, including faculty dinners, university fundraisers, fraternity parties, sporting events and alumni homecoming celebrations.

"It was very, very difficult to stay the course in the face of criticisms," Carothers said later. But binge drinking dropped significantly, applicants' SAT scores rose and the university stopped attracting students seeking a party-school experience, he said. [34]

That was then.

Today, URI students of legal age can have alcohol in their rooms. University sports fans can again drink while tailgating. Alcohol is served in the president's house, the Alumni Center, the University Club, the basketball/entertainment/convention center and the headquarters of the school's fundraising arm, the URI Foundation. Alcohol also is allowed elsewhere on campus, with written permission from a university official. [35]

David M. Dooley, who succeeded Carothers in 2009, said Carothers' policies had achieved their goals and alcohol now could be safely reintroduced to campus. University officials expected the availability of alcohol to increase participation in alumni and foundation events, along with school profits from alcohol sales. [36]

Most colleges have not imposed a campus-wide prohibition. But many are adopting policies to reduce the availability of alcohol.

Campus prohibition would be counterproductive, said Dartmouth President Jim Yong Kim, a public-health expert. "If we ban alcohol on campus, rather than our young people drinking here, they get in cars and drive, which just accentuates the danger," explained Kim, who becomes World Bank president in July. [37]

Nelson of the University of Minnesota agrees that colleges should focus on sources of alcohol in neighborhoods near campus. But, he adds, "Colleges that do ban alcohol have less drinking and drinking problems among their students. At sporting events where alcohol is less available — including in the stadium and tailgating — students are less likely to binge drink."

The CDC task force said there is some evidence that campus prohibition works, but that scholars need to do "more comprehensive evaluation." The task force also called for more research on the effectiveness of banning keg parties, establishing alcohol-free dormitories, prohibiting tailgating with heavy drinking and restricting or banning alcohol at sports events.

Those steps "are particularly appealing because straightforward and relatively brief evaluations should indicate whether they would be successful in reducing high-risk drinking on a particular campus," the task force said. [38]

Some colleges are conducting practical tests of those and other ideas, which Kim said is a good idea.

"Every campus is different," he said. "There are rural campuses where most of the drinking happens on campus. There are city campuses where the big problem is bars that ring the outskirts of the campuses." [39]

Harvard University is pairing stricter oversight of undergraduate drinking with relaxation of one recently instituted ban. Effective in the fall, beer, wine and malt drinks — but not hard liquor such as rum and whiskey — will be permitted at public social events. The events must be registered and can't serve alcohol for more than five hours. Spirits will be allowed at private parties in a student's dorm room, as long as the hosts are at least 21 and they demonstrate to their residence hall tutor a "satisfactory understanding of strategies to create safe social environments."

In announcing that spirits again will be allowed at some formal dances, Harvard officials described the policy as a pilot program to test whether students can drink responsibly. [40]

Thirty-two schools — from Boston University to Stanford, and including Rhode Island and Dartmouth — have joined the Learning Collaborative on High-Risk Drinking to test promising policies. Under the initiative, the schools will implement a variety of programs, measure results, share their findings and try to determine what works best.

"We all have methods of prevention that work some of the time," Cornell President David Skorton said. "By pooling our ideas, we have a better chance of finding solutions that improve our success rates." [41]

St. Mary's College in rural southern Maryland decided to teach responsible drinking this year by opening an on-campus pub where students mingle with faculty and administrators. It followed an alcohol-free first week of classes last fall — to make sure freshmen got a sober introduction to campus — and a year-long responsible-drinking campaign.

"What doesn't work is telling them not to drink," St. Mary's President Joseph Urgo said. "Talking to them about drinking, as adults, helps." [42] ■

BACKGROUND

Taxing Booze

The Chinese began brewing beer more than 7,000 years ago, and a rudimentary form of the beverage has been traced back 10,000 years to the Near East. For a long time it — and, later, other alcoholic drinks — were considered the healthiest beverages. [43]

"Water was very, very unhealthy, so people consumed beer," Belgian economist Johan Swinnen explained. For Europeans, "it wasn't until coffee and tea were imported in the 16th and 17th centuries (and made with boiling water) that people could drink nonpolluted things that were not alcoholic." [44]

Ancient beer would not have appeared healthy to today's Americans. Early brewers tended not to filter their beer, which commonly was served in a large jar and had yeast and hulls floating on the surface, Swinnen wrote in his 2011 book, *The Economics of Beer*. Early drinkers used straws to suck out their beer through the flotsam.

Wine (fermented fruit juice) and mead (fermented honey and water) likely were discovered as early as beer, *Economist* Business Editor Tom Standage writes in his 2006 book, *A History of the World in 6 Glasses*. But beer and its primary ingredient — grain — could be stored more successfully than wine, mead, fruit or honey, and honey was in short supply. So beer became the more practical beverage. [45]

By 3000 B.C. the brewer's art had moved through Mesopotamia into Europe. Ancient Greeks brewed beer. So did the Romans, although they preferred wine, which the Greeks came to prefer as well. Roman conquests spread winemaking throughout much of the continent.

As Europeans began to explore the Americas, they brought stores of beer, assuming the New World's water would be polluted. Although they brought their own brewing technology from the old country, they also discovered some Native Americans brewing their own version of the beverage.

The explorers and traders also packed distilled spirits, which Standage called "alcohol in a compact, durable form ideal for sea transit." [46] For currency in the Atlantic slave trade, Europeans used rum, which was distilled from byproducts of sugar-processing in the Caribbean.

Alcoholic beverages were a regular part of the American diet from the days of the colonists. Even the Pilgrims drank beer. And the Puritan ship *Arbella* listed "42 Tonnes of Beere" — about 10,000 gallons — on its manifest. [47]

But rum became the most popular American drink because it packed a punch, was cheap to make and could be shipped relatively inexpensively from the Caribbean. By the late 17th century, it became even cheaper, as New Englanders imported molasses and distilled the spirit themselves. By the 1730s, Americans were consuming four gallons of rum a year for every adult and child, and children were among the drinkers. The colonists' "rum punch" — rum, water, sugar, lemon juice and spices — was a forerunner of the modern cocktail, Standage writes.

After the American Revolution, more Americans moved west, where homegrown grains were more plentiful than imported molasses. Whiskey, made from grain, soon surpassed rum as the nation's favorite drink.

Alcoholic beverages faced government regulation from early times — for economic rather than health or safety

Continued on p. 512

Chronology

8000-3000 B.C.

Humans make alcoholic beverages, begin using them widely.

8000 B.C.
Simple beer brewed in Near East.

5000 B.C.
Chinese begin brewing beer.

3000 B.C.
Brewing reaches Europe. Governments begin regulating brewing.

1400s-1700s

Alcoholic beverages accompany exploration in the Americas.

1400s-1500s
Fearful of unclean water, European explorers introduce brewing to New World. Spirits serve as currency for Atlantic slave trade. Beer taxes finance European governments.

1600s
Europeans begin distilling rum in the Caribbean; rum becomes Americans' favorite drink, and New Englanders begin distilling it.

Late 1700s
Western settlers distill whiskey from grain; it soon becomes nation's favorite drink.

1791
U.S. government imposes alcohol tax to help pay off Revolutionary War debt. Three years later Western distillers launch anti-tax Whiskey Rebellion.

1860s-1930s

U.S. temperance movements succeed in banning alcohol in a third of the states and territories; later, alcohol is banned nationwide for 14 years.

1860s
States repeal early alcohol bans.

1919
Eighteenth Amendment imposes Prohibition, banning liquor nationwide, beginning in 1920.

1920s
Widespread flouting of Prohibition, rise of organized crime build pressure to repeal 18th Amendment.

1933
Twenty-first Amendment repeals 18th Amendment, leaving alcohol regulation up to the states. Most set legal drinking age at 21.

1936
Liquor producers voluntarily abstain from advertising on radio and in 1948 on TV.

1950s-1980s

Alcoholism is recognized as a disease. States lower drinking age during Vietnam War but raise it again after pressure from mothers' group.

1954
Psychiatrist Morris Chafetz campaigns to define alcoholism as disease.

1956
American Medical Association declares alcoholism a disease.

1966
Mississippi is last state to repeal statewide Prohibition.

Early 1970s
More than two dozen states lower drinking age to 18 or 19. Drunken-driving crashes involving the young increase, triggering campaign to reset drinking age to 21.

1980
Mothers Against Drunk Driving founded.

1984
Federal legislation cuts U.S. highway aid for states with under-21 drinking age. Within four years all states have raised their drinking age to 21. Drunken-driving deaths drop by more than half by 2010.

1990s-2000s

Liquor ads begin on TV, but alcohol use declines.

1996
Seagram airs TV liquor ad on cable sports network and a local Texas broadcast station. Industry drops its broadcast-ad ban, but TV and most radio networks reject liquor ads.

2001
NBC agrees to run TV liquor ads, then backs down under public pressure. Ads increase on cable, local stations.

2011
Except for college students, Americans are drinking and bingeing less than in previous 20 years, but girls are drinking as much or more than boys, partly — experts suggest — due to proliferation of flavored alcoholic beverages. . . . ABC and CBS begin accepting liquor ads on late-night programming.

2012
NBC allows late-night liquor advertising. . . . Governments debate allowing liquor ads in public facilities. . . . Governments, colleges ramp up campaigns against alcohol abuse.

Health Benefits — or Not — of Alcohol

"Alcohol is both a tonic and a poison."

Humans have long had a complex relationship with alcohol. In the Bible, Paul advised Timothy to "no longer drink only water, but use a little wine for the sake of your stomach and your frequent ailments." [1]

The marketing slogan — "A day without orange juice is like a day without sunshine" — was pirated from French author Anthelme Brillat-Savarin, who in 1825 likened a day without sunshine to "a meal without wine." [2] But Jule Renard, another French author, noted in his journal that "to succeed you must add water to your wine until there is no more wine." [3]

Modern science appears equally conflicted about the merits of wine, beer and distilled spirits. Jill U. Adams, a journalist pondering the confusion, began a *Los Angeles Times* story noting recent research that found women who drink moderately are more likely to develop breast cancer and have a higher chance of suffering gastrointestinal problems, but will live longer after a heart attack and suffer from less asthma or dementia. And if they drink wine, they'll have stronger bones.

"Is your head spinning yet?" she asked, as an editor added the helpful sub-headline: "It could drive one to drink." [4]

The Harvard School of Public Health sums up the situation: "It's safe to say that alcohol is both a tonic and a poison." [5]

Some studies, for instance, have found that alcohol postpones or reduces the likelihood of dementia, heart disease, diabetes, early death, arthritis, enlarged prostate, osteoporosis, gallbladder disease, kidney and thyroid cancer, stroke and circulatory problems. [6] Other studies show that consuming alcohol can increase the likelihood of dementia, heart disease, early death, liver disorders, brain disease, fatigue, weight gain, obesity, bloating, broken veins, depression, digestive disorders, sexual difficulties, muscle disease, immune system disorders, pancreatitis and breast, mouth, throat, neck, larynx, bowel and colorectal cancer. [7]

According to the National Institutes of Health, drinking too much can worsen diabetes, high blood pressure, congestive heart failure, liver problems, memory difficulties, depression and anxiety. Alcohol also can decrease the effectiveness of some medicines and make some medicines dangerous or deadly. [8]

Most studies say that moderation — usually defined as one drink a day for women and two for men — is the key to healthy drinking. A drink generally is described as 12 ounces of beer, five ounces of wine or 1.5 ounces of spirits.

Several studies have examined whether the risks increase or decrease with age. According to the NIH, older people are more sensitive to alcohol because their bodies contain less water and break down alcohol more slowly, leaving a higher concentration of alcohol in the blood. [9]

But alcohol appears to have beneficial effects on both older and younger people who are at risk of developing heart disease. For instance, the famed Mayo Clinic in Rochester, Minn., found that the risks from drinking alcohol exceed the benefits until middle age — except for younger people with a particular risk of developing heart disease. [10] *Consumer Reports* also said that drinking — in moderation — seems to benefit those at increased risk of heart disease after age 40 (for men) and 50 (for women). [11] Yet another study, which followed 60- to 79-year-olds for nine years, found that those with low risk of

Continued from p. 510

reasons. Historian Richard Unger traced government oversight of brewing to the Fourth millennium B.C. Beer taxes were the chief income source for many towns and European governments during the Renaissance. In the 15th to 17th centuries, beer taxes raised half the revenue in what is now Belgium and the Netherlands, according to Swinnen. [48]

In 1591, the English ambassador to Russia described Ivan the Terrible encouraging his subjects to drink in order to maximize tax receipts, according to Mark Lawrence Schrad, an assistant professor of political science at Pennsylvania's Villanova University. [49]

In the United States in 1791, the federal alcohol excise tax helped to pay Revolutionary War debt. Treasury Secretary Alexander Hamilton linked the tax to public health as well, suggesting the tax would discourage consumption and be "favourable to the agriculture, to the economy, to the morals and to the health of the society." [50] The tax started at seven cents per gallon and increased with the alcohol content of the drink.

Distillers balked at the levy and launched the Whiskey Rebellion, which drew about 6,000 armed men to a French and Indian-War battlefield near Pittsburgh in 1794. President George Washington dispatched 13,000 militiamen to the scene, but the rebellion had collapsed before the federal troops arrived. In a few years, however, the tax collapsed, too, as Congress repealed the levy and the American whiskey industry grew. Distillers in Bourbon County, Ky., began making whiskey from corn instead of rye, and America's signature drink was born.

Even Washington got into the business, setting up five whiskey stills at his Mount Vernon estate. In 1799, the year of his death, his stills produced 11,000 gallons of rye.

Banning Booze

By early in the next century, Americans' consumption of alcoholic beverages was three times today's rate. And the nation's first temperance move-

heart disease who took two or three drinks daily tended to live longer than teetotalers. Those who took four or more drinks a day had the same death rate as abstainers. And among those at risk of heart disease, even the heavier drinkers fared better than those who didn't drink. [12]

Getty Images/Allsport/Pascal Rondeau

Modern science appears conflicted about the merits of wine, beer and distilled spirits. Some studies indicate alcohol postpones or reduces the likelihood of dementia and other disease; other studies say alcohol increases the likelihood of the same ailments.

One final apparent contradiction: Despite acknowledging the benefits of moderate drinking, many experts recommend that abstainers continue to refrain. "No one should begin drinking or drink more frequently on the basis of potential health benefits," the Mayo Clinic advised. "But if you do drink alcohol and you're healthy, there's probably no need to stop as long as you drink responsibly and in moderation." [13]

— Tom Price

[1] First Timothy, 5:23, Holy Bible, Revised Standard Version, http://quod.lib.umich.edu/cgi/r/rsv/rsv-idx?type=DIV1&byte=5399468.

[2] John Bartlett, *Familiar Quotations* (1968), p. 484.

[3] *Ibid.*, p. 869.

[4] Jill U. Adams, "Women weigh a cocktail of risks," *Los Angeles Times*, Nov. 21, 2011, p. E1.

[5] "Alcohol: Balancing Risks and Benefits," The Nutrition Source, Harvard School of Public Health, www.hsph.harvard.edu/nutritionsource/what-should-you-eat/alcohol-full-story/index.html.

[6] Rose Prince, "Am I drinking too much?" *The* (London) *Telegraph*, Jan. 9, 2012, www.telegraph.co.uk/health/wellbeing/8998675/Am-I-drinking-too-much.html. Also see Adams, *op. cit.*, and "Alcohol: Balancing Risks and Benefits," *op. cit.*

[7] Prince, *op. cit.* Also see Adams, *op. cit.*; "Alcohol Use and Older Adults," National Institutes of Health, http://nihseniorhealth.gov/alcoholuse/alcoholandaging/01.html; Selene Yeager, "Exercise and Alcohol: Running on Empty Bottles," *Women's Health*, March 2012, www.womenshealthmag.com/health/exercise-and-alcohol?page=1; "Alcohol use: If you drink, keep it moderate," Mayo Clinic, www.mayoclinic.com/health/alcohol/SC00024; and "Alcohol: Balancing Risks and Benefits," *op. cit.*

[8] "Alcohol Use and Older Adults," *op. cit.*

[9] *Ibid.*

[10] "Alcohol use: If you drink, keep it moderate," *op. cit.*

[11] "The risks and benefits of drinking alcohol," *Consumer Reports*, June 2010, www.consumerreports.org/health/conditions-and-treatments/the-risks-and-benefits-of-drinking-alcohol/overview/index.htm.

[12] Stanton Peele, "The Hidden Health Benefits of Alcohol?" *The Huffington Post*, Aug. 16, 2010, www.huffingtonpost.com/stanton-peele/the-hidden-health-benefit_b_679321.html.

[13] "Alcohol use: If you drink, keep it moderate," *op. cit.*

ment sought to remove alcohol from the national diet — with substantial success. By 1855, alcohol was illegal in about a third of the states and territories.

Other countries also tried to combat alcohol's ills in different ways. Swedish cities in 1850 began to establish "municipal dispensaries," Villanova's Schrad explains. Leading citizens were given control of alcohol sales and were expected to put sobriety ahead of profit. These local monopolies reduced drinking and drunkenness and became national policy around the turn of the century — the precursors of the distribution monopolies that still exist in some states today, Schrad says.

Nineteenth-century prohibition didn't last long in the United States. States began repealing the bans or failing to enforce them in the 1860s, and some courts found the laws unconstitutional.

Drinking — to get drunk — also became commonplace at many colleges. The University of Virginia's *Cavalier Daily* archive contains the lyrics to "two of the best-known songs of the university." One is a fight song traditionally sung after UVA touchdowns. The other, from "the university's earliest days," celebrates getting drunk. [51] Among its lyrics:

"From Rugby Road to Vinegar Hill,
We're gonna get drunk tonight . . .
So fill your cups, your loving cups,
As full as full can be,
And as long as love and liquor last,
We'll drink to the U. of V. [52]

A prohibition movement arose again in the early 20th century, and the 18th Amendment to the U.S. Constitution banned the manufacture, sale or transportation of intoxicating liquors within the United States in early 1920.

Prohibition did reduce drinking and its harmful side effects. But many Americans continued to imbibe. A gap between ratification of the 18th Amendment in 1919 and its implementation in 1920 gave Americans time to stock up. The Yale Club in New York, for instance, built such a big stockpile that its members drank throughout

Prohibition and had plenty left over after repeal. [53]

Moonshiners distilled illegal spirits, and illegal breweries produced beer. Alcohol was smuggled from Canada, the Caribbean and Europe. "Speakeasies" carried on the nightclub business. And mobsters cleaned up, until Dec. 5, 1933, when the 21st amendment officially ended Prohibition.

"The 18th Amendment was the fastest ever to be ratified, in just over a year," says Schrad, author of *The Political Power of Bad Ideas: Networks, Institutions and the Global Prohibition Wave.* "By 1932-33 you have this avalanche of public support for repeal, and you have repeal happening even faster."

Library of Congress/Sun Newspaper Photograph Collection

Liquor is poured into a sewer following a raid on a bootlegging operation in New York City in 1921, two years after the 18th Amendment banned liquor nationwide. Americans widely flouted Prohibition, which gave rise to organized crime and illicit drinking establishments called speakeasies. In December 1933 the 21st Amendment ended Prohibition, leaving alcohol regulation to the states. Most set the legal drinking age at 21.

Eleven other countries tried prohibition at about the same time, and all replicated the U.S. experience, Schrad says.

Booze did not flow throughout the country after repeal, however. Regulatory power was left with the states, and some chose to remain "dry." Statewide prohibition eventually disappeared, although some states allowed counties or municipalities to remain dry, and some still are. Mississippi was the first state to ratify the 18th Amendment and the last to repeal statewide prohibition (in 1966). [54] Today 34 of Mississippi's 82 counties ban spirits. Four are partially dry and partially wet. Thirty-six ban beer and wine but allow municipalities to choose where to permit beer sales. [55]

Thirteen states still ban Sunday liquor sales; two also ban Sunday beer and wine sales. Four prohibit the sale of alcoholic beverages on election days, but two of them allow local governments to lift the ban. [56]

Regulating Booze

After Prohibition, most states established a legal drinking age of 21. A few chose lower ages — 18 in New York and 20 in Delaware, for example. In Illinois, males couldn't drink until they reached 21, but females could drink at 19, under the theory they were more mature. [57]

Until the 1950s, drunkenness generally was viewed as misbehavior or a crime. Alcoholics were jailed rather than provided medical treatment. In 1954, however, psychiatrist Morris Chafetz launched a campaign to have alcoholism universally recognized as a disease. [58] The American Medical Association did so in 1956. [59]

"I was bound and determined to . . . treat alcoholics as ill human beings who needed treatment, not as bad people who should be ignored and neglected," said Chafetz, who became the first director of the National Institute on Alcohol Abuse and Alcoholism in 1971. [60]

While Chafetz succeeded in revolutionizing the public's understanding of alcoholism, he stirred controversy with some of his healthy-drinking proposals, such as suggesting that grade schools serve children diluted wine to introduce them to responsible drinking. [61]

Generally, the legal drinking age remained at 21 until a raging debate over the Vietnam War fueled a successful drive to lower the voting age to 18 — on the grounds that if 18-year-olds could be drafted into the military, they should have the right to vote. A companion campaign led 29 states to lower the drinking age to 18 or 19 by the early 1970s. [62]

A rise in drunken-driving accidents involving the young inspired the country to revisit that debate, led largely by Mothers Against Drunk Driving (MADD), founded in 1980 by a woman whose 13-year-old daughter was killed by a drunken driver. In 1984 Congress passed, and President Reagan signed, legislation that cut federal highway aid by 10 percent for states that didn't lower their drinking ages to 21. By 1988, all had complied. [63]

Another campaign using the threat of reduced federal highway aid gradually lowered the standard for drunken driving across the states from 0.15 percent blood alcohol content to 0.1 percent and then, in 2000, to today's 0.08. By 2004 all the states had complied with that requirement. [64]

Advertising Booze

Liquor producers abstained voluntarily from advertising on radio, starting in 1936, and on television starting in 1948, although beer and wine producers did advertise. The abstinence began crumbling in the mid-1990s, but it wasn't until the early 2000s that televised liquor advertising really took off, according to Jernigan of the Center on Alcohol Marketing and Youth. "In 2001 there were roughly 1,900 spirits ads on cable," he says. "By 2009, there are more than 62,000." Critics charge the ads, which often feature young adults, encourage drinking, especially by the young — a contention industry representatives dispute.

In March 1996, Seagram aired an ad on a cable sports network and then three months later on a local ABC broadcast in Texas. In October, the Distilled Spirits Council dropped the broadcast-ad ban from its code of conduct, and other distillers said they would purchase broadcast advertisements. [65]

Distilled Spirits Council President Fred Meister explained the policy change as a matter of fairness and necessity. Wine and beer were advertised on television and radio, and liquor's share of U.S. alcohol consumption had declined, he said.

"There are 100 million adults who drink responsibly as part of their normal adult lifestyle," Meister said. "They can't see our products [on TV], but they can see beer and wine." [66]

Despite the council's change of policy, the broadcast television networks and most large radio networks continued to reject liquor ads. In 2001, NBC became the first broadcast television network to accept liquor ads, but heavy criticism soon forced it to reverse course. Ads steadily moved onto cable and local stations, and by 2011 the networks began to drop their bans. First, CBS allowed liquor advertising on late-night programs. ABC then did the same, and NBC followed suit in the spring of 2012. [67] ■

Getty Images/Johannes Simon

Revelers at the annual Oktoberfest beer festival in Munich, Germany, reflect the popularity of drinking in Europe, where the drinking age is 18 or lower. Europe has the world's highest per-capita rate of illness and death caused by alcohol, according to the World Health Organization. Residents of the 27-nation European Union are the world's heaviest drinkers, and binge drinking is common among all age groups across the continent.

CURRENT SITUATION

Banning Ads

When the Massachusetts Bay Transit Authority (MBTA) eliminates alcohol ads from its buses and subway cars this July 1, it will partly be because of the efforts of youngsters like Julia Roberto, a ninth-grader at the elite Boston Latin School.

Alcohol ads are "everywhere," she complained to state transportation officials in December, when she and other Boston school children lobbied against the ads on public transportation. "They're in my face and I can't avoid them," Roberto continued. "The effects of alcohol ads on youth and underage drinking are well-documented, and yet Massachusetts still puts them out there."

The children called MBTA buses and subway cars their "school bus," Massachusetts Transportation Secretary Richard A. Davey said, noting, "We have tens of thousands of kids in the city and in the neighborhoods taking the MBTA to school each day." [68]

Alcohol advertising remains a contentious issue, even though the broadcast television networks now accept ads for spirits on late night programs. Claiming that alcohol promotion encourages underage and excessive drinking, critics want to ban or reduce not only alcohol advertising on television but also alcohol promotion in all forms, especially when it reaches children and youths under 21.

Beverage industry representatives deny that advertising leads to more drinking or more abuse. Many measures of drinking and abuse have declined over the last 20 to 25 years even as alcohol advertising was rising significantly, the Distilled Spirits Council's Cressy points out. "All advertising in the United States is aimed at getting your brand chosen over the other brand or getting your type of alcohol chosen over the other type of alcohol," not at increasing the number of drinkers or the amount of alcohol consumed, he says.

That position was supported by Chafetz, the first head of the National Institute on Alcohol Abuse and Alcoholism. "The claim that advertising can lead anyone down the bottle-strewn garden path, not only to drink alcohol but to abuse it, is pure hokum," he once said. [69]

Underage drinking is down — by some measures to historically low levels. Total U.S. alcohol consumption also has fallen over the last 20 and 25 years. Since spirits producers began television advertising in 1996, however, annual consumption of spirits has risen 18 percent — from 0.63 gallons per person to 0.74. Wine consumption also has increased, while beer consumption has declined. (The figures represent the amount of alcohol within the drinks consumed, not the total amount of beer, wine or whiskey. For example, a 12-ounce beer might contain only 0.6 ounces of alcohol, a 1.5-ounce shot of whiskey the same.)

The spirits and beer industry codes restrict advertising to media in which at least 71.6 percent of the audience is 21 or older. That's the percentage of the U.S. population in that age group, notes Cressy.*

Critics — including the National Research Council, the Institute of Medicine and half the states' attorneys general — prefer an 85-percent standard, says Jernigan of the Center on Alcohol Marketing and Youth, because only 15 percent of Americans are aged 12-20, the group most likely to engage in underage drinking. Under the current codes, many alcohol ads appear in magazines and television programming with a substantial teenage audience, they charge. While youth exposure to alcohol ads in magazines has been declining, exposure to alcohol advertising on television grew by 71 percent between 2001 and 2009, primarily because of spirits advertising on cable networks, which soared by nearly 3,000 percent, according to the center. [70]

Getty Images/Joe Raedle

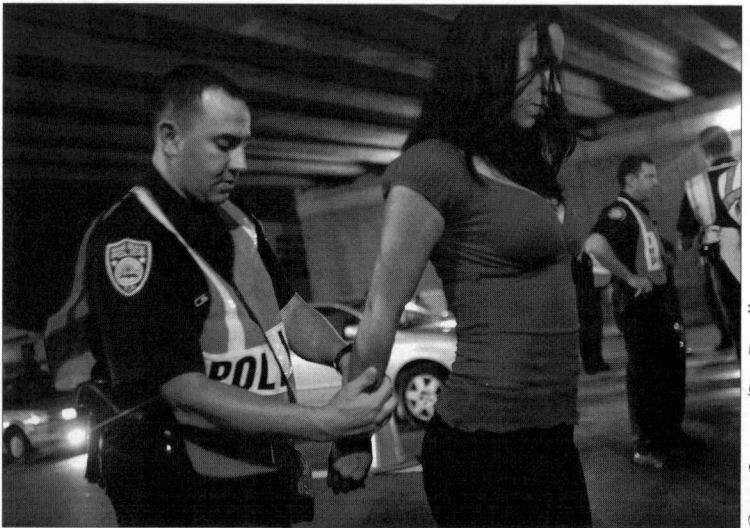

A police officer arrests a woman in Miami after he said she failed a field breathalyzer test. Alcoholism and auto accidents caused by excessive drinking kill 80,000 Americans each year and drain more than $220 billion from the economy.

Discouraging Abuse

Governments, colleges and other private institutions are taking steps to discourage alcohol abuse.

The CDC task force recommends "social norming" exercises, which many campuses are implementing. College representatives show students data about how much drinking really occurs among their classmates and explain the effects of overdrinking. "Students overestimate the amount of drinking that occurs among their peers and then fashion their own behavior to meet this perceived norm," the task force explained. Students also may think drinking makes them attractive, it said, when overdrinking can have the opposite effect. [71]

A growing number of colleges are providing alcohol education to incoming students. Some require students to take online courses at the beginning of their college career or before they arrive on campus. [72] Others address parents as well. [73]

Increasingly popular "medical amnesty" or "alcohol emergency" programs exempt students from punishment if they summon help when they or a companion need medical attention due to overdrinking. Some schools require such underage drinkers to complete education or counseling programs. At Rollins College in Winter Park, Fla., the students also must keep a counselor informed of their drinking habits. "We want to help them

Continued on p. 518

* The Wine Institute Standard is 70 percent.

At Issue:

Would raising alcohol taxes reduce abuse?

PHILIP J. COOK
SENIOR ASSOCIATE DEAN FOR FACULTY SANFORD SCHOOL OF PUBLIC POLICY DUKE UNIVERSITY

WRITTEN FOR *CQ RESEARCHER*, JUNE 2012

yes

Alcohol abuse is a multifaceted problem that requires a diverse portfolio of programs and policies. Adolescent drinking, alcoholism, drunken driving, alcohol-enabled domestic violence and child neglect, crime and public drunkenness all elicit distinct, tailored policy responses. But one policy instrument would help reduce all these problems: alcohol prices. With higher prices come reduced rates of alcohol abuse and improvements in public health and safety.

Government influences alcohol prices in a variety of ways, but most comprehensively through alcohol excise taxes. Unfortunately, Congress has not adjusted alcohol excise rates since 1991, and since then inflation has significantly eroded the impact of those taxes. States also tax alcohol, and those rates also have declined in inflation-adjusted terms, despite some nominal increases. The overall result is cheaper alcohol, more alcohol abuse and more alcohol-related problems of all sorts than would otherwise have occurred.

Concerns that such taxes are regressive, or that they penalize the majority who drink moderately and safely, are off base. In fact, most Americans abstain or drink so little that alcoholic-beverage expenditures are a trivial part of their household budget — yet they would benefit from the extra government revenue (which could take the place of other taxes). Drinking, and hence excise tax payments, are concentrated among the 7 or 8 percent of the population who drink heavily and account for most of the alcohol-related damage. For that group especially, higher taxes would have a moderating effect on consumption.

The scientific evidence showing that prices directly affect abuse levels is strong enough to support a near-consensus among economists who study health behavior. Careful analysis of the effects of raising alcohol taxes bears out the link between higher taxes and reduced alcohol abuse. Most of these changes in price have been small, however, so the effects have been correspondingly small. Relatively large increases, such as Alaska's move to more than double alcohol taxes in 2002, have produced more substantial gains in health and safety.

Of course, prices are by no means the only — or the most important — influence on drinking patterns. The focus on excise tax rates is justified simply because taxes — unlike culture, demographics and other factors — are under the direct control of the government and thus can, at least in principle, be fine-tuned to fit the need.

PETER H. CRESSY, ED.D
PRESIDENT AND CEO DISTILLED SPIRITS COUNCIL OF THE UNITED STATES

WRITTEN FOR *CQ RESEARCHER*, JUNE 2012

no

Raising alcohol taxes doesn't reduce alcohol abuse. Several studies, including a recent analysis supported by the National Institute on Alcohol Abuse and Alcoholism, have concluded that heavy drinkers "are least likely to respond to higher taxes." Moreover, from 1997-2008 — when the affordability index of alcohol increased by 25 percent — underage drinking dropped by nearly 17 percent, according to government data.

Interestingly, during the recession, when disposable income contracted substantially, U.S. per capita alcohol consumption did not. Consumers chose instead to drink at home, a less costly option. Thus, alcohol taxes function as a tax on the hospitality industry, unnecessarily harming thousands of businesses and costing tens of thousands of jobs.

Alcohol taxes are inherently regressive and unfairly penalize moderate drinkers, who are most sensitive to prices and cut back the greatest when prices rise. Government and peer-reviewed research conclude that moderate drinking is associated with a reduced risk of cardiovascular disease, the leading cause of death. Moreover, the federal Dietary Guidelines underscore that moderate drinking can be part of a healthy adult lifestyle. To the extent that moderate consumers would be most affected by this one-size-fits-all approach, those benefits would be lost.

As economist Philip Cook states in *Paying the Tab*, "The goal should be to preserve the benefits of drinking while reducing abuse, all without unwarranted government intrusion."

The overwhelming majority of alcohol consumers drink responsibly and already pay their fair share of taxes. For a typical spirits bottle, 54 percent of the purchase price goes to taxes. It's unfair to punish responsible drinkers with higher taxes to pay for the small percentage who drink irresponsibly.

Alcohol abuse is a serious issue. The best joint efforts of society, government and industry should continue to be applied against this problem. Unfortunately, anti-alcohol advocates and some well-meaning but misguided public health officials often embrace ineffective population-based controls including higher taxes, advertising bans and severe restrictions on access as simple answers to deter alcohol abusers — a small percentage of the overall population.

The better solution is a comprehensive effort that includes tough laws, strong enforcement, educational programs and targeted interventions. These methods are working. Underage drinking — including binge drinking — and drunken driving fatalities are at historic lows, according to government data.

Continued from p. 516

learn from their mistakes," said Diane Willingham, director of community standards and responsibility at the college. [74] A half-dozen states have enacted laws that protect underage drinkers from prosecution if they summon emergency care for someone who has become dangerously ill from drinking. [75]

Virginia has banned alcohol advertising from college newspapers and joined 15 other states that require all convicted drunken drivers to install ignition-interlock systems on their vehicles. The driver must blow into an alcohol-detector before starting the motor vehicle. If the blood-alcohol content is too high, the vehicle won't run. Kurt Erickson, president of the Washington Area Regional Alcohol Program, said studies show the systems cut drunken-driving recidivism by two-thirds. [76]

MADD President Jan Withers says the systems are among the most effective means of fighting drunken driving. Her organization is "working very hard to get those laws on the books in every state," she says.

Another highly effective strategy, she says, is "high-visibility law enforcement," such as publicized sobriety checkpoints and "saturation patrols," during which police agencies deploy a large force to catch large numbers of violators. The tactic not only catches impaired drivers but is "a powerful deterrent," she says.

College students across Alabama have launched a "LessThanUThink" anti-binge-drinking campaign, in which students distribute images of unattractively drunk young people, along with a warning that it doesn't take many drinks to turn into a fool.

"Students think they're invincible," said journalism instructor Morgan Hooper Drinkard, coordinator of Troy University's LessThanUThink campaign. "Scare tactics don't work anymore. They're more afraid of social consequences than they are of getting in their car and having a wreck." [77]

Many attempts to curb child and college drinking also focus on parents, who studies show have the most influence on their offspring's drinking, Withers says. "Parents often fail to fully realize the impact they can have on whether or not their kids are drinking," says Moe, who works with children at the Betty Ford Institute. "Parents who have dinner with their kids multiple times a week, getting fully engaged, make a real difference." Parents also need to monitor their children's behavior, he adds.

Doing must accompany the talking, notes Michael Siegel, a professor of community health sciences at the Boston University School of Public Health. "The way parents use alcohol is going to be the way they teach their kids," he explains. "Kids are going to pay attention to what they see, not what they hear." ■

Getty Images/*New York Daily News Archive*/Debbie Egan-Chin

Family and friends mourn the death of 11-year-old Leandra Rosado, who was killed in October 2009 when an intoxicated driver, Carmen Huertas, the mother of another child, crashed her car full of girls going to a sleepover in New York City. Excessive drinking killed 10,228 people on American roads in 2010. The number has been steadily declining since 1982, when 26,173 died in alcohol-related crashes.

OUTLOOK

Continuing Debate

Activists on alcohol issues don't expect wholesale changes in the foreseeable future. "For the most part, I think it will just be that muddling through, nipping around the edges," Villanova's Schrad says.

Johns Hopkins University's Jernigan sees the trends "cutting both ways in the United States. We're getting a little more alert about bad products," such as caffeine-infused alcoholic beverages. "The most egregious practices," he says, will probably "get fenced in or walled off."

On the other hand, he concedes, "we're in a very deregulatory environment."

Similarly, Duke University's Cook predicts greater availability and lower prices for alcohol. The remaining state monopolies seem to be headed toward privatization, he says. "At least for the time being," he says, "the alcohol industry is riding high, and the public is not eager to raise tax rates of any sort or to have more government intervention, even in an area as dicey as alcohol abuse."

However, Boston University's Naimi says state and local budget squeezes could facilitate higher alcohol taxes. "By doing that, you can offset tax increases in other areas that people object to more and, at the same time, have a positive impact on public health," he explains.

The University of Michigan's Salerno, who works with public schools, foresees a community-based approach to teen alcohol abuse. "People are headed toward developing community support for kids using substances, but also to support not using them," she says, such as providing alternatives to activities that involve alcohol and other drugs. "Coalitions and collaborations across health, education, community-based organizations, police and the juvenile justice system can work together to create an environment that would support more healthy decisions," she says.

Such an approach could create the resources that Moe, of the Betty Ford Institute, says are needed to discourage underage drinking. "To tell young people to say no and not give them alternatives is ludicrous," he says. "We need to give them opportunities to engage in a whole range of activities that are fun and exciting — music, sports, service to others — that don't involve drinking."

Nadel, of the National Youth Rights Association, is "optimistic, ultimately" that the drinking age will be lowered. With the support of college presidents, "we will be able to present this very compelling case to legislators and to the American public," he says.

But the University of Minnesota's Nelson says that campaign "doesn't have a lot of current traction."

Likewise, Frostburg State University President Jonathan Gibralter calls the proposal "dead in the water." Instead, Gibralter expects proven strategies to emerge from the Learning Collaborative on High-Risk Drinking, in which his school participates.

Most attempts to raise taxes, restrict advertising and make alcohol less available won't succeed, predicts the Distilled Spirits Council's Cressy. "I'm confident that science is so much on the side of not going down the path of wholesale population-based controls that they won't be enacted," he says. "Freedom of speech is always going to inhibit what the government can do. That is why self-regulation is so important."

He expects debate about these issues to continue for years and to affect industry policies. "Our industry focuses sharply on having a very tough self-regulatory code," Cressy says. "The pressure from the population-based side will encourage industry to put its energy behind things that have been demonstrated to work."

Like Schrad, Jernigan and Cook, Boston University's Siegel doubts that the current anti-tax, anti-regulatory climate will allow significant new controls on alcohol access. But he admits he could be pleasantly surprised. "Many years ago, if you had asked whether we would be regulating cigarette advertising and raising cigarette taxes, I probably would have said, 'no, tobacco is a very powerful industry.'

"Things can change," he says. "Tobacco has set a model for what could potentially happen in alcohol." ■

Notes

[1] Mary Pat Flaherty, Jenna Johnson and Justin Jouvenal, "George Huguely guilty of second-degree murder," *The Washington Post*, Feb. 22, 2012, www.washingtonpost.com/local/crime/george-huguely-guilty-of-second-degree-murder/2012/02/21/gIQA1ss4TR_story.html.

[2] Lloyd D. Johnston, *et al.*, "Monitoring the Future: National Survey Results on Drug Use, 1975-2010, Volume I, Secondary School Students," University of Michigan Institute for Social Research, 2011, http://monitoringthefuture.org/pubs/monographs/mtf-vol1_2010.pdf.

[3] "Report to Congress on the Prevention and Reduction of Underage Drinking," U.S. Department of Health and Human Services, May 2011, http://store.samhsa.gov/shin/content/SMA11-4645/SMA11-4645.pdf.

[4] *Ibid.*

[5] Tricia Bishop, "Huguely trial highlights alcohol abuse at colleges, universities," *The Baltimore Sun*, Feb. 18, 2012, www.baltimoresun.com/health/bs-md-student-drinking-20120216,0,6950450,full.story.

[6] *Ibid.*

[7] Emily Listfield, "The Underage Drinking Epidemic," *Parade*, June 12, 2011, www.parade.com/health/2011/06/12-teen-drinking-epidemic.html.

[8] "The rise and fall of Four Loko," *The Week*, Nov. 24, 2010, http://theweek.com/article/index/209434/the-rise-and-fall-of-four-loko.

[9] Lloyd D. Johnston, *et al.*, "Monitoring the Future: National Results on Adolescent Drug Use Overview of Key Findings, 2011," University of Michigan Institute for Social Research, 2012, http://monitoringthefuture.org/pubs/monographs/mtf-overview2011.pdf.

[10] Listfield, *op. cit.*

[11] "Women, Girls, and Alcohol," Center on Alcohol Marketing and Youth, Johns Hopkins University School of Public Health, July 2011, www.camy.org/factsheets/sheets/Women_Girls_and_Alcohol.html; Tom Daykin, "Wisconsin Brewers Feeling Effects of 'Alcopops' Backlash," *Milwaukee Journal Sentinel*, May 7, 2006, www.redorbit.com/news/science/494292/wisconsin_brewers_feeling_effects_of_alcopops_backlash; and Michelle Blackston, "Spirited debate: some lawmakers think flavored malt beverages need tighter regulation," *State Legislatures*, Oct. 1, 2009, www.thefreelibrary.com/Spirited+debate%3a+some+lawmakers+think+flavored+malt+beverages+need...-a0211631673.

[12] Listfield, *op. cit.*

[13] "Binge Drinking," Centers for Disease Control and Prevention, Dec. 17, 2010, www.cdc.gov/alcohol/fact-sheets/binge-drinking.htm. Also see "Binge Drinking: Nationwide Problem, Local Solutions," CDC Vital Signs, January 2012, www.cdc.gov/vitalsigns/BingeDrinking/index.html.

[14] Selene Yeager, "Exercise and Alcohol: Running on Empty Bottles," *Women's Health*, March 2012, www.womenshealthmag.com/health/exercise-and-alcohol?page=1.

[15] "Binge Drinking: Nationwide Problem, Local Solutions," *op. cit.*

[16] "Report to Congress on the Prevention and Reduction of Underage Drinking," *op. cit.*

[17] "2010 Motor Vehicle Crashes: Overview," National Highway Traffic Safety Administration, February 2012, www-nrd.nhtsa.dot.gov/Pubs/

811552.pdf. Also see "U.S. Driving Fatalities, Total and Alcohol-Related," infoplease, www.infoplease.com/ipa/A0908129.html.

[18] "Behind Bars II: Substance Abuse and America's Prison Population," National Center on Addiction and Substance Abuse, Columbia University, February 2010, www.casacolumbia.org/articlefiles/575-report2010behindbars2.pdf.

[19] For background, see Kathy Koch, "Drunken Driving," *CQ Researcher*, Oct. 6, 2000, pp. 793-808.

[20] Gordon Jackson, "Military leaders support proposal to lower drinking age on bases, Kingston says," *The Florida Times-Union*, Sept. 10, 2010, http://jacksonville.com/news/georgia/2010-09-10/story/military-leaders-support-proposal-lower-drinking-age-bases-kingston.

[21] "Lower military drinking age would be tough to defend in court," *Anchorage Daily News*, April 18, 2011, www.adn.com/2011/04/18/1816332/drinking-age.html.

[22] "Minimum Age Limits Worldwide," International Center for Alcohol Policies, www.icap.org/Table/MinimumAgeLimitsWorldwide.

[23] "Alcohol Use Facts and Figures," World Health Organization, www.euro.who.int/en/what-we-do/health-topics/disease-prevention/alcohol-use/facts-and-figures.

[24] "The 2011 ESPAD Report," European Monitoring Centre for Drugs and Drug Addiction, 2012, www.espad.org/Uploads/ESPAD_reports/2007/The_2007_ESPAD_Report-FULL_091006.pdf.

[25] Johnston, *et al.*, "Monitoring the Future: National Results on Adolescent Drug Use Overview of Key Findings, 2011," *op. cit.*

[26] For background, see David Hosansky, "Distracted Driving," *CQ Researcher*, May 4, 2012, pp. 401-424.

[27] "UN health agency sounds alarm on alcohol abuse," The Associated Press, Feb. 11, 2011.

[28] "Preventing Excessive Alcohol Consumption," The Community Guide, Centers for Disease Control and Prevention, www.thecommunityguide.org/alcohol/index.html.

[29] "Beer Industry Backs Legislation to Roll Back Unfair Taxes That Threaten Jobs," Beer Institute, May 31, 2011, www.beerinstitute.org/tier.asp?nid=620&archiveyear=2011&bid=102.

[30] Sarah Longwell, "Maryland's alcohol tax: A hard-to-swallow 'victory,' " *The Washington Post*, May 26, 2011, www.washingtonpost.com/opinions/marylands-alcohol-tax-a-hard-to-swallow-victory/2011/05/23/AGbxyLCH_story.html.

[31] Brian Witte, "House panel raises alcohol tax to 9 percent," The Associated Press, April 9, 2011.

[32] Alexander Jackson, "Trade groups urge Busch to reject Maryland alcohol tax," *Baltimore Business Journal*, April 6, 2011.

[33] V. Rammohan, *et al.*, "Effects of dram shop liability and enhanced overservice law enforcement initiatives on excessive alcohol consumption and related harms: Two community guide systematic reviews, Abstract," *American Journal Of Preventive Medicine*, September 2011, www.ncbi.nlm.nih.gov/pubmed/21855749.

[34] Barbara Mantel, "Drinking on Campus," *CQ Researcher*, Aug. 18, 2006, pp. 649-672.

[35] "The University of Rhode Island 2010-2012 Student Handbook," University of Rhode Island, www.uri.edu/judicial/assets/URI_Student_Handbook_2010-2012.pdf.

[36] "In online chat, new URI president lays out his plans," *Providence Journal*, Sept. 17, 2009, p. 9; and Jennifer D. Jordan, "URI president expands drinking policy at events," *Providence Journal*, Nov. 10, 2009, p. 2.

[37] "Dartmouth President Jim Yong Kim on Bloomberg Surveillance," *Analyst Wire*, Oct. 11, 2011.

[38] "4 Tiers," National Institute on Alcohol Abuse and Alcoholism, July 11, 2007, www.collegedrinkingprevention.gov/StatsSummaries/4tier.aspx.

[39] "Dartmouth President Jim Yong Kim on Bloomberg Surveillance," *op. cit.*

[40] Nathalie R. Miraval and Rebecca D. Robbins, "College Releases New Alcohol Policies," *The Harvard Crimson*, March 30, 2012, www.thecrimson.com/article/2012/3/30/college-new-alcohol-regulation.

[41] "U.S. Colleges and Universities Join Forces to Address High-Risk Drinking," Dartmouth College, May 2, 2011, http://now.dartmouth.edu/2011/05/u-s-colleges-and-universities-join-forces-to-address-high-risk-drinking.

[42] Jenna Johnson, "St. Mary's College opens its own pub," *The Washington Post*, May 11, 2012, www.washingtonpost.com/local/education/st-marys-college-opens-its-own-pub/2012/05/11/gIQALS3OIU_story.html.

[43] Unless otherwise noted, information for this historical section was drawn from the following sources: Johan F. M. Swinnen, ed., *The Economics of Beer* (2011); Tom Standage, *A History of the World in 6 Glasses* (2006); Mantel, *op. cit.*; Rich McManus, "Professor Traces Nation's 'Drinking Age Debates,' " *NIH Record*, Sept. 16, 2011, http://nihrecord.od.nih.gov/newsletters/2011/09_16_2011/story1.htm.

[44] Devra First, "The rise of beeronomics," *The Boston Globe*, Feb. 19, 2012, http://articles.boston.com/2012-02-19/ideas/31070405_1_beer-reinheitsgebot-wine.

[45] Standage, *op. cit.*

[46] *Ibid.*, p. 4.

[47] *Ibid.*, p. 114.

[48] First, *op. cit.*

[49] Mark Lawrence Schrad, "Moscow's Drinking Problem," *The New York Times*, April 17, 2011, p. WK 8.

[50] Standage, *op. cit.*, p. 123.

[51] Jenna Johnson and Mary Pat Flaherty, "Boylan Heights bar at center of U-Va. drinking scene," *The Washington Post*, Feb. 21, 2012, www.washingtonpost.com/lifestyle/style/boylan-heights-bar-at-center-of-u-va-drinking-scene/2012/02/17/gIQAcKU9RR_story.html.

[52] "Traditional Songs," *Cavalier Daily Digital Archive*, University of Virginia Library, Sept. 1, 1967, http://scripta.lib.virginia.edu/cgi-textwg/cavdaily.pl?str=a14.3&offset=0&fileid=19670901.

[53] "Whiskey a go-go," *Chicago Tribune*, Oct. 2, 2011, p. C26.

[54] Campbell Robertson, "Voters in 'wettest dry

About the Author

Tom Price, a longtime contributer to *CQ Researcher*, wrote "Assessing the United Nations" for the March 20, 2012, *CQ Global Researcher.* Currently a Washington-based freelancer, he previously was a correspondent in the Cox Newspapers Washington Bureau and chief politics writer for the *Dayton Daily News* and *The Journal Herald* in Dayton. He is author or coauthor of five books, including *Changing The Face of Hunger* and, most recently, *Washington, DC, Free & Dirt Cheap* with his wife Susan Crites Price. His work has appeared in *The New York Times*, *Time*, *Rolling Stone* and other periodicals. He earned a bachelor of science degree in journalism at Ohio University.

county' in Mississippi end beer ban," *The New York Times*, Feb. 6, 2010, http://seattletimes.nwsource.com/html/nationworld/2011004106_beer07.html.

55 "Tobacco, Beer, and Alcohol Frequently Asked Questions," Mississippi Department of Revenue, May 12, 2012, www.tax.ms.gov/info/faqs/TobaccoBeerandAlcohol.html#s.

56 "Current Blue Law States," Distilled Spirits Council, www.prohibitionrepeal.com/legacy/hall.asp.

57 McManus, *op. cit.*

58 William Grimes, "Morris Chafetz, 87, Dies," *The New York Times*, Oct. 21, 2011, p. B12.

59 "Timelines AMA History 1941-1960," American Medical Association, www.ama-assn.org/ama/pub/about-ama/our-history/timelines-ama-history/1941-1960.page.

60 Grimes, *op. cit.*

61 *Ibid.*

62 "History of the 21 Minimum Drinking Age," Mothers Against Drunk Driving, www.madd.org/underage-drinking/why21/history.html.

63 *Ibid.*

64 See Koch, *op. cit.*

65 "Chronology of Broadcast Liquor Advertising," Alcohol Policies Project, Center for Science in the Public Interest, www.cspinet.org/booze/liquor_chronology.htm.

66 "Repealing Ad Prohibition," Online News Hour, PBS, Nov. 12, 1996, www.pbs.org/newshour/bb/business/november96/liquor_11-12.html.

67 "Hard Time: Liquor Advertising Pours Into TV," *Advertising Age*, May 13, 2012, http://adage.com/print/234733.

68 Matt Rocheleau, "Rally touts bill to ban alcohol ads on all state property," *The Boston Globe*, Jan. 27, 2012, http://articles.boston.com/2012-01-27/metro/30667295_1_alcohol-ads-ban-alcohol-state-property.

69 Emily Langer, "Morris E. Chafetz, authority on alcohol abuse, dies at 87," *The Washington Post*, Oct. 22, 2011, www.washingtonpost.com/local/obituaries/morris-e-chafetz-authority-on-alcohol-abuse-dies-at-87-wife-marion-d-chafetz-dies-at-86/2011/10/20/gIQAskhd7L_story.html.

70 "Youth Exposure to Alcohol Ads on TV Growing Faster Than Adults," Center on Alcohol Marketing and Youth, Johns Hopkins University School of Public Health, Dec. 13, 2010, www.camy.org/press/Press_Releases/Youth_Exposure_to_Alcohol_Ads_on_TV_Growing_Faster_Than_Adults.html.

71 "4 Tiers," *op. cit.*

72 Tricia Bishop, "Huguely trial highlights alcohol abuse at colleges, universities," *The Baltimore Sun*, Feb. 18, 2012, www.baltimoresun.com/health/bs-md-student-drinking-20120216,0,6950450,full.story.

73 Amy Bell, "Statistics show binge drinking higher in Michigan than national average," *Daily Tribune*, (Mount Clemens, Mich.), Feb. 13, 2012, http://dailytribune.com/articles/2012/02/13/news/doc4f39380051dea012915465.txt.

74 Denise-Marie Balona, "UCF might go easy if drinkers get counseling," *Orlando Sentinel*, Sept. 26, 2011, p. A1.

75 Brian McVicar, "Underage drinkers would receive amnesty under legislation that passed the State House today," *The Grand Rapids Press*, March 6, 2012, http://blog.mlive.com/grpress/news_impact/print.html?entry=/2012/03/underage_drinkers_would_receiv.html.

76 Justin Jouvenal, "Is Va.'s ignition-interlock rule for first-time DUI offenders too tough?" *The Washington Post*, April 8, 2012, www.washingtonpost.com/local/crime/is-vas-ignition-interlock-rule-for-first-time-dui-offenders-too-tough/2012/04/08/gIQAmFhd4S_story.html.

77 Hannah Wolfson, "University of Alabama students design anti-drinking campaign," *The Birmingham News*, March 12, 2012, http://blog.al.com/spotnews/2012/03/ua_students_design_anti-drinki.html.

FOR MORE INFORMATION

Alcoholics Anonymous, 475 Riverside Dr., 11th Floor, New York, NY 10115; 212-870-3400; www.aa.oprg. An informal society of more than 2 million people who focus on staying sober and supporting each other's quest for sobriety.

Beer Institute, 122 C St., N.W., Suite 350, Washington DC 20001; 202-737-2337; www.beerinstitute.org. Represents the brewing industry before governments and the general public; publishes an advertising and marketing code.

Center on Alcohol Marketing and Youth, 624 N. Broadway, Suite 292, Baltimore, MD 21205; 410-502-6579; www.camy.org. Based at Johns Hopkins University's Bloomberg School of Public Health; monitors the alcoholic beverage industry's marketing practices, publishes reports and calls attention to practices it thinks can entice underage drinkers.

Centers for Disease Control and Prevention, 1600 Clifton Rd., Atlanta, GA 30333; 800-232-4636; www.cdc.gov. Supports research on America's drinking habits, alcohol's impact on health and effective measures for combating alcohol abuse. Web site (www.cdc.gov/Alcohol) contains large amount of information about alcohol and public health.

Community Preventive Services Task Force, 1600 Clifton Rd., N.E., Atlanta, GA 30333; 404-498-6375; www.thecommunityguide.org. Independent, CDC-appointed panel that recommends research-supported measures for improving Americans' health. Panel's alcohol Web site (www.thecommunityguide.org/alcohol) contains recommendations for dealing with alcohol abuse.

Distilled Spirits Council of the United States, 1250 I St., N.W., Suite 400, Washington, D.C. 20005; 202-628-3544; www.discus.org. Trade association representing nearly 70 percent of U.S. liquor brands; advocates the industry's interests before governments and the general public; publishes a "Code of Responsible Practices for Beverage Alcohol Advertising and Marketing."

Interagency Coordinating Committee on the Prevention of Underage Drinking, 1 Choke Cherry Rd., Rockville, MD 20857; 301-407-6798 or 866-419-2514; www.stopalcoholabuse.gov. Composed of representatives from 15 agencies; coordinates U.S. government efforts to prevent or reduce underage drinking.

Mothers Against Drunk Driving, 511 E. John Carpenter Freeway, Suite 700, Irving, TX 75062; 877-275-6233; www.madd.org. Campaigns for legislation and other actions to reduce drunken driving and underage drinking.

Bibliography

Selected Sources

Books

Gately, Iain, *Drink: A Cultural History of Alcohol*, Gotham Books, 2008.

From the discovery of fermentation, brewing and distilling, Gately traces the development and use of alcoholic beverages through history.

Schrad, Mark Lawrence, *The Political Power of Bad Ideas: Networks, Institutions and the Global Prohibition Wave*, Oxford University Press, 2010.

A political scientist shows that Prohibition was an international phenomenon in the early 20th century.

Standage, Tom, *A History of the World in 6 Glasses*, Walker & Company, 2006.

The business editor of *The Economist* applies his journalistic skills to this readable history of beer, wine, spirits, coffee, tea and Coca-Cola and how they affected users.

Swinnen, Johan F. M., ed., *The Economics of Beer*, Oxford University Press, 2011.

A distinguished Belgian economist collects 18 scholarly essays about the role beer has played in the world economy since early civilization. The book features an abundance of statistics, charts and graphs.

Articles

Colman, David, "Challenging the Second 'A' in A.A.," *The New York Times*, May 8, 2011, p. ST-1, www.nytimes.com/2011/05/08/fashion/08anon.html?pagewanted=all.

Recovering alcoholics discuss whether the anonymity of Alcoholics Anonymous is anachronistic or counter-productive.

Crawford, Selwyn, Diane Jennings and Darlean Spangenberger, "Young alcohol abusers often re-offend, avoid treatment," *The Dallas Morning News*, Jan. 3, 2011, p. 1.

The article looks at the unique challenges posed by "minor adults," 17- to 20-year-olds who are too young to drink legally but are treated as adults in drunken driving cases by the Texas judicial system.

Johnson, Jenna, and Mary Pat Flaherty, "Boylan Heights bar at center of U-Va. drinking scene," *The Washington Post*, Feb. 21, 2012, www.washingtonpost.com/lifestyle/style/boylan-heights-bar-at-center-of-u-va-drinking-scene/2012/02/17/gIQAcKU9RR_story.html.

Reporters examine the college drinking culture that helped fuel the romance between George Huguely V and Yeardley Love, and then the drunken rage in which he murdered her.

McCardell, John M., "What Your College President Didn't Tell You," *The New York Times*, Sept. 13, 2004, www.chooseresponsibility.org/filemanager/download/5363.

The former president of Middlebury College lays out his argument for lowering the drinking age to 18 — and challenges some common wisdom about higher education.

Wells, Jon, "He sang with all his heart," *Hamilton Spectator* (Ontario, Canada), March 3, 2012, p. WR1.

A reporter offers a heartbreaking portrait of a brilliant and talented teenager who drank himself to death while the parents of a friend partied with him and after his own parents tolerated his underage drinking at home.

Yeager, Selene, "Exercise and Alcohol: Running on Empty Bottles," *Women's Health*, March 2012, www.womenshealthmag.com/health/exercise-and-alcohol?page=1.

The magazine explores the counter-intuitive research finding that people who exercise more — especially women — drink more, or vice versa.

Reports and Studies

"Behind Bars II: Substance Abuse and America's Prison Population," National Center on Addiction and Substance Abuse, Columbia University, February 2010, www.casacolumbia.org/articlefiles/575-report2010behindbars2.pdf.

Looks at the role alcohol and other drugs play in crime and what happens to the criminals in prison and after release.

"The 2011 ESPAD Report," European Monitoring Centre for Drugs and Drug Addiction, 2012, www.espad.org/Uploads/ESPAD_reports/2011/The_2011_ESPAD_Report_FULL_2012-05-30.pdf.

The European School Survey Project on Alcohol and Other Drugs surveys teenagers in 40 European countries.

"Report to Congress on the Prevention and Reduction of Underage Drinking," U.S. Department of Health and Human Services, May 2011, http://store.samhsa.gov/shin/content/SMA11-4645/SMA11-4645.pdf.

The federal agency summarizes its finding on teen alcohol use and efforts to address it.

Johnston, Lloyd D., *et. al.*, "Monitoring the Future: National Results on Adolescent Drug Use Overview of Key Findings, 2011," University of Michigan Institute for Social Research, 2012, http://monitoringthefuture.org/pubs/monographs/mtf-overview2011.pdf; and Johnston, Lloyd D., *et. al.*, "Monitoring the Future: National Survey Results on Drug Use, 1975-2010, Volume I, Secondary School Students," University of Michigan Institute for Social Research, 2011, http://monitoringthefuture.org/pubs/monographs/mtf-vol1_2010.pdf.

The reports offer results of two decades' worth of annual surveys of high school- and college-age youths and tabulate use of alcohol and many drugs. The 2011 publication addresses only eighth- through 12th-graders.

The Next Step:

Additional Articles from Current Periodicals

Binge Drinking

Finley, Don, "Americans Belly Up to the Bar for Binge Drinking," *San Antonio Express-News*, Jan. 11, 2012, p. A1, www.mysanantonio.com/news/local_news/article/Americans-belly-up-to-the-bar-for-binge-drinking-2457521.php.
Many Americans feel encouraged to engage in binge drinking during special occasions and holidays.

Healey, Katy, "Not Exactly the Toast of the Nation," *Omaha* (Neb.) *World-Herald*, Jan. 11, 2012, p. A1, www.omaha.com/article/20120111/LIVEWELL01/701119872.
Nebraska and Iowa have among the highest binge drinking rates in the United States.

Hogstrom, Erik, "Study: Older Drinkers Binge More," *Telegraph Herald* (Dubuque, Iowa), Jan. 15, 2012, p. A13, www.thonline.com/news/tri-state/article_07cadbab-4954-5a1f-840c-1f193a581d1d.html.
Scientists have found that older binge drinkers get drunk more frequently than younger bingers.

Colleges

Harriman, Peter, "Colleges Rethink Booze," *Argus Leader* (Sioux Falls, S.D.), Feb. 13, 2012, p. A1.
The University of South Dakota has allowed students 21 and older to drink in two residence halls.

Kim, Jim Yong, "Targeting Campus Drinking," *The Washington Post*, Sept. 17, 2011, p. A15.
Administrators from different colleges should work together to address campus drinking instead of trying to solve the problems alone, says the president of Dartmouth College.

Simon, Anne, "Colleges Try to Break Grip of Alcohol Culture Among Students," *Greenville* (S.C.) *News*, March 19, 2012.
Many college administrators advocate a zero tolerance approach to underage drinking and urge those of legal age to drink responsibly.

Drinking Age

Eagen, Margery, "Youths Will Drink Despite All Our Bans," *The Boston Herald*, March 22, 2012, p. 8, bostonherald.com/news/columnists/view/20220322youths_will_drink_despite_all_our_bans.
Many young people say strict rules against under-age drinking are not effective.

Foltz, Madysan, "Lower America's Drinking Age," *Intelligencer Journal* (Lancaster, Pa.), March 31, 2012, p. A6, lancasteronline.com/article/local/615707_TEEN-EDITORIAL--Lower-America-s-drinking-age.html.
Proponents of a lower drinking age say setting it at 21 is inconsistent with the rights already given to 18-year-olds.

Ogilvie, Jessica Pauline, "Is Lowering the Drinking Age Really a Good Idea?" *Los Angeles Times*, May 30, 2011, articles.latimes.com/2011/may/30/health/la-he-drinking-age-20110530.
Opponents of a lower drinking age say roads have become safer since the 1980s, when states raised the threshold to 21.

Health Issues

"Report Urges Review of Safe-Drinking Guide," United Press International, Jan. 9, 2012, www.upi.com/Top_News/World-News/2012/01/09/Report-urges-review-of-safe-drinking-guide/UPI-69871326116319/.
The British House of Commons has expressed skepticism about the health benefits of alcohol.

Graedon, Joe, and Teresa Graedon, "Drinks, Drugs a Lethal Mix," *Buffalo* (N.Y.) *News*, Dec. 19, 2011, p. C5, www.buffalonews.com/life/health-parenting/peoples-pharmacy/article678468.ece.
Even modest alcohol intake can damage the liver for those who are regularly taking painkillers or have chronic health conditions.

Retelny, Victoria Shanta, "A Toast to Your Health," *Chicago Tribune*, Dec. 21, 2011, p. A8, articles.chicagotribune.com/2011-12-21/features/ct-food-1221-drinking-20111221_1_moderate-alcohol-intake-moderate-drinking-alcohol-and-health.
Long-standing studies have shown that moderate alcohol intake can fit into a healthy lifestyle.

CITING *CQ RESEARCHER*

Sample formats for citing these reports in a bibliography include the ones listed below. Preferred styles and formats vary, so please check with your instructor or professor.

MLA STYLE

Jost, Kenneth. "Remembering 9/11," CQ Researcher 2 Sept. 2011: 701-732.

APA STYLE

Jost, K. (2011, September 2). Remembering 9/11. *CQ Researcher, 9*, 701-732.

CHICAGO STYLE

Jost, Kenneth. "Remembering 9/11." *CQ Researcher*, September 2, 2011, 701-732.

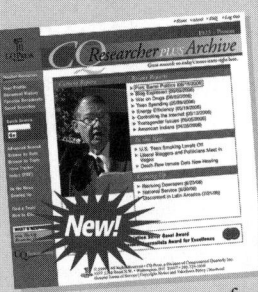

CQ Researcher

Published by CQ Press, an Imprint of SAGE Publications, Inc.

www.cqresearcher.com

Gambling in America

Are states hooked on money from games?

Gambling was once illegal and widely regarded as immoral in most of the United States, but today it is a popular pastime, a $90 billion industry and an important source of revenue for state and local governments and Indian tribes. Lotteries in 43 states and the District of Columbia collectively generate $18 billion in revenue for state and local governments. Commercial casinos contribute $8 billion, while Indian tribes negotiate payments to states for permission to operate casinos on tribal lands. Casino companies promise jobs, economic development and other payoffs, but critics say the benefits are exaggerated and the social costs of gambling ignored. Lottery advocates view the game as a politically palatable revenue source, while critics warn against encouraging compulsive betting by lower-income residents. The criticisms are having little impact, and gambling may become more pervasive with the advent of legal online poker and other games.

Ka-ching! A slot machine pays off at the Aria Resort and Casino in Las Vegas. Commercial and Indian casinos in 38 states account for 65 percent of the revenue from gambling. Lotteries account for nearly 30 percent.

Inside This Report

The Issues 527
Background 534
Chronology 535
Current Situation 540
At Issue........................541
Outlook 543
Bibliography 546
The Next Step 547

CQ Researcher • June 15, 2012 • www.cqresearcher.com
Volume 22, Number 22 • Pages 525-548

CQPRESS

Los Angeles | London | New Delhi
Singapore | Washington DC

Recipient of Society of Professional Journalists Award for Excellence ◆ American Bar Association Silver Gavel Award

Gambling in America

The Issues

527 • Are lotteries a good way for states to raise revenue?
• Do states benefit from casinos?
• Should Internet gambling be legal?

Background

534 **Gambling Debates**
Long-held objections in the early 20th century gradually yielded to relaxed morality and revenue needs.

537 **Betting on Games**
In the 1980s, states and tribes began turning to casinos and lotteries for revenue.

538 **One More Round**
Internet gambling exploded in the 21st century, while casinos and lotteries steadily expanded.

Current Situation

540 **Competing for Customers**
Rivalry is especially fierce in New York and Rhode Island.

542 **Looking Online**
Lawmakers in California and New Jersey are readying proposals to legalize Internet gambling.

Outlook

543 **All About the Money**
Gambling will become less dependable as a revenue source, experts say.

Sidebars and Graphics

528 **Casinos Legal in Most States**
Thirty-eight states have at least one form of casino.

529 **Compulsive Gambling's Warning Signs**
Symptoms include lying and preoccupation with betting.

530 **Tribes Aim to Cash In on Casinos**
"There are haves and have-nots in tribal gaming."

532 **Casino and Lottery Revenues Rose**
Casinos accounted for 65 percent of the growth from 2000 to 2009.

535 **Chronology**
Key events since 1931.

536 **Problem Gamblers Struggle to Beat Habit**
"Each day I make that commitment to not gamble today."

541 **At Issue**
Do lotteries take advantage of the poor?

For Further Research

545 **For More Information**
Organizations to contact.

546 **Bibliography**
Selected sources used.

547 **The Next Step**
Additional articles.

547 **Citing *CQ Researcher***
Sample bibliography formats.

Cover: Getty Images/City Center/Ethan Miller

CQ Researcher

June 15, 2012
Volume 22, Number 22

Managing Editor: Thomas J. Billitteri
tjb@cqpress.com

Assistant Managing Editor: Kathy Koch
kkoch@cqpress.com

Contributing Editor: Thomas J. Colin
tcolin@cqpress.com

Associate Editor: Kenneth Jost

Staff Writer: Marcia Clemmitt

Contributing Writers: Peter Katel, Barbara Mantel, Jennifer Weeks

Design/Production Editor: Olu B. Davis

Assistant Editor: Darrell Dela Rosa

Fact Checker: Michelle Harris

Los Angeles | London | New Delhi
Singapore | Washington DC

An Imprint of SAGE Publications, Inc.

Vice President and Editorial Director, Higher Education Group:
Michele Sordi

Director, Online Publishing:
Todd Baldwin

CQ Researcher (ISSN 1056-2036) is printed on acid-free paper. Published weekly, except: (March wk. 5) (May wk. 4) (July wk. 1) (Aug. wks. 3, 4) (Nov. wk. 4) and (Dec. wks. 3, 4). Published by SAGE Publications, Inc., 2455 Teller Rd., Thousand Oaks, CA 91320. Annual full-service subscriptions start at $1,054. For pricing, call 1-800-834-9020. To purchase a *CQ Researcher* report in print or electronic format (PDF), visit www.cqpress.com or call 866-427-7737. Single reports start at $15. Bulk purchase discounts and electronic-rights licensing are also available. Periodicals postage paid at Thousand Oaks, California, and at additional mailing offices. POSTMASTER: Send address changes to *CQ Researcher*, 2300 N St., N.W., Suite 800, Washington, DC 20037.

Gambling in America

By Kenneth Jost

The Issues

Mega Millions fever was sweeping the country when Merle Butler stopped at a local convenience store on the evening of March 28 in his hometown of Red Bud, Ill., and put down $3 for three chances at the biggest jackpot in U.S. lottery history. The retired computer analyst stuffed the ticket in his billfold without even glancing at the randomly generated numbers on his Easy Pick entry.

Two days later, Butler was watching TV with his wife Patricia when a newscast reported the six numbers on the winning entry: 02, 04, 23, 38, 46 and the 23 Mega Ball. After quickly jotting the numbers down, Butler pulled out the ticket to check — and, then, to double-check.

"After I looked at it for a couple of minutes, I turned to my wife . . . and says, 'We won,' " Butler told a news conference three weeks later. "She kind of looked at me funny, and I says, 'No, we won.' And then she started giggling, and she giggled for four hours." [1]

The Butlers were not alone in their good fortune; they will share the $656 million prize with winners in Kansas and Maryland who — unlike in Illinois — do not have to be publicly identified under state law. The Butlers' share is $218.7 million.

Nor are the Butlers and the other winners alone in winning or sharing nine-figure jackpots in the 10-year history of the giant, 42-state lottery. Since its debut, Mega Millions has awarded nine-figure jackpots 49 times, according to an unofficial count, including the previous record: $390 million shared by two winners in March 2007. [2]

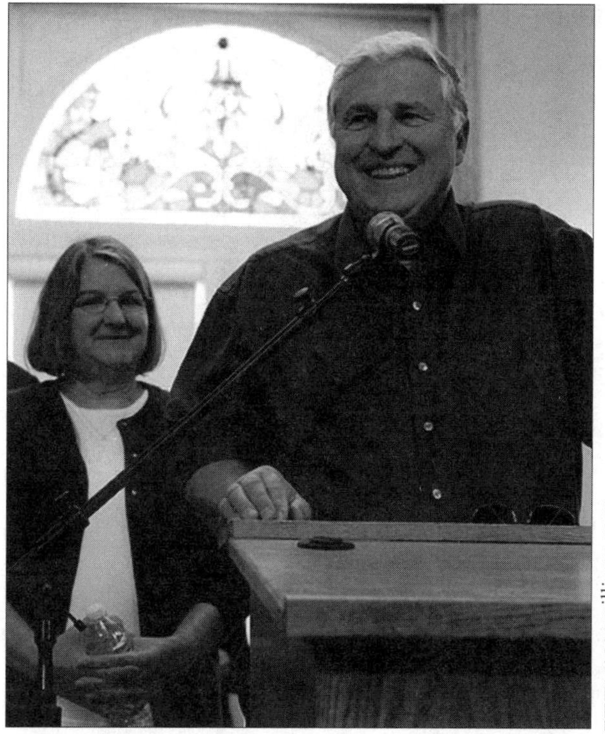

www.megamillions.com

Merle and Patricia Butler meet the press after accepting their $218.7 million share of the $656 Mega Millions jackpot on April 18, 2012, in Red Bud, Ill. For lawmakers and governors, gambling offers a revenue source more politically palatable than new taxes. But gambling critics say the social costs — including the consequences of marketing an addictive product — are unacceptable.

Lotteries were illegal in Illinois and the rest of the country when Butler, 62, was coming of age in tiny Red Bud, 35 miles southeast of St. Louis. Today, they are not only legal but officially sponsored by 43 states and the District of Columbia. The vast majority of Americans play at least occasionally, many of them obsessively: An estimated 100 million people bought tickets for the March 30 drawing. And the proceeds — about one-third of the total take — help finance state and local governments, to the tune of approximately $17.8 billion in 2011. [3]

Casino gambling was also illegal throughout the United States for most of the 20th century except in Nevada, which turned Las Vegas into a gaming mecca for slot machines and table game players not only in the United States but from around the world. Today, casinos operated by private companies or Indian tribes can be found in 38 states. (*See chart, p. 528.*) And they, too, contribute to state finances. Gaming revenues for state and local governments from commercial casinos amounted to $7.9 billion in 2011, according to the American Gaming Association, the trade association for the commercial casino industry. [4]

The spread of lotteries and casinos attests to the dramatic change in Americans' attitudes toward gambling since the mid-20th century. [5] Americans "like to gamble," says Frank Fahrenkopf, the association's president and chief executive officer. Gross revenue from all forms of gambling amounted to $89.3 billion in 2009, according to Christiansen Capital Advisors, a New York-based gaming industry watcher. That represents a recession-related dip from the peak of $92.2 billion the year before. (*See graph, p. 532.*)

In the past, the love of gambling — along with the hope of a winning number or a winning hand — was kept in check by other social forces, including moral or religious objections and fear of the social costs for gamblers and their families as well as society at large. The moral objections have receded in the face of advancing secularization and growing libertarianism in the United States. Concerns about the social costs of gambling have diminished as social safety nets have been established and law enforcement has improved.

The critical reason for gambling's increased acceptance, however, has been its role in providing revenue for state governments. "There's a high acceptance rate of lotteries throughout

Casinos Legal in Most States

Thirty-eight states have at least one of the three types of casinos now in operation: commercial (land-based and riverboat) tribal and "racinos" (casinos at horse-racing tracks). Many states also allow card rooms and electronic gaming devices. Nearly 60 percent of the commercial casinos are in Nevada; a fourth of the tribal casinos are in Oklahoma.

Number of Casinos by Type and State, December 2011

State	Land-based or riverboat casino	Racetrack casino	Tribal casino	Card room	Electronic gaming device
Alabama	0	0	3	0	0
Alaska	0	0	2	0	0
Arizona	0	0	25	0	0
California	0	0	70	89	0
Colorado	40	0	2	0	0
Connecticut	0	0	2	0	0
Delaware	0	3	0	0	0
Florida	0	5	8	24	0
Idaho	0	0	8	0	0
Illinois	10	0	0	0	0
Indiana	11	2	0	0	0
Iowa	15	3	1	0	0
Kansas	2	0	4	0	0
Louisiana	14	4	3	0	2,159
Maine	0	1	0	0	0
Maryland	1	1	0	0	0
Michigan	3	0	24	0	0
Minnesota	0	0	38	2	0
Mississippi	30	0	3	0	0
Missouri	12	0	1	0	0
Montana	0	0	13	288	1,549
Nebraska	0	0	6	0	0
Nevada	256	0	3	0	2,010
New Jersey	11	0	0	0	0
New Mexico	0	5	22	0	0
New York	0	9	7	0	0
North Carolina	0	0	2	0	0
North Dakota	0	0	10	0	0
Oklahoma	0	2	114	0	0
Oregon	0	0	9	0	2,323
Pennsylvania	4	6	0	0	0
Rhode Island	0	2	0	0	0
South Dakota	35	0	11	0	1,498
Texas	0	0	1	0	0
Washington	0	0	34	114	0
West Virginia	1	4	0	0	1,552
Wisconsin	0	0	29	0	0
Wyoming	0	0	4	0	0
Total	**445**	**47**	**459**	**517**	**11,091**

Source: "State of the States: The AGA Survey of Casino Entertainment," American Gaming Association, 2012, p. 4, www.americangaming.org/files/aga/uploads/docs/sos/aga_sos_2012_web.pdf

America," says David Gale, executive director of the North American Association of State and Provincial Lotteries, in Geneva, Ohio. "Their primary role is to generate the revenues for those programs and services that they have been earmarked to support in the states."

State-sponsored lotteries — the first in the modern era was established in 1964 in New Hampshire — "seemed to make other forms of gambling look more acceptable," wrote professors Patrick A. Pierce and Donald E. Miller, of St. Mary's College, in Notre Dame, Ind., in their book *Gambling Politics*. "Once the state engaged in the business of sin, gambling lost part of its stigma." [6]

Fahrenkopf similarly stresses the financial contributions that casino gambling makes to states through taxes as well as economic development. "We're an industry that is taxed very, very high," Fahrenkopf says. Pennsylvania, for example, takes 55 percent of the proceeds from slot machines at the 10 casinos in the state; combined with a 16 percent tax on table game proceeds, the state took in nearly $1.5 billion from the casinos in 2011. [7]

For lawmakers and governors, gambling offers a revenue source more politically palatable than new taxes. "It's much easier to make an argument for expanding gambling than it is for increasing the income tax or sales tax," says Lucy Dadayan, a senior policy analyst with the Rockefeller Institute of Government at the State University of New York-Albany.

The role that gambling has come to play in state government finance sits uncomfortably with those who worry about its social costs. "It's trite to say that state governments have become addicted to gambling, but it's also true," says Keith Whyte, executive director of the National Council on Problem Gambling in Washington, D.C.

"It's a revenue source that is unsustainable," says Les Bernal, executive director of the Washington-based organization Stop Predatory Gambling. "The only way you can increase gambling revenues is for more and more people to lose more and more money."

For most of the past decade, more and more people were in fact losing more money in lotteries and in both commercial and tribal casinos. But the economic recession hit the casino industry hard, according to Eugene Christiansen, chairman of Christiansen Capital Advisors. "The recession was really bad news because people started reducing spending," Christiansen says. In addition, the freezing of credit markets hurt casino companies that had taken on debt to upgrade and modernize facilities in an effort to attract customers in the increasingly competitive market for entertainment dollars.

Today, Christiansen and Fahrenkopf both say the gaming industry is on the upswing again. "The good news is that after a couple of very bad years, things seem to have flattened out and are on an uptick," Fahrenkopf says. Christiansen says the industry is experiencing "a weak recovery."

Tribal casinos are also taking in more money after experiencing a first-ever drop in 2009, according to an annual survey. The report, published by *Casino City Press*, a gaming industry research company, shows Indian casinos with 44 percent of overall casino revenue in 2010, only slightly below the 45 percent share for commercial casinos. "Racinos," which combine horse-race tracks with casinos, account for the remaining 11 percent. [8] *(See sidebar on tribal casinos, p. 530.)*

Overall, revenue from lotteries has continued to increase, according to Gale, in part because the number of states offering lotteries has kept growing. Arkansas became the 43rd state to sponsor a lottery in 2009.

Lotteries and casinos, however, may be hard pressed to continue to grow, according to industry experts. "Lotteries are maturing," says Gale. "There's no doubt about it." None of the seven states without lotteries seems likely to join the club in the foreseeable future. *

Prospects for growth in the casino business are also cloudy, according to Christiansen. "The map is filling up," he says. Fahrenkopf is somewhat less bearish. "The market will tell us when there are too many," he says.

One venue ripe for growth, how-

---

* States without lotteries are Alabama, Alaska, Hawaii, Mississippi, Nevada, Utah and Wyoming.

Compulsive Gambling's Warning Signs

The American Psychiatric Association has recognized pathological gambling as a mental disorder since 1980. Symptoms listed in the association's Diagnostic and Statistical Manual of Mental Disorders *(the so-called* DSM*) include preoccupation with gambling, loss of control and commission of crimes to try to recoup losses. Individuals with at least one of the symptoms are defined as "problem gamblers."*

Symptoms of Pathological Gamblers

Preoccupation — Preoccupied with gambling, such as by reliving past gambling experiences, planning next wagers or thinking about ways to obtain gambling money.

Tolerance — Needs to gamble with increasing amounts of money to achieve desired excitement.

Withdrawal — Restless or irritable when attempting to reduce or quit gambling.

Escape — Gambles to escape problems or relieve an unfavorable mood, such as feelings of helplessness, guilt, anxiety or depression.

Chasing — After losing money on gambling, often returns another day to get even.

Lying — Lies to family members, therapists, others to conceal extent of gambling.

Loss of control — Has made repeated, unsuccessful attempts to control or stop gambling.

Illegal acts — Has committed theft, fraud or other illegal acts to finance gambling.

Risk to significant relationship — Has jeopardized or lost a significant relationship, job or educational or career opportunity because of gambling.

Bailout — Has relied on others to provide money to relieve desperate financial situations caused by gambling.

Source: "DSM-IV Criteria for Pathological Gambling," National Gambling Impact Study Commission, June 1999, pp. 4-2, govinfo.library.unt.edu/ngisc/reports/4.pdf

Tribes Aim to Cash In on Casinos

"There are haves and have-nots in tribal gaming."

Gamblers looking for the biggest casino in the United States need directions not to Las Vegas but to Foxwoods Resort Casino in southeastern Connecticut, midway between Boston and New York City. And the owner of the 6.7 million-square-foot facility — bigger than the Pentagon — is not any of the big names associated with Las Vegas like Harrah's or Caesar's but the Mashantucket Pequot Tribal Nation, a federally recognized Indian tribe with fewer than 1,000 members. [1]

Native American tribes own almost as many casinos in the United States — 459 — as do private companies, which have 492, counting horse track locations. Tribal casino revenues totaled $26.7 billion in 2011, compared to $35.6 billion for commercial casinos. The décor may be different — more Native Americana at tribal facilities — and the locations more out of the way. But the slots and the games are much the same. And, just like the states, Indian tribes have one overriding reason for promoting gambling on tribal lands: money.

Gambling "gives [tribes] enough money to employ people on the reservation, to generate economic activity on the reservation," says Jason Giles, executive director of the National Indian Gaming Association, in Washington. "That's the primary goal of having a gaming operation." [2]

"Gambling has usually been pushed and legalized insofar as it can be relevant to developing government resources," says Kevin Washburn, a gaming-law expert and dean of the University of New Mexico Law School in Albuquerque. "It's similar for tribes. They've built hospitals, roads and schools and increased the level of government services generally."

Indian gaming has been controversial from the beginning of its modern era in the 1980s, when the U.S. Supreme Court rebuffed an effort by state and local authorities to restrict bingo games at Indian reservations in Riverside County, Calif. The court's 6-3 decision in *California v. Cabazon Band* (1987) relied on the federal interest in promoting tribal self-sufficiency to hold that states cannot regulate Indian gaming except as permitted by federal law. Congress responded the next year by passing the Indian Gaming Regulatory Act, which protects tribes' right to allow gambling subject to compacts to be negotiated in good faith with state governments. [3]

Today, 247 tribes — not quite half of the 554 recognized tribes — operate gaming facilities in 29 states. Some are near population centers such as those in California, Connecticut, Florida and Oklahoma; others are more remote, like those in Alaska or Montana. Overall revenues have been steady, according to Giles, despite the 2008 recession and slow recovery since. But the overall figure obscures significant disparities. Forty of the casinos account for more than three-fourths of the revenue, he says, while "the vast majority" of tribes get no revenue from their gaming. "There are haves and have-nots in tribal gaming," Washburn says.

Relations with state governments remain critical and contentious. In Florida, the Seminole Tribe charged the state government in the 1990s with bad faith in negotiations over a gaming compact; the Supreme Court blocked the suit in a 1996 decision. Only in 2010 did the Seminoles and the state finally reach agreement on allowing full casino operations. The

ever, is the Internet. A crucial factor is a Justice Department legal opinion in December 2011 that cleared the way for states to permit online betting except on sports on an intrastate basis. "That's huge," says Anthony Cabot, who heads the gaming law group at a Las Vegas law firm and also teaches at the University of Nevada's Boyd School of Law. Meanwhile, critical observers worry that the social costs from gambling are getting short shrift. "The benefits are easy to measure," says Edward Morse, a professor at Creighton University School of Law in Omaha and co-author of a book on the casino industry. "The costs are harder to measure, and politicians exploit that over time." [9]

As lottery states work to boost sales, casino operators compete for customers and more states consider legalizing casinos, here are some of the questions being debated:

Are lotteries a good way for states to raise revenue?

The Arkansas state constitution first prohibited lotteries in 1836. By 2000, more than 30 states were sponsoring lotteries, but Arkansas voters decisively rejected a ballot initiative that would have amended the constitution to permit lotteries as well as six casinos in the state.

Eight years later, however, the state's voters approved by a 25 percent margin an amendment to permit lotteries with funds earmarked for college scholarships for Arkansas citizens. "It sounded too good to voters," Jerry Cox, president of the anti-lottery Arkansas Family Council Action Committee, acknowledged after the election. [10]

Lotteries were a common means of public financing earlier in American history but fell out of favor from the mid-19th until the mid-20th century. They regained popularity for one reason: money for state governments. "Absolutely," says lottery association executive Gale. "Every lottery in its original bill determines where lottery funds are to be directed," Gale explains — typically for education or, more recently, specifically for scholarships.

compact includes a provision — as in most of the state-tribal agreements — for the tribe to share revenue with the state government.

Until recently, the Pequots were definitely in the "have" category. Foxwoods has produced billions of dollars in revenue for the tribe since full casino operations began in 1992. The proceeds allowed the tribal council to dispense annual stipends to adult tribal members exceeding $100,000 apiece. But the payments have been suspended since the casino hit hard times brought on by the recession, increased competition and overinvestment.

Today, the casino is $2.3 billion in debt and trying to negotiate a severe refinancing with creditors. The tribal council says the community "is pulling together," but a tribal elder was less sanguine in a comment to an Associated Press reporter. "Our stress levels are very high up here," Loretta Libby remarked. "I just don't know what's going to happen."

Nationally, further expansion of Indian gaming may be geographically limited, Washburn says. "There's not a whole lot of undeveloped markets," he says. "Most of the tribes that have markets for gambling have been offering it already."

Felix Stein

Bigger than the Pentagon, the Foxwoods Resort Casino in Connecticut, owned by the tiny Mashantucket Pequot Tribe, is the nation's largest casino.

The lagging economy also poses a challenge, according to Giles. "It's a business that's dependent on consumers and their ability to spend entertainment dollars," he says. "Until the economy gets stronger, we're going to remain where it's at.

"There are plenty of tribes with expansion plans, but the market's going to have to be more secure for the tribes to do that."

— Kenneth Jost

---

[1] Background drawn from Michael Sokolove, "A Big Bet Gone Bad," *The New York Times Magazine*, March 18, 2012, pp. 36ff. See also Michael Melia, "Conn. tribe sees fortune reversal amid casino woes," The Associated Press, March 28, 2012.

[2] For previous coverage, see Peter Katel, "American Indians," *CQ Researcher*, April 28, 2006, pp. 361-384, updated Aug. 5, 2010; "Indian Casinos Rake in Billions," in Patrick Marshall, "Gambling in America," *CQ Researcher*, March 7, 2003, pp. 214-215.

[3] For a full account of legal background, see Kevin K. Washburn, "The Legacy of Bryan v. Itasca County: How an Erroneous $147 County Tax Notice Helped Bring Tribes $200 Billion in Indian Gaming Revenues," *Minnesota Law Review*, Vol. 92, (2008), pp. 919 ff.

Critics find it unseemly, or worse, for state governments to depend on gambling for revenue, especially as more promotion is needed to keep up sales. "The public voice of American government today is lotteries and casinos," says Bernal with Stop Predatory Gambling. Apart from military recruitment, lotteries are virtually the only program that governments routinely advertise. "It's a government program that's based on pushing citizens into deeper personal debt and creating addiction to feed off it," he says.

"Lotteries have become quite aggressive" in their marketing, according to Whyte with the problem-gambling council. "You would never see a billboard saying buy another package of Luckies because we need the revenue," Whyte says. "But that's exactly what you see on state lotteries, operating and profiting from an addictive product."

Morse, the Creighton law professor, finds lotteries especially "pernicious" because they draw players primarily from the less well-educated and the less well-to-do. "If you ask in an office, almost none of the professional staff play," Morse says. "The support staff plays almost every week, and they spend a lot of money." Rockefeller Institute analyst Dadayan similarly calls lotteries "a very regressive tax."

Gale dismisses the criticisms. He emphasizes first that lotteries are strictly voluntary. "If you don't pay your taxes, what happens to you? They may come after you and haul you off to jail," Gale explains. "If you don't buy your lottery ticket, what happens to you? Nothing. It's a choice that people have."

Gaming industry executive Fahrenkopf echoes the point. "Lotteries are a tax on the willing," he says.

Gale also disagrees that lotteries draw primarily from lower socioeconomic classes. "I don't believe it's the lower-income folks who are supporting the games," he says. "Pretty much the demographics of the lottery player tracks the demographics of the state's population." He acknowledges that lower-income players may spend a larger percentage of their income on lotteries than higher-income players do,

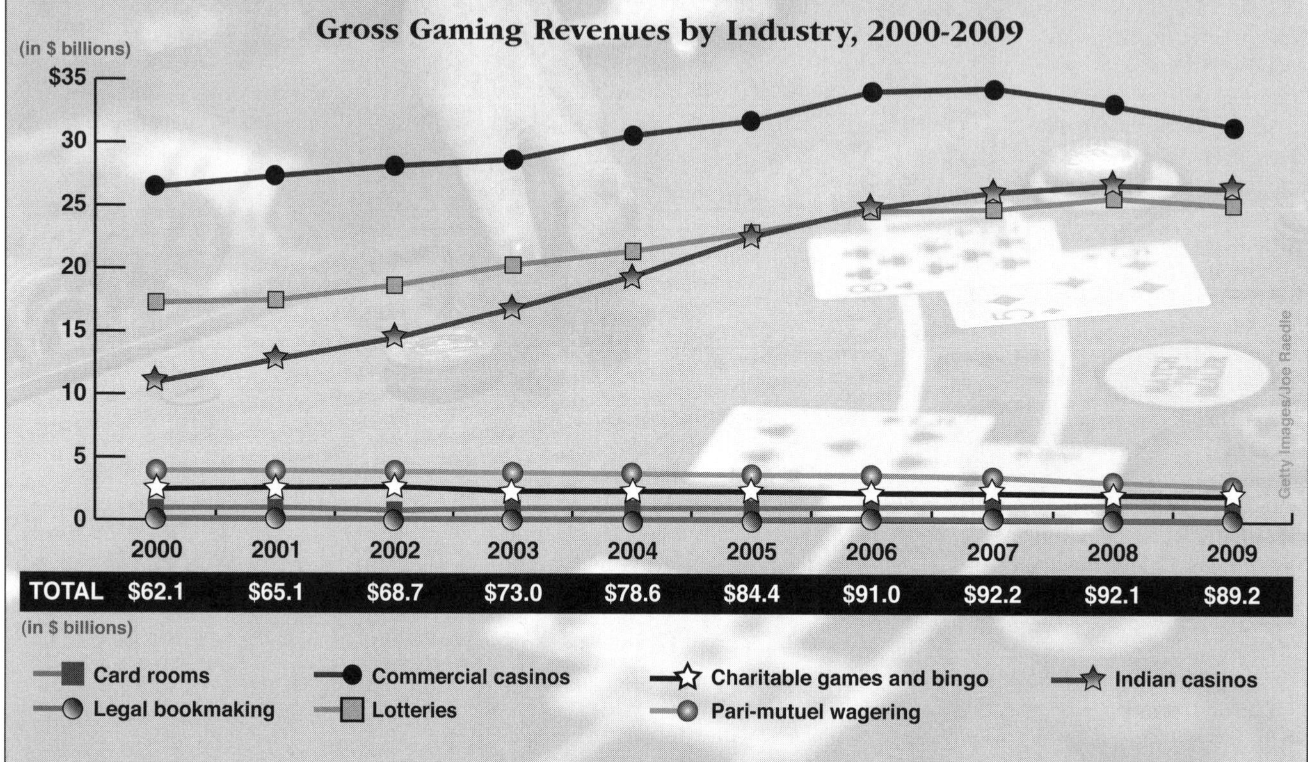
Casino and Lottery Revenues Rose
Total gaming revenues rose nearly 44 percent, from $62 billion in 2000 to about $89 billion in 2009, the latest year for which data are available. They hit $92 billion in 2007 but then dipped during the next two years amid the nation's steep economic downturn. Commercial and tribal casinos accounted for 65 percent — or $58 billion — of 2009 revenue. Lotteries accounted for 28 percent, or $25 billion.
Gross Gaming Revenues by Industry, 2000-2009
(in $ billions)
$35
30
25
20
15
10
5
0
2000
2001
2002
2003
2004
2005
2006
2007
2008
2009
TOTAL $62.1 $65.1 $68.7 $73.0 $78.6 $84.4 $91.0 $92.2 $92.1 $89.2
(in $ billions)
Card rooms
Legal bookmaking
Commercial casinos
Lotteries
Charitable games and bingo
Pari-mutuel wagering
Indian casinos
Getty Images/Joe Raedle
Source: "Gaming Revenue By Industry: 2000 to 2009," U.S. Census Bureau, September 2011, www.census.gov/compendia/statab/2012/tables/12s1259.xls

but he says the same comparison is true for expenditures on groceries or other budget items.

Overall, lottery money represents only a small — and a declining — fraction of state budgets: "niche" revenue, as an expert with the National Conference of State Legislatures once put it. Net proceeds from lotteries amounted to 1.19 percent of total state revenue in 1997; by 2006, they amounted to only 0.97 percent of total state revenue — midway between motor vehicle license taxes (1.07 percent) and tobacco excise taxes (0.82 percent). [11]

For some states, the percentages are higher — more than 7 percent in Rhode Island, South Dakota and West Virginia, according to the nonpartisan Tax Foundation. [12] Whatever the amounts, gambling consultant Christiansen says state governments count on the money. "If you're a state treasurer, I will tell you that numbers like that are meaningful," he says.

Advertising and promotion are "absolutely" essential to keeping up demand, according to St. Mary's political scientist Pierce. "Advertising is really the only way for states to keep their lottery at their current level," he says. "If they didn't do that, they would probably see noticeable drops in revenue."

Gale acknowledges as much. "Lotteries having a product to sell are no different from Coke or Pepsi," he says. "They have to maintain communication with their players." Bigger jackpot games are one draw. "Yes, it's absolutely a way to bring in new players," he says.

The odds against winning or sharing in a nine-figure jackpot are nearly astronomical, of course: 176 million to 1 in the March 30 drawing. But Gale emphasizes the availability of smaller prizes in the games as well. "Lots of people are winning lots of times on all the lottery games," he says.

Despite the efforts of governments to boost gambling revenue, Dadayan warns against relying too much on gambling for state budget needs. "In the long run, the revenues from gambling are much less than the pending needs," she says. "States cannot count on gambling as a sustainable source of revenue for funding education and other services."

Do states benefit from casinos?

When the Iowa legislature authorized riverboat casinos in 1989, it required an initial vote in the county where the vessel was to be docked and subsequent votes every eight years for the operator's license to be renewed. Two decades later, the legislature in 2011 amended the law to eliminate the need for continuing referendums after an initial renewal.

In urging the change, Sen. Jeff Danielson, a Cedar Falls Democrat and floor manager for the legislation, noted that counties with existing casinos had routinely approved gambling referendums by margins of 70 percent or higher. The renewal requirement made it harder for casinos to borrow money, Danielson explained, because banks are reluctant to extend favorable rates to borrowers who need voter approval every eight years to stay in business. [13]

Gaming association president Fahrenkopf points to the development as evidence of the growing acceptance of casinos in communities with gambling operations. Further evidence along the same line comes from a poll of elected officials and civic leaders in casino states other than Nevada, published in the association's most recent annual report.

Eighty-three percent of those surveyed said the overall impact of casinos on their communities has been positive, while only 13 percent said the impact had been negative. And 88 percent said the feared negative impacts cited by casino opponents — crime, prostitution and a bad image generally — had not materialized. [14]

Industry consultant Christiansen says there has been "a huge historic shift" in public opinion toward casinos. "Today, when casinos are proposed in a jurisdiction, the response is, 'Everybody else does. Why haven't we done this already?' "

Casino interests and supporters make their pitch to voters and lawmakers on three major grounds: casinos bring jobs, promote economic development and pay substantial state and local taxes. Overall, commercial casinos employed 339,098 people in 2011 and paid $12.9 billion in wages, according to the gaming association — both figures slightly below the previous year's.* Total taxes paid to 22 states amounted to $406.5 million, up 6 percent from the previous year. Total consumer spending at commercial casinos amounted to $958.7 million, up from the previous year. "We're a mainstream industry," Fahrenkopf says. [15]

Critics respond by minimizing the claimed benefits. They note, for example, that casino revenue may simply "cannibalize" business from other, often locally owned, establishments. They also emphasize what they believe are substantial social costs, chiefly increased crime in casino jurisdictions and increased personal bankruptcies among casino patrons.

The social science research cited by the critics is sharply disputed by the industry. "You can't prove it conclusively to everybody's satisfaction," says Morse, the Creighton law professor. [16]

The leading academic on the issue is Earl Grinols, a professor of economics at Baylor University in Waco, Texas. In a book published in 2004, Grinols calculated that the social costs of gambling — chiefly, derived from problem and pathological gamblers — exceeded the social benefits by a ratio of 3-to-1. Grinols repeats that estimate in a fact sheet that summarizes testimony he gave to Minnesota legislators in 2011 on behalf of the Freedom Foundation of Minnesota, a limited-government advocacy group. [17]

In Grinols' analysis, the principal social cost derives from crimes committed by pathological gamblers, estimated at more than $4,300 per individual. In his book, Grinols cited studies showing that a majority of gamblers in treatment and a majority of members of Gamblers Anonymous had committed illegal acts as a result of their gambling. He also notes a study used by the congressionally created National Impact of Gambling Study Commission in its 1999 report that found pathological gamblers three times more likely to have been incarcerated at some time in their life than individuals who had not gambled.

Other social costs cited by Grinols include lost productivity and work time, bankruptcy, social service costs, illness and family costs in terms of divorce, separation, child abuse and neglect and domestic violence. In addition, he cited an estimated $3,800 per pathological gambler in what he called "abused dollars" — in effect, income put at risk in gambling instead of being used for essential needs.

In a more recent overview, Douglas Walker, an associate professor of economics at the College of Charleston in South Carolina, says the crime estimates cited by Grinols and other gambling industry critics are overstated. He also questions the validity of counting gambling losses or bad debts as a "social" instead of an individual cost. On the other hand, Walker also says the tax revenues from the gambling industry may be overstated. [18]

Fahrenkopf bluntly rejects the claimed social costs. Critics "are out there arguing that the sky is going to fall, that it's going to increase bankruptcy, that crime is going to increase," he says. "That's never proven true in any place where they've made that argument."

* Tribal casinos are not included; tribal casinos do not pay state taxes but typically agree to share revenue with states in order to secure permission to operate.

Morse counters that social costs associated with problem gamblers cannot be denied. "To the extent that you make gambling easily accessible," he says, "it's likely that you're going to exacerbate the problems that problem gamblers have."

Should Internet gambling be legal?

Illinois lottery officials think they have a sure-fire idea for boosting ticket sales: the Internet. Beginning on March 25, Illinois became the first state to allow residents to buy lottery tickets online.

Illinois Lottery Superintendent Michael Jones calls the move the beginning of "a new era" that brings the lottery in line with the growing reality of e-commerce. Northstar, the private company that manages the Illinois Lottery, predicts that online sales will attract 600,000 to 1 million new customers, people who have grown up with the Internet but do not think to buy lottery tickets. The company promises user-friendly ticket buying and a registration process that will inhibit underage and out-of-state play. [19]

Illinois legislators approved Internet lottery sales three years ago, but the move had been on hold pending an answer from the U.S. Department of Justice on whether online sales would violate the 1961 Interstate Wire Act, which prohibits use of any "wire communication facility" for betting on "any sporting event or contest." The Justice Department replied in December 2011 that the act applies only to sports betting. [20]

The Illinois move holds out the prospect of increased sales for the state's 38-year-old lottery but is also stirring concern among the existing network of retail outlets, which fear reduced sales and commissions. But the Justice Department opinion has bigger implications nationwide because it lifts what had been thought to be a broad federal prohibition against Internet gambling, including online poker.

"This is hugely important," says Las Vegas gaming law expert Cabot. "It effectively says to the states that with the exception of sports, you are free to do whatever you want to do on an intrastate basis."

The enthusiasm within the gambling industry is matched by concern among the industry's critics, who fear that the Internet will add to the social costs of problem gambling. "Now the big push is to open a lottery and a casino and a lottery retailer in every home, office, dorm room and smart phone in America," says Bernal with Stop Predatory Gambling. "Internet gambling will be open 24 hours a day, seven days a week, right in your home or office or on your phone."

Online poker, offered by sites based outside the United States, exploded by 2005 into a $2.5 billion industry despite the Justice Department's previous stance against Internet gambling and despite concern on Capitol Hill. [21] Congress responded in 2006 by passing the Unlawful Internet Gambling Enforcement Act, which made it illegal for financial institutions to process payments for online betting. [22]

Some online sites closed down after President George W. Bush signed the measure into law on Oct. 13, 2006. The Justice Department stiffened its stance in April 2011 by obtaining indictments against the operators of three offshore poker sites, two based in Antigua and one on the Isle of Man, for allegedly violating the law. By January 2012, prosecutors had obtained convictions against three of the 10 defendants. [23]

The casino industry has historically resisted Internet gambling, fearing competition but emphasizing concerns about consumer protection. "Millions of Americans have been going online with no consumer protection whatsoever, no jobs being created and no taxes being paid," Fahrenkopf says. But he says the industry now supports federal legislation that would allow states to permit online gambling with sufficient safeguards.

With Internet gambling legislation failing to advance in Congress, however, federal policy is uncertain, and the initiative lies with the states. "The debate now is whether the feds will allow it or will leave it to the states," industry consultant Christiansen says. "The question is difficult to predict because the politics are extremely complex."

States are showing interest but exercising caution. The Iowa Senate approved legislation in March to permit online poker, but the bill was blocked in the House. California and New Jersey legislators are also studying the issue. Meanwhile, Nevada is already accepting applications for online casinos, with decisions expected by the end of the year. [24]

Christiansen says lottery states likely will look to Illinois' experience with online sales before proceeding on their own. New York, which began offering a limited online lottery game in 2005, has plans in the works for two additional jackpot games online.

Despite the legal uncertainties, William Eadington, director of the Institute for the Study of Gambling and Commercial Gaming at the University of Nevada-Reno, says there is "a degree of inevitability" about online gambling. And he discounts the critics' concerns that the Internet will add to the social costs, noting that online gambling is already legal in Britain and several other European countries. "The experience in Europe suggests that it's not going to ravage society," Eadington says. "The social costs are not going to be that different." ■

BACKGROUND

Gambling Debates

Gambling reached its present level of acceptance in the United States only after long-held objections based on religious views and social costs

Continued on p. 536

Chronology

Before 1960

Commercial gambling, lotteries are illegal nationwide as 20th century begins.

1931
Nevada legalizes casinos; Las Vegas becomes tourist mecca for gamblers.

1950-1951
Senate investigative committee documents links between organized crime, gambling.

1960s-1980

First state-sponsored lotteries; New Jersey legalizes casinos.

1964
New Hampshire becomes first state in modern era to sponsor lottery. Three more states follow: New York (1967), New Jersey (1970), and Massachusetts (1974).

1971
North American Association of State and Provincial Lotteries formed.

1972
National Council on Problem Gambling founded.

1976
New Jersey legalizes casinos in bid to revive Atlantic City.

1980
American Psychiatric Association recognizes pathological gambling as mental disorder.

1980s-1990s

More states sponsor lotteries, approve casino gambling; Indian tribes gain conditional right to operate casinos on tribal lands.

1985
National Indian Gaming Association founded.

1987, 1988
Supreme Court says tribes can operate gambling facilities on reservations in states where gambling is legal (1987). . . . Indian Gaming Regulatory Act requires states, tribes to negotiate over gambling operations (1988).

1994
National Coalition Against Legalized Gambling founded; reorganized in 2008 as Stop Predatory Gambling.

1995
American Gaming Association founded.

1996
Supreme Court rules that tribes cannot sue state governments for damages for refusing to negotiate gambling compacts.

1997
Poll finds that a majority of Americans — 52 percent — had played a lottery within previous year.

1999
National Gambling Impact Study Commission calls for rollback in "convenience" gambling; recommendations not acted on.

2000-Present

More state lotteries are launched; casino competition intensifies in Northeast; online poker booms.

2002
Macau permits privately owned casinos; surpasses Las Vegas as world's biggest gambling center by 2007.

2005
U.S. online poker revenue is estimated at $2.5 billion, despite legal curbs.

2006
Unlawful Internet Gambling Enforcement Act prohibits use of credit cards or online payment systems for Internet gambling in United States.

2007-2008
U.S. economy falls into recession; gambling revenues drop.

2008
Arkansas becomes 43rd state to legalize lottery; ballot measure to earmark revenues for college scholarships approved with 63 percent of vote.

2010
Delaware, Pennsylvania permit table games at existing slots casinos. . . . Washington, D.C., quietly approves measure to permit online gambling; after controversy, measure repealed in February 2012.

2011
Massachusetts permits three casinos and one slots-only facility in state (Nov. 22). . . . Nevada Gaming Commission permits online poker (Dec. 22). . . . Justice Department says states can permit intrastate online gambling, except on sports (Dec. 23).

2012
New York legislature gives initial approval to constitutional amendment to legalize casinos. . . . Retired Illinois couple win $218 million share of record $656 Mega Millions jackpot in March 30 drawing; winners in Kansas, Maryland not identified. . . . California, New Jersey legislatures consider online gambling bills. . . . Rhode Island to vote on permitting table games at slot parlors (Nov. 6).

Problem Gamblers Struggle to Beat Habit

"Each day I make that commitment to not gamble today."

Ted Hartwell began playing poker as a youngster, under the tutelage of his father, a professor at Texas Tech University. He played in college, earning enough to get his own apartment, and he played more once he got a job in Las Vegas. Eventually, Hartwell was playing video poker so often that he lied to his family and coworkers about the time spent and the money lost — and lied to himself about his ability to stop.

Carol Hare began gambling two years after moving to Las Vegas to help relieve stress from marital difficulties. The gambling accelerated after her divorce the next year. Video poker became the primary focus of her life. She lost jobs, lost friends and lost time with her three young children. She wrote bad checks to get cash to keep playing, got an eviction notice and contemplated suicide.

Today, Hartwell and Hare are both recovering gambling addicts. Hare has not gambled for 21 years, Hartwell for five. Hare deals daily with the issue as executive director of the Nevada Council on Problem Gaming, a private, nonprofit counseling and referral center. The issue is also constantly on Hartwell's mind. "Each day I make that commitment to not gamble today," Hartwell explains, "recognizing that people who've had a lot more time in recovery than I had have gone back."

Problem gamblers number in the tens of thousands in Nevada and in the millions in the United States. A study commissioned by the Nevada legislature in 2002 estimated that 2.1 percent of the state's population met the definition of "pathological" gamblers laid out in the American Psychiatric Association's clinical guide. (*See box, p. 529.*) Another 3 percent met the broader category of "problem" gambler. [1] Based on the state's current population, that might mean 57,000 pathological gamblers and another 81,000 problem gamblers.

Nationwide, Keith Whyte, executive director of the National Council on Problem Gambling, in Washington, says studies estimate that 1 percent of the population meet the definition of pathological gambling — about 3 million people — with another 3 million to 6 million problem gamblers. The total social cost of problem gambling, Whyte says, is $7 billion per year. [2]

The resources for helping problem gamblers are greater than when Hare began to face her problem in 1991. "There were no billboards, no newspaper stories, no educational programs," Hare recalls. She was guided into counseling by an observant bartender, himself a compulsive gambler.

Today, casinos in Nevada are required by law to post information about the national gamblers hot line. And Nevada is one of 35 states with problem-gambling agencies financed in part with public funds, according to Whyte. But he calls the overall funding "a pittance" — about $60 million per year. In Nevada, Hare says her council's annual budget once was around $500,000, but the public funding was cut in half last year when the legislature diverted half of a $2-per-slot machine fee earmarked for the agency to the state's general fund.

Continued from p. 534

yielded to a relaxed morality and an insistent drive by states and Indian tribes for new revenue sources. At the start of the 20th century, every form of non-social gambling except betting at horse racing tracks was illegal virtually nationwide. Those bans fell over the course of the century — first in a few states and then in a rush to legalization by the end of the 1990s. [25]

Lotteries were a common means of public financing in colonial America and in the first decades of U.S. independence. The colonies used lotteries because England denied them any taxing powers. The earliest American universities — including Harvard, William and Mary and Yale — were funded in part through lotteries. After independence, states used lotteries because no other major tax mechanisms had been created. Recreational gambling was also common, especially in the South and along the Western frontier. But there was also opposition, based on religious beliefs dating from the Puritan era and on more specific concerns over time about crime and corruption and the social inequity of deriving funds from the poor by holding out the promise of easy wealth.

The opposition to gambling gathered strength from the 1830s and became established national policy by the end of the century. States dropped and in many cases specifically banned lotteries, whether public or commercial. The last of the legal lotteries, the state-chartered Louisiana Lottery Company, established in 1864, was so tainted with corruption that Congress passed laws in the 1890s to prohibit interstate mailing or transportation of lottery materials. In upholding the interstate transport ban in 1903, the Supreme Court condemned "the wide-spread pestilence of lotteries." [26] Meanwhile, professional gamblers had given recreational gaming a bad reputation as well, thanks to sometimes shady practices and the seemingly inherent association with alcohol and prostitution. Congress reflected early 20th-century national sentiment by requiring territorial Arizona and New Mexico to prohibit casinos in order to gain statehood.

The modern era of gambling began in Nevada, a state with a history of widespread legal gambling until a legislated ban in 1909. The ban did not eliminate gambling but drove it underground. The legislature then lifted the

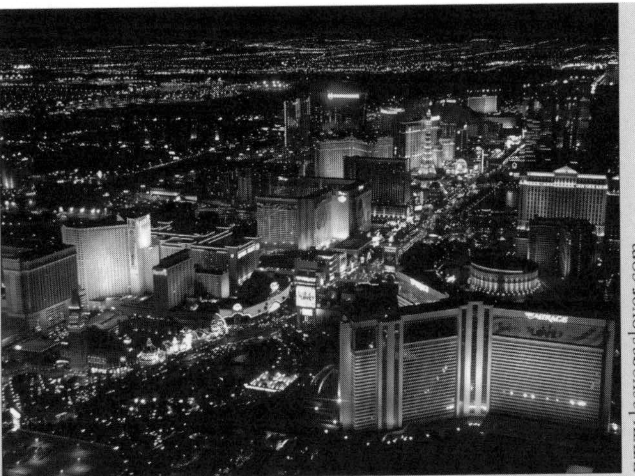
www.lasvegaslover.com

Casinos in Nevada are required by law to post information about the national gamblers hot line. Nevada is one of 35 states with problem-gambling agencies financed in part with public funds. Above, the Las Vegas "Strip."

Scientific understanding of problem gambling has also advanced in the past two decades. Today, gambling addiction is recognized as having a biological basis, according to Whyte. "The features that characterize substance abuse also characterize gambling addiction," he says.

Hartwell recalls how the addiction felt. "It goes beyond a pleasure point to an anesthetic effect," he says. "I was completely checking out when I was gambling compulsively." Today, understanding the physical sensations of addiction is a big help, Hartwell says.

Despite advances in the science, the treatment options are largely what they were two decades ago: cognitive therapy, group sessions and 12-step protocols. "There are no medications approved yet," Whyte say. "But there have been some promising trials in the past decade."

Hare started volunteering with the Nevada council in 1993. Somebody at Harrah's, one of the big casino companies, heard her talk and helped get her hired for two years as a paid consultant on what the company should do about problem gambling. Harrah's decided to help beef up the council, and Hare became a full-time staff member in 1996.

Today, she says the gaming industry recognizes its responsibility to help with prevention and treatment of problem gambling. Frank Fahrenkopf, president of the American Gaming Association, says the industry provides about $20 million per year toward the effort. Says Hare: "We would like for them to do more."

"This is a mental health disorder," she adds. "It's in everybody's interest that more be done."

— Kenneth Jost

[1] Cited in J. Patrick Coolican, "Tony's Story: The pull of a drug, the push to the brink," *Las Vegas Sun*, Nov. 22, 2009.

[2] For a comprehensive though dated overview, see "Problem and Pathological Gambling" in National Impact of Gambling Study Commission (1999), http://govinfo.library.unt.edu/ngisc/reports/4.pdf.

ban in 1931 to allow the little desert town of Las Vegas to profit from the influx of thousands of construction workers building Boulder Dam (now Hoover Dam), about 30 miles to the south. Organized-crime figures provided some of the financing and much of the expertise for the first casinos. The town grew slowly at first, then more rapidly after World War II as tourism boomed in economic good times. With Reno and Tahoe its only competition, Las Vegas rose to become the gambling capital of the nation and, to some extent, the world. [27]

Legal lotteries returned to the United States beginning in 1964, but only after proposals were defeated or failed to come to a vote in several states — including Nevada — and in Congress.

Low-tax New Hampshire debuted with a sweepstakes-style lottery after the legislature authorized a referendum that won approval with 73 percent of the vote. Poorly run — too complicated, not enough outlets — the lottery netted only $2.7 million for state education, short of the projected $4 million. New York followed in 1967, but its lottery also fell short of expectations. New Jersey is credited with launching the first successful modern lottery in 1971, two years after gaining approval with 82 percent of the vote. New Jersey grossed $137 million in sales in its first year — more than five times the projected amount — thanks to aggressive marketing, widespread availability and frequent prizes. Eleven states followed suit by the end of the decade. [28]

Casino gaming had failed to advance, in part because of congressional hearings in the early 1950s documenting the link to organized crime. Proposals to legalize casinos failed in several states, including New Jersey in 1974. Two years later, however, the state's voters narrowly approved a proposal to allow casinos in Atlantic City, a once-prosperous shore resort much in need of revitalization. The first of what would eventually become a dozen casinos opened in 1978, but Atlantic City's hoped-for boom failed to materialize because of Las Vegas's stronger appeal for fun-seeking tourists and the later legalization of state and tribal casinos elsewhere in the East and Mid-Atlantic regions.

Betting on Games

Gambling grew in the 1980s and '90s as one state after another as well as many Indian tribes bet on lotteries or casinos for needed revenue. By the end of the century, lotteries had become a commonplace activity for a majority of Americans. Commercial or tribal casinos were operating in a majority of states. Tens of thousands of electronic gaming devices (EGDs), including slot machines, video poker, video keno and so forth, had been installed in bars, truck stops, convenience stores and other locations — legally in some states, more dubiously in others. And Internet gambling was rapidly increasing after debuting with the birth of the World Wide Web in 1995. [29]

The rapid spread of lotteries in the 1970s continued in the next two decades, with lotteries operating in 37 states and the District of Columbia by 1997 and sales that year totaling $34 billion. A national opinion poll in 1997 found that 52 percent of Americans had played a lottery within the previous year; per capita annual spending on lotteries in states with legal games was put at $150. To boost sales, states adopted more frequent prize drawings. To meet competition from large lotteries, six states and the District of Columbia formed the Multi-State Lottery Association in 1987, joined by nine more, before its Powerball game debuted in 1992. Despite the remote chance of a jackpot, Powerball took in more than $1 billion in the next few years.

Casino gambling advanced less rapidly, abetted by states' desires for revenue but slowed by still strong concerns about the social effects of commercial gaming. The nine states that legalized casinos from 1989 till the end of the century typically confined them to specific locations targeted for economic development, such as "historic" Deadwood in South Dakota's Black Hills region (1989). States along the Upper Mississippi Valley — Iowa, Illinois and Missouri — approved riverboat casinos one after another specifically to draw customers from the state on the river's other side. By 2000, commercial casinos' gross revenue had risen to $26.5 billion, according to Christiansen Capital Advisors' compilation. In a telling bow to revenue needs, Iowa legislators initially set a $5 limit on casino bets but lifted the restriction in 1994.

Indian tribes entered the casino business only after a legal and political battle in the courts and in Congress over their power to allow casinos on tribal reservations. The Supreme Court backed tribes with a 1987 decision allowing them to operate casinos in states that permitted gambling; Congress gave the states significant leverage the next year by passing the Indian Gaming Regulatory Act to require tribes to negotiate with state government over terms of operation. Some states balked, and the Supreme Court in 1996 ruled that tribes could not sue a state for damages for refusing to negotiate.

Despite the difficulties, tribal gaming spread, with 146 tribes operating casinos in 24 states by the end of the decade; revenue ballooned from $212 million in 1988 to $6.7 billion in 1997. Combined with legal states with no tribal operations, casinos could now be found in 28 states altogether.

In addition to lotteries and casinos, stand-alone slot machines, video poker, video keno and other EGDs proliferated in the 1980s and '90s. South Carolina, which legalized cash payoffs from video poker in 1991, had 34,000 machines in operation in 1999, with $2.5 billion in gross receipts and licensing fees to the state totaling $60 million. Even so, the machines were banned in 2001 after the state supreme court blocked a proposed referendum to determine their legality.

Besides South Carolina, several other states had at least 10,000 EGDs, including some such as Alabama, New Jersey and West Virginia, where machines were labeled "for amusement only" and cash payoffs were made surreptitiously. "Such devices provided only minimal revenue and none of the claimed benefits in employment and economic development. In addition, video poker in particular was lastingly stigmatized by clinical psychologist Robert Hunter as "the crack cocaine" of gambling because of the addictive nature of a rapid-fire game with the seeming prospect of skill-based payoffs. [30]

By the mid-1990s, Congress had grown sufficiently concerned to create a commission in 1996 to study the impact of gambling — much like one in the 1970s that had come up with a laundry list of recommendations, few of which were adopted. The report by the new National Gambling Impact Study Commission, released June 18, 1999, set out 76 recommendations, including a moratorium on further expansion of gambling. The report also urged reduced advertising of state lotteries, a ban on Internet gambling and expanded research about and treatment for problem gambling. [31]

Today, commission member Richard Leone, a senior fellow with the Century Foundation, a nonpartisan think tank in New York City, credits the commission with encouraging research and helping prompt Congress to ban use of credit cards for Internet gambling. Otherwise, he says he was "disappointed by the lack of impact."

One More Round

Gambling gained legal status in a few more states in the 21st century, leaving Hawaii and Utah as the only states with no state- or tribal-sponsored or commercial gaming. Internet gambling, especially online poker, grew robustly, even in the face of the federal government's official position that using the Internet to bet across state or national borders was illegal. The old forms of gambling — pari-mutuel wagering on horse or dog racing and charitable games and bingo —

continued to decline, but the take for lotteries and commercial and tribal casinos alike grew steadily except for a dip after the 2008 economic downturn.

State-sponsored lotteries won approval in four Southeastern states in the 2000s after campaigns tied to education funding overcame religious-based opposition. [32] South Carolina voters approved a lottery in 2000 by a comfortable 54 percent to 46 percent margin despite opposition from the state Chamber of Commerce, NAACP and church groups. Tennessee voters followed suit, with 58 percent approval. In North Carolina, the legislature approved a lottery in 2005, with a tie-breaking vote cast by the state's Democratic lieutenant governor. Voter approval of the lottery referendum in Arkansas in 2008 left Alabama and Mississippi as the only holdout states in the Southeast. Religion was seen as the main barrier in Alabama, but in Mississippi fear of competition with casinos was seen as a bigger factor.

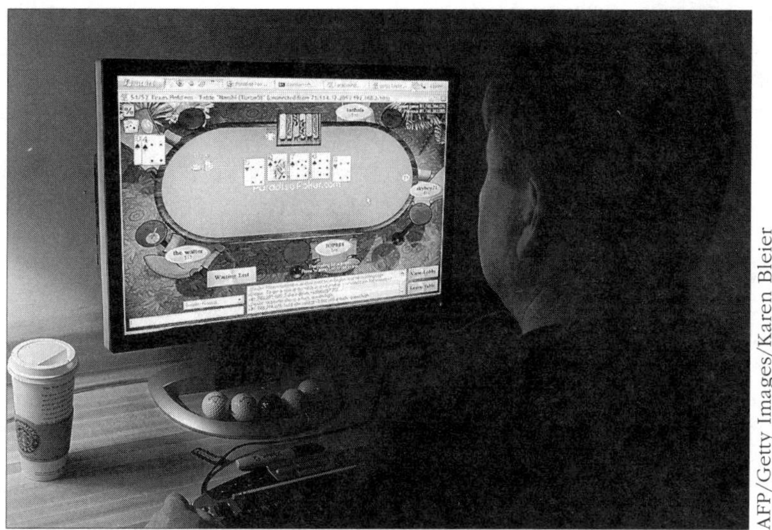

AFP/Getty Images/Karen Bleier

Online poker, offered by sites based outside the United States, exploded by 2005 into a $2.5 billion industry despite Justice Department opposition and concern on Capitol Hill. But last December the department lifted what had been thought to be a broad federal prohibition against Internet gambling, including online poker. States are showing interest but exercising caution. So far, Nevada is the only state with legal rules on the books to allow Internet gaming; online sites may be up and running by the end of 2012.

Meanwhile, casino gaming advanced in the Mid-Atlantic region as neighboring states in the geographically compact area maneuvered either to capture customers outside their borders or hold on to gambling dollars from their own residents. New York touched off the border war in 2002 by approving six new tribal casinos as well as slots at five horse-racing tracks — so-called "racinos." Maryland voters gave 59 percent approval in November 2008 to a constitutional amendment allowing slot machines at five sites. West Virginia approved table games for a horse track in Charles Town, W. Va., late in 2009. Pennsylvania and Delaware both acted in January 2010 to approve table games at existing casinos. The movement reached Maine in November 2010 as voters approved a $165 million casino and resort in a small town near the New Hampshire border. [33]

As lotteries and casino gambling steadily grew, betting on the Internet was exploding despite mixed signals as to its legality. In 2001, Christiansen Capital Advisors estimated online poker revenues at $82 million. By 2005, the figure had increased nearly 30-fold to $2.4 billion. An estimated 1.8 million people were playing nightly, two-thirds of them Americans. [34] Until December 2011, the Justice Department clung to its position that all online gambling was illegal, not just sports betting, even in the face of a federal appeals court opinion in 2002 rejecting the position.

The government had no practical way, however, to go after the estimated 23 million people in the United States betting online or to shut down the offshore Internet sites in such places as Antigua, Barbuda, Gibraltar and the Isle of Man. Congress gave the government a tool with the 2006 credit-card transaction ban, which anti-gambling senators slipped somewhat unnoticed into a port-safety bill with no public hearing. [35] But online poker continued to grow. *Financial Times* estimated revenue in 2008 at $5.9 billion, more than double Christiansen's estimate in 2005. Meanwhile, Antigua was continuing to contest the validity of the U.S. ban before the World Trade Organization. The WTO had issued a mixed ruling in April 2005 that upheld the United States' right to restrict Internet betting but also found the law discriminatory because remote gambling on horse racing was allowed. [36]

U.S. gambling interests also faced another economic threat from overseas: the rise of Macau and Singapore as major gambling meccas drawing not only Asian but also U.S. customers. Macau, the former Portuguese colony that China has overseen since 1999 as a separate administrative region, had been a gambling center since the mid-19th century. By ending a monopoly system for casino franchises, Macau's government opened the door in 2002 to new operators; by 2007, the build-up enabled Macau to surpass Las Vegas as the world's biggest gambling center. Meanwhile, Singapore was also advancing as a gaming resort destination. By mid-2011, it too was being projected to pass Las Vegas. [37]

With overseas competition increasing, U.S. gambling interests took another hit as the country fell into a recession beginning in December 2007. Overall revenue from lotteries and commercial casinos fell in fiscal 2009 for the first time since the late 1970s, according to the Rockefeller Institute. [38]

In response, 10 states enacted measures to expand gambling in fiscal 2010, according to the institute. By the end of 2011, the casino industry was striking an upbeat pose after what it conceded had been "difficult" years. "The slow and steady recovery of the commercial casino industry is well underway," according to the American Gaming Association's annual report. [39] ■

CURRENT SITUATION

Competing for Customers

The competition for gambling patrons is heating up in the Northeast Corridor, with New York and Rhode Island considering moves to legalize full-service casinos to undercut gaming facilities in neighboring states.

Rhode Island voters are being asked to approve two referendums submitted by the state legislature that would allow table games at the state's existing two slot parlors. The Twin River and Newport Grand facilities are both located near the state's border with Massachusetts, which is moving toward opening full-service commercial casinos for the first time.

New York is in an early stage of a plan strongly pushed by Gov. Andrew Cuomo to amend the state's constitution to permit as many as seven full-service casinos in the state. After initial approval by the New York legislature in March, the amendment needs a second legislative vote next year and statewide approval by voters to be adopted. Currently, New York has nine commercial racinos and five tribal casinos.

Rhode Island lawmakers are pushing the plan defensively to avert a potential loss of revenue after Massachusetts opens what are expected to be three "super-casinos" in the compact New England region. The Rhode Island slot parlors already face formidable competition from the giant tribal casino Foxwoods in southern Connecticut. [40]

Gambling revenue amounts to slightly more than 10 percent of Rhode Island's total revenue. Expansion of the existing slot parlors is "an absolute economic necessity," says Gary Sasse, a former state revenue director and now director of the Institute for Public Leadership at Bryant University in Smithfield. "We have to protect that economic base," he says.

Approval of the referendums is regarded as all but certain even though Rhode Island voters rejected a proposal in 2006 to permit a full-scale casino to be operated by the Narragansett tribe. But Leonard Lardaro, an economics professor at the University of Rhode Island in Kingston, calls the move "a quick fix" that will not protect gambling revenue in the long term or address the state's broader economic challenges.

"Once Massachusetts comes on line, we'll lose all the migration from the north of us," Lardaro says. "My worry is that this is going to be seen as a substitute for Rhode Island making the structural changes if Rhode Island is going to be successful going forward."

In New York, Cuomo, a Democrat in the second year of a four-year term, included expanded gambling as one of a series of economic-improvement measures that he recommended to the Democratic-controlled state Assembly and Republican-controlled state Senate in January. The New York Gaming Association, representing the existing racinos, released a report the same month saying that expanded gambling would result in $1.8 billion in construction and eventually generate about $350 million per year in state and local revenues. [41]

New York's gaming establishment already faces competition from casinos in three of the state's biggest neighbors: Connecticut, New Jersey and Pennsylvania, which legalized casinos in 2010. New York legislators gave initial approval to the proposed constitutional amendment as the annual session drew to an end in late March. But Cuomo is now catching flak on the proposal after *The New York Times* disclosed that the gaming association had contributed $2 million in December to the Committee to Save New York, a business and labor coalition closely allied with Cuomo. [42]

Cuomo denied any connection between the contribution and his support for expanded gambling. But Paul Davies, a journalist who writes the blog *GetGovernmentOutofGambling.org* under the auspices of the conservative-leaning Institute for American Values, says the disclosure indicates that "money and influence" are behind the push for gambling. "There's not a whole lot of due diligence or cost-benefit analysis that goes into trying to determine whether states should get into the gambling business," he says.

With a statewide vote still at least a year away, a Siena College poll taken before the legislative vote showed New Yorkers almost evenly split on the proposal: 49 percent opposed, 48 percent in favor. A month earlier, supporters had the edge: 52 percent to 44 percent. [43] Davies concedes that if the measure does get on the ballot, supporters, including gaming interests and labor unions, will be able to outspend any opposition groups that form.

Meanwhile, Maryland is opening a new stage in casino customer chasing with the debut of a mega-facility at a suburban shopping mall popular with

Continued on p. 542

At Issue:

Do lotteries take advantage of the poor?

LES BERNAL
EXECUTIVE DIRECTOR, STOP PREDATORY GAMBLING

WRITTEN FOR *CQ RESEARCHER*, JUNE 2012

After 40 years, only the willfully ignorant and the uninformed still claim government lotteries do not prey on the poor and least educated Americans.

Charles Clotfelter, a Duke University professor considered one of the nation's most respected lottery researchers, has said, "It's one of the easiest things to measure. The lottery is something for poorly educated and lower-income people." And lottery researcher Ross Rubenstein of Syracuse University has said there is no debate among scholars on whether lotteries prey on the poor. "There's simply no disagreement about it," according to Rubenstein.

The only people who claim otherwise are the state lotteries themselves, the gambling-interest groups that support them and the political leaders who approve of the schemes.

It helps explain why in a state such as Massachusetts, which operates one of the most profitable lotteries in America, the lottery's own survey data showed that only 9 percent of the public agreed that "the lottery improves the quality of life for the state's citizens."

To counter this reality, government lotteries have spent enormous sums of public dollars promoting the deception that they are doing a "social good," convincing the mass media to present the lottery program as a great debate rather than as a failed policy in which evidence continues to mount that lotteries prey on low- to middle-income citizens.

In 2008, *The New York Times* revealed lotteries extract 80 percent or more of their profits from 10 percent of their players — money derived from lottery outlets that are heavily concentrated in lower-income areas.

Severe economic times provide lotteries the chance to further intensify their profit making from America's desperate poor. Citizens play the lottery even more when times are tough, according to a study by Yale's Emily Haisley in *The Journal of Behavioral Decision Making*.

Perhaps the biggest indictment of government lotteries is that more than one in five Americans believe playing the lottery represents the most practical way to build wealth. The same 2006 survey by the Consumer Federation of America found the percentage was even higher among lower-income individuals, with 38 percent of those who earn less than $25,000 pointing to the lottery as a solution.

"No taxation without representation" was one of America's founding principles. After 40 years of government using lotteries to prey on its own citizens, the time has come to add the principle of "no taxation by exploitation" right beneath it.

yes

GORDON MEDENICA
PRESIDENT, NORTH AMERICAN ASSOCIATION OF STATE AND PROVINCIAL LOTTERIES; DIRECTOR, NEW YORK LOTTERY

WRITTEN FOR *CQ RESEARCHER*, JUNE 2012

Many myths about lotteries have survived for years. One of the more humorous is that the odds of winning the lottery are worse than getting hit by lightning. The story gets retold by journalists who may only focus on the odds of winning one of the top prizes in a big-jackpot game. In fact, roughly 1,000 people nationwide win at least $1 million from lottery games every year, but only about 250 get hit by lightning.

Another myth is that only poor people play the lottery. One reason many states started lotteries was to stop the illegal numbers rackets that preyed on players and did nothing to raise money for good causes. By making the games legal, credible and honest, states helped both the players and their lotteries' designated good causes.

But lotteries today offer many more games than just the daily numbers games. We have big-jackpot games like Mega Millions and Powerball, local jackpot games like Lotto, social-environment games like Keno and dozens of instant "scratch-off" games at a variety of price points. The lottery industry has become quite sophisticated at reaching all types of players with different kinds of games.

The demographics of lottery players almost perfectly match the demographics of the population at large. With so many people playing lottery games, it's simply not possible for any one segment of the population to dominate.

Another myth is that lottery play is a "regressive tax on the poor." But "regressive" is an economist's term for something that costs a larger percentage of someone's low income. By this definition, all consumer products, from milk to movies, are regressive. And lottery play is voluntary, not a tax.

Playing the lottery is simply an inexpensive form of entertainment. People play for a bit of excitement. Why is it that lotteries are judged by financial standards instead of by the entertainment they provide? The press is filled with stories about "poor odds," "bad investments" and "financial illiteracy" when discussing lotteries, but not when discussing other popular entertainment.

Lotteries provide a very secure, well-run form of entertainment for the large majority of the population that enjoys playing. They also provide much-needed funding for many good causes, such as education, the environment, veterans, local municipalities, old-age programs and scholarships. Lotteries raised almost $20 billion for good causes in North America last year; we are very proud of the contributions we make every day.

no

Continued from p. 540

area residents and interstate travelers. Maryland Live! debuted on June 6 at the Arundel Mills mall, about 15 miles southwest of Baltimore, with about 3,200 slots and other electronic games ready for an anticipated capacity crowd of 12,000. Plans call for 4,750 machines in all when completed. The casino is believed to be the first to be placed at an existing mall outside Nevada, but plans are either in the works or on the drawing boards for more gaming establishments to be placed in urban centers — making them more convenient to walk-in instead of drive-to customers. [44]

Looking Online

Lawmakers in California and New Jersey are moving ahead with proposals to legalize Internet gambling in their states even as bills to allow online gaming are failing to advance in other states. [45]

Meanwhile, family-values advocacy groups are urging Congress to enact a federal ban on Internet gambling. A ban would effectively nullify the Justice Department's late-2011 legal opinion clearing the way for states to allow online wagering on an intrastate basis. [46]

So far, Nevada is the only state with legal rules on the books to allow Internet gaming. The Nevada Gaming Commission approved regulations for online poker on Dec. 22, 2011, coincidentally one day before the Justice Department opinion was publicly announced. Nevada had had a law on the books for years to allow Internet gambling, but had been marking time because of legal doubts and because of opposition from some major gambling companies. Online sites in Nevada may be up and running by the end of 2012. [47]

Both New Jersey and the District of Columbia had moved earlier in 2011 toward permitting online poker, but the moves were thwarted. In New Jersey, Republican Gov. Chris Christie vetoed a bill on March 3 that would have legalized online gambling in the state. Along with criticizing some specifics, Christie contended that a referendum would be required to go beyond the terms of the 1976 ballot measure that allowed casino gambling only in Atlantic City. [48]

In Washington, an online gambling measure was included with little public attention in a budget bill passed late in 2010. The move provoked sharp controversy as D.C. officials began steps to implement it in fall 2011. In February, the D.C. City Council voted 10-2 to repeal the measure. [49]

The online gaming bills in California and New Jersey both have strong support but also face political cross-currents. In New Jersey, the issue pits lawmakers who view online gaming as a way to bolster Atlantic City's sagging casinos against others who want to allow online gambling at the state's horse tracks. In California, the principal bill would allow tribal casinos, card clubs and horse tracks to offer online poker immediately and other games such as 21 later; the state's Indian gaming association wants to allow online poker only, in order to protect brick-and-mortar casinos, while some tribes oppose the bill altogether.

With an estimated 2 million online poker players in the state, California represents a lucrative market for Internet gambling even on an intrastate basis. State Sen. Roderick Wright, a coauthor of the legalization measure, said California is "the leading Internet gaming market in the world" but is making "no money" from the games and has "no [consumer] protections for our citizens who play." [50]

Wright, a Democrat from Los Angeles County, is cosponsoring the bill with the Senate's Democratic leader, Darrell Steinberg of Sacramento. Both men are drawing scrutiny because of campaign contributions from gambling interests: $170,000 in donations to Wright since his 2008 campaign and $1.36 million in the past year to the Democratic Central Committee, which helps finance the party's legislative candidates in the general election. Steinberg says online gaming will bring in at least $200 million a year for the severely cash-strapped state government.

The New Jersey legislation gained approval from the state Assembly's gaming committee on May 10 after having been cleared in early March by the Senate panel with gambling jurisdiction. Democratic Assemblyman John Burzichelli, a sponsor, says online gaming will "rejuvenate our tourist industry" and also increase "employment, capital investment and much needed urban redevelopment." In opposing the bill, Assemblyman Ralph Caputo, also a Democrat, criticized limiting online sites to Atlantic City.

Prospects for the bill are clouded in part because of questions about the views of Christie, often mentioned as a possible running mate for presumptive GOP presidential nominee Mitt Romney. Christie's decision to back out of an address before a state gambling conference in May prompted speculation that he wanted to skirt what is a red-flag issue for some social conservatives. Romney has said he opposes Internet gambling. [51]

Among other states, Utah has protected its gambling-free status by passing preemptive legislation to prohibit online gaming in the state. Republican Gov. Gary Herbert signed the bill into law in late March after a 62-10 vote in the state Assembly and unanimous approval in the state Senate. The measure includes a provision that calls for opting out, if possible, of any federal law that gives blanket permission for Internet gaming. [52] Elsewhere, Internet gaming bills have failed in Hawaii — the nation's only other gambling-free state — and in Iowa and Mississippi.

Despite the limited advances so far, some gambling experts see online gaming as all but inevitable. "If it starts to go on a state-by-state basis, it will roll across the country just like lotteries did," says Las Vegas attorney Cabot. ■

OUTLOOK

All About the Money

The Minnesota Vikings wanted the state to pick up most of the tab for a new and much needed $1 billion football stadium, but the state had no readily available revenue source for its share. So, as part of a protracted political fight, the state legislature hit on the same, pain-free solution that lawmakers in other states have looked to in recent decades to ease fiscal woes: gambling.

The deal, cleared by the legislature on May 10, allows the existing $1 billion charitable games industry — licensed to help fund nonprofit organizations — to initiate electronic gaming on so-called pull-tabs games now played on cardboard. * The hoped-for revenue boost from young, hip customers is intended to generate $348 million in additional state taxes earmarked for the stadium while also providing more money to fund nonprofit organizations. [53]

Minnesota is following the example set by every other state and Indian tribe that has legalized gambling over the past 81 years. Whatever appeal gambling has as entertainment, government officials view it primarily as a source of revenue. But experts, including industry supporters and critics, are now warning that it is becoming harder for states to draw more money out of Americans' urge to gamble.

"Gambling is going to become an increasingly less important source of revenue for governments," says University of Nevada professor Eadington. "There's a cap on how much people are willing to spend on gambling."

Faced with lagging tax flows from gambling, states turn — as in Minnesota — to ideas for attracting new customers or drawing more money from existing customers, according to St. Mary's professor Pierce. The prospect of a decline "makes states desperate to do just about anything to maintain the revenue," he says.

Anti-gambling advocates view the states as partners in an unwholesome alliance with a profitable industry adept at using its political influence to further its ends with little regard for the public interest. "The casino interests spend a ton of money," says Get Government Out of Gambling blogger Davies. "There really is no one on the other side that has the deep pockets to wage a battle. And the media usually doesn't do a very good job of documenting both sides."

Casino interests contribute heavily to political campaigns for an industry of its size, according to data compiled by Citizens for Responsive Politics, a campaign finance monitoring group. Federal campaign contributions for the 2008 election cycle totaled $17.7 million, the group says, about two-thirds to Democrats. For 2012, contributions are already at $20 million, about evenly divided between Democrats and Republicans. [54] "These guys are some of the biggest funders of political campaigns," says Stop Predatory Gambling's Bernal. "They give money to all sides."

The critics say it is unwise for the government to rely on gambling taxes as an important revenue source. "It's a bad way to fund your government," says Davies. Bernal goes further. "It's immoral for government to prey on its own citizens," he says. "Citizens are not calling up legislators demanding more places to lose money," he adds.

Gaming industry chief Fahrenkopf dismisses the critics as out of step with the public. "The people who oppose the gaming industry view it as an illegal industry, as an immoral industry," he says. "But the majority of people don't view it that way."

As for preying on customers, Fahrenkopf says gamblers do not harbor illusions about the odds. "Most people know that when they go to a casino, the odds are in favor of the casino," he says. Fahrenkopf insists the industry does its part to control problem gamblers on the floor and to help fund research and treatment.

The lottery industry also touts its efforts on the issue. "The industry and the individual states are trying to be responsible, reminding people out there that this is a game," says lottery association executive director Gale. The association's home page features this message: "Remember to Play All Lottery Games Responsibly."

The critics are determined to dig in. "The failed government policy of predatory gambling will be one of the biggest issues of this decade," says Bernal. Eadington disagrees. "The anti-gambling movement has lost its punch," he says. "The war is almost over."

Meanwhile, the Mega Millions jackpot started over after the record-busting payout for the March 30 drawing. Some lucky winner or winners in California, unidentified so far, are holding the ticket for the $32 million jackpot from the May 29 drawing. Drawings are held Tuesdays and Fridays, every week, with winning prizes starting at $2. Overall, chances of winning a prize are 1 in 40. ■

* A pull-tab is a gambling ticket with a set of images on the front and perforated windows on the back that conceal images; the player wins, with an instant payout, if the images on the back, once disclosed, match those on the front. An electronic pull-tab adds images and sound and also eliminates the need to physically remove tabs.

Notes

[1] Quote taken from video clip of April 18 news conference by the *Belleville* (Ill.) *News-Democrat*, posted on You Tube: www.youtube.com/watch?v=_-7VVpowVAY. For print coverage, see Stacy St. Clair, "The best-kept Mega secret in Red Bud," *Chicago Tribune*, April 19, 2012, p. C1; Nicholas J. C. Pistor, "A Mega Moment for Red Bud Retirees," *St. Louis Post-Dispatch*, April 19, 2012, p. A1.

[2] See "Mega Millions Jackpot History," www.megamillions.com/winners/jackpothistory.asp.

[3] "State Government Finances: Income and Apportionment of State-Administered Lottery Funds, 2010," U.S. Bureau of the Census, www.census.gov/govs/state/10lottery.html.

[4] "State of the States: The AGA Survey of Casino Entertainment, 2012," American Gaming Association, p. 2, www.americangaming.org/files/aga/uploads/docs/sos/aga_sos_2012_web.pdf.

[5] For previous *CQ Researcher* coverage, see Patrick Marshall, "Gambling in America," March 7, 2003, pp. 201-224, and two reports by Richard L. Worsnop: "Gambling Under Attack," Sept. 6, 1996, pp. 769-792; and "Gambling Boom," March 18, 1994, pp. 241-264.

[6] Patrick A. Pierce and Donald E. Miller, *Gambling Politics: State Government and the Business of Betting* (2004), pp. 2-3, 4. Pierce is a professor of political science; Miller, now deceased, was a professor of mathematics.

[7] Cited in Michael Sokolove, "A Big Bet Gone Bad," *The New York Times Magazine*, March 18, 2012, pp. 36ff. See "State of the States," *op. cit.*, p. 21. Revenues in Pennsylvania are divided between the state gaming fund and general fund, horse racing industry, economic development and local governments.

[8] For highlights, see "Casino City's Indian Gaming Industry Report," 2012 edition, www.casinocitypress.com/gamingalmanac/indiangamingreport/. For coverage, see "American Indian tribes' casinos see turnaround," The Associated Press, March 6, 2012.

[9] Edward A. Morse and Ernest P. Goss, *Governing Fortune: Casino Gambling in America* (2007). Goss is a professor of economics at Creighton.

[10] Quoted in Charlie Frago and Michael R. Wickline, "Passage of all 5 ballot issues stuns some," *Arkansas Democrat-Gazette*, Nov. 6, 2008. The 2008 measure was approved by a vote of 648,122 (62.83%) to 383,467 (37.17%); the vote in 2000 was 309,482 (36.24%) to 544,550 (63.76%). See "Arkansas Secretary of State: Historical Initiative and Referendum Results," www.sos.arkansas.gov/elections/Documents/Initiatives_and_Amendments_1938-2010.pdf.

[11] See "Lotteries as a State Revenue," National Conference of State Legislatures, www.ncsl.org/issues-research/econ/lotteries-as-a-state-revenue.aspx.

[12] "Lottery Revenue as a Percentage of Own-Source Revenue by States, Fiscal Year 2008," Tax Foundation, March 25, 2010, http://taxfoundation.org/article/lottery-revenue-percentage-own-source-revenue-state-fiscal-year-2008.

[13] See William Petroski, "Senate passes proposal to study Internet poker," *Des Moines Register*, April 21, 2011, p. B3.

[14] "State of the States," *op. cit.*, pp. 23-27.

[15] *Ibid.*, pp. 5 (spending), 6 (revenue), 7 (employment).

[16] See Morse and Goss, *op. cit.*, chaps. 4 (economic development), 5 (social costs).

[17] See Earl L. Grinols, *Gambling in America: Costs and Benefits* (2004); Earl L. Grinols, "Gambling Economics: Summary Facts," April 29, 2011, www.freedomfoundationofminnesota.com/Websites/freedomfoundation/Images/Gambling%20Economics-%20Summary%20Facts%20by%20Professor%20Earl%20Grinols,%204.29.11.pdf.

[18] See Douglas M. Walker, "Overview of the Economic and Social Impacts of Gambling in the United States," in Leighton Vaughan Williams and Donald Siegel (eds.), *Handbook on the Economics of Gambling* (forthcoming), http://walkerd.people.cofc.edu/pubs/2012/OxfordCh_dist.pdf.

[19] See "Illinois Lottery Launches Internet Sales on Sunday," press release, March 26, 2012, www.illinoislottery.com/content/dam/ill/documents/subsections/pr/InternetSales.pdf. For coverage, see Jim Jaworski, "Jackpot tickets just a click away," *Chicago Tribune*, March 30, 2012, p. 3.

[20] See "Whether Proposals by Illinois and New York to Use the Internet and Out-of-State Transaction Processors to Sell Lottery Tickets to In-State Adults Violate the Wire Act," U.S. Department of Justice, Sept. 20, 2011, www.justice.gov/olc/2011/state-lotteries-opinion.pdf. The citation for the law is 18 U.S.C. §1084. For coverage, see Edward Wyatt, "Web Gambling Given a Boost in U.S. Ruling," *The New York Times*, Dec. 25, 2012, p. A1; some background drawn from article.

[21] See Brad Stone, "Going All In for Online Poker," *Newsweek*, Aug. 15, 2005, p. 40, www.thedailybeast.com/newsweek/2005/08/14/going-all-in-for-online-poker.html.

[22] See Heather Timmons and Eric Pfanner, "U.S. Law Causing Turmoil in Online Gambling Industry," *The New York Times*, Nov. 1, 2006, p. C3; Eric Pfanner, "Online-Gambling Shares Plunge on Passage of U.S. Crackdown Law," *ibid.*, Oct. 3, 2006, p. C3.

[23] Matt Richtel, "Authorities Crack Down on 3 Poker Sites," *The New York Times*, April 16, 2011, p. B1. For ongoing coverage, see *Internet Gambling News*, www.casinogamblingweb.com/main/other-gambling-news/internet-gambling-bill-news.jsp.

[24] See James Q. Lynch, "Online poker bill is dead, House speaker says," *Quad City Times*, March 15, 2012, p. A1; Tom Jones, "Online Poker Moves Closer in Iowa After Senate Approval," Casino Gambling Web, March 14, 2012, www.casinogamblingweb.com/gambling-news/gambling-law/online_poker_moves_closer_in_iowa_after_senate_approval_57735.html; See Richard N. Velotta, "Nevada approves nation's first regulations for Internet poker play," *Las Vegas Sun*, Dec. 22, 2011.

[25] For compact historical overviews, see Morse and Goss, *op. cit.*, pp 1-12; Pierce and Miller, *op. cit.*, pp. 9-24; Roger Dunstand,

About the Author

Associate Editor **Kenneth Jost** graduated from Harvard College and Georgetown University Law Center. He is the author of the *Supreme Court Yearbook* and editor of *The Supreme Court from A to Z* (both *CQ Press*). He was a member of the *CQ Researcher* team that won the American Bar Association's 2002 Silver Gavel Award. His previous reports include "Celebrity Advocacy" and "Police Misconduct." He is also author of the blog *Jost on Justice* (http://jostonjustice.blogspot.com).

"Gambling in California," California Research Bureau, January 1997, chap. 2, www.library.ca.gov/crb/97/03/crb97003.html#toc.

[26] *Champion v. Ames*, 188 U.S. 321 (1903).

[27] For a recent history, see John L. Smith, *Sharks in the Desert: The Founding Fathers and Current Kings of Las Vegas* (2005).

[28] See Matthew Sweeney, *The Lottery Wars: Long Odds, Fast Money, and the Battle Over an American Institution* (2009), pp. 78-80 (New Hampshire), 82-84 (New Jersey).

[29] Account drawn heavily from *National Gambling Impact Study Commission Final Report* (1999), chap. 2, http://govinfo.library.unt.edu/ngisc/reports/2.pdf.

[30] Hunter quoted in Bennett Liebman, "Not All that It's Cracked Up to Be," *Gaming Law Review*, Vol. 9, No. 3 (2005), p. 446.

[31] For coverage, see Brett Pulley, "Commission on Gambling Prescribes Broad Changes," *The New York Times*, June 19, 1999, p. A9; Edward Walsh, "Panel Urges Pause in Spread of Legalized Gambling," *The Washington Post*, June 19, 1999, p. A2.

[32] For detailed accounts, see Randy Bobbitt, *Lottery Wars: Case Studies in Bible Belt Politics, 1986-2005* (2007).

[33] Some information drawn from Iver Peterson, "And They're Off, as States Race to Add Gambling Sites," *The New York Times*, Nov. 18, 2002, p. B1; Mark Scolforo, "Poker, blackjack now legal at Pa. slots casinos," The Associated Press, Jan. 7, 2010.

[34] Cited in Stone, *op. cit.*

[35] See Frank Ahrens, "New law cripples Internet gambling," *The Washington Post*, Oct. 14, 2006, p. A1.

[36] See Fox Butterfield, "U.S. Limits on Internet Gambling Are Backed," *The New York Times*, April 8, 2005, p. C14; Paul Blustein, "U.S. Claims Victory on Web Betting Ban," *The Washington Post*, April 8, 2005, p. E4.

[37] See Keith Bradsher, "High Rolling Right Past Las Vegas," *The New York Times*, Aug. 28, 2007, p. C1; David Pierson, "Singapore bets big on casinos — and wins," *Los Angeles Times*, June 22, 2011, p. A1.

[38] See Lucy Dadayan and Robert B. Ward, "Back in the Black: States' Gambling Revenues Rose in 2010," Rockefeller Institute, State University of New York-Albany, June 23, 2011, www.rockinst.org/pdf/government_finance/2011-06-23-Back_in_the_Black.pdf.

[39] "State of the States," *op. cit.*, p. 11.

[40] For coverage, see Philip Marcelo, "Spending ramps up on casino issue," *Providence Journal*, May 1, 2012, p. 3.

FOR MORE INFORMATION

American Gaming Association, 1299 Pennsylvania Ave., N.W., Suite 1175, Washington, DC 20004; 202-552-2675; www.americangaming.org. The association, founded in 1995, represents the casino industry.

National Council on Problem Gambling, 730 11th St., N.W., Suite 601, Washington, DC 20001; 202-547-9204; www.ncpgambling.org. The council advocates for programs and services to assist problem gamblers and their families.

National Indian Gaming Association, 224 2nd St., S.E., Washington, DC 20003; 202-56-7711; www.indiangaming.org. The association, founded in 1985, represents organizations, tribes and businesses engaged in tribal gaming enterprises.

National Indian Gaming Commission, 1441 L St., N.W., Suite 9100, Washington, DC 20005; 202-632-7003; www.nigc.gov/. The three-member independent federal commission, established by Congress, regulates gaming activities on Indian lands.

North American Association of State and Provincial Lotteries, One S. Broadway, Geneva, OH 44041; 440-466-5630; www.naspl.org. The association, founded in 1971, represents 52 lottery organizations in the United States and Canada.

Stop Predatory Gambling Foundation, 100 Maryland Ave., N.E., Room 310, Washington, DC 20002; 202-567-6996; http://stoppredatorygambling.org/. The organization, founded in 2008 as the successor to the National Coalition Against Legalized Gambling, seeks to end what it calls the "failed policy of predatory gambling."

[41] "Racetrack Casinos in New York State: Current and Future Economic Impacts of Live Table Games," *Appleseed*, January 2012, New York Gaming Association, www.newyorkgaming.org/Libraries/Appleseed_Statewide_Final_Report_2-28-12/Appleseed_Final_Statewide_Report_2-28-12.sflb.ashx. The report was prepared by Appleseed, an economic development consulting firm.

[42] See Nicholas Confessore, Danny Hakin and Charles V. Bagli, "Gambling Group Gave $2 Million to a Cuomo Ally," *The New York Times*, June 5, 2012, p. A1.

[43] Siena College Poll, March 5, 2012, www.siena.edu/uploadedfiles/home/parents_and_community/community_page/sri/sny_poll/SNY_March_5_2012_ReleaseFINAL.pdf.

[44] See J. Freedom du Lac, "Betting on a $500 million draw," *The Washington Post*, June 7, 2012; Alexandra Berzon, "Casinos Chase Bettor," *The Wall Street Journal*, June 6, 2012, p. C3.

[45] For ongoing coverage, see *Poker News Daily*, www.pokernewsdaily.com/.

[46] Wayne Parry, "Groups in 13 states want US to block Internet bets," The Associated Press, June 7, 2012.

[47] See Chris Sieroty, "Online poker site rules approved," *Las Vegas Review-Journal*, Dec. 23, 2011, p. 1D; Richard N. Velotta, "Nevada approves nation's first regulations for Internet poker play," Dec. 22, 2011. See also Pamela M. Prah, "Nevada Has Head Start as States React to Federal Gambling Decision," *stateline.org*, Jan. 6, 2012, www.pewstates.org/projects/stateline/headlines/nevada-has-head-start-as-states-react-to-federal-gambling-decision-85899375377.

[48] See Megan DeMarco, "Christie vetoes legalized online gaming," *The Star-Ledger* (Newark, N.J.), March 4, 2011, p. 13.

[49] Tim Craig, "D.C. web gambling law is repealed," *The Washington Post*, Feb. 7, 2012, p. B1.

[50] Quoted in Patrick McGreevy, "Offering a cut from Internet poker," *Los Angeles Times*, May 15, 2012, p. AA1. Other background also from story.

[51] See Suzette Parmley, "Politics may be behind Christie's Internet gaming change of heart," *The Philadelphia Inquirer*, May 8, 2012, p. A1.

[52] Earl Burton, "Utah Becomes First State To Opt Out Of Any Federal Online Poker Regulations," *Poker Daily News*, March 25, 2012.

[53] See Jean Hopfensperger, "Minnesota is taking the lead on e-gambling," *Star Tribune* (Minneapolis), May 20, 2012, p. 1A.

[54] "Casinos/Gambling: Long-Term Contribution Trends," Center for Responsive Politics, www.opensecrets.org/industries/totals.php?cycle=2012&ind=N07 (visited June 2012).

Bibliography

Selected Sources

Books

Grinols, Earl, *Gambling in America: Costs and Benefits*, Cambridge University Press, 2004.
An economics professor now at Baylor University calculates that the social costs of casinos — including bankruptcy, crime, family costs and lost productivity — exceed by a factor of three the benefits, chiefly profits and taxes but excluding jobs. The gambling industry sharply challenges the analysis. Includes notes and 10 pages of references.

Haugen, David, *Legalized Gambling*, Facts on File, 2006.
The book gives an overview of the history and current status of legalized gambling in the United States along with a chronology, bibliography, glossary, list of organizations and agencies, guide to research and multiple appendices with pertinent statutes, reports and court decisions.

Light, Steven Andrew, and Kathryn R. L. Rand, *Indian Gaming and Tribal Sovereignty: The Casino Compromise*, University Press of Kansas, 2005 (paperback edition, 2007).
The co-directors of the Institute for the Study of Tribal Gaming Law and Policy at the University of North Dakota examine the history, laws and current politics of Indian gaming and set out recommendations for reform. Includes detailed bibliographical references.

Morse, Edward A., and Ernest P. Goss, *Casino Gambling in America: Governing Fortune*, University of Michigan Press, 2007.
The book traces the evolution of casino gambling in the United States through the first years of the 21st century, with chapters on the economic benefits, tax revenues and social costs associated with gaming and a detailed description of the regulatory environment at the federal, state and tribal levels. Morse is a professor of law and Goss a professor of economics at Creighton University. Includes detailed notes.

Pierce, Patrick A., and Donald E. Miller, *Gambling Politics: State Government and the Business of Betting*, Lynne Riener, 2004.
The book focuses on the politics behind the growth of legalized gambling in the United States, especially in regard to the states' role in promoting gambling as a revenue source. Pierce is a professor of political science at St. Mary's College in Notre Dame, Ind.; Miller was a professor of mathematics at St. Mary's until his death in 2008.

Skolnik, Sam, *High Stakes: The Rising Cost of America's Gambling Addiction*, Beacon Press, 2011.
The deputy editor of the *National Law Journal* and an admitted gambling addict uses his personal experience as the backdrop to informative chapters on, among other topics, the states' reliance on gambling revenues, problem gambling among Asian-Americans and the rise of online poker. Includes notes.

Smith, John L., *Sharks in the Desert: The Founding Fathers and Current Kings of Las Vegas*, Barricade, 2005.
A veteran Las Vegas journalist traces the city's history as a gambling mecca from its initial ties to organized crime to its present-day dominance by corporate moguls.

Sweeney, Matthew, *The Lottery Wars: Long Odds, Fast Money, and the Battle Over an American Institution*, Bloomsbury, 2009.
Sweeney sketches the rise and fall of lotteries from colonial America through the mid-20th century and then turns a critical eye to the pros and cons of their use as a revenue source by state governments. Includes chapter-by-chapter bibliography.

Wolfe, Alan, and Erik C. Owens, eds., *Gambling: Mapping the American Moral Landscape*, Baylor University Press, 2009.
Essays by 21 contributors from various disciplines cover the politics and policy of gambling, individual behavior and social impact, theology and gambling, and the place of gambling in American culture. Includes detailed notes, 41-page bibliography. Wolfe is a professor of political science and Owens an adjunct assistant professor of theology at Boston College and, respectively, director and assistant director of the Boisi Center for Religion and American Public Life.

Articles

"Bottoming Out: Gambling Addiction in Las Vegas," *The Las Vegas Sun*, Nov. 22-24, 2009, www.lasvegassun.com/gambling-addiction/.
The three-part series by reporters J. Patrick Coolican and Liz Benston profiles compulsive gamblers, examines the physiology of gambling addiction and explores the role of game design in the phenomenon. The Web version includes additional multimedia resources.

"Slot Machines: The Big Gamble," CBS News, "60 Minutes," Jan. 9, 2011, www.cbsnews.com/video/watch/?id=7228424n.
Correspondent Lesley Stahl reports on the proliferation of slot machines in the United States — 850,000, more than the number of ATMs — and the increased potential of modern, coinless machines to promote gambling addiction.

Reports and Studies

"Final Report," National Gambling Impact Study Commission, June 18, 1999, http://govinfo.library.unt.edu/ngisc/index.html.
Although dated, the 240-page report by the congressionally created commission provides comprehensive background information about the history and recent development of gambling in the United States. Includes references, contact information, glossary and other appendix material.

The Next Step:

Additional Articles from Current Periodicals

Casino Legalization

Bagli, Charles V., "Rivals Ready Onslaught to Sway Casino Debate," *The New York Times*, Feb. 8, 2012, p. A22, www.nytimes.com/2012/02/08/nyregion/legalizing-casinos-leads-to-fighting-among-factions.html?pagewanted=all.
Democratic New York Gov. Andrew Cuomo says the state should legalize full-scale casino gambling.

Hill, David, "Maryland Struggles to Cash in on Gambling," *The Washington Times*, Jan. 17, 2012, p. A1, www.washingtontimes.com/news/2012/jan/16/maryland-struggles-to-cash-in-on-gambling/?page=all.
Because of a lack of interest from qualified developers, Maryland has struggled to develop slots casinos.

LeBlanc, Steve, "Casino Industry Spent Millions Lobbying in Mass.," The Associated Press, Feb. 20, 2012, boston.cbslocal.com/2012/02/20/casino-industry-spent-millions-lobbying-in-mass/.
The casino industry has spent more than $11 million lobbying for the legalization of casinos in Massachusetts.

Internet Gambling

Bedell, Anita, "Internet Gambling Would Provide More Ways for You to Lose," *Rockford* (Ill.) *Register Star*, Jan. 6, 2012, p.A15, www.rrstar.com/opinions/x735286242/Guest-Column-Internet-gambling-would-provide-more-ways-to-lose.
The problems associated with legalizing Internet gambling far outweigh the benefits, says a church group.

Cooper, Michael, "Mired in Debt, States Pursue Web Gambling," *The New York Times*, Jan. 18, 2012, p. A1, www.nytimes.com/2012/01/18/us/more-states-look-to-legalize-online-gambling.html.
Several states are thinking about trying to plug budget gaps by legalizing, licensing and taxing Internet gambling.

Garcia, Oskar, "World's Richest Casino Exec Opposes Online Wagers," The Associated Press, Dec. 7, 2011.
Sheldon Adelson says he opposes online gambling to prevent young people from wagering.

Lotteries

Ford, Beverly, "Dwindling Lottery Dollars Put Municipal Budgets At Risk," *Lowell* (Mass.) *Sun*, March 25, 2012.
Massachusetts cities and towns are relying more and more on a thinning pool of lottery revenues.

Reitmeyer, John, "Mega Lottery Pays Off for N.J.," *The Record* (Bergen County, N.J.), April 5, 2012, p. A1.
New Jersey collected more than $40 million from its cut of the record-breaking Mega Millions jackpot in March.

Smith, Rick, "Iowa Lottery Is Watching Illinois' New Online Sales," *The Gazette* (Cedar Rapids, Iowa), March 29, 2012, thegazette.com/2012/03/29/iowa-lottery-is-watching-illinois-new-online-sales/.
The Illinois Lottery is the nation's first to permit the online purchase of lottery tickets.

Social Costs

Boyd-Barrett, Claudia, "Training to Address Gambling Problems," *Toledo* (Ohio) *Blade*, March 21, 2012, p. B4, www.toledoblade.com/local/2012/03/20/Seminar-to-help-with-gambling-addiction.html.
Officials in Toledo, Ohio, are hosting a specialized training session on preventing compulsive gambling.

Keilman, John, and Art Barnum, "Priest's $300,000 Theft Puts Spotlight on Gambling Addiction," *Chicago Tribune*, June 12, 2011, articles.chicagotribune.com/2011-06-12/news/ct-met-gambling-priest-0612-20110611_1_gambling-addiction-earl-grinols-regan.
A Chicago-area priest has stolen nearly $300,000 from his church's collection plate to fund his gambling addiction.

Taylor, Gary, "More in State Seek Help, But Gambling-Hotline Funds Cut," *Orlando* (Fla.) *Sentinel*, Nov. 3, 2011, p. A1, articles.orlandosentinel.com/2011-11-02/news/os-gambling-helpline-stats-20111102_1_gambling-problems-compulsive-gambling-treatment-for-problem-gamblers.
More and more Floridians with gambling problems are reaching out for help, but the state has cut funding for its helpline.

CITING *CQ RESEARCHER*

Sample formats for citing these reports in a bibliography include the ones listed below. Preferred styles and formats vary, so please check with your instructor or professor.

MLA STYLE

Jost, Kenneth. "Remembering 9/11," CQ Researcher 2 Sept. 2011: 701-732.

APA STYLE

Jost, K. (2011, September 2). Remembering 9/11. *CQ Researcher, 9*, 701-732.

CHICAGO STYLE

Jost, Kenneth. "Remembering 9/11." *CQ Researcher*, September 2, 2011, 701-732.

CQ Researcher

Published by CQ Press, an Imprint of SAGE Publications, Inc.

www.cqresearcher.com

U.S. Oil Dependence

Is independence from foreign oil possible?

The United States is producing more oil today than it has since 1998, but gasoline prices are still high, averaging more than $3.50 per gallon nationally in early June. New technology is making it possible to extract oil from tar sands and shale rock, but that oil is expensive, and its production causes major environmental impacts. President Obama advocates expanding production of all energy sources, including oil, gas, nuclear power, wind and solar, while warning that the United States can never pump enough oil to sway world prices. Republicans counter that the Obama administration has restricted oil production and that drilling should expand in Western states, the Arctic and coastal waters. Environmentalists want more support for technologies to replace oil, such as electric cars and biofuels. But until those sources become economically competitive with oil, the United States will be subject to price swings in a world oil market that it cannot control.

Demonstrators at the White House on Aug. 25, 2011, oppose the proposed Keystone XL pipeline, which would carry oil from "tar sand" deposits in western Canada to refineries on the U.S. Gulf Coast.

INSIDE THIS REPORT

THE ISSUES 551
CHRONOLOGY 559
BACKGROUND 560
CURRENT SITUATION 563
AT ISSUE........................565
OUTLOOK 567
BIBLIOGRAPHY 570
THE NEXT STEP 571

CQ Researcher • June 22, 2012 • www.cqresearcher.com
Volume 22, Number 23 • Pages 549-572

SAGE Los Angeles | London | New Delhi Singapore | Washington DC | CQPRESS

RECIPIENT OF SOCIETY OF PROFESSIONAL JOURNALISTS AWARD FOR EXCELLENCE ◆ AMERICAN BAR ASSOCIATION SILVER GAVEL AWARD

U.S. OIL DEPENDENCE

THE ISSUES

551 • Will increasing U.S. oil production lower gas prices?
• Should the U.S. use oil from tar sands?
• Can the U.S. achieve independence from foreign oil?

BACKGROUND

560 **America's Dominant Fuel**
Fossil fuels have always powered the nation.

562 **Supply Crisis**
Arab producers shut off exports to U.S. in 1973.

563 **Environmental Impacts**
President Clinton closed off millions of acres from energy production.

563 **From Shock to Trance**
Presidential candidate Obama decried the nation's short energy attention span.

CURRENT SITUATION

563 **Refinery Squeeze**
Lower U.S. oil demand has put refiners under pressure.

564 **New Offshore Drilling**
The administration is considering limited expansion of offshore drilling.

566 **Alt-Fuel Vehicles**
New fuel efficiency standards could boost electric vehicles.

OUTLOOK

567 **No Choice**
Energy efficiency is essential, experts agree.

Cover: Ben Powless

SIDEBARS AND GRAPHICS

552 **Western Hemisphere Provides Most U.S. Oil Imports**
Persian Gulf produces 22 percent, but has most of world's reserves.

553 **Global Events Help Drive Oil Prices**
Prices spiked during the 2008 financial crisis.

554 **Bakken Boom Brings Mixed Blessings**
Social stress tempers the surge in jobs and wealth in North Dakota.

556 **Adding Up the Cost of Gas**
Crude oil comprises two-thirds of the price of a gallon of gasoline.

559 **Chronology**
Key events since 1859.

560 **Arctic Holds Energy Riches — and Environmental Peril**
"Complacency is the biggest threat we have."

565 **At Issue**
Should the Keystone XL pipeline be built?

FOR FURTHER RESEARCH

569 **For More Information**
Organizations to contact.

570 **Bibliography**
Selected sources used.

571 **The Next Step**
Additional articles.

571 **Citing *CQ Researcher***
Sample bibliography formats.

CQ Researcher

June 22, 2012
Volume 22, Number 23

MANAGING EDITOR: Thomas J. Billitteri
tjb@cqpress.com

ASSISTANT MANAGING EDITOR: Kathy Koch
kkoch@cqpress.com

CONTRIBUTING EDITOR: Thomas J. Colin
tcolin@cqpress.com

ASSOCIATE EDITOR: Kenneth Jost

STAFF WRITER: Marcia Clemmitt

CONTRIBUTING WRITERS: Peter Katel, Barbara Mantel, Jennifer Weeks

DESIGN/PRODUCTION EDITOR: Olu B. Davis

ASSISTANT EDITOR: Darrell Dela Rosa

FACT CHECKER: Michelle Harris

Los Angeles | London | New Delhi
Singapore | Washington DC

An Imprint of SAGE Publications, Inc.

VICE PRESIDENT AND EDITORIAL DIRECTOR, HIGHER EDUCATION GROUP:
Michele Sordi

DIRECTOR, ONLINE PUBLISHING:
Todd Baldwin

CQ Researcher (ISSN 1056-2036) is printed on acid-free paper. Published weekly, except: (March wk. 5) (May wk. 4) (July wk. 1) (Aug. wks. 3, 4) (Nov. wk. 4) and (Dec. wks. 3, 4). Published by SAGE Publications, Inc., 2455 Teller Rd., Thousand Oaks, CA 91320. Annual full-service subscriptions start at $1,054. For pricing, call 1-800-834-9020. To purchase a *CQ Researcher* report in print or electronic format (PDF), visit www.cqpress.com or call 866-427-7737. Single reports start at $15. Bulk purchase discounts and electronic-rights licensing are also available. Periodicals postage paid at Thousand Oaks, California, and at additional mailing offices. POSTMASTER: Send address changes to *CQ Researcher*, 2300 N St., N.W., Suite 800, Washington, DC 20037.

U.S. Oil Dependence

BY JENNIFER WEEKS

THE ISSUES

As gasoline hovered near $4 a gallon this past winter, Republican presidential hopeful Newt Gingrich made a bold assertion aimed at frustrated consumers: If elected, he said, he could reduce gas prices to $2.50 a gallon by boosting domestic oil production.

"Drilling here, drilling now so we can pay less and be independent of Middle East oil is just common sense," Gingrich declared. [1]

But President Barack Obama blasted the notion that any president can exert such quick control over what drivers pay at the pump. "It's the easiest thing in the world to make phony election-year promises about lower gas prices," he said. "What's harder is to make a serious, sustained commitment to tackle a problem that may not be solved in one year or one term or even one decade." [2]

The political squabbling — predictable as it may be in an election year — offers a backdrop to an important debate about the nation's energy future, its heavy dependence on petroleum to keep the economy moving and prospects for reducing our reliance on foreign oil.

Underlying that debate is a paradoxical set of facts. Oil currently accounts for 37 percent of U.S. energy use — more than any other fuel source — and 94 percent of transportation fuel. [3] Yet, although oil undergirds the economy, consumption has fallen to a 15-year low, due in part to the steep recession that began at the end of 2007 and rising sales of fuel-efficient cars. At the same time, domestic oil production, aided by technological advances, has cut oil imports from 60 percent of total U.S. consumption in 2005 to 44 percent at the beginning of 2012. [4]

Even as consumption declines and domestic production grows, however, the average price of gasoline was $3.61 per gallon in early June — a sign that Gingrich's focus on boosting production wouldn't have worked.

AFP/Getty Images/Mandel Ngan

President Obama, visiting a pipe storage facility in Cushing, Okla., on March 22, calls for expediting the southern leg of the Keystone XL pipeline, running from Oklahoma to the Gulf, but says the segment from Canada to Oklahoma needs more review. U.S. advocates say the pipeline would generate jobs and increase oil exports from a friendly ally. But environmentalists argue that producing oil from tar sands is harming Canadian forests and rivers and generating high carbon emissions.

Many consumers see a disconnect in these conditions. Why, they ask, should gas prices remain high when oil consumption is down and domestic production is rising? But energy experts say the picture makes sense. Because oil is traded worldwide and prices can be influenced by geopolitical developments anywhere, they say, volatile energy costs are inescapable as long as America relies heavily on oil.

Every president since the 1970s has called for reducing U.S. dependence on oil, especially on imports. Until the 2008 recession drastically slowed world economic growth, imports accounted for a growing share of total U.S. oil consumption. (*See graph, p. 553.*)

Republicans and energy companies say the United States can produce more of its own oil if the federal government relaxes restrictions on exploration and development, especially on public lands in the West and in federal coastal waters. "Many U.S. resources have been off-limits for decades," says Rayola Dougher, a senior adviser with the American Petroleum Institute, the oil industry's main trade group. "We won't be able to secede from the world oil market, but we'd be much more secure, and our balance of trade would be healthier, if U.S. companies could access these areas."

Presumed Republican presidential nominee Mitt Romney contends that the Obama administration has "put in place policies that are designed to reduce our production of fossil-based fuels and drive up the cost of energy" in order to push the nation toward alternative sources like wind and solar power. But although he now stresses production, as recently as 2010 Romney also supported the idea that higher oil prices could have

Western Hemisphere Provides Most U.S. Imports

Although the Middle East produces the largest share of world oil supplies (left), the United States is less dependent on those countries than it used to be. Today the largest share of U.S. imports comes from the Western Hemisphere (right), mainly Canada, Venezuela and Mexico.

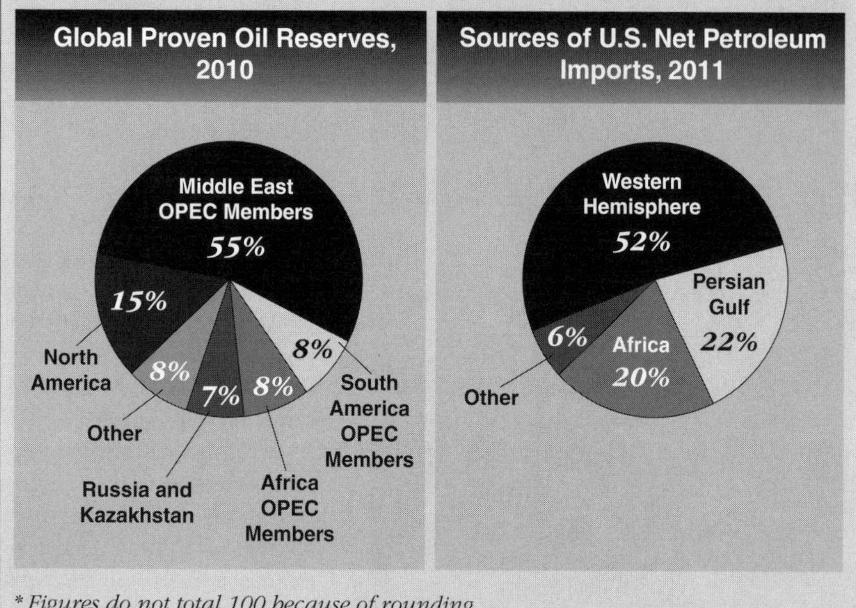

* *Figures do not total 100 because of rounding.*

Source: "How Dependent Are We on Foreign Oil?" Energy Information Administration, May 2012, www.eia.gov/energy_in_brief/foreign_oil_dependence.cfm

a positive impact, motivating consumers to conserve energy and use less oil. [5]

President Obama says the right approach is an "all-of-the-above" policy that expands "responsible" oil and gas development but also reduces oil use and promotes renewable fuels and energy-efficient technologies. [6] In his first two years in office Obama focused on commercializing renewable energy sources and controlling carbon emissions from fossil fuel combustion — the largest driver of global climate change. But even before Republicans gained control of the House and expanded their ranks in the Senate in the 2010 midterm elections, Obama was looking for middle ground.

In April 2010 the president proposed opening the Atlantic Coast to offshore energy production from Maryland south, along with a swath of the eastern Gulf of Mexico and the north coast of Alaska. The administration canceled those plans after the *Deepwater Horizon* oil spill in the Gulf led it to tighten federal oversight of offshore drilling nationwide. [7] Now, however, the Interior Department is considering several leases along Alaska's north coast in the Beaufort and Chukchi seas. (*See sidebar, p. 560.*)

Obama is also under pressure to approve the Keystone XL pipeline, which would carry oil from so-called "tar sand" deposits in western Canada to refineries on the U.S. Gulf Coast. Canada is eager to move the oil, which is a heavy grade of crude, to processors with the specialized technology needed to refine it. And many U.S. advocates say the pipeline would generate jobs and increase oil exports from a friendly ally. But environmentalists strongly oppose the project. They argue that developing tar sand deposits is harming Canadian forests and rivers and generating unusually high levels of carbon emissions. (*See "At Issue," p. 565.*)

The State Department appeared likely to OK the pipeline (which needs federal approval because it crosses an international border) in 2011, but extended the process until after the 2012 election when critics raised problems with its environmental review. [8] Since last November the Republican-controlled House has voted four times to approve the pipeline on a fast track, while the Democratic-controlled Senate has narrowly supported the president.

In March Obama called for expediting the southern leg of the pipeline, which runs from Oklahoma to the Gulf, but argued that the segment from Canada to Oklahoma needed more review. "[A]nybody who suggests that somehow we're suppressing domestic oil production isn't paying attention," Obama said. Republicans countered that the president was taking credit for a project that did not even need federal approval since that segment of the pipeline lay entirely within the United States. [9]

Amid these controversies, the United States is starting to address its near-total reliance on oil for transportation. Last year Obama announced a new agreement with auto companies that will double the average fuel efficiency of U.S. passenger vehicles by 2025, to more than 50 miles per gallon. And Toyota sold its one millionth Prius gas-electric hybrid car in the United States. Since the Prius was introduced in the United States in 2000, 13 other carmakers have brought hybrid models to market. [10]

Now manufacturers are introducing plug-in hybrids, which refuel at recharging stations, and battery-operated electric vehicles that operate entirely on battery power. Auto industry leaders and the Obama administration have hailed new models, like the plug-in Chevy Volt, as evidence that American carmakers are shifting away from gas-guzzling models to more fuel-efficient cars. [11]

However, market prospects for electric cars are uncertain, and could weaken if gasoline prices ease over the next several years. Biofuels are also growing more slowly than many advocates projected, even with strong federal support: Under the Energy Policy Act of 2005 and subsequent laws, oil refiners are required to blend millions of gallons of biofuels into gasoline, and the industry also has received billions of dollars in subsidies. [12]

As the Obama administration, Congress and interest groups debate what kind of energy strategy the United States should pursue, here are some issues they are considering:

Global Events Help Drive Oil Prices

Crude oil prices often are affected by events that have the potential to disrupt the flow of oil to the market. High global commodity prices pushed world oil prices up to $147 per barrel in June 2008, but then the financial crisis deflated them when economic growth stalled. Price shocks also followed the Arab Oil Embargo in 1973 and the start of the Iran-Iraq War in 1980.

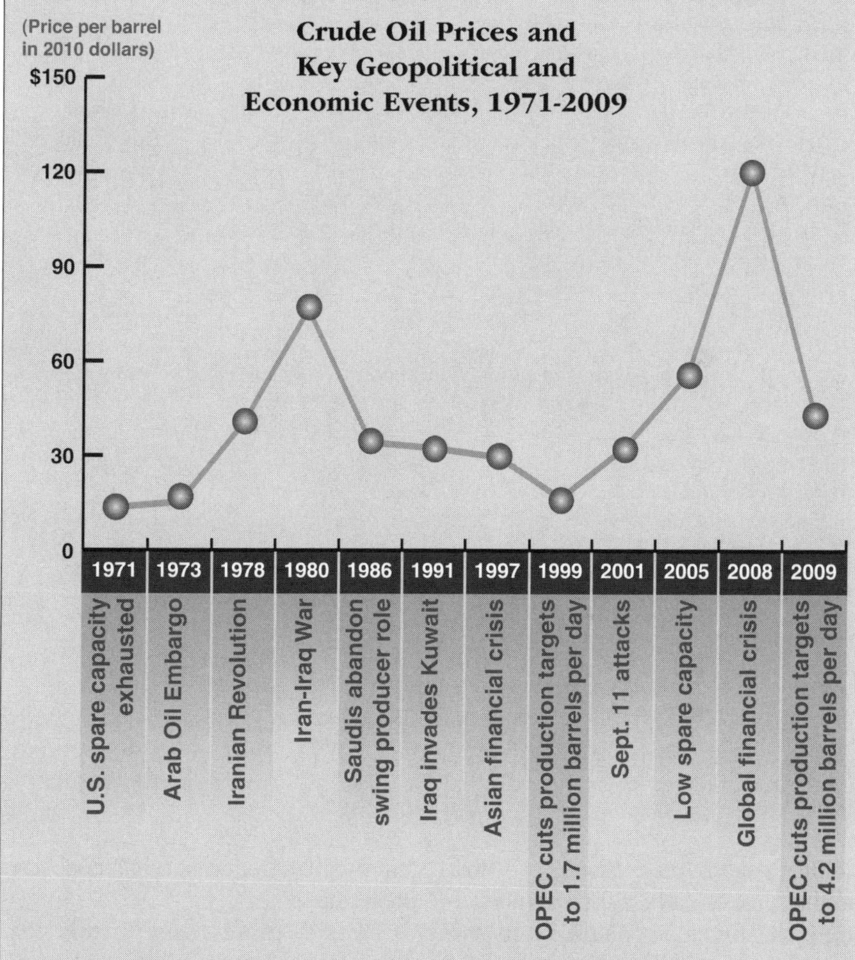

Source: "What Drives Crude Oil Prices?" Energy Information Administration, May 2012, www.eia.gov/finance/markets/spot_prices.cfm

Will increasing U.S. oil production reduce gasoline prices?

Many politicians approach high gasoline prices as a simple supply-and-demand problem, although they frequently disagree on the solution.

Republicans typically argue that more exploration and drilling will lower prices by bringing more oil to the world market. For example, Gingrich this spring proposed a program to increase domestic production and eliminate the Environmental Protection Agency (EPA), which regulates some impacts of oil production. The former House speaker contended that his policies would ensure that "no future [U.S.] president will ever bow to a Saudi king again." [13]

Congressional Republicans also support increasing domestic production and resist tighter environmental regulation of the oil industry. For example, they oppose requirements for new cleaner-burning gasoline blends, known as Tier 3 standards, and new restrictions on emissions from oil refineries.

"None of America's pain at the pump should be self-inflicted, which is why we must do more to increase domestic and North American oil supplies," Rep. Fred Upton, R-Mich., chairman of the House Energy and Commerce Committee, said in March. "Some in Washington claim that producing more domestic oil won't make any difference in prices, but the American people know better." [14]

Yet most mainstream economists say production decisions in the United States cannot affect world oil prices. "Oil is a global market in which America is a big consumer but a small supplier," wrote Richard H. Thaler, an economist at the University of Chicago. "We consume about 20 percent of the world's oil but hold only 2 percent of the oil reserves. That means we are, in eco-

Bakken Boom Brings Mixed Blessings

Social stress tempers surge in jobs and wealth in North Dakota.

California had its Gold Rush in the 1840s and '50s, and now North Dakota and eastern Montana are at the center of their own rush — a pell-mell race for oil riches that has ignited a surge in jobs and tax revenues but also fueled worries about environmental damage and social upheaval.

Beneath the two-state region lies the Bakken Formation, a massive oil shale deposit that is the largest oil resource in the continental United States.

The Bakken contains approximately 3.6 billion barrels of oil, and perhaps as many as 4.3 billion barrels, according to the most recent U.S. Geological Survey (USGS) estimate, completed in 2008. [1] For comparison, the United States consumed roughly 6.8 billion barrels of petroleum products in 2011. [2] USGS is conducting another estimate because recent drilling in the formation suggests that it may hold even more oil. [3]

The Williston Basin, where the Bakken Formation is located, has been a well-known oil production region for decades. Until recently, however, most of the oil in the area was not economically recoverable because it was trapped tightly between rocky layers in shale beds. (In conventional oil formations, oil accumulates in a pool under a dome or vault of impermeable rock and can be pumped out more readily than it can be extracted from shale.)

Now, however, energy companies are using a combination of techniques to produce oil from tight shale. Engineers drill horizontally along seams in the oil-laced rock, then pump in massive quantities of water laced with chemicals to fracture the rock — a technique called hydraulic fracturing, or "fracking." Horizontal drilling and fracking have produced massive yields from U.S. natural gas fields in the past several years. But fracking is controversial because it also has the potential to pollute groundwater and creates huge quantities of wastewater. [4]

In 1995 the USGS estimated that the Bakken Formation contained about 150 million barrels of "technically recoverable oil" — oil that could be extracted with commercially available technology. The agency increased that estimate by a factor of 25 in its 2008 update, based on new insights into the area's geology derived from horizontal drilling.

"Horizontal drilling exposes more of the formation to the wellbore [the vertical shaft drilled from the surface], so you can get a much better picture of the resource," says Stephanie Gaswirth, USGS's task chief for the new assessment of the Williston Basin. "It's important to understand the source rock, which produces the oil, and also how . . . thick [the reservoir] is, whether there are spaces in it, the composition of the rock, how porous and permeable it is, and whether there are trapping mechanisms for oil."

USGS does not drill its own wells when it assesses formations, but the service uses data from energy companies, along with other geologic information such as seismic data. "In cases like the Bakken Formation, where there is a lot of production data, we use as much of it as we can to understand what energy producers are seeing," says Gaswirth. "We have several years to produce an assessment, but some people who work for private companies have been working this formation for their entire careers."

The Bakken boom has brought jobs and tax revenues to North Dakota. Oil companies are hiring hundreds of workers, who spend their earnings (including overtime pay) at local restaurants, bars, stores and motels. Many entry-level jobs in the oil region, such as waiting tables and stocking grocery shelves, pay $12 per hour or more. [5]

---

nomics jargon, 'price takers' " — that is, the United States must pay prevailing prices for its oil. "As producers, we are just too small to matter much," Thaler added. "And even if domestic oil companies further increased production, they would sell to the highest global bidder." [15]

In a statistical analysis of 36 years of monthly, inflation-adjusted gasoline prices and U.S. domestic oil production rates, The Associated Press found no correlation between these two trends. In some years when production was high, prices were also high, and vice versa. Nor were average gasoline prices significantly different under Democratic or Republican presidents. [16]

That's because many factors that drive world oil prices are beyond American control, experts say. "Since 2005 we've had trouble increasing total world oil production, and in emerging economies like China and India consumption has risen drastically. That's a key fundamental, and it's not likely to change any time soon," says James Hamilton, an economist at the University of California-San Diego.

Moreover, Hamilton argues that although technology has helped open up new oil sources, such as Canadian tar sands and deepwater deposits, the gains should be kept in perspective. "These new sources are very expensive places to get oil, and their contribution is relatively modest compared to what we get from mature fields," he says.

Democrats typically put less faith in drilling, except for legislators from oil-producing states such as Louisiana and Alaska. But they also are concerned about the effect of rising gas prices on businesses and consumers, and often call for releasing oil from the Strategic Petroleum Reserve (SPR), a national emergency stockpile created

But energy booms also cause stresses, especially in rural areas. Sudden influxes of workers can lead to housing shortages, traffic jams and rising crime rates. Some rural counties in North Dakota are putting moratoriums on construction of new "man camps," where oil drillers and truckers live in temporary housing compounds. [6]

AFP/Getty Images/Karen Bleier

An oil well is drilled near Tioga, N.D., amid the state's oil-rich Bakken Formation.

One community that has been especially hard-hit by the oil boom is the Fort Berthold Indian Reservation, home to the Mandan, Hidatsa and Arikara nations. Energy companies started leasing rights to develop underground oil and gas from residents of the reservation in 2007, and now many tribal members live on royalties. But critics say the federal Bureau of Indian Affairs — which is legally responsible for verifying that leases are in the best interests of the Indian mineral owners — has rubber-stamped leases that paid less than market value. And the tribe has spent most of its earnings from oil rights held in common on such expenses as repairing roads damaged by heavy trucks, building houses for oil workers and prosecuting energy companies that dump waste illegally. [7]

"These oil projects could dramatically change life on Fort Berthold," *The Bismarck* (N.D.) *Tribune* observed recently. "How that change goes down will be determined largely by how well federal, state and tribal agencies respond to the rapid growth. It will be a challenge all the way around." [8]

— Jennifer Weeks

---

[1] "Assessment of Undiscovered Oil Resources in the Devonian-Mississippian Bakken Formation, Williston Basin Province, Montana and North Dakota, 2008," U.S. Geological Survey, http://pubs.usgs.gov/fs/2008/3021/pdf/FS08-3021_508.pdf.

[2] In 2011 the United States consumed 18.8 million barrels of petroleum per day, which equals approximately 6.862 billion barrels for the year. See, "How dependent are we on foreign oil?" U.S. Energy Information Administration, May 2, 2012, www.eia.gov/energy_in_brief/foreign_oil_dependence.cfm.

[3] "Bakken Formation Oil Assessment in North Dakota, Montana Will Be Updated by U.S. Geological Survey," U.S. Department of the Interior, May 19, 2011.

[4] For background see Daniel McGlynn, "Fracking Controversy," *CQ Researcher*, Dec. 16, 2011, pp. 1045-1072.

[5] Blake Ellis, "Double Your Money in the Middle of Nowhere, North Dakota," CNNMoney, Oct. 20, 2011, http://money.cnn.com/2011/09/28/pf/north_dakota_jobs/index.htm.

[6] A. G. Sulzberger, "Oil Rigs Bring Camps of Men to the Prairies," *The New York Times*, Nov. 25, 2011, www.nytimes.com/2011/11/26/us/north-dakota-oil-boom-creates-camps-of-men.html?pagewanted=all.; Jennifer Oldham, "North Dakota Oil Boom Brings Blight With Growth as Costs Soar," Bloomberg.com, Jan. 25, 2012, www.bloomberg.com/news/2012-01-25/north-dakota-oil-boom-brings-blight-with-growth-as-costs-soar.html.

[7] Sierra Crane-Murdoch, "The Other Bakken Boom: America's Biggest Oil Rush Brings Tribal Conflict," *High Country News*, April 16, 2012, www.hcn.org/issues/44.6/on-the-fort-berthold-reservation-the-bakken-boom-brings-conflict.

[8] "Reservation Oil Issues Look Familiar," *The Bismarck Tribune*, April 6, 2012, http://bismarcktribune.com/news/opinion/editorial/reservation-oil-issues-look-familiar/article_694aaeda-7fec-11e1-aee9-0019bb2963f4.html.

---

after the OPEC oil shocks in the 1970s. Presidents released oil from the SPR in 1991 during the Persian Gulf War; in 2000 when rising world demand caused an oil price spike; and in 2005 after hurricanes Katrina and Rita damaged production facilities along the Gulf Coast.

President Obama released oil from the SPR in June 2011, when concern about political turmoil in Libya drove up world prices. In March 2012, three Northeastern Democratic House members — Reps. Peter Welch of Vermont, Ed Markey of Massachusetts and Rosa DeLauro of Connecticut — urged Obama to tap the reserve again, arguing that concerns about possible hostilities with Iran were triggering speculation on world oil markets and raising gas prices.

"As you know, releasing oil from the SPR has driven down prices in the past," the legislators wrote. "Releasing even a small fraction of that oil could again have a significant impact on speculation in the marketplace and on prices." [17]

Just the rumor that Obama had agreed with Britain in mid-March on a coordinated release of oil reserves caused oil prices to drop temporarily, although they partially recovered after the administration said the reports were wrong. Oil experts said that although a release could cause a "flash crash" in oil prices, it was not a long-term policy. "We do not think a reserve release is a sustainable solution to tame oil prices," said James Zhang, a commodity strategist with the Standard Bank Group in London. [18]

Should the U.S. use oil from tar sands?

The largest single source of U.S. imported crude oil is Canada's tar sands, also known as oil sands. Tar sands contain bitumen — a thick, heavy black form of oil — mixed with sand, clay and water. Canada is eager to devel-

Adding Up the Cost of Gas

Crude oil purchased by refiners comprises two-thirds of the average pump price of a gallon of regular gasoline. Refining costs (15 percent), federal and state taxes (8 percent) and distribution and marketing costs (8 percent) make up the rest.

Cost Components of a Gallon of Regular Gasoline

(at average national retail price of $3.90/gallon, April 2012)

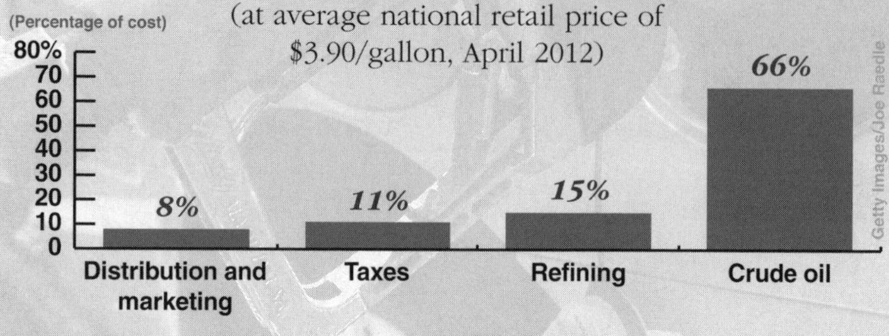

Source: "Gasoline and Diesel Fuel Update," Energy Information Administration, June 2012, www.eia.gov/petroleum/gasdiesel/

op more of its tar sands, and U.S. advocates call them an important new source that can reduce American dependence on other, less reliable suppliers. But critics argue that mining the tar sands and separating the oil consumes huge quantities of water and creates toxic wastes harmful to the environment. Rather than using more oil — especially a dirty form of oil — they say the United States should invest in cleaner sources such as energy efficiency and renewable fuels.

Canada's tar sands, located in Alberta Province north of Montana, extend over an area roughly the size of Florida. The deposits contain an estimated 170 billion barrels of oil — more than the total proven reserves of all other oil-producing countries except Saudi Arabia and Venezuela. But tar sand oil was too costly to develop until the mid-1990s, when the Alberta government slashed royalties and Canada's national government granted the oil industry an array of tax breaks. By 2005 the area was producing a million barrels of oil per day. [19]

Bitumen in tar sands is mingled with other materials, such as sand and clay, and cannot be pumped out like conventional oil. Instead it is mined in two ways. About one-fifth of Canada's tar sands lie near the surface and are dug up with huge mechanical shovels and trucked to factories, where the bitumen is separated using a hot-water process. About two tons of tar sands are needed to produce one barrel of oil using this method. [20] To extract deeply buried tar sands, energy companies inject steam under high pressure into the ground, melting the bitumen so that it flows to an underground reservoir where it can be pumped out.

Heating water to make steam consumes huge quantities of natural gas. Both processes produce massive quantities of wastewater, which energy companies dispose of by injecting it deep underground, and tailings — liquid wastes containing chemicals and trace metals that are toxic to aquatic organisms and mammals. Tailings are stored in huge ponds at mining sites.

Although producing tar sand oil is energy intensive, advocates say, they see Canada's tar sands as a key new source. Canadian oil sands "have become a major engine of global oil supply growth — and the only growing supplier with a land-based connection to the U.S. market," said James Burkhard, managing director at the energy consulting firm IHS CERA. [21] Joe Oliver, Canada's minister of natural resources, called Canada "an emerging energy superpower." [22]

But tar sand development has heavy environmental costs. According to a 2011 summary by Environment Canada, the nation's environmental regulatory agency, they include:

- Excessive water withdrawals that could harm fish habitat in the 765-mile-long Athabasca River, which flows south from the Rocky Mountains through Canada's Jasper National Park;
- Contamination of the river with hydrocarbons and heavy metals that could endanger wildlife and communities downstream;
- Local air pollution from mining operations;
- Damage to forests and loss of habitat for caribou, whooping cranes and other vulnerable species; and
- Rising greenhouse gas emissions from tar sand production. [23]

Tar sand advocates assert that oil companies are improving their production processes so that they use less energy to extract and separate tar sand oil and generate less waste. "As the technology has evolved, it has become more efficient," said Karen Harbert, president of the Institute for 21st Century Energy at the U.S. Chamber of Commerce. "In fact, Albertan oil sands development has become so commonplace that it no longer merits the designation of 'unconventional.' " [24]

U.S. environmentalists want to limit and eventually end imports of oil from tar sands. They strongly oppose the proposed Keystone XL pipeline.

"Over its entire lifecycle the synthetic crude oil from tar sands emits at least 20 percent more global warming pol-

AFP/Getty Images/Gianluigi Guercia

Libyan rebels on July 20, 2011, attend the funeral of comrades killed in the battle for control of the oil-rich town of Brega. President Obama released oil from the Strategic Petroleum Reserve in June 2011, when concern about turmoil in Libya drove up world prices. In March 2012, three Democratic House members urged Obama to tap the reserve again, arguing that concerns about possible hostilities with Iran were triggering speculation on world oil markets and raising gas prices.

lution than conventional oil," the National Wildlife Federation, Sierra Club and four other national environmental groups commented on the initial Keystone XL proposal. "Furthermore, because tar sands oil is a heavier crude, the U.S. refineries that process it will produce higher levels of pollutants that damage human health and lead to more smog, haze and acid rain." [25] Building the pipeline, the groups argued, "would be detrimental to our country's national interests in building a clean-energy economy, curbing climate change and reducing national reliance on oil." [26]

Industry advocates say that if the United States does not approve Keystone XL, Canada will build new pipelines to the West Coast and ship tar sand oil to Asia instead. But Canadian analysts call that scenario unlikely because the pipelines would have to go through British Columbia, where public support for environmental protection is much stronger than in Alberta.

"It will be extremely challenging to build an oil sand pipeline to the West Coast," says Nathan Lemphers, a senior analyst with the Pembina Institute, a Canadian think tank that promotes sustainable energy solutions. Two proposals to expand existing pipelines to the Pacific coast of Canada have generated widespread opposition, especially among aboriginal groups, which have strong legal leverage to intervene in the process. [27]

Since tar sand oil is already flowing to U.S. refineries in the Midwest, Lemphers says the United States should press Canada to clean up its production methods further. "We'd like to see a message to Canada and the oil sand industry that they have to improve their environmental performance if they want to expand," he says. "They're learning that on many fronts." For example, the European Union — which is working to reduce carbon emissions from energy use — is considering a rule that would classify oil from bitumen as more carbon-intensive than conventional crude oil. Canada's government strongly opposes the standard. [28]

"The U.S. has an opportunity to send a clear signal to Canada on managing its oil sands," says Lemphers.

Can the U.S. achieve independence from foreign oil?

For nearly 40 years, since the oil shocks of the 1970s, U.S. presidents and other elected officials have called repeatedly for steps to make the nation less dependent on imported oil. Advocates say cutting reliance on foreign oil would reduce the risk of supply interruptions from countries hostile to the United States or that are destabilized by conflicts, as occurred last year in Libya.

Today, with domestic oil production rising and consumption down, some experts say the United States can substantially reduce oil imports. The U.S. Energy Information Administration projects that imported oil will account for only 36 percent of the nation's liquid fuel supply (including biofuels) by 2035, down from 60 percent in 2005. [29] In a recent survey of energy executives by *Forbes* magazine, 27 percent of respondents said achieving energy independence was either very feasible or somewhat feasible. [30]

"We can probably reduce imports to around 5 million barrels per day, which would be dramatic," says Henry Lee, director of the Environment and Natural Resource Program at the Harvard Kennedy School of Government. In 2010 the United States consumed 19.2 million barrels of oil per day, of which 9.3 million barrels were imported.

In addition to lower oil demand since the recession and rising domestic production, U.S. cars are becoming more fuel efficient. New standards negotiated by the Obama administration and major car manufacturers will boost average passenger car fuel efficiency to more than 50 miles per gallon by 2025 — double the 2010 level. "This is totally different from the perspective we had four years ago," says Lee.

The American Petroleum Institute estimates that constructing the Keystone XL pipeline and expanding access to U.S. oil and gas resources that are currently not open for development could make it unnecessary for the United States to import oil from any source other than Canada by 2024. Because Canada is a neighbor, a democracy and a longtime U.S. ally and trading partner, U.S. energy producers say importing oil from Canada is the next-best alternative to drilling at home.

"For every dollar we spend on Canadian goods, they spend 90 cents in the U.S.," says API's Dougher. "Trade with Canada builds jobs here and expands our economy."

But some argue that even if the United States uses only oil produced in North America, it will still be vulnerable to economic shocks because oil prices are set in a global market. Achieving energy security, they contend, does not mean using less foreign oil. Rather, they say, it means using less oil, period.

"It's a misconception that we depend too much on the wrong suppliers," says Gal Luft, executive director of the Washington-based Institute for the Analysis of Global Security, which focuses on energy security. "We can do easily without Persian Gulf oil, which accounts for about 9 percent of our supply, and we don't import a drop from Iran, but we're still affected if something happens to Iran's oil supplies. There's less chance of embargoes by friendly countries like Canada, but importing from friends doesn't make us more economically secure."

Instead of focusing either on increased production or conservation, Luft and other "energy hawks" say the solution is to create competition for oil and make it less strategically important. To do that, they say, the United States should develop alternative fuels that can substitute for oil — including ethanol from corn and other plant sources and methanol from natural gas — and require auto makers to equip every car sold in the United States to run on any of those fuels, so that drivers can choose the cheapest option at the pump. Bills that would establish this policy, known as an open fuel standard, have been introduced in Congress several times in recent years and are currently pending in both the House and Senate. [31]

"Salt was a strategic commodity for thousands of years, the only way to preserve food until the 19th century," former Director of Central Intelligence R. James Woolsey said last October, comparing salt's role then to oil's today. But, he asserted, household electricity and refrigeration eventually offered a better and cheaper option. "Before that, people went to war over salt mines," Woolsey said. "We can do the same thing with oil. We can make oil boring." [32]

U.S. auto manufacturers oppose an open fuel standard, which they see as an extra regulatory burden, while advocates call it the best way to foster alternatives to oil. [33] Today about eight million cars in the U.S. are "flex-fuel" models that can run on gasoline or ethanol. But since ethanol is sold mainly in the Midwest, where most of it is made, in practice many flex-fuel cars run solely on gasoline. On average, a flex-fuel vehicle in the United States consumes less than 20 gallons yearly of high-blend ethanol (fuel containing mainly ethanol, which is also blended at low concentrations into conventional gasoline).

The U.S. biofuel industry is gradually expanding, although it still produces mainly corn-based ethanol, which offers modest environmental benefits, at best, compared to gasoline. [34] Many plant and waste sources can be used to produce advanced cellulosic biofuels, which have lower carbon footprints than corn ethanol. But cellulosic biofuels cost more to manufacture than corn ethanol because the enzymes that can break down tough plant cell walls are expensive to produce. Corn, in contrast, contains mostly starch, which is easily broken down into sugars and fermented into ethanol. Progress on advanced biofuels has lagged behind early forecasts, even with federal subsidies and mandates, as companies work to bring down costs and find the most efficient production methods. [35]

In 2012 the Renewable Fuel Standard (RFS), established as part of the Energy Independence and Security Act of 2007, requires oil refiners to blend 15.2 billion gallons of renewable fuels into transportation fuels, replacing about 9.2 percent of the total supply. Of this amount, 8.6 million gallons must be cellulosic biofuels. [36] Refiners say the mandate sets unrealistic targets and argue that they should not have to buy "blending credits," as the law requires, to cover their quotas if they fall short.

In March the American Petroleum Institute sued EPA, arguing that the RFS was unachievable because cellulosic biofuels are not being manufactured on a commercial scale yet. EPA projects that manufacturers will be able to make the required amount of cellulosic biofuels in 2012, but acknowledges that it will be difficult. [37]

"We support the idea of using biofuels to diversify our fuel mix, but there's not enough cellulosic ethanol in the market now to meet the target, so refiners are paying a fine for failing to use a supply that doesn't exist," says API's Dougher.

A 2011 study by the National Research Council found that manufacturers were unlikely to meet the long-term RFS target of 36 billion gallons in 2022 without major technology breakthroughs or policy changes. The study also projected that making cellulosic biofuels cost-competitive with petroleum fuels would probably require some combination of high oil prices (well over $100 per barrel) and either a combination of government subsidies and mandates or a price on carbon emissions. [38]

Continued on p. 560

Chronology

1850s-1930s

U.S. oil industry expands from a fledgling venture into the nation's main energy source.

1859
First U.S. oil well drilled in Titusville, Pa.

1870s-1880s
Oil companies begin drilling and building refineries in Southern California.

1911
Supreme Court rules that Standard Oil Co. violates antitrust law and orders it broken into 34 companies.

1923
National Petroleum Reserve established near Prudhoe Bay, Alaska, as a potential emergency oil supply source.

1932
First federal gas tax enacted.

1950s-1960s

U.S. oil consumption swells during post-World War II boom.

1950
Oil surpasses coal as main U.S. energy source.

1956
President Dwight D. Eisenhower signs Federal-Aid Highway Act, authorizing massive investments in a national Interstate Highway System.

1960
Iran, Iraq, Kuwait, Saudi Arabia and Venezuela form Organization of Petroleum Exporting Countries (OPEC) in an effort to influence global oil prices.

1970s-1980s

Arab oil shocks temporarily boost support for conservation and alternative fuels, but reforms fade when oil prices fall.

1970
U.S. oil production peaks at 9.6 million barrels per day and begins a gradual decline, with imports accounting for a growing share of total consumption. . . . environmentalists hold first Earth Day (April 22) in response to events that include a major leak from an undersea oil well near Santa Barbara, Calif.

1973
Arab OPEC members embargo oil exports to the U.S., raising prices and triggering a national energy crisis.

1975
Congress creates Strategic Petroleum Reserve in underground salt caves along the Texas and Louisiana coasts as a buffer against future oil supply disruptions, and adopts fuel-economy (CAFE) standards requiring manufacturers to produce more fuel-efficient cars.

1977
President Jimmy Carter proposes energy conservation programs to reduce dependence on imported oil. . . . Oil from Alaska's North Slope reaches markets via the new Trans-Alaska Pipeline.

1978-1979
Revolution in Iran halts oil exports, triggering a second global oil shock and sharply raising U.S. energy prices.

1989
Exxon Valdez runs aground in Alaska's Prince William Sound, spilling 11 million gallons of oil and contaminating more than 1,000 miles of pristine shoreline.

1990s-Present

U.S. energy policy swings between conservation and production.

1992
Congress passes Energy Policy Act, boosting funds for energy efficiency, renewable energy and alternative fuels.

1997
President Bill Clinton signs Kyoto Protocol, pledging to cut U.S. greenhouse gas emissions 7 percent below 1990 levels by 2012. Senate refuses to ratify the treaty, saying cutting carbon emissions will harm the economy.

2001
George W. Bush administration increases oil production on U.S. lands and offshore.

2008
Global oil consumption slackens as world economy enters a recession.

2010
Blowout at BP's *Deepwater Horizon* offshore well spills more than 200 million gallons of oil into Gulf of Mexico.

2011
Unrest in North Africa and Middle East drives world oil prices above $100 per barrel. . . . President Obama and major automakers agree to double fuel efficiency standards for passenger vehicles. . . . Obama blocks expedited permitting for the Keystone XL pipeline.

2012
TransCanada submits a new Keystone XL proposal that avoids the sensitive Nebraska Sandhills. . . . World oil prices drop below $84 per barrel in May-June.

Arctic Holds Energy Riches — and Environmental Peril

"Complacency is the biggest threat we have."

Rising world demand for oil is converging with another global trend — climate change — to spur competition for Arctic energy reserves. As warmer temperatures at the pole shrink Arctic sea ice, many nations see opportunity to drill for oil and gas that until recently were inaccessible. But environmentalists and many scientists worry that an Arctic oil rush could irreparably harm fragile polar ecosystems.

Scientists broadly agree that the Arctic is warming and that its sea ice — which partially melts during the summer and expands in winter — is shrinking. At its yearly low point from 1979 through 2000, Arctic sea ice covered 2.7 million square miles on average, according to NASA data. Since 2005, however, the ice has contracted to 2.3 million square miles or less each year. In September 2011 it shrank to 1.8 million square miles. [1] The United Kingdom's national weather service, the Met Office, projects that the Arctic could become ice free for part of the year sometime between 2040 and 2060, although scientific estimates vary. [2]

More than 400 onshore oil and gas fields already have been developed north of the Arctic Circle in Russia, Canada and Alaska. The fields contain about 240 billion barrels of oil and oil-equivalent natural gas, counting both what has already been extracted and the reserves that remain in the ground at these sites. But still more large oil and gas deposits in the Arctic may remain to be discovered. In 2008 the U.S. Geological Survey (USGS) published its first appraisal of undeveloped energy resources north of the Arctic Circle, which estimated that the region contained an additional 90 billion barrels of oil; 1.7 quadrillion cubic feet of natural gas; and 44 billion barrels of natural gas liquids — components such as propane and butane that are extracted during processing. Most of these reserves are believed to lie offshore. [3]

As the U.S. prepares to allow Shell to drill test wells off Alaska this summer, other nations also are lining up Arctic ventures. (*See "Current Situation."*) Rosneft, Russia's state-owned oil company, has signed exploration agreements with Exxon Mobil, the Italian energy company Eni and Statoil, Norway's state energy company. [4] Greenland also has opened its onshore and offshore territory to drilling, although no company has recorded a major find yet. [5]

Many scientists say that much more information is needed before oil producers can operate safely in the Arctic Ocean. A 2011 USGS report identified a variety of important needs, including more research on important species, a better understanding of how cumulative impacts from multiple energy exploration projects will add up and a data-management system that allows researchers to share information about trends in many different areas. [6] In January 573 U.S. research scientists wrote to Interior Secretary Ken Salazar urging the Obama administration to act on the USGS's recommendations before approving offshore drilling in the Arctic. [7]

Energy companies say they take the challenges of operating in the Arctic seriously. At a conference last January in Norway, the International Association of Oil and Gas Producers announced a four-year, $20 million research program to address those issues. Because Russia is not participating, however, critics worry that Russian energy projects will fall short of international safety standards. [8]

Insurers also are tracking Arctic energy development. In April Lloyds of London, the world's largest insurer, and Chatham House, a British think tank, warned that cleaning up oil spills in the Arctic would involve unique and challenging risks and that a spill could irreversibly harm Arctic ecosystems. The groups called for major investments in research, infrastructure and monitoring to make development activities in the Arctic safe.

"In many areas — shipping, search and rescue — infrastructure is currently insufficient to meet the expected demands

Continued from p. 558

Ethanol producers respond that the RFS has generated more than 90,000 direct jobs and 311,000 indirect jobs and reduced U.S. gasoline prices in 2011 by $1.09 per gallon. [39] The RFS "has been the most successful energy policy this nation has ever implemented," Renewable Fuels Association President Bob Dinneen said in April. "It should be vigorously defended and maintained and allowed to reach its full potential of 36 billion gallons of clean burning, renewable fuel." [40] ■

BACKGROUND

America's Dominant Fuel

Fossil fuels have powered the U.S. economy through much of the nation's history, enabling Americans to live increasingly comfortable and prosperous lives.

Wood was the main fuel source in the 17th and 18th centuries, but in the 1800s coal became the fuel of choice for powering factories, fueling trains and ships and heating homes. Scientists and entrepreneurs knew, however, that "rock oil" that seeped from the ground in some areas could be burned to generate light and heat. In 1859 the first U.S. well was drilled in Titusville, in northwestern Pennsylvania, making possible large-scale use of oil as fuel.

Because oil contains more energy per unit than coal and as a liquid is easier to transport, the industry grew rapidly, especially after the formation of Standard Oil Co. in 1870 by in-

of economic development," Lloyd's and Chatham House warned. "Full-scale exercises based on worst-case scenarios of environmental disaster should be run by companies with government involvement and oversight" to test what operators know and make them more expert at operating in the Arctic. [9]

Marilyn Heiman, director of the Pew Environment Group's U.S. Arctic Program, points out another useful information source: Alaska, which took steps after the *Exxon Valdez* spill in 1989 to prepare for future disasters. Now industry trains fishermen to respond to oil spills, so that they have relevant qualifications, such as handling hazardous materials. [10]

The Oil Spill Pollution Act of 1990 also created citizen advisory councils after the *Exxon Valdez* disaster. "The councils are a great way to avoid complacency, which is the biggest threat we have," says Heiman. "They look over the shoulders of regulators, who can get complacent too, and provide real vigilance against future events."

— Jennifer Weeks

Drilling Being Considered on Alaska's North Coast

The Interior Department is considering granting several oil exploration leases this summer to Shell Oil Co. along Alaska's north coast in the Beaufort and Chukchi seas.

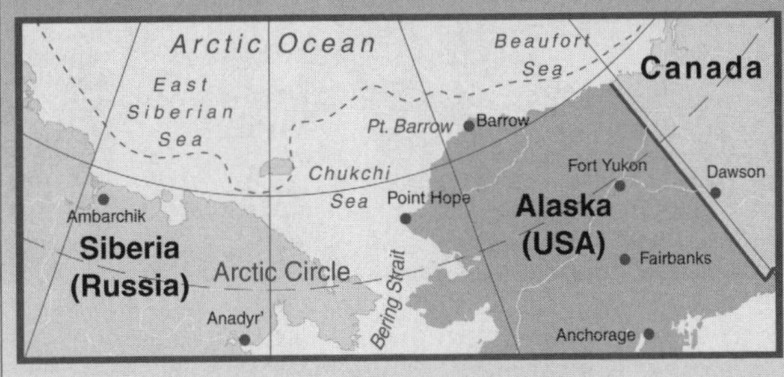

1 "World of Change: Arctic Sea Ice," National Aeronautics and Space Administration, http://earthobservatory.nasa.gov/Features/WorldOfChange/sea_ice.php.

2 Adam Vaughan, "Met Office: Arctic Sea-Ice Loss Linked to Colder, Drier UK Winters," *The Guardian*, March 14, 2012, www.guardian.co.uk/environment/2012/mar/14/met-office-arctic-sea-ice-loss-winter.

3 "Circum-Arctic Resource Appraisal: Estimates of Undiscovered Oil and Gas North of the Arctic Circle," U.S. Geological Survey, 2008, http://pubs.usgs.gov/fs/2008/3049/.

4 Andrew E. Kramer, "Russian-Italian pact Opens Arctic Ocean to Drilling," *The New York Times*, April 25, 2012, www.nytimes.com/2012/04/26/business/global/russian-italian-pact-opens-arctic-ocean-to-drilling.html; Melissa Akin and Vladimir Soldatkin, "Statoil to Drill with Rosneft in Russian Arctic," Reuters, May 5, 2012, www.reuters.com/article/2012/05/05/rosneft-statoil-idUSL5E8G500X20120505.

5 "Greenland: Offshore Drilling's Next Frontier," *24/7 Wall Street*, May 20, 2010, http://247wallst.com/2010/05/20/greenland-offshore-drillings-next-frontier/; Alex Hawkes, "Cairn Fails to Strike Oil Off Greenland," *The Guardian*, Nov. 30, 2011, www.guardian.co.uk/business/2011/nov/30/cairn-fails-oil-greenland/print.

6 Leslie Holland-Bartels and Brenda Pierce, eds., "An Evaluation of the Science Needs to Inform Decisions on Outer Continental Shelf Energy Development in the Chukchi and Beaufort Seas, Alaska," U.S. Geological Survey, 2011, http://pubs.usgs.gov/circ/1370/.

7 Online at www.pewenvironment.org/uploadedFiles/PEG/Publications/Other_Resource/ScientistsLetter-OCSDevelopment.pdf.

8 Quirin Schiermeier, "The Great Arctic Oil Race Begins," *Nature*, Jan. 31, 2012, www.nature.com/news/the-great-arctic-oil-race-begins-1.9932.

9 "Arctic Opening: Opportunity and Risk in the High North," Chatham House, 2011, p. 53, www.lloyds.com/~/media/Files/News%20and%20Insight/360%20Risk%20Insight/Arctic_Risk_Report_20120412.pdf.

10 For example, see Nicole Klauss, "Kodiak Fishermen Get Oil Spill Training," *Kodiak Daily Mirror*, April 7, 2012, www.newsminer.com/view/full_story/18155840/article-Kodiak-fishermen-get-oil-spill-training-?instance=home_news_window_left_bullets.

dustrialist John D. Rockefeller. Over the next several decades Rockefeller built Standard Oil into a massive trust, buying dozens of smaller companies and most of the refining and pipeline capacity across the country. As Rockefeller used his monopoly power to control oil prices, Standard Oil became a reviled symbol of concentrated corporate wealth.

By the early 1900s U.S. oil producers were drilling in the Midwest, California, Oklahoma and Texas. The growing automobile industry created a massive new market for gasoline. America's first gas station opened in Ohio in 1912, just a year after the Supreme Court ordered Standard Oil broken apart to reduce its market power. [41] Oil was in such demand that despite the breakup, Standard's successor companies were soon worth more than the original trust. [42]

In 1929 the U.S. network of gas stations and garages had expanded to 300,000 outlets nationwide. [43] Cars quickly became so central to American life that even bankrupt farmers driven off their land by the Dust Bowl in the 1930s climbed into sedans or trucks to move West looking for work. Oil was the most important strategic resource for all sides during World War II: Germany and Japan, neither of which had large oil reserves, tried but failed to capture oil fields in eastern Europe and Asia, while the United States supplied much of the oil that powered Allied planes, tanks and ships to victory.

Wartime gasoline rationing was lifted in the United States within 24 hours of Japan's surrender in 1945, and in 1950 oil surpassed coal as the primary U.S. energy source. As demand swelled, driven by the postwar economic boom and expansion of the Interstate Highway System, America began to import oil from abroad, mainly from Saudi Arabia. Some U.S. officials, worried about the risks of depending on foreign suppliers, supported research into making synthetic fuels from large domestic coal supplies. But when it became clear that this option would cost several times more than importing cheap foreign oil, the program folded within several years.

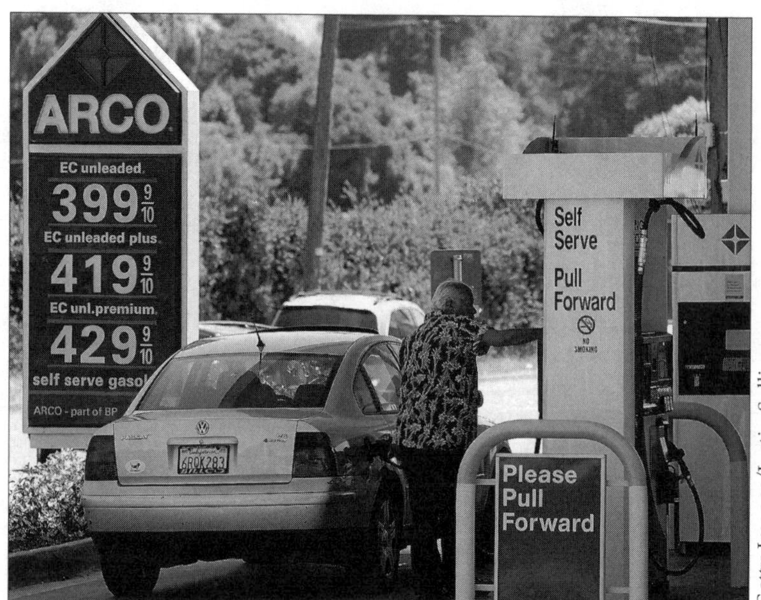

Getty Images/Justin Sullivan

A gas station in Mill Valley, Calif., shows prices above $4 a gallon on June 12. Many consumers ask why gas prices are still high despite lower oil consumption and rising domestic production. But energy experts explain that because oil is traded worldwide and prices can be influenced by geopolitical developments anywhere, volatile energy costs are inescapable as long as the United States relies heavily on oil.

In the late 1950s, as demand for domestic oil swelled, the United States cultivated relationships with oil-exporting countries, aided by American corporations such as Shell and Standard Oil of New Jersey. These linkages helped to expand the global oil industry. Oil prices fell throughout the 1950s and '60s as reserves were developed worldwide, fueling unprecedented international economic growth.

Environmental protection was not a concern for most Americans then, but as the impact of rapid industrial growth became clearer, some advocates began to call for action to reduce air and water pollution. The oil industry came under attack in 1969 when an undersea wellhead off Santa Barbara, Calif., suffered a blowout and, contaminated 35 miles of coastline with 200,000 gallons of oil. The spill helped to catalyze the first Earth Day rally in 1970 and led to state and federal bans on new offshore drilling.

Supply Crises

U.S. domestic oil production peaked in 1970 at 9.6 million barrels per day and began a slow decline. This did not mean that the nation was running out of oil; rather, it signaled that producers were drilling all of the reserves that could be developed profitably with the technology available at the time. [44] Imports filled the widening gap until Oct. 20, 1973, when Arab members of the Organization of Petroleum Exporting Countries (OPEC) shut off oil exports to the United States, responding to U.S. support for Israel in the Yom Kippur War. Oil prices shot up, and the Nixon administration was forced to ration gasoline. The embargo and resulting flow of wealth from Western industrialized countries to Middle East oil exporters triggered a deep economic recession lasting from November 1973 to March 1975.

To reduce America's dependence on imported oil, which accounted for 36 percent of national consumption when the embargo was imposed, the United States began building a pipeline to bring crude oil from Alaska's Prudhoe Bay to the lower 48 states. And in 1975 Congress imposed the first Corporate Average Fuel Economy (CAFE) standards, which required automakers to improve the fuel efficiency of new cars to 27.5 miles per gallon on average (20.7 miles per gallon for light trucks) by 1987. Congress also established the Strategic Petroleum Reserve to safeguard against future supply disruptions.

President Jimmy Carter (1977-1981) labeled the energy crunch a national crisis and called for developing new sources such as wind, solar and nuclear power. Congress created a Cabinet-level Department of Energy and approved new energy-efficiency standards and tax incentives for investments in renewable energy sources. Carter also pressed for deregulation of oil and gas prices to encourage domestic exploration and production.

Before these measures could have much impact, however, a militant fundamentalist Islamic regime took power in Iran in the winter of 1978-79, shutting off Iranian oil exports and triggering a new wave of worldwide panic buying and price spikes. War broke out between Iran and Iraq in 1980, severely damaging both countries' oil industries. High energy prices helped create a condition dubbed "stagflation" (a stagnant economy with high inflation), contributing to Carter's re-election defeat by Ronald Reagan in 1980.

Reagan promised to revive the U.S. economy, but the second oil shock led to a worldwide recession in the early 1980s. One side effect, however, was reduced demand for oil, which undercut OPEC's power to affect world prices. Many industrialized countries turned to other fuels, such as coal, natural gas and nuclear power, and non-OPEC countries such as Britain and Mexico captured growing shares of global oil sales. In late 1985 OPEC abandoned production limits. World oil prices fell to $20 per barrel, rising only temporarily in 1990 when Iraq invaded Kuwait.

Environmental Impacts

As oil prices eased in the late 1980s, U.S. energy consumption once again began to climb. At the same time, however, policy makers began to focus on the environmental impacts of producing and using oil.

President George H. W. Bush (1989-93) supported oil drilling in the Arctic National Wildlife Refuge (ANWR), but public support waned after the *Exxon Valdez* oil tanker ran aground in Alaska's Prince William Sound in 1989, spilling 11 million gallons of oil and contaminating more than 1,000 miles of shoreline. Meanwhile, in the Clean Air Act Amendments of 1990, Congress mandated the use of specially formulated cleaner-burning fuels in cities with severe air pollution, forcing U.S. refineries to produce a wider range of products.

President Bill Clinton (1993-2001) took several steps to limit the environmental impacts of oil production. He opposed opening ANWR to oil exploration; designated nearly 10 million acres of federal lands as wilderness; and signed the Roadless Area Conservation Rule, which classified more than 58 million acres of national forest (at the time about one-third of the total) as roadless areas. These steps put large tracts of land off-limits for energy production, although millions of acres remained available.

Clinton supported increased funding for energy-efficiency programs and renewable fuels, but strong economic growth and low oil prices drove U.S. energy consumption to new highs in the 1990s. Americans shifted away from economy cars to larger, less-efficient models — especially sport utility vehicles (SUVs) and passenger vans, which benefited from a loophole in CAFE standards that classified those vehicles as "light trucks" and thus held them to weaker fuel-economy standards than passenger cars.

From Shock to Trance

In the late 1990s, oil prices started to rise again, driven by rapid economic growth in China and India. President George W. Bush (2001-2009), who had worked in the Texas oil industry early in his career, strongly advocated increasing supplies of oil and other fossil fuels, along with nuclear power. The Bush administration eliminated many regulatory barriers to oil production on public lands and lobbied vigorously for drilling in ANWR. Bush also called for speeding up the siting and construction of oil refineries and pipelines.

Bush cut spending on energy-efficiency programs and development of most renewable energy sources, over strong resistance from congressional Democrats and environmental advocates. Opponents of Bush's policies harshly criticized the administration for emphasizing production over conservation and downplaying environmental impacts of energy development.

High gasoline prices were a major debate topic during the 2008 presidential campaign. Former Alaska Gov. Sarah Palin, the Republican nominee for vice president, called for more domestic oil production, leading chants of "drill, baby, drill!" at campaign rallies. But then-Sen. Barack Obama, D-Ill., the Democratic nominee, argued that promoting cleaner fuels and making cars more fuel-efficient was the right strategy.

"We go from shock to trance. You know, oil prices go up, gas prices at the pump go up, everybody goes into a flurry of activity. And then the prices go back down, and suddenly we act like it's not important, and we start, you know, filling up our SUVs again. And, as a consequence, we never make any progress," Obama said a week after his election. [45]

Within two years, however, Obama was battling Republicans in Congress who argued that his administration was hurting consumers through regulations that limited domestic energy production. In April 2010 Obama proposed expanding offshore oil drilling as part of a broad energy and climate change strategy. That policy was shelved weeks later when the *Deepwater Horizon* oil platform exploded in the Gulf of Mexico, triggering a spill that released nearly five million barrels of oil into some of the nation's richest fishing grounds.

Despite the spill, however, Obama continued to argue that his administration supported more production of all types of fuels, including expanded domestic drilling, while keeping environmentally sensitive areas such as ANWR off limits. "I believe this all-of-the-above approach is the only way we can continue to reduce our dependence on foreign oil and ultimately put an end to some of these gas spikes that we're going through right now," Obama said in March 2012. [46] ■

CURRENT SITUATION

Refinery Squeeze

Flagging U.S. oil demand has put the refining industry under pressure, threatening fuel supplies in some parts of the nation.

Over the past several decades oil companies have closed more than 100 refineries during periods when oil prices were low, and many smaller facilities became unprofitable. In 2011 the nation had 137 operable refineries, down from 254 in 1982. [47] U.S. refining capacity increased very slightly during that time, from 15.7 million barrels per day in 1985 to 17.7 million barrels per day in 2011, but today the U.S. has a smaller fleet of refineries that are clustered in fewer locations compared to the 1970s. [48]

As a result, regions located far from refineries, such as New England, are vulnerable to high gasoline prices and shortages. Several large refineries that service the Northeast have closed in the past year, raising fears of local gasoline shortages this summer. [49] In a surprise move, Delta Air Lines bought one of the refineries and announced that it would operate the plant itself, modifying it to boost its output of jet fuel. [50]

Planning in the refining industry also is complicated by federal policies, such as requiring refiners to produce specially blended "boutique fuels" to address air pollution issues in various areas. Refiners argue that environmental regulations are making it increasingly hard for them to survive in a low-margin industry where demand for oil products is already weak today. For example, the EPA is developing new Tier 3 standards for light-duty vehicle fuels that are designed to reduce a range of conventional air pollutant emissions from cars. A draft rule is scheduled for release in July. [51]

A study commissioned by the American Petroleum Institute estimates that complying with Tier 3 standards — which will require refiners to produce gasoline formulated to burn extremely cleanly — could increase the cost of gasoline by up to 25 cents per gallon, and in an extreme case could force several refineries to close if they were unable to afford the necessary upgrades. "U.S. refineries are under pressure for a combination of reasons, and increased regulatory costs are certainly a factor," API Group Director Robert Greco told Congress's Joint Economic Committee last month. Environmental regulations, Greco contended, "should focus on making regulation more efficient so it materially benefits the environment without impeding economic growth unnecessarily." [52]

But public health advocates argue that tighter air pollution standards for vehicles are worth the cost. "[I]n 2017, Tier 3 will reduce nitrogen oxide emissions by 260,000 tons, the equivalent to taking 33 million cars off our nation's roads," the American Lung Association and other health organizations wrote to EPA in January. "These benefits are a great bargain for the American people, costing less than 1 cent per gallon of gasoline and about one-half of a percent, or $150, of the cost of the average new car." [53]

New Offshore Drilling

Before the *Deepwater Horizon* oil spill in the Gulf of Mexico in 2010, Obama proposed to open large areas of U.S. coastline to offshore drilling, including many areas where drilling had never taken place. That proposal was derailed by the oil spill, which led to an overhaul of the federal office that regulates offshore energy production. Now, however, the administration is considering a much more limited expansion of offshore drilling.

In November 2011 the Interior Department released a proposed five-year plan for offshore oil drilling from 2012-2017, which expands open areas in the Gulf of Mexico and allows oil development off Alaska's north coast and in Cook Inlet on the south coast. Unlike the administration's previous plan, it does not allow drilling along the U.S. East Coast.

"This five-year program will make available for development more than three-quarters of [the] undiscovered oil and gas resources estimated on the [Outer Continental Shelf, OCS], including frontier areas such as the Arctic, where we must proceed cautiously, safely and based on the best science available," said Interior Secretary Ken Salazar. [54]

Conservationists say the United States should move extremely carefully in allowing drilling off the Alaska coast, where operating conditions are harsh and the environment is extremely vulnerable to spills. "In the Arctic you deal routinely with subzero temperatures, long periods of darkness, hurricane-force winds, and 20-foot seas. It's a very challenging place to work and operate equipment," says Marilyn Heiman, director of the Pew Environment Group's U.S. Arctic Program.

Because the Arctic shoreline is frozen for much of the year, there are no docks or infrastructure along the coast to support cleanup operations if a spill occurred offshore. "There are very few roads connecting villages along the coast, and the nearest port is 1,000 miles away. The U.S. Coast Guard has said that massing a spill response in the Arctic would be virtually impossible," says Heiman.

In February the Interior Department approved a spill response plan submitted by Shell Oil to support drilling leases in the Beaufort and Chukchi seas. Shell still needs permits for each individual well it plans to drill but could start operations in the Arctic later this year. [55] The company also has won legal injunctions against the environmental advocacy group Greenpeace, which often sends boats out to protest activities such as whaling and nuclear testing at sea. Greenpeace boats were

Continued on p. 566

At Issue:

Should the Keystone XL pipeline be built?

ALEX POURBAIX
PRESIDENT, ENERGY AND OIL PIPELINES, TRANSCANADA CORP.

FROM TESTIMONY BEFORE THE HOUSE COMMITTEE ON ENERGY AND COMMERCE, SUBCOMMITTEE ON ENERGY AND POWER, DEC. 2, 2011.

yes

When you boil down the debate on this project, I believe it comes down to a simple question for Americans: Do they want secure, stable oil from a friendly neighbor in Canada or do they want to continue importing high-priced conflict oil from unfriendly regions such as the Middle East or Venezuela?

Keystone XL will help secure that stable supply of oil by linking Canadian and U.S. crude supplies with the largest refining markets in the United States. Canada's oil reserves are vast — approximately 175 billion barrels are estimated to be recoverable at today's oil price. This compares to the United States' reserves, which are estimated to be around 19 billion barrels.

While transporting oil from Canada, Keystone XL will also ship domestic U.S. crude oil.

Keystone XL expects to move 100,000 [barrels per day] of American crude production from North Dakota and Montana to Cushing, Okla., or to the Gulf Coast, and further expects to move 150,000 barrels per day of U.S. crude from Cushing to the Gulf Coast. Growing domestic U.S. oil production has long been a goal in the United States. But that production cannot grow effectively if it cannot reach market. Keystone XL encourages domestic U.S. oil production by connecting areas with increased supply in Montana, North Dakota and Cushing, Okla., with the United States' largest refining center in the Gulf Coast. The fact that this pipeline access is needed is apparent in the significant price discount that U.S. inland producers have been receiving for their production compared to the price that Gulf Coast refiners pay for comparable grades of crude oil imported from other countries.

In addition to energy security, our project will also create valuable jobs for Americans. . . . Thousands of direct construction jobs were planned to begin next year, the overwhelming majority of which were union jobs. They would have started only a few months from now. Contracts and subcontracts were awarded to dozens of U.S. companies. Americans were hired and ready to go to work. Those Americans will now need to find other employment while we work through this delay. . . . Who speaks for these thousands of Americans and their families? Canadian crude oil will be produced regardless of whether Keystone XL is built. If it is not exported to the United States, it will be exported to other countries, from which there is no shortage in demand.

JANE FLEMING KLEEB
FOUNDER, BOLD NEBRASKA

FROM TESTIMONY BEFORE THE HOUSE COMMITTEE ON ENERGY AND COMMERCE, SUBCOMMITTEE ON ENERGY AND POWER, DEC. 2, 2011.

no

This pipeline is risky. It is massive, and we literally have no long-term study on how tar sands affect land, water or our health. We have seen first-hand in Michigan, with the awful tar sands spill in the Kalamazoo River, how much more difficult and expensive it is to clean up tar sands and the chemicals mixed with this type of oil. Families have been displaced, and this oil is sticking to the bottom of the riverbed. This is not traditional oil that floats and can be skimmed with booms. We owe it to workers, our families, the environment and our water to do the right study to get us the answers we need.

I am asking for your help in getting a study on how tar sands affect our land, water and health. We need clarity on [whether] traditional pipelines, designed to carry conventional oil, can safely carry corrosive tar sands, especially since we have seen 14 spills in the past year on TransCanada's Keystone 1 when they told us we would see 11 leaks over the lifetime of the pipe. . . . It is hard to rationalize how a pipeline carrying oil across our nation to an unknown final destination can be in our national interest. We all know TransCanada and other tar sands companies need to get their oil to various ports in order to sell it to the highest bidder. In the end, we assume all of the risks and none of the rewards.

Yes, the process has taken a long time. It has been over three years since TransCanada started to contact landowners and threaten eminent domain even though they had no permit for their project, three years of threats from a powerful international company. Our state has been bombarded with misleading ads about the amount of jobs and money this pipeline would bring to our state. We will soon be releasing a report that shows how little in taxes TransCanada actually has paid to our counties compared to their promises. . . .

As a nation, we are facing our next moon challenge. Energy is our moon challenge. I want to look at my three little girls and tell them that I'm doing everything I can to ensure our energy is sustainable, that our energy is helping revitalize our communities, not destroy them, and that our energy is safe.

The TransCanada pipeline simply does not meet the challenge. It sets us on a path backward, not forward. We do not need to figure out ways to approve this pipeline. We need to figure out ways to ensure our land and water are protected . . . as we, together, figure out solutions for our country's energy and job needs.

Continued from p. 564

ordered to stay more than 3,200 feet away from oil rigs and 1,600 feet from support boats nationwide, and the court established a 25-yard safety zone around Shell's oil vessels in Dutch Harbor, Alaska, a staging area for operations in the region. [56]

Heiman argues that Interior has not improved oil spill response planning since the *Deepwater Horizon* spill and that the agency should require lessees to have more detailed spill response plans and gear in place before operations can start.

"We should have equipment and trained personnel in the region, plus containment systems and gear to drill relief wells," she says. "We also need standards for operating in Arctic conditions and responding to a worst-case discharge. There is no requirement now for future operations to have containment systems or relief rigs in the Arctic, or to have tested them in the Arctic."

Shell and Interior Department officials say they are committed to operating safely and protecting Alaska's fragile environment. When the Interior Department approved Shell's spill-response plan in February, Deputy Secretary David J. Hayes said the decision was "based on our new standards and our commitment to ensure the highest standard of safety and environmental preparedness in the world and our commitment to bringing science to all our activities in the Arctic." [57]

On the East Coast, officials and some residents in Virginia want Interior to open areas off the state's coast for drilling. "Energy production in the OCS has vigorous, bipartisan support among Virginians and their political leadership," Democratic U.S. Sens. James Webb and Mark Warner wrote to Salazar in January, citing approval from the state's congressional delegation, legislature, and Republican Gov. Bob McDonnell. Offshore drilling revenues, which are shared by the federal and state governments, could provide "a future source of funding for important State priorities such as transportation, land and water conservation and alternative energy development," the senators wrote. [58]

However, Virginia could face opposition from the Defense Department, which stated in 2010 that about three-quarters of the waters proposed for drilling off Virginia were crucial areas for Navy operations, including training, testing and gunnery exercises. [59] Virginia has large bases representing all four military services. Most notably, hundreds of ships and aircraft are based in the Norfolk/Newport News/Virginia Beach area at the mouth of the Chesapeake Bay, including aircraft carriers, destroyers and submarines.

Alt-Fuel Vehicles

In July 2011 the Obama administration and major auto manufacturers announced new fuel efficiency standards for U.S. cars and light trucks — the second increase during Obama's presidency. Previously, fuel economy standards had not changed since 1985. The new targets will double the average fuel efficiency of cars and light trucks to 54.5 miles per gallon by 2025, when fuel consumption will be an estimated 2.2 million barrels lower per day. [60]

Walter McManus, an economist at Oakland University's School of Business Administration in Michigan and a former market analyst at General Motors, calls the new standards a major breakthrough because they require manufacturers to make every class of vehicles they produce more efficient. Previously, auto makers could average the efficiency of different models across their fleets to meet an overall target, so car companies typically would offset sales of gas guzzlers by also offering smaller, more efficient models.

"Manufacturers will have to make everything lighter across their fleets, downsize engines, turbocharge them, and add features like stop-start systems [which turn engines off when vehicles stop, eliminating engine idling]. They'll have to address all of the ways that today's cars use energy, like tire inflation and wind resistance," says McManus.

The new fuel efficiency standards could boost so-called advanced-drive vehicles — gas/electric hybrids such as the popular Toyota Prius, plug-in hybrids and battery-powered electric vehicles. In November 2011, all of these categories combined accounted for just under 3 percent of monthly U.S. new car sales (27,897 vehicles), with more than two-thirds going to Toyota. [61] Electric vehicles entered mass production at the end of 2010, but started slowly: Combined sales for the Chevy Volt and Nissan Leaf plug-ins totaled about 26,000 cars for their entire first year. [62]

"Electric vehicles depend heavily on high gas prices, and they need to reduce battery costs almost threefold to be cost-competitive, which probably means developing and commercializing a brand-new technology," says Harvard's Lee. "They could make inroads in 2020 to 2030, but I wouldn't bet on it in the next few years."

McManus agrees that electric vehicles could help reduce U.S. oil dependence, but he says it will be in the long term. "If the goal is to use less fuel now, you can argue that the best way is to keep improving internal combustion engines by ratcheting up fuel economy targets, not by picking a technology," he says.

However, McManus does not expect a resurgence of SUVs and other gas-guzzling models in the wake of the recession. "Manufacturers are still making large pickup trucks and [large] SUVs, but they're making them mainly for commercial use. Households still buy pickups, but a lot of those owners are contractors, plumbers and electricians, and they are very concerned about fuel economy. SUVs are waning as a personal-use vehicle," he says. ■

OUTLOOK

No Choice

Over the past several decades Americans have snapped to attention during oil price spikes, then lapsed back into old ways once the crunches eased. But many experts say the recession that started in 2008, combined with rising world energy demand, may permanently alter U.S. attitudes toward oil use.

Energy companies are bullish about new production in the United States, even though domestic sources will not replace those like OPEC. "We're leaders in developing unconventional supplies at home and around the world, which has revolutionized supply," says the American Petroleum Institute's Dougher. She acknowledges that even if the United States becomes independent of oil produced outside North America, it would still pay world prices. Nonetheless, she contends, "What we can do by increasing production is get more control and reliable supplies and give the world more supply from stable sources."

Just because a source is large, however, may not make it reliable. "Energy security isn't just about supply — it's also about environmental impacts," says the Pembina Institute's Lemphers. "Operating costs to produce oil from Canadian tar sands are about four times higher than for Saudi crude oil. If global oil prices drop, this massive supply could become uneconomic to develop."

Although near-term market prospects for plug-in and battery-powered electric cars appear modest, Oakland University's McManus believes U.S. car makers have learned that the era of gas guzzlers is over. "There's been a huge change in attitudes since the gasoline price rise from 2002-2006," he says. "Manufacturers started squeezing their big profit margins on SUVs, but they kept marketing them, which cost them a lot. Eventually they had to cut production dramatically. The only market for SUVs was here in North America, so we took the losses when they became hard to sell."

Now, in contrast, McManus believes that U.S. car companies support the mission of bringing smaller, more fuel-efficient cars to market — particularly Ford. "I think Ford definitely believes in this for the long term and is committed to sustainability because of the Ford family — they want to be in business 100 years from now," he says. "They want to be the fuel economy leader for every market segment that they compete in."

Energy hawks agree that fuel efficiency is important but strongly support an open fuel standard as a way to diversify the U.S. transportation sector away from gasoline. "An open fuel standard would create opportunity for sources like natural gas and methanol, which are much cheaper than oil. It's like switching from $100 per barrel oil to $18 per barrel oil, and it would break oil's monopoly," says Luft of the Institute for Analysis of Global Security. "Utilities switch between different fuels to make electricity, depending on prices, and we should aspire to something like that for transportation."

While experts may disagree on strategies, there is little argument that reducing U.S. oil dependence should be an important national priority. "Expanding world oil production will be very challenging, and demand will keep growing in China, India and other developing countries. We're not going to have a choice about using energy more efficiently," says University of California-San Diego economist James Hamilton. "We're seeing declines in U.S. consumption, and that's an ongoing process." ■

Notes

[1] Brian Montopoli, "Could Gingrich really lower gas to $2.50 per gallon?," CBS News, Political Hotsheet, March 13, 2012, www.cbsnews.com/8301-503544_162-57396671-503544/could-gingrich-really-lower-gas-to-$2.50-per-gallon/.

[2] Kathleen Hennessey, "Obama scoffs at critics on gas prices, defends energy policy," *Los Angeles Times*, Feb. 23, 2012, http://articles.latimes.com/2012/feb/23/nation/la-na-obama-gas-prices-20120224.

[3] "Primary Energy Consumption by Source and Sector, 2010," U.S. Energy Information Administration, http://205.254.135.7/totalenergy/data/annual/pecss_diagram.cfm.

[4] Daniel Yergin, testimony before the Senate Energy and Natural Resources Committee, March 29, 2012, pp. 8-9, www.energy.senate.gov/public/index.cfm/files/serve?File_id=500012a0-c1a5-4c3f-87c4-16d3c06abcff.

[5] Michael D. Shear, "Romney Faults Obama on Energy Costs, but Has cited Benefits of Rising Prices," *The New York Times*, April 2, 2012, www.nytimes.com/2012/04/03/us/politics/romney-faults-obama-for-rising-gas-prices.html?_r=1&pagewanted=print.

[6] "Fact Sheet: Obama Administration's All-of-the-Above Approach to American Energy," Office of the Press Secretary, the White House, March 21, 2012, www.whitehouse.gov/the-press-office/2012/03/21/fact-sheet-obama-administration-s-all-above-approach-american-energy.

[7] For background see Thomas J. Billitteri, "Offshore Drilling," *CQ Researcher*, June 25, 2010, pp. 553-580.

[8] For details see Paul Parformak, *et al.*, "Keystone XL Pipeline Project: Key Issues," Congressional Research Service, R41668 (March 13, 2012), www.fas.org/sgp/crs/misc/R41668.pdf.

[9] Padmananda Rama, "Obama Returns to Oklahoma Talking Oil," NPR, March 22, 2012, www.npr.org/blogs/itsallpolitics/2012/03/22/149161898/obama-returns-to-oklahoma-talking-oil.

[10] "Toyota Sells One-Millionth Prius in the U.S.," Toyota USA Newsroom, April 6, 2011, http://pressroom.toyota.com/article_display.cfm?article_id=2959.

[11] For background see Thomas J. Billitteri, "Auto Industry's Future," *CQ Researcher*, Feb. 6, 2009, pp. 105-128, update, Oct. 3, 2011.

[12] For background see Jennifer Weeks, "Energy Policy," *CQ Researcher*, May 20, 2011, pp. 457-480.

[13] Charles Riley, "Gingrich's $2.50 Gas Promise," CNN Money, Feb. 24, 2012, http://money.cnn.com/2012/02/24/news/economy/gingrich_gas_prices/index.htm.

[14] Rep. Fred Upton, opening statement, March 7, 2012, p. 1, http://republicans.energycommerce.house.gov/Media/file/Hearings/Energy/20120307/HHRG-112-IF03-MState-U000031-20120307.pdf.

[15] Richard H. Thaler, "Why Gas Prices Are Out of Any President's Control," *The New York Times*, March 31, 2012, www.nytimes.com/2012/04/01/business/gas-prices-are-out-of-any-presidents-control.html.

[16] Jack Gillum and Seth Borenstein, "Fact Check: More U.S. Drilling Didn't Drop Gas Price," The Associated Press, March 21, 2012, http://0-news.yahoo.com.precise.petronas.com.my/fact-check-more-us-drilling-didnt-drop-gas-065231245.html.

[17] Letter from Reps. Peter Welch, Ed Markey and Rosa DeLauro to President Barack Obama, March 16, 2012, p. 3, www.welch.house.gov/index.php?option=com_content&task=view&id=1930&Itemid=90.

[18] Sam Fletcher, "Market Watch: Talk of SPR Release Drops Oil Prices," *Oil & Gas Journal*, March 16, 2012, www.ogj.com/articles/2012/03/market-watch-talk-of-spr-release-drops-oil-prices.html.

[19] Andrew Nikiforuk, *Tar Sands: Dirty Oil and the Future of a Continent* (2008), pp. 25-27.

[20] 2012 Oil Shale and Tar Sands Programmatic EIS Information Center, "About Tar Sands," U.S. Department of the Interior, http://ostseis.anl.gov/guide/tarsands/index.cfm.

[21] Testimony before the House Energy and Commerce Committee, Subcommittee on Energy and Power, May 23, 2011, http://press.ihs.com/press-release/energy-power/congressional-testimony-significance-canadas-oil-sands.

[22] "Minister Oliver Promotes Canadian Energy Interests in Kuwait," Marketwire, March 13, 2012, www.marketwatch.com/story/minister-oliver-promotes-canadian-energy-interests-in-kuwait-2012-03-13.

[23] "Environment Canada and the Oil Sands," Environment Canada, May 2011, online at www.scribd.com/doc/76259666/Oilsands-Pollution.

[24] Testimony before the House Committee on Science, Space and Technology, April 17, 2012, www.energyxxi.org/testimony-karen-harbert-house-committee-science.

[25] "Public comments of the Sierra Club, *et al.*, on the TransCanada Keystone XL Pipeline Draft Environmental Impact Statement," July 2, 2010, p. 7, www.nebraskawildlife.org/Documents/NWF%20Comments%20KeystoneXL%20DEIS%207.3.10.pdf.

[26] *Ibid.*, p. 15.

[27] Wendy Stueck, "Native Leaders Vow to Block Northern Gateway Pipeline," *The Globe and Mail*, Dec. 2, 2011, www.theglobeandmail.com/news/national/british-columbia/bc-politics/native-leaders-vow-to-block-northern-gateway-pipeline/article2257573/; Doug Ward, "Feds Likely Could Push Pipelines Through B.C. After Long Legal Struggle," *Montreal Gazette*, May 1, 2012, /www.montrealgazette.com/news/Feds+likely+could+push+pipelines+through+after+long+legal+struggle/6550161/story.html.

[28] Max Paris, "EU Delays 'Anti-Oilsands' Fuel Quality Directive Decision," Canadian Broadcasting Corporation, April 29, 2012, www.cbc.ca/news/politics/story/2012/04/20/pol-fuel-directive-europe-canada.html.

[29] "Annual Energy Outlook 2012; Early Release Overview," U.S. Energy Information Administration, p. 1, http://205.254.135.7/forecasts/aeo/er/pdf/0383er%282012%29.pdf.

[30] "2012 U.S. Energy Sector Outlook," *Forbes Insights*, p. 1, www.forbes.com/forbesinsights/energy_sector_outlook_2012/index.html.

[31] H.R. 1687, introduced by Rep. John Shimkus (R-Ill.), and S. 1603, introduced by Sen. Maria Cantwell (D-Wash.)

[32] "OnPoint," E&E TV, Oct. 13, 2011, www.eenews.net/tv/transcript/1407.

[33] "Automakers Say 'Enough!' on U.S. Flex-Fule Cars," *Biofuels Digest*, June 16, 2011, www.biofuelsdigest.com/bdigest/2011/06/16/automakers-say-enough-on-us-flex-fuel-cars/.

[34] For background see Adriel Bettelheim, "Biofuels Boom," *CQ Researcher*, Sept. 29, 2006, pp. 793-816, and Jennifer Weeks, "Energy Policy," *CQ Researcher*, May 20, 2011, pp. 457-480.

[35] Todd Woody, "New Enzyme Could Make Cellulosic Ethanol Competitive With Fossil Fuels," *Forbes.com*, Feb. 22, 2012, www.forbes.com/sites/toddwoody/2012/02/22/new-enzyme-could-make-cellulosic-ethanol-competitive-with-fossil-fuels/; Jim Lane, "The Enzyme Wars," *Biofuels Digest*, Feb. 24, 2012, www.biofuelsdigest.com/bdigest/2012/02/24/the-enzyme-wars/.

[36] "EPA Finalizes 2012 Renewable Fuel Standards," Environmental Protection Agency Dec. 27, 2011, http://yosemite.epa.gov/opa/admpress.nsf/0/A7CE72844710BE0A85257973006A20F3.

[37] Kelsi Bracmort, "Meeting the Renewable Fuel Standard (RFS) Mandate for Cellulosic Biofuels: Questions and Answers," Congressional Research Service, Jan. 11, 2012, p. 7, www.fas.org/sgp/crs/misc/R41106.pdf.

[38] *Renewable Fuel Standard: Potential Economic and Environmental Effects of U.S. Biofuel Policy* (2011), National Research Council, pp. 3-4, www.nap.edu/openbook.php?record_id=13105&page=3.

[39] "Ethanol Keeps Gasoline Prices $1.09 Cheaper," Renewable Fuels Association, May 2012, http://ethanolrfa.3cdn.net/794558c8d8f4826bb6_alm6i6z9x.pdf, and "Don't Mess with the RFS," March 2012, http://ethanolrfa.3cdn.net/056f576c0cb1b6388f_2om6b9rvl.pdf.

[40] Testimony before the House Energy and Commerce Committee, Subcommittee on Environment and Economy, April 19, 2012, p. 2, http://ethanolrfa.org/page/-/objects/pdf/PublicPolicy/OfficialStatements/Dinneen%20E%26C%20Subcmte%20Testimony%204-19-12.pdf?nocdn=1.

[41] The case is *Standard Oil Co. of New Jersey v. United States*, 221 U.S. 1 (1911).

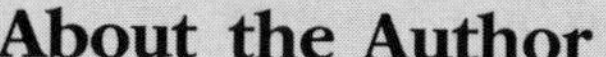

About the Author

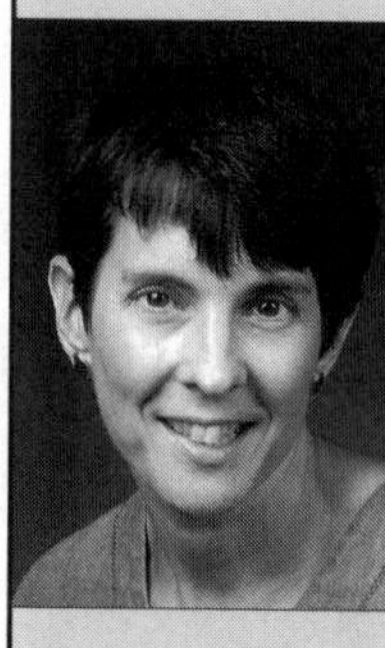

Jennifer Weeks is a Massachusetts freelance writer who specializes in energy, the environment and science. She has written for *The Washington Post, Audubon, Popular Mechanics* and other magazines and previously was a policy analyst, congressional staffer and lobbyist. She has an A.B. degree from Williams College and master's degrees from the University of North Carolina and Harvard. Her recent *CQ Researcher* reports include "Gulf Coast Restoration" and "Energy Policy."

[42] Daniel Yergin, *The Prize: The Epic Quest for Oil, Money & Power* (1991), pp. 112-113.
[43] *Ibid.*, pp. 209-210.
[44] "U.S. Field Production of Crude Oil," U.S. Energy Information Administration, May 30, 2012, www.eia.gov/dnav/pet/hist/LeafHandler.ashx?n=PET&s=MCRFPUS2&f=A.
[45] Andrew Revkin, "Obama on the 'Shock to Trance' Energy Pattern," *The New York Times*, Nov. 17, 2008, http://dotearth.blogs.nytimes.com/2008/11/17/obama-on-shock-to-trance-energy-pattern/.
[46] David Jackson, "Obama: Oil Drilling Has Increased on My Watch," *USA Today*, March 22, 2012, http://content.usatoday.com/communities/theoval/post/2012/03/obama-oil-drilling-up-on-my-watch/1#.T5mGb9USEuc.
[47] "U.S. Number of Operating Refineries as of January 1," U.S. Energy Information Administration, http://205.254.135.7/dnav/pet/hist/LeafHandler.ashx?n=PET&s=8_NA_8OO_NUS_C&f=A.
[48] "U.S. Operable Crude Oil Distillation Capacity," U.S. Energy Information Administration, http://205.254.135.7/dnav/pet/hist/LeafHandler.ashx?n=PET&s=MOCLEUS2&f=M.
[49] Ron Scherer, "Why Gasoline Could Be in Short Supply this Summer on East Coast," *The Christian Science Monitor*, March 28, 2012, www.csmonitor.com/USA/2012/0328/Why-gasoline-could-be-in-short-supply-this-summer-on-East-Coast.
[50] Jad Mouawad, "Delta Buys Refinery to Get Control of Fuel Costs," *The New York Times*, April 30, 2012, www.nytimes.com/2012/05/01/business/delta-air-lines-to-buy-refinery.html?pagewanted=print.
[51] For details see "Control of Air Pollution from Motor Vehicles: Tier 3 Motor Vehicle Emission and Fuel Standards," Environmental Protection Agency, http://yosemite.epa.gov/opei/rulegate.nsf/byRIN/2060-AQ86#1.
[52] Testimony before the Joint Economic Committee, April 26, 2012, p. 4, http://jec.senate.gov/public//index.cfm?a=Files.Serve&File_id=d2c7da82-7987-41e0-a43a-7a86dbea5636.
[53] Letter online at www.lung.org/get-involved/advocate/advocacy-documents/letter-tier3-vechicle.pdf.
[54] "Secretary Salazar Announces 2012-2017 Offshore Oil and Gas Development Program," U.S. Department of the Interior, Nov. 8, 2011, www.doi.gov/news/pressreleases/Secretary-Salazar-Announces-2012-2017-Offshore-Oil-and-Gas-Development-Program.cfm.

FOR MORE INFORMATION

American Petroleum Institute, 1220 L St., N.W., Washington, DC 20005; 202-682-2000; www.api.org. National trade association for the oil and natural gas industry.

Harvard Kennedy School of Government, 79 John F. Kennedy St., Cambridge, MA 02138; 617-495-1100; www.hks.harvard.edu. Graduate school of government and public policy, with research programs on issues including environment and natural resources.

Institute for Analysis of Global Security, 7811 Montrose Rd., Suite 505, Potomac, MD 20854; 866-713-7527; www.iags.org. Nonprofit think tank focused on the connections between energy and national security.

Oak Ridge National Laboratory, P.O. Box 2008, Oak Ridge, TN 37831; 875-574-4160; www.ornl.gov. Multiprogram science and technology laboratory of the U.S. Department of Energy, focusing on clean energy and global security challenges.

Pembina Institute, 219 19th St., N.W., Calgary, Alberta T2N 2H9, Canada; 403-269-3344; www.pembina.org. Canadian think tank that conducts research, education and advocacy to promote sustainable energy solutions.

Pew Environment Group, 901 E St., N.W., Washington, DC 20004; 202-552-2000; www.pewenvironment.org. National environmental research and advocacy group, funded by the Pew Charitable Trusts.

U.S. Geological Survey, 12201 Sunrise Valley Dr., Reston, VA 20192; 703-648-5953; www.usgs.gov. Science agency within the U.S. Department of the Interior that collects, monitors and analyzes information about natural resource conditions, issues and problems.

University of Michigan Transportation Research Institute, 2901 Baxter Rd., Ann Arbor, MI 48109; 734-764-6504; www.umtri.umich.edu. Interdisciplinary research center that works to expand knowledge of transportation systems.

[55] Kim Murphy, "Oil Drilling in Arctic Nears Reality: Shell Emergency Plan OKd," *Los Angeles Times*, Feb. 17, 2012, http://articles.latimes.com/2012/feb/17/nation/la-na-nn-arctic-oilspill-20120217; Sarah Blackman, "Drilling Arctic Oil: Do Shell's Response Plans Hold Water?" *Offshore Technology*, April 24, 2012, www.offshore-technology.com/features/featurethe-race-to-drill-arctic-oil-do-shells-response-plans-hold-water/.
[56] Jim Paulin, "Shell Wins Injunction, Greenpeace Looks at Options," *Arctic Sounder*, April 6, 2012, www.thearcticsounder.com/article/1214shell_wins_injunction_greenpeace_looks_at.
[57] John M. Broder, "Shell Clears Major Drilling Hurdle in Its Bid for New Arctic Drilling," *The New York Times*, Feb. 17, 2012, www.nytimes.com/2012/02/18/science/earth/us-tentatively-approves-shell-spill-plan-for-new-arctic-drilling.html.
[58] Letter online at www.warner.senate.gov/public/index.cfm/pressreleases?ID=defcdc5f-27da-4766-8e3b-7e8d336bb223.
[59] "Virginia Offshore Drilling Hits a Roadblock," *The Washington Times*, May 19, 2010, www.washingtontimes.com/news/2010/may/19/virginia-offshore-drilling-hits-a-roadblock/?page=all.
[60] "Driving Efficiency: Cutting Costs for Families at the Pump and Slashing Dependence on Oil," The White House, 2011, www.whitehouse.gov/sites/default/files/fuel_economy_report.pdf.
[61] John O'Dell, "Hybrid Sales Soar in November," *Edmunds.com*, Dec. 6, 2011, www.edmunds.com/industry-center/analysis/hybrid-sales-soar-in-november.html.
[62] Steve LeVine, "Chevy Volt, Nissan Leaf: Will the Electric Car Ever Be a Success?" *Slate.com*, March 11, 2012, www.slate.com/articles/technology/future_tense/2012/03/chevy_volt_nissan_leaf_will_the_electric_car_ever_be_a_success_.html.

Bibliography

Selected Sources

Books

Coll, Steve, *Private Empire: ExxonMobil and American Power, Penguin*, 2012.
A Pulitzer Prize winner tracks ExxonMobil's meteoric rise, focusing on the leader who remade the company's safety culture after the 1989 *Exxon Valdez* oil spill.

Mitchell, William J., Chris E. Borroni-Bird, and Lawrence D. Burns, *Reinventing the Automobile: Personal Urban Mobility for the 21st Century*, MIT Press, 2010.
A scholar at the Massachusetts Institute of Technology and two General Motors executives propose a new vision for urban transportation that relies on small cars, information technology and clean fuels to make cities cleaner and safer.

Nikiforuk, Andrew, *Tar Sands: Dirty Oil and the Future of a Continent*, Greystone, 2009.
An award-winning Canadian journalist argues that oil production from Alberta's tar sands is causing disastrous environmental, social and political harm and should be capped and limited.

Articles

"Ray Mabus, U.S. Navy Secretary, Defends Biofuels Investment," The Associated Press, March 13, 2012, www.huffingtonpost.com/2012/03/13/ray-mabus-navy-defends-biofuels_n_1341328.html.
The U.S. Navy is experimenting with expensive biofuels to power planes and ships, a strategy that Navy leaders say is a hedge against future oil price shocks.

Broder, John M., and Clifford Krauss, "New and Frozen Frontier Awaits Offshore Oil Drilling," *The New York Times*, May 23, 2012, www.nytimes.com/2012/05/24/science/earth/shell-arctic-ocean-drilling-stands-to-open-new-oil-frontier.html?ref=offshoredrillingandexploration.
The authors vividly describe the challenges of drilling off the Alaskan coast.

Bunkley, Nick, "Payoff for Efficient Cars Takes Years," *The New York Times*, April 4, 2012, www.nytimes.com/2012/04/05/business/energy-environment/for-hybrid-and-electric-cars-to-pay-off-owners-must-wait.html?scp=1&sq=Prius&st=cse.
Hybrids and electric vehicles save owners money on gas, but those savings are offset by high price tags.

Gillum, Jack, and Seth Borenstein, "Fact Check: More U.S. Drilling Didn't Drop Gas Price," The Associated Press, March 21, 2012, www.cbsnews.com/8301-505145_162-57401456/more-us-drilling-didnt-drop-gas-price/.
A statistical analysis of 36 years of monthly, inflation-adjusted gasoline prices shows no relationship between U.S. domestic production levels and fuel costs.

Herron, James, "Citigroup Says Peak Oil is Dead," *Wall Street Journal*, Feb. 17, 2012, http://blogs.wsj.com/source/2012/02/17/citigroup-says-peak-oil-is-dead/.
Citigroup says new oil production from shale could one day make the United States and Canada self-sufficient in oil.

Jaffe, Amy Myers, "The Americas, Not the Middle East, Will Be the World Capital of Energy," *Foreign Policy*, September/October 2011, www.foreignpolicy.com/articles/2011/08/15/the_americas_not_the_middle_east_will_be_the_world_capital_of_energy.
Technical advances are making oil more accessible in the West at a time when political turmoil threatens Middle East production.

Moore, Jina, "After Oil: How We'll Live," *The Christian Science Monitor*, Oct. 10, 2011, www.csmonitor.com/Specials/Future-Focus-Energy.
A package of articles examines alternatives to fossil fuel, including electric cars and biofuels, and the Pentagon's push to reduce the armed forces' oil dependence.

Reports and Studies

"Keystone XL: Undermining Energy Security and Sending Tar Sands Overseas," Oil Change International and Natural Resources Defense Council, 2012, http://priceofoil.org/keystone-xl-undermining-energy-security/.
Two environmental organizations argue that building the Keystone XL pipeline will not improve U.S. energy security.

"Oil and Gas: Interior Has Strengthened Its Oversight of Subsea Well Containment, but Should Improve Its Documentation," U.S. Government Accountability Office, February 2012, www.gao.gov/assets/590/588961.pdf.
Since the 2010 *Deepwater Horizon* spill in the Gulf of Mexico, the Interior Department has tightened policies for managing undersea well blowouts. But drilling off the coast of Alaska poses unique risks.

Lee, Henry, and Grant Lovellette, "Will Electric Cars Transform the U.S. Vehicle Market? An Analysis of the Key Determinants," Discussion Paper 2011-08, Belfer Center for Science and International Affairs, Harvard University, July 2011, www.belfercenter.ksg.harvard.edu/files/LeeLovellette ElectricVehiclesDP2011web.pdf.
For electric cars to reduce U.S. oil use, gasoline prices would have to rise to \$4.50-\$5.50 per gallon and battery technology improve, according to two Harvard scholars.

National Research Council, "Renewable Fuel Standard: Potential Economic and Environmental Effects of U.S. Biofuel Policy," National Academies Press, 2011.
Members of the National Academies of Science find that the United States is unlikely to meet its goals for producing advanced biofuels without major technical breakthroughs or policy changes.

The Next Step:

Additional Articles from Current Periodicals

Arctic

Clanton, Brett, "Arctic Oil Is Luring Majors," *Houston Chronicle*, Oct. 16, 2011, p. A1, www.chron.com/business/energy/article/Oil-beckons-from-the-top-of-the-world-2220860.php.
Technological advances are encouraging many major oil producers to explore the possibility of drilling in the Arctic.

Steiner, Rick, "Offshore Arctic Oil Needs Citizen Input," *Anchorage* (Alaska) *Daily News*, Aug. 3, 2011, p. A13, www.adn.com/2011/08/02/1997621/offshore-arctic-oil-needs-citizen.html.
Citizens should have a say in any decisions to drill in the Arctic, says an environmental consultant in Alaska.

Surrusco, Emilie, "Drilling for Oil in Arctic Ocean Is Fraught With Danger," *The Christian Science Monitor*, Aug. 17, 2011, www.csmonitor.com/Commentary/Opinion/2011/0817/Drilling-for-oil-in-Arctic-Ocean-is-fraught-with-danger.
The Arctic's extreme conditions and remoteness make it a difficult spot for oil drilling, says the Alaska Wilderness League.

Bakken Formation

Donovan, Lauren, "North Dakota's Boom Will Keep On Rolling," *Bismarck* (N.D.) *Tribune*, May 25, 2012, p. A1, bismarcktribune.com/bakken/article_3b0344de-a610-11e1-a890-001a4bcf887a.html.
Top energy executives say North Dakota's oil boom will continue as long as new drilling zones are being discovered.

Howard, Tom, "Banking on the Bakken," *Billings* (Mont.) *Gazette*, Feb. 1, 2012, p. A1.
The Bakken Formation has given a considerable boost to Montana's economy and oil and gas industry.

Tuttle, D. Ray, "Tulsa-Based Oneok Partners to Build Bakken-Cushing Pipeline," *Journal Record* (Okla.), April 9, 2012, journalrecord.com/2012/04/09/oneok-partners-to-build-bakken-cushing-pipeline-energy/.
An Oklahoma-based energy company is planning to build an oil pipeline from North Dakota to Oklahoma.

Gas Prices

Baker, David R., "Rhetoric Fails Reality Check on Gas Prices," *Houston Chronicle*, March 5, 2012, p. B10.
Gas prices are set by a global market based on supply and demand, not just by the amount of U.S. oil produced.

Corredoira, Rafael, "Gas Prices Simply Aren't Up to U.S.," *Philadelphia Inquirer*, April 26, 2012, articles.philly.com/2012-04-26/news/31410993_1_oil-prices-opec-gas-prices.
The influence of the Organization of Petroleum Exporting Countries on gas prices is undervalued, says a professor.

Krumm, Chris, "Natural Gas Market Shows That Drilling Can Lower Gasoline Prices," *Columbus* (Ohio) *Dispatch*, March 17, 2012, p. A13.
Supporters of increasing oil drilling say the practice will lower gasoline prices because the same has happened for natural gas.

Keystone XL Pipeline

Harrison, Pricey, "Should Keystone XL Pipeline Be Built? No.," *Charlotte* (N.C.) *Observer*, March 4, 2012, www.charlotteobserver.com/2012/03/04/3066455/should-keystone-xl-pipeline-be.html.
The Keystone XL pipeline would be hazardous to Americans' health, says a Democrat in the North Carolina House.

Marks, Jay F., "Pipeline Expected to Boost Oil Prices at Cushing's Hub," *The Oklahoman*, Jan. 13, 2012, p. B1, newsok.com/keystone-xl-expected-to-boost-oil-prices-at-cushing/article/3639841.
A Keystone pipeline executive says his company's XL pipeline could boost local oil prices by about $10 a barrel.

Owens, Mackubin Thomas, "Keystone Kops Energy Policy," *The Washington Times*, Jan. 26, 2012, p. B1, www.washingtontimes.com/news/2012/jan/25/keystone-kops-energy-policy/.
President Obama's opposition to the Keystone XL pipeline is indicative of his administration's war on fossil fuels, says a national security professor at the Naval War College in Rhode Island.

Citing *CQ Researcher*

Sample formats for citing these reports in a bibliography include the ones listed below. Preferred styles and formats vary, so please check with your instructor or professor.

MLA STYLE

Jost, Kenneth. "Remembering 9/11," CQ Researcher 2 Sept. 2011: 701-732.

APA STYLE

Jost, K. (2011, September 2). Remembering 9/11. *CQ Researcher, 9*, 701-732.

CHICAGO STYLE

Jost, Kenneth. "Remembering 9/11." *CQ Researcher*, September 2, 2011, 701-732.

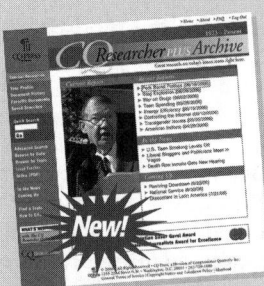

CQ Researcher

Published by CQ Press, an Imprint of SAGE Publications, Inc.

www.cqresearcher.com

Whale Hunting

Should whale and dolphin hunting be outlawed?

For hundreds of years, the United States and countries around the world relentlessly hunted whales and other marine mammals for their oil, blubber and other byproducts. But today whales, dolphins and porpoises are widely viewed as intelligent creatures worthy of conservation and protection from commercial hunters. Scientists describe marine mammals as social animals that share characteristics with humans, including the ability to communicate in sophisticated ways. But Japan, Norway and Iceland still hunt whales, and Japan continues its controversial slaughter of dolphins for their meat, as dramatized by the Academy Award-winning documentary "The Cove." Efforts to ban commercial whaling by the International Whaling Commission have failed because of political bickering and competing national interests. Meanwhile, climate change, entanglement in commercial-fishing gear and ocean noise pollution are adding to the peril facing marine mammals.

Japanese fishermen cut up a bottlenose whale killed off the coast of Tokyo. Several Japanese towns mount commercial hunts for whales not protected by the International Whaling Commission.

INSIDE THIS REPORT

THE ISSUES 575
CHRONOLOGY 583
BACKGROUND 584
CURRENT SITUATION 588
AT ISSUE........................589
OUTLOOK 590
BIBLIOGRAPHY 594
THE NEXT STEP 595

CQ Researcher • June 29, 2012 • www.cqresearcher.com
Volume 22, Number 24 • Pages 573-596

Los Angeles | London | New Delhi
Singapore | Washington DC

RECIPIENT OF SOCIETY OF PROFESSIONAL JOURNALISTS AWARD FOR EXCELLENCE ◆ AMERICAN BAR ASSOCIATION SILVER GAVEL AWARD

THE ISSUES

575 • Should whaling be banned?
• Can cetacean populations be managed internationally?
• Is aboriginal subsistence whaling acceptable?

BACKGROUND

584 **Early Whalers**
By the ninth century, Europeans were whaling in small boats.

586 **Conservation Efforts**
Fifteen whaling countries formed a commission in 1946 to manage whales.

586 **Dolphin Hunts**
Large-scale hunts occur in coastal Japan and the Faroe Islands.

CURRENT SITUATION

588 **More Whale Wars**
Anti-whaling activists and nations continue to battle Japan and other whaling nations.

588 **Other Threats**
Fishing nets, traps and underwater noise take a toll on whales and other cetaceans.

590 **Toxic Waters**
Anti-whaling activists warn that cetacean meat contains mercury and other toxins.

OUTLOOK

590 **New Models**
A cap-and-trade approach to limiting whale hunting has been proposed.

SIDEBARS AND GRAPHICS

576 **Two Sanctuaries Prohibit Commercial Whaling**
Sanctuaries were established in the Indian and Southern oceans in 1979 and 1994, respectively.

577 **Aboriginal Whaling Increased**
The total kill was 406 whales in 2010, versus 282 in 1996.

578 **'Goddess of the Yangtze' Goes Extinct**
The Yangtze River dolphin was among the planet's rarest mammals.

580 **Whale Hunting Declined After Moratorium**
But anti-whaling activists say the ban is ineffective because scientific whaling is allowed.

583 **Chronology**
Key events since 1712.

584 **Sonar Testing Linked to Whale Deaths**
"At some levels there is no way to eliminate the risks."

587 **One BIG Family**
Whales, dolphins and porpoises share two unique characteristics.

589 **At Issue**
Should the International Whaling Commission revise its whaling moratorium?

FOR FURTHER RESEARCH

593 **For More Information**
Organizations to contact.

594 **Bibliography**
Selected sources used.

595 **The Next Step**
Additional articles.

595 **Citing *CQ Researcher***
Sample bibliography formats.

Cover: AFP/Getty Images/Yoshikazu Tsuno

CQ Researcher

June 29, 2012
Volume 22, Number 24

MANAGING EDITOR: Thomas J. Billitteri
tjb@cqpress.com

ASSISTANT MANAGING EDITOR: Kathy Koch
kkoch@cqpress.com

CONTRIBUTING EDITOR: Thomas J. Colin
tcolin@cqpress.com

ASSOCIATE EDITOR: Kenneth Jost

STAFF WRITER: Marcia Clemmitt

CONTRIBUTING WRITERS: Peter Katel, Barbara Mantel, Jennifer Weeks

DESIGN/PRODUCTION EDITOR: Olu B. Davis

ASSISTANT EDITOR: Darrell Dela Rosa

FACT CHECKER: Michelle Harris

INTERN: Kate Irby

Los Angeles | London | New Delhi
Singapore | Washington DC

An Imprint of SAGE Publications, Inc.

VICE PRESIDENT AND EDITORIAL DIRECTOR, HIGHER EDUCATION GROUP:
Michele Sordi

DIRECTOR, ONLINE PUBLISHING:
Todd Baldwin

CQ Researcher (ISSN 1056-2036) is printed on acid-free paper. Published weekly, except: (March wk. 5) (May wk. 4) (July wk. 1) (Aug. wks. 3, 4) (Nov. wk. 4) and (Dec. wks. 3, 4). Published by SAGE Publications, Inc., 2455 Teller Rd., Thousand Oaks, CA 91320. Annual full-service subscriptions start at $1,054. For pricing, call 1-800-834-9020. To purchase a *CQ Researcher* report in print or electronic format (PDF), visit www.cqpress.com or call 866-427-7737. Single reports start at $15. Bulk purchase discounts and electronic-rights licensing are also available. Periodicals postage paid at Thousand Oaks, California, and at additional mailing offices. POSTMASTER: Send address changes to *CQ Researcher*, 2300 N St., N.W., Suite 800, Washington, DC 20037.

Whale Hunting

By Daniel McGlynn

The Issues

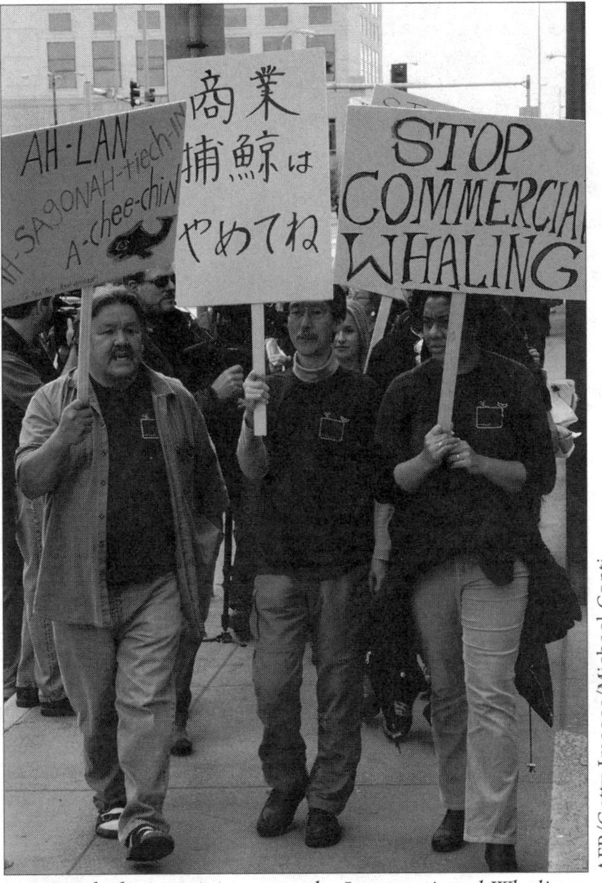

AFP/Getty Images/Michael Conti

Anti-whaling activists urge the International Whaling Commission, meeting in Anchorage, Alaska, in March 2007, to maintain the ban on whale hunting. Environmentalists increasingly argue that whales demonstrate a high level of intelligence, communication and social organization and thus should be protected. Japan, Norway and Iceland all say whaling is part of their cultural identity and that the number of whales they kill — roughly 1,000 annually — is small compared to the total whale population.

For two weeks, the *Bob Barker*, a converted whaling ship manned by anti-whaling activists, pursued the Japanese whaler *Nisshin Maru* and two smaller harpoon vessels. Finally, on March 5, the activists from the Sea Shepherd Conservation Society caught up to the whalers in the icy waters of the Southern Ocean Whale Sanctuary, 60 miles off the Antarctic coast. [1]

The *Nisshin Maru* has been hunting whales in the region since 1986, claiming that the kills are for scientific research — and thus exempt from a ban on whaling in the sanctuary imposed by the International Whaling Commission. [2] But anti-whaling activists, along with some mainstream scientists, say the claims of research are a farce. [3] The whale meat harvested in the sanctuary, they charge, ends up in Japanese shops and restaurants.

When they shipped out last December, the Japanese planned to kill 900 whales, a limit they created for themselves through a loophole in IWC rules. [4] But their mission plans changed after the confrontation with the *Bob Barker*.

As darkness fell and snow pelted the ships, the two sides beamed blinding lights and piercing lasers at each other, tried to foul each other's propellers with heavy ropes and darted perilously close to each other's bows. The tactics had been well-honed over the bitter, eight-year struggle between conservationists and Japanese whalers — confrontations so frequent that they became the subject of the Discovery Channel's "Whale Wars" reality TV series. [5]

In the end, with neither side reporting damage or injuries, the *Nisshin Maru* and its companion vessels headed for home, their take for the 2011-2012 whaling season only 266 minke whales and one endangered fin whale. [6] "It has been a successful campaign," Paul Watson, Sea Shepherd's founder and president, said afterward. "There are hundreds of whales swimming free in the Southern Ocean Whale Sanctuary that would now be dead if we had not been down there for the last three months. That makes us very happy indeed." [7]

The battles in the sanctuary are the most dramatic example, but not the only one, of a much broader fight over protecting marine mammals. (*See map, p. 576.*) Norway kills hundreds of minke whales annually in commercial hunts, and Iceland engages in annual hunts under both commercial and scientific permits. In the North Sea's Danish-controlled Faroe Islands and in Japanese coastal communities, meanwhile, thousands of smaller whales, dolphins and porpoises are slaughtered every year in hunts not regulated by the IWC. [8]

Whales, dolphins and porpoises* comprise a family of marine mammals called cetaceans, whose unifying characteristics are that they breathe air through blowholes, and some species use a form of sonar called echolocation to communicate and forage. [9] Of the three, great whales — the largest animals on Earth — are the most aggressively hunted.

Whales have been hunted intensively for hundreds of years. In the 18th century, sperm, gray and bowhead whales were sought for their ample blubber, which was rendered into oil for lighting, candle wax and other uses, and for their baleen — flexible mouthparts used in women's corsets. [10]

At the turn of the 20th century, wind-powered, square-rigged whale boats gave way to steel-hulled, diesel-powered ships used as floating whale-

---

* Porpoises and dolphins are small toothed whales. Porpoises have rounded heads, while dolphins have pointed snouts or beaks. Both are hunted for meat.

Two Sanctuaries Prohibit Commercial Whaling

The International Whaling Commission has designated two sanctuaries where commercial whaling is prohibited. The Indian Ocean Whale Sanctuary was established in 1979 for a duration of 10 years and has been extended three times. The Southern Ocean Whale Sanctuary was established in 1994 and extended in 2004. Despite the internationally recognized protected status of the sanctuaries, Japan continues its controversial scientific whaling in the Southern Ocean Whale Sanctuary.

Boundaries of the Southern Ocean and Indian Ocean Whale Sanctuaries

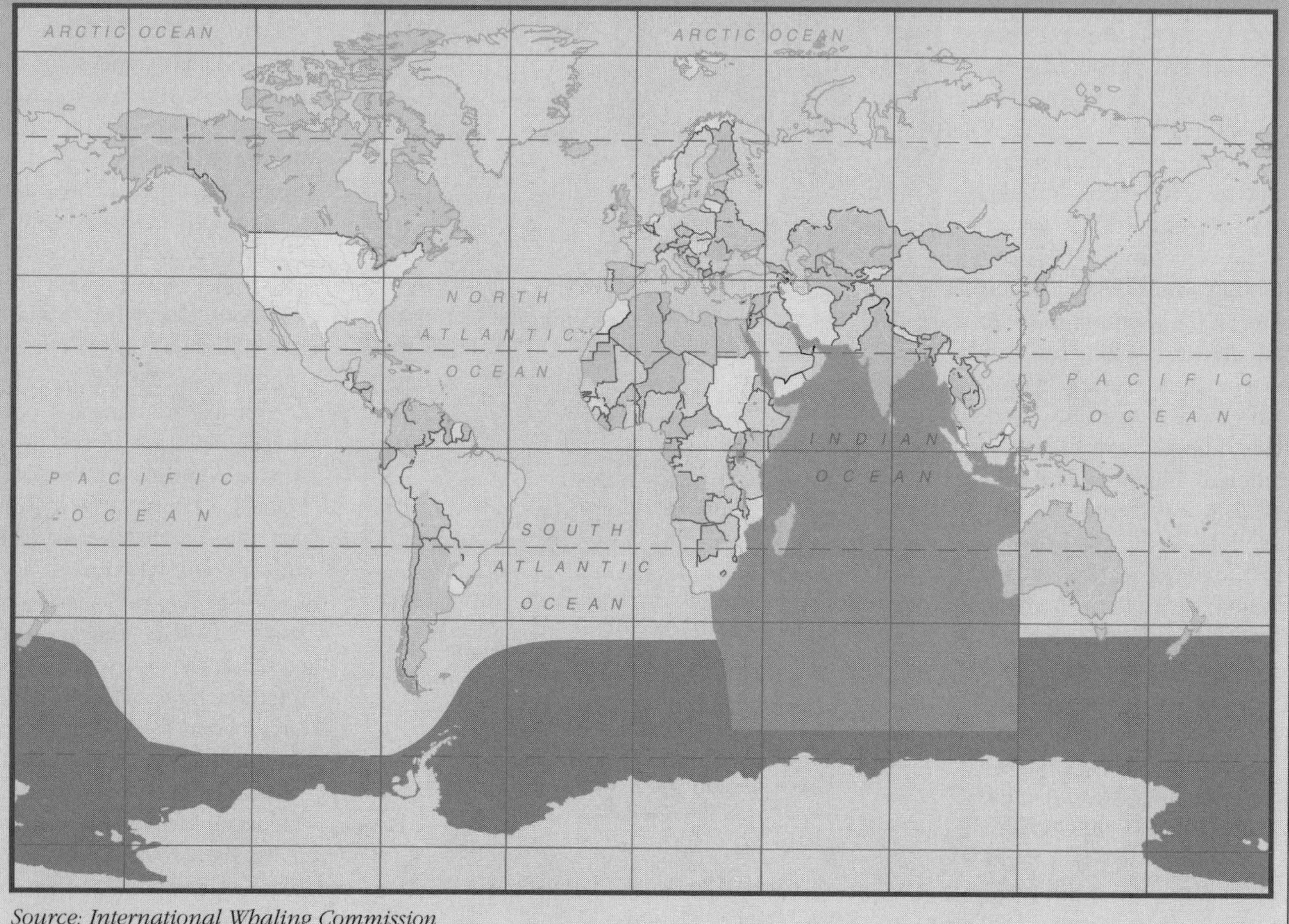

Source: International Whaling Commission

processing factories; at the same time, high-powered cannons and grenade-tipped lances replaced hand-thrown harpoons.

Whale oil remained in use well into the 20th century for specialized industrial lubricants and as a source of hydrogenated oil for margarine. But by the 1960s some whale species had dwindled to near extinction. Meanwhile, whales and other cetaceans became emblematic of a global environmental movement, and many advocacy groups sprang up to protect them. By 1982, the International Whaling Commission (IWC), set up in 1946 to monitor whale populations and ensure a continual harvest, imposed a moratorium on international commercial whaling.

Environmentalists increasingly argue that cetaceans demonstrate a high level of intelligence, communication and social organization and thus should be protected. This year, the American Association for the Advancement of Science, an international organization that promotes scientific collaboration and science-friendly public policy, advocated for a Cetacean Bill of Rights, noting that whales, dolphins and porpoises have similarities to humans in the parts of the brain associated with high cognitive activities. [11]

Not everyone agrees that cetacean hunting should be eradicated, however. Japan, Norway, and Iceland support whaling practices that they say are guided by scientific research and conservation principles. In 2010, Japan's Institute for Cetacean Research, which operates the *Nisshin Maru*, killed 445 whales under a scientific permit. Commercial whalers in Iceland killed 208 and in Norway 464. All three countries say whaling is part of their cultural identity, whale meat is part of their traditional diet and that the number of whales they kill is small compared to the total whale population. [12]

Whale conservation groups charge that the IWC is ineffectual at protecting marine mammals and that the commission's voluntary structure makes its whaling moratorium difficult to enforce. Norway and Iceland filed formal objections to the moratorium and thus are allowed to develop their own annual quotas. Japan continues whaling by making use of a loophole in IWC regulations, claiming its annual hunts are for important scientific research. All three countries say their self-determined annual quotas are calibrated according to known whale populations and are low enough to minimize the impact on hunted species.

Meanwhile, native groups in Siberia, Alaska, Greenland and Saint Vincent and the Grenadines in the Caribbean continue so-called aboriginal whaling as a means to obtain food and assert their traditional cultural identity. The Makah, a Native American tribe in northwest Washington state, are trying to reestablish whale hunting practices for the same reasons. Aboriginal whaling is unopposed by the IWC and most conservation groups.

Debate over protecting cetaceans is part of a larger controversy involving many other types of marine life. For example, sea turtles are being hunted for food in coastal communities worldwide and also are dying in fishing nets. In the United States, all six species of sea turtle are threatened or endangered; 4,600 were snagged in fishing gear, according to a 2011 study. [13] At the same time, thousands of baby sea turtles are lost to habitat destruction, mainly from beach development, which eliminates nesting grounds.

Sharks, too, are being targeted for food. Each year almost 100 million sharks are killed around the world to feed a lucrative shark fin market in Asia. [14]

At the same time, whales and other marine mammals are threatened not only by hunting but also by overfishing — which robs the seas of food sources vital to whales, dolphins and porpoises — and by environmental contamination, which can threaten entire species. (*See sidebar, p. 578.*)

Scientists say a decline in orcas — or killer whales — in the Ross Sea near Antarctica stems from overfishing of the Antarctic toothfish, a main food source for whales in the area. [15] Moreover, researchers found that nearly 700 bottlenose dolphins died after the *Deepwater Horizon* oil rig exploded in the Gulf of Mexico in 2010, spilling more than 200 million gallons of crude oil. [16] And this year, major dolphin and porpoise die-offs were reported in Peru; the cause remains under study. [17]

As cetacean hunting continues, concern also is growing that consumption of whale and dolphin meat will make people sick. Because cetaceans are at the top of the marine food chain, the toxins and heavy metals present in oceans build up in their tissue over time. Of particular concern are high levels of mercury, a byproduct of industrial pollution. In a 2003 study, whale meat sampled in stores around Japan showed mercury levels almost 200 times the allowable limit in some samples. [18]

"More attention is getting focused on new, emerging threats like ocean noise, marine pollution and climate change, says Patrick Ramage, director of the whale program at the International Fund for Animal Welfare, in Yarmouth Port, Mass.

Aboriginal Whaling Increased

Aboriginal subsistence whalers — including Eskimos in Alaska — killed nearly 50 percent more whales in 2010 than 1996. Nearly half of the animals taken in 2010 were minke whales, the most prevalent species. Aboriginal whaling is unopposed by the IWC and most conservation groups.

Aboriginal Subsistence Whaling Catches, 2010

Country	Fin	Humpback	Sei	Gray	Minke	Bowhead	Total
Denmark: West Greenland	5	9	0	0	186	3	203
Denmark: East Greenland	0	0	0	0	9	0	9
St. Vincent and The Grenadines	0	3	0	0	0	0	3
Russia	0	0	0	118	0	2	120
U.S.A.	0	0	0	0	0	71	71
Total	**5**	**12**	**0**	**118**	**195**	**76**	**406**

Source: "Aboriginal Subsistence Whaling Catches Since 1985," International Whaling Commission, January 2012, http://iwcoffice.org/conservation/table_aboriginal.htm

'Goddess of the Yangtze' Goes Extinct

Yangtze River dolphin was among the planet's rarest mammals.

Before it was declared extinct during the past decade, the Yangtze River dolphin, or baiji, was among the planet's rarest mammals. One of the world's four freshwater cetaceans, the so-called "Goddess of the Yangtze" was the first aquatic mammal to go extinct in the last 50 years. [1]

The 3,900-mile-long Yangtze River is one of the longest rivers in the world and the longest in China. It is home to the controversial Three Gorges Dam and vital for irrigation, transportation and fresh water.

Several unique or rare species are found only in the Yangtze, such as the Yangtze sturgeon and the Chinese alligator. But they are endangered, slowly succumbing to the same environmental pressures that may have claimed the baiji, including industrial pollution, agricultural run-off and loss of buffer wetlands. Overfishing has also been a major factor.

In 1997, when researchers mounted an expedition to count baiji, only 14 were left in the river. By December 2006, researchers couldn't find any after a six-week 2,000-mile survey. [2]

"The main reason is overfishing," said August Pfluger, head of the Baiji Foundation, which co-sponsored the expeditions. "The Chinese still use unsustainable fishing methods like dynamite. There's still a lot of illegal fishing, so the dolphins were competing with humans for food." [3]

Increased development and river traffic also likely contributed to the demise of the dolphins, which had poor eyesight and relied on echolocation to forage for food in the shallows. Samples of pollution levels, however, turned out not to be high enough to cause the death of multiple individuals. [4]

Also facing survival pressures are other river dolphins: the Amazon River dolphin, the La Plata River dolphin (South America) and the Indian River dolphin, in India's Ganges River. [5]

"Globally, a pattern has emerged," said researcher Zeb Hogan, a National Geographic fellow and TV personality known for his efforts to protect the world's biggest fish. "These large aquatic animals are disappearing." [6]

— Daniel McGlynn

[1] Ian Sample, "Yangtze river dolphin driven to extinction," *The Guardian*, Aug. 7, 2007, www.guardian.co.uk/environment/2007/aug/08/endangeredspecies.conservation.

[2] Peter Ritter, "Farewell to the Yangtze river dolphin," *Time*, Aug. 10, 2007, www.time.com/time/health/article/0,8599,1651819,00.html.

[3] *Ibid.*

[4] Sample, *op. cit.*

[5] "Chinese River Dolphin, Baiji, Yangtze river dolphin," National Oceanic and Atmospheric Administration, Fisheries Office of Protected Resources, www.nmfs.noaa.gov/pr/species/mammals/cetaceans/chineseriverdolphin.htm.

[6] Stefan Lovgren, "China's rare river dolphin now extinct, experts announce," *National Geographic*, Dec. 14, 2006, http://news.nationalgeographic.com/news/2006/12/061214-dolphin-extinct_2.html.

As conservation groups, international regulators, and nongovernmental organizations debate the future of whaling and dolphin hunting, these are some of the questions they are asking:

Should whaling be banned?

Despite the IWC's efforts to stop large-scale commercial whaling and limit scientific whaling, Norway, Iceland and Japan have advocated for a policy based on the health of targeted species and not a complete ban. They argue that the IWC's original intent was to recommend sound, science-based whale-management practices that did not rule out killing. "Some species need protection and others do not," says Richard Pedersen, counselor for fisheries and oceans in the Norwegian Embassy in Washington.

All three countries have historic and cultural ties to whale meat and products. In their view, whale hunting is an expression of national sovereignty. In addition, consumers — especially in Japan — continue to demand whale meat.

"The total protection of all whales, irrespective of their [population] status, as promoted by some members of the IWC and some environmental and animal welfare organizations, is exclusive of other views and ways of living," said Joji Morishita, Japan's alternate commissioner to the IWC during the group's annual meeting last year. "It is contradictory to the Japanese cultural values where whale meat is still eaten and where whales are still revered through religious ceremonies and festivals." [19]

In Norway, "we have been whaling since the morning of time," says Pedersen. Norway's aging whaling fleet — composed mainly of family-operated cod-fishing vessels rigged for whales during whaling season — killed 533 minke whales last year, fewer than half Norway's self-established quota of 1,286, according to Pedersen.

A dominant part of Iceland's economy, like those of Norway and Japan, has always been fishery and marine-related products. Iceland's whaling industry is similar in size and scope to neighboring Norway's. In 2010, Iceland killed 148 endangered fin whales and 60 minke whales. [20] This past May, however, Iceland announced that it will suspend its fin whale hunt, at least for now, because of lack of demand for whale products and because of a salary disagreement with the fishermen's union. [21]

Ensuring the health of other fisheries is cited as a reason for the continuation of whaling. Because whales consume smaller marine life, allowing more whales in the oceans increases strain on other valuable species, whaling supporters contend. [22]

In 2010, the University of Iceland's Institute for Economic Studies, in a study requested by the Ministry of Fisheries and Agriculture, found that killing 150 fin whales a year would generate the equivalent of $5.8 million in hunting and processing salaries. Moreover, the study found that hunting 150 minke and fin whales would prevent thousands of additional tons of economically valuable fish, such as cod, haddock and capelin, from being consumed by whales. The study also found value in conservation, concluding that whale watching produces about $4 million in taxes for Iceland's economy. [23]

Japan's aggressive whaling continues to draw the most international criticism because it most resembles old-style commercial whaling. To some activists, the *Nisshin Maru*, the mother-ship of Japan's whaling fleet, is a notorious factory whaling ship that is deployed for months and processes and stores whale meat and products supplied by smaller and more nimble harpoon vessels. This arrangement allows whaling expeditions to continue for long periods in the Southern Ocean. [24]

Japan claims its whaling yields valuable scientific data about whale behavior and populations. "More than 100 data items and samples are taken from each whale including ear plugs for age-determination studies, reproductive organs for examination of maturation, reproductive cycles and reproductive rates, stomachs for analysis of food consumption and blubber thickness as a measure of condition," Morishita said. "These data and the analyses of the data provide us with valuable scientific information on whales and the ecosystem of which they are a part." [25]

Critics argue, however, that Japan is using the IWC scientific-research provision as an excuse to continue supplying Japanese markets with whale meat and products. [26] A 2009 report on the economics of whaling sponsored by the WWF (formerly World Wildlife Fund) and the Whale and Dolphin Conservation Society found that the price of whale meat in Japan is dropping and that a large portion of the yearly catch is frozen and stored. That suggests waning Japanese demand for products from Japan's whaling industry, which is heavily subsidized by the government, according to the groups. [27]

Japanese whalers "are supplying products that nobody wants and science that nobody uses," charges Ramage of the International Fund for Animal Welfare.

Since the 1970s, when saving whales began to be synonymous with the modern environmental movement, most animal welfare and conservation groups have rallied around several distinct arguments for permanently banning whale and dolphin hunting.

For one thing, they argue, cetaceans, as large marine mammals, play an important role as indicators of overall ocean health. Despite the near cessation of commercial whaling in recent decades, they contend, the continuation of relatively small-scale whaling strains the populations of endangered great whale species still recovering from heavy hunting in the past.

Other threats include underwater noise pollution, entanglement in fishing gear and climate change.

Conservation organizations also make an economic argument, urging Japan, Iceland and Norway to transition to economic activities based on whale watching rather than whale killing. "We are trying to get them to put down the harpoon and pick up the camera," says Ramage. Whale watching and other ecotourism activities are growing and can become more lucrative, sustainable and better for a whaling nation's image, the WWF and Whale and Dolphin Conservation Society argue. [28] Whale watching is a $2 billion industry that logged 13 million whale watchers in 2008 in 119 countries, according to the International Fund for Animal Welfare. [29]

Cetacean hunting is also opposed on ethical grounds. Critics say whales and dolphins are sentient creatures and that killing them can cause them to suffer a slow, painful death. [30]

Several ethics and animal welfare groups have recommended that cetaceans be viewed as "nonhuman persons" and protected from cruelty, including hunting and capture. "The similarities between cetaceans and humans are such that they, as we, have an individual sense of self," Thomas White, a professor of ethics at Loyola Marymount University in Los Angeles, told a recent meeting of the American Association for the Advancement of Science, where emerging research about cetacean intelligence was presented.

"Dolphins are nonhuman persons," White said. "A person needs to be an individual. If individuals count, then the deliberate killing of individuals of this sort is ethically the equivalent of deliberately killing a human being." [31]

Can cetacean populations be managed internationally?

A comprehensive global plan to manage whale and other cetacean hunting continues to be elusive, mainly because of a lack of enforcement of existing international agreements.

Views about the continuation of whaling at both commercial and subsistence levels vary widely, in part because whales are migratory, traveling across the territorial waters of many nations as well as inhabiting international waters. The United States has some of the oldest and most comprehensive laws protecting marine mammals, but they apply only to species residing within the country and its territorial waters. [32]

Domestically, whales and dolphins are protected by the 1972 Marine Mammal Protection Act (MMPA), which was among the earliest pieces of legislation to look at conservation issues at the more comprehensive ecosystem level rather than the narrower species level.

Whale Hunting Declined After Moratorium

The number of whales killed annually by Japanese, Norwegian and Icelandic crews declined after the International Whaling Commission imposed a moratorium on commercial whaling in 1986. Whaling by aboriginal groups remained fairly constant. The voluntary moratorium, heavily criticized by anti-whaling activists as ineffective, allows whale hunting for scientific purposes or to support aboriginal cultures.

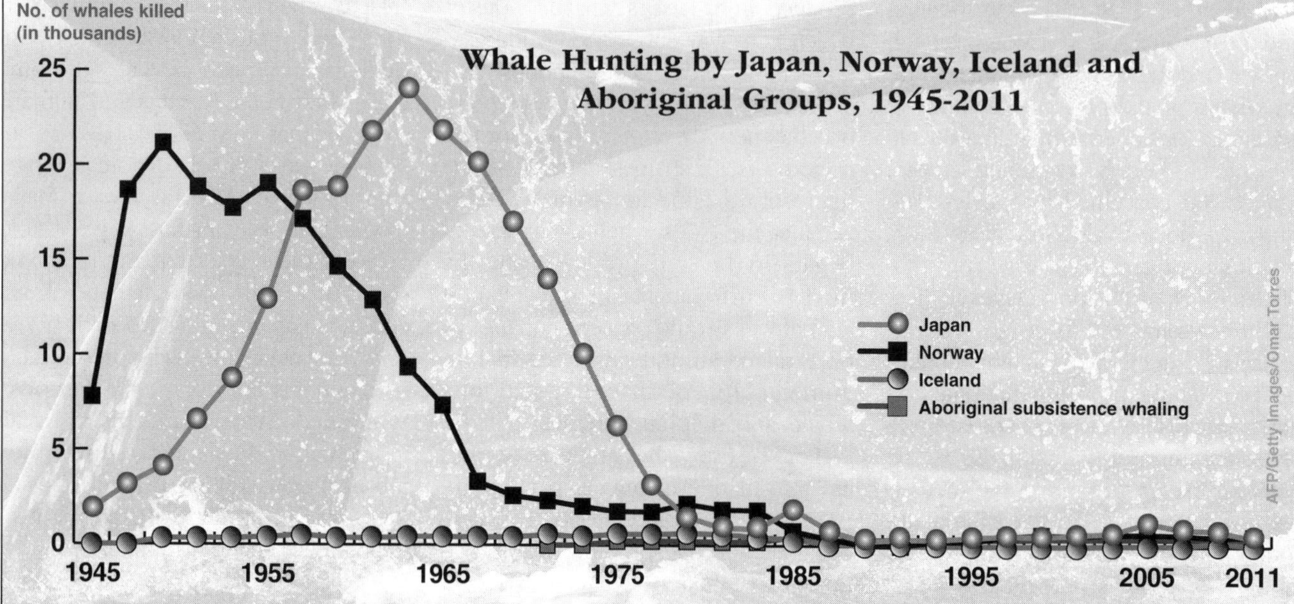

Source: "Whaling in the 21st Century and Before," Whale and Dolphin Conservation Society, 2011, www.wdcs.co.uk/whaling_graphs/main.swf

The act seeks not only to keep marine mammals from becoming extinct but also to keep them from falling below an "optimum sustainable population level." [33]

Seven species of great whales — humpback, blue, fin, sei, southern right, sperm and two species of northern right — are protected by the Endangered Species Act of 1973, which was passed when their populations were low. But conservation efforts seem to be working. In 1960, the worldwide humpback population was estimated at 5,000; today it's more than 60,000. "They appear to be coming back pretty strongly in most of the places we are studying," said Phillip Clapham, a biologist at the National Marine Mammal Laboratory in Seattle. [34] Gray whales were removed from MMPA coverage in 1994 because their populations have rebounded. Fin whales, the second-largest whale in the world after the blue whale, remains endangered. A 2012 study estimates the global blue whale population to be about 14,000. Both the MMPA and the Endangered Species Act are recognized internationally as effective and are used as guidelines for international regulatory efforts. [35]

Meanwhile, the IWC, which oversees international whaling regulation, lacks power because membership is voluntary and there is no enforcement apparatus. The IWC created the commercial whaling moratorium in part so it could study the remnants of the world's great whale stock and determine if a sufficient population allowed for continued hunting. [36] But "what was just a whalers' club more than 60 years ago is becoming a leading whale-conservation organization in the 21st century," says Ramage of the International Fund for Animal Welfare.

Still, some conservationists argue that the limited focus of the IWC on the world's great whales does not go far enough and that smaller whales, along with dolphins and porpoises, also should be better protected. "There is no link between dolphin hunting and IWC regulations," says Hardy Jones, a filmmaker and executive director of the conservation organization BlueVoice.org, based in St. Augustine, Fla.

Both the great whales and smaller cetaceans are also protected by the Convention on International Trade in Endangered Species and Wild Fauna and Flora (CITES), part of the United Nations Environmental Program. Formed in 1973, CITES outlaws the international trade in whale products that come from species listed as in danger of extinction. Trade in other species listed as threatened with extinction, or whose populations are depleted, are subject to heavy regulation. As with the IWC, however, CITES members follow the guidelines and regulations voluntarily; no international enforcement body exists. Instead, member nations are expected to make and enforce national laws that meet CITES guidelines.

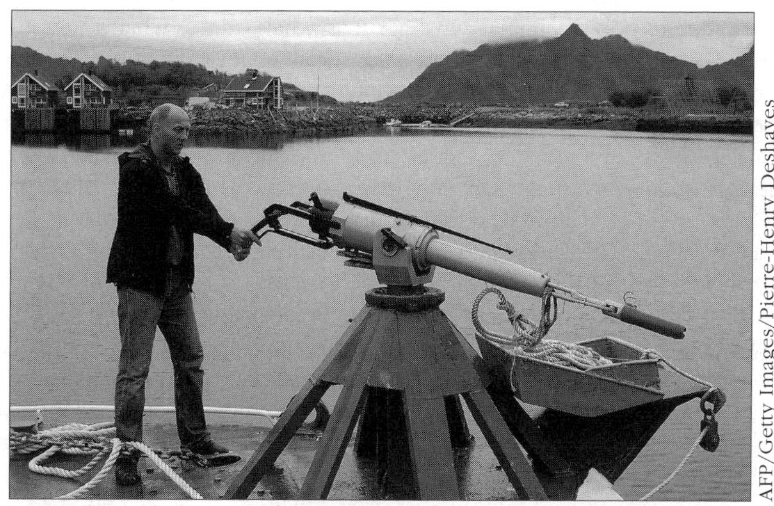

AFP/Getty Images/Pierre-Henry Deshayes

Modern whalers use explosive-tipped harpoons launched by high-powered cannons, such as this harpoon on a ship in Svolvaer, Norway. Norwegian whalers kill hundreds of minke whales annually in commercial hunts, while Iceland hunts under both commercial and scientific permits. In Japanese coastal communities, meanwhile, thousands of smaller whales, dolphins and porpoises are killed every year in hunts not regulated by the International Whaling Commission.

Today, 175 countries belong to CITES, making it one of the largest international environmental agreements. Nonetheless, a market continues for cetaceans — not only for their meat but also for mammals captured alive. A lucrative trade exists, for example, in captured dolphins, which can be sold to private collectors or aquariums in the unregulated captivity trade.

According to the Oscar-winning documentary film "The Cove," fishermen in Taiji, Japan, can make up to $100,000 for selling a single bottlenose dolphin to a collector or aquarium. [37] In the United States, however, "you can be fined $20,000 for even harassing a wild dolphin," says Mark Berman, associate director of the International Marine Mammals Project, a conservation organization.

IWC member nations can set their own whaling catch limits or quotas, as well as issue special permits for scientific research, despite the larger IWC moratorium on commercial whaling.

The trade in whale meat is as politically volatile as whale hunting. In 1986, when the IWC moratorium began, Iceland continued whaling, using a scientific permit and selling the meat to markets in Japan. By the early 1990s international pressure on Iceland to halt whaling and stop selling whale meat was intense, and in 1992 Iceland left the IWC, objecting to the IWC's denial of its 1991 scientific whaling permit. In 2002 Iceland rejoined the IWC and continues to whale under self-created commercial and research quotas.

Norway has always exempted itself from the IWC ban and has set annual quotas for the harvest of minke whales in Norwegian waters. The quota, which has been slowly rising, was set at 1,286 whales a year during the past three years, according to Pedersen, the embassy official. "This is a basic policy point," Pedersen says. "Whatever we catch should be sustainable and based on science. We estimate that there are 150,000 to 200,000 minke whales, so there's a feeling that a quota of 1,286 is not going to affect the stock."

Japan continues to whale under the claim of conducting scientific research in both the Southern Ocean and northern Pacific Ocean.

Often, it is left to international nongovernmental organizations, such as the International Fund for Animal Welfare and WWF, to monitor and report on nations or groups that are not fulfilling their obligations under established agreements. The lack of enforcement can often lead to frustration and backpedaling on international agreements.

To compel action, the United States can use the 1979 Packwood-Magnuson Amendment to the Fisherman's Protective Act of 1967, commonly called the Pelly Amendment, to enact trade sanctions on nations that are violating the IWC agreement. [38] In 2011, the Obama administration instructed American diplomats to encourage Iceland's government to shut down its lone fin whaling company. [39]

Citing the Pelly Amendment, Commerce Secretary Gary Locke recommended increased diplomatic pressure to discourage the growth of commercial whaling. "Iceland's commercial harvest of fin whales escalated dramatically over the past few years," Obama said in a message to Congress "In addition, Iceland recently resumed exporting whale products. Of particular concern to the United States, Iceland harvested 125 endangered fin whales in 2009 and 148 in 2010, a significant increase from the total of seven fin whales it commercially harvested between 1987 and 2007." [40]

Is aboriginal subsistence whaling acceptable?

The IWC currently recognizes the right of five groups to hunt whales for subsistence and cultural reasons under the aboriginal whaling provision: Alaskan Eskimos; Russian Chukotka; Greenlanders; Makah Indians in Washington state; and the residents of Bequia, the largest island in Saint Vincent and the Grenadines, in the Caribbean. [41]

The IWC views subsistence whaling differently from commercial whaling in terms of scale and necessity. Every five years the commission reviews aboriginal subsistence quotas to determine if a need still exists and whether local whale populations can support a hunt.

Besides providing a local source of meat, aboriginal whaling has community and cultural implications, such as increasing a hunter's social status, encouraging sharing and teaching respect for elders and their knowledge. [42] "It's the way of life for the native Eskimos," said Bill Hogarth, former U.S. commissioner to the IWC. "They use [the whales] for everything, for their whole livelihood, and they share the meat between the villages." [43]

Subsistence whalers in Greenland killed 212 whales in 2010, most of them minkes, according to the most recent IWC data. Russian natives in Siberia killed 118 gray whales and two bowheads; Alaskan natives, 71 bowheads; and the residents of Bequia three humpbacks. [44]

Most environmental and animal-welfare groups working to end commercial whaling do not campaign against aboriginal subsistence whaling, focusing instead on whaling for economic gain. "You would be hard-pressed to find any conservation group against aboriginal whaling for nutritional needs," says Ramage of the International Fund for Animal Welfare.

But that doesn't mean aboriginal whaling lacks controversy. The Sea Shepherd Conservation Society, among other anti-whaling groups, says it "is opposed in principle to all whaling by any people, anywhere for any reason." [45]

The same ethical and moral objections to commercial whaling also apply to aboriginal whaling: that whales are sentient, intelligent and social animals that should not be hunted.

Some anti-whaling activists fear that aboriginal whaling can be used to justify more whaling in the future. The Pacific Whale Foundation worries "that the United States' push for 'aboriginal subsistence whaling' will open the door to Japan and other nations asking to hunt whales in their near-shore waters as a form of 'non-commercial' or 'subsistence' whaling. For example, Japan has asked for a quota of minke whales that could be taken through coastal community-based whaling." [46]

A key point of contention for some anti-whaling activists is an attempt by Washington state's Makah Indian tribe to re-establish its ancestral whale hunt after a 70-year break. About 2,000 Makah live along Neah Bay, on the northwest tip of the continental United States. "We are a whaling people for some 3,500 years," says Tribal Council Chairman Micah McCarty. "It's what makes us Makah."

The 1855 Treaty of Neah Bay between the Makah and U.S. government stipulated that the Makah retained the right to hunt whales. By the early 1900s, the Makah had stopped whaling because widespread commercial whaling had depleted the population of eastern North Pacific gray whales that the tribe traditionally hunted.

In the 1990s a group within the tribe decided it was time to hunt again. In 1994 the eastern North Pacific gray whale was delisted from the Endangered Species List, and the following year the Makah Tribal Council notified the U.S. government that it was going to claim its treaty rights and resume whaling.

The tribe asked the United States to represent it at the annual IWC meeting to establish a subsistence quota under the commission's aboriginal subsistence provisions. After approval by the National Marine Fisheries Service, the quota was granted in 1997. "The Makah share a joint, scientifically approved subsistence allocation of gray whales with the natives of the Russian Federation," McCarty says. Native groups in Siberia are allowed to harvest 600 gray whales in a five-year period, while the Makah are allowed 20. [47]

In 1999, under the glare of international media attention and while contending with anti-whaling protests, Makah whalers in a canoe killed a gray whale. In 2000 the Ninth U.S. Circuit Court of Appeals sided with Rep. Jack Metcalf, R-Wash., and a coalition of environmental groups in a suit against the National Oceanic and Atmospheric Administration. Metcalf and the other plaintiffs had claimed the agency violated the National Environmental Protection Act when it granted the Makah permission to resume whaling. [48]

For the past 12 years the Makah's right to hunt gray whales has been in and out of the courts. The Makah continue to argue that their right to whale is established in the Neah Bay treaty. McCarty says resuming whaling will help reestablish the tribe's cultural identity. "We look forward to returning traditional foods like whale meat and blubber to our diet," McCarty says. "As with other cultures, we share a strong interest in reducing processed foods in our diet. We also have an interest in reducing the carbon footprint of our food supply."

The 6,000 Bequian islanders in Saint Vincent and the Grenadines have an IWC quota of four humpbacks a year. Historically, the Bequian relied on a steady harvest of fish and small marine mammals to supplement their diet. During the 19th century, many found work on American and European whaling ships that often stopped in the Caribbean islands for supplies on the way to the Southern Ocean or the Pacific. The Bequian adopted the "Nantucket style" of whaling, in which a crew would pursue and harpoon a whale and then drag it to shore.

Currently, the Bequian use only two wooden, motorless whaleboats of 19th-century design. The six-man crews are

Continued on p. 584

Chronology

1700s-1800s

Whaling industry flourishes.

1712
New England whalers kill their first sperm whale.

1757
The first big square-rigged whaling ship leaves Nantucket, Mass.

1773
Nantucket whaling ships sail for London with whale oil and return to Boston with British tea.

1791
The first New England whaling ship rounds Cape Horn and enters the Pacific whaling grounds.

1848
U.S. whaleships hunt in northern Pacific Ocean and the Arctic.

1870
Technological advances, including grenade harpoon and factory ships, usher in era of modern whaling.

1930s-1940s

Whaling transitions from global enterprise to global concern.

1931
League of Nations proposes whaling standards that are not followed.

1932
Whaling nations adopt blue whale unit (BWU) to measure the oil extracted from a whale.

1945
Whaling resumes after World War II, encouraged during the reconstruction of Japan and Russia as a way to supplement food supplies.

1946
International Convention on the Regulation of Whaling creates International Whaling Commission (IWC) to monitor and regulate dwindling global whale stocks.

1970s-1980s

Nations abandon whaling because of the expense and environmental concerns.

1972
United Nations Conference on the Human Environment passes a 10-year moratorium on commercial whaling. IWC rejects a similar measure, saying that science doesn't support a worldwide moratorium.

1975
The environmental group Greenpeace takes the world's first direct action against whaling when it attempts to use small inflatable boats to stop Soviet whalers. The action, 40 miles off the California coast, is aired on national TV and draws public support for the anti-whaling cause.

1979
IWC creates the Indian Ocean Whale Sanctuary.

1982
IWC establishes a moratorium on commercial whaling; moratorium goes into effect in 1986.

1988
Japanese Whale Research Program Under Special Permit in the Antarctic (JARPA) begins study of minke whales' role in the ecosystem. The Japanese report their findings to the IWC but sell the whale meat commercially.

1990s-Present

Continuing research on cetaceans reveals contemporary threats to their survival.

1994
IWC establishes Southern Ocean Whale Sanctuary.

1999
Makah tribe members in Washington state reestablish gray whale hunting.

2000
Link established between water pollution, whale strandings in Bahamas.

2005
JARPA II begins, with research expanded to include endangered fin and humpback whales.

2008
TV show "Whale Wars" begins documenting the conflict between Japanese whalers and anti-whaling activists.

2009
"The Cove" documentary spotlights Japan's dolphin hunt.

2010
U.S. leads effort to end IWC moratorium, close loopholes in the ban and allow heavily regulated whaling; plan rejected by IWC.

2011
Sea Shepherd Conservation Society begins using drone aircraft to track Japanese whaling fleet.

2012
Creation of South Atlantic Whale Sanctuary, off South America, is proposed at annual IWC meeting. . . . Article in the journal *Nature* advocates cap-and-trade permitting program to promote whale conservation. . . . Sea Shepherd begins anti-whaling campaign in the Faroe Islands.

Sonar Testing Linked to Whale Deaths

"At some levels there is no way to eliminate the risk."

In March 2000, cetacean scientists were alerted to an abnormal whale stranding in the Bahamas. Sixteen whales, from three different beaked whale species, became beached at roughly the same time, at different beaches and islands. [1]

The incident, and the extensive study that followed, established the first connection between underwater military sonar and the deaths of marine mammals. Examination of six of the seven whales that died (the rest were helped back to sea) by a specialist at Harvard Medical School showed damage to the whales' inner ears and throats, in a manner indicating audio trauma. [2]

The study found that the testing and use of underwater sonar by the U.S. Navy and other militaries could be lethal to marine mammals. Since then, numerous other strandings have been linked to nearby sonar testing: In 2004, multiple strandings in the Canary Islands and Japanese waters were linked to U.S. naval exercises. In 2006, a stranding off the coast of Spain was attributed to NATO exercises. [3]

Years of research have proved that sonar and other forms of underwater noise pollution disturb cetaceans. Sonar has been used by modern militaries since World War II. In active sonar, ships send out sound waves and listen for the way the sound changes or echoes to detect underwater objects. [4]

By the 1990s military sonar was becoming more sophisticated and more powerful. Just before scientists started linking cetacean strandings with underwater testing, the Navy spent an estimated $350 million to develop higher intensity and lower frequency sonar. The new technology, developed to track a new generation of submarines that use quieter diesel engines, increases interference with marine mammals' ability to communicate. [5]

Some cetaceans are particularly sensitive to powerful sonar because it interferes with their echolocation, which they use to communicate, navigate and find food. While studies show that many species of marine mammals are disturbed and stressed by underwater sonar, so far only strandings of beaked whales have occurred that can be clearly linked to military testing in the area. [6]

In 2005 the Natural Resources Defense Council (NRDC), an environmental group, sued the Navy, contending that its use of mid-frequency sonar violates the Environmental Protection Act, the Marine Mammal Protection Act and the Endangered Species Act and should not be permitted in areas of high whale populations.

In 2008 the U.S. Supreme Court ruled in the Navy's favor. In the 5-4 decision, Chief Justice John G. Roberts Jr. wrote, "The Navy's need to conduct realistic training with active sonar to respond to the threat posed by enemy submarines plainly outweighs the interests advanced by the plaintiffs." [7]

Cetacean conservationists continue to use the courts to try to compel the Navy to employ effective mitigation strategies. In January, the NRDC sued the National Marine Fisheries Service (NMFS), the federal agency in charge of the environmental oversight and permits for the Navy's activities in national waters. At issue is the latest NMFS environmental impact statement performed in 2010 for the Navy's renewal of its permit to conduct operations on the Pacific Northwest Training Range, off the coasts of Northern California, Oregon and Washington. [8] "That's 126,000

Continued from p. 582

honored for their whaling skill and bravery by Bequian society.

In other parts of the world, such as Alaska and Greenland, the annual subsistence hunts allowed under the IWC's aboriginal whaling provision use modern equipment, including, motorboats, guns and even backhoes and bulldozers. The use of modern tools and technologies leaves aboriginal hunters open to questions about the necessity of their subsistence hunts. "If they are truly important to the culture, then why are they using modern motors and guns?" asks Berman of the International Marine Mammal Project.

"No one can stop what our fathers and forefathers have done for thousands of years. But we're highly adaptable people. We use what tools are available to us to make life easier," said Fenton Rexford, an Alaskan native living near Barrow. [49] ■

BACKGROUND

Early Whalers

Some early civilizations combed beaches looking for stranded whales as a food source. Although no written records survive, archeological evidence shows that indigenous communities around the Arctic Circle, in Russia and Alaska, used whales for food for at least the last 2,000 years. [50]

By the ninth century, Europeans — first in the Basque region in northern Spain and southern France and then elsewhere — began using small boats to chase and kill whales close to shore. These early whalers posted sentries in stone towers along the coast. When whales were spotted, they lit fires to signal boatmen. [51]

By the 12th century, Japanese whalers were using harpoons deployed from small vessels. [52] Alaskan natives and other indigenous cultures in the Pacific Northwest used specialized boats and religious ceremonies that centered around whaling. [53]

The right whale — a baleen whale that is smaller, slower and fatter than some other baleen species and stays closer to shore — was a main target

square miles of open ocean," says Steve Mashuda, an attorney with San Francisco-based Earthjustice, an environmental law firm that is working with the NRDC on the case.

The NRDC contends that the National Marine Fisheries Service rubber-stamped the Navy's permit and, given the recent research about the damage sonar can cause, is not doing enough to develop mitigation strategies. "Their only mitigation strategy right now," Mashuda says, "is to have watch-standers looking out for marine mammals during testing." But since marine mammals spend a majority of their time underwater, that arrangement is problematic. Instead, the NRDC and others want the fisheries service to require the Navy to use passive sonar to listen for whales and dolphins in the vicinity before initiating a test, and for the Navy to limit its activities to locations and times of year that will have less of an impact on marine life.

"The science has gotten to the point now where even the Navy admits that sonar is harmful," Mashuda says, "At some levels there is no way to eliminate the risk, but we can try to minimize it."

The Navy says it is trying to incorporate new science into its policies. "We participate in adaptive management processes with [the National Oceanic and Atmospheric Administration] to ensure that our protective measures are effective based on the best available science," says Kenneth Hess, chief of Naval Operations, Energy and Environmental Readiness in the Division of Public Affairs. "An example of changes made as a result of this process is the fact that following review of a peer-reviewed scientific paper that showed beaked whales may be more sensitive to sound sources than previously thought, the Navy used a more sensitive threshold for estimating the potential effects of sonar on marine mammals."

— Daniel McGlynn

---

[1] "Joint Interim Report Bahamas Marine Mammal Stranding Event of 15-16 March 2000," U.S. Department of Commerce and U.S. Department of the Navy, December 2001, www.nmfs.noaa.gov/pr/pdfs/health/stranding_bahamas2000.pdf.

[2] Rick Weiss, "Whales' deaths linked to Navy sonar tests," *The Washington Post*, Dec. 31, 2001, www.commondreams.org/headlines.shtml?/headlines01/1231-02.htm.

[3] E. C. M. Parsons, *et al.*, "Navy and cetaceans: Just how much does the gun need to smoke before we act?" *Marine Pollution Bulletin*, 2008, pp. 1248-1257, www.co.island.wa.us/commissioners/documents/2011/Navy/NACoRes(Interim)/SonarEffects/EffectsofSonar.pdf.

[4] For background, see "Lethal sounds," Natural Resource Defense Council, www.nrdc.org/wildlife/marine/sonar.asp.

[5] "Whale deaths linked to undersea blasts," *Los Angeles Times*, June 15, 2000, http://articles.latimes.com/2000/jun/15/news/mn-41327.

[6] Brendan Borrell, "Why do whales beach themselves?" *Scientific American*, June 1, 2009, www.scientificamerican.com/article.cfm?id=why-do-whales-beach-themselves.

[7] The case is *Winter v. Natural Resources Defense Council Inc.*, 555 U.S. 7, decided Nov. 12, 2008. See, Brandon Keim, "Supreme Court: National Security trumps whales, environmental law," *Wired*, Nov. 12, 2008, www.wired.com/wiredscience/2008/11/supreme-court-n/.

[8] Gene Johnson, "Groups sue over Navy sonar use off Northwest coast," The Associated Press, Jan. 26, 2012, http://news.yahoo.com/groups-sue-over-navy-sonar-off-northwest-coast-150339575.html.

---

of early whalers. Right whales were easier to hunt and kill than other whale species, and after death they float to the surface, making it possible for whalers in small boats to drag them to shore.

But centuries of hunting right whales depleted their stocks, spurring whalers to use larger vessels that could launch small boats to search farther out in the ocean for other great whale species.

While whalers were organizing missions in larger ships with better equipment, the market for whale products was expanding. Early whalers hunted for meat, but by the 1700s whalers were traveling farther and farther into uncharted waters to kill whales strictly for their baleen and to render their blubber into oil. Often the meat was discarded to make room in cargo holds for barrels of oil. [54]

Sperm whales were particularly valuable because their oil produced a much cleaner and brighter flame in oil lamps. The nation's first energy cartel, the United Company of Spermaceti Chandlers, was created in 1761 by sperm whale oil merchants who tried to control the price of lamp oil. [55]

By the 1800s the United States was quickly becoming the world's leading whaling nation, centered mainly around Nantucket island, 30 miles from Cape Cod, Mass. What began as a modest outpost quickly morphed into a busy port, dispatching crews to whaling grounds in the North Atlantic and beyond, and then sending ships to Boston, New York and London loaded with oil. [56]

Soon, American whaling vessels were circumnavigating the globe on voyages of several years in search of whale oil. In 1848, the first American-based whaling crew entered Arctic waters off the coast of Siberia aboard the *Superior*. The Sag Harbor, N.Y.-based crew killed a bowhead that yielded 120 barrels of oil and baleen 12 feet long. The water was so full of whales that the crew worked around the clock, killing and processing whales until they filled their ship with 1,600 barrels of oil from 11 whales. [57]

But by the 1850s, American whaling was beginning to wane. During California's Gold Rush, San Francisco

Bay became littered with New England whale ships that never made it home because their crews were pursuing their fortunes in the gold fields. Meanwhile, fossil fuels were replacing whale oil for heat and light.

Still, whaling continued into the 20th century, with the oil used for a variety of purposes, including lubrications for industrial machines. Also, hydrogenated whale oil was an important ingredient in margarine. By the 1920s, diesel-powered, steel-hulled vessels replaced sail-powered wooden ships, and grenade harpoons replaced hand-thrown ones. At the same time, several countries, notably Norway and Russia, continued hunting whales for food and to supply the shrinking whale oil market.

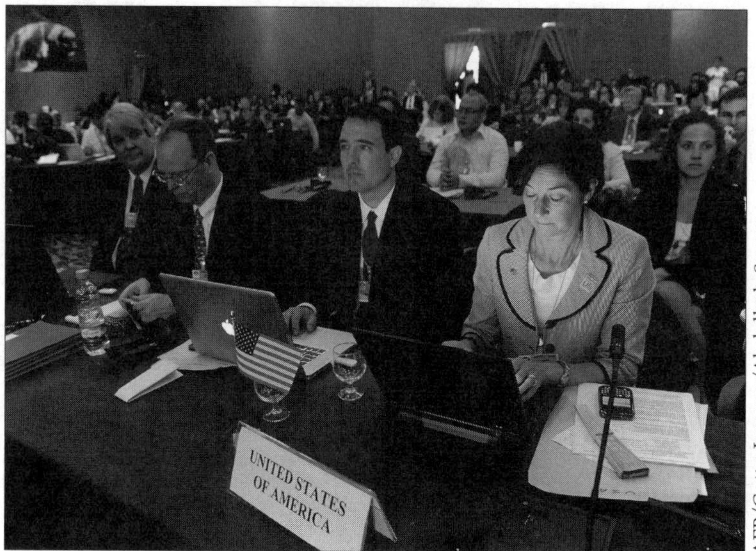

AFP/Getty Images/Abdelhak Senna

The U.S. delegation to the International Whaling Commission attends the IWC's opening session in Agadir, Morocco, on June 21, 2010. The commission imposed a moratorium on international commercial whaling beginning in 1986, but whale conservation groups say the IWC is ineffectual at protecting marine mammals and that its voluntary structure makes the moratorium difficult to enforce.

Conservation Efforts

After World War II, whaling was still seen as a viable economic activity, especially for cultures that ate whale meat. In fact, the Allied forces occupying Japan after the war pushed to restart Japan's traditional whaling industry to help supplement food supplies for the war-ravaged population. [58]

In 1946, the International Convention for the Regulation of Whaling, a group of 15 whaling countries, formed the International Whaling Commission. The organization sought to develop regulations to ensure the world's whale stocks were properly managed so they could continue to be exploited.

During the 1960s the international climate for whaling began to change. The market for whale meat and whale products weakened, and the environmental movement began to promote whales as intelligent creatures and cite ocean health as threatened. The IWC began to reflect the changes, focusing more and more on scientific research, as its membership grew more diverse.

In 1970 whale researcher and anti-whaling activist Roger Payne recorded the sounds of humpback whales communicating with each another. The record album he created, "Songs of the Humpback Whale," helped educate the public about the intelligence and social nature of cetaceans. [59]

In 1972, Congress passed the Marine Mammal Protection Act, making it illegal to hunt or kill cetaceans in U.S. waters. [60] And in 1979, reflecting its growing conservation posture, the IWC created the Indian Ocean Whale Sanctuary, banning commercial whaling within the entire Indian Ocean, from Africa to Australia; and from Southern Asia to the Southern Ocean Whale Sanctuary (established in 1994), which surrounds Antarctica. In 1982, the IWC voted to impose a moratorium on commercial whaling worldwide so that the organization could study the world's whale population, and it devised harvest limits based on scientific research. The moratorium was phased in by 1986.

Thirty years later the moratorium still exists, much to the frustration of several nations — mainly Iceland, Norway and Japan — that continue what are considered, by historical standards, small-scale commercial whale hunts.

In 1992, Denmark's Faroe Islands, Greenland, Iceland and Norway created the Agreement on Cooperation in Research, Conservation and Management of Marine Mammals in the North Atlantic, which in turn created the North Atlantic Marine Mammal Commission (NAMMCO) to address the IWC's perceived shortcomings. NAMMCO's intent is to conduct cetacean research and then recommend management practices and quotas to its members.

In 1994, the IWC created the Southern Ocean Whale Sanctuary, where the "whale wars" between Japan's Institute of Cetacean Research and the Sea Shepherd Conservation Society have occurred annually for the past eight years.

Dolphin Hunts

The IWC regulations apply mainly to the world's great whales — the baleens and the largest of the toothed whales, the sperm whale. However, in recent decades, the need to

One BIG Family

Whales, dolphins and porpoises share two unique characteristics.

Seventy-eight species of whales, dolphins and porpoises make up the scientific order Cetacea. All breathe air through blowholes, and many use a form of sonar called echolocation to communicate and forage. [1]

Cetaceans are divided into two suborders based on the way they capture food. Eleven species are baleen whales, and the rest are toothed whales. A baleen is a large filter-like feeding system that traps krill, which are small shrimp-like crustaceans common in the ocean. [2]

www.wallpaperweb.org

Eleven species of whales use their baleen to filter seawater to catch krill. Above, humpbacks trap krill by creating "bubble nets" in Alaska's Chatham Strait.

The endangered fin whale, one of the larger baleen whales, can filter one ton of krill, its daily nutritional needs, out of seawater every four hours. The baleen has plates arranged like bristles in a brush. [3] Baleen is strong yet flexible, the same consistency of a human fingernail, and was used for a variety of applications, including women's corsets during the 18th and 19th centuries. At some points during the whaling boom years, baleen was more valuable than whale oil, and whalers would lop off the giant heads of the whales they caught and throw the rest back into the ocean. [4]

Cetaceans with teeth, including dolphins and porpoises, are faster swimmers than baleen whales. Because of the structure of their heads and their need to catch fish for food, rather than just filter seawater, they rely more heavily on echolocation.

The 11 species of baleen whales, along with the largest of the toothed whales — the sperm whale — make up a group known as the great whales. The other species of great whale are the bowhead, right, gray, blue, fin, sei, Brydes, minke and humpback.

The great whales were heavily hunted commercially during the 18th and 19th centuries, while the other species of toothed whales, such as killer whales, pilot whales and dolphins, were historically hunted in smaller-scale operations. [5] Today, the Japanese hunt Dall's porpoises and various dolphin species, while residents of the Faroe Islands, which lie between Iceland and Norway, hunt pilot whales.

Cetaceans are found in marine and freshwater ecosystems around the world, from the warm Caribbean to the frigid Arctic and Antarctic. Because of their wide global distribution, numerous nations and cultures once hunted them for food, to render oil from their blubber or for their baleen.

— Daniel McGlynn

[1] For background, see "Cetaceans: whales, dolphins, and porpoises," National Oceanic and Atmospheric Administration, Office of Protected Resources, www.nmfs.noaa.gov/pr/species/mammals/cetaceans/.

[2] *Ibid.*

[3] Carl Zimmer, "Fin whale at feeding time: Dive deep, stop short, open wide," *The New York Times*, Dec. 11, 2010, www.nytimes.com/2007/12/11/science/11gulp.html?_r=2&pagewanted=all.

[4] Eric Jay Dolin, *Leviathan* (2007), pp. 361-363.

[5] For background, see "The Cove," 2009, www.thecovemovie.com.

protect smaller whales, including orcas and dolphins, has become part of the focus of anti-whaling groups. Large-scale hunts for dolphin and pilot whale meat occur in coastal Japan and the Faroe Islands, which lie between Iceland and Norway. In 2010, about 700 pilot whales were killed during the Faroe Island hunt and 20,000 dolphins, pilot whales and porpoises were killed in Japan. [61]

The Japanese dolphin hunts are focused mainly around Taiji, in southeastern Japan. During Taiji's annual dolphin and pilot whale hunt, about 2,000 animals — including entire social groups — are killed. The bloody event received worldwide attention through the 2009 documentary "The Cove." Japan issues about 20,000 permits annually to fisherman in coastal areas to kill small whales and dolphins. [62]

During what is often described in the media as a "slaughter," the dolphins and pilot whales are herded into inlets while hunters bang sticks against the sides of their boats to disrupt the animals' sense of direction and communication. Once driven into shallow water, the animals are stabbed with long lances, loaded onto small boats and taken for processing of their meat. [63]

Japanese officials argue that hunting dolphin is akin to killing cattle for meat. Dolphins are a "resource, just like fish. Killing animals in any way is bloody, unfortunately, just like slaughtering cows and pigs," said Shigeki Takaya, director of the whaling section for the Far Seas Fisheries division at Japan's Fisheries Agency. [64]

Environmentalists and animal welfare activists say that cetaceans are closer to primates than cows and that the Taiji hunt is indicative of similar wrongful dolphin and porpoise hunts in other coastal communities. "This [hunt] is an extreme case of animal cruelty," said Diana Reiss, whose research as an animal behaviorist at Hunter College in New York City shows that dolphins can recognize themselves in a mirror. [65]

Some live animals are captured and sold. "The main markets for captive dolphins are aquariums across Asia," says Jones of BlueVoice.org. A similar hunt also happens every year in the Faroe Islands. Like Greenland, the Faroes are recognized by Denmark as a self-governing country. Faroe whalers mainly hunt pilot whales for food. In 2010, more than 700 whales were harvested. As in Taiji, hunters in small boats herd the whales toward shore and kill them en masse in ankle-deep water. [66] ■

CURRENT SITUATION

More Whale Wars

Despite efforts by the IWC's U.S. delegation in 2010 to eliminate unsanctioned and scientific whaling, some nations continue to hold regular whale hunts — to the dismay of conservationists. [67]

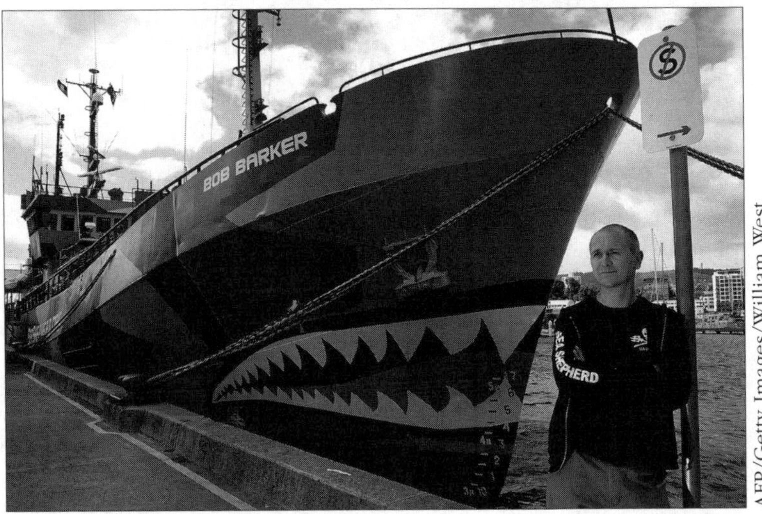

AFP/Getty Images/William West

The anti-whaling ship Bob Barker, *here in Hobart, Australia, in December 2011, with Capt. Alex Cornelissen, chased Japanese whalers to the Southern Ocean Whale Sanctuary last winter in an effort to disrupt the annual whale hunt. The Japanese had planned to kill 900 whales, a limit they created for themselves through a loophole in International Whaling Commission rules, but their take for the 2011-2012 whaling season was only 266 minke whales and one endangered fin whale.*

Sea Shepherd activists promise to return to the Southern Ocean in 2013 and escalate their campaign against Japanese whaling. And between campaigns in the Antarctic they have taken up a new campaign — called Viking Shores — for the new season of the reality TV show "Whale Wars," which began in April. The campaign opposes the annual pilot whale hunt, called the Grind, in the Faroe Islands. Other groups also are taking action against the pilot whale hunt. [68]

Meanwhile, the International Court of Justice — the U.N.'s principal judicial branch, located at The Hague — is hearing an official grievance filed in 2010 by Australia, an outspoken critic of Japan's continued whaling efforts. The grievance seeks judgment on the legality of Japan's whaling in the Southern Ocean under the pretext of scientific research. [69]

"The [Australian] government considers that Japan's whaling is contrary to Japan's international legal obligations, including the global prohibition on commercial whaling, and should stop," said Australia's attorney general, Nicola Roxon. [70]

Japan continues to maintain that scientific whaling expeditions provide beneficial information for understanding the population dynamics of the whales in the Southern Ocean and Northern Pacific. The country argues that its activities are permissible under Article VIII of the International Convention on the Regulation of Whaling, which allows whaling nations to unilaterally set their own quotas for scientific whaling expeditions. [71]

The case is expected to continue into 2013.

Other Threats

In addition to the continuing controversy over hunting cetaceans, other marine mammal conservation issues are becoming equally pressing, particularly entanglement in outdated fishing gear. As the world's fisheries move out of depleted waters to more fertile territory, more and more fishing gear — mainly nets and traps — is fouling whale feeding grounds

Continued on p. 590

At Issue:

Should the IWC revise its whaling moratorium?

MONICA MEDINA
U.S. COMMISSIONER TO THE INTERNATIONAL WHALING COMMISSION AND PRINCIPAL DEPUTY UNDERSECRETARY FOR OCEANS AND ATMOSPHERE, NATIONAL OCEANIC AND ATMOSPHERIC ADMINISTRATION

FROM TESTIMONY BEFORE HOUSE SUBCOMMITTEE ON INTERNATIONAL ORGANIZATIONS, HUMAN RIGHTS, AND OVERSIGHT AND SUBCOMMITTEE ON ASIA, THE PACIFIC, AND THE GLOBAL ENVIRONMENT, MAY 6, 2010.

yes

The United States' biggest concern at the [International Whaling Commission (IWC)] is that more and more whales are being killed. Twenty-four years ago, the international community agreed on a moratorium that was supposed to stop industrialized commercial whaling, but in reality whaling never ended.

Look at the situation today. Just three countries — Japan, Norway, and Iceland — persist in non-indigenous hunting of whales. They justify this by exploiting loopholes in the moratorium. The unfortunate outcome is clear, and growing more dire each year. . . .

In 1990, three countries killed a total of 300 whales. In 1995, they killed 750. By 2000, the annual number topped 1,000 whales. By 2005, it was up to 1,700 whales. And this year, three countries issued themselves quotas . . . to kill more than 3,100 whales annually.

Right now, unfortunately, there is little that the IWC can do about it. Unless something happens, more and more whales will be killed, and there is currently no limit to how many whales will be killed in the future.

Since the [1982] ban on commercial whaling [was phased in by] 1986, more than 35,000 whales have been hunted, and the numbers continue to grow. At the same time, the resulting polarization of the IWC threatens the viability of the organization as the international forum for resolving these issues, for coordinating critical research on other issues and developing international agreements to further whale conservation.

Years, and I do mean years, of protracted and unresolved debate over the proper means to conserve, utilize and study whales have made many IWC members, including the United States, concerned about the body's future relevance in controlling unilateral whaling and conserving whale stocks. I believe a ceasefire is needed. In fact, it is overdue. . . .

While the United States recognizes that some significant achievements have occurred, we are disappointed that the future process has not yet been able to achieve a resolution of some of the key issues facing the commission. Despite this, we believe . . . [a compromise plan, subsequently rejected, to end the IWC moratorium but reduce catch quotas and close other loopholes] represents a step forward, and is a foundation for achieving a functioning IWC and improving the conservation of whales. . . .

PATRICK R. RAMAGE
GLOBAL WHALE PROGRAM DIRECTOR, INTERNATIONAL FUND FOR ANIMAL WELFARE (IFAW)

FROM TESTIMONY BEFORE HOUSE SUBCOMMITTEE ON INTERNATIONAL ORGANIZATIONS, HUMAN RIGHTS, AND OVERSIGHT AND SUBCOMMITTEE ON ASIA, THE PACIFIC, AND THE GLOBAL ENVIRONMENT, MAY 6, 2010.

no

First, as [has been] mentioned, our planet's whales are not saved. They face more threats today than ever before in history.

Second, engaged United States leadership is a prerequisite for effective international whale conservation. The IWC was created here in Washington. Its most important conservation achievements, including the moratorium on commercial whaling adopted in 1982 and the declaration of the Southern Ocean Whale Sanctuary in 1994, were only achieved with creative high-level support and consistent engagement from the United States. . . .

Third, Americans from sea to shining sea . . . are united in their support for whale conservation and their opposition to whaling for commercial purposes by Japan, Norway and Iceland, whether that whaling is conducted in open defiance of the moratorium or under the guise of science. . . .

How, then, did we get to the point where a plan to legitimize the cruel and outmoded commercial whaling industry [by ending the whaling moratorium but closing loopholes] is introduced on the 40th anniversary of Earth Day and is actually being seriously considered? . . .

This is a bad deal for whales and the convention established to conserve them. It ignores the moratorium. It makes a mockery of the Southern Ocean Whale Sanctuary. It grants new rights to Japan, Iceland and Norway to openly kill thousands of whales. It end-runs scientific procedures adopted by consensus to reward the three countries who have refused to play by the rules.

The promised benefits to whales are either nowhere in sight, or the result of sleight of hand. A whale sanctuary is finally established in the South Atlantic, where no whaling exists. A conservation program committee is established, needlessly recreating a conservation committee in place since 2003. Elaborate observer and monitoring schemes, which will be funded by U.S. taxpayers, and an inadequate DNA tracking scheme are also established. . . .

What does change we can believe in look like for whales in the IWC? . . . Ensuring Japan's whaling in the Southern Ocean Whale Sanctuary is brought to an end. Ending international trade in whale products. Adhering to agreed IWC scientific procedures. Ensuring no commercial takes of threatened species and populations. Specific actions to end so-called scientific whaling. And meaningful guarantees regarding objections and enforcement.

Continued from p. 588

and migratory routes. A number of studies in the past decade show that any fishing rig that is anchored in the water or connected with multiple vertical and horizontal lines can entrap or injure a passing cetacean. Newer fishing gear uses weighted lines or is designed to otherwise reduce the risk of entanglement. [72]

Underwater noise pollution is another emerging threat. It is becoming increasingly common because of commercial shipping, seismic surveys and military training disruptive to whales and dolphins. A defining characteristic of most cetaceans is their use of echolocation to locate food and to socialize with other members of their species. Underwater noises disrupt that capability.

"Noisy activities are producing an acoustic fog that prevents whales from maintaining social groups, finding each other for breeding purposes and so forth," said Mark Simmonds, scientific director of the Whale and Dolphin Conservation Society. Veronica Frank, a legal expert at the International Fund for Animal Welfare, estimates that human-caused noise in the ocean has doubled each year for the past 40 years and will keep increasing. [73]

Climate change also threatens cetaceans, especially great whales in the Southern Ocean. If the mean ocean temperature rises even 2 degrees C, as is predicted to occur by 2042, whales that live in or migrate to Antarctica for part of the year will likely be dramatically affected, according to a 2008 WWF study.

Rising seawater temperatures will affect the polar icepack, which will in turn affect whale habitats. Species such as the Antarctic minke whale, which lives close to the ice, will likely be greatly affected by the loss of krill — small marine crustaceans that live in algae blooms at the edge of melting ice. As ice disappears, krill will be harder to find. Migratory species such as the humpback and blue whale will have to travel farther to find food. [74]

"As we learn more and more about cetaceans, a number of threats are proliferating," says Ramage of the International Fund for Animal Welfare.

In some cases, he says, the threats reinforce one another. Climate change will cause the ocean temperature to rise and the water to become more acidic; meanwhile, the Antarctic ice sheet will sink. Research by the Monterey Bay Aquarium in California shows that sound travels farther in an acidic ocean, leading to more social disruption for cetaceans. [75]

Toxic Waters

Anti-whaling activists are increasingly citing the health risks associated with consuming cetacean meat to help turn public perception against whale and dolphin hunts. The activists want the World Health Organization to issue guidelines about toxins found in whale and dolphin meat, such as mercury, polychlorinated biphenyls (PCBs) and heavy metals such as cadmium. [76]

Toxic chemicals are frequently found in the meat of most species of toothed whales, which include smaller whales, dolphins and orcas. The pollution exists at background levels in the marine environment because of past and current industrial pollution. Because dolphins and whales eat other marine life, toxins accumulate in their tissue, eventually making their meat toxic to humans. [77]

Nevertheless, there are no health regulations banning the consumption of cetacean meat. In 2010, American neurologist David Perlmutter told the *Japan Times*, "These levels [of mercury] are dramatically elevated. This practice of serving dolphin meat is tantamount to poisoning people; they may as well serve them arsenic, it would be no less harmful! What they're doing is wrong on every count; it's the wrong thing to do for the people and the wrong thing to do for the dolphins. No matter how you look at this, it's perverse — it's a tragedy and it should be condemned." [78]

Toxicity is also a concern in the Faroe Islands, where every year hundreds of pilot whales are harvested for meat in what local residents say is a traditional hunt that helps them supplement imported meat and the limited meat from island-bred sheep. In 1997, a landmark study found neurological problems in Faroe Islands children whose mothers ate whale meat often. [79]

Still, neither the Faroe Islands nor the Japanese government has limited access to toxic meat. "It is true that pilot whales have very high levels of mercury in the meat and PCBs in the blubber," said Kate Sanderson, director of the Department of Oceans and Environment in the Faroe Islands. "And the relevant health authorities on the Faroes issued a safety recommendation advising people on how much it was safe to eat. And people have taken that advice on board." Even so, the annual hunts and consumption continues. [80] ■

OUTLOOK

New Models

This year the International Whaling Commission celebrates the 30th anniversary of the moratorium on commercial whaling. However, because commercial whaling persists, if only in a handful of places, many groups and nations continue to question the effectiveness of the IWC.

The IWC agreement "might be a broken treaty, but it's the only one we have," says William Rossiter, president of the Cetacean Society International, a conservation group in Georgetown, Conn.

Meanwhile, changes in the IWC are regularly being proposed to address some of the commission's enforcement shortcomings. The most recent idea, which appeared in the January 2012 issue of *Nature*, suggested a cap-and-trade model for issuing whaling permits. Permits to hunt cetaceans would be granted to IWC members, who could in turn give them to whalers, and some permits would be available on the open market. Whalers could then sell the permits to conservation groups. "Whalers could profit from whales without harvesting the animals," the authors of the study, who are marine conservation scientists, wrote. "A market would therefore open the door to reducing mortality without need to battle over whether whaling is honorable or shameful." [81]

Meanwhile, anti-whaling activists are expected to keep using information campaigns and dramatic confrontations with whalers to influence public opinion.

Japan has had to end its Southern Ocean whale hunt early for the past two years because of continued pressure by activists. In May, Iceland announced that it will suspend its fin whale hunt because its only fin whaling operation was unable to come to an agreement with the fishermen's union over wages. And the demand for whale meat in Japan has been depressed since an earthquake and tsunami hit the country in 2011. [82] In other places, such as the Faroe Islands, Taiji, Japan, and coastal communities in Norway, activists are continuing to apply pressure and raise awareness about the threats facing some of the world's endangered whales, as well as the risks associated with eating whale meat.

Pedersen, the Norwegian Embassy official, says that Norway's small, family-run whaling fleet is slipping into obsolescence, which might mean the end of Norwegian whaling on its own, without further regulatory or diplomatic action. "The vessels and whalers are getting older," Pedersen says. "Whaling is a traditional activity, and it's hard to recruit younger fishermen. Maybe it will become less important over time."

As the population of great whales continues to slowly rebound after several centuries of heavy exploitation, the anti-whaling community is stepping up its efforts to educate the public and policy makers about emerging threats to whales, including marine noise pollution, fishing-equipment hazards and climate change.

The extension of international regulations protecting smaller cetaceans also is expected to continue, particularly in the wake of publicity created by "The Cove" documentary. At the same time, as new research reveals the extent of cetaceans' intelligence, social structure and communicative abilities, animal rights activists and ethicists will continue to press for cetaceans to be recognized as "non-human persons" and therefore afforded certain protections.

"We went from seeing the dolphin/whale brain as being a giant amorphous blob that doesn't carry a lot of intelligence and complexity to not only being an enormous brain but an enormous brain with an enormous amount of complexity, and a complexity that rivals our own," said Lori Marino, a psychologist at Emory University in Atlanta. [83] ■

Notes

[1] "The Bob Barker endures a dangerous night attack by the Japanese whaling fleet, Sea Shepherd Conservation Society," March 5, 2012, www.youtube.com/watch?v=5vTKpAfvHkk.

[2] For background, see "Whale Sanctuaries: Establishment of the International Whaling Commission's Sanctuaries," http://iwcoffice.org/conservation/sanctuaries.htm#sanctuaries.

[3] "An open letter to the government of Japan on 'Scientific Whaling,' " *The New York Times*, May 20, 2002, www.baleinesendirect.net/pdf/whaling-letter_to_NY_Times.pdf.

[4] "Japan whale catch falls short," Discovery News, March 11, 2012, http://news.discovery.com/earth/japan-whaling-numbers-short-120310.html.

[5] For background, see "Whale Wars," Animal Planet, http://animal.discovery.com/tv/whale-wars/.

[6] "Japan ends whaling season short of quota," BBC, March 9, 2012, www.bbc.co.uk/.news/world-asia-17312460.

[7] "Sea Shepherd declares victory as Japanese whalers head home," Environmental News Service, March 9, 2012, www.ens-newswire.com/ens/mar2012/2012-03-09-01.html.

[8] For background, see "Fears over Japan porpoise hunt," *Al Jazeera English*, March 12, 2010, www.youtube.com/watch?v=1U8WiGTcc4U; and Patrick Walters, " 'Cove' movie assails dolphin hunt, gets Oscar boost," *National Geographic*, March 8, 2010, http://news.nationalgeographic.com/news/2010/03/100308-cove-movie-oscars-dolphin-hunts-japan/.

[9] For background, see "Cetaceans: whales, dolphins, and porpoises," National Oceanic and Atmospheric Administration, Office of Protected Resources, www.nmfs.noaa.gov/pr/species/mammals/cetaceans/.

[10] Eric Jay Dolin, *Leviathan: History of Whaling in America* (2007), pp. 361-362.

[11] "Whales are people, too," *The Economist*, Feb. 25, 2012, www.economist.com/node/21548150.

[12] Tetsuya Endo, *et al.*, "Mercury Contamination in the Red Meat of Whales and Dolphins Marketed for Human Consumption in Japan," *Environmental Science and Technology*, 2003, http://mounier.univ-tln.fr/rcmo/php_biblio/PDF/4993.pdf.

[13] Bonnie Christian, "Fewer sea turtle killed in US fisheries, but still too many, study finds," *Huffington Post*, Sept. 14, 2011, www.huffingtonpost.com/2011/09/14/sea-turtles-killed-in-fisheries-reduced-90-percent_n_960864.html.

[14] Lisa Ling, "Shark fin soup alters ecosystem," CNN, Dec. 10, 2008, http://articles.cnn.com/2008-12-10/world/pip.shark.finning_1_shark-fin-shark-populations-top-predator?_s=PM:WORLD.

[15] Erik Stokstad, "Killer whales working harder for lunch?" *Science*, May 22, 2012, http://news.sciencemag.org/sciencenow/2012/05/scienceshot-killer-whales-working.html?rss=1.

[16] Noreen Nasir, "Baby dolphin die-offs continue in Gulf," "PBS NewsHour," April 24, 2012, www.pbs.org/newshour/rundown/2012/04/baby-dolphin-die-offs-continue-in-the-gulf.html.

[17] David Jolly and Andrea Zarate, "Peru has no answers on dead dolphins and seabirds," *The New York Times*, May 7, 2012, www.nytimes.com/2012/05/08/world/americas/peru-has-no-answers-on-dead-dolphins-and-seabirds.html?_r=3; Jeanna Bryner, "32 dead porpoises worry wildlife experts," *LiveScience*, May 1, 2012,

www.livescience.com/20021-dead-yangtze-finless-porpoises.html.

[18] "Mercury in packaged whale meat across Japan may be a major health problem," *Science Daily*, May 20, 2003, www.sciencedaily.com/releases/2003/05/030520082803.htm.

[19] "Briefing Note: Joji Morishita, Alternate Commissioner, Delegation of Japan," 63rd Annual Meeting of the International Whaling Commission, July 11-14, 2011, St. Helier, Jersey, UK, www.icrwhale.org/pdf/63BriefingNote.pdf.

[20] Taryn Kiewkow, "U.S. censures Iceland for killing whales," Switchboard, Natural Resources Defense Council, Sept. 15, 2011, http://switchboard.nrdc.org/blogs/tkiekow/us_censures_iceland_for_killing.html.

[21] "Iceland halts fin whaling," *New Europe Online*, May 8, 2012, www.neurope.eu/article/iceland-halts-fin-whaling.

[22] Bryan Walsh, "Will killing whales save the world's fisheries?" *Time*, Feb. 17, 2009, www.time.com/time/health/article/0,8599,1880128,00.html.

[23] "New report says whaling is beneficial for Iceland," *Iceland Review Online*, March 3, 2010, http://icelandreview.com/icelandreview/daily_news/?cat_id=16539&ew _0_a_id=360170.

[24] Andrew Darby, "Anti-whaling activists lay siege to factory ship," *The Sydney Morning Herald*, Feb. 10, 2011, www.smh.com.au/environment/whale-watch/antiwhaling-activists-lay-siege-to-factory-ship-20110210-1anl8.html.

[25] "Briefing Note: Joji Morishita," *op. cit.*

[26] Toko Sekiguchi, "Why Japan's whale hunt continues," *Time*, Nov. 20, 2007, www.time.com/time/world/article/0,8599,1686486,00.html.

[27] Rob Tinch and Zara Phang, "Sink or swim: The economics of whaling today," Whale and Dolphin Conservation Society, June 2009, www.wdcs.org/submissions_bin/economics_whaling_report.pdf.

[28] *Ibid.*

[29] Andrew Revkin, "Whale watching trumps whaling," Dot Earth, *The New York Times*, June 23, 2009, http://dotearth.blogs.nytimes.com/2009/06/23/whale-watching-trumps-whaling/.

[30] Charles Siebert, "Watching whales watching us," *The New York Times Magazine*, July 8, 2009, www.nytimes.com/2009/07/12/magazine/12whales-t.html?pagewanted=all.

[31] Nick Collins, "Dolphins 'should be recognised as non-human persons,'" *The Telegraph*, Feb. 21, 2012, www.telegraph.co.uk/science/science-news/9093407/Dolphins-should-be-recognised-as-non-human-persons.html.

[32] "Whale Conservation and Management: A Future for the IWC," Australian Government, March 4, 2008, http://iwcoffice.org/_documents/commission/future/IWC-M08-INFO11.pdf.

[33] "Marine Mammal Protection Act (MMPA) of 1972," National Oceanic and Atmospheric Administration, Office of Protected Resources, www.nmfs.noaa.gov/pr/laws/mmpa/.

[34] Robert Lee Hotz, "Whale watch: Endangered designation in danger," *The Wall Street Journal*, Nov. 11, 2009, http://online.wsj.com/article/SB125745793337231859.html.

[35] "Annual Report to Congress 1994," Marine Mammal Commission, Jan. 31, 1995, http://mmc.gov/reports/annual/pdf/1994annualreport.pdf.

[36] "Revised Management Scheme: Information on the background and progress of the Revised Management Scheme (RMS)," International Whaling Commission, http://iwcoffice.org/conservation/rms.htm.

[37] "The Cove," 2009, www.thecovemovie.com/.

[38] For background see, "Fisherman's Protective Act of 1967," United States Commission on Ocean Policy, www.oceancommission.gov/documents/gov_oceans/Protective.PDF.

[39] "Fin whale," National Oceanic and Atmospheric Administration, Office of Protected Resources, www.nmfs.noaa.gov/pr/species/mammals/cetaceans/finwhale.htm.

[40] "Message from the President to Congress," The White House, Office of the Press Secretary, Sept. 15, 2011, www.whitehouse.gov/the-press-office/2011/09/15/message-president-congress.

[41] "Aboriginal subsistence whaling," International Whaling Commission, http://iwcoffice.org/conservation/aboriginal.htm.

[42] "Bequian whaling: A statement of need by the government of Saint Vincent and the Grenadines," International Whaling Commission, http://iwcoffice.org/_documents/conservation/IWC-54-AS-7.pdf.

[43] Richard Black, "Cultural claim to whale hunting," BBC News, May 29, 2007, http://news.bbc.co.uk/2/hi/6698501.stm.

[44] "Catches taken: Aboriginal subsistence whaling catches since 1985 (table)," International Whaling Commission, http://iwcoffice.org/conservation/table_aboriginal.htm.

[45] "Whaling around the world," Sea Shepherd Conservation Society, www.seashepherd.org/whales/whaling-around-the-world.html.

[46] "About aboriginal subsistence whaling (ASW): Not always what the name implies," Pacific Whale Foundation, www.pacificwhale.org/content/about-aboriginal-subsistence-whaling-asw.

[47] "Catch limits and catches taken," International Whaling Commission, http://iwcoffice.org/conservation/catches.htm#aborig.

[48] "Metcalf v. Daley," *Lewis and Clark Law School's Environmental Law Online*, www.elawreview.org/summaries/environmental_quality/nepa/Metcalf_v_daley.html.

[49] William Yardley and Erik Olsen, "With powerboat and forklift, a sacred whale hunt endures," *The New York Times*, Oct. 16, 2011, www.nytimes.com/2011/10/17/us/in-sacred-whale-hunt-eskimos-use-modern-tools.html.

[50] "Cultural, traditional, and nutritional needs of the aboriginal population of Chukotka for gray whales and bowhead whales, 2003-2007," Russian Federation, 2002, http://iwcoffice.org/_documents/conservation/IWC-54-AS-5.pdf.

[51] Dolin, *op. cit.*, pp. 21-23.

[52] "Chronology of whaling," Japan Whaling Association, www.whaling.jp/english/history.html.

[53] Ann M. Renker, "Whale Hunting and the Makah Tribe: A Needs Statement," prepared for the IWC, April 2007, http://iwcoffice.org/_documents/commission/IWC59docs/59-ASW%209.pdf.

[54] Dolin, *op. cit.*

[55] *Ibid.*

[56] *Ibid.*

[57] *Ibid.*, p. 230.

[58] "The Convention," International Whaling Commission, http://iwcoffice.org/commission/convention.htm.

About the Author

Daniel McGlynn is a California-based independent journalist who covers science and the environment. His work has appeared in *The New York Times Magazine*, *Earth Island Journal*, *Bay Citizen*, and other publications. He has a master's degree in journalism from the University of California, Berkeley. His last report for *CQ Researcher* was "Fracking Controversy."

[59] "The Cove," *op. cit.*

[60] "The Marine Mammal Protection Act of 1972," National Oceanic and Atmospheric Administration, www.nmfs.noaa.gov/pr/laws/mmpa/.

[61] Katia Moskvitch, "Anti-whaling NGOs warn of 'contaminated' whale meat," BBC News, Aug. 27, 2010, www.bbc.co.uk/news/science-environment-11113887.

[62] "Frequently asked questions," Save Japan Dolphins, http://savejapandolphins.org/take-action/frequently-asked-questions.

[63] "The Cove," *op. cit.*

[64] Coco Masters, "Japan gets its first chance to see 'the Cove,' " *Time*, Sept. 16, 2009, www.time.com/time/world/article/0,8599,1923252,00.html.

[65] Patrick Walters, " 'Cove' movie assails dolphin hunt, gets Oscar boost," *National Geographic*, March 8, 2010, http://news.nationalgeographic.com/news/2010/03/100308-cove-movie-oscars-dolphin-hunts-japan/.

[66] "Faroe Islands Annual Drive Hunt of Pilot Whales," Humane Society International, Aug. 9, 2010, www.hsi.org/news/news/2008/11/faroe_islands_whale_hunt_112008.html.

[67] See Rob Taylor, "IWC draft plan sees end to commercial whaling ban," Reuters, Feb. 23, 2010, www.reuters.com/article/2010/02/23/us-whaling-idUSTRE61M0RF20100223.

[68] "Whale Wars, Viking Shores," Animal Planet, http://animal.discovery.com/tv/whale-wars-viking-shores/.

[69] Rob McGuirk, "Australia sues Japan over whaling," The Associated Press, May 28, 2010, www.huffingtonpost.com/2010/05/28/australia-sues-japan-over_n_593526.html.

[70] "End of Japan's whaling a step closer: Minister," *The Sydney Morning Herald*, May 10, 2012, www.smh.com.au/environment/whale-watch/end-of-japans-whaling-a-step-closer-minister-20120311-1us0x.html.

[71] "Scientific permit whaling: Information on scientific permits, review procedure guidelines and current permits in effect," International Whaling Commission, http://iwcoffice.org/conservation/permits.htm.

[72] "New rules near on whale entanglement," The Associated Press, July 11, 2007, www.usatoday.com/news/nation/2007-07-11-1665403514_x.htm.

[73] "Greenhouse gases make ocean noisier: UN, wildlife groups," Agence France Presse, Dec. 3, 2008, www.google.com/hostednews/afp/article/ALeqM5g8NTkY99XGIPXClMvzjF1AsAcdpw.

[74] Paul Eccleston, "Climate change threat to Antarctic whales," *The Telegraph*, June 19, 2008, www.telegraph.co.uk/earth/earthnews/3344924/Climate-change-threat-to-Antarctic-whales.html.

[75] "Greenhouse gases make ocean noisier: UN, wildlife groups," Agence France-Presse, *op. cit.*

[76] "Dolphins are not food," BlueVoice.org, www.bluevoice.org/news_notfood.php.

[77] "Mercury in Seafood," Oceanic Preservation Society, www.opsociety.org /issues/mercury-in-seafood.

[78] Boyd Harnell, "Experts fear Taiji Mercury tests are fatally flawed," *The Japan Times*, May 23, 2010, www.japantimes.co.jp/text/fe20100523a1.html.

[79] "Mercury in packaged whale meat across Japan may be a major health problem," *Science Daily*, May 20, 2003, www.sciencedaily.com/releases/2003/ 05/030520082803.htm.

[80] Moskvitch, *op. cit.*

[81] Christopher Costello, Steven Gaines and Leah R Gerber, "Conservation science: A market approach to saving the whales," *Nature*, Jan. 12, 2012, www.nature.com/nature/journal/v481/n7380/full/481139a.html.

[82] "Iceland halts fin whaling," *New Europe Online*, May 8, 2012, www.neurope.eu/article/iceland-halts-fin-whaling.

[83] "Dolphins deserve the same rights as humans, scientists say," BBC News, Feb. 21, 2012, www.bbc.co.uk/news/world-17116882.

FOR MORE INFORMATION

Alaska Eskimo Whaling Commission, P.O. Box 570 Barrow, AK 99723; 907-852-2392; www.bluediamondwebs.biz/Alaska-aewc-com/default2.asp. Represents the rights and interests of 10 Inupiat and Siberian Yupik Eskimo whaling communities living in coastal Alaska who continue subsistence whaling.

American Cetacean Society, P.O. Box 1391, San Pedro, CA 90733-1391; 310-548-6279; http://acsonline.org/. Advocacy group that works to educate the public on whale, dolphin and porpoise issues.

BlueVoice.org, 10 Sunfish Drive, St. Augustine, FL 32080; www.bluevoice.org. Conservation organization run by longtime dolphin activist Hardy Jones and supported by actor Ted Danson.

Institute of Cetacean Research, Toyomi Shinko Bldg., 5 F, 4-5 Toyomi-cho, Chuo-ku, Tokyo, Japan 104-0055; 03-3536-652; www.icrwhale.org. Funds and operates Japan's whaling research program.

International Fund for Animal Welfare (IFAW), 1350 Connecticut Ave., N.W., Washington DC 20036; 202-296-3860; www.ifaw.org. International animal-rights organization.

International Whaling Commission, The Red House, 135 Station Rd., Impington, Cambridge, Cambridgeshire CB24 9NP, United Kingdom; 44 (0) 1223 233 971; http://iwcoffice.org/other/contacts.htm. Headquarters of the only international body regulating whaling.

National Oceanic and Atmospheric Administration, National Marine Fisheries Service, NOAA Fisheries Service, 1315 East West Hwy., Silver Spring, MD 20910; 301-427-8003; www.nmfs.noaa.gov. Federal agency charged with monitoring and protecting marine resources.

Natural Resources Defense Council, 40 West 20th St., New York, NY 10011; 212-727-2700; www.nrdc.org; Environmental advocacy group active in the legal battle against marine noise pollution.

Save Japan Dolphins Campaign, Earth Island Institute, 2150 Allston Way, Suite 460, Berkeley, CA 94704-1375; 510-859-9100; www.savejapandolphins.org. Dolphin activist Ric O'Barry's campaign to save dolphins in Taijia and other parts of Japan.

World Wildlife Fund (WWF), 1250 24th St., N.W., P.O. Box 97180 Washington, DC 20090-7180; 202-293-4800; www.worldwildlife.org. International organization focusing on conservation of endangered or threatened wildlife.

Bibliography

Selected Sources

Books

Dolin, Eric Jay, *Leviathan: The History of Whaling in America*, Norton, 2007.
An environmental writer traces the rise of the New England whaling industry and its role in U.S. history.

Morikawa, Jun, *Whaling in Japan: Power, Politics, and Diplomacy*, Columbia University Press, 2009.
A professor of environmental studies at Rakuno Gakuen University in Sapporo, Japan, puts Japan's current position as the world's last big whaling nation into its political and historical context.

Stoett, Peter J., *International Politics of Whaling*, University of British Columbia Press, 1997.
A professor of political science at Concordia University in Montreal, Canada, examines the sometimes contentious international politics of managing the world's whales.

Articles

Blow, Richard, "The Great American Whale Hunt," *Mother Jones*, September/October 1998, www.motherjones.com/politics/1998/09/great-american-whale-hunt.
A reporter joins Makah tribe members in northwestern Washington as they try to resume aboriginal whaling.

Brower, Ken, "Still Blue: Off the Shores of Costa Rica, Scientists Study a Stronghold of Whales that Once Hovered Near Extinction," *National Geographic*, March 2010, http://ngm.nationalgeographic.com/2009/03/blue-whales/brower-text.
A writer searches for an albino blue whale off Costa Rica.

Chadwick, Douglas, "Right Whales: On the Brink, On the Rebound," *National Geographic*, October 2008, http://ngm.nationalgeographic.com/2008/10/right-whales/chadwick-text/1.
An environmental journalist traces how the species, was once the easiest target of the whaling industry, is responding to conservation efforts.

Costello, Christopher, Steven Gaines and Leah Gerber, "Conservation Science: A Market Approach to Saving the Whales," *Nature*, Jan. 12, 2012, www.nature.com/nature/journal/v481/n7380/full/481139a.html.
Three environmental policy professors propose a cap-and-trade system to promote whale conservation.

Norton, Elizabeth, "Nice to Meet eet eet You," *Science*, Feb. 28, 2012, http://news.sciencemag.org/sciencenow/2012/02/nice-to-meet-eet-eet-you.html.
A reporter describes how wild dolphins use signature whistles to communicate and identify one another.

Sekiguchi, Toko, "Why Japan's Whale Hunt Continues," *Time*, Nov. 20, 2007, www.time.com/time/world/article/0,8599,1686486,00.html.
A reporter explains some of the cultural and political reasons behind Japan's insistence on whaling.

Siebert, Charles, "Watching Whales Watching Us," *The New York Times Magazine*, July 8, 2009, www.nytimes.com/2009/07/12/magazine/12whales-t.html?pagewanted=all.
A journalist describes his interactions with whales in Baja's Sea of California.

Reports and Studies

"Blueprint to U.S. Whale Conservation: An Action Plan for the U.S. Government," International Fund for Animal Welfare, 2012, www.ifaw.or/whaleblueprint.
The report summarizes the threats to whale conservation and ways to deal with them.

"Research Plan for Cetacean Studies in the Western North Pacific Under Special Permit (JARPA II)," Government of Japan, 2002, www.icrwhale.org/pdf/SC5402.pdf.
The government's research plan lays out details of Japan's controversial scientific whaling program.

Tinch, Rob, and Zara Phang, "Sink or Swim: The Economics of Whaling Today," World Wildlife Fund and the Whale and Dolphin Conservation Society, June 2009, www.wdcs.org/submissions_bin/economics_whaling_report.pdf.
Two whale conservation groups study the costs and benefits of whale hunting and whale-related tourism in Norway and Japan.

Tynan, Cynthia, and Joellen Russell, "Icebreaker: Pushing the Boundaries for Whales," World Wildlife Fund, 2008, http://awsassets.panda.org/downloads/english_final_proof_final.pdf.
A study explores the projected impact of global climate change — mainly a 2 degree rise in the ocean temperature — on whales in the Southern Ocean.

Documentary Film/TV Series

"The Cove," released 2009, www.thecovemovie.com.
The Academy Award winning documentary profiles environmental activist Ric O'Barry and his crew as they try to sneak into a heavily guarded cove in Taiji, Japan, to film the annual dolphin hunt.

"Whale Wars," released November 2008, http://animal.discovery.com/tv/whale-wars/.
This Discovery Channel documentary-style series follows activists from the Sea Shepherd Conservation Society as they try to stop whaling activities around the world. Its fifth season begins in June 2012.

The Next Step:

Additional Articles from Current Periodicals

International Whaling Commission

Eilperin, Juliet, "Researchers Propose Putting a Price on Whales," *The Washington Post*, Jan. 11, 2012, www.washingtonpost.com/national/health-science/researchers-propose-putting-a-price-on-whales/2012/01/10/gIQAHSH8qP_story.html.

The International Whaling Commission (IWC) is looking into the possibility of selling whaling rights and quotas to both whalers and conservationists as a solution to whaling debates.

Gaines, Richard, "Catch Shares for Whales? Scientists' Protection Proposal Stirs Firestorm," *Gloucester* (Mass.) *Times*, Jan. 19, 2012, www.gloucestertimes.com/fishing/x180453697/Catch-shares-for-whales-Scientists-protection-proposal-stirs-firestorm.

A proposal to sell whaling quotas is sparking protest from animal-rights groups, who say the approach is unethical.

Hennessy, Selah, "Environmentalists Warn of New Dawn in Commercial Whaling," Voice of America (D.C.) News, Feb. 23, 2010, www.voanews.com/content/environmentalists-warn-of-new-dawn-in-commercial-whaling–85068387/112962.html.

A major conservation organization is criticizing the IWC's proposal to end its ban on commercial whaling and introduce quotas.

MacDougall, David, "Anti-Corruption Measures Debated at Whaling Talks," The Associated Press, July 11, 2011, http://seattletimes.nwsource.com/html/businesstechnology/2015575656_apwhaling.html.

Britain is proposing numerous reforms to make the IWC more transparent, including a crackdown on alleged vote-buying.

Marine Mammals

"California Group Seeks Protections for Gray Whale," *Santa Cruz* (Calif.) *Sentinel*, Nov. 7, 2010.

The California Gray Whale Coalition is fighting to put the gray whale back on the endangered species list because the species' population has begun to dwindle.

Loebbecke, Andrea, "Long-Term Ban on Humpback Whaling in Greenland is Lifted," *The Virginian-Pilot*, June 26, 2010.

The IWC approved humpback whaling for the first time since 1986, spurring criticism from environmentalists.

Whiting, Candace Calloway, "Endangered Orcas' Habitat Scheduled for Seismic Tests on June 11th, 2012," *Seattle* (Wash.) *Post-Intelligencer*, June 9, 2012, http://blog.seattlepi.com/candacewhiting/2012/06/09/endangered-orcas-habitat-scheduled-for-seismic-tests-on-june-11th-2012/.

Planned seismic testing, used to predict earthquakes and locate natural gas reserves off the coast of Washington state in fragile marine habitats, is similar to testing done in Peru that killed thousands of orcas.

Whaling

Fackler, Martin, "Japanese Town Mulls Future Without Whaling Industry," *The New York Times*, March 24, 2011, www.nytimes.com/2011/03/25/world/asia/25whale.html?_r=1&pagewanted=all.

Residents of Ayukawahama are experiencing an identity crisis after a tsunami knocked out a major part of their whaling industry.

Fackler, Martin, "With Whaling Ships under Attack, Japan Will Recall Fleet," *The New York Times*, Feb. 18, 2011, www.nytimes.com/2011/02/19/world/asia/19japan.html.

Sea Shepherd vessels disrupted Japanese whaling activities in the Antarctic, cutting short Japan's whale hunting for the year.

MacDougall, David, "Japan, Australia Clash at Whaling Talks," The Associated Press, July 12, 2011, http://abcnews.go.com/Business/wireStory?id=14055609.

Australia is calling for an end to Japan's claimed "scientific" whaling practices.

Taylor, David G., "Incremental Progress at the International Whaling Commission," *Tampa Bay* (Fla.) *Times*, July 21, 2011, www.politifact.com/truth-o-meter/promises/obameter/promise/524/strengthen-international-rules-against-commercial-/.

President Obama says he does not want the IWC to lift its moratorium on commercial whaling.

Citing *CQ Researcher*

Sample formats for citing these reports in a bibliography include the ones listed below. Preferred styles and formats vary, so please check with your instructor or professor.

MLA Style

Jost, Kenneth. "Remembering 9/11," CQ Researcher 2 Sept. 2011: 701-732.

APA Style

Jost, K. (2011, September 2). Remembering 9/11. *CQ Researcher, 9*, 701-732.

Chicago Style

Jost, Kenneth. "Remembering 9/11." *CQ Researcher*, September 2, 2011, 701-732.

In-depth Reports on Issues in the News

Are you writing a paper?

Need backup for a debate?

Want to become an expert on an issue?

For more than 80 years, students have turned to *CQ Researcher* for in-depth reporting on issues in the news. Reports on a full range of political and social issues are now available. Following is a selection of recent reports:

Civil Liberties
Voter Rights, 5/12
Remembering 9/11, 9/11
Government Secrecy, 2/11
Cybersecurity, 2/10

Crime/Law
Criminal Records, 4/12
Police Misconduct, 4/12
Immigration Conflict, 3/12
Financial Misconduct, 1/12
Eyewitness Testimony, 10/11
Death Penalty Debates, 11/10

Education
Arts Education, 3/12
Youth Volunteerism, 1/12
Digital Education, 12/11
Student Debt, 10/11

Environment/Society
U.S. Oil Dependence, 6/12
Gambling in America, 6/12
Celebrity Advocacy, 5/12
Sexual Harassment, 4/12
Internet Regulation, 4/12
Space Program, 2/12

Health/Safety
Alcohol Abuse, 6/12
Traumatic Brain Injury, 6/12
Distracted Driving, 5/12
Patient Safety, 2/12
Military Suicides, 9/11
Teen Drug Use, 6/11
Organ Donations, 4/11

Politics/Economy
U.S.-Europe Relations, 3/12
Attracting Jobs, 3/12
Presidential Election, 2/12

Upcoming Reports

Privatizing Defense, 7/13/12 | Debt Collection, 7/20/12 | Smart Cities, 7/27/12

ACCESS

CQ Researcher is available in print and online. For access, visit your library or www.cqresearcher.com.

STAY CURRENT

For notice of upcoming *CQ Researcher* reports or to learn more about *CQ Researcher* products, subscribe to the free e-mail newsletters, *CQ Researcher Alert!* and *CQ Researcher News*: http://cqpress.com/newsletters.

PURCHASE

To purchase a *CQ Researcher* report in print or electronic format (PDF), visit www.cqpress.com or call 866-427-7737. Single reports start at $15. Bulk purchase discounts and electronic-rights licensing are also available.

SUBSCRIBE

Annual full-service *CQ Researcher* subscriptions—including 44 reports a year, monthly index updates, and a bound volume—start at $1,054. Add $25 for domestic postage.

CQ Researcher Online offers a backfile from 1991 and a number of tools to simplify research. For pricing information, call 800-834-9020, or e-mail librarymarketing@cqpress.com.

CQ RESEARCHER ***PLUS*** *ARCHIVE*

GET ONLINE ACCESS TO VITAL ISSUES FROM 1923 TO THE PRESENT

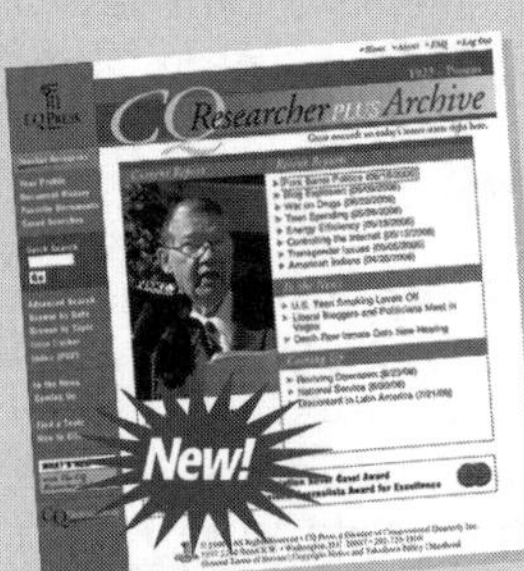

CQ Researcher Plus Archive delivers fast, online access to every *CQ Researcher* report from 1991 to the present, *PLUS* lets you explore the complete archive of *Editorial Research Reports** from 1923-1990. Search and browse more than 3,600 in-depth reports.

Loaded with handy online features, *CQ Researcher Plus Archive* provides the trustworthy reporting and the advanced online functionality today's researchers demand. The new "Issue Tracker" feature provides quick links to past and present reports on the specific topics you need.

For a free trial, visit http://library.cqpress.com/trials.

For pricing information, call 1-800-834-9020, ext. 1906 or e-mail librarymarketing@cqpress.com.

**Editorial Research Reports*, the predecessor to *CQ Researcher*, provides the same expert, nonpartisan reporting on the vital issues that have shaped our society.

CQ Press • 2300 N Street, NW, Suite 800 • Washington, DC 20037

CQ Researcher

Published by CQ Press, an Imprint of SAGE Publications, Inc.

www.cqresearcher.com

Privatizing the Military

Does the U.S. overuse private contractors?

The United States and other nations increasingly rely on private contractors, many of them armed, to guard military bases, protect diplomatic personnel, conduct surveillance of potential military targets and carry out other such duties. Over the past decade, security companies have greatly increased in number and size, becoming a major industry that attracts private-sector clients as well. Multinational corporations hire the same armed contractors that governments use to guard remote mining operations, and shipping companies hire them to fight pirates. Governments and other clients say private guards save money and provide strategic flexibility. Critics argue, however, that using soldiers-for-hire gives governments too much leeway to take armed actions without citizens' or lawmakers' consent. Furthermore, they contend, no system of law — national or international — holds armed contractors or those who hire them fully accountable for human-rights violations.

A private U.S. security guard stands in front of a chilling monument marking a mass grave for victims of dictator Saddam Hussein in Hilla, Iraq. In 2011, the Pentagon employed about 155,000 private security contractors in Iraq and Afghanistan, including some 39,000 Americans.

INSIDE THIS REPORT

The Issues 599
Background 606
Chronology 607
Current Situation 612
At Issue....................613
Outlook 615
Bibliography 618
The Next Step 619

CQ Researcher • July 13, 2012 • www.cqresearcher.com
Volume 22, Number 25 • Pages 597-620

CQPRESS

Los Angeles | London | New Delhi
Singapore | Washington DC

Recipient of Society of Professional Journalists Award for Excellence ◆ American Bar Association Silver Gavel Award

THE ISSUES

599 • Does the U.S. overuse private contractors to conduct missions abroad?
• Has using private contractors worked well in Iraq and Afghanistan?
• Are nations doing enough to hold contractors accountable for fraud or abuse?

BACKGROUND

606 **Private Enterprise**
Foreign soldiers hired for pay have been used throughout history.

608 **Rise of States**
Costly 17th-century wars undercut mercenaries' dominance.

611 **Turning Points**
After the Cold War, mercenaries were again needed.

612 **New Era**
The Iraq War marked a shift in the use of contractors.

CURRENT SITUATION

612 **New Jobs**
Security contracting continues to expand.

614 **Congressional Action**
Proposals would expand civilian courts' jurisdiction over contractors.

OUTLOOK

615 **Regulated or Unregulated?**
Security contractors, governments and human rights groups are working on enforcement rules for a new code of conduct.

SIDEBARS AND GRAPHICS

600 **Most Contractors in Iraq, Afghanistan Are Non-U.S. Citizens**
In Afghanistan, more than half are Afghan nationals.

601 **Comparing Contractor and Troop Casualties**
At least 2,300 contractors died in Iraq and Afghanistan from 2001 through March 2011.

602 **Private Contractors vs. Military Personnel**
Cost comparisons can be hard to calculate.

604 **Iraq Contractors Used Mainly for Base Support**
Security duties comprise only 16 percent of tasks.

607 **Chronology**
Key events since 1989.

608 **Setting Standards for Security Contractors**
New code of conduct sparks many disagreements.

610 **Contracting Takes Unacknowledged Human Toll**
"Everyone believes we're underreporting contractor deaths."

613 **At Issue**
Should Congress increase oversight of private contractors?

FOR FURTHER RESEARCH

617 **For More Information**
Organizations to contact.

618 **Bibliography**
Selected sources used.

619 **The Next Step**
Additional articles.

619 **Citing *CQ Researcher***
Sample bibliography formats.

Cover: AFP/Getty Images/Saeed Khan

CQ Researcher

July 13, 2012
Volume 22, Number 25

MANAGING EDITOR: Thomas J. Billitteri
tjb@cqpress.com

ASSISTANT MANAGING EDITOR: Kathy Koch
kkoch@cqpress.com

CONTRIBUTING EDITOR: Thomas J. Colin
tcolin@cqpress.com

ASSOCIATE EDITOR: Kenneth Jost

STAFF WRITER: Marcia Clemmitt

CONTRIBUTING WRITERS: Peter Katel, Barbara Mantel, Jennifer Weeks

DESIGN/PRODUCTION EDITOR: Olu B. Davis

ASSISTANT EDITOR: Darrell Dela Rosa

FACT CHECKER: Michelle Harris

INTERN: Kate Irby

Los Angeles | London | New Delhi
Singapore | Washington DC

An Imprint of SAGE Publications, Inc.

VICE PRESIDENT AND EDITORIAL DIRECTOR, HIGHER EDUCATION GROUP:
Michele Sordi

DIRECTOR, ONLINE PUBLISHING:
Todd Baldwin

CQ Researcher (ISSN 1056-2036) is printed on acid-free paper. Published weekly, except: (March wk. 5) (May wk. 4) (July wk. 1) (Aug. wks. 3, 4) (Nov. wk. 4) and (Dec. wks. 3, 4). Published by SAGE Publications, Inc., 2455 Teller Rd., Thousand Oaks, CA 91320. Annual full-service subscriptions start at $1,054. For pricing, call 1-800-834-9020. To purchase a *CQ Researcher* report in print or electronic format (PDF), visit www.cqpress.com or call 866-427-7737. Single reports start at $15. Bulk purchase discounts and electronic-rights licensing are also available. Periodicals postage paid at Thousand Oaks, California, and at additional mailing offices. POSTMASTER: Send address changes to *CQ Researcher*, 2300 N St., N.W., Suite 800, Washington, DC 20037.

Privatizing the Military

By Marcia Clemmitt

The Issues

The surveillance operation might never have come to light if the small plane hadn't developed mechanical trouble over the Central African Republic in the summer of 2010. After an emergency landing, the American civilians aboard, along with two military observers from neighboring African countries, were detained by suspicious local officials.

"We felt like we were going to prison," one of the Americans told *The Washington Post*. [1]

As private security contractors working under contract to the Pentagon, the Americans had been hired to watch suspected terrorists. Using contractors, rather than military or CIA personnel, helps the Pentagon keep its expanding African counterterrorism campaign low-profile and provides the government with "deniability" if mishaps occur, explained Peter W. Singer, director of the 21st Century Defense Initiative at the Brookings Institution, a think tank in Washington. [2]

Getty Images/Alex Wong

Kristal Batalona, the daughter of an American security guard who was killed in Iraq, testifies on Feb. 7, 2007, before a congressional committee investigating the use of private military contractors. As the United States increasingly turns to so-called guns for hire, critics argue that private contractors are not fully accountable for human rights violations and that they allow the government to take military action without citizens' or lawmakers' consent.

Indeed, when the detained Americans called the State Department and United Nations for help, both agencies — wanting to avoid being linked to the surveillance effort — declined to intervene. "Eventually," one of the contractors said, "we were able to talk our way out of it." [3]

The episode helps underscore the rapidly expanding role that private security contractors are playing for the Pentagon, CIA, State Department and other agencies in hot spots across the globe.

The government has increasingly turned to security companies over the past two decades to assist in armed and unarmed military operations and help other government agencies working abroad. The trend, originally driven by military downsizing in the wake of the Soviet Union's collapse in the early 1990s, has accelerated sharply in recent years. The wars in Iraq and Afghanistan have fueled it, as has increased public acceptance of privatization as a way to increase quality and efficiency while reducing the number of jobs handled by government.

As of March 2011, approximately 155,000 Department of Defense (DOD) contractors were in Afghanistan and Iraq, comprising more than half of the DOD workforce in the two countries. [4]

The overwhelming majority of private American contractors around the world perform unarmed support duties, such as running food-service operations on military bases or constructing temporary buildings. "Most of the time they don't do sexy stuff," says Joanna Spear, an associate professor of international affairs at George Washington University. "Much of it's boring."

A growing number of contractors, however, over the past decade have taken on delicate, mission-critical jobs, such as surveillance, prisoner interrogation and intelligence gathering to help the military accurately target drones — plus jobs in which the contractors bear arms. In 2011, for example, 10,448 contractors working in Iraq — 16 percent of the total — provided armed security, including in armored vehicles and helicopters. [5]

The rise of armed contractors in the past decade has marked a new era in the long history of military privatization, according to an analysis by RAND, a think tank in Santa Monica, Calif., that studies military issues. While the military hired an increasing number of contractors during the 1990s, including as armed guards in conflict zones and disaster-relief situations, for example, there remained a long-held reluctance to send armed private citizens into actual war zones, RAND noted. Until the 2003 U.S.-led invasion

Most Contractors Are Non-U.S. Citizens

Most private contractors employed by the Pentagon in Afghanistan and Iraq in March 2011 were non-Americans. In Afghanistan, more than half were Afghan nationals, and more than one-fourth were citizens of other countries. In Iraq, 14 percent were Iraqis, and nearly 60 percent came from other countries.

Contractors in Afghanistan

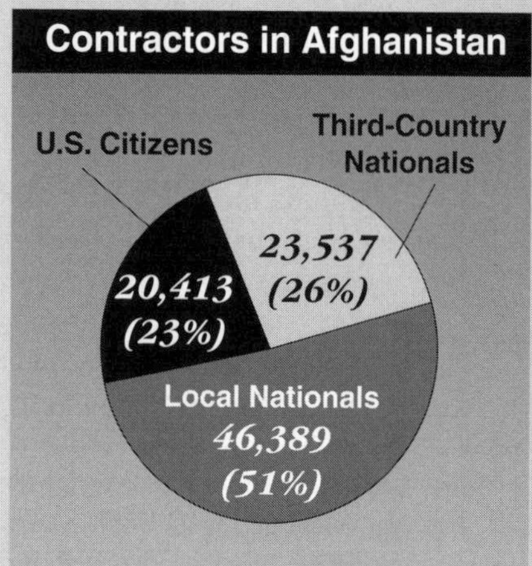

Contractors in Iraq

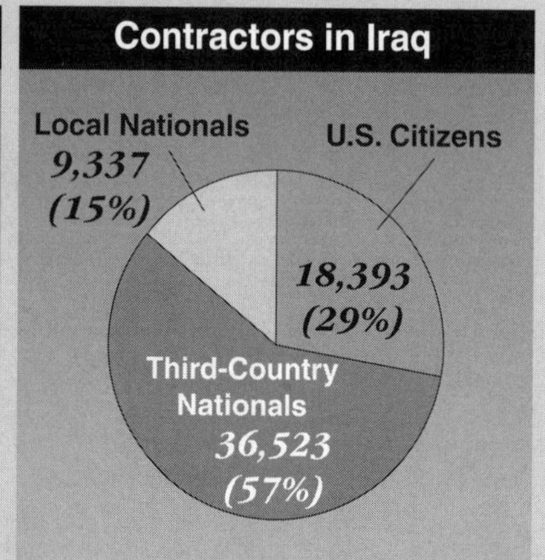

Percentages may not add to 100 because of rounding.

Source: Moshe Schwartz and Joyprada Swain, "Department of Defense Contractors in Afghanistan and Iraq: Background and Analysis," Congressional Research Service, May 13, 2011, pp. 10-11, www.fas.org/sgp/crs/natsec/R40764.pdf

of Iraq, such mercenaries had been rarely used in American history, it said. [6]

The State Department points out that, unlike troops, contractors are under orders to use force only in defense, never in attack mode, and to back off from armed clashes whenever possible. "We run. We go. We do not stand and fight," said Undersecretary for Management Patrick Kennedy, who oversees security for the U.S. Embassy in Baghdad. [7]

But many analysts say that an increasing number of contractor activities skate perilously close to duties that should be performed only by military personnel.

In Iraq and Afghanistan, for example, tens of thousands of armed contractors have defended sensitive military installations, yet they are not part of the tight military chain of command. "They don't get the same intelligence information," said Steven Schooner, a professor of government procurement at the George Washington University Law School. "So when things begin to develop quickly, there's an awful lot of people around with weapons" who will not receive the same commands and information as troops receive, he said. [8]

Most armed private contractors were formerly in the U.S. or another national military. That raises questions about how easily they will obey the far more restrictive rules of force that apply in their private-sector role, said Dov Zahkeim, who worked in the Defense Department under President Ronald Reagan and as a foreign policy adviser to President George W. Bush. "If you're coming under fire and you happen to have a gun in your hand, you're a former military person — are you really going to cut and run?" [9]

Military personnel pledge to uphold the public trust, support the national military mission and respect international law. But military contractors are not bound by that same pledge. Some analysts worry that the widespread use of contractors could erode the commitment of service members to adhere strictly to the military code. Laura Dickinson, a research professor of law at George Washington University, pointed, for example, to the 2004 scandal at U.S.-run Abu Ghraib prison near Baghdad, in which detainees had been severely abused by contractors and service members. The military's own internal report concluded that heavy reliance on contracting had watered down the culture of respect for law and order, contributing to "an environment of lawlessness that resulted in torture," Dickinson wrote. [10]

Contractors fall into a legal gray area that makes them more difficult to prosecute than military personnel for illegal or improper actions. For example, a contractor may be a citizen of one country, work in a second, be employed by a company based in a third and work under contract to the government of a fourth. No international rules stipulate where, how or even if a person in that situation can be tried for a crime, RAND analysts note. [11]

If service members are accused of a crime, they are generally apprehended and subject to court-martial. "But if a contractor shoots someone, he may be out of the country by nightfall," says T. X. Hammes, a retired Marine colonel who served in Iraq and now is a senior research fellow at the Department of Defense's National Defense University in Washington.

Some prosecutions of contractors have gone forward, but progress is slow. In June, for example, the U.S. Supreme Court agreed with an appeals court that four former contractors should be subject to criminal charges in connection with the allegedly unprovoked shooting deaths of 17 Iraqi civilians in Nisour Square, near Baghdad, in 2007. The four were employed by Blackwater Worldwide, a major military contractor now known as Academi. [12]

Comparing Contractor and Troop Casualties

At least 2,300 private military contractors died and more than 50,000 were injured in the Iraq and Afghanistan wars from 2001 through March 2011. U.S. troop fatalities stood at nearly 6,000 for the same period. Because private companies are not required to report contractor deaths or injuries, some experts believe the number of contractor casualties is higher than those reflected here.

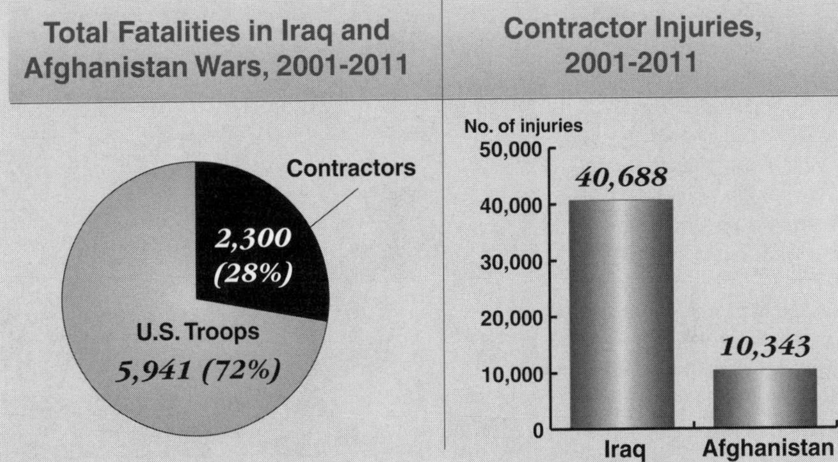

Source: Steven L. Schooner and Collin D. Swan, "Dead Contractors: The Un-Examined Effect of Surrogates on the Public's Casualty Sensitivity," Journal of National Security Law and Policy, *2011, p. 46, www.wartimecontracting.gov/docs/forum2011-05-02_statement-Schooner.pdf*

Military contractors have many defenders, however. Fears that contractors may be more likely than military personnel to commit crimes and human-rights abuses are greatly overblown, wrote independent military-affairs analyst David Isenberg, author of *Shadow Force: Private Security Contractors in Iraq*. Violence is an integral part of war, and "even the worst of classical mercenaries from ancient times or the Middle Ages would have a hard time rivaling the record of human and physical destruction achieved by regular military forces," he said. "Mercenaries did not invent concentration camps, firebomb cities from the air, use chemical or biological weapons or use nuclear weapons on civilian cities." [13]

Contractors can make it possible to carry out some valuable foreign missions that could not be done otherwise, wrote Anna Leander, a professor at Denmark's Copenhagen Business School who studies so-called "non-state actors" in world politics. For example, she said, private security contractors have been "used to break cycles of violence" in countries that experience devastating civil wars or potential ethnic genocides. In North Africa, contractors have assisted international organizations and human-rights groups trying to end a prolonged genocidal conflict in Sudan's Darfur region. When a country torn apart by such violence lacks strategic importance, a powerful nation such as the United States may not want to intervene with military force; however, it might hire contractors to do humanitarian work, avoiding the need for legislative approval or public support to deploy armed troops, she wrote. [14]

Since the end of the Cold War in the early 1990s, "a lot of what [the U.S. government] would like to see done in the world doesn't tie simply to a clear national interest," as it more clearly did when the United States faced off against the Soviet Union, says Deborah Avant, a professor of international security and diplomacy at the University of Denver. That makes contractors a valued option when the White House or Congress believes that an international mission is necessary but fears the public won't support armed intervention.

"If people don't want to use private contractors, the choices are simple: Either scale back U.S. geopolitical commitments or enlarge the military, something that will entail more gargantuan expenditures and even, some argue, a return to the draft down the road," wrote Isenberg. [15]

As private contractors become a standard feature of military and other international operations, here are some of the questions being asked:

Does the United States over-rely on private contractors to conduct missions abroad?

When a group of retired military officers assessed the nature of future military operations back in 2007, they predicted an expanding role for private contractors.

"Whatever threats the Army next faces will be different from the last, but they are likely to be expeditionary" — carried out entirely in foreign countries — "and likely to involve high numbers of contractor personnel," the officers declared. [16]

So far, history has borne out their conclusion. Not only is the U.S. military hiring more and more contractors, but so too are civilian agencies active in foreign countries, including the State Department and the U.S. Agency for International Development (USAID).

Private Contractors vs. Military Personnel

Cost comparisons can be hard to calculate.

Do private contractors save taxpayers money? The answer is something of a toss-up. Some analysts argue that contractors' wages are so much higher than military wages for similar jobs that contracting does not save money and might actually be more expensive than using military personnel.

"In 2007, private security guards working for companies such as Blackwater and DynCorp were earning up to $1,222 a day," wrote Nobel Prize-winning economist Joseph Stiglitz, a professor at Columbia University, and Linda Bilmes, a Harvard University lecturer on budget and public administration. "By contrast, an Army sergeant was earning $140 to $190 a day in pay and benefits." [1]

Corel

Military service members earn far less than many private security guards, according to scholars Joseph Stiglitz and Linda Bilmes.

Such comparisons are flawed, however, according to the nonpartisan Congressional Budget Office (CBO), which provides economic analysis to Congress. The $1,222 a day that Bilmes and Stiglitz cite as a salary is actually a salary plus additional money that goes not to the individual workers but to the company they work for, to cover costs such as overhead, the CBO said. [2]

Hiring a private contractor costs roughly the same as using a comparable military unit, the CBO found. And over the long run, using contractors might actually be cheaper because military units continue to cost the government money during peacetime, while contractors do not, the budget analysts said. [3]

Hiring private security companies to guard embassies in Iraq costs the State Department less in four out of five cases reviewed by the Government Accountability Office (GAO), Congress' nonpartisan auditing agency, than it would have cost to use State Department personnel. The cost difference stems mainly from the fact that State Department guards would serve in Iraq for only a year at a time before rotating to posts in the United States. That means the gov-

Many analysts point out that contractors provide technical expertise that the military may lack and give government the flexibility to expand its forces on short notice. But others warn that the increased use of private contracting makes it easier for presidents to launch foreign missions without robust public discussion or congressional oversight.

Things that go wrong among armed troops can turn lawmakers and the public against a valuable international mission, says Spear of George Washington University. For example, if the military is training troops abroad and a foreign trainee shoots a trainer who is a U.S. service member, even accidentally, the event can destroy legislative support for the mission. But a similar shooting would cause little uproar if the trainer were a private contractor, she maintains.

Because governments often don't anticipate dangerous international situations, contractors give officials the "ability to quickly mobilize and deploy large numbers of personnel," wrote Hammes, the retired Marine colonel. Contractors also offer the possibility of more continuity of staff, since many are willing to stay in a conflict zone longer than the six- to 12-month rotation period that the Pentagon maintains for service members. What's more, private security companies often hire local people, potentially boosting the local economy and enhancing U.S. "nation-building" efforts in countries such as Iraq and Afghanistan, Hammes noted. [17]

Nevertheless, many analysts cite serious potential downsides to contracting. Some argue that contractors' higher salaries and more flexible working schedules not only damage the morale of lower-paid troops but also encourage service members to abandon the military in favor of a private-sector security job.*

"Private military contractors can be a morale deflator for our military guys," said a staff member in the Office of the Secretary of Defense. "They create disincentives for staying with the military." [18] (RAND analysts note,

---

* In 2005, some individual security contractors in Iraq earned $33,000 per month, compared to the $12,000 to $13,000 monthly salaries for Special Operations Forces. Private contractors also had much more liberal leave options, according to the Government Accountability Office.

ernment would have to hire additional guards to cover the Iraq duties while simultaneously paying the State Department personnel for their stateside posts. By contrast, the government does not have to pay any individual contractors unless they're actually on the job. [4]

GAO said it was unable to come up with a similar cost comparison for Department of Defense (DOD) contractors because the DOD couldn't provide enough information about its own costs. DOD said it didn't have information readily available about the number and rank of military personnel that would be required to fulfill a security contractor's duties or about how much it would cost to train service members to do the jobs. [5]

The fact that private contractors are temporary employees whom the government does not have to retain or train certainly makes them a lower-cost option, said Doug Brooks, president of the International Stability Operations Association, a security-contractor industry group. "As soon as the job's over, you stop paying them," he said. Yet the government continues to pay for service members even after they leave the military, providing education benefits through the GI Bill and veterans' health care, for example, he said. [6]

While some analysts say private contractors are cheaper than government or military personnel, however, others say they can wind up costing more. "Warfare is usually characterized by secrecy, heavy time constraints and the imperative of victory," so the government spends little effort on rigorous competitive bidding or cost oversight of contractors, wrote independent military analyst David Isenberg. Between 1998 and 2003, for example, only 40 percent of government contracts were awarded through competitive bidding, and that number has risen only marginally more recently, Isenberg said.

Furthermore, more than half of the contracts aren't monitored to assure that companies fulfill their contractual obligations, he said. "Thus, the market for private security services is only partially competitive," and in some cases it's a near monopoly — hardly the recipe for cost efficiency, Isenberg wrote. [7]

— Marcia Clemmitt

[1] Quoted in "Contractors' Support of U.S. Operations in Iraq," Congressional Budget Office, August 2008, p. 14, www.cbo.gov/sites/default/files/cbofiles/ftpdocs/96xx/doc9688/08-12-iraqcontractors.pdf.

[2] *Ibid.*

[3] *Ibid.*

[4] "Warfighter Support: A Cost Comparison of Using State Department Employees versus Contractors for Security Services in Iraq," Government Accountability Office, March 4, 2010, p. 5, www.gao.gov/assets/100/96571.pdf.

[5] *Ibid.*, p. 2.

[6] Quoted in "Private Warriors," PBS Frontline, www.pbs.org/wgbh/pages/frontline/shows/warriors/interviews/brooks.html.

[7] David Isenberg, "Private Military Contractors and U.S. Grand Strategy," International Peace Research Institute, 2009, p. 23, www.cato.org/pubs/articles/isenberg-private%20military-contractors-2009.pdf.

however, that, while many service members express this view, data don't show that hiring contractors has significantly harmed military retention.) [19]

By using contractors the government can avoid having to justify its foreign policy persuasively enough to make the case for recruiting troops from among the citizenry, says Avant of the University of Denver. As a result, "leaders can become less accountable to the populace. Everything that makes it easier to mobilize armed force means you can have a more aggressive foreign policy."

Accordingly, the use of contractors allows presidents to mislead the public about how serious a military commitment the government is making, says Hammes. Contractors aren't listed in government reports on the number of troops involved in a mission, he notes. In late 2011, for example, when President Obama announced a temporary "surge" of 30,000 troops to Afghanistan, a more accurate number — including contractors — was likely around 130,000, he says. "That might have changed the equation. People might have said, 'No.' So the fundamental question is, 'Is this good for democracy?' "

Contractors help governments escape international scrutiny as well, says Hammes. "There are rumors of a large contingent of Chinese contractors in Africa," for example, but because contractors are involved, the details are unknown. "If they'd moved an infantry division" to Africa, the details would be much more likely to come out and there would be international debate, he says.

Many security companies and other contractors are founded and staffed by high-ranking military officers. That raises the question of how objective Pentagon decision-making involving contractors can be when former staff members submit bids for contracting jobs, and current members mull jobs they might take after retirement.

"Using a previous relationship as an entrée to selling something" creates at least the perception of conflict of interest, suggested William "Buck" Kernan, a retired four-star Army general who once worked for the large Alexandria, Va.-based contractor MPRI. Often, he said, a contractor is a "previous superior" to the contracting officers at the Pentagon to whom he or she is pitching services. That can raise "all kinds

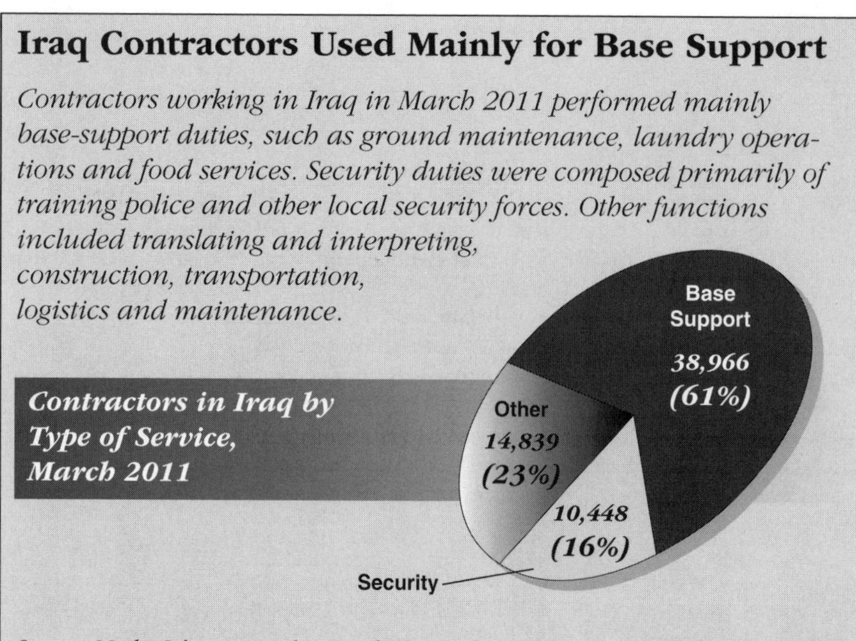

Iraq Contractors Used Mainly for Base Support

Contractors working in Iraq in March 2011 performed mainly base-support duties, such as ground maintenance, laundry operations and food services. Security duties were composed primarily of training police and other local security forces. Other functions included translating and interpreting, construction, transportation, logistics and maintenance.

Source: Moshe Schwartz and Joyprada Swain, "Department of Defense Contractors in Afghanistan and Iraq: Background and Analysis," Congressional Research Service, May 13, 2011, www.fas.org/sgp/crs/natsec/R40764.pdf

of questions" about the objectivity of contracting decisions, he said. [20]

Has using private contractors worked well in Iraq and Afghanistan?

Private contractors have played a large role in the Iraq and Afghanistan wars, doing jobs that would have been difficult without their help, such as keeping supply lines open through the Hindu Kush — the treacherous mountain range between central Afghanistan and northern Pakistan whose name translates to "Hindu killer." However, contractors also have perpetrated high-profile violence against local people that likely harmed U.S. interests — such as the abuse of prisoners at Abu Ghraib prison that came to light in 2004 and the 2007 shooting deaths of 17 Iraqi civilians in Nisour Square by State Department contractors.

In 2007 Gen. David Petraeus, then commanding general of the multinational forces in Iraq, defended the heavy use of armed contractors in Iraq and Afghanistan. Because they guarded bases and performed other routine jobs, he told Congress, service members were available to carry out military missions. "Tens of thousands of contract security forces . . . guard facilities . . . that our forces . . . would otherwise have to guard and secure," said Petraeus, who is now director of the Central Intelligence Agency (CIA). [21]

RAND, the California-based think tank, said it found little evidence that private contractors working for the U.S. government in Iraq had behaved in a reckless fashion. "It does not appear that a majority of either the military or State Department personnel perceive private security contractors to be 'running wild' in Iraq," as some critics charge, said RAND, basing its conclusions on a survey of about 1,000 service members and 1,700 State Department personnel. [22]

While contractors have participated in abuse of civilians, such as at Abu Ghraib, service members have been equally if not more culpable in many incidents, wrote military analyst Isenberg. At Abu Ghraib, for example, while contractors abused prisoners, most abuse was "carried out by regular military forces," he noted. Furthermore, one of the most serious human-rights breaches was the attempt to avoid oversight of activities at the prison, an action in which no contractors were involved, he said. It was government agencies such as the CIA that tried to hide prisoners' records, Isenberg said. [23]

Eleven service members were convicted of abuses at Abu Ghraib; no contractors were criminally charged. Federal courts are still determining whether a civil suit against contractors brought by former Abu Ghraib prisoners can proceed. [24]

Some service members and other government workers surveyed by RAND praised contractors they'd worked with.

"We hired Kroll" bodyguards, and the company did a good job of avoiding negative interactions with Iraqis, a USAID staffer said. "They were former [Special Air Service] guys" from the British army, and "overall they did a pretty good — an excellent job. . . . They learned how to keep a low profile" to help USAID maintain good relations with local people. [25]

New York City-based Kroll ended its bodyguard work in Iraq and Afghanistan in late 2006, after several employees were killed by suicide bombers. [26]

But while private companies may perform well on specific jobs, they are less likely than the military to behave in ways consistent with a larger U.S. mission, some analysts say. For example, contractors have not been as effective as military personnel at winning over the "hearts and minds" of local people in so-called counterinsurgency efforts in Iraq and Afghanistan, they say. [27]

In the RAND survey, 20 percent of service members who said they'd interacted with private contractors in Iraq said they had observed contractors behaving in a "threatening, arrogant or belligerent way" toward Iraqis. Fourteen percent said they'd observed armed contractors taking offensive action, even though private companies are banned from anything but the defensive use of force. [28]

About one-fifth of State Department officials reported having seen armed contractors "often" or "sometimes" mistreating Iraqi civilians, according to RAND analysts. In a mission heavily dependent on winning over Iraqi loyalty to the United States, the number of incidents "does not need to be very high for it to be significant," they said. Furthermore, about half the surveyed State Department officials who'd dealt with contractors told the analysts that they'd had to spend time managing disputes between Iraqis and contractors. [29]

AFP/Getty Images/Ahmad al-Rubaye

Private guards for the Blackwater security firm (now Academi) take positions near the Iranian Embassy in Baghdad, Iraq, following a roadside-bomb attack in July 2005. In 2007, four Blackwater guards working for the State Department were charged with manslaughter in connection with the shooting of 17 Iraqi civilians in Baghdad's Nisour Square. In June 2012, the U.S. Supreme Court held that the former contractors should be subject to criminal charges for the deaths.

In some instances, contractors have flouted international principles of how civilians should be treated, said Mary Picard, senior disaster law officer at the International Federation of Red Cross and Red Crescent Societies, in Geneva, Switzerland. Because local people generally don't distinguish between private-sector and public-sector American workers, such events make it "much more difficult for the military to maintain law and order and to be perceived as doing the right thing." [30]

Military missions require a high degree of coordination between commanders and commanded, but the spread of contracting makes such coordination tougher, some analysts say.

"I didn't even have authority to speak to the contractors" onsite to request changes in procedure, said Hammes, the retired Marine colonel, of his Iraq experience. "I had to call the [company's] home office" in the United States.

Technical barriers also inhibit coordination, said Ian Wing, an associate professor of policing at Charles Sturt University, in Australia, who served with the Coalition Forces' Combined Operations Intelligence Center in Iraq. Troops and contractors "don't have the same radios, they don't have the same procedures," he says. Furthermore, contractors "do what their contract requires, and they won't do anything else." [31]

Being able to rely on contractors makes it easier for governments to say "yes" to some military missions when they should not, and the Afghanistan invasion may be an example, says Hammes. "Foreign militaries have never succeeded in pushing supplies through the Hindu Kush," he says. The United States "has used local contractors to accomplish it. But when you're in a position to absolutely need contractors to do something, you should probably ask yourself, 'Is doing this a good idea?' "

Are nations doing enough to hold contractors accountable for fraud or abuse?

Over the past several years, the United States and other nations have stepped up their efforts to monitor the work of private contractors. (*See sidebar, p. 602.*) However, many analysts argue that both the capacity and the political will to significantly increase oversight may be lacking.

By the late 1990s, Congress recognized that the rapidly growing sector of private security businesses based in the United States but operating abroad fell into a legal gray area. No court — military or civilian — had clear jurisdiction to prosecute criminal activity.

In response, Congress enacted the Military Extraterritorial Jurisdiction Act in 2000 to place contractors working abroad with the military under the jurisdiction of federal criminal law for any offense punishable by more than one year in prison. In 2004, Congress expanded the law to include contractors working abroad with other U.S. agencies during periods of armed conflict. [32]

In 2007, the Uniform Code of Military Justice was amended to allow wider latitude to prosecute contractors in military courts. Previously, only contractors employed during wars declared by Congress could face court-martial, but the amended law includes contractors who work in so-called "contingency operations" — military activity undertaken without a formal congressional declaration of war, such as the wars in Iraq and Afghanistan. [33]

The government has made heroic efforts to pursue cases despite the high price of investigating and prosecuting incidents that happen abroad, says Gary D. Solis, a former Marine prosecutor who is an adjunct professor at Georgetown University Law Center and author of the 2010 book, *The Law of Armed Conflict.* For example, after the 2007 shooting deaths of Iraqi civilians by Blackwater (Academi) contractors at Nisour Square, the government spent millions of dollars to collect and preserve evidence, even "boxing up the vehicles [involved in the case] and shipping them to the United States."

Nevertheless, many analysts say it's still far too easy for contractors to avoid oversight and accountability.

The government's "whole regulatory infrastructure for contracting is sparse," says the University of Denver's Avant. Oversight offices don't have the resources, experience or authority to investigate potential problems before they worsen, she says.

Several years ago, the Pentagon outsourced some contractor oversight to a private company, and the move spurred charges that the company would inevitably have conflicts of interest that would interfere with its work. But the arrangement worked better than the Pentagon's internal oversight system, says Doug Brooks, president of the International Stability Operations Association, a membership group for contractors in the security and disaster-relief fields. The company's contract stipulated that it would take on only a manageable workload, whereas the military's own contract auditors are "often trying to deal with a workload 20 times the reasonable size," Brooks says.

Because "the military is hesitant to apply" its expanded authority under the Uniform Code of Military Justice, the amendment to the code has done little to increase contractor accountability, as evidenced by the fact that hardly any cases have been brought, Solis says. The Pentagon is hesitant to pursue cases under the code for fear that the Supreme Court will strike down the law's expansion, he says. In the 1950s and '60s, the court declared that the military did not have authority to court-martial civilians.

When it comes to Americans charged with crimes abroad, "the United States has always said, 'We will prosecute our own,' partly to assure people a fair trial. But now we seem to have gone further with that approach: We don't prosecute at all," Solis says. What's lacking is "political will," he argues. "The attorney general has to say, 'I don't care how difficult it is. I want somebody in court in 30 days.' "

"Looked at through the lens of partisan politics," however, it's hard to aggressively prosecute Americans who work in dangerous situations abroad, Solis says. "Anyone who started prosecuting civilians would probably be a one-term president."

The issue is not whether contractors are ultimately found innocent or guilty of offenses with which they're charged but whether cases are pursued to conclusion, says Solis. If the government continues its apparent reluctance to see cases through, the result will be an "erosion in the confidence people have in America's ability and willingness to achieve justice." ■

BACKGROUND

Private Enterprise

Armed forces for hire — either individual mercenaries or groups of salaried soldiers working as an army for hire — are nothing new. From ancient times until about 200 years ago, hired guns traveled the world to work for different governments. They were the most common kind of armed force, and, while the trend waned for a time, it never went out of existence. [34]

Before about 1800, few rulers had the ability, or even the inclination, to assemble large armed forces of their own citizens.

Waging war effectively required specialized skills, such as shooting a crossbow or wielding a sword, that were best honed over decades. But few governments needed a standing army or could afford to pay soldiers to keep their skills sharp in peacetime. As late as the 19th century, most governments were either weak or despotic, and most people were poor, making it difficult for rulers to assemble a force of any size from among their citizenry.

Furthermore, until the 19th century there were few nation-states of the kind that we know today, with firm boundaries and stable populations, that citizen armies defended in war. Instead, kings presided over territories with shifting boundaries that they fought to expand into far-ranging empires, employing foreign soldiers-for-hire who were better suited for the task than local farmers or knights.

As a result, "the foreign soldier hired for pay, the mercenary, is an almost ubiquitous type in the entire . . . history of organized warfare," wrote Singer, the Brookings Institution scholar. "Even the Bible tells their tales. The Pharaoh chased the Israelites out of Egypt with an army that included hired foreigners, while [the Israelite King] David and his men . . . were employed in the Philistine army." [35]

But employing freelance warriors had its downside, especially between wars, when the soldiers weren't paid. Mercenary groups lived "off the land," forcing local people to hand over food and money, "leaving the countryside devastated in their wake," wrote Singer. [36]

On the high seas, from the 13th through 19th centuries, armed sailors for hire — known as privateers — served governments in wartime but often terrorized other vessels as pirates in peacetime. At least some rulers "turned a blind eye," probably because piracy honed the skills sailors needed

Continued on p. 608

Chronology

1980s-1990s

Cold War's end increases supply of soldiers for hire.

1989
U.N. circulates treaty pledging signatories to ban mercenary activity.

1990
South Africa begins dismantling apartheid, its brutal segregation system; some ex-government security officers form mercenary companies.

1991
Cold War ends; shrinking defense budgets leave thousands of former military personnel looking for work.

1993
The deaths of 18 elite U.S. forces in Mogadishu, Somalia, in a raid to capture violent rebel leaders, helps turn Americans against foreign military missions.

1995
South Africa-based Executive Outcomes helps Sierra Leone put down a years-long violent uprising.

1999
Contractors working in Bosnia for Virginia-based DynCorp International allegedly buy young girls from organized criminals for prostitution; accused workers are relocated but never charged.

2000s-Present

Security contracting expands into major industry.

2000
Military Extraterritorial Jurisdiction Act (MEJA) extends federal courts' jurisdiction to contractors charged with serious crimes.

2001
The film "Black Hawk Down" is a fictionalized account of the 1993 Mogadishu raid. . . . Pentagon report states that any military job a private company can perform should be outsourced to industry. . . . U.N. anti-mercenary treaty takes effect, ratified by 20 nations; the United States and other highly industrialized nations do not sign.

2002
British government issues regulatory options for security companies; to date, none has been implemented.

2003
U.S. invasion and occupation of Iraq relies heavily on contractors.

2004
Contractors and military personnel accused of abusing detainees at Baghdad's Abu Ghraib prison. . . . Iraqi insurgents in Fallujah kill four Blackwater employees, hang two bodies from bridge; Marines attack the city in response.

2007
Congress expands situations in which contractors may face military court-martial to times when war is not officially declared. . . . Army-commissioned report says all future missions will demand heavy use of private contractors. . . . Blackwater guards charged with manslaughter in connection with deaths of 17 Iraqi civilians in Baghdad's Nisour Square. . . . Responding to congressional inquiries, Pentagon collects and releases data on contractor totals and costs.

2008
United States and 16 other countries sign nonbinding Montreux Document affirming their obligation to protect human rights when using armed contractors.

2010
Contractor deaths in Iraq and Afghanistan in 2010 exceed service-member deaths for first time. . . . Security contractors provide disaster assistance after Haitian earthquake. . . . Pentagon conducts 7,390 contract audits, down from 26,623 in 2004, but says the audits are much more thorough. . . . Afghan President Hamid Karzai declares that a government-controlled Afghan Public Protection Force will replace most armed contractors; shift delayed until 2012.

2011
Congressionally chartered Commission on Wartime Contracting concludes that the government over-relies on contractors. . . . Contractors make up at least 45 percent of Pentagon's Iraq/Afghanistan workforce. . . . U.S. military leaves Iraq, replaced by 15,000 U.S. embassy staff members and 5,000 private security contractors. . . . New government database on contractors includes lawsuit and contract-suspension data.

2012
Supreme Court rules that 2007 Nisour Square shooting case must proceed to trial. . . . Pentagon disburses more than $3 billion in drug war-related contracts. . . . Congressional bills introduced to further expand civilian criminal courts' authority over contractors working abroad, stiffen contract oversight and crack down on contractors' abuse of workers. . . . More than 400 security contractors have signed an International Code of Conduct based on the Montreux Document, but companies, governments and groups representing the public struggle to agree on enforcement procedures.

Setting Standards for Security Contractors

New code of conduct sparks many disagreements.

Differences among nations make it difficult to devise international rules on the use of private security forces. And countries that, until recently, were subjugated colonies are especially fearful that stronger nations can use hired force to make it even easier to impose their wills.

Not surprisingly, George Washington viewed "hired guns" with suspicion, having fought against mercenaries in the Revolutionary War. "Mercenary armies . . . have at one time or another subverted the liberties of almost all the countries they have been raised to defend," the first president said. [1] By the mid-20th century, though, American leaders' views had changed.

The United Nations has always worried that armed contractors could threaten "people's right to self-determination," said José L. Gomez del Prado, former chairman of the U.N. Working Group on the Use of Mercenaries. [2]

Beginning in 1989, the U.N. circulated a treaty to ban mercenary activity. It took effect in 2001 with 20 nations ratifying. The United States and other highly industrialized countries did not sign, however. [3] The United States believed that "we could regulate the companies ourselves, in our own interests," says Deborah Avant, a professor of international security and diplomacy at the University of Denver.

By the mid-2000s, many security contractors were large businesses interested in winning clients by demonstrating professionalism. "The more corporate a company is, the bigger stake they have in showing they're legitimate," says Molly Dunigan, an associate political scientist at RAND, a think tank with offices around the world.

At the same time, the Iraq and Afghanistan wars had led to high-profile reports of alleged human rights abuses by contractors, including unprovoked shootings of civilians. To many, the time seemed ripe to go beyond the traditional U.N. treaty process — in which governments agree to abide by and enforce certain rules — and create a regulatory system devised by security companies themselves in concert with governments, other potential clients such as multinational corporations, and representatives of the public.

Contracting is "a market," says Avant, "so you can accomplish things by changing the way people buy" and "changing the profit equation for companies" so that the most responsible get the most business.

To start, the Swiss government and International Committee of the Red Cross led development of the Montreux Document — a non-legally binding pledge by governments that contractors they hire or that are based in or work in their countries comply with human-rights standards. In September 2008, 17 countries including the United States, the United Kingdom and China announced that they had signed. (Forty-one governments are signatories today.) [4]

Then governments, security companies and so-called civil-society participants representing the interests of the public — such as universities and human-rights organizations — developed an International Code of Conduct (ICOC) for security contractors.

"We're proud of the code" and its "very detailed" statement of companies' responsibilities for fulfilling Montreux Document principles, says Meg Roggensack, senior adviser for the Business and Human Rights Initiative at Human Rights First, a Washington-based nonpartisan advocacy group, and a member of the committee drafting an implementation mechanism for the code. "It represents a real breakthrough."

The toughest job is now under way — creating a credible system to monitor compliance and help people who allege violations by a company to have their complaints resolved through that company's formal grievance mechanism.

Unless an "independent, credible oversight mechanism" is created, the ICOC would remain "just a fig leaf" that unscrupulous

Continued from p. 606

"when serving as the king's wartime privateers," wrote Janice E. Thomson, a retired professor of political science at the University of Washington. [37]

Warfare as business grew steadily larger and by the 17th century had become the "biggest industry in Europe," according to Singer. "European armies of the period often were simple amalgamations of hired mercenary companies, all with their own specialties." Eastern Europeans and Greeks were cavalry specialists, and the Swiss wielded pikes. "'Patriotism' was a meaningless concept to the average soldier," in stark contrast to the strong nationalistic commitment that is a hallmark of modern armies, Singer noted. [38]

During that period, a "new class of military entrepreneurs . . . recruited and equipped military units at their own cost" and leased them to rulers. [39] In addition, countries such as Britain and the Netherlands granted monopolies in international trade to shareholder-owned "mercantile companies" such as the English East India Company. Empowered to develop and manage foreign trade — between India and Europe, for example — the companies received royal permission to conquer territories, make treaties and engage in combat to ensure that the country to which they were bound by contract dominated trade along a designated route.

Rise of States

Some thinkers doubted the wisdom of relying on private armies. In Florence, Italy, political philosopher Nicoló Machiavelli (1469-1527) — author of the influential political treatise *The*

contractors and those who hire them could hide behind, knowing that violations would have no real consequences, says James Cockayne, co-director of the Center on Global Counterterrorism Cooperation, a New York-based policy group.

Early this year, a draft plan was released for comment. Responses revealed numerous disagreements over issues such as the balance of power between contractors and other stakeholders, the degree of confidentiality provided for allegations of wrongdoing and the procedures for dealing with companies that don't quickly remedy their violations. In June, negotiators said they aim for a revised version by year's end. [5]

Such disagreements are no surprise, says Sylvia White, general counsel and board director of the London-based security company Aegis and a member of the drafting panel. A similar process occurred as the code was written, she says. "First, there was lots of interest, then people couldn't necessarily agree on everything, then finally we got a great weight of people agreeing," she says. "I'm hopeful we'll get to that tipping point in the next few months."

White says that the industry is committed to fully implementing the code, partly to end what she calls the widespread misconception "that there are no rules" for how security companies behave.

The enforcement mechanism's feasibility raises questions, however. For example, it's not clear how an industry-funded office to handle grievances could be truly independent, wrote an ex-Marine and security contractor who blogs about security issues under the name "Matt" at his *Feral Jundi* blog. "Isn't it a conflict of interest if a mediator is getting payment by one group in the form of dues/membership fees, and then claiming to help out the other side (the aggrieved) who does not pay dues?" [6]

Strong government commitment is also crucial but not assured, says Laura Dickinson, a research professor of law at George Washington University. "I think the U.S. government should mandate membership [in the ICOC mechanism] before it awards contracts."

Meanwhile, at the Pentagon's request, ASIS International, a membership group for security professionals in Alexandria, Va., has developed business-management standards to help companies conform to the ICOC, says Marc Siegel, commissioner of ASIS's Global Standards Initiative. Companies that sign on will undergo periodic audits to ensure they follow the standards, which stipulate best practices for business functions vital to security contractors, such as accurately evaluating the risks at a job site and hiring staff for jobs that require bearing arms.

"If you're a client hiring a firm for a high-risk environment where people can be hurt and rights violated, it behooves you to look for companies that are well managed," Siegel says.

— Marcia Clemmitt

---

[1] Quoted in Jackson Nyamuya Magogot and Benedict Sheey, "Private Military Companies and International Law: Building New Ladders of Legal Responsibility," *Cardozo Journal of Conflict Resolution*, 2009, Vol. 11, Issue 1, p. 99, http://cojcr.org/vol11no1/index111.html.

[2] José L. Gomez del Prado, "Mercenaries, Private Military and Security Companies and International Law," lecture, University of Wisconsin Law School, Jan. 31, 2008, www.law.wisc.edu/gls/lawwarhumansecurity.html.

[3] *Ibid.*

[4] For background, see Anthony H. Cordesman, "Private Security Forces in Afghanistan and Iraq: The Potential Impact of the Montreux Document," Center for Strategic and International Studies, Nov. 17, 2010, http://csis.org/files/publication/10115_Private_Security_Forces_Afghanistan_Iraq.pdf, and "Participating States of the Montreux Document," Federal Department of Foreign Affairs, web site of the government of Switzerland, www.eda.admin.ch/eda/en/home/topics/intla/humlaw/pse/parsta.html.

[5] Minutes, TSC Meeting, June 5-7, 2012 in Washington, U.S., International Code of Conduct web site, www.icoc-psp.org/uploads/Minutes_TSC_Meeting_5-7_June_2012_Washington_DC.pdf.

[6] Industry Talk: So What IS Going on With the ICoC, *Feral Jundi* blog, Oct. 4, 2011, http://feraljundi.com/3643/industry-talk-so-what-is-going-on-with-the-icoc.

Prince — warned that private armies, by definition, are disloyal. "Mercenary commanders are either skilled in warfare or they are not," Machiavelli wrote. "If they are, you cannot trust them because they are anxious to advance their own greatness by coercing you, their employer. If, however, the commander is lacking in prowess, as often as not, he brings about your ruin." [40]

While mercenary warfare persisted — and even expanded — during the 17th century, the era also saw technological and political trends that decreased mercenaries' dominance.

The Thirty Years War (1618-1648) destroyed towns across Europe, caused famines and drove rulers into bankruptcy as two powerful imperial families — the Hapsburgs and the Bourbons — fought each other and numerous regional opponents, such as the Germans, to control huge swaths of the continent. So damaging was the war that, in the end, "the only conceivable resolution" was to abandon the struggle for imperial power that had dominated European politics to that point and "let each nation decide its own internal matters," wrote Singer.

This principle was enshrined in the Peace of Westphalia treaties that ended the fighting. Afterward, freelancing mercenary armies "began to be replaced by standing state armies made up of citizens" who defended their own borders, he wrote. "The wars of kings finally evolve[d] into the wars of people." [41]

As guns and cannons replaced swords and pikes, combat skills mattered less than sheer numbers of soldiers, another trend that favored temporary conscription of citizens over hiring mercenaries. Furthermore, during

Continued on p. 611

Contracting Takes Unacknowledged Human Toll

"Everyone believes we're underreporting contractor deaths."

As the number of private security companies swells, the death and injury toll for contractors continues to rise, and other contracting-associated problems also are coming to the fore, such as mistreatment of contract workers by the companies who hire them or by labor recruiters.

At least 430 employees of American contractors were killed in Afghanistan in 2011, versus 418 U.S. service members. [1] And the contractor death toll is likely much higher. Until about four years ago, the Department of Defense collected little data of any kind on security companies, including information on contractor deaths. The most reliable mortality data come from the Labor Department, which tallies contractors for whom insurance claims are submitted under a compensation program for federal workers. [2]

"No one believes we're underreporting military deaths. Everyone believes we're underreporting contractor deaths," said Steven L. Schooner, a law professor at George Washington University, in Washington. [3]

The silence surrounding the deaths is disrespectful to the dead and harmful to democracy, argues Schooner. "An honest, accurate tally is important for the public and the nation's elected leaders to understand the true human toll" of wars, in order to reckon their true costs and benefits, he wrote. [4]

The high potential for death is not the only threat facing contractors. Many suffer from traumatic brain injury, post-traumatic stress disorder and other post-service conditions that also plague military personnel. But unlike service members, contractors are ineligible for veterans' care, so their conditions are even more likely to go untreated than those of service personnel.

In addition, contractors have virtually no job security. In hiring private companies, government can quickly staff up for an emergency mission and just as quickly lay off workers when the mission is over. Thus contractors must cope with short-term, unpredictable employment.

Furthermore, while some contractors are covered by health and life insurance while on a job, "coverage usually lapses when they change jobs or return home," says the U.S. Institute of Peace, a congressionally authorized, nonpartisan federal institution that studies and seeks to end armed conflicts. [5]

"There's a moral obligation that's being overlooked. Can the government really send people to a war zone and neglect [its] responsibility to attend to their emotional needs after the fact?" asked Paul Brand, CEO of Mission Critical Psychological Services, a Chicago company that counsels civilians who work in war zones. [6]

Also facing potential hazards are foreign nationals recruited by private companies under contract with the U.S. government to work in Iraq and Afghanistan. Many companies have been caught running bait-and-switch schemes in which workers are promised good salaries, only to face much lower pay, bad living conditions, disrespect, mistreatment and sometimes virtual imprisonment.

In one incident, 35 former Colombian soldiers were flown to Baghdad on the promise of being paid $4,000 a month to work for Virginia-based Blackwater (now Academi). The men were recruited by Colombia-based ID Systems S.A., a Blackwater subcontractor, and by the time they arrived, ID Systems allegedly had cut the wage to $1,000 per month. When the men protested, their tickets home were taken away, and they were told they'd have to find their own way back. [7]

In December 2008, a group of South Asian workers staged protests of their treatment by Kuwait-based Najlaa International Catering Services, a subcontractor to Houston-based KBR, one of the largest Pentagon contractors. After promising jobs to about 1,000 workers, Najlaa held the workers upon their arrival and denied them work or pay for months. [8]

The U.S. government already had a "zero tolerance" policy on such abuses at the time of the 2008 protests by the Najlaa workers, but its commitment to that policy is suspect, charges the Project on Government Oversight (POGO), a Washington-based government-watchdog group. "The U.S. has directly awarded contracts to Najlaa after the . . . protests, including one contract that lasts through 2012," POGO analysts said. [9]

— Marcia Clemmitt

---

[1] Rod Nordland, "Risks of Afghan War Shift from Soldiers to Contractors," *The New York Times*, Feb. 11, 2012, www.nytimes.com/2012/02/12/world/asia/afghan-war-risks-are-shifting-to-contractors.html.

[2] Steven L. Schooner and Collin D. Swan, "Contractors and the Ultimate Sacrifice," *Service Contractor*, September 2010, p. 16, http://papers.ssrn.com/sol3/papers.cfm?abstract_id=1677506.

[3] Quoted in Nordland, *op. cit.*

[4] Schooner and Swan, *op. cit.*, p. 18.

[5] Robert Perito, "The Private Sector in Security Sector Reform," U.S. Institute of Peace, January 2009, www.usip.org/files/resources/USIP_0109.PDF.

[6] T. Christian Miller, "The Other Victims of Battlefield Stress; Defense Contractors' Mental Health Neglected," *ProPublica*, Feb. 26, 2010, www.propublica.org/article/injured-contractors-the-other-victims-of-battlefield-stress-224.

[7] Emily Speers Mears, "Security Privatisation in the Middle East," Global Consortium on Security Transformation," November 2010, p. 7; Peter Krupa, "Vote Tallying Company Also Hired Blackwater Mercenaries," *Lat/Am Daily* blog, March 21, 2010, www.latamdaily.com/2010/03/21/olombian-vote-tallying-company-also-hired-blackwater-mercenaries; "Atrapados en Bagdad," *Semana.com*, Aug. 19, 2006, www.semana.com/nacion/atrapados-bagdad/96550-3.aspx.

[8] David Isenberg and Nick Schwellenbach, "Documents Reveal Details of Alleged Labor Trafficking by KBR Subcontractor," Project on Government Oversight blog, June 14, 2011, http://pogoblog.typepad.com/pogo/2011/06/documents-reveal-details-of-alleged-labor-trafficking-by-kbr-subcontractor.html.

[9] *Ibid.*

Continued from p. 608

the Enlightenment of the 17th and 18th centuries the idea arose that a "social contract" bound rulers and their people in a relationship of mutual responsibilities, rights and duties. As citizens, people were more willing to fight for their countries than when most were mere subjects of all-powerful emperors. In addition, citizens were increasingly viewed as representatives of their home state, leading governments to bar their citizens from fighting abroad, since rulers might be held responsible for harms they inflicted. [42]

Thus, a new norm arose in which governments were considered to hold a "monopoly" on violence, and mercenary fighting became less common.

Weak governments and governments fighting abroad continued to hire some contract soldiers, however. Great Britain famously employed Hessians — troops hailing mainly from the German state of Hesse — to fight against the colonists during the American Revolution.

And while the United States relied mainly on a citizen army during its foreign wars of the 19th and 20th centuries, it gradually expanded the tasks assigned to private companies, from maintaining weaponry to training foreign militaries, such as occurred during the Vietnam War in the 1960s.

Turning Points

In the late 1980s, when the Soviet Union collapsed and the half-century Cold War ended, both the supply of and demand for private military contractors increased.

Many long-simmering power struggles began boiling over in regions once controlled by the Soviets, as independence movements grew and small nations once allied with either the United States or Soviet Union fended off threats. Such conflicts provided new markets for mercenaries. At the same time, mining companies and other international corporations and nonprofit organizations such as environmental groups hired private security personnel to protect staff members working in the unstable states.

In 1995, the government of Sierra Leone, in West Africa, hired several hundred troops from a South Africa-based mercenary company — Executive Outcomes — to put down a four-year-long civil war that government forces were too weak to stop. Executive Outcomes hit rebel forces with precision air and ground attacks, driving them away from the capital and the diamond fields that provided the government with its funding.

During the Cold War, the U.S. government could generally count on public support for military operations abroad, on the grounds that the Soviet Union posed a serious national threat. When that threat vanished, however, making the case for sending troops into armed conflicts or on humanitarian missions grew more difficult. Private contractors increasingly enabled the U.S. government to conduct such operations, however, especially as the supply of potential contractors grew during the past two decades.

In recent years, contractors have come from many countries, but in the 1990s most came from three sources: South Africa, Russia and the other countries that had made up the Soviet Union, and the United States and its allies, such as Australia.

As the United States and the former Soviet Union countries downsized their militaries after the Cold War, thousands of service members searched for jobs, helping to fuel the growth of security-contracting firms. At the same time, South Africa ended apartheid, its brutal racial segregation policy. From the country's large, newly unemployed army of white government security forces arose powerful armed private contractors, such as Executive Outcomes.

With this workforce available, the U.S. government could contract with private security companies to conduct missions abroad — or simply introduce foreign leaders to companies that they might hire. The Clinton administration likely did both as it engineered a series of arms-length interventions in civil and ethnic violence that raged in the Balkan states in the 1990s.

In the mid-1990s, Virginia-based MPRI — Military Professional Resources Inc., (now L-3 MPRI) — provided consulting services under contract to the fledgling state of Croatia that may have included military training and possibly military strategizing. Croatia had declared independence from the former Soviet-allied Yugoslavia at the end of the Cold War. But it faced armed resistance from a Serbian ethnic minority hoping to push Croatia to rejoin Serb-dominated Yugoslavia.

As Croatia's military foundered, ethnic strife left hundreds of thousands dead and millions homeless. But in 1995, the Croats suddenly launched a highly professional strike that quickly ended that phase of the fighting. Many observers argue that there's no way to explain the Croat army's quick transformation without ascribing it to military training from L-3 MPRI. The U.S. government did not hire L-3 MPRI but reportedly brought Croat leaders together with the company, whose founders and staff have included scores of retired top military officers, including a former U.S. Army chief of staff. [43]

"According to European military officers who witnessed the attack, the initial Croatian river crossing into Serb-held territory was a 'textbook U.S. field manual river crossing. The only difference was the troops were Croats,' " wrote Brookings' Singer. [44]

L-3 MPRI, however, says it provided only business-management training. "We don't teach . . . battlefield skills . . . We didn't teach that in Croatia," said Lt. Gen. Ed Soyster, an L-3 MPRI vice president and retired chief of the Defense Intelligence Agency. "We teach general management, . . . planning, programming, . . . budgeting." [45]

Over the past 20 years, a new philosophy of government that advocates privatizing as many jobs as possible has bolstered contracting. A congressionally mandated periodic review of Pentagon priorities declared in 2001 that "only those functions that must be performed by [the Department of Defense] should be kept by DOD. Any function that can be provided by the private sector is not a core government function." [46]

Furthermore, armed security contractors do not work only for governments. As the supply of contractors has grown, multinational corporations have increasingly hired the companies to act as militarily trained, sometimes heavily armed private police forces, protecting mines and other such operations. In some cases, severe human-rights abuses by contractors are alleged. In July 2011, for example, the London- and Hong Kong-based mining company Monterrico Metals paid damages but did not admit liability to settle a lawsuit brought by Peruvian environmental protesters, who alleged that contractors tortured and sexually assaulted them. [47]

New Era

While private security contracting grew during the 1990s, the 2003 Iraq invasion marked a new era, according to analysts at RAND. Before that, while the military hired contractors aplenty, "*armed* contractors had rarely been used in a [U.S.] war zone," they said. [48]

Since the Iraq invasion, the use of contractors has burgeoned, though the Pentagon did not begin gathering and releasing contractor data until the second half of 2007. It says that because of the difficulty of counting subcontractors, all its tallies are estimates. [49]

As of March 2011, DOD counted approximately 155,000 contractors in Afghanistan and Iraq combined, making up slightly more than half of the Defense Department's workforce. [50] In Iraq, 10,448 contractors — 16 percent of the total contracting force — were armed security personnel. [51] Out of the 90,000 contractors Defense counted in Afghanistan, about 20,000 were U.S. citizens, 46,000 were Afghans and 24,000 came from other countries. [52]

While contractors were once hired mainly for support services, such as running food service operations for the military, they have taken on duties closer to core military missions in the Middle East. When a 2010 drone strike killed 15 civilians and injured a dozen more in central Afghanistan, for example, Air Force investigators found that although military personnel operated the drone and made the decision to fire, that "decision was largely based upon intelligence analysis . . . conducted and reported by a civilian contractor," wrote Capt. Keric Clanahan, an Air Force lawyer. [53]

Public awareness of contractors has come mostly from periodic high-profile incidents of alleged misbehavior.

In 1999, the Army asked Falls Church, Va.-based DynCorp International to oust five employees from Bosnia, in the Balkans, after the men were accused of purchasing female sex slaves, some as young as 12, from an organized-crime group and employing them in a prostitution ring. Ultimately, however, neither the U.S. military nor Bosnian police claimed jurisdiction to prosecute, and none of the accused was charged. One worker admitted guilt and left the company. DynCorp fired two whistleblowers who had reported the behavior and moved most of the accused to jobs in other countries. [54]

The incidents demonstrated that DynCorp didn't effectively screen, monitor or discipline employees and may have turned a blind eye to human-rights violations, said independent military analyst Isenberg. But the company "was not particularly hurt by the scandal" and continued to receive security contracts from the United States, Great Britain and others, he said. [55]

In 2009, workers from Arlington, Va.-based ArmorGroup North America — under contract to guard the American Embassy in Kabul — reported misbehavior by coworkers that included illegal brothel visits and sexual hazing of other guards. In one incident, guards hid in abandoned buildings at night, dressed as Afghans and carried illicitly borrowed embassy equipment such as night goggles, apparently acting out a fantasy "reconnaissance mission." [56]

In 2009, the State Department announced it would not renew ArmorGroup's embassy contract, but allegations of wrongdoing by another contractor picked for the job caused repeated delays in the handover. In 2011 ArmorGroup paid the government $7.5 million to settle some charges arising from the incidents. [57] The contract was eventually awarded to London- and Virginia-based Aegis. [58]

In August 2011, the congressionally chartered Commission on Wartime Contracting reported that heavy use of contractors has dangerously diminished the knowledge base within federal agencies and overwhelmed inadequately staffed oversight offices. The government "has come to over-rely" on private companies and should restrict the use of armed contractors, the panel concluded. [59] ■

CURRENT SITUATION

New Jobs

As military contracting continues, Congress and a range of international groups, as well as security

Continued on p. 614

At Issue:

Should Congress increase oversight of private contractors?

LAWRENCE J. KORB
SENIOR FELLOW, CENTER FOR AMERICAN PROGRESS ACTION FUND

FROM A STATEMENT FOR THE RECORD, SENATE HOMELAND SECURITY AND GOVERNMENTAL AFFAIRS COMMITTEE, CONTRACTING OVERSIGHT SUBCOMMITTEE, APRIL 17, 2012

yes

If the U.S. is to protect its vital national interests in a cost-effective manner, the Congress must pass and the president should sign S 2139, the Comprehensive Contingency Contracting Reform Act of 2012, as soon as possible. [The law would increase contract oversight at the Defense and State departments and the U.S. Agency for International Development and require automatic suspension of contractors charged with contracting fraud.] If we do not act expeditiously, we will continue to needlessly squander blood and treasure and undermine our image in current and future conflicts. . . .

S 2139 addresses most of the . . . problems identified by the Commission on Wartime Contracting in Iraq and Afghanistan.

This legislation is necessary because officials in the executive branch have shown that they are unable or unwilling to implement most of the commission's recommendations. If S 2139 is not passed, large amounts of appropriated money will continue to be wasted: In Iraq and Afghanistan at least $31 billion and possibly as much as $61 billion of $200 billion appropriated to contracts has been lost to contractor fraud and waste. Additionally, if S 2139 does not pass, contractors will continue to perform activities that are inherently governmental, thus frequently undermining the mission.

Title I deals with the organization and management of the federal government for contracting for overseas contingency operations. The first title mandates the president [to] include information and the director of the Office of Management and Budget [to] provide the Congress with details of why Overseas Contingency Operations (OCO) funds are needed and subsequently report in detail on how those funds were spent. Hopefully these provisions will limit the various agencies' tendency, exploited in particularly egregious fashion by the Department of Defense, to transfer items more appropriately included in the core budgets into the OCO accounts to hide budget growth and cost overruns. . . .

Title II focuses on transparency, sustainability and accountability. It demands that, unless there is a waiver granted, contracts should be limited to three years for competitively bid contracts and one year for noncompetitive contracts; that contracts have only a single tier of subcontractors; and that the secretaries of State and Defense perform an annual review to determine for which functions it is appropriate to use contractors.

STAN SOLOWAY
PRESIDENT AND CEO, PROFESSIONAL SERVICES COUNCIL

FROM A STATEMENT FOR THE RECORD, SENATE HOMELAND SECURITY AND GOVERNMENTAL AFFAIRS COMMITTEE, CONTRACTING OVERSIGHT SUBCOMMITTEE, APRIL 17, 2012

no

The Comprehensive Contingency Contracting Reform Act of 2012, S 2139, contains some valuable and thoughtful proposals that can enhance future operations. At the same time, we also feel strongly that several provisions in the bill would have precisely the opposite effect.

As various reports have indicated, despite well-documented instances of malfeasance, the vast majority of the challenges and problems in both Iraq and Afghanistan have not been driven by fraud and abuse. Rather, the "waste" that has occurred has been predominantly driven by poor planning, a lack of coordination, and workforce gaps.

What is also clear is that contracting varies significantly based on the nature of the operation. What worked in Iraq and Afghanistan may not be appropriate for operations in East Timor or Haiti. Congress should be careful to avoid legislating for the last contingency and limiting agencies' or contractors' flexibility to respond rapidly to the U.S. government's mission needs.

[The Professional Services Council] strongly opposes Section 113 as currently written. In effect, the provision amounts to a "suspend first, ask questions later" policy that tramples on the due-process rights that all citizens and companies are entitled to. The current Federal Acquisition Regulation (FAR) already allows government suspension and debarment officials (SDO) to take appropriate and immediate actions to suspend a contractor for a broad array of inappropriate behaviors. . . .

The Professional Services Council (PSC) supports initiatives to prevent trafficking in persons, and Section 222 may be helpful. Unfortunately, Section 222 also places excessive requirements on contractors. While contractors may be able to implement prevention and monitoring procedures, it is impossible for them to "certify" with absolute certainty that none of their employees, subcontractors, or recruiters or brokers have engaged in any such activity.

PSC is a strong supporter of the current structure for evaluating contractor past performance. One critical element of the current process is that contractors shall be provided with completed evaluations as soon as practicable; given an opportunity to submit comments or provide additional information; and entitled to an evaluation review at one level above the contracting officer. Section 224 would universally do away with these important protections. Contractors would be left with little recourse for actions taken by an individual contracting officer that posted an unsupported or improper negative past performance evaluation.

Continued from p. 612

companies themselves, are mulling new regulatory mechanisms. But whether rules will be tightened remains unclear. (*See sidebar, p. 608.*)

The U.S. military left Iraq in 2011, and a U.S. Embassy staff of about 15,000 is taking its place in efforts to rebuild the war-ravaged nation. Up to 5,000 armed contractors are assisting the diplomats, driving armored transports and providing protective air cover from armed helicopters. [60]

Afghan President Hamid Karzai announced in 2010 that all armed contractors except those protecting diplomats would be replaced by the central-government-controlled bodyguard group called the Afghan Public Protection Force (APPF). Karzai charged that private contractors cost too much and encourage bribery, nepotism and other corruption. The changeover date has repeatedly slipped as the APPF proved hard to assemble, train and fund. But a gradual phase-in of the public force finally began this spring. [61]

That doesn't necessarily mean that the number of security contractors is on the wane, however. New clients and new kinds of work are emerging.

The Pentagon is rapidly expanding the use of contractors to combat drug trafficking, which it increasingly calls a national-security threat equivalent to terrorism. This year, the Counter Narco-Terrorism Program Office will hand out more than $3 billion in contracts for jobs such as providing helicopter training for Mexico's public-security forces, operating drones and helping governments with surveillance tasks such as analyzing media to spot hidden trends. [62]

Getty Images/Danny La

Former Blackwater guard Paul Slough leaves federal court in Salt Lake City, Utah, with his wife on Dec. 8, 2008. He is among four of the security firm's guards charged with manslaughter in connection with the shooting of 17 unarmed Iraqi civilians in Baghdad in 2007. The guards used machine guns and grenade launchers against the civilians, some with their hands up, federal prosecutors alleged. Blackwater (now Academi) said the guards returned fire after they were ambushed by insurgents while responding to a car bombing.

In the past, nonprofit groups that act as human-rights watchdogs have not hired armed contractors, saying they wanted to avoid compromising their neutrality. Recently, however, violent incidents reportedly have led even staunchly anti-mercenary organizations, including the International Red Cross and Doctors Without Borders, to hire armed guards. [63]

Congressional Action

Even as security contractors proliferate, their legal status remains "opaque," wrote analysts at RAND. "A number of both international and domestic U.S. laws are arguably applicable to private contractors in war zones," but all are difficult to apply with confidence, they wrote. Among other problems, "There is currently no standard formula for prosecuting contractors who come from one country, operate in another country, and work for a firm based in a third country." [64]

Up for consideration in 2012 are congressional proposals first introduced five years ago to expand civilian courts' jurisdiction over contractors working abroad for federal agencies, even when no military mission is occurring there. Current versions of the bills — sponsored by Rep. David Price, D-N.C., and Sen. Patrick Leahy, D-Vt. — would apply to contractors who work abroad for any federal agency, as well as to their dependents, and include federal offenses such as assault, murder, drug or human trafficking, corruption-related crimes such as bribery and treason-related crimes such as providing support to terrorists. [65]

In March, bipartisan bills were introduced in both houses of Congress to crack down on abusive labor practices by contractors, such as seizing workers' passports to trap them in a low-paying or abusive job. The bills would require companies with contracts worth $1 million or more to implement plans to prevent worker abuse and authorize the government to suspend contracts for violations. [66]

The Comprehensive Contingency Contractors Reform Act of 2012, introduced by Democratic Sens. Claire McCaskill of Missouri and Jim Webb of Virginia, would increase contract oversight at DOD, the State Department and USAID and require automatic suspension of contractors charged with contracting fraud. [67]

Meanwhile, the federal Court of Appeals for the Armed Forces is reviewing the constitutionality of the military's expanded authority to prosecute under the Uniform Code of Military Justice (UCMJ), amended by Congress in 2007.

Military courts give the accused fewer rights than do civilian courts — no juries or bail exist, for example — because warfare requires a strictly disciplined force that carries out a mission without deviation. Critics say subjecting civilians to military court jurisdiction is troublesome. It could unduly blur "the line between military and civilian authority — a very real concern of the [country's] Founders" that is evident in both the Declaration of Independence and the Constitution, wrote Stephen Vladeck, a professor at American University's Washington College of Law. [68]

The key question is whether the UCMJ's expansion might subject civilians to harsh military discipline even in nonwar situations that the president or Congress might designate a "national emergency," he said. [69]

But while academics and some courts debate big-picture questions, few officials in the upper hierarchies of government are doing so, argues Hammes, the retired Marine colonel. "I don't think there is a serious discussion at the power centers" such as Congress or the White House, he says.

The law that created the Commission on Wartime Contracting, for example, explicitly limited what the panel could investigate to issues of contract oversight. Congress thereby effectively banned the panel from exploring such questions as whether contractor use might make it too easy for presidents to start wars without public consent or make it harder for officers in the field to command and control a mixed public-private force, he says. ■

OUTLOOK

Regulated or Unregulated?

As the market for armed security expands, the debate over how effectively contractors can be regulated is likely to grow. More than 360 contractors have signed onto the International Code of Conduct for Private Security Service Providers (ICOC), which was completed in late 2010, says Brooks of the International Stability Operations Association. Now representatives of several of the largest companies, governments including those of the United States and the United Kingdom, and other groups, such as nonprofit human-rights watchdog organizations, are working to create an enforcement mechanism. Public comments on a first draft revealed widely varying views of how the mechanism should work, however.

Completion must not be long delayed, warns James Cockayne, co-director of the Center on Global Counterterrorism Cooperation, a New York-based policy group. Otherwise, he argues, public-interest groups will grow "skeptical over whether governments and companies are truly committed to effective international oversight," and contractors may decide that, if governments aren't fully committed, it's not imperative for the industry either.

Failure to fully implement the ICOC would have serious consequences for the U.S. government, which has been a leading participant, Cockayne says. For one thing, he says, "it will give ammunition to countries — especially Cuba — who have long argued that the ICOC will not work and that an international treaty" — rather than a public-private partnership — "is needed to regulate this industry." A collapse of the ICOC would also cast doubt on the future of other U.S.-backed public-private efforts to commit international businesses to human-rights protections, such as worldwide fair labor practices, Cockayne says.

Despite missing an initial, ambitious deadline, however, the ICOC process has strong momentum, says Mark DeWitt, vice president and deputy general counsel of Triple Canopy, a Reston, Va.-based security company, and chair of the enforcement-mechanism drafting panel.

"Now that we've homed in on the main issues" that must be addressed to get buy-in from the stakeholding groups, "it's better to be careful and do it right" than to rush, says DeWitt. "We've gotten to the point of having to talk about and build bridges on the really hard issues. I'd say we're going in the opposite direction from losing credibility."

The ICOC may provide a basis for additional oversight, DeWitt says. For example, he says, a U.N. treaty "could be built on top of multi-stakeholder efforts like this." The U.N.'s working group on mercenaries seems to be seriously considering such an effort, DeWitt says.

Eventually, hiring security companies that fully embrace the code will become the norm, not just for governments but for nongovernmental buyers, such as international corporations that hire contractors to protect mining operations, for example, predicts Sylvia White, general counsel and board director of Aegis, a London-based security company. When the code is fully operational, hiring companies that operate outside it "would be embarrassing for them," she says.

Others are leery about how privatization of government services will affect the military itself. Joining the service has long been viewed as a commitment to professionalism and the upholding of public values, says Jon Michaels, an acting professor of law at the University of California, Los Angeles. As more positions become jobs-for-hire — and pay more than government service itself — "there's a danger that people will stop thinking of [service positions] as careers and start thinking of them as just the credential you need before you can become a contractor." ■

Notes

[1] Quoted in Craig Whitlock, "Contractors Run U.S. Spying Missions in Africa," *The Washington Post*, June 14, 2012, www.washingtonpost.com/world/national-security/contractors-run-us-spying-missions-in-africa/2012/06/14/gJQAvC4RdV_story.html.

[2] Quoted in *ibid.*

[3] Quoted in *ibid.*

[4] Moshe Schwartz and Joyprada Swain, "Department of Defense Contractors in Afghanistan and Iraq: Background and Analysis," Congressional Research Service, May 13, 2011, p. 6, www.fas.org/sgp/crs/natsec/R40764.pdf.

[5] *Ibid.*, p. 16.

[6] Sarah K. Cotton, *et al.*, "Hired Guns: Views About Armed Contractors in Operation Iraqi Freedom," RAND, 2010, p. 11, www.rand.org/pubs/monographs/MG987.html.

[7] Quoted in Tom Bowman, "No U.S. Troops, But an Army of Contractors in Iraq," NPR, Dec. 27, 2011, www.npr.org/2011/12/27/144198497/no-u-s-troops-but-an-army-of-contractors-in-iraq.

[8] Quoted in "Private Warriors," Frontline, PBS, July 2005, www.pbs.org/wgbh/pages/frontline/shows/warriors/interviews/schooner.html.

[9] *Ibid.*

[10] Laura A. Dickinson, *Outsourcing War and Peace: Preserving Public Values in a World of Privatized Foreign Affairs* (2011), p. 19.

[11] Cotton, *op. cit.*, p. 15.

[12] James Vicini, "Supreme Court Rejects Blackwater Iraq Shooting Appeal," Reuters, June 4, 2012, www.reuters.com/article/2012/06/04/us-usa-iraq-blackwater-idUSBRE8530KB20120604.

[13] David Isenberg, "Shadow Force: Private Security Contractors in Iraq," Feb. 16, 2009, www.cato.org/publications/speeches/shadow-force-private-security-contractors-iraq.

[14] Anna Leander, "The Market for Force and Public Security: The Destabilizing Consequences of Private Military Companies," *Journal of Peace Research*, September 2005, p. 605, http://jpr.sagepub.com/content/42/5/605.abstract; Anna Leander and Rens van Muster, "Private Security Contractors in the Debate About Darfur: Reflecting and Reinforcing Neo-Liberal Governmentality," *International Relations*, May 23, 2007, http://ire.sagepub.com/content/21/2/201.short.

[15] Isenberg, *op. cit.*

[16] "Urgent Reform Required: Army Expeditionary Contracting, Commission on Army Acquisition and Program Management and Expeditionary Operations," U.S. Commission on Army Acquisition and Program Management in Expeditionary Operations, 2007, p. 3, www.army.mil/docs/Gansler_Commission_Report_Final_071031.pdf.

[17] T.X. Hammes, testimony before the House Oversight and Government Reform Subcommittee on National Security and Foreign Affairs, June 22, 2010, http://oversight.house.gov/wp-content/uploads/2012/01/20100622Hammes.pdf.

[18] Quoted in. Cotton, *op. cit.*, p. 19.

[19] *Ibid.*, p. 20.

[20] Quoted in Bryan Bender, "From the Pentagon to the Private Sector," *Boston Globe*, Dec. 26, 2010, www.boston.com/news/nation/washington/articles/2010/12/26/defense_firms_lure_retired_generals.

[21] Nominations Before the Senate Armed Services Committee, 110th Congress, First Session, transcript, 2007, www.gpo.gov/fdsys/pkg/CHRG-110shrg42309/html/CHRG-110shrg42309.htm.

[22] Cotton, *op. cit.*, p. 33.

[23] Isenberg, *op. cit.*

[24] "Army Tosses Abu Ghraib Conviction," *USA Today*, Jan. 10, 2008, www.usatoday.com/news/world/2008-01-10-AbuGhraib-me_N.htm; Keith Herting, "Federal Appeals Court Revives Lawsuit Against Abu Ghraib Contractors," *Jurist*, May 13, 2012, http://jurist.org/paperchase/2012/05/federal-appeals-court-revives-lawsuits-against-abu-ghraib-contractors.php.

[25] Cotton, *op. cit.*, p. 28.

[26] For background, see Guy Dinmore and Rebecca Knight, "Kroll to Sell Iraq and Afghan Security Unit," *Financial Times*, Nov. 2, 2006, www.ft.com/intl/cms/s/0/24fa237c-6a13-11db-952e-0000779e2340.html#axzz1xWHZLznq; "Iraq Bomb Blast Killed UK Workers," BBC, Feb. 26, 2007, news.bbc.co.uk/2/hi/uk_news/6397759.stm.

[27] For background, see Thomas J. Billitteri, "Afghanistan Dilemma," *CQ Researcher*, Aug. 7, 2009, updated May 25, 2011.

[28] Cotton, *op. cit.*, p. xiv.

[29] Cotton, *op. cit.*, p. xv.

[30] Quoted in "Private Military Contractors," transcript, "Law Report," ABC Radio National (Australia), Sept. 9, 2008, www.abc.net.au/radionational/programs/lawreport/private-military-contractors/3182656.

[31] Quoted in *ibid.*

[32] For background, see Missye Brickell, "Filling the Criminal Liability Gap for Private Military Contractors Abroad: U.S. v. Slough and the Civilian Extraterritorial Jurisdiction Act of 2010," Legislation and Policy Brief, Spring 2010, http://digitalcommons.wcl.american.edu/cgi/viewcontent.cgi?article=1014&context=lpb.

[33] For background, see Peter W. Singer, Frequently Asked Questions on the UCMJ Change and its Applicability to Private Military Contractors, Brookings Institution website, Jan. 12, 2007, www.brookings.edu/research/opinions/2007/01/12defenseindustry-singer.

[34] For background, see Peter W. Singer, *Corporate Warriors: The Rise of the Privatized Military Industry* (updated edition, 2007).

[35] *Ibid.*, p. 20.

[36] *Ibid.*, p. 29.

[37] Janice E. Thomson, *Pirates, Mercenaries and Sovereigns* (1996), p. 23.

[38] Singer, *op. cit.*, p. 28.

[39] *Ibid.*, p. 29.

[40] Quoted in Singer, *op. cit.*, p. 164.

[41] *Ibid.*, p. 29.

[42] *Ibid.*, pp. 30-31.

[43] Leadership, L-3 MPRI website, www.mpri.com/web/index.php/content/our_company/leadership.

[44] Singer, *op. cit.*, p. 5.

[45] Quoted in David Isenberg, "MPRI Couldn't Read Minds: Let's Sue Them," *Huffington Post*, Aug. 19, 2010, www.huffingtonpost.com/david-isenberg/mpri-couldnt-read-minds-l_b_688000.html.

[46] Quadrennial Defense Review Report, Department of Defense, Sept. 30, 2001, www.defense.gov/pubs/qdr2001.pdf, p. 53.

About the Author

Staff writer **Marcia Clemmitt** is a veteran social-policy reporter who previously served as editor in chief of *Medicine & Health* and staff writer for *The Scientist*. She has also been a high school math and physics teacher. She holds a liberal arts and sciences degree from St. John's College, Annapolis, and a master's degree in English from Georgetown University. Her recent reports include "Internet Regulation" and "U.S.-Pakistan Relations."

[47] *PSMC Bulletin*, Business & Human Rights Resource Centre, Sept. 16, 2011, www.business-humanrights.org/media/documents/pmsc-bulletin-issue-1-16-sep-2011.pdf.
[48] Cotton, *op. cit.*, p. 11.
[49] Schwartz and Swain, *op. cit.*, p. 4.
[50] *Ibid.*, p. 6.
[51] *Ibid.*, p. 16.
[52] *Ibid.*, p. 10.
[53] Keric D. Clanahan, "Drone-Sourcing? United State Air Force Unmanned Aircraft Systems, Inherently Governmental Functions, and the Role of Contractors," *Federal Circuit Bar Journal*, May 4, 2012, http://papers.ssrn.com/sol3/papers.cfm?abstract_id=2051154.
[54] David Isenberg, "Sex and Security in Afghanistan," *Asia Times*, Oct. 6, 2009, http://atimes.com/atimes/South_Asia/KJ06Df03.html.
[55] *Ibid.*
[56] For background, see "POGO Letter to Secretary of State Hillary Clinton Regarding U.S. Embassy in Kabul," Project on Government Oversight website, Sept. 1, 2009, www.pogo.org/pogo-files/letters/contract-oversight/co-gp-20090901.html#clintlett; David Beatson, "Kiwi Connections in Kabul Embassy Scandal," *Pundit* [New Zealand], Dec. 14, 2009, www.pundit.co.nz/content/kiwi-connections-in-kabul-embassy-scandal; and State Department Oversight and Contractor-Employee Conduct, transcript, Commission on Wartime Contracting in Iraq and Afghanistan, Sept. 14, 2009, www.wartimecontracting.gov/images/download/documents/hearings/20090914/CWC_State_Dept_Contractor_Oversight_Transcript_2009-09-14.pdf, p. 29.
[57] "ArmorGroup North American and Its Affiliates Pay $7.5 Million to Remove False Claims Act Allegations," press release, U.S. Department of Justice, July 7, 2011, www.justice.gov/opa/pr/2011/July/11-civ-889.html.
[58] "Audit of the Department of State Process to Award the Worldwide Protective Services Contract and Kabul Embassy Security Force Task Order," Office of Inspector General, U.S. Department of State, December 2011, http://oig.state.gov/documents/organization/180395.pdf.
[59] "Transforming Wartime Contracting: Controlling Costs, Reducing Risks, Commission on Wartime Contracting in Iraq and Afghanistan," Commission on Wartime Contracting in Iraq and Afghanistan, August 2011, www.wartimecontracting.gov.
[60] Tom Bowman, "No U.S. Troops, But an Army of Contractors in Iraq," NPR, Dec. 27, 2011, www.npr.org/2011/12/27/144198497/no-u-s-troops-but-an-army-of-contractors-in-iraq.

FOR MORE INFORMATION

ASIS, 1625 Prince St., Alexandria, VA 22314-2818; 703-519-6200; www.asisonline.org. International membership group for security professionals.

Civilian Contractors in Iraq and Afghanistan, www.americancontractorsiniraq.org. Website run by injured contractors and their families; includes information and commentary on contractor deaths and job-related issues.

Feral Jundi blog, http://feraljundi.com. Provides news and commentary by an ex-Marine and wilderness firefighter who works as a security contractor.

International Code of Conduct for Private Security Service Providers, www.icoc-psp. Website of an international government/security-company/civil-society consortium to create an international regulatory system for activities involving hired security.

International Stability Operations Association, 1634 I St., N.W., Suite 800, Washington, DC 20006; 202-464-7021; http://stability-operations.org. Trade association for companies working in disaster-relief and conflict zones; publishes the *Journal of International Peace Organizations.*

PrivateMilitary.org. Independent website that lists military and security contractors and provides links to academic research and other information.

Private Warriors, "Frontline," PBS website, www.pbs.org/wgbh/pages/frontline/shows/warriors. Website of 2005 television documentary that includes interviews with a range of experts.

Project on Government Oversight/Contract Oversight, 1100 G St., N.W., Suite 500, Washington, DC 20005; 202-347-1122; www.pogo.org/investigations/contract-oversight. Independent government watchdog group.

U.N. Working Group on the Use of Mercenaries, Office of the United Nations High Commissioner for Human Rights (OHCHR), Palais des Nations, CH-1211 Geneva 10, Switzerland; 41-22-917-9220; www.ohchr.org. Monitors mercenary activity and recommends actions to protect human rights in situations involving hired force.

[61] Quil Lawrence, "Afghan Public Protection Force Replaces Contractors," NPR, May 23, 2012, www.npr.org/2012/05/23/153354514/afghan-public-protection-force-profile.
[62] Spencer Ackerman, "Pentagon's War on Drugs Goes Mercenary," Danger Room blog, *Wired*, Nov. 22, 2011, www.wired.com/dangerroom/2011/11/drug-war-mercenary.
[63] Benjamin Perrin, ed., "Private Security Organizations and Humanitarian Organizations: Implications for International Humanitarian Law," *Modern Warfare: Armed Groups, Private Militaries, Humanitarian Organizations* (2012), p. 134.
[64] Cotton, *op. cit.*, p. 15.
[65] Charles Doyle, "Civilian Extraterritorial Jurisdiction Act: Federal Contractor Criminal Liability Overseas," Congressional Research Service, Feb. 15, 2012, www.fas.org/sgp/crs/misc/R42358.pdf. The bills are HR 2136 and S 1145.
[66] Pete Kasperowicz, "GOP, Dems Come Together to Fight Human Trafficking by Contractors in Iraq, Afghanistan," *The Hill*, March 27, 2012, http://thehill.com/blogs/floor-action/house/218353-gop-dems-come-together-to-fight-human-trafficking-by-contractors-in-iraq-afghanistan. The bills are HR 4259 and S 2234.
[67] Neil Gordon and Jake Wiens, "McCaskill, Webb Introduce Wartime Contracting Legislation that Could Save Taxpayers Billions," POGO blog, March 1, 2012, http://pogoblog.typepad.com/pogo/2012/03/mccaskill-webb-introduce-wartime-contracting-legislation-that-could-save-taxpayers-billions.html. The bill is S 2139.
[68] Steve Vladeck, "Can the Military Court-Martial Civilian Contractors?: Reflections on the Oral Argument in the United States v. Ali," *Lawfare blog*, April 12, 2012, www.lawfareblog.com/2012/04/can-the-military-court-martial-civilian-contractors-reflections-on-the-oral-argument-in-united-states-v-ali.
[69] Steve Vladeck, "United States v. Ali and Military Jurisdiction Over Civilians," *Lawfare blog*, Dec. 8, 2011, www.lawfareblog.com/2011/12/united-states-v-ali-and-military-jurisdiction-over-civilians.

Bibliography

Selected Sources

Books

Dickinson, Laura A., *Outsourcing War and Peace: Preserving Public Values in a World of Privatized Foreign Affairs*, Yale University Press, 2011.
A George Washington University law professor contends that increased privatization threatens government accountability and respect for human rights.

Singer, Peter W., *Corporate Warriors: The Rise of the Privatized Military Industry*, Updated Edition, Cornell Studies in Security Affairs, 2007.
A scholar at the centrist Brookings Institution describes the long history of private armed forces.

Articles

"Rise in Mercenary Activities Warrants Urgent Attention, Says UN Expert Group," UN News Centre, UN News Service, Nov. 1, 2011, www.un.org/apps/news/story.asp?NewsID=40270&Cr=mercenar&Cr1.
The U.N. working group on mercenaries says contractors are helping governments subvert peaceful protest.

Ackerman, Spencer, "Pentagon's War on Drugs Goes Mercenary," Danger Room blog, *Wired*, Nov. 22, 2011, www.wired.com/dangerroom/2011/11/drug-war-mercenary.
The Pentagon is handing out more than $3 billion this year to hire contractors to fight illegal narcotics around the world.

Bender, Brian, "From the Pentagon to the Private Sector," *Boston Globe*, Dec. 26, 2010, www.boston.com/news/nation/washington/articles/2010/12/26/defense_firms_lure_retired_generals.
As more military officers join private security companies after retiring, questions arise about whether the prospect of lucrative employment sways Pentagon decision-making.

Cockayne, James, and Emily Speers Mears, "Private Military and Security Companies: A Framework for Regulation," International Peace Institute, March 2009, www.ipacademy.org/publication/policy-papers/detail/81-private-military-and-security-companies-a-framework-for-regulation.html.
Current national and international regulation of security companies is flawed.

Isenberg, David, "The Rise of Private Maritime Security Companies," *Huffington Post*, May 29, 2012, www.huffingtonpost.com/david-isenberg/private-military-contractors_b_1548523.html.
An increase in piracy provides opportunities for private security companies and new legal challenges.

Reports and Studies

"Hired Guns: Views About Armed Contractors in Operation Iraqi Freedom," RAND National Security Research Division, 2010, www.rand.org/pubs/monographs/2010/RAND_MG987.pdf.
A survey of service members finds both support for and concern about contractors' impact in conflict zones.

Gomez del Prado, Jose L., "Why Private Military and Security Companies Should Be Regulated," September 2010, http://198.170.85.29/Gomez-del-Prado-article-on-regulation-of-private-and-military-firms-3-Sep-2010.pdf.
A member of the United Nations working group on mercenaries argues for strong oversight of security companies.

Isenberg, David, "Private Military Contractors and U.S. Grand Strategy," International Peace Research Institute, Oslo, 2009, www.cato.org/pubs/articles/isenberg-private%20military-contractors-2009.pdf.
An independent analyst argues that heavy U.S. reliance on contractors encourages a unilateral approach to international crises.

Mears, Emily Speers, *Security Privatisation in the Middle East, Working Paper No. 10*, Global Consortium on Security Transformation, November 2010, www.securitytransformation.org/images/publicaciones/190_Working_Paper_10_-_Security_privatisation_in_the_Middle_East.pdf.
An analyst for a British nonprofit research and advocacy group on international development describes the range of private security operations in the Middle East.

Schooner, Steven L., and Collin D. Swan, "Dead Contractors: The Un-examined Effect of Surrogates on the Public's Casualty Sensitivity," *Journal of National Security Law & Policy*, April 16, 2012, www.jnslp.com/2012/04/16/dead-contractors-the-un-examined-effect-of-surrogates-on-the-publics-casualty-sensitivity.
Analysts from George Washington University Law School argue that by failing to publicize contractor deaths, the U.S. government misleads the public about the costs of war.

Schwartz, Moshe, and Joyprada Swain, "Department of Defense Contractors in Afghanistan and Iraq: Background and Analysis," Congressional Research Service, May 13, 2011, www.fas.org/sgp/crs/natsec/R40764.pdf.
Analysts for Congress' nonpartisan research office describe contractor use in two wars.

Spear, Joanna, "Market Forces: The Political Economy of Private Military Companies," *Fafo*, 2006, www.fafo.no/pub/rapp/531/531.pdf.
A George Washington University professor discusses the history of security contractors as corporate entities.

The Next Step:

Additional Articles from Current Periodicals

Military Contractors

Glanz, James, "Private Armies a Savior and a Menace: U.S. Military is Reliant on Contractors, who Add to Chaos at Every Turn," *International Herald Tribune*, Oct. 25, 2010.
Critics worry that contractors in Iraq now are adding to chaos in the Middle East.

Nordland, Rod, "Risks of Afghan War Shift from Soldiers to Contractors," *The New York Times*, Feb 11, 2012, www.nytimes.com/2012/02/12/world/asia/afghan-war-risks-are-shifting-to-contractors.html.
Concerns about rising contractor deaths are growing.

Nyden, Paul J., "Manchin Questions Military Officials on Contractors," *The Charleston* (W. Va.) *Gazette*, March 10, 2012, www.wvgazette.com/News/201203090208.
A West Virginia senator has called for military officials to cut the number of contractors instead of regular military personnel.

Schmidt, Michael S., "Military Contractors Are Fined over Aid to China," *The New York Times*, June 28, 2012, www.nytimes.com/2012/06/29/business/global/arms-contractor-pleads-guilty-on-china-exports.html.
A Canadian subsidiary of United Technologies Corp. pleaded guilty to helping the Chinese develop the Z-10 attack helicopter.

Whitlock, Craig, "Pentagon Faces New Budget Reality," *The Washington Post*, Jan. 7, 2011, www.washingtonpost.com/wp-dyn/content/article/2011/01/06/AR2011010606646.html.
Defense Secretary Robert Gates has proposed slashing the number of military contractors by a third over three years to comply with Pentagon budget cuts.

Whitlock, Craig, "U.S. Expands Secret Intelligence Operations in Africa," *The Washington Post*, June 13, 2012, www.washingtonpost.com/world/national-security/us-expands-secret-intelligence-operations-in-africa/2012/06/13/gJQAHyvAbV_story.html.
Military contractors in Africa signify the use of special-operations forces all over the world, not just in war zones.

Nation Building

"Five Principles Critical to Successful Nation Building, Finds History and Global Affairs Scholar," Targeted News Service, Sept. 26, 2011, www.utexas.edu/news/2011/09/26/nation-building/.
A history professor at the University of Texas, Austin, analyzes U.S. attempts at nation-building.

"Painfully Slow Drawdown," *The Palm Beach* (Fla.) *Post*, June 23, 2011, www.palmbeachpost.com/news/news/opinion/painfully-slow-drawdown/nLtTq/.
Despite calls for nation-building at home, many still feel too much of the national budget is spent on the military.

Hallow, Ralph Z., "Libya Action has GOP Rethinking Nation-Building," *The Washington Times*, March 27, 2011, www.washingtontimes.com/news/2011/mar/27/libya-action-has-gop-rethinking-nation-building/.
After 10 years of U.S. nation-building in Afghanistan, some Republican leaders are warning against similar policies in Libya.

Contractor Lawsuits

Brooks, Drew, "Families Sue Military Contractor over Soldier Deaths in Afghanistan," *The Fayetteville* (N.C.) *Observer*, July 12, 2011, www.fayobserver.com/articles/2011/07/12/1107794?sac=Home.
The families of two U.S. soldiers killed by a local interpreter are suing the company for which the interpreter worked.

Liptak, Adam, "State Secrets Block Resolution of Contractor's Suit, Justices Say," *The New York Times*, May 24, 2011, www.nytimes.com/2011/05/24/us/24secret.html.
The Supreme Court ruled it could not resolve a multibillion-dollar dispute between the government and military contractors.

Lundberg, Carol, "Blurring the Battle Lines: Plaintiffs Want to Hold Military Contractors Accountable for Abuses at Abu Ghraib Prison," *Michigan Lawyers Weekly*, May 25, 2012, www.milawyersweekly.com/news/2012/05/25/blurring-the-battlelines/.
Former Abu Ghraib detainees have renewed hope that contractors who allegedly humiliated and tortured them will answer for their actions in court.

CITING *CQ RESEARCHER*

Sample formats for citing these reports in a bibliography include the ones listed below. Preferred styles and formats vary, so please check with your instructor or professor.

MLA STYLE

Jost, Kenneth. "Remembering 9/11," CQ Researcher 2 Sept. 2011: 701-732.

APA STYLE

Jost, K. (2011, September 2). Remembering 9/11. *CQ Researcher, 9*, 701-732.

CHICAGO STYLE

Jost, Kenneth. "Remembering 9/11." *CQ Researcher*, September 2, 2011, 701-732.

CQ Researcher

Published by CQ Press, an Imprint of SAGE Publications, Inc.

www.cqresearcher.com

Debt Collectors

Do consumers need additional safeguards?

Lawsuits filed against debt collectors multiplied in recent years, as have complaints to regulators about abusive collection tactics. Indeed, the Federal Trade Commission (FTC) receives more consumer complaints against debt collectors than any other industry. Collection companies, which recover billions of dollars in delinquent debt for creditors annually, defend their practices and challenge the validity of many of the lawsuits and consumer complaints. Nevertheless, over the past 18 months, the FTC and state attorneys general have stepped up enforcement against collection agencies they believe are breaking consumer-protection laws. Meanwhile, the Internal Revenue Service has drafted rules aimed at curbing aggressive collection methods at nonprofit hospitals, including dunning sick patients for payment in the emergency room. At the same time, the collection industry is bracing for tighter regulation from the newly created Consumer Financial Protection Bureau.

Lung transplant recipient Tom Fuller testifies at a public hearing in St. Paul, Minn., on May 30, 2012, about high-pressure debt collection at a Fairview Health Services hospital. A scathing report by Minnesota's attorney general documents tactics such as asking patients to pay while lying in pain on a gurney.

INSIDE THIS REPORT

THE ISSUES 623
BACKGROUND 630
CHRONOLOGY 631
CURRENT SITUATION 636
AT ISSUE 637
OUTLOOK 639
BIBLIOGRAPHY 642
THE NEXT STEP 643

CQ Researcher • July 20, 2012 • www.cqresearcher.com
Volume 22, Number 26 • Pages 621-644

Los Angeles | London | New Delhi
Singapore | Washington DC

RECIPIENT OF SOCIETY OF PROFESSIONAL JOURNALISTS AWARD FOR EXCELLENCE ◆ AMERICAN BAR ASSOCIATION SILVER GAVEL AWARD

THE ISSUES

623 • Are stronger consumer protections needed?
• Has federal law lagged behind advances in technology?
• Do consumers behind on medical bills deserve special protection?

BACKGROUND

630 **Early Borrowers**
Most Americans relied on credit in the early 19th century.

632 **Credit Transformed**
Installment buying became commonplace in the early 20th century.

634 **Revolving Credit**
In 1938 Bloomingdale's changed the way Americans borrowed.

634 **Regulating Debt Collectors**
Legislation passed in 1977 curbed abusive practices.

634 **Democratizing Credit**
Credit cards became widely available to the poor in the 1980s and '90s.

CURRENT SITUATION

636 **Protecting Consumers**
State attorneys general are increasing enforcement against abusive practices.

638 **Legislative Action**
State legislatures are also targeting debt collectors.

638 **Statute of Limitation**
Collectors are not permitted to sue over old debts.

OUTLOOK

639 **New Rules?**
Disclosure requirements are likely for collection agencies.

SIDEBARS AND GRAPHICS

624 **Medical Bills Pose Burden**
One-third of Americans in families are affected.

625 **Medical Bills Are Half of Debt Collected**
Student loans accounted for about 6 percent.

628 **Suits Against Collectors Rise**
Twelve thousand federal suits were filed in 2011.

630 **Do's and Don'ts for Debt Collectors**
No calls after 9 p.m.

631 **Chronology**
Key events since 1833.

632 **Emergency Room Patients Pressed for Payment**
Officials decry "aggressive" hospital debt collection.

636 **Repeat Calls Top Complaint List**
Consumers also cite false threats, calls at work.

637 **At Issue**
Should the Department of Education stop using debt collectors?

FOR FURTHER RESEARCH

641 **For More Information**
Organizations to contact.

642 **Bibliography**
Selected sources used.

643 **The Next Step**
Additional articles.

643 **Citing *CQ Researcher***
Sample bibliography formats.

Cover: AP Photo/*The Star Tribune*/Richard Tsong-Taatarii

CQ Researcher

July 20, 2012
Volume 22, Number 26

MANAGING EDITOR: Thomas J. Billitteri tjb@cqpress.com

ASSISTANT MANAGING EDITOR: Kathy Koch kkoch@cqpress.com

CONTRIBUTING EDITOR: Thomas J. Colin tcolin@cqpress.com

ASSOCIATE EDITOR: Kenneth Jost

STAFF WRITER: Marcia Clemmitt

CONTRIBUTING WRITERS: Peter Katel, Barbara Mantel, Jennifer Weeks

DESIGN/PRODUCTION EDITOR: Olu B. Davis

ASSISTANT EDITOR: Darrell Dela Rosa

FACT CHECKER: Michelle Harris

INTERN: Kate Irby

Los Angeles | London | New Delhi
Singapore | Washington DC

An Imprint of SAGE Publications, Inc.

VICE PRESIDENT AND EDITORIAL DIRECTOR, HIGHER EDUCATION GROUP:
Michele Sordi

DIRECTOR, ONLINE PUBLISHING:
Todd Baldwin

CQ Researcher (ISSN 1056-2036) is printed on acid-free paper. Published weekly, except: (March wk. 5) (May wk. 4) (July wk. 1) (Aug. wks. 3, 4) (Nov. wk. 4) and (Dec. wks. 3, 4). Published by SAGE Publications, Inc., 2455 Teller Rd., Thousand Oaks, CA 91320. Annual full-service subscriptions start at $1,054. For pricing, call 1-800-834-9020. To purchase a *CQ Researcher* report in print or electronic format (PDF), visit www.cqpress.com or call 866-427-7737. Single reports start at $15. Bulk purchase discounts and electronic-rights licensing are also available. Periodicals postage paid at Thousand Oaks, California, and at additional mailing offices. POSTMASTER: Send address changes to *CQ Researcher*, 2300 N St., N.W., Suite 800, Washington, DC 20037.

BY BARBARA MANTEL

THE ISSUES

It's not uncommon for debt collectors to pressure consumers to pay their bills, but Frank E. Lindstrom Jr. and Kevin Medley crossed the line into harassment and abuse, according to government regulators.

The pair, along with several colleagues, allegedly asked one consumer who was behind on funeral payments for her son how she would feel if his body was dropped outside her door. They allegedly threatened to kill another consumer's dog. The debt collectors were also accused of failing to turn over collected money to clients, threatening supposed debtors with lawsuits never intended to be filed, and harassing them with repeated phone calls and obscene language.

In March, the Federal Trade Commission (FTC) banned Lindstrom and Medley from the debt-collection business. The two did not admit guilt in the case, but as part of a settlement they agreed to a combined judgment of more than $1 million. They will surrender just under $50,000, however, because of their inability to pay. [1]

AP Photo/Chuck Burton

Eleanor Chittum, a convalescent-home resident in Winston-Salem, N.C., fought for a year and a half to stop a collection agency from collecting a $1,439 debt she had already paid. North Carolina law now requires debt buyers — purchasers of older, uncollected debt — to offer more proof they are owed the money before filing collection lawsuits.

The FTC says debt collectors are instrumental in helping creditors collect what they are owed and thus help to keep credit widely available to consumers at low costs. [2] An industry-commissioned study estimates that so-called third-party debt-collection agencies — companies hired by merchants, hospitals, credit-card issuers, utilities and other creditors to collect on past-due accounts — recovered and returned to creditors more than $40 billion in delinquent debt in 2010. [3]

Still, the FTC has stepped up enforcement against collectors it believes have violated the key law governing debt collectors: the 35-year-old Fair Debt Collection Practices Act (FDCPA).

The law applies to third-party debt-collection agencies and to companies that buy old consumer debt for pennies on the dollar and collection agencies those companies sometimes use. The law does not apply to original creditors' in-house debt-collection staff.

The FDCPA:

• Prohibits abusive language, harassing phone calls and deceptive threats of lawsuits;

• Limits the hours that collectors can contact people who owe money;

• Requires collectors to provide consumers with validation of the debt owed upon request; and

• Allows consumers to sue and collect damages for violations of the law. (*See box, p. 630.*)

In the first three months of 2012, about 14 percent of Americans faced collection action for an average $1,500 per person, according to the Federal Reserve Bank of New York. [4]

"Protecting consumers from deceptive or abusive debt collectors is one of the most important things the FTC does," David Vladeck, director of its Bureau of Consumer Protection, said last March. Over the previous 12 months, the FTC had filed or resolved seven debt-collection cases affecting hundreds of thousands of consumers, the highest number of cases in a single year. [5]

Two cases involved record civil penalties. In March 2011, West Asset Management, a major debt collector based in Omaha, Neb., agreed to pay $2.8 million to settle an FTC complaint accusing it of calling consumers "multiple times each day, often regarding accounts that did not belong to them, and sometimes using rude and abusive language." West Asset Management did not admit or deny wrongdoing. [6]

In January 2012, Warren, Mich.-based Asset Acceptance, one of the nation's largest buyers of bad consumer debt, agreed to pay $2.5 million after the FTC accused it of a series of mis-

Medical Bills Burden Families

About one in three Americans lives in a family weighed down by medical bills. A fifth are in families that had problems paying such bills during the previous year, and a one-fourth are in families that are making payments over time.

Persons in Families Burdened by Medical Bills, January-June 2011

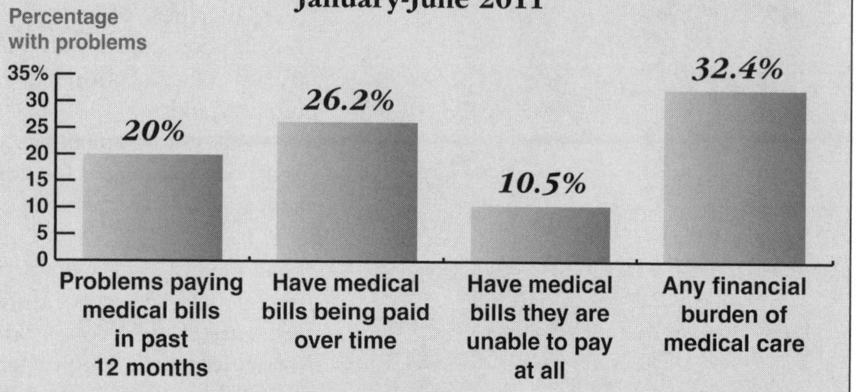

Percentage with problems

Problems paying medical bills in past 12 months	20%
Have medical bills being paid over time	26.2%
Have medical bills they are unable to pay at all	10.5%
Any financial burden of medical care	32.4%

Source: Robin A. Cohen, et al., *"Financial Burden of Medical Care: Early Release of Estimates From the National Health Interview Survey, January-June 2011," Centers for Disease Control and Prevention, March 2012, p. 1, www.cdc.gov/nchs/data/nhis/earlyrelease/financial_burden_of_medical_care_032012.pdf.*

representations, including misleading consumers about the legal status of old debt. [7] Debt collectors may not threaten to sue or sue on debt that is past a state's statute of limitations. Asset Acceptance did not admit or deny the FTC's claims.

In the past few years, the FTC has repeatedly called for tightening of consumer-protection laws and civil court procedures. But consumer advocates, collection agencies and regulators disagree about what reforms are necessary. They debate, for example, whether patients behind on medical debts need special protections, whether debt collectors are bringing bogus lawsuits against consumers and whether consumer attorneys accusing collectors of violations are doing the same. And they disagree on the extent of those violations.

After one FTC enforcement action in April, DBA International, a Sacramento, Calif.-based trade association for the debt-buying industry, said the case "highlights the kind of illegal tactics a few companies employ that give the entire industry a black eye." The association applauded the government "for targeting companies like these that prey on consumers." [8]

But consumer advocates contend the problem extends far beyond a few rogue operators. "This is an industry, according to the FTC, that generates more consumer complaints than any other," says Tena Friery, research director for the Privacy Rights Clearinghouse, a group in San Diego that advocates on behalf of consumers.

Last year the FTC received 142,743 debt-collection complaints, about one-fourth of all complaints to the agency. The top gripe against debt collectors was repeated calls. Misrepresenting the character, amount or status of debt was second, and falsely threatening an illegal or unintended act, such as a lawsuit, was next. [9]

The FTC has said that the number of complaints may actually understate the extent to which debt collectors violate the law. Suzanne Martindale, a staff attorney in the San Francisco office of the advocacy group Consumers Union, agrees. "There are probably a lot of people out there who don't know how to complain or who don't bother to but have nonetheless been harmed."

On the other hand, the FTC acknowledges that it does not verify the accuracy of the vast majority of complaints or whether they involve violations of law. "You could pick up the phone tomorrow and say, 'I have a complaint. Mark's collection agency called me at 9 a.m., and I don't like it.' But that's not a violation," says Mark Schiffman, vice president of public affairs for ACA International, a debt-collection trade association, based in Minneapolis, Minn.

Third-party debt collectors are paid on a contingency basis; they receive an average 25-30 percent of the debt recovered, according to one recent report. [10] The industry employs approximately 148,300 people, and more than half of the debt they collect is health-care related, according to a recent survey. Credit card and other financial debt account for about 20 percent of the debt collected. [11]

The entire industry — third-party collection agencies, debt buyers and law firms in the collection business — "was a boom industry for about 15 years, from around 1993 until 2008 or 2009, driven in large part by the proliferation of credit cards," says Mike Ginsberg, president and CEO of Kaulkin Ginsberg, an industry adviser in Rockville, Md. But the industry was "hit square in the mouth" by the recession, says Ginsberg, as credit-card loans dried up and more consumers began paying off card balances. Just over 11 percent of total credit-card balances were 90 days or more delinquent in the first quarter of this year, down from about 14 percent in early 2010. [12]

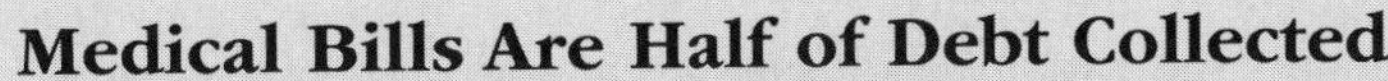

The industry also has a new, more powerful regulator. The 2010 Dodd-Frank Wall Street Reform and Consumer Protection Act created the Consumer Financial Protection Bureau (CFPB), which will share enforcement of the debt-collection law with the FTC. But unlike the FTC, the bureau can issue regulations clarifying the law and, for the first time, supervise and examine "larger" debt-collection and debt-buying companies as well as those it views as a risk to consumers.

"One of the industry's frequent arguments is that violations of the law are not representative of the industry, but you can't really resolve that question through enforcement actions," says Delecia Reynolds Hand, legislative director for the Washington-based National Association of Consumer Advocates, whose members are consumer attorneys. "Now CFPB supervision will provide a whole lot of information about policies and procedures across the industry."

It's not clear yet what supervision will mean: Will the bureau be able to listen in on phone calls to consumers, inspect debt-collectors' scripts or be able to review collectors' procedures for verifying a consumer's identity and delinquency status?

The bureau has preliminarily defined "larger" to capture approximately 175 firms — or 4 percent of companies — that account for 63 percent of the debt-collection market. [13] The industry, however, thinks that is too many firms, while consumer advocates say it is too few.

The CFPB's final decision will come in late July. In the meantime, here are some of the questions that creditors, debt collectors, consumer advocates, regulators and politicians are debating:

Medical Bills Are Half of Debt Collected

Medical bills comprised more than half of the debt collected by collection agencies in 2010. Credit card and other financial debt made up one-fifth of the total.

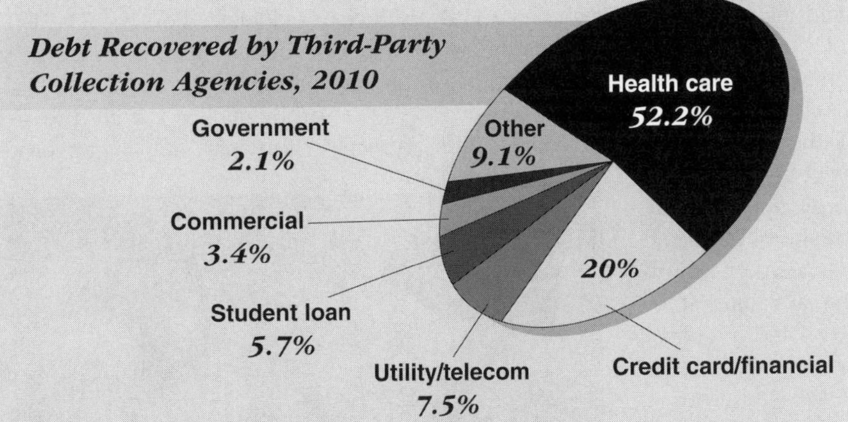

Source: "The Impact of Third-Party Debt Collection on the National and State Economies," Ernst & Young, February 2012, p. 8, www.acainternational.org/files.aspx?p=/images/21594/2011acaeconomicimpactreport.pdf

Are stronger consumer protections needed?

Karen Stevens, a 42-year-old resident of Hagerstown, Md., paid off a delinquent credit-card bill in 2006, but when her bank mistakenly sold her debt soon after a new set of debt collectors began pursuit.

Stevens sent proof that the debt was paid, but "that just didn't seem to be good enough for them," she told *American Banker*. "They still ended up taking me to court." Her debt was sold again, and Stevens ended up countersuing the last debt buyer for violating state and federal debt-collection laws. They settled out of court in 2009. [14]

Debt buying has become one of the fastest-growing parts of the collection business, and "it can be much more profitable" than collecting debt on a contingency basis, according to industry adviser Kaulkin Ginsberg. Debt buyers purchase portfolios of older debt for cents on the dollar, then collect what they can — sometimes "up to three times or more of the original purchase price," Kaulkin Ginsberg said. [15] When a debt buyer cannot collect, it can repackage the debt and sell it to another.

The industry says debt buying is a win for creditors and consumers: Creditors receive money for debt they've written off as uncollectible, and consumers benefit from the low price that debt buyers paid to the original creditors. "Debt buyers are usually much more willing to work out more creative solutions than the original creditor," says Barbara Sinsley, general counsel at DBA International.

But consumer advocates contend that the rapid growth in debt buying has led to an increase in collection actions against the wrong person or involving debts in the wrong amount or that were already settled, and to a surge in poorly documented lawsuits against consumers.

"It's garbage in, garbage out," says Martindale of Consumers Union. "It is all too common for debt buyers to acquire spreadsheets containing inadequate or absent records of payments, disputes or prior exchanges with the consumer — and these spreadsheets are sold and resold repeatedly," Consumers Union told the FTC. [16]

Sinsley disagrees that the problems are widespread. "Debt buyers, when they buy debt, spend a lot of resources on checking the accuracy and integrity of the information," she says. "Debt buyers do not want to be buying or collecting on disputed debt."

Consumer advocates are not convinced and have a laundry list of desired reforms, either through new CFPB rules or federal or state legislation. Chief among them is requiring more and better documentation — such as the name of the original creditor, a copy of the signed contract or credit application, a breakdown of the claimed debt including any interest or fees, and proof of ownership of the debt — before a collection agency or a debt buyer attempts to collect on a consumer debt. And advocates say the information should be given to consumers. [17]

But the industry says the fault is with the original creditors. "At the end of the day, if the bank is not providing the kind of documentation that is needed in the original sale, it's not going to be available later on," says industry adviser Mike Ginsberg. "That's where the regulation needs to be." ACA International wants the federal Truth in Lending Act amended to require original creditors to maintain consumer account information for at least seven years after a debt is written off. [18]

But the chief problem, according to many consumer advocates, is a flood of debt-collection lawsuits. That's a direct result of the proliferation of debt purchasers, according to a U.S. Government Accountability Office report, because they "often use collection law firms as their primary tool for recovery." [19]

"A million or more consumers are sued each year by debt collectors in state courts," says Robert Hobbs, deputy director of the Boston-based National Consumer Law Center, and a substantial portion of those suits have insufficient evidence, he says. The FTC has called debt-collection litigation "a broken system." [20]

The problems start with process servers,* who may not always properly notify consumers of a lawsuit, according to the FTC. From there, the problems build, as many consumers fail to respond to the notices they do receive. While the FTC says there is no empirical data explaining the low response rate, advocates say it is because many indebted consumers are poor and lack access to lawyers. They often are confused about how to navigate the legal system, especially if the notice comes from a debt buyer and not the original creditor, advocates say. [21]

* Process servers deliver notifications, summonses and other relevant paperwork to those who are being sued.

bethsreversemortgageblog.wordpress.com

Credit counselors seek to help consumers with unmanageable debts by negotiating with creditors to establish a plan that may allow for reductions in debt payments, interest and late fees. The Minnesota attorney general recommends finding a reputable counselor through the National Foundation for Credit Counseling.

"They may not understand that even if you don't recognize the name of the plaintiff and you think it is a mistake, you still must respond," says Martindale. "If you don't, you will default, and [collection agencies] can still get a court order to take your money away, even if it is a mistake." Between 60 and 95 percent of consumer debt-collection lawsuits result in default judgments, according to the FTC. [22]

Those judgments, says Hobbs, can be based on flawed affidavits — written sworn statements of fact — submitted by the debt owner to the court. "They can be robo-signed and based on no personal knowledge and no review of the debt because, for the most part, there is no documentation for them to check," says Hobbs.

Sinsley dismisses that argument, however. "I think robo-signing is not the problem it is portrayed to be," she says. "DBA members hire experienced local counsel to assist with local state guidelines."

One year ago, debt buyer Encore Capital Group, based in San Diego, settled a class action lawsuit for $5.2 million in which two subsidiaries were accused of robo-signing affidavits to buttress collection lawsuits. In testimony, an employee was said to be signing hundreds of affidavits a day.

As the case made its way through the courts, Encore amended its methods in 2009 with what it described as "simple process improvements and language changes." After the settlement, it said the "alleged defects in the affidavits had no impact on whether or not the debt was owed." [23]

Consumer advocates would like to see states require debt buyers to provide greater evidence and documentation in court when suing consumers over delinquent debt. In 2009, after North Carolina adopted such a law, collection lawsuits dropped significantly, garnering praise from consumer advocates and protests from the industry that legitimate debts were going uncollected.

Has federal law lagged behind advances in technology?

Collection agencies and debt buyers should be able to contact borrowers more easily on their cellphones and through text messaging and email, the debt collection industry says. But, it complains, outdated federal law, passed long before cellphones and the Internet became standard ways of communicating, hobble debt collectors and hurt consumers. "If you can communicate with a consumer about a debt and understand what they have the ability to pay, I think you would see a decrease in litigation and an increase in payment plans," says Sinsley of DBA International.

"It has become harder to get hold of consumers who have shifted to cellphones and, in many cases, go without a landline at all," says Schiffman of ACA International. To reach consumers on their landlines, debt collectors routinely use recorded messages and automated dialers programmed to predict when a consumer will be home. But the 1991 Telephone Consumer Protection Act does not allow collectors to use predictive dialers to call cellphones unless the consumer has given prior consent — for instance, by putting down a cellphone number as the point of contact in the original credit application.

"We want it to be equal to how I can contact you on a landline phone," says Schiffman. The industry supported a bill introduced in the U.S. House of Representatives last year by Rep. Lee Terry, R-Neb., called the Mobile Information Call Act that would have loosened restrictions on cellphone calls. But 54 state and territorial attorneys general opposed the bill, and it never left committee. *(See "Current Situation," p. 636.)*

The law could result in "a flood of solicitation, marketing, debt collection and other unwanted calls and texts" to consumers' cellphones, they said in a letter to Congress, and "shift the cost of these calls . . . to consumers, placing a significant burden on low-income consumers." [24]

The industry also wants the Consumer Financial Protection Bureau to write specific language that it can use to leave messages on consumers' answering machines and voice mail, technology not much in use when the Fair Debt Collection Practices Act was passed in 1977. Courts have confirmed that collectors must identify themselves when leaving phone messages, but that puts them at risk of disclosing information about the debt to third parties who might overhear the message, something that the FDCPA prohibits.

"It's a huge Catch-22," said Chris Morris, a Minneapolis lawyer who defends collectors accused of violating the FDCPA. [25] As a result, many collectors are no longer leaving messages. When they do, ACA International recommends that they name the party they are trying to reach, instruct anyone else to hang up, and only then proceed to identify themselves as a debt collector.

But, says Sergei Lemberg, a Stamford, Conn., lawyer whose firm specializes in suing collectors for alleged legal violations, "Is there a constitutional right to leave messages? Just because somebody owes a debt doesn't mean that they then have to expose themselves to being embarrassed in front of their roommates or spouses or family members."

Without clarification from regulators, however, collectors say they must call consumers more frequently, risking a lawsuit alleging harassment. Schiffman says consumer attorneys don't want the CFPB to write an allowable script for messages because then they wouldn't be able to sue debt collectors for technical violations of the law.

The number of lawsuits accusing collection agencies, debt buyers and collection law firms of violating the FDCPA has risen steadily, to 12,018 in 2011, nearly four times the total in 2005, according to WebRecon, which tracks such lawsuits and provides the industry with the names of the most litigious consumer lawyers and consumers. *(See graph, p. 628.)* Most cases are settled before trial.

Because consumers do not have to show they were harmed to prove a violation of the FDCPA, many lawsuits are over minor technical violations, such as "calling five minutes after calling is allowed," or that arise from ambiguities in the law, says Jack Gordon, WebRecon's CEO. "Maybe the consumer had their cellphone in a different time zone and the collector had no way to know," leading to a call during prohibited hours.

The Internet has fueled the increase in lawsuits, says Gordon. "There are ads from consumer attorneys imploring you not to pay debt collectors a penny until they give you a free case review," and websites that instruct consumers how to entrap a collector on the phone, says Gordon.

But consumer attorneys say it is the industry's behavior that drives such suits. "The economy is so bad that it's getting more and more difficult for these debt collectors to get money from people who just don't have it," said Tammy Hussin, a Carlsbad, Calif., consumer attorney. "So the collectors are more frustrated, and they're getting more aggressive." [26]

Lemberg agrees. "We don't need marginal cases," he says. "We have dozens of people every day complaining about harassment, abuse, third-party disclosure, getting seven to 10 calls a day and disrespectful collectors."

Suits Against Debt Collectors on Rise

Consumer attorneys filed 12,018 federal lawsuits against debt collectors in 2011 under the Fair Debt Collection Practices Act, nearly four times the total in 2005.

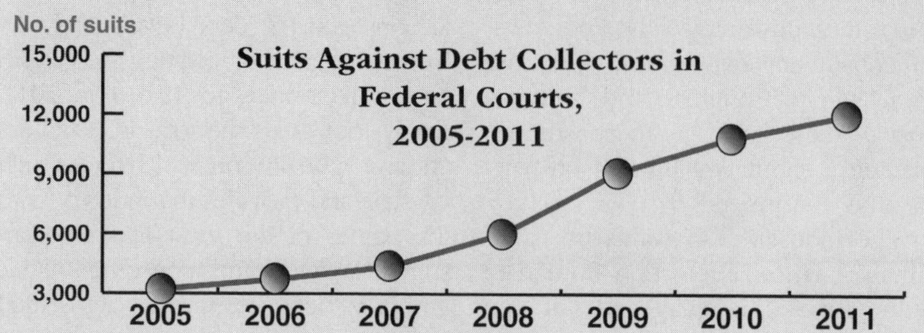

Source: "2011 Litigation Statistics Revised Upward, FDCPA Suits Surpass 12,000," WebRecon LLC, February 2012, www.collectionindustrynews.com/FOR%20IMMEDIATE%20RELEASE%2020120224%202011%20revision.pdf

Consumer attorneys typically take such cases on a contingency basis. If a debt collector is proven to have violated the FDCPA, a consumer can claim reasonable attorney fees, which can be several thousand dollars, statutory damages of up to $1,000 per violation and actual damages, if any.

The industry complains that the consumer lawyers benefit the most from such lawsuits. "Are consumers better off than they were two or three years ago because of all this litigation?" asked Charity Olson, a Michigan attorney who defends debt collectors. "Sadly, I don't think they are. But there are a lot of attorneys who are a lot better off." [27]

"We're not going to deny that there are litigation shops out there that are not very selective," says Reynolds Hand of the National Association of Consumer Advocates. "But our members are not those guys. Our members are contacted by consumers about behavior that is crossing the line, behavior that is outlined in the FDCPA."

To make it more worthwhile for consumers to sue, consumer attorneys and advocates have been asking Congress for years to raise the $1,000 statutory damage award to reflect inflation; it hasn't changed in 35 years. "We've gotten very close in negotiations with the industry to them agreeing to that in exchange for something they wanted," says Hobbs of the National Consumer Law Center. "But it hasn't happened."

Do consumers behind on medical bills deserve special protection?

This spring, in an investigation of the collection practices of Carolinas Healthcare headquartered in Charlotte, N.C., the *Charlotte Observer* found that the nonprofit health-care system sued more than 12,000 patients over a five-year period for bad debt. An in-depth look at some cases found most of the patients in those cases were uninsured and "a significant number of them should have qualified for free hospital care," the newspaper said. [28]

Consumer advocates are pushing for special protections for uninsured and underinsured patients who are behind on their medical bills. "This is not a store credit card that's been overdrawn for consumer goods. This is a vital service," says Mark Rukavina, executive director of The Access Project, an advocacy group in Boston that works to improve health-care access.

Moreover, says Rukavina, "Unlike your mortgage, your monthly credit-card payment and your utility bill, medical bills are "significant expenses that are unanticipated. Generally speaking, you can't predict when you're going to get sick."

Medical debt is a growing problem, according to a survey by The Commonwealth Fund, a New York foundation. Twenty-nine percent of adults ages 19 to 64 — 53 million people — had problems paying or were unable to pay medical bills in 2010, up from 23 percent five years earlier. Sixteen percent, or 30 million people, had been contacted by a collection agency for unpaid medical bills, up from 13 percent in 2005. While the uninsured are most affected, insured patients are increasingly struggling with rising copayments, coinsurance and unaffordable deductibles. [29]

The Affordable Care Act (ACA), which the Supreme Court largely upheld in June, will partly address the problem by increasing the number of Americans with health insurance. In addition, Congress placed rules governing billing and collection in the law, in response to troubling reports of aggressive debt collection at nonprofit hospitals. [30]

The ACA requires nonprofit hospitals to develop and publicize written financial-assistance policies that provide free or partially free care to uninsured or underinsured low-income patients, and to charge those who qualify for partial assistance the same discounted rates for medical care given to insured patients. [31]

"The common practice has been that people who are uninsured are charged a rate that can be three to four times as high," says Jessica Curtis, project director of the Hospital Accountability Project at Community Catalyst, a Boston-based patient-advocacy group.

In addition, the law directs nonprofit hospitals to make a reasonable effort to determine whether a patient qualifies for financial assistance before taking "extraordinary collection actions."

"We supported the law. We thought it made sense," says Melinda Hatton, general counsel at the Chicago-based American Hospital Association, a trade group. But Hatton takes issue with the way it is being implemented.

Last month the Internal Revenue Service (IRS) issued draft rules on the law's billing and collection requirements. For example, the rules lay out detailed procedures for notifying patients of financial-assistance policies. Hatton says they are too rigid.

"You're going to be so focused on making sure that you've got it plastered on the wall in a conspicuous place, that you've got a summary in every single bill, that you've got it available in places that visitors can find it and that you've got it on your website. And as a result, new and better ideas about how to reach patients may fall by the wayside," says Hatton.

Getty Images/Mark Wilson

Richard Cordray heads the new Consumer Financial Protection Bureau, created by the 2010 Dodd-Frank Wall Street Reform and Consumer Protection Act. The bureau can issue regulations clarifying the Fair Debt Collection Practices Act and supervise and examine big debt-collection and debt-buying companies as well as those it views as a risk to consumers.

The IRS also says debt collectors cannot garnish the wages of patients eligible for financial help, place liens on their property or foreclose on their houses, seize their bank accounts or report their bad debts to credit bureaus. [32]

The IRS will hold nonprofit hospitals responsible if third-party collection agencies they hire violate any of these rules, and Hatton says that is not fair. "If hospitals make their best efforts to ensure that third-party collectors comply with their policies and procedures, and those third-parties make a mistake, then the hospital shouldn't be in danger of losing its tax exemption," says Hatton.

In addition, the IRS says nonprofit hospitals must wait up to 240 days to determine whether a patient behind on payments qualifies for financial assistance, during which time it can take no collection action. That's too long and will place a financial burden on nonprofits already squeezed by reduced reimbursement rates and rising costs, says Jeffrey Hausfeld, a physician and managing director of FMS Financial Solutions, a debt-collection agency in Greenbelt, Md. During the five or six or eight months that hospitals' billing staffs are chasing delinquent patients to get them to apply for financial assistance, "they are not working current accounts to get the money in to keep the hospital functioning," says Hausfeld.

Patient advocates, however, are pleased with the ACA's billing and collection requirements but say they go only so far. "It only pertains to nonprofit hospitals," says Rukavina. About half the nation's hospitals are nonprofit, according to the hospital association.

Last month Sen. Al Franken, D-Minn., introduced legislation to extend ACA provisions to all hospitals, and Community Catalyst has written model state legislation that would go even a bit further. While the federal law allows hospitals to set their own eligibility requirements for financial assistance, the model state legislation explicitly spells out the eligibility rules. [33] About a half-dozen states have such laws, including California, Maryland and New York.

But Hatton is not in favor of extending ACA requirements to all hospitals. "Tax-exempt hospitals have a different kind of obligation to their community because of the basis of their tax exemption," she says.

The model state legislation would also require hospital governing boards to expressly approve any extraordinary collection actions, such as placing a lien on a patient's property, garnishing wages or seizing a bank account. [34]

"That is way too onerous," says Hausfeld. "Boards would never get anything else done."

Curtis and Community Catalyst propose that states, or even Congress, ban the sale of medical debt. "You have a third party, possibly a for-profit group, that is profiting from someone's pain and sickness," says Curtis.

But Jim Richards, president and CEO of Capio Partners, a medical-debt purchaser in Sherman, Texas, disagrees. "We most definitely do not believe selling patient debt should be prohibited," he says. "Legislators need to fully understand the negative effect on a hospital's revenue before pursuing such legislation." ■

Do's and Don'ts for Debt Collectors

The Fair Debt Collection Practices Act applies to collection agencies, debt buyers and debt-collection law firms. Under the law:

Debt collectors may not:

- Reveal that a consumer owes a debt when communicating with others to learn the consumer's location. Debt collections also may not contact others more than once to learn the consumer's whereabouts.
- Contact the consumer before 8 a.m. or after 9 p.m. local time without the consumer's permission.
- Contact the consumer at work if the debt collector knows or has reason to know that the employer prohibits such communication.
- Contact a consumer known to be represented by an attorney.
- Harass, oppress or abuse any person in connection with the collection of a debt, including causing the telephone to ring repeatedly.
- Use false, deceptive or misleading information or representation.
- Collect amounts other than authorized by the credit agreement creating the debt.

Debt collectors must:

- Identify themselves as a debt collector in every communication with the consumer.
- Cease communication if the consumer notifies the debt collector in writing that the consumer refuses to pay a debt or wants communication to stop, except to notify the consumer of future remedies, such as a lawsuit.
- Within five days of initial communication, send the consumer a written notice containing the debt amount; creditor's name (or the name of the debt buyer if the debt was sold); a statement that the debt will be assumed valid unless the consumer disputes it within 30 days; a statement that if disputed the collector will mail the consumer verification of the debt; and a statement that the consumer may request the name of the original creditor.
- At the consumer's request, provide verification of the debt, including the amount owed and the name and address of the original creditor.

In addition:

- Consumers may sue a debt collector they believe has violated the law.
- Any debt collector found guilty of a violation is liable to the consumer for any actual damages sustained as a result of the violation, additional damages up to $1,000 to be determined in court, and court costs and reasonable attorney fees.

Source: Federal Trade Commission, www.ftc.gov/bcp/edu/pubs/consumer/credit/cre27.pdf

BACKGROUND

Early Borrowers

In the early 19th century, nearly three-quarters of Americans resided on farms, and most "lived and died by credit," wrote historian Louis Hyman in *Borrow: The American Way of Debt.* "The harvest came but once a year, but they needed goods — farm equipment, clothing, groceries — year-round." [35] So farmers bought from merchants on credit at inflated prices, repaying after the harvest, occasionally in cash, but most often in crops or livestock. For Western farmers, that meant wheat, eggs and hogs. For Southerners, it meant cotton.

The merchant, then, became the middleman, selling the farmer's products in the city and turning a profit. With the development of railroads in the mid- to late 19th century, getting agricultural products to market became much easier, and the number of merchants in farm towns multiplied. The resulting competition drove down the inflated prices farmers had to pay merchants for goods on credit.

Western farmers benefited, but in the South, where control of the land and stores after the Civil War remained concentrated in the hands of a few, the story was different. "Debt kept tenant farmers and sharecroppers in thrall to monopolistic country stores where each year's crop never quite made enough to free them from last year's debt," wrote Hyman. [36]

The Industrial Revolution and a wave of immigration pulled workers to the cities, and by the end of the 19th century, fewer than half of working Americans lived on farms. But many urban workers were poor and could not make ends meet, and they increasingly borrowed money from pawnbrokers and small

Continued on p. 632

Chronology

1800s-1920s

Stores and manufacturers extend installment credit to consumers, and small collection agencies proliferate.

1833
Federal law eliminates imprisonment for debt. Most states follow.

1911
Sears, Roebuck & Co. allows consumer installment payments.

1920s
States raise interest rates lenders can charge consumers for small loans in effort to provide incentive to legitimate lenders and drive out loan sharks. Small lenders thrive, and small collection agencies proliferate. . . . General Motors extends installment credit to car buyers. Ford follows eight years later. By decade's end most goods can be bought on an installment plan.

1930s-1950s

Department stores introduce revolving credit and charge interest on balances due. Banks begin issuing credit cards.

1938
Bloomingdale's is first to offer revolving credit to customers, bundling purchases into one bill and charging interest on overdue balances.

1949
Seventy-five percent of major stores have revolving-credit programs, charging an annual interest rate of 13 percent.

1951
Franklin National Bank in Long Island, N.Y., is first bank to issue a universal credit card, to be used anywhere it is accepted.

1958
Bank of America introduces universal credit card.

1970s-1980s

Congress regulates debt-collection industry; Supreme Court indirectly dismantles usury laws.

1977
Fair Debt Collection Practices Act (FDCPA) prohibits abusive, deceptive or unfair collection practices and allows consumers to sue debt collectors for violations.

1978
Middle Income Student Assistance Act expands student loan eligibility to middle- and upper-income students. . . . Supreme Court says banks can charge credit-card customers nationwide the interest rate in the banks' home state, encouraging banks to flock to states with no interest-rate caps. Credit card interest rates quickly rise.

1979
J.C. Penney is first national department store to accept Visa and then MasterCard. Other stores follow as they realize banks can shoulder bad debts more easily than they can.

1983
Recession ends, and credit card interest rates remain above 18 percent while all other interest rates fall. Banks issue credit cards to riskier consumers.

1986
Tax Reform Act of 1986 phases out deductibility of consumer credit, except mortgages.

1990s-Present

Americans borrow at record levels, and collection industry booms. Credit shrinks in aftermath of 2008 recession.

1990
Newly created Resolution Trust Corp. auctions off nearly $400 billion in assets of failed savings and loan institutions in decade's first half, helping to establish debt-buying industry.

1993
Debt buyers purchase about $6 billion of debt, mostly for credit-card transactions.

2000
Americans' household debt equals personal disposable income for the first time since data collection began.

2003
About one in 10 consumers faces collection action for overdue debt. The average collection amount per person is $900.

2005
Bankruptcy Abuse Prevention and Consumer Protection Act makes it more difficult for consumers to shed bad debts through bankruptcy. . . . Debt buyers purchase more than $110 billion in debt.

2011
Debt collector West Asset Management agrees to pay a record civil penalty of $2.8 million to settle an FTC complaint that it violated the FDCPA.

2012
Bank credit-card balances are 28 percent below their peak of January 2009, but about 14 percent of consumers face collection action, and the average collection amount has almost doubled from nine years earlier to more than $1,500.

Emergency Room Patients Pressed for Payment

Officials decry "aggressive" hospital debt collection.

Some patients were asked to pay while hooked to heart monitors, morphine drips and IVs. Others were dunned while lying naked and in pain on a gurney.

Minnesota attorney general Lori Swanson made those allegations in federal court in June against Chicago-based Accretive Health, one of the nation's largest collectors of medical debt. The complaint accuses Accretive of aggressively collecting late payments and current bills from emergency room patients who, in some cases, had not yet seen a doctor or been stabilized, a violation of the federal Emergency Medical Treatment and Active Labor Act. [1] *

"Accretive used 'bedside collection visits' in other patient hospital rooms besides the emergency room," according to the complaint, pressuring patients scheduled for medically necessary treatment, including time-sensitive surgeries, to pay outstanding bills. [2]

Experts say it is rare — but not unprecedented — for health care companies to pursue bedside payment from emergency-room patients, especially before they've been stabilized and received any treatment, making the allegations against Accretive particularly noteworthy.

"We've certainly heard that this happens anecdotally from some of our state partners, but I am not aware of other active investigations going on at this time," says Jessica Curtis, director of the Hospital Accountability Project at Community Catalyst, a Boston-based advocate for health-care access nationwide.

Swanson's accusations against Accretive are not new. She had made them in a scathing six-volume report in April that documented a culture of high-pressure collection tactics at Minneapolis-based Fairview Health Services, which runs eight nonprofit hospitals. Fairview had turned over its billing and collection to Accretive in 2010. [3]

* On July 30, 2012, Accretive agreed to pay the Minnesota attorney general's office $2.5 million to settle the allegations. The company did not admit wrongdoing.

Swanson also accused Accretive and Fairview employees under Accretive supervision of leading patients to believe that treatment would be withheld if they did not pay.

Alluding to the Accretive investigation, the Internal Revenue Service last month drafted a rule that prohibits debt collection at nonprofit hospitals "in the emergency department or in other hospital venues where collection activities could interfere with treatment."

"In recent months, we have heard concerns about aggressive hospital debt-collection activities, including allowing debt collectors to pursue collections in emergency rooms. These practices jeopardize patient care, and our proposed rules will help ensure they don't happen in charitable hospitals," said Emily McMahon, acting assistant secretary for tax policy at the U.S. Treasury Department. [4]

In an April statement, as well as in a 29-page document in May, Accretive denied all accusations and said the Minnesota attorney general's report was full of "inaccuracies, innuendo and unfounded speculation." The company called any suggestion that it put bedside pressure on patients to pay their medical bills out of pocket "a flagrant distortion of fact." The company said, instead, it worked with insured patients to make sure they were not being over-billed for their share and with uninsured patients to find coverage, including Medicaid, disability or auto insurance and charity.

In addition, "The very serious allegation of denying access to patient care is flatly untrue," said Accretive. [5]

Accretive's contract with Fairview was not its most important. Its biggest is with Missouri-based Ascension Health, the nation's largest Catholic and nonprofit health system. In response to an inquiry from stltoday.com, the online news site of the *St. Louis Post-Dispatch*, neither company would say how many of Ascension's 80 hospitals across the country use Accretive's services. In a written statement provided to the news site, Ascension Health said it "has policies regarding patient accounts that reflect our commitment to recognize the human dignity of our patients and treat them with respect and compassion." [6]

Swanson began investigating Accretive after suing the company in January 2012 for allegedly failing to protect the con-

Continued from p. 630

lenders — loan sharks — charging illegally high interest rates. For those who fell behind in their weekly payments, loan sharks would contact the delinquent borrower first through letters, if possible by telephone, and finally through personal visits. Those visits were made by a female "bawlerout," an employee who trapped "the delinquent borrower before co-workers and family in order to browbeat him publicly for being a sorry deadbeat," wrote historian Lendol Calder in *Financing the American Dream*. [37]

Credit Transformed

In 1928, the Russell Sage Foundation, which worked to improve social and living conditions in the United States, found that licensed pawnbrokers charged annual interest rates of up to 60 percent and loan sharks up to 480 percent, according to economist Charles Geisst in *Collateral Damaged: The Marketing of Consumer Debt to America*. [38]

To drive loan sharks out of business and encourage legitimate lending to middle- and lower-income consumers, the foundation sponsored the Uniform Small Loan Law, which would waive

fidentiality of patient information, as required by state and federal privacy laws. Five months earlier, an employee's laptop computer containing the unencrypted medical records of 23,500 Minnesota patients was stolen from a rental car. [7] The latest charges were added to that lawsuit. Accretive has asked the court to dismiss the entire suit.

The fallout this year has been swift. In January 2012, Fairview dropped Accretive as its debt collector. That decision followed mounting concerns among Fairview employees and officials about Accretive's practices at bedsides and in back offices. For example, in mid-2011, Fairview's chief financial officer, Daniel Fromm, had objected to Accretive's motivational practice of awarding gift cards to top collectors: "Do you also understand that this practice violates our corporate policy?" he asked. Another Fairview official asked Accretive to stop posting employee names with the amounts they collected. [8]

Getty Images/Chip Somodevilla

Sen. Al Franken, D-Minn., introduced legislation in June that would restrict the use of patient medical information for debt-collection purposes.

In April 2012, Fairview severed the last of its ties to Accretive, and, in May Fairview's Board of Directors failed to renew the contract of CEO Mark Eustis, who was instrumental in hiring Accretive. A week later, Charles Mooty, Fairview's board chairman and interim CEO, apologized to patients and offered a "firm commitment on behalf of the entire organization to regain your trust." [9]

Mooty spoke at a congressional hearing held in Minneapolis by Sen. Al Franken, D-Minn., to investigate the Accretive charges. In June, Franken reintroduced an expanded version of his 2011 End Debt Collector Abuse Act. The legislation would restrict the use of patient medical information for debt-collection purposes and apply the consumer protections of the Fair Debt Collection Practices Act to hospital staff.

The Federal Trade Commission, Minnesota Department of Commerce and the federal Centers for Medicare and Medicaid Services are also scrutinizing Accretive for possible violations of state and federal law.

— *Barbara Mantel*

---

1 "State of Minnesota, by its Attorney General Lori Swanson, Plaintiff, v. Accretive Health, Inc., Defendant," Second Amended and Supplemental Complaint, U.S. District Court of Minnesota, June 19, 2012, p. 41, www.ag.state.mn.us/PDF/Consumer/SecondAmendedSupplementaComplaint.pdf.

2 *Ibid.*

3 "Compliance Review of Fairview Health Services' Management Contracts With Accretive Health Inc.," Office of Attorney General Lori Swanson, April 2012, www.ag.state.mn.us.

4 "Treasury Releases Proposed Guidance to Ensure Patient Access to Financial Assistance from Charitable Hospitals," U.S. Department of the Treasury, June 22, 2012, www.treasury.gov/press-center/press-releases/Pages/tg1621.aspx.

5 "Statement from Accretive Health," April 29, 2012, http://phx.corporate-ir.net/phoenix.zhtml?c=234481&p=irol-newsArticle&ID=1688694&highlight=.

6 Jim Doyle, "Ascension Health's ties to embattled debt collector," April 27, 2012, www.stltoday.com/business/local/ascension-health-s-ties-to-embattled-debt-collector/article_6304c69a-8fe2-11e1-b74e-0019bb30f31a.html.

7 "Attorney General Swanson Sues Accretive Health for Patient Privacy Violations," The Office of Attorney General Lori Swanson, Jan. 19, 2012, www.ag.state.mn.us/Consumer/PressRelease/120119AccretiveHealth.asp.

8 Maura Lerner and Tony Kennedy, " 'Money-hungry' tactics raised alarms," *Star Tribune* (Minneapolis), July 9, 2012, www.startribune.com/lifestyle/health/151639735.html?page=2&c=y.

9 "Senator Grills Collection Agency, Health System Executives," *Collections & Credit Risk*, May 31, 2012, www.collectionscreditrisk.com/news/franken-grills-health-care-collection-executives-3010834-1.html.

state usury laws and allow state-licensed personal-finance companies to charge as much as 42 percent annual interest on loans of less than $300. By 1932, 25 states had adopted a version of the law, "a giant step forward toward the creation of a legitimate consumer-loan industry," wrote Calder. [39]

In July of that year, the number of state-licensed personal finance companies totaled 3,667, up from 600 in 1923. Their loans outstanding reached nearly $400 million, compared to $8 million in 1916. [40]

Consumers often used these loans to pay off other debts. But rather than wiping the slate clean with doctors, druggists and grocers as before, consumers were increasingly using the loans to pay off "automobiles, radios, refrigerators, and other goods sold on the installment plan," wrote Calder. [41]

In fact, the nature of consumer credit was rapidly changing in the early 20th century. Buying goods with a small amount of money down and the rest in fixed, monthly installments became acceptable and widespread. Before 1919, cars, for example, were bought with cash. But that year, General Motors created a financial subsidiary to lend money to car dealers and soon began to extend installment credit to consumers as well. Henry Ford resisted the trend, but his Ford Motor Co. eventually followed. By the late 1920s, nearly everything could be bought on an installment plan, from radios to clothes.

With installment credit came delinquencies, and small collection agencies proliferated in the 1920s and '30s. Debt collectors, usually with just a few clients and employees, used phone and mail to reach debtors and if necessary made personal visits, becoming known as "door knockers," according to Kaulkin Ginsberg, the industry adviser. Collectors kept hand-written records on index cards. [42]

Collection industry giant NCO Financial Systems got its start in 1926. The Horsham, Pa.-based company now employs approximately 30,000 people in 11 countries.

Revolving Credit

While most merchants offered customers installment credit, large department stores offered charge accounts to their customers, mostly middle-class consumers. Monthly bills had to be paid promptly and in full. The accounts were not intended as a source of revenue for the store but as a convenience for customers.

In reality, however, many department store customers did not pay promptly, and credit departments became a money pit. Collecting on past-due accounts was a public relations nightmare for department store credit managers, who had to tread carefully between mailing letters asking for payment and making sure not to alienate regular customers, who might complain to friends. "Slow pays and no-pays were all too common but had to be endured for the sake of customer relationships," wrote Hyman. [43]

Then in 1938, Bloomingdale's instituted a new kind of charge account that changed the way Americans borrowed. The New York City department store allowed payment over a six-month period, essentially institutionalizing the existing payment practices of many customers. But for the first time, in exchange for this flexibility, the store charged a small amount of interest on the unpaid balance. Revolving credit was born.

As families moved to the suburbs after World War II, they shopped at newly opened branches of urban department stores in order to fill their empty houses. According to Hyman, revolving credit "bound customers to the stores." Tight budgets "did not have to mean going without." [44] But many consumers were unable to make their monthly payments, and debt collectors followed them to the suburbs. By outsourcing collections to agencies that were paid on a contingency basis, the department stores "could keep annoying debt collectors at arm's length. No self-respecting person would complain about a debt collector coming to her house, even if she might complain about Bloomingdale's refusing her credit." [45]

Soon banks across the country were offering credit cards that could be used at any establishment that accepted them. In the 1960s, BankAmericard — today's Visa — alone claimed 30 million cardholders, who charged $1.7 billion in 1969 and $2.7 billion just a year later. Like the department stores, which gradually came to accept these universal cards in addition to their own store cards, banks would turn to collection agencies when they had no success convincing cardholders to pay their balances. [46]

Regulating Debt Collectors

Health-care practitioners, small businesses, credit-card companies and department stores all used collection agencies to try to recover bad debt. But the industry was largely unregulated when, in 1974, the *Chicago Tribune* sent reporters to work in eight debt-collection agencies during a six-week investigation. In April of that year, the newspaper published a series of stories exposing abuses.

Under headlines such as "Bill Collection Terror Tactics," "Bill Collectors Here Show No Fear of the Law," and "They Try Anything to Catch a Debtor," the *Tribune* described collectors who "posed as police or lawyers, forged court orders and sent collection notices on the fabricated letterhead of a non-existent law firm," noted the National Consumer Law Center. [47] One story focused on a debt collector's harassing phone calls to the workplace of a woman whose health-insurance plan was late in paying a $195 medical bill. Her boss threatened to fire her because the calls were so disruptive. [48]

The *Tribune* exposé had a direct impact. In October 1975, Rep. Frank Annunzio, D-Ill., proposed legislation to curb abusive practices by collection agencies, and in 1977 Congress held hearings in which it found "abundant evidence of the use of abusive, deceptive, and unfair debt collection practices by many debt collectors. Abusive debt-collection practices contribute to the number of personal bankruptcies, to marital instability, to the loss of jobs, and to invasions of individual privacy." [49]

Annunzio's Fair Debt Collection Practices Act was signed into law by President Jimmy Carter on Sept. 20, 1977, with the FTC charged with enforcing the measure. The FDCPA has remained largely unchanged since then.

Democratizing Credit

The nature of credit continued to change after passage of the FDCPA. In the early 1980s, banks found their modest credit-card profits squeezed. To fight inflation, the Federal Reserve had raised interest rates, and banks had to pay a much higher interest rate to borrow money from the Federal Reserve than state usury laws allowed them to charge on credit cards.

However, a 1978 Supreme Court decision, little-noticed at first, allowed Citibank to sidestep state usury laws. The result: a transformation in the credit-card business.

The court ruled that a bank could charge customers nationwide the interest rate in its home state. North Dakota, in search of jobs, repealed its usury law, and Citibank moved its credit-card operations there from New York. Chase Manhattan Bank persuaded Delaware to eliminate its usury law, and Chase, Manufacturer's Hanover and Chemical Bank as well as other banks relocated their credit-card operations there. Banks raised their credit-card rates, and kept them there, charging interest rates over 18 percent long after inflation had subsided and other rates had declined.

Meanwhile, "competition among the credit-card companies led to too many cards being offered and mounting debt by consumers who could not afford to pay it back," wrote Geisst. "The most surprising phenomenon to arise from the democratization of credit cards was the amount of credit made available to the poor. In 1983, one in thirty poor families had a credit card. By 1995, the number had risen to one in eight." [50] Not surprisingly, the percentage of credit-card debt that banks charged off as a loss began to rise sharply that year, reaching 6 percent in 1997, the highest in 25 years. [51]

Still, the bulk of household debt, about 70 percent, was in the form of mortgages in the late 1990s. Credit-card debt accounted for 10 percent, the next largest category; auto loans for 8 percent, and student loans for 2 percent. [52]

As credit was expanding, the debt-collection business was also undergoing significant change. After a crisis in the nation's savings and loan industry left many S&Ls insolvent, the government-owned and newly created Resolution Trust Corp. auctioned off nearly $400 billion in S&L assets in the late 1980s through the mid-1990s. Included in the sales were portfolios of delinquent credit-card debt. These auctions helped to establish the debt-buying industry.

Credit-card companies, hospitals, and other issuers of credit that were owed money could not only hire debt collectors on a contingency basis but also sell portfolios of their most delinquent debt to a growing number of debt purchasers. Debt buyers purchased $12 billion in face value of debt in 1995. More than a decade later, that figure had grown to an estimated $215 billion, most of it credit-card debt. [53]

American Preservation Society

A sign identifies the still-standing colonial-era house in Accomack, Va., that served as a "gaol" for debtors for several years. Imprisonment for debt was outlawed by federal law in 1833, and most states eventually followed suit.

Debt buyers pay pennies on the dollar for delinquent debt. They provide an infusion of cash to creditors and, according to the debt-buying industry, are able to offer consumers more affordable payment plans than the original creditors. But consumer advocates assert that the growth in debt buying has actually led to more aggressive collection tactics, a surge in litigation against consumers and an increase in violations of federal law.

In September 2010, Sens. Franken, the Minnesota Democrat, and George LeMieux, R-Fla., introduced the End Debt Collector Abuse Act. It required debt collectors to provide information to consumers within five days of first contact to help them identify the debt as legitimate; thoroughly investigate consumers' disputes over the debt; and increase penalties on debt collectors who violate the law. [54] The bill died in the Senate Committee on Banking, Housing, and Urban Affairs.

However, that same year Congress passed the Dodd-Frank Wall Street Reform and Consumer Protection Act, which created the Consumer Financial Protection Bureau. The bureau, along with the FTC, enforces federal consumer-protection laws and has the authority to periodically examine the practices of the larger debt-collection agencies or those it considers a risk to consumers. That kind of supervision, which has yet to begin, is unprecedented, and the industry is anxiously waiting to see how the CFPB carries out its authority.

On June 27, 2012, Franken reintroduced his bill, expanded to include new protections for consumers struggling with medical debt. ■

Repeat Calls Top Consumer Complaint List

More than 47,000 complaints of repeated calls by debt collectors were made to the Federal Trade Commission under the Fair Debt Collection Practices Act in 2011, surpassing all other complaint categories. Other common consumer complaints include misrepresentation of debt, false threats and failure to provide written notice.

Complaints Under Fair Debt Collection Practices Act, 2011	
Repeated calls	47,362
Misrepresents debt character, amount or status	46,482
Falsely threatens illegal or unintended act	35,473
No written notice	30,742
Falsely threatens arrest or property seizure	27,027
Fails to identify self as debt collector	20,781
Repeated calls to third parties	20,519
Improperly calls debtor at work	16,895
Uses obscene, profane or abusive language	16,576
Reveals debt to third party	12,636
Calls at inappropriate or inconvenient times	10,488
Refuses to verify debt after written request	10,000
Collects unauthorized fees, interest or expenses	9,314
Calls debtor after getting "cease communication" notice	5,922
Uses or threatens violence	3,977

Note: Callers can make more than one complaint in a single call.

Source: "Fair Debt Collection Practices Act," Consumer Financial Protection Bureau, 2012, Appendix C, files.consumerfinance.gov/f/201203_cfpb_FDCPA_annual_report.pdf

CURRENT SITUATION

Protecting Consumers

As the debt-collection industry evolves, the nation's attorneys general are stepping up their efforts to protect consumers against unscrupulous or abusive collection practices. And as they do, industry officials are watching legislative and regulatory developments carefully.

Rozanne Andersen, chief compliance officer at Muncie, Ind.-based Ontario Systems, which creates debt collection software, is among them. "Perhaps the most alarming news in 2011" for the industry was the joint opposition by 54 U.S. state and territorial attorneys general to the Mobile Information Call Act, which would have loosened restrictions on calls to consumers' cellphones, according to Andersen. [55] "That was unheard of for them to be so organized," she says.

That has not been the only coordinated action of state attorneys general against the debt-collection industry. Thirty-eight attorneys general, along with the FTC, opposed the $5.2 million settlement approved last August between debt buyer Encore Capital Group and 1.4 million consumers in class action lawsuits accusing the company of unfair practices, including using false affidavits to collect on debt.

"Under any interpretation, the ten-dollar-per-class-member settlement is not fair, reasonable, or adequate to address the harm incurred," the attorneys general said in a brief filed in federal court in Ohio. [56] Seven individuals who were part of the class action suits have appealed the settlement to the Sixth U.S. Circuit Court of Appeals in Cincinnati. [57]

Texas, West Virginia and Minnesota filed their own lawsuits against Encore. The company announced last October that it had reached a settlement with Texas but, at the same time, disclosed that North Carolina's attorney general had begun an investigation into Encore's debt-collection practices in that state. [58]

This past February, 19 attorneys general announced they had reached a settlement with NCO Financial Systems, the nation's largest debt collector, over charges of misleading and deceptive debt-collection practices. As part of the settlement, NCO agreed to change certain collection practices, pay $575,000 to the states for consumer enforcement and education efforts and set aside $950,000 to refund customers with valid claims against the company. [59]

A multi-state working group formed by the attorneys general in 2008 "received nearly two thousand complaints from consumers about [NCO Financial's] collection practices," New Mexico Attorney General Gary King said when the settlement was announced. "They include almost every possible violation of the federal Fair Debt Collection Practices Act." [60]

The company did not admit wrongdoing. "We are pleased to resolve the Multi-State Group's concerns, as well

Continued on p. 638

At Issue:

Should the Department of Education stop using debt collectors?

DEANNE LOONIN
DIRECTOR, STUDENT LOAN BORROWER ASSISTANCE PROJECT, NATIONAL CONSUMER LAW CENTER

WRITTEN FOR *CQ RESEARCHER*, JULY 2012

yes

The reliance on private collection agencies has been a disaster for financially distressed borrowers who are desperate for help. Dispute resolution is, obviously, not the primary mission of loan collection agencies. Debt collectors are not adequately trained to understand and administer the complex borrower rights available under the Higher Education Act, and the government does not provide sufficient oversight of their activities.

There are certainly times when a borrower is uncooperative or has exhausted all options. In those cases, the loan holder may have no choice but to focus on collection efforts. Yet there are many borrowers who want to find a solution but are stymied because they cannot get past the rude, harassing and often abusive behavior of a collection agent.

At a minimum, until the government identifies viable alternatives to private collection agencies, it should bring all accounts in-house (and away from collection agencies) for low-income borrowers who are already subject to extreme collection programs such as Social Security seizures. The government should also immediately take the file in-house if a borrower informs a collection agency that he believes he has a defense to the debt, that the amount is wrong or that he wants to request a hardship reduction or waiver.

This will not only help borrowers but also save money. There are significant costs involved in pursuing even the most vulnerable borrowers until they die. Under the current system, lenders and collectors profit as the government pays higher and higher collection fees.

Student borrowers attempting to better their lives face severe consequences if they default on federal student loans. The government has nearly boundless powers to collect student loans, far beyond those of most unsecured creditors. Even in bankruptcy, most student loans must be paid. Unlike any other types of debt, there is no statute of limitations. We see and hear the human toll of the tattered student loan safety net every day from the low-income borrowers we represent.

There comes a point of no return where the government's ceaseless efforts to collect make no sense, monetarily or otherwise. Balancing collection for taxpayers and relief to borrowers can be difficult, but the reality is that the government has consistently favored school, lender and collection industry profits over the needs of struggling borrowers. It is time to do what is right for borrowers.

SHELLY REPP
PRESIDENT, NATIONAL COUNCIL OF HIGHER EDUCATION LOAN PROGRAMS

WRITTEN FOR *CQ RESEARCHER*, JULY 2012

no

For more than three decades the U.S. Department of Education and the guaranty agencies that help it administer the federal student loan programs have utilized the skills and technical expertise of debt collectors to assist in recovering defaulted student loans. The success of this public-private partnership is undeniable — $75 billion recovered in the past decade with more than $12 billion recovered in fiscal 2011. This is reason enough to conclude that the department should continue using private debt collectors, but there are other compelling reasons to maintain this partnership.

Consumer advocates have stated that there should be a balance between the need to collect student loans and the need to assist borrowers. We agree. Average borrower indebtedness has more than doubled in the past decade, and student loan defaults are also on the rise. Congress has provided a number of ways to help defaulted borrowers. Private collection agencies (PCAs) are well-trained to help borrowers find the right solution for their unique financial situations. PCAs invest significant resources to comply with the Fair Debt Collection Practices Act and other applicable laws and use the latest technologies to promote borrower repayment.

The department provides monetary incentives not just based on dollars collected but also to reward superior customer service. It provides significant financial incentives to encourage loan rehabilitation. We expect the department to provide effective oversight. In this regard, the department has established a dedicated website and toll-free hotline to receive borrower complaints, and an active and effective ombudsman office. The Consumer Financial Protection Bureau stands by as a consumer watchdog.

There are some who believe the department should abandon the use of third-party debt collectors. They tout the IRS as an example justifying such a move. But PCA's have helped the Department of Education recover more than 90 percent of the defaulted student loans (after collection costs). On the other hand, since 2000 the IRS's backlog of uncollected debt exploded by 700 percent to more than $70 billion, while during the same period the collection rates on debt it attempted to recover have fallen by half. The government and taxpayers can't afford to replicate that record of loss.

The department's collection portfolio consists of nearly 23 million borrowers. With a program that size, there are bound to be some legitimate borrower complaints. They should be addressed. However, this does not justify ending a successful public-private partnership that benefits borrowers and taxpayers alike.

Continued from p. 636

as upgrade our compliance processes," said Ronald Rittenmeyer, NCO's chief executive. [61]

Legislative Action

State legislatures have been active on the debt-collection front as well. While the FDCPA regulates debt collection at the federal level, states can write their own legislation, and the industry must follow whichever statute is stricter.

North Carolina passed one of the strictest in 2009, aimed particularly at debt buyers. In court, attorneys representing a debt buyer or its collection agency must produce valid documentation that the debt buyer owns the debt; the name of the original creditor; the consumer's account number; a copy of the original credit agreement or similar document; and an itemized accounting of the alleged debt amount.

The law also requires the debt buyer or its collection agency to give 30 days' notice in writing to the consumer of its intent to sue. That notice must include all of the above information.

"It sounds like such a simple request, but the name of the original creditor can be a lot to ask for," says Andersen. "The ability to figure out the name of the first bank can be problematic because of mergers and acquisitions."

Illinois attorney Louis Freedman has a more fundamental objection to the North Carolina law: that the collection industry and its attorneys are being singled out. Freedman, president of the Washington-based National Association of Retail Collection Attorneys, says no other area of law requires such notice. "You are required to give [consumers] every bit of information before you have even filed suit," Freedman says.

But Hobbs of the National Consumer Law Center says the North Carolina law "is a good model for other states. Maryland and Delaware courts have enacted rules which are similar, although they might not be quite as strong."

California has also taken aim at debt buyers. The state Senate approved a bill in February that would require more documentation from debt buyers during the collection process, and on June 28 a committee in the General Assembly approved the measure.

Every state has a law that shields certain property from being claimed by creditors to pay off bad debts, but many of the laws are old. Some states have begun to revise them to reflect inflation and changes in technology.

More than a dozen states have increased the exemption for cars, and about a fifth of states have raised their exemptions for household goods, including computers. The revisions mean that "tens of millions of consumers with judgments over their heads, as they recover from a disability or a long period of unemployment, have the ability to acquire a used car or get a computer to look for a job without having the car seized or their computer taken away," says Hobbs.

The revisions were long overdue, says Hobbs. Before March 2011, Massachusetts law protected two cows, 12 sheep, two swine and a few tons of hay from creditors and exempted a vehicle worth up to $750 from seizure, according to Hobbs. In 2011, the state passed a new law that protected a broader array of items and raised the vehicle cap to $7,500. [62]

Still, says Hobbs, "a lot of states have not significantly improved these laws since the Great Depression."

Statute of Limitations

Debt collectors have a limited number of years to take consumers to court to collect bad debts. This statute of limitations varies from state to state. It's three years in Alabama, for example, five in Florida and eight in Wyoming. [63] But the debt does not go away, and while collectors cannot sue, they are allowed in most states to contact consumers to request payment on debt that has passed the statute of limitations, known as "time-barred" debt. Consumers are often not aware, however, that making a partial payment will reset the clock in most states, giving the debt collector a fresh shot in court.

Even though the FDCPA and state laws forbid collectors to sue on "time-barred debt," consumer advocates say it happens frequently. They say the problem can be missing paperwork that would have spelled out the applicable statute of limitations.

But Schiffman from ACA International disagrees that such lawsuits are commonplace. "It might happen occasionally, and when it does those collectors should be held accountable," he says.

A few states have recently added consumer protections for time-barred debt. New Mexico requires debt collectors to inform consumers if a debt has passed the state's statute of limitations and that they cannot be sued, though collectors can continue to pursue payment by phone or other means. "This rule is intended to ensure that debt collectors provide important information to consumers so that they make informed decisions when they are confronted with a demand to pay an old unenforceable debt," said King, the state's attorney general. [64] New York City and Massachusetts also have such rules.

Laws in Wisconsin and Mississippi go even further by completely extinguishing debt older than their statutes of limitations. The ACA does not want to see that practice spread to other states. "If there is no ability to collect on that debt, there would be a devastating impact on credit granting in the United States. You would make credit almost impossible to get," says Schiffman.

The ACA wants a national statute of limitations, rather than 50 different state statutes, to clear up any confusion during collection lawsuits. The trade association says the limitation period should be seven years. Consumer groups say it should be three. ■

OUTLOOK

New Rules?

The next year or so will be one of uncertainty for debt collectors as the Consumer Financial Protection Bureau (CFPB) rolls out new regulatory rules. But industry insiders say recent enforcement actions by the FTC offer clues to what is coming.

When the FTC settled with Asset Acceptance in January after investigating how the company collected on time-barred debt, it required the company from then on to disclose to consumers if a debt has passed the relevant statute of limitations. It also prohibited the company from suing a consumer after such a disclosure even if the consumer makes a partial payment that otherwise would reset the clock. [65]

Andersen at Ontario Systems, the debt-collection software firm, expects the CFPB to require all debt-collection agencies to notify consumers "that the statute of limitations is either close to an expiration date or has expired." And while the CFPB might not go as far as to prohibit suits against consumers who make a partial payment on time-barred debt, it might require collection agencies to warn consumers of how a debt payment may affect the statute of limitations, Andersen says.

She says she would be surprised if Congress passes legislation to amend the Fair Debt Collection Protection Act (FDCPA) this year or next, whether to raise the $1,000 limit on statutory damages when debt collectors violate the law, add documentation requirements for collectors or shield the industry from consumer lawsuits over debt-related phone messages. "Congress is not going to neuter the CFPB, not our current Senate anyway, by passing FDCPA legislation," Andersen says.

But Curtis of Community Catalyst says Congress might act. "I think there is some interest in strengthening the . . . act," she says, but adds a caveat: "It is also an election year, and that always has interesting implications for Congress."

One debt-related bill before Congress does have broad support. The House passed a version of the Medical Debt Responsibility Act in 2010, and Sen. Jeff Merkley, D-Ore., reintroduced the bill in the Senate in March. The bill would erase medical debt from consumer credit reports within 45 days of being settled or paid. Under current law, consumer debt, including medical debt, can remain on a credit report for seven years, driving down credit scores.

"Medical debt is not a great predictor of a person's creditworthiness, and folks should not be shackled from getting loans to start businesses or buy their dream home because they got very sick," Merkley said. [66]

The bill's support extends beyond patient-advocacy groups, such as Consumers Union and The Access Project, to the Mortgage Bankers Association, American Medical Association and members of the debt-collection industry. "Medical debt is unlike any other type of consumer debt," says Capio CEO Richards. "We totally understand no one plans an accident or illness, which creates medical debt."

Critics of the bill, however, say medical debt is predictive of a consumer's credit worthiness. A spokesman for the Consumer Data Industry Association, which represents the nation's major credit bureaus, told *The New York Times* that it had "deep concerns about deleting any type of accurate, predictive data" before the end of the seven-year period. "Broadly speaking, a precedent of deleting adverse information once a delinquent debt is paid would seriously impinge on the quality of data," he said. [67] ■

Notes

[1] "As a Result of FTC Action, Two Defendants in Abusive Debt Collection Case Are Banned from the Industry, Will Surrender Assets," Federal Trade Commission, March 15, 2012, www.ftc.gov/opa/2012/03/rumson.shtm. "Federal Trade Commission vs. Forensic Case Management," U.S. District Court for the Central District of California, Sept. 12, 2011, pp. 7-8, www.ftc.gov/os/caselist/1123035/110930rumsoncmpt.pdf.

[2] "Repairing a Broken System: Protecting Consumers in Debt Collection Litigation and Arbitration," Federal Trade Commission, July 2010, p. i, www.ftc.gov/os/2010/07/debtcollectionreport.pdf.

[3] "The Impact of Third-Party Debt Collection on the National and State Economies," Ernst & Young, February 2012, p. 2, www.acainternational.org/files.aspx?p=/images/21594/2011acaeconomicimpactreport.pdf.

[4] "Quarterly Report on Household Debt and Credit," Federal Reserve Bank of New York, p. 16, www.newyorkfed.org/research/national_economy/householdcredit/DistrictReport_Q12012.pdf.

[5] "FTC Highlights Expanded Work on Debt Collection Issues over the Past Year," Federal Trade Commission, March 20, 2012, www.ftc.gov/opa/2012/03/cfpb.shtm.

[6] "Leading Debt Collector Agrees to Pay Record $2.8 Million to Settle FTC Charges," Federal Trade Commission, March 16, 2011, www.ftc.gov/opa/2011/03/wam.shtm.

[7] "Under FTC Settlement, Debt Buyer Agrees to Pay $2.5 Million for Alleged Consumer Deception," Federal Trade Commission, Jan. 30, 2012, www.ftc.gov/opa/2012/01/asset.shtm.

[8] "DBA International Supports FTC Enforcement Actions," DBA International, April 16, 2012, www.dbainternational.org/news/ftc-india.asp.

[9] "Fair Debt Collection Practices Act: CFPB Annual Report 2012," Consumer Financial Protection Bureau, March 21, 2012, Appen-

dix B, Appendix C, http://files.consumerfinance.gov/f/201203_cfpb_FDCPA_annual_report.pdf.

[10] "U.S. Debt Collections Industry Worth $12.2. Billion," PRWeb, April 10, 2012, www.prweb.com/releases/2012/4/prweb9383739.htm.

[11] Ernst & Young, *op. cit.*

[12] Federal Reserve Bank of New York, *op. cit.*, p. 10.

[13] "Consumer Financial Protection Bureau proposes rule to supervise larger participants in consumer debt collection and consumer reporting markets," Consumer Financial Protection Board, Feb. 16, 2012, www.consumerfinance.gov/pressreleases/consumer-financial-protection-bureau-proposes-rule-to-supervise-larger-participants-in-consumer-debt-collection-and-consumer-reporting-markets.

[14] Maria Aspan, "Borrower Beware: B of A Customer Repaid Her Bill Yet Faced a Collections Nightmare," *American Banker*, March 29, 2012, www.americanbanker.com/issues/177_62/bofa-credit-cards-debt-collections-delinquent-robo signing-1047991-1.html.

[15] "Evolution of the U.S. Accounts Receivable Management Industry," Kaulkin Ginsberg, October 2006, p. 5.

[16] "Workshop: Debt Collection 2.0: Protecting Consumers," Consumers Union letter to FTC, May 27, 2011, p. 3, www.consumerfed.org/pdfs/Debt_Collection_2_0_wkshop_comment.pdf.

[17] Robert J. Hobbs and Chi Chi Wu, "Model Family Financial Protection Act," National Consumer Law Center, June 2012, p. 14, www.nclc.org/images/pdf/debt_collection/model_family_financial_protection_act.pdf.

[18] "The Path Forward: ACA International's Blueprint for Modernizing America's Consumer Debt Collection System," ACA International, April 2011, p. 18, www.acainternational.org/files.aspx?p=/images/18898/finalblueprint-designedversion.pdf.

[19] "Credit Cards: Fair Debt Collection Practices Act Could Better Reflect the Evolving Debt Collection Marketplace and Use of Technology," Government Accountability Office, September 2009, p. 41, www.gao.gov/assets/300/295588.pdf.

[20] "Repairing A Broken System: Protecting Consumers in Debt Collection Litigation and Arbitration," Federal Trade Commission, July 2010, www.ftc.gov/os/2010/07/debtcollectionreport.pdf.

[21] For background, see Barbara Mantel, "Legal Aid Crisis," *CQ Researcher*, Oct. 7, 2011, pp. 829-852.

[22] "Repairing A Broken System," *op. cit.*

[23] Patrick Lunsford, "Encore Capital Wins Approval of $5.2 million Settlement," *InsideArm*, Aug. 13, 2011, www.insidearm.com/daily/debt-buying-topics/debt-buying/encore-capital-wins-approval-of-5-7-million-settlement.

[24] "Dear Members of Congress," National Association of Attorneys General, Dec. 7, 2011, p. 1, http://signon.s3.amazonaws.com/20111207.signon.Final_HR3035_Letter.pdf.

[25] Chris Serres, "Debtors in court — suing collectors," *StarTribune.com*, Minneapolis-St. Paul, Minn., Aug. 1, 2010, www.startribune.com/investigators/99676349.html?page=5&c=y.

[26] Marjie Lundstromand and Sam Stanton, "Debtors seethe, sue over collector tactics," *The Sacramento Bee*, April 22, 2012, www.sacbee.com/2012/04/22/4432940/debtors-seethe-sue-over-collector.html.

[27] Serres, *op. cit.*

[28] Ames Alexander and David Raynor, "Hospital suits force new pain on patients," *charlotte observercom*, April 23, 2012, www.charlotteobserver.com/2012/04/23/3193509/hospital-suits-force-new-pain.html.

[29] Sara R. Collins, Michele M. Doty, Ruth Robertson and Tracy Garber, "Help on the Horizon: How the Recession Has Left Millions of Workers Without Health Insurance, and How Health Reform Will Bring Relief," The Commonwealth Fund, March 2011, pp. 10-11, www.commonwealthfund.org/~/media/Files/Surveys/2011/1486_Collins_help_on_the_horizon_2010_biennial_survey_report_FINAL_31611.pdf.

[30] For background, see Marcia Clemmitt, "Health Care Reform," *CQ Researcher*, June 11, 2010, updated May 24, 2011, pp. 505-528.

[31] Cheryl Fish-Parcham, Chi Chi Wu, Odette Williamson and Jessica Hiemenz, "Helping Older Americans Cope with Medical Debt," National Consumer Law Center, March 14, 2012, p. 13.

[32] "Additional Requirements for Charitable Hospitals," Internal Revenue Service, June 22, 2012, pp. 80-81, www.irs.gov/pub/irs-drop/reg-130266-11.pdf.

[33] "The Patient Financial Assistance Act," *Community Catalyst*, May 2004, p. 23, www.communitycatalyst.org/doc_store/publications/model_act_and_guide_may04.pdf.

[34] *Ibid.*

[35] Louis Hyman, *Borrow: The American Way of Debt* (2012), p. 21.

[36] *Ibid.*, p. 27.

[37] Lendol Calder, *Financing the American Dream* (1999), p. 54.

[38] Charles R. Geisst, *Collateral Damaged: The Marketing of Consumer Debt to America* (2009), p. 52.

[39] Calder, *op. cit.*, p. 135.

[40] *Ibid.*, p. 147.

[41] *Ibid.*, p. 151.

[42] "Evolution of the U.S. Accounts Receivable Management Industry," *op. cit.*, p. 3.

[43] Hyman, *op. cit.*, p. 104.

[44] *Ibid.*, p. 109.

[45] *Ibid.*, p. 115.

[46] Geisst, *op. cit.*, p. 88.

[47] Rick Jurgens and Robert J. Hobbs, "The Debt Machine: How the Collection Industry Hounds Consumers and Overwhelms Courts," National Consumer Law Center, July 2010, p. 8, www.nclc.org/images/pdf/pr-reports/debt-machine.pdf.

[48] "Fear: the collectors' trump card," *Chicago Tribune*, April 10, 1974, http://expressrecovery.com/uploads/files/90_1-Chicago_Tribune_Bill_Collector_Series_1974.pdf.

[49] The Fair Debt Collections Practices Act, Section 802, www.ftc.gov/os/statutes/fdcpa/fdcpact.shtm.

[50] Geisst, *op. cit.*, p. 105.

[51] Sandra E. Black and Donald P. Morgan, "Meet the New Borrowers," *Current Issues in Economics and Finance*, Federal Reserve Bank of New York, February 1999, p. 1, www.nyfedeconomists.org/research/current_issues/ci5-3.pdf.

[52] Meta Brown, *et. al.*, "The Financial Crisis

About the Author

Barbara Mantel is a freelance writer in New York City. She is a former correspondent and senior producer for National Public Radio and has won several journalism awards, including the National Press Club's Best Consumer Journalism Award and the Front Page Award from the Newswomen's Club of New York for her Nov. 1, 2009, *CQ Global Researcher* report "Terrorism and the Internet." She holds a B.A. in history and economics from the University of Virginia and an M.A. in economics from Northwestern University.

at the Kitchen Table: Recent Trends in Household Debt and Credit," Federal Deposit Insurance Corp., Sept. 15, 2011, p. 9, www.fdic.gov/news/conferences/VanderKlaaw6.pdf.
[53] "Debt Deception: How Debt Buyers Abuse the Legal System to Prey on Lower-Income New Yorkers," The Legal Aid Society, May 2010, p. 4, www.nedap.org/pressroom/documents/DEBT_DECEPTION_FINAL_WEB.pdf.
[54] "Franken, LeMieux Introduce Legislation to End Debt Collector Abuse," Press Release, Sept. 30, 2010, www.franken.senate.gov/?p=press_release&id=1122.
[55] Rozanne M. Andersen, "Eye on the Horizon — 2012: Emerging Legal, Legislative and Regulatory Trends in the Accounts Receivable Industry," Kaulkin Ginsberg, January 2012, p. 2.
[56] "State AGs oppose settlement with Encore unit," Reuters, June 3, 2011, www.reuters.com/article/2011/06/03/encore-settlement-idUSN0316342920110603.
[57] Emily Sachar, "The issue: How far can a debt collector go to pursue its claims?" *AARP Bulletin*, May 2012, http://pubs.aarp.org/aarpbulletin/201205_DC?pg=34#article_id=163864.
[58] "Encore Capital Discloses Another State Investigation as Profits Rise in Q3," insideARM.com, Oct. 27, 2011, www.insidearm.com/daily/debt-buying-topics/debt-buying/encore-capital-discloses-another-state-investigation-as-profits-rise-in-q3.
[59] "Alaska Announces Settlement with Debt Collector NCO Financial Systems," State of Alaska Department of Law, Feb. 6, 2012, www.law.alaska.gov/press/releases/2012/020612-NCFO.html. "States Settle with National Debt Collection Firm," Office of New Mexico Attorney General, Feb. 6, 2012, www.nmag.gov/News-Releases/statessettlewithnationaldebtcollectionfirmagkingmonetaryreliefforvictimizednmconsumers.
[60] *Ibid.*
[61] Patrick Lunsford, "NCO Settles Debt Collection Action with 19 States," insideARM.com, Feb. 7, 2012, www.insidearm.com/daily/collection-laws-regulations/collection-laws-and-regulations/nco-settles-debt-collection-action-with-19-states.
[62] Robert J. Hobbs and Hon. Carol J. Kenner, "How to Protect Your Clients' Cash and Assets Under New Massachusetts Personal Property Exemptions," org??? March 9, 2011, p. 1, www.nclc.org/images/pdf/pr-reports/new-law-protects-cars-wages-bank-accounts.pdf.
[63] "State statutes of limitation for credit card debt," CreditCards.com, www.creditcards.com/credit-card-news/credit-card-state-statute-limitations-1282.php.
[64] New Mexico Attorney General, press release, Dec. 15, 2010, http://creditboards.com/forums/index.php?showtopic=461211.
[65] Federal Trade Commission, Jan. 30, 2012, *op. cit.*
[66] "Merkley Reintroduces Bill to Provide Relief to Americans Struggling with Medical Debt," press release, March 2, 2012, www.merkley.senate.gov/newsroom/press/release/?id=e5b222cf-7804-4b44-8f0d-1310753068e5.
[67] Tara Siegel Bernard, "Discrepancies on Medical Bills Can Leave a Credit Stain," The *New York Times*, May 4, 2012, www.nytimes.com/2012/05/05/your-money/medical-debts-can-leave-stains-on-credit-scores.html?pagewanted=all.

FOR MORE INFORMATION

ACA International, 4040 West 70th St., Minneapolis, MN 55435; 952-926-6547; www.acainternational.org. Trade association for collection agencies, asset buyers, attorneys, creditors and vendor affiliates.

American Hospital Association, 155 N. Wacker Drive, Chicago, IL 60606; 312-422-3000; www.aha.org. Trade association for hospitals and health care networks.

Community Catalyst, 30 Winter St., 10th Floor, Boston, MA 02108; 617-338-6035; www.communitycatalyst.org. Promotes transformation of health system through work with consumer and community leaders.

Consumer Financial Protection Board, 1700 G St., N.W., Washington, DC 20552; 202-435-7000; www.consumerfinance.gov. Federal agency that regulates consumer financial products and services.

Consumers Union, 1535 Mission St., San Francisco, CA 94103; 415-431-6747; www.consumersunion.org. Consumer-protection advocacy organization.

DBA International, 1050 Fulton Ave., Suite 120, Sacramento CA 95825; 916-482-2462; www.dbainternational.org. Trade association for the debt-buying industry.

Federal Trade Commission, 600 Pennsylvania Ave., N.W., Washington, DC 20580; 202-326-2222; www.ftc.gov. Federal agency charged with preventing anti-competitive or deceptive business practices.

National Association of Consumer Advocates, 1730 Rhode Island Ave., N.W., Suite 710, Washington, DC 20036; 202-452-1989; www.naca.net. Membership organization of attorneys and consumer advocates representing consumer interests.

National Association of Retail Collection Attorneys, 601 Pennsylvania Ave., N.W., Washington, DC 20004; 800-633-6069; www.narca.org. Membership organization of law firms engaged in consumer debt collection.

National Consumers Law Center, 7 Winthrop Square, Boston, MA 02110; 617-542-8010; www.nclc.org. Promotes access to quality financial services and protection of family assets from unfair transactions.

National Council of Higher Education Loan Programs, 1100 Connecticut Ave., N.W., Suite 1200, Washington, DC 20036; 202-822-2106, www.nchelp.org. Represents guaranty agencies, lenders, loan servicers, collection agencies and schools involved in the administration and servicing of federal and alternative student loans.

Privacy Rights Clearinghouse, 3108 Fifth Ave., Suite A, San Diego, CA 92103; 619-298-3396; www.privacyrights.org. Advocates for consumers' privacy rights.

Bibliography

Selected Sources

Books

Calder, Lendol, *Financing the American Dream*, Princeton University Press, 1999.
A history professor presents a social and cultural history of the rise of consumer credit in America.

Geisst, Charles R., *Collateral Damaged: The Marketing of Consumer Debt to America*, Bloomberg Press, 2009.
A financial writer examines the policy implications of America's recent credit crisis and proposes how to get the country's fiscal house in order.

Hyman, Louis, *Borrow: The American Way of Debt*, Vintage Books, 2012.
A historian looks at how the rise of consumer borrowing in the past century has altered U.S. culture and the economy.

Articles

Alexander, Ames and David Raynor, "Hospital suits force new pain on patients," *charlotteobserver.com*, April 23, 2012, www.charlotteobserver.com/2012/04/23/3193509/hospital-suits-force-new-pain.html.
Nonprofit North Carolina hospitals are suing patients for bad debts, including some patients who were eligible for hospital financial assistance but did not receive it.

Aspan, Maria, "Borrower Beware: B of A Customer Repaid Her Bill Yet Faced a Collections Nightmare," *American Banker*, March 29, 2012, www.americanbanker.com/issues/177_62/bofa-credit-cards-debt-collections-delinquent-robosigning-1047991-1.html.
A Maryland woman spent a year paying off a delinquent credit card bill, only to be pursued by debt collectors after the credit-card issuer mistakenly sold her settled debt.

Lerner, Maura and Tony Kennedy, " 'Money-hungry' tactics raised alarms at Fairview," *Star Tribune* (Minneapolis), www.startribune.com/lifestyle/health/151639735.html.
Employees of a Minneapolis nonprofit hospital complain about aggressive tactics of a newly hired debt-collection company.

Lundstromand, Marjie and Sam Stanton, "Debtors seethe, sue over collector tactics," *The Sacramento Bee*, April 22, 2012, www.sacbee.com/2012/04/22/4432940/debtors-seethe-sue-over-collector.html.
In the last seven years, the number of lawsuits in California federal courts accusing collectors of violating federal law increased fivefold.

Serres, Chris, "Debtors in court — suing collectors," *Star Tribune.com* (Minneapolis), Aug. 1, 2010, www.startribune.com/investigators/99676349.html?page=1&c=y.
Federal lawsuits by consumers against debt collectors have soared, but collectors say many suits are unsubstantiated.

Reports and Studies

"Additional Requirements for Charitable Hospitals," Internal Revenue Service, June 22, 2012, pp. 80-81, www.ofr.gov/OFRUpload/OFRData/2012-15537_PI.pdf.
The IRS writes draft rules for implementing billing and collection polices at nonprofit hospitals required by the Affordable Care Act.

"Credit Cards: Fair Debt Collection Practices Act Could Better Reflect the Evolving Debt Collection Marketplace and Use of Technology," U.S. Government Accountability Office, September 2009, p. 41, www.gao.gov/assets/300/295588.pdf.
The Government Accountability Office finds that consumer protections should be strengthened in light of growth in debt buying and that decades-old laws should be amended to keep up with communication tools such as email and cellphones.

"Fair Debt Collection Practices Act: CFPB Annual Report 2012," Consumer Financial Protection Bureau, March 21, 2012, Appendix B, Appendix C, http://files.consumerfinance.gov/f/201203_cfpb_FDCPA_annual_report.pdf.
The federal consumer-protection agency reports on progress regulating consumer financial services and on trends in consumer complaints against debt collectors.

"The Path Forward: ACA International's Blueprint for Modernizing America's Consumer Debt Collection System," ACA International, April 2011, p. 18, www.acainternational.org/files.aspx?p=/images/18898/finalblueprint-designedversion.pdf.
A debt-collection industry trade group lays out its blueprint for changes in laws and regulations.

"Repairing a Broken System: Protecting Consumers in Debt Collection Litigation and Arbitration," Federal Trade Commission, July 2010, p. i, www.ftc.gov/os/2010/07/debtcollectionreport.pdf.
After a series of roundtable discussions on litigating and arbitrating debt collectors' claims against consumers, the FTC concludes that the system is broken.

Hobbs, Robert J., and Chi Chi Wu, "Model Family Financial Protection Act," National Consumer Law Center, June 2012, p. 14, www.nclc.org/images/pdf/debt_collection/model_family_financial_protection_act.pdf.
A consumer advocacy group writes a model statue for states to regulate the debt-collection industry and fill gaps it sees in federal law.

The Next Step:

Additional Articles from Current Periodicals

Consumer Protection

Ambrose, Eileen, "Debt Buyers Now Must Back Up Their Lawsuits," *Baltimore Sun*, Jan. 29, 2012, p. C1, articles.baltimoresun.com/2012-01-29/business/bs-bz-ambrose-court-debts-20120129_1_debt-buyers-sonya-smith-valentine-consumer-protection-clinic.

Debt buyers who purchase old consumer debt and then try to collect must now provide greater evidence of their claims when suing consumers in Maryland courts.

Carter, Ted, "Threats, Lies Get Atlanta Debt Collection Company in Very Hot Water in Georgia," *Mississippi Business Journal*, March 1, 2012, msbusiness.com/businessblog/2012/03/01/threats-lies-get-debt-collection-company-in-very-hot-water/.

The Georgia governor's office has ordered an Atlanta collections agency to give up attempts to collect on more than 31,000 accounts because it allegedly used intimidation and lying.

Demarrais, Kevin, "Rules on Debt Collection Are Hazy on What's Harassment," *The Record* (Bergen County, N.J.), April 22, 2012, p. B1, www.northjersey.com/news/business/148419435_Rules_on_debt_collection_are_hazy_on_what_s_harassment.html.

Rules govern when debt collectors may call and what they may say, but there is no definition of what constitutes harassment.

Goforth, Alan, "Getting Bills Paid Can Be a Good Thing, Collectors Say," *Kansas City Star*, Oct. 29, 2011, p. A16.

The Kansas Collectors Association says bill collecting should be handled professionally to help both businesses and consumers.

Medical Bills

Bernard, Tara Siegel, "A Medical Debt's Stain," *The New York Times*, May 5, 2012, p. B1, www.nytimes.com/2012/05/05/your-money/medical-debts-can-leave-stains-on-credit-scores.html?pagewanted=all.

More medical providers are using debt collection services and are turning to them more quickly than they have in the past.

Doyle, Jim, "Ascension Health's Ties to Debt Collection Probe," *St. Louis* (Mo.) *Post-Dispatch*, April 27, 2012, www.stltoday.com/business/local/ascension-health-s-ties-to-embattled-debt-collector/article_6304c69a-8fe2-11e1-b74e-0019bb30f31a.html.

A Chicago-based medical debt collection firm has been accused of illegal collection practices at two Minnesota non-profit hospital systems.

Hart, Patricia Kilday, "Humane Medical Billing — Surely We Can Afford It," *Houston Chronicle*, July 1, 2012, p. B1, www.chron.com/news/kilday-hart/article/Hart-Humane-medical-billing-surely-we-can-3676248.php.

More and more consumers are having their credit scores ruined by delinquent payments on medical bills.

Settlement

Dugas, Christine, "Know Your Options If Seeking Help With Debt," *USA Today*, Nov. 16, 2011, p. B4, www.usatoday.com/money/perfi/credit/story/2011-11-15/debt-relief/51223354/1.

Consumers seeking debt relief should avoid traps and understand their options.

Jowers, Karen, "Do's and Don'ts of Debt Consolidation," *Army Times*, June 21, 2012, www.armytimes.com/money/financial_advice/offduty-consumer-watch-how-to-find-right-path-out-of-financial-trouble-062512w/.

Debt settlement can harm credit scores and require fees from $2,000 to $5,000.

Namee, Roberta, "Look for Red Flags Before Hiring a Credit Repair Company," *Wichita* (Kan.) *Eagle*, May 12, 2012, www.kansas.com/2012/05/12/2332325/look-for-red-flags-before-hiring.html.

Debt settlement and credit-repair companies can often make consumers' financial burdens worse.

Tompor, Susan, "In Many Cases, Consumers Can Fix Their Credit Themselves," *Detroit Free Press*, May 10, 2012, p. B1, www.freep.com/article/20120510/COL07/205100492/Susan-Tompor-Consumers-can-fix-credit-themselves.

Many consumers fail to understand that debt settlement agreements with creditors do not translate into higher credit scores.

Citing *CQ Researcher*

Sample formats for citing these reports in a bibliography include the ones listed below. Preferred styles and formats vary, so please check with your instructor or professor.

MLA Style

Jost, Kenneth. "Remembering 9/11," CQ Researcher 2 Sept. 2011: 701-732.

APA Style

Jost, K. (2011, September 2). Remembering 9/11. *CQ Researcher, 9*, 701-732.

Chicago Style

Jost, Kenneth. "Remembering 9/11." *CQ Researcher*, September 2, 2011, 701-732.

Researcher PLUS Archive
New!

CQ Researcher

Published by CQ Press, an Imprint of SAGE Publications, Inc.

www.cqresearcher.com

Smart Cities

Are futuristic metropolises good investments?

Across the globe, major tech companies and multinational developers are pouring billions of dollars into building futuristic "smart cities" designed to showcase cutting-edge infrastructure and architecture — and serve as models for new cities worldwide. From self-sustaining energy systems and driverless vehicles to software that runs metro areas like operating systems run computers, emerging cities in India, China, South Korea and elsewhere are introducing technology that backers say can reduce common urban problems such as pollution, crime and congestion. For cities to survive and grow, they contend, society must reinvent them. But critics question whether building new metropolises is wise when existing ones need attention. No smart cities are being built from scratch in the United States, but smart-growth strategies designed to make existing communities more livable are taking root from New York to Kansas.

Songdo, South Korea, rises in Incheon on land reclaimed from the Yellow Sea. The New York developer of the project, dubbed the Atlantis of the Far East, says the planned city of 65,000 residents will be among the world's greenest and most technology-rich urban centers — and a model to be replicated worldwide.

INSIDE THIS REPORT

The Issues 647
Background 654
Chronology 655
Current Situation 659
At Issue........................661
Outlook 662
Bibliography 666
The Next Step 667

CQ Researcher • July 27, 2012 • www.cqresearcher.com
Volume 22, Number 27 • Pages 645-668

Los Angeles | London | New Delhi
Singapore | Washington DC

Recipient of Society of Professional Journalists Award for Excellence ◆ American Bar Association Silver Gavel Award

SMART CITIES

THE ISSUES

647 • Does building smart cities make sense when existing cities need attention?
• Can innovations showcased in experimental metropolises be scaled up to benefit large, aging cities?
• Do smart cities over-rely on technology?

BACKGROUND

654 **City Beautiful Movement** Urban-revival efforts began in the late 1800s.

656 **Urban Renewal** Aging buildings, many significant, were demolished beginning in the 1950s.

658 **Mixed Results** Some early efforts at smart growth fared poorly.

658 **Suburban 'Utopias'** Dissatisfaction with urban life led to attempts to recreate small-town America.

659 **Road to Smart Growth** Walt Disney had a grand vision for a futuristic city.

CURRENT SITUATION

659 **Gaining Momentum** Smart cities are being planned around the globe.

660 **Smart Growth Strategies** U.S. cities are focusing on upgrading neighborhoods.

662 **Cautionary Tales** The smart city movement faces numerous problems.

OUTLOOK

662 **Here to Stay?** Demand for new cities is expected to explode.

SIDEBARS AND GRAPHICS

648 **Smart Cities Rising From China to Finland** China is planning at least four smart cities.

649 **Population to Soar** Some 9 billion people will live on Earth by 2041.

652 **Cities Experiencing Explosive Growth** Delhi, India, will grow by 10 million by 2025.

655 **Chronology** Key events since 1893.

656 **Technology Brings New Brainpower to Communities** "The city becomes a platform that allows new forms of innovation."

661 **At Issue** Can smart city technology save ailing cities?

FOR FURTHER RESEARCH

665 **For More Information** Organizations to contact.

666 **Bibliography** Selected sources used.

667 **The Next Step** Additional articles.

667 **Citing *CQ Researcher*** Sample bibliography formats.

Cover: Reuters/Incheon Free Economic Zone/Handout

CQ Researcher

July 27, 2012
Volume 22, Number 27

MANAGING EDITOR: Thomas J. Billitteri tjb@cqpress.com

ASSISTANT MANAGING EDITOR: Kathy Koch kkoch@cqpress.com

CONTRIBUTING EDITOR: Thomas J. Colin tcolin@cqpress.com

ASSOCIATE EDITOR: Kenneth Jost

STAFF WRITER: Marcia Clemmitt

CONTRIBUTING WRITERS: Peter Katel, Barbara Mantel, Jennifer Weeks

DESIGN/PRODUCTION EDITOR: Olu B. Davis

ASSISTANT EDITOR: Darrell Dela Rosa

FACT CHECKER: Michelle Harris

INTERN: Kate Irby

Los Angeles | London | New Delhi
Singapore | Washington DC

An Imprint of SAGE Publications, Inc.

VICE PRESIDENT AND EDITORIAL DIRECTOR, HIGHER EDUCATION GROUP: Michele Sordi

DIRECTOR, ONLINE PUBLISHING: Todd Baldwin

CQ Researcher (ISSN 1056-2036) is printed on acid-free paper. Published weekly, except: (March wk. 5) (May wk. 4) (July wk. 1) (Aug. wks. 3, 4) (Nov. wk. 4) and (Dec. wks. 3, 4). Published by SAGE Publications, Inc., 2455 Teller Rd., Thousand Oaks, CA 91320. Annual full-service subscriptions start at $1,054. For pricing, call 1-800-834-9020. To purchase a *CQ Researcher* report in print or electronic format (PDF), visit www.cqpress.com or call 866-427-7737. Single reports start at $15. Bulk purchase discounts and electronic-rights licensing are also available. Periodicals postage paid at Thousand Oaks, California, and at additional mailing offices. POSTMASTER: Send address changes to *CQ Researcher*, 2300 N St., N.W., Suite 800, Washington, DC 20037.

Smart Cities

BY DAVID HATCH

THE ISSUES

On 1,500 acres of land reclaimed from the Yellow Sea, a gleaming, high-tech metropolis unlike any place on Earth is rising in Incheon, South Korea. Dubbed the Atlantis of the Far East, Songdo offers a glimpse into the future of urban design. [1]

Songdo aspires to be among the world's greenest and most technology-rich cities — and also a utopia devoid of the ills that plague most metropolises. Gale International, a New York development firm, envisions it as a model to be replicated worldwide.

More than halfway toward its 2017 scheduled completion, the new city of 65,000 residents features a dazzling array of innovations:

- More than 10,000 touch screens, developed by Cisco, will be installed in homes and offices and on street corners to enable home tutoring and video phone calls and serve as gateways to city services. [2]
- Wireless sensors track road conditions and congestion, reroute traffic and adjust street lights accordingly.
- Rooftop vegetation absorbs excess heat and reduces storm-water runoff.
- A pneumatic waste-collection system sucks garbage from buildings through pipes.
- And to encourage fitness, parks and other greenery cover 40 percent of the city's footprint. [3]

AP Photo/Kamran Jebreili

Secretary of State Hillary Rodham Clinton meets with project director Sultan Ahmed al-Jaber in Masdar, a smart city being built near Abu Dhabi, United Arab Emirates. A UAE renewable-energy firm building the $19 billion city says it will be among the most sustainable places on the planet. Proponents say new smart cities are necessary because overcrowding and pollution are making the world's biggest metropolises increasingly unsustainable. Skeptics counter that constructing new cities is foolish when existing ones are in dire need of attention.

Songdo, proponents say, will be a full-fledged city with an active economy open to all. Initial demand for housing, secured via a nationwide lottery system, was overwhelming, with an average of eight people vying for each unit. [4]

In a nod to the world's great cities, Songdo borrows from the most notable urban designs. It features the wide, tree-lined boulevards of Paris, a 100-acre commons modeled after New York City's famed Central Park, canals that pay homage to Venice and a convention center inspired by Sydney's iconic Opera House. [5]

With a price tag of $35 billion, it is the largest private real estate venture ever. [6] That figure covers the master plan for the design and construction of Songdo's downtown, where some office tenants were lined up in advance. The Korean government is paying for highways, bridges, a subway extension from Incheon and other public infrastructure.

As Songdo rises, other high-tech cities are sprouting elsewhere. About 10 miles from Abu Dhabi in the United Arab Emirates, the walled metropolis of Masdar, with a planned population of 40,000, conjures images of ancient desert fortresses and swashbuckling Lawrence of Arabia. [7] (The walls are designed to protect against desert winds and not marauders.) [8]

Inspired by ancient cities in what are now Morocco, Syria and Yemen, Masdar broke ground in 2008 but won't be completed until 2025, at a cost that could reach $19 billion. [9] Its designers tout it as carbon-neutral and among the most sustainable places on the planet. Solar energy will power the city, residential buildings will be designed to minimize water and electricity use and treated wastewater will be used for irrigation. [10] Battery-powered, driverless pods that each carry a few passengers run along magnetized tracks. [11]

In Europe, PlanIT Valley, a futuristic city envisioned for northern Portugal, is in the conceptual stage. It won't be ready until 2017 at the earliest, at a potential cost of $12.3 billion if all goes as planned, according to Steve Lewis, CEO of the Portugal-based technology

Smart Cities Rising From China to Finland

China is pursuing the construction of at least four smart cities, which are designed to conserve energy, water and other resources, reduce pollution and traffic congestion and curb other urban ills. Countries building smart cities also include South Korea, the United Arab Emirates, Finland and Portugal.

Notable Smart City Projects

New city (start date)	Nearest major city (distance)	Land size (acres)	Project leader	Estimated cost	Anticipated residents	Use	Completion date and status
Songdo South Korea (2005)	Seoul (40 miles)	1,500	Gale International	$35 billion	65,000	International business district	2017; under construction
Dongtan China (2005)	Shanghai (16 miles)	21,250	Shanghai Industrial Investment Corp.	n/a	25,000 by 2010, 500,000 by 2050	Model sustainable city	Stalled
Masdar United Arab Emirates (2007)	Abu Dhabi (10.5 miles)	1,730	Masdar	$19 billion	40,000	Clean-tech cluster in model sustainable city	2025; six buildings operational with residents; continuing
Tianjin Eco-city China (2007)	Tianjin (25 miles)	7,360	SSTEC	n/a	350,000	Education	2018-2023; continuing
Nanjing eco city China (2008)	Nanjing (4 miles)	1,280	Singapore-Jiangsu Cooperation Council	n/a	n/a	High-tech, smart industries in an ecologically aware environment	2020
PlanIT Valley Portugal (2008)	Porto (20 miles)	1,675	Living PlanIT	$10 billion	220,000	Research	2017; planning
Meixi Lake District China (2009)	Changsha (within city limits)	4,20	Gale International	n/a	180,000	Model future Chinese city	2020; early planning
Low2No Finland (2009)	Helsinki (within city limits)	5.4	Sitra	n/a	60% of space designated residential	Low or no carbon district	2012; in design

Source: Annissa Alusi, et al., *"Sustainable Cities: Oxymoron or the Shape of the Future?" Harvard Business School, March 2011, p. 21, www.hbs.edu/research/pdf/11-062.pdf*

firm Living PlanIT, the developer. The city, with a projected 220,000 residents — half of them researchers, engineers and family members — will be a testing ground for urban projects that Living PlanIT is pursuing in China and other countries. It will be run by an "urban operating system" (OS) — software that controls everything from traffic flow to energy consumption. (*See sidebar, p. 656.*)

These "pop-up" or "instant" cities represent the leading edge of a rapidly expanding global movement to redefine urban space. They are a necessity, proponents say, because the world's biggest metropolises are increasingly viewed as unsustainable due to overcrowding and pollution from factories and fossil fuel.

A century ago, almost 90 percent of humanity resided in rural areas. [12] In 2008, a milestone was reached when more than half of the world's population — for the first time — lived in urban areas. [13] By 2050, the United Nations estimates, the world population, now at 7 billion, will exceed 9 billion, with 70 percent in cities. [14] (*See chart, p. 649.*)

Housing shortages, abject poverty, overcrowding, asthma-inducing pollution and crumbling infrastructures have prompted radical solutions, experts say. Without a drastic rethinking of what a city is, and how it should be designed, these problems will worsen, they warn. "It's very clear that we cannot continue to build cities or use cities in the way that we have over the last several hundred years," says Karen Seto, an associate professor of urban environment at Yale University's School of Forestry and Environmental Studies. The world faces an "urban century" that, without better planning, will further strain cities, she adds.

While most metro areas are a hodgepodge of development and sprawl, nothing is random about a smart city. Every element aims to promote efficiency and health. Intelligent cities deemphasize a hallmark of American cities and most others worldwide: highways. In a smart metropolis, residential areas are near business districts or easily accessible via mass transit to trim commute times and reduce congestion and pollution. Super-fast, ubiquitous Internet connectivity encourages telecommuting.

Skeptics counter that it's folly to spend billions to construct new cities when existing ones are in dire need of attention. "Futuristic technology won't fix many of our basic urban problems," wrote Kaid Benfield, director of the Sustainable Communities and Smart Growth program at the Natural Resources Defense Council, a major environmental organization. "Sprawl will still be sprawl; disinvestment will still be disinvestment; traffic will still be traffic; sprawl-aided obesity will still be obesity." [15]

Anthony Townsend, research director for the Palo Alto, Calif.-based Institute for the Future, a research group that specializes in long-term forecasting, says claims about the level of technological prowess achieved by smart cities are sometimes overblown. The "smart" component of Songdo "is only about 2.9 percent of the construction budget" of what is otherwise a "conventional real estate project," he says. Cisco Systems, the Silicon Valley giant designing much of Songdo's technology infrastructure, declined to comment.

Meanwhile, it remains unclear whether innovations introduced in experimental cities will have real-world applicability and can be scaled to benefit large populations. There are indications that a few technologies — such as urban operating systems — could make the leap. But even smart-city enthusiasts aren't sure others will.

Population to Soar

The world's population will grow from about 7 billion today to 9 billion by 2041 and surpass 10 billion by the end of the century, according to U.N. projections. Sub-Saharan Africa and some nations in Asia, the Pacific Rim and Latin America will account for most of the increase.

Global Population Projections, 2011-2081

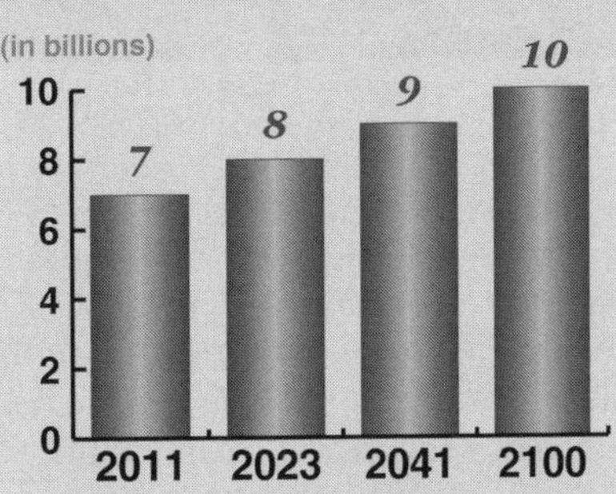

Source: "Global Population to Pass 10 Billion By 2100, UN Projections Indicate," U.N. News Service, May 2011, www.un.org/apps/news/story.asp?NewsID=38253

With their largest urban areas grappling with poverty, pollution and an influx of migrant laborers, China and India are investing heavily in "eco cities" that offer new housing and seek to reduce carbon emissions through wider use of mass transit and renewable energy. Though new, these cities are less futuristic in their designs and innovations, instead emphasizing more practical solutions, such as recycling and energy conservation. [16]

Smart cities raise a host of worries about over-reliance on technology and the outsized influence of major corporations that stand to profit handsomely from lucrative development contracts and service fees. Critics accuse Lavasa, India's signature city of the future, of being too pricey for the masses, and suggest that Masdar was created to deflect attention from the lack of conservation in nearby Abu Dhabi and Dubai. In China, where hundreds of new high-tech cities could be built in the next few decades, concerns are growing that government officials will use the electronic technology to spy on citizens.

While newly planned smart cities are based on cutting-edge technology, many existing cities are adopting more modest "smart growth" revitalization strategies. In a project set to debut in 2014, New York City, for example, is transforming traffic-choked Times Square with expanded pedestrian zones and reduced roadway access. And in 2007 the city released Plan NYC, a blueprint for making the city greener and more livable by 2030. [17] *(See "Current Situation," p. 660.)*

A key driver behind smart cities is economic opportunity, for both host nations and major corporations. International Data Corp. (IDC), a Framingham, Mass.-based firm that analyzes information technology, estimates that spending on smart city technology will surpass $57 billion in 2014. [18] U.S. corporations, meanwhile, are central to the reinvention of urban life. Cisco and IBM are among the technology heavyweights that see a winning combination: huge business potential and the opportunity to dramatically improve lives. Increasingly, developing nations seek their assistance.

In promotional materials, smart cities routinely cast themselves as international economic zones. The trend of new cities being built near or around airports to facilitate business opportunities is so widespread that University of North Carolina business professor John Kasarda coined the term "aerotropolis" to describe the phenomenon — and co-wrote a book about it. [19] Songdo emphasizes on its website that it's just 15 minutes from

AFP/Getty Images/Evaristo Sa

The history of urban planning is littered with visionary schemes that fell short, such as Brazil's capital, Brasília. Completed in 1960, it was heralded by boosters as the first jet-age city. But critics later mocked its sterile architecture and desolate streets — a reputation that lingers today. Critic Benjamin Schwarz said "the city is quite correctly regarded as a colossally wrong turn in urban planning," though he praised it for "some of the most graceful modernist government buildings ever produced."

Incheon Airport. "I believe smart cities become the competitive weapon for the growth economy," says Lewis.

Yet tempering the excitement surrounding new cities is a sobering reality: The history of urban renewal is littered with visionary schemes that fell short. A much-cited example is Brazil's capital, Brasília, heralded by boosters as the first jet-age city upon its inauguration in 1960 but later mocked for its sterile architecture and desolate streets — a reputation that lingers today. [20]

As urban planners, policymakers and academics ponder the future of cities, here are some of the key questions they're debating:

Does building smart cities make sense when existing cities need attention?

Players of the computer game Sim City design breathtaking urban landscapes limited only by the depths of their imaginations. Skyscrapers, roads and industrial zones spring to life with mouse clicks. Of course, these idyllic simulations have imaginary price tags, whereas futuristic cities under construction in Asia and Europe are multibillion-dollar gambles with real-life consequences for investors and others.

Critics say the billions being spent on Songdo, Masdar And PlanIT Valley could go a long way toward improving the crumbling infrastructure of megacities such as Dhaka, Mumbai and Lagos that struggle to provide basics such as electricity and plumbing to shantytowns.

With these large sums at stake, a debate is brewing among urban planners over whether it's better to upgrade existing cities or build new ones. Cisco and IBM highlight the divide: Cisco focuses on constructing new, cutting-edge cities from scratch while IBM emphasizes helping existing urban areas reinvent themselves.

Critics of the rush to build futuristic cities think the exorbitant spending is misguided. "Selling more [information technology] and sophisticated algorithms might help a few of the very fortunate cities," wrote Dan Hoornweg, lead urban adviser at the World Bank. "Being really smart about cities is improving basic service delivery to the one billion urban poor now going without clean water, or the two billion without sanitation," he added. [21]

Smart-city advocates counter that new cities deliver basic amenities more effectively than older ones. "New cities with smart capabilities can provide a level of innovation that I don't think can be achieved by just retrofitting the cities that exist now," says Warren Karlenzig, founder and president of Common Current, a San Anselmo, Calif.-based global consultancy that focuses on sustainability issues.

For example, a smart power grid designed for an intelligent city being built from scratch can "seamlessly" generate, control and distribute energy, allowing for extensive use of renewable fuel, he says. In an aging city, by contrast, the introduction of clean energy requires heavy reliance on fossil fuel as a backup because grids are less efficient, he explains. Smart water systems in new cities automatically detect leaks, account for weather changes and respond instantly during floods — capabilities that may be expensive or cumbersome to replicate in older cities, he says.

The cost of investing in new cities seems less daunting when the expense of the status quo is tallied, reasoned Kai Laursen, a consultant with the Urban Land Institute, a nonprofit educational and research group in Washington. "It can be argued that the cost of urban sprawl is higher, with hidden costs like traffic congestion, pollution and loss of farmland included in the cost/benefit analyses," he wrote. [22]

"With the world population expected to surpass 9 billion by 2050, infill development alone will not come close to meeting future housing needs," Laursen said. "A limited number of new medium-size and large cities makes sense in countries with extreme housing shortages." [23] Noting that China is experiencing "the largest migration in human history" from rural to urban areas, Karlenzig added: "They have to build these cities."

Construction of the next generation of cities and improvements made to older ones should not be viewed as mutually exclusive, some experts contend. "The general consensus is: We're going to need both," says Amy Edmondson, a professor of leadership and management at Harvard Business School and a leading expert on smart cities. "I don't think it's really an either/or" proposition, says Edmondson, a member of Living PlanIT's advisory board since November 2010.

Yale's Seto agrees, but offers this caveat: New cities should rise only in areas experiencing rapid urbanization, such as parts of Asia and Africa. "In the United States, I would argue we don't need to build from scratch," she says.

"China and India, they need new cities," affirms Townsend of the Institute for the Future. "I think these countries deserve a chance to build their utopias — to experiment." Domestically, "our focus needs to be on using all these technologies, all these interesting new business models and new governance models, and applying them to problems that we already have," he says.

If smart cities make sense for overpopulated, impoverished nations, why are they being built in a sparsely populated corner of Portugal, and in South Korea and the United Arab Emirates, among the world's richest nations? Even smart-city proponents acknowledge the projected population figures for Songdo, Masdar and PlanIT Valley are relatively minuscule. [24] "Few places in the world will be able to replicate Masdar," wrote Saskia Sassen, a professor of sociology and cochair of the Committee on Global Thought at Columbia University. "It is a multibillion-dollar investment for 40,000 residents." [25]

Lewis says PlanIT Valley was conceived not as a megacity but as a lab for innovations that can benefit the company's nearly two dozen urban projects in China and elsewhere. Songdo will play a similar role. Gale International, its developer, plans to create at least 20 knock-off versions in China and India. [26]

Common Current's Karlenzig says it's important to look beyond the low population figures because prototype cities will spur new urban models. "It's the beginning of an era," he emphasizes. "These are early days, but they're scaling up," he says, predicting that some new cities breaking ground now will accommodate a million or more residents in five to seven years.

Can innovations showcased in experimental metropolises be scaled up to benefit large, aging cities?

Attend the annual Consumer Electronics Show held every January in Las Vegas and you'll see lots of cool gadgets and designs — including many that will never reach store shelves. Critics contend that the bulk of innovations designed for futuristic cities will meet the same fate: They won't be mass-produced or survive beyond the confines of an experimental urban space.

It's one thing to showcase driverless cars and interactive video screens in a carefully controlled environment, but another to bring such advances to ailing U.S. cities such as Detroit or New Orleans or a sprawling megacity in Asia or Africa with spotty Internet coverage and intermittent electrical power.

Some urban-planning experts, however, see encouraging signs that technologies introduced in fresh, new smart cities will make the leap to older, crumbling ones. "We're probably transitioning to a new place in American history, where a lot of the innovation for urbanization is not happening in the United States, but it's happening elsewhere," Yale's Seto says. "I think that there is really a huge amount that we can learn and really benefit from."

Nevertheless, obstacles abound. "It's very difficult to change laws, zoning codes — the way things are," Seto says. "We are still in the mindset of tinkering on the edges." Existing cities must assess whether it's cost-effective to rip up infrastructure and replace it with newer versions, she explains. Townsend, of the Institute for the Future, notes that innovations that don't require demolishing buildings, digging up streets and rewiring metro areas would be easier for U.S. cities to adopt.

Townsend also offers this caveat: Some innovations that urban reformers are most excited about — such as smart power grids and the ubiquitous use of sensors to monitor services — "are things that may not actually scale very well when you start involving large numbers of disadvantaged people." Lack of education, high-speed Internet access and Internet-enabled devices could put a damper on such investments, Townsend says.

An emergency response center that IBM designed for Rio de Janeiro is an often-cited example of a smart-city innovation that has been successfully adopted by a major city. Colin Harrison, distinguished engineer with IBM's Smarter Cities program, says the company will explore whether this type of center, designed to help Rio respond better to weather catastrophes and other crises,

Cities Experiencing Explosive Growth

Tokyo, already the world's most populous city with about 37 million residents, is expected to reach 39 million by 2025. Delhi, which ranks second with almost 23 million, is projected to grow by more than 10 million over the same period. The New York City-Newark region is expected to drop from fourth to sixth place by 2025, with 15 million fewer residents than Tokyo.

Most Populated Urban Areas, 2011 and 2025 (Projected)
(in millions)

2011			2025		
1.	Tokyo, Japan	37.2	1.	Tokyo, Japan	38.7
2.	Delhi, India	22.7	2.	Delhi, India	32.9
3.	Mexico City, Mexico	20.4	3.	Shanghai, China	28.4
4.	New York-Newark, U.S.	20.4	4.	Mumbai, India	26.6
5.	Shanghai, China	20.2	5.	Mexico City, Mexico	24.6
6.	Sao Paulo, Brazil	19.9	6.	New York-Newark, U.S.	23.6
7.	Mumbai, India	19.7	7.	Sao Paulo, Brazil	23.2
8.	Beijing, China	15.6	8.	Dhaka, Bangladesh	22.9
9.	Dhaka, Bangladesh	15.4	9.	Beijing, China	22.6
10.	Calcutta, India	14.4	10.	Karachi, Pakistan	20.2
11.	Karachi, Pakistan	13.9	11.	Lagos, Nigeria	18.9
12.	Buenos Aires, Argentina	13.5	12.	Calcutta, India	18.7
13.	Los Angeles-Long Beach-Santa Ana, U.S.	13.4	13.	Manila, Philippines	16.3
14.	Rio de Janeiro, Brazil	12.0	14.	Los Angeles-Long Beach-Santa Ana, U.S.	15.7
15.	Manila, Philippines	11.9	15.	Shenzhen, China	15.5
16.	Moscow, Russia	11.6	16.	Buenos Aires, Argentina	15.5
17.	Osaka-Kobe, Japan	11.5	17.	Guangzhou, China	15.5
18.	Istanbul, Turkey	11.3	18.	Istanbul, Turkey	14.9
19.	Lagos, Nigeria	11.2	19.	Cairo, Egypt	14.7
20.	Cairo, Egypt	11.2	20.	Kinshasa, Democratic Republic of the Congo	14.5

Source: "World Urbanization Prospects: The 2011 Revision," United Nations Population Division, March 2012, p. 7, esa.un.org/unpd/wup/pdf/WUP2011_Highlights.pdf

could be scaled for a state or country. Technically, that could be done, though it might be more effective to handle crises at the local level. "Whether that is an effective method of managing, or helping to manage, a crisis," he says of a statewide or nationwide system, "we don't know the answer."

Smart-growth advocates emphasize that Songdo and other innovative cities already are influencing urban redesign projects in older urban areas. McCaffery Interests, a Chicago-based real estate firm, and Cisco are collaborating with Chicago city officials on the Lakeside development, which will transform the site of a former U.S. Steel mill on the south side into a high-tech community that uses green technology for energy and water distribution, waste management and public transit. [27]

The project brings together new development and urban revitalization in a way that is harmonious with the local community, said Wim Elfrink, chief globalization officer and executive vice president of the Emerging Solutions Group at Cisco. [28] *(See "At Issue," p. 661.)*

"The scale of the project is extraordinary," added Chris Raguso, who served as former Mayor Richard M. Daley's deputy chief of staff. "The fact that anybody in this economy still wants to take a shot at developing a site that is basically a landfill and is basing the development on retail and housing is also extraordinary," she said. [29]

Several U.S. cities, including Atlanta, Detroit, Denver, Indianapolis, Milwaukee and Winston-Salem/Greensboro, N.C., are exploring a popular overseas concept, the aerotropolis — an economic zone built around an airport. [30]

Living PlanIT's Lewis is optimistic about prospects for older U.S. cities to adopt smart-city innovations. Still, he says cities would have to adapt the new technologies to existing buildings and infrastructure.

"Los Angeles can't afford to rip out every road" and rewire every building in the city, but smarter technology could be added to the existing landscape to create, for example, an urban operating system that might help L.A. operate more efficiently, he says. It would be unwise, he advises, for older cities to balk at the cost of upgrading their infrastructure. "You can't afford not to do it," he says of today's aging metropolises.

Do smart cities overrely on technology?

In a shocking security breach, hackers infiltrate city-run databases in Chicago and steal sensitive personal information on millions of citizens.

No worries: This is just the plot of "Watch Dogs," an upcoming video game that paints a dystopian portrait of the Windy City as a smart metropolis under siege by nerdy criminals. [31] Yet some experts caution that this doomsday scenario could be real if high-tech wizardry in smart cities crashes or is compromised.

As intelligent cities catch on, more questions are being raised about overreliance on the gadgetry that runs them. Technical glitches, power outages and cyber attacks are a danger for any urban environment, but a hyper-connected city could grind to a halt, critics warn. Another concern is that rogue governments might misuse the wireless sensors and interactive video monitors deployed in new cities to spy on citizens and suppress dissent.

"It's always a risk," acknowledges Living PlanIT's Lewis. "Regardless of how robust you think anything is, it can always be improved," he says. He emphasizes that there are ways to build in redundancy so that fallback systems take control in response to a power failures or other mishaps. "On the one hand," says IBM's Harrison, "we are creating new dependencies" on technology. But he concurs with Lewis that it's possible to mitigate the impact of any failure with secondary systems.

Courtesy of International Business Machines Corp.

The emergency response center that IBM designed for Rio de Janeiro, Brazil, coordinates 30 city departments and is an often-cited example of a smart city innovation that has been successfully adopted by a major city. The company's Smarter Cities program will explore whether the facility, designed to improve Rio's response to weather catastrophes and other crises, could be scaled for a state or country.

Townsend, of the Institute for the Future, is not convinced. "It's going to cost a lot," he says of backup networks. "There's a steep learning curve." He cites the work of Yale sociologist Charles Perrow, who concluded that accidents are inevitable with complex technologies because it's impossible to model every scenario they might encounter. [32] The 1986 meltdown of the Chernobyl nuclear reactor in the former Soviet Union, Townsend says, began with a botched safety test. [33]

Townsend is particularly worried about the impact of a cyber attack. "Every day, new threats are being documented," such as electronic bugs that mess with the operations of infrastructure such as elevators, power lines and water pumps, he says. "It's a whole new category of infrastructure vulnerabilities that nobody anticipated."

Yale's Seto cautions that it's not only technology that can become outmoded or marginalized — it's companies as well. "Technology leaders of two years ago are not the technology leaders today," she says.

Privacy and government surveillance concerns are particularly acute in China, which is rapidly building new cities. With sensors being used in many pilot cities to monitor traffic patterns, power consumption and even pedestrian levels, it's not a giant leap for a government to use these innovations to monitor political opponents and citizen activists, experts say.

"We could slide into a managed space where 'sensored' becomes 'censored,' " warned Sassen, the Columbia professor. [34] "Privacy is a big issue," adds Harvard's Edmondson. "I sometimes look around and think, has the horse already left the barn on that one?" Citizens will have to gauge whether increased risks to their privacy are worth the benefits of innovation, she says.

Lewis, whose company does considerable business with China, says people interact with Living PlanIT's urban software through a "virtual identity" similar to an avatar and control how much personally identifiable information to share. He emphasizes that his company complies with all U.S. export regulations governing which technologies can be distributed to foreign countries and recognizes it has an "ethical responsibility" to deploy smart-city innovations in ways that "benefit society." Still, "There's only so much of that you can physically enforce," he acknowledges.

On a conciliatory note, he thinks some countries are unfairly presumed to have malicious intentions for innovations that can benefit their citizens. "Societies [that] we understand less, we tend to be fearful of," he says. While technology can be used by governments to suppress dissent, it also can be used by citizens to spread democracy, he notes. [35]

Given the swift pace of change, urban planners warn that smart cities risk overreliance on propriety systems that could be difficult to replace or upgrade. Once a city has been wired to the hilt by a Cisco, IBM or Siemens, can it switch to a competing vendor? IBM's Harrison says it's possible, but not easy. Two trends could help facilitate a switch: growing reliance on industrywide standards and cloud-based services that store software and databases on the Internet — rather than on computer hard drives. "These are quite complicated systems, so it's not something you would do over a weekend," he says. "It would require a lot of planning" and take a few months, "but I don't see any absolute obstacle to doing it."

The bottom line: Risk of catastrophic failure of smart-city technology can be minimized but never eliminated. "Since humans are involved in the building process, there will always be errors," Lewis says.

Library of Congress

American urban-planning scholar Jane Jacobs wrote a scathing critique of the urban-renewal policies of the 1950s, The Death and Life of Great American Cities, *published in 1961. Jacobs argued that the monumental structures being built to replace old and often distinguished buildings had a limited impact on the urban landscapes they were supposed to rejuvenate. "Invariably, the ordinary city around [these buildings] ran down instead of being uplifted" and inevitably attracted "an incongruous rim of ratty tattoo parlors and second-hand clothing stores, or else just nondescript, dispirited decay," she wrote.*

BACKGROUND

City Beautiful Movement

Smart cities represent the latest chapter in the history of urban renewal that had its origins at the turn of the 20th century. The City Beautiful movement of the late 1800s and early 1900s was a nationwide effort to strengthen civic pride by sprucing up downtowns with grand architecture and wide boulevards. The effort initially was driven by civic associations and later by city leaders and planners eager to boost property values through redevelopment. [36]

Jane Jacobs, author of *The Death and Life of Great American Cities*, a seminal book on urban revitalization published in 1961, wrote that the aim of the movement was to create "monumental" cities featuring classical architecture. "City after city built its civic center or its cultural center," she wrote. These buildings were "sorted out from the rest of the city, and assembled into the grandest effect thought possible." [37]

Jacobs argued, however, that the imposing architecture had a limited impact on the urban landscapes it was supposed to rejuvenate. "Invariably, the ordinary city around [these buildings] ran down instead of being uplifted" and inevitably attracted "an incongruous rim of ratty tattoo parlors and second-hand clothing stores, or else just nondescript, dispirited decay," she wrote. People also tended to avoid these city centers, despite their new structures. [38]

The remnants of the City Beautiful period can be seen across America, along, for example, Philadelphia's Benjamin Franklin Parkway and at San Francisco's Civic Center. High-minded structures such as the Philadelphia Museum of Art, the Rodin Museum and a statute of Nicolaus Copernicus, the 16th-century

Continued on p. 656

Chronology

1890s-1950s

Urban makeovers aim to beautify cities.

1893
City Beautiful Movement aims to revitalize U.S. cities with grand, inspirational architecture.

1898
Garden City Movement models small towns after quaint English villages.

1949
Housing Act accelerates urban renewal with federal funds to clear slums and replace them with housing developments.

1954
Congress amends the Housing Act to free up more funds for demolition and construction in urban areas.

1960s-1990s

Urban experiments, planned communities have mixed success.

1960
Inauguration of Brazil's ultramodern capital Brasília prompts criticism of the city's desolate streets and imposing architecture.

1961
Briton Robert E. Simon Jr., spearheads creation of Reston, Va., near Washington, D.C., in early example of planned-community design.

1963
American urban planner James Rouse initiates design of Columbia, Md., as cluster of self-contained villages and alternative to suburban sprawl.

1968
New York City contracts with RAND Corp. to predict where fires will occur, but faulty data result in deaths. . . . Urban-renewal efforts coincide with escalation of riots in inner-city neighborhoods.

1974
Brazilian city of Curitiba introduces rapid-transit bus system that functions like a subway.

1982
EPCOT opens as a theme park rather than the futuristic city once imagined by legendary film pioneer Walt Disney.

1992
Agenda 21, a comprehensive plan for reducing human impact on the environment, is adopted by more than 178 nations at U.N. conference.

1997
First residents move to Celebration, Fla., a suburban "utopia" created by the Walt Disney Co. that critics mock as contrived.

2000-2009

Smart Cities and smart-growth movement take shape.

2003
To curb pollution and congestion, London charges drivers who enter business districts during peak periods.

2005
Songdo, South Korea, breaks ground and is heralded as a model for new cities in China and India.

2007
New York City adopts a sweeping environmental plan that seeks to cut greenhouse gases by 30 percent, add parks and overhaul mass transit by 2030.

2008
Construction begins on Tianjin Eco-city in northeast China to add housing for 350,000 people by 2020.

2009
Living PlanIT announces northern Portugal as location for PlanIT Valley, a futuristic city to be run by software. . . . Gujarat International Finance Tec-City, a global financial hub planned for India, selects Cisco to design its tech infrastructure. . . . Gale International and Cisco announce plans for the Meixi Lake District eco city in southeast China.

2010-Present

Futuristic urban development accelerates, particularly in China and India.

2010
IBM establishes data-operations center in Rio de Janeiro that shares crucial information among 30 government agencies.

2011
Economic uncertainty forces Masdar, a futuristic city in the United Arab Emirates, to slash its budget, scale back innovations and delay completion by a decade. . . . Lavasa, a smart city in India, prompts complaints that its housing is too expensive for the country's middle class. . . . Japan commits $4.5 billion to $90 billion Delhi-Mumbai Industrial Corridor in India that will construct 24 cities in six states.

2012
Cisco chosen to create technology master plan for Chicago Lakeside development that will transform a vacant steel-mill site into a high-tech neighborhood.

Technology Brings New Brainpower to Communities

"The city becomes a platform that allows new forms of innovation."

Operating systems such as Windows and Android already run computers, smartphones and tablets — so why not sprawling metropolises?

That's the thinking behind the "urban operating system" (UOS), which uses sensors and software to monitor and analyze the main functions of cities, including traffic levels, power consumption and water usage. The possibilities for this burgeoning technology seem endless: Vehicles instantly rerouted around accidents; office windows automatically tinted at the first hint of sunshine; and excess solar energy diverted to batteries for storage.

Even residents' health could be monitored. Wireless sensors, either placed in homes or worn, could track vital signs such as heart rates and insulin levels to immediately detect medical emergencies.

Steve Lewis, CEO of Living PlanIT, a Portugal-based developer of smart cities that coined the term "urban operating system," likens the technology to the human nervous system. "It senses what's going on around it and acts to support various functions" and maximize resources, he says.

Living PlanIT, which also has offices in Britain and the United States, is working on the software with Microsoft, where Lewis previously was an executive, Cisco and other partners. [1] Living PlanIT is designing a futuristic city in northern Portugal called PlanIT Valley, to be run by a UOS upon its completion, projected for 2017. To be built on uninhabited land, PlanIT Valley is slated to be the third-largest city in Portugal, after Lisbon and Porto, and was designated a "Project of National Interest" by the Portuguese government. Lewis says all construction permits and land rights are in place.

Similar to the software "apps" for Apple's iPhone, apps designed by third parties could supplement the urban software with additional tools and services, Lewis says. "The city becomes a platform that allows new forms of innovation to meet the needs of the citizens," he says. While much of a UOS can be automated, human intervention is sometimes required to analyze the data, Lewis explains.

In Porto, on Portugal's northern coast, Living PlanIT is testing the traffic-related components of its UOS software with the University of Porto. A wider test is under way in the South London district of Greenwich with financial backing from the U.K. government, Lewis says. [2]

Living PlanIT, meanwhile, will add operating systems to cities it is developing in China, and to Almere, an Amsterdam suburb to be reinvented as a "smart society" with help from IBM, Cisco and Royal Philips Electronics, Lewis says. And in South Korea, Songdo, a smart city under construction from scratch along the Incheon waterfront, will be run by similar technology that its designers describe as the city's "brain."

Half a world away, in Rio de Janerio, Brazil, a citywide operations center designed by IBM functions similarly to an urban operating system. Mayor Eduardo Paes sought IBM's help after mudslides and flash floods in the city of 12 million people killed dozens in April 2010 and left Paes without a central command center to oversee the crisis. [3]

The $14 million center, which opened in late 2010 and was expanded a year later, analyzes and shares data about traffic and weather conditions, infrastructure needs, crowds and security among 30 government agencies, including pub-

Continued from p. 654

mathematician and astronomer, line the parkway. In San Francisco, a cluster of historic buildings that includes City Hall, Symphony Hall and the War Memorial Veterans building comprises the Civic Center. [39]

The movement, also known as City Reform, coincided with the Garden City Movement, begun in England in 1898 by British urban planner Ebenezer Howard. It sought to model small towns after quaint English villages. His approach emphasized family homes, gardens and walkable communities. Well-planned, middle-class garden-city suburbs flourished in the United States in the early 1900s, as the idea "soon became the bible for suburban town planning in America," wrote Douglas E. Morris in *It's a Sprawl World After All.* [40] By the late 1930s, the Garden City model was overtaken by other designs, or modified into variants of the original concept. [41]

Urban Renewal

At mid-century, concerns about deteriorating downtowns prompted a wave of urban renewal that resulted in the widespread demolition of aging buildings, many of them architecturally significant but ill-used, as commerce and residential areas shifted to far-flung suburbs. "By the late 1930s and early '40s, it was clear downtown was in trouble," Robert M. Fogelson wrote in *Downtown, Its Rise and Fall, 1880-1950.* In most cities, [the downtown's] daytime population was still below pre-Depression levels. So were its retail sales." [42]

By the 1950s, Americans were hearing a steady stream of alarming stories about the decline of downtowns. Vacant storefronts, decaying buildings, loss of manufacturing and downward spiraling retail sales contributed to the sense of doom, fueling calls for large-scale redevelopment. [43] In response, the federal government provided billions of dollars for highway construction and urban-renewal projects in the 1950s and 1960s. [44]

lic safety and law enforcement. [4] For example, data about a broken water main and corresponding flood is immediately routed to all relevant departments, says Colin Harrison, distinguished engineer with IBM's Smarter Cities program. If police officers detected the break, they could transmit information about it to public works officials and, if necessary, the transit system could reroute buses.

"It just helps everybody to have a common version of the truth," Harrison says. "This is really all about helping people to make decisions."

The center already has been used for crowd control during the annual Carnival festival, serving as a test run for the 2014 World Cup, to be held in Rio and other Brazilian cities, and the 2016 Summer Olympics in Rio. IBM has created similar centers elsewhere, but the one in sprawling Rio is the largest. [5]

While the Rio surveillance is on par with security measures in the United States, urban innovations elsewhere have raised privacy concerns, particularly in China, where some planned cities will deploy ubiquitous wireless sensors, purportedly to monitor traffic and weather, that could be co-opted to spy on citizens.

Living PlanIT SA

Steve Lewis is CEO of Living PlanIT, the Portugal-based developer of PlanIT Valley, a futuristic city envisioned for northern Portugal with a projected 220,000 residents.

As with any technology, challenges abound. For IBM, Rio presents information-gathering hurdles in the form of the city's mountainous topography, dense population and poverty. [6] And it's still too early to gauge whether the software that Living PlanIT envisions will perform as planned. Computer users have long encountered error messages and system crashes, prompting the view in some circles that a UOS won't fare much better.

— David Hatch

[1] For an overview of Living PlanIT's UOS, see http://living-planit.com/UOS_overview.htm.

[2] For background, see Katia Moskvitch, "Will chatting smart cars become a reality soon?" BBC News, July 9, 2012, www.bbc.co.uk/news/technology-18608730. Living PlanIT, "Living PlanIT Led Consortium Receives UK Government Funding for £3m Project," press release, Nov. 10, 2011, http://living-planit.com/pr_SA_TSB_Award.htm.

[3] Natasha Singer, "Mission Control Built for Cities," *The New York Times*, March 3, 2012, www.nytimes.com/2012/03/04/business/ibm-takes-smarter-cities-concept-to-rio-de-janeiro.html?pagewanted=all.

[4] For background, see IBM press release, "City of Rio de Janeiro and IBM Collaborate to Advance Emergency Response System; Access to Real-Time Information Empowers Citizen," Nov. 9, 2011, www-03.ibm.com/press/us/en/pressrelease/35945.wss.

[5] Singer, *op. cit.*

[6] *Ibid.*

Alison Isenberg, author of *Downtown America*, noted a racial and socioeconomic undercurrent to the era's urban restoration, as retailers sought to attract more white, middle-class housewives to downtowns populated mostly by minority and low-income citizens. [45] "Redevelopers persistently argued that the residents of 'slums' adjacent to the downtown threatened to 'cheapen' and ultimately destroy the vitality of urban commercial life," she wrote. [46] Downtown business interests and their allies sought to curb the blight. [47]

The response was to raze downtown storefronts and dilapidated neighborhoods and replace them with housing projects, multilane expressways and large-scale retail developments such as enclosed shopping areas that replicated increasingly popular suburban malls.

Revitalization, however, didn't always achieve its intended goal of restoring ailing cities. "By the late 1950s, as more Main Street buildings fell to renewal, a countermovement invigorated by . . . Jacobs asserted that old, diverse, small stores had economic and aesthetic value," Isenberg recounted. "The contradictions of urban renewal quickly became evident," she wrote. As businesses and governments praised redevelopment, the picture on the ground was less clear. Cities lost longstanding businesses and inner-city neighborhoods, some of which would become the focal point of civil rights riots that destroyed entire blocks in the 1960s. [48]

The demolition of older buildings continued into the 1970s but didn't turn most cities around. In an effort to reinvigorate their downtowns, many cities welcomed shopping malls and mixed-used office developments as they struggled with a growing number of vacant, abandoned storefronts. During this period, a new idea began to take shape that would intensify over the next two decades: preservation of historic buildings and Main Streets designed to reconnect cities with their past and foster nostalgia. [49]

Mixed Results

As urban renewal swept the nation, two early experiments in smart growth — Brazil's much-panned design for its new capital and New York City's unsuccessful use of computers to predict where fires might break out — were precursors to the smart-city experiments of today, with less than impressive results. But a third, in another Brazilian city — Curitiba, founded by Portuguese explorers in 1693 — has been hailed by urban planners as a brilliantly simple and effective idea for cities lacking subways, and an early example of smart growth.

An enduring symbol of a failed urban environment is Brasília, the capital of Brazil, which was heralded by its architects in the early '60s as the first city designed for the jet era. "In an effort to cleanse itself of its colonial past, to flee its burgeoning social afflictions, and to fulfill its long-prophesied emergence as a great power," Brasília's planners designed a capital that was supposed to be a tribute to modernity, *The Atlantic* said. "Here was a city without a traffic light, containing thoroughfares without crosswalks." [50]

The result was a city with few pedestrians and architecture widely regarded as imposing and sterile. Reflecting a widely held view among architectural critics and city planners, the article's author, Benjamin Schwarz, concluded that "the city is quite correctly regarded as a colossally wrong turn in urban planning," though he praised it for "some of the most graceful modernist government buildings ever produced." [51] Added Greg Lindsay, a widely published expert on urbanization, in an essay in *Fast Company*, "Brasília, of course, was an instant disaster: grandiose, monstrously overscale, and immediately encircled by slums." [52]

AFP/Getty Images/Mark Ralston

A bird sanctuary surrounds Dongtan, a so-called eco city planned for China's Chongming Island, near Shanghai. The huge model sustainable city, being developed by the Shanghai Industrial Investment Corp., is slated to have 500,000 residents by 2050. Work on the project, which began in 2005, currently is stalled. Dongtan is one of at least 20 new cities being planned in China.

In 1968, New York City contracted with the RAND Corp. to use computer models to predict the location of fires in an effort to deploy firefighting resources more effectively. Because of inaccurate data and misguided assumptions, the models recommended replacing large firehouses across the city with smaller ones. RAND never foresaw the tragic result: 600,000 residents in low-income areas would lose their homes to fire over the next decade, Lindsay, a visiting scholar at the Rudin Center for Transportation Policy and Management at New York University, wrote in *The New York Times*. [53] Worsening the situation, he said, RAND refrained from cutting services to well-off communities to avoid complaints, forcing poorer areas to compete for limited firefighting resources. [54]

Despite the missteps in Brasília, another urban initiative in Brazil was a success. It occurred in the 1970s in Curitiba, a fast-growing city of almost 1.8 million in southern Brazil near the Atlantic coast. "The mayor came in, and over a very short period of about three years, transformed the transportation sector in that city," says Seto of Yale. Among the most innovative designs, she says, was a low-cost, low-tech solution to congested streets: a rapid-transit system modeled after a subway, but with buses. Riders board on platforms and the bus doors slide open like on a subway, she explains. The buses also operate in dedicated lanes. "This bus design was very innovative because it addressed the issue of why people didn't want to ride the bus" — they're slow and get stuck in traffic, she says. [55]

Suburban 'Utopias'

Suburbs took root more than a century ago and have been expanding ever since. The advent of the automobile and the street car encouraged Americans to move outside cities beginning in the late 1800s and early 1900s. "By 1930 every American city had rings of suburbs like the skins of an onion, and beyond that, usually, other rings of platted fields," observed historian Alan Gowans. [56] As sprawl mushroomed in all directions, some visionaries sought to redefine small-town America in response to growing dissatisfaction with both urban and suburban life. [57]

In the early 1960s, Robert E. Simon Jr., a Briton, led an effort to create a self-contained community in Northern Virginia in which residents would not only live but also work. He persuaded local authorities to cluster homes together to preserve open space, fields and wooded areas. He also urged them to dam streams to create lakes and construct village centers to serve as shopping destinations and gathering places. The result was Reston, located west of Washington, D.C., and considered among the nation's first large-scale planned communities. The Reston Town Center, dedicated in October 1990, furthered Simon's dream with an urban-like center of shops, restaurants, offices and upscale residential buildings. [58]

At about the same time, James Rouse, an American urban planner who later designed the Faneuil Hall marketplace in Boston, was developing the planned community of Columbia, Md., which featured several small villages, each with its own shopping areas. "It's not an attempt at a perfect city or a utopia, but rather an effort to simply develop a better city, an alternative to the mindlessness, the irrationality, the unnecessity of sprawl and clutter as a way of accommodating the growth of the American city," Rouse said in 1982. [59]

In the mid-1990s, the Walt Disney Co. created the planned community of Celebration, Fla., which aspired to be an economically diverse environment, with million-dollar homes next to rental apartments. [60] "The town felt like a movie set," Douglas Frantz and Catherine Collins, husband and wife co-authors of a book about Celebration, wrote in a *New York Times* essay. Rocking chairs sat along the man-made lake, houses were based on a limited number of designs and exterior paint colors were dictated by a community rulebook, wrote the couple, who moved to Celebration with their children in 1997. A return visit a few years ago revealed signs of trouble for the experiment, including encroaching sprawl and home foreclosures. [61]

Road to Smart Growth

Long before Masdar, PlanIT Valley and Songdo, there was film pioneer Walt Disney's grand vision for a city of the future. The Experimental Prototype Community of Tomorrow, or EPCOT, was originally planned as an actual Florida town rather than the tourist attraction it became. Twenty thousand residents would live under an enormous dome and travel by monorail to skyscrapers that would be part of the community. All the residents would rent their housing from the Disney Co. Disney said the town would be "starting from scratch on virgin land and building a special kind of new community that more people will talk about and come to look at than any other area in the world." Disney died in 1966 before he could implement his vision, and EPCOT opened in 1982 as a theme park. [62]

More than two decades later, Dongtan, originally conceived as China's first eco city, is a stark reminder of the risks associated with engineering the next generation of metropolises. Envisioned as a car-free, Manhattan-size city on Chongming Island near Shanghai, the project received a green light from local authorities in 2005 and was supposed to welcome its first inhabitants in time for the 2010 Shanghai World Expo. [63]

Dongtan's troubles started soon after its launch. Other than a wind farm and bridge-and-tunnel connection to Shanghai, little has been built. Construction permits have expired. There's a dispute between Arup, the London-based engineering firm designing the city, and Shanghai Industrial Investment Corp., a state-controlled developer, over who should fund the project. [64] Dongtan took another hit when its main political proponent, former Shanghai Communist Party chief Chen Liangyu, was sentenced on corruption charges in 2008 to 18 years in prison. [65] Today, the project is indefinitely stalled and serves as a lesson on the challenges ahead for smart cities. ■

Current Situation

Gaining Momentum

Futuristic cities and neighborhoods are being planned around the globe — typically in Asia or the Middle East, but increasingly in the Americas and Africa — and often with backing by U.S. developers.

Yet, smart cities face daunting challenges and the reality of scaled-back ambitions. The global economic crisis already has taken a toll, prompting Masdar to trim its budget by 15 percent to $19 billion, delay its completion date by nearly a decade and abandon its dream of being powered exclusively by its own solar panels and other clean-energy technology. [66]

Three years ago, rumors circulated that Songdo, now two years behind schedule, might have been in trouble because of difficulty securing loans. Incheon Mayor Ahn Sang-soo downplayed concerns at the time, saying, "The current global economic crisis won't deter us." At various points, some construction was halted, confirms a spokeswoman with Gale International, Songdo's developer, but the financial situation has since stabilized, she says. [67]

In fact, many smart-city projects were announced "right at the beginning of a global recession," says Karlenzig, the urban consultant. "The timing couldn't have been worse in some ways."

Still, a booming business in smart-city conferences may be the clearest indicator of growing interest in the subject. Recent gatherings include Smart

Cities World, in Dubai; Smart Cities and Communities, in Brussels; Smart Cities Summit, in Durban, South Africa; and City Age, in Toronto. [68]

At least 20 new cities are planned for China. Lewis of Living PlanIT says he expects a private-equity investment fund, in which Living PlanIT is a partner, to help finance 300 more over the next 25 years.

Among the notable projects scheduled in China, India and Russia: [69]

• **Meixi Lake:** An eco city developed by Songdo developers Gale International and Cisco, planned on 1,675 acres in Changsha, the capital of Hunan Province in southeast China. The project will ring a lake but emphasize water conservation. [70]

• **Tianjin Eco-city:** A low-carbon metropolis, rising on once-polluted land less than an hour from Beijing by train. Designed to house 350,000 by 2020, it is a collaboration between the Chinese and Singaporean governments.

• **Lavasa:** India's best-known smart city, located between the economic hubs of Mumbai and Pune and nestled in a lush valley. Guided by the principle of New Urbanism, which promotes sustainable, pedestrian-friendly communities, Lavasa is designed to be walkable and to minimize traffic congestion. [71] At least two other smart cities are under construction in India — SmartCity Kochi and the Gujarat International Finance Tec-city.

• **Delhi-Mumbai Industrial Corridor:** A planned $90 billion project that will create 24 cities in six states with Cisco's participation. [72] The first seven cities are scheduled to open in 2018 or 2019. [73]

• **Skolkovo Project:** An innovation hub near Moscow inspired by Silicon Valley and developed jointly by Cisco and the Russian government. It will house 30,000 entrepreneurs and researchers to facilitate tech start-ups. [74]

Perhaps the boldest urban visions belong to two impoverished, violence-wracked nations: tiny Honduras, in Central America, with the world's highest murder rate due to drug trafficking, gangs and crime, and Nigeria, a major African oil producer at war with Boko Haram, an Islamic terrorist group. Both hope to build versions of Dubai, the ultra-sleek Mideast city known for its stunning architecture and the Burj Khalifa, the world's tallest building.

Nigerian developers want to create Minna Airport City, a self-contained "aerotropolis" in a volatile region 90 miles northwest of the capital, Abuja, that would be safe for foreign workers and their families. [75] Similarly, Honduras is exploring a "charter city" with its own laws and legal system. New York University economics professor Paul Romer espouses the concept, arguing that poor countries saddled by outdated laws and corruption need to create secure business environments that attract foreign investment. [76] Romer told *The New York Times* that some critics have suggested his view "reeks of colonialism" or falls short of what countries need to overcome poverty. [77]

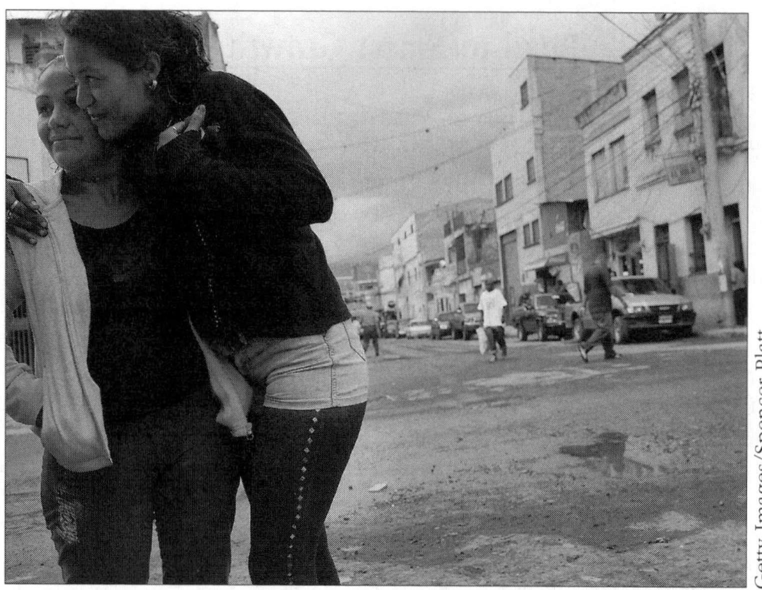

Getty Images/Spencer Platt

Impoverished Honduras envisions the creation of a sleek, new "charter city" with its own legal system. The tiny, Central American nation has the world's highest murder rate due to gangs, drug trafficking, and other crime. New York University economics professor Paul Romer argues that poor countries saddled by outdated laws and corruption need to create secure business environments that attract foreign investment. Above, a decaying neighborhood in Tegucigalpa, the capital.

Smart Growth Strategies

No gleaming city of the future is in the works in the United States. Urban planners cite several reasons: American cities are relatively new, there's a housing oversupply and population growth is stable, leaving little incentive for investors to build new communities from scratch.

As a result, several U.S. cities, large and small, are pursuing so-called smart growth strategies that involve upgrading neighborhoods and infrastructure without building new metropolises from the ground up.

In New York City, a smart-growth plan adopted on Earth Day in 2007 seeks to reduce greenhouse gases 30 percent by 2030 by phasing out dirty heating fuel, expanding and rezoning mass transit and transitioning taxis to cleaner fuel. Other goals include adding green space by turning

Continued on p. 662

At Issue:

Can smart city technology save ailing cities?

WIM ELFRINK
CHIEF GLOBALIZATION OFFICER AND EXECUTIVE VICE PRESIDENT, EMERGING SOLUTIONS, CISCO

WRITTEN FOR *CQ RESEARCHER*, JULY 2012

While no one factor will save an ailing city, Cisco believes that connected technology is key to urban revitalization. With more than 60 percent of the world projected by the U.N. to live in cities by 2030, the challenge of retrofitting cities for future growth is vital.

Two major waves of "network" innovation characterized 20th-century development: In the early 1900s, electrical networks proliferated, and at mid-century the wide availability of transportation systems spurred suburbanization and created transportation networks that facilitated mobility of citizens and more efficient distribution of goods. Today, Internet-enabled communications are as essential as utilities like gas, water and electricity, and there is an opportunity to help build future cities that are capable of meeting population-growth challenges.

Take Chicago as a bold example of urban revitalization. The 470-acre Lakeside project site — the largest undeveloped site in the city — was once home to a U.S. Steel mill that employed more than 30,000 workers. The site, more than 75 percent landfill, is undergoing a 30-year redevelopment that will yield 13,575 market-rate and affordable homes serving 50,000 residents; 17.5 million square feet of retail and commercial space; 125-plus acres of parks; a high school and a marina.

Cisco is the master information and communication technology (ICT) planner and will supply the in-depth ICT infrastructure assessment for the development. The benefits of communities that are smart and connected include alleviating traffic congestion and pollution, helping residents and businesses use energy more efficiently and improving safety and security. We know from other projects worldwide that such communities empower users and create borderless opportunities that can help drive economic development.

Local organizations that know Chicago the best, and have been working to improve it for many years, agree that ICT is a key part of revitalization. Daniel X. O'Neil, executive director of the Smart Chicago Collaborative, wants broadband adoption in Chicago to be as "ubiquitous as the power grid," and the Local Initiatives Support Corp.'s Smart Communities program works to ensure digital access for families, businesses and other organizations.

It's important to note that technology doesn't have to be implemented in spite of citizens' wishes. In fact, as social media have demonstrated, technology can enable citizens to gain more power — including accessing information more quickly and effectively, voicing their opinions on existing services and crowd-sourcing ideas to generate innovation in both private and public spheres.

yes

ANTHONY TOWNSEND
RESEARCH DIRECTOR, INSTITUTE FOR THE FUTURE

WRITTEN FOR *CQ RESEARCHER*, JULY 2012

Cities fall into decline for a host of reasons that don't yield to quick technological fixes. Take Camden, N.J., where I worked in affordable housing many years ago.

Camden is among the nation's poorest cities. Over the last 50 years it has lost its industrial employment base, tax base and human capital. Its schools and health care are inadequate and underfunded. Corruption is rampant, and the infrastructure is crumbling. No technology can reverse that kind of systemic decline overnight. What Camden needs is infrastructure, jobs and a totally new system of government. Or, as in the case of Detroit, it needs to think seriously about planned shrinkage. The city can't even afford its 311 hotline anymore.

The smart solutions being sold by big technology companies can address pieces of these challenges. There are opportunities to cut costs, waste and corruption and improve accountability by tracking municipal assets and service-delivery metrics. But despite big promises and marketing hype from companies like Cisco and IBM, I worry that these improvements are too incremental to reverse steep decline.

We are just beginning to understand the opportunities for innovation in health care and education. But without broadband access, computers and training, declining cities are likely to miss out. We face not one digital divide of access to technology today, but a proliferation of new barriers to literacy.

Industry has focused mostly on growing cities. Rio de Janeiro, Incheon, Amsterdam, New York, San Francisco and other "smart cities" are boomtowns. They are taking off-the-shelf solutions developed over the last 20 years for global logistics — tools for managing expanding businesses — and applying them to the operations of city government. How do you reduce traffic congestion? How do you grow while reducing carbon emissions? These are not problems faced by most cities in decline. If proponents of smart cities have a technology for revitalizing declining urban areas, they are keeping quiet about it.

There is hope, however. City governments and citizens are building smart solutions on their own. Cutting-edge technology today tends to flow from the bottom-up: open-source software and hardware, and open data. Even former corporate smart-city boosters see the opportunity. John Tolva, Chicago's chief technology officer, is re-engineering city government by mining the city's data with open-source statistics software. Ironically, Tolva's previous job was as IBM's chief evangelist for its Smarter Cities initiative.

no

Continued from p. 660

vacant or underused lots into parks and improving energy efficiency in buildings. The city estimates that the proposed changes to mass transit alone could cost $50 billion over the plan's duration. [78] The initiative has received city, state, federal and private funding. [79]

Meanwhile, after a tornado wiped out 95 percent of rural Greensburg, Kan., in 2007, the town of about 1,400 residents has transformed itself into a model of sustainability. Highlights include a wind farm and a solar-powered city hall with a vegetated rooftop. [80]

Holyoke, Mass., which lost its manufacturing base decades ago, has joined with Cisco, EMC Corp. and five universities to create an "innovation district" anchored by an energy-efficient, high-performance computing center operated largely by clean hydroelectricity from a nearby dam. The $95 million center, to be used for research by Boston University, Harvard, MIT, Northeastern University and the University of Massachusetts, is scheduled to be ready in November. [81] To benefit the community, Cisco created a video-conferencing center that allows working students to take college courses remotely.

Cautionary Tales

While the smart-city movement is attracting billions of dollars in investment capital, developers acknowledge the challenges of bringing projects to fruition.

Lewis says the economic downturn has made it tougher to secure financing for PlanIT Valley and says a scaled-down version is possible. With its completion pushed back at least two years, PlanIT Valley will be built in 22 phases, allowing for an easy cessation of construction if funding dries up, he says. "Whether it ends up scaling to its full capacity, I don't know," he says. "We're in the worst economic crisis ever. People are looking at confidence in markets and delaying decisions."

Yet Lewis remains optimistic about the project, in part because it's expected to cost far less than comparable smart cities. He's also bullish about business prospects for his company, particularly in China, because of that country's growth trajectory and insatiable demand for more cities. "Populations are growing dramatically around the world," he adds.

Economic challenges aren't the only hurdle for smart-city developers. In India, critics charge Lavasa with a lack of transparency in the selection of a developer and say housing prices are too expensive for most Indians. [82] The cheapest apartments, between $17,000 and $36,000, are beyond the means of most middle-class Indians. [83] Sensitive to its image, Lavasa addresses these and other critiques on its website in a section called "Facts vs. Misconceptions." It says the city "will cater to the entire spectrum of population" and has not received special treatment from local authorities. [84]

In China, the Tianjin Eco-city is grappling with smog drifting from nearby Beijing. [85] In response to public pressure, authorities set up an air-quality monitoring station to track smog in the region, but the move failed to quell local outrage as the smog continued unabated. [86]

Underscoring the difficulties in building big, new cities, Pegasus Global Holdings scrapped plans in July for a billion-dollar project in southeast New Mexico that was to be used as a test center for solar panels, smart energy grids and other innovations. Pegasus ran into last-minute complications in its efforts to acquire 24 square miles for the site from a private landowner, says Robert Brumley, the company's senior managing director.

Brumley maintains the setback is temporary. "We're just doing a pivot to another site, that's all," he says. He says other New Mexico communities have expressed interest. Still, Brumley acknowledges the challenges of building a city from the ground up.

"Any project of this size, you're going to run into delays," he says. ■

OUTLOOK

Here to Stay?

New smart cities, and retrofits to existing ones, seem destined to play a significant role in shaping the course of urbanization as nations desperately seek an alternative to overcrowding and pollution.

Demand for new cities, particularly in the developing world, is expected to grow significantly as urban populations surge. By 2025, China alone could add another 250 million people to its cities, with more than 200 cities topping one million. [87] These population pressures will coincide, experts say, with the evolution and expansion of smart cities. As a result, Common Current's Karlenzig concludes, new metropolises will be "part of the future in terms of digital infrastructure and energy and water — and our daily lives."

"The real smart cities we're going to see aren't these model cities" like Songdo and Masdar, predicts Townsend of the Institute for the Future. "It's going to be the hundred other big development projects that come in the next five to 10 years that borrow the successful elements of a Songdo or a Masdar and basically harvest the things that actually work."

Urban planners widely agree that new cities will supplement, rather than replace, existing ones, which will gradually become smarter as they adopt newer technologies and designs. Yet impediments remain. Seto of Yale warns that a glut of new cities could stretch investor resources, while one-size-fits-all urban designs might not address cultural and regional needs. A 2011 Harvard Business School report cautions that expensive new cities will need successful economic models to thrive. "Every new city needs an economic foundation based on jobs. Not every new eco city can be a research center whose purpose is the development of new technologies for building other eco cities," the authors wrote. [88]

Of course, the deeper questions that underlie the push to reinvent cities can only be answered with time. It's one thing to pour foundations, erect towers, flood man-made canals and wire every home and office to a digital hub. It's another to create a sense of place — the accents, traditions and styles that instantly distinguish New York from New Orleans. For now, Masdar operates like a theme park, limiting public access from 8:30 a.m. to 10 p.m. [89]

And with architecture drawn from destinations as varied as Savannah and Sydney, Songdo seems at risk of an identity crisis. Plans to use Songdo as a template for at least 20 projects in China and India already are fueling debate over whether cities should be duplicated and commoditized like McDonald's. [90]

It remains unclear whether China or other countries will seize the opportunity presented by hyper-connected cities to surreptitiously monitor citizens and suppress dissent, or if privacy breaches, technical glitches or cyber attacks will wreak havoc. Any of those scenarios could create a public backlash that might dampen public enthusiasm.

In his 2011 book *Triumph of the City*, Edward Glaeser declares that "the era of the industrial city is over." Not every city will succeed, "because not every city has been adept at adapting to the information age, in which ideas are the ultimate creator of wealth," he writes. [91]

Intelligent metropolises seem poised to fill the void, and history may be on their side. Cities, Glaeser notes, have been "engines of innovation since Plato and Socrates bickered in an Athenian marketplace," a view echoed by renowned urbanist Jane Jacobs. She wrote in 1961 that "cities are an immense laboratory of trial and error, failure and success." [92]

The words of Glaeser and Jacobs resonate with dreamers from Silicon Valley to the Arabian Peninsula to the Yellow Sea and beyond, who are staking billions on a wholesale reinvention of one of civilization's most enduring creations: the city. ■

Notes

[1] Gale International, "Korea's Songdo International Business District — One of Asia's Largest Green Developments — Surpasses Milestone of 13 Million Square Feet of LEED Certified Space," press release, June 27, 2012, www.songdo.com/songdo-international-business-district/news/press-releases.aspx/d=386/title=Koreas_Songdo_International_Business_District__One_of_Asias_Largest_Green_Developments__Surpasses_Milestone_of_13_Million_Square_Feet_of_LEED_Certified_Space.

[2] Cisco, "Cisco and New Songdo International City Development Join Forces to Create One of the Most Technologically Advanced Smart+Connected Communities in the World," press release, July 4, 2011, http://newsroom.cisco.com/press-release-content?type=webcontent&articleId=426592.

[3] Charles Arthur, "The Thinking City," BBC Science Focus, January 2012, www.songdo.com/songdo-international-business-district/news/in-the-news.aspx/d=360/title=The_Thinking_City.

[4] David McNeill, "New Songdo: Atlantis of the Far East," *The Independent*, www.independent.co.uk/news/world/asia/new-songdo-city-atlantis-of-the-far-east-1712252.html.

[5] For background, see Songdo's website, www.songdo.com/songdo-international-business-district/why-songdo/a-brand-new-city.aspx.

[6] James Day, "Songdo in South Korea leading charge to become city of the future," *Metro* (U.K.), Jan. 10, 2012, www.metro.co.uk/tech/886852-songdo-in-south-korea-leading-charge-to-become-city-of-the-future.

[7] For background, see Masdar City, Frequently Asked Questions, "What has already been completed and when will the whole city be finished? www.masdarcity.ae/en/110/frequently-asked-questions/.

[8] For more on Masdar's design, see description by World Wildlife Fund, http://wwf.panda.org/?204438.

[9] Cost estimate is from "Frequently asked questions" about Masdar, *op. cit.*

[10] *Ibid.*

[11] Jonathan Glancey, "Inside Masdar City: a Modern Mirage," *The Guardian*, May 10, 2011, www.guardian.co.uk/artanddesign/2011/may/10/inside-masdar-city-modern-mirage.

[12] Adam Davidson, "Who Wants to Buy Honduras?" *The New York Times*, May 8, 2012, www.nytimes.com/2012/05/13/magazine/who-wants-to-buy-honduras.html?pagewanted=all.

[13] See United Nations Population Fund, "Linking Population, Poverty and Development," www.unfpa.org/pds/urbanization.htm.

[14] See U.N. News Centre, "Global population to pass 10 billion by 2100, UN projections indicate," www.un.org/apps/news/story.asp?NewsID=38253, and IDC Government Insights, "Business Strategy: Smart City Strategies" report, April 2012, p. 6, www.idc.com/getdoc.jsp?containerId=prUS23452612 (access to limited to clients).

[15] Kaid Benfield, "Is there a Downside to Intelligent Cities or Smart Cities?" *The Atlantic*, March 8, 2011, www.theatlantic.com/technology/archive/2011/03/is-there-a-downside-to-intelligent-cities-or-smart-cities/72068/.

[16] Malcolm Moore, "Chinese move to their eco-city of the future," *The Telegraph*, March 18, 2012, www.telegraph.co.uk/news/worldnews/asia/china/9151487/Chinese-move-to-their-eco-city-of-the-future.html.

[17] For background, see Michael Grynbaum, "A New Look Is Coming to Times Square: Minimalism," *The New York Times*, Sept. 27, 2011, and the Plan NYC homepage, www.nyc.gov/html/planyc2030/html/home/home.shtml.

[18] See "IDC Predictions 2012: Competing for 2020," http://cdn.idc.com/research/Predictions12/Main/downloads/IDCTOP10Predictions2012.pdf.

[19] John D. Kasarda and Greg Lindsay, *Aerotropolis, The Way We'll Live Next* (2011).

[20] Benjamin Schwarz, "A Vision in Concrete," *The Atlantic*, July/August 2008, www.theatlantic.com/magazine/archive/2008/07/a-vision-in-concrete/6846/.

[21] See Dan Hoornweg, "Smart Cities for Dummies" posting, World Bank Sustainable Cities Blog, Nov. 30, 2011, www.linkedin.com/pub/dan-hoornweg/6/876/627.

[22] Kai Laursen, "Are Satellite Cities the Key to the Future?" *The Atlantic Cities*, March 13, 2012, www.theatlanticcities.com/jobs-and-economy/2012/03/are-satellite-cities-cities-future/1468/.

[23] *Ibid.*

[24] For background on smart city populations, see Annissa Alusi, *et al.*, "Sustainable Cities: Oxymoron or the Shape of the Future?" Harvard Business School, 2011, www.hbs.edu/research/pdf/11062.pdf.

[25] Saskia Sassen, "Talking back to your intelligent city," McKinsey & Co., Feb. 1, 2011, http://whatmatters.mckinseydigital.com/cities/talking-back-to-your-intelligent-city.

[26] Greg Lindsay, "Cisco's Big Bet on New Songdo: Creating Cities From Scratch," *Fast Company*, Feb. 1, 2010, www.fastcompany.com/magazine/142/the-new-new-urbanism.html.

[27] "McCaffery Interests Announces Chicago's Lakeshore Drive Will be Extended Through Chicago Lakeside Development," press release, McCaffery Interests Inc., April 5, 2012, www.prnewswire.com/news-releases/mccaffery-interests-announces-chicagos-lakeshore-drive-will-be-extended-through-chicago-lakeside-development-146355525.html.

[28] "Cisco Selected by Chicago Urban Real Estate Developer to Develop Technology Master Plan for Smart+Connected Communities Project at Chicago Lakeside," press release, Cisco, Feb. 29, 2012, http://newsroom.cisco.com/press-release-content?type=webcontent&articleId=678356.

[29] Robert Sharoff, "Chicago to Redevelop U.S. Steel Site on Lakefront," *The New York Times*, Dec. 28, 2010, www.nytimes.com/2010/12/29/realestate/commercial/29chicago.html?pagewanted=all.

[30] Roger Yu, "Cities build airport cities 'aerotropolises' for growth," *USA Today*, April 20, 2011, http://travel.usatoday.com/flights/2011-04-19-airports-as-commerce-hubs.htm.

[31] Nate Berg, "The Dark Side of the Smart City, in Video Game Form," *The Atlantic Cities*, June 5, 2012, www.theatlanticcities.com/arts-and-lifestyle/2012/06/dark-side-smart-city-video-game/2184/.

[32] For background on Charles Perrow, see www.yale.edu/sociology/faculty/pages/perrow/.

[33] For background on Chernobyl, see www.pbs.org/wgbh/pages/frontline/shows/reaction/readings/chernobyl.html.

[34] Sassen, *op. cit.*

[35] For more on technology and democracy, see José Antonio Vargas, "Spring Awakening: How an Egyptian Revolution Began on Facebook," *The New York Times*, Feb. 17, 2012, www.nytimes.com/2012/02/19/books/review/how-an-egyptian-revolution-began-on-facebook.html?pagewanted=all, and Mark Engler, "The Internet: Tool of Revolution — or Repression?" *Foreign Policy*, April 29, 2011, www.fpif.org/blog/the_internet_tool_of_revolution_or_repression.

[36] Alison Isenberg, *Downtown America, A History of the Place and the People Who Made It* (2004), p. 36.

[37] Jane Jacobs, *The Death and Life of Great American Cities* (1993), p. 33.

[38] *Ibid.*, pp. 33-34.

[39] For background, see websites for Philadelphia's Parkway Museums District, www.parkwaymuseumsdistrictphiladelphia.org, and San Francisco's Civic Center Community Benefit District, http://sfciviccenter.org/.

[40] Douglas E. Morris, *It's a Sprawl World After All* (2005), pp. 6, 176.

[41] *Ibid.*, p. 176.

[42] Robert M. Fogelson, *Downtown, Its Rise and Fall, 1880-1950* (2001), p. 227.

[43] Isenberg, *op. cit.*, pp. 168-169, 171.

[44] *Ibid.*, p. 171. For background on housing legislation in the 1950s and '60s, see the Department of Housing and Urban Development, www.hud.gov/offices/adm/about/admguide/history.cfm.

[45] *Ibid.*, p. 188.

[46] *Ibid.*, p. 167.

[47] Fogelson, *op. cit.*, p. 319.

[48] *Ibid.*, pp. 195, 252-253.

[49] *Ibid.*, p. 256.

[50] Schwarz, *op. cit.*

[51] *Ibid.*

[52] Lindsay, *op. cit.*, *Fast Company.*

[53] Greg Lindsay, "Not So Smart Cities," *The New York Times*, Sept. 24, 2011, www.nytimes.com/2011/09/25/opinion/sunday/not-so-smart-cities.html.

[54] *Ibid.*

[55] For background on Curitiba, visit www.pbs.org/frontlineworld/fellows/brazil1203/.

[56] Dolores Hayden, *Building Suburbia: Green Fields and Urban Growth, 1820-2000* (2003), p. 97.

[57] Douglas Frantz and Catherine Collins, *Celebration U.S.A., Living in Disney's Brave New Town* (1999), p. 28.

[58] History of Reston, Greater Reston Chamber of Commerce, www.restonchamber.org/visiting-reston/History-of-Reston.aspx.

[59] Paul Goldberger, "James W. Rouse, 81, Dies; Socially Conscious Developer Built New Towns and Malls," *The New York Times*, April 10, 1996, www.nytimes.com/1996/04/10/us/james-w-rouse-81-dies-socially-conscious-developer-built-new-townsand-malls.html?pagewanted=all&src=pm.

[60] Frantz, *op. cit.*, p. 29.

[61] Douglas Frantz and Catherine Collins, "It's a Small Town After All," *The New York Times*, Dec. 3, 2010, www.nytimes.com/2010/12/04/opinion/04frantz.html.

[62] Frantz, "Celebration, USA," *op. cit.*, p. 28

[63] Annissa Alusi, *et al.*, "Sustainable Cities: Oxymoron or the Shape of the Future?" Harvard Business School, 2011, pp. 7-8, www.hbs.edu/research/pdf/11062.pdf.

[64] Hillary Brenhouse, "Plans Shrivel for Chinese Eco-City," *The New York Times*, June, 24,

About the Author

David Hatch is a veteran technology journalist based in Arlington, Va., who previously served as a staff writer with the National Journal Group and Crain Communications in Washington, D.C. His publishing credits include *U.S. News & World Report*, *The Daily*, *Dallas Morning News*, *Advertising Age*, Crain's *New York Business* and the *Boston Herald*. Hatch's previous *CQ Researcher* reports include "Google's Dominance," "Drug Company Ethics" and "Media Ownership." He holds a B.A. in English from the University of Massachusetts at Amherst.

2010, www.nytimes.com/2010/06/25/business/energy-environment/25iht-rbogdong.html.

[65] *Ibid.*

[66] Peter Savodnik, "Masdar City Offers Vision of Carbon-Neutral Future Amid Delays, Storms," Bloomberg, Dec. 8, 2011, www.bloomberg.com/news/2011-12-08/masdar-city-a-vision-of-a-greener-future-or-emirati-excess-.html.

[67] "New Songdo City: Atlantis of the Far East," *op. cit.*

[68] For background, see www.terrapinn.com/middle-east/smart-cities-world-mena/index.stm (Dubai); http://eu-smartcities.eu/content/launch-conference-smart-cities-and-communities-com munication (Brussels); www.smartcities-africa.co.za/ (Durban), and www.cityage.org/theinno vationcity/ (Toronto).

[69] Saskia Sassen, "Talking back to your intelligent city," McKinsey & Co., Feb. 1, 2011, http://whatmatters.mckinseydigital.com/cities/talking-back-to-your-intelligent-city, and home page for China's Smart City Fund, www.smartcity fund.com.cn/index.html.

[70] Aleksandr Bierig, "Meixi Lake Master Plan," *Architectural Record*, 2010, http://archrecord.construction.com/ar_china/China_Awards/2010/meixi/default.asp.

[71] For more on Lavasa, see www.lavasa.com; for background on New Urbanism, see Congress for the New Urbanism, www.cnu.org/performs_better.

[72] "Cisco Selected as the Networked Heart of City and Community Developments Around the Globe" press release, Cisco, Feb. 21, 2012, www.marketwire.com/press-release/cisco-selected-as-networked-heart-city-community-developments-around-globe-nasdaq-csco-162 1992.htm.

[73] Arati R. Jerath, "Delhi-Mumbai industrial corridor to spawn 7 'smart' cities," *Times of India*, http://articles.timesofindia.indiatimes.com/2011-01-15/india/28364347_1_delhi-mumbai-industrial-corridor-dmic-development-corporation-industrial-hubs.

[74] Boyd Cohen, "The Skolkovo Project: Can Russia Recreate Silicon Valley?" *Fast Company*, Feb. 27, 2012, www.fastcoexist.com/1679376/the-skolkovo-project-can-russia-recreate-silicon-valley.

[75] David Francis, "Will Nigeria's 'Airport City' Dreams Take Flight?," *Pacific Standard*, Feb. 20, 2012, www.psmag.com/business-economics/will-nigeria-s-airport-city-dreams-take-flight-39836/.

[76] Davidson, *op. cit.*

[77] *Ibid.*

FOR MORE INFORMATION

Congress for the New Urbanism, The Marquette Building, 140 S. Dearborn St., Suite 404, Chicago, IL 60603; 312-551-7300; www.cnu.org. Promotes sustainable, healthy communities and mixed-used development.

Institute for the Future, 124 University Ave., Palo Alto, CA 94301; 650-854-6322; www.iftf.org. Research group that helps organizations make informed decisions about the future.

Masdar City, Khalifa City 'A,' Opposite Presidential Flight, P.O. Box 54115, Abu Dhabi, UAE; +971-2-653-3333; www.masdarcity.ae/en/. Smart city under development near Abu Dhabi.

PlanIT Valley, Living PlanIT, Vale Pisao — Clubhouse, Rua das Laranjeiras, 1, Agua Longa Santo Tirso, 4825-102, Portugal; info@living-planit.com; http://living-planit.com/. Smart city under development by Living PlanIT in northern Portugal.

SENSEable City Laboratory, MIT 9-209, 77 Massachusetts Ave., Cambridge, MA 02139; 617-324-4474; http://senseable.mit.edu/. Research initiative at the Massachusetts Institute of Technology that studies the evolving urban landscape.

Smart Growth America, 1707 L St., N.W., Suite 1050, Washington, DC 20036; 202-207-3355; www.smartgrowthamerica.org. Advocacy group that promotes smart growth practices nationwide.

Songdo, Gale International, Songdo Office, 6-1 Songdo-Dong Yeonsu-Gu, Incheon, South Korea, 406-130; +82-32-850-1500; www.songdo.com. Smart city under development in South Korea.

[78] Ron Scherer, "New York City's mayor wants to turn the city green," *The Christian Science Monitor*, April 23, 2007, www.csmonitor.com/2007/0423/p03s02-usgn.html.

[79] For background on the New York City plan, see www.nyc.gov/html/planyc2030/html/home/home.shtml.

[80] U.S. Department of Energy, "Rebuilding it Better: Greensburg, Kansas," www1.eere.energy.gov/deployment/pdfs/53539.pdf.

[81] Erin Ailworth, "New data center focuses on using less energy," *The Boston Globe*, July 9, 2012, http://articles.boston.com/2012-07-09/business/32586590_1_computer-centers-efficien cy-industrial-site, and Gov. Deval Patrick, "Governor Patrick Celebrates Completion of First Phase of Massachusetts Green High Performance Computing Center," press release, Nov. 29, 2011, www.mass.gov/governor/pressoffice/pressre leases/2011/111129-holyoke-center-toppingoff.html.

[82] Jeremy Kahn, "India Invents a City," *The Atlantic*, June 7, 2011, www.theatlantic.com/magazine/archive/2011/07/india-invents-a-city/8549/, and Makarand Gadgil, "Lavasa Project: CAG report faults Maharashtra govt.," Live Mint.com/*Wall Street Journal*, April 17, 2012, www.livemint.com/2012/04/17235037/Lavasa-Project--CAG-report-fa.html.

[83] Kahn, *op. cit.*

[84] See "Facts v. Misconceptions" about Lavasa, www.lavasa.com/high/facts.aspx.

[85] Moore, *op. cit.*

[86] Shi Jiangtao, "Smog station fails to satisfy public," *South China Morning Post*, Dec. 5, 2011, http://topics.scmp.com/news/china-news-watch/article/Smog-station-fails-to-satisfy-public.

[87] "Urban Sustainability Index," McKinsey & Co., 2011, www.mckinseychina.com/2012/05/07/2011-urban-sustainability-index/.

[88] Alusi, *et al.*, *op. cit.*

[89] For background, see www.masdarcity.ae/en/105/visit-masdar-city/.

[90] Lindsay, *op. cit.*

[91] Edward Glaeser, *Triumph of the City* (2011), p. 40.

[92] *Ibid.*, p. 1, and Jacobs, *op. cit.*, p. 9.

Bibliography

Selected Sources

Books

Ehrenhalt, Alan, *The Great Inversion and the Future of the American City*, Knopf, 2012.
A leading urbanist examines how inner cities, once relegated to the poor, are morphing into high-rent districts, while suburbs are attracting more low-income families.

Glaeser, Edward, *Triumph of the City*, Penguin Press, 2011.
In this contrarian book, a Harvard economics professor argues that cities are generally healthier and greener than most people realize and provide gateways to job opportunities.

Jacobs, Jane, *The Death and Life of Great American Cities*, Random House, 1993.
First published in 1961, Jacobs' critique of urban development was hailed by *The New York Times* as "perhaps the most influential single work in the history of town planning."

Kasarda, John, and Greg Lindsay, *Aerotropolis: The Way We'll Live Next*, Farrar, Straus and Giroux, 2011.
A business professor (Kasarda) and a journalist document the rise of planned cities built around airports.

Articles

Benfield, Kaid, "Is There a Downside to 'Intelligent Cities' or 'Smart Cities'?" *The Atlantic*, March 8, 2011, www.theatlantic.com/technology/archive/2011/03/is-there-a-downside-to-intelligent-cities-or-smart-cities/72068/.
The director of the Sustainable Communities and Smart Growth program at the Natural Resources Defense Council argues that futuristic technology won't solve most urban ills.

Knight, Helen, "The green city that has a brain," *New Scientist*, Oct. 11, 2010, www.newscientist.com/article/mg20827814.800-the-green-city-that-has-a-brain.html (subscription required).
PlanIT Valley, a futuristic city in northern Portugal, will be run by an "urban operating system" that will serve as its "brain."

Lindsay, Greg, "Cisco's Big Bet on New Songdo: Creating Cities From Scratch," *Fast Company*, Feb. 1, 2010, www.fastcompany.com/magazine/142/the-new-new-urbanism.html?page=0%2C4.
Cisco focuses on building state-of-the-art new metropolises around the globe while IBM pursues a different strategy: retrofitting existing cities.

Norton, Leslie P., "Dawn of the Smart City," *Barron's*, Oct. 3, 2011, http://online.barrons.com/article/SB50001424052748704783104576599051649765770.html.
Norton argues that the market for smart cities is set to explode as urban areas undergo major makeovers.

Savodnik, Peter, "Masdar City, Castle in the Sand," *Bloomberg BusinessWeek*, Dec. 8, 2011, www.businessweek.com/magazine/masdar-city-castle-in-the-sand-12082011.html.
A planned utopia rising in the desert near Abu Dhabi must overcome not only the global economic downturn but also relentless sandstorms.

Singer, Natasha, "Mission Control, Built for Cities," *The New York Times*, March 3, 2012, www.nytimes.com/2012/03/04/business/ibm-takes-smarter-cities-concept-to-rio-de-janeiro.html?_r=1&scp=5&sq=smart%20cities&st=Search.
IBM has implemented a citywide system in sprawling Rio de Janeiro, Brazil, that allows 30 agencies to share data and run the metropolis more efficiently.

Reports and Studies

"Is Your City Smart Enough?," Ovum, 2011, www.cisco.com/web/strategy/docs/Is_your_city_smart_enough-Ovum_Analyst_Insights.pdf.
This Cisco-sponsored report by a London-based technology research firm outlines the motivations for building smart cities, such as pollution and congestion control, and highlights major projects under development.

"Smarter Cities Series: A Foundation for Understanding IBM Smarter Cities," IBM, 2011, www.redbooks.ibm.com/redpapers/pdfs/redp4733.pdf.
IBM details its strategy for using technology to help cities overcome challenges ranging from limited availability of water to inefficient use of electricity in buildings.

Alusi, Annissa, *et al.*, "Sustainable Cities: Oxymoron or the Shape of the Future?," Harvard Business School, 2011, www.hbs.edu/research/pdf/11-062.pdf.
Scholars at Harvard University's Business School delineate the goals and challenges of eight major smart-city projects under development around the world.

On the Web

"Designing Healthy Communities," Media Policy Center, 2012, www.designinghealthycommunities.org.
A four-part public television series investigates links between environmental conditions and diseases such as asthma, diabetes and obesity and spotlights cities that are designing healthier, more sustainable environments.

"Smarter Cities," Natural Resources Defense Council, http://smartercities.nrdc.org.
The Web portal features news on smart growth initiatives in the United States and across the globe.

The Next Step:

Additional Articles from Current Periodicals

Spending and Investment

Carter, Jamie, "The Rise of the Smarter, Cleaner City," *South China Morning Post*, March 9, 2012, p. 12.
About $40 billion is expected to be spent on smart city technology worldwide by 2016, a fivefold increase from 2010.

Jung, Jayne, "Utility Endesa Recasts Malaga, Spain As a Smart City," *Institutional Investor*, April 2012, www.institutionalinvestor.com/Article/3007985/Utility-Endesa-Recasts-Mlaga-Spain-as-a-Smart-City.html.
Private investment and government support have helped make Malaga Spain's most energy-smart city.

Singh, Malminderjit, "Nusajaya to Be Turned Into an ICT-Powered Smart City," *Business Times Singapore*, July 28, 2011.
Two investment groups are joining with Cisco to make Nusajaya, Malaysia, a smart city.

Wai, Cheong Suk, "Ideas for a Smarter Singapore," *Straits Times* (Singapore), July 10, 2012.
Singapore has accepted IBM's offer to help turn its Jurong Lake district into a smart city.

Technology

"A Smart Connected City Stimulating Innovation," *Birmingham* (England) *Post*, Feb. 16, 2012, p. 14, www.thefreelibrary.com/A+smart+connected+city+stimulating+innovation.-a0280136460.
The City Council in Birmingham, England, aims to make digital technologies available to all city residents.

McDonald, Mark, "To Build a Better Grid," *The New York Times*, July 29, 2011, p. 10, www.nytimes.com/2011/07/29/business/global/to-build-a-better-grid.html?pagewanted=all.
South Korea hopes linking smart technology and green energy will result in larger power grids for cities.

Pulakkat, Hari, "IT Cos, Developers Embracing Smart Tech in Indian Cities," *Economic Times* (India), Nov. 22, 2011, economictimes.indiatimes.com/opinion/special-report/developers-it-cos-embracing-smart-technologies-in-indian-cities/articleshow/10823415.cms.
An increasing number of Indian cities are using advanced technology to solve problems posed by population growth.

Tanikawa, Miki, "Getting Smart in the Suburbs of Tokyo," *The New York Times*, Nov. 27, 2011, www.nytimes.com/2011/11/28/business/global/28iht-RBOG-SOLAR28.html.
Panasonic is building a Japanese eco town with information-technology systems.

Toda, Yu, "'Smart Cities' Envisioned," *Daily Yomiuri* (Japan), Sept. 13, 2011, p. 6, www.yomiuri.co.jp/dy/business/T110912004466.htm.
Japanese corporations and municipal governments are examining several high-tech green-energy projects to make areas devastated by a 2011 earthquake environmentally smart.

Tuluy, Hasan, "Why Inclusive 'Green' Growth Can Sustain Gains in Latin America," *The Miami Herald*, June 19, 2012, www.miamiherald.com/2012/06/19/2857914/why-inclusive-green-growth-can.html.
Latin America is exploring innovative environmental projects to help cities fight poverty and preserve resources.

Urban Growth

"The Growth of Cities — a Thousand Monsters Stir," U.N. Integrated Regional Information Networks, March 9, 2012, www.irinnews.org/IndepthMain.aspx?InDepthID=63&ReportID=73999.
Increased urbanization often leads to crime and other problems for cities unable to handle population growth.

"Towards a 'Smarter' Nairobi," *The Nation* (Kenya), Nov. 3, 2011, allafrica.com/stories/201111030923.html.
The population of Nairobi, Kenya, is expected to double within the next decade, straining infrastructure and services.

Fitzgibbon, Rebecca, "Smart Move To Redesign Cities," *Hobart* (Australia) *Mercury*, Dec. 16, 2011, p. 42.
The United Nations projects that 70 percent of the world's population will live in cities by 2050, but few cities are prepared to handle the increase, says an Australian columnist.

CITING *CQ RESEARCHER*

Sample formats for citing these reports in a bibliography include the ones listed below. Preferred styles and formats vary, so please check with your instructor or professor.

MLA STYLE

Jost, Kenneth. "Remembering 9/11," CQ Researcher 2 Sept. 2011: 701-732.

APA STYLE

Jost, K. (2011, September 2). Remembering 9/11. *CQ Researcher, 9*, 701-732.

CHICAGO STYLE

Jost, Kenneth. "Remembering 9/11." *CQ Researcher*, September 2, 2011, 701-732.

Researcher PLUS Archive
New!

CQ Researcher

Published by CQ Press, an Imprint of SAGE Publications, Inc.

www.cqresearcher.com

Treating ADHD

Are attention disorders overdiagnosed?

Once viewed chiefly as affecting grade school-age children — chiefly hyperactive boys — attention deficit hyperactivity disorder (ADHD), which makes it difficult to focus attention and control impulses, today is widely seen as a lifelong condition affecting both genders equally. As more and more children, adolescents and adults are diagnosed with ADHD, prescriptions for stimulants such as Ritalin and Adderall to fight the disorder are soaring. Yet many experts say that while stimulants temporarily ease symptoms, they do nothing to improve academic or work performance or social skills, and some worry the condition is being overdiagnosed. At the same time, non-drug treatments remain under-used. The increased availability of stimulants, which are addictive, is fueling prescription-drug abuse among students and others who do not have ADHD but use the drugs as study aids or to get high.

Blake Taylor, a student at the University of California, Berkeley, began taking medication for ADHD at age 5. ADHD is widely seen today as a lifelong condition affecting both genders equally.

INSIDE THIS REPORT

THE ISSUES 671
BACKGROUND 678
CHRONOLOGY 679
AT ISSUE........................685
CURRENT SITUATION 686
OUTLOOK 687
BIBLIOGRAPHY 690
THE NEXT STEP 691

CQ Researcher • Aug. 3, 2012 • www.cqresearcher.com
Volume 22, Number 28 • Pages 669-692

Los Angeles | London | New Delhi
Singapore | Washington DC

RECIPIENT OF SOCIETY OF PROFESSIONAL JOURNALISTS AWARD FOR EXCELLENCE ◆ AMERICAN BAR ASSOCIATION SILVER GAVEL AWARD

TREATING ADHD

THE ISSUES

671 • Is ADHD being over-diagnosed?
• Are too many stimulants being prescribed?
• Are ADHD therapies effective over the long term?

BACKGROUND

678 **Disorder Defined**
Psychiatrists crafted the first definition of ADHD in 1968.

680 **Widening Spectrum**
Most researchers agree ADHD traits lie on a continuum from normal to damaging.

681 **Drug Abuse**
By the 1930s amphetamine decongestants were used to enhance performance.

683 **Under the Influence?**
In the 1960s fears grew that Ritalin and other stimulants could be dangerous.

CURRENT SITUATION

686 **Numbers Rise**
ADHD prescriptions rose 46 percent from 2002 to 2010.

686 **Changing Policies**
ADHD diagnosis guidelines now cover children from ages 4 to 18.

OUTLOOK

687 **Debate Continues**
Brain imaging and genetic profiles eventually may help in diagnosing ADHD.

SIDEBARS AND GRAPHICS

672 **One in 10 Children Diagnosed With ADHD**
Diagnosis rates exceed 14 percent in four states.

673 **Childhood ADHD, Drug Treatment on Rise**
Nine percent of children received ADHD diagnoses between 2008 and 2010.

674 **Cultural Expectations Fuel ADHD Diagnosis**
School pressures help define normal behavior.

676 **More High School Seniors Turning to Adderall**
Nearly twice as many used the drug without a prescription in 2011 as in 2007.

679 **Chronology**
Key events since 1937.

680 **Non-drug Therapies May Help With ADHD**
A change in breathing can have rapid effects on the brain.

682 **Students Abuse ADHD Drugs as Study Aids**
Experts warn of potentially dangerous consequences.

685 **At Issue**
Are ADHD and artificial food dyes linked?

FOR FURTHER RESEARCH

689 **For More Information**
Organizations to contact.

690 **Bibliography**
Selected sources used.

691 **The Next Step**
Additional articles.

691 **Citing *CQ Researcher***
Sample bibliography formats.

Cover: AP Photo/Jeff Chiu

CQ Researcher

Aug. 3, 2012
Volume 22, Number 28

MANAGING EDITOR: Thomas J. Billitteri
tjb@cqpress.com

ASSISTANT MANAGING EDITOR: Kathy Koch
kkoch@cqpress.com

CONTRIBUTING EDITOR: Thomas J. Colin
tcolin@cqpress.com

ASSOCIATE EDITOR: Kenneth Jost

STAFF WRITER: Marcia Clemmitt

CONTRIBUTING WRITERS: Peter Katel, Barbara Mantel, Jennifer Weeks

DESIGN/PRODUCTION EDITOR: Olu B. Davis

ASSISTANT EDITOR: Darrell Dela Rosa

FACT CHECKER: Michelle Harris

INTERN: Kate Irby

Los Angeles | London | New Delhi
Singapore | Washington DC

An Imprint of SAGE Publications, Inc.

VICE PRESIDENT AND EDITORIAL DIRECTOR, HIGHER EDUCATION GROUP:
Michele Sordi

DIRECTOR, ONLINE PUBLISHING:
Todd Baldwin

CQ Researcher (ISSN 1056-2036) is printed on acid-free paper. Published weekly, except: (March wk. 5) (May wk. 4) (July wk. 1) (Aug. wks. 3, 4) (Nov. wk. 4) and (Dec. wks. 3, 4). Published by SAGE Publications, Inc., 2455 Teller Rd., Thousand Oaks, CA 91320. Annual full-service subscriptions start at $1,054. For pricing, call 1-800-834-9020. To purchase a *CQ Researcher* report in print or electronic format (PDF), visit www.cqpress.com or call 866-427-7737. Single reports start at $15. Bulk purchase discounts and electronic-rights licensing are also available. Periodicals postage paid at Thousand Oaks, California, and at additional mailing offices. POSTMASTER: Send address changes to *CQ Researcher*, 2300 N St., N.W., Suite 800, Washington, DC 20037.

Treating ADHD

By Marcia Clemmitt

The Issues

Patricia Quinn, a pediatrician in Washington, D.C., specializes in attention deficit hyperactivity disorder (ADHD), and she has lots of personal experience to back up her medical training. Quinn is a self-described classic example of an adult ADHD sufferer who struggles with organization, focus and time management. She's also the mother of four children, three of whom also have ADHD.

"I've forgotten to pick up my kids from soccer practice," she says. "I interrupt a conversation to finish a conversation we were having three days ago." And without her business partner's help, she says, she'd often commit them to more clients and projects than they could reasonably handle.

Quinn didn't fully realize how hard it was for her to focus her attention until she was in medical school in the 1960s. Despite being a high achiever, "I had to reread and reread and reread" to get the full meaning of texts, she recalls. She didn't identify her problem as ADHD until much later, however.

Getty Images/*The Washington Post*/Caitlin Teal Price

Michelle Suppers, a mother of two in Manassas, Va., gets her eldest son, Anthony, started on his homework as soon as he comes home from school so he doesn't get distracted. When she learned he had ADHD, Suppers also underwent testing and found she too has the condition. Nearly 10 percent of children ages 4-17 have been diagnosed with ADHD at some point in their lives.

That wasn't unusual. In the '60s, doctors were only beginning to identify the mental traits of hyperactivity, impulsiveness and attention-focusing problems as a psychiatric disorder. They called the condition "minimal brain dysfunction" and diagnosed it only in children, primarily below the age of puberty. Today, psychiatry holds a different view. Adults are increasingly diagnosed with ADHD, which many specialists view as a lifelong condition rather than what it used to be considered: a developmental problem that children outgrew in their teens.

Like most mental disorders, ADHD is diagnosed by observations of behavior, not physical abnormalities. Brain imaging and genetic studies have turned up clues about brain regions and functions that may be involved in ADHD, but no consensus exists about its cause.

As more and more adults are diagnosed with ADHD, so too are increasing numbers of children and teens. Driving the increase is growing pressure on children to succeed in school, many scholars say.

Prescriptions for Ritalin, Concerta, Adderall and other stimulant drugs — long the first-line treatment for ADHD — also are increasing. For some medical experts as well as parents, that stirs fears that the amphetamine-like drugs could cause unforeseen health problems, if taken long term. And some worry about an epidemic of stimulant abuse as people without an ADHD diagnosis use the drugs to help them concentrate or to get high.

Over the past three decades, the number of children diagnosed with ADHD has soared, rising nearly eightfold between 1980 and 2007. [1] The percentage of children ages 4 to 17 diagnosed with ADHD increased at an average rate of 5.5 percent a year from 2003 to 2007. [2] In the mid- to late-1990s, the nationwide prevalence of ADHD among American children was estimated at between 4 and 5 percent. [3] By 2007 — the most recent year for which the Centers for Disease Control and Prevention (CDC) has analyzed data — 9.5 percent of children, or 5.4 million, had been diagnosed. [4]

Because young boys are most likely to exhibit hyperactivity, adults and girls with ADHD often have gone undiagnosed in the past, says Quinn. About 13.2 percent of boys have had an ADHD diagnosis, compared to 5.6 percent of girls. [5]

But many specialists now say ADHD is probably about equally prevalent in both genders. They give more weight to attention problems as the hallmark of the condition than in the past, which helps to extend the diagnosis to adults

One in 10 Children Diagnosed With ADHD

Nearly 10 percent of children ages 4 to 17 have been diagnosed with ADHD. Diagnosis rates exceed 14 percent in Alabama, Delaware, Louisiana and North Carolina. Rates are far lower in the West.

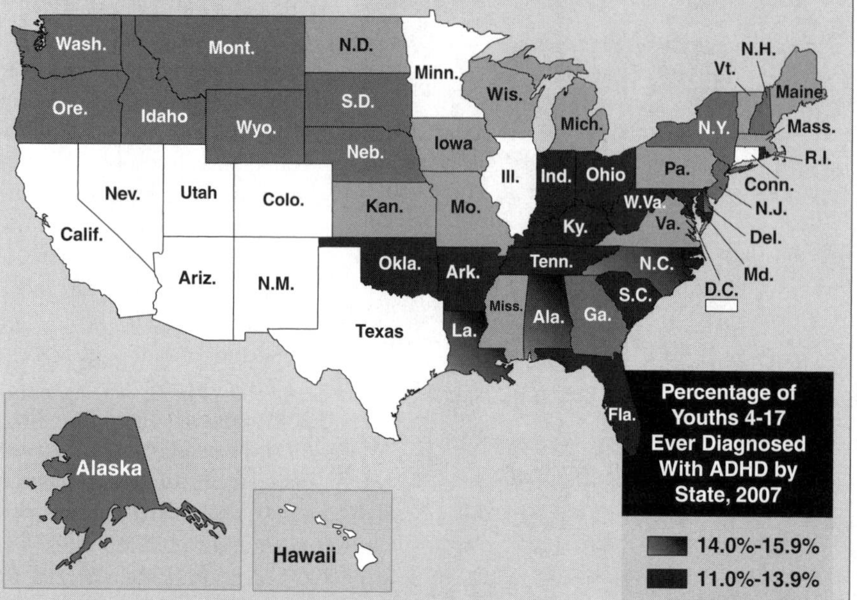

Percentage of Youths 4-17 Ever Diagnosed With ADHD by State, 2007

14.0%-15.9%
11.0%-13.9%
9.6%-10.9%
8.0%-9.5%
5.6%-7.9%

Source: *"State-Based Prevalence Data of ADHD Diagnosis," Centers for Disease Control and Prevention, December 2011, www.cdc.gov/ncbddd/adhd/prevalence.html*

and girls, who are less likely to be perceived as hyperactive, Quinn says.

For as long as ADHD has been diagnosed, however, some clinicians have debated the validity of diagnoses. Today a few clinicians still argue that no matter how many ADHD-type symptoms a person has they do not constitute an actual biological brain disorder that should be treated medically.

"ADHD is defined as involving hyperactivity, inattention and impulsivity. These are not diseases — they are disciplinary and educational problems," wrote Peter R. Breggin, a psychiatrist in Ithaca, N.Y. "Very often these children improve dramatically when parents develop a more consistent, rational and loving plan for discipline. . . . Or the child may be especially full of life and need more opportunity to run, to play and to be creative." [6]

However, most clinicians today seem to agree that at least some people do have traits severe enough to warrant treatment. (*See box, p. 677.*) But intense debate continues over whether doctors are making the diagnosis too freely, whether medical researchers are defining the disorder too broadly and whether ADHD patients' prognosis is far less gloomy than the medical establishment contends.

It's hard to overestimate the areas of life in which children with ADHD may experience — and cause — difficulties, says Richard Milich, a professor of psychology at the University of Kentucky in Lexington. They are more likely to be held back in school, less likely to graduate and "they can be a discouraging presence in the classroom and can disrupt a whole class," he says.

Worse, "these children are often socially rejected by their peers, sometimes within five minutes" of meeting them, Milich says. "The other kids hate them," perhaps because they have poor impulse control. "They act like younger kids. They both give and receive bullying." [7]

Often, "in high school the problems get bigger," encompassing more out-of-school activities, Milich says. For example, when driving skills of young adults with ADHD are tested in a simulator, "their driving is equivalent to the way others drive under the influence of alcohol." Yet, they are "more confident in their driving" than others, he says.

Some experts, however, contend that the new notion of ADHD as a lifetime diagnosis is too extreme. Lawrence Diller, a developmental pediatrician in Walnut Creek, Calif., and author of the 2011 book, *Remembering Ritalin*, interviewed 10 of his former ADHD patients, now young adults, and found they had fewer coping difficulties than one might expect.

"The trend is unmistakable. These kids are getting better," he says. "Some of the most hyperactive kids I've ever seen were in this group," but in their late 20s most are settling into jobs and acquiring stable, productive life patterns "as they're finding what they like to do. One kid was in the penitentiary. But now he's a police officer." Only two of the 10 — "both perfectionists," Diller says — still take medication, while the others haven't taken ADHD drugs for years.

ADHD is no barrier to success. Grammy-winning pop singer Justin Timberlake, comedian Jim Carrey and swimmer Michael Phelps, the most decorated Olympic athlete of all time, for example, all suffer from the condition.

The first line of treatment for ADHD has long been prescription stimulants — amphetamines and similar drugs formulated as relatively low-dose pills such as Ritalin. Seven percent of U.S. children take a psychiatric medication, and most of the prescriptions are for ADHD. [8]

The drugs are effective at temporarily quelling ADHD symptoms such as hyperactivity and lack of mental focus.

Childhood ADHD, Drug Treatment on Rise

Nine percent of children ages 5 to 17 were diagnosed with ADHD between 2008 and 2010, up from 7 percent between 1997 and 1999. Use of ADHD prescription drugs among children rose from less than 1 percent from 1988 to 1994 to 4 percent from 2005 to 2008.

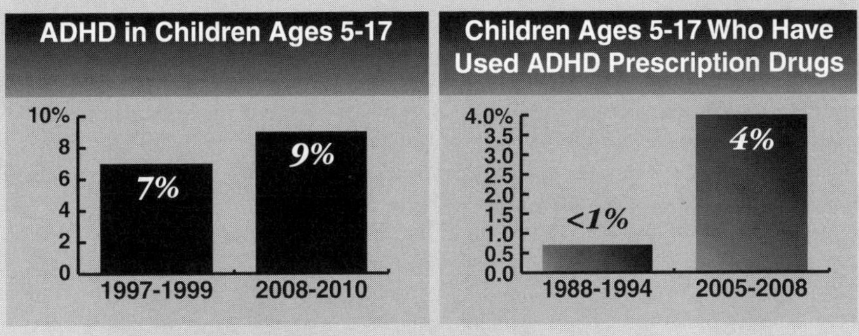

Source: "Health, United States, 2011," National Center for Health Statistics, 2011, p. 29, www.cdc.gov/nchs/data/hus/hus11.pdf

"There are patients who are quite debilitated" by their ADHD symptoms, and stimulants help them "get an even playing field" for school and jobs, says Joshua Israel, a San Francisco psychiatrist and associate clinical professor at the University of California, San Francisco.

But others point out that stimulant drugs can be addictive and may carry cardiovascular risks if used over a long period.

Because many now see ADHD as a long-term illness that also affects adults, the "medications aren't being prescribed the same way they were 20 years ago," says Mark Stein, a professor of psychiatry and pediatrics at the University of Illinois at Chicago. Back then, virtually all prescriptions were written for children, who stopped taking the medications when they hit puberty. Today, Stein says, more people "are taking them for many years," and we "don't have data" on the safety of long-term use or use by adults.

There also is "abundant evidence" that people who have not been diagnosed with ADHD take the drugs as mood elevators and performance enhancers, Nicolas Rasmussen, a professor of the history and philosophy of science at Australia's University of New South Wales, wrote in his 2008 book, *On Speed: The Many Lives of Amphetamine.*

"Reports of medication abuse have increased in step with attention deficit drug prescriptions," he wrote. And "the shift from misusing unprescribed Ritalin as an occasional study aid to straightforward abuse can happen easily." One Harvard student discovered the dangers of Ritalin abuse when she became "an absolute speed-freak — up all night and strung out all day," Rasmussen wrote. [9] (*See sidebar, p. 682.*)

Stimulants can also constitute a too-easy answer to complex behavioral or learning problems, says Milich. While quelling symptoms may be useful, it doesn't help ADHD patients develop appropriate social responses and effective learning strategies, he says. The lack of such skills may be a special problem for ADHD patients as they come of age in today's difficult job market. "In this economy . . . , it's harder and harder to just go out and grab a job," Milich says.

As ADHD diagnoses continue rising for children and adults, here are some of the questions being debated:

Is ADHD being overdiagnosed?

The percentage of children and adults with ADHD has risen steeply for two decades, causing some experts to argue that the condition is overdiagnosed. A minority of critics of the diagnosis go farther, arguing that ADHD-type traits should not be treated as a disease or disorder because the traits would be benign or might disappear altogether with proper response by teachers, parents and others.

Other analysts, however, argue that ADHD is clearly a biological condition and that, while some diagnoses are "false positives," many people who would benefit from treatment have never been told they have ADHD.

No brain scan or other medical test confirms ADHD, say critics of the diagnosis.

"The evidence for an organic basis for most children who are diagnosed with ADHD remains elusive," writes Peter Conrad, a professor of medical sociology at Brandeis University, in Waltham, Mass. He said clinicians who are overdiagnosing ADHD are engaging in a "classic case of the medicalization of deviance" from what is considered normal behavior. "Even if one found some validated biopsychological differences," Conrad wrote, "the sociological question remains: Does difference mean disease?" [10]

Some recent research suggests that careless ADHD diagnoses are occurring. In Germany, where the rate of ADHD increased by 381 percent between 1989 and 2001, a recent survey of nearly 500 therapists found that many of the clinicians diagnosed ADHD based on too few criteria. Clinicians diagnosed ADHD in about 17 percent of the cases deemed by experts not to meet the criteria — compared to about 7 percent of cases in which clinicians missed signs of ADHD. Moreover, boys were incorrectly deemed to have ADHD more often than girls. [11]

(The ADHD rate in Germany for children ages 3-17 is about 5 percent, roughly half the U.S. rate.) [12]

Cultural Expectations Fuel ADHD Diagnosis

School pressures help define normal behavior.

Millions of kids are restless, inattentive, disorganized and impulsive — but does that mean they have a psychiatric disorder?

Some scholars argue that it's wrong to label common childhood traits that way. Doing so, they maintain, is an abdication of the responsibility that parents, society and, especially, schools share to create environments in which children can function effectively.

"Hyperactivity is the most frequent justification for drugging children. The difficult-to-control male child is certainly not a new phenomenon, but attempts to give him a medical diagnosis are the product of modern psychology and psychiatry," wrote Peter R. Breggin, an Ithaca, N.Y., psychiatrist and longtime critic of labeling children as having ADHD. [1]

But Breggin is in the minority. More and more clinicians argue that ADHD has a biological basis, although most also contend that cultural forces play a powerful role in defining ADHD-type traits as a disorder.

The fact that many cases are inherited demonstrates that ADHD is a biological illness, says Russell Barkley, a professor of psychiatry at the Medical University of South Carolina, in Charleston.

Studies of families show that genetics is responsible for about two-thirds of ADHD, he says. Most of the remaining third is due to other biological causes — mainly damage of various kinds to the front portion of young brains, often caused by mothers smoking or drinking alcohol during pregnancy, Barkley says.

Yet, Barkley also maintains that social environment does help determine what mental traits we view as psychiatric illnesses.

Before about the 18th century, when most people couldn't read, "there were no reading disorders," although the traits recognized today as reading disorders certainly existed in people of those times, says Barkley. "The same is true of ADHD," he argues. "Until society demanded that virtually all children and teenagers focus on academics for hours each day," ADHD-type traits existed but were not seen as a problem, he says.

Additional evidence of how academic pressure shapes ADHD diagnoses lies in state variations in ADHD rates, says Stephen Hinshaw, a professor of psychology at the University of California, Berkeley. For example, among 4- to 17-year-olds in North Carolina, 16 percent have had an ADHD diagnosis, compared to only about 6 percent in California — a nearly threefold difference, says Hinshaw. He says that most states with high ADHD rates were among the first to punish schools that did not raise student test scores.

Even the culture of an individual classroom can determine whether a child needs treatment, says Barkley. "If in second grade a child has a great teacher, he may be able to get off medications" for that year but resume treatment in another school year if the nature of the classroom makes concentration tougher, he says.

Still, Barkley maintains that while supportive school environments can make it easier for ADHD students to function without drugs, schools are not obliged to provide such environments. In the Americans With Disabilities Act — which requires institutions to make accommodations to assist disabled people, including those with ADHD — "there is a very important word," Barkley says. "It says that schools must make *reasonable* accommodations. Society can't afford every accommodation that is conceivable. We're not going to design a separate curriculum for every child."

— Marcia Clemmitt

[1] Peter R. Breggin, *Toxic Psychiatry: Why Therapy, Empathy and Love Must Replace the Drugs, Electroshock, and Biochemical Theories of the New Psychiatry* (1994), p. 277.

A recent study of nearly a million children in western Canada found that the youngest in a class are more likely to be diagnosed with ADHD — at a rate of 7.4 percent, compared to 5.7 percent for the oldest children. [13] That result "suggests younger, less mature children are inappropriately being labeled and treated," presumably because their immaturity is mistaken for the disorder, said lead author Richard Morrow, a professor of counseling psychology at the University of British Columbia in Vancouver. [14]

With growing pressure on children to perform well in school, "it's very easy and popular to give this simple diagnosis," says Diller, the California pediatrician. Furthermore, in upscale neighborhoods, private clinics can make good money selling ADHD therapies — proven or not — to parents anxious to raise high achievers, he says.

Other analysts say, however, that fewer people have been diagnosed with ADHD than actually are impaired by it, especially adults and females of all ages.

Once believed to be a condition that affected only children, ADHD is now estimated to afflict 9 million to 10 million U.S. adults, but fewer than 2 million have been diagnosed, says Israel, the San Francisco psychiatrist.

Historically, girls and women have been under-diagnosed because "we've focused on the hyperactivity," which shows up more in males, rather than problems with attention and organizing, says Quinn, the Washington pediatrician. "A lot of people still think girls can't have" ADHD, partly because girls often have quieter symptoms that may cause less trouble in classrooms.

Many experts say misdiagnosis — including both over- and under-diagnosis — is the real problem.

The average diagnosis occurs in "a 10-minute pediatric visit" after a teacher or parent perceives that a child is having problems, says Stephen Hinshaw, a professor of psychology at the University of California, Berkeley. "In a visit like that, you get tons of false positives and tons of false negatives," he says.

For example, under-diagnosis may occur if a doctor concludes that, "Well, it can't be ADHD because the child is sitting still in the [doctor's'] exam room," says Hinshaw. That's because ADHD's "symptoms are context-dependent," and a child's ability to sit still in one situation doesn't rule out having a damaging level of hyperactivity in another.

False-positive diagnoses can occur because doctors don't take the time to rule out the many other conditions besides ADHD that may cause hyperactivity or attention problems, such as seizure disorders or abuse of some kind, Hinshaw says. "It's so easy to prescribe a stimulant," he says. Physicians' professional societies "have good guidelines now" that could prevent most misdiagnosis, "but the guidelines don't have teeth," so they're seldom consulted, Hinshaw says.

But debating the "correct" prevalence of ADHD is beside the point when the real need is to locate the children whose ADHD-type traits are causing them problems and find ways to help them, says William Pelham, a professor of psychology at Florida International University, in Miami. "I've never had a parent say, 'I did a survey [of symptoms], so I brought in my child.' They say, 'I brought him because he won't stay in his seat, he drives the teacher crazy.' For that child, it doesn't mean a hill of beans whether more or fewer children are diagnosed. The important question is: How many children are having problems in school?" Those children should be located and offered help, Pelham says.

Are too many stimulants being prescribed?

Those who argue that ADHD is overdiagnosed worry mainly that stimulants such as Ritalin and Adderall used to treat the condition can create health risks, including addiction. Many ADHD specialists say, however, that stimulants are an important part of ADHD therapy and that studies have not shown significant safety risks. (A few nonstimulant drugs, such as Strattera, also are occasionally prescribed for ADHD; unlike stimulants, they are not believed to be addictive but do carry other health risks. [15])

Up to 80 percent of those diagnosed with ADHD will need medications as part of their treatment, says Russell Barkley, a professor of psychiatry at the Medical University of South Carolina, in Charleston, and author of several books on ADHD. And stimulants are far from the only drug that people abuse, he says. "Are there some students on college campuses using Adderall when they don't have ADHD? Yes. We need to be careful about that, but it's also true for Viagra."

"As a society, it is hard to see why it would be good for us to not let people succeed" when the drugs can help, says Israel, the psychiatrist from San Francisco. "This is not cosmetic pharmacology" aiming to make people "better than well."

The largest long-term study of ADHD — the Multimodal Treatment of Attention Deficit Hyperactivity Disorder Study, funded by the National Institute of Mental Health in the 1990s — found that the medications are largely safe for children. Of 289 children who were randomly assigned to drug treatments, only 4 percent had significant adverse effects, mainly loss of appetite, sleep problems and crying spells. Children also grew somewhat more slowly while taking the drugs. [16]

In both Canada and the United States, some serious health problems among children, including heart attack and stroke — some fatal — have been reported. However, a large 2011 study spurred by the reports found the rates of such cardiovascular problems extremely low. Based on analysis of the medical records of 1.2 million children and young adults, researchers found "no increased risk" for the conditions. [17]

The researchers also analyzed data for about 150,000 people ages 25 to 64 who were currently prescribed ADHD drugs and again found "no evidence of an increased risk" of serious cardiovascular problems. However, because few adults have so far been prescribed the drugs, further study on safety for adults is needed, they said. [18]

Abuse of stimulants has turned some unwary people into "speed" addicts every time doctors began widely prescribing such drugs, says Diller, the Northern California pediatrician. "Every 20 or 30 years we find a reason" to use stimulants for medical purposes, and that's "been followed each time by an epidemic of abuse."

ADHD drugs are classified as "controlled substances" under U.S. and international laws. U.S. law lists the stimulants as Schedule II drugs — drugs that have accepted medical uses but also have "a high potential for abuse which may lead to severe psychological or physical dependence," according to the Drug Enforcement Administration (DEA). [19] Methylphenidate — a stimulant whose commercial forms include Ritalin and Concerta —"produces many of the same effects as cocaine or the amphetamines," the agency says.

Methylphenidate's increased use as an ADHD treatment is paralleled by an increased incidence of abuse, including as a snorted or injected drug, the DEA says. "Binge use, psychotic episodes, cardiovascular complications and severe psychological addiction have all been associated with methylphenidate abuse." [20]

More High School Seniors Turning to Adderall

More than 5 percent of high school seniors admitted in 2011 to taking Adderall without a prescription, nearly double the percentage in 2007. About 1 percent of seniors abused Concerta over the same period. Abuse of Ritalin declined since 2004 but is now trending up.

Non-prescribed ADHD Medication Use Among High School Seniors in Previous 12 Months, 2002-2011

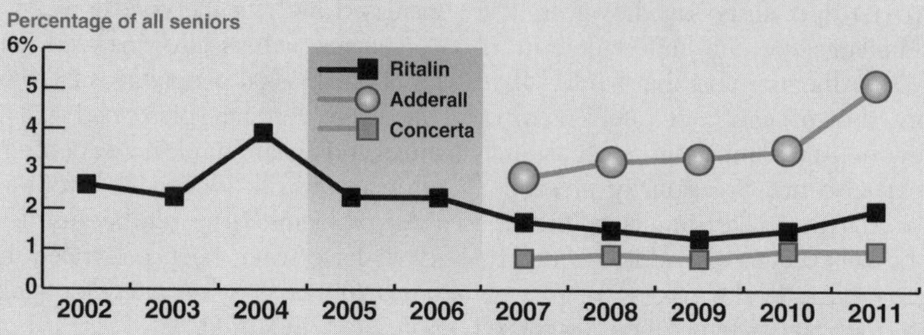

Source: Monitoring the Future, University of Michigan Institute for Social Research, June 2012, p. 751, www.monitoringthefuture.org/pubs/monographs/mtf-vol1_2011.pdf

A United Nations treaty — the Convention on Psychotropic Substances, which took effect in 1971 — urges governments to ban companies from advertising Schedule II drugs directly to consumers. [21]

In 2001, a British company, Celltech Pharmaceuticals, advertised its new methylphenidate-based drug Metadate in American magazines, and the DEA responded with a cease-and-desist order that called the ads a threat "to the public health and safety." [22]

Ultimately, the U.S. government did not ban direct-to-consumer advertising for Schedule II drugs. But the Food and Drug Administration (FDA) has continued to warn companies about misleading ads, and drug makers have confined much of their advertising to smaller outlets, such as websites and cable TV channels. [23] Currently, the FDA is reviewing public comments on a draft plan to require all TV ads for Schedule II drugs to be screened by the FDA before airing. [24]

The ease of prescribing stimulants leads families to neglect deeper problems and longer-term solutions, some analysts contend.

"Stimulant drugs 'work' by suppressing all spontaneous behavior in normal children," a consequence that "looks like an improvement in a classroom or home where the child has seemed uncontrollable," wrote Ithaca, N.Y. psychiatrist Breggin. In fact, when children's behavior becomes "age-inappropriate, excessive or disruptive, the potential causes are limitless, including: boredom, poor teaching . . . and underlying physical illness," and these issues should be examined rather than symptoms merely quelled with medication, he argues. [25]

"Multimodal" treatment — using drugs alongside parental training and training designed to help children foster social skills, learning strategies and the like — is by far the most effective approach to ADHD, many experts say.

Unfortunately, using drugs as the first line of treatment — the usual pattern — may mean the multimodal approach is never tried, says Florida International's Pelham. In one study, a group of children with ADHD was first prescribed stimulants and, later, their parents were offered training in effective techniques for dealing with ADHD. Only 15 percent of those parents ever took the training, Pelham says. By contrast, in families offered training first and prescriptions later, about 90 percent got the training.

"Drugs undermine parents' willingness" to commit themselves to important behavior changes, Pelham says. "Medications are grossly overutilized compared to behavioral treatment." But "there are no gigantic corporations that sell and make a profit on behavioral treatments, so nobody's talking to pediatricians about using these things."

Are ADHD therapies effective over the long term?

Behind every dispute involving ADHD treatments lies the big question: What, if any, therapeutic methods improve the lives of people who have more than average difficulty controlling their impulses and focusing attention on school or work?

Research shows that stimulant drugs effectively quell symptoms, experts say. Research also shows that training in social and learning skills as well as skills training for parents and teachers also help. But drug treatment does not have long-lasting effects against ADHD, and behavior-oriented strategies haven't been fully researched and can be difficult for families and schools to adopt.

"Medications can help improve attention and decrease impulsivity," says the University of Kentucky's Milich. "They work on the symptoms."

But research also shows that drug treatment doesn't make a long-term difference for patients, says Berkeley's Hinshaw, a researcher on the multimodal treatment study. Follow-up research on the study found that a year after being treated with drugs, children with ADHD had "lost 80 percent" of what they'd gained in symptom alleviation; and after two years, their behavior was indistinguishable from that of children with ADHD who'd never received the recommended level of drug treatments, Hinshaw says.

"The moment the medication has worn off, all the benefits are gone," says Pelham, another researcher on the multimodal treatment study. This means that "medication has no long-term benefit at all" when it comes to learning, at least in the studies of grade-school students, whose classroom work is mostly simple drills. "All the studies on learning have failed to show anything" in the way of improvements, he says. It remains unclear whether results would differ for older students, who often perform more complex tasks in the classroom. Pelham says no such research has been done because too few middle school and high school students take the drugs.

In a study of children with ADHD who played baseball, stimulant drugs significantly increased their attention to the game "but didn't do anything for their play," says Milich.

In another study, Milich examined how well children with ADHD understood narrative stories — presented as TV programs to eliminate reading problems as a factor in the scores — before and after drug treatment, compared with children without ADHD. Following a narrative requires grasping the significance of "causal connections," and children with ADHD have been shown to be "somewhat impaired" in that skill, Milich says. After taking medication for two years the children with ADHD had not progressed in their ability to understand narratives, while those without ADHD had, Milich says.

Milich says quelling ADHD symptoms accomplishes nothing in the long term because "until you replace old behaviors with appropriate behaviors" the child hasn't progressed.

On the other hand, behavior-modification strategies, which have been less extensively researched than drug treatments, have demonstrated long-term success in studies, many ADHD scholars say.

Hinshaw believes children with ADHD have abnormalities in the brain's dopamine system, which is thought to respond to rewards and punishments by sending signals that encourage the brain to repeat rewarded behaviors or avoid punished behaviors. "With behaviorally based strategies, you try to motivate kids who have [dopamine-system] problems," he says.

Such strategies may include consistently providing prompt and specific feedback on youngsters' behavior and classwork. Teachers, for example, can be coached to break each academic skill down into small steps and then provide clear and instant feedback as students perform each step.

One technique, called "the daily report card," is "hugely effective," says Stein of the University of Illinois. Children receive a daily assessment about their progress in improving specific behaviors and accumulate points they can later redeem for rewards. Children with ADHD generally have difficulties in social relations with their peers, and Stein runs a summer camp that uses the report card to help. By meeting specific behavior goals related to social interaction, children earn points that they can redeem for a field trip the next week.

"The second week, they quickly realize what they need to do if they didn't get the trip," he says. If parents are trained in the same techniques and use them, the results last, Stein says.

Building new skills and finding effective work-arounds for ADHD-related deficiencies is key to helping adult patients, says Israel, the San Francisco psychiatrist. For example, he says he helps patients find software programs that will help them organize their lives and figure out "where they should keep their keys" so they don't forget them.

Unlike drugs, behavioral interventions have no side effects or health risks,

Symptoms of ADHD

Several behavioral signs have been shown to be characteristic of ADHD. Experts say the number of symptoms matters less than the degree of impairment. Most experts agree that if significant impairment appears in at least five or six of the following behaviors, additional evaluation is advised.

Screening for ADHD	
Resisting distractions	**Persisting toward a goal**
Managing time	**Managing emotions**
Learning from experience	**Completing work or tasks**
Thinking or planning ahead	**Self-monitoring**
Avoiding procrastination	**Accurately reading social cues**
Sustaining effort	**Remembering what to do**
Getting started with work or tasks	**Retaining and retrieving information**
Controlling impulsivity	**Sitting still**
Organizing materials	**Handling transitions**
Demonstrating flexibility	

Source: "Screening Form," Center for Attention Disorders, 2009, www.centerforattentiondisorders.com/downloads/cad-screening-test.pdf

so they have little downside and potentially significant upsides, says Pelham.

Clinicians are careful to point out that today's effective behavioral interventions are not the same as the psychotherapeutic interventions that were widely used beginning in the 1950s in hopes of uncovering hidden emotional roots of ADHD. Diller, the California pediatrician, says the most popular was "play therapy," in which a patient and therapist played together with toys as a way of encouraging a child to uncover and work through anxieties or memories. As early as the 1980s, "it was generally conceded that [play therapy] didn't do anything" for kids with ADHD, Diller says. Despite that, some psychotherapists "continue to waste time and energy doing it," he says.

Many clinicians say the best approach to treating ADHD is combining judiciously prescribed medication with behavioral work carried out with the child and the child's parents and teachers.

In the multimodal treatment study, children who received combination treatment had less anxiety and better academic performance, parent-child relations and social skills, and they needed less medication, than the drug-only group, according to the National Institute of Mental Health. [26]

"The gains can be amazing," but the complexity and cost of such treatment mean that "so few children can get that," says Stein.

But behavioral interventions remain hard to implement. Hinshaw says that to "have a fighting chance" of truly ameliorating serious ADHD problems, behavioral work must be intense. That might mean "catching it at age 3 or 4 and doing 20 hours a week of training," for example.

A further difficulty is that ADHD is often an inherited trait, he says. "You've got to be a super-parent," who scrupulously keeps charts of children's behavior and rewards points, "doing it all calmly and without yelling," he says. That's not easy for anyone, "but what if you're a parent with the same problem?" ■

AFP/Getty Images

Widespread stimulant use in the 1960s led to passage of the 1970 Comprehensive Drug Abuse Prevention and Control Act, signed into law by President Richard M. Nixon, left, here with National Security Adviser Henry Kissinger. The law placed restrictions on prescription stimulants and other drugs, and by the late 1970s stimulant abuse had subsided.

BACKGROUND

Disorder Defined

Over the past half-century, success in American culture has been increasingly defined in terms of educational achievement. It may not be surprising, then, that over the same period traits that make it difficult for children to sit still at a desk or focus on lessons that bore them have increasingly been viewed as a significant disorder.

Yet, psychiatry has long struggled to define ADHD in terms of its key traits. What level of inattentiveness, restlessness or other characteristics is enough to classify someone as having a true psychiatric disorder? The question remains hotly disputed. [27]

Before the 1960s, children with traits such as hyperactivity and a lack of focus were described in the *Diagnostic and Statistical Manual of Mental Disorders* (*DSM*), medicine's mental-health diagnostic bible, as having a "minimal brain dysfunction." But the vagueness of that term didn't lend itself easily to diagnosis or to clear questions that medical researchers could explore.

Gradually, psychiatrists honed the definition in an attempt to "standardize the field so the condition could be recognized as a real entity that people could research because it was no longer amorphous," says Israel, the San Francisco psychiatrist.

The definitions have shifted over the years from a broad description of "a misbehaving child" to "something treatable," says Patricia Gerbarg, an assistant professor of clinical psychiatry at New York Medical College and a specialist in integrative mental health treatment, which promotes alternative therapies such as herbs and breathing exercises alongside traditional ones.

In 1968, the *DSM-II* made the first attempt at a specific definition, emphasizing hyperactivity in what the

Continued on p. 680

Chronology

1930s-1940s

Stimulant drugs gain popularity among college students.

1937
Charles Bradley, a psychiatrist at a Rhode Island mental institution, discovers that the stimulant drug amphetamine calms some severely disturbed children.

1948
College students use the stimulant Benzedrine, sold as a decongestant, as a study aid.

1960s-1980s

Medical interest grows in hyperactivity and attention problems.

1961
Stimulant drug Ritalin first used to treat hyperactivity.

1968
First definition of ADHD appears as "hyperkinetic reaction of childhood" in second edition of American Psychiatric Association's *Diagnostic and Statistical Manual of Mental Disorders* (*DSM*).

1969
Experts declare a "stimulant epidemic" as 10 million Americans use the addictive drugs, either with a prescription or illegally, for weight control, performance enhancement or to get high.

1971
United Nations Convention on Psychotropic Substances seeks government bans on direct-to-consumer ads for stimulant medications.

1973
California allergist Benjamin Feingold tells American Medical Association (AMA) that allergenic foods and synthetic food additives and dyes can cause hyperactivity.

1980
DSM-III shifts emphasis from "hyperkinetic reaction" to problems of inattention, renaming the condition "attention deficit disorder."

1990-Present

Newly named diagnosis of attention deficit hyperactivity disorder (ADHD) gains popularity for children and adults. Use of drugs for performance enhancement also soars.

1991
Activists convince an initially reluctant Department of Education to include ADHD as a disability that qualifies students for extra services.

1994
DSM-IV includes both inattention and hyperactivity in its new term, "attention deficit hyperactivity disorder (ADHD); patients with inattention, hyperactivity or both receive the diagnosis.

1998
Nearly 7 percent of U.S. children ages 5 to 17 diagnosed with ADHD.

1999
National Institutes of Mental Health study finds that stimulant drugs are generally safe for children and that children who receive both medication and behavior therapy do better in school and family relationships than those who get medication alone.

2006
A Food and Drug Administration (FDA) panel recommends that stimulant drugs for ADHD carry a "black box" label — the most serious health caution — warning of cardiovascular risks; FDA rejects the label.

2008
American Academy of Pediatrics recommends that children be assessed for heart conditions before taking stimulants. . . . Sen. Charles Grassley, R-Iowa, accuses three Harvard Medical School ADHD experts — Joseph Biederman, Timothy Wilens and Thomas Spencer — of hiding drug company payments.

2010
ADHD prescriptions for children have risen 46 percent since 2002.

2011
Harvard Medical School disciplines the three ADHD experts for failing to disclose drug company income. . . . FDA rejects calls to ban artificial food dyes, which may trigger hyperactivity in some children.

2012
In a German study, doctors incorrectly diagnosed ADHD in 17 percent of cases where the condition was not present. . . . Canadian researchers report that the youngest children in a school classroom are diagnosed with ADHD much more often than older ones, likely because doctors confused ADHD with immaturity. . . . FDA reviews comments on a plan to require pre-approval before TV ads for Schedule II addictive drugs are aired. . . . Draft of *DSM-5*, due for final release in May 2013, further expands population eligible for ADHD diagnosis. . . . Psychiatrists estimate that between 9 and 10 million U.S. adults have ADHD; under 2 million are diagnosed. . . . Shortages of ADHD medications lead Drug Enforcement Administration (DEA) to raise caps on how much drug manufacturers may produce, despite DEA qualms about drug abuse.

Non-drug Therapies May Help With ADHD

A change in breathing "can have rapid effects on the brain."

Medications such as Ritalin can bring immediate relief from the symptoms of attention deficit hyperactivity disorder (ADHD), but many experts say non-drug therapies are more effective at controlling the condition over the long term.

Yet, those therapies — which range from meditation and diet to one-on-one help from teachers — are often difficult to implement, researchers say, making pills the default choice for many patients.

ADHD problems "manifest themselves at home and school and should be treated in both places" because providing quick feedback that clearly connects behavior with a reward or penalty is crucial, says Julie Owens, an associate professor of psychology at Ohio University.

Researchers have found that classroom-management techniques such as careful, step-by-step instructions are effective for all students. But students who exhibit ADHD symptoms need additional help, such as a "daily report card" that provides instant feedback on student-specific goals. If teachers persist in these methods, "you get month-by-month incremental improvement" in students' behaviors, Owens says.

Getting teachers to apply the techniques consistently isn't easy, however. Teachers face heavy workloads, and many report inadequate training in classroom management, Owens says.

What's more, says Richard Milich, a professor of psychology at the University of Kentucky, "A teacher may even say, 'Why would I invest the effort when I have all these great kids who don't need these extra things?'" Owens points to a study in which all teachers initially used the daily report card. But over the course of a school year, only some continued to do so consistently while others nearly stopped altogether.

Some doctors are training ADHD patients in brain-altering techniques such as "mindfulness" meditation and "mind-body" approaches such as altering breathing patterns to enhance thinking.

ADHD is "a self-regulation disorder" that makes it difficult for sufferers to monitor and control their attention and impulses. Practicing mindfulness meditation — deliberately focusing attention on something specific and immediate, such as the sensations of breathing — can help ADHD suffers stay focused, says Lidia Zylowska, a Los Angeles psychiatrist and a cofounder of the Mindful Awareness Research Center at the University of California, Los Angeles.

"We often recommend exercise for a physical weakness," so it makes sense to do the same for mental capabilities, she says. Research to establish how mindfulness works in ADHD "is still

Continued from p. 678

manual dubbed a "hyperkinetic reaction of childhood." In 1980, the *DSM-III* dubbed the condition attention deficit disorder, or ADD, shifting the definition from hyperactivity to problems in focusing attention, which likely affect more people. In 1994, in *DSM-IV*, the current definition appeared, labeling the illness as ADHD — attention deficit hyperactivity disorder — and distinguishing three subtypes: one consisting mainly of inattentiveness, one of hyperactivity and impulsivity, and one exhibiting all of those traits. [28]

Widening Spectrum

More recently, some ADHD specialists have argued for dubbing ADHD a disorder of the brain's "executive functions."

Calling the condition ADD or ADHD "is like calling autism hand-flapping disorder," says Barkley of the Medical University of South Carolina. "The names of the disease have trivialized it. What you're really finding is a developmental delay in the self-regulating" regions of the brain — the areas, located mostly in the frontal lobe, that control thoughts, emotions and behaviors, he says. The development of those functions to full adult capacity is delayed by two to three years in children with ADHD, Barkley says.

Furthermore, he says brain imaging finds that in children with ADHD, the regions of the brain that perform these functions are 4 to 10 percent smaller and 25 percent less active than in other children. And while the brain structures may catch up in size to those of the average person by the time a person reaches the late teens or 20s, "the function doesn't catch up" but continues to be less robust than in the average person of the same age, Barkley says.

That view strikes a chord with some clinicians. "We're talking about the management, the CEO of the brain — organizing and managing the functions for daily life," says Quinn, the Washington pediatrician. The difference between people with and without ADHD is that "if you have two people whose desks are a mess, one can organize it if she has time, but the ADHD person, no matter how much time you give them, can't organize the desk," she says.

Others remain skeptical. Describing the condition as affecting the brain's "executive function" is another theory into which clinicians try to fit the symptoms they observe, just like earlier definitions, San Francisco psychiatrist Israel says. "But people can't even agree about what [the brain's] executive function is," he notes.

in an early stage," she says. However, studies have demonstrated that meditation can strengthen the brain's prefrontal cortex region, which manages the brain's regulatory functions, according to Zylowska. [1]

A change in breathing "can have rapid effects on the brain," says Patricia Gerbarg, an assistant professor of clinical psychiatry at New York Medical College. A "communication system" called the autonomic nervous system "lets the brain know what's happening in every part of the body" and allows messages coming from the body to affect the brain, she explains.

While the system involves the heartbeat, digestive processes and more, the only function it manages that can be voluntarily changed is breathing, she says. For example, slowing breathing to five steady, rhythmic in-and-out breaths per minute calms anxiety, improves mental focus and allows the brain "to solve problems better," Gerbarg says.

Even children can learn the technique quickly, she says. After one training session, "they can get a CD for 15 bucks and practice at home for free. The kids like it. It doesn't matter what your mind is doing. All you have to do is breathe."

In the early 1970s, when the ADHD diagnosis was in its infancy, Los Angeles-based allergist Benjamin Feingold devised a diet aimed at quelling hyperactivity. The diet eliminates ingredients to which Feingold hypothesized children might be overly sensitive: mainly naturally occurring organic chemicals called salicylates, found in foods such as blueberries and tomatoes, and artificial flavors, dyes and other additives that were new to American diets at the time.

The diet has been studied repeatedly over the years, and some researchers — and many families — have reported that it quiets some children's symptoms. But dietary research is hard to verify, and many analysts speculate that probably few children have these food sensitivities. [2]

The European Union requires foods with certain artificial colors to carry a warning about possible ADHD effects, but the U.S. Food and Drug Administration rejected such a warning last year. [3] (*See "At Issue," p. 685.*)

— Marcia Clemmitt

[1] Stephanie Sarkis, "ADHD & Mindfulness: An Interview with Lidia Zylowska," *Psychology Today*, June 19, 2012, www.psychologytoday.com/blog/here-there-and-everywhere/201206/adhd-mindfulness-interview-lidia-zylowska-md.

[2] For background, see Matthew Smith, *An Alternative History of Hyperactivity: Food Additives and the Feingold Diet* (2011).

[3] "FDA Panel: Studies Needed for Food Dye Side Effects, But No Warnings," AboutLawsuits.com, April 4, 2011, www.aboutlawsuits.com/fda-panel-food-dye-side-effects-17270.

However ADHD's traits are described, most researchers agree that they lie on a continuum, from normal to damaging and difficult to handle. But experts disagree sharply on whether current clinical standards deem too much of that spectrum as illness in need of treatment.

Largely because of the dominance of the pharmaceutical industry, psychiatrists have pushed the ADHD diagnosis beyond impaired people to include many who function normally, charged Allen Frances, a professor emeritus of psychiatry at the Duke University School of Medicine.

ADHD "consists of nonspecific symptoms . . . widely distributed in the general population: poor concentration, distractibility, impulsivity and hyperactivity," wrote Frances, who chaired the panel that assembled the *DSM IV*. "The kid who presents with classic early onset, severe [ADHD] is unmistakable," while "most kids clearly do not have" the disorder, Frances wrote. [29]

In between, however, it's tough to distinguish children with a clinical condition "from normal kids who are no more than extremely frisky and difficult to manage." Those kids in the middle have increasingly been diagnosed with ADHD, Frances wrote. "The epidemic started precisely when aggressive drug company marketing succeeded in 'educating' and sensitizing doctors, parents, and teachers to spot" illness "in kids previously considered to be on the normal side of the . . . boundary." [30]

Drug Abuse

The vast majority of people diagnosed with ADHD are treated at some point with drugs, and most ADHD medications are compounds related to amphetamine — a stimulant first formulated in 1887. The full effects of amphetamine-like drugs on the brain remain unclear. But, among other things, they may enhance the system through which the chemical dopamine — a major neurotransmitter active in functions including attention, memory, motivation, learning and the processing of punishments and rewards — carries messages through the brain. That stimulant drugs are used to treat people who already act overstimulated is an often-noted mystery. But, like most other drugs, stimulants found their medical use through the most common process used for drug discovery: trial and error. Even today, little is known about the actual cellular processes involved in most medical conditions and how chemicals interact with those processes, and ADHD and stimulants are no exceptions.

Students Abuse ADHD Drugs as Study Aids

Experts warn of potentially dangerous consequences.

As a double major at Rhode Island's Brown University, "Sarah" (not her real name) takes a rigorous course load to ensure she'll graduate within four years. Not only that, but she engages in summer internships and plans to study abroad in the fall.

To keep it all going, Sarah, a senior, admits to taking Adderall, a highly addictive amphetamine, twice a week, which she obtains without a prescription from fellow students, whose doctors prescribed it for attention deficit hyperactivity disorder (ADHD).

Illicitly obtained prescription stimulants increasingly are used as study aids — and sometimes to get high — on college campuses. Research conducted at 119 U.S. colleges in 2001 found that, on average, one in 25 students had used Adderall or another prescription stimulant in the past year, with a dozen schools reporting a 10 percent or higher usage rate. [1] Six years later, a study at a large, public research university found that about one in three students said they had illegally used Adderall or some other prescription stimulant. [2]

Sales of Adderall, in a class of stimulants known colloquially as "speed," are regulated because the drug is classified by the U.S. Drug Enforcement Administration as a Schedule II substance, meaning it has a high potential for abuse and psychological and physical dependence.

However, it is readily available for about $3 to $10 per pill from other students, according to Sarah, although prices rise during midterms and finals, when "people are rushing to get it. It's almost a desperation." [3]

Darlene Trew Crist, director of news and communication at Brown, says the university is aware that some students are abusing Adderall and that those caught illegally distributing drugs at Brown are subject to immediate suspension or expulsion. Cases of simple possession of Adderall and other drugs by students are handled on a case-by-case basis. Many students claim prescription stimulants help them stay awake all night without fatigue, providing them with crucial endurance in a competitive college atmosphere.

Sarah says she first used Adderall during the summer before she entered Brown. After procrastinating on a summer reading assignment until the last day, she says, she took the drug at a friend's recommendation. "I finished the assignment so quickly, it was shocking," she recalls.

During her sophomore year, she began using the drug regularly — usually twice a week. Each of her classes required massive amounts of reading, sometimes eight to 12 hours at a stretch. Sarah describes Adderall as a "robotic drug" that makes her so focused on schoolwork that she forgets to eat, drink and go to the bathroom.

One academic study found that many students excuse their illegal use of Adderall by claiming not to use the drug recreationally. In addition, the study found, many students view it as safer than street drugs such as cocaine and ecstasy because Adderall is a prescription medicine manufactured under government supervision. [4]

Even students who say they don't take the drug defend its use. Josh Lundfelt, a recent Ohio University graduate in actuarial science, says people exaggerate Adderall's harmfulness. "People make it out to be some horrible thing, but it's just an aid to accelerate your [academic] process," he says.

However, ADHD drugs may not give the boost to academic performance that students think they provide. According to a 2012 analysis of data on more than 1,200 students conducted by researchers from the University of Maryland, using ADHD

In the early decades of the 20th century, as the fledgling pharmaceutical industry first began to search for "blockbuster drugs" — relatively safe compounds to treat chronic conditions that afflict many people — chemists and clinical researchers spent considerable time testing amphetamines on patients and on themselves, based on hunches about what the drug might do in the body.

By the 1930s, amphetamines and chemically similar drugs were being sold as decongestants, for example.

At the same time, the drugs, which could be bought without a prescription, developed a reputation as remedies for fatigue and as largely overhyped performance enhancers. "During the Second World War, amphetamine and methamphetamine were adopted in the military services on all sides, in quasi-medical efforts to tune mind and body beyond normal human capabilities," wrote Australian medical historian Rasmussen. [31]

Students were among those who bought the drugs — mainly a decongestant sold under the name Benzedrine — for their hoped-for performance-enhancing abilities. In January 1948, for example, *The Harvard Crimson* reported on the "usual semi-annual" influx of "Benzedrine-happy students" who tried to use the stimulant as a study aid for semester exams but sometimes ended up suffering an overdose-fueled disaster. "There is a rumor of the physics major who stayed up three nights in a row and left his exam confident of an 'A,' " said the paper. "Actually, he had filled the blue book with nothing but his name, written over and over."

If a student "takes a little too much, he will fall into a delusional or 'euphoric' state, in which he does everything wrong without ever realizing it," a health professor told *The Crimson.* [32]

drugs without a prescription actually correlates to having a lower grade-point average. [5]

Moreover, Adderall can have serious side effects. Food is "displeasing, even nauseating" when she is using the drug, Sarah says. Her weight dropped from 110 pounds to 97 during her junior year.

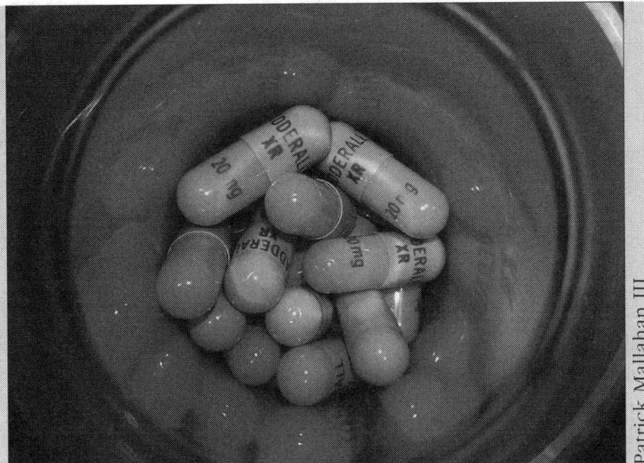

Patrick Mallahan III

The stimulant Adderall — a form of "speed" — is classified as a Schedule II substance because of its high potential for abuse and psychological and physical dependence.

She also experiences lightheadedness, headaches, dehydration and an irresistible desire to smoke cigarettes while on Adderall. "I'd go through a pack every two days," she says, adding that when she isn't taking the drug she smokes only occasionally.

David Goodman, a psychiatrist who is founder and director of the Adult Attention Deficit Disorder Center of Maryland, in Baltimore, says Adderall can be deadly if taken by students with undiagnosed cardiac conditions that could result in an irregular heartbeat or even death.

Doctors and students must take responsibility for controlling Adderall abuse, Goodman says. Because of the drug's popularity with college students who don't have ADHD, he tells students who come to him for prescriptions that he feels he first must call their parents to find out whether they showed signs of ADHD in childhood. "The fakers tend not to want to involve the parent," he says.

Goodman says he also warns patients that selling or giving away prescription medicine is a felony. In Washington, D.C., for example, distributing Adderall is punishable by up to five years in prison and a $50,000 fine. Taking Adderall without a prescription, on the other hand, is a misdemeanor, punishable by up to 180 days in jail and a $1,000 fine. [6] Distributing Adderall in Rhode Island is punishable by up to 30 years in prison and a $100,000 fine. [7]

— Kate Irby

[1] Sean Esteban McCabe, John R. Knight, Christian J. Teter and Henry Wechsler, "Non-medical use of prescription stimulants among US college students: prevalence and correlates from a national survey," Harvard School of Public Health, 2005, www.hsph.harvard.edu/cas/Documents/stimulants/McCabe_2005.pdf.

[2] Alan D. DeSantis and Audrey Curtis Hane, "'Adderall is Definitely Not a Drug': Justifications for the Illegal Use of ADHD Stimulants," *Substance Use & Misuse*, 45:31-46, Informa Healthcare USA, 2010, p. 34, http://andrewvs.blogs.com/files/adderall-is-definitely-not-a-drug.pdf.

[3] For background, see Michelle Trudeau, "More Students Turning Illegally to 'Smart' Drugs," NPR, Feb. 5, 2009, www.npr.org/templates/story/story.php?storyId=100254163.

[4] DeSantis and Hane, *op. cit.*, p. 36.

[5] Laura M. Garnier-Dykstra, *et al.*, "Nonmedical Use of Prescription Stimulants During College: Four-year Trends in Exposure Opportunity, Use, Motives and Sources," *Journal of American College Health*, March 15, 2012, pp. 226-234.

[6] DC Official Code, 2001 Edition, § 48-904.01.

[7] Rhode Island Official Code, Uniform Controlled Substances Act § 21-28-4.01, http://webserver.rilin.state.ri.us/Statutes/TITLE21/21-28/21-28-4.01.HTM.

Under the Influence?

Throughout this period, Benzedrine's manufacturer, the Philadelphia firm Smith, Kline & French, sent many samples of the drug to physicians around the country, to test as a treatment for various conditions. As early as 1937 Charles Bradley, a psychiatrist at a Rhode Island institution for children with severe neurological and emotional problems, was testing the drug as a mental-performance enhancer. In the process, he discovered that it made many children calmer and easier to work with.

Stimulants were not sold commercially as hyperactivity treatments until a quarter-century later, however.

In 1961, Ritalin — methylphenidate — was formulated as a stimulant similar to amphetamine but somewhat gentler and with fewer side effects. At the same time, the diagnosis of hyperactivity was first being applied to significant numbers of children who, unlike Bradley's patients, were not seriously ill. Ritalin soon gained popularity as the treatment of choice for the new diagnosis.

Only in the late 1950s did researchers begin turning up evidence that stimulant drugs can be highly addictive and dangerous. [33] As a result, in the 1960s, for the first time, the government began requiring prescriptions for amphetamine and other stimulant drugs. Despite these new restrictions, however, stimulants remained popular mood lifters and performance enhancers, both as prescribed by physicians and illegally.

By the late '60s, one in 20 American adults had a prescription for a stimulant, and "at least half as many were using 'speed' without prescriptions — altogether around 10 million people, equal to the entire combined populations of New York and Philadelphia at the time," wrote Rasmussen. Stimulant abuse was the leading drug problem of the day. [34]

The 1970 Comprehensive Drug Abuse Prevention and Control Act, signed into law by President Richard M. Nixon, placed restrictions on prescription stimulants along with other drugs, and by the late 1970s stimulant abuse had subsided.

The use of stimulants to treat children with ADHD was just beginning its long ascent, however.

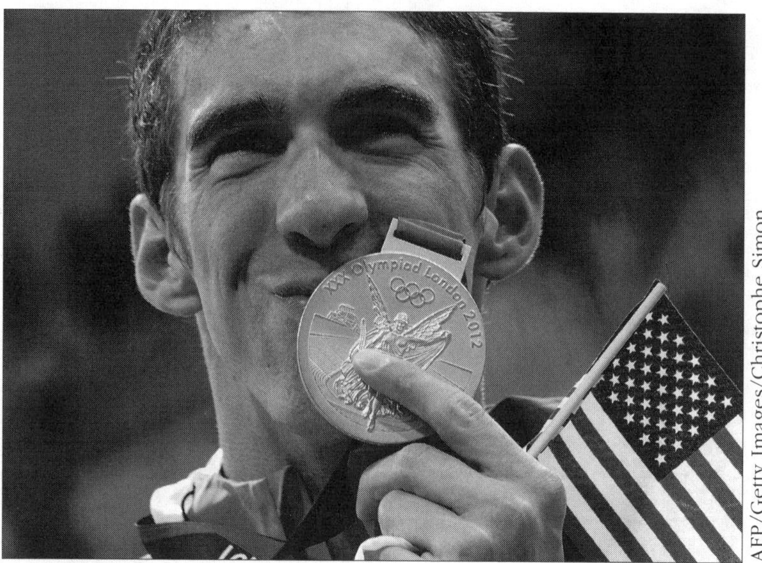

AFP/Getty Images/Christophe Simon

ADHD is no barrier to success. Swimmer Michael Phelps, the most decorated Olympic athlete of all time, Grammy-winning pop singer Justin Timberlake and movie star Jim Carrey, for example, all suffer from the condition. Diagnosed at age 9, Phelps stopped taking medication in seventh grade. His highly structured life as an athlete in training helped keep his symptoms in check, said his mother. "ADHD kids have great passion. It just needs to be funneled," said Debbie Phelps, who used intense behavioral therapy to help her son. Above, Phelps after winning his 19th Olympic medal at the London Summer Games on July 31.

In 1969, at the height of the nation's biggest stimulant epidemic, U.S. drug companies manufactured about 2.5 billion standard doses of prescription stimulants annually, according to Rasmussen. That amount dropped off substantially in the 1970s, but then, as the ADHD diagnosis gained steam, it began rising again, first gradually but then steeply, beginning in the mid-1990s.

Between 1998 and 2009, the percentage of children between ages 5 and 17 who had been diagnosed with ADHD increased from 6.9 percent to around 9 percent. [35] Meanwhile, "America's annual consumption of pharmaceutical "speed" has risen almost tenfold since 1995," and in 2005 it exceeded the number of doses being produced in 1969, Rasmussen said. [36]

In many ways, that's a medical success story, some ADHD experts say.

Many parents are hesitant to expose young children to long-term prescription drug use but change their minds when they discover that other approaches they try don't quell symptoms, says Quinn, the Washington pediatrician. "It's the most difficult thing in the world to put a kid on medications," she says. But "often the families try other things" — such as eliminating sugar from a child's diet — "and then they come back." Even non-drug therapies that do work, such as behavior-modifying techniques, work better when used alongside medications, she says.

But others worry that the rising rate of ADHD diagnosis — and the near-total reliance on drug therapy — is driven as much by drug company influence as by medical understanding.

At most, only one in 10 families with an ADHD child receives parental training on managing the condition, but nine in 10 children diagnosed with ADHD get drugs, says Florida International's Pelham. "Mainly the teacher complains to the parent, the parent goes to the pediatrician, who's not trained to do a full screen" for ADHD, and the simple, well-publicized drug fix is prescribed, he says.

"In recent years, I have come to believe that the individuals who advocate most strongly for medication — both those from the professional community, including the National Institutes of Mental Health, and those from advocacy groups — . . . have major and undisclosed conflicts of interest with the pharmaceutical companies," Pelham said in 2004. [37]

But virtually all medical researchers maintain that they are not influenced by pharmaceutical company funding because as academics their primary interest is in uncovering facts. "My interests are solely in the advancement of medical treatment through rigorous and objective study," and conflict-of-interest issues are something to be taken "very seriously," said Harvard Medical School psychiatry professor Joseph Biederman, an ADHD expert who was sanctioned by the school in 2011 for failing to disclose some payments he got from drug companies. [38]

The nonprofit disease-advocacy group Children and Adults with Attention Deficit/Hyperactivity Disorder (CHADD) says that it is "committed to avoiding conflict of interest or even its appearance in accepting financial support from corporations" with an interest in promoting ADHD-related products. To that end, "for any . . . fiscal year, no more than 30 [percent] of CHADD's revenue can be derived from donations and grants from pharmaceutical companies," and the group will accept donations for education and information campaigns only if it has "complete edi-

Continued on p. 686

At Issue:

Are ADHD and artificial food dyes linked?

MICHAEL F. JACOBSON
EXECUTIVE DIRECTOR, CENTER FOR SCIENCE IN THE PUBLIC INTEREST

WRITTEN FOR *CQ RESEARCHER*, JULY 2012

yes

Without question, food dyes serve a very useful purpose for food manufacturers. They make a wide variety of low-nutrition junk foods — candy, soft drinks, sugary cereals — more appealing to children. Dyes can help disguise the absence of healthy fruit and vegetable ingredients in a product expected to include them, as was the case in a nearly avocado-free "guacamole" dip Kraft used to sell. But given that they provide no nutritive or preservative function, food dyes have quite a high bar to clear when it comes to their safety.

Thanks to numerous controlled studies conducted in the United States, Europe and Australia, we now know that Yellow 5, Red 40, Blue 2 and other petroleum-based food dyes have a powerfully disruptive impact on some children's behavior.

A comprehensive 2004 meta-analysis of the medical literature and two important studies funded by the British government found that dyes (and possibly the preservative sodium benzoate) adversely affect kids' behavior. These studies support what many parents who have placed their hyperactive children on a diet developed by allergist Benjamin Feingold have discovered: that eliminating foods with artificial dyes (and in other cases, other foods) leads to marked improvement in behavior and performance in school.

In 2008, the Center for Science in the Public Interest called on the Food and Drug Administration (FDA) to ban several dyes. At a follow-up 2011 hearing, the FDA agreed that dyes do adversly affect some children.

European food-safety officials are several steps ahead of the FDA and have successfully spurred positive changes in the industry. Thus, a strawberry sundae from a McDonald's in the U.K. gets its red color from strawberries; McDonald's treats its U.S. consumers to strawberries and Red 40.

As it happens, safe natural colorings are abundant. (No European consumers seem to miss the fake ones.) Getting rid of food dyes here would certainly be a safer step than dealing with hyperactivity or other behavioral problems in children with powerful stimulant drugs such as Ritalin. (Irony alert: Some Ritalin pills have Green 3.)

The question I pose to American food-safety regulators and companies is why tolerate any risk, even in just a small percentage of children, from something that serves only a cosmetic purpose in food?

SARAH MECHUM
INTERNATIONAL ASSOCIATION OF COLOR MANUFACTURERS

WRITTEN FOR *CQ RESEARCHER*, JULY 2012

no

The scientific evidence does not support the claims made by the Center for Science in the Public Interest and others linking synthetic color additives and hyperactive behavior in children. Reviews of several studies on hyperactivity and synthetic food color conducted by U.S. experts and international regulatory bodies have found no correlation between the intake of synthetic food colors and hyperactivity among children.

Just last year, the FDA Food Advisory Committee, an expert panel of pediatricians, toxicologists, behavioral scientists, neuroscientists and food scientists, reviewed all of the available evidence and concluded there is no established causal relationship between color additives and hyperactivity in children. The committee voted against recommending additional labeling beyond the name of the color but agreed additional studies are warranted. The International Association of Color Manufacturers supports the committee's conclusions. We are currently conducting a study to further improve the understanding of color additive consumption, and the results will be shared with the FDA.

The color industry takes its responsibility for consumer safety seriously. In addition to complying with FDA regulations and procedures for certification of colors, the industry also sponsors many safety studies, the results of which have been evaluated by the FDA and international regulatory bodies, including the Joint Expert Committee on Food Additives and the European Food Safety Agency. The transparent safety-evaluation process includes commentary from all stakeholders, including regulators, consumers, public health advocates and industry. These studies confirm the safety of FDA-certified colors, and as a result, various coloring additives have been approved for use in food, beverages and other products around the world.

While they are not nutritional, color additives play an important role in food, and they do so without posing a health risk to consumers. Color is one of the principal contributors to the palatability of foods. Color additives enhance colors that occur naturally, correct natural variations in color and provide a colorful identity to foods that would otherwise be virtually colorless. Additionally, they provide a means to identify drugs and dietary supplements, helping to prevent medication errors.

Our industry is vigilant about the safety of our products, and we will continue to stay on top of new scientific developments related to color additive safety. We will continue to work closely with regulatory authorities around the world to ensure that food colors are safe.

Continued from p. 684

torial and managerial control" of the projects.[39]

In his own pharmaceutical-sponsored research, Pelham said he was pressured to delete a portion of an article being prepared for publication "where I was saying it was important to do combined treatments (medication and behavioral)" rather than drugs alone. "It was intimidating to be one researcher and have all these people pushing me to change the text."[40]

Such qualms have been reinforced in the past few years as Biederman and two other leading ADHD experts, all in the psychiatry department of Harvard Medical School, have faced sanctions over failure to disclose payments they've received as consultants to drug companies. NIH requires researchers it supports to report to their universities any outside earnings of $10,000 a year or more, in a bid to make transparent conflicts of interest that may shade the researchers' findings. In 2008, Sen. Charles Grassley, R-Iowa, announced that he'd discovered serious under-reporting of income by Biederman and Harvard professor Timothy Wilens and associate professor Thomas Spencer. Based on the men's disclosure documents, "over the last seven years, it looked like they had taken a couple hundred thousand dollars" from drug companies, when in fact they had received over a million dollars each, Grassley said.[41]

In 2011, Harvard Medical School and Massachusetts General Hospital, where the three are also employed, announced that they were barred from all industry-sponsored outside activities for a year, followed by a two-year probationary period during which they would need approval for such work.[42]

The conflicts of interest in the case involved mostly the psychiatrists' promotion of increased diagnosis of and drug treatment for more severe childhood psychiatric illness than ADHD, such as bipolar disease. But the men's worldwide prominence as ADHD researchers raised questions for many about drug-company influence in that field. An Australian government panel ordered a review of ADHD-treatment guidelines being prepared for the country's national health insurance program following the investigation. At the time, the draft guidelines referred to Biederman's research 50 times, while seven of the 10 people on Australia's guideline-drafting panel also had financial ties to companies such as Swiss-based Ritalin manufacturer Novartis.[43]

Meanwhile, it has remained difficult for researchers to get funding to study behavioral therapies and other non-drug approaches. Pelham, for example, is currently pursuing a federal grant to explore the limitations of drug treatments. He'd prefer to do a study on non-drug therapies, he says, "but NIH doesn't fund those." ■

CURRENT SITUATION

Numbers Rise

The total number of drug prescriptions written for U.S. children and teens has dropped for the past several years, but the rate of ADHD prescriptions continues to climb, according to the Food and Drug Administration.

ADHD prescriptions rose 46 percent between 2002 and 2010 (the latest year examined), the second-highest increase of any category. Contraceptive prescriptions increased 93 percent, while prescriptions for antibiotics and some cough medicines dropped, after new medical guidelines recommended limiting their use.[44]

Driving the increase in ADHD prescriptions has been a steady rise in the number of young people under age 18 diagnosed with the disorder. It grew 66 percent between 2000 and 2010, according to a study this year by researchers at Northwestern University. By 2010, doctors had diagnosed 10.4 million U.S. children and teens, up from 6.2 million in 2000, according to the analysis.[45] (The number of Americans ages 5 through 17 — the prime ages for an ADHD diagnosis — hovered between 53 and 54 million in both years.)[46]

"The magnitude and speed of this shift in one decade is likely due to an increased awareness of ADHD," said study author Craig Garfield, an assistant professor of pediatrics at the Northwestern University Feinberg School of Medicine.[47]

Changing Policies

Late last year, the American Academy of Pediatrics expanded its ADHD diagnosis guidelines to cover children and teens from ages 4 to 18; earlier guidelines had covered only children between 6 and 12. New medical findings about ADHD make it possible to diagnose and treat the broader group, says the academy.

"Treating children at a young age" may "increase their chances of succeeding in school," said Mark Wolraich, lead author of the guidelines and a researcher on neural development at the University of Oklahoma Health Sciences Center, in Oklahoma City.[48]

As for teens, "it's been known for a while" that stopping ADHD drugs at puberty — as recommended in the past — "was a mistake" and that attention problems, in particular, still plague teenagers, says the University of Illinois' Stein.

In the past year, the supply of several ADHD drugs has fallen short of demand. Besides the growing legitimate market, demand is swelling for stimulants as performance enhancers or recreational drugs. Because stimulants are "controlled substances," the Drug Enforcement Agency (DEA) caps the amount that companies can produce, and the combined legitimate and illegal demand has outstripped supply. [49]

"The DEA is tasked with making sure there is enough for legitimate need without making so much [that] it is diverted for illicit purposes," said agency spokesperson Barbara Carreno. This year, DEA has raised the cap for methylphenidate, the basis for such drugs as Ritalin and Concerta, from 50,000 to 56,000 kilograms per year and the cap for amphetamine, used in drugs such as Adderall, from 18,600 to 25,300 kilograms per year. [50]

Meanwhile, implementing school procedures that assist both ADHD students and their teachers continues to be difficult.

Federal legislation is pending to limit schools' leeway in using physical restraints and seclusion to control students, often those with ADHD-related traits. The bills — sponsored by Sen. Tom Harkin, D-Iowa, and Rep. George Miller, D-Calif. — would prohibit schools that receive federal funds from physically restraining a student unless the behavior poses immediate physical harm to the student or others. Restraints can be used only if they allow the student to communicate, and if other means of controlling the behavior have been tried and failed. [51]

Many advocates for the disabled support the bills, but schools are leery. The legislation proposes "an extremely high threshold" that schools must meet before restraints are allowed, said the National School Boards Association. For example, a student whose behavior threatens "to destroy a classroom" — a costly consequence — would not be eligible for restraint under the bills as currently drafted, the group said. [52]

A recent study by the *Chicago Tribune* points to serious inequities between schools in high- and low-income neighborhoods when it comes to making accommodations to help ADHD sufferers and other disabled students. Federal law authorizes schools to make certain adjustments — such as allowing seating in the front of the classroom or providing more time to take tests — to create a level playing field for all students. However, the *Tribune* found that Illinois students who live in higher-income districts got the lion's share of such help. [53]

Statewide, only about 1 percent of public-school students had accommodations in the 2009-2010 school year, according to the paper. But in some wealthy districts near Chicago, 4 to 5 percent of students got accommodations. The 20 school districts with the highest percentages of students with accommodations had student bodies that were 76 percent white and poverty rates well below the state average of 45 percent; the 20 districts with the fewest accommodations were 19 percent white, and the "vast majority had far higher poverty than the state average," the *Tribune* reported. [54] ■

OUTLOOK

Debate Continues

With attention growing on ADHD in adults, teens, preschool children and girls, diagnoses will likely increase for the foreseeable future. Many clinicians hope science can eventually clear up doubts that ADHD is a "real" disorder, but others want researchers to take a closer look at the social trends, such as increasing competitiveness, that lead people to seek achievement-enhancing drugs.

Improvements in brain-imaging technology provide hope that it eventually can diagnose ADHD, says Israel, the San Francisco psychiatrist. Brain images showing clear patterns of aberrant activity in ADHD patients could go a long way toward "clearing up the uncertainty and discomfort people have around the diagnosis," he says.

Studying genetic profiles also may eventually yield valuable information, Israel says. In particular, profiles that show variations among groups of ADHD sufferers may help to "match the right person to the right medications" without trial and error.

The American Psychiatric Association plans to release the *DSM-5* in May 2013. [55] Current *DSM* guidelines state that, to warrant an ADHD diagnosis, a patient must show symptoms by age 7, a threshold that the *DSM-5* will raise to age 12. Drafters say recent research shows that people whose symptoms appear by age 7 aren't any different from people who don't exhibit them until later. Moreover, they say raising the threshold will make it easier to diagnose adults, who seldom remember what they were like before age 7 but do remember what they were like as 12-year-olds. [56]

But some medical professionals worry the change will increase the already skyrocketing rates of ADHD diagnosis and expose too many people to "inappropriate treatment and stigmatization" said Frances, the Duke professor emeritus. [57]

Perhaps most in need of examination, however, is a culture that values achievement to the point that it drives "increasing use of stimulant drugs for enhancement, even among the general population," says Diller, the California pediatrician. ■

Notes

[1] Daniel F. Connor, "Problems of Overdiagnosis and Overprescribing in ADHD," *Psychiatric Times*, Aug. 11, 2011, www.psychiatrictimes.com/adhd/content/article/10168/1926348.

[2] "Attention Deficit/Hyperactivity Disorder, Data and Statistics," Centers for Disease Control and Prevention, www.cdc.gov/ncbddd/adhd/data.html.

[3] Connor, *op. cit.*
[4] "Attention Deficit/Hyperactivity Disorder," *op. cit.*
[5] *Ibid.*
[6] Peter Breggin, "Stimulants for ADHD Shown to Cause Sudden Death in Children," *Huffington Post*, June 17, 2009, www.huffingtonpost.com/dr-peter-breggin/stimulants-for-adhd-shown_b_216912.html.
[7] For background see Thomas J. Billitteri, "Preventing Bullying," *CQ Researcher*, Dec. 10, 2010, pp. 1013-1036; updated May 31, 2012.
[8] Marianne Szegedy-Maszak, "Psychological Science Weighs in on ADHD," *Daily Observations* blog, Association for Psychological Science, June 25, 2012, www.psychologicalscience.org/index.php/publications/observer/obsonline/psychological-science-weighs-in-on-adhd.html.
[9] Nicolas Rasmussen, *On Speed: The Many Lives of Amphetamine* (2008), p. 236.
[10] Peter Conrad, "The Changing Social Reality of ADHD," *Contemporary Sociology*, Oct. 1, 2010, p. 525.
[11] Katrin Bruchmüller, Jürgen Margraf and Silvia Schneider, "Is ADHD Diagnosed in Accord with Diagnostic Criteria? Overdiagnosis and Influence of Client Gender on Diagnosis," *Journal of Consulting and Clinical Psychology*, February 2012, pp. 128-138, http://psycnet.apa.org/index.cfm?fa=buy.optionToBuy&id=2011-30100-001.
[12] M. Huss, *et al.*, "How Often Are German Children and Adolescents Diagnosed with ADHD? Prevalence Based on the Judgment of Health Care Professionals: Results of the German Health and Examination Study," *European Child and Adolescent Psychiatry*, December 2008, www.ncbi.nlm.nih.gov/pubmed/19132304.
[13] Randy Dotinga, "Youngest Kids in Class More Apt to Get ADHD Diagnosis: Study," *HealthDay*, Healthfinder.gov, March 2012, http://healthfinder.gov/news/newsstory.aspx?docID=662425; Richard L. Morrow, *et al.*, "Influence of Relative Age on Diagnosis and Treatment of Attention-Deficit/Hyperactivity Disorder in Children," *CMAJ [Canadian Medical Association Journal]*, March 5, 2012, www.cmaj.ca/content/184/7/755.abstract.
[14] Rick Nauert, "Youngest Kids in Class Get More ADHD Diagnosis, Drugs," *PsychCentral*, March 6, 2012, http://psychcentral.com/news/2012/03/06/youngest-kids-in-class-get-more-adhd-diagnoses-drugs/35621.html.
[15] "Strattera Oral," *WebMD*, www.webmd.com/drugs/drug-64629-Strattera+Oral.aspx?drugid=64629&drugname=Strattera+Oral; *Monitoring the Future*, University of Michigan, 2011, pp. 499-501, http://monitoringthefuture.org/pubs/monographs/mtf-vol1_2011.pdf.
[16] "The Multimodal Treatment of Attention Deficit Hyperactivity Disorder Study (MTA): Questions and Answers," National Institute of Mental Health website, November 2009, www.nimh.nih.gov/trials/practical/mta/the-multimodal-treatment-of-attention-deficit-hyperactivity-disorder-study-mta-questions-and-answers.shtml.
[17] William O. Cooper, Laura A. Habel, *et al.*, "ADHD Drugs and Serious Cardiovascular Events in Children and Young Adults," *New England Journal of Medicine*, Nov. 23, 2011, pp. 1896-1904, www.nejm.org/doi/full/10.1056/NEJMoa1110212.
[18] Laura A. Habel, William O. Cooper, *et al.*, "ADHD Medications and Risk of Serious Cardiovascular Events in Young and Middle-Aged Adults," *JAMA*, Dec. 28, 2011, pp. 2673-2683, www.ncbi.nlm.nih.gov/pubmed/22161946.
[19] "Controlled Substance Schedules," U.S. Drug Enforcement Administration, www.deadiversion.usdoj.gov/schedules/index.html.
[20] "Methylphenidate (Ritalin)," U.S. Drug Enforcement Administration, www.justice.gov/dea/concern/methylphenidate.html.
[21] "Warnings on Packages and Advertising," Article 10, Convention on Psychotropic Substances, 1971, p. 7, www.unodc.org/pdf/convention_1971_en.pdf.
[22] Cease-and-desist order from U.S. DEA to Celltech Pharmaceuticals, purveyor of the control substance methylphenidate, website of Ben Hansen, www.bonkersinstitute.org/medshow/kiddealetter.html; Karen Thomas, "Back to School for ADHD Drugs," *USA Today*, Aug. 8, 2001, www.usatoday.com/life/2001-08-28-adhd.htm.
[23] Ed Silverman, "FDA Warns Five Drugmakers Over ADHD Ads," *Pharmalot blog*, Sept. 26, 2008, www.pharmalot.com/2008/09/fda-warns-five-drugmakers-over-adhd-ads; Marguerite R. Lombardo, "Through the Correct Lens: Understanding Overprescription of Stimulant Drugs, Their Abuse, and Where the Remedies Lie," student paper, Harvard Law School, April 2004, http://leda.law.harvard.edu/leda/data/674/Lombardo.html#fn274; Kevin P. Miller, "FDA Warns ADHD Drugmakers — Again," Kevin P. Miller blog, Sept. 29, 2008, http://kevinpmiller.blogspot.com/2008/09/fda-warns-adhd-drugmaker-again.html.
[24] "Guidance for Industry Direct-to-Consumer Television Advertisements — FDAAA DTC Television Ad Pre-Dissemination Review Program," Food and Drug Administration, March 2012, www.fda.gov/downloads/Drugs/GuidanceComplianceRegulatoryInformation/Guidances/UCM295554.pdf.
[25] Peter R. Breggin, "A Misdiagnosis, Anywhere," Room for Debate blog, *The New York Times*, Oct. 13, 2011, www.nytimes.com/roomfordebate/2011/10/12/are-americans-more-prone-to-adhd/adhd-is-a-misdiagnosis.
[26] *Ibid.*
[27] For background, see Kathy Koch, "Rethinking Ritalin," *CQ Researcher*, Oct. 22, 1999, pp. 905-928.
[28] "Types of ADHD: Making the Diagnosis," *WebMD*, May 15, 2012, www.webmd.com/add-adhd/guide/types-of-adhd.
[29] Allen Frances, "Attention Deficit Disorder Is Over-diagnosed and Over-treated," *Huffington Post*, March 5, 2012, www.huffingtonpost.com/allen-frances/attention-deficit-disorder_b_1206381.html.
[30] *Ibid.*
[31] Rasmussen, *op. cit.*, p. 3.
[32] "Benzedrine-soaked Crammers May Wind Up Behind an 'E,' Bock Warns," *The Harvard Crimson*, Jan. 24, 1948, www.thecrimson.com/article/1948/1/24/benzedrine-soaked-crammers-may-wind-up-behind.
[33] Rasmussen, *op. cit.*, p. 3.
[34] *Ibid.*, p. 4.
[35] Lara K. Akinbami, *et al.*, "Attention Deficit Hyperactivity Disorder Among Children Aged

About the Author

Staff writer **Marcia Clemmitt** is a veteran social-policy reporter who previously served as editor in chief of *Medicine & Health* and staff writer for *The Scientist*. She has also been a high school math and physics teacher. She holds a liberal arts and sciences degree from St. John's College, Annapolis, and a master's degree in English from Georgetown University. Her recent reports include "Traumatic Brain Injury" and "Sleep Deprivation."

5-17 Years in the United States, 1998-2009," National Center for Health Statistics, August 2011, www.cdc.gov/nchs/data/databriefs/db70.PDF.
[36] Rasmussen, *op. cit.*, p. 236.
[37] Quoted in "Leading ADHD Researcher Blows Whistle on Concerta and Chadd," Alliance for Human Research Protection website, Dec. 3, 2004, www.ahrp.org/infomail/04/12/03.php.
[38] Quoted in Gardiner Harris and Benedict Carey, "Researchers Fail to Reveal Full Drug Pay," *The New York Times*, June 8, 2008, www.nytimes.com/2008/06/08/us/08conflict.html?pagewanted=all.
[39] "CHADD Ethical Principles for Acceptance of Corporate and Foundation Support," www.chadd.org/AM/Template.cfm?Section=Home§ion=Privacy_Policy&template=/CM/ContentDisplay.cfm&ContentFileID=1334.
[40] Quoted in Kelly Hearn, "Here, Kiddie, Kiddie," *AlterNet*, Nov. 29, 2004, www.alternet.org/story/20594?page=entire.
[41] Quoted in Harris and Carey, *op. cit.*
[42] Xi Yu, "Three Professors Face Sanctions Following Harvard Medical School Inquiry," *The Harvard Crimson*, July 2, 2011, www.thecrimson.com/article/2011/7/2/school-medical-harvard-investigation.
[43] Nicola Berkovic, "Urgent Review to be Undertaken of 'Tainted' ADHD Guidelines," *The Australian*, Nov. 24, 2009, www.theaustralian.com.au/news/urgent-review-to-be-undertaken-of-tainted-adhd-guidelines/story-e6frg6n6-1225802595063.
[44] Grace Chai, *et al.*, "Trends of Outpatient Prescription Drug Utilization in U.S. Children, 2002-2010," *Pediatrics*, July 2012, http://pediatrics.aappublications.org/content/130/1/23.full.pdf+html.
[45] Erin White, "Diagnosis of ADHD on the Rise," press release, Northwestern University, March 19, 2012, www.northwestern.edu/newscenter/stories/2012/03/adhd-diagnosis-pediatrics.html.
[46] "Resident Population by Sex and Age: 1980 to 2010," Table 7, *Statistical Abstract of the United States, 2012*, U.S. Census Bureau, www.census.gov/compendia/statab/2012/tables/12s0007.pdf.
[47] Quoted in White, *op. cit.*
[48] Quoted in "American Academy of Pediatrics Expands Ages for Diagnosis and Treatment of ADHD in Children," press release, American Academy of Pediatrics, Oct. 16, 2011, www.aap.org/en-us/about-the-aap/aap-press-room/pages/AAP-Expands-Ages-for-Diagnosis-and-Treatment-of-ADHD-in-Children.aspx.
[49] Daniel J. DeNoon, "ADHD Drug Shortages: Why?" *WebMD*, Jan. 3, 2012, www.webmd.com/add-adhd/news/20120103/adhd-drug-shortages-why.
[50] *Ibid.*
[51] "S. 2020: Keeping All Students Safe Act," govtrack.us, www.govtrack.us/congress/bills/112/s2020.
[52] "Statement for the Record: Beyond Seclusion and Restraint: Creating Positive Learning Environments for All Students," National School Boards Association, July 12, 2012, www.nsba.org/Newsroom/Spotlight-On/NSBA-Statement-for-the-Record-on-Senate-Committee-Hearing-on-Keeping-All-Students-Safe-Act-July.pdf.
[53] Diane Rado, "Special Help Starts as Early as Grade School — but Only for Select Students," *Chicago Tribune*, June 6, 2012, http://articles.chicagotribune.com/2012-06-06/news/ct-met-accommodations-folo-20120606_1_disabled-students-time-or-other-accommodations-poorest-schools.
[54] *Ibid.*
[55] "DSM-5: The Future of Psychiatric Diagnosis," American Psychiatric Association, www.dsm5.org/Pages/Default.aspx.
[56] "Rationale for Changes in ADHD in DSM-5," American Psychiatric Association ADHD and Disruptive Behavior Disorders Workgroup, May 3, 2012, www.dsm5.org/ProposedRevisions/Pages/proposedrevision.aspx?rid=383#.
[57] Allen Frances, "DSM 5 Continues to Ignore Criticism From Petitioners," *Huffington Post*, June 20, 2012, www.huffingtonpost.com/allen-frances/dsm-5-petition_b_1610569.html.

FOR MORE INFORMATION

ADDitude, www.additudemag.com/adhd/about-additude.html. Advertising-supported website that provides information about ADHD.

American Academy of Child and Adolescent Psychiatry, 3615 Wisconsin Ave., N.W., Washington, DC 20016-3007; 202-966-7300; www.aacap.org. Membership group for psychiatrists that monitors legislation and policy activities related to children's mental health.

Centers for Disease Control and Prevention, Attention-Deficit/Hyperactivity Disorder, 1600 Clifton Rd., Atlanta, GA 30333; 800-232-4636; www.cdc.gov/ncbddd/adhd. Federal website that posts data and medical information on ADHD.

CHADD (Children and Adults with Attention Deficit Hyperactivity Disorder), 8181 Professional Place, Suite 150, Landover, MD 20785; 800-233-4050; www.chadd.org. Nonprofit membership group that provides information on ADHD; hosts the National Resource Center on ADHD, a federally funded national clearinghouse for evidence-based research on the condition.

DSM-5 Development, American Psychiatric Association, 1000 Wilson Blvd., Suite 1825, Arlington, VA 22209-3901; 703-907-7300; www.dsm5.org. Draft proposal and commentary on the next edition of the *Diagnostic and Statistical Manual of Mental Disorders*.

Feingold Association of the United States, 11849 Suncatcher Dr., Fishers, IN 46037; 800-321-3287; www.feingold.org. Membership group for parents who try to control hyperactivity in children by eliminating food additives from the diet.

Multimodal Treatment of Attention Deficit Hyperactivity Disorder Study, National Institute of Mental Health, 6001 Executive Blvd., Room 8184, MSC 9663, Bethesda, MD 20892-9663; 866-615-6464; www.nimh.nih.gov/trials/practical/mta/multimodal-treatment-of-attention-deficit-hyperactivity-disorder-mta-study.shtml. Federal information website for the largest study of ADHD treatments.

Russell A. Barkley: The Official Site, www.russellbarkley.org. Website of a professor of psychiatry and pediatrics at the Medical University of South Carolina who spearheaded movement to gain recognition for ADHD as a serious affliction with biological causes.

Bibliography

Selected Sources

Books

Barkley, Russell A., *Taking Charge of Adult ADHD*, The Guilford Press, 2010.
A clinical professor of psychiatry and pediatrics at the Medical University of South Carolina describes the relatively new diagnosis of adult ADHD along with drug and non-drug strategies for managing it.

Brown, Richard P., and Patricia L. Gerbarg, *Non-drug Treatments for ADHD: New Options for Kids, Adults and Clinicians*, W.W. Norton & Co., 2012.
An associate clinical professor of psychiatry (Brown) at Columbia College of Physicians and Surgeons, in New York City, and his wife, an assistant clinical professor of psychiatry at New York Medical College, describe a variety of complementary treatments such as dietary changes, herbs, vitamins and mind-body techniques such as breathing exercises, to help manage ADHD.

Diller, Lawrence H., *Remembering Ritalin: A Doctor and Generation Rx Reflect on Life and Psychiatric Drugs*, Perigee, 2011.
A developmental pediatrician and assistant clinical professor of pediatrics at the University of California, San Francisco, recounts the stories of 10 young adults he treated for hyperactivity as children. Diller reflects on whether ADHD is overdiagnosed and says the long-term prognosis for children with the disorder is better than many believe.

Rasmussen, Nicolas, *On Speed: The Many Lives of Amphetamine*, New York University Press, 2009.
A professor of the history and philosophy of medicine at Australia's University of New South Wales chronicles the 100-plus year history of stimulant drugs as medicines, performance enhancers and intoxicants.

Reiff, Michael I., ed., *ADHD: What Every Parent Needs to Know*, 2nd Ed., American Academy of Pediatrics, 2011.
Authors from a pediatricians' professional group describe the current medical thinking on ADHD.

Smith, Matthew, *An Alternative History of Hyperactivity: Food Additives and the Feingold Diet*, Rutgers University Press, 2011.
A research fellow at Britain's University of Exeter says the emergence of ADHD as a diagnosis in the post-World War II era made it almost inevitable that some would ascribe its origins to the presence of chemical additives in food. Skeptics and supporters of that hypothesis continue producing dueling — but ultimately inconclusive — research studies on the question.

Articles

Harris, Dan, and Lana Zak, "Supermom's Secret Addiction: Stepping Out of Adderall's Shadow," ABC News, June 26, 2012, http://abcnews.go.com/Health/adderall-rise-mothers/story?id=16622475.
Middle-aged women, including a mother of four and a nurse, say they became addicted to the ADHD drug Adderall after taking it to enhance their performance in their jobs and as homemakers. Adderall use has risen quickly among adult women, and experts believe many users are obtaining the drug illegally, such as by "doctor shopping" among physicians to get multiple prescriptions.

Rabin, Roni Caryn, "Drugs to Treat ADHD Reach the Preschool Set," *The New York Times*, Oct. 24, 2011, www.nytimes.com/2011/10/25/health/25consumer.html.
The American Academy of Pediatrics has revised its ADHD treatment guidelines, approving the addition of drugs to preschoolers' ADHD treatment if behavioral techniques don't quell their symptoms. The recommendation makes some parents and medical professionals leery, however.

Thurm, Wendy, "Is There an ADHD Epidemic in Major League Baseball?" *SBNation*, June 29, 2012, http://mlb.sbnation.com/2012/6/29/3104332/is-there-an-adhd-epidemic-in-major-league-baseball.
Eight percent of major league baseball players have been diagnosed with ADHD and prescribed stimulant drugs. But the National Institutes of Health estimates that only 4 percent of adults have ADHD, and skeptics wonder whether players are being diagnosed illegitimately. The drugs would otherwise be off-limits to them under baseball's rules forbidding performance-enhancing drugs.

Reports and Studies

"Monitoring the Future: National Results on Adolescent Drug Use," National Institute on Drug Abuse/University of Michigan Institute for Social Research, February 2012, www.monitoringthefuture.org/pubs/monographs/mtf-overview2011.pdf.
The latest edition of a long-running national survey on drug use by high school students describes trends in abuse of the ADHD drugs Ritalin, Concerta and Adderall.

"Teaching Children with Attention Deficit Hyperactivity Disorder: Instructional Strategies and Practices," U.S. Department of Education, 2008, www2.ed.gov/rschstat/research/pubs/adhd/adhd-teaching-2008.pdf.
The Education Department describes how teachers can identify children with ADHD and employ the best classroom strategies to manage their behavior and help them learn.

The Next Step:

Additional Articles from Current Periodicals

Drugs

Bankston, Amanda, "Students Faking ADHD to Get Drugs," *Star Tribune* (Minneapolis), Feb. 17, 2012, p. A1, www.startribune.com/local/139491333.html?refer=y.

University of Minnesota students reportedly are faking ADHD symptoms to obtain prescriptions for Adderall.

Ellison, Katherine, "Mother's New Little Helper," *Los Angeles Times*, Jan. 13, 2012, p. A17.

Experts say some young mothers are taking their children's prescription ADHD drugs to boost their productivity.

Martin, Richard, "ADHD Drugs Dwindle and Parents Scramble," *St. Petersburg* (Fla.) *Times* (now *Tampa Bay Times*), Dec. 3, 2011, p. A1, www.tampabay.com/news/health/adderall-shortage-has-adhd-patients-parents-scrambling-for-answers/1204576.

Doctors say growth in the number of ADHD cases is causing a shortage of a generic form of Adderall.

Non-Drug Treatments

Andazola, Matt, "Struggling to Focus," *Albuquerque* (N.M.) *Journal*, July 25, 2011, p. C1, www.abqjournal.com/main/2011/07/25/health/struggling-to.html.

Alternative ADHD therapies often are preferred to drugs because they don't have side effects such as appetite loss.

Manziello, Evelyn Gilbert, "New Approach to ADD, ADHD," *Poughkeepsie* (N.Y.) *Journal*, Sept. 16, 2011.

Diet, exercise and acupuncture are several ADHD treatments that don't involve drugs.

Yim, Michael, "ADHD — Can the Disorder Be Treated Without Medication?" *The Explorer* (Tucson, Ariz.), Feb. 29, 2012, explorernews.com/northwest_chatter/article_33e0bf8c-6250-11e1-abcd-0019bb2963f4.html.

Many parents of children diagnosed with ADHD prefer alternative treatments.

Prevalence

Hellmich, Nanci, "ADHD Seen As Early As Age 4," *USA Today*, Oct. 17, 2011, p. D4, www.usatoday.com/LIFE/usaedition/2011-10-17-Attention-Deficit_ST_U.htm.

ADHD can be diagnosed in children as young as 4, according to updated diagnostic guidelines from the American Academy of Pediatrics.

Midey, Connie, "Women and ADHD," *Arizona Republic*, Nov. 11, 2011, p. H1, www.azcentral.com/health/news/articles/2011/11/03/20111103adhd-diagnosis-women.html.

ADHD estimates are low among adults because many affected women haven't been properly diagnosed.

Wen, Patricia, "ADHD Rates Low Among Latinos," *The Boston Globe*, Sept. 26, 2011, p. B1, articles.boston.com/2011-09-26/news/30205138_1_adhd-medication-latino-children-latino-youngsters.

Fewer Latino children are diagnosed with ADHD compared to white and black children, according to the Centers for Disease Control and Prevention.

Symptoms

Gerhart, Jacqueline, "Steps to Diagnosing ADHD," *Wisconsin State Journal*, Dec. 13, 2011, p. C3, host.madison.com/wsj/news/local/health_med_fit/dr-jacqueline-gerhart-how-can-a-parent-know-if-child/article_0ef24598-2514-11e1-bbd8-0019bb2963f4.html.

Children should display symptoms for at least six months in two different settings — such as at home and at school — before being diagnosed with ADHD.

Johnson, Tim, "Inside a Teenager's Brain," *Burlington* (Vt.) *Free Press*, April 30, 2012, p. A1, www.burlingtonfreepress.com/article/BT/20120430/NEWS0213/120429012/university-of-vermont-teenage-brain-research.

Behavioral scientists generally agree that ADHD is associated with impulsivity but are unsure whether the impulses make people more prone to drug or alcohol use.

Mascarelli, Amanda, "Profile of ADHD Sharpens in Each School Year," *Los Angeles Times*, Aug. 13, 2011, articles.latimes.com/2011/aug/13/health/la-he-adhd-20110813.

ADHD symptoms can become clearer as children enter classes requiring more attention and organizational skills.

CITING *CQ RESEARCHER*

Sample formats for citing these reports in a bibliography include the ones listed below. Preferred styles and formats vary, so please check with your instructor or professor.

MLA STYLE

Jost, Kenneth. "Remembering 9/11," CQ Researcher 2 Sept. 2011: 701-732.

APA STYLE

Jost, K. (2011, September 2). Remembering 9/11. *CQ Researcher, 9*, 701-732.

CHICAGO STYLE

Jost, Kenneth. "Remembering 9/11." *CQ Researcher*, September 2, 2011, 701-732.

In-depth Reports on Issues in the News

Are you writing a paper?

Need backup for a debate?

Want to become an expert on an issue?

For more than 80 years, students have turned to *CQ Researcher* for in-depth reporting on issues in the news. Reports on a full range of political and social issues are now available. Following is a selection of recent reports:

Civil Liberties
Voter Rights, 5/12
Remembering 9/11, 9/11
Government Secrecy, 2/11

Crime/Law
Debt Collectors, 7/12
Criminal Records, 4/12
Police Misconduct, 4/12
Immigration Conflict, 3/12
Financial Misconduct, 1/12
Eyewitness Testimony, 10/11
Death Penalty Debates, 11/10

Education
Arts Education, 3/12
Youth Volunteerism, 1/12
Digital Education, 12/11
Student Debt, 10/11

Environment/Society
Smart Cities, 7/12
Whale Hunting, 6/12
U.S. Oil Dependence, 6/12
Gambling in America, 6/12
Celebrity Advocacy, 5/12
Sexual Harassment, 4/12

Health/Safety
Alcohol Abuse, 6/12
Traumatic Brain Injury, 6/12
Distracted Driving, 5/12
Patient Safety, 2/12
Military Suicides, 9/11
Teen Drug Use, 6/11

Politics/Economy
Privatizing the Military, 7/12
U.S.-Europe Relations, 3/12
Attracting Jobs, 3/12
Presidential Election, 2/12

Upcoming Reports

Farm Policy, 8/10/12
Genetically Modified Food, 8/31/12
Re-examining the Constitution, 9/7/12

ACCESS

CQ Researcher is available in print and online. For access, visit your library or www.cqresearcher.com.

STAY CURRENT

For notice of upcoming *CQ Researcher* reports or to learn more about *CQ Researcher* products, subscribe to the free e-mail newsletters, *CQ Researcher Alert!* and *CQ Researcher News*: http://cqpress.com/newsletters.

PURCHASE

To purchase a *CQ Researcher* report in print or electronic format (PDF), visit www.cqpress.com or call 866-427-7737. Single reports start at $15. Bulk purchase discounts and electronic-rights licensing are also available.

SUBSCRIBE

Annual full-service *CQ Researcher* subscriptions—including 44 reports a year, monthly index updates, and a bound volume—start at $1,054. Add $25 for domestic postage.

CQ Researcher Online offers a backfile from 1991 and a number of tools to simplify research. For pricing information, call 800-834-9020, or e-mail librarymarketing@cqpress.com.

CQ Researcher **Plus** *Archive*

Get Online Access to Vital Issues from 1923 to the Present

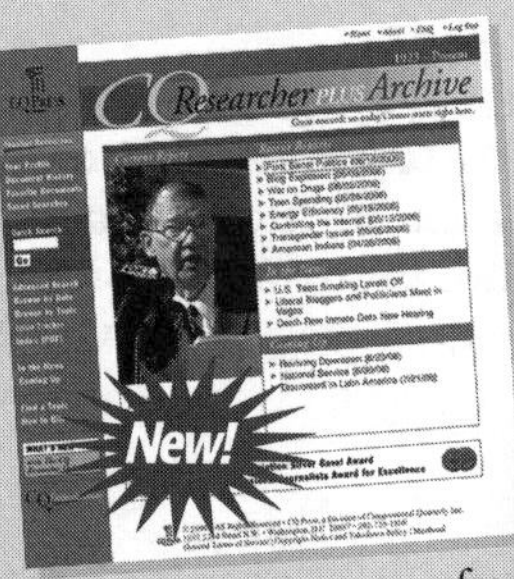

CQ Researcher Plus Archive delivers fast, online access to every *CQ Researcher* report from 1991 to the present, *PLUS* lets you explore the complete archive of *Editorial Research Reports** from 1923-1990. Search and browse more than 3,600 in-depth reports.

Loaded with handy online features, *CQ Researcher Plus Archive* provides the trustworthy reporting and the advanced online functionality today's researchers demand. The new "Issue Tracker" feature provides quick links to past and present reports on the specific topics you need.

For a free trial, visit http://library.cqpress.com/trials.

For pricing information, call 1-800-834-9020, ext. 1906 or e-mail librarymarketing@cqpress.com.

**Editorial Research Reports*, the predecessor to *CQ Researcher*, provides the same expert, nonpartisan reporting on the vital issues that have shaped our society.

CQ Press • 2300 N Street, NW, Suite 800 • Washington, DC 20037

CQ Researcher

Published by CQ Press, an Imprint of SAGE Publications, Inc.

www.cqresearcher.com

Farm Policy

Does U.S. farm policy promote unhealthy eating?

Congress is debating a new farm bill, a sprawling measure typically enacted every five to seven years that sets broad directions for U.S. agriculture policy. Current proposals would eliminate some hotly debated subsidies that mainly benefit large farmers. But the proposed bills would still provide nearly $1 trillion over the next decade for programs including crop insurance, land and water conservation programs, disaster relief and food aid for the poor. Conservatives say the federal government spends too much on agriculture and advocate major cuts to food aid programs, which they see as runaway entitlements. Liberals oppose cutting food aid, which they say provides crucial help for needy Americans during a slow economic recovery. And many public health advocates want more support for production of healthy crops, such as fruits and vegetables, and for local outlets such as farmers markets that connect people directly to food producers.

A vendor prepares a fruit display at a San Francisco farmers market on June 13, 2012. Congress is wrestling with a sprawling new farm bill that strongly influences what Americans eat, how the food is grown and how much it costs.

INSIDE THIS REPORT

THE ISSUES 695
BACKGROUND 701
CHRONOLOGY 703
CURRENT SITUATION 707
AT ISSUE 709
OUTLOOK 711
BIBLIOGRAPHY 714
THE NEXT STEP 715

CQ Researcher • Aug. 10, 2012 • www.cqresearcher.com
Volume 22, Number 29 • Pages 693-716

SAGE | CQ PRESS
Los Angeles | London | New Delhi
Singapore | Washington DC

RECIPIENT OF SOCIETY OF PROFESSIONAL JOURNALISTS AWARD FOR EXCELLENCE ◆ AMERICAN BAR ASSOCIATION SILVER GAVEL AWARD

THE ISSUES

695 • Does U.S. farm policy need major reform?
• Are crop insurance subsidies too large?
• Should SNAP funding be cut?

BACKGROUND

701 **A Nation of Farmers**
In 1862, 90 percent of Americans lived on farms.

702 **Agriculture Transformed**
The Great Depression led to policy changes.

704 **Questioning Growth**
The environmental movement spurred worries about agricultural practices.

706 **Nutrition Debates**
Food stamps grew from an experimental program into the central federal food-aid program.

CURRENT SITUATION

707 **Drought and Delay**
More than 1,400 counties are designated as drought disaster areas.

708 **Conserving Farm Lands**
Preservation programs are under pressure in the new farm bill.

710 **The Disappearing Middle**
"Mid-sized family farms are declining."

710 **Feed Versus Fuel**
The drought's effect on corn crops is revising a debate over ethanol production targets.

Cover: Getty Images/Justin Sullivan

OUTLOOK

711 **Big Shifts**
Experts foresee more organic farming, local food networks.

SIDEBARS AND GRAPHICS

696 **Nutrition Aid Topped 2008 Farm Bill Spending**
The 2008 farm bill cost $248 billion over five years.

697 **Cotton Benefits Most from Federal Insurance**
Crop insurance covers 83 percent of cotton farms.

699 **MyPlate Nutrition Guide Replaces Pyramid**
The Agriculture Department's current guide recommends that fruits and vegetables make up half of every meal.

700 **SNAP Spending Projected to Decline**
Spending for food aid is expected to fall.

703 **Chronology**
Key events since 1862.

704 **'Food Deserts' Provide Few Healthy Eating Options**
Residents must shop at stores that offer few fresh foods.

706 **USDA Seeks New Farmers**
As older farmers retire, beginners need support.

709 **At Issue**
Does U.S. farm policy promote unhealthy eating?

FOR FURTHER RESEARCH

713 **For More Information**
Organizations to contact.

714 **Bibliography**
Selected sources used.

715 **The Next Step**
Additional articles.

715 **Citing *CQ Researcher***
Sample bibliography formats.

CQ Researcher

Aug. 10, 2012
Volume 22, Number 29

MANAGING EDITOR: Thomas J. Billitteri
tjb@cqpress.com

ASSISTANT MANAGING EDITOR: Kathy Koch
kkoch@cqpress.com

CONTRIBUTING EDITOR: Thomas J. Colin
tcolin@cqpress.com

ASSOCIATE EDITOR: Kenneth Jost

STAFF WRITER: Marcia Clemmitt

CONTRIBUTING WRITERS: Peter Katel, Barbara Mantel, Jennifer Weeks

DESIGN/PRODUCTION EDITOR: Olu B. Davis

ASSISTANT EDITOR: Darrell Dela Rosa

FACT CHECKER: Michelle Harris

Los Angeles | London | New Delhi
Singapore | Washington DC

An Imprint of SAGE Publications, Inc.

VICE PRESIDENT AND EDITORIAL DIRECTOR, HIGHER EDUCATION GROUP:
Michele Sordi

DIRECTOR, ONLINE PUBLISHING:
Todd Baldwin

CQ Researcher (ISSN 1056-2036) is printed on acid-free paper. Published weekly, except: (March wk. 5) (May wk. 4) (July wk. 1) (Aug. wks. 3, 4) (Nov. wk. 4) and (Dec. wks. 3, 4). Published by SAGE Publications, Inc., 2455 Teller Rd., Thousand Oaks, CA 91320. Annual full-service subscriptions start at $1,054. For pricing, call 1-800-834-9020. To purchase a *CQ Researcher* report in print or electronic format (PDF), visit www.cqpress.com or call 866-427-7737. Single reports start at $15. Bulk purchase discounts and electronic-rights licensing are also available. Periodicals postage paid at Thousand Oaks, California, and at additional mailing offices. POSTMASTER: Send address changes to *CQ Researcher*, 2300 N St., N.W., Suite 800, Washington, DC 20037.

Farm Policy

By Jennifer Weeks

The Issues

When investigative journalist Tracie McMillan spent a year working in the U.S. food system — cutting garlic in California fields, cleaning produce at Walmart and garnishing plates at a chain restaurant — she learned a hard truth:

Healthy meals were barely affordable on wages of $8 per hour or less. Nutritious choices like fresh fruit and vegetables often were more expensive or less convenient than cheap processed options. And the working-class areas where McMillan lived had fewer grocery stores than did affluent suburbs.

"We're facing a dire public health problem related to poor diet," she writes in her 2012 book, *The American Way of Eating*. "Is it really in America's best interest to maintain a food system where eating well requires one to either be rich or to drive a total of thirty miles?" [1]

Getty Images/Scott Olson

A withered corn plant near Olmsted, Ill., on July 26, 2012, reflects the ravaging effects of a severe drought that has struck corn and soybean harvests throughout the Midwest. As of Aug. 1, 2012, the Agriculture Department had designated 1,452 counties as drought disaster areas. "A bad crop, ruined by a natural disaster or an unpredictable price collapse, can put a hard-working farm family out of business quickly," said Agriculture Secretary Tom Vilsack.

No single cause is to blame, McMillan concluded. Many factors make it hard for Americans to eat well, including "stagnating wages, skyrocketing income inequality and mushrooming health care costs; agricultural policies that pay farmers to exhaust our soils by growing food not to be eaten but to be burned [as biofuels]; an increasingly monopolized food infrastructure that gives the people selling our food little incentive to keep it affordable; and a population so strapped for time, cash and know-how that cooking dinner becomes a Herculean task rather than a simple and necessary chore." [2]

Congress is wrestling with many of those issues as it debates a new farm bill — a sprawling piece of legislation, enacted every five to seven years, that strongly influences what Americans eat, how the food is grown and how much it costs. The 2012 bill will guide hundreds of billions of dollars in federal spending for programs including subsidies for farmers, food aid for needy families, land conservation, rural development and agricultural imports and exports.

Many current farm support programs are rooted in laws passed during the 1930s and '40s to implement President Franklin D. Roosevelt's New Deal. Through the 1980s, farm bills were shaped mainly by agricultural interests, including farm bureaus, trade associations for various crops and large agribusiness companies. More recently the debate has broadened. Today social welfare groups, nutrition advocates and many public officials see the farm bill as an opportunity to tackle food-related health issues that are widespread across the United States.

Food and farming issues "affect the health of residents in urban America because of hunger and food insecurity in low-income populations, lack of access to healthy food in low-income areas, [and] chronic diseases related to poor diet such as obesity, diabetes and cardiovascular diseases," the U.S. Conference of Mayors stated in a June 2012 resolution. [3] The group urged Congress to pass a farm bill that supports nutrition aid, sustainable farming practices and programs to bring more fresh, healthy foods into urban areas. [4]

Environmentalists also are paying increased attention to farm policy. Along with academic experts and advocates for small- and mid-size family farms, they contend that large-scale agriculture focuses too heavily on a few major crops and relies too heavily on synthetic fertilizer, pesticides, herbicides and antibiotics for poultry and livestock.

Instead, environmentalists say, U.S. farm policy should provide more support for sustainable practices that protect the environment, such as farming organically and taking erosion-prone land out of production.

Food Aid Topped 2008 Farm Bill Spending

The most recently enacted farm bill, which expires Sept. 30, was passed in 2008 at a total cost of $284 billion over five years. Most of that spending is for food aid, support for commodity producers, conservation and crop insurance. Smaller programs include rural development, forestry, horticulture and organic agriculture, livestock and research.

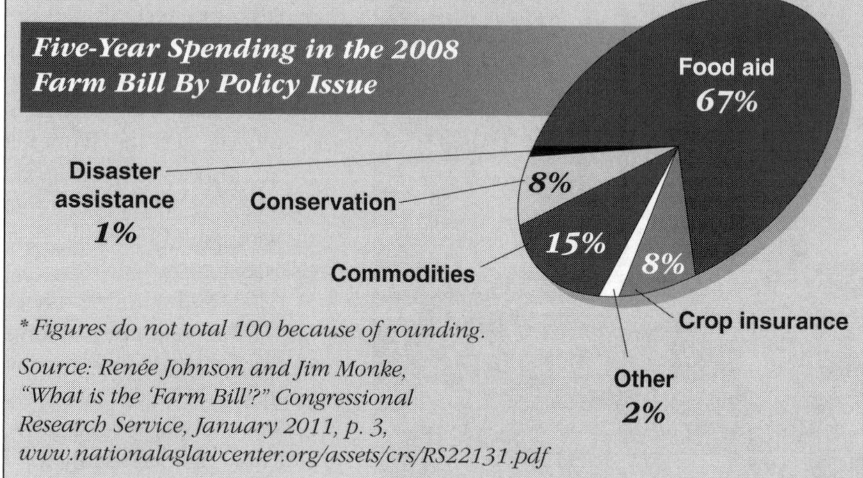

* *Figures do not total 100 because of rounding.*

Source: Renée Johnson and Jim Monke, "What is the 'Farm Bill'?" Congressional Research Service, January 2011, p. 3, www.nationalaglawcenter.org/assets/crs/RS22131.pdf

The last farm bill, enacted in 2008, authorized $24.1 billion over five years for conservation programs on farmland, which environmentalists view as an important and growing priority for the department.

"The Department of Agriculture needs more of a mandate to promote environmental protection," says Rebecca Klein, director of the Public Health and Agriculture Policy Project at Johns Hopkins University's Center for a Livable Future. "Farmers clearly have an interest in protecting water and soil, but they may not always be able to afford conservation measures that they would like to take. We need stronger policies to help make those actions feasible for them."

With billions of dollars at stake, farm bills inevitably generate heated debate about federal spending priorities. The Democratic-led Senate passed a farm bill in June that ends an especially controversial policy: direct subsidies paid for years to farmers and landowners, whether they grew crops or not. Instead, the bill puts greater emphasis on another safety-net measure for farmers: crop insurance subsidies. These programs help farmers qualify for financing by enabling them to pay back loans even if disasters destroy their harvests.

Farm advocacy groups say this shift will make federal agriculture policy more market-based. "We know there are a lot of concerns about direct payments to farmers and payments based on past production," says Dale Moore, deputy policy director with the American Farm Bureau Federation, a trade association for farms of all sizes. "We support an approach that lets producers make decisions based on their reading of markets and doesn't interfere with producers' planting decisions." However, the Farm Bureau says, farmers continue to need strong safety net programs — including crop insurance subsidies and marketing loans — to protect against catastrophes such as droughts and floods. [5]

Critics argue that like direct payments, crop insurance subsidies have outlived their purpose and support mainly large farms and insurance companies. "The federal government pays 60 percent of premiums, and payments are essentially uncapped," says Ariane Lotti, assistant policy director with the National Sustainable Agriculture Coalition. Moreover, she points out, crop insurance subsidies currently do not require farmers to follow conservation rules, although the Senate bill includes a provision that would create such a link. "We should be paying farmers for being good stewards of the land and selling products into their communities, not for their losses," Lotti contends.

Another flash point is the Supplemental Nutrition Assistance Program (SNAP), long known as food stamps, which is the main federal program designed to help low-income families afford adequate and nutritious foods. The Senate farm bill makes what supporters called modest reforms to SNAP, cutting $4.5 billion over 10 years. But House Republicans argue that many recipients abuse the program; the House farm bill, approved by the Agriculture Committee in July, cuts SNAP by $16 billion over 10 years. (*See graphic, p. 700.*)

"SNAP is the first line of defense against hunger," says Eric Olsen, senior vice president of Feeding America, the nation's largest domestic hunger-relief charity. "It's critically important for government to get its budget and spending under control, but past efforts have always exempted the safety net, and we think we can balance the budget without hurting poor people."

But the House recessed in early August without debating its version of the farm bill after Speaker John Boehner, R-Ohio, said the bill lacked enough support to pass. Most House Democrats oppose the bill's large cuts to SNAP funding, while many conservative advocates argue that the measure still spends too much money. The House passed a short-term drought relief package for ranchers, but Senate leaders say they want to debate a full farm bill rather than stopgap measures. [6]

Agriculture is a major sector of the U.S. economy, although the current drought could erode its position. Farm-sector earnings were strong through the 2008-2009 recession and generated a $42.5 billion trade surplus in 2011. The Obama administration's agriculture priorities include maintaining and boosting rural prosperity; conserving natural resources; strengthening local and regional food systems; and combating hunger and obesity, especially in children. Farm advocates say the administration has delivered reasonably well.

"They have not hindered growth in farm income, and many of their rural development and renewable-energy investments have directly contributed to farm income," says Roger Johnson, president of the National Farmers Union, which represents small- to medium-size and family-owned farms. "This administration has presided over a stretch of record farm-income years. Some say [it doesn't] deserve credit, but if prices were low there would be a lot of blame going around."

Presumptive Republican presidential nominee Mitt Romney released names of his agriculture advisory committee in March but did not take positions on specific agriculture issues. "I will work to ensure that our food supply will remain steady, safe and affordable for our citizens," Romney said. [7]

As Congress, advocacy groups and agriculture experts work to shape the 2012 farm bill, here are some issues they are considering:

Does U.S. farm policy need major reform?

The U.S. agricultural system is a vast network of about two million farms and ranches, from small family-owned holdings to huge operations that cover thousands of acres. It also includes agribusiness companies that produce farm equipment, seeds, pesticides, fertilizer and other production materials, as well as food processors and distributors. About 2 percent of all Americans live on farms. [8]

Supporters praise U.S. farmers for efficiently producing abundant quantities of safe and affordable food for both domestic consumption and export. "[T]here are just 210,000 Americans out there who are responsible for 80 percent of U.S. agricultural production," House Agriculture Committee chair Frank Lucas, R-Okla., said last year. "These Americans support our economy, help keep us secure and . . . answer . . . the question of how we are going to feed 9 billion people [worldwide] come the year 2050." [9]

But farm policy has many critics. Budget watchers say the federal government spends too much on farm support programs. Environmental groups want more support for land, water and soil conservation programs. And some public health and nutrition advocates argue that farm policy promotes unhealthy eating by generating vast quantities of cheap processed food, made primarily from heavily subsidized corn and soybeans. Many critics focus on Title I of the farm bill, which provides income support to farmers who raise major agricultural "commodities" such as wheat, corn, soybeans, cotton, rice, peanuts, sugar and dairy products. The 2008 farm bill authorized $41.6 billion for farm commodity support programs, about 15 percent of total spending in the bill. [10]

The critics argue that farm commodity programs have become welfare for large farms, which receive the biggest share of subsidies. [11] Both the Senate and House versions of the 2012 farm bill would save about $50 billion over 10 years by eliminating three commodity programs:

- Direct payments, which are based on past production and paid to farmers whether or not they actually plant crops;
- Countercyclical payments, which farmers receive when market prices fall below certain targets; and

Cotton Farmers Benefit Most from Federal Insurance

More than 80 percent of cotton farms were covered by federal crop insurance in 2009. About 65 percent of farms specializing in peanuts and in such cash grains as corn, wheat and soybeans were covered. Hog and dairy farmers often grow crops to feed their livestock, and those crops are eligible for federal crop insurance.

Percentage of Farms Covered by Federal Crop Insurance, 2009

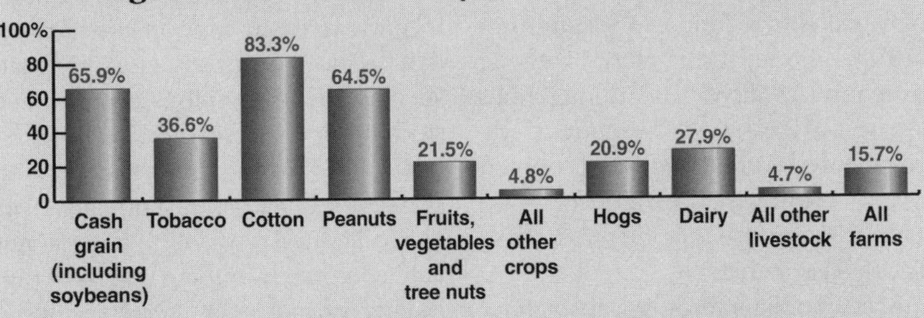

Source: T. Kirk White and Robert A. Hoppe, "Changing Farm Structure and the Distribution of Farm Payments and Federal Crop Insurance," U.S. Department of Agriculture, February 2012, p. 16, www.ers.usda.gov/media/261681/eib91_1_.pdf

• Average Crop Revenue Election payments, which farmers receive when actual revenue falls short of expected revenues. [12]

Instead, the bills increase support to help farmers buy crop insurance, which protects them against natural disasters.

'The most fundamental reform in [the Senate farm bill] is the shift away from direct payments and toward risk management for farmers," Senate Agriculture Committee chair Debbie Stabenow, D-Mich., said during floor debate on the bill. "[T]he current system, focused around direct and counter-cyclical payments, does not focus on actual risks and is no longer defensible or sustainable." [13]

Many public-interest groups want a bigger shift in priorities. "We subsidize too much of the wrong kinds of foods, especially commodity crops, and not enough local and healthy foods," says Justin Tatham, a lobbyist for the Union of Concerned Scientists (UCS), a national environmental advocacy group. The U.S. Department of Agriculture's (USDA's) MyPlate nutrition guidelines, published in 2011, recommend that fruits and vegetables make up 50 percent of every meal, but fruits and vegetables are grown on only about 2 percent of U.S. croplands. [14] (*See graphic, p. 699.*)

Instead, UCS advocates increased funding for farmers markets, production of specialty crops such as fruits and vegetables, organic agriculture and other programs to increase access to healthy foods. The Senate bill takes some steps in this direction, such as offering crop insurance on specialty crops for the first time. "But it doesn't really reform farm policy with respect to supports," Tatham says.

In a 2011 article in the journal *Science*, a dozen university researchers and several sustainable producers outlined a framework for an even broader transformation of U.S. agriculture. Truly sustainable farming, they argued, would provide abundant and affordable products, but also would:

• enhance natural resources and the environment;

• make farming financially viable; and

• promote the well-being of farmers, farm workers and rural communities.

"Most elements of the Farm Bill were not designed to promote sustainability," the authors contended. Farm policy, they argued, should be revised to provide more support for methods that balance all four sustainability goals, such as organic farming, grass-fed livestock production and growing of perennial grains instead of strains that are planted and harvested annually. They also called for reorienting federal agriculture research, arguing that most public and private agricultural science in the United States "is narrowly focused on productivity and efficiency." [15]

"We have the technology and the science right now to grow food in sustainable ways, but we lack the policies and markets to make it happen," lead author John Reganold, a soil scientist at Washington State University, said when the article was published. [16] But advocates of mainstream agriculture do not see the same need for radical change.

"Stretching food dollars to put meals on their tables is consumers' top concern," says the American Farm Bureau Federation's Moore. "We have a growing population around the world, so large-scale production technologies will be critical to help us feed that population."

Are crop insurance subsidies too large?

If a 2012 farm bill is enacted, it is likely to increase funding for crop insurance as an alternative to direct payments. In addition to paying farmers for unexpected losses, crop insurance helps farmers obtain credit to purchase seeds, fertilizer and equipment. When crops are insured, banks are more willing to lend money to farmers and let them use their expected harvests to secure the loans.

Supporters call crop insurance farmers' main shield against events such as the drought currently ravaging corn and soybean harvests. "High input costs mean agriculture will always remain a high risk," Agriculture Secretary Tom Vilsack said last year. "A bad crop, ruined by a natural disaster or an unpredictable price collapse, can put a hard-working farm family out of business quickly. These families rely on a strong safety net."

Sixteen companies have been designated by USDA to provide crop insurance for 2013 under a standard agreement with the Federal Crop Insurance Corp., a unit within USDA. [17] Taxpayers subsidize varying levels of farmers' crop insurance premiums, depending on how much coverage farmers buy. In 2011 subsidies covered about 62 percent of total premiums at a cost of about $7.4 billion (up from $1.5 billion in 2002), plus another $1.3 billion in administrative costs. [18] In contrast to direct payments — which typically were limited to $40,000 per recipient and were phased out for farms earning more than $750,000 — crop insurance subsidies have not had income or payment limits. [19]

Agriculture groups say crop insurance is a structured way of protecting farmers against disasters and market collapses. "Without crop insurance you'd have rampant, unfocused spending after disasters strike — aid programs would be ad hoc, not strategic," says Johnson of the National Farmers Union. "And farmers put some skin in the game — they buy the insurance and pay the premiums, although subsidies make it more affordable."

Moreover, recent farm bills have required farmers to buy crop insurance in order to qualify for disaster relief. "Farmers have been pressured for the past 15 years to use crop insurance instead of relying on government relief, so it's ironic that critics think crop insurance is running

MyPlate Nutrition Guide Replaces Pyramid

MyPlate, the Agriculture Department's current nutrition guide, replaced the nearly two-decade-old food pyramid, which critics said gave too much weight to high-fat foods (mainly dairy products and red meat) and carbohydrates such as white bread, rice and potatoes. The MyPlate guidelines, published in 2011, recommend that fruits and vegetables make up half of every meal. Critics note that those crops are grown on only about 2 percent of U.S. farmland and argue that farm support programs should be more closely aligned with nutrition goals.*

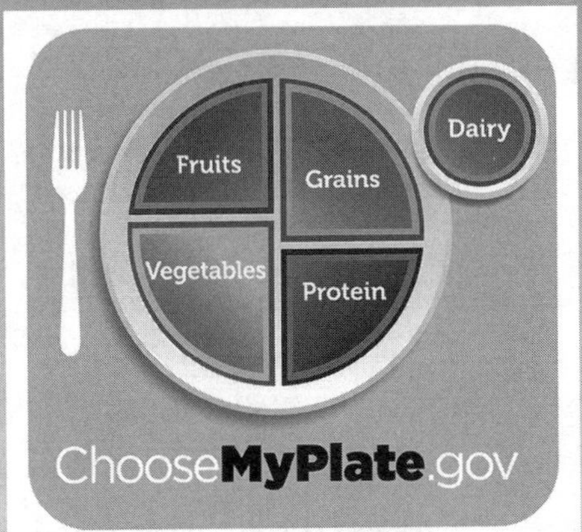

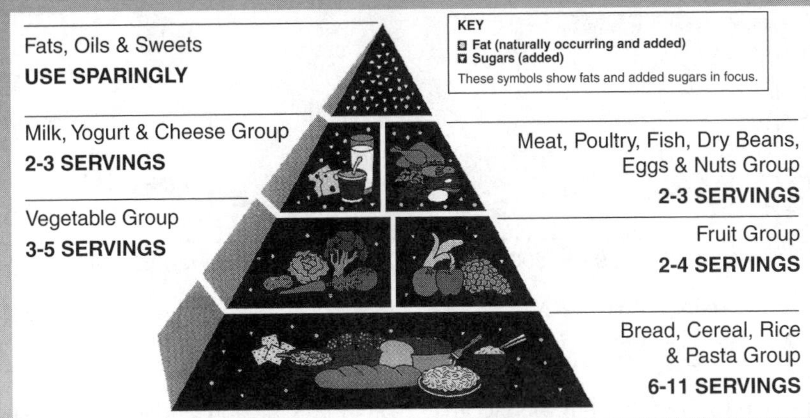

* *A newer version of the food pyramid was introduced in 2005.*

Source: "Food Groups," ChooseMyPlate.gov, U.S. Department of Agriculture, 2012, www.choosemyplate.gov/food-groups/

amok now," says the American Farm Bureau Federation's Moore.

Critics say the federal government spends too much mitigating risk for farmers and that because crop insurance reduces economic risk, it may promote harmful choices such as planting on marginal lands. A study by Iowa State University economist Bruce Babcock concludes that high federal crop insurance subsidies since 2000 (when subsidies were increased) have induced farmers to buy expensive coverage. Babcock argues that Congress could save $4.2 billion yearly by reverting to the old premium structure.

"[F]armers would still have access to the same types of insurance that they buy today, but eliminating the distorted incentives would encourage them to rely more heavily on alternative forms of risk management," Babcock writes. For example, they could vary the types of crops they plant or earn more income from nonfarm activities. [20]

The Senate-passed 2012 farm bill provides $5 billion for crop insurance over 10 years but includes some new limits. Sens. Richard Durbin, D-Ill., and Tom Coburn, R-Okla., offered an amendment cutting premium subsidies available to farmers with incomes over $750,000 by 15 percent, saving an estimated $1.1 billion. And Sen. Saxby Chambliss, R-Ga., offered an amendment requiring farmers to meet conservation compliance requirements in order to qualify for the subsidies. Both measures passed over objections from insurers and most commodity groups. [21]

According to UCS, too much spending for crop insurance goes to large commodity producers. "Organic and local farmers don't have any kind of federally supported risk management system," says UCS agricultural economist Jeffrey O'Hara. "They're managing risk on their own by growing a diverse array of crops, but they need insurance to help them get financing, and a better safety-net system."

USDA offers some crop-specific insurance policies for fruit and vegetable producers, but O'Hara believes more options are needed. "USDA needs to improve its 'whole-farm revenue' insurance program, which covers farmers who grow diverse products," he says. Moreover, many organic farmers are unable to buy insurance that values their crops at the premium prices that organic foods typically bring in the marketplace. "Those rates should be boosted, so farmers can insure their products at prices that reflect their market value," O'Hara says.

Although the National Farmers Union supports crop insurance as a safety net policy, Johnson acknowledges that costs are an issue. "I think Congress is torn between providing price protection through crop insurance or through some other mechanism," he says. "Over the long term Congress

SNAP Spending Projected to Decline

After rising sharply over the past decade, especially during the recent recession, annual federal spending on the Supplemental Nutrition Assistance Program (SNAP) — formerly known as the food stamp program — is projected to decline by 25 percent as the economy improves over the next 10 years, from about $80 billion this year to $60 billion by 2022. The Senate's farm bill would cut $4.5 billion over 10 years, while a House version would cut $16 billion.

Federal Spending on Supplemental Nutrition Assistance Program, FY1990-FY2022

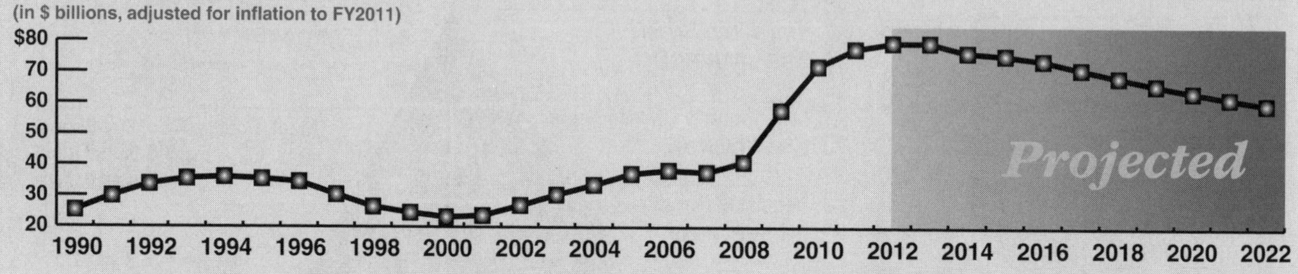

Source: "The Supplemental Nutrition Assistance Program," Congressional Budget Office, April 2012, p. 4, www.cbo.gov/sites/default/files/cbofiles/attachments/04-19-SNAP.pdf

will have to grapple with the fact that crop insurance gets more expensive as prices go higher, because you're insuring the price of the crop as well as production of the crop. We believe that as prices go higher, the need for subsidies goes down. You need to be cautious about changing the system, but cost has to be addressed."

Should SNAP funding be cut?

If the House farm bill comes up for debate, one of the most controversial issues will be funding for the Supplemental Nutrition Assistance Program (SNAP). SNAP is an entitlement program under which anyone who meets eligibility standards can receive benefits. SNAP program costs have grown sharply over the past decade, especially since the 2008-2009 recession. Critics say the program is too expensive, but supporters argue that SNAP is providing vital aid to millions of Americans.

The Senate-passed bill cuts SNAP by $4.5 billion between 2013 and 2022, while the House Agriculture Committee version would reduce SNAP funding by $16 billion. Legislators said the changes were necessary to protect the program's integrity and ensure that benefits went only to truly needy people.

Both bills tighten use of a policy known as "heat and eat," under which many states link the Low-Income Home Energy Assistance Program (LIHEAP) to SNAP benefits. LIHEAP helps poor people pay home energy bills.

Some states allow households that receive as little as $1 to $5 per month from LIHEAP to take a standard deduction for energy costs on their SNAP applications, which typically qualifies them for a higher level of SNAP benefits than they would receive otherwise. But under both pending farm bills, households must receive at least $10 per month from LIHEAP to be able to take the deduction. According to the Congressional Budget Office, this change will save about $4.5 billion in SNAP payments over 10 years and result in about 500,000 households in 15 states losing $90 per month in SNAP benefits. [22]

"[W]e did this in a very careful way to make sure we did not inadvertently hurt families who truly do have significant energy costs," Stabenow said during floor debate.

The House bill also tightens an option called "categorical eligibility," created in the 1996 welfare reform law, that allowed states to declare that families receiving Temporary Aid for Needy Families (TANF) support — the successor to federal welfare payments — were also eligible for SNAP. This approach allowed some low-income working families to qualify for SNAP even though their gross incomes were slightly above SNAP limits, in recognition that these families often spent substantial money on child care in order to work. Like "heat and eat," categorical eligibility was intended to simplify paperwork, align programs and reduce administrative costs for states. [23]

Restricting categorical eligibility in the House bill reduces SNAP costs by $11.5 billion and would eliminate SNAP benefits entirely for 1.8 million to 3 million people. In addition, about 280,000 children who currently receive free school lunches would become ineligible because they qualify for that benefit through their families' participation in SNAP. [24]

House Republicans say that in a tight fiscal climate no programs should be off-limits and emphasize that SNAP costs have risen sharply over the past decade. The number of Americans receiving SNAP benefits rose from 26 million (one in eleven) in 2007 to 45 million (one in seven) in 2011, a roughly 70 percent increase. Total spending on SNAP in 2011 was about $78 billion, the highest in the program's history. [25]

"Some say the cuts we propose to food stamps [SNAP] are not enough, while others say the cuts are too much. I believe most Americans would agree a 2 percent cut to food stamps is reasonable," committee chair Lucas said when the panel marked up its version of the farm bill last month. [26]

Food and nutrition advocates strongly oppose cuts to SNAP, especially at the House levels. They argue that SNAP costs have grown over the past decade mainly because of the punishing 2008-2009 recession. In their view, SNAP worked as designed, expanding as more Americans lost jobs and needed government support to feed themselves and their families. The Congressional Budget Office projects that SNAP costs will fall over the next several years as the U.S. economy gradually recovers. [27]

"We should fix the economy instead of blaming the program or people who need help while the economy is still recovering," says Olsen of Feeding America. The group operates more than 200 food banks across the United States, serving 37 million people annually, including 14 million children.

According to the Congressional Budget Office, the average household receiving SNAP benefits in 2010 had income below the federal poverty guidelines — about $18,500 for a family of three. The average recipient household earned about $8,800 per year, excluding SNAP benefits, which boosted gross monthly income by 39 percent for all households. [28] In other words, typical SNAP recipients are not well off.

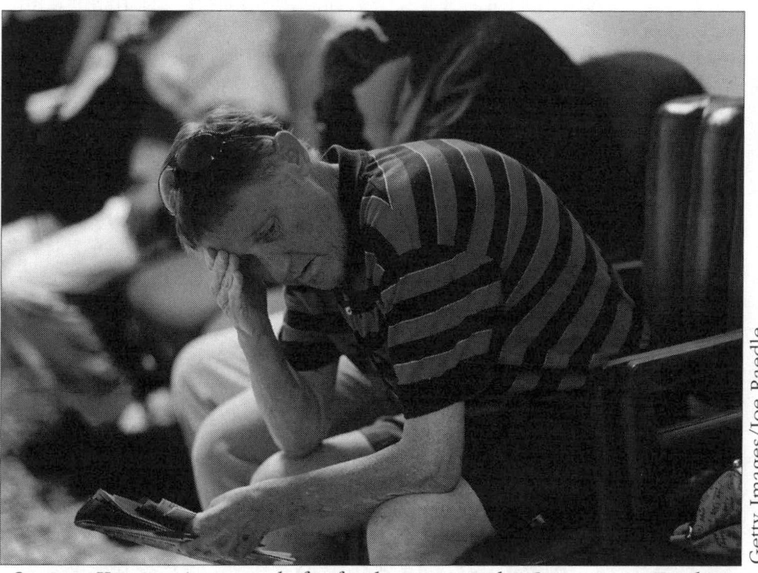

Getty Images/Joe Raedle

Stewart Kern waits to apply for food stamps at the Cooperative Feeding Program in Fort Lauderdale, Fla., on Feb. 10, 2011. Food stamps were first issued on an experimental basis from 1939 through 1942 as a substitute for cash relief payments to hungry families and a way to reduce agricultural surpluses. This year, federal spending on the food stamp program — now known as the Supplemental Nutrition Assistance Program (SNAP) — totals about $80 billion, nearly double the amount in 2008 as the economy sank into recession.

"If your income is low, food competes against everything else in your life, so having a specific budget just for food can be really powerful," says journalist McMillan, who qualified for SNAP for a year while she was writing *The American Way of Eating*. "Healthy food is as important for subsistence as clean water, and we have public programs to make sure everyone gets clean water. We should start thinking about food in that way." ■

BACKGROUND

A Nation of Farmers

When the Department of Agriculture was established in 1862, President Abraham Lincoln called it "the people's department" because 90 percent of Americans lived on farms. [29] Over the next 150 years, as scientific and technical innovation made farming more and more productive, the fraction of Americans living on farms dwindled and the average size of U.S. farms steadily increased.

Farming helped settle the American continent. The Homestead Act of 1862 offered public lands for free (typically in 160-acre claims) west of the Mississippi to settlers who would live on the land and farm it for five years. The law was designed to populate Western territories with small independent farms. More than 270 million acres were "patented" (successfully claimed) under the law over the next 126 years. [30]

But farming was risky, especially in the West: More than half of all homestead efforts failed. [31] Some small farmers had trouble competing with land speculators who exploited loopholes in the law to create large estates. And the federal government encouraged farming in many areas where conditions were not suitable — for example, zones on the High Plains where it was too cold or arid to make a living on 160 acres.

By 1900 the number of Americans employed in agriculture had dropped to 41 percent. Many people moved to cities to escape the drudgery of farm labor and the isolation of rural life. In 1914 USDA created the Cooperative Extension Service, which sent agents into rural communities to help farmers adopt new techniques, based on federally funded agricultural research programs at colleges and universities. The extension service helped to nearly double U.S. wheat acreage during World War I and ease war-related labor shortages on farms at harvest times. [32]

Access to credit was a persistent problem for farmers, who needed money to plant and harvest their crops but had trouble getting long-term loans at low rates. In 1916 Congress passed the Federal Farm Loan Act, which created 12 Federal Land Banks and hundreds of National Farm Loan Associations to help farmers buy land and equipment. But these steps soon were superseded by an even larger problem. Aided by new inventions such as tractors and fertilizer, farmers were producing more goods than U.S. and world markets could absorb. These surpluses pushed down prices and made it hard for farmers to stay in business.

World export demand fell after World War I, causing a collapse in farm prices in 1920-21 that lasted throughout the decade. However, there was little political support for limiting production to balance supply and demand.

"Farmers had two choices: They could cut back, hoping supplies would tighten and prices would rise, or they could plant more as a way to make the same money on higher output," writes journalist Timothy Egan of the years leading to the Dust Bowl — a disaster that began in 1931, when millions of acres of over-plowed prairie soils dried up and blew away during a crippling eight-year drought. "Across the Southern plains, the response was overwhelming: The farmers tore up more grass. They had debts to meet . . . for new tractors, plows, combines and land purchased or rented on credit. The only way for someone who made ten thousand dollars in 1925 to duplicate his earnings in 1929 was to plant twice the amount." [33]

Library of Congress/Arthur Rothstein

A farmer in Cimarron County, Okla., raises his fence to keep it from being buried by drifting sand during the Dust Bowl disaster, when millions of acres of over-plowed prairie soils dried up and blew away during a crippling eight-year drought in the 1930s. Along with the 1929 Wall Street crash and the ensuing Great Depression, the Dust Bowl helped to spur sweeping changes in U.S. farm policy.

Agriculture Transformed

Farmers' plights worsened with the Wall Street crash of 1929, the Great Depression that followed and the Dust Bowl. [34] These blows triggered sweeping changes in U.S. farm policy designed to help farmers earn fair prices for their products and protect them from recessions and natural disasters.

President Franklin D. Roosevelt (1933-1945) introduced a blizzard of legislation upon taking office, including the Agricultural Adjustment Act, passed in 1933 and first amended in 1938, which paid farmers to limit production. The goal was to raise prices of major commodities, including wheat, corn, cotton and tobacco, to the so-called "parity" level, or what farmers would have received in times when agricultural markets were strong. (The Agricultural Act of 1949 provided permanent authority for price supports and set parity levels.)

In the long run, according to historian Paul Conkin, subsidies would make farmland more valuable. That in turn would make it harder for small producers to enter agriculture, speeding the exit of many small farmers. USDA's program mainly benefited large, affluent farmers, who were becoming more dominant in the 1930s and '40s. [35]

Roosevelt also reorganized the farm credit system; established the Rural Electrification Administration, which brought power to many remote areas; and subsidized farmers to carry out soil conservation. USDA created nationwide school lunch and milk programs to use up surplus food. Land-grant universities and USDA's agricultural extension service taught farm families home

Continued on p. 704

Chronology

1860s-1914

Agriculture evolves from small farms and local markets to a national industry.

1862
U.S. Department of Agriculture (USDA) founded. . . . Homestead Act offers free 160-acre claims if applicants live on the land and farm it for five years.

1883
USDA begins conducting agricultural research.

1906
Pure Food and Drug Act gives government power to regulate food safety.

1914
Federal Extension Service is created to educate farmers about agricultural science.

1930-1979

Responding to the Great Depression, new laws guarantee farm income and access to credit. Scientific and technical advances reduce need for farm labor.

1930-33
Tractors begin to replace horse-based plowing. . . . Wall Street crash and Dust Bowl slash farm incomes by more than 50 percent. . . . Agricultural Adjustment Act pays farmers to limit production, authorizes USDA to buy and store food and crops, and creates price supports.

1941
USDA issues first recommended dietary allowances, with specific targets for calories, protein, iron, calcium and several major vitamins.

1945
Farm use of synthetic fertilizer and herbicides begins to rise dramatically.

1954
Agricultural Trade Development Assistance Act, later renamed Food for Peace, authorizes low-cost sales of surplus U.S. crops to foreign countries.

1956
Soil Bank Program pays farmers to take corn, cotton, wheat, tobacco, rice and peanuts out of production and conserve land. The program ends after three years due to farmer opposition.

1964
Congress passes Food Stamp Act of 1964; makes program permanent after several years.

1968
Hunger USA study finds widespread hunger and malnutrition among low-income Americans.

1979
Farmers jam National Mall with tractors to lobby for higher prices.

1980-Present

Vertical concentration increases. Concerns grow about continued viability of small farms.

1985
Farm bill imposes strict rules for conservation grants and revives Conservation Reserve Program.

1990
Organic Foods Production Act creates framework for setting national standards.

1992
Food Pyramid Guide introduced.

1994
Farmers begin using satellite technology to analyze crop conditions and target their use of water and fertilizer.

1996
Freedom to Farm bill is designed to reduce subsidies but boosts federal farm support in 1998-99. . . . Welfare reform legislation requires states to deliver food stamps using electric benefit transfer cards instead of coupons by 2002.

2002
Farm Bill restores most support programs phased out under Freedom to Farm.

2005
Energy Policy Act mandates use of 4 billion gallons of biofuels in motor vehicles, rising to 7.5 billion gallons by 2012.

2007
Expandable Renewable Fuel Standard mandates use of 36 billion gallons of biofuels yearly by 2022.

2008
Federal Food Stamp Program is renamed Supplemental Nutrition Assistance Program (SNAP).

2011
Food Pyramid replaced with MyPlate diagram, recommending that fruits and vegetables make up half of Americans' daily food intake.

2012
Congress debates eliminating direct payments to farmers in 2012 Farm Bill. . . . Worst drought since the 1950s devastates crops. . . . Congress debates reducing SNAP program.

'Food Deserts' Provide Few Healthy Eating Options

Residents are forced to shop at small stores that don't offer fresh foods.

For most Americans, grocery shopping is a routine errand. But millions of consumers, especially people with low incomes, have trouble obtaining affordable and nutritious foods because they live in areas with few, if any, large grocery stores or supermarkets, and they may also lack transportation.

In these so-called food deserts, many health advocates warn that people are likely to eat fewer nutritious foods than recommended, which puts them at risk for such health problems as obesity and diabetes. However, other experts argue that food choices are shaped by many factors, not simply by distance to a supermarket.

In the 2008 farm bill, Congress directed the U.S. Department of Agriculture (USDA) to study the extent and impacts of low access to healthy foods. USDA found that 11.5 million Americans, or 4.1 percent of the U.S. population, have low incomes (at or below 200 percent of federal poverty thresholds) and live more than a mile from a supermarket or large grocery store (10 miles away in rural areas). As a result, people often shop at small markets or convenience stores that do not carry healthy foods such as fresh fruits, vegetables or seafood. And smaller stores typically charge more than supermarkets, so consumers get less food for their money. [1]

According to USDA's online Food Desert Locator, food deserts are widely distributed across the United States, from rural areas such as northern Maine to parts of Chicago, Los Angeles and other large cities. Urban food deserts often are in areas with high percentages of minority residents. [2]

"In North Chicago there are no grocery stores," said Rhonda Moore, who has Type 2 diabetes and struggles to eat a healthy diet. "Buses don't run on weekends. Cabs are expensive. I try to stock up on frozen things. I'd prefer to eat more salads and such, but you can't buy [fresh produce] in bulk. It only lasts so long." [3]

First lady Michelle Obama has made food deserts a focus of her "Let's Move" initiative to improve American health through better diets and exercise. "In so many neighborhoods, if people want to buy a head of lettuce or salad or some fruit for their kid's lunch, they have to take two or three buses, maybe pay for a taxicab, in order to do it," Obama said last October. [4] Large grocers pledged to open more than 1,000 new stores selling fresh produce in underserved areas, but action on that promise has lagged, with one notable exception: Walgreen's, a national pharmacy chain, is opening "food oasis" stores in urban areas that carry fresh produce along with more typical drugstore products. [5]

Still, some experts say the distance to a store is only one of many influences on Americans' food choices. Others include cultural preferences, work schedules and whether consumers have time to cook their own meals. Several recent studies have found only a weak relationship between foods sold near subjects' homes and what those people choose to consume. [6]

"Just because someone lives in a neighborhood doesn't mean they actually shop there. You need to do research on the ground to understand what's happening," says Rebecca Klein, director of the Public Health and Agriculture Policy Project at John Hopkins University's Center for a Livable Future.

Journalist Tracie McMillan, who lived in several areas with relatively few supermarkets while researching her 2012 book *The*

Continued from p. 702

gardening, poultry production, marketing and other skills to help them survive the Depression.

Farm productivity rose sharply after World War II as mechanized equipment and synthetic chemical fertilizers became increasingly available. Antibiotics and artificial insemination enabled poultry and livestock farmers to greatly increase meat production. As meat, poultry and eggs became cheaper, most farmers bought them instead of raising their own animals. National electrification and the introduction of frozen foods reduced the need to grow vegetables and fruit at home. Farms became more specialized, often raising only one or two major crops.

From 1950 through 1970 the pace of change accelerated. Machinery, electrification, pesticides, fertilizers and plant and animal breeding — all supported by federally funded research — made agriculture less labor-intensive than ever. Corn, wheat and cotton yields per acre and milk production per cow all doubled or nearly doubled during this period. And the fraction of employed Americans working on farms fell from 16 percent of the labor force in 1945 to 4 percent in 1970. [36]

Questioning Growth

The transformation of agriculture filled American stores with thousands of food products, including time-savers such as cake mixes, canned soups and frozen "TV dinners" that contained a complete meal in a tray. But as a national environmental movement developed in the 1970s, some Americans began worrying about pesticides, food dyes and additives. [37] Others questioned how large-scale industrial production was affecting farmlands, and farmers.

"That one American farmer can now feed himself and fifty-six other people may be . . . a triumph of technology," Kentucky author and farmer Wendell Berry wrote in 1977. But, Berry argued, the impact on farms and farmers was disastrous. "It has divided all land into two kinds — that which permits the

American Way of Eating, says the issue is more complex than the number of stores in a neighborhood. "The food desert concept is a shorthand for food distribution, which isn't just a matter of counting stores. It's the whole system for getting food into communities," she says. Most of the national transportation and storage systems that move food from farms to plates are controlled by a few large supermarket chains, which historically have not seen investing in low-income communities as a profitable business strategy. But McMillan does not think building more supermarkets in underserved areas will automatically solve the problem.

"Supermarkets do important things really well, but they tend to consolidate power. Their business model depends on offering a lot of processed foods, so you can shop there and buy a completely junk-food diet," McMillan contends. "It's important to bring more retail to communities that don't have enough access. But small grocers and farmers markets may do a better job connecting with people in their neighborhoods and understanding what kinds of foods those people appreciate and want to eat."

— *Jennifer Weeks*

Getty Images/Win McNamee

First lady Michelle Obama and students from Bancroft Elementary School in Washington, D.C., harvest vegetables from the White House kitchen garden on the South Lawn of the White House on June 16, 2009. She has made "food deserts" a focus of her "Let's Move" campaign to improve Americans' health. "In so many neighborhoods, if people want to buy a head of lettuce or salad or some fruit for their kid's lunch, they have to take two or three buses, maybe pay for a taxicab, in order to do it," she said.

[1] "Access to Affordable and Nutritious Food: Measuring and Understanding Food Deserts and Their Consequences," Economic Research Service report summary, U.S. Department of Agriculture, June 2009, p. 2, www.ers.usda.gov/media/242654/ap036_reportsummary_1_.pdf.

[2] USDA Food Desert Locator, www.ers.usda.gov/data-products/food-desert-locator/go-to-the-locator.aspx.

[3] Malcolm Garcia, "For Diabetes Patients, Oases in the Food Desert," *Chicago Tribune*, Feb. 1, 2012, http://articles.chicagotribune.com/2012-02-01/health/ct-x-0201-diabetes-food-desert-20120201_1_food-desert-diabetes-patients-affordable-food.

[4] Steven Yaccino, "In Chicago, Michelle Obama Takes on 'Food Deserts,' " *The New York Times*, Oct. 25, 2011, http://thecaucus.blogs.nytimes.com/2011/10/25/in-chicago-michelle-obama-takes-on-food-deserts/.

[5] Leslie Patton, "Michelle Obama's Food Desert Plans Yield Few New Stores: Retail," Bloomberg.com, May 7, 2012, www.bloomberg.com/news/2012-05-07/michelle-obama-s-food-desert-plan-yields-few-new-stores-retail.html.

[6] Gina Kolata, "Studies Question the Pairing of Food Deserts and Obesity," *The New York Times*, April 17, 2012, www.nytimes.com/2012/04/18/health/research/pairing-of-food-deserts-and-obesity-challenged-in-studies.html.

use of large equipment and that which does not. And it has divided all farmers into two kinds — those who have sufficient 'business sense' and managerial ability to handle the large acreages necessary to finance large machines and those who do not." [38]

Farm production boomed in the 1970s, then ran into a deep economic recession in the first half of the 1980s. Payments to farmers — now based on the difference between target prices set by USDA and market prices — ballooned. In 1983 the Reagan administration instituted an emergency payment-in-kind program in which the government paid farmers who idled their land with USDA-held surplus crops.

Two years later Congress passed a farm bill that reduced price supports, imposed new rules for conserving vulnerable lands and revived the Conservation Reserve Program, an Eisenhower-era measure that paid farmers to set aside vulnerable lands as wildlife habitat.

In the late 1980s and '90s, as politicians and experts grew concerned about curbing federal spending, many started to question whether farm subsidy payments were producing much benefit when most of them went to large landholders. The United States and 116 other nations agreed in 1993 under the General Agreement on Tariffs and Trade (GATT) to reduce domestic farm subsidies and exports of subsidized commodities in order to promote free international trade. And in 1994 Republicans won control of both houses of Congress, pledging to cut federal spending.

These changes set the stage for so-called "Freedom to Farm" legislation in 1996, proposed by Rep. Pat Roberts, R-Kan., which lifted planting restrictions and decoupled farm subsidies from commodity prices in return for declining fixed payments over seven years. Free-market advocates called this the beginning of the end for farm subsidies, but when commodity prices fell shortly after the bill passed, Congress stepped in with billions of dollars in emergency farm assistance. Despite 50 years of radical change in U.S. agriculture, farm policy remained anchored to laws passed in 1938 and 1949.

USDA Seeks New Farmers

As older farmers retire, beginners need many kinds of support.

American agriculture is undergoing a generational shift, as older farmers leave the land and younger ones hoping to take their place confront a wide range of environmental, financial and regulatory challenges.

The average age of farm operators in America has been above 50 since at least 1974, and today more than half are over 55. [1]

"We're facing a major transition right now on our working lands in this country," said Kathleen Merrigan, deputy secretary of Agriculture. "It's not just about farming, it's about food safety, marketing, finance." [2]

Even on small farms, agriculture is a complex business that requires farmers to consider how financing, consumer demand, national and global commodity markets and many other factors will affect their profitability. And despite current record-high revenues, thanks to high world commodity prices, the basic economics of farming are daunting. "Profits are low, and agriculture is very capital-intensive," says National Farmers Union President Roger Johnson. "Both of those factors make it very hard to get started in farming."

The U.S. Department of Agriculture (USDA) defines beginning farmers and ranchers as those who have operated a farm for less than 10 years. About one-fifth of U.S. farms (roughly 450,000) fall into this category. [3]

Beginning farmers represent all age ranges and ethnic groups, but on average they are younger than established farmers. Like veteran farmers, the new farmers are concentrated in the Midwest and South, but also operate in the West and Northeast. On average, beginning farmers hold less land than established farmers (169 acres for a beginning farm, compared to 440 acres for an established one). Beginning farmers also are more likely than experienced farmers to have a college degree, and a larger fraction of their income comes from nonfarm activities. [4]

The 2008 farm bill contained several programs designed to help new farmers, including extra crop insurance subsidies, targeted loans and incentives for retiring farmers to transfer their operations to beginners. [5] Both versions of the 2012 farm bill would increase support for beginning farmers and ranchers, including providing about $50 million for research and outreach programs and $192 million for targeted crop insurance programs over 10 years.

The pending bills also boost support for specialty crops, such as fruits and vegetables, which will help new farmers, says Jeffrey O'Hara, an agricultural economist with the Union of Concerned Scientists. "Local foods are where farmers are coming in, growing the foods that people are demanding but can't get enough of. That's where the opportunities are for them. Supporting healthier foods supports the next generation of farmers."

Growth in local food networks backs that view. The number of farmers markets in the United States has more than quadrupled since 1994, from 1,744 to 7,864, and some markets have waiting lists of farmers seeking sales spaces. [6] (*See graphic, p. 707.*) Moreover, the USDA reported last year that it had been underestimating sales of local foods because it had focused on direct-to-consumer outlets, such as farmers markets and roadside stands, without counting sales to regional distributors, grocery stores and restaurants.

Counting those sales, farmers earned $4.8 billion in 2008 through local food marketing (including $877 million at direct-to-consumer outlets), according to USDA estimates. Local food sales could help promote economic development in many areas, especially near cities, the department said. [7]

Farmers and other agriculture experts were quick to respond early this year to a blog post by journalist Terence Loose, who

Nutrition Debates

As policy makers struggled to guarantee farmers reasonable livings in a boom-and-bust industry, USDA was also shaping debates about nutrition in America. One of its main tasks was administering the food stamp program, as the central federal food aid program was known for decades.

USDA first issued food stamps in an experimental program from 1939 through 1942 as a substitute for cash relief payments to hungry families and a way of reducing agricultural surpluses. The Kennedy administration revived the program in 1961 to address persistent concerns about hunger in America, and Congress made it permanent in 1964, with the overall goal of ensuring that poor families could afford enough food for an adequate and nutritious diet. Participation grew rapidly, from 2.9 million people in 1969 to more than 20 million by the end of the 1970s. [39]

This expansion made the program a political target. President Ronald Reagan (1981-1989) frequently told stories of alleged "welfare queens" and other abusers of entitlement programs who used their benefits to buy goods like steaks and vodka. [40] These charges were often exaggerated, but some food stamp users did sell the coupons for cash. [41] In a 1996 overhaul of welfare policies, Congress ordered states to deliver food stamp benefits via electronic benefit cards instead of paper coupons to reduce fraud and abuse.

USDA also sought to help all Americans understand what types of foods made up a healthy diet, although its efforts were controversial. In 1992 the department published its first Food Pyramid, which recommended how many servings of each of six basic food groups should be eaten daily. Prominent nutrition experts argued that

listed agriculture, horticulture and animal science as three of the top five "useless degrees" for U.S. college students, along with fashion design and theater. He based his views on U.S. Department of Labor projections of job growth in those fields. [8]

Angry rebuttals went viral on the Internet. [9] Merrigan called the blog post "so out of touch with . . . what we know the situation to be," referring to the ongoing generational turnover in agriculture. [10] And a Facebook page titled "I Studied Agriculture and I Have a Job" collected thousands of "likes" within 24 hours of its creation. [11]

— Jennifer Weeks

Boom in Farmers Markets

There are nearly 7,900 farmers markets nationwide, four-and-a-half times more than in 1994 and 10 percent more than last year alone. Supporters of increased funding for farmers markets say they build distribution networks for small farmers and promote the production of fruits, vegetables and other healthy foods.

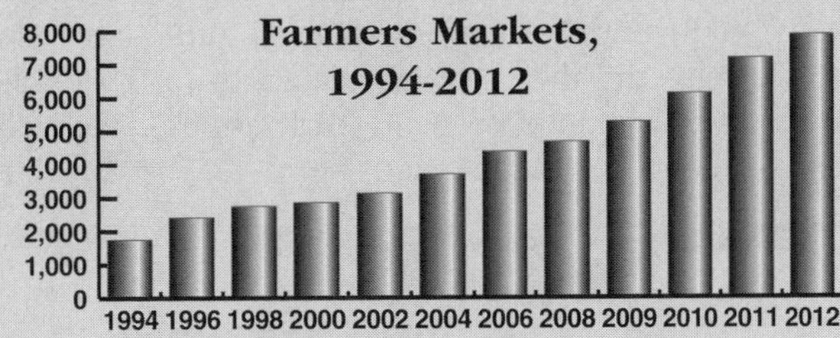

Source: "Farmers Markets and Local Food Marketing," U.S. Department of Agriculture, August 2012, www.ams.usda.gov/AMSv1.0/ams.fetchTemplateData.do?template=TemplateS&leftNav=WholesaleandFarmersMarkets&page=WFMFarmersMarketGrowth&description=Farmers%20Market%20Growth&acct=frmrdirmkt

[1] "Farm Household Well-Being: Labor Allocations and Age," U.S. Department of Agriculture, updated, May 27, 2012, www.ers.usda.gov/topics/farm-economy/farm-household-well-being/labor-allocations-age.aspx.

[2] "Merrigan Stresses Need for Young Leaders in Agricultural Pipeline," *Fresh Cut Magazine*, April 2, 2012, http://freshcut.com/index.php/news/release/16708/.

[3] Mary Clare Ahearn, "Potential Challenges for Beginning Farmers and Ranchers," *Choices*, 2nd Quarter 2011, www.choicesmagazine.org/choices-magazine/theme-articles/innovations-to-support-beginning-farmers-and-ranchers/potential-challenges-for-beginning-farmers-and-ranchers.

[4] "Farm Demographics," U.S. Department of Agriculture, www.start2farm.gov/usda/knowledge; "Farm Household Income and Characteristics: Characteristics of Principal Farm Operator Households by Experience of Operators, 2010," Economic Research Service, U.S. Department of Agriculture, www.ers.usda.gov/data-products/farm-household-income-and-characteristics.aspx.

[5] "2008 Farm Bill side-by-side: Provisions for Traditionally Underserved Groups," Economic Research Service, U.S. Department of Agriculture, http://webarchives.cdlib.org/sw1rf5mh0k/www.ers.usda.gov/FarmBill/2008/Titles/Underserved.htm.

[6] Tracie Cone, "Number of U.S. Farmers Markets Surges," The Associated Press, Aug. 3, 2012, www.timesrecordnews.com/news/2012/aug/03/apnewsbreak-number-us-farmers-markets-surges/.

[7] Sarah A. Low and Stephen Vogel, "Direct and Intermediated Marketing of Local Foods in the United States," Economic Research Report No. 128, U.S. Department of Agriculture, November 2011, pp. 2-3 and 13, www.ers.usda.gov/media/138324/err128_2_.pdf.

[8] Terence Loose, "College Majors That Are Useless," Yahoo.com, http://education.yahoo.net/articles/most_useless_degrees.htm.

[9] See, for example, Rebekah Bowen, "An Open Letter to Terence Loose on the Future of Agricultural Careers," http://rebekahbowen.wordpress.com/2012/01/19/an-open-letter-to-terence-loose-on-the-future-of-agriculture-careers/, and Holly Spangler, "Loose: Not Taking Questions," FarmProgress.com, Jan. 31, 2012, http://farmprogress.com/blogs-loose-taking-questions-2980.

[10] "Merrigan Stresses the Need for Young Leaders," *op. cit.*

[11] "Yahoo's 'Useless Degree' Article Draws Huge Response," Wisconsin Farm Bureau Federation, Jan. 26, 2012, http://wfbf.com/ag-newswire/yahoo%E2%80%99s-%E2%80%98useless-degrees%E2%80%99-article-draws-huge-response/.

the diagram gave too much weight to high-fat foods such as whole milk and red meat, reflecting the influence that large agribusiness companies held over USDA. [42]

In 2005, with obesity reaching record levels across the United States, USDA revised the Food Pyramid, adding a staircase to stress the importance of physical activity. This version was widely denounced as confusing and still overly focused on dairy and meat products. The agency scrapped the pyramid in 2011, replacing it with a new design called MyPlate, which advised that fruits and vegetables should constitute half of every meal. ■

CURRENT SITUATION

Drought and Delay

As much of the United States struggles through intense drought, the Obama administration and farm state legislators are pressing for Congress to pass the 2012 farm bill. Because both the Senate-passed bill and the House Agriculture Committee's version would strengthen crop insurance programs and reauthorize USDA drought and disaster relief programs, advocates argue that enacting them would update important safety-net programs.

"While by no means perfect, this farm bill is needed for producers and those who rely on sound agriculture policy and nutrition programs during difficult economic times," a group of 78 House members (47 Republicans and 31 Democrats) wrote to House leaders on July 19. [43] Minority Leader Nancy Pelosi, D-Calif., echoed that view. "Inaction means economic, nutritional and employment crisis throughout our rural communities," Pelosi said. [44]

But House Speaker Boehner has a record of voting against previous farm bills and has criticized the spending levels in the proposed 2012 bills. "We've got a Soviet-style dairy program in America today, and one of the proposals in the farm bill would actually make it worse," Boehner said in July. [45]

As of Aug. 1, 2012, USDA had designated 1,452 counties as drought disaster areas, with 66 percent of national hay acreage and 73 percent of cattle acreage affected and 48 percent of the corn crop rated as being in poor to very poor condition. [46] Losses of major crops such as corn, wheat, oats and soybeans will drive up the prices of many groceries, including breads, cereals, cooking oils and numerous processed foods that contain corn-based sweeteners. Corn and soybean meal also are major ingredients for animal feeds, so as corn and soybean prices rise, many livestock producers will further reduce their herds to cut costs. Smaller supplies will lead to higher meat, milk and egg prices.

"The bottom line is, food is a necessity," Purdue University agricultural economist Chris Hurt said last month. "[When] food extracts more of our disposable income, that's less dollars to be spent for other things." Hurt predicted that food price inflation caused by the drought could increase overall inflation in the United States by several tenths of a percent, starting this fall. [47]

USDA has limited tools for providing quick relief to farmers hit hard by drought. The department is offering low-interest loans to farmers in drought disaster zones and letting ranchers cut hay and graze cattle on lands protected under the Conservation Reserve Program. Crop insurance will cover about 72 percent of yield and revenue losses for insured farmers, according to Agriculture Secretary Vilsack. "But it's the livestock producers that are in the biggest and most troubled situation because they simply don't have any disaster program, and there's no such thing as a crop insurance program for livestock producers," Vilsack said. [48]

Getty Images/Scott Olson

Agriculture is a major sector of the U.S. economy, but farmers in the nation's midsection have been experiencing one of the worst droughts in more than 50 years. Here, Bill Kirklin sets up an irrigation system in his cornfield near Whiteland, Ind., on July 20, 2012. He and his brother, both sixth-generation farmers, raise about 1,500 acres of corn and soybeans on a farm founded by their family in 1835.

Conserving Farm Lands

Farming can have many negative environmental impacts on soil, water supplies, air quality, wildlife and human health, especially when practiced on a large scale with heavy use of pesticides, herbicides, fertilizers and other chemicals. A 2004 study by Iowa State University economists estimated that the external costs of U.S. agriculture (costs that were not paid by farmers but instead were borne by society) ranged from $5.7 billion to $16.9 billion per year. "We pay for food in our utility bills and taxes and in our declining environmental and personal health," the authors observed. [49]

Environmental groups and sustainable-agriculture advocates have won increasing support for conservation programs in farm bills since 1985, when a conservation title was first added to the bill. Title II of the 2008 farm bill authorized $24.1 billion over five years for conservation programs, which fall into two main categories. Land retirement and easement programs pay farmers to take vulnerable lands out of crop production, while working lands programs help farmers protect natural resources on productive lands.

Now, however, these programs are under pressure. Both versions of the 2012 farm bill cut conservation programs in Title II by more than $6 billion over 10 years and consolidate 23 conservation programs into 13 programs. And market trends are undercutting the largest land retirement initiative: the Conservation Reserve Program (CRP), which pays farmers not to grow crops on sensitive lands, such as prairie wetlands and grasslands. Farmers offer USDA bids to enroll specific parcels of land in the CRP program; the agency awards 10- to 15-year contracts, based on criteria designed to select the most environmentally sensitive lands. The average CRP land rental rate is currently $57.29 per acre, although rates vary widely from state to state. [50]

Continued on p. 710

At Issue:

Does U.S. farm policy promote unhealthy eating?

DAVID LUDWIG
PROFESSOR OF PEDIATRICS, HARVARD MEDICAL SCHOOL; PROFESSOR OF NUTRITION, HARVARD SCHOOL OF PUBLIC HEALTH

FROM "REFORMING THE 2012 FARM BILL," PUBLIC FORUM, OCT. 20, 2011, HARVARD SCHOOL OF PUBLIC HEALTH

yes

In the last century, there's been a progressive transformation to [our] traditional way of eating, such that we now have a massive number of products in our food supply. When you think of all of the prepared breakfast cereals alone, that could be hundreds on a store shelf, together with fast food, sugary drinks [and] a range of processed snacks.

And yet, they're all produced from literally four commodities: corn, wheat, soybeans [and] rice, or the animals that are fed [on] those commodities. That's the majority of calories in our diet now. This profound transformation of the diet has been driven by agricultural policies in general and, to some degree, specifically farm agricultural subsidies of commodities that have made these grains and soybeans that are inherently cheap to produce, even cheaper. . . .

The implications of this policy to public health are increasingly profound, for two reasons. One is that these ultra-processed products, based on commodities, are very dense in calories. Well, the calorie density, by itself, isn't inherently a problem. Nuts are calorie-dense, but they're also nutritious and satiating and have many benefits to health. It's the combination of concentrating calories and removing nutrients and other nutritional properties.

So . . . we might have, 50 years ago, had a child who ate a bowl of strawberries for an afternoon snack that provided 100 calories, [and] those strawberries would also have provided five or more grams of fiber, many vitamins and minerals, antioxidants and phytochemicals, in physiologically relevant doses. Today that child is probably eating strawberry-flavored Fruit Gushers, which have the same 100 calories in a tenth the size, [with] virtually no fiber, vitamins or minerals or anything of value.

The consequence, or what I saw today in the obesity clinic at Children's Hospital, are patients like the 8-year-old girl that I saw who weighed over 200 pounds, with triglycerides of 240, very high, and very low levels of HDL cholesterol, insulin resistance, fatty liver, and pre-diabetes. And this is not genetic; this is dietary. Ultimately, we are going to need to rethink agricultural policy to get us off this dependence primarily on these four products in order to improve the nutritional quality of the food supply, if we're going to do anything about the obesity epidemic and the epidemic of diseases related to obesity in the United States.

JULIAN ALSTON
PROFESSOR OF AGRICULTURAL AND RESOURCE ECONOMICS, UNIVERSITY OF CALIFORNIA, DAVIS; MEMBER, GIANNINI FOUNDATION OF AGRICULTURAL ECONOMICS, UNIVERSITY OF CALIFORNIA

WRITTEN FOR *CQ RESEARCHER*, AUGUST 2012

no

Many people blame federal farm subsidies for America's high obesity rates, but this view is rejected by my work with agricultural economists Brad Rickard and Abigail Okrent. Our careful quantitative analysis indicates that U.S. farm subsidy policies, for the most part, have not made food commodities significantly cheaper and have not had a significant effect on caloric consumption.

First, the effects of farm subsidies on food prices are muted because farm commodities used as ingredients represent a small share of the total cost of retail food products. On average, the farm commodity cost share is approximately 20 percent, but it varies widely: For grains, sugar and oilseeds, it is less than 10 percent; for soda, the share is approximately 2 percent.

Second, the effects on farm commodity prices are small and mixed. Subsidies have at times resulted in lower U.S. prices of some farm commodities, in particular grains, and consequently lower costs of producing breakfast cereal, bread or livestock products. But these effects have been contained by companion policies that restricted acreage. Moreover, U.S. import barriers that support farm prices for many commodities (such as sugar, dairy, orange juice and beef) also increase food prices domestically and discourage consumption. Consequently, eliminating all farm subsidies, including those provided indirectly by trade barriers, may, if anything, lead to an increase in annual per capita consumption of calories and an increase in body weight.

Third, the roles of policies affecting corn are misunderstood. Farm subsidies are responsible for the growth in the use of corn to produce high fructose corn syrup (HFCS) as a caloric sweetener, but not in the way it is often suggested. The culprit here is not corn subsidies; rather, sugar policy has restricted imports, driven up the U.S. price of sugar and encouraged consumers and food manufacturers to replace sugar with alternative caloric sweeteners, especially HFCS. Moreover, U.S. biofuels policy that also subsidizes corn producers has made corn much more expensive for food and feed. On net, corn and sugar policies have made caloric sweeteners more expensive, discouraging obesity.

U.S. farm policies might well be seen as unfair and inefficient. But whether we like these policies or not for other reasons, their effects on obesity are negligible. Farm subsidies are a red herring in the context of obesity, distracting attention from the real causes and potential solutions.

Continued from p. 708

With crop prices rising, many farmers are not renewing CRP contracts. "We recognize that there are seven to 10 million acres in the CRP that could be productive," says the American Farm Bureau Federation's Moore. "The presumption is that farmers who hold expiring CRP contracts won't renew them, because expected returns [from planting on those acres] will be much greater."

Critics say that having crop insurance readily available is also a factor. "Crop insurance decreases risk for farmers, so it will probably motivate some farmers to plant on marginal land," says Johns Hopkins University's Klein. "Making conservation compliance a condition for receiving crop insurance subsidies will create a disincentive to plant those lands."

Some USDA conservation programs have historically been attached to the direct payments to farmers funded in Title I of the farm bill. But if Congress eliminates direct payments, those conservation incentives will no longer apply to the affected lands. These programs include Conservation Compliance, which requires farms operating on highly erodible land to use approved soil conservation techniques; Sodbuster, which bars farmers from plowing up highly erodible land without an approved soil conservation plan; and Swampbuster, which prohibits farms from converting wetlands to croplands. [51]

Instead, advocates say, crop insurance should come with conservation requirements. The American Farm Bureau Federation opposes this approach. "Almost every farmer out there is required to comply with some form of conservation program. But tying conservation to crop insurance raises the possibility that if you're not in compliance because of factors you can't control [for example, a natural disaster], you may not get crop insurance, which is a fundamental risk-management tool," says Moore.

But not all farmers support that position. In a June poll sponsored by the National Farmers Union, 61 percent of farmers surveyed said farmers should be required to meet some environmental standards to receive federal farm benefits such as crop insurance. And 71 percent agreed with the statement, "Conservation programs reduce costs and help farmers' bottom line," compared to 14 percent who believed that "conservation programs are a burden and hurt farmers' bottom line." [52]

The Disappearing Middle

Meanwhile, despite the continuing trend toward consolidation in American agriculture since the 1930s, many observers today say that with local food networks growing and consumers increasingly interested in the sources of their food, small farms are doing quite well overall. The sector of greatest concern is midsize farms — or as a national research initiative dubs them, "Agriculture of the Middle." Farms in this category are typically businesses where:

- Gross yearly sales total $50,000 to $500,000;
- Farming is the household's main income source, and one or more family members make most decisions and provide significant labor; and
- Farms sell to their markets through wholesale supply chains or other organizations such as co-ops, and often operate with high environmental standards. [53]

"We're seeing more really large farms that produce one or two crops on a lot of acres, and more small farms that produce diverse crops for local, regional or organic markets," says Lotti of the National Sustainable Agriculture Coalition. "Midsized family farms are declining — they can't make it with current farm policy and national and international market conditions." These farms often are too large to sell their products directly to consumers through outlets such as farmers markets, but too small to compete with large-scale producers.

Agriculture experts say strengthening local and regional food systems can create more outlets for products from medium-size farms. As one example, the state of Virginia's cooperative extension system recently pointed out that institutions such as colleges and universities, museums, hospitals and corporate cafeterias could not obtain enough locally grown Virginia products to meet customer demand. Better distribution systems could help meet that demand and create "Virginia-based value chains," thereby "linking people to their culture, land, agriculture and natural resources," according to two extension experts. [54]

Feed Versus Fuel

This summer's drought is reviving an intense debate over national production targets for ethanol, a biofuel made mainly from corn. Since 2005, the federal Renewable Fuels Standard (RFS) has required oil refiners to blend specific amounts of ethanol into motor gasoline yearly, a policy designed to reduce U.S. dependence on imported oil and bolster farm communities. Much conventional gasoline sold today across the United States contains 10 percent ethanol, a level that can be used in any car. Some cars and trucks are "flex-fuel" vehicles that can run on either gasoline or blends containing up to 85 percent ethanol.

The ethanol mandate becomes controversial when corn supplies are tight, because it creates competition between using corn to make animal feed or fuel. With the drought driving up corn prices, a coalition of meat and poultry producers petitioned the Environmental Protection Agency on July 30 to waive the RFS for a year. The groups estimated that meeting RFS targets (13.2 billion gallons of corn ethanol in 2012 and 13.98 billion gallons in 2013) could consume up to 40 percent of expected corn crops. [55]

"The combination of the drought and American ethanol policy will lead in many parts of the world to widespread inflation, more hunger, less food security, slower economic growth and political instability, especially in poor countries," University of California-Davis economist Colin Carter and Hoover Institution fellow Henry Miller wrote in support of a waiver. [56]

Ethanol advocates oppose waiving the RFS and say the law offers ways to handle any supply shortage. For example, refiners who earned credits in past years for blending more ethanol than the mandate required can use those credits toward current targets.

Waiving the RFS "will not make it rain in Indiana, bring pastures to life in the Plains, or meaningfully lower corn prices," Renewable Fuels Association President and CEO Bob Dinneen said in response to waiver requests. [57] ■

OUTLOOK

Big Shifts

U.S. agriculture is a vast system that is unlikely to change quickly — rather like turning an ocean liner — so many experts say the system may look much the same in a decade as it does today. "If momentum keeps building, we could get some big shifts within 20 years," says Klein of Johns Hopkins University.

But observers believe certain shifts are likely to continue — particularly the growth of small-scale local food networks and alternative production methods such as organic farming. They also expect increasing support for fruits and vegetables, after decades of focus on commodity crops.

"Ten years ago people thought organic agriculture was a niche market, but now it's much bigger. That's where we are now with local markets," says Robert Guenther, senior vice president of the United Fresh Produce Association. "Our goods go to market within two or three days of harvest, and we have to adjust to consumers' demands and needs. That will be a very important segment of our industry: more local and regional sourcing through outlets like roadside stands and farmers markets."

Growth will also continue at the large end, says Johnson of the National Farmers Union. "Big farms will keep getting larger, more concentrated and more specialized. But consumers will continue wanting to know more about where their food comes from, and that will provide more opportunities for people in areas where smaller operations can do direct marketing — for example, in the Northeastern states."

Much of the current energy in agriculture is at the small-scale end, observers say. Many predict that continued growth in the local and healthy food sector could have a disproportionate impact on health in America. "I expect the local food surge to continue, and it's very positive that people are talking about regional food systems. That's what we really need to achieve a diverse diet," says Klein.

One undervalued aspect of sustainable agriculture, advocates contend, is that it makes farmlands healthier and better able to withstand likely impacts from climate change, such as more frequent droughts. "Organic soils can withstand drought and absorb more water during flooding. On the crop side, if you diversify you have differently timed plantings and crops, so you're buffered against big losses," says Lotti of the National Sustainable Agriculture Coalition. "We should pay farmers for actions that would help mitigate future climate events, instead of just for production or losses the way we do today," she says.

Journalist McMillan says changes are needed beyond farmlands. "We should build more public capacity for quality food distribution and subsidize demand instead of production — for example, increasing programs that provide matching funds for money that low-income consumers spend at farmers markets," she says. "That would make it possible for smaller farmers to sell to smaller grocers in their areas. Small farmers and grocers can't develop cheap distribution systems like the big supermarkets, so a distribution system that brings quality food into communities will make it possible for them to sell directly to people who need it. That would transform the quality of food in a lot of communities, and it would diversify the food system." ■

Notes

1 Tracie McMillan, *The American Way of Eating* (2012), p. 236

2 *Ibid.*, p. 237.

3 For background, see the following *CQ Researcher* reports: Nellie Bristol, "Preventing Disease," Jan. 6, 2012, pp. 1-24; Barbara Mantel, "Preventing Obesity," Oct. 1, 2010, pp. 797-820; Marcia Clemmitt, "Heart Health," Sept. 12, 2008, pp. 721-744; and Alan Greenblatt, "Obesity Epidemic," Jan. 31, 2003, pp. 73-104.

4 "Urging the Passage of a Farm Bill That Supports Healthy, Local, and Regional Food Systems," resolution adopted at 80th annual meeting, U.S. Conference of Mayors, June 13-16, 2012, http://usmayors.org/resolutions/80th_conference/chhs03.asp.

5 For background, see the following *CQ Researcher* reports: Peter Katel, "Water Crisis in the West," Dec. 9, 2011, pp. 1025-1048; and Chanan Tigay, "Extreme Weather," Sept. 9, 2011, pp. 733-756.

6 James Rowley and Derek Wallbank, "House Republicans Pass Drought Relief and Delay Farm Bill," Bloomberg News, Aug. 2, 2012, www.bloomberg.com/news/2012-08-02/house-republicans-seek-drought-relief-while-delaying-farm-bill.html.

7 "Mitt Romney Announces Agriculture Advisory Committee," March 13, 2012, www.mitt

romney.com/news/press/2012/03/mitt-romney-announces-agriculture-advisory-committee.

[8] "Ag 101: Demographics," U.S. Environmental Protection Agency, www.epa.gov/oecaagct/ag101/demographics.html.

[9] Opening statement, House Agriculture Committee hearing, Feb. 17, 2011, http://agriculture.house.gov/statements/lucas-statement-passing-stewart-doan.

[10] Renée Johnson and Jim Monke, "What is the 'Farm Bill?'," Congressional Research Service, Jan. 3, 2011, p. 3, www.nationalaglawcenter.org/assets/crs/RS22131.pdf.

[11] For background, see David Hosansky, "Farm Subsidies," *CQ Researcher*, May 17, 2001, pp. 433-456. Also see Reed Karaim, "Farm Subsidies," *CQ Global Researcher*, May 1, 2012, pp. 205-228.

[12] For Congressional Budget Office (CBO) analyses of the 2012 bills, see www.cbo.gov/sites/default/files/cbofiles/attachments/hr6083.pdf (House bill), and www.cbo.gov/sites/default/files/cbofiles/attachments/s3240Passed.pdf (Senate bill).

[13] Floor statement of Sen. Debbie Stabenow, June 6, 2012, p. 2, www.ag.senate.gov/newsroom/press/release/chairwoman-stabenow-floor-remarks-on-agriculture-reform-food-and-jobs-act-of-2012.

[14] "Plant the Plate," Union of Concerned Scientists, May 1, 2012, www.ucsusa.org/food_and_agriculture/solutions/big_picture_solutions/plant-the-plate.html.

[15] J. P. Reganold, *et al.*, "Transforming U.S. Agriculture," *Science*, vol. 332, May 6, 2011, pp. 670-671, www.sciencemag.org/content/332/6030/670.

[16] "Expert Panel Calls for 'Transforming U.S. Agriculture:' Changes in Markets, Policies and Science Needed for More Sustainable Farming," *Science Daily*, May 5, 2011, www.sciencedaily.com/releases/2011/05/110505142600.htm.

[17] For a list of the companies designated by USDA to provide crop insurance for 2013 and the master agreement, see www3.rma.usda.gov/tools/agents/companies/indexCI.cfm.

[18] "Crop Insurance: Savings Would Result from Program Changes and Greater Use of Data Mining," U.S. Government Accountability Office (GAO), March 2012, pp. 1, 7, http://gao.gov/assets/590/589305.pdf; Bruce Babcock, "Impact of Scaling Back Crop Insurance Premium Subsidies," Environmental Working Group, February 2012, p. 4, http://static.ewg.org/pdf/babcock_cropinsurancesubsidies.pdf.

[19] GAO, *ibid.*, p. 3.

[20] Babcock, *op. cit.*, p. 3.

[21] Chris Clayton, "Senate Votes to Limit Crop Insurance Premium Subsidies," *DTN Progressive Farmer*, June 20, 2012, www.dtnprogressivefarmer.com/dtnag/view/ag/printablePage.do?ID=BLOG_PRINTABLE_PAGE&bypassCache=true&pageLayout=v4&blogHandle=policy&blogEntryId=8a82c0bc37ec102e01380c2a16280148&articleTitle=Senate+Votes+to+Limit+Crop+Insurance+Premium+Subsidies&editionName=DTNAgFreeSiteOnline.

[22] Dorothy Rosenbaum and Stacy Dean, "House Agriculture Committee Farm Bill Would Throw 2 to 3 Million People Off of SNAP," Center on Budget and Policy Priorities, July 12, 2012, www.cbpp.org/files/7-6-12fa.pdf.

[23] For background, see the following *CQ Researcher* reports: Peter Katel, "Child Poverty," Oct. 28, 2011, pp. 901-928; Peter Katel, "Straining the Safety Net," July 31, 2009, pp. 645-668; Thomas J. Billitteri, "Domestic Poverty," Sept. 7, 2007, updated April 27, 2011, pp. 721-744; Tom Price, "Child Welfare Reform," April 22, 2005, pp. 345-368; and Sarah Glazer, "Welfare Reform," Aug. 3, 2001, pp. 601-632.

[24] *Ibid.*, pp. 2, 4, citing Congressional Budget Office estimates.

[25] "The Supplemental Nutrition Assistance Program," Congressional Budget Office, April 2012, pp. 1, 4, http://cbo.gov/publication/43173.

[26] Opening statement of Chairman Lucas, July 11, 2012, http://agriculture.house.gov/statements/opening-statement-chairman-lucas-business-meeting-consider-hr-6083-federal-agriculture.

[27] "The Supplemental Nutrition Assistance Program," Congressional Budget Office, April 2012, p. 4, www.cbo.gov/sites/default/files/cbofiles/attachments/04-19-SNAP.pdf.

[28] "The Supplemental Nutrition Assistance Program," CBO, *op. cit.*, p. 2.

[29] "Troublesome Creek," "American Experience," PBS, www.pbs.org/wgbh/amex/trouble/timeline/index.html.

[30] The Homestead Act was repealed in 1976 everywhere but Alaska, where homesteading continued until 1988.

[31] "Legacy of the Homestead Act and Homesteading," U.S. Department of the Interior, Bureau of Land Management, www.blm.gov/wo/st/en/res/Education_in_BLM/homestead_act/legacy.html.

[32] "Extension," National Institute of Food and Agriculture, U.S. Department of Agriculture, April 19, 2011, www.csrees.usda.gov/qlinks/extension.html#yesterday.

[33] Timothy Egan, *The Worst Hard Time: The Untold Story of Those Who Survived the Great American Dust Bowl* (2006), p. 59.

[34] For a timeline of the Dust Bowl, see "American Experience: Surviving the Dust Bowl," PBS, www.pbs.org/wgbh/americanexperience/features/timeline/dustbowl/.

[35] Paul K. Conkin, *A Revolution Down on the Farm: The Transformation of American Agriculture Since 1928* (2008), pp. 124-125.

[36] Carolyn Dimitri, *et al.*, "The 20th Century Transformation of U.S. Agriculture and Farm Policy," Economic Research Service, Economic Information Bulletin No. 3, U.S. Department of Agriculture, June 2005, http://ageconsearch.umn.edu/bitstream/59390/2/eib3.pdf.

[37] Marian Burros, "Image of an Industry," *The Washington Post*, May 11, 1978, p. E1.

[38] Wendell Berry, *The Unsettling of America: Culture and Agriculture* (1977), p. 33.

[39] Margaret S. Andrews and Katherine L. Clancy, *The Political Economy of the Food Stamp Program in the United States* (1985), pp. 68-69, www.ifpri.cgiar.org/sites/default/files/pubs/pubs/books/ppa93/ppa93ch05.pdf.

[40] Steven V. Roberts, "Food Stamps Program: How It Grew and How Reagan Wants to Cut It Back," *The New York Times*, April 4, 1981, www.

About the Author

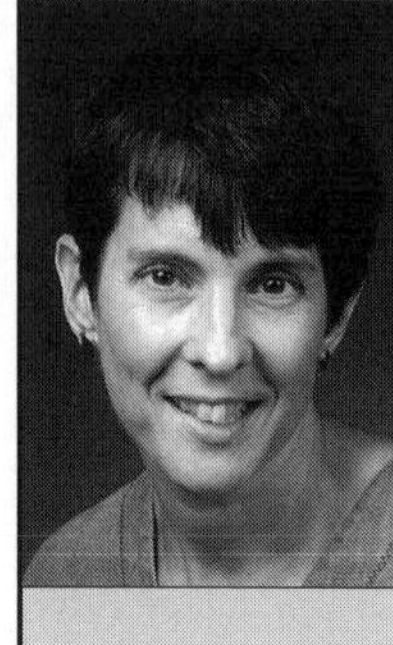

Jennifer Weeks is a Massachusetts freelance writer who specializes in energy, the environment and science. She has written for *The Washington Post*, *Audubon*, *Popular Mechanics* and other magazines and previously was a policy analyst, congressional staffer and lobbyist. She has an A.B. degree from Williams College and master's degrees from the University of North Carolina and Harvard. Her recent *CQ Researcher* reports include "Gulf Coast Restoration" and "Energy Policy."

nytimes.com/1981/04/04/us/food-stamps-program-it-grew-reagan-wants-cut-it-back-budget-targets.html; Donald M. Rothberg, "Senator Says Reagan Missing Point on Issues," The Associated Press, March 2, 1982, http://news.google.com/newspapers?nid=1454&dat=19820302&id=AsssAAAAIBAJ&sjid=YBMEAAAAIBAJ&pg=3500,160234.

41 For background, see "Supplemental Nutrition Assistance Program: Payment Errors and Trafficking Have Declined, But Challenges Remain," GAO-10-956T, U.S. Government Accountability Office, July 28, 2010, www.gao.gov/products/GAO-10-956T.

42 Walter C. Willett and Meir J. Stampfer, "Rebuilding the Food Pyramid," *Scientific American*, January 2003, www.scientificamerican.com/article.cfm?id=rebuilding-the-food-pyram; Marion Nestle, "Why It's Good That the Food Pyramid Became a Plate," *Atlantic.com*, June 3, 2011, www.theatlantic.com/health/archive/2011/06/why-its-good-that-the-food-pyramid-became-a-plate/239889/.

43 "Noem and Welch lead bipartisan group of over 75 urging a vote on Farm Bill," office of Rep. Kristi Noem, U.S. House of Representatives, July 19, 2012, http://noem.house.gov/index.cfm/press-releases?ContentRecord_id=d0013f7a-1d75-4ef7-8c1e-76015e735156.

44 "Pelosi calls for swift action on farm bill before August recess," July 19, 2012, www.democraticleader.gov/news/press?id=2694.

45 Russell Berman, "Speaker Says No Decision Has Been Made on Farm bill Vote," *The Hill.com*, July 12, 2012, http://thehill.com/blogs/on-the-money/1007-other/237557-boehner-no-decision-on-farm-bill-vote.

46 Press release, "Agriculture Secretary Vilsack Announces New Drought Assistance, Designates an Additional 218 Counties as Primary Natural Disaster Areas," U.S. Department of Agriculture, Aug. 1, 2012, www.usda.gov/wps/portal/usda/usdahome?contentid=2012/08/0260.xml&navid=NEWS_RELEASE&navtype=RT&parentnav=LATEST_RE LEASES&edeployment_action=retrievecontent.

47 "Severe Drought Hits the U.S.," "On Point," NPR, July 17, 2012, http://onpoint.wbur.org/2012/07/17/severe-drought.

48 Press briefing by Press Secretary Jay Carney and Secretary of Agriculture Tom Vilsack, U.S. Department of Agriculture, July 18, 2012, www.usda.gov/wps/portal/usda/usdahome?contentid=2012/07/0244.xml.

49 Erin M. Tegtmeier and Michael D. Duffy, "External Costs of Agricultural Production in the United States," *International Journal of Agricultural Sustainability*, Vol. 2, No. 1, 2004, pp. 1-20, www.leopold.iastate.edu/sites/default/files/pubs-and-papers/2004-01-external-costs-agricultural-production-united-states_0.pdf. Quote is from p. 14 of the study.

50 Kent Thiese, "CRP Sign-Up," MinnStar Bank, March 3, 2012, www.minnstarbank.com/blog/2012/03/crp-sign-up.

51 "Farm Bill: Protecting Environmental Compliance Programs: A Public Health Priority," Center for a Livable Future, The Johns Hopkins University, summer 2012, www.jhsph.edu/research/centers-and-institutes/johns-hopkins-center-for-a-livable-future/_pdf/projects/ffp/farm_bill/Protect-Environmental-Compliance.pdf.

52 "U.S. Heartland Farmers Value Conservation Programs and Reject Cutting Farm Bill Conservation Funding," Greenberg Quinlan Rosner Research, June 25, 2012, http://nfu.org/news/201-energy-and-natural-resources/1129-poll-farmers-value-conservation-programs-and-reject-cutting-farm-bill-conservation-funding.

53 "Characterizing Ag of the Middle and Values-Based Food Supply Chains," Agriculture of the Middle, www.agofthemiddle.org/archives/2012/01/characterizing.html#more.

54 Eric Benfeldt and Kenner Love, "Can Virginia Communities and Counties Seize an Economic and Social Opportunity with Farm-based Local and Regional Economic Development?" Virginia Cooperative Extension, Oct. 7, 2009, http://pubs.ext.vt.edu/news/fbmu/2009/10/article_1.html.

55 "Petition Asks EPA for One-Year Waiver of Ethanol Production Mandate," National Cattlemen's Beef Association, July 30, 2012, www.beefusa.org/newsreleases1.aspx?NewsID=2591.

56 Colin A. Carter and Henry I. Miller, "Corn for Food, Not for Fuel," *The New York Times*, July 30, 2012, www.nytimes.com/2012/07/31/opinion/corn-for-food-not-fuel.html.

57 "RFS Waiver Calls 'Premature' and 'Void of Justification,' " Renewable Fuels Association, Aug. 2, 2012, www.ethanolrfa.org/news/entry/rfs-waiver-calls-premature-and-void-of-justification/.

FOR MORE INFORMATION

American Farm Bureau Federation, 600 Maryland Ave., S.W., Suite 1000W, Washington, DC 20024; 202-406-3600; www.fb.org. Trade association for farm and ranch interests.

Feeding America, 35 E. Wacker Dr., Suite 2000, Chicago, IL 60601; 800-771-2303; www.feedingamerica.org. Nationwide network of food banks that advocates for policies to end hunger and food insecurity in the United States.

Harvard School of Public Health, 677 Huntington Ave., Boston, MA 02115; 617-432-8423; www.hsph.harvard.edu. Awards graduate degrees and conducts research on health issues, including nutrition and diet.

National Farmers Union, 20 F St., N.W., Suite 400, Washington, DC 20001; 202-554-1600; www.nfu.org. Advocates on behalf of small farms, ranchers and rural communities.

National Sustainable Agriculture Coalition, 110 Maryland Ave., N.E., Washington, DC 20002; 202-547-5754; www.sustainableagriculture.net. Alliance of grassroots organizations working to support small and midsize family farms, protect the environment and ensure access to healthy, nutritious foods.

Union of Concerned Scientists, 2 Brattle Square, Cambridge, MA 02138; 617-547-5552; www.ucsusa.org. National advocacy group combining scientific research and citizen action to achieve a healthy environment.

United Fresh Produce Association, 1901 Pennsylvania Ave., N.W., Suite 1100, Washington, DC 20006; 202-303-3400; www.unitedfresh.org. Trade association representing producers of fresh fruits and vegetables.

U.S. Department of Agriculture, 1400 Independence Ave., S.W., Washington, DC 20250; 202-720-2791; www.usda.gov. Lead federal agency on agriculture, food and nutrition policy; also manages national forests and grasslands and conducts research in partnership with public and land-grant universities.

Bibliography

Selected Sources

Books

Allen, Will, with Charles Wilson, *The Good Food Revolution: Growing Healthy Food, People, and Communities*, Gotham, 2012.
The son of a sharecropper recounts his journey from professional sports and business to founding one of the nation's premier urban farms in Milwaukee and extols the benefits of strong community food systems.

Conkin, Paul, *A Revolution Down on the Farm: The Transformation of American Agriculture Since 1929*, University Press of Kentucky, 2008.
An emeritus professor of history at Vanderbilt University argues that the greatest industrial revolution in history has occurred in agriculture since 1929.

McMillan, Tracie, *The American Way of Eating: Undercover at Wal-Mart, Applebee's, Farm Fields and the Dinner Table*, Scribner, 2012.
An investigative report into American eating patterns and how they are shaped by employment patterns and incomes.

Salatin, Joel, *Folks, This Ain't Normal: A Farmer's Advice for Happier Hens, Healthier People, and a Better World*, Center Street, 2011.
Local, sustainable food production is the way of the future, argues a third-generation family farmer from Virginia who runs a "beyond organic, grass-fed" farm.

Articles

Bandow, Doug, "It's Time to Kick Farmers Off the Federal Dole," *Forbes*, July 18, 2011, www.cato.org/publications/commentary/its-time-kick-farmers-federal-dole.
A senior fellow at the libertarian Cato Institute calls for reducing direct payments, crop insurance subsidies and other forms of federal support to farmers.

Eligon, John, "Widespread Drought Is Likely to Worsen," *The New York Times*, July 19, 2012, www.nytimes.com/2012/07/20/science/earth/severe-drought-expected-to-worsen-across-the-nation.html?pagewanted=all.
As of mid-July, 55 percent of the continental United States was a federal drought disaster area. Grain prices are spiking because of crop losses, which also will drive up the cost of meat and dairy products.

Eng, Monica, "Politicians, Health Advocates Seek Transparency, Restrictions in Food Stamp Program," *Chicago Tribune*, June 20, 2012, www.chicagotribune.com/news/local/ct-nw-food-stamp-spending-20120620,0,3921977,full.story.
Under current rules participants in SNAP (Supplemental Nutrition Assistance Program) can use federal food credits to buy soda, chips and candy. Health advocates want to change the policy, but the Agriculture Department opposes limiting junk food purchases.

Freeland, Chrystia, "The Triumph of the Family Farm," *The Atlantic*, July/August 2012, www.theatlantic.com/magazine/archive/2012/07/the-triumph-of-the-family-farm/8998/.
Modern technology and global integration have driven most Americans off farms, but those who remain are thriving.

Reports and Studies

"Crop Insurance: Savings Would Result from Program Changes and Greater Use of Data Mining," U.S. Government Accountability Office, March 13, 2012, www.gao.gov/products/GAO-12-256.
Limits on total payments and more review of waste, fraud and abuse could save the federal government more than $1 billion annually in subsidies for crop insurance.

An, Ruopeng, and Roland Sturm, "School and Residential Neighborhood Food Environment and Diet Among California Youth," *American Journal of Preventive Medicine*, Vol. 42, Issue 2, February 2012, www.ajpmonline.org/article/S0749-3797(11)00849-X/abstract.
Rand Corp. researchers find no consistent relationship between the type of food that children and teens choose to eat and what is available nearby, calling into question the theory that living in "food deserts" increases obesity rates.

Carey, John, "The Case for Farm Bill Conservation Programs in the Great Lakes Region," National Wildlife Federation, February 2012, www.nwf.org/News-and-Magazines/Media-Center/Reports/Archive/2012/03-21-12-The-Case-For-Farm-Bill-Conservation-Programs-in-the-Great-Lakes-Region.aspx.
Programs that pay farmers to protect wetlands, manage fertilizer and waste effectively and take other conservation steps help protect the Great Lakes region's multibillion-dollar tourism, fishing and shipping industries and save millions of dollars in cleanup costs.

Carlson, Andrea, and Elizabeth Frazao, "Are Healthy Foods Really More Expensive? It Depends on How You Measure the Price," Economic Information Bulletin EIB-96, U.S. Department of Agriculture, May 2012, www.ers.usda.gov/publications/eib96/.
An analysis by the U.S. Department of Agriculture's Economic Research Service finds that healthy foods are cheaper than unhealthy foods when they are compared based on price by weight or price per average portion, rebutting the belief that healthy foods are expensive.

The Next Step:

Additional Articles from Current Periodicals

Drought

Coleman, Isobel, "U.S. Drought and Rising Global Food Prices," Council on Foreign Relations, Aug. 2, 2012, www.cfr.org/food-security/us-drought-rising-global-food-prices/p28777?cid=nlc-public-the_world_this_week-link5-20120730.
Global food prices are rising partly because of an ongoing drought in the Midwest that has affected U.S. crop production.

Lochhead, Carolyn, "Drought Punishes State's Beef Ranchers," *The San Francisco Chronicle*, July 29, 2012, p. A1, www.sfgate.com/nation/article/State-s-ranchers-hit-by-Midwest-drought-3743945.php.
Ranchers will likely have to endure the financial effects of the Midwest drought a little longer as political bickering delays the passage of a farm bill that would bring economic relief.

Miles, Jack, "Blunt Calls for Federal Funds to Benefit Drought-Hit Farms," *Daily Star-Journal* (Mo.), Aug. 2, 2012.
Sen. Roy Blunt, R-Mo., has called for congressional action to aid livestock farmers in Missouri and other drought-stricken states.

Food Deserts

De Vries, Karl, and Kelly Heyboer, "Broken Food Chain," *Star-Ledger* (Newark, N.J.), Aug. 8, 2011, p. 1, www.nj.com/news/index.ssf/2011/08/stranded_in_food_deserts_hundr.html.
About 340,000 people in New Jersey have limited access to supermarkets and nutritious food, says the USDA.

Dreier, Hannah, "Neighborhoods Served By Small Grocers Called 'Food Deserts,' " *San Jose* (Calif.) *Mercury News*, Sept. 20, 2011.
Residents in "food deserts" often rely on fast-food restaurants to feed their families.

Guy, Sandra, "Report: Chicago Food Desert Shrinks 40 Percent," *Chicago Sun-Times*, Oct. 25, 2011, p. 11, www.suntimes.com/business/8391023-420/report-chicago-food-desert-shrinks-40-percent-end-in-sight.html.
Chicago's "food desert" has shrunk by 40 percent in the past five years, but the number of residents without access to healthy food remains high.

Insurance Subsidies

Casteel, Chris, "Report Recommends Limits on Crop Insurance Subsidies," *The Oklahoman*, April 13, 2012, p. A1, newsok.com/federal-report-calls-for-limits-on-crop-insurance-subsidies/article/3665855.
Congress should consider scaling back federal crop insurance subsidies because high commodity prices lead to higher costs for taxpayers, says the Government Accountability Office.

DeWitte, Dave, "Report Finds Privacy-Shielded Crop Insurance Subsidies Can Be Massive," *The Gazette* (Cedar Rapids, Iowa), May 31, 2012, thegazette.com/2012/05/31/report-finds-privacy-shielded-crop-insurance-subsidies-can-be-massive/.
A report by the environmental organization Environmental Working Group concludes that a disproportionate share of insurance subsidies for premium crops is going to big businesses.

Semple Jr., Robert B., "Where the Trough Is Overflowing," *The New York Times*, June 3, 2012, p. SR12, www.nytimes.com/2012/06/03/opinion/sunday/where-the-trough-is-overflowing.html.
The existing federal crop insurance program is expected to cost $9 billion annually in coming years.

Supplemental Nutrition Assistance Program (SNAP)

Lesley, Bruce, and Scott McCown, "SNAP Is a Program That Helps Kids," *San Antonio Express-News*, July 14, 2012, p. B9, www.mysanantonio.com/opinion/commentary/article/Cutting-child-nutrition-is-wrong-way-to-solve-3705675.php.
SNAP enables 20 million children to get the food they need to stay healthy and focused in school, say the presidents of the First Focus Campaign for Children and the Center for Public Policy Priorities.

Mascaro, Lisa, "Food Stamp Funding May Be Reduced," *Los Angeles Times*, June 20, 2012, p. A6, articles.latimes.com/2012/jun/20/nation/la-na-food-stamps-20120620.
Congressional Republicans are leading efforts to save billions of dollars over the next decade by limiting SNAP eligibility.

CITING *CQ RESEARCHER*

Sample formats for citing these reports in a bibliography include the ones listed below. Preferred styles and formats vary, so please check with your instructor or professor.

MLA STYLE

Jost, Kenneth. "Remembering 9/11," CQ Researcher 2 Sept. 2011: 701-732.

APA STYLE

Jost, K. (2011, September 2). Remembering 9/11. *CQ Researcher, 9*, 701-732.

CHICAGO STYLE

Jost, Kenneth. "Remembering 9/11." *CQ Researcher*, September 2, 2011, 701-732.

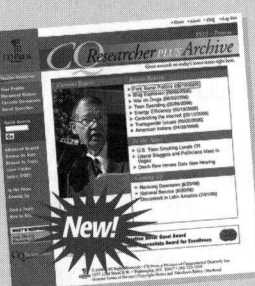

CQ Researcher

Published by CQ Press, an Imprint of SAGE Publications, Inc.

www.cqresearcher.com

Genetically Modified Food

Should labels be required?

California voters will decide in November whether foods produced with genetically modified ingredients — so-called GM foods — should bear special labels. The controversial measure reflects the uneven acceptance of genetically engineered crops since their rise in the 1990s. Organic farmers and other opponents of GM foods contend they may pose health or environmental risks, despite widespread scientific consensus that they are not inherently more risky than other crops. Foes of the labeling referendum, including GM farmers and seed producers, such as Monsanto, say that GM crops are more productive, pest-resistant and environmentally friendly than conventional crops and that the fast-growing organic industry and misguided consumer groups are to blame for confusion about the science behind them. Even as GM crops have been embraced by U.S. commodity growers, Europe remains skeptical. However, eight of the 10 countries with the most acreage in biotech crops are now in the developing world.

Plant breeder Alamgir Hossain is developing Golden Rice for Bangladesh. Supporters of the genetically engineered variety say it could save the lives of up to 2.7 million children a year, but it has yet to be planted commercially; the Philippines may approve it for cultivation in 2013.

INSIDE THIS REPORT

THE ISSUES 719
BACKGROUND 726
CHRONOLOGY 727
CURRENT SITUATION 732
AT ISSUE........................733
OUTLOOK 735
BIBLIOGRAPHY 738
THE NEXT STEP 739

CQ Researcher • Aug. 31, 2012 • www.cqresearcher.com
Volume 22, Number 30 • Pages 717-740

Los Angeles | London | New Delhi
Singapore | Washington DC

RECIPIENT OF SOCIETY OF PROFESSIONAL JOURNALISTS AWARD FOR EXCELLENCE ◆ AMERICAN BAR ASSOCIATION SILVER GAVEL AWARD

GENETICALLY MODIFIED FOOD

THE ISSUES

719 • Were the benefits of GM crops to consumers oversold?
• Have existing GM crops caused environmental harm?
• Should GM foods be labeled?

BACKGROUND

726 **'Green Revolution'** High-yield plants helped spark a boom in agricultural production in the 1960s.

730 **The Roaring '90s** U.S. farmers rapidly switched to new GM varieties.

730 **StarLink Recall** Contamination from GM corn not for human consumption forced a food recall in 2000.

CURRENT SITUATION

732 **In the Pipeline** Drought-resistant corn and soybeans rich in heart-healthy oils are being developed.

734 **Labeling Battle** California's controversial Nov. 6 ballot referendum calls for special labels on GM foods.

OUTLOOK

735 **Conflict Ahead?** Increasing friction between organic farmers and the bio-tech industry over seed-production techniques is seen.

SIDEBARS AND GRAPHICS

720 **Soybeans and Corn Are Among Biggest GM Crops** Commodities, or crops sold on futures exchanges, account for 80 percent of GM crop field trials in the developed world.

721 **Permits for GM Crop-Testing on Rise** Six times as many were issued in 2008 as in 1992.

722 **Genetic Engineering by the Numbers** Key data about GM foods and the industry.

723 **Most Acreage Used for GM Crops** More than 90 percent of U.S. soybeans are herbicide tolerant.

724 **U.S. Leads in Biotech Agriculture** More than 170 million acres of biotech crops are farmed.

727 **Chronology** Key events since 1953.

728 **Is Tampering With DNA Inherently Wrong?** Anti-GM foods ethicist Jeremy Rifkin launched the debate in 1977.

733 **At Issue** Should foods containing genetically modified ingredients be labeled?

FOR FURTHER RESEARCH

737 **For More Information** Organizations to contact.

738 **Bibliography** Selected sources used.

739 **The Next Step** Additional articles.

739 **Citing *CQ Researcher*** Sample bibliography formats.

Cover: International Rice Research Institute

CQ Researcher

Aug. 31, 2012
Volume 22, Number 30

MANAGING EDITOR: Thomas J. Billitteri tjb@cqpress.com

ASSISTANT MANAGING EDITOR: Kathy Koch kkoch@cqpress.com

CONTRIBUTING EDITOR: Thomas J. Colin tcolin@cqpress.com

ASSOCIATE EDITOR: Kenneth Jost

STAFF WRITER: Marcia Clemmitt

CONTRIBUTING WRITERS: Peter Katel, Barbara Mantel, Jennifer Weeks

DESIGN/PRODUCTION EDITOR: Olu B. Davis

ASSISTANT EDITOR: Darrell Dela Rosa

FACT CHECKER: Michelle Harris

Los Angeles | London | New Delhi
Singapore | Washington DC

An Imprint of SAGE Publications, Inc.

VICE PRESIDENT AND EDITORIAL DIRECTOR, HIGHER EDUCATION GROUP: Michele Sordi

DIRECTOR, ONLINE PUBLISHING: Todd Baldwin

CQ Researcher (ISSN 1056-2036) is printed on acid-free paper. Published weekly, except: (March wk. 5) (May wk. 4) (July wk. 1) (Aug. wks. 3, 4) (Nov. wk. 4) and (Dec. wks. 3, 4). Published by SAGE Publications, Inc., 2455 Teller Rd., Thousand Oaks, CA 91320. Annual full-service subscriptions start at $1,054. For pricing, call 1-800-834-9020. To purchase a *CQ Researcher* report in print or electronic format (PDF), visit www.cqpress.com or call 866-427-7737. Single reports start at $15. Bulk purchase discounts and electronic-rights licensing are also available. Periodicals postage paid at Thousand Oaks, California, and at additional mailing offices. POSTMASTER: Send address changes to *CQ Researcher*, 2300 N St., N.W., Suite 800, Washington, DC 20037.

Genetically Modified Food

BY JASON MCLURE

THE ISSUES

When California voters go to the polls Nov. 6, they'll be walking straight into a massive food fight.

On the ballot will be a highly contentious proposal to require special labels on foods produced with genetically modified ingredients — so-called GM foods. The federal government does not require that GM foods be labeled unless they change the nutritional content or add toxic or allergenic properties to food. Labeling advocates want any GM food to be labeled, as more than 40 countries do, including all of Europe, Japan and China.

California's labeling referendum has strong support from environmental and food-safety groups that say GM foods — made from crops that have had genetic material inserted or deleted in a laboratory to give them specific advantages, such as resistance to herbicides — may pose health or environmental risks.

Also among the staunchest labeling supporters are organic farmers, who compete with GM food producers. "People have a right to know what's in the food we eat and feed to our children," said Stacy Malkan, a spokeswoman for California Right to Know, a coalition that has spearheaded the ballot measure. [1]

But GM farming giants and other referendum foes argue that the health and environmental concerns are unfounded, and that the labeling effort is an attempt to demonize a technology with enormous potential benefits. They note that after extensive research, U.S. and international scientific organizations ranging from the National Academy of Science to the World Health Organization have concluded that GM crops don't inherently pose more risk than their conventional counterparts. What's more, they say genetically modified crops are more productive, pest-resistant and environmentally friendly than conventional crops — and they've been consumed by millions of people in the U.S. for nearly two decades without any documented health consequences. [2]

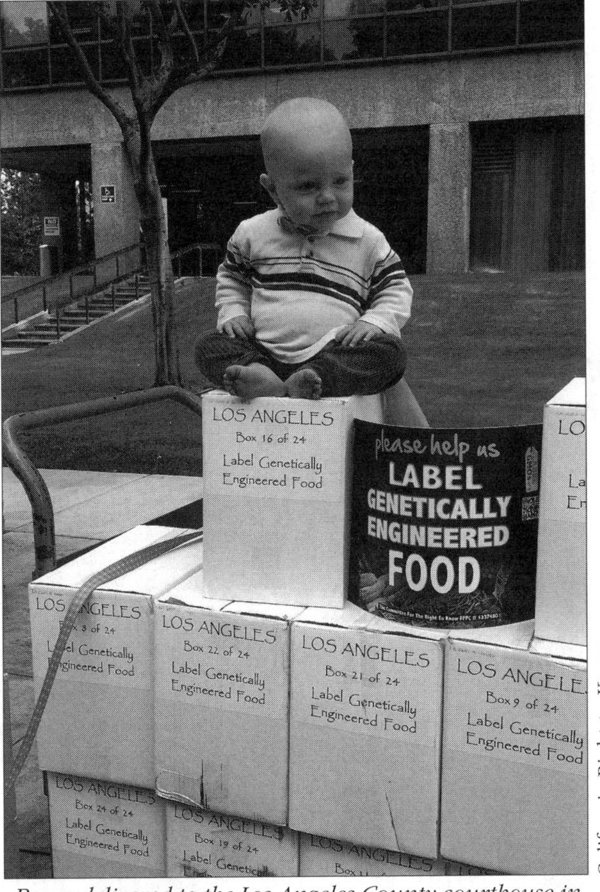

California Right to Know

Boxes delivered to the Los Angeles County courthouse in May hold nearly one million signatures from California voters calling for a ballot initiative in November requiring labeling of genetically modified (GM) foods. Organic farmers and some consumer groups support the initiative, contending GM foods may pose health or environmental risks. The GM farming industry notes that scientific organizations ranging from the National Academy of Science to the World Health Organization say GM crops pose no more risk than conventional foods.

"Do you give the same scientific weight to evolution and creationism?" asks Adrian Dubock, director of the Golden Rice Project, which seeks to cut malnutrition and save millions of lives in the developing world through the use of GM rice varieties enriched with Vitamin A. "There's a point where the scientific controversy is over."

On the contrary, the opposition seems to be growing, says Douglas Gurian-Sherman, a senior scientist with the Union of Concerned Scientists, which favors labeling. "There is clearly more interest and momentum behind it than there was 10 years ago," he says.

Indeed, big agribusiness and biotechnology companies that engineer or produce GM crops are pouring resources into halting that momentum. By mid-August, Monsanto, Dupont Pioneer, Cargill and others had contributed nearly $25 million to defeat the statewide initiative — nearly 10 times the amount raised by supporters. [3]

California is the nation's biggest consumer market, and passage of the referendum could influence GM food policies nationwide. Labeling laws or ballot measures have been proposed in 20 states in the past year, according to the Biotechnology Industry Organization (BIO), a trade group. And more than a million people signed a petition this year urging the Food and Drug Administration (FDA) to require labeling.

California's referendum campaign is part of a much bigger, two-decades-old debate about the safety, effectiveness and commercial viability of agricultural biotechnology. GM supporters argue that abundant peer-reviewed

Field Trials Focus on Corn and Other Big Crops

More than three-quarters of the crop field trials conducted by 24 developed countries (excluding China and India) from 2003-2008 were for big commodity crops, or crops bought and sold on futures exchanges. Only 15 percent of the trials were for GM fruits, vegetables, nuts and other specialty crops, which biotech companies have largely abandoned in favor of industrially grown commodities, such as corn and cotton.

Genetically Modified Crop Field Trials in Developed Countries, 2003-2008

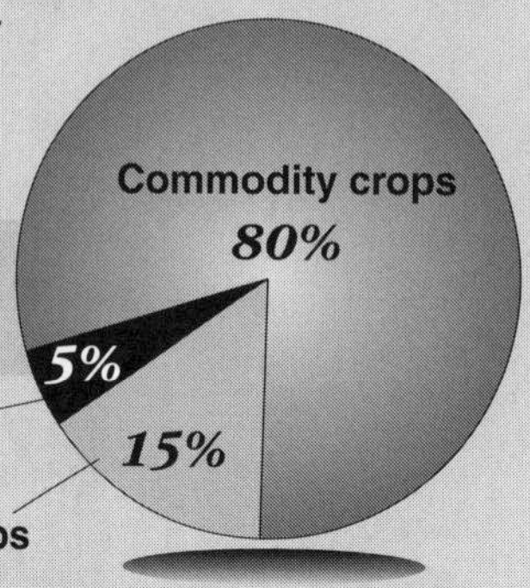

Commodity crops	80%
Specialty crops	15%
Forest tree products	5%

Source: Jamie K. Miller and Kent J. Bradford, "The Regulatory Bottleneck for Biotech Specialty Crops," Nature Biotechnology, *October 2010, p. 1014, www.nature.com/nbt/journal/v28/n10/full/nbt1010-1012.html*

research shows GM crops are safe and that uninformed pressure groups and the organic-farming industry have thwarted GM progress. Opponents argue that the jury is still out on the safety and environmental effects of GM crops and that, at the very least, growers should better inform the public about the use of gene-transferring techniques in food.

The techniques, which have been perfected in laboratories over the past 40 years, include bombarding target cells with heavy metals coated with the gene to be transferred; using a naturally occurring bacterium to transfer genes into the host cell and using a pulse of electricity to introduce genes into the targeted cell. [4]

Two technologies currently dominate the GM farming industry:

• Some crops have been modified to be able to survive the weed-killer glyphosate, commonly sold under Monsanto's Roundup brand. So-called Roundup Ready crops decrease the need to till before planting, saving farmers time and money and reducing erosion and loss of soil moisture. Glyphosate is among the least toxic herbicides that can kill a broad spectrum of weeds, and thus is safer for farmworkers and less environmentally damaging than many chemical alternatives. [5]

• The introduction of genes from the soil bacterium *Bacillus thurengiensis* (Bt) produces a substance toxic to many pests but harmless to humans, wildlife and most beneficial insects, such as bees. While Bt has long been used by organic farmers, scientists have produced GM crops that manufacture their own Bt in the part of the plant susceptible to attack from pests — such as corn-plant roots prone to root-worm attack. Bt has allowed many farmers to reduce the use of harmful insecticides. In China alone, the use of Bt cotton has halved pesticide use since the crop was introduced in 1997, and the population of beneficial pest-eating insects such as ladybugs has increased, because they are resistant to Bt. [6]

The use of GM crops has become widespread among U.S. growers of commodities, or big crops sold on futures exchanges. Eighty-eight percent of corn and 94 percent of cotton, for example, came from GM strains in 2012. [7] Because corn and soy are ubiquitous in processed foods in the United States, from corn syrup-sweetened Coca-Cola to crackers made with soybean oil, it's likely that most Americans consume a product containing a genetically modified ingredient every day.

Nonetheless, GM agriculture has made uneven progress over the past two decades. At the dawn of the GM food revolution in the mid-1990s, scientists and industry officials predicted it would produce healthier food that would be slower to rot, taste better and reduce agriculture's impact on the environment. But some GM crops have failed to produce benefits, and some once-promising research has been abandoned. For instance, researchers have all but given up on developing GM fruits and other so-called specialty crops because the costs of gaining regulatory approval do not justify the potential economic rewards, plant scientists say.

They argue that valuable research has been hindered by consumer resistance to GM foods, due to either misunderstanding or confusion about the safety of the crops. Twenty-one percent of respondents to a 2010 Thomson Reuters and NPR poll thought GM food is safe, while 15 percent said it was unsafe. Nearly two-thirds weren't sure. [8] Some GM proponents contend that opponents resist GM crops because they oppose industrial farming, which is how most GM crops in the United States are grown.

Organic farmers, meanwhile, fear that their non-GM crops could be contaminated by the spread of genetically modified traits by wind and insect cross-pollination. Once those traits are in the agricultural gene pool, they say, there's no way to remove them.

"We believe that this technology doesn't make sense in the long run for the human species," says Bill Duesing, an organic farmer in Oxford, Conn., and Interstate Council president of the 5,000-member Northeast Organic Farming Association. "This is pollution with a life of its own; it spreads forever."

Environmental groups such as the Union of Concerned Scientists say the U.S. Department of Agriculture (USDA) does not adequately examine the environmental impacts of introducing new farming methods on millions of acres, such as possible resistance to Bt and Roundup by weeds and insects. In addition, some scientists complain that biotech companies deny access to their patent-protected GM technology if they suspect researchers may cast doubt on its effectiveness, a charge companies deny. [9]

Meanwhile, some consumers and organic farmers pose philosophical objections to GM plant-breeding methods. "It's the kind of breeding that would never happen in the wild," Duesing says. Resistance to genetic crop engineering ratcheted up a notch this summer after the House passed a version of a new farm bill that critics said would weaken the USDA's regulatory power over the industry while cutting funds for more stringent Environmental Protection Agency (EPA) regulations. The House bill would "create multiple backdoor approval mechanisms that would allow for the premature commercialization of untested biotech traits to enter our food system," charged Colin O'Neil, a policy analyst at the Center for Food Safety, a Washington-based advocacy group. [10]

But biotechnology researchers and industry advocates argue that environmental and food-safety groups are creating public confusion about GM foods long after scientific studies have established that the technology is safe. "We're seeing in the last couple years a vocal opposition to the technology, and food-labeling requirements are just one of the tactics being employed," says Cathleen Enright, vice president for food and agriculture at the Biotechnology Industry Organization.

Labeling initiatives, she says, are "essentially meant not to inform consumers about genetically engineered food but rather to eliminate the technology from agriculture in this country."

Hundreds of Permits Issued for GM Crop Testing

Permits for U.S. field trials of genetically modified (GM) crops totaled 743 in 2008, more than six times the number in 1992. Most permits were for soybeans, corn and other commodity crops, which are far larger than specialty crops such as fruits and vegetables, and thus are more profitable. Successful field trials help the government decide whether to allow GM crops to be commercially produced.

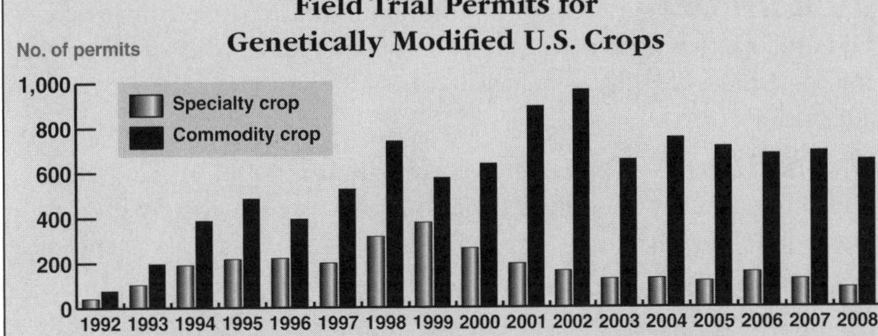

Source: Jamie K. Miller and Kent J. Bradford, "The Regulatory Bottleneck for Biotech Specialty Crops," Nature Biotechnology, *October 2010, p. 1014, www.nature.com/nbt/journal/v28/n10/full/nbt1010-1012.html*

Ironically, for more than a decade some vaccines and life-saving medicines have been genetically engineered in the laboratory by creating new organisms that would never be created in nature — some even made by mixing plant and animal genes. Yet opposition to such products has been much more muted. Likewise, nongenetic engineered plant-breeding methods that would be impossible in nature, such as bombarding plants with radiation or carcinogenic chemicals to induce genetic change, have not attracted such widespread opposition.

Dubock says unfounded opposition to GM foods has caused needless delays in technologies that would potentially save hundreds of thousands of lives. Golden Rice was hailed on the cover of *Time* magazine a dozen years ago as having the potential to save a million children a year. That's because the rice strain was genetically modified to be rich in beta-carotene — a vitamin A precursor — that could help stave off blindness, infections and other maladies among impoverished children in countries like India and Bangladesh. Current estimates say widespread use of the crop could save up to 2.7 million children a year, according to Dubock, but it has not been commercially planted due to suspicion about genetic engineering. That may change soon — the Philippines likely will permit cultivation in 2013.

"The activists have been very successful in promulgating their view," Dubock asserts. "We could have given it to farmers everywhere. We are not able to because of international regulations that prevent us from putting seeds in an envelope and mailing them to people who could use them."

As scientists, environmentalists, consumer advocates and organic farmers debate the effects of GM foods, here are some of the questions being asked:

Were the consumer benefits of GM crops oversold?

The future for genetically modified crops envisioned by biotech advocates

Genetic Engineering by the Numbers

400 million — Acres worldwide planted in genetically modified crops in 2011.

170 million — Acres of GM crops in U.S.

74.8 million — GM acres planted in 2011 by Brazil, the second-largest biotech nation after the U.S.

25 million — Dollars that companies that engineer or produce GM crops had contributed by mid-August to defeat the labeling initiative in California — nearly 10 times the amount raised by supporters.

2.7 million — Impoverished children in countries like India and Bangladesh whose lives could be saved by genetically engineered Golden Rice.

1 million-plus — People who signed a petition this year urging the Food and Drug Administration (FDA) to require labeling of GM foods.

20 — States in which labeling laws or ballot measures have been proposed in the past year.

12 — Percentage of the world's arable land planted in GM crops.

Sources: International Service for the Acquisition of Agri-Biotech Applications, Feb. 7, 2012; Biotechnology Industry Organization; United Nations; U.S. Department of Agriculture

in the 1990s looked substantially different from the GM landscape today.

Developing countries without reliable energy for refrigeration would have an additional supply of food "with no additional cost or environmental effect," Charles Gasser, a cellular biologist at the University of California-Davis and former Monsanto researcher, predicted optimistically in 1994. Biotechnology would provide such countries with slow-ripening fruits and vegetables with shelf lives up to five times longer than regular produce, he said. [11]

Not only have such technologies not been commercialized, but the scale of adoption of genetically modified crops has not matched earlier predictions, such as this one from Val Giddings, vice president for food and agriculture for the Biotechnology Industry Organization (BIO), who said in 1998: "Within five years — and certainly within 10 — some 90 to 95 percent of plant-derived food material in the United States will come from genetically engineered techniques." Furthermore, he predicted, "It'll take a little bit longer for these technologies to penetrate into the organic market, but it will. As the benefits become clearer, . . . opposition will be replaced by understanding, and adoption will follow." [12]

Instead, the organic foods industry — which rebuffed GM crops when they were first commercialized in the mid-1990s — has seen record growth, while GM crop research has slowed markedly. Biotech companies have largely abandoned pursuing genetically modified varieties of fruits, vegetables, nuts and other specialty crops in favor of industrially grown commodities, such as corn and cotton. Between 1994 and 1998, U.S. regulatory authorities approved 17 GM fruits and vegetables, which the USDA calls specialty crops. Over the next decade they approved only three, even though specialty crops account for 40 percent of U.S. agricultural revenues. [13]

Commercialized in 1996, Bt insecticidal crops and so-called Roundup Ready crops tolerant of herbicides became some of the most rapidly adopted agricultural technologies in history. But 16 years later, the two modifications are being used largely in only three row crops: corn, soybeans and cotton, which are grown on a large scale. The three commodities account for 94 percent of the world's acreage planted in GM crops. [14]

Critics of biotechnology say other GM varieties haven't been developed because researchers haven't been able to deliver the beneficial new products they promised. "This technology seems to me to be a fundamentally failed technology, because the science just didn't work," says Andrew Kimbrell, executive director of the Center for Food Safety, a Washington-based consumer group that has opposed GM crops and helped organize the labeling petition to the FDA.

In other words, he explains, while Roundup Ready and Bt insecticidal crops were extremely popular with large-scale commodity farmers, the crops haven't provided an identifiable benefit to consumers. "In 30 years, we've yet to come up with a single [genetic] trait that's advantageous to the consumer," Kimbrell adds. "It's not likely they're going to succeed in the near future."

Both opponents and supporters of the technology agree that the decision by biotech companies to first market herbicide-resistant and insecticidal commodity crops did not help to garner public acceptance and may have lowered perceptions of the potential consumer benefits of the technology.

"It's easy for consumers to reject GMOs [genetically modified organisms], because they don't taste better or smell any better, and they're not noticeably cheaper," says Robert Paarlberg, a political scientist at Wellesley College who researches the debate over biotech foods. "Most of the economic gains are not captured by the consumer but by the farmer and the biotech seed companies."

GM seed producer Monsanto tightly controls use of its product. Farmers who buy Monsanto GM seeds while they are covered by patents are barred from saving them from season to season as they may do with conventional crops.

Some organic farmers, who shun pesticides and GM crops, say the benefits of biotechnology touted by many scientists are illusory. "You keep being told the same promises or propaganda that you heard 20 years ago: It's going to reduce pesticides, it's going to be safer, it's going to produce more food," says Connecticut farmer Duesing.

But he says the way in which genetically engineered crops were developed in the United States — via monoculture industrial farming — has mainly benefited the seed companies. "Nature works because of biodiversity," he says. Growing a single crop on thousands of acres "is the absolute opposite of biodiversity."

Others say the potential benefits of biotechnology to farmers in poor countries have been exaggerated. "Technology is not going to solve the problems of poor farmers," says Rachel Schurman, a sociologist at the University of Minnesota. Farming practices that dramatically boosted agricultural output during the "Green Revolution" in the 1960s and '70s — such as high-yield crop varieties, irrigation and heavy fertilizer and pesticide use — still have not trickled down to many of the poorest farmers in the developing world, she points out. "If they're going to devote all of these resources," she asks, "does it make economic sense to devote them to expensive technologies?"

Most Acreage Used for GM Crops

More than 90 percent of the farmland for soybeans in the United States is dedicated to genetically modified (GM) herbicide-tolerant varieties. Most acreage for cotton and corn is also used for herbicide-tolerant or insect-resistant varieties, or both.

U.S. Acreage Dedicated to GM Crops, 2012

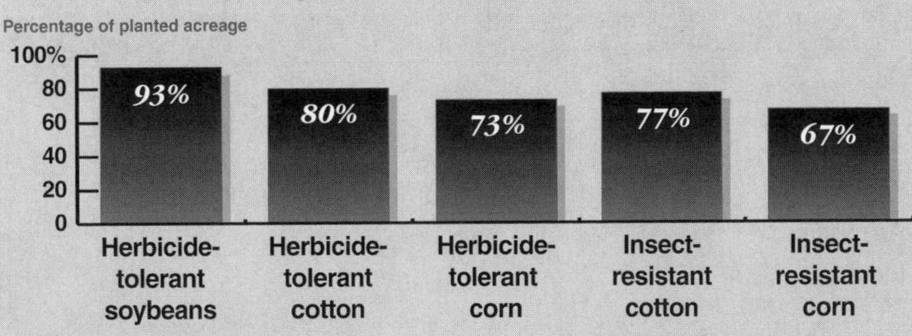

Source: "Adoption of Genetically Engineered Crops in the U.S.," U.S. Department of Agriculture, July 2012, www.ers.usda.gov/data-products/adoption-of-genetically-engineered-crops-in-the-us/recent-trends-in-ge-adoption.aspx

While supporters of biotechnology may have overstated the possibilities of biotech foods, so too did opponents exaggerate the dangers, says Gregory Jaffe, biotechnology project director at the Center for Science in the Public Interest. "I don't think we've seen a lot of detrimental impacts on the environment yet," he says. "Similarly, we haven't seen some of the huge benefits that the industry had also suggested would happen."

Some biotech supporters blame the slow development of new GM varieties on opposition generated by food and environmental groups such as the Center for Food Safety and the Union of Concerned Scientists. The failure is "directly attributable" to "the people who are claiming this as a failure of biotech," says UC's Gasser. "The evidence was we could do it."

Others, like Harry Klee, a former Monsanto scientist who is now at the University of Florida, say progress in developing new crops — especially specialty crops like tomatoes — is impeded by high regulatory costs. Providing research data to make a single genetic alteration in a tomato variety, he says, can cost up to $15 million.

Dubock of the Golden Rice Project says the cost of regulatory approval has kept GM crops out of the hands of all but the best-funded multinational corporations.

"Do we want this technology to be only ruled by multinationals, or do we want it to be accessed by startups and developing countries?" he asks. "It's really a paradox that the attitudes promulgated by the activists against the technology reinforce the status of GM crops as row crops for the industrialized world."

Have existing GM crops caused environmental harm?

Most of the environmental concerns initially raised about biotech crops have not materialized. However, one worry — that the large-scale adoption of GM commodity crops would accelerate the natural development of resistance to the relatively safe Roundup herbicide and Bt insecticide — appears to have become reality.

Researchers have documented cases of resistance to Bt insecticide by the corn borer and corn rootworm, the two main pests killed by Bt corn

U.S Leads in Biotech Agriculture

More than 170 million acres of biotech crops are under cultivation in the United States, more than twice Brazil's acreage, which ranks second. Experts credit faster technological advances, more lenient regulations and expanding economic benefits for the U.S. lead.

Biotech Acreage by Country, 2011

Country	Acres (in millions)	Biotech crops
United States	170.5	Corn, soybean, cotton, canola, sugarbeet, alfalfa, papaya, squash
Brazil	74.9	Soybean, corn, cotton
Argentina	58.6	Soybean, corn, cotton
India	26.2	Cotton
Canada	25.7	Canola, corn, soybean, sugarbeet
China	9.6	Cotton, papaya, poplar, tomato, sweet pepper
Paraguay	6.9	Soybean
Pakistan	6.4	Cotton
South Africa	5.7	Corn, soybean, cotton
Uruguay	3.2	Soybean, corn

Source: Clive James, "Global Status of Commercialized Biotech/GM Crops: 2011," International Service for the Acquisition of Agri-Biotech Applications, 2011, p. 2, www.isaaa.org/purchasepublications/itemdescription.asp?ItemType=BRIEFS&Control=IB043-2011

— and a Roundup-resistant strain of a weed called waterhemp already has spread to 10 states. [15]

"In 2011, we saw glyphosate-resistant waterhemp explode across the Midwest," said Dan Westberg, a technical market manager at BASF, a maker of pesticides and biotech seeds. "It was a tipping point for farmers and another sign that we have to think beyond glyphosate alone for weed control." [16]

Experts say Roundup and Bt have become so widespread that resistant mutations have developed faster than they normally would in conventional crops because other types of controls are absent, an outcome that some GM opponents predicted.

A coalition of environmental groups published a report in 1990 predicting the rise of resistant weeds. [17] "We now know that inside the Trojan horse of biotechnology are just more herbicides and stronger weeds," Margaret Mellon, a biotechnology expert with the Union of Concerned Scientists, wrote in May. [18]

Farmers could have slowed the spread of resistance by planting "refuges," or small plots, of nonbiotech crops, which would allow some of the pests to survive and breed without generating resistance. Yet farmers growing Roundup Ready crops are not required by law to provide refuges, and those growing Bt crops are supposed to provide refuges equivalent to 20 percent of their acreage (or 50 percent for some types of Bt cotton). But a 2009 study found that up to 25 percent of corn farmers were not complying with refuge requirements. [19]

Opponents of biotechnology point out that resistance to existing GM products does not harm biotech multinationals like Monsanto, which already are developing crops resistant to other, more toxic pesticides. It's no coincidence, say the critics, that the new products will be coming on the market just as the patents for Roundup Ready crops expire, in 2014. When the patents expire, other companies can produce seed with the same technology, and farmers can legally plant seed harvested from Roundup Ready plants.

"It's a chemical arms race going backwards," says Kimbrell of the Center for Food Safety. "Now we have to close our eyes and hope we do find this magic, new herbicide. I don't think that's very good policy."

Many biotech supporters are equally worried about resistance to Bt and Roundup. But they say the problem is not biotechnology itself but American-style industrial farming, which allows a single crop to be planted year after year over vast swathes of land, which accelerates resistance to pesticides.

"If people had been smarter — the farmers, the companies and the U.S. Department of Agriculture — they could have easily developed rotations and minimal-use programs to avoid resistance," says Raoul Adamchak, the organic farm coordinator at UC-Davis and co-author of *Tomorrow's Table: Organic Farming, Genetics and the Future of Food*. "Those issues come up with herbicides all the time. If you develop an integrated control strategy, you can put resistance off for many years, or possibly even indefinitely."

Biotech opponents also discount the environmental benefits of replacing more toxic herbicides and pesticides with the relatively safe Roundup and Bt.

"There are now Roundup-resistant weeds on millions of acres that are creating problems for farmers," says Jaffe, of the Center for Science in the Public Interest. "What does that mean? That just means you're going back to other forms of weed killers that are toxic. But we did get 20 years of using the less-toxic weed killer."

The increased productivity provided by biotech crops has also slowed deforestation, say GM proponents. "The reduced environmental impact and abundance in food supply that is offered with genetically engineered seed help to preserve biodiversity," says Enright, of the Biotechnology Industry Organization. "Instead of chopping down the Amazon or other pools of diversity, let's see what we can do on the land that we have." [20]

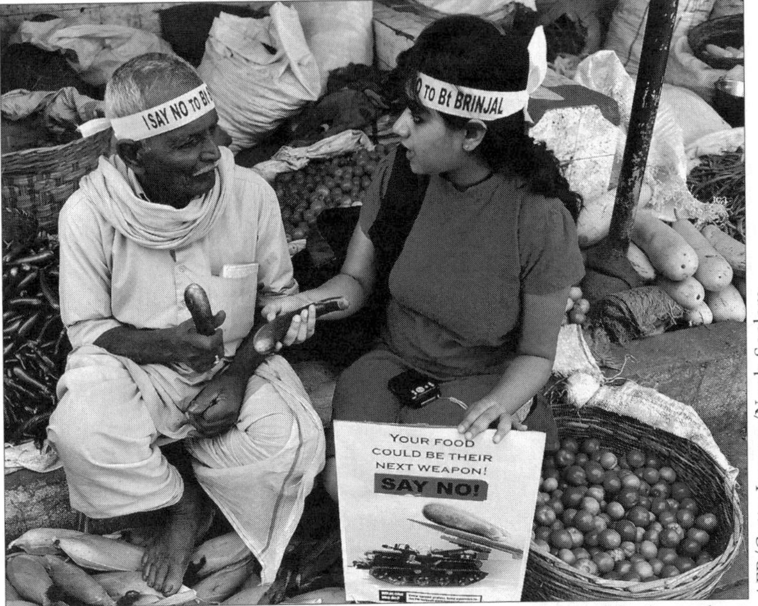

AFP/Getty Images/Noah Seelam

A Greenpeace activist campaigns against genetically modified eggplant (brinjal) at a farmers market in Hyderabad, India, on Jan. 19, 2010. The potential commercialization of a GM variety of the popular vegetable has drawn support and criticism. Cotton is currently the only GM crop permitted in India.

Roundup Ready crops also reduce the need for plowing to clear fields of weeds before planting, which saves topsoil. Bill Olthoff, who farms 1,800 acres of corn and soybeans in Kankakee, Ill., says that since switching to Roundup Ready soybeans he makes three fewer plowing runs over his field per crop, which conserves topsoil and tractor fuel, and he uses less herbicide. Additionally, he says, by using Bt corn he no longer has to use a more toxic insecticide, which can disrupt human and animal neurological systems.

"There's less use of fuel, less man-hours and less pesticide," says Olthoff. [21]

Should GM foods be labeled?

GM opponents say consumers have a right to know what they're eating and feeding their children. "Labeling is obvious — there is a fundamental physical change in the plants that's patented," says Kimbrell of the Center for Food Safety. "There are novel proteins in the plants, never seen before in food."

The Just Label It campaign, which supports California's referendum and organized the labeling petition to the FDA, argues that U.S. consumers are being effectively used as guinea pigs in testing GM foods. "The debate about the benefits and risks of GE crops may go on for a long time," says the group's website, JustLabelIt.org. "Meanwhile, an entire generation will have grown up consuming them. We should all have a choice about whether we want to participate in this grand experiment with our bodies and our environment."

A large majority of consumers agree, according to a poll of 1,000 people commissioned earlier this year by Just Label It. It found that 92 percent support mandatory labeling, a figure that changed only slightly after respondents heard arguments for and against labeling.

Cynthia LaPier, a mental health counselor in Massachusetts, feels she has a right to know whether her food contains genetically modified components. "It just makes me nervous when you take genetic matter from something else that wouldn't have been done in nature and put it into food," she told *The New York Times* earlier this year, having spent part of her morning furtively applying stickers reading "Warning May Contain GMOs" to cereal boxes at her local supermarket. [22]

Just Label It argues that sufficient testing has not yet been done on the technology. The University of Minnesota's Schurman argues that even if there is no specific scientific evidence that GM crops are more harmful than conventional varieties, there is a legitimate case for labeling them.

"I don't think scientific concerns are the only reason we should be concerned about the impact of technology," she says. "We should be able to make decisions about the kind of society we live in, and we can't make those decisions if we don't have information. It's a question of democracy."

Gurian-Sherman, of the Union of Concerned Scientists, says GM crops have helped to push farming more toward industrial agriculture, and consumers who favor more sustainable methods should be able to decide which kinds of foods they want to buy.

"Both Bt and herbicide tolerance work in simplified crop systems," says Gurian-Sherman. "If your aim is to be more and more efficient, you need to make agriculture [simpler], with many, many acres of one crop that is harvested with one type of machinery and simple pest control. All of those things are bad for the environment in a number of different ways."

Biotechnology supporters say labels will mislead consumers into believing there is something harmful to human health about GM foods. That's been the case in Europe, where labeling combined with public suspicion of genetically engineered foods has kept products containing GM crops off grocery store shelves.

Gasser, the UC Davis researcher, likens the debate to that over climate change, in which one side has overwhelming research data on its side but opponents are able to cast doubt on those findings with spurious arguments because the public has little understanding of the complex science involved.

"Climate science is the perfect example, because the anti-biotech people are on the wrong side of the argument both environmentally and scientifically," Gasser says.

He argues that since scientific research over the past two decades has vindicated genetic engineering in plant breeding, opponents are really left only with a philosophical argument about the so-called mutagenic techniques used to manipulate plant genes. Moreover, he says that GM opponents are hypocritical to single out genetic engineering in food crops as "unnatural." There are numerous conventional plant breeding methods that differ radically from how plants reproduce in the wild, including self-pollinating two different plant lines for seven or more generations and then crossing them; and triggering mutations through gamma rays, irradiation and carcinogenic chemicals.

Thousands of products have been developed using mutagenic techniques alone, according to the U.N.'s Food and Agriculture Organization, including more than 800 varieties of rice and familiar fruits such as the Rio Red grapefruit and a variety of the McIntosh apple. [23] Proponents say that, as with GM crops, there is no evidence that crops developed with mutagenic techniques are inherently more harmful to people or the environment than other crops.

"The fact that you're arguing about the one and not the other means your argument is not about safety it's about this religious view you have about biotech," says Gasser. "It's only the people who don't understand it that are scared of it. Unfortunately that's most everyone."

Opponents of labeling also argue that it is unfair to conflate arguments against the environmental harm caused by industrial agriculture with a lab technique for creating better seeds — since farming is damaging to the environment no matter what kind of seeds are used. "If everyone's goal is to have a more sustainable agriculture, to reduce pesticide use and to reduce [fertilizer] run-off, then this labeling campaign doesn't make any improvements," says Adamchak, the UC-Davis organic farmer. "I'd much rather see people putting lots of energy into promoting sustainable agriculture." ■

BACKGROUND

'Green Revolution'

Humans began collecting seeds even before they settled in farming villages millennia ago in the Near East.

Ancient governments often played a major role in introducing new plants to civilizations. An inscription from Mesopotamia tells of the ruler Sargon journeying to Anatolia to collect figs, vines and roses to introduce to his country in the 24th century B.C. In 1495 B.C., Egypt's Queen Hatshepsut sent a team to what is now Ethiopia and Somalia to find the fragrant tree that produces frankincense. [24]

For centuries farmers have selected seeds and cross-bred plants to produce crops that had little in common with wild species. Yet it was not until 1856 that Gregor Johann Mendel, an Augustinian monk in Austria, began his famous study of garden peas that led to the identification of the factors that control heredity. Mendel's work ushered in the study of genetics.

Among other benefits, it laid the groundwork for the birth of modern agriculture in the early 20th century. In 1905 British researcher Roland Biffen showed that a type of wheat resistant to rust fungus could pass the trait on to future generations. Since then dozens of crops, from potatoes to parsnips, have been bred to resist disease and insects. [25]

Government investments in breeding and agricultural technologies helped lead to rapid productivity increases in the 20th century. For example, yields of English wheat took a thousand years to increase from 0.5 to 2 metric tons per hectare,* but jumped from 2 to 6 metric tons in just 40 years during the period. [26]

Beginning in the 1960s, higher yielding plant varieties, combined with increased use of fertilizer, pesticides and irrigation, led to a global boom in agricultural production — especially in the developing world — known as the "Green Revolution."

In the early 1970s scientists first learned how to replicate DNA in the lab and then to introduce foreign genetic material into living organisms, such as bacteria. Initially, concern that transferring genes among organisms could create dangerous microbes led scientists to establish a National Institutes of Health committee to oversee the approval of biotech research. It soon became evident, however, that genetic engineering tended to weaken bacteria rather than strengthen them. The NIH ended restrictions on genetic research in the 1980s, setting the stage for the commercialization of numerous genetically engineered drugs, such as synthetic insulin for diabetics.

In 1992 the commercialization of genetically modified foods was accelerated when limits were put on FDA oversight of GM foods. The new policy meant

* A hectare equals about 2.47 acres; a metric ton equals about 2,200 pounds.

Continued on p. 728

Chronology

1950s-1960s

Scientists identify genes and begin investigating the role of DNA in plant development.

1953
American biochemist James Watson and British biophysicist Francis Crick describe the structure of DNA, setting the stage for mapping the genetic code.

1967
Lenape potato, a new variety bred for making potato chips is withdrawn from experimental production after high levels of toxins are found.

1970s-1980s

Scientists begin experimenting with genetic transformation of plants and animals.

1973
Scientists create first genetically engineered organism.

1983
Researchers transfer new DNA into plants, leading to the creation of genetically modified crops.

1989
Calgene Inc. receives U.S. patent for gene sequence in GM Flavr Savr tomato.

1990s

Biotech foods are marketed to the public despite environmental and health concerns.

1992
FDA decides not to require labeling of most GM foods, sparking mistrust of the technology.

1993
FDA allows cows to be injected with bovine growth hormone (rBGH) made from genetically modified bacteria, setting off consumer protests.

1994
FDA approves Flavr Savr tomato, first GM food approved for sale to consumers.

1996
Monsanto introduces Roundup Ready soybeans, first of several popular herbicide-tolerant or insecticide-producing crops.

1998
European Union (EU) halts approvals of new GM crops in what is termed an "unofficial moratorium."

2000s

Genetically engineered foods face continued criticism despite growing scientific consensus that they do not pose greater safety risks than conventional crops.

2000
Bowing to international demands, U.S. officials agree to label GM commodities for export. . . . Weeds resistant to Roundup discovered in Delaware. . . . Friends of the Earth, a major environmental group, reports that genes from StarLink corn, a GM crop approved only for animal consumption, have been discovered in taco shells. The discovery prompts recalls of corn products and lawsuits, but researchers are unable to document any human health effects. . . . Centers for Disease Control study concludes StarLink did not cause allergic reactions claimed by 28 people.

2002
National Center for Food and Agricultural Policy finds that GM crops in the United States produced four billion pounds of additional food and fiber on the same acreage, improved farm income by $1.5 billion and reduced pesticide use by 46 million pounds. . . . Monsanto announces it will delay introduction of GM wheat amid concerns from farmers that it will harm exports.

2003
Bollworms resistant to the Bt toxin, an insecticide produced by GM cotton, discovered in the South.

2004
Under U.S. pressure, EU drops de facto ban on GM crops but institutes mandatory labeling; many European stores won't stock GM foods because of consumer fears.

2008
Monsanto sells unit that produces rBGH, as major grocers including Walmart, Publix and Kroger decline to sell milk from cows treated with the product.

2010
After approving the sale of GM eggplant, India's environment minister declares a moratorium on the product because of public outcry.

2011
GM crops are grown on 395 million acres of farmland globally, though more than 90 percent is in just three crops: soybeans, corn and cotton.

2012
Anti-GMO groups file petitions containing more than 1 million signatures demanding that the FDA require GM foods be labeled. . . . Californian vote scheduled for Nov. 6 on ballot initiative requiring labeling for GM foods.

Is Tampering With DNA Inherently Wrong?

Ethicists and religious scholars have differing opinions.

Many people recoil instinctively from the idea of taking genes from one plant or animal and inserting them into another — especially if the process inserts an animal gene into a plant's DNA, for instance. Some view the creation of such new part-plant, part-animal organisms as "playing God" or a violation of the natural order.

Several of these objections were first voiced by Jeremy Rifkin, a leading critic of genetic engineering, as early as 1977 when he published a book entitled *Who Should Play God? The Artificial Creation of Life and What it Means for the Human Race.* Rifkin expanded on concerns voiced in that book with later writings on the implications of cloning animals and the creation of plant and animal chimeras, or organisms with genes from both kingdoms.

"The globalization of commerce and trade makes possible the wholesale reseeding of the Earth's biosphere with a laboratory-conceived second Genesis, an artificially produced bioindustrial nature designed to replace nature's own evolutionary scheme," Rifkin wrote. [1] "A global life-science industry is already beginning to wield unprecedented power over the vast biological resources of the planet. Life-science fields ranging from agriculture to medicine are being consolidated under the umbrella of giant 'life' companies in the emerging biotech marketplace."

Ethics research into agricultural biotechnology focuses on two questions: whether the benefits of GM crops outweigh the drawbacks, and whether genetic engineering is inherently wrong. The tangible benefits and drawbacks of genetic engineering are often discussed in the media but the latter question is largely overlooked.

While Rifkin approaches the question from the secular perspective of genetic engineering violating the dignity of nature, theologians have also argued against genetic engineering from a religious perspective. Paul Ramsey, a prominent Christian ethicist who taught at Princeton University in the 1970s and '80s, was a leading advocate of the idea that genetic engineering was inherently unethical and that reducing people and other beings to a collection of genetic traits was a flawed concept. He also argued that since human beings are inherently fallible, they are poor custodians of the building blocks of life.

"We should not play God before we have learned to be men, and as we learn to be men we will not want to play God," Ramsey wrote. [2]

The technology also has implications for religious and dietary traditions established long before the advent of molecular biology. For instance, some vegetarians have questioned whether they can eat a vegetable containing one or more genes taken from an animal.

"The resulting vegetable is no longer a pure vegetable, but instead a chimera with properties taken from the original plant, plus some additional characteristics from an animal," according to Marcus Williamson, a London-based vegetarian who writes for the website www.gmfoodnews.com. [3]

Likewise, the world's 1 billion Hindus — many of whom are vegetarians and all of whom revere cows as sacred — might be concerned about eating a plant containing bovine genes, just as a Jew or Muslim might be concerned about eating a GM food containing pork genes.

Such alterations are potentially within the technology's reach: The use of jellyfish genes to create plant and animal organ-

Continued from p. 726

the agency would give GM crops no more scrutiny than it gave crops produced through conventional breeding.

The FDA's resulting program of "voluntary" consultation set off a controversy that endures today. Activist and economist Jeremy Rifkin, founder and president of the Foundation On Economic Trends, launched the Pure Food Movement, arguing that biotech crops were likely to be harmful to human health and destroy the natural environment. [27] The outcry led biotech companies to universally take part in the voluntary process for reviewing new crops, in addition to mandatory regulation by the Department of Agriculture and in some cases the EPA. Many groups argued that the tests required by federal regulators were insufficient and too reliant on studies supplied by the biotech industry.

Monsanto, a large, St. Louis-based chemical manufacturer, was among the first companies to capitalize on biotechnology for commercial farming. Its scientists inserted cow DNA into bacteria that then worked like millions of tiny factories to produce synthetic bovine growth hormone, known as rBGH or rBST. The hormone was then administered to cows to induce greater milk production. In 1993, the FDA approved the hormone for dairy production after the American Medical Association, National Institutes of Health and American Academy of Pediatrics concluded milk from cows treated with the product was no different from other milk. [28]

Meanwhile, California-based Calgene Inc. developed a tomato that contained an extra bit of tomato DNA that had been altered in the lab. This new gene had been engineered to block production of an enzyme that makes tomatoes grow mushy and rot. Calgene's new Flavr Savr tomato was approved by federal regulators in 1994 and became the first genetically engineered food to be commercialized in the United States. [29]

But Flavr Savr turned out to be a failure. Activists wielding images of a tomato grafted onto a fish head, a reference to a different experimental tomato

isms that "glow" under UV light has been used as a method of "marking" the transference of other genetic traits by researchers. [4]

According to a review of the issue, as of 2008 there was no consensus about biotechnology within the world's three main monotheistic faiths — Islam, Judaism and Christianity — on the ethical and moral issues surrounding GM foods. [5]

Other ethicists see arguments questioning the inherent immorality of genetic engineering as logically flawed. From a religious perspective, those who argue that genetic engineering is a violation of God's creation must explain why genetic engineering is not also an expression of God's will, since God gave humans "free will," including the ability to create technology, according to David Koepsell, a philosophy professor at Delft University of Technology in the Netherlands. [6]

Those who would argue that genetic engineering is a misuse of free will are plagued by a lack of sacred writings supporting that conclusion, says Koepsell. The Bible, for example, says nothing about recombinant DNA.

They must also explain why altering DNA through genetic engineering is bad, but other forms of altering DNA through other techniques are acceptable, given that it is arguably distinct only as a method. "The speed and predictability of the changes brought about by genetic engineering do surpass the speed and predictability of changes accomplished by selective breeding techniques, but that seems a poor argument for saying the former is contrary to God's will, while the latter is acceptable," Koepsell writes. "Is it God's will that modifying nature is acceptable, but only provided we proceed slowly and haphazardly?"

Likewise Koepsell contends that those who argue against genetic engineering from a secular perspective must explain why other forms of genetic change, such as evolution, are not affronts to the "natural" order of things. They also must show that there is an inherent dignity to the current genetic makeup of any given species and why that genetic makeup should only be changed by some forms of genetic alteration and not others.

Still, Koepsell and some other advocates of the technology allow that its effects on our world over the long term are difficult to predict and could yet prove harmful in unexpected ways. In that respect biotechnology is hardly unique: few in the 19th century would have foreseen that the invention of the internal combustion engine would contribute to rising global temperatures, melting polar ice caps and disappearing species 100 years later.

— Jason McLure

---

[1] Jeremy Rifkin, *The Biotech Century: Harnessing the Gene and Remaking the World* (1998), excerpted by *The New York Times*, www.nytimes.com/books/first/r/rifkin-biotech.html.

[2] Paul Ramsey, *Fabricated Man: The Ethics of Genetic Control* (1970), p. 151.

[3] Marcus Williamson, "Genetically Modified Food — Not Suitable for Vegetarians," Connectotel.com, undated, www.connectotel.com/gmfood/gm260401.txt.

[4] "Glowing Proteins — A Guiding Star for Biochemistry," The Royal Swedish Academy of Sciences, The Nobel Prize in Chemistry 2008, Oct. 8, 2008, www.nobelprize.org/nobel_prizes/chemistry/laureates/2008/press.html.

[5] Emmanuel Omobowale, Peter Singer and Abdallah Daar, "The Three Monotheistic Religions and GM Food Technology: An Overview of Perspectives," BMC International Health and Human Rights, 2009, www.biomedcentral.com/1472-698X/9/18.

[6] David Koepsell, "The Ethics of Genetic Engineering," Center for Inquiry, Aug. 28, 2007.

developed by another company that contained a fish gene for cold resistance, portrayed the Calgene product as Frankenfood. The company's bigger problem was that the Flavr Savr was more susceptible than other varieties to pests in the main tomato-growing states of Florida and California, and it could still bruise and become unappealing even without becoming mushy. [30] What's more, many consumers concluded it didn't taste good enough to justify the higher price. By 1997 Flavr Savr was off the market.

rBGH was more successful commercially, though it too faced strong resistance. By 1999, both Canada and the European Union had banned the hormone, citing public opposition to use of hormones on dairy cows and gaps in research.

In the United States, more than a fifth of dairy cows were being injected with the synthetic hormone biweekly by 2002, with milk production rising by about one gallon per day in lactating cows. [31] But advocacy groups opposed the hormone, pointing to studies showing it increased bovine udder infections and led to higher usage of veterinary antibiotics, which potentially could lead to human resistance to the drugs. Other research, including some sponsored by hormone producers, disputed the findings. [32]

Resistance to rBGH helped propel the organic dairy industry's rapid growth. The number of certified organic dairy cows rose to 249,766 in 2008 from zero in 1995, according to the USDA. [33] Companies such as Unilever's Ben & Jerry's Ice Cream and Oakhurst Dairy in Maine successfully marketed their products as rGBH-free.

Meanwhile, rGBH use declined from 22 percent of U.S. dairy cows in 2002 to 17 percent in 2007, and major retailers such as Walmart, Kroger and Publix agreed to stop selling milk made from rBGH-treated cows in their private-label dairy products. With backlash against the hormone growing, Monsanto sold its rBGH division in 2008 to Eli Lilly & Co. [34]

The Roaring 1990s

More significant than the Flavr Savr or rBGH was Monsanto's introduction in 1995 and '96 of genetically engineered soybeans, corn and cotton that were either resistant to Roundup or contained Bt insecticide.

Many farmers rapidly switched to the new crops. In 1996 genetically engineered crops were grown in six countries on 4.2 million acres. By 2000 they were being grown on 109.2 million acres in 13 countries, though 68 percent of that acreage was in the United States, according to the Council for Biotechnology Information, an industry group.

While some food safety and environmental groups in the United States resisted the rapid growth of genetically modified foods, it set off a firestorm of protest in Europe. The reaction was due in part to bad luck: The first shipments of genetically modified soybeans from the United States to the U.K. coincided with a major outbreak of mad cow disease in Britain. The outbreak undermined the credibility of British food-safety officials, who had previously assured Britons that they could not get bovine disease from eating infected beef. [35]

The environmental organization Greenpeace and other groups opposed to GM crops found the European public receptive to arguments that the technology had not been adequately tested and was likely to be harmful in ways not yet understood. "Mad cow disease was immediately used by the anti-biotech groups," says Jaffe, at the Center for Science in the Public Interest. "That was a big disadvantage, to the detriment of biotech. They were able to raise this specter of an unknown that could hurt you."

Emblematic of Europeans' skeptical attitudes was the response to a genetically modified tomato created by Zeneca, a British multinational company. Developed for lower water content to make it more suitable for tomato paste, it was sold in the U.K. from 1996 to 1999. The tomatoes cost 20 percent less than conventional ones used for tomato paste and labeled as genetically engineered. Initially they sold well, but demand collapsed following the airing of a documentary in which a Hungarian researcher said he had found that genetically modified potatoes led to biological changes in rats — research that has since been called into question. [36]

Surveys also indicated that the Europeans were skeptical of Monsanto, the company that led the charge to bring GM crops to Europe. To some, the company was an agent of American corporate imperialism. Many Europeans also perceived the technology as a threat to small farmers, who hold disproportionate political influence.

"In Europe they made a huge misstep by saying, 'Look, we're going to give this to you and you're going to accept it because America makes so much food and if you don't want it you're going to have to pay more for your food,' " says Klee, the former Monsanto researcher.

Resistance may also have reflected European values about the role of farms and nature, which Monsanto did little to address. In Europe, which lacks large forested areas, nature is more closely associated with agricultural land. [37]

"There was a bit of myopia in the industry," says the University of Minnesota's Schurman. "On Monsanto's part, they were so busy trying to get to the patent office that they didn't realize there were people organizing around environmental implications."

Rising resistance to GM crops in Europe led to adoption of the Cartagena Protocol in 2000, a U.N. treaty that updated a 1992 accord on biosafety to permit the use of the so-called precautionary principle in the regulation of biotech crops. That principle holds that when a technology has the potential to cause widespread harm to people or the environment, policymakers should delay approving it until it has been definitively proven safe.

In the wake of the accord, the United Nations Environmental Program began a $60 million training program for governments in the developing world on assessing the risks of biotechnology. Largely funded by European nations skeptical of the technology, the program promoted use of the precautionary principle. It also called for each nation to set up its own system of field trials of GM crops; rules on marketing, transport, packaging, labeling and disposal; and research on the crops' effects on traditional farming practices and implications for cultural and religious interests. [38]

StarLink Recall

A defining moment for GM crops came in 2000, when Taco Bell taco shells were found to contain traces of a genetically engineered corn variety not approved for human consumption, prompting recall of the shells and other consumer products. [39]

Developed by the French biotech company Aventis, the corn variety — known as StarLink — had been approved for animal consumption. But pollen from the corn had drifted into fields with other types of corn. Because one of the proteins in Starlink had not been in the human diet before, it was seen as a possible allergen.

"I view it as a very poignant cautionary tale that our regulatory system is not up to the task of preventing potential problems with genetically engineered food," Joseph Mendelson III, then the legal director of the Center for Food Safety, told *The New York Times*. [40]

Fallout from the controversy led to a temporary halt in U.S. corn exports, a recall of numerous corn products and lawsuits by dozens of consumers — some of whom reported having allergic reactions. However, medical studies have since been unable to document any harms from the protein. [41]

Similarly, in 2006 low levels of ge-

Ethics and Genetically Modified Animals

Is there a difference between GM plants and animals?

In the Gulf of Mexico, a vast oxygen-depleted dead zone as large as New Jersey forms annually due to algae blooms caused by phosphorus and nitrogen run-off from farms in the Midwest. Similar blooms occur in the Great Lakes, killing fish and spoiling scenery. Genetic engineering could help with the problem, as Monsanto, DuPont and BASF are developing corn varieties that are more efficient at utilizing nitrogen fertilizers. A more provocative product is the Enviropig, a genetically modified Yorkshire pig developed in Canada that digests phosphorus more effectively and excretes less polluting nutrients.

The development of genetically modified animals presents just one of a myriad number of ethical problems that would have been hard to fathom even 50 years ago. From corporations patenting genetic sequences to inserting animal genes into plants, biotechnology has stretched into areas that are the province of dystopic novels.

University of Guelph

Genetically modified animals such as the Enviropig, a Yorkshire developed in Canada that excretes less polluting nutrients, raise perplexing scientific and ethical issues.

Evaluating the ethics of creations such as the Enviropig involves weighing environmental benefits — such as a reduction in phosphorus in waterways — against concerns over manipulating the genes of a large mammal that is closely related to humans.

The Biotechnology Industry Organization argues that there is no ethical difference between genetically modified animals and genetically modified plants and that government regulators are wrong to delay approval of the first GM animal. "The market should determine whether there is a market for genetically modified animals," says Cathleen Enright, vice president for food and agriculture at the group.

Yet most societies do treat animals, especially large mammals such as pigs, as different moral beings than plants. No jurisdictions bar cruelty to soybeans. But as genetic engineering pushes further into human health care, it is possible that genetic modification of animals will seem less strange. Insulin produced by genetically engineered organisms has been used for diabetes patients since the early 1980s. Genetic engineering is expanding rapidly in health care, and people will likely benefit from therapeutic cloning of skin cells, heart tissue and even bones. [1]

U.S. consumers are unlikely to be eating genetically modified animal products anytime soon. The Enviropig project was recently terminated due to a lack of commercial interest, and a salmon genetically engineered to grow nearly twice as fast as existing breeds is still awaiting approval nearly two years after the FDA reached a preliminary finding that it is safe for people and the environment. Yet some fear that continued resistance will cause the United States to fall behind other countries. Researchers in China are already studying transgenic sheep that produce more wool, cows resistant to foot-and-mouth disease and pigs that contain healthy omega-3 fatty acids in their meat. [2]

— Jason McLure

[1] "The Value of Therapeutic Cloning," Biotechnology Industry Organization, May 25, 2010, www.bio.org/articles/value-therapeutic-cloning-patients.

[2] Andrew Pollack, "An Entrepreneur Bankrolls a Genetically-Modified Salmon," *The New York Times*, May 21, 2012, www.nytimes.com/2012/05/22/business/kakha-bendukidze-holds-fate-of-gene-engineered-salmon.html?pagewanted=all.

netic material from a herbicide-resistant GM rice known as LibertyLink, which was not approved for human consumption, appeared in other U.S. rice. That led to a plunge in rice prices and temporary bans on imports of U.S. rice by Japan and the EU. The following year the Department of Agriculture concluded that LibertyLink posed no identifiable concerns for human health and the environment and approved it for human consumption, but farmers suffered extensive economic damage. [42] In 2011, Bayer CropScience, which had developed the rice, settled a class action suit with farmers for $750 million. [43]

Two other factors helped keep biotech agriculture in the spotlight. Monsanto, Dupont and Novartis — three of the biggest developers of biotech crops — all began buying up regional seed companies, greatly increasing their ability to spread the technology but also expanding their clout in the market. Their growing dominance raised concerns that a handful of large businesses would gain too much control over global agriculture.

Also controversial has been a decision by Monsanto to sue its own customers over the use of seeds gathered and saved from crops that originally were sown with the company's patented GM seeks. Saving and using seeds from subsequent crops violates contracts that farmers sign with the company.

To gather evidence against the farmers, Monsanto sent "seed police" to gather samples from fields that it suspected illegally contained plants with its patented genetic sequence. Since 1997, Monsanto says it has filed suit against 145 U.S. farmers — a relatively small number considering the 250,000 American farmers who buy the company's seed each year. [44] Monsanto sees itself as defending a technology it spent tens of millions of dollars to develop.

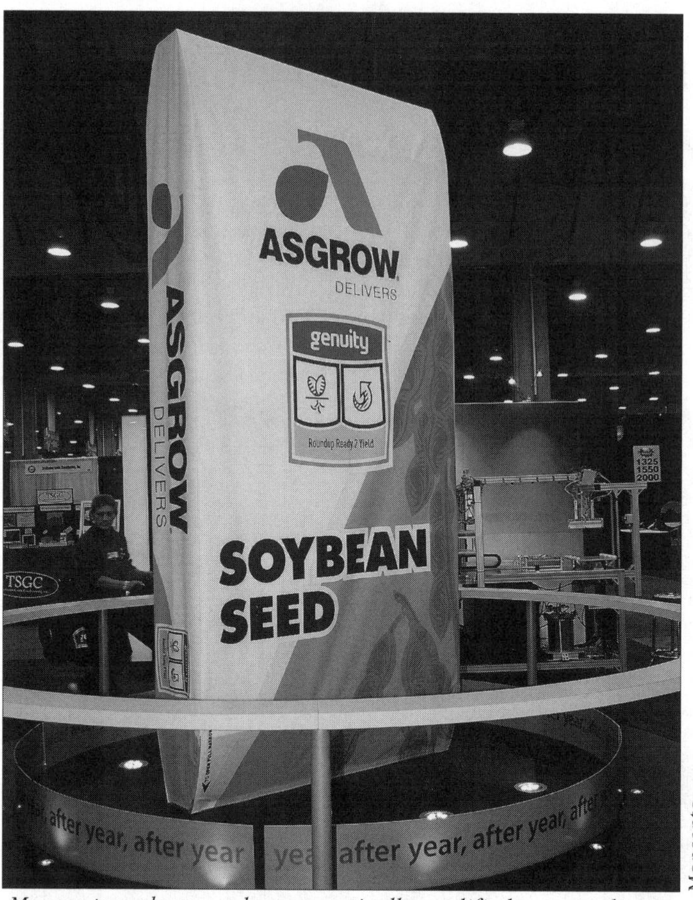

Monsanto

Monsanto soybean seeds are genetically modified to resist disease and provide more yield per bushel. In the mid-1990s, the St. Louis agribusiness giant introduced GM soybeans, corn and cotton that were either resistant to Roundup or contained Bt insecticide. Environmental groups say the Department of Agriculture does not adequately examine the potential impacts of introducing GM farming methods on millions of acres, such as weed and insect resistance to Roundup and Bt.

A spokesman for Monsanto declined to be interviewed for this article. However, on its website the company says it sues "to ensure a level playing field for the vast majority of honest farmers who abide by their agreements, and to discourage using technology illegally to gain an unfair advantage."

But critics see a corporate Goliath bullying farmers.

Gary Rinehart, a Missouri farmer suspected by Monsanto of violating a seed contract, said their message was: "Monsanto is big. You can't win. We will get you. You will pay." [45] ■

CURRENT SITUATION

In the Pipeline

With patents for common GM seeds, such as Roundup Ready crops, expiring, biotechnology companies are focusing on GM's next generation. Monsanto has recently gained regulatory approval for an early variety of drought-resistant corn, and both it and Syngenta are about five to seven years from commercializing additional drought-resistant strains, which could potentially aid farmers in the developing world and help mitigate the effects of increasingly frequent droughts linked to climate change.

Dupont's Pioneer Hi-Bred division and Monsanto also anticipate marketing GM soybean varieties rich in heart-healthy oils such as omega-3 fatty acids. Researchers also are in the advanced stage of developing new forms of Bt corn seed that provide non-Bt refuges for insects so as to slow the development of resistance. Virus-resistant strains of potatoes and beans are also less than a decade away, according to the industry's trade association. [46]

Other products could potentially be more environmentally damaging than today's GM crops, analysts say. These include corn and soybean varieties being developed by Dow AgroSciences that would be resistant to the herbicide 2,4-D. The new crops are being developed to provide farmers an alternative herbicide-resistant crop to battle Roundup-resistant weeds.

Yet 2,4-D is categorized as "moderately hazardous" by the World Health Organization, two steps more toxic than Roundup, which is considered "unlikely to present acute hazard" to people. Opponents of biotech note that the chemical was an ingredient in Agent Orange, a controversial defoliant used by the U.S. military during the Vietnam War that caused significant health problems — including cancer and birth defects — among Vietnamese villagers and U.S. soldiers exposed during the

Continued on p. 734

At Issue:

Should foods containing GM ingredients be labeled?

GARY HIRSHBERG
CHAIRMAN AND FOUNDING PARTNER, JUST LABEL IT; CHAIRMAN AND CO-FOUNDER, STONYFIELD FARM

WRITTEN FOR *CQ RESEARCHER*, AUGUST 2012

yes

Unlike more than 40 other countries — including all of Europe, Japan and China — the United States has no laws requiring labeling of genetically engineered (GE) foods. Yet most polls show that the vast majority (90 percent) of Americans believe GE foods should be labeled. For 20 years, however, we've been denied that right.

Reasons for wanting to know what's in our food vary, but the belief that it's our right unifies us. Without labeling, we can't make informed choices about our food. The Just Label It (JLI) campaign, a national coalition of more than 500 diverse organizations, was created to advocate for GE foods labeling.

Americans want labeling for many reasons, including health, safety, environmental and religious considerations, as well as the belief that the right to know is a core American value.

The Federal Food, Drug, and Cosmetic Act requires the Food and Drug Administration to prevent consumer deception by clarifying that a food label is misleading if it omits significant "material" information. In 1992 an FDA policy statement defined "material" as the ability to be sensed by taste, smell or other senses. The FDA determined that GE foods were "substantially equivalent" to conventional foods, so no labeling was required.

Twenty years later, this outdated policy remains in effect. This means a GE salmon designed to continuously produce hormones is not materially different from a non-GE salmon because it does not taste, smell or feel different, according to the FDA.

Mounting demand for the right to make informed decisions is responsible for the unprecedented success of Just Label It. In only 180 days, JLI generated more than 1.2 million comments on the FDA's labeling petition — the most comments on a food petition in the agency's history.

Despite the overwhelming support for GE foods labeling, our elected officials in the greatest democracy on earth have chosen to deny this right for the very people they represent. People on all sides of the political spectrum are voicing concern and distrust with how government and companies are making decisions.

We're living in a new era of transparency, and government can no longer justify keeping us in the dark. GE foods must be labeled so consumers can have the information they need to make informed decisions about the foods they eat and feed their families.

PHILIP NELSON
PRESIDENT, ILLINOIS FARM BUREAU

WRITTEN FOR *CQ RESEARCHER*, AUGUST 2012

no

Recently, there's been a lot of talk about the need to label foods that contain genetically modified organisms, or GMOs, as activist groups negatively label them. But why? After all, the Food and Drug Administration (FDA) provides science-based labeling guidelines for all food and drugs produced and sold in the United States.

That's why the Illinois Farm Bureau supports FDA's guidelines. In particular, we support the fact that no special labeling is required unless a food is significantly different than its traditional counterpart or where a specific component is altered.

We also support FDA's use of nutritional information on labels, particularly where health effects of an ingredient are medically proven, including, for example, information on salt, trans fat and caffeine content and whether a food is calcium-enriched. Moreover, we support voluntary use of special labeling for specific characteristics of a food product or when certain ingredients are used to preserve the characteristics of a product throughout production and distribution, as they are in USDA-certified organic foods and even in some non-GMO foods.

The key is that we support voluntary labeling.

FDA guidelines do not require labeling for products of biotechnology — so-called GMOs. One reason is that biotechnology is not a product — it is a process that speeds up plant breeding. A second is that biotech products are not significantly different from conventional counterparts, nor are they allergens, which do require labeling. Biotech crops have been researched, grown and consumed for nearly 30 years. In that time, not a single allergy, sickness or reaction has occurred. What's more, thousands of scientists have attested to their safety.

The government determines how best to provide labels that protect consumers while also informing them. That is why details on labels are science-based and why most companies have additional information on their websites or information hotlines.

Finally, the organic industry does not include biotech production methods in its certification. Therefore, if people do not want to eat anything that includes GMO foods, they can choose organic products.

To start labeling for reasons other than science is a slippery slope that will result in less useful information, greater confusion and higher prices. Moreover, mandatory labeling of GM products will reduce organic market share and potentially decimate a market that farmers and the food industry alike worked to build.

Continued from p. 732

war. The USDA recently received 365,000 public comments opposing the approval of 2,4-D-resistant crops. [47]

Enright, of the Biotechnology Industry Organization, argues that such products will extend the life of Roundup by ridding fields of Roundup-resistant weeds with an herbicide sold under a variety of brand names such as Ortho's Weed B Gon Max. "Now what we're hearing is that farmers are going to be using Agent Orange. That's not true," says Enright. "Is 2,4-D new to consumers? No, they put it on their lawns every day."

Enright said she did not have enough information about 2,4-D to determine whether it would be worse for the environment if sprayed on the same scale as Roundup.

Others, however, are concerned about the prospect of a dramatic increase in 2,4-D spraying. "2,4-D is a much more toxic material," says Adamchak, the UC-Davis organic farm coordinator, who supports biotech research. "If the next generation is 2,4-D resistant, that's not making progress; that's going backwards."

Labeling Battle

The frontlines of the current debate are now in California, where the November ballot measure would require foods containing biotech crops to be labeled as "Partially Produced with Genetic Engineering," or "May Be Partially Produced with Genetic Engineering." Should it pass, the measure could have a broad impact nationwide if some food processors choose to stop using GM ingredients in order to avoid the stigma of a label in America's most populous state.

Supporters of the measure have momentum. It took them just 10 weeks to gather 971,126 signatures to put the question before voters.

The supporters argue labeling will put California in line with other developed nations. "More than 40 other countries — including all of Europe, Japan and even China — already label genetically engineered food," said Grant Lundberg, CEO of Lundberg Family Farms, a large, organic rice grower and processor. "Californians deserve to be able to make informed choices too." [48]

Consumers Union, publisher of *Consumer Reports* magazine, also supports labeling, arguing that there is uncertainty about the molecular characterization of some GM crops and researchers' ability to detect potential allergens. The issue is one of consumers' ability to make choices about their products and protect themselves from potential harms, the group says.

"If foods are not labeled, it would be very difficult to even identify an unexpected health effect resulting from a [GM] food," Michael Hansen, a researcher with the group, wrote to the American Medical Association (AMA) this year. [49]

The California ballot measure includes several assertions that are misleading or at odds with peer-reviewed scientific research. "Government scientists have stated that the artificial insertion of DNA into plants, a technique unique to genetic engineering, can cause a variety of significant problems with plant foods," the ballot measure reads. "Such genetic engineering can increase the levels of known toxicants in foods and introduce new toxicants and health concerns."

It also states that the FDA "does not require safety studies of such food" and argues that some consumers — such as vegetarians, Muslims, Jews and Hindus — "can unknowingly violate their own dietary and religious restrictions" by eating genetically modified foods that might be created using animal genes.

Opponents of the measure point out that it doesn't explain that the FDA, World Health Organization, numerous national science academies and other prestigious research organizations have determined that GM crops aren't inherently less safe than other foods, which also aren't required to go through safety studies — nor does it mention that every product currently on the market has gone through FDA's voluntary regulatory process or that crops also are required to be approved by the USDA and in some cases the EPA. They also question concerns about violating religious dietary restrictions, given that no products on the market are made using genetic material from animals, nor have major Christian, Jewish or Muslim leaders raised significant opposition to the technology. [50]

In June the AMA opposed labeling and called for the FDA to strengthen pre-market safety testing for new GM products. "There is no scientific justification for special labeling of bioengineered foods, as a class, and voluntary labeling is without value unless it is accompanied by focused consumer education," the group said. [51]

The labeling referendum is likely to come down to a funding battle. Monsanto and other multinationals, for instance, spent $5.5 million campaigning against a similar measure in Oregon in 2002. Food processors and biotech giants have already dwarfed that figure, raising $25 million through Aug. 15, including seven-figure contributions from Monsanto, DuPont, PepsiCo., BASF Plant Science and Conagra Foods. This money is being largely spent on advertisements calling the labeling proposal a costly and needless burden on food companies.

Despite being outspent, labeling proponents include some heavy hitters. Organic food sales in the United States topped $31.5 billion in 2011, [52] nearly three times Monsanto's $11.8 billion in global biotech sales in 2011. [53] The board of directors of Just Label It, which is spearheading the California effort, includes representatives of Stonyfield Farms, an organic yogurt company that is majority-owned by Groupe Danon, the world's largest dairy company; Organic Valley, the largest U.S. organic dairy co-op with $715 million in sales; and the Organic Trade Association, a coalition of 6,500 organic businesses.

The growing political clout of the organic industry rankles conventional farmers like Olthoff, who say labeling unfairly demonizes GM crops. "I believe in testing; I want everything to be right, but I don't want people to bad-mouth biotech just to make money," he says.

Proponents have crafted the California measure more narrowly than Oregon's. The California initiative would allow several exemptions, including:

- restaurants;
- meat from animals fed GM crops;
- milk from cows injected with rBGH;
- food unintentionally contaminated with GM material;
- alcoholic beverages (such as wine made with genetically modified yeast); and
- cheeses and other foods made using genetically engineered enzymes.

"It's cleverly crafted to exempt those interests in California that could most readily influence consumers to reject the initiative," says Enright, of the biotech industry trade group.

The effectiveness of the FDA labeling petition, meanwhile, seems uncertain. Although organizers say more than a million people have sent comments and signed petitions to the agency, the FDA says it has only received 394 official comments. Even if thousands of people sign a form letter or a petition, the agency explains, their signatures are only counted as one person or "comment."

After the March deadline to respond to the petition passed, the agency said it needed more time to consider its response. ■

OUTLOOK

Conflict Ahead?

Some opponents of biotechnology foresee a difficult future for the seed-development technique.

Duesing, of the Northeast Organic Farming Association, predicts growing conflict between organic farmers and the biotech industry, particularly as GM alfalfa and sweet corn are grown in the Northeast, where small farms are often clustered closely together. Should GM varieties pollinate with nearby organic fields, organic farmers could lose their organic certification — and thus their price premium.

Duesing expects such situations to trigger an even stronger backlash against biotech companies, benefitting small farmers. "They've got their vision for the food system," he says. "They want control, and they don't want any other messy thing. Once we move away from Monsanto's technologies, people will be breeding for local conditions."

The Center for Food Safety's Kimbrell foresees greater environmental damage from GM crops and the expanded use of older and more toxic herbicides to fight Roundup-resistant weeds.

"I think the past is the future," he says. "You can't base good agriculture on bad science. That doesn't mean the corporations . . . won't keep pushing it."

Others predict that biotechnology will be able to achieve only modest gains in the near future as researchers struggle with the scientific challenges of producing higher-yielding and more drought-resistant crops. "We think breeding will considerably outpace genetic engineering for five to 10 years," says Gurian-Sherman, of the Union of Concerned Scientists. "For the foreseeable future I see genetic engineering being useful at the margins for society."

Some grain farmers disagree. "As far as we've come, I think we'll go further again, we'll double it," says Olthoff, the Illinois corn and soybean farmer. "I know Monsanto is working on drought-tolerant corn, which will be a boon for us and a boon for Africa."

Klee, the University of Florida molecular biologist, predicts research into fruit and vegetable crops likely will remain stymied for the foreseeable future by consumer resistance — even as crops that are components of processed foods are more widely adopted. "When someone picks up a GM fruit or vegetable and someone points out to them that this is a genetically modified food, there is a different attitude," says Klee.

The only exception is when specialty crops face crises, as when ringspot virus cut production by more than half in Hawaii's papaya industry, says Klee.

"In the late 1980s [the virus] took over everybody, and we were chopping down trees," says Ken Kamiya, a director of the Hawaii Papaya Industry Association. That led to the development of the Rainbow papaya, bred to be virus resistant. "Without GMOs we basically wouldn't have a papaya industry," he says.

The fact that public sentiment, spurred by advocacy groups and the rapidly growing organic sector, may be strong enough to pass a GM labeling law in California has the industry rethinking its public relations approach.

"They have a problem with industrial agriculture or with processed food," says Enright, of the industry trade group. "So to argue against either one of those they criticize biotech, because it's an easy target." The growth of social media has helped fuel anti-GM sentiment, she adds. "What we're all reconsidering right now is how do we talk about genetically engineered food. One of the results of all these calls for mandatory labeling has been to make us think about how we want our food products to be perceived."

Golden Rice may be the product that changes the dynamics of the debate, should it end up saving the lives, or sight, of hundreds of thousands of Vitamin A-deficient malnourished children each year. The Philippines now appears likely to approve the product for its first commercial planting in 2013, and China, Vietnam and Bangladesh may eventually approve it.

The Golden Rice Project's Dubock says researchers in the future will be able to create grain varieties that include nutrients such as folic acid. Deficiencies of the B-complex vitamins in pregnant women can lead to birth defects.

"It's important for a project like Golden Rice to be successful," says Dubock. "Twenty years from now, people will look back on it and say, 'What was all the fuss about?' " ■

Notes

[1] Elizabeth Weise, "Fight over genetically engineered crops on Calif. ballot," *USA Today*, June 12, 2012, www.usatoday.com/news/health/story/2012-06-12/genetically-engineered-food-california/55558352/1.

[2] "20 questions on genetically modified foods," World Health Organization, 2012, www.who.int/foodsafety/publications/biotech/20questions/en/.

[3] "Ag Giants Spend Big to Defeat Labeling Initiative," The Associated Press, Aug. 15, 2012, www.nytimes.com/aponline/2012/08/15/us/ap-us-california-food-labeling.html?hp.

[4] Safety of Genetically Engineered Foods: Approaches to Assessing Unintended Health Effects, National Research Council and Institute of Medicine of the National Academies (2004), pp. 191-195.

[5] Stephen Duke and Stephen Powle, "Glyphosate: A Once In a Century Herbicide," *Pest Management Science*, April 2008, http://ddr.nal.usda.gov/bitstream/10113/17918/1/IND44034731.pdf.

[6] Damian Carrington, "GM Crops Good for the Environment, Study Finds," *The Guardian*, June 13, 2012, www.guardian.co.uk/environment/2012/jun/13/gm-crops-environment-study.

[7] "Recent Trends in GE Adoption," Economic Research Service, U.S. Department of Agriculture, 2012, www.ers.usda.gov/data-products/adoption-of-genetically-engineered-crops-in-the-us/recent-trends-in-ge-adoption.aspx.

[8] "National Survey of Healthcare Consumers: Genetically Engineered Food," Thomson Reuters PULSE, October 2010, www.factsforhealthcare.com/pressroom/NPR_report_GeneticEngineeredFood.pdf.

[9] Andrew Pollack, "Crop Scientists Say Biotech Research Companies are Thwarting Research," *The New York Times*, Feb. 19, 2009, www.nytimes.com/2009/02/20/business/20crop.html.

[10] "Statement by Center for Food Safety at National Press Club Event Challenging House Farm Bill Biotech Riders," Center for Food Safety, July 17, 2012, www.centerforfoodsafety.org/2012/07/17/statement-by-center-for-food-safety-at-national-press-club-event-challenging-house-farm-bill-biotech-riders/. For background on the farm bill, see Jennifer Weeks, "Farm Policy," *CQ Researcher*, Aug. 10, 2012, pp. 693-716.

[11] Quoted in Susan C. Phillips, "Genetically Engineered Foods," *CQ Researcher*, Aug. 5, 1994, pp. 673-696.

[12] For background, see Kathy Koch, "Food Safety Battle: Organic Vs. Biotech," *CQ Researcher*, Sept. 4, 1998, pp. 761-784.

[13] Jamie Miller and Kent Bradford, "The Regulatory Bottleneck for Biotech Specialty Crops," *Nature Biotechnology*, October, 2010.

[14] Clive James, "Global Status of Commercialized Biotech/GM Crops: 2011," International Service for the Acquisition of Agri-Biotech Applications, 2011, p. 8 (web link in graphic on p. 724).

[15] Dan Charles, "Insect Experts Issue 'Urgent' Warning on Using Biotech Seeds," NPR, March 9, 2012, www.npr.org/blogs/thesalt/2012/03/08/148227668/insect-experts-issue-urgent-warning-on-using-biotech-seeds.

[16] "Survey: Waterhemp Top Weed to Watch in Midwest," Croplife.com, July 9, 2012, www.croplife.com/article/29047/survey-waterhemp-top-weed-to-watch-in-midwest.

[17] Rebecca Goldburg, Jane Rissler, Hope Shand and Chuck Hassebrook, "Biotechnology's Bitter Harvest: Herbicide-Tolerant Crops and the Threat to Sustainable Agriculture," Biotechnology Working Group, March 1990, http://blog.ucsusa.org/wp-content/uploads/2012/05/Biotechnologys-Bitter-Harvest.pdf.

[18] Margaret Mellon, "The Trojan Horse of Biotechnology," Union of Concerned Scientists, May 10, 2012, http://blog.ucsusa.org/the-trojan-horse-of-biotechnology/.

[19] Gregory Jaffe, "Complacency on the Farm: Significant Noncompliance with EPA's Refuge Requirements Threatens the Future Effectiveness of Genetically Engineered Pest-Protected Corn," Center for Science in the Public Interest, November 2009, http://cspinet.org/new/pdf/complacencyonthefarm.pdf.

[20] For background, see Doug Struck, "Disappearing Forests," *CQ Global Researcher*, Jan. 18, 2011, pp. 27-52.

[21] For information on pesticides and toxicity see the Pesticide Action Network Database: www.pesticideinfo.org/.

[22] Amy Harmon and Andrew Pollack, "Battle Brewing Over Labeling of Genetically Modified Food," *The New York Times*, May 25, 2012, www.nytimes.com/2012/05/25/science/dispute-over-labeling-of-genetically-modified-food.html?_r=2&ref=geneticallymodifiedfood.

[23] For additional information on mutagenic crops see the International Atomic Energy Agency and the Food and Agriculture Organization's database on mutant-enhanced crops at http://mvgs.iaea.org/Search.aspx.

[24] Calestous Juma, *The Gene Hunters* (1989), pp. 37-38.

[25] See David Hosansky, "Biotech Foods" *CQ Researcher*, March 30, 2001, pp. 249-272.

[26] B. R. Hazell, "Green Revolution: Curse or Blessing?" International Food Policy Research Institute, 2002, www.ifpri.org/pubs/ib/ib11.pdf.

[27] Hosansky, *op. cit.*

[28] Susan C. Phillips, "Genetically Engineered Foods, *CQ Researcher*, Aug. 5, 1994, pp. 673-696.

[29] Phillips, *op. cit.*

About the Author

Jason McLure is a New Hampshire-based correspondent for Thomson Reuters. Previously he was an Africa correspondent for Bloomberg News and *Newsweek* and worked for *Legal Times* in Washington, D.C. His writing has appeared in publications such as *The Economist*, *The New York Times* and *Business Week*. His last *CQ Global Researcher* was "Russia in Turmoil." His work has been honored by the Washington, D.C., chapter of the Society for Professional Journalists, the Maryland-Delaware-District of Columbia Press Association and the Overseas Press Club of America Foundation. He is also coordinator of the Committee to Free Eskinder Nega, a jailed Ethiopian journalist.

[30] Mark Youngblood Herring, *Genetic Engineering* (2005) pp. 71-73.

[31] Andrew Pollack, "Maker Warns of Hormone in Dairy Cows," *The New York Times*, Jan. 27, 2004, www.nytimes.com/2004/01/27/business/maker-warns-of-scarcity-of-hormone-for-dairy-cows.html.

[32] See also I. R. Dohoo, *et. al.*, "A Meta-Analysis Review of the Effects of Recombinant Bovine Somatotropin," *Canadian Journal of Veterinary Research*, October 2003, www.ncbi.nlm.nih.gov/pmc/articles/PMC280708/?tool=pmcentrez, and Richard Raymond, *et al.*, "Recombinant Bovine Somatotropin (rbST): A Safety Assessment," ADSA-CSAS-ASAS Joint Annual Meeting, July 14, 2009, www.ads.uga.edu/documents/rbstexpertpaper-6.26.09-final.pdf.

[33] "Organic Production Statistics," Economic Research Service, U.S. Department of Agriculture, www.ers.usda.gov/data-products/organic-production.aspx.

[34] Andrew Martin and Andrew Pollack, "Monsanto Looks to Sell Dairy Hormone Business," *The New York Times*, Aug. 6, 2008, www.nytimes.com/2008/08/07/business/07bovine.html; Mike Barris, "Lilly to Pay $300 Million for Dairy-Hormone Business," *The Wall Street Journal*, Aug. 20, 2008, http://online.wsj.com/article/SB121923768836656505.html.

[35] Sandra Blakeslee, "British Mad Cow Toll Rises, but the Cause is Unclear," *The New York Times*, March 19, 1999, www.nytimes.com/1999/03/19/world/british-mad-cow-disease-toll-rises-but-the-cause-is-unclear.html. For additional background, see Mary H. Cooper, "Mad Cow Disease," *CQ Researcher*, March 2, 2001, pp. 161-184.

[36] G. Bruening and J. M. Lyons, "The Case of the FLAVR SAVR Tomato," *California Agriculture*, July-August, 2000, http://ucanr.org/repository/CAO/landingpage.cfm?article=ca.v054n04p6&fulltext=yes.

[37] Michael Hertz, "Monsanto Europe, Case A: Monsanto Introduces GMOs to Europe with Unexpected Results: Draft," University of Virginia Darden School Foundation, May 17, 2001, www.docstoc.com/docs/50820240/Monsanto-Europe.

[38] Robert Paarlberg, *Starved for Science: How Biotechnology is Being Kept Out of Africa* (2008), pp. 127-132.

[39] Andrew Pollack, "Kraft Recalls Taco Shells With Bioengineered Corn," *The New York Times*, Sept. 23, 2000, www.nytimes.com/2000/09/23/business/kraft-recalls-taco-shells-with-bioengineered-corn.html?pagewanted=all&src=pm.

[40] *Ibid.*

FOR MORE INFORMATION

Biotechnology Industry Organization, 1201 Maryland Ave., S.W., Suite 900, Washington, DC 20024; 202-962-9200; www.bio.org. Trade group for agricultural and medical biotechnology companies.

Center for Science in the Public Interest, 1220 L St., N.W., Suite 300, Washington, DC 20005; 202-332-9110; www.cspinet.org. Food-safety group that advocates science-based government policies.

Greenpeace USA, 702 H St., N.W., Suite 300, Washington, DC 20001; 202-462-1177; www.greenpeace.org. Major global environmental group that opposes agricultural biotechnology.

International Food Policy Research Institute, 2033 K St., N.W., Washington, DC 20006-1002; 202-862-5600; www.ifpri.org. Group supported by governments, foundations and international organizations that provides research and policy advice on regulation of biotech crops.

National Academy of Sciences, 500 Fifth St., N.W., Washington, DC 20001; 202-334-2000; www.nasonline.org. Society of scientists and engineers created by Congress to advise the government on scientific issues. NAS has published a number of reports assessing the risks of agricultural biotechnology.

Union of Concerned Scientists, Two Brattle Square, Cambridge, MA 02138-3780; 617-547-5552; www.ucsusa.org. Environmental group critical of agricultural biotechnology.

[41] Andrew Pollack, "Study Raises Doubt About Allergy to Genetic Corn," *The New York Times*, Nov. 10, 2003, www.nytimes.com/2003/11/10/business/study-raises-doubt-about-allergy-to-genetic-corn.html.

[42] "Conclusion on Rice Investigation," Animal and Plant Health Inspection Service, U.S. Department of Agriculture, October 2007.

[43] Robert Patrick, "Genetic Rice Lawsuit in St. Louis Settled for $750 Million," *St. Louis Post-Dispatch*, July 2, 2011, www.stltoday.com/news/local/metro/genetic-rice-lawsuit-in-st-louis-settled-for-million/article_38270243-c82f-5682-ba3b-8f8e24b85a92.html.

[44] "Saved Seed and Farmer Lawsuits," Monsanto.com, www.monsanto.com/newsviews/Pages/saved-seed-farmer-lawsuits.aspx.

[45] Donald Barlett and James Steele, "Monsanto's Harvest of Fear," *Vanity Fair*, May 2008, www.vanityfair.com/politics/features/2008/05/monsanto200805.

[46] "Plant Biotechnology Pipeline: PowerPoint Presentation," Biotechnology Industry Organization, May 2011.

[47] "USDA Receives Over 365,000 Public Comments Opposing Approval of 2,4-D Resistant, Genetically Engineered Corn," Center for Food Safety, April 26, 2012, www.centerforfoodsafety.org/2012/04/26/usda-receives-over-365000-public-comments-opposing-approval-of-24-d-resistant-genetically-engineered-corn/.

[48] "California Voters to Decide on GMO Labeling," California Right to Know press release, June 12, 2012, www.carighttoknow.org/california_voters_to_decide_on_gmo_labeling.

[49] Michael Hansen, "Reasons for Labeling Genetically Engineered Foods," letter to American Medical Association Council on Science and Public Health, Consumers Union, March 19, 2012, http://truthinlabelingcoalition.org/AMA.GE.resolution.3.19.12[1]%20(1).pdf.

[50] Emmanuel Omobowale; Singer, Peter and Daar, Abadallah, "The Three Main Monotheistic Religions and GM Food Technology: An Overview of Perspectives," BMC International Health & Human Rights, 2009, www.biomedcentral.com/1472-698X/9/18.

[51] Rosie Mestel, "GMO Foods Don't Need Special Labels, American Medical Association Says," *Los Angeles Times*, June 21, 2012, http://articles.latimes.com/2012/jun/21/news/la-heb-gmo-foods-medical-association-20120620.

[52] "Consumer-Driven U.S. Organic Market Surpasses $31 billion in 2011," Organic Trade Association, April 23, 2012, www.organicnewsroom.com/2012/04/us_consumerdriven_organic_mark.html.

[53] Carey Gillam, "UPDATE 1 — DuPont Urges U.S. to Curb Monsanto Seed Monopoly," Reuters, Jan. 8, 2010, www.reuters.com/article/2010/01/08/monsanto-antitrust-idUSN087196620100108.

Bibliography

Selected Sources

Books

Brunk, Conrad, and Harold Coward, eds., *Acceptable Genes? Religious Traditions and Genetically Modified Foods*, State University of New York Press, 2009.
Brunk, a philosopher, and Coward, a historian, have gathered views on how practices such as the insertion of fish genes into tomatoes fit with religious dietary and ethical codes.

Engdahl, William F., *Seeds of Destruction: The Hidden Agenda of Genetic Manipulation*, Global Research, 2007.
Engdahl documents the effort by multinational companies and governments to exert greater control over the world's food supply through genetic engineering.

Federoff, Nina, and Nancy Marie Brown, *Mendel in the Kitchen: A Scientist's View of Genetically Modified Food*, Joseph Henry Press, 2006.
A molecular biologist and member of the National Academy of Sciences (Federoff) and a science writer (Brown) argue that biotechnology will help feed humanity for generations.

McHughen, Alan, *Pandora's Picnic Basket*, Oxford University Press, 2000.
A molecular geneticist at the University of California-Riverside clearly and objectively discusses the technologies underlying genetically modified food and the controversy over, among other things, labeling of GM foods.

Paarlberg, Robert, *Starved for Science: How Biotechnology is Being Kept Out of Africa*, Harvard University Press, 2008.
A Wellesley College political scientist argues that non-science-based fears about genetically modified crops in wealthy countries are slowing the adoption of beneficial crops in Africa.

Ronald, Pamela, and Raoul Adamchak, *Tomorrow's Table: Organic Farming, Genetics and the Future of Food*, Oxford University Press, 2010.
Combining memoir with argument, a California plant geneticist (Ronald) and an organic farmer (Adamchak) argue that the organic movement should adopt biotechnology in the interest of feeding the world's population sustainably.

Schurman, Rachel, and William Munro, *Fighting for the Future of Food: Activists Versus Agribusiness in the Struggle Over Biotechnology*, University of Minnesota Press, 2010.
A sociologist (Schurman) and a political scientist (Munro) explore differing views of the biotech industry.

Articles

Borrell, Brendan, "Food Fight: The Case for Genetically Modified Food," *Scientific American*, April 11, 2011, www.scientificamerican.com/article.cfm?id=food-fight.
The author argues in favor of increased use of genetically modified crops.

Levaux, Ari, "The Very Real Danger of Genetically Modified Foods," *The Atlantic*, Jan. 9, 2012, www.theatlantic.com/health/archive/2012/01/the-very-real-danger-of-genetically-modified-foods/251051/.
A food blogger argues that new research shows that genetically modified foods can be dangerous and merit greater regulation. The article generated extensive rebuttals from science writers at *Scientific American* and *Slate*.

Pollack, Andrew, "That Fresh Look, Genetically Buffed," *The New York Times*, July 12, 2012, www.nytimes.com/2012/07/13/business/growers-fret-over-a-new-apple-that-wont-turn-brown.html?pagewanted=all.
A GM apple that doesn't bruise or turn brown has met resistance from others in the apple industry.

Willingham, Emily, "The Very Real Paranoia Over Genetically Modified Foods," *Slate*, Jan. 17, 2012, www.slate.com/articles/health_and_science/medical_examiner/2012/01/genetically_modified_foods_ari_laux_s_alarmism_in_the_atlantic.html.
A science writer attacks Levaux's widely read critique of GMO foods in *The Atlantic*. Her article led the magazine to admit "scientific inconsistencies" in his piece.

Reports and Studies

"A Decade of EU Funded GMO Research: 2001-2010," European Commission, Directorate-General for Research and Innovation, 2010, http://ec.europa.eu/research/biosociety/pdf/a_decade_of_eu-funded_gmo_research.pdf.
A 262-page overview of 50 research projects on GM organisms concludes that food biotechnology carries no more environmental or health risks than other plant breeding methods.

"Genetically Engineered Food: An Overview," *Food & Water Watch*, 2012, www.foodandwaterwatch.org/reports/genetically-engineered-food/.
Genetically modified food should be labeled, and the U.S. government should stop approving new GM crops, an advocacy group argues.

"Impact of Genetically Modified Crops on Farm Sustainability in the United States," National Academy of Sciences, 2010, www.nap.edu/catalog.php?record_id=12804.
The nation's most prestigious scientific body concludes that genetically engineered crops offer farmers substantial environmental and economic benefits.

The Next Step:

Additional Articles from Current Periodicals

Effects

Bittman, Mark, "Profits Before Environment," *The New York Times*, Aug. 31, 2011, p. A27, opinionator.blogs.nytimes.com/2011/08/30/profits-before-environment/.

The Obama administration continues to enact policies that benefit the genetically modified food industry regardless of the environmental consequences, says a columnist.

Burns, Greg, "A Plant of Last Resort," *Chicago Tribune*, Oct. 2, 2011, p. A27, articles.chicagotribune.com/2011-10-01/news/ct-oped-1002-cassava-20110930_1_cassava-genetic-engineering-famine.

Americans have consumed genetically modified food ingredients for years with no ill effects thus far.

Davies, Peter, "GM Crops Are a Boon to All of Us," *Ithaca* (N.Y.) *Journal*, Jan. 19, 2012, www.courier-journal.com/article/CB/20120119/VIEWPOINTS02/201190328/Guest-Viewpoint-GM-crops-boon-all-us.

U.S. production of GM foods is helping to feed other parts of the world, says a Cornell biology professor.

Kraft, Jessica Carew, "The Rapid Growth of GMOs," *East Bay* (Calif.) *Express*, Oct. 26, 2011, www.eastbayexpress.com/ebx/the-rapid-growth-of-gmos/Content?oid=3025056.

Many facets of daily life, such as clothes and food, are infected with genetically modified organisms.

Labeling

Bauers, Sandy, "Labeling the Modified Foods," *Philadelphia Inquirer*, Feb. 20, 2012, p. D1, articles.philly.com/2012-02-20/news/31079947_1_gmo-crops-interest-in-organic-food-organic-farmers.

The genetically modified food industry says GM foods are safe to eat and do not require special labeling.

Dininny, Shannon, "Some Washington Farmers Support Labeling Genetically Modified Foods," *Lewiston* (Idaho) *Morning Tribune*, Jan. 30, 2012.

Washington State wheat farmers want genetically modified wheat to be labeled if its production is approved by the federal government so that unlabeled GM wheat doesn't undermine their market.

Finston, Susan K., "FDA Shouldn't Order Costly GMO Labels," *Fresno* (Calif.) *Bee*, July 7, 2012, www.fresnobee.com/2012/07/07/2900980/susan-k-finston-fda-shouldnt-order.html.

The Food and Drug Administration should not adopt costly labeling requirements for GM foods just to satisfy those without scientific knowledge of the products, says a former director of the American BioIndustry Alliance.

Finz, Stacy, "Modified Food on Voters' Menu," *Houston Chronicle*, Aug. 12, 2012, p. 1, www.chron.com/business/article/Modified-food-will-be-on-voters-menu-3780299.php.

California voters will decide in November whether their state will be the first to require labels on GM foods.

Harmon, Amy, and Andrew Pollack, "Battle Brewing Over Labeling of Genetically Modified Food," *The New York Times*, May 25, 2012, p. A1, www.nytimes.com/2012/05/25/science/dispute-over-labeling-of-genetically-modified-food.html/.

Labeling bills have been proposed in more than a dozen states since 2011.

Singer, Stephen, "Organic Farmers Hope for Boost With Rivals' Labels," The Associated Press, April 15, 2012, www.boston.com/news/local/connecticut/articles/2012/04/15/organic_farmers_hope_for_boost_with_rivals_labels/.

Organic farmers say they will benefit if genetically modified food is labeled.

Superweeds

Lochhead, Carolyn, "Modified Crops Battle Steps Up as Doubts Grow," *The San Francisco Chronicle*, April 30, 2012, p. A1.

Many corn and soybean farmers want new genetically engineered seeds because those now in use have spawned superweeds.

Winchester, Cody, " 'Superweeds' Sprout Trouble in S.D. Fields," *Argus Leader* (Sioux Falls, S.D.), May 22, 2012, p. A1.

Superweeds are increasing farming costs in South Dakota, and some farmers are using more potent chemicals to combat them.

Citing *CQ Researcher*

Sample formats for citing these reports in a bibliography include the ones listed below. Preferred styles and formats vary, so please check with your instructor or professor.

MLA Style

Jost, Kenneth. "Remembering 9/11," CQ Researcher 2 Sept. 2011: 701-732.

APA Style

Jost, K. (2011, September 2). Remembering 9/11. *CQ Researcher, 9*, 701-732.

Chicago Style

Jost, Kenneth. "Remembering 9/11." *CQ Researcher*, September 2, 2011, 701-732.

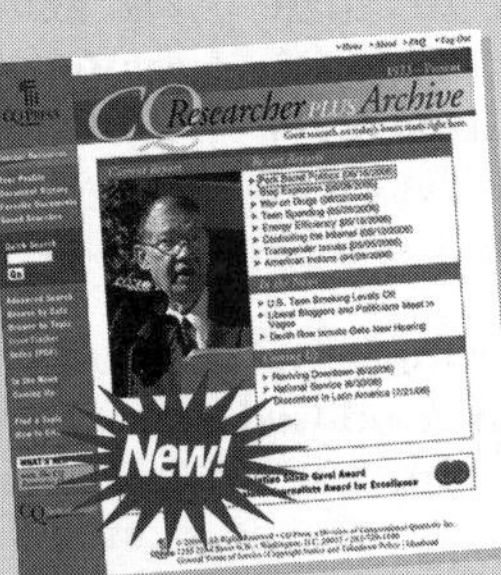

Researcher PLUS Archive
New!

CQ Researcher

Published by CQ Press, an Imprint of SAGE Publications, Inc.

www.cqresearcher.com

Re-examining the Constitution

Are major changes needed?

The 225th anniversary of the U.S. Constitution finds Americans in a less celebratory mood than they were during the Bicentennial a quarter-century ago. The Constitution's intricate system of checks and balances and separation of powers is sometimes blamed for the political gridlock in Washington. Some of the basic structural features are also viewed as outmoded, such as the Electoral College, equal representation for each state in the Senate and life tenure for Supreme Court justices. And many conservatives and libertarians, including the Tea Party movement, complain that the federal government has taken on powers beyond what the Constitution was intended to allow. Simmering discontent on both the left and the right has led to efforts to force Congress to call a convention to propose constitutional amendments. Public opinion polls indicate, however, that most Americans view the Constitution favorably.

The Declaration of Independence and Constitution are preserved at the National Archives in Washington. As the Constitution's 225th anniversary approaches, Americans appear more divided about the nation's founding document than they were 25 years ago.

INSIDE THIS REPORT

THE ISSUES 743
BACKGROUND 750
CHRONOLOGY 751
CURRENT SITUATION 756
AT ISSUE........................757
OUTLOOK 760
BIBLIOGRAPHY 762
THE NEXT STEP 763

CQ Researcher • Sept. 7, 2012 • www.cqresearcher.com
Volume 22, Number 31 • Pages 741-764

Los Angeles | London | New Delhi
Singapore | Washington DC

RECIPIENT OF SOCIETY OF PROFESSIONAL JOURNALISTS AWARD FOR EXCELLENCE ◆ AMERICAN BAR ASSOCIATION SILVER GAVEL AWARD

Re-Examining the Constitution

The Issues

743 • Should the structure of Congress under the Constitution be changed?
• Should the election of the president under the Constitution be changed?
• Should the tenure of Supreme Court justices under the Constitution be changed?

Background

750 **An Imperfect 'Miracle'?**
The Constitution grew out of the Framers' ability to craft compromises.

754 **Progressive Eras**
In its second century, the Constitution became an instrument of sweeping changes.

755 **Constitution in Turmoil**
Partisan polarization and public discontent have marked the Constitution's third century.

Current Situation

756 **Convention Talk**
Interest in amending the Constitution is growing, but changes are unlikely.

759 **Constitution Talk**
Americans know little about the nation's founding document.

Outlook

760 **The 'Durable' Constitution**
Only 27 amendments have been passed in 225 years.

Sidebars and Graphics

744 **The Framers' Constitution: 'A More Perfect Union'**
Seven articles lay out the structure and powers of the national and state governments.

745 **'Leave It Alone'**
Most Americans view the Constitution favorably.

746 **The Bill of Rights: Protections and Prohibitions**
The amendments are largely applicable to state and local governments.

748 **Most Dislike Electoral College System**
A majority of Americans favor election of the president by popular vote.

751 **Chronology**
Key events since 1776.

752 **Rewriting the Constitution: Some Modest Proposals**
Online readers and scholars weigh in.

755 **The 'Second Constitution'**
Three post-Civil War amendments had a profound effect on the nation.

757 **At Issue**
Should a constitutional convention be called?

For Further Research

761 **For More Information**
Organizations to contact.

762 **Bibliography**
Selected sources used.

763 **The Next Step**
Additional articles.

763 **Citing *CQ Researcher***
Sample bibliography formats.

Cover: Getty Images/Alex Wong

CQ Researcher

Sept. 7, 2012
Volume 22, Number 31

Managing Editor: Thomas J. Billitteri
tjb@cqpress.com

Assistant Managing Editor: Kathy Koch
kkoch@cqpress.com

Contributing Editor: Thomas J. Colin
tcolin@cqpress.com

Associate Editor: Kenneth Jost

Staff Writer: Marcia Clemmitt

Contributing Writers: Peter Katel, Barbara Mantel, Jennifer Weeks

Design/Production Editor: Olu B. Davis

Assistant Editor: Darrell Dela Rosa

Fact Checker: Michelle Harris

Los Angeles | London | New Delhi
Singapore | Washington DC

An Imprint of SAGE Publications, Inc.

Vice President and Editorial Director, Higher Education Group:
Michele Sordi

Director, Online Publishing:
Todd Baldwin

CQ Researcher (ISSN 1056-2036) is printed on acid-free paper. Published weekly, except: (March wk. 5) (May wk. 4) (July wk. 1) (Aug. wks. 3, 4) (Nov. wk. 4) and (Dec. wks. 3, 4). Published by SAGE Publications, Inc., 2455 Teller Rd., Thousand Oaks, CA 91320. Annual full-service subscriptions start at $1,054. For pricing, call 1-800-834-9020. To purchase a *CQ Researcher* report in print or electronic format (PDF), visit www.cqpress.com or call 866-427-7737. Single reports start at $15. Bulk purchase discounts and electronic-rights licensing are also available. Periodicals postage paid at Thousand Oaks, California, and at additional mailing offices. POSTMASTER: Send address changes to *CQ Researcher*, 2300 N St., N.W., Suite 800, Washington, DC 20037.

Re-examining the Constitution

BY KENNETH JOST

THE ISSUES

Tours at the National Constitution Center in Philadelphia end in Signers' Hall, where visitors can stand shoulder to shoulder with life-size statues of 42 of the delegates who assembled in the summer of 1787 to rewrite the governing charter for the infant republic. There they are: George Washington, president of the four-month-long convention; Benjamin Franklin, the elder statesman; James Madison, the young politician later dubbed "the father of the Constitution"; Roger Sherman, author of the crucial compromise between large and small states; and 38 other delegates representing all of the 13 states except tiny Rhode Island, including the three who refused to sign. *

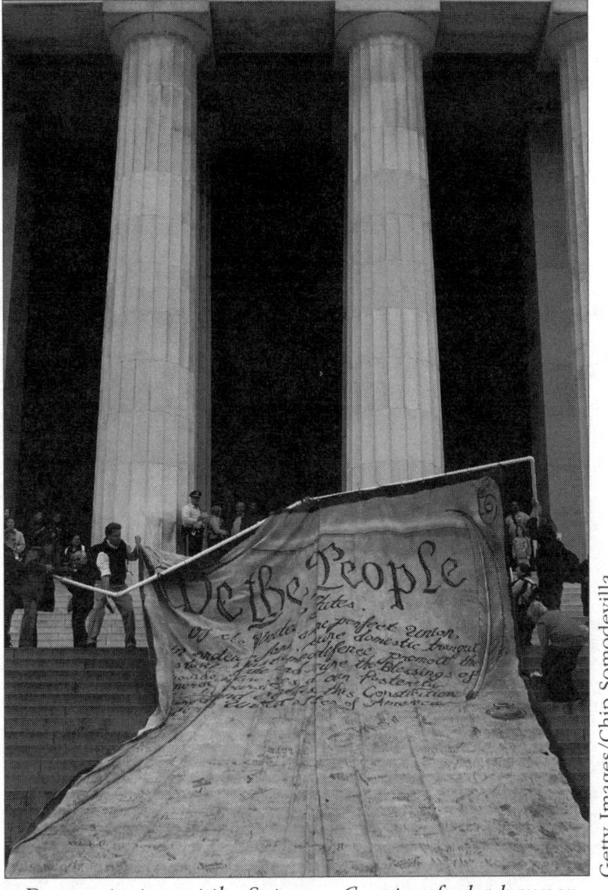

Getty Images/Chip Somodevilla

Demonstrators at the Supreme Court unfurl a banner depicting the Constitution on Oct. 20, 2010, to protest the court's Citizens United *decision allowing unlimited corporate spending in political campaigns. Some liberals want to amend the Constitution to undo the controversial decision.*

Visitors to the center learn of the dangers besetting the new nation under the existing Articles of Confederation: threat of foreign invasion, economic rivalries between states and widespread unrest and disorder. The delegates to the so-called Federal Convention had gathered to revise the charter but ended by replacing it with something new and groundbreaking: a "Constitution for the United States of America." [1] *(See p. 744.)*

Once in Signers' Hall, visitors are invited to sign their names alongside a reproduction of the Constitution — "in support of constitutional government everywhere." Millions of visitors have done so since the independent, publicly and privately supported center opened on July 4, 2003. But when University of Texas law professor and constitutional scholar Sanford Levinson came to Philadelphia for the center's grand opening, he decided not to sign.

Levinson balked because he thinks the Constitution is out of date, given "our own twenty-first century norms." As he relates in his book *The Undemocratic Constitution*, he hopes for "a national conversation" about the Constitution in place of the automatic acceptance of it for current times. [2]

Then and even today, Levinson's book stirred debate in legal and academic circles, respectful but often negative. Polls show that, despite controversies, the Constitution still holds a special place in public opinion as well. *(See poll, p. 745.)* Yet, as the Constitution's milestone 225th anniversary on Sept. 17 approaches, Americans appear more ambivalent or divided about the Constitution than they were 25 years ago. During the Bicentennial, the only prominent dissent came from Supreme Court Justice Thurgood Marshall, who criticized the Constitution for perpetuating slavery. [3]

"We're very much divided as a nation about what we see as the appropriate role of the government," says David Bodenhamer, a professor of history at Indiana University's School of Liberal Arts in Indianapolis and author of a more celebratory book, *The Revolutionary Constitution*. "We're forced to think once again about what those fundamental assumptions of the relationship of the government to the individual are." [4]

"We have in this country people, on both sides, feeling that the Constitution has let them down," says Gloria Browne-Marshall, an associate professor of constitutional law at John Jay College in New York City. "When it's there for them, they think the Constitution is a wonderful document. And when it isn't, they think the Constitution needs to be amended."

Debates about the Constitution have topped the political agenda ever since the closely contested 2000 presidential race between Republican George W. Bush and Democrat Al Gore gave the nation a crash course in the

Continued on p. 745

* In all, 70 delegates were selected to represent the 12 participating states at the convention; 55 of those actually attended sessions; only 39 signed the final document.

The Framers' Constitution: 'A More Perfect Union'

The Constitution drafted in 1787 began with a "Preamble" followed by seven articles. The first three outlined the structure and powers of Congress, the president and the judiciary.

The next three pertained to the powers and responsibilities of the states, the amendment process and the powers of the national government. The final article set out the requirements for ratification. Here are some of the major provisions:

Preamble

"We the People of the United States, in Order to form a more perfect Union, establish Justice, insure domestic Tranquility, provide for the common defence, promote the general Welfare, and secure the Blessings of Liberty to ourselves and our Posterity, do ordain and establish this Constitution for the United States of America."

Article I

Vests "all legislative Powers herein granted" in "a Congress," to consist of a Senate, with two members from each state, and a House of Representatives, with members apportioned by population; age, residency requirements set out; slaves to be counted as three-fifths of a person for apportionment.

Requires approval by each chamber of Congress and signature by president for enactment of law; if "returned" by president, bill may be become law after two-thirds vote in each chamber.

Makes each chamber exclusive judge of qualifications and elections of members; no member to be "questioned in any other Place" for "any Speech or Debate."

Grants Congress so-called "enumerated" powers (sec. 8), including power to tax and spend, regulate interstate and foreign commerce, declare war, raise and support armies and "make all Laws . . . necessary and proper" for executing "foregoing Powers."

Bars restriction on importation of slaves until 1808.

Bars states from entering any treaty with another country or laying duties on imports or exports without consent of Congress.

Article II

Vests "the executive Power" in "a President of the United States of America."

Prescribes election of president by "electors" to be "appoint[ed]" by each state as directed by legislature; each state to have number of electors equal to the state's "whole Number of Senators and Representatives;" meeting of electors, counting of ballots detailed; election by House of Representatives, with one vote per state, if no candidate has majority.

Makes president "commander in chief" of Army and Navy.

Grants president power to nominate, with "Advice and Consent" of Senate, ambassadors, judges and (most) "Officers of the United States."

Permit removal of president and vice president after impeachment (by House) and conviction (by Senate) of "Treason, Bribery, or other high Crimes and Misdemeanors."

Article III

Vests "the judicial Power" in "one supreme Court" and inferior courts to be created by Congress; judges to hold offices "during good Behaviour;" compensation not to be diminished.

Extends judicial power to, among others, cases arising under Constitution, federal laws, treaties; cases where United States is party; controversies between two states or between citizens of different states; Supreme Court to have original jurisdiction in limited number of cases, appellate jurisdiction in all others.

Article IV

Requires states to give "Full Faith and Credit" to official actions of other states, recognize "all Privileges and Immunities" of citizens of other states and extradite persons accused of crime in another state upon request of executive authority of that state.

Requires states to deliver escaped slaves upon claim by owner.

Permits admission of new states; no state to be divided or joined with another without consent of affected state or states and of Congress.

Article V

Permits amendments to be proposed by two-thirds vote of both houses of Congress or by a convention called for by two-thirds of the state legislatures; amendments effective when ratified by three-fourths of the states by legislatures or conventions as Congress directs.

Bars until 1808 any amendment to restrict importation of slaves.

Prohibits depriving any state of equal representation in Senate without state's consent.

Article VI

Accepts all debts of states as "valid against the United States."

Makes the Constitution and laws and treaties of the United States "the supreme Law of the Land."

Bars any religious test for any office of the United States.

Article VII

Requires ratification by nine states to establish the Constitution "between the States so ratifying."

Continued from p. 743

Electoral College and the House of Representatives' back-up role in the event of a deadlock, as spelled out in the Constitution. [5] Bush came under nearly continual criticism throughout his eight years in the White House from liberals and libertarians for stretching presidential powers in what he called the "global war on terrorism." President Obama and congressional Democrats have been under all but constant criticism from conservatives and libertarians for stretching the federal government's powers in the new health care law.

Levinson broadly views what he sees as the Constitution's faults as among the causes of the growing discontent with politics generally and the declining public confidence in all three branches of the federal government. "There is just generally a much greater level of dissatisfaction with the state of American politics," Levinson says today. "What drives me crazy is the inability to engage in connecting the dots to recognize that the Constitution itself bears part of the blame."

Some constitutional scholars agree. "There is a fairly general perception that the constitutional structure that we regarded as normal 25 years ago isn't working," says Glenn Reynolds, a professor at the University of Tennessee College of Law in Knoxville and a conservative commentator on his Instapundit.com website and in other media.

Others say the concerns about dysfunctional government stem more from the political culture in Washington and partisan polarization nationwide than from the Constitution. "I agree that the Constitution is a deeply imperfect instrument, but I don't believe that the imperfections are tightly tied to our current predicament," says Akhil Reed Amar, a law professor at Yale University in New Haven, Conn., and prolific author on constitutional topics. [6] "I don't see what dots there are to be connected," he adds.

'Leave It Alone'

More than half of Americans say the Constitution should be left alone, and two-thirds say it has a positive impact on life in the United States. Forty-three percent, however, think the Constitution does not place enough restrictions on what government can do.

Which best describes your view toward changing the Constitution?	
Leave it alone	57%
Make minor changes	39%
Make major changes	3%

Does the Constitution place too many or not enough restrictions on what government can do?	
Not enough	43%
Right amount	33%
Too many	15%

How do you rate the U.S. Constitution in terms of how it impacts life today?	
Excellent or good	67%
Poor	7%

Source: Rasmussen Reports, June 2012, www.rasmussenreports.com/public_content/politics/general_politics/june_2012/57_say_constitution_should_be_left_alone

Levinson favors rewriting significant provisions in each of the Constitution's first three articles dealing with Congress, the president and the judiciary. Among other changes, Levinson would enlarge the Senate to give bigger states more senators, replace the Electoral College with direct popular election of the president and limit the lifetime tenure of Supreme Court justices.

Amar says he favors or could be open to some of those changes, but discounts their importance. "I think those things tidy up the democratic project in ways that make the project more aesthetically appealing, but I don't think they change the system," he says.

Some constitutional scholars, on the other hand, flatly oppose any tinkering with the constitutional infrastructure. "What makes America exceptional is that we rejected a majoritarian form of democracy in favor of a limited-power republic," says Randy Barnett, a professor at Georgetown Law School in Washington and a libertarian critic of the federal government's expanding role since the 1930s. "I don't favor amending the Constitution to reverse those structural features."

Barnett, author of *Restoring the Lost Constitution*, has his own ideas for amending the Constitution, including limiting Congress' powers under the Commerce Clause more in keeping with what he regards as the provision's true meaning. [7] Barnett played a major role in crafting the legal and intellectual argument behind the court challenge to Obama's health care plan. Another of his proposals would allow a vote by legislatures in two-thirds of the states to repeal a law passed by Congress. [8]

The Framers — as the delegates to the convention have come to be called — included a procedure for amendments in Article V of the Constitution, but it is difficult, more difficult than provisions in other countries' governing charters. Some experts see the difficulty as fostering stability. "Perhaps it's good not to amend it too easily," says Caroline Fredrickson, president of the American Constitution Society, a progressive advocacy group.

Levinson complains that the procedure used for all 27 amendments so far — proposals submitted by Congress to state legislatures for ratification — imposes a daunting impediment in practice because members of Congress have little interest in or time for constitutional revision. He favors use of the second route set out in Article V: a convention called by Con-

The Bill of Rights: Protections and Prohibitions

Congress and the states approved 10 amendments to the Constitution, known as the Bill of Rights, in the first two years of the new national government. Originally, the provisions applied only to the federal government, but the Supreme Court has now held almost all of them applicable to state and local governments under the so-called incorporation doctrine.

First Amendment

Prohibits any law "respecting an establishment of religion, or prohibiting the free exercise thereof;" protects freedom of speech and press; guarantees right to "peaceably assemble" and to "petition the Government for redress of grievances."

Second Amendment

Protects "right of the people to keep and bear arms."

Third Amendment

Prohibits quartering of soldiers in private homes during peacetime.

Fourth Amendment

Prohibits "unreasonable searches and seizures" of "persons, houses, papers, and effects;" requires probable cause for warrants, which must specify place to be searched and person or things to be seized.

Fifth Amendment

Requires grand jury indictment (not incorporated against states); prohibits double jeopardy; establishes privilege against self-incrimination; requires due process; prohibits taking of private property for public use except with "just compensation."

Sixth Amendment

Protects, in all criminal prosecutions, right to "speedy and public trial" by jury, with rights to be informed of charges, confront witnesses and be represented by counsel.

Seventh Amendment

Protects right to jury trial in "suits at common law" (not applicable to states).

Eighth Amendment

Prohibits "excessive bail," "excessive fines," "cruel and unusual punishments."

Ninth Amendment

Specifies that enumeration of rights "shall not be construed to deny or disparage others retained by the people."

Tenth Amendment

Provides that powers "not delegated to the United States . . . nor prohibited . . . to the States" are "reserved to the States respectively, or to the people."

gress when requested by two-thirds of the states, with ratification required from three-fourths of the states by their legislatures or specially called conventions. That idea draws mixed responses from scholars, advocates and politicians. (*See "At Issue," p. 757.*)

However difficult the amendment process may be, interest in constitutional tinkering appears to be spiking in this anniversary year. *The New York Times* compiled a diverse list of possible changes from various invited experts this summer. The online magazine *Slate* drew a wider array of ideas when it threw the topic out for crowd sourcing. (*See sidebar, p. 752.*)

Historian Carol Berkin finds no fault with the current interest in possible changes despite the laudatory account of the convention in her book *A Brilliant Solution*. [9] The Framers "would not have been upset if we changed the Constitution," says Berkin, a professor at Baruch College, City University of New York. "These were ordinary men, and what makes them extraordinary is that they compromised every day. They knew that they had to give up something in order to save the country."

As Sept. 17 approaches, schools nationwide are required under a law passed in 2004 to provide educational programming that day on the history of the Constitution. The Philadelphia center is marking the anniversary with various events, including its annual Liberty Medal ceremony on Sept. 13; the 2012 awardee is Muhammad Ali, the former professional boxer, who is being honored as an "outspoken fighter for religious and civil rights." [10] As these observances take place, here are some of the questions being discussed:

Should the structure of Congress under the Constitution be changed?

The Constitutional Convention came close to collapsing in June 1787 over the structure of the legislative body for the new government. The Virginia

Plan, favored by Madison and other strong nationalists, called for two houses of Congress with the number of members in each chamber based on each state's population. Small states, led by New Jersey's delegation, wanted a unitary legislature with one vote per state, just as in the Articles of Confederation.

With each side having threatened to pull out of the convention over the issue, the Connecticut delegation — Roger Sherman and Oliver Ellsworth — offered the compromise that saved the project: proportional representation in the House of Representatives, equal representation by state in the Senate. With voting by states, the plan carried by a single vote, 5-4, with two delegations split and New York delegate Alexander Hamilton absent. [11]

More than two centuries later, the Connecticut Compromise remains the cornerstone of congressional architecture. But Levinson at the University of Texas is one of many academics who say the rule giving each state two senators without regard to population is utterly undemocratic. "Why should you be stuck to eternity with a compromise that was explainable only because of political considerations then and that hasn't worked out well?" he asks.

In his book, Levinson illustrates the results of small states' disproportionate voting power in the Senate. As one example, he quotes a study showing that in 2005, the Senate could have passed a bill with the votes of 51 Republican senators whose total votes amounted to less than 20 percent of the total national vote "The equal-vote rule in the Senate makes an absolute shambles of the idea that in the United States the majority of the people rule," Levinson writes. [12]

Indeed, full-throated defenses of the equal-vote rule appear to be hard to find among constitutional law experts. "I prefer a proportionally representative system," says Yale professor Amar. A change, he says, might make "a smallish difference." Historian Bodenhamer calls the Senate's composition "a real structural flaw that in some sense probably should be addressed."

"I can't figure out what damage it has, the current system," counters Donald Lutz, a professor of philosophy at the University of Houston who has studied national constitutions in the United States and other countries. "It's worked so well so far. What exactly is broken except for some people's sensibilities?"

Whatever the pros and cons, the rule appears impossible to change because of a specific provision agreed to at the convention that prohibits depriving any state of its "equal suffrage" in the Senate without the state's consent. "No small state is going to vote to do that," says Bodenhamer. Levinson agrees. "That's not going to happen in my lifetime," he says. "It probably won't happen in my grandchildren's lifetime."

Levinson has other complaints about the Senate — in particular, the current filibuster rule that, in operation today, effectively requires a 60-vote majority for a bill to pass. Amar agrees. "The Senate is ungovernable at 60," he says. But Amar quickly notes that no constitutional amendment is needed to change the Senate rules.

Other constitutional changes in Congress' structure currently being discussed seem almost as unlikely of adoption as any change in the equal-vote rule. One proposal pushed by elements of the Tea Party movement and other states' rights advocates is to repeal the 17th Amendment, which established direct election of senators in place of election by state legislatures as provided in the original Constitution. "Senators were emissaries of state government," says Adam Freedman, a conservative commentator and author of the recently published *The Naked Constitution*. "That was key to the original design." [13]

Levinson acknowledges the reasons supporters of state autonomy vis-à-vis the federal government favor the change. But he calls the idea of returning to election of senators by state legislatures "remarkably stupid, guaranteed to make the Senate even more egregiously parochial than it is now."

At least four current Republican candidates for the Senate have signaled interest in the idea. But even sympathetic constitutional law experts acknowledge that change is unlikely. "The 17th Amendment weakened the states' ability to resist the expansion of federal powers," writes John Yoo, a conservative law professor at the University of California-Berkeley and former Justice Department official in the George W. Bush administration. "The problem is that there is no point to trying to fix this problem — an effort to amend the Constitution will be fruitless." [14]

University of Tennessee professor Reynolds offers a more novel structural change: a new, third house of Congress empowered only to repeal existing federal laws. "Right now, there's no body that has an incentive to repeal laws," he says. Levinson disagrees. "We already have a third house of Congress," he says. "It's called the White House, with its power to veto and, therefore, to shape legislation. Or some might say that the Supreme Court plays that role, on occasion."

Should the election of the president under the Constitution be changed?

Delegates to the Constitutional Convention struggled to decide how to elect the president, who was to head the executive branch of the new government. Popular election was proposed but had scant support. Instead, delegates first voted in favor of election by the Senate. With persistent doubts about potential conflicts of interest, however, the convention referred the issue in August to the catchall Committee on Postponed Matters.

Most Dislike Electoral College System

More than 60 percent of Americans say the Constitution should be amended to allow U.S. presidents to be elected by popular vote rather than through the Electoral College system, reflecting a view that has prevailed since at least 1944. Critics of the Electoral College say candidates can win the White House without gaining a popular majority. Supporters say the system ensures that the winning candidate has support from a broad, nationwide coalition.

Do you prefer to amend the Constitution to elect presidents by popular vote or keep the current Electoral College system?

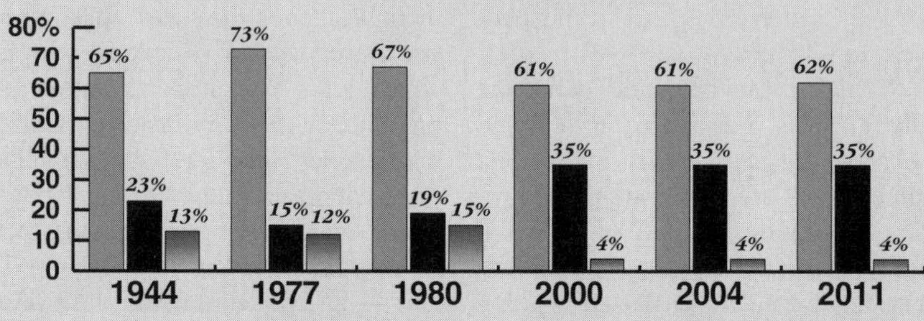

** Poll results in 1944, 1968, 1977 and 1980 include responses of "no opinion." All others include responses of "both," "neither," and "no opinion." Figures may not total 100 because of rounding.*

Sources: "Americans Have Historically Favored Changing Way Presidents Are Elected," Gallup, November 2000, www.gallup.com/poll/2323/Americans-Historically-Favored-Changing-Way-Presidents-Elected.aspx; Lydia Saad, "Americans Would Swap Electoral College for Popular Vote," Gallup, October 2011, www.gallup.com/poll/150245/americans-swap-electoral-college-popular-vote.aspx

The committee's recommendation, submitted on Sept. 4, set out the hybrid system that came to be called the Electoral College. Electors were allotted to each state based on the number of representatives and senators, to be chosen by the state legislature in whatever manner it chose. Each elector was to vote for two candidates. Each state legislature was to send the results to the Senate, which would open and count the ballots and declare a winner if a candidate received a majority; the runner-up was to be vice president. If no candidate received a majority, the election would go to the House, where each state would have one vote. [15]

The system malfunctioned in the nation's third and fourth presidential elections. In 1796 Federalist John Adams was elected president and his political foe Thomas Jefferson, the runner-up, as vice president. In 1800 no candidate had a majority, and the election was thrown into the House, which required 36 ballots to choose Jefferson. The 12th Amendment, ratified in 1804, established the current system of separate balloting for president and vice president.

Even with that change, the Framers would be hard pressed to recognize the current system of nationwide, media-intensive campaigns organized by political parties, with anonymous electors chosen by popular vote. Yet the superstructure remains, to the dismay of many experts and seemingly a majority of Americans, who would replace it with direct popular election. "I think the Electoral College is the most outmoded piece in the Constitution," says historian Berkin.

"Popular election, this is what we expect from other countries," says Browne-Marshall, the John Jay professor. "I think we are being hypocrites in allowing the Electoral College."

Opponents of the Electoral College point in particular to the four presidential elections in which the winner did not come in first in the popular vote — most recently, Bush's election over Gore. (The others: John Quincy Adams, 1824; Rutherford B. Hayes, 1876; Benjamin Harrison, 1888.) Levinson shares that concern, but in his book he sets out several other flaws at length. [16]

For one thing, Levinson says, the system results in candidates' focusing disproportionately on "battleground" or "swing" states and virtually writing off states with solid majorities for one party or the other. "As someone who lives in both Massachusetts and Texas, I saw nothing at all of the 2004 campaign," he writes.

Worse, Levinson says, is the possibility of an Electoral College deadlock being thrown into the House — on a one vote per state basis. "This provision," he writes, "is a national constitutional crisis waiting to happen."

Yale law professor Amar struck the same ominous note in a law review article in the mid-1990s, describing the Electoral College as "a constitutional accident waiting to happen." [17] Today, however, he voices less concern about the system. "I like direct election," he says, but then adds that he doubts that a change would make a significant difference in political campaigns. "You change the metric," he says. "You don't change the system."

Supporters of the Electoral College see one major advantage to the system: greater certainty than with a popular vote in a close election, with all but inevitable voting irregularities and errors in countless voting places. "Every time the presidential election is within 3 percent, you don't know who wins," says Lutz, the University of Houston professor. "The Electoral College gives us a winner — and what looks like a big winner because of the way it's counted."

Reynolds, the University of Tennessee professor, is tentative on the issue but sees a similar advantage in reducing the likelihood of vote recounts and contests. "There are reasons to think that the Electoral College compartmentalizes fraud," he says. "Under the Electoral College, once a state's won, extra votes don't matter. In a national popular-vote system, any extra vote created by fraud anywhere could conceivably tip the result."

Barnett, the Georgetown professor, opposes direct election for a different reason. He says a popular-vote system would shift power to populous, liberal states. "California would swamp a good deal of the rest of the country," he says.

Among other changes affecting the presidency, Levinson favors shortening the two-and-a-half-month transition period between the election and inauguration. (The transition was even longer until the 20th Amendment in 1933 moved the inauguration from March 4 to Jan. 20.) In a more sweeping change, Levinson would provide for a president to be removed from office by a vote of confidence by two-thirds majorities in each chamber of Congress.

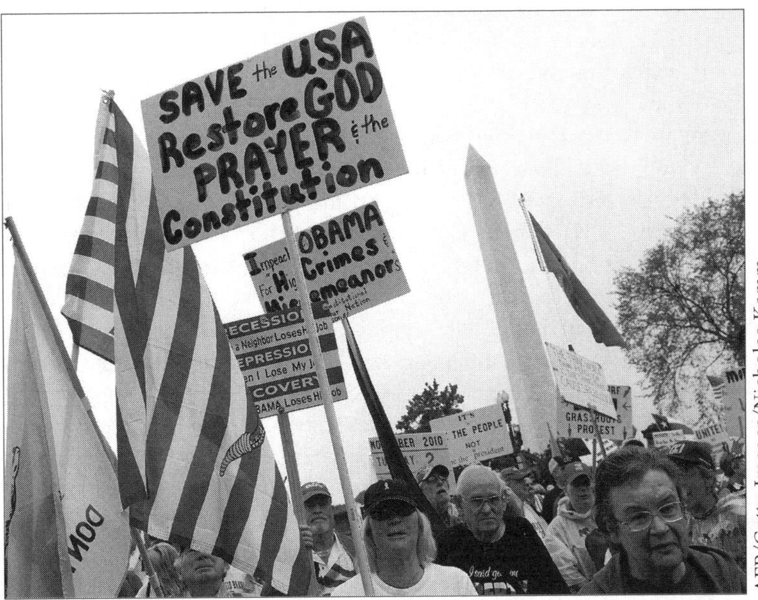

AFP/Getty Images/Nicholas Kamm

Tea Party backers rally in Washington in opposition to the growth of the federal government on Sept. 12, 2010. Elements of the Tea Party movement and other states' rights advocates are pushing to repeal the 17th Amendment, which established direct election of senators in place of election by state legislatures, as the Constitution originally stipulated.

Barnett forcefully disagrees. "The Framers' Constitution did not give us that form of government," he says.

Of Levinson's various proposals, only replacing the Electoral College with popular election has received widespread attention; it has consistently registered majority support in public opinion polls over several decades.[18] "Every poll has shown majority support for getting rid of the Electoral College," Levinson says. "But it's not going anywhere."

Should the tenure of Supreme Court justices under the Constitution be significantly changed?

Delegates to the Constitutional Convention devoted less time to establishing the judicial branch of the new government than they did with regard to Congress and the president. There was also less controversy. The only major point of contention came over a proposal to give the judiciary a veto over legislation passed by Congress — a proposal advanced to strengthen the president's power but eventually rejected for fear of weakening both Congress and the president.[19]

The judicial article is also the sparest of the first three. It vests "the judicial power" in a supreme court and "such inferior courts" as Congress decides to establish. The courts' power was defined, significantly, to extend to "all" cases arising under federal law as well as to other categories of cases. And the Framers protected judges from control by the other branches by giving them tenure "during good behavior" and barring pay cuts while in office.

The Supreme Court had little to do in its first decade, but in 1803 Chief Justice John Marshall turned a partisan dispute over a judicial appointment in Washington, D.C., into the landmark ruling *Marbury v. Madison*, which established the court's power to declare acts of Congress unconstitutional. President Thomas Jefferson criticized the ruling as a judicial power grab. Despite continuing criticism in some conservative circles, the power of judicial review is now firmly established.

Like the Framers, Levinson devotes less attention to the judiciary than to Congress or the president. And he endorses only one significant structural change: an end to what he calls the "indefensible system of life tenure for judges," especially for Supreme Court justices. Life tenure, he writes, "is an idea whose time has passed."[20]

Civics textbooks typically treat the constitutional provision for life tenure for federal judges as essential to an independent judiciary. But the idea of changing life tenure for Supreme Court justices has drawn support over the past decade from a surprising number of law professors representing a range of ideological views. Concerns about the mental and physical capacity of aging justices are one motivation for the proposal, but — as Levinson explains — "not the main one."

Instead, limiting justices' tenure is aimed at promoting more frequent and more regular turnover on the court. With long tenure, Levinson argues, justices may stay wedded to legal views dating from an earlier era. In addition, regular turnover could reduce what he calls the "*sturm und drang*" (storm and stress) of contemporary Supreme Court confirmation fights and eliminate the justices' political maneuvering to time their retirements so that a like-minded president names their successor.

One reason for increased interest in revising lifetime tenure is the trend toward justices serving longer than in the past. Justices who served from 1789 to 1970 served an average of 14.9 years, according to data compiled by Northwestern University professors Steven Calabresi and James Lindgren. Justices from 1970 through Justice Sandra Day O'Connor's retirement in 2006 served considerably longer on average: 26.1 years. [21]

The most concrete proposals currently under discussion call for 18-year term limits for justices. Calabresi and Lindgren propose instituting the change by constitutional amendment. Paul Carrington, a professor at Duke Law School, and Roger Cramton, a professor at Cornell Law School, have an alternative that they believe could be enacted by statute. Under their plan, justices would have 18-year terms of active service on the court. Thereafter, a justice would be available to serve on lower federal courts or the Supreme Court itself to substitute for justices forced to disqualify themselves from an individual case. [22]

Lutz, the University of Houston professor, sees no rationale for the 18-year term limit, but looks favorably on a mandatory retirement age. "That would make more sense for me," Lutz says. "I think the Supreme Court should turn over every once in a while."

Lifetime tenure still has supporters, however, even from a strong critic of contemporary Supreme Court jurisprudence such as Barnett. "I strongly support lifetime tenure," the Georgetown professor says. "I am not a huge fan of the Supreme Court. [But] I don't think the problem is lifetime tenure. The problem is who gets put on the court."

Historian Bodenhamer also questions the need to revise life tenure to ensure the court's responsiveness to changing political conditions. "Most historians of the court would argue that the court has changed over time and that it continues to be responsive to significant shifts of opinion in the American electorate," he says.

"It's quite clear that the court does follow the election returns," Bodenhamer continues. "Unfortunately, the appointment process has become really embroiled in the political process. It's not that the court is in some sense unresponsive. It is quite responsive. It looks dysfunctional at times because the politics of the moment has made it harder for the president to pick justices." ■

BACKGROUND

An Imperfect 'Miracle'?

The "Constitution for the United States of America" emerged from a convention called to rewrite, not replace, the existing Articles of Confederation. Built on crucial compromises on such issues as states' rights and slavery, the new charter won ratification only after sharp debates between supporters who called themselves Federalists and their opponents, who got stuck with the moniker Anti-Federalists; votes in several of the states were very close.

Ten amendments — the Bill of Rights — were needed immediately afterward to quiet the Anti-Federalists' concerns about individual rights. (*See box, p. 746.*) Two more amendments were added in a little over a decade. But the Constitution was most seriously tested by the Framers' attempt to skirt the slavery issue. The failure of constitutional politics to settle it brought on a bloody Civil War — and three additional amendments that, over time, fundamentally transformed individual rights and state versus federal powers. [23]

The Framers' ability to craft the compromises needed to reach agreement on the proposed Constitution has been celebrated time and again — most famously, in the title *Miracle at Philadelphia* that historian Catherine Drinker Bowen gave to her detailed account. But George Washington, who presided over the convention, wrote afterward that the charter was "not free of imperfections." [24] Today, historian Berkin stresses that the delegates were "terrified" that the country would disappear without a stronger national government to replace the confederation, with its rivalries among states and sections. "They compromised every day," Berkin says. "They knew that they had to give up something in order to save the country."

The Bill of Rights fulfilled the promise made by supporters of the Constitution during the ratification debates to add provisions protecting individual liberties from encroachment by the new national government. The 11th Amendment was added quickly in 1795, after an unpopular Supreme Court decision, to protect states from being sued in federal courts. The 12th Amendment followed a more dramatic demonstration of the Framers' lack of foresight. The emergence of political parties during Washington's presidency made it

Continued on p. 752

Chronology

1776-1791
U.S. Constitution is drafted and ratified.

1776-1787
Articles of Confederation drafted (1776), sent to states for ratification (1777), ratified by 13 states (1781).

1787-1788
Convention to revise Articles of Confederation meets in Philadelphia, drafts new Constitution with stronger central government; signed by 39 delegates (Sept. 17, 1787); sent to states for ratification; ratified by 11 states (December 1787-July 1788).

1791
Bill of Rights ratified; 10 amendments establish individual rights.

1800s *Turmoil over slavery, Civil War, Reconstruction.*

1804
Twelfth Amendment separates election of president, vice president.

1861-1865
Civil War breaks out after Southern states secede over slavery, states' rights.

1865-1870
Thirteenth Amendment abolishes slavery (1865); 14th Amendment prohibits states from violating due process, equal-protection rights (1868); 15th Amendment prohibits racial discrimination in voting (1870).

1900s *Federal government expands in size, scope; Bill of Rights applied to states.*

1913
Sixteenth Amendment authorizes federal income tax. . . . Seventeenth Amendment establishes direct election of U.S. senators; amendment was proposed by Congress after nationwide campaign to force action on issue.

1919
Nineteenth Amendment grants women right to vote nationwide.

1920s, '30s
First Supreme Court decisions applying Bill of Rights provisions (freedom of speech, press, religion, assembly) to states.

1933-1936
Supreme Court strikes down parts of President Franklin D. Roosevelt's New Deal program.

1937-1941
Roosevelt fails with "court-packing" plan (1937); succeeds in shifting court's ideological balance with new appointments as vacancies arise.

1951
Twenty-Second Amendment limits president to two full terms.

1954-1969
Supreme Court decisions under Chief Justice Earl Warren stir constitutional debates over desegregation, civil liberties, school prayer, reapportionment, criminal procedure; efforts to curb rulings by constitutional amendment fail.

1971
Twenty-Sixth Amendment guarantees 18-year-olds right to vote.

1973
Abortion-rights ruling in *Roe v. Wade* provokes opposition; protracted campaign to overturn decision by constitutional amendment fails.

1980s
Balanced budget amendment proposed, falls short.

1997-1998
President Bill Clinton impeached by House on obstruction, perjury counts; acquitted by Senate.

2000-Present
Constitutional confrontations under presidents Bush, Obama.

2000
Supreme Court ruling in *Bush v. Gore* assures election of George W. Bush as president; election contest highlights pitfalls of Electoral College system.

2001-2009
Bush tests presidential power after al Qaeda's Sept. 11, 2001, attacks; domestic surveillance expanded by USA Patriot Act; courts rebuff legal challenges to Patriot Act; Supreme Court decisions require habeas corpus review for Guantánamo detainees.

2009-Present
Obama retreats from broad claims of presidential power but leaves some policies in place; Obama, congressional Democrats assailed by conservatives, Republicans over constitutionality of Affordable Care Act; Supreme Court upholds legislation but rejects broadest claims for congressional power.

2012
Calls for amending major features of Constitution continue as its 225th anniversary on Sept. 17 approaches; some groups on left and right favor new convention to consider changes.

Rewriting the Constitution: Some Modest Proposals

When the online magazine Slate *asked readers this summer to propose amendments to the Constitution, 343 people rose to the challenge. Based on more than 6,000 votes in the so-called "Constitution Smackdown,"* Slate *picked a set of winners and runners-up whose ideas ranged from requiring term limits for politicians to allowing states to secede. Meanwhile,* The New York Times *tapped a bevy of scholars for their views on the Constitution, and they too did not hold back. Here are edited excerpts from both publications.*

From Slate:

"Telecommute, Congress!" by MeterReader

"Why are there quorum requirements still in place for Congress? Why must members of Congress be present in the Capitol to vote on legislation? . . . The current process creates huge waste in travel, security, staff and other support expenses. It also facilitates the kind of 'backroom' deals, concentrated lobbying and lack of transparency that voters hate. Send Congress home, but give them the tools to do their job from there."

"Abolish Geographic Representation" by Steve Robertson

"In a global economy, the idea that we should have representatives of New York or Wyoming, as opposed to representatives of union workers, gays or cat fanciers, seems completely arbitrary. At least one house of the legislature should be composed of anyone who can collect enough online votes (yes, this proposal would have to wait for something like universal broadband) to reach a threshold for representation that is pegged off the census."

"Elect the President and V.P. by Direct Vote — No More Electoral College" by RadOwl

"The Electoral College system for electing the president skews the national focus to a few all-important states and their issues. By replacing the Electoral College with direct election of the president and V.P., campaigns would have to treat states more equally. Plus, the ability to influence national results through corruption at the state level would be reduced."

"Supermajority To Overturn Laws" by KC64

"A supermajority of at least seven Supreme Court Justices should be required to overturn laws as unconstitutional. When a law is passed by Congress or a state legislature, and signed by a governor or the president, it has already been deemed constitutional by all those who approved it. If the law is to be deemed unconstitutional, it shouldn't be a close call. It should be obvious."

"Weight Voting by Age with Younger Voters' Votes Having More Weight" by Winn

"By giving the votes of younger voters greater weight than those of their older counterparts, the membership of the executive and legislative branches can be structured to look out for the long-term health of the country rather than for the short-term benefits of older voters at the cost of the long-term health of the country and the future earnings of younger voters. The mechanism through which this will work is that the vote of an 18-year-old . . . will count 100 times more than the vote of someone who somehow makes it to age 118 or older. The vote of a 19-year-old will be worth 99 percent that of an 18-year-old, the vote of a 43-year-old will be worth 75 percent of that of an 18-year-old, the vote of a 68-year-old will be worth half of that of an 18-year-old, and so on."

From *The New York Times*

Akhil Reed Amar (Professor of Law, Yale University), *"Allow Naturalized Citizens to be President" www.nytimes.com/roomfordebate/2012/07/08/another-stab-at-the-us-constitution/revisiting-the-constitution-allow-naturalized-citizens-to-be-president.*

"[M]odern-day naturalized citizens are barred from the presidency simply because they were born in the wrong place to the wrong parents. . . . Opening the door of presidential eligibility to naturalized Americans will redeem the Constitution's

Continued from p. 750

absurd to elect as vice president the runner-up in the balloting for president — as happened in 1796 with the election of rivals Adams and Jefferson in the two offices. The 12th Amendment separated the two contests, but it left the House's deadlock-breaking role in place and made no move toward popular election.

The slavery issue unsettled American politics for a half-century despite the Framers' make-peace accord. Congress banned the importation of slaves in 1808; the Missouri Compromise of 1820 went further by prohibiting slavery in new territories north of Missouri's southern border. But the slave-holding states used their power in Congress to stifle any discussion of abolishing the practice and to win enactment of a strengthened Fugitive Slave Act in 1850 as part of another attempted compromise on the issue. The Supreme Court's infamous *Dred Scott* decision in 1857 undid the compromise by ruling that, under the Constitution, Congress could not limit slavery nor recognize blacks — slave or free — as citizens. Inflamed abolitionist sentiment spurred fearful Southern states to secede and then to provoke the armed confrontation that drew the North into a war to save the Union. "The Founders' Constitution failed," Yale's Amar writes. [25]

With the Union victorious in the Civil War, three Reconstruction Congresses approved and states ratified

grand trajectory, adding a new chapter true to the spirit of the story thus far. The founders promised more equality than had existed in 1775; later amendments brought blacks and women into the fold; and full equality for naturalized Americans is the logical next step."

Melynda Price (Associate Professor, University of Kentucky College of Law), *"Get Rid of the Right to Bear Arms," www.nytimes.com/roomfordebate/2012/07/08/another-stab-at-the-us-constitution/revisiting-the-constitution-do-we-really-need-the-second-amendment.*

"I am not naïve enough to believe that doing away with the Second Amendment would do away with gun violence, but I know firsthand the impact of guns and gunshots on children. This nation was constructed and reconstructed in the aftermath of violent and bloody conflicts. Still, the Framers believed that not only the Constitution, but also the peaceful way the document was created, would penetrate the Americans' minds. . . . The Second Amendment acknowledged the vulnerability of a nation in its infancy but could not predict a world where some would move through life feeling more like targets than citizens."

Rachel E. Barkow (Professor of Regulatory Law and Policy, N.Y.U.), *"Clarify What's Cruel and Unusual" www.nytimes.com/roomfordebate/2012/07/08/another-stab-at-the-us-constitution/revisiting-the-constitution-clarify-whats-cruel-and-unusual-punishment.*

"Sometimes prison sentences — even the most severe — are a rational response to crime. But often, sentences are the product of a political process in which politicians are scared of appearing soft on crime so they do not even question the reasonableness of a proposed criminal law. . . . The Constitution has failed to check this pathological process. The Eighth Amendment bans 'cruel and unusual punishments.' But some justices do not think this bans excessive prison terms. And the requirement that a sentence be 'unusual' has meant that the justices often do little more than count up states with similar sentences without looking at how states reached those outcomes. . . . [C]larifying and expanding the Eighth Amendment could help. It should specifically state that excessive terms of incarceration are prohibited, just as it bans excessive fines. It should expressly prohibit mandatory sentences so that every case gets the benefit of individualized attention by a judge. And it should insist that legislatures create a record showing that they considered empirical evidence about the law's likely impact."

Pauline Maier (Professor of American History, M.I.T.), *"Rewrite the First Amendment" www.nytimes.com/roomfordebate/2012/07/08/another-stab-at-the-us-constitution/revisiting-the-constitution-rewrite-the-first-amendment.*

" 'Congress shall make no law' is a peculiarly stingy way to begin an amendment that protects the rights of conscience, speech, press, assembly and petition. James Madison proposed more capacious language for those rights. He would have said, for example, that 'the civil rights of none shall be abridged on account of religious belief or worship, nor shall any national religion be established, nor shall the full and equal rights of conscience be in any manner, or on any pretext infringed.' He would also have stated that 'the people shall not be deprived of their right to speak, to write, or to publish their sentiments; and the freedom of the press, as one of the great bulwarks of liberty, shall be inviolable.' . . . Keeping Madison's language would make the First Amendment like most of the first eight amendments, which affirm basic rights in general terms, not as restrictions on the federal government."

Sources: Kevin Bleyer, "The Winners of Constitution Smackdown," *Slate*, July 5, 2012, http://hive.slate.com/hive/how-can-we-fix-constitution/article/the-winners-of-constitution-smackdown; "Room for Debate: Another Stab at the Constitution," *The New York Times*, July 8, 2012, www.nytimes.com/roomfordebate/2012/07/08/another-stab-at-the-us-constitution/revisiting-the-constitution-rewrite-the-first-amendment.

successive amendments that collectively have been called the nation's "Second Founding." (*See box, p. 755.*) The 13th Amendment, abolishing slavery, was ratified less than eight months after the war's end. The 14th was more complex and more contentious. Congress approved it on a party-line vote and declared it ratified in July 1868 only by counting the votes of military governments installed in Southern states that had previously rejected it. The amendment granted citizenship to all persons "born or naturalized" in the United States and laid the groundwork for federal supervision of state laws with the Privileges and Immunities, Due Process and Equal Protection clauses. The 15th Amendment, added in 1870, prohibited the states from denying the right to vote on the basis of race. It said nothing about women's suffrage.

Significantly, each Reconstruction amendment included a section authorizing Congress to enforce its provisions through "appropriate" legislation. Congress exercised the power first in 1866 with a law — the first ever enacted over a presidential veto — aimed at guaranteeing blacks the same contract and property rights as whites. Two subsequent civil rights acts, in 1870 and 1871, sought to safeguard blacks in exercising voting and other political rights; an 1875 law barred racial discrimination in public accommodations. But Congress and the president stepped away from Reconstruction policies after 1876. And the Supreme

Court ruled the public accommodations statute unconstitutional in 1883.

Despite the limitations now apparent, the nation was in a self-confident and self-congratulatory mood as it marked the Constitution's centennial in 1887. President Grover Cleveland embodied the national sentiment as he spoke of the Constitution's "trials" and "triumphs" at a celebration staged in front of Independence Hall in Philadelphia. The Constitution "has been found sufficient in the past," Cleveland declared. "And in all the future years it will be found sufficient if the American people are true to their sacred trust." [26]

Progressive Eras

The Constitution, in its second century, became an instrument of sweeping changes in a succession of progressive eras broken up by periods of political and legal backlash. The federal government grew in size and scope, with the Supreme Court's constitutional blessing. Mass politics emerged with the extension of the right to vote to women and the successful struggle to make real the right to vote for African-Americans. The Constitution itself became a subject of political debate as grassroots movements lobbied for amendments — sometimes successfully, sometimes not — and politicians regularly invoked it to justify their positions or criticize their opponents'.

Congress and the states approved four constitutional amendments in the first two decades of the 20th century; each represented the culmination of hard-fought political struggles by mass political movements. The Sixteenth, authorizing a federal income tax, was ratified in 1913 to overturn the Supreme Court's 1895 decision barring such a levy. Also that year the 17th instituted direct election of senators nationwide, a goal of the Progressive movement that had already been adopted in a majority of states. The temperance movement won ratification of the ill-fated 18th Amendment — Prohibition — in 1919, only to see it repealed 14 years later. The women's suffrage movement achieved a more lasting success the next year, with ratification of the 19th Amendment — again, after many states had already acted to give women the right to vote.

The Supreme Court became the focal point of intensified constitutional debates during the next two decades as a conservative majority struck down economic regulations supported by labor and opposed by business. Two decisions, in 1918 and 1922, striking down federal laws to ban child labor nationwide led to an unsuccessful effort to overturn the rulings by constitutional amendment. Labor unions and progressive groups also supported an unsuccessful constitutional amendment pushed by Sen. Robert M. La Follette Sr., of Wisconsin, to allow Congress itself to override a Supreme Court decision striking down a federal law simply by re-enacting it.

The court continued to take a narrow view of Congress' powers under the Commerce or Tax and Spending clauses in the 1930s as it struck down several major parts of President Franklin D. Roosevelt's New Deal program. The clash inspired FDR's unsuccessful "Court-packing" scheme in 1937 — Roosevelt's transparent effort to change the balance of power on the court by providing for the appointment of additional justices for any over the age of 70. The plan failed in Congress, but a series of vacancies beginning that year allowed the president to remake the court into a tribunal more supportive of federal power and more protective of individual rights.

Beginning in the 1950s, the Supreme Court became the target of a conservative backlash tied to liberal rulings on diverse issues including desegregation, internal security, school prayer, reapportionment, criminal procedure and abortion — all based on new interpretations of constitutional provisions. As early as the 1950s, the court under Chief Justice Earl Warren prompted efforts to curb its powers with rulings that limited Congress' power in internal-security investigations; bills to limit the court's jurisdiction over such cases were introduced but failed. The reapportionment rulings of the 1960s prompted unsuccessful proposals to overturn them by constitutional amendment. Opponents of the Warren Court's school prayer rulings and the later abortion-rights ruling by the court under Chief Justice Warren E. Burger have waged more protracted fights to overturn them by constitutional amendment, but those too have fallen short.

By contrast, the Constitution was amended three times in a decade to enlarge voting rights. The 23rd Amendment (1961) gave the District of Columbia three electoral votes in presidential and vice presidential balloting; broader proposals to grant statehood or give the District voting representation in Congress have failed. The 24th (1964) abolished poll taxes. And the 26th (1971) gave 18-year-olds the right to vote, nationwide; Congress had passed a law in 1970 lowering the voting age to 18, but the Supreme Court ruled Congress had no authority to set age requirements for state and local elections. In the meantime, Congress had passed the Voting Rights Act of 1965, a law enacted under the 15th Amendment's enforcement clause that gave the federal government broad powers to break down racial barriers to voting in state and local elections.

Four other 20th-century constitutional amendments reflected urges to tinker. The 20th (1933) moved the inauguration of the president from March 4 to Jan. 20, shortening the post-election lame-duck period. The 22nd (1951) limits the president to two full terms — a return to George Washington's precedent after FDR's elections to third and fourth terms. The 25th (1967), approved in the wake of the assassination of

President John F. Kennedy, provides for a new president to nominate and Congress to confirm a vice president after the death of the president; it also establishes a mechanism for the vice president to act as president in the event the president is disabled. And the 27th, proposed in 1789 as part of the Bill of Rights but ratified only in 1992, prevents a pay raise for Congress from taking effect until after the next congressional election.

The flurry of amendments and proposed amendments suggested a measure of discontent with the governing charter. But the Bicentennial observances in 1987 were almost uniformly celebratory, climaxing in a nationally televised parade and gala in Philadelphia. Speaking outside Independence Hall, President Ronald Reagan recalled the country's perilous state as the Framers met to lay the foundation of a new, stronger national government. In a real sense, Reagan said, the American Revolution truly began in 1787. It was only with the writing of the Constitution, he said, "that the hopes and dreams of the revolutionists could become a living, enduring reality." [27]

The 'Second Constitution'

Three amendments passed soon after the Civil War — during Reconstruction — have been called "the Second Constitution" because of the profound effects they had, over time, in recognizing individual rights and in subordinating the powers of the states to federal law. Each of the amendments significantly included a final section specifying that Congress has the power to enforce the amendment "by appropriate legislation." Here are the amendments, with dates of ratification and major provisions:

Thirteenth (Dec. 6, 1865): Prohibits "slavery or involuntary servitude," except as punishment for crime, within the United States "or any place subject to their [sic] jurisdiction."

Fourteenth (July 9, 1868):

Section 1: Recognizes "all persons born or naturalized in the United States, and subject to the jurisdiction thereof" as citizens of the United States and their state of residence; prohibits any state from abridging "the privileges or immunities" of citizens of the United States, depriving any person of life, liberty, or property without due process of law, or denying any person "the equal protection of the law."

Section 2: Apportions members of the House of Representatives according to population "counting the whole number of persons in each State, excluding Indians not taxed;" basis of representation to be reduced proportionately if suffrage was denied or abridged to "any male inhabitants," age 21 or older.

Section 3: Bars anyone who "engaged in insurrection or rebellion" against the United States, or gave "aid or comfort" to enemies of the United States, from serving as member of Congress, elector for president or vice president or other civil or military officer of the United States; Congress "may remove such disability" by two-thirds vote of each chamber.

Section 4: Validates all public debts of the United States incurred in Civil War, including pensions and bounties; rejects as "illegal and void" all public debts of the Confederacy and "any claim for the loss or emancipation of any slave."

Fifteenth (Feb. 3, 1870): Prohibits any state from denying or abridging the right of U.S. citizens to vote "on account of race, color, or previous condition of servitude."

Constitution in Turmoil

The Constitution has been in turmoil for much of its third century, an era marked by divided government, partisan polarization and public discontent. Congress and the president have clashed almost continuously over fiscal policy, twice taking the government to the edge of a fiscal cliff. The Supreme Court defined limits of presidential power in politically charged cases involving two chief executives: Republican George W. Bush and his Democratic predecessor, Bill Clinton. The court was also thrust into deciding the razor's-edge 2000 election between Bush and Gore. And critics of presidential and congressional power have found frequent fault with Obama and Congress, focused most dramatically on Obama's health care plan as enacted by a Democratically controlled Congress.

Divided political control of the White House and Congress, once the exception in U.S. history, has been the norm under the last four presidents, two from each major political party. Neither of the Bush presidents nor Clinton served with a Congress with both chambers controlled by his party for most of his time in the White House; Obama faces the same fate even if re-elected, unless Democrats can defy the oddsmakers and regain control of the House.

The partisan divisions have contributed to the growing sense of a "dysfunctional" federal government. An ABC-*Washington Post* poll in February 2011 found only 26 percent of respondents optimistic about "our government and how well it works" — the lowest figure since the question was first asked in 1974. [28]

The partisan divisions have played out most dramatically in budget battles between Democratic presidents and Republicans in Congress. A budget impasse between Clinton and Republicans, who then controlled both the House and the Senate, resulted in two government shutdowns, in late 1995 and early 1996, totaling 28 days. In summer 2011, Obama and the GOP-controlled House locked horns over a debt limit increase, reaching agreement only barely in time to avert the first ever federal government default. Throughout the period, Republicans and some Democrats urged passage of a proposed balanced budget constitutional amendment. The House approved an amendment in January 1995, but the measure fell just short of the needed two-thirds majority in the Senate. The House voted on the issue in November 2011, but it fell short of a two-thirds majority (261-165).

Clinton also faced politically charged investigations raising constitutional issues during much of his presidency that included an inquiry by an independent counsel, a sexual harassment lawsuit and, ultimately, the second presidential impeachment in U.S. history. The Supreme Court in 1997 rejected Clinton's effort to defer the sexual harassment lawsuit while he was president. Independent counsel Kenneth Starr summoned Clinton before a federal grand jury to answer allegations of sexual behavior with a White House intern. Starr submitted his conclusion that Clinton had committed perjury to the House, which voted in December 1998 to impeach him on two counts: perjury and obstruction of justice. The Senate trial, with Chief Justice William H. Rehnquist presiding, ended in February 1999 with Clinton's acquittal on both counts.

The close partisan divisions played a part in exposing the potential pitfalls in the Electoral College system when Bush and Gore fought to a near draw in the 2000 presidential election. [29] The outcome hinged on Florida's 25 electoral votes, but Bush's apparent election night victory was narrowed to only 327 votes after a recount. Gore contested the results, spawning litigation that reached the Supreme Court twice. Gore won the popular vote nationwide, but news coverage during the litigation noted that Florida's GOP-controlled legislature could award the electoral votes without regard to the vote tabulation in the state or that the election could wind up in the House of Representatives. The Supreme Court's 5-4 decision to cut off the recount in Florida effectively ended the election with Bush the winner.

Just nine months after his inauguration, Bush faced a test of presidential leadership that turned into a test of presidential power: al Qaeda's Sept. 11, 2001, terrorist attack on the United States. Bush responded by winning congressional approval of legislation, the USA Patriot Act, expanding domestic surveillance powers. He also launched a war in Afghanistan that resulted in the capture of hundreds of prisoners who were brought to the U.S. Naval Base at Guantánamo Bay, Cuba. Civil liberties groups and others unsuccessfully challenged provisions of the Patriot Act in court, but they won some modifications when it was renewed in 2006. Human-rights lawyers representing the Guantánamo prisoners won a Supreme Court decision establishing the right to judicial review, but as Bush left the White House more than 200 were still being held. [30]

Obama took office in 2009 promising to undo some of the Bush administration's anti-terrorism policies, but he disappointed civil liberties and human-rights groups by continuing to claim broad presidential authority to detain foreigners suspected of anti-American terrorism. He arguably went beyond Bush's policies by claiming the power to direct lethal attacks against U.S. citizens abroad if linked to al Qaeda. In domestic politics, Obama and congressional Democrats have been under nearly constant attack for three years over the health care bill, enacted in March 2010 as the Patient Protection and Affordable Care Act. Constitutional attacks centered on provisions requiring individuals to obtain health insurance and expanding coverage of the joint state-federal Medicaid program.

Legal challenges that spanned two full years ended on June 28 with a closely divided Supreme Court leaving the law largely intact while rejecting the administration's major rationale for the insurance mandate. Obama claimed victory with the ruling, while conservatives and Republicans consoled themselves by pointing to aspects of the court's ruling suggesting limits on Congress' commerce and spending powers. [31] ■

CURRENT SITUATION

Convention Talk

Interest in calling a convention to amend the Constitution is stirring among some unlikely political bedfellows on the left and the right, but the odds still appear to be heavily against the first-ever use of this alternate process of writing and ratifying a constitutional amendment.

Some conservatives want to use the convention route to limit federal spending policies by adding a balanced

Continued on p. 758

At Issue:

Should a constitutional convention be called?

SANFORD LEVINSON
PROFESSOR OF LAW, UNIVERSITY OF TEXAS

WRITTEN FOR *CQ RESEARCHER*, SEPTEMBER 2012

yes

We very much need a new constitutional convention, for two reasons. The first is simply that our 18th-century Constitution, remarkably unchanged with regard to our basic institutional structures, contributes to the widespread perception, across political and ideological lines, that our political system is "broken," "dysfunctional" or "pathological." Many causes are assigned to the contemporary unhappiness with our politics — 24-hour confrontational news programs, the ever-bigger role of money and ever-stronger "partisanship," where loyalty to one's political party often seems to take precedence over genuinely striving to work for the public good (if credit might go to members of the other party). All bear some of the blame, but it is past time to realize that the Framers, drafting a constitution for a substantially different world, made their own contribution to today's dysfunction.

They would not be surprised to learn that the Constitution might need changing. Article V speaks to the certainty of imperfections in the design by providing a mechanism for change, including, crucially, a new constitutional convention. James Madison, even when supporting ratification of the new constitution, emphasized the necessity of paying strong attention to "the lessons of experience" that might suggest ways of improving our system. One might expect the Framers to be shocked that so many modern Americans treat them as demigods, making decisions for all time, rather than gifted, but necessarily imperfect, men doing their best in troubled times to solve what they thought was the crisis facing the young country at the time. We best honor their spirit by asking the tough questions they did in 1787 — precisely what might need to be changed in order to confront our own challenges?

But there is a second reason for a convention: It is foolish to expect Congress to take the time to address the multiple and complex questions that a convention would have to confront. Even if one suspends all cynicism about whether political "ins" would ever seriously contemplate changes that would threaten their own power, they just don't have the time. Congress is faced with too many other issues to expect them to suspend their regular work to take off a year for serious debate about how to make the Constitution more functional for the 21st century. Only an independent body — a constitutional convention — with no legislative or executive duties could take the time for study, hearings and intense debate that We the People would legitimately expect before embarking on needed constitutional changes.

MEG PENROSE
PROFESSOR OF LAW, TEXAS WESLEYAN LAW SCHOOL

WRITTEN FOR *CQ RESEARCHER*, SEPTEMBER 2012

no

We live in very interesting times. The federal government appears to be failing. The state governments are not faring much better. And the political parties seem broken beyond repair. Amid this dysfunctional backdrop are calls for change. Radical change. Scholars and activists alike are calling for resort to a little known constitutional provision, Article V.

Since the first constitutional convention in 1787, Article V has lain dormant. Article V provides states with an avenue to amend the Constitution when the federal government is unable or unwilling to do so. Many welcome the current gridlock as an opportunity to call an untested, unregulated and unconfined Article V constitutional convention ("Con-Con"). A growing chorus sees the Con-Con as the solution to our failing government. I do not.

I strongly oppose wading into the Con-Con experiment during the current political climate. My opposition is based on the fact that under any Article V Con-Con experiment, Congress — and all its toxicity — will undoubtedly play a significant role in the convention process. Congress, not the states, will be the first to interpret Article V and establish the Con-Con parameters. And when the states challenge Congress' role, as they assuredly would, they would be forced to turn to an equally divided, and divisive, branch of our government, the Supreme Court. This process, undertaken at this particular time, has all the markings of a true constitutional crisis.

Our Constitution has endured for generations because, while large on democratic ideas and principles, it has always remained short on detail. The Constitution, including Article V, is but a rough outline of an ideal government. It was intentionally crafted to be difficult to amend.

The Con-Con advocates cannot assure us what an Article V convention would look like, who would be in charge or how business would be conducted. There are no guarantees that the Con-Con would be limited to amendments upon which the requisite states agree, or whether it would be open to the sentiments of the attendees and their respective agendas.

The problem, quite simply, is that there is no way to predict how this revolutionary idea would take shape. After all, the only constitutional convention this country has witnessed, the original Constitutional Convention, immediately abandoned its limited mandate and proved to be the very runaway convention that Con-Con opponents now fear. If history repeats itself, we have reason to be fearful.

Continued from p. 756

budget provision to the Constitution or, in a more recent proposal, requiring approval by state legislatures to increase the national debt ceiling. Some liberals want to amend the Constitution to enact campaign finance reform — most specifically, to overrule the Supreme Court's controversial *Citizens United* decision to allow limits on corporate spending in political campaigns. [32]

Both sides want to use the convention route because they despair of winning approval of their proposals from two-thirds majorities in both chambers of Congress, as required in the procedure used for all 27 amendments to date. "Congress is captured by so many interests," David Segal, a former Democratic state representative from Rhode Island, said as he opened a two-day conference on a constitutional convention at Harvard Law School in late September 2011. [33]

Advocates of a constitutional convention, however, run up against opposition from others on both the left and the right, who raise fears of a "runaway convention" that would repeal rights-protecting provisions viewed as sacrosanct by one side or the other: free speech for the left, gun rights for the right. "This is almost literally the first thing you hear," says Levinson, the University of Texas professor who has been a leading proponent of a convention.

The Harvard conference featured speakers from such conservative and libertarian organizations as the Cato Institute, the Arizona-based Goldwater Institute and the Tea Party Patriots and others from liberal groups such as Common Cause and the Green Party.

In opening the conference, Lawrence Lessig, a left-leaning professor at the law school, said the Framers deliberately included the convention route to an amendment to allow circumventing roadblocks in Congress. "The Framers recognized that there might be times when Congress might not be capable of proposing the kinds of amendments that the nation needs," Lessig said.

Getty Images/Alex Wong

President Obama signs the Patient Protection and Affordable Care Act on March 23, 2010. Constitutional attacks on the law centered on provisions requiring individuals to obtain health insurance and expanding coverage of Medicaid. On June 28 a closely divided Supreme Court left the law largely intact while rejecting the administration's major rationale for the insurance mandate. Conservatives and Republicans consoled themselves by pointing to aspects of the court's ruling suggesting limits on Congress' commerce and spending power.

The conference was co-sponsored by Tea Party Patriots, largest of the Tea Party organizations. Mark Meckler, a California attorney and co-founder of the group, told the gathering that he was "neither for or against a convention." But he batted away concerns about a runaway convention. Meckler said he was "confident" that debate at the convention would be both "reasoned" and "heated," but "in the end we would do the right thing."

Only minimal concrete progress has been made in getting states to request Congress to call a convention, as the Article V amendment procedure outlines. The Goldwater Institute lobbied in 26 states over the past two legislative seasons in favor of calling a convention to consider the national-debt amendment, but only two approved the proposal: Louisiana and North Dakota. Nick Dranias, director of constitutional studies for the Goldwater Institute, says the proposal was "overwhelmingly" opposed by two other conservative groups: the Eagle Forum and the John Birch Society. "They proved to be quite the foe," he says.

On the left, Segal, who also served as a Green Party representative on the Providence, R.I., City Council, also acknowledges scant progress on the issue. "A few resolutions have passed, but activity isn't as robust as one might hope, given the intransigence of Congress," he says. Segal says he wants to see the convention address "election reform and money in politics — very worthy causes."

Further complicating the push for a convention are the many unknowns associated with a procedure never successfully invoked. Questions discussed but left unresolved at the conference include whether a convention could be limited in scope, how the rules for the convention would be established and how delegates would be elected.

Supporters of a convention note, however, that pushing the procedure could itself pressure Congress into acting. They note that Congress approved the 17th Amendment, which established direct election of U.S. senators, after proponents of the change had gotten nearly enough states to call for a convention to force Congress to act.

Despite the interest from different ideological groups, many constitutional experts remain profoundly skeptical, especially on the political left. "I have trust issues," says Browne-Marshall, the John Jay College professor. "I do not trust those people in that room to put the interests of the country above their own or whatever group to which they owe their allegiance."

Interest appears to be somewhat greater among conservative constitutional experts. "I've sort of come to a conclusion that it's not such a bad idea," says Reynolds, the University of Tennessee professor. "We really need to focus on why our system is not working."

"A convention might lead to useful change even if were a failure," Reynolds adds. "That's not a failure. That might be a success in that it would cause people to focus on [needed constitutional changes]."

Constitution Talk

Interest in the Constitution is spiking as the 225th anniversary approaches, but many experts say Americans fall short in their knowledge and understanding of a founding document that they nevertheless celebrate and revere.

"Americans appear to love and absolutely revere the Constitution, to regard it as the thing that defines who they are and what we stand for in this nation," says Richard Beeman, a professor of history at the University of Pennsylvania in Philadelphia and author of a recent history of the writing of the Constitution, *Plain Honest Men*. [34]

Even so, Beeman says, "Americans' ignorance of the specifics of the Constitution is quite vast." For that reason, he sees "a kind of obvious disjunction about what Americans know and their apparent reverence for it."

Baruch College historian Berkin agrees. "I'm willing to bet you that 99 and 44 one-hundredths of a percent of Americans have never read the Constitution," Berkin says. "There's just so much uninformed discussion that it makes your head spin."

The ignorance and misunderstandings about the Constitution extend to matters both small and large, the historians say. Berkin says she once had an argument with someone who insisted Abigail Adams was a delegate to the Philadelphia convention. She was not, nor was her husband John Adams or Adams' later political rival, Jefferson. They were both posted abroad in 1787 as ambassadors to Britain and France, respectively.

More broadly, Beeman says Americans misunderstand the Framers' basic reason for establishing a new national government. "For most Americans, the Constitution is the Bill of Rights — those amendments that speak about what Congress is not allowed to do," he explains. Beeman agrees that the Framers had "a healthy distrust of concentrations of power," but says the delegates "gathered to establish a stronger government."

"The best statement of that is in the preamble," Beeman continues, referring to the six grand purposes set out at the start of the Constitution. "To do the things in the preamble, you needed a strong, central government."

Conservative experts and commentators view the purpose of the Constitution differently. "The pushback against the great expansion of government spending and regulations that began in the Bush administration and continued in the Obama administration is being organized around the Constitution as the main argument against these measures," says Barnett, the Georgetown law professor. Author Freedman sees a need to amend the Constitution "in a way that is likely to produce results consistent with the original design."

Americans interested in viewing the original Constitution itself can see it on display in the central rotunda of the National Archives building in Washington along with the Declaration of Independence and the Bill of Rights. The Archives museum receives about 1 million visitors per year, a spokeswoman says.

The National Constitution Center in Philadelphia drew 817,727 visitors in 2011, according to a spokeswoman. The center is sited across Independence Mall from Independence Hall, the former Pennsylvania statehouse where the Constitutional Convention met.

The center's introductory presentation for visitors, entitled "Freedom Rising," tells the history of the Constitution in celebratory tones but recognizes some aspects less worthy of celebration. A live narrator acknowledges that the Framers' commitment to equality "did not include all the people." The Constitution left slavery up to the states, without ever using the word itself. It took 75 years and a Civil War to abolish slavery, the narrator says, and another century to overcome racial segregation. Women were not granted the vote nationwide until the 20th century.

Some visitors on a recent weekend in August picked up on some of the points. "It's amazing to me as a woman that we weren't able to vote until 1920," said Mary Wicker, a homemaker from Runnemede, N.J. All the delegates, she said, "were rich, white males." Floyd Smith, an African-American security officer visiting from Chicago, said he would have voted against the pro-slavery provisions if he had been a delegate, even at the risk of some slave-holding states walking out.

Other visitors left with fewer reservations about the Framers' work. "It's really quite amazing how they figured it out," said Pat Aurand, a teacher in Philadelphia. "They were up against some tough stuff." Wicker also ended with approving remarks. The Constitution, she said, "is the thing that ties us together." ■

OUTLOOK

The 'Durable' Constitution

The Constitution is "the oldest governing document still in existence today," actor-commentator Ben Stein tells visitors to the National Constitution Center in a video. The important point, Stein adds, "is not how old it is, but how durable it is."

With only 27 amendments in 225 years, the Constitution does appear to have stood up remarkably well over time. But it has also been the focus of all but continuous struggle from the moment it was written up to the present day. "The history of the Constitution shows that it has been a constant focus of the American people in the question of who we are as a nation and who do we want to become," says Frederickson with the American Constitution Society.

The debates over ratification themselves were contentious and the outcome far from certain as the delegates left Philadelphia in September. [35] Three states ratified before the end of the year. But when New Hampshire became the ninth to ratify on June 21, 1788, two states crucial to the Union — Virginia and New York — remained to be heard from. Virginia voted to ratify on June 25 and New York on July 26, but the margins were close in both states. The last two states, North Carolina and Rhode Island, voted to ratify only after the new government had been formed. And the price for winning ratification was the Bill of Rights, the package of amendments proposed and submitted to the states by the First Congress in order to satisfy the fears of the Anti-Federalists of an overreaching central government.

Echoes of the debates between the Federalists and Anti-Federalists can be heard in the sharp arguments in Washington and across the nation today over the scope and powers of the federal government. Historian Bodenhamer finds the arguments neither surprising nor disturbing. "The Constitution invites us to struggle over issues of power and rights," Bodenhamer says. "This is what makes the Constitution a radical document. It puts the responsibility of that struggle back on the people because we hold popular sovereignty."

Fellow historian Beeman is disturbed, however, by the tone of some of the arguments. "A lot of the passion that one hears in the current debate over how to interpret the Constitution is generated by the fact that Americans may feel very strongly about it but don't know much about it," he says. "They don't know what's in it."

The Constitution is also taking some of the blame for the political gridlock in Washington — wrongly in the view of some of the experts. "We have a terrible political culture in this country," says University of Tennessee professor Reynolds. "It's difficult to blame the Constitution for that." Yale law professor Amar agrees. "Am I critical of our system?" he asks, rhetorically. Yes, he says, but "more of our culture than the formal world of the Constitution."

The Framers themselves had only limited hopes for the Constitution, historian Berkin notes. "They knew that all Republics devolve into tyranny," she says. "What they wanted to do is to delay this as long as possible." She says they would be surprised at how long it has lasted with so few changes. "They didn't envision that changing the Constitution would be so extraordinarily difficult," she says.

Those who favor changing the Constitution have a decidedly uphill struggle to do so. "It's hard for me to imagine any major structural changes," Bodenhamer says. Reynolds tentatively agrees. A quarter-century from now, he says, "I would say it would look more like what we have today than something different."

Still, the arguments go on. "Americans have been arguing about the Constitution from the very, very beginning," says Penn professor Beeman. "I regard that in general as a sign of its health rather than its infirmity." ■

About the Author

Associate Editor **Kenneth Jost** graduated from Harvard College and Georgetown University Law Center. He is the author of the *Supreme Court Yearbook* and editor of *The Supreme Court from A to Z* (both *CQ Press*). He was a member of the *CQ Researcher* team that won the American Bar Association's 2002 Silver Gavel Award. His previous reports include "States and Federalism" and "Abortion Debates." He is also author of the blog *Jost on Justice* (http://jostonjustice.blogspot.com).

Notes

[1] The full text of the original Constitution is on the National Archives' website: www.archives.gov/exhibits/charters/constitution_transcript.html. For a compact account of the Constitutional Convention, see Robert K. Landers, "Bicentennial of the Constitution," *Editorial Research Reports*, March 27, 1987, http://library.cqpress.com/cqresearcher/document.php?id=cqresrre1987032700&type=hitlist&action=print.

[2] Sanford Levinson, *Our Undemocratic Constitution: Where the Constitution Goes Wrong (and How We the People Can Correct It)* (2006), pp. 4-7. See also Sanford Levinson, *Framed: America's 51 Constitutions and the Crisis of Governance* (2012).

[3] Text of Marshall's speech, May 6, 1987, to the San Francisco Patent and Trademark Law Association, www.thurgoodmarshall.com/speeches/constitutional_speech.htm. For coverage, see Stuart Taylor Jr., "Marshall Sounds Critical Note on Bicentennial," *The New York Times*, May 7, 1987, p. A1.

[4] David J. Bodenhamer, *The Revolutionary Constitution* (2012).
[5] See Kenneth Jost and Greg Giroux, "The Electoral College," *CQ Researcher*, Dec. 8, 2000, pp. 977-1008.
[6] See Akhil Reed Amar, *The Unwritten Constitution: The Precedents and Principles We Live By* (2012); *America's Constitution: A Biography* (2005).
[7] Randy E. Barnett, *Restoring the Lost Constitution: The Presumption of Liberty* (2004).
[8] See Maggie Clark, "States Look to Article V to Limit Federal Power," in Kenneth Jost, "States and Federalism," *CQ Researcher*, Oct. 15, 2010, pp. 845-868.
[9] Carol Berkin, *A Brilliant Solution: Inventing America's Constitution* (2002).
[10] "Muhammad Ali: 2012 Liberty Medal Recipient," National Constitution Center, http://constitutioncenter.org/libertymedal/recipient_2012.html.
[11] Account drawn from Berkin, *op. cit.*, pp. 96-112.
[12] Levinson, *op. cit.,* pp. 58-59. The study is "The Potential for Minority Rule in U.S. Congressional Elections," FairVote: The Center for Voting and Democracy, February 2005, http://archive.fairvote.org/library/geog/congress/minorityrule2004.htm.
[13] Adam Freedman, *The Naked Constitution: What the Founders Said and Why It Still Matters* (2012). Freedman covers legal affairs for Ricochet.com, a conservative news site.
[14] See Niels Lesniewski, "GOP Senate Candidates Advocate 17th Amendment Repeal," *Roll Call*, Aug. 13, 2012, www.rollcall.com/news/GOP-Senate-Candidates-Advocate-17th-Amendment-Repeal-216856-1.html; John Yoo, "Repeal the 17th Amendment?," *National Review Online*, Oct. 22, 2010, www.nationalreview.com/corner/250726/repeal-17th-amendment-john-yoo.
[15] Account drawn from Berkin, *op. cit.*, pp. 136-146.
[16] See Levinson, *op. cit.*, pp. 85-98.
[17] Akhil Reed Amar, "A Constitutional Accident Waiting to Happen," *Constitutional Commentaries*, Vol. 12, p. 143 (summer 1995), www.law.yale.edu/documents/pdf/1995Constitutional.pdf.
[18] See "Americans Would Swap Electoral College for Popular Vote," Gallup, Oct. 24, 2011, www.gallup.com/poll/150245/Americans-Swap-Electoral-College-Popular-Vote.aspx.
[19] See Berkin, *op. cit.*
[20] Levinson, *op. cit.*, pp. 123-139.
[21] Steven G. Calabresi and James Lindgren, "Term Limits for the Supreme Court: Life Tenure Reconsidered," *Harvard Journal of Law and Public Policy*, Vol. 12 (summer 2006), pp. 770-877, http://epstein.usc.edu/research/supctLawCalabresi.pdf.
[22] See Linda Greenhouse, "New Focus on the Effects of Life Tenure," *The New York Times*, Sept. 10, 2007, p. A20. See also Paul Carrington and Roger C. Cramton (eds.), *Reforming the Court: Term Limits for Supreme Court* (2005). Levinson was one of the contributors to the volume; it also includes an earlier version of Calabresi and Lindgren, *op. cit.*
[23] For longer accounts of the Constitutional Convention, see Berkin, *op. cit.*; Catherine Drinker Brown, *Miracle at Philadelphia: The Story of the Constitutional Convention, May to September 1787* (1986: first published 1966). Some subsequent background drawn from Amar, *op. cit.*
[24] Washington's letter to his nephew (and future Supreme Court justice) Bushrod Washington is quoted in Levinson, *op. cit.*, p. 21.
[25] Amar, *op. cit.*, p. 360.
[26] *Public Papers of Grover Cleveland* (1889), pp. 263-264, http://books.google.com/books?id=p35RAAAAYAAJ&pg=PA266&lpg=PA266&dq=constitution+centennial+celebration+1887+grover+cleveland&source=bl&ots=B-MMDTeqJF&sig=T_XjMmHeNSq7JnVxkgdZjUJlkFY&hl=en#v=onepage&q=constitution%20centennial%20celebration%201887%20grover%20cleveland&f=false.
[27] *Public Papers of Ronald Reagan*, Sept. 17, 1987, www.reagan.utexas.edu/archives/speeches/1987/091787a.htm.
[28] "Economy, Gas, Partisanship and War Gang Up on Confidence in Government," ABC News-*Washington Post* poll, March 15, 2011, www.langerresearch.com/uploads/1121a2%202011%20Politics.pdf.
[29] For a comprehensive account, see Kenneth Jost, *Supreme Court Yearbook 2000-2001*.
[30] The case is *Boumediene v. Bush*, 553 U.S. 723 (2008). See Kenneth Jost, *Supreme Court Yearbook 2007-2008*.
[31] The case is *National Federation of Independent Business v. Sebelius*, 567 U.S.—(2012). For a comprehensive account, see Kenneth Jost, *Supreme Court Yearbook 2011-2012* (forthcoming).
[32] The decision is *Citizens United v. Federal Election Commission*, 558 U.S. 50 (2010). For an account, see Kenneth Jost, *Supreme Court Yearbook 2009-2010*.
[33] Account and quotes taken from the archived proceedings. See "Conference on the Constitutional Convention," Harvard Law School, Sept. 24-25, 2011, www.conconcon.org/archive.php. For coverage, see James O'Toole, "Constitutional Convention Call Gains Traction," *Pittsburgh Post-Gazette*, Dec. 12, 2011, p. A1; Gregory Korte, "Balanced budget push brews debate," *USA Today*, Nov. 30, 2011, p. 4A.
[34] Richard Beeman, *Plain Honest Men: The Making of the American Constitution* (2009).
[35] For a history, see Pauline A. Maier, *Ratification: The People Debate the Constitution, 1787-1788* (2011).

FOR MORE INFORMATION

American Constitution Society, 1333 H St., N.W., 11th Floor, Washington, DC 20005; 202-393-6181; www.acslaw.org. Liberal-leaning organization promoting constitutional values of individual rights and liberties, equality, access to justice, democracy and rule of law.

Cato Institute, 1000 Massachusetts Ave., N.W., Washington, DC 20001; 202-842-0200; www.cato.org. Libertarian think tank supporting limited government and free markets.

Constitution Project, 1200 18th St., N.W., Suite 1000, Washington, DC 20036; 202-580-6920; www.constitutionproject.org. Nonprofit think tank seeking bipartisan consensus on constitutional and legal issues.

The Federalist Society, 1015 18th St., N.W., Suite 425, Washington, DC 20036; 202-822-8138; www.fed-soc.org. Organization of conservatives and libertarians seeking to reform the American legal system in accordance with an originalist interpretation of the Constitution.

National Constitution Center, Independence Mall, 525 Arch St., Philadelphia, PA 19106; 215-409-6600; constitutioncenter.org. Independent nonprofit institution — largely funded by federal and state government entities — dedicated to educating the American public about the Constitution.

Bibliography

Selected Sources

Books

Amar, Akhil Reed, *America's Constitution: A Biography*, Random House, 2005.

The well-known Yale law professor "seeks to reacquaint twenty-first century Americans with the written Constitution" in a comprehensive "biography" from its birth to the present. Includes illustrations, detailed notes. Amar's most recent book is *America's Unwritten Constitution: The Precedents and Principles We Live By* (Basic Books, 2012).

Barnett, Randy E., *Restoring the Lost Constitution: The Presumption of Liberty*, Princeton University Press, 2004.

A Georgetown law professor who later played a major role in the legal challenges to President Obama's health care plan forcefully argues that courts have read key provisions of the Constitution in a way that reduces or eliminates protections for liberty against governmental power. Includes notes.

Beeman, Richard, *Plain, Honest Men: The Making of the American Constitution*, Random House, 2009.

A history professor at the University of Pennsylvania provides a detailed, day-to-day account of the Constitutional Convention. Includes detailed notes.

Berkin, Carol, *A Brilliant Solution: Inventing the American Constitution*, Harcourt, 2002.

A historian at Baruch College, City University of New York, gives a compact account of events from the call for the Federal Convention and the writing of the Constitution through ratification and the inauguration of President George Washington. Includes short biographies of all delegates to the Constitutional Convention.

Bodenhamer, David J., *The Revolutionary Constitution*, Oxford University Press, 2012.

A professor of history at Indiana University traces the evolution of the Constitution from its ratification to the present day in regard to such "core concepts" as federalism, equality, rights and security. Includes notes.

Freedman, Adam, *The Naked Constitution: What the Founders Said and Why It Still Matters*, Broadside, 2012.

A conservative commentator argues for returning to what he calls the "original meaning" of the Constitution and for calling a new constitutional convention to limit the growth of government. Includes select bibliography.

Levinson, Sanford, *Our Undemocratic Constitution: Where the Constitution Goes Wrong (and How We the People Can Correct It)*, Oxford University Press, 2006.

A law professor at the University of Texas-Austin argues in favor of considering major structural changes to provisions in the Constitution regarding Congress, the president, the Supreme Court and the amendment process. Includes notes.

Liu, Goodwin, Pamela S. Karlan and Christopher Schroeder, *Keeping Faith With the Constitution*, American Constitution Society, 2009, www.acslaw.org/pdf/ACS_KeepFaith_FNL.pdf.

The book examines, from a progressive perspective, application of the Constitution in such areas as equality, democracy, criminal justice and liberty. Liu was a law professor at the University of California-Berkeley and is now a justice on the California Supreme Court; Karlan is a professor at Stanford Law School, Schroeder a professor at Duke University School of Law.

Maier, Pauline A., *Ratification: The People Debate the Constitution, 1787-1788*, Simon & Schuster, 2010.

A prominent history professor at the Massachusetts Institute of Technology provides the first comprehensive history of what she calls "one of the greatest and most probing public debates in American history." Includes detailed notes.

Monk, Linda R., *The Words We Live By: Your Annotated Guide to the Constitution*, Hyperion, 2003.

A constitutional scholar illustrates the Constitution, section by section, with historical and contemporary accounts of issues and controversies arising under the provisions. Includes illustrations, notes, selected bibliography.

On the Web

"Centuries of Citizenship: A Constitutional Timeline," National Constitution Center, http://constitutioncenter.org/timeline/.

The online resource traces significant events in U.S. constitutional history from the signing of the Magna Carta in 1215 to the present day.

"Charters of Freedom," National Archives, www.archives.gov/exhibits/charters/.

The site allows a virtual visit to the principal exhibit at the National Archives in Washington with its displays of the Declaration of Independence, Constitution and Bill of Rights and exhibit cases tracing the "making" of the charters and their impact. Includes links to additional historical material.

From CQ Press

Maddex, Robert L., *The U.S. Constitution A to Z* (2d ed.), CQ Press, 2008.

The 731-page volume provides easy-to-find entries examining provisions of the Constitution and their application in U.S. society today. Includes selected bibliography, online resources, other appendix material. Maddex is an attorney specializing in constitutional law. The book is part of CQ Press' five-volume American Government A to Z series. Other titles are *Congress A to Z*, *Presidency A to Z*, *Supreme Court A to Z* and *Elections A to Z*.

The Next Step:

Additional Articles from Current Periodicals

Constitutional Convention

Korte, Gregory, "Balanced Budget Push Brews Debate," ***USA Today*, Nov. 30, 2011, p. A4, www.usatoday.com/NEWS/usaedition/2011-11-30-constitutional-convention_ST_U.htm.**

Supporters of a balanced-budget amendment believe a constitutional convention is the best hope for passage.

O'Toole, James, "Constitutional Convention Call Gains Traction," ***Pittsburgh Post-Gazette*, Dec. 12, 2011, p. A1, www.post-gazette.com/stories/news/us/constitutional-convention-call-gains-traction-223813/.**

A growing number of scholars and activists are calling for a constitutional convention to curb political bickering.

Shea, Christopher, "Unconventional Meeting of Minds," ***The Chronicle of Higher Education*, Sept. 18, 2011, chronicle.com/article/An-Unconventional-Meeting-of/129048/.**

Tea Party members say Americans don't have to agree on what a constitutional convention should do in order to call for one.

Electoral College

Lane, Charles, "Keep the Electoral College," ***The Washington Post*, Jan. 24, 2012, p. A19, www.washingtonpost.com/opinions/electoral-college-may-not-be-popular-but-it-works/2012/01/23/gIQApsj6LQ_story.html.**

The Electoral College helps stabilize U.S. politics by encouraging a two-party system, says a columnist.

Southwick, Albert B., "Is Electoral College History?" ***Telegram & Gazette* (Mass.), June 21, 2012, p. A9, www.telegram.com/article/20120621/COLUMN21/106219838/0.**

The National Popular Vote movement doesn't call for an amendment to the Constitution but provides an agreement among states to bypass provisions of the Electoral College.

Tryon, Thomas, "Electoral College and Primary Systems Need to Change," ***Sarasota* (Fla.) *Herald Tribune*, Oct. 9, 2011, p. A18, www.heraldtribune.com/article/20111009/COLUMNIST/111009658.**

The Electoral College skews the results of presidential elections because it does not allow Americans to directly elect the president, says an opinion editor.

Prospects

Dinan, Stephen, "Don't Hold Your Breath for a 28th Amendment," ***The Washington Times*, Nov. 14, 2011, p. A1, www.washingtontimes.com/news/2011/nov/13/dont-hold-your-breath-for-a-28th-amendment/?page=all.**

Political gridlock in Washington makes any amendments to the Constitution unlikely anytime soon, says a political scholar.

Gorham, Will Short, "Of 11,000 Attempts to Amend U.S. Constitution, Only 27 Amendments Have Passed," ***Tampa Bay* (Fla.) *Times*, Aug. 30, 2011, www.politifact.com/truth-o-meter/statements/2011/aug/30/xavier-becerra/11000-attempts-amend-us-constitution-only-27-amend/.**

Amendments are approved by Congress and ratified by states only when there is broad national consensus on an issue.

Levinson, Sanford, "Our Imbecilic Constitution," ***The New York Times*, May 29, 2012, p. A23, campaignstops.blogs.nytimes.com/2012/05/28/our-imbecilic-constitution/.**

Article V makes the Constitution the most difficult to amend of any in the world, says a University of Texas law professor.

Supreme Court

"Term Limits for Judiciary Intriguing Idea," ***Albany* (Ga.) *Herald*, Feb. 21, 2012, www.albanyherald.com/news/2012/feb/21/term-limits-for-judiciary-intriguing-idea/.**

It is difficult to believe that the Founders expected Supreme Court justices to serve up to 40 years on the bench, says an editorial board.

Cohn, Douglas, and Eleanor Clift, "The Founding Fathers Got It Wrong," ***Evening Telegram* (N.Y.), April 9, 2012, p. 4.**

Supporters of abolishing lifetime tenure for Supreme Court justices say the current system does not create a politically free high court.

Gillman, Todd J., "Perry Is Building His Case for High Court Term Limits," ***Dallas Morning News*, Aug. 30, 2011, p. A1.**

Republican Gov. Rick Perry of Texas says lifetime tenure should be abolished for Supreme Court justices.

Citing *CQ Researcher*

Sample formats for citing these reports in a bibliography include the ones listed below. Preferred styles and formats vary, so please check with your instructor or professor.

MLA Style

Jost, Kenneth. "Remembering 9/11," CQ Researcher 2 Sept. 2011: 701-732.

APA Style

Jost, K. (2011, September 2). Remembering 9/11. *CQ Researcher, 9*, 701-732.

Chicago Style

Jost, Kenneth. "Remembering 9/11." *CQ Researcher*, September 2, 2011, 701-732.

In-depth Reports on Issues in the News

Are you writing a paper?

Need backup for a debate?

Want to become an expert on an issue?

For more than 80 years, students have turned to *CQ Researcher* for in-depth reporting on issues in the news. Reports on a full range of political and social issues are now available. Following is a selection of recent reports:

Civil Liberties
Voter Rights, 5/12
Remembering 9/11, 9/11
Government Secrecy, 2/11

Crime/Law
Debt Collectors, 7/12
Criminal Records, 4/12
Police Misconduct, 4/12
Immigration Conflict, 3/12
Financial Misconduct, 1/12
Eyewitness Testimony, 10/11
Death Penalty Debates, 11/10

Education
Arts Education, 3/12
Youth Volunteerism, 1/12
Digital Education, 12/11
Student Debt, 10/11

Environment/Society
Genetically Modified Food, 8/12
Smart Cities, 7/12
Whale Hunting, 6/12
U.S. Oil Dependence, 6/12
Gambling in America, 6/12
Sexual Harassment, 4/12

Health/Safety
Farm Policy, 8/12
Treating ADHD, 8/12
Alcohol Abuse, 6/12
Traumatic Brain Injury, 6/12
Distracted Driving, 5/12
Teen Drug Use, 6/11

Politics/Economy
Privatizing the Military, 7/12
U.S.-Europe Relations, 3/12
Attracting Jobs, 3/12
Presidential Election, 2/12

Upcoming Reports

Solitary Confinement, 9/14/12
Health Care Law, 9/21/12
European Debt Crisis, 9/28/12

ACCESS

CQ Researcher is available in print and online. For access, visit your library or www.cqresearcher.com.

STAY CURRENT

For notice of upcoming *CQ Researcher* reports or to learn more about *CQ Researcher* products, subscribe to the free e-mail newsletters, *CQ Researcher Alert!* and *CQ Researcher News*: http://cqpress.com/newsletters.

PURCHASE

To purchase a *CQ Researcher* report in print or electronic format (PDF), visit www.cqpress.com or call 866-427-7737. Single reports start at $15. Bulk purchase discounts and electronic-rights licensing are also available.

SUBSCRIBE

Annual full-service *CQ Researcher* subscriptions—including 44 reports a year, monthly index updates, and a bound volume—start at $1,054. Add $25 for domestic postage.

CQ Researcher Online offers a backfile from 1991 and a number of tools to simplify research. For pricing information, call 800-834-9020, or e-mail librarymarketing@cqpress.com.

CQ RESEARCHER **PLUS** ARCHIVE

GET ONLINE ACCESS TO VITAL ISSUES FROM 1923 TO THE PRESENT

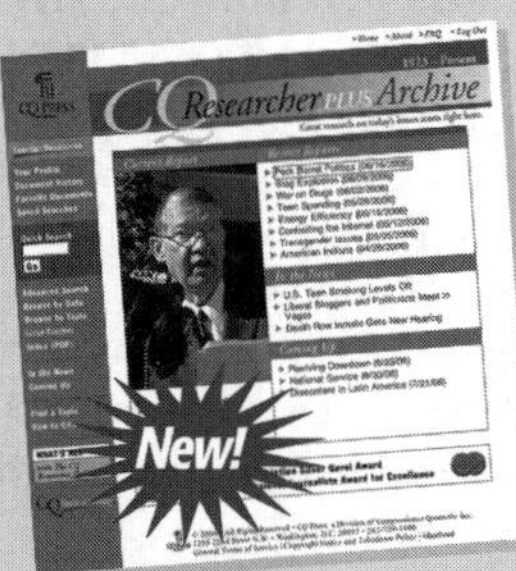

CQ Researcher Plus Archive delivers fast, online access to every *CQ Researcher* report from 1991 to the present, *PLUS* lets you explore the complete archive of *Editorial Research Reports** from 1923-1990. Search and browse more than 3,600 in-depth reports.

Loaded with handy online features, *CQ Researcher Plus Archive* provides the trustworthy reporting and the advanced online functionality today's researchers demand. The new "Issue Tracker" feature provides quick links to past and present reports on the specific topics you need.

For a free trial, visit http://library.cqpress.com/trials.

For pricing information, call 1-800-834-9020, ext. 1906 or e-mail librarymarketing@cqpress.com.

**Editorial Research Reports*, the predecessor to *CQ Researcher*, provides the same expert, nonpartisan reporting on the vital issues that have shaped our society.

CQ Press • 2300 N Street, NW, Suite 800 • Washington, DC 20037

CQ Researcher

Published by CQ Press, an Imprint of SAGE Publications, Inc.

www.cqresearcher.com

Solitary Confinement

Is long-term isolation of prisoners inhumane?

Debate is growing over the isolation of U.S. prison inmates in virtually round-the-clock solitary confinement. When the practice began booming in the late 1980s, politicians and some prison administrators — many supporting the construction of special "supermax" facilities — said prison safety demanded that "the worst of the worst" inmates be held in prolonged isolation. But even some supporters of long-term solitary acknowledge that many prison systems have used the strategy to warehouse mentally ill inmates. A growing number of federal court decisions prohibit placing the mentally ill in strict isolation, citing evidence that it aggravates their condition. Recently, some states have reduced the number of prisoners in long-term isolation. But in Illinois, guards protesting the planned closure of a supermax argue that transferring inmates to a conventional prison poses grave danger.

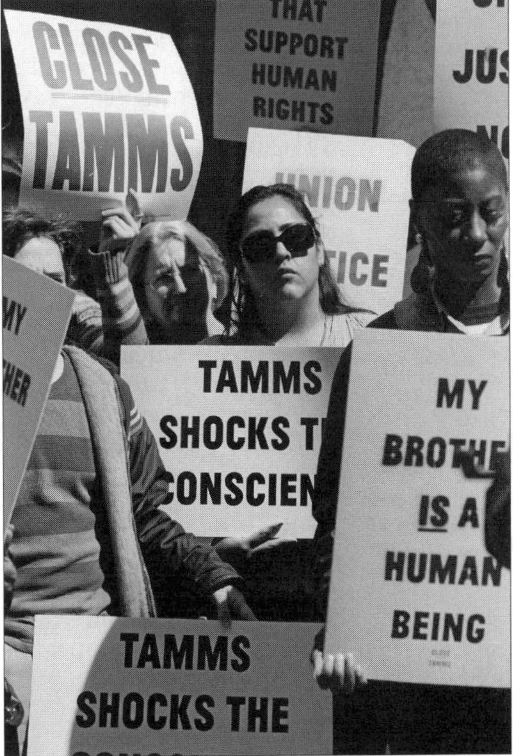

Relatives of inmates at the Tamms supermax prison in Illinois support Gov. Pat Quinn's plan to close the facility. Union officials representing prison guards say closure would cost 250 jobs and raise the danger level in institutions to which Tamms prisoners would be transferred.

Inside This Report

The Issues 767
Background 773
Chronology 775
Current Situation 780
At Issue........................781
Outlook.......................783
Bibliography 786
The Next Step 787

CQ Researcher • Sept. 14, 2012 • www.cqresearcher.com
Volume 22, Number 32 • Pages 765-788

Los Angeles | London | New Delhi
Singapore | Washington DC

Recipient of Society of Professional Journalists Award for Excellence ◆ American Bar Association Silver Gavel Award

THE ISSUES

767 • Does long-term solitary confinement constitute torture?
• Is separating the "worst of the worst" from other prisoners beneficial?
• Does long-term solitary confinement make normal prisoners mentally ill?

BACKGROUND

773 **Repentance in Isolation**
Early prisons adopted solitary confinement to encourage penitence.

774 **Supreme Displeasure**
In 1890 the Supreme Court said a condemned man couldn't be held in solitary.

774 **Institutionalizing Solitary**
Alcatraz, opened as a federal penitentiary in 1934, was the forerunner of supermax prisons.

778 **Constitutional Issues**
A judge's 1995 ruling excoriated isolation policies at California's Pelican Bay prison.

CURRENT SITUATION

780 **Fight Over Supermax**
A legal battle is raging over efforts to close Illinois' Tamms prison.

780 **New Litigation**
Lawsuits challenge supermax prisons in several states.

OUTLOOK

783 **'Losing Favor'**
Prison experts think use of strict isolation will continue to decline.

SIDEBARS AND GRAPHICS

768 **Solitary Confinement Under Scrutiny Nationwide**
Lawsuits and prison officials are challenging policies.

769 **Tight Quarters and Total Isolation**
Supermax prisoners are generally kept in their cells 23 hours a day.

775 **Chronology**
Key events since 1787.

776 **Controversial Study Fuels Supports Use of Solitary**
Inmates claim no ill effects, but critics cite flaws in the research.

778 **Some States Rethinking Solitary Confinement**
Trend began with inmate lawsuit over Ohio supermax.

781 **At Issue**
Should solitary be limited to one year?

FOR FURTHER RESEARCH

785 **For More Information**
Organizations to contact.

786 **Bibliography**
Selected sources used.

787 **The Next Step**
Additional articles.

787 **Citing *CQ Researcher***
Sample bibliography formats.

Cover: AP Photo/Kiichiro Sato

CQ Researcher

Sept. 14, 2012
Volume 22, Number 32

MANAGING EDITOR: Thomas J. Billitteri
tjb@cqpress.com

ASSISTANT MANAGING EDITOR: Kathy Koch
kkoch@cqpress.com

SENIOR CONTRIBUTING EDITOR:
Thomas J. Colin
tcolin@cqpress.com

ASSOCIATE EDITOR: Kenneth Jost

STAFF WRITER: Marcia Clemmitt

CONTRIBUTING WRITERS: Peter Katel, Barbara Mantel, Jennifer Weeks

SENIOR PROJECT EDITOR: Olu B. Davis

ASSISTANT EDITOR: Darrell Dela Rosa

FACT CHECKER: Michelle Harris

Los Angeles | London | New Delhi
Singapore | Washington DC

An Imprint of SAGE Publications, Inc.

VICE PRESIDENT AND EDITORIAL DIRECTOR, HIGHER EDUCATION GROUP:
Michele Sordi

DIRECTOR, ONLINE PUBLISHING:
Todd Baldwin

CQ Researcher (ISSN 1056-2036) is printed on acid-free paper. Published weekly, except: (March wk. 5) (May wk. 4) (July wk. 1) (Aug. wks. 3, 4) (Nov. wk. 4) and (Dec. wks. 3, 4). Published by SAGE Publications, Inc., 2455 Teller Rd., Thousand Oaks, CA 91320. Annual full-service subscriptions start at $1,054. For pricing, call 1-800-834-9020. To purchase a *CQ Researcher* report in print or electronic format (PDF), visit www.cqpress.com or call 866-427-7737. Single reports start at $15. Bulk purchase discounts and electronic-rights licensing are also available. Periodicals postage paid at Thousand Oaks, California, and at additional mailing offices. POSTMASTER: Send address changes to *CQ Researcher*, 2300 N St., N.W., Suite 800, Washington, DC 20037.

Solitary Confinement

BY PETER KATEL

THE ISSUES

Brutal aggression. Unbridled rage. Self-mutilation. Desolation and despair. Descent into madness. Texas prisoner Anthony C. Graves saw it all among inmates locked down in extreme solitary confinement — an ordeal he himself endured for 18 years while awaiting execution for murders he later was exonerated of committing. * [1]

"I would watch guys come to prison totally sane and in three years they don't live in the real world anymore," Graves told a Senate Judiciary subcommittee in June. "I know a guy who would sit in the middle of the floor, rip his sheet up, wrap it around himself and light it on fire. Another guy would go out in the recreation yard, get naked, lie down and urinate all over himself. He would take his feces and smear it all over his face." [2]

AP Photo/Pat Sullivan

Anthony C. Graves is free after 18 years in solitary confinement in Texas for a crime he didn't commit. "I would watch guys come to [isolation] totally sane, and in three years they don't live in the real world anymore," Graves told a Senate subcommittee in June. The rise in supermax prisons in recent years has sparked questions over whether extended strict isolation is humane and effective in keeping order in prisons.

Accounts of bizarre and self-destructive behavior by prisoners have multiplied as long-term solitary confinement has become commonplace in the U.S. prison system over the past two decades. Mental-health experts who have interviewed prisoners in solitary disagree on whether prolonged isolation robs mentally healthy people of their sanity. But virtually no one doubts that prisoners already mentally ill when they enter solitary tend to deteriorate severely.

Questions about psychological effects are part of a larger debate in criminal-justice and human-rights circles over whether confining anyone for long periods in strict isolation is humane and whether isolation is effective in keeping order in prisons while protecting prison workers, other inmates and the public once prisoners are released.

Prison officials impose solitary confinement in a variety of ways and under a variety of names. The best-known may be short-term confinement for rule-breaking — often known as "disciplinary segregation." [3]

But debate centers on prolonged solitary confinement, or "administrative segregation," which is used in so-called "supermax" prisons, though long-term solitary confinement also is used in conventional prisons. Supermaxes are built specifically to house inmates considered extremely dangerous. The prisoners are locked in individual cells, usually with solid steel doors, for 23 hours a day. They are fed in their cells, through a slot in the door, and chained and guarded when they leave for any reason. Like Graves, some prisoners spend a decade or longer in isolation, with even out-of-cell exercise taken alone in cage-like settings. (Supermaxes may also hold prisoners who are not kept in strict solitary.) [4]

"Increasing the use of high-security segregation is counterproductive, often causing violence inside facilities, contributing to recidivism after release," Sen. Richard J. Durbin, D-Ill., chairman of the Senate Judiciary Committee's Constitution, Civil Rights and Human Rights Subcommittee, said in opening the June hearing. [5]

The controversy over solitary confinement has gone international. Last year, Juan E. Méndez, a former senior staff member for Human Rights Watch who is now the United Nations Human Rights Commission's investigator on mistreatment of prisoners, * concluded that long-term solitary confinement can amount to torture in some circumstances. He proposes a time limit of 15 days. [6]

---

* Graves was convicted as an accomplice in the 1992 murders of six members of a Somerville, Texas, family. Recanted testimony by the admitted killer, along with prosecutorial misconduct, led to his exoneration in 2010.

* Méndez's full title is special rapporteur on torture and other cruel, inhuman or degrading treatment or punishment.

Solitary Confinement Under Scrutiny Nationwide

Lawsuits by inmates in a number of states are challenging solitary confinement practices, while in other states penal authorities are reviewing policies on prisoner isolation.

Colorado — Prisoners in federal supermax suing over alleged long-term solitary confinement of mentally ill inmates. . . . State prison system cuts population in solitary and closes new prison designed mainly for solitary.

Illinois — State revising system to send fewer prisoners to solitary. . . . Temporary restraining order bars closure of state supermax; prison guard union argues closure would be dangerous.

Ohio — Prison system redesigns solitary confinement to ensure prisoners receive behavioral programs.

Maine — Prison system reduces population in solitary by nearly 70 percent, to 45 inmates at most, and slashes time spent in solitary to days instead of months.

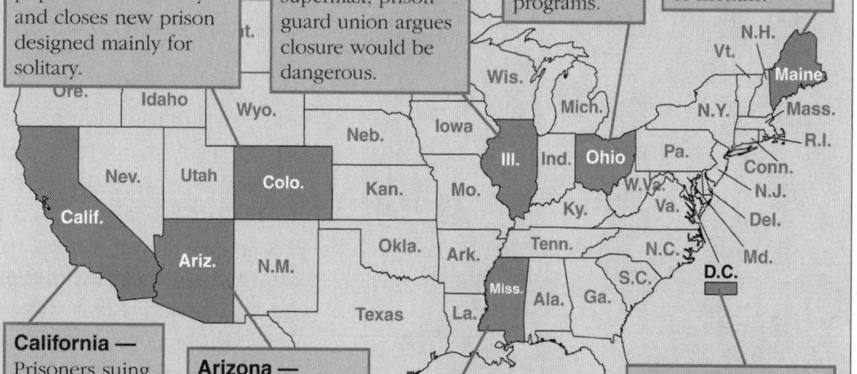

California — Prisoners suing over inmate placement in long-term solitary and conditions in isolation units.

Arizona — Inmates suing state over medical care and other issues affecting general prison population and those in solitary.

Mississippi — Prison system director lauds massive reduction in long-term solitary population.

Washington, D.C. — Senate Judiciary Subcommittee on the Constitution, Civil Rights and Human Rights holds first major congressional hearing on long-term solitary confinement.

Sources: Various news reports and court documents

Virtually round-the-clock isolation existed before supermaxes started going up. But the U.S. controversy over long-term solitary confinement began during a supermax boom starting in the 1990s. By the early 2000s, supermaxes in at least 44 states were estimated to hold about 25,000 prisoners. Experts believe that number is now declining because a series of court decisions — as well as the higher expenses involved in running super-secure institutions — are leading some states to reduce or end supermax use. [7]

In June, Illinois Gov. Patrick Quinn, a Democrat, announced the imminent closure of his state's supermax, Tamms Correctional Institution, though that politically controversial move was delayed by an Illinois state judge in early September. (*See "Current Situation," p. 780.*)

And in recent years, following litigation over conditions in long-term solitary, Mississippi reduced its supermax population by 89 percent, and Ohio by 85 percent. Maine, which hadn't been sued but faces potential litigation, reduced its long-term solitary population by about 70 percent. Joseph Ponte, Maine's corrections commissioner, said the new policy resulted in "substantial reductions in violence," reductions in use of force, chemicals and restraint chairs, and "reductions in inmates cutting [themselves] up — which was an event that happened every week or at least every other week." [8]

Supermax supporters describe such prisons, and their use of strict solitary confinement, as essential for public safety and management of potentially explosive prison populations. Strict solitary keeps highly dangerous inmates in conditions in which they're less able to harm prison staff or other inmates or induce other prisoners to commit violent acts.

"It takes someone whose behavior amounts to a threat and incapacitates their ability to do such things," says Eugene Atherton, a consultant on prison management who was warden of two Colorado prisons and assistant director of the Colorado prison system. "Physically, they can't put their hands on other people, and it's easier to monitor their communications if they are about sending directions to other associates to do harm."

But like other prison professionals, Atherton acknowledges that supermaxes in many states have expanded beyond their intended purpose, making what should be, in his view, a standard prison-management tool a matter of controversy. "A lot of wardens were locking guys up who were headaches but manageable under normal circumstances," he says. "That's a huge error."

Some supermax critics agree that a small number of extremely dangerous prisoners should be isolated from other inmates. Federal courts, though they have placed some restrictions on long-term solitary confinement, have not outlawed it.

The U.S. Supreme Court ruled unanimously in 2005 that prison inmates have a constitutional right to challenge an order transferring them to a supermax because, the court said, strict, long-term solitary confinement isn't ordinary imprisonment. "Almost all human contact is prohibited, even to the point that conversation is not permitted from cell to cell; his cell's light may be dimmed, but is on for 24 hours; and he may exercise only one hour per day in a small indoor room," Justice Anthony Kennedy wrote for the court. Along with the fact prisoners were sent to supermax for indefinite periods, "These conditions impose an atypical and significant hardship." [9]

Whether supermaxes necessarily suppress prison violence remains a matter of debate. In Mississippi, prison system officials acknowledged that they had gone overboard in assigning prisoners to the notorious isolation wing of the state penitentiary at Parchman. The wing, known as Unit 32, produced more instead of less violence among prisoners, as well as assaults on staff. "From May in 2007 to August 2007, three homicides," the state's corrections commissioner, Michael Epps, told Durbin's subcommittee. "Highly unusual. One suicide. That's highly unusual in any prison environment. In addition to that, inmates was throwing urine and feces on staff." [10]

Though the facility's purpose was to prevent exactly those sorts of events, experts later said that the accumulation of hostility by prisoners — including seriously mentally ill inmates — housed there unjustly, along with security lapses, allowed the violence to happen. The events persuaded Epps to begin working with prisoner-rights lawyers to massively reduce his state's strict isolation population. [11] (*See sidebar, p. 778.*)

Tight Quarters and Total Isolation

Long-term solitary confinement differs from prison to prison, but its common denominators are isolation and maximum security:

- Prisoners are generally kept in their cells for 23 hours a day, let out only for exercise — taken alone — and showers.
- Cells measure 6 or 7 feet wide by 8 to 10 feet deep. Some have a barred door that allows a view of immediate surroundings. Others have a solid steel door with only a small opening for meal delivery.
- Some prisons allow televisions in cells, possibly restricted to educational or behavioral programming. Rules on reading material, visits and other diversions vary. At the Florence, Colo., supermax, prisoners in the highly restricted Special Housing Unit can talk with family members or other approved visitors by video only and are escorted to the visiting room in hand and leg restraints, including a belly chain.
- In federal supermax prisons, prolonged solitary is considered a disciplinary measure for grave misconduct, such as murdering another inmate, or for being an "extraordinarily extreme" flight risk. In California, gang members and suspected members are automatically placed in long-term isolation. In states such as Michigan, Mississippi and Oklahoma, prisoners considered a threat to staff or other inmates are locked up in long-term solitary.

Sources: Urban Institute; Journal of Law and Policy; National Institute of Corrections; California Department of Corrections and Rehabilitation; Senate Judiciary Subcommittee on the Constitution, Civil Rights and Human Rights, June 19, 2012; Oklahoma Department of Corrections; Michigan Department of Corrections; United States Penitentiary, Administrative Maximum Facility.

Mississippi aside, hard data don't exist on whether supermaxes reduce prison violence, researchers say. "What states did was assume that violence stemmed from what certain inmates were doing or incited others to do," says Daniel P. Mears, a criminology professor at Florida State University in Tallahassee. That case is unproven, he says, partly because standards for tracking prison violence are inconsistent. "The leeway about whether an incident is recordable or not is considerable," Mears says. "It might be recorded as simple assault or aggravated assault," depending on the prison or the officer.

Also unclear is the average length of stay in isolation. While some inmates are isolated for only days or weeks, others spend years alone in their cells. A class-action lawsuit filed this year by a group of prisoners at California's Pelican Bay supermax reports isolation periods of 11 to 25 years. [12]

Only a handful of states have gathered figures on time spent in isolation, as well as other key prison statistics. In Colorado, prisoners with no mental health problems spent an average of 19.5 months in isolation according to 2011 data; inmates with mental health needs spent about 14.1 months. Nationwide, "Basic data as to the functioning of systems for isolation — the reasons for admission, the duration of stays, the prevalence of mental illness and recidivism rates — are unavailable," two Yale Law School professors wrote to the Durbin subcommittee. [13]

Still, a wealth of evidence exists on the effects of long-term solitary on people with mental illnesses. The evidence has persuaded a number of federal judges who have ruled in prisoners' lawsuits against supermax conditions. "Every federal court to consider the question has held that 'supermax' confinement of the seriously mentally ill is unconstitutional," David C. Fathi, executive director of the ACLU National Prison Project, wrote in 2004. [14]

The ACLU prison project is representing inmates at the federal supermax at Florence, Colo., who have suffered from severe mental illness and spent long periods in the prison's high-security unit. According to the lawsuit, one of them amputated some of his fingers, a testicle, scrotum and earlobes. Acts by other prisoner-plaintiffs include: swallowing a razor blade to persuade medical staff to amputate his right leg, where he suffered a gunshot wound long ago (he succeeded); amputating a finger, adding it to a bowl of ramen noodle soup and eating it; and swallowing broken glass. [15]

Federal Bureau of Prison lawyers haven't yet responded to the lawsuit. But episodes of extreme self-harm, as well as feces-smearing, are common enough among mentally ill prisoners in solitary that mental-health professionals have developed explanations.

Jeffrey Metzner, a psychiatry professor at the University of Colorado medical school in Denver, says self-mutilation seems to be an attempt to feel something, in a setting in which outside stimulation is nearly absent.

Feces-smearing is a way of asserting control by doing something that authorities are unable to stop. "It's also a way of expressing significant anger," says Metzner, a critic of long-term solitary confinement of the mentally ill who has reported on mental-health conditions in prisons on assignment by federal judges and court-appointed monitors.

That issue resonates beyond supermax cell walls. Contrary to what many in the public may think, a large number of prisoners who have served lengthy terms in solitary are released from prison. In a comprehensive study published in 2006, Mears reported that Texas alone released an average of 1,400 prisoners a year directly from strict solitary to the street. [16]

"If I were locked down 24-7 for many years, with little human contact and little to do," says Chase Riveland, former corrections director in Colorado and Washington state, "I'd probably be a little bit angry when I got out."

As judges, penologists, prison officials and human-rights activists debate the role of solitary confinement in prisons, here are some of the questions they are asking:

Does long-term solitary confinement constitute torture?

Last year's U.N. report avoided categorically denouncing solitary confinement as torture, but it said solitary imprisonment that lasts for years, and that includes severe restrictions on all human contact, can legitimately be defined that way.

"The longer the duration of solitary confinement or the greater the uncertainty regarding the length of time, the greater the risk of serious and irreparable harm to the inmate that may constitute cruel, inhuman or degrading treatment or punishment or even torture," wrote Méndez, the special investigator. [17]

Similar concerns led the American Bar Association to propose in 2010 that "only the most severe disciplinary cases" should lead to solitary confinement of more than 30 days, with a limit of one year in all cases. [18]

In Wisconsin in 2006, three federal judges on the Seventh U.S. Court of Appeals likened long-term solitary confinement to the inhumane world of a labor camp in the former Soviet Union.

Writing in a decision on a prisoner's lawsuit, the judges described the inmate's harsh existence : "Stripped naked in a small prison cell with nothing except a toilet; forced to sleep on a concrete floor or slab; denied any human contact; fed nothing but 'nutri-loaf;' and given just a modicum of toilet paper — four squares — only a few times." The judges, ruling in the prisoner's favor, added: "Although this might sound like a stay at a Soviet gulag in the 1930s, it is, according to the claims in this case, Wisconsin in 2002." The prisoner was kept naked for his first three days of isolation, and then for two more days, for alleged misconduct. [19]

Some human-rights advocates insist on defining long-term solitary, as practiced in the United States, as torture plain and simple. They have backing from some physicians, among them Atul Gawande, a surgeon, professor of health policy and management at Harvard School of Public Health and a journalist-author. He and other medical professionals point to evidence that prolonged isolation from human contact does deep and lasting psychological damage.

"In much the same way that a previous generation of Americans countenanced legalized segregation, ours has countenanced legalized torture," Gawande wrote in *The New Yorker* in 2009. "And there is no clearer manifestation of this than our routine use of solitary confinement — on our own people, in our own communities." [20]

But prison administrators deny the torture allegation, arguing that prisoners in solitary are, in fact, in regular contact with prison staff. "We seek to ensure that these inmates are not completely isolated as that term may be typically understood," Charles E. Samuels Jr., director of the Federal Bureau of Prisons, told the Senate Judiciary Committee in June. [21]

Atherton, the former Colorado warden and state prison official, also rejects the torture label. "What you are describing is a version of solitary confinement created by prison reform groups out of California, and Human Rights Watch, that have chosen isolated confinement as an issue for the last 20 years," he says. "They have fabricated every possible mythology of what confinement means."

American prisoners in solitary confinement "are not really isolated at all," Atherton says. "They communicate with staff constantly. They have case managers, medical providers talking to them; that is an American Correctional Association standard." Atherton spoke from Afghanistan, where he is a State Department contractor advising the Afghan and U.S. governments on the Afghan prison system.

Prisoner advocates counter that those communications are cursory at best, however. "Three times a day, a guard comes through and slides a food tray through the slot," says the ACLU's

Fathi. "You may occasionally have a mental health person come by and shout through the crack between the steel cell door and the door frame; in my experience, mental health checks are overwhelmingly conducted that way."

The issue of actual compliance with policies and standards aside, "What's damaging about solitary confinement is not the absence of literally all human contact," Fathi says. "What's damaging is the lack of meaningful human interaction. A prisoner can go weeks, months or years without meaningful human interaction." As with physical torture, he says, the effects can damage a prisoner for life.

Riveland, the former corrections boss in Colorado and Washington state and now a consultant on prison issues, argues that it's a mistake to apply the "torture" label across the board. "I'm sure there are instances where some people have undergone treatment that you would label torture," he says. But misclassification of prisoners is a more widespread problem, Riveland says — "widening the net too much on who stays in solitary and how long, without a serious professional review on, 'Can we get this person into some other setting?' "

Others argue for keeping the focus on conditions they call inhumane. "I'm not given to hyperbole," says Fred Cohen, co-editor of the penology trade journal *Correctional Law Reporter* and editor of *Correctional Mental Health Report*, "but I see things so bad that it's not too much to say that it's wholesale torture being practiced, in some states more than others."

AP Photo/*Belleville News-Democrat*/George Pawlaczyk

Former inmate Chris Marcum shows scars from cutting himself while in isolation at the Tamms supermax prison in Illinois. Several states recently have reduced their supermax populations following litigation over conditions in long-term solitary. In Maine, a prison official said the state's new policy reduced violence and instances of inmates cutting themselves. Jeffrey Metzner, a psychiatry professor at the University of Colorado medical school, says self-mutilation seems to be an attempt to feel something in a setting where outside stimulation is nearly absent.

Cohen, who has served as a court-appointed monitor in litigation over prison conditions, cites prisoners confined in solitary for a decade or longer. "One guy told me, 'I don't know who I am.' You're surrounded by people smearing themselves with feces, eating their own flesh. I met a guy in Illinois who ate his own shoulder."

Is separating the "worst of the worst" from other prisoners beneficial?

The rationale for constructing supermax prisons would seem clear and straightforward. As some prison officials and politicians pose the issue, certain prisoners are so dangerous to other inmates and to staff that there is no way to house them in general prison populations.

As examples, prison professionals often cite gang leaders who order murders and gang members who are sworn to carry out those orders. "Perhaps the most successful gang-control strategy, from a viewpoint of reducing violence and disorder, has been the isolation of gang members, making it more difficult for them to influence and prey on the general prison population," three Texas university criminologists wrote in the American Correctional Association's monthly magazine in 2006. [22]

Nevertheless, the strategy has drawbacks, wrote Chad R. Trulson and Soraya K. Kawucha of the University of North Texas and James W. Marquart of the University of Texas at Dallas. A missing gang member can be replaced, they noted. And there may be better ways to deal with "peripheral or inactive" gang members, the scholars said: Encourage them to renounce their affiliation, transfer them out of state or enroll them in behavior-change programs. [23]

But academics may not make the best guides to the realities of prison administration, argues Gary W. DeLand, former director of the Utah corrections department. "If you have actual knowledge of a serious threat to safety, order or to an individual, and you fail to take action, you are liable," he says, citing a 1994 U.S. Supreme Court ruling that found that federal prison officials had acted with "deliberate indifference" in failing to protect a transsexual prisoner from rape. [24]

"What happens if you know you've got a heavy risk, if you know you have people who are dangerous to staff and to other prisoners?," DeLand asks rhetorically. "What do you do with them? Put them in suspended animation?" Segregation and isolation is the only practical solution, he argues.

Yet, Florida State's Mears, who has written a series of detailed studies of supermax confinement — including an evaluation of results — argues that the case for segregating the "worst of the worst" is less definitive than it appears. [25] "I did phone interviews and state-by-state visits and I'd hear, 'It's worst-of-the-worst control,' " Mears says. "So my response [was], 'What outcomes would you use to show you're controlling the worst of the worst?' "

Supermax prisoners can still assault guards, Mears notes, citing so-called "cell extraction" operations after an inmate breaks rules in some way. "They're also not incapacitated from ordering assaults," he says, noting that prisoners can send out mail and may be able to receive visits, even if they are not face-to-face. A "savvy leader" can use those occasions to send out directives, Mears notes. And Mississippi's experience at Unit 32 in 2007, when three prisoners died during an outbreak of violence between gangs, shows that prisoners can cause violence even when confined in solitary. [26]

Still, some prison officials say segregating dangerous prisoners in supermax-type settings has improved safety for staff and other prisoners in standard prison housing. In Illinois, following the 1998 opening of the Tamms Correctional Center supermax, "Incidents of inmate-on-inmate assaults, inmate-on-staff assaults, gang-related activities, the number of lockdown days . . . have all gone down," Michael Randle, then the director of the Illinois corrections department, said during December 2009 testimony in a prisoner lawsuit over conditions at Tamms. [27]

Charles E. Samuels Jr., Federal Bureau of Prisons director, echoed Randle's safety argument last June. "If you have individuals who have the propensity to harm others and in many cases who have killed other individuals," he told the Constitution, Civil Rights and Human Rights Subcommittee, "these are individuals who have proven that they're going to require a restrictive form of confinement until . . . we are comfortable to ensure the safety of the facility putting them back into general population." [28]

Prisoner advocates don't entirely condemn the idea of separating extremely dangerous prisoners. But these inmates don't account for most of those in supermax-type units, critics of solitary argue. "People who end up in solitary, most of them, are not the worst of the worst, they're the sickest of the sick," says Fathi of the ACLU.

The result is that the supermax effect on the overall safety of prison systems is minimal, Fathi argues. "In every system you can find a handful of prisoners who are truly dangerous and require physical separation from others," he says. Despite their small numbers, "They are the only justification for building these cruel and extraordinarily expensive facilities."

Does long-term solitary confinement make normal prisoners mentally ill?

Many prison professionals say long-term solitary confinement is no place for mentally ill prisoners — but that they often end up there anyway. "Every class-action case I've ever worked on, they're over-represented in segregation," says Steve J. Martin of Austin, Texas, a lawyer and ex-prison officer with long experience as a court-appointed prison monitor. "And they're over-represented in terms of use of force and disciplinary infractions. Those things are all linked. If you engage in the type of behavior that requires staff use of force, that typically leads to long-term segregation."

Moreover, Martin says, the controversy over long-term solitary grows out of the increased use of supermax-type confinement for mentally ill prisoners. "American prisons have always held a certain number of prisoners in 22- to 23-hour-a-day lockup," he says. But the widespread use of it for mentally ill prisoners is relatively recent.

A string of court decisions and settlement orders has barred about a half-dozen prison systems from sending mentally ill inmates to long-term solitary. These started with a 1995 federal court order to remove mentally ill inmates from the Security Housing Unit of California's Pelican Bay supermax. *(See "Background," p. 777.)*

More recently, U.S. District Judge G. Patrick Murphy of East St. Louis, Ill., went further, concluding that supermax confinement could psychologically damage any prisoner. Murphy said in a 2010 ruling concerning Tamms Correctional Center that "a number of inmates who testified to experiencing severe depression and other disturbances while confined at Tamms testified also to significant improvement in their mental health after being transferred to the less restrictive conditions" at another state prison. [29]

Murphy wrote that prisoners were entitled to hearings before being sent to Tamms. Conditions there "inflict lasting psychological and emotional harm on inmates confined there for long periods," he wrote. [30]

The issue is on some politicians' minds as well. "Some [inmates] are already seriously mentally ill before they're confined" in isolation, Durbin said at the Senate Judiciary subcommittee hearing in June. "Others who may not have had any psychological problems before isolation can be driven into a psychosis or a suicidal state." [31]

Durbin was echoing the conclusions of one of the subcommittee's witnesses, Craig Haney, a psychology professor at the University of California, Santa Cruz, and a veteran researcher on the effects of long-term supermax-type confinement. Extreme cases of self-mutilation aside, Haney testified, "Solitary confinement places all prisoners exposed to it at grave risk of harm." [32]

All prisoners in solitary, Haney said, may find "this environment . . . so painful, so bizarre and impossible to make sense of, that they create their own reality." In addition, "The deprivations, restrictions, the totality of control, and the prolonged absence of any real opportunity for happiness or joy fills many prisoners with intolerable levels of frustration that, for some, turns to anger, and then even to uncontrollable and sudden outbursts of rage." [33]

Nevertheless, some supermax defenders dispute the idea that long-term solitary confinement can do lasting mental health damage to a psychologically fit prisoner. "I've seen nothing, and I've been in this business now for about four decades," says DeLand. "I've yet to run into anything that one could solidly point to as a person without serious emotional problems being affected in a negative way by being isolated."

During his stint as Utah corrections director, DeLand says, systematic audits he ordered to spot problems that could lead to lawsuits never picked up evidence of solitary confinement driving prisoners into mental illness. "I am not familiar with any study that's been done that would indicate that being locked in isolation for some period of time is going to cause mental health problems."

Cohen of *Correctional Mental Health Report* says he is not aware of any studies that objectively assess the mental health of people before and after solitary confinement. But, he adds, "In the last 25 years, I've been to probably 100 prisons. I have seen guys that I have known before they went in [to solitary] who became hopelessly mad."

Some prisoners could be faking insanity, Cohen acknowledges. But he says that would be hard to imagine "for guys who come in from the street as dudes, who are fastidious, who smear themselves with feces."

But Metzner of the University of Colorado, who also has a long track record in prison work and opposes solitary confinement for mentally ill inmates, argues that prolonged isolation doesn't induce mental illness, except in unusual cases.

Long-term solitary can make anyone depressed, Metzner says. And "that can be harmful even without mental illness. But it's uncommon for people to become psychotic if they're in segregation, absent existing mental illness." ■

BACKGROUND

Repentance in Isolation

Long-term solitary confinement as a penal strategy dates back to the formation of American prisons.

In 1787, the Pennsylvania legislature ordered that a wing of a jail on Walnut Street in Philadelphia be converted to a "penitentiary house," where convicts would be held in isolation for the length of their sentences. Lawmakers believed that without the distraction of cellmates, prisoners could reflect on their errors and repent for them — hence the term "penitentiary," which eventually passed into common usage as a synonym for prison. [34]

In 1821, New York state adopted the isolation strategy for a recently built prison at Auburn, about 35 miles west of Syracuse. Eighty convicts considered in special need of repentance were locked in dark isolation cells with only a Bible for company.

Whatever progress the prisoners made in repairing their souls, their bodies suffered. By early 1823, five had died of consumption, as tuberculosis was then known, and 41 were gravely ill. Others lost their minds.

Auburn shifted to a system in which prisoners were allowed out of their cells to work, though they weren't allowed to talk to each other. "Industry, obedience, silence" was the institution's doctrine.

Elsewhere, the idea of redemption through isolation still appealed to state officials. When Pennsylvania built Eastern Penitentiary outside Philadelphia in 1829, the idea was to keep all prisoners — not a select group — in total, permanent isolation.

Isolation at Eastern was so complete that prisoners were brought in with black hoods over their heads, so that they'd be unable to see even the prison grounds. The prisoners never left their cells, until death or end of sentence.

Unlike modern solitary, prisoners were required to work. Looms or workbenches were part of cell furniture. Still, a prisoner's separation from other people was all but total. Food was passed through a slot designed so that even glimpsing the guard delivering the tray was impossible. The only exceptions were occasional visitors — not family or friends, but officials and a few foreign researchers.

Among those researchers were the French social thinker Alexis de Tocqueville and his friend, Gustave de Beaumont. They visited Eastern in 1831 during an American tour that produced Tocqueville's classic two-volume *Democracy in America* (1835, 1840). Tocqueville seemed impressed by what he saw. One prisoner told him and Beaumont, sincerely or not, that he considered "being brought to the Penitentiary as a signal benefit of Providence." [35] Another prisoner sobbed incessantly, Tocqueville reported. The man said he hoped he would be accepted back into society upon release.

For their part, the prison's official inspectors defended solitary as redemptive. "The sense of shame and feelings of remorse drives them to some source of consolation," they wrote, "and the ordinary means of stifling an actively reproving conscience being denied by reason of their solitariness, the comforts of the Bible and the peace of religion are eagerly sought for." [36]

The British novelist Charles Dickens, who spent a day at Eastern in 1842, took away a different impression. He concluded, "This slow and daily tampering with the mysteries of the brain [is] immeasurably worse than any torture of the body . . . because its ghastly signs and tokens are not so palpable to the eye and sense of touch as scars upon the flesh." [37]

Supreme Displeasure

In September 1889, a Colorado jury convicted James J. Medley of murdering his wife the previous May. He was sentenced to hang. [38]

The sentence, handed down in November of that year, included a provision called for by a newly enacted law: Medley was to be held in solitary confinement until his execution. [39]

Colorado's new homicide law had been enacted in April 1889. But under the Colorado constitution, laws took effect 90 days after passage. Thus, the crime had been committed when the previous homicide law was in effect — a law that didn't require solitary confinement for prisoners awaiting execution.

Medley's lawyer filed a habeas corpus petition seeking the prisoner's release. It reached the U.S. Supreme Court in 1890. The high court decided in Medley's favor, ruling that the convicted man's sentencing violated the constitutional prohibition on "ex-post-facto" laws, which apply a new statute to an offense committed when a previous law was in effect.

The court cited a history of "serious objections" to solitary confinement. In Pennsylvania and other states that followed its example, "A considerable number of the prisoners fell, after even a short confinement, into a semi-fatuous condition, from which it was next to impossible to arouse them," the court said, "and others became violently insane; other still committed suicide while those who stood the ordeal better were not generally reformed." [40]

The court also called solitary confinement "an additional punishment of the most important and painful character [that is] therefore forbidden" under the Constitution's ex-post-facto provision. [41] Moreover, because the homicide law in force when Medley committed his crime was no longer in effect, the Supreme Court reasoned that it could not simply send him back for a new trial. "James J. Medley is entitled to have his liberty."

Accordingly, the court ordered him freed from prison.

To this day, solitary confinement critics quote Medley's passage about the effects of solitary confinement. Most recently, Hope Metcalf, director of Yale Law School's Arthur Liman Public Interest Program, and Judith Resnik, a Yale law professor, cited the description in testimony to the Senate Judiciary subcommittee hearing in June. [42]

Nevertheless, Cohen, the *Correctional Law Reporter* co-editor, noted that the high court didn't reject solitary confinement as inherently unconstitutional. "It was merely found to be sufficiently harsh to be an ex-post-facto (that is, not then authorized) punishment," Cohen wrote. [43]

He further argued that Medley suffers from a built-in weakness. "The majority's reliance on the much older Philadelphia system of silence and the mental suffering it caused seems quite misplaced where a death sentenced inmate was to be kept in mandatory solitary for about four weeks, with guaranteed access by various visitors, and with no mention whatsoever of the particular conditions of confinement." [44]

Institutionalizing Solitary

The country's first prison for the hardest of hard-core criminals was a federal prison opened on Alcatraz Island in San Francisco Bay in 1934. Its inmates included the Prohibition-era gangster Al Capone and other notorious criminals, as well as prisoners known for escape or for assaulting fellow inmates or officers. Alcatraz is "commonly recognized as the forerunner of today's supermax facilities," wrote Riveland, the former Washington state corrections director, in a 1999 guide to supermax administration. [45]

Even so, Alcatraz prisoners were housed one to a cell but weren't confined nearly full-time to those cells, as are many supermax prisoners in today's institutions. Round-the-clock solitary confinement was used as punishment — limited to 14 days, with an interval of 14 days required before officials could impose it again. [46]

The U.S. government closed Alcatraz in 1963 because it was nearly three times more expensive to run than any other federal prison, due to its island location. [47]

Continued on p. 776

Chronology

1787-1842

Round-the-clock isolation of prisoners begins in Pennsylvania and New York in the belief that enforced solitude encourages repentance.

1787
Pennsylvania turns a wing of a Philadelphia jail into a "penitentiary house," where prisoners are kept in their cells.

1821
New York imposes isolation regime at a new state prison in Auburn.

1829
Eastern Penitentiary, designed to completely isolate prisoners, opens outside Philadelphia.

1842
British novelist Charles Dickens visits Eastern and reports that long-term solitary confinement was "immeasurably worse than any torture of the body."

1890-1963

U.S. Supreme Court expresses skepticism about solitary confinement but doesn't reject it.

1890
High court frees a Colorado man sentenced to hang for his wife's murder, saying he'd been punished with solitary confinement under a law that shouldn't have been applied to him.

1934
Federal government opens prison for hard-core prisoners on Alcatraz Island in San Francisco Bay, considered the predecessor of supermax prisons.

1963
After Alcatraz is closed as too expensive, the government opens a replacement in Marion, Ill.

1983-1998

Supermax era begins as prisons are built to hold the "worst of the worst" in strict solitary confinement; prisoner-rights lawyers begin challenging the strategy.

1983
Prisoners kill two guards at the federal prison at Marion, prompting a lockdown of all prisoners.

1989
California opens Pelican Bay prison with Security Housing Unit (SHU) designed to hold prisoners in their cells for 23 hours a day.

1995
Federal judge in San Francisco prohibits confinement of mentally ill prisoners at the SHU and concludes that conditions were close to intolerable even for the mentally healthy.

1998
Illinois opens Tamms Correctional Center, which became a target of prisoners' litigation and a center of political controversy.

2001-2012

Prisoner lawsuits, combined with tightened finances for states, increase pressures to restrict supermax confinement.

2001-2002
Supermax prisoners in Ohio, Mississippi and Wisconsin sue over their conditions of confinement.

2004
Nationwide, 44 state supermaxes hold an estimated 25,000 prisoners.

2005
U.S. Supreme Court rules in Ohio lawsuit that prisoners have a right to challenge orders transferring them to supermax and to qualify for release from solitary.

2006
U.S. Appeals Court ruling on Wisconsin suit likens supermax conditions to those in the Soviet gulag in the 1930s.

2007
Violence in Mississippi's supermax prompts state immediately to lay groundwork for reducing supermax population.

2010
Ruling on a lawsuit by Illinois supermax prisoners, federal judge writes that conditions at the prison cause lasting psychological damage. . . . American Bar Association proposes one-year limit on strict solitary confinement.

2011
U.N. investigator says long-term solitary confinement can amount to torture, proposes 15-day limit.

2012
Prisoner-rights lawyers file lawsuits alleging inhumane conditions at federal supermax in Florence, Colo., and state supermaxes in California and Arizona. . . . Senate subcommittee holds hearing on long-term solitary confinement. . . . Illinois Gov. Patrick Quinn orders Tamms supermax closed. Prison guards' union says decision threatens safety at prisons to which Tamms inmates are to be transferred. . . . Illinois state judge temporarily blocks Tamms closing.

Controversial Study Supports Use of Solitary

Inmates claim no ill effects, but critics cite flaws in research.

Until recently, supporters of long-term solitary confinement had little academic research to back up what their experience told them: that placing inmates in isolation for long periods — is an indispensable tool in running a prison system.

Now, a controversial study based on research among Colorado prisoners is filling the gap — at least as far as advocates of solitary confinement are concerned.

The results, published in 2010 by the Justice Department's National Institute of Justice, are based on psychological tests administered to about 250 Colorado prisoners — some mentally ill — in both solitary and in the prison system's general population. The average length of a stay in solitary in Colorado is two years, but the study doesn't say how long each study participant in solitary had spent there. The tests included prisoners' self-assessments of their own psychological condition. [1]

A report on the study, co-written by Maureen L. O'Keefe, research director for the Colorado Department of Corrections, concluded that "there was initial improvement in psychological well-being across all study groups." What's more, it said "elevations in psychological and cognitive functioning that were evident at the start of the study remained present at the end of the study." [2]

The report noted that researchers had not expected these results and that the study's conclusions contradicted "the bulk of literature" indicating that solitary confinement "is extremely detrimental to inmates with and without mental illness." [3]

"People who rail against isolated confinement were very disappointed in the outcome of the report," says Eugene Atherton, a Pueblo, Colo.-based prison management consultant and former Colorado warden. "The research showed the opposite of what they had hoped would be proved." Atherton, now working for the State Department to advise the Afghan government on development of a prison system, spoke from Kabul.

Advocates of solitary confinement have used the study to support their view that isolating prisoners for long periods — usually known in the field as "administrative segregation" or "ad seg" — is a legitimate form of punishment and necessary for maintaining control of inmate populations.

Last June, Charles E. Samuels Jr., director of the Federal Bureau of Prisons, told the Senate Judiciary Committee's Constitution, Civil Rights and Human Rights Subcommittee that the study found that "no negative effect on individuals in restrictive housing has occurred." [4]

But opponents of solitary confinement argue that the study is flawed and should not be used to shape prison policy.

O'Keefe and study adviser Jeffrey L. Metzner, a University of Colorado psychiatry professor and longtime expert on mental health in prison, acknowledged that the report shouldn't be taken as conclusive evidence that applies to all long-term solitary nationwide. "This study may not generalize to other prison systems, especially those that have conditions of confinement more restrictive and/or harsher than CSP [Colorado State Penitentiary]," they wrote last year in a professional journal, *Correctional Mental Health Report.* [5]

Writing separately, Metzner said, "Such results should not be interpreted to indicate that there is little harm associated with housing inmates with mental illness on a long-term basis in" solitary confinement. Metzner served as an adviser on the study. Others included Jamie Fellner, a senior adviser to the U.S. program of Human Rights Watch, an advocacy group that is critical of long-term solitary confinement. [6]

Despite the caveats, the report has generated a furious response from corrections experts, who have concluded that isolation damages prisoners who were either mentally ill to start with or mentally healthy when their isolation began.

Continued from p. 774

Its replacement was the federal prison at Marion, Ill., which opened in 1964. There, the only prisoners initially kept in their cells 23 hours a day were those locked in the prison's "control unit," which was reserved for 35 inmates considered especially dangerous. [48]

In October 1983, during a period of rising tension, two control unit prisoners killed two guards in a 10-hour span. Each prisoner was being escorted to his cell when he turned on a guard and stabbed him to death. Rules then in effect didn't require control-unit prisoners to be handcuffed when outside their cells. [49]

After the killings, the federal Bureau of Prisons put Marion on permanent "lockdown." When an inmate was let out of his cell, he was chained, handcuffed and escorted by three guards. Visitors saw inmates only through a Plexiglas window and spoke to them over a telephone. Work programs ceased. (Today, Marion is a medium-security prison, without permanent solitary.) [50]

The killings prompted a call to reestablish a federal death penalty, which the U.S. Supreme Court had rejected in 1972. "Locking some men up will not stop them from injuring others," Bureau of Prisons Director Norman Carlson said shortly after the homicides. "They use virtually anything to make deadly weapons, and they spend their days plotting murder. We can keep them in their cells for 23 hours a day, but we can't weld the bars shut. For these few, the death penalty is the only answer." [51]

Congress passed a new federal capital punishment law in 1988 and expanded its application in 1994. Among politicians, the debate over that move

Stuart Grassian and Terry Kupers, psychiatrists with long professional track records in correctional mental health, argued, for example, that relying on prisoners to assess their own psychological conditions constitutes a fundamental flaw of the study. The testing materials the researchers used weren't designed specifically for prison inmates, Grassian and Kupers wrote. Prisoners in the study sample were told that the purpose was to research adjustment to prison life.

"Anyone with a background in corrections knows that is not the kind of information an inmate would likely expose," Grassian and Kupers wrote. "It could harm him, even surreptitiously, for example at a parole hearing or in hearings to determine whether he could progress to higher levels in [administrative segregation]." [7]

Grassian, a retired Harvard Medical School professor, and Kupers, a professor at the Wright Institute in Berkeley, Calif., a postgraduate clinical psychology school, also wrote that the study failed to evaluate test results in light of prison mental-health records. These would have provided data, they wrote, against which to assess the test results. [8]

The study's critics may have feared that it would be used to justify maintaining or even expanding the number of prisoners in solitary confinement. But that has not been the result, at least in Colorado. After the report was issued, the legislature last year ordered the state corrections department to report annually on progress in removing mentally ill or developmentally disabled prisoners from solitary confinement. The bill imposing the requirement was prompted by an increase in the number of mentally ill prisoners placed in solitary. [9]

But changes in the prison system went deeper. Administrators have been sending fewer prisoners of any kind to solitary confinement. Along with a general decrease in the prison population, partly resulting from lowered penalties for some drug crimes, the decline in the solitary population led this year to closure of the brand-new Colorado State Penitentiary in Canon City. It had been used mainly for strict solitary confinement of the long-term type, with virtually round-the-clock isolation and limited human contact. [10]

The $162 million prison, opened in 2010 with room for 948 administrative-segregation prisoners, has housed only 316 inmates since it opened. [11]

Atherton acknowledges the report hasn't settled the issue. "On goes this battle," he says, "with those who know little or nothing about correctional institutions and criminal behavior who are applying their own suburban standards to prisons."

— Peter Katel

---

[1] Maureen L. O'Keefe, "One Year Longitudinal Study of the Psychological Effects of Administrative Segregation," Colorado Department of Corrections, University of Colorado, Colorado Springs, Oct. 31, 2010, pp. v-vi, 11, www.ncjrs.gov/pdffiles1/nij/grants/232973.pdf.

[2] *Ibid.*, p. ii.

[3] *Ibid.*

[4] "Sen. Richard J. Durbin Holds a Hearing on Reassessing Solitary Confinement," *CQ Transcriptions*, June 19, 2012.

[5] Jeffrey L. Metzner and Maureen L. O'Keefe, "Psychological Effects of Administrative Segregation: The Colorado Study," *Correctional Mental Health Report*, May/June, 2011, p. 1, www.civicresearchinstitute.com/online/article_abstract.php?pid=14&iid=512&aid=3553.

[6] *Ibid.*, p. 14 and "Acknowledgements" page.

[7] Stuart Grassian and Terry Kupers, "The Colorado Study vs. the Reality of Supermax Confinement," *Correctional Mental Health Report*, *op. cit.*, p. 9.

[8] *Ibid.*, p. 10.

[9] "DOC gets report on solitary confinement review," The Associated Press, Nov. 18, 2011.

[10] Kristen Wyatt, "Colorado closing Canon City prison," The Associated Press, March 19, 2012.

[11] Tracy Harmon, "Reduced crime means less need for state prisons," *Pueblo Chieftain* (Pueblo, Colo.), March 21, 2012; Tracy Harmon, "$162 million prison opens," *Pueblo Chieftain*, Aug. 26, 2010.

---

overshadowed, for a time, arguments about the wisdom, cost and ethics of confining prisoners in solitary for periods of years. [52]

In fact, the Marion lockdown became the template for supermax prisons nationwide. At the federal level, the administrative maximum (ADX) prison in Florence, Colo., which opened in 1994, was built to enable a regime of permanent lockdown. By then, too, the Marion model had started spreading to state prison systems.

The best-known state supermax, the Security Housing Unit (SHU) of Pelican Bay State Prison in California, opened in 1989. SHU prisoners were locked in their cells for all but about one hour a day. Massachusetts followed suit in 1991, with a supermax on the grounds of the state prison at Walpole, where prisoners were locked in cells for 22 hours a day. "This unit sends a message to both existing inmates and potential criminals that disruptive behavior is not going to be tolerated in the Massachusetts prison system," Gov. William Weld said. [53]

By 1998, about 20,000 prisoners were housed under supermax conditions in 34 states — either in newly built institutions or in existing prisons or prison wings retrofitted as supermaxes. [54]

Virtually as soon as the wave of supermax construction began, some corrections professionals began questioning whether the facilities were needed, at least on such a broad scale. "Fad, trend or wise investment?," Riveland, the former Washington state prison system director, asked in a 1999 report published by the Justice Department's National Institute of Corrections. [55]

Some States Rethinking Solitary Confinement

Trend began with inmate lawsuit over Ohio supermax prison.

The prison world has a new buzzword: "reclassification." High costs, litigation and controversy involving long-term solitary confinement are prompting politicians and prison officials to question whether prisoner isolation has been overused. As a result, some states are revamping their security classifications under which certain prisoners are segregated in round-the-clock lockdown.

The reclassification trend, so far limited to a few states, got its first major impetus from Ohio's decision in the early 2000s to drastically reduce its population housed in long-term solitary with little human contact in the state's supermax prison, the Ohio State Penitentiary. At the time, the state was embroiled in a lawsuit by prisoners challenging their transfer to the supermax. In 2005, the U.S. Supreme Court upheld prisoners' right to challenge such transfers. [1]

But by the time the court ruled, Ohio already had changed its classification system. By 2008, only 53 of 533 prisoners who had been in supermax in the early 2000s remained there. The others had been reclassified to lower security levels, a move that took them out of solitary. [2]

The most dramatic shift in state policy came in Mississippi in 2007. Prompting the change was an increase in violence in the notorious isolation wing of the state penitentiary at Parchman — Unit 32, which held only prisoners in round-the-clock solitary — made possible by a breakdown in isolation security procedures. [3]

At the time, the Mississippi prison system was being sued by prisoners represented by the National Prison Project of the American Civil Liberties Union (ACLU). The lawsuit had already led to talks between prison system officials and lawyers for inmates on changing the classification system. Following the violence, officials quickly accepted changes in the system proposed by the ACLU's classification expert, James Austin (who had also worked on the Ohio revamping). A few months later, about three-quarters of Unit 32 prisoners had been reclassified for transfer to the prison's general population. [4]

Austin had concluded that under the old classification system, some prisoners were sent to Unit 32 immediately after they began their sentences, without having broken any rules. Many prisoners remained in the unit for years though they had not committed any misconduct there and should have been eligible for transfer. "Required reassessments were not being done . . . [and] the caseload for case managers was so large that they could not have adequate contact with prisoners," said a study by experts including Austin, other ACLU staff members and Mississippi prison officials. [5]

As prisoners were reclassified, the population of Unit 32 plummeted from about 1,000 to fewer than 150. [6]

The Ohio and Mississippi reclassifications are now being used as a template for other states. The Vera Institute of Justice, a New York-based criminal justice system think tank and advocacy organization, is working with Illinois, Maryland and New Mexico on revamping their classification systems. [7]

The projects are designed to develop new standards for releasing prisoners from segregation, strengthening programs by which prisoners can move out of solitary confinement and improving conditions in solitary. "Vera aims to demonstrate that states can reduce the numbers of prisoners they hold in segregation without jeopardizing institutional or public safety," Michael Jacobson, Vera's president, told the Senate Judiciary Committee's Constitution, Civil Rights and Human Rights Subcommittee last June. The organization also hopes to create a "replicable model" that other states can use. [8]

Work on the project so far shows that many prisoners are sent to solitary for minor rule-breaking, three Vera Institute reclassification specialists wrote last year. These offenses include "unauthorized movement, failure to report to work or school, insolence or talking back and disobeying a direct order," the

Riveland didn't answer the question directly. But he wrote that supermaxes were significantly more expensive to build and operate, their conditions raised ethical and constitutional issues of inhumane treatment and effects on staff as well as prisoners could be negative. "When there is little interaction except in control situations," Riveland wrote, "the adversarial nature of the relationships tends to be one of dominance and, in return, resistance on both sides." [56]

Constitutional Issues

As supermaxes proliferated, prisoner advocates and human-rights activists began a campaign to limit their use, or abolish them altogether.

The first major lawsuit over supermax conditions was a 1993 federal case that combined more than 300 individual suits by inmates at California's Pelican Bay prison. A trial featured harrowing testimony from prison experts about systematic brutality and mistreatment of inmates throughout the prison and in its SHU supermax wing — testimony cited in detail in a 345-page ruling by U.S. District Judge Thelton E. Henderson in 1995. [57]

Henderson ruled that prison system officials "cross the constitutional line when they force certain subgroups of the prison population, including the mentally ill, to endure the conditions in the SHU, despite knowing that the likely consequence for such inmates is serious injury to their mental health." Another subgroup, Henderson ruled, was made up of inmates

experts wrote. "Confinement to segregation is often out of scale for these violations." [9]

The Illinois corrections department reported that Vera's analysis showed that 85 percent of prisoners were in long-term, limited-human-contact solitary for "less severe" infractions. "It was also found that those who spent less time in segregation were not more likely to commit new violations during the first 12 months of release into general prison population," the department reported in comments that Jacobson relayed to the Senate subcommittee. [10]

Overall, Illinois officials reported, "The mantra of the program has been to determine if we are mad at the offender or scared of them when making recommendations for segregation time and transfer." [11]

In Mississippi, meanwhile, reclassification has improved conditions in the prison system, according to a top official. "When we started moving people to lower security levels, we found that there was no increase in violence," Deputy Corrections Commissioner Emmitt Sparkman wrote on the Vera Institute's blog. "We've been conditioned that 23-hour lockdowns make it safer, make it better for staff and other offenders and for the system. In Mississippi, we've found that's not necessarily true." [12]

The Ohio story has been more complicated. The most recent prison system director, Gary Mohr, said that when he took over last year he found dangerously high levels of violence. In response, he announced a new classification system early this year that would house an estimated 300 to 500 gang members and other dangerous prisoners in "control" units or special prisons. [13]

Those units include cells for virtually round-the-clock solitary confinement. But officials made a point of stressing differences between their system and previous versions of long-term solitary confinement. They said "control" prisoners would be able to earn a way into less restrictive conditions and would be enrolled in behavioral programs. "Control prisons are not designed as disciplinary centers," the department said in its annual report for last year. "Offenders in control units will still have access to programming designed to change their way of thinking." [14]

— Peter Katel

[1] *Wilkinson v. Austin*, 544 U.S. 74 (2005), www.law.cornell.edu/supct/html/04-495.ZS.html.

[2] "Examples of supermax prisons whose purposes have changed," The Associated Press, April 5, 2008.

[3] Terry A. Kupers, *et al.*, "Beyond Supermax Administrative Segregation," *Criminal Justice and Behavior*, July 21, 2009, p. 4, https://www.aclu.org/images/asset_upload_file359_41136.pdf.

[4] *Ibid.*

[5] *Ibid.*, p. 5.

[6] *Ibid.*, p. 5.

[7] "Segregation Reduction Project," Vera Institute of Justice, undated, www.vera.org/project/segregation-reduction-project.

[8] Michael Jacobson, written testimony, Senate Judiciary Committee, Subcommittee on the Constitution, Civil Rights and Human Rights, June 19, 2012, www.vera.org/files/michael-jacobson-testimony-on-solitary-confinement-2012.pdf.

[9] Angela Browne, Alissa Cambier and Suzanne Agha, "Prisons Within Prisons: The use of Segregation in the United States," *Federal Sentencing Reporter*, October 2011, p. 29, www.jstor.org/discover/10.1525/fsr.2011.24.1.46?uid=3739816&uid=2129&uid=2&uid=70&uid=4&uid=3739256&sid=21101142915511.

[10] Jacobson, *op. cit.*

[11] *Ibid.*

[12] Emmitt Sparkman, "Mississippi DOC's Emmitt Sparkman on reducing the use of segregation in prisons," *Current Thinking* (blog), Vera Institute of Justice, Oct. 31, 2011, www.vera.org/blog/mississippi-docs-emmitt-sparkman-reducing-use-segregation-prisons.

[13] "Prisoners with gang links to be isolated," *Dayton Daily News* (Ohio), Feb. 15, 2012 p. A1; "Annual Report, 2011," Ohio Department of Rehabilitation and Correction, undated,www.drc.ohio.gov/web/Reports/Annual/Annual%20Report%202011.pdf.

[14] *Ibid.*, "Annual Report," p. 4.

with mental conditions — chronic depression and brain damage effects, among them — who would severely deteriorate in solitary. In December 1995, Henderson followed up by ordering the removal of 100 severely mentally ill prisoners from the SHU by year's end. [58]

Nevertheless, Henderson explicitly refrained from concluding that conditions in the SHU were unconstitutional across the board. They "may well hover on the edge of what is humanly tolerable for those with normal resilience, particularly when endured for extended periods of time," Henderson wrote. "They do not, however, violate exacting Eighth Amendment standards." [59] The amendment, which prohibits "cruel and unusual punishments," is central to analyzing the constitutionality of prison conditions. [60]

The Pelican Bay ruling led to a series of federal lawsuits by the American Civil Liberties Union (ACLU) on behalf of prisoners confined in solitary in Wisconsin, Ohio, Connecticut, New Mexico and Indiana. (The New Mexico case began in state court.) By 2007, those suits led to settlements or court orders prohibiting confinement of seriously mentally ill prisoners in supermax facilities. [61]

When another supermax lawsuit reached the U.S. Supreme Court in 2005, the justices also refrained from defining long-term solitary as unconstitutional. But the decision did uphold prisoners' arguments that they'd been denied due process when they were sent to the Ohio supermax. Likewise, once in solitary, the court said, prisoners had a constitutional right to periodic review of their cases, with the possibility of earning transfer out of solitary. [62]

Following the high court action, prisoners argued in a lower federal court that the prison system wasn't actually carrying out the due-process proceedings, despite what officials had told the Supreme Court. In 2007, a federal district judge ruled that Ohio was still denying prisoners an effective procedure to win release from the supermax. [63]

Meanwhile, opposition to long-term solitary confinement was intensifying in the domestic and international human-rights community. The ACLU, in addition to litigating for years over conditions for prisoners in prolonged solitary confinement, launched a campaign to "stop solitary." Among the reasons was solitary's effect on mental health, among both mentally ill prisoners and those who'd been mentally stable before being locked in prolonged isolation. Argued the ACLU, "The clinical impacts of isolation can actually be similar to that of physical torture." [64] ■

CURRENT SITUATION

Fight Over Supermax

In early September, Associate Circuit Judge Charles Cavaness of Alexander County, Ill. (Cairo), issued a temporary restraining order halting Gov. Quinn's planned closure of the Tamms supermax. The action had the potential to make "the prisons that remain more dangerous for employees," the judge said. [65]

That conclusion echoed arguments by union prison guards and other staff, who have been fighting Democrat Quinn's plan to close Tamms, a conventional prison for women and some centers for juvenile offenders.

The judge's order followed an arbitrator's decision upholding the union's position that Quinn's decision violated the employees' labor contract. Both sides were ordered to negotiate a solution within 30 days. The judge's decision effectively maintains the status quo until a deal is reached.

The legal battle between Quinn and the American Federation of State, County and Municipal Employees union (AFSCME) demonstrates the complications of the debate over supermax prisons. Among the big issues in Illinois: jobs, safety in the state's remaining prisons, state spending on an institution running at far below capacity because of a court ruling and longstanding human-rights concerns over supermax confinement.

Ever since Quinn began publicly weighing the possibility of shutting Tamms, AFSCME leaders have insisted that the move — in addition to costing 250 jobs in economically struggling southern Illinois — would raise the danger level in institutions to which Tamms prisoners would be transferred. "Conditions are already volatile and dangerous in the prison system, which is jammed," Henry Bayer, AFSCME's executive director in Illinois, said in early August. [66]

When he spoke, the confrontation between the union and Quinn had been heating up. In late July, The Associated Press reported that the state corrections department ordered pat-down searches of employees as they left work at about 15 state prisons. Union members alleged that the search order was designed as retaliation for leaks to a newspaper about plans to transfer as many as nine Tamms inmates to prisons in other states. Union leaders said the reported plan to send dangerous inmates out of state showed that Illinois officials were aware that the supermax was the only safe place to house those inmates within the boundaries of their own state. [67]

Among the nine reportedly considered for transfer was Henry Brisbon, who entered prison on a 1,000- to 3,000-year sentence for killing an engaged couple in 1973. In prison, he was sentenced to death for stabbing another inmate to death. His death sentence was commuted to life imprisonment when, in 2000, Republican Gov. George Ryan declared a moratorium on the death penalty, which the Illinois legislature later abolished. [68]

Inmates classified as extremely dangerous may have been the only ones left at Tamms in the wake of the 2010 federal court ruling that prisoners had a constitutional right to challenge transfer to Tamms. By this year, according to a budget summary by Quinn's office, Tamms had a prisoner population of 389, or slightly more than half the prison's 753-inmate capacity. The prison's annual operating cost is $62,000 per prisoner, compared with the state average of $21,405. [69]

When Quinn disclosed his plan in June to close Tamms, he said he hoped the legislature would channel the savings into the Department of Children and Family Services, which had suffered a $50 million budget cut that would eliminate 375 jobs. "I think the priority is children, not a half-empty prison," he said. [70]

Alan Mills, legal director for the nonprofit Uptown People's Law Center in Chicago, which represented prisoners in the case that led to the federal court ruling, says the court decision strongly influenced the governor's decision. The judge forced a "recognition that penologically you don't need Tamms," Mills says.

New Litigation

Recent lawsuits against federal and state supermaxes continue a legal offensive under way virtually since the first such prison opened. Lawsuits filed

Continued on p. 782

At Issue:

Should solitary confinement be limited to one year?

DAVID C. FATHI
DIRECTOR, ACLU NATIONAL PRISON PROJECT

WRITTEN FOR *CQ RESEARCHER*, SEPTEMBER 2012

yes

"It's an awful thing, solitary," Sen. John McCain wrote of his time as a prisoner of war in Vietnam. "It crushes your spirit and weakens your resistance more effectively than any other form of mistreatment." McCain spent about two years in solitary; in the United States today, many prisoners are held in continuous solitary confinement for five years, 10 years or longer.

It's undisputed that solitary confinement is profoundly and sometimes irreparably damaging, and the damage becomes more severe with increasing duration. In 2010, a federal judge reviewing conditions at Illinois' Tamms supermax prison concluded that "Tamms imposes drastic limitations on human contact, so much so as to inflict lasting psychological and emotional harm on inmates confined there for long periods." And in 2005, a group of mental health experts told the U.S. Supreme Court that "no study of the effects of solitary or supermax-like confinement that lasted longer than 60 days failed to find evidence of negative psychological effects." Some effects, such as a slowing of brain activity, are detectable after as little as one week.

On the other side of the ledger, there's little proof that solitary confinement promotes prison or public safety, and a growing body of evidence indicates that it's actually counterproductive. A 2006 study found that opening a supermax prison had no effect on prisoner-on-prisoner violence in Arizona, Illinois and Minnesota. Indeed, Mississippi Corrections Commissioner Christopher Epps recently testified before a U.S. Senate subcommittee that when his state slashed its solitary population by 75 percent, violent incidents fell by half. And a 2004 study from Washington state found that prisoners who had experienced solitary confinement were more likely to commit new crimes upon release, and also committed more serious crimes, than similar prisoners who had not been in solitary.

No one denies that some prisoners sometimes require physical separation so they don't harm others. But physical separation can be achieved without the extreme social isolation and sensory deprivation that are the hallmarks of solitary confinement. Based on the overwhelming evidence of its harmful effects, the United Nations Special Rapporteur on Torture in 2011 recommended a global ban on solitary confinement lasting more than 15 days. But even a one-year limit would dramatically reduce the suffering and damage caused by solitary confinement as it's practiced in the United States today. It should be adopted without delay.

GARY W. DELAND
EXECUTIVE DIRECTOR, UTAH SHERIFFS ASSOCIATION, FORMER DIRECTOR, UTAH DEPARTMENT OF CORRECTIONS

WRITTEN FOR *CQ RESEARCHER*, SEPTEMBER 2012

no

In the debate over whether solitary confinement is beneficial or hostile to prisoner management, legal considerations have received insufficient attention.

The Supreme Court has repeatedly ruled that officials have a duty to take reasonable measures to protect prisoners from violence. But to provide reasonable measures to protect safety, officials must be able to control prisoners' mobility, interaction with other prisoners and capability to harm others. Hands-on methods of control (i.e., grappling, fighting) provide a high risk of injury. Restraint methods such as pepper spray, electronic restraint devices and restraint chairs provide safer force options. Despite abundant data demonstrating the safety benefits, detractors are campaigning to ban their use.

Solitary confinement is effective for managing prisoners who are a serious threat to others. However, the well-established effectiveness and safety benefits of solitary — just as with pepper spray or restraint chairs — have become targets of self-styled reformers. There are many operational justifications to support the value of solitary confinement; however, one that justifies attention is the litigation threat to corrections officials if they fail to protect prisoners from violence when the officials know of a serious or excessive risk of prisoner-on-prisoner violence.

The Supreme Court has ruled that if officials know of a substantial risk of harm to a prisoner, but knowingly disregard the risk by failing to take reasonable measures to abate it, and the prisoner suffers serious harm, the officials may be found deliberately indifferent and thus liable for the harm to the prisoner. When officials know a prisoner is a gang member, a predator or has other violent propensities, assigning that prisoner to general housing and permitting the prisoner to have direct interaction with other inmates pose a strong potential to create a substantial threat of violence to other prisoners. Solitary limits prisoner violence by limiting physical contact with other inmates and staff. Simply put, limiting or controlling violent prisoners' interaction with other prisoners greatly limits the potential for violence.

A time limit on confinement is appropriate in cases where the aim is to discipline a rule-breaking inmate. But when the isolation is based on a prisoner's history of being a violent predator or violent gang member, the time frame for solitary confinement should be indefinite. A few months in isolation do not change a highly dangerous individual into an easily manageable prisoner. Solitary confinement of such prisoners is, in many cases, essential to the safety of other inmates and staff.

Continued from p. 780

in recent months against the federal supermax at Florence, Colo., the California supermax at Pelican Bay and the Arizona state prison system, including its long-term solitary unit, present a long list of charges against officials of the three systems.

None of the systems has yet filed a detailed response to the allegations. However, Federal Bureau of Prisons Director Samuels in effect countered the federal lawsuit's allegations that the Florence supermax housed deeply mentally ill prisoners and denied them effective treatment. "Only a very small proportion of offenders are held in more restricted housing, and most for only brief periods of time," Samuels said.

Referring to the strict-solitary wing, Samuels said placement "is restricted to inmates who clearly pose an extreme safety risk and need stringent restrictions to maintain safety for other inmates, staff, institutional operations and the public." [71]

The lawsuit against the Florence prison, filed on behalf of five inmates by Arnold & Porter, a prominent Washington law firm, and the Washington Lawyers' Committee for Civil Rights and Urban Affairs, lays out a harrowing account of untreated mental illness in the most restrictive of the solitary confinement units.

"Even where prisoners . . . are properly identified as having a serious mental illness," the lawsuit states, "many are not given appropriate treatment, including either counseling or medication." In allegedly withholding treatment, the bureau is ignoring its own rules, the lawsuit says. [72]

The lawsuit's lengthy and highly detailed accounts of self-mutilation and other self-destructive behavior prompted a similarly detailed and impassioned denunciation of the supermax by Andrew Cohen, a contributing editor at *The Atlantic* magazine and a legal analyst for CBS News' "60 Minutes."

"For these inmates," Cohen wrote of mentally ill prisoners in strict solitary, "the prison is a gulag, a place of unspeakable cruelty and state-sponsored wickedness, run by officials who ignore their own policies and seem to revel in humiliating prisoners by depriving them of basic human dignities." [73]

A separate but related lawsuit filed last May centers on the suicide of an allegedly severely mentally ill inmate at Florence in 2010. José Martin Vega, who was serving four consecutive life sentences on a 1995 conviction for racketeering and armed drug trafficking, had been diagnosed as a paranoid schizophrenic, the lawsuit alleges. [74]

Vega's brother, Raymond, represented by an Arnold & Porter lawyer, is suing warden Blake R. Davis over the suicide, alleging that prison staff chained Vega, sometimes for 10 days or more at a time, instead of treating him. "The behavior claimed by the BOP (Bureau of Prisons) to justify such abuse was a product of Vega's untreated mental illness," the lawsuit states, without specifying Vega's behavior. [75]

Vega was found dead in his cell. A coroner ruled he had hanged himself.

Treatment of mentally ill prisoners, including those held in long-term solitary, is also a major issue in a federal class-action lawsuit filed in March against Arizona prison officials for allegedly seriously deficient medical care, including mental health care, throughout the state's prison system. [76]

Lawyers for the state deny specific allegations. And, they wrote in their first response to the lawsuit, they specifically rejected the claim that prison officials "are deliberately indifferent to a substantial risk of serious physical or psychiatric harm" to prisoners in solitary. Further, they said that prisoners are kept in solitary only for unspecified short periods of time, except for prison gang members. The latter, the state said, can exit solitary by providing information about gang activities and renouncing membership. [77]

And California's Pelican Bay supermax is the target of a class-action lawsuit filed last May that centers on gang members and alleged members. California prison policy, the lawsuit alleges, is to confine these prisoners in strict solitary unless they "debrief" with prison staff — that is, provide information on other inmates' gang activities. Informing on fellow prisoners, the lawsuit says, would invite retaliation on the informants and their families. "Accordingly, for those many prisoners who refuse or are unable to debrief, defendants' policies result in 'effectively permanent' solitary confinement," the lawsuit says. [78]

Moreover, according to the lawsuit, evidence of gang affiliation for at least some of the prisoners is sketchy. One plaintiff, George Ruiz, has been in solitary confinement for 22 years "based on nothing more than his appearance on lists of alleged gang members discovered in some unnamed prisoners' cells and his possession of allegedly gang-related drawings." [79]

The lawsuit, filed by lawyers of the New York-based Center for Constitutional Rights, followed a hunger strike last year by prisoners in the Pelican Bay long-term solitary unit. Among other issues, they were protesting the debriefing requirement. In response, California's undersecretary of corrections, Scott Kernan, told prisoners that the state would assess the criteria by which prisoners are categorized as gang members, as well as the debriefing procedure. [80]

After the lawsuit was filed, the department declined to comment. But a spokesman told a reporter that the department was still designing a system under which prisoners could "demonstrate their ability to refrain from criminal gang behavior" and would undergo preparation for living in "housing in a less restrictive environment." Prisoners still in solitary would get added privileges if they "refrain from criminal gang behavior." [81] ■

OUTLOOK

'Losing Favor'

Prison experts generally concur that supermaxes and the strict isolation they represent will keep declining in use. "It's losing favor as a result, to some extent, of litigation," says Martin, the Texas-based prison consultant and monitor. Driving the supermax decline, he says, are judicial prohibitions on keeping mentally ill prisoners in strict solitary.

Aside from the fact that mentally ill prisoners typically make up a large percentage of supermax inmates, Martin says, "There is growing acknowledgement by prison administrators that we need to be more careful in choosing to put people in segregation and need to be more careful in how long we keep them. Systems are learning to operate without such a reliance on segregation."

Atherton, the Colorado prison consultant, also sees a trend, but argues that it won't and shouldn't lead to complete abolition of long-term solitary. Financial pressures to close supermaxes are real, he says, and politicians may want to close isolation units to build support among prison critics. "They'll close administrative segregation and say, 'Look what a wonderful person I am.' Or they will be judicious and preserve the ways in which wardens can put bad people in lockup."

Strict solitary confinement won't disappear, Atherton argues. "Wardens and correctional professional associations will rise up and preserve the ability to provide administrative segregation, which by law is constitutional." However, he says, "It might be used less because of the cost."

Cohen, the Arizona penology editor, also says further supermax closings are likely — but only "if you can pitch it in a way that says you're not compromising safety inside or out."

One danger of continuing a relatively high use of strict solitary, he says, is that prisoners will come to depend on court rulings prohibiting that form of imprisonment for the mentally ill. "You end up putting a premium on mental illness: 'If it takes being crazy to stay out, I'll be crazy.' "

DeLand, the former Utah corrections official and a defender of strict solitary confinement, concedes that supermax construction became a "fad." But, he says, "You have to recognize you have certain prisoners" who require round-the-clock lockdown.

"You want your very best people running these operations," DeLand says. Under those circumstances, he says, "They work pretty well."

Nonetheless, says the ACLU's Fathi, financial and legal pressures to decrease use of long-term solitary are becoming overwhelming. "This is an enormously expensive way to house people," he says. "As states are experiencing fiscal pressure, they are taking a long-overdue second look at whether this is an appropriate use of scarce public dollars."

Meanwhile, prison professionals are increasingly recognizing that supermax-type confinement "is overused and that there are people there who don't belong there."

Mills of the Uptown People's Law Center in Chicago, whose litigation against the Tamms supermax in Illinois helped set the stage for the governor's order to close the prison, says that move represents an irreversible trend. "In 10 to 15 years, I don't think that more than one or two will be left."

Supermaxes, Mills says, "were an experiment that never had an evidentiary basis in the first place. There is no empirical evidence that they make prisons systems any safer. The economy no longer gives states the money to experiment." ■

Notes

[1] Maurice Possley, "Anthony Graves," *National Registry of Exonerations*, undated, www.law.umich.edu/special/exoneration/Pages/casedetail.aspx?caseid=3253.

[2] Anthony C. Graves, written testimony, Senate Judiciary Subcommittee on the Constitution, Civil Rights and Human Rights, June 19, 2012, www.judiciary.senate.gov/pdf/12-6-19GravesTestimony.pdf.

[3] Michael Jacobson, written testimony, Senate Subcommittee on the Constitution, Civil Rights and Human Rights, June 19, 2012, www.vera.org/pubs/michael-jacobson-testimony-solitary-confinement-us-senate-committee-judiciary.

[4] Chase Riveland, "Supermax Prisons: Overview and General Considerations," 1999 National Institute of Corrections, pp. 5-6, http://static.nicic.gov/Library/014937.pdf.

[5] "Sen. Richard J. Durbin Holds a Hearing on Reassessing Solitary Confinement," Senate Committee on the Judiciary, Subcommittee on Constitution, Civil Rights and Human Rights, *CQ Transcriptions*, June 19, 2012.

[6] Juan E. Méndez, "Torture and other cruel, inhuman or degrading treatment of punishment," United Nations General Assembly, Aug. 5, 2011, p. 17, http://solitaryconfinement.org/uploads/SpecRapTortureAug2011.pd; "Juan E Méndez," American University, faculty biographies, undated, www.wcl.american.edu/faculty/bio/jmendez.pdf.

[7] Daniel P. Mears, "Evaluating the Effectiveness of Supermax Prisons," Urban Institute, March, 2006, pp. 1, 3, www.urban.org/UploadedPDF/411326_supermax_prisons.pdf.

[8] Michael Jacobson, written testimony, *op. cit.* Quoted in Alex Barber, "Less restriction equals less violence at Maine State Prison," *Bangor Daily News*, June 15, 2012, http://bangordailynews.com/2012/06/15/news/state/less-restriction-equals-less-violence-at-maine-state-prison/; Lance Tapley, "Reducing solitary confinement," *Portland Phoenix*, Nov. 2, 2011, http://portland.thephoenix.com/news/129316-reducing-solitary-confinement/?page=1#TOPCONTENT/.

[9] The case is *Wilkinson v. Austin*, 544 U.S. 74 (2005), www.law.cornell.edu/supct/html/04-495.ZS.html.

[10] "Sen. Richard J. Durbin Holds a Hearing . . . ," *op. cit.*

[11] Terry A. Kupers, *et al.*, "Beyond Supermax Administrative Segregation," *Criminal Justice and Behavior*, July 21 2009, p. 4, www.aclu.org/

images/asset_upload_file359_41136.pdf.

[12] *Ruiz, et al., v. Brown, et al.*, U.S. District Court, Northern District of California, Case No 4:09-cv-05796-CW, Second Amended Complaint, May 31, 2012, www.clearinghouse.net/chDocs/public/PC-CA-0054-0001.pdf.

[13] Hope Metcalf and Judith Resnik, written testimony, Senate Subcommittee on the Constitution, Civil Rights and Human Rights, June 19, 2012, http://solitarywatch.com/wp-content/uploads/2012/06/hope-metcalf-and-judith-resnik-yale-law-school.pdf; "Administrative Segregation and Classification System Analysis and Review Process," Colorado Department of Corrections, January 2012, p. 7, www.aclu.org/files/assets/co_adseg_rept_jan2012.pdf.

[14] David C. Fathi, "The Common Law of Supermax Litigation," *Pace Law Review*, Spring 2004, p. 681, http://digitalcommons.pace.edu/cgi/viewcontent.cgi?article=1209&context=plr.

[15] *Bacote, et al., v. Federal Bureau of Prisons, et al.*, Case 1:12-cv-01570, Complaint, June 18, 2012, www.clearinghouse.net/chDocs/public/PC-CO-0019-0001.pdf.

[16] Mears, *op. cit.*, p. 33.

[17] Méndez, *op. cit.*, p. 17.

[18] "Standard 23-4.3 Disciplinary Sanctions," *Standards on Treatment of Prisoners*, American Bar Association, February 2010, www.americanbar.org/publications/criminal_justice_section_archive/crimjust_standards_treatmentprisoners.html#23-2.9.

[19] *Gillis v. Litscher, et al.*, U.S. Court of Appeals for the Seventh Circuit, No. 06-2099, Nov. 14, 2006, http://caselaw.findlaw.com/us-7th-circuit/1035106.html; Martha Nell, "Longtime 7th Circuit Judge Terence Evans Is Dead After Sudden Illness," *ABA Journal*, Aug. 11, 2011, www.abajournal.com/news/article/7th_circuit_judge_terence_evans_is_dead/.

[20] Atul Gawande, "Hellhole," *The New Yorker*, March 30, 2009, www.newyorker.com/reporting/2009/03/30/090330fa_fact_gawande?printable=true¤tPage=all#ixzz22sGDYqKK.

[21] Written testimony, Charles E. Samuels, Federal Bureau of Prisons, Subcommittee on the Constitution, Civil Rights and Human Rights, Senate Judiciary Committee, June 19, 2012, www.judiciary.senate.gov/pdf/12-6-19SamuelsTestimony.pdf.

[22] Chad R. Trulson, James W. Marquart and Soraya K. Kawucha, "Gang Suppression and Institutional Control," *Corrections Today*, American Correctional Association, April 2006, p. 30, www.aca.org/fileupload/177/prasannak/Trulson1.pdf.

[23] *Ibid.*

[24] *Farmer v. Brennan*, 511 U.S. 825 (1994), http://scholar.google.com/scholar_case?case=2417836767044325448&hl=en&as_sdt=2&as_vis=1&oi=scholarr.

[25] Daniel P. Mears, "An Assessment of Supermax Prisons Using an Evaluation Research Framework," *The Prison Journal*, March, 2008, http://tpj.sagepub.com/content/88/1/43.abstract.

[26] Kupers, *et al.*, *op. cit.*, p. 4.

[27] *Westefer, et al., v. Snyder, et al.*, U.S. District Court for the Southern District of Illinois, Case 00-162-GPM, Dec. 9, 2009.

[28] "Sen. Richard J. Durbin Holds a Hearing . . . ," *op. cit.*

[29] "Memorandum and Order," *Westefer, et al. v. Snyder, et al.*, *op. cit.*, July 20, 2010, www.leagle.com/xmlResult.aspx?xmldoc=in%20fdco%2020100720b93.xml&docbase=cslwar3-2007-curr.

[30] *Ibid.*

[31] "Sen. Richard J. Durbin Holds a Hearing . . . ," *op. cit.*

[32] Craig Haney, written testimony, Senate Judiciary Subcommittee on the Constitution, Civil Rights and Human Rights," June 19, 2012, www.judiciary.senate.gov/pdf/12-6-19HaneyTestimony.pdf.

[33] *Ibid.*

[34] Except where otherwise noted, this subsection is drawn from Scott Christianson, *With Liberty For Some: 500 Years of Imprisonment in America* (1998), pp. 133-138.

[35] Quoted in *ibid.*, p. 135.

[36] Quoted in *ibid.*, p. 136.

[37] Quoted in *ibid.*, p. 138.

[38] Except where otherwise indicated, information in this subsection is drawn from Medley, Petitioner, 134 U.S. 160 (1890), http://supreme.justia.com/cases/federal/us/134/160/case.html; Stuart Grassian, "Psychiatric Effects of Solitary Confinement," *Journal of Law and Policy*, 2006, pp. 329-330, http://law.wustl.edu/journal/22/p325grassian.pdf.

[39] Quoted in Medley *op. cit.*

[40] "Samuel F. Miller, 1862-1890," The Supreme Court Historical Society, undated, www.supremecourthistory.org/history-of-the-court/associate-justices/samuel-miller-1862-1890/.

[41] Quoted in *ibid.*

[42] Metcalf and Resnik, *op. cit.*, p. 9,

[43] Fred Cohen, "Isolation in Penal Settings: The Isolation-Restraint Paradigm," *Journal of Law and Policy*, 2006, p. 317, http://law.wustl.edu/Journal/22/p295Cohen.pdf.

[44] *Ibid.*

[45] Riveland, *op. cit.*, p. 5; Erwin N. Thompson, *The Rock: A History of Alcatraz Island 1847-1972* (undated), National Park Service, pp. 387, 414, www.nps.gov/alca/photosmultimedia/upload/TheRock-web.pdf.

[46] *Ibid.*, p. 334.

[47] "A Brief History of Alcatraz," Federal Bureau of Prisons, undated, www.bop.gov/about/history/alcatraz.jsp.

[48] Peter M. Carlson and Judith Simon Garrett, *Prison and Jail Administration: Practice and Theory* (1999), p. 255; E. R. Shipp, "Killings Tighten Rule At Tough Prison," *The New York Times*, Jan. 20, 1984, p. A14.

[49] *Ibid.*, Shipp; "Racist Inmates Who 'Kill for Sport' Are Suspects in Slayings," The Associated Press, Oct. 30, 1983.

[50] Carlson and Garrett, *op. cit.*, p. 255; *Admission and Orientation Handbook*, United States Penitentiary, Marion, Illinois," Federal Bureau of Prisons, updated October 2010, www.bop.gov/locations/institutions/mar/MAR_aohandbook.pdf.

[51] Quoted in "Racist Inmates Who Kill . . .," *op. cit.*

[52] "The Federal Death Penalty System: Supplementary Data, Analysis and Revised Protocols for Capital Case Review," U.S. Justice Department, June 6, 2001, www.justice.gov/dag/pubdoc/deathpenaltystudy.htm#feddeathpenaltylaw.

About the Author

Peter Katel is a *CQ Researcher* contributing writer who previously reported on Haiti and Latin America for *Time* and *Newsweek* and covered the Southwest for newspapers in New Mexico. He has received several journalism awards, including the Bartolomé Mitre Award for coverage of drug trafficking, from the Inter-American Press Association. He holds an A.B. in university studies from the University of New Mexico. His recent reports include "Prisoner Reenty" and "Downsizing Prisons."

[53] Quoted in Scot Lehigh, "Weld opens 'super' secure prison unit," *Boston Globe*, Aug 6, 1991, p. 21; Mary Bosworth, *Explaining U.S. Imprisonment* (2010), p. 141.

[54] Mears, "Evaluating the Effectiveness of Supermax Prisons," *op. cit.*, pp. 69-70 (Tables 1, 2).

[55] Riveland, *op. cit.*, p. 1.

[56] *Ibid.*, p. 2.

[57] *Madrid v. Gomez*, Jan. 10, 1995, Findings of Fact, Conclusions of Law, and Order, http://ca.findacase.com/research/wfrmDocViewer.aspx/xq/fac.19950110_0000003.NCA.htm/qx.

[58] *Ibid.*; Bill Wallace, "Conditions at Pelican Bay Prison Ruled Unconstitutional, But Judge Says Isolation Unit Can Remain," *San Francisco Chronicle*, Jan. 12, 1995, p. A17; Susan Sward and Bill Wallace, "No More Solitary Confinement for Prison's Mentally Ill," *San Francisco Chronicle*, Dec. 20, 1995, p. A17, www.sfgate.com/news/article/No-More-Solitary-Confinement-for-Prison-s-3018055.php.

[59] *Madrid v. Gomez*, *op. cit.*

[60] Jules Lobel "Prolonged Solitary Confinement and the Constitution," *Journal of Constitutional Law*, December 2008, www.supermaxed.com/NewSupermaxMaterials/Prolonged-Solitary-Constitution-Lobel.pdf.

[61] "Solitary Confinement Called 'Inappropriate' for Mentally Ill Prisoners in Indiana," ACLU (press release), Jan. 30, 2007, www.aclu.org/prisoners-rights/solitary-confinement-called-inappropriate-mentally-ill-prisoners-indiana; Fathi, *op. cit.*, p. 679.

[62] *Wilkinson v. Austin*, 544 U.S. 74 (2005), June 13, 2005, www.law.cornell.edu/supct/html/04-495.ZS.html; Lobel, *op. cit.*, pp. 127-129.

[63] *Ibid.*, pp. 128-129.

[64] "Stop Solitary — Mental Health Resources," ACLU, regularly updated, www.aclu.org/prisoners-rights/stop-solitary-mental-health-resources.

[65] Quoted in John J. O'Connor, "Illinois judge bars Quinn from closing prisons," The Associated Press, Sept. 4, 2012, www.businessweek.com/ap/2012-09-05/illinois-judge-bars-quinn-from-closing-prisons.

[66] Quoted in John O'Connor, "Ill. Agrees to stop prison transfers temporarily," The Associated Press, Aug. 8, 2012, http://bigstory.ap.org/article/ill-agrees-stop-prison-transfers-temporarily; Sal Rodriguez, "Testimony From Hearing on Closure of Tamms Supermax Prison," *Solitary Watch*, April 21, 2012, http://solitarywatch.com/2012/04/21/testimony-from-hearing-on-closure-of-tamms-supermax-prison; Jim Suhr, "To Tamms, prison closure means pain, betrayal," The Associated Press (*SFGate*, July 15, 2012), www.sfgate.com/news/article/To-Tamms-prison-closure-means-pain-betrayal-3677158.php.

FOR MORE INFORMATION

ACLU National Prison Project, 915 15th St., N.W., 7th Floor, Washington, DC 20005; 212-549-2500; www.aclu.org/prisoners-rights. Litigates on behalf of prisoners in solitary confinement and is campaigning to end the practice.

American Correctional Association, 206 N. Washington St., Alexandria, VA 22314; 703-224-0000; www.aca.org. Provides material on solitary confinement.

Civil Rights Litigation Clearinghouse, University of Michigan Law School, 625 South State St., Ann Arbor, MI 48109; 734-647-2160; http://clearinghouse.net. National repository of litigation documents, many from major lawsuits over conditions in solitary confinement.

National Institute of Justice, 810 7th St., N.W., Washington, DC 02531; 202-307-0703; www.nij.gov/nij/topics/corrections/institutional/welcome.htm#. Justice Department's research arm; includes a library of studies on prison issues.

Segregation Reduction Project, Vera Institute of Justice, 1100 First St., N.E., Suite 950, Washington, DC 20002; 202-465-8900; www.vera.org/project/segregation-reduction-project. Advocacy effort that aims to lower the number of prisoners in long-term solitary confinement, conducted with state corrections departments.

Solitary Watch, PO Box 11374, Washington, DC 20008; http://solitarywatch.com. Anti-solitary confinement advocacy group co-led by a veteran muckraking journalist.

[67] John O'Connor, "AP Exclusive: Shakedowns of prison staff ordered," The Associated Press, July 30, 2012, http://bigstory.ap.org/article/ap-exclusive-guards-7-ill-prisons-searched-0.

[68] Emily Wilkerson, "Ultimate confinement doesn't change most violent inmate," *State Journal-Register* (Springfield, Ill), Oct. 23, 1995, p. 1, local section; "Death Row inmate receives life," *Chicago Tribune*, Jan. 12, 2003, www.chicagotribune.com/media/flash/2003-01/6205019.pdf; Don Babwin, "Illinois Death Row Shuts Down," The Associated Press (*The Huffington Post*), July 2, 2011, www.huffingtonpost.com/2011/07/01/illinois-death-row_n_888516.html; "Governor Ryan Declares Moratorium on Executions," press release, Illinois Government News Network, Jan. 31, 2000, www.illinois.gov/pressreleases/showpressrelease.cfm?subjectid=3&recnum=359.

[69] "Quinn Staying with Dwight, Tamms, Closures," Illinois Public Media, July 17, 2012, http://will.illinois.edu/news/spotstory/quinn-staying-with-dwight-tamms-closures/; "Efficiencies Fact Sheet — FY 2013 Budget," Illinois governor's office, June 30, 2012, http://capitolfax.com/63012EfficienciesFactSheet.pdf.

[70] Quoted in Bill Ruthhart, "Quinn's budget swap," *Chicago Tribune*, June 30, 2012, p. A1.

[71] Charles E. Samuels Jr., written testimony, *op. cit.*

[72] *Bacote v. Federal Bureau of Prisons*, *op. cit.*, p. 21.

[73] Andrew Cohen, "An American gulag — the Mentally Ill at Supermax," *The Atlantic*, June 20, 2012, www.theatlantic.com/personal/archive/2012/06/an-american-gulag-0151-the-mentally-ill-at-supermax/258818/.

[74] *Vega v. Davis*, U.S. District Court for the District of Colorado, Case 1:12-cv-01144-RPM, May 1, 2012, www.clearinghouse.net/chDocs/public/PC-CO-0020-0001.pdf; Andrew Cohen, "Death, Yes, But Torture at Supermax?," *The Atlantic*, June 4, 2012, www.theatlantic.com/national/archive/2012/06/death-yes-but-torture-at-supermax/258002/.

[75] *Vega v. Davis*, *op. cit.*, pp. 8-9.

[76] *Gamez, et al. v. Ryan, et al.*, United States District Court, District of Arizona, CV-20-2070-PHX-JWS, www.aclu.org/files/assets/gamez_v_ryan_final_complaint.pdf.

[77] "Amended Answer to Class Action Complaint," *Gamez v. Ryan*, June 4, 2012, p. 17.

[78] *Ruiz, et al., v. Brown, et al.*, *op. cit.*, pp. 2-3.

[79] *Ibid.*, p. 2.

[80] Rina Palta, "Civil rights group sues California over the state's Security Housing Unit at Pelican Bay State Prison," KPCC, May 31, 2012, www.scpr.org/blogs/news/2012/05/31/6410/civil-rights-group-sues-california-over-states-sec.

[81] *Ibid.*

Bibliography

Selected Sources

Books

Bosworth, Mary, *Explaining U.S. Imprisonment*, SAGE, 2010.
Writing from a critical perspective, an American criminologist at Britain's University of Oxford provides historical context for the rise of long-term solitary confinement.

Christianson, Scott, *With Liberty For Some: 500 Years of Imprisonment in America*, Northeastern University Press, 1998.
A journalist specializing in criminal justice provides a narrative history of U.S. prison systems.

Articles

Cohen, Andrew, "An American Gulag — the Mentally Ill at Supermax," *The Atlantic*, June 20, 2012, www.theatlantic.com/personal/archive/2012/06/an-american-gulag-0151-the-mentally-ill-at-supermax/258818/.
A journalist specializing in legal affairs writes a detailed and impassioned condemnation of conditions at the federal supermax in Florence, Colo. The article is part of a continuing series.

Gawande, Atul, "Hellhole," *The New Yorker*, March 30, 2009, www.newyorker.com/reporting/2009/03/30/090330fa_fact_gawande.
An influential article by a prominent physician-writer argues that long-term solitary confinement amounts to torture.

Goldberg, Jamie, "Prison solitary called inhumane," *Florida Sun-Sentinel* (Fort Lauderdale), June 22, 2012, p. A9.
A brief report — and one of very few — on a Senate subcommittee's hearing on long-term solitary confinement.

Goode, Erica, "Prisons Rethink Isolation, Saving Money, Lives and Sanity," *The New York Times*, March 10, 2012, www.nytimes.com/2012/03/11/us/rethinking-solitary-confinement.html?pagewanted=all.
A national correspondent chronicles the supermax-reduction trend, focusing largely on Mississippi.

Goode, Erica, "Fighting a Drawn-Out Battle Against Solitary Confinement," *The New York Times*, March 30, 2012, www.nytimes.com/2012/03/31/us/battles-to-change-prison-policy-of-solitary-confinement.html?pagewanted=all.
In a follow-up article, *The Times* reports on California's controversial policy of segregating and locking down suspected gang members.

Smyth, Julie Carr, "Supermax lockups adjust to decreasing demand," The Associated Press, April 5, 2008.
Toward the end of the previous decade, financial and legal pressures were forcing the closing of supermax prisons, a state government correspondent reported.

Reports and Studies

Fathi, David C., "The Common Law of Supermax Litigation," *Pace Law Review*, Spring, 2004, http://digitalcommons.pace.edu/plr/vol24/iss2/13.
The director of the ACLU National Prison Project summarizes the effects of major court decisions on solitary confinement.

Grassian, Stuart, "Psychiatric Effects of Solitary Confinement," *Journal of Law & Policy*, 2006, http://law.wustl.edu/journal/22/p325grassian.pdf.
A leading researcher and critic of long-term solitary confinement examines the effects of isolation.

Mears, Daniel P., "Evaluating the Effectiveness of Supermax Prisons," Urban Institute, March 2006, www.urban.org/UploadedPDF/411326_supermax_prisons.pdf.
In one of the most comprehensive and dispassionate examinations of long-term solitary confinement, a Florida State University scholar concludes that justifications for supermaxes are not clear-cut.

Méndez, Juan E., "Torture and other cruel, inhuman or degrading treatment of punishment," United Nations General Assembly, Aug. 5, 2011, p. 17, http://solitaryconfinement.org/uploads/SpecRapTortureAug2011.pdf.
A "special rapporteur" for the U.N. Human Rights Council concludes that solitary confinement can amount to torture.

Metzner, Jeffrey L., and Jamie Fellner, "Solitary Confinement and Mental Illness in U.S. Prisons: A Challenge for Medical Ethics," *Journal of the American Academy of Psychiatry and the Law*, March 1, 2010, www.hrw.org/sites/default/files/related_material/Solitary%20Confinement%20and%20Mental%20Illness%20in%20US%20Prisons.pdf.
A wealth of evidence shows prolonged solitary confinement deeply damages mentally ill prisoners.

O'Keefe, Maureen L., "One Year Longitudinal Study of the Psychological Effects of Administrative Segregation," Colorado Department of Corrections, University of Colorado, Colorado Springs, Oct. 31, 2010, www.ncjrs.gov/pdffiles1/nij/grants/232973.pdf.
The Colorado prison system's research director found no evidence of systemic psychological damage to prisoners, including the mentally ill, in solitary confinement.

Riveland, Chase, "Supermax Prisons: Overview and General Considerations," National Institute of Corrections, January 1999, http://static.nicic.gov/Library/014937.pdf.
The report by a prison management consultant — a former corrections director in two states — provides perspective on why supermax prisons have proved so popular and on the challenges they present for penology.

The Next Step:

Additional Articles from Current Periodicals

Colorado

Maes, Denise, "Solitary Confinement Reform Is Welcome Sign of Progress," *The Gazette* (Colo.), Jan. 28, 2012, www.gazette.com/articles/solitary-132524-prison-confinement.html.
Colorado's decision to move 300 inmates out of solitary confinement is safer, less costly and more humane, says the public policy director of the state's ACLU office.

Mitchell, Kirk, "Inmate Isolation Reviewed," *Denver Post*, Nov. 27, 2011, p. B10, www.denverpost.com/news/ci_19419191.
More mentally ill prisoners are in solitary confinement in Colorado than in any other state.

Mental Illness

Hult, John, "Release From Isolation to Public Called Risky," *Argus Leader* (S.D.), July 11, 2011, www.argusleader.com/article/20111118/NEWS/111180003/Release-from-isolation-public-called-risky.
A transitional period between the isolation and release of prisoners is essential for public safety, says a psychiatrist.

Matthews, Cara, "Mental Health Treatment at Prisons Faces Scrutiny," *Ithaca* (N.Y.) *Journal*, Dec. 7, 2011.
New York state law requires inmates with serious mental illnesses to be removed from solitary confinement.

Ortega, Bob, "Arizona Accused of Abuses in Prisons," *Arizona Republic*, April 3, 2012, p. A1, www.azcentral.com/news/articles/2012/04/02/20120402arizona-accused-abuses-prisons.html.
Serious mental illnesses among Arizona prisoners in solitary confinement are often undiagnosed, says an Amnesty International report.

Results

Ortega, Bob, "Deaths in 'Solitary' Point to Problems," *Arizona Republic*, June 3, 2012, p. A6, www.azcentral.com/news/articles/2012/06/02/20120602arizona-prison-suicide-rate.html.
Nineteen Arizona inmates — many of whom were in solitary confinement — committed suicide in the past two years.

Weiser, Benjamin, "Pondering Solitary Future for Gangster Held in Isolation for Years," *The New York Times*, July 9, 2012, p. A13, www.nytimes.com/2012/07/09/nyregion/concerns-keep-the-gang-leader-peter-rollock-isolated-in-supermax-prison.html?pagewanted=all.
The leader of a narcotics gang has remained well-behaved since being placed in solitary confinement in 2000.

Torture

Gorman, Anna, "Activists Call Solitary Confinement Torture," *Los Angeles Times*, March 21, 2012, p. B4, articles.latimes.com/2012/mar/21/local/la-me-0321-solitary-20120321.
California treats several thousand prisoners the same way the United States treats suspected terrorists detained in Guantánamo, says an attorney representing hundreds of California inmates.

Kochakian, Charles, "Solitary Confinement May Be Crueler Than Death Penalty?" *New Haven* (Conn.) *Register*, April 8, 2012, p. B3.
Solitary confinement can be as distressing as physical torture, says the American Academy of Psychiatry and the Law.

Kumar, Anita, "Va. Plans to Modify Prisoner Isolation," *The Washington Post*, March 31, 2012, p. A1, www.washingtonpost.com/local/dc-politics/virginia-plans-changes-in-prisoner-isolation-process/2012/03/30/gIQAMzpFmS_story.html.
Virginia is reconsidering how it administers solitary confinement at the state's only supermax prison amid criticism that the practice equates to torture.

Yates, Riley, "Execution Delays Have Created a Different Form of Punishment," *Morning Call* (Pa.), Aug. 5, 2012, p. A18, articles.mcall.com/2012-08-04/news/mc-pennsylvania-death-row-cruel-unusual-20120804_1_death-row-inmates-critics-of-capital-punishment-death-row.
Several Pennsylvania death row inmates have spent decades in solitary confinement.

Citing *CQ Researcher*

Sample formats for citing these reports in a bibliography include the ones listed below. Preferred styles and formats vary, so please check with your instructor or professor.

MLA STYLE

Jost, Kenneth. "Remembering 9/11," CQ Researcher 2 Sept. 2011: 701-732.

APA STYLE

Jost, K. (2011, September 2). Remembering 9/11. *CQ Researcher, 9*, 701-732.

CHICAGO STYLE

Jost, Kenneth. "Remembering 9/11." *CQ Researcher*, September 2, 2011, 701-732.

CQ Researcher

Published by CQ Press, an Imprint of SAGE Publications, Inc.

www.cqresearcher.com

Assessing the New Health Care Law

Will it improve care and reduce spending?

In June, the Supreme Court upheld most of the Obama administration's 2010 health care law, allowing the government to fine people who decline to buy medical insurance. But the court barred cutting off Medicaid funds for states that refuse to participate in a new program expanding health care for the poor. Some Republican governors have balked at the expanded coverage, undermining the administration's goal of adding 30 million people to the health insurance rolls. Meanwhile, GOP presidential nominee Mitt Romney, along with many congressional Republicans, vows to repeal the entire Affordable Care Act, arguing it is too costly and abridges individual freedoms. The law's supporters, however, say its benefits already are evident, as children with pre-existing illnesses can no longer lose coverage and young adults can enroll in their parents' health plans.

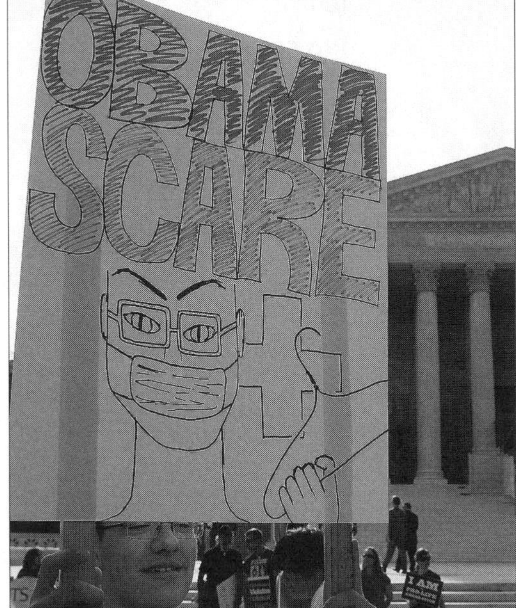

An opponent of President Obama's health care plan — derisively known as Obamacare — protests at the Supreme Court on June 28, 2012, the day the court largely upheld the controversial law aimed at reducing health care expenses and expanding coverage to some 30 million Americans without insurance.

INSIDE THIS REPORT

THE ISSUES 791
BACKGROUND 798
CHRONOLOGY 799
CURRENT SITUATION 803
AT ISSUE........................805
OUTLOOK 806
BIBLIOGRAPHY 810
THE NEXT STEP 811

CQ Researcher • Sept. 21, 2012 • www.cqresearcher.com
Volume 22, Number 33 • Pages 789-812

Los Angeles | London | New Delhi
Singapore | Washington DC

RECIPIENT OF SOCIETY OF PROFESSIONAL JOURNALISTS AWARD FOR EXCELLENCE ◆ AMERICAN BAR ASSOCIATION SILVER GAVEL AWARD

Assessing the New Health Care Law

The Issues

791 • Should the health care law be repealed?
• Will Americans be better off because of the law?
• Will the law cost too much?

Background

798 **The Mandate**
The new law's "individual mandate" requires most Americans to obtain insurance or pay a penalty.

800 **The Poor**
The law can't penalize states that don't expand Medicaid.

801 **The Court**
The individual mandate was narrowly upheld, but the justices compromised on Medicaid expansion.

Current Situation

803 **Uncertain Future**
Most of the new law's provisions are a year or more from implementation.

804 **Court Fallout**
Numerous state officials say they won't expand Medicaid, but many analysts predict they will eventually.

806 **Only a Beginning**
The states and the federal government are not meeting the law's implementation schedule.

Outlook

806 **Voting on Health**
Voters worry more about jobs than the new law.

Sidebars and Graphics

792 **Biggest States Have High Rates of Uninsured**
California, Texas and Florida have some of the largest percentages of uninsured residents.

793 **Medical Expenses Worry Younger Adults**
One in three under age 65 has delayed health care because of financial concerns.

794 **Views on the Affordable Care Act**
Slightly more have an unfavorable opinion than favorable.

796 **Coverage of Young Adults Rises**
Those under 26 can now obtain health coverage through parents' policies.

799 **Chronology**
Key events since 2006.

800 **Caring for the Poorest and Sickest**
Expanding Medicaid challenges would-be reformers.

802 **Trying to Trim the Waste From Health Care**
Conservatives and liberals both take a "big picture" approach.

805 **At Issue**
Should the Affordable Care Act be repealed?

For Further Research

809 **For More Information**
Organizations to contact.

810 **Bibliography**
Selected sources used.

811 **The Next Step**
Additional articles.

811 **Citing *CQ Researcher***
Sample bibliography formats.

Cover: Getty Images/Mark Wilson

CQ Researcher

Sept. 21, 2012
Volume 22, Number 33

Managing Editor: Thomas J. Billitteri
tjb@cqpress.com

Assistant Managing Editor: Kathy Koch
kkoch@cqpress.com

Senior Contributing Editor:
Thomas J. Colin
tcolin@cqpress.com

Associate Editor: Kenneth Jost

Staff Writer: Marcia Clemmitt

Contributing Writers: Peter Katel, Barbara Mantel, Jennifer Weeks

Senior Project Editor: Olu B. Davis

Assistant Editor: Darrell Dela Rosa

Fact Checker: Michelle Harris

Los Angeles | London | New Delhi
Singapore | Washington DC

An Imprint of SAGE Publications, Inc.

Vice President and Editorial Director, Higher Education Group:
Michele Sordi

Director, Online Publishing:
Todd Baldwin

CQ Researcher (ISSN 1056-2036) is printed on acid-free paper. Published weekly, except: (March wk. 5) (May wk. 4) (July wk. 1) (Aug. wks. 3, 4) (Nov. wk. 4) and (Dec. wks. 3, 4). Published by SAGE Publications, Inc., 2455 Teller Rd., Thousand Oaks, CA 91320. Annual full-service subscriptions start at $1,054. For pricing, call 1-800-834-9020. To purchase a *CQ Researcher* report in print or electronic format (PDF), visit www.cqpress.com or call 866-427-7737. Single reports start at $15. Bulk purchase discounts and electronic-rights licensing are also available. Periodicals postage paid at Thousand Oaks, California, and at additional mailing offices. POSTMASTER: Send address changes to *CQ Researcher*, 2300 N St., N.W., Suite 800, Washington, DC 20037.

Assessing the New Health Care Law

By Marcia Clemmitt

The Issues

Caleb Medley, a 23-year-old aspiring stand-up comic, was at a midnight showing of "The Dark Knight Rises" in Aurora, Colo., on July 20, when a gunman entered the theater and shot 70 people, killing 12. Shot in the eye, Medley remained in a medically induced coma for more than a month. He has endured multiple brain surgeries, but is slowly improving, according to his family. [1] On Sept. 12, Medley was transferred from the hospital to a long-term-care facility. [2] Meanwhile, his wife, Katie, gave birth to the couple's first child a few days after the shootings.

Getty Images/Dennis Brack

Cancer patient Gail O'Brien greets President Obama during a backyard discussion of his administration's proposed health care reform law in Falls Church, Va., on Sept. 22, 2010. The Supreme Court on June 28, 2012, upheld the law's requirement that uninsured people buy medical insurance or pay a penalty. Conservative justices objected to forcing healthy young people to buy insurance they may not need.

The Medleys have no health insurance. To help with what doctors said could amount to $2 million in medical bills, Michael West, a longtime family friend, is soliciting donations through a website he set up. "Caleb . . . needs to get better because he needs to be a dad," said West. [3]

Stories of uninsured people who unexpectedly incur high medical bills have figured heavily in debates over the Obama administration's controversial health care law, the 2010 Patient Protection and Affordable Care Act (ACA). Ideological arguments over the legislation came into sharp focus June 28, when the U.S. Supreme Court upheld most of the ACA, whose main provisions take effect in 2014, but said states could opt out of a key provision aimed at expanding Medicaid coverage for the poor. [4]

The court rendered its decision in two parts:

- In a 5-4 ruling dominated by court liberals, with Chief Justice John G. Roberts unexpectedly providing the swing vote, the justices upheld the ACA's requirement that uninsured people buy medical insurance or pay a penalty — a stipulation in the law known as an "individual mandate." Conservative justices objected that it is unfair to force healthy young people to buy insurance they may not need.
- In a 7-2 vote dominated by court conservatives, plus two liberal justices, the court greatly narrowed the ACA's requirement that states either accept new federal grants to pay for expanded Medicaid coverage or risk losing all the money they receive from Washington for their Medicaid programs. The court said states can refuse the expansion grants without giving up their existing Medicaid funding. [5]

The Supreme Court's philosophical and legal differences over the health care law reflected a broad national divide over the measure since its enactment in March 2010.

In their dissenting opinion, the court's four conservative justices, who voted to strike down the entire law, asserted that Congress exceeded its constitutional authority by requiring every American to purchase health insurance or pay a penalty. Moreover, they wrote that healthy young people "may decide that purchasing health insurance is not an economically sound decision" — especially, they said, because the ACA allows them to purchase it in later years at the same cost, even if they have developed a pre-existing medical condition by then. [6]

But Justice Ruth Bader Ginsburg, a liberal who voted to uphold the ACA in its entirety, argued that getting everyone — even healthy young people — to buy insurance is the only way to ensure that there is enough money to pay for every American's care. "A victim of an accident or unforeseen illness will consume extensive medical care immediately, though scarcely expecting to do so," Ginsburg wrote. If that person hasn't bought coverage, others have to pick up the tab, she argued. [7]

Ultimately, the ACA's impact on health care costs and insurance coverage remains unclear. With implementation of the law's major provisions more than a year away, much of the debate is still driven by theories rather than data. But the ACA's

Biggest States Have High Rates of Uninsured

The Affordable Care Act and any other attempt to overhaul the health care system to increase insurance coverage will face daunting challenges. Not least is the fact that three of the nation's four most populous states — California, Texas and Florida — have among the highest rates of uninsured residents. Texas leads the pack with one in four residents uninsured.

Percentage of Population Without Health Insurance
(2009-2010)

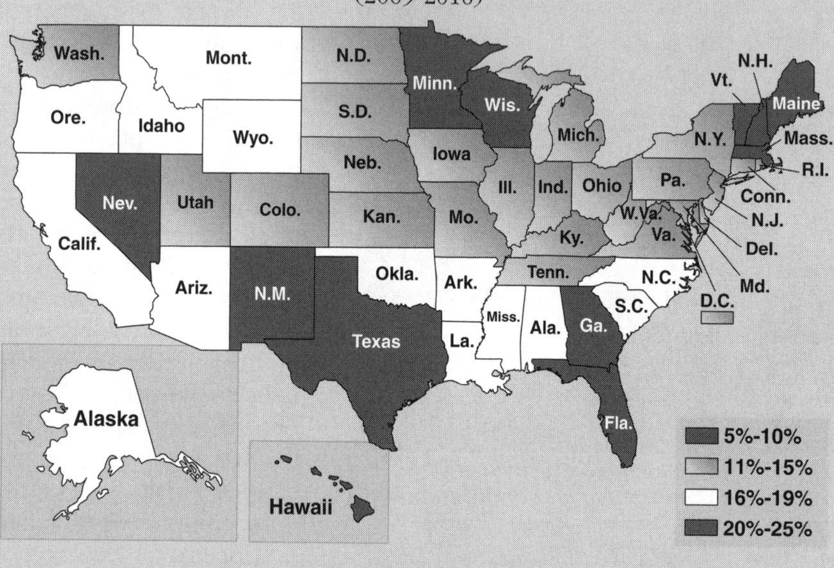

Source: "Health Insurance Coverage of the Total Population, States (2009-2010), U.S. (2010)," Henry J. Kaiser Family Foundation, 2012, www.statehealthfacts.org/comparetable.jsp?ind=125&cat=3&sub=39&yr=252&typ=2&rgnhl=1

supporters and detractors have long given voice to the issues raised by the Supreme Court.

President Obama said the court's affirmation of the law is a boon for average Americans. "Insurance companies no longer have unchecked power to cancel your policy, deny you coverage or charge women more than men," he said. Furthermore, "soon, no American will ever again be denied care or charged more due to a pre-existing condition, like cancer or even asthma." [8]

But GOP presidential nominee Mitt Romney, who derides the new law as "Obamacare," has vowed to repeal it if he is elected president in November. He has said he would replace it with another plan that relies more on the private sector to deal with many of the same problems the ACA addresses. [9] "Obamacare puts the federal government between you and your doctor," potentially limiting a physician's options for treating patients, Romney has said. [10] As governor of Massachusetts in 2006, Romney worked with Democrats to enact a plan similar to the ACA, but he has since said health care should be left to the states. [11]

Supporters say the ACA is structured in a way that will make the American health care system more effective and efficient and eventually save hundreds of millions of dollars annually in unnecessary or misdirected care. To keep insurance premiums for older, sicker people from becoming unaffordable, the ACA will subsidize them by raising premiums somewhat for young, healthy people.

And in an attempt to ensure that health coverage is worth its costs, the law also will require that all insurance plans cover a basic but comprehensive slate of benefits, essentially eliminating some bare-bones, low-cost plans available today. Beginning in 2014, four tiers of coverage will be available to individual purchasers, ranging from low-cost plans providing only basic benefits to comprehensive coverage, but at higher premiums. [12]

The ACA represents "tremendous progress towards reshaping our health system into one that saves the lives of at least 44,000 people who die annually simply because they do not have health insurance that could keep them healthy," said Georges Benjamin, executive director of the American Public Health Association. [13]

But many ACA opponents argue that it forces people to buy insurance they don't want and may not need. "Never before has the federal government coerced its citizens to purchase a personal commodity for private use," said Brooks Wicker, a Kentucky Republican running for a U.S. House seat. "I'll work to repeal the mandate through legislation and to return [to] the American people the full measure of freedom taken from them." [14]

Meanwhile, some young adults complain that they are being required to buy a minimum level of coverage and, in their view, overpay for it to help hold down premiums for older, sicker people.

The law is biased against young people, who will be forced "to shoulder the burden of the entire health system," complained Ryan Fazio, a columnist for Northwestern University's *Daily Northwestern*, in Evanston, Ill. [15] Richard Cooper, a 26-year-old lawyer in Miami, said requiring all health plans to include basic coverage for such services as mental health treatment and maternity care is "one of the things I'm sort of leery about. I'm going to be paying for things I don't need." [16]

But both young and old will get far more comprehensive coverage from even the cheapest plans than many people find in the insurance they can buy today, said Paul Ginsburg, president of the Center for Studying Health System Change, a nonpartisan research group in Washington. "That's worth something." [17]

While much of the controversy over the ACA has centered on the individual mandate, the law's Medicaid provision has been equally contentious.

Medicaid is a program financed jointly by the states and the federal government that covers health care, including nursing home care, for some groups of poor people — children, their custodial parents, pregnant women and the blind, disabled and elderly. The ACA expansion provision was designed to broaden coverage to include some 17 million poor, able-bodied, childless adults.

States leery about expanding their Medicaid rolls worry that doing so will bust their budgets, despite the fact that under the law most costs will be covered by federal grants. [18]

But Stan Dorn, a senior fellow at the Urban Institute, a nonpartisan think tank in Washington that studies poverty and health care, says the ACA's Medicaid provision would help states save money and improve health care efficiency. Today states reimburse hospitals for care they provide to uninsured people and for mental-health care provided to low-income adults. The federally funded Medicaid expansion would pay for that care up front, at least as efficiently as today's fragmented programs do, he says.

"It's mind-boggling to see the opposition," given the way the law is structured, says Dorn. "There are lots of ways that states can actually save money on the expansion."

Medical Expenses Worry Younger Adults

The inability to pay medical bills or afford necessary health care services is of greatest concern to adults under age 65, when Medicare eligibility begins. About one in three adults 18-64 has delayed a medical procedure or doctor's visit because of financial concerns.

Health Care Problems and Worries by Age, 2012

Problem or worry	Age 18-29	Age 30-49	Age 50-64	Age 65+
Problems with paying medical bills in past 12 months	29%	30%	26%	17%
Put off or postponed necessary health care	30%	34%	32%	15%
Worried about not being able to afford health care services you think you need	25%	30%	26%	15%

Source: "Health Security Watch," Henry J. Kaiser Family Foundation, June 2012, p. 7, www.kff.org/healthpollreport/CurrentEdition/security/upload/8322.pdf

As lawmakers, health care providers and the public ponder the ACA's impact, here are some of the questions being asked:

Should the health care law be repealed?

The ACA's opponents in Washington argue that nothing short of repeal will stop the law from damaging free-market economics and the American health care system. Central to their criticism is the law's individual-mandate provision requiring every American to buy health insurance or pay a financial penalty. [19]

But the law's supporters argue that it is that very mandate that holds the key to the law's success. By requiring universal coverage, they contend, the law prevents insured people from having to shoulder the cost of treating the uninsured, often through costly emergency room visits.

Senate Minority Leader Mitch McConnell, R-Ken., has said that if Republicans gain control of the Senate in November, he will schedule a vote to erase the ACA from the books. Ultimately, that may not work, he acknowledges, unless Republicans also win the White House and control of the House. Still, McConnell says most Americans agree with him that the law should go. "I'm confident they're going to give us the votes to repeal it," he said. [20]

Michael D. Tanner, director of health and welfare studies at the Cato Institute, a think tank in Washington that promotes a philosophy of individual liberty and limited government, said the "individual mandate crosses an important line" because it enshrines in law the principle "that it is the government's responsibility to ensure that every American has health insurance. It opens the door to widespread regulation of the health care industry and political interference in personal health care decisions. The result will be a slow but steady spiral downward toward a government-run national health care system." [21]

Others argue that the ACA usurps responsibilities that rightly belong to the states.

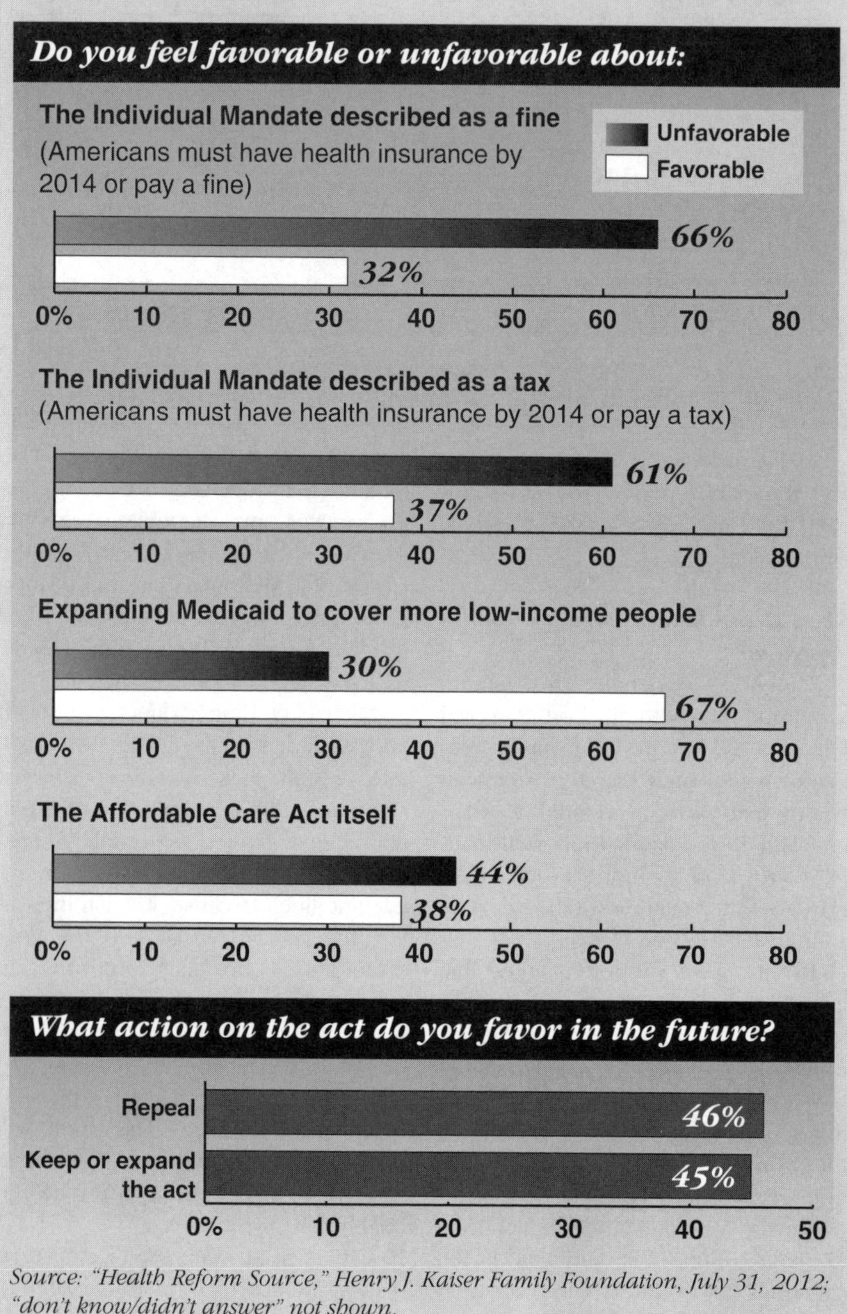

Views on the Affordable Care Act
Roughly the same percentages of people oppose the individual mandate requiring Americans to obtain health coverage or pay a penalty whether it is described as a fine or a tax. The act's plan to expand Medicaid is favored by two-thirds of Americans and opposed by fewer than a third. Overall, slightly more Americans have unfavorable views of the act than favorable, and almost the same percentages favor repeal or keeping the law.
Do you feel favorable or unfavorable about:
The Individual Mandate described as a fine
(Americans must have health insurance by 2014 or pay a fine)
Unfavorable
Favorable
66%
32%
0% 10 20 30 40 50 60 70 80
The Individual Mandate described as a tax
(Americans must have health insurance by 2014 or pay a tax)
61%
37%
0% 10 20 30 40 50 60 70 80
Expanding Medicaid to cover more low-income people
30%
67%
0% 10 20 30 40 50 60 70 80
The Affordable Care Act itself
44%
38%
0% 10 20 30 40 50 60 70 80
What action on the act do you favor in the future?
Repeal
46%
Keep or expand the act
45%
0% 10 20 30 40 50

Source: "Health Reform Source," Henry J. Kaiser Family Foundation, July 31, 2012; "don't know/didn't answer" not shown.

"States shouldn't be forced by the federal government to adopt a one-size-fits-all health care plan," said Sen. Scott Brown, R-Mass., whose home state, under Romney, adopted a health care system similar to the ACA in 2006. "Each state's health care needs are different." [22]

Thomas Miller, a resident fellow at the American Enterprise Institute (AEI), a conservative think tank in Washington that opposes the health care law, instead wants legislation that facilitates development of a nationwide market offering a wide variety of private medical plans for purchase.

Miller says the ACA will undermine the development of free-market dynamics in the health insurance field and force states to accede to federal dictates. At first, he says, states may be able to shape their own insurance exchanges through which people purchase health coverage. But that is simply because Washington made certain "concessions" to the states to induce them to back the law, he says. Once the new health regime is deeply rooted, he predicts, "the long-term dynamics will very much have Washington in control rather than having open markets."

But ACA supporters say the individual mandate — and the fact that the law is national, not limited to some states — ensure that health care will be available to as many people as possible. Furthermore, they say, states will have flexibility to shape their own insurance markets under the law.

Most states aren't willing or able to resolve the problem of the uninsured on their own because states rightly fear bankrupting themselves if they offer universal coverage and other states don't, Justice Ginsburg wrote. She quoted an earlier court ruling that described a universal state coverage program as a potential "bait to the needy and dependent elsewhere, encouraging them to migrate and seek a haven of repose." States that took the lead in offering universal coverage would be "placing themselves in a position of economic disadvantage as compared with neighbors or competitors," she wrote. [23]

The ACA does not create the one-size-fits-all nightmare for states that critics fear, says the Urban Institute's Dorn. The Obama administration's implementation rules for the law permit "a huge amount" of flexibility in the kind of insurance exchanges — markets — states may set up, thus accommodating "hugely different visions," both liberal and conservative, of how the health care market should operate.

"You can have a tightly managed exchange and allow only three health plans to come in and sell only a particular set of benefits" or "simply say that any company can come in" and give consumers a wide choice of health plans, Dorn says.

The ACA's supporters also say that the new law will relieve some of the pressure on workers' compensation and other parts of the health care system that have been strained in recent decades by the lack of universal insurance coverage.

Workers' compensation insurance — mostly state-based programs that pay for injuries workers suffer on the job — will function better under the law, according to Joseph Paduda, a Connecticut-based consultant on managed care and workers' compensation insurance. Because so many people lack regular health insurance, workers' comp often ends up paying for care that has nothing to do with on-the-job injuries, he wrote.

Getty Images/David Greedy

Republican presidential nominee Mitt Romney has vowed to repeal the new health care law if he is elected president in November. He has said he would replace it with a plan that relies more on the private sector to deal with many of the same problems the law addresses. "Obamacare puts the federal government between you and your doctor," potentially limiting a physician's options for treating patients, Romney contends.

In states such as Texas and Florida with high percentages of residents without insurance (*see map, p. 792*), a person who tears a rotator cuff on the job, for example, may also need treatment for unrelated maladies, such as diabetes or high blood pressure, before having rotator cuff surgery. The ACA's widespread insurance coverage will cut costs and red tape for the workers' comp system, he said. [24]

Will Americans be better off because of the health care law?

With the ACA still in early stages of implementation, researchers have been unable to collect much data that either prove or refute claims of the law's success. Supporters point to millions of additional Americans who will gain insurance coverage. Opponents argue that new taxes and regulations will cripple innovation by medical firms such as health insurers and pharmaceutical companies.

Regardless of the ACA's merits, the changes it brings will cause some problems in the early going, even the law's supporters acknowledge. For example, expanded coverage and the emphasis on preventive care mean "there will (very) likely be an access problem over the near term as primary care providers are inundated with new patients, and over the medium term for specialists as folks who've long avoided care because they could not afford it now get those problems resolved — knee replacements, etc.," wrote insurance consultant Paduda. [25]

Meanwhile, supporters tout an ACA provision requiring insurers to spend a minimum percentage of premium payments on patient care or refund the money to employers and consumers. But many conservatives say this so-called Medical Loss Ratio rule will run insurance companies out of business. Sen. Charles Grassley, R-Iowa, said one insurer, the American Enterprise Group, left the business in Iowa and Nebraska last year, dropping thousands from its rolls and laying off 110 employees, and the "culprit is the new Medical Loss Ratio regulation." [26]

That's because selling health insurance to individuals and very small businesses is an economically tricky enterprise that works much differently than selling insurance to large-employer groups, Grassley said. The medical needs of an individual or employees at a small business are much harder for insurers to estimate than those of workers at a large employer, where the group's health status tends to mirror that of the general population. As a result, individual and small-group insurers must set each year's premiums high enough to ensure coverage of hard-to-predict costs, said Grassley. The Medical Loss Ratio rule, which

Coverage of Young Adults Rises

A provision of the Affordable Care Act that took effect in 2010 allows adult children under age 26 to obtain health care coverage through their parents' policies. Experts credit the provision with increasing the share of young adults covered by medical insurance in 2011.

Percentage of Adults Ages 19 Through 25 With Private Insurance Coverage, 2010-2011

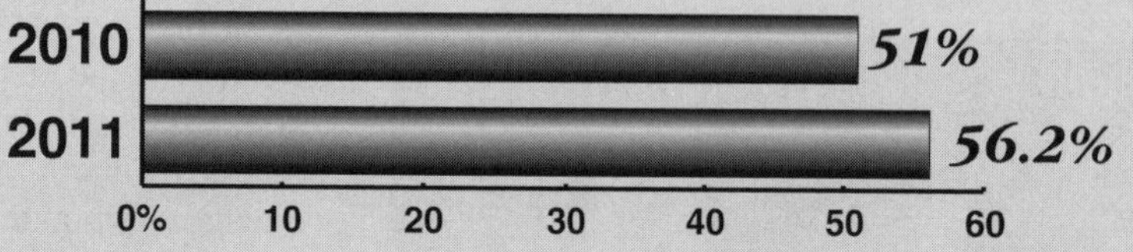

Source: Matt Broaddus, "The Census Bureau's Upcoming Report on Health Insurance Coverage in 2011: What to Watch For," Center on Budget and Policy Priorities, September 2012, www.cbpp.org/cms/index.cfm?fa=view&id=3830

penalizes insurers in any year the government deems their premiums are too high compared to spending on patient care, simply makes the risks of the insurance business "too great," he said. [27]

Opponents of the ACA point to what they see as other ill effects of the law. To help pay for expanded coverage, the ACA imposes new taxes that threaten research-and-development budgets and medical innovation, said Sally Pipes, president of the San Francisco-based Pacific Research Institute, a think tank that promotes a limited-government philosophy. "Excise taxes on drug-company sales are already in effect," Pipes wrote. "In 2013, there will be a new 2.3 percent excise tax on medical-device companies." As a result, she said, some firms have announced work-force cuts. "These industries are job creators and will no longer be unless the Affordable Care Act is repealed and replaced." [28]

John Goodman, a conservative analyst who heads the National Center for Policy Analysis, in Dallas, has found particular fault with efforts to expand Medicaid, the ACA's main means of insuring the poor. Medicaid, he argued, provides such low-quality care that "the Supreme Court has done a lot of families a big favor" by ruling that states can't be penalized for failing to expand coverage. As an example of what he sees as Medicaid's failings, he said 16 states cap the number of prescriptions Medicaid patients can get, with Mississippi limiting patients to two brand-name drugs and Arkansas limiting adult enrollees to six medications a month. [29]

Supporters of the law are just as vocal as opponents in their views about the ACA's impact on consumers.

Ron Pollack, founding executive director of the national consumer-advocacy group Families USA, says many people will be better off under the law and that some already are. "Right now, a significant but still clear minority of the benefits are already in effect," he says, and "we're hearing from people who've already gotten significant help."

Among those who have benefited are enrollees in Medicare, which provides health insurance for people age 65 and older, Pollack says. Under the ACA, they now receive additional government help with prescription-drug expenses, he says. Young adults also have benefited, Pollack notes. They now can remain on their parents' insurance plans until age 26.

And Pollack cites a host of other benefits: When insurers spend too little premium revenue on health care, they must provide rebates; children with pre-existing illnesses must be offered health coverage; preventive services such as diabetes and cervical-cancer screening are available without deductibles or copayments; and small businesses receive tax credits for providing worker coverage.

A study published in July in the *New England Journal of Medicine* concludes that previous Medicaid expansions similar to what the ACA calls for have resulted in decreased death rates. Researchers from the Harvard School of Public Health examined mortality data from three states — New York, Maine and Arizona — that added low-income, nondisabled adults with no children to their Medicaid programs in the past decade and found that the death rate for people age 20 to 64 decreased in the five years following the expansion. [30]

While the study included all deaths in the states, not just those among low-income people, the mortality rate dropped most for nonwhites and people living in poor counties, suggesting a Medicaid connection. Meanwhile, death rates rose in four neighboring states that didn't expand Medicaid. The coverage expansions are associated with a 6.1 percent decrease in death rates, or about 2,840 fewer deaths per year for each additional 500,000 adults insured. [31]

Some analysts say the ACA will provide economic as well as health benefits. "If basic insurance is made universally available on the individual market," the country could see a substantial drop in so-called job-lock — "people staying in jobs that might not be the best for them" simply because those jobs are the only potential source of health insurance, said

Jonathan Kolstad, a professor of health care management at the University of Pennsylvania's Wharton School. Job-lock not only keeps workers from advancing in their careers but also hurts the economy by inhibiting innovation and productivity, he said. [32]

Will the health care law cost too much?

ACA opponents say both the government and individuals will pay too much for health care under the new law. Supporters say expanded insurance coverage is worth its costs and that provisions aimed at creating a more efficient, prevention-focused system will eventually help to tame soaring medical expenses.

The ACA "virtually ignored the health care cost crisis facing this country and instead imposes billions of dollars in new mandates" — such as requiring insurers to devote a minimum amount of premium dollars to patient care — "and taxes that will increase the costs of coverage," said Robert Zirkelbach, a vice president of America's Health Insurance Plans, the main association representing health insurers in Washington. [33]

"Even accepting the law's assumptions about how the health care system should be reformed, actually putting all the pieces in place is exceptionally expensive," said Joseph Antos, who studies health and retirement policy at the free-market-oriented American Enterprise Institute in Washington. Furthermore, "the Supreme Court decision on Medicaid will . . . drive up federal spending" even more because in states that decline to participate "the alternative is expanded enrollment in subsidized [private] insurance through the [state insurance] exchanges," and private insurance costs more than Medicaid, Antos said. [34]

Meanwhile, liberal ACA critics argue that by relying on private insurance companies, rather than making the government the single payer for all insured people, the law forgoes most cost savings it might have achieved. Insurance companies "only add cost and complexity" to the system without improving care, said Bill Mahan, a political activist and retiree in Lexington, Ky., who advocates a switch to a single-payer system. [35]

But ACA supporters point to analysis by the Congressional Budget Office, Congress' nonpartisan budget-analysis agency, which has repeatedly found that the law will actually lower government health care spending and pare federal deficits because cost-saving provisions will offset the price of expanded coverage. In 2011, the CBO estimated that the law's coverage expansion would cost the federal government $1.1 trillion between 2012 and 2021, but that the law as a whole would end up saving the government money. That's because the cost of the coverage expansion will be offset by ACA provisions aimed at trimming unnecessary and wasteful health-care spending. As a result, the ACA will lower federal deficits by about $210 billion in that period, CBO said. [36]

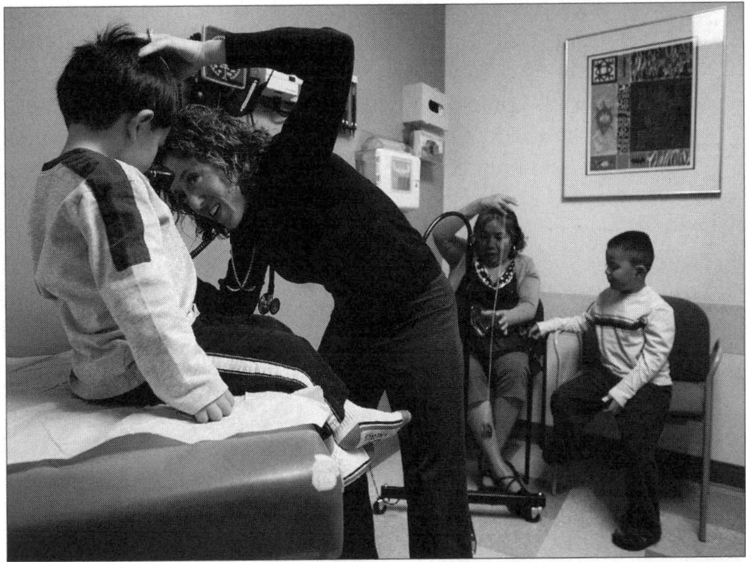

Getty Images/John Moore

A youngster receives a check-up at a community health center in Lakewood, Colo., for low-income people. Passage of the new health care law will mean additional federal subsidies for such clinics as well as health care insurance coverage for as many as 30 million people.

The fact that the law saves taxpayers some cash means that a Republican repeal of the ACA "would cause a net increase in federal budget deficits of $109 billion over the 2013-2022 period" — that is, repealing the law would cost money, not save it, as repeal supporters had hoped, the CBO wrote to House Speaker John Boehner, R-Ohio, in July. [37]

The law also invests heavily in studies designed to establish definitively which treatments are most successful. Many analysts believe that, eventually, the federal investment in such "comparative-effectiveness" research will discourage doctors from prescribing costly treatments that don't work. That's "good news indeed for [workers'] comp payers," for example, who are "saddled with back surgeries" that many experts now believe don't help but whose ineffectiveness hasn't yet been established by research, said insurance consultant Paduda. [38]

Few promise that cost savings will come easily, however. Besides comparative-effectiveness research, the law also will launch experiments on potential cost-control measures such as paying health care providers based on whether they keep people from getting sick rather than for rendering individual services. But because neither public nor private health care entities have yet seriously explored such techniques, "it will be at least 10 years" before it's known whether they work, says Robert Laszewski, an Alexandria, Va.-based insurance industry consultant. ■

BACKGROUND

The Mandate

In their bid to expand coverage to 30 million of the approximately 50 million uninsured Americans, the drafters of the Affordable Care Act (ACA) proposed two strategies: [39]

• Medicaid would be expanded, through a federal-state effort, to cover everyone in households earning less than 138 percent of the federal poverty level (FPL), or $26,344 for a family of three.

• The law would require everyone whose earnings exceed that threshold either to carry employer-sponsored insurance or to buy it from a new, federally subsidized government-regulated insurance market or else pay a financial penalty for not doing so. [40]

Both provisions are controversial. Opponents — largely Republicans — argue that states opting into the Medicaid expansion would be unreasonably burdened financially and that the individual mandate violates Americans' freedom by forcing them to buy a product — insurance — they may not want. Because the U.S. Supreme Court significantly altered the Medicaid provision, the CBO projects that about 3 million fewer people will be covered by the ACA than originally estimated. [41]

The individual mandate is a practical necessity to create a working insurance system, its defenders say. At any given time, only relatively few have high medical costs, and different people experience high costs in different years, wrote David Cole, a professor at Georgetown University Law Center in Washington. Because predicting when and whom serious accident or illness will strike is virtually impossible, it's crucial to bring everyone into the insurance pool so that premiums paid by the currently healthiest can subsidize care for the currently sick and injured, said Cole. [42]

State experience proves that without a mandate, attempts to provide affordable coverage for all will collapse, Cole wrote. In 1994, for example, Kentucky enacted a law similar to the ACA, requiring insurers to cover people with pre-existing health conditions at affordable prices, "but without an individual mandate." Quickly, "costs rose so steeply that they became untenable," insurers left the market and Kentucky had to repeal its law, Cole said. [43]

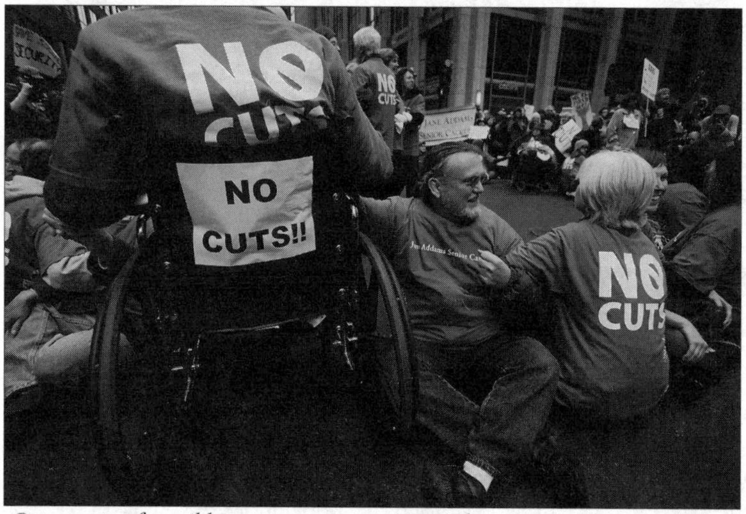

Getty Images/Scott Olson

Opponents of possible cuts to government entitlement programs, including Medicaid, block a downtown Chicago intersection on Nov. 7, 2011. About 40 of several hundred protesters were arrested. The Affordable Care Act could increase the size of the Medicaid program to cover some 17 million poor, able-bodied, childless adults. But many state officials say they'll reject federal funds to expand health coverage in this way, saying it would strain their already tight budgets.

Ironically, many conservatives have proposed health-system overhauls over the past quarter-century that included a mandate.

"In our scheme, every person would be required to obtain basic coverage, through either an individual or a family insurance plan," Mark Pauly, a professor of health care management at the University of Pennsylvania's Wharton School, wrote in 1991. Pauly, along with other conservative scholars, devised a plan they hoped President George H. W. Bush could use to expand coverage. [44]

"It is reasonable" to impose "a requirement on individuals to enroll themselves and their dependents in at least a basic health plan — one that at a minimum should protect the rest of society from large and unexpected medical costs incurred by the family," Stuart Butler, director of the Center for Policy Innovation at the conservative Heritage Foundation, told a congressional panel in 2003. [45]

In 2004, Senate Majority Leader Bill Frist, R-Tenn., a transplant surgeon and heir to the founders of the large for-profit hospital chain Hospital Corp. of America, said "higher-income Americans today have a societal and a personal responsibility to cover in some way themselves and their children." [46]

Recently, though, most conservatives have turned against the mandate, arguing that requiring healthy people to buy insurance to subsidize the sick is an attack on individual freedom.

"The mandate's proponents call it an 'individual responsibility' requirement. But its real aim is to force young people to cover up for irresponsible government policies" — mainly gov-

Continued on p. 800

Chronology

2006-2018

Congress enacts legislation to expand health insurance coverage; controversies dog the law.

2006
Massachusetts, under Republican Gov. Mitt Romney, enacts mandatory, universal health coverage with bipartisan support, requiring residents to buy insurance in a state-regulated market.

2007
As of July 1, all Massachusetts residents must purchase health insurance.

2009
To control costs, Massachusetts officials consider paying doctors and hospitals flat, up-front fees to provide care. . . . In December, U.S. Senate passes the Affordable Care Act (ACA) 60-39, but with no Republicans voting in favor; House scheduled to take up the bill in spring 2010.

2010
House passes Affordable Care Act (ACA) 219-212, with no Republican support. . . . President Obama signs the law March 23; it aims to expand coverage to 30 million people and trim costs while maintaining quality. . . . States and private groups challenge the ACA's constitutionality in court. . . . Federal government opens "high-risk" health plan, in which people with preexisting health conditions can get affordable coverage; sign-up is slow because premiums remain costly. . . . Adults under 26 become eligible for coverage on their parents' health plans. . . . Health insurers must cover children with pre-existing illnesses.

2011
Some Medicare enrollees get ACA rebates for prescription drug expenses. . . . Very small businesses become eligible for tax credits for insuring workers. . . . Newly elected House Republican majority repeatedly votes to repeal or defund the ACA, but Democrat-controlled Senate declines to consider the bills. . . . Federal appeals courts consider challenges to the ACA, upholding some but rejecting others; matter heads to the Supreme Court, which agrees to examine the ACA's "individual mandate" provision requiring people to buy insurance coverage or pay a penalty and the law's Medicaid-expansion provision. . . . Primary-care doctors treating Medicare patients get payment boost. . . . Copayments waived for some preventive-health services under Medicare. . . . High-income Medicare beneficiaries pay higher premiums. . . . States get grants to improve Medicaid care for chronic-disease patients. . . . Payments cut for private "Medicare Advantage" health plans. . . . Medicare Independent Payment Advisory Board (IPAB) established. Beginning in 2015, Medicare must implement cost-control measures recommended by IPAB, absent a two-thirds "no" vote by Congress.

2012
Supreme Court declares ACA's individual mandate constitutional but makes Medicaid expansion optional for states. . . . Republican governors and state legislatures say they might not expand Medicaid to cover poor adults. . . . Health plans that spend too little on medical care must give cash rebates to enrollees. . . . With bipartisan support, Massachusetts clamps down on health care cost growth and adopts incentives to pay doctors and hospitals for "bundles" of high-quality care, rather than "fees for service." . . . GOP presidential nominee Mitt Romney and many congressional Republicans vow to repeal the ACA if they win November elections. . . . More than 2,000 hospitals lose some Medicare payments because of below-standard patient care. . . . Makers and importers of some brand-name drugs must pay new fees to help finance the law.

2013
Primary-care doctors get Medicaid payment boost. . . . Taxpayers who itemize medical expenses must meet a higher threshold to claim a deduction. . . . Federal sales tax imposed on some medical devices. . . . Payroll tax on Medicare Part A, which pays for hospital services, rises. . . . With the ACA set to extend coverage to more uninsured people, special hospital reimbursements for providing free care to the uninsured are phased out.

2014
ACA's Medicaid expansion and individual mandate slated to begin. . . . Individuals may buy federally subsidized insurance in state- or federally managed markets, called exchanges. . . . Insurers banned from imposing annual dollar limits on individuals' health spending. . . . Fees imposed on large employers who do not offer health coverage. . . . Insurers must sell coverage to people with pre-existing health conditions. . . . New fees imposed on health insurers.

2018
Tax imposed on insurers offering employer-sponsored coverage costing more than $10,200 for individuals or $27,500 for families.

Caring for the Poorest and Sickest

Expanding Medicaid challenges would-be reformers.

Regardless of what happens to the Affordable Care Act (ACA) — whether it rolls out as planned over the next several years or is repealed under a new Republican administration — American health care still will face perhaps its biggest challenge: caring for the sickest and the poorest. Analysts from across the ideological spectrum agree on the urgency of the challenge, but solutions remain elusive.

Today, Medicaid, which is funded jointly by states and the federal government, provides care for poor families with children as well as many people with severe disabilities; it also provides long-term-care, mostly in nursing homes, for the low-income elderly. But as the costs of care have risen far faster than incomes, more Americans who fall outside these coverage categories continue to lose access to care. In 2010, 49.1 million Americans were uninsured. [1] (As of June 2011, 52.6 million people were covered by Medicaid. [2])

"You can be penniless" and yet receive no assistance in getting health coverage, says Ron Pollack, founding executive director of the national consumer-advocacy group Families USA. "We have 42 states that don't do anything for adults without children," making the Medicaid safety net "more holes than webbing," he says. But the ACA aims to remedy the problem by expanding Medicaid to low-income childless adults.

Some liberals have long predicted that such an expansion would not only provide much-needed access to care but also save money. The savings would come from poor people getting preventive health care rather than ending up seeking expensive emergency room treatment after long-untreated medical conditions worsened. Some conservative commentators, on the other hand, scoff at the ACA expansion, arguing that Medicaid is such a skimpy program and pays doctors and hospitals so little that the new Medicaid enrollees will gain almost nothing of value.

"There's a lot of rhetoric on both sides" of the Medicaid-expansion question, says Katherine Baicker, a professor of health policy at the Harvard School of Public Health. She says new data she and other scholars collected show clearly that the most extreme claims of both proponents and detractors miss the mark.

The scholars, who also include Amy Finkelstein, a Massachusetts Institute of Technology economics professor, conducted the first-ever research on insurance coverage using the most rigorous standards of scientific evidence, says Baicker. In the study, nearly 90,000 very low-income Oregonians, ages 19 to 64, signed up for a lottery that randomly assigned them either to the Oregon Health Plan or left them uninsured. [3] The research, which is ongoing, ultimately will examine and compare the health care usage, health status and financial situations of both the group covered under the state health plan and those in the uninsured control group.

The data show that, after one year, those who gained Medicaid coverage gave their health status better marks than did their uninsured peers, and they also faced far fewer struggles with medical bills, says Baicker. The newly insured were more

Continued from p. 798

ernment regulations on health care — "that make insurance too expensive," charged Avik Roy, a senior fellow at the conservative Manhattan Institute in New York. [47]

Mandate supporters, however, insist that buying insurance while healthy is essentially a prepayment plan for the unpredictable but inevitable day when illness or accident strikes. In rejecting mandates — as most Americans do in public-opinion polls — "Americans believe they have a moral right to critically needed health care, whether or not they can pay for it, but also believe that they should be free not to make financial provision for that event beforehand," wrote Princeton University economics professor Uwe Reinhardt. [48]

The Poor

The ACA's other proposed coverage mechanism — Medicaid — also stirs controversy, mainly because many states worry about the program's rising costs and federal rules imposed on it.

Enacted in 1965, Medicaid replaced two federal grant programs that helped states provide medical care to the poor elderly and to people on welfare. Eventually, Medicaid used combined state and federal funds to provide health coverage for very poor families with children, long-term care and other services for low-income elderly and disabled people and, as a state option, coverage for other groups such as poor, childless adults.

States can choose whether or not to participate in Medicaid, and indeed not all states jumped on the Medicaid bandwagon at first. Arizona didn't start a Medicaid program until the 1980s, for example. Today, every state provides Medicaid, although eligibility rules vary widely. [49] In Alabama and Louisiana, for example, parents with dependent children who make more than 11 percent of the federal poverty level — about $2,100 a year for a family of three — are ineligible for Medicaid, while in Minnesota the same family could earn more than $41,000 and receive benefits. [50]

Before the Supreme Court altered the ACA's Medicaid provision, the law essentially required states to help the federal government expand Medicaid coverage or risk losing the federal Medicaid funds they already received, a penalty intended to ensure that all states would participate. [51]

likely to describe their health as good and improving and themselves as happier than did the uninsured, she says.

In addition, the newly insured were 25 percent less likely to have had an unpaid medical bill sent to a collection agency and 40 percent less likely to have had to borrow money or leave other bills unpaid to pay their medical bills.

These findings prove that "expanding Medicaid has real benefits," not just for health but for people's financial status as well, says Baicker. The findings should effectively end speculation by Medicaid's critics that the program would be of no help to people if it were expanded, she says.

The data don't "tell you whether it's a good idea to expand Medicaid, but they do give you information about what the effects are," on individuals and on government budgets, Baicker says.

Nevertheless, the same data also dampens expectations by Medicaid-expansion supporters that hospital use might decline, along with expenses, if more people receive Medicaid coverage, says Baicker. Instead, she says, "we found a substantial increase [in hospital use], at least in the first year," she says. Still, she says, the increase came in scheduled hospital care such as non-emergency surgeries, not in pricey emergency-room visits that sometimes result from neglected preventive care.

Meanwhile, conservative economists who hope to see the ACA repealed and replaced with a less-regulated, more market-oriented system also acknowledge the importance — and trickiness — of serving the poorest and sickest people while allowing a free market to flourish in health care for the rest of the population.

"Sometimes there's a tendency to think only in dollar terms, but that's not the be-all and end-all," says Thomas Miller, a resident fellow at the free-market-oriented American Enterprise Institute. Miller says "you need a health care system that works for people" — both the poorest and sickest, who need more assistance than others, and the rest of the population, who are best served by having a health care market that offers them choices.

"You need first to acknowledge that the very poor or the very sick must get more" help to meet costs, Miller says. But at the same time, he adds, "you want to allow a wider variety of choices" for others so that savvy consumers can drive the market toward better quality and lower cost. Subsidies are required for the poor under any system, but the ACA's subsidies are too rich and reach people who earn too much, thereby undercutting the incentives for wiser spending, he says.

— Marcia Clemmitt

[1] "The Uninsured: A Primer," Kaiser Commission on Medicaid and the Uninsured, October 2011, p. 1, www.kff.org/uninsured/upload/7451-07.pdf.

[2] "Medicaid Enrollment: June 2011 Data Snapshot," Kaiser Commission on Medicaid and the Uninsured, June 2012, www.kff.org/medicaid/upload/8050-05.pdf.

[3] For background, see Amy Finkelstein, *et al.*, "The Oregon Health Insurance Experiment: Evidence from the First Year," National Bureau of Economic Research, 2011, www.rwjf.org/files/research/72577.5294.oregon.nber.pdf.

States provide a hefty share of the funding for traditional Medicaid. In fiscal 2010, for example, they spent a total of $126 billion, supplemented by $263 billion in federal funds. [52] The federal contribution to the ACA's Medicaid expansion is much bigger, with the government picking up 100 percent of costs from 2014 through 2016, then gradually shifting more costs to states until the federal share drops to 90 percent in 2020 and thereafter. [53]

About half of the people who were expected to gain coverage under the ACA were expected to gain it through the Medicaid program, said Alan Weil, executive director of the National Academy for State Health Policy, which helps states improve their health systems. "This is not a small change to Medicaid, and it's also not a small part of the Affordable Care Act." [54]

The Court

As soon as the law was enacted, both the individual mandate and Medicaid-expansion mechanisms came under legal challenge. Twenty-six states eventually joined an anti-ACA lawsuit filed in Florida on March 23, 2010, the same day President Obama signed the act into law. In this and other suits, states and private groups charged that Congress had overstepped its constitutional authority by requiring individuals to buy health insurance or pay a penalty and by requiring states to expand Medicaid or lose federal Medicaid funding altogether.

Some of the first cases reached the U.S. Supreme Court in its 2011-2012 session, and the Court agreed to examine both the mandate and the Medicaid issues. [55]

On June 28, the Court issued a mixed ruling that pleased ACA's defenders and left the law's critics with little to do but vow to try to repeal it.

The ACA's supporters and even some conservative legal commentators have argued that Congress has the power to require individuals to buy health insurance because the Constitution's Commerce Clause gives federal lawmakers the right to impose rules on business dealings that cross state boundaries. "The health industry is of course an interstate business; there is a continuous flow of health insurance payments, health insurance

Trying to Trim the Waste From Health Care

Conservatives and liberals both take "big picture" approach.

In this campaign season of extreme political bickering, Democrats and Republicans agree on one thing: the pressing need to slow ever-rising health care costs. In 2010, U.S. spending, public and private, on health care totaled nearly $2.6 trillion, more than 10 times the cost in 1980. [1]

Moreover, conservative and liberal economists take essentially the same big-picture cost-cutting approach — setting annual budgets and giving them teeth by forcing an entity such as an insurance company or hospital-and-physician group to pick up the tab for cost overruns, says Michael Chernew, a professor of health care policy at Harvard Medical School.

In conservatives' preferred model — sometimes called a "voucher" or a "premium-support" system — the annual budget comes in the form of a capped payment that insurers receive in exchange for keeping an individual healthy for a year, says Chernew. (GOP vice presidential candidate Paul Ryan proposes such a plan as a new model for Medicare, for example.)

Under this kind of capped-payment plan, the government — or an employer — calculates what it deems fair for a year's worth of health care and hands each person a check to shop for an insurance plan at that price. Individuals must choose wisely, and insurers must provide adequate care at the set price, since extra spending won't be reimbursed, Chernew explains.

Chernew says left-leaning analysts favor a similar fixed-price approach, but with health-care providers, such as integrated hospital-physician practice groups, rather than insurers getting the cash. The Affordable Care Act (ACA) dubs such groups Accountable Care Organizations (ACOs). In this model, a group of providers, rather than an insurer, gets a "bundled" payment to provide all needed health services. The providers must provide adequate care at that price or else pick up the tab for additional services patients need.

Both models are intended to "change the nature of the good that's being bought" in the health care market from "specific services that are sold at certain fees" to "care overall" — a total package of care to keep people healthy, Chernew says.

The current system of buying one health service at a time encourages consumers to purchase unneeded, or even harmful, medical services, since health-care organizations profit by selling as many services as possible, says Robert Laszewski, an insurance consultant in Alexandria, Va. Both proposed capped-payment systems have promise and pitfalls, though, and which one a policymaker opts for is still largely a matter of ideology, since little evidence exists about either plan's effectiveness.

Chernew says he believes the conservative plan of offering insurers capped payments would encourage competition in the insurance industry. But many questions remain. For example, it is unclear how effective it would be to shape the health care system around consumers' ability to "shop around," Chernew says. Among other issues, such an approach makes it crucial for the government to prevent any insurers from gaining monopoly power, because only with a wide range of buying options can consumers run an overpriced or low-quality health plan out of business.

On the ACO side, too, "we know enough to be somewhat optimistic, but not enough to be sure," Chernew says.

Massachusetts, which enacted a universal health-coverage program similar to the ACA in 2006, has been experimenting

reimbursements, drugs, doctors, patients, donations to hospitals, research money, etc., across state boundaries," wrote Richard Posner, a conservative judge on the Seventh U.S. Circuit Court of Appeals and a lecturer at the University of Chicago Law School. [56]

But conservative justices, including Chief Justice Roberts, rejected that argument, maintaining that uninsured people to whom the mandate primarily would apply are not actually participants in the health care market and therefore may not be subjected to rules under the Commerce Clause.

Roberts, however, ultimately added his vote to those of the court's four liberal justices to uphold the mandate by a 5-4 majority, despite rejecting the idea that the Commerce Clause authorizes Congress to impose it. He concluded instead that the ACA's financial penalty for failing to buy insurance falls under Congress' power to levy taxes.

The penalty raises revenue for the government — the distinguishing mark of a tax — even though it is "plainly designed to expand health insurance coverage," Roberts wrote. "But taxes that seek to influence conduct" — such as by heavily taxing alcoholic beverages or imported goods to dissuade people from buying them — "are nothing new" and are allowable, he said. [57]

But the court struck down the harsh penalty the ACA sought to impose on states unwilling to expand Medicaid, thus effectively transforming the provision from a requirement into a voluntary program. ACA opponents argued that the law's expansion plan as a whole should be struck down because the stiff penalty attached to it violated a basic constitutional principle — that the federal government can't compel states to either enact or administer any federal regulatory program. [58] The Obama administration, on the other hand, contended that the expansion plan falls under a provision in current law that requires states that participate in Medicaid to go along with any future changes Congress may make in the program or cease receiving federal Medicaid funds.

with a version of ACOs — called Alternative Quality Contracts (AQCs). In an AQC, a hospital or physicians' group negotiates a set price from an insurer to cover the entire cost of care for all the insurer's patients whom the health care providers serve. If the provider group goes over budget, it must pay the difference. That gives it a financial stake in avoiding problems such as untreated chronic conditions that worsen until costly emergency care is needed. [2]

So far, evidence is mixed on AQCs. One study last year found no savings while another reported "modest" savings. [3] A 2012 study, however, concluded that the average AQC spent 1.9 percent less than control groups in the first year of operation and 3.3 percent less in the second year, while providing better chronic-disease and preventive-health care. [4]

Liberal proposals generally set strict rules to prevent an organization receiving a capped payment from skimping on care, while conservatives believe that a robust market will perform that function, says Laszewski. That difference gets to the heart of the debate over the competing models, says Laszewski. "Some people fear big business and prefer to be protected from it by the government, and others fear the government" and its potential to strangle choice and innovation with rules.

Whatever plan economists or lawmakers may propose to slow the growth in medical costs, consumers or the health care industry can undermine the effort. Consumers may balk at cost-cutting, fearing it deprives them of care. And providers, from medical-device manufacturers to individual physicians, have routinely pushed back against such efforts to avoid losing income. In Massachusetts, that dynamic is playing out with AQCs, said Eric Beyer, president of Boston's Tufts Medical Center, which holds an AQC contract. Contrary to policymakers' hopes, "employers are not signing up for the [AQC] plans in droves — in fact, more of our population is moving toward products that have no requirement for paying providers for quality over quantity," Beyer said. [5]

Meanwhile, fearing they'll lose their clout as the government becomes more aggressive about demanding cost-efficient and high-quality care, doctors and hospitals are linking up into very large medical groups, says Stan Dorn, a senior fellow at the Urban Institute, an independent domestic-issues research group in Washington. Ideally, such arrangements could provide better integrated care, but "big systems can also extract high prices," Dorn says.

— Marcia Clemmitt

[1] "U.S. Healthcare Costs," Kaiser Family Foundation, www.kaiseredu.org/Issue-Modules/US-Health-Care-Costs/Background-Brief.aspx; for background, see Marcia Clemmitt, "Rising Health Costs," *CQ Researcher*, April 7, 2006, pp. 289-312.

[2] Dan Diamond, "To Gauge ObamaCare Impact, Ignore CBO and Focus on AQC," *California Healthline*, July 25, 2012, www.californiahealthline.org/road-to-reform/2012/to-gauge-obamacare-impact-ignore-cbo-and-focus-on-aqc.aspx.

[3] *Ibid.*

[4] Zirui Song, *et al.*, "The 'Alternative Quality Contract,' Based on a Global Budget, Lowered Medical Spending and Improved Quality," *Health Affairs*, July 2012, http://content.healthaffairs.org/content/early/2012/07/09/hlthaff.2012.0327.abstract.

[5] Eric Beyer, "State Needs to Take Stock Before Expanding Health Payment Methods Employers Are Rejecting," *The Boston Globe*, July 18, 2012, www.bostonglobe.com/opinion/2012/07/18/state-needs-take-stock-before-expanding-health-payment-methods-employers-methods-rejecting-state-needs-take-stock-before-expanding-health-payment/12nbA6ag2uUOCihzjFk7OI/story.html.

A seven-member court majority, led by Roberts, issued a split decision, allowing the Medicaid coverage proposal to stand, but only as a voluntary program that states could take or leave without penalty. Roberts concluded that the proposal was outside established Medicaid rules, meaning states' pledges to go along with all legislated changes in the program don't apply.

Medicaid "was designed to cover medical services for . . . particular categories of the needy: the disabled, the blind, the elderly, and needy families with dependent children," and previous Medicaid amendments "merely altered and expanded . . . these categories," Roberts wrote. The coverage expansion, by contrast, is not "a program to care for the neediest among us, but . . . an element of a comprehensive national plan to provide universal health insurance coverage." [59] ■

Current Situation

Uncertain Future

The Supreme Court's June ruling has not ended the legal controversy surrounding the ACA. Church-run institutions are claiming in new lawsuits that a requirement in the ACA that health plans provide contraception coverage violates the Constitution's guarantee of religious freedom.

The main ACA story of 2012, though, is uncertainty, as most of the law's provisions are a year or more from implementation and the Supreme Court ruling has made Medicaid expansion voluntary for states.

This year, several groups, including colleges run by the Roman Catholic Church and some conservative Protestant churches, as well as at least seven states and some for-profit businesses whose owners strongly oppose contraception out of religious conviction, have filed lawsuits seeking to exempt employers from the contraception mandate. [60] (Churches, but not employers such as church-run hospitals and schools, already are exempt.)

"We're very clear on the sanctity of life, and this insurance mandate goes against our conscience," said Philip Graham Ryken, president of Wheaton College, an evangelical Protestant institution in Wheaton, Ill. [61]

The Obama administration announced a compromise plan last February. Women who work at nonprofit, church-affiliated entities can go directly to the insurance companies that administer their employer-based health plans and get contraceptive coverage — free — so that employers can avoid acting as go-betweens. Under the ACA, insurers face stricter government rules than in the past on what coverage they offer and what they charge for it. In this case, the administration argues that insurers may not demand that women pay a higher premium to get contraceptive coverage because contraceptives are a preventive-health measure that reduces overall health spending. [62]

But opponents contend that the compromise still implicates employers in immoral activity.

"We have a president who, for the first time in American history, is directly assaulting the First Amendment and freedom of religion," said former Sen. Rick Santorum, R-Pa., in a campaign speech on behalf of Romney. President Obama, he said, is "forcing business people right now to do things that are against their conscience." [63]

Court Fallout

Since the Supreme Court rendered its decision, numerous Republican governors and state lawmakers have expressed doubt about whether their states will undertake a Medicaid expansion. Officials in states including Mississippi, Nebraska, Missouri, Idaho, Texas, Wisconsin, Florida, Indiana, South Carolina, Iowa, Louisiana and Kansas have suggested they might reject the expansion funds, thus reducing by millions the number of people covered under the law. [64] About 1.8 million uninsured people who were expected to gain Medicaid coverage live in Texas alone, and nearly 1 million reside in Florida. [65]

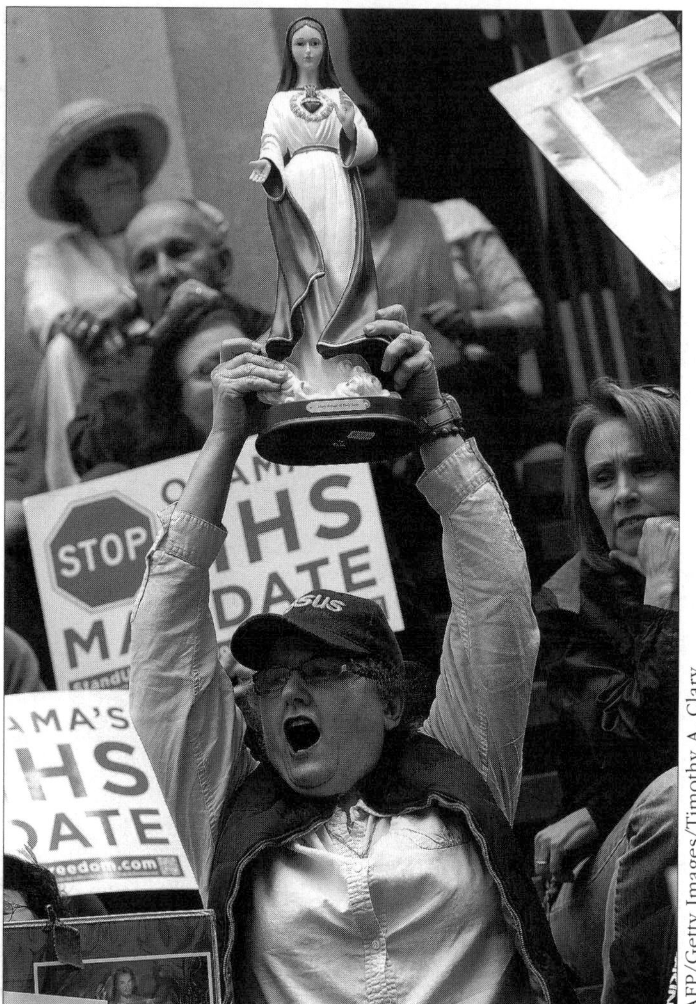

AFP/Getty Images/Timothy A. Clary

Demonstrators in New York City on March 23, 2012, protest a requirement of the health care law that most employers provide health insurance coverage for contraception. Several groups, including colleges run by the Roman Catholic Church, at least seven states and business owners who strongly oppose contraception out of religious conviction, have filed lawsuits seeking to exempt employers from the contraception mandate.

Some officials have flatly announced that the expansion is a no-go. "I don't see any chance" of Missouri participating, said Ryan Silvey, a budget committee chairman in that state's Republican-dominated legislature. [66]

Opposition, by and large, is not about money, and that's why it will stick, argued Andrew Koppelman, a professor of law and political science at Northwestern University. Because the state funding share is so low — the federal government will pick up 100 percent of costs through 2016, gradually dropping to 90 percent in 2020 — the objections amount to "states refusing to spend federal money to help people that they do not want to help," he contends. "The temptation to trash Obamacare will be irresistible." [67]

However, many analysts expect states eventually to back away from their hard-line resistance and adopt the program.

"I'm really excited about the ruling" because by freeing states to turn down the program altogether, it gives them leverage to bargain with the federal government for looser rules about how they structure it, says insurance consultant Laszewski. "I believe that states will implement the law, but [Louisiana's Republican Gov.] Bobby Jindal will do it

Continued on p. 806

At Issue:

Should the Affordable Care Act be repealed?

THOMAS MILLER
RESIDENT FELLOW, AMERICAN ENTERPRISE INSTITUTE

WRITTEN FOR *CQ RESEARCHER*, SEPTEMBER 2012

YES

The Affordable Care Act (ACA) — also known as "Obamacare" — was unpopular, unwise and unsustainable when enacted in March 2010. Another two years of stumbling implementation and real-world analysis, amid fierce battles in the courts, on Capitol Hill and throughout the states, provided further evidence of the health law's flaws. The law is too costly to finance, too difficult to administer, too burdensome on health care practitioners and too disruptive of health care arrangements that many Americans prefer.

The ACA is not just too misguided to succeed. It's too dangerous to maintain and far too flawed to fix on a piecemeal basis. The law will jeopardize future economic growth, distort health care delivery and limit access to quality care. It doubles down on our already unsustainable entitlement spending for health care, transferring dedicated funds from one overcommitted program (Medicare) to expand another (Medicaid) and establish a new one — the subsidies the ACA provides consumers to buy insurance in government-run exchanges.

The ACA will further erode meaningful limits on the powers of the federal government. Its maze of current and future mandates, regulatory edicts and arbitrary bureaucracy undermines political accountability and the rule of law.

Obamacare was built on faulty premises, then disguised with accounting fictions and narrowly approved through cynical dealmaking. Repealing it in whole is necessary to clear the way for the lasting reforms of health care we so desperately need.

The long overdue journey to health policy that drives sustainable health care improvement must be centered on better incentives, information, choices, competition, personal responsibilities and trust in the decisions of individuals and their families. It should not be guided by top-down mandates, arbitrary budgetary formulas and bureaucratic buck-passing. We won't improve our health until we move personal health care decisions out of politics and back into the hands of patients and physicians.

Repeal of the ACA is not enough by itself. But it opens the door to a more decentralized and market-based alternative that will work and improve the lives of Americans. The country needs a more competitive health care marketplace that encourages more entry and less command-and-control regulation, while retargeting our tax-funded resources on protecting the most vulnerable individuals and their families.

Rebalancing our resources, our values, our hopes and our fears is too important, complex and personal to leave in the hands of the many politicians, experts and entrenched interests that have failed us in the past.

RON POLLACK
FOUNDING EXECUTIVE DIRECTOR, FAMILIES USA

WRITTEN FOR *CQ RESEARCHER*, SEPTEMBER 2012

NO

In June, the Supreme Court upheld the constitutionality of the Affordable Care Act. Just last week, however, its theatrical opponents in the House of Representatives staged their 34th loud, divisive and utterly futile vote to repeal it. Afterward, nothing changed; it remains the law of our land. The benefits and protections it grants consumers are real, and many are already in place. Soon, even strident opponents will put aside their showmanship and recognize the positive impact and value of the law.

The law makes sure that insurance companies treat people fairly. Under the law, it will be illegal for insurers to discriminate against women by charging higher premiums simply because of their gender. Nobody — male or female — will be denied coverage or charged higher premiums because of a pre-existing condition, such as asthma or diabetes. No one will live in fear of their insurance being cancelled. People will no longer be subject to arbitrary lifetime or annual caps in what insurers pay out, thereby denying coverage when it is needed the most.

The act also comes with much-needed direct help for middle-class families. They will receive substantial subsidies to make health insurance premiums affordable. Seniors will no longer fall into the huge prescription drug coverage gap in Medicare euphemistically named the "doughnut hole." Comprehensive preventive care will be available at no cost for women, including mammograms and contraception.

A significant number of these benefits, and many others, already are being provided in whole or in part, such as the millions of young adults (under age 26) who are staying on their parents' policies. As more and more people feel the direct protections and benefits of the new law, repealing the Affordable Care Act will increasingly be considered an absurdity.

At its heart, the ACA is about keeping people healthy and giving Americans the peace of mind that health care will always be there when they need it. Irrespective of changes in any person's life circumstances — the desire to switch jobs or start a business, being laid off from work, changes in marital status or the sudden loss of income — the Affordable Care Act ensures the availability of quality, affordable health care.

Instead of playing politics with the act, it's time to fully implement it across the country. In fact, Democrats and Republicans should come together to build on the ACA so that additional steps can be taken to moderate health care costs for America's families and businesses.

Continued from p. 804

in a different way than in New York" under Democratic Gov. Andrew Cuomo.

The result will be a variety of natural experiments carried out around the country that will test how different coverage models work, from single-payer systems to the most loosely regulated private markets, he says. Conducting such experiments has always been a good idea, "but the problem is that you need gobs of federal money" for states to do them, which the ACA now offers, he says.

"Virtually every state" will implement the expansion "after the rhetorical season" of the November election is over, says Pollack of Families USA. Some "very influential" health care sectors, such as hospitals, already are urging states to take the funding to help eliminate the unpaid medical bills they struggle with, he says.

"ACA provided a carrot and a stick" for the expansion, and "although the stick is gone, the very big carrot remains," he says.

Only a Beginning

Because many aspects of health care are state responsibilities, such as setting and enforcing rules for health insurance sold to individuals and small businesses, the ACA puts additional burdens on state governments. However, the law allows the federal government to step in if states don't fulfill these responsibilities effectively and on time.

"A few states — including Massachusetts, California and Maryland — appear to be well along in their implementation activities" for the insurance exchanges through which individuals will buy health coverage using ACA subsidies, said Antos of the American Enterprise Institute. Nationwide, however, given the present rate of progress, both the states and the federal government are doomed to fall behind the aggressive schedule the law requires, he said.

For example, 37 states have not yet enacted enabling legislation or issued an executive order to establish an insurance exchange through which citizens can buy coverage, Antos noted. Citizens of those states risk becoming liable for the ACA's mandate-related tax penalty in January 2014 — before their states have managed to set up the exchanges through which affordable coverage is supposed to be available, he wrote. What's more, it's "doubtful that the federal government . . . will be capable of stepping in" to help states get their insurance exchanges up and running, he said. "The task is too large, the time is too short." [68]

But ACA supporter Pollack says the law's opponents are secretly rooting for the law to stumble hard out of the gate. He calls their predictions that lagging ACA implementation will harm citizens "wishful thinking." Even "a lot of governors who actually oppose the law and joined the lawsuit [against it] are still working quietly with folks to get ready" to implement it, he says. That's partly because many Republican governors hope to shape the exchanges according to their own ideas — not the Obama administration's — about how the insurance market should work he says. "It would put a conservative governor in an ironic situation — letting the federal government decide what goes on in the state."

Besides expanding insurance coverage, the ACA also is intended to reshape the way health care is delivered and paid for, with the goal to hold down cost increases while maintaining quality. The law includes a wide range of possible cost-control measures, such as establishment of an independent board empowered to make cost-saving changes to Medicare. It also offers financial incentives to induce physicians and hospitals to provide preventive care. But all these measures "have to be built" before it becomes clear whether they actually work, says insurance consultant Laszewski.

Furthermore, much more must be attempted on the cost-control front, Laszewski says. "This law didn't take a really serious shot at it" — not surprising, given the controversy that surrounds any attempt to reduce medical costs, he says. Massachusetts, which enacted a close-to-universal coverage system similar to the ACA in 2006, "just passed their cost-control bill this year," a full six years into the program's operation, Laszewski says. ■

OUTLOOK

Voting on Health

Parts of the ACA, if not the law as a whole, undoubtedly will have some impact in the November elections. The ACA provisions intended to trim some wasteful Medicare spending, for example, could undermine President Obama's popularity among older voters. Meanwhile, many congressional Republicans continue to say they'll cut implementation funding for the law and repeal it in January if they have the power.

On July 18, 127 members of the House GOP caucus — more than half its members — wrote House Speaker Boehner and House Majority Leader Eric Cantor, R-Va., expressing "outrage" over the Supreme Court's upholding of the health care law. They pledged to "continue efforts to repeal the law in its entirety this year, next year, and until we are successful." [69] Romney has repeatedly made the same vow in his campaign for the White House.

Still, says Robert Blendon, a professor of health policy and political analysis at the Harvard School of Public Health, the ACA may not be foremost on voters' minds this fall. "The polling is pretty clear," he says. "The economy and jobs are the main issues for voters, but if the election is within three or four points, then other issues matter." Health care counts high among those other issues, but in that category it is mainly Medicare that has voters concerned, Blendon says.

Ryan, the GOP vice presidential nominee, wants to provide future Medicare recipients with a fixed government payment and let them choose among private Medicare plans, Blendon notes. But the idea "has not done well in any poll," he says.

That doesn't mean the Medicare issue is friendly to Obama, however, Blendon says. The Romney campaign "is trying to do something quite politically sophisticated" by taking Medicare and reframing it in campaign ads, speeches and interviews to depict Obama as Medicare's chief foe, he says. Romney charged in an August TV ad and in an interview that in the ACA, Obama "cuts Medicare by $716 billion, takes that money out of the Medicare trust fund and uses it to pay for Obamacare." [70]

But the ACA's defenders argue that the cuts don't trim Medicare benefits but shift the payments in ways aimed at reducing wasteful spending. For example, the law trims payments to so-called Medicare Advantage private health plans that cost more than traditional Medicare. It also lowers payments to hospitals that discharge too many patients too quickly, only to readmit them to treat conditions that could have been prevented with better patient management. If those changes save money, as many expect they will, the savings will fund new Medicare benefits — such as free preventive care — as well as other ACA provisions, PolitiFact Florida, a fact-checking website run by the *Tampa Bay Times*, reported. [71]

Nevertheless, Republican ads and speeches condemning the cuts are successfully harming Obama's standing with senior voters, at least for now, says Blendon. "Just the one big number" — $716 billion — is enough "to make people very nervous," while details that could make the number sound less frightening "are awfully complex to explain to people." In states such as Florida and Ohio, where the presidential vote will be close, the Medicare ads could win the day for Republicans, he says.

In polls, most voters continue to say they dislike the ACA, despite expressing support for some of its provisions, such as its guarantee that people with pre-existing illnesses can buy insurance at a relatively affordable price. Public opposition stems in large part from people's lack of knowledge about what the law does, some analysts argue.

The Urban Institute's Dorn describes a conversation he had with a small-business owner who doesn't provide health insurance for his mainly low-wage workers and buys his personal coverage in the private market. "I said, 'Your own premiums will come down a lot" once the ACA kicks in in 2014, "and your low-wage workers will get subsidies" from the government to help them buy coverage, too. The man responded that he hadn't heard of these ACA features and wasn't sure he believed they existed, Dorn says.

Nevertheless, the ACA has set in motion some changes that will go forward, whatever the election results, says Dorn. For example, states are using ACA funds to automate and streamline their Medicaid administrative procedures, which may trim costs and make it easier for poor people to get access to all the state services they need. And some hospitals and doctors are shifting their focus to preventive care, in anticipation of ACA payment changes that will reward prevention.

"Even if Republicans sweep the table" in November, says Dorn, "they can't take all of those things away." ■

Notes

[1] "Support Caleb," Facebook, www.facebook.com/supportcalebmedley.

[2] Jeremy P. Meyer, "Caleb Medley, Last Shooting Victim at CU Hospital, Released," *Denver Post*, Sept. 13, 2012, www.denverpost.com/breakingnews/ci_21528421/caleb-medley-last-shooting-victim-at-cu-hospital.

[3] Quoted in John Blackstone, "Aurora Shooting May Ruin One Victim's Finances," CBS News, July 23, 2012, www.cbsnews.com/8301-18563_162-57478303/aurora-shooting-may-ruin-one-victims-finances.

[4] The decision is *National Federation of Independent Business v. Sebelius*, 567 U.S. 2— (June 28, 2012), www.supremecourt.gov/opinions/11pdf/11-393c3a2.pdf; For an account, see Kenneth Jost, "Health Care Law Upheld in Fractured Ruling," *CQ Researcher* Blog, June 28, 2012, http://cqresearcherblog.blogspot.com/2012_06_01_archive.html.

[5] Phil Galewitz and Marilyn Werber Serafini, "Ruling Puts Pressure on States to Act," *Kaiser Health News*, June 28, 2012, www.kaiserhealthnews.org/stories/2012/june/28/pressure-on-states-to-act-after-supreme-court-ruling.aspx.

[6] *NFIB v. Sebelius*, *op. cit.* (opinion of Scalia, Kennedy, Thomas, and Alito dissenting), p. 6.

[7] *NFIB v. Sebelius*, *op. cit.*, (opinion of Ginsburg, J.), fn 5, p. 19.

[8] Nancy-Ann DeParle, "Supreme Court Upholds President Obama's Health Care Reform," *The White House Blog*, June 28, 2012, www.whitehouse.gov/blog/2012/06/28/supreme-court-upholds-president-obamas-health-care-reform.

[9] For background, see Julie Rovner, "Mitt Romney's Shifting Stance on Health Care," *Shots blog*, NPR, Sept. 10, 2012, www.npr.org/blogs/health/2012/09/10/160898409/mitt-romneys-shifting-stance-on-health-care.

[10] Robin Abcarian and Maeve Reston, "Romney Uses Healthcare Ruling to Motivate Voters Against Obama," *Los Angeles Times*, June 28, 2012, http://articles.latimes.com/2012/jun/28/news/la-pn-romney-uses-healthcare-ruling-to-motivate-voters-against-obama-20120628.

[11] For background, see Mitt Romney, "Romney: As First Act, Out With Obamacare," *USA Today*, May 11, 2011, www.usatoday.com/news/opinion/forum/2011-05-11-Romney-on-fixing-health-care_n.htm.

[12] For background, see "Plan Levels/Standardization of Coverage," American Cancer Society, www.acscan.org/pdf/healthcare/imple

mentation/background/PlanLevelsStandardizationofCoverage.pdf.

13 Quoted in Kim Krisberg, "Public Health Reacts to Supreme Court's ACA Ruling: 'Surprised and Then Ecstatic,' " *The Pump Handle blog*, June 28, 2012, http://scienceblogs.com/thepumphandle/2012/06/28/public-health-reacts-to-supreme-courts-aca-ruling-surprised-and-then-ecstatic.

14 "On ObamaCare," Wicker for Congress website, www.brookswicker.com/on-obamacare.

15 Ryan Fazio, "Health Care Reform Biased Against Youth," *The Daily Northwestern*, Feb. 13, 2012, www.dailynorthwestern.com/mobile/forum/fazio-health-care-reform-biased-against-youth-1.2700776.

16 Quoted in Jeffrey Young, "Health Care Reform Will Remake Health Insurance Market for Young Adults," *Huffington Post*, Aug. 1, 2012, www.huffingtonpost.com/2012/08/01/health-care-reform-young-adults_n_1711376.html.

17 Quoted in *ibid.*

18 For background, see Michael Cooper, "Many Governors Are Still Unsure About Medicaid Expansion," *The New York Times*, July 14, 2012, www.nytimes.com/2012/07/15/us/governors-face-hard-choices-over-medicaid-expansion.html?pagewanted=all.

19 For background, see "The Requirement to Buy Coverage Under the Affordable Care Act," *Health Reform Source*, Henry J. Kaiser Family Foundation, http://healthreform.kff.org/the-basics/Requirement-to-buy-coverage-flowchart.aspx.

20 "Mitch McConnell: Odds Are Against Health Law Repeal," The Associated Press/*Huffington Post*, July 2, 2012, www.huffingtonpost.com/2012/07/02/mitch-mcconnell-health-care-law_n_1644466.html.

21 Michael D. Tanner, "Individual Mandates for Health Insurance: Slippery Slope to National Health Care," *Policy Analysis No. 565*, Cato Institute, April 5, 2006, www.cato.org.

22 Quoted in Sarah Kliff, "Scott Brown, Ron Wyden Offering Health Care Revision," *Politico*, Nov. 17, 2010, www.politico.com/news/stories/1110/45316.html.

23 *NFIB v. Sebelius*, (opinion of Ginsburg, J.), *op. cit.*, p. 7.

24 Joseph Paduda, "Update — Health reform, the Supreme Court decision and workers comp," *Managed Care Matters*, June 29, 2012, www.joepaduda.com/archives/002363.html.

25 *Ibid.*

26 Quoted in Steve O'Keefe, "Loss Ratio Means Lost Care for Millions," *Health Care Compact Blog*, Nov. 14, 2011, http://healthcarecompact.org/blog/2011-11-14/loss-ratio-means-lost-care-millions.

27 *Ibid.*

28 Quoted in Kathryn Jean Lopez, "Post-Court Report: Sally Pipes on the Future of Health-Care Reform in America," *National Review Online*, March 29, 2012, www.nationalreview.com/critical-condition/294752/post-court-report-sally-pipes-future-health-care-reform-america-kathryn-je.

29 John Goodman, "The Supreme Court May Have Saved Lives," *The Health Care Blog*, July 30, 2012, http://thehealthcareblog.com/blog/2012/07/30/the-supreme-court-may-have-saved-lives.

30 Pam Belluck, "Medicaid Expansion May Lower Death Rates, Study Says," *The New York Times*, July 25, 2012, www.nytimes.com/2012/07/26/health/policy/medicaid-expansion-may-lower-death-rate-study-says.html?pagewanted=all; Benjamine D. Sommers, *et al.*, "Mortality and Access to Care Among Adults After State Medicaid Expansions," *The New England Journal of Medicine*, July 25, 2012, www.nejm.org/doi/full/10.1056/NEJMsa1202099.

31 Belluck, *op. cit.*

32 Quoted in "The Supreme Court Health Care Ruling: Now What?" *Knowledge at Wharton*, June 28, 2012, http://knowledge.wharton.upenn.edu/article.cfm?articleid=3038.

33 John Rossomando, "ObamaCare Forcing Americans out of Their Health Plans," *Human Events*, July 8, 2011, www.humanevents.com/2011/07/08/obamacare-forcing-americans-out-of-their-health-plans.

34 Joseph Antos, "After the Supreme Court, Higher Cost and Unrealistic Timeline Will Force Major Changes," *Health Affairs blog*, July 2, 2012, http://healthaffairs.org/blog/2012/07/02/after-the-supreme-court-higher-cost-and-unrealistic-timeline-will-force-major-changes.

35 Quoted in Tom Eblen, "Commentary: Medicare for Everyone," McClatchy/*Lexington Herald Leader* [KY], Aug. 7, 2012, www.mcclatchydc.com/2012/08/07/160417/commentary-medicare-for-everyone.html.

36 "Testimony on Last Year's Major Health Care Legislation," Congressional Budget Office, March 30, 2011, www.cbo.gov/publication/25155.

37 Douglas W. Elmendorf, letter to Rep. John Boehner, Congressional Budget Office, July 24, 2012, http://cbo.gov/sites/default/files/cbofiles/attachments/43471-hr6079.pdf.

38 Paduda, *op. cit.*

39 "Overview of the Uninsured in the United States: A Summary of the 2011 Population Survey," Assistant Secretary for Planning and Evaluation, U.S. Dept. of Health and Human Services, September 2011, http://aspe.hhs.gov/health/reports/2011/CPSHealthIns2011/ib.shtml.

40 For background, see Marcia Clemmitt, "Health-Care Reform," *CQ Researcher*, June 11, 2010 (updated May 24, 2011), pp. 505-528, and Marcia Clemmitt, "Health-Care Reform," *CQ Researcher*, Aug. 28, 2009, pp. 693-716.

41 "Estimates for the Insurance Coverage Provisions of the Affordable Care Act Updated for the Recent Supreme Court Decision," Congressional Budget Office, July 2012, p. 3, http://cbo.gov/sites/default/files/cbofiles/attachments/43472-07-24-2012-CoverageEstimates.pdf.

42 David Cole, "Is Health Care Reform Unconstitutional?" *The New York Review of Books*, Feb. 24, 2011, www.nybooks.com/articles/archives/2011/feb/24/health-care-reform-unconstitutional/?pagination=false.

43 *Ibid.*

44 Mark V. Pauly, Patricia Damon, Paul Feldstein and John Hoff, "A Plan for 'Responsible National Health Insurance,' " *Health Affairs*, Spring 1991, p. 10, http://hc.wharton.upenn.edu/danzon/html/CV%20pubs/1991_Danzon-PaulyFesteinHoff_APlanForResponsibleNationalHealthInsurance_HA%20Spring%201991.pdf.

45 Stuart Butler, testimony before the Senate Special Committee on Aging, March 10, 2003, www.heritage.org/research/testimony/laying-the-groundwork-for-universal-health-care-coverage.

About the Author

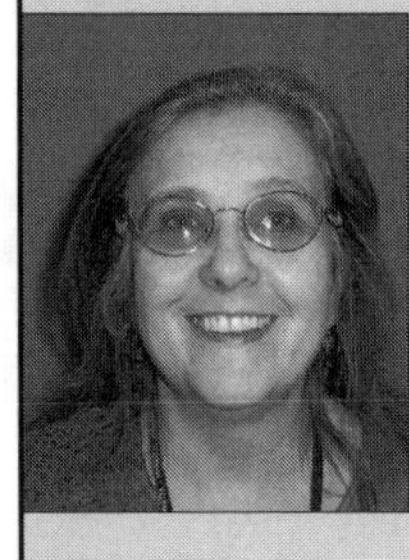

Staff writer **Marcia Clemmitt** is a veteran social-policy reporter who previously served as editor in chief of *Medicine & Health* and staff writer for *The Scientist*. She has also been a high school math and physics teacher. She holds a liberal arts and sciences degree from St. John's College, Annapolis, and a master's degree in English from Georgetown University. Her recent reports include "National Debt" and "Internet Regulation."

[46] Quoted in Marcia Clemmitt, "Frist: Limit Tax Exclusion for Employer-Based Coverage," *Medicine and Health*, July 19, 2004.

[47] Avik Roy, "Opposing View: Individual Mandate Masks and Ugly Deal," *USA Today*, March 28, 2012, www.usatoday.com/news/opinion/story/2012-03-27/supreme-court-individual-mandate/53815712/1.

[48] Uwe E. Reinhardt, "The Supreme Court and the National Conversation on Health Care Reform," *Economix blogs, The New York Times*, March 30, 2012, http://economix.blogs.nytimes.com/2012/03/30/the-supreme-court-and-the-national-conversation-on-health-care-reform.

[49] Galewitz and Serafini, *op. cit.*; for background, see Elicia J. Herz, "Medicaid: A Primer," Congressional Research Service, Jan. 11, 2011, www.ncsl.org/documents/health/MAPrimer.pdf.

[50] "Eligibility Levels in Medicaid & CHIP for Children, Pregnant Women, Parents, and Childless Adults," Georgetown University Health Policy Institute, Center for Children and Families, January 2012, http://ccf.georgetown.edu/wp-content/uploads/2012/04/Eligibility-by-State.pdf.

[51] "Who Benefits from the ACA Medicaid Expansion," The Kaiser Commission on Medicaid and the Uninsured, June 20, 2012, www.kff.org/medicaid/quicktake_aca_medicaid.cfm.

[52] "Federal and State Share of Medicaid Spending FY2010," statehealthfacts.org, Kaiser Family Foundation, www.statehealthfacts.org/comparemaptable.jsp?ind=636&cat=4.

[53] "Summary of New Health Reform Law," Kaiser Family Foundation, www.kff.org/healthreform/upload/8061.pdf.

[54] Quoted in Julie Rovner, "Medicaid Expansion Goes Overlooked in Supreme Court Anticipation," *Shots blog*, NPR, June 27, 2012, www.npr.org/blogs/health/2012/06/27/155861308/medicaid-expansion-goes-overlooked-in-supreme-court-anticipation.

[55] Galewitz and Serafini, *op. cit.*

[56] Richard Posner, "Entry 17: The Commerce Clause Was Clearly Enough to Uphold the Affordable Care Act," *Supreme Court Year in Review, Slate*, June 28, 2012, www.slate.com/articles/news_and_politics/the_breakfast_table/features/2012/_supreme_court_year_in_review/affordable_care_act_upheld_why_the_commerce_clause_should_have_been_enough_.html.

[57] *NFIB v. Sebelius*, (opinion of Roberts, C. J.), *op. cit.*, p. 36.

[58] *Ibid.*, p. 45.

[59] *Ibid.*, p. 53.

[60] For background, see Robin Marty, "Hobby Lobby Files Suit Opposing Affordable Care Act Birth Control Benefit," *RH Reality Check*, Sept. 13, 2012, www.rhrealitycheck.org/article/2012/09/13/hobby-lobby-lawsuit-opens-new-realm-in-opposing-afforable-care-act.

[61] Quoted in "Evangelical College Joins Suit Against ObamaCare Contraception Mandate," FoxNews.com, July 18, 2012, www.foxnews.com/politics/2012/07/18/evangelical-college-joins-suit-against-obamacare-contraception-mandate.

[62] David Brown, "U.S. Bishops Blast Obama's Contraception Compromise," *The Washington Post*, Feb. 11, 2012, www.washingtonpost.com/national/health-science/us-bishops-blast-obamas-contraception-compromise/2012/02/11/gIQAlGVO7Q_story.html.

[63] Quoted in Andrew Rafferty, "Santorum Says Government Forcing Catholics to Sin," First Read, NBCNews.com, Aug. 15, 2012, http://firstread.nbcnews.com/_news/2012/08/15/13303104-santorum-says-government-forcing-catholics-to-sin?lite.

[64] Galewitz and Serafini, *op. cit.*; N.C. Aizenman and Sandhya Somashekhar, "More State Leaders Considering Opting Out of Medicaid Expansion," *The Washington Post*, July 3, www.washingtonpost.com/national/health-science/more-state-leaders-considering-opting-out-of-medicaid-expansion/2012/07/03/gJQADvMsLW_story.html. John Celock, "Health Care Reform Battles Taking Shape at State Level," *Huffington Post*, June 29, 2012, www.huffingtonpost.com/2012/06/28/health-care-reform-battle-states_n_1635545.html.

[65] Galewitz and Serafini, *ibid.*

[66] Quoted in *ibid.*

[67] Andrew Koppelman, "Terrible Arguments Prevail!" *Salon*, June 28, 2012, www.salon.com/2012/06/28/terrible_arguments_prevail.

[68] Antos, *op. cit.*

[69] Letter to Reps. John Boehner and Eric Cantor, July 18, 2012, http://rsc.jordan.house.gov/UploadedFiles/Defund_ObamaCare_Letter_July_18.pdf.

[70] Quoted in "Romney Says Obama 'Cuts' $716 Billion from Medicare to Pay for Obamacare," *PolitiFact Florida*, Aug. 20, 2012, www.politifact.com/florida/statements/2012/aug/20/mitt-romney/romney-says-obama-cuts-716-medicare-pay-obamacare.

[71] *Ibid.*

FOR MORE INFORMATION

ACA Litigation Blog, http://acalitigationblog.blogspot.com. Blog of Bradley Joondeph, a professor of law at the Santa Clara University School of Law in northern California, that chronicles legal challenges to the Affordable Care Act (ACA).

Alliance for Health Reform, 1444 Eye St., N.W., Suite 910, Washington, DC 20005; 202-789-2300; www.allhealth.org. Nonpartisan group that calls on health care experts representing a wide range of opinions to provide information about the ACA and other issues.

American Enterprise Institute, 1150 17th St., N.W., Washington, DC 20036; 202-862-5800; www.aei.org/issue/health/healthcare-reform/beyond-repeal-and-replace-series. Conservative think tank providing information and analysis on developing a more market-oriented health care system.

Center on Budget and Policy Priorities, 820 First St., N.E., Suite 510, Washington, DC 20002; 202-408-1080; www.cbpp.org. Liberal think tank that analyzes how economic policies, including the ACA, affect individuals and state and federal budgets.

Families USA, 1201 New York Ave., N.W., Suite 1100, Washington, DC 20005; 202-628-3030; www.familiesusa.org. Liberal consumer-advocacy group that is tracking the progress and effects of the ACA's rollout.

Health Affairs Blog, http://healthaffairs.org/blog. Blog run by an academic journal covering health policy that presents a range of opinion on the ACA.

Healthcare.gov, U.S. Department of Health and Human Services, 200 Independence Ave., S.W., Washington, DC 20201; www.healthcare.gov/law/index.html. Federal government website providing summaries and information about how the ACA is being implemented.

Henry J. Kaiser Family Foundation, Health Reform Source, http://healthreform.kff.org. Website of a nonpartisan foundation that provides information about U.S. health care and the ACA, including a law summary.

Bibliography

Selected Sources

Books

McDonough, John E., *Inside National Health Reform*, California/Milbank Books on Health and the Public, 2011.
A Harvard professor of public health who supports the 2010 Affordable Care Act explains its background and why he believes it will improve American health.

Starr, Paul, *Remedy and Reaction: The Peculiar American Struggle over Health Care Reform*, Yale University Press, 2011.
A Princeton professor of sociology and public affairs chronicles legislative attempts to overhaul the U.S. health-care system over the past three decades and the vested interests of health-care practitioners, insurers and the public that have made those attempts so difficult.

Turner, Grace-Marie, James C. Capretta, Thomas P. Miller and Robert E. Moffit, *Why ObamaCare Is Wrong for America: How the New Health Care Law Drives Up Costs, Puts Government in Charge of Your Decisions, and Threatens Your Constitutional Rights*, Broadside Books, 2011.
Analysts from the free-market-oriented think tanks Galen Institute (Turner) and American Enterprise Institute argue that the Affordable Care Act (ACA) relies on government regulation rather than market competition to address health-system problems and say alternative approaches would allow consumer choice to determine how the health care market develops.

Articles

Keck, Anthony, "South Carolina's View: The Affordable Care Act's Medicaid Expansion Is the Wrong Approach," *Health Affairs Blog*, Sept. 6, 2012, http://healthaffairs.org/blog/2012/09/06/south-carolinas-view-the-affordable-care-acts-medicaid-expansion-is-the-wrong-approach.
The director of South Carolina's Medicaid program argues that eliminating waste in the medical system and changing how health care providers are reimbursed can help his state provide care to more poor people than by accepting federal funds under the ACA to expand Medicaid.

Rau, Jordan, "Medicare to Penalize 2,211 Hospitals for Excess Readmissions," *Kaiser Health News*, Aug. 13, 2012, www.kaiserhealthnews.org/Stories/2012/August/13/medicare-hospitals-readmissions-penalties.aspx.
As ACA provisions aimed at trimming ineffective health care spending and improving care quality take effect, more than 2,000 hospitals will lose some Medicare payments because too many of their elderly patients were readmitted for conditions that could have been prevented during their hospital stay. ACA supporters argue that such penalties prevent hospitals from profiting from readmissions and protect patients from ineffective care. But hospitals that serve low-income neighborhoods contend they're being unfairly penalized because their patient populations tend to need more care than do wealthier people.

Reinhardt, Uwe E., "Health Care: Solidarity vs. Rugged Individualism," *Economix blogs*, *The New York Times*, June 29, 2012, http://economix.blogs.nytimes.com/2012/06/29/health-care-solidarity-vs-rugged-individualism.
A Princeton University professor of economics describes the differences between what he calls the European "social-solidarity" approach to health care and the American "libertarian" approach and why he considers the European view more practical.

Reports and Studies

"The Affordable Care Act: A Brief Summary," National Conference of State Legislatures, March 2011, www.ncsl.org/portals/1/documents/health/HRACA.pdf.
A nonpartisan group that provides information to and about state governments offers a plain-language summary of the 2010 health-care law.

Hahn, Jim, and Christopher M. Davis, "The Independent Payment Advisory Board," Congressional Research Service, March 12, 2012, http://assets.opencrs.com/rpts/R41511_20120312.pdf.
Analysts from Congress' nonpartisan research office explain the workings of the ACA's highly controversial expert board that will develop payment and care-delivery changes to trim Medicare costs.

Lunder, Erika K., and Jennifer Staman, "NFIB v. Sebelius: Constitutionality of the Individual Mandate," Congressional Research Service, Sept. 3, 2012, www.fas.org/sgp/crs/misc/R42698.pdf.
Lawyers at Congress' nonpartisan research arm explain the Supreme Court's ruling upholding the 2010 Affordable Care Act's requirement that individuals buy health insurance.

Smith, Mark, Robert Saunders, Leigh Stuckhardt and J. Michael McGinnis, eds., "Best Care at Lower Cost: The Path to Continuously Learning Health Care in America," Institute of Medicine, September 2012, www.nap.edu/catalog.php?record_id=13444.
Experts on improving health care quality say 30 cents of every dollar in health care spending is wasted on useless services. To stem soaring medical costs, the United States should pay medical practitioners based on health outcomes rather than "per service rendered," they contend. Quick adoption of information technology also would help keep doctors up to date on which treatments are supported by science and on patients' medical histories, they also say.

The Next Step:

Additional Articles from Current Periodicals

Cost

Berwick, Donald M., "Why Obamacare Works," *The Washington Post*, June 22, 2012, p. A17, www.washingtonpost.com/opinions/putting-health-care-on-the-right-track/2012/06/21/gJQAtBGltV_story.html.

The Affordable Care Act (ACA) reduces health care costs by providing better care and promoting better health, says a former administrator of the Centers for Medicare and Medicaid Services.

Calmes, Jackie, "Patients Would Pay More If Romney Restores Medicare Savings, Analysts Say," *The New York Times*, Aug. 22, 2012, p. A18, www.nytimes.com/2012/08/22/us/politics/costs-seen-in-romneys-medicare-savings-plan.html?pagewanted=all.

If the ACA is repealed, $716 billion in potential Medicare savings would be lost and elderly Americans would pay more for health care, according to analysts at the American Institutes for Research.

Norquist, Grover, "With a Gavel Bang, Obamacare Is Obamatax," *The Washington Times*, July 5, 2012, p. B1, www.washingtontimes.com/news/2012/jul/4/with-a-gavel-bang-obamacare-is-obamatax/?page=all.

President Obama's health care law was supposed to reduce health insurance costs, but it imposes six taxes on Americans who are already insured, says the president of Americans for Tax Reform.

Medicaid

Levey, Noam N., "Medical Plan for Poor Is Targeted for Cuts," *Los Angeles Times*, July 31, 2012, p. A1, www.latimes.com/news/nationworld/nation/la-na-medicaid-rollback-20120731,0,1410769.story.

Republican critics of Medicaid hope to shrink the program if their party wins the presidential election.

Lyon, John, "Beebe Says He Fully Supports Medicaid Expansion," *Arkansas News*, Sept. 11, 2012, arkansasnews.com/sections/news/arkansas/beebe-says-he-fully-supports-medicaid-expansion.html.

Gov. Mike Beebe, D-Ark., says he favors expanding Medicaid under the federal Affordable Care Act and will seek legislative support.

Sharockman, Aaron, "Rick Scott Says Medicaid Expansion Will Cost State $1.9 Billion," *Tampa Bay Times*, July 2, 2012.

Gov. Rick Scott, R-Fla., says his state will not expand its Medicaid program because doing so would cost an additional $1.9 billion annually.

Supreme Court

Burdick, James, "Universal Care on the Horizon," *The Baltimore Sun*, July 13, 2012, p. A19, articles.baltimoresun.com/2012-07-12/news/bs-ed-universal-coverage-20120712_1_health-care-affordable-care-act-universal-coverage.

The Supreme Court ruling in favor of Obama's health care law puts the United States on a positive path toward universal coverage, says a Johns Hopkins professor of surgery.

Grant, David, "Why Republicans See a Loss in the Supreme Court as a Win at the Polls," *The Christian Science Monitor*, June 28, 2012, www.csmonitor.com/USA/DC-Decoder/2012/0628/Why-Republicans-see-a-loss-in-the-Supreme-Court-as-a-win-at-the-polls.

The Supreme Court's decision to uphold health care reform gives Republicans another opportunity to call for its repeal leading up to the November elections.

Kersten, Katherine, "Obamacare Is a Disaster, So, No, the Fight Isn't Over," *Star Tribune* (Minneapolis), July 1, 2012, p. OP3.

Flaws in Obama's health care law ensure that battles over medical care will continue well past the Supreme Court decision, says a fellow at the Center of the American Experiment, a conservative think tank in Minneapolis.

Kopicki, Allison, "Americans Split on Health Ruling," *The New York Times*, July 4, 2012, p. A13, query.nytimes.com/gst/fullpage.html?res=9D00E1DA153DF937A35754C0A9649D8B63.

Americans are divided over the Supreme Court's ruling on health care reform, as they have been since the law was enacted in 2010.

Citing *CQ Researcher*

Sample formats for citing these reports in a bibliography include the ones listed below. Preferred styles and formats vary, so please check with your instructor or professor.

MLA Style

Jost, Kenneth. "Remembering 9/11," CQ Researcher 2 Sept. 2011: 701-732.

APA Style

Jost, K. (2011, September 2). Remembering 9/11. *CQ Researcher, 9*, 701-732.

Chicago Style

Jost, Kenneth. "Remembering 9/11." *CQ Researcher*, September 2, 2011, 701-732.

CQ Researcher

Published by CQ Press, an Imprint of SAGE Publications, Inc.

www.cqresearcher.com

Supreme Court Controversies

Has Chief Justice Roberts led an activist court?

The Supreme Court opens a new term on Oct. 1 with a major affirmative action case from the University of Texas set for argument the next week. Chief Justice John G. Roberts Jr. is starting his eighth year on a court that is divided on many issues between five generally conservative Republican appointees and four liberal Democratic appointees. Court watchers are still debating the implications of Roberts' surprising vote in late June to join the liberal bloc in upholding President Obama's controversial health care law. Despite that decision, liberal critics continue to accuse the Roberts Court of political decision making, judicial activism and a pro-business orientation. The court's defenders say the justices are acting without regard to politics and following judicial restraint. Besides the affirmative action case, the justices may also tackle marriage equality and voting rights cases before the term ends next June.

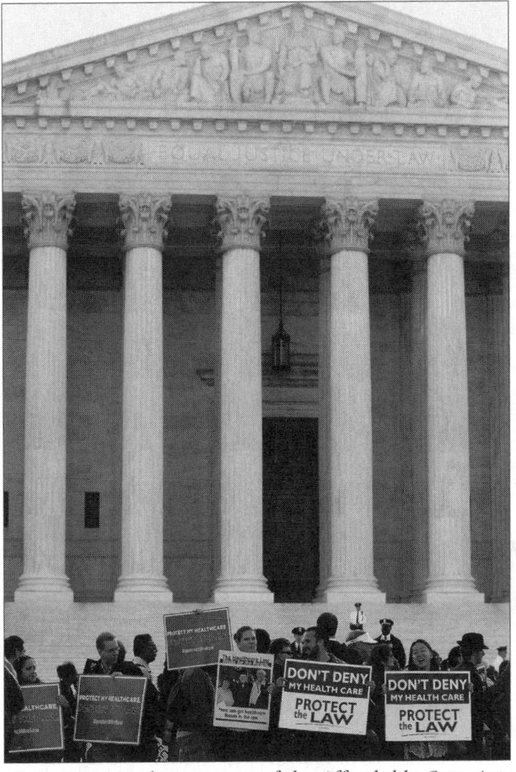

Supporters and opponents of the Affordable Care Act demonstrate at the Supreme Court on March 26, 2012. The court's surprise decision to uphold the health care law on June 28 — with Chief Justice Roberts voting with the court's liberal bloc — focused new attention on the high court.

INSIDE THIS REPORT

THE ISSUES 815
BACKGROUND 824
CHRONOLOGY 825
CURRENT SITUATION 831
AT ISSUE........................833
OUTLOOK 835
BIBLIOGRAPHY 838
THE NEXT STEP 839

CQ Researcher • Sept. 28, 2012 • www.cqresearcher.com
Volume 22, Number 34 • Pages 813-840

Los Angeles | London | New Delhi Singapore | Washington DC

RECIPIENT OF SOCIETY OF PROFESSIONAL JOURNALISTS AWARD FOR EXCELLENCE ◆ AMERICAN BAR ASSOCIATION SILVER GAVEL AWARD

Supreme Court Controversies

The Issues

815 • Has the Roberts Court based decisions on the justices' political views?
• Is the Roberts Court biased in favor of business interests?
• Has the Roberts Court engaged in judicial activism?

Background

824 **Political Target**
Slavery and social and economic reforms roiled the court in the 19th century.

828 **Partisan Fights**
Bitter confirmation battles were frequent in the late 20th century.

829 **Roberts' Court?**
Conservatives and liberals have traded victories.

Current Situation

831 **'Hefty' Docket**
The new term begins with several important cases.

832 **Vanishing Issue?**
The court is getting little attention on the campaign trail.

Outlook

835 **Watershed Term?**
Scholars doubt the court will temper its conservative instincts on the upcoming affirmative action case and other major issues.

Sidebars and Graphics

816 **Meet the Roberts Court**
Justices share Ivy League credentials but are ideologically divided.

818 **Key Roberts Court Decisions**
Issues range from gun control to campaign spending to Guantánamo.

820 **Major Cases Before the Supreme Court**
Thirty-one cases are scheduled for oral arguments in October, November and December, including a major affirmative action case.

823 **Key Decisions Sway Views of High Court**
The public's assessments have hit peaks and valleys since 1985.

825 **Chronology**
Key events since 2000.

826 **Use of Race Challenged in University Admissions**
Justice Kennedy could hold key to Texas decision.

833 **At Issue**
Should the Supreme Court prohibit racial preferences in university admissions?

For Further Research

837 **For More Information**
Organizations to contact.

838 **Bibliography**
Selected sources used.

839 **The Next Step**
Additional articles.

839 **Citing *CQ Researcher***
Sample bibliography formats.

Cover: Getty Images/Chip Somodevilla

CQ Researcher

Sept. 28, 2012
Volume 22, Number 34

Managing Editor: Thomas J. Billitteri
tjb@cqpress.com

Assistant Managing Editor: Kathy Koch
kkoch@cqpress.com

Senior Contributing Editor: Thomas J. Colin
tcolin@cqpress.com

Associate Editor: Kenneth Jost

Staff Writer: Marcia Clemmitt

Contributing Writers: Peter Katel, Barbara Mantel, Jennifer Weeks

Senior Project Editor: Olu B. Davis

Assistant Editor: Darrell Dela Rosa

Fact Checker: Michelle Harris

Los Angeles | London | New Delhi
Singapore | Washington DC

An Imprint of SAGE Publications, Inc.

Vice President and Editorial Director, Higher Education Group:
Michele Sordi

Director, Online Publishing:
Todd Baldwin

CQ Researcher (ISSN 1056-2036) is printed on acid-free paper. Published weekly, except: (March wk. 5) (May wk. 4) (July wk. 1) (Aug. wks. 3, 4) (Nov. wk. 4) and (Dec. wks. 3, 4). Published by SAGE Publications, Inc., 2455 Teller Rd., Thousand Oaks, CA 91320. Annual full-service subscriptions start at $1,054. For pricing, call 1-800-834-9020. To purchase a *CQ Researcher* report in print or electronic format (PDF), visit www.cqpress.com or call 866-427-7737. Single reports start at $15. Bulk purchase discounts and electronic-rights licensing are also available. Periodicals postage paid at Thousand Oaks, California, and at additional mailing offices. POSTMASTER: Send address changes to *CQ Researcher*, 2300 N St., N.W., Suite 800, Washington, DC 20037.

Supreme Court Controversies

BY KENNETH JOST

THE ISSUES

Abby Fisher graduated from Louisiana State University in May with a business degree and landed a job as a financial analyst in Austin in her home state of Texas. But LSU was not Fisher's first choice for college.

Back in 2008, Fisher had hoped to enroll at the University of Texas' flagship Austin campus but was turned down — just like more than three-fourths of the 30,000 applicants that year. Fisher's rank in her high school class in Sugar Land, an affluent Houston area suburb, was too low to qualify for automatic admission to UT under a state law guaranteeing slots to all students in the top 10 percent of their class. And her grades and test scores were significantly below the 3.5 "academic index" level needed for admission under the university's scoring system.

Barack Obama takes the oath of office as president from Chief Justice John G. Roberts Jr. at the Capitol on Jan. 20, 2009. Roberts presides over a Supreme Court that is sharply divided on legal and judicial philosophies. The court has handed down several controversial rulings, including upholding the Affordable Care Act and striking down campaign finance laws, during his seven years leading the court. A major affirmative action case tops the list of issues facing the justices in the new term beginning Oct. 1.

Unlike other unsuccessful applicants, Fisher turned her rejection into a federal court case that has now reached the U.S. Supreme Court. Supported by a longtime opponent of racial preferences, Fisher, who is white, filed a suit in April 2008 challenging UT's use of race as a factor in admissions decisions. Two lower courts rejected her challenge, but the high court agreed on Feb. 21, 2012, to hear the suit. The action set up a showdown on a legal issue that has divided the justices and the nation for more than 40 years. [1] (*See sidebar, p. 826; "At Issue," p. 833.*)

Fisher's case, to be argued Oct. 10, will help provide a high-profile opening for the Supreme Court's new term, which begins on Oct. 1 — the traditional First Monday in October. When the justices convene that day, it will be the first time for the nine to be together in public since the dramatic end-of-term decision to uphold President Obama's health care reform plan. [2]

The June 28 ruling to uphold the Affordable Care Act, *National Federation of Independent Business v. Sebelius*, came with Americans focused on the Supreme Court more intensely than at any time since the court effectively decided the 2000 presidential election in the still controversial decision *Bush v. Gore*. It also came as President George W. Bush's choice to lead the court, John G. Roberts Jr., ended his seventh year as chief justice of the United States.

The Roberts Court has made its share of waves in legal and political waters since Roberts assumed the court's center seat on Oct. 3, 2005 — at age 50, the youngest chief justice in more than 200 years.* Seven years later, Roberts appears to have aged hardly at all. All but invariably, Roberts enters the courtroom with a half-smile on his face and an active glint in his eyes. He presides with a light touch, cracks jokes occasionally and admonishes lawyers or his colleagues without ever raising his voice. [3]

Yet Roberts is merely the first among equals on a court that is sharply divided on legal and judicial philosophies. Roberts joins four other justices appointed by Republican presidents to form a conservative majority on some of the most closely divided issues. Four justices appointed by Democratic presidents — including Obama's two appointees, Sonia Sotomayor and Elena Kagan — form a liberal bloc that winds up in dissent in most of the court's 5-4 decisions. The balance of power often rests with Justice Anthony M. Kennedy, the moderate conservative appointed by President Ronald Reagan in 1987 after the Democratic-controlled Senate rejected Reagan's first choice for the vacancy: the doggedly conservative Robert Bork. (*See justices' biographies, p. 816.*)

Until the health care ruling, conservatives had mostly warm feelings about the Roberts Court's general course. "It's been largely positive," says Curt Levey, president of the Committee for Justice, a conservative court-watching advocacy group. Levey cites decisions striking down campaign finance laws on First Amendment grounds, limiting use of race in pupil assignments and cutting

* John Marshall was 45 years old when he became chief justice on Jan. 31, 1801.

Meet the Roberts Court

Justices share Ivy League credentials but are ideological opposites.

The Roberts Court consists of five justices appointed by Republican presidents and four by Democrats. Eight were federal appeals courts judges at the time of their appointments; Elena Kagan was solicitor general of the United States. All are graduates of Ivy League law schools. Here are brief biographies of the justices showing their dates and places of birth, education, Senate confirmation dates and votes and selected major opinions since September 2005.

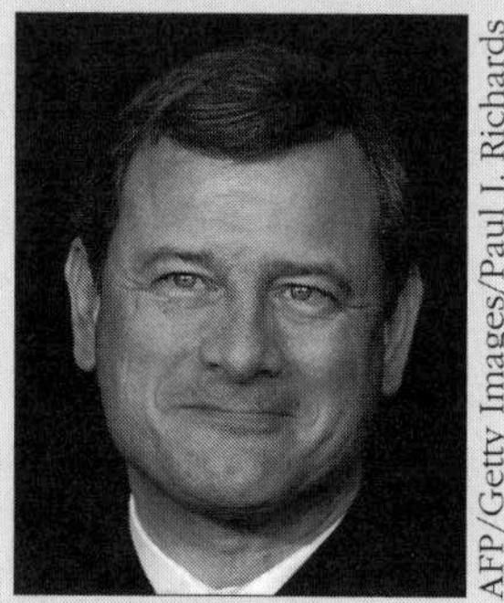
AFP/Getty Images/Paul J. Richards

John G. Roberts Jr., chief justice: born Jan. 27, 1955, Buffalo, N.Y.; Harvard, Harvard Law School; appointed by President George W. Bush; confirmed Sept. 29, 2005 (78-22). Major opinions: *Parents Involved in Community Schools v. Seattle School District* (school integration); *Arizona Free Enterprise v. Bennett* (campaign finance); *National Federation of Independent Business v. Sebelius* (Affordable Care Act).

AFP/Getty Images/Paul J. Richards

Antonin Scalia, associate justice born March 11, 1936, Trenton, N.J.; Georgetown, Harvard Law School; appointed by President Ronald Reagan; confirmed Sept. 17, 1986 (98-0). Major opinions: *Wal-Mart Stores v. Dukes* (class actions); *Boumediene v. Bush* (dissent, Guantánamo); *District of Columbia v. Heller* (gun rights); *Arizona v. United States* (dissent, immigration).

AFP/Getty Images/Paul J. Richards

Anthony McLeod Kennedy, associate justice: born July 23, 1936, Sacramento, Calif.; Stanford, Harvard Law School; appointed by President Ronald Reagan; confirmed Feb. 3, 1988 (97-0). Major opinions: *Gonzales v. Carhart* (abortion); *Boumediene v. Bush* (Guantánamo); *Citizens United v. Federal Election Commission* (campaign finance); *Arizona v. United States* (immigration).

AFP/Getty Images/Paul J. Richards

Clarence Thomas, associate justice: born June 23, 1948, Pin Point, Ga.; Holy Cross, Yale Law School; appointed by President George H. W. Bush; confirmed Oct. 15, 1991 (52-48). Major opinions: *Hamdan v. Rumsfeld* (dissent, Guantánamo); *McDonald v. Chicago* (concurrence, gun rights).

Getty Images/Mark Wilson

Ruth Joan Bader Ginsburg, associate justice: born March 15, 1933, Brooklyn, N.Y.; Cornell, Columbia Law School; appointed by President Bill Clinton; confirmed Aug. 3, 1993 (96-3). Major opinions: *Gonzales v. Carhart* (dissent, abortion); *Ledbetter v. Goodyear Tire & Rubber Co.* (dissent, job discrimination); *Wal-Mart Stores v. Dukes* (dissent, class actions).

back on criminal procedure protections for defendants and suspects.

Offsetting those positives, Levey says, are two trends viewed critically by conservatives. The court has stood still on federalism issues after favorable rulings for states under Roberts' predecessor, Chief Justice William H. Rehnquist. And the court has imposed new limits on criminal sentencing, typically with Roberts in dissent. Levey also acknowledges that the favorable trend has been "overshadowed" by the ruling to leave the Affordable Care Act almost completely intact.

Liberal groups find much to pan and little to praise. Nan Aron, president of the progressive Alliance for Justice, criticizes the court for favoring "a limited role for the federal government," adopting "conservative views on social issues" and "tilting the court in a pro-corporate direction."

"We have seen him shift the court in a pro-corporate direction at the expense of everyday people," says Aron, after noting that the alliance opposed Roberts' confirmation. "There is a consistent theme in his opinions, a predisposition to rule in favor of large corporations."

Academic experts differ along ideological lines in assessing the Roberts

AFP/Getty Images/B. Smialowski

Stephen Gerald Breyer, associate justice: born Aug. 15, 1938, San Francisco; Stanford, Magdalen College (Oxford), Harvard Law School; appointed by President Bill Clinton; confirmed July 29, 1994 (87-9). Major opinions: *Parents Involved in Community Schools v. Seattle School District* (dissent, school integration); *McDonald v. Chicago* (dissent, gun rights).

Getty Images/Mark Wilson

Sonia Maria Sotomayor, associate justice: born June 25, 1954, Bronx, N.Y.; Princeton, Yale Law School; appointed by President Barack Obama; confirmed Aug. 6, 2009 (68-31). Major opinion: *Southern Union Co. v. United States* (criminal fines).

AFP/Getty Images/Paul J. Richards

Samuel Anthony Alito, Jr., associate justice: born April 1, 1950, Trenton, N.J.; Princeton, Yale Law School; appointed by President George W. Bush; confirmed Jan. 31, 2006 (58-42). Major opinions: *Ledbetter v. Goodyear Tire & Rubber Co.* (job discrimination); *McDonald v. Chicago* (plurality, gun rights); *Miller v. Alabama* (dissent, criminal sentencing).

AFP/Getty Images/Tim Sloan

Elena Kagan, associate justice: born April 28, 1960, New York, N.Y.; Princeton, Oxford, Harvard Law School; appointed by President Barack Obama; confirmed Aug. 5, 2010 (63-37). Major opinions: *Arizona Free Enterprise v. Bennett* (dissent, campaign finance); *Miller v. Alabama* (criminal sentencing).

— Kenneth Jost

Court's decisions even if they agree in describing the court's general orientation. "Overall, the Roberts Court has been what we expected," says Erwin Chemerinsky, dean of the University of California-Irvine Law School and an outspoken liberal critic of many of the court's decisions. "When the court's ideologically divided, the conservative position prevails much more than the liberal position."

Jonathan Adler, a professor at Case Western Reserve University School of Law in Cleveland who has been affiliated with conservative organizations, agrees. "It is a moderately conservative court," Adler says. "On most issues, the court is going to lean in a conservative direction." (*See decisions, p. 818.*)

To some extent, however, the term that ended on June 28 belied that pattern. [4] In addition to upholding Obama's health care law, the court also cheered liberal groups with a decision to strike down several provisions of Arizona's widely copied crackdown on undocumented immigrants. Kennedy wrote the majority opinion in the case, *Arizona v. United States*, joined by Roberts and three liberal justices. Immigrant-rights groups were disappointed, however, that the court unanimously left standing the most controversial provision in the Arizona law: the so-called "show me your papers" section. That provision instructs state and local police to conduct immigration status checks during an arrest or stop if they suspect the individual is in the country illegally. [5]

Civil liberties and criminal defense groups also counted several victories during the term, including a final-week decision written by Kagan to bar mandatory life-without-parole sentences for juvenile murderers. Earlier, Kennedy had written companion decisions that allow defendants to challenge criminal convictions if they reject a favorable plea bargain based on bad or inadequate advice from their lawyers. Kennedy also wrote a decision striking down a federal law, the Stolen Valor Act, making it a crime to lie about having received military medals. The ruling continued the Roberts Court's general pattern of pro-free speech decisions.

Business groups fared well during the term, but the victories came in relatively minor cases. A year earlier, however, the headline decision of the term was the 5-4 ruling, split along ideological lines, that threw out a broad sex discrimination suit against Walmart, the nation's largest private employer. The ruling established new require-

Key Roberts Court Decisions

Issues range from gun rights to campaign spending to Guantánamo. Most of these decisions came on 5-4 votes reflecting the court's conservative-liberal split.

	Name of Case	Vote	Holding
2006	*Hudson v. Michigan*	5-4	Violation of knock-and-announce rule does not require suppressing evidence
	Hamdan v. Rumsfeld	5-3	Military tribunals for Guantánamo detainees violate military law, Geneva Conventions
2007	*Gonzales v. Carhart*	5-4	Upholds federal "partial-birth" abortion ban
	Ledbetter v. Goodyear Tire & Rubber Co.	5-4	Requires employees to file pay bias complaint within statutory deadline after last intentional act of discrimination; rejects "paycheck accrual rule"
	FEC v. Wisconsin Right to Life	5-4	Eases law limiting pre-election "issue-advertising" by unions, corporations
	Parents Involved in Community Schools v. Seattle School Dist. No. 1	5-4	Limits use of race to assign students to promote racial diversity; permits some other "general policies"
2008	*Boumediene v. Bush*	5-4	Strikes down Military Commissions Act; extends habeas corpus to Guantánamo detainees
	Kennedy v. Louisiana	5-4	Bars death penalty for child rape
	Davis v. FEC	5-4	Throws out "Millionaire's Amendment" in campaign finance reform law
	District of Columbia v. Heller	5-4	Strikes down D.C. gun ban
2009	*Ricci v. DeStefano*	5-4	Requires employers to have a "substantial basis" to fear disparate-impact liability before adopting race-conscious policies to avoid liability
	United States v. Herring	5-4	Limits use of exclusionary rule to reckless/intentional mistakes by police
	Northwest Austin Municipal Utility District No. 1 v. Holder	8-1	Expands eligibility for municipalities to "bail out" of preclearance requirement in Voting Rights Act; constitutional challenge left unresolved

ments for class actions — mass lawsuits favored by lawyers representing consumers and workers but feared by attorneys representing big companies. A second ruling that year allowed companies to enforce arbitration agreements to prevent customers from transforming individual complaints into class actions. [6]

The dramatic ruling in the health care case on June 28 was followed by an extraordinary leaked account from inside the court that Roberts had initially voted to strike down the law but changed his mind midway through the opinion-writing process. CBS's chief legal correspondent Jan Crawford, who has good sources in Republican and conservative circles, attributed her July 1 scoop to "two sources with specific knowledge of the deliberations." Kennedy conducted a "relentless" effort to bring Roberts back around, according to Crawford. The dissent jointly authored by Kennedy and three other conservatives — Antonin Scalia, Clarence Thomas and Samuel A. Alito Jr. — reflected their anger with Roberts over his decision, Crawford reported. [7]

The University of Texas affirmative action case is now being eyed as a likely headline-grabber for the court's new term. "Universities all over the nation are looking at this case," says Dean Sparlin, a lawyer representing the Association for Affirmative Action, which filed a brief supporting the university. Roger Clegg, president and general counsel of the Center for Equal Opportunity, which filed a brief supporting Fisher's position, says he is "cautiously optimistic" that the court will rule flatly that racial preferences in college and university admissions are unconstitutional. (*See "At Issue," p. 833.*)

The court's calendar includes several other closely watched cases, including one to be argued on the opening day that tests federal courts' jurisdiction over suits for human rights violations committed in other countries. And two other major issues are waiting in the wings: gay marriage and the federal Voting Rights Act. (*See calendar, p. 820.*)

Year	Name of Case	Vote	Holding
2010	*Citizens United v. FEC*	5-4	Permits corporations to spend own money on political campaigns
	Berghuis v. Thompkins	5-4	Requires suspect to claim right of silence to suppress later incriminatory statement
	McDonald v. Chicago	5-4	Applies Second Amendment gun rights to state and local governments
2011	*Brown v. Plata*	5-4	Orders California prisons to reduce overcrowding to improve health services
	Wal-Mart Stores, Inc. v. Dukes	5-4	Rejects class action sex discrimination suit against Wal-Mart
	Arizona Free Enterprise Club v. Bennett	5-4	Strikes down "matching-fund" provision in Arizona public campaign financing law
2012	*United States v. Jones*	9-0	Defines extended GPS tracking of suspect's vehicle as search for Fourth Amendment purposes
	FCC v. Fox Television Stations, Inc.	8-0	Sets aside FCC order against TV networks for fleeting expletives, adult nudity
	Southern Union Co. v. United States	6-3	Requires jury finding beyond reasonable doubt to find facts to raise criminal fine
	Miller v. Alabama	5-4	Bars mandatory life-without-parole sentence for juvenile murderers
	Arizona v. United States	5-3	Strikes three parts of state immigration law; allows immigration status checks (8-0)
	National Federation of Independent Business v. Sebelius	5-4	Upholds Affordable Care Act; narrows enforcement of Medicaid expansion (7-2)

Source: Kenneth Jost, Supreme Court Yearbook *(annual series)*

On gay marriage, the justices are being asked to review decisions that strike down on equal protection grounds the federal Defense of Marriage Act, which bars marriage-like benefits under federal law to same-sex couples even if they are legally married in their states. Separately, opponents of gay marriage are seeking to reinstate California's Proposition 8 that barred recognition of same-sex couples. The federal appeals court for California ruled the 2008 initiative unconstitutional earlier this year. [8]

The challenges to the Voting Rights Act focus on section 5 of the 1965 law. It requires states and localities with a history of discrimination in voting to "preclear" any change in election procedure with the U.S. Department of Justice or a federal court in Washington. Two municipalities — Kinston, N.C., and Shelby County (suburban Birmingham), Ala. — have appeals pending at the Supreme Court challenging the provision as an improper intrusion on state sovereignty. [9]

As the justices prepare to convene for the new term, here are some of the competing assessments of the Roberts Court being heard:

Has the Roberts Court based decisions on the justices' political views?

The Supreme Court split the difference on the hot-button issue of immigration on June 25 by striking down parts of the Arizona law while upholding the "show me your papers" provisions. But in a sharply worded dissent that he emphasized by summarizing it from the bench, Justice Antonin Scalia single-mindedly defended the state's right to control its own borders. For good measure, he added a tart criticism of Obama's decision 10 days earlier to grant temporary status to immigrants under age 30 brought to the United States as children.

Critics denounced Scalia's comments on Obama's actions as political. Jeffrey Rosen, a professor at George Washington University Law School in Washington, said Scalia "is sounding more like a conservative blogger or Fox News pundit than a justice." Scalia, in television interviews, dismissed the criticism. Appearing on "Fox News Sunday" a month later, Scalia said he was merely making the point that "Arizona is being prevented from enforcing federal immigration law." [10]

Scalia's dissenting bench slap at Obama came after a succession of other high-profile rulings in which the court had rejected the administration's

Continued on p. 821

Major Cases Before the Supreme Court

The Supreme Court opens the 2012-2013 term with 31 cases scheduled for oral arguments during three two-week sessions that begin on Oct. 1, Oct. 29 and Nov. 26. Here are some of the major upcoming cases:

Case	Date of Oral Arguments	Issue
Kiobel v. Royal Dutch Petroleum Co.	Oct. 1	Federal court jurisdiction over suits for human rights violations abroad
Ryan v. Gonzales; Tibbals v. Carter	Oct. 9	Right to mental competency for death row inmates in habeas corpus proceedings
Fisher v. University of Texas at Austin	Oct. 10	Constitutionality of University of Texas' use of race in undergraduate admissions
Clapper v. Amnesty International USA	Oct. 29	Standing for plaintiffs challenging global terrorism wiretapping program
Florida v. Jardines	Oct. 31	Use of drug-sniffing dog at front door of house to justify search
Florida v. Harris	Oct. 31	Use of drug-sniffing dogs' "alerts" for probable cause for vehicle search
Comcast v. Behrend	Nov. 5	Evidence required for availability of class-wide damages to certify class action
Amgen Inc. v. Connecticut Retirement Plans and Trust Funds	Nov. 5	Evidence required to certify securities fraud class action based on "fraud-on-the-market" theory
Vance v. Ball State University	Nov. 26	Supervisory liability in hostile work environment suits
Decker v. Northwest Environmental Defense Center, Georgia-Pacific West v. Northwest Environmental Defense Center	Dec. 3	Environmental Protection Agency jurisdiction over channeled runoff from forest logging roads

Major cases awaiting the justices' decisions whether to grant review:

Case	Issue
National Organization for Marriage, Inc. v. McKee	Constitutionality of campaign finance regulations on nonprofit organizations participating in ballot measure campaigns
Mount Holly v. Mt. Holly Gardens Citizens in Action	Liability under Fair Housing Act for unintentional ("disparate impact") discrimination
Bipartisan Legal Advisory Group of the United States House of Representatives v. Gill; Department of Health and Human Services v. Massachusetts; Office of Personnel Management v. Golinski; Windsor v. United States	Constitutionality of section 3 of federal Defense of Marriage Act (DOMA)
Nix v. Holder; Shelby County v. Holder	Constitutionality of 2006 reauthorization of section 5 of federal Voting Rights Act (preclearance provision)
Hollingsworth v. Perry	Constitutionality of California's Proposition 8 defining marriage as union between a man and a woman.
Maryland v. King	Constitutionality of state law allowing collection of DNA samples from arrestees

Compiled by Rob Silverblatt, Niccolo Barber

Continued from p. 819

legal position. In the most dramatic instance, the court in the *Citizens United* decision in January 2010 struck down a major provision of a federal campaign finance law defended by the then solicitor general, Kagan. The ruling opened the door to unlimited campaign spending by corporations and unions. Six days afterward, Obama criticized the decision in his State of the Union speech, with six of the justices seated below him in the House chamber. Obama said the ruling would open the door to unlimited political spending by foreign corporations. In the television coverage, Justice Samuel A. Alito Jr. could be seen at that point shaking his head and mouthing the words "not true." [11]

Citizens United is one in a series of Roberts Court decisions striking down or narrowing campaign finance laws. The rulings — with Republican appointees Roberts, Scalia, Kennedy, Thomas and Alito in the majority — are widely seen as favoring Republicans to Democrats' disadvantage. *Citizens United* "ensures that corporations can give unlimited amounts of money," says Alliance for Justice president Aron. The dissenters in the 5-4 ruling included three Democratic appointees — Ruth Bader Ginsburg, Stephen G. Breyer and Sotomayor — and the liberal Republican-appointed justice, John Paul Stevens. Kagan was nominated to succeed the retiring Stevens four months later.

Case Western's Adler is one of many experts who defend the campaign finance decisions at the same time that they minimize their impact. "A lot of people overstate the implications," Adler says. He goes on to deny any partisan motivation on the justices' part. "There are easier ways to explain the pattern of the court's decisions that don't require impugning motivations or suggesting anything other than fealty to their judicial oaths," he says.

Others on the political right agree. "It's not being political to say that different theories of constitutional interpretation correlate to the party of the president who appoints the justices," says Ilya Shapiro, a senior fellow in constitutional studies at the libertarian Cato Institute and editor in chief of *Cato Supreme Court Review*. Levey with the Committee for Justice also maintains that the criticism is unfair because the same groups that praise other rights-expanding decisions criticize rulings in the opposite direction. "When conservatives try to rein that in, it's political," Levey says. "I think it's a very, very one-sided term."

Some critics of the Roberts Court also reject the description of the court as political. "I'm very hesitant to assume that the court acts out of partisan political motives," says Steven Shapiro, national legal director of the American Civil Liberties Union (ACLU). "The majority is conservative, and that ideology more often lines up with Republicans than with Democrats. But I don't think of the court as overtly political in the way others might."

Chemerinsky of UC-Irvine echoes that view. "The court's not political at all in the sense of lobbying, trading votes or responding to pressure," he says. He adds that the court has always been "ideological," dating to its earliest days. But he says the Roberts Court differs from those of previous years in one respect: "The ideology [of the justices] exactly corresponds to the political party of the president who appointed them."

In fact, until recently presidents of both parties have appointed ideologically diverse justices to the court. Republican Dwight D. Eisenhower appointed liberal justices Earl Warren and William J. Brennan Jr. as well as the moderate conservatives John Marshall Harlan and Potter Stewart. Democrat John F. Kennedy named Byron R. White, who took conservative positions on many issues, as well as the solidly liberal Arthur J. Goldberg.

For his part, however, Scalia, a Reagan appointee, finds actions by today's court completely unsurprising. "I don't think the court is political at all," he said on the "Fox News Sunday" broadcast. The current alignment, he continued, "doesn't show they are voting politics. It shows that they had been selected because of their judicial philosophy.

"The Republicans have been looking for, you know, originalist and textualist and restrained judges for 50 years. And the Democrats have been looking for the opposite, for people who believe in *Roe v. Wade*. Why should it be a surprise that after, you know, assiduously trying to get people with these philosophies, they end up with [these] philosophies?" [12]

Is the Roberts Court biased in favor of business interests?

Business groups cheered when the Supreme Court blocked a major sex-discrimination suit against Walmart later that month. But when the term ended in late June, the U.S. Chamber of Commerce counted up only 12 wins in the 21 cases in which it participated. Robin Conrad, executive director of the National Chamber Litigation Center, said the middling record disproved what she called "the silly myth" of a pro-business Supreme Court.

A year later, the Chamber had a better record: eight wins and no outright defeats. Neil Weare, senior counsel of the consumer-oriented Constitutional Accountability Center, said the record demonstrated "the roaring success" that the Chamber has enjoyed throughout the Roberts Court period: 60 wins out of 88 cases, according to the center's count. But Conrad was still poor-mouthing the record. She stressed that the justices had skirted rulings on some of the business group's issues. [13]

Liberal court watchers agree in labeling the Roberts Court pro-business. "This is the most pro-business court since the 1930s," says Chemerinsky, referring to the court that struck down several major laws enacted as part of President Franklin D. Roosevelt's New Deal program. In its compilation, the Constitutional Accountability Center says the Chamber's 68 percent success rate with the Roberts Court is higher than its win-loss records in the final years of either the Burger Court (43 percent) or Rehnquist Court (56 percent).

The Roberts Court "has been a friend to big business," says the ACLU's Shapiro. "The court is sympathetic to the anti-regulatory claims that business brings to the court."

Conservative court watchers are unconvinced. "I think the court is pretty balanced on this," says Levy with the Committee on Justice. "For the crowd that sees the court's job as standing up for the little guy, the court is failing. That's not what I see as the court's role."

Adler acknowledges that the court has taken up somewhat more business-related cases than in the past. Roberts was a successful Supreme Court advocate with a big corporate law firm in Washington for more than a decade before being appointed to the federal appeals court in 2003, and he cheered business groups by hinting in his confirmation hearing that he favored the court's increasing the number of cases it agreed to decide. But Adler thinks business groups' win-loss record is mixed. "Business has gotten very little from this court," Adler says.

The Chamber essentially sat out the past term's two highest-profile cases. It took no position on Arizona's immigration law and argued in the health care case only for striking down the entire law if any parts were ruled invalid. The eight victories came in non-headline cases, but several reflected general themes seen in past Roberts Court rulings.

In two separate rulings, for example, the court favored business interests by invoking the federal preemption doctrine, which blocks states from overriding or interfering with federal regulatory schemes. One decision struck down a California law regulating slaughterhouses as conflicting with federal law; the other barred asbestos-exposure suits in state courts against locomotive manufacturers because of a 1915 federal law. The court's record in previous preemption cases is mixed, but business won several of the more important, including a 5-4 decision in 2011 blocking state court product liability suits against generic drug manufacturers.

The court this year made it somewhat harder for shareholders to sue corporate insiders for profits improperly made on stock trades shortly after new stock offerings. The ruling was in line with other rulings limiting securities litigation, including a 5-3 decision in 2008 that made it harder to sue a company's suppliers or customers for helping it to perpetrate securities fraud.

Employers have fared well in many Roberts Court decisions, including a 5-4 ruling this year that spared drug companies from paying overtime to their sales representatives. Earlier, the court in 2009 had raised the burden of proof for plaintiffs in federal age discrimination suits. And in 2007 the court in the so-called *Ledbetter* case had made it harder for workers to obtain back pay for long-standing equal pay violations. Those two decisions also came on 5-4 votes. Congress effectively overruled the *Ledbetter* decision in the first weeks of Obama's administration. [14]

Business interests also won an important criminal law decision this year with a 6-3 ruling calling for juries, not judges, to make any factual findings needed to raise criminal fines. The ruling, which set aside an $18 million fine for a federal environmental violation, follows a line of other decisions generally strengthening juries' fact-finding roles in criminal cases.

Getty Images/Chip Somodevilla

Lily Ledbetter, a supervisor at a Goodyear tire plant in Gadsden, Ala., sued the firm for paying her less than her male counterparts. In 2006 the Supreme Court rejected her claim, making it harder for workers to obtain back pay for long-standing equal-pay violations. The court's 5-4 decision — one of many Roberts Court rulings seen as pro-business — was effectively overruled by Congress in the first weeks of the Obama administration.

Among the various pro-business rulings, defeats have come mostly in lesser cases. The most significant setback came in 2007 when Kennedy joined the liberal bloc in backing the Environmental Protection Agency's power to regulate so-called greenhouse gases.

Adler acknowledges the court leans against plaintiffs' interests in civil litigation. "The court is less willing to rubber stamp or green light new, creative plaintiffs' theories," he says. But he says the court has not issued any broad ruling limiting punitive damages, a major issue for business groups. "This is not a court that is altering the law in a pro-business direction," he says. "It's much more a status-quo court on business issues than anything else."

Has the Roberts Court engaged in judicial activism?

Early in the days of federal antitrust law, the Supreme Court issued a decision in 1911 that flatly prohibited a manufacturer from dictating the price that retailers could set for its products. The per se rule against "resale price maintenance" stood for nearly a century, untouched by Congress, until 2007 when the Roberts Court voted 5-4 to overrule it.

For the majority, Kennedy said the earlier ruling was poorly reasoned, had come under criticism from economists and others and actually hurt rather than helped competition. Writing for four liberal dissenters, Breyer argued for keeping the precedent. "I do not believe," Breyer wrote, "that the majority has shown new or changed conditions to warrant overruling a decision of such long standing." [15]

Reversals of prior rulings are one practice cited by legal experts as an example of judicial activism. Another are decisions to overturn federal, state or local laws as unconstitutional. Some legal experts also label rulings as activist if a court reaches out to decide an issue despite procedural hurdles or decides a case more broadly than necessary.

Legal experts offer these types of court actions to try to give objective substance to a politically charged term that many insist is simply a pejorative label people use for decisions with which they disagree. "I've long believed that judicial activism is the label we use for the decisions that we don't like," says UC-Irvine's Chemerinsky. The Cato Institute's Shapiro says activism is "an empty term without any meaning."

As Chemerinsky notes, the Roberts Court's decision in *Citizens United* fits the attempt at an objective definition of judicial activism. The court could have decided the case on a narrower ground than it did; in fact, a recent account by legal journalist Jeffrey Toobin of CNN and *The New Yorker* says Roberts favored a narrow ruling but went along with a broader decision favored by the other four conservatives. The decision invalidated a major provision of the Bipartisan Campaign Reform Act, enacted only seven years earlier, and had to

Key Decisions Sway Views of High Court

The public's view of the Supreme Court has hit peaks and valleys over the past three decades (top). Favorability ratings dipped in 2005 after the court allowed local governments to take property and transfer it to another owner for redevelopment. Ratings dipped again amid a slew of conservative decisions in 2007 involving abortion, campaign finance and school integration, and again this summer after the court upheld President Obama's health care law. Favorability was highest in summer 1994, after the court ended its term with no "blockbuster" rulings. Overall, Americans believe the Supreme Court's ideology is "middle of the road," but a significant number of Republicans believe the court is liberal while many Democrats view it as conservative (chart at bottom).

Americans' View of the Supreme Court, 1985-2012

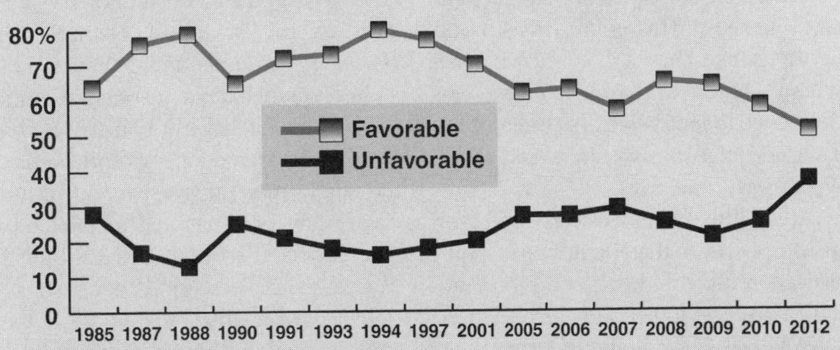

Americans' Perception of the Supreme Court's Ideology, 2012

Ideology	Total	Republicans	Democrats	Independents
Conservative	24%	9%	39%	21%
Middle of the road	41	45	39	41
Liberal	23	36	12	24
Don't know	12	9	10	13

Source: "Obama Holds Lead; Romney Trails on Most Issues," Pew Research Center, July 2012, www.people-press.org/2012/07/12/obama-holds-lead-romney-trails-on-most-issues/

overrule two recent Supreme Court precedents to do so. [16]

The *Citizens United* decision is exhibit No. 1 for Roberts Court critics to use in describing the court as activist. In a critical law review article, Geoffrey Stone, a prominent liberal law professor at the University of Chicago, says the decision represents "an aggressively activist approach." [17] Chemerinsky points to two other high-profile rulings, in 2008 and 2010, that recognized a personal right under the Second Amendment to possess firearms for self-defense in the home. The rulings struck down handgun bans in Washington, D.C., and Chicago. [18]

The ACLU's Shapiro says the activist label applies. "This is an activist court in the sense that it has shown itself willing, ready and able to give less deference to legislative enactments than a version of conservatism would otherwise apply," he says.

Adler, the Case Western professor, insists, however, that the Roberts Court's overall record is less, not more, activist than previous courts as measured by reversals of rulings and laws held unconstitutional. He cites statistics compiled by Supreme Court expert Lee Epstein in 2010 — at the end of the Roberts Court's fifth tem — showing fewer such decisions than the rate for the court during Rehnquist's 19 years as chief justice.

Epstein counted eight reversals of precedents in the Roberts Court's first five years, for an average of about one-and-a-half per year; the Rehnquist Court had 45 reversals in 19 years — more than two per year. Epstein counted 15 Roberts Court rulings declaring laws unconstitutional, or three per year; the Rehnquist Court averaged more than six per year: 120 rulings in 19 years. [19]

"If you're going to label the court as activist, you can't just look at one decision," Adler says today. "You have to look at the overall trend. And if you look at the overall trend, it's doing this less often than its predecessors."

Levey with the Committee for Justice again argues that liberals use the label unfairly in criticizing the Roberts Court. "For years, liberals were viewed as the activists because they were the one who thought that the court should help the Constitution evolve," Levey says. "I think they've tried to change the definition to mean not giving enough deference to the federal government. Conservatives generally favor deference, but conservatives also say it is very much the province of the court to strike down laws that are unconstitutional."

The liberal critique is also undercut by the number of Roberts Court decisions striking down laws that liberal groups called unconstitutional. Adler cites as the strongest example the *Boumediene* decision in 2008 that guaranteed Guantánamo prisoners the right to use federal habeas corpus to challenge their detention. "*Boumediene* is the single most aggressive use of judicial review of a national security measure endorsed by both political branches that we have seen," Adler says. [20]

The court also invalidated state sentencing laws when it barred life-without-parole for juvenile murders this year and outlawed the death penalty for child rape in 2008. And in a series of First Amendment decisions, the court has struck down a California law banning violent video games for minors (2011), a federal statute prohibiting depictions of animal cruelty (2010) and another federal law this year making it a crime to lie about having received military medals.

Adler also says Roberts "likes to save statutes when possible." He notes that Roberts in 2009 helped skirt a constitutional challenge to the federal Voting Rights Act. [21] Roberts' role in upholding the health care law fits that pattern, but the ACLU's Shapiro says it is too soon to know what the ruling signifies for the future. "Whether we are entering a phase two of the Roberts Court, I don't know the answer to that," he says. "Only time will tell." ■

BACKGROUND

Political Target

The Supreme Court was formed in 1789 with its powers undefined and no cases to hear. Through the 19th century the court gained in influence, most significantly by supporting a broad view of federal powers and its own power under Chief Justice John Marshall. The court also became the target of political attacks — notably from abolitionists over the slavery issue before the Civil War and from progressives and organized labor over social and economic reforms at the turn of the 20th century. The court's influence increased through the century along with political attacks, which peaked in response to the mid-century explosion of judicial activism under Chief Justice Earl Warren (1953-1969). [22]

The Constitution listed the kinds of cases federal courts could hear but did not specify the powers they could exercise. The Supreme Court opened its first session in New York City on Feb. 1, 1790, with only three of the six justices present and nothing on the docket. Over the next decade, the court had so little stature that Chief Justice John Jay resigned in 1795 to be governor of New York and refused President John Adams' reappointment in 1800. The post went instead to Marshall, who established the court as a powerful institution during his record 34-year tenure (1801-1835). The Marshall Court's precedent-setting decisions established the court's power to declare an act of Congress unconstitutional and to reverse state court decisions; other rulings supported a broad view of Congress' powers vis-à-vis the states. Several of the rulings drew strong criticism from advocates of states' prerogatives.

Continued on p. 826

Chronology

Supreme Court scholars use the term "natural court" to define the time period with no personnel changes on the court. The Roberts Court has had four "natural courts" so far.

Rehnquist Court (1986-2006)

Chief Justice William H. Rehnquist leads conservative court; Sandra Day O'Connor and Anthony M. Kennedy are swing votes.

2004
Rehnquist operated on for thyroid cancer (Oct. 23).

2005
Bush nominates John G. Roberts Jr. to succeed retiring O'Connor (July 19). . . . Rehnquist dies (Sept. 3) . . . . Bush nominates Roberts for post (Sept. 5). . . . Senate confirms Roberts (Sept. 29).

Roberts 1 (2005-2006)

A new chief justice.

2005-2006
Roberts presides as new term opens (Oct. 3). . . . Bush nominates Samuel A. Alito Jr. for O'Connor's seat (Oct. 31). . . . Alito confirmed by Senate (Jan. 31).

Roberts 2 (2006-2009)

Alito solidifies conservative bloc.

2006
Alito provides crucial vote, after case reargued, in decision to limit exclusionary rule (June 15). . . . With Roberts recused, court rebuffs Bush, Congress on military tribunals for Guantánamo prisoners (June 29).

2006-2007
Court hardens conservative positions in 5-4 decisions on major issues: upholds federal ban on "partial birth" abortions (April 18, 2007). . . . eases rules on campaign-season issue advertising by corporations (June 25) . . . limits use of race in K-12 pupil assignments (June 28).

2007-2008
Conservatives, liberals count wins in close cases: Court guarantees habeas corpus right for Guantánamo prisoners (June 12) . . . bars death penalty for child rape (June 25) . . . recognizes gun rights for self-defense in home (June 26).

2008-2009
Barack Obama elected president (Nov. 4). . . . Roberts flubs oath at inauguration (Jan. 20, 2009). . . . Obama nominates Sonia Sotomayor to succeed David H. Souter (May 26). . . . Court skirts ruling on Voting Rights Act despite doubts from conservatives (June 22). . . . Sotomayor confirmed (Aug. 6).

Roberts 3 (2009-2010)

Sotomayor joins liberal bloc.

2009-2010
Court recognizes First Amendment right for corporations, unions to spend unlimited amounts on political campaigns (Jan. 21, 2010); Obama criticizes ruling in State of the Union speech (Jan. 27). . . . Obama nominates Elena Kagan to succeed John Paul Stevens (May 10). . . . Court extends gun rights ruling to limit state, local laws (June 28). . . . Kagan confirmed (Aug. 5).

Roberts 4 (2010-Present)

Kagan seated; three women on court.

2010-2011
Court convenes with three female justices for first time in history (Oct. 4). . . . Court requires California to reduce prison overcrowding (May 23, 2011). . . . rejects major sex-discrimination suit against Walmart (June 20).

2011-2012
Appeals on Obama's health care law granted (Nov. 14), argued (March 26-28, 2012). . . . Court bars life-without-parole sentences for juvenile murderers (June 25); strikes parts of Arizona immigration law but upholds provision for status checks at arrests, stops (June 25); upholds individual insurance mandate as tax, narrows penalty for states rejecting Medicaid expansion (June 28). . . . Court's approval rating falls in polls (May, July). . . . Ginsburg, Scalia squelch any talk of retirement (August).

2012-2013
Court to convene on First Monday in October (Oct. 1). . . . Challenge to University of Texas-Austin affirmative action plan to be argued (Oct. 10). . . . Marriage equality, Voting Rights Act cases awaiting. Presidential, congressional elections (Nov. 6). . . . Justices end oral arguments for term (April 24). . . . Term will end in late June 2013; final decisions due.

Use of Race Challenged in University Admissions

Justice Kennedy could hold key to Texas decision.

The Supreme Court is returning to the hot-button issue of affirmative action just 10 years after it issued a closely divided decision upholding the limited use of race in university admissions.

The justices will take on the issue in a case from the University of Texas (UT), which has been in and out of the courts over the past 20 years defending and refining its efforts to increase enrollment of African-American and Hispanic students at its flagship Austin campus. [1]

Opponents of affirmative action hope, and supporters fear, that the Supreme Court will use the UT case to narrow or possibly prohibit altogether consideration of race in university admissions. The reason: Justice Sandra Day O'Connor, who wrote the 5-4 decision upholding affirmative action in a case from the University of Michigan, has been replaced by Samuel A. Alito Jr., who has voted against race-conscious policies in several cases since joining the court in 2006.

UT tweaked its admission policies in 2004, the year after the University of Michigan case. Most of the slots in UT's incoming freshman class — about 75 percent today — are filled under a 1997 law that guarantees a seat to anyone who graduates from a Texas high school in the top 10 percent of the class. The remaining slots are filled through an admissions process, as revised in 2004, that evaluates applicants on the basis of grades and test scores as well as personal background and characteristics, including race or ethnicity.

UT's current system represents the evolution of legal developments dating from 1992, when unsuccessful white applicants challenged the admissions policies then being used. As the university now acknowledges, race was directly considered at that time and was often a controlling factor in admissions decisions.

The federal appeals court for Texas in 1996 ruled the procedures unconstitutional as a violation of equal protection. The ruling by the Fifth U.S. Circuit Court of Appeals in *Hopwood v. Texas* was the first federal court decision striking down use of racial preferences in college or university admissions. The Supreme Court declined to hear Texas' appeal after the university changed the system. [2]

UT says its previous admissions policy helped boost minority enrollment at the Austin campus to about 4.1 percent for African-Americans and 14.5 percent for Hispanics. After *Hopwood*, the number of African-Americans admitted for the entering class in 1997 dropped sharply by 40 percent; the number of Hispanics fell slightly, by 5 percent.

The university sought to increase recruiting of African-American and Hispanic students, but it also urged the legislature to pass the "Top Ten Percent" law as an ostensibly race-neutral policy that could pass muster under *Hopwood*. The law — signed by then-Gov. George W. Bush — was explicitly aimed at increasing minority enrollment by admitting top students from predominantly African-American and Hispanic schools without regard to other admissions criteria.

The policy had only limited effect, the university says today. In fall 2002, African-American and Hispanic enrollment remained below the 1996 levels; in 2004, the numbers were slightly higher: 4.5 percent African-American enrollment, 16.9 percent Hispanic enrollment. The increase in Hispanic enrollment was far less than the overall increase in the state's Hispanic population.

The Supreme Court's decision in the Michigan case, *Grutter v. Bollinger* (2003), gave UT officials the opening to reintroduce some consideration of race in its admissions policies. The ruling allowed colleges and universities to use an applicant's race or ethnicity as a factor in admissions decisions as long as it was part of a "holistic" evaluation of the applicant and not tied to a specific racial or ethnic quota. The ruling explicitly recognized racial and ethnic diversity as a "compelling interest" for public colleges and universities. The four dissenters included three justices still on the court: Antonin Scalia, Anthony M. Kennedy and Clarence Thomas. [3]

UT contends its current policies conform precisely to the "holistic" consideration of applicants allowed by *Grutter*. Race or ethnicity is one of many personal factors, along with grades and test scores, that go into a "personal achievement index" (PAI) used for final admissions decisions. Race is, as the university describes it, "a factor of a factor of a factor of a factor." Today, in UT's incoming freshman class of 8,092 students, Hispanics account for about 18.4 percent of the class, African-Americans 4.5 percent. [4]

The challenge to the UT policies comes from Abigail Fisher, an unsuccessful white applicant in 2008 from the affluent Houston suburb of Sugar Land. Fisher's father is a longtime friend of Edward Blum, a UT graduate who created the Project on Fair Representation to challenge race-conscious public policies. Through the project, Blum is funding Fisher's lawsuit and also supporting pending constitutional challenges to the federal Voting Rights Act.

Fisher, who has not given interviews during the litigation, did not qualify for admission to UT under either of the available routes. With a 3.65 GPA, she ranked at the 12th percentile in her graduating class of 674 students at Stephen F. Austin High School in Sugar Land. Her "academic index" score, based on grades and test scores alone, was 3.1 — below the 3.5 level needed to qualify.

Continued from p. 824

The court under Chief Justice Roger Taney (1836-1864) drew political fire from a different source: abolitionists opposed to the court's condoning of slavery. Despite the Taney Court's deference to states' rights, the court issued two controversial rulings (in 1842 and 1859) that enforced the federal Fugitive Slave Act in the face of state laws seeking to shield escaped slaves. And the court in the infamous *Dred*

And her PAI was below six — the level that might have qualified her for admission, according to the university. (The exact score is sealed.) But she contends that the use of race allowed less qualified minority applicants to be admitted to UT ahead of her.

www.praag.org

Abigail Fisher contends that the use of race allowed less qualified minority applicants to be admitted to the University of Texas ahead of her.

Two lower courts rejected Fisher's suit. U.S. District Court Judge Sam Sparks ruled in August 2009 that the admissions policy satisfied the criteria in *Grutter* that it be "narrowly tailored to further a compelling government interest." A three-judge Fifth Circuit panel affirmed that decision in January 2011, but in a splintered opinion. The Supreme Court agreed to hear Fisher's appeal on Feb. 21, 2012, in time for the case to be argued early in the court's next term. By the end of August, 92 friend-of-the-court briefs had been filed with the court: 17 on Fisher's side from conservative groups and individuals opposed to racial preferences and 73 supporting UT from national organizations such as the American Bar Association, more than a dozen *Fortune* 500 companies and a host of education and traditional civil rights groups.

The Obama administration is also supporting the university. In its brief, the government argues that the United States "has a critical interest in ensuring that educational institutions are able to provide the educational benefits of diversity." The government's involvement in the case is affecting the composition of the court that will decide it. Liberal Justice Elena Kagan has recused herself, presumably because she participated in the case as U.S. solicitor general before joining the court in 2010.

Two other friend-of-the-court briefs take no direct position on the case. In one, the Equal Employment Advisory Council, an employers group, cautions the court against any decision that would make it harder for government contractors to comply with affirmative action guidelines on hiring and promotions. In the other, UCLA law professor Richard Sander and lawyer-journalist Stuart Taylor Jr. argue, in a statistics-laden brief, that racial preferences in university admissions actually hurt the minority students the policies are intended to benefit. A group of social scientists filed an opposing brief sharply disputing Sanders' and Taylor's so-called "mismatch" thesis.

As a result of Kagan's recusal, the court will hear the case with eight justices. Based on their previous votes in race-related cases, liberal justices Ruth Bader Ginsburg, Stephen G. Breyer and Sonia Sotomayor are seen as likely votes to uphold UT's admissions policies, while Chief Justice John G. Roberts Jr., Scalia, Thomas and Alito are thought likely to rule for Fisher. In an earlier case that limited the use of race in pupil assignments in K-12 education, Roberts ended the main opinion in the 5-4 decision by writing, "The way to stop discrimination on the basis of race is to stop discriminating on the basis of race." Scalia, Thomas, and Alito joined the opinion, but not Kennedy. [5]

Based on that history, all eyes will be on Kennedy in the UT case. "What happens depends on psychoanalyzing Anthony Kennedy," says Louis Michael Seidman, a professor at Georgetown University Law Center in Washington. Kennedy could join the other conservatives in limiting race-conscious admissions policies. If he joins the liberal bloc, a 4-4 vote would affirm the Fifth Circuit's decision and leave UT's policies intact. The decision would be due by the end of June 2013.

— ***Kenneth Jost***

---

[1] Background is drawn from legal materials in the Supreme Court case, *Fisher v. University of Texas*, 11-345, which are compiled on the websites for the organization representing the plaintiff, the Project on Fair Representation (www.projectonfairrepresentation.org/current-litigation) and the university (www.utexas.edu/vp/irla/Fisher-V-Texas.html).

[2] The citation is 78 F.3d 932 (5th Cir. 1996). See Linda Greenhouse, "Justices Decline Affirmative-Action Case," *The New York Times*, July 2, 1996, p. A12.

[3] The citation is 539 U.S. 306 (2003). In a companion decision, the court struck down, by a 6-3 vote, the admissions policies for University of Michigan graduates because race played a greater role in decisions. *Gratz v. Bollinger*, 539 U.S. 244 (2003). For a comprehensive account of the cases, see Kenneth Jost, *Supreme Court Yearbook 2002-2003*.

[4] "The University of Texas at Austin Releases Preliminary Enrollment Data," Sept. 19, 2012, www.utexas.edu/news/2012/09/19/2012-preliminary-enrollment-data/.

[5] The decision is *Parents Involved in Community Schools v. Seattle School District No. 1*, 551 U.S. 701 (2007). For a full account, see Kenneth Jost, *Supreme Court Yearbook 2006-2007*.

Scott decision (1857) emphatically declared slaves ineligible for citizenship and barred Congress from limiting slavery in territories or newly admitted states. The future president Abraham Lincoln criticized the ruling as "erroneous" and vowed to do what he could to overrule it. The decision was overturned after the Civil War by the 14th Amendment, which extended citizenship to "all persons born or naturalized" in the United States.

With the Civil War over, the court entered a 70-year-long conservative era marked by a generally pro-business orientation even as progressive forces and organized labor gained political influence. The court's solicitude for business can be seen in a trio of rulings in 1895 that limited the still new Sherman Antitrust Act, barred a federal income tax and authorized federal judges to block strikes. A year later, the court in the infamous decision *Plessy v. Ferguson* upheld legally enforced racial segregation in public accommodations. The court shifted somewhat in 1917 by ruling racial segregation ordinances unconstitutional, but its pro-business orientation continued — exemplified by two decisions striking down federal laws to prohibit child labor. Political opposition to the court's rulings prompted the successful drive to ratify the 16th Amendment authorizing a federal income tax and unsuccessful efforts to adopt amendments overturning the child labor decisions or limiting the Supreme Court's power to nullify congressional statutes.

The ideological storm over the court intensified in the 1930s as a conservative majority struck down several major parts of President Franklin D. Roosevelt's New Deal program. Roosevelt railed against the "nine old men" and crafted a proposal after his landslide re-election in 1936 to "pack" the court by appointing new justices for each member of the court past the age of 70. Faced with strong public opposition to Roosevelt's power grab, the Senate rejected the plan. But Roosevelt got his chance to remake the court in a more liberal image with eight appointments over the next four years. Even earlier, however, the court had moved toward a more assertive role in protecting individual rights with decisions applying provisions of the Bill of Rights to the states and reviewing some criminal law convictions for constitutional violations — most notably, the notorious rape case against the so-called Scottsboro Boys, black youths wrongly accused in Alabama of assaulting a white girl.

The Warren Court expanded on these precursors of judicial activism with rulings that brought more sustained political attacks on the court than ever before or since. The landmark school desegregation ruling in *Brown v. Board of Education* (1954) prompted a decade of "massive resistance" in the South and opposition to what critics called "forced integration" that continues to this day. The court's rulings in the 1950s limiting anti-subversive laws prompted an unsuccessful effort in the Senate to strip the court of jurisdiction over internal-security cases. Opponents of the court's decisions in the early 1960s to bar government-sponsored prayer in public schools tried for decades to overturn them by constitutional amendment. State officials mobilized against the court's "one-man, one-vote" reapportionment rulings. And the Warren Court's so-called criminal law revolution — exemplified in the famous *Miranda* decision in 1966 establishing guidelines for police interrogation — became a major issue in Richard M. Nixon's successful presidential campaign in 1968. As president, Nixon followed through on his campaign promises by appointing four justices, including a new chief justice, Warren E. Burger, expected to steer the court to the right.

Partisan Fights

The Supreme Court was lastingly shifted to the right from the 1970s on thanks to appointments of conservative justices by three Republican presidents: Nixon, Ronald Reagan and George H. W. Bush. With the court's balance of power at stake, Democrats and liberal advocacy groups mounted efforts to block Senate confirmation of some of the nominees; they succeeded three times and fell only four votes short in one other fight. In early rulings, the Burger Court broke new ground on abortion rights and the death penalty, but in later decisions both the Burger and Rehnquist courts generally staked out conservative positions on those and other issues, including affirmative action.

Partisan confirmation fights became frequent occurrences in the late 1900s. Senate Republicans had flexed their muscles in 1968 by blocking a vote on President Lyndon B. Johnson's lame-duck nomination of Justice Abe Fortas to succeed Warren as chief justice. Burger's appointment as chief justice sailed through the Senate, but Democrats defeated Nixon's two choices for the next vacancy (Clement Haynsworth and G. Harrold Carswell) before the president settled on Harry A. Blackmun. Rehnquist was confirmed in 1971, but with 26 votes cast against him; 15 years later, he won confirmation as chief justice with 33 no votes — the most ever cast against a chief justice. Two more tumultuous confirmation fights followed: the 58-42 rejection of the hard-line conservative Bork in 1987 — that seat went to Kennedy instead — and the narrow 52-48 confirmation of Clarence Thomas in 1991 after the dramatic airing of still unresolved accusations of sexual harassment.

With Warren Court holdovers still in the majority, the early Burger Court issued liberal rulings on three major issues: upholding the use of busing in school desegregation cases (1970), invalidating existing death sentences (1972) and recognizing a qualified right to abortion (1973). The court backed away from those rulings as the conservative bloc gelled. On the death penalty, the court in 1976 allowed states to adopt capital punishment if the death penalty was limited to well-defined crimes, and juries had full discretion to consider aggravating and mitigating circumstances. In later rulings, the court barred the death penalty for some offenses — notably, rape —

but it rejected the broadest attacks against capital punishment.

On reproductive rights, the 7-2 ruling in *Roe v. Wade* provoked the strongest backlash against a court decision since *Brown v. Board of Education.* Anti-abortion groups mounted efforts to overrule the decision by constitutional amendment or limit it by legislative action in Washington or in state capitals. The court sustained many of the newly enacted restrictions, typically in closely divided decisions. Most significantly, the court upheld laws prohibiting the use of Medicaid funds to pay for abortions for poor women. By the late 1980s, anti-abortion forces thought they were close to a majority of justices willing to overrule *Roe v. Wade* outright. But in 1992 the court largely reaffirmed *Roe* in a pivotal opinion jointly authored by three Republican appointees: Sandra Day O'Connor, Kennedy and David H. Souter.

On racial issues, the court began retreating on school desegregation within a few years of the busing decision and adopted a skeptical position toward affirmative action in the first cases to reach the justices. The significant milestones included a 1974 ruling that blocked courts from combining urban and suburban school districts in desegregation orders. Four years later, in the *Bakke* decision — *Regents of the University of California v. Bakke* — the court gave only a limited green light to racial preferences in university admissions. In later rulings, the Burger and Rehnquist courts set limits on affirmative action policies by government employers and minority preferences in government contracting. In the 1990s, the Rehnquist Court issued a series of decisions significantly limiting federal courts' role in desegregation suits. Most of the rulings were closely divided, often by 5-4 votes.

Getty Images/Time Life Pictures/Carl Iwasaki

The parents of these and other black children filed the suits that eventually led to the Supreme Court's 1954 Brown v. Board of Education *ruling overturning public school segregation. The landmark decision prompted a decade of massive resistance in the South and opposition to what critics called "forced integration" that continues to this day.*

The Rehnquist Court staked out new conservative positions in two other major areas: federalism and church-state issues. On federalism, the court limited Congress' ability to pass laws intruding on states' prerogatives and protected states from private damage suits for violating federal laws. On church-state issues, the justices relaxed restrictions on display of religious messages in public sites and moved to allow use of public funds for pupils at church-affiliated schools. Those decisions culminated in a 2002 ruling upholding a broad tuition-voucher program for pupils at parochial and other private schools. Major decisions again came on 5-4 votes.

None of the Rehnquist Court's 5-4 decisions had more impact or stirred more partisan criticism than the ruling in December 2000 that effectively cinched the presidential election for George W. Bush. The ruling in *Bush v. Gore* ended a ballot recount in Florida that Democrat Al Gore had asked for in hopes of reversing Bush's apparent edge for the state's crucial 27 electoral votes. The conservative majority said Florida courts had failed to establish consistent rules for recounting votes; the liberal dissenters said the recount should have been allowed to continue. Critics said the ruling conflicted with the majority's customary deference to state courts; supporters said the court had to step in to settle the issue. In the years since, Justice Scalia has repeatedly defended the ruling in public comments. To critics, Scalia has a blunt answer: "Get over it." [23]

Roberts' Court?

Two presidents — the Republican Bush and the Democrat Obama — filled vacancies on the Supreme Court with like-minded justices who first fortified the court's conservative bloc and then re-energized the liberal wing. All four of the new justices — Roberts, Alito, Sotomayor and Kagan — first had to survive partisan confirmation fights in the Senate that emphasized the polarized atmosphere surrounding the court. Roberts and Alito made their marks in their first two terms with a burst of conservative rulings at odds with prior decisions. Over the next five terms, the conservative and liberal blocs traded victories, with Kennedy most often casting the decisive vote until Roberts played that role in the dramatic showdown over Obama's health care law. [24]

Bush nominated Roberts initially to succeed O'Connor as an associate justice and then picked him to succeed Rehnquist as chief justice just two days after Rehnquist died of cancer on Sept. 3, 2005. Roberts made an impressive appearance in his confirmation hearing but still drew 22 Democratic votes against his confirmation later that month. Among those voting against Roberts was Obama, then the junior senator from Illinois, who said he thought Roberts "has far more often used his formidable skills on behalf of the strong in opposition to the weak." [25]

Digital image ©1998 Missouri Historical Society, St. Louis

The Supreme Court under Chief Justice Roger Taney (1836-1864) drew fire from abolitionists opposed to the court's condoning of slavery. The court issued two controversial rulings, in 1842 and 1859, that enforced the federal Fugitive Slave Act in the face of state laws seeking to shield escaped slaves. And in the infamous Dred Scott *decision (1857), the court emphatically declared Scott (above) and other slaves ineligible for citizenship and barred Congress from limiting slavery in territories or newly admitted states.*

O'Connor agreed to stay on until a successor was confirmed; Alito won confirmation, by a narrower 58-42 margin, in late January 2006, with both Obama and his future vice president, Joe Biden, voting no. Alito made an identifiable impact by casting decisive votes in three cases that were reargued after O'Connor's departure — presumably because the remaining eight justices were evenly divided. In one of the reargued cases, the court voted 5-4 to limit application of the exclusionary rule — the doctrine that bars the use of illegally obtained evidence in criminal trials.

The conservatives flexed their muscles more dramatically in the first full term with Roberts and Alito on the court. In rulings that either overturned or diverged from prior decisions, the court in 2007 upheld a federal ban on so-called partial-birth abortions, limited taxpayer suits challenging government spending on church-state grounds and eased campaign finance restrictions on issue-oriented advertising. Other decisions limited punitive damages and — in the *Ledbetter* case — made it harder for employees to win back pay in job discrimination suits. The term ended with a ruling overturning a century-old antitrust doctrine and a final decision, announced by Roberts, limiting the use of race in pupil assignments in K-12 public education. Except for the punitive damages case, the rulings came on 5-4 votes with Kennedy and the other conservatives in the majority. "Conservatives got everything they could reasonably have hoped for," remarked Thomas Goldstein, a frequent Supreme Court advocate and publisher of *SCOTUSBlog*, a comprehensive compendium of court-related materials. [26]

Conservatives claimed many more victories over the next four terms, but they were offset by some significant liberal rulings. Among the most dramatic decisions were 5-4 rulings in 2008 and 2010 by the conservative majority that established a Second Amendment right to possess firearms in the home for self-defense. The rulings struck down handgun bans first in a case from Washington, D.C., and then in a case from Chicago that applied to state and local governments nationwide. The conservative bloc showed its distaste for campaign finance laws not only with the *Citizens United* decision but with rulings in 2008 and 2011 that struck down a federal provision and an Arizona law intended to help candidates facing high-spending, privately financed opponents. But Roberts apparently helped divert conservatives in 2009 from a clear ruling on the constitutionality of the Voting Rights Act; instead, he led an 8-1 decision favoring the challenger on a narrow ground and voicing doubts about the law's continuing validity without resolving the question.

The liberal wing won its most important victories thanks to pivotal support from Kennedy. Kennedy wrote the 5-4 decision in 2008 that guaranteed Guantánamo prisoners the right to challenge their detention in federal courts — the third rebuff to Bush's handling of suspected enemy combatants. In the same year, Kennedy wrote the ruling that barred the death penalty for child rape as a violation of the Eighth Amendment's Cruel and Unusual Punishment Clause. Three years later, Kennedy again relied on the Eighth Amendment in a 5-4 decision requiring California to reduce severe overcrowding in its prison system.

The court opened its new term in October 2011 with the politically contentious challenges to the Affordable Care Act and the Arizona immigration law at its doorstep. The justices agreed to hear both controversial cases, setting aside three full mornings in late March for arguments in the health care case. By then, the court had cheered privacy advocates with a unanimous ruling setting some, but unspecified, limits on law enforcement use of global positioning systems (GPS) to track criminal suspects. Liberals won other significant victories, including decisions in two companion cases strengthening the right to counsel for defendants in plea bargaining. The ruling to strike down some parts of Arizona's immigration law came on June 25 as the court began its final week; on the same day Kennedy also provided the crucial vote to bar mandatory life-without-parole sentences for juvenile murderers.

The ruling on the Affordable Care Act three days later ended the term in dramatic and unexpected fashion. Summarizing an opinion that no other justice joined in toto, Roberts began by rejecting the administration's main rationale for the law's individual mandate requiring most people to have health insurance or pay a financial penalty, but he then ended by upholding the provision as a tax measure. Kennedy followed with a stern delivery of the joint dissent by four conservatives arguing that the law should be struck down in its entirety. Ginsburg concluded the session by summarizing her opinion defending both the mandate and the law's Medicaid-expansion provision, which the majority upheld but narrowed somewhat.

Obama hailed the ruling, while his Republican opponent, Mitt Romney, stressed that the court had upheld the law without endorsing it; he promised to work to repeal it if elected. For court watchers, however, the big story was the chief justice. "Roberts Straddles Ideological Divide," a *Wall Street Journal* headline declared. A *New York Times* headline said Roberts had emerged as the "court's fulcrum." To *SCOTUSBlog*'s Goldstein, the decision was Roberts' "signature statement that he is not a partisan." [27] ■

CURRENT SITUATION

'Hefty' Docket

The Supreme Court is starting a new term with a major affirmative action case set for early argument and high-profile cases on voting rights and gay marriage expected to be granted review by the end of the year.

The justices will open the term on Oct. 1 with a case testing whether federal courts can hear suits by foreign nationals against a foreign-headquartered multinational company with U.S. operations for human rights violations committed abroad. A month later, the court will hear arguments on whether human rights groups, journalists and lawyers can challenge the constitutionality of the foreign electronic surveillance program crafted by Congress and the George W. Bush administration in Bush's last full year in the White House.

Other issues already teed up for the justices include use of drug-sniffing dogs by police and rules for high-impact class action suits against corporations. In all, the court has accepted 39 cases for review during the term, including six added on Sept. 25 after an all-day conference the previous day to review appeals that had accumulated over the summer.

The court will likely add 30 to 40 more cases by early January to be argued next year and to be decided by late June, continuing the Roberts Court's output of 75 or fewer decisions per term. The docket "is sparse but not without heft," says the Cato Institute's Shapiro. [28]

The affirmative action case, *Fisher v. University of Texas*, revives an issue the court last dealt with in 2003, when it upheld the use of race as one of several factors in admissions at the University of Michigan School of Law. Lawyers representing unsuccessful UT applicant Fisher argue that the school's use of race goes beyond what was authorized in the Michigan decision, *Grutter v. Bollinger*; alternatively, they urge that *Grutter* be overruled. Lawyers for UT, backed by the Obama administration, defend both the admissions system and the court's prior ruling. The case has drawn more than 90 friend-of-the-court briefs: 17 on Fisher's side, 73 for the school and two others ostensibly filed on behalf of neither side. The Oct. 10 argument features prominent Washington attorney Bert Rein for Fisher and former U.S. solicitor general Gregory Garre for the university.

The human rights case, *Kiobel v. Royal Dutch Petroleum Co.*, stems from allegations by 12 Nigerian nationals now living in the United States that the multinational oil company aided Nigeria's military government in a brutal campaign in the 1990s to put down opposition to oil drilling in the country's Ogoni region. The court initially heard arguments in the case on Feb. 28 on the question whether a corporation could be sued under the federal Alien Tort Statute. But the justices asked for a second round of arguments on the broader question whether federal courts have any jurisdiction over such suits, whether against an individual or corporation. The action was an ominous sign for human rights lawyers, who have used the 220-year-old law to try to bring human rights violators to justice in U.S. courts.

The foreign intelligence surveillance case, *Clapper v. Amnesty International USA*, to be argued Oct. 29, is before the justices on the preliminary question whether opponents of the super-secret program have legal standing just to get into court with their challenge. The government keeps tight wraps on the program, which Congress authorized in 2008 to replace the warrantless terrorism surveillance the Bush administration instituted as part of its war on terrorism in 2001. The various plaintiffs say they fear their conversations with individuals or groups overseas may be subject to surveillance, but the government says they have failed to show the kind of actual injury needed to have standing for a federal court suit.

Two cases from Florida test the rules for using trained dogs to sniff for evidence of drugs. In *Florida v. Jardines*, the justices have to decide whether police can use a dog at the front door of a private house to try to detect drugs inside. In *Florida v. Harris*, the issue is what police have to show about a dog's training to use the dog's reaction — a so-called "alert" — as the evidence needed to get a search warrant. Both cases are to be argued on Oct. 31.

Getty Images/Mario Tama

The Supreme Court's Boumediene *decision in 2008 gave the court's liberal wing one of its most important victories. The 5-4 vote, with pivotal support from Justice Anthony M. Kennedy, guaranteed terrorists being held at the Guantánamo Bay prison in Cuba the right to challenge their detention in federal court.*

The class action cases both represent efforts by corporate defendants to tighten the rules for plaintiffs to get a suit certified for treatment as collective litigation. In *Amgen v. Connecticut Retirement Plans and Trust Fund*, the big biotech company argues that investors in a securities fraud suit must first prove that alleged misstatements about the safety of its products actually influenced the investors to buy or hold the company's stock. In *Comcast v. Behrend*, the big cable company is seeking to prevent class certification of an antitrust suit over rate increases to up to 2 million subscribers. The two cases are to be argued on Nov. 5.

The gay marriage issue all but certain to be taken up by the justices is the constitutionality of the provision in the Defense of Marriage Act (DOMA), section 3, that denies federal benefits to same-sex couples even if legally married in their states. Judges in three separate cases have ruled the law unconstitutional on equal-protection grounds. Also pending is the appeal by supporters of California's Proposition 8 seeking to reinstate the ban on gay marriage that was invalidated by the federal appeals court for California on Feb. 7. Many court watchers expect the justices to defer action on the Prop. 8 case until after ruling on one or more of the DOMA challenges.

The justices are also widely expected to agree to review the constitutionality of the federal Voting Rights Act after diverting a challenge to the act in 2009. The most likely vehicle is a broad attack on the law filed in 2010 by Shelby County, Ala., contending that the formula enacted in 1965 to determine the states and local jurisdictions that have to get "preclearance" for any election law change is now out of date. The federal appeals court for the District of Columbia rejected the challenge in a 2-1 decision on May 18.

Vanishing Issue?

Obama and Romney are campaigning on party platforms with sharply divergent views on legal issues, but the Supreme Court itself is getting virtually no attention so far out on the campaign trail.

Continued on p. 834

At Issue:

Should the Supreme Court prohibit racial preferences in university admissions?

ROGER CLEGG
PRESIDENT AND GENERAL COUNSEL, CENTER FOR EQUAL OPPORTUNITY

WRITTEN FOR *CQ RESEARCHER*, SEPTEMBER 2012

yes

The Supreme Court should prohibit racial preferences in university admissions because the Constitution and federal statutes say so. The Constitution says, "No State" — and that includes state universities — ". . . shall abridge the privileges or immunities of citizens of the United States . . . nor deny to any person . . . the equal protection of the laws," and foremost in the Framers' minds at that time (1868) was racial discrimination.

Congress said, more recently and even more clearly, that in any institution receiving federal funding (and, again, that includes the University of Texas), "No person in the United States shall, on the ground of race, color, or national origin, . . . be subjected to discrimination. . . ." Congress has also said, "All persons within the jurisdiction of the United States shall have the same right . . . to make and enforce contracts" without regard to race, and the Supreme Court has expressly held that this includes school admissions and tuition.

The only justification offered by universities for ignoring all this is that some academics say there are "educational benefits" to interracial campus conversations. Seriously — that's it. Role-model and historical and societal discrimination arguments have, rightly, been rejected by the Court already.

This shaky benefit doesn't justify ignoring federal law, nor does it outweigh the many costs of admissions discrimination:

It's personally unfair, passes over better qualified students and sets a disturbing legal and moral precedent in allowing racial discrimination;

It creates resentment;

It stigmatizes the supposed beneficiaries in the eyes of their classmates, teachers and themselves, as well as future employers, clients and coworkers;

It mismatches African-Americans and Latinos with institutions, setting them up for failure;

It fosters a victim mentality, removes the incentive for academic excellence and encourages separatism;

It compromises the academic mission of the university and lowers the academic quality of the student body;

It creates pressure to discriminate in grading and graduation;

It breeds hypocrisy among college officials;

It obscures the real problem of why so many African-Americans and Latinos are academically uncompetitive; and

It involves states and schools in unsavory activities such as deciding which minorities will be favored and which ones (e.g., Asians) not, and how much blood is needed to establish group membership — an untenable legal regime as America becomes increasingly multiracial and multiethnic.

SHIRLEY J. WILCHER
EXECUTIVE DIRECTOR, AMERICAN ASSOCIATION FOR AFFIRMATIVE ACTION

WRITTEN FOR *CQ RESEARCHER*, SEPTEMBER 2012

no

If the term "racial preferences" means equal opportunity through diversity programs, the answer is an unequivocal "no." The Supreme Court, which will decide the *Fisher v. University of Texas at Austin* case this year, should agree if it follows its own cases.

In *Regents of the University of California v. Bakke* (1978) and *Grutter v. Bollinger* (2003), the court made clear that "student body diversity is a compelling state interest that can justify the use of race in university admissions." The benefits that flow from racial and ethnic diversity as well as other factors, including grades and scores, study abroad, fluency in several languages, the ability to overcome personal hardship and other considerations contribute to achieving a student body that is varied, rich and intellectually challenging.

To minimize the burden on nonminority applicants, the law requires that diversity admissions programs be narrowly tailored and that the university consider race-neutral alternatives to achieve the same goal.

In *Grutter*, the court embraced a "holistic," individualized view of the student. Use of quotas, set asides or other numerical factors was prohibited. At the University of Michigan as well as the University of Texas, nonminority students with lower grades and test scores than those of under-represented minority applicants were admitted as part of an individualized review.

The *Grutter* Court believed that including diverse perspectives improved the quality of the educational process. Student body diversity also better prepared students as professionals because it helped to remove stereotypes and promoted better understanding of individuals of different races.

According to the U.S. Census Bureau, racial and ethnic minorities constituted the majority of babies born in 2011. Some states, including Texas, have already become "majority minority." Diversity is not only desirable, it is essential if, in the Supreme Court's words, the "dream of one Nation, indivisible, is to be realized."

In a recent survey 11 percent of admissions directors said they admit male applicants (presumably nonminority) with below-average credentials because women are becoming the majority of college students. Prohibiting diversity could affect the aspirations of men as well.

It would be unfortunate to close the educational gateway to the intended beneficiaries of the 14th Amendment's Equal Protection Clause by prohibiting race and ethnicity as factors in higher education admissions. This nation's future depends on keeping that gateway open — for everyone.

Continued from p. 832

"It's quite remarkable to me that the talk about the Supreme Court has been entirely absent from the presidential campaign as compared to past years," says the ACLU's Shapiro. "I have literally not heard it mentioned, not even once."

The Democratic platform cites Obama's appointments of "two distinguished jurists," Sotomayor and Kagan, to the Supreme Court and promises to continue appointment of "men and women of unquestionable talent and character" to the federal bench. The Republican platform calls for appointment of "constitutionalist jurists, who will interpret the law as it was originally intended rather than make it." It goes on to praise GOP senators for opposing Obama's nomination of "activist judges." [29]

Both party documents emphasize economic issues, but they also lay out clear differences on issues that have been and are likely to return to the court's docket. Democrats say the party "strongly and unequivocally supports *Roe v. Wade* and a woman's right to make decisions regarding her pregnancy"; Republicans say they oppose abortion because it "endangers the health and well-being of women." The Democratic platform notes that the Affordable Care Act guarantees insurance coverage of contraception; the GOP platform says the law "has promoted the notion of abortion as health care."

The Republican platform promises to protect "traditional marriage," while the Democrats say they support "marriage equality" and "the movement to secure treatment under law for same-sex couples." The GOP platform says a Republican administration "will fulfill its responsibility to defend all federal laws in court, including the Defense of Marriage Act."

The Democrats say the party "will preserve Americans' Second Amendment right to own and use firearms," but add that the right "is subject to reasonable regulation." The GOP platform calls the Second Amendment right "fundamental" and implicitly criticizes the District of Columbia for enacting an overly restrictive gun law after the Supreme Court rejected its handgun ban.

The parties also differ on immigration. The Democrats call for "comprehensive immigration reform," while the Republicans say Obama's approach "has undermined the rule of law." On another issue, Democrats say they favor campaign finance reform "by constitutional amendment if necessary," while Republicans "oppose any restrictions or conditions that would discourage Americans from exercising their constitutional right to enter the political fray."

Despite the limited discussion of the court so far, it is likely though not certain that the winning candidate in November will have the opportunity to name one new justice during his presidency. Three justices — Ginsburg, Scalia and Kennedy — will reach age 80 by the end of the next president's term in January 2017. [30]

Of the three, Ginsburg is the oldest at 79 and the only one to have set a target date for her retirement. Ginsburg has said several times, most recently in an interview with Reuters' Joan Biskupic, that she wants to serve at least until she reaches 82 — the age at which her judicial hero, Louis Brandeis, retired from the Supreme Court. [31]

Scalia and Kennedy are both 76. Scalia batted away any talk of retirement in an interview this summer. "My wife doesn't want me hanging around the house, I know that," Scalia said on "Fox News Sunday." Kennedy is not known to have addressed the subject publicly. [32]

Ginsburg, a two-time cancer survivor, cracked two ribs in a fall at her home in June but says she is in good health. Scalia and Kennedy are not known to have any health problems. Of the other justices, Breyer is 74, Thomas and Alito are in their early 60s, and Roberts, Sotomayor and Kagan are in their 50s.

At least since 1970, justices have timed their retirements to coincide with a like-minded president in the White House unless forced to step down by health issues. The Democrat-appointed White and the liberal Republican appointee Blackmun retired in good health with Democrat Clinton in the White House. O'Connor stepped down after George W. Bush's re-election. Stevens and Souter, liberals on the court despite their

Getty Images/Mark Wilson

Anti-abortion advocates protest on Capitol Hill on July 13, 2009, before the start of Senate confirmation hearings for President Obama's first Supreme Court nominee, Sonia Sotomayor. She was confirmed along party lines, 68-31. Sotomayor and another Obama appointee, Elena Kagan, join Clinton appointees Ruth Bader Ginsburg and Stephen Breyer to form a liberal bloc that dissents in most of the court's 5-4 decisions.

Republican backgrounds, waited until Obama was in the White House.

If that practice continues, Ginsburg might be considered likely to retire in 2015 if Obama is re-elected but to try to extend her tenure if Romney is president. Scalia and Kennedy could be thought of as potential retirees if Romney wins but unlikely to step down if Obama is still in the White House. ■

OUTLOOK

Watershed Term?

Every time a new justice is appointed, "it's a different court," Byron White famously remarked. [33] By that standard, John Roberts is now presiding over his fourth court in only seven years — a dizzying series of transformations after nearly 11 years with no changes in court personnel before his appointment in September 2005.

Roberts presided first over a transitional court with O'Connor in her final half-term in a swing justice's seat and then over a court with his fellow Reagan administration alumnus Alito helping to fortify a general conservative majority. Roberts' third and fourth courts came with the appointment of Sotomayor, as the first Hispanic justice, and Kagan's selection to bring the number of women on the court to three for the only time in history.

Each of the new justices changed the court, just as White suggested. Roberts brought a younger face and lighter touch to the center chair than his predecessor, Rehnquist. Alito is credited with asking penetrating questions from a conservative perspective, less argumentative than those from the loquacious Scalia. Sotomayor, who grew up in a housing project in the Bronx, sometimes injects a real world perspective into oral arguments, while Kagan, a former Harvard Law School dean, is winning praise for insightful questions from the bench and clear yet forceful writing in her opinions.

With Roberts' surprising vote in the health care case, some court watchers question whether the new term will see the emergence of Roberts 4.1 — a court that further tempers its conservative instincts to try to lower its political profile in a politically polarized country. But the answer from many appears to be no.

"Liberals should have no illusion that Roberts is in the midst of an ideological conversion," *Newsweek* special correspondent and former managing editor Daniel Klaidman writes. "In the coming year, the safe bet is that he will side with conservatives on affirmative action, gay marriage and voting rights." [34]

Rosen, the George Washington University Law School professor and legal affairs editor for *The New Republic*, suggests that Roberts' vote in the health care case may encourage him to harden his conservative stance on issues. "His health care votes may embolden him to join the conservatives in striking down only affirmative action and the Voting Rights Act next year, but in enforcing other limits on federal power in the future," Rosen wrote. [35]

Largely in agreement, Adam Winkler, a professor at UCLA Law School, says Kennedy, not Roberts, remains the court's most essential justice. "My own view is that things have not changed radically on the ground on who the swing justice is," Winkler says. "It's still Justice Kennedy."

Still, the Cato Institute's Shapiro contends — counter to the court's liberal critics — that Roberts has guided the court toward "minimalist" decisions. "The court is very deliberate," he says. "They don't go out of their way to reach issues or pronounce sweeping opinions that aren't called for."

Based on that view, Shapiro is among several court watchers who predict a narrow, Texas-specific decision in the new term's affirmative action case that will leave the precedent in the Michigan case largely untouched. Court watchers are less certain about what the court will do with the Voting Rights Act case. The justices could decline to hear the case, leaving the law unchanged; if they accept the case, they could keep a low profile by upholding the law or crafting a narrow decision or, more perilously, expose the court to sharp political attack by invalidating the preclearance provision in whole or in part.

As for gay marriage, many court watchers on the left confidently predict that Kennedy will join the liberal bloc in ruling DOMA unconstitutional. But several experts from across the ideological spectrum see the Proposition 8 case as likely to be resolved narrowly or deferred in some way. With gay marriage recognized in only six states and the District of Columbia, the court is seen as nowhere near establishing a constitutional rule on the subject. "We're not going to get a decision where the Supreme Court says the state of Mississippi has to recognize same-sex marriage," says Georgetown law professor Louis Michael Seidman.

The court's role will re-emerge as a national issue when the next vacancy arises. Levey with the Committee for Justice forecasts another partisan confirmation fight, no matter who is president or which party controls the Senate. "It's now become a very acrimonious issue on both sides," he says. "I don't know how to get out of it."

For Roberts, the political attention may be unwelcome, but Case Western professor Adler suggests it is inevitable. "He wanted to extricate the court from these political fights, but that's really hard to do." ■

Notes

[1] The case is *Fisher v. University of Texas*, 11-345. For comprehensive coverage and compilation of materials, see *SCOTUSBlog*, www.scotusblog.com/case-files/cases/fisher-v-university-of-texas-at-austin/?wpmp_switcher=desktop. Some additional materials on the website of the Project for Fair Representa-

tion: www.projectonfairrepresentation.org/current-litigation/. For coverage, see Adam Liptak, "Justices Take Up Race as a Factor in College Entry," *The New York Times*, Feb. 22, 2012, p. A1; Ralph K. M. Haurwitz, "High court to hear race case," *The Austin American-Statesman*, Feb. 22, 2012, p. A1 (includes timeline). For background, see Peter Katel, "Affirmative Action," *CQ Researcher*, Oct. 17, 2008, updated June 19, 2012.

[2] See Kenneth Jost, "Health Law Upheld in Fractured Ruling," *CQ Researcher Blog*, June 28, 2012, http://cqresearcherblog.blogspot.com/2012_06_01_archive.html. See also Marcia Clemmitt, "Assessing the New Health Care Law," *CQ Researcher*, Sept. 21, 2012, pp. 789-812.

[3] For profiles, see Daniel Klaidman, "How Chief Justice John Roberts Will Handle Obamacare," *The Daily Beast*, Sept. 10, 2012, www.thedailybeast.com/newsweek/2012/09/09/how-chief-justice-john-roberts-will-handle-obamacare.html; Jeffrey Rosen, "Big Chief: How to understand John Roberts," *The New Republic*, Aug. 3, 2012, pp. 13-14.

[4] See Kenneth Jost, "Supreme Court Blurred Ideological Lines in Momentous Term," *CQ Researcher Blog*, July 2, 2012, http://cqresearcherblog.blogspot.com/2012/07/scotus-2011-12-wrap-up.html.

[5] For background, see Kenneth Jost, "Immigration Conflict," *CQ Researcher*, March 9, 2012, pp. 229-252.

[6] See "CQ Press Major Cases," in Kenneth Jost, *Supreme Court Yearbook 2010-2011*; and Kenneth Jost, "Class Action Lawsuits," *CQ Researcher*, May 13, 2011, pp. 433-456.

[7] Jan Crawford, "Roberts switched views to uphold health care law," CBS News, July 1, 2012, www.cbsnews.com/8301-3460_162-57464549/roberts-switched-views-to-uphold-health-care-law/.

[8] See Lyle Denniston, "Same-sex marriage cases: made simple," *SCOTUSBlog*, Sept. 13, 2012, www.scotusblog.com/2012/09/same-sex-marriage-cases-made-simple/; Kenneth Jost, "Anti-Gay Marriage Measure Struck Down," *CQ Researcher Blog*, Feb. 7, 2012, http://cqresearcherblog.blogspot.com/2012/02/anti-gay-marriage-measure-struck-down.html.

[9] See Lyle Denniston, "Voting Rights Act cases: made simple," *SCOTUSBlog*, Sept. 7, 2012, www.scotusblog.com/2012/09/voting-rights-cases-made-simple/.

[10] Rosen quoted in David G. Savage, "Did Justice Scalia go too far this time?," *Los Angeles Times*, June 27, 2012, p. A13; Scalia interview transcript, "Fox News Sunday," July 29, 2012, www.foxnews.com/on-air/fox-news-sunday/2012/07/29/justice-antonin-scalia-issues-facing-scotus-and-country?page=4#ixzz26jXrEcqc.

[11] The decision is *Citizens United v. Federal Election Commission*, 558 U.S. 50 (2010). See Adam Liptak, "A Rare Rebuke, in Front of the Nation," *The New York Times*, Jan. 29, 2010, p. A12. For a full account of the case, see *Supreme Court Yearbook 2009-2010, op. cit.* See also, Kenneth Jost, "Campaign Finance Debates," *CQ Researcher*, May 28, 2010, pp. 457-480.

[12] "Fox News Sunday," *op. cit.*

[13] See "2011 Term — Cases of Interest to Business," National Chamber Litigation Center, www.chamberlitigation.com/scotus/2011%20Term (undated, June 2012, before completion of term); Neil Weare, "U.S. Chamber Quietly Completes Undefeated 7-0 Term," Constitutional Accountability Center, June 29, 2012, http://theusconstitution.org/text-history/1503/us-chamber-quietly-completes-undefeated-7-0-term-success-versus-solicitor-general. The center's 7-0 count does not include the court's summary reversal of the Montana Supreme Court's decision to uphold a state law banning independent political spending by corporations. Quotes from pertinent editions of *Supreme Court Yearbook, op. cit.* Descriptions of cases discussed also drawn from *Supreme Court Yearbook.*

[14] The decision is *Ledbetter v. Goodyear Tire & Rubber Co.*, 550 U.S. 618 (2007). For a full account, see *Supreme Court Yearbook 2006-2007.* For legislation, see Robert Pear, "Congress Relaxes Rules on Suits Over Pay Inequality," *The New York Times*, Jan. 29, 2009, p. A14, www.nytimes.com/2009/01/28/us/politics/28rights.html. See also Thomas J. Billitteri, "Gender Pay Gap," *CQ Researcher*, March 14, 2008, pp. 241-264.

[15] The decision is *Leegin's Creative Leather Products v. PSKS*, 551 U.S. 887 (2007). For a full account, see *Supreme Court Yearbook 2006-2007, op. cit.*

[16] For Toobin's account, see "Money Unlimited: How John Roberts orchestrated the Citizens United decision," *The New Yorker*, May 21, 2012, www.newyorker.com/reporting/2012/05/21/120521fa_fact_toobin, excerpted from his book *The Oath: The Supreme Court and the Obama White House* (2012).

[17] Geoffrey R. Stone, "Citizens United and Conservative Judicial Activism," *University of Illinois Law Review* (2012), p. 486, http://illinoislawreview.org/wp-content/ilr-content/articles/2012/2/Stone.pdf.

[18] The decisions are *Heller v. District of Columbia*, 554 U.S. 570 (2008), and *McDonald v. Chicago*, 561 U.S. — (2010). For accounts, see the pertinent editions of *Supreme Court Yearbook.*

[19] Epstein, now a professor at the University of Southern California in Los Angeles, provided the statistics to *The New York Times* for use in an article by Adam Liptak, "The Roberts Court: The Most Conservative Court in Decades," July 25, 2010, p. A1, www.nytimes.com/2010/07/25/us/25roberts.html?pagewanted=all. Adler commented on the figures on the legal blog *The Volokh Conspiracy.* See Jonathan H. Adler, "Roberts Court Is Most Restrained in Decades," *The Volokh Conspiracy*, Aug. 1, 2010, www.volokh.com/2010/08/01/court-under-roberts-is-most-restrained-in-decades/.

[20] The decision is *Boumediene v. Bush*, 553 U.S. 723 (2008). For a full account, see *Supreme Court Yearbook 2007-2008, op. cit.* For background, see Kenneth Jost, "Closing Guantánamo," *CQ Researcher*, Feb. 27, 2009, pp. 177-200.

[21] The decision is *Northwest Austin Municipal Utility District No. 1 v. Holder*, 557 U.S. 193 (2009). For an account, see *Supreme Court Yearbook 2008-2009.*

[22] For a compact historical overview, see David G. Savage, *Guide to the U.S. Supreme*

About the Author

Associate Editor **Kenneth Jost** graduated from Harvard College and Georgetown University Law Center. He is the author of the *Supreme Court Yearbook* and *The Supreme Court from A to Z* (both *CQ Press*). He was a member of the *CQ Researcher* team that won the American Bar Association's 2002 Silver Gavel Award. His previous reports include "Reexamining the Constitution" and "States and Federalism." He is also author of the blog *Jost on Justice* (http://jostonjustice.blogspot.com). Research assistants Rob Silverblatt and Niccolo Barber contributed to this report.

Court (5th ed., 2010), pp. 3-84. See also "Historic Milestones" in Kenneth Jost, *Supreme Court A to Z* (5th ed., 2012), pp. 591-593.

[23] See, e.g., "60 Minutes," CBS News, April 24, 2008.

[24] Account drawn from ongoing reporting for *Supreme Court Yearbook, op. cit.*

[25] Quoted in Toobin, *The Oath, op. cit.*, p. 36.

[26] Quoted in *Supreme Court Yearbook 2006-2007, op. cit.* See also Linda Greenhouse, "In Steps Big and Small, Supreme Court Moved Right," *The New York Times*, July 1, 2007, p. A1. Scalia and Thomas joined Ginsburg and John Paul Stevens in dissent in the punitive damages case, *Philip Morris Co. v. Williams*.

[27] See Ashby Jones and Brent Kendall, "Roberts Straddles Ideological Divide," *The Wall Street Journal*, June 29, 2012, p. A1, http://online.wsj.com/article/SB10001424052702303561504577494723149538572.html; Adam Liptak, "Roberts's Delicate Twist: Surprise From Conservative Chief Justice Marks His Emergence as Court's Fulcrum," *The New York Times*, June 29, 2012, p. A1; Goldstein was quoted on "CBS Evening News," June 29, 2012.

[28] For an overview, see Kannon K. Shanmugam and James M. McDonald, "Looking Ahead: October Term 2012," in *Cato Supreme Court Review*, September 2012, pp. 393-417. Exposition drawn from *SCOTUSBlog* and Supreme Court preview briefings conducted by, among others, Georgetown University Law Center, Cato Institute, American Civil Liberties Union, American Constitution Society, Washington Legal Foundation, American Bar Association and National Chamber Litigation Center. Videos of all but the ACLU session are available on the respective websites.

[29] The Democratic platform is here: www.democrats.org/democratic-national-platform; the Republican platform, here: www.gop.com/news/press-releases/rnc-releases-2012-republican-party-platform/.

[30] See Mark Sherman, "Why It Matters: 1 New Justice Could Change a Lot," The Associated Press, Sept. 20, 2012, www.google.com/hostednews/ap/article/ALeqM5jqfEtAAtj2Fgtu8–P38X-yJbDlg?docId=5c8c9b4dd2c448efaafcc65f38c2eaaa.

[31] Joan Biskupic, "Exclusive: Justice Ginsburg shrugs off rib injury," Reuters, Aug. 8, 2012, www.reuters.com/article/2012/08/09/us-usa-court-ginsburg-idUSBRE87801920120809.

[32] "Justice Scalia on issues facing SCOTUS and the country," "Fox News Sunday," July 29, 2012, www.foxnews.com/on-air/fox-news-sunday/2012/07/29/justice-antonin-scalia-issues-facing-scotus-and-country.

FOR MORE INFORMATION

Alliance for Justice, 11 Dupont Circle, N.W., Suite 200, Washington, DC 20036; 202-822-6070; www.afj.org. Works to ensure that the federal judiciary advances core constitutional values and administers justice fairly.

American Association for Affirmative Action, 888 16th St., N.W., Suite 800, Washington, DC 20006; 202-349-9855; www.affirmativeaction.org. Promotes affirmative action to achieve equal opportunity.

American Civil Liberties Union, 125 Broad St., 18th Floor, New York, NY 10004; 212-549-2500; www.aclu.org. Works to protect rights and liberties guaranteed by the Constitution.

American Constitution Society, 1333 H St., N.W., 11th Floor, Washington, DC 20005; 202-393-6181; www.acslaw.org. Liberal-leaning organization promoting constitutional values of individual rights and liberties, equality and access to justice.

Cato Institute, 1000 Massachusetts Ave., N.W., Washington, DC 20001; 202-842-0200; www.cato.org. Libertarian think tank supporting limited government and free markets.

Center for Equal Opportunity, 7700 Leesburg Pike, Falls Church, VA 22043; 703-442-0066; www.ceousa.org. Conservative think tank focusing on issues related to affirmative action and immigration.

Committee for Justice, 722 12th St., N.W., Fourth Floor, Washington, DC 20005; 202-270-7748; www.committeeforjustice.org. Promotes a neutral interpretation of established law and opposes the creation of new laws through judicial activism.

Constitutional Accountability Center, 1200 18th St., N.W., Suite 501, Washington, DC 20036; 202-296-6889; theusconstitution.org. Think tank, law firm and action center opposing the influence of politics and special interests in the judiciary.

Criminal Justice Legal Foundation, 2131 L St., Sacramento, CA 95816; 916-446-0345; www.cjlf.org. Public interest law organization supporting a balance of rights between crime victims and the criminally accused.

Federalist Society, 1015 18th St., N.W., Suite 425, Washington, DC 20036; 202-822-8138; www.fed-soc.org. Conservatives and libertarians seeking to reform the American legal system in accordance with an originalist interpretation of the Constitution.

Freedom to Marry, 155 W. 19th St., Second Floor, New York, NY 10011; 212-851-8418; www.freedomtomarry.org. Coalition campaigning for same-sex marriage rights.

National Association of Criminal Defense Lawyers, 1660 L St., N.W., 12th Floor, Washington, DC 20036; 202-872-8600; www.nacdl.org. Criminal defense organization promoting a fair and proper administration of criminal justice.

National Organization for Marriage, 2029 K St., N.W., Suite 300, Washington, DC 20006; 1-888-894-3604; www.nationformarriage.org. Nonprofit political organization opposing the legalization of same-sex marriage.

U.S. Chamber of Commerce, 1615 H St., N.W., Washington, DC 20062; 202-659-6000; www.uschamber.com. Lobbying group representing the interests of businesses and trade associations.

[33] See Linda Greenhouse, "Every Justice Creates a New Court," *The New York Times*, May 26, 2009, p. A27, www.nytimes.com/2009/05/27/opinion/27greenhouse.html?pagewanted=all.

[34] Klaidman, *op. cit.*

[35] Rosen, *op. cit.*

Bibliography

Selected Sources

Books

Biskupic, Joan, *American Original: The Life and Constitution of Supreme Court Justice Antonin Scalia*, Sarah Crichton Books, 2009.

The veteran Supreme Court correspondent, now with Thomson Reuters, provides a comprehensive account of Scalia's life with insightful analysis of his judicial philosophy.

Breyer, Stephen, *Active Liberty: Interpreting Our Democratic Constitution*, Knopf, 2005.

The Supreme Court justice argues that courts should resolve issues of constitutional and statutory interpretation with an eye to encouraging popular participation in democratic government. Includes notes.

Colucci, Frank J., *Justice Kennedy's Jurisprudence: The Full and Necessary Meaning of Liberty*, University Press of Kansas, 2009.

An associate professor of political science at Purdue University identifies Justice Anthony Kennedy's "core belief" in liberty as essential to understanding his role, votes and opinions on the Supreme Court. For a somewhat parallel evaluation, see Helen Knowles, *The Tie Goes to Freedom: Justice Anthony M. Kennedy on Liberty* (Rowman & Littlefield, 2009).

Greenburg, Jan Crawford, *Supreme Conflict: The Inside Story of the Struggle for Control of the United States Supreme Court*, Penguin, 2007.

The CBS News correspondent — now reporting as Jan Crawford — provides a well-sourced account of President George W. Bush's nominations and the Senate confirmations of John Roberts and Samuel Alito to the Supreme Court.

Scalia, Antonin, and Bryan A. Garner, *Reading Law: The Interpretation of Legal Texts*, West, 2012.

The Supreme Court justice coauthors with the noted legal lexicographer a book detailing and demonstrating the philosophy of "textualism" in statutory construction. Includes glossary, bibliography.

Toobin, Jeffrey, *The Oath: The Obama White House and the Supreme Court*, Doubleday, 2012.

The CNN legal analyst and *New Yorker* writer weaves together the stories of the Roberts Court and the Obama White House up through the court's upholding of Obama's health care law in June. Toobin's earlier work is *The Nine: Inside the Secret World of the Supreme Court* (Anchor, 2007).

Articles

Klaidman, Daniel, "How Chief Justice John Roberts Will Handle Obamacare," *The Daily Beast*, Sept. 10, 2012, www.thedailybeast.com/newsweek/2012/09/09/how-chief-justice-john-roberts-will-handle-obamacare.html.

The veteran *Newsweek* correspondent depicts Roberts' pivotal vote to uphold President Obama's health care law as the culmination of his struggle between "his staunch conservatism" and "his attachment to predictability, social harmony, decorum, and propriety."

Liptak, Adam, "Supreme Court Moving Beyond Its Old Divides," *The New York Times*, July 1, 2012, p. A1.

The *Times*' Supreme Court correspondent saw "good evidence" in the 2011-2012 term's decisions that Chief Justice Roberts had "worked hard to insulate his institution from the charge that it has political motivations."

Rosen, Jeffrey, "Big Chief: How to understand John Roberts," *The New Republic*, Aug. 3, 2012, pp. 13-14.

The George Washington University law professor and *New Republic* legal affairs editor views Roberts' "deft performance" in the health care case as a possible prelude to taking bold conservative stands in "decades" to come.

Shanmugam, Kannon K., and James M. McDonald, "Looking Ahead: October Term 2012," *Cato Supreme Court Review*, September 2012.

The article previews the major cases on the Supreme Court's calendar and those awaiting the justices' decisions whether to grant review.

On the Web

The Supreme Court's website provides access to docket information, schedules, argument transcripts and decisions (**www.supremecourt.gov/**). The site also includes a link to the American Bar Association's Preview website for links to briefs filed in Supreme Court cases from the 2003-2004 term to the present (**www.americanbar.org/publications/preview_home/alphabetical.html**).

SCOTUSBlog, sponsored by Bloomberg Law, compiles coverage and materials on Supreme Court cases (**www.scotusblog.com**). The Legal Information Institute at Cornell University Law School is another online resource for Supreme Court materials (**www.law.cornell.edu/supct/**).

From CQ Press

CQ Press has an extensive catalogue of print and online resources about the Supreme Court. Titles include ***The Supreme Court Yearbook***, an online annual series; ***The Supreme Court A to Z*** (5th ed., 2012); the two-volume ***Guide to the U.S. Supreme Court*** (5th ed., 2010); ***Supreme Court Compendium: Data, Decisions, and Developments*** (5th ed., 2011); and ***The Supreme Court Justices: Illustrated Biographies, 1789-2012*** (3d ed., forthcoming 2012).

The Next Step:

Additional Articles from Current Periodicals

Affirmative Action

Browne-Marshall, Gloria, "America's Affirmative Action Dilemma," *Bay State Banner* (Mass.), April 12, 2012, p. 16, www.baystatebanner.com/natl15-2012-04-12.
The Supreme Court will perpetuate inequality if it decides that affirmative action in higher education is unconstitutional, says a constitutional law expert.

Schmidt, Peter, "Texas Lawsuit Complicates Presidential Race," *The Chronicle of Higher Education*, July 30, 2012, chronicle.com/article/U-of-Texas-Admissions-Case/133203/.
A lawsuit questioning a Texas undergraduate admissions policy has landed in the Supreme Court, likely adding the politics of affirmative action to the presidential race.

Ware, Leland, "Affirmative Action's Future May Rest With Justice Kennedy," *News Journal* (Del.), March 19, 2012.
The outcome of *Fisher v. University of Texas* will likely rest with the vote of Justice Anthony Kennedy.

Business Interests

Liptak, Adam, "Court Declines to Revisit Its Citizens United Decision," *The New York Times*, June 26, 2012, p. A14, www.nytimes.com/2012/06/26/us/supreme-court-declines-to-revisit-citizens-united.html?_r=0.
Critics of the Supreme Court's campaign finance rulings say they have led to unprecedented levels of corporate money pouring into presidential and congressional campaigns.

Savage, David G., "Chief Justice Roberts Signals That Supreme Court Remains Independent," *Los Angeles Times*, June 30, 2012, articles.latimes.com/2012/jun/30/nation/la-na-roberts-20120630.
Chief Justice John G. Roberts considers it an insult when he hears that the Supreme Court is playing politics or pandering to business interests.

Weiner, Rachel, "Supreme Court's Montana Decision Strengthens Citizens United," *The Washington Post*, June 25, 2012, www.washingtonpost.com/blogs/the-fix/post/supreme-courts-montana-decision-strengthens-citizens-united/2012/06/25/gJQA8Vln1V_blog.html.
The high court has struck down a Montana law regulating corporate political spending, ruling that Citizens United applies to state and local elections.

Judicial Activism

Hays, Michael, "Judicial Activism By Professedly Conservative Jurists," *Las Cruces* (N.M.) *Sun-News*, April 21, 2012.
Republicans and Democrats often accuse courts of judicial activism when they dislike a decision.

Knight, Robert, "Obama's Bullying Pulpit," *The Washington Times*, April 9, 2012, p. B3, www.washingtontimes.com/news/2012/apr/6/obamas-bullying-pulpit/?page=all.
President Obama's positions on several Supreme Court decisions undermine his opposition to judicial activism.

Steiden, Bill, "Faulting Judges Is Hardly New," *Atlanta Journal-Constitution*, April 8, 2012, p. A4.
Conservatives have long complained about judicial activism, but now a Democratic president is voicing similar concerns.

Politics

Clyne, Reginald J., "The Importance of a Free-Thinking Court," *The Miami Times*, July 4, 2012, p. A3, miamitimesonline.com/the-importance-of-a-free-thinking-court/.
The Supreme Court is not an impartial arbiter of the law but rather a group of Democratic and Republican appointees voting along party lines, says a legal columnist.

Greenhouse, Linda, "What We Think About When We Think About the Court," *The New York Times*, Dec. 28, 2011, opinionator.blogs.nytimes.com/2011/12/28/what-we-think-about-when-we-think-about-the-court/.
Judging at the Supreme Court level involves a complicated blend of considerations, says a columnist.

Rodricks, Dan, "What's Broccoli Got to Do With It?" *The Baltimore Sun*, April 1, 2012, p. A23, articles.baltimoresun.com/2012-04-02/news/bs-ed-rodricks-obamacare-20120331_1_justice-scalia-justice-breyer-obamacare.
The Supreme Court's legitimacy would be enhanced if Americans could believe that ideology hasn't played a role in the court's deliberations over the Affordable Care Act, says a columnist.

CITING *CQ RESEARCHER*

Sample formats for citing these reports in a bibliography include the ones listed below. Preferred styles and formats vary, so please check with your instructor or professor.

MLA STYLE

Jost, Kenneth. "Remembering 9/11," CQ Researcher 2 Sept. 2011: 701-732.

APA STYLE

Jost, K. (2011, September 2). Remembering 9/11. *CQ Researcher, 9*, 701-732.

CHICAGO STYLE

Jost, Kenneth. "Remembering 9/11." *CQ Researcher*, September 2, 2011, 701-732.

Researcher PLUS Archive
New!

CQ Researcher

Published by CQ Press, an Imprint of SAGE Publications, Inc.

www.cqresearcher.com

Euro Crisis

Should the U.S. help ease Europe's economic woes?

Amid Europe's continuing economic troubles, riots erupted in several nations last month, notably Spain and Greece, as citizens protested radical government efforts to cut spending and raise taxes. Rising debt has damaged the euro currency and pushed many nations into deep recession, high unemployment and widespread poverty. Some experts say Europe's economic woes are holding back economic recovery in the United States by undermining consumer confidence, exports and investments and that the U.S. government should do more to help Europe fix its problems. Otherwise, they warn, a new global economic crisis on the scale of the 2008 crash could hit Europe, the United States and the rest of the world. Other experts argue, however, that it is not in the United States' interest to help rescue the European economy.

A policeman in Madrid confronts a demonstrator on Sept. 25, as thousands of Spaniards protest tax increases and spending cuts imposed to help solve Spain's sovereign debt crisis. Europe's economic troubles already have hit U.S. exports and forced many American banks to trim overseas investments. But if the euro collapses, some analysts say the repercussions in the United States could be severe.

INSIDE THIS REPORT

THE ISSUES 843
BACKGROUND 850
CHRONOLOGY 851
CURRENT SITUATION 854
AT ISSUE........................857
OUTLOOK 858
BIBLIOGRAPHY 862
THE NEXT STEP 863

CQ Researcher • Oct. 5, 2012 • www.cqresearcher.com
Volume 22, Number 35 • Pages 841-864

CQPRESS

RECIPIENT OF SOCIETY OF PROFESSIONAL JOURNALISTS AWARD FOR EXCELLENCE ◆ AMERICAN BAR ASSOCIATION SILVER GAVEL AWARD

THE ISSUES

843 • Is the euro crisis slowing the U.S. recovery?
• Would a euro collapse be as bad as doomsayers predict?
• Should the United States provide more aid to help Europe?

BACKGROUND

850 **Dreams of a United Europe**
The European Coal and Steel Community was a precursor of the eurozone.

853 **The Golden Years**
Initially, Europe's single currency promoted more trade, growth and wealth.

854 **Sovereign Debt Crisis**
Europe's government debt problems emerged in 2009.

CURRENT SITUATION

854 **Hoping for Salvation**
European bankers think they have solved the debt crisis, at least temporarily.

856 **U.S. Reverberations**
American exports and corporate investments in Europe are down.

OUTLOOK

858 **Eyeing Italy**
Some experts say that if Italians elect anti-austerity politicians, Italy and the eurozone could be doomed.

SIDEBARS AND GRAPHICS

844 **Five Eurozone Members Face Crises**
Seventeen European Union members have adopted the euro.

845 **EU Is America's Second-Biggest Customer**
Canada buys the most U.S. products.

847 **Euro's Path: Promise to Uncertainty**
Introducing the euro spurred economic growth for about a decade.

848 **Euro Crisis Devastated EU Growth**
Greece's economy has declined the most.

851 **Chronology**
Key events since 1951.

852 **How Wall Street Helped European Nations Cheat**
New economic problems may reveal more scandals.

855 **Preparing for the Worst in Greece**
Many U.S. firms are hedging against a euro crash.

857 **At Issue**
Should the U.S. government bail out Europe's financial system?

FOR FURTHER RESEARCH

861 **For More Information**
Organizations to contact.

862 **Bibliography**
Selected sources used.

863 **The Next Step**
Additional articles.

863 **Citing *CQ Researcher***
Sample bibliography formats.

Cover: AFP/Getty Images/Pierre-Philippe Marcou

CQ Researcher

Oct. 5, 2012
Volume 22, Number 35

MANAGING EDITOR: Thomas J. Billitteri
tjb@cqpress.com

ASSISTANT MANAGING EDITOR: Kathy Koch
kkoch@cqpress.com

SENIOR CONTRIBUTING EDITOR:
Thomas J. Colin
tcolin@cqpress.com

ASSOCIATE EDITOR: Kenneth Jost

STAFF WRITER: Marcia Clemmitt

CONTRIBUTING WRITERS: Peter Katel, Barbara Mantel, Jennifer Weeks

SENIOR PROJECT EDITOR: Olu B. Davis

ASSISTANT EDITOR: Darrell Dela Rosa

FACT CHECKER: Michelle Harris

Los Angeles | London | New Delhi
Singapore | Washington DC

An Imprint of SAGE Publications, Inc.

VICE PRESIDENT AND EDITORIAL DIRECTOR, HIGHER EDUCATION GROUP:
Michele Sordi

DIRECTOR, ONLINE PUBLISHING:
Todd Baldwin

CQ Researcher (ISSN 1056-2036) is printed on acid-free paper. Published weekly, except: (March wk. 5) (May wk. 4) (July wk. 1) (Aug. wks. 3, 4) (Nov. wk. 4) and (Dec. wks. 3, 4). Published by SAGE Publications, Inc., 2455 Teller Rd., Thousand Oaks, CA 91320. Annual full-service subscriptions start at $1,054. For pricing, call 1-800-834-9020. To purchase a *CQ Researcher* report in print or electronic format (PDF), visit www.cqpress.com or call 866-427-7737. Single reports start at $15. Bulk purchase discounts and electronic-rights licensing are also available. Periodicals postage paid at Thousand Oaks, California, and at additional mailing offices. POSTMASTER: Send address changes to *CQ Researcher*, 2300 N St., N.W., Suite 800, Washington, DC 20037.

Euro Crisis

BY CHRISTOPHER HACK

THE ISSUES

Riots overseas don't usually cause jitters on Wall Street, but when civil unrest in late September in Greece and Spain led to sell-offs in the world's major stock markets U.S. exchanges suffered too.

More than 100,000 Greeks marched through downtown Athens, some throwing Molotov cocktails at police. In Madrid, truncheon-wielding Spanish riot police fired rubber bullets as tens of thousands of Spaniards gathered near parliament to protest government austerity measures. The demonstrations were only the latest protests at government efforts to balance their books, including drastic spending cuts and tax hikes.

The protests worried Wall Street because Greece's debt crisis has dragged down the European economies that share the single euro currency, and some analysts fear that the troubles in the eurozone could knock the weak U.S. recovery off course — or even put the country back in recession.

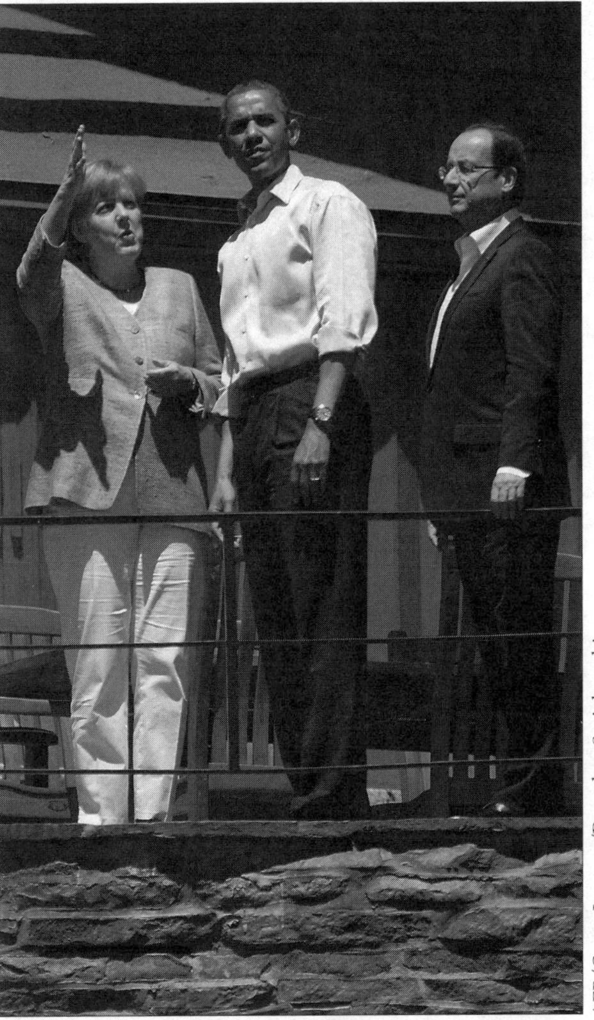

AFP/Getty Images/Brendan Smialowski

President Obama visits informally with German President Angela Merkel and French President François Hollande following a G-8 summit meeting on May 19 at Camp David, the presidential retreat in rural Maryland. With the U.S. presidential election just weeks away, the Obama administration is urging European leaders to intensify efforts to resolve their economic problems. Many experts agree that if troubled nations, such as Greece, exit the eurozone, the effect on the U.S. economy could be disastrous.

The European Union is the second-largest purchaser of American exports, and many U.S. banks do a large portion of their business either in Europe or in conjunction with European banks. The problems in Europe already have hit U.S. export income and forced banks to retrench. But, in an increasingly globalized world, and one in which the economies of Europe and the United States are often said to be joined at the hip, many economists worry that Europe's problems could undermine Americans' fragile confidence in the U.S. economic recovery — even for individuals and companies that don't deal directly with the continent.

The strong economic ties between the United States and Europe are well known. With mutual investments worth $2.71 trillion, the United States and the 27-member European Union (EU) have the world's most integrated economic relationship. The "transatlantic economy" supports 15 million jobs and accounts for 45 percent of the world's annual output, or gross domestic product (GDP), according to the U.S. Chamber of Commerce. In trade terms alone, the EU bought 18 percent of all U.S. exports last year, second only to Canada's 19 percent. [1]

But the relationship is deeper than just trade, with many large companies investing and operating on both sides of the Atlantic, says Jacob Kirkegaard, a research fellow at the Peterson Institute for International Economics in Washington, who says up to 70 percent of U.S. foreign investments are in Europe.

In 2002, 17 EU members gave up their individual currencies to create a shared currency, the euro. The move was part of a long-term plan to create a "united states of Europe" that would lead to a greater sense of cohesion after two world wars tore the continent apart. It was also designed to boost business, trade and prosperity, just as adopting a central currency shared by all the states aided America's fledgling economy at the end of the 18th century.

Initially, the euro was credited with creating solid growth and lower costs, as companies saved up to $33 billion per year just by not having to exchange currencies. [2]

But the euro also created massive problems, unforeseen by most proponents at the outset. By joining the 17-nation eurozone, some less-prosperous countries — notably Greece, Ireland,

Continued on p. 845

Five Eurozone Members Face Crises

Seventeen of the 27 European Union (EU) members — representing a population of about 330 million — have adopted the euro currency. Seven others are scheduled to join the eurozone by 2017. Sweden, Denmark and the United Kingdom have declined to join the eurozone. Portugal, Ireland, Italy, Greece and Spain are experiencing sovereign debt crises, largely because of profligate government borrowing and spending during the early 2000s.

The European Union and the Eurozone

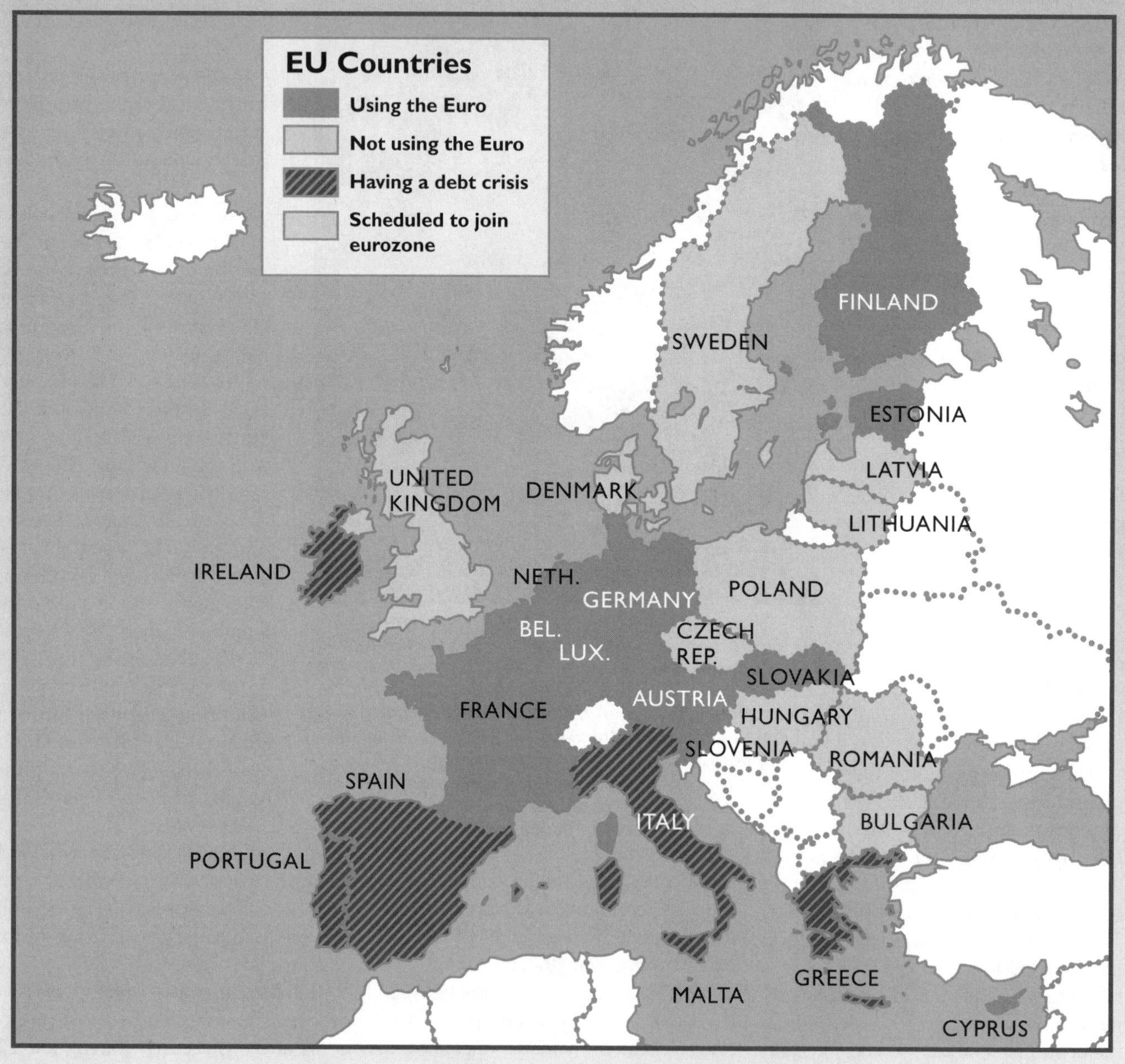

Source: European Commission. Map by Lewis Agrell

Continued from p. 843

Portugal, Spain and Italy — suddenly had access to cheap credit. Greece's borrowing costs, for instance, dropped from about 8 percent to less than 4 percent. [3] The governments and people from those countries went on borrowing sprees, racking up huge debts.

Meanwhile, the poorer countries' less-efficient economies could not compete with the productivity of powerhouses such as Germany. German workers, for instance, produce on average about $55 worth of output per hour, compared to $34 in Greece. [4] And social benefits are higher in the poorer states. Germans typically retire at age 67 on 50 percent of their former salaries, while Greeks retire at 65 with 93 percent of their salaries. [5] With such diverse countries now locked together in a single currency, business and wealth began to shift from the poorer countries in the south to wealthier nations in the north.

After the global recession hit in 2007-2008, international lenders sharply raised lending rates for the weaker euro countries, pushing them to the verge of bankruptcy. EU authorities and the International Monetary Fund (IMF) offered cheap loans to rescue the indebted countries, provided they cut spending, raised taxes and increased productivity. [6]

After three years of such austerity, affected countries are seeing massive job and wage cuts and sharply rising taxes. Official figures show average unemployment in the eurozone reached 11.4 percent in August, compared to 8.1 percent in the United States for the same month. With unemployment comparatively low in the prosperous countries such as Germany, the averages reflect very high levels in the periphery countries. Greece, for instance, has 24.4 percent unemployment, while Spain is at 25.1 percent. [7] The Greek economy is expected to shrink 4.7 percent in 2012, after contracting 6.9 percent last year. [8]

Austerity is provoking anger, demonstrations, riots and swings toward extremist political parties. Some economists question whether slashing spending and jobs is the right way to dig the continent out of its troubles. "There has been so much austerity that in most of those countries being hit, there is going to be absolutely no growth in 2013," says Scheherazade Rehman, director of the European Union Research Center at The George Washington University in Washington.

Meanwhile, in the euro's wealthier countries, bailouts for nations viewed as spendthrift and feckless are unpopular. German voters especially feel they are picking up the tab for others. An opinion poll in Germany in June found that 51 percent thought the country would be better off leaving the euro, while 71 percent wanted Greece out. [9] In addition to the German public's anger over bailouts, the German economy is being dragged down by the European recession. The IMF forecasts that the economy will grow by just 1 percent in 2012, and some analysts fear it may slip into recession.

International investors remain skeptical, continuing to demand high interest rates despite the austerity programs. Spain — seen as financially well managed but with high debt levels — saw its borrowing costs on 10-year debt rising to 7.5 percent, from about 4 percent. That triggered a bold move in early September by the European Central Bank (ECB). It promised to buy up any eurozone country's debt that could not be sold in the international financial markets. Effectively, this meant the ECB was agreeing to bail out the indebted nations, which angered the Germans. To placate them, the ECB said it would agree to buy the debt only if the marginal countries stuck to their austerity plans — but few believed that. [10]

All these measures have affected U.S. exports to Europe, which were down 4.8 percent as of April, and undermined the earnings of U.S. companies. [11] U.S. multinational companies such as GM, Ford, Dow and IBM are attributing lower

EU Is America's Second-Biggest Customer

The 27-member European Union (EU) was the second-largest buyer of U.S. products in 2011, just behind Canada. Exports to all the major U.S. trading partners increased between 2002 and 2011, led by China, where U.S. exports nearly quintupled.

Most Important Destinations for U.S. Exports

(2002-2011)

U.S. Exports (in $ billions)

$600, 500, 400, 300, 200, 100, 0

2002, 2011

Canada, European Union, Mexico, China, Japan, Korea, Rest of world

Source: U.S. Department of Commerce, 2012

earnings this year to Europe's debt crisis. "The majority of global holdings or global subsidiaries of U.S. companies are in Europe, which means it's not so much U.S. exports that are hurt, but it's the earnings of U.S. multinationals," says Kirkegaard.

Analysts also say the crisis is hitting confidence at home, with some suggesting that the U.S. recovery is being held back by Europe's troubles. With a presidential election only weeks away, the Obama administration is urging European leaders to move more quickly to get the crisis under control. "People in the administration and the Treasury want to see more aggressive action by the Europeans to resolve this in an orderly manner, rather than this slow unraveling of the crisis," says Ethan Ilzetzki, a professor of economics at the London School of Economics. "But the influence any administration has is limited."

Experts say the euro crisis will end either with the weaker economies being reformed and returned to growth or with one or more being forced out. Some suggest the latter could be achieved in a managed way, to limit the fallout, but almost all agree that if forced exits lead to panic — as was the case in 2008 with the collapse of the giant American investment bank Lehman Brothers — the effect on the U.S. economy could be disastrous.

"A meltdown in European financial markets would — because of the role of European banks in American money markets and the role of the U.S. banks in European money markets — be quite significant for some time, but you're talking here about a pretty extreme event," explains Martin Wolf, chief economics commentator at London's *Financial Times*.

As efforts continue to focus on keeping the weaker economies afloat, attention is turning to upcoming political events — notably parliamentary elections in Italy next April. Some fear that the unpopularity of Italy's austerity program could lead voters to choose extremist parties advocating a breakup of the euro, with potentially devastating effects on the United States and the world.

"Everybody has their eye on Italy . . . we are tied in so many ways to them, either through interest rates, trade, exchange rates, credit threats, borrowing costs. There is no way around it," says George Washington University's Rehman.

As American leaders, economists and consumers watch developments in the eurozone, here are some of the questions being debated:

Is the euro crisis slowing the U.S. recovery?

U.S. exports, banking, investment and economic confidence are feeling the effects of the European debt crisis, although experts disagree on the extent of the impact on American businesses, investors and consumers.

The EU bought 18 percent of all American exports last year, much of it from the aircraft, computer and pharmaceutical industries. [12] With Europe in recession and its economies shrinking, Europeans are expected to buy fewer American goods this year. How that will affect the U.S. economy, however, is a matter of debate.

Rehman, of the European Union Research Center at George Washington University, foresees trouble for the American economy. "The U.S. and the EU growth patterns — if you look at them over time — have mirrored each other," he says. "Clearly any slowdown or crisis or worsening of what's happening in the euro is going to slow us down."

But others suggest that, even if exports take a hit in Europe, U.S. companies can look to wider markets. "The world's emerging economies, led by China and India, account for half of the global economy and will continue to expand . . . , keeping the global economy — including the United States — churning for some time," said Fred Bergsten, director of the Peterson Institute for International Economics in Washington. [13] Indeed, the United States sold $1.48 trillion worth of goods and services overseas in 2011, up 15.8 percent over the previous year. All of Europe only accounted for about 20 percent of that total.

Ilzetzki, at the London School of Economics, says the domestic side of the U.S. economy is so big that a slowdown in global trade would not have as large an impact as some might expect. "The U.S. is a relatively closed economy," he says. "Total trade — exports plus imports — is approximately 30 percent of [the economy], which is very, very low compared to most other economies." Instead of focusing on increasing or maintaining European trade, U.S. policymakers should concentrate on the "real problem" of creating jobs at home, he says.

But others say the European crisis is worrisome for exporters such as the United States. They note that European banks, which often finance foreign purchases of U.S. goods, are contracting, raising the specter of a major slowdown in foreign trade — not just to Europe but to emerging markets such as Asia and Africa. "European banks, which have traditionally been the main financiers of emerging-market trade and are a huge presence in the global economy, are retrenching," says David Smick, a global economic policy strategist in Washington and publisher of the journal *International Economy*. "So, that's not great for the U.S. export sector."

European banks financed about three-fourths of Boeing's $40 billion in international sales in 2011, and the euro crisis could undermine sales this year, the company says. [14] That is because many international sales of big-ticket U.S. exports such as commercial aircraft are financed by European banks, which are more willing to lend to purchasers such as the governments of developing countries. And now, with the European banks retrenching, those governments can't get financing to buy the U.S. exports.

The euro crisis also could hurt U.S. banks because, as Rehman says, American and European banks have large investments in one another. If those on either side of the Atlantic are having financial trouble, it immediately affects those on the other side. And while American banks have taken measures to recover from the 2008 financial crash, they are still exposed to problems in the eurozone through their links to European banks.

U.S. multinational corporations also have major investments, including manufacturing and services subsidiaries, in Europe. "The majority of global subsidiaries of U.S. companies are in Europe, which means it's not so much U.S. exports that are hurt but the earnings of U.S. multinationals," says Kirkegaard at the Peterson Institute. "The economic relationship between the U.S. and Europe is closer than just trade. It's investments; it's companies like General Motors." Reduced earnings at such U.S. multinationals have a greater impact on the U.S. economy than lower exports, he says. This problem is hidden in companies' lower earnings figures rather than being in published trade data, he adds.

Ordinary American investors are also on the hook, some say, because their savings are invested in pension and hedge funds that often invest heavily in European companies, many of which have seen lower returns as a result of the euro crisis.

Economic confidence may be among the biggest casualties of Europe's troubles. "It used to be that most Americans really didn't understand or didn't worry about these issues," says Uri Dadush, director of the International Economics Program at the Carnegie Endowment for International Peace. "But in the last two years — and in the last year particularly — the euro crisis has become very, very present in the minds not just of business people and investors but families and consumers" as well. Lack of confidence in the economy affects people's decisions to spend and invest.

Euro's Path: Promise to Uncertainty

Creation of the euro in 1999 spurred economic growth in the eurozone. The euro-to-dollar exchange rate — showing the strength of the euro against the dollar — peaked in 2007. But the sovereign debt crisis that began in 2008 has sent the exchange rate down, reflecting a weaker euro and concern about struggling European nations.

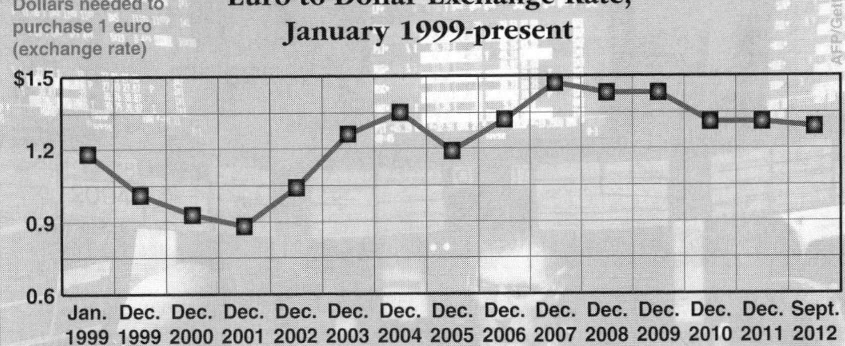

Source: "Exchange Rates," European Central Bank, September 2012, www.ecb.int/stats/exchange/eurofxref/html/eurofxref-graph-usd.en.html

That is especially noticeable in the corporate sector, Kirkegaard says. U.S. businesses have at least $1 trillion on their balance sheets "just sitting there that they could be investing," he says, but many are holding back on hiring new workers and making sizeable capital investments. "I think it has to do with the uncertainty in the global economy — linked to Europe," Kirkegaard says. "Rightly or wrongly, a lot of U.S. businesses are worried about the euro. And you don't need to be a multinational to be affected."

In one area — interest rates — the euro crisis is helping the U.S. economy, analysts agree. European anxiety is encouraging global investors to put their money into U.S. government bonds, which are seen as one of the world's safest currencies. Because demand is up for those bonds, authorities don't have to offer high interest rates to get investors to buy them. So global investors effectively are lending money to the U.S. government at a cheaper rate, and interest rates for American borrowers thus remain low.

"This is a little bit of a positive effect that should not be ignored," says Dadush.

Would a euro collapse be as bad as doomsayers predict?

If the euro collapses, it could be another "Lehman moment" for the United States, say some analysts — referring to the 2008 bankruptcy of the giant U.S. investment bank Lehman Brothers, whose fall helped push the United States into its steepest recession since the 1930s.

To prevent the U.S. and global financial system from collapsing in the wake of Lehman's failure, the U.S. Treasury Department, Federal Reserve and central banks and governments around the world undertook an unprecedented multitrillion-dollar rescue effort. Doomsayers predict a financial

Euro Crisis Devastated EU Growth

Declining growth in Europe's biggest economies in the last seven years reflects the impact of the euro crisis across the European Union (EU). Greece's gross domestic product (GDP) growth rate has fallen the furthest, followed by Spain and Ireland.

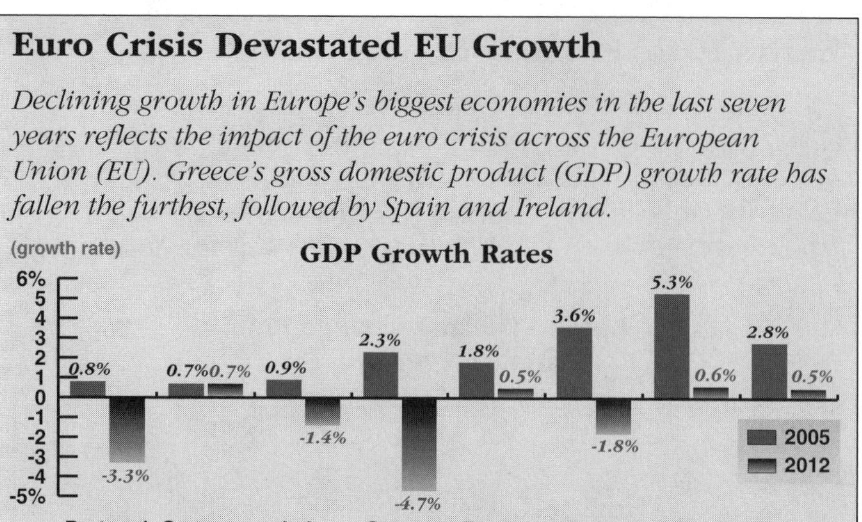

Source: Eurostat, the official EU statistical agency

collapse in Europe today would similarly threaten the global financial system, including American banks.

But things have changed since 2008, insist U.S. banks, the Fed and the Obama administration. Wall Street institutions have built a financial firewall by increasing the amount of capital set aside to cover bad loans and by reducing their exposure to loan risk in the eurozone. In other words, bankers and policy makers say, the U.S. economy would be protected from a euro collapse because Wall Street firms have cut their lending to European institutions. [15]

Economist Ed Yardeni, an independent analyst who previously worked for the Federal Reserve and U.S. Treasury, agrees. "My sense is that the U.S. banks are not greatly exposed to the European banks. U.S. banks have been able to issue a lot of the bonds and raise money in the equity markets since early 2009, and the money markets are still open to U.S. banks."

Some analysts say it is important to be clear on what a financial "collapse" means. In a much-discussed scenario, Greece would become either unwilling or unable to keep paying interest on its debts. This "default" would prevent it borrowing money, so it would leave the eurozone and print a new currency in order to keep paying employees — a chain of events dubbed "Grexit."

The Carnegie Endowment's Dadush says that if this were a well-managed, "not too messy" divorce, then the effect on the United States could be limited.

Ilzetzki, at the London School of Economics, says Europe would suffer, but the United States could ride it out. "This would not be a shock of the magnitude of Lehman Brothers to the United States," he says. "For the U.S. the exposure would be big enough, given the already weak recovery, to tip the scales towards another recession. There could be political ramifications — the presidential race is close enough that any economic bad news could tip the scales — but it would not be another Lehman for the U.S."

Much would depend on the mechanics of a "Grexit." Analyst say the Greek government could introduce a new currency "virtually overnight." [16] That currency would then fall against the euro and the dollar, allowing Greece to start growing again. [17] But the devaluation would decimate the wealth of Greek individuals and companies — and European banks that hold Greek debt.

What would happen next is unclear. The markets could restabilize or an international financial panic could ensue. The latter scenario could lead investors to withdraw their money from banks across Europe and force larger countries, such as Spain and Italy, into default — by which time the crisis could be too big to stop.

This worst-case scenario, dubbed "contagion," would bankrupt even heavyweight European banks, a crisis that in turn could hit U.S. banks in a domino effect, since many of these European banks owe large sums of money to American banks. "If the exit of Greece was very messy and disputed, the first impact would be on the rest of Europe, Spain and Italy, and the contagion could become very serious," says Dadush. "The effect on the U.S. would be huge and disastrous," undermining thousands of businesses and consumers and eventually putting the country "back into recession."

The key is whether the exit of one or two smaller countries could be contained, the Peterson Institute's Kirkegaard says. "Direct U.S. exposure to Greece, Ireland and Portugal is very, very small; maybe $10 billion. But U.S. exposure to Spain and Italy is in the multi-hundred billions of dollars," he says. "In the worst-case scenario, it would destroy large parts of the euro area financially, and that would have an immediate effect on the United States, reminiscent of what happened after Lehman. And that is something U.S. authorities should be worried about."

American banks say their net exposure to the troubled countries of Europe — Portugal, Ireland, Italy, Greece and Spain, known collectively as the "PIIGS" — is limited. In June filings to the Securities and Exchange Commission, Bank of America put its exposure at $9.7 billion (down from $16.7 billion in June last year), Citigroup was at $17.5 billion, and JPMorgan Chase at $6.2 billion.

But Dadush says all the firewalls erected by the banks could amount to nothing in the event of contagion. "I never bought the idea that the U.S. banks are insulated from the euro crisis," he says, explaining that American banks only report their "net exposure" to the eurozone. Banks across the world lend each other billions of dollars on a daily basis as part of their routine transactions. But instead of saying, for example, that an American bank owes a European bank $100 million, and that the European bank owes them $100 million, they cancel the figures out and say that they have a "net exposure" of zero. In a global financial crisis, however, if a European bank can't pay the $100 million it owes, the fact that an American bank owes it some money in return becomes meaningless, because both debts could be left unpaid. So measuring this "net exposure" becomes meaningless.

AFP/Getty Images/Filippo Monteforte

Students demonstrate in Rome on Sept. 28 against spending cuts by the Italian government aimed at bringing Italy back from the brink of economic collapse. Some experts fear that the unpopularity of Italy's austerity program could lead voters in parliamentary elections next April to choose extremist parties advocating a breakup of the eurozone, which could have devastating effects on the United States and the world.

"A lot of exposures that you read about are concluded on the 'net basis' . . . but in a systemic crisis, gross exposures matter a lot," explains Dadush. "The fact that people owe you money cannot be offset against the fact that you owe them money, because you cannot be sure that you are going get your money back."

Bank analyst Christopher Wolfe, a managing director at Fitch Ratings, a New York-based credit-rating agency, says there are always risks. "You can look at the published numbers, in terms of who holds what sovereign [government] and corporate debt in the eurozone, and come up with the numbers and gross and net, but that's not the concern. It's what happens if there are some very disorderly actions in the eurozone. No one can predict that."

Smick, the global economic policy strategist in Washington, says there also are questions about how strong the big European banks are. "Nobody believes the balance sheets of the European banks," he says. "So much of the stuff on the balance sheets is junk." Many loans recorded as assets may be worthless, because a borrower has either stopped making repayments or is close to stopping repayments, he says. "That's a lot of concern."

While American banks are well protected in the current situation, Yardeni says, if the euro crisis leads to contagion, then all bets are off. "If there is a financial meltdown in Europe, the trouble at Lehman will seem like just a warm-up act."

Should the United States provide more aid to help Europe?

Given the risks the euro crisis poses to the U.S. economic recovery, some economists say Washington should do more to rescue Europe.

For instance, the administration could pledge more money to the IMF to ensure that it has sufficient funds to prevent another global crisis. "The U.S. is running a big risk in Europe," says the Carnegie Endowment's Dadush, who criticizes Congress for blocking an expansion of IMF funding. "Their response has not been adequate. By not contributing to the expansion of IMF resources, they have let everybody else off the hook — China and others."

Since the Lehman collapse, the IMF has sought to increase its funding in case there is a new international crisis. At the beginning of 2012, for example, Christine Lagarde, the new IMF managing director, sought to raise $500 billion and urged the United States to play a role, saying: "If the European economy falters, the American recovery and American jobs would be in jeopardy." [18]

The United States, which provides about one-fifth of the IMF's funding, already underwrites part of the euro bailout program, which is jointly financed by the IMF and the EU. But so far Congress has refused to approve a proposed temporary boost in the U.S. share of the institution's funding by $63 billion. In addition, in May 2010 Congress blocked IMF funds from being used to directly bail out debtor nations. [19]

When Washington said no, much of the money to increase the IMF's emergency funding reserve came from European and emerging nations, with $43 billion from China. [20]

"It is a tremendous mistake by Congress to not have authorized the IMF capital expansion," says the Peterson Institute's Kirkegaard. "It is in very strong American interest to make sure the IMF is strong and well capitalized."

It is also a strategic mistake at a geopolitical level, he says, for Washington to allow China to play a bigger role. "The IMF was essentially designed by the U.S. and has been run by the United States and Europe since inception and is more dominated by the United States and Europe than any alternative organization that could be created today. If the Asian countries decided to create an Asian monetary fund, U.S. influence on that would be a lot smaller. So it is in the direct U.S. national interest to ensure the IMF remains the indispensable, unambiguous global body. Congress has made a huge mistake. The Chinese can [now] put a lot of money into the IMF, and say 'Look, give us a lot more influence.' And that influence is going to come at the direct expense of Europe and the U.S."

But former Federal Reserve official Yardeni says the United States is right to limit its role: "If you start going down that road, you may find that it's a black hole and you have committed yourself to being involved in a rescue that is not in our interest. The Europeans got themselves into this mess; they're going to have to work themselves out."

Policy strategist Smick says he is surprised that the euro issue has not featured more in the presidential campaign. "If I were running as a Republican, I'd be talking about Greece every day. I would be quoting European policy officials who said not that long ago that this kind of massive debt is manageable. You would say, 'Here is a group who thought they could finance their way around it using central-bank tricks. Has it worked? We risk going into that at some point.' "

Ilzetzki at the London School of Economics says the policy will be largely unchanged no matter who is in the White House. "There tends to be continuity in international affairs, and even more so in international economic affairs," he says. "So I would not expect a big change. And even if there was the desire, it's not clear that there is much that the United States could really do." ■

BACKGROUND

United States of Europe

Merging Europe's economies and currencies has been a dream for centuries. But after World War II, which devastated Europe for the second time in less than 40 years, policymakers increasingly saw economic integration as the best way to end centuries of bloodshed on the continent.

Part of the pressure came from the United States, which launched its four-year Marshall Plan in 1947 to reconstruct the continent's war-torn economies. [21] Another step came in 1951, when France, Germany, Italy, the Netherlands, Belgium and Luxembourg agreed to operate their coal and steel industries under a common umbrella organization called the European Coal and Steel Community. The idea was that none of the six countries could then go to war against a fellow member because steel is essential for the manufacture of weapons. War would be "not only unthinkable, but materially impossible," France's foreign minister said at the time. [22]

In a precedent-setting move, the six nations agreed to surrender some sovereignty to the new organization. Six years later they signed the Treaty of Rome creating the European Economic Community (EEC), which aimed to remove trade barriers and allow the free movement of goods, services and people across borders. [23]

Over time, trade and cooperation grew in this "Common Market," and more European countries joined, with Britain, Denmark and Ireland signing up in 1973, Greece in 1980 and Portugal and Spain in 1985.

While many proponents saw the EEC as merely a vehicle to boost trade, others — notably French leaders, European intellectuals and, increasingly, EEC officials and advisers — had an unwavering desire for an "ever-deeper union," which became the EU motto. France sought to reinforce its own political status while weakening Germany's economic dominance and saw a merging of political and economic sovereignty as a means to that end. In 1986, the Single European Act committed member states to "economic and monetary union" — but with no deadline, since some countries — especially Britain — preferred to maintain the EEC as little more than a trading bloc.

In 1989, the fall of the Berlin Wall separating East and West Germany raised the prospect of a reunified Germany for the first time since World War II. [24] But German reunification required the consent of the four post-war occupying powers: France, Britain, the United States and Russia. France seized the opportunity to advance its dream of a unified Europe, agreeing to German reunification in exchange for an unwavering pledge by German officials to support monetary union — and to end Germany's powerful deutschemark currency.

"Now that Germany's land area, population and economic capacity were set to expand at a stroke, it became even more urgent to lock it into Europe," writes Barry Eichengreen, a University of California economist. [25] Germany, in effect, sacrificed the deutschemark for reunification.

On Feb. 7, 1992, a new treaty was signed at Maastricht, in the Netherlands, by members of the renamed European Union. It established rules for a single currency and a 1999 deadline for introducing the "euro." Because of strong domestic resistance —

Continued on p. 852

Chronology

1950s-1970s

European nations cooperate after World War II to prevent future conflicts and foster growth.

1951
To prevent future weapons build-ups, France, Germany, Italy, the Netherlands, Belgium and Luxembourg agree to operate coal and steel industries under a common pact.

1957
The six nations create the European Economic Community (EEC) allowing free movement of goods and people.

1968
EEC members remove all customs duties between themselves; trade and prosperity accelerates.

1973
Denmark, Ireland and United Kingdom join EEC.

1980s ***EEC membership grows; Berlin Wall falls; Germany agrees to monetary union in exchange for national reunification.***

1981
Greece becomes 10th nation to join EEC, followed five years later by Portugal and Spain.

1988
Single Market Act commits members to "monetary union" — creating a single European currency — but resistance slows setting final date.

1989
Collapse of communism leads to fall of Berlin Wall; France reluctantly approves reunification of East and West Germany in exchange for German agreement to push for creation of euro.

1990s-2003

Euro is established; economies enjoy strong growth as huge credit bubble develops.

1992
Maastricht Treaty, signed in the Netherlands, commits countries to monetary union by 1999. Stability Pact later sets debt and budget targets but is not enforced.

1999
Eleven countries abandon their currencies and adopt euro; Britain balks. Greece joins currency two years later, but its financial qualifications turn out to have been falsified.

2002
Euro currency is introduced, national currencies phased out. Cheap credit lifts heavily borrowing poorer countries, but real estate and debt bubbles grows.

2003
Germany and France override EU budget rules, join others in running large budget deficits; rules are eventually abandoned.

2008-2012

World financial crisis leads investors to withdraw funds; indebted nations face crisis.

2008
Lehman Brothers collapses in wake of U.S. subprime crisis; financial panic spreads to Europe as investors run from highly indebted banks, companies and nations. European governments pour money into local banks to keep them afloat, incurring even more so-called sovereign debt.

2009
Greece reveals its budget deficit is twice what it previously reported, prompting fear the country will go bankrupt and bring down the euro.

2010
EU and International Monetary Fund (IMF) bail out Greece and Ireland and set up European Financial Stability Facility. Across Europe, countries pledge to end credit binge, cut spending and raise taxes.

2011
EU and IMF bail out Portugal and agree to second bailout for Greece (May). . . . European leaders persuade banks that lent money to Greece to accept 50 percent cut in value of loans (October); European rescue fund is raised to €1 trillion ($1.3 trillion, at today's exchange rate).

2012
Voters across Europe, angry at cuts and higher taxes, elect anti-austerity politicians (May); socialist François Hollande becomes French president, and Greeks choose extremist parties offering utopian solutions. But the parties are unable to form a government, leading to new elections. As fears grow afresh for the euro, Greek voters elect centrists who back the austerity program. . . . Pressure grows on larger economies, such as Spain and Italy. . . . In September, the European Central Bank calms nerves when it pledges to bail out any eurozone state that adopts strict austerity measures.

How Wall Street Helped European Nations Cheat

New economic problems may reveal more scandals.

When economic times turn bad, it's not hard to spot the investors with poor judgment or those who took excessive risks. As billionaire investor Warren Buffett colorfully puts it, "After all, you only find out who is swimming naked when the tide goes out."

Buffett could have been describing the fallout from the current euro crisis. In one of his legendary annual letters to his investors, Buffett illustrates how unacceptable practices and nefarious deals in the eurozone came to light only after the crash — many involving Wall Street investment banks. [1]

In 2000, for example, euro membership was seen as a symbol of success, modernity and pride, and the Greek government was desperate to join. But EU rules stipulated that government debt be no more than 60 percent of a country's economy, or gross domestic product (GDP), or at least "approaching" that figure. Greece's debt was 94 percent of GDP that year, and with state funds pouring into preparations for the 2004 Olympics in Athens the debt figure was going in the wrong direction. [2]

But Goldman Sachs, the Wall Street investment bank, came to the rescue in 2001, lending Greece €2.80 billion ($3.64 billion) disguised in a complicated foreign-currency transaction. [3] The secret loan made Greece's debt ratio appear to be improving enough to allow it to join the euro.

As Buffet essentially predicted, the full details of the transaction came to light in 2010, only after the euro debt crisis began. [4] The already indebted Greek government had indeed agreed to pay Goldman €600 million ($540 million at the time) in fees and interest for the deal. But by 2005, the total cost had risen to €5.1 billion ($6.1 billion) — contributing towards Greece's downfall. Martin Wolf, the chief economics commentator at London's *Financial Times*, described the deal as "completely legal and completely scandalous." [5]

Greece was not alone in cooking its books to meet the euro entry criteria. Italy in 1996 engaged in a similar transaction with JP Morgan, another Wall Street bank. [6] Similar deals have come to light across the continent, from Portugal to France. As recently as 2009 — as the euro crisis was unfolding — Goldman was back in Athens offering the troubled government a way to stretch its health-care costs over a longer period to make debt figures look better. [7] This time Greece declined.

Banks also have manipulated the international interest rates on which much European debt is calculated. Again, the shenanigans only emerged this summer, "when the tide went out," as Buffett would say. The issue concerns the London interbank offer rate, or "Libor," which is used to set the interest rate on millions of international loans.

Continued from p. 850

in part because of British nationalism and fears of continental socialism — Britain refused to join and retained its pound currency. [26] After a referendum on the issue in 2000, Denmark also chose to stay outside the eurozone. [27]

Adopting the euro offered many economic benefits, including a massive trade boost, much as the creation of the original EEC had done in 1957. But creating a single currency for independent nations with different political and economic systems also raised the prospect of intra-continental tension. To ensure that one country did not drag the others down, politicians reluctantly agreed that member countries would need similar economic policies. Germany, which had the strongest economy, insisted that all members maintain debt and budget deficits similar to its own stringent standards.

Euro countries adopted a set of "Maastricht criteria" stipulating that countries seeking to join the euro maintain deficits of no more than 3 percent of the country's annual income [or gross domestic product (GDP)] and public debt of no more than 60 percent of GDP. For Germany, the biggest hurdle was the need to abandon the iconic deutschemark.

But Germany also recognized a huge potential economic reward from joining a single currency: a vast market for its famed industrial goods, made by BMW, Mercedes, Bosch, Braun and others, without having to deal with constantly fluctuating exchange rates.

Although a single European currency was created for economic reasons, it was also done as a political move. Many European political figures and intellectuals rode roughshod over dissenting voices, urging them to believe in the single currency as the embodiment of the European ideal, as something almost mythical. Skeptical economists and center-right politicians who opposed the euro were portrayed as narrow-minded Luddites. [28] Pro-euro politicians insisted that "political will" would overcome any economic problems. [29]

However, the new eurozone rules for how European economies should be managed were routinely broken, even by Germany. After reunification, the high cost of rebuilding East Germany drove up Germany's borrowing, leading to a budget deficit of 4 percent in 2004, and forced the government to ask the EU for permission to break the rules it had itself demanded.

That left the rules in tatters, but politicians across the continent were swept up in the desire to expand the eurozone. "Policymakers wanted the new currency to succeed . . . allowing weaker economies to join without

Libor is announced daily, by drawing together data from many banks on the interest rate they are charging and being paid in loans between themselves. Many consumer, auto and housing loans, for example, charge interest at the current "Libor rate" with the addition of a fixed percentage, such as "Libor + 4 percent." So if Libor goes down, a consumer's repayments go down, and vice versa. But in July it emerged that this rate for years had been artificially fixed so that banks could profit from it, with the finger pointing at Bank of America, Citigroup, JPMorgan Chase, the Swiss bank UBS and Barclays in the U.K. [8] Moreover, knowledge of the scandal went right to the top. It was revealed, for example, that Treasury Secretary Timothy Geithner knew about the scandal as far back as 2008, but did little. [9]

Despite American bankers' claims that they are now "fully protected," should the euro collapse, the Libor scandal highlights how little is known of their real exposure to European markets.

With fears growing that the euro crisis could get dramatically worse in coming months — possibly forcing one or more countries out of the single currency — it's likely that still other bankers were "swimming naked."

— Christopher Hack

1 Warren E. Buffet, "Chairman's Letter," Berkshire Hathaway, Feb. 28, 2002, www.berkshirehathaway.com/2001ar/2001letter.html.

2 See Christopher Hack, "Hosting the Olympics," *CQ Global Researcher*, July 3, 2012, pp. 305-328.

3 Nicholas Dunbar and Elisa Martinuzzi, "Goldman Secret Greece Loan Shows Two Sinners as Client Unravels," Bloomberg, March 6, 2012, www.bloomberg.com/news/2012-03-06/goldman-secret-greece-loan-shows-two-sinners-as-client-unravels.html.

4 Beat Balzil, "How Goldman Sachs Helped Greece to Mask its True Debt," *Der Spiegel*, Aug. 2, 2010, www.spiegel.de/international/europe/greek-debt-crisis-how-goldman-sachs-helped-greece-to-mask-its-true-debt-a-676634.html.

5 Aaron Task, "Greece-Goldman Sachs Deals Were 'Completely Scandalous' — And Perfectly Legal: Martin Wolf," *The Huffington Post*, May 2, 2010, www.huffingtonpost.com/2010/03/02/greece-goldman-sachs-deal_n_482001.html.

6 Louise Story, Landon Thomas Jr. and Nelson D. Schwartz, "Wall St. Helped to Mask Debt Fueling Europe's Crisis," *The New York Times*, Feb. 13, 2010, www.nytimes.com/2010/02/14/business/global/14debt.html?pagewanted=all.

7 Robert Scheer, "It's Greek to Goldman Sachs," *The Huffington Post*, Feb. 17, 2010, www.huffingtonpost.com/robert-scheer/its-greek-to-goldman-sach_b_465134.html.

8 Mark Gongloff, "Citigroup Manipulated Libor More Than Any Other U.S. Bank: Reports," *The Huffington Post*, July 20, 2012, www.huffingtonpost.com/mark-gongloff/libor-scandal-citigroup_b_1689853.html.

9 Margaret Hartmann, "With Release of 2008 Memo, Focus Shifts to Geithner in Libor Scandal," *New York Magazine*, July 13, 2012, nymag.com/daily/intel/2012/07/focus-shifts-to-geithner-in-libor-scandal.html.

due scrutiny," writes Mary Elise Sarotte, a professor of international relations at the University of Southern California. [30] "Such laxness allowed the entry of members [Belgium and Italy] with debt-to-GDP ratios well in excess of 60 percent but also applicants such as Greece, which not only flouted the rules but also falsified its records." [31]

The Golden Years

In 1999 the euro was introduced as the currency for commercial transactions in 11 countries. Then three years later, with great fanfare, bank teller machines were stocked with new euro notes for the first time on Jan. 1, 2002.

The "European dream" became real. Aside from promoting more trade, growth and wealth, the single currency created a new sense of oneness, or social integration, on the continent. Rather than the EU being about distant meetings of ministers, or a new law, it was something physical, in Europeans' pockets.

The early European integration period is forever linked to the emergence of an elite group of young, highly educated, multilingual graduates from across the continent who had participated in the "Erasmus program," a university-level European student-exchange program. [32] This "Erasmus generation" effortlessly crossed borders and language barriers, taking well-paid white-collar jobs in Brussels, the capital of the EU. It was seen as the embodiment of the new Europe and the rootstock of a new generation of leaders on the continent.

Through the mid-2000s, a huge wave of prosperity spread across the continent, especially in once-marginalized Ireland, Greece, Portugal and Spain. Ireland, which became known as the "Celtic Tiger," enjoyed mushrooming manufacturing and service industries and a massive housing boom. Greece poured money into new infrastructure, roads, railways and airports in preparation for hosting the 2004 Olympics. Spain and Italy enjoyed boom years previously unimagined.

The new investments were the product of a little-discussed factor. Before the creation of the euro, international banks lent to each government in Europe at different exchange rates, charging risky governments the most. With the arrival of the euro, all European economies were considered as safe as the safest nation: Germany. As a result, borrowing costs fell for the more marginal nations. Like a teenager getting his first credit card, once countries were accepted into the union, they could borrow vast amounts at very low interest rates. Greece, for example, had previously paid about

8 percent to borrow money using a 10-year bond. After the introduction of the euro, that rate fell below 4 percent. [33] National spending sprees ensued. With few countries sticking to the rules, many borrowed vast amounts during the 2000s, and some countries became hugely indebted.

The single currency also exacerbated another perennial problem: imbalances among nations. German workers are very productive, receive few pay rises, retire late on a relatively low pension and enjoy low inflation rates. Workers in southern Europe typically have low productivity levels, retire early on high pensions, receive frequent pay rises and are accustomed to high inflation rates. Before the euro, such trends were unimportant when it came to their respective economies and the effect on exports, because each country had its own currency, and the weaker currencies usually fell in value compared to the deutschemark. As a result, the price of an item made in Greece, for instance, continued to rise steadily measured in the drachma. But when exported, the steady devaluation of the drachma meant that when the price of the item converted into deutschemarks, it had not gone up. So Greek exports remained affordable in Germany, despite steadily rising wages and inflation at home.

The arrival of the euro changed all that. The Greek government could no longer allow a steady decline in the exchange rate of its currency against its neighbors. Wages, costs and inflation rose in Greece, but rose more slowly in Germany. So with every passing year, Greek exports became more expensive in Germany and elsewhere in Europe, progressively destroying the country's economy.

During the same early period, roughly from 2002-2007, many peripheral countries, such as Ireland, Spain and Greece, experienced massive real estate booms, fed by the lower borrowing costs. In Ireland, for example, average house prices nearly doubled between 2000 and 2006, and the Irish economy became increasingly dependent on the construction sector. When the mortgage bubble burst and the Irish government bailed out its banks, it took over all of their debts, undermining Ireland's position in the euro. [34]

Sovereign Debt Crisis

In early 2007, when it became clear that home loans had been made to millions of people who could not afford to pay them back, the U.S. subprime mortgage crisis went largely unnoticed in Europe, where it was seen as an "Anglo-Saxon problem" — standard EU jargon for the free-market economics embraced by the United States and Britain.

But in 2008, after the situation morphed into a global banking crisis, European banks began to look hard at how much they had lent to individuals, companies and governments across the continent and began asking questions about heavily indebted countries such as Greece and Ireland.

Europe's government — or "sovereign" — debt crisis emerged at the end of 2009, when Greece's new prime minister, George Papandreou, revealed that his country's budget deficit was nearly four times worse than reported by his predecessor. Instead of being 3.7 percent of GDP, he said, the deficit was 12.7 percent. [35] And worse, government debt was an astounding 120 percent of GDP in 2010. [36] Global financial markets panicked as investors began to demand higher interest rates on government bonds to keep lending to Greece.

Bond rating agencies downgraded Greek government debt to "junk" status, in essence advising clients that lending to Greece was a gamble with no guarantee the money would ever be repaid. [37] Although the government desperately cut spending and raised taxes, it wasn't enough. High interest costs on government debt were beginning to swallow up a larger proportion of state income. Declaring Greece "a sinking ship," Papandreou asked the EU for help. [38]

Countless summits between the governments of Europe, senior figures in the European Union, the European Central Bank and IMF resulted in a series of bailouts, in which the EU and IMF agreed to lend the indebted countries enough to keep them afloat while they sorted out their financial problems. Greece initially received €110 billion ($146 billion), Portugal €78 billion and Ireland €85 billion. With the IMF involved in the lending, some of the money was effectively being put up by U.S. taxpayers.

But when governments desperately cut spending and raised taxes to balance their books, a backlash erupted across Europe, with demonstrations, strikes, riots and — in some countries — a swing towards extreme leftist politics. The chaos in Europe has had pronounced economic effects on the United States. Exporters sending goods to Europe have seen their order books shrink, affecting jobs at home. American banks, worried about how much they have already lent to European countries, have tightened up their lending, and fears have grown about what would happen to the U.S. recovery if the crisis in Europe gets worse. ■

CURRENT SITUATION

Hoping for Salvation

Almost three years after the euro debt crisis began, the situation today seems little changed, although

Preparing for the Worst in Greece

Many American firms are staying but hedging against a euro crash.

The shaky euro has American companies operating in Greece preparing for the worst. To protect their funds if Greece suddenly abandons the euro, U.S. and other international companies routinely sweep money out of Greek banks every evening and into accounts in countries outside the eurozone, such as the U.K. and Switzerland. Then, every morning, they transfer it back in so that they can do business.

"These sorts of measures are expensive, but American and other foreign companies are nervous now," says a Greek business journalist in Athens, who asked not to be named. He says many U.S. companies also are simply pulling up stakes. "They have been leaving for about four or five years now, and it is continuing. Every now and then you hear that another company has gone."

AFP/Getty Images/Louisa Gouliamaki

A gas mask-wearing protester runs from tear gas fired by riot police in Athens on Sept. 26 during a 24-hour general anti-austerity strike that turned violent.

Analysts warn that a Greek exit from the euro would temporarily freeze all bank accounts in the country. Funds in euro accounts would then be converted into a new national currency, which would then plummet in value by at least half, they predict. And a euro exit would affect even dollar accounts in Greece, because the government would be expected to impose "capital controls" to prevent a hemorrhage of wealth out of the country, thus trapping all moveable foreign assets.

"It is irrational for anyone, whether a corporation or an individual, to be leaving money in Greek financial institutions, so long as there is a credible prospect of a eurozone exit," said Ian Clark, a London attorney.

Meanwhile, American firms across the eurozone are subtly changing their business practices. When negotiating new contracts, for example, some seek payment in dollars or British pounds instead of the euro; others are storing dollars in eurozone countries to pay local workers in case of a breakdown in the currency union. [1]

Sandra Cohen, an assistant professor in the Department of Business Administration at the Athens University of Economics and Business, who is Greek, says such moves are to be expected. At the same time, she notes, many American companies are staying and doing good business: "Some are leaving, but many companies have chosen to stay and keep trading here, including big American firms like Proctor & Gamble and Johnson & Johnson.

"Of course, they are making contingency plans — it is their money, and they want to be prepared," she continues. "But they still see opportunities." Since parliamentary elections in June brought a pro-reform coalition to power, she says, "there is a much more optimistic feel in the country," noting for example that the General Index of the Athens Stock Exchange has almost doubled in three months, from 476 at the beginning of June to 770 in mid-September. "The Greeks are a proud people, and we take any opportunity to be positive and hopeful."

The business journalist adds that despite the generally negative international view of the country's finances, plenty of investment opportunities exist. "Salaries have gone down, labor laws have been reformed, assets are very cheap, rents are low. This can be a good place to do business now, but there are still risks, and funding of course is difficult." He says that some markets for foreign goods also are being tested by a shift in favor of domestically produced products — a consumer initiative to "buy Greek."

"Some American brands are suffering, but that is not deliberate," he says. "It is the German brands that are being deliberately left on the shelves."

— Christopher Hack

[1] Heidi N. Moore, "U.S. firms prep for Greece exit from euro," American Public Media, Sept. 7, 2012, www.marketplace.org/topics/business/european-debt-crisis/us-firms-prep-greece-exit-euro.

the mood is brighter in Brussels — the EU capital — where a new plan to buy bonds from heavily indebted countries has lifted spirits.

Still, the situation in the peripheral countries — Greece, Portugal, Ireland, Spain and Italy — remains grim. To be able to continue making payments on their huge amounts of debt, governments are cutting spending, raising taxes and trying to improve competitiveness. But the austerity measures are slashing economic growth and personal incomes. The Greek economy is expected to shrink by "only" 4.7 percent in 2012, according to the IMF, an improvement from 2011, when it dropped 6.9 percent. [39]

And popular anger is growing. In Athens, protesters took to the streets again in September, with demonstrations that in some cases descended into widespread rioting. But the anger was not just coming from rebellious youth. In one week in September alone, for example, doctors and teachers took to the streets to protest funding cuts; [40] 2,000 retired military officers marched through Athens against pension cuts; [41] local government workers announced a two-day strike; [42] and pensioners stormed the health ministry protesting reductions to spending on pharmaceuticals and plans to reduce their benefits. [43]

AFP/Getty Images/Saul Loeb

A Boeing 787 Dreamliner undergoes finishing touches in Everett, Wash., on Feb. 17. European banks financed about three-fourths of Boeing's $40 billion in international sales in 2011, but the euro crisis could undermine sales this year, the company says. European banks finance many purchases of big-ticket U.S. exports, especially to developing countries. With European banks retrenching, it is harder for Boeing's customers to buy U.S.-made planes.

Darker forces also are emerging. In the same week, surveys showed that support for Golden Dawn, a neo-fascist party, reportedly had climbed to 10.5 percent, making it the third most popular political party in the country. [44] Greek President Karolos Papoulias summed up the national mood: "The Greek people have suffered great sacrifices. I think they have reached their limit. . . . We have sustained merciless whipping. I think we have paid for our mistakes enough." [45]

In Brussels, however, officials are more optimistic. Mario Draghi, the new president of the European Central Bank (ECB), announced in September that the bank would start buying unlimited quantities of the most indebted euro countries' government bonds, which had become increasingly unattractive to investors. [46] The announcement has reassured analysts that, no matter how bad things get, no European government will be allowed to go bankrupt because it cannot sell bonds. Investors are reassured, stock markets have risen and the interest rates indebted governments must pay to raise money have eased.

Rehman, of George Washington University, welcomes Draghi's move. "It is calming the markets, easing the pressure and stating that they will do anything to keep Spain and Italy solvent," she says. "That is exactly what we need to hear, because there is a crisis in confidence."

Economic policy strategist Smick echoes her sentiment. "The fact that the ECB is now going to buy everything probably takes some of the threat away," he says. "Now they feel like they have probably bought some time."

But the move has triggered fresh anger in Germany, where it is perceived as letting the peripheral countries avoid tackling their profligate spending habits. Although Draghi has said the purchases will occur only if the indebted governments stick to their austerity programs, many Germans are skeptical.

The ECB move is "tantamount to financing governments by printing bank notes," railed the head of the German central bank, which for nearly half a century had built the deutschemark into a powerful currency by acting cautiously and avoiding inflation. [47] His comment echoed the popular opinion among many Germans that the ECB move would lead to rampant inflation and decimate the wealth of hard-working German savers, while letting work-shy spendthrifts off the hook.

U.S. Reverberations

While EU politicians and bankers struggle to keep the euro alive, Europe's economies continue to stagnate, which is damaging the American economic recovery, say some analysts. Although there are no reliable indicators of how the crisis is affecting American business, investor and consumer confidence, published figures indicate that exports and corporate investments in Europe are down.

During the year that ended in April, U.S. exports to the EU dropped 4.8 percent, according to the U.S. Commerce Department, the worst performance in three years. The effects are being felt in sectors such as auto, aircraft, chemicals and pharmaceutical manufacturing. And analysts say the decline in European demand is only just beginning to show up in trade data because it typically takes three to six months for goods to be shipped after an order is placed. [48]

Continued on p. 858

At Issue:

Should the U.S. bail out Europe's financial system?

URI DADUSH
DIRECTOR, INTERNATIONAL ECONOMICS PROGRAM, CARNEGIE ENDOWMENT FOR INTERNATIONAL PEACE

WRITTEN FOR *CQ RESEARCHER*, SEPTEMBER, 2012

yes

The United States is running a big risk in Europe, and the American response so far has been inadequate. Even given the European Central Bank's recent decision to buy the bonds of troubled countries, the euro's survival is far from assured. It is in America's interest for Congress to increase U.S. contributions to the International Monetary Fund (IMF) for a contingency fund to support countries in the European periphery and across the world.

A collapse of the euro would be a calamity for Europe but also a disaster for the United States. A failure of banks in the core European countries could have implications for U.S. banks similar to the failure of Lehman Brothers. Other U.S. financial institutions would be hit, including money market funds and insurance and pension companies.

A crisis that called into question the existence of the euro would also generate the mother of all flights to the dollar, causing a big dollar appreciation. Global demand for U.S. goods would plummet. The Organisation for Economic Co-operation and Development (OECD) calculates that disorderly sovereign defaults in some euro countries could cut U.S. gross domestic product (GDP) by more than 2 percent. But in a systemic crisis, official projections cannot be trusted, because they tend to shy away from the direst possibilities.

The IMF has about $250 billion in unused lending capacity, but it needs it to support the whole world and may need another $1 trillion in the event of a generalized European crisis. The U.S. share would be about $160 billion, if the United States took the lead. It would be a loan that may never be disbursed, but it would help restore confidence and contain the crisis. By deciding not to support a large IMF expansion, Congress let everybody else off the hook, including China.

But the message to Congress remains. This is not a question of whether the United States will pay for the euro crisis. It will. The question is how. Congress needs to be convinced that a failure to act could have catastrophic implications. If the euro breaks apart and Europe becomes politically unstable, that could induce Congress to act. But it would be better to act well in advance, in the interest of stability, rather than take that risk. If not, we may well have a Lehman repeat, or perhaps worse. The debts are much bigger, and so much fiscal and monetary ammunition has been spent already.

REP. RON PAUL, R-TEXAS
U.S. HOUSE OF REPRESENTATIVES

WRITTEN FOR *CQ RESEARCHER*, SEPTEMBER, 2012

no

The United States should not consider bailing out the European financial system. The economic establishment in this country has come to the conclusion that it is not a matter of "if" the United States must intervene, but "when" and "how." Newspapers are full of assertions that the breakup of the euro would result in a worldwide depression and that economic assistance is the only way to prevent this.

These assertions are yet again more scaremongering, just as we witnessed during the 2008 crisis. The real cause of economic depression — and every boom and bust — is loose monetary policy. Yet it is precisely what political and economic elites, in both Europe and the United States, are prescribing as a resolution for this crisis, with a multitrillion-dollar bailout.

The euro was built on an unstable foundation. Its creators tried to establish a dollar-like currency for Europe while forgetting that it took nearly two centuries for the dollar to devolve from a defined unit of silver to so-called fiat currency completely unbacked by a commodity such as gold. The euro had no such history. Europe's economic depression is the result of the euro's very structure, a fiat money system that allowed member governments to spend themselves into oblivion and expect someone else to pick up the tab.

A bailout of European banks by the European Central Bank and the Federal Reserve would only exacerbate the crisis. What is needed is for bad debts to be liquidated. Banks that invested in sovereign debt need to take their losses rather than socializing these and prolonging their balance-sheet adjustments. If this were done, the correction would be painful but quick. Bailing out profligate European governments will only ensure that no correction will take place.

The Federal Reserve already has pumped trillions of dollars into the U.S. economy with nothing to show for it. Just considering Fed involvement in Europe is ludicrous. The U.S. economy is in horrible shape precisely because of too much government debt and too much money creation; the European economy is destined to flounder for the same reasons. We have an unsustainable amount of debt at home; it is hardly fair to U.S. taxpayers to take on Europe's debt as well. That will only ensure an accelerated erosion of the dollar and a lower standard of living for all Americans.

Continued from p. 856

U.S. manufacturing subsidiaries in Europe also are seeing lower profits and returns on investment. "Anecdotally, companies in the second quarter did blame some of their earning disappointments on Europe. And investors weren't surprised to hear that," says economist Yardeni.

The auto industry is a classic case. GM Europe and Ford Europe have manufacturing plants in Germany, Spain, Belgium and the U.K. With demand in Europe down due to the euro crisis, many subsidiary plants on the continent are reducing capacity, which is hitting the companies' global profits.

For example, General Motors in August attributed a 38 percent drop in net global profits in the second quarter of 2012 to losses in Europe. [49] Industry analysts expect GM Europe to spend at least $1 billion shutting some of its 11 European factories. [50] At Ford, which gets a quarter of its sales from Europe, net global income was down 57 percent in the second quarter of 2012 due in part to losses in Europe. [51]

European losses also are having an effect on U.S. operations, the analysts add. "The European market has been dragging everyone's balance sheets down," said Rebecca Lindland, a research director for IHS Automotive, a forecasting company. "Ford and General Motors are feeling that just as much as anyone else," with fewer profits reinvested in American jobs, new models or more efficient factories. [52]

Similar gloom clouds the chemical sector in Europe. Dow Chemical, which has several plants in Europe that manufacture Styrofoam, reported a 34 percent fall in overall profits for the second quarter due to falling sales in Europe and currency conditions. The company says it will close or idle five factories in Europe. Closing plants overseas has ripple effects in the United States: The company needs fewer support staff back in the United States, and it brings back fewer profits from abroad, so it can't hire or invest at home. [53]

In the technology sector, similar trends are emerging. IBM, with plants across Europe, reported a 3 percent fall in global sales for the second quarter, blaming conditions in Europe, where sales were down 9 percent. [54]

Meanwhile, pharmaceutical companies such as Pfizer and Bristol-Myers Squibb say European governments are cutting back on buying drugs for health care, which could force companies to consolidate European operations.

It is difficult to calculate other potential effects on the U.S. economy. Kris Bledowski, a senior economist at the Virginia-based Manufacturers Alliance for Productivity and Innovation, said the effects extend to the U.S. supply chain, because Europe supplies important components, such as car engines and plastic parts, to many U.S. manufacturers.

"The feedback I'm getting is a concern over the logistical issues that may arise in Europe due to labor issues or economic paralysis there," said Bledowski. [55]

Other analysts discount these effects, saying that most events in the European economy have only a limited impact on the United States. "Demand in Europe is clearly weak. There is no question of that, but it hasn't collapsed," says Wolf, at London's *Financial Times*. Moreover, he says, U.S. exports to Europe represent only about 2 percent of U.S. GDP. "As long as the crisis is contained, and you don't have a real meltdown, then the effect on the U.S. of the eurozone crisis is pretty small."

The effect on U.S. confidence is limited as well, he contends. The eurozone crisis will be near the bottom on a "top 20" list of "things Americans might not be confident about," he says. At the top of the list, he says, are future U.S. tax policy, who will be running U.S. economic policy and the health of the domestic financial system. "These are all obviously vastly more important." ■

OUTLOOK

Eyeing Italy

In the long term, the euro debt crisis can be resolved in only one of two ways: Either the economic problems in the marginal countries are fixed and the eurozone returns to growth and prosperity, or the eurozone disintegrates, one or more countries leaves the single currency and the European Union fragments.

Optimists suggest that due to the ECB's recent promise to buy all marginal countries' government debt — coupled with the existing bailouts of Greece, Portugal and Ireland — the countries will remain solvent as they cut spending, raise taxes and improve competitiveness. Antonis Samaras, the Greek prime minister, who is committed to the country's austerity program, has predicted that Greece will return to economic growth in 2014.

"Over this year we will begin to contain the recession, and by the beginning of 2014 we will be able to move towards recovery. . . . We will prove that Greece can pleasantly surprise both friends and opponents, and even itself," he said. [56] His optimism is supported by the Organization for Economic Co-operation and Development, which represents the world's industrialized countries. It says Greece's efforts to cut wages and make exports more competitive will see results by 2013, and lead to a return to positive growth. [57]

However, the World Bank's new chief economist thinks the European debt crisis could adversely affect the world economy for years, prompting policy makers to consider new approaches to restarting growth and creating new jobs.

The global economy "is not doing well," said Kaushik Basu, a former top

Indian government official who went on leave from Cornell University to take the bank's top economics post on Oct. 1. "The difficult phase will live with us for a while." [58]

Meanwhile, the EU is pushing for a new treaty that will bind member states into a tighter economic union, allowing Brussels to more directly control spending so as to avoid the problems that precipitated the current crisis. But some countries are resisting the loss of yet more sovereignty. [59] And in Greece, criticism is taking on a nationalist edge, portraying the EU austerity program as German colonialism by another name. [60]

More rational skeptics of the EU plan say the ECB move only buys time, and that the Greeks and citizens of other marginal countries are not prepared to suffer the growing poverty required to return their countries to growth. Citigroup has predicted, for example, a "90 percent" chance that Greece will leave the eurozone before 2014. [61]

If that occurs, the question is: Will it be a managed exit, or will it be messy, leading to the destruction of many European banks, and possibly some in the United States? The key is what happens in Spain and Italy. EU authorities believe they can cope with the financial fallout from a default by Greece, Ireland or Portugal, but not if it spreads to the larger troubled European economies — Spain and Italy.

Thus, attention is focused on next April's parliamentary elections in Italy. If populist politicians are elected, they could tear up the austerity program, potentially bringing down the whole eurozone. "Italy is too big to fail, and it is too big to save," says Rehman of George Washington University. "If Italy starts to go south then we are in real trouble, and if you thought that the Greek election [June 2012] was bad for the market, I want to hide under the bed for the Italian elections."

Her concern stems from Italy's history of electing politicians "who are not taken very seriously," she continues. "And if you look at the Italian economy, we know it is contracting. We know they have a terrible year ahead of them, and you look at the aging population, and you look at the way Italians vote. You could get another Berlusconi-type figure, and that would a death sentence for Italy," she said, referring to Italy's former populist prime minister, Silvio Berlusconi, who was widely blamed for allowing the country to fall into high levels of debt by avoiding tough economic policies that were needed.

The United States, she says, is basically powerless. "Our hands are tied. We can try to assure ourselves that the best possible way is to make sure there is enough liquidity in our system and try to get job growth going," she says. "But other than that, you really can't do much against what happens in Europe." ■

Notes

1 "Why Europe matters: facts and figures," U.S. Chamber of Commerce, www.uschamber.com/international/europe/facts-and-figures-why-europe-matters.

2 "The euro — Business Benefits," *EUBusiness.com*, Oct. 1, 2009, www.eubusiness.com/topics/euro/business.

3 "Greece Government Bond 10Y," *Trading Economics*, www.tradingeconomics.com/greece/government-bond-yield.

4 "Labour productivity levels in the total economy," Organisation for Economic Co-operation and Development, http://stats.oecd.org/Index.aspx?DatasetCode=LEVEL.

5 For background, see Brian Beary, "Future of the EU," *CQ Global Researcher*, April 17, 2012, p. 188; and Roland Flamini, "U.S.-Europe Relations," *CQ Researcher*, March 23, 2012, pp. 277-300.

6 "Troika demanding increase to working week, retirement age," *Ekathimerini* (newspaper), Sept. 12, 2012, www.ekathimerini.com/4dcgi/_w_articles_wsite1_1_12/09/2012_460867.

7 David Jolly and Raphael Minder, "Unemployment in Euro Zone at Record High," *The New York Times*, Oct. 1, 2012, www.nytimes.com/2012/10/02/business/global/unemployment-in-euro-zone-rose-to-new-high-in-august.html?_r=1&emc=eta1.

8 "Greece and the IMF," International Monetary Fund, Aug. 30, 2012, www.imf.org/external/country/GRC/index.htm.

9 "Germans say they're 'better off without euro': poll," France24.com/AFP, July 29, 2012, www.france24.com/en/20120729-germans-say-theyre-better-off-without-euro-poll.

10 Robin Wigglesworth, "Spanish borrowing costs reach record level," *The Irish Times*, July 24, 2012, www.irishtimes.com/newspaper/finance/2012/0724/1224320708393.html.

11 Ian Katz and Cheyenne Hopkins, "Europe Imperils U.S. Sales from Chemicals to PCs: Economy," Bloomberg, June 18, 2012, www.bloomberg.com/news/2012-06-18/europe-crisis-imperils-u-s-sales-from-chemicals-to-pcs-economy.html.

12 "Trade in Goods with European Union," U.S. Census Bureau, September 2012, www.census.gov/foreign-trade/balance/c0003.html.

13 Fred C. Bergsten, "Five myths about the euro crisis," *The Washington Post*, Sept. 7, 2012, www.washingtonpost.com/opinions/five-myths-about-the-euro-crisis/2012/09/07/9b8d1412-f6db-11e1-8253-3f495ae70650_story.html.

14 Peter Whoriskey, "U.S. exporters brace for cutbacks in European bank lending," *The Washington Post*, Dec. 22, 2012, www.washingtonpost.com/business/economy/us-exporters-brace-for-cutbacks-in-european-bank-lending/2011/12/21/gIQA3n8KAP_story.html. Also see Andrew Parker, "Banks withdraw from aircraft financing," *Financial Times*, Dec. 6, 2011, www.ft.com/cms/s/0/097a515c-2003-11e1-8462-00144feabdc0.html#axzz25XNdCt9s.

15 Dan Fitzpatrick and Victoria McGrane, "Stress Test Buoys US Banks," *The Wall Street Journal*, March 14, 2012, http://online.wsj.com/article/SB10001424052702304537904577279720671471152.html. Also see Craig Torres and Josh Zumbrun, "Fed says 15 of 19 banks pass stress tests," *The Washington Post*, March 13, 2012, www.washingtonpost.com/business/economy/fed-says-15-of-19-banks-pass-stress-tests/2012/03/13/gIQAIdg99R_story.html; and Richard Wolf, "Five ways the European debt crisis could affect the U.S.," *USA Today*, Oct. 28, 2011, www.usatoday.com/money/world/story/2011-10-27/eurozone-crisis-deal/50963370/1.

16 "Who, What, Why: How would Greece switch currencies?" BBC News, June 12, 2012,

www.bbc.co.uk/news/magazine-18279522.
[17] Shawn Tully, "Greece: The anatomy of a default," *CNN Money*, May 16, 2012, http://finance.fortune.cnn.com/2012/05/16/greece/.
[18] "IMF chief Christine Lagarde urges US to give more cash to fight European debt crisis," *The Telgraph*/AFP, April 3, 2012, www.telegraph.co.uk/finance/financialcrisis/9183884/IMF-chief-Christine-Lagarde-urges-US-to-give-more-cash-to-fight-European-debt-crisis.html.
[19] Ambrose Evans-Pritchard, "Congress blocks indiscriminate IMF aid for Europe," *The Telegraph*, May 18th, 2010, http://blogs.telegraph.co.uk/finance/ambroseevans-pritchard/100005734/congress-blocks-indiscriminate-imf-aid-for-europe/.
[20] "IMF wins pledges of $456bn for crisis fund," *The Telegraph*, June 19, 2012, www.telegraph.co.uk/finance/financialcrisis/9340480/IMF-wins-pledges-of-456bn-for-crisis-fund.html.
[21] "The Marshall Plan," National Archives, www.archives.gov/exhibits/featured_documents/marshall_plan/. Also see F. Van Schaick, "Conditions for American Aid," *Editorial Research Reports*, Aug. 17, 1947, available at *CQ Researcher Plus Archive*.
[22] Robert Schuman, "The Schuman Declaration — 9 May 1950," European Union, europa.eu/about-eu/basic-information/symbols/europe-day/schuman-declaration/index_en.htm.
[23] For background, see B. W. Patch, "European Economic Union," *Editorial Research Reports*, March 27, 1957, available at *CQ Researcher Plus Archive*.
[24] For background, see Mary H. Cooper, "A Primer on German Reunification," *Editorial Research Reports*, Dec. 22, 1989, available at *CQ Researcher Plus Archive*.
[25] Barry Eichengreen, *Exorbitant Privilege* (2011), pp. 88-89.
[26] Under Conservative Prime Minister John Major, Britain had participated in an earlier version of monetary union, the European Monetary System. But after a speculators' attack on the pound, Britain took its currency out of the joint system in 1992. "Tony Blair could credit his victory in the 1997 general election to the damage done to the Conservative government of John Major by the 1992 crisis," Eichengreen writes.
[27] The €110 billion package, formally agreed to May 10, 2010, consists of €80 billion from euro area countries and €30 billion from the IMF.
[28] Daniel Hannan, "Black Wednesday: Britain was free, but we Tories were done for," *The Telegraph*, Sept. 11, 2012, www.telegraph.co.uk/news/politics/9535659/Black-Wednesday-Britain-was-free-but-we-Tories-were-done-for.html.
[29] Roger Bootle, "Unraveling an economy with an interlinked crisis," *The Telegraph*, Oct. 16, 2011, www.telegraph.co.uk/finance/comment/rogerbootle/8830079/Unravelling-an-economy-with-an-interlinked-crisis.html.
[30] Mary Elise Sarotte, "Eurozone Crisis as Historical Legacy," *Foreign Affairs*, Sept. 29, 2010, www.foreignaffairs.com/print/66715?page-2.
[31] *Ibid.*
[32] "The ERASMUS Program — studying in Europe and more," The European Commission, http://ec.europa.eu/education/lifelong-learning-programme/erasmus_en.htm.
[33] "Greece Government Bond 10Y," *op. cit.*
[34] "Irish Construction output at 23 percent of GNP in 2007; 416,000 employed in construction related activity — 19 percent of workforce; Up to 30,000 job losses by 2009," *Finfacts Ireland*, Sept. 25, 2007, www.finfacts.ie/irishfinancenews/article_1011255.shtml.
[35] Dan Bilefsky and Niki Kitsantonis, "Greek Statistician Is Caught in Limelight," *The New York Times*, Feb. 13, 2010, www.nytimes.com/2010/02/14/world/europe/14greek.html. Also see William L. Watts, "Greece's revised 2009 deficit tops 15 percent of GDP: Eurostat lifts reservations over Greek methodology," MarketWatch, Nov. 15, 2010, 6:36 a.m. EST, www.marketwatch.com/story/greeces-revised-2009-deficit-tops-15-of-gdp-2010-11-15.
[36] "Greek debt to reach 120.8 pct of GDP in '10 — draft," Reuters News Agency, Nov. 5, 2009, www.reuters.com/article/2009/11/05/greece-budget-debt-idUSATH00496420091105. Also see "A very European crisis: The sorry state of Greece public finances is a test not only for the country policymakers but also for Europe," *The Economist*, Feb. 4, 2010, www.economist.com/node/15452594?story_id=15452594.
[37] "Greek bonds rated 'junk' by Standard & Poor's," BBC News, April 27, 2010, news.bbc.co.uk/1/hi/business/8647441.stm.
[38] Jessica Pressler, "Greece's Economy Is a 'Sinking Ship,' Prime Minister Says in Asking for Aid," *The New York Times*, April 23, 2010, nymag.com/daily/intel/2010/04/greeces_economy_is_a_sinking_s.html.
[39] "Greece and the IMF," *op. cit.*
[40] Nicholas Paphitis, "Greece faces more anti-austerity strikes, protests," The Associated Press, Sept. 12 2012, www.google.com/hostednews/ap/article/ALeqM5gpnG2yszLfyfOf3DqbSdfqlpJG_A?docId=15ee557e881c4a0d8a9a09ffe9de0344.
[41] "Athens: Members of Greek Armed Forces Protest Wages and Pensions Cuts," keeptalkinggreece.com, Sept. 12, 2012, www.keeptalkinggreece.com/2012/09/12/athens-members-of-greek-armed-forces-protest-wages-and-pensions-cuts/.
[42] "Municipalities to begin two-day strike on Wednesday," *Ekathimerini* (newspaper), Sept. 12, 2012, www.ekathimerini.com/4dcgi/_w_articles_wsite1_1_11/09/2012_460666.
[43] "Pensioners storm Health Ministry," *Ekathimerini* (newspaper), Sept. 4, 2012, www.ekathimerini.com/4dcgi/_w_articles_wsite1_1_04/09/2012_459616.
[44] "Support for Golden Dawn rises, poll shows," *Ekathimerini* (newspaper), Sept. 12, 2012, www.ekathimerini.com/4dcgi/_w_articles_wsite1_1_06/09/2012_459953.
[45] " 'Enough merciless whipping' of Greece, says president,' *Ekithimerini* (newspaper), Sept. 11, 2012, www.ekathimerini.com/4dcgi/_w_articles_wsite1_1_11/09/2012_460758.

About the Author

Christopher Hack is a London-based freelance writer and economic analyst working for *The Economist* Intelligence Unit and *The Observer* and *Guardian* newspapers, among others. He writes on contemporary events in Britain and Europe and is a former foreign correspondent in Beirut, Lebanon, for the BBC and *Time*. He earned a Joint Honors degree in politics and economics in 1993 at the University of London.

[46] Michael Steen, "ECB signals resolve to save euro," *Financial Times*, Sept. 6, 2012, www.ft.com/cms/s/0/b70ff9a8-f84c-11e1-b0e1-00144feabdc0.html#axzz263MhkteO.
[47] Gavin Hewitt, "Eurozone crisis: From deutschmark to lira?" BBC News, Sept. 7, 2012, www.bbc.co.uk/news/world-europe-19516810.
[48] Ian Katz and Cheyenne Hopkins, "Europe Imperils U.S. Sales From Chemicals to PCs: Economy," Bloomberg, June 18, 2012, www.bloomberg.com/news/2012-06-18/europe-crisis-imperils-u-s-sales-from-chemicals-to-pcs-economy.html.
[49] Jeff Bennett, "Europe's Woes Hamper GM," *The Wall Street Journal*, Aug. 2, 2102, http://online.wsj.com/article/SB100008723963904436875045775646942758064 10.html.
[50] Mathew Phillips, "How Europe's Contagion May Hit the U.S. Economy," Bloomberg, June 7, 2012, www.businessweek.com/articles/2012-06-07/how-europes-contagion-may-hit-the-u-dot-s-dot-economy#p2.
[51] Dee-Ann Durbin, "Ford's second quarter earnings hobbled by European losses," *Denver Post*, www.denverpost.com/business/ci_21159253/fords-second-quarter-earnings-hobbled-by-european-losses.
[52] Richard Wolf, "Five ways the European debt crisis could affect the US," *USA Today*, Oct. 28, 2011, www.usatoday.com/money/world/story/2011-10-27/eurozone-crisis-deal/50963370/1.
[53] Jack Kaskey, "Dow Chemical to Close Five Plants on Slower European Economy," Bloomberg, April 2, 2012, www.bloomberg.com/news/2012-04-02/dow-chemical-to-close-five-plants-on-slower-european-economy-2-.html. Also see Viktor Puskorius, "Weakness in Europe Leads to Weak Earnings for Dow Chemical," *Benzinga*, July 26, 2012, www.benzinga.com/news/earnings/12/07/2779225/weakness-in-europe-leads-to-weak-earnings-for-dow-chemical.
[54] Erin Kim, "IBM sales fall, dragged down by Europe," *CNN Money*, July 18, 2012, http://money.cnn.com/2012/07/18/technology/ibm-earnings/index.htm.
[55] Matthew Philips, "How Europe's Contagion May Hit the U.S. Economy," *Bloomberg Business Week*, June 7, 2012, www.businessweek.com/articles/2012-06-07/how-europes-contagion-may-hit-the-u-dot-s-dot-economy.
[56] "Greek PM Samaras Predicts Economic Growth by 2014," *VOA News*, July 24, 2012, blogs.voanews.com/breaking-news/2012/07/24/greek-pm-samaras-predicts-economic-growth-by-2014.
[57] "OECD sees Greek recession lasting through 2013," *Ekathimerini* (newspaper), Sept. 13, 2012, www.ekathimerini.com/4dcgi/_w_articles_wsite2_1_22/05/2012_443265.
[58] Sudeep Reddy, "World Bank Sees Long Crisis Effect," *The Wall Street Journal*, Oct. 2, 2012, p. A9, http://online.wsj.com/article_email/SB10000872396390443862604578030841318692174-lMyQjAxMTAyMDAwMjAwODI3Wj.html?mod=wsj_valetleft_email.
[59] Luke Baker and Mark John, "Europe moves ahead with fiscal union, UK isolated," Reuters, www.reuters.com/article/2011/12/09/eurozone-idUSL5E7N900120111209.
[60] "Greeks brand Germans 'Nazis' for driving through painful cuts and 'taking control of their economy,' " *Daily Mail*, Feb. 15, 2012, www.dailymail.co.uk/news/article-2101614/Greece-debt-crisis-Greeks-brand-Germans-Nazis-taking-control-economy.html#ixzz26LfVRlq6.
[61] Cheyenne Hopkins, "Citigroup Sees 90 percent Chance That Greece Leaves Euro," Bloomberg, July 26, 2012, www.bloomberg.com/news/2012-07-25/citigroup-sees-90-chance-that-greece-leaves-euro.html.

FOR MORE INFORMATION

Centre for Economic Policy Research, 77 Bastwick St., London EC1V 3PZ, U.K.; +44 20 7183 8801; www.cepr.org. A network of more than 700 European researchers who study economic issues, such as the future of the euro.

European Council, Rue de la Loi 175, B-1048 Brussels, Belgium; +32 2 281-6111; www.european-council.europa.eu. Composed of the heads of member states of the European Union; defines the political directions and priorities of the EU.

European Policy Centre, Résidence Palace, 155 rue de la Loi, B-1040, Brussels, Belgium; +32 2 231-0340; www.epc.eu. An independent Brussels think tank devoted to European integration.

European Union, http://europa.eu/index_en.htm. Web portal that links to all EU agencies.

European Union Delegation to the United States of America, 2175 K St., N.W., Washington, DC 20037; 202-862-9500; www.eurunion.org/eu. Provides information about the EU for Americans.

European Union Research Center, The George Washington University, 2121 Eye St., N.W., Washington, DC 20052; 202-994-1000; www.business.gwu.edu/eurc. Promotes research and analysis on the EU and EU-US relations.

European-American Business Council, 919 18th St., N.W., Suite 220, Washington, DC 20006; 202-828-9104; www.eabc.org. Promotes investment, innovation and integration between the U.S. and EU business communities.

Open Europe, 7 Tufton St., London SW1P 3QN, U.K.; +44 207 197 2333; www.openeurope.org.uk. An independent think tank with offices in London and Brussels.

Peterson Institute for International Economics, 1750 Massachusetts Ave., N.W. Washington, DC 20036-1903; 202-328-9000; www.iie.com. A private, nonprofit, nonpartisan research institution devoted to the study of international economic policy.

Trans-Atlantic Business Dialogue, 1717 Pennsylvania Ave., N.W., Suite 1025, Washington, DC 20006; 202-559-9299; hwww.tabd.com. Works to improve economic relations between the United States and Europe.

Bibliography

Selected Sources

Books

Lewis, Michael, *Boomerang: The Meltdown Tour*, Penguin, 2011.
The co-author of *Barbarians at the Gate* and other best-sellers about the financial world explains entertainingly and clearly how the global financial crisis spread to Europe.

Manolopoulos, Jason, *Greece's Odious Debt: The Looting of the Hellenic Republic by the Euro, the Political Elite and the Investment Community*, Anthem, 2011.
A Greek investment banker offers a detailed analysis of Greece's experience with the euro, from birth to bailout.

Marsh, David, *The Euro: The Battle for the New Global Currency*, Yale, 2011.
A business consultant who has written extensively on European finance analyzes the birth and plight of the euro.

Soros, George, *Financial Turmoil in the United States and Europe: Essays*, PublicAffairs, 2012.
The global financier looks at what went wrong with the euro and the global economy, and ruminates on how the financial system can be fixed.

Van Overtveldt, Johan, *The End of The Euro: The Uneasy Future of the European Union*, Agate, 2011.
A Belgian economic journalist analyzes what has happened with the single currency and where it is heading.

Articles

Dadush, Uri, Shimelse Ali and Zaahira Wyne, "What Does the US Election Mean for the World Economy?" Carnegie Endowment for International Peace, Aug. 2, 2012, www.carnegieendowment.org/2012/08/02/what-does-u.s.-election-mean-for-world-economy/d5mp.
The director of Carnegie's International Economics Program and two writers contemplate the implications of the U.S. presidential election for the euro crisis and other global issues.

Eichlers, Alexander, "The European Debt Crisis: A Beginner's Guide," *The Huffington Post*, Dec. 21, 2011, www.huffingtonpost.com/2011/12/21/european-debt-crisis_n_1147173.html.
A business reporter explains the euro crisis and its importance.

Elliott, Douglas, "What the Euro Crisis Means for Taxpayers and the U.S. Economy," Brookings Institution, Dec. 15, 2011, www.brookings.edu/research/testimony/2011/12/15-euro-crisis-elliott.
A former investment banker testifies before the House Subcommittee on TARP, Financial Services and Bailouts of Public and Private Programs.

Gongloff, Mark, "Eurozone Crisis Explainer That Will Finally Make You Care," *The Huffington Post*, June 12, 2012, www.huffingtonpost.com/2012/06/12/eurozone-crisis-explainer_n_1590446.html.
The Huffington Post's chief financial writer offers a readable account of how the continuing euro crisis can affect the U.S. economy.

McNamara, Kathleen R., "Can the Eurozone be Saved?" *Foreign Affairs*, April 7, 2011, www.foreignaffairs.com/articles/67710/kathleen-r-mcnamara/can-the-eurozone-be-saved.
The director of Georgetown University's Mortara Center for International Studies says the eurozone has failed to create the kind of unified federal government necessary for a monetary union to work.

Tankersley, Jim, "How the Euro Crisis Could Destroy the U.S. Economy," *The Atlantic*, Dec. 2, 2011, www.theatlantic.com/business/archive/2011/12/how-the-euro-crisis-could-destroy-the-us-economy/249392/.
An economics correspondent explains how America could be dragged into the euro crisis.

Wolf, Richard, "Five ways the European debt crisis could affect the US," *USA Today*, Oct. 28, 2011, www.usatoday.com/money/world/story/2011-10-27/eurozone-crisis-deal/50963370/1.
A financial journalist examines the specific threat from the euro crisis to various aspects of the U.S. economy.

Reports and Studies

"Europe Will Work," Nomura, March 2011, www.nomura.com/europe/resources/pdf/Europe%20will%20work%20FINAL_March2011.pdf.
An Asian investment bank concludes that the euro zone probably will not break up but needs to strengthen its governance.

Bergstein, Fred, and Jacob Kirkegaard, "The Coming Resolution of the European Crisis," Peterson Institute for International Economics, June 2012, www.iie.com/publications/interstitial.cfm?ResearchID=2158.
Two leading academics examine the factors driving the European sovereign debt crisis.

Tilford, Simon, "How to Save the Euro," Centre for European Reform, September 2010, www.cer.org.uk/about_new/about_cerpersonnel_tilford_09.html.
The gap between the rhetoric of economic integration in Europe and the reality of national interests is proving lethal to the eurozone, argues the chief economist for a London think tank.

The Next Step:

Additional Articles from Current Periodicals

Euro Collapse

DiLorenzo, Sarah, "Debt Crisis Could Make the Euro a Failure," *Chicago Sun-Times*, Jan. 1, 2012, p. 16.
Few European citizens maintain confidence in the euro amid the continent's latest debt crisis.

Morici, Peter, "Almost Time for E.U. to Abandon Euro," *Providence* (R.I.) *Journal*, Nov. 30, 2011, p. 6.
European leaders are seeking treaty amendments that would limit national budget deficits to prevent the euro from collapsing.

Rahn, Richard W., "How the Debt Crisis Will End," *The Washington Times*, Dec. 13, 2011, p. B3, www.washingtontimes.com/news/2011/dec/12/how-the-debt-crisis-will-end/.
Europe's debt crisis will likely lead to financial collapse and the creation of a new economic order, says a senior fellow at the libertarian Cato Institute.

Taylor, Paul, "With Ruling, Europe Edges Toward Stability," Reuters, Sept. 13, 2012.
The German constitutional court's decision to allow the creation of a permanent bailout fund could help stabilize the eurozone.

U.S. Assistance

Alderman, Liz, and David Barboza, "China Is Asked for Investment in Euro Rescue," *The New York Times*, Oct. 29, 2011, p. A1, www.nytimes.com/2011/10/29/world/asia/europe-seeks-chinese-investment-in-euro-rescue.html?pagewanted=all.
China could supplant the United States as the world's pivotal economic power if it decides to provide Europe with financial assistance to solve its debt crisis.

Pace, Julie, "U.S. Will Not Help Pay for Europe's Debt Woes," The Associated Press, Nov. 28, 2011, news.yahoo.com/us-not-help-pay-europes-debt-woes-202103993.html.
President Obama says the United States is ready to help Europe with its debt crisis but has ruled out any financial contributions from U.S. taxpayers.

Samuelson, Robert J., "Who Will Take the Wheel?" *The Washington Post*, Nov. 4, 2011, p. A17.
The United States is unable to help Europe with its debt crisis because of its own sluggish economy, mounting government debt and constant political bickering.

U.S. Recovery

Browne, John, "Europe's Crisis Ricochets Toward U.S.," *Pittsburgh Tribune Review*, Oct. 9, 2011, triblive.com/x/pittsburghtrib/opinion/columnists/browne/s_760771.html#axzz27c1Wyn3T.
The European Union's woes affect the United States and the rest of the world because of the increased interdependence of the world's financial institutions.

Lee, Don, and Henry Chu, "Europe's Woes Put a Drag on World Growth," *Los Angeles Times*, May 25, 2012, p. A1.
The European debt crisis threatens the U.S. economy because Europe is a major market for American exports.

Mufson, Steven, "Ailing E.U. Banks Could Hamper U.S.," *The Washington Post*, Dec. 23, 2011, p. A17.
Many economists say European banks play a much larger role in the U.S. economy than has been generally thought.

Norris, Floyd, "Recovery in U.S., Though Lackluster, Trumps Europe's," *The New York Times*, Aug. 18, 2012, p. B2, www.nytimes.com/2012/08/18/business/economy/us-recovery-though-lackluster-trumps-european-stagnation.html.
The United States has been slow to recover from the recession, but its economic progress has been faster than that of many European countries.

O'Connor, Brian J., "Europe's Problems a Drag on U.S. Economy," *Detroit News*, June 14, 2012, p. A17, detnews.gmti.com/article/20120614/AUTO01/206140381/1148/Europe%E2%80%99s+problems+a+drag+on+U.S.+economy.
The European debt crisis is dragging down the continent's demand for products manufactured by U.S.-based multinational corporations.

CITING *CQ RESEARCHER*

Sample formats for citing these reports in a bibliography include the ones listed below. Preferred styles and formats vary, so please check with your instructor or professor.

MLA STYLE

Jost, Kenneth. "Remembering 9/11," CQ Researcher 2 Sept. 2011: 701-732.

APA STYLE

Jost, K. (2011, September 2). Remembering 9/11. *CQ Researcher, 9*, 701-732.

CHICAGO STYLE

Jost, Kenneth. "Remembering 9/11." *CQ Researcher*, September 2, 2011, 701-732.

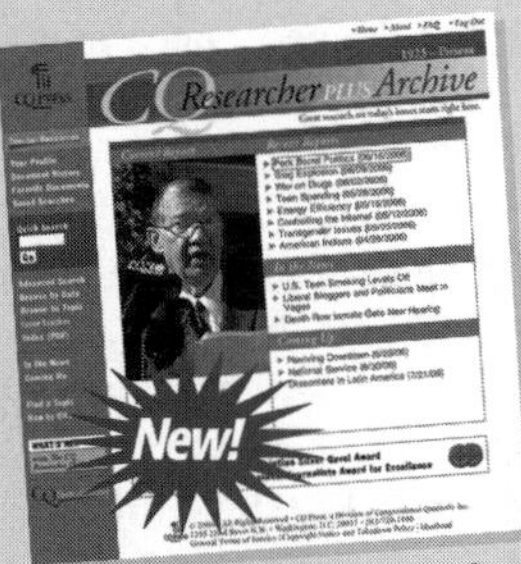
Researcher PLUS Archive
New!

CQ Researcher

Published by CQ Press, an Imprint of SAGE Publications, Inc.

www.cqresearcher.com

Social Media and Politics

Do Facebook and Twitter influence voters?

Social media, including Facebook, Twitter and YouTube, have become major battlegrounds in this year's elections. Candidates are using the platforms to identify and organize supporters and raise funds. They bypass traditional news media to send their messages unfiltered to the public. They target niche audiences with growing precision, contact hard-to-reach voters, extend their influence as online supporters forward their messages and carry out many campaign tasks at much lower cost than before. The increasing ability of campaign strategists to collect and analyze information about individual voters has raised privacy concerns, and many worry that the social networks' insular nature contributes to political polarization. But social media's low cost, ease of use and wide reach also raise hopes that they can level the campaign-spending playing field.

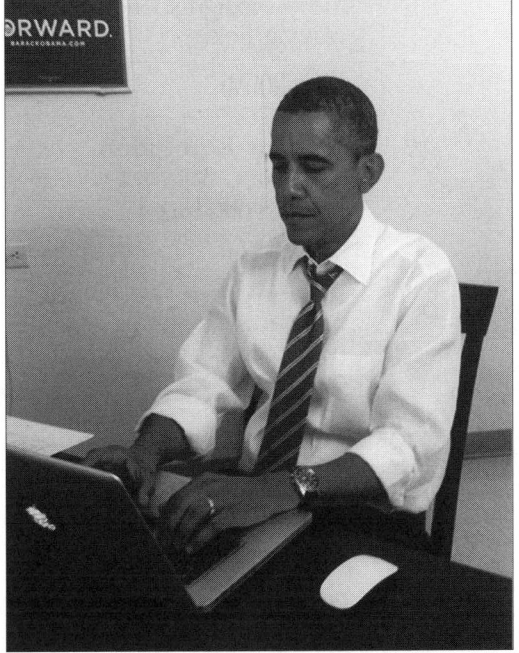

President Obama takes social media campaigning to a new level, answering questions on reddit during the Republican National Convention on Aug. 29. The half-hour live session, designed to draw attention away from his rival party's big event, generated 5,266 queries and comments. By Aug. 31, the discussion had logged nearly 5.3 million page views and netted Obama 10,000 potential volunteers.

INSIDE THIS REPORT

The Issues 867
Background 874
Chronology 875
Current Situation 879
At Issue 881
Outlook 883
Bibliography 886
The Next Step 887

CQ Researcher • Oct. 12, 2012 • www.cqresearcher.com
Volume 22, Number 36 • Pages 865-888

Los Angeles | London | New Delhi
Singapore | Washington DC

Recipient of Society of Professional Journalists Award for Excellence ◆ American Bar Association Silver Gavel Award

THE ISSUES

867 • Does online data mining threaten voters' privacy?
• Do social media cause political polarization?
• Do social media level the campaign-spending playing field?

BACKGROUND

874 **Nascent Revolution** UCLA and Stanford computers linked in 1969 to launch the Internet Age.

876 **Empowering the People** Online campaigning offers new method of grassroots outreach.

878 **Conservative Victories** Social media helped make the Tea Party a political force in 2010.

CURRENT SITUATION

879 **Courting 'Likes'** Obama and Romney boast millions of online supporters, but experts question the data.

880 **Incumbency Edge** YouTube and Facebook videos magnify the president's voice.

882 **Close and Personal** New social media like Pinterest help candidates connect with voters.

OUTLOOK

883 **Creative Approaches** Candidates may end the election year with big social media campaigns.

SIDEBARS AND GRAPHICS

868 **Many Voters Ignore Internet Comments** More consideration is given to family and friends.

869 **Strongest Views Dominate Political Posts** Highly partisan social media users "like" political posts the most.

871 **Social Media Use Drops With Age** Users 18-29 were twice as active as those over 65.

872 **Social Media Lag in Trustworthiness** Traditional news sources are trusted more.

875 **Chronology** Key events since 1991.

876 **Twitter: A New Political Weathervane** "We have never had a way to peer into discussions before."

878 **Social Media Give a Dark Horse the Edge** "The Internet allowed him to compete with someone with deep pockets."

881 **At Issue** Should government restrict online data collection to protect voters' privacy?

FOR FURTHER RESEARCH

885 **For More Information** Organizations to contact.

886 **Bibliography** Selected sources used.

887 **The Next Step** Additional articles.

887 **Citing *CQ Researcher*** Sample bibliography formats.

Cover: Reddit

CQ Researcher

Oct. 12, 2012
Volume 22, Number 36

MANAGING EDITOR: Thomas J. Billitteri
tjb@cqpress.com

ASSISTANT MANAGING EDITOR: Kathy Koch
kkoch@cqpress.com

SENIOR CONTRIBUTING EDITOR: Thomas J. Colin
tcolin@cqpress.com

ASSOCIATE EDITOR: Kenneth Jost

STAFF WRITER: Marcia Clemmitt

CONTRIBUTING WRITERS: Peter Katel, Barbara Mantel, Tom Price, Jennifer Weeks

SENIOR PROJECT EDITOR: Olu B. Davis

ASSISTANT EDITOR: Darrell Dela Rosa

FACT CHECKER: Michelle Harris

Los Angeles | London | New Delhi
Singapore | Washington DC

An Imprint of SAGE Publications, Inc.

VICE PRESIDENT AND EDITORIAL DIRECTOR, HIGHER EDUCATION GROUP: Michele Sordi

DIRECTOR, ONLINE PUBLISHING: Todd Baldwin

CQ Researcher (ISSN 1056-2036) is printed on acid-free paper. Published weekly, except: (March wk. 5) (May wk. 4) (July wk. 1) (Aug. wks. 3, 4) (Nov. wk. 4) and (Dec. wks. 3, 4). Published by SAGE Publications, Inc., 2455 Teller Rd., Thousand Oaks, CA 91320. Annual full-service subscriptions start at $1,054. For pricing, call 1-800-834-9020. To purchase a *CQ Researcher* report in print or electronic format (PDF), visit www.cqpress.com or call 866-427-7737. Single reports start at $15. Bulk purchase discounts and electronic-rights licensing are also available. Periodicals postage paid at Thousand Oaks, California, and at additional mailing offices. POSTMASTER: Send address changes to *CQ Researcher*, 2300 N St., N.W., Suite 800, Washington, DC 20037.

Social Media and Politics

BY TOM PRICE

THE ISSUES

As Republicans sought to boost Mitt Romney's then-flagging presidential campaign during their August nominating convention in Tampa, this message popped up on the social media website reddit on Aug. 29:

"I am Barack Obama, President of the United States — AMA" (reddit shorthand for "ask me anything"). [1]

For the next half hour, Obama fielded questions from reddit participants, generating 5,266 queries and comments. By the morning of Aug. 31, the discussion had logged nearly 5.3 million page views. He wrapped up the unprecedented online session — complete with a photo of him at his computer, shirtsleeves rolled up, tie loosened, to prove he was really answering questions — with a pitch for voting and a link to an online voter-registration form. [2]

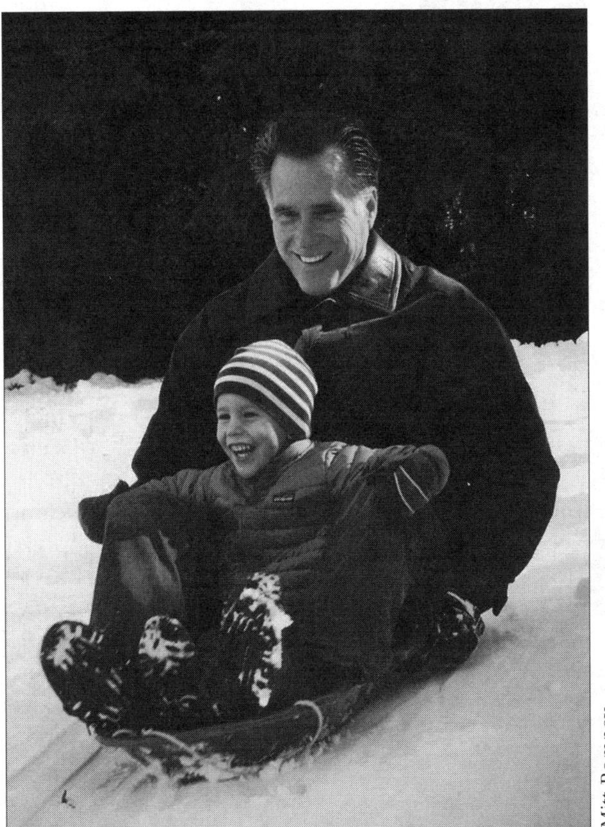

Mitt Romney

Republican presidential candidate Mitt Romney sleds with one of his grandsons in a family photo posted on Pinterest by his wife, Ann. Mrs. Romney and Michelle Obama, as well as the candidates themselves, have posted recipes, family photographs and other personal information on the site in an effort to humanize the candidates and forge closer links to voters.

In the process, the president asserted his affinity for the rapidly growing world of social media and enrolled more than 10,000 reddit users as potential campaign volunteers, Obama chief digital strategist Joe Rospars said. The president also served notice that he would not allow Romney a solo moment in the sun, even during the GOP convention.

Obama's command of the Internet proved a key to his victory over Arizona Sen. John McCain in 2008. This year, all candidates are striving to emulate Obama's 2008 online success, but there are differences:

- The president's 2012 campaign is doing much more online than it did four years ago.
- The buzz now is about social media such as Facebook, Twitter, YouTube and the many less-prominent platforms such as reddit, all of which had far less impact — or didn't even exist — in 2008.
- And Romney's camp is determined to keep up.

"The tools people can use to get messages to their friends are much more powerful than they were in 2008," says Joe Trippi, architect of former New Hampshire Gov. Howard Dean's 2004 campaign for the Democratic presidential nomination, which tapped the powers of the Internet more than any candidate had done before. [3] "The sheer size of the networks has exploded. [Prominent Democratic strategist James] Carville used to say: 'It's the economy, stupid.' Now 'It's the networks, stupid.' "

One proof of social media's growing importance, says Vincent Harris, who ran GOP presidential hopeful Newt Gingrich's online activities in some of this year's primaries, is its incorporation as an integral component of many campaigns' operations. No longer is the "new-media guy" sent to a corner to manage the Internet in isolation from the rest of the staff, Harris explains.

Other proof is in the numbers. Twitter users posted 1.8 million tweets on Election Day in 2008, the kind of event that spurs social media activity. Now tweets average 340 million a day — nearly 200 times as much. [4] This year's Republican National Convention generated more tweets the day before it opened than the 2008 convention did during its full run, according to Adam Sharp, head of Twitter's government, news and social innovation operations.

"More tweets are sent every two days today than had had been sent in total from Twitter's creation in 2006 to the 2008 election," he told a panel at the Democratic National Convention in early September. Registered voters who use Facebook today outnumber those who actually voted in the 2008 general election, says Katie Harbath, a Facebook manager who helps Republicans use the platform.

Overall, nearly two-thirds of U.S. adults say they use social media regularly. [5] And "they don't skew as young as you may think," says Michael Reilly, a partner in the Democratic campaign consulting firm Murphy Vogel Askew Reilly in Alexandria, Va.

Many Voters Ignore Internet Comments

Two-thirds of voters say they are taking little or no account of comments posted on social media and Internet forums before voting for president in November. More consideration is given to conversations with family and friends and opinions voiced by experts on major news outlets.

How much do you consider the following in deciding whom to vote for in the November presidential election?

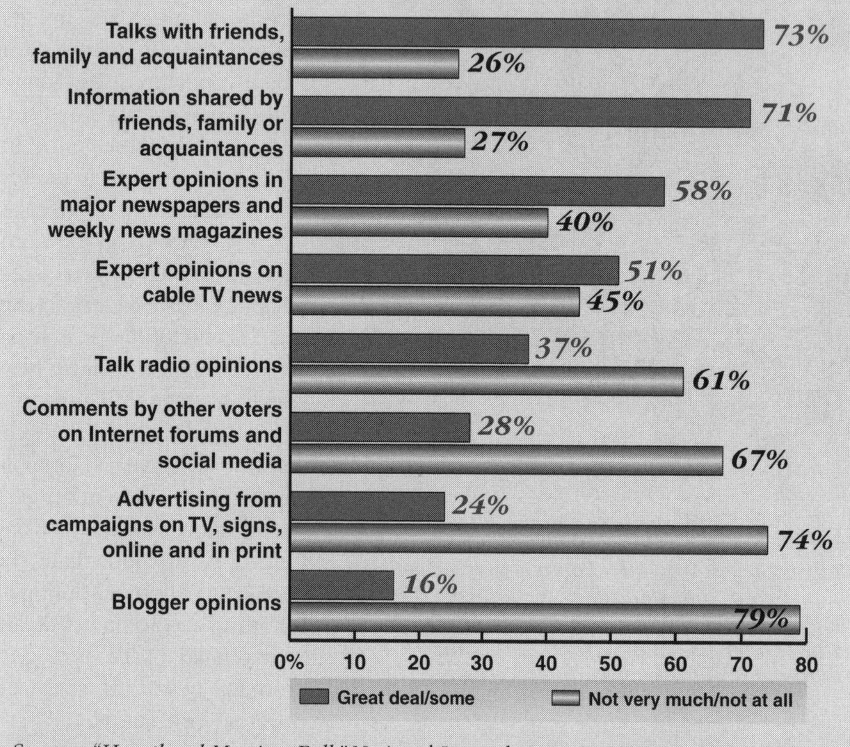

Source: "Heartland Monitor Poll," National Journal, *June 9, 2012, p. 24, www.allstate.com/Allstate/content/refresh-attachments/Heartland_monitor_XIII_topline.pdf*

While younger people are more likely to use social media, the contingent of older adults is growing most rapidly. Eighty-six percent of 18- to 29-year-olds use social media, compared with about a third of those 65 and older. But participation nearly quintupled among those 50 and older between 2008 and 2012. Nearly three times as many 30- to 49-year-olds use social media now as in 2008. Among 18- to 29-year-olds, the increase was just 19 percent, with the same proportion using social media this year as two years ago. [6] (*See graph, p. 871.*)

That growing participation increases social media's attractiveness to politicians, who use the platforms to identify and organize supporters, raise funds and spread their messages. Candidates bypass traditional news media to send unfiltered communication to the public. They target recipients of their messages with growing precision. They contact hard-to-reach voters — especially the young — who record television programs and fast-forward through the commercials. They use online communication to organize phone banks, door-to-door canvassing and other offline activities. And they tap into what is believed to be the most effective form of persuasion: friend-to-friend conversation.

Social media's interactive nature allows candidates to engage in what can be — or can appear to be — conversations with individual voters. Those voters can forward the candidates' posts to their friends, extending the candidates' reach and adding the endorsement of the people who pass the messages on.

But the increasing ability of online campaign strategists to collect and analyze detailed personal information about individual voters has raised privacy concerns.

Polled in May about information sources they tap when deciding how to vote, Americans put family, friends and acquaintances at the top. Bloggers ranked at the bottom, just below advertisements and online comments by people voters don't know. [7] (*See graph at left.*)

Each social medium offers its own political tools. Trying to label one more valuable than the other is "sort of like asking which is your favorite child," says Phil Noble, a Democratic online political consultant since the 1990s. "Advantage," says George Washington University political scientist Michael Cornfield, "goes to people who can use all of them."

But one network clearly dominates. "Facebook is the 800-pound gorilla," with its large number of users and friend-to-friend networks, Harris says. Politicians communicate with journalists through Twitter and use its brief messages for rapid response to political attacks. Television news media often pick up YouTube videos and give them wider distribution.

These interactive media's greatest value comes from how they interact with each other, says Ken Deutsch, who manages the digital practice at the Jones Public Affairs communications firm's Boston office. "If YouTube wasn't shared on Facebook and Twitter and blogs and those other places, it would have no [political] value," Deutsch explains. "If you couldn't link newspaper articles to Twitter, Twitter would have no value."

Social media enable individuals to enter the public political debate in ways previously reserved to politicians and the traditional news outlets. That poses a challenge to candidates, who can't control their messages once social media users start passing them around and commenting on them. But candidates also benefit when supporters rise to the candidates' defense after a social media attack.

Indeed, the millions of citizen postings create an unending barrage of attacks, defenses and counterattacks that demand rapid responses from campaigns. That heightens the likelihood of gaffes, which in turn get amplified in online repostings, adding to the cacophony, and the allure, of social media.

Smart phones and other mobile devices increase the speed and ubiquity of the debate, which individuals can enter whenever they want from wherever they happen to be. The devices' cameras also enable individuals to record candidates' gaffes and post them online instantly.

As campaign 2012 races to its conclusion on Nov. 6, here are some questions being raised about social media's impact on the American political process:

Strongest Views Dominate Political Posts

Social media users who identify themselves as "very liberal" or "very conservative" are more likely than those who identify themselves as less partisan to "like" political posts, write positive comments or "friend" those who share their political views.

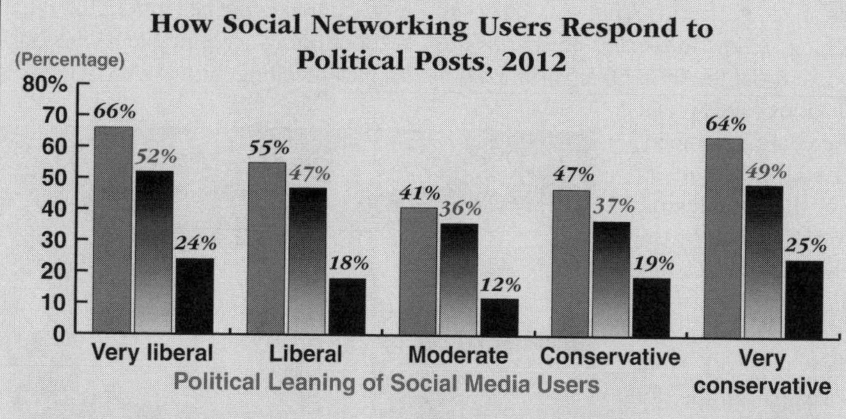

Source: "Social Networking Sites and Politics," Pew Research Center, March 2012, p. 8, www.pewinternet.org/~/media//Files/Reports/2012/PIP_SNS_and_politics.pdf

Does online data mining threaten voters' privacy?

Political operatives and political scientists are talking about "Big Data" a lot this year.

The phrase refers to political organizations' ability to collect enormous amounts of information about individual voters — through social media and traditional means — then crunch it and use the results to send finely tuned messages to narrowly targeted audiences. Some critics worry that it's also a highly intrusive invasion of privacy. (*See "At Issue," p. 881.*)

By gathering material from social media, other websites and offline sources, campaigns can identify individuals' browsing habits, online purchases, social media discussions, data about friends and friends' interests and other information. [8]

When people signed up for a smart phone app that was to notify them of Romney's vice presidential pick, the campaign gathered their email addresses and other data. [9] Those who joined Obama's campaign by clicking "I'm in" on Facebook gave the campaign their Facebook data plus information on their Facebook friends, according to Trippi, the architect of Howard Dean's Internet-dependent 2004 campaign. "People would want to turn their machines off if they knew everything these campaigns know about them," he says, only partly in jest.

When campaigns target voters now, Democratic online consultant Noble says, "it's not [an anonymous] white male voter in this precinct. It's James Q. Smith on Grand Street."

That so-called "microtargeting" is quite valuable, according to Mike Zaneis, senior vice president of the Interactive Advertising Bureau, a New York-based trade group for companies that sell online advertising. In the commercial sector, he says, targeted ads are 2.5 times as effective as nontargeted ones.

Directly addressing a voter's precise interests through social media allows a campaign to "engage people in detail on issues you might not otherwise have had the time or resources to talk about through traditional media," says Reilly, the Democratic campaign consultant.

"If you want to reach people who are interested in a particular topic, there are groups and sub-groups for everything in social media with their own thought leaders that you can identify and either advertise to or reach out to directly," Deutsch of Jones Public Affairs notes.

The practice carries "great potential for abuses of privacy," according to John Allen Hendricks, chair of the mass communication department at Stephen F. Austin State University in Nacogdoches, Texas, and co-editor of a book about the 2008 Obama campaign. "I don't know that there are prominent enough disclaimers on the politicians' websites to inform the electorate that they are giving up a lot of information that they may not want revealed in the future," he explains. "We do not know what the campaigns will do with that data after the election is over."

Jeffrey Chester, executive director of the Center for Digital Democracy, a consumer-protection and privacy advocacy group in Washington, D.C., argues that the privacy threat is especially serious because it involves voting. "It's not about selling books and music and T-shirts," he says. "It's about the heart of the democratic process. Do we really want giant political parties and well-funded special interest groups like the Super PACs compiling millions of dossiers on voters and becoming a series of private National Security Agencies or FBIs?"

Chester wants the federal government to adopt "new rules that enable the voters to make the decisions about how their data can be collected and used." Voters should have to give permission before organizations could gather information about them online, he says. "Retention limits" should allow data to be used only for a short time and not be archived or sold, he adds.

He also worries that microtargeting will enable politicians to distribute false campaign pitches "under the radar, without being accountable to the public fact-checking process."

AP Photo/Evan Vucci

Republican presidential candidate Mitt Romney works online aboard his bus after a campaign stop in Council Bluffs, Iowa, on June 8. In an effort to enhance his social media presence, Romney urged his Facebook friends on Aug. 21: "We're almost to 5 million likes — help us get there! 'Like' and share this with your friends and family to show you stand with Mitt!" By the second week of October, Romney had 8.6 million "likes."

Zaneis calls Chester's under-the-radar warning "a bit of a red herring. It's no more of a potential problem in the digital world than it is in the offline world," he says, pointing out that direct-mailers have targeted individuals with postal mail for decades.

Gingrich online director Harris notes that "there's a reason people who subscribe to *Guns* magazine get direct-mail pieces about the Second Amendment."

"If somebody wants to deceive," Zaneis says, "they're going to be able to do that in any medium."

The Interactive Advertising Bureau's code allows consumers to opt out of being tracked and targeted online, he says, although that doesn't apply to political organizations that don't belong to the organization. An opt-in requirement would hinder the operations of the $35-billion online advertising industry, which supports 3 million jobs, he says. Most consumers wouldn't bother to opt in, even though most also don't bother to opt out, he says.

"I'm not sure why the Internet should be the redheaded stepchild of the media," he adds. "You can collect data about people all over the place" offline.

Jim Harper, director of information policy studies at the libertarian Cato Institute, says federal legislation would be too blunt an instrument.

"Legislation is going to produce privacy protection that is too high for many people and too low for many people," he says. "My argument is that privacy is a product of personal responsibility. You don't share what information you don't want others to have. That way you get custom privacy protection, because you've done it yourself."

Douglas Pinkham, president of the Public Affairs Council, an association of public affairs professionals that studies online political activity, observes that many younger Americans are comfortable revealing information on the Internet because they "just don't care about privacy as much as middle-aged and older people do."

Do social media cause political polarization?

"It's constitutional. B----es," Democratic National Committee Executive Director Patrick Gaspard tweeted crudely when the Supreme Court upheld Barack Obama's signature health-care legislation in June. [10]

After Republicans attacked him for the intemperate remark, Gaspard tweeted an apology, explaining that "I let my excitement [at the Supreme Court's ruling] get the better of me." Then he let his Twitter feed go silent for six weeks. [11]

Gaspard's gaffe is just one example of the polarization and hostility that seem to characterize some online political communication. And the ill feelings are not restricted to political leaders.

A woman in the Houston, Texas, area became so disturbed about the tone of political debate that she declared her Facebook page to be a "Politics-Free zone." "Let's all take a deep breath, step back and remember that we are friends — in spite of our political views," Sandy Mansfield posted. [12]

More than a third of social media users in a Pew Research Center study this year reported receiving a "strong negative reaction" after they posted a political comment. [13]

Explanations for the phenomenon range from the overall polarized political climate to the nature of social media themselves.

The brevity of social media messages tends to "tweak people's impulses rather than cause them to think," said Bill Shireman, president of Future 500, a San Francisco consulting firm that helps businesses work with activist groups. "So prejudice and group-think can appear very quickly with few restraints." [14]

Social media worsen polarization that already exists in American politics, says Deutsch, the online communications manager at Jones Public Affairs. "People follow people they agree with. On Facebook, you're seeing news put up by friends who are reinforcing your own views."

ComScore Inc., which measures online activity, this year released a study that found people tend to visit Internet sites that share their political leanings. Some Republicans visit the liberal TalkingPointsMemo.com, for instance, but Democrats account for 70 percent of the time spent at the site. Conversely, Democrats account for just 9 percent of the time spent at the conservative DailyCaller.com site. [15]

Aaron Smith, who studies politics and the Internet at the Pew Research Center, says most political posts in social media are made by activists with strong views. In one Pew survey, for instance, 66 percent of "very liberal" people said they had "liked" a political post, as did 64 percent of "very conservative" people. Only 41 percent of self-described "moderates" did so. Pew found the same pattern when asking if people had posted political comments. [16]

"They come to this [online] world with a certain set of attitudes and a team mentality, and social networking sites provide a way for them to support their team," Smith says of the activists. "While you can see ways social networking sites can exacerbate [polarization], in a way they're only reflecting that broader political culture."

Social media promote nationalization of politics, just as cable TV news and the Internet in general do, Democratic campaign consultant Reilly says. Nationalization then promotes polarization, as ideological activists from around the country jump into local political debates, he explains.

"No matter where you're running," he says, "the challenge to make it about [often-less-polarized] local issues and local candidates is tremendous," Reilly says.

Former House Speaker Thomas P. "Tip" O'Neill, D-Mass., famously proclaimed that "all politics is local," Reilly noted, but the media now are making it more accurate to say that "all politics is national."

Social Media Use Declines With Age

More than 70 percent of adults under age 50 say they use social networking sites, with usage highest among those 18 to 29. Only about a third of those 65 and older use social media. Experts say a lower level of technological literacy among seniors is the reason for less social media use, but their participation is increasing rapidly.

Social Networking Use by Age Group, 2012

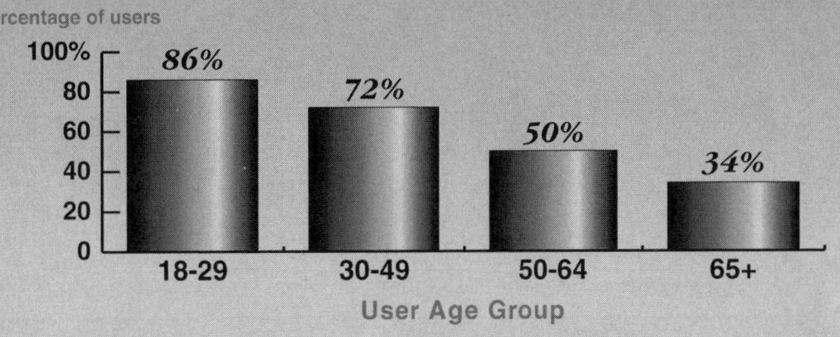

Source: "Older Adults and Internet Use," Pew Research Center, June 2012, p. 9, www.pewinternet.org/~/media//Files/Reports/2012/PIP_Older_adults_and_internet_use.pdf

Social Media Lag in Trustworthiness

Americans find traditional news outlets such as public television and newspapers as the most trustworthy sources of news. More than half of those surveyed say social media platforms as well as blog and online forums — which allow anybody to post content — are not very trustworthy.

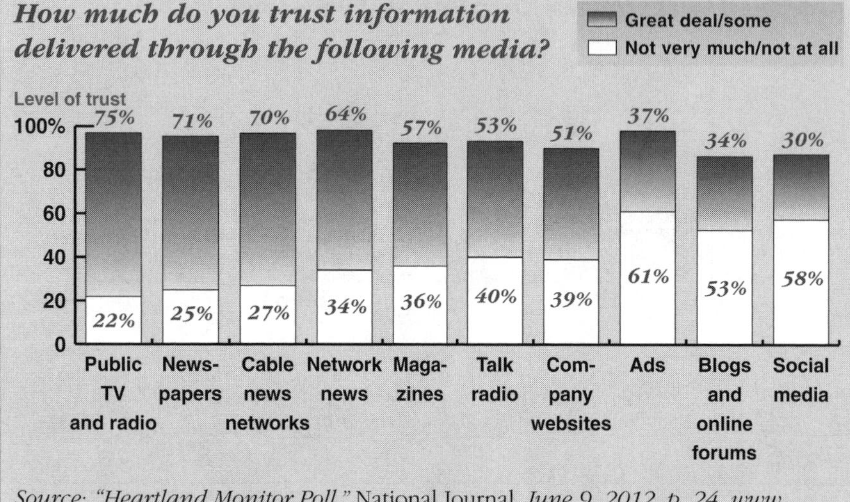

Source: "Heartland Monitor Poll," National Journal, *June 9, 2012, p. 24, www.allstate.com/Allstate/content/refresh-attachments/Heartland_monitor_XIII_topline.pdf*

Social media amplify the heated, negative campaigning that often appears in polarized debates, Reilly says. But well-funded independent organizations tend to drive the negativity through the offline advertisements that they purchase, he adds.

Other aspects of social media can combat polarization and negativity.

While Twitter requires micro-comments and Facebook encourages brevity, tweets and Facebook postings can link to longer documents, and long videos can be posted on YouTube, for example.

"On television, you're limited to the sound bite you can get on the news and the 30-second ad," Reilly notes. "On social media, you can be posting as much as you want every day. It's an avenue for getting more information to people that wasn't available before social media came about."

Although people tend to associate with others who have similar beliefs, few people's networks are devoid of diversity.

Asked in a May survey about the political orientation of their social media contacts, 24 percent of those polled said most were the same as their own, 9 percent said most were different, and 60 percent said there was an even mix. The rest didn't know or didn't answer. [17]

"There are plenty of echo chambers, but there also are lots of tunnels among the echo chambers," the Cato Institute's Harper says.

"People are on social media to interact with the drama of their lives," not to form political organizations, Harris says. Their networks tend to be comprised of family and friends. And "not everyone in a family or at a high school or in college agrees on all the same political points." As a result, he says, "the average person on Facebook is friends with people of diverse political views, religions and backgrounds."

Do social media level the campaign-spending playing field?

Mark McKinnon, chief media adviser for George W. Bush's presidential campaigns, has become an Internet evangelist.

"Americans are leveraging technology to more fully engage in the political process," McKinnon proclaimed earlier this year. "Voters have become more than just passive consumers of these digital messages. . . . 'We the people' can now compete against the near-deafening influence of unlimited campaign contributions." [18]

McKinnon is not alone in his optimism. Low cost and ease of use have led many to view social media as weapons that underfunded candidates and common citizens can use to combat the enormous campaign spending of millionaires and billionaires that was unleashed by the Supreme Court's *Citizens United* decision in 2010. [19] They also view social media as an inexpensive tool for solving problems that defy traditional media.

Social media are "good for niche issues," Democratic online consultant Noble says, noting that television is too expensive for addressing topics of interest to small groups. Social media offer effective access to young people, who watch less television than their elders, Democratic campaign consultant Reilly says. Because the young are less likely to vote, as well, their cost-per-vote in television advertising can be prohibitive, he adds.

Social media also open an avenue of influence that can't be tapped by traditional, geographically bound media, according to Deutsch of Jones Public Affairs.

Presidential campaigns concentrate their television spending in the handful of states where the race is close. But "most of us are influenced by people who live outside the media market we live in — our friends, our classmates, our colleagues," as well as by advertising and by people who live nearby, Deutsch points out. Social media enable those people to be in touch with each other and allow campaigns to try to influence them no matter where they live, he says.

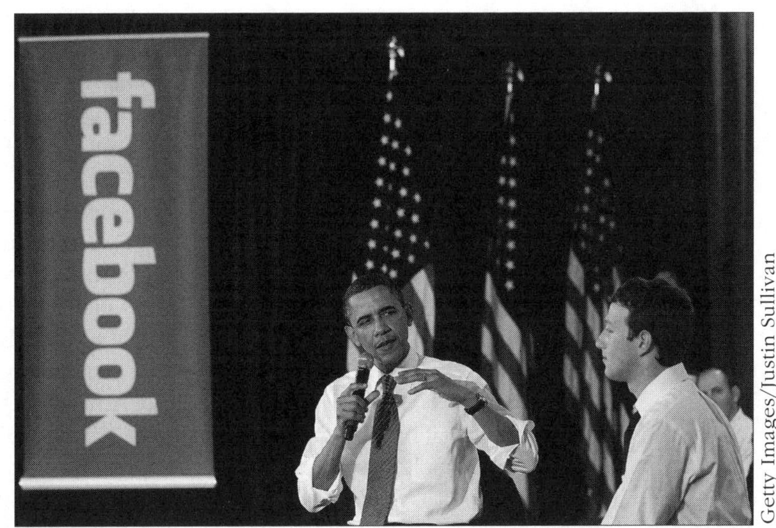

Getty Images/Justin Sullivan

President Obama talks with Facebook CEO Mark Zuckerberg during a town hall meeting at the social media company's headquarters in Palo Alto, Calif., on April 20, 2011. A majority of young adults 18 to 29 say Facebook is their top news source, and a fifth name Comedy Central's Jon Stewart and Stephen Colbert, according to a recent survey.

Social media also have become a leveling tool as television advertising becomes less effective.

Zac Moffatt, digital director of the Romney campaign, has identified "off-the-gridders" — people who avoid television commercials by not watching programs when they're broadcast. Instead, they record shows and fast-forward through the ads later, or they get their commercial-free entertainment from such sources as Netflix.

Surveys found that a third of the residents of Ohio and Virginia — key swing states — fall into that category, watching only sporting events at their scheduled broadcast time, Moffatt said in a panel discussion during the Republican Convention. Advertising that runs next to online search results or in social media offers ways to reach these potential voters, Moffatt said. In addition, he noted, recipients of online advertising can share it with friends, thus extending its reach.

Social media will not replace traditional news sources anytime soon, however. One important reason: Other than information they receive from friends and relatives, people — including young people — don't trust what they're told on social media as much as they trust what traditional news outlets tell them.

In a May *National Journal* survey, three-quarters of Americans polled said they have some or a great deal of trust in public television and public radio. Newspapers and cable news followed close behind with 71 and 70 percent. Next came network news (64 percent), magazines (57) and talk radio (53). Social media finished dead last, with just 30 percent. [20] (*See graph, p. 872.*)

Television also topped a 2011 Public Affairs Council survey that asked Americans where they get most of their news. Print newspapers or magazines stood second at 12 percent, well below TV's 70 percent. Just 1 percent picked social media. [21]

In an August survey for the *Los Angeles Times* and the University of Southern California's Annenberg communication school, a majority of young adults ages 18 to 29 said Facebook is their top news source, and a fifth listed Jon Stewart and Stephen Colbert, the Comedy Central cable station's fake news anchor and commentator. But those sources finished below traditional news media in trust. [22]

"An insurgent candidate with little money can use the Web to catch fire," former Gingrich online coordinator Harris says. "But every survey continues to show that television is where people are spending most of their time. So, until those numbers change, television will continue to take the lion's share of the media money."

The candidates with the lion's share of the money will be able to buy the lion's share of television time, which limits social media's ability to level the field, Deutsch says.

"In a world where there was some regulation of size of donations, social media may have leveled it," he says. "But, at this point, with the number of individual donors you have to have to make up for the wealthiest donors who support PACs, I don't think it can be."

Hendricks of Stephen F. Austin State University agrees that "the wealthy's ability to spend unlimited amounts on campaigns may overcome the Internet's people power." But Cornfield of George Washington University suggests that the enormous amount of cash being poured into this year's campaigns may, ironically, limit money's impact in the closing weeks before the election.

"I'm hearing that we're going to see, because of the rise of Super PACs, much less advertising space available, especially in broadcast and cable TV and radio," he says. "All the time's been bought up. That's forcing campaigns to rely more on Web ads. And there are starting to be anticipated shortages on the favorite Web ad spaces."

BACKGROUND

Nascent Revolution

Today's global Internet can trace its birth to the transmission of one word — "log" — from a computer at the University of California, Los Angeles to a computer at Stanford University about 360 miles up the California coast. [23] The UCLA computer was logging into the Stanford computer on Oct. 29, 1969, to create the first link in a network that now serves about 2 billion users. [24]

The $19,800 contract that funded the first Internet research was paid for by the federal government's Defense Advanced Research Projects Agency (ARPA) to facilitate information exchange among military research facilities. As more computers joined the network, it became known as ARPANET.

To facilitate civilian research, the federal government's National Science Foundation (NSF) created the Computer Science Network (CSNET) in 1981. Five years later, the foundation established the faster NSFNET. As these early networks began to link to each other, they created a network of networks that became known as the Internet.

The general public didn't acquire Internet access until the late 1980s, when MCI Mail and CompuServe began selling email services. Earlier in the '80s, companies offered slow phone-line connections to private networks. In 1989, a service called "The World" offered the public its first full-service access to the Internet.

Hints at the Internet's eventual wide popularity appeared in the early '90s, when companies were allowed to conduct commercial operations online and scientists invented the point-and-click navigation system and the graphical browser — a web browser that allows interaction with both graphics and text.

The Internet found an early congressional advocate in Tennessee Sen. Al Gore, who helped turn the Web into a campaign tool when he joined presidential nominee Bill Clinton on the Democratic ticket in 1992. Shortly after they took office in 1993, Clinton and Gore launched the first White House website. Two years later, the Library of Congress created an online legislative information system named "Thomas," after President Thomas Jefferson, who sold his personal book collection to the library after British troops burned it during the War of 1812. Following the White House lead, members of Congress began to create websites and use email.

Political use of the Web was spreading by the time Clinton and Gore ran for re-election in 1996. Candidates' websites now contained graphic elements, links to other sites and capabilities for exchanging email with voters. The Republican presidential nominee, Sen. Bob Dole of Kansas, became the first candidate to promote a website on television, doing so during a debate with Clinton.

Two years later, professional wrestler Jesse Ventura demonstrated the Internet's political value when he used it in running a successful upstart campaign for Minnesota governor. To help overcome doubts about his qualifications, he posted detailed position papers online. He raised $50,000 in cyberspace — nearly 10 percent of his treasury — and used email to help manage far-flung volunteers.

"We didn't win the election because of the Internet," Phil Madsen, Ventura's webmaster, said. But Ventura "could not have won the election without the Internet." [25]

The Federal Election Commission (FEC) greatly boosted the Internet's political value in 1999 when it ruled that campaign contributions charged to credit cards online would be eligible for matching federal funds. Sen. Bill Bradley of New Jersey raised more than $600,000 online that year as he prepared to challenge Gore in the 2000 Democratic presidential primaries, and Arizona Sen. John McCain raised $260,000 in the runup to the GOP contest. McCain then raised $2.7 million online in three days following his upset win over George W. Bush in the Feb. 2 New Hampshire primary.

Gore and Bush won the nomination, but the losers demonstrated the Web's political potential, which Howard Dean exploited dramatically in 2004.

Dean made the Internet central to his campaign, using its ever-strengthening capabilities to organize, motivate and manage his paid and volunteer workers. His supporters organized meetings at Meetup.com. He used the Internet to become the most prolific Democratic fundraiser in history up to that point.

Massachusetts Sen. John Kerry won the nomination but learned from Dean's Internet prowess. He and Bush both developed sophisticated websites with video and audio files, search capabilities and interactive features. In addition to raising funds online, they recruited volunteers, encouraged supporters to bring their friends and neighbors into the campaign, distributed good news about themselves and attacked their opponent.

Kerry and Bush also:

• Used their Senate and White House websites to supplement their campaigns' online activities;

• Placed targeted advertising on others' websites;

• Used email to deploy workers shortly before and on Election Day; and

Continued on p. 876

Chronology

1990s The Internet becomes a political instrument.

1991
Commercial activities are allowed on the Internet. . . . Point-and-click navigation invented. . . . World Wide Web name coined.

1992
Clinton-Gore campaign uses Internet to reach out to prospective voters.

1994
First graphical browser invented. . . . White House website introduced.

1995
Library of Congress creates www.thomas.gov site, named after President Thomas Jefferson, to put legislative information online.

1996
More campaigns go online. . . . Center for Responsive Politics puts campaign finance information on the Web.

1998
Professional wrestler Jesse Ventura demonstrates Internet's value to the underdog by winning Minnesota governorship as a third-party candidate.

1999
Federal Election Commission allows matching federal campaign funds for online credit-card donations. . . . Napster music-sharing network founded. . . . New Jersey Sen. Bill Bradley raises more than $600,000 online in unsuccessful campaign for 2000 Democratic presidential nomination.

2000s Online campaigning expands, and social media enter politics.

2000
After upset victory in New Hampshire primary, Republican presidential candidate John McCain raises $2.7 million online in three days.

2001
Accused of violating copyrights, Napster goes offline and is later reborn as a legal online music store.

2002
LinkedIn business networking site and Friendster, a prototypical social networking platform, launched; Friendster later morphs into a gaming website.

2003
Exploiting Internet's fundraising and voter outreach capabilities, former New Hampshire Gov. Howard Dean becomes frontrunner for 2004 Democratic presidential nomination but ultimately loses to Sen. John Kerry.

2004
TheFacebook (later just Facebook) begins business as a networking platform for Harvard undergraduates. . . . Flickr photo-sharing platform created. . . . Dean's 2004 campaign taps power of Internet fundraising as never before.

2005
YouTube video-sharing platform founded. Facebook expands on college campuses and allows some high school students to participate.

2006
After expanding to more college campuses, Facebook is opened to anyone 13 and older. . . . Twitter established.

2007
CNN and YouTube sponsor Democratic and Republican debates during which viewers submit video questions.

2008
Barack Obama wins presidency after raising $500 million online and conducting most-ever campaign activities online. . . . Twitter records 1.8 million tweets on Election Day.

2009
White House begins posting photos to Flickr. . . . Grassroots conservatives tap social media to find like-minded activists and grow the decentralized Tea Party movement.

2010
Social media contribute to conservative election victories at all levels of government.

2011
In run-up to 2012 election, all major political candidates campaign on social media; GOP presidential candidates debate on Twitter; Obama hosts "Twitter Town Hall" from White House.

2012
Social media play larger campaign role than ever; Twitter averages 340 million tweets a day; U.S. Facebook users outnumber 2008 total voters; Obama leads Romney in most measures of social media activity, but some think Romney's social media supporters may be more engaged; online data-mining raises privacy concerns; researchers study social media activity to evaluate political campaigns' effectiveness. . . . Candidates use social media for on-the-fly tests of campaign tactics' effectiveness. . . . Companies create fake social media followers to inflate apparent size of campaigns' online support.

Twitter: A New Political Weathervane

"We have never had a way to peer into discussions before."

Can social media conversations predict election results? A growing number of organizations are trying to find out.

Twitter launched the Twitter Political Index — or Twindex — on Aug. 1. [1] It's an attempt to measure Twitter users' opinions about the leading presidential candidates by evaluating their tweets.

The index was developed in partnership with two prominent political pollsters — Democrat Mark Mellman and Republican Jon McHenry — and a firm that analyzes social media activity, Topsy.

Topsy uses software to evaluate the sentiments expressed about people or things in tweets by Americans each day. It then compares the results with tweets about Barack Obama and Mitt Romney. Finally, it creates a 0-100 ranking that resembles an SAT percentile. An 80 score means tweets about the candidate were more positive than tweets about 80 percent of all people and things that were tweeted about that day. A score of 20 means the candidate's tweets were more negative than 80 percent of the others.

Computing Obama's Twindex scores for the previous two years, Topsy said they often paralleled his approval ratings in Gallup polls. [2]

Adam Sharp, Twitter's head of government, news and social innovation, said the index offers a peek into "conversations that just an election cycle ago were limited to coffee shops, dinner tables and water coolers." [3]

The most influential conversations are among friends, relatives and colleagues, Mellman said, but "we have never really had a way to peer into those discussions before."

The index can't claim the precision of scientific surveys, both pollsters said. But the way the index has paralleled Obama's Gallup ratings suggests that "what we're seeing in these conversations is not radically divorced from what we're seeing in the country as a whole," Mellman said. [4]

Mining the conversations reveals nuances that aren't captured in yes-or-no or multiple-choice questions in a poll, Sharp said. [5] A campaign could find the Twindex data helpful if the data could show which topics link a candidate to more positive conversations, McHenry said. [6]

Twindex might offer a "leading indicator" of opinion, Sharp said during the Democratic National Convention. In the days following the spike of American good feeling caused by Osama bin Laden's death in May 2011, for instance, Obama's Twindex score dropped more quickly than his approval ratings in polls, "as the Twitter conversation returned to being more focused on economic issues," Sharp said at the index's launch. [7]

Twindex has obvious weaknesses, says Brad Fay, chief operating officer of the Keller Fay Group, a research and consulting firm that specializes in word-of-mouth marketing. For one thing, three-quarters of conversations occur face-to-face and 15 percent by phone, he says. Only about 10 percent occur online, and just a fraction of those on Twitter, he says.

"We know that the Twitter universe skews young whereas the voting universe skews a little older," he says. "Some people participate at a much higher frequency rate than other people. You could tweet once a month or 10 times a day, but on Election Day everyone gets just one vote."

Fay's firm has teamed with *National Journal* to evaluate conversations offline as well as online by conducting weekly surveys of people who match the demographics of the total U.S. adult population. They are asked the topics of conversations they had face-to-face, over the phone and online and whether the tone was positive or negative.

An interesting finding of "Conversation Nation," as the project is called: Political polling results tend to be stable while

Continued from p. 874

• Guided their canvassers with information about individual voters that was gleaned from analyzing huge computer databases.

By voting day, they — along with nearly every other serious effort to influence the election — campaigned online.

Empowering the People

Steve Murphy — managing partner at Murphy Vogel Askew Reilly, the Democratic campaign consulting firm — described online campaigning as a new, more effective way to conduct old-style grassroots campaigning.

"You can't call them on the phone any more because nobody wants to talk on the phone because they've been inundated by telemarketers," he said. "You can't knock on the door anymore because nobody's ever home. But everybody's always home on the Internet." [26]

Bush press secretary Scott Stanzel agreed. "Our Internet effort empowers people to go to their neighbors and distribute information on their email lists," he said. "So we are bringing the campaign back to a very grassroots, neighbor-to-neighbor effort." [27]

Four years later, then-Sen. Barack Obama of Illinois took Internet campaigning to heights not dreamed of by the 2004 activists. McKinnon, the Bush media adviser, called Obama's 2008 campaign a "seminal, transformative race" and "the year campaigns leveraged the Internet in ways never imagined." [28]

Obama turned down public financing, which, according to FEC rules,

"we find the conversation changes quite a bit," Fay says. [8]

The project does not pretend to be predictive, Fay says. But when Keller Fay did the same surveying as an R&D project four years ago, Obama "was running away with the conversation, both in the amount of conversation and the positive nature of the conversation. It was very clear in that data who was leading on Election Day."

CQ Press/Screenshot

Mitt Romney's Twitter site registers more than 1.3 million followers. The new Twitter Political Index attempts to measure Twitter users' opinions about the presidential candidates by evaluating their tweets.

For the week ending Sept. 30, Fay's survey found 52 percent of conversations about Romney were mostly negative, 23 percent mostly positive and the rest neutral or mixed. It was the Republican's most negative score since the surveying began in late May. Obama recorded his highest positive score, 47 percent, to 30 percent negative. [9]

The Twitter index showed tweets about the candidates were much more negative than all tweets on Sept. 30. Obama scored higher than Romney, 20-19, and led for most of the entire preceding week.

Others attempting to measure online sentiment include CNN, in a collaboration with Facebook, and NBC News.

CNN's "Election Insights" simply reports the number of Facebook posts about the presidential and vice presidential candidates, broken down by state and various demographics. [10] Obama and Romney ran close together through most of the week ending Sept. 30, with each spiking occasionally. GOP vice presidential nominee Paul Ryan inspired many more posts than Vice President Joe Biden.

NBC analyzes social media posts using a tool developed by Crimson Hexagon, a Boston firm that monitors and analyzes social media activity. The analysis appears on the network's "Politics" page. [11] On Sept. 29, Romney received more expressions of support than Obama in all tweets and a sample of Facebook posts.

— Tom Price

[1] "The Twitter Political Index," https://election.twitter.com.

[2] "Topsy Analytics for Twitter Political Index," Topsy, http://about.topsy.com/election.

[3] Adam Sharp, "A new barometer for the election," Twitter Blog, Aug. 1, 2012, http://blog.twitter.com/2012/08/a-new-barometer-for-election.html.

[4] Ariel Edwards-Levy and Mark Blumenthal, "Twindex, New Twitter Polling System, Tracks Opinions On Presidential Candidates," *The Huffington Post*, Aug. 1, 2012, www.huffingtonpost.com/2012/08/01/twindex-twitter-polling-candidates_n_1730488.html.

[6] *Ibid*.

[5] *Ibid*.

[7] Sharp, *op. cit*.

[8] "Conversation Nation," http://nationaljournal.com/conversation-nation.

[9] "Conversation Nation," *National Journal*, Oct. 3, 2012, http://nationaljournal.com/conversation-nation.

[10] www.cnn.com/election/2012/facebook-insights.

[11] "NBC Politics," www.msnbc.msn.com/id/3032553/#.UGoWZVGruSq.

would have limited his spending to $126 million in the primary and general elections, and raised $745 million, including $500 million online — unheard-of figures. [29]

Obama collected more than 13 million email addresses and compiled a million-member audience for text messages. He hired 90 people to run his online operations — Web developers, bloggers, videographers and others — and put them to work on communication, fundraising, grassroots organizing and other tasks. (GOP nominee John McCain hired four.) [30] Obama spent tens of millions of dollars on Internet ads. He campaigned on Facebook, Twitter and YouTube, as well as on lesser-known sites such as AsianAvenue and BlackPlanet. He even bought ads in video games, such as billboards along the highways of the Xbox racing game "Need for Speed: Carbon." [31] He also "killed public financing for all time," in the words of Steve Schmidt, McCain's chief campaign strategist. [32]

Although social media had far less reach in 2008 than 2012, they offered hints of their potential. Black Eyed Peas singer will.i.am's "Yes We Can" video and "I've Got a Crush on Obama" composed and sung by Leah Kauffman and lip-synched by actress Amber Lee Ettinger (better known as "Obama Girl") went spectacularly viral. On a more serious note, Hollywood film producer Robert Greenwald created several videos showing McCain contradicting himself. Dean's online manager Trippi says the songs showed, importantly, that social media enable private citizens to become a notable

Social Media Give a Dark Horse the Edge

"The Internet allowed him to compete with someone with deep pockets."

Lt. Gov. David Dewhurst was supposed to be the next U.S. senator from Texas, succeeding the retiring Kay Bailey Hutchison. He had money. He had experience. He had name recognition and the support of Gov. Rick Perry and the rest of the state's Republican establishment.

Paul Burka, longtime columnist for *Texas Monthly* magazine, questioned if the race would be worth covering.

"Dewhurst has the money and the name I.D. Dewhurst has already driven most of the hopefuls out of the race," Burka wrote in mid-2011 as candidates jockeyed for positions in the 2012 campaign. "He will win in November. . . . The only way Dewhurst loses is if someone with more money and better conservative credentials than he has gets into the race. And that would be . . . who?" [1]

It turns out that would be Ted Cruz, a 40-year-old lawyer who had never held elected office, was not well known to the public, who might have had better conservative credentials but who certainly didn't have more money. Cruz won the GOP nomination for many reasons, one of the most important being his mastery of social media.

"For Ted Cruz to be outspent in the huge state of Texas, people thought he could never win," says Vincent Harris, digital consultant to Cruz's campaign. "But the Internet allowed him to raise money in small-dollar donations and to compete with someone with deep pockets."

Katie Harbath, an associate manager for policy in Facebook's Washington office, says Cruz's GOP primary victory demonstrates that "just having a ton of money doesn't matter. He used Facebook and other social media to help build up his ID and to talk to voters, and he ended up winning."

Cruz understood the power of social media from the beginning and integrated them throughout his campaign, says Harris, a Texas-based consultant who ran online operations for Perry and then Newt Gingrich in this year's Republican presidential primaries. Eventually the campaign dedicated three staff members to digital operations and received frequent help from Harris' consulting firm.

The campaign tapped social media and other online resources to raise money, recruit and engage supporters, organize campaign activities, distribute Cruz's messages and respond to opponents' attacks, Harris says. Cruz was especially effective in connecting with Tea Party members, who tend to be quite active online, Harris says.

Cruz announced his candidacy during a conference call with conservative Texas bloggers at the beginning of 2011, then tweeted the announcement. [2] He maintained an active relationship with the bloggers throughout the campaign, meeting with them individually and encouraging them to keep in touch with his staff. [3]

To engage supporters from the beginning, Cruz conducted an online poll to choose the campaign bumper sticker. As Cruz began to collect endorsements from prominent conservatives

part of the campaign discussion with no assist from the candidates.

Conservative Victories

In the 2010 elections, social media contributed to many conservative victories at all levels of government. ComScore said Twitter "played a key role, providing a broadcast channel for candidates to voice their thoughts, ideas and opinions directly to their constituents and public at large." [33]

According to Facebook's Harbath, social media helped unhappy, unorganized conservatives locate each other and make the Tea Party a political force. "There wasn't a single group that said: 'Let's create the Tea Party,'" she said. "It was a lot of people finding themselves through social media." [34]

YouTube and Facebook had cosponsored debates with CNN and ABC during the 2008 presidential campaign, and the YouTube sessions included viewer questions submitted through the platform. They cosponsored debates again during the 2012 GOP presidential campaign, with Facebook also enabling viewer-submitted questions. In addition, an entire GOP debate took place on Twitter. The candidates made two or three 140-character Twitter posts in response to the questions. [35]

The GOP candidates made extensive use of social media, and some political analysts say that probably helped keep this year's Republican primary contest going for an unusually long time.

"Chunks of the Republican base, including Tea Partiers, anti-abortion activists and evangelicals, are using social media to form self-reinforcing factions within the larger party that are less and less susceptible to what nominal party leaders may want them to do," according to Micah Sifry, a networking consultant who studies how the Internet and other technologies are changing politics. [36] As a result, the various conservative factions were less likely to heed pleas to unite around frontrunner Romney, Sifry said.

That's not the sole reason the primary race lasted so long, Harbath says, but "it allowed [less-established] candidates like Herman Cain a lot of momentum because of something they said that was spread on social media."

According to Deutsch of Jones Pub-

and conservative organizations — such as former vice presidential candidate Sarah Palin, U.S. Sen. Jim DeMint of South Carolina, the Club for Growth and FreedomWorks — the campaign would place search engine ads around their names and Facebook ads directed at users who liked them. The ads promoted Cruz's candidacy and solicited donations.

The campaign used advertising on search engines to respond to attacks. The ads — containing Cruz's answer to an attack — appeared with results that would likely be found by someone searching for information about the attack.

In addition, Cruz's supporters used social media on their own to respond to attacks.

Online advertising tends to raise more money than it costs — a key advantage, Harris says. "When was the last time a television advertisement raised money back?" he asks.

On election days — the initial primary and a two-candidate runoff — the campaign used social media posts and ads to encourage supporters to vote. Supporters were invited to virtually join Cruz's victory celebration when he wrapped up the nomination by watching live streaming of his election-night party on his Facebook page. [4]

Cruz had to use social media effectively, Harris says, because he didn't have the money to compete with Dewhurst in television advertising early in the race. Eventually Cruz "caught fire" and raised enough funds to compete on TV as well, Harris says. Substantial contributions from conservative organizations added to the small donations the campaign received online.

Cruz finished second in the May primary with 34 percent of the vote to Dewhurst's 45 percent in a field of nine. [5] Cruz won the runoff with 57 percent. [6] He's favored in the general election against Democrat Paul Sadler, a former state legislator.

"Ted Cruz is the Barack Obama of 2012," University of Texas political scientist Sean Theriault said, referring to Obama's groundbreaking use of the Internet in 2008. "It is a great case study of using these tools in politics." [7]

— Tom Price

[1] Paul Burka, "The Senate race," *Texas Monthly*, July 5, 2011, www.texasmonthly.com/blogs/burkablog/?p=10803.

[2] Steve Friess, "Ted Cruz's secret: Mastering social media," *Politico*, July 31, 2012, http://dyn.politico.com/printstory.cfm?uuid=0BC9A312-8A76-4517-B003-7BBF5AA4613D.

[3] Rick Dunham, "Q&A with Vincent Harris, the mastermind behind Ted Cruz's social media success," *The Houston Chronicle*, Aug. 6, 2012, http://blog.chron.com/txpotomac/2012/08/qa-with-vincent-harris-the-mastermind-behind-ted-cruzs-social-media-success.

[4] Alicia M. Cohn, "Ted Cruz wins social media victory," *The Hill*, Aug. 1, 2012, http://thehill.com/blogs/twitter-room/other-news/241643-ted-cruz-wins-social-media-victory.

[5] Friess, *op. cit.*

[6] Anna M. Tinsley, "A Texas stunner: Cruz beats Dewhurst in Senate runoff," *Fort Worth Star-Telegram*, Aug. 1, 2012, www.star-telegram.com/2012/08/01/4145441/a-texas-stunner-cruz-beats-dewhurst.html.

[7] Friess, *op. cit.*

lic Affairs, social media enabled underdogs to continue raising money, finding supporters and engaging with them.

Rep. Michele Bachmann, R-Minn., for instance, credited Facebook with playing an important role in her surprise victory in the Iowa straw poll. Former Republican Pennsylvania Sen. Rick Santorum created a Facebook page for every state and used the pages to organize supporters. He also used Fundly, a social media fundraising site, to collect more than $230,000 through nearly 3,000 supporters who created Fundly pages of their own to seek contributions from friends. [37] And Gingrich created the #250 Twitter category to promote his promise to lower gasoline prices to $2.50 a gallon.

But candidates don't get to campaign by themselves in social media. Obama bought advertising that sent an Obama tweet on energy policy to everyone who searched for #250 gas. [38] Similarly, Romney bought Google advertising that displayed criticism of Gingrich to anyone who searched for information on the former House speaker. [39] ■

CURRENT SITUATION

Courting 'Likes'

As the Nov. 6 election draws near, Obama and Romney are locked in battle to rack up as many YouTube subscribers, Facebook "likes" and Twitter retweets as possible. But political analysts view the importance of such metrics in different ways, and some say the data can be unreliable or even bogus.

Trying to enhance his social media presence, Romney sent a plea to his Facebook friends on Aug. 21: "We're almost to 5 million likes — help us get there! 'Like' and share this with your friends and family to show you stand with Mitt!" [40]

That same day, Obama's Facebook page boasted more than 27 million likes — more than five times Romney's and just one piece of evidence that the president is running far ahead of his Republican challenger in online popularity. [41]

By the second week of October, Obama had 29.4 million Facebook "likes" to Romney's 8.6 million, 20.7 million Twitter followers to Romney's 1.3 million and 237,000 YouTube subscribers to Romney's 23,000. [42]

Moffatt, the digital director of Romney's campaign, dismisses those statistics as "vanity metrics" that don't tell how much effect the candidate's online efforts are having. "List size has no bearing," he said during the GOP convention. "It really doesn't matter how many people you have following you if you don't have people really engaged with your campaign."

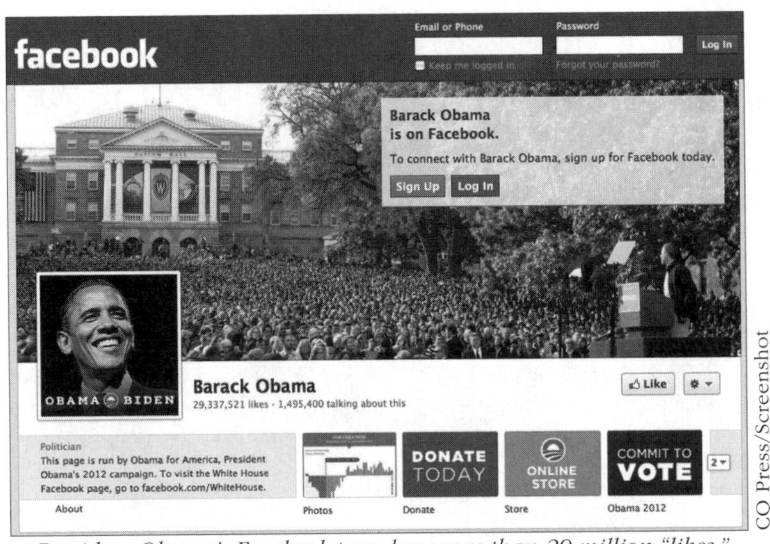

CQ Press/Screenshot

President Obama's Facebook page has more than 29 million "likes." Candidates this year are using social media sites such as Facebook, Twitter and YouTube to identify and organize supporters and raise funds. Using such platforms also allows them to bypass traditional news media and send their messages unfiltered to the public.

Moffatt prefers measures such as Facebook's "talking about" metric, which is the weekly total of the number of unique visitors who interact with a Facebook page by taking such actions as "liking," commenting or sharing, plus the viral effect of their friends doing such things as resharing. [43] At the beginning of October, Romney's "talking about" number was 1.7 million, Obama's 1.4 million. But on Oct. 8 Obama had pulled ahead, 3.2 million to 2.9 million.

Moffatt also likes to compare those kinds of statistics with the candidate's fan base. Those 2.9 million interacting with Romney's site represented 34 percent of his likes, compared with Obama's 11 percent. [44]

Complicating assessments of the campaigns' relative standing in social media are companies that will create fake Twitter followers for as little as a penny apiece. [45] Two companies say they have developed methods for detecting fake followers.

Barracuda Labs, a threat-assessment firm, said most of a 117,000 jump in Romney followers in one day in July were fake. [46] StatusPeople, which develops tools for managing use of social networks, alleged that 30 percent of Obama's followers are fake and 40 percent are inactive. For Romney it's 15 percent fake and 31 percent inactive, StatusPeople said. [47]

Both campaigns deny buying followers, and others have questioned the accuracy of the analysis. Barracuda research scientist Jason Ding said it is impossible to determine who is responsible for buying the fake followers — the campaigns, campaign supporters or opponents trying to embarrass the campaigns. [48]

As hazy as social media metrics may sometimes seem, both Obama and Romney have made huge strides in building online support, though Obama is widely perceived as still having the edge.

It appears Republicans have made "a great amount of progress in closing the technology gap," says Hendricks of Stephen F. Austin State University. "But I do not believe Romney and the Republicans have quite caught up with the Obama campaign."

Costas Panagopoulos, an assistant professor of political science at Fordham University and editor of the book *Politicking Online*, says counting Obama's social media contacts may overstate the president's current Internet strength. "Much of Obama's online following is a result of the 2008 election cycle," and some may no longer be in his camp, Panagopoulos notes.

But having the older operation can give Obama a head start on activities that matter now, Hendricks points out, saying that Obama released a smart-phone app to promote his campaign in 2010, something Romney's organization didn't do until 2012. This year, Obama distributed an app that gives door-to-door canvassers access to voter registration lists, neighborhood maps, talking points and the ability to process contributions. [49]

Incumbency Edge

And Obama benefits from incumbency online as well as off. His weekly radio addresses also appear as videos on YouTube, where they can be viewed at any time. Press briefings and other White House events also are posted to YouTube. Videos are made available at the White House Facebook site as well.

Obama also leads in other recent statistical measures.

His convention acceptance speech generated 52,756 tweets in the minute following its conclusion, the highest

Continued on p. 882

At Issue:

Should government restrict online data collection to protect voters' privacy?

JEFFREY CHESTER
EXECUTIVE DIRECTOR, CENTER FOR DIGITAL DEMOCRACY

WRITTEN FOR *CQ RESEARCHER*, OCTOBER 2012

yes

A political campaign sends a striking digital ad personalized to your age, gender, race, spending habits, location and favorite musician or TV show. That interactive ad later appears on your mobile device, gaming platform and computer screen as you surf the Web. Its message and visual content keep changing, as if it learned about you — including what you had most recently done online. Your best friend gets an ad from the same candidate, but with a different message. It seems you care about the economy, your friend about the Middle East.

Such scenarios are no longer fantasy. Campaigns, candidates and special-interest groups, tapping into the personalized data-mining capabilities of digital marketing, now can "shadow" or track voters wherever they go or whatever they do online — including using their mobile phones. Political groups can buy individual profiles that contain information culled from both online and offline data brokers, producing a "road map" to the specific issues likely to sway a particular voter.

Our digital dossier can include our race and ethnicity, gender, relationships, events that have affected us (a loan application or a medical treatment, for example), favorite websites and even our past actions (products purchased or videos viewed). It can access the torrent of social media information that tells not only about us but also about our relations with friends. New, interactive multimedia tools perfected for selling cars, computers and entertainment on websites and mobile phones make data-enabled voter ads even more effective.

We shouldn't allow voter decisions to be influenced by digital micro-targeting tactics that invade our privacy and set the stage for potential manipulation. As campaigns increasingly have the ability to tell each of us what they think we want to hear, the truth can easily become a victim. As tens of millions of finely tuned, personalized interactive ads are delivered to mobile phone screens, how will news organizations and other watchdogs effectively monitor the information to say what's right or misleading?

We are allowing powerful special interests — campaigns, candidates, super Pacs and the like — to build a vast data mining and targeting apparatus that is transforming our political process without public debate. Congress must step in to both protect the rights of voters and enact fair ground rules for digital political campaigns. Voters — not the K Street complex — should have the power to decide what online information can be collected and used.

JIM HARPER
DIRECTOR, INFORMATION POLICY STUDIES, CATO INSTITUTE

WRITTEN FOR *CQ RESEARCHER*, OCTOBER 2012

no

Just like marketers do year in and year out, political campaigns are doing everything they can at election time to learn the interests of voters and how to reach them. Is democracy better served by campaigns that know less about voters or by campaigns that know more?

Nobody loves the tawdry tone of electoral politics, and some of the obscure techniques campaigns use to gather voter information leave us squirming. But this is hardly a justification for laws that could blinder our political system.

Political privacy is an interesting beast. Some people are reticent to speak even with family members about their politics and their votes. Others put on garish costumes and post signs on their lawns and cars to advertise what they think. No law regulating how campaigns can collect and use information would hit the right notes for communities this diverse.

Instead of taking privacy off the table as a campaign issue, why not push it forward? This problem should be put to the politicians vying for votes. Their tact and skill in handling voter information is a signal of how they might handle things they oversee, such as government agencies' collection and use of citizen data.

It's not likely to be a top issue, but the use of data in campaigns might sway privacy-sensitive voters. A campaign data law would prevent this competition. Voters couldn't learn which candidates demonstrate sensitivity toward personal information. These are skills elected officials should have.

The best way to learn voters' preferences, just like consumers' preferences, is to hash things out through real-world experience. Rather than having lawmakers decide for all of us how data can be used in society, let voters and consumers render their judgments, casting their ballots and dollars with the candidate or marketer who satisfies them the most.

Privacy regulation is impossible to write well, easy to sidestep and, in the campaign area, contrary to free-speech principles, if not the actual First Amendment. The long-term solution for privacy problems has always been consumer empowerment and awareness, so that sensitive voters can hide their politics online as well as off.

Over time, people will learn how their electronic devices work to protect or expose them. Social practices will catch up with the rapid advance of personal information technology. And people will have political privacy to the extent they want it.

Continued from p. 880

per-minute rate ever recorded for a political event, while Romney's acceptance speech generated 14,289. The figures were 28,003 when the president joined Michelle Obama on stage in the first minute following her speech, 6,195 when Romney joined his wife Ann. [50]

As of Sept. 24, Obama's acceptance speech had been viewed 4.9 million times on YouTube, compared with Romney's 1.1 million. Michelle Obama's convention speech had outdrawn Ann Romney's YouTube audience, 3.2 million to 560,000. Perhaps even more troubling for Romney: Clint Eastwood's lecture to an empty chair drew three times the YouTube viewers as Romney's speech, as did the surreptitiously recorded video that shows Romney saying 47 percent of Americans don't "take personal responsibility" for their own lives. [51]

One of the most interesting developments in this election, according to George Washington University's Cornfield, is the campaigns' ability to use social media and powerful computers to conduct on-the-fly experiments that can lead to rapid changes in campaign tactics.

Likening it to medical research, Cornfield describes a campaign delivering a message to a "treatment group" while a "control group" doesn't get the message. The campaign then measures how well the message worked. Or the campaign tries variations on a message with more than one group and determines which works better. "It's hard to know, when a campaign switches from message to message, whether they're undisciplined or experimenting," Cornfield says.

Moffatt, Romney's digital director, termed Facebook "a way for us to test messages for online advertising and other platforms, because it's instant feedback." [52] Twitter, also, "helps us keep our finger on the pulse of the fast-moving pace of new media," Romney spokesman Ryan Williams said. [53]

The campaigns use the experiments' findings to guide advertising in all media. Both have sophisticated strategies for advertising beside the results of online searches. [54] Keeping an ear to what people were talking about earlier this year, for instance, Obama bought advertising beside Google results for "Warren Buffett," "Obama singing," "Obama birthday" and "Obama [NCAA basketball tournament] bracket." [55]

That strategy isn't restricted to presidential campaigns, notes Deutsch of Jones Public Affairs. After Rep. Todd Akin, R-Mo., sparked a nationwide furor by saying victims of "legitimate rape" don't get pregnant, Sen. Claire McCaskill, his Democratic opponent in the Missouri U.S. Senate race, put fundraising solicitations next to searches on Akins' name, Deutsch says.

Obama even repeated his 2008 tactic of advertising on video games — this year in the "Madden NFL 13" football game, the free online game site Pogo.com and mobile phone games such as "Tetris." [56]

Close and Personal

Candidates are tapping new social media to connect with voters on a personal level.

At Pinterest — which resembles a scrapbook or a refrigerator door and appeals primarily to women — Ann Romney and Michelle Obama emphasize their roles as wife and mother. Romney identifies herself as "Mom of five boys, Grandmother of 18." Among her posts are recipes, crafts and family photographs. [57] Michelle Obama also posts recipes and family photos as well as pictures of "people who inspire me." [58]

The candidates also created Pinterest pages. Romney's includes lists of his favorite movies, television shows and books — including the science fiction novel *Battlefield Earth* by Scientology founder L. Ron Hubbard. Obama's includes family photos but focuses primarily on the campaign.

Gingrich online director Harris called Pinterest "a great way to humanize a candidate. The Romney campaign has done a very good job of using Pinterest to showcase that Ann Romney's interests are very similar to the interests of average female voters in this country."

Both candidates also post favorite songs on the music site Spotify and participate on other social media, Hendricks of Stephen F. Austin State University says. "Both the Democrats and the Republicans realize that they need to adopt those platforms and reach the demographic groups who are using them," he says.

During the presidential campaign's last big events — the October debates — social media provided platforms for users to watch, evaluate and discuss the clashes while they were in progress. The first debate, on Oct. 3, for instance, generated more than 10 million tweets during its 90-minute run, making it the most-tweeted-about event in U.S. politics. [59]

The debates illustrate one challenge to traditional news media that Twitter's Adam Sharp noticed during the conventions. Tweets would spike at points during a speech, peak in the first minute after the speech ended, then decline rapidly over 10 or 15 minutes, he said in a panel discussion during the Democratic convention.

During the first debate, tweeting peaked when Obama and Romney clashed with moderator Jim Lehrer over control of the proceedings and when they discussed Medicare. [60]

"By the time the pundits have actually gotten on the air and are sitting around the round table talking about it, the audience's conversation has already moved on," Sharp said. "Viewers are no longer waiting for that post-game analysis. They are participating in it in real time." ■

OUTLOOK

Creative Approaches

Candidates are poised to end this election year with a big bang as they deploy social media to get voters to the polls.

"I expect we're going to see a social-media-based campaign geared toward turnout that is like something we've never seen before," says Pinkham of the Public Affairs Council. "There probably will be a lot of creative approaches to how social media can be used to get people to show up to vote. They'll be saving some of their best ideas for last."

"It's not just connecting people online," says Trippi, the architect of Democrat Howard Dean's 2004 presidential campaign. "It's connecting the online army to do the hard work of getting out in the community, knocking on doors and making phone calls."

The effort will be especially important for Democrats, Trippi says, because of recently enacted voter-ID laws and cutbacks in early voting that are expected to make voting more difficult for Democrat-leaning young people, minorities and the elderly. [61]

"I suspect this is going to be a very close election," Trippi says, "and the ability of Obama to activate his network could very well be the difference in Ohio or Florida," which are viewed as key swing states. "If Romney's beating Obama by 10 points" — which polls indicate is unlikely — "no social network makes that up."

Experts say it's difficult to foresee what's likely to occur in future elections.

"One thing we know for sure is that the social media landscape is continually changing and evolving," Panagopoulos of Fordham University points out, "and campaigns and political parties will have to adapt to the changing circumstances."

Trippi envisions "a lot of kids in their garages who are working on really compelling technology. We're going to wake up in two months and there will be something that will totally change and empower people in a completely different way from what Twitter has. These networks, as big as they are, are going to be dwarfed four years from now."

Because of the technology they've developed, Obama, Romney and their social media experts will remain influential by helping candidates in future campaigns, Hendricks of Stephen F. Austin State University says.

"The Obama camp has been constantly building on and improving their platform," he notes. "They'll continue to do that beyond the 2012 campaign, and the Republicans will continue to build on what they started this year. This does not end after 2012."

Trippi also sees a "lasting impact" from this year's campaigns. "The Dean campaign had a lasting impact, and I think it laid the foundation for Obama," he says. "They took that and went far higher in orbit than we ever did. We were like the Wright brothers, and they landed a guy on the moon."

Technological developments will continue to make nuts-and-bolts campaigning more effective and efficient, says Harris, the Gingrich campaign's online director. For example, he says, "Campaign advertising is going to get to a degree of accuracy that was almost unimaginable when direct mail was started in the '80s."

"Big Data" will grow even bigger, Trippi says. Panagopoulos sees online fundraising becoming more dominant. Rapid improvement in mobile devices will continue, and their popularity will continue to grow, Pew's Smith says. As a result, campaigns will acquire continually improving capabilities for "getting out political messages and encouraging people to take action where they are."

At some point, Trippi says, "an independent candidacy or a new party is going to happen, [because] there are only two reasons left to be in a party from a tactical point of view: money and organization." Both increasingly can be addressed outside the old institutions, he notes.

Television's influence will diminish gradually, and the Internet's importance will increase, Harris says. But Smith warns against predicting television's demise any time soon.

"People layer the new things on top of their existing communication," Smith says. "Just because we have text messaging doesn't mean people don't talk on the phone anymore. All of these things fit into the same big basket, and people pick the tool that's right for them based on their needs of the moment."

Hendricks says that won't happen until social media "are perceived by the citizens as being a reliable source of information," which they aren't now.

All of this will make old-fashioned campaigning more important, Pinkham says. "More and more money is going to be allocated toward the ground game to encourage turnout and to get volunteers who will try to help persuade undecided voters." But much of that will occur through social media.

"Personal contact still matters," Pinkham adds. "There's still no substitute for the candidate making personal appearances. What Obama did on reddit was the social media equivalent of making a personal appearance." ■

Notes

[1] "President Obama," reddit, undated, www.reddit.com/user/PresidentObama.

[2] "POTUS IAMA Stats," reddit, Aug. 31, 2012, http://blog.reddit.com/2012/08/potus-iama-stats.

html; www.reddit.com/user/PresidentObama.
[3] See Tom Price, "Cyberpolitics," *CQ Researcher*, Sept. 17, 2004, pp. 757-780.
[4] Jake Tapper, Richard Coolidge and Sherisse Pham, "#Campaign: How Twitter is Playing Politics in 2012," *Yahoo News*, May 7, 2012, http://news.yahoo.com/blogs/power-players-abc-news/campaign-twitter-playing-politics-2012-101813518.html;_ylt=A0LkuK2N6adPPD0AyACs0NUE;_ylu=X3oDMTNtdDY0NGs2BG1pdANKdW1ib3Ryb24gRlAEcGtnA2Q3YzBkNDE1LTU0YzUtM2JhNi1hNGU5LWU1MzFiZWJlNWM4NgRwb3MDMQRzZWMDanVtYm90cm9uBHZlcgNmN-TQ2OTc2MC05ODJkLTExZTEtOWU3Zi00YmJiODJmODVmZjA-;_ylg=X3oDMTFlamZvM2Zl-BGludGwDdXMEbGFuZwNlbi11cwRwc3RhaWQDBHBzdGNhdAMEcHQDc2VjdGlvbnM-;_ylv=3.
[5] Ronald Brownstein, "Communications is changing the relationship between business, government, and individuals," *National Journal*, June 7, 2012, http://nationaljournal.com/magazine/how-the-internet-is-reshaping-us-and-our-government-20120607?page=1. Jenna Wortham, "Winning Social Media Votes," *The New York Times*, Oct. 8, 2012, p. B1, www.nytimes.com/2012/10/08/technology/campaigns-use-social-media-to-lure-younger-voters.html?_r=1.
[6] Pew Research Center Internet & American Life surveys, www.pewinternet.org/~/media/Files/Reports/2011/PIP-SNS-Update-2011.pdf and www.pewinternet.org/~/media/Files/Reports/2012/PIP_Older_adults_and_internet_use.pdf.
[7] Allstate/*National Journal* Heartland Monitor Poll XIII, Conducted May 19-23, 2012, www.allstate.com/Allstate/content/refresh-attachments/Heartland_XIII_data.pdf.
[8] T. W. Farnam, "Obama has aggressive Internet strategy to woo supporters," *The Washington Post*, April 6, 2012, www.washingtonpost.com/politics/obama-has-aggressive-internet-strategy-to-woo-supporters/2012/04/06/gIQAavB2zS_story.html.
[9] Adam Mazmanian, "The Underdogs? Inside the Romney Campaign's Digital Efforts," *The Atlantic*, Aug. 22, 2012, www.theatlantic.com/politics/archive/2012/08/the-underdogs-inside-the-romney-campaigns-digital-efforts/261435.
[10] For background, see Marcia Clemmitt, "Assessing the New Health Care Law," *CQ Researcher*, Sept. 21, 2012, pp. 789-812.
[11] Patrick Gaspard, https://twitter.com/patrickgaspard, and David Nakamura, "In a vicious campaign year, apologies are in the air," *The Washington Post*, Aug. 3, 2012, www.washingtonpost.com/politics/in-a-vicious-campaign-year-apologies-are-in-the-air/2012/08/03/cfe47e14-dd70-11e1-8e43-4a3c4375504a_story.html.
[12] Alyson Ward, "The politics of friendship: Have you unfriended someone over their views?," *The Houston Chronicle*, Sept. 24, 2012, p. 1, www.chron.com/life/article/The-politics-of-friendship-Have-you-unfriended-3881766.php.
[13] "Politics on Social Networking Sites," Pew Research Center, Sept. 4, 2012, p.19, http://pewinternet.org/~/media//Files/Reports/2012/PIP_PoliticalLifeonSocialNetworkingSites.pdf.
[14] Tom Price, "Beyond Control: How Social Media and Mobile Communication Are Changing Public Affairs," Foundation for Public Affairs, 2011, http://pac.org/system/files/FINAL%20Beyond%20Control%20Report_0.pdf.
[15] "The Digital Politico," ComScore Inc., April 2012, www.comscore.com/Press_Events/Press_Releases/2012/4/comScore_Releases_The_Digital_Politico_Report.
[16] "Social networking sites and politics," Pew Research Center, March 12, 2012, p. 8, http://pewinternet.org/~/media//Files/Reports/2012/PIP_SNS_and_politics.pdf.
[17] Allstate/*National Journal* Heartland Monitor Poll, *op. cit.*
[18] Mark McKinnon, "How a Tweet Can Beat a PAC," *The Daily Beast*, April 1, 2012, www.thedailybeast.com/articles/2012/04/01/how-a-tweet-can-beat-a-pac-social-media-gives-voters-muscle-in-politics.html.
[19] For background, see Kenneth Jost, "Campaign Finance Debates," *CQ Researcher*, May 28, 2010, pp. 457-480.
[20] Brownstein, *op. cit.*
[21] "2011 Public Affairs Pulse Survey," Public Affairs Council, http://pac.org/pulse/report.pdf.
[22] James Rainey, "Voters still tuned in to traditional news media, poll finds," *Los Angeles Times*, Aug. 24, 2012, latimes.com/news/nationworld/nation/la-na-media-poll-20120824,0,3396454.story.
[23] Except where noted, information in this historical section was drawn from the following: Price, "Cyberpolitics," *op. cit.* Marcia Clemmitt, "Social Networking," *CQ Researcher*, Sept. 17, 2010, pp. 749-772; and John Allen Hendricks and Robert E. Denton Jr., *Communicator-in-Chief: How Barack Obama Used New Media Technology to Win the White House* (2010).
[24] Josh Catone, "The Staggering Size of the Internet," *Mashable*, Jan. 25, 2011, http://mashable.com/2011/01/25/internet-size-infographic.
[25] Price, "Cyberpolitics," *op. cit.*
[26] *Ibid.*
[27] *Ibid.*
[28] Adam Nagourney, "The '08 Campaign: Sea Change for Politics as We Know It," *The New York Times*, Nov. 4, 2008, p. 1, www.nytimes.com/2008/11/04/us/politics/04memo.html.
[29] "2008 Election: Presidential Candidate Barack Obama," Center for Responsive Politics, www.opensecrets.org/pres08/summary.php?cycle=2008&cid=N00009638. Chris Cillizza, "Is Obama overrated as a candidate?" *The Washington Post*, Oct. 7, 2013, www.washingtonpost.com/politics/decision2012/is-obama-overrated-as-a-candidate/2012/10/07/316c40f6-1087-11e2-ba83-a7a396e6b2a7_story.htm.
[30] Philip Rucker, "Romney advisers, aiming to pop Obama's digital balloon, pump up online campaign," *The Washington Post*, July 13, 2012, www.washingtonpost.com/politics/romney-advisers-aiming-to-pop-obamas-digital-balloon-pump-up-online-campaign/2012/07/13/gJQAsbc4hW_story.html.
[31] Sami Yenigun, "Presidential Campaigns Rock The Gamer Vote," "All Things Considered,"

About the Author

Tom Price, a Washington-based freelance journalist and *CQ Researcher* contributing writer, has written about the Internet's impact on public affairs since the mid-1990s. Last year the Foundation for Public Affairs published his report, "Beyond Control: How Social Media and Mobile Communication Are Changing Public Affairs." Before he began freelancing, Price was a correspondent in the Cox Newspapers Washington Bureau and chief politics writer for the *Dayton Daily News* and *The* (Dayton) *Journal Herald*. He is author or coauthor of five books, including *Changing The Face of Hunger* and, most recently, *Washington, DC, Free & Dirt Cheap* with his wife Susan Crites Price.

NPR, Oct. 1, 2012, www.npr.org/2012/10/01/162103528/presidential-campaigns-rock-the-gamer-vote.

[32] Nagourney, *op. cit.*

[33] "The Digital Politico," ComScore Inc., April 30, 2012, www.comscore.com/DigitalPolitico.

[34] Price, "Beyond Control," *op. cit.*

[35] Jason Donner, "GOP Presidential Candidates to Debate in the 'Twitter-Sphere,' " foxnews.com, July 15, 2011, http://politics.blogs.foxnews.com/2011/07/15/gop-presidential-candidates-debate-twitter-sphere.

[36] Micah Sifry, "How grass-roots social media are extending the GOP race," CNN, March 1, 2012, http://articles.cnn.com/2012-03-01/tech/tech_social-media-gop-sifry_1_social-media-conservative-voters-and-activists-social-networking?_s=PM:TECH.

[37] *Ibid.*

[38] Daniel Malloy, "Gingrich engages his 'tweeples' on social media," *The Atlanta Journal-Constitution*, March 10, 2012, www.ajc.com/news/news/local-govt-politics/gingrich-engages-his-tweeples-on-social-media/nQR5x.

[39] Mazmanian, *op. cit.*

[40] Romney-Ryan campaign, www.mittromney.com/we039re-almost-5-million-likes-x2013-help-us-get-there-quotlikequot-and-share.

[41] Mazmanian, *op. cit.*

[42] Data taken from the following sources: www.facebook.com/barackobama?ref=ts&fref=ts; www.facebook.com/mittromney; https://twitter.com/BarackObama; https://twitter.com/MittRomney; www.youtube.com/user/BarackObamadotcom?feature=g-all-a; and www.youtube.com/user/mittromney?feature=results_main.

[43] Brittany Darwell, " 'People Talking About This' defined," *Inside Facebook*, Jan. 10, 2012, www.insidefacebook.com/2012/01/10/people-talking-about-this-defined.

[44] "Inside Network," *PageData*, Sept. 30, 2012, http://pagedata.appdata.com/pages/leaderboard/fc/fan_count/type/78.

[45] Alex Fitzpatrick, "Obama Has Millions of Fake Twitter Followers," *Mashable*, Aug. 24, 2012, http://mashable.com/2012/08/24/obama-has-13-million-fake-twitter-followers-report.

[46] Dara Kerr, "Mitt Romney suspiciously gets 116K Twitter followers in one day," CNET, Aug. 6, 2012, http://news.cnet.com/8301-1023_3-57487861-93/mitt-romney-suspiciously-gets-116k-twitter-followers-in-one-day.

[47] Fitzpatrick, *op. cit.*

[48] Kerr, *op. cit.*

[49] Mazmanian, *op. cit.*

[50] Simon Owens, "No Strong Evidence Romney Is Beating Obama in Digital Media," *U.S. News & World Report*, Sept. 7, 2012, www.usnews.com/opinion/articles/2012/09/07/no-strong-evidence-romney-is-beating-obama-in-digital-media; Leigh Ann Caldwell, "Ann Romney created buzz on Twitter," CBS News, Aug. 29, 2012, www.cbsnews.com/8301-503544_162-57502597-503544/ann-romney-created-buzz-on-twitter.

[51] Henry Blodget, "Romney's 47% Video Has Been Viewed 3 Times As Often As His Convention Speech," *Business Insider*, Sept. 28, 2012, www.businessinsider.com/romneys-47-viewed-more-than-convention-speech-2012-9; Brad Plumer, "Romney versus the 47 percent," *The Washington Post*, Sept. 17, 2012, www.washingtonpost.com/blogs/ezra-klein/wp/2012/09/17/romney-my-job-is-not-to-worry-about-those-people.

[52] Jennifer Moire, "How Mitt Romney Upgraded to Facebook Timeline," *AllFacebook*, March 15, 2012, www.allfacebook.com/facebook-timeline-romney-2012-03.

[53] Beth Fouhy, "Twitter plays outsize role in 2012 campaign," The Associated Press, May 7, 2012, http://news.yahoo.com/twitter-plays-outsize-role-2012-campaign-073847636.html;_ylt=Am7NGDL.3RobLkBs3JIjnwqs0NUE;_ylu=X3oDMTNhMXFvNXZqBG1pdAMEcGtnAzRmN2M3NzVlLWU0MWItMzA3Yy1hODBiLTI4NzQxMDAyN2M3NQRwb3MDNgRzZWMDbG5fQVBfZ2FsBHZlcgMwNzMyNGZlOS05ODU3LTExZTEtYmZiZi02NTMzZWYxYTZlZGQ-;_ylv=3.

[54] Rucker, *op. cit.*

[55] Farnam, *op. cit.*

[56] Yenigun, *op. cit.*

[57] Ann Romney, http://pinterest.com/annromney.

[58] Michelle Obama, http://pinterest.com/michelleobama.

[59] Adam Sharp, "Dispatch from the Denver debate," Twitter Blog, Oct. 4, 2012, http://blog.twitter.com/2012/10/dispatch-from-denver-debate.html.

[60] *Ibid.*

[61] For background see Peter Katel, "Voter Rights," *CQ Researcher*, May 18, 2012, pp. 449-476.

FOR MORE INFORMATION

Association of Internet Researchers, 910 W. Van Buren St., #142, Chicago, IL 60607; www.aoir.org. Cross-disciplinary international academic association of scholars who study the Internet; conducts conferences and makes some research papers available for free on its website.

Berkman Center for Internet and Society at Harvard University, 23 Everett St., 2nd Floor, Cambridge, MA 02138; 617-495-7547; www.cyber.law.harvard.edu. Research center for studying the Internet and its impact on society; associates include faculty, students, fellows, entrepreneurs, lawyers and Internet practitioners.

Center for Democracy and Technology, 1634 I St., N.W., #1100, Washington, DC 20006; 202-637-9800; www.cdt.org. Advocacy group that promotes Internet freedom and individual privacy.

Center for Digital Democracy, 1621 Connecticut Ave., N.W., Suite 550, Washington, DC 20009; 202-986-2220; www.democraticmedia.org. Research, education and advocacy organization that promotes consumer protection and privacy.

Congressional Management Foundation, 513 Capitol Court, N.E., Suite 300, Washington, DC 20002; 202-546-0100; www.congressfoundation.org. Nonprofit organization that provides advice aimed at improving the way Congress works; publications include periodic reports on how Congress is — and should be — using the Internet.

Interactive Advertising Bureau, 116 East 27th St., 7th Floor, New York, NY 10016; 212-380-4700; www.iab.net. Trade association for companies that sell online advertising; website contains information about industry codes, public policy positions and research.

Personal Democracy Media, www.personaldemocracy.com. Promotes discussion about technology's impact on government, politics and society; publishes news and information on its website.

Bibliography

Selected Sources

Books

Hendricks, John Allen, and Robert E. Denton Jr., eds., *Communicator in Chief: How Barack Obama Used New Media Technology to Win the White House*, Lexington Books, 2010.

This collection of scholarly essays looks at specific aspects of President Obama's 2008 campaign online, from email and YouTube to Twitter and video games.

Issenberg, Sasha, *The Victory Lab: The Secret Science of Winning Campaigns*, Crown Publishers, 2012.

A Washington journalist reveals the practical side of winning elections in the age of the Internet and powerful computers. One fascinating vignette: how, in the age of electronic communication, the Obama campaign decided to buy cardboard ads on buses on certain routes in 10 cities.

Panagopoulos, Costas, ed., *Politicking Online: The Transformation of Election Campaign Communications*, Rutgers University Press, 2009.

This collection of scholarly essays about politics and the Internet addresses campaigns in 2008 and earlier and elections in Europe as well as in the United States.

Trent, Judith S., Robert V. Friedenberg and Robert E. Denton Jr., *Political Campaign Communication: Principles and Practices*, Rowman & Littlefield Publishers, 2011.

Three communications scholars explore the full range of political communication, including various kinds of speeches, fundraising appeals, debates, advertising, communication among voters and use of the Internet.

Articles

Darwell, Brittany, "Does Romney have a better Facebook strategy than Obama?" *Inside Facebook*, Aug. 28, 2012, www.insidefacebook.com/2012/08/28/does-romney-have-a-better-facebook-strategy-than-obama.

Darwell, lead writer for an online magazine that covers all things Facebook, looks at Mitt Romney's and President Obama's Facebook operations and concludes that Romney is ahead.

McKinnon, Mark, "How a Tweet Can Beat a PAC," *The Daily Beast*, www.thedailybeast.com/articles/2012/04/01/how-a-tweet-can-beat-a-pac-social-media-gives-voters-muscle-in-politics.html.

A campaign communication adviser to both Democrats and Republicans argues that social media have the potential to "return power to all of the people."

Nagourney, Adam, "The '08 Campaign: Sea Change for Politics as We Know It," *The New York Times*, Nov. 4, 2008, p. 1, www.nytimes.com/2008/11/04/us/politics/04memo.html.

Writing on the eve of the 2008 general election, a veteran reporter reflects on how much the 2008 race changed campaigning.

Sifry, Micah, "How grass-roots social media are extending the GOP race," CNN, March 1, 2012, http://articles.cnn.com/2012-03-01/tech/tech_social-media-gop-sifry_1_social-media-conservative-voters-and-activists-social-networking?_s=PM:TECH.

An expert on politics and the Internet argues that social media played a key role in lengthening the race for the 2012 Republican presidential nomination.

Owens, Simon, "No Strong Evidence Romney Is Beating Obama in Digital Media," *U.S. News & World Report*, Sept. 7, 2012, www.usnews.com/opinion/articles/2012/09/07/no-strong-evidence-romney-is-beating-obama-in-digital-media.

The magazine's assistant managing editor examines the major presidential candidates' digital campaigns and concludes that despite Romney's best efforts, Obama has the edge.

Ward, Alyson, "The politics of friendship: Have you unfriended someone over their views?" *The Houston Chronicle*, Sept. 24, 2012, p. 1, www.chron.com/life/article/The-politics-of-friendship-Have-you-unfriended-3881766.php.

Texans describe how they're coping with the sometimes not-so-friendly political conversations encountered on Facebook and other social media.

Reports and Studies

"The Digital Politico: 5 Ways Digital Media is Shaping the 2012 Presidential Election," ComScore Inc., April 2012, www.comscore.com/Press_Events/Press_Releases/2012/4/comScore_Releases_The_Digital_Politico_Report.

ComScore, a firm that measures online activity, analyzes the impact of social media, digital advertising, Internet fundraising and actions online that earn coverage from traditional news organizations.

Price, Tom, "Beyond Control: How Social Media and Mobile Communication Are Changing Public Affairs," Foundation for Public Affairs, 2011, http://pac.org/system/files/FINAL%20Beyond%20Control%20Report_0.pdf.

The research and educational foundation examines how social media and mobile communications are causing businesses and activist groups to accept a more freewheeling world of public affairs. The author also is the author of this *CQ Researcher*.

Rainie, Lee, and Aaron Smith, "Social networking sites and politics," Pew Research Center, March 12, 2012, http://pewinternet.org/Reports/2012/Social-networking-and-politics.aspx; and "Politics on Social Networking Sites," Pew Research Center, Sept. 4, 2012, http://pewinternet.org/~/media//Files/Reports/2012/PIP_PoliticalLifeonSocialNetworkingSites.pdf.

Companion reports, based on a public opinion survey conducted early this year, explore how Americans use social media for political purposes.

The Next Step:

Additional Articles from Current Periodicals

Campaigns

Borreca, Richard, "Candidates All Atwitter Over Social Media's Reach," *Honolulu Star-Advertiser*, Jan. 10, 2012, www.staradvertiser.com/s?action=login&f=y&id=136986823&id=136986823.

Social media can be both offensive and defensive weapons for political campaigns, says a political columnist.

Man, Anthony, "Facebook, Twitter Reshaping Political Campaigns," *Sun-Sentinel* (Fla.), Jan. 13, 2012, weblogs.sun-sentinel.com/news/politics/broward/blog/2012/01/facebook_twitter_reshaping_pol.html.

Facebook and Twitter are changing how people obtain political information and politicians interact with voters.

Merl, Jean, "Anonymous Web Attacks Can Stick," *Los Angeles Times*, March 27, 2012, p. A1, articles.latimes.com/2012/mar/27/local/la-me-opposition-websites-20120327.

Social media allow politicians to smear their opponents in ways that are anonymous and difficult to combat.

Schneider, Mary Beth, and Chris Sikich, "Social Media Are a Game-Changer in Politics," *Indianapolis Star*, April 29, 2012, p. A1, www.indystar.com/article/20120429/NEWS0502/304290002/-b-Election-2012-b-Social-media-now-game-changer-politics.

Few campaigns have figured out how to maximize the potential of Facebook and other social media.

Data Mining

Korte, Gregory, "Web Pioneer Providing Voter Database for Free," *USA Today*, Sept. 13, 2012, p. A7, www.usatoday.com/story/news/politics/2012/09/13/web-pioneer-providing-voter-database-for-free/1422626/.

An Internet pioneer has mined more than 170 million voter-registration records and is giving them to grassroots political groups for free.

McQueary, Kristen, "A Revolution in Canvassing Among Voters," *The New York Times*, Nov. 20, 2011, p. A33, www.nytimes.com/2011/11/20/us/a-revolution-in-canvassing-among-voters.html.

Republicans and Democrats are harnessing information about social media users to target them for mailings and phone calls.

Using Social Media

Atkins, Kimberly, "In Politics, Twitter's for the Birds," *The Boston Herald*, Aug. 20, 2012, p. 4, bostonherald.com/news/columnists/view/20220820in_politics_twitters_for_the_birds_rivals_phony_followers_inflate_numbers_in_web_popularity_contest.

Many of President Obama's and Republican challenger Mitt Romney's Twitter "followers" come from fake accounts, according to a study by a technology firm.

Moore, Martha T., "Conventions Gone Wild," *USA Today*, Aug. 23, 2012, p. A1, usatoday30.usatoday.com/news/politics/story/2012-08-22/democratic-republican-convention-twitter/57221846/1.

Political conventions have embraced Twitter as a way to engage and excite supporters back home.

Pacheco, Walter, "On Facebook, Politics Can Become Minefield," *Orlando* (Fla.) *Sentinel*, Sept. 7, 2012, p. A1, articles.orlandosentinel.com/2012-09-06/news/os-facebook-politics-20120907_1_social-media-users-unfriend-facebook-users.

One in five social media users blocks or hides the political comments posted by others who post too frequently or who have different political views.

Parker, Ashley, "For Campaigns, Twitter is Both an Early-Warning System and a Weapon," *The New York Times*, Jan. 29, 2012, p. A15, www.nytimes.com/2012/01/29/us/politics/twitter-is-a-critical-tool-in-republican-campaigns.html?pagewanted=all.

Twitter is a real-time engagement mechanism, and campaigns must use it continuously, says Romney's digital director.

Tumulty, Karen, "140 Characters Say a Lot About Modern Politics," *The Washington Post*, April 27, 2012, p. A1, www.washingtonpost.com/politics/twitter-becomes-a-key-real-time-tool-for-campaigns/2012/04/26/gIQARf1TjT_story.html.

Twitter's political influence has less to do with the number of users than who those users are.

Citing *CQ Researcher*

Sample formats for citing these reports in a bibliography include the ones listed below. Preferred styles and formats vary, so please check with your instructor or professor.

MLA Style

Jost, Kenneth. "Remembering 9/11," CQ Researcher 2 Sept. 2011: 701-732.

APA Style

Jost, K. (2011, September 2). Remembering 9/11. *CQ Researcher, 9*, 701-732.

Chicago Style

Jost, Kenneth. "Remembering 9/11." *CQ Researcher*, September 2, 2011, 701-732.

In-depth Reports on Issues in the News

Are you writing a paper?

Need backup for a debate?

Want to become an expert on an issue?

For more than 80 years, students have turned to *CQ Researcher* for in-depth reporting on issues in the news. Reports on a full range of political and social issues are now available. Following is a selection of recent reports:

Civil Liberties
Solitary Confinement, 9/12
Re-examining the Constitution, 9/12
Voter Rights, 5/12
Remembering 9/11, 9/11
Government Secrecy, 2/11

Crime/Law
Supreme Court Controversies, 9/12
Debt Collectors, 7/12
Criminal Records, 4/12
Police Misconduct, 4/12
Immigration Conflict, 3/12

Education
Arts Education, 3/12
Youth Volunteerism, 1/12
Digital Education, 12/11
Student Debt, 10/11

Environment/Society
Genetically Modified Food, 8/12
Smart Cities, 7/12
Whale Hunting, 6/12
U.S. Oil Dependence, 6/12
Gambling in America, 6/12
Sexual Harassment, 4/12

Health/Safety
New Health Care Law, 9/12
Farm Policy, 8/12
Treating ADHD, 8/12
Alcohol Abuse, 6/12
Traumatic Brain Injury, 6/12

Politics/Economy
Euro Crisis, 10/12
Privatizing the Military, 7/12
U.S.-Europe Relations, 3/12
Attracting Jobs, 3/12
Presidential Election, 2/12

Upcoming Reports

Mormonism, 10/19/12
Mexico's Future, 10/26/12
Wildfires, 11/2/12

ACCESS

CQ Researcher is available in print and online. For access, visit your library or www.cqresearcher.com.

STAY CURRENT

For notice of upcoming *CQ Researcher* reports or to learn more about *CQ Researcher* products, subscribe to the free e-mail newsletters, *CQ Researcher Alert!* and *CQ Researcher News*: http://cqpress.com/newsletters.

PURCHASE

To purchase a *CQ Researcher* report in print or electronic format (PDF), visit www.cqpress.com or call 866-427-7737. Single reports start at $15. Bulk purchase discounts and electronic-rights licensing are also available.

SUBSCRIBE

Annual full-service *CQ Researcher* subscriptions—including 44 reports a year, monthly index updates, and a bound volume—start at $1,054. Add $25 for domestic postage.

CQ Researcher Online offers a backfile from 1991 and a number of tools to simplify research. For pricing information, call 800-834-9020, or e-mail librarymarketing@cqpress.com.

CQ Researcher ***Plus*** *Archive*

Get Online Access to Vital Issues from 1923 to the Present

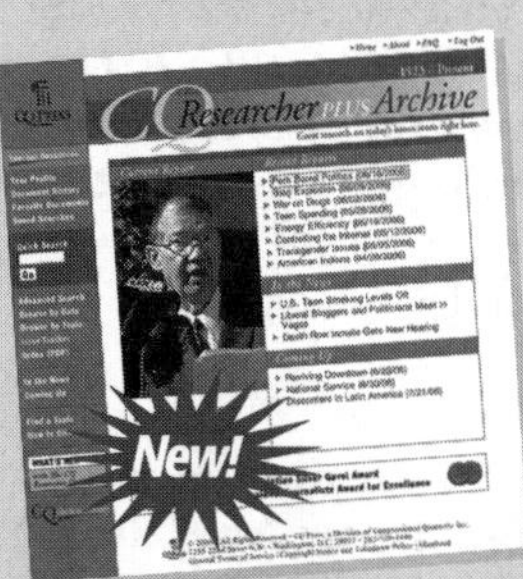

CQ Researcher Plus Archive delivers fast, online access to every *CQ Researcher* report from 1991 to the present, *PLUS* lets you explore the complete archive of *Editorial Research Reports** from 1923-1990. Search and browse more than 3,600 in-depth reports.

Loaded with handy online features, *CQ Researcher Plus Archive* provides the trustworthy reporting and the advanced online functionality today's researchers demand. The new "Issue Tracker" feature provides quick links to past and present reports on the specific topics you need.

For a free trial, visit http://library.cqpress.com/trials.

For pricing information, call 1-800-834-9020, ext. 1906 or e-mail librarymarketing@cqpress.com.

**Editorial Research Reports*, the predecessor to *CQ Researcher*, provides the same expert, nonpartisan reporting on the vital issues that have shaped our society.

CQ Press • 2300 N Street, NW, Suite 800 • Washington, DC 20037

CQ Researcher

Published by CQ Press, an Imprint of SAGE Publications, Inc.

www.cqresearcher.com

Understanding Mormonism

Has it become a mainstream religion?

As the first Mormon to win the Republican Party's nomination for president, Mitt Romney has focused new attention on the Church of Jesus Christ of Latter-day Saints. Built in 1830 upon what founder Joseph Smith said was God's word delivered on golden tablets by an angel, the church is deeply rooted in American history. Yet only half of Americans view the faith as Christian despite its regard of Christ as divine. Adding to Mormonism's struggle for acceptance are its legacy of polygamy (disavowed by the church in 1890), its treatment of blacks (banned from the priesthood until 1978) and its treatment of women (still barred from almost all leadership positions). Yet, many scholars say Mormonism has become a mainstream faith, and prominent Americans from Senate Majority Leader Harry Reid to TV pundit Glenn Beck are members.

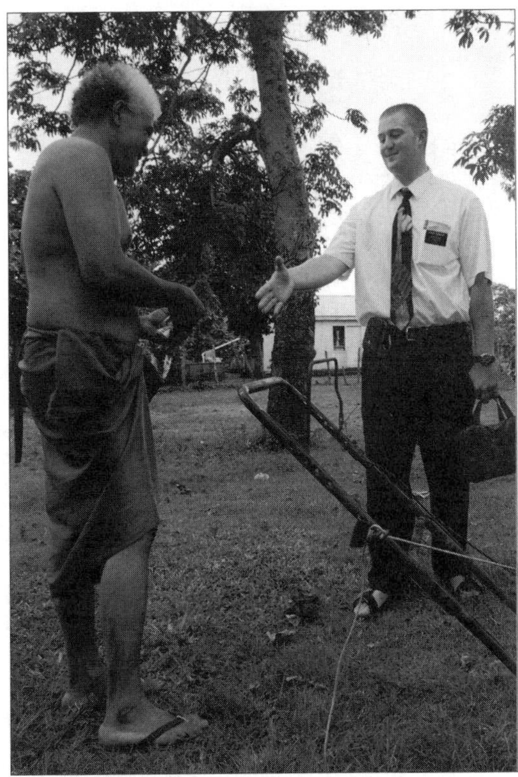

A young Mormon missionary says good-bye to a villager in Ha'apai, Tonga, after spending two years in the South Pacific nation seeking converts. As a young man, GOP presidential candidate Mitt Romney spent his missionary stint in France.

Inside This Report

The Issues 891
Background 898
Chronology 899
At Issue........................905
Current Situation 906
Outlook 907
Bibliography 910
The Next Step 911

CQ Researcher • Oct. 19, 2012 • www.cqresearcher.com
Volume 22, Number 37 • Pages 889-912

Los Angeles | London | New Delhi
Singapore | Washington DC

Recipient of Society of Professional Journalists Award for Excellence ◆ American Bar Association Silver Gavel Award

UNDERSTANDING MORMONISM

THE ISSUES

891 • Are Mormons Christians? • Should the Mormon faith be an election issue? • Are charges of racism against the Mormon Church valid?

BACKGROUND

898 **American Dream** The fledgling U.S. democracy spawned new sects, including Joseph Smith's Mormons.

898 **The Outsiders** The insular Mormons were viewed as a threat in Ohio and Missouri.

900 **West to Utah** The Mormons left Illinois after a mob killed Smith.

903 **Plural Marriage** Polygamy, introduced by Smith, fueled distrust of Mormonism.

CURRENT SITUATION

906 **Political Clout** Mormons will wield more congressional power in 2013.

906 **High Growth?** The church's expansion claims have been challenged.

OUTLOOK

907 **Confronting Modernism** Science-based scholarship subjects Mormon revelations to scrutiny.

SIDEBARS AND GRAPHICS

892 **U.S. Mormons Concentrated in West** Only 19 percent of the estimated 3.2 million Mormons live east of the Mississippi.

893 **Public Divided Over Mormonism** Half of Americans regard it as a Christian religion.

896 **Mormon Church Expands Globally** The church claims almost 14 million members worldwide, including more than 10 million in North and South America.

899 **Chronoolgy** Key events since 1823.

900 **Mormon Women Seek a Bigger Voice** "They don't feel they are really exercising their spiritual power."

902 **Mormon Faith Steeped in Rituals** Revelations and sacred temples are sources of strength and strife.

905 **At Issue** Should a candidate's Mormon beliefs be an election issue?

FOR FURTHER RESEARCH

909 **For More Information** Organizations to contact.

910 **Bibliography** Selected sources used.

911 **The Next Step** Additional articles.

911 **Citing *CQ Researcher*** Sample bibliography formats.

Cover: Getty Images/Amy Toensing

CQ Researcher

Oct. 19, 2012
Volume 22, Number 37

MANAGING EDITOR: Thomas J. Billitteri tjb@cqpress.com

ASSISTANT MANAGING EDITOR: Kathy Koch kkoch@cqpress.com

SENIOR CONTRIBUTING EDITOR: Thomas J. Colin tcolin@cqpress.com

ASSOCIATE EDITOR: Kenneth Jost

STAFF WRITER: Marcia Clemmitt

CONTRIBUTING WRITERS: Peter Katel, Barbara Mantel, Tom Price, Jennifer Weeks

SENIOR PROJECT EDITOR: Olu B. Davis

ASSISTANT EDITOR: Darrell Dela Rosa

FACT CHECKER: Michelle Harris

Los Angeles | London | New Delhi
Singapore | Washington DC

An Imprint of SAGE Publications, Inc.

VICE PRESIDENT AND EDITORIAL DIRECTOR, HIGHER EDUCATION GROUP: Michele Sordi

DIRECTOR, ONLINE PUBLISHING: Todd Baldwin

CQ Researcher (ISSN 1056-2036) is printed on acid-free paper. Published weekly, except: (March wk. 5) (May wk. 4) (July wk. 1) (Aug. wks. 3, 4) (Nov. wk. 4) and (Dec. wks. 3, 4). Published by SAGE Publications, Inc., 2455 Teller Rd., Thousand Oaks, CA 91320. Annual full-service subscriptions start at $1,054. For pricing, call 1-800-834-9020. To purchase a *CQ Researcher* report in print or electronic format (PDF), visit www.cqpress.com or call 866-427-7737. Single reports start at $15. Bulk purchase discounts and electronic-rights licensing are also available. Periodicals postage paid at Thousand Oaks, California, and at additional mailing offices. POSTMASTER: Send address changes to *CQ Researcher*, 2300 N St., N.W., Suite 800, Washington, DC 20037.

Understanding Mormonism

BY MARCIA CLEMMITT

THE ISSUES

Not since John F. Kennedy's Catholicism became an issue in his successful 1960 bid for the White House has a candidate's religion sparked as much interest as Mitt Romney's Mormonism.

Just as Kennedy did 52 years ago, Republican presidential nominee Romney has sought to dampen concerns that his private beliefs might shape his governance. At the same time, his candidacy has introduced Mormonism to a nation largely unfamiliar with one of its largest and most influential faiths — the Church of Jesus Christ of Latter-day Saints (LDS). Popularly known as the Mormon church, it has deep roots in America's history and its quest for religious freedom.

In a "Meet the Press" appearance on Sept. 9, Romney referred to his faith as a reason for his candidacy. "An absolute conviction that we are all sons and daughters of the same God and therefore in a human family is one of the reasons I am doing what I am doing," he said.

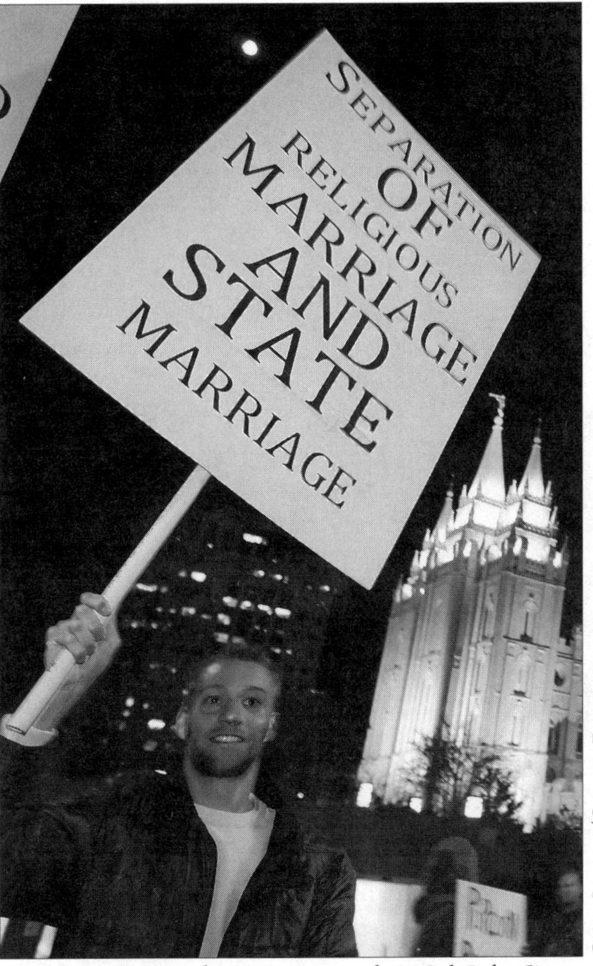

A young man at the Mormon temple in Salt Lake City, Utah, protests passage on Nov. 4, 2008, of California's Proposition 8, a state constitutional amendment barring gay marriage that the Mormon church actively supported. Presidential candidate Mitt Romney has strongly denied that the church dictates monolithic policy-related views to its members, pointing to the fact that both Democratic and Republican LDS members serve in Congress and often support sharply different policies.

Moreover, he cast his candidacy as a testament to Mormon belief in American religious pluralism. "I'm sure a number of members of my faith are proud of the fact that someone of . . . our faith is able to run for president," he said. [1]

In fact, the 2012 election cycle has seen two Mormons in the presidential race — Romney and former Utah Gov. Jon Huntsman, who briefly contended for the GOP nomination. And while Romney's father, Michigan Gov. George Romney, actively sought the 1968 GOP presidential nomination, Mitt Romney is the first LDS member to win a major party's nomination. To many observers, that's a sign that the 180-year-old faith has reached a level of mainstream status that previously eluded the church. Nevertheless, about one in five Americans have routinely told pollsters over the past half-century that they would not vote for even a well-qualified Mormon presidential candidate, and that percentage remains largely unchanged today.

Antipathy toward Mormonism was long fueled at least in part by early church leaders' practice of polygamy, and distrust of the church still runs strong for some more than a century after it banned plural marriage. In addition, some conservative Protestants say that despite Mormons' belief in the divinity of Christ, elements of LDS theology — such as the belief that God the Father has a physical body — are so at odds with mainstream Christian belief that they disqualify a Mormon as a national leader.

For others, such as gay and lesbian activists, a successful, highly organized 2008 campaign by California Mormons to ban recognition of gay marriage in the state raises qualms about whether church leaders would have the power to shape the policies of a Mormon president.

The church also has an early history of racial bias, including banning black men from leadership positions. While it reversed the ban in 1978, concerns about the policy's legacy persist in some quarters. [2]

Some scholars of religion argue, however, that anxieties about Mormonism stem from the same fears of the unknown that led earlier generations of American Protestants — then as now America's dominant religious group — to express similar distrust of Catholics and Jews.

The LDS Church was founded in 1830 in upstate New York by Joseph Smith, a young farmhand who published a set of scriptures called the

U.S. Mormons Concentrated in West

An estimated 3.2 million Mormons live in the United States, but the Mormon population is heavily concentrated in a few areas. Only 19 percent of Mormons live east of the Mississippi River. Mormons are most concentrated in two states. In Utah, more than half of the total population are Mormons; in Idaho, nearly a quarter.

Mormons in America, 2008

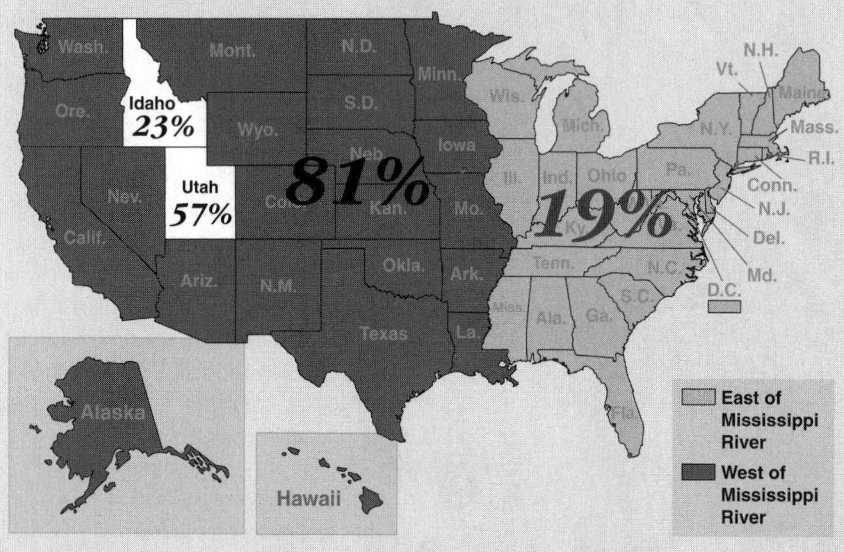

Source: Ryan T. Cragun and Rick Phillips, "Mormons in the United States 1990-2008: Socio-Demographic Trends and Regional Differences," Trinity College, 2008, p. 2, commons.trincoll.edu/aris/files/2011/12/Mormons2008.pdf

Book of Mormon that he said had been revealed to him by an angel. Like most Protestant churches at the time, Smith's church embraced Christian millennialism — the belief in the imminent return of Jesus Christ to establish the kingdom of God on Earth.

Unlike many other millennialists, however, Smith and his followers set about building literal cities of believers to prepare for Christ's return. Smith, charismatic and eloquent though uneducated, quickly gained converts, and the church's rapid growth, as well as the LDS belief that its new scriptures came from contemporary divine revelation, caused many to view the young sect with alarm.

LDS members, as well as some non-Mormon religion scholars, generally regard Mormons as Christians. But many analysts argue that differences in belief between the LDS Church and other Christian denominations are too great to place them in the same category.

As many as 70 percent of Protestant ministers "don't consider [the LDS Church] a part of Christianity," says Robert Jeffress, pastor of First Baptist Church in Dallas. Among other differences are the Mormon beliefs in "three realms of heaven," rather than one, with "no hell to speak of," and "works-oriented" — rather than faith-oriented — salvation, he says.

"To trivialize important theological issues is frankly an insult to the earliest Christians, many of whom died" for their specific beliefs, wrote Ben Witherington III, a professor of New Testament doctoral studies at Asbury Theological Seminary in Wilmore, Ky., an interdenominational Protestant institution with roots in the Methodist tradition. [3]

But David Howlett, a postdoctoral fellow in the religions of North America at Bowdoin College in Brunswick, Maine, says that "the best way to think of [Mormonism] is as a kind of Christianity." LDS members "definitely believe" in Christ and believe that the goal of the church Joseph Smith founded based on his revelations was to restore the world to the true, original understanding of Christianity, he says.

Over the years, polls have suggested that the vast majority of Americans would be willing to vote for a Mormon presidential candidate. A June 2012 poll, for example, found only 18 percent of Americans unwilling to vote for a well-qualified Mormon presidential candidate, virtually unchanged from the 17 percent registered in 1967 when Romney's father unsuccessfully sought the Republican nomination. [4] By contrast, 43 percent of those surveyed in the June 2012 poll said they would not vote for an atheist, 40 percent for a Muslim and 30 percent for a gay or lesbian candidate. [5]

Not everyone is convinced that such attitude surveys tell the full story, though. "Most people will contend that evangelicals will support Romney to the degree that they support" other Republican candidates, says Mark Silk, director of the Leonard Greenberg Center for the Study of Religion in Public Life at Trinity College, a private non-church-affiliated college in Hartford, Conn. "But the big question is still whether they'll actually show up" at the polls for such a candidate.

Some conservative Christians are skeptical of separating Romney's religious beliefs from his political platform. "The prevailing wisdom . . . says that Romney's Mormonism will not be, or should not be, a factor in the election," but "you can't have it 'both ways' when it comes to Romney's faith. You can't say that his religious beliefs don't matter, but his 'values' do," wrote Warren Cole

Smith, an evangelical Christian publisher and editor. "If the beliefs are false, then the behavior will eventually — but inevitably — be warped." [6]

For his part, Romney has strongly denied that the Mormon church has monolithic policy-related views that its members follow, pointing for evidence to the fact that both Democratic and Republican LDS members serve in Congress. "There's no church-directed view," he said during his first campaign for the GOP presidential nomination, in 2007. "How can you have [Senate Majority Leader] Harry Reid, [D-Nev.], on one side and [Sen.] Orrin Hatch, [R-Utah], on the other without recognizing that the church doesn't direct political views?" [7]

Asked whether LDS doctrines and policies, such as the church's stances on gay marriage and women's roles, may make Mormon beliefs a valid electoral issue, the church's public-affairs office referred *CQ Researcher* to its official website statement that the LDS Church is "neutral in matters of party politics. . . . In the United States . . . it is customary for the Church at each national election to issue a letter to be read to all congregations encouraging its members to vote, but emphasizing the Church's neutrality in partisan political matters." [8]

Because some Mormon theological beliefs seem "peculiar — even bizarre" — to members of larger, mainstream American churches, "some . . . are convinced Mormons secretly await an opportunity to take over the world" and therefore regard them with "unease and distrust," wrote Laurie Maffly-Kipp, a professor of religious history at the University of North Carolina-Chapel Hill. That's despite the fact that the Mormon community is generally regarded as hard-working, patriotic, "clean-cut, wholesome and polite" — qualities that Americans usually value highly in elected officials and others, said Maffly-Kipp. [9]

"The history of Mormons really illuminates many basic questions we have in general about religion in the United States," says Patrick Mason, chair of Mormon studies at Claremont Graduate University, a private research university in California. "What are the boundaries of religious freedom," and what rights do states and the federal government have to curb it? "How do we deal with religious faiths that don't agree to just be private" but act on their beliefs in the same way Muslim women wear the veil despite workplace prohibitions or other believers reject vaccines?, Mason asks. "How does religion operate in the public sphere?"

"To say that religions should just stay home makes no sense," Mason says. In the end, "everything about politics is ultimately about values. Voters will bring it to the ballot box."

As more Americans learn about the LDS Church through its increasing prominence on the national stage, here are some of the questions being asked:

Are Mormons Christians?

The United States has never had an official church, but Protestant belief was a strong component of American culture from the beginning. [10] Against this backdrop of relative religious

Public Divided Over Mormonism

About half of Americans regard Mormonism as a Christian religion, and 41 percent say they are comfortable with Republican presidential nominee Mitt Romney's Mormon faith. About a third say they simply are unfamiliar with it. Mormons tend to be more conservative than Americans generally, and they almost uniformly view their religion as Christian.

Is Mormonism a Christian religion? (2011)

Group	Yes	No	Don't know
U.S. Mormons	97%	2%	1%
U.S. general public	51%	32%	17%

Political Views of U.S. Mormons Compared to American General Public (2011)

Group	Conservative	Moderate	Liberal	Don't know
Mormons	66%	22%	8%	4%
General public	37%	37%	22%	4%

Are you comfortable with Mitt Romney's religious faith? (2012)

Comfortable	Uncomfortable	Doesn't matter/ don't know	Don't know his religion
41%	13%	14%	32%

Source: "Mormons in America," Pew Forum on Religion and Public Life, January 2012, pp. 10, 14, 22, www.pewforum.org/uploadedFiles/Topics/Religious_Affiliation/Christian/Mormon/Mormons%20in%20America.pdf; "Little Voter Discomfort With Romney's Mormon Religion," Pew Forum, July 2012; www.pewforum.org/Politics-and-Elections/2012-romney-mormonism-obamas-religion.aspx

uniformity, others, including Catholics, faced uphill struggles to reassure the dominant majority that they were part of the American mainstream.

Debate over whether members of the LDS Church can accurately deem themselves Christians — and thus part of America's most mainstream religious group — has been heated since the 19th century. Most Mormons assert that they are Christians, but others argue that the theology of the LDS Church veers too far from that of other Christian sects to qualify.

"Formally, Mormonism is not Christian because it has a different creed and a different canon of scripture," says Brian Lee, pastor of Christ Reformed Church, a Protestant congregation in Washington, D.C. "Regarding salvation, [in the LDS Church] there is no Christian teaching of grace, understood as the free pardon of all sins on the basis of Christ's death on the cross, but rather one is saved by obedience to the Law" as laid out in Mormon scriptures, which include the Bible, he says.

Although many Mormons today say they are Christians, LDS founder Smith set his new church firmly apart from the Christian churches of his day. He taught "that all extant Christian churches [of the time] were false and apostate," Lee says.

"The key sticking point for evangelicals and actually for many [others] is the issue of the Trinity," said Rick Warren, founder of the evangelical Saddleback Church, a 22,000-member megachurch in Lake Forest, Calif. [11] "Orthodox Christians, Catholic Christians, Protestant Christians, evangelical Christians and Pentecostal Christians all believe in the Trinity . . . that God is three-in-one," he said. [12]

Mormons do "reject the traditional concept of the Trinity, the idea that Father, Son and Holy Ghost are different forms of one entity whose ethereal substance fills the entire universe," wrote Mormons Jana Riess and Christopher Kimball Bigelow in the book *Mormonism for Dummies*. The Mormon interpretation of the Trinity is "a godhead staffed by three individual beings — called personages — who are one in mind and purpose." [13]

However, "vehemently and to a person, Mormons will say, 'We are Christians.' We believe that [Jesus Christ] came to Earth and died for our sins and that there is no saving but through his atonement," says Matthew Bowman, a visiting assistant professor of religion at Virginia's Hampden-Sydney College. Bowman is a Mormon and author of the 2012 book *The Mormon People: The Making of an America Faith*.

"The single biggest reason" that others consider Mormons not Christian is that Mormons believe God the Father is a god but also a human being, "flesh and bone," which makes interpretation of the Trinity as a single entity impossible, Bowman says. "If God and Jesus each has a body, then [God and Jesus] are not the same" being, as the most widely used formal statement of Christian theology and belief, the Nicene Creed, by contrast, asserts. [14] Because of that difference, "people will look at the [LDS description of the Father and Jesus] and say, 'This doesn't match the creed,' " Bowman says.

Thinking in terms of such abstract doctrine is largely foreign to the LDS Church, in which "there is no real, formal creed," unlike other Christian churches, Bowman says. Instead, the church bases its assertion of being a strong Christian faith on the overall content of its scriptures, including the *Book of Mormon*. The overarching story of that book and of Smith's teaching is "profoundly Christocentric," depicting, for example, "ancient American prophets talking about [the coming of] Jesus," Bowman says.

"A lot of Mormons would be okay with being viewed as heretical Christians" — believers who hold non-orthodox views that other believers consider wrong or even dangerous — but are distressed by being called non-Christians, Bowman says.

In the view of Stephen H. Webb, a professor of religion and philosophy at Wabash College in Crawfordsville, Ind., Mormons are Christian heretics mainly because they believe that Christ has a physical body that

Getty Images/Justin Sullivan

Republican presidential candidate Mitt Romney and his wife, Ann, campaign in Port St. Lucie, Fla., with state Attorney General Pam Bondi, right, on Oct. 7. In addition to Senate Majority Leader Harry Reid, D-Nev., and Senate veteran Orrin Hatch, R-Utah, 13 other Mormons — three Democrats and 10 Republicans — serve in Congress this year.

exists eternally, rather than being a spiritual entity who temporarily assumed a material body. But, Webb argued, the Mormon heresy is relatively benign and to some degree even helpful when compared to some of today's more common heresies.

Unlike some contemporary Christian churches, "Mormonism is obsessed with Christ," and what actually "gives Christianity its identity is its commitment to the divinity of Jesus," Webb wrote. "On that ground Mormons are more Christian than many mainstream Christians who do not take seriously the astounding claim that Jesus is the son of God. Everything that [Mormonism] teaches is meant to awaken, encourage and expand faith in him. It adds to the plural but coherent portrait of Jesus that emerges from the four Gospels in a way, I am convinced, that does not significantly damage or deface that portrait." [15]

One common argument for excluding Mormons from the ranks of true Christians is that the LDS Church considers the *Book of Mormon* and a few other Mormon texts as legitimate, sacred scriptures, on a par with the Old and New Testaments, Bill Hamblin, a history professor at Brigham Young University — a Mormon institution in Provo, Utah — wrote on the website of the Foundation for Apologetic Information and Research, a Mormon group that publishes analyses defending the faith.

But this scriptural-canon argument doesn't hold up, in Hamblin's view, because many Christian groups disagree about exactly which books make up the Bible. For example, the Protestant Bible excludes seven books that appear in the Catholic and Greek Orthodox Bibles because Protestants do not consider them legitimate, sacred texts, Hamblin wrote. And "what of the Ethiopian Bible, which includes the Book of Enoch and Jubilees? Are the Ethiopians therefore not Christians?" [16]

Should the Mormon faith be an electoral issue?

Ever since Romney and former Utah Gov. Huntsman announced they would seek the 2012 Republican nomination for president, there's been debate over whether Americans would vote a Mormon into the White House and how much weight voters should give candidates' religious beliefs and practices in their electoral decision making.

One reason LDS members could remain at something of an electoral disadvantage compared to candidates who belong to other churches is that they "are geographically concentrated in the mountainous West," said David Campbell, an associate professor of political science at the University of Notre Dame. "There is an immense amount of data supporting that Americans get along across religious lines because we have made relationships with people of other religions," having "neighbors, close friends or extended family members of a different religious background," Campbell said. But their geographical concentration has left Mormons "less likely to have friends and family members in other religions, and that works against them." [17]

The dispute over what role candidates' religious beliefs should play in voters' electoral decisions is long-running, especially when it comes to nonmainstream beliefs. Some liberals and some conservatives point to voter resistance to Mormon beliefs as particularly challenging for a presidential candidate to overcome.

"As [President] Theodore Roosevelt said, the presidency is a 'bully pulpit,' " wrote evangelical Christian publisher Smith. "Placing a Mormon in that pulpit . . . would serve to normalize the false teachings of Mormonism the world over. . . . A false religion should not prosper with the support of Christians. The salvation of souls is at stake." [18]

The LDS Church is one of only a few that still excommunicate members perceived to act against the faith's principles and interests, and it has a long-standing reputation for prowess at organizing large projects — from holiday pageants with thousands of performers to a massive welfare-assistance network that provides food and other necessities to members down on their luck. The combination of organizational ability and tightly controlled doctrinal positions makes the church an especially worrisome foe to some progressives and liberals, such as gay-rights advocates.

Mormons' organizational abilities were on full display in 2008 when the church helped spearhead passage of California's Proposition 8 ballot initiative, amending the state constitution to ban government recognition of gay marriages. [19] Given the LDS Church's demonstrated unity of action and purpose, a President Romney, "an obedient, faithful Mormon his whole life," would likely follow church leaders' guidance without question in such cases, said Fred Karger, a Republican political consultant and gay-rights activist. [20] (Romney has said he supports a federal constitutional amendment banning gay marriage. [21])

Specific beliefs of the LDS Church aside, "the overarching question is, does a candidate's faith matter to voters?" says Jeffress, the Dallas pastor. While there is an ironclad and well-justified constitutional prohibition against a "governmental litmus test" that would bar candidates with particular belief from office, "individual voters are allowed to examine candidates in any way they choose," and it's "absolutely absurd to consider faith off-limits" in those personal deliberations. "Any candidate who would say that faith didn't shape his views is either very weak in that faith" or not telling the truth, he argues.

But others argue that voters should scrutinize candidates' values and behavior, not their theological opinions, to guide their voting. They contend that emphasizing a candidate's nonmainstream religious beliefs can too easily slide into religious bigotry.

Mormon Church Expands Globally

Almost 14 million people worldwide identify themselves as Mormon, 45 percent of whom live in the United States or elsewhere in North America. Overseas missionary work, a tradition of the church from its founding in the 1830s, has helped the religion grow nearly ninefold since 1960.

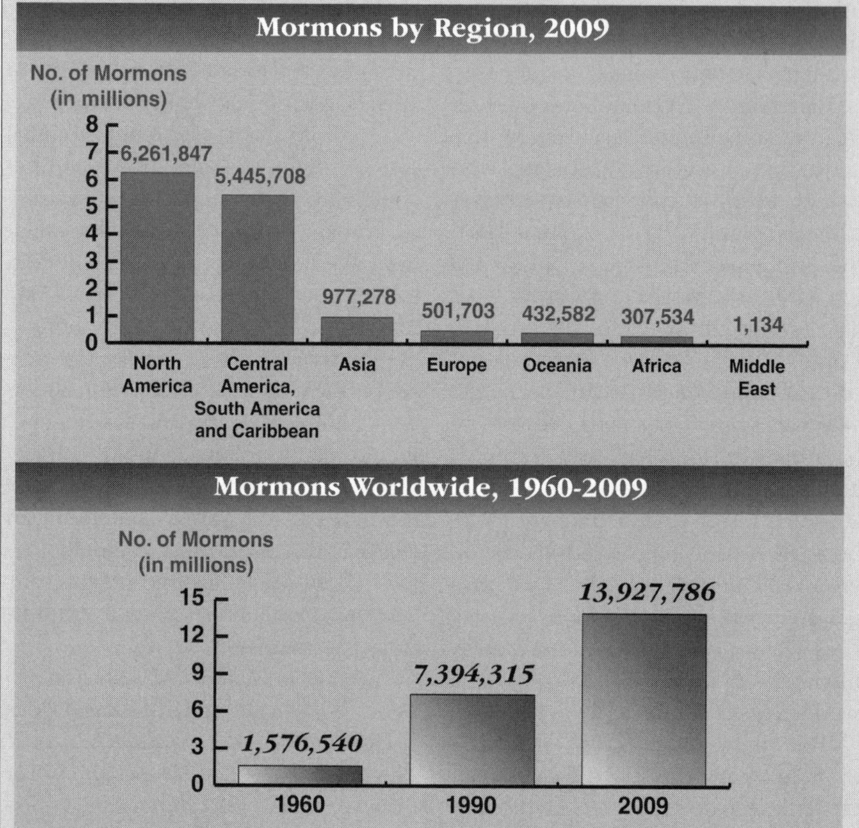

Source: Ryan T. Cragun and Ronald Lawson, "Comparing the Geographic Distributions and Growth of Mormons, Adventists, and Witnesses," Journal for the Scientific Study of Religion, *June 2012, p. 224*

In fact, elected officials from minority faiths would have a much bigger check on their behavior in office than others, argued Grant Hardy, a Mormon and professor of history and religious studies at the University of North Carolina-Asheville. "In the event that Romney were elected president, both [Democrats and Republicans] would be anxiously looking for any signs that he was promoting his faith or doing the bidding of the LDS hierarchy," said Hardy. "Any reaching out to [fellow Mormon] Harry Reid would be carefully scrutinized for indications of putting religious ties above party loyalty." [22]

Opinion polls suggest that evangelical Protestant voters are among the most likely to reject Mormon candidates because of religion. [23] But if those voters were to scrutinize Mormon values rather than theological beliefs, they would — and should — come to the opposite conclusion, argued Mormon writer Riess. "Mormons uphold many of the exact values" that conservative Protestants embrace, such as commitment to long-term marriage and to making family a top priority, wrote Riess. "I wish that . . . my evangelical brothers and sisters would do Mormons the favor of looking beyond theological differences and cast their votes on the basis of record, public service and character." [24]

Are charges of racism against the Mormon church valid?

For more than a century, the Mormon church embraced certain policies and practices that have led to charges of discrimination and bigotry. Notably, from the late 19th century until 1978, black men were barred from leadership positions such as the lay priesthood that serves local congregations. [25] (Women have gender-specific roles in LDS life but may not serve as priests. *See sidebar, p. 900.*) Each successive head — that is, president — of the LDS Church is considered a prophet whose revelations from God govern church policy. In 1978, President Spencer W. Kimball announced a revelation ordering abandonment of the old church rule barring the priesthood to blacks. [26]

Debates persist, however, about whether this history has left the LDS Church with a persistent strain of racial bias or whether the church has successfully left racial bias behind.

The ban itself did not stem from specific revelation but was based on numerous policy statements by the second LDS president, Brigham Young, and others that reflected a longstanding folk interpretation of scripture. The idea that blacks were unsuited to the priesthood sprang from passages in Mormon scriptures — as well as some biblical passages — that imply that all black Africans come from a single descendant of the Old Testament figure Cain, who murdered his brother, Abel, and are a cursed race. This idea popped up repeatedly in Jewish, Christian and even Muslim folklore over the centuries, and in the 19th century Young focused on the story. "Any man having one drop of the seed of [Cain] in him cannot hold the priesthood," said Young. He also fiercely condemned black-white intermarriage, saying that one could atone for it only by having "his head cut off." [27]

The Cain mythology as justification for the priesthood ban persisted as a widespread Mormon folk belief at least until well into the 20th century, wrote Armand Mauss, a professor emeritus of sociology and religious studies at Washington State University, in Pullman, and a visiting scholar in religion at Claremont Graduate University. "As late as the 1960s, my surveys of Mormons in Salt Lake City and San Francisco revealed a widespread popular acceptance" of this view, Mauss wrote. Furthermore, recent editions of books by early LDS writers have been published without expunging this racist "theological folklore" so that it "lingers in the popular Mormon grapevine," he wrote. [28]

Even when the priesthood ban was lifted in 1978, the church "neither repudiated . . . nor apologized for" its past views on race, as many other churches have done, wrote John Turner, a non-Mormon assistant professor of religious studies at George Mason University in Fairfax, Va., and author of a 2012 biography of Brigham Young. That's mainly because leaders of a faith based on the principle that divine revelation continues in the present day worry that repudiating past church proclamations might cause the faithful to doubt the validity of all revelations, including current ones, said Turner. Despite these qualms, though, he said, LDS leaders today should offer a clear apology because the historical ban causes continued "pain to church members of African descent" and may give cover to members who hold racist views as individuals. [29]

In an interview earlier this year with *The Washington Post*, Randy Bott, a religion professor at Mormon-run Brigham Young University, raised eyebrows with an apparently approving reference to the priesthood ban. Bott suggested that the mid- and late-19th century statements by church leaders that effectively barred blacks from full participation in the church were an example of God wisely giving to each person only the degree of responsibility that he or she can handle.

In Mormon belief, people who misuse the powers of the priesthood end up in the lowest rungs of hell, and by denying the priesthood to blacks God was protecting them from the awful consequences of assuming such responsibility when they were not ready to handle it, Bott said. "In reality . . . blacks not having the priesthood was the greatest blessing God could give," just as a parent protects a young child by not handing over the keys to the family car, he said. [30]

Bott later said that he had been misquoted. [31] But "he provided similar justification for the priesthood ban in a blog post from 2008 that was only taken down" after his 2012 comments were published, according to Max Perry Mueller, a doctoral candidate in the study of religion at Harvard University and associate editor of the online journal *Religion and Politics*. [32]

The experiences of some black Mormons suggest that the church's racial history may have helped perpetuate racist views among certain individual members. "The first time ever in my life that I was called a nigger to my face was in the Salt Lake Temple, inside of the temple" in 1993, said Tamu Smith, a Utah homemaker who, along with her grandparents, joined the church at age 11 in California. She was one of several African-Americans who recounted their experiences as LDS members in a 2008 documentary film, "Nobody Knows: The Untold Story of Black Mormons." [33]

Nevertheless, scholars point out that racism was rampant in 19th-century America, when the LDS Church was born, and that the church's history is mixed on the issue.

LDS founder Smith advocated abolition of slavery, for example, says Turner. Furthermore, prior to Smith's death, at least one and perhaps a handful of black men held leadership positions in the church.

Smith actually ran for president of the United States in 1844 and emphasized civil rights for blacks as part of his campaign, says Mason of Claremont Graduate University.

Young, the second LDS leader, expressed racial bias from early in his tenure, which began in 1844. But to some degree he was merely "expressing the racism of his time" — which was rampant across the United States and sometimes particularly virulent in the frontier areas where Mormons settled, says Turner.

The Mormon faith's emphasis on sending out missionaries to gain new converts — a practice it shares with other churches that look forward to the imminent second coming of Christ — changed the church's views of race during the 20th century, wrote Mauss. For one thing, the ban on priests of African descent clearly conflicted with the church's "aspirations for a worldwide Mormon presence," he said. In the early 1960s, for example, "a very promising opportunity for . . . expansion into West Africa had to be aborted when the Nigerian government refused entry to Mormon missionaries" because of the priesthood ban. [34]

Then, gradually, the experience of "missionizing among [a] great variety of the world's peoples brought about a change in the racial teachings and attitudes" of the church, Mauss said in an email interview with *CQ Researcher.*

Meanwhile, some African-American Mormons say the church offers them enough sustenance to make membership worthwhile despite the fact that remnants of the old views linger. Darius Gray, a founding member of the Genesis Group, a church-sponsored support group for black Mormons in Salt

Lake City, joined the church in the 1960s and remains a committed believer. That's despite some racially charged incidents, such as when white church members whom Gray characterizes as well-meaning but racially tone-deaf reassured him that, if he lived a worthy life, "you will find your skin will become lighter and lighter," Gray said. [35]

Mormon scripture itself is strongly non-discriminatory, said Don Harwell, another Genesis Group member. God "denieth none that come unto him, black and white, bond and free," he said, quoting the *Book of Mormon*. [36] ■

BACKGROUND

American Dream

In the first half of the 19th century, when Joseph Smith spread the word about what he called angelic revelations that formed the basis of his Church of Jesus Christ of Latter-day Saints, the American landscape was already bristling with new religious sects, divine revelations and a zealous hope for the imminent return of Jesus.

In short order, though, the LDS Church became not only one of the largest but perhaps the most controversial of the new churches. The group's size, cohesion and commitment to building a community on Earth to prepare for Christ's return all stoked long-running suspicions and, often, open hostilities between Mormons and the nation's evangelical Protestant majority. [37]

Smith, a farmhand and treasure hunter, founded the LDS Church in 1830 in upstate New York and published a set of scriptures called the *Book of Mormon*. Smith said that in one of a series of revelations he received over several years, beginning in the 1820s, an angel led him to two buried golden plates containing the scriptures written in an unknown language.* Buried along with the scriptures, he said, were stones containing a key he used to translate the religious history of an ancient people: Israelites who had traveled from the Middle East to North America long before Christ's birth.

Smith, who at age 25 was charismatic and eloquent but uneducated, quickly gained converts. He sent missionaries across the United States the year the church was founded and to Canada, Europe, India, Australia and South America before the mid-1840s. In 1831, he began moving his followers west, initially to the northeast Ohio town of Kirtland, and then to Missouri.

Life in a fledgling democracy with no government-established church meant that many Americans saw "exciting possibilities for everyone to make their own religious choices," which encouraged the growth of new sects, says Howlett of Bowdoin College. At the same time, the religious openness caused public anxiety, leading some to yearn for structure, which Smith's church satisfied, he says. From the LDS Church's earliest days, for example, Smith set up a multilayered leadership structure in which many, perhaps most, male members played roles. He also established a Relief Society run by women who cared for children and the Mormon needy.

The Outsiders

In both Ohio and Missouri, however, non-Mormons grew alarmed when large numbers of Mormons flocked into their towns, bought up land and formed cohesive, highly organized communities.

In 1831, an LDS group settled in Independence, Mo., which, according to Smith, God had decreed as an end-of-the-world gathering place for all Mormons. According to Smith's revelations, the group was to establish an American Zion, or "New Jerusalem," there — an American counterpart to the Old Testament's Mount Zion, which had served as a spiritual dwelling place for God and his people. Clashes soon erupted between the LDS settlers and locals.

The Mormons "voted as a bloc and worked economically as a bloc," living out a communitarian vision — a philosophy that emphasizes individuals' ties to the larger group — and soon were perceived as a threat, says Mason of Claremont Graduate School.

Missouri was still a frontier state, and in the early 1800s "extra-judicial violence was common" in such areas, Mason says. "There was no effective law enforcement, so settlers took things into their own hands."

In August 1838, non-Mormons in western Missouri attempted to block LDS settlers from voting. On the LDS side, church theologian Sidney Rigdon promised in a Fourth of July address "a war of extermination" against any "mob that comes . . . to disturb us." Vowed Rigdon: "We will follow them, till the last drop of their blood is spilled, or else they will have to exterminate us." [38]

In October, Missouri Gov. Lilburn Boggs deemed the Mormons enemies of the state and ordered them driven out or killed. Later that month — in an incident historians say was unrelated to Boggs' proclamation — a local militia killed 17 LDS members, including some children.

Smith sought federal government help to end Boggs' evict-or-kill order. At the time, however, the Bill of Rights was understood to protect only against federal abridgements of freedom, says Mason. (Only in the 20th century did the Supreme Court firmly rule that the Bill of Rights protects against in-

Continued on p. 900

---

* Smith said he reburied the plates after translating their contents. No plates have ever been found.

Chronology

1820s-1830s

New York farmhand Joseph Smith founds Church of Jesus Christ of Latter-day Saints (LDS).

1823
Smith says an angel told him of buried golden plates that reveal North America's status as home to exiled Israelites.

1830
The Book of Mormon, which Smith says he translated from the golden plates, is published.

1831
Mormons settle in Kirtland, Ohio, and Independence, Mo.

1833
Non-Mormons drive the Mormans from Independence.

1837
Mormon missionaries begin conversion efforts in England.

1838
Missouri's governor authorizes citizens to drive the Mormons out or kill them; most flee to Illinois.

1840s-1850s

LDS members move west to the Utah Territory.

1840
Mormons establish Nauvoo, Ill., which rivals Chicago in population.

1844
Smith runs for president, advocating increased federal power to protect religious and other minorities. . . . Angry because Smith is taking multiple wives, former associates start a newspaper to denounce him; he destroys its printing press and is jailed. . . . An angry mob kills Smith. . . . Brigham Young becomes head of the church.

1846
Young leads Mormons to Mexico-controlled Utah, serves as territorial governor.

1848
After a two-year war, Mexico cedes Utah and other Western regions to the U.S.

1852
LDS Church embraces polygamy as church doctrine; Young states that black men may not be priests.

1857
Worried by reports that Utah is a theocracy, President James Buchanan sends a non-Mormon governor to replace Young, along with 2,500 troops to head off trouble. . . . A Mormon militia murders 120 non-Mormon men, women and children at Mountain Meadows in southern Utah.

1858
Buchanan offers Utah Mormons amnesty for treasonous acts in exchange for accepting new governor; armed standoff with federal troops ends.

1860s-1890s

Federal government pressures Mormons to disavow polygamy.

1862
Federal Morrill Anti-Bigamy Act criminalizes polygamy in U.S. territories.

1879
Supreme Court upholds Morrill Act.

1882
Edmunds Act makes polygamy a felony.

1887
Edmunds-Tucker Act dissolves LDS Church and confiscates its property.

1890
Mormon leaders renounce polygamy; church assets returned in 1893.

1900s-Present

Church influence grows.

1907
After years of debate, Senate votes to seat Sen. Reed Smoot, an LDS leader elected in 1903 to represent Utah.

1978
LDS President Spencer Kimball announces divine revelation that all Mormon males, including blacks, may serve as priests.

1993
Mormon church excommunicates five writers and intellectuals whose works contradict church doctrine; a sixth, one of three feminists in the group dubbed the September Six, receives a lesser punishment.

2008
Mormons help push California's Proposition 8 banning gay marriage to electoral victory.

2012
Two LDS members, former Mass. Gov. Mitt Romney and former Utah Gov. Jon Huntsman, vie for the Republican presidential nomination; Romney becomes the nominee. . . . To boost the number of Mormon missionaries, the church drops eligibility age for men from 19 to 18 and for women from 21 to 19.

Mormon Women Seek a Bigger Voice

"They don't feel that they are really exercising their spiritual power."

Strictly defined gender roles and lasting heterosexual marriages have been a hallmark of Mormon communities, winning the Church of Jesus Christ of Latter-day Saints (LDS) plaudits from religious and social conservatives for upholding traditional values. But today some Mormon women are balking at the church's longstanding practice of barring them from leadership roles in their congregations.

From the church's earliest days in the 1830s, LDS founder Joseph Smith established an elaborate leadership system composed not of professional pastors but of male lay members, who ministered to the faithful and set church policies. Women did not get formal roles in the church until 1842 — and then only as leaders of an all-female Mormon organization called the Relief Society.

Women are automatically enrolled at age 18 in the Relief Society, which continues today to aid the poor, sick and needy in the LDS community. Over the years, the society has helped set up hospitals and other institutions, including the church's efficient welfare-assistance program for members facing hard times. In recent years, the Relief Society has focused mainly on helping individual families in need. [1]

The society has helped create a strong "women's culture" in the LDS church, although it has not had the "institutional impact" of the many church jobs held by men, says Susanna Morrill, an associate professor of religious studies at Lewis & Clark College in Portland, Ore. Nevertheless, says Morrill, a non-Mormon scholar who extensively researched the LDS women's community, LDS men as well as women have always considered women's caregiving activities "as a spiritual practice with great religious significance."

In 1995, even as women's roles worldwide were expanding beyond traditional caregiving, top LDS leaders issued their most explicit statement ever on the role of women in the church, expressing a commitment to maintain traditional gender roles whenever possible, according to LDS members Jana Riess and Christopher Kimball Bigelow, authors of *Mormonism for Dummies*. [2]

"The Family: A Proclamation to the World" states in part that "the primary duty of fathers is to preside over their families and provide for their material needs, while the first responsibility of mothers is to nurture their children." While it "doesn't pronounce dire punishments on women who work outside the home . . . the general idea is clear," write Riess and Bigelow. [3]

For many LDS women, these caregiving roles are reassuring, says Morrill. "You know what your place is. It's really clear, and a lot of the women do love that," she says. Furthermore, "despite what outsiders may think" about the consequences of maintaining such role boundaries, "I have not met many Mormon women who are very shy and retiring. They have a pretty good sense of confidence."

Some LDS women, however, "are really frustrated," Morrill says. "They don't feel that they are really exercising their spiritual power to direct how the church is run" because they are barred from actual leadership positions.

By some accounts, struggles over women's desire to have a real say in church policies go back nearly to the faith's beginning. In a 1984 biography of Smith's first wife, Emma, for ex-

Continued from p. 898

fringement by state governments as well. [39]) Accordingly, President Martin van Buren told a frustrated Smith that he had no power to help.

Ultimately, thousands of Mormons fled Missouri for Illinois, where they soon built and populated the city of Nauvoo — a name that Smith said was derived from a Hebrew word meaning a beautiful place. By 1844 Nauvoo rivaled Chicago as Illinois' largest city.

From their Missouri experience, "the [Latter-day Saints] really learned their civics lesson about the dangers of popular democracy" to minority groups, says Mason. In fact, in early 1844 Smith launched an independent campaign for the presidency as "an early nationalist," Mason says. "One of Smith's complaints was 'Why have a federal government if they can't protect anybody?' "

West to Utah

Later that same year, strife among Smith's followers, some disaffected Mormons and local non-Mormons in Illinois reached a fever pitch, and in June Smith and his brother Hyrum were killed by an angry mob. In 1846, the majority of members followed new leader Brigham Young on a grueling 1,200-mile trek west toward the Great Basin — the intermountain desert mostly comprising Utah and Nevada — then controlled by Mexico. Disappointed by their inability to create Zion in the United States, the group hoped to build it in this largely uninhabited territory beyond the reach of states and the U.S. government.

The Mexican-American War, which began in 1846, intervened, however. In 1848, the treaty ending the war handed Utah and Nevada, along with California and much of the rest of the Southwest, including Colorado and parts of New Mexico and Arizona, to the United States. With territories now extending from sea to sea, the federal government cast a wary eye on potential rival power centers in the West, says Mason. The government pushed

ample, historians Linda King Newell and Valeen Tippetts Avery, both Mormons, concluded that Emma's successful attempt to rally the Relief Society to speak out against church leaders' increasing acceptance of polygamy led to a temporary shutdown of the group. In 1844, "when Emma had the women take a public oath with their hands raised in support of virtue, she caused enough consternation in the men's councils to stop the Relief Society meetings . . . for more than a decade," they wrote. [4]

Official church documents, however, state that the society was suspended from 1844 until 1867 not to squelch women's outspokenness on policy but because of traumatic times the church was enduring, including Smith's murder and the church's move to Utah. [5]

Over the ensuing century-and-a-half, the emphasis on traditional gender roles "has become more complicated because American culture has shifted away from a Victorian patriarchy," says Morrill.

In 1979, Sonia Johnson, a mother of four and a feminist, was excommunicated after she actively protested church leaders' campaign against the Equal Rights Amendment (ERA), a proposed — but never ratified — constitutional amendment aimed at guaranteeing equal rights for women. Johnson said she first became aware that the church squelched women's voices when a 1967 proclamation by the LDS president barred women from leading congregations in prayer during sacramental meetings. (The proclamation was rescinded in 1978.) [6]

But some Mormon women say they never felt punished for backing gender rights. "I, too, was for the ERA," and the church never declared such support an offense, says Kathleen Flake, an associate professor of religious history at Vanderbilt University. Johnson's mistake was taking her protest too far, says Flake. She crossed the line when she "rejected the church's authority and led others astray" by suggesting, for example, that people actively protest the church by refusing to admit LDS missionaries into their homes.

Some Mormon women are seeking new ways to obtain a voice in church affairs. Margaret Young, who teaches English at LDS-run Brigham Young University in Provo, Utah, said many LDS women are troubled by the gender-role definition laid out in the 1995 Proclamation. "Might that be a document," she asked, that "could use some female input and even a rewrite," with women's voices included in the process? [7]

— Marcia Clemmitt

[1] Jana Riess and Christopher Kimball Bigelow, *Mormonism for Dummies*, Kindle Location 2152.

[2] *Ibid.*, Kindle Location 3510.

[3] *Ibid.*, Kindle Location 3525.

[4] Linda King Newell and Valeen Tippetts Avery, *Mormon Enigma: Emma Hale Smith*, 2nd edition (1994), p. 174.

[5] Richard L. Jensen, "Forgotten Relief Societies, 1844-1867," *Dialogue*, Winter 1982, p. 105, www.dialoguejournal.com/wp-content/uploads/sbi/articles/Dialogue_V16N01_107.pdf.

[6] Kay Gaisford, "Guest Post: Sonia Johnson — Mormon Feminist Role Model or Cautionary Tale?" *The Exponent blog*, July 25, 2009, www.the-exponent.com/sonia-johnson-mormon-feminist-role-model-or-cautionary-tale.

[7] Quoted in Peggy Fletcher Stack, "Mormon Women Seeking Middle Ground to Greater Equality," *Salt Lake Tribune*, Aug. 16, 2012, www.sltrib.com/sltrib/lifestyle/54704413-08/church-equality-female-general.html.csp.

Native Americans onto reservations, strictly limited Chinese immigration and sought to limit Mormon power in Utah.

"I think it's clear that the LDS expected Jesus to arrive in the 19th century," and they took the belief to its logical political end: "We're going to set up the kingdom of God before he comes so that we can hand it over to Jesus," Mason says. In this virtual theocracy — a government by church leaders or others who believe their policies are divinely guided —"there was a democratic structure. But the church would decide who was going to be on the ballot, and all the Mormons voted for him." Non-Mormons in Utah were a minority, and when matters came down to a vote, "essentially it was rigged."

The U.S. government's uneasy relationship with the LDS approached a crisis — known as the Utah War — when in the spring of 1857 President James Buchanan appointed a non-Mormon, Alfred Cumming, to replace Young as territorial governor. Already facing threats from Southern states to secede and believing that the LDS community might resist the posting, Buchanan sent 2,500 soldiers along with Cumming in hopes of ensuring a peaceful transition.

But the administration never informed Young that the force was on its way. Utah leaders learned about the troops' approach from rumors. Already primed to expect hostility from non-Mormon America, the Latter-day Saints took an armed defensive stance, although Young also sent emissaries to the government to seek a diplomatic solution. Although no actual battle between Mormons and federal troops occurred, a tense standoff went on for more than a year. Neither Buchanan nor Young wanted the ugly consequences of a shooting war, and the standoff ended in the summer of 1858, when Young accepted an offer to pardon any earlier acts of sedition committed by the LDS settlers in Utah in exchange for their accepting Cumming as governor.

A troubling event that occurred during — though not really as part of — the Utah War cemented many Americans' anti-Mormon feelings.

Mormon Faith Steeped in Rituals

Revelations and sacred temples are sources of strength and strife.

The highly structured faith that Joseph Smith bequeathed to his followers includes many elements that helped Mormons develop strong, lasting connections to the Church of Jesus Christ of Latter-day Saints (LDS). But Mormonism's roots in revelations that Smith said he received from angels have proved a stumbling block for some.

A compelling aspect of Mormon belief is the sacred temples that the LDS Church has built in every region containing a significant Mormon population.

Smith was "assiduously literal in his reading of scripture," says David Howlett, a postdoctoral fellow in the religions of North America at Bowdoin College in Brunswick, Maine, so "Mormons have temples because temples are there in the Bible," especially the Old Testament.

Unlike an ordinary Mormon chapel, a temple is set aside as a place for the most important rituals of the faith. Temples symbolize "God's entire plan of salvation and provide a safe, private place" for performing the faith's most sacred rituals, according to Mormon authors Jana Riess and Christopher Kimball Bigelow. Moreover, temples are designed for "maximum beauty and reverence" because Mormons envision a temple as "the literal house of the Lord." [1]

In establishing the temples, Smith was "one of the first Protestant Americans to respond to people's need for sacred space" — something that Catholic shrines and cathedrals addressed, but that many Protestants downplayed as part of reforms instituted by early Protestants such as Martin Luther, says Howlett.

Non-Mormons and Mormon children under age 12 generally are not allowed inside the approximately 140 temples worldwide. [2] And even adult believers must "meet certain standards" before gaining admittance, explains Matthew Gowans, a visiting assistant professor of religious studies at DePaul University, a Catholic institution in Chicago. Before authorizing a member to enter, a church official asks questions about "whether you're living up to the code," such as by practicing chastity, being good to one's children and following dietary restrictions such as eschewing alcohol, he says.

"For Mormons, the temple" — and its exclusivity — "reinforced the sense of it as a super-holy and sacred place," says John Turner, an assistant professor of religious studies at George Mason University in Fairfax, Va. However, the very privacy that conveyed a sense of the sacred to LDS believers was "antithetical to what Americans think about churches, where everyone is welcome," and increased public hostility toward Mormons, says Turner.

In the temples, Mormons perform their most important rituals — "temple work" — that they envision as truly "sacred work, done for God," says Turner.

Mormons admitted to the temple wear special, modest undergarments as a tangible sign of their bonds to God. [3] While "Mormon underwear" has been ridiculed by non-members, the use of special church garb isn't unusual, says Laurie Maffly-Kipp, a professor of religious history at the University of North Carolina-Chapel Hill. "Would you make fun of the yarmulke [the skullcap worn by Orthodox and Conservative Jewish men]?" she asks.

Baptism is part of the sacred work carried out in temples — not just of living Mormons but of the dead, from virtually every religion and from anywhere on Earth. Mormons believe that many people who have died either never got the chance to hear the full Gospel or chose to reject Christian salvation. By baptizing the dead into what they regard as the true faith, Mormons believe they are providing a chance to accept salvation after death and enjoy the full benefits of heaven.

The LDS church's effort to assemble a list of all the dead has led to creation of a massive database of public records that has become a treasure trove for amateur and professional historians and genealogists, who may search the records for

In September 1857, a California-bound wagon train from Arkansas was brutally attacked in Utah. The so-called Mountain Meadows massacre ended with 120 travelers slaughtered and only 17 of the youngest children spared. "Women's hair . . . hung to the sage-brushes. . . . For at least a mile . . . there gleamed, bleached white by the weather, the skulls and other bones of those who had suffered," ran the account of the government's investigator, Army Brevet Major J. H. Carleton. [40]

Initially, Native Americans got the blame, but Carleton soon concluded that Mormon settlers had engineered the killings, disguised themselves as Native Americans to carry them out and possibly persuaded some members of the local Paiute nation to join in. Indictments were issued against several men, most of whom fled into the desert. Ultimately, only one of the accused, John D. Lee, was tried and, in 1877, executed.

Whether Brigham Young himself was involved in or had foreknowledge of the massacre has long been debated.

"I conclude that there isn't sufficient evidence to indict him for ordering it," says George Mason's Turner. However, Young "created a climate" in which the massacre was possible, such as by engaging in loose talk about "getting the Indians to attack a wagon train," he says.

Also unclear is what role, if any, the church's history in Arkansas played in the massacre. Arkansas was the scene of the May 1857 murder of Parley P. Pratt, patriarch of a prominent LDS family. Like many early church leaders, Pratt practiced plural marriage — polygamy — eventually having 12 wives, some of whom were also married to other men. [41]

free.[4] But people of other faiths have been angered by the baptisms. In March, the LDS Church ordered members to stop baptizing Jewish Holocaust victims, for example, after complaints that the practice is disrespectful.[5]

While temples stand as tangible reminders to Mormons of their beliefs, the source of the faith is the personal revelation that Smith, especially, but also subsequent LDS leaders said they received from God. In fact, unlike most other churches today, the LDS church teaches that God still imparts revelations not only to church leaders but to members as well.

Joseph Smith was a 24-year-old farmhand in New York state when he founded the Mormon Church in 1830.

A revelation's applicability is tied to the scope of the person's authority, says Gowans. Any Mormon may receive a revelation applicable to self or family, for example. But only a local congregation's official leadership may state that revelations they receive apply to the whole congregation, and only top church officials receive revelations that apply to the church as a whole, he says.

One consequence of having continuing revelations as a basis for the faith is that "Mormons are good at accepting that some things simply haven't been fully explained yet" by God, says Maffly-Kipp. That includes aspects of scripture that trouble skeptics, such as the idea that in the afterlife, all believers have the potential to grow to be like God, she says.[6]

However, over the past century scientific and historical evidence has cast doubt on many revelations reported by Smith, and a growing number of Mormons struggle to reconcile this scholarship with church teaching.

Smith, for example, reported translating Mormon scriptures from golden plates he received from an angel. But the plates have never been found, and historical accounts from witnesses suggest that no one besides Smith ever actually saw them, wrote Kay Burningham, an ex-Mormon and author of the 2011 book *An American Fraud: One Lawyer's Case Against Mormonism.*

Members of Smith's family only reported touching the plates when the objects were covered with a cloth, while men designated by Smith as witnesses to the golden-plate revelations later described viewing the plates only with " 'spiritual eyes' or 'eyes of faith,' as in a vision," Burningham wrote.[7]

— Marcia Clemmitt

[1] Jana Riess and Christopher Kimball Bigelow, *Mormonism for Dummies* (2011), Kindle Location 2258 and 2271.

[2] Temples, LDS Church Temples.com, www.ldschurchtemples.com/temples.

[3] Riess and Bigelow, *op. cit.*, Kindle Location 470.

[4] *Ibid.*, Kindle Locations 790 and 1679.

[5] Peggy Fletcher Stack, "Mormons Warned Against Baptizing Holocaust Victims," *USA Today*/Religion News Service, March 5, 2012, http://usatoday30.usatoday.com/news/religion/story/2012-03-05/mormons-proxy-baptism-holocaust-jews/53372816/1.

[6] For background, see "Mormonism and the nature of God/deification of man/Gods of their own planets," FAIR website, http://en.fairmormon.org/Mormonism_and_the_nature_of_God/Deification_of_man/Gods_of_their_own_planets.

[7] Kay Burningham, *An American Fraud: One Lawyer's Case Against Mormonism* (2011), Kindle Location 3318-3322.

(Pratt was a true patriarch of the Mormon community, even as it exists today. Mitt Romney is a Pratt great-great grandson and former Utah governor and erstwhile GOP presidential candidate Jon Huntsman is a great-great-great grandson.[42])

Plural Marriage

Quietly introduced into Mormon life by Smith, perhaps as far back as 1831, plural marriage fueled much of the public distrust of the religion, although official church statements before 1852 declared the practice unacceptable.

Pratt was shot and stabbed to death in Van Buren, Ark., by the legal husband of the 12th woman to join his family, Eleanor McLean, who had left Hector McLean after she converted to Mormonism and he did not. Whether the Mountain Meadows killings were related to Pratt's murder is unknown, although there was widespread suspicion that they were. "It was in accordance with Mormon policy to hold every Arkansan responsible for Pratt's death," wrote William Alexander Linn, a non-Mormon historian and journalist in a popular 1902 history of the church.[43]

There's virtually no agreement about exactly what motivated Smith — and, following his example, other church leaders — to take multiple wives.

To many of its critics, polygamy was mainly a matter of powerful men taking what they wanted, including teenage girls and other men's wives, regardless of morality. Oliver Cowdery, a longtime Smith friend who was later excommunicated, for example, condemned the married Smith's relationship in the 1830s with Fanny Alger, a teenage servant in his home, as a "dirty, nasty, filthy affair." [44]

By contrast, Benjamin F. Johnson, a one-time secretary to Smith, stated that "without doubt in my mind Fanny Alger was . . . the Prophet's first plural wife." [45]

Smith described plural marriage as a harkening back to God's covenants with patriarchs of the Old Testament. "I, the Lord, justified my servants Abraham, Isaac and Jacob, . . . Moses, David and Solomon . . . as touching the principle and doctrine of their having many wives and concubines," runs Smith's account of his revelation on the subject. [46]

The terms "polygamy" or "plural marriage" are essentially a translation into the common parlance of the "celestial marriage" or "patriarchal marriage" that Mormon leaders envisioned as a sacrament to "seal" families together for eternity and link them to the divine, says Kathleen Flake, an LDS member and an associate professor of American religious history at Vanderbilt University, in Nashville. Most "celestial marriages" were not polygamous, however, and in the mid- to late 19th century, when the rate of plural marriage was at its height, only 20 to 25 percent of Mormons — mostly church leaders — maintained polygamous families. "You had to have permission from the highest authority" for the unions, she says.

Disapproval among non-Mormons soon led to legislative action. In 1862, the Morrill Anti-Bigamy Act banned polygamy in U.S. territories, but the law was not enforced, partly because the Civil War was in progress. In 1879, the Supreme Court upheld the law, ruling that the First Amendment protects religious beliefs but not necessarily religious practices. [47] In 1882, the Edmunds Act deemed participation or even avowed belief in plural marriage a felony punishable by jail and loss of voting rights and eligibility to serve on a jury or in public office.

As a result, fathers went to jail, and poverty spread throughout Mormon communities, with all believers facing "loss of all civil rights" simply by belonging to the church, says Flake. Soon "the church faced dissolution," forcing leaders to act.

In 1890, church President Wilford Woodruff issued "The Manifesto," stating that "we are not teaching polygamy or plural marriage, nor permitting any person to enter into its practice." Said Woodruff, "I now publicly declare that my advice to the Latter-day Saints is to refrain from contracting any marriage forbidden by the law of the land." [48]

Nevertheless, the "practice had a 50-year history," and polygamous families could not simply be dismantled at will, Flake says. "After holding this up as the spiritual model" for not only the earthly but the eternal lives of members, church leaders couldn't disavow it in an instant. "It took 20 years" to fully sever the church's ties with the plural-marriage tradition, Flake says.

During that time church leaders "were saying one thing in public and another to families and close friends," whom they reassured that celestial marriage, including the plural variety, remained a spiritual principle of the faith, Flake says.

Some polygamous families sought refuge over the border with Mexico or Canada or in remote areas of the intermountain West. Some apparently received the tacit blessing of church leaders during their exile while others broke off into dissenting sects, some of which still exist and practice polygamy. [49]

Struggles between Latter-day Saints and America's Protestant majority continued into the 20th century.

Between 1904 and 1907, the Senate conducted hearings debating whether to seat Sen. Reed Smoot, R-Utah, a Mormon apostle. Arguing that Smoot's high rank in the church implicated him in a conspiracy to continue thwarting anti-polygamy laws, a large coalition of Protestant churches fought a vigorous — ultimately losing — battle against admitting him to Congress. [50]

Despite — or perhaps because of — its struggles, the LDS Church survived and grew in the 20th century, even though "history suggests that the overwhelming majority of religious movements fail to survive even one generation," wrote Mauss of Claremont Graduate School. [51]

New religious groups form because their beliefs differ from those of existing churches, and they often have an exceptionally strong hold on their members, who must cope with more differences and surmount more difficulties to belong. Over time, however, young sects typically adapt themselves to the religious mainstream, "with an accompanying loss of fervency, commitment and distinctiveness," Mauss says.

The LDS Church pursued such assimilation until the mid-20th century, says Mauss. Many members moved quickly up the economic and social ladder, and the church accepted modern intellectual trends such as reconciling scriptural history with evolutionary science. [52]

Unlike most churches, however, which never look back once assimilation begins, the LDS Church "retrenched" near the end of the 20th century in "an apparent effort to stop . . . the erosion of the . . . Mormon identity . . . as a 'peculiar people,' " Mauss writes. Among other things, rote learning of church doctrine received greater emphasis. In addition, some Mormon intellectuals found their analytical writings on LDS doctrine and history questioned. And, in some cases, those scholars were accused of veering too far toward dissent. [53] ■

Continued on p. 906

At Issue:

Should a candidate's Mormon beliefs be an election issue?

KAY BURNINGHAM
***AUTHOR,* AN AMERICAN FRAUD: ONE LAWYER'S CASE AGAINST MORMONISM**

WRITTEN FOR *CQ RESEARCHER*, OCTOBER 2012

YES

All candidates' beliefs, religious and otherwise, should be legitimate election issues, including Mitt Romney's faithfulness to Mormonism and its secretive practices.

Mormonism uses a religious fable — golden tablets delivered by an angel — as a pretext for the annual collection of billions in tithes, which are then invested into its global financial empire. Though some funds are spent on buildings and religious education, much of the profit benefits the Mormon elite. In exchange for donations, tithe-payers attend services and may participate in Masonic-like temple ceremonies. Previously compliant adherents may also receive warehoused foods and a limited income supplement during hard times.

Mormon plagiarism of the Bible, Egyptian funeral text and other sources has been recognized since the church's birth in 1830. However, once indoctrinates become leaders, any good-faith questioning of Mormon theology is moot. All time, money and resources are consecrated to the Church of Jesus Christ of Latter-day Saints for building up the Kingdom of God on Earth, leaving little time for introspection. This can be seen in Utah, a de facto theocracy where Mormons rule through heavily biased public education and news reporting.

Mitt Romney's character was formed by lifelong allegiance to the church and its focus on wealth, control and exclusion. At 19 and repeatedly thereafter, he made and renewed the temple vow of consecration. Romney spent two-and-a-half years as a French missionary, where controls for sleep, work schedules, dress, personal associations and conversion records were top-down ordered and supervised. After his mission he returned to study not at Stanford but Mormon-run Brigham Young University. There, his immersion into Mormonism was completed.

Misrepresentations documented during the Romney campaign parallel the church's historical revisionism. Romney's policy opinions change like Mormonism's historic reworkings of its theology regarding marriage, racism and Christianity. Romney avoids tax return disclosure much like the church fails to disclose financial statements to its members. What appears to many as a huge character failing is simply an individual example of what the Mormon hierarchy has done for decades, because according to LDS leaders, "lying for the lord," is sometimes necessary.

If Romney is elected, economic elitism will continue. Civil rights will be circumscribed and a national theocracy based on religious fundamentalism will be more than a remote risk. In Mormonism, as with Romney himself, the ends justify the means.

Is there any doubt those beliefs must be an election issue?

LAURIE F. MAFFLY-KIPP
PROFESSOR OF RELIGIOUS STUDIES, UNIVERSITY OF NORTH CAROLINA AT CHAPEL HILL

WRITTEN FOR *CQ RESEARCHER*, OCTOBER 2012

NO

Since the nation's founding, Americans have advocated the separation of church and state. But they have never been successful at separating religion and politics, or even willing to do so. This may be a good thing, in part because knowledge of a candidate's religious background provides a significant way to judge the kind of engagement he or she might exercise on political issues. It seems just as germane as any other set of loyalties as voters try to predict the commitments a candidate will bring into office.

That said, religious beliefs are also a notoriously elusive target of analysis. History is enough of a guide to suggest that knowing about President Richard Nixon's Quaker upbringing would not have been the best predictor of his escalation of the Vietnam War; nor would John F. Kennedy's Catholicism point in any straight-line way to his social policies. Conservative evangelicals were hopeful in 1976 when Jimmy Carter allowed that he had experienced conversion, but they were disappointed by the leftward spin of his actions as president. Professed religious beliefs rarely predict policy with any precision.

Mitt Romney's candidacy, though, presents another challenge. Not only are his religious beliefs not well known to most Americans, they are puzzling, odd and even vaguely threatening because of their links to a Mormon faith that has come into violent conflict with the government and non-Mormons in the past. They stretch a commitment to religious tolerance to new levels. For very different reasons, both conservative Christians (who share many social values with most Mormons but reject their theology) and liberals (who believe in religious toleration but are put off by a tradition that has remained geographically isolated and proudly "peculiar") are wary of the injection of the Mormon faith into the political arena.

Romney has been reticent about his faith, exhibiting an evasiveness that, while intended to reduce popular discomfort with unusual beliefs, also exacerbates it by feeding into the narrative of Mormons as overly secretive. A Mormon candidate brings Americans face to face with their own long history of fear about religious difference and its limits in a democratic society. These are not unreasonable fears, just as the Mormon wariness of engagement has been won honestly by a history of violence against the faith. Religion is a force we cannot ignore, but we don't know fully how to incorporate it. It may be one case where actions speak much louder than words ever could.

Continued from p. 904

CURRENT SITUATION

Political Clout

Whether Romney wins or loses in November, this might still be the year that Mormonism achieves a new level of political influence in America, some observers say.

"Next year could be a banner one for Mormons in the nation's capital," declared a July headline in *The Hill*, a newspaper for Capitol Hill insiders. "Depending on who controls the Senate, it will have either . . . a Mormon Senate majority leader in Harry Reid, D-Nev., or a Mormon president pro tempore in Sen. Orrin Hatch, R-Utah." [54] (President pro tem is the majority party's second-highest officer, held by the longest-serving senator of that party.)

Reid emerged this year as one of the most vociferous opponents of GOP presidential nominee Romney. Furthermore, Reid's opposition stems from his intense disagreement with Romney on the policy implications of their shared Mormon faith, said Jim Manley, a former top aide to the majority leader. Reid's "faith is very important to him," and he firmly believes that Romney's public-policy positions are at odds with church teachings on compassion and the importance of caring for those in need, Manley said. [55]

Besides Reid and Hatch, 13 other Mormons — two Democrats and 10 Republicans — serve in Congress this year, representing California, Idaho, New Mexico and Utah, along with a Democratic non-voting delegate from American Samoa. [56]

If Romney wins the presidency, there might be an outcry by "a fairly large minority that does view America as a Christian nation" and therefore believes the White House must be in orthodox Christian hands, says Lee, the D.C. pastor.

Nevertheless, "a Romney presidency would inevitably move Mormonism further into the mainstream of American religious life," and that ultimately would be a good thing for Christians, Lee argues. "I believe that it is healthy for the church to seek their savior in heaven, not in the White House. Ultimately, I think orthodox Christianity will be strengthened and made more vibrant as it is further disabused of the notion that American citizenship is akin to a Christian birthright," he said in an email interview.

Getty Images/Timothy Hiatt

Donny and Marie Osmond, among the nation's most prominent Mormons, perform at Chicago's Ford Oriental Theatre on Dec. 6, 2011. Other well-known American Mormons include singer Gladys Knight, Washington Nationals outfielder Bryce Harper, talk show host Glenn Beck and Senate Majority Leader Harry Reid, D-Nev. An estimated 3.2 million Americans are Mormon.

High Growth?

In 1984, sociologist Rodney Stark, co-director of the Institute for Studies of Religion at Baylor University in Waco, Texas, famously speculated that Mormonism might well be on track to become the next "major world faith." If growth trends continued, Stark said, the LDS Church would have at least 60 million and potentially as many as 265 million members by 2080. [57]

Growth has been considerably slower than Stark projected but healthy nonetheless, swelling to 14.1 million members worldwide by the end of 2010, according to the church's count. [58]

"They continue building buildings" — both chapels for local congregations and larger regional spiritual sites called temples — which demonstrates continued growth, says Vanderbilt's Flake. [59]

The church's worldwide expansion has been driven mostly by high growth in a few areas, says Ryan Cragun, an assistant professor of the sociology of religion at the University of Tampa. "In several parts of Africa, the LDS Church is growing fairly well, and they are still building buildings there," for example, he says.

Nevertheless, the number of active LDS Church members in the United States is considerably lower than membership figures reported by the church, according to Cragun, who studies Mormon demographics using data from the "American Religious Identification Survey," which regularly polls 53,000 Americans. The 2008 survey put the number of Mormons at about 3.1 million — 1.3 percent of the U.S. population — rather than nearly 6 million, as the church reports, Cragun says.

The discrepancy occurs because the LDS Church reports nearly everyone who has been baptized into the faith as a current member, Cragun says. Thus, LDS self-reported numbers are likely inflated, unlike membership data from some other churches that periodically clear their rolls of people who don't attend services, he says.

In the United States and other highly industrialized countries, the church is growing only "at the same rate as the population, or maybe even a bit slower," rather than seeing conversions increase, Cragun says. Furthermore, some demographic groups are leaving the church at high rates, he says. For example, 80 percent of single women ages 18 to 30 are no longer active, "and my guess is that it's even higher for men," he says.

Dropout rates after initial conversion may be even higher in other countries than in the United States. Data from nations that tally religious affiliation show this in many cases, Cragun says. In Brazil, for example, the 2010 census found that 225,695 people identified as Latter-day Saints, compared to the 1.1 million members whom the church reported baptizing there, the *Salt Lake Tribune* reported. [60] ■

OUTLOOK

Confronting Modernism

A world increasingly attuned to science-based scholarship is and may continue to be a difficult place for faiths based on continuing revelation, especially a faith of relatively recent origin.

"Miracle stories about the origins of the LDS Church are harder to accept" today compared with equivalent miracles surrounding the formation of older faiths such as Islam and Christianity, says Mauss of Claremont Graduate School. "There are original records and testimonies of both Mormon converts and anti-Mormons that are available in public archives, so that they can be questioned, compared, and evaluated," for historical accuracy, says Mauss. "This makes Mormonism and its founding prophet more vulnerable to sneers" and doubts, he says.

Simon Southerton, an ex-Mormon plant geneticist in Brisbane, Australia, sees contradiction in the way LDS Church leaders treat some modern scientific findings. An example, he says, is DNA research pointing to Asian, rather than Israelite, origins for Native Americans, contrary to Mormon scripture. Southerton says LDS Church leaders apparently support the DNA scholarship and, at the same time, continue to tell members that the scriptural accounts are factual. The contradiction "becomes very troubling for ordinary members of the church," Southerton said. [61]

As the church matures, such controversies will fade, as they have for other faiths, predicts Bowman of Hampden-Sydney College. "In 500 to 1,000 years, Joseph Smith will be looked upon as like Muhammad," he says. "Nobody argues at dinner parties whether Muhammad really saw the angel Gabriel."

No one knows, of course, whether the LDS Church will maintain its influence and current share of the population, realize the predictions for its robust growth or fade like some mainline Protestant churches have.

Up to now, at least, the church's "bureaucratic charisma" — linking strong organizational structure with the possibility of vibrant new divine revelations — has sustained the institution, says Vanderbilt's Flake, a Mormon. At some point, "this may prove unable to continue," she says. "But they've been at it for nearly 200 years."

Mormon beliefs about issues such as gay marriage could change with time, says Matthew Gowans, a Mormon assistant professor of philosophy at DePaul University, a Catholic institution in Chicago. Because of the idea that continuing revelation is possible, Mormons tend to have a fluid and open view of the future. "If leaders pray about an issue and a new revelation comes," members tend to be open to that, he says.

"I would expect Mormonism to be eventually assimilated like all the other new religions that began as radical 'sects' or 'cults,' but just to take longer in doing so than, say, the Methodists have done," says Mauss. "That would be my assessment as a social scientist. As a believer, I would expect that divine revelation through the LDS prophets would determine whatever the church would look like in 200 years." ■

Notes

1 "September 9: Mitt Romney, Ann Romney, Julian Castro, Peggy Noonan, E. J. Dionne, Bill Bennett, Chuck Todd," transcripts from "Meet the Press," www.msnbc.msn.com/id/48959273/ns/meet_the_press-transcripts/t/september-mitt-romney-ann-romney-julian-castro-peggy-noonan-ej-dionne-bill-bennett-chuck-todd/#.UG2D-a5vCUk.

2 For background, see John G. Turner, "Why Race Is Still a Problem for Mormons," *The New York Times*, Aug. 18, 2012, www.nytimes.com/2012/08/19/opinion/sunday/racism-and-the-mormon-church.html.

3 Ben Witherington III, "Why Mormonism Is Not Christianity — the Issue of Christology,"

Patheos, Aug. 27, 2012, www.patheos.com/blogs/bibleandculture/2012/08/27/why-mormons-are-not-christians-the-issue-of-christology.

4 Elizabeth Hartfield, "Americans Least Likely to Vote for Atheist, Muslim Presidential Candidates, Poll Finds," "The Note," ABC News, June 21, 2012, http://abcnews.go.com/blogs/politics/2012/06/americans-least-likely-to-vote-for-atheist-muslim-presidential-candidates-poll-finds.

5 "Atheists, Muslims See Most Bias as Presidential Candidates," Gallup, June 21, 2012, www.gallup.com/poll/155285/Atheists-Muslims-Bias-Presidential-Candidates.aspx?utm_source=alert&utm_medium=email&utm_campaign=syndication&utm_content=morelink&utm_term=All%20Gallup%20Headlines%20-%20Politics.

6 Warren Cole Smith, "A Vote for Romney Is a Vote for the LDS Church," *Patheos*, May 24, 2011, www.patheos.com/Resources/Additional-Resources/Vote-for-Romney-Is-a-Vote-for-the-LDS-Church-Warren-Cole-Smith-05-24-2011.html.

7 Quoted in Adam Nagourney and Laurie Goodstein, "Mormon Candidate Braces for Religion as Issue," *The New York Times*, Feb. 8, 2007, p. A1, www.nytimes.com/2007/02/08/us/politics/08romney.html?pagewanted=all.

8 "Political Neutrality," Church of Jesus Christ of Latter-day Saints website, www.mormonnewsroom.org/official-statement/political-neutrality.

9 Laurie Maffly-Kipp, "Mormons' Double Legacy," Room for Debate, *The New York Times*, Jan. 30, 2012, www.nytimes.com/roomfordebate/2012/01/30/what-is-it-about-mormons/the-double-legacy-of-mormons.

10 For background, see Marcia Clemmitt, "Protestants Today," *CQ Researcher*, Dec. 7, 2007, pp. 1009-1032, and Thomas J. Billitteri, "Government and Religion," *CQ Researcher*, Jan. 5, 2010, pp. 25-48.

11 "Defining a Megachurch," Christiantimelines.com, 2009, www.christiantimelines.com/Megachurches.htm.

12 Quoted in Billy Hallowell, "Pastor Rick Warren: Mormons' Views on 'The Trinity' Are a Sticking Point," *The Blaze*, April 9, 2012, www.theblaze.com/stories/pastor-rick-warren-mormons-views-on-the-trinity-are-a-sticking-point.

13 Jana Riess and Christopher Kimball Bigelow, *Mormonism for Dummies* (2011), Kindle Location 911.

14 The Nicene Creed, www.creeds.net/ancient/nicene.htm.

15 Quoted in Joseph Walker, "Mormonism Is Different, but Is it too Christian?" *Deseret News*, June 7, 2012, www.deseretnews.com/article/865557055/Mormonism-is-different-but-is-it-too-Christian.html?pg=all.

16 Bill Hamblin, "Are Mormons Christians? Witherington Says No," *FAIR blog*, Aug. 31, 2012, www.fairblog.org/2012/08/31/are-mormons-christians-witherington-says-no.

17 Quoted in Rachel Bracker, "Professor Discusses Role of Religion in 2012 Election," *Daily Trojan* [University of Southern California], Feb. 21, 2012, http://dailytrojan.com/2012/02/21/professor-discusses-role-of-religion-in-2012-election.

18 Smith, *op. cit.*

19 Latter-day Saints and California Proposition 8, The FAIR Wiki, Foundation for Apologetic Information & Research website, http://en.fairmormon.org/Church_involvement_in_politics/Latter-day_Saints_and_California_Proposition_8.

20 Quoted in Matt Canham, "Would LDS Church Influence Romney if President?" *Salt Lake Tribune*, Jan. 5, 2012, www.sltrib.com/sltrib/home2/53185712-183/church-romney-lds-faith.html.csp.

21 Michael Foust, "Election 12: Obama & Romney on Gay Marriage," Baptist Press, Oct. 5, 2012, www.sbcbaptistpress.org/BPnews.asp?ID=38868.

22 Quoted in Canham, *op. cit.*

23 For background, see "Romney's Mormon Faith Likely a Factor in Primaries, Not in General Election," Pew Forum on Religion and Public Life, Nov. 23, 2011, www.pewforum.org/Politics-and-Elections/Romneys-Mormon-Faith-Likely-a-Factor-in-Primaries-Not-in-a-General-Election.aspx.

24 Jana Riess, "Can a Candidate Be Too Perfect?" "Room for Debate," *The New York Times*, Jan. 30, 2012, www.nytimes.com/roomfordebate/2012/01/30/what-is-it-about-mormons/are-mormon-candidates-just-too-perfect.

25 For background, see Riess and Bigelow, *op. cit.*, p. 181.

26 For background, see "Mormonism and Racial Issues/Blacks and the Priesthood," The FAIR Wiki, FAIR website, http://en.fairmormon.org/Mormonism_and_racial_issues/Blacks_and_the_priesthood; "Blacks and the Priesthood," MormonThink blog, http://mormonthink.com/blackweb.htm.

27 Quoted in Turner, *op. cit.*

28 Armand L. Mauss, "Mormonism's Worldwide Aspirations and its Changing Conceptions of Race and Lineage," *Dialogue: A Journal of Mormon Thought*, Fall-Winter 2001, pp. 117, 124.

29 Turner, *op. cit.*

30 Quoted in Jason Horowitz, "The Genesis of a Church's Stand on Race," *The Washington Post*, Feb. 28, 2012, www.washingtonpost.com/politics/the-genesis-of-a-churchs-stand-on-race/2012/02/22/gIQAQZXyfR_story.html.

31 Joseph Walker, "LDS Church Condemns Past Racism 'Inside and Outside the Church,' " *Deseret News* [Salt Lake City], Feb. 29, 2012, www.deseretnews.com/article/765555339/LDS-Church-condemns-past-racism-inside-and-outside-the-church.html?pg=all.

32 Max Perry Mueller, "Is Mormonism Still Racist?" *Slate*, March 2, 2012, www.slate.com/articles/life/faithbased/2012/03/mormon_church_and_racism_a_new_controversy_about_old_teachings_.html.

33 Darius Aidan Gray, "0608 Vignettes," *Daily Herald* [Provo, Utah], June 8, 2003, www.heraldextra.com/lifestyles/article_499651ac-9eef-5955-a9ea-b173b7c2d1c1.html, and Sharon Haddock, "Film Explores Stories of Black Mormons," *Deseret News* [Salt Lake City], Jan. 24, 2008, www.deseretnews.com/article/695246634/Film-explores-stories-of-black-Mormons.html?pg=all.

34 Mauss, *op. cit.*, p. 123.

35 Horowitz, *op. cit.*

36 *Ibid.* The scriptural citation is 2 Nephi 26:33, The Book of Mormon, www.lds.org/scriptures/search?lang=eng&type=verse&query=black+white+bond+free.

About the Author

Staff writer **Marcia Clemmitt** is a veteran social-policy reporter who previously served as editor in chief of *Medicine & Health* and staff writer for *The Scientist*. She has also been a high school math and physics teacher. She holds a liberal arts and sciences degree from St. John's College, Annapolis, and a master's degree in English from Georgetown University. Her recent reports include "U.S.-Pakistan Relations" and "Youth Volunteerism."

[37] For background, see Matthew Bowman, *The Mormon People: The Making of an American Faith* (2012), and Ryan Cragun and Rick Phillips, *Could I Vote for a Mormon for President? An Election-year Guide to Mitt Romney's Religion* (2012).

[38] Sidney Rigdon, "Oration Delivered by Mr. S. Rigdon, Far West, Caldwell, Co., MO, 1838," SidneyRigdon.com, www.sidneyrigdon.com/rigd1838.htm.

[39] Richard C. Cortner, "The Nationalization of the Bill of Rights: An Overview," American Political Science Association website, www.apsanet.org/imgtest/Nationalization_Bill.pdf.

[40] Brevet Major J. H. Carleton, "Special Report on the Mountain Meadows Massacre," May 25, 1859, http://law2.umkc.edu/faculty/projects/ftrials/mountainmeadows/carletonreport.html.

[41] Terryl L. Givens and Matthew J. Grow, *Parley P. Pratt: The Apostle Paul of Mormonism* (2011), p. 403.

[42] "Romney, Huntsman Compete in Mormon Primary," Fox News/Associated Press, June 23, 2011, www.foxnews.com/us/2011/06/23/romney-huntsman-compete-in-mormon-primary.

[43] William Alexander Linn, *The Story of the Mormons: From the Date of Their Origin to the Year 1901* (1902), pp. 519-520, http://books.google.com/books?id=QDdAAAAAYAAJ&printsec=frontcover#v=onepage&q=Arkansan&f=false.

[44] Quoted in Todd M. Compton, *In Sacred Loneliness: The Plural Wives of Joseph Smith* (1997), p. 28.

[45] *Ibid.*

[46] "The Doctrine and Covenants," Section 132, Church of Jesus Christ of Latter-day Saints website, www.lds.org/scriptures/dc-testament/dc/132.7?lang=eng

[47] The case is *Reynolds v. United States*, 98 U.S. (8 Otto.) 145 (1878), www.oyez.org/cases/1851-1900/1878/1878_0.

[48] "Official Declaration — I, Doctrine and Covenants," The Church of Jesus Christ and Latter-day Saints, www.lds.org/scriptures/dc-testament/od/1?lang=eng.

[49] For background, see Nick Miroff, "In Besieged Mormon Colony, Mitt Romney's Mexican Roots," *The Washington Post*, July 23, 2011, www.washingtonpost.com/politics/in-besieged-mormon-colony-mitt-romneys-mexican-roots/2011/07/21/gIQAFGOXVI_story.html; D. Michael Quinn, "Plural Marriage and Mormon Fundamentalism," *Dialogue: A Journal of Mormon Thought*, Summer 1998, www.dialoguejournal.com/wp-content/uploads/sbi/articles/Dialogue_V31N02_19.pdf.

FOR MORE INFORMATION

American Religious Identification Survey, Institute for the Study of Secularism in Society & Culture, Trinity College, 300 Summit St., Hartford, CT 06106; 860-297-2381; http://commons.trincoll.edu/aris. Website for largest U.S. survey on religious affiliation; contains statistics and analysis.

The Church of Jesus Christ of Latter-day Saints (LDS), www.lds.org. Official church website; publishes news and background information about church doctrines and practices.

The Foundation for Apologetic Information and Research (FAIR), P.O. Box 491677, Redding, CA 96049; www.fairlds.org. Website run by Mormons but not officially affiliated with the LDS Church; publishes research and analysis to answer criticisms of LDS doctrines and practices.

LDS Living Magazine, P.O. Box 30178, Salt Lake City, UT 84130; http://ldsliving.com. Mormon-run, advertising-supported magazine with news and feature articles related to LDS families and communities.

Mormon Stories Podcast, http://mormonstories.org. Website run by Mormon John Dehlin that includes in-depth interviews with LDS members and other experts on faith-related issues, including some members' struggles over remaining in the church.

MormonThink, www.mormonthink.com. Website run by LDS members who question whether church leaders and media accounts accurately portray Mormon historical events.

Patheos, www.patheos.com. Advertising-supported website that carries news and commentary on many faith traditions, including Mormonism.

The Pew Forum on Religion and Public Life, 1615 L St., N.W., Suite 700, Washington, DC 20036-5610; 202-419-4550; www.pewforum.org. Foundation-supported group that provides public-opinion polling, information and analysis on religion's role in American life, including extensive information on Mormonism.

[50] For background, see Kathleen Flake, *The Politics of American Religious Identity* (2004).

[51] Armand Mauss, *The Angel and the Beehive* (1994), p. ix.

[52] For background, see Armand Mauss, "The Mormon Struggle With Assimilation and Identity: Trends and Developments Since Midcentury," *Dialogue: A Journal of Mormon Thought*, Spring 1994, www.dialoguejournal.com/wp-content/uploads/sbi/articles/Dialogue_V27N01_141.pdf.

[53] *Ibid.*

[54] Cameron Joseph, "Mormons on Cusp of New Powerful Era," *The Hill*, July 23, 2012, http://thehill.com/homenews/campaign/239379-mormons-on-cusp-of-new-powerful-era-in-the-nations-capital-.

[55] Quoted in John Stanton, "Why Harry Reid Hates Mitt Romney," *Buzzfeed*, Oct. 8, 2012, www.buzzfeed.com/johnstanton/why-harry-reid-hates-mitt-romney.

[56] Joseph, *op. cit.*

[57] Rodney Stark, *The Rise of Mormonism* (2005), p. 2.

[58] Rachel Bruner, "Mormon World Population," About.com, http://lds.about.com/od/mormons/a/church_membership.htm.

[59] For background, see LDS Church Growth blog, http://ldschurchgrowth.blogspot.com.

[60] Peggy Fletcher Stack, "Brazil Mystery: Case of the Missing Mormons (913,045 of Them, to Be Exact)," *Salt Lake Tribune*, July 16, 2012, www.sltrib.com/sltrib/blogsfaithblog/54497395-180/church-census-reported-latter.html.csp.

[61] Quoted in Patty Henetz, "DNA Research and Mormon Scholars Changing Basic Beliefs," *USA Today*/Associated Press, July 26, 2004, http://usatoday30.usatoday.com/tech/news/2004-07-26-dna-lds_x.htm.

Bibliography

Selected Sources

Books

Bowman, Matthew B., *The Mormon People: The Making of an American Faith*, Random House, 2012.

A practicing Mormon and visiting assistant professor of history at Hampden-Sydney College in Virginia recounts the history of the Church of Jesus Christ of Latter-day Saints (LDS) from its founding to the present day.

Brooks, Joanna, *The Book of Mormon Girl: A Memoir of an American Faith*, Free Press, 2012.

A professor of literature at San Diego State University describes growing up in a happy Mormon household and struggling as an adult to reconcile her feminism with the tenets of the church.

Burningham, Kay, *An American Fraud: One Lawyer's Case Against Mormonism*, Amica Veritatis, 2011.

An ex-Mormon discusses her reasons for leaving the church she was raised in and what she views as inconsistencies and ethical problems surrounding the LDS Church's accounts of its history.

Campbell, David E., and J. Quin Monson, "Dry Kindling: A Political Profile of American Mormons," in J. Matthew Wilson, ed., From *Pews to Polling Places: Faith and Politics in the American Religious Mosaic*, Georgetown University Press, 2007, pp. 105-129.

A professor of political science at the University of Notre Dame (Campbell) and an associate professor of political science at Brigham Young University find that between the 1970s and 1990s Mormon voters became more closely identified with the Republican Party. Over the period, LDS members followed a political trajectory similar to that of Catholics and Southern Baptists, but with an even more marked turn toward the GOP.

Cragun, Ryan T., and Rick Phillips, *Could I Vote for a Mormon for President? An Election-year Guide to Mitt Romney's Religion*, Strange Violin Editions, 2012.

Sociologists at the University of Tampa (Cragun) and the University of North Florida, both raised as Mormons (although Cragun has left the church), describe LDS beliefs about theology and social issues.

Turner, John G., *Brigham Young: Pioneer Prophet*, Belknap Press of Harvard University Press, 2012.

A non-Mormon assistant professor of religious studies at George Mason University in Fairfax, Va., chronicles the life of Brigham Young, the LDS Church's second leader, who led his followers to the Utah Territory and established a thriving theocracy there.

Articles

Walker, Joseph, "Criticism Follows Businessweek Cover on Mormon Church Finances," *Deseret News* [Salt Lake City], July 12, 2012, www.deseretnews.com/article/865558976/Criticism-follows-Businessweek-cover-on-Mormon-Church-finances.html?pg=all.

In this report by the *Deseret News*, whose management company is owned by the LDS Church, LDS members and religion scholars criticize as offensive and insensitive a *Business Week* cover that depicts John the Baptist advising church founder Joseph Smith to "own stock in Burger King." The cover highlights an article on church finances by Caroline Winter (see below) that LDS members call biased.

Wallace-Wells, Benjamin, "Mitt's Stake," *New York*, Oct. 1, 2012, http://nymag.com/news/features/mitt-romney-mormonism-2012-10.

As a lay bishop who oversaw a dozen Mormon congregations in Massachusetts, Mitt Romney served the local LDS community with energy and compassion, Wallace-Wells says. However, he argues that Romney's record as a politician suggests that his embrace of Mormonism's communal spirit may not extend far beyond his fellow LDS members.

Winter, Caroline, "How the Mormons Make Money," *Bloomberg Businessweek*, July 18, 2012, www.businessweek.com/articles/2012-07-10/how-the-mormons-make-money.

Winter describes the LDS church's billions of dollars in business holdings, which include mega-malls, for-profit real estate holding companies and large agricultural operations. The church's entrepreneurial success, which dates back to pioneer days, stems at least partly from its determination to provide a self-contained welfare system for members, but the extent of its business holdings is a closely guarded secret.

Reports and Studies

Mauss, Armand, "The Mormon Struggle with Assimilation and Identity: Trends and Developments Since Mid-century," *Dialogue: A Journal of Mormon Thought*, Spring 1994, www.dialoguejournal.com/wp-content/uploads/sbi/articles/Dialogue_V27N01_141.pdf.

A Mormon professor emeritus of sociology and religious studies at Washington State University in Pullman describes the maturing church's 20th-century history as, first, a strong movement toward becoming a mainstream church, adopting many of the values of the larger society, followed by a somewhat surprising turn toward re-adopting some of its older, more patriarchal ways, similar to those of fundamentalist Christian groups.

The Next Step:

Additional Articles from Current Periodicals

Christianity

Burke, Daniel, "Are Mormons Christian? It's Complicated," Religion News Service, Jan. 19, 2012.
Mormons believe they belong to a Christian church, but nearly a quarter of Americans are unconvinced.

Mason, David V., "I'm a Mormon, Not a Christian," *The New York Times*, June 13, 2012, p. A27, www.nytimes.com/2012/06/13/opinion/im-a-mormon-not-a-christian.html?_r=0.
Setting Mormonism apart from Christianity would give Mormons a better chance of creating their own historical legacy.

Poling, Jason, "Evangelicals and Mormons: Can We Talk?" *The Baltimore Sun*, Feb. 1, 2012, p. A19, articles.baltimoresun.com/2012-01-31/news/bs-ed-mormons-20120131_1_mormons-theological-differences-religious-movements.
Many unbridgeable theological gaps exist between evangelical Christians and Mormons, says a Maryland pastor.

Politics

Brunner, Jim, "Delegates Don't See Romney's Mormon Faith as Issue Now," *Seattle Times*, Aug. 31, 2012, p. A1, seattletimes.com/html/localnews/2019032749_localconvention31m.html.
Most voters who know about Mitt Romney's Mormon faith are comfortable with his religion or don't consider it a concern.

Landsberg, Mitchell, "Mixed Blessing for Mormons," *Los Angeles Times*, Feb. 3, 2012, p. A1, articles.latimes.com/2012/feb/02/nation/la-na-mormons-20120203.
Mormon leaders say Romney's presidential candidacy brings more attention to their church but that public backlash can occur when the church takes controversial positions on issues.

Lane, Charles, "In November, a Verdict on the 'Mormon Question'?" *The Washington Post*, Jan. 17, 2012, p. A13, www.washingtonpost.com/opinions/a-verdict-on-the-mormon-question/2012/01/13/gIQANY753P_story.html.
The November election will test whether a Mormon candidate can become president.

Toeplitz, Shira, "Mormons See Rise on Campaign Trail," *Roll Call*, Nov. 17, 2011, www.rollcall.com/issues/57_61/Mormons-See-Rise-on-Campaign-Trail-210420-1.html.
Higher Mormon concentrations in the West have created unprecedented opportunities for Mormon candidates.

Racism Charges

Man, Anthony, "Broward Pastor Blasts Mitt Romney, Mormon Religion," *Sun-Sentinel* (Fla.), March 12, 2012, weblogs.sun-sentinel.com/news/politics/broward/blog/2012/03/broward_pastor_blasts_mitt_rom.html.
A black Florida pastor has urged Republican presidential candidate Mitt Romney to "renounce his racist Mormon religion."

Turner, John G., "Why Race Is Still a Problem for Mormons," *The New York Times*, Aug. 19, 2012, p. SR5, www.nytimes.com/2012/08/19/opinion/sunday/racism-and-the-mormon-church.html.
Mormon leaders generically criticize past and present racism but avoid specific criticism of past church presidents.

Weathersby, Ronald W., "Black Mormons Say History of African Americans and Their Church Is Misunderstood," *Tennessee Tribune*, Nov. 24, 2011, p. A1.
Black Mormons say most people are unaware that the church has had black members since its earliest days.

Women

Stack, Peggy Fletcher, "Mormon Women Seeking Middle Ground to Greater Equality," *Salt Lake Tribune*, Aug. 16, 2012, www.sltrib.com/sltrib/lifestyle/54704413-80/church-equality-female-general.html.csp.
Mormon feminists say they want to play a greater role in the church without undermining what they believe are divinely ordained differences between men and women.

Walker, Joseph, "New Study Confirms Many LDS Stereotypes," *Deseret* (Utah) *Morning News*, Dec. 14, 2011, www.deseretnews.com/article/700207176/New-study-confirms-many-LDS-stereotypes.html?pg=all.
Mormon women are just as educated as other American women but less likely to work outside the home.

CITING *CQ RESEARCHER*

Sample formats for citing these reports in a bibliography include the ones listed below. Preferred styles and formats vary, so please check with your instructor or professor.

MLA STYLE

Jost, Kenneth. "Remembering 9/11," CQ Researcher 2 Sept. 2011: 701-732.

APA STYLE

Jost, K. (2011, September 2). Remembering 9/11. *CQ Researcher, 9*, 701-732.

CHICAGO STYLE

Jost, Kenneth. "Remembering 9/11." *CQ Researcher*, September 2, 2011, 701-732.

CQ Researcher

Published by CQ Press, an Imprint of SAGE Publications, Inc.

www.cqresearcher.com

Mexico's Future

Can the country's new president stop the drug cartels?

Following years of grisly drug-related violence, Mexico's next president, Enrique Peña Nieto, is hinting that he will adopt a new anti-crime strategy when he takes office Dec. 1. Instead of using a military-style offensive to kill or capture the leaders of Mexico's drug cartels — the approach of outgoing president Felipe Calderón — Peña Nieto has suggested that he will focus on protecting civilians from crimes committed by cartel underlings and their allies in Mexico's security forces. The cartels pose strategic and political risks for both Mexico and the United States. Drug violence has raised tensions along the U.S.-Mexico border and complicated Mexico's trade relationships with the United States. At the same time, Mexico complains that the cartels are using guns smuggled from the United States and are supported by American appetites for illegal narcotics.

Journalists and students protest on April 29, 2012, after the murder of Mexican journalist Regina Martínez Pérez in Xalapa, Veracruz state. The veteran crime reporter covered Mexico's violent drug cartels for the newsmagazine Proceso. *At least 59 journalists and media workers have been killed in Mexico since 2006.*

INSIDE THIS REPORT

THE ISSUES 915
BACKGROUND 923
CHRONOLOGY 925
CURRENT SITUATION 930
AT ISSUE........................931
OUTLOOK 932
BIBLIOGRAPHY 937
THE NEXT STEP 938

CQ Researcher • Oct. 26, 2012 • www.cqresearcher.com
Volume 22, Number 38 • Pages 913-940

SAGE | CQPRESS
Los Angeles | London | New Delhi
Singapore | Washington DC

RECIPIENT OF SOCIETY OF PROFESSIONAL JOURNALISTS AWARD FOR EXCELLENCE ◆ AMERICAN BAR ASSOCIATION SILVER GAVEL AWARD

MEXICO'S FUTURE

THE ISSUES

915 • Is the U.S.-aided Mexican drug war hurting Mexicans more than helping them?
• Would legalizing marijuana scale back Mexico's drug war?
• Is U.S. border-control policy heightening tensions with Mexico?

BACKGROUND

923 **Election Crisis**
Voter fraud helped the Revolutionary Institutional Party (PRI) hold power in 1988.

924 **High Drama**
Marred by scandal, Carlos Salinas de Gortari's term marked the end of PRI domination.

927 **Transition**
The center-right National Action Party's Vicente Fox defeated the PRI candidate in 2000.

929 **Untamed Mexico**
Drug-trafficking violence escalated under presidents Fox and Calderón.

CURRENT SITUATION

930 **'Fast and Furious'**
The flawed U.S. effort to track smuggled guns embarrassed the Obama administration.

932 **Privatizing Pemex**
President Enrique Peña Nieto plans to open up Mexico's state-controlled oil industry.

OUTLOOK

932 **Corruption and Cartels**
Improving the reliability of security agencies will be among Peña Nieto's biggest challenges.

SIDEBARS AND GRAPHICS

916 **Powerful Drug Cartels Dominate Mexico**
Each gang controls a section of the country.

917 **Drug Killings on the Rise**
More than 12,000 people died in drug violence in 2011.

918 **Son's Murder Sparks Father's Crusade**
"This war is lost. It's burning our house."

920 **Marijuana Dominates Drug Seizures**
More than 3 million pounds of illegal drugs were seized along the border in 2010.

925 **Chronology**
Key events since 1988.

926 **NAFTA Stirs Conflict on Both Sides of Border**
From tomatoes to toilet paper, trade stakes are huge.

931 **At Issue**
Is legalization a better approach than the drug war for fighting drugs in Mexico?

FOR FURTHER RESEARCH

936 **For More Information**
Organizations to contact.

937 **Bibliography**
Selected sources used.

938 **The Next Step**
Additional articles.

939 **Citing *CQ Researcher***
Sample bibliography formats.

Cover: AFP/Getty Images/Sergio Hernandez

CQ Researcher

Oct. 26, 2012
Volume 22, Number 38

MANAGING EDITOR: Thomas J. Billitteri
tjb@cqpress.com

ASSISTANT MANAGING EDITOR: Kathy Koch
kkoch@cqpress.com

SENIOR CONTRIBUTING EDITOR:
Thomas J. Colin
tcolin@cqpress.com

ASSOCIATE EDITOR: Kenneth Jost

STAFF WRITER: Marcia Clemmitt

CONTRIBUTING WRITERS: Peter Katel, Barbara Mantel, Tom Price, Jennifer Weeks

SENIOR PROJECT EDITOR: Olu B. Davis

ASSISTANT EDITOR: Darrell Dela Rosa

FACT CHECKER: Michelle Harris

Los Angeles | London | New Delhi
Singapore | Washington DC

An Imprint of SAGE Publications, Inc.

VICE PRESIDENT AND EDITORIAL DIRECTOR, HIGHER EDUCATION GROUP:
Michele Sordi

DIRECTOR, ONLINE PUBLISHING:
Todd Baldwin

CQ Researcher (ISSN 1056-2036) is printed on acid-free paper. Published weekly, except: (March wk. 5) (May wk. 4) (July wk. 1) (Aug. wks. 3, 4) (Nov. wk. 4) and (Dec. wks. 3, 4). Published by SAGE Publications, Inc., 2455 Teller Rd., Thousand Oaks, CA 91320. Annual full-service subscriptions start at $1,054. For pricing, call 1-800-834-9020. To purchase a *CQ Researcher* report in print or electronic format (PDF), visit www.cqpress.com or call 866-427-7737. Single reports start at $15. Bulk purchase discounts and electronic-rights licensing are also available. Periodicals postage paid at Thousand Oaks, California, and at additional mailing offices. POSTMASTER: Send address changes to *CQ Researcher*, 2300 N St., N.W., Suite 800, Washington, DC 20037.

Mexico's Future

By Peter Katel

The Issues

When Enrique Peña Nieto takes over as president of Mexico on Dec. 1, he will face a choice whose outcome could shape his country's future — and U.S.-Mexican relations — for years to come.

Should he continue his predecessor's military-style assaults against violent drug cartels that control wide swaths of Mexico? Or is a broader policy needed, one aimed at protecting citizens from the widespread lawlessness that has taken at least 50,000 Mexican lives — and possibly far more — over the past six years?

Peña Nieto has hinted he favors the broader approach, provoking concern among some U.S. officials that the new government may be planning to seek an accommodation with Mexico's drug lords.

Such concerns are unfounded, Peña Nieto, a lawyer and former governor of the state of Mexico, has suggested. "The fight by the government will be against organized crime, drug trafficking in all its forms and shapes, but we have to focus especially on reducing violence," he said following his July election. [1]

The United States has a huge stake in the outcome. Outgoing President Felipe Calderón received major help from the Obama and George W. Bush administrations in pursuing the frontal-assault strategy. That's only fair, from the Mexican government's perspective, because American drug users provide most of the cartels' revenue, and American gun dealers supply many of their firearms.

AFP/Getty Images/Justin Tallis

When he takes office Dec. 1, President-elect Enrique Peña Nieto will face many issues of critical importance to the United States, including Mexico's violent drug cartels and corruption in its police and security forces. Above, the 46-year-old lawyer addresses the news media on Oct. 16.

Mexico's major cartels produce, smuggle and sell marijuana, heroin, cocaine, methamphetamine and other narcotics, bringing in from $4.7 billion to $29 billion a year. [2] (The Drug Enforcement Administration (DEA) says that up to 80 percent of the methamphetamine in the United States now comes from Mexican "superlabs." The cartels have no compunction about using hangings, decapitations and indiscriminate massacres to thwart rival drug syndicates or intimidate Mexican authorities and ordinary citizens. [3]

Complicating the picture is the fact that a long history of collusion between security forces and cartels has not ended. Mexican authorities have charged police and prison officials in northern Coahuila state with complicity in a mass prison break and the murder of a politician's relative. And reports of torture and other human-rights abuses against citizens by security agencies are on the increase. [4]

The Obama and Bush administrations have spent more than $1.9 billion on military and police hardware, training and other assistance to Mexico since 2007 to help in the anti-cartel fight. [5] But U.S. politicians and officials who follow Latin American affairs wonder about the extent to which Peña Nieto will continue to allow the United States to help shape Mexico's anti-drug strategy.

Their doubt arises in part from the fact that the 46-year-old Peña Nieto represents the Revolutionary Institutional Party (PRI), which, during its authoritarian rule from 1929 to 2000, effectively allowed government and security officials to share profits with the drug traffickers while ensuring that violence didn't touch ordinary citizens.

Citing Peña Nieto's emphasis on reducing crime and making Mexican policy not "subordinate to the strategies of other countries," Rep. James Sensenbrenner, R-Wis., chairman of the House Crime, Terrorism and Homeland Security Subcommittee, said in June. "This sounds like a reversion to the PRI politics of old." [6]

But political analyst Andrés Rozental, a former senior career Mexican

Powerful Drug Cartels Dominate Mexico

Each of Mexico's major drug cartels dominates a part of the country, with the Sinaloa and Zetas organizations exerting the greatest influence. Recent arrests and killings of cartel chieftains are expected to realign territories and prompt formation of new crime organizations. The cartels traffic in marijuana, heroin, cocaine, methamphetamine and other narcotics, bringing in from $4 billion to $29 billion a year. The gangs use extreme violence to thwart rival drug syndicates and intimidate Mexican authorities and citizens.

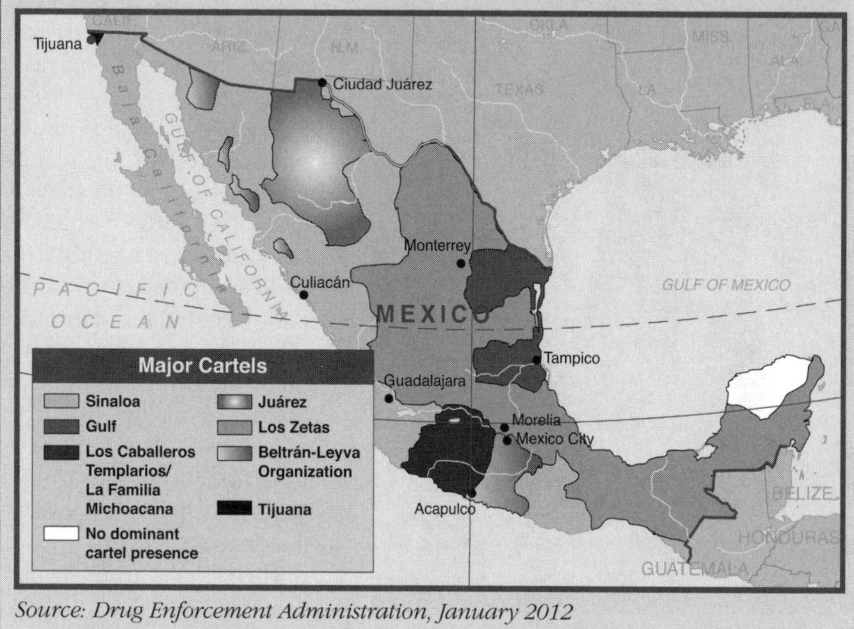

Source: Drug Enforcement Administration, January 2012

diplomat, argued that a strategic shift from trying to wipe out organized-crime groups doesn't mean making deals with them. "You can dedicate the scarce resources that Mexico has to protecting Mexicans and reducing violence in Mexico," he said. "If you deal with organized crime on the basis of a declared war where your objective is to annihilate it, you provoke a violent response." [7]

Rozental and other analysts point to additional factors suggesting that Peña Nieto will not follow past PRI policies. For example, they say, he is laying the groundwork for trying to reverse Mexico's 1938 nationalization of the oil industry, long a pillar of the PRI and considered untouchable. (*See "Current Situation," p. 932.*)

In addition, free elections and a press largely free of government control seem to be in place to stay (though at least 59 journalists and media workers have been killed since 2006, with the motives unclear in some cases). [8]

What's more, Mexico has been governed for a dozen years by two democratically elected, non-PRI presidents — outgoing President Felipe Calderón and his predecessor, Vicente Fox. Peña Nieto would face heavy resistance if he tried to backpedal, said Rozental. "Even if he wanted to maintain the PRI the way it used to be, he wouldn't be able to," he said. [9]

For the United States, Mexico's proximity makes some of the key issues between the two countries — immigration, U.S. drug consumption and U.S. gun control, among them — domestic matters, and highly charged political ones at that. In August, two CIA agents driving near Mexico City in an armored SUV with diplomatic license plates were wounded after they came under heavy fire from Mexican federal police officers who U.S. officials suspect were working for a cartel. [10]

On the other side of the coin, the U.S.-based Spanish-language Univision TV network reported that guns allowed to be smuggled into Mexico by the U.S. Bureau of Alcohol, Tobacco, Firearms and Explosives' botched "Fast and Furious" operation were used in a notorious 2010 massacre of Mexican high school students.

Of course, U.S. ties to Mexico go far beyond the countries' joint efforts to bring the cartels to heel. The two countries are huge trading partners, for instance. Since the North American Free Trade Agreement (NAFTA) took effect in 1994 between the United States, Mexico and Canada, U.S. exports to Mexico more than tripled to $223 billion last year, and imports from Mexico rose nearly fivefold to $277 billion. (*See sidebar, p. 926.*) [11]

"We buy more U.S. exports than Germany, Italy, the Netherlands and the UK combined," Arturo Sarukhan, Mexico's ambassador to the United States, said in July. "We buy more U.S. exports than China and Japan put together. . . . This is a stunning, stunning two-way trade relationship." [12]

Yet, despite the economic and strategic ties and tensions between the two nations, U.S.-Mexico relations rarely seem to get the level of attention from policy experts that, say, the Middle East or China command.

Mexico "is arguably the most important relationship the United States has in the world," says Michael Shifter, president of Inter-American Dialogue, a nonpartisan think tank in Washington. "But when people are doing all the assessments of administration foreign policy, Mexico doesn't appear.

It's not considered part of the foreign-policy agenda."

For instance, Shifter says, the United States has been reinforcing the U.S.-Mexico border since 1993 purely for domestic reasons, without "even a consideration for how that will affect Mexico." Since 2007 the United States has spent about $3.5 billion on fences and anti-illegal entry technology along the border, plus about $20 billion on the U.S. Border Patrol, mostly for personnel and other costs. [13]

While curbing illegal immigration is a chief U.S. policy aim, so too is keeping Mexico's drug wars from spilling across the border. Outgoing president Calderón reaped some success from his strategy of targeting "capos" of the major crime groups. As of the beginning of 2012, at least 22 of 37 kingpins had been killed or captured. [14] Just this month, Mexican authorities said they had killed Heriberto Lazcano, founder of the feared Zetas cartel which is active in a huge swath of the country, from the U.S. border to the Yucatán Peninsula. (Authorities initially said they were sure of Lazcano's identification, but doubts persist because the body of the man believed to be him was stolen from a funeral home.) [15]

Eliminating cartel capos hasn't stopped crime in Mexico, however. Often, lower-ranking members of the cartels have turned to extortion, kidnapping and other money-making ventures after their bosses were killed, some experts say.

Still, killings do seem to be on the decline nationwide, according to Alejandro Hope, director of the "Less Crime, Less Punishment" project of the Mexican Institute for Competitiveness and "México Evalúa," both nonpartisan think tanks. He noted that "malicious homicides" overall fell 8.2 percent nationwide in the first eight months of 2012, from the same period last year — though rising by double-digit percentages in some states. [16]

Drug-Related Killings on the Rise

Tensions among rival Mexican drug cartels have resulted in a sharp increase in cartel-related killings since 2006. More than 12,000 people died in drug violence in 2011, about six times the total in 2006. The statistics do not include the unkown number of victims who have "disappeared." Other sources cite higher numbers of victims.

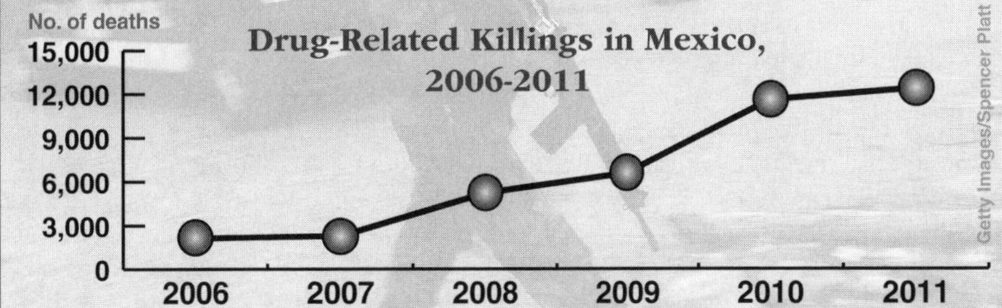

Source: "Justice in Mexico News Report," Trans-Border Institute, February 2012, p. 5, justiceinmexico.files.wordpress.com/2011/02/2012-02-february-news-report.pdf

"We're continuing a trend of gradual reduction from very high levels," wrote Hope, a former senior official in Mexico's domestic intelligence agency. "In other words, we're in bad shape, but we're not getting worse." [17]

But other Mexican experts argue that the level of killings amounts to a profound and continuing national emergency. "In Mexico we are living through an unbearable human tragedy," said Sergio Aguayo, a prominent political scientist and democracy advocate. "We need external support, and in the United States that requires combating indifference and denial." [18]

As Mexico seeks to balance its security and economic interests with the United States, here are some of the questions being asked:

Is the U.S.-aided Mexican drug war hurting Mexicans more than helping them?

From his first days in office, outgoing President Calderón embraced a policy of confronting the cartels with all the power at his command.

Calderón not only ordered major military deployments in cities and states plagued by hyper-violent turf battles between rival drug-trafficking organizations but also dressed in military fatigues to underscore his anti-cartel strategy. In doing so, he broke a longtime precedent in a country whose 20th-century political life was defined by a rejection of military strongmen and dictators. (*See "Background," p. 924.*)

But Calderón's military assault on cartel power was very much in keeping with the anti-drug approach favored by the United States in Colombia and other drug-producing and drug-transit countries, especially under the George W. Bush administration. Under the Mérida Initiative, a 2007 counter-drug security-assistance pact between the United States and Mexico (named after the Yucatán Peninsula city where Calderón had met with President Bush to discuss strategy), the United States has provided about $1 billion in helicopters, scanners and other equipment, as well as technical assistance and training to Mexico. [19]

In addition, the Defense Department has a separate "counternarcotics" aid program to Mexico, under which the department spent nearly $76 million in fiscal 2009-2010, nearly $85 million in 2010-2011 and an estimated $100 million in 2011-2012. [20]

The Obama administration has focused its aid under the Mérida program on professionalizing Mexican

Son's Murder Sparks Father's Crusade

"This war is lost. It's burning our house."

Juan Francisco Sicilia, a soccer-playing, 24-year-old student of health care administration, went to a nightclub last year in Cuernavaca, south of Mexico City, with a couple of friends to try to recover a friend's digital camera, stolen from his car by a club parking attendant.

The club owner, who had ties to a criminal gang, grew angry at the young men and held them at gunpoint. Then he panicked. Fearing they would identify him, he paid an associate 300,000 pesos (about $23,000) to kill them.

Javier Sicilia, Juan Francisco's father, told the story last September at the Woodrow Wilson Center for International Scholars in Washington. He called his son's death the result of a failed strategy by Mexican leaders to mount a military-style assault on the country's drug syndicate kingpins — a strategy he said has sparked more and more violence throughout Mexico and fractured the cartels into criminal gangs like the one that killed his son. Sicilia believes the drug trade will not go away and that instead of pursuing a quixotic goal of ridding Mexico of its big drug organizations, the government should focus its resources on protecting civilians from all forms of crime.

The kingpin strategy "has diversified crime, because these armies of criminals now aren't handling drugs — because the drugs are controlled by the big bosses — so they live on extortion, on kidnapping," Sicilia said. "No one controls them. My son is a victim of this." [1]

Sicilia, a white-bearded, chain-smoking intellectual, had been known as a poet and novelist inspired by Catholic mysticism before tragedy struck his family. In the aftermath, he turned to activism, forming a citizens' movement around the slogan, Estamos hasta la madre, a colloquial form of, "We've had it up to here." [2]

His appearance at the Wilson Center in Washington marked the last stop on a "peace caravan" tour of the United States, which Sicilia led in hopes of showing Americans the human cost of Mexico's war on drugs and the role that American drug users play in fueling it. [3]

The caravan, which included relatives of other victims, received relatively little attention in the United States on a route that began in the border states. In Albuquerque, N.M., Sicilia and others talked about the Mexican drug war to a crowd of about 200 outside Holy Family Parish. "The war has left hundreds of thousands of widows and orphans," he said. "Part of the responsibility for this war lies here. . . . It's your addicts that have generated this war. The U.S. government wants to prevent your addicts from continuing to consume drugs."

In Mexico, the anti-drug war message resonates with far more force. A caravan tour of Mexico that Sicilia led last year, followed by a march from Cuernavaca to Mexico City, captivated public attention and brought out crowds of tens of thousands. [4]

"Mexican society is fighting back, defending itself," says political scientist Sergio Aguayo, who has been working with Sicilia and joined the caravan. "Democracy is in crisis, and the Sicilia movement . . . is an expression of dissatisfaction by many Mexicans toward what is going on." Aguayo, who teaches at El Colegio de México, a graduate school and think tank, has a long record of activism in pro-democracy and human rights movements.

The Sicilia movement has become powerful enough that the leading candidates for president felt obliged to attend a meeting organized by Sicilia about five weeks before last July's election. Relatives of drug-war victims told their stories, and Sicilia tore into all the candidates, delivering his harsh judgments to their faces.

"You represent a party that after 12 years leaves a huge graveyard of a country as an inheritance," he told Josefina Vázquez Mota of the National Action Party (PAN), to which outgoing president Felipe Calderón and his predecessor belong. [5]

Sicilia was equally unsparing of left-wing candidate Andrés Manuel López Obrador and of Enrique Peña Nieto of the Revo-

security forces and intelligence sharing, with less money spent on expensive military and police equipment. [21]

Some U.S. and Mexican experts say the past two years have seen a better use of intelligence in anti-cartel operations. But the strategy under Calderón remains focused on capturing or killing crime syndicate kingpins.

The major cartels, some weakened over the past year, include: the Tijuana, Sinaloa, Gulf and Zetas cartels; the Beltrán Leyva Organization and La Familia Michoacana/Los Caballeros Templarios (Knights Templar). [22] (*See map, p. 916.*)

Precisely how many Mexicans have been killed or "disappeared" in the violence involving these organizations and military and civilian security agencies is unknown. The Calderón government has been less than forthcoming with statistics on organized crime-related murders, which are categorized that way by characteristics including the use of automatic weapons, and signs of torture on a victim. To date, official figures stop after the third quarter of 2011. From 2007 until then, the number of these homicides totaled 47,515. *Reforma*, a respected Mexico City-based newspaper chain, has made a more conservative estimate of 40,155 through the end of 2011. [23]

Milenio, another daily in the capital city, counted about 54,000 dead from the beginning of Calderón's presidency through last March. Molly Molloy, a research librarian at New Mexico State University at Las Cruces, cites reports by Mexico's National Institute of Statistics and Geography, as well as data from the National Institute of

lutionary Institutional Party (PRI), who won the vote and is now president-elect. "How many criminals have gone unpunished and are still in the ranks of your party?," Sicilia asked, referring to the once-ruling party's long record of tolerating corruption. [6]

Peña Nieto reiterated his campaign pledge to bring down violence — an implicit rejection of the outgoing government's strategy of targeting drug cartel leaders. [7]

What lasting effect the citizens' movement will have on Peña Nieto's administration remains to be seen. Some analysts say Sicilia's uncompromising approach could limit the movement's possibilities. Other, smaller organizations of crime victims "were ready to sit down at the table with the government to negotiate the kinds of changes they wanted to see," says Federico Estévez, a political scientist at the Instituto Tecnológico Autónomo de México, a private university. "Sicilia has been very wary of doing that. It's difficult for the movement; you may be losing the opportunity to make change."

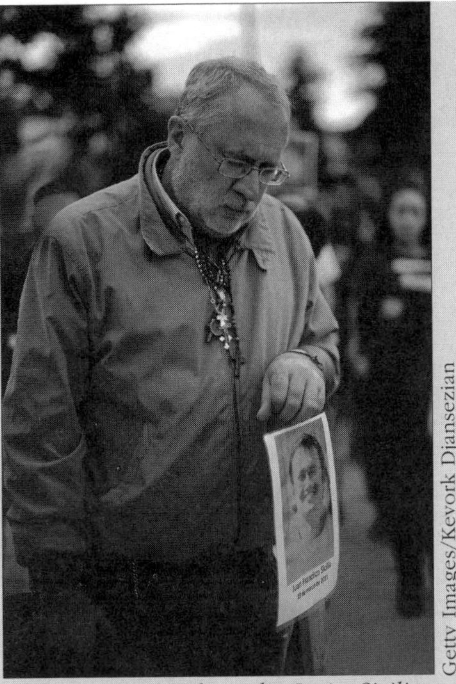

Getty Images/Kevork Djansezian

Mexican poet and novelist Javier Sicilia became an anti-drug war activist after his son's murder.

Nevertheless, Michael Shifter, president of Inter-American Dialogue, a think tank in Washington, argues that Sicilia's blasts at all of the conventional politicians ensures credibility with ordinary Mexicans. "People are more willing to grant him the benefit of the doubt to the extent that he has pried himself away from partisan commitment."

David A. Shirk, director of the University of San Diego's Trans-Border Institute, also argues that the movement's autonomy is a strength. "You had a society where interests were either part of the establishment or marginalized," he says. "Now you have a society where independent citizens' groups are mobilized, and politicians pay attention and make efforts to address those concerns, though not always satisfactorily."

Whatever effect the citizens' movement has had on Mexican anti-crime strategy, there's little sign yet that it has influenced U.S. policy. But in Washington, Sicilia insisted that American politicians and citizens ignore the Mexican crisis at their peril.

"This war is lost," he says. "It's burning our house. It's going to burn you as well."

— Peter Katel

---

[1] "The Peace Movement in Mexico: Efforts to bring justice to the victims of violence in the country," Woodrow Wilson International Center for Scholars, web video, Sept. 11, 2012, www.wilsoncenter.org/event/the-peace-movement-mexico-efforts-to-bring-justice-to-the-victims-violence-the-country-0.

[2] Tim Padgett, "Why I Protest: Javier Sicilia of Mexico," *Time*, Dec. 14, 2011, www.time.com/time/specials/packages/article/0,28804,2101745_2102138_2102238,00.html.

[3] "U.S. Peace Caravan Route," Global Exchange, undated, www.globalexchange.org/mexico/caravan/route.

[4] Enrique Krauze, "Can This Poet Save Mexico?," *The New York Times*, Oct. 2, 2011, Opinion Section, p. 6; Ken Ellingwood, "Poet an emblem of nation's mayhem," *Los Angeles Times*, May 21, 2011, p. A3.

[5] Quoted in Ioan Grillo, "Drug war victims; families blast Mexican candidates," Reuters, May 28, 2012, www.reuters.com/article/2012/05/29/us-mexico-election-drugs-idUSBRE84S00420120529.

[6] Quoted in *ibid.*

[7] *Ibid.*

Public Security, to arrive at about 99,000 deaths. [24]

The disparate data in themselves are revealing, argues political scientist Aguayo. "The social cost is enormous, and the indifference of the [Mexican] federal government is offensive," he says. "The government doesn't report the number of casualties. It's as if the Pentagon didn't report the number of casualties in Afghanistan."

What is clear, Aguayo says, is that the war has spread from a few states to nearly all 31. [25] "There is certainly no doubt that Calderón launched the war without having a plan," he says. "He is a very mediocre commander in chief with very mediocre results." Aguayo, a professor at El Colegio de México, a graduate school and think tank, is also associated with Propuesta Cívica (Civic Proposal), a human-rights and democracy promotion organization.

Hope, at Less Crime, Less Punishment, acknowledges that murders and other forms of violence have increased. "On the flip side," he adds, "it is also the case that the large drug organizations have fragmented and in some ways no longer pose an existential threat to the Mexican state. They do pose a significant threat to the life, liberty and property of many Mexicans, but that is a different question."

Looking ahead, Hope argues that the incoming government's goal of reducing violence is possible. "What you see is a lot of people profiting from disorder and from high levels of fear, extorting money from people" by posing as cartel members, he says. "If and when

Marijuana Dominates Drug Seizures

More than 1.7 million kilograms of illegal drugs — primarily marijuana, the heaviest of these products — were seized along the U.S.-Mexico border in 2010. Some experts credit greater investment in border security for the rise in drug seizures. Others say that stepped-up security has deterred illegal immigrants but not drug traffickers.

U.S. Illegal Drug Seizures Along Southwest Border
(in kilograms, 2005-2010)*

Drug	2005	2006	2007	2008	2009	2010
Cocaine	22,653	28,284	22,656	16,755	17,583	18,623
Heroin	228	489	404	556	839	1,062
Marijuana	1,034,102	1,146,687	1,472,536	1,253,054	1,859,258	1,718,424
Ecstasy	23	16	39	92	80	59
Methamphetamine	2,918	2,798	1,860	2,201	3,788	5,253
Total	**1,059,924**	**1,178,274**	**1,497,495**	**1,272,658**	**1,881,548**	**1,743,421**

* *A kilogram is equal to 2.2 pounds.*

Sources: Kristin M. Finklea, et al., *"Southwest Border Violence: Issues in Identifying and Measuring Spillover Violence," Congressional Research Service, August 2011, p. 5, www.fas.org/sgp/crs/homesec/R41075.pdf; Adam Isacson and Maureen Meyer, "Beyond the Border Buildup: Security and Migrants Along the U.S.-Mexico Border," Washington Office on Latin America, El Colegio de la Frontera Norte, April 2012, p. 7, www.borderfactcheck.com*

conditions of security are re-established, a lot of that will go away."

But David A. Shirk, director of the University of San Diego's Trans-Border Institute, argues that the two most powerful drug organizations pose major threats. The Sinaloa cartel, led by Joaquín "El Chapo" (Shorty) Guzmán, likely has "tentacles that reach relatively high in the Mexican government," Shirk says. "It is a national security threat."

The Zetas fall in the same category, Shirk said before the syndicate's leader was reported killed. That organization "has captured significant spaces in Mexico, operating as an almost paramilitary force, preying on ordinary Mexican citizens in a way that previous generations of organized crime groups in Mexico in the 1990s and early 2000s didn't do."

One argument in Calderón's favor, says Shifter of Inter-American Dialogue: "It's hard to know what the Mexicans could have done differently. There has been no shortage of critics, many of them justified, but I haven't seen anything very compelling of what an alternative would have looked like."

To be sure, Shifter adds, "It's hard to call the [anti-cartel] approach a success. The numbers we've seen are nothing to get very enthusiastic about." But one possibility remains, he says: "Maybe the results will come later, and people will say this was necessary."

Would legalizing marijuana scale back Mexico's drug war?

Peña Nieto will take office at a time when a dozen U.S. states have already decriminalized marijuana and 14 (including six of the decriminalizing states) permit the sale of "medical marijuana" or the growing by individuals of marijuana plants for medical use. Three of the four border states — the exception is Texas — are on the medical marijuana list. Meanwhile, some Latin American presidents are starting to turn away from the U.S.-initiated drug war. Perhaps surprisingly, those leaders include outgoing Mexican President Calderón. [26]

Calderón is the most cautious of his colleagues in urging that anti-drug strategy be re-evaluated. But in a speech to the U.N. General Assembly in September, he called for the U.N. to open debate on the "progress and limits of the current prohibitionist approach, which has led to the results we've achieved thus far." [27]

Other chief executives have been more direct. And one has already proposed legislation. President José Mujica of Uruguay is backing a bill to legalize and regulate the entire marijuana business, from growing to selling to consumption. [28]

At the Summit of the Americas in Cartagena, Colombia, last April, Colombian President Juan Manuel Santos used a public discussion with President Obama to bring up the idea of replacing prohibitionism. In a pre-summit interview Santos hinted at a preference for what he called an intermediate approach — "decriminalizing consumption, but continuing to pursue narcotraffickers." [29]

Obama called debating drug policy "legitimate," but added, "I personally, and my administration's position is, that legalization is not the answer." Legalized trafficking, he said "could be just as corrupting if not more corrupting than the status quo." [30]

For now, Peña Nieto is effectively going no further than Obama, though with more pointed language about drug-war results. "We have more drug consumption and drug use and drug trafficking," the president-elect told PBS' "NewsHour" in July. "That means that we're not moving in the right direction. Things are not working. And I'm not saying that we should legalize; it's exactly the opposite. I'm against legalization, but with a debate where countries in the hemisphere — and especially the U.S. — should participate in this broad debate to redefine the way in which we fight drug trafficking." [31]

Debate is already well under way in the United States. "I expect that we're going to significantly decriminalize, legalize and regulate marijuana consumption," says Shirk of the Trans-Border Institute. "That's a really game-changing path that we're headed down. It will significantly undermine organized-crime groups in Mexico."

Shirk acknowledged that estimates attribute only 25 percent or less of Mexican organized-crime revenues to marijuana. But, he adds, "If Apple posted a 25 percent loss in business, they'd have to rethink their strategy."

For the rest of Mexico and its government, argues political scientist Aguayo, creeping legalization in the United States demands a strategy reassessment as well. "In some states," he says, "you are finding a solution to the problem of federal prohibition — and we are not even discussing legalization of marijuana in Mexico."

Mexico could rise to the occasion with solutions of its own, Aguayo says. "Why not put Mexican medical marijuana stores along the border?" he asks. "We can fill prescriptions for Americans."

Nevertheless, some Mexican analysts question how extensive the effects would be if the United States softens its drug laws. "You would probably lower violence figures," says Federico Estévez, a political scientist at the Instituto Tecnologico Autónomo de México (ITAM), an elite private university in Mexico City. "But the big, savage violence . . . is not really associated with marijuana, but with hard drugs."

Raúl "Lucky" Hernandez Lechuga, an alleged member of the Zetas drug cartel, is paraded before the news media on Dec. 13, 2011, after his capture. Widespread violence and lawlessness spawned by the cartels that control Mexico have led to at least 50,000 deaths in Mexico, and possibly far more, over the past six years. U.S. officials worry that President-elect Peña Nieto may seek an accommodation with the cartels, rather than continuing a military-style assault on the traffickers, in an effort to protect citizens from further violence.

Estévez acknowledges, however, that the disconnect between U.S. federal marijuana prohibition and medical-marijuana laws in some states poses a challenge for Mexico. "After all, we're dying like flies in the heat so that officially you Americans can deny cancer patients pain relief," he says. "I'm sorry, that's just weird."

Nevertheless, says Hope, the former intelligence official, federal marijuana legalization in the United States is at least some years away. If Mexico legalized marijuana before then, the price of marijuana would drop in Mexico while remaining expensive across the border. "So now we've given the drug traffickers a bigger incentive to smuggle into the United States," Hope says. Even if the U.S. price eventually fell as Mexican pot flooded the market, he says, "In the meantime you have just given a hell of a lot of money to Chapo Guzmán."

Legalization is likely in Mexico, Hope says, but not ahead of the United States. "But [Mexican legalization] will disappoint its promoters, because in terms of whatever metric you choose, marijuana is not the major source of harm. And the amount of [Mexican] resources devoted to marijuana enforcement is not that extensive, so the notion that there is a huge reserve of enforcement resources waiting to be redirected from marijuana is not quite true."

Is U.S. border-control policy heightening tensions with Mexico?

The Obama administration has continued a border-reinforcement buildup that began in 1993 as an anti-illegal immigration and drug-interdiction measure and escalated after the Sept. 11 attacks into anti-terrorist protection. "The plain fact of the matter is that there's more manpower and technology at that border than ever before," Homeland Security Secretary Janet Napolitano said in September. [32]

The number of people apprehended while crossing the border illegally has dropped to about 327,000, or about 20 percent of the 1.68 million total in 2000, Homeland Security officials report, describing that trend as a result of stepped-up border security. Last year the Obama administration reported that 7.7 million pounds of illegal drugs had been seized along the border during the previous two fiscal years. [33]

Most seizures, however, occur at legal border crossings — "ports of entry" — where most major drug shipments occur.

Some drugs are smuggled by illegal immigrants. But "the extent of this practice is impossible to determine," write the authors of a recent border security report for the liberal Washington Office on Latin America and a Mexican border-studies think tank, El Colegio de la Frontera Norte. They added: "One El Paso law enforcement official voiced skepticism that drug organizations would entrust an unknown migrant with thousands of dollars worth of product." [34]

Getty Images/George Frey

Mourners gather for the funeral of U.S. Border Patrol agent Nicholas Ivie on Oct. 11 in Orem, Utah. Ivie was killed late at night near Bisbee, Ariz., about five miles north of the Mexican border, after responding with two fellow agents to an alert triggered by a ground sensor in a zone favored by smugglers. The FBI reported that Ivie was accidentally shot by one of the agents as they approached the sensor site from different directions.

Arizona Gov. Jan Brewer, a Republican who is the administration's most prominent border-region critic, insists that most illegal immigrants are drug transporters and that the U.S. side of the line remains unsafe. In early October, following the death from friendly fire of a U.S. Border Patrol agent, Nicholas Ivie, in southern Arizona, she decried "the federal failure and political stalemate that has left our border unsecured and our Border Patrol in harm's way." [35]

Ivie was shot and killed late at night about five miles north of the Mexican border, seven miles east of Bisbee, Ariz., after responding with two fellow agents to an alert triggered by a ground sensor in a zone favored by smugglers. The FBI reports that Ivie was accidentally hit by one of those fellow agents as they approached the sensor site from different directions. [36]

Notwithstanding criticism by Brewer and others that the border remains unsafe, the barren boundary area is much more closely guarded than in past years. Ivie was part of an 18,000-officer Border Patrol that is nearly twice the size of the force of 10,000 in 2004. Along with ground sensors, the Homeland Security Department has deployed 250 remote video surveillance cameras, designed to give agents an around-the-clock view of active illegal crossing points. And nearly 40 truck-mounted monitoring systems that include infrared cameras and radar are roving the border, while 134 helicopters, airplanes and drones patrol overhead. [37]

Safety is becoming an issue on the Mexican side of the line as well. Border Patrol agents have killed 18 people since 2010, 16 of them along the border, the *Arizona Republic* reported, citing the ACLU's Regional Center for Border Rights, in Las Cruces, N.M. In eight of those cases, the agents reported coming under attack by rock-throwers. Six of those killed were on the Mexican side of the border and shot from the U.S. side. The most recent episode of these fatalities occurred in October when a 16-year-old boy was killed by shots fired through the border fence in Nogales, Ariz., by agents who said they were being targeted by rock-throwers during a confrontation that began over a marijuana-smuggling attempt. [38]

The use of airborne surveillance contributes to the impression of militarized border enforcement, though the Obama administration has made only temporary use of a sizeable body of actual soldiers. In 2010, the president sent 1,200 National Guard troops to the border. Yet, not counting 300 Guard troops on aviation duty, the deployment lasted only 19 months, during which time a major Border Patrol personnel increase was under way. [39]

The use of active-duty soldiers on the border is a sensitive issue — not only for Americans but for Mexican officials, the U.S. government acknowledged. "Department of State and DOD [Department of Defense] officials expressed concerns that greater or extended use of military forces on the border could create a perception of a militarized U.S. border with Mexico," the Government Accountability Office (GAO) reported in April, "especially when Department of State and Justice officials are helping support civilian law enforcement institutions in Mexico to address crime and border issues." [40]

In Mexico, those issues are playing out most prominently over illegal trafficking of firearms from the United States to cartels south of the border. Concern over that flow intensified this fall, after Univision reported Sept. 30 that guns the ATF allowed to be smuggled to Mexico in the botched "Fast and Furious" operation had been used in a massacre of high school students. [41]

But George Grayson, a professor of government at the College of William and Mary in Williamsburg, Va., and a longtime scholar of Mexican politics and security policy, has written that U.S. weapons aren't essential to the Mexican cartels because they also buy guns smuggled from Central America and Asia.

Grayson argues that both the American and Mexican governments' border-safety rhetoric evades uncomfortable realities. U.S.-Mexico relations experts in both countries might dislike border militarization, he says, but in the United States, "Public opinion polling shows that people would like to have the National Guard back." Some survey data do show that the Guard deployment was popular, though not universally. [42]

Grayson also accuses Mexican politicians of exploiting U.S. border policy for their own purposes. "The elites in Mexico have used border policy as an escape valve to dodge reforming education, reforming health care, creating jobs, collecting taxes, fighting corruption," he says. "Then they shake their fists every time a Border Patrol officer bloodies the nose of an illegal immigrant."

John Bailey, a political science professor at Georgetown University in Washington, where he directs the school's Mexico Project, reads public opinion in Mexico as broadly accepting the U.S. border buildup as inevitable. "I get symptoms of tensions in the human-rights community, and there are complaints on the left, [but] in the mainstream my sense is that Mexicans look at this as a sequel of 9/11."

Bailey adds that the United States does show some concern for Mexican response to the border enforcement escalation, which involves worry over cartel activities in Mexico as much as it does immigration. "Drones and those sorts of things — the fact that the Americans are talking about them tells me they are trying to move to less obtrusive ways of monitoring."

Whether Mexicans view the border buildup as genuinely effective is another issue. Though illegal migration has dropped, says Estévez of ITAM, the private university in Mexico City, "At the same time it appears that overall drug trans-shipments have increased."

The bottom line, Estévez says, is "an effective border against people — that part of it seems to work well, while the drug part doesn't. For Mexico, that is an odd signal."

In any event, some U.S. and Mexican experts remain uncertain of how effective the anti-immigrant side of border enforcement really is. "I don't think that immigrants are necessarily dissuaded by the difficulty of crossing," says Shirk of the Trans-Border Institute. "It's a hypothesis that we hopefully will be able to test as the U.S. economy improves. My sense is that for every undocumented immigrant we stop, there are three to four who get through."

Effective against illegal migrants and drug smugglers or not, the border enforcement escalation has a clear political effect, Shirk says. "It doesn't send a very good message to Mexico that you're building a big, ugly wall between your countries." ■

BACKGROUND

Election Crisis

For most of the 20th century, the PRI controlled Mexico by means of a political system that combined elements of monarchy, democracy, iron-fisted repression and populism. Mario Vargas Llosa, the Nobel laureate Peruvian novelist, famously called it "the perfect dictatorship." [43]

During the 71-year PRI monopoly on political power, after a period of violent turmoil following the 1910 revolution, the party's leaders espoused a fiercely nationalistic rhetoric while cultivating Mexico's powerful neighbor to the north. In the 1960s and early '70s, that accommodation included close relationships with the CIA, so close that two Mexican presidents, Adolfo López Mateos (1958-1964) and Gustavo Díaz Ordaz (1964-1970), were paid sources for the agency. [44]

Paradoxically, the PRI also owed its long tenure to its record — real if uneven — as protector of the poor and guarantor of social justice. The embodiment of that element of PRI political culture, and the single most popular figure in modern Mexican history, was Lázaro Cárdenas, an ex-general who came to power in 1934.

So when Cárdenas' son, Cuauhtémoc (named after a rebellious Aztec ruler executed by the Spanish conquerors of Mexico) challenged the PRI candidate for president of Mexico in 1988, a clash of major proportions ensued.

The younger Cárdenas had joined a handful of other PRI members in breaking with the party in 1987. They argued that the long-ruling PRI had betrayed its own revolutionary heritage, embodied by President Cárdenas.

The PRI candidate, Carlos Salinas de Gortari, represented the U.S.-influenced, pro-international-business current that had become powerful in the PRI.

Salinas* boasted Ivy League credentials — two master's degrees from Harvard University's Kennedy School of Government and a 1978 doctorate in economics from Harvard. [45]

Salinas also had served as planning minister in President Miguel de la Madrid's administration (1982-1988), which was dominated by budget cuts and foreign-debt woes. That administration had also been discredited by its flailing response to a massive 1985 earthquake that killed an estimated 10,000 people and leveled thousands of buildings in Mexico City. [46]

The disaster ratcheted up discontent that had been building for years, fed by PRI officials' attitude that they had an inalienable right to govern.

On presidential election day in July 1988, early results available only to senior government officials showed that they were facing defeat at the hands of Cárdenas supporters.

In a panic, officials blocked release of early voting data, alleging computer troubles. They then cooked the books in thousands of precincts, often simply adding zeros to the count for Salinas. For example, in one documented case in the state of Puebla, 73 votes for Salinas became 730. [47]

* Like many Mexicans, Salinas is commonly referred to on second reference by his paternal last name only; in Mexico, the second last name is the maternal one and is usually left out on second reference.

By then, Salinas had already acknowledged what the entire country realized. "The era dominated in practice by a single party is ending," he said in his first post-election speech. [48]

High Drama

Salinas' assessment proved correct, but not immediately. One-party rule didn't finally end until after his term and that of his successor. Salinas' six years in office were marked by the country's opening to foreign trade; a localized armed uprising; major financial crisis; and two political assassinations, one of them opening the door to a linked series of government-related scandals marked by nepotism, fratricide, murder, suicide and the discovery of tens of millions of dollars in hidden cash. [49]

Nearly all of these events bore a connection to Mexico's relationship with the United States. The largely untapped value of that relationship was the basis of the case for the North American Free Trade Agreement (NAFTA), which took effect in 1994, ending decades of Mexican protectionism that had strictly limited foreign trade.

In Mexico, the trade pact was strongly identified with Salinas' wing of the PRI and strongly opposed by the Mexican left. But NAFTA in the United States was a bipartisan affair, pushed strongly by President George H. W. Bush and his successor, President Bill Clinton, who obtained congressional ratification over opposition from unions and union-backed Democrats in Congress.

AFP/Getty Images/Hector Guerrero

Mexican soldiers burn marijuana plants in El Llano, Jalisco state, on Sept. 27. In addition to marijuana, the country's major drug cartels sell heroin, cocaine, methamphetamine and other narcotics, bringing in from $4 billion to $29 billion a year. More than 1.7 million kilograms (about 3.7 million pounds) of illegal drugs — primarily marijuana — were seized along the U.S.-Mexico border in 2010.

In Mexico, the trade agreement was overshadowed by an armed uprising in the southern state of Chiapas, which had a long history of conflict growing out of oppression of the Indian majority. The Zapatista National Liberation Army — named after Mexican revolutionary leader Emiliano Zapata — briefly took over the state's colonial-era city of San Cristóbal de las Casas, calling for an uprising against the government that had ushered in NAFTA.

In 1996, the Zapatistas were effectively granted an autonomous zone in Chiapas, which they still occupy. The group, which has long enjoyed the support of "solidarity" activists in the United States and Europe, also has in effect renounced armed struggle. [50]

By March of 1994, the Zapatistas were themselves overshadowed by an act that shook Mexico to its core: the assassination of the hand-picked PRI candidate for president, Luis Donaldo Colosio, shot to death during a

Continued on p. 926

Chronology

1988-2000 *Institutional Revolutionary Party (PRI) comes under sustained pro-democracy pressure for first time since its political monopoly began in 1929.*

1988
Cuauhtémoc Cárdenas, son of a legendary PRI president, runs for president as left-wing candidate. . . . Result-tampering apparently steals victory from him. . . . Declared winner is pro-business, U.S.-influenced Carlos Salinas de Gortari.

1993
United States begins reinforcing border to deter drug smugglers and illegal immigrants.

1994
North American Free Trade Agreement (NAFTA) takes effect after campaign for ratification by Salinas, President Bill Clinton and his predecessor, George H. W. Bush. . . . Left-wing guerrillas of Zapatista National Liberation Army take over part of southern Mexico state of Chiapas, protesting NAFTA and oppression of Mexico's Indian population. . . . PRI presidential candidate Luis Donaldo Colosio assassinated. . . . Replacement PRI candidate Ernesto Zedillo wins election. . . . PRI secretary-general assassinated.

1995
Former Attorney General Mario Ruiz Massieu, brother of the assassinated PRI official, arrested at airport in Newark, N.J., with $40,000 in cash. . . . Ruiz Massieu later charged with arranging smuggling of $9 million in bribe money into United States. . . . Peso devaluation crisis prompts Clinton administration to advance $5 billion of credit, arrange $52 billion bailout package.

2000
Farmer and former Coca Cola executive Vicente Fox, supported by many on left, wins election as president, running on center-right National Action Party (PAN) ticket as alternative to un-democratic PRI.

2001-2006 *First non-PRI president presides over escalating crime and drug violence.*

2001
Drug lord Joaquín "Chapo" Guzmán escapes from Mexican prison.

2004
Anti-crime march in Mexico City draws 200,000 protesters.

2005
Drug cartel violence kills more than 1,500.

2006
PAN Party's Felipe Calderón becomes second non-PRI president. . . . More than 2,000 die in cartel-linked violence.

2007-2012 *War among cartels and by government against cartels intensifies.*

2007
Calderón sends military to Michoacán state, Juárez and Tijuana to battle drug cartels. . . . "Mérida Initiative" offers U.S. aid to Mexico's anti-cartel efforts.

2008
Mexican congress approves constitutional amendment to replace non-public trials with U.S.-style adversarial court system. . . . Mexico allows foreign and private participation in oil projects, but no ownership stake.

2009
"Fast and Furious" weapons-tracing operation allows guns to be smuggled from United States into Mexico. . . . Mexico puts tariffs on potatoes, other commodities, following U.S. refusal to allow Mexican trucks to travel throughout United States.

2010
Fifteen high school students are killed by cartel members at party in Juárez. . . . Calderón retracts initial statement that some victims had cartel ties. . . . President Obama sends 1,200 National Guard troops to border. . . . Secretary of State Hillary Rodham Clinton warns of cartel violence turning into insurgency.

2011
Mexican writer Javier Sicilia launches influential anti-drug war movement following murder of his son by cartel members. . . . Mexican government announces that drug war death toll during Calderón administration is 47,515 through third quarter of year; other estimates are considerably higher. . . . U.S. and Mexico settle trucking dispute.

2012
PRI candidate Enrique Peña Nieto wins presidential election, hints at shifting drug-war focus to preventing violence rather than targeting kingpins. . . . U.S.-based Univision TV network reports that "Fast and Furious" weapons were used in Juárez student massacre. . . . Sicilia leads caravan through United States to spark awareness of U.S. connection to Mexican drug violence. . . . Mérida Initiative aid to Mexico reaches $1.2 billion. . . . U.S. spending on border fences and related technology since 2007 reaches $3.5 billion.

NAFTA Stirs Conflict on Both Sides of Border

From tomatoes to toilet paper, trade stakes are huge.

American shoppers who have gotten used to inexpensive vine-ripened tomatoes can thank Mexican farmers. Florida tomato growers respond a little differently.

Mexico ships $1.8 billion worth of tomatoes a year to the United States under a 1996 deal prompted by the North American Free Trade Agreement (NAFTA), which took effect in 1994. [1]

The 1996 accord set minimum prices for Mexican tomatoes. Florida growers had complained that their Mexican competitors were taking unfair advantage of NAFTA's elimination of tariffs on tomatoes, allowing Mexican farmers to sell their produce below cost in the United States — and to take over the U.S. tomato market. But the Florida growers say the price deal isn't working, and the Obama administration is listening.

Last September, the Floridians persuaded the U.S. Commerce Department to consider scrapping the tomato price agreement. The Florida Tomato Exchange said its growers' revenues have dropped by half since the 1996 deal, from as much as $500 million a year to as little as $250 million. [2]

Commerce officials have until next May to decide. Meanwhile, Mexico is unhappy at the possibility of a hit to its tomato industry, which accounts for about 350,000 jobs. "We are very disappointed," the country's top trade official, Francisco de Rosenzweig, said. [3]

Important as the tomato price skirmish may be to farmers in Florida and Mexico, it is but one battle in a much bigger war over NAFTA, which opened each country's economy to the other. A Commerce decision in Florida's favor could lead Mexico to retaliate, intensifying an already simmering NAFTA conflict.

Agricultural economists are doing the math on the effects of a Mexican counter-action. U.S. pork producers, for example, would lose an estimated $14 per pig if Mexico slapped tariffs on pork. "We're already having one of the worst financial periods ever because of high grain prices, and if we were to lose a major market like Mexico, it would be like Armageddon," Nick Giordano, vice president of the National Pork Producers Council, told *The New York Times*. [4]

Recent precedent suggests such concern is well-founded. In 2009-2011, during a fight over whether Mexican cargo trucks could travel into the United States farther than 25 miles north of the border, Mexico imposed tariffs not only on pork but also on such commodities as potatoes, peanuts, onions and toilet paper. U.S. potato exports alone dropped 35 percent, costing farmers $64 million during the first year of the fight. All told, Mexico put tariffs on $2.4 billion worth of U.S. goods. [5]

Opponents of allowing Mexican trucks full access to U.S. highways argued that the vehicles and drivers aren't safe enough. [6]

As with other U.S.-Mexico trade disputes, American interest groups fought each other. Opposing full access for Mexican trucks were such unions as the Teamsters, whose cargo-handling members would lose work if Mexican goods no longer needed to be offloaded and transferred to U.S. trucks. "This cheap-labor program comes at too high a risk and at too large a cost to middle-class American workers who work long, hard hours to help maintain a safe commerce system in our nation," said Ed Sills, a spokesman for the Texas AFL-CIO. [7]

But Texas' agriculture commissioner focused on lost business for farmers from Mexico's retaliatory moves. "Texas agriculture should not be penalized because Congress broke a 17-year-old agreement," Todd Staples told *The New York Times*, referring to NAFTA. [8]

Mexico dropped the punitive tariffs last year as part of a deal in which the U.S. Department of Transportation established a pilot program for Mexican trucking in the United States. The first Mexican truck in the program crossed the border on Oct. 21, 2011. [9]

Continued from p. 924

campaign stop in Tijuana. The killing was taken as a return to the era of political killings that had helped inspire creation of the PRI. Throughout the country, the belief took hold that Colosio had been ordered killed by an enemy or enemies within his own party. (Investigators later concluded the lone gunman acted on his own.)

In any event, the assassination forced Salinas to pick a new successor. He settled on another technocrat, who had been planning minister and education minister in his cabinet. Ernesto Zedillo, like Salinas and others in his circle, had Ivy League credentials: master's and doctoral degrees in economics from Yale. But he also had political credibility as Colosio's ex-campaign manager.

After an election marked by few accusations of fraud and an astonishing 78 percent turnout, Zedillo was declared the winner with 50.1 percent of the vote.

But Salinas-era drama hadn't ended. Before Zedillo was sworn in, PRI secretary-general José Francisco Ruiz Massieu was assassinated on a Mexico City street. Salinas appointed the dead man's brother, Attorney General Mario Ruiz Massieu, to investigate the killing.

The gunman was arrested at the scene, but the attorney general found evidence of a phone call from a suspected mastermind, a PRI politician, to Salinas' brother, Raúl. But a week before Salinas' term ended, the attorney general resigned from the case, saying that forces within the PRI were blocking his investigation.

Mexico wasn't entirely closed to foreign businesses before NAFTA, but entering the market was a long and complicated process. After the trade pact, direct investment in Mexico by U.S. companies increased from $17 billion in 1994 to $91.4 billion last year, a 440 percent increase. [10]

Wal-Mart is a major player in the NAFTA-enabled trade and investment boom. As of last April, the company was operating more than 2,000 stores and restaurants in Mexico, or one in five of the company's stores, *The New York Times* reported. One engine of that expansion, the paper reported on the basis of internal company documents and interviews, was bribery of local officials to ignore zoning and other regulations that might slow the company's plans. [11]

NAFTA was controversial in both countries from the time it was proposed, and it remains so. Florida's tomato growers aside, many American unions and their allies view the pact as a device that facilitates the export of U.S. jobs to a country where workers are paid less. Paradoxically, many small-scale Mexican farmers were done in by NAFTA, as cheap food imports from the United States slashed demand for local produce. [12]

Mexican critics also note that NAFTA proponents' promise that the agreement would curb emigration to the United States by providing jobs at home never materialized. Instead, as food imports hit Mexican agriculture, displaced Mexican farmers headed north over the border. Rural Mexicans accounted for only 25 percent of the country's population but 44 percent of migrants to the United States. [13]

One reason for that imbalance, some economists said, was the low-wage nature of the jobs NAFTA did produce in Mexico. "The main thing that would have stemmed the flow of people across the border was a rapid increase in wages in Mexico," Dani Rodrik, an economist and trade specialist at Harvard University's John F. Kennedy School of Government, told *The New York Times* in 2007. "And that certainly has not happened." [14]

— Peter Katel

---

1 Stephanie Strom and Elisabeth Malkin, "Ammunition for a Trade War Between U.S. and Mexico," *The New York Times*, Sept. 27, 2012, www.nytimes.com/2012/09/28/business/global/tomatoes-are-ammunition-for-a-trade-war-between-us-and-mexico.html?pagewanted=all.

2 *Ibid.*

3 Quoted in Tracy Wilkinson and Ricardo Lopez, "Tomato fight might splatter U.S. shoppers," *The Chicago Tribune*, Oct. 5, 2012, p. 2.

4 Quoted in Strom and Malkin, *op. cit.*

5 *Ibid.*

6 Clare Ribando Seelke, "Mexico: Issues for Congress," Congressional Research Service, p. 35, www.fas.org/sgp/crs/row/RL32724.pdf; Robert J. Carbaugh, "NAFTA and the U.S.-Mexican Trucking Dispute," *Journal of International and Global Economic Studies*, June 2011, www2.southeastern.edu/orgs/econjournal/index_files/JIGES%20JUNE%202011%20NAFTA%20and%20the%20U.S.-Mexican%20Trucking%20Dispute.pdf.

7 Quoted in Julian Aguilar, "U.S.-Mexico Trucker Dispute Takes a Step Forward," *The New York Times*, Jan. 22, 2011, www.nytimes.com/2011/01/23/us/23tt-truckers.html.

8 Quoted in *ibid.*

9 Seelke, *op. cit.*, pp. 34-35.

10 *Ibid.*, p. 33.

11 David Barstow, "Vast Mexico Bribery Case Hushed Up by Wal-Mart After Top-Level Struggle," *The New York Times*, April 22, 2012, www.nytimes.com/2012/04/22/business/at-wal-mart-in-mexico-a-bribe-inquiry-silenced.html; Andrew Martin, "Wal-Mart Vows to Fix Its Controls," *The New York Times*, April 24, 2012, www.nytimes.com/2012/04/25/business/wal-mart-says-it-is-tightening-internal-controls.html.

12 Elisabeth Malkin, "Nafta's promise, unfulfilled," *The New York Times*, March 23, 2009, www.nytimes.com/2009/03/24/business/worldbusiness/24peso.html?_r=1&pagewanted=all.

13 *Ibid.*

14 Quoted in Louis Uchitelle, "Nafta Should Have Stopped Illegal Immigration, Right?," *The New York Times*, Feb. 18, 2007, www.nytimes.com/2007/02/18/weekinreview/18uchitelle.html.

Transition

After Zedillo was inaugurated on Dec. 1, 1994, the Ruiz Massieu scandal morphed into an astounding series of events. Among other consequences, the unfolding drama put Salinas, a darling of the U.S. and international business community, into a most unflattering light.

The events included the arrest of Raúl Salinas for Ruiz Massieu's murder, the arrest in Switzerland of Raúl's wife after she tried to access money, stored in a safe-deposit box, that the Swiss government suspected was the proceeds of drug trafficking. The government seized $130 million that she and her husband had deposited in banks there. [51]

These arrests led to events that might have seemed far-fetched if they'd been fiction. In 1999, Raúl Salinas was convicted of plotting the Ruiz Massieu assassination, apparently because of rivalries over bribery income, and sentenced to 50 years in prison (later reduced to 27 1/2 years). The outcome once would have been unthinkable for such a well-connected figure. [52]

By then, Mario Ruiz Massieu — the former attorney general and brother of the man killed — had been arrested at Newark Liberty International Airport on his way to Madrid with $40,000 in cash in his luggage. Later, U.S. authorities said that when Ruiz Massieu had been in government, he had shipped $9 million to the United States in duffel bags. In a civil case, the money was confiscated on grounds that it came from drug traffickers' bribes. In 1999, after he was indicted in Houston on 25 counts

AFP/Getty Images/Jesus Alcazar

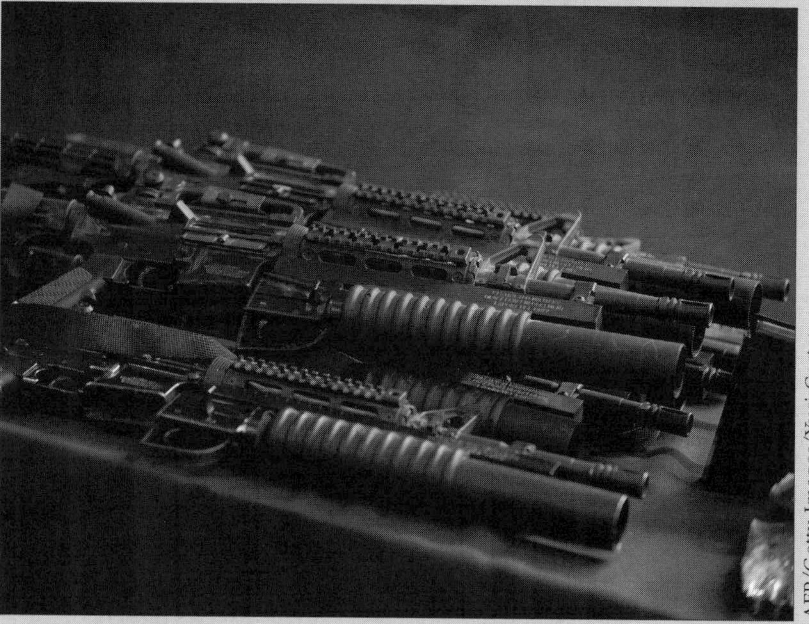

AFP/Getty Images/Yuri Cortez

Violence to Guns

Thousands of weapons seized from drug cartel members are destroyed by the Mexican Army on Feb. 16 (top). U.S.-made grenade launchers were part of a cartel arsenal seized on March 9 in Guadalajara (bottom). The botched "Fast and Furious" gun-trafficking investigation run by the U.S. Bureau of Alcohol, Tobacco, Firearms and Explosives focused new attention on the source of weapons used by the cartels. Some experts say U.S.-made weapons aren't essential to the gangs because they also can buy guns smuggled from Central America and Asia.

of drug and money-laundering charges, Ruiz Massieu committed suicide while under house arrest.

The scandals played out against the backdrop of a catastrophic drop in the value of the peso. When Zedillo and his team took over, they found that the previous administration's accounting had papered over some serious weaknesses in government finances. That discovery, along with a short-lived intensification of conflict with the Zapatistas, forced Zedillo and his advisers to order a lowering of the peso's value. Panic seized Wall Street, and the government was left unable to pay what it owed to bondholders.

The Clinton administration stepped in with a $5 billion emergency line of credit. Months later, the administration assembled a $52 billion bailout package.

For ordinary Mexicans, the peso devaluation was disastrous. Middle-class Mexicans saw their savings plunge in value. And poorer Mexicans saw prices on basic foods soar as businesses ignored government price controls.

As Zedillo hammered out a new economic program, which eventually restored stability, he broke with PRI political traditions. He oversaw establishment of a modern and trustworthy vote-counting system. And he refused to hand-pick his successor, insisting instead that the party hold a primary election.

With the 2000 election approaching, the most promising challenger to the PRI came from the center-right National Action Party (PAN). Vicente Fox, a 6-foot-6-inch cowboy-boot-wearing farmer and former Coca-Cola executive, presented himself as a modern, forward-looking alternative to a ruling party that had by then enjoyed a political monopoly for 71 years.

Fox portrayed himself as a non-ideological pragmatist. Sensing his appeal, prominent left-wing intellectuals, including Jorge G. Castañeda, a political scientist and prolific journalist and author — now a professor at New York University — forged an alliance with Fox. Under their influence, Fox accepted the idea that government should ensure social justice, a left-wing tenet that the PRI had adopted.

His message hit home. Fox won 43 percent of the vote, against 36 percent for PRI candidate Francisco Labastida and 17 percent for Cárdenas. Labastida's only wins came in the country's most rural states.

Untamed Mexico

PRI operatives had always said their party acted as a bulwark against *Mexico bronco* — the untamed Mexico that would be unleashed if the long-ruling party's grip on power slipped.

The presidency of Fox, and of his PAN successor, Calderón, did suggest the PRI operatives weren't completely wrong, even though they'd been arguing from self-interest.

To be sure, Fox's major legislative initiatives were blocked because the PAN didn't enjoy a congressional majority. And he inherited from his predecessors a criminal-justice system riddled with corruption and incompetence. In 2001, for example, Sinaloa cartel head Guzmán escaped — seemingly effortlessly — from a maximum-security prison after Mexico's Supreme Court made his extradition to the United States likely. As of early October, Guzmán remained at large. [53]

The escape infuriated U.S. officials, who had placed great hope in Fox's administration. And by later in 2001, the United States had helped Mexico form a 117-member organized crime unit of agents who had been carefully vetted to eliminate anyone with links to drug traffickers. But even then, drug-war analyst and author Michael Massing told *The New York Times*, "I'd be surprised if these changes lead to a substantial decrease in drugs going to the U.S. or a decrease in the violence and power of the cartels." [54]

Indeed, drug-trafficking remained a major enterprise during Fox's administration despite a series of arrests of high-level traffickers. And criminality in general was on the rise, with intensifying levels of violence that touched growing numbers of ordinary citizens. In 2004, a nationwide protest against crime brought an estimated 200,000 people into the streets of Mexico City.

The call to march drew so much support that Fox endorsed it, though the demonstrators were protesting what they saw as government ineffectiveness. "Society is right to affirm that governments have only reached partial solutions in the fight against crime and that we have to do much more," he said, implicitly including state and municipal administrations, many of them in the hands of PRI politicians. [55]

By November, 2006, the last month of Fox's administration, authorities estimated that 2,000 killings that year grew out of a war between cartels for control of key "plazas" — drug-traffickers' lingo meaning turf critical for shipping drugs north to the United States. [56]

Calderón won office in 2006, with his victory disputed by left-wing candidate Andrés Manuel López Obrador, a fiery populist. Between his election and his swearing-in on Dec. 1, 2006, the cartels killed an estimated 1,000 or more people. Over the entire year, killings increased to 2,120 from 1,537 in 2005. [57]

Calderón's central-Mexico home state of Michoacán was one of the worst-hit, as cartels disputed turf in a prized territory that includes a major Pacific port (Lázaro Cárdenas), which is an entry point for cocaine and for chemical precursors of methamphetamine shipped from Asia. Ciudad Juárez, across the border from El Paso, Texas, and Tijuana, across the border from the outskirts of San Diego, Calif., were also suffering from a war between trafficking organizations. [58]

Calderón had campaigned on a moderate center-right platform much like Fox's, emphasizing job creation and poverty reduction. But crime fighting soon took priority.

By early 2007, Calderón had dispatched more than 7,000 federal police and Army troops to Michoacán, where drug violence had claimed more than 500 lives. He also sent 2,600 troops and 110 federal police to Tijuana, whose local police were reported to be colluding with, or afraid of, drug gangs. The federal force underlined its presence by confiscating firearms from all local police. Troops also were dispatched to the Pacific resort city of Acapulco and other theaters of combat between cartels. [59]

The Mexican government's efforts soon shifted elsewhere in border country, to Ciudad Júarez, the scene of a brutal fight between the Sinaloa and Juárez cartels for control of a key drug-transit point.

But the troops failed to quell the violence. Calderón didn't help matters when he suggested that some of the 15 high school students massacred at a party in January, 2010, might have had drug-gang connections. He later apologized, but when he visited Júarez the following month to acknowledge that military and police efforts had to be accompanied by social programs, he was greeted by street demonstrators with signs including, "Apologize, then resign!" [60]

The following year, 2011, may have represented a peak in violence. "In absolute terms, it was probably the year with the most homicides in the country's history (periods of civil war excepted)," wrote security analyst Alejandro Hope. [61]

That was the context for the 2012 election campaign, in which Peña Nieto was opposed by López Obrador on the left, and by Josefina Vázquez Mota, a congresswoman from the PAN. The widely shared view that Calderón's anti-cartel strategy had led to more violence rather than less helped Peña Nieto of the once-discredited PRI win the vote. ■

CURRENT SITUATION

"Fast and Furious"

"Fast and Furious," the flawed ATF gun-tracking operation that supplied a weapon that killed U.S. Border Patrol agent Brian Terry in 2010, is seen in the United States as a political embarrassment for the Obama administration. [62]

But Mexicans now know the controversial U.S. operation as the source of weapons in one of the most notorious events in the bloody saga of the Mexican drug war — the slaying of the 15 high school students in Juárez. [63]

As a result, Mexican as well as U.S. politicians are demanding more information on what the outgoing government may have known about the operation.

Phoenix-based ATF agents and federal prosecutors had intended to let weapons bought in the United States "walk" across the border to cartels in order to make cases against weapons-suppliers for the cartels. But the operation fell apart when the ATF lost track of nearly 2,000 weapons once they were smuggled over the border. [64]

On Oct. 4 Mexico's lower house, the Chamber of Deputies, passed a resolution demanding that Mexico's attorney general's office and foreign ministry "make public all the information available" concerning "Fast and Furious." [65]

The left-wing Democratic Revolutionary Party (PRD) and the PRI pushed through the resolution. Members of the PAN — the party of outgoing President Calderón — opposed the move, arguing that investigations of "Fast and Furious" are under way in both countries.

Meanwhile, the Sept. 30 Univision report on the operation prompted the Mexican attorney general's office — roughly the equivalent of the U.S. Justice Department — to disclose that it is investigating Mexican arms traffickers who may have handled some of the "Fast and Furious" guns, including those used in the Juárez massacre. *Reforma*, a major Mexican newspaper chain, reported that sources in the agency said some suspects had been arrested and detained in maximum-security prisons. [66]

Univision's chief investigative reporter, Gerardo Reyes, found that three of the weapons used in the massacre were among the 1,961 weapons that the ATF allowed to cross into Mexico. "The ATF was frustrated at only arresting straw buyers, the simple middlemen who buy the weapons illegally in return for a commission," Reyes reported. "They wanted to catch the big narcos who received them." [67]

Comparing a list of guns that the ATF allowed to cross the border with lists of guns seized at crime scenes in Mexico, Univision found 57 firearms that investigators for the Justice Department's Office of Inspector General hadn't been able to trace. [68]

In addition to the weapons used at the high school party massacre, other weapons were found in the possession of a commander of hit teams for the Juárez cartel, José Antonio Acosta, who confessed to having ordered another massacre, at a drug rehabilitation center where he believed gunmen from the rival Sinaloa cartel were hiding out. Eighteen young men were killed there in 2009. [69]

The Univision report also prompted Rep. Darrell Issa, R-Calif., chair of the House Over-

Continued on p. 932

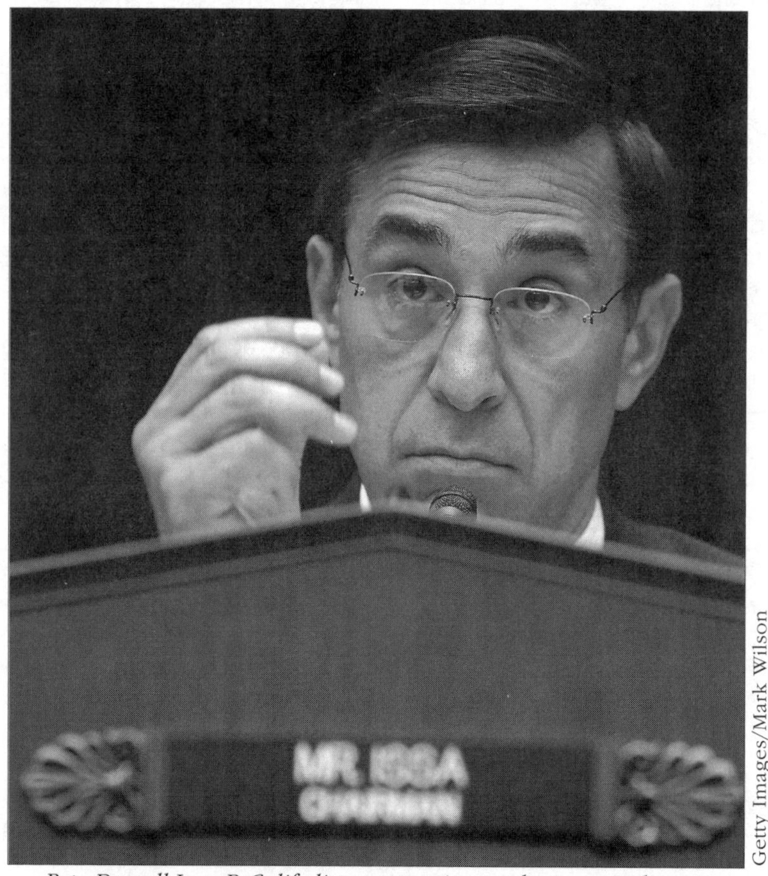

Getty Images/Mark Wilson

Rep. Darrell Issa, R-Calif., listens to testimony during a Judiciary Committee hearing on Sept. 20 about the controversial "Fast and Furious" gun-tracking investigation. The flawed U.S. effort to follow weapons smuggled to Mexican cartels supplied the gun that killed a Border Patrol agent in 2010 as well as weapons used in the slaying by cartel gangsters of 15 high school students in Juárez.

At Issue:

Is legalization a better approach to fighting drugs in Mexico than the drug war?

JORGE G. CASTAÑEDA
GLOBAL DISTINGUISHED PROFESSOR OF POLITICS AND LATIN AMERICAN AND CARIBBEAN STUDIES, NEW YORK UNIVERSITY; FORMER FOREIGN MINISTER OF MEXICO (2000-2003)

FROM REMARKS AT A COUNCIL ON FOREIGN RELATIONS SYMPOSIUM, MAY 1, 2012

yes

Most Latin American presidents know this [drug war] doesn't work. I'm absolutely convinced that this is a complete failure, that the price we've paid in Mexico is just outrageous and that the results are very meager. I mean, 60,000 deaths in exchange for what?

So the question is, do you go on with this? . . . Where do you go from here?

For those who don't like legalization, the best way of shooting it down is by saying, if you think legalization is a panacea, well, it's not. But nobody thinks it's a panacea. Legalization can be part of an alternative policy; it's certainly not an alternative policy in itself. If anything, it's a corollary, in the case of Mexico, to an alternative policy that emphasizes fighting violence that affects society — kidnapping, extortion, assassinations, automobile theft. . . .

If that's going to be your priority, then your non-priority is obviously going to be drug trafficking. What that means is you are not going to devote all the money and the troops and the police and the effort to combating drug trafficking. What are you going to do?

You're going to let it go through. Now, you don't want to do that, because you are encouraging a culture of illegality in Mexico by so doing. And that's something that has done the country an enormous amount of damage over the years. So what's the best way to let it go through without encouraging a culture of illegality? Make it legal.

Canadians, during Prohibition, broadened the tires on the trucks that would ride across the lakes in the winter on the ice so they could take more scotch to Chicago and Detroit. They taxed them. And they never thought of contributing to American Prohibition. What they thought of doing — mainly the government of Ontario — was to benefit as much as possible from a great opportunity, which was: "These crazy Americans have prohibition on alcohol, and we can make it here. Well, let's give them all the liquor they want."

This is one of the issues that perhaps can begin to be talked about by a second-term president in the United States and by someone like [President-elect] Peña Nieto in Mexico, who does not feel constricted or bound by [outgoing] President Calderón's policies.

SHANNON O'NEIL
SENIOR FELLOW FOR LATIN AMERICA STUDIES, COUNCIL ON FOREIGN RELATIONS

FROM REMARKS AT A COUNCIL ON FOREIGN RELATIONS SYMPOSIUM, MAY 1, 2012

no

Legalization is a perfect soundbite. It's the silver bullet that will solve the problems. It will take the money out of it, supposedly, and that will get rid of the violence.

That is simple but wrong. If you look at the United States' struggles with legalization, or the way the United States' markets work, it has some lessons for Latin America.

When you look at the one drug that we have legalized through the end of Prohibition, alcohol, it hasn't all been sweetness and light for the United States. It is a huge cost for our society. That's one cautionary note. People, families are destroyed by the addiction to alcohol. We see huge public health costs from what alcohol does to people's bodies when they are addicted to alcohol. And we see huge costs to total strangers who are killed by drunk drivers.

In the United States, the fastest growing drug problem we have, and the drugs that kill the most individuals, are prescription drugs. These are legal drugs. They're being used illegally.

But if you were to take cocaine or heroin or marijuana or meth, or whatever the pharmacy cabinet is, and legalize them . . ., you could get them with your Pepsi or Coke at McDonald's? If it becomes a prescription drug, you have the same problem you have with all these other drugs that are being abused in the United States.

Those lessons of how our market works cautions those who say legalization would solve many of these problems.

The transit [of drugs] is causing much of the violence, but Latin American countries are becoming consumer countries, so they have some of these public health and criminal problems that we have as well.

What I think the United States can do is to focus on strengthening the [law enforcement] institutions. Where are drugs most expensive? Where is most of the drug money? And where are most of the guns?

Well, they're in the United States, but we don't have the violence problem, right? But here's where the profits are and here's where most of the guns are, even though Mexico has the problem. So, what is the problem in Mexico or Colombia or other places? It's these weak institutions. When we talk about strengthening institutions, it is training police officers to do their job, but it's also putting in the institutional checks and balances to incentivize cops to stay clean and to incentivize these forces to be cleaner.

Continued from p. 930

sight Committee, and Sen. Charles Grassley, R-Iowa, the top Republican on the Senate Judiciary Committee, to demand more information from the Justice Department. [70]

In an Oct. 2 letter to Attorney General Eric Holder, the two Republicans requested all information that the department has concerning weapons used in violent incidents in Mexico, including the Juárez massacre. "Why did the department fail to report these weapons to Congress?," the legislators asked. [71]

Privatizing Pemex

In addition to grappling with the drug cartels, Peña Nieto also will face major economic and trade challenges. He is making clear that he will try to keep a campaign promise to open up Mexico's oil industry, which has been a state monopoly since President Cárdenas' 1938 nationalization of petroleum and expropriation of U.S. and British oil companies.

Peña Nieto's top economic adviser said the president-elect and his team have been researching the possibility of ending the oil exploration and refining monopoly held by Petróleos Méxicanos (Pemex) without the need for a constitutional amendment. That would require a two-thirds majority in the Mexican Congress, which could be difficult to get. [72]

The 1938 nationalization has long been considered politically untouchable. Mexicans celebrate the March 18 anniversary of the move every year as a demonstration of national pride.

But Pemex, though the world's fourth-largest oil producer, is considered to be badly in need of capital. Production fell from 3.38 million barrels a day in 2004 to 2.55 million barrels in 2011, and Pemex doesn't have the money on its own to start pumping oil from the Gulf of Mexico. [73]

Writing of that deficiency in an op-ed published earlier this year on the nationalization anniversary, Peña Nieto wrote that changing times and circumstances demand that Mexico "take daring measures and rid ourselves of ideological hindrances." [74]

Peña Nieto wouldn't completely privatize Pemex, he wrote. But legal or constitutional changes would be required to allow foreign investors to have equity. Mexico in 2008 started allowing private and foreign companies to put money in exploration and production but barred them from an ownership stake. Those arrangements "are not as attractive as joint ventures," Antonio Szabo, an oil industry specialist and chief executive officer of Stone Bond Technologies of Houston, a research firm, told Bloomberg in April. [75]

Whatever the scale of Mexico's need for private investment in oil, the politics may remain tricky. Earlier this year, following Peña Nieto's campaign statements, his advisers argued that the political landscape had changed. "The taboo has been broken," Hector Moreira, a Pemex board member, told Bloomberg. "People are talking about private stakes — it's a first step. And it's a step that's not prompting a negative reaction from the public." [76]

Jorge Chabat, a political science professor at the Center for Economic Research and Teaching, a major Mexico City think tank and university, made a similar assessment. "This is the first time the topic is discussed in a presidential campaign, at least in such an explicit way." Speaking in April, he said a Peña Nieto victory and awareness of Pemex's problems could overcome traditional resistance to weakening the Pemex monopoly. [77]

Nevertheless, with Peña Nieto's transition team now talking of avoiding the constitutional amendment route, the congressional dynamic of reinventing Mexico's oil industry may look more challenging than ever. Ildefonso Guajardo, a top economic adviser to the president-elect, said a new approach would be shaped according to "a technical analysis of how far we can get without a constitutional change." [78]

The left-wing Revolutionary Democratic Party (PRD) is presumed to stand in the way of a constitutional amendment, and it's not clear all members of Peña Nieto's PRI would favor it. Already, the PRD and PRI are opposing legislation by outgoing President Calderón that would change workplace rules and curb the power of Mexico's powerful unions. [79]

Still, Mexicans do recognize the oil industry's importance. Pemex's tax payments account for one-third of the government budget. Peña Nieto in his op-ed pitched his proposal in terms designed to appeal to ordinary citizens. Mexico has to "take advantage of petroleum resources in order to improve Mexicans' quality of life" in the present economic environment, he wrote. [80] ■

OUTLOOK

Corruption and Cartels

However much Peña Nieto may improve Mexicans' living standards, the reliability of security agencies is likely to remain his biggest hurdle. Two recent instances of apparent law enforcement collusion with the Zetas cartel suggest the scope of the challenge: In Coahuila state, prison employees are suspected of helping 132 prisoners to escape, and police officers allegedly participated in the murder of the governor's nephew. [81]

Distrust extends into police agencies themselves. A survey of the Juárez municipal police last year by the Trans-Border Institute and several Mexican nongovernmental and governmental organizations found that only 11 percent of officers said no corruption existed in the department; 18 percent said corruption was extensive. Further, 44 percent said corruption was most prevalent at the command level. [82]

An earlier survey in Guadalajara, one of Mexico's major cities, showed even more pronounced results, with 68 percent of respondents pointing to corruption at senior levels. [83]

Against this backdrop, experts are especially interested in the outcomes of changes already under way in the courts. In 2008, the Mexican Congress approved a constitutional amendment to change from a system of trials conducted largely out of view to a U.S.-style adversarial system open to the public. The transition is scheduled to be completed by 2016. [84]

"Three states have already completed the transition, five more are partially there and 10 more will start the transition phase soon," former intelligence official Hope said in Washington. "It will take a while and will not reflect itself initially in crime indicators, but will provide a sense of transparency that is wholly lacking." [85]

In an interview, Hope sees reason for qualified optimism in other areas. "We are going to see a decline in the more brutal forms of violence," he says. "We'll continue to have relatively high levels of criminal violence, but this will be more local. We'll be in a better place in 10 years, but how much better is difficult to say."

Along the same lines, Shirk of the Trans-Border Institute sees the major cartels disintegrating. Former members "will go into other areas of criminal activity that will have a greater effect on ordinary folks, but that will be easier to stop with a more efficient police force," he says.

Shirk also sees reason to hope that as the U.S. and Mexican economies improve the resulting bigger volume of trade will force U.S. officials to make border crossing easier. "We are taxing ourselves at the border with unnecessary wait times and hassles," he says.

Still, continued deterioration of safety and security would provide incentive to maintain or increase — not reduce — border security. But Bailey of Georgetown University also foresees a decline in violence. "It can't hold at this level," he says. "I'm thinking like an epidemiologist; once a fever has gone through a population, there would be a mechanism to control it. I don't think it would continue to get worse at the pace it has," he says. "There is no good, strong evidence for it."

But even those who see violence trending downward don't predict quick improvements. "This war in Mexico is here for a long time, — another 10 or 15 years given the strength of the organized-crime cartels and the ineptitude and corruption of the Mexican government," Aguayo of El Colegio de México said in Washington. "We have to do what we can to achieve justice for those who have died and prevent others from dying." ■

Statement of Ownership Management, Circulation

Act of Aug. 12, 1970: Section 3685, Title 39, United States Code

Title of Publication: CQ Researcher. Date of filing: October 5, 2012. Frequency of issue: Weekly (Except for 3/30, 5/25, 7/6, 8/17, 8/24, 11/23, 12/21, 12/28/12). No. of issues published annually: 44. Annual subscription price for high schools: $977. Annual subscription price for college/university: $1,054. Location of known office of publication: SAGE Publications, Inc., 2455 Teller Road, Thousand Oaks, CA 91320. Names and addresses of publisher, editor and managing editor: Publisher, SAGE Publications, Inc., 2455 Teller Road, Thousand Oaks, CA 91320; Managing Editor, Thomas J. Billitteri, CQ Press, 2300 N Street, N.W., Suite 800, Washington, D.C. 20037. Owner: SAGE Publications, Inc., McCune Inter-Vivos Trust, David F. McCune, 2455 Teller Road, Thousand Oaks, CA 91320. Known bondholders, mortgagees and other security holders owning or holding 1 percent or more of total amount of bonds, mortgages or other securities: None.

Extent and Nature of Circulation	Average Number of Copies of Each Issue During Preceding 12 months	Actual Number of Copies of Single Issue Published Nearest to Filing Date
A. Total number of copies printed (Net press run)	858	772
B. Paid and/or requested circulation		
(1) Paid/requested outside-county mail subscriptions stated on Form 3541	667	577
(2) Paid in-county subscriptions stated on Form 3541	0	0
(3) Sales through dealers and carriers, street vendors, counter sales, and other non-USPS paid distribution	0	0
(4) Other classes mailed through the USPS	0	0
C. Total paid and/or requested circulation	667	577
D. Free distribution by mail (Samples, complimentary, and other free copies)		
(1) Outside-county as stated on Form 3541	0	0
(2) In-county as stated on Form 3541	0	0
(3) Other classes mailed through the USPS	0	0
E. Free distribution outside the mail (Carriers or other means)	0	0
F. Total free distribution	0	0
G. Total distribution	667	577
H. Copies not distributed	191	195
I. Total	858	772
J. Percent paid and/or requested circulation	100%	100%

Notes

1 "PBS 'NewsHour' Interview With Mexican President-Elect Enrique Peña Nieto," Federal News Service, July 3, 2012, www.pbs.org/newshour/bb/world/july-dec12/mexico_07-03.html.

2 June S. Beittel, "Mexico's Drug Trafficking Organizations: Source and Scope of the Rising Violence," Congressional Research Service, Aug. 3, 2012, p. 36, www.fas.org/sgp/crs/row/R41576.pdf.

3 "Mexican meth pours into US cities, negates effort to curb US drug production," The Associated Press, Oct. 11, 2012, www.washingtonpost.com/national/ap-impact-mexican-meth-pours-into-us-cities-negates-effort-to-curb-us-drug-production/2012/10/11/e5920b0e-1372-11e2-9a39-1f5a7f6fe945_story.html.

4 "Known Abusers, But Victims Ignored: Torture and Ill-Treatment in Mexico," Amnesty International, October 2012, www.amnesty.org/

en/library/asset/AMR41/063/2012/en/74354a01-4946-4301-b922-8d048782bfef/amr410632012en.pdf; "Neither Rights Nor Security: Killings, Torture and Disappearances in Mexico's 'War on Drugs,' " Human Rights Watch, 2011, www.hrw.org/sites/default/files/reports/mexico1111webwcover_0.pdf. For background, see Peter Katel, "Mexico's Drug War," *CQ Researcher*, Dec. 12, 2008, pp. 1009-1032.

[5] Clare Ribando Seelke, "Mexico: Issues for Congress," Congressional Research Service, p. 16, www.fas.org/sgp/crs/row/RL32724.pdf; "Judicial and Police Reforms in Mexico: Essential Building Blocks For a Lawful Society," Senate Foreign Relations Committee, majority staff report, July 9, 2012, p. 4, http://mexicoinstitute.files.wordpress.com/2012/07/senate-foreign-relations-mexico-7-12.pdf.

[6] "Rep. F. James Sensenbrenner Jr. Holds a Hearing on Drug Enforcement Administration," House Committee on the Judiciary, Subcommittee on Crime, Terrorism and Homeland Security, *CQ Transcriptions*, June 20, 2012.

[7] "Mexico's Next Sexenio: What Lies Ahead," Inter-American Dialogue, July 26, 2012, webcast, https://thedialogue.adobeconnect.com/_a994606385/p45z9hri2ld/?launcher=false&fcsContent=true&pbMode=normal.

[8] "27 Journalists Killed in Mexico since 1992/Motive Confirmed," Committee to Protect Journalists, updated regularly, http://cpj.org/killed/americas/mexico.

[9] "Mexico's Next Sexenio," *op. cit.*

[10] "AP Exclusive: Official says organized crime possible in attack on CIA agents in Mexico," The Associated Press (*The Washington Post*), Oct. 2, 2012, www.washingtonpost.com/world/the_americas/us-official-strong-evidence-of-organized-crime-in-attack-on-cia-agents-in-mexico/2012/10/02/be3984c8-0cc0-11e2-97a7-45c05ef136b2_story.html.

[11] "Office of the United States Trade Representative, Mexico," undated, www.ustr.gov/countries-regions/americas/mexico.

[12] "The Woodrow Wilson Center Holds a Discussion on Policy Recommendations for U.S.-Mexico Relations," *CQ Transcriptions*, July 11, 2012.

[13] Marc R. Rosenblum, "Border Security: Immigration Enforcement Between Ports of Entry," Congressional Research Service, Jan. 6, 2012, pp. 12-17, http://fpc.state.gov/documents/organization/180681.pdf.

[14] "Mexico: Issues for Congress," *op. cit.*, Congressional Research Service, p. 16; "Judicial and Police Reforms in Mexico: Essential Building Blocks For a Lawful Society," *op. cit.*, p. 6.

[15] Randal C. Archibold, "Mexico Kills a Drug Kingpin, but the Body Gets Away," *The New York Times*, Oct. 9, 2012, www.nytimes.com/2012/10/10/world/americas/mexico-zetas.html?pagewanted=all; E. Eduardo Castillo and Michael Weissenstein, "Official: Gunmen stole Zeta leader's body," The Associated Press (*The Miami Herald*), Oct. 8, 2012, www.miamiherald.com/2012/10/08/v-print/3040496/cartel-suspect-blamed-for-jailbreak.html.

[16] Alejandro Hope, "No está creciendo la violencia," *Plata o Plomo* (blog), Sept. 23, 2012, www.animalpolitico.com/blogueros-plata-o-plomo/2012/09/23/no-esta-creciendo-la-violencia.

[17] *Ibid.*

[18] "The Peace Movement in Mexico: Efforts to bring justice to the victims of violence in the country," Woodrow Wilson International Center for Scholars, Sept. 11, 2012, www.wilsoncenter.org/event/the-peace-movement-mexico-efforts-to-bring-justice-to-the-victims-violence-the-country-0. Aguayo and others spoke in Spanish. For an English-language version of his talk: Sergio Aguayo, "Remarks at the Woodrow Wilson Center, The Neighboring Societies of Mexico and the United States," Caravan for Peace, Sept. 20, 2012, www.caravanforpeace.org/caravan/?p=3570.

[19] *Op. cit.*, "Judicial and Police Reforms in Mexico: Essential Building Blocks For a Lawful Society," p. 4; Elizabeth Dickinson, "Fighting the Last War," *Washington Monthly*, January-February 2012, www.washingtonmonthly.com/magazine/january_february_2012/features/fighting_the_last_war034573.php#.

[20] "Mexico: Issues for Congress," *op. cit.*, p. 16.

[21] "Judicial and Police Reforms . . .," *op. cit.*, p. 5.

[22] "Mexico's Drug Trafficking Organizations . . .," *op. cit.*, pp. 8-17.

[23] Cory Molzahn, Viridiana Ríos and David A. Shirk, "Drug Violence in Mexico: Data and Analysis Through 2011," Trans-Border Institute, University of San Diego, March 2012, pp. 5-14, http://justiceinmexico.files.wordpress.com/2012/03/2012-tbi-drugviolence.pdf; *ibid.*, "Mexico's Drug Trafficking Organizations . . .," pp. 22-26. Damien Cave, "Mexico Updates Death Toll in Drug War to 47,515, but Critics Dispute the Data," *The New York Times*, Jan. 11, 2012, www.nytimes.com/2012/01/12/world/americas/mexico-updates-drug-war-death-toll-but-critics-dispute-data.html?_r=0.

[24] "50 mil muertes en la guerra contra el narco en México," *Milenio*, May 14, 2012, www.milenio.com/cdb/doc/noticias2011/1db22ab7d4f97d7491d79e46da56c4cf; Molly Molloy, "Mexican Toll in Drug War Likely Higher Than Reported," *Phoenix New Times*, July 26, 2012, www.phoenixnewtimes.com/2012-07-26/news/mexico-s-unknown-drug-war-death-toll; Damien Cave, "Mexico Updates Death Toll in Drug War to 47, 515, but Critics Dispute the Data," *The New York Times*, Jan. 11, 2012, www.nytimes.com/2012/01/12/world/americas/mexico-updates-drug-war-death-toll-but-critics-dispute-data.html.

[25] "Waves of violence: an interactive guide to drug crime in Mexico," *The Economist*, June 6, 2012, www.economist.com/blogs/graphicdetail/2012/06/mexican-drug-war.

[26] "State info," (State marijuana law information), NORML, undated, http://norml.org/states.

[27] "Felipe Calderón Hinojosa, president of the United Mexican States, Delivers Remarks at the General Assembly of the United Nations," *CQ Transcriptions*, Sept. 26, 2012.

[28] Damien Cave, "South America Sees Drug Path to Legalization," *The New York Times*, July 29, 2012, www.nytimes.com/2012/07/30/world/americas/uruguay-considers-legalizing-marijuana-to-stop-traffickers.html?pagewanted=all.

[29] Quoted in "Santos propone método para debatir legalización de drogas en Cumbre," *El Tiempo*, March 13, 2012, www.eltiempo.com/politica/ARTICULO-WEB-NEW_NOTA_INTER

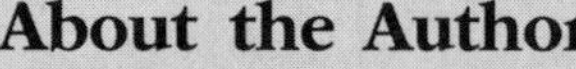

About the Author

Peter Katel is a *CQ Researcher* contributing writer who previously reported on Haiti and Latin America for *Time* and *Newsweek* and covered the Southwest for newspapers in New Mexico. He has received several journalism awards, including the Bartolomé Mitre Award for coverage of drug trafficking, from the Inter-American Press Association. He holds an A.B. in university studies from the University of New Mexico. His recent reports include "Prisoner Reenty" and "Downsizing Prisons."

IOR-11344841.html.

[30] Quoted in Christi Parsons and Matea Gold, "Obama says no to legalizing drugs," *Los Angeles Times*, April 14, 2012, http://articles.latimes.com/2012/apr/14/world/la-fg-obama-summit-20120415.

[31] "PBS 'NewsHour' Interview with Mexican President-Elect Enrique Peña Nieto," Federal News Service, July 3, 2012.

[32] Discussion with Janet Napolitano, Secretary of Homeland Security . . . Reviewing the U.S.-Mexico Security Relationship," Federal News Service, Sept. 17, 2012.

[33] "National Southwest Border Counternarcotics Strategy," Office of National Drug Control Policy, 2011, p. 2, www.whitehouse.gov/sites/default/files/ondcp/policy-and-research/swb_counternarcotics_strategy11.pdf. Rosenblum, "Border Security: Immigration Enforcement. . . .," *op. cit.*, p. 21.

[34] Adam Isacson and Maureen Meyer, "Beyond the Border Buildup: Security and Migrants Along the U.S.-Mexico Border," Washington Office on Latin America, April, 2012, p. 7, www.wola.org/files/Beyond_the_Border_Buildup_FINAL.pdf.

[35] Quoted in "Reaction to the death of slain Border Patrol Agent Nicholas Ivie," abc15.com, Oct. 2, 2012, www.abc15.com/dpp/news/region_central_southern_az/other/Reaction-to-the-death-of-slain-Border-Patrol-Agent-Nicholas-Ivie; J.J. Hensley, "Immigrants' activity in drug trade uncertain," *Arizona Republic*, July 6, 2010, www.azcentral.com/arizonarepublic/news/articles/2010/07/06/20100706illegal-immigration-drug-trade.html.

[36] Brady McCombs, "Sheriff: 'Friendly fire' killed agent Ivie," *Arizona Daily Star*, Oct. 6, 2012, http://azstarnet.com/news/local/crime/sheriff-friendly-fire-killed-agent-ivie/article_7ea6147e-fb0b-57f0-9658-3edd27737185.html; Lizbeth Diaz and David Schwartz, "Mexican troops arrest two in killing of U.S. border agent: officials," Reuters, Oct. 3, 2012, www.reuters.com/article/2012/10/03/us-usa-border-shooting-idUSBRE89203P20121003; Written testimony, Homeland Security Department, House Homeland Security Subcommittee on Border and Maritime Security, March 11, 2011, www.dhs.gov/news/2011/03/15/written-testimony-cbp-house-homeland-security-subcommittee-border-and-maritime.

[37] *Ibid.*, written testimony.

[38] Bob Ortega, "Border Patrol scrutinized over teen's shooting death," *Arizona Republic*, Oct. 18, 2012, www.azcentral.com/arizonarepublic/news/articles/2012/10/17/20121017border-patrol-scrutinized-teen-shooting-death.html.

[39] Brian Bennett, "National Guard withdrawing 900 troops from border," *Los Angeles Times*, April 18, 2012, http://articles.latimes.com/2012/apr/18/news/la-pn-national-guard-withdrawing-900-troops-from-the-usmexico-border-20120418.

[40] Brian J. Lepore, "Border Security: Observations on Costs, Benefits, and Challenges of a Department of Defense Role in Helping to Secure the Southwest Land Border," Government Accountability Office, written testimony, April 17, 2012, p. 10, www.gao.gov/assets/600/590173.pdf.

[41] Gerardo Reyes and Santiago Wills, "Fast and Furious Scandal: New Details Emerge on How the U.S. Government Armed Mexican Drug Cartels," ABC News, Univision, Sept. 30, 2012, http://abcnews.go.com/ABC_Univision/News/fast-furious-scandal-details-emerge-us-government-armed/story?id=17352694&singlePage=true#.UG2k3rR8uJU.

[42] Nick Miroff, "Mexican cartel violence prompts calls for bigger National Guard deployment along the border," *The Washington Post*, Jan. 4, 2011, www.washingtonpost.com/wp-dyn/content/article/2011/01/04/AR2011010404811_pf.html. CNN Poll: Support for border crackdown grows," CNN, May 26, 2010, http://politicalticker.blogs.cnn.com/2010/05/26/cnn-poll-support-for-border-crackdown-grows/.

[43] Quoted in Julia Preston and Samuel Dillon, *Opening Mexico: The Making of a Democracy* (2004), p. 424. Except where otherwise noted, this subsection is drawn from the book.

[44] "Our Man in Mexico," Jefferson Morley, undated (promotional website for book), www.ourmaninmexico.com/documents_mexican-pres.html; Jefferson Morley, "Litempo: The CIA's Eyes on Tlatelolco," National Security Archive, Oct. 18, 2006, www.gwu.edu/~nsarchiv/NSAEBB/NSAEBB204/index.htm.

[45] Carlos Salinas de Gortari, LinkedIn profile, undated, www.linkedin.com/pub/carlos-salinas-de-gortari/31/766/47.

[46] Shannon K. O'Neil, "Earthquake in Mexico: Why the Country Was Ready This Time," *The Atlantic*, March 21, 2012, www.theatlantic.com/international/archive/2012/03/earthquake-in-mexico-why-the-country-was-ready-this-time/254855.

[47] Quoted in Preston and Dillon, *op. cit.*, p. 173.

[48] Quoted in *ibid.*, p. 170.

[49] Except where otherwise noted, this subsection is drawn from Preston and Dillon, *op. cit.*

[50] Geoffrey Ramsey, "How Mexico's Zapatista guerrillas stayed clear of organized crime," *Latin America Monitor* (blog), *The Christian Science Monitor*, Jan. 10, 2012, www.csmonitor.com/World/Americas/Latin-America-Monitor/2012/0110/How-Mexico-s-Zapatista-guerrillas-stayed-clear-of-organized-crime; "Zapatismo," Mexico Solidarity Network, 2012, www.mexicosolidarity.org/programs/alternativeeconomy/zapatismo/en.

[51] Except where otherwise noted, this subsection is drawn from Preston and Dillon, *op. cit.*

[52] Julia Preston, "Raul Salinas's Sentence in Mexico Murder is Cut to 27 1/2 Years," *The New York Times*, July 17, 1999, www.nytimes.com/1999/07/17/world/raul-salinas-s-sentence-in-mexico-murder-is-cut-to-27-1-2-years.html?ref=raulsalinasdegortari.

[53] Malcolm Beith, *The Last Narco: Hunting El Chapo, the World's Most Wanted Drug Lord* (2010), pp. 1-19; Randal C. Archibold, "Mexico Announces Capture of Gulf Cartel's Top Leader," *The New York Times*, Sept. 13, 2012, www.nytimes.com/2012/09/14/world/americas/el-coss-head-of-gulf-cartel-captured-mexico-says.html.

[54] Quoted in Tim Weiner, "Mexico's New Anti-Drug Team Wins the Trust of U.S. Officials," *The New York Times*, July 18, 2001, p. A1, www.nytimes.com/2001/07/18/world/mexico-s-new-anti-drug-team-wins-the-trust-of-us-officials.html?pagewanted=all&src=pm.

[55] Quoted in Ginger Thompson, "Hundreds of Thousands in Mexico March Against Crime," *The New York Times*, June 28, 2004, p. A6, www.nytimes.com/2004/06/28/world/hundreds-of-thousands-in-mexico-march-against-crime.html?pagewanted=all&src=pm.

[56] Manuel Roig-Franzia, "Surge in Violence Shocks Even Weary Mexico," *The Washington Post*, Nov. 29, 2006, p. A18, www.washingtonpost.com/wp-dyn/content/article/2006/11/28/AR2006112801579.html; Manuel Roig-Franzia, "In Mexican Drug War, a Desperate Measure," *The Washington Post*, April 30, 2006, p. A12, www.washingtonpost.com/wp-dyn/content/article/2006/04/29/AR2006042901216.html.

[57] George W. Grayson, *Mexico: Narco-Violence and a Failed State?* (2010), pp. 97-98.

[58] "Familia Michoacana," *InSight Crime*, undated, www.insightcrime.org/groups-mexico/familia-michoacana/.

[59] Quoted in James C. McKinley Jr., "Mexico's New President Sends Thousands of Federal Officers to Fight Drug Cartels," *The New York Times*, Jan. 7, 2007, p. A6; Grayson, *op. cit.*, pp. 97-117, www.nytimes.com/2007/01/07/world/americas/07mexico.html.

[60] Quoted in Tracy Wilkinson, "Calderon visits Juarez," *Los Angeles Times*, Feb. 12, 2010, p. A10, http://articles.latimes.com/2010/feb/12/world/la-fg-mexico-juarez12-2010feb12.

[61] Alejandro Hope, "Más muertos, más números," *Plata o Plomo* (blog), Aug. 22, 2012, www.animalpolitico.com/blogueros-plata-o-plomo/2012/08/22/mas-muertos-mas-numeros.

[62] Sari Horwitz, "Inspector general's report on 'Fast and Furious' criticizes Justice Department, ATF," *The Washington Post*, Sept. 19, 2012, www.washingtonpost.com/world/national-security/justice-ig-critical-of-atf-in-gun-operation/2012/09/19/379daf18-0273-11e2-8102-ebee9c66e190_print.html.

[63] Reyes and Wills, *op. cit.*; Ken Ellingwood, "Four found guilty in massacre of 15 at teen party," *Los Angeles Times*, July 8, 2011, p. A3, http://articles.latimes.com/2011/jul/07/world/la-fg-mexico-massacre-20110708.

[64] Horwitz, *op. cit.*; "A Review of ATF's Operation Fast and Furious and Related Matters," Office of Inspector General, Justice Department, September 2012, pp. 1-2, 132-138, www.justice.gov/oig/reports/2012/s1209.pdf.

[65] Claudia Salazar and Érika Hernández, "Exige Cámara informe de Rápido y Furioso," *Reforma.com*, Oct. 4, 2012, www.reforma.com/congreso/articulo/674/1347537/default.asp.

[66] Anabel Barajas, "Va PGR por ligados a 'Rápido y Furioso,' " *Reforma.com* (Terra), Oct. 4, 2012, http://noticias.terra.com.mx/mexico/seguridad/pgr-va-por-ligados-a-operacion-rapido-y-furioso,e32bc44e9bb2a310VgnVCM4000009bcceb0aRCRD.html.

[67] Reyes and Wills, *op. cit.*

[68] *Ibid.*

[69] *Ibid.*; "Operacíon Rápido y Furioso, armando al enemigo, parte 2: La Masacre de Aliviane, Sept. 30, 2012, http://noticias.univision.com/aqui-y-ahora/videos/video/2012-09-30/operacion-rapido-furioso-aqui-ahora-parte-2-masacre-aliviane.

[70] Santiago Wills and Gerardo Reyes, "Univision News' Fast and Furious Investigation Prompts Congressional Inquiry," ABC, Univision, Oct. 4, 2012, http://abcnews.go.com/ABC_Univision/News/univision-news-fast-furious-investigation-prompts-congressional-inquiry/story?id=17397156#.UHQYQrR8uJU.

[71] *Ibid.*

[72] Eric Martin and Nacha Cattan, "Peña Nieto Ponders Easier Way to Open Mexican Oil Industry," Bloomberg, Oct. 4, 2012, www.bloomberg.com/news/2012-10-04/pena-nieto-ponders-easier-way-to-open-up-mexican-oil-industry.html; Ron Buchanan, "Mexico's Calderon backs successor's oil sector plans," *Platts Oilgram News*, July 17, 2012.

[73] *Ibid.*; Whitney Eulich and Sara Miller Llana, "Brazil, Venezuela, and Mexico: three ways to nationalize oil," *The Christian Science Monitor*, May 12, 2012, www.csmonitor.com/layout/set/print/World/Americas/2012/0512/Brazil-Venezuela-and-Mexico-three-ways-to-nationalize-oil. Carlos Manuel Rodriguez and Adrian Lopez Caraveo, "Mexico Oil Opening First Time Since 1938 Shows Revival: Energy," Bloomberg, April 26, 2012, www.bloomberg.com/news/2012-04-25/mexico-oil-opening-first-time-since-1938-shows-revival-energy.html.

[74] Enrique Peña Nieto, "México, potencia energética," transitition website, March 18, 2012, www.enriquepenanieto.com/dia-a-dia/entrada/mexico-potencia-energetica.

[75] Quoted in Carlos M. Rodriguez and Adriana Lopez Caraveo, "Mexico Oil Opening First Time Since 1938 Shows Revival: Energy," Bloomberg, April 25, 2012, www.bloomberg.com/news/2012-04-25/mexico-oil-opening-first-time-since-1938-shows-revival-energy.html.

[76] Quoted in *ibid.*

[77] Quoted in *ibid.*

[78] Quoted in "Peña Nieto Ponders. . . .," *op. cit.*

[79] Tracy Wilkinson, "Mexico workers protest labor overhaul proposal," *Los Angeles Times*, Sept. 27, 2012, p. A11; "Mexico's Calderon backs. . . .," *op. cit.*

[80] "Mexico, potencia energética," *op. cit.*

[81] Oscar Villalba, "Mexico: 132 inmates escape from border prison," The Associated Press, Sept. 18, 2012; Alfredo Corchado, "Violence flares during political limbo," *Dallas Morning News*, Sept. 23, 2012, p A1; "Mexican probe: Cop helped kill governor's nephew," The Associated Press, Oct. 8, 2012, http://abclocal.go.com/kfsn/story?section=news/national_world&id=8814537.

[82] Marcos Pablo Moloeznik, *et al.*, "A Comprehensive Assessment of the Municipal Police of Ciudad Juárez," Justice in Mexico Project, 2011, p. 37, http://justiceinmexico.files.wordpress.com/2011/09/jb-cj_report_eng.pdf.

[83] *Ibid.*; Justice Barometer Survey: Guadalajara Metropolitan Zone," 2009, http://justiceinmexico.files.wordpress.com/2011/03/executive-summary.pdf.

[84] "Judicial and Police Reforms in Mexico," *op. cit.*, p. 9.

[85] "Mexico's Next Sexenio . . .," *op. cit.*

FOR MORE INFORMATION

Border Fact Check, Washington Office on Latin America, 1666 Connecticut Ave., N.W., Suite 400, Washington, DC 20009; 202-797-2171; www.borderfactcheck.com. Blog on border issues by a think tank and advocacy organization focusing on social justice and human rights in Mexico and the rest of Latin America.

Frontera List, http://fronteralist.org. Blog maintained by a New Mexico State University research librarian who has a special interest in drug-war developments.

InSight Crime, 4545 42nd St., N.W., Suite 308, Washington DC 20016; www.insightcrime.org. Nonprofit think tank that analyzes organized crime trends in Mexico and five other Latin American countries.

Mexico Institute, Woodrow Wilson Center for International Scholars, Ronald Reagan Building and International Trade Center, One Woodrow Wilson Plaza, 1300 Pennsylvania Ave., N.W., Washington, DC 20004; 202-691-4000; www.wilsoncenter.org/program/mexico-institute. Think tank that sponsors research on trade, infrastructure development, security and politics.

Plato o Plomo, Alejandro Hope, www.animalpolitico.com/blogueros-plata-o-plomo. Spanish-language blog by a leading researcher on organized crime in Mexico.

Inter-American Dialogue, 1211 Connecticut Ave., N.W., Washington, DC 20036; 202-822-9002; www.thedialogue.org/page.cfm?pageID=69. Think tank whose work on Mexico includes, articles, studies and videos of panel discussions, with a special focus on political trends.

Trans-Border Institute, University of San Diego, Joan B. Kroc School of Peace Studies, 5998 Alcala Park, San Diego, CA 92110; 619-260-4600; www.sandiego.edu/peacestudies/tbi. Publishes an annual analysis of drug-war violence trends, as well as research on immigration issues and other topics.

Bibliography

Selected Sources

Books

Beith, Malcolm, *The Last Narco: Hunting El Chapo, the World's Most Wanted Drug Lord*, Penguin, 2010.
A journalist formerly based in Mexico City describes the dramatic search for the head of the Sinaloa cartel.

Grayson, George W., *Mexico: Narco-Violence and a Failed State?*, Transaction, 2011.
A political scientist at the College of William and Mary examines the drug war and its links to Mexican politics.

Preston, Julia, and Samuel Dillon, *Opening Mexico: The Making of a Democracy*, Farrar, Straus and Giroux, 2004.
Two longtime *New York Times* correspondents chronicle Mexico's recent political transformation, including the coming to light of major drug-related corruption.

Villalon, Oscar, ed., *Blood Calls to Blood: Mexican Writers on the Drug War*, ZYZZYVA/Byliner, 2012.
Some of Mexico's leading young authors fill this electronic book with vivid, up-close reporting on the drug war.

Articles

Eulich, Whitney, and Sara Miller Llana, "Brazil, Venezuela, and Mexico: three ways to nationalize oil," *The Christian Science Monitor*, May 12, 2012, www.csmonitor.com/World/Americas/2012/0512/Brazil-Venezuela-and-Mexico-three-ways-to-nationalize-oil.
Reporters examine the regional context in which Mexico might loosen restrictions on foreign participation in its state-owned oil monopoly.

Hope, Alejandro, "Is a Wave of Violence Reversing Progress in Mexico?," *InSight Crime*, Aug. 15, 2012, www.insightcrime.org/news-analysis/alejandro-hope-mexico-violence-rising.
A recent uptick in violence doesn't necessarily upset what has been a slow downward trend, argues a leading Mexican security analyst.

Johnson, Tim, "Mexico's new leader, Enrique Peña Nieto, will need rivals' help to enact his agenda," McClatchy Newspapers, July 2, 2012, www.mcclatchydc.com/2012/07/02/154773/mexicos-new-leader-enrique-pena.html.
Lacking a clear congressional majority, Peña Nieto will forge compromises with the right or the left, depending on the issue, a Mexico-based correspondent reports.

Miroff, Nick, and William Booth, "Middle-class Mexicans snap up more products 'Made in USA,' " *The Washington Post*, Sept. 9, 2012, www.washingtonpost.com/world/the_americas/middle-class-mexicans-snap-up-more-products-made-in-usa/2012/09/09/27c9d1b4-f212-11e1-892d-bc92fee603a7_story.html.
The penetration of major U.S. chains, including Costco and Wal-Mart, has changed Mexican buying habits.

Martin, Eric, and Nacha Cattan, "Peña Nieto Ponders Easier Way to Open Mexican Oil Industry," Bloomberg, Oct. 4, 2012, www.bloomberg.com/news/2012-10-04/pena-nieto-ponders-easier-way-to-open-up-mexican-oil-industry.html.
Mexico's incoming president is looking for alternatives to a constitutional amendment to relax the government oil monopoly, a top adviser says.

Molloy, Molly, "Mexican Death Toll in Drug War Likely Higher Than Reported," *Phoenix New Times*, July 26, 2012, www.phoenixnewtimes.com/2012-07-26/news/mexico-s-unknown-drug-war-death-toll.
An influential researcher argues that the effects of the violence are far worse than most sources admit.

Padgett, Tim, "Why I Protest: Javier Sicilia of Mexico," *Time*, Dec. 14, 2011, www.time.com/time/specials/packages/article/0,28804,2101745_2102138_2102238,00.html.
Mexico's leading anti-drug war campaigner tells how he became an activist following his son's murder.

Robbins, Ted, "U.S. Grows an Industrial Complex Along the Border," NPR, Sept. 12, 2012, www.npr.org/2012/09/12/160758471/u-s-grows-an-industrial-complex-along-the-border.
A veteran border-country journalist reports on the massive expansion of border reinforcements.

Reports and Studies

Beittel, June S., "Mexico's Drug Trafficking Organizations: Source and Scope of the Rising Violence," Congressional Research Service, Aug. 3, 2012, www.fas.org/sgp/crs/row/R41576.pdf.
Congress' nonpartisan research agency provides a comprehensive status update on the drug war.

Molzahn, Cory, Viridiana Ríos and David A. Shirk, "Drug Violence in Mexico: Data and Analysis Through 2011," Trans-Border Institute, University of San Diego, March 2012, http://justiceinmexico.files.wordpress.com/2012/03/2012-tbi-drugviolence.pdf.
Specialists at a leading think tank offer a detailed examination of the war's expansion and toll.

Seelke, Clare Ribando, "Mexico: Issues for Congress," Congressional Research Service, Sept. 24, 2012, www.fas.org/sgp/crs/row/RL32724.pdf.
Congressional researchers analyze the major Mexico-related questions facing Congress.

The Next Step:

Additional Articles from Current Periodicals

Border Control

Coleman, Michael, "N.M. Dems Reject Border Changes," *Albuquerque* (N.M.) *Journal*, June 22, 2012, p. C1, www.abqjournal.com/main/2012/06/22/news/nm-dems-reject-border-changes.html.
New Mexico's congressional delegation is nearly unanimous in its opposition to a bill that would allow Border Patrol agents to monitor vast wilderness areas in vehicles because of potential harm to the environment.

Dibble, Sandra, "U.S., Mexico Program to Fly Deportees to Hometowns," *San Diego Union-Tribune*, Feb. 29, 2012, p. A4, www.utsandiego.com/news/2012/feb/29/tp-us-mexico-program-to-fly-deportees-to-hometowns/?print&page=all.
The U.S. and Mexican governments are exploring a new program that flies deportees to their hometowns to avoid overcrowding in Mexican border communities.

Ellingwood, Ken, "No Work, No Reason to Go North," *Los Angeles Times*, Nov. 15, 2011, p. A3, articles.latimes.com/2011/nov/15/world/la-fg-mexico-migration-20111115.
Mexican census statistics show that fewer people are going to the United States because of a lack of job prospects, while many more are returning home.

Jacobson, Louis, "Barack Obama Touts High Border Agents," *Tampa Bay* (Fla.) *Times*, Oct. 17, 2012, www.politifact.com/truth-o-meter/statements/2012/oct/17/barack-obama/barack-obama-touts-record-high-border-agents-lowes/.
President Obama says his administration has put more agents on the U.S.-Mexico border than at "any time in history," leading to the lowest level of illegal immigration from Mexico in 40 years.

Marosi, Richard, and Richard Fausset, "Border Patrol Assailed for Teen's Fatal Shooting," *Los Angeles Times*, Oct. 13, 2012, p. A16, articles.latimes.com/2012/oct/13/nation/la-na-border-shooting-20121013.
The fatal shooting of a Mexican teenager suspected of throwing rocks at U.S. Border Patrol agents has prompted condemnation from Mexican officials and human rights groups.

Miroff, Nick, "Does the 'American Great Wall' Need to Be Longer?" *The Washington Post*, Jan. 1, 2012, p. A10.
Republican politicians have proposed extending the barricade along the entire length of the U.S.-Mexico border.

Powell, Stewart M., "Border Patrol Steps Up Penalties," *Houston Chronicle*, Jan. 18, 2012, p. A1, www.chron.com/news/houston-texas/article/Border-Patrol-steps-up-punishment-for-illegal-2590036.php.
The U.S. Border Patrol is planning to impose harsher penalties on illegal immigrants from Mexico to replace a revolving-door approach that amounts to little more than catch-and-release.

Drug War

"Kingpin Bowling," *The Economist*, Oct. 20, 2012, p. 34, www.economist.com/news/americas/21564897-most-wanted-men-mexico-are-tumbling-will-crime-follow-suit.
The capture of Mexican drug kingpins has often led to violent feuds among their deputies.

Booth, William, and Nick Miroff, "Closer Ties to U.S. on Horizon," *The Washington Post*, July 6, 2012, p. A8.
Mexican President-elect Enrique Peña Nieto says he wants to expand his country's anti-drug partnership with the United States but doesn't want American agents in Mexico.

Corchado, Alfredo, "Probe Sought on U.S. Role in Drug War," *Dallas Morning News*, Dec. 7, 2011, p. A17.
The Mexican Senate has asked the government to investigate the increasing role of U.S. narcotics agencies in Mexico.

Dibble, Sandra, "Drug-Linked Violence Falls Along the Border," *San Diego Union-Tribune*, March 3, 2012, p. A1, www.utsandiego.com/news/2012/mar/03/tp-usd-report-drug-linked-violence-falls-along/?print&page=all.
Mexico's northern border saw a reduction in drug-related violence in 2011, while violence increased in the rest of the country.

Escalona, Alejandro, "The War on Drugs Isn't Working," *Chicago Sun-Times*, Sept. 6, 2012, p. 26, www.suntimes.com/news/escalona/14959165-452/the-war-on-drugs-isnt-working.html.
The United States must stop the flow of assault weapons into Mexico and go after banks that launder drug money, says a columnist.

Goldberg, Jamie, "Mexican Left in Dark on Fast and Furious, Ambassador Says," *Los Angeles Times*, June 1, 2012, articles.latimes.com/2012/jun/01/nation/la-na-fast-furious-20120601.
Mexico's ambassador to the United States says the "Fast and Furious" gun-tracking operation failed because of a lack of understanding of how criminal groups operate.

Licon, Adriana Gomez, "Mexican Judges Involved in Drug Cases Suspended," The Associated Press, June 3, 2012, www.huffingtonpost.com/2012/06/02/mexico-drug-cases-judges-_n_1565262.html.
Mexican court authorities have suspended two federal judges who presided over high-profile drug cases because of questionable decisions in prior ones.

Martinez, Guillermo, "Mexican President's Stance on Drug War May Affect U.S.," *Sun-Sentinel* (Fla.), July 5, 2012, p. A11, articles.sun-sentinel.com/2012-07-05/news/fl-gmcol-mexico-drug-war-martinez-0705-20120705_1_cartels-mexican-election-mexico-elections.

U.S. politicians are throwing their support behind Mexican President Felipe Calderón in his country's drug war to prevent conflict from crossing into the United States.

Porter, Eduardo, "Numbers Tell of Failure in Drug War," *The New York Times*, July 4, 2012, p. B1, www.nytimes.com/2012/07/04/business/in-rethinking-the-war-on-drugs-start-with-the-numbers.html?pagewanted=all.

Mexico's drug trade has pushed the U.S. street price of cocaine to its lowest level in 30 years.

Prada, Juan Blanco, "Latin America Breaking Ranks on Drug War," *Philadelphia Inquirer*, April 14, 2012, articles.philly.com/2012-04-14/news/31342327_1_drug-war-cartels-unwinnable-war.

Several Latin American nations have been engulfed in drug violence since President Richard M. Nixon declared a war on drugs in the 1970s, says a columnist.

Romo, Rene, "Poet, Tour Seek Peace in Mexico," *Albuquerque* (N.M.) *Journal*, Aug. 18, 2012, p. C1, www.abqjournal.com/main/2012/08/18/news/poet-tour-seek-peace-in-mexico.html.

Mexican poet Javier Sicilia has emerged as a powerful critic of the war on drugs since his son died as a bystander during a fight between drug cartels.

Weiner, Robert, and George Clingan, "U.S. Must Boost Drug-War Aid to Stop the Cartels," *Arizona Republic*, July 3, 2012, p. B9, www.azcentral.com/arizonarepublic/opinions/articles/2012/06/28/20120628weiner-clingan-us-must-boost-drug-war-aid-stop-cartels.html.

The United States should double its anti-drug aid to Mexico to prevent cartels from winning the drug war, says a former spokesman for the White House Office of National Drug Policy.

Wilkinson, Tracy, and Ken Ellingwood, "Mexico Lacks a Plan to End Its Drug War," *Los Angeles Times*, June 24, 2012, p. A1, articles.latimes.com/2012/jun/24/world/la-fg-mexico-election-security-20120624.

Critics say Mexico's government has not presented any practical strategies to end the violent drug war.

NAFTA

Blodgett, Bonnie, "What Global Capitalists Didn't Foresee," *Star Tribune* (Minnesota), Sept. 2, 2012, p. OP3, www.startribune.com/opinion/commentaries/168200756.html?refer=y.

The North American Free Trade Agreement lowered U.S.-Mexico trade barriers but has also been responsible for costing American jobs, says a columnist.

Hendricks, David, "Looking Ahead After 20 Years of NAFTA," *San Antonio Express-News*, May 9, 2012, p. C1, www.mysanantonio.com/business/business_columnists/david_hendricks/article/Looking-ahead-after-20-years-of-NAFTA-3543595.php.

Trade across North America has more than tripled since NAFTA went into effect in January 1994.

Miroff, Nick, and William Booth, "Mexicans Snap Up 'Made in U.S.A.,' " *The Washington Post*, Sept. 10, 2012, p. A8, www.washingtonpost.com/world/the_americas/middle-class-mexicans-snap-up-more-products-made-in-usa/2012/09/09/27c9d1b4-f212-11e1-892d-bc92fee603a7_story.html.

Most Mexican politicians are in favor of expanding NAFTA because of the trade surplus it has created with the United States.

Pacheco, Jerry, "NAFTA Lifts Mexico, But Problems Linger," *Albuquerque* (N.M.) *Journal*, March 5, 2012, p. 7, www.abqjournal.com/main/2012/03/04/biz/outlook/nafta-lifts-mexico-but-problems-linger.html.

The success of NAFTA is putting pressure on Mexico's educational institutions to increase the job skills of its workforce.

Pastor, Robert A., "We're Neglecting Our North American Neighbors," *The Miami Herald*, Nov. 14, 2011.

President Obama should focus on building more trade partnerships with Mexico and Canada because of the benefits provided by NAFTA, says a professor of international relations at American University.

Taylor, Guy, "NAFTA Key to Economic, Social Growth in Mexico," *The Washington Times*, May 15, 2012, p. A8, www.washingtontimes.com/news/2012/may/14/nafta-key-to-economic-social-growth-in-mexico/?page=all.

NAFTA has been the key driver of Mexico's economic and social transformation over the past two decades, say analysts from the Woodrow Wilson International Center for Scholars.

Citing *CQ Researcher*

Sample formats for citing these reports in a bibliography include the ones listed below. Preferred styles and formats vary, so please check with your instructor or professor.

MLA STYLE

Jost, Kenneth. "Remembering 9/11," CQ Researcher 2 Sept. 2011: 701-732.

APA STYLE

Jost, K. (2011, September 2). Remembering 9/11. *CQ Researcher, 9*, 701-732.

CHICAGO STYLE

Jost, Kenneth. "Remembering 9/11." *CQ Researcher*, September 2, 2011, 701-732.

In-depth Reports on Issues in the News

Are you writing a paper?

Need backup for a debate?

Want to become an expert on an issue?

For more than 80 years, students have turned to *CQ Researcher* for in-depth reporting on issues in the news. Reports on a full range of political and social issues are now available. Following is a selection of recent reports:

Civil Liberties
Solitary Confinement, 9/12
Re-examining the Constitution, 9/12
Voter Rights, 5/12
Remembering 9/11, 9/11
Government Secrecy, 2/11

Crime/Law
Supreme Court Controversies, 9/12
Debt Collectors, 7/12
Criminal Records, 4/12
Police Misconduct, 4/12
Immigration Conflict, 3/12

Education
Arts Education, 3/12
Youth Volunteerism, 1/12
Digital Education, 12/11
Student Debt, 10/11

Environment/Society
Understanding Mormonism, 10/12
Genetically Modified Food, 8/12
Whale Hunting, 6/12
U.S. Oil Dependence, 6/12
Gambling in America, 6/12
Sexual Harassment, 4/12

Health/Safety
New Health Care Law, 9/12
Farm Policy, 8/12
Treating ADHD, 8/12
Alcohol Abuse, 6/12

Politics/Economy
Social Media and Politics, 10/12
Euro Crisis, 10/12
Privatizing the Military, 7/12
U.S.-Europe Relations, 3/12
Attracting Jobs, 3/12
Presidential Election, 2/12

Upcoming Reports

Wildfires, 11/2/12 | Indecency on Television, 11/9/12 | U.S. Demographics, 11/16/12

ACCESS

CQ Researcher is available in print and online. For access, visit your library or www.cqresearcher.com.

STAY CURRENT

For notice of upcoming *CQ Researcher* reports or to learn more about *CQ Researcher* products, subscribe to the free e-mail newsletters, *CQ Researcher Alert!* and *CQ Researcher News*: http://cqpress.com/newsletters.

PURCHASE

To purchase a *CQ Researcher* report in print or electronic format (PDF), visit www.cqpress.com or call 866-427-7737. Single reports start at $15. Bulk purchase discounts and electronic-rights licensing are also available.

SUBSCRIBE

Annual full-service *CQ Researcher* subscriptions—including 44 reports a year, monthly index updates, and a bound volume—start at $1,054. Add $25 for domestic postage.

CQ Researcher Online offers a backfile from 1991 and a number of tools to simplify research. For pricing information, call 800-834-9020, or e-mail librarymarketing@cqpress.com.

CQ Researcher

Published by CQ Press, an Imprint of SAGE Publications, Inc.

www.cqresearcher.com

Managing Wildfires

Can they be controlled in a warming world?

Record-setting heat and intense drought have made 2012 one of the worst wildfire seasons in a decade of intense fires. Climate change, residential development in fire-prone rural areas and the impact of past firefighting policies have combined to put many areas of the United States at risk, especially in the West. Federal agencies spend more than $2.5 billion yearly to control wildfires, and the cost is rising. Scientists widely agree that fire plays an important ecological role, and federal land managers are working to reintroduce fire in controlled settings to regenerate forests and reduce combustible brush that can cause wildfires to burn out of control. Public officials are under heavy pressure to fight fires that threaten homes, but few are willing to make homeowners bear more of the costs to protect their property. Using fire-resistant building materials and clearing brush around homes can reduce fire risks. Some advocates want to go further and bar new development in fire-prone areas.

Firefighters battle a brushfire in the Meadowlands in Carlstadt, N.J., on April 11, 2012. Drought, low humidity and strong winds were blamed for a rash of wildfires throughout the country this year.

INSIDE THIS REPORT

The Issues 943
Background 949
Chronology 951
Current Situation 954
At Issue....................957
Outlook....................958
Bibliography....................962
The Next Step 963

CQ Researcher • Nov. 2, 2012 • www.cqresearcher.com
Volume 22, Number 39 • Pages 941-964

CQ PRESS

Los Angeles | London | New Delhi
Singapore | Washington DC

Recipient of Society of Professional Journalists Award for Excellence ◆ American Bar Association Silver Gavel Award

MANAGING WILDFIRES

THE ISSUES

943 • Should some wildfires be allowed to burn?
• Should development be limited in fire-prone areas?
• Can logging reduce fire hazards?

BACKGROUND

949 **Fire on the Frontier**
As colonists moved West, they altered fire patterns.

949 **Suppressing Fire**
President Theodore Roosevelt established the U.S. Forest Service in 1905.

950 **New Attitudes**
In the 1960s scientists began to argue that fire can be beneficial.

953 **Fire in the Exurbs**
A 2001 study found severe fire risks where development adjoins wildland.

CURRENT SITUATION

954 **Budget Shortfall**
Intense wildfires have drained fire-fighting budgets.

955 **Hotter and Drier**
Scientists worry that climate change will intensify fire risks.

956 **Using Fire**
The Nature Conservancy advocates controlled burning for land restoration.

OUTLOOK

958 **"Common Vision"**
"We should be talking about land-use planning."

Cover: Getty Images/Michael Bocchieri

SIDEBARS AND GRAPHICS

944 **Wildfire Funding Down from Peak**
Federal wildfire appropriations fell sharply beginning in 2008.

945 **West Is Wildfire Hotspot**
More than 5 million acres in Texas, New Mexico and Arizona burned in 2011.

947 **Wildfires' Deadly Toll**
More than 300 firefighters and other personnel died battling wildfires from 1990 to 2007.

948 **Wildfires Consume More Acreage**
Fires burned an average of 6.8 million acres annually since 2000.

951 **Chronology**
Key events since the 1860s.

952 **Wildfires Threaten Air, Water Quality**
Smoke and erosion lead to safety concerns.

954 **Wildfires Offer Both Risks and Rewards**
"A lot of fires do good ecological work."

957 **At Issue**
Should Congress allow more logging to reduce wildfire threats?

FOR FURTHER RESEARCH

961 **For More Information**
Organizations to contact.

962 **Bibliography**
Selected sources used.

963 **The Next Step**
Additional articles.

963 **Citing *CQ Researcher***
Sample bibliography formats.

CQ Researcher

Nov. 2, 2012
Volume 22, Number 39

MANAGING EDITOR: Thomas J. Billitteri
tjb@cqpress.com

ASSISTANT MANAGING EDITOR: Kathy Koch
kkoch@cqpress.com

SENIOR CONTRIBUTING EDITOR:
Thomas J. Colin
tcolin@cqpress.com

ASSOCIATE EDITOR: Kenneth Jost

STAFF WRITER: Marcia Clemmitt

CONTRIBUTING WRITERS: Peter Katel, Barbara Mantel, Tom Price, Jennifer Weeks

SENIOR PROJECT EDITOR: Olu B. Davis

ASSISTANT EDITOR: Darrell Dela Rosa

FACT CHECKER: Michelle Harris

Los Angeles | London | New Delhi
Singapore | Washington DC

An Imprint of SAGE Publications, Inc.

VICE PRESIDENT AND EDITORIAL DIRECTOR, HIGHER EDUCATION GROUP:
Michele Sordi

DIRECTOR, ONLINE PUBLISHING:
Todd Baldwin

CQ Researcher (ISSN 1056-2036) is printed on acid-free paper. Published weekly, except: (March wk. 5) (May wk. 4) (July wk. 1) (Aug. wks. 3, 4) (Nov. wk. 4) and (Dec. wks. 3, 4). Published by SAGE Publications, Inc., 2455 Teller Rd., Thousand Oaks, CA 91320. Annual full-service subscriptions start at $1,054. For pricing, call 1-800-834-9020. To purchase a *CQ Researcher* report in print or electronic format (PDF), visit www.cqpress.com or call 866-427-7737. Single reports start at $15. Bulk purchase discounts and electronic-rights licensing are also available. Periodicals postage paid at Thousand Oaks, California, and at additional mailing offices. POSTMASTER: Send address changes to *CQ Researcher*, 2300 N St., N.W., Suite 800, Washington, DC 20037.

Managing Wildfires

BY JENNIFER WEEKS

THE ISSUES

As temperatures cool and trees change colors in autumn, millions of Americans head outdoors to hike and camp or go fishing, hunting or bird-watching. But fall is less carefree in much of the United States this year. Across Washington state, for example, after an August without measurable rainfall and the third-driest September on record, the National Weather Service warned that conditions were ideal for wildfires.

"We have not seen wildfire conditions this bad in October in a lifetime," said Peter Goldmark, Washington's commissioner of public lands. [1]

With four large, uncontained wildfires burning across the state, Washington's Department of Natural Resources issued rules in early October to prevent more fires on state-managed lands: no campfires, no smoking outside of an enclosed vehicle, no target shooting except on established ranges, no chainsaw use and no operating vehicles off-road, where heat from exhaust systems could ignite dry grass. [2]

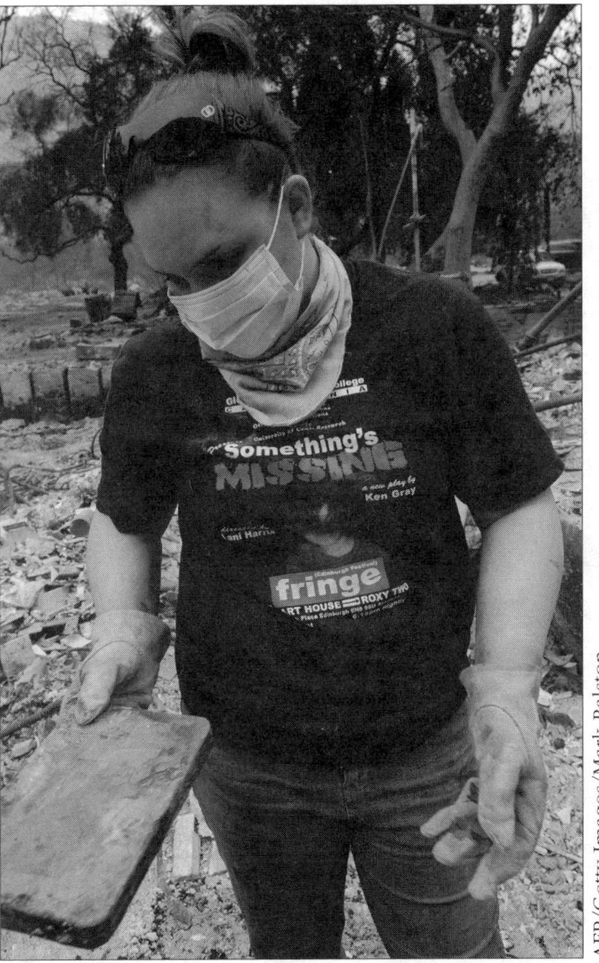

AFP/Getty Images/Mark Ralston

Tiffany Brain salvages items from her uncle's cabin, destroyed in the Station Fire in Angeles National Forest near Los Angeles on Sept. 2, 2009. The fire, started by an arsonist, burned more than 160,000 acres and claimed the lives of two firefighters. Experts say wildfires pose a growing threat to lives, property and natural resources throughout the United States because of development encroaching on wild areas and changing climate conditions.

As of late October, wildfires had burned nearly 9 million acres across the United States in 2012 — the third highest total in a decade of large and intense fires. (*See graph, p. 948.*) In the 1960s about 4.5 million acres on average burned each year; from 2002 through 2011 the yearly average was 7 million acres. [3]

"When I first started fighting fires in California in 1970, we wouldn't get too gunned up until nearly the 4th of July, and we'd go through Thanksgiving," says Tom Harbour, director of fire and aviation management for the U.S. Forest Service. "Today the wildland fire season starts in the Southeast early in the spring and may last through New Year's Day or longer in Southern California."

The Forest Service, which is part of the U.S. Department of Agriculture, manages fire on 193 million acres of national forests and grasslands. It shares this mission with other agencies that manage public lands: the National Park Service, Bureau of Land Management, Bureau of Indian Affairs and the U.S. Fish and Wildlife Service, plus state forestry managers. [4] In recent years the Forest Service has received about 70 percent of federal funding for wildfire control. (*See graph, p. 944.*) [5]

Experts say wildfires pose a growing threat to lives, property and natural resources in many parts of the United States, due to several factors:

- Climate change is making many parts of the nation hotter and drier.
- For most of the past century federal policy called for fighting every wildfire on public lands, instead of letting smaller and more isolated outbreaks burn naturally. This strategy allowed brush and dense stands of trees to accumulate, creating huge potential fuel stocks.
- Americans are moving from cities into fire-prone rural areas, where they expect firefighters to protect their homes and property from nearby wildfires.

Impacts are most severe in Western states, which have large expanses of public wildlands. But wildfires also occur regularly in the Plains and Southeast. (*See chart, p. 945.*) "Fire was a very well known historic visitor in all of our trusts and territories. We think about it the most in the West, but it was very common in the East at the time of early settlement," says Harbour.

Several multiyear droughts have worsened fire conditions in the West and central Plains states over the past decade, extending fire seasons and increasing supplies of dry fuel. With more combustible material on the ground,

Wildfire Funding Down from Peak

U.S. Forest Service and Interior Department wildfire appropriations, which fluctuate year to year depending largely on the severity of the preceding fire season, peaked in 2008 before falling sharply as congressional Republicans pushed for cuts in federal spending. Wildfire funding trended upward over the past decade following efforts by President Bill Clinton in 2000 to increase funding.

Wildland Fire Management Appropriations, 1994-2012

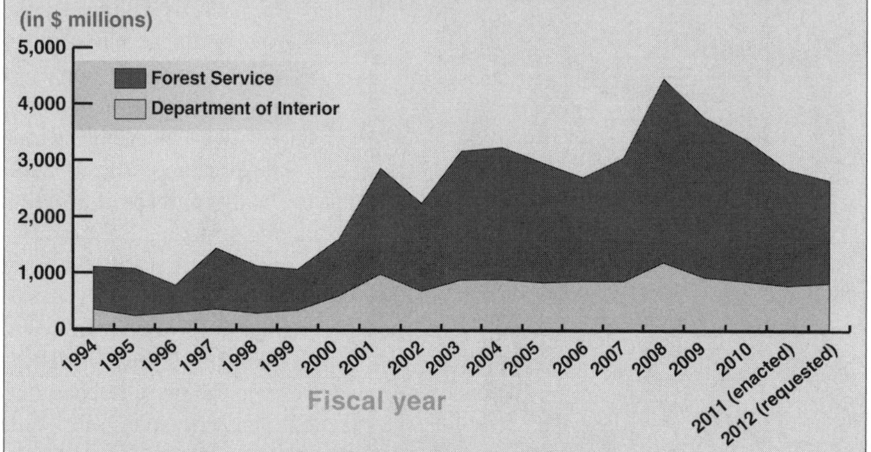

(in $ millions)
5,000
4,000
3,000
2,000
1,000
0
Forest Service
Department of Interior
1994 1995 1996 1997 1998 1999 2000 2001 2002 2003 2004 2005 2006 2007 2008 2009 2010 2011 (enacted) 2012 (requested)
Fiscal year

Source: Ross W. Gorte, "Federal Funding for Wildlife Control and Management," Congressional Research Service, July 2011, p. 4, www.fas.org/sgp/crs/misc/RL33990.pdf

and more people living near wild areas, the cost of suppressing wildfires has risen from $1.1 billion in 1994 to $2.7 billion in 2011.* And since agencies cannot forecast precisely how much money they will need to fight fires in an upcoming year, federal land managers must shift funds from other accounts and seek reimbursement from Congress during intense fires seasons.

"There's a real funding crisis. Firefighting is eating up a bigger and bigger share of the Forest Service's total budget," says Stephen Pyne, a professor of life sciences at Arizona State University and an expert on the history of fire. "You have to respond to fires, but nobody wants to pay for them. It's similar to health care: We pay obscene amounts of money for emergency services, but we won't fix the system."

Led by the National Park Service, federal land agencies have been working since the 1970s to restore fire gradually to wild lands, both through planned burns and by letting some wildfires burn themselves out under careful supervision. Scientists and land managers say fire can produce many benefits, such as thinning dense undergrowth and making room for native plant species. "It's the best way to make forests more resilient," says Scott Stephens, an associate professor of fire sciences at the University of California at Berkeley.

Others, including timber industry leaders and some politicians from rural areas, argue that the way to reduce fire risks is to allow more logging and grazing on overgrown public lands — an approach sometimes referred to as "active management." In their view, laws such as the Endangered Species Act that limit logging and grazing block land managers from taking steps that would generate revenues and make adjoining communities safer.

"Fire behavior is affected by weather, terrain and fuels. Fuels are the only piece of that equation that humans can modify in a short time through active management," Gov. C. L. "Butch" Otter, R-Idaho, wrote in an October newspaper column, noting that 1.7 million acres had burned in his state in 2012, of which 93 percent was public land. "Removing fuel by logging or grazing isn't the answer for every acre of public land, but it should certainly be considered where it's needed," Otter asserted. [6]

But environmentalists strongly oppose this approach and say today's fire hazards are partly due to decades of fire suppression — not allowing wildfires to burn. "Fire suppression has removed 'good' fire that naturally thinned forests," says Andy Stahl, executive director of Forest Service Employees for Environmental Ethics (FSEEE), a watchdog group that promotes land stewardship in the national forest system.

"From an ecological perspective, we have too little fire on the landscape. The acres burning today are a tenth of what burned before fire suppression started," Stahl contends. Moreover, he argues, many large wildfires occur on non-federal lands not subject to federal environmental laws. (*See "At Issue," p. 957.*)

Federal, state, local and tribal governments and nongovernmental organizations are working together to develop a National Cohesive Wildland Fire Management Strategy that will set priorities for managing wildfire threats and costs. Pyne calls the initiative, which Congress mandated in 2009 after years of recommendations from the U.S. Government Accountability Office, an attempt to create a "fire constitution."

* The figures are not adjusted for inflation.

"We have to redefine the political structure for making these decisions," he says.

As federal land agencies, Congress and advocacy groups debate how to manage wildfire risks, here are some issues they are considering:

Should some wildfires be allowed to burn?

From the early 1900s through the 1960s, federal land managers sought to suppress wildfires on public lands as soon as the fires were detected. Today the policy is different. Agencies allow some wildfires to burn, or they control them in areas near homes and people but let them progress naturally in remoter zones.

"Fire protection requires an appropriate response to wildfire — not only suppression, but also, where safe and beneficial, the use of fire for management purposes," Forest Service chief Tom Tidwell said in September. [7]

Yet, the Forest Service had officially suspended that policy four months earlier for the 2012 fire season, based on forecasts that the costs of fighting full-scale wildfires during this year's intense drought could exceed the agency's budget. Wildfires could be allowed to burn only with approval at a senior level, Deputy Chief James E. Hubbard instructed regional foresters and directors on May 25. "I acknowledge that this is not a desirable approach in the long run," he added. [8]

Many observers assumed that the order sought to control costs by stamping out small burns before they could explode into mega-fires. But Tidwell asserted that the order was issued because of unusually high fire risks. "It's not a change of policy. It's not about saving money. It's about recognizing the conditions we have this year," Tidwell said in August. [9]

Stahl of Forest Service Employees for Environmental Ethics (FSEEE) suggests another motive. "It may be a political strategy, so that if suburbs are overrun by fire, the administration can argue that it didn't happen because of a fire that was allowed to burn," he says. FSEEE has criticized the Forest Service for putting too much emphasis on firefighting at the expense of other missions. The group also has successfully sued the agency to force it to assess environmental impacts of firefighting tactics, such as dumping flame retardant from airplanes.

"When the Forest Service attacks a fire in a wilderness area with bulldozers, there's no environmental review or any post hoc assessment of whether it was worth it. Those impacts are just seen as a casualty of the campaign," Stahl says.

Many scientists are studying the ecology of various wildland areas, particularly in Western states, seeking to measure what role fire played in those zones before government agencies began suppressing wildfires. By analyzing multiple sources — including historical records, fire scarring on older trees and charcoal deposits in soil — researchers can draw conclusions about how often and how intensely different areas burned.

Stephens at the University of California-Berkeley, for example, has analyzed Forest Service records from 1911 that describe areas in the Sierra Nevada Mountains in and around what is now Yosemite National Park. "These forests used to burn about every seven to 15 years, but now they haven't burned for something like a century," he says.

West Is Wildfire Hotspot

Wildfires burned more than 5 million acres in Texas, New Mexico and Arizona combined in 2011. Wildfires occur more frequently in the West but are not uncommon in the Great Plains and Southeast.

Most Acres Burned by Wildfires by State, 2011

Texas	2,722,623
New Mexico	1,286,487
Arizona	1,016,428
Nevada	424,170
Idaho	384,103
Florida	299,991
Oklahoma	293,381
Alaska	293,018
Oregon	285,712
Montana	168,010
Colorado	161,167
Georgia	149,222
Wyoming	135,878
Minnesota	135,650
California	126,854
North Carolina	119,482
Kansas	111,128

Source: "National Report of Wildland Fires and Acres Burned by State," National Interagency Fire Center, 2011, www.predictiveservices.nifc.gov/intelligence/2011_statssumm/fires_acres.pdf

Because they were more fire-prone before they came under human management, those forests looked very different in 1911 from today, Stephens says. "In 1911 the canopy [the area where crowns of trees meet] shaded about 27 percent of the forest floor. Now it ranges between 55 and 70 percent. If we walked through those 1911 forests, we'd need hats and sunscreen," he says. "Tree diameters used to be much bigger, and stands were dominated by more oaks and ponderosa pines, which are fire-tolerant species." In his view, Americans have significantly changed U.S. forests by suppressing fires for most of the past century. Many forests are less healthy and resilient today than they were in the past, Stephens says.

But other scientists contend that limited forest thinning (logging some trees) and prescribed low-level fires — the Forest Service's general strategy up to the 2012 fire season — may not be the right way to reduce fire risks across the West. A recent study at the University of Wyoming, based on records kept by 19th-century land surveyors, concluded that large, intense fires were more the norm in many parts of the West. According to this view, which is considered a minority position among fire researchers, thinning and prescribed burns may not actually help prevent mega-fires, and they could harm ecosystems. [10]

Forest managers know about the study but can point to areas where thinning and low-level prescribed burns have helped save homes from wildfires. Many factors determine whether low- or high-intensity fires are more suited to a given area, including local plant and tree species, elevation, topography and moisture levels. "I have to take it all into consideration," said Linda Wadleigh, a Forest Service fire ecologist in fire-prone northern Arizona. [11]

Getty Images/Tom Pennington

A wildfire threatens a home in Strawn, Texas, on April 19, 2011. Dry conditions, high winds and low humidity fueled the fire. More than 2.7 million acres burned in Texas in 2011, the most of any state.

Should development be limited in fire-prone areas?

Over the past 50 years, residential development has dramatically increased in zones near wild areas — the so-called wildland-urban interface (WUI). Protecting homes in the WUI is a key factor driving up firefighting costs.

Nearly 17 million new homes were built in the United States between 1990 and 2008, of which 10 million were in the WUI, according to a recent study by CoreLogic, a California-based financial research company. The report estimates that more than 740,000 homes in Western states, valued at more than $136 billion, are in areas where the risk of wildfire is high. [12]

Official responsibility for fire protection on non-federal lands falls to states or, if states choose not to provide protection, to local governments or private landowners. However, federal agencies are responsible for preventing fires that start on federal lands from spreading onto private or state lands. And when agencies decide how to fight wildfires, they are required to consider whether buildings or other resources are at risk. "I have to treat a fire differently when I know there are people or structures on those acres then when they are uninhabited," says the Forest Service's Harbour.

Many experts, including economists and analysts at the Government Accountability Office, say the federal government pays a disproportionate share of fire-management costs. [13] States can apply to the Federal Emergency Management Agency (FEMA) for grants that pay 75 percent of the costs of fighting major fires on public or private lands. [14] The Forest Service provides about $100 million annually in fire protection support to state and local governments. [15] And the Healthy Forest Restoration Act of 2003 requires that at least half of federal funds for fuel treatment (removing excess grasses, trees and brush to reduce fire risks) must be used in the WUI. [16]

Critics want to shift more responsibility to state and local governments and landowners. "People who make decisions about land use aren't directly accountable for the costs of their actions," says Ray Rasker, executive director of Headwaters Economics, a nonprofit research group in Montana. Analyzing firefighting data from Montana, California and Oregon, Headwaters Economics has found that protecting a single home within one to six miles of a wildfire can cost hundreds of thousands of dollars, especially if the home is in an isolated area. [17]

Wildfires' Deadly Toll

More than 300 firefighters and other personnel died battling wildfires from 1990 to 2007. Common causes of death are burnovers, in which firefighters are overrun by flames, and falling trees, vehicle accidents and heart attacks. The most deadly year for wildfires was 1910, when 78 firefighters died in fires that swept across 3 million acres in Idaho and Montana. That so-called "Big Blowup" led to heightened government efforts to extinguish wildfires, improve prevention strategies and make firefighting safer.

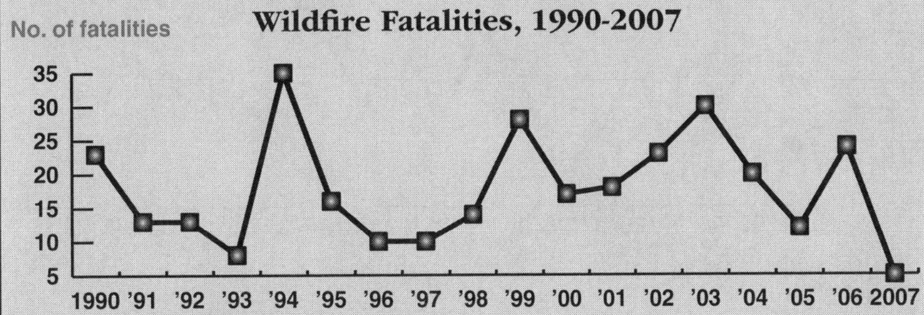

Source: "Wildland Fire Fatalities by Year," National Interagency Fire Center, 2011, www.nifc.gov/safety/reports/year.pdf

"Local officials should consider issues like road access and water hookups before they permit developments in wooded areas. But if it's next to Forest Service or BLM land, they assume costs of firefighting will be borne by the feds," says Rasker.

The Forest Service and Interior Department co-sponsor Firewise, an education program managed by the National Fire Protection Association that encourages homeowners, community leaders, planners and developers to take steps that will reduce wildfire risks. [18] More than 800 neighborhoods and sites in 40 states have become "Firewise Communities" by encouraging members to limit flammable vegetation near homes and use fire-resistant building materials. [19]

However, Firewise standards are voluntary in most communities that have adopted them. California, Oregon and Utah have adopted statewide codes for construction or vegetation management in WUI zones and either require or offer incentives to local governments to enforce those standards. [20] Elsewhere, however, WUI development is regulated at the city or county level, and policies vary widely.

Rasker agrees that Firewise upgrades can help make existing houses in fire-prone areas less vulnerable, but he says regulators should have the power to bar new construction where fire risks are very high. "Firewise isn't fireproofing. We don't tell people that it's OK to build on river flood plains as long as they put their houses on stilts," he contends. "Firewise is the easiest conversation to have because everyone can agree on it, but encouraging people to build in fire-prone areas is dangerous."

But property-rights advocates say the choice should be up to individuals and that development in WUI zones does not need more regulation. "People already bear the full risk of their choices, except when the Forest Service comes in and puts fires out," says Randal O'Toole, a senior fellow with the Cato Institute, a Washington-based think tank that promotes libertarian views on public policy issues. "If private landowners want to build on land near forests, they should recognize that it's not the Forest Service's responsibility to protect their homes."

Most regulations governing WUI development apply only to new construction projects, and sometimes to major renovations, but not to existing homes. "Broad-based initiatives to apply newer, safer standards to existing properties are extremely rare, not only because they are generally unpopular with voters, but because they tend to be expensive," a 2011 review of community fire protection regulations observed. [21]

Ironically, surviving a raging wildfire may be the biggest motivator to adopt stricter fire regulations. Diane Paton, a Colorado Springs resident, had been considering replacing her cedar roof with a fire-resistant version last June but had not scheduled the project. Then her home was destroyed in this summer's Waldo Canyon fire, Colorado's most-damaging wildfire on record. It burned 392 homes, killed two people and caused $350 million in property damage. "When you see your grand piano — something so solid and big — destroyed, you can't believe how hot this fire must have burned," she said. [22]

Can logging reduce fire hazards?

Timber industry representatives and many officials from rural areas have long argued that logging lowers wildfire risks by reducing the amount of combustible fuel, especially when it targets dead or damaged trees (a method called salvage logging). Currently, logging advocates are particularly concerned about widespread outbreaks of bark beetles, tiny wood-boring insects, about the size of a grain of rice, that are native across the West and periodically spread in massive outbreaks. Since 1997 bark beetles have killed or damaged millions of pine, spruce, fir and other

Wildfires Consume More Acreage

Wildfires have burned an average of 6.8 million acres annually since 2000, more than twice the annual average of the previous decade. Experts attribute the increase to climate change, which has made certain areas hotter, drier and more fire-prone, and to high fuel loads that built up for decades as wildfires were suppressed.

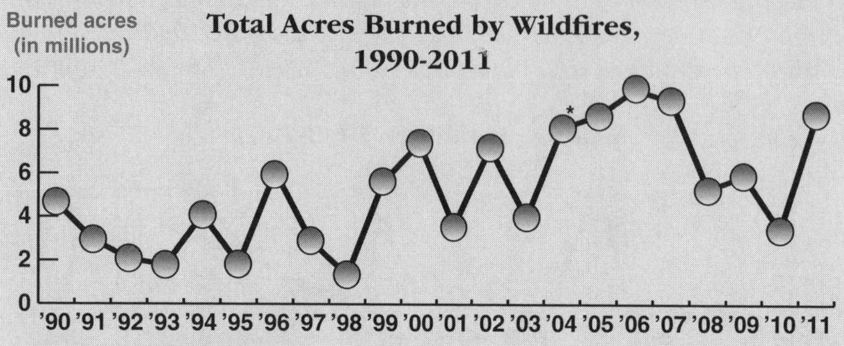

* *Does not include North Carolina state lands*

Source: "Total Wildland Fires and Acres (1960-2009)," National Interagency Fire Center, 2012, www.nifc.gov/fireInfo/fireInfo_stats_totalFires.html

trees over more than 41 million acres in Western states. [23]

Logging advocates and many Western politicians argue that large swaths of standing dead trees will burn readily and feed wildfires. In July, after two intense wildfires, six Western Republicans introduced a bill that would let state and local land managers log damaged trees in designated "high-risk" areas even if they are federal land. [24] "I believe that local communities know their forests best and know what needs to be done to restore them to healthy conditions," Rep. Scott Tipton, the bill's main sponsor, said in October. [25]

But Forest Service and academic scientists say the relationship between bark beetle attacks and wildfires is complex and that beetle-killed trees are not always more flammable than healthy trees. When bark beetles kill pine or spruce trees, the trees turn reddish-brown and retain their dried-out needles for one or two years. Then, three to five years after the insect attack, needles turn gray and fall to the ground. Later, dead trees begin toppling. Fire dangers vary with each of these stages, researchers say.

"One big debate in fire science is whether red needles enhance crown fires" — hot, intense fires that can spread rapidly between treetops, says University of Wisconsin zoologist Monica Turner, who has conducted extensive research on ecosystems in the Greater Yellowstone region of the northern Rocky Mountains. "Red needles are drier and more flammable than green ones, so the issue is what relative effect they have. The question is not whether beetle-killed forests will burn, it's how much more flammable they are compared to healthy forests."

In a 2011 study Turner and her colleagues analyzed factors that affected fire risk, such as fuel quantities, moisture levels and soil surface temperatures, in Rocky Mountain lodgepole pine forests severely affected by mountain pine beetles. [26] "Our results suggested that beetle kills don't increase risks of crown fire, and in some cases they may actually reduce it by thinning out the canopies," Turner says.

Separately, Forest Service scientists and others recently reviewed several dozen studies on bark beetle kills and wildfires and found that while beetle outbreaks increased some fire factors, the outbreaks decreased or did not affect others. Moreover, the researchers pointed out, time passage between beetle outbreaks and fire mattered because risks were different in red-needle and grey-needle phases. The scientists concluded that more study in different types of forests was needed and warned against generalizing about the relationship between beetle attacks and fire risks. [27]

Another longstanding controversy centers on the impacts of logging after large-scale fires. Forest managers have many concerns after fires: They want to ensure that trees will regenerate; preserve enough growth for animals and birds that return to the burned area (*see sidebar, p. 954*); reduce the likelihood that insects will infest fire-damaged trees; and minimize chances that the forests will burn again. They also want to recover valuable timber before it begins to rot.

President George W. Bush's administration (2001-2009) approved salvage logging after the 2002 Biscuit Fire in Oregon's Siskiyou National Forest, including in old-growth and roadless areas that previously had been protected from logging. Opponents demonstrated against the plan, and timber companies were less enthusiastic about logging in the burned areas than advocates had expected because many of the trees had been damaged by fire. [28]

A study later found that trees regenerated more slowly in areas that had been logged after the Biscuit Fire than in non-logged areas. Logging disturbed the soil and smothered seedlings. [29] Another study concluded that the Biscuit Fire caused more severe damage in areas that had been logged after an earlier major wildfire, the 1987 Silver Fire, than in areas that had not been logged. [30]

Forest Service research suggests that the length of time since a forest last burned has more influence on the risk of future fires than post-fire logging. Fires can reach from the surface to crowns of trees if "fuel ladders" are present — fallen branches or young trees that the fire can climb. "A one-size-fits-all story of how fire behaves in the forests is not possible," said Forest Service researcher Tom Spies, an author of the study comparing impacts from the Silver and Biscuit fires. [31] ■

Getty Images/David McNew

Residents in Porter Ranch, Calif., evacuate their homes as an approaching wildfire fills the air with smoke and haze on Oct. 13, 2008. The fire began when high winds downed a power line that ignited dry brush. It burned more than 14,000 acres.

BACKGROUND

Fire on the Frontier

Fire has been present in North American ecosystems for millions of years. Before European settlers arrived, Native Americans used it extensively for cooking, shaping tools, clearing fields, hunting and waging war. Many Native Americans were nomadic, so if their living area burned from lightning strikes or manmade fire, they moved and started over.

Colonists used fire in many of the same ways but also altered fire patterns across the continent. Along the East Coast, farmers cleared large tracts and drained wetlands, leaving huge piles of brush that could fuel wildfires. Later, as settlers moved west in the 1800s, they grazed sheep and cattle on the prairies. Overgrazing reduced fire on the plains by stripping native grasses that fueled small-scale local fires, and it allowed tough woody plants such as mesquite to take over. [32]

"This disruption of fire regimes put fire into landscapes where it had not been significant before and removed fire from landscapes where it had been common," writes Arizona State's Pyne. [33] Some of the biggest recorded fires in 19th-century America were in the East and Midwest. In 1825 the Miramichi Fire burned 3 million acres and killed 160 people in Maine and Canada. And on Oct. 8, 1871, fires in Wisconsin and Michigan burned more than 3.7 million acres and killed 1,182 people, on the same day that the Great Chicago Fire killed 250 people and destroyed more than 17,000 buildings. [34]

As the country's population exploded in the late 1800s, conservationists and some national leaders recognized that unrestricted use could harm scenic places and damage valuable resources. In 1872 Congress created Yellowstone National Park in Wyoming, followed by other parks in the Sierra Mountains of California. And in 1891 the Forest Reserve Act authorized the president to create national forest reserves on public lands.

The 1897 Organic Act stated three purposes for these reserves: producing timber and protecting forests and watersheds, which are large areas where all streams and rivers merge and flow to one outlet. Experts recognized that healthy forests were important sources of clean drinking water because they filtered and cooled water as it flowed through. Moreover, keeping lands planted with trees, shrubs and grasses protected against erosion, which could carry silt into rivers and streams.

Suppressing Fire

Initially Congress did not specify who would manage national parks and forests or how to protect them from fires and other threats. But in 1905 President Theodore Roosevelt (1901-09) — an avid conservationist who embraced the idea of preserving and actively protecting valuable lands — established the U.S. Forest Service within the Department of Agriculture to operate the national forest system.

Gifford Pinchot, the service's first chief, believed that preventing fires was crucial. In a 1905 manual, he argued that "probably the single greatest benefit derived by the community and the nation from forest reserves is insurance against destruction of property, timber resources, and water supply by fire." [35]

In the Forest Fires Emergency Act of 1908, Congress gave the Forest Service an unusual power for a public agency: It could spend any amount necessary in emergency fire situations and Congress would reimburse it with supplemental funds. But even with a blank check from Congress, the Forest Service was unprepared to stop enormous wildfires that swept across Idaho and Montana in 1910, killing 78 firefighters and nine civilians and burning more than 3 million acres.

After the "Big Blowup," as it was called, the Forest Service committed to an intensive strategy that cast fire as an enemy to be vanquished. Agency leaders opposed some experts' view that moderate fires could benefit forests by burning away undergrowth and reducing the risk of larger fires.

In 1926 the service adopted a policy that wildfires should be extinguished before they reached 10 acres in size. And in 1935 it added a goal of suppressing every fire by 10 a.m. on the day after it was reported (or if not, by 10 a.m. the next day, and so on). The rule had a scientific basis: it concentrated firefighting efforts during the night and early morning, when temperatures were typically lower and winds calmer. It also set a clear operating guideline for forest crews across the nation.

In 1944 the Forest Service launched a campaign to educate the public about ways in which humans caused fires, such as throwing away lit cigarettes or leaving campfires smoldering. The Smokey Bear campaign became the longest-running public service advertising campaign in U.S. history, best known for the catchphrase it carried from 1947 through 2001: "Remember . . . Only YOU Can Prevent Forest Fires." [36]

Initially foresters fought fires with axes, saws and shovels, cutting trees and removing brush to create firebreaks — open areas without combustible fuel. But the Forest Service constantly sought new tools and strategies. In 1930 it developed the first modern bulldozer, designed to create fire protection roads in steep backcountry areas. [37] During the 1930s thousands of young men belonging to the Civilian Conservation Corps — a Depression-era public works relief program set up by President Franklin D. Roosevelt — built fire roads and lookout towers and fought fires on public lands.

Getty Images/Tom Pennington

A California Department of Forestry plane drops fire retardant on the Station Fire near Los Angeles on Aug. 29, 2009. Forest Service Employees for Environmental Ethics, a watchdog group, has successfully sued the Forest Service to force it to assess environmental impacts of dumping flame retardant chemicals from airplanes.

In 1939 the Forest Service began training "smokejumpers" to parachute into remote areas to fight fires. And in the 1940s and '50s, as surplus military equipment became available after World War II and the Korean War, the Forest Service began using helicopters and tanker planes to drop water on wildfires. In the 1960s firefighters began large-scale drops of chemical retardant, which was developed to slow the spread of fires so that they could be fought more effectively on the ground.

Firefighting was a dangerous job. Although the 78 fatalities of 1910 were never equaled, another 255 people died fighting wildfires between 1911 and 1960. The most common cause was burnovers, which occur when fires overrun firefighters. Other hazards include falling trees, vehicle accidents and health issues such as heart attacks. [38]

New Attitudes

In the 1960s attitudes toward wildfire began to change. Conservationists and some researchers — notably at the nonprofit Tall Timbers Research Station and Land Conservancy in Tallahassee, Fla. — argued that fire had a place in wild systems and that not every wildfire should automatically be suppressed. Scientists began discussing "fire ecology," the study of how fire affects plants, birds and animals in different settings. In many cases, they found, fire was beneficial: It helped plants germinate and bloom, reduced infestations of forest pests and created new habitat for animals and birds. (*See sidebar, p. 954.*)

These ideas were buoyed by a growing conservation movement. In 1964 Congress passed the Wilderness Act, which directed federal land managers to maintain large, undeveloped tracts of federal lands in a wild condition.

Continued on p. 952

Chronology

1600s-1900

As settlers move across North America, fire evolves from a tool to a threat.

1860s-1890s
The spread of livestock grazing across the West strips native grasses that fueled small-scale local fires and allows tough, woody plants such as mesquite to take over.

1872
Congress creates Yellowstone National Park in Wyoming, the first U.S. national park, for conservation and public enjoyment.

1891
Forest Reserve Act authorizes the president to set aside publicly held forests as timber sources.

1900s-1950s

Federal policy emphasizes fire suppression.

1905
U.S. Forest Service established within Department of Agriculture to manage forest reserves.

1908
Forest Fires Emergency Act allows unlimited spending by Forest Service for fire suppression.

1910
Wildfires burn more than 3 million acres in Idaho and Montana, killing 78 firefighters. In response, Forest Service leaders commit to an intensive firefighting strategy.

1935
Forest Service sets goal of suppressing fires by 10 a.m. the day after they are reported.

1944
Wartime Advertising Council introduces Smokey Bear as fire prevention symbol.

1956
Tanker planes first used to quench fires.

1960s-1995

Fire policy shifts away from suppression and toward the use of fire to clear combustible underbrush and make areas less prone to uncontrollable burns.

1962
Tall Timbers Research Station in Tallahassee, Fla., holds first conference focusing on wildfires' effect on the environment and forest ecology.

1964
Wilderness Act mandates protection for wild sections of federal lands.

1967
National Park Service drops 10 a.m. suppression policy and endorses use of fire to clear excess growth and underbrush, reducing risks of large-scale wildfires.

1978
Forest Service changes its strategy from controlling to managing wildfires. . . . Congress repeals Forest Fires Emergency Act and begins providing annual appropriations for fire fighting.

1988
Amid a multiyear drought, massive summertime wildfires burn nearly 800,000 acres in Yellowstone National Park, more than a third of the park's area; firefighting agencies spend $120 million and use 25,000 people to fight the fires.

1995
Agriculture and Interior departments adopt Federal Fire Policy calling for the use of controlled burns on public wildlands whenever safe as a means of restoring a zone's natural habitat.

2000-Present

Firefighters grapple with heat, drought and the legacy of decades of fire suppression.

2000
Prescribed burns at National Park Service sites in Arizona and New Mexico expand out of control, forcing public evacuations.

2002
President George W. Bush's Healthy Forests Initiative promotes logging and thinning in national forests to reduce fire risks, over opposition from environmental groups.

2009
With the FLAME Act, Congress creates reserve funds to help pay for firefighting.

2011
Congress rescinds $600 million from Forest Service and Department of Interior fire suppression and management funds to help plug budget gaps. . . . Wildfires cause record-setting damage in Arizona and New Mexico.

2012
Congress rescinds $192 million in Forest Service fire management funds. . . . Record-setting wildfires destroy hundreds of homes in Colorado. . . . Forest Service receives $400 million in emergency funds to manage intense wildfire season.

Wildfires Threaten Air, Water Quality

Smoke and erosion lead to widespread safety concerns.

Damage from wildfires often extends beyond blackened trees, destroyed houses and dead or displaced wildlife. Fires generate smoke and other emissions that harm human health either directly or when they combine to form atmospheric haze. Wildfires also threaten nearby water supplies, which can become polluted when burned-over areas erode and debris washes into waterways. And in some areas wildfires help create conditions for dangerous landslides.

Smoke is a complex mixture of particulate matter, water vapor, carbon dioxide, carbon monoxide and other chemicals, which vary depending on such factors as the type of fuel, weather and temperature. Of greatest concern to human health are fine particles, with diameters of 2.5 micrometers or less — a fraction of the width of a human hair. Small enough to be absorbed deeply into the lungs, these particles can worsen respiratory problems such as asthma and increase heart attack and stroke risks. [1]

Carbon monoxide alone is a serious health threat. The odorless, colorless gas is produced when wood or fossil fuels do not burn completely. Exposure to high concentrations can cause dizziness, headaches, poor concentration, and, in extreme cases, loss of consciousness or even death. In wildfires the highest carbon monoxide risks occur very close to smoldering fires.

Other chemicals in wildfire smoke include nitrogen oxides, ozone and volatile organic compounds — substances that would be regulated as air pollutants if released from a factory. [2]

Large forest fires that burn for long periods can cause serious regional air quality problems when wind transports the smoke over long distances. Such fires have taken a toll worldwide, especially in tropical Africa, the Amazon, Siberia and Southeast Asia. Pollution from fires in Indonesia causes recurring health and visibility problems in Malaysia, Thailand and other neighboring countries. [3]

In the United States, smoke from Western wildfires earlier this year was visible from space and triggered widespread air-quality alerts from public health agencies advising people who lived near fire zones to stay indoors. [4] Forest fires on the Alaska-Canada border in 2004 worsened air pollution in Houston, more than 3,000 miles away. [5]

Wildfires can also pollute drinking water supplies and damage water treatment facilities. Fires release soil chemicals such as nitrate, which is harmful in high concentrations in drinking water, and phosphorus, a nutrient that causes algae blooms in waterways. [6] And burned-over areas are vulnerable to erosion. Without layers of leaf litter and other natural debris on the ground to soak up rainfall, or shrubs to anchor the soil, rain detaches soil particles and carries them away. Sediments, ash, charcoal and debris wash into rivers, muddying waters and killing fish.

Other pollutants also can be picked up in runoff. For example, tailings — waste materials left over from processing metal ores — are present around abandoned mine sites in many Western states. After the 2010 Fourmile Canyon fire in Boulder, Colo., the U.S. Geological Survey (USGS) found elevated levels of aluminum, iron and manganese from mine waste washing into local drinking water. These materials did not pose a health threat, but concentrations were strong enough to affect the water's taste and odor. [7]

Continued from p. 950

Three years later the National Park Service announced that it would end the 10 a.m. goal for suppressing wildfires in national parks. Instead, it would use planned burns — fires designed and ignited by forest managers to destroy brush and other fuel that could lead to a bigger conflagration — or let wildfires burn in situations where fire was expected to have positive effects.

Over the next decade Congress rewrote the laws governing the Forest Service and other public-land agencies. The National Forest Management Act (1976) required the Forest Service to develop plans for managing forests, with public input. And the Federal Lands Policy and Management Act (1976) directed the Interior Department's Bureau of Land Management (BLM) to manage public lands for multiple uses while protecting their environmental quality. Reflecting this growing focus on ecology and natural processes, the Forest Service and BLM adopted a new policy: Naturally occurring fires — those not started by humans — would be allowed to burn themselves out, when it could be done safely.

This approach, sometimes referred to as "let it burn," received little notice at first. But throughout the summer of 1988, during a multiyear drought, massive wildfires burned nearly 800,000 acres in Yellowstone National Park, 36 percent of the park's area. Initially park managers let the fires burn, but after dry conditions and winds fanned the flames, they switched to fire suppression. Firefighting agencies spent $120 million and used 25,000 people to fight the fires, but the burn was not permanently extinguished until snow fell in September. [39]

Some critics argued that the Park Service had failed to do its job, but federal officials emphasized that fire was an important part of the ecosystem and would not ruin park lands. Field studies over the next several decades supported their view. But some experts began to worry that after decades of fire suppression, the West was overgrown with massive fuel loads that could spark more large-scale fires. Intense wildfires in Oakland, Calif.

Post-fire erosion can also threaten public safety. In the Southwest, fall wildfires and heavy winter rains create a dangerous form of erosion called a debris flow. Massive landslides, sometimes big enough to crush houses, occur when wet soil washes down fire-hardened mountain slopes. Nature writer John McPhee described this process in Los Angeles, where wildfires and flash floods are endemic and many neighborhoods are built high up on hillsides:

"Debris flows amass in stream valleys and more or less resemble fresh concrete," McPhee wrote. "They consist of water mixed with a good deal of solid material, most of which is above sand size. Some of it is Chevrolet size. Boulders bigger than cars ride long distances in debris flows. Boulders grouped like fish eggs pour downhill in debris flows." [8]

Massive debris flows occurred in Colorado in 1994 and '95 after the South Canyon fire near Glenwood Springs. Debris washed onto Interstate Highway 70 in four places, engulfing 30 cars (with only minor injuries) and spilling into the Colorado River, where it blocked nearly half of the river channel. [9] Last August the USGS estimated that a high risk for debris flows existed in New Mexico's Gila National Forest, where a major wildfire occurred earlier in the year. In several areas of the forest USGS calculated that flows could exceed 500,000 cubic meters — enough to fill the Olympic Aquatics Centre in London. [10]

— Jennifer Weeks

---

[1] U.S. Environmental Protection Agency, "Particle Pollution and Health," 2012, www.epa.gov/pm/2012/fshealth.pdf.

[2] "Wildfires, Weather and Climate," University Corporation for Atmospheric Research, 2012, www2.ucar.edu/news/backgrounders/wildfires-weather-climate.

[3] Liz Gooch, "Malaysia Haze Points to a Regional Problem," *The New York Times*, June 23, 2012, www.nytimes.com/2012/06/24/world/asia/smoky-haze-over-malaysia-signals-a-regional-problem.html; "Gas from Pollutants, Forest Fires at Potentially Toxic Levels," *Science Daily*, July 16, 2012, www.sciencedaily.com/releases/2012/07/120716214857.htm.

[4] "New Mexico Fire Visible From Space," NBC Nightly News, June 1, 2012, http://video.msnbc.msn.com/nightly-news/47653300#47653300; "NASA Satellite Sees Several Western U.S. Fires Blazing," National Air and Space Administration, June 22, 2012, www.nasa.gov/mission_pages/fires/main/western-us.html; Russell Contreras, "Smoke from Huge Wildfire Envelops Parts of New Mexico, Ariz.," The Associated Press, May 26, 2012, www.boston.com/news/nation/articles/2012/05/26/smoke_from_wildfire_envelops_parts_of_new_mexico_ariz/.

[5] "NASA Study: Alaskan Fires Affected Houston Air Quality in 2004," Rice University, Sept. 21, 2006, http://news.rice.edu/2006/09/21/nasa-study-alaskan-fires-affected-houston-air-quality-in-2004/.

[6] "Water Quality and Erosion Following Wildfires," University of Wyoming College of Agriculture, October 2006, www.uwyo.edu/barnbackyard/_files/documents/resources/fire/fire-recovery-water-quality-1006.pdf.

[7] "Wildfire Effects on Source-Quality Water — Lessons from Fourmile Canyon Fire, Colorado, and Implications for Drinking-Water Treatment," U.S. Geological Survey, July 2012, http://pubs.usgs.gov/fs/2012/3095/.

[8] John McPhee, "Los Angeles Against the Mountains," reprinted in *The Control of Nature* (1989), p. 185.

[9] "Geologic Mapping Along the I-70 Corridor in Western Colorado," U.S. Geological Survey, updated April 15, 2010, http://esp.cr.usgs.gov/info/i70/index.html.

[10] "Estimated Probability of Postwildfire Debris Flows in the 2012 Whitewater-Baldy Fire Burn Area, Southwestern New Mexico," U.S. Geological Survey, 2012, p. 8, http://pubs.usgs.gov/of/2012/1188/ofr2012-1188.pdf; "Amount of waste flytipped each year would fill Olympics Aquatics Centre, says ESA," Environmental Services Association, July 25, 2012, www.esauk.org/reports_press_releases/press_releases/120725_Amount_of_waste_flytipped_each_year_would_fill_Olympics_Aquatics_Centre_says_ESA.pdf.

(1991); Malibu, Calif. (1993); and Storm King Mountain, Colo. (1994) fueled these concerns.

In response, the Agriculture and Interior departments adopted a unified Federal Fire Policy in 1995 that called for restoring fire on public lands wherever it could be done without increasing risk for firefighters or nearby residents. "Catastrophic wildfire now threatens million of wildland acres," the policy stated. "Enormous public and private values are at risk, and our nation's capability to respond to this threat is becoming overextended." The new policy called wildland fire "a critical natural process [that] must be reintroduced into the ecosystem." [40]

It also spotlighted an important and growing factor adding to wildfire risks: the growth of wildlife-urban interface areas where human development adjoins wild lands. The report estimated that federal agencies had spent $250 million to $300 million in 1994 protecting these areas and called for clearer plans, more public education and greater cost-sharing with state and local governments to reduce fire risks in these zones. [41]

Fire in the Exurbs

Fire threats appeared to outrun national strategy over the next several years. In 1998 wildfires in Florida forced more than 80,000 people to evacuate their homes. And in 2000, two prescribed burns at National Park Service sites — the North Rim of the Grand Canyon in Arizona and Bandelier National Monument in New Mexico — spread out of control, forcing evacuations. [42] A 2001 review of the national fire policy concluded that fire hazards on overgrown lands were "worse than previously understood" and risks in the WUI zones were "more complex and extensive" than understood in the original fire plan. [43]

President George W. Bush's administration focused on reducing fuel loads with its 2002 Healthy Forests Initiative, which authorized tree thinning and logging to reduce fire risks on public lands. [44] Congress passed

Wildfires Offer Both Risks and Rewards

"A lot of fires do good ecological work."

The headlines are often predictable: A wildfire has become a "catastrophic natural disaster" that has "ravaged" a pristine forest and "devastated" trees, plants and wildlife.

But such characterizations can be greatly exaggerated, experts say. Some fires burn only parts of the areas they move through. What's more, many plants and animals derive surprising benefits from fire.

"A lot of fires do good ecological work, even if they also cause ecological harm," says Scott Stephens, an associate professor of fire science at the University of California-Berkeley. "We need to stop characterizing all fire in ecosystems as negative."

Surface fires move along the ground, mainly burning shrubs and underbrush, and are usually the least-intense type of fire. Understory fires rise higher, but not to the tops of trees, and are more intense. However, trees often survive fires even after being partially scorched, especially if fire moves through an area quickly and does not heavily damage trees' trunks and roots. [1] Crown fires are usually the most intense: They move through the tops of trees and typically kill all trees that burn. Wind, terrain and moisture levels affect where a fire moves: Wildfires can leave untouched patches of green next to burned areas.

One well-studied case is Yellowstone National Park, where researchers have found that most forests and meadows recovered naturally from massive wildfires in 1988. "The 1988 fires were really large and very severe, but they were not remotely an ecological catastrophe as some people said," says Monica Turner, a professor of zoology at the University of Wisconsin-Madison who has done extensive research on the ecology of the Greater Yellowstone region.

"A lot of grasses, wildflowers and shrubs survived. It looked as though everything was dead, but a year later plants were re-sprouting. The fires didn't burn very deeply into the soil, so many roots were still alive after the fire. Two years later they flowered profusely — it was just beautiful."

Some plants and animals actually need fire to grow and reproduce successfully. For example:

- Lodgepole pine trees, which grow throughout the Rockies and Pacific Northwest, produce seeds that are enclosed in waxy cones. After wildfires melt the coating, the seeds fall onto ashy ground, where they can sprout without heavy competition from other plants.
- Fireweed, a tall grass with bright pink flowers, grows across much of the northern United States and Canada. It spreads quickly in burned-over forests, where its roots stabilize the soil and its leaves shade less sun-tolerant plants. Fireweed is consumed by many grazing animals and produces nectar for bees. [2]
- Some insects, including wood wasps and numerous species of wood-boring beetles, actually are attracted to forest fires, which they detect by the smell of burning foliage or the fires' heat. The insects bore into burned trees and lay their eggs. [3]

the program in 2003 over protests from environmental groups. They argued that the plan was an excuse to increase logging in protected areas, such as old-growth forests, and would not reduce fire risks. [45]

However, no high-level actions were taken to restrict development in WUI zones, driven in many areas by wealthy second-home buyers. According to one analysis, between 2000 and 2005 the Forest Service and Bureau of Land Management spent an average of $630 million to $1.2 billion to protect private property from wildfires. [46] In 2006 and 2007, more than 9 million acres burned each year — more than in any fire season since the 1960s.

As the Forest Service worked to control wildfires, it repeatedly overspent its funding for fire suppression and was forced to transfer money from other activities, such as maintaining trails or planting new trees. In 2009 Congress passes the FLAME Act, which sought to address the rising cost of fighting fires by creating two reserve funds at the Agriculture and Interior departments for fire suppression. But when Republicans gained strength in Congress after the 2010 elections and confronted the Obama administration over federal spending, Congress took back $600 million from the suppression fund and other wildfire management accounts in fiscal 2011 and an additional $192 million in fiscal 2012 to help pay for compromise budget cuts. [47]

"The FLAME Act set up a reserve account for Interior and the Forest Service so that in milder fire years unspent money could be banked for more intense years," says Jake Donnay, policy director for the National Association of State Foresters, which supported the FLAME Act. "Obviously, when times are tough you have to decide where to cut, but this year the FLAME account has been drained. It's not a perfect system." ■

CURRENT SITUATION

Budget Shortfall

Just three years after Congress passed the FLAME Act in an effort to prevent funding shortfalls, fire-suppression budgets are drained again because of this year's intensive wildfire season.

• Many types of birds, including kestrels, woodpeckers and flickers, nest in dead trees, known as snags, and feed on wood-boring insects. Some species, such as the black-backed woodpecker, seek out burned-over sites. [4]

• Small mammals such as chipmunks, mice and squirrels move into the holes that birds create in dead trees and forage on fresh plants that sprout in newly open areas. In turn, these animals draw predators such as foxes and coyotes back to the area.

www.firepix.nifc.gov

Wildfires can devastate forests, but they also can help regenerate natural areas. Here, new growth sprouts in the shadow of a burned tree.

Wildfires also affect the health of ecosystems in many other ways. They can make soil either more or less fertile, depending on the intensity of the fire. Fires also kill off forest pests and pathogens, although insect outbreaks can occur after a fire in weakened and damaged trees.

Over time, scientists can learn about the strengths and weaknesses of different ecosystems by studying how they recover after fires. "The 1988 Yellowstone fires may end up being a very valuable benchmark," says Turner. "There will be more fire in the future, so we can use what we've learned since the 1988 fires to predict how the area will respond next time."

— *Jennifer Weeks*

[1] For details see Peter F. Kolb, "After Wildfire," Section 4, Montana State University Extension Service, 2002, http://forestandrange.org/modules/after wildfire/pdfs/tree.pdf.

[2] "Index of Species Information," U.S. Forest Service, www.fs.fed.us/database/feis/plants/forb/chaang/all.html; Jackson Hole Land Trust, "Field Notes," www.jhlandtrust.org/fieldnotes/fieldnotes_details.php?fieldnotes_id=79

[3] Daniel S. Burgess, "Bugs Lead the way to Better Detectors," *Photonics Spectra*, June 2001, www.photonics.com/Article.aspx?AID=9319; "Fire-Chasing Beetles Sense Infrared Radiation From Fires Hundreds of Kilometres Away," *Discovermagazine.com*, May 27, 2012, http://blogs.discovermagazine.com/notrocketscience/2012/05/27/fire-chasing-beetles-sense-infrared-radiation-from-fires-hundreds-of-kilometres-away/.

[4] Cornell Laboratory of Ornithology, www.allaboutbirds.org/guide/Black-backed_Woodpecker/lifehistory; "Managing Forests After Fire," U.S. Forest Service, Pacific Northwest Research Station, Summer 2007, p. 6, www.fs.fed.us/pnw/pubs/science-update-15.pdf.

On Aug. 27, Forest Service chief Tidwell warned agency managers that the service was likely to overspend its $948 million fire-suppression budget for fiscal 2012 and was making plans to transfer $400 million from other accounts. In the meantime, Tidwell instructed agency chiefs and directors to defer all non-critical travel, purchases and contracts.

"I recognize that this direction will have a significant effect on agency operations," Tidwell wrote. "[H]owever, we must be in a position to protect life and property from wildfire, and do so within the funds available to the agency." [48]

In response, a coalition of conservation, recreation, forestry, timber and wildlife organizations wrote to Congress and the Agriculture Department asking for $400 million in emergency supplemental funds for the Forest Service. The groups called transfers from other Forest Service accounts "a short-term solution that will reduce the ability of the Forest Service and collaborators to treat forests and reduce wildfire dangers and risks in the future." [49]

Congress included the $400 million in a continuing resolution enacted in late September to fund the government through March 2013. The act also increases fire-suppression funding for the same period. But forest advocates say firefighting agencies need more sustained long-term support.

"The intent of the FLAME Act was that the Forest Service should budget for fire suppression based on a 10-year average of past costs, and Congress should fund it at that level, with a reserve account that would let the Interior Department and the Forest Service bank any unspent funds left over after mild fire years," says Donnay of the National Association of State Foresters. "We support the intent of the act, but we expect a commitment from Congress and the administration to bank reserve funds."

Hotter and Drier

Scientists widely agree that climate change will make much of the United States — especially the West — hotter and drier in coming decades, which will intensify fire risks.

In a study published in August James Hansen — a prominent climate expert and head of NASA's Goddard Institute for Space Studies — reported that extreme heat covered 4 to 13 percent of Earth during the months of June, July and August from 2006 through 2011, compared to just 0.2 percent of the planet during summers from 1951 through 1980. Based on this finding, Hansen and his co-authors argued that extreme heat waves during the past several years were a direct consequence of climate change because it was extremely unlikely that they would have occurred in the absence of such warming. [50]

Hansen, whose outspoken demands for action on climate change have made him controversial, asserted in interviews that climate change was also the likely cause of this year's crippling drought across much of the United States. Some scientists agreed with his argument about patterns of increasing warmth, but others were skeptical. "Perception is not a science," said Martin P. Hoerling, a climate researcher with the National Oceanic and Atmospheric Administration (NOAA). [51]

Another study, by University of California researchers, used 16 different climate change models to assess how warming could alter wildfire patterns. In many parts of the world, including the Western United States, the scientists projected that wildfires will become more frequent. "We need to learn how to coexist with fire," said Max Moritz, a cooperative-extension specialist at the University of California and lead author of the study. [52]

In some areas, more frequent fires could change ecosystems drastically. In Greater Yellowstone, for example, average summer temperatures are predicted to increase by as much as 6 degrees Fahrenheit in the coming century, but effects on rainfall are uncertain. "If we get higher temperatures and the same amount of precipitation that we have today, there will be more drought, which will push the system into a zone associated with big fires," says Turner of the University of Wisconsin. "Our modeling suggests that there will be fewer years without fire. At some point, fires could come so quickly that forests don't have enough time to regrow in between them."

If that scenario occurs, the mix of plants growing in the Yellowstone area would change. "More area would be occupied by young forests. We would expect to see dry conifers like Douglas fir and aspen expanding to higher elevations, and high-elevation species like whitebark pine and Engelmann spruce declining," says Turner. "At lower elevations we would have more sagebrush and grassland habitat in zones that are forested now. The key question is whether climate and fire regimes will change enough to cause forested areas to shift to non-forests. If drought years follow fire years, that could keep tree seedlings from regenerating," she says.

Getty Images/David McNew

Flames from the Porter Ranch fire near Los Angeles threaten homes on Oct. 13, 2008. Over the past 50 years, residential development has dramatically increased in zones near wild areas — the so-called wildland-urban interface (WUI). Protecting homes in the WUI is a key factor driving up firefighting costs. Nearly 17 million new homes were built in the United States between 1990 and 2008, of which 10 million were in the WUI, according to CoreLogic, a California-based financial research company.

University of California fire science professor Scott Stephens agrees that climate change and more frequent fires could significantly alter U.S. forests, but he believes action now could help slow the process. "The next 10 to 30 years will be a critical time for restoring forests and making them more resilient to fire," he says. "After that, climate change could make it impossible. We're not doing enough fuel treatment," such as thinning trees, shredding brush mechanically and using prescribed fire to burn away excess growth, he adds. "Right now the Forest Service is doing about one-fifth of what we should be doing yearly. Foresters need to find new ways of doing business."

Using Fire

Amid debates about federal fire policy, some conservation groups are working with government agencies to use fire safely as a conservation tool. The Nature Conservancy, an environmental advocacy group that works to protect ecologically important lands in the United States and worldwide, has long advocated controlled burning as a cost-effective land restoration tool. In 2011 the Conservancy carried out planned burns on

Continued on p. 958

At Issue:

Should Congress allow more logging to reduce wildfire threats?

U.S. REP. PAUL GOSAR, R-ARIZ.

FROM TESTIMONY BEFORE HOUSE SUBCOMMITTEE ON NATIONAL PARKS, FORESTS AND PUBLIC LANDS, JULY 20, 2012

yes

Last year, our communities were victims [of] some of the largest forest fires in recorded history. The Wallow Fire grew to over 800 square miles, over just a few short weeks, charring in its wake some of the most treasured parts of our Ponderosa Pine country. The Horseshoe Fire, the Murphy Complex, the Stanley Fire and the Monument Fire blackened another 200,000-plus acres. This year's fire season has not been any better. Over 900 fires have charred nearly 6,000 square miles in Arizona, California, Colorado, Nevada, New Mexico, Oregon and Utah. Over 50,000 of those acres are in Arizona alone. . . . Our ecosystems are suffocating. Where we once had 10 to 25 trees per acre, we now have hundreds. Roughly 80 million acres of forests across the West are overgrown and ripe for catastrophic wildfire, according to the [federal] Landfire multiagency database. Our forests have been mismanaged for a long time, and it is way past due to change our strategy.

The current federal system continues to prioritize fighting fires. Although the need to suppress fires is never going to go away, we must shift priority towards pro-active management. We simply cannot afford to do otherwise.

Catastrophic wildfires are difficult to control and cost the federal government millions of dollars in immediate fire response and many millions more in restoration and rehabilitation. The Western Forestry Leadership Coalition, a state and federal government partnership, estimates the costs [of post-fire rehabilitation and restoration] are two to 30 times the reported [fire] suppression costs. Last year, the Forest Service spent a record . . . $48 million on burned-area recovery work, [and] $25 million has already been spent to prepare for the immediate aftermath of this year's wildfires, putting the U.S. Forest Service on track for another possible record year of spending on burned-area recovery efforts.

Forest thinning works! In eastern Arizona, the areas that were treated as part of the White Mountain Stewardship Project, a contract designed to thin the Apache-Sitgreaves National Forest and White Mountain Apache tribal lands, and the areas managed locally by the Apache Tribe and the state of Arizona, were properly cleared. Today there are still healthy trees with burned underbrush. In the lands that were untouched by thinning practices — the majority of the U.S. Forest Service-administered land in the state — fire has left only scorched earth behind. We simply need to make ecological restoration easier.

ANDY STAHL
EXECUTIVE DIRECTOR, FOREST SERVICE EMPLOYEES FOR ENVIRONMENTAL ETHICS

WRITTEN FOR *CQ RESEARCHER*, OCTOBER 2012

no

Would repealing federal environmental laws to allow increased logging reduce wildfire size, intensity and home losses, as some in Congress suggest? Consider Texas. In 2011, 27,976 fires burned 3.9 million acres, destroying 2,862 homes. All of these destructive fires were on private land, where federal environmental laws do not regulate land practices. In 1991, California's Oakland Hills Fire, the most destructive fire in dollar value of property damage in U.S. history, burned on private, municipal and state-owned land not subject to federal environmental laws. The firestorm was fueled by non-native eucalyptus trees planted after unregulated private-land logging had removed the original fire-resistant forests.

The relevant federal environmental laws — the National Environmental Policy Act, Endangered Species Act and National Forest Management Act — were enacted in the 1970s. If these laws are the cause of destructive fires or have contributed to them, one would expect few such fires in the decades preceding these laws. Not so. In 1970, the Laguna Fire in San Diego County, Calif., burned over 280,000 acres as it swept 30 miles through the Cleveland National Forest, destroying 382 homes and killing eight people. Between World War II and 1970, the Cleveland National Forest alone saw major fires in 1944, 1947, 1950, 1956, 1958, 1967 and 1969.

In every case cited above — and for every other major wildland fire — the conditions that led to the conflagration are unaffected by federal environmental laws. Firefighters throughout the world know these conditions well. They are drought and wind. Alone, drought or wind is manageable. Ignition on a windy day during damp conditions poses little catastrophic risk. Under calm conditions, fire burning through tinder-dry vegetation creeps along slowly and is easily contained. Combined, however, drought and wind create fire conditions that are deadly and uncontrollable.

Blaming destructive wildfires on environmental laws risks overlooking real policy solutions. Forest Service research shows that 90 percent of homes lost to wildland fires could have been saved by lessening flammable vegetation within 150 feet of the house and building homes with a fire-resistant design and materials. These "Firewise" policies are being adopted by local and state governments throughout the nation because they work. The federal government and Congress should support these efforts instead of seeking to use fire to burn away environmental laws that have protected our nation's water, fish, wildlife and recreation for a generation.

Continued from p. 956

130,000 acres of conservation lands. [53]

Some of that work took place in the Shawangunks, a forested mountain ridge in New York state west of the Hudson River. The Conservancy's local chapter conducts planned burns jointly with other groups to reduce the amount of leaves, litter and wood on the forest floor. "We want to keep the forest healthy and resilient and reduce risk for people who live around the ridge," explains Cara Lee, director of the group's Shawangunk Ridge Program. "People around here recognize that using prescribed fire makes firefighters and neighbors safer because it reduces the risk of large, intense wildfires."

Without fire, forests in the Shawangunk preserve would gradually change from a mix of oaks and pitch pines to maples, according to Gabe Chapin, the preserve's forest ecologist and fire manager. "Oaks provide acorns, which are an important food source for wildlife, and they store a lot of carbon, so we want to maintain them," he says. Both oaks and pitch pines have thick bark and very deep root systems, so they are adapted to resprout after fires. "They grow well in a post-fire environment, where they have more light and growing space and less competition," Chapin says.

For each planned burn, the Conservancy and local partners review the target zone's ecology and reasons for using fire. Then the groups write a detailed blueprint that spells out acceptable conditions for the burn, such as temperature, humidity, wind speed and direction and fuel moisture levels. The plan also assesses what local emergency-response services will be needed to manage the operation. Burn plans are reviewed and approved by state regulators.

AFP/Getty Images/Robyn Beck

Firefighters take a break as they monitor smoldering "hot spots" in areas burned in the Waldo Canyon Fire west of Colorado Springs on June 29, 2012. The fire killed two people, destroyed more than 300 homes and burned more than 18,000 acres in the Pike National Forest and in Colorado Springs.

For a burn to take place, all of the experts listed in the plan have to be present, including forest rangers. Often, operators light a test fire and watch how the smoke and fire behaves. "We'll set up an ignition pattern that will let the fire burn toward the center of the land unit and effectively burn itself out when all the fuel is used up," says Chapin. "And we watch smoke very carefully to make sure it's lifting above the ground and dispersing away from houses and roads. There's no such thing as a fire without any risk, but all of the planning, managing and crew training that go into this process mitigate the risk, and we don't proceed unless we're very comfortable with the way the fire is behaving."

Fire historian Pyne lauds the Nature Conservancy for its expertise in using fire for land management and for working with government agencies and conservation groups on fire projects. "The Conservancy is creating working landscapes where people are present and doing things with fire, and they are using it for good purposes," he says. ■

OUTLOOK

"Common Vision" Needed

Land managers, scientists and other experts widely agree that it will take more than money and equipment to manage wildfires in a warming world. "We won't ever get ahead of the problem at the federal level just by throwing money at it," says Harbour of the Forest Service. "We need a common vision about the responsibility of homeowners, communities and government."

Harbour and others point to development in the wildland-urban interface as a critical issue. Rasker of Headwaters Economics points out that about 80 percent of WUI land is still undeveloped. He argues that growth in those areas should be restricted before it drives fire-suppression costs even higher over the next several decades.

"No one seems to want to have a conversation about what we should be doing with the rest of our WUI land, what kind of development we want there and who will bear responsibilities," says Rasker. "We should be talking about land-use planning and getting the incentives right to keep people from building in dangerous areas. Insurance companies won't come up with the answer — they benefit from the federal subsidy [for fire suppression], which lowers their risk."

Many experts also say that American attitudes toward fire will have to evolve as it becomes more unavoidable in many regions. "We've created an ecological insurgency" — fuel buildups on public lands — "and we're not going to bomb it out," says Arizona State University's Pyne.

Stahl of Forest Service Employees for Environmental Ethics agrees that Americans will have to become more used to fire, and says part of the problem lies with politicians and journalists. For example, he says, officials often call for tankers to drop fire retardant on big, wind-blown fires near towns and cities. "That's not the scenario where it's effective — it was designed to slow down low-level fires creeping through remote wilderness areas, so firefighters would have time to get to them," Stahl says. "But now, if you don't do [dramatic] 'CNN drops' on big fires, politicians get upset and homeowners want to know why the Forest Service isn't using everything it's got."

"Firefighting is eating up a bigger and bigger share of the Forest Service's total budget. You have to respond to fires, but nobody wants to pay for them."

— Stephen Pyne

Professor of Life Sciences,

Arizona State University

Land managers such as the Nature Conservancy's Chapin want to see controlled burns applied more widely. "Wildfires in the United States are becoming more severe and hard to put out," Chapin says. "Controlled burns are a tool we can use to manage that threat." The University of California's Stephens agrees. "Most people who talk to Congress about 'active management' of forests are talking about mechanical means like thinning trees and shredding brush. But managing wildfires is an active decision, too, and can have great benefits," he says.

After intense fire seasons like this year's, Americans who visit national forests and parks will have many opportunities to see fire's impacts. That should not deter them, says David Nimkin, Southwest regional director for the National Parks Conservation Association.

"It's exciting to see how land changes," Nimkin says. He cites Mesa Verde National Park, a popular destination located on a high, forested plateau in southwest Colorado. "Wildfires over the past several years have opened up the mesa. There are scarred tree trunks, but the fires opened up extraordinary views from the plateau that are a really new experience," Nimkin says. ■

Notes

[1] Washington State Department of Natural Resources, "Dry Conditions and Extreme Wildfire Risk Lead to Burn Ban Extensions by DNR," Oct. 4, 2012, www.dnr.wa.gov/RecreationEducation/News/Pages/2012_10_04_dry_conditions_nr.aspx.

[2] Washington State Department of Natural Resources, "Severe Fire Conditions We Have Not Seen in Our Lifetimes," and "Fire Prevention Guide," posted at *Ear to the Ground*, Oct. 4, 2012, http://washingtondnr.wordpress.com/.

[3] National Fire Information Center, "Total Wildland Fires and Acres," www.nifc.gov/fireInfo/fireInfo_stats_totalFires.html.

[4] For background see Jennifer Weeks, "Managing Public Lands," *CQ Researcher*, Nov. 4, 2011, pp. 929-952.

[5] Ross W. Gorte, "Federal Funding for Wildfire Control and Management," Congressional Research Service, RL33990, July 5, 2011, p. 6, www.fas.org/sgp/crs/misc/RL33990.pdf.

[6] "Otter Calls for More Logging, Grazing on Public Land to Prevent Wildfire," *Spokane Spokesman-Review*, Oct. 4, 2012, www.spokesman.com/blogs/boise/2012/oct/04/otter-calls-more-logging-grazing-public-land-prevent-wildfire/.

[7] "State of the Forest Service," Sept. 18, 2012, www.fs.fed.us/news/2012/speeches/09/state_of_fs.shtml.

[8] Online at www.documentcloud.org/documents/407523-2012-wildfire-guidance-memo-may-25.html; for an analysis, see Richard Manning, "In a Major Policy Reversal, the Forest Service Is Fighting Every Fire This Year — But at What Cost?", *On Earth*, Aug. 7, 2012, www.onearth.org/article/forest-service-fire-fighting-policy-reversal.

[9] Rocky Barker, "Debt Standoff Makes Agency Fight All Fires," *Idaho Statesman*, Aug. 23, 2012, www.idahostatesman.com/2012/08/23/2241641/debt-standoff-makes-agency-fight.html.

[10] Jim Robbins, "Forest Fire Research Questions the Wisdom of Prescribed Burns," *The New York Times*, Sept. 17, 2012, www.nytimes.com/2012/09/18/science/earth/forest-survey-questions-effect-of-prescribed-burns.html?pagewanted=all; Emily Guerin, "Fire Scientists Fight Over What Western Forests Should Look Like," *High Country News*, Sept. 17, 2012, www.hcn.org/issues/44.16/fire-scientists-fight-over-what-western-forests-should-look-like.

[11] Laurel Morales, "Fire Study Stirs Controversy," Fronteras.org, Sept. 28, 2012, www.fronterasdesk.org/news/2012/sep/28/fire-study-stirs-controversy/.

[12] "2012 CoreLogic Wildfire Hazard Risk Report," CoreLogic, 2012, www.corelogic.com/about-us/researchtrends/wildfire-hazard-risk-report-2012.aspx, pp. 7, 9.

[13] "Wildland Fire Management: Federal Agencies Have Taken Important Steps Forward, but Additional, Strategic Action Is Needed to Capitalize on Those Steps," U.S. Government Accountability Office, September 2009; Gwenlyn Busby and Heidi J. Albers, "Wildfire Risk Management on a Landscape with Public and Private Ownership: Who Pays for Protection?" *Environmental Management*, Vol. 45 (2010), pp. 296-310; Timothy Ingalsbee, "Getting Burned: A Taxpayer's Guide to Wildfire Suppression Costs," Firefighters United for Safety, Ethics and Ecology, 2010, www.idahoforests.org/img/pdf/FUSEE.pdf.

[14] "Fire Management Assistance Grant Program," Federal Emergency Management Agency, www.fema.gov/fire-management-assistance-grant-program.

[15] Gorte, *op. cit.*

[16] Busby and Albers, *op. cit.*

[17] For dollar figures, see "Northern California, Homes and Cost of Wildfires," Headwaters Economics, http://headwaterseconomics.org/wildfire/northern-california-homes-and-cost-of-wildfires/, and "Oregon Homebuilding, Higher Temperatures Drive Price Tag Ever Higher," http://headwaterseconomics.org/wildfire/oregon-homes-and-cost-of-wildfires/.

[18] For details see "Firewise," www.firewise.org.

[19] "Firewise Communities," www.firewise.org/communities.aspx.

[20] "Addressing Community Wildfire Risk: A Review and Assessment of Regulatory and Planning Tools," Clarion Associates, December 2011, p. 27, www.nfpa.org/assets/files/Research%20Foundation/RFWUIRegulatoryAssessment.pdf.

[21] *Ibid.*, p. 11.

[22] Fred Durso, Jr., "After Waldo Canyon," *NFPA Journal*, September/October 2012, p. 4, www.nfpa.org/publicColumn.asp?categoryID=2644&itemID=58466.

[23] U.S. Forest Service, "Western Bark Beetle Strategy," July 11, 2011, p. 6, www.fs.fed.us/publications/bark-beetle/bark-beetle-strategy-appendices.pdf. For background, see Jennifer Weeks, "Invasive Species," *CQ Researcher*, Feb. 17, 2012, pp. 153-176.

[24] H.R. 6089, the Healthy Forest Management and Wildfire Prevention Act.

[25] "Congressman Scott Tipton Addresses 2012 Colorado Forest Summit," press release, Oct. 12, 2012, http://tipton.house.gov/press-release/congressman-scott-tipton-addresses-2012-colorado-forest-summit; Valerie Richardson, "Calls for Removing Beetle-Kill Trees Intensify," *The Colorado Observer*, July 10, 2012, http://thecoloradoobserver.com/2012/07/calls-for-removing-beetle-kill-trees-intensify/.

[26] Martin Simard, *et al.*, "Do Mountain Pine Beetle Outbreaks Change the Probability of Active Crown Fire in Lodgepole Pine Forests?" *Ecological Monographs*, Vol. 81, No. 1 (2011), pp. 3-24.

[27] Jeffrey A. Hicke, *et al.*, "Effects of Bark Beetle-Caused Tree Mortality on Wildfire," *Forest Ecology and Management*, Vol. 271 (2012), pp. 81-90.

[28] Blaine Harden, ""Salvage Logging a Key Issue in Oregon," *The Washington Post*, Oct. 15, 2004, www.washingtonpost.com/wp-dyn/articles/A33571-2004Oct14.html; Kathie Durbin, "Unsalvageable," *High Country News*, May 16, 2005, www.hcn.org/issues/298/15501.

[29] D.C. Donato, *et al.*, "Post-Wildfire Logging Hinders Regeneration and Increases Fire Risk," *Science*, Vol. 311, Jan. 20, 2006, p. 352.

[30] "Managing Forests After Fire," U.S. Forest Service, Pacific Northwest Research Station, Summer 2007, p. 5, www.fs.fed.us/pnw/pubs/science-update-15.pdf.

[31] *Ibid.*

[32] Mary Ramos, "The Ubiquitous Mesquite," *Texas Almanac*, www.texasalmanac.com/topics/science/ubiquitous-mesquite.

[33] Stephen J. Pyne, *America's Fires: A Historical Context for Policy and Practice* (2010), p. 11.

[34] "U.S. Major Wildfires Timeline," Forest History Society, www.foresthistory.org/Education/Curriculum/activity/activ9/Wildfire%20Timeline.pdf; "Large Fires and Fatalities," National Park Service, www.nps.gov/fire/wildland-fire/learning-center/fireside-chats/history-timeline.cfm#text.

[35] Quoted in Pyne, *op. cit.*, p. 26.

[36] In 2001 the line was changed to "Only You Can Prevent Wildfires," www.smokeybear.com/vault/history_main.asp.

[37] Howard R. Jones, "The Modern Bulldozer: A Forest Service Project," Forest History Society, www.foresthistory.org/ASPNET/Publications/region/1/early_days/4/sec28.htm.

[38] National Interagency Fire Center, "Wildland Fire Fatalities by Year," www.nifc.gov/safety/reports/year.pdf.

[39] "The Yellowstone Fires of 1988," National Park Service, 2008, www.nps.gov/yell/naturescience/upload/firesupplement.pdf.

[40] "Federal Wildland Fire Management Policy & Program Review, Final Report," Dec. 18,

About the Author

Jennifer Weeks is a Massachusetts freelance writer who specializes in energy, the environment and science. She has written for *The Washington Post*, *Audubon*, *Popular Mechanics* and other magazines and previously was a policy analyst, congressional staffer and lobbyist. She has an A.B. degree from Williams College and master's degrees from the University of North Carolina and Harvard. Her recent *CQ Researcher* reports include "Gulf Coast Restoration" and "Energy Policy."

1995, p. iii, www.nwcg.gov/branches/ppm/fpc/archives/fire_policy/mission/1995_fed_wildland_fire_policy_program_report.pdf.
[41] *Ibid.*, pp. 21-27.
[42] "U.S. Major Wildfires Timeline," Forest History Society, www.foresthistory.org/Education/Curriculum/activity/activ9/Wildfire%20Timeline.pdf.
[43] "Review and Update of the 1995 Federal Wildland Fire Management Policy," January 2001, p. ii, www.nwcg.gov/branches/ppm/fpc/archives/fire_policy/history/index.htm.
[44] "Healthy Forests," http://georgewbush-whitehouse.archives.gov/infocus/healthyforests/.
[45] Anthony Ambrose, "Logging Without Laws: Bush's 'Healthy Forests Initiative,' " Sierra Club Redwood Chapter newsletter, December/January 2003, www.redwood.sierraclub.org/articles/December_02/LoggingWOLaws.html; "Native Forest Network Statements Regarding President Bush's 'Healthy Forest Initiative,' " Aug. 22, 2002, www.nativeforest.org/press_room/release_8_22_02.htm.
[46] Patricia Gude, Ray Rasker and Jeff van den Noort, "Potential for Future Development on Fire-Prone Lands," *Journal of Forestry*, June 2008, pp. 200, 203, http://headwaterseconomics.org/pubs/wildfire/PGude_2008_Forestry.pdf.
[47] Gorte, *op. cit.*
[48] Letter provided by Andy Stahl, executive director, Forest Service Employees for Environmental Ethics.
[49] "Partners Caucus on Fire Suppression Funding Solutions," letter to Sens. Jack Reed and Lisa Murkowski, Sept. 10, 2012, www.stateforesters.org/sites/default/files/publication-documents/Simpson-Moran%20FLAME%20Letter%20with%20Groups%20Sep%2010.pdf.
[50] James Hansen, Makiko Sato and Reto Ruedy, "Perception of Climate Change," *Proceedings of the National Academy of Sciences*, published online Aug. 6, 2012, www.nature.com/nature_education.
[51] Justin Gillis, "Study Finds More of Earth is Hotter and Says Global Warming Is at Work," *The New York Times*, Aug. 6, 2012, www.nytimes.com/2012/08/07/science/earth/extreme-heat-is-covering-more-of-the-earth-a-study-says.html.
[52] "Climate Change to Alter Global Fire Risk," *Science Daily*, June 12, 2012, www.sciencedaily.com/releases/2012/06/120612144805.htm.
[53] Blane Heumann, "Reflections on 50 Years of Burning in the Nature Conservancy," The Nature Conservancy, April 26, 2012, http://blog.nature.org/2012/04/reflections-on-50-years-of-burning-in-the-nature-conservancy/.

FOR MORE INFORMATION

Cato Institute, 1000 Massachusetts Ave., N.W., Washington, DC 20001; 202-842-0200; www.cato.org. Think tank promoting principles of individual liberty, limited government and free markets.

Forest Service Employees for Environmental Ethics, P.O. Box 11615, Eugene, OR 97440; 541-484-2692; www.fseee.org. Watchdog group that includes present, former and retired U.S. Forest Service employees and works to hold the agency accountable for responsible land stewardship.

Goddard Institute for Space Studies, 2880 Broadway, New York, NY 10025; 301-286-8955; www.giss.nasa.gov. A NASA agency that studies Earth and space-based issues, including atmospheric and climate change.

Headwaters Economics, P.O. Box 7059, Bozeman, MT 59771; 406-570-8937; www.headwaterseconomics.org. Independent, nonprofit research group working to improve community development and land management decisions in the West.

National Association of State Foresters, 444 N. Capitol St., N.W., Suite 540, Washington, DC 20001; 202-624-5415; www.stateforesters.org. Represents officials who manage and protect state and private forests across the United States and its territories.

National Center for Atmospheric Research, P.O. Box 3000, Boulder, CO 80307; 303-497-1000; www.ncar.ucar.edu. Federally funded research and development center focusing on service, research and education in the atmospheric sciences, including weather, climate, and atmospheric pollution.

National Fire Protection Association, 1 Batterymarch Park, Quincy, MA 02169-7471; 617-770-3000; www.nfpa.org. Develops, publishes and disseminates more than 300 fire codes and standards intended to minimize the possibility and effects of fire and other risks.

National Oceanic and Atmospheric Administration (NOAA), 1305 East-West Highway, Silver Spring, MD 20910; 301-713-4248; www.noaa.gov. U.S. government agency that oversees coastal and marine resources.

National Parks Conservation Association, 777 Sixth St., N.W., Washington, DC 20001; 202-223-6722; www.npca.org. Private, nonprofit organization that works to protect and enhance America's national parks.

The Nature Conservancy, 4245 North Fairfax Dr., Suite 100, Arlington, VA 22203; 800-628-6860; www.nature.org. U.S.-based group that works to preserve lands and waters at home and in 33 countries abroad.

Tall Timbers Research Station and Land Conservancy, 13093 Henry Beadel Dr., Tallahassee, FL 32312; 850-893-4153; www.talltimbers.org. Private organization that studies fire ecology and forestry and protects land in north Florida.

U.S. Forest Service, 1400 Independence Ave., S.W., Washington, DC 20250-0003; 202-720-8732; www.fs.fed.us. Department of Agriculture agency that manages 193 million acres of national forests and grasslands and receives the largest share of federal funding for wildfire management.

Western Forestry Leadership Coalition, 2850 Youngfield St., 4th floor, Denver, CO 80215; 303-445-4362; www.wflccenter.org. Alliance of 34 state and federal forestry agencies that promotes science-based forest management.

Bibliography

Selected Sources

Books

Connors, Philip, *Fire Season: Field Notes from a Wilderness Lookout*, Ecco, 2011.
A former *Wall Street Journal* editor recounts his experience as a seasonal fire lookout in Gila National Forest.

DeBuys, William, *A Great Aridness: Climate Change and the Future of the American Southwest*, Oxford University Press, 2011.
A New Mexico writer examines the likely harsh impact of climate change in the Southwest.

Egan, Timothy, *The Big Burn: Teddy Roosevelt and the Fire That Saved America*, Houghton Mifflin, 2009.
A journalist tells how the disastrous 1910 wildfires prompted major investments in the national forest system.

Articles

Barker, Rocky, "Memo Orders Forest Service to Fight Fires to Save Money," *Arizona Daily Sun*, Aug. 24, 2012, http://azdailysun.com/news/national/memo-orders-forest-service-to-fight-fires-to-save-money/article_ff972874-b880-51a4-9e59-207130096df3.html.
The Forest Service's deputy chief ordered forest managers to suppress all wildfires immediately because of a high danger that burns would escalate in hot, dry conditions.

Bryan, Susan Montoya, "Scientists Scrutinize Beetle-Fire Interplay," *Seattle Times*, July 2, 2012, http://seattletimes.com/html/nationworld/2018585228_firebeetles03.html.
Scientists are studying whether a massive outbreak of bark beetles across the West is increasing wildfire risks, with mixed evidence so far.

Draper, Electa, "Black Sludge Coats Poudre River After High Park Fire," *Denver Post*, July 13, 2012, www.denverpost.com/breakingnews/ci_21069966/black-sludge-left-poudre-river-after-high-park?source=pkg.
Long-term impacts of wildfire can include erosion, soil damage and fish kills.

Fattig, Paul, "The Biscuit Fire: Ten Years Later," *The Mail Tribune* (Medford, OR), July 8, 2012, www.mailtribune.com/apps/pbcs.dll/article?AID=/20120708/NEWS/207080320.
Ten years after a massive wildfire in the Siskiyou National Forest in southern Oregon, both positive and negative effects are evident.

Peterson, Jodi, "Good Policy and Good Intentions Won't Stop Big Wildfires," *High Country News*, Oct. 17, 2011, www.hcn.org/issues/43.17/good-policy-and-good-intentions-wont-stop-big-destructive-wildfires/article_view?b_start:int=0&-C=.
Federal agencies have adopted science-based fire policies but need to apply them at much larger scales.

Wald, Matthew L., "U.S. is Urged to Change its Firefighting Air Fleet," *The New York Times*, July 30, 2012, www.nytimes.com/2012/07/30/us/forest-service-urged-to-update-firefighting-fleet.html?_r=1&ref=forestandbrushfires.
The Forest Service is rejecting a study it commissioned that recommends replacing its aging tanker planes with modern "scooper" aircraft that use water from local lakes and rivers.

Weidensee, Derek, "Clearcuts Don't Burn," *Range Magazine*, Fall 2011, www.rangemagazine.com/features/fall-11/range-fa11-clearcuts.pdf.
A land surveyor and former logger argues that clear-cutting is an effective way to reduce fire risks in Western forests.

Zuckerman, Laura, "Smoke from Idaho Wildfire Poses Health Risk: Officials," Reuters, Sept. 12, 2012, www.reuters.com/article/2012/09/12/us-usa-wildfires-idUSBRE88B03M20120912.
Smoke from a long-burning fire in Idaho causes symptoms that include fatigue, headaches and chronic coughing.

Reports and Studies

"Forest Service: Continued Work Needed to Address Persistent Management Challenges," U.S. Government Accountability Office, March 10, 2011, www.gao.gov/assets/130/125695.pdf.
To fight wildfires effectively, the Forest Service needs a clear strategy and goals that will help it spend limited funds effectively.

"Wildfire Effects on Source-Quality Water — Lessons from Fourmile Canyon Fire, Colorado, and Implications for Drinking-Water Treatment," U.S. Geological Survey, July 2012, http://pubs.usgs.gov/fs/2012/3095/.
Forest fires lead to flooding and erosion, which can degrade drinking water quality and damage water treatment systems.

"Wildfire Hazard Risk Report," CoreLogic, 2012, www.corelogic.com/about-us/researchtrends/wildfire-hazard-risk-report-2012.aspx.
A Santa Ana, Calif., company estimates that more than 740,000 homes in 13 Western states, valued at more than $136 billion, are at high risk from wildfires.

Pyne, Stephen J., "America's Fires: A Historical Context for Policy and Practice," Forest History Society, 2010.
An Arizona State University professor who has written widely on fires throughout history provides an overview of fire issues and policies in the United States.

The Next Step:

Additional Articles from Current Periodicals

Development

Kodas, Michael, and Burt Hubbard, "Policies Put More Coloradans at Risk of Losing Homes to Wildfire," *Daily Camera* (Colo.), June 30, 2012, www.dailycamera.com/state-west-news/ci_20980375/red-zone-policies-put-more-coloradans-at-risk.

Forested Colorado areas zoned for future development are at greater risk of wildfire, a geography professor has found.

Kraft, Michael E., "Wildfires: Climate Change and Home Construction Likely Causes," *Centre Daily Times* (Pa.), Sept. 24, 2012, www.centredaily.com/2012/09/24/3347313/climate-change-and-home-construction.html.

Home construction near forested areas has led to the construction of power lines that can cause fires, says an environmental affairs professor.

Wickham, Shawne K., "Wildfire Risk Keeps NH Vigilant," *Union Leader* (N.H.), July 29, 2012, p. A1, www.unionleader.com/article/20120729/NEWHAMPSHIRE03/707299977.

Supporters of development in forested areas say roads often serve as natural fire breaks.

Ecological Benefits

Bien, Walter, "Fire Vital to Pinelands Ecology," *Asbury Park* (N.J.) *Press*, Nov. 15, 2011.

Wildfires historically have helped New Jersey's Pine Barrens regenerate after beetle infestations, says a columnist.

Finley, Bruce, "Things Looking Up," *Denver Post*, Sept. 5, 2012, p. A1.

Wildfires release nutrients into soil and allow light to reach places where forests were unnaturally dense.

Knudson, Tom, "In an Environmental Exchange, Some Ancient Trees Are Killed to Help Others," *Sacramento* (Calif.) *Bee*, Aug. 12, 2012, p. A1, www.sacbee.com/2012/08/12/4717554/in-an-environmental-exchange-some.html#storylink=misearch.

Wildfires have helped conifers and aspen trees spread throughout the Sierra Nevadas over thousands of years.

Health Risks

Dodge, John, "Thurston County Air Quality Risky for Some as Fire Smoke Drifts In," *The Olympian* (Wash.), Sept. 13, 2012, www.theolympian.com/2012/09/13/2249841/thurston-county-air-quality-risky.html.

A wildfire has caused air quality to plummet to unhealthy levels in certain parts of Washington state.

O'Malley, Jaclyn, "Smoke From Calif. Wildfires Continues to Choke Reno," *Reno* (Nev.) *Gazette-Journal*, Aug. 23, 2012.

Pregnant women, children, the elderly and those suffering from heart or lung disease face the greatest risk from inhaling wildfire smoke.

Palmer, Brian, "Wildfire Management: A Costly Oxymoron," *The Washington Post*, July 10, 2012, p. E2.

Water quality can be compromised up to 100 miles from wildfires.

Logging

Boxall, Bettina, "New Blueprint for Sequoia Monument," *Los Angeles Times*, Sept. 5, 2012, p. B3, articles.latimes.com/2012/sep/05/local/la-me-sequoia-monument-20120905.

The U.S. Forest Service has unveiled a plan allowing the cutting of young sequoia trees around the Giant Sequoia National Monument in California to reduce wildfire risks.

Cockerham, Sean, "Otter Says No Logging Puts State at Risk," *Lewiston* (Idaho) *Morning Tribune*, Feb. 29, 2012, lmtribune.com/northwest/article_cea58c1b-9b5e-533d-973a-3234af5c7150.html.

Gov. C. L. "Butch" Otter, R-Idaho, says his state is at risk of a catastrophic wildfire because the U.S. Forest Service isn't thinning forests enough.

Erhard, Evelyn Madrid, "Pearce Cuts Funding, Then Blames Forest Service," *Las Cruces* (N.M.) *Sun-News*, July 15, 2012.

Rep. Steve Pearce, R-N.M., says increased logging could have prevented a recent string of intense wildfires in the state.

Citing *CQ Researcher*

Sample formats for citing these reports in a bibliography include the ones listed below. Preferred styles and formats vary, so please check with your instructor or professor.

MLA STYLE

Jost, Kenneth. "Remembering 9/11," CQ Researcher 2 Sept. 2011: 701-732.

APA STYLE

Jost, K. (2011, September 2). Remembering 9/11. *CQ Researcher, 9*, 701-732.

CHICAGO STYLE

Jost, Kenneth. "Remembering 9/11." *CQ Researcher*, September 2, 2011, 701-732.

In-depth Reports on Issues in the News

Are you writing a paper?

Need backup for a debate?

Want to become an expert on an issue?

For more than 80 years, students have turned to *CQ Researcher* for in-depth reporting on issues in the news. Reports on a full range of political and social issues are now available. Following is a selection of recent reports:

Civil Liberties
Solitary Confinement, 9/12
Re-examining the Constitution, 9/12
Voter Rights, 5/12
Remembering 9/11, 9/11
Government Secrecy, 2/11

Crime/Law
Supreme Court Controversies, 9/12
Debt Collectors, 7/12
Criminal Records, 4/12
Police Misconduct, 4/12
Immigration Conflict, 3/12

Education
Arts Education, 3/12
Youth Volunteerism, 1/12
Digital Education, 12/11
Student Debt, 10/11

Environment/Society
Understanding Mormonism, 10/12
Genetically Modified Food, 8/12
Whale Hunting, 6/12
U.S. Oil Dependence, 6/12
Gambling in America, 6/12
Sexual Harassment, 4/12

Health/Safety
New Health Care Law, 9/12
Farm Policy, 8/12
Treating ADHD, 8/12
Alcohol Abuse, 6/12

Politics/Economy
Social Media and Politics, 10/12
Euro Crisis, 10/12
Privatizing the Military, 7/12
U.S.-Europe Relations, 3/12
Attracting Jobs, 3/12
Presidential Election, 2/12

Upcoming Reports

Indecency on Television, 11/9/12 U.S. Demographics, 11/16/12 Sugar Controversy, 11/30/12

ACCESS

CQ Researcher is available in print and online. For access, visit your library or www.cqresearcher.com.

STAY CURRENT

For notice of upcoming *CQ Researcher* reports or to learn more about *CQ Researcher* products, subscribe to the free e-mail newsletters, *CQ Researcher Alert!* and *CQ Researcher News*: http://cqpress.com/newsletters.

PURCHASE

To purchase a *CQ Researcher* report in print or electronic format (PDF), visit www.cqpress.com or call 866-427-7737. Single reports start at $15. Bulk purchase discounts and electronic-rights licensing are also available.

SUBSCRIBE

Annual full-service *CQ Researcher* subscriptions—including 44 reports a year, monthly index updates, and a bound volume—start at $1,054. Add $25 for domestic postage.

CQ Researcher Online offers a backfile from 1991 and a number of tools to simplify research. For pricing information, call 800-834-9020, or e-mail librarymarketing@cqpress.com.

CQ RESEARCHER ***PLUS*** *ARCHIVE*

GET ONLINE ACCESS TO VITAL ISSUES FROM 1923 TO THE PRESENT

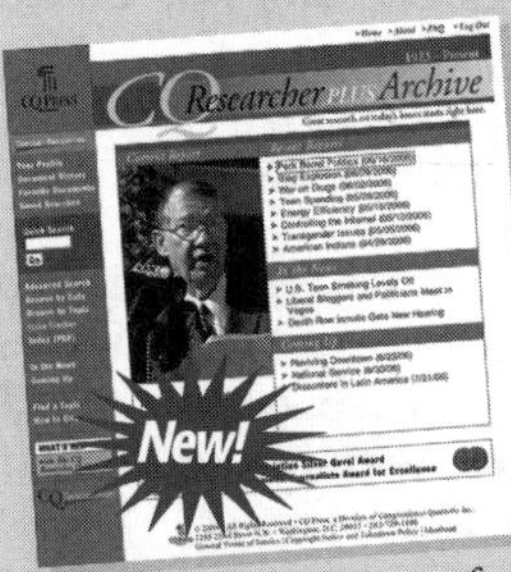

CQ Researcher Plus Archive delivers fast, online access to every *CQ Researcher* report from 1991 to the present, *PLUS* lets you explore the complete archive of *Editorial Research Reports** from 1923-1990. Search and browse more than 3,600 in-depth reports.

Loaded with handy online features, *CQ Researcher Plus Archive* provides the trustworthy reporting and the advanced online functionality today's researchers demand. The new "Issue Tracker" feature provides quick links to past and present reports on the specific topics you need.

For a free trial, visit http://library.cqpress.com/trials.

For pricing information, call 1-800-834-9020, ext. 1906 or e-mail librarymarketing@cqpress.com.

**Editorial Research Reports*, the predecessor to *CQ Researcher*, provides the same expert, nonpartisan reporting on the vital issues that have shaped our society.

CQ Press • 2300 N Street, NW, Suite 800 • Washington, DC 20037

CQ Researcher

Published by CQ Press, an Imprint of SAGE Publications, Inc.

www.cqresearcher.com

Indecency on Television

Should the FCC crack down or give up?

The protracted legal fight over broadcast indecency is continuing after the Supreme Court wiped out penalties against three TV networks but left the constitutionality of the Federal Communications Commission's policy unresolved. Now, the FCC faces pressures from broadcasters and free-speech advocates on one side and anti-indecency groups on the other over how to deal with a backlog of 1.5 million pending complaints about sex and vulgarity on radio and television. Federal law prohibits obscenity, indecency or profanity on broadcast channels, though not on cable or satellite systems. The FCC tightened its policy in recent years to prohibit even a "fleeting" use of the F- or S-word and began imposing costly penalties against stations in indecency cases. Broadcasters say the policy limits their ability to compete with cable systems, but anti-indecency groups say over-the-air television should be kept as family-friendly as possible. Many legal experts say, however, that the proliferation of other media may lead the courts eventually to strike down the law.

The prime-time CBS show "How I Met Your Mother" is rated by the Parents Television Council, an anti-indecency advocacy group, as "inappropriate for youngsters" because of its "heavy" sexual content.

Inside This Report

The Issues 967
Background 974
Chronology 975
Current Situation 980
At Issue........................981
Outlook 983
Bibliography 986
The Next Step 987

CQ Researcher • Nov. 9, 2012 • www.cqresearcher.com
Volume 22, Number 40 • Pages 965-988

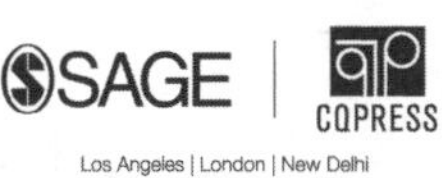

Recipient of Society of Professional Journalists Award for Excellence ◆ American Bar Association Silver Gavel Award

Indecency on Television

The Issues

967 • Is there too much sex and vulgarity on television?
• Should the FCC relax enforcement of its indecency rules?
• Should the FCC regulate indecency on cable TV?

Background

974 **Loss of Innocence**
Radio and TV began pushing sexual boundaries in the 1960s.

977 **"Chilling" Effect?**
The FCC fined broadcasters $4 million in 2006 for airing graphic sex scenes and "fleeting expletives."

979 **Longtime Wait**
Legal challenges by broadcasters brought FCC indecency enforcement to a stand-still after 2006.

Current Situation

980 **FCC's Full Plate**
Indecency may be less important than other issues.

982 **Broadcasters' Woes**
Major broadcast networks are more concerned about sagging ratings than about the FCC's next moves on indecency.

Outlook

983 **"Heinously Difficult" Job**
The FCC has no easy path on indecency enforcement, but courts may eventually throw the law out.

Cover: CBS Entertainment

Sidebars and Graphics

968 **Many Prime-Time Shows Fail Parents' Group Test**
No program was rated "family friendly" in a recent survey.

969 **Indecency Complaints to FCC Declined**
Complaints peaked after Janet Jackson's Super Bowl "wardrobe malfunction" in 2004.

971 **Indecency Complaints Can Lead to Big Penalties**
CBS' 2006 drama "Without a Trace" drew $3.6 million in fines.

972 **FCC's Indecency Policy: A Work in Progress**
A Supreme Court ruling in June left modification of the policy to the commission.

975 **Chronology**
Key events since 1934.

976 **TV Violence Remains Unregulated**
"There would be enormous hurdles" in regulating it.

981 **At Issue**
Should FCC regulation of broadcast indecency be eliminated?

For Further Research

985 **For More Information**
Organizations to contact.

986 **Bibliography**
Selected sources used.

987 **The Next Step**
Additional articles.

987 **Citing *CQ Researcher***
Sample bibliography formats.

CQ Researcher

Nov. 9, 2012
Volume 22, Number 40

Managing Editor: Thomas J. Billitteri
tjb@cqpress.com

Assistant Managing Editor: Kathy Koch
kkoch@cqpress.com

Senior Contributing Editor:
Thomas J. Colin
tcolin@cqpress.com

Associate Editor: Kenneth Jost

Staff Writer: Marcia Clemmitt

Contributing Writers: Peter Katel, Barbara Mantel, Tom Price, Jennifer Weeks

Senior Project Editor: Olu B. Davis

Assistant Editor: Darrell Dela Rosa

Fact Checker: Michelle Harris

Los Angeles | London | New Delhi
Singapore | Washington DC

An Imprint of SAGE Publications, Inc.

Vice President and Editorial Director, Higher Education Group:
Michele Sordi

Director, Online Publishing:
Todd Baldwin

CQ Researcher (ISSN 1056-2036) is printed on acid-free paper. Published weekly, except: (March wk. 5) (May wk. 4) (July wk. 1) (Aug. wks. 3, 4) (Nov. wk. 4) and (Dec. wks. 3, 4). Published by SAGE Publications, Inc., 2455 Teller Rd., Thousand Oaks, CA 91320. Annual full-service subscriptions start at $1,054. For pricing, call 1-800-834-9020. To purchase a *CQ Researcher* report in print or electronic format (PDF), visit www.cqpress.com or call 866-427-7737. Single reports start at $15. Bulk purchase discounts and electronic-rights licensing are also available. Periodicals postage paid at Thousand Oaks, California, and at additional mailing offices. POSTMASTER: Send address changes to *CQ Researcher*, 2300 N St., N.W., Suite 800, Washington, DC 20037.

Indecency on Television

By Kenneth Jost

The Issues

The Fox television network's hit animated comedy "Family Guy" prides itself on "outrageous humor" and a "cult status" among millions of fans nationwide. But on March 8, 2009, the Emmy-nominated show went so far over the top that nearly 180,000 non-fans complained to the Federal Communications Commission (FCC) that the program violated the federal law against indecency on broadcast radio or television.

As part of a convoluted plot, the early prime-time show that Sunday included a depiction of bestiality — a horse licking the bare behind of the taste-challenged patriarch Peter Baker — and a gay orgy scene with one graphic term unsuitable for straight company.

The anti-indecency advocacy group Parents Television Council rose up in indignation on its website. "This is the kind of 'entertainment' Fox thinks is ideal for your kids to see on a Sunday night cartoon," the e-alert read. Website visitors were provided links to file a complaint with the FCC, contact their local Fox station or make a donation to the council.

The council's Internet alarm apparently paid off, according to figures from the FCC, the federal agency that regulates broadcasters and to a lesser degree other telecommunications services. The commission received 179,997 indecency complaints that month — compared to only 505 in the previous month. [1] (*See graph, p. 969.*)

Getty Images/Christopher Polk

M.I.A. performs at halftime during the Super Bowl in Indianapolis last Feb. 5. When the British singer raised her middle finger at the crowd, some TV stations used taped delays to block the gesture, but it appeared on many other stations, intensifying calls by anti-indecency advocacy groups for more stringent policing of indecency on TV by the Federal Communications Commission.

For broadcasters, the parents group has been an unwelcome thorn in the side since its formation in 1995. "I don't think we're ever going to please the Parents Television Council," says Dennis Wharton, executive vice president for communications at the National Association of Broadcasters (NAB). "We respect what they do," Wharton continues. "But let's not kid ourselves. They use these campaigns to bring in more revenue for their cause."

The council's leaders bristle at the insinuation that the complaints are not genuine. "The broadcast networks and their surrogates like to pretend that these are ginned up," says Dan Isett, the council's Washington-based director of public policy. "We can't force anybody to file a complaint."

The complaints against the "Family Guy" episode have now lain with the FCC for more than three years, part of an estimated backlog of 1.5 million complaints left unacted on during a protracted legal challenge to the agency's indecency policy. The legal uncertainty continues despite a Supreme Court decision on June 21 that threw out indecency rulings in three separate cases against the Fox and ABC networks but left a constitutional challenge to the FCC policy unresolved.

The decision marked the Supreme Court's first substantive ruling on the issue since 1978, when it tenuously upheld the agency's power to penalize broadcasters for indecency aired when children were likely to be in the audience. The earlier ruling, *FCC v. Pacifica Foundation*, upheld the FCC's decision to reprimand a New York City radio station for a mid-afternoon broadcast of a recorded monologue by the late comedian George Carlin that satirized what he described as seven "filthy words" that "you couldn't say on the public airwaves." [2]

The FCC's authority stems from the very first law regulating radio broadcasting in 1927. The provision, as added to the U.S. criminal code in 1948, said that anyone who "utters any obscene, indecent, or profane language by means of radio communication" can be punished by up to two years' imprisonment and a fine of up to $10,000.

Many Prime-Time Shows Fail Parents' Group Test

The Parents Television Council's "Family Guide to Prime Time Television" rates programs by color: red for those "unsuitable for children" because of "gratuitous sex, explicit dialogue, violent content or obscene language"; yellow for those "inappropriate for youngsters" because of "adult-oriented themes and dialogues"; and green for "family-friendly" programs that promote "responsible themes and traditional values." In the last week of October, no prime-time program was rated green, though some — such as sports programs — were unrated. Here are the council's ratings for some of the most popular programs (broadcast times, Eastern time zone):

Program (Network, Time)	Rating	Description
America's Next Top Model (CW/reality: 8 pm Friday)	☆ Red	Foul language "common"; sex discussed
The Big Bang Theory (CBS: 8 pm Thursday)	☆ Red	"Frequent sexual content"
Criminal Minds (CBS: 10 pm Wednesday)	☆ Red	Violence "frequent," "often extreme"
Dancing With the Stars (ABC: 8 pm, Monday, Tuesday)	Yellow	"Harsh" language; "suggestive" dancing
Family Guy (Fox: 9 pm Sunday)	☆ Red	"Vile, offensive content"
How I Met Your Mother (CBS: 8:30 pm Monday)	☆ Red	"Heavy" sexual content
Modern Family (ABC: 9 pm Wednesday)	Yellow	"Innuendo and mild references to sex"
Person of Interest (CBS: 9 pm Thursday)	☆ Red	Violence; "ambiguous morality"
The Simpsons (Fox: 8:30 pm Sunday)	☆ Red	"Steadily more graphic" over time
Two and a Half Men (CBS: 8:30 pm Thursday)	☆ Red	"Constant barrage" of sexual scenes, jokes
30 Rock (NBC: 8 pm Thursday)	Yellow	"Sexual innuendo and language"
The Voice (NBC: 8 pm Monday, Tuesday)	Yellow	"Sexual innuendo and references"

☆ Red ⬭ Yellow

Source: Parents Television Council, www.parentstv.org/PTC/familyguide/weekly.asp

Congress in 2006 raised the fine that the FCC could levy against an individual station to $325,000 per violation or a maximum of $3 million for a continuing violation.

For 25 years, the FCC treated the *Pacifica* case as authorizing it to punish radio or television broadcasters only for extended or repetitive vulgarity or sexual material, not for brief nudity or what came to be called a "fleeting expletive," such as a vulgar word uttered accidentally. [3] But the commission shifted its stance in March 2004 to permit a sanction for a single use of the F-word. A later decision extended the same prohibition to any use of the S-word. (*See box, p. 972.*)

The policy change came six weeks after the halftime show at the 2004 Super Bowl provoked a contentious national debate about nudity on television. Viewers of the musical extravaganza that night caught a glimpse of the singer Janet Jackson's exposed right breast after fellow pop star Justin Timberlake dislodged one side of her bustier. Jackson famously blamed the incident on a "wardrobe malfunction." Both CBS, which broadcast the show, and MTV, which produced it, apologized, but the FCC in September 2004 fined CBS stations a total of $550,000 for the incident. (*See FCC enforcement record, p. 971.*)

The Supreme Court rejected the FCC's effort to uphold the fine against CBS in a brief order on June 29. That action came eight days after the court had similarly rejected FCC pleas to uphold the indecency findings against Fox and ABC.

The Fox cases stemmed from seemingly unscripted uses of the F- and S-words by entertainers during live broadcasts of separate music awards programs in 2002 and 2003. The ABC case stemmed from brief nudity in a 2003 episode of the police drama "NYPD Blue." ABC stations were fined a total of $1.24 million for the incident; the Fox stations were only warned.

In rejecting the FCC's effort to uphold the fines and warnings, however, the Supreme Court said broadcasters had no advance notice of the more restrictive policy. "The Commission failed to give Fox or ABC fair notice prior to the broadcasts in question that fleeting expletives and momentary nudity could be found actionably indecent," Justice Anthony M. Kennedy wrote in *FCC v. Fox Television Stations.* [4]

The broadcasters had urged the court to go further, however. They wanted the justices to rule the "fleeting expletive" policy itself unconstitutionally vague or prohibit the FCC from punishing sexual depictions and language altogether unless the material met the stricter definition of legal obscenity. Instead, Kennedy closed his opinion for seven justices by saying it was up to the FCC to decide whether to modify its policy — and up to the courts to rule on any future enforcement actions. In a separate opinion concurring in the result, Justice Ruth Bader Ginsburg called for overruling *Pacifica*, a position urged in a brief filed on behalf of a bipartisan group of six former FCC officials. [5] (*See "At Issue," p. 981.*)

The decision disappointed broadcasters and many media law experts who had hoped for a more definitive ruling. "There's still a lack of clarity, obviously, given the non-decision decision that came from the court," says the NAB's Wharton. But the parents group cheered what it viewed as an affirmation of the FCC's underlying policy. "From our perspective, it was a pretty complete win," says Isett. "It was a status quo ruling that took everything back to where we had been."

The five FCC commissioners all responded to the court's decision by promising, with varying emphasis, to enforce the law. Four months later, however, the only hint of action from the agency is a Sept. 21 directive by the current FCC chairman, Julius Genachowski, that the agency's enforcement bureau focus on "the strongest cases that involve egregious indecency violations." [6]

The mountain of pending complaints reflects the success of the Parents Television Council in mobilizing viewers and listeners concerned about sex and vulgarity on television and radio. The public concern in turn reflects the evolution of television in particular from a supposedly sex-free golden age in the 1950s and '60s to today's franker and more frequent depictions of sex.

Sex now is discussed and depicted on television matter-of-factly — whether marital, premarital or extramarital. Bedroom scenes are frequent, pajamas a thing of the past and gays and lesbians out of the closet. "A lot of the advocacy groups would like television to be like it was in the 1950s," says Robert Thompson, a professor of popular culture and director of the Bleier Center for Television and Popular Culture at Syracuse University.

The FCC's indecency authority extends, however, only to over-the-air radio and television broadcasters, not to cable television with its much looser standards or to the Internet, video games, mobile apps and other media. "Broadcast indecency enforcement feels largely irrelevant today," says Paul Gallant, a media industry analyst in Washington with the investment firm Guggenheim Partners.

Some industry observers say the competition from new media is helping to drive decency standards down to a low common denominator. "Sex sells," as James P. Steyer, head of the children's advocacy group Common Sense Media, wrote in his book *The Other Parent.* [7]

Both the Parents Television Council and Common Sense Media rate many of the prime-time programs on broadcast television as unsuitable for youngsters. (*See chart, p. 968.*) Both groups say that sex as well as violence on TV harms impressionable young viewers. "Children become sexually interested

Indecency Complaints to FCC Declined

Indecency complaints received by the Federal Communications Commission (FCC) peaked in 2004 at more than 1.4 million after many Super Bowl viewers objected to singer Janet Jackson's "wardrobe malfunction" during the game's halftime show. The number of complaints plummeted in 2005 because the FCC dismissed many complainst that did not fall within FCC guidelines. Complaints rose in 2006 after advocacy groups urged their members to flood the FCC with objections against particular shows. The number of complaints sent to the agency fell significantly in 2011 and 2012 as a legal battle over the constitutionality of the FCC's policy was moving toward the Supreme Court. The court's ruling in late June threw out penalties in three cases but left the legal issue unresolved.

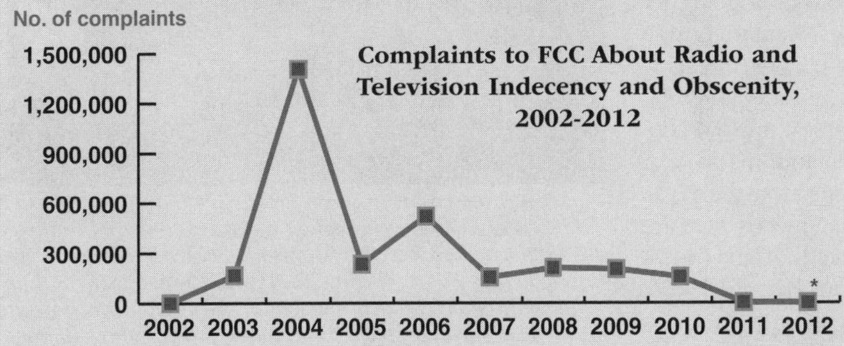

* *January-June 2012*

Source: "Quarterly Reports — Consumer Inquiries and Complaints," FCC, 2012

and sexually active at younger ages," says Isett. "If kids are encouraged to be sexually active younger, that has a long-term effect."

Many experts disagree. "The media follow changing social norms and mores rather than leading," says Frank Couvares, a professor of history and American studies at Amherst College in Massachusetts. "I'm very skeptical that if you let the media broadcast certain kinds of images or words, it's going to significantly corrupt or change morals."

As media companies, media critics and media experts await the FCC's next moves, here are some of the questions being debated:

© Fox Broadcasting

Fox Television's animated comedy hit "Family Guy" is embraced by millions of fans — and reviled by others — for its "outrageous humor." The show's March 8, 2009, episode, which included a gay orgy scene, drew nearly 180,000 complaints that the program violated the federal law against broadcast indecency. The complaints have now lain with the FCC for more than three years, part of an estimated backlog of 1.5 million complaints unacted upon during a protracted legal challenge to the agency's indecency policy.

Is there too much sex and vulgarity on television?

Parents looking for family-friendly programming on prime-time television are pretty much out of luck, according to the Parents Television Council. The council's color-coded guide to the broadcast networks' prime-time schedules rates the vast majority of programs either red ("unsuitable for children") or yellow ("may be inappropriate for youngsters"). Some shows, including sports programs, are unrated, but in the last full week of October not a single program was green-lighted as "promoting responsible themes and traditional values."

The council's reports over the years have documented what it calls a shocking increase in sex and vulgarity on television. A report at the start of the fall 2010 television season found a roughly 70 percent increase in profanity on the five commercial networks compared to five years earlier; the report counted bleeped use of the F- or S-words and unbleeped anatomical references such as "balls" and "boobs." [8]

"The amount of adult content has gone up year after year for years," says the council's Isett. "There is simply more of this type of content than there ever was before."

Other advocates and experts generally agree on the trend, but they view it with less alarm and question the government's role in dealing with the issue. "There are a lot of things that are on television that I am not comfortable with," says Syracuse University professor Thompson. "But to regulate the content of a medium because you and your kids find it offensive or because you don't want your kids to watch is not a very good argument."

"There's more acceptance of violent and sexual imagery in popular culture than there used to be," says Alan Simpson, Common Sense Media's vice president of public policy. "But it's also in part a competition for viewers."

Jonathan Rintels, executive director of the Center for Creative Voices, an organization representing writers and other professionals in the creative community, similarly sees changing tastes among viewers as a reason for more sex and graphic language on TV. "The reason we have it is it's in demand," Rintels says. As a parent himself, Rintels views government regulation as contributing to "parental complacency" about what their children see. "It's given parents a false sense of security that something off-color won't reach their children when they're watching television," he says.

Broadcasters acknowledge the change in TV offerings but accuse other media of purveying more sex than they do. "It would be naïve of us not to concede that the envelope moves," says the NAB's Wharton, "but we often get lumped in with programs that air on other platforms: cable, pay cable and satellite. We don't have naked people cavorting across the screen."

In any event, Wharton says viewers should be free to decide for themselves what to watch or listen to. "We're not living in a 'Leave It to Beaver' world anymore," he says. "The proper approach is to let parents decide what's appropriate for their kids to watch or hear on the radio."

The cable industry — with no indecency regulation — similarly emphasizes customer tastes and customer choice over any governmental role. "We provide programming of interest to a broad variety of people," says Jill Luckett, senior vice president for program network policy at the National Cable and Telecommunications Association (NCTA). "There's something for everyone. That includes a wide variety of networks and genres, including what some people would find inappropriate for their families but also a lot of children and family programming for everyone."

The laissez-faire approach does not come naturally, however, to government officials. Members of Congress seized on the Super Bowl broadcast within a week to criticize CBS and begin pushing legislation to increase penalties for broadcast indecency. "Some broadcasters are engaged in a race to the bottom," Rep. Fred Upton, a Michigan Republican and chair of the House Commerce Subcommittee on Telecommunications and the Internet, said as he opened a hearing on his legislation to raise fines for indecency.

FCC Chairman Michael Powell used the same metaphor to describe broadcasters' changed practices. The Super Bowl broadcast "is just the latest example in a growing list of deplorable incidents over the nation's airwaves," Powell told the subcommittee. "We must take action to protect our nation's children." [9]

Despite the tough talk, the FCC has been something of a paper tiger on the indecency enforcement front. The commission got big news coverage in March 2006 when it imposed penalties totaling about $4 million in seven indecency cases, but the omnibus order rejected indecency complaints in 17 others.

Still, Thompson sees the clamor about indecency as irrational. "The idea that a great communication medium like television in a country like the United States is actually having a conversation about an exposed breast, I find amusing," he says.

Indecency Complaints Can Lead to Big Penalties

The Federal Communications Commission issues Notices of Apparent Liability (NALs) when it finds television or radio stations liable for indecency violations. The number of NALs hit a peak of 12 in 2004, and total penalties nearly topped $8 million. Television licensees of the Fox reality show "Married by America" were fined about $1.2 million that year. Similarly, three media companies — Viacom, Clear Channel and Emmis — agreed to consent decrees totaling nearly $4.3 million that same year. Penalties totaled about $4 million in 2006 when licensees of the CBS drama "Without a Trace" were ordered to pay $3.6 million.

FCC Indecency Penalties, 1993-2010

Year	Number of Notices of Apparent Liability (NALs)	$ Amount of NALs
1993	5	$665,000
1994	7	$674,500
1995	1	$4,000
1996	3	$25,500
1997	7	$35,500
1998	6	$40,000
1999	3	$49,000
2000	7	$48,000
2001	7	$91,000
2002	7	$99,400
2003	3	$440,000
2004	12	$7,928,080*
2005	0	$0
2006	7	$3,962,500
2007	0	$0
2008	0	$0
2009	0	$0
2010	1	$25,000

** Includes amounts from three separate consent decrees.*

Sources: "Indecency Complaints and NALs: 1993-2006," FCC, 2010

Should the FCC relax enforcement of its indecency rules?

The Public Broadcasting Service (PBS) garnered attention and appreciative reviews in fall 2003 for a seven-part documentary series, "The Blues," executive-produced by the acclaimed director Martin Scorsese. Two-and-a-half years later, however, a small public television station in San Mateo, Calif., landed in trouble with the FCC for having broadcast one of the programs that contained what the agency determined to be "gratuitous" use of the S- and F-words.

The FCC in March 2006 fined San Mateo Community College, the licensee for station KCSM, $15,000 for violating the federal ban on broadcast indecency. The penalty was part of nearly $4 million in fines that the FCC imposed on seven broadcasters as it resolved complaints in 28 cases altogether. The Parents Television Coun-

FCC's Indecency Policy: A Work in Progress

The Federal Communications Commission has authority under the Communications Act of 1934 to prohibit "obscene, indecent, or profane language" on broadcast radio or television. The Supreme Court upheld the FCC's power to penalize broadcasters for violating the ban in a case involving repeated use of seven vulgar words. The FCC in 2004 ruled that the prohibition also applies to a single use of the F-word — a so-called "fleeting expletive." After a protracted legal battle, the Supreme Court in June ruled that the stricter policy could not be applied to earlier broadcasts. The court left it up to the FCC to decide whether to modify the policy. Here are excerpts from key laws, FCC pronouncements and court rulings on broadcast indecency:

"Whoever utters any obscene, indecent, or profane language by means of radio communication shall be fined not more than $10,000 or imprisoned not more than two years, or both."
18 U.S. Code § 1464 (enacted 1948)

Broadcast indecency is defined as follows: "Language or material that depicts or describes, in terms patently offensive as measured by contemporary community standards for the broadcast medium, sexual or excretory activities or organs."
New Indecency Enforcement Standards, 2 F.C.C.Rcd. 2726 (1987)

"We now clarify . . . that the mere fact that specific words or phrases are not sustained or repeated does not mandate a finding that material that is otherwise patently offensive to the broadcast medium is not indecent."
In re "Golden Globe Awards," 19 F.C.C.Rcd. 4975 (2004)

"[T]he amount of any forfeiture penalty determined under this subsection [for a broadcast licensee or applicant] shall not exceed $325,000 for each violation or each day of a continuing violation, except that the amount assessed for any continuing violation shall not exceed a total of $3,000,000 for any single act of failure to act."
Broadcast Decency Enforcement Act of 2006

"[T]his opinion leaves the Commission free to modify its current indecency policy in light of its determination of the public interest and applicable legal requirements. And it leaves the courts free to review the current policy or any modified policy in light of its content and application."
FCC v. Fox Television Stations, U.S. Supreme Court (2012)

cil applauded the crackdown, but KCSM and other penalized broadcasters vowed to appeal. And in a partial dissent, FCC Commissioner Jonathan Adelstein sharply criticized the finding on "The Blues," contrasting it with the commission's earlier no-indecency rulings on the World War II movies "Saving Private Ryan" and "Schindler's List" despite their graphic language or nudity. [10]

The FCC's indecency enforcement came to a virtual halt after the 2006 order as broadcasters, including KCSM, challenged the actions in court. The commission's only major cases were seven-figure, nudity-related penalties against ABC stations for the "NYPD Blue" episode and against 169 Fox stations for an April 2003 episode of "Married by America" that featured male and female strippers. Now, the Supreme Court's decision in the long-running *Fox* case clears the way for the FCC to take on the huge backlog of complaints that have continued to pile up.

The Parents Television Council is eager for the FCC to get to work even if many of the complaints are on their face invalid. "It's time to adjudicate this enormous backlog," says Isett. "What the Supreme Court said is that the networks didn't have ample notice" of the change in FCC policy in March 2004, Isett explains. "There's no question that they haven't had advance notice now."

Broadcasters similarly want the backlog reduced, but for different reasons. Hundreds of license renewals for stations have been held up because of pending indecency complaints, the NAB's Wharton explains. Many of the complaints can be dismissed readily, Wharton says, because they are too old or because they relate to programs aired during the 10 p.m. to 6 a.m. "safe harbor" period for adult viewers when the indecency regulation does not apply. "I'm sure there are defective cases, cases that don't meet the very narrow definition of indecency," Isett acknowledges from the other side, "but some of them surely do."

The FCC commissioners appear to agree on the goal, but they spoke only in generalities after the Supreme Court's decision. Chairman Genachowski, a Democrat appointed by President Obama at the start of his term in 2009, vowed to "carry out Congress's directive to protect young TV viewers" in a manner "[c]onsistent with First Amendment principles." The commission's senior Republican, Robert McDowell, called on the commission to act "expeditiously . . . to put an end to years of litigation and uncertainty."

The uncertainty about the FCC's definition of indecency is one of the major criticisms of its policy advanced by broadcasters and their free-speech-oriented allies. "Unless we know what's safe and what's not safe, we can't comply," says Rintels with the Center for Creative Voices. Critics note that even though the F- and S-words are treated as presumptively indecent, other references to sexual or excretory organs are not. "It seems utterly arbitrary under current FCC practice," Rintels says.

Getty Images/Donald Miralle

Janet Jackson ignited a national debate about nudity on TV after a so-called "wardrobe malfunction" briefly exposed one of her breasts during her Super Bowl halftime performance with Justin Timberlake in Houston on Feb. 1, 2004. Both CBS, which broadcast the show, and MTV, which produced it, apologized, but the FCC in September 2004 fined CBS stations a total of $550,000 for broadcasting the incident. The penalty was thrown out in the courts.

Fox and ABC emphasized what they called the vagueness of the FCC's policy in their legal arguments before the Supreme Court. So did other groups. As one example, the Reporters Committee for Freedom of the Press acknowledged that the FCC had created an exception for "bona fide newscasts," but argued that the exception is "unworkable" because of "the increased blurring of the distinction between news and entertainment programming." In its brief, the NAB contended that broadcasters "are left to guess at how the policy will apply to them."

Isett at the Parents Television Council mocks the argument. "It's a very recent phenomenon that broadcasters have decided that they don't understand the rules," he says. "There are tests, and they make a lot of sense," Isett concludes. "The idea that broadcasters are absolutely clueless doesn't hold water."

For its part, Common Sense Media supports the FCC's role in regulating indecency. "We've given a lot of money and a lot of benefit to broadcasters," Simpson says. "They're using public airwaves, aren't there still public obligations that go with that?" But he also stresses parents' role in monitoring their children's viewing habits. "Parents are the essential players," he says.

Should the FCC regulate indecency on cable television?

Online film reviewer James Berardinelli fondly recalls sneaking peeks at *Playboy* magazine as a teenager in the 1980s. But he got his real guilty pleasures thanks to a neighbor who gave him the run of his cable-wired house on Friday nights. There, beyond parental supervision, Berardinelli regularly tuned in to "Cinemax After Dark," the soft-porn channel created by HBO in 1984 that now runs seven nights a week. [11]

Before the Internet, cable was for porn — hard and soft — as well as mainstream programming with not-so-fleeting glimpses of nudity and sexual activity that could not be shown on broadcast channels. Today, cable channels, especially premium pay channels such as HBO and Showtime, continue to offer more skin and more salty language than broadcast stations, at least in part because the FCC has no power to regulate indecency on cable.

The cable industry defends its regulation-free status. "Cable is a private subscription service that doesn't use the government's airwaves to transmit programming that's available to all," says Brian Dietz, NCTA's vice president for communication. "Customers make a choice to subscribe to cable. The industry is built on an entirely different model than broadcasting."

Broadcasters bristle at living under FCC regulation that does not cover their cable competitors. "It's serious why we should be singled out when 85 percent of all homes get broadcast programming through a pay TV platform," says the NAB's Wharton. Broadcasters would prefer "responsible self-regulation" by both industries, Wharton says, but he adds: "If it's good for broadcasting, why shouldn't it apply to other media outlets?"

Historically, the indecency law does not apply to cable for the simple reason that cable was not invented until the late 1940s and did not reach a majority of U.S. households until the 1980s. At the time of the Supreme Court's ruling in the *Pacifica* case in 1978, cable service was not "pervasive" nor "uniquely accessible to children" — the two factors that the court cited in upholding the indecency regulation for broadcasters.

Today, media watchers note what TV viewers know from their daily lives: For cable-subscribing households, there is no practical difference between a broadcast channel and a cable channel. "Parents don't make the distinction as to whether [programming] is coming from broadcasting or cable," says Simpson with Common Sense Media.

"The idea that parents can place a kid in front of a television set and leave them without supervision and expect they will only be watching shows that don't have any potential for off-color material is not justified," says Rintels with the Center for Creative Voices. "Nearly 90 percent of Americans subscribe to cable television, and in cable those rules don't apply."

The legal distinction remains, however. Michael Schooler, a deputy general counsel with the NCTA, explains that the Supreme Court has twice struck down federal laws aimed at regulating sexually explicit material on cable. Schooler says the court noted in both cases that there were less restrictive ways to limit children's access to sexually explicit material. He points to moves supported by industry such as use of the so-called "v-chip" to block age-inappropriate programs and ratings advisories to identify programs with sexual, violent or other questionable content.

The cable industry came under pressure as Congress considered legislation to crack down on indecency on television after the 2004 Super Bowl episode. A proposal to extend the indecency regulations to cable operators' expanded basic subscription offerings failed on an 11-12 vote in the Senate Commerce Committee on March 9 even as the panel voted to increase penalties for broadcasters and subject performers to indecency penalties as well. [12]

Two committee leaders — Chairman John McCain, Republican of Arizona, and ranking Democrat Ernest Hollings of South Carolina — floated a narrower proposal to help subscribers screen out indecent programming. The proposal would have required cable operators to offer "a la carte pricing" plans that allow customers to subscribe on a per-channel basis instead of choosing among bundled service packages. A consortium of independent cable channels warned that the proposal could result in fewer choices and higher prices for subscribers. Hollings withdrew the proposal without seeking a vote, saying the issue would have complicated passage of the main bill. [13]

The cable industry continues to warn that a la carte pricing would reduce diversity in programming. After he became FCC chairman in 2005, Kevin Martin pushed a narrower proposal to require cable systems to offer customers an indecency-free "family tier" subscription package. Some cable companies promised to offer such plans, in part to kill interest in a la carte pricing or ward off mandated family-tier packages.

NCTA officials say some cable companies continue to offer such plans, but Isett with the Parents Television Council — which favors the idea — says the plans are not promoted. "It sort of exists in some markets to some extent," he says. "There's no market for it, and they don't market it even if there were."

With cable exempted from indecency regulation, Rintels says the reasons for regulating broadcasters simply fail. "The growth of cable really negates this whole idea that the government can create an environment in which parents can rely on television not to be off-color at any moment," he says. ■

BACKGROUND

Loss of Innocence

Congress gave the FCC authority to regulate indecency when it established the commission in 1934. The power went unused, however, until the 1960s when first radio and then television began pushing the sexual boundaries for mass entertainment media. With the FCC's encouragement, the existing three commercial television networks adopted a "family viewing hour" policy in the 1970s that reserved the first hour of the prime-time schedule for programs suitable for children. Meanwhile, several challenges to sexually explicit material on talk radio culminated with the Supreme Court's *Pacifica* decision in 1978 upholding the FCC's authority to penalize broadcasters for indecency on programming aired when children were likely to be in the audience. [14]

The Communications Act of 1934 established the FCC with broad but undefined power to regulate what was then only radio broadcasting "in the public interest, convenience, and necessity." The act's Section 326 prohibited the commission from exercising any power of censorship but did authorize it to prohibit "obscene, indecent, or profane language." In 1948, the prohibition was recodified as a stand-alone provision in the U.S. criminal code, with punishment of up to two years' imprisonment or a fine of up to $10,000 per violation. The commission also had the power to punish obscenity, indecency or profanity with administrative fines up to a maximum of $10,000; the amount was raised in 1994 and again in 2006 to its present level of $325,000 per violation.

As television emerged in the 1950s as the nation's dominant entertainment medium, broadcasters treated sexual matters with kid gloves. A voluntary code of conduct adopted in 1951 called on broadcasters not to "emphasize anatomical details indecently" and to use "good taste and delicacy" in depicting locations "closely associated with sexual life or with sexual sin." Lucy Ricardo, the ditzy character played by Lucille Ball, gave birth to little Ricky on the hit situation-comedy "I Love

Continued on p. 976

Chronology

Before 1960

Sex is treated gingerly on radio, television.

1934
Communications Act of 1934 creates Federal Communications Commission to regulate radio (later, television); Section 326 prohibits "obscene, indecent, or profane" language on broadcasts.

1948
Prohibition against obscenity, indecency or profanity enacted in U.S. criminal code, with penalty of up to two years' imprisonment and/or up to $10,000 fine.

1950s
Television becomes dominant entertainment medium; broadcasters adopt voluntary ethics code requiring "good taste and delicacy" in treating sexual matters.

1960s-1970s

Television becomes more venturesome on sexual matters; "topless radio" draws FCC's attention; Supreme Court upholds FCC authority over indecency.

1964
FCC rejects indecency complaints against Pacifica radio stations for sex-related programs. . . . Racy prime-time soap opera "Peyton Place" debuts on ABC, runs five seasons.

1971
Blue-collar situation comedy "All in the Family" debuts; breaks taboos on sexual matters; runs eight seasons on CBS.

1973
FCC fines Illinois radio station $2,000 for discussion of oral sex on call-in show; federal appeals court upholds decision in 1974.

1975
Three major TV networks, under pressure from FCC, adopt "Family Viewing Hour" policy; federal judge cites FCC pressure in invalidating policy in 1976; networks readopt it "voluntarily."

1978
Supreme Court upholds FCC authority to penalize stations for indecency when children likely to be in audience; decision backs FCC warning to Pacifica station in New York City for broadcasting George Carlin monologue "Seven Filthy Words."

1980s-1990s

Radio, TV bust through limits on sexual matters; FCC, courts settle on late-night "safe harbor" for adult-oriented programming.

1985
Shock-jock Howard Stern signs with Infinity Broadcasting; morning talk show wins top ratings in national syndication.

1989
"The Simpsons" debuts on Fox network; graphic content increases over time.

1993
Federal appeals court bars FCC indecency enforcement from 10 p.m. to 6 a.m. to ensure adults have access to legally protected material; ruling comes after years of back and forth between FCC, Congress and courts.

1995
Infinity Broadcasting fined $1.7 million over complaints about Howard Stern show. . . . Parents Television Council founded.

2000-Present

FCC, Congress crack down on indecency; long legal challenge over "fleeting expletives" ends inconclusively at Supreme Court.

2001
FCC says context, multiple factors important in indecency cases.

2004
Janet Jackson's breast briefly exposed in Super Bowl halftime show (Feb. 1); episode becomes cause célèbre. . . . FCC, in shift, says isolated use of F-word is indecent (March 18). . . . CBS stations fined $550,000 for Super Bowl broadcast (Sept. 22).

2006
FCC imposes $4 million in fines in indecency cases; CBS stations hit for $3.6 million for graphic sex scene in "Without a Trace"; Fox network warned for fleeting expletives by Cher, Nicole Richie on Billboard Music Awards programs in 2002, 2003. . . . Broadcast Decency Enforcement Act raises maximum fine for indecency to $325,000 per violation (June 15).

2009
Supreme Court says FCC acted properly in adopting ban on "fleeting expletives"; sends *Fox* case back for ruling on constitutional challenge (April 28); FCC penalty against ABC for brief nudity in "NYPD Blue" later added to case.

2012
Supreme Court throws out penalties against Fox, ABC; lack of notice cited; constitutional issue unresolved (June 21); penalty in Super Bowl case thrown out eight days later, but Chief Justice Roberts says FCC policy stands. . . . FCC faces backlog of 1.5 million indecency complaints.

Violence on TV Remains Unregulated

"There would be enormous hurdles" in regulating it.

Five years ago, the Federal Communications Commission unanimously approved a report concluding that the agency could regulate violence on television if Congress gave it that authority. Lawmakers on communications policy applauded the report, but Congress has never acted on the proposal.

Today, the issue appears largely dormant at the FCC and on Capitol Hill. The two major industry groups, the National Association of Broadcasters and the National Cable and Telecommunications Association, continue to oppose any government regulation of violent programming. And the Parents Television Council, a leading critic of both sex and violence on television, itself favors other approaches to the problem.

"There would be enormous hurdles" to government regulation of violence on TV, says Dan Isett, the council's director of public policy. Isett says the council instead favors pressuring advertisers not to support programs with excessively violent content.

Broadcasters say regulating violence would be even more difficult for the FCC than trying to police sex-related indecency. "It's really difficult to define," says Dennis Wharton, the National Association of Broadcasters' (NAB) executive vice president for communication. "Are we talking about 'Three Stooges' violence or Arnold Schwarzenegger violence or 'Sopranos'-like violence?" ("The Sopranos" was a critically acclaimed HBO series, now in syndication, about an organized crime leader and his family.)

The FCC ducked the problem of how to define violence when it approved the report on TV violence on April 26, 2007. Despite acknowledged "obstacles," the 38-page report concluded that "Congress likely has the ability and authority to craft a sustainable definition." The report also endorsed studies finding that exposure to violence on television "can increase aggressive behavior in children, at least in the short term." [1]

The FCC action, endorsed in separate statements by each of the five commissioners, came three months after the Parents Television Council had published its own report documenting what it characterized as a nearly eightfold increase in violence on broadcast television over the previous eight years. [2] The council has not published a more recent study, but Isett says the trend continues. "There's still an enormous amount of violent content on broadcast television," he says.

NAB's Wharton disagrees. Violence is "far less explicit than what you find on pay-TV platforms," he says. "You don't find 'Sopranos'-like violence on broadcast television. We don't air explicitly violent Hollywood movies uncut."

In the 2007 report, the FCC said that use of the v-chip to block objectionable programming and the industry rating system for designating violent programs had been "ineffective." Instead,

Continued from p. 974

Lucy" without using the word "pregnant" over seven episodes. Into the 1960s, TV families were all but invariably intact, children angelic and mostly asexual and marital bedrooms furnished with twin beds. ABC's risqué prime-time soap opera "Peyton Place," which debuted in 1964, presaged changing policies, with its bed-hopping among married partners. In the same year, however, NBC shelved as "inappropriate for family viewing" an already-produced two-part dramatic episode about a teenager who contracts syphilis. [15]

Radio became the first indecency battleground, beginning in the mid 1960s. In 1964 the FCC rejected indecency complaints filed by listeners challenging renewal of the Pacifica Foundation's liberal radio stations; five programs drew complaints, including readings by authors and a discussion about gay life among eight homosexuals. Six years later, however, the commission fined the Philadelphia educational station WHUY $100 for an obscenity-laced interview with Jerry Garcia, leader of the acid rock band the Grateful Dead. In a more substantive action, the commission in 1973 imposed a $2,000 penalty on an Illinois radio station for a call-in talk show — the genre was then known as "topless radio" — that included vivid discussion of oral sex. The federal appeals court in Washington in 1974 upheld the commission's finding that the program was obscene. [16]

Television, meanwhile, was in the beginning of a paradigm shift on indecency, marked by the 1971 debut of the hit situation comedy "All in the Family," a program sprinkled with ethnic and sexual references and bathroom humor. As the three networks pushed the envelope on sex and violence, public and official concern grew. FCC Chairman Richard Wiley used his office to push the networks into adopting a "family viewing policy" that set aside the first hour of prime time for programs appropriate for all ages. The policy bumped "All in the Family" from its 8 p.m. Saturday time slot, helping to prompt producer Norman Lear along with the Writers Guild of America to challenge it as a government-induced free-speech violation. A federal judge in Los Angeles sustained the challenge in 1976, but the networks responded by adopting it again. [17]

The indecency issue reached the Supreme Court in a case stemming from a single complaint about the broadcast of Carlin's "filthy words" monologue by WBAI, the Pacifica radio station in New York City. The complainant was a New York man who heard the program one afternoon while

the report urged broadcasters to voluntarily keep violent programming out of the first hour of the prime-time schedule, when small children are likely to be watching, or limit violent programming overall.

For cable and satellite systems, the FCC report said customers should be given greater freedom to "select the channels they want to pay for and to opt out of those that they do not." The cable industry has strongly opposed so-called a la carte pricing, saying that the current practice of bundled subscription packages allows more diversity in programming at more affordable cost.

Robert Thompson, a professor of popular culture and director of the Bleier Center for Television and Popular Culture at Syracuse University, seconds the NAB's view that critics overstate the amount of violence on broadcast television. "Yes, we have all these 'CSIs,' where all these people die," he says. "But when one compares it to the movies or video games or for that matter cable or pay-cable, I think the level of violence on broadcast TV is quaint."

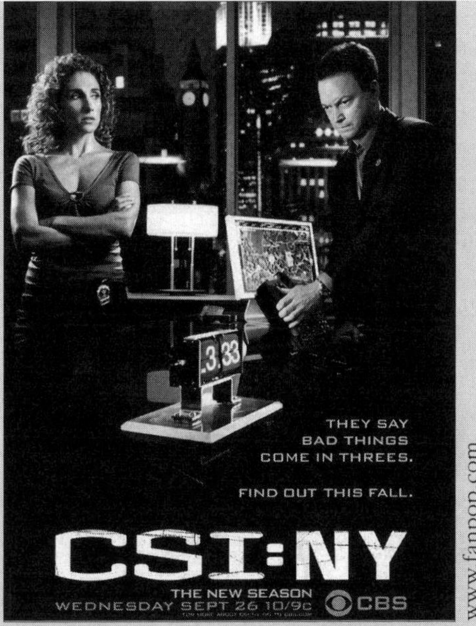

Shows such as "CSI" are tame compared to movies and cable shows, says Robert Thompson, director of the Bleier Center for Television and Popular Culture at Syracuse University.

But Alan Simpson, vice president for policy for the children's advocacy group Common Sense Media, says that even if violence is not graphically presented, children can be affected by the sight of bodies. "Gore is pretty scary for young kids," Simpson says. "If you're talking about a 5-year-old or 7-year-old, seeing the results of a murder is pretty scary. Your young kids are going to have nightmares."

— *Kenneth Jost*

[1] See "Violent Programming on Television and Its Impact on Children," April 26, 2007, http://hraunfoss.fcc.gov/edocs_public/attachmatch/FCC-07-50A1.doc. For coverage, see John Eggerton, "FCC to Congress: Take Action on Violence," *Broadcasting & Cable*, April 30, 2007, p. 10.

[2] See Parents Television Council, "Dying to Entertain: Violence on Prime Time Broadcast Television 1998-2006," January 2007, www.parentstv.org/ptc/publications/reports/violencestudy/DyingtoEntertain.pdf.

driving in his car with his young son. The FCC found the program indecent and entered a reprimand in the station's file. On a 5-4 vote, the Supreme Court upheld the FCC's action. For the majority, Justice John Paul Stevens said broadcasters could be penalized for what would be legally protected sex-related material in other media because broadcasting had "a uniquely pervasive presence in the lives of all Americans" and was "uniquely accessible to children, even those too young to read." In a dissent, Justice William J. Brennan Jr. chided the majority justices for "their fragile sensibilities." [18]

Only a few days later, the FCC gave broadcasters an encouraging signal by renewing the license of the Boston public television station WGBH despite a pending indecency complaint by the advocacy group Morality in Media. Speaking to New England broadcasters, FCC Chairman Charles Ferris depicted the Carlin case as limited. The case "should show that the FCC is not going to become a censor," Ferris said. "And hopefully it will prevent an outpouring of audience complaints based on occasional words." [19]

"Chilling" Effect?

The FCC did nothing at first with its officially validated authority over broadcast indecency, but it moved toward a more aggressive stance beginning in the late 1980s under pressure from citizens' groups. A succession of court cases in the 1990s eventually established a safe harbor for broadcast indecency between 10 p.m. and 6 a.m. but left the anti-indecency rule in place for the rest of the day. After the turn of the century, the FCC stiffened its position — first by ruling that a single "fleeting expletive" could be penalized and then by imposing fines totaling millions of dollars on programs found to be indecent.

From the 1980s on, the sexual revolution has been broadcast with fewer and fewer limits on radio and on both broadcast and cable television. "Shock jock" talk radio programs — exemplified by the flamboyantly raunchy Howard Stern — featured franker and franker discussions of sexual matters. The major commercial broadcasters, including the boundary-defying Fox network created in 1986, made sex an all but constant theme on many situation comedies — for example, "That 70's Show" — and such prime-time dramas as "L.A. Law" and "NYPD Blue." Fox also broke new ground with sexual themes on its animated shows, first "The Simpsons" and later "Family Guy." Cable television went further, with such sex-saturated programs as MTV's reality show "Real World," HBO's smash hit comedy "Sex and the City" and Showtime's "Queer as Folk."

The FCC responded to the change in media practices in fits and starts. The commission took on radio first. In coordinated rulings in April 1987, the commission found two stations and Stern's Infinity Broadcasting Network guilty of indecency but, because of the change in enforcement policy, withheld any penalty and issued only a warning for the stations' files. On appeal, the D.C. Circuit Court in 1988 vacated the two decisions involving late-night programs but upheld the commission's finding against Infinity for Stern's daytime program. The appeals court ruling effectively required the FCC to establish a "safe harbor" time period for indecency when children are not in the audience.

ABC Television

"Leave It to Beaver," a popular TV situation comedy in the late 1950s and early '60s, avoided sexual matters, like other shows of the period. A voluntary code of conduct adopted in 1951 called on broadcasters to use "good taste and delicacy" in depicting locations "closely associated with sexual life or with sexual sin." Into the 1960s, TV families were all but invariably intact, children angelic and mostly asexual and marital bedrooms furnished with twin beds.

Congress responded by passing a law requiring the commission to prohibit indecency around the clock. The FCC obliged, but the appeals court in 1991 ruled the law unconstitutional. The court relied on a Supreme Court decision in 1989 that safeguarded adults' right to access non-obscene material on so-called "dial-a-porn" phone services. Congress stepped in again, enacting a law that established a midnight to 6 a.m. safe harbor for commercial stations and 10 p.m. to 6 a.m. for public broadcasters. In a final appeal, the D.C. Circuit in 1993 found no basis for the distinction and effectively required the FCC to recognize the 10 p.m. to 6 a.m. safe harbor now in effect. [20]

Congress also tried to limit children's access to sexual material on cable television and the Internet, but the Supreme Court blocked major provisions of the laws enacted. In 1996 the court invalidated a provision of a 1992 cable TV law that required cable operators to "segregate" channels with "offensive programming" and "block" the channels except upon a customer's request. In the same year, Congress included in the Telecommunications Act of 1996 a provision requiring that pay cable channels with sex-related programming be "scrambled" to avoid unintended access for children. The law also included a complex of provisions aimed at preventing children's access to sexually explicit material on the Internet. The court ruled the Internet law unconstitutional the very next year; Congress' rewrite was eventually struck down as well after a drawn out appellate battle. The Supreme Court ruled the scrambling provision unconstitutional in 2000. [21]

The FCC's continuing battles with shock radio resulted in a $1.7 million penalty against Infinity, agreed to by the broadcaster, in 1995 and a new $375,000 fine in 2003 for 13 stations that broadcast a live description of a couple having sex in St. Patrick's Cathedral in New York City. Meanwhile, as part of a settlement with Evergreen Media, the FCC in 2001 issued a policy statement aimed at giving broadcasters guidance on the indecency rules. The guidelines cited three factors as "significant" on the issue: whether the material was explicit or graphic, whether it dwelt on or repeated sexual depictions, and whether the material was used to pander or titillate. Broadcasters generally found the guidance still too vague. [22]

The issue came to a head beginning in 2004 after the uproar over the Super Bowl halftime show. Congress initiated hearings that led two years later to legislation raising the penalty for indecency to $325,000 per violation or a maximum of $3 million. Meanwhile, the commission, reversing its previous policy, released its decision on March 18 holding that a single use of the F-word could be ruled indecent. The shift came on a complaint against NBC for the use of the word as an adjective by the singer Bono during the 2003 broadcast of the Golden Globes award program. Citing the change, the commission decided not to impose a fine. [23]

By contrast, the FCC later that year imposed stiff fines on several broadcasters; the cases included a $1.75 million fine against the Clear Channel radio network, agreed to by the network, for programming that included Howard Stern's show and a $3.5 million fine in November against Viacom for sex-related programming on several stations in its Infinity Broadcasting chain. In a well-publicized protest, Stern left over-the-air broadcasting for the subscription satellite radio network Sirius XM. And in September the commission imposed a $550,000 fine against CBS stations for the Super Bowl broadcast. [24]

Two years later, the commission on March 15, 2006, imposed fines totaling about $4 million as it disposed of "hundreds of thousands" of complaints in decisions that penalized some broadcasters, withheld fines in some other cases and cleared broadcasters in many others. The biggest penalty hit 111 CBS stations for $32,500 apiece for a December 2004 broadcast of a program, "Without a Trace," that included a graphic sex scene. No penalties were imposed in two prominent cases that figured in the later Supreme Court litigation: use of the F-word by the singer Cher in the 2002 "Billboard Music Awards" program and ad-libbed patter with both the F- and S-words by the TV personality Nicole Richie in the same program a year later. Of the other cases with fines, four dealt with sexual themes; the fifth was the penalty against KCSM in San Mateo for its broadcast of "The Blues: Godfathers and Sons."

In a statement, FCC Chairman Martin said the decisions "demonstrate the Commission's continued commitment to enforcing the law prohibiting the airing of obscene, indecent, and profane material." TV writer-producer Steven Bochco of "L.A. Law" and "NYPD Blue" fame called the FCC action "goddamn chilling." [25]

Long-time Wait

The FCC's indecency enforcement came to a virtual standstill after 2006 as broadcasters and free-speech advocates challenged the fleeting expletive policy in two successive trips to the U.S. Supreme Court. The federal appeals court in New York City twice struck down the policy — first for administrative law reasons and then, after getting the case back from the Supreme Court, on constitutional grounds. The justices appeared divided along liberal-conservative lines during the court's second round of arguments in January. But they reached a unanimous decision on June 21 to throw out the sanctions against Fox and ABC while leaving it up to the FCC to modify the policy or keep it as is. [26]

Despite the legal challenges, broadcasters responded to the FCC's crackdown to ward off potential penalties and curry public favor in the seemingly changed environment. Networks and stations instituted brief tape delays on live broadcasts to guard against unscripted expletives. Broadcasters also generally defended their programs, insisting that they strove to avoid giving offense even while adapting to changing public standards on language and sex. For its part, however, the Parents Television Council viewed broadcasters as driving standards down. In successive reports, the council documented increases in profanity on prime-time TV, in what it called the "sexualization" of teen-aged girls, and in depictions of sex, drugs and profanity on prime-time animated programs on cable channels.

The broadcasters' challenge to the FCC's crackdown went up and down the federal court system twice before the Supreme Court's ruling in June. In an initial detour, the FCC decided to drop two no-fine cases from its 2006 order: one against CBS's "Early Show" for use of the S-word by a cast member from the program "Survivor," and the other against ABC's "NYPD Blue" for use of the F- and S-words in various episodes. With the case pared down to Fox's two broadcasts of the "Billboard Music Awards," the Second U.S. Circuit Court of Appeals issued a limited ruling in June 2007 holding that the FCC had failed to justify its changed policy of treating a single, fleeting expletive as indecent.

The Supreme Court agreed to hear the FCC's appeal seeking to reinstate the policy. By a 5-4 vote, the court held on April 28, 2009, that the commission had adequate grounds for the changed policy. For the majority, Justice Antonin Scalia said the FCC could reasonably consider "more stringent broadcast regulation" helpful to parents because of the "pervasiveness of foul language" and "the coarsening of public entertainment in other media such as cable." Two of the justices in the majority, Kennedy and Clarence Thomas, voiced reservations about the ruling. And among the four dissenters was Stevens, who had authored the *Pacifica* decision three decades earlier. The stricter policy would never have been accepted at that time, Stevens said.

The court sent the case back to the Second Circuit to rule on Fox's constitutional challenge. In July 2010, the appeals court ruled that the FCC policy was unconstitutionally vague. The judges said the FCC gave broadcasters too little guidance on what words would be found offensive and adopted exceptions with "little rhyme or reason." In the meantime, the FCC in February 2008 had ruled the Feb. 23, 2003, episode of "NYPD Blue" indecent because of an opening shower scene with a female character's bare breast and buttocks visible. The commission fined 45 ABC affiliates $27,500 apiece for a total of $1,237,500. A separate Second Circuit panel in January 2011 applied the court's ruling from the Fox case to throw the penalty out.

The FCC appealed the Fox and ABC cases to the Supreme Court, which heard the cases together on Jan. 10, 2011. Once again, conservative justices, including Chief Justice John G. Roberts Jr., appeared to support the FCC's policy, while liberal justices voiced doubts. (Justice Sonia Sotomayor recused herself; she had been on the Second Circuit when the Fox case was before that court.) Roberts, part of the majority in the earlier case, suggested the government had good reason to set aside "a few channels" where children would not be exposed to the F- or S-words or nudity. Ginsburg, a dissenter in the earlier ruling, said the FCC had been arbitrary in recognizing exceptions for some programs — she mentioned "Saving Private Ryan" and "Schindler's List" — but not others.

The court's decision on June 21 was short — only 18 pages — and anticlimactic. Writing for seven justices, Kennedy said the networks had "no notice . . . that a fleeting expletive or a brief shot of nudity could be found actionably indecent." Ruling solely on due process grounds, the court passed over the issues of whether the FCC's policy was too vague or whether *Pacifica* should be overruled. The commission was free, Kennedy continued, to modify the policy "in light of its determination of the public interest and applicable legal requirements." But he added pointedly that the courts would still be free to review the policy, whether modified or unchanged. Ginsburg wrote separately to call for overruling *Pacifica*.

Eight days later, the court on June 29 turned aside the FCC's effort to salvage the penalties against CBS for the Super Bowl halftime show. But Roberts took the opportunity to emphasize that the FCC's policy remained intact. "It is now clear that the brevity of an indecent broadcast — be it word or image — cannot immunize it from FCC censure," Roberts wrote. In a brief rejoinder, Ginsburg again called for overruling *Pacifica*. ■

CURRENT SITUATION

FCC's Full Plate

The FCC is beginning to work on a mountain of indecency complaints with no direct guidance from the Supreme Court, unresolved doubts about its current policy and an agenda of other pressing telecommunications issues.

The commission has no official count of the number of complaints or the subjects of the complaints, according to spokesman Justin Cole. But McDowell, a Republican appointed by President George W. Bush in 2006 and reappointed by Obama in 2009, put the number at 1.5 million in a statement following the Supreme Court's decision in June. McDowell said the complaints involve 9,700 broadcasts and affect 700 pending license renewal applications. [27]

The indecency issue moved up on the FCC's agenda under two Bush-appointed chairmen: Powell, who led the response to the 2004 Super Bowl broadcast, and then Martin. It has not been a priority for Genachowski, a technology-oriented lawyer and businessman who took office on June 29, 2009. "Right now, the FCC seems to be focused on other priorities," says Amy Sanders, an assistant professor at the University of Minnesota Law School in Minneapolis who is researching the history of the FCC's indecency regulation.

Despite the attention received by the Fox and ABC cases, the FCC since 2000 has rejected more indecency complaints than it has sustained, according to an unofficial count of cases on the commission's website. [28] The commission lists 41 "notices of apparent liability," including the omnibus March 2006 order, which sustained complaints on the Fox and ABC programs and seven others. Listed on a separate page are 17 "complaint denial orders," including two orders on Jan. 24, 2005, that rejected complaints filed by the Parents Television Council against 40 programs in all. The March 2006 order rejected complaints in 17 cases — bringing the number of cases turned down to 72.

Of the 50 sustained complaints, more than half appear to involve local radio stations that broadcast shock-jock sex talk or songs with X-rated lyrics. The penalties imposed ranged from $7,000 to $27,500. The FCC began imposing bigger penalties in 2003 with the $357,500 penalty against Infinity Broadcasting for the Aug. 15, 2002, "Opie and Anthony" program that included a listener's account of having sex in St. Patrick's Cathedral in New York City. Other six-figure penalties were imposed in 2004 for stations that broadcast "Bubba the Love Sponge" and the "Howard Stern Show."

The first big penalty in a TV case came in October 2004 against Fox stations that broadcast a "Married by America" program that the FCC said "featured strippers and various sexual situations." The 169 stations were fined $1,183,000 in all.

Many of the rejected complaints were filed against programs with sexually suggestive scenes or dialogues but with no nudity and no use of the F- or S-words. Other anatomical language passed muster with the FCC, including "dick" and "ass," as did profanity such as "hell" and "damn." And when it rejected a complaint against stations that broadcast "Saving Private

Continued on p. 982

At Issue:

Should FCC regulation of broadcast indecency be eliminated?

BERIN SZOKA
PRESIDENT, TECHFREEDOM, A TECH POLICY THINK TANK

WRITTEN FOR *CQ RESEARCHER*, NOVEMBER 2012

yes

Does the First Amendment permit the FCC to censor "indecent" content on daytime broadcast TV — the occasional curse word or brief glimpses of a bare butt? The Supreme Court has now twice struck down the FCC's indecency standards as unconstitutionally vague. But each time, the Court has dodged the hard question: Should broadcasters have the same First Amendment rights as, say, cable operators or website publishers to offer content that some might find offensive — but isn't obscene (pornographic)?

The Court created a special exception to the First Amendment's protection of free speech in its 1978 *Pacifica* decision because it deemed broadcasting (1) "uniquely pervasive in the lives of Americans" and (2) "uniquely accessible to children" — i.e., parents had little control over what their children could watch on TV. But today, less than 8-15 percent of American households rely on over-the-air broadcasting. Most use cable, FiOS, satellites or Internet services like Hulu. While broadcasting might have been considered an "intruder in the home" in 1978, these modern services are very much invited guests — and so, the Court has held, cannot be censored.

Today, parents can choose from, and filter, a range of video programming options unimaginable in 1978. A variety of tools empower parents to decide what broadcast content their children can access. Since 2000, every television larger than 13 inches has come with the v-chip. This free technology empowers parents to block content based on ratings that include age-based designations as well as several specific content descriptors (coarse language, sex, violence, etc.). A wide variety of other tools have empowered parents, such as DVD players, digital video recorders and video-on-demand services. Parents can now build, and even pre-screen, libraries of preferred programming for their children. Similar tools are available for cable content, video games, movies and the Internet.

It's only a matter of time before the Supreme Court ends the FCC's censorship of broadcasting, just as it ended cable indecency censorship back in 2000, when it held:

"[I]t is no response that voluntary blocking requires a consumer to take action, or may be inconvenient, or may not go perfectly every time. A court should not assume a plausible, less restrictive alternative would be ineffective; and a court should not presume parents, given full information, will fail to act . . . Technology expands the capacity to choose; and it denies the potential of this revolution if we assume the Government is best positioned to make these choices for us."

DAN ISETT
DIRECTOR OF PUBLIC POLICY, PARENTS TELEVISION COUNCIL

WRITTEN FOR *CQ RESEARCHER*, NOVEMBER 2012

no

Broadcast decency law has existed since the dawn of the medium for one purpose alone: to protect children from material that is clearly inappropriate or even harmful to them. Broadcasters, in exchange for free use of the publicly owned airwaves, must abide by the law, which simply channels patently offensive sexual or excretory content to the times of day when children are much less likely to be in the audience.

In 1996, Congress required that most televisions be equipped with a v-chip that families could use to block programming based on a rating assigned to that program by the networks themselves. Unfortunately, the conflict of interest inherent in the existing system has yielded poor results for families. Study after study conducted by the Parents Television Council and others has concluded that there are major inconsistencies in the application of the TV ratings system. Inaccuracies abound, and those inaccuracies yield only one result: More graphic content is consistently misrated as appropriate for a younger audience.

When the rating applied to a program is inaccurate, the v-chip cannot work as intended, leaving even the most diligent parents without the tools necessary to enforce their own rules about media content. Even worse, the TV Parental Guidelines Monitoring Board, designated to field consumer complaints about the TV ratings system, meets only in private, and its membership is not publicly available. Clearly, this is a system in dire need of reform.

The Communications Act of 1934, which created the FCC, mentions the "public interest" well over 100 times. Do the broadcast networks and their allies expect the American people to believe that unlimited indecent content, broadcast over the airwaves that they own, in front of their own children, is in their interest?

For years, the networks argued in federal court that broadcast decency law should be overturned and that they should have free rein to air unlimited indecent material at any time of day, no matter the audience. However, the Supreme Court ruled against them last summer, for the second time, and left the time-honored law intact.

The focus now shifts back to the FCC, where more than 1.5 million indecency complaints have languished. There has been no enforcement of broadcast decency law for years, and with no further legal challenges to the law, the time for the FCC to act is now.

Continued from p. 980

Ryan," the commission specifically found that the rough language was "not gratuitous."

The FCC's case-by-case adjudication leaves broadcasters at sea, according to Douglas Linder, a First Amendment expert at the University of Missouri Law School in Kansas City. "They haven't provided the kind of guidance that broadcasters have been looking for," Linder says. "Broadcasters just want to know what they can do, what they cannot do."

Clearing out the backlog of cases could take a year or longer even though many can be disposed of quickly, according to Rosemary Harold, a communications lawyer in Washington and former media legal adviser to McDowell. Some of the complaints, she says, are too old; others fall outside the FCC's jurisdiction, such as complaints about depictions of violence or complaints against programs on cable. She suggests the commission also should dismiss cases that involve "fleeting expletives" or "fleeting body parts." With those cases out of the way, Harold says, the commission should set a goal of resolving the remaining cases within 12 months and issue enforcement updates periodically while moving toward that goal.

Like Sanders, Harold says the indecency issue ranks low on the FCC's list of priorities. "I wouldn't say it's in the top three issues that any one of the FCC commissioners gets excited about," Harold says. Genachowski has focused his attention on a national broadband plan that includes reallocating airwaves for mobile communications and overhauling the fund that now supports phone service to one to help subsidize access to broadband.

ABC/Adam Taylor

ABC's prime-time show "Dancing With the Stars" rates a yellow warning — "inappropriate for youngsters" — from the Parents Television Council's "Family Guide to Prime Time Television" because of its "harsh" language and "suggestive" dancing. No programs rated in late October (not counting sports shows) received green ("family friendly") designations.

Harold also agrees with Linder and Sanders that the long-term constitutionality of the FCC's authority over broadcast indecency is very much in doubt. But she says the FCC has no choice but to enforce the law as long as it is on the books. "Unless and until a court puts it out of its misery, it's going to be in this business for a while," Harold says.

Broadcasters' Woes

The major broadcast television networks are greeting the fall season with more concern about sagging ratings and bearish investors than about the FCC's next moves on indecency.

The big four networks — ABC, CBS, Fox and NBC — drew 15 percent fewer viewers in the age 18-49 demographic in the first two weeks of the 2012/2013 season than they drew in the same period for the previous year, according to the Nielsen rating service. The overall decline among all adults was put at 11 percent. [29]

Prominent media industry analysts cited the declines in cautionary reports for investors. "There is little doubt that early 2012/2013 network results have been disappointing," Michael Nathanson, an analyst with Nomura Securities, said in a report. Anthony DiClemente of Barclays Equity Research blamed the decline on weaknesses in the new prime-time offerings. "Without top-quality new programs to augment the success of past hits, we believe aggregate network ratings have suffered," DiClemente wrote. [30]

In terms of audience, broadcasters, who are subject to the FCC's indecency authority, continue to enjoy a substantial lead over cable channels, which are not regulated. The top 20 prime-time programs on the broadcast networks during the week of Oct. 22-28 all drew at least 11 million viewers; the top-rated program, CBS's crime drama "NCIS," had 17.7 million viewers. The top-rated cable program, Fox News Channel's broadcast of the presidential debate, drew 11.5 million viewers; ESPN's "Sunday Night Football" had 10.7 million. Cable's leading dramatic offering is AMC's "The Walking Dead," broadcast on Sunday nights, which had 10.5 million viewers that week. [31]

Despite the broadcasters' audience advantage, Syracuse University professor Thompson says cable channels enjoy a creative edge because they have no indecency police looking over their shoulders. "You've got this flowering of wonderful programs on cable," Thompson says, citing HBO's "The Wire," Showtime's "Dexter" and AMC's "Breaking Bad" as examples.

"Most of these programs are filled with language, sexuality and other things that are at the center of indecency rules," Thompson says. "Broadcasters have to rely on stupid reality shows to get their audience or double entendres and that kind of coded stuff," he continues. "The indecency rule encourages a lot of what we get on broadcast television."

Financial analyst Gallant agrees, to an extent. "Broadcasters are handicapped in competing for audience by the indecency limits," he says. But he predicts that broadcasters would continue to show restraint even if the indecency rules are overturned. "There's a certain kind of limit that the public has come to expect of broadcasters," Gallant says.

The new season's ratings slump is a snapshot of what may be a broader, overall decline in television viewing, especially among young people. In May 2012, Nielsen reported that for the last three months of 2011 the average American with a TV set at home spent 153 hours and 19 minutes per month watching television the traditional way — rather than on a computer or tablet. That represented a decline of 46 minutes — or 0.5 percent — from the same period in 2010. The decline was sharper among viewers age 12-17: a 5 percent drop from about 105 hours to 100 hours. [32]

Nielsen says its ratings capture the vast majority of television viewers, but harder-to-measure nontraditional viewing is evidently on the rise. Broadcasters sought to play down the significance of the new season's rating slump by pointing to the growing practice of using digital video recorders (DVRs) to record and watch a program after its original broadcast. Recorded viewing can increase a show's audience, in some cases it is said, by as much as 50 percent. [33]

Mobile viewing may become an even more important factor. Smart-phone manufacturers are competing with each other on the quality of video their devices can deliver. The broadcast networks are catching on, reminding viewers that their programs can also be watched on computers and tablets. But mobile video also means that broadcasters have even more competition for viewers — from video-producing new media such as *Huffington Post* to the video-sharing website You Tube.

The increasingly crowded video marketplace underlines what broadcasters feel to be the unfairness of being singled out for indecency regulation, according to the NAB's Wharton. "Given the fragmentation of the audience, given the competition, given the fact that broadcasters and only broadcasters are subject to these rules, over time there is a very good chance that the courts will eliminate these rules altogether," he says. ■

OUTLOOK

"Heinously Difficult" Job

Michael Powell was at a neighbor's house watching the 2004 Super Bowl halftime show when he saw something that was not supposed to be seen on broadcast television. More than 100 million other viewers also saw Janet Jackson's exposed right breast, but the glimpse of something shocking had special meaning for the chairman of the FCC. "Tomorrow's going to really suck," Powell told his wife after he got back home. "And it did."

Recalling the crackdown-launching episode on a C-SPAN program with two other former FCC chairmen — fellow Republican Martin and Reed Hundt, the Democratic-appointed chair in the mid-1990s — Powell said he never much cared for the commission's role as anti-indecency enforcer. "The problem is the job proves heinously difficult to do because it's fraught with ambiguity and subjective choices and trying to maintain consistency of decisions across ever-changing content," Powell remarked. "I never found it a particularly enjoyable part of the job in any way, shape or form."

Hundt quickly agreed. "I don't think anybody ever did," he said. Tellingly, Martin, who became identified with the indecency issue during his tenure, let Hundt's remark pass. [34]

Like the job or not, the FCC appears to have no choice at present but to begin whittling down a huge backlog of indecency complaints one way or another. The courts may look askance at the FCC's existing policy, but the commission's congressional overseers seem unlikely to let the agency off the hook. "Indecency is an issue that no public official wants to be on the wrong side of," says media industry analyst Gallant. "Washington will probably continue to make all the appropriate noises about how indecency enforcement continues to be important policy."

Other experts, however, say the role is totally unimportant given the proliferation of media choices for 21st-century viewers. "If you banned [indecency] from broadcasting, it would be on the Internet," says Amherst professor Couvares. "It's like trying to hold back the tide," he adds. "Not that I don't sympathize with parents who would like to hold back the tide."

The FCC's enforcement record to date hardly suggests an agency hell-bent to police the airwaves. But Rintels with the Center for Creative Voices cites his own experience as a screenwriter for television back in the 1980s to demonstrate the impact of the FCC's authority even if only rarely exercised.

Rintels was one of the writers of the critically acclaimed made-for-TV movie "Lena: My 100 Children," an account of a Holocaust survivor's search for missing family members. He recalls that producers decided not to show concentration camp prisoners fully nude. "Would it have more strongly conveyed the horror and impacted people more deeply?" he asks today. "We'll never know."

The FCC confronted the issue in 1997 when a Michigan viewer complained about the depiction of full-frontal nudity in the broadcast of the Holocaust movie "Schindler's List." FCC staff quickly rejected the complaint, but the viewer asked for reconsideration. The full commission took more than two years before formally rejecting the complaint. The five-page order concluded that the broadcast was not indecent based on "the subject matter of the film, the manner of its presentation, and the warnings that accompanied the broadcast of this film." [35]

"The Supreme Court put the ball back in the FCC's court," Rintels says. "They're going to have to determine what rules they want to apply. This will be a battle that will be fought in court for many, many more years unless the FCC comes up with some rules that will provide real clarity as to what they will and will not consider violations of indecency rules." ■

About the Author

Associate Editor **Kenneth Jost** graduated from Harvard College and Georgetown University Law Center. He is the author of the *Supreme Court Yearbook* and *The Supreme Court from A to Z* (both *CQ Press*). He was a member of the *CQ Researcher* team that won the American Bar Association's 2002 Silver Gavel Award. His previous reports include "Children's Television" and "The Future of Television." He is also author of the blog *Jost on Justice* (http://jostonjustice.blogspot.com).

Notes

[1] The Parents Television Council's undated e-alert is here: www.parentstv.org/ptc/action/familyguy/Content.asp; the description of "Family Guy" is drawn from the program's website: www.fox.com/familyguy/. For statistics on indecency complaints to the Federal Communications Commission, see Matthew Lasar, "Did Family Guy cause 179,997 FCC indecency complaints?," arstechnica.com, Sept. 9, 2009, http://arstechnica.com/tech-policy/2009/09/did-the-family-guy-cause-a-jump-in-fcc-indecency-complaints/.

[2] The official citation is 438 U.S. 726 (1978); the decision is available on the Find Law website: http://caselaw.lp.findlaw.com/cgi-bin/getcase.pl?court=us&vol=438&invol=726. A transcript of the monologue appears as an appendix to the opinion. For an account of the case, see Paul Finkelman and Melvin L. Urofsky, *Landmark Decisions of the United States Supreme Court* (2d. ed, 2008), pp. 494-495.

[3] The FCC has a summary of its policy, including procedures for filing a complaint, on its website: www.fcc.gov/guides/obscenity-indecency-and-profanity. For previous coverage, see William Triplett, "Broadcast Indecency," *CQ Researcher*, April 16, 2004, pp. 321-344.

[4] The official citation, not yet paginated, will be 567 U.S. — (2012); the opinion is available here: www.supremecourt.gov/opinions/11pdf/10-1293f3e5.pdf. For coverage, see Adam Liptak, "For now, 2 networks win ruling on indecency," *The New York Times*, June 22, 2012, p. B1; for a complete account of the case, see Kenneth Jost, *Supreme Court Yearbook 2011-2012* (online).

[5] The former FCC officials included former chairmen Newton Minow, a Democrat, and Mark Fowler, a Republican. For coverage, see John Eggerton, "Former FCC Chairs Slam Commission's 'Victorian Crusade,' " *Broadcasting & Cable*, Nov. 10, 2011, www.broadcastingcable.com/article/476529-Former_FCC_Chairs_Slam_Commission_s_Victorian_Crusade_.php. The brief is available from an American Bar Association website: www.americanbar.org/content/dam/aba/publications/supreme_court_preview/briefs/10-1293_respondentamcufmrfccofficials.authcheckdam.pdf.

[6] Quoted in John Eggerton, "DOJ, FCC Drop Pursuit of Fox 'Married by America' Indecency Fine," *Broadcasting & Cable*, Sept. 24, 2012, www.broadcastingcable.com/article/489505-DOJ_FCC_Drop_Pursuit_of_Fox_Married_by_America_Indecency_Fine.php.

[7] James P. Steyer, *The Other Parent: The Inside Story of the Media's Effect on Our Children* (2002), p. 44.

[8] Parents Television Council, "Habitat for Profanity: Broadcast TV's Sharp Increase in Foul Language," Nov. 9, 2010, www.parentstv.org/PTC/publications/reports/2010ProfanityStudy/study.pdf.

[9] Quotes from David Zurawik, "TV, radio get static from Congress," *The Baltimore Sun*, Feb. 12, 2004, p. 3A.

[10] See "Complaints Regarding Various Television Broadcasts Between Feb. 2, 2005, and March 8, 2005," March 15, 2006, http://transition.fcc.gov/eb/Orders/2006/FCC-06-17A1.html; "Complaints Against Various Television Licensees Concerning Their December 31, 2004 Broadcast of the Program 'Without a Trace,' " March 15, 2006, http://transition.fcc.gov/eb/Orders/2006/FCC-06-18A1.html. For coverage, see Julie Bosman, "TV Stations Fined Over CBS Show Deemed to Be Indecent," *The New York Times*, March 16, 2006, p. C2.

[11] See James Berardinelli, "The 2011 Nudity Column," *ReelThoughts*, April 14, 2011, www.reelviews.net/reelthoughts.php?identifier=663.

[12] Amol Sharma, "Senate Panel Toughens Broadcast Indecency Bill," *CQ Today*, March 9, 2004, www.oncongress.cq.com/doc/news-1047451?wr=bGFldXRDRDVoeHFZTjhweGxUektMdw.

[13] Susan Crabtree, "Solons scramble on smut," *Daily Variety*, March 10, 2004, p. 2. See also Ted Hearn, "McCain files a la carte amendment," *Multichannel News*, March 8, 2004, www.multichannel.com/content/mccain-files-la-carte-amendment.

[14] For legal background, see T. Barton Carter, Marc A. Franklin, Amy Kristin Sanders and Jay B. Wright, *The First Amendment and the Fourth Estate: The Law of Mass Media* (11th ed., 2012).

[15] See Louis Chunovic, *One Foot on the Floor:*

The Curious Evolution of Sex on Television from I Love Lucy *to* South Park (2000), pp. 19 (broadcasting code), 33-37 ("I Love Lucy"), 47 ("Peyton Place"), 48-49 (syphilis). The two-part episode about syphilis was to have been on two dramatic series: "Mr. Novak" and "Dr. Kildaire."

[16] The cases are *Pacifica Foundation*, 36 F.C.C. 147 (1964), *Eastern Educational Radio* (WHUY-FM), 24 F.C.C. 2d 408 (1970), *Illinois Citizens Committee for Broadcasting v. FCC*, 515 F.2d 397 (D.C. Cir. 1974), discussed in Carter, *et al., op. cit.*, pp. 486-489.

[17] For a full account, see Geoffrey Cowan, *See No Evil: The Backstage Battle over Sex and Violence in Television* (1979).

[18] The majority included Chief Justice Warren E. Burger and Associate Justices Harry A. Blackmun, Lewis F. Powell Jr., William H. Rehnquist and Stevens. Brennan's dissent was joined by Justice Thurgood Marshall. Separately, four justices — Potter Stewart, Brennan, Byron R. White and Marshall — argued in a dissent written by Stewart that the term indecent "should properly be read as meaning no more than 'obscene.' "

[19] Quoted in Cowan, *op. cit.*, p. 286.

[20] The Supreme Court's decision is *Sable Communications v. FCC*, 492 U.S. 115 (1989). The D.C. Circuit's three decisions are all entitled *Action for Children's Television v. FCC*, abbreviated as *ACT I*, *ACT II* and *ACT III*.

[21] The Supreme Court cases are *Denver Area Educational Television Consortium v. FCC*, 518 U.S. 727 (1996); *Reno v. American Civil Liberties Union*, 521 U.S. 844 (1997); and *United States v. Playboy Entertainment Group*, 529 U.S. 803 (2000).

[22] Industry Guidance on the Commission's Case Law Interpreting 18 U.S.C. § 1464 and Enforcement Policies Regarding Broadcast Indecency, 16 F.C.C.Rcd. 7999 (2001).

[23] "Complaints Against Various Broadcast Licensees Regarding Their Airing of the 'Golden Globes Awards' Program," http://transition.fcc.gov/eb/Orders/2004/FCC-04-43A1.html.

[24] "Complaints Against Various Television Licensees Concerning Their Feb. 1, 2004, Broadcast of the Super Bowl XXXVIII Halftime Show," http://transition.fcc.gov/eb/Orders/2004/FCC-04-43A1.html.

[25] See "Complaints Regarding Various Television Broadcasts" Between Feb. 2, 2002, and March 8, 2005, March 15, 2006, http://transition.fcc.gov/eb/Orders/2006/FCC-06-17A1.html; "Complaints Against Various Television Licensees Concerning Their Dec. 31, 2004 Broadcast of the Program 'Without a Trace,' " March 15, 2006, http://transition.fcc.gov/eb/Orders/2006/FCC-06-18A1.html; Bocho quoted in John Eggerton, "FCC's Full Frontal Assault on TV," *Broadcasting & Cable*, March 20, 2006, p. 18.

[26] For accounts of the two Supreme Court cases, see Kenneth Jost, *Supreme Court Yearbook 2008-2009*, and *Supreme Court Yearbook 2011-2012* (online).

[27] Quoted in John Eggerton, "FCC's McDowell: Time to Get Moving on Indecency," *Broadcasting & Cable*, July 9, 2012, www.broadcastingcable.com/article/486919-FCC_s_McDowell_Time_to_Get_Moving_on_Indecency.php.

[28] See "FCC Actions," http://transition.fcc.gov/eb/oip/Actions.html (visited Nov. 1, 2012).

[29] Figures quoted in Christopher S. Stewart and John Jannarone, "Viewership Declines for the Fall TV Season," *The Wall Street Journal*, Oct. 12, 2012, p. B1.

[30] Quoted in Joe Flint, "Wall Street is disappointed with fall television lineups," *Los Angeles Times*, Oct. 12, 2012, p. B3. See also David Lieberman, "Wall Street Grows Anxious About Dreary Initial Fall TV Season Ratings," "Deadline New York," Oct. 11, 2012, www.deadline.com/2012/10/wall-street-concern-prime-time-tv-ratings/.

[31] See "TV by the Numbers," www.zap2it.com/zap-weekly-ratings,0,2436061.htmlstory (broadcasters); tvbythenumbers.zap2it.com/2012/10/30/cable-top-25-monday-night-football-again-tops-cable-viewership-for-the-week-ending-october-28-2012/155129/ (cable).

[32] See two posts by Brian Stelter on "Media Decoder," a *New York Times* blog: "Nielsen Reports a Decline in Television Viewing;" Young People Are Watching TV Less, Though Still 100 Hours a Month," both May 3, 2012.

[33] See Flint, *op. cit.* Flint cites no source for the statement.

[34] "The Communicators: Former FCC Chairmen Reed Hundt, Michael Powell, and Kevin Martin," C-SPAN, Oct. 29, 2010, www.c-span.org/Events/Former-FCC-Chairmen-Reed-Hundt-Michael-Powell-and-Kevin-Martin/19249/.

[35] See In Matter of WBPN/WTOM License Subsidiary, Jan. 14, 2000, http://transition.fcc.gov/eb/Orders/fcc0010.doc.

FOR MORE INFORMATION

American Family Association, 107 Park Gate Dr., Tupelo, MS 38803; 662-844-5036; www.afa.net. Christian advocacy organization that promotes morality in popular culture, including television.

Bleier Center for Television and Popular Culture, S.I. Newhouse School of Public Communications, Syracuse University, Syracuse, NY 13244-2100; 315-443-4077; http://tvcenter.syr.edu. A leading academic center for scholarship, commentary and education in the areas of television and popular culture.

Center for Creative Voices in Media, P.O. Box 331, Keswick, VA 22947; 202-903-4081; www.creativevoices.us. Advocacy group representing the creative community in support of artistic freedom and diversity.

Common Sense Media, 650 Townsend St., Suite 435, San Francisco, CA 94103; 415-553-6728; www.commonsensemedia.org/. Nonprofit organization seeking to improve lives of kids and families through information, education and advocacy.

Family Research Council, 801 G St., N.W., Washington, DC 20001; 800-225-4008; www.frc.org. Advocacy group seeking to advance faith, family and freedom in public policy and culture from a Christian worldview.

Media Access Project, 1625 K St., N.W., Washington, DC 20006; 202-232-4300; www.mediaccess.org. Nonprofit public interest law firm and advocacy organization.

National Association of Broadcasters, 1771 N St., N.W., Washington, DC 20036; 202-429-5300; www.nab.org. Trade association for radio and television broadcasters.

National Cable and Telecommunications Association, 25 Massachusetts Ave., N.W., Suite 100, Washington, DC 20001; 202-222-2300; www.ncta.com/. Trade association for the cable and telecommunications industry.

Parents Television Council, 707 Wilshire Blvd., #2075, Los Angeles, CA 90017; 213-403-1300; www.parentstv.org/. Nonpartisan education organization advocating responsible entertainment.

Bibliography

Selected Sources

Books

Carter, T. Barton, Marc A. Franklin, Amy Kristin Sanders and Jay B. Wright, *The First Amendment and the Fourth Estate: The Law of Mass Media* (11th ed.), Foundation Press, 2012.
The law school casebook includes a 48-page section detailing the major legal developments at the Federal Communications Commission and in the courts on regulating indecency on broadcast television. Carter is a professor of communication and law at Boston University, Franklin a professor emeritus at Stanford Law School, Sanders an assistant professor of mass communication and law at the University of Minnesota-Twin Cities and Wright a professor of public communications at Syracuse University.

Chunovic, Louis, *One Foot on the Floor: The Curious Evolution of Sex on Television from* I Love Lucy *to* South Park, TV Books, 2000.
A former television journalist provides a discursive account of television's changing standards and practices regarding sex, from the black-and-white days of the 1950s through the franker and smirkier depictions by broadcasters and cable channels in the late 20th century. Includes illustrations.

Cowan, Geoffrey, *See No Evil: The Backstage Battle over Sex and Violence on Television*, Simon & Schuster, 1979.
The book recounts the history of the television networks' "family viewing hour" policy in the1970s from its adoption under pressure from the FCC through the invalidation of the policy by a federal court and its later "voluntary" readoption by the networks. Cowan was an attorney who advised the Writers Guild of America during the litigation; he later was a law professor at the University of Southern California and is now president of the Annenberg Foundation Trust at Sunnylands in California.

Steyer, James P., *The Other Parent: The Inside Story of the Media's Effect on Our Children*, Atria Books, 2002.
A former Stanford University professor who now heads the advocacy group Common Sense Media forcefully criticizes television and other media for bombarding children with sex, violence and commercialism and recommends steps for parents and citizen activists to counter the media's influence. Includes notes.

Articles

"FCC Seen Unlikely to Give Indecency Guidance," *Communications Daily*, June 27, 2012.
FCC and industry officials are predicting that the agency will begin disposing of the backlog of 1.5 million indecency complaints without providing any broad guidance for broadcasters. For earlier coverage in the respected trade journal, see "No Appetite in Congress to Take Up Broadcast Indecency, Hill Staffers Say" (June 25, 2012) and "Supreme Court Tossing ABC, Fox Indecency Actions Turns Focus Back on FCC" (June 22, 2012).

Denniston, Lyle, "Opinion recap: TV indecency policy awaits next round," SCOTUSblog, June 21, 2012, www.scotusblog.com/?p=147158.
The veteran Supreme Court reporter says the court's limited decision in *FCC v. Fox Television Stations* signaled that the FCC's indecency policy would not survive another round before the justices. The site provides a complete history of the litigation with links to legal materials, including all briefs filed with the Supreme Court.

Elwood, John P., Jeremy C. Marwell and Eric A. White, "FCC, Fox, and That Other F-Word," *Cato Supreme Court Review 2011-2012*, September 2012, pp. 281-305.
The article traces the history of the case that ended with the Supreme Court's decision in *FCC v. Fox Television Stations*, analyzes the June 21 ruling and predicts further litigation over the FCC's broadcast-indecency regime. Elwood and White filed an amicus brief in the case on behalf of the Cato Institute and other groups that advocated overruling the court's seminal ruling on the issue, *FCC v. Pacifica Foundation* (1978).

Reports and Studies

"Cartoons Are No Laughing Matter: Sex, Drugs and Profanity on Primetime Animated Programs," Parents Television Council, Aug. 16, 2011, www.parentstv.org/PTC/publications/reports/animation/Report.pdf.
The council's analysts reported finding 1,487 incidents of explicit sex, drug use and/or offensive language in 123 episodes of prime-time animated programs, representing about 57 hours of program time altogether. The 41-page report details the findings by category. The council's other reports include "Sexualized Teen Girls: Tinseltown's New Target," Dec. 15, 2010, http://issuu.com/parentstv.org/docs/sexualized_teen_girls?mode=embed&layout=http%3A%2F%2Fskin.issuu.com%2Fv%2Flight%2Flayout.xml&showFlipBtn=true, and "Habitat for Profanity: Broadcast TV's Sharp Increase in Foul Language," Nov. 9, 2010, www.parentstv.org/PTC/publications/reports/2010ProfanityStudy/study.pdf.

Rintels, Jonathan, "Big Chill: How the FCC's Indecency Decisions Stifle Free Expression, Threaten Quality Television, and Harm America's Children," Center for Creative Voices, November 2006, www.creativevoices.us/cgi-upload/news/news_article/CVPaperFINAL092106.pdf.
The 34-page report argues that the FCC's "inconsistent and confusing" decisions in indecency cases, combined with the then newly enacted tenfold increase in possible fines for broadcast stations, creates a strong chilling effect on writers, directors and producers of television programming. Rintels is the center's executive director.

The Next Step:

Additional Articles from Current Periodicals

Cable Television

Lawrence, Blake, "FCC Regulations Are Outdated," ***Daily Oklahoman*****, July 28, 2012, p. A9, newsok.com/its-long-past-time-for-fcc-to-change-its-broadcast-tv-rules/article/3696018.**

The Federal Communications Commission's indecency regulations are unfair to cable, says an Oklahoma attorney.

Maerz, Melissa, "The Creeping of Bleeping," ***Los Angeles Times*****, June 12, 2011, p. D1, articles.latimes.com/2011/jun/12/entertainment/la-ca-bleeping-20110612.**

TV networks are skirting the rules of indecency to compete with cable television, says a communications professor.

Children

Blundo, Joe, "Government a Poor Judge of Trashy TV," ***Columbus*** **(Ohio)** ***Dispatch*****, Jan. 15, 2012, p. E1, www.dispatch.com/content/stories/life_and_entertainment/2012/01/15/government-a-poor-judge-of-trashy-tv.html.**

Parents, not the government, should be in charge of protecting their children from television indecency, says a columnist.

Peyser, Andrea, "TV Teaches the Slut Life," ***New York Post*****, Dec. 15, 2011, p. 27, www.nypost.com/p/news/local/tv_teaches_the_slut_life_aulGLBbVz4tzFcq3wiDKOI.**

Experts say teenagers often adopt the sexual and violent behavior that they watch on reality television shows.

Winter, Tim, "Our Children Deserve Protection," ***USA Today*****, Jan. 11, 2012, p. A8, usatoday30.usatoday.com/news/opinion/story/2012-01-10/FCC-decency-Supreme-Court/52488728/1.**

Children should be protected from all forms of broadcast indecency, says the president of the Parents Television Council.

Ratings System

Askar, Jamshid Ghazi, "A 15-Year Failure?" ***Deseret*** **(Utah)** ***Morning News*****, Oct. 18, 2012, www.deseretnews.com/article/865564776/A-15-year-failure-Parents-Television-Council-says-TV-content-ratings-are-flawed.html?pg=all.**

TV content ratings are flawed because many shows aren't properly rated, says the Parents Television Council.

Kang, Cecilia, "Mobile Apps Lack Ratings Standards," ***The Washington Post*****, Oct. 15, 2011, p. A1.**

Television violence and nudity are being presented without a ratings standard on mobile applications aimed at children.

Stelter, Brian, "TV Ratings System Expected to Expand Online," ***The New York Times*****, June 11, 2012, p. B6, query.nytimes.com/gst/fullpage.html?res=940DE6DF1E30F932A25755C0A9649D8B63.**

Content ratings are expanding to the Internet streams of shows regularly shown on television.

Regulations

Perkins, Tony, "Keep the Public Airwaves Clean," ***USA Today*****, June 22, 2012, p. A8, usatoday30.usatoday.com/news/opinion/story/2012-06-21/FCC-Family-Research-Council/55749750/1.**

Broadcasters should be able to figure out what's "indecent" without consulting FCC regulations, says the president of the Family Research Council.

Richey, Warren, "Are Tough FCC Indecency Laws Obsolete?" ***The Christian Science Monitor*****, Jan. 10, 2012, www.csmonitor.com/USA/Justice/2012/0110/Are-tough-FCC-indecency-laws-obsolete-Supreme-Court-hears-free-speech-case.**

Fox and ABC say tougher FCC indecency regulations against broadcasters are discriminatory.

Wolfgang, Ben, "FCC's Policy on Obscenity on TV 'Vague,' " ***The Washington Times*****, June 22, 2012, p. A6, www.washingtontimes.com/news/2012/jun/21/supreme-court-fccs-indecency-rules-too-vague/.**

The Supreme Court has provided little guidance on whether TV indecency standards violate the First Amendment.

Wyatt, Edward, "Can You Say That on TV? Broadcasters Aren't Sure," ***The New York Times*****, June 22, 2012, p. B6.**

Broadcasters have little grasp of what constitutes indecency because the FCC has not pursued many complaints.

Citing *CQ Researcher*

Sample formats for citing these reports in a bibliography include the ones listed below. Preferred styles and formats vary, so please check with your instructor or professor.

MLA Style

Jost, Kenneth. "Remembering 9/11," CQ Researcher 2 Sept. 2011: 701-732.

APA Style

Jost, K. (2011, September 2). Remembering 9/11. *CQ Researcher, 9*, 701-732.

Chicago Style

Jost, Kenneth. "Remembering 9/11." *CQ Researcher*, September 2, 2011, 701-732.

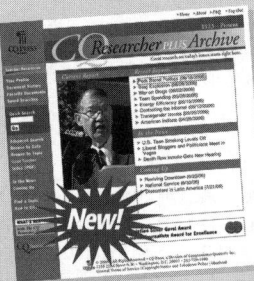

CQ Researcher

Published by CQ Press, an Imprint of SAGE Publications, Inc.

www.cqresearcher.com

Changing Demographics

Will the rising minority population benefit the economy?

The nation is undergoing one of the most important demographic transitions in its history. For the first time, minority babies outnumbered white newborns last year, and Census estimates predict that by 2042 non-Hispanic whites will no longer be in the majority. Already, more than a third of Americans are minorities, and non-whites accounted for 92 percent of population growth between 2000 and 2010, a trend driven by rising Hispanic immigration. Meanwhile, as millions of baby boomers retire, the nation is growing older. More than a fifth of Americans will be 65 or older by 2030, compared with one in eight today. Seismic changes also are occurring on the religious front: Protestants are no longer in the majority, and millions have abandoned religion altogether. And, in a striking trend of reverse migration, millions of blacks are moving back to the South.

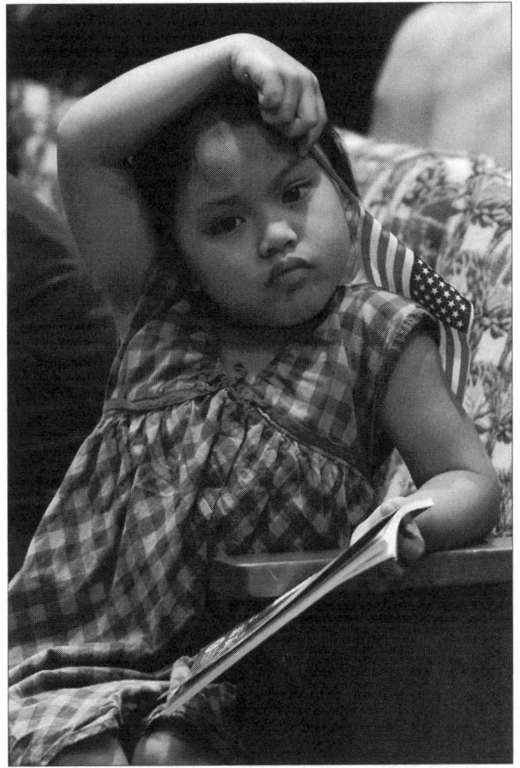

Happy Citizenship Day! A youngster rests after joining other local children who attended a naturalization ceremony in Los Angeles on Sept. 19, 2012. Some 40 million Americans — about one in eight — are foreign-born.

INSIDE THIS REPORT

THE ISSUES 991
BACKGROUND 997
CHRONOLOGY 999
CURRENT SITUATION 1004
AT ISSUE 1005
OUTLOOK 1006
BIBLIOGRAPHY 1010
THE NEXT STEP 1011

CQ Researcher • Nov. 16, 2012 • www.cqresearcher.com
Volume 22, Number 41 • Pages 989-1012

Los Angeles | London | New Delhi
Singapore | Washington DC

RECIPIENT OF SOCIETY OF PROFESSIONAL JOURNALISTS AWARD FOR EXCELLENCE ◆ AMERICAN BAR ASSOCIATION SILVER GAVEL AWARD

Changing Demographics

The Issues

991 • Will changing demographics affect American values?
• Will the nation's demographic changes benefit the U.S. economy?
• Will changing demographics affect future U.S. elections?

Background

997 **Pioneering Blacks** The first blacks in North America were traders who helped settle the continent.

998 **Early Immigrants** Political upheaval abroad fueled 19th-century U.S. immigration.

998 **Expanding Equality** Major demographic changes swept the nation in the 20th century.

1002 **New Newcomers** Strict immigration quotas gave way to expanding diversity.

Current Situation

1004 **Immigration Standstill** Net immigration from Mexico has dropped to zero.

1004 **Dayton Model** Some cities are trying to attract immigrant workers and entrepreneurs.

1006 **Aging in Place** Communities are preparing for a sharp rise in elderly residents.

Outlook

1006 **Political Changes** The 2012 election underscored the important role of demography.

Sidebars and Graphics

992 **More Americans Religiously Unaffiliated** A fifth say they are unattached to a faith group.

993 **Religion and the 2012 Election** Evangelicals overwhelmingly supported Mitt Romney.

996 **Older Population on Rise** Seventy million Americans will be at least 65 years old by 2030.

999 **Chronology** Key events since 1670.

1000 **Black Migration Makes a U-Turn** Millions of African-Americans are returning to the South.

1002 **Boomers More Conservative but Still Feisty** Mistrust of government still spurs the '60s generation.

1005 **At Issue** Is large-scale immigration good for the U.S. economy?

For Further Research

1009 **For More Information** Organizations to contact.

1010 **Bibliography** Selected sources used.

1011 **The Next Step** Additional articles.

1011 **Citing *CQ Researcher*** Sample bibliography formats.

Cover: Getty Images/Kevork Djansezian

CQ Researcher

Nov. 16, 2012
Volume 22, Number 41

Managing Editor: Thomas J. Billitteri
tjb@cqpress.com

Assistant Managing Editor: Kathy Koch
kkoch@cqpress.com

Senior Contributing Editor:
Thomas J. Colin
tcolin@cqpress.com

Associate Editor: Kenneth Jost

Staff Writer: Marcia Clemmitt

Contributing Writers: Peter Katel, Barbara Mantel, Tom Price, Jennifer Weeks

Senior Project Editor: Olu B. Davis

Assistant Editor: Darrell Dela Rosa

Fact Checker: Michelle Harris

Los Angeles | London | New Delhi
Singapore | Washington DC

An Imprint of SAGE Publications, Inc.

Vice President and Editorial Director, Higher Education Group:
Michele Sordi

Director, Online Publishing:
Todd Baldwin

CQ Researcher (ISSN 1056-2036) is printed on acid-free paper. Published weekly, except: (March wk. 5) (May wk. 4) (July wk. 1) (Aug. wks. 3, 4) (Nov. wk. 4) and (Dec. wks. 3, 4). Published by SAGE Publications, Inc., 2455 Teller Rd., Thousand Oaks, CA 91320. Annual full-service subscriptions start at $1,054. For pricing, call 1-800-834-9020. To purchase a *CQ Researcher* report in print or electronic format (PDF), visit www.cqpress.com or call 866-427-7737. Single reports start at $15. Bulk purchase discounts and electronic-rights licensing are also available. Periodicals postage paid at Thousand Oaks, California, and at additional mailing offices. POSTMASTER: Send address changes to *CQ Researcher*, 2300 N St., N.W., Suite 800, Washington, DC 20037.

Changing Demographics

BY BILL WANLUND

THE ISSUES

The nation is undergoing a profound population makeover, a transformation so sweeping that just about every aspect of American life will be affected in coming years, from economic growth and electoral politics to social-welfare policies and religious affiliation.

Growing ethnic and racial diversity is the most striking sign of change. For the first time in U.S. history, minority babies outnumbered white newborns last year, a trend driven by rising Hispanic immigration. [1] By 2042, non-Hispanic whites will cease to be in the majority. Already, more than a third of Americans are minorities, and nonwhites accounted for 92 percent of population growth between 2000 and 2010. [2]

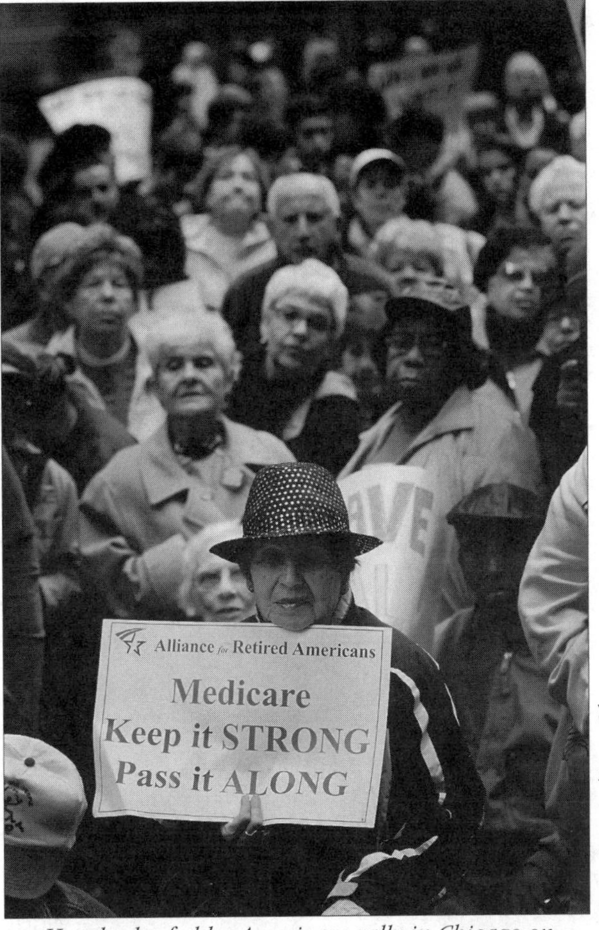

Getty Images/Scott Olson

Hundreds of older Americans rally in Chicago on Nov. 7, 2011, against cuts in programs that benefit the elderly. Each day for the next 19 years, 10,000 baby boomers will reach the traditional retirement age of 65. By 2030, more than one in five Americans will be 65 or older, compared with about one in eight today. The number of older Americans is expected to more than double between now and 2050, to about 84 million.

The pace of demographic change in the nation, whose population has grown to about 315 million, has stunned even the experts. "It was always predicted that we would be diverse, but it's happened faster than anyone predicted," said Cheryl Russell, former editor in chief of *American Demographics* magazine and now editorial director of New Strategist Publications. "Diversity and the rapid growth in diversity is one of the reasons we have a black president today. That's one thing that would never have been predicted." [3]

Nowhere have the effects of diversity been more evident than in this month's presidential election. In his Nov. 6 victory over GOP contender Mitt Romney, President Obama garnered an estimated 71 percent of the Hispanic vote, according to election day polling by the Pew Hispanic Center. [4] Asian-Americans, who supported Obama by about 47 percentage points, made up 3 percent of the 2012 electorate, up a full point from 2008. [5] "The nonwhite vote has been growing — tick, tick, tick — slowly, steadily," said Paul Taylor, executive vice president of the nonpartisan Pew Research Center. "Every four-year cycle the electorate gets a little bit more diverse. And it's going to continue." [6]

That diversity extends to Capitol Hill. Next year's 113th Congress will include 28 Latinos in the House of Representatives, the largest Latino class in U.S. history, and a third Latino will join the U.S. Senate. [7]

The nation's demographic evolution goes far beyond ethnicity, race and politics, however. For example:

- By 2030, more than one in five Americans will be age 65 or older, compared with about one in eight today. (*See chart, p. 996.*)
- More than one-fourth of Americans have left the religious denomination of their childhood and either joined a different faith or abandoned organized religion altogether.
- For the first time, Protestants are a minority in the United States: Only 48 percent of Americans identify themselves as Protestants — down from 53 percent in 2007. [8] (*See chart, p. 992.*)

The nation's shifting demographic profile has huge implications for many facets of American life, noted Laura B. Shrestha and Elayne J. Heisler, researchers for the Congressional Research Service, which advises Congress on policy issues. "There is ample reason to believe that the United States will be able to cope with the current and projected demographic changes if policy makers accelerate efforts to address and adapt to the changing population profile as it relates to . . . work, retirement and pensions, private wealth and income security — and the health and well-being of the aging population," they wrote. [9]

Indeed, the rise in the average age of the U.S. population is among the benchmarks demographers and econ-

More Americans Religiously Unaffiliated

The percentage of Americans who classify themselves as religiously unaffiliated has steadily increased since 2007, to nearly 20 percent, and Protestants comprise less than half the population for the first time in U.S. history. Experts say fewer and fewer young adults are embracing the religious traditions of their elders and that more Americans are choosing to remain unaffiliated with any faith group.

Religious Affiliation Among Americans, 2007-2012

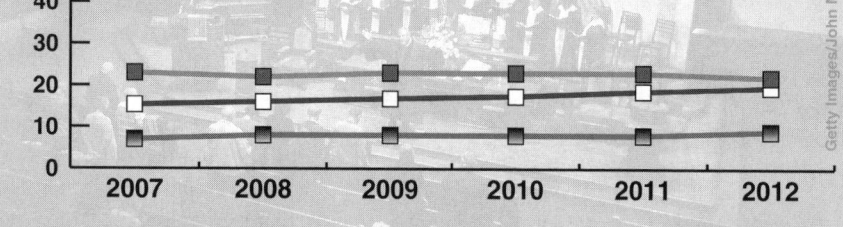

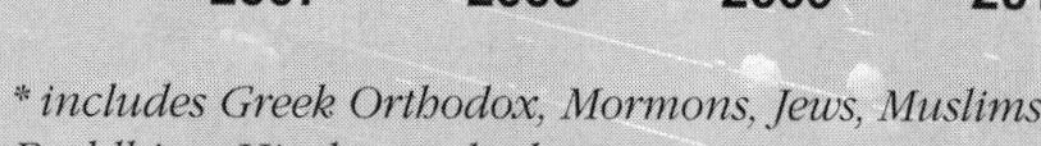

* *includes Greek Orthodox, Mormons, Jews, Muslims, Buddhists, Hindus and others*

** *includes atheists, agnostics and those who believe nothing in particular*

Source: " 'Nones' on the Rise: One-in-Five Adults Have No Religious Affiliation," Pew Research Center, October 2012, p. 13, www.pewforum.org/uploadedFiles/Topics/Religious_Affiliation/Unaffiliated/NonesOnTheRise-full.pdf

omists are watching most closely. The number of Americans 65 or older is expected to more than double between now and 2050 — from 40 million to 84.5 million. On Jan. 1, 2011, the first of the 78 million Americans born between 1946 and 1964 — the baby boomers — reached the traditional retirement age of 65. For the next 19 years, 10,000 more will cross that threshold every day, according to the Pew Research Center. [10]

Experts note that as a nation's citizens age out of the workforce, its tax base declines, reducing the amount of money available for pensions and publicly supported medical and residential needs. What's more, older people generally spend less on consumer goods, putting less money into the economy.

Yet, while an aging U.S. population poses challenges for social-welfare programs targeted at the elderly, including Medicare and Social Security, experts say the nation retains an economic advantage over Europe, Japan and China, all of which are aging faster than the United States. [11] The reason for the U.S. edge, they say, is immigration. The Census Bureau estimates that 14 million immigrants came legally or illegally to the U.S. between 2000 and 2010 — the largest decennial influx in history. Some 40 million Americans — about one in eight — are foreign-born. [12]

"If the U.S. depended on white births alone, we'd be dead," said Dowell Myers, a professor of policy, planning and demography at the University of Southern California. "Without the contributions from all these other groups, we would become too top-heavy with old people." [13]

Myers noted that countries with low immigration rates, such as Japan, can end up with young, working-age populations too small to support the larger group of aging citizens.

Along with immigration, birth rates also are keeping America younger than other industrialized countries. Between 2000 and 2010, the Hispanic population — now the nation's largest minority — grew 43 percent, to more than 50 million, partly because the birth rate among Hispanics is 60 percent higher than among whites. The Asian-American population grew at about the same rate, reaching 17 million, while the black population rose 15.4 percent, to 42 million.

For some whites, predictions that minorities will grow to more than half of the U.S. population come as a jolt. They feel as though they had gone "from being a privileged group to all of a sudden becoming whites, the new victims," said Charles Gallagher, a sociologist at La Salle University in Pennsylvania who researches racial attitudes among whites. [14] In fact, a 2011 joint survey by the Brookings Institution and the Public Religion Research Institute, both in Washington, found that nearly half of whites believe discrimination against them is now as big a problem as discrimination against minorities. [15]

Meanwhile, "non-affiliated" is now the fastest-growing category in the nation's religious profile. Twenty percent of Americans say they have no church affiliation — up from 15 percent five years ago, according to a study by the Pew Forum on Religion and Public Life released in October. "Young people today are coming of age at a time when they are less religious than at any time before in our polling," says Greg Smith, a lead researcher on the study. (*See graphs, pp. 992, 993.*)

In what Smith calls a "churn" taking place in American religion, 28 percent of adults have left the faith in which they were raised to join another religion — or to practice no religion at all. Roughly 44 percent have either switched religious affiliation, rejoined a church after being unaffiliated or dropped out of organized religion altogether. [16]

The Protestant decline marks an important transition point, says Randall Balmer, chairman of the religion department at Dartmouth College. But he adds, "The U.S. has always been a pluralistic country in terms of religion, and this is simply another indication that we are a religiously diverse people."

The Catholic Church has lost the most followers of any major denomination in the United States: Four Catholics leave the Church for every individual who converts to the faith. [17]

Nevertheless, about 25 percent identify themselves as Catholic, a proportion that has remained steady for decades, Smith notes. "Immigration from Latin America is boosting the size of the Catholic population, and it's mostly responsible for the Catholic share of the population holding steady," he says.

As demographic changes bring sweeping changes to American society, here are some of the questions being debated:

Religion and the 2012 Election

White evangelicals and white Catholics largely backed GOP contender Mitt Romney in this year's presidential election, as did most members of his Mormon faith. Black Protestants and Hispanic Catholics largely supported President Obama's re-election. Experts say the ethnic identity of minority voters, who traditionally support Democratic candidates, often trumps religious affiliation at the polls. Religiously unaffiliated voters overwhelmingly backed Obama.

Presidential Vote by Religious Affiliation and Race, 2012
(by percentage of voters)

Religion	Barack Obama	Mitt Romney
Total Percentage	**50%**	**48%**
Protestant/other Christian	**42**	**57**
White Protestant/other Christian	30	69
Born-again/evangelical	20	79
Non-evangelical	44	54
Black Protestant/other Christian	95	5
Catholic	**50**	**48**
White Catholic	40	59
Hispanic Catholic	75	21
Jewish	**69**	**30**
Mormon	**21**	**78**
Other faiths	**74**	**23**
Religiously unaffiliated	**70**	**26**

Source: "How the Faithful Voted: 2012 Preliminary Analysis," Pew Forum on Religion and Public Life, November 2012.

Will changing demographics affect American values?

The late Harvard University political scientist Samuel P. Huntington feared that America was losing its way. He was particularly concerned about the influx of Hispanic immigrants, specifically from Mexico. Huntington feared that their sheer numbers and the rise of multiculturalism in the United States would be a challenge to America's "core culture." [18]

But Joel Kotkin, distinguished presidential fellow in urban futures at Chapman University in Orange, Calif., took a different view of immigrants. "America's ability to absorb newcomers represents . . . a new paradigm, where race itself begins to matter less than culture, class and other factors," he wrote. "Rather than a source of national decline, the new Americans represent the critical force that can provide the new markets, the manpower, and, perhaps most important, the youthful energy to keep our country vital and growing. [19]

Attitudes toward abortion and gay marriage are often seen as a yardstick of religious values. Hispanics — many of whom are Catholic — are more conservative than the U.S. population overall on abortion, according to a 2012 survey by the Pew Hispanic Center. Slightly more than half of Hispanics believe abortion should be illegal in all or most cases, compared to 41 percent of the general population.

Americans' support for same-sex marriage has been gradually increasing, and in 2011, according to the Pew Research Center, the public was evenly divided on whether gay and lesbian couples should be allowed to marry. A slim majority of Hispanics believes same-sex marriage should be legal. [20]

Pew also found that Asian-Americans' views on abortion and homosexuality largely mirror those of the nation at large. Like Hispanics, Asians are more likely to call themselves liberal — 31 percent do so — and less likely than the overall population to describe themselves as conservative. [21]

"Another measure of Americans' acceptance of diversity is the increase in interracial marriage, which demographers typically interpret to mean that race relations are improving, says Cornell University sociology professor Daniel Lichter. "It means the things that promote intimacy between racial and ethnic groups — for example, residential proximity or economic equality or similar levels of education — have taken place," Lichter says.

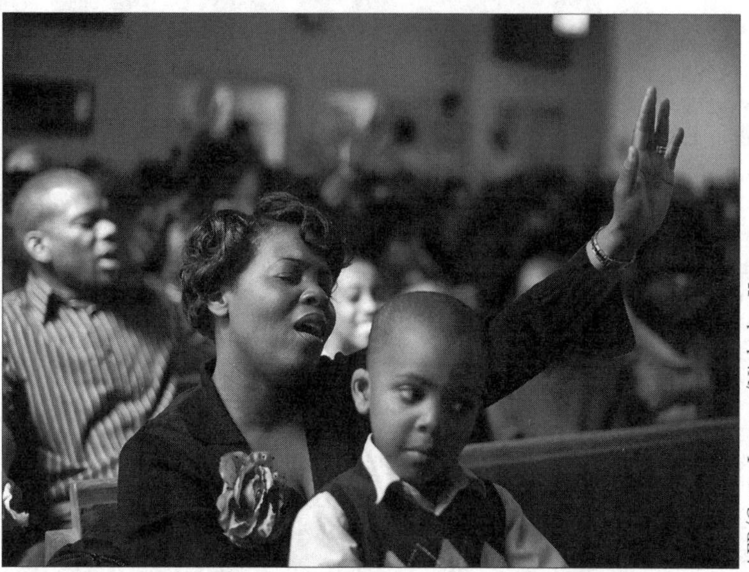

Worshippers at the First Church of Seventh-day Adventists in Washington, D.C., on March 31, 2012, pray for the families of slain Florida teenager Trayvon Martin and the neighborhood watch volunteer who killed him. More than a fourth of Americans have left the religious denomination of their childhood and either joined a different faith or abandoned organized religion.

AFP/Getty Images/Nicholas Kamm

A 2012 study by the Pew Research Center showed that about 15 percent of all new marriages in the United States in 2010 were between spouses of different races or ethnicity, more than double the 6.7 percent share in 1980. [22]

However, "This doesn't mean that we're in a post-racial society," Lichter says. "We've made great strides, but we have an awfully long way to go before race doesn't matter in this culture." [23]

Twenty-eight percent of Asians married people of another race, the highest percentage of all ethnic groups. "The rate of intermarriage in the Asian-American, especially the Japanese-American, community is definitely having a cultural impact," says Lane Hirabayashi, a professor of Asian-American studies at the University of California, Los Angeles.

However, Hirabayashi also notes that the rate of increase of Asian interracial marriage has slowed. "Increasing immigration from Asia gives immigrants a larger pool of potential partners from the same ethnic group," he says.

John Nieto-Phillips, a history professor at Indiana University who specializes in Latino studies, says, "Latinos are comfortable with marrying a person of another heritage or background. Latinos are less comfortable, however, defining their own identity by existing racial categories. The 'browning of America' by way of intermarriage portends the blurring of conventional racial boundaries, though it may not mitigate the social or structural inequalities that tend to sustain boundaries."

Pew found that 43 percent of Americans feel that having more interracial marriages has been a change for the better, and nearly two-thirds say it "would be fine" with them if a member of their own family were to marry someone outside their own racial or ethnic group. In 1986, only one-third viewed intermarriage as acceptable. [24]

Pew Research Center researcher Kim Parker, who worked on the intermarriage study, says increased immigration over the past 40 years has helped spur the attitudinal change. "With greater diversity, there's more opportunity for people of different ethnic backgrounds to interact," Parker says. "As people get to know each other, the pool of 'candidates' becomes larger. And as an individual gains familiarity with people from different backgrounds, the degree of acceptance may rise."

It's difficult to generalize about baby boomers' impact on values. Some formed their political consciousness during the turbulent anti-Vietnam War movement, while many others were influenced by the conservative "Reagan Rebellion" of the early 1980s.

In general, however, according to a 2011 Pew survey, boomers appear to be nudging the values needle leftward. On issues such as abortion and same-sex marriage, they are somewhat less conservative than their parents' generation but less liberal than their children. Still, Pew found, in recent years "more boomers have come to call themselves conservatives [and] many . . . express reservations about the changing face of America. . . . Boomers' current attitudes bear little imprint from coming of age in an era of great social change." [25] *(See sidebar, p. 1002.)*

American University communications professor Leonard Steinhorn, author of *The Greater Generation: In Defense of the Baby Boom Legacy*, believes embracing diversity may be the boomers' chief lasting contribution to America. "It used to be that the white men who ran our businesses could exclude women and minorities with a wink and a nod," he says. "That's no longer acceptable. [Boomers] have made diversity a moral value. And they have created a cultural norm that says prejudice and discrimination are immoral; they have created new norms, and the children they have raised under those norms have internalized them."

Still, says Brookings Institution demographer William Frey, "Demography marches on. It's the younger population that [will] be living, working and building communities with each other in a very different kind of America. They are developing a different set of values, in terms of their acceptance of diversity — from having more mixed race and racially diverse friends, dating partners, spouses — and are generally more accepting of new social trends including same-sex couples, alternative religions, etc. They will also be more globally conscious due to their associations with more new Americans and their greater ability to "network" across the country and globally through social media. . . . [A]s we move into the next decade or two we're going to be much more about the people who are under age 30 than the people who are over age 50."

Will the nation's demographic changes benefit the U.S. economy?

As the U.S. population ages, economists see both trouble and opportunity ahead.

The number of Americans 65 or older is expected to more than double by 2050, to about 84 million, and today's 65-year-old can expect to live another 20 years, up from 13 years in 1950. [26]

Increased longevity and a desire to remain active are spurring many older workers to remain in the labor force. But so too are economic pressures, stemming in part from the loss of trillions of dollars in retirement assets during the recent recession.

Researchers Frank W. Heiland and Zhe Li of Boston College's Center for Retirement Research found that nearly 23 percent of men over age 65 were working in 2010, compared to 16.8 percent in 1994. The participation rate for women over 65 nearly doubled, from 7.4 percent in 1988 to 13.8 percent. [27]

As more older workers remain on the job, some experts believe they may be preventing younger workers from finding employment. One of the reasons [that young people can't find jobs is] because older people are not leaving the workforce," said Sung Won Sohn, an economist at California State University-Channel Islands. [28] But others disagree with the view that older workers are hurting the prospects of younger ones. There is "no evidence that increasing the employment of older persons reduces the job opportunities or wage rates of younger persons," said Alicia Munnell, director of the Center for Retirement Research. In fact, she said, "greater employment of older persons leads to better outcomes for the young in the form of reduced unemployment, increased employment and a higher wage." [29]

"Younger workers come into the labor force with a different vintage of education, and they don't have work experience. So, you don't often find old and young workers clamoring for the same low-wage McDonald's job," said Jeffrey Zax, a professor at the University of Colorado who specializes in labor economics. Moreover, Zax said, "A senior worker with experience might allow a company to hire more junior employees because you have someone who can manage them." [30]

Inevitably, aging Americans will require medical care and specialized living and transportation accommodations — which will open up job opportunities for younger workers, says Sara Rix, senior strategic policy adviser at the AARP Public Policy Institute.

"The proportion of older people living in nursing homes is declining, but we are going to see a substantial increase in the 'very, very old' — people in their upper 90s and 100s — many of whom . . . will need assisted-living facilities." As a result, Rix says, construction workers will be needed to build and upgrade assisted-living facilities, and doctors, nurses and home health care workers will be needed to care for the elderly.

Even so, America's aging population poses deep challenges for the health care system. For example, a projected nursing shortage is expected to grow worse as baby boomers grow older and care needs grow. [31]

As policy makers debate the implications of America's aging population, they also are studying the impact of immigration — particularly the influx of undocumented workers — on the economy.

The Federation for American Immigration Reform (FAIR), a group in Washington that promotes reduced immigration, argues that by curbing illegal immigration, "there would be many more jobs available to native workers — jobs that paid higher wages and offered better working conditions." [32]

Pia Orrenius, an assistant vice president and senior economist with the Federal Reserve Bank of Dallas, says illegal immigration might have some adverse effects on employment among specific groups — native-born teenagers, for example. "It looks like if employers have the choice of an undocumented, somewhat higher-skilled 23- or 24-year-old, they'll take that person over a 16- to 19-year-old." But, she adds, "the effects are modest."

Julie Hotchkiss, a research economist and policy adviser at the Federal Reserve Bank of Atlanta, researched undocumented workers in Georgia. "Our research shows that newly arriving undocumented workers appear to displace only earlier-arriving undocumented workers," she said. "This makes sense since undocumented workers are going to be the closest substitutes for each other." [33]

Many economists say that immigrant workers have a positive effect on the economy. "There is no evidence that immigrants crowd out U.S.-born workers in either the short or long run," wrote Giovanni Peri, an economics professor at the University of California-Davis. "The economy absorbs immigrants by expanding oppor-

Older Population on Rise

The number of Americans age 65 or older is projected to surpass 70 million by 2030. Experts cite two key reasons for the rise: the aging of the post-World War II baby boom generation and medical advances that have increased average life expectancy.

Americans Age 65 or Older, 1900-2030

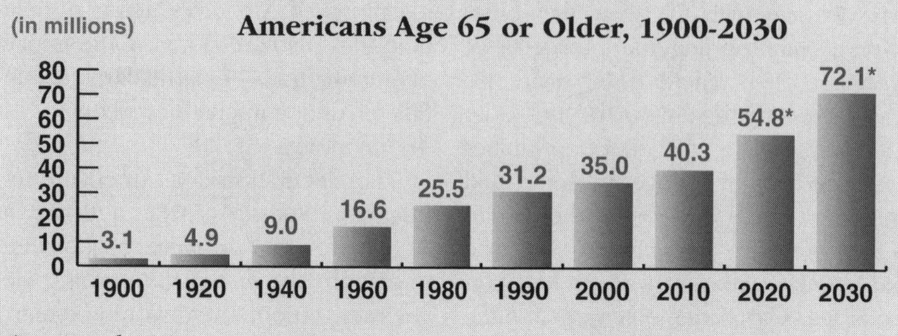

**projected*

Source: "A Profile of Older Americans: 2011," Administration on Aging, U.S. Department of Health and Human Services, 2011, p. 3, www.aoa.gov/aoaroot/aging_statistics/Profile/2011/docs/2011profile.pdf

tunities rather than by displacing U.S.-born workers. Data show that, on net, immigrants expand the U.S. economy's productive capacity, stimulate investment and promote specialization that in the long run boosts productivity." [34]

Moreover, Peri says in an interview, in the short run the loss of immigrant workers would cause an economic contraction. And while the economy might recover, the loss of immigrant labor could turn out to be "quite costly.

"If we don't have people picking vegetables and fruit in California, for example, we'll end up importing [those products]. Other jobs can't be outsourced — such as construction workers or waiters. We have seen very few natives taking these jobs, especially at the low end . . . a lot of businesses will have to slim down or substitute with imports or pay more wages."

Will changing demographics affect future U.S. elections?

Obama's victory in this year's presidential election was due, in the words of *The Hill*, a Washington newspaper that covers national politics, to "at least three concrete, demographic reasons" — the president's "broad advantage among female voters," his negation of the erroneous view "that black enthusiasm for Obama would taper off this year" and the fact that "Latinos went for Obama by even bigger margins than they did in 2008." [35]

While Obama may be particularly popular among female, black and Latino voters, many experts view the influence of those demographic groups in the 2012 election as a harbinger of how demographics might shape political destiny in campaigns of the future.

Ruy Teixeira, a senior fellow at the Center for American Progress, a liberal think tank in Washington, says a growing minority population and a shrinking white working class — a traditionally Republican-voting demographic — point to growing minority influence in future elections, a force he said would favor liberal candidates. However, he cautioned, "There is no guarantee that demographic trends will automatically lead to [electoral] dividends. . . . Parties always have to deliver." [36]

While the expected majority-minority tipping point for the general population is still 30 years off, it will come by 2023 for the younger sector of the population, primarily because of the rapid growth in the Hispanic population, according to Census Bureau estimates. Among children under age 17, about 17 million, or 23 percent, were Latinos, a rise of 39 percent in a decade, according to the Pew Hispanic Center. [37]

Brookings Institution demographer Frey said minorities' electoral influence is just becoming apparent. He pointed to the relative youth of the minority population: Currently, only 44 percent of Hispanics, 69 percent of African-Americans and 53 percent of Asians are eligible to vote, compared with 78 percent of whites. "It's because they are disproportionately below age 18, and among Hispanics and Asians, are less likely to be citizens," he says.

Whites still comprise 71 percent of the electorate, Frey pointed out, and will outnumber minority voters "well beyond" the 2012 election. Nevertheless, he added, "the handwriting is on the wall." In coming elections, as today's minority children reach the voting age of 18, "minority votes will matter, and both parties need to pay attention," Frey observed. [38]

Alan Abramowitz, a political science professor at Emory University in Atlanta, predicts that the minority electorate, which stood at 13 percent in 1992, will comprise more than a third of voters by the 2020 election. [39]

Cornell University's Lichter, who also directs the Cornell Population Center, believes the divide between older and younger voters is an issue to watch. He says, "In the 2012 elections, we saw a large, aging, mostly white population voting in one direction, and a mostly minority population voting differently. The question is, how will an older, aging, white population vote and what will it support? When older people vote, are they going to vote to support children of people who might not share the same culture?

"In 15 or 20 years, today's minorities are going to be America's taxpayers and leaders," Lichter points out. "They're going to be replacing the white baby boom generation. Will they vote to support pension and health care programs for older, American, white baby boomers? And will boomers support the kind of education, employment and social programs that help make these groups good citizens?"

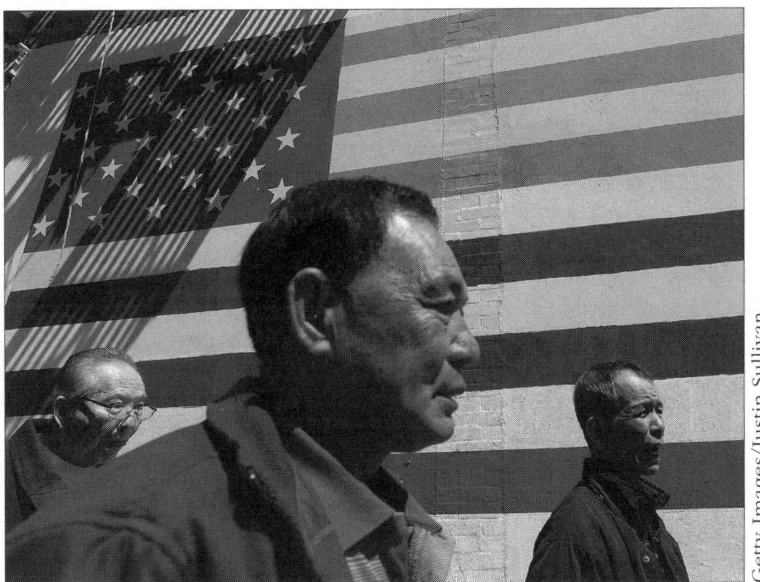

Getty Images/Justin Sullivan

Pedestrians pass an American flag mural in San Francisco's Chinatown on June 19, 2012. In 2011, the number of Asian immigrants who came to the United States outnumbered Hispanics for the first time: 438,000 came from East and South Asia and the Middle East, compared with 404,000 who arrived from Central or South America or the Caribbean.

Raw numbers aren't the only measure of minority voters' influence; another is location. Teixeira and Frey wrote that minorities are strongly influencing election outcomes in "swing states," where races are particularly hotly contested. Between 2008 and 2012, the minority share of eligible voters rose 9 percent in Nevada, 4 percent in Florida and North Carolina, 3 percent in Colorado and Wisconsin, 2 percent in Pennsylvania and Michigan, and 1 percent in Virginia. At the same time, the share of white voters in those states declined by between 1 and 3 percent. [40] And of those states, all but North Carolina voted for Obama in 2012. As for the electorate's changing religious makeup, some scholars say that just because Hispanic immigrants are predominantly Catholic does not mean they constitute a Catholic voting bloc. Indeed, said presidential scholar John Kenneth White, a professor of politics at Catholic University (CU) in Washington, the "Catholic vote" has effectively vanished. "For Hispanics, ethnic identity trumps Catholic identity," he said at a Sept. 27, 2012, forum at the university.

In 2004 more Catholics voted for George W. Bush, an evangelical Christian, than for Catholic John Kerry. William Dinges, a CU professor of religion and culture, agrees there is no such thing as a Catholic vote any more. "People are becoming more independent," he said at the CU forum. "They can support a candidate or party who supports ideas not consistent with teachings of the faith. And, the church hierarchy can't force votes the way it once could."

For example, the tide appears to be changing with regard to gay marriage, which Catholic leaders and evangelical Protestants have strongly opposed. After voters rejected same-sex marriage in 32 state referendums since the late 1990s, a measure to legalize it passed on Nov. 6 in three states (Maine, Maryland and Washington), and a constitutional amendment to define marriage as between a man and a woman failed in Minnesota. [41]

According to a Pew Forum on Religion & Public Life analysis of exit polls, traditionally Republican groups such as white evangelicals and weekly churchgoers strongly backed Republican Mitt Romney, while traditionally Democratic groups such as black Protestants, Hispanic Catholics, Jews and the religiously unaffiliated backed Obama by large margins. Obama's support among white Catholics fell 7 percentage points from 2008 but gained 3 points among Hispanic Catholics. Meanwhile, his support among white evangelicals fell by 6 percentage points. [42]

The apparent growing electoral support for same-sex marriage indicates to some analysts that the political power of white evangelicals may be on the wane. Dartmouth's Balmer, an evangelical himself, says that while the religious right will continue to be a force in U.S. politics, its influence may be less apparent in coming elections.

"I think it's going to be a bit less forceful, less dramatic than it was in the 1980s and '90s and the first decade of the 21st century," Balmer says. ■

BACKGROUND

Pioneering Blacks

The first blacks who came to North America hundreds of years ago were not slaves — far from it.

In 1613, João Rodrigues — son of a Portuguese sailor and an African woman — served as a translator on a Dutch trading ship that had sailed to the North American island known as Manhatta. When the ship returned to Europe, Rodrigues stayed behind to start a trading post selling hatchets and knives provided by the ship's captain. He also served as an interpreter and facilitator for Dutch merchants who came to the island to trade with the Indians. That's how a black man became the first non-native American to live and do business in what was to become New York City.

A little over 150 years later, Jean Baptiste Point Sable — son of a French father and African mother and probably born in the Caribbean in what is now the Dominican Republic — established himself in North America as a trader at the mouth of a river in an area called Eschecagou. Point Sable, a black man, is regarded as the first non-Indian to set up permanent residence in present-day Chicago.

And in 1781, 26 full or mixed-race blacks were among the 44 Mexicans who settled the little pueblo that would become Los Angeles.

Far better known, of course, is the tragic history of the blacks who came to North America under extreme duress. England began taking captured Africans to serve as slaves in its Carolina colony in 1670. During the colonial period, an estimated 600,000 African slaves were brought to America. In 1808, Congress banned the importation of slaves, but the law was not seamlessly enforced. It did effectively end the transatlantic slave trade — though not the practice of slavery in the colonies. By 1860, the slave population in the United States was about 4 million.

With the end of the Civil War and ratification in 1865 of the 13th amendment abolishing slavery, blacks were granted citizenship. Black males gained the right to vote with ratification of the 15th Amendment in 1870. The postwar Reconstruction period saw improved educational and economic opportunities for Southern blacks, and many even were elected to public office. In the Carolinas alone, nearly 100 black legislators were elected during Reconstruction, including 22 who were elected to Congress between 1870 and 1901. [43] Tens of thousands of African-Americans living in the North moved south to become teachers or farmers or just to reunite with families.

By 1876, however, the federal government's commitment to protect the rights of black citizens was wavering. States enacted harsh "Jim Crow" laws that institutionalized racial segregation in schools and other public places, and black voting was blocked by fraud, intimidation or worse. In 1896, a nearly unanimous U.S. Supreme Court, in the infamous *Plessy v. Ferguson* decision, upheld the concept that state laws could require separate facilities for blacks and whites, as long as the facilities were equivalent. But equivalence was left undefined. The ruling in effect conferred constitutionality to the South's Jim Crow caste system.

Early Immigrants

In the first years of the democracy, immigration to the United States was relatively slight; even so, one of the early legislative acts of the cautious Founding Fathers was the Naturalization Act of 1790, which limited naturalized citizenship to "free white persons" of "good moral character."

Immigration gathered momentum in the early 19th century. During the 1820s, 143,000 immigrants were reported; in the following decade, immigration — mostly by Irish and Germans — more than quadrupled. The 1840s recorded 1,713,000 immigrants, nearly half of them from Ireland escaping the 1845-49 potato famine. Politics also helped swell the immigrant tide, as unsuccessful European revolutions in 1848 spurred large numbers of intellectuals and political activists to flee their homelands. By 1850 foreign-born residents made up 9.7 percent of America's 23 million population.

While early post-colonial America was largely a Protestant nation, large numbers of Catholics were absorbed with the acquisition of the Louisiana Purchase from France in 1803, Florida from Spain in 1819, and territory in what is now New Mexico and California in 1847 as a result of the Mexican-American War.

The second half of the century saw the Catholic population triple, in large part the result of immigration from Europe — notably Ireland, Italy, and Poland. By 1906, there were 14 million Catholics in America, 17 percent of the total population. [44]

Asian immigrants were rare in North America until 1849, when Chinese workers were recruited to work in the California gold fields, and later to help build the transcontinental railway system and work in other, mostly menial, jobs. As the Chinese population grew, racial prejudice and distrust increased among whites, and in 1882 Congress passed the Chinese Exclusion Act, which ended immigration by Chinese laborers. The law also made Chinese immigrants already in the country ineligible for citizenship.

Expanding Equality

The 20th century saw the United States experience major demographic changes. The start of World War I (1914-1918) helped spark the mass South-to-North movement of African-Americans, and the end of World War II (1939-1945) led to the birth of the baby boom generation — the largest population bulge in the nation's history. In addition, after the United States loosened immigration restrictions, a flood of new citizens dramatically altered the country's ethnic mixture. All these forces began to come together around the middle of the 20th century, ultimately changing the way Americans perceived each other and their own values.

Meanwhile, the black population, which had reached 8.8 million by 1900

Continued on p. 1000

Chronology

1600s-1700s

Slavery is introduced to North America.

1670-1783
England begins importing African slaves to its Carolina colony. Some 600,000 African slaves are brought to America during the colonial period.

1790
Congress restricts naturalized citizenship to "free white persons" of "good moral character."

1800s

Slavery is abolished, and new rights are granted to African-Americans.

1808
Congress bans the transatlantic slave trade but not slavery.

1849
Chinese laborers recruited for California gold fields.

1863
President Abraham Lincoln issues the Emancipation Proclamation, declaring slaves in the Confederate states to be free.

1865
Thirteenth Amendment to Constitution is ratified Dec. 1, freeing all slaves.

1866
Congress enacts legislation giving blacks full citizenship.

1870
Fifteenth Amendment gives black men the right to vote.

1876
First "Jim Crow" laws in South mandate segregated public facilities.

1882
Chinese Exclusion Act forbids immigration by Chinese laborers.

1896
Supreme Court upholds "separate but equal" doctrine for whites and blacks in *Plessy v. Ferguson*.

1900s-1945

Congress seeks "homogeneity" by favoring immigrants from northern and western Europe while severely restricting everyone else. U.S. blacks migrate northward for jobs and rights.

1915
Blacks begin "Great Migration" from the South to the North.

1924
Immigration Act of 1924 essentially limits citizenship to immigrants from northern and western Europe.

1943
Congress repeals Chinese Exclusion Act (but 1924 Immigration Act is still in force).

1946-2000

Postwar baby boom creates huge population "bulge." Immigrant pool expands. Civil Rights Movement makes major advances.

1946
First of 78 million post-World War II baby boomers are born.

1963
March for Jobs and Freedom attracts up to 300,000 demonstrators to Washington in pivotal moment for the Civil Rights Movement.

1964
President Lyndon B. Johnson signs Civil Rights Act, outlawing segregation in public places.

1965
Immigration and Nationality Act opens citizenship to Asians, Hispanics, Africans and others largely excluded by the 1924 Immigration Act. The Supreme Court, in *Loving v. Virginia*, unanimously rules that restrictions on interracial marriage are unconstitutional."

1970s
Rev. Jerry Falwell and other leaders call on conservative Christians to become politically active; the Religious Right becomes political force.

2000s

America contemplates "majority-minority" status. Baby boomers enter old age.

2001
U.S. Hispanic population reaches 37 million, making Latinos the largest ethnic minority.

2008
Census Bureau projects that by 2042 whites will no longer be majority in the United States.

2011
Minority births outnumber white newborns. . . . Net Mexican immigration to United States falls to zero, mostly in response to Great Recession that began in 2007. First baby boomers reach retirement age of 65.

2012
Religion survey indicates that for the first time Protestants comprise less than half of Americans.

Black Migration Makes a U-Turn

Millions fled the South, but many are returning.

Demographers and historians call it the "Great Migration," an extraordinary exodus of blacks from the South to the urban North throughout much of the 20th century. Now that epic shift is reversing, bringing millions of African-Americans back to a region that once shunned or tormented them and their ancestors.

Between 1916 and 1975, an estimated 6 million African-Americans left the South in search of greater economic opportunity and social freedom in cities such as Chicago, Detroit, Cleveland and New York. But in the 1990s demographers began to notice something remarkable: Millions of black Americans were leaving their homes and jobs in the North and returning to their roots in the South.

Census data released in 2011 show that 57 percent of American blacks now live in the South, the highest percentage since 1960. Michigan and Illinois, home to large concentrations of African-Americans, both lost black population for the first time, according to the 2010 census, and Atlanta replaced Chicago as the city with the second-largest African-American population, after New York. More than one million blacks now living in the South were born in the Northeast, a 10-fold increase since 1970. [1]

"This is the decade of black flight," Brookings Institution demographer William Frey told *The New York Times* last year. [2]

Frey credited the return of many blacks to the South to an improved racial and economic climate there, along with "the strong cultural and economic ties that the South holds for blacks." Even so, he noted that "blacks, by and large, are not settling in the Deep South states that registered the greatest out-migration of blacks in the 1960s" and where discriminatory "Jim Crow" laws restricted blacks' freedom. [3]

That out-migration began in earnest in the second decade of the 20th century, driven by the demand for workers in Northern munitions factories during World War 1. Between 1916 and 1919, half a million African-Americans came North.

Yet, jobs were far from the only lure for Southern blacks. Isabel Wilkerson, author of the Pulitzer Prize-winning portrait of the Great Migration, *The Warmth of Other Suns*, frames the migration as a flight from racial hatred and abuse.

"This was . . . a defection from a system that had held [black] Americans in an artificial hierarchy that restricted their every move . . .," Wilkerson told *CQ Researcher* in an e-mail interview. "They were, in effect, seeking political asylum from a caste system that limited every aspect of their lives and [that] was enforced with such brutality that, in the two decades leading up to the Migration, an African-American was lynched in a public spectacle every four days for some perceived breach of that caste system."

The economic impact the South faced from the exodus of blacks wasn't apparent at first. Some Southerners gloated: "As the North grows blacker, the South grows whiter," the New Orleans *Times-Picayune* wrote. [4]

Then, as the implications of the loss of so much of the South's agricultural workforce became clear, worry set in. Southern authorities tried to stem the hemorrhaging of cheap farm labor by invoking "anti-enticement" laws to discourage agents from northern companies from recruiting blacks. [5] But it was too late: The Great Migration was on. And it kept going long after the lure of Northern jobs ended following World War I.

"Those in the World War I-era wave of the Great Migration didn't see their move as permanent — they thought when the war was over, they'd go back home," says Lorenzo Morris, a political science professor at Howard University in Washington. "But when the war ended, although it was difficult to stay [in the North], to return was intolerable."

During the post-war 1920s, the industrial economy kept booming, and so did the migration: Nearly a million more blacks headed North during the decade, and nearly half a million more left the South during the Depression era of the 1930s.

Continued from p. 998

— 90 percent of whom lived in the South — began to change rapidly in the early to mid-1900s. Jobs were being created in the rapidly industrializing North, while the South's oppressive Jim Crow laws were spurring a mass exodus known as the Great Migration. Over six decades, an estimated 6 million blacks left the South for new lives in the North and West. (*See sidebar, above.*)

Mexican migration also began to accelerate in the early to mid-20th century. It had begun in the late 1800s with the building of the railroads across the American Southwest. By 1900, half a million Mexicans were living in the United States. Though they weren't treated as well as Northern European immigrants, Mexicans didn't experience the same exclusion as Asians. All Mexicans living in territories acquired from Mexico were granted citizenship. In 1897, a U.S. district court ruled that the skin color of Mexicans should not be a factor in determining eligibility for citizenship.

The vast majority, however, had no interest in citizenship. "Why bother to become an American citizen when the land one loved, the land of family, language and *la raza* (the people or race), was so close by?," wrote historian Lawrence H. Fuchs. [45]

But eligibility for citizenship didn't stop discrimination, of course. "The Mexican-American has been the black man of the Southwest," wrote Ronnie

Schomburg Center for Research in Black Culture

An estimated 6 million African-Americans left the South between 1916 and 1975 in search of greater economic opportunity and social freedom, settling in such cities as Chicago, Detroit, Cleveland and New York. Today, many blacks are leaving the North and returning to their Southern roots.

The exodus continued — 1.6 million in the 1940s, 1.4 million in the '50s, another million in the '60s. When the Great Migration began, one in 10 American blacks lived outside the South; by the 1970s, nearly one in two did. [6] Within the migration statistics is evidence of an evolution in American society, culture and politics. "Many leading figures in American culture — from [writers] Toni Morrison and August Wilson to [performers] Miles Davis and Aretha Franklin to [sports figures] Jesse Owens and Jackie Robinson — are people whose names we likely would never have known had there been no Great Migration," Wilkerson said in the e-mail interview. "Each one of them was a child of this Migration, whose life chances were altered because their parents or grandparents chose to escape the restrictions of the South."

The Great Migration came to a close in the 1970s after its over-arching catalyst — a caste system sanctioned by law — ended with passage of landmark civil rights legislation during the previous decade. By the 1990s, the Great Migration had turned around. But its legacy lives on.

"Perhaps one of the least recognized effects of the migration was its role, unintended though it was, in helping bring the South into mainstream culture and ultimately helping it open up to the rest of the country," Wilkerson said in the e-mail interview. "The upending of the caste system brought the South more in line with the rest of the country and made it a more welcoming place for white Northerners and for immigrants who might never have considered living there under the old regime, as well as for the children and grandchildren of black Southerners who had fled in previous generations.

"The return migration of many of the children and grandchildren of the Great Migration is, in my view, one of the legacies of the Great Migration itself," Wilkerson continued. "The people who left, by their heartbreaking decision to leave, helped to change the region they had been forced to flee and make it a more welcoming place for everyone, including immigrants from other parts of the world, for white Northerners who might never have considered living in the South and for the migrants' own descendants."

— Bill Wanlund

[1] Sabrina Tavernise and Robert Gebeloff, "Many U.S. Blacks Moving to South, Reversing Trend," *The New York Times*, March 24, 2011, www.nytimes.com/2011/03/25/us/25south.html?pagewanted=all.

[2] Quoted in *ibid.*

[3] William Frey, "The New Great Migration: Black Americans' Return to the South, 1965-2000", The Brookings Institution, May 2004, www.brookings.edu/~/media/research/files/reports/2004/5/demographics%20frey/20040524_frey.

[4] Isabel Wilkerson, *The Warmth of Other Suns: The Epic Story of America's Great Migration* (2010), p. 162.

[5] *Ibid.*

[6] *Ibid.*, p. 8.

Lopez, executive assistant to former Arizona Democratic Gov. Bruce Babbitt. "There have been rapings and lynchings. . . . People's land was taken from them." [46]

The immigrant waves of the first quarter of the century brought another 750,000 legal immigrants from Mexico. The flow ebbed during the Great Depression, when many recent Mexican arrivals voluntarily returned to their homeland, and the United States tightened its immigration policy. Some 400,000 Mexicans — including many born in the United States — were deported. Mexican immigration to the United States picked up again — though slightly — in the 1940s, spurred by wartime labor shortages. In 1942, the nation initiated the "Bracero" guestworker program, under which large numbers of temporary workers were transported north. The program was supposed to end with the war but lasted until Congress refused to renew it in 1964. The Mexican guestworkers — 4.8 million over the life of the program — worked in at least 38 states, mostly picking fruit and vegetables in the Southwest. [47]

By the 1960s, public sympathy for the Civil Rights Movement was spreading across the country, giving President Lyndon B. Johnson (1963-1969) the support he needed to push through the 1964 Civil Rights Act, which outlawed segregation in public places. A year later, Johnson signed the Voting

Boomers More Conservative but Still Feisty

Mistrust of government still spurs '60s generation.

Forty years ago, the anti-establishment protests of the baby boom generation helped end the Vietnam War. Today, many of those same boomers form the core of the conservative Tea Party movement.

The Tea Party phenomenon reflects a general move to the right by many of the 78 million Americans born between 1946 and 1964, pollsters and demographers say. In 2008, 12 percent of boomers identified themselves as liberal, compared with 30 percent in 1972, according to the American National Election Survey. Meanwhile, the percentage calling themselves conservative more than doubled, from 21 percent to 46 percent. [1]

Still, many experts say the ideological transformation of the boomer generation is not inconsistent with its formative ideals in the 1960s.

"Tea Partiers are mistrustful of authority," says Leonard Steinhorn, a communications professor at American University in Washington who has studied the boomers. "In many ways that distrust of any sort of power or authority is not so dissimilar to what so many boomers throughout the years have expressed against either unchecked power or illegitimate authority, which many felt was exercised during the Vietnam War."

The Pew Research Center, which tracks Americans' social and political attitudes, says many boomers who pushed for sweeping societal change in the '60s are feeling uncomfortable with demographic and cultural shifts occurring in society today.

"Many boomers express reservations about the changing face of America," the Pew Research Center said in a report outlining the results of a survey on political views. "Boomers' current attitudes bear little imprint from coming of age in an era of great social change." [2]

Citing the Pew report, William Frey, a demographer at the Brookings Institution, a Washington think tank, noted boomers' attitudes on immigration. "[Twenty-three] percent of baby boomers regard the country's growing population of immigrants as a change for the better," he wrote. "Forty-three percent saw it as a change for the worse. Almost half of white boomers said the growing number of newcomers from other countries represented a threat to traditional U.S. customs and values." [3]

The conservative shift belies boomers' popular image — honed by the counterculture of the 1960s — as left-wing idealists whose motto was "don't trust anyone over 30."

Under that banner, boomers challenged the "establishment" over issues such as the Vietnam War, racial and sexual equality and matters of faith. More than 60 percent left organized

Rights Act of 1965, significantly improving blacks' access to the polls.

The new laws were the crowning legislative achievements of the Civil Rights Movement and reflected its successful effort to mobilize public support for its cause. The movement's success also inspired other groups that felt they were treated unfairly. Feminist scholar Jo Freeman wrote, "During the fifties and early sixties, the Civil Rights Movement captured the public imagination and educated it on the immorality of discrimination and the legitimacy of mass protest . . . . For women, it provided not only a model for action but a very different world view from that of the 'separate spheres' [for women and men], which had been the reigning ideology for the previous century." [48]

Lessons from the Civil Rights Movement also helped to frame the push for gay rights. Bayard Rustin, a civil rights leader and a key organizer of the landmark 1963 March on Washington, later turned the lessons he had learned to promoting gay rights. "Today, blacks are no longer the litmus paper or the barometer of social change," he said in 1986. "The new 'niggers' are gays. . . . It is in this sense that gay people are the new barometer for social change." [49]

The New Newcomers

The Exclusion Act, which prohibited Chinese and most other Asians from immigrating to the United States, was repealed in 1943, when China was an American ally in World War II. However, another strict law — the Immigration Act of 1924, which put annual quotas on the number of immigrants from each country who could be accepted into the United States — was still in effect.

In a later analysis, the State Department historian's office wrote, "The most basic purpose of the 1924 Immigration Act was to preserve the ideal of American homogeneity." [50] To do so, the act tied the quotas to numbers from the 1890 census, in a thinly disguised attempt to limit a new flood of immigrants — many of them poor and uneducated — from Eastern and Southern Europe. So, while the law allowed immigration by about 51,000 Germans and 62,000 people from Great Britain and Ireland, it permitted fewer than 4,000 Italians and around 2,000 Russians to enter. In fact, 86.5 percent of the yearly immigrant quota of 164,667 was to come from northwest Europe and Scandinavia. [51]

With only minor modifications, the act remained in force for 40 years. Then, reflecting the growing atmosphere of tolerance in the 1960s, Congress passed the Immigration and Nationality Act of 1965, which abolished the national origins quota sys-

religion, most while in their teens or early 20s, though about a third of those eventually returned. [4]

A 2009 survey by pollster John Zogby found that 36 percent of boomers thought their generation would be remembered for its self-indulgence, compared with 31 percent who said its legacy would be social change. [5]

Still, in gauging the boomer generations' legacy, it's important to see the nation's transformation in the past four decades in a positive light, Steinhorn says.

"We are a far better, more inclusive, more equal, more free, more environmentally conscious and less bigoted and prejudiced society than we have ever been in our nation's history," he says. "And given that our nation's original sin was built on bigotry and discrimination . . ., we have come a very long way in just a few decades."

— Bill Wanlund

AFP/Getty Images/Kimihiro Hoshino

Some 78 million Americans, known as the baby boom generation, were born between 1946 and 1964. In 2008, 12 percent of boomers identified themselves as liberal, compared with 46 percent who said they were conservative.

[1] Survey cited by Karlyn Bowman and Andrew Rugg, "As the Baby Boomers Turn," *Los Angeles Times*, Sept. 12, 2011, www.latimes/news/opinion/commentary/la-oe-bowman-baby-boomers-more-conservative-20010912,0,4867587.story.

[2] "The Generation Gap and the 2012 Election," Pew Research Center for the People and the Press, Nov. 3, 2011, p. 11, www.people-press.org/2011/11/03/the-generation-gap-and-the-2012-election/3.

[3] William Frey, "Baby Boomers Had Better Embrace Change," *The Washington Post*, June 8, 2012, www.brookings.edu/research/opinions/2012/06/08-baby-boomers-frey.

[4] Research by Prof. Wade Clark Roof, cited in Leonard Steinhorn, *The Greater Generation* (2006).

[5] John Zogby, "The Baby Boomers' Legacy," *Forbes.com*, July 23, 2009, www.forbes.com/2009/07/22/baby-boomer-legacy-change-consumer-opinions-columnists-john-zogby.html.

tem. The new law limited to 170,000 the total number of immigrants allowed into the country but eliminated regional quotas and tied immigration to immigrants' skills and family relationships with citizens or U.S. residents.

"This is not a revolutionary bill," President Johnson said at the time. "It does not affect the lives of millions. . . . It will not reshape the structure of our daily lives or add importantly to either our wealth or our power." [52]

Johnson may have underestimated the impact of the law, or he may have been understating the case to ease the fears of nervous nationalists. In any event, 30 years after the law went into effect, the United States had admitted more than 18 million new immigrants, more than three times the number who had entered over the previous three decades.

This time, instead of northern Europeans, immigrants from Latin America topped the list. While European immigrants made up nearly 60 percent of the United States' total foreign population in 1970, they accounted for only 15 percent by the end of the century. The percentage of immigrants from Latin America, however, grew from less than 19 percent to more than 50 percent in the same period. [53]

In recent years the United States has admitted more than a million new immigrants annually. Today, Hispanics make up the lion's share of the immigrant population. Nearly 22 million, or around 55 percent of foreign-born Americans, came from Central or South America or the Caribbean; about 404,000 arrived in 2011 alone, or about 37 percent of the total.

However, in 2011, for the first time, Asian immigrants outnumbered Hispanics: Some 438,000 came from East and South Asia and the Middle East, representing 41 percent of new immigrants. About 8.4 percent of American immigrants came from Europe, another 9.1 percent from Africa and the remainder, around 5.1 percent, from "other regions" — principally, Canada and Oceania. [54]

Overall, the U.S. population is aging. In 1950, when the baby boom was just getting under way, 8.2 percent of Americans were 65 or older; now, with the boomers reaching that age, 13.3 percent are in that age bracket. [55] Meanwhile, the birth rate is declining: The United States recorded 4 million births in 2010, down 3 percent from the previous year, continuing a recent trend. [56]

These factors, along with increasing longevity (expected life span in the United States now is about 78.5 years), pushed the median age of Americans to 37.2 in 2010 — up from 35.3 in 2000. "The aging of the baby boom population, along with stabilizing birth rates and longer life expectancy, have contributed to the increase in median age," according to the Census Bureau.[57] ■

CURRENT SITUATION

Immigration Standstill

Once a flood, the flow of immigrants from Mexico into the United States has come to a halt.

In April, the Pew Hispanic Center reported that since 2007 net immigration from Mexico — the single largest source of immigrants to the United States — had dropped to zero. Mexicans are still emigrating to the United States, the center said, but just as many, and maybe more, are returning home.

"The standstill appears to be the result of many factors, including the weakened U.S. job and housing construction markets, heightened border enforcement, a rise in deportations, the growing dangers associated with illegal border crossings, the long-term decline in Mexico's birth rates and broader economic conditions in Mexico," Pew said.[58]

Audrey Singer, a senior fellow at the Metropolitan Policy Program at the Brookings Institution, believes the decline is due largely to developments in Mexico. "They've been sending labor to the U.S. for one or two generations, but now they have a shrinking supply themselves. Fertility rates are dropping, and they have a birthrate close to ours. Moreover, Mexican education levels are rising, and people are deciding not to come who may have taken a chance before."

The immigration pause is not likely to continue, however, she says. "We can probably assume that when our economy begins to pick up, immigration from Mexico will resume."

Even with the recent slowdown, America has about 12 million Mexican immigrants — more immigrants than from all other countries combined. Roughly 10 percent of people born in Mexico currently reside in the United States.[59]

Getty Images/Kevork Djansezian

Young people at the Coalition for Humane Immigrant Rights of Los Angeles on Aug. 15, 2012, hear about a new federal program under which eligible undocumented young people can avoid deportation and obtain work permits. Many economists argue that immigrant workers have a positive effect on the economy, but others contend that curbing immigration would leave more jobs for U.S.-born workers.

However, more than half of the Mexicans in the United States are undocumented, according to the Department of Homeland Security, a fact that stirs heated debate, especially in the Border States.[60] Cities and states have adopted a variety of measures to deal with illegal immigration, including a controversial law adopted by Arizona in 2010 aimed at driving illegal immigrants away. Known as SB 1070, the measure requires law enforcement officials to check the immigration papers of suspected undocumented workers.[61]

Under challenge in the courts, SB 1070 is regarded as at least partly responsible, along with high unemployment rates, for a sharp decline in the number of undocumented immigrants in Arizona, from 560,000 in 2008 to 360,000 in 2011.[62]

"The greatest effect of the bill is its deterrent effect," said Republican state Rep. John Kavanagh, a sponsor of SB 1070. "It probably scared a lot of illegal immigrants from coming here in the first place or staying if they were here." Kavanagh said the loss of illegal immigrants opened up job opportunities for U.S. citizens and legal immigrants at a time when the state's unemployment rate is 9.5 percent. "So losing 100,000 or 200,000 workers who were undercutting legal workers and depressing wages is a big plus, as far as I am concerned," he said. "Good riddance."[63]

But the Center for American Progress, a liberal Washington, D.C., research organization that opposes the legislation, estimates that if all undocumented workers were expelled from Arizona, the state would lose $29.5 billion in pre-tax salary and wage earnings, $4.2 billion in tax revenue and more than 500,000 jobs for both legal and undocumented workers.[64]

Dayton Model

In some places, especially cities far removed from the Border States,

Continued on p. 1006

At Issue:

Is large-scale immigration good for the U.S. economy?

AUDREY SINGER
SENIOR FELLOW, THE BROOKINGS INSTITUTION

WRITTEN FOR *CQ RESEARCHER*, NOVEMBER 2012

yes

The typical way of viewing immigration's impact on the economy is through costs and benefits derived from their presence in the labor market.

While economists debate how best to address this issue, there is some agreement that immigrants are a net benefit as measured by national GDP.

A benefit of a steady flow of immigrant workers to the United States is that they are responsive to labor-market changes and can go where workers are needed. This is especially so for newcomers, who tend to be most flexible on where to locate. The plateauing of immigration to the United States in response to declining jobs following the recession is an important illustration at the national level; many local areas mirror this trend.

It is not surprising, then, that the greatest economic impact of immigrants is at the state and local levels, where the brunt of costs to schools, health care systems and law enforcement is borne.

In the past two decades, immigrant settlement patterns have shifted significantly. Between 1930 and 1990, half of all immigrants in the United States lived in just five metropolitan areas, primarily in the Northeast and Midwest. Since then, the share in the top five places has declined to 40 percent, as immigrants have found opportunities in new places, particularly in the South and West.

Areas with new immigrant streams are more focused on the costs of immigration because, at least in the pre-recession economy, these areas attracted low-wage undocumented workers at a fast pace.

Estimates summarized by the Congressional Budget Office in 2007 show that in the aggregate and over the long term, tax revenues paid by immigrants are greater than the services they use. However, unauthorized immigrants use more state and local services than they pay for because of the types of services provided and because of the eligibility rules.

For example, while the percentage of school-age children of unauthorized immigrants is small nationally, this population tends to be concentrated at the very local level, and thus its impact can be swift.

The long-term view brings an important economic benefit into focus. Most of the future growth of the U.S. labor force will come from immigrants and their offspring. This next generation of workers will support the large cohort of baby boom retirees that now looms large. This is a reward that the United States should reap — with proper investments — as the next economy and workforce take shape.

MADELEINE SUMPTION
SENIOR POLICY ANALYST, MIGRATION POLICY INSTITUTE

WRITTEN FOR *CQ RESEARCHER*, NOVEMBER 2012

no

The assertion that large-scale immigration is good for the U.S. economy implies that more immigration is inherently better than less. This is not necessarily true. The types of immigrants a country has — and whether their skills meet U.S. labor market needs — arguably matters much more than raw numbers.

Most economists believe that immigration to the United States has raised average incomes (albeit recognizing the gains are not universal), and that immigrants — through their tax contributions — make it easier to provide public services without raising tax rates. Other research suggests immigrants have contributed disproportionately to innovation and productivity. But these findings come with caveats.

First, not all immigration is the same, and the benefits of some types of immigration are more clear-cut than others. The greatest economic gains come from highly skilled immigrants, many of whom compete for the tiny share of permanent visas available for employment-based immigration. (Most U.S. green cards are issued on the basis of family ties, not prospective economic value.)

Low-skilled immigrants bring some economic benefits, such as lower prices for goods and services like food and child care. But these overwhelmingly low-paid workers also draw on public services such as education. More selective policies to admit and retain the low-skilled workers best able to support themselves might help shift this calculus. Balancing current costs and benefits, the overall economic impact of low-skilled workers today is probably close to zero.

The green card lottery, known as the diversity visa, is also likely to have a low economic return, since its annual 50,000 beneficiaries fare relatively poorly in the U.S. labor market. A similar argument applies to some refugees and to the parents and adult siblings of U.S. citizens. These types of immigration are almost certainly not economically detrimental, and there are plenty of noneconomic arguments in their favor (like the value of family unity and the moral obligation to protect people fleeing persecution). The economic arguments, however, are not particularly compelling.

Immigration policies are adopted with more than economic benefit in mind — and for good reason. But if the goal is purely economic gain, simply opening the immigration spigot is not the best strategy. Rather than a bottom-line focus on numbers, a more reliable approach for making immigration an engine for economic growth would be to create more thoughtful, predictable and transparent policies to select the immigrant workers who will succeed here.

Continued from p. 1004

public officials are encouraging immigration instead of discouraging it.

For instance, the once-thriving manufacturing center of Dayton, Ohio, started losing population in the 1970s after businesses began relocating to Sun Belt states with cheaper, non-union labor. General Motors closed a large assembly plant in 2008, eliminating 2,400 jobs; NCR, born in Dayton in 1884 as the National Cash Register Co., moved to Atlanta in 2009, eliminating another 1,000 jobs. Dayton's population plunged 42 percent between 1970 and 2010, sinking to 141,000. Unemployment is currently over 10 percent.

Hoping to end the downward spiral, civic leaders in 2011 introduced the "Welcome Dayton" initiative to attract immigrant entrepreneurs and workers. Welcome Dayton serves as a catalyst for public institutions such as police, libraries and community-service organizations to help brand the city as immigrant-friendly. For instance, the city's teachers are offered classes in Spanish, Arabic, Turkish and Swahili to make it easier for them to work with immigrant students.

Dayton also helped to establish a center to provide education, recreation and other services to immigrants for the region's Ahiska Turkish community. Officials plan to authorize grants to help immigrants establish businesses, and the city's First Annual World Soccer Tournament, held in September, featured local adult and youth teams representing the international community.

Tom Wahlrab, who retired in January as director of the city's Office of Human Rights, says, "Two things are fueling Welcome Dayton: The need for economic development and the human factor. Many of those who are coming are refugees with a lot of needs. Unless we recognize those needs and do what we can to help them gain a foothold in our community, they're going to be a burden. They won't be productive, and they're going to cost the community in terms of the social services we'll need to provide."

It's too early to measure concrete results, although Dayton in 2011 added 600 new residents, Wahlrab says — a small gain, but the first population increase after 40 years of steady decline. Still, other localities are taking notice. Financially strapped Detroit, which launched "Global Detroit" in 2010 with the slogan, "Welcoming and Connecting the World to Our City," invited Wahlrab to come and discuss Dayton's experiences. "There is a certain elegance and opportunity in the plan that Dayton has put together," said Steve Tobocman, director of Global Detroit. "They've done certain things so profoundly right that I think we have a lot to learn from it." [65]

Aging in Place

As cities and states try to adjust to immigration trends, they also are beginning to taking steps — albeit haltingly in some cases — to accommodate the transportation, housing, health and other needs of the aging population. In eight years, one-fourth of residents in half of Ohio's counties will be at least 60 years old, and Arizona and Pennsylvania are projecting that a quarter of their residents will top age 60 by 2020. [66]

Some cities are stepping up to the challenge. For example:

- New York City, where more than one in eight residents are over 60, established Age-Friendly New York City, which officials describe as "promoting an 'age-in-everything' lens across all aspects of city life. The initiative asks the city's public agencies, businesses, cultural, educational and religious institutions, community groups and individuals to consider how changes to policy and practice can create a city more inclusive of older adults and more sensitive to their needs." The effort, formed in 2009, is part of a broader Age-friendly Cities project sponsored by the World Health Organization. [67]
- In Atlanta, where one-fifth of residents will be over age 60 by 2030, the Atlanta Regional Commission created a Lifelong Communities Initiative aimed at promoting housing and transportation options, encouraging healthy lifestyles and expanding information and access to services tailored to older residents. [68]

Still, many localities are ill-prepared to accommodate the coming wave of older residents, experts say. A 2005 survey of communities by the National Association of Area Agencies on Aging found that while many communities had some programs for older people, "few had undertaken a comprehensive assessment to create a 'livable community' for all ages." A 2011 follow-up survey found "only limited progress" toward that goal, the group said. Indeed, as a result of the recent recession, "most communities have been able only to 'hold the line' — maintaining policies, programs and services already established," the association said. "They have not been able to move forward to the degree needed to address the nation's current 'age wave.' " [69]

"The bottom line is, the baby boomers are hitting," Charles Gehring, president and CEO of LifeCare Alliance, an agency that serves seniors in central Ohio, told the *Columbus Dispatch*. "Are communities prepared for this? No." [70] ■

OUTLOOK

Political Changes

The 2012 presidential election underscored in dramatic fashion the crucial role that demographic changes are having in political and policy circles. Experts expect that role to grow even stronger in coming years as the profile of the electorate continues to evolve.

Many analysts believe the Republican Party fared poorly in this year's election in part because it did not do enough to address the interests of the nation's burgeoning Hispanic population. "The Hispanic population will grow faster than any other demographic, meaning this political problem is growing for Republicans," GOP strategist Matt Mackowiak told *The Hill* after the Nov. 6 elections. "We need more Hispanic candidates, more Hispanic outreach and less bellicose language on immigration." [71]

Former Secretary of State Condoleezza Rice, who served in the administration of Republican George W. Bush, said Republicans had sent "mixed messages" on immigration and women's issues and must do a better job of adapting to changing U.S. demographics.

"Right now for me, the most powerful argument is that the changing demographics in the country really necessitate an even bigger tent for the Republican Party," she said. "But when you look at the composition of the electorate, clearly we are losing important segments of that electorate, and what we have to do is to appeal to those people not as identity groups but understanding that if you can get the identity issues out of the way, then you can appeal on the broader issues that all Americans share concerns for." [72]

The demographic challenges facing policy makers in coming years cross party lines, however. Dealing with the burgeoning ranks of seniors and adequately funding Social Security, Medicare and Medicaid — which pays for nursing home care for low-income elderly people — are among the biggest challenges.

More than 56 million Americans now receive Social Security benefits, and 23 percent of married couples and about 46 percent of unmarried persons who are 65 years old or older rely on Social Security for 90 percent or more of their income. [73]

In 2010, for the first time, Social Security collected less in taxes than it paid out in benefits. The Social Security Board of Trustees told Congress that the combined assets of the two trust funds from which Social Security benefits are paid will be exhausted in 2033. [74]

Meanwhile, some question whether Obama's re-election, along with the growing prominence of minorities in the nation's demographic profile, means that policy makers no longer need to pay the same degree of attention to race and ethnicity as in the past.

Brian Smedley, vice president of the Joint Center for Political and Economic Studies, a Washington-based research organization dealing with minority public policy issues, doesn't think so.

"One of the most significant challenges for the Civil Rights Movement today is to somehow tackle the notion that the United States is now color-blind or post-racial," he says. He fears the nation is in danger of leaving behind the ideals of racial equality.

"There are many who believe that because we have [elected] an African-American president, and people of color are leading *Fortune* 500 companies, etc., race no longer matters in our society. Of course, we've made tremendous progress in race relations in the United States over the past 50-plus years, and that should be celebrated," he says. "It's remarkable that we have created a society that is much more egalitarian, and we're moving closer to our ideal as a nation where people truly are judged by the content of their character and not by the color of their skin.

"However," he continues, "many people of color still face profound inequities across a host of dimensions . . . such as health, wealth, educational status, income, home ownership, you name it. It's more critical than ever that we focus the nation's attention on these problems because the demographic shifts that are coming suggest that we need to be very mindful of what our nation will look like and how the inequities will hurt everyone in this country unless we solve them." ■

Notes

1 "Most Children Younger Than Age 1 are Minorities, Census Bureau Reports", U.S. Census Bureau news release, May 17, 2012, www.census.gov/newsroom/releases/archives/population/cb12-90.html.

2 "An Older and More Diverse Nation by Midcentury", U.S. Census Bureau news release, Aug. 14, 2008, www.census.gov/newsroom/releases/archives/population/cb08-123.html.

3 Haya El Nasser and Paul Overberg, "Census tracks 20 years of sweeping change," *USA Today*, Aug. 10, 2011, http://usatoday30.usatoday.com/news/nation/census/2011-08-10-census-20-years-change_n.htm.

4 Mark Hugo Lopez and Paul Taylor, "Latino Voters in the 2012 Election," Pew Hispanic Center, Nov. 7, 2012, www.pewhispanic.org/2012/11/07/latino-voters-in-the-2012-election/.

5 Michael D. Shear, "Demographic Shift Brings New Worry for Republicans," *The New York Times*, Nov. 7, 2012, www.nytimes.com/2012/11/08/us/politics/obamas-victory-presents-gop-with-demographic-test.html?ref=politics.

6 "Obama Win Shows Demographic Shifts," *op. cit.*

7 Press release, "Latino Candidates Make History on Election Night," National Association of Latino Elected and Appointed Officials Education Fund, Nov. 7, 2012, www.prnewswire.com/news-releases/latino-candidates-make-history-on-election-night-177729141.html.

8 " 'Nones' on the Rise: One-in-Five Adults Have No Religious Affiliation", Report by the Pew Research Center Forum on Religion & Public Life, Oct. 9, 2012, www.pewforum.org/Unaffiliated/nones-on-the-rise.aspx.

9 Laura B. Shrestha and Elayne J. Heisler, "The Changing Demographic Profile of the United States", Congressional Research Service, March 31, 2011, www.fas.org/sgp/crs/misc/RL32701.pdf.

10 D'Vera Cohn and Paul Taylor, "Baby Boomers Approach Age 65 — Glumly," Pew Research Center, Dec. 20, 2010, http://pewresearch.org/pubs/1834/baby-boomers-old-age-downbeat-pessimism.

11 For background see Alan Greenblatt, "The Graying Planet," *CQ Global Researcher*, March 15, 2011, pp. 133-156.

12 2010 Census Data, U.S. Census Bureau, http://2010.census.gov/2010census/data/.

13 Sabrina Tavernise, "Whites Account for Under Half of Births in U.S.," *The New York Times*, May 17, 2012, www.nytimes.com/

2012/05/17/us/whites-account-for-under-half-of-births-in-us.html?pagewanted=all.

[14] John Blake, "Are Whites Racially Oppressed?", CNN, March 4, 2011, www.cnn.com/2010/US/12/21/white.persecution/index.html.

[15] Daniel Cox; E.J. Dionne, Jr.; William A. Galston; Robert P. Jones, "What it Means to be an American," Brookings Institution, Sept. 6, 2011, www.brookings.edu/research/reports/2011/09/06-american-attitudes.

[16] "U.S. Religious Landscape Survey", Pew Forum on Religion and Public Life, February 2008, http://religions.pewforum.org/pdf/report-religious-landscape-study-full.pdf.

[17] *Ibid.*

[18] Samuel P. Huntington, *Who Are We? The Challenges to America's National Identity* (2004), p. 18.

[19] Joel Kotkin, "Minority America," Newgeography.com, Aug. 20, 2008, www.newgeography.com/content/00175-minority-america.

[20] Paul Taylor, Mark Hugo Lopez, Jessica Hamar Martinez and Gabriel Velasco, "When Labels Don't Fit: Hispanics and Their Views of Identity," Pew Hispanic Center, April 4, 2012, "Two-Thirds of Democrats Now Support Gay Marriage," Poll, Pew Forum on Religion and Public Life, July 31, 2012, www.pewforum.org/Politics-and-Elections/2012-opinions-on-for-gay-marriage-unchanged-after-obamas-announcement.aspx.

[21] "The Rise of Asian Americans," Pew Research Center, June 19, 2012, www.pewsocialtrends.org/2012/06/19/the-rise-of-asian-americans/.

[22] Wendy Wang, "The Rise of Intermarriage," Pew Research Center, Feb. 16, 2012, www.pewsocialtrends.org/2012/02/16/the-rise-of-intermarriage/?src=prc-headline.

[23] For background, see Haya El Nasser, "Black-white marriages on the rise," *USA Today*, Sept. 20, 2011, http://usatoday30.usatoday.com/news/nation/story/2011-09-19/interracial-marriages/50469776/1.

[24] Wang, *op. cit.*

[25] "The Generation Gap and the 2012 Election," The Pew Research Center, Nov. 3, 2011, www.people-press.org/2011/11/03/the-generation-gap-and-the-2012-election-3/.

[26] Linda A. Jacobsen, *et al.*, "America's Aging Population," *Population Bulletin 66*, no. 1 (2011), Population Reference Bureau.

[27] Frank W. Heiland and Zhe Li, "Changes in Labor Force Participation of Older Americans and Their Pension Structures: A Policy Perspective," Boston College Center for Retirement Research, August 2012, http://crr.bc.edu/working-papers/changes-in-labor-force-participation-of-older-americans-and-their-pension-structures-a-policy-perspective-2.

[28] Don Lee, "More older workers making up labor force," *Los Angeles Times*, Sept. 4, 2012, http://articles.latimes.com/2012/sep/04/business/la-fi-labor-seniors-20120903.

[29] Alicia H. Munnell and April Yanyuan Wu, "Will Delayed Retirement by the Baby Boomers Lead to Higher Unemployment Among Younger Workers?", Center for Retirement Research at Boston College, October 2012, http://crr.bc.edu/working-papers/will-delayed-retirement-by-the-baby-boomers-lead-to-higher-unemployment-among-younger-workers/.

[30] Mark Miller, "Are Older Workers Getting in the Way of the Young?," Reuters, Jan. 6, 2012, www.reuters.com/article/2012/01/06/retirement-jobs-idUSN1E80507520120106.

[31] Press release, American Association of Colleges of Nursing, "Nursing Shortage," www.aacn.nche.edu/media-relations/fact-sheets/nursing-shortage.

[32] "Immigration, Poverty and Low-Wage Earners: The Harmful Effects of Unskilled Immigrants on American Workers," Federation for American Immigration Reform, July 2010 (revised Feb. 2011), www.fairus.org/publications/immigration-poverty-and-low-wage-earners-the-harmful-effects-of-unskilled-immigrants-on-american-wor.

[33] "Georgia Data Quantify Impact of Undocumented Workers," Southwest Economy, Federal Reserve Bank of Dallas, second quarter 2012, www.dallasfed.org/assets/documents/research/swe/2012/swe1202e.pdf.

[34] Giovanni Peri, "The Effect of Immigrants on U.S. Employment and Productivity," Federal Reserve Bank of San Francisco Economic Letter, August 30, 2010, www.frbsf.org/publications/economics/letter/2010/el2010-26.html.

[35] Niall Stanage, "Women, minorities propel Obama victory," *The Hill*, Nov. 7, 2012, http://thehill.com/homenews/campaign/266485-women-minorities-propel-obama-victory.

[36] Quoted in Dylan Scott, "Political Demographic Trends Brighter for Democrats," *Governing*, April 11, 2012, www.governing.com/blogs/politics/gov-political-demographic-trends-brighter-for-democrats.html.

[37] Jeffrey Passell, D'Vera Cohn and Mark Hugo Lopez, "Hispanics Account for More than Half of Nation's Growth in Past Decade," Pew Hispanic Center, March 24, 2011, www.pewhispanic.org/2011/03/24/hispanics-account-for-more-than-half-of-nations-growth-in-past-decade/.

[38] William H. Frey, "Will 2012 be the Last Hurrah for Whites?," *National Journal*, "The Next America," June 13, 2012, http://nationaljournal.com/thenextamerica/demographics/will-2012-be-the-last-hurrah-for-whites--20120613.

[39] Alan I. Abramowitz, "Beyond 2010: Demographic Change and the Future of the Republican Party," University of Virginia Center for Politics, "Larry J. Sabato's Crystal Ball," March 11, 2010, www.centerforpolitics.org/crystalball/articles/aia2010031101/.

[40] Ruy Teixeira and William Frey, "New Data on Obama's Massive Demographic Advantage," *The New Republic*, July 9, 2012, www.tnr.com/blog/plank/104746/how-much-will-demographic-changes-help-obama-in-swing-states.

[41] Lila Shapiro, "Gay Marriage Victory In Maine, Maryland; Minnesota Votes Down 'Traditional' Amendment (UPDATE)," *The Huffington Post*, Nov. 7, 2012, www.huffingtonpost.com/2012/11/07/gay-marriage-victory_n_2085900.html.

[42] "How the Faithful Voted: 2012 Preliminary Analysis," Pew Forum on Religion & Public Life, Nov. 7, 2012, www.pewforum.org/Politics-and-Elections/How-the-Faithful-Voted-2012-Preliminary-Exit-Poll-Analysis.aspx.

[43] "Black Americans in Congress," Office of the Clerk, U.S. House of Representatives, http://baic.house.gov/historical-essays/essay.html?intID=1&intSectionID=11.

[44] Roger Finke and Rodney Starke, *The Churching of America, 1776-2005: Winners and Losers in Our Religious Economy* (2002), p. 123.

[45] Lawrence H. Fuchs, *The American Kaleidoscope: Race, Ethnicity, and the Civic Culture* (1990), p. 134.

About the Author

Bill Wanlund is a freelance writer in the Washington, D.C., area. He is a former foreign service officer, with service in Europe, Asia, Africa and South America. He holds a journalism degree from The George Washington University and has written for *CQ Researcher* on drone warfare and downtown development.

[46] Rodman D. Griffin, "Hispanic Americans," *CQ Researcher*, Oct. 30, 1992.

[47] For background, see Congressional Quarterly, *Congress and the Nation Vol. I* (1965), pp. 762-767.

[48] Jo Freeman, "From Suffrage to Women's Liberation: Feminism in Twentieth Century America," published in Jo Freeman, ed., *Women: A Feminist Perspective* (5th ed., 1995), excerpted at www.uic.edu/orgs/cwluherstory/jofreeman/feminism/suffrage.htm.

[49] Rev. Osagyefo Uhuru Sekou, "Killing the Buddha" blog, http://killingthebuddha.com/mag/damnation/gays-are-the-new-niggers/.

[50] U.S. State Department, Office of the Historian, Milestones 1921-1936, http://history.state.gov/milestones/1921-1936/ImmigrationAct.

[51] "Who Was Shut Out?: Immigration Quotas, 1925-1927," History Matters, http://historymatters.gmu.edu/d/5078/.

[52] Remarks by President Lyndon B. Johnson at the Signing of the Immigration Bill, Liberty Island, New York, Oct. 3, 1965, www.lbjlib.utexas.edu/johnson/archives.hom/speeches.hom/651003.asp.

[53] "U.S. Historical Immigration Trends," Migration Policy Institute, www.migrationinformation.org/datahub/historicaltrends.cfm#source.

[54] "The Newly Arrived Foreign-Born Population of the United States: 2010," American Community Survey Brief, U.S. Census Bureau, November 2011, www.census.gov/prod/2011pubs/acsbr10-16.pdf.

[55] "USA Quick Facts", US Bureau of the Census, http://quickfacts.census.gov/qfd/states/00000.html.

[56] "Births: Final Data for 2010", Joyce Martin, M.P.H., *et al.*, National Center for Health Statistics, August 2012, www.cdc.gov/nchs/births.htm.

[57] "2010 Census Shows Nation's Population is Aging ", News Release, US Census Bureau, May 26, 2011, http://2010.census.gov/news/releases/operations/cb11-cn147.html.

[58] Jeffrey Passel, D'Vera Cohn and Ana Gonzalez-Barrera, "Net Migration from Mexico Falls to Zero-and Perhaps Less," Pew Hispanic Center, April 23, 2012, www.pewhispanic.org/2012/04/23/net-migration-from-mexico-falls-to-zero-and-perhaps-less/.

[59] Jeffrey Passel, *et al.*, "Net Migration from Mexico Falls to Zero-and Perhaps Less", Pew Hispanic Center, April 23, 2012, www.pewhispanic.org/2012/04/23/net-migration-from-mexico-falls-to-zero-and-perhaps-less/.

[60] Michael Hoefer, Nancy Rytina and Bryan Baker, "Estimates of the Unauthorized Immigrant Population Residing in the United States: January 2011," Report of the Department of Homeland Security, March 2012, www.dhs.gov/files/statistics/publications/estimates-unauthorized-immigrant-population.shtm.

[61] For background, see Kenneth Jost, "Immigration Conflict," *CQ Researcher*, March 9, 2012, pp. 229-252.

[62] Daniel González, "Arizona's illegal-immigration population plunges," *The Arizona Republic*, March 23, 2012, www.azcentral.com/arizonarepublic/news/articles/2012/03/23/20120323arizona-illegal-migrant-population-plunges.html.

[63] Daniel Gonzalez, "Arizona immigration law: A look at bill's impact 1 year later," *The Arizona Republic*, April 23, 2011, www.azcentral.com/news/election/azelections/articles/2011/04/23/20110423arizona-immigration-law-impact-year-later.html.

[64] Raul Hinojsa-Ojeda and Marshall Fritz, "A Rising Tide or a Shrinking Pie: The Economic Impact of Legalization Versus Deportation in Arizona," Center for American Progress, March 2011, www.americanprogress.org/wp-content/uploads/issues/2011/03/pdf/rising_tide.pdf.

[65] Andrew O'Reilly, "Dayton's Immigration Strategy for Growth is Drawing Notice", Fox News Latino, May 10, 2012, http://latino.foxnews.com/latino/news/2012/05/10/dayton-immigration-strategy-for-growth-is-drawing-notice/.

[66] "Few U.S. cities are ready for aging Baby Boomer population," Associated Press, March 25, 2012, http://usatoday30.usatoday.com/news/health/story/health/story/2012-03-25/Few-US-cities-are-ready-for-aging-baby-boomer-population/53765292/1.

[67] "Age-Friendly NYC," Nov. 9, 2012 www.nyam.org/agefriendlynyc/.

[68] "Lifelong Communities," Atlanta Regional Commission, Nov. 9, 2012, www.atlantaregional.com/aging-resources/lifelong-communities-llc.

[69] "The Maturing of America: Communities Moving Forward for an Aging Population," National Association of Area Agencies on Aging, June 2011, pp. i, ii, www.n4a.org/files/MOA_FINAL_Rpt.pdf.

[70] Quoted in "Few cities are ready . . .," *op. cit.*

[71] Stanage, *op. cit.*

[72] "Condoleezza Rice: GOP Sent 'Mixed Messages' On Immigration And Women's Issues," The Associated Press/*The Huffington Post*, Nov. 9, 2012, www.huffingtonpost.com/2012/11/09/condoleezza-rice_n_2099505.html.

[73] "Social Security Basic Facts," Social Security Administration fact sheet, July 30, 2012, www.ssa.gov/pressoffice/basicfact.htm.

[74] "The 2012 Annual Report of the Board Of Trustees of the Federal Old-Age and Survivors Insurance and Federal Disability Insurance Trust Funds", April 25, 2012, U.S. Government Printing Office 73-947, Washington, DC.

FOR MORE INFORMATION

American Association of Retired Persons, 601 E St., N.W., Washington, DC 20009; 888-687-2277; www.aarp.org. Membership organization that advocates for people 50 years of age and older.

Brookings Institution, 1775 Massachusetts Ave., N.W., Washington, DC 20036; 202-797-6000; www.brookings.edu. Research organization focusing on wide range of issues, including economics, social policy, urban affairs and politics.

Center for Immigration Studies, 1629 K St., N.W., Suite 600, Washington, DC 20006; 202-466-8185; www.cis.org. Research organization that supports lower levels of immigration.

Center for Retirement Research at Boston College, Hovey House, 258 Hammond St., Chestnut Hill, MA 02467; 617-552-1762; www.crr.bu.edu. Research institution focusing on retirement issues.

Pew Research Center, 901 E St., N.W., Washington, DC 20004-2008; 202-552-2000; www.pew.org. Arm of the Pew Charitable Trusts that conducts research on such topics as Hispanics in America and the role of religion in public life.

Urban Institute, 2100 M St., N.W., Washington, DC 20037; 202-833-7200; www.urban.org. Non-partisan research organization focusing on social and economic issues.

U.S. Social Security Administration, Windsor Park Building, 6401 Security Blvd., Baltimore, MD 21235; 800-772-1213; www.ssa.gov. Federal agency that administers the Social Security retirement, disability and survivors' benefits programs.

Bibliography

Selected Sources

Books

Ehrenhalt, Alan, *The Great Inversion and the Future of the American City*, Alfred A. Knopf, 2012.
The executive editor of Stateline news service and former executive editor of *Governing* magazine explores how American cities are changing and the implications for the future.

Huntington, Samuel P., *Who Are We? The Challenges to America's National Identity*, Simon & Shuster, 2004.
The late Harvard University political scientist (1927-2008) examines the impact of immigrants and their cultural values on American society.

Putnam, Robert D., and David E. Campbell, *American Grace: How Religion Divides and Unites Us*, Simon & Schuster, 2010.
A professor of public policy at Harvard (Putnam) and a political science professor at the University of Notre Dame (Campbell) examine how religion, politics and culture intersect.

Steinhorn, Leonard, *The Greater Generation: In Defense of the Baby Boom Legacy*, Thomas Dunne Books, 2006.
A professor of communications at American University argues that the postwar generation shaped America for the better.

Wilkerson, Isabel, *The Warmth of Other Suns: The Epic Story of America's Great Migration*, Random House, 2010.
A journalist and Boston University professor provides a Pulitzer Prize-winning account of the exodus of 6 million African-Americans from the South to the urban North and West between 1915 and 1970.

Articles

Brownstein, Ron, "Do Immigrants Threaten American Values?" *National Journal*, June 14, 2012, www.nationaljournal.com/thenextamerica/immigration/do-immigrants-threaten-american-values--20120614.
A journalist dissects a decade of Pew research polling that reveals consistent divides among whites over the impact of immigrants on American society.

Castañeda, Jorge G., and Douglas S. Massey, "Do-it-Yourself Immigration Reform," *The New York Times*, June 1, 2012, www.nytimes.com/2012/06/02/opinion/do-it-yourself-immigration-reform.html?_r=1&ref=jorgegcastaneda.
A former Mexican foreign minister (Castañeda) and a Princeton sociology and public affairs professor (Massey) discuss the causes and effects of the current stasis in immigration from Mexico.

"A Contentious Flock," *The Economist*, July 7, 2012, pp. 33-34.
The reporter examines polarization and diversity among American Catholics.

Frey, William, "Baby Boomers Had Better Embrace Change," *The Washington Post*, June 8, 2012, www.brookings.edu/research/opinions/2012/06/08-baby-boomers-frey.
A demographer at the Washington, D.C.-based think tank discusses population and attitudinal trends.

Howe, Neal, "What Makes Boomers the Boomers?" *Governing.com*, September 2012, www.governing.com/generations/government-management/gov-what-makes-boomers.html.
A demographer, historian, author and consultant on generational transitions investigates the myths about and realities of the baby boom generation.

Reports and Studies

"Immigration, Poverty and Low-Wage Earners: The Harmful Effect of Unskilled Immigrants on American Workers (2011)," Federation for American Immigration Reform, 2011, www.fairus.org/issue/immigration-poverty-and-low-wage-earners-the-harmful-effect-of-unskilled-immigrants-on-american-work.
A national nonprofit organization that seeks stricter limits on immigration argues that unskilled immigrant labor harms native-born Americans.

"State of Metropolitan America: On the Front Lines of Demographic Transformation," Metropolitan Policy Program, Brookings Institution, 2010.
The Washington-based public policy think tank analyzes the impact of recent demographic changes on U.S. metropolitan areas.

Funk, Cary, and Greg Smith, " 'Nones' on the Rise: One-in-Five Adults Have No Religious Affiliation," Pew Forum on Religion and Public Life, Oct. 9, 2012, www.pewforum.org/Unaffiliated/nones-on-the-rise.aspx.
A nonpartisan research organization examines trends in American religious belief and practice.

Jacobsen, Linda A., *et al.*, "America's Aging Population," Population Reference Bureau, 2011, www.prb.org/pdf11/aging-in-america.pdf.
The think tank report examines the costs and implications of an aging population.

Myers, Dowell, and John Pitkin, "Assimilation Tomorrow: How America's Immigrants will Assimilate by 2030," Center for American Progress, November 2011, www.americanprogress.org/issues/immigration/report/2011/11/14/10583/assimilation-tomorrow/.
A demographer/urban planner (Myers) and a demographer/economist from the University of Southern California (Pitkin) examine the outlook for American immigrants.

The Next Step:

Additional Articles from Current Periodicals

Black Migration

Diaz, John, "Quiet Exodus From the City," ***The San Francisco Chronicle*****, Dec. 4, 2011, p. E3, www.sfgate.com/opinion/diaz/article/The-quiet-exodus-of-African-Americans-from-S-F-2345107.php.**

Blacks recently have been moving out of major cities often because of positive factors, says a Brookings Institution report.

DiSalvo, Daniel, "The Great Reverse Migration," ***Pittsburgh Post-Gazette*****, Sept. 30, 2012, p. B1, www.post-gazette.com/stories/opinion/perspectives/the-great-reverse-migration-african-americans-are-abandoning-the-northern-cities-that-have-failed-them-655514/.**

Many blacks are returning to the South because the Great Migration trapped many of them in urban ghettos for several generations.

Jackson, Maurice, "Pricing the Soul Out of Washington, D.C.," ***The Chronicle of Higher Education*****, June 18, 2012, chronicle.com/article/Pricing-the-Soul-Out-of/132259/.**

Many blacks are migrating out of the nation's capital because of rising home costs and a lack of upward mobility.

Economy

Aguilera, Elizabeth, "Fewer Whites in Workforce by End of Decade," ***San Diego Union-Tribune*****, March 4, 2012, p. C1, www.utsandiego.com/news/2012/mar/04/tp-fewer-whites-in-workforce-by-end-of-decade/?print&page=all.**

The nation's growing Latino population will make up about three-quarters of the predicted growth in the labor market by 2020, says the Bureau of Labor Statistics.

Censer, Marjorie, "Graying Workforce Creates More Complex World for Employers," ***The Washington Post*****, Feb. 20, 2012, p. A19.**

Companies must navigate the changing demographics of the labor force as more employees reach retirement age.

Ontiveros, Sue, "So Much for the Myth Latinos Are a Drain on Local Economy," ***Chicago Sun-Times*****, Nov. 20, 2011, p. A29, www.suntimes.com/news/ontiveros/8875319-452/so-much-for-the-myth-latinos-are-a-drain-on-local-economy.html.**

Latinos — including both U.S. citizens and undocumented immigrants — add $5 billion in tax revenues to metropolitan Chicago and use $3.9 billion worth of public services.

Politics

Gergi, Bassam, "Republican References to 'Real Americans' Incite Division and Fear," ***The Christian Science Monitor*****, July 31, 2012, www.csmonitor.com/Commentary/Opinion/2012/0731/Republican-references-to-real-Americans-incite-division-and-fear.**

The Republican Party must abandon divisive language and embrace more unifying racial messages in order to remain relevant amid changing demographics, says a comparative government student at Oxford University.

Helms, Ann Doss, "Changing Demographics Leave South's Political Future in Flux," ***Charlotte*** **(N.C.)** ***Observer*****, Sept. 2, 2012, www.charlotteobserver.com/2012/09/03/3498928/unc-panel-changing-demographics.html.**

The changing racial composition of the Southern states may determine which political party becomes more influential in the future, says at panel of experts at the University of North Carolina at Chapel Hill.

Malveaux, Julianne, "Blacks Must Adjust to Changing Times," ***USA Today*****, Feb. 17 2012, p. A9, usatoday30.usatoday.com/news/opinion/forum/story/2012-02-16/black-history-month/53122698/1.**

Black politicians in urban areas can no longer rely strictly on the black vote to win elections because of demographic shifts in their neighborhoods, says the president of Bennett College for Women in North Carolina.

O'Toole, James, "Do New Realities Alter Voting Patterns?" ***Pittsburgh Post-Gazette*****, Jan. 21, 2012, p. A1, www.post-gazette.com/stories/news/politics-national/republican-party-deals-with-changing-demographics-in-south-carolina-primary-218595/?print=1.**

Republican politicians are constantly changing campaign strategies to respond to the changing demographics of their voter base, says a columnist.

CITING *CQ RESEARCHER*

Sample formats for citing these reports in a bibliography include the ones listed below. Preferred styles and formats vary, so please check with your instructor or professor.

MLA STYLE

Jost, Kenneth. "Remembering 9/11," CQ Researcher 2 Sept. 2011: 701-732.

APA STYLE

Jost, K. (2011, September 2). Remembering 9/11. *CQ Researcher, 9*, 701-732.

CHICAGO STYLE

Jost, Kenneth. "Remembering 9/11." *CQ Researcher*, September 2, 2011, 701-732.

In-depth Reports on Issues in the News

Are you writing a paper?

Need backup for a debate?

Want to become an expert on an issue?

For more than 80 years, students have turned to *CQ Researcher* for in-depth reporting on issues in the news. Reports on a full range of political and social issues are now available. Following is a selection of recent reports:

Civil Liberties
Solitary Confinement, 9/12
Re-examining the Constitution, 9/12
Voter Rights, 5/12
Remembering 9/11, 9/11
Government Secrecy, 2/11

Crime/Law
Supreme Court Controversies, 9/12
Debt Collectors, 7/12
Criminal Records, 4/12
Police Misconduct, 4/12
Immigration Conflict, 3/12

Education
Arts Education, 3/12
Youth Volunteerism, 1/12
Digital Education, 12/11
Student Debt, 10/11

Environment/Society
Indecency on Television, 11/12
Managing Wildfires, 11/12
Understanding Mormonism, 10/12
Genetically Modified Food, 8/12
Whale Hunting, 6/12
U.S. Oil Dependence, 6/12

Health/Safety
New Health Care Law, 9/12
Farm Policy, 8/12
Treating ADHD, 8/12
Alcohol Abuse, 6/12

Politics/Economy
Social Media and Politics, 10/12
Euro Crisis, 10/12
Privatizing the Military, 7/12
U.S.-Europe Relations, 3/12
Attracting Jobs, 3/12
Presidential Election, 2/12

Upcoming Reports

Sugar Controversy, 11/30/12 — 3-D Printing, 12/7/12 — Housing Industry, 12/14/12

ACCESS

CQ Researcher is available in print and online. For access, visit your library or www.cqresearcher.com.

STAY CURRENT

For notice of upcoming *CQ Researcher* reports or to learn more about *CQ Researcher* products, subscribe to the free e-mail newsletters, *CQ Researcher Alert!* and *CQ Researcher News*: http://cqpress.com/newsletters.

PURCHASE

To purchase a *CQ Researcher* report in print or electronic format (PDF), visit www.cqpress.com or call 866-427-7737. Single reports start at $15. Bulk purchase discounts and electronic-rights licensing are also available.

SUBSCRIBE

Annual full-service *CQ Researcher* subscriptions—including 44 reports a year, monthly index updates, and a bound volume—start at $1,054. Add $25 for domestic postage.

CQ Researcher Online offers a backfile from 1991 and a number of tools to simplify research. For pricing information, call 800-834-9020, or e-mail librarymarketing@cqpress.com.

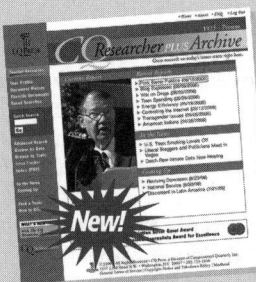

CQ Researcher

Published by CQ Press, an Imprint of SAGE Publications, Inc.

www.cqresearcher.com

Sugar Controversies

Should government restrict sugar consumption?

When New York City announced in September it will ban sugary beverages larger than 16 ounces in restaurants, sports arenas and other public venues, critics complained that the city has no right to meddle with individual food choices. Many public-health advocates, however, praised the move as an important step toward slowing the nation's decades-long rise in obesity rates. Sugar-sweetened drinks add an average 300 calories a day to teens' diets without providing any nutrition, they say. Some scientists even hypothesize that fructose, the main sweetener used in sodas, may trigger diseases such as Type 2 diabetes, which is also on the rise. Other nutrition experts, however, say sugar can't be the only or even the primary culprit in the nation's skyrocketing obesity rates, since they have doubled since 1980 while sugar in sodas and other packaged foods has increased by a much smaller percentage over that period.

Oversize drinks will be illegal in restaurants, movie theaters and other public venues in New York City beginning next March. Mayor Michael Bloomberg pushed the ban to reduce obesity-related health problems, which cost the city $4 billion a year. Critics say it won't cut obesity but will erode personal freedom.

INSIDE THIS REPORT

The Issues 1015
Background 1021
Chronology 1023
Current Situation 1028
At Issue 1029
Outlook 1030
Bibliography 1034
The Next Step 1035

CQ Researcher • Nov. 30, 2012 • www.cqresearcher.com
Volume 22, Number 42 • Pages 1013-1036

SAGE | CQPRESS
Los Angeles | London | New Delhi
Singapore | Washington DC

Recipient of Society of Professional Journalists Award for Excellence ◆ American Bar Association Silver Gavel Award

SUGAR CONTROVERSIES

THE ISSUES

1015 • Is eliminating excess sugar the best solution to the obesity epidemic?
• Is fructose more harmful than other sugars?
• Should the government do more to limit sugar consumption?

BACKGROUND

1021 **Sweet Eating**
Public policies have made sugary foods cheap and abundant.

1022 **Rise of Corn**
Farm policies boosted the use of high-sugar corn syrup.

1024 **Low-Fat Craze**
Cutting fat resulted in more sugar in processed foods.

1027 **Limiting Sugar**
Governments are restricting sugar in schools and public places.

CURRENT SITUATION

1028 **Shrinking Drinks?**
Banning gigantic sodas is aimed at counteracting beverage marketing.

1030 **Studying Sugar**
Scientists question whether sugar calories are more dangerous than others.

OUTLOOK

1030 **Focusing on Sugar**
Some scientists question the evidence for discouraging sugar consumption.

SIDEBARS AND GRAPHICS

1016 **Childhood Obesity Most Common in South**
Obesity rates are among the nation's highest.

1017 **Sodas and Juices Are High in Sugar**
Cranberry juice "cocktail" has more sugar than soda.

1019 **Childhood Obesity Triples**
U.S. childhood obesity rates are the world's highest.

1020 **Schools Crack Down on Candy Sales**
Many states have banned candy from vending machines in an effort to fight obesity.

1023 **Chronology**
Key events since 1900.

1024 **Artificial Sweeteners Raise Hope — and Concern**
They may help with weight loss, but are they safe?

1026 **Path to Better Eating Strewn with Traps**
Salad for lunch? Count the added sugars.

1029 **At Issue**
Should government try to cut sugary drink consumption?

FOR FURTHER RESEARCH

1033 **For More Information**
Organizations to contact.

1034 **Bibliography**
Selected sources used.

1035 **The Next Step**
Additional articles.

1035 **Citing *CQ Researcher***
Sample bibliography formats.

Cover: Getty Images/Mario Tama

CQ Researcher

Nov. 30, 2012
Volume 22, Number 42

MANAGING EDITOR: Thomas J. Billitteri
tjb@cqpress.com

ASSISTANT MANAGING EDITOR: Kathy Koch
kkoch@cqpress.com

SENIOR CONTRIBUTING EDITOR:
Thomas J. Colin
tcolin@cqpress.com

ASSOCIATE EDITOR: Kenneth Jost

STAFF WRITER: Marcia Clemmitt

CONTRIBUTING WRITERS: Peter Katel, Barbara Mantel, Tom Price, Jennifer Weeks

SENIOR PROJECT EDITOR: Olu B. Davis

ASSISTANT EDITOR: Darrell Dela Rosa

FACT CHECKER: Michelle Harris

Los Angeles | London | New Delhi
Singapore | Washington DC

An Imprint of SAGE Publications, Inc.

VICE PRESIDENT AND EDITORIAL DIRECTOR, HIGHER EDUCATION GROUP:
Michele Sordi

DIRECTOR, ONLINE PUBLISHING:
Todd Baldwin

CQ Researcher (ISSN 1056-2036) is printed on acid-free paper. Published weekly, except: (March wk. 5) (May wk. 4) (July wk. 1) (Aug. wks. 3, 4) (Nov. wk. 4) and (Dec. wks. 3, 4). Published by SAGE Publications, Inc., 2455 Teller Rd., Thousand Oaks, CA 91320. Annual full-service subscriptions start at $1,054. For pricing, call 1-800-834-9020. To purchase a *CQ Researcher* report in print or electronic format (PDF), visit www.cqpress.com or call 866-427-7737. Single reports start at $15. Bulk purchase discounts and electronic-rights licensing are also available. Periodicals postage paid at Thousand Oaks, California, and at additional mailing offices. POSTMASTER: Send address changes to *CQ Researcher*, 2300 N St., N.W., Suite 800, Washington, DC 20037.

Sugar Controversies

BY MARCIA CLEMMITT

THE ISSUES

Starting in March, super-thirsty residents of New York City — at least those who like their beverages super-sized — will be out of luck. Thanks to Mayor Michael Bloomberg, they will be able to buy sugar-sweetened beverages — sodas, sports and energy drinks, teas and sweetened juices — only in 16-ounce or smaller containers at restaurants, food carts and entertainment venues. [1]

The new rule, adopted in September by the New York City Board of Health, is designed to "help save lives" and help stem the rising health and financial cost of high obesity rates, said Bloomberg, who proposed it. [2] * Medical costs directly related to obesity are said to cost the city $4 billion a year. [4]

The ban has triggered angry complaints that it curtails consumers' and businesses' freedoms. "It's sad that the board wants to limit our choices. We are smart enough to make our own decisions about what to eat and drink," said Liz Berman, chairperson of New Yorkers for Beverage Choices, a coalition consisting mainly of national and local businesses and business groups who, along with individual New Yorkers, say the ban will hurt them. [5]

Getty Images/ABC/Craig Sjodin

An overweight woman works out on ABC's "Extreme Makeover: Weight Loss Edition." About 36 percent of Americans are obese, which some scientists blame on overconsumption of overly sweetened foods and drinks — especially those with high fructose corn syrup.

The flap is part of a growing debate over the role of sugar in America's obesity crisis. Some analysts say excess calories from sugar in processed foods and, especially, beverages are the key culprit in the nation's sky-high obesity rates and may play additional roles in triggering the rise in obesity-related diseases such as Type 2 diabetes and heart disease.** Thus, they argue, public policies aimed at limiting sugar are justified and harmless, since sugars have no nutritional value.

Other experts say, however, that the scientific evidence so far is lacking to deem sugar consumption the top reason that more than a third of Americans are obese — the highest rate in the developed world. [6] And public policies implemented with insufficient scientific foundation are likely to fail, they contend.

Experts agree that obesity threatens people's lives and costs the nation precious dollars.

In October, state Comptroller Tomas P. DiNapoli reported that New York residents' obesity-related problems cost public and private payers of medical bills about $11.8 billion annually — $4.3 billion through Medicaid and $7.5 billion through Medicare, private insurers and other sources. [7]

Some scientists and policy-makers see good reason to focus on so-called "added sugars" — sweeteners added to processed foods and drinks, rather than those found naturally in fruit and milk — as the key driver of obesity rates. In recent decades, manufacturers have put added sugars — such as high fructose corn syrup — into foods ranging from bread and cereal to ketchup and spaghetti sauce. Up to 80 percent of the 600,000 processed-food items sold in America may have added sugars, according to one study. [8]

At about the same time that the amount of sugar consumed annually by the average American jumped by

* New York City's adult obesity rate of more than 23 percent is actually significantly lower than the national average of about 36 percent. However, while the city's obesity rate among children ages 6 to 11 has dropped recently, at 21.3 percent it's still higher than the national average of 19.6 percent. [3]

** Excess calories are defined as the calories one consumes in a day beyond the number one burns off through exercise. Type 2 diabetes — also known as adult-onset diabetes — is characterized by "insulin resistance" or an inability of the cells to use insulin, a hormone that regulates the body's conversion of food to energy.

Childhood Obesity Most Common in South

Southern states have childhood overweight and obesity rates above 30 percent, among the nation's highest. Some research suggests that excessive consumption of sugar, particularly in sodas and other sugary beverages, could be a primary cause for the nation's obesity epidemic. Obesity rates doubled nationwide to about one-third today at about the same time that the amount of sugar consumed annually by the average American jumped 42 percent — from about 110 pounds to 152 pounds.

Percentage of Overweight or Obese Children Ages 10 to 17, 2007

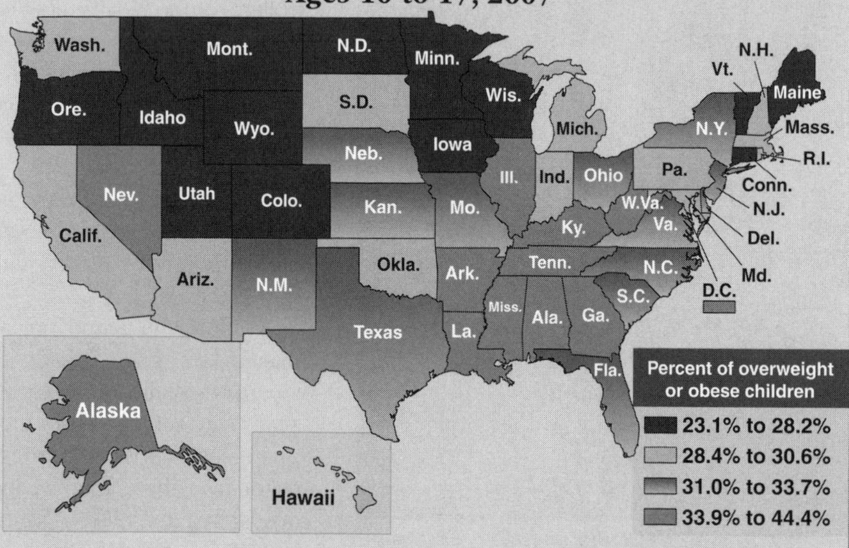

Source: "Percent of Children (10-17) Who Are Overweight or Obese, 2007," Henry J. Kaiser Family Foundation, 2012, www.statehealthfacts.org/comparemaptable.jsp?cat=2&ind=51

42 percent — from 110 pounds in the 1950s to 152 pounds in 2000 — obesity rates doubled, from around 15 percent in the 1960s. [9]

New research also shows that added sugars, such as fructose — a sugar found in both table sugar (sucrose) and the high fructose corn syrup (HFCS) used to sweeten many processed foods today — produces "unique adverse metabolic effects" in the body, according to Frank Hu, a professor of nutrition at the Harvard School of Public Health. Experimental studies show that higher fructose consumption increases the production of free fatty acids — substances that circulate in the blood and may play a role in the development of Type 2 diabetes, Hu says in an email interview.

Such facts make the focus on sugar crucial, said Robert Lustig, a professor of pediatric endocrinology at the University of California, San Francisco (UCSF), and author of the 2012 book, *Fat Chance: Beating the Odds Against Sugar, Processed Food, Obesity and Disease.* "We were not designed to eat all this sugar," said Lustig, perhaps the most well-known scientist leading the anti-sugar charge. [10]

Calories in sugar-sweetened beverages may be the most pernicious, many researchers say, because beverages don't make people feel full the way solid foods do.

"Human beings are designed to get our calorie requirements from solids and our liquid requirements from liquids," so people are generally unaware of the calories they consume when drinking a soda, for example, says David Ludwig, director of the New Balance Foundation Obesity Prevention Center at Boston Children's Hospital. "A child might drink for hydration or socially, and the calories come along for the ride."

The beverage industry, among others, strongly disputes these arguments. Sugar-sweetened beverages contribute only about 7 percent of the calories in the average American's diet and "play a small and declining role" in the American diet overall, said the American Beverage Association (ABA). [11] "We know, and science supports, that obesity is not uniquely caused by any single food or beverage," said the ABA. [12]

Some scientists agree that focusing on sugar oversimplifies the nation's obesity problem.

The cause of obesity is 100 times more scientifically complicated than that of heart disease, so focusing on any one food as the key driver of higher obesity rates is not intellectually serious, said Mike Gibney, a professor of food and health at University College Dublin in Ireland. [13]

Moreover, a group of medical scholars and statisticians who reviewed existing research argued that excessive focus on sugar consumption and declining exercise rates have diverted research attention from other potential obesity causes. Those include infections, sleep deprivation, exposure to environmental chemicals and side effects of common medications such as antidepressants and other psychotropic drugs and some treatments for high blood pressure and diabetes. [14]

Nevertheless, some analysts say there's reason enough to craft anti-obesity policies with an eye to limiting sugar consumption. The average adolescent ages 12 to 19 gets about

Sodas and Juices Are High in Sugar

Cranberry juice cocktail contains 12 teaspoons of sugar per 12-ounce serving. Other high-sugar beverages include orange juice and soda. Nutritionists recommend drinking beverages with far less sugar content, such as water, tea, seltzer and coffee.

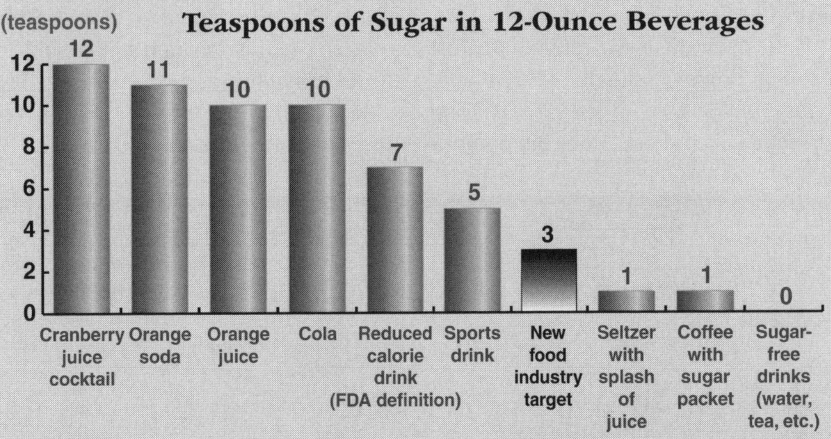

Source: "The Nutrition Source: How Sweet Is It?" School of Public Health, Harvard University, 2009, www.hsph.harvard.edu/nutritionsource/healthy-drinks/how-sweet-is-it/index.html

300 calories per day from sugared beverages, says Sara Bleich, an assistant professor of health policy and management at the Johns Hopkins University Bloomberg School of Public Health. Thus, beverages are the single largest contributor of excess sugar calories "and the easiest to eliminate," she says.

Steve Gortmaker, a professor of the practice of health sociology at the Harvard School of Public Health, says schools and local governments are trying a variety of simple, easy-to-replicate measures, such as Boston's recent move to eliminate all sugar-sweetened beverages from the public schools. [15]

As Americans ponder the potential effects of sugar-laden diets, here are some of the questions being asked:

Is eliminating excess sugar the best solution to the obesity epidemic?

Both obesity and some obesity-related diseases such as Type 2 diabetes have soared over the past half-century. Obesity rates doubled between the 1960s and 2000s, for example, and the rate of Type 2 diabetes doubled between the 1970s and 1990s. [16] As these trends continue to escalate, debate has intensified over what causes such health changes and how to reverse them.

Recently, some researchers have suggested that the key culprit is added sugars in processed foods and beverages. Other analysts, however, say obesity-related health problems likely stem from many causes. In addition, they say, little of the data indicting sugar as a particularly dangerous source of extra calories come from randomized, double-blind trials — the only type of study that can reliably demonstrate cause-and-effect relationships.

However, opponents of added-sugar consumption point out that evidence for their theory is expanding. A just-released, randomly controlled trial, for instance, studied 224 overweight and obese adolescents who regularly drank sugar-sweetened beverages. Some were randomly assigned to a group that received counseling or other assistance to help them switch to low-calorie drinks and some to a control group that continued consuming sugared drinks. After one year, the teens who got the help had stopped drinking sugar-sweetened beverages almost entirely and their weight had dropped. [17] "We got a four-pound differential in body weight," says Ludwig of Boston Children's Hospital, a study author.

In addition, an analysis of a very large, nearly three-decades-long observational study in the Minneapolis/St. Paul area — the Minneapolis Heart Survey — showed that increased consumption of added sugars correlated closely with weight gain. [18]

When it comes to sugars consumed in sugar-sweetened beverages, "It boils down to the question of, 'Is a calorie always a calorie?' " — whether it comes in liquid or solid form, says Richard Mattes, a professor of foods and nutrition at Purdue University in West Lafayette, Ind. At the molecular level, the answer is certainly "yes," he says. When the body metabolizes sugar — turns it into energy — "you break a certain [chemical] bond and you get energy" of the same amount, he says, regardless of whether a person drank or ate the sugar.

But "at the food level the question becomes, 'which makes you feel fuller?' " because the feeling of fullness helps regulate how much people eat, he continues. Beverages don't make people feel full. They bypass digestive-system processes that trigger the feeling of fullness that comes from eating solid food. So with sugar-sweetened beverages in the diet, "our total consumption [of calories] tends to go up," he says.

Some researchers say sugar not only adds excess calories but also metabolizes differently from similar foods — such as starches — so that when consumed in large quantities, it can trigger chronic diseases such as Type 2 diabetes.

Unlike with other foods, the liver takes on a large part of the job of metabolizing sugar, with negative consequences for long-term health, says UCSF's Lustig. Among other things, metabolizing sugars creates fatty deposits in the liver, eventually compromising its functioning, he says.

But other analysts caution against blaming primarily sugar — especially sugary beverages — for obesity. The current research base "does not demonstrate conclusively that [sugar-sweetened beverage] consumption has uniquely contributed to obesity or that reducing [it] will reduce BMI [body mass index] levels in general," wrote Mattes and others in a 2010 review of the research. [19]

Data suggest that added sugar can't bear the lion's share of responsibility for rising obesity, wrote Stephan Guyenet, a research fellow in the Division of Metabolism, Endocrinology and Nutrition at the University of Washington. Americans' weight rose slowly throughout the 20th century — until fairly recently. The proportion of American adults who are obese, for example, rose from just below to just above 15 percent during the 1960s and through the 1970s, for example. Then the obesity rate more than doubled between 1978 and 2004, rising from 15 to 33 percent. Meanwhile, however, the percentage of added sugars consumed by the average American grew from 86 pounds to 101 pounds annually, a 17 percent increase that Guyenet says isn't nearly enough to account for the obesity increase. [20]

Research suggests that "even if you have people drink a liter a day" of sugar-sweetened drinks, "they don't gain as much weight as you'd expect," says Kathryn Kaiser, an instructor in the statistical genetics department of the School of Public Health at the University of Alabama, Birmingham, and a coauthor on Mattes' 2010 research review. The group is currently preparing a new analysis that will include the Ludwig study cited above and another study that appeared in the same issue of the *New England Journal of Medicine* last month.

> **"Our consumption of high fructose corn syrup has gone from less than half a pound [per person] per year in 1970 to 56 pounds per year" in 2011.**
>
> ***— Robert Lustig***
>
> ***Professor of Pediatric Endocrinology, University of California, San Francisco, and author of*** **Fat Chance: Beating the Odds Against Sugar, Processed Food, Obesity and Disease**

Is fructose more harmful than other sugars?

Recently, some researchers have pointed to fructose as the cause of sugar's health dangers.

Fructose is a simple sugar that is found in many plants and is a substantial component of both sucrose (table sugar) and high fructose corn syrup (HFCS), which comes from corn. Critics say fructose is dangerous because it metabolizes solely in the liver, which leads to health problems. Glucose — the other main simple sugar humans consume, and which is also found in plants, including corn — is metabolized in every cell of the body.*

There is a good, historical reason to suspect fructose, said Lustig. "Our consumption of HFCS has gone from less than half a pound [per person] per year in 1970 to 56 pounds per year" in 2011, he said. [21] During the same period, the percentage of obese 12- to 19-year-olds nearly tripled, from 6.1 percent to 17.4 percent. [22]

Beginning in the mid-1970s, HFCS became a standard ingredient in many processed foods, and in 1980 its use skyrocketed when it became the sweetener of choice for sodas and other beverages, Lustig says. "You can actually trace the prevalence of childhood obesity to 1980 when this change was made."

Lustig goes so far as to call sugars containing fructose "toxic." When ingested at a high enough dose, he says, "anything can be a poison" — even something as innocuous-seeming as water. (Drinking too much water can lead to mental confusion, brain swelling and possibly death.) He believes fructose-containing sugars likely have now passed the dose threshold to be toxic to at least some people. For example, sugar-sweetened sodas, once sold in six-and-a-half or eight-ounce cans, are now routinely consumed as 32-ounce — one quart — drinks, he notes.

However, sugar is not the kind of toxin that quickly kills outright, like arsenic,

* Sucrose (table sugar) is a 50-50 combination of fructose and glucose. The high fructose corn syrup used in the United States today is 55 percent fructose and only 45 percent glucose.

Lustig says, but rather is a "chronic" poison that damages the liver over time.

Among other things, fructose may activate a mechanism that produces fat directly in the liver to a greater degree than other sugars and carbohydrates and similarly to how alcohol behaves in the liver, he contends. In some cases, a fatty liver can lead to serious, even fatal, diseases, although the mechanisms of these conditions and whether any relate to fructose consumption is unknown. [23] Some studies suggest that fat in the liver could cause insulin resistance — a reduction in cells' ability to take up glucose and convert it to energy, which is a precursor of Type 2 diabetes. [24]

Rats fed large amounts of fructose over the long term develop insulin resistance within and outside the liver, obesity, Type 2 diabetes and high blood pressure, according to Luc Tappy, a physiologist at the University of Lausanne, in Switzerland. [25]

"I think there's something to the fructose concerns, although only when fructose is present in large amounts, which it often is," says Marion Nestle, a professor of food studies, nutrition and public health at New York University in New York City, in an email interview. A well-known author and advocate of healthy eating, Nestle is a former senior nutrition policy advisor in the Department of Health and Human Services and was editor of the "Surgeon General's Report on Nutrition and Health."

But others say existing research doesn't allow firm conclusions about fructose. Some scientists, for example, point out that most research on fructose has been conducted on animal, not human, subjects and involves feeding higher amounts of the sugar than real-world diets contain.

While some studies suggest unusual health effects, there is "no unequivocal evidence that fructose intake at moderate doses is directly related with adverse metabolic effects," said Tappy. [26]

Childhood Obesity Triples

Obesity among young children and teenagers jumped more than threefold between 1980 and 2008, reaching nearly 20 percent in both age groups — the highest rate in the world. Rising consumption of sugary sodas and beverages — the biggest source of excess sugar in the American diet — may account for much of the increase, experts say. Other likely causes include a lack of exercise and excessive consumption of other unhealthy foods.

Childhood Obesity* Rates by Age, 1980 and 2008

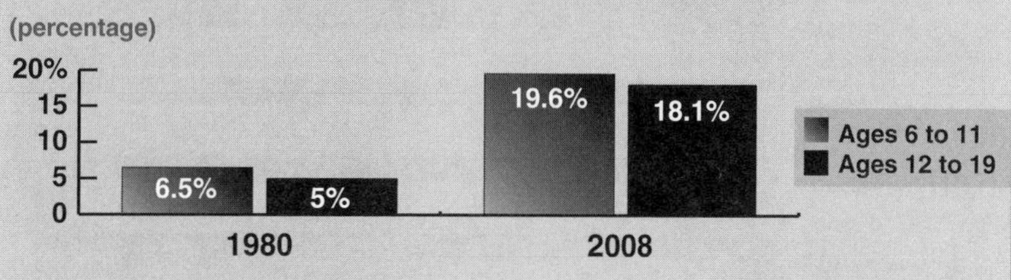

** Obesity is defined as having a body mass index — a number calculated from a person's weight and height — at or above the 95th percentile for children of the same age and sex.*

Source: "Reducing Access to Sugar-Sweetened Beverages Among Youth," Centers for Disease Control and Prevention, June 2011, www.cdc.gov/features/healthybeverages/

Those who argue that fructose poses particular dangers base their contention on the fact that when the liver metabolizes fructose, the body's vital insulin response — which regulates the conversion of food to energy — is not triggered, says Purdue's Mattes. But that may not matter, he says, because fructose is virtually always consumed along with some glucose, which does trigger the insulin response.

Analysis of existing studies demonstrates that, like other sugars, fructose causes health problems only if it provides extra calories in the diet beyond those we need, said John Sievenpiper, a resident physician in medical biochemistry at McMaster University in Hamilton, Ontario. Researchers have discovered biological mechanisms through which fructose metabolism might produce the harms observed in rats, Sievenpiper said. But when scientists have substituted fructose for another sugar in otherwise equivalent diets, the increased blood pressure and other negative consequences have not appeared, he said. [27]

Animals also metabolize fructose and other carbohydrates differently from the way humans do, so while fructose may be "bad for rats or mice . . . it doesn't seem that it's the case in humans," Sievenpiper said. [28]

Should the government do more to limit sugar consumption?

Few doubt that excess calories, many provided by sugars, are at least partially to blame for rising obesity rates. Disagreements are intense, however, over whether the evidence for sugars' role is compelling enough to justify government action, such as heavily taxing some sugary foods.

Trying to dissuade people from consuming extra sugar calories, especially in beverage form, should be an obvious strategy because it "does no harm," said Harvard's Hu. And virtually all health experts agree that most Americans would benefit from consuming fewer calories. [29]

But other analysts warn that imposing limits on people's pleasures

Schools Crack Down on Candy Sales

To help cut sugar consumption, many states have banned candy from high school vending machines. In 2010 only a quarter of secondary schools nationwide allowed students to buy candy on campus — down from more than half in 2002. Alabama had the largest decline over the eight-year period — more than 64 percentage points.

States with the Largest Declines in Percentage of High Schools Selling Non-chocolate Candy*

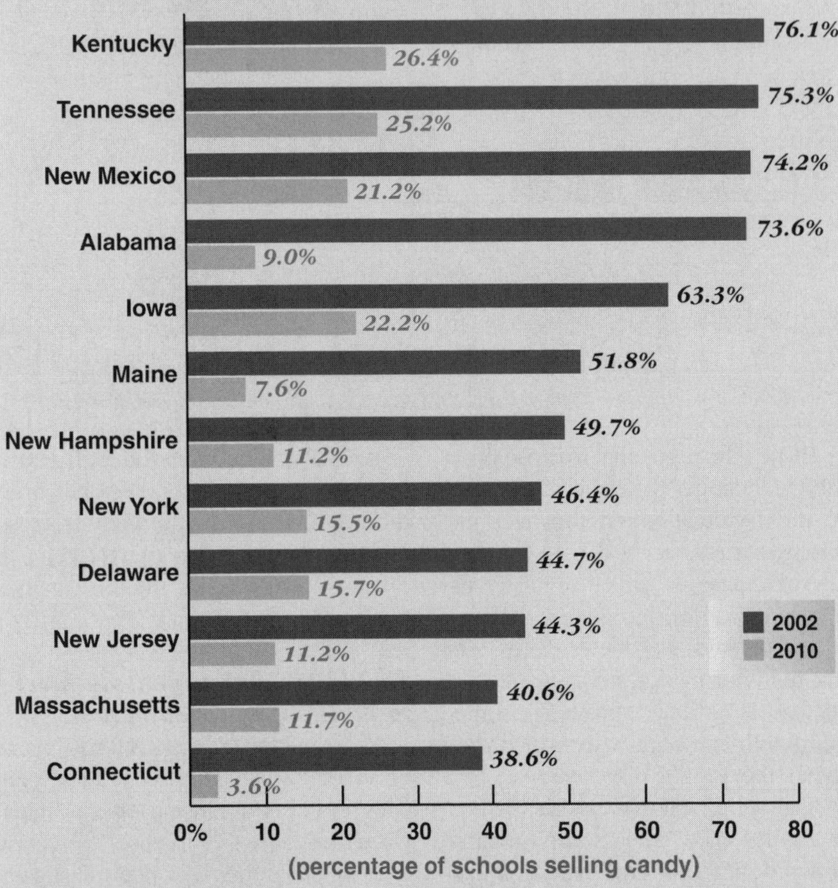

** Similar declines were seen in sales of chocolate candy on campus.*

Source: "Out of Balance: A Look at Snack Foods in Secondary Schools Across the States," Robert Wood Johnson Foundation, October 2012, p. 19, www.rwjf.org/content/dam/farm/reports/reports/2012/rwjf402345

based on insufficient evidence could backfire, potentially causing them to rebel against other, truly urgent science-based laws and regulations later.

Whether enough evidence to warrant policy action already exists "depends on which action [is taken], in which regulatory context and according to whose tastes and moral values," said David Allison, director of the Nutrition Obesity Research Center at the University of Alabama, Birmingham. [30]

The public costs of the obesity epidemic justify public action to limit sugar consumption, said the University of California's Lustig. Treating obesity-related health problems such as Type 2 diabetes, he said, is throwing $147 billion a year in public funds "down a rat hole." [31]

"Given the large proportion of people who claim that they want to lose weight and the small proportion who are actually able to do so," it's clear that people do, in fact, need help to improve their diets, wrote Deborah A. Cohen, a senior natural scientist at the Santa Monica branch of the RAND Corp. think tank, and Susan H. Babey, a senior research scientist at the UCLA Center for Health Policy Research. Simple changes, such as banning the sale of sugar-heavy junk foods near supermarket checkout counters could help people make better eating decisions, they suggest. [32]

Tax increases that raise prices and thus dissuade some people from buying unhealthy products have worked in the past, say proponents of raising taxes on sugary beverages. For example, a 10 percent price increase on cigarettes has been found to reduce sales by about 3 percent overall and by 7 percent among teenagers. [33]

"Even though there is more to learn, we know enough to be giving firm dietary advice and taking policy actions" to dissuade people from consuming so much sugar, says Walter Willett, chair of the Department of Nutrition at the Harvard School of Public Health. "These dietary and beverage patterns can be encouraged and supported by many different policies, from local to national," he says. "Of course, each of these policies needs to be monitored and evaluated for impact, but we can't afford to wait and do nothing just because we don't have long-term data on the impact of each policy."

But other analysts say sugar's harms aren't fully proven and that limiting people's pleasures can backfire. The analogy between tobacco bans or taxes and similar measures related to sugar-sweetened beverages isn't valid, wrote Robbin S. Johnson, a research fellow at the University of Minnesota's Hubert H. Humphrey School of Public Affairs and a retired senior vice president of the Minneapolis-based food conglomerate Cargill, Inc., which sells sugar and HFCS. [34] Smoking is "hazardous to one's health under any circumstances," but sugar-sweetened beverages "are not intrinsically hazardous or even problematic. . . . Behavior, not bad food," should be the target of obesity-related policy interventions, he wrote. [35]

Furthermore, "there is nothing about a soda tax per se that contributes to the growth in understanding that would lead most directly to the kind of behavior change needed to arrest and reverse obesity," wrote Johnson. [36]

Product bans have been tried "before, with more evidence to back [them] than in the case of sugar-sweetened beverages (and with fewer potential costs in terms of freedom), and we have failed to change behavior," wrote Cornell University's David R. Just, an associate professor of behavioral economics, and Brian Wansink, a professor of marketing. "Prohibition, for instance, was intended to wipe out the ills of alcohol, but it could not withstand the violent backlash, subversion and illegal consequences that quickly followed." [37]

They suggest milder approaches, such as encouraging stores to move sugar-sweetened drinks to less prominent locations. "Simple behavioral nudges, such as making soft drinks less visible and less convenient, can have a big effect on consumption," they write. [38]

"One of the most interesting things coming out right now is that youngsters are substituting other sweetened drinks," such as sweetened juices or lemonade and sports drinks — which many teens believe are healthier — when a school system bans sodas, making the school bans useless, says Daniel Taber, a postdoctoral research associate at the Institute for Health Research and Policy at the University of Illinois, Chicago. "Unless you comprehensively ban all sugar-sweetened beverages," the likelihood of limiting sugar consumption is low, he says.

Getty Images/Alex Wong

U.S. first lady Michelle Obama and celebrity cook Rachael Ray (far left) visit Parklawn Elementary School in Alexandria, Va., on Jan. 25, 2012, to promote the Department of Agriculture's new nutrition standards, which limit added sugars in school lunches. Many kids won't eat the low-sugar, low-fat foods, however, leading parents and school officials to complain that students are not eating enough to get through the day.

At least partly because of such dietary substitutions, little correlation seems to exist between the level of soft-drink taxes and obesity, said Jason Fletcher, an associate professor of health policy and administration at the Yale University School of Public Health. That's probably because, unlike with cigarettes, when higher prices discourage soda buying, people have other equally high-calorie options to turn to, he said. [39] ■

BACKGROUND

Sweet Eating

Humans are biologically programmed to seek out sweet tastes. In nature, sweetness signals ripe, wholesome fruit or energy-boosting honey. In a world of hunting and gathering or simple farming, however, sweet tastes were hard to come by.

Industrialization has turned that principle on its head. Over the past three centuries, and partly as a result of public policies to keep food costs in check and boost economies, sugary tastes have grown ever cheaper and more readily available. [40]

Added sugars have risen continually as a component of U.S. diets for at least 200 years, wrote Guyenet, of the University of Washington. In 1822, the average American ate 6.3 pounds of added sugars a year. By 2004, it was 101 pounds. Over the past three decades, especially, sugar has been added to thousands of processed foods and beverages. [41]

Meanwhile, industrialized nations' health concerns have shifted from infectious diseases toward chronic ills such as heart disease and Type 2 diabetes, which are associated with obesity, at least in some cases. In turn, not surprisingly, sugar has come under scrutiny as a potential cause.

Sugar consumption by Europeans and North Americans began rising in about 1700, as huge sugar-cane plantations were established in places such as Brazil and the West Indies to satisfy a growing public desire for sweet tastes. By 1865 in Brisbane, Australia, for example, plantations produced about 2,200 pounds of sugar every day. Even so, the sweet treat "was still expensive, and wasn't being eaten every day by anyone but Queen Victoria and her mates," wrote David Gillespie, the Australian author of the 2008 book *Sweet Poison: Why Sugar Is Making Us Fat.*

By the turn of the 20th century, however, sugar was becoming a daily menu item for the working and middle classes. Many cheap sweet treats were invented around this time, such as Hershey's chocolate bars and Life Savers. [42]

Rise of Corn

In the 1970s, a new sugar option came on the market. Food scientists figured out how to mass-produce and use high fructose corn syrup, especially in commercial cooking. Unlike older sugars, which came from sugar cane and sugar beets and had as much of the simple sugar glucose as fructose, HFCS was derived mainly from corn, a quintessential and plentiful North American crop whose adaptability to multiple uses makes it a highly valuable export product.

Ounce for ounce, HFCS is sweeter than the other sugars, lowering the cost of sweetening food. It helps keep foods from drying out, is less likely to ruin foods by quickly crystallizing, fends off spoilage and works well in frozen foods and beverages.

Federal farm policies initiated in the 1970s boosted the use of HFCS, after President Richard M. Nixon "appropriately saw high food prices as a cause of potential unrest" among citizens and sought ways to keep them low, says Lustig, the pediatric endocrinologist at the University of California-San Francisco.

Most farm policy involves subsidies and price supports to ensure that farmers consistently earn enough income to encourage them to keep farming. [43] Prior to the Nixon era, the government achieved that mainly by paying farmers to keep some land unplanted. That kept the food supply tight so crop commodity prices wouldn't fall too low.

Nixon Agriculture Secretary Earl Butz, however, encouraged dense planting, especially of foods with multiple uses such as corn, to provide cheap food and to bolster American agribusiness exports. By providing billions of dollars in subsidies over the years to farmers to grow as much corn as their acreage allows, the government has kept corn prices low while ensuring that farmers could earn a good income. And with corn so cheap, food processors were motivated to incorporate more corn sweeteners into products.

Ironically, according to the Institute for Agriculture and Trade Policy (IATP), which promotes family farms and sustainable agriculture, as the U.S. government was encouraging massive increases in production of corn and other grains, it did not subsidize healthier foods such as fruits and vegetables to the same degree. "For the past 50 years, U.S. farm policy has been increasingly directed toward driving down the price of farm commodities, including corn and soybeans," says an IATP fact sheet entitled, "Food Without Thought: How U.S. Farm Policy Contributes to Obesity." "At the same time, prices for fruits and vegetables, grown with relatively little government support, have steadily increased." [44]

As a result, "The low cost of commodities . . . makes sugars and fats some of the cheapest food substances to produce," the IATP continues. "Whether by intention or not, current farm policy has directed food industry investment into finding ways of using these cheap food additives in processed foods. Not coincidentally, U.S. consumers are now eating many more added sweeteners and oils than is healthy."

Lustig sums up the problem succinctly: "A calorie has become very cheap."

Soon corn sweeteners found their way into "things that never had sugar before, like hamburger buns, hamburger meat, barbeque sauce, ketchup, salad dressing," Lustig said. Our biologically programmed craving for sweetness added few calories when sweet foods were scarce and pricey, but when corn became cheap and plentiful, "the food industry figured it out . . . and hijacked our taste buds" to make their wares more appealing, said Lustig. [45]

Over the same period, obesity and related diseases were on the rise. In 1900, the average college-age man weighed 133 pounds and a woman, 122 pounds. By 2000, those averages had risen to 166 and 144 pounds. (Men's average height also increased slightly, but not enough to fully account for the weight gain.) [46]

Heart disease was also on the rise, and long-term surveys of very large groups of people showed that, although thin people also develop heart disease, obesity is perhaps the strongest risk factor for the condition. Exactly how obesity leads to heart disease remains unclear, although scientists now know that, rather than being an inert part of the body, at least some body fat actually affects the way our metabolism operates. [47]

In public-health circles, concern arose about whether changing diets were fueling obesity-related disease, and some initial suspicion fell on sugar. In 1972, John Yudkin, a British physiologist, published *Pure, White and Deadly*, a book proposing that added sugars were a key cause of heart disease. [48]

In 1973, Sen. George McGovern, D-S.D., convened a hearing of the Select Committee on Nutrition and Human Needs to discuss potential links between sugar and disease. Some witnesses testified that differences in added-sugar consumption most likely

Continued on p. 1024

Chronology

1900s-1950s

After centuries as a luxury item, sugar becomes a diet staple.

1900
Hershey's chocolate bar introduced.

1912
Peppermint flavored Life Savers are introduced.

1955
McDonald's begins selling Coke in seven-ounce servings.

1957
High fructose corn syrup (HFCS) is invented but without a method to mass produce it.

1970s ***Mass-produced corn sweeteners lower the cost of sugared food and drinks.***

1972
In *Pure, White and Deadly*, British physiologist John Yudkin argues that added sugars lead to heart disease.

1973
Senate Select Committee on Nutrition and Human Needs hears testimony on possible links between added sugars and diabetes. . . . Agriculture Secretary Earl Butz introduces corn subsidies and fencerow-to-fencerow planting to ensure plentiful low-priced corn.

1980s-1990s

Americans adopt low-fat and nonfat diets, but more foods have added sugar. Obesity rises steeply.

1980
HFCS is rapidly becoming the main sweetener in sodas.

1988
"Surgeon General's Report on Nutrition and Health" declares fat the unhealthiest food item.

1994
Men take in 90 percent more calories from snacks than in 1978, women 112 percent. . . . Nearly 23 percent of adults are obese.

2000s ***Obesity-rate increases slow. Schools cut back on the amount of sugary food and drinks they sell and serve.***

2000
On average, a college-age man weighs 166 pounds, a college-age woman, 144 pounds — up from 133 and 122 pounds in 1900.

2004
More than 17 percent of 12- to 19-year-olds are obese — up from 6 percent in the 1970s. . . . Adult obesity rates top 33 percent. . . . The average American consumes more than 100 pounds of added sugars annually — up from 86 pounds in 1978.

2005
Kraft Foods stops advertising sugary snacks during TV shows for young children.

2009
"Sugar: The Bitter Truth," a lecture posted online by University of California, San Francisco, pediatric endocrinologist Robert Lustig, argues that too much sugar is toxic; it becomes a YouTube sensation, garnering nearly 3 million views by 2012.

2010
Between January 2009 and May 2010, 17 states file proposals for new soda taxes. . . . Eighty-eight percent of high schools and 63 percent of middle schools sell sugared drinks, down from 95 percent and 78 percent in 2006. . . . Department of Agriculture's Dietary Guidelines recommend that no more than 15 percent of calories come from added sugar and solid fats; the average American gets about 15 percent from added sugars alone.

2011
Four federal agencies propose, then withdraw, voluntary guidelines urging companies to market healthier, lower-sugar foods to kids. . . . Working with the Better Business Bureau, 16 food companies commit to marketing healthier food to kids, including limiting sugar. . . . KFC introduces 64-ounce sodas.

2012
New York City Mayor Michael Bloomberg and the city's Board of Health limit sugared drinks sold in restaurants, entertainment venues and food carts to 16 ounces or smaller; restaurant and beverage associations challenge the policy in court. . . . Obesity-related health care for New York state residents costs $11.8 billion a year. . . . Average 12- to 19-year-old gets 300 calories a day from sugared drinks. . . . Cambridge, Mass., Washington, D.C., and Los Angeles mull limiting sugary-drink sales. . . . Food and Drug Administration considers listing added-sugar totals on food labels. . . . Voters in Richmond and El Monte, Calif., defeat proposed soda taxes. . . . National Institutes of Health plans to study health effects of fructose.

Artificial Sweeteners Raise Hope — and Concern

They may help with weight loss, but are they safe?

Not all Americans guzzle sugary drinks by the barrel. In 2008 around a quarter of weight-conscious American adults and more than 12 percent of children said they regularly drank artificially sweetened, or "diet," sodas instead. [1]

On the weight-loss front, that's undeniably good news. "The evidence is now clear from randomized trials that artificial sweeteners can help reduce weight if they replace standard sugar-sweetened beverages," Walter Willett, chair of the Department of Nutrition at the Harvard School of Public Health, said in an email interview.

Nevertheless, artificial sweeteners are relatively new products, so the effects of consuming large amounts of them for decades isn't fully understood, prompting scientists to advise using them in moderation. Artificial sweeteners "are not the ideal long-term solution," said Willett, but they can "be useful in helping some people withdraw from products that are seriously harmful to their health."

The Food and Drug Administration (FDA) has approved for human consumption five so-called artificial sweeteners that consist of manmade molecules: saccharin, aspartame, acesulfame potassium, sucralose and neotame. (*See box for brand names.*) [2] A sixth approved non-caloric sweetener, rebaudioside A, is a natural extract from the stevia plant.

The FDA banned a seventh sweetener, cyclamate (Sucaryl), in 1969 based on studies suggesting it caused bladder cancer in rats. Worried about a surge in sales of diet soda sweetened with much cheaper artificial sweeteners, the sugar industry was one of the loudest groups sounding the alarm about potential health dangers from cyclamate. [3]

"If anyone can undersell you nine cents out of 10, you'd better find some brickbat you can throw at him," remarked John Hickson, vice president of the sugar-industry-affiliated International Sugar Research Foundation. [4]

A subsequent study 20 years later found that monkeys fed massive amounts of cyclamate remained cancer-free, raising serious doubts about the applicability of the rat findings to humans and other primates. "With cyclamate we made a mistake," said Robert Scheuplein, an FDA scientist who headed the agency's toxicology office in the early 1990s. [5]

Cyclamate remains banned in the United States, but it is sold in Canada — as SugarTwin — and throughout Europe. Research has produced no clear evidence that any approved artificial sweetener is associated with human cancers, says the National Cancer Institute. [6]

Aspartame comes under fire from food-additive opponents in part because, in storage and during digestion, it breaks down into methanol (wood alcohol) and then formaldehyde, best known as an embalming chemical. [7] Toxicologists point out, however, that most fruits and vegetables break down into the same chemicals and that the body makes use of them without allowing toxins to accumulate. [8]

Plenty of questions remain about artificial sweeteners' effects on the body, however. The San Antonio Heart Study, for example, which followed 3,682 adults for eight years, found that those who consistently used artificially sweeteners weighed more. [9] Such results leave some scientists wondering whether the sweet taste of noncaloric sweeteners might stimulate the appetite more than sugar.

In search of answers, researchers use brain imaging to discover how humans respond to calorie-laden and no-calorie sweet tastes and observe rats that are fed both sugar and artificial sweeteners.

A typical diet — which includes both calorie-rich and no-calorie sweets — may confuse the brain, said Susan Swithers, a professor of behavioral neuroscience at Purdue University in West Lafayette, Ind. "The brain normally uses a learned relationship between sweet taste and the delivery of calories" to regulate eating by switching off hunger pangs after consuming sugar.

Continued from p. 1022

explained the increases in diabetes among certain population groups. [49]

The Sugar Association, a powerful food-industry lobbying group, fought back. Scientists affiliated with the association argued that, while some studies suggested a connection between sugar and chronic disease, other research found no link. Lawmakers were reluctant to slow the economy-boosting success of American farmers and food processors and largely accepted the association's view of sugar as benign. [50]

Low-Fat Craze

Soon consensus formed around dietary fats as the likely culprit in rising obesity.

In the mid-1980s, the National Institutes of Health began counseling Americans to cut out fats. In 1988, the massive "U.S. Surgeon General's Report on Nutrition and Health" declared fat the single unhealthiest food in the American diet. The American Heart Association opined that if low-fat eating became the norm, atherosclerosis — fat-clogged arteries — would be a thing of the past by 2000. [51]

Low-fat and fat-free products soon were everywhere, but because the fat had provided flavor, manufacturers began adding more sugars in order to boost the appeal of fat-free foods. Obesity rates kept rising throughout the '90s. "With more fat-free products than ever, Americans got fatter," says Harvard's Willett.

The proportion of Americans who are overweight but not obese has

But when one eats both no-calorie and calorie-rich sweeteners, the appetite-suppression mechanism may go haywire and lead to overeating, she hypothesized. [10]

Another recent study, however, found no link between artificial sweeteners and appetite, said its lead author, Bjørn Richelsen, a professor of endocrinology and metabolism at Denmark's Aarhus University.

In a test of how hungry people were after drinking water, milk, Coke or Diet Coke, "we found if you're drinking soft drinks without calories it behaves [on the appetite] exactly like drinking water," Richelsen said. [11]

— Marcia Clemmitt

[1] Allison C. Sylvetsky, *et al.*, "Low-calorie Sweetener Consumption Is Increasing in the United States," *The American Journal of Clinical Nutrition*, September 2012, pp. 640-646, http://ajcn.nutrition.org/content/96/3/640.abstract.

[2] "Fact Sheet: Artificial Sweeteners and Cancer," National Cancer Institute, Aug. 5, 2009, www.cancer.gov/cancertopics/factsheet/Risk/artificial-sweeteners.

[3] Gary Taubes and Cristin Kearns Couzens, "Sweet Little Lies," *Mother Jones*, November/December 2012, p. 35, www.motherjones.com/environment/2012/10/sugar-industry-lies-campaign.

[4] Quoted in *ibid.*

[5] Quoted in *ibid.*; also see Robert J. Scheuplein, Ph.D., Keller and Heckman LLP, www.khlaw.com/Robert-Scheuplein.

[6] "Artificial Sweeteners and Cancer," National Cancer Institute, www.cancer.gov/cancertopics/factsheet/Risk/artificial-sweeteners.

[7] Christina Dambra, "What Are the Dangers of Aspartame?" LIVESTRONG, June 12, 2010, www.livestrong.com/article/146748-what-are-the-dangers-of-aspartame.

[8] Bernadene Magnuson, "Relationship Between Aspartame, Methanol and Formaldehyde Explained," Evidence Analysis Library, Academy of Nutrition and Dietetics, http://andevidencelibrary.com/topic.cfm?cat=4089&auth=1; Methanol, United Nations Environment Programme, www.inchem.org/documents/ehc/ehc/ehc196.htm#SubSectionNumber:5.1.3.

[9] Qing Yang, "Gain Weight by 'Going Diet'? Artificial Sweeteners and the Neurobiology of Sugar Cravings," *Yale Journal of Biology and Medicine*, June 2010, pp. 101-108, www.ncbi.nlm.nih.gov/pmc/articles/PMC2892765.

[10] Quoted in Janet Raloff, "Diet Sodas May Confuse Brain's 'Calorie Counter,' " *Science News*, July 14, 2012, www.sciencenews.org/view/generic/id/341424/title/Diet_sodas__may_confuse_brains_calorie_counter.

[11] Allison Aubrey, "Swapping Out Sugary Soda for Diet Drinks May Help Tip the Scale In Your Favor," NPR, Oct. 22, 2012, http://m.npr.org/news/Health/163260960.

Brand Names of Sugar Alternatives

Artificial sweeteners — which contain few or no calories — can help reduce weight when used to replace sugar-sweetened beverages, but scientists advise using them in moderation because the effects of consuming large amounts of them over the long term are not fully understood.

Artificial Sweeteners (derived from man-made substances):

Acesulfame Potassium — Sunnett, Sweet One

Aspartame — Nutrasweet, Equal

Neotame — no brand name; used as an additive by food processors

Saccharin — Sweet 'N Low, Sweet Twin, SugarTwin

Sucralose — Splenda

Natural Noncaloric sweetener (derived from the stevia plant):

Rebaudioside A — PureVia, Steviva, A Sweet Leaf, Sun Crystals, Truvia

Source: American Diabetes Association and Sharecare, www.sharecare.com/question/what-common-brand-artificial-sweeteners

hovered at around a third of the population since the 1960s, but obesity rates have soared, rising from around 15 percent in the 1960s and '70s to more than a third of the population today. [52] (A 5'9" tall adult is overweight if he weighs 169-202 pounds and obese at 203 pounds or more, for example.) [53]

It seems likely that added sugars bear much of the blame, but the issue is complicated.

Over the past three decades, Americans have increased their average daily calorie intake by between 150 and 300 calories, with approximately half coming from sweetened beverages. [54] In 2000, the average American consumed 152 pounds of calorie-containing sweeteners annually, up from about 110 pounds in the 1950s. [55]

Another statistic seems to link obesity and added sugar: Between about 1999 and 2008, as consumption of added sugars declined — mostly because people drank fewer sugar-sweetened sodas — obesity rates began to stabilize. [56] "There is a positive correlation between the obesity trends and increasing consumption of sugar, but this correlation needs to be interpreted with caution because many other things have happened during the same time period," says Harvard's Hu. For example, more people today have sedentary jobs and drive rather than walk to work or school.

With regard to diets, consumption of other high-caloric foods has risen along with sugar consumption. Cheese consumption, for instance, jumped 287 percent between the 1950s and 2000 — from about 8 pounds per

Path to Better Eating Strewn with Traps

Salad for lunch? Better count the added calories.

From sugar-laden processed foods to supersized sugary sodas, the American diet provides abundant opportunities for people to consume more calories than they realize. And trying to figure out the sugar content on a food label can be challenging, say nutrition experts, because the true sugar content is often obscured.

Most packaged foods and beverages — from salad dressings and bread to sports drinks — contain added sugars, often quite a bit. Over the years, those added sugars — separate from sugar that occurs naturally in fruits and milk — have become a larger and larger source of calories in the American diet. But unlike fruits and milk, added sugars lack nutritional value — they only provide flavoring and calories.

The American Heart Association recommends getting only about 100 to 150 calories a day from added sugars. [1] But abiding by that limit is challenging, because while finding out the total amount of sugar in a food is easy, spotting the added sugars can be devilishly difficult.

That's because food nutrition labels don't list added sugars separately. They list only the total sugar — stated in grams — contained in the food or drink. If there are no fruit or milk products in the food, the "total sugar" listed on the label is the amount of added sugar. [2]

For food containing fruit or milk, scrutinizing the ingredient list can provide some clues as to whether the food contains large amounts of added sugar. By law, manufacturers must list ingredients by weight, so those at the top of the list are present in the largest quantities. But manufacturers "know people are reading labels to find out how much sugar is in the product," explained Jonny Bowden, a weight-loss coach in Woodland Hills, Calif. "So they mix in a small amount of lots of different sugars. That way, no single kind of sugar is the main ingredient by weight. [But] add them all up, and sugar outweighs anything else in the recipe." [3]

In an ingredient list, sugars go by many names. Besides the word "sugar" — such as "turbinado sugar" (a form of brown sugar) — other sugars might be listed as corn syrup, dextrin, honey, corn sweetener, evaporated cane juice, high fructose corn syrup, malt, molasses, fruit juice concentrate, molasses and sorghum. And any word that ends with "ose" — such as dextrose, lactose, maltose, sucrose, polydextrose and galactose — is likely a sugar. [4]

Added sugars can add up quickly. A light lunch of a green salad spiced up with a couple of tablespoons of low-fat salad dressing (5 grams of added sugars) and accompanied by half a bottle of sweetened vitamin water (15 grams) contains 20 grams of sugar. Since all sugars contain about four calories per gram, that's 80 calories from added sugars, fast approaching the heart association's daily recommendation of no more than 150 calories. And that doesn't include dessert. [5]

Sugar-sweetened beverages pose another label trap. One bottle generally contains two to four "servings" of a drink, but the calorie count on the nutrition label is for just one serving, says Joanne Slavin, a nutrition professor at the University of Minnesota-Twin Cities. In an ideal world, she says, "labels would list the full number of calories in the bottle, not per-serving calories." But unless that happens, consumers must figure out that downing a bottle of energy drink or soda may provide two to three times as many calories as they imagine, Slavin says.

People are more likely to consume hefty amounts of sugar and calories via beverages than in foods, say nutrition scientists, because beverages don't trigger the same sensations of fullness that solid foods do. So cutting down on sugar-sweetened beverages is a good place to start to bring into better balance the energy one consumes and the energy one expends, says Sara Bleich, an assistant professor of health policy and management at the Johns Hopkins University Bloomberg

person annually to nearly 30 pounds. And consumption of added fats rose from about 45 pounds per person per year to 74.5 pounds in 2000. [57]

And between-meal snacking has also increased. Between 1977-78 and 1994-96, the average man's daily calorie intake from snacks grew by 90 percent, the average woman's by 112 percent. People compensate to some degree by eating less for dinner, but, overall, total daily calorie intake over the period increased by 268 calories for men, and 143 calories for women. [58]

Contemporary diets also include many highly processed foods — with natural fiber removed — another change likely related to obesity, the University of California's Lustig argues.

Removing fiber gives some perishable foods a longer shelf life, but at a cost to health, Lustig says. Oranges, for example, are perishable and are ruined by freezing, he says. "But if you squeeze the orange" — removing the fiber — "it can last forever," in the form of frozen juice, which is mostly sugar.

Humans digest fiber-free foods differently than foods high in fiber, Lustig says. When unprocessed foods — such as fruits — are eaten, the sugars are accompanied by fiber. Among other effects, fiber reduces the rate at which the bloodstream absorbs sugar from the gut, avoiding the blood-sugar spike that occurs when one drinks fiberless juice, and it causes the food to move faster through the intestine, which triggers an "I'm full" signal sooner. "The removal of fiber was as important as sugar" in creating what Lustig calls the modern obesity-driving diet.

School of Public Health. "Sugar from beverages is the biggest single" contributor of excess sugar calories and therefore "the easiest to eliminate," she says. And cutting out sugary drinks doesn't risk eliminating important nutrients from the diet, she notes.

Being more aware of one's blind spots can also foster more thoughtful eating and drinking. For example, research shows that most people underestimate both the size and calorie count of what they consume. In a recent study, Pierre Chandon, a professor of marketing at INSEAD, an international graduate school of business in Paris, found that study participants estimated that large-sized soda cups held between 20 and 40 percent less liquid than they actually did. In another study, trained dieticians consistently underestimated — by 13 to 26 percent — the number of calories in fast-food meals. [6]

But there's yet another mental quirk that leads to overconsumption: It takes more food or drink to satisfy the palate when it's served in larger containers. In one study, people served stale movie popcorn ate 34 to 45 percent more of the mediocre snack when it was served in "extra-super-size ginormous buckets" than in regular-sized containers, said Brian Wansink, a professor of consumer behavior at Cornell University. And people poured 37 percent more beverage into short, wide glasses than into tall skinny ones of equal volume, he found, and children poured twice as much cereal into 16-ounce bowls as into 8-ounce ones. [7]

His takeaway? To avoid such "mindless eating," serve meals on salad plates rather than dinner plates.

CQ Press/Olu Davis

Food labels often list sugars by different names, making it difficult for the consumer to figure out exactly how much sugar is in the product. A single frosted strawberry Pop-Tart, for instance, contains 16 grams of "sugars," including corn syrup, high fructose corn syrup, dextrose and sugar.

— Marcia Clemmitt

---

[1] "Sugars and Carbohydrates," American Heart Association, June 11, 2012, www.heart.org/HEARTORG/GettingHealthy/NutritionCenter/HealthyDietGoals/Sugars-and-Carbohydrates_UCM_303296_Article.jsp.

[2] *Ibid.*

[3] Jonny Bowden, "Sugar and Processed Foods: Finding the Hidden Sugars," iVillage UK, www.ivillage.co.uk/sugar-and-processed-foods-finding-the-hidden-sugars/77330#ixzz2C8Qqy1Qu.

[4] Becky Hand, "The Hunt for Hidden Sugar," Sparkpeople, www.sparkpeople.com/resource/nutrition_articles.asp?id=616; and Kathy A. Johnson, "How to Spot Hidden Sugars in Your Everyday Foods," *She Knows Health and Wellness*, March 28, 2012, www.sheknows.com/health-and-wellness/articles/826561/how-to-spot-hidden-sugars-in-your-everyday-foods.

[5] *Ibid.*, (Johnson).

[6] Tara Parker-Pope, "Well; How Can a Big Gulp Look So Small?" *The New York Times*, June 24, 2012, http://query.nytimes.com/gst/fullpage.html?res=9905E0D8163BF937A15755C0A9649D8B63.

[7] Quoted in Charlene Laino, "Ways to Combat Mindless Eating," WebMD, Aug. 5, 2011, www.webmd.com/diet/news/20110805/ways-combat-mindless-eating.

"The more processed the food got, the fatter we got," he says.

Limiting Sugar

Policies to limit sugar consumption have increased, especially in the past decade.

In the past, states have taxed sugary foods such as soda and candy, but initially such taxes aimed to generate revenue, not to discourage consumption. For instance, revenue from the nation's first sugary soda tax — levied in 1917 on ingredients used to manufacture soda — was used to help pay for fighting World War I. [59]

But as obesity rates rose, states began to view soda taxes as a public-health measure. [60] Between 1989 through 2006, for instance, up to two dozen states in any given year imposed taxes on soft drinks, with average rates ranging from 4.1 to 5.1 percent. [61] Between January 2009 and May 2010, at least 17 states proposed — though few passed — new soft-drink taxes. [62]

Some jurisdictions have banned sugary food and drink sales from school grounds. In the 2006-2007 school year, 95 percent of high school, 78 percent of middle-school and 17 percent of elementary-school students could buy sugar-sweetened beverages at school. By 2010-2011, those percentages had dropped to 88 percent, 63 percent and 12 percent, respectively. [63]

Some states and school districts, such as California and Arkansas, have aggressively limited junk-food sales, says Taber of the University of Illinois.

America's highest obesity rates are in the South, and those states "have realized what a problem obesity is for them," he says. (*See map, p. 1016, and graph, p. 1020.*)

In 2011, four federal agencies — the Department of Agriculture, Centers for Disease Control and Prevention, Federal Trade Commission (FTC) and Food and Drug Administration — proposed voluntary guidelines for food companies to follow in curtailing the marketing of high-sugar and other less healthy foods to children and promoting healthier foods more actively.

"The proposal is designed to support, not supplant, moms and dads," said Rep. Jan Schakowsky, D-Ill. "The more marketing that kids see for foods that make up a healthy diet, [the more] kids will start asking for healthier foods." [64]

Congressional Republicans quickly denounced the plan as an encroachment on companies' and families' freedom. The guidelines were "so extreme" they would prevent companies from marketing to children some foods that most parents try to get their kids to eat, such as yogurt sweetened with sugar, said Rep. Fred Upton, R-Mich. [65] Early this year, FTC Chairman Jon Leibowitz suggested that the voluntary guidelines will likely be withdrawn. [66]

Meanwhile, food companies have taken some steps on their own to discourage overconsumption of sugars. For instance, in 2005, Northfield, Ill.-based Kraft Foods announced it would stop advertising snack foods such as Oreo cookies during TV shows aimed at young children. [67]

In summer 2011, some food companies agreed to voluntarily stop marketing some less healthy foods to kids. For example, the companies have vowed that by January 2014 they would market to children only cereals with 10 grams or less of sugar per serving. [68]

But the Environmental Working Group (EWG), a Washington-based health advocacy organization, noted that that's still more sugar than in three Nabisco Chips Ahoy! Cookies. [69]

"Kids need healthy food, not hyped junk," says EWG. [70] ■

CURRENT SITUATION

Shrinking Drinks?

With about two-thirds of Americans obese or overweight, some government officials hope new public-health policies will help people resist the lure of sugar. [71] One strategy for shrinking Americans' waistlines is to shrink the size of their sugared drinks.

New York City's ban on extra-large sugar-sweetened beverages is expected to get New Yorkers accustomed to smaller servings as their new normal — not just for sodas but also for sports and energy drinks, teas, coffees and sweetened juices. [72]

The policy "is the single biggest step any gov't has taken to curb #obesity. It will save lives," Bloomberg tweeted. [73]

Such policies "are designed to counteract the environmental risk of beverage marketing," such as getting vendors to place sodas in highly visible spots and using "volume-based discounting to encourage consumers to 'trade up' to larger sizes," wrote New York City Commissioner of Health Thomas Farley. [74]

Industry groups have challenged the ban in court, saying it "burdens consumers and unfairly harms small businesses" and that the city doesn't have the authority to impose it. But the mayor says the Board of Health has authority because the ban is a public-health measure. [75]

Policies to limit sugar consumption are being considered elsewhere. Government panels in Cambridge, Mass., and Washington, D.C., are mulling New York-style bans. And a Los Angeles panel is considering a ban on sodas in vending machines in city parks and libraries. [76] The Portland, Maine, school district has banned on-campus soda sales at all school events, including sports events. [77]

A backlash has developed against such measures in some communities. On Nov. 6, voters in two California towns — Richmond, near San Francisco, and El Monte, near Los Angeles — defeated proposed soda taxes, with 67 percent and 77 percent, respectively, voting against the measures. [78]

At the federal level, the Food and Drug Administration recently received public comments on a proposal to include "added sugars" — sugars that do not occur naturally in foods — as a separate category on food nutrition labels. [79] (*See sidebar, p. 1024.*) In January, the U.S. Department of Agriculture (USDA) released new — controversial — nutrition rules for public-school lunches and breakfasts, championed by first lady Michelle Obama. Among other things, the rules forbid serving frozen fruits that contain added sugars or canned fruits packed in heavy, high-sugar-content syrup; they limit grain-based desserts such as cake or granola bars to two per week because of their high added-sugar and solid-fat content. [80]

But many kids are refusing to eat many of the low-sugar, low-fat, high-fiber foods being served, so they're not eating enough to get through the day, complain many parents and school officials. "Our trash cans are overflowing with fruits and vegetables the students don't want," said Rich Prall, nutrition director of Utah's Granite School District. [81]

Some nongovernment institutions also are limiting sugared drinks. Four Vanguard hospitals in the Chicago area are replacing sugar-sweetened beverages in cafeterias and vending machines with healthier options such as bottled water. In Boston, 10 hospitals are cutting out some sugary beverages from soda fountains and patient meal trays and are

Continued on p. 1030

At Issue:

Should government try to cut sugary-drink consumption?

yes

MICHAEL F. JACOBSON
FOUNDER AND EXECUTIVE DIRECTOR, CENTER FOR SCIENCE IN THE PUBLIC INTEREST

WRITTEN FOR *CQ RESEARCHER*, NOVEMBER 2012

A great many things contribute to America's horrific obesity epidemic, and it's going to take a wide range of government policies to help Americans eat better (and less) and exercise much more. But at the top of any serious policy maker's list should be a concerted effort to reduce Americans' out-of-control consumption of soda and other sugary drinks.

Soda plays a unique role in promoting obesity and other diet-related conditions such as heart disease and diabetes. Unlike most foods, soda has no redeeming protein, vitamins, minerals or dietary fiber — just sugar, usually in the form of high fructose corn syrup, and sometimes questionable chemicals. Sugary sodas are the largest single contributor of excess calories in American diets and have been proven in studies to consistently cause weight gain. These drinks are a problem because so many Americans consume huge volumes of them, and because, unlike the calories in solid foods, the calories in soda aren't fully recognized by the body — meaning that people don't compensate by eating or drinking less of other things. All in all, it's as if soda were engineered for the specific purpose of promoting obesity: a time-delayed metabolic bioweapon.

Fortunately, we've seen progress. Schools have largely expelled soda (though not high-calorie Gatorade-type "sports" drinks). Calorie counts coming to menu boards will remind consumers of soda's heavily caloric payload. Mayors in Boston, Philadelphia, San Antonio, San Francisco and elsewhere have eliminated or reduced soda in vending machines on public property. New York City has instituted a sensible 16-ounce cap on the size of sodas sold in the city's restaurants. And cash-strapped city and state governments are considering taxes on soft drinks — both for the desperately needed revenue and to reduce consumption.

Government could also end a subsidy to the soda industry that might be as high as $4 billion a year by testing the effectiveness of prohibiting the use of Supplemental Nutrition Assistance Program (SNAP) benefits (formerly food stamps) to buy sugary drinks. The program already excludes other products that don't make nutritional sense, such as tobacco, dietary supplements and ready-to-eat hot foods. Simultaneously, the SNAP program could subsidize the purchase of fresh produce and perhaps other especially healthful foods.

To do nothing — while sugary drinks fuel an epidemic of obesity and other expensive diseases — would be reckless from a public health and a fiscal standpoint.

no

KATHERINE MANGU-WARD
***MANAGING EDITOR,* REASON MAGAZINE**

WRITTEN FOR *CQ RESEARCHER*, NOVEMBER 2012

As any student of history knows, Americans can get pretty testy when the government tries to meddle with their beverage of choice. While it's hard to imagine modern Bostonians dumping cans of Coca-Cola Classic into the harbor in protest, Americans still don't like government telling them what to drink.

When it comes to curbing soda consumption, governments at all levels tend to tax first, ask questions later. But where soda taxes have been implemented, the consumption of sugary drinks hasn't gone down. Instead, state revenues have gone up. And that's not a coincidence. Soda drinkers tend to be poorer than nondrinkers — making any such tax regressive — but they aren't terribly price sensitive when it comes to that large Pepsi. After all, there's already a free alternative out there waiting to quench thirst. Meanwhile, there are no serious proposals afoot to apply a similar tax to Jamba Juice, Starbucks pumpkin lattes or similarly sugary drinks preferred by wealthier consumers.

Awareness campaigns are an easier sell. What's wrong with giving consumers more information? But government-funded ad campaigns about the contribution of soda to obesity have their limits as well. They're not exactly conveying breaking news, for one thing: No one thinks that a full-sugar soda is a health food. To compensate, public awareness campaigns tend to overstate their case in their zeal to do good and drive the message home. The New York City Department of Health ran ads in January showing a black and white photo of an obese man whose right leg appeared to have been amputated behind a reminder to drink smaller cups of soda. Just one problem: The chunky man in the ad actually has two healthy legs. One was photoshopped out for propaganda purposes. New York Mayor Michael Bloomberg defended the decision, saying: "You can't have it both ways. Do you want to help people or do you not want to annoy people?"

But the main reason government shouldn't fiddle with our drink orders is one that those guys who once dumped tea in the Boston Harbor would understand: People should be free to make their own choices and their own mistakes. People engage in all kinds of "unhealthy" behaviors like eating jellybeans and "forgetting" to floss. Some of those behaviors cost taxpayers money and some don't, but just because something is a terrible idea doesn't mean it is the business of the state to advise against, restrict, tax or otherwise limit it.

Continued from p. 1028

requiring calorie counts on the labels of drinks sold in the hospital. [82]

Similar policies are under consideration or being implemented outside the United States as well. In October, the United Kingdom unveiled new front-of-the-package nutrition labels that highlight calorie counts and total sugar amounts. The labels, which will be voluntary for the food industry, will debut in 2013. [83]

In Denmark, however, lawmakers are considering repealing two new junk-food taxes: those on high-fat foods — already in effect — and on sugary foods, set to begin next year. Businesses complained that they'd lost revenues as Danes drive to nearby countries such as Germany to buy lower-priced goodies. Fewer than 5 percent of Danes approve of higher prices for sugared goods such as sweetened yogurt and jam, but nearly half say they'd be willing to pay more for sugary drinks. [84]

Studying Sugar

No one doubts that if people consume more calories than they burn, they'll gain weight and potentially could develop diseases such as Type 2 diabetes. The jury is still out, however, on whether calories from sugar are more to blame than other calories, and new research is beginning to test that proposition.

Earlier this month, the National Institutes of Health convened experts to begin designing a research agenda for determining how the body digests and uses fructose and whether the process has negative health effects. [85]

"Taking in too much energy" — calories — "that is not burned off at the end of the day" is a known risk factor for heart disease, but some recent research suggests that calories from sugar may increase the risk even more, says Christina M. Shay, an assistant professor of biostatistics and epidemiology at the University of Oklahoma College of Public Health in Oklahoma City.

In one rigorous study, all the participants lost weight after being put on diets, but those who reduced their consumption of sugar-sweetened beverages saw the greatest reductions in blood pressure, Shay says. In this study and others, she says, the evidence has been "pretty convincing" that sugar consumption causes other health risks besides excess calorie intake. But the studies have had very small sample sizes, so additional research is needed, she says. If the results hold up, it could open the door to improving blood-pressure control by, for example, limiting intake of high fructose corn syrup (the main sweetener used in most sodas today), she notes.

Researchers now are reanalyzing data collected in older, large, long-term observational studies of nutrition and health, says Shay. "Now we're going back and looking at the data we have" to see if adverse health effects correlate with HFCS consumption. "The older observational data are gold mines" for further testing of some new hypotheses about the effects of sugar, Shay says.

Such analyses, along with "gold-standard" randomized control trials and laboratory studies of cellular mechanisms involved in sugar metabolism, will be needed to develop solid answers, scientists say.

It's difficult — and expensive — to get solid answers from nutrition research, says Kaiser of the University of Alabama. To truly verify what people have eaten, for example, it's usually necessary to confine them in a research center, a pricey proposition that makes it hard to get study volunteers, she says. Otherwise, ordered not to drink a sugar-sweetened beverage, "they may decide they need a Snickers bar" instead, without telling researchers, she says.

Another avenue of current study involves the possible relationship between glucose and cancer-cell growth. All human cells, including tumor cells, use the simple sugar glucose as their primary fuel.

Nearly a third of some common cancers — including breast and colon cancers — have so-called insulin receptors on their surface, according to Lewis Cantley, head of the Cancer Center at Weill Cornell Medical College in New York City, who hopes to find a drug that can cut off cancer cells' glucose supply. Insulin binds to these receptors and signals the tumor to start consuming glucose. [86]

The role, if any, of dietary sugar in cancer development is unknown. However, some scientists studying the question offer the same dietary advice as many others who study the health effects of sugars: Consume them with care.

"I have eliminated refined sugar from my diet and eat as little as I possibly can," said Craig Thompson, president of Memorial Sloan-Kettering Cancer Center in New York, who has also studied the insulin-tumor link. "I believe, ultimately, it's something I can do to decrease my risk of cancer." [87] ■

OUTLOOK

Focusing on Sugar

Many scientists caution that more rigorous research is needed in order to conclude that sugars are — or aren't — the key to cutting obesity and reducing disease risk. Others, however, argue that, since added sugars don't actually add nutrients to anyone's diet and excess calories clearly are a problem, governments are justified in adopting public-health efforts to restrict added-sugar consumption.

Purdue's Mattes contends that rigorous studies must be conducted before concluding that restricting sugar is the key to conquering obesity. Without solid research, later science could end up debunking the link between sugar and adverse health effects, he says.

And reporters and policymakers should be careful not to over-interpret early studies, says the University of

Alabama's Kaiser. "Statistics are only the arbiter of proof" when they are validated by additional studies, she says. One study — no matter how strong and impressive it seems — "does not an answer make."

Some analysts predict that policies to discourage overconsumption of sugar-sweetened beverages will move ahead anyway. "We'll see a lot of movement" toward new taxes on sugar-sweetened drinks, says Johns Hopkins' Bleich, adding that soda taxes could be "a huge revenue generator" for cash-strapped states.

But Ludwig of Boston Children's Hospital believes progress by states and local governments in limiting sugary drinks in schools or raising soda taxes will be slow because "the industry has a lot of influence." Nevertheless, evidence is accumulating that limiting consumption of sugar-sweetened beverages helps curb obesity. "Ultimately, the truth does prevail" in such matters, he says. "The question is, How much delay will there be?"

One "obvious place to begin," he says, would be to remove sugar-sweetened beverages from items that can be purchased with food stamps. "We estimate that about $4 billion in taxpayer money is being used to buy sugary beverages" for food stamp recipients, he says. As a result, "the public is likely to pay twice" when obesity-related health problems occur in those populations, because Medicaid and Medicare end up paying for many of those costs, Ludwig says.

In any event, some voluntary industry actions will soon take effect. The American Beverage Association, for example, has promised to provide healthier beverages at schools, says the University of Illinois' Taber.

Replacing low-fiber, sugary, processed foods with high-fiber, low-sugar foods such as fresh vegetables, fruits and grass-fed beef is already feasible, said Lustig. "Years ago we couldn't [make that switch] because we didn't have the distribution system to be able to do it. We have it now," he said. [88]

But food sales are a major economic engine, and for the government to admit that it's pushing the food system in a new direction because the older one wasn't very healthy would have serious repercussions for international sales, Lustig says.

"The question is, When does health finally win out?" asks Lustig. "When is the tipping point?" ■

Notes

[1] Dylan Stableford, "Bloomberg's Big-soda Ban Approved by NYC Health Board," Yahoo!News, Sept. 13, 2012, http://news.yahoo.com/blogs/lookout/nyc-soda-ban-bloomberg-163224412.html.

[2] Quoted in *ibid.*

[3] For background, see "Reversing the Epidemic: The New York City Obesity Task Force Plan to Prevent and Control Obesity," New York City, May 31, 2012, p. 12, www.nyc.gov/html/om/pdf/2012/otf_report.pdf; "Adult Obesity Facts," Centers for Disease Control and Prevention, www.cdc.gov/obesity/data/adult.html.

[4] Nadia Arumugam, "Why Soda Ban Will Work in Fight Against Obesity; Food Regulations Have Proven Record," *Forbes*, Sept. 14, 2012, www.forbes.com/sites/nadiaarumugam/2012/09/14/why-soda-ban-will-work-in-fight-against-obesity-food-regulations-have-a-proven-record.

[5] "Board of Health Rubberstamps Mayor's Ban, Goes Against Wishes of New Yorkers," New Yorkers for Beverage Choice, Sept. 13, 2012, http://nycbeveragechoices.com/news.

[6] "Adult Obesity," Harvard School of Public Health, www.hsph.harvard.edu/obesity-prevention-source/obesity-trends/obesity-rates-worldwide/index.html.

[7] "Soaring Health Care Costs Highlight Need to Address Childhood Obesity," Office of the State Comptroller, New York, October 2012, http://osc.state.ny.us/reports/obesity_and_child_obesity_10_23_12.pdf.

[8] "Robert Lustig: Transcript," "Here's the Thing with Alec Baldwin," WNYC Radio, July 2, 2012, www.wnyc.org/shows/heresthething/2012/jul/02/transcript.

[9] "Profiling Food Consumption in America," *Agriculture Fact Book 2000*, Chapter 2, pp. 16-17, www.usda.gov/factbook/chapter2.pdf.

[10] "The Obesity Epidemic," transcript, "Health Report," ABC Radio National [Australia], July 9, 2001, www.abc.net.au/radionational/programs/healthreport/the-obesity-epidemic/3240406.

[11] "Beverage Industry Addresses Sugar-Sweetened Beverages and Obesity Articles in the *New England Journal of Medicine*," American Beverage Association, Sept. 21, 2012, www.ameribev.org/news-media/news--releases--statements/more/285.

[12] *Ibid.*

[13] Quoted in Trevor Butterworth, "The Sugar Wars: Science's Fierce, Geeky Debate Over Soda," *The Awl*, Oct. 8, 2012, www.theawl.com/2012/10/the-sugar-wars.

[14] Emily J. McCallister, *et al.*, "Ten Putative Contributors to the Obesity Epidemic," *Critical Reviews in Science and Nutrition*, Dec. 2, 2009.

[15] Angie L. Cradock, *et al.*, "Effect of School District Policy Change on Consumption of Sugar-sweetened Beverages Among High School Students, Boston, Massachusetts, 2004-2006," *Preventing Chronic Disease*, July 2011, www.cdc.gov/pcd/issues/2011/jul/10_0149.htm.

[16] Caroline S. Fox, *et al.*, "Trends in the Incidence of Type 2 Diabetes Mellitus From the 1970s to the 1990s: Framingham Heart Study," *Circulation*, June 27, 2006, pp. 2914-2918.

[17] Cara B. Ebbeling, *et al.*, "A Randomized Trial of Sugar-Sweetened Beverages and Adolescent Body Weight," *The New England Journal of Medicine*, Oct. 11, 2012, p. 1407.

[18] "Not So Sweet: Increased Added Sugars Intake Parallels Trends in Weight Gain," *Science Daily*/American Heart Association, March 25, 2011, www.sciencedaily.com/releases/2011/03/110324162229.htm.

[19] Richard D. Mattes, *et al.*, "Nutritively Sweetened Beverage Consumption and Body Weight: A Systematic Review and Meta-analysis of Randomized Experiments," *Obesity Reviews*, 2010.

[20] Stephan Guyenet, "Is Sugar Fattening?" Whole Health Source: Ancestral Nutrition and Health blog, Feb. 22, 2012, http://wholehealthsource.blogspot.com/2012/06/new-study-demonstrates-that-sugar-has.html; for background, see "National Health and Nutrition Examination Study," Centers for Disease Control and Prevention, www.cdc.gov/nchs/nhanes/about_nhanes.htm.

[21] "The Obesity Epidemic," *op. cit.*

[22] Cynthia Ogden and Margaret Carroll, "Prevalence of Obesity Among Children and Adolescents: United States, Trends 1963-1965 Through 2007-2008," National Center for Health Statistics, Health E-Stat, Centers for Disease Control and Prevention, www.cdc.gov/nchs/data/hestat/obesity_child_07_08/obesity_child_07_08.htm.

[23] For background, see "Fatty Liver Disease," WebMD, www.webmd.com/hepatitis/fatty-liver-disease.
[24] For background, see Elisa Fabbrini, *et al.*, "Intrahepatic Fat, Not Visceral Fat, Is Linked With Metabolic Complications of Obesity," *PNAS* [Proceedings of the National Academy of Sciences of the United States], Sept. 8, 2009, www.pnas.org/content/106/36/15430.
[25] Luc Tappy, "Metabolic Effects of Fructose and the Worldwide Increase in Obesity," *Physiology Review*, January 2010, pp. 23-46.
[26] *Ibid.*
[27] Quoted in David Despain, "Fate of Fructose: Interview with Dr. John Sievenpiper," Evolving Health blog, May 26, 2012, http://evolvinghealthscience.blogspot.com/2012/05/fate-of-fructose-interview-with-dr-john.html.
[28] *Ibid.*
[29] Quoted in Butterworth, *op. cit.*
[30] Quoted in *ibid.*
[31] "Robert Lustig: Transcript," *op. cit.*
[32] Deborah A. Cohen and Susan H. Babey, "Candy at the Cash Register — A Risk Factor for Obesity and Chronic Disease," *The New England Journal of Medicine*, Oct. 11, 2012, www.nejm.org/doi/full/10.1056/NEJMp1209443.
[33] Nicholas D. Kristof, "Miracle Tax Diet," *The New York Times*, Dec. 17, 2008, www.nytimes.com/2008/12/18/opinion/18kristof.html.
[34] "Ingredient Portfolio," Cargill, Inc., p. 17, www.cargillfoods.com/wcm/groups/public/@cseg/@food/@all/documents/document/na3046087.pdf.
[35] Robbin S. Johnson, "Caloric Sweetened Beverage Taxes: The Good Food/Bad Food Trap," *Choices*, October 2011, www.choices-magazine.org/choices-magazine/policy-issues/caloric-sweetened-beverage-taxes-the-good-foodbad-food-trap.
[36] *Ibid.*
[37] David R. Just and Brian Wansink, "Do Not Support Regulation of Sugar-Sweetened Beverages," *The New England Journal of Medicine*, Oct. 11, 2012, p. 1465.
[38] *Ibid.*
[39] Jason Fletcher, "Soda Taxes and Substitution Effects: Will Obesity Be Affected?" *Choices Magazine*, Agricultural and Applied Economics Association, 3rd Quarter 2011, www.choicesmagazine.org/magazine/pdf/cmsarticle_188.pdf.
[40] For background see Kenneth F. Kiple and Kriemhild Conee Ornelas, eds., "Sugar," Chapter II.F.2, *The Cambridge World History of Food*, www.cambridge.org/us/books/kiple/sugar.htm; Barbara Mantel, "Preventing Obesity," *CQ Researcher*, Oct. 1, 2010, pp. 797-820.
[41] Guyenet, *op. cit.*
[42] "History of Candy Including a Candy History Time Chart," B. W. Clifford, Inc., www.bwcliffordcandy.com/historyofcandyincludingacandyhistorytimechart.aspx.
[43] For background, see Tom Philpott, "A Reflection on the Lasting Legacy of 1970s USDA Secretary Earl Butz," *Grist*, Feb. 8, 2008, http://grist.org/article/the-butz-stops-here.
[44] "Fact Sheet, Food Without Thought: How U.S. Farm Policy Contributes to Obesity," Institute for Agriculture and Trade Policy, www.nffc.net/Learn/Fact%20Sheets/Obesity%20and%20Ag.pdf.
[45] "Robert Lustig: Transcript," *op. cit.*
[46] Jeffrey Kluger, "How America's Children Packed on the Pounds," *Time*, June 12, 2008, www.time.com/time/magazine/article/0,9171,1813985,00.html.
[47] For background, see Obesity, World Heart Federation website, www.world-heart-federation.org/cardiovascular-health/cardiovascular-disease-risk-factors/obesity; Kathleen Doheny, "The Truth About Fat," WebMD, July 13, 2009, webmd.com/diet/features/the-truth-about-fat.
[48] For background, see Jacques Peretti, "Why Our Food Is Making Us Fat," *Guardian* [UK], June 11, 2012, www.guardian.co.uk/business/2012/jun/11/why-our-food-is-making-us-fat, and Gary Taubes and Cristin Kearns Couzens, "Sweet Little Lies," *Mother Jones*, November/December 2012, p. 35, www.motherjones.com/environment/2012/10/sugar-industry-lies-campaign.
[49] Taubes and Couzens, *op. cit.*, p. 37.
[50] *Ibid.*
[51] Gary Taubes, "The Soft Science of Dietary Fat," *Science*, March, 30, 2001, pp. 2536-2545.
[52] "Adult Obesity Facts: Obesity is common, serious and costly," Centers for Disease Control and Prevention, www.cdc.gov/obesity/data/adult.html. Also see "Obesity and Overweight," FastStats, Centers for Disease Control and Prevention, www.cdc.gov/nchs/fastats/overwt.htm.
[53] "Defining Overweight and Obesity," U.S. Centers for Disease Control and Prevention, www.cdc.gov/obesity/adult/defining.html.
[54] John Craig, "Leading the War on Obesity," *On Wisconsin*, Spring 2012, http://onwisconsin.uwalumni.com/features/leading-the-war-on-obesity.
[55] "Profiling Food Consumption in America," Chap. 2, *Agriculture Fact Book 2000*, pp. 16-17, www.usda.gov/factbook/chapter2.pdf.
[56] Jean A. Walsh, *et al.*, "Consumption of Added Sugars Is Decreasing in the United States," *American Journal of Clinical Nutrition*, September 2011, pp. 726-734; Genevra Pittman, "Little Change in U.S. Obesity Rates in Recent Years," Reuters, Jan. 17, 2012, www.reuters.com/article/2012/01/17/us-obesity-rates-idUSTRE80G1J320120117.
[57] "Profiling Food Consumption in America," *op. cit.*
[58] David M. Cutler, Edward L. Glaeswer and Jesse M. Shapiro, "Why Have Americans Become More Obese," *Journal of Economic Perspectives*, Summer 2003, pp. 93-118, http://dash.harvard.edu/bitstream/handle/1/2640583/cutler_obese.pdf?sequence=2.
[59] Scott Drenkard, "Overreaching on Obesity: Governments Consider New Taxes on Soda and Candy," Tax Foundation, October 2011, http://taxfoundation.org/article/overreaching-obesity-governments-consider-new-taxes-soda-and-candy.
[60] Fletcher, *op. cit.*; also see Jason M. Fletcher, David E. Frisvold and Nathan Tefft, "The Effects of Soft Drink Taxes on Child and Adolescent Consumption and Weight Outcomes," *Journal of Public Economics*, Sept. 17, 2010.
[61] Fletcher, *et al.*, *ibid.*
[62] Fletcher, *op. cit.*; *ibid.*
[63] "Beverages Sold in Public Schools, Bridging the Gap," August 2012, www.bridgingthegapresearch.org/_asset/7jf02g/BTG_competitive_beverage_brief_final-8-7-12.pdf.

About the Author

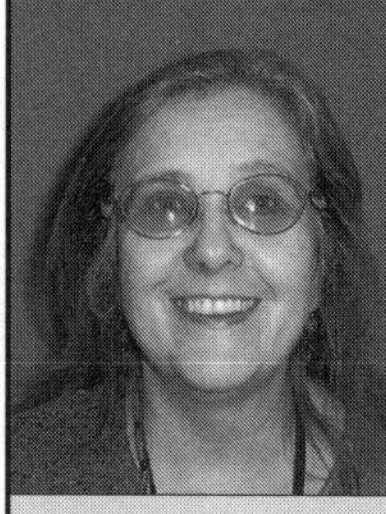

Staff writer **Marcia Clemmitt** is a veteran social-policy reporter who previously served as editor in chief of *Medicine & Health* and staff writer for *The Scientist*. She has also been a high school math and physics teacher. She holds a liberal arts and sciences degree from St. John's College, Annapolis, and a master's degree in English from Georgetown University. Her recent reports include "Treating ADHD" and "Traumatic Brain Injury."

FOR MORE INFORMATION

American Beverage Association, 1101 16th St., N.W., Washington, DC 20036; 202-463-6732; www.ameribev.org. Membership group that promotes the interests of companies that produce non-alcoholic beverages.

Caloric Calculator, http://caloriccalculator.org/calc. Developed at Columbia University's Mailman School of Public Health to show how different food, exercise choices and policy interventions would affect child and teen obesity rates.

Health Policy Center, University of Illinois at Chicago, Institute for Health Research and Policy, (MC 275), Westside Research Office Building, 5th floor, 1747 West Roosevelt Rd., Chicago, IL 60608; 312-996-7222; www.ihrp.uic.edu/center/health-policy-center. Studies the effects of policies to limit sugar consumption.

The Obesity Society, 8757 Georgia Ave., Suite 1320, Silver Spring, MD 20910; 301-563-6526; www.obesity.org. Membership group for scientists studying obesity's causes, treatment and prevention.

Rudd Center for Food Policy and Obesity, Yale University, P.O. Box 208369, New Haven, CT 06520-8369; 203-432-6700; www.yaleruddcenter.org. University-based center that studies and advocates for policy interventions to prevent obesity, improve diets and decrease stigmatization based on weight.

The Skinny on Obesity, UCTV, Youtube/University of California. Documentary series by University of California, San Francisco, pediatric endocrinologist Robert Lustig, who argues that sugar and processed foods are the primary causes of the obesity epidemic.

The Sugar Association, 1300 L St., N.W., Suite 1001, Washington, DC 20005; 202-785-1122; www.sugar.org. Sugar-industry group that promotes sugar as a wholesome dietary component.

Trust for America's Health, 1730 M St., N.W., Suite 900, Washington, DC 20036; 202-223-9870; http://healthyamericans.org. Nonpartisan group that promotes preventive health care as a national priority; publishes annual "F as in Fat" report on trends in Americans' weight status, diet and exercise.

[64] "Food Marketing: Can 'Voluntary' Government Restrictions Improve Children's Health?" Preliminary Transcript, joint hearing, House Energy and Commerce Subcommittees on Commerce, Manufacturing and Trade and Health, Oct. 12, 2011, http://democrats.energycommerce.house.gov/sites/default/files/image_uploads/Transcript_10.12.11_Hearing_CMT-HE_0.pdf.

[65] Quoted in *ibid.*

[66] Quoted in E. J. Schultz, "FTC Attempt to Limit Food Marketing to Kids Loses Steam," *Advertising Age*, May 7, 2012, http://adage.com/article/news/ftc-attempt-limit-food-marketing-kids-loses-steam/234583.

[67] Quoted in "Ronald McDonald — Ambassador of Goodwill — or Purveyor of Poor Health?" *Knowledge at Wharton Today*, May 19, 2011, https://knowledgetoday.wharton.upenn.edu/tag/ronald-mcdonald.

[68] "Children's Food and Beverage Advertising Initiative," Council of Better Business Bureaus, July 2011, www.bbb.org/us/storage/16/documents/cfbai/CFBAI-Category-Specific-Uniform-Nutrition-Criteria.pdf.

[69] Quoted in Margo Wootan and David Ludwig, "Sugary Cereal: Breakfast Candy or Obesity Cure?" *The Atlantic*, April 24, 2012, www.theatlantic.com/health/archive/2012/04/sugary-cereal-breakfast-candy-or-obesity-cure/256293.

[70] "Kids Need Healthy Food, Not Hyped Junk," Environmental Working Group, http://action.ewg.org/p/dia/action/public/?action_KEY=1943&tag=foodmarketingfb.

[71] "Obesity and Overweight," Centers for Disease Control and Prevention, www.cdc.gov/nchs/fastats/overwt.htm.

[72] Stableford, *op. cit.*

[73] Quoted in *ibid.*

[74] Thomas Farley, "Support Regulation of Sugar-Sweetened Beverages," *The New England Journal of Medicine*, Oct. 11, 2012, p. 1464.

[75] David McLaughlin, "NYC Big Soda Ban Challenged in Court by Industry Groups," Bloomberg News, Oct. 13, 2012, www.bloomberg.com/news/2012-10-12/nyc-big-soda-ban-challenged-in-court-by-industry-groups-1-.html.

[76] Mike DeBonis, "A Bloomberg-style Soda Ban for DC?" *Washington Post blogs*, Oct. 22, 2012, www.washingtonpost.com/blogs/mike-debonis/wp/2012/10/22/a-bloomberg-style-soda-ban-for-d-c; Jennifer Delgado, "Many Are No Longer Sweet on Soft Drinks," *Chicago Tribune*, July 8, 2012, http://articles.chicagotribune.com/2012-07-08/news/ct-talk-sugary-drink-bans-0708-20120708_1_sugary-drinks-soft-drinks-american-beverage-association.

[77] "Portland Schools Ban Soda Sales, Aim for Healthier Snacks," WCSH News 6, Aug. 17, 2012, www.wcsh6.com/news/local/story.aspx?storyid=211089.

[78] Sam Allen, "Voters Reject Tax on Sugary Drinks in 2 California Cities," *Los Angeles Times*, Nov. 8, 2012, http://articles.latimes.com/2012/nov/08/local/la-me-soda-tax-20121108.

[79] Rosie Mestel, "An 'Added Sugar' Label on Foods? Stop! You're Confusing Me!" *Los Angeles Times*, Aug. 3, 2012, www.latimes.com/health/boostershots/la-heb-fda-added-sugar-label-foods-20120803,0,7009961.story.

[80] "Nutrition Standards in the National School Lunch and School Breakfast Programs," *Federal Register*, Jan. 26, 2012, www.gpo.gov/fdsys/pkg/FR-2012-01-26/pdf/2012-1010.pdf.

[81] Quoted in Benjamin Wood, "Students, Parents, Educators Displeased With New School Lunch Standards," *Deseret News*, Sept. 27, 2012, www.deseretnews.com/article/865563339/Students-parents-educators-displeased-with-new-school-lunch-standards.html?pg=all.

[82] Delgado, *op. cit.*

[83] Florence Derrick, "New Food Labeling System Revealed," *Resource Magazine* [UK], Oct. 24, 2012, www.resource.uk.com/article/Retailers/New_food_labelling_system_revealed-2355#.ULJbfeOe-pE.

[84] Asbjørn Kristensen Høgsbro, "Slim Chances for Denmark's 'Fat Tax,' " Bertelsmann Stiftung, July 24, 2012, http://futurechallenges.org/local/slim-chances-for-denmark%E2%80%99s-%E2%80%98fat-tax%E2%80%99.

[85] "Clinical Researcher Strategies for Fructose Metabolism," National Institute of Diabetes and Digestive and Kidney Diseases, www2.niddk.nih.gov/News/Calendar/FructoseMetab2012.htm.

[86] Quoted in "Is Sugar Toxic?" Transcript, CNN/"60 Minutes," April 28, 2012, http://transcripts.cnn.com/TRANSCRIPTS/1204/28/hcsg.01.html.

[87] Quoted in Gary Taubes, "Is Sugar Toxic?" *The New York Times*, April 13, 2011, www.nytimes.com/2011/04/17/magazine/mag-17Sugar-t.html?pagewanted=all&_r=0.

[88] "Robert Lustig: Transcript," *op. cit.*

Bibliography

Selected Sources

Books

Abbott, Elizabeth, *Sugar: A Bittersweet History*, Overlook, 2011.

A research associate at the University of Toronto recounts the history of humanity's quest for a sugary diet, including the role sugar played in the expansion of slavery and Europeans' conquest of lands suitable for growing sugarcane.

Lustig, Robert H., *Fat Chance: Beating the Odds Against Sugar, Processed Foods, Obesity and Disease*, Hudson Street Press, 2012.

A pediatric endocrinologist at the University of California-San Francisco argues that increased consumption of sugars and highly processed foods is the key cause of the rise in obesity and obesity-related diseases.

Articles

Begley, Sharon, "RPT-Can It! Soda Studies Cite Stronger Link to Obesity," Reuters, Sept. 21, 2012, www.reuters.com/article/2012/09/22/health-obesity-soda-idUSL1E8KLFUC20120922.

New, randomized clinical trial data suggest that sugar-sweetened beverages have played a substantial role in the obesity epidemic.

Butterworth, Trevor, "The Sugar Wars: Science's Fierce, Geeky Debate Over Soda," *The Awl*, Oct. 8, 2012, www.theawl.com/2012/10/the-sugar-wars.

The keynote session of this year's annual meeting of the Obesity Society featured a discussion of whether the current science on sugar's relationship to obesity is strong enough to justify policy actions such as taxes and restrictions on sugar consumption.

Cohen, Deborah A., and Susan H. Babey, "Candy at the Cash Register — A Risk Factor for Obesity and Chronic Disease," *The New England Journal of Medicine*, Oct. 11, 2012, p. 1381, www.nejm.org/doi/full/10.1056/NEJMp1209443.

Health-policy analysts at the RAND Corp. think tank (Cohen) and the University of California, Los Angeles, (Babey) argue that public-health agencies should consider restricting the marketing of sugary foods in order to curb impulse buying of unhealthy products.

Guyenet, Stephan, "Is Sugar Fattening?" Whole Health Source blog, Feb. 22, 2012, http://wholehealthsource.blogspot.com/2012/02/is-sugar-fattening.html.

A University of Washington nutrition researcher discusses the evolutionary history of humans' sugar consumption and what it suggests about the findings of recent research on sugar and obesity.

Peretti, Jacques, "Why Our Food Is Making Us Fat," *The Guardian* [UK], June 11, 2012, www.guardian.co.uk/business/2012/jun/11/why-our-food-is-making-us-fat.

As early as the 1970s, some scientists and policymakers favored policies to encourage lower sugar consumption, but the industry's economic clout made governments reluctant to act. That may be changing as the health and financial burdens of obesity rise, however.

Reports and Studies

"F As in Fat: How Obesity Threatens America's Future 2012," Trust for America's Health, September 2012, http://healthyamericans.org/assets/files/TFAH2012FasInFatFnlRv.pdf.

Obesity-prevention efforts are increasing in the United States, especially for children and teens, according to a foundation-funded group that promotes disease prevention. If rising obesity trends are not slowed, coronary heart disease, Type 2 diabetes and stroke rates could jump tenfold by 2020, the group says.

Drenkard, Scott, "Overreaching on Obesity: Governments Consider New Taxes on Soda and Candy," Tax Foundation, October 2011, http://taxfoundation.org/article/overreaching-obesity-governments-consider-new-taxes-soda-and-candy.

An analyst for a corporation-founded think tank that favors a flat, simple tax structure and low tax rates recounts the history of taxes levied on sugar-sweetened food. He argues that increasing such taxes would unfairly burden even people who don't consume enough sugar to become obese and could lead to unintended consequences, as when tobacco-tax increases led to smuggling.

McCallister, Emily J., *et al.*, "Ten Putative Contributors to the Obesity Epidemic," *Critical Reviews in Science and Nutrition*, Dec. 2, 2009.

A focus on high fructose corn syrup consumption and declining exercise has diverted attention from other potential causes of obesity, says a group of medical scholars and statisticians. Contributing causes may include certain infections; a lack of adequate sleep and environmental toxins that lead to hormone imbalances.

Wang, Y. Claire, *et al.*, "A Penny-per-ounce Tax on Sugar-sweetened Beverages Would Cut Health and Cost Burdens of Diabetes," *Health Affairs*, January 2012, pp. 199-207.

Biostatistics and health-policy scholars from New York's Columbia University and the University of California-San Francisco argue that soda taxes are justified because current beverage prices don't take into account the costs to society of consuming them.

The Next Step:

Additional Articles from Current Periodicals

Artificial Sweeteners

Chang, Kenneth, "Artificial Sweeteners: Doubts by the Teaspoonful," *Honolulu Star-Advertiser*, June 12, 2012, www.staradvertiser.com/news/20120612_Artificial_sweeteners_Doubts_by_the_teaspoonful.html?id=158538665.

The scientific community disagrees on the safety and long-term health effects of artificial sweeteners.

Choi, Candice, "Coke, Pepsi Racing for a Better No-Calorie Soda," The Associated Press, July 26, 2012, www.huffingtonpost.com/2012/07/26/coke-pepsi-no-calories-soda_n_1705083.html.

Coca-Cola and Pepsi are trying to develop a soda with no calories or artificial sweeteners.

Komaroff, Anthony, "Natural Sources of Sweetness Are Better Than Artificial," *Lake County* (Ill.) *News-Sun*, May 21, 2012, newssun.suntimes.com/lifestyles/komaroff/12658749-423/natural-sources-of-sweetness-are-better-than-artificial.html.

Artificial sweeteners may promote long-term weight gain by discouraging people from eating less sweet — but healthier — foods such as fruits and vegetables, says a medical columnist.

Fructose

Lazarus, David, "A Sour Note for Sweetener Makers," *Los Angeles Times*, June 5, 2012, p. B1, articles.latimes.com/2012/jun/05/business/la-fi-lazarus-20120605.

The Food and Drug Administration has rejected a request from the Corn Refiners Association to change the name of high fructose corn syrup to "corn sugar."

Ungar, Laura, "Is High Fructose Corn Syrup Ruining Your Health?" *Courier-Journal* (Ky.), June 20, 2012, p. A1, www.courier-journal.com/article/20120620/prime06/306200001/Is-high-fructose-corn-syrup-ruining-your-health-.

There is no conclusive evidence that identifies high fructose corn syrup as a primary cause of obesity and diabetes.

Obesity

Connor, Erinn, "Debate Over Soda Made Complex by a Variety of Factors," *Herald News* (N.J.), June 24, 2012, p. E1, www.northjersey.com/news/160154785_Debate_over_soda_made_complex_by_variety_of_factors.html.

Regular soda consumption will not increase body weight if other healthy habits are maintained, says a New Jersey nutritionist.

Healy, Melissa, "Expanding on Soda's Role in Growing Obesity," *Los Angeles Times*, Sept. 22, 2012, p. A1, articles.latimes.com/2012/sep/21/science/la-sci-obesity-soda-link-20120922.

Removing sugary drinks from kids' diets slows weight gain in overweight teens and reduces the risk that normal-weight children will become obese, studies show.

Hellmich, Nanci, "Is Sugar to Blame for Obesity?" *USA Today*, June 12, 2012, p. B10, usatoday30.usatoday.com/LIFE/usaedition/2012-06-12-War-on-sugar-sidebarART_ST_U.htm.

Sugar is only one cause of obesity, but it is the biggest cause for many people, says a nutrition professor.

Regulation

Amante, Maria, "Banning Large Sodas? New York Will, But Brown County Won't," *Green Bay* (Wis.) *Press-Gazette*, Sept. 19, 2012.

Brown County, Wis., plans to promote better health through education instead of bans on sugary beverages.

Brody, Jane E., "In Fighting Obesity, Drink Sizes Matter," *The New York Times*, Oct. 23, 2012, p. D7, well.blogs.nytimes.com/2012/10/22/in-fight-against-obesity-drink-sizes-matter/.

Other cities may follow New York's lead in limiting the size of sugary beverages.

Rogers, Robert, "Voters Resoundingly Reject Richmond 'Soda' Tax," *San Jose* (Calif.) *Mercury News*, Nov. 6, 2012, www.mercurynews.com/news/ci_21944292/richmond-soda-tax-gets-off-rough-start.

Voters in Richmond, Calif., have rejected a soda tax.

CITING *CQ RESEARCHER*

Sample formats for citing these reports in a bibliography include the ones listed below. Preferred styles and formats vary, so please check with your instructor or professor.

MLA STYLE

Jost, Kenneth. "Remembering 9/11," CQ Researcher 2 Sept. 2011: 701-732.

APA STYLE

Jost, K. (2011, September 2). Remembering 9/11. *CQ Researcher, 9*, 701-732.

CHICAGO STYLE

Jost, Kenneth. "Remembering 9/11." *CQ Researcher*, September 2, 2011, 701-732.

In-depth Reports on Issues in the News

Are you writing a paper?

Need backup for a debate?

Want to become an expert on an issue?

For more than 80 years, students have turned to *CQ Researcher* for in-depth reporting on issues in the news. Reports on a full range of political and social issues are now available. Following is a selection of recent reports:

Civil Liberties
Solitary Confinement, 9/12
Re-examining the Constitution, 9/12
Voter Rights, 5/12
Remembering 9/11, 9/11
Government Secrecy, 2/11

Crime/Law
Supreme Court Controversies, 9/12
Debt Collectors, 7/12
Criminal Records, 4/12
Police Misconduct, 4/12
Immigration Conflict, 3/12

Education
Arts Education, 3/12
Youth Volunteerism, 1/12
Digital Education, 12/11
Student Debt, 10/11

Environment/Society
Indecency on Television, 11/12
Managing Wildfires, 11/12
Understanding Mormonism, 10/12
Genetically Modified Food, 8/12
Whale Hunting, 6/12
U.S. Oil Dependence, 6/12

Health/Safety
New Health Care Law, 9/12
Farm Policy, 8/12
Treating ADHD, 8/12
Alcohol Abuse, 6/12

Politics/Economy
Social Media and Politics, 10/12
Euro Crisis, 10/12
Privatizing the Military, 7/12
U.S.-Europe Relations, 3/12
Attracting Jobs, 3/12
Presidential Election, 2/12

Upcoming Reports

3D Printing, 12/7/12 Housing Industry, 12/14/12 Plagiarism, 1/4/13

ACCESS

CQ Researcher is available in print and online. For access, visit your library or www.cqresearcher.com.

STAY CURRENT

For notice of upcoming *CQ Researcher* reports or to learn more about *CQ Researcher* products, subscribe to the free e-mail newsletters, *CQ Researcher Alert!* and *CQ Researcher News*: http://cqpress.com/newsletters.

PURCHASE

To purchase a *CQ Researcher* report in print or electronic format (PDF), visit www.cqpress.com or call 866-427-7737. Single reports start at $15. Bulk purchase discounts and electronic-rights licensing are also available.

SUBSCRIBE

Annual full-service *CQ Researcher* subscriptions—including 44 reports a year, monthly index updates, and a bound volume—start at $1,054. Add $25 for domestic postage.

CQ Researcher Online offers a backfile from 1991 and a number of tools to simplify research. For pricing information, call 800-834-9020, or e-mail librarymarketing@cqpress.com.

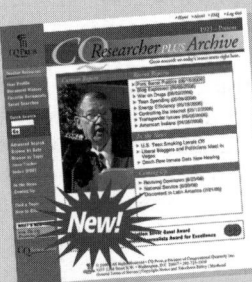

CQ Researcher

Published by CQ Press, an Imprint of SAGE Publications, Inc.

www.cqresearcher.com

3D Printing

Will it revolutionize manufacturing?

Used for years to make instant industrial prototypes, medical devices and other finished parts, 3D printers now are available in desktop models or inexpensive build-it-yourself kits — allowing anyone to create an object from a digital blueprint. Some Web-based companies provide 3D printing of customer-designed products, and Staples is even planning to install 3D printers in some stores in Europe. The surging activity surrounding 3D printing reminds many observers of the exciting early days of personal computing. Indeed, some experts see a decentralized manufacturing revolution in the making. Others caution that such cottage industry networks are a long way from replacing industrial-size factories. And with small-scale producers capable of making exact duplicates of objects, experts predict legal collisions with corporate patent-holders. Some experts also fear proliferation of 3D-printed weapons. But the steady expansion of 3D printing appears unstoppable.

3D printers, once largely limited to making prototypes for industry, now are used to turn out a growing number of products, including replacement parts for medicine and dentistry. Bre Pettis, CEO of Makerbot Industries, in Brooklyn, N.Y., manufactures small, inexpensive printers increasingly used in homes, offices and small-scale manufacturing firms.

INSIDE THIS REPORT

THE ISSUES 1039
BACKGROUND 1046
CHRONOLOGY 1047
CURRENT SITUATION 1052
AT ISSUE 1053
OUTLOOK 1055
BIBLIOGRAPHY 1058
THE NEXT STEP 1059

CQ Researcher • Dec. 7, 2012 • www.cqresearcher.com
Volume 22, Number 43 • Pages 1037-1060

Los Angeles | London | New Delhi
Singapore | Washington DC

RECIPIENT OF SOCIETY OF PROFESSIONAL JOURNALISTS AWARD FOR EXCELLENCE ◆ AMERICAN BAR ASSOCIATION SILVER GAVEL AWARD

THE ISSUES

1039 • Can 3D printing revive U.S. manufacturing?
• Will intellectual-property disputes slow the evolution of 3D printing?
• Does 3D printing of weapons pose a major security threat?

BACKGROUND

1046 **Forerunners**
In the 1820s, manufacturers and artists made machines that reproduced objects.

1048 **Mass Production**
American inventors made the United States a manufacturing leader.

1050 **Computers and CADs**
New technologies revolutionized office work and design in the 1950s.

1051 **Computer-aided Consumers**
3D printer kits for hobbyists have been available for several years.

CURRENT SITUATION

1052 **Printing Sanitation**
University of Washington students won $100,000 for a 3D-produced toilet.

1052 **Government Boost**
A new center is fostering 3D technology advances.

1054 **Bloomberg's Dream**
New York's mayor hopes 3D manufacturing will spark a high-tech boom.

OUTLOOK

1055 **Only the Beginning**
3D printing is the first stage of a manufacturing revolution.

SIDEBARS AND GRAPHICS

1040 **Use of Personal 3D Printers Skyrocketed**
More than 23,000 were owned worldwide in 2011.

1041 **Professional 3D Printing Continues to Grow**
Nearly 6,500 professional-grade 3D printers were sold in 2011.

1042 **3D Printing Pushes Medical Boundaries**
Applications range from artificial livers to hip implants.

1044 **3D Revenues Exploded**
Revenue from sales and service hit $1.7 billion in 2011.

1047 **Chronology**
Key events since 1819.

1048 **Magic of 3D Printing Captures Students' Interest**
"It was almost like a bucket of water being dumped on my head."

1053 **At Issue**
Is a new "micro-patent" needed to protect 3D innovators?

FOR FURTHER RESEARCH

1057 **For More Information**
Organizations to contact.

1058 **Bibliography**
Selected sources used.

1059 **The Next Step**
Additional articles.

1059 **Citing *CQ Researcher***
Sample bibliography formats.

Cover: Reuters/Handout

CQ Researcher

Dec. 7, 2012
Volume 22, Number 43

MANAGING EDITOR: Thomas J. Billitteri
tjb@cqpress.com

ASSISTANT MANAGING EDITOR: Kathy Koch
kkoch@cqpress.com

SENIOR CONTRIBUTING EDITOR:
Thomas J. Colin
tcolin@cqpress.com

ASSOCIATE EDITOR: Kenneth Jost

STAFF WRITER: Marcia Clemmitt

CONTRIBUTING WRITERS: Peter Katel, Barbara Mantel, Tom Price, Jennifer Weeks

SENIOR PROJECT EDITOR: Olu B. Davis

ASSISTANT EDITOR: Darrell Dela Rosa

FACT CHECKER: Michelle Harris

Los Angeles | London | New Delhi
Singapore | Washington DC

An Imprint of SAGE Publications, Inc.

VICE PRESIDENT AND EDITORIAL DIRECTOR, HIGHER EDUCATION GROUP:
Michele Sordi

DIRECTOR, ONLINE PUBLISHING:
Todd Baldwin

CQ Researcher (ISSN 1056-2036) is printed on acid-free paper. Published weekly, except: (March wk. 5) (May wk. 4) (July wk. 1) (Aug. wks. 3, 4) (Nov. wk. 4) and (Dec. wks. 3, 4). Published by SAGE Publications, Inc., 2455 Teller Rd., Thousand Oaks, CA 91320. Annual full-service subscriptions start at $1,054. For pricing, call 1-800-834-9020. To purchase a *CQ Researcher* report in print or electronic format (PDF), visit www.cqpress.com or call 866-427-7737. Single reports start at $15. Bulk purchase discounts and electronic-rights licensing are also available. Periodicals postage paid at Thousand Oaks, California, and at additional mailing offices. POSTMASTER: Send address changes to *CQ Researcher*, 2300 N St., N.W., Suite 800, Washington, DC 20037.

3D Printing

By Peter Katel

The Issues

Imagine an old-fashioned computer printer with an ink-squirting head that moves back and forth across a page printing text. Now imagine that instead of ink the head is discharging melted plastic, and the platform under it is moving to follow programmed commands from a three-dimension digital blueprint of an object. [1] The printer builds the object up from the bottom — applying successive layers of plastic or other material until the object is finished.

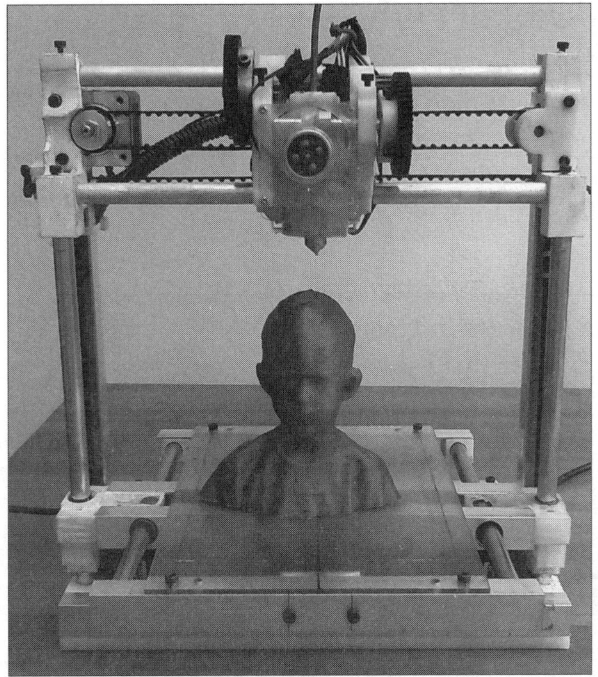

printxel.blogspot.com

3D printing is known as additive manufacturing (AM) because printers build up objects from the bottom — applying successive layers of liquid plastic or other material until an object, such as this bust of a child, is finished. This $300 hobbyist's 3D printer kit is made by Adjunct Engineering, a small firm in Iowa City. Other types of 3D printers use lasers or electron beams to form plastic or metal objects.

Though it sounds like science fiction, 3D printing is no imaginary concept. Indeed, the revolutionary method of producing products — even those with moving parts — is spreading far beyond research labs, garage workshops and factory prototype shops:

- A University of Pennsylvania bioengineer recently used a 3D printer to "print" a blood vessel system made of crystallized sugar in which liver cells could survive. (*See sidebar, p. 1042.*)
- A design firm based in Seattle and Munich recently "printed" out a pair of stereo headphones using a 3D printer;
- University of Washington students won a $100,000 international prize for developing a "printable" composting toilet made of recycled plastic, which could be produced in farming regions of developing countries. [2]

Known to industrial users as additive manufacturing, 3D printing has been used to make prototypes in factories for about 20 years, and somewhat more recently to produce dental replacements and surgical tools and models. [3] Now it is migrating into homes, conventional offices, science laboratories and small-scale manufacturing firms. And a printer that can spit out finished, three-dimensional products is inspiring 3D innovators to see limitless possibilities ahead.

Hod Lipson, director of Cornell University's Creative Machines Lab in Ithaca, N.Y., likens trying to envision future uses and societal impacts of 3D printing today to trying to imagine 40 years ago how computers would evolve. "If you put yourself back in the '70s, trying to think about which industries computers were going to affect, you would say the payroll industry, because it requires a lot of calculating done quickly; military technology, which has to predict ballistic trajectory; and maybe NASA. But e-commerce, Facebook — there was no equivalent in the '70s for those kinds of things."

Some say 3D printing could revolutionize manufacturing. "The 'killer app' in digital fabrication, as in computing, is personalization, producing products for a market of one person," writes physicist Neil Gershenfeld, director of the Massachusetts Institute of Technology's Center for Bits and Atoms, in Cambridge, Mass., where students used 3D printers to make products such as a hard-to-turn-off alarm clock for heavy sleepers. [4]

3D printing has unleashed a wave of cottage-industry enthusiasts and entrepreneurs, known as "makers," sometimes working out of nonprofit "fab[rication] labs." But now the fledgling industry may be poised for bigger things.

Amid growing concern over a decades-long decline in U.S. manufacturing, the Obama administration announced in March 2012 that it would help fund a consortium of universities, government agencies and private companies in Pennsylvania, West Virginia and Ohio that is researching innovations and applications for 3D printing. The effort is designed to promote investment in "the cutting-edge technologies and skills our manufacturers need to compete," the Commerce Department said following the announcement. (*See "Current Situation," p. 1054.*) [5]

Meanwhile, interest in the technology is rising worldwide. Terry Wohlers, president of a Fort Collins, Colo., consulting firm specializing in 3D printing, says so many conferences are being held in so many places — from South Africa to Canada to Germany — that he can't attend them all. "It's through the roof," he says.

Use of 3D Printers Rising Rapidly

More than 23,000 personal 3D printers were in use worldwide in 2011, nearly four times the number a year earlier. Manufacturers have long used 3D printers to develop prototypes, but now, with more accessible technology, individuals are using them to make a variety of products, including jewelry and toys.

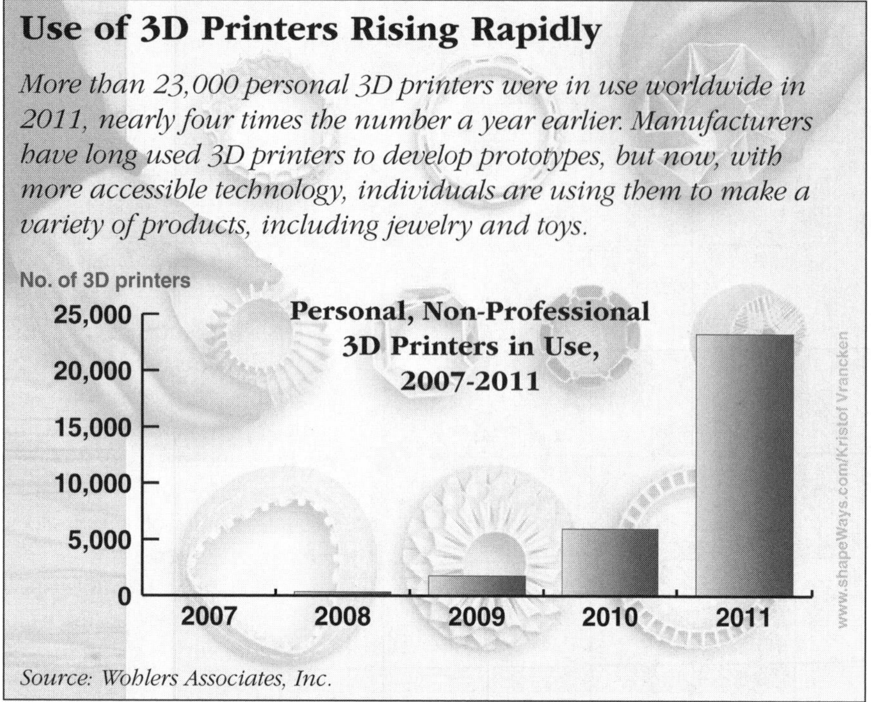

Source: Wohlers Associates, Inc.

A veteran industrial analyst, however, urges a dose of caution. "There is great potential for the technology," says Richard McCormack, editor and publisher of *Manufacturing & Technology News*. "But it's still a tiny industry, a niche. It hasn't reached a tipping point."

Matthew Rogge, an engineering student who spearheaded the composting toilet project, narrows down the computer revolution analogy to a precise point in time: "Right now, we're in the same phase that computers were in when we had the Apple II. Clubs at schools like the one I'm in had computers, then 10 years later everybody's got one." [6]

The Apple II, the first computer designed for the general public, went on sale in 1977 for $1,298 to $2,638, depending on memory capacity. Today, 3D printers aimed at the consumer market cost about $1,500 to $2,000, with build-it-yourself kits available for just a few hundred dollars. [7]

But 3D machines that use a wider range of materials or more precise production methods, which can include laser-beam systems, cost in the hundreds of thousands of dollars and demand far more technical skill to operate — leading some to predict that 3D printers might not become standard household items anytime soon. "Before we see household printers, we'll see neighborhood locations with machines — what I call the Walgreens' photo-printing model," says David L. Bourell, a professor of mechanical engineering and materials science and engineering at the University of Texas at Austin.

Weeks after Bourell spoke, the office supplies superstore Staples announced the beginning of exactly that service in its stores based in the Netherlands and Belgium. Plans for possible on-demand 3D printing in the United States were not announced. [8]

What might a 3D printer-equipped store create? One widely voiced prediction: replacement parts. "Imagine you have, say, a Hoover [vacuum cleaner] in your home and it has broken down," Lisa Harouni, CEO and co-founder of Digital Forming, a British company that designs software allowing easy individual customization of products, told a TED Talks conference in 2011. "You need a spare part, but you realize that Hoover's been discontinued. Can you imagine going online . . . and finding that spare part from a database of geometries of that discontinued product and downloading that information, that data, and having the product made for you at home, ready to use, on your demand?" [9]

3D machines for the consumer market would utilize "material extrusion" — the process of squirting soft plastic from a printer head. Additive Manufacturing (AM) — the technical term for 3D printing, based on construction in successive layers — also uses other materials. They all follow instructions from three-dimensional blueprint software, known generically as computer aided design (CAD) programs, which have been widely used in architectural design for decades. [10]

More complex and expensive forms of AM use materials that harden when exposed to a laser beam or other light source — known as stereolithography. Another system "prints" powdered metal that is then fused by a laser or electron beam, allowing production of titanium parts or objects. [11] Such machines can cost around $1 million. [12]

But even the less costly AM technologies cannot simply replace traditional manufacturing methods, at least for now. For one thing, the plastics and other materials the machines use are relatively expensive. And 3D printing is slow, which is impractical for mass production.

"That's one barrier that has to be overcome," says Denis Cormier, a professor of industrial and systems engineering at the Rochester Institute of Technology in New York. "There are a lot of companies working on chipping away at that."

Others predict that brick-and-mortar factories will continue mass producing commodity items, such as nuts and bolts, while small-scale manufacturers can supply more complicated or customized parts using AM technologies.

Chris Anderson, former editor in chief of *Wired*, quit his job in November to devote himself to his San Diego-based start-up firm, 3D Robotics, which plans to make civilian drone aircraft. "Manufacturing new products is no longer the domain of the few, but the opportunity of the many," Anderson wrote in a new book. "Rather than selling to factories that control the path to market, today's maker-style cottage industries sell directly to consumers around the world online, on their own websites or through marketplaces like Etsy or eBay." [13] Etsy is a website featuring handcrafted items.

"We're pretty excited that this technology is open-source," * says Jordan S. Miller, a postdoctoral fellow in bioengineering at the University of Pennsylvania, who led the successful effort to produce the sugar-based blood vessel system. "You get collaborators all over the world working to solve similar problems."

It is unclear whether the open-source spirit can survive, given traditional legal protections for intellectual property. The future of AM technology is equally unclear, even though most observers agree that the expanding uses of 3D printing are bound to be immense.

"You can't point your finger at one industry that is going to be changed," says Cornell's Lipson. "This is an infrastructural change, which takes a while to happen."

As researchers and entrepreneurs contemplate the vast potential of 3D printing, here are some of the questions being debated:

Can 3D printing revive U.S. manufacturing?

The buzz over 3D printing coincides with growing concern over the future of American manufacturing, which historically has been the pillar of U.S. economic power.

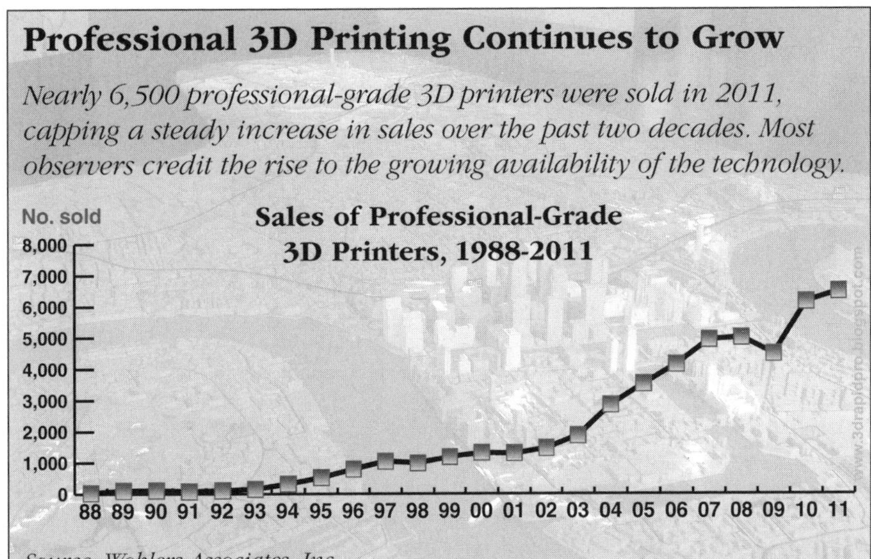
Professional 3D Printing Continues to Grow
Nearly 6,500 professional-grade 3D printers were sold in 2011, capping a steady increase in sales over the past two decades. Most observers credit the rise to the growing availability of the technology.
No. sold
Sales of Professional-Grade 3D Printers, 1988-2011
8,000
7,000
6,000
5,000
4,000
3,000
2,000
1,000
0
88 89 90 91 92 93 94 95 96 97 98 99 00 01 02 03 04 05 06 07 08 09 10 11
www.3drapidpro.blogspot.com
Source: Wohlers Associates, Inc.

U.S. manufacturing has remained relatively strong, even in today's recession-recovery environment. Early this year, manufacturing companies were adding jobs for the second year in a row, and U.S. products account for about 17 percent of manufacturing worldwide. [14]

However, American manufacturing occupies a substantially smaller share of the domestic economy — 11 percent of gross domestic product (GDP) — than the 25 percent it represented in 1960. [15] As low-skilled, repetitive-labor jobs have moved to China and other low-wage countries, U.S. manufacturing jobs have dropped from 17 million in the 1990s to fewer than 12 million last year. [16] At the same time, manufacturers say they can't find enough employees trained to operate the computer-controlled machinery that is a key element in modern American factories. [17]

The idea that 3D printing could help spark a new phase of innovation in the United States clearly appeals to the Obama administration, especially since manufacturers and researchers worldwide are refining and using the technology. In March, the administration announced establishment of the National Additive Manufacturing Innovation Institute, an effort to link government, higher education and industry to research and develop AM and its applications.

Parallel to the work of the institute, research projects and business ventures are popping up around the country — and around the world — that use 3D printing in small-scale manufacturing or in medical and other research projects. (*See sidebar, p. 1042.*)

Whether the spurt of research activity on the one hand and DIY (do-it-yourself) enthusiasm on the other signals an imminent revitalization of American manufacturing remains to be seen.

Bourell at the University of Texas notes that AM is already well-established in two key manufacturing industries, aerospace and biomedical. The technology is suitable in both cases because neither industry requires millions of identical parts, which would be time-consuming and expensive for AM machines. "Where additive processes make cost sense is for objects that have complicated geometry and where the production run is short," Bourell says.

Aircraft makers use AM machines that use laser or electron beams to produce titanium parts, adds Bourell, a specialist in "sintering," or fusing powdered

* Open-source refers to the free sharing of technical or other information, allowing collaborative efforts in developing or improving products.

3D Printing Pushes Medical Boundaries

Applications range from artificial livers to hip implants.

Bioengineer Jordan S. Miller had a problem. He and his colleagues from the University of Pennsylvania and Massachusetts Institute of Technology (MIT) were trying to build an artificial liver, a first step toward making one that could replace a patient's failed organ.

But livers, unlike thin-tissue organs such as bladders and corneas, must have blood-vessel networks running through them in order to keep the cells alive. To study how liver cells function inside an artificial liver, the scientists needed to build a blood-vessel system. [1]

Fabricating such a vascular system is theoretically possible, but liver cells are too delicate to survive the fabrication process.

Finally, Miller, a postdoctoral fellow at Penn, decided to see if liver cells could survive in hardened sugar, a material that could be dissolved without harming the cells. After the sugar was printed, a tissue-like gel containing the liver cells would be poured around the sugar structure, which served as a mold of the network. The sugar could then be dissolved in water, leaving the vascular network, complete with cells.

Using a RepRap — an open-source kit printer used by hobbyists to make plastic jewelry, toys and other objects — Miller and his colleagues modified it to discharge hardened sugar, which they then used to print the blood vessel network.

The experiment's success attracted considerable attention from scientists and 3D printing enthusiasts. "The idea of 3D printing has been around for several years, and certainly it is possible to print virtually anything," Martin Birchall, a surgeon at University College, London, told the BBC. "I'm fascinated by their proposals. . . . It is certainly very exciting." [2]

Nonscientists, for their part, were excited by the open-source nature of the 3D printer modification. "If you had asked the RepRap community the day before he announced his project what the next 5 or 10 or 50 applications of 3D printing would be, it is unlikely that they would have said 'printing vasculature out of sugar to help grow cells,' " says Michael Weinberg, vice president of the Institute of Emerging Technologies at Public Knowledge, an organization that seeks to "ensure universal access to affordable and safe networks." "However, since the RepRap is open, they did not have to anticipate it. Jordan could just appear out of nowhere, find the project and tweak it to do what he needed to be done."

Meanwhile, 3D printing is becoming established in nonexperimental medicine as well. Michael Mauldin, an Albuquerque, N.M.-based territory manager for MCAD Technologies, which sells Israeli-made 3D printers, says doctors and dentists make up one of his two biggest customer sectors (the other is scientists and engineers at Sandia and Los Alamos national laboratories).

Dentists, he says, "can just scan your mouth, pull the scan into software to create a [blueprint] and send it to a lab to print it." The result is a more accurate model of a patient's teeth than the traditional mold-casting method, he says.

Invisalign, a San Jose, Calif., company that makes customized, transparent teeth-straightening devices, uses 3D printing to make each one. "They print 50,000 a day," says Hod Lipson, an engineering professor at Cornell University and a leading expert on 3D printing. "They are probably the biggest application story in 3D printing." The company uses printing machines developed by 3DSystems, which produced the first 3D printers. [3]

Doctors are printing out medical instruments for one-time use in surgery, Andrew M. Christensen, president of Medical Modeling, in Golden, Colo., wrote last year in a paper for the National Academy of Engineering. And a titanium hip replacement made by an Italian company using advanced 3D technology has been implanted in more than 15,000 patients in Europe in the past three years. [4]

In the United States, the Food and Drug Administration has approved at least four 3D-printed metal implants for spines and hips, Christensen wrote. Walter Reed Army Medical Center and

metals into solids. The Boeing 787 Dreamliner has at least 30 AM-produced pieces, most of them as part of ductwork — and not all of them metal — he says. And some companies are using 3D printers to produce "copings," metal bases for human replacement teeth. Other industries also could use AM to customize parts.

"It's not a technical holdup," Bourell says. "It's a business decision."

Significantly, a note of caution comes from someone with a vested interest in the AM industry's growth, Michael Mauldin, a sales executive in Albuquerque, N.M., for MCAD Technologies. The company sells AM machines made by Objet Geometries, an Israeli company whose printers range from $31,000 desktop models to full-standing machines that cost about $270,000 and can use a wide range of materials. "We are not to the point of rapid manufacture yet," Mauldin says, because the plastics and other materials used in most printers don't have sufficient strength to withstand years of use in machinery. And sintering machines that use AM technology to produce titanium parts cost millions and require highly skilled operators.

Overall, "There's no justification in mass producing parts on a printer because it takes longer and costs so much," he says. "The real advantage is prototyping. You get a true-to-design part; you're trying to avoid being wrong and tooling an entire manufacturing line based on a mistake."

Likewise, Catarina Mota, a visiting scholar at New York University's post-graduate Interactive Telecommunications

the National Naval Medical Center have considered using 3D-printed titanium implants for war-wounded veterans with major skull injuries. [5]

So far, however, the use of 3D-printed implants remains relatively rare. The 15,000 hip replacements represent only about 1 percent of the 1.4 million such operations performed in 2010. [6] But some researchers see the fabrication of customized replacement body parts as a major new field for 3D printing. "With an aging population, that is becoming an increasing issue," says David L. Bourell, a professor of mechanical engineering and materials science and engineering at the University of Texas at Austin.

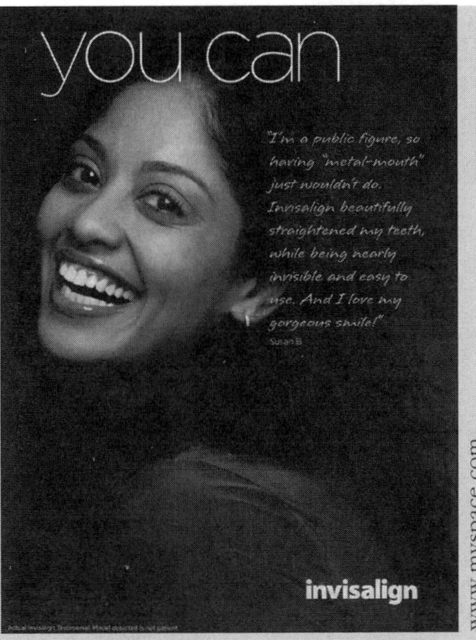

www.myspace.com

3D printing is used by Invisalign, a San Jose, Calif., company, to make transparent, custom teeth-straightening devices.

Meanwhile, the use of the technology is well-established in surgical planning. Back in 2002, surgeons at the University of California, Los Angeles' Mattel Children's Hospital used 3D-printed models of the conjoined brains of Guatemalan twins María Teresa and María de Jesús Quiej Alvarez to map out the successful operation to separate them. A Boston company, Biomedical Modeling, used the scans to produce three 3D-printed models — one of each twin's skull and a third of the area where the twins' brains and skulls were fused.

"The third biomodel [enabled] the surgeons to easily see the architecture of arteries and veins," a British engineering journal reported at the time. "The surgeons were able to meticulously plan the operation, [which] took 22 hours to complete. But similar operations in the past have taken as long as 97 hours." [7]

The 3D printing of major body organs, however, remains further out on the horizon. "It's going to be several more decades before we have good control over the variables," says Miller, the Penn bioengineer. But, the use of 3D printing is making the work easier, he says. "We will be able to change the vascular architecture very easily."

— Peter Katel

---

[1] "Penn Researchers Improve Living Tissues With 3D Printed Vascular Networks Made From Sugar," University of Pennsylvania, press release, July 1, 2012, www.upenn.edu/pennnews/news/penn-researchers-improve-living-tissues-3d-printed-vascular-networks-made-sugar; Gabor Forgacs, "Perfusable vascular networks," *Nature Materials*, September 2012, www.nature.com/nmat/journal/v11/n9/full/nmat3412.html.

[2] Quoted in "3D-printed sugar network to help grow artificial liver," BBC News, July 2, 2012, www.bbc.co.uk/news/technology-18677627; Jon Bardin, "Sweet technique makes blood vessels using sugar and 3-D printer," *Los Angeles Times, Science Now* (blog), July 2, 2012, http://articles.latimes.com/2012/jul/02/science/la-sci-sn-new-technique-makes-blood-vessels-from-sugar-using-3d-printer-20120702.

[3] "Digital Dentistry," Biosystesms, 3Dsystems, undated, http://production3dprinters.com/digital-dentistry; Charles Hull, "Hit Rewind . . . The History of 3D Printing," *3D Innovations* (blog), March 22, 2012, www.3d-innovations.com/blog/?tag=charles-hull.

[4] Andrew M. Christensen, "Additive Manufacturing Is Changing Surgery," Frontiers of Engineering: Reports on Leading-Edge Engineering from the 2011 Symposium," National Academy of Engineering, pp. 25-31, www.nap.edu/openbook.php?record_id=13274&page=1.

[5] *Ibid.*

[6] *Ibid.*

[7] Dave Wilson, "Conjoined twins benefit from rapid prototyping," *The Engineer*, Oct. 2, 2002, www.theengineer.co.uk/in-depth/conjoined-twins-benefit-from-rapid-prototyping/280686.article.

Program (ITP) who is doing doctoral research at the University of Lisbon, Portugal, on open-source development of products, argues that 3D printing alone is too limited to revolutionize manufacturing. But when small-scale producers use AM together with computer-controlled cutting and milling machines, she says, the potential is enormous.

"Access to these technologies will create a different landscape in manufacturing," she says. "So far, customers have accepted mass manufacture because it's cheap and available, but once the option is there for more local products or more customizable goods, we will probably see a replacement of one by the other."

Mota notes that already, two firms — Local Motors, in Chandler, Ariz., and Wikispeed of Lynnwood, Wash., — allow buyers to custom-design cars and motorcycles (though not the engines or transmissions) that the firms build at their plants. [18] "Giant companies and multinationals" likely will stay in business, Mota says, but they will exist alongside "little companies that are networked and form a supply chain."

Willy Shih, a professor of management practice at Harvard Business School, acknowledges that manufacturers can use AM to produce quickly domestically instead of outsourcing. But Shih, co-author of an influential book on American manufacturing weaknesses, points out that technology doesn't entirely compensate for Asian manufacturers' vast, low-cost labor force, which typically works from dawn to dusk. [19] "If you get to the question: Will I ever be able to make 5 million iPhones for the first weekend of sales in the United States — you'll never get people in the United States to work like that."

And technological advances aren't geographically restricted, Shih adds. "To the extent that all the know-how is embodied in a tool, don't you think Chinese manufacturers will buy the same tools?"

Will intellectual-property disputes slow the evolution of 3D printing?

A pioneering 3D printing firm charged in a lawsuit in November that a Cambridge, Mass., startup is using the older firm's patented technology in a new desktop printer. 3D Systems filed the lawsuit against Formlabs in federal court in Rock Hill, S.C. [20]

Patent lawsuits are nothing new in the high-tech or manufacturing fields, but the South Carolina suit drew special attention because it also named the widely used fundraising website Kickstarter as a defendant. "This could set an awful precedent that could put future hardware funding at risk," Nick Pinkston, a 3D printing entrepreneur, told *Wired*. "I hope that fallout from this doesn't affect the ability of others to raise funding for their projects on Kickstarter." [21] Neither Formlabs nor Kickstarter has yet responded publicly to the suit.

Most of the concern over 3D printing's implications for intellectual-property law focuses not on the technology itself, but on its application. Inventors can harness digital technology for making exact, three-dimensional blueprints of their creations, then producing them on printers. And anyone with less originality can use the same technology to make exact replicas of objects that others have designed.

Back in the late 1990s musicians and record and movie companies were the first to realize the implications on their businesses of mass Internet connectivity and the democratization of recording technology. By 2001, record labels reported selling 20 million fewer albums a year in the United States alone, a startling trend blamed in large part on digital piracy. [22]

None of them came up with a solution, however. Then the late Steve Jobs' firm, Apple Inc., invented the iPod and its iTunes software, which created a mechanism for consumers to buy digital files of songs, albums, movies and TV shows. Jobs realized that music and video piracy would be unstoppable unless someone created a simple, accessible alternative. "If protection of intellectual property begins to disappear, creative companies will disappear or never get started," Jobs told his biographer. [23]

Google, for its part, was sued by publishers and authors after it announced plans to digitize and provide online access to every book in the world. In October, Google reached a legal settlement with the Association of American Publishers. But litigation is still under way between the search giant and the Authors Guild. Both lawsuits center on whether the Google Library Project amounts to a mammoth series of copyright violations. [24]

But concerns over intellectual-property protection transcend the worlds of scholarship, arts and entertainment. U.S. manufacturers and their foreign counterparts have been complaining for years about unfair competition from counterfeiters producing imitations of every imaginable kind of product, from pharmaceuticals to handbags. Last year, the Homeland Security Department's two customs agencies seized about $179 million worth of counterfeit goods. [25]

Cormier of Rochester Institute of Technology expects the use of digital-rights management (DRM) software that could prevent, for example, the buyer of a digital file of instructions for making a replacement part from sharing that file with others. "The company that now would sell the replacement from a warehouse is not going to give away that revenue stream," he says.

"There's no question in my mind that there will be some version of digital-rights management incorporated into files, probably sooner rather than later," Cormier says.

But Michael Weinberg, vice president of the Institute for Emerging Innovation at Public Knowledge, an advocacy organization for loosening restrictions on information over the Internet, argues that DRM has already proved a failure. "Ask the movie studios if DRM on DVDs has prevented illegal copies of movies on the Internet," he says. "What it ends up doing is stopping otherwise legal uses of works protected by copyright. If I wanted to make a video that criticized a movie, and wanted to use clips from the movie, I'd have to break DRM to do so."

Weinberg acknowledges that some companies may follow the entertain-

3D Revenues Exploded

Revenues for products and services associated with professional and consumer 3D printing exceeded $1.7 billion in 2011, a 17-fold increase over revenues in 1993.

Revenues for 3D Printing Products and Services, 1993 and 2011

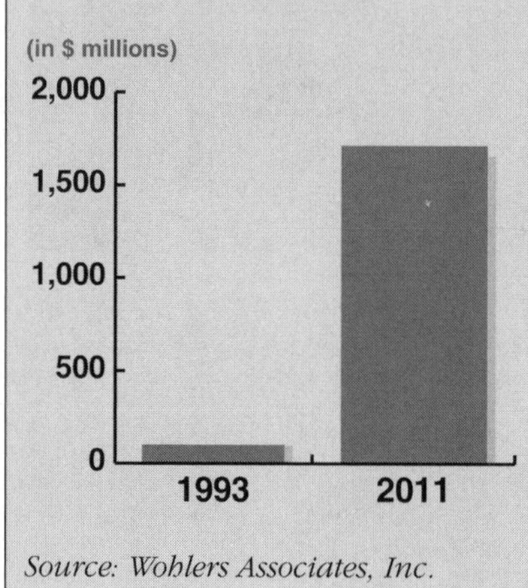

Source: Wohlers Associates, Inc.

ment industry's lead in trying to impose technological restrictions on copying. An alternative approach would be to build ties to creative copiers — such as LEGO fans who devise new block shapes, using Lego's connecting system. "People who are spending their time on that are LEGO super-fans," he says. "These are people they don't want to sue, but want to encourage."

Still, says Wohlers, the Colorado-based AM consultant, corporations such as the Walt Disney Co. that typically sue counterfeiters may continue the practice for those who use 3D technology. "If one of [Disney's] characters gets copied, they go after you," he notes. However, "When thousands or millions of people do it, I don't know how they control it." Especially, he notes, if the counterfeiters are located abroad.

Wohlers is skeptical about the efficacy of DRM. But he believes the widespread practice of sharing files for 3D designs online does create a new environment for copyright and patent holders. "We've dealt with 3D-modeled data for a very long time, but we're now seeing a lot more uploaded on the Web. The difference now is the ease with which you can copy."

Large corporations aren't the only players with an interest in protecting intellectual-property rights, says Lipson, at Cornell's Creative Machines Lab. "Even kids who come to Cornell for summer camp — they design something and offer it for sale; the first question is, 'What if someone copies my thing?' "

Hence, "It's not Disney versus the small inventor," Lipson says. "It's maker versus maker. That's different from what it used to be."

Yet small-scale producers don't need patent-style protection, argues Mota of New York University's Interactive Telecommunications Program (ITP), who participates in do-it-yourself fabrication networks in New York and Portugal.[26] "With all the open-source work and collaboration we see online, people don't necessarily need monopolies," she says.

AR15.com/HaveBlue

A 3D printer was used to create plastic parts of this operational AR-15 rifle. In a separate project, University of Texas law student Cody R. Wilson sparked controversy recently when he sought to raise money to develop and make 3D-produced weapons. The owner of the 3D printer he had leased took the machine back, and an online fund-raising site revoked his membership.

Mota cites the experience of a friend who founded an electronics parts business. "The moment he launches a product and publishes the plans, he knows that he has six weeks until it's cloned," Mota says. "He says the open-source system keeps him on his toes."

Does printing weapons using 3D technology pose a major security threat?

Like any technology, 3D printing can be turned to evil purposes as well as good.

For instance, the advent of color laser copiers and printers prompted alarm within the U.S. Secret Service that counterfeiters would use the technology to make fake bills. To overcome this threat, the printer manufacturers agreed to install software that left telltale, virtually invisible yellow dots on every page printed by laser.[27]

But with 3D printers, worries over security transcend the fabrication of counterfeit money. In late September, Stratasys, an Eden, Minn., 3D printing industry leader, seized a machine it had leased to Cody R. Wilson, a law student at the University of Texas at Austin. Wilson heads a project to produce a 3D-printed firearm.

"It is the policy of Stratasys not to knowingly allow its printers to be used for illegal purposes," the company wrote to Wilson, who replied that he didn't think he would be breaking the law against unlicensed firearms manufacture because he wouldn't be selling the gun. But the argument didn't change the company's mind.[28]

Earlier in September, Indiegogo, a Web-based platform for raising investment funds by mass appeal, expelled Wilson's "Wiki Weapon Project" and refunded individuals' contributions. Wilson had been trying to raise $20,000 through the service. Indiegogo told the would-be firearms innovator that the Wiki Weapon Project had violated Indiegogo's prohibition on the sale of "ammunition, firearms, or certain firearm parts or accessories." After moving his fundraising to his own site, Defense Distributed, Wilson raised more than his $20,000 goal.[29]

In a video interview in September, Wilson noted that 3D blueprint files for firearms are easily accessible on the Web, where they can be used by people with access to computer numerical control (CNC) milling machines to make weapons. Those factory-grade machines are far too expensive for most people, but 3D printers — including kits for so-called RepRap machines that replicate some of their own parts — are becoming widely accessible. "I might have a $500 RepRap one day," he said. "You can get the file, click print — run it through your software — and then you've got a gun." [30]

As to why he would provide that assistance, Wilson characterized the project as a philosophical, political and artistic challenge to legal prohibitions and restrictions. "What this project is about — f--- your laws," he said. "You know what, I don't like this legal regime. I neatly step outside of it." [31]

Some manufacturing experts consider the hubbub over Wilson's project as exaggerated. Reliable firearms, says consultant Wohlers, "are pretty difficult to do with additive manufacturing," and relatively easy to make for anyone with access to traditional machine tools.

Nevertheless, Wohlers says, 3D printing does offer dangerous possibilities that should be monitored by government agencies. "In theory, you could design a product with a cavity in it and print it so that it was completely sealed," he says, "and put explosive in it or a listening device. Our intelligence community needs to know about that — and maybe use it."

But Mota of ITP argues that all technology can be turned to bad ends. And she notes that proliferation doesn't necessarily lead to disaster. "Back in the 1940s, only the United States had the atomic bomb," she says. "Now everyone does. Is that better or worse? I don't know."

The problem isn't technology, Mota argues, but human nature. "Somebody who wants to destroy will find a way to do it." As for restricting production devices in the name of safety, she asks, "Would it be safer if technology were only in the hands of a few? I don't think so."

Lipson of Cornell argues for a moderate dose of regulation, citing rules governing biological experiments on humans as a possible approach. "Doing scientific experiments is a good thing," he says, "but there is an approval process."

At the same time, Lipson argues against making security concerns a priority.

"There have been mills and lathes and other manufacturing tools for a long time; you can use them to make weapons just as easily," he says. "You can argue, 'Let's not teach chemistry because people will know it doesn't take a lot to make explosives.' " ■

BACKGROUND

Reproducing Firearms

A machine that reproduces the exact shapes of objects has long been a dream of both manufacturers and artists.

In the 1820s members of both groups made progress toward developing such a machine. In the arts, progress began with early attempts at photography. A French pioneer in the field, Joseph Nicéphone Niépce, made an exact copy of an engraving of Pope Pius VII on a glass plate coated with a light-sensitive chemical. [32]

The reproduction was closer to a modern photograph than to a duplicated object, but the use of light-sensitive material was the key to later processes for reproducing three-dimensional objects.

In 1819, Thomas Blanchard, an American inventor, developed a duplicating lathe, which enabled uniform production of items such as gunstocks. The machine meant that craftsmen no longer had to individually shape each stock by hand.

Blanchard's lathe worked essentially like a modern key-cutting tool, in which one part follows a model's contour while a connected cutter or shaper mimics each move on a piece of wood, ensuring that the second piece becomes a duplicate of the model. Earlier, Blanchard had invented a machine that produced identically formed musket barrels. By the early 1820s, the new country's two national armories were using the machine, along with related Blanchard inventions. [33]

In the ensuing decades, another influential series of innovations also centered on the firearms industry. Samuel Colt invented machines to make parts for a new kind of gun, a revolver. With bullets held in a rotating cylinder, the gun could fire six rounds in a row without reloading. And as manufacturers at an 1851 exhibition in London saw to their amazement, the pistols were made from interchangeable parts — a system that later was adopted by manufacturers of all kinds of other products. [34]

Rifle and pistol production methods may have helped create modern manufacturing, but the roots of 3D printing lie in two fields of handcrafted work — portraiture and mapmaking.

Sculptors were seeking a way to make exact, three-dimensional reproductions of a subject's head. As early as 1860, a French portraitist, François Willème, designed a method of producing such exact models. The subject was placed in a circular room, surrounded by 24 cameras that simultaneously took pictures of each segment in front of each camera. A craftsman then used each photograph as a guide to carving each of the sections of the subject's head. [35]

But the time-consuming nature of Willème's method led to refinements. One, patented in the United States in 1904, used a light-sensitive gelatin that expanded according to how much light it received. The method was called "photosculpture." [36]

Meanwhile, mapmakers wanted to reproduce precise, three-dimensional shapes for topographical charts. In 1892, mapmaker J. E. Blanther received a patent for a method of making topographical maps using layers of wax plates. The idea is considered

Continued on p. 1048

Chronology

1822-1892 *Early attempts made at three-dimensional (3D) copying and manufacturing in U.S. and France.*

1819
American inventor Thomas Blanchard receives patent for a lathe that can copy irregularly shaped pieces of wood, such as rifle stocks.

1822
French photography pioneer Joseph Nicéphone Niépce precisely copies an engraving using a glass plate coated with light-sensitive chemical.

1852
Gunmaker Samuel Colt exhibits firearms made of identical, interchangeable parts — a first.

1860
French portraitist François Willème invents process to produce exact, three-dimensional model of a subject's head, using 24 cameras.

1892
American mapmaker J. E. Blanther patents system for making topographical maps using layers of wax plates.

1911-1945 *Mass production methods make U.S. an industrial powerhouse.*

1911
American engineer Frederick Taylor develops systems engineering for making factory workers efficient.

1913
Henry A. Ford installs moving assembly line in his new Detroit factory, turning out nearly five times more cars as closest competitor.

1917
Ford builds massive factory in Dearborn, Mich., which eventually turns out a car every 49 seconds.

1946-1970s *As U.S. transitions from industrial to service economy, advances in copying and data-processing transform office work.*

1946
Electronic Numeral Integrator and Computer (ENIAC), considered the first U.S. computer, is unveiled at the University of Pennsylvania.

1950
3M Corp. introduces office copier requiring chemically coated paper.

1950s
U.S. Army lends 120 new computer-operated factory machines to defense contractors to encourage adoption.

1959
First office copier using standard paper, Haloid Xerox 914, unveiled.

1960
Sketchpad computer software leads to computer aided design (CAD) programs and graphical user interface (GUI) for computers.

1970
Xerox establishes Palo Alto Research Center (PARC) for developing high-tech innovations.

1977
Apple introduces Apple II, first computer aimed at non-hobbyists, with its own keyboard and screen.

1979
Apple co-founder Steve Jobs makes deal with Xerox to use GUI in future Apple models.

1984-Present *Computer technology and manufacturing continue converging, spurred by 3D printing.*

1984
American inventor Charles Hull patents stereolithography, the first industrial 3D printing method.

1988
3D Systems, founded by Hull, produces first commercial 3D printer.

1993
Researchers at Massachussetts Institute of Technology (MIT) patent 3D printer that uses a printer head to discharge object-building material.

2002
California surgeons use 3D printer-produced model of conjoined twins' brains to prepare operation to separate them.

2003
MIT professor opens fabrication lab in inner-city Boston.

2006
Open-source 3D printer developers in Britain produce initial plans for "RepRap" printer, a machine that produces parts to replicate itself.

2012
Obama administration establishes National Additive Manufacturing Innovation Institute. . . . Composting toilet designed by University of Washington students wins international 3D competition. . . . University of Pennsylvania and MIT scientists use 3D printer to produce experimental blood vessel network. . . . 3D printer-maker Stratasys reclaims a machine from University of Texas student who planned to make firearms.

Magic of 3D Printing Captures Students' Interest

"It was almost like a bucket of water being dumped on my head."

The future impact of 3D printing on the U.S. economy may be uncertain, but if 15-year-old Riley Myers is any gauge, the technology is already showing promise as a recruiting tool. Myers, a sophomore at Las Cruces High School in New Mexico, recalls a tour of nearby New Mexico State University when he was in middle school.

"They showed us a rapid prototyping machine," he says, using an alternate term for 3D printing, "and a wrench they had printed out on it. It was an adjustable wrench that really worked."

That demonstration, Myers says, "is one of the things that really got me interested in engineering in the first place."

3D printers are becoming increasingly prevalent in college engineering departments. Matthew Rogge, a student at the University of Washington, credits a 3D printing course with setting him on the path that led him and fellow students to win a $100,000 prize for designing a socially useful 3D printer application.

University of Washington mechanical engineering professor Mark Ganter suggests that colleges have no choice but to introduce students to the popular technology, which he says will either "get to the ubiquity of Kinko's, or lots of people are going to have them in their house," he told *The Chronicle of Higher Education*. [1]

Indeed, even within universities, 3D printers are beginning to see uses far beyond traditional engineering functions. At New York University's postgraduate Interactive Telecommunications Program, Marko Manriquez designed a 3D printer to produce . . . burritos. "Any food that can be converted into paste form can be extruded and hence 3D printed," Manriquez told the Web magazine *Co.design*. "That's because the printer uses syringes to push/print the food material just like a normal printer uses ink cartridges. The main limitation in this design is that the ingredients have to have that paste-like (or Play Dough) consistency to go through the printer's syringe." [2]

Using artistic rather than culinary or engineering language, Manriquez said although the printed burritos were merely OK, "More to the point is to deliver a conceptual burrito creating a dialogue about food issues." [3]

Food creation may turn out to be the best way to use 3D printers to excite students. One of Ganter's classes "printed" 8,000 edible cookies for middle and high school students visiting the campus for an engineering open house. The cookies and their manufacturing process were the No. 1 attraction. [4]

At Cornell University, engineering professor and 3D expert Hod Lipson reports similar experiences. Food may be the "killer app" for 3D printing as an educational tool, he says. "When you show kids you can write a simple formula that makes a flower-shaped cookie, they get interested more than from any other way you can explain why they should get interested in math. I saw kids in fourth grade that couldn't care less about math or manufacturing become interested when you print chocolate."

The government's Defense Advanced Research Projects Agency doesn't mention food engineering in describing its project to distribute 3D printers to high schools. (*See main story, p. 1052.*) But the culinary explorations do fit with a drive by some engineers to emphasize the enjoyability of their field to young people.

Continued from p. 1046

an early, manual version of additive manufacturing. [37]

Attempts to further refine photochemical methods for exact reproduction of three-dimensional objects continued well into the 20th century.

How widespread these methods became isn't clear. In any event, they lacked the key elements that would arrive only with digital technology in the late 20th century — three-dimensional blueprints and computer-controlled production machines.

Mass Production

Long before those developments amounted to anything more than science fiction, American inventors and industrialists had created machines and methods that made the United States the world leader in mass production. A key chapter took place in the 19th century, when more efficient ways of fabricating steel promoted the development of national railway networks, which in turn enabled raw materials and finished products to be shipped nationwide.

In the early 20th century, Henry A. Ford devised a new form of factory production. He borrowed from 19th-century methods used in Midwestern slaughterhouses and bicycle factories, where each worker had a specific task or set of tasks. But he took things a crucial step further. In 1913, in a Detroit automobile plant he built for his Ford Motor Co., he built a 135-foot-long moving assembly line, with room on both sides for 140 workers, each of whom performed a specified task on unfinished cars as they moved past. The method allowed the factory to turn out nearly 203,000 cars that year, more than five times as many as Ford's closest competitor. [38]

Four years later Ford began building the mammoth River Rouge auto plant in nearby Dearborn. It embodied his strategy of making — instead of buying — everything needed for auto production, from the steel to the glass and upholstery. At its peak in the 1930s, the factory employed more than 100,000 people and rolled out a car every 49 seconds.

General Motors, which became Ford's main competitor, copied Ford's

Traditionally, introductory math and science courses force students to go on "a math-science death march," said David E. Goldberg, a professor emeritus of engineering at the University of Illinois. "Instead of starting with the creative part, we start teaching them the abstract stuff and lose up to 50 percent of the people who enter engineering." Goldberg is co-founder of Big Beacon, an advocacy group to transform engineering education. [5]

Students from the University of Washington pose with their faculty adviser after winning a $100,000 prize for their development of a 3D-produced composting toilet for use in developing countries. In the foreground is Big Red, a 3D printer that turns recycled plastic into new objects.

Puzzles offer another interesting recruiting possibility. At Las Cruces High School, which has its own 3D printer, Myers and other members of an engineering class used the machine to create the pieces of a Rubik's Cube-like puzzle — comparing the printed versions with pieces that they carved by hand. The school obtained the printer through Project Lead the Way, an initiative by high-tech companies to promote interest in science and engineering. One of the companies is 3D printer manufacturer Stratasys. [6]

As the son of an architect and an artist — both of whom use computer aided design (CAD) software, which is used in 3D printing — Myers might have headed into engineering even without his early 3D printing experience.

But the printed wrench caught his imagination. "It was so totally outside of what I had seen before," he says. "It was almost like a bucket of water being dumped on my head to see the possibilities that this one handy tool opened up."

— Peter Katel

[1] Angela Chen, "3-D Printers Spread From Engineering Departments to Designs Across Disciplines," *The Chronicle of Higher Education*, Sept. 17, 2012, http://chronicle.com/article/3-D-Printers-Arent-Just-for/134440/.

[2] Quoted in Neal Ungerleider, "Burritobot: A 3-D Printer That Spits Out Burritos," *Co.Design, Fast Company*, 2012, www.fastcodesign.com/1670070/burritobot-a-3-d-printer-that-spits-out-burritos#1.

[3] Quoted in *ibid.*

[4] Chen, *op. cit.*

[5] Quoted in Andrés Oppenheimer, "U.S., Latin America need more engineers," *The Miami Herald*, Nov. 17, 2012, www.miamiherald.com/2012/11/17/3101173/us-latin-america-need-more-engineers.html.

[6] "Project Lead the Way," www.pltw.org/partners-sponsors/partners; also see "Las Cruces High School," Project Lead the Way, http://lascruces.lcps.k12.nm.us/pltw.shtml.

production methods. GM provided more model choices to consumers by creating distinct brands — Chevrolet, Cadillac and others. But many of the models used the same parts, in another reflection of GM's debt to Ford's mass production doctrine.

World War II, which generated enormous demand for warplanes, tanks and other weapons, provided an enormous boost to U.S. factory output. In the last quarter of 1940, before the United States entered the war, only 514 military aircraft were produced. In 1944, the military received 96,000 airplanes, and aircraft production capacity had increased 20-fold. [39]

After the war, a major part of U.S. industry turned to consumer items demanded by the emerging middle class, ranging from cars and refrigerators to radios and TVs. The postwar industrial boom depended on the same assembly-line methods pioneered by Ford at the beginning of the century.

Mass production also owed a large debt to Frederick Taylor, a mechanical engineer who founded the discipline of systems engineering. In a 1911 treatise, Taylor argued that most factory workers deliberately under-performed, reasoning that if they increased their output, management would need fewer workers.

Taylor argued that "scientific" management techniques would ensure that workers performed at the highest level. Greater productivity would mean more sales, which in turn would boost demand, he reasoned. Of his system, he said, "It would insure higher wages and make shorter working hours and better working and home conditions possible." [40]

While arguing that workers would better their lives by working harder, Taylor saw them as performing nothing more than rote, simple functions that they could be trained to carry out as efficiently as possible. But classic U.S. mass production methods assumed that numerous errors would occur, making extensive post-production quality control essential.

In the 1970s, Japanese manufacturers, notably Toyota, adapted the Ford and Taylor methods into a system that put far greater emphasis on workers' contribution to making goods correctly the first time around. Because Japanese companies were also devoted to keep-

www.mocoloco.com

© Propshop Modelmakers Ltd

Custom Printing From A to Z

Products made by 3D printers run the gamut from fanciful plastic shoes (top) to models of the priceless Aston Martin DB5 (bottom) used by Daniel Craig — aka James Bond — in the new movie "Skyfall." The actual historic car was far too valuable to be blown up in one of the movie's dramatic scenes, so the moviemakers turned to three-quarter-size replicas made by 3D printing.

ing machinery costs down, workers there were also trained to do more than one task, as opposed to the U.S. system of one worker performing one job.

Japanese manufacturers also pioneered a "just in time" production system that kept inventory down and depended on speedy communication with parts suppliers to deliver their products exactly when they were needed, but not before. Over time, U.S. manufacturers adopted the Japanese versions, which had evolved out of American production methods.

Computers and CADs

Paradoxically, during the same century that the United States was becoming a world manufacturing power, Americans were increasingly employed in offices, stores and classrooms instead of in factories. Professional, managerial, sales and service jobs accounted for a quarter of all workers in 1910 — and three-quarters in 2000. [41]

Virtually all of these employees worked in environments that generated and received tremendous numbers of documents of all kinds, from sales reports to income tax filings to trial transcripts and legal briefs — all of which had to be reproduced. A typist could use carbon paper to produce multiple copies, but that didn't work for all documents, such as copies coming from another office.

In 1950, the 3M company introduced the Thermo-Fax, which produced copies by way of an infrared light that shone through the original onto a chemically coated sheet of paper. Other companies produced similar machines. But, like the 3M model, all required special paper. [42]

By then, inventor Chester Carlson had been toiling alone for years on a radical new way of making copies on ordinary, untreated paper. Haloid Co., a Rochester, N.Y., firm that bought the rights to the idea and eventually hired

Carlson, called the process xerography — based on Greek for "dry" and "writing." The company later changed its name to a version of the same word — Xerox. [43]

The company's Haloid Xerox 914, introduced in 1959, revolutionized office work worldwide. Carlson had foreseen in the 1950s that a company might need to turn out as many 100 copies a day. Instead, the machine's first users were soon cranking out as many 3,000 copies daily. [44]

Another development during the same decade would unleash huge changes in office work methods and in the world economy. World War II had prompted a major demand for intensive computing power for, among other reasons, breaking enemy codes. Indeed, cracking German encryption machines was the objective of the first programmable "logic calculator" built by Britain in 1943.

By that time, work on similar devices had been under way in the United States for some time. In 1943-1945, two Americans at the University of Pennsylvania built the electronic numerical integrator and computer — ENIAC, considered the first U.S. computer.

In the 1950s and '60s, as the Cold War between the United States and the Soviet Union kept the U.S. military searching for new technologies, the Defense Department and its contractors were racing to develop computers, in part to use in the new space program but also for designing the complicated guidance systems of ballistic missiles and nuclear submarines.

A major development came in 1954, when engineers replaced glass vacuum tubes with transistors. ENIAC had used 17,648 vacuum tubes and 6,000 manual switches and weighed 30 tons. In the 1990s, a team at the University of Pennsylvania recreated ENIAC on a single silicon microchip containing 174,569 transistors. The chip completed in three minutes calculations that had taken ENIAC 24 hours.

As engineers and scientists refined computers, the military began encouraging manufacturers to use parts-producing tools that were computer controlled. Producing precision parts became faster and cheaper because the machines reduced the amount of human labor involved. Manufacturers were wary at first, but the U.S. Army — which depended on a reliable supply chain from defense contractors — bought 120 of the so-called computer numerical control (CNC) machines in the 1950s and lent them to various companies. [45]

The 1950s also saw the beginnings of the design software system that became known as computer aided design (CAD). In 1960, Ivan Sutherland, a doctoral candidate at MIT, invented the Sketchpad computer program, which led to both CAD and the graphical user interface (GUI), which allowed computer screens to display graphics as well as words and digits.

During the 1960s engineers and computer scientists continued improving CAD, making it less expensive; early versions had cost $500,000 each. And their counterparts at Xerox's Palo Alto Research Center, established in 1970, began doing the same. In 1979 a young entrepreneur named Steve Jobs, who was seeking new ideas for his Apple computer company, saw GUI demonstrated at the center. He arranged for Xerox to allow Apple to use the graphics system. [46]

GUI also became the foundation of the Windows operating system released in 1985 by Microsoft, co-founded by Jobs' rival and sometime partner, Bill Gates.

Consumer Printers

The computer revolution that Jobs, Gates and others helped unleash was the necessary prelude to what the 3D printing community today views as the looming transformation of manufacturing.

In the same way that computers began as enormous machines used only by a few government agencies, big corporations and universities, the first additive manufacturing (AM) printers were expensive devices meant only for industrial use, mainly for making prototypes. [47]

The wave of innovation that led to the present 3D boom began in 1984, when Charles Hull, a physicist specializing in photographic processes, patented a stereolithography device. It aimed a laser beam at a vat of liquid photopolymer, which hardens in reaction to the laser light. Following a digital blueprint and working layer by layer, the machine traces a shape with the laser hardening the material that will form the object. [48]

Hull went on to found 3D Systems, a company that produced the first commercial 3D printer in 1988. [49] By then engineers and scientists elsewhere were developing other versions of the additive reproduction system. In 1993, MIT researchers patented an AM machine that resembled an inkjet computer printer — a technology that grew out of the computer revolution. Another digital revolution — the invention and expansion of the Internet — enabled the next phase of 3D printing development.

In 2006 British "open source" developers — spreading and sharing their ideas freely over the Web — produced the first plans for the RepRap 3D printer, which essentially could replicate itself by reproducing its own plastic parts. The first version of a self-manufacturing 3D printer was produced in 2008. [50]

The following year, the U.S. Society of Manufacturing Engineers included "personal fabrication" on an annual list of six innovations likely to change manufacturing. [51] During the two years that followed, startup companies began selling kits to assemble desktop 3D printers based on the RepRap model. Prices ranged from $950 to $3,900. In 2010, a Chinese firm began selling a fully assembled desktop 3D printer for

$2,990. The following year, a British firm offered another assembled printer for about $2,700. [52]

Another trend that began in the early 2000s drew on 3D printing's power to excite youthful imagination and spurred use of the technology. In 2003 Sherry Lassiter, an MIT professor, organized a 3D fabrication lab — dubbed the "fab lab" — at the South End Technology Center, in a poor section of Boston. Neighborhood youths used the lab to make crafts that they sold at a street fair.

The idea then spread to Ghana, South Africa and Detroit, among other places. As of November, about 100 such labs were up and running, "democratizing access to the modern means to make things," wrote Gershenfeld of MIT. [53] ■

CURRENT SITUATION

Printing Sanitation

A group of University of Washington engineering students is making plans to set up a 3D printer in rural Mexico. Aided by a $100,000 prize they won in October for their proposal, the three students from the Washington Open Object Fabricators (WOOF) group envision helping people in Oaxaca set up small businesses producing the composting toilets devised by the students.

The prize for the best 3D printing-based project was awarded by Trade4all Limited, a British charity focused on technological approaches to fighting poverty in developing countries. "Our interest focused on the potential for 3D printing technology to overcome some of the challenges faced in countries with poor infrastructure and a lack of a traditional manufacturing base," the organization said in describing its so-called 3D4Dcontest. [54]

As an anti-poverty worker in rural Ghana, Panama and Bolivia — mostly as a Peace Corps volunteer — WOOF member Rogge, 37, had six years of experience dealing with development challenges in poor countries. During that time, he learned to appreciate the importance of basic water and sanitation services. "My experience with water systems and pumps made me realize it wasn't trivial to make pumps precise enough to work."

But once enrolled as an engineering student at the University of Washington for his second undergraduate degree (he has a B.S. in chemistry and a master's in education), Rogge took a class in 3D printing. There he saw that AM machines could make precisely sized parts, eliminating his problems in the field of trying to adapt parts to the systems he was building.

Meanwhile, he was working with a nonprofit, Water for Humans, which had started a project in Oaxaca to make composting toilets. They store waste in vaults for a year to allow time for pathogens to die, before the waste is spread in fields as fertilizer.

The original plan called for the toilets to be cast in concrete. "If you do that in town and you're working your way up the mountains in Oaxaca where you can't even use pack animals, you'd have to carry a 75-pound object up a mountain," Rogge says.

He hit on the idea of using a 3D printer to make a toilet that weighs far less than a concrete model. "We'll set up a shop in Oaxaca that will build the printers themselves," Rogge says of the prize-winning project. "When someone else in town wants to get in on latrine printing, we'll lease them printers. The shop will continue to have a vested interest in the printers to ensure that they're kept running."

Rogge and his fellow WOOF members — Bethany Weeks and Brandon Bowman — found a way around the high cost of the plastic raw material used by 3D printers. The expense could have doomed the idea of adapting the technology for poverty-stricken farmers.

So WOOF members rounded up a load of empty milk containers and had a recycler reduce them to plastic flakes. The students designed a printer-head feeder that could heat the plastic chips, then use the melted material to "print" a seven-foot-long, one-person boat. With that experiment under their belts, the students turned to looking for a 3D4D contest entry that would use the recycled-plastic innovation.

Now involved in the nuts and bolts of their Oaxaca project, the WOOF team is trying to find a way around another potential problem, the sometimes tricky adjustments that 3D printers require. "We want to train a group in Oaxaca to be expert at that," Rogge says. "An entrepreneur on his own is going to struggle with that. They'll need support."

Government Boost

Establishment of the National Additive Manufacturing Innovation Institute — the first of up to 15 programs designed to accelerate and expand manufacturing modernization — continues a long government (mostly military) tradition of encouraging technological innovation.

The nonprofit National Center for Defense Manufacturing and Machining, in Blairsville, Pa., will manage the $69 million initiative, which is designed to speed up improvements in 3D printing technology and encourage companies to adopt them. Established by the Defense Department, the center is designed to develop manufacturing innovations for the Pentagon and its private contractors.

Where 3D printing is concerned, the goals of both the center and the new institute are "to cross the technological valley of death" — the gap between research and commercialization, says Bourell of the University of Texas, who had joined in an effort to get the in-

Continued on p. 1054

At Issue:

Is a new "micro-patent" needed to protect 3D innovators?

HOD LIPSON
***ASSOCIATE PROFESSOR OF ENGINEERING, CORNELL UNIVERSITY; CO-AUTHOR,* FABRICATED: THE NEW WORLD OF 3D PRINTING**

WRITTEN FOR *CQ RESEARCHER*, NOVEMBER 2012

yes

In his novel *Makers*, science fiction author Cory Doctorow paints a riveting picture of a future world in which 3D printers are commonplace. Eventually, the economy crashes as businesses fall apart under an onslaught of high-speed counterfeiting. And large corporations in search of new, profitable ventures launch aggressive intellectual-property lawsuits that eventually cripple what's left of the economy.

Today, 3D printing does not fall neatly into traditional intellectual-property categories. If a copied product's technology is not covered by an active patent, there is no patent violation. Likewise, if no registered trademark is embedded in the created object, no trademark is violated. And if the object has some utility, it is not covered by copyright.

Intellectual-property (IP) rights are becoming critical. If nothing is done, small inventors, unable to afford expensive patents, will suffer. Yet, if copyright law is simply extended to all physical things, it could stifle innovation. A careful balance must be struck between the freedom to create and the protection of ideas. Open-source licenses, while successful in software and electronics, may be difficult to enforce in mechanical devices and materials. Perhaps what's needed is a new form of IP — call it a micro-patent — that facilitates innovation yet is friendlier to small businesses and solo inventors.

Here's how such patents would work. An inventor would submit, for a few hundred dollars, a document describing his invention to a centralized government micro-patent repository. The document would be time-stamped and then immediately released to the public.

Its lifespan would be shorter — perhaps five years rather than the traditional 20 — and only for demonstrated fields of use. In order to prevent patent trolling, it would protect only objects being sold commercially. Like a patent, it would cover a utilitarian application. Like a copyright, it would be easy and straightforward to obtain and would be tested only upon dispute.

By filing a micro-patent document, the inventor would be granted an immediate, implicit, short-term exclusive right to the disclosed idea, and only in case of a dispute by two *practicing* commercial entities would the case be evaluated.

In a global financial economy, micro-loans have given many entrepreneurs the financial tools to establish a small business. Micro-patents could similarly level the IP playing field, affording small entrepreneurs the intellectual-property protection needed to compete in a global innovation economy.

MICHAEL WEINBERG
VICE PRESIDENT, INSTITUTE FOR EMERGING INNOVATION, PUBLIC KNOWLEDGE

WRITTEN FOR *CQ RESEARCHER*, NOVEMBER 2012

no

Attempting to create a new short-term patent to benefit small-scale creators could end up doing more harm than good. So-called micro-patents are not needed to protect 3D-printed products. In fact, digital-manufacturing techniques may make patents *less* necessary by making it easier for creators to bring products to market themselves. Additionally, inventors using 3D printing are not waiting for a new intellectual-property right to innovate, and there is nothing to suggest that they will lack adequate incentives to create in the future. Finally, expanding the scope of intellectual-property protection tends to favor large, well-funded interests.

Small inventors have always existed. In the past, they were forced to find partners to turn their ideas into mass-produced products and to get them to market. Patents, though expensive and time-consuming to obtain, could help protect them from ceding all control to their more sophisticated partners. 3D printing allows small-scale inventors to create and perfect objects themselves. That gives them the choice to enter a market themselves and allows them to do so economically on a small scale.

Expanding intellectual-property rights comes at a cost. That cost can be worthwhile if it spurs innovation. However, it is not worthwhile if that innovation would happen without expanded intellectual-property rights. Numerous creative industries, including fashion, food and stand-up comedy, show that innovation and intellectual-property rights are not inexorably linked. The innovation surrounding 3D printing provides additional proof. Simply put, there is a lot of it. Even the relatively unsophisticated 3D printers available to the public today are fueling an explosion in innovation. The lack of an additional type of patent does not seem to be holding these inventors back.

There also are unintended consequences to consider, which can be especially pernicious in intellectual-property discussions. The expansion of patent rights could make it harder for inventors to innovate by expanding the existing patent thicket. It is already daunting for a small inventor to search prior art and existing patents before bringing a product to market. Creating an additional type of protection — potentially less formally documented and therefore even harder to search — runs the risk of imposing more roadblocks on an innovator who simply wants to bring an invention to market.

Continued from p. 1052

stitute based in his state. The long-range goal is to "create jobs and get people employed," he adds.

More than 50 entities — universities, community colleges in Ohio, Pennsylvania and West Virginia and large- and small-scale manufacturers — are participating. Institutions and companies involved include Carnegie Mellon University in Pittsburgh, Case Western Reserve University in Cleveland, the Society of Manufacturing Engineers and firms such as IBM, 3D Systems (which pioneered commercial 3D printing), Boeing and Lockheed Martin. [55]

The Pentagon is keenly interested in keeping U.S. manufacturing efficient and up to date, especially where AM is concerned, experts say, largely because of the military's large fleet of aging aircraft. "The military has an acute need for keeping these airplanes serviceable," says Cormier of the Rochester Institute of Technology. "The Defense Department has been a big driver in the recent explosive interest" in 3D printing.

That interest isn't limited to the newly formed institute. The Defense Advanced Research Projects Agency (DARPA) — which pioneered creation of the Internet — has begun installing up to 1,000 3D printers and other digitally controlled manufacturing machines in public high schools around the country, according to Cornell's Lipson and co-author Melba Kurman.

"The goal is to encourage students across clusters of schools to collaborate via social networking media to jointly design and build systems of moderate complexity, such as mobile robots, go-carts, etc., in response to prize challenges," DARPA said on its website. [56]

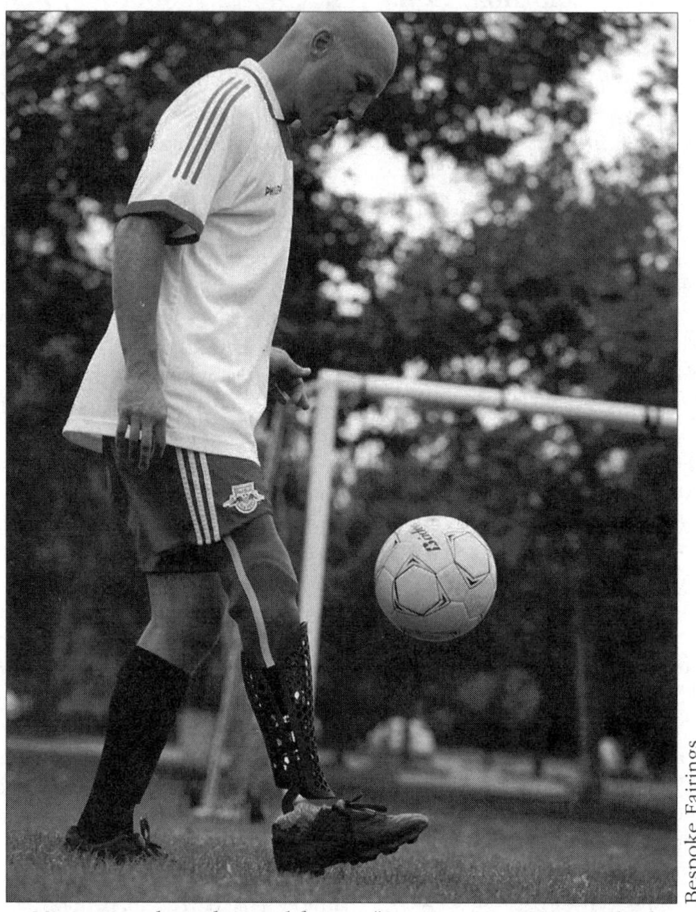

Bespoke Fairings

Motivational speaker and former "Survivor" contestant Chad Crittenden, who lost a leg to cancer, wears a custom-made plastic cover, or sport fairing, over his traditional prosthesis. By scanning an amputee's remaining limb, the manufacturer, Bespoke Fairings, is able to recreate the body's natural contour using 3D printing technology.

Bloomberg's Dream

New York City Mayor Michael Bloomberg hopes to make 3D manufacturing part of a high-tech boom in his city, which once boasted countless factories.

In October, Bloomberg announced a contest, "New York's Next Top Makers," aimed at encouraging inventors and designers with ideas for producing products on AM machines. "This contest will make sure New York City stays on the cutting edge of 3D printing, an exciting new industry with virtually unlimited potential," Bloomberg said. [57]

Bloomberg spoke at the opening of a factory for Shapeways, a company founded in the Netherlands that produces 3D designs submitted by customers, and helps market them. The event's big photo-op was Bloomberg's use of a pair of 3D-printed plastic scissors to cut the ribbon on Shapeways' 25,000-square-foot factory. [58]

Located in Long Island City, a neighborhood in Queens across the East River from Manhattan, the Shapeways facility is scheduled to be fully operational by January, with up to 50 3D printers in operation. The company says it has nearly 200,000 customers for its printing services. And more than 7,000 makers use the Shapeways site to sell their products — including jewelry, crafts and toys — over the Web. [59]

Shapeways' new neighborhood had housed industrial producers as long ago as the Civil War era. But when New York deindustrialized in the 1970s, the district was left with empty factories. [60]

Bloomberg's red-carpet greeting for Shapeways reflected his strategy of transforming New York into an East Coast version of Silicon Valley. "Over the last few years, what we've seen over and over again is a commitment to make New York City a viable alternative to Silicon valley and a place where true innovation occurs," Eric Schmidt, executive chairman of Google, said after meeting with Bloomberg in October. [61]

In addition to Google, Facebook and eBay have opened major offices in Manhattan. And startups such as Foursquare, Tumblr, Kickstarter and Gilt Groupe were founded in New York. [62]

The "makers" contest, organized by the city's Economic Development Corp., is part of a larger effort that includes a $22.5 million startup investment fund and other incentives to lure high-tech businesses to New York. The city also made a 12-acre site available, along with $100 million in improvements, for a high-tech graduate school. Cornell University and the Technion-Israel Institute of Technology won the bid to operate the school, which will offer advanced degreess to 2,500 students. [63]

What role 3D printing research and development might play in the school's curriculum isn't clear from initial descriptions. But faculty and students at Cornell and Technion are active in the field. [64]

In announcing the "makers" contest, Bloomberg called AM "an exciting new industry with virtually unlimited potential, and which could completely revolutionize manufacturing." [65] ■

OUTLOOK

Only the Beginning

Asked to forecast the future of 3D printing, most experts veer between caution and excitement about the technology's potential. For those most closely involved in pushing the process forward, the biggest danger lies in underestimating the effects of AM as its use expands.

After all, one of the most notorious analyses in technology history is a 1977 sentence by Ken Olsen, the founder and then-CEO of the once high-flying and now-defunct Digital Equipment Corp.: "There is no reason for any individual to have a computer in his home." [66]

Olsen later said he was talking about computers that would essentially operate a household. But the one-liner lives on. Lipson of Cornell and co-author Kurman quote a version of it in a 2010 report on 3D printer-based manufacturing. [67]

And Lipson seems to have taken the Olsen example to heart. "You can expect lots of dispersed groups making things," he says. "Maybe the automobile industry is not going to change, but the supply chain is going to be reorganized. There will be a lot of opportunities for small businesses to participate in the supply chain, which previously was reserved for a few large companies."

Relying on hundreds of small makers instead of one large supplier likely will prove more reliable, Lipson says, likening that shift to using remote Internet-connected servers ("the cloud") to store data, instead of relying on an individual hard drive. "One thousand people manufacturing 1,000 parts is much more robust, because if one machine goes down, it's not noticed," he says.

And, says Mota of New York University's ITP, small makers who produce customized items don't have to entirely replace industrial producers in order to carve out a place for themselves in manufacturing. "I don't see that they will supply the entire world," she says.

However, even conventional manufacturers are likely to take advantage of AM technology and its digitally controlled cousins to produce some items that need quick turnaround. "3D printers are only one piece of this," she says. "I'm talking about factories having several technologies. I don't think 3D printing alone will replace a lot of manufacturing, but I think the whole family will change manufacturing."

McCormack of *Manufacturing & Technology News* says that change may be on the distant horizon. If the need for continuing scientific and engineering work on 3D printing is a mountain, he says, "We're maybe one-third of the way up."

AM production is suitable for some non-machine parts, he acknowledges. But a major obstacle to immediate 3D production of engine parts — instead of just prototypes — in heavy industry is the nature of the materials used in 3D printers. "It's hard to create a part that has a high level of ability to withstand constant pressure or force," he says. "I don't want to be on an airplane with a 3D-printed turbine blade."

For now, at least, MIT's Gershenfeld notes that advanced and traditional technology can coexist comfortably. "Glowing articles about 3-D printers read like stories in the 1950s that proclaimed that microwave ovens were the future of cooking," he wrote. "Microwaves are convenient, but they don't replace the rest of the kitchen." [68]

But, he adds, 3D printers are only the beginning — not the end — of transformative manufacturing technology. At MIT and other research centers, he wrote, scientists and engineers are already moving beyond "printing" objects to assembling them.

"A key difference between existing 3-D printers and these assemblers is that the assemblers will be able to create complete functional systems in a single process," Gershenfeld wrote recently. Eventually, "they will be able to integrate fixed and moving mechanical structures, sensors and actuators and electronics. Think a jumbo jet that can flap its wings." [69] ■

Notes

[1] Brent Stucker, "Additive Manufacturing Technologies: Technology Introduction and Business Implications," National Academies of Sciences, *Frontiers of Engineering 2011*, pp. 5-12, www.nap.edu/openbook.php?record_id=13274&page=1.

[2] "Penn Researchers Improve Living Tissues with 3D Printed Vascular Networks Made From Sugar," *Penn News*, July 1, 2012, www.upenn.edu/pennnews/news/penn-researchers-improve-living-tissues-3d-printed-vascular-networks-made-sugar; "Prototype as Product: 13:30 Printable Headphones," Teague Labs, Oct. 1, 2012, http://labs.teague.com/2012/10/01/prototype-as-product-1330-printable-headphones/; "WOOF wins the 3D4D Challenge," 3D4D Challenge, press release, Oct. 20, 2012, www.3d4dchallenge.org/woof-wins-the-3d4d-challenge/.

[3] Stucker, *op. cit.*

[4] Neil Gershenfeld, "How to Make Almost Anything: The Digital Fabrication Revolution," *Foreign Affairs*, November-December, 2012, www.foreignaffairs.com/articles/138154/neil-gershenfeld/how-to-make-almost-anything.

[5] "NCDMM is Chosen to Manage National Additive Manufacturing Innovation Institute," National Center for Defense Manufacturing and Machining, press release, Aug. 16, 2012, http://ncdmm.org/2012/08/14/namii-press-release/; "Obama Administration Announces New Public-Private Partnership to Support Manufacturing Innovation, Encourage Investment in America," U.S. Commerce Department, press release, Aug. 16, 2012, www.commerce.gov/news/press-releases/2012/08/16/obama-administration-announces-new-public-private-partnership-support.

[6] "WOOF wins the 3D4D Challenge," *op. cit.*

[7] Makershed.com, www.makershed.com/default.asp; Walter Isaacson, *Steve Jobs* (2011), pp. 71-80; "Apple II — 1977," oldcomputers.net, http://oldcomputers.net/appleii.html.

[8] Mike Senese, "Staples Announces In-Store 3-D Printing Service," *Wired*, Nov. 29, 2012, www.wired.com/design/2012/11/staples-goes-3-d/.

[9] Lisa Harouni, "A primer on 3D printing," "TED Talks," November 2011, www.ted.com/talks/lisa_harouni_a_primer_on_3d_printing.html.

[10] Stucker, *op. cit.*, pp. 6-10.

[11] *Ibid.*

[12] Steve Rengers, "Electron Beam Melting [EBM] vs. Direct Metal Laser Sintering [DMLS]," Midwest Society for the Advancement of Material and Process Engineering [search in site], November 2012, www.midwestsampe.org/?u=/content/pages/home&f=0.

[13] Chris Anderson, *Makers: The New Industrial Revolution* (2012), location 739, Kindle edition; Laura Hazard Owen, "Chris Anderson leaves *Wired* for his robotics startup," paidContent, Nov. 2, 2012, http://paidcontent.org/2012/11/02/chris-anderson-leaves-wired-for-his-robotics-startup/.

[14] Floyd Norris, "Manufacturing Is Surprising Bright Spot in U.S. Economy," *The New York Times*, Jan. 5, 2012, www.nytimes.com/2012/01/06/business/us-manufacturing-is-a-bright-spot-for-the-economy.html.

[15] Michael Ettlinger and Kate Gordon, "The Importance and Promise of American Manufacturing: Why It Matters if We Make It in America and Where We Stand Today," Center for American Progress, April 2011, p. 11, www.americanprogress.org/wp-content/uploads/issues/2011/04/pdf/manufacturing.pdf.

[16] *Ibid.*, pp. 10-11.

[17] Byron Pitts, "3 Million Open Jobs," "60 Minutes," CBS News, Nov. 11, 2012, www.cbsnews.com/video/watch/?id=50134943n; Adam Davidson, "Making It in America," *The Atlantic*, January-February 2012, www.theatlantic.com/magazine/archive/2012/01/making-it-in-america/308844/.

[18] Wikispeed, http://main.wikispeed.softlaunch.352media.com; Local Motors, www.localmotors.com.

[19] Gary P. Pisano and Willy C. Shih, *Producing Prosperity: Why America Needs a Manufacturing Renaissance* (2012).

[20] Joseph Flaherty, "3D Systems Sues Formlabs and Kickstarter for Patent Infringement," *Wired*, Nov. 21, 2012, www.wired.com/design/2012/11/3d-systems-formlabs-lawsuit/.

[21] Quoted in *ibid.*

[22] Jeff Leeds, "Lackluster sales add to problems at firms already battling web piracy, soaring expenses and eroding profits," *Los Angeles Times*, Dec. 26, 2001, part 3, p. 1.

[23] Quoted in Isaacson, *op. cit.*, p. 396.

[24] Claire Cain Miller, "Google Deal Gives Publishers a Choice: Digitize or Not," *The New York Times*, Oct. 4, 2012, www.nytimes.com/2012/10/05/technology/google-and-publishers-settle-over-digital-books.html. Also see Barbara Mantel, "Academic Publishers Seek to Enforce Electronic Copyrights," in "Future of Libraries," *CQ Researcher*, July 29, 2011, pp. 625-652.

[25] "CPB, ICE Release Report on 2011 Counterfeit Seizures," U.S. Customs and Border Protection, press release, Jan. 9, 2012, www.cbp.gov/xp/cgov/newsroom/news_releases/national/01092012.xml; Jayne O'Donnell, "Counterfeit products are a growing, and dangerous problem," *USA Today*, June 6, 2012, http://usatoday30.usatoday.com/money/perfi/columnist/odonnell/story/2012-06-01/confident-consumer-jayne-odonnell/55406774/1.

[26] Catarina Mota research notebook, www.researchnotebook.cc/?page_id=2.

[27] Gershenfeld, *op. cit.*

[28] Quoted in Robert Beckhusen, "3-D Printer Company Seizes Machine From Desktop Gunsmith," *Danger Room* blog, Oct. 1, 2012, www.wired.com/dangerroom/2012/10/3d-gun-blocked/.

[29] Quoted in Andy Greenberg, "3D-Printable gun Project Hits Its Fundraising Goal Despite Being Booted Off Indiegogo," *Forbes*, Sept. 20, 2012, www.forbes.com/sites/andygreenberg/2012/09/20/3d-printed-gun-project-hits-its-fundraising-goal-despite-being-booted-off-indiegogo.

[30] "Should We Print Guns? Cody R. Wilson Says 'Yes,' " *Slashdot* (video), Sept. 5, 2011, http://hardware.slashdot.org/story/12/09/04/1837209/should-we-print-guns-cody-r-wilson-says-yes-video.

[31] *Ibid.*

[32] Paulo Jorge Bártolo and Ian Gibson, "History of Stereolithographic Processes," in P. J. Bártolo, ed., *Stereolithography: Materials, Processes and Applications* (2011), pp. 37-52; Helmut Gernsheim, "The 150th Anniversary of Photography," January 1977, Harry Ransom Center, University of Texas, www.hrc.utexas.edu/exhibitions/permanent/wfp/heliography.html.

[33] "Thomas Blanchard (1788-1864)," Springfield Armory, National Park Service, undated, www.nps.gov/spar/historyculture/upload/Thomas-Blanchard.pdf.

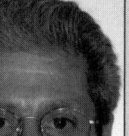

About the Author

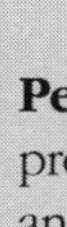

Peter Katel is a *CQ Researcher* contributing writer who previously reported on Haiti and Latin America for *Time* and *Newsweek* and covered the Southwest for newspapers in New Mexico. He has received several journalism awards, including the Bartolomé Mitre Award for coverage of drug trafficking, from the Inter-American Press Association. He holds an A.B. in university studies from the University of New Mexico. His recent reports include "Mexico's Future" and "Voter Rights."

[34] For background, see Peter Katel, "Reviving Manufacturing," *CQ Researcher*, July 22, 2011, pp. 601-624.

[35] David L. Bourell, *et al.*, "A Brief History of Additive Manufacturing and the 2009 Roadmap for Additive Manufacturing: Looking Back and Looking Ahead," presented at RapidTech 2009, U.S.-Turkey Workshop on Rapid Technologies, Istanbul Technical University, http://iweb.tntech.edu/rrpl/rapidtech2009/bourell.pdf.

[36] *Ibid.*

[37] *Ibid.*

[38] Except where otherwise noted, this subsection is drawn from Vaclav Smil, *Transforming the Twentieth Century: Technical Innovations and Their Consequences* (2006).

[39] *Ibid.*, p. 177.

[40] Frederick W. Taylor, "The Principles of Scientific Management, 1911," in *Modern History Sourcebook*, www.fordham.edu/halsall/mod/1911taylor.html.

[41] Ian D. Wyatt and Daniel E. Hecker, "Occupational changes during the 20th century," *Monthly Labor Review*, Bureau of Labor Statistics, March 2006, www.bls.gov/opub/mlr/2006/03/art3full.pdf.

[42] David Owen, "Making Copies," *Smithsonian*, August 2004, www.smithsonianmag.com/history-archaeology/copies.html.

[43] *Ibid.*

[44] *Ibid.*

[45] "CNC Machine and Computer Numerical Control History," *CNC Cookbook*, undated, www.cnccookbook.com/CCCNCMachine.htm.

[46] Marian Bozdoc, "The History of CAD," mb solutions, 2003, www.mbdesign.net/mbinfo/CAD-History.htm; Isaacson, *op. cit.*, pp. 94-101.

[47] Bourell, *op. cit.*

[48] Charles Hull, "Hit Rewind . . . The History of 3D Printing," *3D Innovations* (blog), March 22, 2012, www.3d-innovations.com/blog/?tag=charles-hull; Bártolo and Gibson, *op. cit.*; "3D Systems Founder and Inventor of Stereolithography, Charles Hull Announces Retirement," *Business Wire*, Feb. 5, 1999.

[49] *Ibid.*, Hull.

[50] Sean Dodson, "The machine that copies itself," *The Guardian*, July 2, 2008, www.guardian.co.uk/technology/2008/jul/03/copy.machine.reprap.

[51] Terry Wohlers, "Innovations That Could Change the Way You Manufacture," *Manufacturing Engineering*, Society of Manufacturing Engineers, March 2009, www.sme.org/Tertiary.aspx?id=19290.

[52] Catarina Mota, "The Rise of Personal Fabrication," *Research Notebook*, undated, www.researchnotebook.cc/?p=6#3dprinters.

[53] Gershenfeld, *op. cit.*

[54] "About the 2012 Challenge," Trade4All Limited, 2012, www.3d4dchallenge.org.

[55] "NCDMM is Chosen . . .," *op. cit.*

[56] "The Manufacturing Experimentation and Outreach (MENTOR)," Defense Advanced Research Project Agency, undated, www.darpa.mil/Our_Work/TTO/Programs/Manufacturing_Experimentation_and_Outreach_(MENTOR).aspx.

[57] Quoted in Matthew Lysiak and Corky Siemaszko, "Shape Shift City Boosts '3-D Printing' Biz," *New York Daily News*, Oct. 19, 2012, p. 10; "New York's Next Top Makers," New York City Economic Development Corp., undated, http://nexttopmakers.com.

[58] *Ibid.*; "Shapeways Announces Manufacturing Facility in New York City That Can 3D Print Up To 5 Million Products a Year," PR Newswire, Oct. 18, 2012, www.prnewswire.com/news-releases/shapeways-announces-manufacturing-facility-in-new-york-city-that-can-3d-print-up-to-5-million-products-a-year-174798981.html.

[59] *Ibid.*

[60] Kenny Greenberg, "A Brief History of LIC," LIC Web, 1996, www.licweb.com/history.html.

[61] Quoted in Jennifer Peltz, "NYC sees progress in quest to become tech capital," The Associated Press (Malone, *N.Y. Telegram*), Oct. 22, 2012.

[62] *Ibid.*

[63] Richard Pérez-Peña, "Cornell Alumnus Is Behind $350 Million Gift to Build Science School in City," *The New York Times*, Dec. 19, 2011, www.nytimes.com/2011/12/20/nyregion/cornell-and-technion-israel-chosen-to-build-science-school-in-new-york-city.html?_r=0.

[64] "3D Print the Impossible! Turning Escher Drawings Into Real 3D Models," *It's a 3D World* (blog), *Objet*, Aug. 28, 2012, http://blog.objet.com/2012/08/28/3d-print-the-impossible-turning-escher-drawings-in-real-3d-models/; "Cornell Creative Machines Lab," undated, http://creativemachines.cornell.edu.

[65] Quoted in "Mayor Bloomberg and Economic Development Corporation Launch Competition," press release, Office of the Mayor, New York City, Oct. 18, 2012, www.nyc.gov/portal/site/nycgov/menuitem.c0935b9a57bb4ef3daf2f1c701c789a0/index.jsp?pageID=mayor_press_release&catID=1194&doc_name=http%3A%2F%2Fwww.nyc.gov%2Fhtml%2Fom%2Fhtml%2F2012b%2Fpr361-12.html&cc=unused1978&rc=1194&ndi=1.

[66] "Ken Olsen," Snopes.com, Sept. 21, 2004, www.snopes.com/quotes/kenolsen.asp.

[67] Hod Lipson and Melba Kurman, "Factory @ Home: The Emerging Economy of Personal Manufacturing," Cornell University, December 2010, p. 30, http://web.mae.cornell.edu/lipson/FactoryAtHome.pdf.

[68] Gershenfeld, *op. cit.*

[69] *Ibid.*

FOR MORE INFORMATION

Cornell Creative Machines Lab, http://creativemachines.cornell.edu/front. A leading research center on advanced technology of all kinds; provides detailed information on 3D printing, including "Fab@Home," an open-source, virtual community centered on small-scale manufacturing.

Interactive Telecommunications Program, New York University, 721 Broadway, 4th Floor, New York, NY 10003; 212-998-1880; http://itp.nyu.edu/itp/. The home of the 3D printer-based "Burritobot" and other innovative uses of the technology.

MIT Center for Bits and Atoms, Room E15-401, 20 Ames St., Cambridge, MA 02139; 617-253-0392; http://cba.mit.edu. A major research lab on digital fabrication; website provides a wealth of information on innovative fabrication projects using 3D printing and other technologies.

National Additive Manufacturing Innovation Institute, 236 Boardman St., Youngstown, OH 44503; 724-539-8811; http://namii.org. The new government-education-industry initiative to improve 3D technology and its applications.

Open 3D Printing, Solheim Additive Manufacturing Laboratory, University of Washington; http://open3dp.me.washington.edu. A 3D printing website that provides information on completed projects, accessible information sources and more.

Public Knowledge, 1818 N St., N.W., Suite 410, Washington, DC 20036; 202-861-0020; www.publicknowledge.org. Advocacy organization for open information access on the Internet; monitors intellectual-property issues involving 3D printing.

Bibliography

Selected Sources

Books

Anderson, Chris, *Makers: The New Industrial Revolution*, Crown Business, 2012.
Wired magazine's former editor in chief — a leading theoretician and advocate of decentralized manufacturing and a startup entrepreneur himself — contends that 3D printers and other digital tools are transforming manufacturing.

Lipson, Hod, and Melba Kurman, *Fabricated: The New World of 3D Printing*, Wiley, 2013.
A leader in developing 3D technology, Cornell engineering and computer science professor Lipson and technology policy specialist Kurman explore the present and future effects of vastly expanded use of 3D printing.

Articles

"Difference Engine: The PC all over again?" *The Economist* (*Babbage* blog), Sept. 9, 2012, www.economist.com/blogs/babbage/2012/09/3d-printing.
The British news magazine reports on concerns about the potential effects of intellectual-property law on 3D printer-based production.

Chen, Angela, "3-D Printers Spread From Engineering Departments to Designs Across Disciplines," *The Chronicle of Higher Education*, http://chronicle.com/article/3-D-Printers-Arent-Just-for/134440.
Colleges and universities are seeing art majors, among others, using 3D printers for purposes beyond science and engineering.

Davidson, Paul, "3-D printing could remake U.S. manufacturing," *USA Today*, July 10, 2012, http://usatoday30.usatoday.com/money/industries/manufacturing/story/2012-07-10/digital-manufacturing/56135298/1.
A business correspondent covers the growing interest in 3D printing as an economic force.

Drumm, Brook, "Report: First Ever 3D Printshow London 2012," *Make* magazine, Oct. 25, 2012, http://blog.makezine.com/2012/10/25/report-first-ever-3d-printshow-london-2012/.
An on-scene report from a major 3D-printing industry exhibition in London offers yet more evidence of strong British involvement in the technology.

Excell, Jon, and Stuart Nathan, "The rise of additive manufacturing," *The Engineer*, May 24, 2010, www.theengineer.co.uk/in-depth/the-big-story/the-rise-of-additive-manufacturing/1002560.article.
Anticipating the present booming interest in 3D printing, a British engineering journal explores the field in depth, with special attention to activity in Britain.

Gershenfeld, Neil, "How to Make Almost Anything: The Digital Fabrication Revolution," *Foreign Affairs*, November-December 2012, www.foreignaffairs.com/articles/138154/neil-gershenfeld/how-to-make-almost-anything.
The head of an MIT lab explains, in readable prose, the importance of the 3D revolution.

Igoe, Tom, and Catarina Mota, "A Strategist's Guide to Digital Fabrication," *strategy + business*, Autumn 2011, www.strategy-business.com/article/11307?gko=63624.
A visiting scholar at New York University's Interactive Telecommunications Program (MOTA) analyzes the business possibilities of 3D printing and digital fabrication.

Kessler, Sarah, "Shapeways' New 3-D-Printing Factor Brings Manufacturing Jobs Into The Tech Scene," *Fast Company*, Oct. 24, 2012, www.fastcompany.com/3002303/shapewayss-new-3-d-printing-factory-brings-manufacturing-jobs-tech-scene.
The business magazine reports on the move to New York City by a firm pioneering Web-based 3D printer fabrication.

Vance, Ashlee, "3-D Printing Spurs a Manufacturing Revolution," *The New York Times*, Sept. 13, 2010, www.nytimes.com/2010/09/14/technology/14print.html?pagewanted=all.
A correspondent specializing in 3D printing reports on an upsurge in niche manufacturing using the technology.

Reports and Studies

"Frontiers of Engineering: Reports on Leading-Edge Engineering from the 2011 Symposium," National Academy of Engineering, 2012, www.nap.edu/openbook.php?record_id=13274&page=1.
The first 44 pages of these collected papers by leaders in the field focus on 3D-printing applications in aerospace, surgery and other fields.

Lipson, Hod, and Melba Kurman, "Factory @ Home: The Emerging Economy of Personal Manufacturing," Cornell University, December 2010, http://web.mae.cornell.edu/lipson/FactoryAtHome.pdf.
In an early version of their new book, Lipson and Kurman survey progress in the field and its implications for the manufacturing economy

Weinberg, Michael, "It Will Be Awesome If They Don't Screw It Up: 3D Printing, Intellectual Property, and the Fight Over the Next Great Disruptive Technology," Public Knowledge, November 2010, www.publicknowledge.org/files/docs/3DPrintingPaperPublicKnowledge.pdf.
A leading advocate of open-source methodology explores the potential problems that intellectual-property law enforcement poses for the expanded use of 3D-printing technology.

The Next Step:

Additional Articles from Current Periodicals

Manufacturing

Brennan, Pat, "3D Printing May Help Carve Healthier Future," *Orange County* (Calif.) *Register*, Oct. 27, 2012, www.ocregister.com/articles/printing-375880-manufacturing-madou.html.
An engineering professor at the University of California at Irvine hopes to rejuvenate U.S. manufacturing by expanding the uses of 3D printing.

Davidson, Paul, "More Goods Come From 3-D Printing," *USA Today*, July 11, 2012, p. B1, usatoday30.usatoday.com/money/industries/manufacturing/story/2012-07-10/digital-manufacturing/56135298/1.
Manufacturing employment is expected to increase as more companies relocate to the United States to pursue 3D printing.

Kirby, Carrie, "Boon to Entrepreneurs," *The San Francisco Chronicle*, Nov. 26, 2012, p. D1, www.sfgate.com/business/article/3-D-printing-a-boon-to-entrepreneurs-4065697.php.
3D printing is allowing small businesses to develop products that can't be created using traditional manufacturing processes.

Wadhwa, Vivek, "Manufacturing Returns to America," *Pittsburgh Post-Gazette*, Aug. 12, 2012, p. B1, www.post-gazette.com/stories/opinion/perspectives/manufacturing-is-returning-to-america-648616/.
Advances in 3D printing, robotics and artificial intelligence will lead to a manufacturing renaissance in the United States, says a columnist.

Medicine

Chan, Marcus, "Helping Amputees to Walk Tall," *The San Francisco Chronicle*, May 31, 2011, p. D1, www.sfgate.com/business/article/Bespoke-creates-prosthetic-leg-case-using-3-D-tech-2370108.php.
A California company is using 3D printing to develop prosthetic limbs that allow patients to give their prostheses personalized touches such as patterns and graphics.

Chen, Angela, "3-D Printers Spread From Engineering Departments to Designs Across Disciplines," *The Chronicle of Higher Education*, Sept. 17, 2012, chronicle.com/article/3-D-Printers-Arent-Just-for/134440/.
3D printing has the potential to expand the possibilities of bioengineering and several medical fields.

Robbins, Christopher, "Clarkson Scientist Honored for Tissue-Engineering Work," *Watertown* (N.Y.) *Daily Times*, July 29, 2012, p. B6, www.watertowndailytimes.com/article/20120726/DCO01/707269876.
A German think tank has honored a New York scientist for his work on the three-dimensional bioprinting of human tissues.

Robbins, Gary, "Engineering School Adding Huge New Facility," *San Diego Union-Tribune*, Sept. 10, 2012, p. A1, www.utsandiego.com/news/2012/sep/10/tp-engineering-school-adding-huge-new-facility/.
The University of California at San Diego engineering school has created an $83 million facility that will, among other things, test medical devices and perform the 3D printing of artificial blood vessels.

Security

Bilton, Nick, "Just Print the Gun Now," *The New York Times*, Oct. 8, 2012, p. B1, bits.blogs.nytimes.com/2012/10/07/with-a-3-d-printer-building-a-gun-at-home/.
The Bureau of Alcohol, Tobacco, Firearms and Explosives is keeping a close watch on 3D printers because of their ability to make homemade guns.

Kurtz, Ced, "3-D Printers Can Produce Homemade Guns," *Pittsburgh Post-Gazette*, Oct. 21, 2012, p. D4, www.post-gazette.com/stories/business/technology/techman-3-d-printers-can-produce-homemade-guns-658493/?print=1.
Guns are one of the unintended consequences brought about by 3D printing, says a columnist.

Ulloa, Jazmine, "Student in Gun-Printing Drama," *Austin* (Texas) *American-Statesman*, Oct. 4, 2012, p. B1, www.statesman.com/news/news/crime-law/online-collective-aims-to-print-plastic-guns/nSSqt/.
A University of Texas law student is at the center of a legal controversy involving the printing of homemade guns.

CITING *CQ RESEARCHER*

Sample formats for citing these reports in a bibliography include the ones listed below. Preferred styles and formats vary, so please check with your instructor or professor.

MLA STYLE

Jost, Kenneth. "Remembering 9/11," CQ Researcher 2 Sept. 2011: 701-732.

APA STYLE

Jost, K. (2011, September 2). Remembering 9/11. *CQ Researcher, 9*, 701-732.

CHICAGO STYLE

Jost, Kenneth. "Remembering 9/11." *CQ Researcher*, September 2, 2011, 701-732.

CQ Researcher

Published by CQ Press, an Imprint of SAGE Publications, Inc.

www.cqresearcher.com

Future of Homeownership

Should government do more to help homeowners?

The housing market is finally showing signs of recovery after the housing crash and Great Recession of the late 2000s. The number of foreclosed homes is shrinking, sales of homes are climbing, prices are rebounding and builders are ramping up construction. Yet the share of Americans who own their homes dropped to 65.5 percent in the third quarter — the lowest since 1997. Many of today's buyers are investors who are snapping up houses in some of the hardest-hit neighborhoods and converting them into rentals, which experts say is a new trend. Analysts wonder whether many Americans are permanently rejecting homeownership in favor of renting. Meanwhile, policymakers are weighing how much the government should help the millions of remaining distressed homeowners and how to reform mortgage financing to avoid another housing debacle.

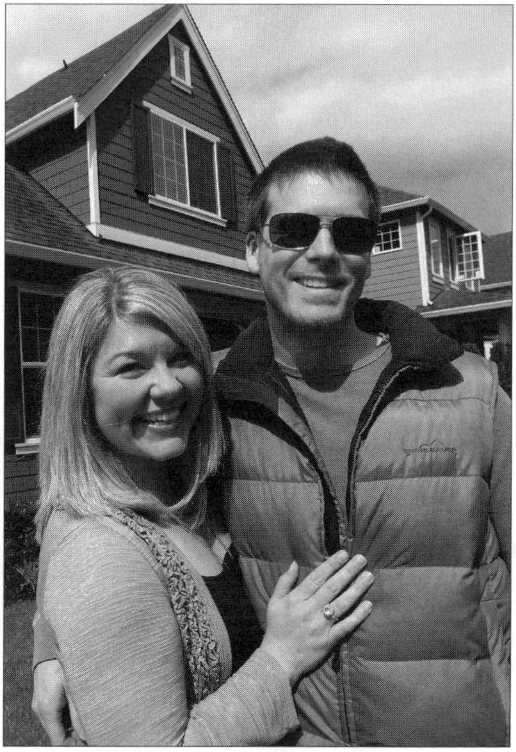

Public relations worker Laura Young, 29, and her husband, Andre Gjerde, 31, a translator, were able to buy a new Seattle-area house, thanks to the weak housing market. "We were just shocked we were able to get it" at such a low price, says Young of their 2011 purchase.

INSIDE THIS REPORT

THE ISSUES 1063

CHRONOLOGY 1071

BACKGROUND 1073

CURRENT SITUATION 1076

AT ISSUE......................1077

OUTLOOK 1079

BIBLIOGRAPHY 1082

THE NEXT STEP 1083

CQ Researcher • Dec. 14, 2012 • www.cqresearcher.com
Volume 22, Number 44 • Pages 1061-1084

CQPRESS

Los Angeles | London | New Delhi
Singapore | Washington DC

RECIPIENT OF SOCIETY OF PROFESSIONAL JOURNALISTS AWARD FOR EXCELLENCE ◆ AMERICAN BAR ASSOCIATION SILVER GAVEL AWARD

THE ISSUES

1063 • Does homeownership benefit society?
• Should the government do more to help distressed homeowners?
• Should the federal government get out of the mortgage business?

BACKGROUND

1073 **Early Suburbs**
After the Civil War, home builders promised escape from the problems of urban living.

1074 **Housing Collapses**
After the stock market crash, defaults exploded.

1075 **Homeownership Rises**
No-down-payment mortgages enabled World War II veterans to purchase homes.

1075 **Securities and the Crash**
Mortgage defaults revealed the financial system's exposure to subprime mortgages.

1076 **Clean-up**
Five major banks agreed to new consumer safeguards.

CURRENT SITUATION

1076 **Reforms Disappoint**
The five banks are making reforms too slowly, consumer groups say.

1078 **Discrimination**
Housing activists accuse banks of poorly maintaining foreclosed houses in communities of color.

OUTLOOK

1079 **Big Decisions**
Regulators will soon set new rules on getting a mortgage.

SIDEBARS AND GRAPHICS

1064 **Glossary of Real Estate Terms**

1065 **Hispanics' Homeownership Grew the Most**
Rate grew 5 percentage points since 1994.

1066 **Home of the Future Is Here**
Accessing "smart" home systems online is confusing.

1068 **Homeownership Rate Hit New Low**
The decline was the largest since the Great Depression.

1071 **Chronology**
Key events since 1927.

1072 **More Americans Are Renting**
But the cost is out of reach for many poor families.

1074 **Value of Mortgage Originations Is Rising**
Increases began after prices bottomed out in 2008.

1077 **At Issue**
Should Congress phase out the mortgage interest deduction?

FOR FURTHER RESEARCH

1081 **For More Information**
Organizations to contact.

1082 **Bibliography**
Selected sources used.

1083 **The Next Step**
Additional articles.

1083 **Citing *CQ Researcher***
Sample bibliography formats.

Cover: AP Photo/Elaine Thompson

CQ Researcher

Dec. 14, 2012
Volume 22, Number 44

MANAGING EDITOR: Thomas J. Billitteri
tjb@cqpress.com

ASSISTANT MANAGING EDITOR: Kathy Koch
kkoch@cqpress.com

SENIOR CONTRIBUTING EDITOR:
Thomas J. Colin
tcolin@cqpress.com

ASSOCIATE EDITOR: Kenneth Jost

STAFF WRITER: Marcia Clemmitt

CONTRIBUTING WRITERS: Peter Katel, Barbara Mantel, Tom Price, Jennifer Weeks

SENIOR PROJECT EDITOR: Olu B. Davis

ASSISTANT EDITOR: Darrell Dela Rosa

FACT CHECKER: Michelle Harris

Los Angeles | London | New Delhi
Singapore | Washington DC

An Imprint of SAGE Publications, Inc.

VICE PRESIDENT AND EDITORIAL DIRECTOR, HIGHER EDUCATION GROUP:
Michele Sordi

DIRECTOR, ONLINE PUBLISHING:
Todd Baldwin

CQ Researcher (ISSN 1056-2036) is printed on acid-free paper. Published weekly, except: (March wk. 5) (May wk. 4) (July wk. 1) (Aug. wks. 3, 4) (Nov. wk. 4) and (Dec. wks. 3, 4). Published by SAGE Publications, Inc., 2455 Teller Rd., Thousand Oaks, CA 91320. Annual full-service subscriptions start at $1,054. For pricing, call 1-800-818-7243. To purchase a *CQ Researcher* report in print or electronic format (PDF), visit www.cqpress.com or call 866-427-7737. Single reports start at $15. Bulk purchase discounts and electronic-rights licensing are also available. Periodicals postage paid at Thousand Oaks, California, and at additional mailing offices. POSTMASTER: Send address changes to *CQ Researcher*, 2300 N St., N.W., Suite 800, Washington, DC 20037.

Future of Homeownership

BY BARBARA MANTEL

THE ISSUES

Danielle and Robert Burke moved into their four-bedroom, three-bath house in August. The 50-year-old Dutch colonial in Princeton Junction, N.J., is the first home the young couple, married a little more than two-and-a-half years, has owned together. Prior to closing, they had been renting a much smaller two-bedroom, one-bath apartment.

"It's really nice to come home to something that we are making ours," says Danielle, 27, who teaches middle school in a neighboring town. Her 31-year-old husband, an engineer, commutes to work in New York City. Renting, however, had its appeal, says Danielle. "I did love that if anything broke, they took care of it."

The Burkes considered moving to a larger rental. "But if we want to buy our 'forever' home, what better time than now, when we can afford to get into this area and get a really low interest rate?" asks Danielle. They have a 30-year, fixed-rate mortgage at just 3.7 percent interest. The only surprise, so far, has been the number of hours they spend on home-improvement projects. "Sometimes we're wondering where our time goes," she says.

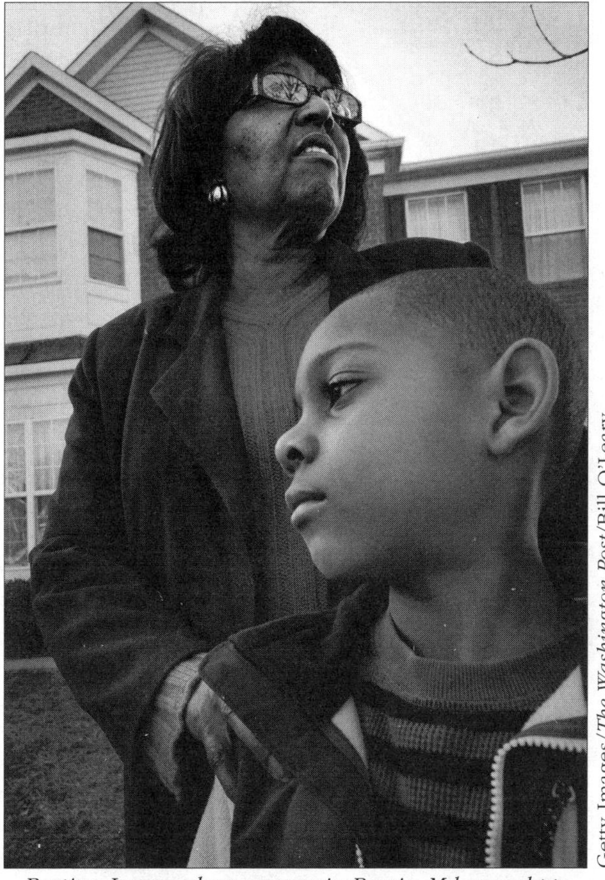

Getty Images/*The Washington Post*/Bill O'Leary

Bertina Jones, a homeowner in Bowie, Md., sought to avoid foreclosure with help from a nonprofit housing group. The sharp drop in home prices between 2006 and early 2012 has wiped out more than $8 trillion in wealth for homeowners. Delinquencies and foreclosures on home mortgages reached levels not seen since the Great Depression.

Just before the housing bubble burst nearly seven years ago, when home prices were peaking and mortgage rates averaged more than 6 percent, renting typically cost less than owning. Now, as the Burkes discovered, the opposite is generally true. [1]

"Nationally, the cost of owning is 45 percent less than the cost of renting, if you stay in your home for seven years," which is the typical duration, says Jed Kolko, chief economist at Trulia, an online real estate site. That's assuming a homeowner has a 3.5 percent mortgage rate, is in the 25 percent tax bracket and itemizes to take advantage of the home mortgage interest deduction.*

"Even if you're not itemizing, it is still cheaper to own than rent," says Kolko, whose firm has an interactive map that calculates the rent-vs.-own equation for different mortgage rates, tax brackets and expected home tenure. [2]

The sharp drop in home prices between 2006 and early 2012 — more than 30 percent nationally and up to 60 percent in the hardest-hit cities — has made buying a home more affordable for newcomers. But it also has wiped out more than $8 trillion in wealth for homeowners. Delinquencies and foreclosures on home mortgages reached levels not seen since the Great Depression. [3] As a result, the homeownership rate had fallen to 65.5 percent in the third quarter of 2012, the lowest since 1997. [4] (*See graph, p. 1068.*)

"The severity of the housing crash has raised important questions about the short- and long-term impacts of this experience on the demand for homeownership," wrote Rachel Bogardus Drew and Christopher Herbert, economists with Harvard University's Joint Center for Housing Studies. Many now are wondering whether homeownership will rebound as the economy recovers, or whether a fundamental shift is occurring, with more Americans choosing to rent for the long haul. [5]

Some are questioning the government's continued promotion of homeownership through tax breaks and the long-held belief that homeownership benefits communities more than renting. In addition, federal officials are butting heads about the government's responsibility to ease the burdens of homeowners who find themselves

---

* Trulia factors in costs of homeownership such as closing costs, maintenance, insurance and taxes; costs of renting, such as renter's insurance and a security deposit; and the opportunity cost of putting money into housing rather than into other investments.

Glossary of Real Estate Terms

Adjustable-rate mortgage — a loan to a homebuyer that has an initial interest rate that is fixed for a period of time but then is reset periodically.

Conforming mortgage — a loan purchased by Fannie Mae and Freddie Mac from the lender; the mortgage must conform to Fannie and Freddie guidelines establishing a maximum loan amount, borrower credit and income requirements, down payment and suitable properties. The loan limit is currently $417,000, although it is more in high-cost areas.

Conventional mortgage — a loan that is not insured by the government's Federal Housing Administration (FHA). A conventional loan can be conforming or non-conforming.

Delinquent mortgage — a loan whose monthly payment has not been made by the due date, usually the first of the month. Most lenders give borrowers a grace period, usually one to two weeks after the official due date, to send in a payment without incurring a late fee.

Fixed-rate mortgage — a loan with a fixed interest rate for the entire term of the loan, traditionally 30 years.

Foreclosure — a legal process by which a bank, mortgage company or other creditor takes a homeowner's property in order to satisfy a debt. The foreclosure process usually begins once the borrower is 90 or more days late with payment.

Jumbo mortgage — a loan above the maximum loan amount established by Fannie and Freddie. The two GSEs (government-sponsored enterprises) do not purchase jumbo loans from lenders.

Mortgage-backed security — a bond backed by payments from a collection or "bundle" of mortgages.

Mortgage default — when the monthly payment is 30 days or more late.

Mortgage origination — the creation of a new mortgage, including all the steps from taking a loan application through disbursal of funds.

Mortgage principal — the amount of money the homeowner has borrowed.

Mortgage servicer — a company that manages a mortgage, including collecting mortgage payments from the homeowner, negotiating mortgage modification if the homeowner defaults and supervising the foreclosure process when necessary.

Redlining — discrimination that occurs when lenders refuse to extend financial services to an entire poor, often minority neighborhood without taking into account an individual borrower's qualifications and creditworthiness. The practice is illegal under the 1974 Equal Credit Opportunity Act and the 1968 Fair Housing Act.

Self-amortizing mortgage — a loan for which the monthly payments consist of both principal and interest so that the loan is paid off by the end of its term.

Strategic default — the practice of not making monthly mortgage payments despite having the financial ability to pay. Homeowners who are "underwater" may decide to strategically default and walk away from the home.

Underwater mortgage — when the homeowner owes more than the home is currently worth.

"underwater" — owing more on their mortgages than their homes are currently worth. From 11 million to 14 million households are underwater nationwide, but their ranks are shrinking as the economy and housing market slowly recover. [6]

In October, home prices nationwide increased by 6.3 percent over the same time last year, according to CoreLogic, a provider of financial and real estate data in Irvine, Calif. That is the eighth consecutive price increase and the biggest since June 2006, when prices peaked.

"The recovery is geographically broad-based with almost all markets experiencing some appreciation," said Mark FLeming, the firm's chief economist. Only three states — Delaware, Alabama, and New Jersey — saw home prices fall in October. Arizona was the best performer, with home prices rising nearly 17 percent in October. [7]

Other news also indicates that the housing market is healing. Construction of single-family homes is climbing, existing and new home sales are also up and consumer mortgage default rates are reaching new lows.

Owner-occupants are not the only ones buying homes. Investors, from mom-and-pop operations to large corporations, are purchasing foreclosed homes and turning them into rentals. That helps to account for the large price increases in cities that were hardest hit during the housing bust, such as Phoenix. In fact, some investors are buying foreclosed properties in bulk, and that has drawn criticism.

"We need home buyers in the properties," said Sharon Bowler, chairwoman of the California Association of Realtors' Distressed Property Task Force. "When you put this amount of rentals in one community, your housing values are going to drop." On the other hand, empty homes invite vandalism and depress values. "It's surely a lot better to have a renter in a property than have a property that's vacant," said Ingrid Gould Ellen, co-director of New York University's Furman Center for Real Estate and Urban Policy. [8]

Either way, a sustained housing recovery is far from assured. New household formation drives the housing market, but young people aren't striking out on their own in the usual numbers and instead are choosing to live longer with parents and roommates, a trend due, in part, to the weakest economic recovery since the Great Depression.

"Given the demographic profile of the country, we'd expect to be seeing 1.2 million extra households forming every year," says Harvard economist Christopher Herbert. But in the last few years, only 600,000 to 700,000 new households have formed annually, and while recent census data suggest that figure has increased to about 900,000, it is still below trend, says Herbert.

Obtaining a mortgage is more difficult too. Lenders have ended the era of loose credit, while potential homebuyers in a weak economy struggle to save for a down payment. As a result, the number of mortgage originations has fallen by nearly two-thirds since the 2003 peak. [9] (*See graph, p. 1074.*)

Some housing advocates complain that lending has become too restrictive, but Herbert says that's not clear. Tighter credit may have "simply removed the excesses of the boom, when income wasn't documented, very high debt-to-income ratios were allowed and borrowers with very low credit scores were approved," he says. In any case, the government's Federal Housing Administration (FHA) continues to insure mortgages that have less stringent income and down payment requirements,* and its share of the mortgage market has more than doubled over the past decade to 14 percent. [10]

* FHA rules require a minimum down payment of 3.5 percent of a home's purchase price.

Hispanic Homeownership Grew the Most

Nearly three-quarters of white American households own their home, compared to less than half of blacks and Hispanics. Since 1994, however, Hispanics' homeownership rate grew the most — more than 5 percentage points.

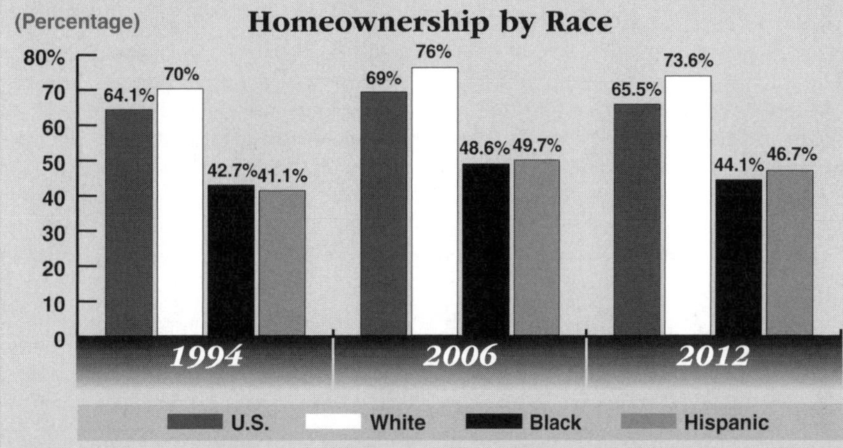

Note: percentages are for the third quarter.

Source: Current Population Survey/Housing Vacancy Survey, Bureau of the Census

Nevertheless, minority homebuyers are being hurt, says Robert Gnaizda, former general counsel for the Berkeley, Calif.-based Greenlining Institute, which promotes racial and economic justice. For one thing, the average credit score required for an FHA-insured loan has risen substantially.

"Government policies and bank policies inadvertently are creating a form of redlining that is far more vicious in its impact than any deliberate actions," he says.

Redlining occurs when lenders refuse to extend financial services to an entire poor, minority neighborhood without taking into account an individual's qualifications and creditworthiness. The practice is illegal under the 1974 Equal Credit Opportunity Act and the 1968 Fair Housing Act.

Gnaizda says only 5 percent of all home loans are originating in primarily minority areas. Yet some research shows that lower-income, minority homebuyers are a relatively good credit risk when placed in affordable, fixed-rate, 30-year mortgages, even with low down payments. [11]

In addition to tighter credit, the housing recovery also is threatened by the "shadow inventory," the millions of homes that are in, or in danger of entering, foreclosure. Although that number is declining, the recovery in housing prices could be dampened if banks quickly put many of those homes up for sale. In addition, as home prices continue to rise and more homeowners get above water, many may decide to sell, flooding the market and causing home prices to reverse course.

Finally, one more major unknown hangs over the housing market: The automatic government spending cuts and tax increases, known as the "fiscal cliff," scheduled to go into effect in early 2013 unless Congress and President Obama agree on an alternative plan to reduce the federal deficit. The Congressional Budget Office estimates that the automatic measures would cause a recession next year. [12]

Against this backdrop of uncertainty, here are some of the questions that regulators, politicians, economists and

Home of the Future Is Here

But for many, accessing "smart" home systems is overwhelming.

Imagine being able to control your home's air conditioning, heat, exterior lights, burglar alarm and front door lock from anywhere in the world. [1]

Such "smart" home amenities already are available, for about $2,500 for installation and $50 a month for a smart phone application. But the cost can climb into the hundreds of thousands of dollars if you add multiple zones in your home, security cameras, motion sensors, and controls for your pool or hot tub, interior lighting, audio/visual equipment and motorized window treatments.

When working properly — and experts say that can be a big if — smart systems not only offer convenience but also save energy. And in the future, they may not even be controlled by the homeowner. Electric utilities, for instance, already are installing "smart meters" in individual homes to monitor energy use. Eventually, utility companies could use such meters to remotely adjust a home's temperature, lighting and appliances to reduce energy use during peak demand.

Down the road, such monitoring might be offered by cable companies or Google, Apple or Amazon. "Expect large battles [between] companies to try to own this space by offering free or subsidized devices and/or apps," said Los Angeles-based consultant Steven Swimmer. [2]

Or maybe not. Swimmer was one of 1,021 technology stakeholders and critics who participated in a survey released by the Pew Research Center's Internet & American Life Project last summer. The experts are nearly evenly split between pessimists and optimists about the future of the smart home.

Some 51 percent agreed with this statement: "By 2020, the connected household has become a model of efficiency, as people are able to manage consumption of resources (electricity, water, food, even bandwidth) in ways that place less of a burden on the environment while saving households money."

And 46 percent agreed with the opposite statement: "By 2020, most initiatives to embed IP-enabled devices in the home have failed due to difficulties in gaining consumer trust and because of the complexities in using new services. As a result, the home of 2020 looks about the same as the home of 2011 in terms of resources consumption and management." [3]

Survey respondents could also share their comments. "Smart homes and smart devices will become a necessity if we are to preserve and wisely consume remaining fossil fuel resources," wrote David Lowe, innovation and technology manager for the National Telecommunications Cooperative Association, a nonprofit organization based in Arlington, Va. [4]

But Lowe was the rare optimist to share his thoughts. Naysayers dominated the comments, asserting that the home of the future "will continue to be mostly a marketing mirage." [5]

"People don't want this stuff very much. They like their homes

housing advocates are debating about homeownership:

Does higher homeownership benefit society?

Despite the housing crash, nearly 90 percent of American adults expect to buy a home sometime in the future, according to a Harvard analysis of national survey data. The top four reasons given are related to lifestyle: Owning a home provides a good place to raise children, a safe place to live, more space and greater control over that space. [13]

The federal government has been encouraging homeownership since the Great Depression, when President Herbert Hoover told a national conference in 1931 that homeownership "makes for happier married life, it makes for better children . . . it makes for better citizenship." Soon after, he signed legislation making mortgages more widely available. [14]

Since then, promoting homeownership has been a bipartisan goal. For President Bill Clinton, expanding homeownership would "reinforce family values in America" and "encourage two-parent households." [15] President George W. Bush said it would "put light where there's darkness, and hope where there's despondency." [16]

To promote greater homeownership, the federal government insures mortgages, supports affordable housing programs, provides billions of dollars in tax breaks to homeowners and guarantees payments to investors holding mortgage-backed securities — bonds backed by payments from a collection of mortgages. But are the underlying assumptions about homeownership correct?

Former Greenlining Institute general counsel Gnaizda says yes. "It creates a more stable family life. Children do better in school," he says.

A recent study sponsored by Habitat for Humanity and the Mortgage Bankers Association supports that view. The study found that the children of homeowners were more likely to remain in school than the children of renters, and daughters of homeowners were less likely to become teenage mothers. [17]

No one knows for sure why kids do better when their parents own their home. Homeowners do, on average, stay longer in their homes than renters, but that wasn't the reason, said the study's authors. The children of homeowners outperformed the children of renters with similar tenure. [18]

"If you own a home, it takes a lot of planning. What kind of mortgage is best, what size house is best, what is the best neighborhood for my

to be dumb," said Tracy Rolling, a product user-experience expert for Nokia. "How many people do you know who have bought one of those alarm-clock coffee pots, loved them for a month, and then stopped using the alarm clock feature altogether? Smart homes are like that on a grand scale."

Mike Leibhold, senior researcher at the Institute for the Future, a Palo Alto-based research center, wrote that "people seem to resist the idea of smart grid, top-down monitoring and control of resource consumption as invasive." [6]

There is also the high cost of smart systems and their complexity, a problem that has already plagued some cars. "A few years back, BMW and Mercedes-Benz had to turn off some of the onboard electronics on their high-end cars because complexity gremlins were making things break," said Jerry Michalski, president of Sociate, a San Francisco-based independent consultancy. "It also opens the door to hacking scenarios we seem to not want to contemplate." [7]

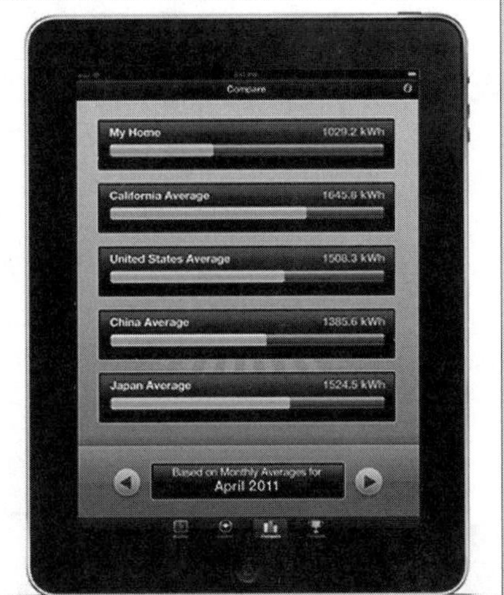

www.LPAinc.com

Homeowners can use their iPads and other devices to monitor heating, air conditioning and other systems in their "smart" homes.

The lack of standardization appears to be a major stumbling block. "My iPhone won't want to talk to my GE smart toaster, and my Bosch smart refrigerator won't connect to my generic smart coffee maker," said Rolling. "This is not going to take off for a very, very long time." [8]

— Barbara Mantel

[1] Jerold Leslie, "5 smart-home systems: From cheap to ultraluxe," *msn Real Estate*, Oct. 20, 2011, http://realestate.msn.com/5-smart-home-systems-from-cheap-to-ultraluxe.

[2] Janna Anderson and Lee Rainee, "The Future of Smart Systems," Pew Internet & American Life Project, June 29, 2012, p. 4, http://pewinternet.org/Reports/2012/Future-of-Smart-Systems/Overview.aspx.

[3] *Ibid.*, p. 2.

[4] Janna Anderson and Lee Rainee, "The Future of Smart Systems — Credited Responses," Pew Internet & American Life Project, June 29, 2012, www.elon.edu/e-web/predictions/expertsurveys/2012survey/future_smart_systems_Internet_IOT_2020_cred.xhtml.

[5] Anderson and Rainee, "The Future of Smart Systems," *op. cit.*

[6] *Ibid.*, p. 3.

[7] *Ibid.*, p. 4.

[8] *Ibid.*, p. 4.

family, and that probably reflects the planning that goes into all of home life," says Paul Bishop, vice president of research at the Washington-based National Association of Realtors. Some researchers theorize that maintaining a home — hiring plumbers and electricians and pestering city hall for better services — causes homeowners to become better managers, both of their home and their children.

Homeowners may also be more involved citizens. Researchers Denise DiPasquale and Edward Glaeser found that, after controlling for age, race, gender, marital status, children, income, education and city size, homeowners were approximately 10 percent more likely to work to solve local problems; 13 percent more likely to know the identity of their local school board head; and 16 percent more likely to vote in local elections. [19]

DiPasquale and Glaeser, however, found that these differences *were* largely a result of homeowners' tendency to stay longer in one place than renters. "If you compare renters and homeowners of the same tenure, the benefits become very small," says Stephanie Stern, a professor at the Illinois Institute of Technology's Chicago-Kent College of Law, who has reviewed the literature.

Societal benefits of homeownership are often exaggerated, says Stern, and significant negatives are often ignored, particularly concerning labor mobility. "That is what we are seeing now: homeowners who cannot move even though they need to because they have lost a job and have to find a new one somewhere else," says Stern. They may own a home they cannot sell for a price that would allow them to move, or they may be underwater and unable to convince the bank to accept less than what it is owed.

"With a high degree of owner-occupation, everything slows. Folk get stuck," said Andrew Oswald, an economist in England who studies the link between homeownership and employment. "The most successful, stable, attractive country in the Western world is one in the centre of Europe: Switzerland," he said. "Does it have high homeownership rates? Absolutely not. In Switzerland, about seven in 10 of the population are renters." [20]

So should the federal government be encouraging homeownership by allowing homeowners to deduct their mortgage interest from their taxes? Eliminating the popular mortgage interest deduction is one of the proposals being debated as solutions to the national debt problem. The program costs the federal government more than $100 billion

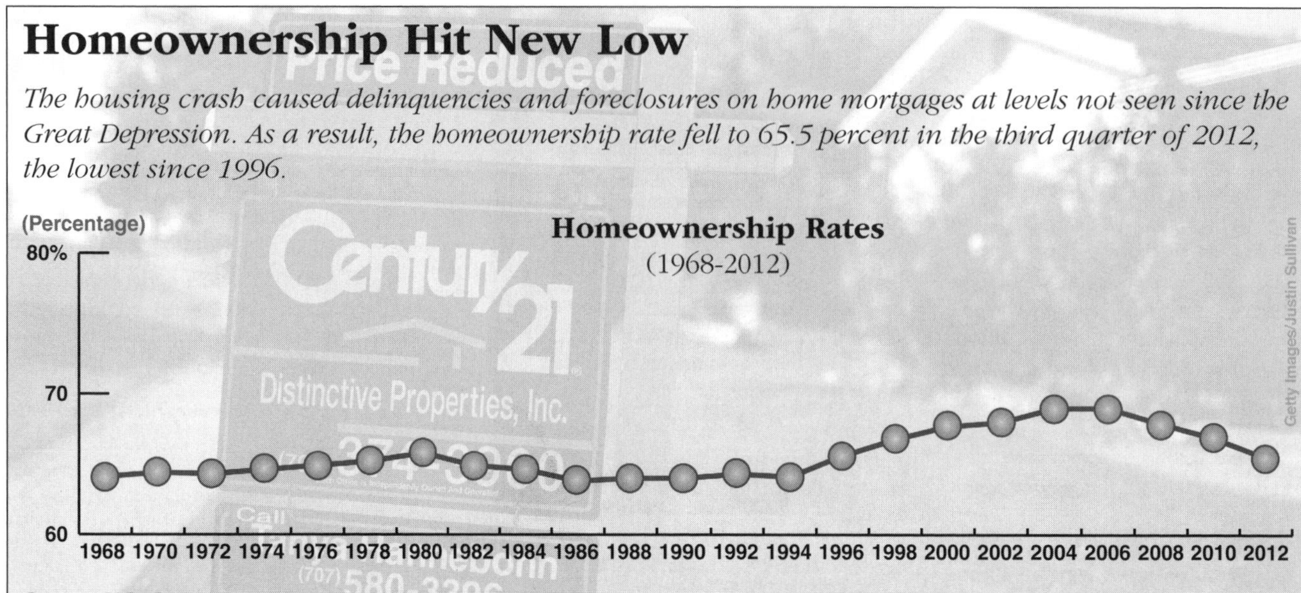

Homeownership Hit New Low

The housing crash caused delinquencies and foreclosures on home mortgages at levels not seen since the Great Depression. As a result, the homeownership rate fell to 65.5 percent in the third quarter of 2012, the lowest since 1996.

Source: U.S. Census Bureau

a year in lost revenue. And even many who believe there are significant societal benefits from homeownership don't like the mortgage interest deduction.

"The bulk of the benefits go to fairly rich people who aren't particularly close to the margin between owning and not owning," said Glaeser. "It mainly serves to induce prosperous people to buy bigger homes and pay more for those homes." [21] The bigger the mortgage, the more interest there is to deduct. And the higher the tax bracket, the more that deduction is worth.

Gnaizda would like to see the government do away with the home mortgage interest deduction. "I would recommend that if the government wants to help potential homeowners, it should start at the bottom and provide small subsidies in the form of a tax credit," says Gnaizda.*

The National Low Income Housing Coalition, a Washington-based advocacy group, wants the government to convert the home mortgage interest deduction to a tax credit. Under its proposal, homeowners would receive a credit of 20 percent of their annual mortgage interest payments applied against their federal income tax bill, and they would not have to itemize their tax deductions as is required to take the mortgage interest deduction. Eligible mortgages would be capped at $500,000.

The coalition estimates its proposal would increase the number of mortgage-holding homeowners who would get a tax break from 43 million to 60 million while saving the federal government $20 billion to $40 billion a year. The coalition recommends the savings be used to build and rehabilitate rental housing. [22]

The National Association of Realtors and other industry groups oppose changing the deduction. "About 65 percent of the households who claim the home mortgage interest deduction earn less than $100,000, and 91 percent earn less than $200,000," says Bishop. "It's not the stereotype that you often see from the critics. It's the solid middle and upper-middle class."

Should the government do more to help distressed homeowners?

A very public fight has been taking place over how far the government should go to help financially struggling homeowners avoid foreclosure. U.S. Treasury Department officials are pushing for more action while a powerful regulator is saying no.

The dispute revolves around a nearly four-year-old program called the Home Affordable Modification Program (HAMP). Under HAMP, Treasury makes incentive payments to financial firms that manage mortgage loans and agree to modify them so homeowners' monthly payments don't exceed 31 percent of their monthly pre-tax income. Such a firm — known as a mortgage servicer — might lower a loan's interest rate, extend the term of the loan or delay payments on a portion of the amount borrowed — called the principal — until the end of the mortgage term.

To qualify, a homeowner must have a mortgage written before 2009, suffer a financial hardship, be either delinquent or close to it and have sufficient, documented income to support the reduced payments. [23]

In 2010, the government added a twist to HAMP, called the Principal Reduction Alternative (PRA). Under the program, mortgage servicers are encouraged to forgive — that is, permanently reduce — some of the principal owed by qualified

* Tax credits are subtracted directly from a taxpayer's tax bill and don't require taxpayers to itemize. Tax deductions are subtracted from a taxpayer's total income on an itemized return, reducing the taxpayer's taxable income.

homeowners who are underwater.

But this summer, Edward DeMarco, the acting director of the Federal Housing Finance Agency (FHFA), refused to allow two major financial institutions currently under FHFA conservatorship to participate in the principal forgiveness program. "After much study, I have concluded that Fannie Mae and Freddie Mac's adoption of HAMP PRA would not make a meaningful improvement in reducing foreclosures in a cost-effective way for taxpayers," DeMarco wrote to the Senate Committee on Banking, Housing and Urban Affairs on July 31. [24]

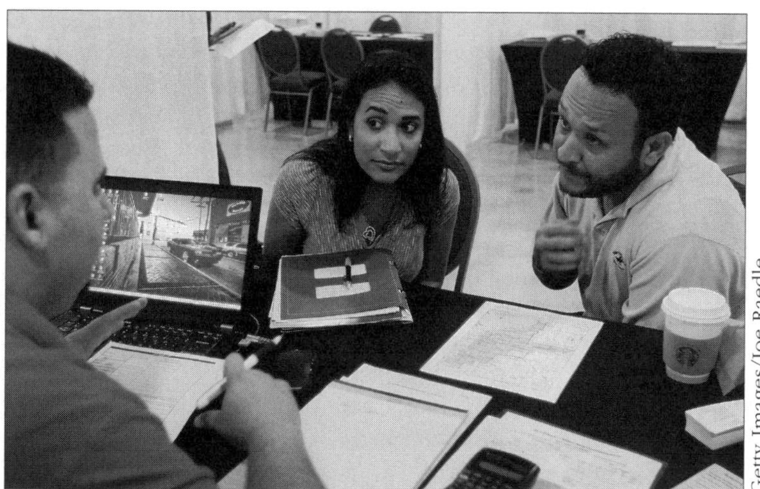

Getty Images/Joe Raedle

Prospective homebuyers Michelle and Nilson Ruiz discuss obtaining a down payment assistance grant from Wells Fargo bank. Obtaining a mortgage is more difficult in the wake of the housing crisis. Lenders have ended the era of loose credit, while potential homebuyers in a weak economy struggle to save for a down payment. As a result, the number of new mortgages has fallen by nearly two-thirds since the 2003 peak.

Fannie Mae and Freddie Mac are quasi-private companies, chartered by Congress. They purchase home mortgages from lenders and repackage them as guaranteed, mortgage-backed securities to sell to investors or hold in their own portfolios. This keeps money flowing to lenders so people can get credit and buy homes.

But the government had to bail out Fannie and Freddie during the housing crash, leaving taxpayers on the hook, and the so-called government-sponsored enterprises (GSEs) are now under FHFA control. The two companies own or back slightly less than half of all underwater mortgages. The rest are owned by the original lenders or by investors who bought mortgage-backed securities packaged and sold by commercial banks and investment banks.

U.S. Treasury Secretary Timothy Geithner immediately blasted DeMarco's decision, publicly accusing him of using selective data and urging him to reconsider. "I do not believe it is the best decision for the country," Geithner said. [25]

John Taylor, president and CEO of the Washington-based National Community Reinvestment Coalition, which works to bring banking services to underserved communities, says DeMarco should reverse his decision. "It's a voluntary program, and frankly, a lot of these banks are sitting on the sidelines and saying, 'Why should I do this principal reduction when nearly 50 percent of the mortgages are held by the government, and they're not doing it.' "

Between 80 and 85 percent of underwater homeowners are current on their mortgage payments and so would not qualify for principal forgiveness. But it is still important for hard-hit communities and cities, say advocates. "It doesn't take very many homes in foreclosure to move house prices significantly down," says Andrew Jakabovics, senior director of policy development and research at Enterprise Community Partners, a nonprofit in Columbia, Md., that invests in affordable housing nationwide.

Most everyone agrees that principal forgiveness is often less expensive for the lenders and investors who own the mortgages than foreclosure, which may involve maintaining a vacant property, making repairs, paying taxes and selling at a loss. And no financial firm would agree to place a homeowner in HAMP PRA if it weren't cheaper than foreclosure in that instance.

But there is disagreement about how much taxpayers would save if Fannie and Freddie were allowed to participate. DeMarco's agency estimates it would be between $500 million and $1.8 billion compared to the standard mortgage modification program. [26] Geithner has said FHFA's own internal data show the savings could be as high as $3.6 billion and could help up to half a million households. [27]

Nevertheless, DeMarco has said it is not worth the risks. The publicity alone "could give borrowers who are current on their mortgages a message that the government endorses forgiving a portion of mortgage debt if hardship can be demonstrated, creating a broad incentive for underwater borrowers to seek ways to become eligible," DeMarco wrote. That could include not making monthly mortgage payments despite having the financial ability to pay, called a strategic default. [28]

"We'd have a stampede. Everybody would go late on their mortgages so they could get a principal reduction," says Anthony Sanders, a senior scholar at the Mercatus Center, a free-market oriented research organization at George Mason University in Arlington, Va.

But advocates of principal reduction say the risk of such strategic default is overblown. First of all, defaulting homebuyers would have no guarantee that they would get their principal reduced; they might get the interest rate lowered or the term of the mortgage extended instead. In addition, "You can set eligibility such that you had to have been in default by some previous date," says Jakabovics.

"There could be circuit breakers in place, that's true. But that's not the headline," says Sanders. "The headline is Fannie and Freddie will lower your principal. That's what people will focus on."

Taylor says another safeguard could be to carefully verify a homeowner's income and expenses to make sure they meet all the qualifications. But Sanders says the amount of fraud would be "horrific."

Of even greater concern to DeMarco is the message that principal reduction would send the financial markets. "Forgiving debt owed pursuant to a lawful, valid contract risks creating a longer-term view by investors that the mortgage contract is less secure than ever before," said DeMarco. This, he said, could lead to a decreased willingness of investors to buy mortgage-backed securities and, as a result, higher mortgage rates and fewer mortgage loans. [29]

The Financial Times has reported that the Obama administration may try to replace DeMarco while Congress is in recess. [30]

Should the federal government get out of the mortgage business?

Today, Fannie Mae and Freddie Mac back nearly nine out of every 10 new mortgages in America, largely because most commercial and investments banks have withdrawn from the business. But the Obama administration plans to wind down the two, long-established government-sponsored enterprises (GSEs), although it has not yet decided what will replace them. That decision could affect the kind of mortgages available to homeowners and their cost.

Few experts from across the political spectrum want a return to the status quo before the bailout of Fannie and Freddie. For decades, Fannie Mae and Freddie Mac enjoyed special tax treatment and lower capital requirements* than private firms that bought mortgage loans. In addition, investors, believing that the federal government would bail the two enterprises out in a crisis, were willing to accept lower yields on GSE-issued securities in exchange for less risk.

Fannie and Freddie took the resulting savings and "gave it to their managers, or employees or shareholders," says Dwight Jaffee, a professor at the University of California's Haas School of Business at Berkeley, and passed only about half onto homeowners in the form of lower interest rates on mortgages.

"Why would we do that again?" asks Barry Zigas, director of housing policy at the Consumer Federation of America, a Washington-based association of consumer groups.

In addition, just as the housing bubble was about to burst, Fannie and Freddie began taking enormous risks. Traditionally, the two GSEs bought and repackaged only high-quality mortgages for lower- and middle-income borrowers, a market they dominated. Commercial and investment banks stuck to buying and securitizing riskier mortgages and the jumbo mortgages that Fannie and Freddie, by law, could not touch.

But in the mid-2000s, Fannie and Freddie began buying and securitizing riskier mortgages as well in order to boost profits and recover market share. As home prices plummeted and default rates reached alarming levels, Fannie's and Freddie's losses mounted. Since the 2008 bailout, they have received nearly $188 billion from the Treasury and paid back $46 billion in dividends to the government, according to *The Wall Street Journal.* [31]

* The amount of cash and easily liquidated assets that regulators require banks keep on hand.

The two GSEs have recently returned to profitability and, under a revised agreement with the government, will stop paying dividends in January. Instead, they will turn over all profits to the U.S. Treasury. Still, the government plans to phase them out, and there's a healthy debate about what should come next.

"The idea that we need government-provided mortgage subsidies for the average American homeowner is ludicrous," says Jaffee, who would like to see the government phase out Fannie Mae and Freddie Mac by lowering the size limit on mortgages that they are allowed to buy. That so-called conforming loan limit is currently $417,000 for a single-family home, although it's larger in high-cost areas such as California, New York City and Washington, D.C.

"I would just keep lowering it by $100,000 a year for four or five years," says Jaffee. "As the conforming loan limit comes down, the private market will return." In Jaffee's plan, the FHA and the Veterans Administration would continue to support mortgages for lower-income families and veterans, respectively, and if there were hiccups in private mortgage finance, the FHA could expand its operations.

This mostly private system would mean higher mortgage rates, but not by much, says Jaffee. "I think mortgage rates would rise only modestly for prime mortgages, maybe only 10 to 25 basis points [0.1 of a percentage point to 0.25 of a percentage point] at most," he says, and "the fixed-rate, 20 percent down payment mortgage would be the dominant mortgage."

But Zigas strongly disagrees and says there would be two possible outcomes from such a system: Political pressure from consumers, builders and real estate agents would cause the FHA footprint to expand. "Then all of the risk will be on the taxpayer," says Zigas, since the FHA is a government agency.

Continued on p. 1072

Chronology

1920s-1960s

Federal government starts programs to support homeownership.

1927-1932
Congress loosens real estate lending restrictions on national banks; homeownership climbs to nearly 48 percent of households. . . . Stock market crash of 1929 and banking system collapse trigger national housing crisis; many homeowners default.

1933
Banks are foreclosing on 1,000 homes a day. . . . New federal Home Owners' Loan Corporation buys mortgages in default from lenders, then refinances loans for homeowners.

1934
Federal Housing Administration (FHA) is created to insure new kind of residential mortgage: fixed-rate, self-amortizing long-term loans.

1938
Federal National Mortgage Association — Fannie Mae — is founded to buy FHA-insured mortgages, freeing up funds for lenders to make more home loans.

1944
Servicemen's Readjustment Act — the "GI Bill" — creates a no-down-payment loan program for veterans.

1950-1960
Homeownership rate climbs from 55 percent to more than 60 percent.

1968
Congress converts Fannie Mae into a quasi-private, shareholder-owned company allowed to purchase conventional mortgages. . . . Congress creates Government National Mortgage Association — Ginnie Mae — to take over Fannie's role of purchasing government-insured loans.

1970s-1990s

Secondary mortgage market and homeownership grow.

1970
Federal Home Loan Mortgage Corporation — Freddie Mac — joins Fannie Mae as a quasi-private purchaser of conventional mortgages. . . . Freddie and Ginnie begin buying and packaging mortgage loans into mortgage-backed securities to sell to investors.

1974
Equal Credit Opportunity Act prohibits discrimination against credit applicants.

1981
Fannie Mae starts packaging and selling mortgage-backed securities.

1986
Tax Reform Act of 1986 phases out deductibility of interest on consumer credit, except for mortgages.

1999
Homeownership rate reaches 67 percent of households.

2000s-Present

Housing industry booms as government encourages financial firms to expand lending. Use of subprime loans grows. Housing bubble bursts, sending economy into deep recession.

2001-2006
Housing prices in 20 major U.S. cities more than double. . . . Subprime loans make up growing share of new residential mortgages.

2003
President George W. Bush signs American Dream Downpayment Assistance Act, which helps low-income households with down payments.

2005
Homeownership rate reaches a peak of 69.1 percent.

2006-2011
Housing bubble bursts as mortgage defaults climb, battering financial industry, which heavily invested in mortgage-backed securities. . . . Home prices fall by a third in 20 major U.S. cities over six-year period. . . . Percentage of mortgage loans in foreclosure increases from half a percent to more than 4 percent.

2008
Government takes over Fannie Mae and Freddie Mac through a legal process known as conservatorship after their losses reach catastrophic levels.

2009
Government's Home Affordable Refinance Program (HARP) helps homeowners refinance if they are current on mortgages owned by Fannie or Freddie; Home Affordable Modification Program (HAMP) encourages mortgage servicers to modify mortgages of qualified borrowers who are behind on payments.

2012
Housing market begins slow recovery. . . . Forty-nine states and the federal government reach a $25 billion settlement with five big banks after investigation into abusive foreclosure practices. . . . National Fair Housing Alliance accuses some banks of discrimination in maintenance of foreclosed homes in poor, minority neighborhoods.

More Americans Are Renting

But rising rents are out of reach for many families.

The percentage of Americans who rent their homes is climbing, either by choice or because a weak economy, bad credit or a previous foreclosure has put homeownership out of reach.

"I'm still trying to figure out career decisions and where I want to be," said 22-year-old financial analyst Chris Mahannah, who recently rented a two-bedroom apartment in the heart of Miami. "I definitely want to own a home one day, but until I figure those things out, I think I'm just going to continue to keep renting." [1]

From 2005 through 2011, annual growth in the number of renter households averaged 730,000 — nearly three times the average in the 1990s. Mahannah's age group — adults under 25 — helped fuel the growth but not nearly as much as they typically had in the past. Due to the weak economy, many in his age group are choosing to live with their parents.

Instead, 25-34-year-olds accounted for almost 90 percent of new renter households — a group that in other times would typically be buying their first homes. [2] And many are opting for houses rather than apartments. In fact, single-family detached homes now are capturing a growing share of the rental market, at about 28 percent, according to Fannie Mae. [3]

"We've never seen anything like this," said John Burns, CEO of an eponymous real estate consulting firm in Irvine, Calif. Burns estimates that between 2010 and 2015 the ongoing foreclosure crisis will drive 3 million former homeowners to rent single-family homes. [4]

As more people enter the rental market, builders are responding. In 2011, construction began on 178,000 apartments in multi-unit buildings. That's expected to increase to 235,000 units this year and 320,000 in 2014, according to New York-based research firm Zelman & Associates. [5]

But it can take years for such construction to be completed, so supply remains tight in the meantime. Vacancy rates for rental housing — both apartments and single-family homes — is 8.6 percent, the lowest in a decade. [6]

Not surprisingly, rents have been rising. The largest annual increase — 4.8 percent — was measured at the end of last year. In the third quarter of this year, rents still rose a healthy 3.3 percent compared to the same period in 2011. [7] But incomes have been stagnating, leading to a growing proportion of households — more than half — spending at least 30 percent of their pre-tax income on housing, a level the federal government considers unaffordable. [8] The poor have been hit the hardest.

"The housing bust and Great Recession helped to swell the ranks of low-income renters in the 2000s, increasing the already intense competition for a diminishing supply of low-cost units," according to Harvard economists. In 2001, they found, 8.1 million low-income renters competed for 5.7 million affordable units, leaving a gap of 2.4 million units. A decade later, that gap had more than doubled. "With rents on most newly constructed units well out of reach, the recent jump in multifamily production will do little to alleviate the shortage," they wrote. [9]

That leaves the Low-Income Housing Tax Credit as the primary method of increasing the number of rental apartments that are affordable for low-income families. Each year, the Internal Revenue Service issues these tax credits to the states, which in turn award them to developers to subsidize construction of new or refurbished affordable housing. The program has provided 2.5 million affordable rental units in the United States since 1986.

Continued from p. 1070

"An alternative outcome is that the FHA serves a very small portion of the marketplace, and everyone else, to the extent that they can get mortgages at all, will only be able to get adjustable-rate mortgages and potentially very expensive, high-priced, fixed-rate mortgages," says Zigas. In an adjustable-rate mortgage, the interest rate can move up or down over the life of the loan, thus shifting interest rate risk from lenders to borrowers.

Zigas says some form of federal guarantee is necessary "if we are going to have a stable, deep and liquid mortgage market that offers consumers long-term, fixed-rate financing."

There are several versions of such a proposal. Basically, they entail having one or several private firms buy mortgages and package them into mortgage-backed securities to sell to investors. These issuers would have to hold a minimum level of capital determined by a federal regulator. Investors would pay a premium for catastrophic insurance, which would be administered and guaranteed by the federal government.

If there were another housing crisis, the government would make insurance payments to investors only after the private issuers of mortgage-backed securities used up all their capital to pay back investors. The government would not bail out the private issuers, as it bailed out Fannie Mae and Freddie Mac.

"Investors would provide money to borrowers through this system at very low interest rates because they know that if worst came to worst there would be a government backstop," says Janneke Ratcliffe, executive director of the Center for Community Capital at the University of North Carolina in Chapel Hill.

But a government guarantee would eliminate investor concern about both the quality of underlying mortgages and the financial health of the issuers, wrote Peter Wallison, a financial scholar at the American Enterprise

But the program's future is not secure. Congressional efforts to cut the federal budget deficit could have "serious implications" for the program, according to the U.S. Department of Housing and Urban Development. [10] Congress could shrink, or even eliminate, the credit.

But even if the program survives, the credits have not been large enough to close the affordability gap.

"The lack of affordable housing in the United States means that for many families, homeless shelters have become a surrogate for low-income housing," said Ralph da Costa Nunez, president of the Institute for Children, Poverty and Homelessness, a nonprofit research organization based in New York City. [11]

Getty Images/*The Boston Globe*/Suzanne Kreiter

Boston social media consultant Sarah Dussault, 28, is reluctant to take on a mortgage and instead rents an apartment. Rather than set aside money for a down payment, she is putting a lot of her disposable income into her business and also saving for retirement. Just before the housing bubble burst nearly seven years ago, mortgage rates averaged more than 6 percent, and renting typically cost less than owning. Now, the opposite is generally true.

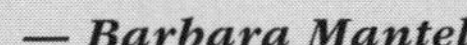

— Barbara Mantel

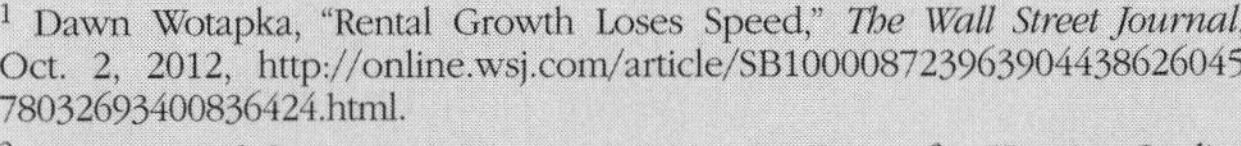

1 Dawn Wotapka, "Rental Growth Loses Speed," *The Wall Street Journal*, Oct. 2, 2012, http://online.wsj.com/article/SB10000872396390443862604578032693400836424.html.

2 "The State of the Nation's Housing 2012," Joint Center for Housing Studies of Harvard University, p. 22, www.jchs.harvard.edu/sites/jchs.harvard.edu/files/son2012_rental_housing.pdf.

3 "Rental Resurgence Marked by Single-Family Expansion and Diverging Affordability Trends for Owners and Renters," *Fannie Mae Housing Insights*, Vol. 2, Issue 5, Nov. 15, 2012, p. 2, www.fanniemae.com/resources/file/research/datanotes/pdf/housing-insight-1112.pdf.

4 Julie Schmit, "Home rentals: the new American Dream?" *USA Today*, June 5, 2012, http://usatoday30.usatoday.com/money/economy/housing/story/2012-06-05/are-home-rentals-the-new-american-dream/55402648/1.

5 Wotapka, *op. cit.*

6 "Housing Vacancies and Homeownership: Rental Vacancy Rate Times Series," U.S. Census Bureau, www.census.gov/econ/currentdata/dbsearch?program=HV&startYear=1956&endYear=2012&categories=RATE&dataType=RVR&geoLevel=US&adjusted=0¬Adjusted=1&errorData=.

7 "U.S. Apartment Market Report," MPF Research, www.realpage.com/apartment-market-research/u.s.-apartment-report-trends/us-performance-highlights.

8 "Rental Resurgence Marked by Single-Family Expansion and Diverging Affordability Trends for Owners and Renters," *op. cit.*

9 "The State of the Nation's Housing 2012," *op. cit.*

10 "Enterprise Webinar: At the Fiscal Cliff: The 2013 Budget and Its Implications for Low Income Housing and Community Development Programs — Online," U.S. Department of Housing and Urban Development, Nov. 15, 2012, https://hudnsphelp.info/index.cfm?do=viewEventdetails&EventID=9F15DD56-D521-9C1D-B0255843B2BF3816&View=month&linkDate=November%2024%2C%202012.

11 "Lack of Affordable Housing Adds to Homelessness," multifamilybiz.com, Sept. 17, 2012, www.multifamilybiz.com/News/4266/Lack_of_Affordable_Housing_Adds_to_Homelessness.

Institute, a conservative think tank in Washington. So the government would have to rely on regulation to prevent the issuer from taking excessive risk, said Wallison, and he doesn't think that would work. [32]

Meanwhile, Jaffee says, "I reluctantly have come to believe that a purely privatized system will not happen because the mortgage industry and the home building industry and politicians have strong concerns that it will not work." So he's devising a compromise that would include a government backstop to be activated only after a greater loss of private capital than in some of the other proposed plans. In other words, says Jaffee, the private issuers of mortgage-backed securities would have higher minimum-capital requirements.

"The point at which government support begins must be sufficiently high to give private-sector lenders incentive to make safe mortgages and to protect taxpayers from losses in all but truly catastrophic circumstances," says Jaffee.

The U.S. Treasury is weighing the pros and cons of the various options. Geithner has said that whatever plan Treasury and Congress choose, it would take from five to seven years to implement. [33] ■

BACKGROUND

Early Suburbs

In the early 1800s, nearly three-quarters of Americans lived on farms, and most of the rest lived in cities. But after the Civil War, home builders began developing suburbs. In brochures and newspaper advertisements, they promised "an escape from the problems of poor health, social unrest and vice associated with urban life," wrote architectural historian Gwendolyn Wright in *Building the Dream.*

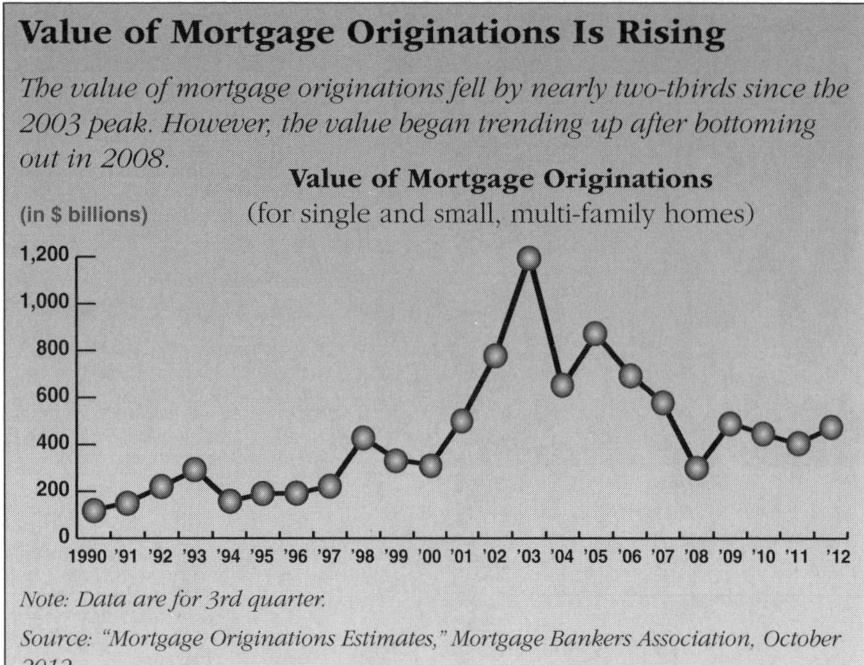
Value of Mortgage Originations Is Rising
The value of mortgage originations fell by nearly two-thirds since the 2003 peak. However, the value began trending up after bottoming out in 2008.
Value of Mortgage Originations
(for single and small, multi-family homes)
(in $ billions)
1,200
1,000
800
600
400
200
0
1990 '91 '92 '93 '94 '95 '96 '97 '98 '99 '00 '01 '02 '03 '04 '05 '06 '07 '08 '09 '10 '11 '12
Note: Data are for 3rd quarter.
Source: "Mortgage Originations Estimates," Mortgage Bankers Association, October 2012

"Subdivisions of small or moderate-sized lots, near transit lines, were intended to attract the families of salesmen, schoolteachers, clerks and carpenters." Larger plots in leafier suburbs drew upper-middle-class professionals. [34]

By 1880, construction was booming outside cities such as Boston, New York, Philadelphia and Milwaukee. One successful builder, Chicago's Samuel Eberly Gross, "developed sixteen towns and 150 subdivisions, built and sold over seven thousand houses, all between 1880 and 1892," wrote Wright. [35]

Technology spurred the rapid growth. The introduction of the cable car in San Francisco in 1882, the electric trolley in Richmond, Va., in 1888 and the elevated railroad in Chicago in 1892 made commuting cheaper and faster. By the turn of the century, more than a 1,000 cities had installed electric streetcar lines that extended to the suburbs, covering 10,000 miles. [36]

But the suburban boom could not have happened without changes to mortgage lending. For much of the 19th century, nationally chartered banks were prohibited from making real estate loans, and state-chartered banks required at least a 50 percent down payment for loans that matured in three to five years. "These terms meant that buying a home often required years of saving and typically wasn't an option for young families," wrote R. Daniel Wadhwani, a business professor at University of the Pacific in Stockton, Calif. [37]

Late in the century, states began allowing the establishment of building-and-loan associations, which working-class families could join to borrow mortgage money at lower interest rates. Philadelphia alone had more than four hundred associations by 1874. [38]

In 1922, after a slight dip in homeownership during World War I, then-Commerce Secretary Herbert Hoover launched the Own Your Own Home campaign, pressing builders to expand residential construction and encouraging renters to buy homes. In 1927, at Hoover's urging, Congress loosened real estate lending restrictions on national banks, and over the next two years their mortgage lending increased by 45 percent. By 1930, the homeownership rate had climbed to nearly 48 percent of American households compared to 45 percent a decade earlier. [39] Government studies from the time suggest that the expansion in home buying was linked to increasing investment in children's education and a decline in reliance on income from child labor. [40]

Housing Collapses

"But beneath the surface were disquieting signs. For as homeownership grew, so did the rate of foreclosures," said Steven Malanga, a senior fellow at the New York-based Manhattan Institute, a conservative think tank. Banks foreclosed on just 2 percent of their mortgage loans in 1922, but foreclosures rose to 11 percent by 1927. The Own Your Own Home Campaign had encouraged many Americans to take on "mortgages far beyond their reach," according to Malanga. [41]

After the stock market crashed in October 1929, panicked depositors withdrew money from banks, and banks stopped making loans. Homeowners, who typically had short-term mortgages with large final payments (so-called balloon payments) that they frequently had to roll over into new mortgages, were shut off from credit. Defaults exploded, and by 1933 — the Depression's peak — about 1,000 homes were being foreclosed every day. [42]

By 1934, the construction industry had shrunk to a 10th of its size five years earlier. The repercussions were felt throughout the economy: by factories that had manufactured building materials; by the railroads that had transported those materials and by skilled laborers who put it all together. "Clearly, restoring the economy turned on restoring the construction industry," wrote Louis Hyman in *Debtor Nation*. To encourage new construction, the new administration of President Franklin D. Roosevelt focused on the housing sector "because it had fallen so hard and so fast." [43] It would be the first time that the federal government had provided financial support for homeownership.

In 1933 Congress and Roosevelt passed legislation creating the Home Owners' Loan Corp. (HOLC), which sold lenders long-term bonds in exchange for mortgages in danger of foreclosure. It then refinanced the mortgages for homeowners, extending the terms up to 15 years. "The hope was that by lowering the monthly payments owners could meet their obligations," wrote Hyman. Within a year, nearly 10 percent of all home mortgages were held by the HOLC. The hemorrhaging of the value of housing was stopped, and other New Deal policies were able to step in to get construction started again. [44]

In 1934, to stimulate residential construction, Congress created the Federal Housing Administration (FHA) to insure a new kind of loan: fixed-rate, self-amortizing mortgages with a down payment as low as 20 percent and maturity of 20 years or more. (Self-amortizing means the loan is completely paid off at the end of the term through regular principal and interest payments.) The interest rate could not exceed 5 percent, and the amount of the mortgage was capped, initially at $20,000.

In 1938, Congress established the Federal National Mortgage Association, later known as Fannie Mae, to purchase FHA-insured mortgages, which kept money flowing to banks and other financial institutions, thus allowing them to make more home loans than just their deposits would allow.

Homeownership Rises

After World War II, returning soldiers who were starting families were able to purchase homes with new, no-down payment mortgages backed by the Veterans' Administration. "Home ownership surged, rising from 44 percent of households in 1940 to 55 percent by 1950," according to Mark Zandi, chief economist at New York-based Moody's Analytics, the economics research arm of the Moody's credit-rating agency. [45]

The expansion of the national highway system also played a large role. Soldiers returning from the Korean War in the early 1950s also took advantage of the VA-insured loans, and, by 1960 the homeownership rate had passed 60 percent. To provide liquidity to the mortgage market, Fannie Mae was now purchasing both VA- and FHA-insured mortgages.

But by then lenders were finding it profitable to write mortgages without government insurance, and the market for these so-called "conventional" mortgages grew. Eventually states passed laws allowing private companies to issue mortgage insurance, ending the FHA's and VA's monopoly.

The government programs were not without problems. "VA appraisers passed on houses and entire developments with faulty sewer lines, no street paving and jerry-built construction," wrote Wright. In the suburbs, the FHA encouraged the use of restrictive covenants that limited certain neighborhoods to whites to ensure, in the words of an FHA manual, "harmonious, attractive neighborhoods." The National Association for the Advancement of Colored People accused the FHA of "fostering black ghettos." But even after the Supreme Court outlawed restrictive covenants in 1948, FHA officials continued to accept unwritten restrictive agreements in the neighborhoods whose mortgages it insured until 1968, according to Wright. [46]

The government also began to loosen the lending standards on the mortgages it insured, as rising home prices after World War II made home buying too costly for many middle-class Americans. It cut the percentage required for down payments and extended the terms of mortgages.

"By attracting riskier home buyers, these moves provoked a surge in foreclosures on government-backed mortgages," wrote Malanga. Between 1950 and 1960, the failure rate on FHA-insured loans increased fivefold and nearly doubled on VA-backed loans. "By contrast, the foreclosure rate on conventional mortgages barely increased." [47]

In 1968, Congress converted Fannie Mae into a shareholder-owned government-sponsored enterprise (GSE) allowed to purchase conventional mortgages that met certain underwriting standards, and created Ginnie Mae (Government National Mortgage Association), a government agency, to take over the role of purchasing government-insured loans. Freddie Mac (Federal Home Loan Mortgage Corp.) was created in 1970 to provide competition for Fannie by also purchasing mortgages.

Securities and the Crash

In the early 1970s, both Ginnie Mae and Freddie Mac began packaging the loans they purchased into mortgage-backed securities to sell to investors such as banks and pension funds. Fannie Mae began to do the same in 1981.

Soon, large commercial banks and investment banks were buying mortgages and selling mortgage-backed securities to investors as well, staking out the jumbo loans and riskier loans off-limits to Fannie and Freddie. During the 1990s and 2000s, as these securities became more sophisticated with different grades of risk, they attracted a broader group of investors, including mutual funds, life insurance companies and foreigners.

As investors poured trillions of dollars into mortgage-backed securities and increased the amount of funds available for lending, "mortgage lenders avidly courted home buyers," wrote Moody's Zandi. "Borrowers with less than perfect credit history — or no credit history — could now get a loan. Of course, a subprime borrower needed a sizable down payment and a sturdy income — but even that changed quickly." [48]

Policy measures also helped to fuel the housing boom. In the 1990s, regulators under President Clinton aggressively enforced 1970s-era legislation requiring mortgage originators to lend to traditionally excluded groups. In 2003, President George W. Bush signed the American Dream Downpayment Assistance Act, which helped low-income households with down payments and closing costs. As part of its housing goals, the Bush administration also pressured Fannie Mae and Freddie Mac to expand their purchases of riskier mortgages made to lower-income individuals. [49]

Between 1994 and early 2005, the homeownership rate increased from 64 percent to a peak of 69 percent. [50] Owner-occupants were joined by speculators looking to "flip" homes for a quick profit. By mid-decade, "house sales, construction and prices were all shattering records," wrote Zandi. [51]

When housing prices began to fall in 2006 and the number of defaults on mortgages accelerated to historic highs in 2007, "the extent of the financial system's exposure to the subprime mortgages came into relief," wrote Zandi. "By summer 2007, the subprime financial shock was reverberating across the globe." [52]

In 2008, the federal government stepped in to bail out Fannie Mae and Freddie Mac, which continued to buy mortgages and issue securities, but private capital left the market because most banks stopped issuing mortgage-backed bonds, especially those backed by subprime loans. The FHA increased the number of mortgages it insured, but there are concerns that its activities are not sustainable as its own losses mount.

Clean-up

In February, 49 states and the federal government reached a $25 billion agreement with five of the country's largest banks to settle an investigation into abusive and fraudulent foreclosure practices during the collapse of the housing market. At issue is the mortgage servicing industry — dominated by banks — which processes mortgage payments for the lenders and investors who own mortgages.

In 2010, the multistate task force of state attorney's general and state banking regulators began investigating the flawed procedures used by mortgage servicers to create documents to support foreclosure, including the widespread signing of documents without verifying their accuracy, which came to be known as "robo-signing."

Bank of America, JPMorgan Chase, Citigroup, Wells Fargo and Ally Financial have agreed to collectively spend a minimum of $17 billion in principal reduction and other loan modifications for distressed homeowners. Another $1.5 billion is expected to be distributed to some 750,000 borrowers who lost their homes to foreclosure by one of the five servicers from 2008 through 2011.

Under the National Mortgage Settlement, the five banks have also agreed to a series of new consumer protections, including providing struggling borrowers with a single point of contact, streamlining reviews for loan modifications, providing timely written communication to homeowners and banning "dual tracking," a confusing practice in which mortgage servicers pursue foreclosure while simultaneously evaluating borrowers for loan modification. [53]

Meanwhile, the federal government launched programs designed to stem the foreclosure tide. In addition to HAMP, which pays mortgage servicers that modify mortgages of qualified borrowers who are behind on their payments, the Home Affordable Refinance Program (HARP) helps homeowners who are current on their Fannie- or Freddie-owned mortgages refinance.

But HAMP has underperformed expectations. As of July, servicers participating in the program have permanently modified a little more than 1 million loans, a quarter less than what the government had projected. [54] To encourage participation in HARP, the Obama administration has loosened eligibility requirements several times, and this year refinancings under that program have surged. ■

CURRENT SITUATION

Reforms Disappoint

The five banks that agreed to the National Mortgage Settlement have three years to meet their commitments or face a $1 million penalty for each violation. Ten months in, legal groups working with distressed homeowners complain that change has been too slow.

"Our office has seen an increase in the number of principal reductions being offered homeowners to resolve foreclosures," says Julie Robie, managing attorney for consumer law at the Legal Aid Society of Cleveland. "However, the timing, amount and availability of those principal reductions has been unpredictable."

Robie also says high turnover among bank employees has meant that so-called single points of contact appear and disappear in rapid succession. "One homeowner we recently assisted got a series of four letters from four different customer service representatives," Robie says, "each claiming to be the 'single point of contact' for the account."

In addition, dual tracking continues "with vigor," says Alys Cohen, a staff attorney in the Washington office of the National Consumer Law Center. "Many homeowners seeking a modification still face the start of a foreclosure or even the wrongful sale of their home while they are waiting to find out if they qualify."

The settlement applies only to the five large banks and the loans that they own and service themselves. The

Continued on p. 1078

At Issue:

Should Congress phase out the mortgage interest deduction?

ANTHONY RANDAZZO
DIRECTOR OF ECONOMIC RESEARCH, REASON FOUNDATION

WRITTEN FOR *CQ RESEARCHER*, DECEMBER 2012

yes

The mortgage interest deduction (MID) has wrongly been hailed as a social good — a subsidy to help more middle-class families achieve the American dream of home ownership. It has become so entrenched that mere suggestions for eliminating it spur inaccurate worries that homeownership rates and housing prices would tumble. In reality, it disproportionately benefits the wealthy and has only a fairly small upward impact on housing prices — 2-3 percent. And any impact it does have on keeping housing prices higher just means the MID is creating a housing price bubble and artificial value. It's time to phase it out.

In 2010, only 23.5 percent of taxpayers — 33 million Americans — used the mortgage interest deduction, and very few were low-income families or seniors. Claims that the mortgage deduction reduces the cost of homeownership for the middle class just don't stand up to the math. Households with incomes over $100,000 filed 54 percent of tax returns that claimed the mortgage deduction in 2010. That same year, households making $75,000 or less received only 10.7 percent of the total tax savings from the MID combined. So how is the MID so vital for middle-class homeownership?

In 2010 the average MID tax savings for households earning from $50,000 to $75,000 was only $1,192 — or $99.35 a month off the mortgage. For most middle-class families, that's not the deciding factor in home affordability.

If the mortgage deduction were eliminated, the government would collect around $100 billion in new revenues. A revenue-neutral elimination of the MID would put all of those dollars toward lowering individual tax rates by 8 percent, benefiting all tax filers — not just the 23.5 percent using the deduction — without adding a dime to the budget deficit.

Alternatively, as some deficit hawks favor, a portion of the revenues could be used to reduce the deficit. Or Congress could lower tax rates for those few in the middle class whose tax bill would rise as the MID is phased out and apply the remaining revenues to deficit reduction.

The average homeowner moves or refinances a mortgage every seven years, so phasing out the deduction over a seven-year period would allow those who depend on it to adjust their budgets accordingly.

Eliminating the mortgage deduction is an important step in simplifying our tax code and jettisoning unnecessary subsidies. What is Congress waiting for?

BARRY RUTENBERG
CHAIRMAN, NATIONAL ASSOCIATION OF HOME BUILDERS

WRITTEN FOR *CQ RESEARCHER*, DECEMBER 2012

no

For decades, the mortgage interest deduction (MID) has supported society's desire to promote homeownership and a strong middle class. And at a time when housing is once again a generator of jobs and economic growth, cutting the tax benefits associated with homeownership would reverse this policy and place the emerging but sluggish economic recovery at risk.

Increasing the cost of a mortgage would reduce housing demand and weaken home values. While the negative economic impacts from weakening the deduction vary by proposal, it is certain that every 1 percentage point decline in home prices would reduce total household net worth by $164 billion. Thus, even only a 6 percentage point decline would wipe out $1 trillion in net worth — a disastrous outcome given the state of the economy in the wake of the Great Recession.

Critics argue that the MID benefits only those few homeowners who itemize on their taxes. This is false. In a given year, approximately 80 percent of mortgage interest paid by homeowners is claimed as a deduction. Most of the remaining 20 percent is paid by homeowners in the later years of a mortgage, when interest payments are low and principal payments are large. Those homeowners most likely claimed the MID in previous years.

The official data from Congress' Joint Committee on Taxation also demonstrate how the MID benefits the middle class, with two-thirds of the tax benefit being collected by households — many with dual incomes — with income less than $200,000.

Some have suggested that deductions such as the MID should be sacrificed in order to lower marginal tax rates. This is a dangerous political bargain, particularly for prospective home buyers. Lower marginal tax rates do not imply lower tax bills. And history suggests that lower tax rates do not persist. The late 1980s experience is informative: The top marginal rate declined to 28 percent in 1988 but within five years had increased to 39.6 percent.

Moreover, housing is a jobs catalyst. Building 100 single family homes creates 305 full-time jobs and generates $8.9 million in federal, state and local taxes.

Raising taxes on homeowners is not the answer to dealing with tax reform or resolving the nation's fiscal woes. Stabilizing the housing market is a major way to achieve sustained economic growth.

Continued from p. 1076

federal government estimates those accounts for about 20 percent of the U.S. mortgage market. [55]

Earlier this year, the federal government's new Consumer Financial Protection Bureau (CFPB) proposed consumer-protection rules similar to the ones in the National Mortgage Settlement. While the bureau's rules would be permanent and extend to servicers beyond the five banks, they are "much weaker," complains Cohen.

For instance, the settlement requires the five banks to finish reviewing a homeowner for loan modification before starting the foreclosure process. But the bureau's proposal "allows a servicer to start a foreclosure and proceed all the way to the moment before sale without stopping to finish a modification review," says Cohen.

In addition, the settlement requires that mortgage servicers apply homeowners' payments promptly and limits the use of so-called suspense accounts. Servicers place a homeowner's payment in a "suspense" account if they have questions about the payment. Many times the borrower is not notified.

"In our experience, a servicer may place in suspense a payment that is only a few cents short — possibly due to a typographical mistake on a borrower's money order — rather than crediting the payment as timely and working with the borrower to correct the very minor error," Robie, along with lawyers from several other Ohio legal aid organizations, wrote to the CFPB. "This over-use of suspense accounts can lead to unnecessary loan delinquencies," said the group, and even foreclosure.

The legal aid organizations want the CFPB to adopt rules that mirror the language of the National Mortgage Settlement. For instance, "servicers should be required to accept and to apply at least two partial payments when the payments come within $50 of the scheduled payment," they wrote. [56]

The CFPB will issue its final mortgage servicing rules in January. Robert Davis, executive vice president of the American Bankers Association, has warned that small banks may be harmed. "Requiring duplicate disclosures and mounds of documentation for simple one-to-one conversations may push some banks out of the servicing business, which doesn't benefit borrowers," said Davis. [57]

Getty Images/Alex Wong

President Obama discusses his plan to aid struggling homeowners during a speech in Falls Church, Va., on Feb. 1, 2012. To stem the foreclosure tide the government's Home Affordable Modification Program (HAMP) pays mortgage servicers that modify mortgages of qualified borrowers who are behind on their payments. The Home Affordable Refinance Program (HARP) helps struggling homeowners refinance if they are current on their Fannie Mae- or Freddie Mac-owned mortgages.

Discrimination

This past spring, the National Fair Housing Alliance released the results of an investigation of how banks have cared for 1,036 foreclosed homes in cities across the country. The alliance, a Washington-based consortium of fair-housing organizations and state and local civil rights agencies, said its investigation "revealed a pattern of consistently poorer maintenance in communities of color than in white communities" and that properties in white communities "were more likely to be marketed with professional for-sale signs." [58]

The alliance filed a discrimination complaint against Wells Fargo bank and U.S. Bancorp with the U.S. Department of Housing and Urban Development (HUD). This fall it filed a series of similar complaints against Bank of America.

"If you have eyesores in the community, it's going to drag down the appeal of the neighborhood, and it's going to curb the appraised values of all the properties in the neighborhood," says Lisa Rice, vice president of the alliance. "Rectifying these property maintenance issues are critical to the survival of communities that have been waylaid by the foreclosure crisis."

Rice says the banks are not properly monitoring the vendors they hire to clean out and maintain vacant properties. Many times a vendor will clean out a house and "dump the trash in the backyard or the driveway instead of taking it to the dump," says Rice. "Neighbors have told me that companies doing the cleanup will dump the trash in their yards." Some vendors may even be stripping homes of copper pipes and other valuable items to sell and make more money, she says.

Rice suggests that the banks may be designating homes in high-foreclosure, lower-income minority communities as properties to be sold to investors who will rent them out and homes in predominantly white communities as properties to be sold to owner-occupants, who are going to demand homes in better shape. "If you treat a community as an 'investor' community, it will become an 'investor community,' " says Rice.

All three banks vigorously deny the alliance's charges. U.S. Bancorp says it is not responsible for property maintenance because it is not the mortgage servicer but is merely the trustee for investors who own the securities backed by the foreclosed mortgages. Wells Fargo also says it is only a trustee, at least in some cases. For mortgages that it does own and service, Wells Fargo says it conducts monthly inspections of the properties, resolves violations, fines or fees with localities, completes maintenance work and secures and winterizes the homes. And it does so, it says, "in a fair and consistent manner without regard to race or national origin."

Bank of America says it stands behind its property-maintenance and marketing practices and also denies that it was responsible for many of the properties publicly identified in the alliance's announcement of its discrimination complaint. Some have been sold and others conveyed back to investors, according to Rick Simon, a Bank of America spokesman. Rice says that may be true today, but at the time of the alliance's investigation, she says the bank was responsible for the properties.

"HUD takes this matter very seriously. All three cases — Bank of America, Wells Fargo and U.S. Bancorp — are in active investigation regarding all cities," says Shantae Goodloe, a HUD spokeswoman. If HUD determines there is reasonable cause to believe unlawful discrimination has occurred, it can refer the case to an administrative law judge or a court. Relief can include damages for victims, policy changes, training and monitoring of conduct.

But first HUD tries to call conciliation meetings between the parties. "The conciliation meetings are confidential, and I don't know legally if I can tell you with whom we have met," says Rice. ■

OUTLOOK

Big Decisions

The near-term outlook for homeownership is uncertain, according to analysts. On the one hand, loans are cheap. "Mortgage rates are likely to stay below 4 percent through the middle of 2013," forecasts the Mortgage Bankers Association, largely because the Federal Reserve is continuing to buy large amounts of mortgage-backed securities, pumping money into mortgage finance. [59]

On the other hand, banks have tightened credit requirements, in part because Fannie Mae and Freddie Mac have stopped buying loans with lower credit scores.* Fannie and Freddie "have tightened their credit scores into the upper 700s. During the height of the housing bubble, the [lower] limit was 660," says Sanders of the Mercatus Center. "You cannot have a mortgage-fueled housing recovery with a 100-point change in credit scores."

Regulators will soon be making decisions that will also affect who can obtain mortgages and at what cost. Under the 2011 Dodd-Frank Wall Street Reform and Consumer Protection Act, "a creditor may not make a mortgage loan without first determining that the borrower has a reasonable ability to repay the loan. Penalties for violating this test include fines, civil liability, and potentially class action liability," explains *American Banker*. [60] By January, the Consumer Financial Protection Bureau will define what Dodd-Frank calls a "qualified mortgage," or one that is presumed to meet the law's ability-to-pay requirement.

"Lenders probably will only make qualified mortgages, because if the loans ever go into default, they could be sued by disgruntled borrowers," said Zandi. The Dodd-Frank legislation already assumes that mortgages purchased by Fannie Mae and Freddie Mac are qualified, so the CFPB's definition will apply to all other mortgage loans.

"If the government defines 'qualified' too tightly, mortgages will become even harder to get than they are now," said Zandi. "Minority, lower-income and first-time home buyers will have the most trouble, and many will be blocked from homeownership." [61]

While obtaining a mortgage is difficult, it's not the biggest barrier to home buying at the moment, says Trulia's Kolko. "When we survey consumers who are renting now and who want to own, they say the biggest barrier is saving enough for a down payment." That is a function of the weak economy, says Kolko.

In the longer term, housing analysts say demographics bode well for homeownership because of the echo boom generation — the nearly 80 million children of the baby-boom generation, born between 1982 and 1995. They may be late in forming their own households, but eventually they will have to find their own housing. The echo boom population "is already larger than the baby boom at the same ages and so should fuel solid demand for both rental housing and starter homes over the coming decade," says Harvard's Herbert. That's especially true if it gets a boost from an increase in immigration, he adds. [62]

The echo boomers are much more racially and ethnically diverse than previous generations. As a result, Herbert's group at Harvard is predicting that minorities will account for more than 70 percent of net household growth in 2010-2020.

* A credit score is based on an individual's credit history and is designed to predict the risk of delinquency on loan payments. The FICO credit score, the most commonly used, ranges from 300 to 850, with risk decreasing as the number rises.

Moreover, they have far different tastes and desires from their parents, and the housing market will have to adjust, says the National Association of Realtors.

"Smaller houses that are closer to work are often desirable because echo boomers tend to prefer a walking or biking commute instead of long drives on congested expressways," according to the association. "Perhaps another reason echo boomers prefer urban areas is that they tend to stay in jobs for less than two years, so they need to live in a market where there is access to new career opportunities — career opportunities that they happen to be looking for on social media." [63] ■

Notes

[1] For background, see the following *CQ Researcher* reports: Marcia Clemmitt, "Mortgage Crisis," Nov. 2, 2007, pp. 913-936 (updated, Aug. 9, 2010); and Thomas J. Billitteri, "Financial Bailout," Oct. 24, 2008, pp. 865-888 (updated, July 30, 2010); and Marcia Clemmitt, "Financial Industry Overhaul," July 30, 2010, pp. 629-652.

[2] "Rent vs. Buy: Which is Cheaper for You?" Trulia, http://trends.truliablog.com/vis/rentvs-buy-summer2012.

[3] Rachel Bogardus Drew and Christopher Herbert, "Post-Recession Drivers of Preferences for Homeownership," August 2012, p. 1, www.jchs.harvard.edu/research/publications/post-recession-drivers-preferences-homeownership.

[4] "Homeownership Rates for the U.S.: 1965-2012," U.S. Census Bureau, www.census.gov/housing/hvs/data/q312ind.html.

[5] Drew and Herbert, *op. cit.*, p. 1.

[6] CoreLogic Reports Number of Residential Properties in Negative Equity Decreases Again in Second Quarter of 2012, CoreLogic, Sept. 12, 2012, www.corelogic.com/about-us/news/corelogic-reports-number-of-residential-properties-in-negative-equity-decreases-again-in-second-quarter-of-2012.aspx; also see "The U.S. Housing Crisis: Where are home loans underwater?" Zillow, www.zillow.com/visuals/negative-equity/#10/37.1811/-93.0363.

[7] "CoreLogic Home Price Index Marks Eighth Consecutive Month of Year-Over-Year Gains," CoreLogic, Dec. 4, 2012, www.corelogic.com/about-us/news/corelogic-home-price-index-marks-eighth-consecutive-month-of-year-over-year-gains.aspx.

[8] Meghan Hoyer, "Investment firms look to single-family rentals," *USA Today*, Oct. 21, 2012, www.usatoday.com/story/money/business/2012/10/21/investors-single-family-homes/1634689.

[9] "FHA Single Family Insurance Activity," Table 2, Federal Housing Administration, http://portal.hud.gov/hudportal/documents/huddoc?id=fhamktq2_2012.pdf.

[10] *Ibid.*

[11] Allison Freeman and Janneke Ratcliffe, "Setting the Record Straight on Affordable Homeownership," Center for Community Capital, University of North Carolina, May 2012, p. 3, http://ccc.unc.edu/documents/Set.Record.Str8.Aff.HO.May2012.WP.pdf.

[12] "Economic Effects of Policies Contributing to Fiscal Tightening in 2013," Congressional Budget Office, Nov. 8, 2012, www.cbo.gov/publication/43694.

[13] Drew and Herbert, *op. cit.*, pp. 7-9.

[14] President Herbert Hoover, "Address to the White House Conference on Home Building and Home Ownership," Dec. 2, 1931, www.presidency.ucsb.edu/ws/index.php?pid=22927.

[15] President Bill Clinton, "Remarks on the National Homeownership Strategy," June 5, 1995, www.presidency.ucsb.edu/ws/index.php?pid=51448.

[16] Jo Becker, Sheryl Gay Stolberg and Stephen Labaton, "Bush drive for home ownership fueled housing bubble," *The New York Times*, Dec. 21, 2008, www.nytimes.com/2008/12/21/business/worldbusiness/21iht-admin.4.18853088.html?pagewanted=all.

[17] Richard K. Green, Gary D. Painter and Michelle J. White, "Measuring the Benefits of Homeowning: Effects on Children Redux," Research Institute for Housing America, Aug. 10, 2012, p. 33, www.housingamerica.org/RIHA/RIHA/Publications/82405_11693_RIHA_Children_Report.pdf.

[18] *Ibid.*, p. 17.

[19] Denise DiPasquale and Edward L. Glaeser, "Incentives and Social Capital: Are Homeowners Better Citizens?" National Bureau of Economic Research, Working Paper 6363, January 1998, p. 3, www.nber.org/papers/w6363.pdf?new_window=1.

[20] "Home-ownership: Should home-ownership be discouraged?" *The Economist*, Sept. 19, 2012, www.economist.com/debate/days/view/882.

[21] Stephen Slivinski, "House Bias: The economic consequences of subsidizing homeownership," Region Focus, Federal Reserve Bank of Richmond, Fall 2008, p. 14, www.richmondfed.org/publications/research/region_focus/2008/fall/pdf/cover_story.pdf.

[22] "About the MID," National Low Income Housing Coalition, http://nlihc.org/issues/mid/about.

[23] "Home Affordable Modification Program," www.makinghomeaffordable.gov/programs/lower-payments/Pages/hamp.aspx.

[24] DeMarco letter, July 31, 2012, p. 1, www.fhfa.gov/webfiles/24110/PF_LettertoCong73112.pdf.

[25] Geithner letter, July 31, 2012, p. 1, www.treasury.gov/connect/blog/Documents/letter.to.demarco.pdf.

[26] "Review of Options Available for Underwater Borrowers and Principal Forgiveness," Federal Housing Finance Agency, July 31, 2012, p. 11, www.fhfa.gov/webfiles/24108/PF_FHFApaper73112.pdf.

[27] Geithner letter, *op. cit.*

[28] DeMarco letter, *op. cit.*

[29] *Ibid.*, p. 4.

[30] Shahien Nasiripour, "White House seeks removal of Fannie regulator," *Financial Times*, Oct. 24, 2012, www.ft.com/intl/cms/s/0/ef7bd3a6-191d-11e2-af88-00144feabdc0.html#axzz2CeAEFYP8.

[31] Nick Timiraos, "Cost of Bailing Out Fannie and Freddie Expected to Fall Sharply," *The Wall Street Journal*, Oct. 26, 2012, http://online.

About the Author

Barbara Mantel is a freelance writer in New York City. She is a 2012 Kiplinger Fellow and has won several journalism awards, including the National Press Club's Best Consumer Journalism Award and the Front Page Award from the Newswomen's Club of New York for her Nov. 1, 2009, *CQ Global Researcher* report "Terrorism and the Internet." She holds a B.A. in history and economics from the University of Virginia and an M.A. in economics from Northwestern University.

wsj.com/article/SB10001424052970204598504578080770443540656.html.

[32] Peter J. Wallison, "A New Housing Finance System for the United States," House of Cards, p. 55, http://mercatus.org/sites/default/files/House_of_Cards_March_2012.pdf.

[33] Jon Prior, "Treasury provides three options to replace Fannie, Freddie," *HousingWire*, Feb. 11, 2011, www.housingwire.com/news/treasury-provides-three-options-replace-fannie-freddie.

[34] Gwendolyn Wright, *Building the Dream* (1983), pp. 96, 98.

[35] *Ibid.*, pp. 99-100.

[36] *Ibid.*, p. 104.

[37] R. Daniel Wadhwani, "Origins of the Indebted American Homeowner," Bloomberg, April 20, 2012, www.bloomberg.com/news/2012-04-20/origins-of-the-indebted-american-homeowner.html.

[38] Wright, *op. cit.*, p. 104.

[39] Steven Malanga, "Obsessive Housing Disorder," *City Journal*, Manhattan Institute, Spring 2009, www.city-journal.org/2009/19_2_homeownership.html.

[40] Wadhwani, *op. cit.*

[41] Malanga, *op. cit.*

[42] David C. Wheelock, "The Federal Response to Home Mortgage Distress: Lessons from the Great Depression," *Review*, Federal Reserve Bank of St. Louis, May/June Part 1, 2008, p. 138, http://research.stlouisfed.org/publications/review/08/05/Wheelock.pdf.

[43] Louis Hyman, *Debtor Nation: The History of America in Red Ink* (2011), p. 49.

[44] *Ibid.*, pp. 49-50.

[45] Mark Zandi, *Financial Shock: A 360° Look at the Subprime Mortgage Implosion, and How to Avoid the Next Financial Crisis*, p. 47.

[46] Wright, *op. cit.*, pp. 247-248.

[47] Malanga, *op. cit.*

[48] Zandi, *op. cit.*, pp. 13-14.

[49] Celia Chen, "Homeownership in the U.S.: A Return to the Old Normal," *Regional Finance Review*, Moody's Analytics, September 2012, pp. 13-14.

[50] "Homeownership Rates for the U.S.," *op. cit.*

[51] Zandi, *op. cit.*, p. 15.

[52] *Ibid.*, p. 22.

[53] "State Attorneys General, Feds Reach $25 Billion Settlement with Five Largest Mortgage Servicers on Foreclosure Wrongs," National Association of Attorneys General, Feb. 9, 2012, http://naag.org/state-attorneys-general-feds-reach-25-billion-settlement-with-five-largest-mortgage-servicers-on-foreclosure-wrongs.php.

[54] Chen, *op. cit.*, p. 14.

FOR MORE INFORMATION

Consumer Federation of America, 1620 I St., N.W., Suite 200, Washington, DC 20006; 202-387-6121; www.consumerfed.org. Association of nonprofit consumer organizations conducting research, advocacy and education.

Federal Home Loan Mortgage Corp. (Freddie Mac), 8200 Jones Branch Dr., McLean, VA 22102; 703-903-2000; www.freddiemac.com. Government-sponsored enterprise that buys and securitizes mortgage loans originated by lenders; created in 1970 to provide competition for Fannie Mae.

Federal National Mortgage Association (Fannie Mae), 3900 Wisconsin Ave., N.W., Washington, DC 20016; 800-732-6643; www.fanniemae.com. Government-sponsored enterprise that buys and securitizes mortgage loans originated by lenders.

Joint Center for Housing Studies at Harvard University, 1033 Massachusetts Ave., 5th Fl., Cambridge, MA 01238; 617-495-7908; www.jchs.harvard.edu. Investigates housing's role in the economy and in communities.

Mercatus Center at George Mason University, 3351 Fairfax Dr., 4th Fl., Arlington, VA 22201; 703-993-4930; http://mercatus.org. Develops market-based solutions to housing issues and other problems.

National Association of Home Builders, 1201 15th St., N.W., Washington, DC 20005; 202-266-8200; www.nahb.org. Trade association that analyzes housing policies and advocates for its members.

National Association of Realtors, 430 N. Michigan Ave., Chicago, IL 60611; 800-874-6500; www.realtor.org. Trade association representing more than 1 million members involved in the residential and commercial real estate industries.

National Community Reinvestment Coalition, 727 15th St., N.W., Suite 900, Washington, DC 20005; 202-628-8866; www.ncrc.org. Association of more than 600 community-based organizations working to increase the flow of private capital into traditionally underserved communities.

National Fair Housing Alliance, 1101 Vermont Ave., N.W., Suite 710, Washington, DC 20005; 202-898-1661; www.nationalfairhousing.org. National organization dedicated solely to ending discrimination in housing.

U.S. Department of Housing and Urban Development, 451 7th St., S.W., Washington, DC 20410; 202-708-1112. Oversees home mortgage lending practices.

[55] National Association of State Attorneys General, *op. cit.*

[56] "2012-10-09 FINAL Comments to CFPB," Ohio legal aid organizations, Oct. 9, 2012, p. 6, www.regulations.gov/#!documentDetail;D=CFPB-2012-0034-0134.

[57] Kate Berry, "CFPB Unveils Revamp of Mortgage Servicing Standards," *American Banker*, Aug. 13, 2012.

[58] "The Banks Are Back — Our Neighborhoods Are Not: Discrimination in the Maintenance and Marketing of REP Properties," National Fair Housing Alliance, 2012, www.nationalfairhousing.org/Portals/33/REO%20powerpoint%20Webinar.pdf.

[59] "Forecast Commentary Oct 2012," Mortgage Bankers Association, Oct. 24, 2012, www.mortgagebankers.org/files/Bulletin/InternalResource/82425_.pdf.

[60] Raymond Natter, "Dodd-Frank's 'Qualified Mortgage' Was Intended to Be Broad," *American Banker*, April 25, 2012, www.americanbanker.com/bankthink/dodd-frank-qualified-mortgage-was-intended-to-be-broad-1048714-1.html.

[61] Mark Zandi, "Defining a 'qualified' mortgage," *The Washington Post*, Aug. 24, 2012, http://articles.washingtonpost.com/2012-08-24/news/35492116_1_mortgage-loans-disgruntled-borrowers-mortgage-market.

[62] For background, see Bill Wanlund, "Changing Demographics," *CQ Researcher*, Nov. 16, 2012, pp. 989-1012.

[63] "Who Are the Echo Boomers and Why Should REALTORS(r) Care?" "The Member's Edge" blog, National Association of Realtors, Aug. 2, 2012, http://themembersedge.blogs.realtor.org/2012/08/02/who-are-echo-boomers-why-should-realtors-care.

Bibliography

Selected Sources

Books

Hyman, Louis, *Borrow: The American Way of Debt*, Vintage Books, 2012.
A historian examines how the rise of consumer borrowing in the 20th century has altered the United States.

Wright, Gwendolyn, *Building the Dream*, Pantheon Books, 1981.
An architectural historian traces the social history of Americans' homes from the Puritans through suburban sprawl.

Zandi, Mark, *Financial Shock: A 360° Look at the Subprime Mortgage Implosion, and How to Avoid the Next Financial Crisis*, FT Press, 2009.
An economist explains the causes of the recent financial crisis and how to prevent it from recurring.

Articles

"Home-ownership: Should home-ownership be discouraged?" *The Economist*, Sept. 19, 2012, www.economist.com/debate/days/view/882.
Two economists debate whether homeownership is good for society.

Berry, Kate, "CFPB Unveils Revamp of Mortgage Servicing Standards," *American Banker*, Aug. 13, 2012, www.americanbanker.com/issues/177_154/cfpb-unveils-revamp-of-mortgage-servicing-standards-1051725-1.html.
The new Consumer Financial Protection Bureau has proposed rules to protect distressed homeowners fighting to keep their homes.

Hoyer, Meghan, "Investment firms look to single-family rentals," *USA Today*, Oct. 21, 2012, www.usatoday.com/story/money/business/2012/10/21/investors-single-family-homes/1634689.
Large corporate investors are buying single-family homes as rental properties.

Nasiripour, Shahien, "White House seeks removal of Fannie regulator," *Financial Times*, Oct. 24, 2012, www.ft.com/intl/cms/s/0/ef7bd3a6-191d-11e2-af88-00144feabdc0.html#axzz2CeAEFYP8.
The Obama administration may replace the powerful regulator of Fannie Mae and Freddie Mac.

Timiraos, Nick, "Cost of Bailing Out Fannie and Freddie Expected to Fall Sharply," *The Wall Street Journal*, Oct. 26, 2012, http://online.wsj.com/article/SB10001424052970204598504578080770443540656.html.
Fannie Mae and Freddie Mac will repay the government for their bailout faster than initially expected.

Reports and Studies

"The Banks Are Back — Our Neighborhoods Are Not: Discrimination in the Maintenance and Marketing of REP Properties," National Fair Housing Alliance, 2012, www.nationalfairhousing.org/Portals/33/REO%20powerpoint%20Webinar.pdf.
Civil rights agencies says banks maintain foreclosed homes better in white neighborhoods.

"Review of Options Available for Underwater Borrowers and Principal Forgiveness," Federal Housing Finance Agency, July 31, 2012, www.fhfa.gov/webfiles/24108/PF_FHFApaper73112.pdf.
Fannie Mae and Freddie Mac can't reduce mortgage principals for homeowners who owe more than their homes are worth.

Anderson, Janna and Lee Rainee, "The Future of Smart Systems," Pew Internet & American Life Project, June 29, 2012, http://pewinternet.org/Reports/2012/Future-of-Smart-Systems.aspx.
Technology experts are evenly divided about whether the smart home of the future is on the horizon or a marketing mirage.

DiPasquale, Denise, and Edward L. Glaeser, "Incentives and Social Capital: Are Homeowners Better Citizens?" National Bureau of Economic Research, Working Paper 6363, January 1998, www.nber.org/papers/w6363.pdf?new_window=1.
Two researchers say homeowners are more involved in their local communities than renters.

Drew, Rachel Bogardus, and Christopher Herbert, "Post-Recession Drivers of Preferences for Homeownership," Joint Center for Housing Studies at Harvard University, August 2012, www.jchs.harvard.edu/research/publications/post-recession-drivers-preferences-homeownership.
Researchers analyze factors that drive Americans' decisions on whether to purchase or rent a home.

Freeman, Allison, and Janneke Ratcliffe, "Setting the Record Straight on Affordable Homeownership," Center for Community Capital, University of North Carolina, May 2012, http://ccc.unc.edu/documents/Set.Record.Str8.Aff.HO.May2012.WP.pdf.
Researchers say lower-income homeowners are good credit risks when placed in affordable, fixed-rate, long-term mortgages.

Green, Richard K., Gary D. Painter and Michelle J. White, "Measuring the Benefits of Homeowning: Effects on Children Redux," Research Institute for Housing America, Aug. 10, 2012, www.housingamerica.org/RIHA/RIHA/Publications/82405_11693_RIHA_Children_Report.pdf.
Researchers say children of homeowners stay longer in school and better avoid pregnancy than renters' children.

The Next Step:

Additional Articles from Current Periodicals

Benefits

Druse, Fran, "Housing Is Critical to Family, U.S. Economy," *Mobile* (Ala.) *Register*, March 2, 2012, p. 8.
Homeownership promotes social stability and creates wealth and financial security for individual households, says a columnist.

Ventry, Dennis, "Homeownership Myths Have Now Been Fully Debunked," *The Sacramento* (Calif.) *Bee*, Aug. 12, 2012, p. E5, www.sacbee.com/2012/08/12/4715349/what-are-some-lessons-of-the-housing.html#storylink=misearch.
Homeownership is not always a good investment and does not always lead to prosperity, says a columnist.

Mortgage Interest Deduction

Eavis, Peter, "A Tax Break Once Sacred Is Now Seen as Vulnerable," *The New York Times*, Nov. 27, 2012, p. B1, dealbook.nytimes.com/2012/11/26/mortgage-interest-deduction-once-a-sacred-cow-is-seen-as-vulnerable/.
The mortgage interest deduction could be eliminated as Congress and President Obama work to reduce the budget deficit.

Harrop, Froma, "Time to Retire Home Loophole?" *Des Moines* (Iowa) *Register*, Sept. 16, 2012.
Letting homeowners deduct mortgage interest from taxable income encourages taking on more debt, says a columnist.

Kalfus, Marilyn, "Capping Mortgage Deduction Worries Realtors," *Orange County* (Calif.) *Register*, Oct. 5, 2012, www.ocregister.com/articles/mortgage-373717-deduction-realtors.html.
Many California realtors worry that combining the mortgage interest deduction with other deductions as part of a cap could hurt the state's housing recovery.

Recovery

Fletcher, Michael A., "Housing Market Continues to Hobble Economic Recovery," *The Washington Post*, Feb. 29, 2012, p. A13, www.washingtonpost.com/business/economy/housing-prices-fell-in-december-continue-to-hurt-economic-recovery/2012/02/28/gIQAwnK3gR_story.html.
Falling home prices have cast a shadow over what has otherwise been a steady economic recovery.

Hazard, Carol, "Va. Home Sales Go Up," *Richmond* (Va.) *Times Dispatch*, July 24, 2012, p. A1, www.timesdispatch.com/business/home-sales-increase-seen-as-positive-sign-for-richmond-region/article_78e80eda-b904-52ca-bb10-1c9c0f999bba.html.
Central Virginia home sales have reached levels that haven't been seen since 2007.

Mullaney, Tim, "Analysis: Recovery Begins to Look Normal," *USA Today*, Oct. 11, 2012, p. B4, usatoday30.usatoday.com/MONEY/usaedition/2012-10-11-Analysis-Hopeful-signs-in-everhalting-recovery_ST_U.htm.
An improving housing market and lower consumer debt are signs that the U.S. economy is recovering.

Regulations

Kashkari, Neel, "Saving Homes Requires Work," *The Washington Post*, April 29, 2012, p. A17, www.washingtonpost.com/opinions/why-homeowner-bailout-plans-dont-work/2012/04/27/gIQAhplImT_story.html.
Political constraints have forced many government housing programs to target homeowners in need of just a moderate amount of assistance.

Reagor, Catherine, "Plan Seeks Refinancing on Private Mortgages," *Arizona Republic*, Jan. 28, 2012, p. D1, www.azcentral.com/business/realestate/articles/2012/01/26/20120126reagor-plan-seeks-refinancing-private-mortgages.html.
President Obama has announced a plan to introduce legislation that would extend the federal government's refinancing program to homeowners with private loans.

Stiglitz, Joseph E., and Mark Zandi, "The One Housing Solution Left: Mass Mortgage Refinancing," *The New York Times*, Aug. 13, 2012, p. A17, www.nytimes.com/2012/08/13/opinion/the-one-housing-solution-left-mass-mortgage-refinancing.html?_r=0.
The government needs to find a way to facilitate mass mortgage refinancing to reduce homeowners' monthly payments and free up money to spend on other things.

CITING *CQ RESEARCHER*

Sample formats for citing these reports in a bibliography include the ones listed below. Preferred styles and formats vary, so please check with your instructor or professor.

MLA STYLE

Jost, Kenneth. "Remembering 9/11," CQ Researcher 2 Sept. 2011: 701-732.

APA STYLE

Jost, K. (2011, September 2). Remembering 9/11. *CQ Researcher, 9*, 701-732.

CHICAGO STYLE

Jost, Kenneth. "Remembering 9/11." *CQ Researcher*, September 2, 2011, 701-732.

Published by CQ Press, an Imprint of SAGE Publications, Inc.

www.cqresearcher.com

Index

January 1991–December 2012

- *CQ Researcher* reports are indexed by title under boldface topic headings.
  - Titles are followed by the date the report appeared and the first page number of its print version.
  - Page numbers followed by an asterisk refer to a sidebar or the "At Issue" (Pro/Con) feature.
  - Page numbers preceded by a double asterisk refer to an issue that has been updated.
- This index is updated monthly and available at: http://www.cqpress.com/docs/cqrindex.pdf
- *CQ Researcher* can be accessed online at: www.cqresearcher.com

Published by CQ Press, an Imprint of SAGE Publications, Inc.

	Date	Page
Abortion. ***See also Birth control***		
Abortion Clinic Protests	04/07/95	297
Abortion Debates	03/21/03	249
Abortion Debates	09/10/10	725
Abortion Showdowns	09/22/06	769
Catholic Church in the U.S.	09/08/95	784*
Embryo Research	12/17/99	1065
Feminism's Future	02/28/97	181*
Fetal Tissue Research	08/16/91	561
Population and the Environment	07/17/98	607*
Population Growth	07/16/93	601
Religion and Politics	07/30/04	637
Reproductive Ethics	04/08/94	289
Roe v. Wade at 25	11/28/97	1033
Supreme Court's Future	01/28/05	77
Supreme Court Preview	09/17/93	817
Teenagers and Abortion	07/05/91	441
Teen Pregnancy	03/26/10	265*
Women and Human Rights	04/30/99	367*
Abu Musab al-Zarqawi		
Global Jihad	10/14/05	857
Accidents. ***See Occupational health and safety; Safety; Traffic accidents***		
Acquired immune deficiency syndrome. ***See AIDS disease***		
Addiction. ***See Drug abuse***		
Adolescents and youth. ***See also Colleges and universities; Elementary and secondary education; Children's health and safety***		
Advertising Overload	01/23/04	49
Arts Education	03/16/12	253
Boys' Emotional Needs	06/18/99	521
Broadcast Indecency	04/16/04	321
Changing U.S. Electorate	05/30/08	**457
Childhood Depression	07/16/99	593
Child Poverty	04/07/00	281
Child Welfare Reform	04/22/05	345
Chronic Fatigue Syndrome	04/05/02	289
Combating Plagiarism	09/19/03	773
Community Prosecution	12/15/00	1016*
Consumer Debt	11/15/96	1009
Cosmetic Surgery	04/15/05	317
Covering the Uninsured	06/14/02	521
Cyberbullying	05/02/08	385
Cyber-Predators	03/01/02	169
Cyber Socializing	07/28/06	625
Declining Crime Rates	04/04/97	289
Digital Education	12/02/11	1001
Draft Debates	08/19/05	661
Drug Safety	03/11/05	221
Eating Disorders	02/10/06	**121
Extreme Sports	04/03/09	297
Financial Literacy	09/04/09	717
The Future of Baseball	09/25/98	839*
Future of Books	05/29/09	**473
Future of the GOP	03/20/09	249
Future of Marriage	05/07/04	397
Future of the Music Industry	11/21/03	989
Gang Crisis	05/14/04	421
Gender and Learning	05/20/05	445
Hazing	01/09/04	1
Highway Safety	07/14/95	609
Home Schooling Debate	01/17/03	25
Homework Debate	12/06/02	993
HPV Vaccine	05/11/07	409
Human Trafficking and Slavery	03/26/04	273
Illegal Immigration	05/06/05	393
Impact of the Internet on Thinking	09/24/10	773
Increase in Autism	06/13/03	**545
Juvenile Justice	02/25/94	169
Juvenile Justice	11/07/08	913
Kids in Prison	04/27/01	345
Mental Illness Medication Debate	02/06/04	101
Mothers' Movement	04/04/03	297
Movie Ratings	03/28/03	273
National Service	06/30/06	577
Native Americans	05/08/92	400
No Child Left Behind	05/27/05	469
Parental Rights	10/25/96	950*
Preventing Bullying	12/10/10	**1013
Preventing Juvenile Crime	03/15/96	217
Preventing Obesity	10/01/10	797
Prostitution Debate	05/23/08	433
Reality TV	08/27/10	677
Reforming Big-Time College Sports	03/19/04	249
Rising College Costs	12/05/03	1013
School Desegregation	04/23/04	345
School Violence	10/09/98	881
School Vouchers Showdown	02/15/02	121
Sentencing Debates	11/05/04	925
Sex Offenders	09/08/06	721
Sex on Campus	11/04/94	961
Sexual Abuse and the Clergy	05/03/02	393
Sexually Transmitted Diseases	12/03/04	997
Soccer in America	04/22/94	337
Social Networking	09/17/10	749
Student Journalism	06/05/98	481
Students Under Stress	07/13/07	577
Teenage Suicide	06/14/91	369
Teen Driving	01/07/05	1
Teen Drug Use	06/03/11	481
Teen Pregnancy	03/26/10	265*
Teen Sex	09/16/05	761
Teen Spending	05/26/06	457
Tobacco Industry	12/10/04	**1025
The Value of a College Education	11/20/09	981
Video Games	11/10/06	**937
Violence in Schools	09/11/92	785

 *Indicates sidebar or "At Issue" report section. **Indicates an updated report.

	Date	Page
Youth Gangs	10/11/91	753
Youth Suicide	02/13/04	125
Adolescents and youth — Alcohol and drug use		
AB and IP Programs	03/03/06	193
Alcohol Advertising	03/14/97	217
Athletes and Drugs	07/26/91	513
Bullying	02/04/05	101
Celebrity Culture	03/18/05	245
Drinking on Campus	03/20/98	241
Drinking on Campus	08/18/06	649
Drug-Policy Debate	07/28/00	610*
Drug Testing	11/20/98	1006*
High School Sports	09/22/95	825
Juvenile Justice	11/07/08	913
Marijuana Laws	02/11/05	125
Medical Marijuana	08/20/99	711*
Medication Abuse	10/09/09	837
Methamphetamine	07/15/05	589
Preventing Teen Drug Use	07/28/95	657
Preventing Teen Drug Use	03/15/02	217
Reforming Big-Time College Sports	03/19/04	249
Rethinking Ritalin	10/22/99	922*
Sports and Drugs	07/23/04	618*
Teen Driving	01/07/05	1
Underage Drinking	03/13/92	217
War on Drugs	03/19/93	254*
War on Drugs	06/02/06	481
Youth Violence	03/05/10	193*
Adolescents and youth — Employment		
Closing In on Tobacco	11/12/99	977
Fast-Food Shake-Up	11/08/91	825
Future Job Market	01/11/02	1
High-Tech Labor Shortage	04/24/98	370*
Job Stress	08/04/95	695*
National Service	06/25/93	553
The Value of a College Education	11/20/09	981
Youth Apprenticeships	10/23/92	905
Adolescents and youth — Pregnancy		
Abortion Debates	03/21/03	249
Abortion Showdowns	09/22/06	769
Birth-Control Debate	06/24/05	565
Child Welfare Reform	04/22/05	345
Encouraging Teen Abstinence	07/10/98	577
Infant Mortality	07/31/92	652
Preventing Teen Pregnancy	05/14/93	409
Sexually Transmitted Diseases	12/03/04	997
Teenagers and Abortion	07/05/91	441
Teen Pregnancy	03/26/10	265*
Tobacco Industry	12/10/04	**1025
Welfare, Work and the States	12/06/96	1069*
Adoption		
Abortion Debates	03/21/03	249
Adoption	11/26/93	1033
Adoption Controversies	09/10/99	777

	Date	Page
Child Welfare Reform	04/22/05	345
Foster Care Reform	01/09/98	1
Gay Marriage	09/05/03	721
Gay Rights	03/05/93	210*
Gay Rights Update	04/14/00	305
Native Americans' Future	07/12/96	617*
Advanced Placement (AP)		
AB and IP Programs	03/03/06	193
Racial Diversity in Public Schools	09/14/07	**745
Students Under Stress	07/13/07	577
Advertising. *See also Political advertising*		
Advertising Overload	01/23/04	49
Advertising Under Attack	09/13/91	657
Alcohol Advertising	03/14/97	217
Celebrity Culture	03/18/05	245
Centennial Olympic Games	04/05/96	289
Children's Television	08/15/97	734*
The Consumer Culture	11/19/99	1007*
Dietary Supplements	09/03/04	709
Digital Commerce	02/05/99	98*
Drinking on Campus	03/20/98	253*
Drug Company Ethics	06/06/03	521*
Future of Newspapers	01/20/06	49
The Growing Influence of Boycotts	01/04/91	1
The New Corporate Philanthropy	02/27/98	186*
Online Privacy	11/06/09	**933
Preventing Teen Drug Use	07/28/95	663*
Reforming Big-Time College Sports	03/19/04	249
Regulating the Internet	06/30/95	568*
Regulating Tobacco	09/30/94	852*
Sex, Violence and the Media	11/17/95	1025*
Soccer in America	04/22/94	342*
Teen Driving	01/07/05	1
Teen Drug Use	06/03/11	481
Teens and Tobacco	12/01/95	1065
Television's Future	02/16/07	145
Tobacco Industry	12/10/04	**1025
Underage Drinking	03/13/92	217
Affirmative action		
Affirmative Action	09/21/01	737
Affirmative Action	10/17/08	**841
The Black Middle Class	01/23/98	49
Diversity in the Workplace	10/10/97	889
Getting into College	02/23/96	169
Race in America	07/11/03	603*
Racial Diversity in Public Schools	09/14/07	**745
Racial Quotas	05/17/91	277
Racial Tensions in Schools	01/07/94	1
Rethinking Affirmative Action	04/28/95	369
Supreme Court Controversies	09/28/12	813
Afghanistan		
Afghanistan Dilemma	08/07/09	**669*
America at War	07/23/10	**605
Caring for Veterans	04/23/10	361

	Date	Page
Civil Liberties in Wartime	12/14/01	1017
Closing Guantánamo	02/27/09	**177
Cost of the Iraq War	04/25/08	361*
Drone Warfare	08/06/10	653
Exporting Democracy	04/01/05	269
Foreign Aid and National Security	06/17/11	529
Government Secrecy	02/11/11	121
Intelligence Reforms	01/25/02	49
International Law	12/17/04	1049
Interrogating the CIA	09/25/09	789
Islamic Fundamentalism	03/24/00	241
Military Suicides	09/23/11	781*
New Defense Priorities	09/13/02	721
The Obama Presidency	01/30/09	73
Policing the Borders	02/22/02	145
Privatizing the Military	07/13/12	597
Prosecuting Terrorists	03/12/10	**217*
Remembering 9/11	09/02/11	701*
Treatment of Detainees	08/25/06	673
U.S.-British Relations	11/05/10	917*
U.S.-Pakistan Relations	08/05/11	653*
War on Terrorism	10/12/01	817
Weapons of Mass Destruction	03/08/02	193
Women and Human Rights	04/30/99	353
Women in the Military	11/13/09	957
Wounded Veterans	08/31/07	697
Africa		
Aiding Africa	08/29/03	697
AIDS Update	12/04/98	1062*
Assisting Refugees	02/07/97	104*
Battling HIV/AIDS	10/26/07	889
Children in Crisis	08/31/01	657
Democracy in Africa	03/24/95	241
Ecotourism	10/20/06	865
Ending Poverty	09/09/05	733
Famine in Africa	11/08/02	921
Foreign Aid and National Security	06/17/11	529
Foreign Aid After Sept. 11	04/26/02	361
Global AIDS Crisis	10/13/00	809
Global Food Crisis	06/27/08	553
Global Jihad	10/14/05	857
Global Refugee Crisis	07/09/99	569
Global Water Shortages	12/15/95	1113
Homegrown Jihadists	09/03/10	701
Human Rights in China	07/25/08	601
Human Rights Issues	10/30/09	909
Human Trafficking and Slavery	03/26/04	273
Oil Diplomacy	01/24/03	49
Philanthropy in America	12/08/06	1009
Religious Persecution	11/21/97	1009
Sexually Transmitted Diseases	12/03/04	997
South Africa's Future	01/14/94	25
Stopping Genocide	08/27/04	685
Water Shortages	08/01/03	649

	Date	Page
Women and Human Rights	04/30/99	353
World Hunger	10/25/91	814
African-Americans		
Adoption	11/26/93	1033
Adoption Controversies	09/10/99	777
Affirmative Action	10/17/08	**841
Asian Americans	12/13/91	960
Asthma Epidemic	12/24/99	1093*
Black Colleges	12/12/03	1045
The Black Middle Class	01/23/98	49
Breast Cancer	04/02/10	289
Census Controversey	05/14/10	433
Changing Demographics	11/16/12	989
Changing U.S. Electorate	05/30/08	**457
Charter Schools	12/20/02	1033
College Football	11/18/11	977
College Sports	08/26/94	745
Consumer Debt	03/02/07	193
Debate Over Immigration	07/14/00	580*
Democracy in Africa	03/24/95	246*
Discipline in Schools	02/15/08	145
Diversity in the Workplace	10/10/97	889
Domestic Poverty	09/07/07	**721
Drug-Policy Debate	07/28/00	612*
Electing Minorities	08/12/94	697
Encouraging Teen Abstinence	07/10/98	594*
Evaluating Head Start	08/26/05	685
Fighting Crime	02/08/08	121
Financial Literacy	09/04/09	717
The Future of Baseball	09/25/98	839*
Future of the GOP	03/20/09	249
Gun Control Debate	11/12/04	949
Hate Crimes	01/08/93	1
Hate Groups	05/08/09	421
Hispanic Americans	10/30/92	935
Historic Preservation	10/07/94	876*
Housing Discrimination	02/24/95	169
Intelligence Testing	07/30/93	649
The Jury System	11/10/95	993
Juvenile Justice	11/07/08	913
Mortgage Crisis	11/02/07	**913
Muslims in America	04/30/93	361
New Military Culture	04/26/96	361
The Obama Presidency	01/30/09	73
Obesity Epidemic	01/31/03	78*
Peace Corps' Challenges in the 1990s	01/25/91	49
Police Corruption	11/24/95	1041
Police Misconduct	04/06/12	301
Policing the Police	03/17/00	209
Preventing Teen Pregnancy	05/14/93	409
Protestants Today	12/07/07	1009
Public Defenders	04/18/08	337*
Public Housing	09/10/93	793
Race and Politics	07/18/08	577

 *Indicates sidebar or "At Issue" report section. **Indicates an updated report.

	Date	Page
Race in America	07/11/03	593
Racial Diversity in Public Schools	09/14/07	**745
Racial Quotas	05/17/91	277
Racial Tensions in Schools	01/07/94	1
Reassessing the Nation's Gun Laws	03/22/91	157
Rebuilding New Orleans	02/03/06	97
Redistricting Disputes	03/12/04	221
Redistricting: Drawing Power with a Map	02/15/91	97
Reforming Big-Time College Sports	03/19/04	249
Reparations Movement	06/22/01	529
Rethinking Affirmative Action	04/28/95	382*
Rethinking School Integration	10/18/96	913
Revising No Child Left Behind	04/16/10	337
School Desegregation	04/23/04	345
School Vouchers	04/09/99	281
School Vouchers Showdown	02/15/02	121
Sentencing Debates	11/05/04	925
Sexually Transmitted Diseases	12/03/04	997
Should the U.S. Reinstate the Draft?	01/11/91	17
Student Aid	01/25/08	73
Teaching History	09/29/95	849
Teens and Tobacco	12/01/95	1082*
Upward Mobility	04/29/05	369
Worker Retraining	01/21/94	62*
Wrongful Convictions	04/17/09	**345
Youth Violence	03/05/10	193*
Zero Tolerance	03/10/00	185
Agency for International Development		
Aiding Africa	08/29/03	697
Famine in Africa	11/08/02	921
Foreign Aid After Sept. 11	04/26/02	361
Reassessing Foreign Aid	09/27/96	841
Trouble in South America	03/14/03	225
Aging. ***See Elderly***		
Agriculture. ***See also Forests and forestry***		
Animal Rights	05/24/91	316*
Animal Rights	01/08/10	1
Biofuels Boom	09/29/06	793
Biotech Foods	03/30/01	249
Bush and the Environment	10/25/02	865
California: Enough Water for the Future?	04/19/91	221
Child Labor and Sweatshops	08/16/96	732*
Coastal Development	08/21/98	739*
Consumer Safety	10/12/07	841
Crisis on the Plains	05/09/03	417
Factory Farms	01/12/07	25
Farm Policy	12/02/94	1057
Farm Policy	08/10/12	693
Farm Subsidies	05/17/02	433
Fighting over Animal Rights	08/02/96	673
Food Safety	11/01/02	897
Food Safety	12/17/10	1037
Food Safety Battle: Organic v. Biotech	09/04/98	761

	Date	Page
Genetically Modified Food	08/31/12	717
Global Food Crisis	06/27/08	553
Global Water Shortages	12/15/95	1113
Illegal Immigration	05/06/05	393
The New Environmentalism	12/01/06	985
Reforming the Corps	05/30/03	497
Regulating Pesticides	01/28/94	73
Regulating Pesticides	08/06/99	665
Slow Food Movement	01/26/07	73
Tobacco Industry	12/10/04	**1025
U.S. Trade Policy	01/29/93	84*
Water Crisis in the West	12/09/11	1025
Water Shortages	08/01/03	649
Water Shortages	06/18/10	529
World Hunger	10/25/91	818
AIDS disease		
Aiding Africa	08/29/03	697
AIDS Update	12/04/98	1049
Alternative Medicine	01/31/92	79*
Battling HIV/AIDS	10/26/07	889
Birth Control Choices	07/29/94	649
Birth-Control Debate	06/24/05	565
Blood Supply Safety	11/11/94	985
Children in Crisis	08/31/01	657
Combating AIDS	04/21/95	345
Famine in Africa	11/08/02	935*
Fighting over Animal Rights	08/02/96	677*
Gay Rights	03/05/93	204*
Global AIDS Crisis	10/13/00	809
Infant Mortality	07/31/92	651
New Military Culture	04/26/96	377*
Philanthropy in America	12/08/06	1009
Privacy in the Workplace	11/19/93	1023*
Prostitution	06/11/93	505
Prostitution Debate	05/23/08	433
Sexually Transmitted Diseases	12/03/04	997
Women and AIDS	12/25/92	1121
Air pollution. ***See also Global warming***		
Acid Rain: New Approach to Old Problem	03/08/91	129
Air Pollution Conflict	11/14/03	965
Alternative Energy	02/25/05	173
Asbestos Litigation	05/02/03	398*
Bush and the Environment	10/25/02	865
Climate Change	01/27/06	73
Coal's Comeback	10/05/07	817
Crackdown on Smoking	12/04/92	1066*
Electric Cars	07/09/93	577
Environmental Movement at 25	03/31/95	280*
Flexible Work Arrangements	08/14/98	715*
The Greening of Eastern Europe	11/15/91	849
Indoor Air Pollution	10/27/95	945
Human Rights in China	07/25/08	601
Jobs vs. Environment	05/15/92	422

	Date	Page
Lead Poisoning	06/19/92	537
Managing Wildfires	11/02/12	941
New Air Quality Standards	03/07/97	193
The New Environmentalism	12/01/06	985
Oil Imports	08/23/91	585
SUV Debate	05/16/03	460*
Traffic Congestion	05/06/94	385
Air transportation		
Airline Industry Problems	09/24/99	825
Airline Safety	10/08/93	865
Future of the Airline Industry	06/21/02	545
Future of the Airlines	03/07/08	217
Homeland Security	09/12/03	749
Homeland Security	02/13/09	129
Re-examining 9/11	06/04/04	493
Alcohol		
Advertising Overload	01/23/04	49
Alcohol Advertising	03/14/97	217
Athletes and Drugs	07/26/91	519*
Combating Addiction	02/09/07	121
Crime on Campus	02/04/11	97
Diet and Health	02/23/01	129
Drinking on Campus	03/20/98	241
Drinking on Campus	08/18/06	649
Drug-Policy Debate	07/28/00	599*
Drug Testing	11/20/98	1001
Drunken Driving	10/06/00	793
Ending Homelessness	06/18/04	541
Hazing	01/09/04	1
Highway Safety	07/14/95	609
Native Americans	05/08/92	394*
Native Americans' Future	07/12/96	608*
Preventing Teen Drug Use	03/15/02	217
Socially Responsible Investing	08/29/08	673
Teen Driving	01/07/05	1
Treating Addiction	01/06/95	14*
Underage Drinking	03/13/92	217
Youth Suicide	02/13/04	125
Alternative fuels		
Alternative Energy	07/10/92	573
Alternative Energy	02/25/05	173
Confronting Warming	01/09/09	1
Biofuels Boom	09/29/06	793
Bush and the Environment	10/25/02	865
Electric Cars	07/09/93	577
Energy and Climate	07/24/09	621
Energy Efficiency	05/19/06	433
Energy Security	02/01/02	84*
Future of the Airlines	03/07/08	217
Modernizing the Grid	02/19/10	145
Oil Diplomacy	01/24/03	49
Oil Imports	08/23/91	599
Oil Production in the 21st Century	08/07/98	682*
Renewable Energy	11/07/97	961

	Date	Page
SUV Debate	05/16/03	449
Alternative medicine		
Alternative Medicine	01/31/92	73
Alternative Medicine's Next Phase	02/14/97	121
Chronic Fatigue Syndrome	04/05/02	289
Dietary Supplements	07/08/94	590*
Dietary Supplements	09/03/04	709
Drug-Resistant Bacteria	06/04/99	489*
Homeopathy Debate	12/19/03	1069
Marijuana Laws	02/11/05	125
Prayer and Healing	01/14/05	25
Rethinking Ritalin	10/22/99	905
Alternative sentences		
Civic Renewal	03/21/97	252*
Community Prosecution	12/15/00	1009
Juvenile Justice	02/25/94	180*
Prison-Building Boom	09/17/99	801
Prison Overcrowding	02/04/94	105*
Punishing Sex Offenders	01/12/96	25
Sentencing Debates	11/05/04	925
American Indians. *See Native Americans*		
American Library Association		
The Future of Libraries	05/23/97	457
Hard Times for Libraries	06/26/92	553
Americans with Disabilities Act, 1990		
The Disabilities Act	12/27/91	993
Implementing the Disabilities Act	12/20/96	1105
Mental Health Policy	09/12/97	793
Amtrak. *See Railroads*		
Animals. *See also Endangered species; Wildlife*		
America's Pampered Pets	12/27/96	1129
Animal Intelligence	10/22/10	869
Animal Rights	05/24/91	301
Animal Rights	01/08/10	1
Biology and Behavior	04/03/98	295*
The Cloning Controversy	05/09/97	409
'Designer' Humans	05/18/01	433*
Disappearing Species	11/30/07	985
Factory Farms	01/12/07	25
Fighting over Animal Rights	08/02/96	673
Hunting Controversy	01/24/92	49
Invasive Species	10/05/01	785
Invasive Species	02/17/12	153
Marine Mammals vs. Fish	08/28/92	737*
Organ Transplants	08/11/95	705
Protecting Wetlands	10/03/08	793*
Prozac Controversy	08/19/94	734*
Zoos in the 21st Century	04/28/00	353
Anorexia nervosa. *See Eating disorders*		
Anti-Ballistic Missile Treaty, 1972. *See Treaties and international agreements; International relations — U.S. foreign policy*		

	Date	Page
Antitrust law. ***See also Business and industry***		
Airline Industry Problems	09/24/99	825
Antitrust Policy	06/12/98	505
The Business of Sports	02/10/95	121
Digital Commerce	02/05/99	89
Google's Dominance	11/11/11	953
Paying for College	11/20/92	1017*
Reforming Big-Time College Sports	03/19/04	249
Aquaculture		
Fish Farming	07/27/07	625
Saving the Oceans	11/04/05	933
Arab-Americans		
Middle East Tensions	10/27/06	**889
Muslims in America	04/30/93	361
Race in America	07/11/03	612*
Understanding Islam	11/03/06	913
War on Terrorism	10/12/01	817
Arafat, Yasser. ***See Middle East***		
Archaeology		
Archaeology Today	05/24/02	457
Historic Preservation	10/07/94	870*
Is America Allowing Its Past to Be Stolen?	01/18/91	33
Arctic National Wildlife Refuge		
Bush and the Environment	10/25/02	865
Domestic Energy Development	09/30/05	809
Energy Efficiency	05/19/06	433
Energy Policy	05/25/01	441
Energy Security	02/01/02	73
Oil Imports	08/23/91	601*
Armed forces. ***See Military service***		
Arms control		
Arms Sales	12/09/94	1081
Banning Land Mines	08/08/97	697
Bush's Defense Strategy	09/07/01	703*
Chemical and Biological Weapons	01/31/97	73
Confronting Iraq	10/04/02	793
Defense Priorities	07/30/99	658*
Ethics of War	12/13/02	1013
Future of NATO	02/28/03	177
Gun Rights Debates	10/31/08	**889
Haiti's Dilemma	02/18/05	149
Missile Defense	09/08/00	689
Non-Proliferation Treaty at 25	01/27/95	73
North Korean Crisis	04/11/03	321
Nuclear Arms Cleanup	06/24/94	553
Nuclear Proliferation	06/05/92	481
Nuclear Proliferation and Terrorism	04/02/04	297
U.S. Policy in Asia	11/27/92	1025
U.S.-Russia Relations	01/18/02	32*
U.S.-Russian Relations	05/22/98	457
The United Nations and Global Security	02/27/04	173
United Nations at 50	08/18/95	745*
Weapons of Mass Destruction	03/08/02	193
Army Corps of Engineers		
Coastal Development	08/21/98	721
Reforming the Corps	05/30/03	497
Army, U.S. ***See Military service***		
Artificial intelligence		
Artificial Intelligence	11/14/97	985
Artificial Intelligence	04/22/11	361
Future of Computers	05/26/00	449
Insurance Fraud	10/11/96	906*
Arts		
Arts Education	03/16/12	253
Arts Funding	10/21/94	913
Stolen Antiquities	04/13/07	313
Asbestos		
Asbestos Litigation	05/02/03	393
Indoor Air Pollution	10/27/95	957*
Science in the Courtroom	10/22/93	922*
Worker Safety	05/21/04	445
Asia		
Battling HIV/AIDS	10/26/07	889
China After Deng	06/13/97	505
China Today	08/04/00	625
Deflation Fears	02/13/98	121
Democracy in Asia	07/24/98	625
Ecotourism	10/20/06	865
Emerging India	04/19/02	329
Fighting SARS	06/20/03	569
Future of Korea	05/19/00	425
Global AIDS Crisis	10/13/00	814*
Human Trafficking and Slavery	03/26/04	273
International Monetary Fund	01/29/99	65
New Era in Asia	02/14/92	121
Religious Persecution	11/21/97	1009
Taiwan, China, and the U.S.	05/24/96	457
U.S.-Europe Relations	03/23/12	277
U.S. Policy in Asia	11/27/92	1025
U.S.-Vietnam Relations	12/03/93	1057
Asian-Americans		
Asian Americans	12/13/91	945
Debate Over Immigration	07/14/00	580*
Electing Minorities	08/12/94	711*
Gang Crisis	05/14/04	421
Hate Crimes	01/08/93	1
The New Immigrants	01/24/97	49
Race in America	07/11/03	593
Racial Quotas	05/17/91	285*
School Desegregation	04/23/04	356*
Assisted suicide		
Assisted Suicide	02/21/92	145
Assisted Suicide Controversy	05/05/95	393
Caring for the Dying	09/05/97	769
Right to Die	05/13/05	421
Asylum. ***See Political asylum***		

	Date	Page
Athletes. ***See Sports***		
Attention deficit disorder		
Rethinking Ritalin	10/22/99	905
Australia		
Caring for the Dying	09/05/97	782*
Gun Control Standoff	12/19/97	1116*
Reparations Movement	06/22/01	529
Automobiles and automobile industry. ***See also Highways and roads; Traffic accidents***		
Aggressive Driving	07/25/97	649*
Air Pollution Conflict	11/14/03	965
Alternative Energy	07/10/92	584*
Alternative Energy	02/25/05	173
Auto Industry's Future	01/21/00	17
Auto Industry's Future	02/06/09	**105
Auto Safety	10/26/01	873
Biofuels Boom	09/29/06	793
Business Bankruptcy	04/10/09	321
Buying Green	02/29/08	193
Cell Phone Safety	03/16/01	201
Confronting Warming	01/09/09	1
Distracted Driving	05/04/12	401
Electric Cars	07/09/93	577
Energy and the Environment	03/03/00	174*
Energy Efficiency	05/19/06	433
Energy Security	02/01/02	73
Future of Amtrak	10/18/02	841
Global Warming Update	11/01/96	966*
High-Speed Trains	05/01/09	**397
Labor Movement's Future	06/28/96	571*
Mass Transit Boom	01/18/08	49
The New Environmentalism	12/01/06	985
Oil Imports	08/23/91	585
Oil Jitters	01/04/08	**1
Recession's Regional Impact	02/01/91	74*
Reducing Your Carbon Footprint	12/05/08	985
Renewable Energy	11/07/97	972*
SUV Debate	05/16/03	449
Teen Driving	01/07/05	1
Traffic Congestion	05/06/94	385
Traffic Congestion	08/27/99	729
Transportation Policy	07/04/97	577
The U.S. and Japan	05/31/91	342*
U.S. Auto Industry	10/16/92	881
U.S. Trade Policy	01/29/93	73
Avian Flu		
Avian Flu Threat	01/13/06	25
Aviation. ***See Air transportation***		
Baby Boomers		
Aging Baby Boomers	10/19/07	865
Aging Population	07/15/11	577
Baby Boomers at Midlife	07/31/98	649
Budget Deficit	12/09/05	1029
Caring for the Dying	09/05/97	787*
Caring for the Elderly	02/20/98	160*
Medicare Reform	08/22/03	673
The New Corporate Philanthropy	02/27/98	184*
Overhauling Social Security	05/12/95	417
Pension Crisis	02/17/06	145
Preventing Memory Loss	04/04/08	289*
Religion in America	11/25/94	1033
Retirement Security	05/31/02	481
Saving Social Security	10/02/98	857
Smart Growth	05/28/04	469
Social Security Reform	09/24/04	781
Balkans		
Democracy in Eastern Europe	10/08/99	865
Economic Sanctions	10/28/94	954*
Ethics of War	12/13/02	1013
Europe's New Right	02/12/93	121
Foreign Policy Burden	08/20/93	721
Future of NATO	02/28/03	177
Privatizing the Military	06/25/04	565
Torture	04/18/03	345
The United Nations and Global Security	02/27/04	173
War Crimes	07/07/95	585
Bankruptcy		
Accountants Under Fire	03/22/02	241
Auto Industry's Future	02/06/09	**105
Business Bankruptcy	04/10/09	321
Consumer Debt	11/15/96	1009
Consumer Debt	03/02/07	193
Financial Literacy	09/04/09	717
Future of the Airline Industry	06/21/02	545
Pension Crisis	02/17/06	145
Regulating Credit Cards	10/10/08	817*
Teen Spending	05/26/06	457
Banks and banking		
Business Bankruptcy	04/10/09	321
Cyber-Crime	04/12/02	305
The Federal Reserve	09/01/00	673
Holocaust Reparations	03/26/99	257
Housing Discrimination	02/24/95	169
Jobs in the '90s	02/28/92	179
Mortgage Crisis	11/02/07	**913
Mutual Funds	05/20/94	449*
Recession's Regional Impact	02/01/91	75*
Regulating Credit Cards	10/10/08	817*
Y2K Dilemma	02/19/99	137
Battered women. ***See Domestic violence***		
Bilingual education		
Bilingual Education	08/13/93	697
Debate over Bilingualism	01/19/96	49
Hispanic Americans	10/30/92	946*
Hispanic-Americans' New Clout	09/18/98	809

 *Indicates sidebar or "At Issue" report section. **Indicates an updated report.

	Date	Page
Bin Laden, Osama		
Civil Liberties in Wartime	12/14/01	1017
Democracy in the Arab World	01/30/04	73
Future of NATO	02/28/03	177
The Future of U.S.-Russia Relations	01/18/02	25
Hating America	11/23/01	869
Intelligence Reforms	01/25/02	49
Islamic Fundamentalism	03/24/00	241
New Defense Priorities	09/13/02	721
Policing the Borders	02/22/02	145
Rebuilding Afghanistan	12/21/01	1041
Re-examining 9/11	06/04/04	493
Smallpox Threat	02/07/03	105
Treatment of Detainees	08/25/06	673
War on Terrorism	10/12/01	817
Weapons of Mass Destruction	03/08/02	193
Bioethics. ***See Medical ethics***		
Biological diversity. ***See Environmental protection***		
Biological weapons		
Chemical and Biological Weapons	01/31/97	73
Confronting Iraq	10/04/02	793
Ethics of War	12/13/02	1013
Future of NATO	02/28/03	177
Homeland Security	09/12/03	749
Homeland Security	02/13/09	129
Smallpox Threat	02/07/03	105
Weapons of Mass Destruction	03/08/02	193
Biology — Study and teaching		
Animal Intelligence	10/22/10	869
Animal Rights	05/24/91	308*
Evolution vs. Creationism	08/22/97	745
Fighting over Animal Rights	08/02/96	689*
Fighting SARS	06/20/03	569
Gender and Learning	05/20/05	445
Biotechnology		
Biofuels Boom	09/29/06	793
Biology and Behavior	04/03/98	306*
Blood Supply Safety	11/11/94	985
'Designer' Humans	05/18/01	425
Famine in Africa	11/08/02	921
Food Safety	06/04/93	497*
Food Safety	11/01/02	897
Food Safety Battle: Organic v. Biotech	09/04/98	761
Gene Therapy	10/18/91	777
Gene Therapy's Future	12/08/95	1089
Human Genome Research	05/12/00	401
Organ Shortage	02/21/03	153
Stem Cell Research	09/01/06	**697
Birth control. ***See also Abortion***		
Abortion Debates	03/21/03	249
Birth Control Choices	07/29/94	649
Birth-Control Debate	06/24/05	565
Catholic Church in the U.S.	09/08/95	777
Encouraging Teen Abstinence	07/10/98	577
Parental Rights	10/25/96	937
Population and the Environment	07/17/98	601
Population Growth	07/16/93	601
Preventing Teen Pregnancy	05/14/93	409
Sexually Transmitted Diseases	12/03/04	997
Teen Pregnancy	03/26/10	265*
The United Nations and Global Security	02/27/04	173
Welfare Reform	08/03/01	606*
Women's Health	11/07/03	941
Birth defects		
Human Genome Research	05/12/00	401
Infant Mortality	07/31/92	652
Right to Die	05/13/05	421
Blacks. ***See African-Americans***		
Blogs		
Blog Explosion	06/09/06	**505
Press Freedom	02/05/10	97
Bonds. ***See Stocks and bonds***		
Books. ***See also Libraries***		
Combating Plagiarism	09/19/03	773
The Future of Books	06/23/00	545
Reading Crisis?	02/22/08	169
Bosnia		
Ethics of War	12/13/02	1013
Foreign Policy and Public Opinion	07/15/94	601
Foreign Policy Burden	08/20/93	726*
Privatizing the Military	06/25/04	565
Stopping Genocide	08/27/04	685
The United Nations and Global Security	02/27/04	173
United Nations at 50	08/18/95	729
War Crimes	07/07/95	585
Boycotts		
Advertising Under Attack	09/13/91	657
The Growing Influence of Boycotts	01/04/91	1
Threatened Fisheries	08/02/02	624*
Brady bill		
Gang Crisis	05/14/04	421
Gun Control	06/10/94	505
Gun Control Debate	11/12/04	949
Gun Control Standoff	12/19/97	1119*
Reassessing the Nation's Gun Laws	03/22/91	157
States and Federalism	09/13/96	793
Suburban Crime	09/03/93	780*
Brain. ***See also Mental health and illness***		
Alzheimer's Disease	07/24/92	617
Alzheimer's Disease	05/15/98	433
Animal Intelligence	10/22/10	869
Artificial Intelligence	11/14/97	985
Biology and Behavior	04/03/98	289
Chronic Fatigue Syndrome	04/05/02	289
Embryo Research	12/3/99	1078*

	Date	Page
Gender and Learning	05/20/05	445
Impact of the Internet on Thinking	09/24/10	773
Increase in Autism	06/13/03	**545
Intelligence Testing	07/30/93	649
Learning Disabilities	12/10/93	1081
Mental Health Insurance	03/29/02	265
Professional Football	01/29/10	**73
Prozac Controversy	08/19/94	721
Rethinking Ritalin	10/22/99	905
Right to Die	05/13/05	421
Sleep Deprivation	06/26/98	553
Sleep Deprivation	02/12/10	121
Youth Suicide	02/13/04	125
Branch Davidians. ***See Cults***		
Brazil		
Biofuels Boom	09/29/06	793
Broadcasting. ***See Television and radio***		
Budget deficit		
Assessing the New Health Care Law	09/21/12	789
Budget Deficit	12/09/05	1029
Health-Care Reform	06/11/10	**505
The National Debt	11/14/08	937
National Debt	03/18/11	241
Budget surplus		
Budget Surplus	04/13/01	297
Bush's Defense Strategy	09/07/01	689
The National Debt	11/14/08	937
National Debt	03/18/11	241
Buildings and construction industry		
Aging Infrastructure	09/28/07	**793
Asbestos Litigation	05/02/03	393
Confronting Warming	01/09/09	1
Earthquake Research	12/16/94	1105
Implementing the Disabilities Act	12/20/96	1105
Property Rights	03/04/05	197
Recession's Regional Impact	02/01/91	74*
Smart Growth	05/28/04	469
Worker Safety	05/21/04	445
Bulimia. ***See Eating disorders***		
Bush, George		
Business' Role in Education	11/22/91	873
Confronting Iraq	10/04/02	793
Disaster Response	10/15/93	906*
Ethics of War	12/13/02	1013
Presidential Libraries	03/16/07	241
Presidential Power	11/15/02	945
Privatizing Government Services	08/09/96	712*
Racial Quotas	05/17/91	277
Redistricting Disputes	03/12/04	221
School Choice	05/10/91	253
U.S.-Vietnam Relations	12/03/93	1070*

	Date	Page
Bush, George W.		
Abortion Debates	03/21/03	249
Abortion Showdowns	09/22/06	769
Affordable Housing	02/09/01	104*
Aiding Africa	08/29/03	697
Air Pollution Conflict	11/14/03	965
Alternative Energy	02/25/05	173
Biofuels Boom	09/29/06	793
Birth-Control Debate	06/24/05	565
Budget Deficit	12/09/05	1029
Budget Surplus	04/13/01	297
Bush Presidency	02/02/01	65
Bush's Defense Strategy	09/07/01	689
Campaign Finance Showdown	11/22/02	969
Change in Latin America	07/21/06	601
Civil Liberties Debates	10/24/03	893*
Climate Change	01/27/06	73
Coal Mining Safety	03/17/06	241
Confronting Iraq	10/04/02	793
Corporate Crime	10/11/02	817
Cost of the Iraq War	04/25/08	361*
Cyberpolitics	09/17/04	757
Dealing With the "New" Russia	06/06/08	481
Democracy in the Arab World	01/30/04	73
Democrats in Congress	06/08/07	505
Disaster Preparedness	11/18/05	**981
Draft Debates	08/19/05	661
Drug Company Ethics	06/06/03	521
Electing the President	04/20/07	337
Electoral College	12/08/00	977
Ending Homelessness	06/18/04	541
Ending Poverty	09/09/05	733
Energy Efficiency	05/19/06	433
Energy Policy	05/25/01	447*
Energy Security	02/01/02	73
Ethics of War	12/13/02	1013
Evaluating Head Start	08/26/05	685
Exporting Democracy	04/01/05	269
Faith-Based Initiatives	05/04/01	377*
Farm Subsidies	05/17/02	433
Free-Press Disputes	04/08/05	293
Future of the GOP	03/20/09	249
Future of Marriage	05/07/04	397
Future of NATO	02/28/03	177
Gay Marriage	09/05/03	721
Government Secrecy	12/02/05	1005
Homeland Security	09/12/03	749
Human Trafficking and Slavery	03/26/04	273
Identity Theft	06/10/05	517
Illegal Immigration	05/06/05	393
Interrogating the CIA	09/25/09	789
Judges and Politics	07/27/01	577
Medical Malpractice	02/14/03	129

 *Indicates sidebar or "At Issue" report section. **Indicates an updated report.

	Date	Page
Medicare Reform	08/22/03	673
Mental Illness Medication Debate	02/06/04	101
Middle East Peace	01/21/05	53
Middle East Tensions	10/27/06	**889
New Defense Priorities	09/13/02	721
New Strategy in Iraq	02/23/07	169
No Child Left Behind	05/27/05	469
North Korean Crisis	04/11/03	321
Nuclear Energy	03/10/06	217
Nuclear Proliferation and Terrorism	04/02/04	297
The Obama Presidency	01/30/09	73
Oil Diplomacy	01/24/03	49
The Partisan Divide	04/30/04	373
Political Conventions	08/08/08	649
Port Security	04/21/06	337
Presidential Libraries	03/16/07	241
Presidential Power	11/15/02	945
Presidential Power	02/24/06	169
Preventing Teen Drug Use	03/15/02	217
Privacy in Peril	11/17/06	961
Race in America	07/11/03	593
Rebuilding Afghanistan	12/21/01	1041
Rebuilding Iraq	07/11/03	625*
Redistricting Disputes	03/12/04	221
Re-examining 9/11	06/04/04	493
Reforming the Corps	05/30/03	497
Religion and Politics	07/30/04	637
Religion in Schools	01/12/01	1
Remembering 9/11	09/02/11	701*
Retirement Security	05/31/02	481
Revising No Child Left Behind	04/16/10	337
Right to Die	05/13/05	421
Rising Health Costs	04/07/06	289
School Desegregation	04/23/04	345
Science and Politics	08/20/04	661
Sexually Transmitted Diseases	12/03/04	997
Smallpox Threat	02/07/03	105
Social Security Reform	09/24/04	781
Stem Cell Research	09/01/06	**697
Stimulating the Economy	01/10/03	1
Supreme Court's Future	01/28/05	77
Teacher Shortages	08/24/01	633
Teen Sex	09/16/05	761
Testing in Schools	04/20/01	321
Transatlantic Tensions	07/13/01	533
Treatment of Detainees	08/25/06	673
Treatment of Veterans	11/19/04	973
Trouble in South America	03/14/03	225
Unemployment Benefits	04/25/03	369*
The United Nations and Global Security	02/27/04	173
Upward Mobility	04/29/05	369
U.S.-British Relations	11/05/10	917*
U.S.-Mexico Relations	11/09/01	921
U.S. Policy on Iran	11/16/07	961

	Date	Page
Voting Controversies	09/15/06	745
War in Iraq	10/21/05	881
War on Drugs	06/02/06	481
Weapons of Mass Destruction	03/08/02	193
Wounded Veterans	08/31/07	697

Business and industry. ***See also Antitrust law; Corporate mergers; Employment and unemployment; International trade; Privatization; Wages and salaries***

	Date	Page
3D Printing	12/07/12	1037
Accountants Under Fire	03/22/02	241
Airline Industry Problems	09/24/99	825
Air Pollution Conflict	11/14/03	965
Airline Safety	10/08/93	865
Alternative Energy	07/10/92	573
Alternative Energy	02/25/05	173
Antitrust Policy	06/12/98	505
Arms Sales	12/09/94	1081
Artificial Intelligence	04/22/11	361
Asbestos Litigation	05/02/03	393
Attracting Jobs	03/02/12	205
Auto Industry's Future	02/06/09	**105
Big-Box Stores	09/10/04	733
Broadcast Indecency	04/16/04	321
Business Bankruptcy	04/10/09	321
Business Ethics	05/06/11	409
The Business of Sports	02/10/95	121
Buying Green	02/29/08	193
Campaign Finance Debates	05/28/10	457
Celebrity Culture	03/18/05	245
Centennial Olympic Games	04/05/96	289
Charitable Giving	11/12/93	993*
Child-Care Options	05/08/98	409
Child Labor and Sweatshops	08/16/96	721
Civic Renewal	03/21/97	241
Class Action Lawsuits	05/13/11	433
Coal Mining Safety	03/17/06	241
College Football	11/18/11	977
Computer Hacking	09/16/11	757*
Consumer Safety	10/12/07	841
Corporate Crime	10/11/02	817
Corporate Social Responsibility	08/03/07	649
Cosmetic Surgery	04/15/05	317
Crisis on the Plains	05/09/03	417
Curbing CEO Pay	03/09/07	217
Cyber-Crime	04/12/02	305
Cybersecurity	09/26/03	811*
Cybersecurity	02/26/10	169
Debating Hip-Hop	06/15/07	529
Democrats' Future	10/29/10	893
Dietary Supplements	09/03/04	709
Digital Commerce	02/05/99	89
Distance Learning	12/07/01	993
Downward Mobility	07/23/93	625
Drug Company Ethics	06/06/03	521

	Date	Page
Drug Safety	03/11/05	221
Emerging China	11/11/05	957
Energy and Climate	07/24/09	621
Energy Policy	05/20/11	457
Energy Security	02/01/02	73
Euro Crisis	10/05/12	841
Executive Pay	07/11/97	601
Exporting Jobs	02/20/04	149
Fairness in Salaries	05/29/92	457
Fast-Food Shake-Up	11/08/91	825
Financial Bailout	10/24/08	**865
Financial Crisis	05/09/08	409
Financial Industry Overhaul	07/30/10	629
Financial Misconduct	01/20/12	53
Fracking Controversy	12/16/11	1049
Future Job Market	01/11/02	1
Future of the Airline Industry	06/21/02	545
Future of the Airlines	03/07/08	217
The Future of Baseball	09/25/98	833
Future of Books	05/29/09	**473
Future of Journalism	03/27/09	**273
Future of Libraries	07/29/11	625
Future of Newspapers	01/20/06	49
Future of Telecommunications	04/23/99	329
The Future of Television	12/23/94	1129
Genetically Modified Food	08/31/12	717
The Glass Ceiling	10/29/93	937
Google's Dominance	11/11/11	953
The Growing Influence of Boycotts	01/04/91	1
Gulf Coast Restoration	08/26/11	677*
Health-Care Reform	08/28/09	693*
Human Spaceflight	10/16/09	861
Identity Theft	06/10/05	517
Illegal Immigration	05/06/05	393
Impact of the Internet on Thinking	09/24/10	773
Implementing the Disabilities Act	12/20/96	1105
Income Inequality	04/17/98	337
Internet Regulation	04/13/12	325
Jobs in the '90s	02/28/92	169
Journalism Standards in the Internet Age	10/08/10	821
Journalism Under Fire	12/25/98	1121
Judicial Elections	04/24/09	373
Labor Unions' Future	09/02/05	**709
Limiting Lawsuits	12/19/08	1033
Managing Public Lands	11/04/11	929
Media Ownership	10/10/03	**845
Mental Illness Medication Debate	02/06/04	101
Minimum Wage	12/16/05	1053
Nanotechnology	06/11/04	517
NASA's Future	05/23/03	489*
New Challenges in Space	07/23/99	617
The New Corporate Philanthropy	02/27/98	169
The New Volunteerism	12/13/96	1081
The Obama Presidency	01/30/09	73
'Occupy' Movement	01/13/12	25
Offshore Drilling	06/25/10	553
Online Privacy	11/06/09	**933
Pension Crisis	02/17/06	145
Port Security	04/21/06	337
Prescription Drug Prices	07/17/92	610*
Preventing Disease	01/06/12	1
Privatizing the Military	06/25/04	565
Privatizing the Military	07/13/12	597
Professional Football	01/29/10	**73
Property Rights	06/16/95	513
Property Rights	03/04/05	197
Protecting Whistleblowers	03/31/06	265
Public-Works Projects	02/20/09	153
Puerto Rico: The Struggle over Status	02/08/91	81
Race in America	07/11/03	593
Reading Crisis?	02/22/08	169
Rebuilding Iraq	07/11/03	637*
Reducing Your Carbon Footprint	12/05/08	985
Reforming School Funding	12/10/99	1052*
Reforming the FDA	06/06/97	481
Regulating Nonprofits	12/26/97	1129*
Regulating the Internet	06/30/95	561
Regulating Toxic Chemicals	01/23/09	49
Restructuring the Electric Industry	01/17/97	25
Revitalizing the Cities	10/13/95	910*
Reviving Manufacturing	07/22/11	601
Science and Politics	08/20/04	661
School Reform	04/29/11	385
Smart Cities	07/27/12	645
Social Networking	09/17/10	749
Social Security Reform	09/24/04	781
Socially Responsible Investing	08/29/08	673
Software Piracy	05/21/93	433
Space Program	02/24/12	177
Space Program's Future	12/24/93	1143*
Stimulating the Economy	01/10/03	1
The Stock Market	05/02/97	385
Stock Market Troubles	01/16/04	25
Student Debt	10/21/11	877
Supreme Court Controversies	09/28/12	813
SUV Debate	05/16/03	449
Tax Reform	03/22/96	241
Threatened Fisheries	08/02/02	617
Tobacco Industry	12/10/04	**1025
Too Many Lawsuits?	05/22/92	433
Transatlantic Tensions	07/13/01	566*
Underground Economy	03/04/94	193
Unemployment Benefits	04/25/03	369
Upward Mobility	04/29/05	369
U.S. Auto Industry	10/16/92	881
U.S.-China Relations	05/07/10	**409
Whistleblowers	12/05/97	1057

 *Indicates sidebar or "At Issue" report section. **Indicates an updated report.

	Date	Page
Women and Sports	03/25/11	265
Work, Family and Stress	08/14/92	689
Worker Safety	05/21/04	445
Y2K Dilemma	02/19/99	137
Youth Apprenticeships	10/23/92	905
Business and industry — Environmental issues		
Acid Rain: New Approach to Old Problem	03/08/91	129
Air Pollution Conflict	11/14/03	965
Alternative Energy	02/25/05	173
Asbestos Litigation	05/02/03	393
Auto Industry's Future	02/06/09	**105
Biofuels Boom	09/29/06	793
Bush and the Environment	10/25/02	865
Buying Green	02/29/08	193
Cleaning Up Hazardous Wastes	08/23/96	745
Crisis on the Plains	05/09/03	434*
The Economics of Recycling	03/27/98	265
Energy and the Environment	03/03/00	161
Energy Security	02/01/02	73
Environmental Justice	06/19/98	529
Food Safety Battle: Organic v. Biotech	09/04/98	761
Future of the Airlines	03/07/08	217
Garbage Crisis	03/20/92	241
Global Warming Treaty	01/26/01	53*
Global Warming Update	11/01/96	961
The Growing Influence of Boycotts	01/04/91	1
Historic Preservation	10/07/94	865
Jobs vs. Environment	05/15/92	409
Modernizing the Grid	02/19/10	145
Nanotechnology	06/11/04	517
New Air Quality Standards	03/07/97	193
The New Environmentalism	12/01/06	985
Nuclear Energy	03/10/06	217
Oil Spills	01/17/92	25
Ozone Depletion	04/03/92	289
Reforming the Corps	05/30/03	497
Renewable Energy	11/07/97	961
Saving the Rain Forests	06/11/99	512*
SUV Debate	05/16/03	460*
Threatened Fisheries	08/02/02	617
Traffic Congestion	05/06/94	401*
Water Shortages	08/01/03	649
Cable television		
Alcohol Advertising	03/14/97	217
Broadcast Indecency	04/16/04	321
Future of Journalism	03/27/09	**273
The Future of Telecommunications	04/23/99	329
The Future of Television	12/23/94	1129
Indecency on Television	11/09/12	965
Media Ownership	10/10/03	**845
Pay-Per-View TV	10/04/91	729
Public Broadcasting	09/18/92	809

	Date	Page
California		
Assisted Suicide	02/21/92	145
Assisted Suicide Controversy	05/05/95	406*
Big-Box Stores	09/10/04	733
Bilingual Education	08/13/93	712*
California: Enough Water for the Future?	04/19/91	221
Celebrity Culture	03/18/05	245
Crackdown on Smoking	12/04/92	1062
Cracking Down on Immigration	02/03/95	97
Downsizing Prisons	03/11/11	217
Drug-Policy Debate	07/28/00	593
Earthquake Research	12/16/94	1105
Earthquake Threat	04/09/10	313
Gay Marriage Showdowns	09/26/08	**769
Getting into College	02/23/96	169
Global Water Shortages	12/15/95	1128*
Gridlock in Washington	04/30/10	385
Gun Control Standoff	12/19/97	1120*
High-Speed Rail	04/16/93	328*
High-Speed Trains	05/01/09	**397
Hispanic-Americans' New Clout	09/18/98	809
Identity Theft	06/10/05	517
Illegal Immigration	05/06/05	393
Immigration Reform	09/24/93	841
Jobs vs. Environment	05/15/92	409
Latinos' Future	10/17/03	869
Learning to Read	05/19/95	441
Mandatory Sentencing	05/26/95	480*
Marijuana Laws	02/11/05	125
Medical Marijuana	08/20/99	716*
Networking the Classroom	10/20/95	926*
Oil Imports	08/23/91	599*
Prisoner Reentry	12/04/09	1005
Redistricting Disputes	03/12/04	221
Redistricting: Drawing Power with a Map	02/15/91	108
Rethinking Affirmative Action	04/28/95	386*
Rethinking the Death Penalty	11/16/01	960*
State Budget Crises	10/03/03	827*
State Budget Crisis	09/11/09	741
Testing Term Limits	11/18/94	1016*
Three-Strikes Laws	05/10/02	427*
Traffic Congestion	05/06/94	385
Water Shortages	08/01/03	649
Year-Round Schools	05/17/96	447*
Campaign finance		
Campaign Finance Debates	05/28/10	457
Campaign Finance Reform	02/09/96	121
Campaign Finance Reform	03/31/00	257
Campaign Finance Reform	06/13/08	505
Campaign Finance Showdown	11/22/02	969
China After Deng	06/13/97	516*
Corporate Crime	10/11/02	817

	Date	Page
Cyberpolitics	09/17/04	757
Electing the President	04/20/07	337
Income Inequality	12/03/10	989
Judicial Elections	04/24/09	373
Low Voter Turnout	10/20/00	833
The New Immigrants	01/24/97	56*
The Partisan Divide	04/30/04	384*
Presidential Election	02/03/12	101
Presidential Libraries	03/16/07	241
Regulating Nonprofits	12/26/97	1129
Social Media and Politics	10/12/12	865
Supreme Court Controversies	09/28/12	813
Canada		
Acid Rain: New Approach to Old Problem	03/08/91	129
Blood Supply Safety	11/11/94	998*
Courts and the Media	09/23/94	830*
Deepening Canadian Crisis over Quebec	04/12/91	205
Fighting SARS	06/20/03	569
Gay Marriage	09/05/03	721
Marijuana Laws	02/11/05	125
Movie Ratings	03/28/03	279*
Native Americans	05/08/92	396*
Oil Diplomacy	01/24/03	63*
Quebec Sovereignty	10/06/95	873
Rethinking NAFTA	06/07/96	481
Retiree Health Benefits	12/06/91	937*
U.S. Trade Policy	01/29/93	83*
Cancer		
Advances in Cancer Research	08/25/95	753
Alternative Medicine	01/31/92	73
Asbestos Litigation	05/02/03	393
Biology and Behavior	04/03/98	294*
Birth Control Choices	07/29/94	649
Breast Cancer	06/27/97	553
Breast Cancer	04/02/10	289
Cancer Treatments	09/11/98	785
Cell Phone Safety	03/16/01	201
Diet and Health	02/23/01	129*
Electromagnetic Fields	04/26/91	237
Gene Therapy's Future	12/08/95	1095*
Indoor Air Pollution	10/27/95	945
Marijuana Laws	02/11/05	125
Preventing Cancer	01/16/09	25
Regulating Pesticides	01/28/94	73
Tobacco Industry	12/10/04	**1025
Women's Health	11/07/03	941
Women's Health Issues	05/13/94	409
Worker Safety	05/21/04	445
Capital punishment. *See Death penalty*		
Carbon dioxide emissions. *See Global warming*		
Careers. *See Job training; Wages and salaries*		
Carpal tunnel syndrome		
Repetitive Stress Injuries	06/23/95	537
Cars. *See Automobiles and automobile industry*		
Catholic Church		
Abortion Debates	03/21/03	249
Birth-Control Debate	06/24/05	565
Castro's Next Move	12/12/97	1081
Catholic Church in the U.S.	09/08/95	777
Child Sexual Abuse	01/15/93	32*
Future of the Catholic Church	01/19/07	49
Future of the Papacy	02/26/99	161
Latinos' Future	10/17/03	869
Religion and Politics	07/30/04	637
Sex Offenders	09/08/06	721
Sexual Abuse and the Clergy	05/03/02	393
Catholic schools		
Boys' Emotional Needs	06/18/99	534*
School Vouchers	04/09/99	281
School Vouchers Showdown	02/15/02	121
Cattle. *See Livestock and ranching*		
Celebrities		
Celebrity Advocacy	05/11/12	425
Celebrity Culture	03/18/05	245
Medication Abuse	10/09/09	837
Offshore Drilling	06/25/10	553
Philanthropy in America	12/08/06	1009
Sex Scandals	01/22/10	49
Cellular telephones		
Cell Phone Safety	03/16/01	201
Distracted Driving	05/04/12	401
Future of Recycling	12/14/07	1033
Rising College Costs	12/05/03	1026*
Censorship		
Controlling the Internet	05/12/06	409
Debating Hip-Hop	06/15/07	529
Free-Press Disputes	04/08/05	293
Google's Dominance	11/11/11	953
Movie Ratings	03/28/03	273
The Obscenity Debate	12/20/91	969
Press Freedom	02/05/10	97
School Censorship	02/19/93	145
Sex, Violence and the Media	11/17/95	1017
Shock Jocks	06/01/07	**481
Student Journalism	06/05/98	481
U.S.-China Relations	05/07/10	**409
Census. *See also Population, Redistricting*		
Census 2000	05/01/98	385
Census Controversey	05/14/10	433
Crisis on the Plains	05/09/03	417
Helping the Homeless	01/26/96	78*
The Homeless	08/07/92	665
Illegal Immigration	04/24/92	366*

	Date	Page
Latinos' Future	10/17/03	869
Native Americans	05/08/92	389*
Redistricting Debates	02/25/11	169
Redistricting Disputes	03/12/04	221
Religion in America	11/25/94	1040*
Central America		
Debate Over Immigration	07/14/00	582*
Foreign Aid After Sept. 11	04/26/02	361
Gang Crisis	05/14/04	421
Illegal Immigration	04/24/92	372
Central Intelligence Agency		
Civil Liberties Debates	10/24/03	893
Cybersecurity	09/26/03	797
Government Secrecy	12/02/05	1005
Homeland Security	09/12/03	749*
Intelligence Reforms	01/25/02	49
Interrogating the CIA	09/25/09	789
The New CIA	12/11/92	1073
Policing the Borders	02/22/02	145
Privacy in Peril	11/17/06	961
Re-examining 9/11	06/04/04	493
Reforming the CIA	02/02/96	97
Torture	04/18/03	345
Treatment of Detainees	08/25/06	673
Charities and nonprofit organizations. ***See also Voluntarism***		
Arts Funding	10/21/94	913
Assisting Refugees	02/07/97	97
Blighted Cities	11/12/10	941*
Celebrity Advocacy	05/11/12	425
Charitable Giving	11/12/93	985
Corporate Social Responsibility	08/03/07	649
Fairness in Salaries	05/29/92	470*
Faith-Based Initiatives	05/04/01	377
Foreign Aid After Sept. 11	04/26/02	361
Future of Journalism	03/27/09	**273
Haiti's Dilemma	02/18/05	149
Helping the Homeless	01/26/96	73
The Homeless	08/07/92	665
National Service	06/30/06	577
The New Corporate Philanthropy	02/27/98	169
The New Volunteerism	12/13/96	1081
Philanthropy in America	12/08/06	1009
Reassessing Foreign Aid	09/27/96	841
Regulating Nonprofits	12/26/97	1129
Role of Foundations	01/22/99	49
School Choice Debate	07/18/97	632*
Sexual Abuse and the Clergy	05/03/02	393
Socially Responsible Investing	08/29/08	673
Straining the Safety Net	07/31/09	645
Tax Reform	03/22/96	241
Youth Volunteerism	01/27/12	77
Charter schools		
Attack on Public Schools	07/26/96	656*
Charter Schools	12/20/02	1033

	Date	Page
Fixing Urban Schools	04/27/07	**361
Home Schooling Debate	01/17/03	25
Private Management of Public Schools	03/25/94	282*
Revising No Child Left Behind	04/16/10	337
School Reform	04/29/11	385
School Vouchers	04/09/99	281
School Vouchers Showdown	02/15/02	121
Special Education	11/10/00	905
Chechnya		
The Future of U.S.-Russia Relations	01/18/02	37*
Russia and the Former Soviet Republics	06/17/05	541
Russia's Political Future	05/03/96	399*
Chemical weapons		
Chemical and Biological Weapons	01/31/97	73
Confronting Iraq	10/04/02	793
Ethics of War	12/13/02	1013
Weapons of Mass Destruction	03/08/02	193
Chemicals and chemical industry		
Breast Cancer	04/02/10	289
Ozone Depletion	04/03/92	289
Regulating Pesticides	01/28/94	73
Regulating Pesticides	08/06/99	665
Regulating Toxic Chemicals	01/23/09	49
Chesapeake Bay		
Water Quality	11/24/00	953
Child abuse		
Catholic Church in the U.S.	09/08/95	792*
Children in Crisis	08/31/01	657
Child Sexual Abuse	01/15/93	25
Child Welfare Reform	04/22/05	345
Cyber-Predators	03/01/02	169
Eating Disorders	12/18/92	1108
Foster Care Crisis	09/27/91	705
Foster Care Reform	01/09/98	1
Human Trafficking and Slavery	03/26/04	273
Infant Mortality	07/31/92	652
Parental Rights	10/25/96	937
Prayer and Healing	01/14/05	25
Punishing Sex Offenders	01/12/96	25
Recovered-Memory Debate	07/05/96	577
Sex Offenders	09/08/06	721
Sexual Abuse and the Clergy	05/03/02	393
Treating Anxiety	02/08/02	97
Violence in Schools	09/11/92	785
Women and Human Rights	04/30/99	353
Child care		
Child Care	12/17/93	1105
Child-Care Options	05/08/98	409
Child Welfare Reform	04/22/05	345
Future of Feminism	04/14/06	313
Mothers' Movement	04/04/03	297
State Budget Crises	10/03/03	832*

	Date	Page
Child custody and support		
Child Custody and Support	01/13/95	25
Children and Divorce	06/07/91	358*
Children and Divorce	01/19/01	25*
Child Poverty	10/28/11	901
Child Welfare Reform	04/22/05	345
Gay Rights	03/05/93	210*
Mothers' Movement	04/04/03	297
Child welfare		
Adoption	11/26/93	1033
Child Poverty	04/07/00	281
Child Poverty	10/28/11	901
Children in Crisis	08/31/01	657
Child Welfare Reform	04/22/05	345
Foster Care Crisis	09/27/91	705
Foster Care Reform	01/09/98	1
The Homeless	08/07/92	675*
Kids in Prison	04/27/01	345
Treating Addiction	01/06/95	6*
Welfare, Work and the States	12/06/96	1057
Children. ***See also Adolescents and youth; Adoption; Elementary and secondary education; Family***		
Children — Health and safety		
Aggressive Driving	07/25/97	649
Asthma Epidemic	12/24/99	1092*
Boys' Emotional Needs	06/18/99	521
Bullying	02/04/05	101
Childhood Depression	07/16/99	593
Childhood Immunizations	06/18/93	529
Child Labor and Sweatshops	08/16/96	721
Child Poverty	04/07/00	281
Children in Crisis	08/31/01	657
Children's Legal Rights	04/23/93	337
Children's Television	08/15/97	721
Child Welfare Reform	04/22/05	345
Chronic Fatigue Syndrome	04/05/02	289
Closing in on Tobacco	11/12/99	977
Combating Infectious Diseases	06/09/95	505*
Consumer Safety	10/12/07	841
Covering the Uninsured	06/14/02	521
Cyberbullying	05/02/08	385
Cyber-Predators	03/01/02	169
Dieting and Health	04/14/95	321
DNA Databases	05/28/99	466*
Drug-Resistant Bacteria	06/04/99	479*
Drug Safety	03/11/05	221
Eating Disorders	12/18/92	1109
Fatherhood Movement	06/02/00	473
Fighting Superbugs	08/24/07	673
Food Safety	11/01/02	897
Future of Marriage	05/07/04	397
Gun Rights Debates	10/31/08	**889
Gun Violence	05/25/07	457
Head Start	04/09/93	297*
Highway Safety	07/14/95	623*
Homework Debate	12/06/02	993
HPV Vaccine	05/11/07	409
Hunger in America	12/22/00	1050*
Increase in Autism	06/13/03	**545
Indecency on Television	11/09/12	965
Infant Mortality	07/31/92	641
Internet Privacy	11/06/98	967*
Job Stress	08/04/95	695*
Kids in Prison	04/27/01	345
Lead Poisoning	06/19/92	525
Marriage and Divorce	05/10/96	409
Medicaid Reform	07/16/04	589
Mental Illness Medication Debate	02/06/04	106*
Mothers' Movement	04/04/03	297
Movie Ratings	03/28/03	273
Obesity and Health	01/15/99	40*
Obesity Epidemic	01/31/03	73
Physical Fitness	11/06/92	953
Prayer and Healing	01/14/05	25
Preventing Bullying	12/10/10	**1013
Preventing Teen Drug Use	07/28/95	670*
Reality TV	08/27/10	677
Reforming the FDA	06/06/97	496*
Regulating Pesticides	01/28/94	73
Regulating Tobacco	09/30/94	841
Rethinking Ritalin	10/22/99	905
Right to Die	05/13/05	421
School Violence	10/09/98	881
Sex Offenders	09/08/06	721
Sexual Abuse and the Clergy	05/03/02	393
Sexually Transmitted Diseases	12/03/04	997
Sleep Deprivation	06/26/98	553
Sleep Deprivation	02/12/10	121
Social Networking	09/17/10	749
Sugar Controversies	11/30/12	1013
Teen Driving	01/07/05	1
Teens and Tobacco	12/01/95	1065
Tobacco Industry	12/10/04	**1025
Treating Anxiety	02/08/02	97
TV Violence	03/26/93	265
Vaccine Controversies	08/25/00	641
Violence in Schools	09/11/92	785
Women and AIDS	12/25/92	1121
Work, Family and Stress	08/14/92	689
Youth Fitness	09/26/97	841
Youth Violence	03/05/10	193*
Chile		
Foreign Aid After Sept. 11	04/26/02	361
Rethinking NAFTA	06/07/96	497*
Saving Social Security	10/02/98	865*
Trouble in South America	03/14/03	225

 *Indicates sidebar or "At Issue" report section. **Indicates an updated report.

	Date	Page
China		
China After Deng	06/13/97	505
China Today	08/04/00	625
Coal's Comeback	10/05/07	817
Consumer Safety	10/12/07	841
Controlling the Internet	05/12/06	409
Cybersecurity	02/26/10	169
Democracy in Asia	07/24/98	625
Emerging China	11/11/05	957
Exporting Jobs	02/20/04	149
Fighting SARS	06/20/03	569
Foreign Aid and National Security	06/17/11	529
Foreign Aid After Sept. 11	04/26/02	361
Future of Recycling	12/14/07	1033
Google's Dominance	11/11/11	953
Human Rights in China	07/25/08	601
Human Rights Issues	10/30/09	909
Illegal Immigration	04/24/92	376
New Challenges in Space	07/23/99	634*
New Era in Asia	02/14/92	121
Oil Jitters	01/04/08	**1
Panama Canal	11/26/99	1017
Religious Persecution	11/21/97	1009
Reviving Manufacturing	07/22/11	601
Smart Cities	07/27/12	645
Space Program	02/24/12	177
Taiwan, China, and the U.S.	05/24/96	457
Torture	04/18/03	345
The United Nations and Global Security	02/27/04	173
U.S.-China Relations	05/07/10	**409
U.S.-China Trade	04/15/94	313
U.S.-Europe Relations	03/23/12	277
U.S. Policy in Asia	11/27/92	1025
Weapons of Mass Destruction	03/08/02	193
Christian Coalition		
Bullying	02/04/05	101
Parental Rights	10/25/96	937
Protestants Today	12/07/07	1009
Religion and Politics	10/14/94	889
Rise of Megachurches	09/21/07	769
Teaching Values	06/21/96	529
Christians. ***See also Catholic Church***		
Abortion Showdowns	09/22/06	769
Birth-Control Debate	06/24/05	565
Cloning Debate	10/22/04	877
Embryo Research	12/17/99	1065
Evangelical Christians	09/14/01	713
Faith-Based Initiatives	05/04/01	377
Gay Marriage	09/05/03	721
Global AIDS Crisis	10/13/00	809
Government and Religion	01/15/10	25
Home Schooling Debate	01/17/03	25
The New Millennium	10/15/99	889
Parental Rights	10/25/96	937
Prayer and Healing	01/14/05	25
Protestants Today	12/07/07	1009
Religion and Politics	10/14/94	889
Religion and Politics	07/30/04	637
Religion in America	11/25/94	1033
Religion in Schools	01/12/01	1
Religion in the Workplace	08/23/02	649
Religious Persecution	11/21/97	1009
Right to Die	05/13/05	421
Rise of Megachurches	09/21/07	769
School Censorship	02/19/93	145
Science and Politics	08/20/04	661
Searching for Jesus	12/11/98	1073
Sexual Abuse and the Clergy	05/03/02	393
Sexually Transmitted Diseases	12/13/04	997
Teaching Values	06/21/96	529
Understanding Mormonism	10/19/12	889
Church-state separation. ***See First Amendment***		
Churches. ***See Religion***		
Cigarettes. ***See Tobacco***		
Cities and towns		
Big-Box Stores	09/10/04	733
Blighted Cities	11/12/10	941*
Census Controversey	05/14/10	433
Downtown Renaissance	06/23/06	**553
Ending Homelessness	06/18/04	541
Fighting Crime	02/08/08	121
Fixing Urban Schools	04/27/07	**361
Housing the Homeless	12/18/09	1053
Mass Transit Boom	01/18/08	49
Property Rights	03/04/05	197
Smart Cities	07/27/12	645
Smart Growth	05/28/04	469
Civil rights and liberties. ***See Democracy; First Amendment***		
Academic Freedom	10/07/05	833
Affirmative Action	10/17/08	**841
Birth-Control Debate	06/24/05	565
Campaign Finance Showdown	11/22/02	969
Charter Schools	12/20/02	1033
Children's Legal Rights	04/23/93	337
Civic Renewal	03/21/97	241
Civil Liberties Debates	10/24/03	893
Civil Liberties in Wartime	12/14/01	1017
Closing Guantánamo	02/27/09	**177
Combating Terrorism	07/21/95	633
Courts and the Media	09/23/94	817
Crackdown on Smoking	12/04/92	1049
Crime Victims' Rights	07/22/94	625
Cyberbullying	05/02/08	385
Cyber-Crime	04/12/02	305
Cyber-Predators	03/01/02	169
Death Penalty Debate	03/10/95	193

	Date	Page
Death Penalty Debates	11/19/10	965
Death Penalty Update	01/08/99	1
Declining Crime Rates	04/04/97	306*
DNA Databases	05/28/99	449
Domestic Partners	09/04/92	761
Drug-Policy Debate	07/28/00	612*
Drug Testing	11/20/98	1001
Electing Minorities	08/12/94	697
Environmental Justice	06/19/98	529
Exporting Democracy	04/01/05	269
The FBI Under Fire	04/11/97	313
Fighting SARS	06/20/03	569
Future of the Airline Industry	06/21/02	545
Gay Marriage Showdowns	09/26/08	**769
Gay Rights	03/05/93	193
The Growing Influence of Boycotts	01/04/91	1
Gun Control	06/10/94	505
Gun Control Debate	11/12/04	949
Haiti's Dilemma	02/18/05	149
Hate Crimes	01/08/93	1
Hate Groups	05/08/09	421
Helping the Homeless	01/26/96	89*
Homeland Security	09/12/03	749
Illegal Immigration	04/24/92	361
Illegal Immigration	05/06/05	393
Immigration Conflict	03/09/12	229
Kids in Prison	04/27/01	345
Latinos' Future	10/17/03	869
Legal-Aid Crisis	10/07/11	829
Libraries and the Internet	06/01/01	465
The Obscenity Debate	12/20/91	969
Parental Rights	10/25/96	937
Plea Bargaining	02/12/99	127*
Police Brutality	09/06/91	633
Police Misconduct	04/06/12	301
Policing the Borders	02/22/02	145
Presidential Power	11/15/02	945
Preventing Bullying	12/10/10	**1013
Prison Overcrowding	02/04/94	102*
Privacy in Peril	11/17/06	961
Prostitution	06/11/93	505
Public Defenders	04/18/08	337*
Punishing Sex Offenders	01/12/96	25
Race in America	07/11/03	593
Racial Diversity in Public Schools	09/14/07	**745
Racial Quotas	05/17/91	277
Reassessing the Nation's Gun Laws	03/22/91	157
Redistricting Disputes	03/12/04	221
Redistricting: Drawing Power with a Map	02/15/91	97
Re-examining 9/11	06/04/04	493
Religion in Schools	02/18/94	145
Religion in Schools	01/12/01	1
Remembering 9/11	09/02/11	701*

	Date	Page
School Desegregation	04/23/04	345
School Vouchers Showdown	02/15/02	121
Sentencing Debates	11/05/04	925
Serial Killers	10/31/03	917
Sexual Harassment	08/09/91	537
Student Rights	06/05/09	501
Supreme Court Preview	09/17/93	817
Torture	04/18/03	345
Treatment of Detainees	08/25/06	673
War on Terrorism	10/12/01	817

Clean Air Act Amendments, 1990. *See Air pollution; Global warming*

Climate change. *See Global warming*

Clinton, Bill

	Date	Page
Air Pollution Conflict	11/14/03	965
Bush Presidency	02/02/01	82*
Campaign Finance Showdown	11/22/02	969
Closing In on Tobacco	11/12/99	991*
Cyberpolitics	09/17/04	757
Drug Company Ethics	06/06/03	521
Electing the President	04/20/07	337
The Federal Judiciary	03/13/98	217
Foreign Policy and Public Opinion	07/15/94	601
Foreign Policy Burden	08/20/93	721
Gays in the Military	09/18/09	**765
Gun Control Debate	11/12/04	949
Independent Counsels	02/21/97	145
Independent Counsels Re-examined	05/07/99	377
Line-Item Veto	06/20/97	529
Missile Defense	09/08/00	689
National Education Standards	05/14/99	401
National Service	06/25/93	553
National Service	06/30/06	577
Non-Proliferation Treaty at 25	01/27/95	86*
North Korean Crisis	04/11/03	321
Northern Ireland Cease-Fire	09/15/95	801
Partisan Divide	04/30/04	373
Partisan Politics	03/19/99	233
Philanthropy in America	12/08/06	1009
Political Conventions	08/08/08	649
Political Scandals	05/27/94	457
Politicians and Privacy	04/17/92	337
Presidential Libraries	03/16/07	241
Re-examining 9/11	06/04/04	493
Reforming the CIA	02/02/96	97
Reinventing Government	02/17/95	145
Religion and Politics	10/14/94	889
Saving Open Spaces	11/05/99	953
Social Security Reform	09/24/04	781
Talk Show Democracy	04/29/94	361
Tax Reform	03/22/96	241
U.S.-British Relations	01/30/98	73
U.S.-British Relations	11/05/10	917*

 *Indicates sidebar or "At Issue" report section. **Indicates an updated report.

	Date	Page
U.S.-China Trade	04/15/94	313
U.S.-Russian Relations	05/22/98	457
U.S. Trade Policy	01/29/93	88*
Welfare Experiments	09/16/94	793
Welfare, Work and the States	12/06/96	1057
Clinton, Hillary Rodham		
Campaign Finance Debates	05/28/10	457
Changing U.S. Electorate	05/30/08	**457
Children's Legal Rights	04/23/93	348*
Electing the President	04/20/07	337
First Ladies	06/14/96	505
Independent Counsels Re-examined	05/07/99	377
Mental Illness	08/06/93	673
Political Conventions	08/08/08	649
Political Scandals	05/27/94	457
Talk Show Democracy	04/29/94	374*
Teaching Values	06/21/96	534*
U.S.-China Relations	05/07/10	**409
Women and Human Rights	04/30/99	353
Women in Politics	03/21/08	265
Cloning		
The Cloning Controversy	05/09/97	409
Embryo Research	12/17/99	1065
Food Safety	11/01/02	897
Mass Extinction	09/15/00	728*
Organ Shortage	02/21/03	153
Clothing and dress		
Animal Rights	05/24/91	311*
Child Labor and Sweatshops	08/16/96	721
Preventing Juvenile Crime	03/15/96	224*
Coaching. ***See Sports***		
Coal		
Acid Rain: New Approach to Old Problem	03/08/91	129
Air Pollution Conflict	11/14/03	965
Alternative Energy	07/10/92	573
Alternative Energy	02/25/05	173
Coal Mining Safety	03/17/06	241
Coal's Comeback	10/05/07	817
Confronting Warming	01/09/09	1
Energy and Climate	07/24/09	621
Energy Policy	05/25/01	455*
Energy Policy	05/20/11	457
Energy Security	02/01/02	73
Mine Safety	06/24/11	553
The Politics of Energy	03/05/99	185
Renewable Energy	11/07/97	961
Coastal areas		
Climate Change	01/27/06	73
Coastal Development	08/21/98	721
Disaster Preparedness	11/18/05	**981
Rebuilding New Orleans	02/03/06	97
Reforming the Corps	05/30/03	497

	Date	Page
Threatened Coastlines	02/07/92	97
Water Shortages	08/01/03	649
Cocaine. ***See Drug abuse***		
Cold fusion. ***See Nuclear fusion***		
Cold War		
Dealing With the "New" Russia	06/06/08	481
Colleges and universities		
AB and IP Programs	03/03/06	193
Academic Freedom	10/07/05	833
Academic Politics	02/16/96	145
Affirmative Action	09/21/01	737
Affirmative Action	10/17/08	**841
Archaeology Today	05/24/02	457
Black Colleges	12/12/03	1045
Career Colleges	01/07/11	1
Cheating in Schools	09/22/00	745
Combating Plagiarism	09/19/03	773
Combating Scientific Misconduct	01/10/97	1
Community Colleges	04/21/00	329
Contingent Work Force	10/24/97	948*
Crime on Campus	02/04/11	97
Cults in America	05/07/93	402*
Cyber-Crime	04/12/02	305
Cyber Socializing	07/28/06	625
Discipline in Schools	02/15/08	145
Distance Learning	12/07/01	993
Drinking on Campus	03/20/98	241
Drinking on Campus	08/18/06	649
Education and Gender	06/03/94	481
Future of Books	05/29/09	**473
Future of the Music Industry	11/21/03	989
Gender and Learning	05/20/05	445
Getting into College	02/23/96	169
Grade Inflation	06/07/02	505
Gun Rights Debates	10/31/08	**889
Gun Violence	05/25/07	457
Hate Crimes	01/08/93	1
Hazing	01/09/04	1
Home Schooling Debate	01/17/03	39*
Hospitals' Financial Woes	08/13/99	697*
Illegal Immigration	05/06/05	393
Immigration Debate	02/01/08	**97
Income Inequality	12/03/10	989
Internet Accuracy	08/01/08	625
Jobs Outlook	06/04/10	481
Liberal Arts Education	04/10/98	313
Living-Wage Movement	09/27/02	782*
National Service	06/25/93	553
Paying for College	11/20/92	1001
Prayer and Healing	01/14/05	25
Preventing Teen Drug Use	03/15/02	217
Race in America	07/11/03	603*
Racial Quotas	05/17/91	277

	Date	Page
Racial Tensions in Schools	01/07/94	1
Rethinking Affirmative Action	04/28/95	375*
Rising College Costs	12/05/03	1013
Science in America	01/11/08	25
Science and Politics	08/20/04	661
Sex on Campus	11/04/94	961
Sexual Harassment	04/27/12	377
Single-Sex Education	07/12/02	569
Social Networking	09/17/10	749
Special Education	11/10/00	919*
State Budget Crisis	09/11/09	741
Student Activism	08/28/98	745
Student Aid	01/25/08	73
Student Debt	10/21/11	877
Student Journalism	06/05/98	481
Teacher Education	10/17/97	913
Treating Anxiety	02/08/02	97
Treatment of Veterans	11/19/04	984*
Underage Drinking	03/13/92	217
Upward Mobility	04/29/05	369
Women and Sports	03/25/11	265
Worker Retraining	01/21/94	55*
Year-Round Schools	05/17/96	446*
Youth Volunteerism	01/27/12	77
Colleges and universities — Sports		
Athletes and Drugs	07/26/91	513
College Football	11/18/11	977
College Sports	08/26/94	745
Eating Disorders	12/18/92	1103
Gender and Learning	05/20/05	445
Gender Equity in Sports	04/18/97	337
Getting into College	02/23/96	186*
Press Freedom	02/05/10	97
Reforming Big-Time College Sports	03/19/04	249
Repetitive Stress Injuries	06/23/95	548*
Shock Jocks	06/01/07	**481
Soccer in America	04/22/94	350*
Sports and Drugs	07/23/04	**613
Sportsmanship	03/23/01	225
Student Aid	01/25/08	73
The Value of a College Education	11/20/09	981
Women and Sports	03/06/92	193
Colombia		
Children in Crisis	08/31/01	657
Democracy in Latin America	11/03/00	896*
Privatizing the Military	06/25/04	565
Reforming Big-Time College Sports	03/19/04	249
Trouble in South America	03/14/03	241*
Colorado		
Cleaning Up Hazardous Wastes	08/23/96	745
Parental Rights	10/25/96	937
Redistricting Disputes	03/12/04	221
Reforming Big-Time College Sports	03/19/04	249

	Date	Page
Saving Open Spaces	11/05/99	965*
Urban Sprawl in the West	10/03/97	865
Water Shortages	08/01/03	661*
Columbine High School. *See Littleton, Colo.*		
Communication. *See Telecommunications*		
Communism and communist countries		
Aid to Russia	03/12/93	217
Castro's Next Move	12/12/97	1081
China After Deng	06/13/97	505
Cuba in Crisis	11/29/91	897
Cuba's Future	07/20/07	601
Dealing With the "New" Russia	06/06/08	481
Democracy in Eastern Europe	10/08/99	876*
Emerging China	11/11/05	957
Emerging India	04/19/02	329
The Greening of Eastern Europe	11/15/91	849
New Era in Asia	02/14/92	121
Policing the Borders	02/22/02	145
Religious Persecution	11/21/97	1009
Russia and the Former Soviet Republics	06/17/05	541
Russia's Political Future	05/03/96	385
U.S.-China Relations	05/07/10	**409
Community colleges		
Community Colleges	04/21/00	329
Distance Learning	12/07/01	993
Nursing Shortage	09/20/02	757*
Paying for College	11/20/92	1018*
Worker Retraining	01/21/94	55*
Community service. *See Voluntarism*		
Commuting. *See also Telecommuting*		
Affordable Housing	02/09/01	94*
Smart Growth	05/28/04	469
Traffic Congestion	05/06/94	385
Traffic Congestion	08/27/99	729
Computers. *See also Internet*		
3D Printing	12/07/12	1037
Artificial Intelligence	11/14/97	985
Artificial Intelligence	04/22/11	361
Computer Hacking	09/16/11	757*
Controlling the Internet	05/12/06	409
Cyberbullying	05/02/08	385
Cyber-Crime	04/12/02	305
Cyber-Predators	03/01/02	169
Cybersecurity	09/26/03	797
Cyber Socializing	07/28/06	625
Digital Education	12/02/11	1001
Distance Learning	12/07/01	993
Employee Benefits	02/04/00	65
Examining Forensics	07/17/09	597
Future of Computers	05/26/00	449
Future of the Music Industry	11/21/03	989
Future of Recycling	12/14/07	1033

 *Indicates sidebar or "At Issue" report section. **Indicates an updated report.

	Date	Page
The Future of Television	12/23/94	1136*
Hard Times for Libraries	06/26/92	565*
High-Tech Labor Shortage	04/24/98	361
Identity Theft	06/10/05	517
Impact of the Internet on Thinking	09/24/10	773
Internet Accuracy	08/01/08	625
Internet Regulation	04/13/12	325
Nanotechnology	06/11/04	517
Networking the Classroom	10/20/95	921
Online Privacy	11/06/09	**933
Preventing Bullying	12/10/10	**1013
Reading Crisis?	02/22/08	169
Recession's Regional Impact	02/01/91	75*
Redistricting Disputes	03/12/04	221
Redistricting: Drawing Power with a Map	02/15/91	101*
Regulating the New Economy	10/19/01	849
Repetitive Stress Injuries	06/23/95	537
Rising College Costs	12/05/03	1026*
Smart Cities	07/27/12	645
Social Media and Politics	10/12/12	865
Social Networking	09/17/10	749
Software Piracy	05/21/93	433
Teacher Education	10/17/97	926*
Television's Future	02/16/07	145
Video Games	11/10/06	**937
Work, Family and Stress	08/14/92	703*
Worker Safety	05/21/04	451*
Y2K Dilemma	02/19/99	137

Congress, U.S.

	Date	Page
Campaign Finance Reform	02/09/96	121
Campaign Finance Showdown	11/22/02	969
Census 2000	05/01/98	403*
Census Controversey	05/14/10	433
Civic Renewal	03/21/97	246*
Democrats in Congress	06/08/07	505
Democrats' Future	10/29/10	893
Domestic Energy Development	09/30/05	809
Domestic Violence	01/06/06	1
Draft Debates	08/19/05	661
Drug Testing	11/20/98	1015*
Electing Minorities	08/12/94	697
Evaluating Head Start	08/26/05	685
Foreign Aid After Sept. 11	04/26/02	361
Future of the GOP	03/20/09	249
Governing Washington, D.C.	11/22/96	1033
Gridlock in Washington	04/30/10	385
Homeland Security	09/12/03	749
Independent Counsels	02/21/97	145
Interrogating the CIA	09/25/09	789
Lies and Politics	02/18/11	145
Line-Item Veto	06/20/97	529
Lobbying Boom	07/22/05	613
Medicaid Reform	07/16/04	589
Mental Illness Medication Debate	02/06/04	101
Middle East Tensions	10/27/06	**889
Minimum Wage	12/16/05	1053
NASA's Future	05/23/03	473
New Strategy in Iraq	02/23/07	169
The Partisan Divide	04/30/04	384
Partisan Politics	03/19/99	233
Political Scandals	05/27/94	457
Pork Barrel Politics	06/16/06	529
Presidential Power	11/15/02	945
Rebuilding Iraq	07/11/03	625
Rebuilding New Orleans	02/03/06	97
Redistricting Debates	02/25/11	169
Redistricting Disputes	03/12/04	221
Re-examining the Constitution	09/07/12	741
Re-examining 9/11	06/04/04	493
Reforming the Corps	05/30/03	497
Right to Die	05/13/05	421
Science and Politics	08/20/04	661
Sex Scandals	01/22/10	49
Sexual Harassment	08/09/91	551*
States and Federalism	10/15/10	845
Supreme Court's Future	01/28/05	77
Tea Party Movement	03/19/10	**241*
Term Limits	01/10/92	1
Testing Term Limits	11/18/94	1009
Treatment of Veterans	11/19/04	973
U.S.-British Relations	11/05/10	917*
War in Iraq	10/21/05	881
Women in Politics	03/21/08	265

Congress, U.S. — Legislative outlooks

	Date	Page
Abortion Debates	03/21/03	265*
Abortion Debates	09/10/10	725
Abortion Showdowns	09/22/06	769
Afghanistan Dilemma	08/07/09	**669*
Age Discrimination	08/01/97	687*
Aging Infrastructure	09/28/07	**793
Aiding Africa	08/29/03	697
Air Pollution Conflict	11/14/03	965
Alzheimer's Disease	05/15/98	433
America at War	07/23/10	**605
American Indians	04/28/06	**361
Animal Rights	01/08/10	1
Asbestos Litigation	05/02/03	393
Assessing the New Health Care Law	09/21/12	789
Auto Industry's Future	02/06/09	**105
Biofuels Boom	09/29/06	793
Birth-Control Debate	06/24/05	565
Blighted Cities	11/12/10	941*
Breast Cancer	04/02/10	289
Broadcast Indecency	04/16/04	321
Business Bankruptcy	04/10/09	321
Business Ethics	05/06/11	409
Buying Green	02/29/08	193

	Date	Page
Campaign Finance Debates	05/28/10	457
Caring for the Dying	09/05/97	784*
Caring for Veterans	04/23/10	361
Celebrity Advocacy	05/11/12	425
Child-Care Options	05/08/98	423*
Child Custody and Support	01/13/95	39*
Children and Divorce	06/07/91	362
Child Poverty	10/28/11	901
Child Welfare Reform	04/22/05	345
Civil Liberties Debates	10/24/03	893
Cleaning Up Hazardous Wastes	08/23/96	745
Coal Mining Safety	03/17/06	241
Coal's Comeback	10/05/07	817
Coastal Development	08/21/98	736*
Combating Addiction	02/09/07	121
Combating Terrorism	07/21/95	633
Computer Hacking	09/16/11	757*
Confronting Iraq	10/04/02	793
Consumer Safety	10/12/07	841
Cost of the Iraq War	04/25/08	361*
Crime on Campus	02/04/11	97
Crisis on the Plains	05/09/03	438*
Cuba's Future	07/20/07	601
Curbing CEO Pay	03/09/07	217
D.C. Voting Rights	04/11/08	313*
Death Penalty Debate	03/10/95	206*
Debate over Bilingualism	01/19/96	49
Debt Collectors	07/20/12	621
Democrats in Congress	06/08/07	505
Dietary Supplements	07/08/94	577
Dietary Supplements	09/03/04	709
Distracted Driving	05/04/12	401
Domestic Poverty	09/07/07	**721
Downsizing Prisons	03/11/11	217
Drug Company Ethics	06/06/03	521
Drugmakers Under Siege	09/03/99	753
Drug Safety	03/11/05	221
Earthquake Threat	04/09/10	313
Electing the President	04/20/07	337
Embryo Research	12/17/99	1065
Ending Homelessness	06/18/04	541
Energy and Climate	07/24/09	621
Energy Efficiency	05/19/06	433
Energy Policy	05/20/11	457
Environmental Movement at 25	03/31/95	273
Executive Pay	07/11/97	615*
Exporting Jobs	02/20/04	149
Extreme Weather	09/09/11	733*
Farm Policy	12/02/94	1057
Farm Policy	08/10/12	693
Farm Subsidies	05/17/02	433
Financial Bailout	10/24/08	**865
Financial Crisis	05/09/08	409
Financial Industry Overhaul	07/30/10	629

	Date	Page
Fish Farming	07/27/07	625
Fixing Urban Schools	04/27/07	**361
Foreign Aid and National Security	06/17/11	529
Fracking Controversy	12/16/11	1049
Free-Press Disputes	04/08/05	293
Future of the Airlines	03/07/08	217
Future of Homeownership	12/14/12	1061
The Future of Television	12/23/94	1129
Gang Crisis	05/14/04	421
Gays in the Military	09/18/09	**765
Google's Dominance	11/11/11	953
Gulf Coast Restoration	08/26/11	677*
Gun Control Debate	11/12/04	949
Gun Control Standoff	12/19/97	1105
Gun Rights Debates	10/31/08	**889
Gun Violence	05/25/07	457
Health-Care Reform	08/28/09	693*
Health-Care Reform	06/11/10	**505
Helping the Homeless	01/26/96	90*
High-Speed Trains	05/01/09	**397
High-Tech Labor Shortage	04/24/98	378*
Highway Safety	07/14/95	622*
Homeland Security	09/12/03	749
The Homeless	08/07/92	676
Housing the Homeless	12/18/09	1053
Human Rights Issues	10/30/09	909
Human Spaceflight	10/16/09	861
Human Trafficking and Slavery	03/26/04	273
Identity Theft	06/10/05	517
Illegal Immigration	05/06/05	393
Immigration Conflict	03/09/12	229
Immigration Debate	02/01/08	**97
Income Inequality	12/03/10	989
Increase in Autism	06/13/03	**553*
Independent Counsels	02/21/97	145
Independent Counsels Re-examined	05/07/99	377
Indoor Air Pollution	10/27/95	960*
Infant Mortality	07/31/92	658
Insurance Fraud	10/11/96	904*
Intelligence Reforms	01/25/02	49
Internet Regulation	04/13/12	325
IRS Reform	01/16/98	25
Jobs vs. Environment	05/15/92	409
Jobs Outlook	06/04/10	481
Lead Poisoning	06/19/92	542
Legalizing Marijuana	06/12/09	**525
Limiting Lawsuits	12/19/08	1033
Managed Care	04/12/96	329*
Managing Nuclear Waste	01/28/11	73
Managing Public Lands	11/04/11	929
Managing Wildfires	11/02/12	941
Media Ownership	10/10/03	**845
Medical Malpractice	02/14/03	129
Medicare Reform	08/22/03	673

 *Indicates sidebar or "At Issue" report section. **Indicates an updated report.

	Date	Page
Mexico's Drug War	12/12/08	1009
Middle-Class Squeeze	03/06/09	201
Military Suicides	09/23/11	781*
Mine Safety	06/24/11	553
Mortgage Crisis	11/02/07	**913
The National Debt	11/14/08	937
National Debt	03/18/11	241
National Education Standards	05/14/99	401
Native Americans	05/08/92	398
Nuclear Disarmament	10/02/09	**813
Nuclear Energy	03/10/06	217
Nuclear Power	06/10/11	505
Nuclear Proliferation and Terrorism	04/02/04	297
The Obama Presidency	01/30/09	73
Offshore Drilling	06/25/10	553
Oil Jitters	01/04/08	**1
Online Privacy	11/06/09	**933
Overhauling Social Security	05/12/95	417
Patent Disputes	12/15/06	1033
Patients' Rights	02/06/98	112*
Patient Safety	02/10/12	125
Pension Crisis	02/17/06	145
Policing the Borders	02/22/02	145
Port Security	04/21/06	337
Presidential Libraries	03/16/07	241
Presidential Power	11/15/02	952*
Press Freedom	02/05/10	97
Preventing Cancer	01/16/09	25
Preventing Obesity	10/01/10	797
Primary Care	03/17/95	234*
Prison Reform	04/06/07	289
Privacy in Peril	11/17/06	961
Privatizing the Military	06/25/04	565
Privatizing the Military	07/13/12	597
Property Rights	06/16/95	513
Protecting Endangered Species	04/19/96	337
Protecting Wetlands	10/03/08	793*
Protecting Whistleblowers	03/31/06	265
Real ID	05/04/07	385
Reassessing Foreign Aid	09/27/96	841
Reducing Your Carbon Footprint	12/05/08	985
Regulating Credit Cards	10/10/08	817*
Regulating Nonprofits	12/26/97	1129
Regulating Pesticides	01/28/94	73
Regulating Pesticides	08/06/99	682*
Regulating Toxic Chemicals	01/23/09	49
Religious Persecution	11/21/97	1009
Renewable Energy	11/07/97	978*
Repetitive Stress Injuries	06/23/95	537
Rethinking Affirmative Action	04/28/95	369
Rethinking Retirement	06/19/09	549
Revising No Child Left Behind	04/16/10	337
Revitalizing the Cities	10/13/95	909*
Rising Health Costs	04/07/06	289

	Date	Page
Roe v. Wade at 25	11/28/97	1033
Saving Open Spaces	11/05/99	966*
School Reform	04/29/11	385
School Vouchers Showdown	02/15/02	121
Sentencing Debates	11/05/04	925
Sex Offenders	09/08/06	721
Shock Jocks	06/01/07	**481
Social Networking	09/17/10	749
Space Program	02/24/12	177
Stem Cell Research	09/01/06	**697
Stimulating the Economy	01/10/03	17*
The Stock Market	05/02/97	401*
Straining the Safety Net	07/31/09	645
Student Aid	01/25/08	73
Student Debt	10/21/11	877
Supreme Court's Future	01/28/05	77
Teacher Education	10/17/97	930*
Testing Term Limits	11/18/94	1009
Treating Depression	06/26/09	573
Three-Strikes Laws	05/10/02	417
Transportation Policy	07/04/97	577
Treatment of Detainees	08/25/06	673
Underage Drinking	03/13/92	217
Unemployment Benefits	04/25/03	369
United Nations at 50	08/18/95	729
Universal Coverage	03/30/07	265
Upward Mobility	04/29/05	369
U.S.-Pakistan Relations	08/05/11	653*
U.S. Policy on Iran	11/16/07	961
Vanishing Jobs	03/13/09	225
Voter Rights	05/18/12	449
Voting Controversies	09/15/06	745
Water Shortages	06/18/10	529
Weapons of Mass Destruction	03/08/02	193
Whistleblowers	12/05/97	1072*
Wind Power	04/01/11	289
Women in the Military	11/13/09	957
Worker Safety	05/21/04	445
The Working Poor	11/03/95	984*
Wounded Veterans	08/31/07	697
Youth Violence	03/05/10	193*

Conservation. ***See also Endangered species; Environmental Protection***

	Date	Page
Alternative Energy	02/25/05	173
Archaeology Today	05/24/02	457
Bush and the Environment	10/25/02	865
Buying Green	02/29/08	193
California: Enough Water for the Future?	04/19/91	221
Crisis on the Plains	05/09/03	439*
Disappearing Species	11/30/07	985
Ecotourism	10/20/06	865
Endangered Species Act	06/03/05	**493
Energy and the Environment	03/03/00	161

	Date	Page
Energy Efficiency	05/19/06	433
Energy Security	02/01/02	73
Farm Policy	08/10/12	693
Global Water Shortages	12/15/95	1113
Hunting Controversy	01/24/92	49
Mass Transit Boom	01/18/08	49
National Forests	10/16/98	905
National Parks	05/28/93	457
National Parks Under Pressure	10/06/06	817
Oil Jitters	01/04/08	**1
Protecting the National Parks	06/16/00	521
Public Land Policy	06/17/94	529
Reducing Your Carbon Footprint	12/05/08	985
Reforming the Corps	05/30/03	497
Saving Open Spaces	11/05/99	953
Saving the Forests	09/20/91	681
Saving the Rain Forests	06/11/99	497
Smart Growth	05/28/04	469
SUV Debate	05/16/03	449
Threatened Fisheries	08/02/02	617
Water Shortages	08/01/03	649
Constitution, U.S. ***See also Civil rights and liberties; First Amendment***		
Affirmative Action	10/17/08	**841
Campaign Finance Showdown	11/22/02	985*
Civil Liberties Debates	10/24/03	893
Closing Guantánamo	02/27/09	**177
Cyberbullying	05/02/08	385
Death Penalty Debates	11/19/10	965
Free-Press Disputes	04/08/05	293
Future of Marriage	05/07/04	397
Gay Marriage Showdowns	09/26/08	**769
Gender Pay Gap	03/14/08	241
Gun Control Debate	11/12/04	949
International Law	12/17/04	1049
Line-Item Veto	06/20/97	529
Presidential Power	11/15/02	945
Presidential Power	02/24/06	169
Preventing Bullying	12/10/10	**1013
Property Rights	06/16/95	513
Public Defenders	04/18/08	337*
Racial Diversity in Public Schools	09/14/07	**745
Reassessing the Nation's Gun Laws	03/22/91	157
Redistricting Disputes	03/12/04	221
Re-examining the Constitution	09/07/12	741
School Vouchers Showdown	02/15/02	121
Sentencing Debates	11/05/04	925
Supreme Court Controversies	09/28/12	813
Term Limits	01/10/92	1
Testing Term Limits	11/18/94	1009
Three-Strikes Laws	05/10/02	417
Consumerism		
Advertising Overload	01/23/04	49
Alternative Energy	02/25/05	173
Buying Green	02/29/08	193
Celebrity Culture	03/18/05	245
Consumer Debt	03/02/07	193
The Consumer Culture	11/19/99	1001
Financial Literacy	09/04/09	717
Limiting Lawsuits	12/19/08	1033
Professional Football	01/29/10	**73
Reducing Your Carbon Footprint	12/05/08	985
Rise of Megachurches	09/21/07	769
Teen Spending	05/26/06	457
Consumer prices		
America's Pampered Pets	12/27/96	1129
Big-Box Stores	09/10/04	733
Child Labor and Sweatshops	08/16/96	721
Civic Renewal	03/21/97	241
Drugmakers Under Siege	09/03/99	753
The Economics of Recycling	03/27/98	265
Energy Security	02/01/02	73
Fast-Food Shake-Up	11/08/91	825
Jobs in the '90s	02/28/92	182*
Liberal Arts Education	04/10/98	313
Managed Care	04/12/96	313
Mental Illness Medication Debate	02/06/04	101
Oil Production in the 21st Century	08/07/98	673
Paying for College	11/20/92	1001
Prescription Drug Prices	07/17/92	597
Restructuring the Electric Industry	01/17/97	25
Rethinking NAFTA	06/07/96	481
Rising College Costs	12/05/03	1013
Space Program's Future	04/25/97	372*
Stimulating the Economy	01/10/03	1
U.S. Auto Industry	10/16/92	881
Consumer protection		
Advertising Overload	01/23/04	49
Advertising Under Attack	09/13/91	657
Airline Industry Problems	09/24/99	825
Animal Rights	05/24/91	301
Antitrust Policy	06/12/98	510*
Caring for the Elderly	02/20/98	145
Class Action Lawsuits	05/13/11	433
Consumer Debt	03/02/07	193
Consumer Safety	10/12/07	841
Corporate Crime	10/11/02	817
Cosmetic Surgery	04/15/05	317
Cyber-Crime	04/12/02	305
Cyber-Predators	03/01/02	169
Debt Collectors	07/20/12	621
Dietary Supplements	07/08/94	577
Dietary Supplements	09/03/04	709
Drugmakers Under Siege	09/03/99	753
Drug Safety	03/11/05	221
Electromagnetic Fields	04/26/91	237
Fighting over Animal Rights	08/02/96	673
Financial Misconduct	01/20/12	53

 *Indicates sidebar or "At Issue" report section. **Indicates an updated report.

	Date	Page
Food Irradiation	06/12/92	505
Food Safety	06/04/93	481
Genetically Engineered Foods	08/05/94	673
The Growing Influence of Boycotts	01/04/91	1
High-Impact Litigation	02/11/00	93*
Homeopathy Debate	12/19/03	1069
Identity Theft	06/10/05	517
Insurance Fraud	10/11/96	889
Managing Managed Care	04/16/99	305
Mortgage Crisis	11/02/07	**913
Mutual Funds	05/20/94	433
Nanotechnology	06/11/04	517
Obesity and Health	01/15/99	25
Regulating Credit Cards	10/10/08	817*
Regulating Pesticides	01/28/94	73
Regulating Pesticides	08/06/99	665
Stock Market Troubles	01/16/04	25
Student Debt	10/21/11	877
Whistleblowers	12/05/97	1057
Contraceptives. ***See Birth control***		
Copyright		
Clashing over Copyright	11/08/96	985
Combating Plagiarism	09/19/03	773
Copyright and the Internet	09/29/00	769
Cyber-Crime	04/12/02	305
Future of Libraries	07/29/11	625
Future of the Music Industry	11/21/03	989
Internet Regulation	04/13/12	325
Regulating the Internet	06/30/95	566*
Software Piracy	05/21/93	433
Corporate mergers. ***See also Business and industry***		
Antitrust Policy	06/12/98	505
Baby Boomers at Midlife	07/31/98	649
Business Bankruptcy	04/10/09	321
Corporate Crime	10/11/02	817
Cosmetic Surgery	04/15/05	317
Financial Bailout	10/24/08	**865
Financial Crisis	05/09/08	409
Financial Industry Overhaul	07/30/10	629
Future of Journalism	03/27/09	**273
The Future of Telecommunications	04/23/99	329
Journalism Under Fire	12/25/98	1135*
The Politics of Energy	03/05/99	200*
Cosmetics — Testing. ***See Animals***		
Cosmetic Surgery		
Celebrity Culture	03/18/05	245
Cosmetic Surgery	04/15/05	317
Courts. ***See also Supreme Court***		
Abortion Debates	03/21/03	249
Abortion Debates	09/10/10	725
Abortion Showdowns	09/22/06	769
Advertising Overload	01/23/04	49
Air Pollution Conflict	11/14/03	965

	Date	Page
Asbestos Litigation	05/02/03	393
Assisted Suicide	02/21/92	145
Assisted Suicide Controversy	05/05/95	393
Birth-Control Debate	06/24/05	565
Boys' Emotional Needs	06/18/99	538*
Breast Cancer	04/02/10	289
Cameras in the Courtroom	01/14/11	25
Campaign Finance Debates	05/28/10	457
Campaign Finance Showdown	11/22/02	980*
Caring for the Dying	09/05/97	769
Children's Legal Rights	04/23/93	337
Child Welfare Reform	04/22/05	345
Civil Liberties Debates	10/24/03	893
Class Action Lawsuits	05/13/11	433
Closing Guantánamo	02/27/09	**177
Closing In on Tobacco	11/12/99	977
Cosmetic Surgery	04/15/05	317
Courts and the Media	09/23/94	817
Crackdown on Sexual Harassment	07/19/96	625
Crime Victims' Rights	07/22/94	625
Cyber-Crime	04/12/02	305
Death Penalty Controversies	09/23/05	785
Death Penalty Update	01/08/99	1
Debt Collectors	07/20/12	621
DNA Databases	05/28/99	449
Domestic Partners	09/04/92	761
Downsizing Prisons	03/11/11	217
Drug-Policy Debate	07/28/00	593
Drug-Policy Debate	07/28/00	599*
Environmental Justice	06/19/98	529
Examining Forensics	07/17/09	597
Eyewitness Testimony	10/14/11	853
The Federal Judiciary	03/13/98	217
Foster Care Reform	01/09/98	6*
Free-Press Disputes	04/08/05	293
Future of the Music Industry	11/21/03	989
Gay Marriage	09/05/03	721
Gay Marriage Showdowns	09/26/08	**769
Google's Dominance	11/11/11	953
Helping the Homeless	01/26/96	73
High-Impact Litigation	02/11/00	89
Homegrown Jihadists	09/03/10	701
International Law	12/17/04	1049
Judges and Politics	07/27/01	1003*
Judicial Elections	04/24/09	373
The Jury System	11/10/95	993
Juvenile Justice	02/25/94	169
Juvenile Justice	11/07/08	913
Legal-Aid Crisis	10/07/11	829
Limiting Lawsuits	12/19/08	1033
Marijuana Laws	02/11/05	125
Medical Malpractice	02/14/03	129
Mental Health Policy	09/12/97	793
Mine Safety	06/24/11	553

	Date	Page
No Child Left Behind	05/27/05	469
Patent Disputes	12/15/06	1033
Plea Bargaining	02/12/99	113
Presidential Power	11/15/02	945
Prison Reform	04/06/07	289
Property Rights	06/16/95	513
Property Rights	03/04/05	197
Prosecuting Terrorists	03/12/10	**217*
Prosecutors and the Law	11/09/07	937
Prosecutors and Politics	06/22/07	553
Public Defenders	04/18/08	337*
Punishing Sex Offenders	01/12/96	25
Race in America	07/11/03	593
Redistricting	02/16/01	113
Redistricting Debates	02/25/11	169
Redistricting Disputes	03/12/04	221
Redistricting: Drawing Power with a Map	02/15/91	97
Reforming School Funding	12/10/99	1041
Rethinking School Integration	10/18/96	913
Right to Die	05/13/05	421
School Censorship	02/19/93	145
School Choice Debate	07/18/97	630*
School Desegregation	04/23/04	345
School Funding	08/27/93	745
School Vouchers Showdown	02/15/02	121
Science and Politics	08/20/04	661
Science in the Courtroom	10/22/93	913
Sentencing Debates	11/05/04	925
Serial Killers	10/31/03	917
Sex Offenders	09/08/06	721
Sexual Abuse and the Clergy	05/03/02	393
Sexual Harassment	04/27/12	377
Sleep Deprivation	06/26/98	570*
Solitary Confinement	09/14/12	765
States and Federalism	09/13/96	798*
Stock Market Troubles	01/16/04	25
Supreme Court Controversies	09/28/12	813
Supreme Court's Future	01/28/05	77
Three-Strikes Laws	05/10/02	417
Tobacco Industry	12/10/04	**1025
Too Many Lawsuits?	05/22/92	433
Transgender Issues	05/05/06	385
Vaccine Controversies	08/25/00	650*
Voting Controversies	09/15/06	745
War Crimes	07/07/95	585
Women and Sports	03/25/11	265
Wrongful Convictions	04/17/09	**345
Creationism		
Evolution vs. Creationism	08/22/97	745
Intelligent Design	07/29/05	637
Religion in Schools	01/12/01	11*
Credit cards		
The Consumer Culture	11/19/99	1001
Consumer Debt	11/15/96	1009
Consumer Debt	03/02/07	193
Cyber-Crime	04/12/02	305
Debt Collectors	07/20/12	621
Identity Theft	06/10/05	517
Student Aid	01/25/08	73
Teen Spending	05/26/06	457
Crime and criminals		
Accountants Under Fire	03/22/02	241
Biology and Behavior	04/03/98	289
Business Ethics	05/06/11	409
Cameras in the Courtroom	01/14/11	25
Child Sexual Abuse	01/15/93	25
Child Welfare Reform	04/22/05	345
Civic Renewal	03/21/97	252*
Combating Terrorism	07/21/95	633
Community Policing	02/05/93	97
Community Prosecution	12/15/00	1009
Computer Hacking	09/16/11	757*
Corporate Crime	10/11/02	817
Courts and the Media	09/23/94	817
Crime on Campus	02/04/11	97
Crime Victims' Rights	07/22/94	625
Criminal Records and Employment	04/20/12	349
Cyber-Crime	04/12/02	305
Cyber-Predators	03/01/02	169
Cybersecurity	02/26/10	169
Death Penalty Debate	03/10/95	193
Death Penalty Debates	11/19/10	965
Death Penalty Update	01/08/99	1
Declining Crime Rates	04/04/97	289
Democracy in Latin America	11/03/00	881
DNA Databases	05/28/99	449
Downsizing Prisons	03/11/11	217
Drug-Policy Debate	07/28/00	593
Examining Forensics	07/17/09	597
Eyewitness Testimony	10/14/11	853
Fighting Crime	02/08/08	121
Financial Misconduct	01/20/12	53
Free-Press Disputes	04/08/05	293
Future of the Music Industry	11/21/03	989
Gambling in America	03/07/03	201
Gambling Under Attack	09/06/96	785*
Gang Crisis	05/14/04	421
Government Secrecy	02/11/11	121
Gun Control	06/10/94	505
Gun Control Debate	11/12/04	949
Gun Control Standoff	12/19/97	1105
Gun Rights Debates	10/31/08	**889
Gun Violence	05/25/07	457

 *Indicates sidebar or "At Issue" report section. **Indicates an updated report.

	Date	Page
Hate Crimes	01/08/93	1
Hazing	01/09/04	1
Human Trafficking and Slavery	03/26/04	273
Identity Theft	06/10/05	517
Illegal Immigration	04/24/92	361
Illegal Immigration	05/06/05	393
Insurance Fraud	10/11/96	889
Internet Regulation	04/13/12	325
Is America Allowing Its Past to Be Stolen?	01/18/91	33
Job Stress	08/04/95	688*
The Jury System	11/10/95	993
Juvenile Justice	02/25/94	169
Juvenile Justice	11/07/08	913
Kids in Prison	04/27/01	345
Labor Unions' Future	09/02/05	**709
Legalizing Marijuana	06/12/09	**525
Mafia Crackdown	03/27/92	265
Mandatory Sentencing	05/26/95	465
Marijuana Laws	02/11/05	125
Medical Marijuana	08/20/99	721*
Mental Illness	08/06/93	673
Mexico's Future	10/26/12	913
The Obscenity Debate	12/20/91	969
Plea Bargaining	02/12/99	113
Police Misconduct	04/06/12	301
Policing the Borders	02/22/02	145
Policing the Police	03/17/00	209
Pork Barrel Politics	06/16/06	529
Preventing Juvenile Crime	03/15/96	217
Prison-Building Boom	09/17/99	801
Prison Overcrowding	02/04/94	97
Prison Reform	04/06/07	289
Prisoner Reentry	12/04/09	1005
Privatizing the Military	06/25/04	565
Prosecutors and the Law	11/09/07	937
Prostitution	06/11/93	505
Protecting Whistleblowers	03/31/06	265
Public Defenders	04/18/08	337*
Public Housing	09/10/93	793
Punishing Sex Offenders	01/12/96	25
Recovered-Memory Debate	07/05/96	577
Reforming Big-Time College Sports	03/19/04	249
Regulating the Internet	06/30/95	561
Science in the Courtroom	10/22/93	920*
School Violence	10/09/98	881
Sentencing Debates	11/05/04	925
Serial Killers	10/31/03	917
Sex Offenders	09/08/06	721
Sex on Campus	11/04/94	961
Sexual Abuse and the Clergy	05/03/02	393
Software Piracy	05/21/93	433
Solitary Confinement	09/14/12	765
Sports and Drugs	07/23/04	**613

	Date	Page
Stock Market Troubles	01/16/04	25
Stolen Antiquities	04/13/07	313
Suburban Crime	09/03/93	769
Supreme Court Preview	09/17/93	817
Teen Driving	01/07/05	1
Teen Drug Use	06/03/11	481
Three-Strikes Laws	05/10/02	417
Treating Addiction	01/06/95	17*
TV Violence	03/26/93	279*
Violence Against Women	02/26/93	169
Violence in Schools	09/11/92	785
War Crimes	07/07/95	585
War on Drugs	03/19/93	241
War on Drugs	06/02/06	481
Wrongful Convictions	04/17/09	**345
Youth Gangs	10/11/91	753
Youth Violence	03/05/10	193*
Cuba		
Castro's Next Move	12/12/97	1081
Closing Guantánamo	02/27/09	**177
Cuba in Crisis	11/29/91	897
Cuba's Future	07/20/07	601
Economic Sanctions	10/28/94	937
Oil Production in the 21st Century	08/07/98	689*
Cults		
Cults in America	05/07/93	385
The FBI Under Fire	04/11/97	313
Cyber Politics		
Campaign Finance Reform	06/13/08	505
Czech Republic and Czechoslovakia		
Democracy in Eastern Europe	10/08/99	865
Expanding NATO	05/16/97	433
The Greening of Eastern Europe	11/15/91	849
Dance		
Arts Education	03/16/12	253
Arts Funding	10/21/94	913
Centennial Olympic Games	04/05/96	297*
Date rape		
Preventing Teen Drug Use	03/15/02	217
Sex on Campus	11/04/94	961
Violence Against Women	02/26/93	169
Day care. *See Child care*		
"Deadbeat Dads." *See Child custody and support*		
Dean, Howard		
Cyberpolitics	09/17/04	757
Death penalty		
Crime Victims' Rights	07/22/94	625
Death Penalty Controversies	09/23/05	785
Death Penalty Debate	03/10/95	193
Death Penalty Debates	11/19/10	965
Death Penalty Update	01/08/99	1
Human Rights	11/13/98	982*

	Date	Page
Juvenile Justice	11/07/08	913
Kids in Prison	04/27/01	361*
Public Defenders	04/18/08	337*
Race in America	07/11/03	593
Rethinking the Death Penalty	11/16/01	945
Sentencing Debates	11/05/04	925
Transatlantic Tensions	07/13/01	564*
Wrongful Convictions	04/17/09	**345

Defense. ***See Military policy***

Democracy

	Date	Page
Aid to Russia	03/12/93	217
Aiding Africa	08/29/03	697
The British Monarchy	03/08/96	193
China After Deng	06/13/97	513*
Civic Journalism	09/20/96	817
Confronting Iraq	10/04/02	806*
Conspiracy Theories	10/23/09	885
Cuba's Future	07/20/07	601
Democracy in Africa	03/24/95	241
Democracy in Asia	07/24/98	625
Democracy in Eastern Europe	10/08/99	865
Democracy in Latin America	11/03/00	881
Democracy in the Arab World	01/30/04	73
Emerging India	04/19/02	329
Exporting Democracy	04/01/05	269
Future of Journalism	03/27/09	**273
Human Rights in China	07/25/08	601
Human Rights Issues	10/30/09	909
Islamic Fundamentalism	03/24/00	241
Judicial Elections	04/24/09	373
Mexico's Emergence	07/19/91	489
'Occupy' Movement	01/13/12	25
Race in America	07/11/03	593
Reform in Iran	12/18/98	1097
Rethinking Foreign Policy	02/02/07	97
Russia and the Former Soviet Republics	06/17/05	541
Russia's Political Future	05/03/96	385
South Africa's Future	01/14/94	25
Taiwan, China, and the U.S.	05/24/96	457
Trouble in South America	03/14/03	225
Voting Controversies	09/15/06	745

Democratic Party

	Date	Page
Air Pollution Conflict	11/14/03	965
Black Middle Class	01/23/98	66*
Campaign Finance Debates	05/28/10	457
Campaign Finance Reform	02/09/96	134*
Changing Demographics	11/16/12	989
Changing U.S. Electorate	05/30/08	**457
Cyberpolitics	09/17/04	757
D.C. Voting Rights	04/11/08	313*
Democrats in Congress	06/08/07	505
Democrats' Future	10/29/10	893
Feminism's Future	02/28/97	183*
Future of the GOP	03/20/09	249
Gridlock in Washington	04/30/10	385
Health-Care Reform	08/28/09	693*
Hispanic-Americans' New Clout	09/18/98	809
Labor Movement's Future	06/28/96	553
Lies and Politics	02/18/11	145
National Debt	03/18/11	241
The New Immigrants	01/24/97	56*
The Obama Presidency	01/30/09	73
'Occupy' Movement	01/13/12	25
The Partisan Divide	04/30/04	373
Partisan Politics	03/19/99	233
Political Conventions	08/08/08	649
Presidential Election	02/03/12	101
Prosecutors and Politics	06/22/07	553
Race and Politics	07/18/08	577
Redistricting Debates	02/25/11	169
Redistricting Disputes	03/12/04	221
Redistricting: Drawing Power with a Map	02/15/91	97
Religion and Politics	07/30/04	637
Rethinking Affirmative Action	04/28/95	369
Rising College Costs	12/05/03	1013
Social Media and Politics	10/12/12	865
Tax Reform	03/22/96	241
Term Limits	01/10/92	1
Third-Party Prospects	12/22/95	1137
Voting Controversies	09/15/06	745
Women in Politics	03/21/08	265
Wounded Veterans	08/31/07	697

Depression, Mental. ***See Mental health and illness***

Deregulation. ***See Regulation and deregulation***

Developing countries

	Date	Page
Aiding Africa	08/29/03	697
Arms Sales	12/09/94	1088*
Change in Latin America	07/21/06	601
Cheating in Schools	09/22/00	758*
Childhood Immunizations	06/18/93	546*
Child Labor and Sweatshops	08/16/96	721
Children in Crisis	08/31/01	657
Democracy in Africa	03/24/95	241
Democracy in the Arab World	01/30/04	73
Drug Company Ethics	06/06/03	534*
Ending Poverty	09/09/05	733
Exporting Democracy	04/01/05	269
Exporting Jobs	02/20/04	149
Fair Trade Labeling	05/18/07	433
Famine in Africa	11/08/02	921
Foreign Aid and National Security	06/17/11	529
Foreign Aid After Sept. 11	04/26/02	361
Global AIDS Crisis	10/13/00	809
Global Refugee Crisis	07/09/99	569
The Greening of Eastern Europe	11/15/91	865*
Human Trafficking and Slavery	03/26/04	273

	Date	Page
International Monetary Fund	01/29/99	65
Mexico's Emergence	07/19/91	489
Nuclear Proliferation	06/05/92	481
Ozone Depletion	04/03/92	289
Peace Corps' Challenges in the 1990s	01/25/91	49
Philanthropy in America	12/08/06	1009
Population Growth	07/16/93	601
Puerto Rico: The Struggle over Status	02/08/91	81
Reassessing Foreign Aid	09/27/96	841
Rebuilding Iraq	07/11/03	625
Saving the Forests	09/20/91	681
Saving the Rain Forests	06/11/99	497
Sexual Abuse and the Clergy	05/03/02	393
Three-Strikes Laws	05/10/02	417
Trouble in South America	03/14/03	225
Water Shortages	08/01/03	649
World Hunger	10/25/91	801

Diet. ***See Food and nutrition***

Disabled

	Date	Page
Arts Education	03/16/12	253
Asbestos Litigation	05/02/03	393
Centennial Olympic Games	04/05/96	306*
Charter Schools	12/20/02	1033
Child-Care Options	05/08/98	422*
Covering the Uninsured	06/14/02	521
Cracking Down on Immigration	02/03/95	109*
The Disabilities Act	12/27/91	993
Election Reform	11/02/01	908*
Implementing the Disabilities Act	12/20/96	1105
Learning Disabilities	12/10/93	1081
Medical Malpractice	02/14/03	129
Mental Health Policy	09/12/97	793
Mental Illness	08/06/93	679*
No Child Left Behind	05/27/05	469
Rethinking Ritalin	10/22/99	905
Retirement Security	05/31/02	481
Right to Die	05/13/05	421
Special Education	11/10/00	905
Treatment of Veterans	11/19/04	973

Disadvantaged. ***See Poverty***

Discrimination

	Date	Page
Age Discrimination	08/01/97	673
Asian Americans	12/13/91	945
Biology and Behavior	04/03/98	289
Black Colleges	12/12/03	1045
The Black Middle Class	01/23/98	49
Charter Schools	12/20/02	1033
Civil Liberties Debates	10/24/03	893
Crackdown on Sexual Harassment	07/19/96	625
Crackdown on Smoking	12/04/92	1063*
Criminal Records and Employment	04/20/12	349
Diabetes Epidemic	03/09/01	192*
The Disabilities Act	12/27/91	993
Diversity in the Workplace	10/10/97	889
Domestic Partners	09/04/92	761
Educating Gifted Students	03/28/97	265
Education and Gender	06/03/94	481
Education Standards	03/11/94	217
Future of the Airline Industry	06/21/02	557*
Gay Rights	03/05/93	202*
Gender and Learning	05/20/05	445
Gender Pay Gap	03/14/08	241
Getting into College	02/23/96	169
The Glass Ceiling	10/29/93	937
Housing Discrimination	02/24/95	169
Illegal Immigration	04/24/92	361
Implementing the Disabilities Act	12/20/96	1105
Latinos' Future	10/17/03	869
Medicare Reform	08/22/03	681*
Mental Health Policy	09/12/97	793
Northern Ireland Cease-Fire	09/15/95	812*
Policing the Borders	02/22/02	145
Privacy Under Attack	06/15/01	505
Race in America	07/11/03	593
Racial Diversity in Public Schools	09/14/07	**745
Racial Quotas	05/17/91	277
Racial Tensions in Schools	01/07/94	1
Reforming the CIA	02/02/96	110*
Religion in the Workplace	08/23/02	649
Rethinking Affirmative Action	04/28/95	369
School Choice	05/10/91	253
School Desegregation	04/23/04	345
Sexual Harassment	08/09/91	537
Sexual Harassment	04/27/12	377
Women and AIDS	12/25/92	1138
Women and Sports	03/06/92	193
Women and Sports	03/25/11	265
Women in the Military	09/25/92	833

Diseases and health problems. ***See also AIDS disease; Cancer; Drug abuse; Medical care; Mental health and illness; Tobacco***

	Date	Page
Alzheimer's Disease	07/24/92	617
Alzheimer's Disease	05/15/98	433
American Indians	04/28/06	**361
Asbestos Litigation	05/02/03	393
Assisted Suicide	02/21/92	145
Asthma Epidemic	12/26/99	1089
Avian Flu Threat	01/13/06	25
Battling HIV/AIDS	10/26/07	889
Biotech Foods	03/30/01	249
Birth-Control Debate	06/24/05	565
Blood Supply Safety	11/11/94	985
Breast Cancer	04/02/10	289
Caring for the Elderly	10/13/06	841
Cell Phone Safety	03/16/01	201
Childhood Immunizations	06/18/93	529
Child Welfare Reform	04/22/05	345

	Date	Page
Chronic Fatigue Syndrome	04/05/02	289
Combating Infectious Diseases	06/09/95	489
Cosmetic Surgery	04/15/05	317
Covering the Uninsured	06/14/02	521
Diabetes Epidemic	03/09/01	185
Diet and Health	02/23/01	129
Dietary Supplements	09/03/04	709
Dieting and Health	04/14/95	321
The Disabilities Act	12/27/91	997*
Drug-Resistant Bacteria	06/04/99	473
Drug Safety	03/11/05	221
Eating Disorders	12/18/92	1097
Eating Disorders	02/10/06	**121
Embryo Research	12/17/99	1065
Ending Poverty	09/09/05	733
Fighting SARS	06/20/03	569
Fighting Superbugs	08/24/07	673
Food Safety	06/04/93	481
Food Safety	11/01/02	897
Food Safety	12/17/10	1037
Genes and Health	01/21/11	49
Gene Therapy	10/18/91	777
Gene Therapy's Future	12/08/95	1089
Heart Health	09/12/08	721
Human Genome Research	05/12/00	401
Impact of the Internet on Thinking	09/24/10	773
Increase in Autism	06/13/03	**545
Indoor Air Pollution	10/27/95	945
Infant Mortality	07/31/92	641
Invasive Species	10/05/01	785
Lead Poisoning	06/19/92	525
Limiting Lawsuits	12/19/08	1033
Mad Cow Disease	03/02/01	161
Marijuana Laws	02/11/05	125
Medicaid Reform	07/16/04	589
Medical Malpractice	02/14/03	129
Medical Mistakes	02/25/00	137
Mental Health Insurance	03/29/02	265
Mental Illness Medication Debate	02/06/04	101
Military Suicides	09/23/11	781*
Native Americans	05/08/92	399
Obesity and Health	01/15/99	25
Obesity Epidemic	01/31/03	73
Organ Donations	04/15/11	337
Organ Shortage	02/21/03	153
Organ Transplants	08/11/95	705
Patient Safety	02/10/12	125
Prayer and Healing	01/14/05	25
Preventing Cancer	01/16/09	25
Preventing Disease	01/06/12	1
Preventing Memory Loss	04/04/08	289*
Preventing Obesity	10/01/10	797
Prison Health Care	01/05/07	1
Privacy in the Workplace	11/19/93	1023*

	Date	Page
Professional Football	01/29/10	**73
Prolonging Life	09/30/11	805*
Prostitution	06/11/93	505
Prostitution Debate	05/23/08	433
Regulating Pesticides	01/28/94	73
Regulating Pesticides	08/06/99	665
Regulating Toxic Chemicals	01/23/09	49
Repetitive Stress Injuries	06/23/95	537
Rethinking Ritalin	10/22/99	905
Right to Die	05/13/05	421
Sexually Transmitted Diseases	12/03/04	997
Sleep Deprivation	06/26/98	553
Sleep Deprivation	02/12/10	121
Smallpox Threat	02/07/03	105
Stem Cell Research	09/01/06	**697
Students Under Stress	07/13/07	577
Sugar Controversies	11/30/12	1013
Threatened Fisheries	08/02/02	634*
Tobacco Industry	12/10/04	**1025
Treating ADHD	08/03/12	669
Treating Alzheimer's	03/04/11	193
Treating Anxiety	02/08/02	97
Treating Depression	06/26/09	573
Treatment of Veterans	11/19/04	973
Universal Coverage	03/30/07	265
Vaccine Controversies	08/25/00	641
Water Quality	02/11/94	121
Weapons of Mass Destruction	03/08/02	193
Women's Health	11/07/03	941
District of Columbia		
D.C. Voting Rights	04/11/08	313*
Downtown Renaissance	06/23/06	**553
Foster Care Crisis	09/27/91	719*
Governing Washington, D.C.	11/22/96	1033
Gun Control Debate	11/12/04	949
Infant Mortality	07/31/92	647*
Public Housing	09/10/93	793
Student Journalism	06/05/98	498*
Diversity awareness training		
Diversity in the Workplace	10/10/97	894*
Police Corruption	11/24/95	1058*
Policing the Police	03/17/00	209
Race in America	07/11/03	593
Religion in the Workplace	08/23/02	649
Divorce. ***See Family***		
DNA analysis		
Biology and Behavior	04/03/98	289
DNA Databases	05/28/99	449
Eyewitness Testimony	10/14/11	853
Genes and Health	01/21/11	49
Human Genome Research	05/12/00	401
Mass Extinction	09/15/00	728*
Privacy in the Workplace	11/19/93	1023*

 *Indicates sidebar or "At Issue" report section. **Indicates an updated report.

	Date	Page
Public Defenders	04/18/08	337*
Science in the Courtroom	10/22/93	924*
Serial Killers	10/31/03	917
Wrongful Convictions	04/17/09	**345
Doctors. ***See Physicians***		
Domestic partners. ***See Family***		
Domestic violence		
Domestic Violence	01/06/06	1
Future of Marriage	05/07/04	397
Gay Marriage	09/05/03	736*
Treating Anxiety	02/08/02	97
Violence Against Women	02/26/93	169
Women and Human Rights	04/30/99	366*
"Downsizing." ***See Corporate mergers***		
Draft. ***See Military service***		
Drinking. ***See Alcohol; Drunken driving***		
Drinking water		
Bush and the Environment	10/25/02	865
Fracking Controversy	12/16/11	1049
Global Water Shortages	12/15/95	1113
Water Quality	02/11/94	121
Water Shortages	08/01/03	649
Drought		
Global Food Crisis	06/27/08	553
Drug abuse. ***See also Alcohol***		
AIDS Update	12/04/98	1055*
American Indians	04/28/06	**361
Athletes and Drugs	07/26/91	513
Centennial Olympic Games	04/05/96	289
Childhood Depression	07/16/99	593
Child Poverty	10/28/11	901
Combating Addiction	02/09/07	121
Combating AIDS	04/21/95	350*
Community Prosecution	12/15/00	1014*
Downsizing Prisons	03/11/11	217
Drug-Policy Debate	07/28/00	593
Ending Homelessness	06/18/04	541
Faith-Based Initiatives	05/04/01	382*
High School Sports	09/22/95	825
Infant Mortality	07/31/92	650
Legalizing Marijuana	06/12/09	**525
Marijuana Laws	02/11/05	125
Medical Marijuana	08/20/99	705
Methamphetamine	07/15/05	589
Mexico's Drug War	12/12/08	1009
Preventing Teen Drug Use	03/15/02	217
Prison Health Care	01/05/07	1
Prostitution	06/11/93	505
Prostitution Debate	05/23/08	433
Regulating Tobacco	09/30/94	841
Rethinking Ritalin	10/22/99	905
Sports and Drugs	07/23/04	**613
Student Rights	06/05/09	501
Teen Driving	01/07/05	1
Teen Drug Use	06/03/11	481
Three-Strikes Laws	05/10/02	417
Treating Addiction	01/06/95	1
Treating ADHD	08/03/12	669
War on Drugs	03/19/93	241
War on Drugs	06/02/06	481
Women and AIDS	12/25/92	1121
The Working Poor	11/03/95	982*
Drug abuse — Testing		
Drug Testing	11/20/98	1001
Medication Abuse	10/09/09	837
Privacy in the Workplace	11/19/93	1021*
Sentencing Debates	11/05/04	925
Drug traffic		
Afghanistan Dilemma	08/07/09	**669*
Change in Latin America	07/21/06	601
Declining Crime Rates	04/04/97	289
Democracy in Latin America	11/03/00	896*
Drug-Policy Debate	07/28/00	593
Foreign Aid After Sept. 11	04/26/02	383*
Gangs in the U.S.	07/16/10	581
Haiti's Dilemma	02/18/05	149
Legalizing Marijuana	06/12/09	**525
Mandatory Sentencing	05/26/95	465
Mexico's Drug War	12/12/08	1009
Mexico's Future	09/19/97	817
Mexico's Future	10/26/12	913
Prison-Building Boom	09/17/99	801
Prisoner Reentry	12/04/09	1005
Reassessing the Nation's Gun Laws	03/22/91	157
Rethinking Ritalin	10/22/99	922*
Sentencing Debates	11/05/04	925
Three-Strikes Laws	05/10/02	417
Treating Addiction	01/06/95	10*
Underground Economy	03/04/94	193
U.S.-Mexico Relations	11/09/01	921
War on Drugs	03/19/93	241
War on Drugs	06/02/06	481
Youth Gangs	10/11/91	753
Drugs and pharmaceutical industry		
Advances in Cancer Research	08/25/95	753
Advertising Overload	01/23/04	56*
AIDS Update	12/04/98	1049
Alternative Medicine's Next Phase	02/14/97	121
Alzheimer's Disease	05/15/98	433
Assisted Suicide Controversy	05/05/95	406*
Asthma Epidemic	12/24/99	1096*
Avian Flu Threat	01/13/06	25
Baby Boomers at Midlife	07/31/98	649
Biology and Behavior	04/03/98	307*
Birth Control Choices	07/29/94	649
Birth-Control Debate	06/24/05	565
Cancer Treatments	09/11/98	785

	Date	Page
Childhood Depression	07/16/99	593
Childhood Immunizations	06/18/93	529
Chronic Fatigue Syndrome	04/05/02	289
Combating AIDS	04/21/95	345
Cosmetic Surgery	04/15/05	317
Covering the Uninsured	06/14/02	521
Depression	10/09/92	857
Dietary Supplements	09/03/04	709
Dieting and Health	04/14/95	339*
Drug Company Ethics	06/06/03	521
Drugmakers Under Siege	09/03/99	753
Drug-Resistant Bacteria	06/04/99	473
Drug Safety	03/11/05	221
Gene Therapy's Future	12/08/95	1089
Legalizing Marijuana	06/12/09	**525
Limiting Lawsuits	12/19/08	1033
Marijuana Laws	02/11/05	125
Medical Marijuana	08/20/99	705
Medicare Reform	08/22/03	673
Medication Abuse	10/09/09	837
Mental Illness Medication Debate	02/06/04	101
Nanotechnology	06/11/04	517
The New Corporate Philanthropy	02/27/98	174*
Obesity and Health	01/15/99	25
Organ Shortage	02/21/03	153
Organ Transplants	08/11/95	713*
Patent Disputes	12/15/06	1033
Prescription Drug Prices	07/17/92	597
Preventing Cancer	01/16/09	25
Prozac Controversy	08/19/94	721
Punishing Sex Offenders	01/12/96	32*
Reforming the FDA	06/06/97	481
Rethinking Ritalin	10/22/99	905
Rising Health Costs	04/07/06	289
Saving the Rain Forests	06/11/99	497
Science in the Courtroom	10/22/93	913
Sexually Transmitted Diseases	12/03/04	997
Sleep Deprivation	06/26/98	553
Treating Addiction	01/06/95	16*
Treating Alzheimer's	03/04/11	193
Treating Anxiety	02/08/02	104*
Vaccine Controversies	08/25/00	641
Women's Health	11/07/03	941
Youth Suicide	02/13/04	125
Drunken driving		
Drinking on Campus	03/20/98	241
Drinking on Campus	08/18/06	649
Drunken Driving	10/06/00	793
Highway Safety	07/14/95	609
Teen Driving	01/07/05	1
Underage Drinking	03/13/92	217
E-mail		
Advertising Overload	01/23/04	49
Cyber-Predators	03/01/02	169
Cybersecurity	09/26/03	797
Privacy in the Workplace	11/19/93	1013*
Regulating the Internet	06/30/95	561
Earmarks		
Pork Barrel Politics	06/16/06	529
Earth Day		
Bush and the Environment	10/25/02	865
Environmental Movement at 25	03/31/95	273
Earthquakes		
Disaster Response	10/15/93	889
Earthquake Research	12/16/94	1105
Earthquake Threat	04/09/10	313
Eastern Europe		
Blighted Cities	11/12/10	941*
Democracy in Eastern Europe	10/08/99	865
Europe 1992	06/28/91	417
Expanding NATO	05/16/97	433
Future of NATO	02/28/03	177
The Greening of Eastern Europe	11/15/91	849
Human Trafficking and Slavery	03/26/04	273
Peace Corps' Challenges in the 1990s	01/25/91	49
Privatizing Government Services	08/09/96	708*
Russia's Political Future	05/03/96	385
Eating disorders		
Depression	10/09/92	869
Eating Disorders	12/18/92	1097
Eating Disorders	02/10/06	**121
Obesity Epidemic	01/31/03	73
Prozac Controversy	08/19/94	721
Women's Health	11/07/03	941
Economic conditions		
3D Printing	12/07/12	1037
Affordable Housing	02/09/01	89
Aging Baby Boomers	10/19/07	865
Aging Population	07/15/11	577
America's Border Fence	09/19/08	745
Antitrust Policy	06/12/98	505
Arms Sales	12/09/94	1097*
Assessing the New Health Care Law	09/21/12	789
Attracting Jobs	03/02/12	205
Auto Industry's Future	02/06/09	**105
Big-Box Stores	09/10/04	733
Budget Surplus	04/13/01	307*
Business Bankruptcy	04/10/09	321
Changing Demographics	11/16/12	989
Child Poverty	10/28/11	901
Confronting Warming	01/09/09	1
The Consumer Culture	11/19/99	1001
Consumer Debt	11/15/96	1009
Cost of the Iraq War	04/25/08	361*
Covering the Uninsured	06/14/02	521
Criminal Records and Employment	04/20/12	349
Crisis on the Plains	05/09/03	417

 *Indicates sidebar or "At Issue" report section. **Indicates an updated report.

	Date	Page
Curbing CEO Pay	03/09/07	217
Cyber-Crime	04/12/02	321*
Debate Over Immigration	07/14/00	569
Debt Collectors	07/20/12	621
Democracy in Latin America	11/03/00	881
Democrats' Future	10/29/10	893
Deflation Fears	02/13/98	121
Domestic Poverty	09/07/07	**721
Downtown Renaissance	06/23/06	**553
Downward Mobility	07/23/93	625
Ending Homelessness	06/18/04	541
Euro Crisis	10/05/12	841
Exporting Jobs	02/20/04	149
Famine in Africa	11/08/02	921
The Federal Reserve	09/01/00	673
Financial Bailout	10/24/08	**865
Financial Crisis	05/09/08	409
Financial Industry Overhaul	07/30/10	629
Financial Literacy	09/04/09	717
Financial Misconduct	01/20/12	53
Fracking Controversy	12/16/11	1049
Future of the Airline Industry	06/21/02	545
Future of Homeownership	12/14/12	1061
Future Job Market	01/11/02	1
Hate Groups	05/08/09	421
Health-Care Reform	06/11/10	**505
High-Speed Trains	05/01/09	**397
Housing the Homeless	12/18/09	1053
Identity Theft	06/10/05	517
Illegal Immigration	04/24/92	361
Illegal Immigration	05/06/05	393
Immigration Conflict	03/09/12	229
Income Inequality	04/17/98	337
Income Inequality	12/03/10	989
Internet Regulation	04/13/12	325
Jobs in the '90s	02/28/92	169
Jobs Outlook	06/04/10	481
Latinos' Future	10/17/03	869
Legal-Aid Crisis	10/07/11	829
Middle-Class Squeeze	03/06/09	201
Mortgage Crisis	11/02/07	**913
Mutual Funds	05/20/94	433
The National Debt	11/14/08	937
National Debt	03/18/11	241
The Obama Presidency	01/30/09	73
'Occupy' Movement	01/13/12	25
Oil Jitters	01/04/08	**1
Presidential Election	02/03/12	101
Public-Works Projects	02/20/09	153
Puerto Rico: The Struggle over Status	02/08/91	81
Racial Diversity in Public Schools	09/14/07	**745
Recession's Regional Impact	02/01/91	65
Regulating Credit Cards	10/10/08	817*
Rethinking Retirement	06/19/09	549
Retirement Security	05/31/02	481
Reviving Manufacturing	07/22/11	601
Rise of Megachurches	09/21/07	769
Saving Social Security	10/02/98	857
Science in America	01/11/08	25
State Budget Crises	10/03/03	821
State Budget Crisis	09/11/09	741
Stimulating the Economy	01/10/03	1
The Stock Market	05/02/97	385
Stock Market Troubles	01/16/04	25
Straining the Safety Net	07/31/09	645
Student Aid	01/25/08	73
Student Debt	10/21/11	877
Tax Reform	03/22/96	241
Teen Pregnancy	03/26/10	265*
Truck Safety	03/12/99	209
Underground Economy	03/04/94	193
Unemployment Benefits	04/25/03	369
Upward Mobility	04/29/05	369
U.S. Auto Industry	10/16/92	884*
The Value of a College Education	11/20/09	981
Vanishing Jobs	03/13/09	225
Water Crisis in the West	12/09/11	1025
Welfare Reform	04/10/92	327
The Working Poor	11/03/95	969
Economic conditions — International		
Aid to Russia	03/12/93	217
Aiding Africa	08/29/03	697
Castro's Next Move	12/12/97	1081
China After Deng	06/13/97	505
Declining Birthrates	11/21/08	961
Deflation Fears	02/13/98	121
Democracy in the Arab World	01/30/04	73
Earthquake Threat	04/09/10	313
Emerging China	11/11/05	957
Euro Crisis	10/05/12	841
European Monetary Union	11/27/98	1025
Exporting Jobs	02/20/04	149
Fair Trade Labeling	05/18/07	433
Famine in Africa	11/08/02	921
Fighting SARS	06/20/03	581*
The Future of U.S.-Russia Relations	01/18/02	25
Global Food Crisis	06/27/08	553
The Greening of Eastern Europe	11/15/91	849
Haiti's Dilemma	02/18/05	149
Holocaust Reparations	03/26/99	257
International Monetary Fund	01/29/99	65
Japan in Crisis	07/26/02	593
Mexico's Future	09/19/97	817
The New CIA	12/11/92	1073
Oil Jitters	01/04/08	**1
Privatization	11/13/92	991*
Reform in Iran	12/18/98	1097
Reforming the CIA	02/02/96	97

	Date	Page
Reviving Manufacturing	07/22/11	601
Saving Social Security	10/02/98	871*
Smart Cities	07/27/12	645
South Africa's Future	01/14/94	25
Student Aid	01/25/08	73
Russia's Political Future	05/03/96	385
Trouble in South America	03/14/03	225
Underground Economy	03/04/94	206*
U.S.-Europe Relations	03/23/12	277
U.S.-Russian Relations	05/22/98	457
Y2K Dilemma	02/19/99	137
Economic development		
Aiding Africa	08/29/03	697
Change in Latin America	07/21/06	601
Coastal Development	08/21/98	721
Declining Birthrates	11/21/08	961
Democracy in the Arab World	01/30/04	73
Downtown Renaissance	06/23/06	**553
Earthquake Threat	04/09/10	313
Emerging India	04/19/02	329
Energy Security	02/01/02	73
Exporting Jobs	02/20/04	149
Famine in Africa	11/08/02	921
Farm Subsidies	05/17/02	438*
Gambling Under Attack	09/06/96	769
Global Water Shortages	12/15/95	1113
Historic Preservation	10/07/94	865
Jobs vs. Environment	05/15/92	409
National Parks	05/28/93	457
Native Americans	05/08/92	400
Native Americans' Future	07/12/96	601
Population and the Environment	07/17/98	601
Property Rights	03/04/05	197
Protecting Endangered Species	04/19/96	337
Puerto Rico: The Struggle over Status	02/08/91	81
Reassessing Foreign Aid	09/27/96	841
Regulating the New Economy	10/19/01	849
Revitalizing the Cities	10/13/95	897
Saving Open Spaces	11/05/99	953
Stimulating the Economy	01/10/03	1
Threatened Coastlines	02/07/92	97
Trouble in South America	03/14/03	225
Upward Mobility	04/29/05	369
Water Crisis in the West	12/09/11	1025
Economic espionage		
The New CIA	12/11/92	1089
Reforming the CIA	02/02/96	97
Economic sanctions		
Economic Sanctions	10/28/94	937
Reform in Iran	12/18/98	1097
South Africa's Future	01/14/94	39*
U.S.-Vietnam Relations	12/03/93	1068*

	Date	Page
Ecotourism		
Ecotourism	10/20/06	865
Panama Canal	11/26/99	1031*
Saving the Rain Forests	06/11/99	506*

Education. ***See Colleges and universities; Education standards; Elementary and secondary education; Libraries; Preschool education; Special education; Student aid***

	Date	Page
Education Amendments Act, 1972 (Title IX)		
College Sports	08/26/94	745
Future of Books	05/29/09	**473
Gender Equity in Sports	04/18/97	337
High School Sports	09/22/95	825
Reforming Big-Time College Sports	03/19/04	249
Revising No Child Left Behind	04/16/10	337
Single-Sex Education	07/12/02	580*
Soccer in America	04/22/94	351*
State Budget Crisis	09/11/09	741
Women and Sports	03/06/92	193
Women in Sports	05/11/01	401
Women and Sports	03/25/11	265
Youth Fitness	09/26/97	846*
Education standards		
AB and IP Programs	03/03/06	193
Affirmative Action	10/17/08	**841
American Indians	04/28/06	**361
Bilingual Education vs. English Immersion	12/11/09	1029
Career Colleges	01/07/11	1
Charter Schools	12/20/02	1033
Cheating in Schools	09/22/00	745
College Football	11/18/11	977
Combating Plagiarism	09/19/03	773
Digital Education	12/02/11	1001
Educating Gifted Students	03/28/97	265
Education Standards	03/11/94	217
Fixing Urban Schools	04/27/07	**361
Future of Libraries	07/29/11	625
Gender and Learning	05/20/05	445
Government and Religion	01/15/10	25
Grade Inflation	06/07/02	505
Home Schooling Debate	01/17/03	25
Homework Debate	12/06/02	993
Impact of the Internet on Thinking	09/24/10	773
Internet Accuracy	08/01/08	625
Low Voter Turnout	10/20/00	833
National Education Standards	05/14/99	401
No Child Left Behind	05/27/05	469
Racial Diversity in Public Schools	09/14/07	**745
Reading Crisis?	02/22/08	169
Reforming Big-Time College Sports	03/19/04	249
Reforming School Funding	12/10/99	1047*
Revising No Child Left Behind	04/16/10	337

 *Indicates sidebar or "At Issue" report section. **Indicates an updated report.

	Date	Page
School Funding	08/27/93	760*
School Reform	04/29/11	385
School Vouchers	04/09/99	281
School Vouchers Showdown	02/15/02	121
Science in America	01/11/08	25
Student Aid	01/25/08	73
Student Debt	10/21/11	877
Students Under Stress	07/13/07	577
Teacher Education	10/17/97	913
Teaching History	09/29/95	849
Teaching Math and Science	09/06/02	697
Upward Mobility	04/29/05	369
The Value of a College Education	11/20/09	981
Youth Volunteerism	01/27/12	77
Egypt		
Archaeology Today	05/24/02	457
Democracy in the Arab World	01/30/04	73
Exporting Democracy	04/01/05	269
Foreign Aid After Sept. 11	04/26/02	361
Reassessing Foreign Aid	09/27/96	848*
Understanding Islam	11/03/06	913
Elderly. ***See also Social Security***		
Age Discrimination	08/01/97	673
Alzheimer's Disease	07/24/92	617
Alzheimer's Disease	05/15/98	433
Assisted Suicide	02/21/92	145
Baby Boomers at Midlife	07/31/98	649
Cancer Treatments	09/11/98	803*
Caring for the Elderly	02/20/98	145
Caring for the Elderly	10/13/06	841
Changing Demographics	11/16/12	989
Covering the Uninsured	06/14/02	521
Cracking Down on Immigration	02/03/95	109*
Drug Company Ethics	06/06/03	521
Flexible Work Arrangements	08/14/98	715*
Medicare Reform	08/22/03	673
Medicaid Reform	07/16/04	589
National Service	06/30/06	577
Patients' Rights	02/06/98	108*
Preventing Memory Loss	04/04/08	289*
Prolonging Life	09/30/11	805*
Retiree Health Benefits	12/06/91	921
Retirement Security	05/31/02	481
Right to Die	05/13/05	421
Rising Health Costs	04/07/06	289
Treating Alzheimer's	03/04/11	193
Youth Fitness	09/26/97	858*
Elections. ***See also Campaign finance; Presidential elections; Term limits; Voting and voting rights***		
Judicial Elections	04/24/09	373
Electric cars. ***See Automobiles and automobile industry***		
Electric power		
Acid Rain: New Approach to Old Problem	03/08/91	129
Aging Infrastructure	09/28/07	**793
Air Pollution Conflict	11/14/03	965
Alternative Energy	07/10/92	573
Alternative Energy	02/25/05	173
Buying Green	02/29/08	193
Coal's Comeback	10/05/07	817
Confronting Warming	01/09/09	1
Electromagnetic Fields	04/26/91	237
Energy and the Environment	03/03/00	161
Energy Policy	05/20/11	457
Modernizing the Grid	02/19/10	145
Nanotechnology	06/11/04	517
Nuclear Power	06/10/11	505
The Politics of Energy	03/05/99	185
Reducing Your Carbon Footprint	12/05/08	985
Renewable Energy	11/07/97	961
Restructuring the Electric Industry	01/17/97	25
Setting Environmental Priorities	05/21/99	438*
Will Nuclear Power Get Another Chance?	02/22/91	113
Wind Power	04/01/11	289
Electromagnetic waves		
Airline Safety	10/08/93	882*
Archaeology Today	05/24/02	457
Electromagnetic Fields	04/26/91	237
Science in the Courtroom	10/22/93	913
Electronic surveillance		
Cyber-Crime	04/12/02	305
Nanotechnology	06/11/04	517
Privacy in the Workplace	11/19/93	1009
Privacy Under Attack	06/15/01	505
Elementary and secondary education		
AB and IP Programs	03/03/06	193
Advertising Overload	01/23/04	49
Arts Education	03/16/12	253
Arts Funding	10/21/94	921*
Attack on Public Schools	07/26/96	649
Bilingual Education	08/13/93	697
Bilingual Education vs. English Immersion	12/11/09	1029
Boys' Emotional Needs	06/18/99	521
Bullying	02/04/05	101
Business' Role in Education	11/22/91	873
Catholic Church in the U.S.	09/08/95	791*
Charter Schools	12/20/02	1033
Cheating in Schools	09/22/00	745
Childhood Depression	07/16/99	593
Children's Television	08/15/97	721

	Date	Page
Child Welfare Reform	04/22/05	345
Combating Plagiarism	09/19/03	779*
Consumer Debt	11/15/96	1020*
Debate over Bilingualism	01/19/96	49
Diabetes Epidemic	03/09/01	192*
The Digital Divide	01/28/00	58*
Discipline in Schools	02/15/08	145
Distance Learning	12/07/01	993
Educating Gifted Students	03/28/97	265
Education and Gender	06/03/94	481
Education Standards	03/11/94	217
Encouraging Teen Abstinence	07/10/98	577
Evolution vs. Creationism	08/22/97	745
Faith-Based Initiatives	05/04/01	391*
Financial Literacy	09/04/09	717
Fixing Urban Schools	04/27/07	**361
Free-Press Disputes	04/08/05	293
Gangs in the U.S.	07/16/10	581
Gay Rights	03/05/93	207*
Gender and Learning	05/20/05	445
Gender Equity in Sports	04/18/97	337
Getting into College	02/23/96	169
Head Start	04/09/93	289
High School Sports	09/22/95	825
Hispanic Americans	10/30/92	929
Hispanic-Americans' New Clout	09/18/98	823*
Home Schooling	09/09/94	769
Home Schooling Debate	01/17/03	25
Homework Debate	12/06/02	993
Implementing the Disabilities Act	12/20/96	1105
Intelligence Testing	07/30/93	649
Intelligent Design	07/29/05	637
Jobs in the '90s	02/28/92	169
Kids in Prison	04/27/01	350*
Learning Disabilities	12/10/93	1081
Learning to Read	05/19/95	441
Libraries and the Internet	06/01/01	477*
National Debt	03/18/11	241
National Education Standards	05/14/99	401
National Service	06/25/93	564*
Networking the Classroom	10/20/95	921
The New Volunteerism	12/13/96	1086*
No Child Left Behind	05/27/05	469
Parental Rights	10/25/96	937
Parents and Schools	01/20/95	49
Patriotism in America	06/25/99	545
Physical Fitness	11/06/92	958*
Preventing Juvenile Crime	03/15/96	217
Preventing Teen Drug Use	07/28/95	657
Private Management of Public Schools	03/25/94	265
Privatization	11/13/92	988*
Professional Football	01/29/10	**73
Public Broadcasting	09/18/92	827*
Public-Employee Unions	04/08/11	313
Racial Diversity in Public Schools	09/14/07	**745
Racial Tensions in Schools	01/07/94	1
Reforming School Funding	12/10/99	1041
Religion in Schools	01/12/01	1
Rethinking School Integration	10/18/96	913
Revising No Child Left Behind	04/16/10	337
School Censorship	02/19/93	145
School Choice Debate	07/18/97	625
School Desegregation	04/23/04	345
School Funding	08/27/93	745
School Reform	04/29/11	385
School Violence	10/09/98	881
School Vouchers	04/09/99	281
School Vouchers Showdown	02/15/02	121
Science in America	01/11/08	25
Single-Sex Education	07/12/02	569
Sexually Transmitted Diseases	12/03/04	997
Sleep Deprivation	06/26/98	553
Special Education	11/10/00	905
Student Journalism	06/05/98	481
Student Rights	06/05/09	501
Teacher Education	10/17/97	913
Teacher Shortages	08/24/01	633
Teaching History	09/29/95	849
Teaching Math and Science	09/06/02	697
Teaching Values	06/21/96	529
Teenage Suicide	06/14/91	385*
Teen Driving	01/07/05	1
Teen Sex	09/16/05	761
Testing in Schools	04/20/01	321
Treating ADHD	08/03/12	669
Upward Mobility	04/29/05	369
Violence in Schools	09/11/92	785
Year-Round Schools	05/17/96	433
Youth Apprenticeships	10/23/92	905
Youth Fitness	09/26/97	841
Youth Violence	03/05/10	193*
Zero Tolerance	03/10/00	185

Embryos. ***See Fetal tissue research***

Employee-assistance programs

	Date	Page
Job Stress	08/04/95	681
Retirement Security	05/31/02	481
Treating Addiction	01/06/95	15*
Unemployment Benefits	04/25/03	369

Employment and unemployment. ***See also Discrimination; Job stress; Job training; Occupational health and safety; Pensions; Social Security; Wages and salaries***

	Date	Page
Accountants Under Fire	03/22/02	252*
Affirmative Action	10/17/08	**841
America's Border Fence	09/19/08	745
Arms Sales	12/09/94	1089*
Artificial Intelligence	04/22/11	361

 *Indicates sidebar or "At Issue" report section. **Indicates an updated report.

	Date	Page
Attracting Jobs	03/02/12	205
Auto Industry's Future	02/06/09	**105
Bilingual Education	08/13/93	734*
Business Bankruptcy	04/10/09	321
Business Ethics	05/06/11	409
Career Colleges	01/07/11	1
Child-Care Options	05/08/98	409
Child Labor and Sweatshops	08/16/96	721
Class Action Lawsuits	05/13/11	433
Contingent Work Force	10/24/97	937
Crackdown on Smoking	12/04/92	1049
Criminal Records and Employment	04/20/12	349
Curbing CEO Pay	03/09/07	217
Debate Over Immigration	07/14/00	569
Diversity in the Workplace	10/10/97	889
Domestic Partners	09/04/92	761
Domestic Poverty	09/07/07	**721
Downward Mobility	07/23/93	625
Drug Testing	11/20/98	1001
Employee Benefits	02/04/00	65
Exporting Jobs	02/20/04	149
Fairness in Salaries	05/29/92	457
Fast-Food Shake-Up	11/08/91	825
Flexible Work Arrangements	08/14/98	697
Future Job Market	01/11/02	1
Future of Feminism	04/14/06	313
Future of the European Union	10/28/05	909
High-Tech Labor Shortage	04/24/98	361
Illegal Immigration	04/24/92	361
Illegal Immigration	05/06/05	393
Immigration Debate	02/01/08	**97
Immigration Reform	09/24/93	841
Implementing the Disabilities Act	12/20/96	1105
Income Inequality	12/03/10	989
Intelligence Testing	07/30/93	649
Job Stress	08/04/95	681
Jobs in the '90s	02/28/92	169
Jobs vs. Environment	05/15/92	409
Jobs Outlook	06/04/10	481
Labor Movement's Future	06/28/96	553
Latinos' Future	10/17/03	869
Liberal Arts Education	04/10/98	313
Living-Wage Movement	09/27/02	769
Managing Managed Care	04/16/99	317*
Middle-Class Squeeze	03/06/09	201
Minimum Wage	12/16/05	1053
Mothers' Movement	04/04/03	297
National Service	06/25/93	553
'Occupy' Movement	01/13/12	25
Paying for College	11/20/92	1001
Prison-Building Boom	09/17/99	813*
Prisoner Reentry	12/04/09	1005
Privacy in the Workplace	11/19/93	1009
Public-Employee Unions	04/08/11	313
Public-Works Projects	02/20/09	153
Recession's Regional Impact	02/01/91	65
Rethinking NAFTA	06/07/96	481
Rethinking Retirement	06/19/09	549
Retirement Security	05/31/02	481
Reviving Manufacturing	07/22/11	601
Rising College Costs	12/05/03	1013
Science in America	01/11/08	25
Sexual Harassment	04/27/12	377
Should the U.S. Reinstate the Draft?	01/11/91	17
Sleep Deprivation	06/26/98	561*
Stimulating the Economy	01/10/03	1
Straining the Safety Net	07/31/09	645
Too Many Lawsuits?	05/22/92	440
Transatlantic Tensions	07/13/01	566*
Underground Economy	03/04/94	193
Unemployment Benefits	04/25/03	369
Upward Mobility	04/29/05	369
U.S. Auto Industry	10/16/92	895
The Value of a College Education	11/20/09	981
Vanishing Jobs	03/13/09	225
Welfare Reform	04/10/92	313
Welfare, Work and the States	12/06/96	1057
Whistleblowers	12/05/97	1057
Work, Family and Stress	08/14/92	689
Worker Retraining	01/21/94	49
The Working Poor	11/03/95	969
Youth Apprenticeships	10/23/92	905
Endangered species		
Animal Rights	01/08/10	1
Bush and the Environment	10/25/02	865
Disappearing Species	11/30/07	985
Ecotourism	10/20/06	865
Endangered Species	06/21/91	393
Endangered Species Act	10/01/99	849
Endangered Species Act	06/03/05	**493
Environmental Movement at 25	03/31/95	283*
Hunting Controversy	01/24/92	49
Jobs vs. Environment	05/15/92	409
Marine Mammals vs. Fish	08/28/92	737
Mass Extinction	09/15/00	713
National Parks Under Pressure	10/06/06	817
Property Rights	06/16/95	513
Protecting Endangered Species	04/19/96	337
Protecting Wetlands	10/03/08	793*
Public Land Policy	06/17/94	542*
Saving the Forests	09/20/91	697*
Saving the Rain Forests	06/11/99	497
Science and Politics	08/20/04	661
Setting Environmental Priorities	05/21/99	425
Slow Food Movement	01/26/07	73
Threatened Fisheries	08/02/02	617

	Date	Page
Energy policy. ***See also Coal; Electric power; Nuclear power plants; Petroleum***		
Air Pollution Conflict	11/14/03	965
Alternative Energy	07/10/92	573
Alternative Energy	02/25/05	173
Biofuels Boom	09/29/06	793
Bush and the Environment	10/25/02	865
Buying Green	02/29/08	193
Climate Change	01/27/06	73
Coal's Comeback	10/05/07	817
Confronting Iraq	10/04/02	793
Confronting Warming	01/09/09	1
Dealing With the "New" Russia	06/06/08	481
Domestic Energy Development	09/30/05	809
Energy and Climate	07/24/09	621
Energy and the Environment	03/03/00	161
Energy Efficiency	05/19/06	433
Energy Policy	05/25/01	441
Energy Policy	05/20/11	457
Energy Security	02/01/02	73
Fracking Controversy	12/16/11	1049
Future of Recycling	12/14/07	1033
The Future of U.S.-Russia Relations	01/18/02	40*
Global Warming Treaty	01/26/01	41
Gulf Coast Restoration	08/26/11	677*
Homeland Security	09/12/03	761*
Jobs Outlook	06/04/10	481
Managing Nuclear Waste	01/28/11	73
Managing Public Lands	11/04/11	929
Modernizing the Grid	02/19/10	145
Nuclear Energy	03/10/06	217
Nuclear Power	06/10/11	505
The Obama Presidency	01/30/09	73
Offshore Drilling	06/25/10	553
Oil Diplomacy	01/24/03	49
Oil Imports	08/23/91	585
Oil Jitters	01/04/08	**1
The Politics of Energy	03/05/99	185
Reducing Your Carbon Footprint	12/05/08	985
Renewable Energy	11/07/97	961
Socially Responsible Investing	08/29/08	673
SUV Debate	05/16/03	449
Utility Deregulation	01/14/00	1
Wind Power	04/01/11	289
English language. ***See Official English***		
Enron Corp. Scandal		
Accountants Under Fire	03/22/02	241
Corporate Crime	10/11/02	817
Financial Misconduct	01/20/12	53
Stock Market Troubles	01/16/04	25
Environmental protection		
Acid Rain: New Approach to Old Problem	03/08/91	129
Advertising Under Attack	09/13/91	671*
Affordable Housing	02/09/01	103*
Aging Infrastructure	09/28/07	**793
Air Pollution Conflict	11/14/03	965
Alternative Energy	07/10/92	573
Alternative Energy	02/25/05	173
Animal Intelligence	10/22/10	869
Asbestos Litigation	05/02/03	393
Biofuels Boom	09/29/06	793
Biotech Foods	03/30/01	249
Bush and the Environment	10/25/02	865
Buying Green	02/29/08	193
Cleaning Up Hazardous Wastes	08/23/96	745
Climate Change	01/27/06	73
Coal's Comeback	10/05/07	817
Coastal Development	08/21/98	721
The Consumer Culture	11/19/99	1005*
Disappearing Species	11/30/07	985
Domestic Energy Development	09/30/05	809
Downtown Renaissance	06/23/06	**553
The Economics of Recycling	03/27/98	265
Ecotourism	10/20/06	865
Electric Cars	07/09/93	577
Endangered Species	06/21/91	393
Endangered Species Act	10/01/99	849
Endangered Species Act	06/03/05	**493
Energy and Climate	07/24/09	621
Energy and the Environment	03/03/00	161
Energy Policy	05/25/01	441
Energy Policy	05/20/11	457
Energy Security	02/01/02	73
Environmental Justice	06/19/98	529
Environmental Movement at 25	03/31/95	273
Extreme Sports	04/03/09	297
Famine in Africa	11/08/02	921
Farm Policy	12/02/94	1057
Farm Policy	08/10/12	693
Farm Subsidies	05/17/02	433
Food Safety Battle: Organic v. Biotech	09/04/98	761
Future of Amtrak	10/18/02	841
Future of Recycling	12/14/07	1033
Garbage Crisis	03/20/92	241
Genetically Engineered Foods	08/05/94	686*
Genetically Modified Food	08/31/12	717
Global Warming Treaty	01/26/01	41
Global Warming Update	11/01/96	961
Global Water Shortages	12/15/95	1113
The Greening of Eastern Europe	11/15/91	849
The Growing Influence of Boycotts	01/04/91	1
Gulf Coast Restoration	08/26/11	677*
Human Rights in China	07/25/08	601
Indoor Air Pollution	10/27/95	945
Invasive Species	10/05/01	785
Invasive Species	02/17/12	153

 *Indicates sidebar or "At Issue" report section. **Indicates an updated report.

	Date	Page
Jobs vs. Environment	05/15/92	409
Managing Public Lands	11/04/11	929
Managing Wildfires	11/02/12	941
Marine Mammals vs. Fish	08/28/92	737
Mass Extinction	09/15/00	713
Mass Transit Boom	01/18/08	49
Mexico's Emergence	07/19/91	503*
Mine Safety	06/24/11	553
Modernizing the Grid	02/19/10	145
National Forests	10/16/98	905
National Parks	05/28/93	457
National Parks Under Pressure	10/06/06	817
New Air Quality Standards	03/07/97	193
The New CIA	12/11/92	1085*
The New Environmentalism	12/01/06	985
Nuclear Arms Cleanup	06/24/94	553
Nuclear Fusion	01/22/93	59*
Offshore Drilling	06/25/10	553
Oil Imports	08/23/91	585
Oil Spills	01/17/92	25
Ozone Depletion	04/03/92	289
Population and the Environment	07/17/98	601
Population Growth	07/16/93	601
Preventing Cancer	01/16/09	25
Property Rights	06/16/95	513
Protecting Endangered Species	04/19/96	337
Protecting the National Parks	06/16/00	521
Protecting Wetlands	10/03/08	793*
Public Land Policy	06/17/94	529
Reducing Your Carbon Footprint	12/05/08	985
Reforming the Corps	05/30/03	497
Regulating Pesticides	01/28/94	73
Regulating Pesticides	08/06/99	665
Renewable Energy	11/07/97	961
Restructuring the Electric Industry	01/17/97	31*
Saving Open Spaces	11/05/99	953
Saving the Forests	09/20/91	681
Saving the Oceans	11/04/05	933
Saving the Rainforests	06/11/99	511*
Science and Politics	08/20/04	661
Setting Environmental Priorities	05/21/99	425
Smart Cities	07/27/12	645
Smart Growth	05/28/04	469
Socially Responsible Investing	08/29/08	673
SUV Debate	05/16/03	449
Threatened Coastlines	02/07/92	97
Threatened Fisheries	08/02/02	617
Traffic Congestion	08/27/99	739*
Urban Sprawl in the West	10/03/97	865
Utility Deregulation	01/14/00	8*
Water Quality	02/11/94	121
Water Quality	11/24/00	953
Water Shortages	08/01/03	649
Water Shortages	06/18/10	529
Will Nuclear Power Get Another Chance?	02/22/91	113
Wind Power	04/01/11	289
Equal Employment Opportunity Commission		
Age Discrimination	08/01/97	673
Crackdown on Sexual Harassment	07/19/96	625
Latinos' Future	10/17/03	869
Mental Health Policy	09/12/97	793
Sexual Harassment	08/09/91	537
Ergonomics		
Worker Safety	05/21/04	456*
Espionage. ***See Intelligence service***		
Ethanol		
Global Food Crisis	06/27/08	553
Ethical and moral issues. ***See also Ethics in government; Medical ethics; Religion***		
Accountants Under Fire	03/22/02	241
Animal Rights	05/24/91	301
Broadcast Indecency	04/16/04	321
Bullying	02/04/05	101
Business Ethics	05/06/11	409
Catholic Church in the U.S.	09/08/95	777
Cell Phone Safety	03/16/01	208*
Cheating in Schools	09/22/00	745
Civic Renewal	03/21/97	241
The Cloning Controversy	05/09/97	409
Combating Plagiarism	09/19/03	773
Combating Scientific Misconduct	01/10/97	1
Computer Hacking	09/16/11	757*
The Consumer Culture	11/19/99	1001
Disappearing Species	11/30/07	985
Drug Company Ethics	06/06/03	521
Drug Safety	03/11/05	221
Encouraging Teen Abstinence	07/10/98	577
Ethics of War	12/13/02	1013
Financial Misconduct	01/20/12	53
Free-Press Disputes	04/08/05	293
Future of the Catholic Church	01/19/07	49
Future of the Music Industry	11/21/03	989
Gays in the Military	09/18/09	**765
Genetically Modified Food	08/31/12	717
High School Sports	09/22/95	825
Human Trafficking and Slavery	03/26/04	273
Hunting Controversy	01/24/92	49
Interrogating the CIA	09/25/09	789
Journalism Standards in the Internet Age	10/08/10	821
Journalism Under Fire	12/25/98	1129*
Lead Poisoning	06/19/92	529*
Marriage and Divorce	05/10/96	409
Mothers' Movement	04/04/03	297
Parental Rights	10/25/96	937
Patriotism in America	06/25/99	545

	Date	Page
Prayer and Healing	01/14/05	25
Protestants Today	12/07/07	1009
Punishing Sex Offenders	01/12/96	25
Race in America	07/11/03	593
Reforming Big-Time College Sports	03/19/04	249
Reproductive Ethics	05/15/09	449
Right to Die	05/13/05	421
Sentencing Debates	11/05/04	925
Sex on Campus	11/04/94	961
Sexually Transmitted Diseases	12/03/04	997
Sports and Drugs	07/23/04	**613
Sportsmanship	03/23/01	225
Stock Market Troubles	01/16/04	25
Stopping Genocide	08/27/04	685
Teaching Values	06/21/96	529
Three-Strikes Laws	05/10/02	417
Tobacco Industry	12/10/04	**1025
Torture	04/18/03	345
Understanding Mormonism	10/19/12	889
Ethnic groups. ***See Minorities***		
Ethics in government		
Drug Safety	03/11/05	221
Fighting SARS	06/20/03	569
Independent Counsels	02/21/97	145
Political Scandals	05/27/94	457
Politicians and Privacy	04/17/92	337
Pork Barrel Politics	06/16/06	529
Privatizing the Military	06/25/04	565
Property Rights	03/04/05	197
Protecting Whistleblowers	03/31/06	265
Europe and European Union		
Avian Flu Threat	01/13/06	25
Declining Birthrates	11/21/08	961
Democracy in Eastern Europe	10/08/99	865
Drinking on Campus	08/18/06	649
Euro Crisis	10/05/12	841
Europe 1992	06/28/91	417
European Monetary Union	11/27/98	1025
Europe's New Right	02/12/93	121
Expanding NATO	05/16/97	433
Exporting Democracy	04/01/05	269
Food Safety Battle: Organic v. Biotech	09/04/98	768*
Future of NATO	02/28/03	177
Future of the European Union	10/28/05	909
Future of Marriage	05/07/04	405*
Global Jihad	10/14/05	857
The Greening of Eastern Europe	11/15/91	866
Internet Privacy	11/06/98	962*
Mad Cow Disease	03/02/01	161
Middle East Tensions	10/27/06	**889
Missile Defense	09/08/00	700*
NATO's Changing Role	08/21/92	713
Oil Spills	01/17/92	36*
Population and the Environment	07/17/98	612*
Religious Persecution	11/21/97	1009
Revitalizing the Cities	10/13/95	902*
Russia and the Former Soviet Republics	06/17/05	541
Transatlantic Tensions	07/13/01	553
U.S. Auto Industry	10/16/92	894
U.S.-British Relations	01/30/98	73
U.S.-British Relations	11/05/10	917*
U.S.-Europe Relations	03/23/12	277
Euthanasia		
Assisted Suicide	02/21/92	145
Assisted Suicide Controversy	05/05/95	393
Caring for the Dying	09/05/97	780*
Right to Die	05/13/05	421
Everglades		
Invasive Species	02/17/12	153
Jobs vs. Environment	05/15/92	423*
National Parks	05/28/93	462*
Reforming the Corps	05/30/03	497
Evolution		
Evolution vs. Creationism	08/22/97	745
Intelligent Design	07/29/05	637
Religion in Schools	01/12/01	11*
Teaching Math and Science	09/06/02	697
Executions. ***See Death penalty***		
Exercise. ***See Physical fitness***		
Export controls		
Internet Privacy	11/06/98	961*
Non-Proliferation Treaty at 25	01/27/95	89*
Nuclear Proliferation	06/05/92	481
Exports. ***See International trade***		
Extraterrestrial life		
Pursuing the Paranormal	03/29/96	265
The Search for Extraterrestrials	03/05/04	197
Family. ***See also Adoption; Parents***		
Alzheimer's Disease	07/24/92	630*
Alzheimer's Disease	05/15/98	433
Birth-Control Debate	06/24/05	565
Child Care	12/17/93	1122*
Children and Divorce	06/07/91	349
Children and Divorce	01/19/01	25
Children's Legal Rights	04/23/93	337
Child Sexual Abuse	01/15/93	25
Child Welfare Reform	04/22/05	345
Declining Birthrates	11/21/08	961
Domestic Partners	09/04/92	761
Domestic Violence	01/06/06	1
Foster Care Crisis	09/27/91	705
Foster Care Reform	01/09/98	1
Future of Feminism	04/14/06	313
Future of Marriage	05/07/04	397

 *Indicates sidebar or "At Issue" report section. **Indicates an updated report.

	Date	Page
Gay Marriage	09/05/03	721
Gay Marriage Showdowns	09/26/08	**769
Marriage and Divorce	05/10/96	409
Mothers' Movement	04/04/03	297
New Military Culture	04/26/96	378*
Preventing Teen Pregnancy	05/14/93	409
Primary Care	03/17/95	217
Prostitution Debate	05/23/08	433
Recovered-Memory Debate	07/05/96	577
Religion in America	11/25/94	1033
Reproductive Ethics	05/15/09	449
Right to Die	05/13/05	421
Teen Pregnancy	03/26/10	265*
Family — Economic aspects		
Black Middle Class	01/23/98	63*
Caring for Veterans	04/23/10	361
Charitable Giving	11/12/93	991*
Child-Care Options	05/08/98	409
Child Poverty	04/07/00	281
Child Poverty	10/28/11	901
Children and Divorce	06/07/91	358*
Child Welfare Reform	04/22/05	345
Consumer Debt	11/15/96	1009
Covering the Uninsured	06/14/02	521
Declining Birthrates	11/21/08	961
Ending Homelessness	06/18/04	541
Future of Homeownership	12/14/12	1061
Gender Pay Gap	03/14/08	241
Getting into College	02/23/96	169
Income Inequality	04/17/98	337
Middle-Class Squeeze	03/06/09	201
Mothers' Movement	04/04/03	297
Paying for College	11/20/92	1001
Paying for Retirement	11/05/93	961
School Vouchers	04/09/99	281
School Vouchers Showdown	02/15/02	121
Straining the Safety Net	07/31/09	645
Tax Reform	03/22/96	241
Underground Economy	03/04/94	197*
Vanishing Jobs	03/13/09	225
Welfare Experiments	09/16/94	793
Welfare Reform	04/10/92	313
Welfare, Work and the States	12/06/96	1066*
Work, Family and Stress	08/14/92	689
The Working Poor	11/03/95	969
Wounded Veterans	08/31/07	697
Famine		
Global Food Crisis	06/27/08	553
Farming. ***See Agriculture***		
Fast-food restaurants		
Fast-Food Shake-Up	11/08/91	825
Obesity and Health	01/15/99	25
Obesity Epidemic	01/31/03	73

	Date	Page
Fathers		
Adoption	11/26/93	1033
Child Care	12/17/93	1119*
Domestic Violence	01/06/06	1
Fatherhood Movement	06/02/00	473
Gay Marriage	09/05/03	732*
Federal Bureau of Investigation		
Civil Liberties Debates	10/24/03	893
Combating Terrorism	07/21/95	633
Cyber-Crime	04/12/02	305
Cyber-Predators	03/01/02	169
Cybersecurity	09/26/03	797
The FBI Under Fire	04/11/97	313
Future of the Airline Industry	06/21/02	545
Gang Crisis	05/14/04	421
Homegrown Jihadists	09/03/10	701
Homeland Security	09/12/03	749
Identity Theft	06/10/05	517
Insurance Fraud	10/11/96	901*
Intelligence Reforms	01/24/02	49
Policing the Borders	02/22/02	145
Presidential Power	11/15/02	945
Re-examining 9/11	06/04/04	493
Serial Killers	10/31/03	917
War on Terrorism	10/12/01	817
Weapons of Mass Destruction	03/08/02	193
Federal Communications Commission		
Broadcast Indecency	04/16/04	321
Children's Television	08/15/97	721
The Future of Telecommunications	04/23/99	329
The Future of Television	12/23/94	1129
Indecency on Television	11/09/12	965
Media Ownership	10/10/03	**845
Pay-Per-View TV	10/04/91	729
Reality TV	08/27/10	677
Shock Jocks	06/01/07	**481
Talk Show Democracy	04/29/94	377*
Transition to Digital TV	06/20/08	529
Federal Election Commission		
Campaign Finance Reform	02/09/96	126*
Campaign Finance Showdown	11/22/02	969
Voting Controversies	09/15/06	745
Federal Emergency Management Agency		
Disaster Preparedness	11/18/05	**981
Rebuilding New Orleans	02/03/06	97
Federal government. ***See also Congress, U.S.; Regulation and deregulation; specific agencies and programs***		
Aging Infrastructure	09/28/07	**793
Air Pollution Conflict	11/14/03	965
American Indians	04/28/06	**361
Census Controversey	05/14/10	433
Conspiracy Theories	10/23/09	885
Cosmetic Surgery	04/15/05	317

	Date	Page
Democrats' Future	10/29/10	893
Disaster Preparedness	11/18/05	**981
Drone Warfare	08/06/10	653
Drug Safety	03/11/05	221
Ending Homelessness	06/18/04	541
Exporting Democracy	04/01/05	269
Financial Bailout	10/24/08	**865
Financial Industry Overhaul	07/30/10	629
Free-Press Disputes	04/08/05	293
Future of the Airline Industry	06/21/02	545
Future of Homeownership	12/14/12	1061
Gangs in the U.S.	07/16/10	581
Gridlock in Washington	04/30/10	385
Homeland Security	09/12/03	749
Homeland Security	02/13/09	129
Human Spaceflight	10/16/09	861
Legal-Aid Crisis	10/07/11	829
Managing Nuclear Waste	01/28/11	73
Medicaid Reform	07/16/04	589
Nanotechnology	06/11/04	517
The National Debt	11/14/08	937
National Debt	03/18/11	241
National Service	06/25/93	553
The Obama Presidency	01/30/09	73
Patent Disputes	12/15/06	1033
Policing the Borders	02/22/02	145
Privatizing Government Services	08/09/96	697
Prosecutors and Politics	06/22/07	553
Prostitution Debate	05/23/08	433
Protecting Whistleblowers	03/31/06	265
Public-Employee Unions	04/08/11	313
Public-Works Projects	02/20/09	153
Pursuing the Paranormal	03/29/96	265
Re-examining the Constitution	09/07/12	741
Reinventing Government	02/17/95	145
Renewable Energy	11/07/97	961
Reviving Manufacturing	07/22/11	601
Smart Growth	05/28/04	469
Space Program	02/24/12	177
State Budget Crises	10/03/03	837*
States and Federalism	09/13/96	793
States and Federalism	10/15/10	845
Tea Party Movement	03/19/10	**241*
Three-Strikes Laws	05/10/02	417
Water Shortages	08/01/03	665*
Y2K Dilemma	02/19/99	137
Water Crisis in the West	12/09/11	1025
Wind Power	04/01/11	289
Federal lands		
Bush and the Environment	10/25/02	865
Domestic Energy Development	09/30/05	809
Energy Security	02/01/02	73
Environmental Movement at 25	03/31/95	286*
Managing Public Lands	11/04/11	929
National Forests	10/16/98	905
National Parks	05/28/93	457
National Parks Under Pressure	10/06/06	817
Public Land Policy	06/17/94	529
Reforming the Corps	05/30/03	497
Saving Open Spaces	11/05/99	953
Setting Environmental Priorities	05/21/99	440*
Federal Reserve		
Deflation Fears	02/13/98	121
The Federal Reserve	09/01/00	673
Financial Bailout	10/24/08	**865
Financial Crisis	05/09/08	409
Financial Industry Overhaul	07/30/10	629
The National Debt	11/14/08	937
National Debt	03/18/11	241
Stimulating the Economy	01/10/03	1
The Stock Market	05/02/97	385
Federalism		
Deepening Canadian Crisis over Quebec	04/12/91	205
Marijuana Laws	02/11/05	125
National Education Standards	05/14/99	401
No Child Left Behind	05/27/05	469
Setting Environmental Priorities	05/21/99	431*
States and Federalism	09/13/96	793
Fetal tissue research		
Embryo Research	12/17/99	1065
Fetal Tissue Research	08/16/91	561
Organ Shortage	02/21/03	153
Organ Transplants	08/11/95	718*
Film. *See Movies*		
Firearms. *See also Arms control; Weapons*		
3D Printing	12/07/12	1037
Arms Sales	12/09/94	1092*
Declining Crime Rates	04/04/97	289
Discipline in Schools	02/15/08	145
Fighting Crime	02/08/08	121
Future of the Airline Industry	06/21/02	561*
Gang Crisis	05/14/04	421
Gangs in the U.S.	07/16/10	581
Gun Control	06/10/94	505
Gun Control Debate	11/12/04	949
Gun Control Standoff	12/19/97	1105
Gun Rights Debates	10/31/08	**889
Gun Violence	05/25/07	457
Haiti's Dilemma	02/18/05	149
High-Impact Litigation	02/11/00	89
Hunting Controversy	01/24/92	49
Juvenile Justice	02/25/94	169
Mexico's Drug War	12/12/08	1009
Mexico's Future	10/26/12	913
Reassessing the Nation's Gun Laws	03/22/91	167*

 *Indicates sidebar or "At Issue" report section. **Indicates an updated report.

	Date	Page
School Violence	10/09/98	881
Suburban Crime	09/03/93	782*
Violence in Schools	09/11/92	785
Youth Gangs	10/11/91	753
Youth Suicide	02/13/04	131*
First Amendment		
Abortion Debates	03/21/03	255*
Advertising Overload	01/23/04	49
Advertising Under Attack	09/13/91	657
Broadcast Indecency	04/16/04	321
Campaign Finance Debates	05/28/10	457
Campaign Finance Reform	02/09/96	121
Computer Hacking	09/16/11	757*
Courts and the Media	09/23/94	817
Crackdown on Sexual Harassment	07/19/96	642*
Cults in America	05/07/93	385
Cyberbullying	05/02/08	385
Cyber-Predators	03/01/02	169
Digital Commerce	02/05/99	89
Evolution vs. Creationism	08/22/97	749*
Faith-Based Initiatives	05/04/01	377
Free-Press Disputes	04/08/05	293
Future of Journalism	03/27/09	**273
Government and Religion	01/15/10	25
Government Secrecy	02/11/11	121
Hate Crimes	01/08/93	1
Libraries and the Internet	06/01/01	465
Movie Ratings	03/28/03	273
The Obscenity Debate	12/20/91	969
'Occupy' Movement	01/13/12	25
Press Freedom	02/05/10	97
Preventing Bullying	12/10/10	**1013
Protestants Today	12/07/07	1009
Regulating the Internet	06/30/95	561
Religion and Politics	10/14/94	889
Religion in Schools	02/18/94	145
Religion in Schools	01/12/01	1
Rise of Megachurches	09/21/07	769
School Censorship	02/19/93	145
School Choice Debate	07/18/97	630*
School Vouchers	04/09/99	281
Sex, Violence and the Media	11/17/95	1017
Sexual Harassment	08/09/91	537
Student Journalism	06/05/98	481
Student Rights	06/05/09	501
First Ladies		
First Ladies	06/14/96	505
Fish and fishing		
Acid Rain: New Approach to Old Problem	03/08/91	129
Coastal Development	08/21/98	739*
Disappearing Species	11/30/07	985
Endangered Species	06/21/91	406*
Endangered Species Act	10/01/99	854*
Endangered Species Act	06/03/05	**493
Fish Farming	07/27/07	625
Food Safety	06/04/93	481
Gulf Coast Restoration	08/26/11	677*
Invasive Species	02/17/12	153
Marine Mammals vs. Fish	08/28/92	737
Offshore Drilling	06/25/10	553
Protecting Endangered Species	04/19/96	337
Protecting Wetlands	10/03/08	793*
Saving the Oceans	11/04/05	933
Threatened Fisheries	08/02/02	617
Water Shortages	06/18/10	529
Fitness. *See Physical fitness*		
Flag desecration		
Patriotism in America	06/25/99	545
Floods		
Coastal Development	08/21/98	721
Disaster Response	10/15/93	889
Extreme Weather	09/09/11	733*
Farm Policy	12/02/94	1072*
Global Food Crisis	06/27/08	553
Reforming the Corps	05/30/03	497
Threatened Coastlines	02/07/92	97
Water Shortages	08/01/03	649
Florida		
Bilingual Education	08/13/93	708*
Cuba in Crisis	11/29/91	908*
Cuba's Future	07/20/07	601
Disaster Response	10/15/93	889
Electoral College	12/08/00	977
High-Speed Rail	04/16/93	327*
Kids in Prison	04/27/01	364*
Reforming the Corps	05/30/03	497
Rethinking the Death Penalty	11/16/01	960*
Water Quality	11/24/00	967*
Food and Drug Administration, U.S.		
Birth-Control Debate	06/24/05	565
Cancer Treatments	09/11/98	785
Closing In on Tobacco	11/12/99	977
Consumer Safety	10/12/07	841
Cosmetic Surgery	04/15/05	317
Dietary Supplements	07/08/94	577
Dietary Supplements	09/03/04	709
Drug Company Ethics	06/06/03	521
Drugmakers Under Siege	09/03/99	753
Drug Safety	03/11/05	221
Fish Farming	07/27/07	625
Food Irradiation	06/12/92	505
Food Safety	06/04/93	481
Food Safety	11/01/02	897
Food Safety	12/17/10	1037
Genetically Engineered Foods	08/05/94	673

	Date	Page
Marijuana Laws	02/11/05	125
Obesity Epidemic	01/31/03	73
Prescription Drug Prices	07/17/92	606*
Preventing Obesity	10/01/10	797
Prozac Controversy	08/19/94	721
Reforming the FDA	06/06/97	481
Regulating Tobacco	09/30/94	841
Regulating Toxic Chemicals	01/23/09	49
Tobacco Industry	12/10/04	**1025
Women's Health	11/07/03	941
Food and nutrition		
Advances in Cancer Research	08/25/95	760*
Advertising Overload	01/23/04	49
Biotech Foods	03/30/01	249
Children in Crisis	08/31/01	671*
Child Poverty	10/28/11	901
Consumer Safety	10/12/07	841
Diet and Health	02/23/01	129
Dietary Supplements	07/08/94	577
Dietary Supplements	09/03/04	709
Dieting and Health	04/14/95	321
Drugmakers Under Siege	09/03/99	767*
Drug-Resistant Bacteria	06/04/99	482*
Eating Disorders	12/18/92	1097
Factory Farms	01/12/07	25
Fair Trade Labeling	05/18/07	433
Farm Policy	08/10/12	693
Fast-Food Shake-Up	11/08/91	825
Fish Farming	07/27/07	625
Food Irradiation	06/12/92	505
Food Safety	06/04/93	481
Food Safety	11/01/02	897
Food Safety	12/17/10	1037
Food Safety Battle: Organic v. Biotech	09/04/98	761
Genetically Engineered Foods	08/05/94	673
Genetically Modified Food	08/31/12	717
Heart Health	09/12/08	721
Lead Poisoning	06/19/92	539
Mad Cow Disease	03/02/01	161
Obesity and Health	01/15/99	25
Obesity Epidemic	01/31/03	73
Preventing Disease	01/06/12	1
Preventing Obesity	10/01/10	797
Prolonging Life	09/30/11	805*
Regulating Pesticides	01/28/94	73
Regulating Pesticides	08/06/99	665
Rethinking Ritalin	10/22/99	916*
Slow Food Movement	01/26/07	73
Sugar Controversies	11/30/12	1013
Threatened Fisheries	08/02/02	634*
Treating ADHD	08/03/12	669
Treating Alzheimer's	03/04/11	193

	Date	Page
Food stamps		
Child Poverty	10/28/11	901
Farm Policy	08/10/12	693
Hunger in America	12/22/00	1033
Welfare, Work and the States	12/06/96	1062*
Food supply		
Animal Rights	05/24/91	301
Factory Farms	01/12/07	25
Farm Policy	12/02/94	1057
Farm Subsidies	05/17/02	433
Food Safety	11/01/02	897
Food Safety	12/17/10	1037
Fighting over Animal Rights	08/02/96	673
Future of Recycling	12/14/07	1033
Hunger in America	12/22/00	1033
Marine Mammals vs. Fish	08/28/92	737
Population and the Environment	07/17/98	601
Slow Food Movement	01/26/07	73
World Hunger	10/25/91	801
Football. ***See Sports***		
Foreign aid		
Aid to Russia	03/12/93	217
Aiding Africa	08/29/03	697
Assisting Refugees	02/07/97	97
Calculating the Costs of the Gulf War	03/15/91	145
Democracy in Africa	03/24/95	241
Emerging India	04/19/02	329
Ending Poverty	09/09/05	733
Euro Crisis	10/05/12	841
Famine in Africa	11/08/02	921
Foreign Aid and National Security	06/17/11	529
Foreign Aid After Sept. 11	04/26/02	361
The Greening of Eastern Europe	11/15/91	849
Haiti's Dilemma	02/18/05	149
Hating America	11/23/01	969
Israel at 50	03/06/98	193
North Korean Crisis	04/11/03	321
Population Growth	07/16/93	601
Reassessing Foreign Aid	09/27/96	841
Rebuilding Afghanistan	12/21/01	1041
Rebuilding Iraq	07/11/03	625
Russia's Political Future	05/03/96	396*
Trouble in South America	03/14/03	225
U.S.-Pakistan Relations	08/05/11	653*
World Hunger	10/25/91	801
Foreign languages		
Bilingual Education	08/13/93	697
Bilingual Education vs. English Immersion	12/11/09	1029
Debate over Bilingualism	01/19/96	49
Electing Minorities	08/12/94	704*
Future of Language	11/17/00	929

 *Indicates sidebar or "At Issue" report section. **Indicates an updated report.

	Date	Page
Foreign policy. ***See International relations***		
Foreign relations. ***See International relations***		
Forests and forestry		
Acid Rain: New Approach to Old Problem	03/08/91	129
Bush and the Environment	10/25/02	865
Disappearing Species	11/30/07	985
Endangered Species	06/21/91	393
Endangered Species Act	06/03/05	**493
Jobs vs. Environment	05/15/92	409
Managing Public Lands	11/04/11	929
Managing Wildfires	11/02/12	941
National Forests	10/16/98	905
Protecting Endangered Species	04/19/96	337
Protecting the National Parks	06/16/00	521
Public Land Policy	06/17/94	529
Saving the Forests	09/20/91	681
Former Soviet Union. ***See Soviet Union (Former)***		
Fossil fuels. ***See Coal; Petroleum***		
Foster care		
Adoption	11/26/93	1033
Foster Care Crisis	09/27/91	705
Foster Care Reform	01/09/98	1
France		
Blood Supply Safety	11/11/94	997*
Future of NATO	02/28/03	177
Future of the European Union	10/28/05	909
High-Speed Rail	04/16/93	313
NATO's Changing Role	08/21/92	729*
The United Nations and Global Security	02/27/04	173
Fraternities		
Drinking on Campus	08/18/06	649
Hazing	01/09/04	1
Fraud		
Aiding Africa	08/29/03	708*
Alternative Medicine's Next Phase	02/14/97	138*
Business Ethics	05/06/11	409
Caring for the Elderly	02/20/98	145
Cheating in Schools	09/22/00	745
Combating Scientific Misconduct	01/10/97	1
Consumer Debt	11/15/96	1018*
Cyber-Crime	04/12/02	305
Digital Commerce	02/05/99	106*
The Disabilities Act	12/27/91	1005*
Identity Theft	06/10/05	517
Insurance Fraud	10/11/96	889
Real ID	05/04/07	385
Reforming Big-Time College Sports	03/19/04	249
Regulating Nonprofits	12/26/97	1129
Stock Market Troubles	01/16/04	25
Voter Rights	05/18/12	449
Whistleblowers	12/05/97	1057

	Date	Page
Free Speech		
Campaign Finance Reform	06/13/08	505
Free trade and protection		
Aiding Africa	08/29/03	697
Deepening Canadian Crisis over Quebec	04/12/91	214*
Europe 1992	06/28/91	429
Fair Trade Labeling	05/18/07	433
Foreign Aid After Sept. 11	04/26/02	361
Mexico's Emergence	07/19/91	489
New Era in Asia	02/14/92	137*
Rethinking NAFTA	06/07/96	481
World Trade	06/09/00	497
Freedom of Information Act		
The FBI Under Fire	04/11/97	328*
Government Secrecy	12/02/05	1005
Press Freedom	02/05/10	97
Privacy in Peril	11/17/06	961
Freedom of speech. ***See First Amendment***		
Freedom of the press. ***See First Amendment***		
Fuel. ***See Gasoline; Petroleum***		
Gambling		
American Indians	04/28/06	**361
Combating Addiction	02/09/07	121
Gambling Boom	03/18/94	241
Gambling in America	03/07/03	201
Gambling Under Attack	09/06/96	769
Native Americans	05/08/92	391*
Native Americans' Future	07/12/96	601
Gangs		
Community Prosecution	12/15/00	1016*
Declining Crime Rates	04/04/97	289
Discipline in Schools	02/15/08	145
Fighting Crime	02/08/08	121
Gang Crisis	05/14/04	421
Gangs in the U.S.	07/16/10	581
Mexico's Drug War	12/12/08	1009
Preventing Juvenile Crime	03/15/96	217
School Violence	10/09/98	892*
Violence in Schools	09/11/92	797
Youth Gangs	10/11/91	753
Garbage. ***See Waste products; Landfills***		
Gasoline		
Alternative Energy	02/25/05	173
Auto Industry's Future	02/06/09	**105
Biofuels Boom	09/29/06	793
Lead Poisoning	06/19/92	536
Oil Diplomacy	01/24/03	49
The Politics of Energy	03/05/99	192*
SUV Debate	05/16/03	449
Transportation Policy	07/04/97	593*
Gays. ***See Homosexuals***		

	Date	Page
Gender equity		
Boys' Emotional Needs	06/18/99	521
Class Action Lawsuits	05/13/11	433
College Sports	08/26/94	759*
Debating Hip-Hop	06/15/07	529
Education and Gender	06/03/94	481
Gender and Learning	05/20/05	445
Gender Equity in Sports	04/18/97	337
Gender Pay Gap	03/14/08	241
Future of Feminism	04/14/06	313
Income Inequality	04/17/98	346*
Mothers' Movement	04/04/03	297
Saving Social Security	10/02/98	863*
Single-Sex Education	07/12/02	569
Treating Anxiety	02/08/02	100*
Understanding Mormonism	10/19/12	889
Women in Politics	03/21/08	265
Women in the Military	11/13/09	957
Women's Health Issues	05/13/94	409
General Agreement on Tariffs and Trade (GATT)		
Farm Policy	12/02/94	1071*
U.S. Trade Policy	01/29/93	73
Generation X		
Feminism's Future	02/28/97	169
Low Voter Turnout	10/20/00	833
Mothers' Movement	04/04/03	302*
Overhauling Social Security	05/12/95	417
Religion in America	11/25/94	1033
Retirement Security	05/31/02	481
Genetics. *See also DNA analysis*		
Advances in Cancer Research	08/25/95	753
Alzheimer's Disease	05/15/98	441*
Biology and Behavior	04/03/98	289
Biotech Foods	03/30/01	249
Birth-Control Debate	06/24/05	565
Cancer Treatments	09/11/98	785
Cell Phone Safety	03/16/01	201
The Cloning Controversy	05/09/97	409
'Designer' Humans	05/18/01	425
Diabetes Epidemic	03/09/01	185
Drugmakers Under Siege	09/03/99	770*
Drug-Resistant Bacteria	06/04/99	473
Embryo Research	12/17/99	1065
Famine in Africa	11/08/02	921
Fish Farming	07/27/07	625
Food Safety Battle: Organic v. Biotech	09/04/98	761
Gay Rights	03/05/93	193
Gender and Learning	05/20/05	445
Genes and Health	01/21/11	49
Gene Therapy	10/18/91	777
Gene Therapy's Future	12/08/95	1089
Genetically Engineered Foods	08/05/94	673
Genetically Modified Food	08/31/12	717
Human Genome Research	05/12/00	401
Increase in Autism	06/13/03	**545
Intelligence Testing	07/30/93	649
Obesity and Health	01/15/99	25
Organ Shortage	02/21/03	153
Privacy Under Attack	06/15/01	505
Prolonging Life	09/30/11	805*
Reproductive Ethics	04/08/94	289
Sports and Drugs	07/23/04	624*
Treating Alzheimer's	03/04/11	193
Vaccine Controversies	08/25/00	641
Genocide		
Stopping Genocide	08/27/04	685
The United Nations and Global Security	02/27/04	173
Geology		
Earthquake Research	12/16/94	1105
Geothermal energy		
Alternative Energy	07/10/92	587
Renewable Energy	11/07/97	961
Germany		
The Economics of Recycling	03/27/98	276*
Ethics of War	12/13/02	1013
Europe's New Right	02/12/93	121
Future of NATO	02/28/03	177
Future of the European Union	10/28/05	909
Holocaust Reparations	03/26/99	257
Sports and Drugs	07/23/04	**613
War Crimes	07/07/95	585
Year-Round Schools	05/17/96	440*
Youth Apprenticeships	10/23/92	917*
Gifted and talented children		
AB and IP Programs	03/03/06	193
Bilingual Education	08/13/93	702*
Educating Gifted Students	03/28/97	265
Grade Inflation	06/07/02	505
Intelligence Testing	07/30/93	654*
Gingrich, Newt		
Campaign Finance Reform	02/09/96	135*
Glass ceiling. *See Discrimination; Sex discrimination*		
Globalization		
Aiding Africa	08/29/03	697
Auto Industry's Future	02/06/09	**105
Child Labor and Sweatshops	08/16/96	732*
Contingent Work Force	10/24/97	937
Corporate Social Responsibility	08/03/07	649
Cracking Down on Immigration	02/03/95	104*
Emerging India	04/19/02	329
European Monetary Union	11/27/98	1025
Expanding NATO	05/16/97	433
Exporting Jobs	02/20/04	149
Foreign Aid After Sept. 11	04/26/02	361

	Date	Page
Future of Language	11/17/00	929
Future of the European Union	10/28/05	909
Globalization Backlash	09/28/01	761
Global Refugee Crisis	07/09/99	569
Human Rights	11/13/98	933*
Human Rights in China	07/25/08	601
International Monetary Fund	01/29/99	65
Oil Production in the 21st Century	08/07/98	678
Population and the Environment	07/17/98	601
Reassessing Foreign Aid	09/27/96	841
Rethinking NAFTA	06/07/96	481
Saving the Rain Forests	06/11/99	512*
Setting Environmental Priorities	05/21/99	432*
Transatlantic Tensions	07/13/01	533
Upward Mobility	04/29/05	369
U.S. Trade Policy	01/29/93	73
World Trade	06/09/00	497
Global warming. ***See also Air pollution***		
Air Pollution Conflict	11/14/03	965
Alternative Energy	07/10/92	573
Alternative Energy	02/25/05	173
Bush and the Environment	10/25/02	865
Buying Green	02/29/08	193
Celebrity Advocacy	05/11/12	425
Climate Change	01/27/06	73
Coal's Comeback	10/05/07	817
Confronting Warming	01/09/09	1
Corporate Social Responsibility	08/03/07	649
Disappearing Species	11/30/07	985
Ecotourism	10/20/06	865
Endangered Species Act	06/03/05	**493
Energy and Climate	07/24/09	621
Energy and the Environment	03/03/00	161
Extreme Weather	09/09/11	733*
Future of Recycling	12/14/07	1033
Global Warming Treaty	01/26/01	41
Global Warming Update	11/01/96	961
Global Water Shortages	12/15/95	1127*
Invasive Species	02/17/12	153
National Parks Under Pressure	10/06/06	817
The New Environmentalism	12/01/06	985
Nuclear Energy	03/10/06	217
Oil Diplomacy	01/24/03	63*
Ozone Depletion	04/03/92	294
The Politics of Energy	03/05/99	202*
Public-Works Projects	02/20/09	153
Reducing Your Carbon Footprint	12/05/08	985
Renewable Energy	11/07/97	974*
Saving the Forests	09/20/91	681
Science and Politics	08/20/04	661
Setting Environmental Priorities	05/21/99	425
Socially Responsible Investing	08/29/08	673
Threatened Coastlines	02/07/92	97
Water Shortages	08/01/03	657*

	Date	Page
Water Shortages	06/18/10	529
Will Nuclear Power Get Another Chance?	02/22/91	113
Gore, Al		
Electoral College	12/08/00	977
Reinventing Government	02/17/95	145
Setting Environmental Priorities	05/21/99	425
Voting Controversies	09/15/06	745
Great Britain		
The British Monarchy	03/08/96	193
DNA Databases	05/28/99	461*
Future of the European Union	10/28/05	909
Gun Control Standoff	12/19/97	1116*
Middle East Tensions	10/27/06	**889
Northern Ireland Cease-Fire	09/15/95	801
Taiwan, China, and the U.S.	05/24/96	468*
U.S.-British Relations	01/30/98	73
Greenhouse effect. ***See Global warming***		
Greenspan, Alan		
The Federal Reserve	09/01/00	673
Social Security Reform	09/24/04	781
Gulf War. ***See Persian Gulf War***		
Gun control. ***See also Firearms***		
Gun Violence	05/25/07	457
Gypsies. ***See Roma***		
Habeas corpus reform		
Death Penalty Controversies	09/23/05	785
Death Penalty Debate	03/10/95	193
Death Penalty Update	01/08/99	1
Habitat for Humanity		
Affordable Housing	02/09/01	103*
Haiti		
Economic Sanctions	10/28/94	937
Foreign Aid After Sept. 11	04/26/02	361
Foreign Policy and Public Opinion	07/15/94	601
Haiti's Dilemma	02/18/05	149
Illegal Immigration	04/24/92	361
Handguns. ***See Firearms***		
Handicapped. ***See Disabled***		
Hate crimes		
Asian Americans	12/13/91	960
Bullying	02/04/05	101
Europe's New Right	02/12/93	121
Hate Crimes	01/08/93	1
New Military Culture	04/26/96	361
Race in America	07/11/03	593
Hazing		
Hazing	01/09/04	1
Hawaii		
Marriage and Divorce	05/10/96	420*
Native Americans' Future	07/12/96	612*

	Date	Page
Hazardous substances. ***See also Nuclear waste; Pesticides; Tobacco; Waste products***		
Acid Rain: New Approach to Old Problem	03/08/91	129
Asbestos Litigation	05/02/03	393
Blood Supply Safety	11/11/94	985
Breast Cancer	06/27/97	560*
Cleaning Up Hazardous Wastes	08/23/96	745
Drug Safety	03/11/05	221
Electromagnetic Fields	04/26/91	237
Environmental Justice	06/19/98	529
Environmental Movement at 25	03/31/95	288*
Food Irradiation	06/12/92	505
Food Safety	06/04/93	481
Food Safety Battle: Organic v. Biotech	09/04/98	761
Garbage Crisis	03/20/92	241
Genetically Engineered Foods	08/05/94	673
The Greening of Eastern Europe	11/15/91	849
Indoor Air Pollution	10/27/95	945
Lead Poisoning	06/19/92	525
Nanotechnology	06/11/04	517
Ozone Depletion	04/03/92	289
Panama Canal	11/26/99	1031*
Policing the Borders	02/22/02	145
Regulating Toxic Chemicals	01/23/09	49
Science in the Courtroom	10/22/93	923*
Setting Environmental Priorities	05/21/99	425
Tobacco Industry	12/10/04	**1025
Water Quality	02/11/94	121
Weapons of Mass Destruction	03/08/02	193
Head Start. ***See Preschool education***		
Health. ***See Diseases and health problems; Food and nutrition; Medical care; Physical fitness***		
Health-care reform. ***See also Medical Care — costs control***		
Abortion Debates	09/10/10	725
Covering the Uninsured	06/14/02	521
Democrats' Future	10/29/10	893
Drug Company Ethics	06/06/03	521
First Ladies	06/14/96	505
Gridlock in Washington	04/30/10	385
Health-Care Reform	08/28/09	693*
Lies and Politics	02/18/11	145
Medicaid Reform	07/16/04	589
Medical Malpractice	02/14/03	129
Medicare Reform	08/22/03	673
The Obama Presidency	01/30/09	73
Primary Care	03/17/95	217
Prison Health Care	01/05/07	1
Prozac Controversy	08/19/94	736*
Retirement Security	05/31/02	481
Rising Health Costs	04/07/06	289
States and Federalism	10/15/10	845
Tea Party Movement	03/19/10	**241*
Universal Coverage	03/30/07	265

	Date	Page
Health insurance		
Abortion Debates	09/10/10	725
Advances in Cancer Research	08/25/95	770*
Aging Baby Boomers	10/19/07	865
Aging Population	07/15/11	577
Alternative Medicine	01/31/92	88
Alzheimer's Disease	07/24/92	617
Baby Boomers at Midlife	07/31/98	657*
Birth-Control Debate	06/24/05	565
Breast Cancer	04/02/10	289
Cancer Treatments	09/11/98	794*
Caring for the Elderly	02/20/98	162*
Caring for Veterans	04/23/10	361
Covering the Uninsured	06/14/02	521
Domestic Partners	09/04/92	761
Drug Company Ethics	06/06/03	521
Eating Disorders	02/10/06	**121
Emergency Medicine	01/05/96	1
Employee Benefits	02/04/00	65
Fighting Superbugs	08/24/07	673
Health-Care Reform	08/28/09	693*
Insurance Fraud	10/11/96	889
Managed Care	04/12/96	313
Managing Managed Care	04/16/99	305
Medicaid Reform	07/16/04	589
Medical Malpractice	02/14/03	129
Medicare Reform	08/22/03	673
Mental Health Insurance	03/29/02	265
Mental Health Policy	09/12/97	793
Mental Illness	08/06/93	673
Mental Illness Medication Debate	02/06/04	101
Middle-Class Squeeze	03/06/09	201
The Obama Presidency	01/30/09	73
Organ Shortage	02/21/03	153
Patients' Rights	02/06/98	97
Prescription Drug Prices	07/17/92	597
Prison Health Care	01/05/07	1
Reproductive Ethics	04/08/94	289
Reproductive Ethics	05/15/09	449
Rethinking Retirement	06/19/09	549
Retiree Health Benefits	12/06/91	921
Retirement Security	05/31/02	481
Rising Health Costs	04/07/06	289
Treating Anxiety	02/08/02	97
Treating Depression	06/26/09	573
Universal Coverage	03/30/07	265
Women and AIDS	12/25/92	1138
Wounded Veterans	08/31/07	697
Youth Suicide	02/13/04	125
Health maintenance organizations		
Covering the Uninsured	06/14/02	521
Drugmakers Under Siege	09/03/99	753
Emergency Medicine	01/05/96	1
Health-Care Reform	08/28/09	693*

 *Indicates sidebar or "At Issue" report section. **Indicates an updated report.

	Date	Page
Managed Care	04/12/96	313
Managing Managed Care	04/16/99	305
Patients' Rights	02/06/98	97
Primary Care	03/17/95	217
Universal Coverage	03/30/07	265
Heart disease		
Breast Cancer	06/27/97	558*
Obesity Epidemic	01/31/03	73
Organ Shortage	02/21/03	153
Organ Transplants	08/11/95	705
Physical Fitness	11/06/92	967*
Tobacco Industry	12/10/04	**1025
Women's Health Issues	05/13/94	409
High-speed rail. ***See Railroads***		
Highways and roads		
Aggressive Driving	07/25/97	649
Aging Infrastructure	09/28/07	**793
Auto Safety	10/26/01	873
Distracted Driving	05/04/12	401
Future of Amtrak	10/18/02	841
Highway Safety	07/14/95	609
Mass Transit Boom	01/18/08	49
National Forests	10/16/98	921*
Privatization	11/13/92	992
Privatizing Government Services	08/09/96	713*
Public-Works Projects	02/20/09	153
Smart Growth	05/28/04	469
SUV Debate	05/16/03	449
Teen Driving	01/07/05	1
Traffic Congestion	05/06/94	385
Traffic Congestion	08/27/99	729
Transportation Policy	07/04/97	577
Truck Safety	03/12/99	209
Hispanics		
Affirmative Action	09/21/01	737
Affirmative Action	10/17/08	**841
Alcohol Advertising	03/14/97	221*
America's Border Fence	09/19/08	745
Bilingual Education vs. English Immersion	12/11/09	1029
Census Controversey	05/14/10	433
Changing U.S. Electorate	05/30/08	**457
Cuba in Crisis	11/29/91	908*
Debate over Bilingualism	01/19/96	49
Debate Over Immigration	07/14/00	580*
Democrats' Future	10/29/10	893
Diversity in the Workplace	10/10/97	889
Domestic Poverty	09/07/07	**721
Electing Minorities	08/12/94	697
Evaluating Head Start	08/26/05	685
Fighting Crime	02/08/08	121
Hate Groups	05/08/09	421
Hispanic Americans	10/30/92	929
Hispanic-Americans' New Clout	09/18/98	809
Illegal Immigration	05/06/05	393
Immigration Debate	02/01/08	**97
Latinos' Future	10/17/03	869
Mortgage Crisis	11/02/07	**913
No Child Left Behind	05/27/05	469
Police Misconduct	04/06/12	301
Protestants Today	12/07/07	1009
Race and Politics	07/18/08	577
Race in America	07/11/03	593
Racial Diversity in Public Schools	09/14/07	**745
Racial Tensions in Schools	01/07/94	1
Redistricting Disputes	03/12/04	221
Redistricting: Drawing Power with a Map	02/15/91	97
Rethinking School Integration	10/18/96	918*
School Desegregation	04/23/04	345
School Vouchers Showdown	02/15/02	121
Sexually Transmitted Diseases	12/03/04	997
Student Aid	01/25/08	73
Worker Retraining	01/21/94	62*
History — Study and teaching		
Archaeology Today	05/24/02	457
Black Colleges	12/12/03	1056*
Conspiracy Theories	10/23/09	885
Historic Preservation	10/07/94	865
School Censorship	02/19/93	159*
Searching for Jesus	12/11/98	1073
Teaching History	09/29/95	849
HIV infection. ***See AIDS disease***		
HMOs. ***See Health maintenance organizations***		
Holistic medicine		
Alternative Medicine's Next Phase	02/14/97	133*
Drug-Resistant Bacteria	06/04/99	489*
Prayer and Healing	01/14/05	25
Hollywood. ***See Movies***		
Holocaust		
Ethics of War	12/13/02	1013
Holocaust Reparations	03/26/99	257
Reparations Movement	06/22/01	529
Stopping Genocide	08/27/04	685
Home Schooling		
Home Schooling	09/09/94	769
Home Schooling Debate	01/17/03	25
Parental Rights	10/25/96	942
Homeland Security		
Civil Liberties Debates	10/24/03	893
Confronting Iraq	10/04/02	793
Cyber-Crime	04/12/02	305
Cybersecurity	09/26/03	797
Cybersecurity	02/26/10	169
Energy Security	02/01/02	73
Exporting Democracy	04/01/05	269

	Date	Page
Future of the Airline Industry	06/21/02	545
Homeland Security	09/12/03	749
Homeland Security	02/13/09	129
Illegal Immigration	05/06/05	393
New Defense Priorities	09/13/02	721
Policing the Borders	02/22/02	145
Port Security	04/21/06	337
Presidential Power	11/15/02	945
Presidential Power	02/24/06	169
Privacy in Peril	11/17/06	961
Remembering 9/11	09/02/11	701*
Smallpox Threat	02/07/03	105
Torture	04/18/03	345
War on Terrorism	10/12/01	817
Weapons of Mass Destruction	03/08/02	193
Homeless persons		
Charitable Giving	11/12/93	996*
Declining Crime Rates	04/04/97	289
Ending Homelessness	06/18/04	541
Hard Times for Libraries	06/26/92	562
Helping the Homeless	01/26/96	73
The Homeless	08/07/92	665
Housing the Homeless	12/18/09	1053
Treatment of Veterans	11/19/04	973
Homeopathic medicine. ***See Alternative medicine***		
Homosexuals		
Adoption Controversies	09/10/99	782*
Biology and Behavior	04/03/98	298*
Bullying	02/04/05	101
Catholic Church in the U.S.	09/08/95	788*
Diversity in the Workplace	10/10/97	900*
Domestic Partners	09/04/92	761
Employee Benefits	02/04/00	72*
Future of the Catholic Church	01/19/07	49
Gay Marriage	09/05/03	721
Gay Marriage Showdowns	09/26/08	**769
Gay Rights	03/05/93	193
Gay Rights Update	04/14/00	305
Gays in the Military	09/18/09	**765
Hate Crimes	01/08/93	1
Human Rights Issues	10/30/09	909
Marriage and Divorce	05/10/96	420*
New Military Culture	04/26/96	361
Politicians and Privacy	04/17/92	351*
Revitalizing the Cities	10/13/95	908*
School Censorship	02/19/93	145
Sexual Abuse and the Clergy	05/03/02	393
Sexually Transmitted Diseases	12/03/04	997
Teaching Values	06/21/96	529
Transgender Issues	05/05/06	385
Women and AIDS	12/25/92	1121
Women and Sports	03/06/92	199
Women in the Military	09/25/92	850*

	Date	Page
Hong Kong		
China After Deng	06/13/97	510*
Taiwan, China, and the U.S.	05/24/96	468*
U.S.-China Trade	04/15/94	327*
Hormone-replacement therapy		
Baby Boomers at Midlife	07/31/98	660*
Breast Cancer	06/27/97	553
Women's Health	11/07/03	941
Women's Health Issues	05/13/94	423*
Hospices		
Assisted Suicide Controversy	05/05/95	400*
Caring for the Dying	09/05/97	769
Hospitals		
Caring for Veterans	04/23/10	361
Covering the Uninsured	06/14/02	521
Drug-Resistant Bacteria	06/04/99	473
Emergency Medicine	01/05/96	1
Fighting SARS	06/20/03	569
Fighting Superbugs	08/24/07	673
Hospitals' Financial Woes	08/13/99	689
Managing Managed Care	04/16/99	305
Medical Malpractice	02/14/03	129
Medicare Reform	08/22/03	673
Organ Shortage	02/21/03	153
Patient Safety	02/10/12	125
Prayer and Healing	01/14/05	25
Right to Die	05/13/05	421
Treatment of Veterans	11/19/04	973
Wounded Veterans	08/31/07	697
Housing. ***See also Public housing***		
Affordable Housing	02/09/01	89
Blighted Cities	11/12/10	941*
Buying Green	02/29/08	193
Consumer Debt	03/02/07	193
Downward Mobility	07/23/93	643*
Ending Homelessness	06/18/04	541
Financial Bailout	10/24/08	**865
Financial Crisis	05/09/08	409
Financial Industry Overhaul	07/30/10	629
Future of Homeownership	12/14/12	1061
Helping the Homeless	01/26/96	73
The Homeless	08/07/92	665
Housing Discrimination	02/24/95	169
Housing the Homeless	12/18/09	1053
Implementing the Disabilities Act	12/20/96	1117*
Indoor Air Pollution	10/27/95	945
Lead Poisoning	06/19/92	525
Middle-Class Squeeze	03/06/09	201
Mortgage Crisis	11/02/07	**913
The Obama Presidency	01/30/09	73
Racial Tensions in Schools	01/07/94	1
Reducing Your Carbon Footprint	12/05/08	985
Regulating Credit Cards	10/10/08	817*

 *Indicates sidebar or "At Issue" report section. **Indicates an updated report.

	Date	Page
Smart Growth	05/28/04	469
Urban Sprawl in the West	10/03/97	865
Human Genome Project. *See Genetics*		
Human rights		
Castro's Next Move	12/12/97	1081
Celebrity Advocacy	05/11/12	425
China After Deng	06/13/97	505
Democracy in Asia	07/24/98	625
Democracy in Eastern Europe	10/08/99	876*
Emerging China	11/11/05	957
Ethics of War	12/13/02	1013
Human Rights	11/13/98	977
Human Rights in China	07/25/08	601
Human Rights Issues	10/30/09	909
Human Trafficking and Slavery	03/26/04	273
International Law	12/17/04	1049
Religious Persecution	11/21/97	1009
Stopping Genocide	08/27/04	685
Torture	04/18/03	345
Treatment of Detainees	08/25/06	673
U.S.-China Relations	05/07/10	**409
U.S.-China Trade	04/15/94	313
War Crimes	07/07/95	585
Women and Human Rights	04/30/99	353
Hungary		
Expanding NATO	05/16/97	433
The Greening of Eastern Europe	11/15/91	849
Peace Corps' Challenges in the 1990s	01/25/91	49
Hunger		
Celebrity Advocacy	05/11/12	425
Famine in Africa	11/08/02	921
Foreign Aid and National Security	06/17/11	529
Hunger in America	12/22/00	1033
World Hunger	10/25/91	801
Hunting		
Endangered Species Act	06/03/05	**493
Hunting Controversy	01/24/92	49
Hurricanes and storms		
Aging Infrastructure	09/28/07	**793
Coastal Development	08/21/98	721
Disaster Response	10/15/93	889
Extreme Weather	09/09/11	733*
Rebuilding New Orleans	02/03/06	97
Threatened Coastlines	02/07/92	97
Youth Volunteerism	01/27/12	77
Hydroelectric power		
Renewable Energy	11/07/97	961
Setting Environmental Priorities	05/21/99	438*
Hypnosis		
Recovered-Memory Debate	07/05/96	577
Treating Anxiety	02/08/02	97

	Date	Page
Illegal aliens. *See Immigration and emigration*		
Immigration and emigration		
Adoption Controversies	09/10/99	787*
America's Border Fence	09/19/08	745
Asian Americans	12/13/91	945
Assisting Refugees	02/07/97	110*
Bilingual Education	08/13/93	697
Castro's Next Move	12/12/97	1093*
Catholic Church in the U.S.	09/08/95	785*
Census Controversey	05/14/10	433
Changing Demographics	11/16/12	989
Civil Liberties in Wartime	12/14/01	1029*
Cracking Down on Immigration	02/03/95	97
Cuba in Crisis	11/29/91	908*
Cuba's Future	07/20/07	601
Debate Over Bilingualism	01/19/96	49
Debate Over Immigration	07/14/00	569
Declining Birthrates	11/21/08	961
Drone Warfare	08/06/10	653
Europe's New Right	02/12/93	121
Exporting Jobs	02/20/04	149
Gangs in the U.S.	07/16/10	581
Global Refugee Crisis	07/09/99	569
Haiti's Dilemma	02/18/05	149
High-Tech Labor Shortage	04/24/98	361
Hispanic Americans	10/30/92	929
Hispanic-Americans' New Clout	09/18/98	809
Homeland Security	09/12/03	749
Homeland Security	02/13/09	129
Human Trafficking and Slavery	03/26/04	273
Illegal Immigration	04/24/92	361
Illegal Immigration	05/06/05	393
Immigration Conflict	03/09/12	229
Immigration Debate	02/01/08	**97
Immigration Reform	09/24/93	841
Insurance Fraud	10/11/96	893*
Latinos' Future	10/17/03	869
Mexico's Emergence	07/19/91	499*
Mexico's Future	09/19/97	832*
The New Immigrants	01/24/97	49
Policing the Borders	02/22/02	154*
Population and the Environment	07/17/98	609*
Population Growth	07/16/93	601
Race in America	07/11/03	593
Real ID	05/04/07	385
Re-examining 9/11	06/04/04	493
Science in America	01/11/08	25
States and Federalism	10/15/10	845
Underground Economy	03/04/94	207*
U.S.-Mexico Relations	11/09/01	921
War on Terrorism	10/12/01	817
Welfare, Work and the States	12/06/96	1062*
The Working Poor	11/03/95	975*

	Date	Page
Impeachment		
The Federal Judiciary	03/13/98	234*
Partisan Politics	03/19/99	250*
Imports. ***See International trade***		
Incest. ***See Sex crimes***		
Income. ***See Wages and salaries***		
Income tax		
Age Discrimination	08/01/97	684*
Calculating the Costs of the Gulf War	03/15/91	153*
Governing Washington, D.C.	11/22/96	1049*
Income Inequality	04/17/98	345*
Income Inequality	12/03/10	989
IRS Reform	01/16/98	25
Marriage and Divorce	05/10/96	414*
Social Security: The Search for Fairness	04/05/91	189
Stimulating the Economy	01/10/03	1
Tax Reform	03/22/96	241
Underground Economy	03/04/94	193
The Working Poor	11/03/95	969
Independent counsels		
Independent Counsels	02/21/97	145
Independent Counsels Re-examined	05/07/99	377
Partisan Politics	03/19/99	233
Political Scandals	05/27/94	474*
Independent political candidates		
The Partisan Divide	04/30/04	389*
Partisan Politics	03/19/99	242*
Third-Party Prospects	12/22/95	1137
India		
Coal's Comeback	10/05/07	817
Democracy in Asia	07/24/98	625
Emerging India	04/19/02	329
Exporting Jobs	02/20/04	149
Human Trafficking and Slavery	03/26/04	273
Nuclear Proliferation	06/05/92	481
Nuclear Proliferation and Terrorism	04/02/04	297
Oil Jitters	01/04/08	**1
Weapons of Mass Destruction	03/08/02	193
Individual retirement accounts (IRAs)		
IRS Reform	01/16/98	38*
Overhauling Social Security	05/12/95	417
Paying for Retirement	11/05/93	961
Saving Social Security	10/02/98	857
Social Security: The Search for Fairness	04/05/91	201*
Indonesia		
Democracy in Asia	07/24/98	625
Industry. ***See Business and industry***		
Infant mortality		
Infant Mortality	07/31/92	641
Native Americans	05/08/92	399
Infertility		
The Cloning Controversy	05/09/97	409
Embryo Research	12/17/99	1065
Reproductive Ethics	04/08/94	302*
Inflation		
Affordable Housing	02/09/01	89
Deflation Fears	02/13/98	121
The Federal Reserve	09/01/00	673
Insomnia. ***See Sleep disorders***		
Insurance. ***See also Health insurance***		
Caring for the Elderly	10/13/06	841
Coastal Development	08/21/98	721
Disaster Response	10/15/93	889
Farm Policy	08/10/12	693
Holocaust Reparations	03/26/99	257
Insurance Fraud	10/11/96	889
Medical Malpractice	02/14/03	129
Medicare Reform	08/22/03	673
Reproductive Ethics	05/15/09	449
Too Many Lawsuits?	05/22/92	440
Universal Coverage	03/30/07	265
Intellectual property rights		
Clashing over Copyright	11/08/96	985
Cyber-Crime	04/12/02	305
Future of the Music Industry	11/21/03	989
Software Piracy	05/21/93	433
U.S. Trade Policy	01/29/93	84*
Intelligence service		
Cybersecurity	09/26/03	797
Gay Rights	03/05/93	202*
Homeland Security	09/12/03	749
Intelligence Reforms	01/25/02	49
The New CIA	12/11/92	1073
Policing the Borders	02/22/02	145
Presidential Power	02/24/06	169
Re-examining 9/11	06/04/04	493
Reforming the CIA	02/02/96	97
Torture	04/18/03	345
Weapons of Mass Destruction	03/08/02	193
Intelligence tests		
Artificial Intelligence	04/22/11	361
Intelligence Testing	07/30/93	649
Intelligent design		
Intelligent Design	07/29/05	637
Internal Revenue Service, U.S.		
IRS Reform	01/16/98	25
Regulating Nonprofits	12/26/97	1129
Underground Economy	03/04/94	193
International Atomic Energy Agency (IAEA)		
The United Nations and Global Security	02/27/04	173

	Date	Page
International Baccalaureate (IB)		
AB and IP Programs	03/03/06	193
Racial Diversity in Public Schools	09/14/07	**745
International courts		
Ethics of War	12/13/02	1025*
Government Secrecy	02/11/11	121
Human Rights	11/13/98	933*
International Law	12/17/04	1049
Stopping Genocide	08/27/04	685
Torture	04/18/03	345
War Crimes	07/07/95	585
International Monetary Fund		
Deflation Fears	02/13/98	127*
Famine in Africa	11/08/02	937*
Globalization Backlash	09/28/01	761
International Monetary Fund	01/29/99	65
Trouble in South America	03/14/03	225
International relations. ***See also Military policy; Treaties and international agreements***		
Adoption Controversies	09/10/99	787*
America's Border Fence	09/19/08	745
Assisting Refugees	02/07/97	97
Confronting Iraq	10/04/02	793
Death Penalty Update	01/08/99	14*
Democracy in Eastern Europe	10/08/99	865
Democrats in Congress	06/08/07	505
Ethics of War	12/13/02	1013
Euro Crisis	10/05/12	841
Europe 1992	06/28/91	417
European Monetary Union	11/27/98	1025
Expanding NATO	05/16/97	433
Exporting Democracy	04/01/05	269
Famine in Africa	11/08/02	921
Future of NATO	02/28/03	177
Global AIDS Crisis	10/13/00	809
Global Refugee Crisis	07/09/99	569
Global Warming Update	11/01/96	961
Global Water Shortages	12/15/95	1113
Government Secrecy	02/11/11	121
Haiti's Dilemma	02/18/05	149
Hating America	11/23/01	969
Human Rights	11/13/98	977
International Law	12/17/04	1049
International Monetary Fund	01/29/99	65
Israel at 50	03/06/98	193
Mexico's Drug War	12/12/08	1009
Mexico's Future	10/26/12	913
Middle East Conflict	04/06/01	273
Middle East Peace	01/21/05	53
NATO's Changing Role	08/21/92	713
North Korean Crisis	04/11/03	321
The Obama Presidency	01/30/09	73
Oil Jitters	01/04/08	**1

	Date	Page
Privatizing the Military	07/13/12	597
Prospects for Mideast Peace	08/30/02	673
Race in America	07/11/03	593
Rise in Counterinsurgency	09/05/08	697
United Nations at 50	08/18/95	729
U.S.-China Relations	05/07/10	**409
U.S.-Europe Relations	03/23/12	277
U.S.-Pakistan Relations	08/05/11	653*
War Crimes	07/07/95	585
Weapons of Mass Destruction	03/08/02	193
International relations — U.S. foreign policy		
Aid to Russia	03/12/93	217
Aiding Africa	08/29/03	697
Air Pollution Conflict	11/14/03	965
America at War	07/23/10	**605
Calculating the Costs of the Gulf War	03/15/91	145
Castro's Next Move	12/12/97	1081
Change in Latin America	07/21/06	601
China After Deng	06/13/97	505
China Today	08/04/00	625
Combating Terrorism	07/21/95	633
Confronting Iraq	10/04/02	793
Cuba in Crisis	11/29/91	897
Cuba's Future	07/20/07	601
Defense Priorities	07/30/99	641
Democracy in Africa	03/24/95	258*
Democracy in Asia	07/24/98	625
Democracy in Eastern Europe	10/08/99	872*
Democracy in the Arab World	01/30/04	73
Democrats in Congress	06/08/07	505
Drone Warfare	08/06/10	653
Economic Sanctions	10/28/94	937
Expanding NATO	05/16/97	433
Exporting Democracy	04/01/05	269
First Ladies	06/14/96	508*
Foreign Aid and National Security	06/17/11	529
Foreign Aid After Sept. 11	04/26/02	361
Foreign Policy and Public Opinion	07/15/94	601
Foreign Policy Burden	08/20/93	721
Future of Korea	05/19/00	425
Future of NATO	02/28/03	177
The Future of U.S.-Russia Relations	01/18/02	25
Government Secrecy	02/11/11	121
Haiti's Dilemma	02/18/05	149
International Law	12/17/04	1049
Israel at 50	03/06/98	193
Japan in Crisis	07/26/02	593
Mexico's Emergence	07/19/91	489
Mexico's Future	09/19/97	817
Middle East Peace	01/21/05	53
Middle East Tensions	10/27/06	**889
The New CIA	12/11/92	1073
New Era in Asia	02/14/92	121
New Strategy in Iraq	02/23/07	169

	Date	Page
North Korean Crisis	04/11/03	337*
Northern Ireland Cease-Fire	09/15/95	801
Nuclear Proliferation and Terrorism	04/02/04	297
Oil Diplomacy	01/24/03	49
Oil Production in the 21st Century	08/07/98	678*
The Palestinians	08/30/91	623
Panama Canal	11/26/99	1017
Peace Corps' Challenges in the 1990s	01/25/91	49
Policing the Borders	02/22/02	145
The Politics of Energy	03/05/99	199*
Presidential Power	11/15/02	945
Prospects for Mideast Peace	08/30/02	673
Quebec Sovereignty	10/06/95	873
Reassessing Foreign Aid	09/27/96	841
Rebuilding Iraq	07/11/03	625
Reform in Iran	12/18/98	1097
Reforming the CIA	02/02/96	97
Religious Persecution	11/21/97	1009
Rethinking Foreign Policy	02/02/07	97
Rise in Counterinsurgency	09/05/08	697
Russia and the Former Soviet Republics	06/17/05	541
Russia's Political Future	05/03/96	385
South Africa's Future	01/14/94	39*
Soviet Republics Rebel	07/12/91	465
Stopping Genocide	08/27/04	685
Taiwan, China, and the U.S.	05/24/96	457
Torture	04/18/03	345
Treatment of Detainees	08/25/06	673
Trouble in South America	03/14/03	225
Understanding Islam	11/03/06	913
United Nations at 50	08/18/95	729
U.S.-British Relations	01/30/98	73
U.S.-British Relations	11/05/10	917*
U.S.-China Relations	05/07/10	**409
U.S.-China Trade	04/15/94	313
U.S.-Pakistan Relations	08/05/11	653*
U.S. Policy in Asia	11/27/92	1025
U.S. Policy on Iran	11/16/07	961
U.S.-Russian Relations	05/22/98	457
U.S.-Vietnam Relations	12/03/93	1057
War in Iraq	10/21/05	881
Weapons of Mass Destruction	03/08/02	193
Women and Human Rights	04/30/99	353
International trade — Issues and problems		
Aiding Africa	08/29/03	697
Asbestos Litigation	05/02/03	409*
Child Labor and Sweatshops	08/16/96	721
China After Deng	06/13/97	521*
Cuba's Future	07/20/07	601
The Consumer Culture	11/19/99	1006*
Deflation Fears	02/13/98	121
Economic Sanctions	10/28/94	937
Emerging China	11/11/05	957
Endangered Species Act	10/01/99	856*
Fair Trade Labeling	05/18/07	433
Food Safety	11/01/02	897
Foreign Aid After Sept. 11	04/26/02	361
Foreign Policy Burden	08/20/93	721
Global Food Crisis	06/27/08	553
Human Rights in China	07/25/08	601
Identity Theft	06/10/05	517
International Law	12/17/04	1049
Mexico's Future	10/26/12	913
The New Corporate Philanthropy	02/27/98	182*
New Era in Asia	02/14/92	138*
Port Security	04/21/06	337
Recession's Regional Impact	02/01/91	65
Reforming the CIA	02/02/96	97
Religious Persecution	11/21/97	1025*
Rethinking NAFTA	06/07/96	481
Trouble in South America	03/14/03	225
Truck Safety	03/12/99	222*
U.S. Trade Policy	01/29/93	73
World Trade	06/09/00	497
International trade — Products and services		
Airline Industry Problems	09/24/99	836*
Airline Safety	10/08/93	865
Arms Sales	12/09/94	1081
Cuba's Future	07/20/07	601
Emerging India	04/19/02	329
Exporting Jobs	02/20/04	149
Fair Trade Labeling	05/18/07	433
Farm Policy	12/02/94	1057
Fast-Food Shake-Up	11/08/91	839
Food Safety	11/01/02	897
Food Safety	12/17/10	1037
Nuclear Proliferation	06/05/92	481
Oil Imports	08/23/91	585
Oil Production in the 21st Century	08/07/98	673
Oil Spills	01/17/92	25
The Politics of Energy	03/05/99	185
Prostitution	06/11/93	516*
Protecting Endangered Species	04/19/96	348*
Regulating Pesticides	01/28/94	73
Regulating Tobacco	09/30/94	847*
Reviving Manufacturing	07/22/11	601
Software Piracy	05/21/93	433
U.S. Auto Industry	10/16/92	881
U.S.-British Relations	11/05/10	917*
Internet. *See also Computers*		
Adoption Controversies	09/10/99	790*
Alcohol Advertising	03/14/97	234*
Blog Explosion	06/09/06	**505
Broadcast Indecency	04/16/04	326*
Cameras in the Courtroom	01/14/11	25
Campaign Finance Reform	03/31/00	269*
Cheating in Schools	09/22/00	754*

	Date	Page
Civil Liberties in Wartime	12/14/01	1017
Clashing over Copyright	11/08/96	985
Combating Plagiarism	09/19/03	773
Computer Hacking	09/16/11	757*
Computers and Medicine	10/27/00	857
Controlling the Internet	05/12/06	409
Copyright and the Internet	09/29/00	769
Criminal Records and Employment	04/20/12	349
Cyberbullying	05/02/08	385
Cyber-Crime	04/12/02	305
Cyberpolitics	09/17/04	757
Cybersecurity	09/26/03	797
Cybersecurity	02/26/10	169
Cyber-Predators	03/01/02	169
Cyber Socializing	07/28/06	625
Digital Commerce	02/05/99	89
Digital Education	12/02/11	1001
Distance Learning	12/07/01	993
The Digital Divide	01/28/00	41
Drugmakers Under Siege	09/03/99	762*
Energy and the Environment	03/03/00	173*
Examining Forensics	07/17/09	597
Free-Press Disputes	04/08/05	304*
Future of Books	05/29/09	**473
Future of Journalism	03/27/09	**273
Future of Language	11/17/00	929
The Future of Libraries	05/23/97	457
Future of Libraries	07/29/11	625
Future of Marriage	05/07/04	409*
The Future of Telecommunications	04/23/99	329
Future of the Music Industry	11/21/03	989
Future of Newspapers	01/20/06	49
Gambling in America	03/07/03	201
Google's Dominance	11/11/11	953
Government Secrecy	02/11/11	121
Homeland Security	09/12/03	749
Human Rights in China	07/25/08	601
Identity Theft	6/10/05	517
Impact of the Internet on Thinking	09/24/10	773
Internet Accuracy	08/01/08	625
Internet Privacy	11/06/98	953
Internet Regulation	04/13/12	325
IRS Reform	01/16/98	36*
Journalism Standards in the Internet Age	10/08/10	821
Journalism Under Fire	12/25/98	1121
Libraries and the Internet	06/01/01	465
Lies and Politics	02/18/11	145
Low Voter Turnout	10/20/00	844*
Medication Abuse	10/09/09	837
Online Privacy	11/06/09	**933
Press Freedom	02/05/10	97
Preventing Bullying	12/10/10	**1013
Privacy Under Attack	06/15/01	505
Prostitution Debate	05/23/08	433
Reading Crisis?	02/22/08	169
Regulating the Internet	06/30/95	561
Regulating the New Economy	10/19/01	849
Rising College Costs	12/05/03	1026*
Smart Cities	07/27/12	645
Social Media and Politics	10/12/12	865
Social Networking	09/17/10	749
Student Journalism	06/05/98	499*
Student Rights	06/05/09	501
Television's Future	02/16/07	145
U.S.-China Relations	05/07/10	**409
Video Games	11/10/06	**937
Iran		
Computer Hacking	09/16/11	757*
Economic Sanctions	10/28/94	944*
Exporting Democracy	04/01/05	269
Hating America	11/23/01	969
Islamic Fundamentalism	03/24/00	241
Middle East Tensions	10/27/06	**889
New Strategy in Iraq	02/23/07	169
Nuclear Disarmament	10/02/09	**813
Nuclear Energy	03/10/06	217
Nuclear Proliferation and Terrorism	04/02/04	297
Oil Jitters	01/04/08	**1
Oil Production in the 21st Century	08/07/98	673
Reform in Iran	12/18/98	1097
Rethinking Foreign Policy	02/02/07	97
Understanding Islam	11/03/06	913
The United Nations and Global Security	02/27/04	173
U.S.-Europe Relations	03/23/12	277
U.S. Policy on Iran	11/16/07	961
War on Terrorism	10/12/01	817
Women and Human Rights	04/30/99	353
Iran-contra affair		
Independent Counsels	02/21/97	158*
Political Scandals	05/27/94	470*
Reforming the CIA	02/02/96	111*
U.S. Policy on Iran	11/16/07	961
Iraq		
Alternative Energy	02/25/05	173
America at War	07/23/10	**605
Assisting Refugees	02/07/97	109*
Calculating the Costs of the Gulf War	03/15/91	145
Caring for Veterans	04/23/10	361
Celebrity Culture	03/18/05	245
Chemical and Biological Weapons	01/31/97	84*
Confronting Iraq	10/04/02	793
Cost of the Iraq War	04/25/08	361*
Democracy in the Arab World	01/30/04	73
Democrats in Congress	06/08/07	505
Draft Debates	08/19/05	661
Drone Warfare	08/06/10	653

	Date	Page
Economic Sanctions	10/28/94	937
Examining Forensics	07/17/09	597
Exporting Democracy	04/01/05	269
Foreign Aid and National Security	06/17/11	529
Future of NATO	02/28/03	177
Global Jihad	10/14/05	857
Government Secrecy	12/02/05	1005
Government Secrecy	02/11/11	121
Hating America	11/23/01	969
International Law	12/17/04	1049
Interrogating the CIA	09/25/09	789
Middle East Tensions	10/27/06	**889
Military Suicides	09/23/11	781*
New Defense Priorities	09/13/02	735*
New Strategy in Iraq	02/23/07	169
Nuclear Proliferation	06/05/92	481
Nuclear Proliferation and Terrorism	04/02/04	297
The Obama Presidency	01/30/09	73
Oil Diplomacy	01/24/03	49
Oil Jitters	01/04/08	**1
Oil Production in the 21st Century	08/07/98	673
Privatizing the Military	06/25/04	565
Privatizing the Military	07/13/12	597
Prosecuting Terrorists	03/12/10	**217*
Rebuilding Iraq	07/11/03	625
Remembering 9/11	09/02/11	701*
Rethinking Foreign Policy	02/02/07	97
Rise in Counterinsurgency	09/05/08	697
Smallpox Threat	02/07/03	118*
Stolen Antiquities	04/13/07	313
Stopping Genocide	08/27/04	685
Torture	04/18/03	345
Treatment of Detainees	08/25/06	673
Treatment of Veterans	11/19/04	973
Understanding Islam	11/03/06	913
The United Nations and Global Security	02/27/04	173
U.S. Policy on Iran	11/16/07	961
War in Iraq	10/21/05	881
War on Terrorism	10/12/01	817
Women in the Military	11/13/09	957
Wounded Veterans	08/31/07	697
IRAs. ***See Individual retirement accounts***		
Ireland		
Northern Ireland Cease-Fire	09/15/95	801
Irradiation. ***See Radiation***		
Islam		
Democracy in the Arab World	01/30/04	73
Emerging India	04/19/02	329
Future of the European Union	10/28/05	909
Global Jihad	10/14/05	857
Hating America	11/23/01	969
Homegrown Jihadists	09/03/10	701
Islamic Fundamentalism	03/24/00	241
Middle East Tensions	10/27/06	**889
Muslims in America	04/30/93	361
Oil Diplomacy	01/24/03	49
Policing the Borders	02/22/02	145
Rebuilding Iraq	07/11/03	625
Reform in Iran	12/18/98	1097
Religious Persecution	11/21/97	1009
Remembering 9/11	09/02/11	701*
Russia and the Former Soviet Republics	06/17/05	541
Understanding Islam	11/03/06	913
U.S. Policy on Iran	11/16/07	961
War on Terrorism	10/12/01	817
Women and Human Rights	04/30/99	353
Israel		
Confronting Iraq	10/04/02	793
Democracy in the Arab World	01/30/04	73
Foreign Aid and National Security	06/17/11	529
Foreign Aid After Sept. 11	04/26/02	361
Global Water Shortages	12/15/95	1113
Human Rights Issues	10/30/09	909
Israel at 50	03/06/98	193
Middle East Conflict	04/06/01	273
Middle East Peace	01/21/05	53
Middle East Tensions	10/27/06	**889
Oil Diplomacy	01/24/03	49
The Palestinians	08/30/91	609
Prospects for Mideast Peace	08/30/02	673
Reassessing Foreign Aid	09/27/96	848*
Torture	04/18/03	345
Understanding Islam	11/03/06	913
Japan		
Asian Americans	12/13/91	945
Auto Industry's Future	01/21/00	26*
Chemical and Biological Weapons	01/31/97	86*
Declining Birthrates	11/21/08	961
Deflation Fears	02/13/98	133*
Earthquake Research	12/16/94	1122*
Ethics of War	12/13/02	1013
Europe 1992	06/28/91	432
Japan in Crisis	07/26/02	593
New Era in Asia	02/14/92	121
Nuclear Fusion	01/22/93	66*
The Obama Presidency	01/30/09	73
The U.S. and Japan	05/31/91	325
U.S. Auto Industry	10/16/92	881
U.S. Policy in Asia	11/27/92	1025
U.S. Trade Policy	01/29/93	73
War Crimes	07/07/95	585
Year-Round Schools	05/17/96	440*
Jews		
Hate Crimes	01/08/93	1
Holocaust Reparations	03/26/99	257

 *Indicates sidebar or "At Issue" report section. **Indicates an updated report.

	Date	Page
Israel at 50	03/06/98	202*
Middle East Peace	01/21/05	53
Middle East Tensions	10/27/06	**889
Prospects for Mideast Peace	08/30/02	673
Religion and Politics	07/30/04	642*
Religion in Schools	02/18/94	159*
Reparations Movement	06/22/01	529
Searching for Jesus	12/11/98	1084*
Job discrimination. ***See Discrimination***		
Job stress		
Flexible Work Arrangements	08/14/98	705*
Job Stress	08/04/95	681
Jobs in the '90s	02/28/92	169
Work, Family and Stress	08/14/92	689
Job training		
Business Ethics	05/06/11	409
Career Colleges	01/07/11	1
Domestic Poverty	09/07/07	**721
Future Job Market	01/11/02	1
Income Inequality	04/17/98	353*
Jobs Outlook	06/04/10	481
Liberal Arts Education	04/10/98	313
Nursing Shortage	09/20/02	745
Straining the Safety Net	07/31/09	645
Student Journalism	06/05/98	481
Teacher Education	10/17/97	913
Upward Mobility	04/29/05	369
The Value of a College Education	11/20/09	981
Vanishing Jobs	03/13/09	225
Welfare Experiments	09/16/94	793
Worker Retraining	01/21/94	49
Youth Apprenticeships	10/23/92	905
Jobs. ***See Employment and unemployment***		
Journalism		
Blog Explosion	06/09/06	**505
Business Bankruptcy	04/10/09	321
Celebrity Culture	03/18/05	245
Child Sexual Abuse	01/15/93	36*
Civic Journalism	09/20/96	817
Civil Liberties Debates	10/24/03	893
Civil Liberties in Wartime	12/14/01	1017
Combating Plagiarism	09/19/03	773
Copyright and the Internet	09/29/00	783*
Courts and the Media	09/23/94	817
Crime Victims' Rights	07/22/94	638*
Evangelical Christians	09/14/01	718*
Fairness in Salaries	05/29/92	466*
Feminism's Future	02/28/97	176*
Free-Press Disputes	04/08/05	293
Foreign Policy and Public Opinion	07/15/94	601
Future of Journalism	03/27/09	**273
Future of Newspapers	01/20/06	49
Globalization Backlash	09/28/01	775*
Human Rights in China	07/25/08	601
Internet Accuracy	08/01/08	625
Journalism Standards in the Internet Age	10/08/10	821
Journalism Under Fire	12/25/98	1121
Lies and Politics	02/18/11	145
Media Ownership	10/10/03	**845
The Partisan Divide	04/30/04	373
Partisan Politics	03/19/99	233
Patriotism in America	06/25/99	551
Political Conventions	08/08/08	649
Political Scandals	05/27/94	457
Politicians and Privacy	04/17/92	337
Press Freedom	02/05/10	97
Pursuing the Paranormal	03/29/96	272*
Religion in America	11/25/94	1050*
School Censorship	02/19/93	153*
Serial Killers	10/31/03	920*
Sex Scandals	01/22/10	49
Social Media and Politics	10/12/12	865
Student Journalism	06/05/98	481
Talk Show Democracy	04/29/94	361
TV Violence	03/26/93	282*
Women in Politics	03/21/08	265
Women and Sports	03/06/92	200*
Judicial system. ***See Courts***		
Justice Department, U.S.		
Antitrust Policy	06/12/98	505
Civil Liberties in Wartime	12/14/01	1017
Closing In on Tobacco	11/12/99	977
Corporate Crime	10/11/02	817
Cyber-Predators	03/01/02	169
Eyewitness Testimony	10/14/11	853
Gang Crisis	05/14/04	421
Government Secrecy	02/11/11	121
Homegrown Jihadists	09/03/10	701
Independent Counsels Re-examined	05/07/99	377
Interrogating the CIA	09/25/09	789
Legal-Aid Crisis	10/07/11	829
Mafia Crackdown	03/27/92	265
Policing the Borders	02/22/02	145
Presidential Power	11/15/02	945
Prosecuting Terrorists	03/12/10	**217*
Prosecutors and Politics	06/22/07	553
Race in America	07/11/03	593
Redistricting Disputes	03/12/04	221
Juvenile delinquency		
Bullying	02/04/05	101
Childhood Depression	07/16/99	611*
Death Penalty Update	01/08/99	7*
Declining Crime Rates	04/04/97	289
Gang Crisis	05/14/04	421
Juvenile Justice	02/25/94	169

	Date	Page
Juvenile Justice	11/07/08	913
Kids in Prison	04/27/01	345
Preventing Juvenile Crime	03/15/96	217
Preventing Teen Drug Use	03/15/02	217
School Violence	10/09/98	881
Teen Driving	01/07/05	1
Underage Drinking	03/13/92	217
Violence in Schools	09/11/92	785
Youth Gangs	10/11/91	753
Kerry, John		
Cyberpolitics	09/17/04	757
Social Security Reform	09/24/04	781
Kevorkian, Jack		
Assisted Suicide	02/21/92	145
Assisted Suicide Controversy	05/05/95	393
Klu Klux Klan		
Hate Groups	05/08/09	421
Korea (North)		
Economic Sanctions	10/28/94	945*
Foreign Aid After Sept. 11	04/26/02	361
Future of Korea	05/19/00	425
New Era in Asia	02/14/92	121
Non-Proliferation Treaty at 25	01/27/95	87*
North Korean Crisis	04/11/03	321
Nuclear Proliferation	06/05/92	481
Nuclear Proliferation and Terrorism	04/02/04	297
Rethinking Foreign Policy	02/02/07	97
U.S. Policy in Asia	11/27/92	1025
Weapons of Mass Destruction	03/08/02	193
Korea (South)		
Democracy in Asia	07/24/98	625
Foreign Aid After Sept. 11	04/26/02	361
Future of Korea	05/19/00	425
New Era in Asia	02/14/92	121
North Korean Crisis	04/11/03	321
U.S. Policy in Asia	11/27/92	1025
Kosovo		
Defense Priorities	07/30/99	641
Ethics of War	12/13/02	1013
Global Refugee Crisis	07/09/99	569
Stopping Genocide	08/27/04	685
The United Nations and Global Security	02/27/04	173
Kyoto Protocol on global warming		
Air Pollution Conflict	11/14/03	965
Alternative Energy	02/25/05	173
Bush and the Environment	10/25/02	865
Global Warming Treaty	01/26/01	41
Setting Environmental Priorities	05/21/99	425
The United Nations and Global Security	02/27/04	173
Labeling in packaging		
Consumer Safety	10/12/07	841
Dietary Supplements	09/03/04	709
Fair Trade Labeling	05/18/07	433
Fast-Food Shake-Up	11/08/91	840
Food Safety	06/04/93	498*
Food Safety	11/01/02	897
Food Safety Battle: Organic v. Biotech	09/04/98	761
Genetically Engineered Foods	08/05/94	687*
Genetically Modified Food	08/31/12	717
The Obscenity Debate	12/20/91	982*
Labor. ***See Employment and unemployment***		
Labor unions		
Attracting Jobs	03/02/12	205
Auto Industry's Future	02/06/09	**105
Big-Box Stores	09/10/04	733
The Business of Sports	02/10/95	121
Child Labor and Sweatshops	08/16/96	721
Contingent Work Force	10/24/97	937
Curbing CEO Pay	03/09/07	217
Exporting Jobs	02/20/04	149
Fairness in Salaries	05/29/92	468*
Future of the Airline Industry	06/21/02	545
The Growing Influence of Boycotts	01/04/91	1
Labor Movement's Future	06/28/96	553
Labor Unions' Future	09/02/05	**709
Living-Wage Movement	09/27/02	769
'Occupy' Movement	01/13/12	25
Privatizing Government Services	08/09/96	697
Public-Employee Unions	04/08/11	313
Regulating Nonprofits	12/26/97	1142*
Rethinking NAFTA	06/07/96	481
Retiree Health Benefits	12/06/91	921
School Reform	04/29/11	385
Teacher Education	10/17/97	929*
Upward Mobility	04/29/05	369
Worker Safety	05/21/04	445
Youth Apprenticeships	10/23/92	909*
Land mines		
Banning Land Mines	08/08/97	697
Land use policy		
Big-Box Stores	09/10/04	733
Crisis on the Plains	05/09/03	417
Energy Security	02/01/02	73
Public Land Policy	06/17/94	529
Reforming the Corps	05/30/03	497
Saving Open Spaces	11/05/99	953
Smart Growth	05/28/04	469
Traffic Congestion	05/06/94	393*
Urban Sprawl in the West	10/03/97	865
Landfills		
The Economics of Recycling	03/27/98	265
Future of Recycling	12/14/07	1033
Garbage Crisis	03/20/92	241
Languages. ***See Foreign languages; Official English***		

 *Indicates sidebar or "At Issue" report section. **Indicates an updated report.

	Date	Page
Latin America		
Change in Latin America	07/21/06	601
Cuba's Future	07/20/07	601
Democracy in Latin America	11/03/00	881
Ecotourism	10/20/06	865
Foreign Aid After Sept. 11	04/26/02	361
Globalization Backlash	09/28/01	761
Mexico's Drug War	12/12/08	1009
Oil Diplomacy	01/24/03	49
Oil Jitters	01/04/08	**1
Policing the Borders	02/22/02	145
Privatizing Government Services	08/09/96	708*
Rethinking NAFTA	06/07/96	481
Saving the Forests	09/20/91	681
Saving the Rain Forests	06/11/99	497
Torture	04/18/03	356*
Trouble in South America	03/14/03	225
Latinos. ***See Hispanics***		
Law enforcement. ***See Police and law enforcement***		
Lawyers. ***See also Independent counsels***		
Asbestos Litigation	05/02/03	393
Combating Scientific Misconduct	01/10/97	1
Death Penalty Debates	11/19/10	965
Eyewitness Testimony	10/14/11	853
Fairness in Salaries	05/29/92	464*
Fighting over Animal Rights	08/02/96	680*
High-Impact Litigation	02/11/00	89
Judicial Elections	04/24/09	373
The Jury System	11/10/95	993
Legal-Aid Crisis	10/07/11	829
Limiting Lawsuits	12/19/08	1033
Medical Malpractice	02/14/03	129
Prosecuting Terrorists	03/12/10	**217*
Prosecutors and the Law	11/09/07	937
Prosecutors and Politics	06/22/07	553
Public Defenders	04/18/08	337*
Too Many Lawsuits?	05/22/92	433
Wrongful Convictions	04/17/09	**345
Lead poisoning		
Indoor Air Pollution	10/27/95	957*
Lead Poisoning	06/19/92	525
New Air Quality Standards	03/07/97	193
Learning disabilities		
Boys' Emotional Needs	06/18/99	521
Homework Debate	12/06/02	993
Implementing the Disabilities Act	12/20/96	1105
Learning Disabilities	12/10/93	1081
Lebanon		
Middle East Tensions	10/27/06	**889
Leisure		
Ecotourism	10/20/06	865
Gambling Under Attack	09/06/96	769
National Forests	10/16/98	905

	Date	Page
National Parks	05/28/93	457
National Parks Under Pressure	10/06/06	817
Protecting the National Parks	06/16/00	521
Work, Family and Stress	08/14/92	689
Year-Round Schools	05/17/96	433
Lesbians. ***See Homosexuals***		
Libertarian Party		
Testing Term Limits	11/18/94	1020*
Third-Party Prospects	12/22/95	1144*
Libraries		
Civil Liberties Debates	10/24/03	893
Clashing over Copyright	11/08/96	985
Distance Learning	12/07/01	993
Future of Books	06/23/00	545
Future of Books	05/29/09	**473
The Future of Libraries	05/23/97	457
Future of Libraries	07/29/11	625
Hard Times for Libraries	06/26/92	549
Libraries and the Internet	06/01/01	465
Presidential Libraries	03/16/07	241
Reading Crisis?	02/22/08	169
Regulating the Internet	06/30/95	561
School Censorship	02/19/93	145
Library of Congress		
The Future of Libraries	05/23/97	457
Hard Times for Libraries	06/26/92	554*
Libya		
Economic Sanctions	10/28/94	945*
Nuclear Proliferation and Terrorism	04/02/04	297
Liquor. ***See Alcohol***		
Literacy and illiteracy		
Impact of the Internet on Thinking	09/24/10	773
Internet Accuracy	08/01/08	625
Learning to Read	05/19/95	441
The New Volunteerism	12/13/96	1088*
No Child Left Behind	05/27/05	469
Reading Crisis?	02/22/08	169
Video Games	11/10/06	**937
Littleton, Colo., school shootings, 1999		
Boys' Emotional Needs	06/18/99	521
Bullying	02/04/05	101
Childhood Depression	07/16/99	593
Discipline in Schools	02/15/08	145
Gang Crisis	05/14/04	421
Gun Rights Debates	10/31/08	**889
Gun Violence	05/25/07	457
School Violence	10/09/98	881
Smart Growth	05/28/04	469
Livestock and ranching		
Biotech Foods	03/30/02	262*
The Cloning Controversy	05/09/97	409
Crisis on the Plains	05/09/03	417
Drug-Resistant Bacteria	06/04/99	473

	Date	Page
Farm Subsidies	05/17/02	433
Food Safety	11/01/02	897
Genetically Engineered Foods	08/05/94	673
Mad Cow Disease	03/02/01	161
Public Land Policy	06/17/94	529
Water Shortages	08/01/03	649
Lobbying and lobbyists		
Covering the Uninsured	06/14/02	521
Dietary Supplements	09/03/04	709
Fairness in Salaries	05/29/92	466*
Pork Barrel Politics	06/16/06	529
Regulating Nonprofits	12/26/97	1129
Regulating Tobacco	09/30/94	841
Stock Market Troubles	01/16/04	25
The U.S. and Japan	05/31/91	341*
Local government. ***See Cities and towns***		
Logging. ***See Forests and forestry***		
Long-term health care		
Alzheimer's Disease	05/15/98	433
Caring for the Elderly	02/20/98	145
Caring for the Elderly	10/13/06	841
Drug Company Ethics	06/06/03	521
Medicaid Reform	07/16/04	589
Los Angeles, Calif.		
Community Policing	02/05/93	97
Drug Company Ethics	06/06/03	521
Gang Crisis	05/14/04	421
Police Brutality	09/06/91	633
Prison Reform	04/06/07	289
Water Shortages	08/01/03	649
Lotteries. ***See Gambling***		
Louisiana		
Electing Minorities	08/12/94	714*
Rebuilding New Orleans	02/03/06	97
Threatened Coastlines	02/07/92	109*
Low income. ***See Poverty***		
Magnet schools		
Rethinking School Integration	10/18/96	924*
School Choice	05/10/91	259*
School Desegregation	04/23/04	345
School Vouchers Showdown	02/15/02	121
Malcolm X		
Muslims in America	04/30/93	361
Mammography		
Advances in Cancer Research	08/25/95	764*
Breast Cancer	06/27/97	553
Women's Health Issues	05/13/94	423*
Managed medical care		
Caring for the Dying	09/05/97	777*
Caring for the Elderly	02/20/98	145
Caring for the Elderly	10/13/06	841

	Date	Page
Covering the Uninsured	06/14/02	521
Emergency Medicine	01/05/96	1
Hospitals' Financial Woes	08/13/99	689
Managed Care	04/12/96	313
Managing Managed Care	04/16/99	305
Medicare Reform	08/22/03	673
Mental Health Insurance	03/29/02	281*
Mental Health Policy	09/12/97	804*
Patients' Rights	02/06/98	97
Right to Die	05/13/05	421
Mandatory sentencing		
Drug-Policy Debate	07/28/00	593
Mandatory Sentencing	05/26/95	465
Prison-Building Boom	09/17/99	801
Prison Overcrowding	02/04/94	97
Sentencing Debates	11/05/04	925
Three-Strikes Laws	05/10/02	417
War on Drugs	03/19/93	252*
Mandela, Nelson		
South Africa's Future	01/14/94	31*
Marijuana		
Alternative Medicine's Next Phase	02/14/97	121
Drug-Policy Debate	07/28/00	593
Drug Testing	11/20/98	1001
Legalizing Marijuana	06/12/09	**525
Marijuana Laws	02/11/05	125
Medical Marijuana	08/20/99	705
Medication Abuse	10/09/09	837
Mexico's Future	10/26/12	913
Preventing Teen Drug Use	07/28/95	657
Preventing Teen Drug Use	03/15/02	233*
Teen Drug Use	06/03/11	481
Treating Addiction	01/06/95	8*
War on Drugs	06/02/06	481
Marriage. ***See Family***		
Mars		
Human Spaceflight	10/16/09	861
NASA's Future	05/23/03	473
Space Program	02/24/12	177
Space Program's Future	04/25/97	361
Uncertain Future for Man in Space	03/29/91	173
Mass transit		
Future of Amtrak	10/18/02	841
Mass Transit Boom	01/18/08	49
Smart Growth	05/28/04	469
Traffic Congestion	08/27/99	729
Mbeki, Thabo		
Global AIDS Crisis	10/13/00	821*
McCain, John		
Campaign Finance Reform	06/13/08	505
McCain-Feingold Act		
Campaign Finance Reform	06/13/08	505

 *Indicates sidebar or "At Issue" report section. **Indicates an updated report.

	Date	Page
McDonald's		
Fast-Food Shake-Up	11/08/91	825
Historic Preservation	10/07/94	882*
Meat. ***See Food and nutrition***		
Media. ***See Journalism; Television and radio***		
Medicaid		
Aging Baby Boomers	10/19/07	865
Aging Population	07/15/11	577
AIDS Update	12/04/98	1063*
Alzheimer's Disease	05/15/98	433
Assessing the New Health Care Law	09/21/12	789
Birth-Control Debate	06/24/05	565
Caring for the Elderly	02/20/98	145
Caring for the Elderly	10/13/06	841
Covering the Uninsured	06/14/02	521
Emergency Medicine	01/05/96	1
Health-Care Reform	08/28/09	693*
Health-Care Reform	06/11/10	**505
Infant Mortality	07/31/92	641
Medicaid Reform	07/16/04	589
Mental Illness Medication Debate	02/06/04	101
Organ Donations	04/15/11	337
Right to Die	05/13/05	421
State Budget Crises	10/03/03	821
States and Federalism	10/15/10	845
Medical care. ***See also Diseases and health problems; Health insurance***		
Aging Baby Boomers	10/19/07	865
Aging Population	07/15/11	577
AIDS Update	12/04/98	1049
Alternative Medicine	01/31/92	73
Alternative Medicine's Next Phase	02/14/97	121
Alzheimer's Disease	07/24/92	617
Asbestos Litigation	05/02/03	393
Assessing the New Health Care Law	09/21/12	789
Assisted Suicide Controversy	05/05/95	393
Banning Land Mines	08/08/97	710*
Battling HIV/AIDS	10/26/07	889
Cancer Treatments	09/11/98	803*
Caring for the Dying	09/05/97	769
Caring for the Elderly	02/20/98	145
Caring for the Elderly	10/13/06	841
Caring for Veterans	04/23/10	361
Childhood Immunizations	06/18/93	529
Combating AIDS	04/21/95	345
Computers and Medicine	10/27/00	857
Cosmetic Surgery	04/15/05	317
Covering the Uninsured	06/14/02	521
Debt Collectors	07/20/12	621
Drug Company Ethics	06/06/03	521
Drug Safety	03/11/05	221
Emergency Medicine	01/05/96	1
Fighting SARS	06/20/03	569
Fighting Superbugs	08/24/07	673
Genes and Health	01/21/11	49
Head Start	04/09/93	297*
Health-Care Reform	08/28/09	693*
Health-Care Reform	06/11/10	**505
Homeopathy Debate	12/19/03	1069
Increase in Autism	06/13/03	**545
Infant Mortality	07/31/92	641
Legalizing Marijuana	06/12/09	**525
Managing Managed Care	04/16/99	305
Medicaid Reform	07/16/04	589
Medical Malpractice	02/14/03	129
Medical Mistakes	02/25/00	137
Medicare Reform	08/22/03	673
Mental Illness Medication Debate	02/06/04	101
Middle-Class Squeeze	03/06/09	201
Native Americans' Future	07/12/96	608*
Nursing Shortage	09/20/02	745
Organ Donations	04/15/11	337
Organ Shortage	02/21/03	153
Patients' Rights	02/06/98	97
Patient Safety	02/10/12	125
Prayer and Healing	01/14/05	25
Preventing Cancer	01/16/09	25
Preventing Disease	01/06/12	1
Preventing Memory Loss	04/04/08	289*
Primary Care	03/17/95	217
Prison Health Care	01/05/07	1
Rating Doctors	05/05/00	377
Re-examining the Constitution	09/07/12	741
Reforming the FDA	06/06/97	481
Right to Die	05/13/05	421
Sexually Transmitted Diseases	12/03/04	997
Supreme Court Controversies	09/28/12	813
Torture	04/18/03	352*
Treating ADHD	08/03/12	669
Treating Anxiety	02/08/02	97
Treating Depression	06/26/09	573
Treatment of Veterans	11/19/04	973
Universal Coverage	03/30/07	265
Vaccine Controversies	08/25/00	641
Women in the Military	11/13/09	957
Women's Health	11/07/03	941
Women's Health Issues	05/13/94	409
Wounded Veterans	08/31/07	697
Youth Suicide	02/13/04	125
Medical care — Cost control		
Alzheimer's Disease	05/15/98	433
Assessing the New Health Care Law	09/21/12	789
Assisted Suicide	02/21/92	145
Assisted Suicide Controversy	05/05/95	399*
Asbestos Litigation	05/02/03	393
Childhood Immunizations	06/18/93	529
Closing In on Tobacco	11/12/99	977

	Date	Page
Cost of the Iraq War	04/25/08	361*
Covering the Uninsured	06/14/02	521
Drug Company Ethics	06/06/03	521
Emergency Medicine	01/05/96	1
Health-Care Reform	08/28/09	693*
Health-Care Reform	06/11/10	**505
Heart Health	09/12/08	721
Hospitals' Financial Woes	08/13/99	689
Managed Care	04/12/96	313
Managing Managed Care	04/16/99	305
Medicaid Reform	07/16/04	589
Medical Malpractice	02/14/03	129
Medicare Reform	08/22/03	673
Mental Health Insurance	03/29/02	265
Mental Illness Medication Debate	02/06/04	101
Middle-Class Squeeze	03/06/09	201
Nursing Shortage	09/20/02	745
Organ Shortage	02/21/03	153
Patients' Rights	02/06/98	97
Prescription Drug Prices	07/17/92	597
Preventing Cancer	01/16/09	25
Preventing Disease	01/06/12	1
Preventing Teen Pregnancy	05/14/93	409
Primary Care	03/17/95	217
Retiree Health Benefits	12/06/91	930*
Rising Health Costs	04/07/06	289
Talk Show Democracy	04/29/94	374*
Too Many Lawsuits?	05/22/92	443
Treatment of Veterans	11/19/04	973
Medical ethics		
Abortion Debates	03/21/03	249
Advances in Cancer Research	08/25/95	769*
Assisted Suicide	02/21/92	145
Assisted Suicide Controversy	05/05/95	393
Biology and Behavior	04/03/98	289
Caring for the Dying	09/05/97	769
The Cloning Controversy	05/09/97	409
Cosmetic Surgery	04/15/05	317
Covering the Uninsured	06/14/02	521
'Designer' Humans	05/18/01	425
Drug Company Ethics	06/06/03	521
Drug Safety	03/11/05	221
Embryo Research	12/17/99	1065
Fetal Tissue Research	08/16/91	561
Fighting SARS	06/20/03	576*
Gene Therapy	10/18/91	777
Gene Therapy's Future	12/08/95	1089
Health-Care Reform	08/28/09	693*
Homeopathy Debate	12/19/03	1069
Human Genome Research	05/12/00	401
Internet Privacy	11/06/98	966*
Managed Care	04/12/96	313
Marijuana Laws	02/11/05	125
Medical Malpractice	02/14/03	129
Medical Mistakes	02/25/00	137
Medication Abuse	10/09/09	837
Organ Donations	04/15/11	337
Organ Shortage	02/21/03	158*
Organ Transplants	08/11/95	705
Patients' Rights	02/06/98	103*
Prayer and Healing	01/14/05	25
Preventing Memory Loss	04/04/08	289*
Privacy Under Attack	06/15/01	505
Professional Football	01/29/10	**73
Reproductive Ethics	04/08/94	289
Right to Die	05/13/05	421
Stem Cell Research	09/01/06	**697
Teen Drug Use	06/03/11	481
Too Many Lawsuits?	05/22/92	443
Medical research		
3D Printing	12/07/12	1037
Abortion Debates	09/10/10	725
Advances in Cancer Research	08/25/95	753
Alternative Medicine	01/31/92	73
Alzheimer's Disease	07/24/92	622*
Alzheimer's Disease	05/15/98	433
Animal Rights	05/24/91	301
Animal Rights	01/08/10	1
Baby Boomers at Midlife	07/31/98	649
Battling HIV/AIDS	10/26/07	889
Biology and Behavior	04/03/98	289
Birth-Control Debate	06/24/05	565
Blood Supply Safety	11/11/94	985
Breast Cancer	06/27/97	553
Breast Cancer	04/02/10	289
Cancer Treatments	09/11/98	785
Childhood Depression	07/16/99	593
Chronic Fatigue Syndrome	04/05/02	289
The Cloning Controversy	05/09/97	409
Combating AIDS	04/21/95	345
Combating Infectious Diseases	06/09/95	489
Combating Scientific Misconduct	01/10/97	1
Depression	10/09/92	857
Diabetes Epidemic	03/09/01	185
Drug Company Ethics	06/06/03	521
Drugmakers Under Siege	09/03/99	753
Drug Safety	03/11/05	221
Electromagnetic Fields	04/26/91	237
Embryo Research	12/17/99	1065
Examining Forensics	07/17/09	597
Fetal Tissue Research	08/16/91	561
Fighting over Animal Rights	08/02/96	673
Fighting SARS	06/20/03	569
Fighting Superbugs	08/24/07	673
Genes and Health	01/21/11	49
Gene Therapy	10/18/91	777
Gene Therapy's Future	12/08/95	1089
Human Genome Research	05/12/00	401

	Date	Page
Increase in Autism	06/13/03	**545
Lead Poisoning	06/19/92	529*
Mad Cow Disease	03/02/01	161
Medical Marijuana	08/20/99	705
Mental Health Insurance	03/29/02	265
Mental Illness Medication Debate	02/06/04	101
Nanotechnology	06/11/04	517
New Air Quality Standards	03/07/97	193
Organ Donations	04/15/11	337
Organ Shortage	02/21/03	153
Organ Transplants	08/11/95	705
Patient Safety	02/10/12	125
Prayer and Healing	01/14/05	25
Preventing Cancer	01/16/09	25
Preventing Memory Loss	04/04/08	289*
Reforming the FDA	06/06/97	481
Reproductive Ethics	04/08/94	289
Saving the Forests	09/20/91	697*
Science in America	01/11/08	25
Science and Politics	08/20/04	661
Sexually Transmitted Diseases	12/03/04	997
Sleep Deprivation	06/26/98	553
Sleep Deprivation	02/12/10	121
Space Program's Future	12/24/93	1133*
Stem Cell Research	09/01/06	**697
Treating ADHD	08/03/12	669
Treating Alzheimer's	03/04/11	193
Treating Anxiety	02/08/02	97
Treating Depression	06/26/09	573
Treatment of Veterans	11/19/04	973
Women and AIDS	12/25/92	1121
Women's Health	11/07/03	941
Medicare		
Aging Baby Boomers	10/19/07	865
Alzheimer's Disease	05/15/98	433
Assessing the New Health Care Law	09/21/12	789
Caring for the Elderly	02/20/98	145
Caring for the Elderly	10/13/06	841
Covering the Uninsured	06/14/02	521
Drug Company Ethics	06/06/03	521
Drugmakers Under Siege	09/03/99	753
Health-Care Reform	08/28/09	693*
Health-Care Reform	06/11/10	**505
Hospitals' Financial Woes	08/13/99	689
Managing Managed Care	04/16/99	323*
Medicaid Reform	07/16/04	589
Medicare Reform	08/22/03	673
National Debt	03/18/11	241
Patients' Rights	02/06/98	109*
Prescription Drug Prices	07/17/92	607
Retiree Health Benefits	12/06/91	930*
Retirement Security	05/31/02	481
Right to Die	05/13/05	421
Social Security Reform	09/24/04	781
Medvedev, Dmitry		
Dealing With the "New" Russia	06/06/08	481
Melatonin		
Alternative Medicine's Next Phase	02/14/97	132*
Baby Boomers at Midlife	07/31/98	660*
Sleep Deprivation	06/26/98	564*
Mental health and illness		
Adoption	11/26/93	1044*
Advances in Cancer Research	08/25/95	766*
Aggressive Driving	07/25/97	649
Alternative Medicine	01/31/92	73
Alzheimer's Disease	07/24/92	617
American Indians	04/28/06	**361
America's Pampered Pets	12/27/96	1129
Boys' Emotional Needs	06/18/99	521
Child Sexual Abuse	01/15/93	25
Childhood Depression	07/16/99	593
Children and Divorce	06/07/91	349
Children and Divorce	01/19/01	25
Chronic Fatigue Syndrome	04/05/02	289
Combating Addiction	02/09/07	121
Death Penalty Debate	03/10/95	199*
Death Penalty Debates	11/19/10	965
Depression	10/09/92	857
Disaster Response	10/15/93	902*
Downward Mobility	07/23/93	625
Drug Safety	03/11/05	221
Eating Disorders	12/18/92	1097
Eating Disorders	02/10/06	**121
Educating Gifted Students	03/28/97	273*
Ending Homelessness	06/18/04	541
Gambling Boom	03/18/94	241
Gambling Under Attack	09/06/96	776*
Gun Rights Debates	10/31/08	**889
Gun Violence	05/25/07	457
Helping the Homeless	01/26/96	73
The Homeless	08/07/92	681*
Increase in Autism	06/13/03	**545
Job Stress	08/04/95	681
Marriage and Divorce	05/10/96	409
Mental Health Insurance	03/29/02	265
Mental Health Policy	09/12/97	793
Mental Illness	08/06/93	673
Mental Illness Medication Debate	02/06/04	101
Military Suicides	09/23/11	781*
Prayer and Healing	01/14/05	25
Politicians and Privacy	04/17/92	346*
Preventing Memory Loss	04/04/08	289*
Professional Football	01/29/10	**73
Prozac Controversy	08/19/94	721
Punishing Sex Offenders	01/12/96	25
Recovered-Memory Debate	07/05/96	577
Rethinking the Death Penalty	11/16/01	953*
Serial Killers	10/31/03	917

	Date	Page
Sexual Abuse and the Clergy	05/03/02	407*
Sleep Deprivation	02/12/10	121
Solitary Confinement	09/14/12	765
Students Under Stress	07/13/07	577
Teenage Suicide	06/14/91	369
Torture	04/18/03	352*
Transgender Issues	05/05/06	385
Treating ADHD	08/03/12	669
Treating Alzheimer's	03/04/11	193
Treating Anxiety	02/08/02	97
Treating Depression	06/26/09	573
Treatment of Veterans	11/19/04	973
Whistleblowers	12/05/97	1064*
Youth Suicide	02/13/04	125
Mercenaries. ***See Private Military Contractors (PMCs)***		
Mergers. ***See Corporate mergers***		
Methamphetamine		
Methamphetamine	07/15/05	589
War on Drugs	06/02/06	481
Methanol. ***See Alternative fuels***		
Mexican Americans		
America's Border Fence	09/19/08	745
Hispanic Americans	10/30/92	929
Hispanic-Americans' New Clout	09/18/98	809
Immigration Debate	02/01/08	**97
Mexico		
America's Border Fence	09/19/08	745
Change in Latin America	07/21/06	601
Debate Over Immigration	07/14/00	582*
Democracy in Latin America	11/03/00	881
Exporting Jobs	02/20/04	149
Illegal Immigration	04/24/92	361
Illegal Immigration	05/06/05	393
Immigration Debate	02/01/08	**97
International Law	12/17/04	1049
Mexico's Drug War	12/12/08	1009
Mexico's Emergence	07/19/91	489
Mexico's Future	09/19/97	817
Mexico's Future	10/26/12	913
Policing the Borders	02/22/02	145
Rethinking NAFTA	06/07/96	481
Truck Safety	03/12/99	222*
U.S.-Mexico Relations	11/09/01	921
Worker Retraining	01/21/94	66*
Microsoft Corp.		
Antitrust Policy	06/12/98	505
Cybersecurity	09/26/03	797
Exporting Jobs	02/20/04	149
Online Privacy	11/06/09	**933
Middle class		
Affordable Housing	02/09/01	89
The Black Middle Class	01/23/98	49

	Date	Page
Middle-Class Squeeze	03/06/09	201
Student Aid	01/25/08	73
Vanishing Jobs	03/13/09	225
Middle East		
Archaeology Today	05/24/02	457
Blighted Cities	11/12/10	941*
Calculating the Costs of the Gulf War	03/15/91	145
Civil Liberties in Wartime	12/14/01	1017
Confronting Iraq	10/04/02	793
Democracy in the Arab World	01/30/04	73
Democrats' Future	10/29/10	893
Energy Security	02/01/02	73
Exporting Democracy	04/01/05	269
Foreign Aid After Sept. 11	04/26/02	361
Global Jihad	10/14/05	857
Global Refugee Crisis	07/09/99	572*
Global Water Shortages	12/15/95	1113
Hating America	11/23/01	969
Israel at 50	03/06/98	193
Middle East Conflict	04/06/01	273
Middle East Peace	01/21/05	53
Middle East Tensions	10/27/06	**889
New Strategy in Iraq	02/23/07	169
Nuclear Proliferation	06/05/92	493
Nuclear Proliferation and Terrorism	04/02/04	297
Oil Diplomacy	01/24/03	49
Oil Jitters	01/04/08	**1
The Palestinians	08/30/91	609
Policing the Borders	02/22/02	145
The Politics of Energy	03/05/99	199*
Prospects for Mideast Peace	08/30/02	673
Rebuilding Iraq	07/11/03	625
Reform in Iran	12/18/98	1097
Religious Persecution	11/21/97	1009
Rethinking Foreign Policy	02/02/07	97
Rise in Counterinsurgency	09/05/08	697
Understanding Islam	11/03/06	913
The United Nations and Global Security	02/27/04	173
War in Iraq	10/21/05	881
War on Terrorism	10/12/01	820*
Water Quality	02/11/94	138*
Weapons of Mass Destruction	03/08/02	193
Military police		
Haiti's Dilemma	02/18/05	149
Military policy		
Afghanistan Dilemma	08/07/09	**669*
America at War	07/23/10	**605
Artificial Intelligence	04/22/11	361
Assisting Refugees	02/07/97	103*
Banning Land Mines	08/08/97	697
Bush's Defense Strategy	09/07/01	689
Chemical and Biological Weapons	01/31/97	73

	Date	Page
Civil Liberties in Wartime	12/14/01	1017
Closing Guantánamo	02/27/09	**177
Costs of the Gulf War	03/15/91	145
Confronting Iraq	10/04/02	793
Cybersecurity	09/26/03	808*
Cybersecurity	02/26/10	169
Defense Priorities	07/30/99	641
Democrats in Congress	06/08/07	505
Disaster Preparedness	11/18/05	**981
Drone Warfare	08/06/10	653
Ethics of War	12/13/02	1013
Expanding NATO	05/16/97	433
Exporting Democracy	04/01/05	269
Foreign Policy and Public Opinion	07/15/94	611*
Foreign Policy Burden	08/20/93	721
Future of NATO	02/28/03	177
Gays in the Military	09/18/09	**765
Global Refugee Crisis	07/09/99	569
Government Secrecy	02/11/11	121
International Law	12/17/04	1049
Interrogating the CIA	09/25/09	789
Israel at 50	03/06/98	209*
Military Suicides	09/23/11	781*
Missile Defense	09/08/00	689
NATO's Changing Role	08/21/92	713
New Challenges in Space	07/23/99	631*
The New CIA	12/11/92	1073
New Defense Priorities	09/13/02	721
New Era in Asia	02/14/92	121
New Strategy in Iraq	02/23/07	169
North Korean Crisis	04/11/03	321
Nuclear Disarmament	10/02/09	**813
Nuclear Proliferation and Terrorism	04/02/04	297
Panama Canal	11/26/99	1017
Presidential Power	11/15/02	945
Privatizing the Military	06/25/04	565
Privatizing the Military	07/13/12	597
Prosecuting Terrorists	03/12/10	**217*
Pursuing the Paranormal	03/29/96	265
Reassessing Foreign Aid	09/27/96	847*
Rebuilding Afghanistan	12/21/01	1057*
Reforming the CIA	02/02/96	97
Rise in Counterinsurgency	09/05/08	697
Sexual Harassment	04/27/12	377
Treatment of Detainees	08/25/06	673
U.S. Policy in Asia	11/27/92	1025
U.S.-British Relations	01/30/98	81*
U.S.-China Relations	05/07/10	**409
U.S.-Europe Relations	03/23/12	277
The U.S. and Japan	05/31/91	325
U.S.-Pakistan Relations	08/05/11	653*
War in Iraq	10/21/05	881
Weapons of Mass Destruction	03/08/02	193
Women in the Military	11/13/09	957

	Date	Page
Military service		
America at War	07/23/10	**605
Calculating the Costs of the Gulf War	03/15/91	145
Draft Debates	08/19/05	661
Drone Warfare	08/06/10	653
Gay Rights	03/05/93	193
Gay Rights Update	04/14/00	305
Gays in the Military	09/18/09	**765
Legacy of the Vietnam War	02/18/00	113
Military Suicides	09/23/11	781*
New Military Culture	04/26/96	361
Privatizing the Military	06/25/04	565
Treating Depression	06/26/09	573
Treatment of Veterans	11/19/04	973
Upward Mobility	04/29/05	369
Women in the Military	09/25/92	850*
Millennium		
The New Millennium	10/15/99	889
Mineral resources and mining		
Asbestos Litigation	05/02/03	393
Cleaning Up Hazardous Wastes	08/23/96	745
Coal Mining Safety	03/17/06	241
Energy Security	02/01/02	73
Public Land Policy	06/17/94	529
Worker Safety	05/21/04	445
Minimum wage		
Domestic Poverty	09/07/07	**721
Ending Homelessness	06/18/04	541
Income Inequality	04/17/98	337
Living-Wage Movement	09/27/02	769
Minimum Wage	12/16/05	1053
The Working Poor	11/03/95	977*
Minorities		
Affirmative Action	09/21/01	737
Affirmative Action	10/17/08	**841
Aging Population	07/15/11	577
AIDS Update	12/04/98	1049
Alcohol Advertising	03/14/97	221*
Arts Education	03/16/12	253
Asian Americans	12/13/91	945
Bilingual Education	08/13/93	697
Bilingual Education vs. English Immersion	12/11/09	1029
Birth-Control Debate	06/24/05	565
Black Colleges	12/12/03	1045
The Black Middle Class	01/23/98	49
Census 2000	05/01/98	385
Census Controversey	05/14/10	433
Changing Demographics	11/16/12	989
Changing U.S. Electorate	05/30/08	**457
Charter Schools	12/20/02	1033
Chronic Fatigue Syndrome	04/05/02	289
Cleaning Up Hazardous Wastes	08/23/96	752*

	Date	Page
Consumer Debt	03/02/07	193
Criminal Records and Employment	04/20/12	349
Debate over Bilingualism	01/19/96	49
Debating Hip-Hop	06/15/07	529
Discipline in Schools	02/15/08	145
Diversity in the Workplace	10/10/97	889
Domestic Poverty	09/07/07	**721
Educating Gifted Students	03/28/97	265
Education Standards	03/11/94	217
Electing Minorities	08/12/94	697
Environmental Justice	06/19/98	529
Europe's New Right	02/12/93	121
Eyewitness Testimony	10/14/11	853
Fixing Urban Schools	04/27/07	**361
Foster Care Reform	01/09/98	14*
The Future of Baseball	09/25/98	839*
Future of the Airline Industry	06/21/02	545
Future of the GOP	03/20/09	249
Future of Homeownership	12/14/12	1061
Gangs in the U.S.	07/16/10	581
Getting into College	02/23/96	169
The Glass Ceiling	10/29/93	937
Grade Inflation	06/07/02	505
Hate Crimes	01/08/93	1
Hispanic Americans	10/30/92	929
Hispanic-Americans' New Clout	09/18/98	809
Housing Discrimination	02/24/95	169
Immigration Conflict	03/09/12	229
Infant Mortality	07/31/92	641
Intelligence Testing	07/30/93	654*
Living-Wage Movement	09/27/02	769
Mafia Crackdown	03/27/92	270*
Muslims in America	04/30/93	361
National Education Standards	05/14/99	401
Native Americans	05/08/92	385
Native Americans' Future	07/12/96	601
The New Immigrants	01/24/97	49
New Military Culture	04/26/96	361
No Child Left Behind	05/27/05	469
Obesity Epidemic	01/31/03	78*
Organ Donations	04/15/11	337
Police Misconduct	04/06/12	301
Policing the Borders	02/22/02	145
Prisoner Reentry	12/04/09	1005
Property Rights	03/04/05	197
Puerto Rico: The Struggle over Status	02/08/91	81
Race in America	07/11/03	593
Racial Diversity in Public Schools	09/14/07	**745
Racial Quotas	05/17/91	277
Racial Tensions in Schools	01/07/94	1
Redistricting	02/16/01	113
Redistricting Debates	02/25/11	169
Redistricting Disputes	03/12/04	221
Reproductive Ethics	05/15/09	449
Rethinking Affirmative Action	04/28/95	369
Rethinking School Integration	10/18/96	913
Revitalizing the Cities	10/13/95	904*
School Choice	05/10/91	253
School Desegregation	04/23/04	345
School Vouchers Showdown	02/15/02	121
Shock Jocks	06/01/07	**481
Soviet Republics Rebel	07/12/91	465
Straining the Safety Net	07/31/09	645
Student Aid	01/25/08	73
Talk Show Democracy	04/29/94	379*
Teacher Shortages	08/24/01	633
Three-Strikes Laws	05/10/02	417
Upward Mobility	04/29/05	369
Voter Rights	05/18/12	449
Women and Human Rights	04/30/99	353
Women and Sports	03/06/92	206*
Youth Gangs	10/11/91	753
Youth Violence	03/05/10	193*
Missile-defense systems		
Bush's Defense Strategy	09/07/01	689
Defense Priorities	07/30/99	641
Missile Defense	09/08/00	689
New Challenges in Space	07/23/99	631*
New Defense Priorities	09/13/02	721
Nuclear Proliferation and Terrorism	04/02/04	297
Transatlantic Tensions	07/13/01	533
Weapons of Mass Destruction	03/08/02	193
Mobile phones. ***See Cellular telephones; Telecommunications***		
Monetary policy		
Deflation Fears	02/13/98	121
Euro Crisis	10/05/12	841
European Monetary Union	11/27/98	1025
Financial Bailout	10/24/08	**865
Financial Crisis	05/09/08	409
Financial Industry Overhaul	07/30/10	629
The National Debt	11/14/08	937
National Debt	03/18/11	241
Stimulating the Economy	01/10/03	1
Monopoly. ***See Antitrust law; Economic conditions***		
Montreal Protocol		
Global Warming Update	11/01/96	969*
Ozone Depletion	04/03/92	299*
Setting Environmental Priorities	05/21/99	439*
Morals. ***See Ethical and moral issues***		
Mothers Against Drunk Driving		
Alcohol Advertising	03/14/97	230*
Drunken Driving	10/06/00	793
Teen Driving	01/07/05	1
Movie industry		
Attracting Jobs	03/02/12	205
Clashing over Copyright	11/08/96	985

 *Indicates sidebar or "At Issue" report section. **Indicates an updated report.

	Date	Page
Copyright and the Internet	09/29/00	769
Fairness in Salaries	05/29/92	463*
Movie Ratings	03/28/03	273
Pay-Per-View TV	10/04/91	729
Movies		
Artificial Intelligence	11/14/97	990*
Asian Americans	12/13/91	959*
The Cloning Controversy	05/09/97	420*
Encouraging Teen Abstinence	07/10/98	588*
The FBI Under Fire	04/11/97	318*
Helping the Homeless	01/26/96	86*
Internet Regulation	04/13/12	325
Mafia Crackdown	03/27/92	276*
Mental Illness	08/06/93	684*
Movie Ratings	03/28/03	273
Muslims in America	04/30/93	361*
The Obscenity Debate	12/20/91	980*
Searching for Jesus	12/11/98	1087*
Sex, Violence and the Media	11/17/95	1017
Teaching History	09/29/95	862*
Youth Gangs	10/11/91	765*
Multicultural education		
Academic Politics	02/16/96	145
Liberal Arts Education	04/10/98	313
Racial Tensions in Schools	01/07/94	17*
Teaching History	09/29/95	849
Museums		
Archaeology Today	05/24/02	473*
Is America Allowing Its Past to Be Stolen?	01/18/91	33
Native Americans	05/08/92	399
Stolen Antiquities	04/13/07	313
Teaching History	09/29/95	858*
Music		
Clashing over Copyright	11/08/96	985
Copyright and the Internet	09/29/00	769
Debating Hip-Hop	06/15/07	529
Fairness in Salaries	05/29/92	463*
Future of the Music Industry	11/21/03	989
Internet Regulation	04/13/12	325
The Obscenity Debate	12/20/91	969
Pay-Per-View TV	10/04/91	733*
Sex, Violence and the Media	11/17/95	1028*
Teenage Suicide	06/14/91	381*
TV Violence	03/26/93	276*
Mutual funds		
Mutual Funds	05/20/94	433
Socially Responsible Investing	08/29/08	673
Stock Market Troubles	01/16/04	25
NAACP. ***See National Association for the Advancement of Colored People***		
NAFTA. ***See North American Free Trade Agreement***		
Nanotechnology		
Nanotechnology	06/11/04	517
Narcotics. ***See Drug abuse; Drug traffic***		
National Aeronautics and Space Administration (NASA)		
NASA's Future	05/23/03	473
Networking the Classroom	10/20/95	926*
New Challenges in Space	07/23/99	617
Ozone Depletion	04/03/92	289
The Search for Extraterrestrials	03/05/04	197
Space Program	02/24/12	177
Space Program's Future	12/24/93	1129
Space Program's Future	04/25/97	361
Uncertain Future for Man on Space	03/29/91	173
National Association for the Advancement of Colored People (NAACP)		
The Black Middle Class	01/23/98	61*
Redistricting Disputes	03/12/04	221
School Desegregation	04/23/04	345
National Collegiate Athletic Association (NCAA)		
Reforming Big-Time College Sports	03/19/04	249
National Education Association		
Charter Schools	12/20/02	1033
Grade Inflation	06/07/02	505
Teacher Education	10/17/97	924*
National Endowment for the Arts		
Arts Funding	10/21/94	913
National Highway Traffic Safety Administration		
SUV Debate	05/16/03	454*
Teen Driving	01/07/05	1
Truck Safety	03/12/99	209
National Institutes of Health, U.S.		
Alternative Medicine	01/31/92	73
Alternative Medicine's Next Phase	02/14/97	121
Avian Flu Threat	01/13/06	25
Chronic Fatigue Syndrome	04/05/02	289
Combating Scientific Misconduct	01/10/97	1
Embryo Research	12/17/99	1065
Fetal Tissue Research	08/16/91	561
Fighting SARS	06/20/03	569
Gene Therapy	10/18/91	777
Gene Therapy's Future	12/08/95	1089
Increase in Autism	06/13/03	**545
Science and Politics	08/20/04	672*
Stem Cell Research	09/01/06	**697
Women's Health Issues	05/13/94	416*
Nationalism		
Centennial Olympic Games	04/05/96	289
Deepening Canadian Crisis over Quebec	04/12/91	205
Democracy in the Arab World	01/30/04	73
Europe's New Right	02/12/93	121
Quebec Sovereignty	10/06/95	873

	Date	Page
Soviet Republics Rebel	07/12/91	465
U.S.-Russian Relations	05/22/98	474*
National Labor Relations Board		
Future of the Airline Industry	06/21/02	545
Labor Movement's Future	06/28/96	564*
National Parks		
Bush and the Environment	10/25/02	865
Is America Allowing Its Past to Be Stolen?	01/18/91	33
Managing Public Lands	11/04/11	929
National Parks	05/28/93	457
National Parks Under Pressure	10/06/06	817
Protecting the National Parks	06/16/00	521
National Performance Review		
Reinventing Government	02/17/95	145
National Public Radio		
Public Broadcasting	09/18/92	821*
National Rifle Association		
Gun Control Debate	11/12/04	949
Mexico's Drug War	12/12/08	1009
National Science Foundation		
Combating Scientific Misconduct	01/10/97	1
National service. ***See Voluntarism***		
Native Americans		
Adoption	11/26/93	1047*
Alcohol Advertising	03/14/97	221*
American Indians	04/28/06	**361
Archaeology Today	05/24/02	457
Bilingual Education vs. English Immersion	12/11/09	1029
Crisis on the Plains	05/09/03	417
Environmental Justice	06/19/98	534*
Gambling Boom	03/18/94	241
Gambling in America	03/07/03	201
Gambling Under Attack	09/06/96	769
Is America Allowing Its Past to Be Stolen?	01/18/91	33
Native Americans	05/08/92	385
Native Americans' Future	07/12/96	601
Parental Rights	10/25/96	942*
Quebec Sovereignty	10/06/95	887*
Religion in the Workplace	08/23/02	649
Reparations Movement	06/22/01	536*
NATO. ***See North Atlantic Treaty Organization***		
Natural gas		
Air Pollution Conflict	11/14/03	976*
Alternative Energy	07/10/92	584
Alternative Energy	02/25/05	173
Electric Cars	07/09/93	582*
Energy Policy	05/25/01	454*
Energy Policy	05/20/11	457
Fracking Controversy	12/16/11	1049
Renewable Energy	11/07/97	961

	Date	Page
Natural resources. ***See Agriculture; Conservation; Energy policy; Forests and forestry; Water resources; Wildlife***		
Navy, U.S. ***See Military service***		
Nazis		
Ethics of War	12/13/02	1013
Holocaust Reparations	03/26/99	257
Reparations Movement	06/22/01	529
Stopping Genocide	08/27/04	685
War Crimes	07/07/95	598*
Neo-Nazis		
Europe's New Right	02/12/93	121
Netherlands		
Aggressive Driving	07/25/97	662*
Assisted Suicide	02/21/92	158*
Assisted Suicide Controversy	05/05/95	404*
Caring for the Dying	09/05/97	780*
Nevada		
Nuclear Waste	06/08/01	489
Prostitution	06/11/93	505
New England. ***See Northeastern states***		
New York		
Community Policing	02/05/93	110*
Death Penalty Debate	03/10/95	193
Declining Crime Rates	04/04/97	289
The Homeless	08/07/92	676
Mafia Crackdown	03/27/92	265
Policing the Police	03/17/00	209
Re-examining 9/11	06/04/04	493
News media, Newspapers. ***See Journalism***		
Noise pollution		
Indoor Air Pollution	10/27/95	958*
Nonprofit organizations. ***See Charities and nonprofit organizations***		
North American Free Trade Agreement (NAFTA)		
Deepening Canadian Crisis over Quebec	04/12/91	214*
Exporting Jobs	02/20/04	149
Illegal Immigration	04/24/92	379
Immigration Reform	09/24/93	854*
Income Inequality	04/17/98	352*
International Law	12/17/04	1049
Mexico's Emergence	07/19/91	501*
Mexico's Future	09/19/97	817
Mexico's Future	10/26/12	913
Quebec Sovereignty	10/06/95	880*
Rethinking NAFTA	06/07/96	481
Truck Safety	03/12/99	222*
U.S. Auto Industry	10/16/92	897*
U.S.-Mexico Relations	11/09/01	921
U.S. Trade Policy	01/29/93	73
Worker Retraining	01/21/94	66*
Worker Safety	05/21/04	445

	Date	Page
North Atlantic Treaty Organization (NATO)		
Afghanistan Dilemma	08/07/09	**669*
Dealing With the "New" Russia	06/06/08	481
Defense Priorities	07/30/99	641
Expanding NATO	05/16/97	433
Foreign Policy Burden	08/20/93	721
Future Job Market	01/11/02	1
Future of NATO	02/28/03	177
Global Refugee Crisis	07/09/99	569
NATO's Changing Role	08/21/92	713
Russia's Political Future	05/03/96	401*
Stopping Genocide	08/27/04	685
U.S.-Europe Relations	03/23/12	277
U.S.-Russian Relations	05/22/98	457
North Korea. *See Korea (North)*		
Northeastern states		
Marine Mammals vs. Fish	08/28/92	747
Recession's Regional Impact	02/01/91	65
Northern Ireland		
Northern Ireland Cease-Fire	09/15/95	801
U.S.-British Relations	01/30/98	84*
Northern spotted owl		
Endangered Species	06/21/91	409*
Jobs vs. Environment	05/15/92	409
Protecting Endangered Species	04/19/96	337
Public Land Policy	06/17/94	542*
Nuclear fusion		
Energy and the Environment	03/03/00	165*
Nuclear Fusion	01/22/93	49
Will Nuclear Power Get Another Chance?	02/22/91	119*
Nuclear power plants		
Air Pollution Conflict	11/14/03	976*
Alternative Energy	07/10/92	582*
Energy Policy	05/25/01	455*
Energy Security	02/01/02	73
Managing Nuclear Waste	01/28/11	73
Nuclear Energy	03/10/06	217
Nuclear Fusion	01/22/93	49
Nuclear Waste	06/08/01	489
The Politics of Energy	03/05/99	193*
U.S. Policy on Iran	11/16/07	961
Will Nuclear Power Get Another Chance?	02/22/91	113
Nuclear test ban treaties		
Emerging India	04/19/02	329
Non-Proliferation Treaty at 25	01/27/95	73
Nuclear Arms Cleanup	06/24/94	553
Nuclear Proliferation	06/05/92	497*
Nuclear Proliferation and Terrorism	04/02/04	297
Weapons of Mass Destruction	03/08/02	193

	Date	Page
Nuclear waste		
Food Irradiation	06/12/92	511
Managing Nuclear Waste	01/28/11	73
Nuclear Arms Cleanup	06/24/94	553
Nuclear Energy	03/10/06	217
Nuclear Power	06/10/11	505
Nuclear Waste	06/08/01	489
The Politics of Energy	03/05/99	193*
Will Nuclear Power Get Another Chance?	02/22/91	123*
Worker Safety	05/21/04	445
Nuclear weapons		
Confronting Iraq	10/04/02	793
Emerging India	04/19/02	329
Ethics of War	12/13/02	1013
The Future of U.S.-Russia Relations	01/18/02	32*
Homeland Security	02/13/09	129
Managing Nuclear Waste	01/28/11	73
Middle East Tensions	10/27/06	**889
Missile Defense	09/08/00	689
New Defense Priorities	09/13/02	726*
Non-Proliferation Treaty at 25	01/27/95	73
North Korean Crisis	04/11/03	329*
Nuclear Arms Cleanup	06/24/94	553
Nuclear Disarmament	10/02/09	**813
Nuclear Proliferation	06/05/92	481
Nuclear Proliferation and Terrorism	04/02/04	297
Policing the Borders	02/22/02	145
Rethinking Foreign Policy	02/02/07	97
Russia and the Former Soviet Republics	06/17/05	541
The United Nations and Global Security	02/27/04	173
U.S. Policy on Iran	11/16/07	961
U.S.-Russian Relations	05/22/98	457
Weapons of Mass Destruction	03/08/02	193
Nursing		
Nursing Shortage	09/20/02	745
Primary Care	03/17/95	230*
Nursing homes		
Caring for the Elderly	02/20/98	145
Caring for the Elderly	10/13/06	841
Medicaid Reform	07/16/04	589
Retirement Security	05/31/02	481
Worker Safety	05/21/04	445
Nutrition. *See Food and nutrition*		
Obama, Barack		
Afghanistan Dilemma	08/07/09	**669*
America at War	07/23/10	**605
Campaign Finance Reform	06/13/08	505
Closing Guantánamo	02/27/09	**177
Conspiracy Theories	10/23/09	885

	Date	Page
Democrats' Future	10/29/10	893
Financial Industry Overhaul	07/30/10	629
Gays in the Military	09/18/09	**765
Gridlock in Washington	04/30/10	385
Hate Groups	05/08/09	421
Health-Care Reform	08/28/09	693*
High-Speed Trains	05/01/09	**397
Human Rights Issues	10/30/09	909
Human Spaceflight	10/16/09	861
Interrogating the CIA	09/25/09	789
Lies and Politics	02/18/11	145
Nuclear Disarmament	10/02/09	**813
The Obama Presidency	01/30/09	73
Presidential Election	02/03/12	101
Revising No Child Left Behind	04/16/10	337
Social Media and Politics	10/12/12	865
Space Program	02/24/12	177
States and Federalism	10/15/10	845
Supreme Court Controversies	09/28/12	813
U.S.-British Relations	11/05/10	917*
U.S.-China Relations	05/07/10	**409
U.S.-Europe Relations	03/23/12	277
The Value of a College Education	11/20/09	981
Vanishing Jobs	03/13/09	225
Obesity		
Diabetes Epidemic	03/09/01	185
Dieting and Health	04/14/95	321
Eating Disorders	12/18/92	1097
Hunger in America	12/22/00	1046*
Obesity and Health	01/15/99	25
Obesity Epidemic	01/31/03	73
Physical Fitness	11/06/92	964*
Preventing Disease	01/06/12	1
Smart Growth	05/28/04	474*
Sugar Controversies	11/30/12	1013
Women's Health	11/07/03	941
Obscenity. *See Pornography*		
Obsessive-compulsive disorders		
Prozac Controversy	08/19/94	721
Occupational health and safety		
Child Labor and Sweatshops	08/16/96	721
Coal Mining Safety	03/17/06	241
Crackdown on Smoking	12/04/92	1049
Drug Testing	11/20/98	1001
Electromagnetic Fields	04/26/91	237
Indoor Air Pollution	10/27/95	953*
Job Stress	08/04/95	681
Labor Unions' Future	09/02/05	**709
Lead Poisoning	06/19/92	534*
Mine Safety	06/24/11	553
Nuclear Power	06/10/11	505
Prison Reform	04/06/07	289
Privacy in the Workplace	11/19/93	1013*
Regulating Pesticides	08/06/99	678*
Repetitive Stress Injuries	06/23/95	537
Worker Safety	05/21/04	445
Occupations. *See Employment and unemployment; Wages and salaries*		
Oceans		
Climate Change	01/27/06	73
Fish Farming	07/27/07	625
Marine Mammals vs. Fish	08/28/92	737
Oil Spills	01/17/92	25
Renewable Energy	11/07/97	975*
Saving the Oceans	11/04/05	933
Threatened Coastlines	02/07/92	97
Threatened Fisheries	08/02/02	617
Water Shortages	08/01/03	649
Official English		
Bilingual Education	08/13/93	713*
Bilingual Education vs. English Immersion	12/11/09	1029
Debate over Bilingualism	01/19/96	49
Future of Language	11/17/00	929
Latinos' Future	10/17/03	869
Puerto Rico's Status	10/23/98	936*
Oil industry. *See Petroleum*		
Oklahoma City, Okla., bombing, 1995		
Combating Terrorism	07/21/95	633
Treating Anxiety	02/08/02	97
Old age. *See Elderly*		
Olympic games		
Athletes and Drugs	07/26/91	513
Centennial Olympic Games	04/05/96	289
Extreme Sports	04/03/09	297
Gender Equity in Sports	04/18/97	337
Human Rights in China	07/25/08	601
Pay-Per-View TV	10/04/91	729
Sports and Drugs	07/23/04	**613
Women and Sports	03/06/92	193
OPEC. *See Organization of Petroleum Exporting Countries*		
Operation rescue		
Abortion Clinic Protests	04/07/95	297
Abortion Debates	03/21/03	249
Oregon		
Assisted Suicide Controversy	05/05/95	393
Caring for the Dying	09/05/97	769
Jobs vs. Environment	05/15/92	409
Medicaid Reform	07/16/04	589
Prison Overcrowding	02/04/94	111*
Right to Die	05/13/05	421
Smart Growth	05/28/04	469

	Date	Page
Organ transplants		
Fetal Tissue Research	08/16/91	561
Fighting over Animal Rights	08/02/96	673
Organ Donations	04/15/11	337
Organ Shortage	02/21/03	153
Organ Transplants	08/11/95	705
Organic farming and food		
Buying Green	02/29/08	193
Crisis on the Plains	05/09/03	417
Factory Farms	01/12/07	25
Farm Subsidies	05/17/02	433
Fish Farming	07/27/07	625
Food Safety	11/01/02	897
Food Safety Battle: Organic v. Biotech	09/04/98	761
Reducing Your Carbon Footprint	12/05/08	985
Regulating Pesticides	01/28/94	73
Regulating Pesticides	08/06/99	665
Slow Food Movement	01/26/07	73
Organization of American States		
Democracy in Latin America	11/03/00	893*
Organization of Petroleum Exporting Countries (OPEC)		
Air Pollution Conflict	11/14/03	976*
Energy Security	02/01/02	73
Oil Diplomacy	01/24/03	49
Oil Imports	08/23/91	585
Oil Jitters	01/04/08	**1
Oil Production in the 21st Century	08/07/98	673
Ozone		
Bush and the Environment	10/25/02	865
New Air Quality Standards	03/07/97	193
Ozone Depletion	04/03/92	289
Pacific Northwest		
Jobs vs. Environment	05/15/92	409
Marine Mammals vs. Fish	08/28/92	750
Packaging		
Fast-Food Shake-Up	11/08/91	825
Garbage Crisis	03/20/92	241
The Obscenity Debate	12/20/91	982*
Pain management		
Assisted Suicide Controversy	05/05/95	406*
Caring for the Dying	09/05/97	769
Marijuana Laws	02/11/05	125
Pakistan		
Afghanistan Dilemma	08/07/09	**669*
Emerging India	04/19/02	329
Exporting Democracy	04/01/05	269
Homegrown Jihadists	09/03/10	701
Middle East Tensions	10/27/06	**889
Nuclear Proliferation	06/05/92	481
Nuclear Proliferation and Terrorism	04/02/04	297
U.S.-Pakistan Relations	08/05/11	653*
Weapons of Mass Destruction	03/08/02	193

	Date	Page
Palestinians		
Democracy in the Arab World	01/30/04	73
Global Water Shortages	12/15/95	1113
Human Rights Issues	10/30/09	909
Israel at 50	03/06/98	193
Middle East Conflict	04/06/01	273
Middle East Peace	01/21/05	53
Middle East Tensions	10/27/06	**889
The Obama Presidency	01/30/09	73
The Palestinians	08/30/91	609
Prospects for Mideast Peace	08/30/02	673
Understanding Islam	11/03/06	913
Panama Canal		
Panama Canal	11/26/99	1017
Panhandling. ***See Homeless persons***		
Paralympic Games		
Centennial Olympic Games	04/05/96	306*
Implementing the Disabilities Act	12/20/96	1118*
Paranormal phenomena		
Pursuing the Paranormal	03/29/96	265
Parents — Rights. ***See also Family***		
Abortion Showdowns	09/22/06	769
Adoption	11/26/93	1033
Bullying	02/04/05	101
Charter Schools	12/20/02	1033
Child Care	12/17/93	1105
Child Custody and Support	01/13/95	25
Children's Television	08/15/97	721
Child Welfare Reform	04/22/05	345
Cyberbullying	05/02/08	385
Cyber Socializing	07/28/06	625
Drinking on Campus	03/20/98	241
Encouraging Teen Abstinence	07/10/98	592*
Fatherhood Movement	06/02/00	473
Future of Feminism	04/14/06	313
Gay Marriage	09/05/03	732*
Gay Rights	03/05/93	210*
Gay Rights Update	04/14/00	305
Head Start	04/09/93	289
Home Schooling	09/09/94	769
Home Schooling Debate	01/17/03	25
Increase in Autism	06/13/03	**545
Infant Mortality	07/31/92	657*
Mothers' Movement	04/04/03	297
Movie Ratings	03/28/03	273
Parental Rights	10/25/96	937
Parents and Schools	01/20/95	49
Preventing Bullying	12/10/10	**1013
Preventing Juvenile Crime	03/15/96	217
Right to Die	05/13/05	421
School Censorship	02/19/93	145
School Choice Debate	07/18/97	625
School Vouchers Showdown	02/15/02	121

	Date	Page
Sex, Violence and the Media	11/17/95	1017
Sportsmanship	03/23/01	225
Students Under Stress	07/13/07	577
Teaching Values	06/21/96	529
Teenagers and Abortion	07/05/91	441
Teen Driving	01/07/05	1
Treating Addiction	01/06/95	6*
Treating Anxiety	02/08/02	108*
Unemployment Benefits	04/25/03	385*
Underage Drinking	03/13/92	217
Video Games	11/10/06	**937
Youth Fitness	09/26/97	854*
Patents		
3D Printing	12/07/12	1037
Drugmakers Under Siege	09/03/99	753
Future of Books	05/29/09	**473
Genes and Health	01/21/11	49
Gene Therapy's Future	12/08/95	1089
Patent Disputes	12/15/06	1033
Software Piracy	05/21/93	433
U.S. Trade Policy	01/29/93	73
PATRIOT Act		
Civil Liberties Debates	10/24/03	893
Civil Liberties in Wartime	12/14/01	1017
Homeland Security	09/12/03	749
Intelligence Reforms	01/24/02	49
Policing the Borders	02/22/02	145
Presidential Power	11/15/02	945
Presidential Power	02/24/06	169
Patriotism		
Patriotism in America	06/25/99	545
Pay. ***See Wages and salaries***		
Payroll taxes. ***See Social Security***		
Peace Corps		
National Service	06/25/93	553
National Service	06/30/06	577
Peace Corps' Challenges in the 1990s	01/25/91	49
Peacekeeping		
Privatizing the Military	06/25/04	565
The United Nations and Global Security	02/27/04	173
Pedestrian safety		
Aggressive Driving	07/25/97	649
Transportation Policy	07/04/97	577
Pensions. ***See Social Security; Retirement***		
Rethinking Retirement	06/19/09	549
People for the Ethical Treatment of Animals		
Animal Rights	05/24/91	301
Fighting over Animal Rights	08/02/96	673
People's Republic of China. ***See China***		
Perot, Ross		
Third-Party Prospects	12/22/95	1137

	Date	Page
Persian Gulf War, 1991		
Calculating the Costs of the Gulf War	03/15/91	145
Chemical and Biological Weapons	01/31/97	73
China Today	08/04/00	633*
Confronting Iraq	10/04/02	793
Defense Priorities	07/30/99	641
Democracy in the Arab World	01/30/04	73
Oil Diplomacy	01/24/03	49
Oil Imports	08/23/91	585
Oil Spills	01/17/92	25
The Palestinians	08/30/91	609
Recession's Regional Impact	02/01/91	65
Should the U.S. Reinstate the Draft?	01/11/91	17
Weapons of Mass Destruction	03/08/02	193
Women in the Military	09/25/92	833
Peru		
Democracy in Latin America	11/03/00	881
Privatizing the Military	06/25/04	565
Trouble in South America	03/14/03	225
Pesticides		
Breast Cancer	06/27/97	560*
Food Safety	06/04/93	481
Food Safety Battle: Organic v. Biotech	09/04/98	761
Regulating Pesticides	01/28/94	73
Regulating Pesticides	08/06/99	665
Petroleum		
Air Pollution Conflict	11/14/03	976*
Alternative Energy	07/10/92	573
Calculating the Costs of the Gulf War	03/15/91	145
Cost of the Iraq War	04/25/08	361*
Democracy in the Arab World	01/30/04	73
Domestic Energy Development	09/30/05	809
Energy and Climate	07/24/09	621
Energy Policy	05/25/01	454*
Energy Policy	05/20/11	457
Energy Security	02/01/02	73
The Future of U.S.-Russia Relations	01/18/02	40*
Gulf Coast Restoration	08/26/11	677*
Hating America	11/23/01	982*
Lead Poisoning	06/19/92	536
Mass Transit Boom	01/18/08	49
Mexico's Emergence	07/19/91	497
Offshore Drilling	06/25/10	553
Oil Diplomacy	01/24/03	49
Oil Imports	08/23/91	585
Oil Jitters	01/04/08	**1
Oil Production in the 21st Century	08/07/98	673
Oil Spills	01/17/92	25
The Politics of Energy	03/05/99	185
Rebuilding Iraq	07/11/03	632*
Reform in Iran	12/18/98	1110*
Renewable Energy	11/07/97	961

 *Indicates sidebar or "At Issue" report section. **Indicates an updated report.

	Date	Page
Socially Responsible Investing	08/29/08	673
SUV Debate	05/16/03	449
Pets		
America's Pampered Pets	12/27/96	1129
Animal Intelligence	10/22/10	869
Caring for the Elderly	02/20/98	150*
Fighting over Animal Rights	08/02/96	691*
Invasive Species	02/17/12	153
Philanthropy. ***See Charities and nonprofit organizations; Voluntarism***		
Philippines		
U.S. Policy in Asia	11/27/92	1025
Phonics. ***See Reading***		
Physical fitness		
Aging Baby Boomers	10/19/07	865
Aging Population	07/15/11	577
Baby Boomers at Midlife	07/31/98	649
Diabetes Epidemic	03/09/01	185
Dieting and Health	04/14/95	321
Eating Disorders	12/18/92	1097
Heart Health	09/12/08	721
Obesity Epidemic	01/31/03	86*
Physical Fitness	11/06/92	953
Preventing Disease	01/06/12	1
Preventing Obesity	10/01/10	797
Professional Football	01/29/10	**73
Prolonging Life	09/30/11	805*
Sports and Drugs	07/23/04	**613
Treating Alzheimer's	03/04/11	193
Youth Fitness	09/26/97	841
Physicians. ***See also Medical malpractice***		
Alternative Medicine	01/31/92	73
Assisted Suicide	02/21/92	145
Assisted Suicide Controversy	05/05/95	393
Caring for the Dying	09/05/97	769
Computers and Medicine	10/27/00	863*
Cosmetic Surgery	04/15/05	317
Fairness in Salaries	05/29/92	464*
Fighting Superbugs	08/24/07	673
Health-Care Reform	08/28/09	693*
Homeopathy Debate	12/19/03	1069
Managed Care	04/12/96	313
Managing Managed Care	04/16/99	305
Marijuana Laws	02/11/05	125
Medicaid Reform	07/16/04	589
Medical Malpractice	02/14/03	129
Medical Mistakes	02/25/00	137
Medication Abuse	10/09/09	837
Mental Illness	08/06/93	690*
Mental Illness Medication Debate	02/06/04	101
Patients' Rights	02/06/98	97
Primary Care	03/17/95	217
Rating Doctors	05/05/00	377

	Date	Page
Right to Die	05/13/05	421
Smallpox Threat	02/07/03	105
Plastics		
The Economics of Recycling	03/27/98	265
Future of Recycling	12/14/07	1033
Garbage Crisis	03/20/92	253*
Plutonium		
Nuclear Arms Cleanup	06/24/94	553
Nuclear Proliferation	06/05/92	496*
Poland		
Democracy in Eastern Europe	10/08/99	865
Expanding NATO	05/16/97	433
The Greening of Eastern Europe	11/15/91	849
Peace Corps' Challenges in the 1990s	01/25/91	49
Police and law enforcement		
Age Discrimination	08/01/97	673
Aggressive Driving	07/25/97	649
Combating Terrorism	07/21/95	633
Community Policing	02/05/93	97
Crime on Campus	02/04/11	97
Crime Victims' Rights	07/22/94	636*
Cyber-Predators	03/01/02	169
Cyber Socializing	07/28/06	625
Declining Crime Rates	04/04/97	289
DNA Databases	05/28/99	449
Drug-Policy Debate	07/28/00	593
Examining Forensics	07/17/09	597
Eyewitness Testimony	10/14/11	853
The FBI Under Fire	04/11/97	313
Fighting Crime	02/08/08	121
Future of the Airline Industry	06/21/02	545
Gang Crisis	05/14/04	421
Gangs in the U.S.	07/16/10	581
Globalization Backlash	09/28/01	761
Gun Control Debate	11/12/04	949
Haiti's Dilemma	02/18/05	149
Homeland Security	09/12/03	749
Human Trafficking and Slavery	03/26/04	273
Identity Theft	06/10/05	517
Illegal Immigration	04/24/92	361
Illegal Immigration	05/06/05	393
Immigration Conflict	03/09/12	229
Mafia Crackdown	03/27/92	265
Methamphetamine	07/15/05	589
Police Brutality	09/06/91	633
Police Corruption	11/24/95	1041
Police Misconduct	04/06/12	301
Policing the Borders	02/22/02	145
Policing the Police	03/17/00	209
Presidential Power	11/15/02	945
Preventing Teen Drug Use	03/15/02	217
Property Rights	06/16/95	524*
Prostitution	06/11/93	505

	Date	Page
Prostitution Debate	05/23/08	433
Punishing Sex Offenders	01/12/96	25
Pursuing the Paranormal	03/29/96	280*
Race in America	07/11/03	593
Reforming the CIA	02/02/96	97
Serial Killers	10/31/03	917
Sexual Abuse and the Clergy	05/03/02	393
Sleep Deprivation	02/12/10	121
State Budget Crises	10/03/03	821
Stock Market Troubles	01/16/04	25
Suburban Crime	09/03/93	769
Three-Strikes Laws	05/10/02	417
Torture	04/18/03	345
Underage Drinking	03/13/92	217
War on Drugs	03/19/93	241
Youth Gangs	10/11/91	753
Political action committees		
Campaign Finance Reform	02/09/96	121
Campaign Finance Reform	03/31/00	257
Campaign Finance Showdown	11/22/02	969
Electing the President	04/20/07	337
Tea Party Movement	03/19/10	**241*
Political advertising		
Advertising Under Attack	09/13/91	668*
Campaign Finance Showdown	11/22/02	969
Cyberpolitics	09/17/04	757
Electing the President	04/20/07	337
Labor Movement's Future	06/28/96	568*
Political Consultants	10/04/96	865
Regulating Nonprofits	12/26/97	1135*
Political asylum		
Assisting Refugees	02/07/97	111*
Europe's New Right	02/12/93	121
Global Refugee Crisis	07/09/99	576*
Illegal Immigration	04/24/92	361
Illegal Immigration	05/06/05	393
"Political correctness"		
Academic Politics	02/16/96	145
Racial Quotas	05/17/91	292*
Racial Tensions in Schools	01/07/94	13*
Political ethics. ***See Ethics in government***		
Politics. ***See also Special interest groups***		
Birth-Control Debate	06/24/05	565
Blog Explosion	06/09/06	**505
Campaign Finance Reform	02/09/96	121
Campaign Finance Reform	03/31/00	257
Campaign Finance Showdown	11/22/02	969
Celebrity Culture	03/18/05	256*
Change in Latin America	07/21/06	601
Changing Demographics	11/16/12	989
Changing U.S. Electorate	05/30/08	**457
Computer Hacking	09/16/11	757*
Conspiracy Theories	10/23/09	885
Cost of the Iraq War	04/25/08	361*
Cyberpolitics	09/17/04	757
D.C. Voting Rights	04/11/08	313*
Debating Hip-Hop	06/15/07	529
Democrats in Congress	06/08/07	505
Downsizing Prisons	03/11/11	217
Drug Testing	11/20/98	1015*
Electing the President	04/20/07	337
Evangelical Christians	09/14/01	713
First Ladies	06/14/96	505
Gay Marriage	09/05/03	742*
Gay Rights	03/05/93	203*
Gridlock in Washington	04/30/10	385
Independent Counsels	02/21/97	145
Independent Counsels Re-examined	05/07/99	377
Internet Accuracy	08/01/08	625
Judges and Politics	07/27/01	577
Judicial Elections	04/24/09	373
Latinos' Future	10/17/03	869
Lies and Politics	02/18/11	145
Lobbying Boom	07/22/05	613
'Occupy' Movement	01/13/12	25
The Partisan Divide	04/30/04	373
Partisan Politics	03/19/99	233
Political Consultants	10/04/96	865
Political Conventions	08/08/08	649
Political Scandals	05/27/94	457
Politicians and Privacy	04/17/92	337
Pork Barrel Politics	06/16/06	529
Presidential Election	02/03/12	101
Prosecutors and Politics	06/22/07	553
Protestants Today	12/07/07	1009
Public-Employee Unions	04/08/11	313
Race and Politics	07/18/08	577
Race in America	07/11/03	598*
Redistricting Debates	02/25/11	169
Redistricting Disputes	03/12/04	221
Redistricting: Drawing Power with a Map	02/15/91	97
Religion and Politics	07/30/04	637
Science and Politics	08/20/04	661
Sex Scandals	01/22/10	49
Social Media and Politics	10/12/12	865
State Budget Crises	10/03/03	821
Supreme Court Controversies	09/28/12	813
Tea Party Movement	03/19/10	**241*
Term Limits	01/10/92	1
Third-Party Prospects	12/22/95	1137
Understanding Mormonism	10/19/12	889
Voter Rights	05/18/12	449
Women in Politics	03/21/08	265
Pollution. ***See Air pollution; Hazardous substances; Water pollution***		

	Date	Page
Popular culture		
Celebrity Culture	03/18/05	245
Cosmetic Surgery	04/15/05	317
Reality TV	08/27/10	677
U.S.-British Relations	11/05/10	917*
Population. ***See also Census***		
Blighted Cities	11/12/10	941*
Census Controversey	05/14/10	433
Crisis on the Plains	05/09/03	417
Debate Over Immigration	07/14/00	580*
Declining Birthrates	11/21/08	961
Emerging India	04/19/02	342*
Foreign Aid After Sept. 11	04/26/02	361
Latinos' Future	10/17/03	869
Population and the Environment	07/17/98	601
Population Growth	07/16/93	601
Reassessing Foreign Aid	09/27/96	841
Redistricting Debates	02/25/11	169
Smart Growth	05/28/04	469
Water Shortages	08/01/03	649
Women and Human Rights	04/30/99	365*
World Hunger	10/25/91	801
Pornography		
Broadcast Indecency	04/16/04	326*
Crackdown on Sexual Harassment	07/19/96	642*
Cyber-Predators	03/01/02	169
Digital Commerce	02/05/99	89
The Future of Libraries	05/23/97	472*
Libraries and the Internet	06/01/01	465
The Obscenity Debate	12/20/91	969
Regulating the Internet	06/30/95	561
Sex, Violence and the Media	11/17/95	1017
Violence Against Women	02/26/93	177*
Postal Service, U.S.		
Job Stress	08/04/95	688*
Privatizing Government Services	08/09/96	697
Poverty		
AB and IP Programs	03/03/06	193
Abortion Debates	03/21/03	249
Affordable Housing	02/09/01	89
American Indians	04/28/06	**361
Asthma Epidemic	12/24/99	1089
Birth-Control Debate	06/24/05	565
Change in Latin America	07/21/06	601
Charitable Giving	11/12/93	985
Childhood Immunizations	06/18/93	529
Children in Crisis	08/31/01	657
Child Poverty	04/07/00	281
Child Poverty	10/28/11	901
Child Welfare Reform	04/22/05	345
Community Prosecution	12/15/00	1009
Consumer Debt	03/02/07	193
Covering the Uninsured	06/14/02	521
Cyberpolitics	09/17/04	757
Debating Hip-Hop	06/15/07	529
Declining Crime Rates	04/04/97	289
Democracy in Latin America	11/03/00	881
The Digital Divide	01/28/00	41
Distance Learning	12/07/01	993
Domestic Poverty	09/07/07	**721
Educating Gifted Students	03/28/97	265
Emergency Medicine	01/05/96	1
Ending Poverty	09/09/05	733
Environmental Justice	06/19/98	529
Evaluating Head Start	08/26/05	685
Fighting Crime	02/08/08	121
Fixing Urban Schools	04/27/07	**361
Haiti's Dilemma	02/18/05	149
Head Start	04/09/93	289
Helping the Homeless	01/26/96	73
The Homeless	08/07/92	665
Human Trafficking and Slavery	03/26/04	273
Hunger in America	12/22/00	1033
Income Inequality	04/17/98	337
Infant Mortality	07/31/92	641
Lead Poisoning	06/19/92	531
Legal-Aid Crisis	10/07/11	829
Living-Wage Movement	09/27/02	785*
Medicaid Reform	07/16/04	589
Middle-Class Squeeze	03/06/09	201
Networking the Classroom	10/20/95	931*
The New Volunteerism	12/13/96	1081
No Child Left Behind	05/27/05	469
Philanthropy in America	12/08/06	1009
Preventing Obesity	10/01/10	797
Preventing Teen Pregnancy	05/14/93	409
Public Defenders	04/18/08	337*
Public Housing	09/10/93	793
Puerto Rico: The Struggle over Status	02/08/91	81
Reforming School Funding	12/10/99	1041
Revising No Child Left Behind	04/16/10	337
School Vouchers	04/09/99	281
School Vouchers Showdown	02/15/02	121
Sexually Transmitted Diseases	12/03/04	997
Should the U.S. Reinstate the Draft?	01/11/91	17
State Budget Crises	10/03/03	832*
Straining the Safety Net	07/31/09	645
Student Aid	01/25/08	73
Teacher Education	10/17/97	918*
Trouble in South America	03/14/03	225
Unemployment Benefits	04/25/03	369
Upward Mobility	04/29/05	369
Welfare Experiments	09/16/94	793
Welfare Reform	08/03/01	601
Welfare, Work and the States	12/06/96	1057
The Working Poor	11/03/95	969
Youth Volunteerism	01/27/12	77

	Date	Page
POWs/MIAs. ***See Prisoners of war***		
Prayer		
Prayer and Healing	01/14/05	25
Pregnancy. ***See also Abortion; Adolescents and youth — Pregnancy***		
Abortion Debates	03/21/03	249
Abortion Showdowns	09/22/06	769
AIDS Update	12/04/98	1064*
Birth Control Choices	07/29/94	649
Electromagnetic Fields	04/26/91	244*
Gene Therapy	10/18/91	790*
Infant Mortality	07/31/92	641
Lead Poisoning	06/19/92	534*
Mothers' Movement	04/04/03	297
Reproductive Ethics	04/08/94	289
Reproductive Ethics	05/15/09	449
Teen Pregnancy	03/26/10	265*
Women's Health	11/07/03	941
Preschool education		
Child Care	12/17/93	1105
Evaluating Head Start	08/26/05	685
Head Start	04/09/93	289
School Vouchers Showdown	02/15/02	121
Presidency, U.S.		
Bush Presidency	02/02/01	65
Campaign Finance Reform	02/09/96	132*
Campaign Finance Reform	03/31/00	257
Democrats in Congress	06/08/07	505
Electing the President	04/20/07	337
First Ladies	06/14/96	505
Line-Item Veto	06/20/97	529
The Partisan Divide	04/30/04	373
Partisan Politics	03/19/99	250*
Political Conventions	08/08/08	649
Politicians and Privacy	04/17/92	344
Presidential Election	02/03/12	101
Presidential Libraries	03/16/07	241
Presidential Power	11/15/02	945
Presidential Power	02/24/06	169
Prosecutors and Politics	06/22/07	553
Re-examining the Constitution	09/07/12	741
Religion in America	11/25/94	1044*
Social Media and Politics	10/12/12	865
State Budget Crises	10/03/03	821
Tea Party Movement	03/19/10	**241*
Term Limits	01/10/92	12
Presidential elections		
Political Conventions	08/08/08	649
Presidential election, 1996		
China After Deng	06/13/97	516*
Labor Movement's Future	06/28/96	553
The New Immigrants	01/24/97	56*
Political Consultants	10/04/96	865
Rethinking NAFTA	06/07/96	481
Tax Reform	03/22/96	241
Presidential election, 2000		
Cyberpolitics	09/17/04	757
Electoral College	12/08/00	977
Election Reform	11/02/01	897
Legacy of the Vietnam War	02/18/00	128*
The Partisan Divide	04/30/04	373
Voting Controversies	09/15/06	745
Presidential election, 2004		
Blog Explosion	06/09/06	**505
Cyberpolitics	09/17/04	757
Electing the President	04/20/07	337
Exporting Jobs	02/20/04	149
The Partisan Divide	04/30/04	373
Religion and Politics	07/30/04	637
Social Security Reform	09/24/04	781
Worker Safety	05/21/04	445
Voting Controversies	09/15/06	745
Presidential election, 2008		
Changing U.S. Electorate	05/30/08	**457
Political Conventions	08/08/08	649
Race and Politics	07/18/08	577
Women in Politics	03/21/08	265
Presidential election, 2012		
Presidential Election	02/03/12	101
Press. ***See Journalism***		
Preventive medicine		
AIDS Update	12/04/98	1049
Asthma Epidemic	12/24/99	1089
Prisoners of war (POWs/MIAs)		
Ethics of War	12/13/02	1013
Presidential Power	11/15/02	945
Torture	04/18/03	345
Treatment of Detainees	08/25/06	673
U.S.-Vietnam Relations	12/03/93	1057
War Crimes	07/07/95	585
Prisons and prisoners		
Census Controversey	05/14/10	433
Closing Guantánamo	02/27/09	**177
Death Penalty Update	01/08/99	1
Downsizing Prisons	03/11/11	217
Gangs in the U.S.	07/16/10	581
Interrogating the CIA	09/25/09	789
Juvenile Justice	11/07/08	913
Kids in Prison	04/27/01	345
Mandatory Sentencing	05/26/95	465
Mental Illness Medication Debate	02/06/04	112*
Organ Shortage	02/21/03	167*
Policing the Borders	02/22/02	145
Prison-Building Boom	09/17/99	801
Prison Health Care	01/05/07	1

 *Indicates sidebar or "At Issue" report section. **Indicates an updated report.

	Date	Page
Prison Overcrowding	02/04/94	97
Prison Reform	04/06/07	289
Prisoner Reentry	12/04/09	1005
Privatization	11/13/92	985*
Privatizing Government Services	08/09/96	710*
Public Defenders	04/18/08	337*
Sentencing Debates	11/05/04	925
Solitary Confinement	09/14/12	765
State Budget Crisis	09/11/09	741
Torture	04/18/03	345
War on Drugs	03/19/93	241
Women and Human Rights	04/30/99	368*
Wrongful Convictions	04/17/09	**345
Privacy		
Adoption Controversies	09/10/99	777
AIDS Update	12/04/98	1049
Artificial Intelligence	04/22/11	361
Civic Renewal	03/21/97	257*
Computers and Medicine	10/27/00	857
Cyber-Predators	03/01/02	169
Cybersecurity	02/26/10	169
DNA Databases	05/28/99	449
Drug Testing	11/20/98	1001
Gay Rights	03/05/93	205*
Google's Dominance	11/11/11	953
Identity Theft	06/10/05	517
Internet Privacy	11/06/98	953
Online Privacy	11/06/09	**933
Patients' Rights	02/06/98	104*
Policing the Borders	02/22/02	159*
Politicians and Privacy	04/17/92	337
Privacy in Peril	11/17/06	961
Privacy in the Workplace	11/19/93	1009
Privacy Under Attack	06/15/01	505
Regulating the Internet	06/30/95	561
Sex Scandals	01/22/10	49
Social Media and Politics	10/12/12	865
Social Networking	09/17/10	749
Private Military Contractors (PMCs)		
Privatizing the Military	06/25/04	565
Privatization		
Business' Role in Education	11/22/91	887
Foster Care Reform	01/09/98	1
Hard Times for Libraries	06/26/92	555
Health-Care Reform	08/28/09	693*
Prison-Building Boom	09/17/99	801
Private Management of Public Schools	03/25/94	265
Privatization	11/13/92	977
Privatizing Government Services	08/09/96	697
Privatizing the Military	06/25/04	565
Public Broadcasting	09/18/92	825*
Public Land Policy	06/17/94	539*
Reassessing Foreign Aid	09/27/96	849*
Reforming the FDA	06/06/97	497*

	Date	Page
Reinventing Government	02/17/95	145
Saving Social Security	10/02/98	857
Social Security Reform	09/24/04	781
Social Security:The Search for Fairness	04/05/91	189
Space Program's Future	04/25/97	375*
Welfare, Work and the States	12/06/96	1070*
Product liability		
Consumer Safety	10/12/07	841
Regulating Tobacco	09/30/94	854*
Teens and Tobacco	12/01/95	1078*
Tobacco Industry	12/10/04	**1025
Too Many Lawsuits?	05/22/92	433
Professional sports. *See Sports*		
Property rights		
California: Enough Water for the Future?	04/19/91	231*
Endangered Species Act	10/01/99	849
Global Water Shortages	12/15/95	1129*
Government and Religion	01/15/10	25
Native Americans' Future	07/12/96	601
Property Rights	06/16/95	513
Property Rights	03/04/05	197
Saving Open Spaces	11/05/99	953
School Funding	08/27/93	761*
Smart Growth	05/28/04	469
Stolen Antiquities	04/13/07	313
Threatened Coastlines	02/07/92	97
Urban Sprawl in the West	10/03/97	865
Prostitution		
Prostitution	06/11/93	505
Prostitution Debate	05/23/08	433
Women and Human Rights	04/30/99	353
Prozac. *See Mental health and illness*		
Psychiatry. *See Mental health and illness*		
Public broadcasting		
Public Broadcasting	09/18/92	809
Public Broadcasting	10/29/99	929
Public health		
AIDS Update	12/04/98	1049
Asbestos Litigation	05/02/03	393
Asthma Epidemic	12/24/99	1089
Birth-Control Debate	06/24/05	565
Breast Cancer	06/27/97	553
Combating Infectious Diseases	06/09/95	489
Covering the Uninsured	06/14/02	521
Dietary Supplements	09/03/04	709
Disaster Preparedness	11/18/05	**981
Drug Company Ethics	06/06/03	521
Drugmakers Under Siege	09/03/99	760*
Drug-Resistant Bacteria	06/04/99	473
Fighting SARS	06/20/03	569
Food Safety	11/01/02	897
Homeopathy Debate	12/19/03	1069

	Date	Page
Increase in Autism	06/13/03	**545
Obesity Epidemic	01/31/03	73
Smallpox Threat	02/07/03	105
Sexually Transmitted Diseases	12/03/04	997
Tobacco Industry	12/10/04	**1025
Public housing		
Housing the Homeless	12/18/09	1053
Public Housing	09/10/93	793
Public lands. *See Federal lands*		
Public opinion		
Foreign Policy and Public Opinion	07/15/94	601
Legacy of the Vietnam War	02/18/00	116*
Public schools. *See Elementary and secondary education*		
Public utilities		
Alternative Energy	07/10/92	590
Homeland Security	09/12/03	761*
Modernizing the Grid	02/19/10	145
Public-Works Projects	02/20/09	153
Restructuring the Electric Industry	01/17/97	25
Utility Deregulation	01/14/00	1
Publishing Industry		
Future of Books	05/29/09	**473
Puerto Rico		
Hispanic Americans	10/30/92	944*
Prescription Drug Prices	07/17/92	610*
Puerto Rico: The Struggle over Status	02/08/91	81
Puerto Rico's Status	10/23/98	929
Putin, Vladimir		
Dealing With the "New" Russia	06/06/08	481
Quebec		
Deepening Canadian Crisis over Quebec	04/12/91	205
Quebec Sovereignty	10/06/95	873
Racial profiling		
Civil Liberties in Wartime	12/14/01	1033*
Extreme Sports	04/03/09	297
Police Misconduct	04/06/12	301
Race in America	07/11/03	593
Understanding Islam	11/03/06	913
Racism		
Affirmative Action	09/21/01	737
Asian Americans	12/13/91	945
Black Colleges	12/12/03	1045
Black Middle Class	01/23/98	49
Death Penalty Update	01/08/99	1
Debating Hip-Hop	06/15/07	529
Discipline in Schools	02/15/08	145
Drug-Policy Debate	07/28/00	612*
Environmental Justice	06/19/98	529
Hate Crimes	01/08/93	1

	Date	Page
Hate Groups	05/08/09	421
Income Inequality	04/17/98	344*
The Jury System	11/10/95	993
Native Americans' Future	07/12/96	601
New Military Culture	04/26/96	361
Police Brutality	09/06/91	633
Police Corruption	11/24/95	1041
Policing the Borders	02/22/02	145
Policing the Police	03/17/00	209
Property Rights	03/04/05	197
Prosecutors and the Law	11/09/07	937
Race and Politics	07/18/08	577
Race in America	07/11/03	593
Racial Diversity in Public Schools	09/14/07	**745
Racial Tensions in Schools	01/07/94	1
Reality TV	08/27/10	677
School Desegregation	04/23/04	345
Shock Jocks	06/01/07	**481
Suburban Crime	09/03/93	769
Understanding Mormonism	10/19/12	889
Radiation		
Electromagnetic Fields	04/26/91	237
Food Irradiation	06/12/92	505
Nuclear Power	06/10/11	505
Nuclear Waste	06/08/01	497*
Ozone Depletion	04/03/92	289
Will Nuclear Power Get Another Chance?	02/22/91	113
Radio. *See Television and radio*		
Railroads		
Future of Amtrak	10/18/02	841
High-Speed Rail	04/16/93	313
Traffic Congestion	08/27/99	742*
Transportation Policy	07/04/97	593*
Rain forests		
Ecotourism	10/20/06	865
Saving the Forests	09/20/91	681
Ranching. *See Livestock and ranching*		
Rap music. *See Music*		
Rape. *See Sex crimes*		
Reading. *See Literacy and illiteracy*		
Real estate		
Blighted Cities	11/12/10	941*
Downtown Renaissance	06/23/06	**553
Financial Bailout	10/24/08	**865
Financial Crisis	05/09/08	409
Financial Industry Overhaul	07/30/10	629
Housing Discrimination	02/24/95	169
Indoor Air Pollution	10/27/95	951*
Recession's Regional Impact	02/01/91	65
Smart Growth	05/28/04	469

 *Indicates sidebar or "At Issue" report section. **Indicates an updated report.

	Date	Page
Recession. ***See Economic conditions***		
Recreation. ***See Leisure; Sports***		
Recycling		
The Economics of Recycling	03/27/98	265
Environmental Movement at 25	03/31/95	288*
Future of Recycling	12/14/07	1033
Garbage Crisis	03/20/92	241
Lead Poisoning	06/19/92	537
Managing Nuclear Waste	01/28/11	73
Red Cross		
Blood Supply Safety	11/11/94	985
Ethics of War	12/13/02	1013
First Ladies	06/14/96	505
National Service	06/30/06	577
Philanthropy in America	12/08/06	1009
Redistricting. ***See also Census***		
Census Controversey	05/14/10	433
The Partisan Divide	04/30/04	373
Race in America	07/11/03	598*
Redistricting	02/16/01	113
Redistricting Debates	02/25/11	169
Redistricting Disputes	03/12/04	221
Redistricting: Drawing Power with a Map	02/15/91	97
Refugees		
Assisting Refugees	02/07/97	97
Ethics of War	12/13/02	1013
Europe's New Right	02/12/93	121
Global Refugee Crisis	07/09/99	569
Human Trafficking and Slavery	03/26/04	273
Middle East Peace	01/21/05	53
Regulation and deregulation		
Accountants Under Fire	03/22/02	257*
Advertising Overload	01/23/04	49
Airline Industry Problems	09/24/99	825
Airline Safety	10/08/93	865
Air Pollution Conflict	11/14/03	965
Alternative Energy	02/25/05	173
Antitrust Policy	06/12/98	505
Auto Safety	10/26/01	873
Biology and Behavior	04/03/98	299*
Broadcast Indecency	04/16/04	321
Bush and the Environment	10/25/02	880*
Bush Presidency	02/02/01	82*
Career Colleges	01/07/11	1
Caring for the Elderly	02/20/98	152*
Child-Care Options	05/08/98	409
The Cloning Controversy	05/09/97	409
Combating Scientific Misconduct	01/10/97	1
Corporate Crime	10/11/02	817
Cosmetic Surgery	04/15/05	317
Debt Collectors	07/20/12	621
Dietary Supplements	07/08/94	577
Dietary Supplements	09/03/04	709
Digital Commerce	02/05/99	89
The Digital Divide	01/28/00	57*
Drugmakers Under Siege	09/03/99	767*
Drug Safety	03/11/05	221
Drunken Driving	10/06/00	793
Embryo Research	12/17/99	1065
Endangered Species Act	10/01/99	849
Environmental Movement at 25	03/31/95	273
Financial Bailout	10/24/08	**865
Financial Crisis	05/09/08	409
Financial Industry Overhaul	07/30/10	629
Financial Misconduct	01/20/12	53
Fracking Controversy	12/16/11	1049
Future of the Airlines	03/07/08	217
The Future of Telecommunications	04/23/99	329
The Future of Television	12/23/94	1129
Future of the Music Industry	11/21/03	989
Gene Therapy's Future	12/08/95	1102*
Genetically Engineered Foods	08/05/94	684*
Homeopathy Debate	12/19/03	1069
Home Schooling	09/09/94	769
Indecency on Television	11/09/12	965
Internet Privacy	11/06/98	953
Managing Managed Care	04/16/99	305
Marijuana Laws	02/11/05	125
Media Ownership	10/10/03	**845
Mental Illness Medication Debate	02/06/04	101
Mine Safety	06/24/11	553
Modernizing the Grid	02/19/10	145
Nuclear Power	06/10/11	505
The Politics of Energy	03/05/99	185
Privatizing the Military	07/13/12	597
Property Rights	06/16/95	513
Reforming the FDA	06/06/97	481
Regulating Nonprofits	12/26/97	1129
Regulating Pesticides	08/06/99	665
Regulating Tobacco	09/30/94	841
Regulating Toxic Chemicals	01/23/09	49
Regulating the Internet	06/30/95	561
Regulating the New Economy	10/19/01	849
Renewable Energy	11/07/97	961
Restructuring the Electric Industry	01/17/97	25
Right to Die	05/13/05	421
Role of Foundations	01/22/99	49
School Vouchers	04/09/99	281
School Vouchers Showdown	02/15/02	121
Sleep Deprivation	06/26/98	553
Smart Growth	05/28/04	469
Stimulating the Economy	01/10/03	1
The Stock Market	05/02/97	393*
Stock Market Troubles	01/16/04	25
Sugar Controversies	11/30/12	1013
Tea Party Movement	03/19/10	**241*

	Date	Page
Teen Driving	01/07/05	1
Teens and Tobacco	12/01/95	1065
Tobacco Industry	12/10/04	**1025
Truck Safety	03/12/99	209
Underground Economy	03/04/94	193
Utility Deregulation	01/14/00	1
Water Crisis in the West	12/09/11	1025
Wind Power	04/01/11	289
Women's Health	11/07/03	957*
Worker Safety	05/21/04	445
Rehnquist, William H.		
Supreme Court Preview	09/17/93	817
Supreme Court's Future	01/28/05	77
Religion. *See also Ethical and moral issues*		
Alternative Medicine	01/31/92	87*
Birth-Control Debate	06/24/05	565
Castro's Next Move	12/12/97	1085*
Catholic Church in the U.S.	09/08/95	777
Changing Demographics	11/16/12	989
Charitable Giving	11/12/93	1002*
Cults in America	05/07/93	385
Democracy in the Arab World	01/30/04	73
Disappearing Species	11/30/07	985
Domestic Partners	09/04/92	761
Embryo Research	12/17/99	1077*
Emerging India	04/19/02	351*
Evangelical Christians	09/14/01	713
Evolution vs. Creationism	08/22/97	745
Faith-Based Initiatives	05/04/01	377
Future of the Catholic Church	01/19/07	49
Future of the Papacy	02/26/99	161
Gay Marriage	09/05/03	726*
Global Jihad	10/14/05	857
Government and Religion	01/15/10	25
Helping the Homeless	01/26/96	73
Home Schooling Debate	01/17/03	25
Islamic Fundamentalism	03/24/00	241
Israel at 50	03/06/98	206*
Marriage and Divorce	05/10/96	409
Muslims in America	04/30/93	361
The New Millennium	10/15/99	889
Northern Ireland Cease-Fire	09/15/95	812*
Parental Rights	10/25/96	937
Population Growth	07/16/93	610*
Prayer and Healing	01/14/05	25
Prison-Building Boom	09/17/99	815*
Protestants Today	12/07/07	1009
Religion and Politics	10/14/94	889
Religion and Politics	07/30/04	637
Religion in America	11/25/94	1033
Religion in Schools	02/18/94	145
Religion in Schools	01/12/01	1
Religion in the Workplace	08/23/02	649
Religious Persecution	11/21/97	1009
Rise of Megachurches	09/21/07	769
School Censorship	02/19/93	157*
School Choice	05/10/91	256
School Choice Debate	07/18/97	625
School Vouchers	04/09/99	281
School Vouchers Showdown	02/15/02	121
The Search for Extraterrestrials	03/05/04	197
Searching for Jesus	12/11/98	1073
Sexual Abuse and the Clergy	05/03/02	393
Student Rights	06/05/09	501
Supreme Court Preview	09/17/93	817
Teaching Values	06/21/96	529
Understanding Islam	11/03/06	913
Understanding Mormonism	10/19/12	889
Women and Human Rights	04/30/99	353
Renewable energy resources		
Air Pollution Conflict	11/14/03	976*
Alternative Energy	07/10/92	573
Alternative Energy	02/25/05	173
Biofuels Boom	09/29/06	793
Bush and the Environment	10/25/02	865
Energy Efficiency	05/19/06	433
Energy Policy	05/25/01	455*
Energy Policy	05/20/11	457
Energy Security	02/01/02	73
Jobs Outlook	06/04/10	481
Managing Public Lands	11/04/11	929
Modernizing the Grid	02/19/10	145
Nanotechnology	06/11/04	517
The Politics of Energy	03/05/99	185
Renewable Energy	11/07/97	961
Vanishing Jobs	03/13/09	225
Water Crisis in the West	12/09/11	1025
Wind Power	04/01/11	289
Reparations		
Holocaust Reparations	03/26/99	257
Reparations Movement	06/22/01	529*
Repetitive stress injuries		
Repetitive Stress Injuries	06/23/95	537
Reproduction. *See Pregnancy*		
Republic of China. *See Taiwan*		
Republican Party		
Abortion Debates	09/10/10	725
Academic Freedom	10/07/05	833
Air Pollution Conflict	11/14/03	965
Assessing the New Health Care Law	09/21/12	789
Birth-Control Debate	06/24/05	565
The Black Middle Class	01/23/98	66*
Budget Deficit	12/09/05	1029
Campaign Finance Debates	05/28/10	457
Campaign Finance Reform	02/09/96	134*
Changing Demographics	11/16/12	989

 *Indicates sidebar or "At Issue" report section. **Indicates an updated report.

	Date	Page
Changing U.S. Electorate	05/30/08	**457
Cracking Down on Immigration	02/03/95	112*
Cyberpolitics	09/17/04	757
D.C. Voting Rights	04/11/08	313*
Democrats in Congress	06/08/07	505
Democrats' Future	10/29/10	893
Environmental Movement at 25	03/31/95	290*
Exporting Democracy	04/01/05	269
The Federal Judiciary	03/13/98	217
Feminism's Future	02/28/97	184*
Future of the GOP	03/20/09	249
Gridlock in Washington	04/30/10	385
Health-Care Reform	06/11/10	**505
Hispanic-Americans' New Clout	09/18/98	809
Housing Discrimination	02/24/95	184*
Labor Movement's Future	06/28/96	553
Lies and Politics	02/18/11	145
Lobbying Boom	07/22/05	613
Minimum Wage	12/16/05	1053
National Debt	03/18/11	241
Non-Proliferation Treaty at 25	01/27/95	90*
The Obama Presidency	01/30/09	73
The Partisan Divide	04/30/04	373
Partisan Politics	03/19/99	233
Political Conventions	08/08/08	649
Presidential Election	02/03/12	101
Prosecutors and Politics	06/22/07	553
Protestants Today	12/07/07	1009
Race and Politics	07/18/08	577
Redistricting Debates	02/25/11	169
Redistricting: Drawing Power with a Map	02/15/91	97
Regulating Nonprofits	12/26/97	1129
Reinventing Government	02/17/95	145
Religion and Politics	10/14/94	889
Religion and Politics	07/30/04	637
Rethinking Affirmative Action	04/28/95	369
Revitalizing the Cities	10/13/95	909*
Rising College Costs	12/05/03	1013
Science and Politics	08/20/04	661
Social Media and Politics	10/12/12	865
State Budget Crises	10/03/03	821
States and Federalism	09/13/96	793
Tax Reform	03/22/96	241
Tea Party Movement	03/19/10	**241*
Term Limits	01/10/92	1
Third-Party Prospects	12/22/95	1137
Voting Controversies	09/15/06	745
Women in Politics	03/21/08	265
Wounded Veterans	08/31/07	697
Respiratory diseases		
Air Pollution Conflict	11/14/03	965
Fighting SARS	06/20/03	569
New Air Quality Standards	03/07/97	193

	Date	Page
Restaurants		
Crackdown on Smoking	12/04/92	1049
Fast-Food Shake-Up	11/08/91	825
Food Safety	06/04/93	481
Food Safety Battle: Organic v. Biotech	09/04/98	766*
Historic Preservation	10/07/94	870*
Obesity Epidemic	01/31/03	94*
Threatened Fisheries	08/02/02	617
Retail trade		
Big-Box Stores	09/10/04	733
Child Labor and Sweatshops	08/16/96	721
The Consumer Culture	11/19/99	1001
Digital Commerce	02/05/99	89
Drugmakers Under Siege	09/03/99	762*
Future of the Music Industry	11/21/03	989
Jobs in the '90s	02/28/92	182
Religion in the Workplace	08/23/02	665*
Retirement		
Accountants Under Fire	03/22/02	252*
Age Discrimination	08/01/97	673
Aging Baby Boomers	10/19/07	865
Aging Population	07/15/11	577
Budget Deficit	12/09/05	1029
Corporate Crime	10/11/02	817
Declining Birthrates	11/21/08	961
Employee Benefits	02/04/00	65
Middle-Class Squeeze	03/06/09	201
Overhauling Social Security	05/12/95	417
Paying for Retirement	11/05/93	961
Pension Crisis	02/17/06	145
Rethinking Retirement	06/19/09	549
Retiree Health Benefits	12/06/91	921
Retirement Security	05/31/02	481
Rising Health Costs	04/07/06	289
Saving Social Security	10/02/98	857
Smart Growth	05/28/04	469
Social Security Reform	09/24/04	781
Socially Responsible Investing	08/29/08	673
State Budget Crisis	09/11/09	741
Rights. ***See Civil rights and liberties; Property rights***		
Ritalin. ***See Attention Deficit Disorder***		
Roads. ***See Highways and roads***		
Robotics		
Artificial Intelligence	11/14/97	985
Future Job Market	01/11/02	13*
Nanotechnology	06/11/04	517
Space Program's Future	04/25/97	361
Roma (Gypsies)		
Democracy in Eastern Europe	10/08/99	882*
Roman Catholics. ***See Catholic Church***		
Romania		
The Greening of Eastern Europe	11/15/91	849

	Date	Page
Ruby Ridge, Idaho, shootout		
The FBI Under Fire	04/11/97	315*
Russia. ***See also Soviet Union (Former)***		
Aid to Russia	03/12/93	217
Bush's Defense Strategy	09/07/01	689
Defense Priorities	07/30/99	641
Democracy in Eastern Europe	10/08/99	873*
Expanding NATO	05/16/97	433
Exporting Democracy	04/01/05	269
Future of NATO	02/28/03	177
The Future of U.S.-Russia Relations	01/18/02	25
Human Spaceflight	10/16/09	861
International Monetary Fund	01/29/99	65
Missile Defense	09/08/00	689
NASA's Future	05/23/03	473
New Challenges in Space	07/23/99	617
Nuclear Disarmament	10/02/09	813
Nuclear Proliferation and Terrorism	04/02/04	297
Oil Diplomacy	01/24/03	49
Religious Persecution	11/21/97	1009
Russia and the Former Soviet Republics	06/17/05	541
Russia's Political Future	05/03/96	385
Soviet Republics Rebel	07/12/91	465
Space Program	02/24/12	177
Space Program's Future	12/24/93	1129
Space Program's Future	04/25/97	361
U.S.-Russian Relations	05/22/98	457
Weapons of Mass Destruction	03/08/02	193
Rwanda		
Assisting Refugees	02/07/97	97
Ethics of War	12/13/02	1013
Famine in Africa	11/08/02	921
Foreign Policy and Public Opinion	07/15/94	601
Stopping Genocide	08/27/04	685
The United Nations and Global Security	02/27/04	173
War Crimes	07/07/95	585
Saddam Hussein		
Confronting Iraq	10/04/02	793
Democracy in the Arab World	01/30/04	73
Economic Sanctions	10/28/94	937
Ethics of War	12/13/02	1013
Future of NATO	02/28/03	177
Hating America	11/23/01	969
New Defense Priorities	09/13/02	721
Nuclear Proliferation	06/05/92	481
Oil Diplomacy	01/24/03	49
Oil Production in the 21st Century	08/07/98	673
Presidential Power	11/15/02	945
Rebuilding Iraq	07/11/03	625
Reform in Iran	12/18/98	1097
Stopping Genocide	08/27/04	685
War Crimes	07/07/95	585

	Date	Page
War on Terrorism	10/12/01	817
Weapons of Mass Destruction	03/08/02	193
Safety. ***See also Occupational health and safety; Traffic accidents***		
3D Printing	12/07/12	1037
Aging Infrastructure	09/28/07	**793
Airline Safety	10/08/93	865
Auto Safety	10/26/01	873
Cell Phone Safety	03/16/01	201
Consumer Safety	10/12/07	841
Cybersecurity	02/26/10	169
Earthquake Threat	04/09/10	313
Extreme Sports	04/03/09	297
Managing Wildfires	11/02/12	941
Nanotechnology	06/11/04	517
Nuclear Power	06/10/11	505
Patient Safety	02/10/12	125
Prison Reform	04/06/07	289
Sleep Deprivation	02/12/10	121
Teen Driving	01/07/05	1
Salaries. ***See Wages and salaries***		
Sales tax		
Digital Commerce	02/05/99	89
IRS Reform	01/16/98	38*
Tax Reform	03/22/96	241
Salmonella		
Food Irradiation	06/12/92	505
Food Safety	06/04/93	481
Food Safety	11/01/02	897
SAT tests		
Attack on Public Schools	07/26/96	649
Education and Gender	06/03/94	488*
Getting into College	02/23/96	169
Grade Inflation	06/07/02	505
Implementing the Disabilities Act	12/20/96	1116*
Learning to Read	05/19/95	446*
Students Under Stress	07/13/07	577
Testing in Schools	04/20/01	328*
Scholarships. ***See Student aid***		
School choice		
Attack on Public Schools	07/26/96	662*
Business' Role in Education	11/22/91	885*
Charter Schools	12/20/02	1033
Home Schooling Debate	01/17/03	25
No Child Left Behind	05/27/05	469
Private Management of Public Schools	03/25/94	265
Privatization	11/13/92	988*
Racial Diversity in Public Schools	09/14/07	**745
Religion in Schools	01/12/01	1
School Choice	05/10/91	253
School Choice Debate	07/18/97	625
School Desegregation	04/23/04	345

	Date	Page
School Vouchers	04/09/99	281
School Vouchers Showdown	02/15/02	121
School funding		
Advertising Overload	01/23/04	49
Arts Education	03/16/12	253
Charter Schools	12/20/02	1033
Fixing Urban Schools	04/27/07	**361
No Child Left Behind	05/27/05	469
Reforming School Funding	12/10/99	1041
Schools. ***See Elementary and secondary education***		
Science and technology. ***See also Medical research***		
3D Printing	12/07/12	1037
Acid Rain: New Approach to Old Problem	03/08/91	132*
Alternative Energy	07/10/92	573
Alternative Energy	02/25/05	173
Animal Intelligence	10/22/10	869
Artificial Intelligence	04/22/11	361
Animal Rights	01/08/10	1
Artificial Intelligence	11/14/97	985
Biofuels Boom	09/29/06	793
Biotech Foods	03/30/01	249
Breast Cancer	04/02/10	289
California: Enough Water for the Future?	04/19/91	224*
Cell Phone Safety	03/16/01	213*
Cheating in Schools	09/22/00	754*
Combating Scientific Misconduct	01/10/97	1
Crisis on the Plains	05/09/03	430*
Cyber-Crime	04/12/02	305
Cyberpolitics	09/17/04	757
Cybersecurity	09/26/03	797
Cybersecurity	02/26/10	169
Debt Collectors	07/20/12	621
Digital Education	12/02/11	1001
Distracted Driving	05/04/12	401
Drug Company Ethics	06/06/03	521
Earthquake Research	12/16/94	1105
Earthquake Threat	04/09/10	313
Emerging India	04/19/02	329
Energy and Climate	07/24/09	621
Examining Forensics	07/17/09	597
Extreme Weather	09/09/11	733*
Future of Books	05/29/09	**473
Future of Homeownership	12/14/12	1061
Future of Libraries	07/29/11	625
The Future of Television	12/23/94	1129
Future of the Music Industry	11/21/03	989
Gender and Learning	05/20/05	445
Genes and Health	01/21/11	49
Genetically Modified Food	08/31/12	717
Global Water Shortages	12/15/95	1113
High-Tech Labor Shortage	04/24/98	361
Homeopathy Debate	12/19/03	1069
Human Genome Research	05/12/00	401
Human Spaceflight	10/16/09	861
Internet Regulation	04/13/12	325
Journalism Standards in the Internet Age	10/08/10	821
Mine Safety	06/24/11	553
Modernizing the Grid	02/19/10	145
Nanotechnology	06/11/04	517
NASA's Future	05/23/03	473
The New CIA	12/11/92	1073
Nuclear Arms Cleanup	06/24/94	564*
Nuclear Disarmament	10/02/09	**813
Nuclear Fusion	01/22/93	49
Nuclear Proliferation and Terrorism	04/02/04	297
Oil Production in the 21st Century	08/07/98	685*
Online Privacy	11/06/09	**933
Organ Donations	04/15/11	337
Patient Safety	02/10/12	125
Preventing Memory Loss	04/04/08	289*
Prolonging Life	09/30/11	805*
Pursuing the Paranormal	03/29/96	265
Reading Crisis?	02/22/08	169
Reality TV	08/27/10	677
Regulating Toxic Chemicals	01/23/09	49
Reproductive Ethics	05/15/09	449
Science in America	01/11/08	25
Science in the Courtroom	10/22/93	913
Science and Politics	08/20/04	661
The Search for Extraterrestrials	03/05/04	197
Smart Cities	07/27/12	645
Space Program	02/24/12	177
Space Program's Future	12/24/93	1129
Space Program's Future	04/25/97	361
Stem Cell Research	09/01/06	**697
Teaching Math and Science	09/06/02	697
Television's Future	02/16/07	145
Transition to Digital TV	06/20/08	529
Treating Alzheimer's	03/04/11	193
Uncertain Future for Man in Space	03/29/91	173
Weapons of Mass Destruction	03/08/02	193
Wrongful Convictions	04/17/09	**345
Scientists		
Animal Rights	01/08/10	1
Combating Scientific Misconduct	01/10/97	1
Gender and Learning	05/20/05	445
NASA's Future	05/23/03	473
Nuclear Proliferation	06/05/92	486*
The Search for Extraterrestrials	03/05/04	197
Science in America	01/11/08	25
Science and Politics	08/20/04	661
Second Amendment. ***See Firearms***		
Secondhand smoke. ***See Tobacco***		

	Date	Page
Segregation. ***See Civil rights and liberties; Discrimination***		
Self-employment		
Aging Baby Boomers	10/19/07	865
Contingent Work Force	10/24/97	937
The Glass Ceiling	10/29/93	947*
Sentencing guidelines. ***See also Alternative sentences***		
Mandatory Sentencing	05/26/95	465
Plea Bargaining	02/12/99	125*
Prosecutors and the Law	11/09/07	937
Punishing Sex Offenders	01/12/96	25
Sentencing Debates	11/05/04	925
Sept. 11, 2001		
Academic Freedom	10/07/05	833
Afghanistan Dilemma	08/07/09	**669*
Civil Liberties Debates	10/24/03	893
Civil Liberties in Wartime	12/14/01	1017
Conspiracy Theories	10/23/09	885
Foreign Aid After Sept. 11	04/26/02	361
Future of the Airline Industry	06/21/02	545
Government Secrecy	12/02/05	1005
Hating America	11/23/01	969
Homegrown Jihadists	09/03/10	701
Homeland Security	09/12/03	749
Homeland Security	02/13/09	129
Intelligence Reforms	01/25/02	49
International Law	12/17/04	1049
Interrogating the CIA	09/25/09	789
New Defense Priorities	09/13/02	721
Port Security	04/21/06	337
Presidential Power	11/15/02	945
Presidential Power	02/24/06	169
Prosecuting Terrorists	03/12/10	**217*
Real ID	05/04/07	385
Re-examining 9/11	06/04/04	493
Remembering 9/11	09/02/11	701*
Torture	04/18/03	345
Treatment of Detainees	08/25/06	673
Understanding Islam	11/03/06	913
War in Iraq	10/21/05	881
War on Terrorism	10/12/01	817
Weapons of Mass Destruction	03/08/02	193
Serbia		
Ethics of War	12/13/02	1013
Stopping Genocide	08/27/04	685
War Crimes	07/07/95	585
SETI Institute		
The Search for Extraterrestrials	03/05/04	197
Sex crimes. ***See also Child abuse***		
College Football	11/18/11	977
Cyber-Predators	03/01/02	169
Cyber Socializing	07/28/06	625
DNA Databases	05/28/99	449
Feminism's Future	02/28/97	182*
Human Trafficking and Slavery	03/26/04	273
The Obscenity Debate	12/20/91	985
Prosecutors and the Law	11/09/07	937
Prostitution	06/11/93	505
Prostitution Debate	05/23/08	433
Punishing Sex Offenders	01/12/96	25
Reforming Big-Time College Sports	03/19/04	249
Serial Killers	10/31/03	917
Sex Offenders	09/08/06	721
Sex on Campus	11/04/94	961
Sexual Abuse and the Clergy	05/03/02	393
Treating Anxiety	02/08/02	97
Violence Against Women	02/26/93	169
War Crimes	07/07/95	590*
Women and Human Rights	04/30/99	353
Sex discrimination. ***See also Sexual harassment***		
Crackdown on Sexual Harassment	07/19/96	625
Democracy in the Arab World	01/30/04	73
Education and Gender	06/03/94	481
Feminism's Future	02/28/97	169
Gender and Learning	05/20/05	445
Gender Equity in Sports	04/18/97	337
The Glass Ceiling	10/29/93	937
Lead Poisoning	06/19/92	534*
Mothers' Movement	04/04/03	297
Prostitution Debate	05/23/08	433
Racial Quotas	05/17/91	277
Reforming the CIA	02/02/96	110*
Transgender Issues	05/05/06	385
Women and Sports	03/06/92	193
Women in the Military	09/25/92	833
Women in the Military	11/13/09	957
Sex education		
Abortion Showdowns	09/22/06	769
Battling HIV/AIDS	10/26/07	889
Encouraging Teen Abstinence	07/10/98	577
Gay Rights	03/05/93	207*
HPV Vaccine	05/11/07	409
Parental Rights	10/25/96	946*
Preventing Teen Pregnancy	05/14/93	409
Sexually Transmitted Diseases	12/03/04	997
Teaching Values	06/21/96	534*
Teen Pregnancy	03/26/10	265*
Teen Sex	09/16/05	761
Sexual behavior. ***See also Homosexuals; Pornography; Pregnancy***		
AIDS Update	12/04/98	1049
Battling HIV/AIDS	10/26/07	889
Broadcast Indecency	04/16/04	321
Catholic Church in the U.S.	09/08/95	777
Children's Television	08/15/97	721
Cyber-Predators	03/01/02	169
Encouraging Teen Abstinence	07/10/98	577
Feminism's Future	02/28/97	183*

	Date	Page
Future of Marriage	05/07/04	397
Future of the Catholic Church	01/19/07	49
Global AIDS Crisis	10/13/00	809
HPV Vaccine	05/11/07	409
Indecency on Television	11/09/12	965
Marriage and Divorce	05/10/96	409
Political Scandals	05/27/94	457
Politicians and Privacy	04/17/92	337
Preventing Teen Pregnancy	05/14/93	409
Prostitution	06/11/93	505
Prostitution Debate	05/23/08	433
Sex on Campus	11/04/94	961
Sex Scandals	01/22/10	49
Sex, Violence and the Media	11/17/95	1017
Sexually Transmitted Diseases	12/03/04	997
Teen Pregnancy	03/26/10	265*
Teen Sex	09/16/05	761
TV Violence	03/26/93	176*
Women and AIDS	12/25/92	1121
Sexual harassment		
Academic Politics	02/16/96	162*
Bullying	02/04/05	101
Crackdown on Sexual Harassment	07/19/96	625
Crime on Campus	02/04/11	97
Cyber-Predators	03/01/02	169
Education and Gender	06/03/94	494*
New Military Culture	04/26/96	370*
Political Scandals	05/27/94	462*
Sexual Harassment	08/09/91	537
Sexual Harassment	04/27/12	377
Women and Sports	03/06/92	200*
Women in the Military	09/25/92	833
Women in the Military	11/13/09	957
Sexually transmitted diseases. *See also AIDS disease*		
Battling HIV/AIDS	10/26/07	889
Encouraging Teen Abstinence	07/10/98	577
HPV Vaccine	05/11/07	409
Prostitution Debate	05/23/08	433
Sexually Transmitted Diseases	12/03/04	997
Sharon, Ariel. *See Middle East*		
Simpson, O.J.		
Courts and the Media	09/23/94	817
The Jury System	11/10/95	993
Single-parent families. *See Family*		
Single-sex education		
Boys' Emotional Needs	06/18/99	521
Education and Gender	06/03/94	481
Racial Tensions in Schools	01/07/94	18*
Single-Sex Education	07/12/02	569
Sinn Fein. *See Ireland*		
Sleep disorders		
Chronic Fatigue Syndrome	04/05/02	289
Homework Debate	12/06/02	1002*

	Date	Page
Sleep Deprivation	06/26/98	553
Sleep Deprivation	02/12/10	121
Truck Safety	03/12/99	209
Small business		
Aging Baby Boomers	10/19/07	865
Asian Americans	12/13/91	945
The Glass Ceiling	10/29/93	947*
Implementing the Disabilities Act	12/20/96	1105
Smoking. *See Tobacco*		
Social Security		
Age Discrimination	08/01/97	682*
Aging Baby Boomers	10/19/07	865
Aging Population	07/15/11	577
Budget Deficit	12/09/05	1029
Middle-Class Squeeze	03/06/09	201
National Debt	03/18/11	241
Overhauling Social Security	05/12/95	417
Privatizing Government Services	08/09/96	704*
Rethinking Retirement	06/19/09	549
Retirement Security	05/31/02	481
Saving Social Security	10/02/98	857
Social Security Reform	09/24/04	781
Social Security: The Search for Fairness	04/05/91	189
Social services. *See Welfare and social services*		
Soft Money		
Campaign Finance Reform	06/13/08	505
Solar energy		
Alternative Energy	07/10/92	586
Confronting Warming	01/09/09	1
Nanotechnology	06/11/04	517
Renewable Energy	11/07/97	961
Solid waste. *See Waste products*		
Somalia		
Famine in Africa	11/08/02	921
Foreign Policy Burden	08/20/93	721
Privatizing the Military	06/25/04	565
South Africa		
Democracy in Africa	03/24/95	252*
Economic Sanctions	10/28/94	942*
South Africa's Future	01/14/94	25
South America		
Foreign Aid After Sept. 11	04/26/02	361
Saving the Rain Forests	06/11/99	497
War on Drugs	06/02/06	481
South Dakota		
Abortion Showdowns	09/22/06	769
South Korea. *See Korea (South)*		
Soviet Union (Former). *See also Russia*		
Aid to Russia	03/12/93	217
Conspiracy Theories	10/23/09	885
Cuba in Crisis	11/29/91	897
Defense Priorities	07/30/99	641

	Date	Page
Democracy in Eastern Europe	10/08/99	873*
Expanding NATO	05/16/97	433
Global Refugee Crisis	07/09/99	574*
Missile Defense	09/08/00	689
NATO's Changing Role	08/21/92	713
The New CIA	12/11/92	1073
New Challenges in Space	07/23/99	617
Non-Proliferation Treaty at 25	01/27/95	73
Nuclear Arms Cleanup	06/24/94	553
Nuclear Disarmament	10/02/09	**813
Nuclear Proliferation	06/05/92	481
Nuclear Proliferation and Terrorism	04/02/04	297
Oil Production in the 21st Century	08/07/98	673
Religious Persecution	11/21/97	1009
Russia and the Former Soviet Republics	06/17/05	541
Russia's Political Future	05/03/96	385
Soviet Republics Rebel	07/12/91	465
Space Program's Future	12/24/93	1129
Space Program's Future	04/25/97	361
Uncertain Future for Man in Space	03/29/91	173
U.S.-Russian Relations	05/22/98	457
Will Nuclear Power Get Another Chance?	02/22/91	113
Weapons of Mass Destruction	03/08/02	193
Space programs		
Conspiracy Theories	10/23/09	885
Human Spaceflight	10/16/09	861
NASA's Future	05/23/03	473
New Challenges in Space	07/23/99	617
The Search for Extraterrestrials	03/05/04	197
Space Program	02/24/12	177
Space Program's Future	12/24/93	1129
Space Program's Future	04/25/97	361
Uncertain Future for Man in Space	03/29/91	173
U.S.-Russian Relations	05/22/98	468*
Spanish		
Bilingual Education	08/13/93	697
Hispanic-Americans' New Clout	09/18/98	809
Puerto Rico's Status	10/23/98	936*
Special education		
Air Pollution Conflict	11/14/03	965
Charter Schools	12/20/02	1044*
Child-Care Options	05/08/98	422*
Educating Gifted Students	03/28/97	265
Home Schooling Debate	01/17/03	25
Increase in Autism	06/13/03	**558*
Learning Disabilities	12/10/93	1081
No Child Left Behind	05/27/05	469
Special Education	11/10/00	905
Special-interest groups		
Animal Rights	01/08/10	1
Campaign Finance Reform	02/09/96	121
Campaign Finance Reform	03/31/00	257
Campaign Finance Showdown	11/22/02	969
Crackdown on Smoking	12/04/92	1049
Cyberpolitics	09/17/04	757
D.C. Voting Rights	04/11/08	313*
Environmental Movement at 25	03/31/95	284*
Feminism's Future	02/28/97	183*
The Growing Influence of Boycotts	01/04/91	1
Gridlock in Washington	04/30/10	385
Hunting Controversy	01/24/92	49
Judicial Elections	04/24/09	373
Lobbying Boom	07/22/05	613
Media Ownership	10/10/03	**850*
Patriotism in America	06/25/99	558*
Regulating Nonprofits	12/26/97	1129
Religion and Politics	10/14/94	889
Religion in Schools	02/18/94	145
School Censorship	02/19/93	145
Student Activism	08/28/98	745
Talk Show Democracy	04/29/94	361
Tea Party Movement	03/19/10	**241*
Testing Term Limits	11/18/94	1020*
Special olympics		
Centennial Olympic Games	04/05/96	306*
Special prosecutors. *See Independent counsels*		
Sport-utility vehicles		
Alternative Energy	02/25/05	173
Auto Industry's Future	01/21/00	17
Auto Safety	10/26/01	873
Oil Diplomacy	01/24/03	49
SUV Debate	05/16/03	449
Traffic Congestion	08/27/99	739*
Sports		
Athletes and Drugs	07/26/91	513
Attracting Jobs	03/02/12	205
The Business of Sports	02/10/95	121
Centennial Olympic Games	04/05/96	289
College Football	11/18/11	977
College Sports	08/26/94	745
Drug Testing	11/20/98	1012*
Eating Disorders	12/18/92	1097
Executive Pay	07/11/97	608*
Extreme Sports	04/03/09	297
Fairness in Salaries	05/29/92	462*
The Future of Baseball	09/25/98	833
Gambling Boom	03/18/94	241
Gender Equity in Sports	04/18/97	337
Getting into College	02/23/96	186*
Hazing	01/09/04	1
High School Sports	09/22/95	825
Hunting Controversy	01/24/92	49
Implementing the Disabilities Act	12/20/96	1118*
Marine Mammals vs. Fish	08/28/92	751*

 *Indicates sidebar or "At Issue" report section. **Indicates an updated report.

	Date	Page
Native Americans	05/08/92	388
Organ Transplants	08/11/95	708*
Pay-Per-View TV	10/04/91	729
Physical Fitness	11/06/92	953
Professional Football	01/29/10	**73
Reforming Big-Time College Sports	03/19/04	249
Soccer in America	04/22/94	337
Sports and Drugs	07/23/04	**613
Sportsmanship	03/23/01	225
Women and Sports	03/06/92	193
Women and Sports	03/25/11	265
Women in Sports	05/11/01	401
Youth Fitness	09/26/97	841
Starr, Kenneth W.		
Independent Counsels	02/21/97	145
Independent Counsels Re-examined	05/07/99	377
State government		
Abortion Debates	09/10/10	725
Abortion Showdowns	09/22/06	769
Adoption Controversies	09/10/99	780*
Affirmative Action	10/17/08	**841
Air Pollution Conflict	11/14/03	965
Animal Rights	01/08/10	1
Assessing the New Health Care Law	09/21/12	789
Assisted Suicide Controversy	05/05/95	396*
Attack on Public Schools	07/26/96	666*
Attracting Jobs	03/02/12	205
Bilingual Education	08/13/93	711*
Biofuels Boom	09/29/06	793
Birth-Control Debate	06/24/05	565
Blighted Cities	11/12/10	941*
Budget Surplus	04/13/01	312*
Cameras in the Courtroom	01/14/11	25
Campaign Finance Reform	03/31/00	270*
Census Controversey	05/14/10	433
Child Poverty	10/28/11	901
Child Welfare Reform	04/22/05	345
Cleaning Up Hazardous Wastes	08/23/96	748*
Closing In on Tobacco	11/12/99	977
Coal Mining Safety	03/17/06	241
Confronting Warming	01/09/09	1
Cracking Down on Immigration	02/03/95	97
Crime Victims' Rights	07/22/94	637*
Criminal Records and Employment	04/20/12	349
Cyberbullying	05/02/08	385
D.C. Voting Rights	04/11/08	313*
Death Penalty Controversies	09/23/05	785
Death Penalty Debates	11/19/10	965
Death Penalty Update	01/08/99	5*
Debate over Bilingualism	01/19/96	52*
Democrats' Future	10/29/10	893
Discipline in Schools	02/15/08	145
Distracted Driving	05/04/12	401
Domestic Partners	09/04/92	761
Downsizing Prisons	03/11/11	217
The Economics of Recycling	03/27/98	268*
Educating Gifted Students	03/28/97	268*
Education Standards	03/11/94	217
Electing Minorities	08/12/94	710*
Energy and Climate	07/24/09	621
Extreme Sports	04/03/09	297
Evolution vs. Creationism	08/22/97	745
Fighting Crime	02/08/08	121
Free-Press Disputes	04/08/05	293
Future of the Airlines	03/07/08	217
Future of Libraries	07/29/11	625
Future of Recycling	12/14/07	1033
Gambling Boom	03/18/94	241
Gambling in America	03/07/03	201
Gangs in the U.S.	07/16/10	581
Garbage Crisis	03/20/92	241
Gay Marriage Showdowns	09/26/08	**769
Gay Rights	03/05/93	208*
Genetically Modified Food	08/31/12	717
Government and Religion	01/15/10	25
Gridlock in Washington	04/30/10	385
Gulf Coast Restoration	08/26/11	677*
Gun Control Standoff	12/19/97	1105
Gun Rights Debates	10/31/08	**889
Gun Violence	05/25/07	457
Hard Times for Libraries	06/26/92	549
Hate Crimes	01/08/93	13*
Health-Care Reform	06/11/10	**505
High-Speed Trains	05/01/09	**397
Home Schooling	09/09/94	776*
Homeland Security	09/12/03	749
The Homeless	08/07/92	665
Housing the Homeless	12/18/09	1053
HPV Vaccine	05/11/07	409
Immigration Conflict	03/09/12	229
Immigration Debate	02/01/08	**97
Immigration Reform	09/24/93	841
Infant Mortality	07/31/92	641
Insurance Fraud	10/11/96	894*
Judges and Politics	07/27/01	577
Judicial Elections	04/24/09	373
Juvenile Justice	11/07/08	913
Legal-Aid Crisis	10/07/11	829
Legalizing Marijuana	06/12/09	**525
Limiting Lawsuits	12/19/08	1033
Line-Item Veto	06/20/97	529
Living-Wage Movement	09/27/02	769
Managing Managed Care	04/16/99	318*
Mandatory Sentencing	05/26/95	469*
Marijuana Laws	02/11/05	125
Marriage and Divorce	05/10/96	409
Mass Transit Boom	01/18/08	49
Medicaid Reform	07/16/04	589

	Date	Page
Medical Marijuana	08/20/99	708*
Mental Health Policy	09/12/97	800*
Mental Illness Medication Debate	02/06/04	101
Mexico's Drug War	12/12/08	1009
Middle-Class Squeeze	03/06/09	201
Mine Safety	06/24/11	553
National Education Standards	05/14/99	401
New Air Quality Standards	03/07/97	193
The New Environmentalism	12/01/06	985
No Child Left Behind	05/27/05	469
Parental Rights	10/25/96	940*
Port Security	04/21/06	337
Preventing Bullying	12/10/10	**1013
Preventing Juvenile Crime	03/15/96	230*
Prison-Building Boom	09/17/99	801
Prison Overcrowding	02/04/94	97
Prisoner Reentry	12/04/09	1005
Private Management of Public Schools	03/25/94	265
Privatizing Government Services	08/09/96	697
Property Rights	06/16/95	517*
Prosecuting Terrorists	03/12/10	**217*
Prosecutors and the Law	11/09/07	937
Prostitution Debate	05/23/08	433
Protecting Wetlands	10/03/08	793*
Public Defenders	04/18/08	337*
Public-Employee Unions	04/08/11	313
Punishing Sex Offenders	01/12/96	28*
Race and Politics	07/18/08	577
Real ID	05/04/07	385
Rebuilding New Orleans	02/03/06	97
Redistricting Debates	02/25/11	169
Redistricting: Drawing Power with a Map	02/15/91	97
Re-examining the Constitution	09/07/12	741
Reforming School Funding	12/10/99	1041
Reinventing Government	02/17/95	145
Renewable Energy	11/07/97	976*
Restructuring the Electric Industry	01/17/97	25
Revising No Child Left Behind	04/16/10	337
Roe v. Wade at 25	11/28/97	1040*
Right to Die	05/13/05	421
Saving Open Spaces	11/05/99	953
School Choice Debate	07/18/97	628*
School Funding	08/27/93	745
School Reform	04/29/11	385
School Vouchers Showdown	02/15/02	121
Sex Offenders	09/08/06	721
Sex Scandals	01/22/10	49
Sleep Deprivation	02/12/10	121
Smart Growth	05/28/04	469
Solitary Confinement	09/14/12	765
State Budget Crises	10/03/03	821
State Budget Crisis	09/11/09	741
States and Federalism	09/13/96	793

	Date	Page
States and Federalism	10/15/10	845
Stem Cell Research	09/01/06	**697
Stimulating the Economy	01/10/03	12*
Teacher Education	10/17/97	921*
Teen Drug Use	06/03/11	481
Testing Term Limits	11/18/94	1009
Threatened Coastlines	02/07/92	97
Too Many Lawsuits?	05/22/92	433
Transportation Policy	07/04/97	577
Urban Sprawl in the West	10/03/97	881*
Vanishing Jobs	03/13/09	225
Voter Rights	05/18/12	449
Voting Controversies	09/15/06	745
Water Crisis in the West	12/09/11	1025
Water Shortages	06/18/10	529
Welfare Experiments	09/16/94	793
Welfare Reform	04/10/92	313
Welfare, Work and the States	12/06/96	1057
Women in Politics	03/21/08	265
The Working Poor	11/03/95	969
Wrongful Convictions	04/17/09	**345
Year-Round Schools	05/17/96	436*
Steel industry		
The Economics of Recycling	03/27/98	265
Recession's Regional Impact	02/01/91	67*
Stem cells		
Embryo Research	12/17/99	1065
Organ Shortage	02/21/03	153*
Stem Cell Research	09/01/06	**697
Steroids		
Athletes and Drugs	07/26/91	513
Centennial Olympic Games	04/05/96	289
Sports and Drugs	07/23/04	**613
Stocks and bonds		
Accountants Under Fire	03/22/02	241
Aging Baby Boomers	10/19/07	865
Business Ethics	05/06/11	409
Corporate Crime	10/11/02	817
Curbing CEO Pay	03/09/07	217
Executive Pay	07/11/97	601
Fairness in Salaries	05/29/92	462
Financial Bailout	10/24/08	**865
Financial Crisis	05/09/08	409
Financial Literacy	09/04/09	717
Financial Industry Overhaul	07/30/10	629
Financial Misconduct	01/20/12	53
Mutual Funds	05/20/94	433
Nanotechnology	06/11/04	517
Overhauling Social Security	05/12/95	422*
Rethinking Retirement	06/19/09	549
Retirement Security	05/31/02	481
Saving Social Security	10/02/98	857
Stimulating the Economy	01/10/03	1
The Stock Market	05/02/97	385

 *Indicates sidebar or "At Issue" report section. **Indicates an updated report.

	Date	Page
Socially Responsible Investing	08/29/08	673
Stock Market Troubles	01/16/04	25
Tax Reform	03/22/96	241
Storms. ***See Hurricanes and storms***		
Strikes		
The Future of Baseball	09/25/98	848*
Labor Movement's Future	06/28/96	570*
Student aid		
Caring for Veterans	04/23/10	361
Consumer Debt	03/02/07	193
Financial Literacy	09/04/09	717
Getting into College	02/23/96	169
National Service	06/25/93	553
Paying for College	11/20/92	1001
Regulating Credit Cards	10/10/08	817*
Rising College Costs	12/05/03	1013
School Vouchers	04/09/99	281
School Vouchers Showdown	02/15/02	121
Student Aid	01/25/08	73
Student Debt	10/21/11	877
Upward Mobility	04/29/05	369
The Value of a College Education	11/20/09	981
Women and Sports	03/06/92	193
Wounded Veterans	08/31/07	697
Suburban areas		
The Black Middle Class	01/23/98	55*
Census Controversey	05/14/10	433
Changing U.S. Electorate	05/30/08	**457
Downtown Renaissance	06/23/06	**553
Revitalizing the Cities	10/13/95	897
Rise of Megachurches	09/21/07	769
Saving Open Spaces	11/05/99	953
School Funding	08/27/93	745
Setting Environmental Priorities	05/21/99	442*
Smart Growth	05/28/04	469
Suburban Crime	09/03/93	769
Traffic Congestion	08/27/99	729
Urban Sprawl in the West	10/03/97	865
Sudan		
Human Rights Issues	10/30/09	909
Human Trafficking and Slavery	03/26/04	273
Stopping Genocide	08/27/04	685
Sudden Infant Death Syndrome		
Infant Mortality	07/31/92	651*
Suicide. ***See also Assisted suicide***		
Childhood Depression	07/16/99	593
Drug Safety	03/11/05	221
Homework Debate	12/06/02	993
Gun Control	06/10/94	514*
Middle East Peace	01/21/05	53
Military Suicides	09/23/11	781*
Native Americans	05/08/92	400
Prospects for Mideast Peace	08/30/02	686*

	Date	Page
Teenage Suicide	06/14/91	369
Youth Suicide	02/13/04	125
Superfund		
Asbestos Litigation	05/02/03	393
Cleaning Up Hazardous Wastes	08/23/96	745
Supreme Court		
Abortion Showdowns	09/22/06	769
Advertising Overload	01/23/04	49
Affirmative Action	09/21/01	737
Affirmative Action	10/17/08	**841
Age Discrimination	08/01/97	673
Alcohol Advertising	03/14/97	229*
Antitrust Policy	06/12/98	505
Broadcast Indecency	04/16/04	326*
Cameras in the Courtroom	01/14/11	25
Campaign Finance Debates	05/28/10	457
Campaign Finance Showdown	11/22/02	969
Caring for the Dying	09/05/97	769
Civil Liberties Debates	10/24/03	893
Class Action Lawsuits	05/13/11	433
Death Penalty Debate	03/10/95	193
Death Penalty Debates	11/19/10	965
Downsizing Prisons	03/11/11	217
Electing Minorities	08/12/94	697
Eyewitness Testimony	10/14/11	853
Free-Press Disputes	04/08/05	293
Gay Marriage	09/05/03	721
Gays in the Military	09/18/09	**765
Gender Pay Gap	03/14/08	241
Government and Religion	01/15/10	25
The Growing Influence of Boycotts	01/04/91	9*
Gun Control Standoff	12/19/97	1119*
Hate Crimes	01/08/93	1
High School Sports	09/22/95	825
Immigration Conflict	03/09/12	229
Indecency on Television	11/09/12	965
International Law	12/17/04	1049
Learning Disabilities	12/10/93	1081
Limiting Lawsuits	12/19/08	1033
Line-Item Veto	06/20/97	544*
Marijuana Laws	02/11/05	125
Parental Rights	10/25/96	950*
Plea Bargaining	02/12/99	122*
Police Brutality	09/06/91	643*
Police Misconduct	04/06/12	301
Policing the Borders	02/22/02	145
Policing the Police	03/17/00	209
Presidential Power	11/15/02	945
Presidential Power	02/24/06	169
Press Freedom	02/05/10	97
Property Rights	06/16/95	513
Property Rights	03/04/05	197
Prosecuting Terrorists	03/12/10	**217*
Prosecutors and Politics	06/22/07	553

	Date	Page
Public Defenders	04/18/08	337*
Racial Diversity in Public Schools	09/14/07	**745
Racial Quotas	05/17/91	288*
Re-examining the Constitution	09/07/12	741
Re-examining 9/11	06/04/04	493
Reforming Big-Time College Sports	03/19/04	249
Religion in Schools	02/18/94	145
Religion in Schools	01/12/01	1
Religion in the Workplace	08/23/02	649
Rethinking Affirmative Action	04/28/95	381*
Rethinking School Integration	10/18/96	913
Rethinking the Death Penalty	11/16/01	945
Right to Die	05/13/05	421
Roe v. Wade at 25	11/28/97	1033
School Choice	05/10/91	260*
School Desegregation	04/23/04	345
School Vouchers	04/09/99	281
School Vouchers Showdown	02/15/02	121
Science in the Courtroom	10/22/93	913
Sentencing Debates	11/05/04	925
Sexual Harassment	04/27/12	377
Solitary Confinement	09/14/12	765
States and Federalism	10/15/10	845
Stem Cell Research	09/01/06	**697
Student Journalism	06/05/98	481
Student Rights	06/05/09	501
Supreme Court Controversies	09/28/12	813
Supreme Court Preview	09/17/93	817*
Supreme Court's Future	01/28/05	77
Testing Term Limits	11/18/94	1009
Threatened Coastlines	02/07/92	111*
Three-Strikes Laws	05/10/02	417
Treatment of Detainees	08/25/06	673
Voting Controversies	09/15/06	745
Surveillance. ***See Electronic surveillance***		
Sweatshops		
Child Labor and Sweatshops	08/16/96	721
Corporate Social Responsibility	08/03/07	649
Taiwan		
China Today	08/04/00	625
New Era in Asia	02/14/92	121
Taiwan, China, and the U.S.	05/24/96	457
U.S.-China Trade	04/15/94	320*
U.S. Policy in Asia	11/27/92	1025
Tariffs		
Mexico's Emergence	07/19/91	489
U.S.-China Trade	04/15/94	313
U.S. Policy in Asia	11/27/92	1041*
U.S. Trade Policy	01/29/93	73
Tax evasion		
IRS Reform	01/16/98	34*
Tax Reform	03/22/96	241
Underground Economy	03/04/94	193

	Date	Page
Taxation. ***See also Business and industry; Taxation; Income tax; User fees***		
Alternative Energy	07/10/92	589*
Attracting Jobs	03/02/12	205
Budget Deficit	12/09/05	1029
Budget Surplus	04/13/01	297
Business Bankruptcy	04/10/09	321
Child-Care Options	05/08/98	409
Energy Policy	05/20/11	457
Gambling Boom	03/18/94	241
Historic Preservation	10/07/94	865
Income Inequality	12/03/10	989
Legalizing Marijuana	06/12/09	**525
Line-Item Veto	06/20/97	543*
National Debt	03/18/11	241
Public-Works Projects	02/20/09	153
Reforming School Funding	12/10/99	1041
Regulating Nonprofits	12/26/97	1129
Saving Open Spaces	11/05/99	953
School Vouchers	04/09/99	281
School Vouchers Showdown	02/15/02	121
State Budget Crises	10/03/03	821
State Budget Crisis	09/11/09	741
Stimulating the Economy	01/10/03	1
Tax Reform	03/22/96	241
Tea Party Movement	03/19/10	**241*
Tobacco Industry	12/10/04	**1025
Teachers. ***See Elementary and secondary education***		
Technology. ***See Science and technology***		
Teenagers. ***See Adolescents and youth***		
Telecommunications. ***See also Cellular telephones***		
Advertising Overload	01/23/04	49
Cyber-Crime	04/12/02	305
The Future of Telecommunications	04/23/99	329
New Challenges in Space	07/23/99	617
Regulating the New Economy	10/19/01	849
Telecommuting		
Flexible Work Arrangements	08/14/98	697
Traffic Congestion	05/06/94	390*
Work, Family and Stress	08/14/92	706*
Television and radio		
Advertising Overload	01/23/04	49
Advertising Under Attack	09/13/91	657
Alcohol Advertising	03/14/97	217
Assisting Refugees	02/07/97	105*
Broadcast Indecency	04/16/04	321
The Business of Sports	02/10/95	132*
Cameras in the Courtroom	01/14/11	25
Celebrity Culture	03/18/05	245
Centennial Olympic Games	04/05/96	289
Children's Television	08/15/97	721
College Sports	08/26/94	754*
The Consumer Culture	11/19/99	1007*

	Date	Page
Cosmetic Surgery	04/15/05	317
Courts and the Media	09/23/94	817
Cyberbullying	05/02/08	385
Death Penalty Debate	03/10/95	210*
Emergency Medicine	01/05/96	8*
Extreme Sports	04/03/09	297
Food Safety Battle: Organic v. Biotech	09/04/98	772*
Foreign Policy and Public Opinion	07/15/94	601
Free-Press Disputes	04/08/05	293
Future of Journalism	03/27/09	**273
The Future of Television	12/23/94	1129
The Growing Influence of Boycotts	01/04/91	1
Hispanic-Americans' New Clout	09/18/98	818*
Indecency on Television	11/09/12	965
Journalism Standards in the Internet Age	10/08/10	821
Journalism Under Fire	12/25/98	1121
Lies and Politics	02/18/11	145
Media Ownership	10/10/03	**845
Obesity Epidemic	01/31/03	86*
The Obscenity Debate	12/20/91	983
The Partisan Divide	04/30/04	373
Patriotism in America	06/25/99	545
Pay-Per-View TV	10/04/91	729
Political Conventions	08/08/08	649
Political Scandals	05/27/94	457
Preventing Bullying	12/10/10	**1013
Public Broadcasting	09/18/92	809
Public Broadcasting	10/29/99	929
Pursuing the Paranormal	03/29/96	265
Reading Crisis?	02/22/08	169
Reality TV	08/27/10	677
Reassessing the Nation's Gun Laws	03/22/91	157
Reforming Big-Time College Sports	03/19/04	249
School Violence	10/09/98	888*
Sex Scandals	01/22/10	49
Sex, Violence and the Media	11/17/95	1017
Shock Jocks	06/01/07	**481
Soccer in America	04/22/94	354*
Talk Show Democracy	04/29/94	361
Television's Future	02/16/07	145
Transition to Digital TV	06/20/08	529
TV Violence	03/26/93	265
Violence in Schools	09/11/92	802*
Women and Sports	03/06/92	200*
Women and Sports	03/25/11	265
Term limits		
Term Limits	01/10/92	1
Testing Term Limits	11/18/94	1009
Terrorism		
Academic Freedom	10/07/05	833
Afghanistan Dilemma	08/07/09	**669*
Airline Safety	10/08/93	874*
America at War	07/23/10	**605
Chemical and Biological Weapons	01/31/97	73
Civil Liberties Debates	10/24/03	893
Civil Liberties in Wartime	12/14/01	1017
Closing Guantánamo	02/27/09	**177
Combating Terrorism	07/21/95	633
Cost of the Iraq War	04/25/08	361*
Cyber-Crime	04/12/02	322*
Cybersecurity	09/26/03	797
Cybersecurity	02/26/10	169
Death Penalty Update	01/08/99	1
Democracy in the Arab World	01/30/04	73
Drone Warfare	08/06/10	653
Energy Security	02/01/02	73
Exporting Democracy	04/01/05	269
Fighting Crime	02/08/08	121
Food Safety	11/01/02	897
Future of Amtrak	10/18/02	853*
Future of NATO	02/28/03	177
Future of the Airline Industry	06/21/02	545
Global Jihad	10/14/05	857
Government Secrecy	12/02/05	1005
Hating America	11/23/01	969
Homegrown Jihadists	09/03/10	701
Homeland Security	09/12/03	749
Homeland Security	02/13/09	129
Illegal Immigration	05/06/05	393
Intelligence Reforms	01/25/02	49
International Law	12/17/04	1049
Interrogating the CIA	09/25/09	789
Middle East Peace	01/21/05	53
Middle East Tensions	10/27/06	**889
Muslims in America	04/30/93	361
Nuclear Proliferation and Terrorism	04/02/04	297
The Obama Presidency	01/30/09	73
Policing the Borders	02/22/02	145
Port Security	04/21/06	337
Presidential Power	11/15/02	945
Prosecuting Terrorists	03/12/10	**217*
Protecting Whistleblowers	03/31/06	265
Puerto Rico: The Struggle over Status	02/08/91	91*
Real ID	05/04/07	385
Re-examining 9/11	06/04/04	493
Remembering 9/11	09/02/11	701*
Smallpox Threat	02/07/03	118*
Torture	04/18/03	361*
Treating Anxiety	02/08/02	97
Treatment of Detainees	08/25/06	673
Understanding Islam	11/03/06	913
U.S.-Pakistan Relations	08/05/11	653*
U.S. Policy on Iran	11/16/07	961
War on Terrorism	10/12/01	817
Weapons of Mass Destruction	03/08/02	193
Worker Safety	05/21/04	445

	Date	Page
Texas		
Death Penalty Debates	11/19/10	965
Debate over Bilingualism	01/19/96	60*
High School Sports	09/22/95	837*
High-Speed Rail	04/16/93	327*
Illegal Immigration	05/06/05	393
Protecting Endangered Species	04/19/96	337
Redistricting Disputes	03/12/04	221
Rethinking the Death Penalty	11/16/01	960*
Testing in Schools	04/20/01	332*
Textbooks		
Education and Gender	06/03/94	496*
Evolution vs. Creationism	08/22/97	745
Government and Religion	01/15/10	25
Home Schooling Debate	01/17/03	30*
Teaching History	09/29/95	849
School Censorship	02/19/93	145
School Funding	08/27/93	756*
Thailand		
Human Trafficking and Slavery	03/26/04	273
Prostitution	06/11/93	516*
Thalidomide		
Cancer Treatments	09/11/98	798*
Reforming the FDA	06/06/97	493*
Third World. ***See Developing countries***		
Timber industry. ***See Forests and forestry***		
Title IX. ***See Education Amendments Act***		
Tobacco		
Advertising Overload	01/23/04	49
Advertising Under Attack	09/13/91	657
Closing In on Tobacco	11/12/99	977
Crackdown on Smoking	12/04/92	1049
Drug-Policy Debate	07/28/00	599*
High-Impact Litigation	02/11/00	102*
Indoor Air Pollution	10/27/95	945
Limiting Lawsuits	12/19/08	1033
Preventing Cancer	01/16/09	25
Preventing Disease	01/06/12	1
Preventing Teen Drug Use	07/28/95	657
Prolonging Life	09/30/11	805*
Reforming the FDA	06/06/97	481
Regulating Tobacco	09/30/94	841
Science and Politics	08/20/04	661
Socially Responsible Investing	08/29/08	673
Teens and Tobacco	12/01/95	1065
Tobacco Industry	12/10/04	**1025
Women's Health	11/07/03	952*
Torture. ***See Violence; War crimes***		
Toxic substances. ***See Hazardous substances***		
Trade. ***See International trade***		

	Date	Page
Traffic accidents		
Aggressive Driving	07/25/97	649
Aging Infrastructure	09/28/07	**793
Auto Safety	10/26/01	873
Distracted Driving	05/04/12	401
Drinking on Campus	03/20/98	241
Drunken Driving	10/06/00	793
Highway Safety	07/14/95	609
Sleep Deprivation	06/26/98	553
Sleep Deprivation	02/12/10	121
SUV Debate	05/16/03	454*
Teen Driving	01/07/05	1
Too Many Lawsuits?	05/22/92	440
Truck Safety	03/12/99	209
Underage Drinking	03/13/92	217
U.S. Auto Industry	10/16/92	896*
U.S.-Mexico Relations	11/09/01	921
Traffic congestion		
Flexible Work Arrangements	08/14/98	697
Mass Transit Boom	01/18/08	49
Smart Growth	05/28/04	469
Traffic Congestion	05/06/94	385
Traffic Congestion	08/27/99	729
Transportation Policy	07/04/97	577
Transit Systems		
High-Speed Trains	05/01/09	**397
Transportation. ***See also Air transportation; Automobiles and auto industry; Railroads; Highways and roads***		
Affordable Housing	02/09/01	94*
Future of Amtrak	10/18/02	841
Future of the Airline Industry	06/21/02	545
Future of the Airlines	03/07/08	217
High-Speed Rail	04/16/93	313
High-Speed Trains	05/01/09	**397
Mass Transit Boom	01/18/08	49
Public-Works Projects	02/20/09	153
Transportation Policy	07/04/97	577
Truck Safety	03/12/99	209
U.S.-Mexico Relations	11/09/01	921
Transsexuals		
Transgender Issues	05/05/06	385
Travel and tourist trade. ***See also Ecotourism***		
Airline Industry Problems	09/24/99	842*
Castro's Next Move	12/12/97	1081
Coastal Development	08/21/98	721
Ecotourism	10/20/06	865
Future of the Airline Industry	06/21/02	545
Gambling Boom	03/18/94	245*
Historic Preservation	10/07/94	865
National Forests	10/16/98	905

	Date	Page
National Parks	05/28/93	457
Prostitution	06/11/93	516*
Treaties and international agreements. ***See also North American Free Trade Agreement; International relations***		
Air Pollution Conflict	11/14/03	965
Banning Land Mines	08/08/97	697
Chemical and Biological Weapons	01/31/97	73
Children's Legal Rights	04/23/93	345*
Endangered Species Act	06/03/05	**493
Ethics of War	12/13/02	1013
European Monetary Union	11/27/98	1025
Future of NATO	02/28/03	177
Human Rights	11/13/98	977
Human Trafficking and Slavery	03/26/04	273
International Law	12/17/04	1049
Invasive Species	10/05/01	785
Kids in Prison	04/27/01	361*
Missile Defense	09/08/00	689
Native Americans' Future	07/12/96	610*
Nuclear Arms Cleanup	06/24/94	553
Nuclear Proliferation	06/05/92	481
Nuclear Proliferation and Terrorism	04/02/04	297
Panama Canal	11/26/99	1017
Setting Environmental Priorities	05/21/99	425
Sports and Drugs	07/23/04	**613
Stopping Genocide	08/27/04	685
Women and Human Rights	04/30/99	353
Trucks and trucking		
Auto Safety	10/26/01	873
Highway Safety	07/14/95	620*
Sleep Deprivation	06/26/98	553
SUV Debate	05/16/03	449
Truck Safety	03/12/99	209
U.S.-Mexico Relations	11/09/01	921
Tuberculosis		
Battling HIV/AIDS	10/26/07	889
Combating Infectious Diseases	06/09/95	496*
Women and AIDS	12/25/92	1134
Tuition vouchers		
Attack on Public Schools	07/26/96	662*
Private Management of Public Schools	03/25/94	276*
Privatization	11/13/92	988*
School Choice	05/10/91	253
School Choice Debate	07/18/97	625
School Desegregation	04/23/04	345
School Vouchers	04/09/99	281
School Vouchers Showdown	02/15/02	121
Turkey		
Future of the European Union	10/28/05	909
UFOs		
Pursuing the Paranormal	03/29/96	265
The Search for Extraterrestrials	03/05/04	197

	Date	Page
Unemployment. ***See Employment and unemployment***		
Unification Church		
Cults in America	05/07/93	385
Unions. ***See Labor unions***		
United Nations		
Aiding Africa	08/29/03	697
Childhood Immunizations	06/18/93	546*
Children in Crisis	08/31/01	657
Confronting Iraq	10/04/02	793
Economic Sanctions	10/28/94	937
Emerging India	04/19/02	329
Ending Poverty	09/09/05	733
Ethics of War	12/13/02	1013
Foreign Aid After Sept. 11	04/26/02	361
Foreign Policy Burden	08/20/93	721
Global Food Crisis	06/27/08	553
Haiti's Dilemma	02/18/05	149
Human Rights	11/13/98	977
Human Rights Issues	10/30/09	909
International Law	12/17/04	1049
Middle East Tensions	10/27/06	**889
Non-Proliferation Treaty at 25	01/27/95	73
Nuclear Disarmament	10/02/09	**813
Population Growth	07/16/93	601
Privatizing the Military	06/25/04	565
Rebuilding Afghanistan	12/21/01	1057*
Rebuilding Iraq	07/11/03	625
Stopping Genocide	08/27/04	685
Torture	04/18/03	345
Treatment of Detainees	08/25/06	673
The United Nations and Global Security	02/27/04	173
United Nations at 50	08/18/95	729
War Crimes	07/07/95	585
Weapons of Mass Destruction	03/08/02	193
Women and Human Rights	04/30/99	353
United States		
Dealing With the "New" Russia	06/06/08	481
Universities. ***See Colleges and universities***		
Urban areas. ***See Cities and towns***		
User fees		
Hard Times for Libraries	06/26/92	553
National Parks	05/28/93	457
Reforming the FDA	06/06/97	481
Transportation Policy	07/04/97	580*
Utilities. ***See Public utilities***		
Vaccines		
AIDS Update	12/04/98	1049
Avian Flu Threat	01/13/06	25
Childhood Immunizations	06/18/93	529
Combating AIDS	04/21/95	345

	Date	Page
Combating Infectious Diseases	06/09/95	489
Fighting Superbugs	08/24/07	673
HPV Vaccine	05/11/07	409
Increase in Autism	06/13/03	**561*
Sexually Transmitted Diseases	12/03/04	997
Smallpox Threat	02/07/03	105
Vaccine Controversies	08/25/00	641
Values. ***See Ethical and moral issues***		
Vegetarianism		
Animal Rights	05/24/91	318*
Veterans		
Caring for Veterans	04/23/10	361
Wounded Veterans	08/31/07	697
Veterinary medicine		
America's Pampered Pets	12/27/96	1129
Drug-Resistant Bacteria	06/04/99	473
Prozac Controversy	08/19/94	734*
Victims' rights. ***See Crime and criminals***		
Video games		
Digital Education	12/02/11	1001
Reading Crisis?	02/22/08	169
Video Games	11/10/06	**937
Vietnam		
Global Refugee Crisis	07/09/99	574*
Legacy of the Vietnam War	02/18/00	113
New Era in Asia	02/14/92	121
Privatizing the Military	06/25/04	565
Should the U.S. Reinstate the Draft?	01/11/91	17
Treatment of Veterans	11/19/04	973
U.S.-Vietnam Relations	12/03/93	1057
Weapons of Mass Destruction	03/08/02	193
Wounded Veterans	08/31/07	697
Violence		
Aggressive Driving	07/25/97	649
Biology and Behavior	04/03/98	289
Boys' Emotional Needs	06/18/99	521
Bullying	02/04/05	101
Childhood Depression	07/16/99	593
Children in Crisis	08/31/01	657
Children's Television	08/15/97	721
Child Welfare Reform	04/22/05	345
Combating Terrorism	07/21/95	633
Cyberbullying	05/02/08	385
Democracy in Latin America	11/03/00	881
Discipline in Schools	02/15/08	145
Europe's New Right	02/12/93	121
Extreme Sports	04/03/09	297
Fighting Crime	02/08/08	121
Gang Crisis	05/14/04	421
Gangs in the U.S.	07/16/10	581
Gun Control	06/10/94	505
Gun Control Debate	11/12/04	949

	Date	Page
Gun Rights Debates	10/31/08	**889
Gun Violence	05/25/07	457
Haiti's Dilemma	02/18/05	149
Hate Crimes	01/08/93	1
Hate Groups	05/08/09	421
Hazing	01/09/04	1
Indecency on Television	11/09/12	965
Job Stress	08/04/95	688*
Juvenile Justice	02/25/94	186*
Mental Illness	08/06/93	678*
Mexico's Future	10/26/12	913
Middle East Peace	01/21/05	53
Movie Ratings	03/28/03	273
Northern Ireland Cease-Fire	09/15/95	801
Patriotism in America	06/25/99	558*
Police Misconduct	04/06/12	301
Preventing Bullying	12/10/10	**1013
Preventing Juvenile Crime	03/15/96	217
Prison Overcrowding	02/04/94	97
Privatizing the Military	07/13/12	597
Prozac Controversy	08/19/94	737*
Reassessing the Nation's Gun Laws	03/22/91	157
School Violence	10/09/98	881
Serial Killers	10/31/03	917
Sex, Violence and the Media	11/17/95	1017
Soccer in America	04/22/94	349*
Socially Responsible Investing	08/29/08	673
South Africa's Future	01/14/94	25
Suburban Crime	09/03/93	769
Treating Depression	06/26/09	573
TV Violence	03/26/93	265
Violence Against Women	02/26/93	169
Violence in Schools	09/11/92	785
Women and Human Rights	04/30/99	353
Youth Violence	03/05/10	193*
Zero Tolerance	03/10/00	185
Violence Against Women Act (VAWA)		
Domestic Violence	01/06/06	1
Vitamins and minerals. ***See Food and nutrition***		
Voluntarism. ***See also Charities and nonprofit organizations***		
Celebrity Advocacy	05/11/12	425
Civic Renewal	03/21/97	244*
Corporate Social Responsibility	08/03/07	649
Ending Homelessness	06/18/04	556*
Future Job Market	01/11/02	8*
Invasive Species	10/05/01	796*
National Service	06/25/93	553
National Service	06/30/06	577
The New Corporate Philanthropy	02/27/98	169
The New Volunteerism	12/13/96	1081
Parents and Schools	01/20/95	49
Peace Corps' Challenges in the 1990s	01/25/91	49
Youth Volunteerism	01/27/12	77

 *Indicates sidebar or "At Issue" report section. **Indicates an updated report.

	Date	Page
Voting and voting rights		
Asian Americans	12/13/91	962
Campaign Finance Showdown	11/22/02	969
Changing Demographics	11/16/12	989
Changing U.S. Electorate	05/30/08	**457
D.C. Voting Rights	04/11/08	313*
Electing Minorities	08/12/94	697
Electing the President	04/20/07	337
Election Reform	11/02/01	897
Future of the GOP	03/20/09	249
Haiti's Dilemma	02/18/05	149
Hispanic-Americans' New Clout	09/18/98	809
Lies and Politics	02/18/11	145
Low Voter Turnout	10/20/00	833
Partisan Politics	03/19/99	233
Political Conventions	08/08/08	649
Presidential Election	02/03/12	101
Prison-Building Boom	09/17/99	817*
Race and Politics	07/18/08	577
Race in America	07/11/03	593
Real ID	05/04/07	385
Redistricting Debates	02/25/11	169
Redistricting Disputes	03/12/04	221
Redistricting: Drawing Power with a Map	02/15/91	97
Re-examining the Constitution	09/07/12	741
Term Limits	01/10/92	1
Third-Party Prospects	12/22/95	1137
Voter Rights	05/18/12	449
Voting Controversies	09/15/06	745
Wages and salaries		
Auto Industry's Future	02/06/09	**105
Big-Box Stores	09/10/04	733
The Business of Sports	02/10/95	121
Child Care	12/17/93	1105
Child Labor and Sweatshops	08/16/96	721
College Football	11/18/11	977
Contingent Work Force	10/24/97	937
Corporate Crime	10/11/02	817
Corporate Social Responsibility	08/03/07	649
Curbing CEO Pay	03/09/07	217
Domestic Poverty	09/07/07	**721
Downward Mobility	07/23/93	629*
Employee Benefits	02/04/00	65
Executive Pay	07/11/97	601
Fairness in Salaries	05/29/92	457
The Future of Baseball	09/25/98	833
Future of Feminism	04/14/06	313
Gender Pay Gap	03/14/08	241
The Glass Ceiling	10/29/93	937
Health-Care Reform	08/28/09	693*
High-Tech Labor Shortage	04/24/98	361
Illegal Immigration	05/06/05	393
Immigration Debate	02/01/08	**97
Income Inequality	04/17/98	337
Income Inequality	12/03/10	989
Jobs in the '90s	02/28/92	169
Labor Unions' Future	09/02/05	**709
Living-Wage Movement	09/27/02	769
Middle-Class Squeeze	03/06/09	201
Minimum Wage	12/16/05	1053
'Occupy' Movement	01/13/12	25
Paying for College	11/20/92	1006*
Paying for Retirement	11/05/93	961
Public-Employee Unions	04/08/11	313
Overhauling Social Security	05/12/95	417
Rethinking Retirement	06/19/09	549
Reviving Manufacturing	07/22/11	601
Rising College Costs	12/05/03	1013
Social Security Reform	09/24/04	781
Stimulating the Economy	01/10/03	1
Stock Market Troubles	01/16/04	25
Teacher Shortages	08/24/01	640*
Universal Coverage	03/30/07	265
Upward Mobility	04/29/05	369
Vanishing Jobs	03/13/09	225
Worker Retraining	01/21/94	56*
The Working Poor	11/03/95	969
Youth Apprenticeships	10/23/92	918*
Wall Street. *See Stocks and bonds*		
War crimes		
Closing Guantánamo	02/27/09	**177
Ethics of War	12/13/02	1013
Famine in Africa	11/08/02	921
International Law	12/17/04	1049
Interrogating the CIA	09/25/09	789
Rebuilding Iraq	07/11/03	625
Stopping Genocide	08/27/04	685
War Crimes	07/07/95	585
Women and Human Rights	04/30/99	353
Washington, D.C. *See District of Columbia*		
Washington (State)		
Assisted Suicide	02/21/92	145
Assisted Suicide Controversy	05/05/95	406*
Gun Control Standoff	12/19/97	1120*
Jobs vs. Environment	05/15/92	409
Punishing Sex Offenders	01/12/96	25
School Choice Debate	07/18/97	629*
Waste products. *See also Nuclear waste*		
The Economics of Recycling	03/27/98	265
Environmental Movement at 25	03/31/95	288*
Fast-Food Shake-Up	11/08/91	825
Future of Recycling	12/14/07	1033
Garbage Crisis	03/20/92	241
Panama Canal	11/26/99	1031*
Renewable Energy	11/07/97	970*
Setting Environmental Priorities	05/21/99	438*

	Date	Page
Water pollution. *See also Water resources*		
Acid Rain: New Approach to Old Problem	03/08/91	129
Bush and the Environment	10/25/02	865
Coastal Development	08/21/98	739*
Environmental Movement at 25	03/31/95	283*
Farm Subsidies	05/17/02	433
Fish Farming	07/27/07	625
Fracking Controversy	12/16/11	1049
The Greening of Eastern Europe	11/15/91	849
Gulf Coast Restoration	08/26/11	677*
Jobs vs. Environment	05/15/92	423
Lead Poisoning	06/19/92	538
Managing Wildfires	11/02/12	941
Marine Mammals vs. Fish	08/28/92	754
Offshore Drilling	06/25/10	553
Oil Spills	01/17/92	25
Protecting Wetlands	10/03/08	793*
Reforming the Corps	05/30/03	497
Saving the Oceans	11/04/05	933
Setting Environmental Priorities	05/21/99	425
Threatened Coastlines	02/07/92	107
Threatened Fisheries	08/02/02	617
Water Quality	02/11/94	121
Water Quality	11/24/00	953
Water Shortages	08/01/03	649
Water Shortages	06/18/10	529
Water resources. *See also Water pollution*		
Aging Infrastructure	09/28/07	**793
California: Enough Water for the Future?	04/19/91	221
Crisis on the Plains	05/09/03	434*
Farm Policy	08/10/12	693
Farm Subsidies	05/17/02	433
Fish Farming	07/27/07	625
Global Water Shortages	12/15/95	1113
Protecting Wetlands	10/03/08	793*
Public-Works Projects	02/20/09	153
Reforming the Corps	05/30/03	497
Urban Sprawl in the West	10/03/97	880*
Water Crisis in the West	12/09/11	1025
Water Shortages	08/01/03	649
Water Shortages	06/18/10	529
Watergate scandal. *See Independent counsels*		
Weapons. *See also Arms control; Firearms*		
Arms Sales	12/09/94	1081
Banning Land Mines	08/08/97	697
Calculating the Costs of the Gulf War	03/15/91	145
Chemical and Biological Weapons	01/31/97	73
Confronting Iraq	10/04/02	793
Defense Priorities	07/30/99	641
Future of NATO	02/28/03	177
Gun Control Debate	11/12/04	949
Gun Rights Debates	10/31/08	**889
Gun Violence	05/25/07	457
Homeland Security	09/12/03	764*
Missile Defense	09/08/00	689
New Challenges in Space	07/23/99	631*
North Korean Crisis	04/11/03	321
Nuclear Proliferation and Terrorism	04/02/04	297
Panama Canal	11/26/99	1031*
Policing the Borders	02/22/02	145
Rise in Counterinsurgency	09/05/08	697
Smallpox Threat	02/07/03	105
War on Terrorism	10/12/01	833*
Weapons of Mass Destruction	03/08/02	193
Welfare and social services		
Assisting Refugees	02/07/97	97
Caring for Veterans	04/23/10	361
Child-Care Options	05/08/98	409
Child Poverty	04/07/00	281
Child Poverty	10/28/11	901
Child Welfare Reform	04/22/05	345
Cost of the Iraq War	04/25/08	361*
Covering the Uninsured	06/14/02	521
Domestic Poverty	09/07/07	**721
Encouraging Teen Abstinence	07/10/98	577
Ending Homelessness	06/18/04	541
Faith-Based Initiatives	05/04/01	377
Future of Marriage	05/07/04	397
Head Start	04/09/93	289
Helping the Homeless	01/26/96	73
The Homeless	08/07/92	665
Hunger in America	12/22/00	1033
Illegal Immigration	04/24/92	361
Immigration Reform	09/24/93	841
National Debt	03/18/11	241
National Service	06/25/93	553
Native Americans' Future	07/12/96	601
The New Immigrants	01/24/97	49
The New Volunteerism	12/13/96	1081
Preventing Teen Pregnancy	05/14/93	409
Privatization	11/13/92	983*
Race in America	07/11/03	593
State Budget Crisis	09/11/09	741
States and Federalism	09/13/96	793
Straining the Safety Net	07/31/09	645
Teen Pregnancy	03/26/10	265*
Upward Mobility	04/29/05	369
Welfare Experiments	09/16/94	793
Welfare Reform	08/03/01	601
Welfare, Work and the States	12/06/96	1057
The Working Poor	11/03/95	969
Wounded Veterans	08/31/07	697
West Bank		
Global Water Shortages	12/15/95	1113
Israel at 50	03/06/98	193

 *Indicates sidebar or "At Issue" report section. **Indicates an updated report.

	Date	Page
Middle East Conflict	04/06/01	273
Middle East Peace	01/21/05	53
The Palestinians	08/30/91	609
Prospects for Mideast Peace	08/30/02	673
Wetlands		
Endangered Species	06/21/91	393
Reforming the Corps	05/30/03	513*
Saving the Oceans	11/04/05	933
Threatened Coastlines	02/07/92	97
Whistleblowers		
Accountants Under Fire	03/22/02	241
Combating Scientific Misconduct	01/10/97	6*
Corporate Crime	10/11/02	817
Government Secrecy	12/02/05	1005
Protecting Whistleblowers	03/31/06	265
Stock Market Troubles	01/16/04	25
Whistleblowers	12/05/97	1057
Whitewater scandal. ***See Independent counsels***		
Wildlife		
America's Pampered Pets	12/27/96	1140*
Animal Intelligence	10/22/10	869
Animal Rights	01/08/10	1
Crisis on the Plains	05/09/03	439*
Disappearing Species	11/30/07	985
Endangered Species	06/21/91	393
Endangered Species Act	10/01/99	849
Environmental Movement at 25	03/31/95	286*
Hunting Controversy	01/24/92	49
Invasive Species	02/17/12	153
Managing Public Lands	11/04/11	929
Managing Wildfires	11/02/12	941
Marine Mammals vs. Fish	08/28/92	737
Protecting Endangered Species	04/19/96	337
Protecting Wetlands	10/03/08	793*
Threatened Fisheries	08/02/02	617
Zoos in the 21st Century	04/28/00	353
Women		
Academic Politics	02/16/96	145
Aiding Africa	08/29/03	712*
Boys' Emotional Needs	06/18/99	521
Changing U.S. Electorate	05/30/08	**457
Children and Divorce	06/07/91	357
Cosmetic Surgery	04/15/05	317
Crime on Campus	02/04/11	97
Democracy in the Arab World	01/30/04	73
Domestic Violence	01/06/06	1
Education and Gender	06/03/94	481
Emerging India	04/19/02	338*
Exporting Democracy	04/01/05	269
Feminism's Future	02/28/97	169
First Ladies	06/14/96	505
Foreign Aid and National Security	06/17/11	529
Future of Feminism	04/14/06	313
Future of Marriage	05/07/04	397
Gender and Learning	05/20/05	445
Gender Pay Gap	03/14/08	241
Global Refugee Crisis	07/09/99	586*
Human Trafficking and Slavery	03/26/04	273
Japan in Crisis	07/26/02	604*
Jobs Outlook	06/04/10	481
Marriage and Divorce	05/10/96	409
Mothers' Movement	04/04/03	297
The Obscenity Debate	12/20/91	969
Prostitution	06/11/93	505
Racial Quotas	05/17/91	277
Rebuilding Afghanistan	12/21/01	1048*
Reform in Iran	12/18/98	1103*
Retirement Security	05/31/02	496*
Saving Social Security	10/02/98	863*
Single-Sex Education	07/12/02	569
Teaching History	09/29/95	860*
Understanding Mormonism	10/19/12	889
Violence Against Women	02/26/93	169
War Crimes	07/07/95	590*
Welfare Reform	04/10/92	313
Women and Human Rights	04/30/99	353
Women in Politics	03/21/08	265
Women and Sports	03/25/11	265
Women in Sports	05/11/01	401
Women in the Military	11/13/09	957
Women athletes		
College Sports	08/26/94	745
Eating Disorders	12/18/92	1102
Eating Disorders	02/10/06	**121
Gender Equity in Sports	04/18/97	337
High School Sports	09/22/95	825
Soccer in America	04/22/94	351*
Women and Sports	03/06/92	193
Women and Sports	03/25/11	265
Youth Fitness	09/26/97	846*
Women — Employment		
Big-Box Stores	09/10/04	733
Child Care	12/17/93	1105
Class Action Lawsuits	05/13/11	433
Contingent Work Force	10/24/97	937
Crackdown on Sexual Harassment	07/19/96	625
Diversity in the Workplace	10/10/97	889
Fairness in Salaries	05/29/92	457
Feminism's Future	02/28/97	169
Foreign Aid After Sept. 11	04/26/02	370*
Future of Feminism	04/14/06	313
Future of Marriage	05/07/04	397
Gender and Learning	05/20/05	445
Gender Pay Gap	03/14/08	241
The Glass Ceiling	10/29/93	937
Income Inequality	04/17/98	346*

	Date	Page
Mothers' Movement	04/04/03	297
Paying for Retirement	11/05/93	978*
Rethinking Affirmative Action	04/28/95	369
Sexual Harassment	08/09/91	537
Sexual Harassment	04/27/12	377
Women and Sports	03/06/92	204*
Work, Family and Stress	08/14/92	689
Women — Health. ***See also Abortion; Pregnancy***		
Abortion Debates	03/21/03	249
Advances in Cancer Research	08/25/95	753
Battling HIV/AIDS	10/26/07	889
Birth Control Choices	07/29/94	649
Birth-Control Debate	06/24/05	565
Breast Cancer	06/27/97	553
Chronic Fatigue Syndrome	04/05/02	289
Cosmetic Surgery	04/15/05	317
Dieting and Health	04/14/95	331*
Eating Disorders	12/18/92	1097
Sexually Transmitted Diseases	12/03/04	997
Treating Anxiety	02/08/02	97
Women and AIDS	12/25/92	1121
Women's Health	11/07/03	941
Women's Health Issues	05/13/94	409
Women — Military service		
New Military Culture	04/26/96	361
Should the U.S. Reinstate the Draft?	01/11/91	17
Women in the Military	09/25/92	833
Women in the Military	11/13/09	957

	Date	Page
World Bank		
Emerging India	04/19/02	329
Famine in Africa	11/08/02	937*
Foreign Aid After Sept. 11	04/26/02	361
Globalization Backlash	09/28/01	761
Global Water Shortages	12/15/95	1113
Trouble in South America	03/14/03	225
World Trade Organization		
China After Deng	06/13/97	518*
China Today	08/04/00	625
Foreign Aid After Sept. 11	04/26/02	361
Globalization Backlash	09/28/01	761
International Law	12/17/04	1049
World Trade	06/09/00	497
World Wide Web. ***See Internet***		
Youth. ***See Adolescents and youth***		
Yugoslavia		
Defense Priorities	07/30/99	641
Democracy in Eastern Europe	10/08/99	865
Economic Sanctions	10/28/94	945*
Europe's New Right	02/12/93	121
Global Refugee Crisis	07/09/99	569
NATO's Changing Role	08/21/92	713
Stopping Genocide	08/27/04	685
United Nations at 50	08/18/95	729
War Crimes	07/07/95	585